Blairsville High School Library
Blairsville, Pennsylvania

P9-DCZ-633

THE DICTIONARY OF DATES

THE MACMILLAN COMPANY
NEW YORK · CHICAGO
DALLAS · ATLANTA · SAN FRANCISCO
LONDON · MANILA

THE MACMILLAN COMPANY
OF CANADA, LIMITED
TORONTO

THE DICTIONARY OF DATES

By HELEN REX KELLER

IN TWO VOLUMES

VOLUME I
THE OLD WORLD

3377

THE MACMILLAN COMPANY

NEW YORK   MCMLV

Blairsville High School Library
Blairsville, Pennsylvania

902

Copyright, 1934, by

THE MACMILLAN COMPANY

All rights reserved—no part of this book may be reproduced in any form without permission in writing from the publisher, except by a reviewer who wishes to quote brief passages in connection with a review written for inclusion in magazine or newspaper.

Set up and electrotyped. Published, November, 1934.

Second Printing, 1955

PRINTED IN THE UNITED STATES OF AMERICA

PREFACE

This history of the world by dates is a record from earliest times through the year 1930 arranged under countries, giving a digest of information contained in many books, encyclopedias, and yearbooks. It is an outline of events and is also intended to be used as a supplementary aid to histories written from the modern standpoint which stresses subjects rather than dates.

Part I, the Old World (Europe, Africa, Asia), and Australasia, includes the World War, the Peace Conference, the League of Nations, International Labor Organization, Permanent Court of International Justice, and general international affairs since the War.

Part II, the New World, begins with the discovery of America, and contains the history of the exploration and development of the United States, Canada, Mexico, Central and South America, and the Arctic and Antarctic regions.

Haydn's "Dictionary of Dates," the well known English reference book, with addenda including October 1910, is used as a basis for Part I, with Great Britain, Africa, and some other sections rewritten from a more international standpoint. For the all-important events of the following twenty years the compiler has relied upon the indexes of events in the "Political Science Quarterly," "American Journal of International Law," "Survey on Foreign Affairs," "Documents on Foreign Affairs," the "Annual Register," "Statesman's Yearbook," "Current History Magazine," "International Conciliation," pamphlets of the "World Peace Foundation," and the yearbooks of the different countries, as of China, India (by the Bureau of Public Information), Union of South Africa, Australia, etc., in addition to the standard histories. The treaties listed have been checked with the "British and Foreign State Papers," Hertslet's "The Map of Africa by Treaty," and the "Documents on International Affairs." For the World War the chronology published by the Committee on Imperial Defense (Great Britain), and the British "Official History of the War" have been used, supplemented by many other accounts in the large literature of the subject, for the economic history, the "Economic and Social History of the War," published by the "Carnegie Endowment for International Peace," and for the period immediately following the War, Temperley's "A History of the Peace Conference in Paris." For the countries, colonies and mandated regions of Africa works consulted included the "Handbooks prepared under the direction of the Historical Section of the (British) Foreign Office," the official reports, N. D. Harris, "Intervention and Colonization in Africa," R. L. Buell, "The Native Problem in Africa," L. S. Woolf, "Empire and Commerce in Africa," J. N. L. Baker, "A History of Geographical Discovery and Exploration," "Histoires des colonies françaises," edited by Gabriel Hanotaux and Alfred Martineau, and "Germany's Colonial Empire," by M. E. Townsend.

The sources of Part II are the standard histories of the United States, Winsor, Bancroft, Adams, Schouler, Channing, Rhodes, Wilson, the "American Nation" series, and for the later period, McMaster, Bassett, Muzzey, Oberholtzer, Hackett, and Kendrick, the "American Year Book," the "New International Yearbook," "Americana Annual," and "Survey of American Foreign Relations," and for

v

treaties the "Subject Index of the Treaty Series," published by the State Department. The general Latin-American histories of W. S. Robertson, H. G. James, H. G. James and P. A. Martin, J. F. Rippy, C. E. Chapman, R. R. Merriman, C. E. Akers, A. Helps, C. R. Markham, B. Mitre, and Bernard Moses have been used for South America, and the national histories; for Canada, "Canada and its Provinces," edited by Adam Shortt and A. D. Doughty, "The Chronicles of Canada," "The Makers of Canada," "Cambridge History of the British Empire," Canada volume, and the histories of William Kingsford, George Bryce, J. C. Bracq, A. P. Cockburn, J. C. Dent, C. Wittke, and for the early period, F. X. Charlevoix, H. P. Biggar, G. M. Wrong, J. B. Brebner, and the publications of the Champlain Society, and for current history, the "Canada Year Book," and "Canadian Annual Review of Public Affairs"; for Mexico, the histories of H. H. Bancroft, and H. I. Priestley, Callahan's "American Foreign Policy in Mexico," and the "Mexican Year Book."

The collection of accurate dates is made difficult by the abundance of material, since as Anatole France points out in the preface to "Penguin Island," the account of historical events as related by two or more witnesses tends to be contradictory and irreconcilable. For example there is the greatest discrepancy in the dates given for laws, without explanation whether the date used is the day the law passed the legislature, the date published, proclaimed or promulgated, when it came into effect, or the date signed by the President or assented to by the King, which is the official date. The lists of cabinets of France differ in excellent authorities because the date used is often the date of publication in the newspaper rather than the official announcement in the "Journal Officiel." E. Le Chartier lists 54 ministries for the period from Sept. 4, 1870 to Jan. 1, 1914, Léon Muel, 56 for the same period, and Lavaud and the *Société d'Histoire*, 52, the difference due to the fact that some authorities count as a separate ministry a cabinet which holds over into the term of a new president of the Republic as in the case of M. Briand in 1913.

The dates of the Old Style and New Style Calendar are both given in this list in a number of cases to avoid confusion, indicated by ( ) or a / between the dates. The Pilgrim Fathers landed from the "Mayflower" at Plymouth, Dec. 11 O.S. and Dec. 21 N.S., written Dec. 11(21) or Dec. 11/21. Many authorities give Dec. 22 as the date of the New Style adding erroneously 11 days to Dec. 11, Old Style, instead of 10 as was used in the seventeenth century to correct the calendar.

The statistics of population and area of countries, and the names of kings, rulers and presidents, are of the year 1930 unless otherwise stated.

In a work covering this large field and compiled from many sources there are bound to be inconsistencies, but every effort has been made to verify dates supplied.

CONTENTS

EUROPE

AFRICA

ASIA

AUSTRALASIA AND OCEANIA

CONTENTS

ASIA

AUSTRALASIA AND OCEANIA

THE OLD WORLD

THE OLD WORLD

EUROPE

Europe, the northwestern continent of the Old World, the most important historically and politically, and the smallest except Australia, with an area of 3,988,500 square miles. It may be regarded as a peninsula on the continent of Asia, the Ural Mountains and the Caspian Sea forming the eastern boundary, the Black Sea and Sea of Marmora and Ægean on the southeast, the Arctic Ocean the northern boundary, the Atlantic Ocean the western boundary, and the Mediterranean Sea on the south separating Europe from Africa. The greatest distance from north to south, the North Cape in Norway to Cape Tarifa in Spain is 2,400 miles, and from east to west from Cape da Roca in Portugal to a point in the Ural Mountains is 3,300 miles. The World War resulted in a redistribution of the countries of Europe, Sweden, Norway, Luxemburg, Holland, Switzerland, Great Britain, Portugal, and Spain remained the same, but France recovered Alsace and that part of Lorraine lost in 1871; Belgium recovered the cantons lost in 1815 under the Treaty of Vienna; Denmark recovered the Danish part of Schleswig; Serbia, Rumania, Poland, and Italy were enlarged by annexation of districts of former Austro-Hungarian Empire, the new State of Czechoslovakia was created, Austria and Hungary becoming small, separate States; Poland, Finland, Estonia, Latvia, and Lithuania separated from Russia became independent States, and Poland received parts of German territory. For further statement of the New Europe *see* the Peace Treaties, p. 561 *et seq.*

ÆGEAN ISLANDS

Ægean Islands, in the Ægean Sea, divided in possession between Greece and Italy, and Turkey. Certain islands were occupied by Italy in 1912 during the war with Tripoli, and by the Treaty of Lausanne which came into effect Aug. 6, 1924, Turkey ceded islands of the Northeast Ægean to Italy (*see* Dodecanese Islands) including the Dodecanese and Castellorizo. The Conference of London (Feb. 13, 1914) assigned to Greece the Ægean islands occupied by Greece during the Balkan Wars including Lemnos, Samos, Chios, Mytilene, Samothrace, and Nikaria except Tenedos, and Imbros which were retroceded to Turkey by the Treaty of Lausanne which recognized Greek sovereignty over remaining islands as assigned by the Powers in 1914. (*See also* Greece.) Between the Cyclades (Greek) and the Dodecanese are 6 or more islands or minor groups ceded by Turkey to the Allied Powers by Article 16 of the Treaty, namely: Lebinthos, Kinaros, Adelphi, or Zaphrania, Syrnos, Tria-nisia, and the southwestern Zaphrania, of undetermined status. The small Rabbit Islands were retained by Turkey as part of the defenses of the Dardanelles.

ÅLAND ISLANDS

Åland Islands, archipelago of nearly 300 islands across the entrance to the Gulf of Bothnia between Finland and Sweden, distant from Finland about 15 miles, and under sovereignty of Finland by decision of the League of Nations of June 24, 1921; area 551 square miles, population 1928 27,156. About 80 of the islands are inhabited, the rest being rocks forming a granite reef along the southern coast. With Finland the Åland Islands were incorporated with Sweden by the Peace of Nöteberg in 1323, and in 1634 the Islands made a department of the Government of Finland by Sweden. By the Treaty of Fredrikshavn of Sept. 17, 1809 the Islands with Finland were ceded to Russia by Sweden.

1854

Fortress of Bomersund begun in 1835 was destroyed by Anglo-French force in the Crimean War

1856

March 30, Åland Convention, an annex to the Treaty of Paris, provided for demilitarization of Islands, no fortifications to be built or military or naval establishments to be maintained or created. The

1

question of fortification was discussed in 1906 and 1907 and 1908 in connection with new North Sea Agreements but Russia did not actually fortify the Islands until 1914

1917

Aug. 20, Communal Assembly held by Islanders to consider the question of reunion with Sweden

Dec. 25–29, Plebiscite held and 95% of the inhabitants voted for reunion with Sweden

Dec. 31, Appeal signed by 7,135 persons presented to King of Sweden asking for reunion on Feb. 3, 1918

1918

March 2, German forces landed at Islands at request of Finnish (White) Government and Swedish force which had been sent to aid against the Bolsheviks withdrawn

March 3, Treaty of Brest-Litovsk, Russia to evacuate Islands

March 7, Agreement of Germany, Sweden, and Finland not to fortify the Islands

March 9, Decree of Finnish Government constituted Islands a province with a civil and a military Governor

June 27, Agreement of Finland, Sweden, and Germany for demolition of fortifications

Nov. 9, Appeal of the Islanders to the United States, France, and Great Britain for reunion with Sweden

1919

March 18, Sweden brought the question of the Islands before the Peace Conference

May 7, Finland granted the Islands autonomy

May 26, Sweden asked the Peace Conference to allow the Islands to decide by plebiscite whether they should belong to Sweden or Finland

1920

June 10 and 12, Finland and Sweden exchanged Notes on the question of the Islands

June 19, Great Britain called attention of the League of Nations to dispute of Finland and Sweden as to the Islands

July 12, The Council of the League of Nations referred the question of the Islands to an international commission of 3 jurists which held sessions from Aug. 3– Sept. 5 and declared the League of Nations competent to deal with the matter

Sept. 20, A new international commission appointed by the League notwithstanding the protests of Finland who regarded the Islands as a domestic question

Nov. 27–Feb. 25, 1921, The Commission conducted inquiry visiting Stockholm, Helsingfors, and the Islands

1921

May 10, The Commission recommended that the Åland Islands be awarded to Finland

June 24, Decision of the League of Nations that the Islands should remain under the sovereignty of Finland, but to be neutralized with respect to military matters and guaranteed full autonomy

June 27, Resolution of the Council of the League adopted pledge that Finland should guarantee autonomy under Finnish law of May 7, 1920

Oct. 10–20, Conference on the Åland Islands held at Geneva

Oct. 20, Convention providing for the neutralization and non-fortification of the Islands signed by representatives of Finland, Sweden, Germany, Denmark, Estonia, France, Great Britain, Italy, Latvia, and Poland

1922

Jan. 11, The Council of the League of Nations formally undertook to guarantee the neutralization of the Islands

April 6, The Convention came into effect

ALBANIA

The territory known as Albania (Shqiperia) is made up of the old Turkish Provinces of Scutari and of Yanina, and of parts of those of Kossovo and Monastir. The Albanian, from the point of view of their language are divided into two principal groups—the Ghegs, who live to the north of the River Shkumbi, and the Tosks in the south.

Little is known of their early history. From 1431, when the Turks captured Yanina and Scutari, the Albanians remained under Turkish rule, except for two brief periods of independence, first between 1443 and 1468, under Prince George Castriot II, surnamed Skanderbeg, and again in the eighteenth century, under the Tosk, Ali Tepelen of Yanina, in the south, and the Bushati Dynasty of Scutari, in the north, both of whom reigned as suzerains of the Ottoman Empire. In 1878 the short-lived Albanian League was founded, and ruled Albania for two years, making an unsuccessful effort to obtain independence.

The independence of Albania was proclaimed at Valona on November 28, 1912.

The area of the country is 10,629 square miles, while the population, according to the Census held on May 25, 1930, was 1,003,068. The capital is Tirana.

Zog I, Reigning King, born October 8, 1895, a Moslem by religion and hereditary chieftain of the Mati clan, proclaimed king September 1, 1928.

1878–1898

Sept. 7, 1878, An Albanian league (favored by the Turks) formed to resist the cession of any part of the country to Austria and Montenegro in April, said to have caused the death of Mehemet Ali

April, 1879, The country semi-independent

April, 1880, Army formed rebels against Turkey

The league forces defeated in an attack on Dervish Pasha in Uskub between Pristina and Prisrend April 19; he reported the country settled, but asked for reinforcements; more fighting; Albanians said to be defeated, and struggle almost over May 12, 1881

Revolt of chiefs, severe fights, June 2, 3, 1883. Turks defeated with loss; reported dispersion of the chiefs about June 8. Continued fighting June 12 *et seq.* The Turks successful in fight; the Albanians submit, announced June 21. Unsettled June 25. Insurrection subsiding about July 19. Albanians appeal to the Powers for annexation to Greece, about Nov. 3.

General disorder and much brigandage reported, Aug., 1884

May, 1889, The Albanian society established at Bucharest for the political, moral, and intellectual development of the Albanians has been reorganized, and the Sultan has been asked to accept the protectorate

July, Aug., 1890, Albanian attacks on Montenegro, &c., checked by the Turks

Nov., 1891, League of Albanian chiefs formed to resist the Turks

Dec., 1891, Martial law established on the confines of Montenegro

Rebel Arnauts attack and loot Prisrend, demanding its autonomy; the Turkish garrison retreat into the citadel, Nov. 1; rising suppressed, Nov. 6, 1893

March 7, 1896, Conflicts with the Turks, reported

Demonstration of Albanians against taxation, &c.; at Elbassan, reported Jan. 8, 1897; outbreak in Divra, Jan. 11, 1897; denied by the Porte, March 9, 1897

Revolt in Ipek and Diakova; conflict, heavy loss on both sides, Nov., 1897; the Albanians agitate for autonomy Jan., 1898; severe border warfare, many Christian villages burnt in the Berane district, June, 1898

1899

Fight among Albanian nobles near Ipek, a village burnt, a Serbian woman killed, April 20; Serbian frontier guard near Vronya attacked by a band of Albanians, 1 Serbian killed, May 17, 21

Dec. 19, Outrages on Christians by Mohammedan Albanians round Ipek and other places, reported

1901

June 30, Fighting on the frontier, 7 Christians killed, reported

Oct., Continued outrages on Christians reported

Nov. 16, 22, Kiazim Pasha, Vali for 4 years, resigns, succeeded by General Shakir Pasha

1902–1903

March 29, Further disturbances and great unrest reported

Sept., 1902–April, 1903, The appointment of a Russian vice-consul at Mitrovitza disallowed, Sept. 1; revolt against reforms, many lives lost

1904

Feb. 18, Shemsi Pasha with 2,500 troops, besieged by Albanians at Babaj-Hoshi, is relieved by reinforcements, besieging force routed, 800 killed and wounded; Albanians lose 500 killed and wounded in a fight near Liuma

Three battalions forming garrison of Jakova surrounded and attacked by Albanians, Feb. 16; Shemsi and Shakir Pashas relieve the garrison; district round Jakova, Prinzen, Ipek, Mitrovitza, and Verisovich occupied by 25 battalions of Turkish troops, Feb. 20

Submission of the two Albanian chiefs Suleiman Batusha and Shaban; Albanian movement reported to be at an end, early April

1905

June 1, Earthquake at Scutari, 100 killed, 250 injured

1910

April 3, Collision between Turks and Albanians in the Prishtina district when a meeting was held outside the town to protest against the "Octroi"

[Turkish losses in the action on the Lyab River were 200 killed and wounded and 40 prisoners]

April 25, Turkish troops ambushed by Albanians at the Tchernalova pass; over 200 Albanians killed, reported

April 28–29, Turkish troops recapture the Katchanik Elesham pass from the insurgents after hard fighting, with a loss of 142 killed and wounded

June 6, The rising reported at an end

1911

March, Revolt against Turkish rule

April 3, Turks defeated Albanians at Scutari

1912

June 25, Troops at Monastir joined the revolt in the Balkans

July 21, Insurgents captured Prishtina

Aug. 16, Massacre of Albanian Christians near frontier of Montenegro

Aug. 20, Announcement that Turkey had granted reforms demanded at conference at Prishtina, the 12 demands including recognition of Albanian nationality, use of Albanian language in schools and administration

Nov. 28, Assembly at Valona (Avlona) summoned by Ismael Kemal proclaimed the independence of Albania and made declaration of neutrality in the Balkan War. Provisional Government established headed by Ismael Kemal

Dec. 20, Conference of the Powers in London accepted principle of autonomy of Albania and guaranteed Serbia commercial access to the sea

1913

Jan. 13, Hazan Riza, Commandant at Scutari, assassinated at instigation of Essad Pasha

April 7, Announcement of decision of the Powers of frontiers of Albania by Lord Grey

April 22, Surrender of Scutari to Montenegrins by Essad Pasha. (See Balkan Wars.)

May 30, Treaty of London provided that the status and boundaries of Albania should be determined by the Powers. Two international commissions sent to Albania to delimit boundaries

May 5, Scutari evacuated by Montenegrins and occupied by international force

July 29, Decision of Powers that Albania should be governed by a prince and an international commission should manage its affairs until a ruler appointed

Aug. 11, Southern boundary with Serbia settled. Not accepted by Serbia

Aug. 19, Note of Powers demanded withdrawal of Serbian troops from Albania

Sept. 21, Serbs at Dibra executed 48 prominent Albanians

Sept. 22, Albanians capture Dibra which was recovered by Serbs

Oct. 25, Serbian troops withdrawn after ultimatum from Austria-Hungary

Nov. 23, Prince William Frederick Henry of Wied, German Protestant Prince related to the Queen of Rumania an officer in the Prussian army, offered the throne

Dec. 17, Protocol of Florence signed defined southern boundary

1914

Jan. 11, Essad Pasha, who had established a government at Tirana after the surrender of Scutari, in engagement with troops of Provisional Government of Ismael Kemal

Jan. 15, Ismael Kemal resigned the Government to International Commission

Feb. 8, William Prince of Wied negotiated loan of £500,000 with Austria-Hungary and Italy

Feb. 13, Note of Powers demanded that Greece withdraw troops from southern Albania. Accepted by Greece Feb. 22

Feb. 21, Deputation of Albanians headed by Essad Pasha offered crown to Prince William of Wied and received his formal acceptance

Feb. 28, C. Zographos, Greek leader, elected President of Government of Northern Epirus

March 2, Independence of Northern Epirus declared at Argyrocastro

March 7, Prince William of Wied arrived at Durazzo. Essad Pasha appointed a general

March 18, First Cabinet formed headed by Turkhan Pasha, Essad Pasha, Minister of War and of the Interior

April 28, Greeks withdrew army of occupation from Northern Epirus

May 17, Revolt in Northern Epirus ended by concessions as to language and religion, the " Agreement of Corfu "

May 19, Armed forces surrounded house of Essad Pasha charged with leading revolt against William I. Essad Pasha escaped to Italian warship and proceeded to Italy

May 24–26, William I took refuge on Italian warship during rising of followers of Essad Pasha

June 15, Durazzo besieged by insurgents

June 22–24, Armistice conference without agreement

June 23, Insurgents in successful engagement with Government troops

July 9, Epirotes insurgents captured Koritza, Klesura, and Terpelen

July 19, Meeting of citizens at Valona resolved to ask Powers for government by an international commission

Aug. 31, Insurgents occupied Valona and attacked Durazzo

Sept. 4, Prince William left the country

Sept. 4, International Commission of Control took over the Government at Durazzo

Sept. 13, Italian troops landed at Valona

Sept. 27, Prince Burhan-ed-Din, son of Abdul Hamid former sultan, and leader of revolt, proclaimed head of Government by Senate

Oct. 4, Essad Pasha entered the capital at head of army

Oct. 5, Essad Pasha elected President by the Senate

Oct. 26, Italian marines occupied Valona

Oct. 31, Italians occupied Saseno Island. Greeks retaliated by occupation of Santi Quaranta, Premedi, and Argyrocastro

Dec. 25, Italian troops established occupation at Durazzo because of revolt against Essad Pasha

1915

Jan. 3, Insurgents (Mussulman Committee) attacking Durazzo checked by Italians

March 25, Moslem insurgents again attack Durazzo

May 29, Italians landed additional troops at Valona

June 21, Serbs invaded Albania occupying Elbassan and advanced on Durazzo

June 26, San Giovanni di Medua occupied by Montenegrins

July 4, Italians occupied Durazzo

July 17, Treaty of Alliance of Bulgaria with Central Powers provided for cession of Albania to Bulgaria

July 17, Serbs evacuated Durazzo on request of Italian Government

July 29, The Entente Allies notified Montenegro that Montenegrin occupation of Albanian territory would not be recognized

Dec. 3, Serbs established a Government at Scutari

Dec. 16, Italians occupied Valona

Dec. 20, Italians occupied Durazzo

1916

Jan. 25, Austrians captured San Giovanni di Medua

Jan. 23, Austrians took Scutari

Feb. 17, Austrians took Berat

Feb. 24, Government of Essad Pasha left Durazzo retiring to Naples

Feb. 27, Austrians took Durazzo evacuated by Italians

Feb. 28, Essad Pasha established Provisional Government at Naples

Sept. 20, Provisional Government of Essad Pasha established at Salonika

Dec. 10, The French occupied Korçe (Koritsa) evacuated by Greek troops and established a Provisional Government declaring independence of Albania under French military protection

Dec. 12, The Entente Allies proclaimed the independence of Albania

1917

March 10, Austrians declared Albania an autonomous State under protection of Austria-Hungary

June 3, Italy proclaimed independence of Albania under protection of Italy

June 19, Statement of Baron Sonnino that Italy would annex Avlona (Valona)

1918

Feb. 18, Statement of Mr. Balfour that arrangements of 1913 had ceased to have force

July 6, Italian offensive in Albania begun. *See* World War

Nov. 11, After the armistice an Inter-Allied Commission administered affairs at Scutari, Korçe occupied by the French, Yugoslavs occupied the northeast, and Italians most of the rest of the country

Dec. 25, A National Assembly at Durazzo elected Turkhan Pasha President and Prenk Bib Doda Vice-President and elected a delegation to the Peace Conference headed by Turkhan Pasha

1919

Feb. 12, Memorandum to Peace Conference asked " restoration to the Albanian State of 1913 "

March 7, Letter of Turkhan Pasha to Clemenceau asked for an American mandate for Albania and a plebiscite

March 17 and April 14, Albanians protested against Treaty of London of 1915 which gave Valona to Italy, and considered as possible the repartition of northern and southern districts between Montenegro, Serbia, and Greece

April, Manager Bumci made head of the delegation at the Peace Conference in Paris and the pro-Italian members replaced

1920

Jan. 28, National Assembly met at Lushnja and appointed new Government headed by Suleiman Bey Delvina, and 4 constitutional regents appointed, Manager Bumci, Dr. Tourtuli, Abdi Toptani, and Afik Pasha, representing the 4 religious sects, and selected Tirana as capital

April 7, Independence recognized by Italy

May, French troops withdrew from Koritsa an Albanian Committee taking charge

June 6, Rising on the coast against Italian troops headed by Bairam Tsuri drove them into Valona district

June 13, Essad Pasha assassinated in Paris by Albanian youth, Aveni Rustam

Aug. 2, Convention with Italy signed by which Italy recognized the independence of Albania and agreed to surrender Valona and evacuate Albania except the Island of Saseno

Sept. 2, Last Italian troops left Albania occupied since 1914, except Saseno Island

Dec. 17, Albania admitted to membership of the League of Nations

Dec. 31, Earthquake destroyed Elbassan

1921

June 25, Albanians presented request for intervention of League of Nations to the Council in dispute with Greece and Yugoslavia as to boundaries. No action taken

June, " Mirdite Republic" proclaimed at Prizrend supported by Yugoslavs

July 7, Protest of Government to League of Nations against invasion of Yugoslavs in northern Albania

July 13, Conference of Ambassadors fixed boundary with Yugoslavia

Oct. 2, Declaration regarding protection of minorities signed

Oct. 6, Commission of Inquiry on Yugoslav invasion of Albania appointed by League of Nations

Oct. 17, Resignation of Elias Vrioni, Prime Minister. Succeeded by Pandeli Evangeli

Nov. 7, Great Britain recognized independence of Albania

Nov. 9, Conference of Ambassadors announced decision as to frontiers fixed as in 1913 with minor rectifications in favor of Yugoslavia and appointed a Yugoslav-Albanian Mixed Commission to trace the frontiers

Nov. 12, De jure recognition given Albania by Great Britain, France, Italy, and Japan

Nov. 19, League of Nations Commission of Inquiry arrived in Albania

Nov. 28, Political amnesty declared

Dec. 7, Hassan Prishtina became Prime Minister

Dec. 10, De jure recognition given by Belgium

——, Yugoslav troops began evacuation of Albanian territory

Dec. 22, New Cabinet formed by Djafer Ypi, with Fan Noli, Foreign Affairs, and Ahmed Zogu, Interior

1922

Feb. 25, Customs tariff enacted

March 8–10, Irredentist Insurrection against the Government headed by Elez Jussorf took Tirana. Suppressed by Government troops

March 24, De jure recognition given by Yugoslavia

May 25, De jure recognition given by Portugal

June 19, Recognition of Government by Greece with reservations

July 4, De jure recognition given by Czechoslovakia

July 27, Government formally recognized by the United States and Spain

Sept. 10, National Albanian Church pronounced independent

Dec. 3, Ahmed Zogu became Prime Minister

Dec. 6, Conference of Ambassadors assigned Monastery of Svet Naum to Albania. Decision announced Dec. 23

1923

April 17, J. D. Hunger appointed Financial Adviser to Albania by the Council of the League of Nations. Arrived at Tirana May 31

April, Congress of Moslems abolished polygamy and the compulsory wearing of the veil by women

1924

Jan. 20, Treaty of commerce and navigation with Italy signed

Jan. 21, Constituent Assembly met

Feb. 29, Consular and establishment Convention with Italy signed

——, Contract with J. D. Hunger, Financial Adviser, canceled by the Government

June 10, Revolutionists headed by Bishop Fan Noli entered Tirana and overthrew the Government, Zogu fled from the country

June 12, "National Provisional Government" with Bishop Fan Noli at head proclaimed

Sept. 4, Advisory opinion of Permanent Court of International Justice upheld decision of Council of League of Nations of Dec. 6, 1922 assigning monastery of Svet Naum to Albania

Oct. 31, 14 villages awarded to Albania Nov. 9, 1921 evacuated by Greeks

Dec. 12, Insurrection against Government organized in Yugoslavia

Dec. 19, Protest of Government to League of Nations against Yugoslav interference in internal affairs

Dec. 21, Agreement with Yugoslavia as to policy of non-interference in Albania

Dec. 23, Noli fled from Tirana and established a Government at Valona

Dec. 24, Revolutionists led by Ahmed Bey Zogu captured Tirana

Dec. 27, Noli left the country proceeding to Italy

1925

Jan. 6, Ahmed Zogu became Prime Minister

Jan. 15, Constituent Assembly of Jan., 1924, met and resumed work on constitution

Jan. 19, National Assembly convoked by Zogu

Jan. 21, National Assembly proclaimed Republic

Jan. 31, Constituent Assembly elected Ahmed Zogu President

Feb. 20, Assembly ratified oil exploitation grant to Anglo-Persian Oil Company

March 2, Constituent Assembly adopted Constitution

March 20, Legislative decree prohibited entrance of alien workers

March 28, Greek Metropolitan of Paramythia expelled from Constantinople under Convention for exchange of populations

June 10, Provisional Commercial Agreement with Great Britain concluded

Sept. 2, National Bank of Albania established in Rome with branches in Tirana, Durazzo, Valona, and Scutari

Sept. 22, Cabinet resigned and was reorganized

Oct. 15, Government accepted decision of Conference of Ambassadors of Aug. 6 which assigned Monastery of Svet Naum to Yugoslavia reversing former decision of Dec. 22

Oct. 20, Amnesty granted to those who had taken up arms against Zogu

Nov., Resignation of 20 of the 26 elected senators

1926

Jan. 19, Provisional Commercial Agreement with Czechoslovakia signed

June 22, Treaty of commerce and navigation with Yugoslavia signed

July 30, Final Act delimiting boundaries of Albania signed by Albania in Paris and Great Britain, France, Greece, Italy, Japan, and Yugoslavia

Aug. 7, Treaty of friendship, conciliation, and judicial settlement with Spain

Sept. 16, Treaty of friendship with Rumania signed

Oct. 13, Three Conventions with Greece signed, commerce and navigation, consular and establishment, and nationality

Nov. 20, Revolt of Catholic tribes in northern Albania, the Malissors of Dukagjin north and east of Scutari. Support by Yugoslavs charged

Nov. 26, Insurrection defeated by Government forces

Nov. 27, Treaty of friendship and security with Italy signed at Tirana, by which Italy undertook to guarantee the territorial integrity of Albania

Dec. 29, Treaty of arbitration and conciliation with Germany signed

1927

Jan. 14, Provisional Commercial Agreement with Rumania signed

Feb. 8, Treaty with Italy of Nov. 27, 1926, registered with League of Nations with letter stating that Italy could not interfere in the affairs of Albania except at request of Albania

March 19, Italian Government notified Great Britain, France, and Germany of information of preparations made by Yugoslavia to invade Albania and overthrow the Government. International crisis averted by intervention of Powers

April 14, Provisional Commercial Agreement with Austria signed

May 27, Arrest at Durazzo of Vuko Juraskovic, employed at Yugoslav legation, on charge of espionage for Yugoslavia

May 30, Protest of Yugoslav Government demanded release of Juraskovic in Note which was resented by Albanian Government as offensive

June 4, Yugoslav charge d'affaires left Tirana because of refusal to release Juraskovic

June 16, Albanian Minister to Yugoslavia left Belgrade

June 23, Joint Note of Great Britain, France, and Italy to Albania and Yugoslavia

July 3, Dispute with Yugoslavia settled by intervention of the Powers, the Yugoslav Note modified and Juraskovic released

Oct. 14, Assassination of Tsena Bey Kryeziu, Minister to Yugoslavia and Czechoslovakia assassinated at Prague

Nov. 4, Provisional Commercial Agreement with Hungary signed

Nov. 22, Defensive alliance with Italy signed for 20 years which provided for military coöperation if efforts to maintain peace proved ineffective

1928

Jan. 13, Resignation of Prime Minister Kotta in disagreement as to budget and Parliament dissolved

March 28, New Civil Code adopted

June 2, Navigation Agreement with Hungary concluded

June 17–Aug. 16, First general election ever held in the country for National Assembly

Aug. 25, Constituent Assembly met for the purpose of changing the Republic into a Monarchy

Sept. 1, Amendments to Constitution voted and Ahmed Zogu proclaimed King assumed the title as Zog I

Sept. 4, New Government recognized by Greece and Hungary, by the United States Sept. 12, by Yugoslavia Sept. 18, by Rumania Sept. 20, by France Sept. 21, by Great Britain Sept. 22, by Germany Sept. 24, by Spain Sept. 26, and by Czechoslovakia Sept. 26

Oct. 22, Treaties of arbitration and conciliation with the United States signed

Nov. 22, Constituent Assembly drafted and ratified new monarchical Constitution and resolved itself into Chamber of Deputies

Dec. 11, First Parliament under the Monarchy assembled

1929

Jan. 1, New Civil Code based on that of Switzerland and new Penal Code based on that of Italy came into effect

Jan. 16, Council of Ministers appointed by the King headed by Kostaq Kotta as Prime Minister and Minister of the Interior

June 20, Most favored nation commercial Agreement with Switzerland signed

Oct. 4, Diplomatic relations with Turkey severed because no Minister sent from Turkey to Albania since the accession of King Zog

1930

March 5, Kotta Cabinet resigned in dispute over arrangements as to coinage of currency taken over by the National Bank

March 6, Pandeli Evangeli became Prime Minister

May 25, Census gave population as 1,003,068

ANDORRA

Andorra, a small autonomous State on the Franco-Spanish border forming one large valley of 191 square miles in the eastern Pyrenees, maximum length 17 miles, and width, 18 miles, population, 5,231 scattered in 6 villages. The independence of the Republic is ascribed to Charlemagne. The political status was regulated by the

Paréage of 1278, according to which the territory was placed under the joint suzerainty of the head of the French State and the Spanish Bishop of Urgel. It is governed by a Council of 24 members elected for 4 years by the heads of families in each of the 6 parishes, half of the members being re-elected every 2 years, and executive power is vested in a First Syndic elected by the Council to preside over its deliberations. The capital is Andorra.

AUSTRIA

Austria, Republic of central Europe, proclaimed Nov. 12, 1918 after the revolution which followed the World War from the predominantly German-speaking lands of the former Austro-Hungarian Empire. The area of Austria in 1910 was 115,882 square miles, with population of 28,571,934, reduced by the Peace Treaties to 32,369 square miles with no seacoast, with population of 6,534,481 according to Census of March 7, 1923. It is bounded on the north by Germany and Czechoslovakia, and on the south by Italy and Yugoslavia, by Germany and Switzerland on the west and Hungary and Czechoslovakia on the east. Vienna is the capital. For a statement of the boundaries according to the Treaty of St. Germain *see* STATESMAN'S YEAR-BOOK for 1920, pp. 674-675.

PROVINCES	AREA, ENGLISH SQUARE MILES	POPU-LATION (CENSUS 1923)
Vienna	107	1,865,780
Burgenland	1,532	285,609
Lower Austria	7,452	1,480,449
Upper Austria	4,626	876,074
Salzberg	2,762	223,023
Styria	6,323	978,845
Carinthia	3,680	370,817
Tirol	4,882	313,885
Vorarlberg	1,005	139,999
Total	32,369	6,534,481

PROVINCES	AREA, ENGLISH SQUARE MILES	CENSUS POPU-LATION, DEC. 31, 1910
Lower Austria	7,658	3,531,814
Upper Austria	4,628	853,006
Salzburg	2,763	214,737
Styria	8,662	1,444,157
Carinthia	3,989	396,200
Carniola	3,845	525,995
Coast land	3,078	893,797
Tirol and Vorarlberg	11,312	1,092,021
Bohemia	20,065	6,769,548
Moravia	8,584	2,622,271
Silesia	1,988	756,949
Galicia	30,321	8,025,675
Bukovina	4,033	800,098
Dalmatia	4,956	645,6661
Total	115,882	28,571,934

Doctor Wilhelm Mikias, President, elected Dec. 5, 1928.

1919

Jan. 20, Tyrolese Diet passed resolution refusing to recognize cession of South Tirol

Feb. 1, Unemployed numbered 162,000

Feb. 16, General election held for National Constituent Assembly on basis of universal and proportional suffrage, 72 Social Democrats, 69 Christian Socialists, 26 German Nationalists, 3 others, total 170, no elections being held in territories held by Czechoslovakia, Italy, and Yugoslavia

Feb. 27, Law empowered Minister of Finance to stamp Austrian bank notes separating currency from that of the "succession States"

March 4, National Constituent Assembly met in Vienna

March 14, Republican Constitution adopted and a Government Commission on Nationalization adopted

——, Act passed regarding measures preparatory to socialization of industry

March 15, Government reconstituted by election from the National Assembly, Dr. Karl Renner appointed first Chancellor, Otto Bauer, Secretary of Foreign Affairs

March 24, The Emperor Charles and his family left Austria taking residence in Switzerland

March 26-28, Strike of railroad employees for increase in wages

April 3, Law reorganized judiciary and created a Constitutional Court to decide controverted constitutional questions

April 17, Unemployment riots in Vienna

May 1, Maximum of 186,000 unemployed reached

May 14, Austrian Delegation headed by Dr. Renner arrived at St. Germain

——, Act prohibited night work for women and young persons

May 15, Law established industrial councils

May 19, From this date employers who on April 26 employed a minimum of 15 persons were compelled to employ additional workmen up to $1/5$ of their previous establishment and replace workers whose work ended

May 28, Yugoslavs began hostilities against Austrians in Carinthia

June 2, Preliminary Draft Peace Treaty submitted to Austrian Delegation. *See* p. 561

June 6, Communist riots in Vienna

——, Armistice with Yugoslavia became effective

June 15, Communist demonstration in Vienna

July 20, Second draft of Peace Treaty handed to Austrian Delegation

July 25, Otto Bauer resigned as Minister of Foreign Affairs because of defeat of his policy of union with Germany forbidden by Peace Treaty Article 88, and the cession of Southern Tirol to Italy. Chancellor Renner assumed direction of Foreign Affairs

July 28, Act passed as to employment of young persons and women in mines, Sunday rest, &c.

July 29, Law on socialistic enterprises provided for transfer of existing private and public undertakings in business to control of socialistic institutions representing employers, workmen, and consumers

July 30, Workers' Holiday Act passed

Aug. 6, Austrian Delegation presented final observations on the Peace Treaty

Sept. 6, National Assembly voted 97 to 23 to accept Treaty of St. Germain

Sept. 8, Austrian Delegation authorized to sign Treaty of St. Germain

Sept. 10, Treaty of Peace signed at St. Germain. Independence of Hungary, Czechoslovakia, Poland, and Yugoslavia recognized, Trentino, the Tirol, Istria and a part of Dalmatia, and Islands in Adriatic ceded to Italy, army to be reduced to 30,000, rights of minorities guaranteed, Austria not to become a part of the German Republic, provision for reparations, Austria guaranteed free access by railroad to the Adriatic

Oct. 1, Law defined frontiers according to Treaty of St. Germain

Oct. 17, National Assembly ratified Treaty of St. Germain and adopted law changing name from German-Austrian Republic to Austrian Republic as required by Treaty

——, Government reconstituted, Herr Reisch becoming Finance Minister, and J. Fink, Vice-Chancellor

Oct. 21, National Assembly eliminated from Constitution clause declaring Austria a component part of Germany

Oct. 25, President Seitz signed the Peace Treaty

Nov. 2, 87,000 persons listed as unemployed

Nov. 12, Decree provided for coming into effect for provisions for Sunday rest of law of 1895 and July, 1919

Dec. 18, Act legalized collective bargaining and labor mediation

Dec. 27, All passenger trains on railroads stopped for one week to save coal

Dec. 30, Acute food shortage in Vienna. Bread ration of 4 ounces a week

1920

Jan. 6, Death of Professor Heinrich Lammasch, former Premier

Jan. 9, Provisional Agreement with Poland providing for reciprocal treatment of nationals in respect of property

Jan. 28, Commercial Agreement with Hungary signed

Feb. 26, Act ordered formation of Chambers of workers and clerks

March 17, Commercial Convention with Poland signed

March 24, Unemployment Insurance Act

April 17, The Austrian Section of the Reparations Commission met in Vienna to consider measures to relieve destitution of the country

June 7, Treaty and final Protocol signed with Czechoslovakia for settlement of questions of citizenship and protection of minorities

June 11, Renner Cabinet resigned. Dr. Michael Mayr succeeded as Chancellor heading a "Proportional Cabinet" representing all parties

June 27, Provisional Commercial Agreement concluded with Yugoslavia which was prolonged by later Agreements

July 3, Dr. Mayr assumed office as Prime Minister, Dr. Renner remaining in Cabinet as Minister of Foreign Affairs

July 16, Treaty of St. Germain came into force

July 28, Eight Hour Day Act passed

Aug. 2, Financial Agreement with Czechoslovakia signed at Prague

Aug. 3, Convention with France signed as to settlement of Austrian debts to French nationals under Article 248 of the St. Germain Treaty

Aug. 14, Commercial Agreement concluded with Rumania

Aug. 23, Supplementary Protocol signed with Czechoslovakia regarding citizenship and protection of minorities

Sept. 1, Commercial and financial Agreement with Germany signed

Oct. 1, New Constitution adopted declared Austria a Federal Republic of 8 provinces and the city of Vienna, provided for a President chosen by the 2 Houses for 4 years, an Assembly (Nationalrat) and a first Chamber (Bundesrat) with advisory powers

Oct. 4, Convention with Belgium signed regarding application of the economic clauses of the Treaty of St. Germain

Oct. 5, Constitution of the Republic proclaimed

Oct. 10, Plebiscite held in the Klagenfurt region of Carinthia gave decision in favor of Austria, 60% of votes cast against union with Yugoslavia

Oct. 14, Yugoslav troops occupied part of Klagenfurt area

Oct. 17, Election held a victory for moderate policy of Christian Socialists who obtained 82 seats; Pan-Germans, 19; Peasants League, 7; Bourgeois-Labor, 1

Oct. 20, Ultimatum of Conference of Ambassadors demanded withdrawal of Yugoslav troops from Klagenfurt Basin

Nov. 1, Scheme for reconstruction of Austrian finances submitted to Reparation Commission

Nov. 10, Constitution came into effect

Nov. 18, Klagenfurt district handed over to Austria

Dec. 9, Dr. Michael Hainisch elected first constitutional President by the National Assembly

——, New Cabinet constituted under Dr. Michael Mayr

Dec. 15, Austria admitted to membership in the League of Nations

Dec. 19, Further Commercial Agreement with Hungary signed

Dec. 31, The dollar quoted in Vienna at 668 kronen as compared to 5 kronen in pre-War times

1921

Jan. 8, Supplementary Commercial Agreement with Poland signed

Feb. 9, Decision of Conference of Ambassadors allowed Austria to retain the Klagenfurt Basin

Feb. 26, Death of Karl Menger, economist

March 4, Death of Rudolf Pöch, anthropologist

March 10, Agreement as to frontiers with Czechoslovakia signed

——, Regulations as to employment of domestic servants and agricultural labor enacted, Upper Austria

March 17, Allied Powers decided to suspend provisional claims against Austria for reparations and relief credits

March 22, Act provided regulations for labor in Lower Austria

March 26, Return of former Emperor Charles to Hungary. *See* Hungary

April 14, Anti-Habsburg law enacted

——, Allies declared that all agitation for union with Germany must end on penalty of end of proposed financial relief

April 24, Plebiscite held in Tirol voted for union with Germany

April 30, "Austrian Section" of the Reparations Commission left Vienna, the finances of Austria being turned over to management of the League of Nations

May 4, Commercial Convention with Czechoslovakia signed

——, Death of Dr. Alfred Hermann Fried, pacifist

May 29, People of Salzburg voted for union with Germany

June 21, Johann Schober, Police President of Vienna, headed new Cabinet of Christian Socialists and German Nationalists

July 2, War with Austria declared at end by the United States

July 26, The Burgenland officially became Austrian Territory

Aug. 6, Allied Commission to supervise the transfer of Burgenland (West Hungary) to Austria under Treaty of Trianon met at Oedenburg

Aug. 21, League of Nations appointed two commissions to work out scheme for reconstruction of Austria

Aug. 24, Treaty with the United States established friendly relations.

Aug. 28, Austrian troops taking possession of Burgenland resisted by Hungarian forces and driven out

Sept. 27, Burgenland proclaimed an independent State by former War Minister Herr Friedrich

Sept. 30, Commercial Agreement with Rumania signed

Oct. 13, Protocol with Hungary signed at Venice by which Hungarian troops to be withdrawn from Burgenland and Austria agreed to plebiscite in Oedenburg (Sopron)

Oct. 22–24, Second return of ex-Emperor Charles to Hungary. *See* Hungary

Dec. 1, Extradition Convention with the Netherlands revived that of Nov. 24, 1880

——, Riots in Vienna because of the high cost of living, prices of bread and meat had increased 100%

Dec. 7, Treaty with Russia signed renewal of political and economic relations

Dec. 14–17, Plebiscite at Oedenburg (Sopron) declared in favor of Hungary by 65% of votes cast. Not accepted by Austria

Dec. 16, Treaty of Lana (Lany) signed with Czechoslovakia, political agreement for 5 years, both Governments undertaking to loyally carry out terms of the Peace Treaty, to support each other against all revolutionary movements and to submit all disputes to arbitration

Dec. 17, Supplementary financial Convention with Czechoslovakia signed

Dec. 21, Decision of Conference of Ambassadors allowed Hungary to retain district near Oedenburg (Sopron) as result of plebiscite

——, Act of National Council required owners of foreign currency, or credit abroad to be deposited with the Government in exchange for 5% bonds

1922

Jan. 1, Control of Burgenland assumed

——, The krone 10,000 to the dollar

　Prices trebled since October increasing the cost of living especially in Vienna and 30,000 unemployed

Feb. 4, Agreement with Czechoslovakia signed by which Austria to receive a loan of 500 million crowns (approximately £2,300,000)

Feb. 8, Great Britain and France promised credit to Austria in various amounts

——, Commercial Agreement with Hungary signed

Feb. 18, Great Britain gave Austria credit of £2,000,000

Feb. 25, Austria agreed to recognize cession of Oedenburg to Hungary

March 9, Commercial Agreements concluded with Bulgaria and the Netherlands by exchange of notes

March, 90,000 unemployed of whom 50,000 in Vienna

April 5, Industrial Court law enacted

April 6, At Conference in Rome Austria signed 6 Conventions as to financial, judicial, and other matters

May 18, Resignation of Dr. Gürtler, Finance Minister

May 24, Schober Cabinet forced to resign by withdrawal of support of German Nationalists because of rapprochement with Czechoslovakia member of the Little Entente

May 31, Ignaz Seipel (Christian Socialist) headed an anti-Socialist coalition Cabinet of Christian Socialists and German Nationalists; Dr. Felix Frank (Pan-German), Vice-Chancellor and Interior; Dr. Alfred Grüberger, Foreign Affairs

June 27, Commercial Agreement with Hungary signed

July 12, Commercial Treaty with Yugoslavia indefinitely prolonged

July 22, Reparation Commission notified Austria of final removal of reparations liens to serve instead as security for new Bank of Issue

July 27, Parliament gave approval to statutes of new Bank of Issue

Aug. 18, The mark 336,000 to pound sterling

Aug. 24, Conference with representatives of Italy discussed economic union, presented details of desperate financial situation of Austria, rise in prices and danger from communists and anarchists in Vienna

Aug. 25, Italian delegates to Conference declared union of Austria with Little Entente would be considered cause of war

Aug. 29, Italian delegates to Conference recommended Italian financial coöperation

Sept. 6, Chancellor Seipel appealed to Council of League of Nations for financial aid for Austria

Sept. 19, Decision as to frontier with Hungary by League of Nations

Sept. 25, Supplementary Commercial Agreement with Poland signed

Oct. 4, Protocols signed with Great Britain, France, Italy, and Czechoslovakia instituting plan of League of Nations for financial reconstruction of Austria, independence of Austria guaranteed, Austrian State bonds to be issued for not more than 650 million gold crowns, gradual reform of taxation and civil service, guaranteed by customs and tobacco monopoly

Oct. 20, Agreement to maintain Austrian-Hungarian-Bulgarian Convention for judicial assistance and extradition of May 31, 1911

Nov. 6, Government deficit over 5,000 milliards marks

Nov. 27, National Council passed Reconstruction Bill based on Protocols for reconstruction of finances. Ratified Dec. 3

Dec. 4–Jan. 16, 1923, Internal loan floated resulted in 30 million gold kronen from the banks and 21 million from the public

Dec. 15, Dr. Zimmermann appointed High Commissioner under reconstruction scheme by League of Nations arrived at Vienna

1923

Jan. 2, New Bank of Issue opened in Vienna, Dr. Reisch, President, took over affairs of former Austrian-Hungarian Bank

Jan. 18, Frontier Agreement with Czechoslovakia signed supplementing that of March, 1921

Jan. 19, Announcement of internal loan of 280 milliard of Austrian paper kronen. Closed with subscription of about two-thirds

Jan. 23, The Reparation Commission divided old unsecured debts of the Empire between Austria and the Succession States

Feb. 1, Preliminary loan of £3,500,000 authorized by League of Nations

Feb. 3, Unemployment Insurance Act amended

Feb. 5, Death of Erich von Kielmansegg

Feb. 8, Credit Convention with Czechoslovakia signed

Feb. 21, Reparation Commission renounced for 20 years all rights to Austrian property and revenues under the Treaty of St. Germain

Feb. 24, Protocol signed with Yugoslavia abolished sequestrations of property belonging to Austrian subjects

Feb. 26, Agreement with Hungary signed provided for arbitration to settle disputes financial and otherwise as to Burgenland

March 29, Agreement as to tariff concessions signed with Italy

April 3, Anti-Semitic demonstration in Vienna, several workmen killed

April 6, Allied Powers asked Austria to dissolve and disarm anti-Semitic Swastika Society and expel foreign agitators

April 10, Arbitration Treaty with Hungary signed

April 28, Commercial Treaty with Italy signed and regarding traffic through Trieste

May 4, Clash between Fascists and Communists, a score or more of persons wounded

May 31, Unemployed persons 109,000

June 11, Loan authorized by League of Nations effected through bankers of Europe and the United States for 650 million gold crowns guaranteed by the following Powers: Great Britain, 24½%; France, 24½%; Czechoslovakia, 24½%; Italy, 20½%; Belgium, 2%; Sweden, 2%; Denmark, 1%; Netherlands, 1%; American bankers $25,000,000

June 22, Commercial Convention with France concluded

June 29, Protocol signed with Succession States of the old Empire for division of pre-War debts

June 30, Agreement with Denmark for provisional application of Commercial Convention of March 4, 1887

July 19, Federal law provided for " the creation of a corporation in Vienna for the purpose of conducting the operations of the federal railroads " to reduce the railroad deficit by giving up government administration while retaining government control

July 21, Provisional Commercial Agreement with Portugal signed

July 29, Austro-Hungarian Bank liquidated according to Treaty of St. Germain

Aug. 26, Provisional Commercial Agreement with Belgium signed

Sept. 5, Commercial Treaty with the Netherlands signed

Oct. 2, Commercial Agreement with Japan concluded

Oct. 20, General elections for Parliament a victory for the bourgeois element, the Christian Socialists and Conservatives defeating the Social Democrats and Pan-Germans

Nov. 13, Arbitration Agreement with Poland signed

Nov. 19, University of Vienna closed because of attacks on Jewish students because of refusal of University Senate to limit number as demanded by the Nationalist students

Nov. 22, Tax increases announced included doubling of the income tax, and quadrupling the tax on shares, and trebling the turn-over tax

——, Six Conventions with Yugoslavia signed as to frontiers

Dec. 14, Further Commercial Agreement with Belgium signed

Dec. 15, Commercial Agreement with Hungary signed

Dec. 18, Further provisional Commercial Agreement with Portugal signed

1924

Jan. 28, Treaty of friendship and commerce and navigation with Turkey signed

Feb. 13–March 7, Strike of bank employees of Vienna against overtime

March 19, Juridical Agreement with Poland signed

May 22, Treaty of commerce and navigation with Great Britain signed

June 1, Chancellor Seipel shot and seriously wounded by a mental defective

June 20, Agreement with Norway provided for maintenance of certain former treaties

July 12, Additional Commercial Agreement with Germany signed

July 26, Two financial Conventions with Hungary signed

July 29, Conventions with Roumania signed provided for settlement of financial and other questions under Treaty of St. Germain

Aug. 9, Commercial Treaty with Latvia signed

Aug. 19, Protocols signed with Hungary adjusted frontier

Aug. 24, Aërial Navigation Agreement with Hungary signed

Sept. 8–17, Strike of 60,000 metal workers for increase of wages and guarantee of eight-hour day

Sept. 16, Report on Austria presented to League of Nations

Oct. 11, Treaty of conciliation with Switzerland signed

Nov. 7–12, Strike of railroad workers gained increase in wages, in early part of month

Nov. 10, Agreement continued Treaty of commerce and navigation of Nov. 3, 1873 with Sweden and Norway

Nov. 17, Resignation of Chancellor Seipel whose health had been injured by attack on his life. Succeeded by Dr. Rudolf Ramek who carried on his policy

Nov. 19, Treaty with Switzerland for straightening of the Rhine River

Nov. 20, Dr. Ramek took office as Chancellor

Nov. 26, Agreement with the United States for appointment of a claims commission

Nov. 27, Supplementary Commercial Agreement with Czechoslovakia

Dec. 3, Provisional Commercial Agreement with Norway signed

Dec. 9, Dr. Michael Hainisch reëlected President

Dec. 20, New "Schilling" Act passed fixed gold value and made use of the schilling obligatory in public accounts from July 1, 1925

1925

Jan. 21, Protocol regarding customs tariff with Italy signed

Feb. 3, Commercial *modus vivendi* with Spain arranged

Feb. 17, Juridical Convention with Rumania signed

Feb. 23, Agreement with Italy signed provided for settlement of questions as to interests in the Tirol

March 1, All public offices, railroads, banks, post offices, and customhouses adopted the "shilling standard," 1 Austrian shilling to 10,000 crowns

March 3, Death of Heinrich Oskar Lenz (77), explorer

March 23, Decree reëstablished free dealing in foreign exchange

April 18, The Government asked the League of Nations to appoint experts to investigate economic position of Austria

——, Provisional Commercial Agreement with Greece signed

May 6, Aërial Navigation Agreement with Poland signed

May 19, Aërial Navigation Agreement with Germany signed

June 4, A "German People's League" with membership of a million formed to further the project of union of Austria with Germany

June 30, Mr. Layton and M. Rist appointed by League of Nations (June 9), to investigate economic position of Austria arrived in Vienna

July 17 and Aug. 16, Anti-Semitic riots in Vienna

July 27, Supplementary Commercial Agreement with Czechoslovakia signed

July 30, Constitution amended strengthened the federal principle, the administrative authority being transferred from the federal state departments to the provincial governments

——, Nationality law enacted as to acquisition and loss of federal and provincial citizenship

Aug. 26, Death of Field Marshal Conrad von Hoetzendorff

Sept. 3, Commercial Agreement with Yugoslavia signed

Sept. 4, Report of economic experts (Layton and Rist) on Austria submitted to the League of Nations

Sept. 10, Decision of League of Nations to relinquish control of Austrian finances by July, 1926

——, Three hour strike of 10,000 federal employees in Vienna for salary increases

Sept. 16, Death of Leo Fall, composer

Oct. 3, Customs Convention with Germany signed

Sept. 22, Strike of 4,000 metal workers Donauwitz factory

Oct. 14, Resolution of Parliament accepted conditions of League of Nations for ending financial control

Oct. 19, Commercial Treaty with China signed

Oct. 21, Death of Heinrich Angeli, Artist (85)

Oct. 27, Death of Wilhelm Gericke, musical conductor

Nov. 3–6, Strike of 7,000 Vienna bakers for increase in wages settled by agreement to accept award which gave 5%

Nov. 18, Reduction in municipal taxes in Vienna, theater tickers from 40% to 10%, hotel rooms from 60% to less than 20%

Dec. 9, Resolution of the Council of the League of Nations as to termination of financial control held Austrian budget to be permanently balanced and the remainder of loan transferred to Austrian Government

1926

Jan. 1, Modified control of Austrian finances by League of Nations came into effect

Jan. 6, Ramek Cabinet resigned

Jan. 6, Commercial Treaty with Switzerland signed

Jan. 8, Social Insurance Agreement with Germany signed

Jan. 15, Ramek Cabinet reorganized, Dr. Leopold Weber becoming Vice-Chancellor and Minister of Justice

Feb. 6, Agreement with Norway signed modified Commercial Agreement of Dec., 1924

March 5, Arbitration and conciliation Treaty with Czechoslovakia signed

March 22, Additional Protocol to Treaty of commerce with Italy of April, 1923, signed

April 6, Death of Franz Klein, jurist

April 9, Supplementary Commercial Agreement with Hungary signed

April 16, Arbitration Convention with Poland signed

May 18, Customs Convention with Switzerland signed

May 28, Arbitration Convention with Sweden signed

June 3, Customs Agreement with the Netherlands signed

June 12, Financial Convention with Czechoslovakia signed

June 18, Resignation of Dr. Schneider, Minister of Education, in issue as to removal of religious education from the schools

June 30, Control of Austrian finances by League of Nations ended

Aug. 4, Customs Agreement with the Netherlands concluded

Sept. 24, Death of Dr. Paul Kammerer, biologist

Oct. 15, Ramek Cabinet resigned because of bank scandals, the collapse of the Zentralbank deutscher Sparkassen, and Austrian Post Office Savings Bank which had to be reorganized by the Government to make good losses incurred by speculation

Oct. 20, New Coalition Cabinet headed by Dr. Ignaz Seipel, with Dr. Victor Kienböck, Minister of Finance; Vice-Chancellor, Dr. Franz Dinghofer; Education, Dr. Richard Schmitz; Social Welfare, Dr. Joseph Resch; Commerce and Communications, Dr. Hans Schuerff; Agriculture, Andreas Thaler

Dec. 26, Ordinance as to salaried employees under labor law

——, Sick Funds (Organization) Act passed

Dec. 28, Act created Post Office Savings Bank

1927

Jan. 30, Clash of Fascists and Republican Defense League in Burgenland, 2 Social Democrats killed

Feb. 5, Two legal Conventions with Germany signed

Feb. 15, Air Convention with Czechoslovakia signed

Feb. 22, Unemployment Insurance Act amended replaced that of March, 1920

April 1, Workers' Insurance Act enacted

April 19, Customs Agreement with Switzerland signed

April 24, General elections gave the Government (anti-Socialist Coalition) 94 seats against Socialist 71

May 19, Chancellor Seipel in address opening Parliament spoke in favor of union of Austria with Germany

May 23, Land League declared for economic union with Germany

June 8, Customs Agreement with Yugoslavia signed

July 14, Acquittal of 3 Fascists of murder of 2 Social Democrats in clash in preceding January in Burgenland led to Socialist riots in Vienna

July 15, General strike called by Socialists. Riots in Vienna in which the Palace of Justice was burned. Police fired on crowd 57 civilians killed and 6 policemen

July 16–17, Troops restored order in Vienna, martial law proclaimed

July 26, Association of Property Owners voted to join German association

July 29, Ordinance of the Municipal Council provided for permanent establishment of armed municipal police formed during riots of July 15–19

Aug. 8, Commercial Treaty with Finland signed

Aug. 18, Armed municipal police disbanded on demand of the Liquidation Commission as contravening Treaty of St. Germain

Sept. 19, Agreement with Great Britain signed provided for settlement of War debt

Oct. 27, Protocol signed with Conference of Ambassadors as to air régime

Nov. 19, Agreement with Rumania signed as to War debt

Nov. 26, Attempt of unemployed youth to assassinate Dr. Karl Seitz, Socialist mayor of Vienna

Dec. 2, Frau Olga Rudel-Zeynek took office as president of the Upper House

Dec. 2, Decision of Conference of Ambassadors that Liquidation Commission should cease Jan. 31, 1928

Dec. 17, Act regarding old age pensions for aged domestic servants out of employment passed

1928

Jan. 17, Additional Agreement as to debt signed with Rumania

Jan. 31, Allied Liquidation Commission withdrawn

Feb. 23, Speech of Chancellor Seipel on the forced Italianization of the Germans in South Tirol (Upper Adige) Resolution adopted expressing sympathy for the German minority in Italy

March 23, Clash at Feldkirch between Fascists (Heimwehr) and Socialist Defense League

April 6, Commercial Convention for Iceland signed with Denmark

April 26, Bela Kun arrested in Vienna charged with entrance to country on false passport

May 16, Commercial Agreement with France signed

May 24, Rioting at Innsbruck, Italian consulate attacked

June 11, Arbitration and Conciliation Convention with Spain signed

June 14, Additional Commercial Convention with Hungary signed

June 17, Provisional Commercial Convention with Persia signed

June 19, Treaty of friendship, commerce, and consular rights with the United States signed

June 26, Bela Kun sentenced to 3 months imprisonment in Vienna for conspiracy against the State

July 9, Supplementary Commercial Convention with Yugoslavia signed

July 18, Accident and invalidity insurance extended to agricultural labor and foresters

Aug. 16, Arbitration and Conciliation Treaties with Austria signed

Sept. 19–Oct. 19, Unsuccessful strike of dockers

Oct. 5, Commercial Convention with Lithuania signed

Oct. 7, Government troops prevented conflict of Socialists and Heimwehr (Fascists) at Wiener Neustadt where rival parades planned

Nov. 11, Anti-Jewish demonstration by students at University of Vienna

Nov. 12, Pan-German Manifesto endorsing union with Germany signed by leading Austrians

Dec. 2–8, "Passive resistance" strike of postal, telegraph, and telephone officials

Dec. 5, Wilhelm Miklas elected second President of the Republic by Parliament. Took office Dec. 10

Dec. 11, Treaty of Commerce with Estonia signed

1929

Feb. 3, Conflict of Socialists and Fascists at Gloggnitz near Vienna. Police intervened

Feb. 14, Government raid on Socialist headquarters at Vienna. Police seized rifles, machine gun parts, and ammunition

Feb. 24, Parade of 6,000 Fascists in Vienna and counter parade of 18,000 Socialists in different districts

March 9, Accident Insurance Act consolidating all laws since 1894 promulgated

March 24, Fascist and Socialist workmen in clash in Vienna

April 3, Resignation of Chancellor Seipel

April 30, Dr. Ernst Streeruwitz appointed Chancellor and Minister of Foreign Affairs, Karl Vaugoin, Minister of War

May 14, Heimwehr (Fascists) and Socialists marched in parades in Vienna, 10,000 police kept order

July 18, Accident Insurance Act amended and Industrial Court Act

Aug. 18, Fascists and Socialists in clash, 1 person killed and 62 wounded

Sept. 25, Resignation of Dr. Streeruwitz, Chancellor

Sept. 26, Johann Schober, president of the Vienna police, appointed Chancellor asked to take office by a coalition of Pan-German, Agrarian, and Christian Socialists to maintain order between Fascists and Socialists

Sept. 29, Parade of 28,000 Fascists around Vienna

Dec. 7, Constitutional Reform Bill passed Chamber and became law Dec. 10

Dec. 31, Aviation Treaty with the Netherlands

1930

Jan. 18, Agreement signed with Belgium as to sections as to debts, property, &c., of the Treaty of St. Germain

Jan. 20, Agreement with Poland signed as to pre-War debts

Feb. 6, Treaty of friendship and arbitration with Italy signed for 10 years

April 1, March of Heimwehr (Fascists) and counter parade of Socialists in Triesting Valley. Police intervention necessary

April 2, "Anti-Terrorist" Bill passed limiting powers of Socialist trade unions

April 4, Heimwehr parade near Vienna at St. Pölten

April 12, Commercial Treaty with Germany signed

April 14, Republican Defense Corps parade of about 40,000 members in counter-demonstration against Fascists

May 25, Death of Archduke Rainer Karl

June 13, Disarmament Bill passed by vote of 82 to 76 defeating Fascists

June 14, Major Waldemar Pabst (German) working for Fascists in Austria under name of Peters arrested near Vienna and deported by aëroplane the following day

——, Treaty of Commerce with Hungary signed

June 16, Resignation of Michael Hainisch as protest against Commercial Treaty with Hungary

June 17, Arms Licensing Bill aimed at the "private

armies" of the Heimwehr and Defense Corps passed third reading. Transferred the private possession of arms and munitions to the federal authorities and increased penalties for violation of the arms laws

June 26, Treaty of friendship, arbitration, and conciliation with Greece signed

July 14, Bank for International Settlement made trustee of foreign loan of $100,000,000

Aug. 4, "Civil war rehearsal" by Heimwehr at St. Pölten near Vienna

Aug. 16, Commercial Treaty with Japan signed

Sept. 4, Prince Ernst Rüdiger von Starhemberg became commander of the Heimwehr

Sept. 25, Chancellor Schober and his non-partisan Cabinet overthrown because of friction over the appointment of Dr. Strafella, a Fascist, as managing director of the State railways

Sept. 30, Karl Vaugoin (Christian Socialist), Vice-Chancellor and Minister of Defense in former Cabinet became Chancellor, Ignaz Seipel becoming Minister of Foreign Affairs, Prince Ernst Rüdiger von Starhemberg, Minister of the Interior

Oct. 1, Arbitration and conciliation Treaty with Norway signed

Nov. 4, Government search of Socialist clubs, houses and seized 20 machine guns and much ammunition

Nov. 9, Election for Parliament gave Social Democrats, 72 seats; Christian Socialists, 66; Economic Party, 19; Fascists, 8; a defeat for the reactionary Clerical Party and the Fascists

Nov. 29, The Vagouin minority Cabinet resigned

Dec. 3, Dr. Otto Ender (Christian Socialist) appointed Prime Minister with Johann Schober as Vice-Chancellor and Minister of Foreign Affairs. Herr Vagouin remained as Minister of War; Dr. Hans Schurff, Justice; Dr. Engelbert Dollfuss, Agriculture and Forestry; Dr. Otto Juch, Finance; Dr. Eduard Heindl, Commerce and Communications; Dr. Emmerich Czermak, Education; Franz Winkler, Interior

Dec. 31, Public debt of the Republic in schillings: Pre-War, 271,282,534; War, 281,969; incurred by the Republic, 1,715,749,810

AUSTRIA-HUNGARY

Austria-Hungary, Empire in central and eastern Europe, established by Constitution of Feb. 26, 1861, dissolved after World War in 1918, and territories partitioned between Austria, Hungary, Czechoslovakia, Poland, Hungary, Rumania, and Yugoslavia. The total area of the Dual Monarchy was 261,259 square miles divided as follows; Austria, 115,882 square miles; Hungary, 125,609 square miles; Bosnia and Herzegovina added Oct., 1908, 19,768 square miles. The total population according to the Census of Dec. 31, 1910 was 51,604,464, of which 28,818,928 was in Austria, and 20,886,487 in Hungary, and 1,898,044 in Bosnia and Herzegovina. Vienna was the capital. On Nov. 11, 1918 the Emperor renounced all part in the government of Austria though not his crown, but abdicated as Emperor of Austria Nov. 12, and on Nov. 13 withdrew from public affairs in Hungary. The last Emperor was Charles I, Emperor of Austria and King of Hungary, succeeding on death of Francis Joseph I on Nov. 21, 1916. He died in exile April 1, 1922.

1246–1804

June 15, 1246, Frederic II, the last male of the house of Bamberg, killed in battle with the Hungarians

1247, Disputed succession: the Emperor Frederic II sequestered the provinces, appointing Otto, Count of Eberstein, Governor in the name of the Emperor; they are seized by Ladislaus, Margrave of Moravia, in right of his wife, Frederic's niece, Gertrude: he died childless

1250, Herman, Margrave of Baden, marries Gertrude, and holds the provinces till his death

1254, Premislas Ottocar, of Bohemia, acquires the provinces

1260, Compelled to cede Styria to Hungary, he makes war and recovers it, in consequence of a great victory he inherits Carinthia, 1263; refuses to become Emperor of Germany, 1272; and to render homage to Rodolph of Habsburg, elected Emperor 1273

1274, War against Ottocar as a rebel: he is compelled to cede Austria, Carinthia, and Styria to Rodolph

Aug. 26, 1278, The war renewed: Ottocar perishes in the battle of Marchfeld

Dec. 27, 1282, The Emperor Rodolph establishes the Duchy of Austria, &c.

May 1, 1308, Albert I assassinated by his nephew while attempting to enslave the Swiss

1307–09, Successful revolt of the Swiss

Nov. 15, 1315, They totally defeat the Austrians under Duke Leopold, at Morgarten

1363, The Tirol acquired

July 9, 1386, The Duke Leopold imposes a toll on the Swiss; which they resist with violence: he makes war on them, and is defeated and slain at Sempach

1437, Duke Albert V obtains Bohemia and Hungary, and is elected Emperor of Germany

Jan. 6, 1453, The Emperor Frederic III, as head of the house of Habsburg, creates the Archduchy of Austria with sovereign power

1457, Austria divided between him and his relatives; war ensues between them till 1463

1477, The Low Countries accrue to Austria by the marriage of Maximilian with Mary, the heiress of Burgundy

1496, Also Spain, by the marriage of Philip I of Austria, with the heiress of Arragon and Castile

1526, Bohemia and Hungary united to Austria under Ferdinand I

1529–45, Austria harassed by Turkish invasions

1556, Charles V, reigning over Germany, Austria, Bohemia, Hungary, Spain, the Netherlands, and their dependencies (*see* Spain) abdicates

1618–48, The destructive Thirty Years' War

1701–13, War of Spanish Succession

Jan. 3, 1708, Mantua ceded to the Emperor

April 11, 1713, By Treaty of Utrecht he obtains part of the Duchy of Milan

1714, By Treaty of Rastadt he acquires the Netherlands

Nov. 15, 1715, Naples, &c., added to his dominions

1718, Further additions on the east (Temeswar, &c.) by the Peace of Passarowitz

1735, Naples and Sicily given up to Spain

Oct. 20, 1740, Death of Charles VI, the last sovereign of the male line of the house of Habsburg; his daughter, Maria Theresa, becomes Queen of Hungary

1740-42; 1744-45, Silesian wars

1741, Maria Theresa is attacked by Prussia, France, Bavaria, and Saxony; but supported by Great Britain

1745, Francis, Duke of Lorraine, who had married Maria Theresa in 1736, elected Emperor

Oct. 18, 1748, Peace of Aix-la-Chapelle: Parma, Milan, &c., ceded to Spain

1745-63, Seven Years' War; Silesia ceded to Prussia

1772, Galicia, &c., acquired from Poland

1792-97, War with France

Oct. 17, 1797, By the Treaty of Campo Formio, the Emperor gives up Lombardy and obtains Venice

Feb. 1, 1801, Treaty of Luneville (more losses)

Aug. 11, 1804, Francis II, Emperor of Germany, becomes Francis I of Austria: declared hereditary Emperor of Austria

1805

Aug. 5, His declaration against France

Oct. 20, Capitulation of his army at Ulm

Nov. 14, War: Napoleon enters Vienna

Dec. 2, Austrians and Russians defeated at Austerlitz

1806

Jan. 1, By Treaty of Presburg, Austria loses Venice and the Tirol

Jan. 12, Vienna evacuated by the French

Aug. 6, Dissolution of the Germanic Confederation, and formal abdication of the Emperor

1809

May 13, The French again take Vienna

Oct. 14, But restore it at the peace

1810-1838

April 1, Napoleon marries the Archduchess Maria Louisa, the daughter of the Emperor

Oct. 2, 1814, Congress at Vienna

Feb. 25, 1815, Treaty of Vienna
[Italian provinces restored with additions—Lombardo-Venetian kingdom established, April 7.]

March 2, 1835, Francis I dies; Ferdinand I succeeds

July 3, 1838, New treaty of commerce with England

1848

March 13, Insurrection at Vienna; flight of Metternich

March 18, Insurrection in Italy

May 15-17, Another insurrection at Vienna; the Emperor flees to Innsbruck

May 29, Archduke John appointed Vicar-General of the Empire

Sept. 11, Revolution in Hungary, *see* Hungary

Oct. 6, Insurrection of Vienna; murder of Count Latour

Dec. 2, The Emperor abdicates in favor of his nephew, Francis Joseph

1851-1856

Dec. 31, The Emperor revokes the constitution of March 4, 1849

April 4, 1852, Death of Prince Schwartzenburg, Prime Minister

Feb. 18, 1853, Attempted assassination of the Emperor by Libenyi; who was executed Feb. 28

Aug., 1854, Austrians enter Danubian principalities

Dec. 2, 1854, Alliance with England and France relative to eastern question

June 24, 1855, Great reduction of the army

Aug. 18, 1855, By a Concordat the Pope acquires great power in the Empire

July 12, 1856, Amnesty for political offenders of 1848-49

1857-1858

Feb. 10, Austria remonstrates against the attacks of the free Sardinian press

Feb. 20, Firm reply of Count Cavour

March, Austrians quit the Danube principalities

March 23-30, Diplomatic relations between Austria and Sardinia broken off in consequence

May, Emperor and Empress visit Hungary

Jan. 5, 1858, Death of Marshal Radetzky (aged 92)

1859

Jan. 1, Excitement throughout Europe, caused by the address of the Emperor Napoleon III to the Austrian Ambassador

Jan. 30, Prince Napoleon Bonaparte marries Princess Clotilde of Sardinia

Feb. & March, Austria prepares for war; enlarges her armies in Italy; and strongly fortifies the banks of the Ticino, the boundary of her Italian provinces, and Sardinia

Feb. 27, Lord Cowley at Vienna on a "mission of peace"

March & April, Intervention of Russia—proposal for a congress; disputes respecting the admission of Sardinia—Sardinia and France prepare for war

April 23, Austria demands the disarmament of Sardinia and the dismissal of the volunteers from other states within three days

April 26, This demand rejected

———, The Austrians cross the Ticino

April 27, The French troops enter Piedmont

May 3, The French Emperor declares war (to expel the Austrians from Italy)

May 13-18, Resignation of Count Buol, Foreign Minister; appointment of Count Rechberg

May 20, The Austrians defeated at Montebello; at Palestro, May 30-31; at Magenta, June 4; at Malegnano (Marignano), June 8

June 11, Prince Metternich dies, aged 86 (he had been actively engaged in the wars and negotiations of Napoleon I)

June 24, Austrians defeated at Solferino (near the Mincio); the Emperors of Austria and France and King of Sardinia present

July 6, Armistice agreed upon; the Emperors meet, July 11; the preliminaries of peace signed at Villa Franca (Lombardy given up to Sardinia, and an Italian confederation proposed to be formed), July 12

July 12, Manifesto justifying the peace issued to the army; to the people July 15

Aug. 8 to Sept., Conference between the envoys of Austria and France at Zurich

Nov. 10, Treaty of Zurich, confirming the preliminaries of Villa Franca, signed

1860

Jan. 6, 10, Feb. 18, Decrees removing Jewish disabilities

March 5, Patent issued for the summoning the great imperial council (Reichsrath), composed of representatives elected by the provincial diets

March, Discovery of great corruptions in the army financial arrangements, a deficiency of about 1,700,000*l*. discovered; General Eynatten commits suicide; 82 persons arrested

———, Austria protests against the annexation of Tuscany, &c., by Sardinia

April 20, Baron Brück, suspected of complicity in the army frauds, dismissed; commits suicide April 23

May 30, The Reichsrath assembles; addressed by the Emperor June 1

July 26, Friendly meeting of the Emperor and the Regent of Prussia at Töplitz

Aug. & Sept., Free debates in the Reichsrath; strictures on the concordat, the finances, &c.; proposals for separate constitutions for the provinces

Sept. 29, The Reichsrath adjourned

Oct 20, Diploma conferring on the Reichsrath legislative powers, the control of the finances, &c., a manifesto issued to the populations of the Empire (not well received)

Oct. 20–26, Meeting of the Emperor with the Emperor of Russia and Prince Regent of Prussia at Warsaw: no important result

Oct. & Nov., The Government professes non-intervention in Italy, but increases the army in Venetia

Dec., Sale of Venetia, publicly spoken of, is repudiated

Dec. 13, Ministerial crisis: M. Schmerling becomes Minister—more political concessions

    The proscribed Hungarian, Count Teleki, at Dresden, is given up to Austria, which causes general indignation, about Dec. 20; he is released on parole, Dec. 31

1861

Jan. & Feb., Reactionary policy of the court leads to increased general disaffection

Feb. 26, The statutes of the new constitution for the Austrian Monarchy published

April 8, Civil and political rights granted to Protestants, throughout the Empire except in Hungary and Venice

April 29, Meeting of Reichsrath—no deputies present from Hungary, Croatia, Transylvania, Venetia, or Istria

1862

April 26, At an imperial council, the Emperor present, the principle of ministerial responsibility is resolved on

June, Deficiency of 1,400,000l. in financial statement—indignation of the Reichsrath

Dec., Reduction in the army assented to; and a personal liberty law (resembling habeas corpus act) passed

1863

April, Insurrection in Russian Poland, Jan.; Austria joins in the intercession of England and France

Aug. 16–31, Meeting of the German sovereigns (except Kings of Prussia, Holland, and Denmark) with the Emperor of Austria at Frankfort, by his invitation; the draft of a reform of the federal constitution agreed to

1864

Jan., Austria joins Prussia in war with Denmark (see Denmark)

Feb. 29, Galicia and Cracow declared to be in a state of siege

April 10, The Archduke Maximilian becomes Emperor of Mexico (see Mexico)

June 22, The Emperor and the King of Prussia meet at Carlsbad

Oct. 30, Peace with Denmark, signed at Vienna

Nov. 14, Emperor opens Reichsrath; great freedom of debate; the state of siege in Galicia censured, Dec.

Dec., Austria supports the Confederation in the dispute respecting the duchies

1865

Jan., Apparent reunion between Austria and Prussia

——, Great financial difficulty; proposed reduction in the army by the chambers

April, Contest between the Government and the chambers

June, Reported failure of Mr. Hutt's mission to Vienna, to promote free trade

Aug. 14, Convention of Gastein (see Prussia) signed

Sept. 21, Emperor's rescript suppressing the constitution, with the view of giving autonomy to Hungary (see s.v.)

Nov., Dec., Rejoicings in Hungary but dissatisfaction in Austria, Croatia, &c.

Dec. 16, Treaty of commerce with Great Britain signed

1866

Jan. 1, Amnesty for Italy issued

Jan., March, Warm disputes with Prussia (aggressive), respecting the settlement of Holstein

March, Preparations for war begin

May 6, The Archduke Albrecht made commander of the southern army; Benedek of the northern May 12

June 18, War declared by Prussia; by Italy (see s.v.) June 20

June 18, The Austrians enter Silesia; and the Prussians Bohemia June 24

June 24, The Italians defeated by the Archduke Albrecht, at Custozza

June 27–29, Prussian victories at Nachod, &c.

July 3, Benedek totally defeated at Königgrätz or Sadowa

    (For details of the war see Prussia and Italy.)

July 4, The Emperor cedes Venetia to the Emperor Napoleon, and requests intervention

July 26, Preliminaries of peace signed at Nikolsburg

Aug. 23, Treaty of peace between Austria and Prussia signed at Prague (by its articles Austria consented to the breaking up of the Germanic Confederation, and to Prussia's annexing Hanover, Hesse Cassel, Nassau, and Frankfort; and gave up Holstein, and her political influence in North Germany), and North Schleswig to Denmark if the people vote for it (the last not cårried out)

Oct. 3, Treaty of peace with Italy signed at Vienna, ceding Venetia. The iron crown given up Oct. 11

Oct. 11–19, The Quadrilateral and Venice surrendered to the Italians

Dec. 11, Commercial treaty with France (to commence Jan. 1, 1867), signed

Dec., Great dissension among the nationalities of the Empire

1867

Jan. 3, Extraordinary diet convoked (for Feb. 25)

Feb. 4, Establishment of autonomy for Hungary announced, mainly the work of Von Beust; resignation of Belcredi; Von Beust made president of the council Feb. 7

Feb. 17, Rescript restoring a separate ministry for Hungary, Count Andrassy president

Feb., Death of Archduke Stephen (Palatine of Hungary in 1848)

April 23, Commercial treaty with Italy signed

May & July, The Czechs (of Bohemia and Moravia), Croats, Slavonians, Serbs, Roumans (of Transylvania), and Russinians (of Galicia), protest against absorption, and demand national legislative powers

June 8, The Emperor and Empress crowned King and Queen of Hungary at Buda
July 27–Aug. 1, The Sultan visits Vienna
Aug. 18–23, The Emperors of Austria and France meet at Salzburg
Sept. 23, Arrangements for the dividing the financial affairs of Austria and Hungary signed
Oct. 22, Emperor of Austria and King of Prussia meet at Oos, near Baden-Baden
Oct. 23, Emperor arrives at Paris; leaves Nov. 5
Dec. 21, Dualism accepted by the Reichsrath at Vienna
Dec. 30, New Austrian ministry under Prince Auersperg constituted

1868

May 25, Civil marriage law enacted
Oct. 11, Von Beust justifies the maintenance of an army of 800,000; is made a count Dec.

1869

Feb. 20, The frigate *Radetsky* blown up, about 340 lives lost
Oct. 7, The Crown Prince of Prussia visits Vienna
Nov. 10, The Emperor visits the East;—at Jerusalem; present at the opening of the Suez Canal Nov. 16
Nov., Successful insurrection against the conscription in Dalmatia, Oct.; ceased

1870

Jan., Ministerial crisis: the Cis-Leithan ministry resigns; Count Potocki, Prime Minister April 4
July 18, Neutrality in the Franco-Prussian War announced
July 30, The Concordat with Rome declared to be suspended in consequence of the promulgation of the doctrine of papal infallibility
Sept. 29, Oct., Dissension between the federal and national parties
Nov., The Ministry support Great Britain in opposing the Russian repudiation of the Treaty of Paris (*see* Russia)

1871

Jan., The new German Empire recognized by the Emperor
Feb., Dismissal of Potocki; Count Hohenwart, Minister
April 7, Death of Admiral Tegethoff
July 26, First meeting of "Old Catholics" at Vienna
Sept. 6–8, Meeting of Emperor with Emperor William
Sept. 14, Meeting of 17 provincial diets; struggle between the (Slavonian) conservatives and the (German) constitutionalists renewed
Oct. 25, Political crisis: dissension between German and Slavonian parties, Oct.; resignation of the Hohenwart Ministry
Nov. 4, A ministry formed under Baron Kellersperg
Nov. 6, Resignation of Count Beust, the Arch-Chancellor; much excitement
Nov. 13–14, Count Andrassy (*see* Hungary, 1849, *et seq.*), having opposed Von Beust's policy of alliance with France, succeeds him as Minister of the Imperial Household and of Foreign Affairs; Von Beust to be Ambassador at London; Lonyay, Premier of Hungarian Ministry
About Nov. 25, New Austrian Ministry formed by Prince Auersperg

1872

March 13, New constitutional law promulgated, giving the Emperor power to order new elections of the chambers
Sept. 6–12, Meeting of the Emperor with the Emperor of Germany and other sovereigns at Berlin

1873

March 10, Reform bill passed changing the Reichsrath into a national representative assembly
May 1, Great international exhibition at Vienna; opening
    Visits to Vienna; the Prince of Wales, April 28; the Czar of Russia, June 1; the Shah of Persia, July 30; the King of Italy, Sept. 17; the Emperor of Germany, Oct. 17

1874

Feb. 13, The Emperor at St. Petersburg
March 7, Encyclical letter from the Pope condemning the new ecclesiastical laws
April, Protest of the Austrian bishops; adoption by both parties of Cavour's cry, "A free church in a free state"

1875

Feb. 27, Ofenheim, railway financier connected with Messrs. Brassey, after long trial for fraud, acquitted at Vienna
April 5, The Emperor warmly received at Venice by the King of Italy
May 30, Inauguration of the new bed of the Danube by the Emperor
June 28, The Czar meets the Emperor at Eger
June 20, Death of the ex-Emperor Ferdinand
Nov. 24, Death of Cardinal Rauscher, Prince Bishop of Vienna

1876–1877

July 8, The Czar and the Emperor meet at Reichstadt; agree to neutrality in the Serbo-Turkish War
Dec. 5, New treaty of commerce with Great Britain signed
June 26, 1877, Declaration of neutrality in Russo-Turkish War by Austrian and Hungarian Ministers; foreign policy to be for "the interest of the Monarchy, to the exclusion of all antipathies and sympathies," M. de Tisza (Hungarian)

1878–1880

Feb. 19, Prince Auersperg announces disagreement with the proposed Russian conditions of peace
March 8, Death of Archduke Francis Charles, the Emperor's father
June 13–July 13, Count Andrassy at the Berlin Conference
July 13, Austria to occupy and administer Bosnia and Herzegovina, by Treaty of Berlin
July 29, The Austrians enter, and war ensues
Oct., Bosnia occupied (except Novi Bazar)
Sept. 21–24, 1879, Bismarck's visit to Vienna; warmly received
June 8, 1880, Opening of all the diets of the Empire

1881

May 10, Marriage of the Archduke Rodolph and the Princess Stephanie of Belgium
Oct. 10, Sudden death of Baron Haymerle

Oct. 28–31, The King and Queen of Italy warmly received at Vienna
About Dec. 27, Temporary rupture with Rumania respecting the Danube

1882

Insurrection in Herzegovina, &c.; several small engagements with Austrians, Jan. 16–31; insurgents defeated
About Feb. 9, Provisional government said to have been formed by insurgents
Feb. 16 *et seq.*, Alleged defeat of insurgents at Glavalicevo and in other small engagements
Feb. 25, Severe conflict at Cettinje; alleged great loss by Austrians; small loss by insurgents
Feb., Mohammedans sympathize with Christian insurgents
March 14, Successful advance of the Austrians; capture of Dragali announced
About May 12, Insurgents adopting guerilla warfare
Oct. 26, Insurrection suppressed, announced
Dec. 20, Execution of Overdank, a soldier, for attempted assassination of Emperor
Dec. 27, 600th anniversary of the establishment of the house of Habsburg celebrated throughout the Empire

1883

Aug.–Sept., Slavonic agitation against Germans and the Magyars and taxation, *see* Croatia; conciliatory policy adopted by the government, Sept.

1884

Jan., Much social disaffection at Vienna; two detective policemen assassinated, Hlubek, Bloch
Jan. 25, Corporal Hermann Stellmacher, assassin of Bloch, captured; a great conspiracy suspected; law decreed by Count Taaffe repressing public meetings, the press, trials by jury, &c., Jan. 30; many arrested or expelled
Feb. 9, Another policeman murdered
Feb. 15, Government measures adopted by the chambers
About March 15, 700 expelled at Vienna
Aug. 8, Stellmacher executed
Oct. 3, Hans Makart, historical painter, died
Dec., Heavy bank frauds; suicide of culprits

1885

Jan. 5, Prince Adolph Auersperg, statesman, died
April 30, Imperial assent given to the reform act of the upper house
Aug. 25–26, Cordial meeting of the Emperor and the Czar at Kremsier in Moravia

1886

About June 2, Political crisis relating to duties on Russian petroleum, end of May, settled
Oct. 24, Death of Count F. von Beust, great liberal statesman, ex-Chancellor

1887

Feb. 26, Increased army estimates voted
March 13, Treaty of alliance with Germany and Italy signed
March 28, Anarchists sentenced to imprisonment for dynamite plot
Sept., Successful military manœuvers in Transylvania

Dec. 16–17, Panic at the Bourse at Vienna, through article in the *Invalide Russe* (*see* Russia)
Dec. 19, Money granted for war preparations

1888

Defensive treaty with Germany against Russian or other aggression, Oct. 7, 1879; Feb. 3, first published
Oct. 3, Visit of the German Emperor William II, at Vienna

1889

Jan. 30, Suicide of the Archduke Rodolph, heir to the throne
April 29, Catholic congress of nobles and clergy met at Vienna
May 20, Death of Count Alfred Potocki, statesman, aged 72, about
Aug. 12–15, The Emperor and his nephew visit Berlin

1890

Jan. 17–19, Temporary reconciliation of the Czechs and Germans in Bohemia in a conference, by the intervention of the Emperor
Feb., Formation of the Anglo-Austrian printing and publishing company in Vienna (Lord Mayor Isaacs and others, directors)
Feb. 18, Count Julius Andrassy dies in Istria
March 12, Thirty-two persons out of 62 charged, convicted of criminal practices in Galicia connected with emigration; four months' trial; sentence, 4½ years and other terms of imprisonment
April 23, Riot of about 1,000 workmen at Biala on the Galician frontier, suppressed by military; 3 men killed and about 14 died of wounds
April, Labor agitation, strikes with rioting in different provinces, gradually subsides May
July 31, Marriage of the Emperor's youngest daughter, Archduchess Marie Valérie, to her cousin, the Archduke Francis Salvator
Aug. 10, Edward von Bauernfeld, poet and dramatist, dies, aged 88
Aug. 11, Austrian fleet under Archduke Stephen, reviewed by Queen Victoria off Cowes, Isle of Wight
Sept. 17–20, Cordial meeting of the Austrian and German Emperors at Rhonstock in Silesia, at Vienna Oct. 1–8
Oct., The Archduke John of the Tuscan branch, who resigned his dignities and took the name of Johann Orth, Oct., 1889, became captain of a merchant ship, the *St. Margaret*, supposed to have been lost off the coast of S. America Aug., reported
Nov. 30, The compromise between the Germans and the Czechs in Bohemia not effected, through the opposition of the Young Czechs; *see* Bohemia

1891

Feb., The Archduke Franz Ferdinand d'Este, heir to the Emperor, warmly received at St. Petersburg; at Moscow Feb. 14
June 28, The Triple Alliance renewed
Dec. 6, New treaty of commerce between Austria-Hungary and Germany, signed at Vienna

1892

Jan. 25, New commercial treaty with Germany, Italy, and Belgium adopted by the lower house, Jan. 19, by the senate
March, Conference of Austrian bishops at Vienna

May 27, Currency reform bill passed

Dec. 14, Tour of the Archduke Franz Ferdinand, the heir-presumptive, starts; visits Ceylon, Jan. 5; Bombay, Jan. 17; Hyderabad, Jan. 24; Calcutta, Feb. 1; Sydney, May 16; Hongkong, July; Yokohama, Aug. 2

1893

Jan. 1, The new Bourse tax passed, Sept. 18, 1892; comes into operation

March 13, Meeting of Christian Socialists, many eminent persons, at Vienna

June 12, Strike of 5,000 miners at Kladno reported

Nov. 11, Resignation of Premier Taafe; succeeded by Prince Alfred Windischgrätz

1894

Jan. 15, The *Omladina*, a political society, active in 1893, trial began; many sentenced to various terms of imprisonment for treason and other serious offenses, Feb. 21

Feb. 19–23, Trial of anarchists (14); 8 sentenced to various terms of imprisonment, 6 acquitted

March 20, Ottokar, Dolezal, Franz Dragoum, and Joseph Kriz, members of the *Omladina*, charged with the murder of Mrva, an official at Prague, Dec. 23, 1893; sentenced to ten years' penal servitude

March 29, Meeting of the Austrian and German Emperors at Abbazia

July 6, Commercial treaty between Austria-Hungary and Russia, ratified

1895

Feb. 18, Death of the Archduke Albrecht; eminent in the army, liberal and popular; born, 1817, son of Archduke Charles

March 1, Death of Prince Richard Metternich, diplomatist

March 13, 26 students tried at Tarnopol, Galicia, for high treason, and conspiring for the independence of Poland, March 4; all acquitted

June 19, Resignation of Ministry. Count Badeni succeeded Oct. 2

Sept., Death of the Archduke Ladislaus by an accident while hunting

Anti-Semitic movement; 1895–96

Nov. 9, Financial crisis at Vienna and Budapest in relation to Turkey

Nov. 29, Death of Count Taaffe, ex-Premier, aged 63

1896

March 13, The Emperor and Empress received by Queen Victoria at Nice

April 14, Visit of the German Emperor and Empress at Vienna

May 19, Death of the Archduke Karl Ludwig, heir-presumptive

May 28, Electoral reform bill passed by the Reichsrath, and adopted by the peers

June 29, German Progressist Party founded

July 19, Differences between Austria and Hungary settled by compromise at a meeting of the Ministers in Vienna

Nov. 5, The Archduchess Maria Dorothea niece of the Emperor married to the Duke of Orleans at Vienna

1897

March 21, The railway laborers' association dissolved by government order

April 22, Grand military review by the Emperors Francis Joseph and William II

April 27–30, The Emperor arrives at St. Petersburg, received by the Czar

Aug. 29, Agrarian association founded at Vienna

Sept. 25, Duel between Count Badeni the Premier and Herr Wolf in consequence of insulting language used by the latter, the Count wounded

Nearly 24 hrs. debate in the Reichsrath on the renewal of the *Ausgleich* with Hungary; 12 hrs. speech by Dr. Lecher, Oct. 28–29; long sitting, bill read 1st time, amidst great disorder, Nov. 5; violent scenes, Socialists expelled by the police, Nov. 24–26; Reichsrath prorogued, Nov. 27; Count Badeni resigns, Nov. 28; Baron Gautsch forms a new Ministry, Nov. 30; deadlock, Dec. 12; the Reichsrath closed by decree, Dec. 29

1898

Feb. 13, Count Kalnoky, born, Dec. 29, 1832, Foreign Minister from 1881–95; died

Feb. 27, Political agitation, large meetings in Styria and Bohemia

March 5, Baron Gautsch resigns; new Cabinet formed by Count Thun, March 7

March 7, Prince Ferdinand received by the Emperor at Vienna

March 31, Increase of the navy determined on; 30,000,-000*fl.* demanded for fortifications, May

April 20, Bills for the renewal of the *Ausgleich* with Hungary introduced

May 8, Jubilee of the Emperor's reign celebrated, exhibition opened

June 1 *et seq.*, Reichsrath reassembled (deadlock); prorogued, June 13

June 24–28, Anti-Semitic outrages, &c., in W. Galicia, houses plundered in 30 villages, troops called out, outbreak spreading; martial law and other strong measures adopted with good effect, June 29

Sept. 10, Assassination of the Empress Elizabeth (born Dec. 27, 1837) at Geneva by Luigi Luccheni (aged 25), an Italian anarchist, about 2 P.M.

Nov. 10, Luccheni sentenced to life imprisonment

Nov. 21, Increasing agrarian revolt against clerical interference in secular affairs; *see* Hungary

Nov. 29, Count Thun protests against the expulsion of Austrians from Prussia

Dec. 31, The Austro-Hungarian *Ausgleich* renewed for 1899 by imperial rescript

1899

Jan. 17, Crisis of disorderly scenes in the Reichsrath, Dec. 15 *et seq.*

Jan. 27, Violent scene in the Reichsrath

Feb. 1, Reichsrath prorogued

Feb. 6, Mass meetings of social democrats in Vienna; manifesto against the Germans by the young Czechs, issued Feb. 11

Feb. 25, Count Rechberg, diplomatist, born 1806, died

April 12, Conference of Roman Catholic bishops of Vienna, at Austria, on the "emancipation from Rome" movement; repressive measures; 4 societies dissolved in Vienna; reported

April 26, Count Karl Hohenwart, ex-Premier, federalist, died aged 75

May 24, Negotiations respecting the Austro-Hungarian *Ausgleich;* a bill passed 2nd reading, July 4

June 3, Johann Strauss, "Walzerkönig," popular composer, died, aged 73

June 29, Chevalier von Blumencorn (ex-soldier, musician, and diplomatist), editor of the *Fremdenblatt*, died, aged 95

July, Agitation against the government increasing, meetings violently suppressed

Sept. 23, Count Thun's Ministry promulgates the outstanding portions of the *Ausgleich*, and resigns; Count Clary forms a cabinet Oct. 1

Sept. 26–27, Prince Ferdinand of Bulgaria received with honors at Vienna

Oct. 7, Jewish meeting at Vienna to protest against the charge of ritual murder revived against their creed

Oct. 18, Reichsrath meets, Premier states neutral policy; stormy scene, sitting closed Oct. 24

Oct. 22–24, Fatal Czech riots in Moravia, German and Jewish houses looted, troops called out

Nov., Anti-Semitism and agitation against the use of German as the official language in the army, rioting in Bohemia and Moravia

Nov. 9–10, Disorder in the Reichsrath, provoked by the Czechs and Anti-Semites; crisis averted by the Emperor, Nov. 20–21

Dec. 1, The Austro-Hungarian delegates received by the Emperor with a speech from the throne; deadlock in the Reichsrath continues Dec. 19

Dec. 21, Count Clary's cabinet resigns; Dr. von Wittek forms a " provisional" ministry, Dec. 22

1900

Jan. 13, The Emperor intimates firmly to Dr. Stransky, a Czech leader, that the language of the army must remain German

Jan. 23, Coal-miners' strike, 91,000 men involved, commission of inquiry appointed, reported

Feb. 5, Nationality conference (Czechs and Germans) on the language question, Dr. von Körber, Premier, present; closed, sub-committee appointed, March 22

Feb. 22, Reichsrath meets, Dr. von Körber, Premier, declares the cabinet to be neutral

May 8, New language bills for Bohemia and Moravia introduced, noisy scene in the Reichsrath

June 9, Deadlock continues, session closed by the Emperor's order

Aug. 7, Sir Francis Plunkett appointed ambassador at Vienna

Sept. 7, Dissolution of the Reichsrath

Sept. 13, The Emperor attends the army manœuvers in Galicia, receives a Polish parliamentary deputation, threatens the suspension of the constitution if obstruction continues

Sept. 20, The Shah of Persia visits the Emperor

Nov. 14, Leopold Hilsner, a Jew (22), sentenced to death for complicity in the murder of a Christian girl, Oct., 1899; sentence quashed May, 1900; 2nd trial at Pisek, Bohemia, for another murder, Oct. 25; again found guilty and sentenced to death (ritual murder theory rejected)

1901

Jan. 3, Elections, defeat of Clericals and Anti-Semites, reported Jan. 15; the Reichsrath opened, Jan. 31

Feb. 4, The Emperor's speech from the throne, proposes industrial, economic, and social reforms, and earnestly protests against the strife of nationalities

April 23–24, Stormy debates in the Reichsrath on the action of the Archduke Franz Ferdinand assuming

the protectorate over the Catholic schools' association

May 5, Pan-Germanic union advocating emancipation from Rome meets in Vienna

June 1, Canal bill and government railway bill read 3rd time by the Reichsrath

June 12–18, The Emperor visits Prague

July 2, Dr. Lueger and the Anti-Semitic Party beaten at the polls in Lower Austria

Oct. 17, Reichsrath meets, the Premier protests against the nationality strife

Nov. 7, The Emperor interviews the King of Greece and Prince George of Crete

Nov. 19, Manifesto against obstruction issued by the Germans in the Reichsrath

1902

Feb. 7, Archduke Franz Ferdinand visits the Czar

March 18, Reichsrath: Pan-Germanic demonstration; uproar over the language question, April 9

April 10, Count von Bülow, German Imperial Chancellor, received by the Emperor

May 21, 22, and 26, Conference of Austrian and Hungarian premiers at Budapest on the *Ausgleich* and tariff questions; Vienna, July 10 and Aug. 22

June 28, The Triple Alliance renewed

Aug. 2, The King of Roumania visits Austria

Sept, Riots in Agram (*see* Croatia)

Nov. 11, 13, Violent scenes between Czechs and Germans

Dec. 31, Reichsrath meets. Renewal of *Ausgleich* for 10 years agreed to

1903

Feb. 16, Debt conversion bill passed

Aug. 31, King Edward VII visits Vienna

Sept. 3, Death of Count Deym, Austro-Hungarian Ambassador to Great Britain, from Oct. 8, 1888

Sept. 9, Inter-parliamentary conference at Vienna adopt resolution in favor of a new international congress to consider the disarmament schemes formulated by Russia in 1898

Sept. 26, Austro-Hungarian army bill virtually repealed by the adoption of a Polish amendment to a German urgency motion sanctioning the enrollment of the ordinary Austrian contingent of 54,024 recruits

Sept. 30, Czar visits the Emperor at Vienna; Imperial conference on Macedonian affairs, Oct. 2

Oct. 3, Battleship *Erzherzog Karl* launched at Trieste

Oct. 22, Austro-Russian instructions for the executions of the reforms in Macedonia presented to the Sultan; reform scheme accepted by the Porte, Nov. 25

1904

March 7, Count Khuen Hedervary, ex-Ban of Croatia, and ex-Premier of Hungary, takes the oath as Hungarian Minister resident in Vienna

March 8, Reichsrath meets: Dr. von Körber, Premier, states that 60 important imperial ordinances, and many bills, were awaiting the sanction of parliament as the consequence of the continued obstruction of parliamentary business

March 10, Grave riots at Prague and in Vienna between German and Slav students; University of Vienna closed by the authorities

March 22, Obstructive tactics resumed in the Reichsrath; violent scenes; Reichsrath adjourns without electing Austrian delegations; estimates for previous year neither discussed nor indemnity granted

March 23, Colonel von Grünzweig and Colonel von Törvek sentenced to 5 and 2 months close arrest respectively for breach of army regulations in connection with the death of soldiers from heat apoplexy during a forced march in the autumn

April 19, Prince and Princess of Wales arrive at Vienna on a visit to the Emperor

May 2, Emperor leaves Vienna for Budapest, is enthusiastically greeted by the people

May 10, Reichsrath again adjourned by government *sine die*, legislation being prevented by the continuous obstruction of the Czechs

June 1, Austrian delegation passes the extraordinary credits required by ministries of war and marine, 88,000,000 kronen (3,666,666*l*.) army; 77,000,000 kronen (3,208,333*l*.) for the navy

Aug. 11, Centenary of the promulgation of the pragmatic law, which created for the head of the house of Habsburg the title and dignity of Emperor of Austria

Aug. 16, Emperor visits King Edward VII at Marienbad

Sept. 12, Prince Ferdinand of Bulgaria arrives at Vienna, and is received by the Emperor

Sept. 22, Provisional agreement between Austria-Hungary and Italy signed after long negotiations covering the period from Oct. 15, 1904, to Dec. 31, 1905, when the new commercial treaty between the two nations, the draft of which is agreed upon, will come into operation

Oct. 26, Reconstruction of the cabinet, Dr. Mansuetus Kosel, Finance Minister, Count Ferdinand Buquoy, Minister of Agriculture

Nov. 3, Serious riot at Innsbruck between German and Italian law students at the celebration of inauguration of a new and separate law faculty for Italian students; troops called out, several lives lost

Dec. 5, Ultimatum presented to the Porte demanding the dismissal and punishment of Turkish officials at Scutari who had forcibly prevented the dispatch of the Austro-Hungarian mails; naval demonstration threatened in event of non-compliance

1905

Jan. 1, Baron Gautsch von Frankenthurn, Premier in succession to Dr. von Körber

——, Cardinal Pyzyna, Bishop of Cracow, who pronounced the Austrian veto against the election of Cardinal Rampolla, as Pope, receives the Grand Cross of the Order of St. Stephen, the highest Austro-Hungarian decoration

Jan. 25, New Austro-German commercial treaty signed at Berlin

May 8, Count Tisza, acting Premier of Hungary, leaves Vienna after another fruitless attempt to persuade the crown to relieve him and his colleagues of their duties

June 13, Death of the Archduke Joseph Karl Ludwig of Austria

June 21, In the Reichsrath, Baron Gautsch declares that the Austrian Government would remain as long as possible upon the basis of the laws which regulate Austrian relations to Hungary; but that the Austrian Government was prepared for any and every eventuality, and would not fail energetically to defend Austrian interests in any and every situation

Nov. 2, Proposal for universal suffrage for Hungary arouses much popular excitement in Austria; great socialist demonstration in favor of universal suffrage held in Vienna; serious conflict between police and people

1906

Feb. 5, Breakdown of the negotiations between the crown and the coalition, announced

Feb. 12, Commercial treaty with Belgium signed in Vienna

Feb. 13, Violent attack on the government made in the lower house by Count Sternberg, on a motion of urgency proposed by the Pan-Germans in favor of the separation of the common Austro-Hungarian army; motion rejected by 117 votes to 25

Feb. 22, Chamber adopts the new Austro-Italian commercial treaty

Feb. 23, Franchise and parliamentary reform bills presented to the lower house by Baron Gautsch; by these bills every male citizen of 24 years of age, who is not under any legal disability, is entitled to be registered as a voter after residence for one year in an electoral district; number of seats raised from 425 to 455; in the new chamber, elected according to the proposed reform, there would be 205 Germans, 99 Czechs, 95 Poles and Ruthenians, 35 Southern Slavs, 17 Italians, and 4 Rumanians

March 9, Treaty of commerce with Switzerland signed

April 4, Royal decree published, calling to the colors the supplementary reserves of the 1904 contingent of Honved troops, in consequence of the failure of Parliament to pass the recruiting bill

April 9, Death of M. Franz Stockinger, Austro-Hungarian Consul-General in London

April 28, Polish Party reaffirms its standpoint that any acceptable suffrage reform must give Galicia 110 mandates, and that suffrage reform must go hand in hand with an extension of provincial self-government

May 3, Resignation of Baron Gautsch, who is succeeded by Prince Conrad von Hohenlohe-Schillingsfürst as Premier

May 28, Prince Hohenlohe resigns, being unable to acquiesce in the Emperor's wish to agree to the Hungarian demand that the economic compact should be replaced by a commercial treaty

May 30, Reichsrath protests by 240 votes to 8 against the concession to Hungary of the right to enact a separate tariff

June 1, New ministry united on the basis of prompt suffrage reform and thorough revision of the economic relationship to Hungary, formed by Baron Max Vladimir von Beck as Premier

June 6, Visit of the German Emperor to the Emperor Joseph at Vienna, July 6 and 7; the two Emperors send to the King of Italy, "their faithful ally," a joint expression of unalterable friendship

June 7, Baron von Beck presents himself and his colleagues to the chamber, and makes an important statement of policy; Government requests the support of the house, which gives the Government a majority of 180 votes against 91

June 10, Violent demonstration made by a Vienna mob against the Hungarian ministry in the Bankgasse, where the Hungarian delegation was sitting

Oct. 21, Count Goluchowski, Foreign Minister to the Dual Monarchy, tenders his resignation to the Emperor

Oct. 24, Baron von Aehrenthal, Austro-Hungarian Ambassador at St. Petersburg, accepts the post vacated by Count Goluchowski

Nov. 25, The Emperor intervenes personally in favor of maintaining universal suffrage as the basis of franchise reform in Austria

1907

Jan. 21, Statute amendment bill, modifying the constitution of 1867 in accordance with the universal suffrage law, adopted in the Austrian upper chamber

March 18, Strike among dressmakers and ladies' tailors for increased wages, involving 9,000 women and girls and 3,000 men, begins in Vienna

May, General election under new law, 4,615,020 voting as compared with 1,217,993 in 1897

Aug. 4, The Emperor Francis Joseph receives Prince Ferdinand of Bulgaria in audience

Aug. 15, Meeting between King Edward and the Emperor Francis Joseph at Ischl

Oct. 8, New customs treaty with Hungary signed

1908

Jan. 17, Death of Duke Ferdinand IV of Tuscany, Archduke of Austria, age 72

Mar. 13, Serious fighting at Budapest between the police and a crowd of socialists who had organized a demonstration in favor of universal suffrage

March 14, New commercial treaty between Austria and Serbia signed

May 7, Arrival of the German Emperor and Empress, with a deputation of German princes

May 23, Baron von Aehrenthal, Minister for Foreign Affairs, and General von Schönaich, War Minister, tender their resignations to the Emperor

Aug. 12, King Edward meets the Emperor Francis Joseph at Ischl

Sept. 18 and 20, Anti-German riots at Laibach; troops fire a volley, killing 2 and wounding 4 persons

Sept. 23, Arrival of Prince Ferdinand and Princess Eleonora of Bulgaria on a state visit to the Emperor Francis Joseph

Oct. 1, Visit of King Alfonso and Queen Victoria of Spain to Budapest

Oct. 7, Annexation of Bosnia and Herzegovina proclaimed

Nov. 6, The Emperor William visits the Emperor Francis Joseph at Schönbrunn

Nov. 29, Riots at Prague, mob attacked German students and professors and tore down Austrian flag

Dec. 2, Celebration of the 60th anniversary of the accession of the Emperor Francis Joseph takes place in Vienna and throughout Austria

1909

April 26, Dr. Wekerle, the Premier, announces the resignation of the Hungarian coalition ministry appointed in April, 1906

April–Oct., Agram trials in connection with the "Greater Serbia conspiracy"

May 14–15, Visit of the German Emperor and Empress to Vienna

Sept. 25, Dr. Wekerle tenders the resignation of his cabinet

Oct. 5, The high treason trial at Agram concluded; 31 of the accused condemned to terms of penal servitude ranging from 5 to 12 years, the remaining 22 being acquitted

Dec. 31, All, except two, of the prisoners condemned in the Agram trial, set at liberty pending the decision of their appeal to the supreme court

1910

Jan 3, The Chinese naval mission, with Prince Tsaihsun, received by the Emperor Francis Joseph

Jan. 4, Dr. de Lukacs appointed Hungarian Premier

Jan. 11, Dr. de Lukacs resigns the Hungarian premiership and Count Khuen-Hedervary appointed in his stead

Jan. 28, Defeat of the Khuen-Hedervary cabinet, the chamber prorogued until March 24

Feb. 15, The newly formed government party in Hungary assumes the name of "National Party of Work"

Feb. 22, Fundamental statutes for Bosnia and Herzegovina promulgated

March 10, Death of Dr. Karl Lueger (65) founder of the Christian Socialist Party in Austria

April 2, The sentences on the 31 defendants in Agram high treason trial annulled by the Croatian supreme court

April 12, Launching of the battleship, *Zrinyi*, at Trieste

April 15, Mr. Roosevelt, American ex-President, received in Vienna by the Emperor Francis Joseph; at Budapest April 18–20

May 28, Lieutenant Hofrichter, who in November, 1909, sent poisonous pills to several officers of the Austrian general staff, and caused the death of one of them, was sentenced to death

July 1, Conflict between Ruthene and Polish students at Lemberg University, 120 Ruthene students arrested

July 16, Arbitration Convention with Great Britain signed

Sept. 20, Visit of the German Emperor

Oct. 24, Bank rate raised from 4 to 5%

1911

Jan 9, Ministry of Baron Bienerth reconstructed, Dr. Meyer succeeding Dr. Bilinski as Minister of Foreign Affairs

Jan. 10, Scheme for reorganization of military and naval forces published in Vienna and Budapest

Jan. 24, Austro-Hungarian-Serbian Treaty of Commerce signed in 1910 became effective

Jan. 30, Students at Cracow University protested against appointment of a German professor and refused to attend classes. University closed by the Government

Feb. 4, Bank rate reduced to 4½% from 5%

Feb. 9, Agreement with Great Britain to submit to Hague Tribunal any dispute over existing treaties that could not be settled by diplomacy

Feb. 23, Bank rate reduced to 4%

March 24, Visit of Emperor and Empress of Germany to Vienna

March 30 Lower House of Reichsrat dissolved

June 1, Civil law reformed

June 13–20, General election resulted in defeat of the Christian Socialist Party of the Government. Lower House: German Nationalists, 100; Christian Socialists (German), 73; German Social Democrats, 49; United Bohemian Club, 84; Bohemian Social Democrats, 25; Poles, 70; Polish Social Democrats, 9; Ukraine Union, 28; Croatio-Slavonian Club, 27; Dalmatians, 7; Uniolatina, 21; Independents, 23

June 19, Resignation of Bienerth Ministry

June 26, Ministry of Baron Paul Gautsch von Franken-
thurn succeeded
Sept. 17, Riots in Vienna protesting against the high
cost of living
Sept. 18, Vienna placed under martial law
Sept. 22, Bank rate raised to 5%
Oct. 28, Resignation of Premier Baron Gautsch
Nov. 3, Count Stürgkh, Minister of Education, became
Prime Minister; Cabinet reorganized Nov. 30, Prince
Hohenlohe-Schillingsfürst, Interior; Ritter von Leth,
Finance; Herr von Spitzmüller, Commerce
Dec., Demonstration before Parliament against provi-
sion of Civil Code which made remarriage of divorced
persons of Catholic and mixed Catholic marriages
illegal

1912

Feb. 17, Death of Count Aloys Lexa von Aehrenthal,
Minister of Foreign Affairs since Oct. 24, 1906.
Succeeded by Count Leopold Berchtold
Oct. 25, Bank rate raised to 5½%
Nov. 16, Bank rate raised to 6%
Dec. 5, Triple Alliance renewed
Dec. 10, General Krobatin appointed Minister of War

1913

May 12, Austria annexed Island of Ada Keleh in Dan-
ube (Turkish)
July 26, Imperial letters patent suspended autonomy of
Bohemia
Nov. 27, Bank rate reduced to 5½%
Public debt $2,152,000,000
Outcome of the Balkan Wars a loss of prestige for
Austro-Hungarian Monarchy in the Balkan Penin-
sula

1914

Jan. 20, Bank rate reduced to 5%
Feb. 3, Bank rate reduced to 4½%
Feb. 24 and March 6, Prosecution and conviction of
3 former officers charged with espionage for Russia.
Sentenced to imprisonment
March 3, Trial of persons charged with activities against
the Government among Ruthenians of East Galicia
and Hungary ended and 32 persons given prison
sentences
March 9, Trial of Ruthenians accused of espionage in
favor of Russia ended in acquittal
March 12, Bank rate reduced to 4%
June 12, Visit of William II of Germany accompanied
by Admiral von Tirpitz to the Archduke Francis
Ferdinand at Konopicht
June 21, Death of Baroness Bertha von Suttner, author
and pacifist
June 22, Memorandum of Conrad von Hötzendorff,
Chief of the General Staff, described existing conditions in the Balkans as intolerable
June 28, Assassination of Archduke Francis Ferdinand,
heir-presumptive to the throne, and his morganatic
wife, the Duchess of Hohenberg, at Bosnian capital
of Serajevo, by student, Gavrilo Princip, member of
Serbian secret society, the "Narodna Odbrana,"
organized to carry on pro-Serb revolutionary propaganda in provinces of Bosnia and Herzegovina
July 14, Decision of Council of Ministers to send Serbia
an ultimatum with a short time limit
July 23, Note to Serbia formulated 10 demands and
stated that Serbia had failed to fulfill promises of the
Declaration of March 31, 1909, that the assassina-

tions had been planned in Belgrade, and gave 48
hours for acceptance
July 25, Serbian Note to Austria accepted most of
demands but made reservations as to participation
of Austro-Hungarian representatives in judicial inquiry to be held in Serbia, and dismissal of officers and
officials compromised, and proposed that any points
in dispute should be referred to the decision of the
Hague Court or to the Powers who took part in the
drawing up of the Declaration of March 31, 1909
——, Austro-Hungarian Minister severed diplomatic
relations with Serbia leaving Belgrade as Serbia had
not yielded absolutely and unqualifiedly to the
Austro-Hungarian demands
——, Cabinet decree transferred a number of offenses
and crimes from local courts to military courts
July 27, Bank rate raised from 4 to 5%; stock exchange
closed
July 28, Austria refused to consider negotiations on
basis of Serbian reply
——, War declared on Serbia. See World War
July 31, General mobilization ordered
——, Bank rate raised to 6%, and moratorium de-
clared
Aug. 2, Bank rate raised to 8%
Aug. 4, Bank Act suspended by imperial ordinance
Aug. 5, Montenegro declared war on Austria-Hungary
Aug. 6, Austria declared war on Russia
Aug. 9, Austria declared war on Montenegro
Aug. 10, France and Austria severed diplomatic rela-
tions
Aug. 12, Great Britain declared war on Austria-Hungary
Aug. 13, France declared war on Austria-Hungary
Aug. 14, An organization created for supplying labor
based on labor exchanges
Aug. 15, Manifesto of Polish Parties declared in favor
of performing their duty to the State
Aug. 20, Bank rate reduced to 6%
Aug. 22, War declared on Belgium
Aug. 25, Japan declared state of war with Austria-
Hungary
Aug. 27, Severance of diplomatic relations with Japan
Aug. 31, The krone 5.12 to the American dollar
Oct. 7 and 13, Decrees passed deprived of citizenship
all subjects abroad suspected of working against the
interests of the monarchy, their families to be de-
ported
Oct. 24, Declaration of the Czech Union "It is true
that we have been against one Government or
another, but never against the State"
Oct. 26, Gavrilo Princip and 23 accomplices found
guilty of treasonable conspiracy against the life of
Archduke Franz Ferdinand
Nov. 4, Decree gave military courts competence in
parts of Empire where because of the War the civil
courts had ceased to function
Nov. 15, Patriotic manifesto of Czech Parties in
Moravia
Nov. 23, Manifesto of 30,000 Rumanian peasants of
the Bukovina in favor of the Emperor and the
Empire
Nov., First war loan of 5½% Treasury Bills due at par
April 1, 1920, and Hungary, 6% stock redeemable
Nov. 1, 1920

1915

Jan. 1, Death of Carl Goldmark, composer
Jan. 13, Resignation of Count Berchtold, Minister of

Foreign Affairs. Succeeded by Baron Stephen Burian, a Hungarian

Feb. 24, All stocks of grain and flour in the country taken over by the Government

March 9, Baron Burian expressed willingness to discuss with Italy cession of Austrian territory as price of neutrality

March 27, Offer of territory in South Tirol including Trentino to Italy

April 16, 25, and 29, Italy's terms refused by Austria but cession of part of Tirol inhabited by Italians, western bank of the Isonzo where the population Italian and town of Gradisca. Refused cession of islands along the Dalmation coast

May 3, The Triple Alliance denounced by Italy

May 21, Note to Italy offered important concessions

May 23, Italy declared war on Austria-Hungary

May, Second war loan 5½% stock at 95¼ redeemable in 1925. Hungary offered as alternative 6% stock redeemable 1921

Aug. 30, Sir Edward Grey, British Foreign Minister, declares that Allies could guarantee the eventual freedom and self-determination of Bosnia, Herzegovina, Slavonia, South Dalmatia, and Croatia

Sept. 6, Treaty of alliance with Bulgaria signed

Oct., Third war loan 5% Treasury Bills redeemable Oct. 1, 1930, Hungary offering 6% Rente, redeemable May 1, 1921

Nov. 30, Changes in the Cabinet, Prince Hohenlohe-Schillingsfürst appointed Minister of the Interior, Herr von Spitzmüller, Commerce; Ritter von Leth, Finance; Dr. Viktor von Hochenburger, Justice; Dr. Max von Hussarek, Instruction; Dr. Zdenko Baron Forster, Railways; Franz Zenker, Agriculture; General Friedrich Baron Georgi, National Defense; Ottokar Trnka, Labor; Ladislaus von Dlugosz, Minister without Portfolio

1916

Jan. 13, Death of Professor Count Lützow

Jan. 28, Negotiations begun at Budapest for new *Ausgleich*

Feb. 24, Central Securities Board established

March 15, Declaration of war on Portugal

April 16, Decree imposed taxes on war profits

May, Fourth war loan, 5½ Treasury Bills repayable at par June, 1923, and 5½% bonds to run for 40 years, Hungary offering 6% Rente redeemable Nov. 1, 1921 and 5½% Treasury Bills redeemable June 1, 1926. War loans issued about every 6 months until end of War thereafter

May 12–27, Commission of Austro-Hungarians and Germans met in Berlin to make a uniform tariff schedule for the 2 countries

Aug. 27, Rumania declared war on Austria-Hungary

Oct. 21, Count Karl Stürgkh, Prime Minister, fatally shot by Socialist youth, Friedrich Adler, son of Deputy Ludwig Adler, because of his refusal to convene Parliament

Oct. 27, Dr. Ernst von Körber became Prime Minister and also ruled without Parliament

Nov. 4, Rescript of Emperor Francis Joseph on future organization of the Kingdom of Galicia issued

Nov. 5, Joint rescript of Emperors of Austria-Hungary and Germany announced creation of Kingdom of Poland. *See* Poland

Nov. 14, Office of Food Control established

Nov. 21, Death of Emperor Francis Joseph I. Suc-

ceeded by his grand-nephew Archduke Charles (Karl Franz Joseph)

Dec. 12, Peace proposals of Quadruple Alliance announced. *See* World War

Dec. 13, Resignation of Prime Minister Körber

Dec. 20, Count Clam-Martinitz succeeded as Prime Minister

Dec. 23, Count Czernin became Minister of Foreign Affairs succeeding Baron Burian resigned

Dec. 30, Charles I crowned King of Hungary at Budapest as Charles IV

1917

Jan. 5, Ministry of Food established

Jan. 11, Note repudiating responsibility for continuance of war. *See* World War

Jan. 12, Entente Note in reply to Note of President Wilson of Dec. 11, referred to liberation of the "oppressed" peoples of Austria

Jan. 17, Croatian representatives proclaimed allegiance to house of Habsburg in answer to Note of Jan. 12

Jan. 23, The Czech Union by unanimous resolution of its governing committee rejected suggestions of Entente Powers as insinuations based on erroneous premises

Jan. 24, Rumanian Club made declaration of allegiance

Jan. 26, Agreement between Austria and Hungary known as the Ausgleich renewed for 20 years. Changes made in favor of Hungary

March 21, Decree gave the Government right to commandeer all supplies and fix prices

March 22, Austria-Hungary associated itself with the German-Turkish Agreements of Sept. 28, 1916 and Jan. 11, 1917

March 24, Letter of Emperor Charles to his brother-in-law Prince Sixtus of Bourbon Parma empowered him to declare to President Poincaré of France that to obtain peace he would support the just claims of France to Alsace-Lorraine

March 27, Agreement signed by Count Czernin with the German Chancellor Bethmann Hollweg provided for a minimum and maximum program of peace

April, War Minister Baron von Krobatin resigned. Succeeded by General Svon von Steinstatten

April 3, Count Czernin proposed to German Emperor at Homburg that Germany make cession of Alsace-Lorraine and take Poland and Galicia as compensation. Refused

April 8, Austria-Hungary broke off diplomatic relations with the United States

April 14, Proposals to Revolutionary Government of Russia of a separate peace refused

——, Memorandum of Count Czernin to the German Emperor on desperate internal situation of Austria-Hungary

May 17–18, Kreuznach Agreement with Germany by which Austria-Hungary to receive large annexations of territory in the Balkans and surrender her interests in Poland to Germany

May 30, The Reichsrat assembled for first time in more than 3 years. The Czechs and Southern Slavs demanded creation of autonomous States

June 19, Resignation of Count Clam-Martinitz as Prime Minister

June 24, Dr. Ritter von Seidler appointed Prime Minister

June 27, Greece declared state of war to exist

July 2, Amnesty granted to Czech political offenders

July 20, Declaration of Corfu establishing the Serb-Croat-Slovene State

July 23–Aug. 4, German-Austrian-Hungarian Tariff Commission began sessions at Vienna

Aug. 14, China declared war on Austria-Hungary

Aug. 31, Cabinet reorganized

Sept. 18, German-Austrian-Hungarian Tariff Commission met at Budapest

Nov. 5–Dec. 5, German-Austrian-Hungarian Tariff Commission met at Budapest

Nov. 18, Provisional Treaty continued old *Ausgleich* due to lapse on Dec. 31

Dec. 7, The United States declared war on Austria-Hungary

Dec. 20, The Lower House adopted a Resolution calling for peace on basis of no indemnities or annexations

1918

Jan. 6, Convention of Czechoslovaks at Prague made demand for sovereign State

Jan. 12, Resolution of Czechoslovak deputies at Prague declared the Bohemian question would receive an international solution at the Peace Conference

Jan. 16–17, Strikes in Vienna

Jan. 22, Germans demanded a province of their own in German Bohemia

Jan. 24, Address of Count Czernin, Minister of Foreign Affairs, regarding the "Fourteen Points"

Feb. 1, Sailors in rebellion organized demonstrations in Pola and near Cattaro raising the red flag

March 2, Second Pan-Slavic Conference at Agram

March 3, Demand of Ruthenians for establishment of East Galicia as Ukraine

March 5, Preliminary Peace Treaty with Rumania signed

April 8–10, Congress of "oppressed nationalities" of Austro-Hungarian Empire met in Rome. Pact of Rome adopted April 10. *See* Yugoslavia

April 15, Resignation of Count Czernin as Minister of Foreign Affairs after publication by Clemenceau of letter of Charles to Prince Sixtus of March, 1917

April 16, Baron Burian appointed Minister of Foreign Affairs

May 4, Reichsrat closed by Emperor

May 7, Final Treaty of Peace with Rumania signed at Bucharest

May 12, Treaty of political and military alliance with Germany signed

May 29, Declaration of Secretary of State Lansing "that the nationalistic aspirations of the Czechoslovaks and the Yugoslavs for freedom" had the sympathy of the Government of the United States

——, Peace Treaty with Finland signed

May 30, Treaty with Turkey signed as to the capitulations

June 15, Czechs set up national committee headed by Kramarz and adopted program of a "Czecho-Slovak State sovereign and independent"

June 16, New Parliament summoned

June 20–21, Food riots in Vienna

July 9, German-Austrian-Hungarian Commission at Salzburg completed negotiations for an economic treaty

July 14, Resignation of Field Marshal Count Conrad von Hötzendorff from active service. Succeeded by Colonel Metzger

July 22, Resignation of Prime Minister von Seidler

July 25, Baron Max Hussarek appointed Prime Minister

July 26, Reichsrat adjourned

Sept. 15, Austrian Note to all belligerent nations urged ending War by diplomatic negotiations

Sept. 15, Austrian Note to President Wilson

Oct. 1, Announcement of Government of recognition of rights of nationalities to self-determination and national autonomy, Polish independence, and union of the Southern Slavs by constitutional means

Oct. 4, Central Powers' Peace Note to President Wilson

Oct. 7, The Poles in Warsaw proclaimed independence

Oct. 11, Manifesto of Emperor announced union of Croatia, Slavonia, Bosnia, and Herzegovina into one State

Oct. 14, Czech Government formed in Paris

Oct. 16, Manifesto of the Emperor proclaimed conversion of Austria into a Federal State composed of free nations each to establish its own body politic on the territory occupied by it

Oct. 17, Czechs proclaimed republic at Prague, Magyars in Budapest

Oct. 18, Resignation of Baron Burian, Foreign Minister

——, Note of President Wilson recognized state of war between Czechoslovaks and the Empire

Oct. 19, Ukraine National Council set up at Lemberg

Oct. 21, German-Austrians made declaration of independence at Vienna and formed Provisional Assembly

Oct. 23, Independence of Austrian Ukraine proclaimed

Oct. 24, Count Julius Andrassy appointed Minister of Foreign Affairs

Oct. 27, Dr. Heinrich Lammasch succeeded Hussarek, resigned, as Prime Minister

——, Second Note to President Wilson asked for immediate armistice and request to Italy for armistice

Oct. 29, Croatia established itself as a separate State

Oct. 30, Demonstration of workers and students in Vienna against the House of Habsburg

——, German-Austrian Provisional Assembly adopted fundamental laws

Oct. 31, Revolution in Budapest and Vienna

——, Fleet turned over to Yugoslav National Council by Emperor

——, The krone 11.83 to the American dollar

——, Lammasch Ministry, the last imperial Cabinet resigned

Nov. 1, Count Stephen Tisza, former Hungarian Prime Minister, assassinated

——, Administration of Carniola taken over by Slovene leaders

Nov. 3, Armistice signed with Italy to go into effect Nov. 4, unconditional surrender

Nov. 11, Manifesto of Emperor Charles announced his withdrawal from all part in the Government of Austria but did not renounce crown. He retired to Eckartsau

Nov. 12, Republic proclaimed by National Assembly at Vienna and draft Constitution passed

——, Abdication of Charles as Emperor but not as King of Hungary

Nov. 13, Rescript of King Charles announced withdrawal from public affairs in Hungary and willingness to recognize form of Government adopted

Nov. 16, Republic proclaimed in Hungary. *See also* Hungary

Nov. 19, The Austrian Ukraine (Ruthenians) proclaimed independence

Nov. 22, Fundamental law of National Assembly assumed sovereignty over the German-speaking territory of the old Empire

Dec. 18, Electoral law passed

For further events, *see* Austria

RULERS

MARGRAVES OF AUSTRIA

Leopold I, 982; Albert I, 1018; Ernest, 1056; Leopold II, 1075; Leopold III, 1096; Albert II, 1136; Leopold IV, 1136; Henry II, 1142 (made a duke, 1156)

DUKES

1156. Henry II

1177. Leopold V. He made prisoner Richard I of England when returning incognito from the crusade, and was compelled to surrender him to the Emperor Henry VI

1194. Frederic I, the Catholic

1198. Leopold VI, the Glorious. Killed in battle

1230. Frederic II, the Warlike. Killed in a battle with the Hungarians, June 15, 1246

Interregnum

1276. Rodolph I

1282. Albert I and his brother Rodolph II. Albert becomes Emperor of Germany, 1298

1308. Frederic I and Leopold I

1326. Frederic I

1330. Albert II and Otho, his brother

1339. Albert II

1358. Rodolph IV

1365. Albert III and Leopold II or III (killed at Sempach)

1395. William I and brothers, and their cousin Albert IV

1411. The same. The provinces divided into the duchies of Austria and Carinthia, and the county of Tirol

1411. Albert V, Duke of Austria; obtains Bohemia and Moravia; elected King of Hungary and Emperor, 1437; dies, 1439; succeeded by his posthumous son

1439. Ladislaus, who dies childless, 1457

1457. The Emperor Frederic III and Albert VI

1493. Maximilian I, son of Frederick III (Archduke), Emperor; *see* Germany

EMPERORS

1804. Francis I (late Francis II of Germany), styled Emperor of Austria only, Aug. 11, 1804; resigned Empire of Germany, Aug. 6, 1806; died March 2, 1835

1835. Ferdinand, his son, March 2; abdicated in favor of his nephew (his brother Francis Charles having renounced his rights), Dec. 2, 1848; died June 29, 1875

1848. Francis Joseph (son of Francis Charles), born Aug. 18, 1830; succeeded, Dec. 2, 1848; married April 24, 1854, to Elizabeth of Bavaria; crowned King of Hungary, June 8, 1867; died Nov. 21, 1916; their son, the Archduke Rodolph, born Aug. 21, 1858; married to Princess Stephanie Clotilde of Belgium May 10, 1881; suicide, Jan. 30, 1889

Heir-presumptive, brother, Archduke Charles Louis, born July 30, 1833; his son, Archduke Francis Ferdinand, born Dec. 18, 1862; assassinated June 23, 1914

1916. Charles (Karl) I (son of Archduke Otto, younger brother of Francis Ferdinand); abdicated Nov. 12, 1918

AZORES

Azores, archipelago belonging to Portugal in the Atlantic Ocean, 8,000 miles east of Cape da Roca; area 922 square miles, population 232,012 (census 1920). They include St. Michael (São Miguel) the largest island with area of 297 square miles, St. Mary (Santa Maria), Formigas, Fayal, Pico, St. George, Terceira, Graciosa, Flores, and Corvo. The Azores are found on a map of 1531. The Portuguese navigator, Cabral, discovered and named Santa Maria in 1432 and in 1444 took possession of St. Michael's. The capital is Ancra on Terceira Island, the chief ports are Angra, Ponta Delgada, and Horta.

BALEARIC ISLANDS

Balearic Islands, archipelago of 4 islands in the Mediterranean Sea off the east coast of Spain, a province of Spain, total area 1,935 square miles, population (1929) 352,926. Palma, on the island of Majorca, is the capital.

BALKAN WARS, 1912–1913

The First Balkan War began in October, 1912, Bulgaria, Greece, Serbia, and Montenegro as Allies attacking and defeating the Turks, and ended with signing of the Treaty of London May 30, 1913. The Second Balkan War due to dispute over division of Macedonia, Serbia demanding from Bulgaria revision of secret Treaty of 1912 and part of Macedonia because intervention of the Powers had prevented Serbia from having Durazzo and southern Albania as agreed. Bulgaria began hostilities June 30, 1913, and was defeated by Serbia, Greece, Montenegro, and Rumania; war ended with signing of Treaty of Bucharest Aug. 10, 1913.

1912

Feb. 29, March 13, Political Treaty of Alliance between Bulgaria and Serbia and secret annex directed against any Great Power which should occupy any territory in the Balkan Peninsula. Spheres of influence in Macedonia designated, Serbia to receive Durazzo and a large part of Albania

May 16, Secret Treaty of alliance between Bulgaria and Greece

June 19, Military Agreement between Bulgaria and Serbia

Aug. 14, Note of Austria-Hungary to other European Powers proposed "progressive decentralization" of Macedonia, maintenance of the *status quo* in the Balkans, and the strengthening of Turkey

Aug., Understanding between Montenegro and Bulgaria as to Balkan affairs

Sept. 22, Military Agreement between Bulgaria and Greece

Sept. 28, Bulgaria announced contrary to treaties that only one division instead of three would be available for operation with Serbians in Macedonia

Blairsville High School Library
Blairsville, Pennsylvania

FIRST BALKAN WAR

Sept. 30–Oct. 1, Mobilization of armies of the Balkan League, Bulgaria, Serbia, Montenegro, and Greece

Oct. 1, Mobilization of Turkey

Oct. 4, France proposed that the European Powers should act jointly to prevent war in the Balkans

Oct. 7, Great Britain, Russia, and Austria accepted French proposals

Oct. 8, Austro-Russian Note presented to Governments of the different Balkan States informing them that the Powers would take collective action at Constantinople, that the question of reforms in Macedonia would be taken up, and in case of war would not allow any changes in the Balkan territorial *status quo*

——, Montenegro declared war on Turkey and sent an army across the frontier

Oct. 9, Montenegrins bombarded Turks out of fortified positions on Podgoritza heights

Oct. 12, Montenegrins defeated Turks near Scutari and invested Tarabosch

Oct. 13, Note of Bulgaria, Serbia, and Greece to Turkey demanded reforms within 6 months and the " ethnic autonomy of the nationalities of the Empire" and demobilization of the Turkish army in the Balkans

——, Note of Bulgaria, Serbia, and Greece acknowledged Note of Powers of Oct. 8

Oct. 14, Montenegrins captured Tuzi (Tushi)

Oct. 16, Turkey announced withdrawal of its representatives from the Balkan capitals

——, Montenegrins captured Berane

Oct. 17, Bulgaria, Serbia, and Greece declared war on Turkey and Turkey declared war on Bulgaria, Serbia, and Greece

Oct. 18, Bulgarians captured Mustapha Pasha near Adrianople

Oct. 19, Turkish fleet bombarded Verna, Bulgarian port on Black Sea

——, Greeks captured Elassona in Epirus

——, Montenegrins captured Gusinje

Oct. 20, Greeks announced blockade of coast of Epirus

Oct. 21, Greek troops landed at Island of Lemnos and occupied the capital

Oct. 22–24, First great battle at Kirk Kilisse near Adrianople won by Bulgarians

Oct. 22–25, Battle of Kumanovo won by Serbians

Oct. 22, Greeks commanded by Crown Prince Constantine defeated Turks at Sarandoporus

——, Serbians captured Prishtina evacuated by Turks

——, Bulgarians in battle of Seliolu defeated Turks

Oct. 23, Serbians occupied Novi Bazar having captured the Turkish works the night before

——, Bulgarians occupied Petra evacuated by Turks

Oct. 24, Bulgarians occupied Kirk Kilisse evacuated the night before by Turks

Oct. 25, Greeks occupied Koziani, and Selfidje (Serbia) and advanced on Monastir and Salonica

——, Siege of Adrianople begun by Bulgarians, Kartal Tepe captured

Oct. 26, Uskub abandoned by Turks entered by Serbians, national capital of the Serbians lost 400 years before at the battle of Kovno, at once renamed Skoplje, Turks retreating to Ovtche Polye. Senitza also taken

——, Montenegrins began investment of Scutari

——, M. Dragoumis appointed Governor of Crete in name of the King of Greece

——, Greeks took Luros

Oct. 27, Serbians captured Istib and Kuprulu

——, Bulgarians captured Baba Eski

——, Montenegrins began bombardment of Scutari

Oct. 28, Serbians entered Kumanovo and captured Sienitza and Mitrovista

——, Greeks occupied Eleutherochori and Verria and Katerina on Gulf of Salonika

Oct. 28–31, General Savov commanding Bulgarians defeated main Turkish army in battle of Lule Burgas forcing Turks under Nazim Pasha to fall back to Tchataldja lines before Constantinople

Oct. 29, Serbs and Montenegrins captured Pleolye

Oct. 31, Ipek (Pech) taken by Montenegrins

——, Serbians captured Prizrend

——, Greeks occupied Grevena. Turkish battleship sunk in Salonika harbor by Greek torpedo

Nov. 1, Greeks took Samothrace Island

——, Bulgarians reached Nevrokop and same day railway station at Buk taken isolating Macedonia from Thrace

——, Turks evacuated Kuprulu falling back on Monastir

Nov. 2, Djakova captured by Serbians and Montenegrins

Nov. 2–3, Greeks repulsed in attack on Turkish position at Yenije Vardar and flank troops defeated by Turks at Banitsa and Kastoria

Nov. 3, The Greeks captured Prevesa, Epirus

Nov. 5, The Greeks captured Yenije Vardar forcing Turks to retire to Salonika and Serbs forced Babuna Pass reaching Prilep after battle

Nov. 4, Turkey asked the Powers to mediate

Nov. 8, Salonika surrendered to Greeks and occupied by Constantine the following day

Nov. 9, Bulgarians occupied Seres

Nov. 14, Negotiations for armistice begun by Powers

Nov. 16, San Giovanni di Medua on the Adriatic occupied by Montenegrins

Nov. 17, Serbians occupied Allessio

Nov. 17–18, Bulgarian attack on Turkish fortified position, the Tchataldja lines repulsed with heavy loss

Nov. 18, Serbians captured Monastir after desperate battle

Nov. 19, Armistice terms offered Turkey included surrender of Adrianople

——, Serbs dislodged Turks from Oblakovo northwest of Monastir

Nov. 20, Turkey refused to accept terms for armistice

Nov. 21, Greeks captured Mytilene

Nov. 24, After naval battle off Varna the Greeks occupied the Island of Chios

Nov. 28, Serbians and Montenegrins occupied Durazzo

Dec. 3, Valona (Avlona) shelled by Greeks

——, Armistice at Tchataldja lines signed by all Balkan States except Greece

Dec. 6, Greeks took Doiran and entered Seres

Dec. 16, Peace Conference opened in London

Dec. 18, Greeks captured Nevrokop

Dec. 20, Autonomy of Albania accepted by Powers at London Conference with guarantee to Serbia of commercial access to the Adriatic Sea

Dec. 23, Balkan Allies demanded cession of Turkey in Europe west of line from Rodosto on the Sea of Marmora to Cape Malatra on Black Sea except Gallipoli Peninsula and small strip around Constantinople

Dec. 28, Turkey offered counter proposals

1913

Jan. 3, Turks in interior of Chios surrendered
——, Balkan Allies rejected terms offered by Turkey
Jan. 6, Balkan Allies rejected revised Turkish proposals and suspended the discussions
Jan. 9, Serbia announced she would withdraw from the Adriatic on the signing of peace thus ending military preparations of Austria in Hungary and Croatia which had been answered by military preparations in Russia
Jan. 15, The Turkish war vessel *Hamidich* ran the Blocade out of the Dardanelles and raided Ægean ports
Jan. 17, Greek and Turkish fleets in engagement off Lemnos
——, Note of the Powers to Turkey advised cession of Adrianople and to leave the question of the Ægean Islands to the Powers
Jan. 22, Turkish National Assembly decided to accept conditions of peace offered by the Powers
Jan. 23, *Coup d'état* of Young Turks overthrew the Government and denounced the armistice
Jan. 29, Balkan Allies in London gave notice of termination of negotiations
Jan. 30, Balkan Allies denounced the armistice
——, Protocol signed in London stated Rumanian territorial demands on Bulgaria and Bulgarian concessions, a "rectification of frontier" between Silistria and the Black Sea at Kavarna
——, Turkish Note to Powers offered part of Adrianople on right bank of Maritza
Feb. 1, London Conference ended without agreement
Feb. 3, Hostilities resumed
Feb. 4, Adrianople forts attacked by Bulgarians
——, Bulgarians victorious at Bulair near Gallipoli
Feb. 6, Montenegrins and Serbians began three day attack on Scutari with no result
March 1, Renewed offer of mediation by the Powers accepted by Turkey
March 6, Jannina (Yannina) in Epirus besieged by the Greeks surrendered
March 10, Island of Samos occupied by the Greeks
March 25, Serb artillery forced surrender of Ekmetchikei
March 26, Surrender of Adrianople compelled by attacks of Bulgarians and Serbians
——, Powers in London agreed to incorporate Scutari into Albania
March 31, Montenegrins attacked fortress of Tarabosh near Scutari and were repulsed with heavy loss
April 1, The Powers notified the King of Montenegro that he must raise the siege of Scutari and allow that city to be incorporated in Albania
——, Turkey accepted terms of peace proposed by the Powers
——, Montenegrins attacked fortress of Tarabosh without success
April 7–May 9, Greco-Bulgarian Commission in conference to discuss priority of occupation of territory in dispute broke up without result
April 10, Formal declaration of blocade of Montenegrin ports by the Powers of Europe
April 13, Serbians withdrew from before Scutari fearing international complications
April 16, Armistice concluded between Bulgaria and Turkey
April 20, Armistice concluded between Turkey and all the Balkan States except Montenegro

April 21, Balkan Allies accepted unconditional mediation of the Powers
April 22, Scutari surrendered to Montenegrins, Essad Pasha signing the capitulation with General Vukovitch
April 24, Austria-Hungary demanded that Scutari be given to Albania at once
April 30, Note of Montenegro to the Powers regarding evacuation of Scutari
May 1, Austria-Hungary announced she would proceed against Montenegro if Montenegro did not withdraw from Scutari
May 5, King Nicholas yielded withdrawing troops from Scutari
May 7, Agreement of Bulgaria and Rumania for cession of town of Silistria to Rumania
May 14, Scutari occupied by international force in the name of Albania
May 15, Protocol signed by Rumania and Bulgaria regarding cession of territory
May 20–June 9, Second Peace Conference in London
May 25, Balkan Financial Commission met in Paris
May 28, Serbia demanded of Bulgaria revision of territorial commitments of Treaty of 1912 to compensate her for loss of territory due to creation of an autonomous Albania
May 30, Treaty of Peace between Balkan Allies and Turkey signed in London, Turkey ceding to the four Balkan Allies Crete and all European territory west of Enos-Midia line, the delimitation of Albania, and settlement of Ægean Islands to be decided by the five European Powers
June 1, Greece and Serbia concluded an offensive and defensive alliance against Bulgaria for 10 years
June 8, The Tsar of Russia offered to arbitrate territorial dispute between Bulgaria and Serbia
June 9, Break up of London Peace Conference
June 10, Serbia demanded revision of territorial agreements of the Treaty of Feb. 29 with Bulgaria in view of Bulgaria's non-fulfillment of the Military Agreement of June 19, 1912. *See* Sept. 28, 1912 and May 28, 1913
June 24, Serbia severed diplomatic relations with Bulgaria
June 29, Bulgarians attacked Serbian positions on right bank of the Zlatovo River between Kratovo and Kotchana without declaration of war as an occupation of territory

SECOND BALKAN WAR

June 30, Second Balkan War begun, the Battle of Bregalnitsa, by attack of Bulgarians on Serbian and Greek positions reaching the Vardar at Krivolak forcing Serbians back between Krivolak and Kriva Palanka, and captured heights Car-Vrh and Redki-Buki, and driving Greeks back all along the line, their right from near Kavala across the Struma, their center from Nigrita almost to Lanzaza and their left from Gyevgli southward
July 1, End of Bulgarian offensive
——, Serbia declared war on Bulgaria, and Greece declared state of war existed
July 2–4, Serbs attacked Bulgarians driving them back to the upper Bregalnitsa and recaptured Redki Buki and the hills between Drenek and Istib
July 2, Counter-offensive attack of Greeks begun which captured Gyevgli, Kilkish, and drove Bulgarians

back on Negrita and eastward on the Seres road (July 3-4)

July 3, Rumania mobilized

July 5, France asked the Powers to declare against intervention in the Second Balkan War

——, Montenegro joined Serbia and Greece against Bulgaria

——, Serbians occupied Kotchana

July 6, Montenegro and Greece withdrew their ministers from Bulgaria

July 6-7, The Greeks reached the Salonika-Drama railway and carried the pass over the Belashitsa leading to Strumitsa cutting Bulgarian General Ivanov from the railway and forcing his retreat inland towards Bulgaria by the narrow Struma Valley

July 8, Bulgarians abandoned Istib

July 9, Kavala occupied by a landing party of Greek marines

——, Bulgarians abandoned Radovishta (Raitchanski), occupied by Serbians

July 10, Greeks occupied Demirhassar

——, Rumania declared war on Bulgaria invading that country on the north and east

——, Bulgarian offensive against Serbia ended

July 12, Turks began reoccupation of Thrace

——, Rumanians occupied Silistria

——, Serbians occupied Pataritza

July 15, New Allied offensive begun along line Golemi-Vhr, Sivakobila-Obochna

July 17, Bulgaria asked Rumania for an armistice

July 20, Turks recaptured Adrianople

July 24, Bulgaria protested to the Powers against Turkish invasion

July 25-27, Battle of Semitli, Bulgarian attack on Greek Struma column before the main body of troops was through the Kresna defile repelled

July 30, Peace Conference opened at Bucharest

July 31, Armistice signed

Aug. 7, Joint Note of Powers asked Turkey to observe the provisions of the Treaty of London

Aug. 10, Treaty of Bucharest signed between Bulgaria and Serbia, Greece, Montenegro, and Rumania; Rumania gained extension of southeastern frontier to a line from Turtukai on the Danube River to Balchik on the Black Sea; Greece gained Salonika, Doiran, Demirhassar, Seres, Drama and Kavala, and Crete; Serbia received Kotchana, Istib, and Radovishta; Montenegro received a part of the Sanjak of Novi Bazar including towns of Plevlye, Bielopolie, Ipek, and Jacova. Secret annex guaranteed new boundaries. *See also* Bulgaria

Aug. 19, International Commission appointed by Carnegie Endowment for International Peace to investigate atrocities of the Balkan War

Aug. 30, Treaty of Bucharest ratified by the Powers

Sept. 17, Agreement between Bulgaria and Turkey as to settlement of frontiers

Sept. 29, Treaty of Constantinople between Turkey and Bulgaria adjusted frontiers following the course of the Maritza River from its mouth to a point near Mandra thence due north to Mustapha Pasha and easterly to the Black Sea giving Turkey double the territory awarded her under Treaty of London (May, 1913), which ended the First Balkan War

Oct. 9, Austro-Russian Note to Balkan Allies on Balkan War and the division of Turkey in Europe

Nov. 4, Treaty of Belgrade between Montenegro and Serbia

Nov. 13, Treaty between Turkey and Greece settled questions arising out of Balkan Wars

1914

Feb. 13 and 14, Notes of Powers to Greece and Turkey stated decision that Greece should be allowed to keep Ægean Islands except Tenedos, Imbros, and Castellorizo

BELGIUM

Belgium (Royaume de Belgique—Koniglijk Belgie), Kingdom of western Europe, with northwest coast on the North Sea, bounded by the Netherlands on the north, by France on the southwest, and Germany and Luxemburg on the east, area including the districts of Eupen and Malmédy ceded by the Treaty of Versailles 11,755 square miles. Brussels is the capital. The Kingdom of Belgium formed itself into an independent State in 1830, having from 1815 been a part of the Netherlands. The secession was decreed on October 4, 1830, by a Provisional Government, established in consequence of a revolution which broke out at Brussels, on August 25, 1830. A National Congress elected Prince Leopold of Saxe-Coburg King of the Belgians on June 4, 1831; he ascended the throne July 21, 1831. On his death in 1865 he was succeeded by his son, Leopold II, who reigned until 1909.

By the Treaty of London, Nov. 15, 1831, the neutrality of Belgium was guaranteed by Austria, Russia, Great Britain, and Prussia. It was not until after the signing of the Treaty of London, April 19, 1839, which established peace between King Leopold I and the King of the Netherlands, that all the States of Europe recognized the Kingdom of Belgium.

Area and population of provinces:—

PROVINCES	AREA, ENG. SQ. MILES	POPULATION	
		Census Dec. 31, 1920	Estimated Dec. 31, 1928
Antwerp (Anvers)	1,093	1,016,963	1,158,752
Brabant	1,268	1,521,699	1,661,684
Flanders } West	1,249	803,687	880,900
Flanders } East	1,158	1,107,325	1,134,291
Hainaut	1,437	1,220,271	1,262,702
Liége	1,119	863,092	962,664
Limburg	930	300,455	358,453
Luxemburg	1,706	223,739	222,749
Namur	1,413	348,338	353,363
Eupen and Malmédy	382	60,213	—
Total	11,755	7,465,782	7,995,558

Albert, Reigning King, born April 8, 1875, son of the late Prince Philippe of Saxe-Coburg and Gotha and of Flanders (died November 17, 1905), and of the late Princess Marie de Hohenzollern-Sigmaringen (died Nov. 27, 1912); married Oct. 2, 1900, to Princess Elizabeth of Bavaria; succeeded his uncle, Leopold II, Dec. 17, 1909.

Children of the King.—(1) Prince Leopold, Duke of Brabant, born Nov. 3, 1901; married on Nov. 4, 1926, to Princess Astrid of Sweden. Offspring:— Josephine Charlotte, born October 11, 1927. Prince Baudouin, born September 7, 1930. (2) Prince Charles, Count of Flanders, born Oct. 10, 1903. (3) Princess Marie-José, born Aug. 4, 1906, married to Prince Umberto, heir-apparent to the crown of Italy, on January 8, 1930.

1830

Aug. 25, The revolution commences at Brussels
Oct. 4, The provisional government declares Belgium independent (M. Van de Weyer, active)
Dec. 23, Antwerp taken (except the citadel)
Dec. 26, Belgian independence acknowledged by the allied Powers

1831

Feb. 3, Duc de Nemours elected King (his father, the French king, refused his consent)
Feb. 24, Surlet de Chokier is elected Regent
July 12, Leopold, Prince of Saxe-Coburg, accepted the crown; enters Brussels July 19
Aug. 3, War with the Netherlands commences
Aug., France sends 50,000 troops to assist Belgium, and an armistice ensues
Nov. 15, Conference of Ministers of the five great powers held in London: acceptance of 24 articles of pacification

1832

Oct. 22, Convention between England and France against Holland
Nov. 30, Antwerp besieged; the citadel taken by the French Dec. 23
Dec. 27, The French army returns to France

1833–1853

May 21, 1833, Preliminary convention with Holland signed
April 5, 1834, Riot at Brussels
April 19, 1839, Treaty * between Holland and Belgium signed in London
1842, Clerical education bill passed; made teaching of religion obligatory in all elementary schools which received grants from the Government, and under the charge of the clergy
May 10, 1853, Increase of army to 100,000 men voted

1857

June, Opposition to religious charities' bill †
Nov. 9, A new ministry under M. Charles Rogier
Dec. 10, The chambers dissolved; reassembled

* This treaty arose out of the conference held in London on the Belgian question; by the decision of which, the treaty of Nov. 15, 1831, was maintained, and the pecuniary compensation of sixty millions of francs offered by Belgium for the territories adjudged to Holland was declared inadmissible.

† At the revolution in 1830, the Roman Catholic clergy lost the administration of the public charities, which they have struggled to recover ever since. In April, 1857, M. Decker, the head of the ministry, brought in a bill for this purpose, but was compelled to withdraw it, and eventually to resign.

1859

May, The King proclaims Belgium neutral in the Italian war
June 12, Birth of Prince Leopold Ferdinand
July 22, Death of M. Potter

1860

June, The King visits England
June 13, Vague rumors of annexation to France produce warm loyal addresses to the King
July 21, The octrois abolished
Aug., Successful military volunteer movement

1861

May 1, Commercial treaty with France signed

1862

Aug. 22, Commercial treaty with Great Britain adopted by the chamber
Aug., Great distress through decay of trade

1864

Jan., Fierce dissensions through Roman Catholics, the ministry resigns, but resumes office, Feb. 4; dissolution of the chambers, July 17; the Protestants superior in the election, Aug.

1865

Dec. 10, Death of Leopold I; accession of Albert

1868

Jan. 3, New ministry (under M. Frère-Orban); liberal
March 25–29, Serious riots in the mining districts; put down by the military; 10 lives lost
Nov. 6–13, Intern. Congress of workmen at Brussels

1869

Jan. 22, The Crown Prince Leopold Ferdinand, Duke of Brabant, died
Feb. 13, Concession of a Luxemburg railway to a French railway company, without the assent of the State, prohibited by the assembly; dispute with the French Government arranged May

1870

About June 19, Resignation of Frère-Orban ministry
July 3, M. d'Anethan's Ministry announced
Aug. 9, Treaty for the neutrality of Belgium between Great Britain and Prussia, signed; and France, signed Aug. 11
Sept. 1–2, After surrender of Sedan many French soldiers enter Belgium; disarmed and interned
Nov. 22–25, Strong opposition to the Ministry by M. Barra and others; riots at Brussels

1871–1873

Dec. 7, 1871, Resignation of D'Anethan; M. Malou (a moderate) forms a ministry
Feb. 17, 1872, The Comte de Chambord arrives at Antwerp; compelled to quit Belgium through popular demonstrations, Feb. 27
March 29, 1872, The French Government denounce the treaty of commerce with Belgium
Feb. 5, 1873, Treaty of commerce with France signed

1874

May 23, M. Van de Weyer, statesman; active during the revolution of 1830; ambassador to England 1831–67; died

July 27–Aug. 28, International conference at Brussels respecting rights of neutrals during war—no results

1875

Feb. 1, April 15, Notes from the German Government, complaining of publications favoring the censured German ecclesiastics; respecting the *Duchesne's* proposal to the Archbishop of Paris to assassinate Bismarck

March and May, Dignified Belgian replies

May, The court at Liége cannot interfere; modification of the criminal law proposed, June

1876

About June 16, 17, Catholic successes in the elections; riots against them at Brussels and Antwerp

Sept. 27–Oct. 2, International congress respecting hygiene, &c., held at Brussels

1878

June 13, 14, Catholic minority in elections; the Malou ministry resign; M. Frère-Orban forms a liberal ministry, June 20

July 28, Gigantic weir for water distribution at La Gileppe, near Verviers, inaugurated by the king

Dec. 3, Eugene T' Kindt de Rooden Veke, a clerk, convicted of embezzlement of 20,000,000 francs of the Bank of Belgium (149 thefts); the governor, Fortamps, of fraudulently repurchasing shares, &c.

1879

July 1, The King sanctions the new law of public instruction; Education Act abolished religious instruction in the schools. A year after this law was passed the Catholic Church had founded 2,064 free schools for education of Catholic children

Sept., Pastoral of the Roman Catholic hierarchy against the government plan of mixed education (sacraments to be refused to teachers and parents, &c.) published in Germany

1880

March, Archduke Rodolph of Austria betrothed to the Princess Stephanie

June 1, Permanent international exhibition opened at Brussels

——, Elections: clerical majority, June; the new senate and chamber unite to form a constituent assembly to consider the revision of the constitution

Sept. 9, Henri Conscience, eminent national Flemish poet and novelist, died, aged 73

Sept. 29, Death of Cardinal Deschamps, Archbishop of Mechlin, the primate

1884

Aug. 9, Great meeting of burgomasters at Brussels to oppose M. Jacobs' new reactionary education bill, which is accepted by the deputies (80–49), Aug. 30; by the senate (40–25), Sept. 10

Sept. 7, Liberal riots at Brussels and Antwerp

Sept. 13, New education law restored teaching of religion in the schools

1885

May 2, King Leopold proclaimed sovereign of the new Congo State

May 2, Universal exhibition opened at Antwerp by the King

May 27, Death of Charles Rogier (aged 85), member of the provisional government in 1830, six times Minister

1886–1889

March 22–29, 1886, Riotous strikes in the coal districts between Namur and Liége and collision with the military, many killed and wounded; convents, country houses, factories, &c., pillaged, works stopped

March 27–29, Liége quieted by vigorous action; great disorder in Charleroi, Mons, &c.

May 31, 1887, Revival of strikes; arrival of French dynamitards; universal suffrage demanded; the strikes subside about

May, 1889, State trials of 27 socialists at Mons, nearly all acquitted, May 25; the minister of justice was censured for the prosecution

1890

Jan. 13, Great colliery strike at Charleroi, &c., about 20,000 men out; settled by compromise

July, Loan to Congo State, *see* Congo

Aug. 22, Strike of about 10,000 miners at Mons; strike over, Sept. 1

1891

Jan. 23, Death of Prince Baudouin, aged 21

About May 2, Great political strike of colliers at Mons, Charleroi, and other places, with rioting; state of siege in the Liége district, about 100,000 men out, May 7

About May 10, Strike of the metallurgists in Charleroi district, the Progressist Party demand the revision of the constitution

July 9, End of the coal-miners' strike of 70 days

1892

Jan 3, Death of M. Emile de Laveleye, eminent publicist and writer, aged 69

Jan. 28, The commercial treaties with Austria-Hungary and Germany adopted by the chamber; by the senate, Feb. 1

Feb. 2, Discussion in the chamber on the revision of the constitution of 1831

June, Elections: clerical majority; the new senate and chamber unite to form a constituent assembly to consider the revision of the constitution, July 12 *et seq.*

Nov. 7, 8, Riotous meetings at Ghent and Brussels demanding universal suffrage, quelled by police

Nov. 8, The chambers opened by the King, who advocates revision of the constitution; universal suffrage rejected, Nov. 18

1893

Feb. 26, Referendum: manhood suffrage voted for at Brussels

April 12, All revision proposals rejected by the chamber; consequent large strike of workmen in the Mons district, etc., April 13 *et seq.*; rioting at Brussels, April 14; the civic guard at Mons fires on the miners, 4 men killed; above 1,000 dockers on strike at Antwerp, April 17

April 18, Manhood suffrage with plural voting for some persons adopted by the chamber (119–14); by the senate, April 27

April 18 *et seq.*, The strikes end; order restored

Sept. 28, Strike of miners in the center coal fields and the Charleroi district reported; closed by compromise, Oct. 10

Nov. 1, The Flemish volksraad (people's council) opposed to predominance of French influence, annual meeting at Brussels

1894

Feb. 17, New electoral bill passed by the chamber

March 25, Resignation of M. Beernaert the Premier, and M. Le Jeune, Minister of Justice. New ministry, M. de Burlet, Premier

May 5, Exhibition opened at Antwerp

May 28, Marriage of the Princess Josephine, daughter of the Count of Flanders, to Prince Charles of Hohenzollern-Sigmaringen at Brussels

May 12, Treaty with Great Britain respecting the Congo

Oct. 21, Parliamentary elections: 104 Catholics, 19 Liberals, 29 Socialists and Radicals

1895

Jan. 4, Annexation of the Congo State proposed by the Government

Feb. 13, The chamber of representatives adopt the bill for conversion of the 3½%, rente into 3% stock

March 26–30, General strike ordered by the labor syndicates against the communal electoral bill; stopped by the leaders

March 30, Rioting at Renaix, collision with the police, one man killed

March 31, The masters yield to men's demands

May 26, Readjustment of the Ministry; M. de Burlet becomes Foreign Minister

June 27, 28, Proposed payment of the debt of the Congo State voted

July 28, National demonstration against the government education bill (religious instruction made compulsory) at Brussels

Sept. 5, Annexation of the Congo State postponed

Nov. 12, Parliament opened, with an address by M. Beernaert

1896

Jan. 2, M. Frère-Orban, eminent liberal statesman, born, 1812; died

Feb. 25, Resignation of M. de Burlet; succeeded by M. de Smet de Naeyer Feb. 26

June 19, Royal warrant withdrawing the proposal for the annexation of the Congo State, read in the chamber

July 13, New chamber of deputies: 111 Clericals, 12 Liberals, 29 Socialists; reported

Oct. 31, Jan Verhas, eminent painter, died, aged 63

Nov. 9, General Brassine, Minister of War, resigns, on his scheme of military reform being rejected; chambers opened Nov. 10

1897

Feb. 5, Official use of Flemish ordered

June 30, Coal-miners' strike, 16,500 men out, round Mons; reported

Aug. 1, The Anglo-Belgian commercial treaty (1862) to be annulled in 1898 announced

1898

Dec. 26, Georges Rodenbach, novelist and poet, died, aged 44

1899

March 29, Stormy scene in the chamber, soldiers called in

June 28–30, Rioting in Brussels, agitation against the electoral reform bill, 1 death

June 28, 29, Socialist obstruction in the chamber, sitting suspended; conciliation offered by the Premier, chamber adjourns, June 30

July 31, Electoral reform bill rejected by the chamber; the cabinet resigns, Aug. 1; new Ministry; M. de Smet de Naeyer, Premier and Finance Minister, proposes the adoption of proportional representation; long debate in the chamber, Aug. 8; motion for considering the revision of the constitution rejected by the deputies (59–31), Aug. 31

1900

April, The King presents his real estate to the nation

May, Parliamentary elections: new chamber, 85 Clericals, 33 Liberals, and 33 Radicals

Nov. 20, 21, Debate in the chamber on the extradition of Sipido from Paris (Oct. 26)

1901

April 7, 8, Socialist and anarchist meetings held in Liége and Brussels in favor of universal suffrage

May 17, Angry scene in the chamber on the proposal for restoring temporal power to the Pope

May 20, Charleroi glass-workers' strike, began Aug. 1 1900, closed

July 17, Congo State bill passed by the chamber; annexation postponed

Early Aug., Old age pensions act comes into operation, 175,000 applications

——, Mathilde Ramboux, "Hilda Ram," popular Flemish poetess, died aged 43

Sept. 27, Miners' strike in the Liége basin begins, closed Oct.

1902

Jan. 24, Military reform bill passed the chamber; the senate, March 20

Jan. 30, Debate on the prosecution of M. Smeets for using seditious language at a meeting; wild uproar, sitting suspended, many arrests

March 22, Anti-gambling bill finally passed (Ostend and Spa granted 7,000,000f. as indemnity, May 7)

April 8–12, Socialist agitation for electoral reform at Brussels, Liége, and elsewhere; general strike; fatal rioting

April 18, Eight rioters killed at Louvain; strikes closed, except in the coal district, April 22

——, Revision of the suffrage question, rejected in the chamber; government majority (20)

April 25, Budget passed; session closed May 20

May 25, Elections: Catholic majority increased to 24 in the chamber

Sept. 19, Death of the Queen at Spa

Oct. 12–14, Frontier riots between French and Belgian miners

Nov. 15, Attempt to assassinate King Leopold by Rubino, an anarchist (sentenced to life imprisonment Feb. 10, 1903)

1903

Feb. 4, Dynamite outrage in Brussels by Vandermeuben (sentenced to 10 years' imprisonment)

June 1, International congress of miners at Brussels

July 1, Interpellation on the Congo by M. Vandervelde; debates closed, M. Woeste's order of the day passed (91–35), July 8

Aug. 19, British note opposing grant of monopolies, employment of forced labor, &c., in the Congo Free State, presented

Sept. 4, Visit of the King to Paris, received by M. Loubet

Sept. 19, Reply of the King to the Powers; denies charges of cruelty to natives in the Congo Free State, and rejects proposed arbitration

Sept. 27, Demonstration in Brussels against British attacks on the government of the Congo

Oct. 10, Official reply to the British note

1904

Feb. 5, Protracted debate in the chamber over liberal and socialist demand for compulsory education, and the abolition of subsidized schools; motion defeated; budget of public instruction voted by large majority

Feb. 29, Law suit arising out of the will of the late Queen comes before the probate division of the law courts at Brussels, the King being sued by the creditors of his daughter, Princess Louise of Coburg, who claimed that the Belgian law, setting up a joint partnership of property, applied to the estates of the King and the late Queen; judgment given in favor of the King against the claims of the Princess Louise, and her sister, Princess Stephanie, the marriage contract being held to be in the nature of a diplomatic treaty, and the administration of the late Queen's will to proceed on this basis, April 20

March 18, Bomb explosion at Liége in doorway of the office of the chief of police, 7 persons injured, 2 well-known French anarchists, Lambin and Gudefin, arrested

March 23, Report of Mr. Casement, British consul, containing a damaging indictment of the methods of the officials of the Congo, partly confirmed by Lord Cromer's report on the condition of the Upper Nile border country, created much excitement and indignation in Belgium; government appoint 3 non-Belgian inspectors-general

May 5, Motion by M. Féron, leader of the Radical Party, to abolish plural voting in favor of universal suffrage, rejected by 15 majority

May 29, Election for one-half of the members of the chamber and the senate; opposition gain 5 seats in the chamber, 2 seats in the senate

June 23, Commercial treaties with Germany and Holland signed

July 23, Commission of 3 appointed to inquire into the condition of the natives of the Congo

Aug. 7, Fifty Swedish sub-officers appointed for service in the Congo State

Aug. 30, Anglo-Belgian commission for the delimitation of the Uganda-Congo State frontier reports that Lake Albert Edward lies entirely within Congo territory

Nov. 3, Arbitration treaty concluded with Russia

1905

Jan. 23, Coal-miners' strike in the Mons district

Feb. 5, General strike proclaimed in the Mons and Charleroi districts by the national miners' federation

Feb. 20, Members of commission of inquiry, Congo Free State, leave Boma on return home end of Feb. Two committees, one Anglo-Belgian, the other Belgo-German, reported at work on delimitation of eastern frontier in region of lakes Tanganyika and Kivu; revolt of the Bakubas in Kassai district suppressed, still much trouble in French Congo; Great Lakes railway has reached 80th kilometer

Feb. 22, Further extension of the coal strike in Charleroi district reported, 34,000 men on strike; pit owners refuse any concession. M. Verhaegen's motion ad-

mitting in principle the settlement of labor disputes by boards of conciliation without active interference on the part of the government with respect to present strike, passed in the chamber by large majority

Feb. 25, International conference on maritime law holds its final sitting; draft convention signed by the respective delegates before ratification by the legislatures of the governments interested

Feb. 26, End of strike at Liége

March 6, Death of Baron Lambermont, veteran diplomatist, aged 86

Early March, End of coal strike in Mons and Charleroi districts, work resumes at all the chief pits; none of the men's demands granted

March 24, M. Bertrand's motion to reduce the war budget by 400,000fr. (16,000l.) in respect of salaries paid to Belgian officers on foreign service defeated by a large majority. Motion directed against pensions paid to agents of the Congo State

April 10, International committee of master cotton spinners and manufacturers' associations meet in Brussels, under the presidency of Mr. C. W. Macara

April 14, New Belgo-German treaty of commerce ratified by the chamber

——, Death of M. Constantine Meunier, member of the Belgian academy of fine arts, sculptor and painter, aged 75

April 26, Arbitration treaty between Denmark and Belgium, signed at Brussels

May 17, Antwerp communal council passes a resolution accepting the government scheme for the extension of the port of Antwerp; the undertaking will, it is stated, greatly increase the shipping accommodation of the port, and make Antwerp the first port in the world. Estimated cost, 10,000,000l., guaranteed by the State; 10 years will be required for its construction

June 28, Parliamentary committee passes by 5 votes to 2 that portion of the bill for the extension of the port of Antwerp which provides a sum of 108,000,000f. (4,320,000l.) for reërecting the forts of Antwerp on an enlarged scale; the entire bill, including the construction of a maritime canal and the dock extension, voted by 6 to one

June 30, House of representatives rejects by large majority the proposal to postpone until Nov. the discussion of the government bill for the extension of the port of Antwerp, and decides debate shall begin in July

July 1, Official celebration of the 75th anniversary of Belgian independence, inaugurated by the laying by King Leopold of the foundation stone of a new Ecole Mondiale, or colonial institute, in the park of Tervueran, Brussels. Institute built and maintained at the expense of the Congo State

July 5, Death of M. Elisse Reclus, eminent French geographer and philosopher, at Thournet, near Bruges, aged 75

Aug. 29, Inter-parliamentary conference meets at Brussels; concludes its sittings

1906

Jan. 24, Port of Antwerp bill, including both the commercial and the military portions of the scheme, passed by the chamber and becomes law

Jan. 25, Supreme court gives final judgment for the King, in the law suit arising out of the will of the late Queen of the Belgians

Feb. 12, Commercial treaty with Austria-Hungary signed in Vienna

March 1, Final sitting of the Congo commission

May 9, An arrangement, signed in London, by Sir E. Grey and Baron von Setvelde, ending the difficulty between Great Britain and the Congo State in respect to the territory on the Upper Nile

May 27, Polling throughout Belgium to supply vacancies in the chamber of representatives, half of whom seek a renewal of their mandates at the end of four years, results in the reduction of the clerical majority from 20 to 12. New chamber will contain 89 Catholics, 47 Liberals, 28 Socialists, and 1 Christian Democrat

Sept. 17–Nov. 2, Strike of manufacturers at Verviers

Sept. 25, Death of M. Leon Verhaeghe de Naeyer, Belgian Minister to the Quirinal

Nov. 28, Debate on the administration of the Congo Free State, opened in the chamber

1907

April 11, Government defeated in the chamber by 76 to 70 votes, on a question of the length of the working day in the mines

May 2, New cabinet formed with M. de Trooz as Premier; M. Liebaert, Finance; M. Renken, Justice; M. Helleputte, Railways; M. Hubert, Industry and Labor; M. Descamps, Arts and Science; General Hellebaut, War; M. Davignon, Foreign Affairs; and M. Delbeke, Public Works

July 23, New port of Zeebrugge, the sea terminus of the Bruges Ship Canal, opened by King Leopold

Sept. 2, Strikes in Antwerp; men handling coal and minerals, and porters cease work; riots, damage done to the amount of 160,000l., Sept. 4–5; men decide to resume work under promise of an increase in wages, Sept. 24

Nov. 28, Treaty of cession between Belgium and the Congo Free State concluded; text published Dec. 6

Dec. 31, Death of M. de Trooz, Prime Minister

1908

Jan. 8, M. Schollaert appointed Minister of the Interior, in succession to the late M. de Trooz

1909

Aug. 20, The Congo treaty of annexation, and the colonial law passed in the chamber; adopted by the senate, Sept. 9

Dec. 14, The military service bill passed by the senate

Dec. 23, King Albert takes the oath of accession

Dec. 23–24, Severe floods; overflow of the Senne causes hundreds of houses to be surrounded by water; several factories closed

1910

Jan. 29, M. Renken announces that forced labor in the Congo is to be abandoned

Feb. 27, Overflow of the Meuse and the Sambre; the valley inundated at Liége; and also at Jemeppe and Flemalle-Grande; quays and promenades under water at Namur; factories flooded, and thousands thrown out of work at Marchienne

April 23, Brussels exhibition opened by King Albert

1911

Jan. 9–17, Strike of 22,000 coal miners near Liége for reduction of hours

May 9–11, Visit of President Fallières of France

June 4, Partial election for senate gave Catholic majority

June 8, Resignation of Schollaert Ministry because of failure to obtain a majority for his Education Bill providing for giving Catholic schools the same financial support as the communal schools

June 9, Bill passed provided for old age pensions for coal miners to go into effect Jan. 1, 1912

June 14, New Cabinet formed by Baron de Broqueville as Prime Minister and Minister of Railways

June 16–25, Strike of seamen for recognition of union

July 26, Visit of Queen Wilhelmina and Prince Henry of the Netherlands

Aug. 15, Great demonstration against new Education Bill in Brussels by Democrats, Liberals, and Socialists

Oct. 15, Municipal elections a victory for Liberals and Socialists

1912

Jan. 1, Old Age Pension Act came into effect

Jan., Strike of 24,480 coal miners as protest against payment of wages fortnightly instead of weekly which ended Feb. 15

Feb. 13, Act requiring weekly payment of wages passed

March 29, Successful strike of 2,200 dockers for increase of wages

April 3, General Michel appointed Minister of War replacing General Hellebaut resigned

May 15, Law established a petty code of childrens' law and a childrens' magistracy

June 2, Elections for Parliament gave majority to Catholic Clerical Party obtaining 101 seats in new Chamber, Liberals, 45; Socialists, 38; and Christian Democrats, 2

Oct. 6, Death of Auguste Beernaert, former Prime Minister (83)

Nov. 10, General Michel, Minister of War resigned, the portfolio taken by the Prime Minister

Nov. 26, Death of Dowager Queen Marie, mother of King Albert

1913

April 14–24, General political strike for reform of franchise law

April 22, Resolution of Chamber to appoint commission to frame "a suffrage system superior to that now in force"

April 26, International Exposition at Ghent opened by King Albert

May 26, Commission for Electoral Reform of 31 members of Parliament appointed

June 22, Opening of the Terneuzen Canal

Aug. 30, Army Bill enacted, provided for general compulsory service in place of recruiting and of taking of one son from each family of law of Dec. 14, 1909 and created 8 new regiments and new division staffs; service in infantry for 15 months, field artillery 21 months, cavalry 24

Dec. 23, Miners' Pension Bill passed by chamber gave $70 a year to all miners over 55 who had worked underground 40 years

1914

Feb. 28, M. Davignon appointed Minister of Foreign Affairs, Baron de Broqueville, Minister of War

May 19 and June 15, Compulsory Education laws passed, education of children to begin at 6 years and extend over 8 years

May 24, Election gave Catholic Party 99 seats in chamber, Liberals, 46; Socialists, 40; Christian Democrats, 2

July 27, Stock exchange closed

July 29, Army placed on a reënforced peace footing

July 31, Army mobilized

——, France officially pledged herself to respect Belgian neutrality

Aug. 2, German ultimatum to Belgium demanded free passage of troops through Belgium, in case of refusal after 12 hours Belgium to be considered as an enemy

Aug. 3, Belgium replied to Germany that her neutrality would be defended

——, Appeal of the King to Great Britain to safeguard neutrality of Belgium

——, Offer of 5 French army corps not accepted

Aug. 4, German invasion of Belgium. *See* World War

——, Germany declared war on Belgium. Government handed German Minister his passports

——, Speech of King Albert to Parliament affirmed country's decision for unyielding resistance before he left for headquarters

Aug. 14, Government rationed bread

Aug. 16, The Government and the Queen and the royal children left Brussels for Antwerp on approach of the Germans

Aug. 22, German levy of £8,000,000 on Brussels

——, Austria-Hungary declared war on Belgium

Aug. 24, Lille declared an open town and evacuated

Aug. 30, Belgian mission left for the United States headed by Carton de Wiart, Minister of Justice, and including M. de Sadeleer, Emile Vandervelde, and Paul Hymans. Received by President Wilson, Sept. 16

Sept. 2, General von der Goltz took office as German Governor General

Sept. 3, First meeting of the *Comite Central Secours et d'Alimentation* at Brussels which opened canteens and food depots

Sept. 19, The British and French Governments guaranteed the integrity of the Belgian colonies

Oct. 7, The Government moved to Ostend

Oct. 13, Government established at Havre, France

——, Germans levied £20,000,000 on Antwerp

Oct. 22, Committee for Relief in Belgium organized by the American and Spanish Ambassadors in London and Brussels

Dec. 2, Baron von Bissing appointed German Governor General of Belgium

Dec. 3, Functions of provincial governors transferred to German military governors

Dec. 10, War contribution of 40 million francs a month imposed by order of German Government

Dec. 25, Pastoral letter of Cardinal Mercier to be read in churches Jan. 3 on patriotism and endurance in which he protested against cruelties inflicted on Belgian population

Dec., Declaration of stocks of benzine, petrol, alcohol, glycerine, oils, fats, rubber, and motor tires required

1915

Jan. 2, Proclamation of General von Bissing forbade reading of the pastoral letter of Cardinal Mercier in the churches and the Cardinal arrested

Jan. 3, Arrest of Cardinal Mercier

Jan. 25, Declaration of stocks of lead, copper, aluminum, zinc, nickel, &c., required

Feb. 2, *La Libre Belge* appeared and was thereafter published each week and distributed until the Armistice in spite of efforts of Germans

Feb. 3, Decree abolished law concerning responsibility of communes pillaged by force or violence setting up special arbitration courts

Feb. 5, General von Bissing established a judicial system giving German governors of provinces unlimited power to institute penalties and penalties transferred to other persons in default of the offenders themselves

Feb. 15, Report of War Relief Committee of the Rockefeller Foundation published

Feb. 17, Sequestration of all industrial and business concerns of Belgians or nationals of countries at war with Germany

March 1, Belgian Government at Havre called all Belgians between ages of 18 and 25 to the colors for service in army

March 16, Royal decree established workshops, munitions factories, storehouses, &c., at Havre

April 24, The coal "Central" (*Kohkenzentrale*) established requisitioned entire output of mines to provide coal for railroads and German army

May 12, Bryce Report published on German occupation in Belgium

June 3, Oil "Central" established to control supply for German purposes and the surplus for export trade to neutral countries by German Government of occupation

June 16, Tax decreed on Belgian absentees who did not return by March 1 and seizure of property if not paid

July 26, The "Central" for water, gas, and electricity established placing these services under German control

Aug. 5, Strike of Belgian coal miners. Fired on by German troops

Aug. 14 and 15, Decrees prescribed penalties for persons who refused to work for German authorities

Oct. 12, Execution of Edith Cavell, English nurse in Brussels, shot after German court martial for harboring Allied soldiers and aiding them to escape

1916

Jan. 10 and Oct. 10, Official orders prohibited more than 24 hours per week in the textile and bootmaking trades

Jan. 18, Baron Beyens became Minister of Foreign Affairs in Belgian Cabinet

Jan. 28, Paul Hymans, Count Goblet d'Alviella, and Emile Vandervelde sworn in as members of the Cabinet at Havre

March 15, Order of German Government that all lectures in the University of Ghent should be given in the Flemish language

April 5, The German Chancellor in the Reichstag outlined policy of establishment of a protectorate over Flemish people

April 29, France, Great Britain, Italy, Russia, and Japan made declaration guaranteeing integrity of the Belgian Congo

May 15, Decree of General von Bissing required unemployed Belgians to accept work for German authorities even if such work to the advantage of the German cause

June 26, Death of Emile Waxweiler, sociologist

July 21, All Belgians aged 18 to 40 in Allied or neutral States called to military service

Oct. 3, Decree of General von Bissing stated that unemployed Belgians might be called to work outside the place where they were living and called on the communal authorities to furnish lists of unemployed which they refused to do

Oct. 24, By this date 15,000 Belgians had been deported to Germany

Nov. 9, Protest of Belgian Parliament to General von Bissing against the deportation to Germany of Belgians and to the legations of neutral nations

Nov. 13, Cardinal Mercier addressed an appeal to the civilized world against the deportation of Belgians to Germany

Nov. 22, Belgian Government protested to Neutral Powers against the deportations and forced labor

Nov. 27, Death of Emile Verhaeren

Nov. 29, Appeal of the Pope to the German Government on behalf of the deported Belgians without effect

Dec. 1, By this date nearly 100,000 Belgians deported to Germany

1917

Feb. 4, "Council of Flanders" constituted by separatists

Feb. 14, Committee of representative Belgians addressed letter to the German Emperor demanding repatriation of deported Belgians

Feb. 17 and July 21, Decrees of German Government of occupation prohibited work in workshops and factories except by authorization of the administration

March 3, The "Council of Flanders" sent commission headed by A. Borms and P. Tack to Germany to petition for the independence of Flanders which was received by the Emperor

March 21, German decree divided Belgium into 2 administrative districts with administrative centers at Brussels and Namur, French becoming the official language in the Walloon district, Flemish in the west

April 18, Death of General von Bissing. Succeeded by General von Falkenhausen

May 29, New tax announced of 10 million francs making total tax levied on Belgium 720 million francs

June 1, Belgians in Germany repatriated but those who were returned had to accept work in requisitioned Belgian factories or be again deported

Aug. 4, Baron de Broqueville became Minister of Foreign Affairs, and General de Ceuninck of War

Aug. 9, Flemish proclaimed the official language of Flanders by German decree

Oct. 12, Ministry of Economic Affairs constituted for reconstruction after the War by Belgian Government

Oct. 13, An Economic Council of experts outside Belgium created by royal decree for reconstruction after the War

Dec. 22, The Council of Flanders proclaimed the independence of Flanders

Dec. 24, King Albert replied to Peace Note of the Pope

1918

Jan. 1, M. Hymans appointed Minister of Foreign Affairs

Jan. 8, Point 7 of President Wilson's Fourteen Points demanded evacuation and restoration of Belgium

Feb. 11, Great demonstration in Brussels against the Council of Flanders and attempt to organize a Flemish State under German protection

April 7, German courts established and the Belgian courts suppressed by decree

May 31, M. Cooreman succeeded M. de Broqueville as Prime Minister of Belgian Government at Havre

July 6, Belgian provincial councils suppressed by decree

Sept. 14, German Government made peace offer to Belgium on basis of no indemnity or reparations

Oct. 16, Retreat of the Germans from western Belgium begun

Oct. 17, Belgians occupied Ostend

Oct. 19, Belgians occupied Bruges and Zeebrugge evacuated by Germans

Oct. 20, The entire coast evacuated by Germans

Nov. 10, Decree of the Belgian Government ordered sequestration of all property belonging to subjects of enemy countries

Nov. 11, Germans evacuated and Belgians entered Ghent

Nov. 13, King Albert formally entered Ghent

Nov. 17, Brussels evacuated by Germans and Burgomaster Max reassumed office after 50 months of captivity in Germany

Nov. 19, Formal entry of the King and Queen into Antwerp

Nov. 21, Resignation of General de Ceuninck as Minister of War. Succeeded by M. Masson

Nov. 22, Formal entry of the King and Queen into Brussels

Dec. 17, Decree regulated sale of butter

Dec. 27, Decree regulated trade in meat

1919

Feb. 28, Royal order coördinated legislation regarding the employment of women and children

March 3, Tax placed on war profits progressive to 10% and railway fares doubled

April 11, Universal male suffrage and partial female suffrage adopted in chamber

May 4, System of unemployment benefits became effective

May 9, Electoral law establishing universal male suffrage and giving vote to certain women enacted

May 17, Official announcement that damage suffered by Belgium estimated as $7,600,000,000 of which $1,705,000 represented losses suffered by industry

May 30, Agreement with Great Britain as to division of German East Africa, Belgium receiving mandate for Ruanda and Urundi

June 1, Hours of labor in steel manufactories and mines reduced to 8½ hours a day

June 4, Decision of Supreme Council announced after consideration of Report of Belgian Affairs Commission of March 8 that the Treaties of 1839 should be revised and an international commission appointed to make proposals "which imply neither the transfer of territorial sovereignty nor the creation of international servitudes"

June 28, By the Treaty of Versailles, Belgian neutrality abolished, and Germany ceded rights over Eupen and Malmédy and Moresnet

July 30, Law established a commercial commission to secure sufficient supply of cereals

Aug. 8, Decision of the Government to temporarily take over farms in the devastated regions to be worked by scientific methods, owners to be paid 5% on pre-War valuation

Aug. 12, Belgian troops occupied Malmédy and formal possession taken Aug. 25

Aug. 19, Decree required that all cereals not absolutely needed by farmers must be handed over to the Commission created July 30

Aug. 21, Belgian mandate over Ruanda-Urundi accepted by Supreme Council

Aug. 29, Law prohibited sale of alcohol in public

Sept. 5, National foundation of child welfare established

Sept. 7, August Borms and 44 other Flemish separatists sentenced to various severe terms of imprisonment, the death sentence for Borms commuted later to life imprisonment

Sept. 9, Arrival of Cardinal Mercier in New York to express the gratitude of the Belgian nation for American aid

Sept. 15, Law attached Eupen and Malmédy and Prussian Moresnet to the arrondissement of Verviers, La Calamine formerly neutral Moresnet changed to Commine de La Calamine

Oct. 11, New inheritance law imposed tax which varied with decree of kinship of heir from 1 to 50%, and inheritance from an intestate beyond the fourth decree abolished in favor of the State. New taxes placed on beer, tobacco, alcohol, and cinemas

Oct. 25, Law provided for option of Belgian nationality

Oct. 28, King Albert with the Queen and Crown Prince arrived in Washington on a visit to the United States

Nov. 16, Elections under new universal male suffrage law gave Catholics 73 seats in Chamber; Socialists, 70; Liberals, 34; Christian Democrats, 4; minor parties, 7; the Catholics losing majority it had held since 1884

Nov. 21, New coalition Cabinet headed by M. Delacroix (Catholic) with Hymans (Liberal) as Minister of Foreign Affairs

Dec. 1, Hours of labor reduced to eight hours per day

1920

Jan. 10, Proclamation of sovereignty over Eupen and Malmédy

——, Belgium became original member of the League of Nations

Jan. 11, Colonial School established at Antwerp

Jan. 13, Agreement with the Netherlands to appoint a commission to settle questions in dispute as to the Scheldt, and the Ghent-Terneuzen

Jan. 22, Declaration signed with Portugal modified commercial arrangements of 1897

Jan. 26, Belgian High Commissioner made formal entry into Eupen and Malmédy

Feb. 6, Eight Socialists expelled from Senate and seats declared vacant because of failure to meet income tax requirements previous to election

March 10, Bill granting suffrage to women in municipal elections passed in Chamber, and Senate April 14

April 4–21, First annual commercial fair held in Brussels

April 8, Royal decree reorganized higher agricultural education

April 15, Electoral law enacted gave Belgians over 21, without distinction of sex, who have been domiciled for at least 6 months the right to vote in communal elections

May 19, Decree regulated cultivation of farms and required a declaration by all farmers of details of crops, cultivated lands, cattle, &c.

May 26, Negotiations with Holland as to the Scheldt broken off without agreement

June 1, Royal order provided for supervision of health of young persons employed

June 18, Bill passed Chamber making women eligible for election to Parliament

July 1, Bill granting unrestricted suffrage to women defeated in Chamber

July 25, Economic Agreement with Luxemburg signed

July 29, Soldiers invaded Chamber to protest against neglect of Government demanding a bonus

Aug. 19, *Académie de la langue française* inaugurated at Brussels

Aug. 20, Royal order coördinated Acts as to old age pensions

Aug. 29, Law prohibited sale of alcohol in public

Sept. 1, Economic Agreement with Germany signed

Sept. 7, Military Agreement with France signed

Sept. 20, Decision of the League of Nations confirmed sovereignty of Belgium over Eupen and Malmédy and Prussian Moresnet

Oct. 30–Nov. 1, Workmen's Party Convention rejected Third International by vote of 493,000 to 76,000

Nov. 2, Strike of coal miners in Charleroi district for increase in wages spread to other mining centers

Nov. 13, Commercial Convention with Brazil signed

Nov. 19, New coalition Cabinet headed by Carton de Wiart succeeded Delacroix Ministry, H. Jaspar (Clerical) Minister of Foreign Affairs, E. Vandervelde, Justice

Dec. 30, Royal order respecting unemployment insurance

1921

Feb. 5, The right to sequestrate property of Germans in case of default of Treaty obligations renounced to further trade relations

Feb. 9, Workmens' Compensation Convention with the Netherlands concluded

March 15, Convention with Great Britain signed as to Belgian traffic through East Africa

March 23, Parliament passed 50% Tariff Bill on German imports

June 14, Act established eight-hour day and forty-eight-hour week

July 7, Commercial *modus vivendi* with Spain concluded. Prolonged Dec. 21

July 25, Economic Convention with Luxemburg signed by which the customs barriers between the 2 countries to be abolished for 50 years and railway systems unified to take effect May 1, 1922

Aug. 7, Workmens' Compensation Amendment Act replaced that of Dec. 24, 1903

Aug. 10, Agreement signed with Egypt modified Treaty of commerce and navigation of June 24, 1891

Aug. 12, Law established use of Flemish language in administrative affairs

Nov. 15, Convention signed with France, Brazil, and 9 other nations established an International Patent Bureau in Brussels

Nov. 20–28, Elections gave Catholic Party a majority in chamber, Mme Marie Spaak-Janson, Socialist Senator, the first woman elected to Parliament

Dec. 14, Georges Theunis appointed Prime Minister

Dec. 31, Population estimated as 7,478,840 exclusive of Eupen and Malmédy with a population of about 60,000

1922

Jan. 1, Law passed in August, 1921, provided for use of both Flemish and French as official languages in administration

May 15, New naturalization law passed

Oct. 25, Commercial Agreement with Rumania signed

Dec. 30, Commercial Agreement with Poland signed

1923

Jan. 11, Belgian troops joined French force in occupation of the Ruhr Valley to force German fulfillment of the Treaty of Versailles

May 12, Commercial Agreement with France signed

June 14, Theunis Ministry resigned because of defeat in Senate of Bill to substitute the Flemish for the French language in the University of Ghent, and division of Cabinet on Army Bill

July 3, Premier Theunis withdrew resignation

July 20, Army Bill passed provided for recruiting by means of annual calls to the colors and by voluntary enlistments; military service compulsory for those called to the colors, 10 months service in infantry, artillery and engineers and 12 months cavalry

July 27, Nolf-Theunis Bill introducing Flemish language in Ghent University passed Chamber by vote of 87 to 75 with 8 not voting

July, Election gave the Right 31 seats and the Left 19

Aug. 3, Enlargement of Ruanda-Urundi mandated territory made effective by an Agreement with Tanganyika

Aug. 26, Provisional Commercial Agreement with Austria signed

Aug. 31, Modification of boundaries between British and Belgian mandated territories in East Africa approved by League of Nations Council

Oct. 16, University of Ghent opened under new régime using Flemish as well as French, Dr. Heymans becoming new rector

Nov. 11, Colonial University constituted by union of the School of Tropical Medicine and the Colonial School

Dec. 14, Commercial Treaty with Austria signed

Dec. 15, New boundaries with Belgium proclaimed by Germany

Dec. 31, Kisha territory in East Africa ceded by Great Britain

1924

Feb. 12, Commercial Agreement with Finland concluded

Feb. 27, Theunis Ministry resigned defeated in Parliament. The Chamber rejected Commercial Agreement with France signed in May, 1923

March 10, M. Theunis formed new Cabinet, Paul Hymans, Minister of Foreign Affairs

April 12–16, Flemish Congress at Louvain

June 3, Mixed Arbitral Tribunal decided in favor of Belgium in test case of Loriaux as to payment by Germany to labor deported during the War. By later agreement (July, 1925), Germany paid 24,000,000 francs

June 27, Commercial Treaty with Japan signed

July 3, Commercial Convention with Canada signed

July 12, Commercial Agreement with Germany signed

Aug. 18, Debt Agreement with the United States signed

Sept. 1, Loan of $30,000,000 negotiated with American bankers

Sept. 30, Commercial *modus vivendi* with Hungary concluded

Oct. 11, Strike of miners ended

Oct. 24, Provisional Commercial Agreement with France signed

Nov. 7, Commercial Treaty with Guatemala signed

Dec. 10, Compulsory old age insurance for workers earning less than 12,000 francs a year voted

Dec. 12, Provisional Commercial Agreement with Spain signed

1925

Feb. 13, Treaty of conciliation and arbitration with Switzerland signed

March 6, Decree joined Eupen and Malmédy to Liége

March 10, Old age insurance regulations as to salaried employees promulgated

April 3, Treaty with the Netherlands as to the Scheldt signed, settled controversy regulating navigation and intention stated of cancellation of Treaty of April 19, 1839

April 4, Colonial Trade Agreement with Germany signed

——, Supplementary Commercial Agreement with France signed

April 5, Election for Parliament gave Socialists a majority with 79 seats in Chamber instead of 68; Catholics, 78; Liberals, 22; Communists, 2

——, Resignation of Theunis Cabinet

April 24 and Oct. 26, Further provisional Commercial Agreements with Spain

May 13, Cabinet formed by Aloys Van de Yyvere

May 22, Resignation of Van de Yyvere Cabinet

May 23, Burgomaster Max invited to form Cabinet but was not successful

June 3, Viscount Poulet formed coalition Cabinet of Catholics and Socialists

June 13, Poulet Cabinet defeated resigned

June 17, Poulet Cabinet reconstituted

June 28, Customs Tariff Agreement with Greece signed

July 1, Strike of 60,000 metal workers against proposed wage reduction of 5%

July 8, Treaty of commerce and navigation with Latvia signed

July 19, Strike of newspaper printers for increase of 12.50 francs (62 cents) a week

Aug. 18, Debt Agreement with the United States concluded funded at $727,830,500 to be repaid by 1987 by means of annuities

Aug. 27, Announcement of end of strike of metal workers, terms of settlement accepted by workers

Sept. 1, Agreement with Poland signed as to scientific, literary, and scholastic relations

Nov. 9, Results of provincial elections gain for Liberals and Catholics

Dec. 1, Treaty of Arbitration with Germany

Dec. 3, Resignation of M. Tschoffen, Minister of Finance. Succeeded by M. Poulet, Prime Minister

Dec. 9, Liquor smuggling Treaty with the United States signed

Dec. 28, Commercial Treaty with Czechoslovakia signed

Dec. 31, Agreement with Great Britain concluded by which total debt of Belgium and the Belgian Congo of £12,600,000 to be paid within 30 years, interest 5%

1926

Jan. 14, Resignation of General Kesten, Minister of War, refusing to reduce period of military training

Jan. 23, Death of Cardinal Mercier

Feb. 8, Provisional Commercial Agreement with Bulgaria signed

Feb. 22, Finance Committee of Senate adopted financial stabilization measures passed by Chamber including ratification of American loan of $150,000,000

Feb. 25, Failure of Crédit Foncier, large Antwerp bank, with deficit estimated at 40,000,000 francs

March 14, Fall of Belgian franc because of failure to obtain foreign loan

April 6, Treaty of Nov. 2, 1865, with China denounced by Peking Government. *See also* China, Nov. 5 and 6

April 30, Treaty of arbitration and conciliation with Sweden signed

May 5, Resignation of Baron Rolin Jacquemyns, Minister of Interior, over financial policy

May 11, Ministry resigned

May 17, Exchange of Notes with Great Britain acceptance of boundary of Tanganyika with Ruanda-Urundi

May 20, Henri Jaspar formed Cabinet as Prime Minister and Minister of Foreign Affairs; Emile Vandervelde (Socialist); without Portfolio, Emile Francqui; Justice, Paul Hymans (Liberal); Education, Camille Huysmans (Socialist); Finance and Colonies, Baron Houtart (Catholic); Agriculture and Public Works, Henri Baels (Catholic); Industry and Labor and Social Insurance, Joseph Wauters (Socialist); Railways, Marine, Posts and Telegraphs, and Aëronautics, Edouard Anseele (Socialist); National Defense, Comte de Broqueville (Catholic)

May 22, Treaty with Great Britain, the Netherlands and France signed abrogated Treaty of 1839

——, Air Navigation Agreement with Germany signed

June 7, Act passed provided for new taxes to yield one and a half milliards

July 3–9, Strike of Antwerp dock workers for increase in wages

July 12, The franc at 240 to the English pound sterling

July 13, Treaty of friendship, commerce, and navigation with Siam concluded

July 16, Dictatorial powers voted to King Albert for 6 months during financial crisis

July 23, Management of railroads turned over to a national railway company by the State

July 31, Royal decree consolidated floating debt, creditors of the State given Treasury bonds against shares in railway company

Aug., Offer of Germany of a milliard and a half gold marks for Eupen and Malmédy rejected

Aug. 14, Law providing for taxing of foreigners went into effect increasing tax on lodgings from 10 to 20%, and daily tax of 10 francs required for foreign automobiles

Sept. 10, Provisional Commercial Agreement with Greece signed

Sept. 17 and Dec. 16, Provisional Commercial Agreements with Yugoslavia signed

Sept. 28, Treaty of commerce and navigation with Estonia signed

Oct. 20, Labor Treaty with Luxemburg signed

Oct. 25, Franc stabilized at 174.30 to the English pound, 36 to the dollar on gold basis and new currency unit, the belga, introduced equal to 5 paper francs, 35 belgas equal to one pound gold. A stabilization loan of $100,000,000 contracted for for 30 years

Oct. 27, New metal currency placed in circulation

Nov. 4, Marriage of Crown Prince Leopold to Princess Astrid of Sweden

Nov. 15, Resignation of M. Francqui, Finance Minister

Nov. 26, Belgium instituted proceedings against China before Permanent Court of International Justice because of abrogation of Treaty of 1865

1927

Jan. 6, Provisional Commercial Agreement with Portugal signed

Jan. 19, Death of Princess Charlotte, sister of Leopold II and the former Empress of Mexico

Feb. 5, Treaty of arbitration and conciliation with Switzerland signed

Feb. 8, Consular Convention with Estonia signed

March 3, Treaty of arbitration and conciliation with Denmark signed

March 4, Treaty of arbitration and conciliation with Finland signed

June 21, Italian ambassador recalled as protest against anti-Fascist position of Emile Vandervelde, Minister of Foreign Affairs

July 9, Treaty of arbitration and conciliation with Portugal signed

——, Financial Agreement with Germany signed

July 19, Treaty of conciliation, arbitration, and judicial settlement with Spain signed

July 22, Convention with Portugal regarding Belgian Congo and Angola signed cession of territory

Aug. 28, Commercial Treaty with Turkey signed

Sept. 30, Total Belgian public debt 56,190,000,000 francs (£320,000,000), consolidated debt 90% of this total 51 billion francs, internal debt approximately 27,500,000,000, foreign debt 28,700,000,000

Oct. 18, Arbitration Treaty with Luxemburg signed

Nov. 21, Jaspar Ministry resigned defeated on question of military service

Nov. 22, Jaspar formed new Ministry: Henri Jaspar (Catholic), Prime Minister and Minister of the Colonies; Paul Hymans (Liberal), Foreign Affairs; M. Janson (Liberal), Justice; Maurice Vauthier (Liberal), Education; Baron Houtart (Catholic), Finance; Henri Baels (Catholic), Agriculture and Public Works; M. Heyman (Christian Democrat), Industry and Labor and Social Insurance; M. Lippens (Liberal), Railways, Marine, Posts and Telegraphs, and Aëronautics; Comte de Broqueville (Catholic), National Defense; M. Carnoy (Christian Democrat), Interior

1928

Feb. 23, Commercial Agreement with France signed

April 14, "Family Allowances" law passed provided for payment over and above regular wages to workers with children

June 5–Aug. 31, Visit of the King and Queen to the Belgian Congo

June 12, Consular Convention with Poland signed

June 20, Strike of 10,000 dockers for wage increase

July 4, Dedication of new Library at Louvain University replacing the library burned by the Germans in 1914

——, Labor Agreement with France signed

Aug. 16, Provisional Commercial Agreement with Lithuania signed

Oct. 25, Treaty of arbitration and conciliation with Poland signed

Nov. 22, Treaty of amity and commerce with China signed by which Belgium agreed to surrender of extraterritoriality

Dec. 15, Commercial Agreement with Spain signed

Dec. 27, Floods inundated 15 villages along the Scheldt River making 8,000 persons homeless

1929

May 23, Treaty of friendship and arbitration with Persia signed

May 26, Elections for Parliament gave Catholics 77 seats in Chamber; Socialists, 70; Liberals, 28; minor parties, 12; and for the Senate Catholics, 70; Liberals, 23; Socialists, 55; and minor parties, 12

June 25, Arbitration Treaty with Greece signed

July 13, Agreement with Germany signed as to sequestrated German property and German marks left in the country after the War in exchange for Belgian francs confiscated

Aug. 26, Commercial Agreement with Switzerland signed

Aug. 31, Agreement with China signed for retrocession of Belgian concession at Tientsin

Oct. 15, Death of Leon Delacroix, former Premier

Oct. 18, Cabinet reconstituted on resignation of M. Carnoy, Minister of the Interior

——, Three new Ministries added

Nov. 25, Cabinet resigned

Dec. 4, Cabinet reconstituted: Henri Jaspar (Catholic), Prime Minister; Paul Hymans (Liberal), Minister of Foreign Affairs; M. Janson (Liberal), Justice; Maurice Vauthier (Liberal), Education; Baron Houtart (Catholic), Finance; Henri Baels (Catholic), Agriculture, Home Affairs and Hygiene; M. Heyman (Christian Democrat), Industry and Labor and Social Insurance; M. Lippens (Liberal), Railways, Marine, and Aëronautics; Comte de Broqueville (Catholic), National Defense; M. Henri Jaspar (acting), Colonies; M. Forthomme, Posts and Telegraphs; M. van Caenegem, Public Work

Dec. 30, Workers Industrial Compensation Act for seamen passed

1930

Jan. 16, Convention signed with Germany regarding financial questions arising under Treaty of Versailles

——, Amnesty law passed under which Dr. August Borms, leader of Flemish separatist movement, released from prison the following day

Jan. 18, Agreement with Austria signed as to property rights and debts

Feb. 27, Bill passed Chamber making Flemish the language of University of Ghent, hitherto bilingual

March 25, Arbitration, conciliation, and judicial settlement Convention signed with Yugoslavia

May 31, First sod in Liége-Antwerp Canal turned by King Albert which when completed will enable boats to cover distance in 30 hours instead of 8 days

June 18, Old Age Insurance Act for salaried employees of 1925 amended and Workmens' Compensation Act

July 4, Strike of 25,000 coal miners against old age pensions regulations

July 8, Treaty of arbitration, conciliation, and judicial settlement with Rumania signed

Aug. 1, Miners Retirement Pension Act promulgated

Sept. 24, Treaty of arbitration, conciliation, and judicial settlement with Lithuania signed

Oct. 25, Decree established Government control of imports to prevent dumping at request of Farmers' Union, licenses instituted on certain classes of goods including wheat, barley, oats, rye, wines, hides, and pelts

Nov. 11, Cabinet resigned in clash over use of French and Flemish languages after resignation of 5 Liberal Ministers but remained in office reconstituted

Dec. 4–6, Fog in Valley of the Meuse near Liége caused death of 67 persons and loss of cattle

Dec. 15, Court of Appeals reversed decision of lower court which had ordered the inscription of the American architect, Whitney Warren, "Destroyed by German fury; restored by American generosity" to be placed on the Balustrade of the Louvain University Library

KINGS

1831. Leopold, first King of the Belgians; born Dec. 16, 1790; inaugurated July 21, 1831, at Brussels; married, Aug. 9, 1832, Louise, eldest daughter of Louis Philippe, King of the French (she died Oct. 11, 1850). He died Dec. 10, 1865.

1865. Leopold II, son; born April 9, 1835; married Archduchess Maria Henrietta of Austria, Aug. 22, 1853 (she died Sept. 19, 1902, aged 66); died Dec. 17, 1909.
Daughter, Princess Louise, born Feb. 18, 1858; married Duke Philip of Saxony, Feb. 4, 1875.

1909. Albert, nephew; born April 8, 1875; married Elizabeth, Duchess of Bavaria, Oct. 2, 1900; heir, son, Leopold, born Nov. 3, 1901

BERLIN CONFERENCES

BERLIN CONFERENCE (June 16–July 1, 1880)

July 15, The ambassadors for Great Britain and France, and the German Foreign Minister, agree to a collective note presented to the Sultan of Turkey (urging the surrender of Dulcigno and cession of provinces to Greece), which is presented

1890

Berlin Conference respecting the condition of the working classes proposed by the German Emperor, Feb. 4. The delegates meet March 15

[The conference opened March 15, closed March 29, 1890. Subjects discussed: regulation of labor in mines, of Sunday labor, and of the labor of children and youths. Recommendations adopted referred to the respective legislatures.]

BERLIN CONGRESS ON THE EASTERN QUESTION

Representatives (with resident ambassadors): Germany, Prince Bismarck, President; Russia, Prince Gortschakoff; Turkey, Alexander Carathéodori; Great Britain, Lord Beaconsfield and Marquis of Salisbury (Lord Odo Russell, Ambassador); Austria, Count Andrassy; France, M. Waddington; Italy, Count Corti

1878

June 13, First meeting; 20th and last meeting, treaty signed, July 13

Articles 1–12. Bulgaria constituted an autonomous principality, tributary to the Sultan; the Balkans southern limit; the Prince to be elected by the population, approved by the Sultan and other Powers; public laws, and other details

" 13–22. New province of Eastern Rumelia constituted; partially autonomous; boundaries defined; Christian governor general to be appointed by the Sultan; to be organized by an Austrian commission; a Russian army of occupation to remain nine months

" 23. Bosnia and Herzegovina to be occupied and administered by Austria-Hungary.

" 24–30. Montenegro to be independent; new frontiers; Antivaria annexed

" 31–39. Serbia to be independent, with new frontiers

" 40–49. Rumania to be independent, losing part of Bessarabia to Russia, with compensation

" 50–54. Regulation of navigation of the Danube, &c.

" 55–57. Legal reforms in Crete, &c.

" 58. The Porte cedes to Russia Ardahan, Kars, and Batum, and settles boundaries

" 59. Batum to be a free commercial port.

" 60. Alasgird and Bayazid restored to Turkey.

" 61–62. The Porte engages to realize legal reforms, and to grant religious liberty, &c.

" 63. The Treaty of Paris (March 30, 1856), and of London (March 13, 1871), maintained when not modified by this treaty

" 64. Treaty to be ratified in three weeks time. Ratified Aug. 3

1880

May, Circular respecting delay in fulfilling the treaty from Earl Granville, the British Foreign Secretary, to the foreign powers

BOER WAR

See South African War.

BOHEMIA

Bohemia, a province of Czechoslovakia, former province and crown land of Austria-Hungary, once powerful independent kingdom and from 1253 to 1278, the reign of Ottocar II, extended from the Elbe to the Adriatic. In 1278 Ottocar was defeated and slain in battle with Rudolph of Habsburg. *See* Czechoslovakia.

ca. 400 to 1889

About 5th century, The Czechs (Slavonians) conquer Bohemia

759, City of Prague founded

894, Introduction of Christianity

1041, Bohemia conquered by the Emperor Henry III who spreads devastation through the country

1198, Ottocar (Premislas) I, first King of Bohemia

1253, Ottocar II rules over Austria, and obtains Styria, &c.; refuses the imperial crown, 1272

1277, Ottocar vanquished by the Emperor Rudolph and deprived of Austria, Styria, and Carniola; killed at Marchfeld, Aug. 26, 1278

1346, King John (blind), slain at the battle of Crécy

1415, 1416, John Huss and Jerome of Prague, two of the first reformers, burnt for heresy; which occasions an insurrection

July 14, 1420, Ziska, leader of the Hussites, takes Prague; dies of the plague, 1424

1438, Albert, Duke of Austria, marries the daughter of the late Emperor and King, and receives the crowns of Bohemia and Hungary

1440–1458, The succession infringed by Ladislas, son of the King of Poland, and George Podiebrad, a protestant chief

1471, Ladislas, King of Poland, elected King of Bohemia on the death of Podiebrad

1527, The Emperor Ferdinand I marries Anne, sister of Louis the late King, and obtains the crown

Sept. 5, 1610, The Emperor Ferdinand II, oppressing the Protestants, is deposed, and Frederic the Elector-Palatine, elected King

Nov. 9, 1620, Frederic, totally defeated at Prague, flees to Holland

1648, Bohemia secured to Austria by treaty

1742, Silesia and Glatz ceded to Prussia

1744, Prague taken by the Prussians

May 6, 1757, Prussians defeat Austrians at Prague

1775, Revolt of the peasantry

1781, Edict of Toleration promulgated

1806, The French occupy Prague

1848, Insurrection at Prague, June 12; submission, state of siege raised, July 20

June 23, 1866, The Prussians enter Bohemia, which becomes the seat of war (*see* Germany, 1866)

1867, autumn, Agitation of the Czechs, who require the Emperor to be crowned King of Bohemia with the crown of St. Wenceslas at Prague

Oct. 10, 1868, Riots at Prague; habeas corpus act suspended

Sept. 14 and Oct. 5, 1870, Bohemian agitation for self-government; addresses to the Emperor

Sept. 14, 1871, Manifesto of the Emperor

Dec., Bohemian deputies absent from the Reichsrath

July, 1874, The "Young Czech" Party defeated in the elections

Oct. 8, 1879, Czech deputies enter Reichsrath

Nov. 6, 1889, The motion of the Young Czechs in the assembly for the coronation of the Emperor as King of Bohemia negatived, after several days' warm debate

1890

Jan. 17–19, Peaceful settlement of the disputes between Czechs and Germans, in a conference, by the intervention of the Emperor

May 19, Peace confirmed at a meeting of the diet

May 19–20, Strike of about 6,000 miners at Nürschau; fight with military; five men killed

Oct., The diet reopened Oct. 14, the Young Czechs obstruct legislation

Nov., Meeting of the diet; the Young Czech Party obstructive; the reconciliation of Germans and Czechs delayed

Nov. 30, The Brüx mine inundated through heavy rains, 87 colliers perish, announced

Middle Dec., The Emperor intervenes to promote the passing of the compromised bill by the diet; the Young Czechs require autonomy like Hungary

Dec., Gradual dissolution of the Old Czech Party (moderates)

1891

Jan. 5, The Austrian Government determine to make no more concessions to the Czechs; announced to the diet

About Jan. 16, Useful legislation in the diet obstructed by the Young Czechs

March 2–4, The Young Czechs victorious in the elections; Dr. Rieger, the venerable leader of the Old Czechs, and his party, totally defeated; he retires from public life (died March 3, 1903)

Sept. 26–Oct. 1, The Emperor visits Prague to promote peace between the Germans and Czechs

Sept. 30, Explosion of a bridge at Rosenthal, over which the Emperor was expected to pass

1892

March 24, The government compromise discussed in the diet and strongly opposed

May 31, Fire in the great silver mine, Birkenberg, near Przibram, about 319 deaths

1893

May 17, Disagreements in the diet; ordered to be closed

June 18, Disturbances of workmen at Prague and Brünn, suppressed

About Sept. 12, Repression of the Young Czech agitation in Prague

1895

Nov. 5, Amnesty granted for political offenses; announced

1898

Jan., New language ordinance issued

June 19, Death of Palacky (Czech) historian

1899

June 25, Death of Cardinal Count Schoenborn, Archbishop of Prague

Oct. 17, Language ordinances repealed

1901

Oct. 17, Diet elections completed, Czech majority

1904

May 1, Death of A. Dvorak, composer

KINGS

1198. Premislas Ottocar I
1230. Wenceslas III
1253. Premislas Ottocar II
1278. Wenceslas IV, King of Poland
1305. Wenceslas V
1306. Rudolph of Austria
1307. Henry of Carinthia
1310. John of Luxemburg (killed at Crécy)
1346. Charles I, Emperor (1347)
1378. Wenceslas VI, Emperor
1419. Sigismund I, Emperor
1438. Albert of Austria, Emperor
1440. Ladislas V
1458. George von Podiebrad
1471. Ladislas VI, King of Hungary (in 1490)
1516. Louis, King of Hungary (killed at Mohatz)
1526. Bohemia united to Austria under Ferdinand I elected King

BOUVET ISLAND

This uninhabited island in the Southern Atlantic (43° 10′ S.) was discovered in 1739 by a Frenchman, Pierre Bouvet, but no flag was hoisted till, in 1825, Captain Norris raised the Union Jack.

A neighboring island, Thompson Island, has been reported but its existence is seriously doubted. In 1928 a diplomatic dispute arose between Great Britain as to the claim to Bouvet, particularly in connection with the occupation since December, 1927, by a Norwegian whaling expedition, and the Norwegian decision to erect a wireless station on the island, and Great Britain decided in November, 1928, to waive its claim. By law of February 27, 1930, it is stated that Bouvet Island belongs to Norway as a dependency.

BRITISH EMPIRE

British Empire consists of Great Britain and Northern Ireland, Channel Islands and Isle of Man, the Irish Free State, India, the Dominions including Canada, Australia, New Zealand, Newfoundland, and South Africa, and Colonies, Protectorates, and Dependencies, including in Europe, Gibraltar and Malta, in America, Bermuda, Falkland Islands, British Guiana, British Honduras, Labrador, and the British West Indies. London is the capital. *See also* Africa; Asia.

BULGARIA

Bulgaria (Blgariya), Kingdom of southeastern Europe with eastern coast on the Black Sea, with Rumania on the north, Yugoslavia on the west and Greece and Turkey in Europe on the south, area 103,146 square kilometers, or 39,814 English square miles, and the census population on December 31, 1926, was 5,483,125 (2,748,060 males and 2,735,065 females), as against 4,846,971 (2,420,784 males and 2,426,187 females) in the Census of 1920. Population on December 31, 1928, was estimated at 5,596,800 (2,806,700 males and 2,790,100 females).

Population of districts, according to Census of December 31, 1926:—

DISTRICT	AREA IN SQ. MILES	POPULATION	PER SQ. MILE
Burgaz	5,257	484,759	92.2
Haskovo	1,916	245,354	128.1
Kustendil	1,532	243,493	158.9
Mastanly	1,523	183,828	120.7
Pashmakly	1,067	68,860	64.5
Petritch	2,624	186,040	70.9
Pléven	2,948	431,804	146.4
Plovdiv	3,823	561,021	146.7
Ruse	1,905	341,648	179.4
Shumen	2,313	359,485	150.5
Sofia	3,567	641,135	179.7
Stara Zagora	2,561	326,285	127.4
Tirnovo	3,010	505,251	168.0
Varna	1,472	230,121	156.6
Vidin	1,635	276,904	169.4
Vratza	2,661	392,753	147.3
Total	39,814	5,478,741	137.7

According to the Census of 1926, the population comprised 2,743,025 males and 2,735,716 females. On January 1, 1930, population was estimated at

5,824,900 (2,920,000 men and 2,904,900 women); 20.7% of the population was urban and 79.3% rural.

The capital is the city of Sofia, with a population (Census, 1926) of 213,002. The other principal towns, with population in 1926, are Philippopolis (Plovdiv), 84,655; Varna, 60,563; Ruschuk (Ruse), 45,788; Slivno (Sliven), 29,263; Plévna (Pléven), 28,775; Stara Zagora, 28,957; Shumen, 25,137; Burgaz, 31,157; Jambol, 23,037; Haskovo, 26,256; Pazarjik, 21,578; Vidin, 18,507; Vratza, 15,672; Kustendil, 15,440.

By the Peace Treaty of Neuilly, signed on November 27, 1919, Bulgaria ceded Thrace to the Allied and Associated Powers and the Strumnitsa line and a strip of territory on the northwest frontier to Serbia. Bulgaria was deprived of its Ægean littoral, but an efficient economic outlet to the same sea was promised to her by the Treaty, but has not yet been put into effect.

On October 5, 1908, Bulgaria declared her independence of Turkey, and the Powers recognized Bulgarian independence, and the title of "King of the Bulgarians" assumed by Prince Ferdinand. On September 18, 1885, the province of Eastern Rumelia was united with Bulgaria.

Boris III, reigning King (Tsar), eldest son of Ferdinand of Saxe-Coburg and Gotha, and of the late Marie Louise (died January 31, 1899), eldest daughter of Robert the last reigning Duke of Parma, born January 30, 1894, succeeded to the throne on the abdication of his father, October 3, 1918, married October 25, 1930, to Princess Giovanna of Savoy, daughter of King Victor Emanuel III of Italy.

1876

May–Sept., Insurrection in Bulgaria, quickly suppressed with great cruelty; see Turkey
Oct. 9, Zankoff and Balabanow, Bulgarian delegates, received in London

1878

July 13, Bulgaria constituted an autonomous principality, tributary to the Sultan, by the Berlin Treaty (see s.v.)

1879

Feb. 22, First parliament (or sobranje) opened at Tirnova by Prince Dondoukoff Korsakoff; the new constitution brought forward
April 29, Prince Alexander of Hesse elected Prince as Alexander I
June 5, Visits the European courts; received by Queen Victoria
July 9, Takes the oaths to the constitution at Tirnova
July 17, Bulgaria said to be quitted by the Russians
Dec. 18, Ministerial difficulties; parliament dissolved

1881

May 9, The Prince announces the summoning a national assembly, and threatens to resign
June 21, Zankoff and other liberal Ministers arrested for insulting the Prince in their election addresses (soon released)

June 27 et seq., Elections for national assembly; voters said to be coerced
July 13, Meeting of the assembly; the Prince's proposals unanimously accepted; he promises reforms and adherence to the constitution
About July 23, The late liberal Ministers, Zankoff and Slaviekoff, temporarily arrested
Sept. 12, Amnesty for political offenses proclaimed

1883

March 15, New ministry under General Skobeloff and M. Kypriak
Sept. 16, The Prince virtually dictator; opposes Russia, under whose influence a liberal reaction against the Prince takes place, and a new constitution is proposed; the national assembly meets
Sept. 20, Manifesto of the Prince restoring the Tirnova constitution; Zankoff Minister
Oct. 26, Colonel Redigher, War Minister, and other Russian officers summarily dismissed by the Prince
About Nov. 15, Peaceful relations with Russia re-established

1884

May, June, Disputes with Serbia respecting refugees and boundaries
July, M. Zankoff's Ministry resigns; succeeded by Karaveloff
Sept., Oct., Raids of Serbians repelled; the Bulgarian Government protests
Dec., Disputes with Serbia unsettled

1885

About Oct. 15, Reunion with Rumelia (termed South Bulgaria, April, 1886) declared; about Sept. 18; all Bulgaria arming; action suspended on advice of the Powers of Europe
Nov. 13, Declaration of war by Serbia; circular to the Powers alleging Bulgarian aggression; denied by Prince Alexander; Bulgaria invaded at four points; skirmishes, several killed and wounded, and small places occupied by Serbians; Prince Alexander appeals to Turkey for help, Nov. 14
Nov. 15, The Bulgarians bravely defend the Dragoman pass, attacked by 40,000 Serbians, but retire at night
——, Desperate fighting: Serbians take positions at Raptcha, Bulgarians retreat to Slivnitza; 400 Bulgarians captured; 50 Serbians killed
Nov. 16, Serbian attack repulsed; renewed with artillery with success, many Bulgarian prisoners, Nov. 17
Nov. 17, Bulgarians defeated between Kula (Adlie) and Widdin
Nov. 17–19, Prince Alexander and the Bulgarians attack the Serbians at Slivnitza; severe fighting; King Milan and the Serbians retire, leaving 400 prisoners
Nov. 17–21, Estimated Serbian loss 6,000 killed and wounded
Nov. 19, Prince Alexander submits to the Porte and orders evacuation of Eastern Rumelia
Nov. 21–22, Bulgarians totally defeat the Serbians near the Dragoman pass; near Zaribrod, which is occupied by Prince Alexander Nov. 23
Nov. 24, Serbians retreat to Pirot; Prince Alexander enters Serbia, defeats Serbians and occupies Pirot after severe conflict, Nov. 26–27; siege of Widdin, Bulgarian sally repulsed Nov. 27
Nov. 28, Cessation of hostilities through Austrian intervention

About Dec. 2, Serbian proposals rejected

Nov.–Dec., Sir W. M. White at Constantinople supports the Bulgarian union

Dec. 21, Protocol signed by International Commission; Pirot in Serbia and Widdin in Bulgaria to be evacuated; armistice to last till March 1

1886

About Jan. 16, The Powers in a collective note call upon the Balkan rulers to disarm; refused by Greece and Serbia

Jan., Virtual (not nominal) union of Eastern Rumelia with Bulgaria; Prince Alexander representing the Sultan, his Suzerain, for five years; decree promulgated Feb. 2

March 3, Peace between Bulgaria and Serbia signed at Bucharest; ratified March 17; by the Sultan March 13

About March 15, Prince Alexander demands governorship for life; not agreed to, March

April 5, The conference of Powers at Constantinople; Turko-Bulgarian convention protocol nominating Prince Alexander Governor of Eastern Rumelia for five years signed; accepted with reservation by Prince Alexander, April 8

Aug. 21, Provisional government formed by M. Zankoff and others

Their proclamation disavowed by the army and people at Sofia, Philippopolis, and other places

M. Stefan Stamboloff a lawyer, an ardent Bulgarian, elected deputy at Tirnova, 1879, president of the sobranje

Aug. 21–23, Conspiracy at Sofia, Prince Alexander carried off a prisoner

Dec. 23, A loyalist provisional government formed at Tirnova by Stamboloff and others, which issues manifesto in the Prince's name

The Prince landed at Keni Russi in Russian Bessarabia

Conflicts with M. Zankoff's supporters

Aug. 25, The rebel government prisoners or fugitives

Aug. 29, Return of Prince Alexander; triumphant reception at Rustchuk: he issues a proclamation; arrives at Philippopolis, Sept. 1; at Sofia Sept. 3. M. Zankoff and others released; Prince Alexander submits to Russia, announces his intention to abdicate, Sept. 4; regency appointed Stamboloff, Mutkuroff, and Karaveloff, Sept. 6

Sept. 8, Prince Alexander leaves Sofia with simple dignity; Sofia in a state of siege

About Sept. 8, The revolting soldiers degraded and officers arrested

Sept. 25, Arrival of General Kaulbars as Russian agent, intimidating policy

Sept. 30, M. Tisza, Hungarian Prime Minister, declares for maintenance of the Treaty of Berlin and Bulgarian independence

Oct., M. Radoslavoff, Premier, and Ministry, firmly resist General Kaulbars, Oct. 4; his mission in the provinces unsuccessful

Oct. 10, Elections for the sobranje (parliament); majority for the regency (about 400 to 20), 78 Zankoffists

Oct. 20, Gadban Effendi, Turkish envoy, impugns the elections and requires delay of the meeting of the sobranje; resisted by the regency

Oct. 28, Russian warships at Varna; state of siege renewed at Sofia

Nov. 1, The sobranje opened; the rebel officers released

Nov. 1, 2, General Kaulbars threatens to retire if Russians are ill treated; 100 Russian sailors land at Varna

Nov. 4, Captain Nabokoff's attempt to create an insurrection in favor of the Tzar at Bourgas quickly suppressed

Nov. 10, Prince Waldemar of Denmark elected Prince by the sobranje (declined Nov. 13); resignation of the Regent M. Karaveloff Nov. 10; succeeded by M. Zivkoff Nov. 13

Nov. 13, Important speeches of the Marquis of Salisbury (Nov. 9) and of Count Kalnoky against Russian aggression

Nov. 20 et seq., General Kaulbars' ultimatum unanswered; he and Russian consuls quit Bulgaria

Dec. 15, Prince Ferdinand of Saxe-Coburg invited for election as Prince by Bulgarian delegates; Prince Nicholas of Mingrelia recommended by Russia

The delegates (MM. Stoiloff, Grekoff, and Caltcheff) visit various courts; not received at St. Petersburg; received unofficially at Vienna and Berlin, Dec.; London (favorably), Dec. 29, 1886; Paris, Jan. 9; Rome, Jan. 18; Constantinople, Jan. 29, 1887

1887

March 1, 2, Military revolt at Silistria, Colonel Kristeff shot; quickly suppressed

March 3, Military insurrection at Rustchuk; fighting, many killed and wounded; suppressed by the militia and people, March 4; several ringleaders executed, March 6; many imprisoned, March 8–9

March 4, Sofia in a state of siege; MM. Karaveloff, Nikoforoff, and 22 others arrested; released April 6

March 11, Reported execution of 14 rebels at Rustchuk

March 31, M. Mantoff, Prefect of Rustchuk, shot at Bucharest

About June 12, Prince Alexander definitely declines reelection

July 4, Meeting of the sobranje at Tirnova; unanimous election of Prince Ferdinand of Saxe-Coburg and Gotha as Prince, July 7; he accepts conditionally, July 8; the ministers and regency resign, announced July 9. M. Stoiloff forms a ministry, July 12; the regency on request withdraw resignation about July 14

Aug. 14, Prince Ferdinand arrives at Tirnova, and signs the constitution, &c., and issues a proclamation; the Russian Government protests against this, Aug. 15

Aug. 21, The Prince well received at Philippopolis; and at Sofia, Aug. 22

Aug. 22, The Sultan declares Prince Ferdinand's position illegal

Aug., The Bulgaria publishes a libellous statement respecting the German Consul, Herr Loper; contradiction published by intervention of the Bulgarian Government, and the paper suppressed, Sept.; matter referred to the German Government about Sept. 14; pacific settlement announced Sept. 21

Sept. 1, Stamboloff forms a strong ministry

Sept., Proposed mission of General Ernroth (Russian) opposed by the Powers

Sept., State of siege closed; the opposition to the Government active

Oct. 9, Elections for the sobranje; majority for the ministry (260–32); riots at Plevna, suppressed with bloodshed, 10 killed

Oct. 27, Sobranje opened by the Prince

Nov. 16, Insurrection at Eski-Zagra suppressed, 17 soldiers killed, announced

1888

Middle Feb.–March, Russian note to the Sultan and the Powers declaring the illegality of Prince Ferdinand's position, Russia supported by France and Germany; Austria, England, and Italy maintain reserve; the Porte telegraphs to M. Stamboloff that Prince Ferdinand's position is illegal, March 6; no answer returned, March

Aug. 14, Prince Ferdinand's first anniversary

1889

Feb. 5–6, About 60 eminent men arrested by M. Stamboloff for petitioning the Exarch at Constantinople, as favoring M. Zankoff

Sept. 15, Death of Zacharia Stoianoff, president of the sobranje, eminent patriot, at Paris

Oct. 8, Prince Ferdinand visits Germany [M. Stamboloff appointed Regent]

Oct. 8–12, The Russian Prince Dolgoroukoff visits Sofia, intrigues with the Zankoffists, and is expelled

Oct. 20, Loan of 25,000,000 francs at 6% obtained on the railways announced

Nov. 3, Prince Ferdinand, after a successful tour, during which he visited Paris, Oct. 16, Vienna, Oct. 27, returns to Sofia; the parliament opened

1890

Jan., Russian circular note to the Powers stating that the terms of the loan are contrary to the Treaty of Berlin; this is denied by the Bulgarian Government; the loan fully subscribed for five or six times at Vienna, Berlin, &c.

Feb. 1, Major Panitza, a high army official, and six others arrested on a charge of plotting against the Prince and Government (in 1887 *et seq.*)

Feb. 7, More arrests; M. Stamboloff acts as prefect of police

June 19, Trial of Major Panitza and 14 others, charged with conspiring to overthrow the Government and assassinate Prince Ferdinand and his Ministers; 9 officers, 4 civilians, and Captain Kalobkoff, a Russian, also arraigned. Court martial opened May 15; sentences, Major Panitza to be shot; Captain Kalobkoff nine years' imprisonment; Lieutenant Rifoff and M. Arnodoff six years, 4 officers three years, one man five months, the rest acquitted May 30; sentences confirmed on appeal

June 26, The Government sends a courteous but firm note to the Porte requesting the recognition of Prince Ferdinand and religious autonomy to the Macedonian Bulgarians

[Answer deferred, July, 1890]

June 28, Major Panitza shot at Sofia

About July 31, 3 Bulgarian bishops in Macedonia appointed by the Porte

About Aug. 5, Disapproved by the Greek patriarch, who resigns

About Aug. 25, Kalobkoff, the Russian intriguer, released and expelled from Bulgaria

Sept., Elections: great majority for the Government

Oct. 27, The Prince opens the sobranje with a firm speech

1891

Feb. 5, He is partially recognized by the Porte

March 17, Detection of a plot by Major Bendereff against the Government reported

March 27, M. Beltcheff, Minister of Finance, assassi-

nated in the street in the presence of M. Stamboloff (for whom it was thought he was taken) about 8 P.M.; many arrests, March 28

March 28, Connection with Major Bendereff's conspiracy suspected; above 150 arrests up to April

Aug. 30, Archiepiscopal palace at Sofia searched by order of M. Stamboloff; documents and letters carried off

Dec. 13, The sobranje votes by acclamation a pension of 50,000 francs to Prince Alexander of Battenberg (Count Hartenau), reported

Dec. 15, Rupture with France, on account of the expulsion of M. Chadourne, a journalist, accused of publishing injurious intelligence

1892

About Jan. 21, Rupture with France settled by explanation and apology

Feb. 26, Dr. Vulkovitch, Bulgarian agent at Constantinople, stabbed Feb. 24; died

April 13, Government note to the Porte complaining of plots, &c., delivered

April, May, Plot at Rustchuk; bombs discovered, April 22; many arrests

June 30–July 18, Trial of 18 persons connected with the conspiracy against Prince Ferdinand and the assassination of M. Beltcheff (March 27, 1891); sentences, imprisonment: M. Petko Karaveloff, ex-Premier and Regent, 5 years; Ghorghi Velikoff, 15 years; three persons, 9 years; one, 5 years; one, 3 years; one, 16 months; six acquitted; Sweetoslaw Milaroff, Constantin Popoff, Toma Gheorghieff, and Alexander Karaguloff sentenced to death, July 18; executed, July 27

Aug. 12–14, M. Stamboloff, invited by the Sultan, warmly received at Constantinople

Aug. 27, First Bulgarian exhibition opened at Philippopolis by Prince Ferdinand; closed Nov. 13

Sept. 21 *et seq.*, Dispute with Greece respecting Greek schools and the new Bulgarian education law; the question referred to the Powers, about Sept. 27; the schools reopened, Oct. 1

Oct. 27, The sobranje opened by the Prince with a cheerful speech

About Nov. 22, Loan of 142,780,000 francs for railways authorized

Dec. 16, Revision of the constitution; Ferdinand and his heirs to remain Roman Catholics; bill introduced

Dec. 19, The bill passed permitting Prince Ferdinand and his first successor to be Romanists, the next to belong to the Greek church

1893

About Feb. 24, M. Zankoff issues a fruitless manifesto against the Prince and Government

Feb. 26, The Metropolitan Clement arrested for exciting the people against the Government in a sermon at Tirnova

About March 15, Russian circular to the Powers against Bulgarian changes

March 22, Ilia Gheorghieff convicted as an accomplice in the murder of M. Beltcheff

[Acquitted and discharged, Nov. 3]

April 20, Marriage of Prince Ferdinand to Princess Marie Louise of Parma at Florence

May 15, Meeting of the grand sobranje; the new constitution passed May 27; proclaimed May 29

June 10, 11, Public entrance of the Prince and Princess into Sofia; great festivities

July 22, The Metropolitan, M. Clement, sentenced to banishment for his sermon (Feb. 26); commuted to 3 years' imprisonment, Nov. 10

July 30, Government majority in the elections

Aug. 29, The first Bulgarian steamship navigation company inaugurated at Varna

Oct. 27, The sobranje opened by Prince Ferdinand

Dec. 1, Discovery of a plot to assassinate Prince Ferdinand; arrest of Lieutenant Ivanoff and others reported

1894

Jan. 1, Bill restricting the press passed; the sobranje adjourns

Jan. 30, Trial of Lieutenant Luka Ivanoff and Stojan Ivanoff began Jan. 26; Luka sentenced to 15 years' and Stojan Ivanoff to 3 years' imprisonment

March 15, Archbishop Clement's appeal dismissed, Feb. 21; pardoned by the prince

June 1, Rioting at Sofia, checked by the police

June 12, Prince Ferdinand, in a warm complimentary rescript, expresses deep regret at the retirement of M. Stamboloff

Sept. 5, M. Stamboloff, for uttering remarks against Prince Ferdinand, is prosecuted and jailed

Oct. 27, The sobranje opened by Prince Ferdinand

Dec. 21, M. Stoiloff reconstitutes his Ministry

Dec. 30, Amnesty for political offenses granted, with some exceptions

1895

Jan. 4, M. Zankoff returns to Sofia; warmly received by the people; and the Prince, Jan. 9

May, Prosecution of M. Stamboloff; in ill health; his passport refused

June 19, Frontier conflicts and disputes with Turkey, Macedonian agitation reported

June 23, Rupture with Turkey, M. Dimitroff (Minister) recalled

July 8, Bulgarian note to the Powers

July 15, M. Stamboloff with his friend M. Petkoff attacked and dreadfully wounded in his carriage by three assassins; he dies 3 A.M., July 18; sympathy expressed to Madame Stamboloff by Queen Victoria and other foreign Powers

July 17, Bulgarian mission well received by the Tzar at St. Petersburg; no reconciliation with Prince Ferdinand; returns to Sofia, Aug. 4

1896

Feb. 8, Communication of reconciliation of the Russian Government with Prince Ferdinand, in consequence of his assent to the conversion of Prince Boris to the Greek church

Feb. 9, M. Stoiloff honorably received by the Sultan, who sends representatives to the Prince's conversion; conversion of Prince Boris from the Roman to the Greek church; solemn ceremony; the Tzar as sponsor represented by General Kutuzoff, Feb. 14; the sobranje presents 500,000 francs to Prince Boris, to remain in the bank till his majority, Feb. 14

Feb. 19, Prince Ferdinand recognized by all the Powers; announced

Dec. 21, Trial of persons implicated in the murder of M. Stamboloff; Mme Stamboloff summoned to the court, asserts the innocence of the prisoners, and

that the real assassins are known to the court, Dec. 27; 1 prisoner acquitted, and 2 others sentenced to 3 years' imprisonment, Dec. 30

1898

Jan. 31 and Feb. 3, Strong appeals to the Sultan respecting torturing of prisoners, outrages, &c., at Kossova, and demanding the dismissal of Turkish officials; rejected by the Porte, Feb. 12

Dec. 20, The public debt converted into a 3% loan of about 290,000,000f.

1899

Jan., The Macedonian committee memorialize the Powers in favor of reforms, autonomy, &c.

Jan. 31, M. Stoiloff's Ministry resigns, Jan. 28; M. Grekoff forms a conciliation cabinet

——, Death of Princess Marie Louise

Oct. 13, Cabinet crisis: M. Grekoff, Premier, resigns, early Oct.; new ministry, M. Ivantchoff, Premier and Foreign Minister

Nov. 20, New railway, branch line to the Danube between Roman, Plevna, and Shumla, opened by the Prince

1900

Early May, Fatal rioting round Rustchuk quelled by the military, martial law proclaimed

July, Aug., Lawlessness and reign of terror against resident Rumanians in Sofia, many political murders; see Rumania

Oct. 21, New railway from Rustchuk to Tirnova, opened by Prince Ferdinand

1901

Jan. 1, New French loan, 120,000,000f., reported

Feb. 26, Turkish troops ordered to the frontier owing to the Macedonian agitation

April 5, The Porte demands the dissolution of the Macedonian committee, March; the leaders are arrested in Sofia

April 6, M. Stoiloff, ex-Premier, born 1856, dies

May 24, Impeachment of ex-ministers by the budget committee

July 12, Visit of the Grand Duke Alexander and Russian fleet, at Varna

Aug. 12, 14, Sarafof, ex-president of the Macedonian committee, and 3 others charged with assassination (see Rumania), tried, and acquitted

Sept. 6, M. Ivantcheff, ex-Premier, and 3 colleagues impeached on charges of treason, &c., by the sobranje, which closed Sept. 8

Dec. 16, Contract for a loan of 125,000,000f. from a Paris bank, signed, Dec. 13; withdrawn government resigns

Dec. 24, 27, Financial and ministerial crisis; proposed French loan rejected, the sobranje suspended; the ministry resigns

1902

Jan. 3, M. Daneff forms a cabinet; supplies rejected, the sobranje dissolved, Jan. 5

Middle Jan., Conflict with Turkish troops in Kossova, 10 Bulgarians killed

Feb. 6, M. Kantcheff, Minister of Public Instruction, assassinated by a discharged schoolmaster, who afterwards committed suicide

March 22, Cabinet (Zankoffists) reconstructed, M. Daneff Premier and Foreign Minister

July 3, Bulgarian band destroyed by Turkish troops at Patili; reported

Aug. 8, Budget passed, deficit over 6,000,000f.

Aug. 10, Split in the Macedonian congress at Sofia, Colonel Zoutcheff president

Middle. Aug., Macedonian band captured near Sofia

Sept. 1, 2, Colonels Zoutcheff and Nicoloff charged with aiding revolutionary bands, arrested; escaped Sept. 23

Oct. 9, 11, Bulgarian raids into Macedonia

Nov. 4, Anti-Greek riots at Varna

Nov. 11, Visit of King of Rumania

Dec. 26, 28, Count Lamsdorff, Russian Foreign Minister, negotiates on the Macedonian question

1903

Feb. 6, M. Karaveloff, thrice Premier, died, aged 58

Feb. 14, Macedonian committees in Sofia suppressed, leaders arrested

March 7, General Paprikoff (War) resigns, crisis; the ministry resigns, March 27, but returns, with Colonel Savoff War Minister, March 31

March 11, Fatal rioting near Sofia

About April 7, General Paprikoff created inspector-general of the army

May–June, Anti-Greek revolt suppressed with great severity

Sept. 14, Bulgarian Government addresses note to the great Powers, protesting against the cruelties of the Porte in Macedonia, and threatening action unless the Powers intervene, reported

Sept. 16, Joint note from the Powers warning the Government against any action leading to war

Sept. 13–20, Troops mobilized on the frontier

Sept. 22, Turko-Bulgarian negotiations respecting Macedonia, concessions offered

Oct. 7, Elections, Government victory; Zankovists defeated, sobranje opened by the Prince, Nov. 15

Oct. 11, Public demonstration in favor of the Macedonians, Sofia, Aug. 15, and frontier post and village near Kottendail attacked by Albanians, Oct. 8; Bulgaria demands satisfaction

Middle Oct., About 22,000 Macedonian refugees reported

Oct. 18, Agreement with Turkey, mutual disarmament of troops reported

Nov. 14, Boris Sarafoff, Macedonian leader, welcomed in Sofia

1904

Middle Jan., New press laws introduced in the sobranje providing for the punishment of authors of attacks on Prince Ferdinand and the members of his family in Bulgarian newspapers, by imprisonment for 2 to 10 years, and by fines up to 10,000fr.

April 8, Turko-Bulgarian agreement signed at Sofia

Nov., New loan of 4,000,000l. at 5% issued

Nov. 30, Sobranje passes vote for an extraordinary credit of 1,708,000l. for military purposes

1905

Aug. 6, Tender (14,500,000fr.) for constructing the Trans-Balkan railway linking up the valleys of the Danube and the Naritza accepted

1906

Jan. 2, Death of M. Todor Ivanchoff, formerly Prime Minister of Bulgaria

May 31, New port of Varna opened

Aug. 13, Anchialos, a town on the Black Sea, completely destroyed by fire

Aug. 19, Great citizen meeting, from all parts of Bulgaria, held at Philippopolis; resolution, adopted, to ask the government to use all the means at the country's disposal for the application, in Macedonia, of art. 23 of the Treaty of Berlin

Nov. 4, The Bulgarian Government refuses the Greek demand for compensation, for losses suffered by the Greeks in Bulgaria, during the recent anti-Greek movement, saying that the movement was provoked by Greek bands

Nov. 5, General Petroff, Prime Minister and Minister for Foreign Affairs, resigns, and is succeeded in the premiership by M. Petkoff, who retains the portfolio of the Interior, and in the foreign ministry by Dr. Stancioff, Bulgarian diplomatic agent in St. Petersburg, announced

1907

Jan. 12, New Turko-Bulgarian commercial treaty signed

Feb. 16, Princess Clémentine of Coburg, mother of Prince Ferdinand, aged 89, died

March 11, Assassination of M. Petkoff, Premier

March 16, New ministry formed, Dr. Gudeff, Premier

July 4, Petroff, murderer of M. Petkoff, sentenced to death

1908

Jan. 21, Resignation of the cabinet

Jan. 29, M. Malinoff, chief of the Democratic Party, forms a cabinet with himself as Premier and Minister of Communications, General Paprikoff, Minister for Foreign Affairs, and General Nikolaieff for War

Feb. 28, Marriage of Prince Ferdinand with Princess Eleanora of Reuss-Köstritz

June 28, Prince Ferdinand opens the newly elected sobranje

Sept. 23, Prince Ferdinand and Princess Eleonora visit the Emperor Francis Joseph

Oct. 5, Prince Ferdinand declares the independence of Bulgaria and assumes the title of King

1909

Feb. 21, Prince Ferdinand arrives in St. Petersburg for the funeral of the Grand Duke Vladimir and is received with royal honors

April 19, Russo-Bulgarian agreement for settling the question of Bulgaria's pecuniary liability to Turkey under an arrangement arrived at between the Porte and the Sofia government; protocol signed in St. Petersburg

——, Turko-Bulgarian protocol disposing of all questions pending between Turkey and Bulgaria, and providing for the recognition of Bulgaria's independence by Turkey, signed at Constantinople

May 25, Sir George Buchanan, British Minister to Bulgaria, leaves Sofia

1910

March 13, Riot at Rustchuk arising from the elopement of a Moslem girl with a Bulgarian; 15 persons were killed and a large number wounded

1911

March 5, Visit of King Ferdinand to Emperor Francis Joseph, the first since 1908 and independence of Bulgaria

March 22, Malinov Cabinet fell and Guesov, leader of Nationalist Party, became Premier

May 31, Convention of judicial assistance and extradition with Austria signed

July 10, The Grand Sobranje (Parliament) confirmed title of King

July 21, Bill for modification of the Constitution adopted vesting succession to the throne in first born male descendant of Ferdinand and re civil list

Sept. 19, Elections for Parliament gave Nationalists 190 seats; Agrarians, 5; National Liberals, 6; Democrats, 6; Young Liberals, 1

Nov. 2, Provisional Commercial Agreement with Turkey signed

1912

Feb. 29, March 13, Treaty of alliance with Serbia signed directed against any Great Power which should occupy territory in the Balkan Peninsula; secret annex by which all "territorial gains acquired by combined action" to be the common property of the two allies and Serbia recognized Bulgarian right to "territory east of the Rhodope Mountains and the Struma River" and Bulgaria recognized "right of Serbia to territory north and west of the Shar Mountains" in Macedonia subject to approval of the Tsar of Russia

May 16, 29, Treaty of alliance with Greece concluded

June 19, Military Agreement with Serbia signed

July 14, Article 17 of Bill for amendment of Constitution passed Chamber giving King right to conclude secret political treaties

Aug. 2, Massacre of Bulgarians by Mohammedans at Kochana, Turkey

Aug. 21, Mass meeting at Philippopolis protested against massacre of Bulgarians by Turks at Istib, Kotchana, and other places and demanded liberation of Macedonia

Sept. 22, Military Agreement with Greece concluded

Sept. 30, Mobilization against Turkey ordered

Oct. 13, Bulgaria joined Serbia and Greece in ultimatum to Turkey demanding reforms. See Balkan Wars

Oct. 17, Declaration of war against Turkey. See Balkan Wars, p. 25, for military operations

Dec. 3, Armistice signed

Dec. 16, Peace Conference opened in London. See Balkan Wars

1913

Feb. 3, Hostilities resumed. See Balkan Wars

April 16 and 19, Armistice with Turkey signed

May 7, Agreement with Rumania as to cession of Silistria to Rumania

May 30, Treaty of Peace signed with Turkey in London ——, Resignation of Guesov

June 14, Dr. Danev became Prime Minister

June 29, Bulgarians invaded territory under military occupation of Greece and Serbia under Treaty of London of May 30

June 30, Second Balkan War begun. See Balkan Wars

July 15, Danev Ministry resigned and Radoslavov succeeded as Premier

Aug. 10, Treaty of Bucharest signed with Serbia, Greece, Rumania, and Montenegro by which Balkan War ended, Rumania receiving the southern Dobruja which had been Bulgarian since 1878 from Turtukai on the Danube to Balchik on the Black Sea. Bulgaria received the mountainous district of the Pirin

and Dospat down to the Ægean and the port of Dedeagatch and Port Lagos

Sept. 16, 29, Treaty of Constantinople with Turkey signed as to boundaries. See Balkan Wars

Sept. 17, Announcement of agreement with Turkey as to frontiers

Dec. 10, Exarch Joseph, head of Bulgarian Church, removed from Constantinople to Sofia

Dec. 27, Resignation of Genadiev, Minister of War

1914

Jan. 5, Cabinet reappointed Premier, and Minister for Foreign Affairs, M. Radoslavoff; Finance, M. Toncheff; Interior, M. Christo Popoff; Justice and Education, M. Pecheff; War, General Naïdenoff; Commerce, M. Bakaloff; Public Works, M. Dincheff; Railways, M. Apostoloff

Feb. 17, Diplomatic relations with Serbia resumed

March 10, Elections held for the Sobranje gave Ministerialists 126 seats; Democrats, 31; Agrarians, 51; Socialists, 21; Nationalists, 9; Radicals, 5; Zankovists, 2

July 29, Declaration of neutrality in World War

July, Loan of 500,000,000 leva negotiated from Germany

1915

Feb. 3, German loan of $3,000,000 to Bulgaria

May 16, The Entente Powers offered Kavalla to Bulgaria as price of neutrality

June 14, Bulgarian Note to Entente Powers asked for specific guarantees as to territory

June 22, Turkey ceded a strip of land on Thracian frontier to Bulgaria

July 17, Visit of Prince Hohenlohe (Germany)

July 26, Turkey ceded to Bulgaria Turkish territory west of the Maritsa River including Demotika and large final section of Dedeagatch-Adrianople Railroad

Aug. 3, British Minister at Sofia offered Bulgaria Kavalla and an undefined part of hinterland in Macedonia to declare war on Turkey

Aug. 6, New loan of 400,000,000 francs from Austro-German banks concluded

Aug. 9, Bulgaria asked for Serbian Macedonia, Greek Macedonia, and Silistria

Aug. 18, Resignation of Minister of War, General Fichev. Succeeded by General Jekov

Aug. 29, Visit of Duke of Mecklenburg-Schwerin on mission from Germany

Sept. 6, Military Convention signed with the Central Powers at Pless providing for common action against Serbia

Sept. 12, Manifesto protesting against Government policy issued by the Opposition

Sept. 15, The Entente Powers offered Bulgaria part of Macedonia unconditionally if she would declare war on Turkey

Sept. 21, Bulgaria mobilized

Sept. 22, Protocol with Turkey the Dedeagatch Agreement provided for cession of territory

Oct. 4, Russian ultimatum to Bulgaria declared severance of diplomatic relations within 24 hours unless the military officers of hostile belligerent countries were sent out of the country

Oct. 5, Russian Minister, Savinski, asked for his passports on receipt of unsatisfactory reply from Government as did other Entente Ministers

Oct. 11, Bulgarian troops crossed the Serbian frontier northeast of Nish

Oct. 14, Bulgaria declared war on Serbia

Oct. 15, Great Britain declared war on Bulgaria, and Montenegro declared state of war existed. Bulgaria declared war on Great Britain

Oct. 16, France and Serbia declared war on Bulgaria

Oct. 18, Bulgaria declared war on France

Oct. 19, Italy and Russia declared war on Bulgaria

1916

Sept. 1, Bulgaria declared war on Rumania

Dec. 30, Note to the United States accepted peace proposals

1917

Oct., Visit of the German Emperor to Sofia

1918

May 7, Treaty of Bucharest with Rumania gave Bulgaria territory ceded to Rumania in 1913

June 16, Radoslavov resigned as Prime Minister

June 19, Malinov became Prime Minister

Sept. 24 and 27, Bulgaria asked for an armistice

Sept. 25, Stamboliski with other Agrarian deputies in prison since 1915 released

Sept. 30, Armistice signed with Entente Powers, unconditional surrender

Oct. 4, King Ferdinand abdicated in favor of his eldest son Boris, and left the country

Nov. 2, Peasant Government established by Stamboliski at Tirnova and republic proclaimed

Nov. 28, Malinov resigned and Todorov assumed office as Prime Minister forming a coalition Cabinet

1919

Feb. 28, Blockade of Bulgaria raised

Aug. 17, General election gave 85 seats to the Agrarian Party of Stamboliski, Democrats, 28; Conservatives, 19; Socialists, 39; Communists, 47; and other minor parties, 19

Sept. 19, Draft Peace Treaty handed to Bulgarian Delegation to the Peace Conference

Oct. 6, Todorov resigned and Alexander Stamboliski became Premier

Oct. 24, Bulgarian Reply and comments on Treaty presented

Nov. 4, All ex-Ministers of the Radoslavov War Cabinet except Radoslavov himself who had fled to Germany after abdication of Ferdinand imprisoned charged with having countersigned the declaration of war without consent of the National Assembly

Nov. 27, Treaty of Peace with the Allied and Associated Powers signed at Neuilly by which Bulgaria ceded the southern Dobruja to Rumania, the towns of Tsaribod and Strumitsa to Serbia, and to the Allied Powers territory in Thrace which at San Remo Conference was assigned to Greece except a part of East Thrace given to Turkey, and reparations provided for, and disarmament and reduction of army

——, Convention with Greece signed as to reciprocal emigration of national minorities

1920

March 28, Elections gave Agrarians 110 seats out of 229, Communists receiving 50 and Democrats, 24

Aug. 9, Peace Treaty of Neuilly ratified came into force

Sept., Commercial Treaty with Czechoslovakia signed

Oct. 22, Minorities clauses of Treaty of Neuilly placed under guarantee of the League of Nations

Dec. 16, Bulgaria admitted as member of League of Nations

1921

Feb. 7, Demand of Yugoslavia for delivery of cattle under the Treaty of Neuilly

Feb. 19, Provisional Commercial Agreement with Germany signed

Feb. 23, Reparation Committee arrived in Sofia

April 14, Commercial Agreement with Sweden signed

June 28, Order of Council removed 3 letters from the Bulgarian alphabet

July 8, Reparation Commission agreed to postpone for one year reparations payments from Bulgaria

Sept. 3, Commercial Agreement with Hungary concluded

Sept. 20, Conference of Ambassadors granted permission for temporary frontier guards and police of 13,000

Sept. 22, Death of Ivan Vazov, poet

Oct. 11, Trial of members of the Radoslavov Cabinet begun charged with responsibility for the War

Oct. 22, Assassination of Dimitrov, Minister of War

1922

Feb. 24, Commercial *modus vivendi* with Spain concluded

March 9, Commercial Agreements with Austria and the Netherlands signed

April 3, Reparations Commission fixed Bulgarian payments for 1922 and 1923

June 14, Joint Note of Governments of Yugoslavia, Rumania, and Greece protested against raids across borders

June 28, Railroad Convention with Rumania

July 11, Agreement with Denmark renewed Treaty of commerce and navigation of 1909

July 21, Interallied Commission informed Government that time limit had expired and demanded payment of 112 millions in gold francs

July 27, Bulgaria asked Reparation Commission for 3 years moratorium because of inability to pay

Aug. 18, Preliminary Protocol with Yugoslavia defined boundaries

Oct. 20, Agreement with Austria to maintain Convention of judicial assistance and extradition of May 31, 1911

Dec. 4, Town of Kustendil occupied by bands of Macedonian Revolutionary Organization of Todor Alexandrov

Dec. 6, Final Boundary Treaty with Yugoslavia signed

Dec. 17, Referendum on indictment of former Ministers of the War Cabinet gave 681,970 votes guilty, 251,185 not guilty

1923

Feb. 4, Bomb thrown in attempt on life of Premier Stamboliski

Feb. 10, Premier Stamboliski reconstructed Cabinet

March, Cabinet reconstructed, Stoyanov appointed Minister of the Interior; Mouraviev, War; Obov, Agriculture; Pavlov, Public Works; Dupaninov, Justice; Yanev, Finance; Athanassov, Railways

March 21, Agreement as to reparations payments signed with Interallied Commission at Sofia and approved by the Reparation Commission, May 1 by which

Bulgarian payments reduced from 2,250,000,000 gold francs to 550,000,000 immediate payment of 5,000,000 francs and annual payments thereafter

April 22, Elections held gave Premier's party, the Agrarians, 212 seats out of 245; the Bourgeoisie, 15 seats; Communists, 16; Socialists, 2

May 31, Agreement with France signed as to payment of private debts to French creditors

June 9, Military *coup d'état* overthrew the Agrarian Stamboliski Government and arrested the Ministers. A bourgeois bloc Ministry formed, headed by Professor Alexander Tzankov (Zankov) the following day

June 14, Stamboliski shot and killed in alleged attempt to escape

June 29, The new Government recognized by members of the Little Entente, Czechoslovakia, Yugoslavia, and Rumania

July 17, Appeal to peasants and workers by Executive Committee of Third International to overthrow the new Government

Aug. 10, Union of parties formed new party, the " Democratic Entente"

Aug. 11, Of 85 Communists accused of conspiracy with Moscow Communists to overthrow the Government, 4 sentenced to death, the others to terms of imprisonment

Aug. 26, Daskalov, former Minister to Czechoslovakia, and friend of Stamboliski, assassinated at Prague

Sept. 12, Arrest of all Communist leaders ordered

Sept. 22, Parliament dissolved by the King and a state of siege declared because of insurrection

Sept. 26–28, Battle of Government troops with Communists ended revolt

Oct. 30, Nicola Gennadiev, former Minister of Foreign Affairs, assassinated

Nov. 18, Election gave Government (bourgeois) Party 185 seats against 62 for the Opposition of Agrarians and Communists

Nov. 19, Frontier Convention with Rumania signed

Nov. 23, Naturalization Treaty with the United States signed

1924

March 6, Social Insurance Act passed

March 11, Death of Ivan Guesov, former Minister

March 19, Treaty of extradition with the United States signed

March 28, Protocol signed with France, Italy, and Great Britain as to costs of occupation

April 7, Commercial Treaty with Czechoslovakia signed

April 9, Members of the Stamboliski Government who had been imprisoned on charges of murder, bribery, and incitement to riot were acquitted

July 17, Amnesty for members of the Vasail Radoslavov Cabinet voted by Parliament

July 26–27, Frontier incident on Macedonian border of Greece, Greeks arrested 70 Bulgarians and murdered several of their prisoners

July 26, Agreement with Yugoslavia as to deliveries in kind by Bulgarians as reparations

Aug. 22, Tariff Agreement with Switzerland concluded

Aug. 31, General Todor Alexandrov, leader of the Macedonian Revolutionary Organization assassinated

Sept. 29, Protocols with Greece for protection of minorities signed at Geneva. Ratified by Parliament, Dec. 29

Oct. 2, Commercial Agreement with Norway signed

1925

Feb. 3, Greek National Assembly refused to ratify Protocol of Sept. 29, 1924 with Bulgaria as to protection of minorities

Feb. 13, Professor Nicola Milev murdered in railroad station in Sofia by Communist

Feb. 24, State of siege declared in 12 provinces on Yugoslav frontier because of clashes on frontier

Feb. 25, Mixed Commission of Yugoslavs and Bulgarians appointed to investigate frontier incidents

March 20, Six Communist members expelled from Parliament

April 10, Conference of Ambassadors granted request of Government of March 11, to allow enrollment of 3,000 volunteer troops to suppress Communists

April 14, Attempt made on life of King Boris by Communists

April 15, General Gherorghiev assassinated

April 16, At funeral of General Gherorghiev held in the Cathedral at Sofia a bomb was exploded which killed 123 persons and wounded 323

April 20, Captain Ninkov, leader of Communist plot which exploded bomb in the Cathedral, killed resisting arrest by the police

April 22, Conference of Ambassadors authorized a further increase of militia to 7,000

April 30, Treaty of commerce and navigation with Poland signed

May 4, All Communists outlawed by the Government

May 11, Peter Zadgorski, sacristan, and Tolhers, sentenced to death for Sofia Cathedral bomb outrage

May 27, Zadgorski, Friedman, and Koev hanged for Sofia Cathedral bomb outrage

June 10, Perchemliev hanged in connection with Sofia Cathedral bomb outrage, and the sentences of French citizens Mme Nicolava and Leger commuted to life imprisonment

July 9, Transit Convention with Yugoslavia signed

Oct. 16, Commercial Treaty with Czechoslovakia signed

Oct. 18, Treaty of friendship with Turkey signed

Oct. 19, Border clash with Greeks near Demirhassar. A Greek soldier killed

——, Martial law in force since April 16 ended

Oct. 21, Greek ultimatum to Bulgaria demanded apology, indemnity, and punishment of offenders

Oct. 22, Commercial Agreement with France signed

Oct. 22–23, Greek troops occupied 70 square miles of Bulgarian territory and bombarded Petritch

Oct. 23, Bulgaria appealed to the League of Nations against Greek invasion

Oct. 26, Council of League of Nations meeting in Paris ordered cessation of hostilities between Greece and Bulgaria and withdrawal of Greek troops from Bulgarian territory

Oct. 27, Provisional Commercial Agreement with Italy concluded

Oct. 28, Protocol signed with Greek officers ended hostilities and provided for evacuation of Greek troops

Oct. 29, Greek troops withdrawn from Bulgaria

Nov. 12, Provisional Commercial Agreement with Great Britain signed

Nov. 19, Cabinet crisis, all Ministers resigned except Colonel Vulkov, War

Dec. 14, League of Nations Council decision imposed fine on Greece of about $219,000 to be paid to Bulgaria as indemnity

Dec. 29, Failure of Prime Minister to form new Cabinet

Dec. 30, Interallied military control ended in Bulgaria

1926

Jan. 2, Tsankov Government resigned

Jan. 4, André Liaptchev appointed Prime Minister, Premier and Minister of Interior, André Liaptchev; Education, Nicholas Naidenov; Justice, Dr. Kulev; Commerce, M. Bobotchevsky; Finance, Vladimir Mollov; Public Works, Slaveico Vassilev; Posts and Railways, Kimon Georghiev; Foreign Affairs, Athanase Burov; Agriculture, Dimitri Christov; War, General Ivan Volkov

Feb. 4, Amnesty Bill passed third reading, 6,325 political offenders affected, Communists excluded

Feb. 8, Provisional Commercial Agreement with Belgium and Luxemburg

Feb. 15, Greece paid first installment of 30,000,000 levas on account of invasion of 1925 and the other half March 1

March 8, Trial of more than 100 Communists and Agrarians resulted in death sentence for 8 persons

May 27, Frontier incident, one Greek soldier killed and one Bulgarian

June 10, Council of the League of Nations approved request of Bulgaria for a loan for the settlement of Bulgarian refugees

July 28, Raid of Bulgarian revolutionary bandits near Kriva, Palanka

July 29, Raid of revolutionary bandits into Yugoslav territory

Aug. 11, Joint Note of Greece, Rumania, and Yugoslavia presented to Bulgaria demanded adequate protection against border raids of Bulgarian bandits by frontier guards and prosecution of bandits

Aug. 25, Provisional Agreement with Bank of England signed by which £400,000 advanced to Bulgaria for destitute Bulgarian refugee settlement

Aug. 28, Provisional Commercial Agreement with Turkey signed

Nov. 12, Husrey Bey, first official representative from Turkey since the War, received by the King

Dec. 11, Arrangement concluded with bondholders of Bulgarian pre-War debt

Dec. 26, Foreign loan offered in London and New York for £2,400,000 and $4,500,000

Dec. 31, Census gave population as 5,460,000, an increase of 12.8% since 1920

1927

Feb. 28, Provisional Commercial Agreement with Greece signed

April 10, Frontier clash, Bulgarians on Yugoslav territory attacked and 3 killed

May 29, Election gave Government Coalition 168 seats, Agrarians, 48; Macedonian Independents, 11; National Liberals, 14; Democrats, 12; Radicals, 2; Social Democrats, 10; others, 8; 40,000 candidates stood for 273 seats

May 31, Allied Military Control Commission withdrawn

June 17, Agreement with Great Britain for dissolution of Anglo-Bulgarian Mixed Arbitration Commission

June 19, Bulgarian bandits attacked Yugoslav custom post near Bosilovgrad and Yugoslavs in retaliation shelled village of Izvor

Oct. 7, Yugoslav Government asked dissolution of Macedonian Revolutionary Organization after series of outrages

Oct. 10, Martial law proclaimed in districts of Kustendil and Petric to suppress Macedonian Revolutionary Organization

Nov. 20, Yugoslav freight train bombed by Bulgarian bandits

Dec. 5, Attempt of Macedonians to assassinate commander of Yugoslav garrison at Strumitsa

1928

Feb. 11, Commercial Agreement with Estonia concluded

Feb. 12, Treaty of commerce and navigation with Turkey signed

March 10, Protocol signed at Geneva for international stabilization loan of $25,000,000 to strengthen Bulgarian banks and currency

April 14–18, Earthquake shocks in southern Bulgaria destroyed more than 30,000 houses

July 7, General Protogerov, head of Macedonian Revolutionary Organization, assassinated in Sofia

Aug. 10, Joint Anglo-French diplomatic interview with the Government as to the activities of the Macedonian Revolutionary Organization

Aug. 18–Sept. 12, Cabinet crisis and reform

Sept. 12, Liaptchev Cabinet reorganized: Premier and Minister of Interior, André Liaptchev; Education, Nicholas Naidenov; Justice, Dr. Theodore Kulev; Commerce, M. Tzvetco Bobotchevsky; Finance, Vladimir Mollov; Public Works, Slaveico Vassilev; Posts and Railways, R. Madjarov; Foreign Affairs, Athanase Burov; Agriculture, Dimitri Christov; War, General Vulkov

Nov. 1, Agreement signed in London for loan issued in New York and London, Nov. 20

Nov. 22, Preliminary Treaty of friendship and commerce with China signed

Dec. 5, Reconstitution of Liaptchev Cabinet, General Vulkov, Macedonian, and supporter of Macedonian Revolutionary Organization, retained as Minister of War

1929

Jan. 2, Resignation of General Vulkov, Minister of War

Jan. 11, General Bakardjiev appointed Minister of War

Jan. 21, Treaty of arbitration and of conciliation with the United States signed

Feb. 26–March 17, Conference of Bulgarian-Yugoslav Mixed Commission at Pirot on frontier questions

March 6, New Treaty of neutrality, conciliation, and arbitration with Turkey signed

May 24, Pact of Paris for renunciation of war ratified by Chamber

July 22, Arbitration Treaty with Hungary signed

Aug. 15, Announcement that ban of ex-communication against Greek Church of half a century would be canceled

Sept. 4, Yugoslav troops crossed frontier into Bulgaria and fired on Bulgarian post near Tun

Sept. 23–Oct. 2, Conference with Yugoslavs at Pirot resumed

Sept. 26, Protocol signed by Mixed Commission at Pirot dealing with frontier régime, &c.

Oct. 21, Death of Vassili Radoslavov, former Premier in exile at Berlin, Germany

Nov. 15, Conference with Yugoslavs resumed at Sofia to discuss a neutral zone, and liquidation of divided properties

Dec. 31, Arbitration and conciliation Treaty with Poland signed

1930

Jan. 20, Agreement with Italy signed, provided for Mixed Arbitration Tribunal to settle questions in dispute as to frontier and property, &c.

Feb. 14, Two Agreements with Yugoslavia signed regarding liquidation of frontier property and maintenance of order on the frontier and other matters

Feb. 16, Municipal and county elections a victory for the Government

March 4, Vassail Poundev, editor of Macedonian newspaper *Vardar* assassinated in Sofia, and same day bomb explosion by Macedonian revolutionists at Pirot killed 1 person and injured 25

March 15 and 20, Yugoslav Minister to Bulgaria protested and asked punishment for Macedonian revolutionists raiding Yugoslav border villages

May 14, Resignation of 4 Ministers either Macedonians or sympathetic to the I.M.R.O. (Internal Macedonian Revolutionary Organization)

——, Treaty of friendship, non-aggression, and peaceful settlement signed with Czechoslovakia

May 16, Liaptchev Cabinet reconstituted: Premier and Minister of Interior, André Liaptchev; Foreign Affairs, Athanase Burov; Education, Alex. Tzankov; Justice, Kantcho Milanov; Commerce, Dimitri Michaïkov; Finance, Vladimir Mollov; Public Works, Gheorghi J. Danaïlov; Posts and Railways, Petko Stainov; Agriculture, Grigor Vassilev; War, General Kissiov (January 31, 1931)

July 18, Order for arrest of Ivan Mihailov, leader of Macedonian Revolutionary Organization

Aug. 11, Action against the I.M.R.O. begun by Government by arrest of Ivan Mihailov and other Macedonian leaders charged with assassination of General Protogerov in 1928

Oct. 25, King Boris III married at Assissi, Italy, to Princess Giovanna, third daughter of the King of Italy

KINGS

Prince Alexander (Joseph) I (son of Prince Alexander, uncle of Louis IV, Grand Duke of Hesse), born April 5, 1857; elected April 29, 1879; deposed Sept. 4th, 1886; declines reëlection June 12, 1887; dies Nov. 17, 1893

Ferdinand, Duke of Saxe-Coburg and Gotha, born Feb. 26, 1861; elected July 7; married Princess Marie Louise (daughter of Robert, Duke of Parma, born, Jan. 17, 1870; died Jan. 31, 1899), April 20, 1893; heir, Boris (son), born, Jan. 18, 1894; Cyril, born Nov. 17, 1895; Clementina, born Jan. 30, 1899

Oct. 3, 1918, Boris III, succeeded to throne on abdication of Ferdinand

CONFEDERATION OF THE RHINE

Confederation of the Rhine, the League of the Germanic States, formed by Napoleon Bonaparte, July 12, 1806, when he abolished the Holy Roman Empire, and the Emperor of Germany became Emperor of Austria. In Dec. it consisted of France, Bavaria, Württemberg, Saxony, and Westphalia; seven grand duchies; six duchies; and twenty principalities. The princes collectively engaged to raise 258,000 troops to serve in case of war, and established a diet at Frankfort. This league terminated with the career of Bonaparte in 1814, and in 1815 it was replaced by the Germanic Confederation.

CORSICA

Corsica, Mediterranean Island, forming a department of France since 1815, situated north of Sardinia from which it is separated by the Strait of Bonifacio, area 3,367 square miles, population (1926) 289,890. It is famous as the birthplace of Napoleon Bonaparte. The island was colonized by Phocæans from Ionia in 560 B.C., and afterwards held by the Etruscans who were driven out by the Carthaginians, from whom it was taken by the Romans about the middle of the second century B.C. During the break-up of the Roman Empire the island was held by Vandals, A.D. 456, by Saracens 852, by Pisans, 1077, and was dependent on Genoa from 1559 to May 15, 1768 when it was ceded to France. Pasquale Paoli, Corsican patriot, appealed to Great Britain for assistance against the French which resulted in a British occupation and government, June 17, 1794 to Oct. 22, 1796, when Bonaparte sent an expedition against Corsica, and French authority was accepted by Corsica.

COUNCILS OF THE CHURCH

The following are among the most memorable. Those numbered are the Œcumenica or General Councils. Sir Harris Nicolas in his CHRONOLOGY OF HISTORY, enumerates 1604 councils, and gives an alphabetical list.

Of the church at Jerusalem (*Acts* xv), 50

    Of the western bishops at Arles, in France, to suppress the Donatists; three fathers of the English church attended, 314

I. First Œcumenical or General, at Nice (Constantine the Great presided), decreed the consubstantiality of the Son of God, condemned Arianism, and composed the Nicene creed, 325

    At Tyre, against Athanasius, 335

    The first at Constantinople, when the Arian heresy gained ground, 337

    At Rome, in favor of Athanasius, 342

    At Sardis: 370 bishops attended; Arians condemned, 347

    At Rimini: 400 bishops attended; Constantine obliged them to sign a new confession, 359

II. Constantinople: oriental council; 150 orthodox bishops present when it met; presided over 1st by Meletius, 2nd by Gregory Nazianzen, 3rd by Nectarius; added to the Nicene creed; declared the Bishop of Constantinople next in rank to Rome; Constantinople being New Rome, 381

III. Ephesus: Cyril of Alexandria presided; anathematized and deposed Nestorius; protested against any addition to the original Nicene creed, 431

IV. Chalcedon: 520 bishops present; declared the two natures of Christ, Divine and Human, as defined by Leo of Rome; accepted and decreed the Constantinopolitan addition to the Nicene creed, 451

V. Constantinople: Eutyches, Patriarch of Constantinople, presided; condemned the three chapters (written by Theodore of Mopsuestia, Theodoret, and others); Vigilius, Bishop of Rome, protested, but afterwards assented, 553

VI. Constantinople: Pope Agatho presided; against Monothelites, Nov. 7, 680 to Sept. 16, 681

  Authority of the six general councils reëstablished by Theodosius, 715

VII. Second Nicene: 350 bishops attended; against Iconoclasts, Sept. 24 to Oct. 23, 787

VIII. Constantinople: the Emperor Basil attended; against Iconoclasts and heresies, Oct. 5, 869, to Feb. 28, 870

  At Clermont, convened by Urban II to authorize the crusades: 310 bishops attended, 1095

IX. First Lateran: right of investiture settled by treaty between Pope Calixtus II and the Emperor Henry V, March 18 to April 5, 1123

X. Second Lateran: Innocent II presided; preservation of temporalities of ecclesiastics, the principal subject; 1,000 fathers of the church attended, April 20, 1139

XI. Third Lateran, against schismatics, March 5 to 19, 1179

XII. Fourth Lateran: 400 bishops and 1,000 abbots attended; Innocent III presided; against Albigenses, &c., Nov. 11 to 30, 1215

XIII. Lyons; under Pope Innocent IV: Emperor Frederick II deposed, June 28 to July 17, 1245

XIV. Lyons; under Gregory X: temporary union of Greek and Latin churches, May 7 to June 17, 1274

XV. Vienne in Dauphiné: Clement V presided, and the Kings of France and Aragon attended; order of Knights Templars suppressed, Oct. 16, 1311; April 3 and May 6, 1312

XVI. Pisa: Gregory XII and Benedict XIII deposed; Alexander elected, March 5 to Aug. 7, 1409

XVII. Constance: Martin V elected Pope; and John Huss and Jerome of Prague condemned to be burnt, 1414–1418

XVIII. Basel, 1431–1443

  Ferrara—Florence, met 1438. Proclaimed 1439 reunion of Latin and Greek churches

XIX. Fifth Lateran: begun by Julius II, 1512

  Continued under Leo X for the suppression of the pragmatic sanction of France, against the council of Pisa, &c., till 1517

XX. Trent: held to condemn the doctrines of the reformers, Luther, Zuinglius, and Calvin. (*See* Trent), Dec. 13, 1545 to Dec. 3, 1563

XXI. Vatican, at Rome: summoned by an encyclical letter, Sept. 8, 1868; met Dec. 8, 1869

  Present: 6 archbishop-princes, 49 cardinals, 11 patriarchs, 680 archbishops and bishops, 28 abbots, 29 generals of orders—803 in all

  There were held four public sessions, and between 90 and 100 congregations. New canons were issued April 24, 1870, and after much discussion and opposition, the infallibility of the pope as head of the Church was affirmed by 547 placets against 2 nonplacets, and promulgated, July 18, 1870

  Many bishops withdrew from the discussion. The council then adjourned to Nov. 11 (*see* Rome)

CRETE

Candia, the mediæval name (now disused) of Crete, of which Candia is the capital, an island in the Mediterranean Sea, mythically celebrated for its 100 cities, its center Mount Ida, the laws of its King Minos, and its labyrinth to secure the Minotaur. It was conquered by the Romans 68 B.C.

The Island of Crete was under Venetian rule from 1211 to 1669, when it fell beneath the Ottoman power. Thenceforth (with the exception of about 10 years, 1830–40, when it was ruled by the Viceroy of Egypt) it was governed as a Turkish vilayet. After more than 70 years of almost continuous insurrection, the 4 Powers—Great Britain, Russia, France, and Italy—intervened, and in 1898 constituted the Island, with the adjacent islets, an autonomous State under a High Commissioner of the Powers, subject to the suzerainty of the Porte, paying, however, no tribute. From August 14, 1906, the right of the King of the Hellenes to propose the High Commissioner was recognized by the protecting Powers, under whose sanction Greek officers took over the direction of the Gendarmerie and Militia.

In 1908 after many years' agitation Crete declared its annexation to Greece. The agitation went on until October, 1912, when the Cretan deputies were admitted into the Greek Parliament at Athens, and after the declaration of war against Turkey the annexation to the kingdom became an accomplished fact. The treaty of peace between Greece and Turkey, November 1 (14), 1913, formally handed over the Island to Greece, and the Greek annexation was recognized by the Powers in December, 1913.

823–1859

823, Seized by the Saracens
961, Retaken by the Greeks
Aug., 1204, Sold to the Venetians
1364, Rebelled; reduced
1669, Gained by the Turks, after a twenty-four years' siege, during which about 30,000 men perished
1830, Ceded to the Egyptian Pasha
1840, Restored to Turkey
1858, Insurrections suppressed, 1841; by conciliation
July 31, 1859, Persecution of the Christians

1866

June, The Christians demand redress of grievances
Aug. 12, They establish a "sacred battalion"
Aug. 21, Publish an address to the Powers protecting Greece
Sept. 2, The Cretan General Assembly proclaim the abolition of the Turkish authority in Crete, and union with Greece
Sept. 11, Commencement of hostilities: the Turkish army commanded by Mustapha Pasha
Sept. and Oct., Greeks victorious in several conflicts
Oct., The Greek steamer *Panhellenion* begins to convey volunteers, &c., to Crete

Nov. 26, Monastery of Arkadi besieged; blown up by the defenders; great loss on both sides

1867

March 28, Proposition of Austria, Prussia, Italy, and Switzerland to the Sultan to give up Crete; declined, March 31

June 15, Collective note from Russia and other Powers urging the Porte to suspend hostilities

Aug. 19, The *Arkadi*, Greek steamer, after running the blockade 22 times, landing Greek volunteers, and bringing away women and children, destroyed by the Turkish vessel *Izeddin*

Sept. 22, Assembly of delegates meet the Vizier

Sept. 28, Insurrection subsides; the grand vizier arrives; proclaims an amnesty, and promises reforms, Nov. 5

Nov., Successful blockade-running by the Greeks; Omar Pasha, the Turkish General, resigns his command in the Island

Dec. 11, The delegates' demands granted

1868

Feb., The war renewed (indecisive)

Dec. 26, The *Petropaulakes* landed about 2,500 men on opposite sides of the isle, Dec. 10, but failed in their attempt to unite; after several skirmishes, in which they lost about 650 men, all surrendered (and were sent to Greece)

Dec. 30, The provisional government surrendered

1869–1877

March 8, 1869, The new Turkish Governor, Omer Fenizi, arrived, and the blockade ended

About 1871, The "Organic statute," a scheme of reform, compiled

About Dec. 20, 1877, Insurrection announced, with provisional government

1878

Jan. 31, Union with Greece proclaimed; decreed by a general assembly, Feb. 11

July 13, Insurrection unsubdued; anarchy; Berlin treaty declares for enforcing legal and political reforms

Oct., Pacification by Mukhtar Pasha through concession of self-government, &c.

Nov., The Pact of Halepa, drawn up under British influence, sanctioned by the Porte

1884

Feb. 8, Insurrection on account of religious difficulties

About March 1, The Christian notables appeal to the Sultan for a Christian governor, and to Greece and other powers for mediation

March 6, Photiades, reappointed Governor for five years announced

1887

May 1–6, Temporary disturbances, order restored

1889

May–June, Anarchy through party strife of Christians and Mohammedans; Turkish troops sent to Crete, June 13; provisional government formed to restore order, June 13

June 14 *et seq.*, Mahmoud Djellalledin Pasha, Turkish Commissioner, well received; agitation calmed by his inquiries. An insurgent assembly demands a constituent assembly, judicial reforms, and dismissal of the governor, the people neutral about July 1; the Sultan sends 20,000*l.* T., July 6; Mahmoud Djellalledin Pasha informs a deputation that their demands must be referred to the Sultan, July 8; he is suddenly recalled, July 8

July 22, Asserted influence of Greek agitators; insurrection increasing; call for annexation to Greece, or British protection, about July 25; Djavad Pasha arrives to take command of the troops, Aug. 1

Aug. 4, Riza Pasha appointed temporary governor, with extra powers for repressing disorder

Aug. 5, Fighting going on, villages burnt reported

Aug. 6, Note from the Greek Government to the Powers, urging intervention in Crete; they decline, leaving the settlement to the Sultan, Aug. 9–12; about 17,000 Turkish troops in Crete, reported Aug. 7

Aug. 14, Riza Pasha, the Governor, recalled; replaced by Shakir Pasha, who arrives with plenary powers, Aug. 13; proclaims martial law

Aug. 17, Partial submission of the insurgents; amnesty promised

Sept., Tranquillity gradually restored by Turkish moderate firmness

1890

Jan. 28, The Notables address the Sultan, thanking him for his good government

March 6, Turkish circular to the great Powers, reporting the pacification of Crete; amnesty, except to 18 persons convicted of crimes, announced March 11

About May 10, Great return of refugees from Greece

About July 7, Djevad Pasha appointed governor, in place of Shakir Pasha

1891–1894

Sept. 8, Mahmoud Djellalledin Pasha appointed governor (Djevad Pasha having been made Grand Vizier)

Oct. *et seq.*, 1892, Disturbances; several conflicts with the Turkish troops

Aug. 13, 1894, Turkhan Pasha appointed governor; discontent among the people reported

1895

March, Alexander Karatheodory Pasha (a Christian) appointed governor

Nov. 12, Reforms demanded by the assembly; refusal of the Porte reported

Nov. 20, Sanguinary conflict between Turkish troops and Cretans at Kampos

Dec. 10, Turkish troops defeated with heavy loss at Vryses, in Apokorona

Dec. 26, Reinforcements sent; prisoners released by request of the Greek consul; reported

1896

Feb. 23, Renewed conflicts and murders between Turks and Christians, intervention of the Greek Government; reported

Feb. 27, Karatheodory, Governor General, resigns; succeeded by Turkhan Pasha, March 6

March 18, General amnesty proclaimed

April 23, Serious conflicts between Turks and Christians, many killed; reported

May 7, Krape, in the mountains of Sphakia, held by the Cretan reform committee; negotiations between the Greek Government and the Porte; reported

May 17, Turkish garrison besieged at Vamos; continued hostilities; siege raised by Abdullah Pasha, the new Governor, May 30

May 21, Turkhan Pasha recalled

May 24, Massacre of Christians in Canea without provocation by the Turkish soldiery

May 26 *et seq.*, H.M.S. *Hood* and other foreign warships arrive

June 1, Turkish troops burn and sack Tsivara and other villages; reported

June 4, Anarchy and destruction over the western portion of the Island; increased excesses by the Turks; state of siege proclaimed; reported

June 11, Turkish troops defeated at Aghia

June, Galata and other villages looted and burnt by the Turks, June 6–10; subscriptions at Alexandria for relief of the sufferers

June 12, Protest of the foreign consuls submitted to the Governor General

June 15, The Cretan relief committee at Athens appeal to the world for assistance

June 19, The Turkish proclamation promising reforms, &c., discredited; the Cretans demand securities

June 19–21, Frequent encounters and massacres by Turkish troops reported

June 28, Georgi Pasha Berovitch, Prince of Samos, appointed Governor General of Crete, reported

June 29, The Cretan committee issue a circular calling for a provisional government and union with Greece

July 3, The Powers recommend that the Porte should grant a Christian governor general, the revival of the Halepa constitution, the immediate convocation of the Assembly, and a general amnesty; all granted

July 11–12, The Christian deputies arrive at Canea

July 13, The Assembly opened by the Governor

July, Desultory fighting near Candia, Retimo, and other places

Aug. 3, Villages destroyed; anarchy and rioting at Heraklion, Aug. 4; 30,000 Mohammedans enter the town, flight of Christians, Aug. 5–9

Aug. 8, The monastery of St. John at Anopolis attacked and burnt, 32 men, women, and children and 3 monks killed, churches and other villages burnt

Aug. 9, Reform committee dissolved; new revolutionary assembly formed at Canea; they profess submission to the premier and deputies, and await the action of the Powers

Aug. 11, Four Christian villages and two monasteries sacked

Aug. 13, Zihni Pasha, Special Commissioner, and Ibrahim Pasha, Military Commander, arrive in Canea

Aug. 16, Fighting at Tenedos in Candia, reported

Aug. 16 *et seq.*, Greek officers and volunteers land on the W. and E. coasts

Aug. 24, Turkish troops besieged by Christians at Kasteli, reported

Aug. 25, 29, The ambassador's scheme of reforms; political independence of the island, &c.; Christian governor for 5 years to be appointed; accepted by the Porte; by the Cretan deputies, Sept. 1, and by the insurgents, Sept. 6

Aug. 29, Devastation and massacre at Platania, near Canea, reported

Sept. 2, New "organic statute" comprising the scheme of reforms promulgated

Sept. 11, Georgi Pasha Berovitch reappointed as the first Christian Governor General, reported

Sept. 27, Three villages looted and burnt in Monofatsi by armed Mohammedans from Candia, reported

Dec. 15, Saadeddin Pasha, the Sultan's envoy, recalled through the remonstrances of the ambassadors, announced

1897

Jan. 13, Organization of temporary gendarmerie proceeding

Jan. 14–Feb. 5, Anarchy and murders at Heraklion, Retimo, Galata, and Canea, villages burnt

Feb. 6–7, Exodus of 5,000 refugees in foreign war vessels to the Piræus and Greek islands

Canea desolate; 2 entire streets, the bishop's house and schools destroyed, 20 lives lost; fires suppressed by bluejackets from the British fleet

Feb. 7, Major Bor appointed commandant of the gendarmerie; arrives and takes active measures; chief offices guarded by marines

——, Mohammedans capture rifles from the arsenal at Heraklion; panic among the Christians

——, Desperate fight at Kisamo Kasteli; women and children killed; 22 Mohammedans killed

Feb. 9–10, H.M.S. *Revenge*, flagship of Rear-Admiral Harris, arrives at Retimo and H.M.S. *Trafalgar* at Heraklion; conflicts at Sitia, villages burnt and eastern districts blockaded by Christians, reported

Feb. 11, Mohammedans plunder Heraklion

Feb. 12, Desultory fighting; flotilla of torpedo boats, under Prince George of Greece, arrives at Canea

——, Halepa declared neutral territory by the Cretan insurgents and the foreign consuls, announced

Feb. 13, Georgi Pasha Berovitch, Governor General, resigns to Mushavir Ismail Bey, and takes refuge on the Russian flagship off Halepa; Ibrahim Pasha, Military Governor, also resigns, Feb. 14

Feb. 14, The Greek consuls leave Canea and other places; Canea bombarded by the Christians, frequent conflicts, with much bloodshed

Feb. 15, Naval occupation of Canea, Heraklion, and Retimo by the allied powers; the Greek commodore called on to withdraw

——, Greek forces, under Colonel Vassos, land at Columbari; fighting reported near Heraklion

Feb. 16, Colonel Vassos issues a proclamation in the name of King George; the fort of Aghia attacked and captured, 400 Mohammedans taken prisoners, two Greek officers killed

——, The Porte appeals to the Powers to intervene

Feb. 17, The Italian admiral, on behalf of the Powers, warns the Greek commodore that any attack on the seaports will be repelled by force; the Greek Government concurs and the Greek consulate is reopened; the Greek army remains in the interior

Feb. 18, Massacre of prisoners at Sitia by Christians

——, Photiades Karatheodery Pasha made governor, and Saadeddin Pasha military commander; Turkey preparing for war

——, Massacre of 104 Mohammedans at Sarakina in Selino, including 23 women and 61 children, reported

Feb. 19, The Greek army attacks the Turkish outposts at Platania; the tower of Bukolies captured by the Greeks, 7 Greeks killed, reported

——, The foreign consuls reject the proclamation of Colonel Vassos concerning the annexation of Crete by Greece

——, Circular note from Lord Salisbury to the Powers recommending autonomy for Crete announced

Feb. 20, Colonel Vassos proclaims the occupation of Crete by Greece at Retimo and Candia

Feb. 21, Insurgents take possession of the heights above Halepa, and are fired on from the Turkish outposts and bombarded by the foreign squadron, 3 men killed (Turks afterwards declared to be the aggressors); constant firing kept up by the Turks on the insurgents and on the Greek outposts at Platania but not returned, Feb. 22, 23

Feb., Turks and Mohammedans (2,000) besieged at Candano

Feb. 22, Seven days' armistice agreed to in Selino

Feb. 25, The zone of protection under the Powers extended

——, The Christians blockaded at Hierapetra, liberated by the Italian warship *Etna;* announced

Feb. 27, 28, Sharp fight at Malaxa and near Retimo with bloodshed

Feb. 28, Union with Greece demanded by the insurgents; Tewfik Pasha, new Military Governor, arrives

March 1, Fort Stavros captured by the Cretans, 3,000 Turks prisoners; reported

March 2, Mutiny of the Turkish gendarmerie at Canea suppressed; Suleiman Bey (Colonel) and 2 others killed

——, Collective and identical note from the Powers informing the Greek Government of their decision to give autonomy to Crete under Turkish suzerainty, and withdrawal of the Greek forces within 6 days demanded

——, Death of Manager Timotheos, Archbishop of Crete, on landing at the Piraeus

March 4, Declaration of neutrality and unanimity by the foreign admirals

March 8, The Greek Government declines to accede to the request of the Powers

——, Turkish outrages continue

——, Colonel Vassos ordered by his government to avoid conflicts, desultory fighting at Akrotiri, on the east coast; Greeks ordered to quit Canea

March 9, Sir A. Biliotti, British consul, with a mixed foreign force under Captain Rainier, of H.M.S. *Rodney*, rescues the besieged Mohammedans (about 2,000) in Candano

March 11, Greek volunteers (500) landed

March 12, The fortress of Spinalonga bombarded by insurgents and Greeks

March 14, The interior of Crete held by Greeks and insurgents; Mohammedans rescued by detachments from the warships from Kisamo Kasteli

March 15, International gendarmerie disbanded, Colonel Bor leaves Canea

March 16, The Greek fleet leaves Cretan waters

March 16–23, Conflicts near Candia, Malaxa, and Retimo

March 17, Autonomy proclaimed in Crete

——, Colonel Chermside appointed British military commissioner in Crete

March 21, Blockade of the island by the six Powers begun; the Greek Government protests March 26

March 23–24, British and foreign troops landed

March 25, Desperate fighting between Turks and insurgents at Malaxa; Malaxa bombarded by the foreign fleet

March 28, Turkish troops fire on a body of insurgents with a flag of truce

March 29, Fort Butsunaria occupied by a foreign contingent

March 30, 31, Desultory fighting near Retimo and Canea; insurgents driven back, 2 killed, by the foreign bombardment; Fort Izedin occupied by a foreign contingent; villages burnt by Turkish troops

April 3–4, Mohammedans attack the insurgents near Canea, and are afterwards disarmed by European troops

April 5, Turks repulsed near Retimo

April 8–18, Fruitless negotiations

April 9, Insurgents bombarded by the warships at Kisamo-Kasteli; refugees taken away by foreign ships

April 15, Insurgents bombarded by the Turkish warships, Kalyves destroyed

——, Bashi-Bozouks disarmed at Canea

April 24–28, Relaxation of the blockade; 65,000 persons in receipt of relief

May 9–26, Greek army recalled; leaves

——, Insurgents retire after a severe conflict with Bashi-Bozouks at Elia; Major Mustapha Bey killed

May, Insurgents gradually disarming

May 29, Mohammedan raid from Candia, Christian village burnt, 14 persons killed

June 2, The insurgents institute a provisional government; reported

June 22–25, Mohammedan outrages on Christians near Candia, Kani-Kasteli and other places burnt, many killed; another raid, July 7

July 13, Conflicts between Bashi-Bozouks and Christians; reported

July 14, The Christian delegates style their body at Armeni the "General insurrectionary assembly of Cretans," Dr. Sphakianaki, President, and present a document to the foreign admirals announcing their constitution

July 15, 16, Mohammedan outrages, murders, &c.

July 16, Mohammedans prohibited from carrying arms; 20 arrested and taken on board five European ships, July 18

July 24, Djevad Pasha arrives as military commander at Canea

Aug. 1, An assembly of deputies proclaim their acceptance of autonomy; notified to the admirals, Nov.

Aug. 15, An international commission appointed as a court of summary jurisdiction for the Island reported; M. Vandenbrook (France), President, Aug. 21

Sept. 21, The Porte protests to the Powers against the commission; announced

Sept. 26, Suda placed under the jurisdiction of Captain Amoretti; reported

Oct. 22, Colonel Schäffer chosen by the Powers as Governor General of Crete; reported; opposed by the Porte, Oct. 27; and dropped, Nov. 29

Nov. 3, International court holds its first sitting at Canea

Dec. 6, Appeal from the Cretan Assembly to the Powers for relief from tribute to the Sultan through poverty; reported; again, Dec. 27

Dec. 8, Perivolaki besieged by insurgents to avenge a murder; reported

Dec. 13, Great excitement in Canea through the murder of a Christian merchant; public funeral, Dec. 15

About Dec. 19, International committee of consuls agree to Bozo Petrovitch (Montenegrin), proposed as governor; rejected; Prince George of Greece proposed by Russia, Great Britain, and France, Dec. 29; opposed by the Sultan, Germany, and Austria, Jan., 1898 (deferred)

Dec., Distress in the Island increasing

Dec. 28, Fifteen Christians killed by an ambuscade of Bashi-Bozouks; announced

1898

Jan., The Cretan Assembly address a memorial to the Powers against the ambassadors' proposals for the government of the Island

Jan. 20, Crete pillaged by Bashi-Bozouks; reported; 20 of them taken prisoners and embarked on H.M.S. *Hood*; Edhem Pasha appointed governor of Candia

Jan. 23, in consequence of the protests of the admirals

Jan. 24, Memorial from the Cretan Assembly respecting the raids, &c., to the admirals

Jan. 31, Mohammedan raids at Retimo, and great distress; reported

Feb., Refugees (506) starving near Candia, relief afforded by officers and men of H.M.S. *Anson*

March 16 and April 12, German and Austrian troops withdrawn from Canea

April 2, Turkish cordon removed from Canea; outposts taken by international troops; peaceable meetings of Christians and Mohammedans at markets instituted by Sir A. Biliotti, near Candia, under British protection, April 6 *et seq.*

April 10, The admirals decide that the Island shall be divided into 4 provinces under the 4 Powers; military tribunals instituted, May

June, *Modus vivendi* committee of the national Assembly, under supervision of the admirals, carries on the government; the Porte protests against the provisional régime arranged by the 4 Powers (the Cretan Assembly to govern the interior and the admirals the coast towns), July 8

Sept. 6, British troops attacked in Candia by Mohammedans and Turkish troops dissatisfied with the measures taken by the admirals, 4 hours' fighting, Lieutenant Robert Haldane and 12 British soldiers and marines killed, 42 (6 mortally) wounded, about 500 Christians massacred, 29 Bashi-Bozouks and 4 Turkish soldiers killed; Mr. L. A. Calocherino, British Vice-Consul, and his servants, massacred, the town looted and set fire to by Bashi-Bozouks; foreign consulates looted and burnt, Sept. 7; Edhem Pasha, the Governor, held responsible for the massacre by his inaction (succeeded by Colonel Chevki, Sept. 29); foreign reinforcements landed, martial law proclaimed, Sept. 9

Sept. 10, Two British soldiers murdered by Bashi-Bozouks

Sept. 12, Admiral Noel (K.C.M.G., Nov.) in H.M.S. *Revenge*, arrives; British ultimatum: surrender of ringleaders, Turkish disarmament, &c., Sept. 13; demands acceded to, reinforcements arrive, Sept. 14; prisoners transferred to British warships, Sept. 16; a stringent ultimatum dispatched to the Sultan by the 4 Powers, Oct. 5; accepted, Oct. 16, 20; 17 murderers hanged at Candia by British authority Oct. 19, 29, Nov. 7; 2 shot, Nov. 22; others sentenced to life imprisonment, Nov. 30

Oct. 19–Nov., Turkish troops evacuate the Island

Nov. 7, Exodus of Mohammedans

Nov. 11, Ismail Bey, ex-civil Governor General of Crete, leaves

Nov. 21, General peace and order; British administration in Candia and 6 provinces very successful

——, International court martial opened at Candia, 3 Turks sentenced to death

Nov. 26, Prince George of Greece appointed by the 4 Powers High Commissioner of Crete for 3 years under the Sultan's suzerainty; agreed to by the Porte, Dec. 7

Dec. 5, Blockade of Crete abolished

Dec. 6, Mohammedan petition to the Queen, begging for British protection, and that Sir H. Chermside may remain

Dec. 7, The executive committee resign, their demands being granted

Dec. 21, Prince George well received at Canea; the Christians express gratitude to England and the Queen

1899

Jan. 12, Commission appointed to draw up a constitution, inaugural meeting, Prince George presides

Feb. 20, 21, Prince George opens the Assembly; new constitution voted; M. Sphakianaki elected president

April, Amnesty granted to political offenders (between Sept. 16, 1896 and Dec. 9, 1898), with some exceptions

April 8, M. de Bloney, a Swiss, financial adviser to Prince George, arrives

April 27, Loan of 9,000,000 drachma, 3%, voted by the Assembly, reported

April 30, The first administrative (autonomous) council (4 Christians and 1 Mohammedan) formed

May, Mohammedan emigration continues

July 21, The British resign; Cretan Government begins at Candia, July 24; the Russians evacuate Retimo, July 27

1900

Oct., Prince George visits Europe to negotiate for union with Greece; returns, Dec. 15

1901

Feb. 22, Union with Greece rejected by the Powers

April, M. Venezelos, councilor, suggests a temporary principality in Crete; is dismissed from office

Prince George opens the Assembly; resolution appealing for union with Greece passed by the chamber, May 31; again refused by the Powers, the *status quo* to be maintained, June 18

Dec. 15, Prince George reappointed high commissioner for 3 years

1903

Early April, Elections give the Government a majority

May 4, Union with Greece again appealed for by the chamber of deputies

1904

Middle July, 17 friends and relatives of M. Malintrebos, who was sentenced in May to 15 months imprisonment for using disrespectful language about Prince George, force open the doors of the town hall of Lakkos and tear down the national flag

1905

Feb. 21, Protecting powers, France, Italy, Great Britain, and Russia, in reply to representations made by Prince George of Greece in his tour to the chief European courts in favor of the annexation of Crete by Greece, intimate that they will not tolerate the annexation of Crete by any power without the consent of the inhabitants, but express willingness to withdraw the European guards and permit Cretan authorities to impose higher dues

March 30, Insurgents at Therisso set up a national assembly with a president, who announces to the foreign consuls, the union of Crete with Greece. Prince George issues a proclamation to the Cretan people deploring the revolutionary movement, and declaring that it will impair the national interests of the Island. In a further proclamation the Prince appeals to the revolutionaries at Therisso to lay down their arms

April 20, Cretan Assembly meets; the high commissioner, opening the third session, refers to the inability of the Powers to modify at present the political status of Crete, adding that the insurgent movement " may injure the national cause of a clever and virtuous people." After departure of the Prince the Assembly passes a resolution proclaiming the union of Crete with Greece; president at once submits the resolution to the Prince at the palace

April 21, Declaration of the Assembly evokes great enthusiasm in the Island, Greek flag is flown on many buildings in Canea and Candia

April 24, Conference at Rome between Italian Foreign Minister and the British, French, and Russian ambassadors results in a declaration that in present circumstances the annexation of Crete to Greece cannot be permitted

April 25, Cretan chamber passes a resolution abiding by its decree of union; insurgents propose to establish a provisional government in the interior and to levy taxes

April 28, Conflict at Bukolies, in which 3 gendarmes, 2 insurgents, and 4 unarmed peasants are killed. Authorities informed by consuls that they must replace the Cretan flag on the public buildings; on their refusal, the international troops replace flags at Canea

May 5, Insurgents occupy Castelli on the N. coast between Retimo and Candia and seize the customhouse

May 24, Prince George declares the one issue to the situation is union with Greece. Chamber issues an appeal to the Cretans stating that they will endeavor to persuade the Powers that the solution of the Cretan question is union with Greece

End May, Cretan chamber passes a resolution again appealing to the Powers to assent to the union of the Island with Greece, and temporarily suspends its sittings; detachments of British troops sent to various points to restore order

June 26, Prince George's advisers tender their resignations, on the ground that the denial of union with Greece renders government impossible; resignations not accepted, reported

See Greece

June 30, Serious engagement lasting many hours between the insurgents and Russian troops; Russians occupy village of Platania

July 12, Insurgents in the district of Retimo besiege Russian detachments in the villages of Margarites and Rustika; skirmish near Arkhanæs between insurgents and British troops, supporting the Cretan gendarmerie in a search for arms

July 15, Consuls issue proclamation giving the insurgents 15 days to lay down their arms, an amnesty being granted to all who conform within that time, martial law to be applied if necessary in the case of non-submission; subsequent meeting of consuls and insurgents, who justify their armed movement and insist on the modification of the political status in the direction of union with Greece, and declare they will only yield to force

Middle July, Chamber reduces salaries, abolishes unnecessary posts, and dismisses the Italian gendarmerie officers

July 31, Martial law proclaimed in the British section

1906

Jan. 10, Sir Fitzgerald Law appointed British representative on the international commission to inquire into the question of financial and administrative reforms

End May, Elections result in the government party obtaining 78 seats, the opposition 36 seats, in a chamber of 130 members, of which number 16 are Mussulman deputies

Sept. 5, In view of the unrest caused by his resignation, Prince George issues a message to the Cretans urging them to show " patience, peace and prudence"

Sept. 25, Departure of Prince George

Sept. 29, Investiture of M. Zaimis as High Commissioner of Crete

1908

May 12, Following on the good influence of M. Zaimis, the High Commissioner, the 4 protecting Powers agree to withdraw the international troops in the course of a year

At Knossos, a small palace unearthed adjoining the great one; relics found indicate the date to be of the 17th century B.C.; account by Dr. Evans, *see Times*, Aug. 27

Oct. 7, Union with Greece proclaimed by the people throughout the Island

1909

July 26, Departure of the troops of the protecting Powers; the transports sail from Canea

See Greece

CRIMEAN WAR

See Russo-Turkish War, 1853

CROATIA

Croatia, included since 1918 in the Serb-Croat-Slovene State (Yugoslavia), conquered by Coloman, King of Hungary, in 1102, was with that country united to Austria in 1526.

1861

Nov., The Croatian Diet abolished

1867

May 25, The Croats protest against incorporation with Hungary

May 27, Their Diet (including Croatia and Sclavonia), at Agram dissolved

1868

May 27, The union of Croatia with Hungary recognized by a Croatian deputation

Nov. 24, Croatian delegates enter the Hungarian Diet

1883

Aug., Riots in Agram and other places against the Jews, complicated with Slavonic jealousy of Hungary, and desire for autonomy; the Ban superseded by General Ramberg, Special Commissioner, about Sept. 6

Sept. 8–10, Conflicts with the military; ten rioters killed Sept. 20

About Sept. 22, Agitation increasing; demand for separation from Hungary

Sept. 30, 38 rioters sentenced to imprisonment, &c.

Dec. 4, Count Khün-Hedervary appointed Ban

1887

Nov., The separatist movement said to be totally quelled by the Ban after much resistance

1895 to 1908

Middle Oct., 1895, Visit of the Emperor to Agram; warmly received

Sept. 29, 1897, Disturbances, agitation against the Magyars; 3 officials murdered by peasants in Lasinia, martial law reported

Aug. 31, Riots in Agram, houses and shops wrecked, troops called out, over 100 persons injured

Sept. 1, 1902, Captain Wittas beaten by the mob, martial law proclaimed, Sept. 3

March 27–30, 1903 and later in July, Further rioting. *See* Hungary, 1904–05

Jan. 15, 1908, Baron Paul Rauch, the new Ban of Croatia meets hostile reception at Agram

1909

April–Oct., Agram (Zagreb) treason trials. *See* Austria-Hungary

1910

July 17, Baron Rauch resigned and was succeeded as Ban by Dr. Tomacic

1911

Nov. 7, Diet dissolved by royal rescript. Elections in Dec. a defeat for Government

1912

April 3, The Croatian Constitution suspended and Eduard von Cuvaj appointed Dictator

Dec. 27, Cuvaj resigned

1913

Nov. 27, Baron Skerlecz appointed Ban and the dictatorship ended

1917

July 20, Pact of Corfu signed. *See* Yugoslavia

Oct. 10, Yugoslav National Council transferred to Zagreb

Oct. 29, Declaration of independence. *See* Yugoslavia

CYPRUS

Cyprus, British Crown Colony, island in the Mediterranean 44 statute miles from the coast of Asia to the north, and 69 miles from Syria to the east, area 3,584 square miles, exceeded in size only by Sicily and Sardinia of the Mediterranean islands, population at 1921 census 310,709 including 61,422 Mohammedans (Ottoman Turks), population of Nicosia, the capital, 18,461.

At a very early date important Greek and Phœnician colonies were established in Cyprus, and later it formed part of the Persian and Roman Empires. Its government frequently changed hands until 1571, when the Turks conquered the island from the Venetians, and retained possession of it until its cession to England for administrative purposes under a convention concluded with the Sultan at Constantinople, June 4, 1878. On the outbreak of hostilities with Turkey on November 5, 1914, the island was annexed. On May 1, 1925, the island was given the status of a colony by Letters Patent, and the High Commissioner became Governor.

Sir Ronald Storrs, Governor.

CZECHOSLOVAKIA

Czechoslovakia, Republic of central Europe formed out of the Slav regions of the former Austro-Hungarian Empire (Bohemia, Moravia, and part of Silesia) of the old Kingdom of Bohemia, Slovakia, the Slovak territory of former Hungary, the autonomous territory of Carpathian Ruthenia, and part of Teschen district. It is bounded on the north by Germany and Poland and projects into Germany on the west, and Austria, Hungary, and Rumania form the southern boundary, Rumania to the southeast. Prague is the capital.

	AREA IN SQUARE KILOMETERS	AREA IN ENGLISH SQUARE MILES	POPULATION FEB. 15, 1921	POPULATION PER SQUARE MILE, 1921	ESTIMATED POPULATION DEC. 31, 1929	POPULATION PER SQUARE MILE, 1929
Bohemia	52,064	20,102	6,670,582	331.8	6,995,427	348.0
Moravia and Silesia	26,738	10,324	3,335,152	323.0	3,598,902	348.6
Slovakia	48,936	18,895	3,000,870	158.8	3,300,749	174.7
Ruthenia	12,656	4,886	606,568	124.1	713,334	146.0
Total	140,394	54,207	13,613,172	251.1	14,608,412	269.5

Of the Czechoslovak citizens 8,760,937 are Czechoslovaks, 3,123,568 Germans, 745,431 Magyars, 461,849 Ruthenians, 75,853 Poles, 180,855 of Jewish nationality, and 25,871 others. There were besides 238,808 aliens.

Census population, Dec., 1930, 14,723,214.

The population of the principal towns with more than 20,000 inhabitants in 1921 was:—

Prague	. .	676,663	Cheb (Eger) . .	27,524
Brno .	. .	221,758	Most . . .	27,239
Ostrava. M.	. .	113,709	Jablonec n/N	
Plzen .	. .	108,023	(Gablonz a.d.	
Bratislava		93,189	Neisse) . .	26,929
Olomouc .	. .	57,206	Pardubice. .	25,162
Kosice .	. .	52,898	Ostrava Sl. .	22,890
Budejovice Ceske		44,022	Prerov. .	21,416
Usti n/L (Aussig)		39,830	Znojmo . .	21,197
Liberec (Reichen-			Krnov (Zagern-	
berg)	. .	34,985	dorf) . .	21,129
Opava.	. .	33,457	Chomutov (Ko- .	
Prostejov .	. .	31,092	motau) . .	21,123
Teplice-Sanov			Mukacevo . .	20,865
(Teplitz-			Uzhorod . .	20,601
Schonau)	. .	28,892	Varnsdorf. .	20,328
Jihlava	. .	28,179		

The term Czechoslovaks comprises two branches of the same Slav nation: the Czechs (pronounced Tschechs) of Bohemia, Moravia, and Silesia, and the Slovaks of Slovakia.

The Czechoslovak State came into existence on October 28, 1918. On that day the *Narodni Vybor* (National Council) took over the government of the Czechoslovak countries, including Bohemia, Moravia, Silesia, and Slovakia, which had hitherto belonged to the former Austro-Hungarian Monarchy. On November 14, 1918, the Czechoslovak National Assembly met in Prague, and formally declared the Czechoslovak State to be a Republic, with Professor T. G. Masaryk as its first President.

By the Treaty of Peace of September 10, 1919 (the Treaty of St. Germain), the Allied and Associated Powers formally recognized the Czechoslovak Republic, declaring that "the peoples of Bohemia, of Moravia, and of part of Silesia, as well as the peoples of Slovakia, have decided of their own free will to unite . . . for the purpose of forming a single sovereign independent state under the title of the Czecho-Slovak Republic." For the sake of brevity the Czechoslovak Republic is designated Czechoslovakia.

Thomas Garrigue Masaryk, President, reëlected May 27, 1927, for a period of 7 years.

1915

Nov. 14, Revolutionary manifesto issued by T. G. Masaryk and Durich, Czech leaders, first official pronouncement of Czechs abroad against Austria-Hungary in favor of an independent Czechoslovak State. Signed by Czechs and Slovaks in the United States, Great Britain, France, and Russia. A revolutionary committee formed, the Czechoslovak National Council, Masaryk, President, Benes, Secretary

1917

Jan. 10, Allied Note to President Wilson, statement of war aims, included demand for liberation of Slavs and Czechoslovaks

May 30, The Czech deputies in meeting of Reichsrat at Vienna, Austria, demanded establishment of a Federal State with equal rights for different nationalities

July 2, After Zborov where Czech regiments distinguished themselves Kerensky allowed troops to be raised from the Czech prisoners of war

Dec. 16, Decree permitted organization of Czech army in France under military control of France but under political control of the National Council in Paris, and Dec. 19 recognized as "autonomous army"

1918

Jan. 6, Convention of Czechs and Slovaks at Prague made demand for sovereign State and liberation from Magyar rule

Jan. 8, Point 10 of President Wilson's Fourteen Points stipulated peoples of Austria-Hungary should have opportunity of autonomous development

Jan. 12, Resolution of Czechoslovak deputies at Prague declared that the Bohemian question would receive an international solution at the Peace Conference

March 2, Second Pan-Slavic Conference at Agram

April 8–10, Congress of subject nationalities of the Austro-Hungarian Empire held at Rome. Anti-Austrian resolution adopted

April 13 and 16, Czechoslovak Congress met at Prague and demanded sovereign State

April 21, Italy recognized the Czechoslovak National Council as a *de facto* Government

May 22, Statement of Lord Robert Cecil recognized right of Czechoslavak nation to independence

May 29, Statement of Secretary of State Lansing declared sympathy with the United States with the aspirations of the Czechoslovaks. *See also* Austria

May 30, Czechs in the United States (at Pittsburgh) where Masaryk had proceeded from England to organize his countrymen promised Slovaks complete autonomy in the future State

June 3, Declarations of premiers of Great Britain, France, and Italy declared sympathy with the national aims of the Czechoslovaks, and Yugoslavs and Poles

June 15, The Czechs set up a national committee at Prague which adopted resolution for a "Czechoslovak State sovereign and independent"

June 30, First Czechoslovak on western front received flag formally presented by President Poincaré and recognition of independence of nation
———, Treaty with Italy signed

July 13, Czech National Council at Prague reorganized under leadership of Kramar as a complement to the National Council established at Paris

Aug. 3, American-Japanese Agreement for intervention in Siberia and aid to Czech regiments in Russia

Aug. 9, Declaration of the British Government recognized "the Czechoslovaks as an Allied nation and recognizes the unity of the three Czechoslovak armies as an Allied and belligerent army waging a regular warfare against Austria-Hungary and Germany . . ."

Aug. 13, The Czechoslovaks declared war on Germany
———, Declaration of the British Government of recognition of the Czechoslovaks as a nation reaffirmed

Sept. 2, The United States recognized the Czechoslovaks as a nation

Sept. 9, Japan recognized the Czechoslovaks as a nation

Sept. 11, Telegram of Lloyd George thanked Czech legions for service to Allies

Oct. 14, The Czechoslovak National Council in Paris constituted as a Provisional Government, Dr. Masaryk, President; Dr. Benes, Minister of Foreign Affairs; and Colonel Stebjanik, Minister of War

Oct. 15, Provisional Government recognized by France

Oct. 16, Manifesto of Emperor of Austria offered Federal State. *See* Austria

Oct. 17, Proclamation of the Czechoslovak Republic in Prague

Oct. 18, Czechoslovak declaration of independence formally proclaimed by the National Council

——, Note of President Wilson to Austria recognized the independence of the Czechoslovaks and Yugoslavs and stated that no negotiations could be undertaken except on basis of their independence

Oct. 27, Austro-Hungarian Government recognized the rights of the Czechoslovaks

Oct. 28, The National Council took over the administration of the Czechoslovak countries including Bohemia, Moravia, Silesia, and Slovakia bringing the Czechoslovak State into existence

Oct. 29, Meeting of Slovak National Council at Turciansky, voted with Czechs for union

Oct. 30, Declaration of union of Slovaks with Czechs in single State

Nov. 9, Czech forces at Ekaterinburg proclaimed the national independence

Nov. 10, Professor T. G. Masaryk, President of the National Council, elected first President of the Republic by representatives of 8 political parties assembled at Geneva, Switzerland, Dr. Karl Kramar chosen Prime Minister, and Voita Benes, Minister of Foreign Affairs

Nov. 13, Provisional Constitution adopted by the Prague Government

Nov. 14, National Assembly met in Prague, and formally declared the State to be a Republic with Professor Masaryk as first President

Dec. 10, Law enacted to provide aid for unemployed demobilized soldiers

Dec. 19, Law established the eight-hour day and 48-hour week

Dec. 21, President Masaryk arrived in Prague

Dec. 22, Inauguration of President Masaryk

1919

Jan. 18, Czech representatives admitted to Peace Conference

Jan. 24–28, Czechs in conflict with the Poles in Galicia because of announcement of Poland of election of deputies from occupied part of Teschen

Jan. 26, The Czechs captured Oderberg from the Poles

Jan. 28, The Czechs captured Karvin mining region from the Poles

Jan. 31, Supreme Council appointed a commission to investigate Teschen in dispute between Poles and Czechs

Feb. 1, Slovak Government formally installed at Bratislava

Feb. 5, Armistice with Poland and Polish and Czech zones defined

Feb. 20, Law defined customs frontiers and provided for collection of duties at rates of autonomous tariff of 1906

Feb. 25, Law of National Assembly empowered Minister of Finance to stamp bank notes to distinguish currency from Austrian

March 12, Treaty with Austria as to freedom of transit Trieste

March 20, Enactment constituted a Board of Audit and Control charged with superintendence of State economy, State property, and the national debt

April 1, and March 17, 1921, Laws limited freedom of migration

April 3, State supervision for private schools provided for

April 16, Land Reform Bill passed provided for expropriation of the large estates to be sold to peasants at low price, owners to be compensated

April 23, Formal recognition of the Republic by the United States

May 8, National Central Council of the Ruthenians met at Uzhorod and adopted resolution formally approving incorporation with Czechoslovakia as an autonomous region

May 15, Law provided for compulsory labor insurance as to sick benefits

May 18, Clash with Poles in Teschen

May 23, Law authorized loans for building

May 27, Law provided for purchase of land by renters of cultivated land if it has been farmed by renter continuously from Oct. 1, 1901

June 11, Law defined duties of Land Office

June 13, Permanent boundaries with Rumania published by the Supreme Council

June 15, Municipal elections held gave Social Democrats 934,801 votes; the National Democrats (Government Party), 256,336; Socialists, 484,743; and Agrarians, 637,013

June 28, Peace Treaty with Germany recognized independence of Czechoslovakia

June 30, Law provided for protection of children

July 1, Hungarian Red troops began evacuation of Czechoslovakia which they had invaded

July 5, The Kramar Cabinet resigned

July 8, Vlastimil Tusar (Social Democrat) formed a coalition Cabinet

July 17, Child Labor law adopted, promulgated July 28

Sept. 10, Treaty of Peace with Austria signed recognized independence of Czechoslovakia and defined boundaries, and Minorities Treaty which guaranteed the rights of minorities in Czechoslovakia

Sept. 15, Land Office organized

Sept. 27, Decision of Supreme Council to hold plebiscite for Duchy of Teschen including the territories of Spisz (Zips) and Orava (Arva) in dispute between Poland and Czechoslovakia

Oct. 30, Law regarding shortage of houses authorized taking over property if necessary

Dec. 17, Law provided for taking over land

1920

Jan. 10, Czechoslovakia an original member of the League of Nations

Jan. 21, Decree established four regions of production of sugar beets, cereals, cereals and potatoes, and for pasture

Feb. 5, Pensions reclassified and extended

Feb. 12, Land law provided regulations for dealing with lands expropriated

Feb. 19, Armistice concluded with Poles in Teschen

Feb. 24, Coal Agreement with Germany signed

Feb. 25, Law provided for participation of employees

of mines in administration of mining enterprises and of their participation in the net benefits

Feb. 29, Constitution adopted by National Assembly

March 6, Commercial Agreement with Switzerland signed

March 7–11, Conflict with the Poles in Teschen

March 11, Law established a system of farm credits to enable purchase of land by persons of small means

March 19, Law provided for assistance to private building enterprises

——, Law regulated service in the army

April 8, Land law gave new rules of procedure for taking over expropriated lands and made provision for indemnification of owners

April 14, Banking law enacted authorized a national bank

April 15, Constituent Assembly dissolved

April 18, First election for Parliament held on basis of universal compulsory suffrage, 8,000,000 of a population of approximately 13,000,000 voting, Socialists gaining 77 seats in Chamber and non-Socialists 177

May 18, Serious riot in town of Teschen

May 21, Strike of Polish miners in Karvin district, Teschen

May 24, Tusar reconstructed Cabinet with 7 Social Democrats, 3 Czechoslovak Socialists, 3 Agrarians; Benes again Minister of Foreign Affairs; Englis, Finance; Hotowetz, Commerce

May 28, Masaryk reëlected President

June 4, Treaty of Peace with Hungary signed gave the Hungarian Slovak provinces to Czechoslovakia

June 7, Treaty and final Protocol with Austria signed for settlement of questions of citizenship and protection of minorities

June 24, Foreign Trade Bureau authorized. Abolished Jan. 19, 1922

June 29, Commercial Agreement with Germany signed

July 28, Conference of Ambassadors announced boundary line for Teschen, Spisz (Zips), and Orava as between Poland and Czechoslovakia and appointed a Delimitation Commission to trace the boundaries. Javorina assigned to Czechoslovakia the Karvin mining district and the Oderburg-Jablunkov Railroad

Aug. 2, Financial Agreement with Austria signed

Aug. 10, Treaty of frontiers signed with Great Britain, France, Italy, and Japan

Aug. 14, Convention with Yugoslavia signed provided for mutual help in case of unprovoked attack, a defensive alliance against Hungary

Aug. 23, Supplementary Agreement with Austria signed as to citizenship and protection of minorities

Sept. 15, Tusar Ministry resigned, and Jan Cerny became Prime Minister, Benes, Englis, and Hotowetz remaining in the Cabinet

Oct. 18, Commercial Agreement with Yugoslavia signed

Nov. 4, Commercial Treaty with France signed

Nov. 9, Agreement with Poland signed as to nationality and cognate matters

Nov. 29, Convention with Poland signed as to options, civil rights, schools and languages, &c.

——, Minorities Treaty placed under guarantee of the League of Nations

Dec. 6, Death of Karel Kovarovic, musician

Dec. 20, Law as to compulsory sick benefits amended and extended

Dec. 25, General strike called by Communists in Prague and mining centers

Dec. 27, Hungarian plot to raid Pressburg prevented by police

1921

Jan. 18, Agreement with France regarding sequestration signed

Feb. 15, Census gave total population as 13,595,730, and 1,933,776 houses

Feb. 16, Principle for payment of compensation of expropriated land established

March 10, Boundary Convention with Austria signed

March 23, Commercial Treaty with Italy

April 23, Convention of alliance with Rumania signed joining that of Aug., 1920, with Yugoslavia forming the "Little Entente," and Commercial Convention

May 4, Commercial Convention with Austria signed

May 21, Ordinance established system of exchange surtaxes modeled on French tariff

Aug. 12, Law provided for unemployment benefit

Sept. 27, New Cabinet formed by Dr. Benes as Prime Minister, and Foreign Affairs; Dr. Cerny, Interior; Dr. Novak, Finance

Oct. 20, Commercial Treaty with Poland signed

Oct. 27, Mobilization begun because of return of Charles to Hungary

Nov. 6, Political Convention with Poland signed

Nov. 19, Commercial Treaty with Spain signed

Dec. 16, Treaty of guarantee and arbitration with Austria signed, and loan to Austria

1922

Jan. 20, Juridical Agreement with Germany signed

Feb. 2–10, Strike of coal miners against a 25% wage cut settled by compromise

Feb. 4, Statute for Silesian Teschen, Orava, and Spisz signed with Poland

Feb. 12, Emigration Act passed

April 6, Twelve Agreements signed with the Succession States of Austria-Hungary

May 8, Extradition Agreement with Germany signed

May, Strike in the metal industry

June 5, Trade Agreement with Russia signed

June 6, Trade Agreement with the Ukraine

July 13, Agreement with Hungary signed as to double taxation and pre-War debt

July 20, Juridical Convention with Germany signed

Aug. 31, Treaty of alliance with Yugoslavia renewed and extended for 5 years

Sept. 9, Proclamation announced reduction of tariff rates

Sept. 15, Commercial Agreement with Yugoslavia signed

Sept. 21, Decree provided for assessment of valuation of land increase not to exceed 5% for land without buildings, 10% with buildings, 15% buildings

Oct. 5, Resignation of Benes Cabinet

Oct. 7, Commercial Agreement with Latvia signed and Convention for legal protection and assistance with France

Oct. 8, M. Svehla, leader of Agrarian Party formed Cabinet

Oct. 14, Agreement with Roumania regarding separation of public records formerly Austro-Hungarian

Oct. 20, Commercial Treaty with Poland signed

Oct. 28, Boundary with Hungary fixed except Salgo-Targan district

Nov. 22, Commercial Agreement with Hungary signed

Dec. 11, Commercial Treaty with Portugal signed

Dec. 21, Agreement with Italy signed as to the port of Trieste

1923

Jan. 1, New prefectoral divisions for Slovakia came into effect

Jan. 10, Commercial Treaty with Greece signed

Jan. 18, Supplementary Convention with Austria signed as to frontier relations

Jan. 20, Commercial Treaty with the Netherlands signed

Jan. 25, Act for encouragement of building established industrial arbitration courts

Feb. 8, Credit Convention with Austria signed

Feb. 15, Death of Dr. Alois Rasin, Finance Minister, from wound received Jan. 5 from assassin

Feb. 26, Bohdan Bechka succeeded Rasin as Finance Minister

March 7, Bill for Protection of the Republic passed

March 8, Agreement with Hungary signed as to frontier stations and railroad traffic

April 5, Further Commercial Agreement with Yugoslavia

April 20, Czech soldier killed in clash with Hungarians on frontier at Him-Pereny

April 27, Commercial Treaty with Lithuania signed

May 7, Defensive military alliance with Rumania signed renewing that of April, 1921

July 13, Agreement with Hungary signed as to double taxation and pre-War debts

July 14, Commercial Treaty with Great Britain signed

Aug. 17, Commercial Treaty with France signed

Aug. 20–Oct. 6, Coal strike which was settled with agreement for reduction of wages 13%

Oct. 15–27, State visit of President Masaryk and Dr. Benes to Paris, Brussels, and London

Oct. 29, Commercial Treaty with the United States signed

Oct. 30, Commercial Agreement with Norway

Dec. 17, Decision of Council of League of Nations that Javorina should be retained by Czechoslovakia

1924

Jan. 20, Treaty of commerce with Albania signed

Jan. 25, Treaty of political alliance with France signed

Jan. 31, Provisional commercial Agreement with Denmark signed

Feb. 10, Protocol signed with Hungary as to frontiers in Salgo-Tarjan district

March 12, Frontier as to Javorina district accepted by League of Nations, Poland, and Czechoslovakia

March 16, First election for National Assembly held by the Carpathian Ruthenians

May 16, Protocol signed with Poland settled dispute over Javorina

——, Treaty of friendship with Italy signed

May 30, Commercial Agreement with Poland signed

July 5, Pact of cordial collaboration with Italy signed

July 31, Commercial Agreement with Germany signed

Aug. 18, Supplementary Commercial Agreement with France signed

Aug. 28, Coal Agreement with Germany signed

Oct. 9, Workers' Insurance Act passed

Oct. 11, Treaty of friendship with Turkey signed

Oct. 15, Protocol with Hungary signed as to frontier relations

Nov. 11, Extradition Treaty with Great Britain signed

Nov. 27, Supplementary Commercial Agreement with Austria signed

1925

March 6, Agreement with Poland signed as to mutual judicial assistance

April 7, Commercial Agreement with Poland signed

April 8, Commercial Agreement with Greece signed

April 16, Convention with Roumania signed as to frontier communications and property rights

April 18, Further Commercial Agreement with Denmark signed

April 23, Treaty of arbitration and conciliation, of commerce and 3 financial Conventions with Poland signed

May 7, Treaty of extradition and judicial assistance with Rumania signed

July 2, Extradition Convention with the United States signed

July 6, Celebration of the anniversary of John Huss, religious reformer, as a State holiday. Regarded by Vatican as an act of hostility and recall of Papal Nuncio, Manager Marmaggi

July 27, Commercial Agreement and supplementary customs tariff Agreement with Austria signed

Aug. 14, Treaty of commerce and navigation with Sweden signed

Sept. 30, Commercial Agreement with Switzerland modified by exchange of notes

Oct. 13, War debt Agreement with the United States signed on a basis of $115,000,000 to be paid over a period of 62 years

Oct. 16, Parliament dissolved

Oct. 27, $25,000,000 bond issue offered by New York City and Amsterdam (Holland) banks

Oct. 30, Commercial Treaty with Japan signed

Nov. 3, War debt Agreement with Great Britain provided for immediate repayment of £80,000 and future payment of £900,000 in 10 annual installments

Nov. 15 and 22, Elections held for second Parliament a victory for the Government receiving 159 seats in Chamber, the Opposition, 141; Senate (150 members):—Czechoslovak Coalition, 80 (Agrarians, 23; Clericals, 16; Social Democrats, 14; Czechoslovak Socialists, 14; National Democrats, 7; Middle Class Party, 6); Slovakian Clericals, 12; German and Magyar Agrarians, 14; Social Democrats, 9; Christian Socialists, 7; Nationalists, 5; National Socialists, 3; Communists, 20

Dec. 9, Anthony Svehla reconstituted Cabinet

Dec. 28, Commercial Treaty with Belgium signed

1926

Jan. 2, Conciliation and arbitration Treaty with Sweden signed

Feb. 8, Official recognition of Soviet Government of Russia

March 5, Conciliation and arbitration Treaty with Austria signed

March 11, Tourist Convention with Poland signed

March 17, Resignation of the Svehla Ministry

March 18, Dr. Jan Cerny appointed Prime Minister

April 1, National Bank of Czechoslovakia opened taking over the functions of the "Banking Office of the Finance Ministry" established in 1919

April 11 and Sept. 30, Commercial Agreements with Turkey signed

April 15, Air navigation Agreement with Poland signed

June 12, Financial Convention with Austria signed

——, Customs Tariff Bill passed

June 13, Little Entente Treaties renewed

July 1, Social Insurance Act came into effect

July 6, Judicial Convention with Latvia signed

Aug. 26, Provisional Commercial Treaty with Hungary signed

Oct. 12, Resignation of the Cerny Cabinet. Succeeded by third Svehla Cabinet based on collaboration of Czech and German bourgeois parties: Dr. Eduard Benes, Minister of Foreign Affairs; Dr. Karel Englis, Finance; J. Cerny, Interior; F. Peroutka, Commerce; Dr. Fr. Spina, Public Works; Josef Najman, Railways; Jan Sramek, Social Welfare; Dr. Robert Mayr-Harting, Justice; Dr. Otakar Srdinko, Agriculture; Dr. Milan Hodza, Education; Frantisek Udrzal, National Defense; Dr. Frantisek Nosek, Posts and Telegraphs; M. Tiso (Jan., 1927), Health; M. Gazhik, Unification of Laws

Nov. 30, Arbitration Treaty with Denmark signed

Dec. 20, Provisional Trade Agreement with Canada signed

Dec. 29, Death of Raimer M. Rilke, writer

1927

Jan. 15, Gazic and Joseph Tizo entered the Government as representatives of the Slovak Peasant Party

Jan. 22, Air navigation Agreement with Germany signed

Feb. 15, Air navigation Agreement with Austria signed

Feb. 16, Commercial Treaty with Switzerland signed

March 2, Commercial Treaty with Finland signed

May 27, Thomas G. Masaryk reëlected President for second term of 7 years

May 31, Commercial Treaty with Turkey and with Hungary signed

June 20, Commercial Treaty with Estonia signed

July 1, Act of administrative reform passed introduced provincial status and divided country for administrative purposes into the four parts of Bohemia, Moravia, Slovakia, and Carpatho-Russia

Dec. 17, *Modus vivendi* with the Vatican signed. Came into effect Feb. 2, 1928

1928

Feb. 19, Strike of coal miners for increase in wages and better conditions

March 22, Frontier Agreement with Germany signed

May 7, Extradition Treaty with France signed

May 11, Labor Agreement with Germany signed

July 2, Commercial Agreement with France signed

July 16, Naturalization Treaty with the United States signed

Aug. 16, Arbitration and Conciliation Treaties with the United States signed

Oct. 1, Strike of coal miners for wage increase

Nov. 8, Workers' Insurance Act amended

Nov. 16, Arbitration Convention with Spain signed

Dec. 2, Election a victory for the Agrarian Party of Premier Svehla

Dec. 13, Commercial Agreement with Spain signed

Dec. Professor Vojtech Tuka, Deputy, leader of Slovak Peoples' Party, arrested charged with treason and espionage

1929

Feb. 1, Resignation of Premier Svehla because of ill health. Succeeded by Franz Udrzal (Agrarian), Minister of War

Feb. 20, Dr. Benes, Minister of Foreign Affairs, stated that Czechoslovakia would not pay award to Archduke Frederick as granted by decision of Court at The Hague

Feb. 21, Act regarding pension insurance for salaried employees passed

Feb. 26, Trotsky refused permission by the Government to reside in the country

March 2, Alexander Mach, Secretary of the Slovak national organization, arrested charged with treason

May 21, The Little Entente Treaties of alliance by Czechoslovakia, Yugoslavia, and Rumania

June 8, Treaty of friendship, conciliation, and arbitration with Greece signed

July 2, Arrest of Czechoslovak citizens as spies on Hungarian territory at Hidasne-meti. Settled by exchange of notes July 8

July 9, Treaty of conciliation and arbitration with Estonia signed

July 24, Railroad to Hungary reopened

July 29, Trial of Dr. Tuka begun charged with giving aid to Hungarian irredentist propaganda in Slovakia. Convicted Oct. 5 and sentenced to 15 years imprisonment for his political activities

Sept. 9, Treaty of arbitration with Norway signed

Sept. 14, Treaty of arbitration and conciliation with the Netherlands signed

Sept. 20, Treaty of arbitration and friendship with Switzerland signed

Oct. 8, Resignation of M. Labay and Dr. Tiszo, Slovaks, from the Cabinet

Oct. 27, Elections gave Government only 143 seats in total of 300, gain for Socialists and defeat of bourgeois parties as follows:—Czech Agrarian, 46; Czech Socialist Democrats, 39; Czech National Socialists, 32; Communists, 30; Czech Clericals, 25; German Social Democrats, 21; Slovak Clericals, 19; German Agrarian and Middle Class Parties, 16; Czech National Democrats, 15; German Christian Socialists, 14; Czech Small Traders, 12; Hungarian Christian Socialists, 9; German National Socialists, 8; German Nationals, 7; Poles and Jews, 4; League for Election Reform, 3

Dec. 7, Bourgeois-Socialist Ministry constituted under Prime Minister Udrzal, 12 Czechs, 2 Slovaks, and 2 Germans: Frantisek Udrzal (Czech Agrarian), Prime Minister; Dr. Eduard Benes (Czech National Socialist), Minister of Foreign Affairs; Dr. K. Viskovsky (Czech Agrarian), National Defense; Karl Trapl (April 16, 1931), Finance; Dr. J. Slavik (Czech Agrarian), Interior; Dr. Josef Matousek (Czech National Democrat), Commerce; Dr. Franz Spina (German Agrarian), Health; Rudolph Mlcoch (Czech Small Traders), Railways; Dr. Ludwig Czech (German Social Democrat), Social Welfare; Dr. Alfred Meissner (Czech Social Democrat), Justice; Bohumil Bradac (Czech Agrarian), Agriculture; Dr. Ivan Derer (Czech Social Democrat), Education; Dr. Emil Franke (Czech National Socialists), Posts and Telegraphs; Jan Dostalek (Czech Clerical), Public Works; Dr. Jan Sramek (Czech Clerical), Unification of Laws; Rudolf Bechyne (Czech Social Democrat), Food

Dec. 13, Four Communist senators and 23 Communist

deputies barred from next few sittings of Parliament because of disorder; refused to obey order of suspension and were carried out by police in general fight

1930

Jan. 20, Financial Agreement with Italy signed
Jan. 21, Agreement with France concluded as to War debt
March 8, Treaty of arbitration, conciliation, and judicial settlement with Lithuania signed
May 14, Treaty of non-aggression, friendship, &c., with Bulgaria signed
June 27, Commercial Treaty with Rumania signed
Aug. 18, Voluntary surrender to avoid confiscation by Prince of Liechtenstein and Order of Teutonic Knights of 150,000 acres of land at nominal price for redistribution
Sept. 11, Anti-Italian demonstration stoned the Italian Legation at Prague
Oct. 29, Treaty of friendship and Convention as to treatment of nationals with Persia signed

DANZIG

Danzig, Free City, constituted in accordance with the provisions of the Treaty of Versailles of June 28, 1919, Articles 100–108, the decision of the Conference of Ambassadors dated Oct. 27, 1920 "constituting Danzig a Free City," and the Treaties between Danzig and Poland signed Nov. 9, 1920 and Oct. 24, 1921. Danzig was formerly part of German West Prussia, area about 754 square miles, population in 1928 390,000. By Article 102 of the Treaty of Versailles, the Principal Allied and Associated Powers undertook to establish the Town of Danzig with the surrounding territory as a Free City, to be placed under the protection of the League of Nations. The League of Nations also appoints a High Commissioner.

The proclamation of the Freedom of the City and adjacent territory, as well as the coming into force of the Danzig-Polish Treaty, in accordance with Article 104 of the Treaty of Versailles, took place on November 9, 1920. According to this Treaty Danzig and Poland form a single customs territory. Since January 1, 1922, the Polish-German customs frontier extends to the sea, *i.e.*, Danzig is a unit in the Polish customs administration.

The Constitution (approved by the League of Nations on May 11, 1922) provides for a *Volkstag* or Diet of 120 members elected for 4 years, and a Senate. This consists of a President, as Chairman, a Vice-President, and 20 Senators, the President and 7 Senators in main office being elected by the *Volkstag* for 4 years, the Vice-President and the other 13 Senators for the duration of the *Volkstag*. Election is by majority of votes.

Count Manfred Gravina, High Commissioner, appointed September 22, 1928.

DENMARK

Denmark, Kingdom of northern Europe, occupying the greater part of the Jutland peninsula (11,408 square miles), and a group of islands dividing the Baltic and North seas, the largest of which are Zealand and Funen, total area 16,568 square miles, the Faroe Islands, lying between Scotland and Iceland and administratively a part of Denmark, 540 square miles. Iceland is an autonomous State under the Danish Monarchy. Greenland is the only colonial possession of Denmark, area 46,740 English square miles. The total population according to Census of Nov. 5, 1925 was 3,434,555 including North Slesvig with 1,502 square miles and 176,433 inhabitants. The population for 1930 was 3,542,210. Capital, Copenhagen.

The crown of Denmark was elective from the earliest times. In 1448 after the death of the last male scion of the Princely House of Svend Estridsen the Danish Diet elected to the throne Christian I, Count of Oldenburg, in whose family the royal dignity remained for more than four centuries, although the crown was not rendered hereditary by right till the year 1660. The direct male line of the House of Oldenburg became extinct with the sixteenth King, Frederik VII, on November 15, 1863. In view of the death of the King without direct heirs, the Great Powers of Europe, "taking into consideration that the maintenance of the integrity of the Danish Monarchy, as connected with the general interests of the balance of power in Europe, is of high importance to the preservation of peace," signed a treaty at London on May 8, 1852, by the terms of which the succession to the crown of Denmark was made over to Prince Christian of Schlesvig-Holstein-Sonderburg-Glücksburg, and to the direct male descendants of his union with the Princess Louise of Hesse Cassel, niece of King Christian VIII of Denmark. In accordance with this treaty, a law concerning the succession to the Danish crown was adopted by the Diet, and obtained the royal sanction July 31, 1853.

Christian X, reigning King, born September 26, 1870; son of King Frederick VIII and Queen Louisa; married April 26, 1898, to Princess Alexandrine of Mecklenburg; succeeded to the throne on the death of his father, May 14, 1912.

60 B.C. to 1846

60 B.C., Reign of Skiold, alleged first King
794 A.D., The Danish chronicles mention 18 kings to the time of Ragnar Lodbrog, killed in an attempt to invade England
1016–28, Canute the Great conquers Norway
July 12, 1397, By the union of Calmar, Denmark, Norway, and Sweden made one kingdom under Margaret
1440, Copenhagen made the capital
1448, Accession of Christian I (of Oldenburg), from whom the late royal family sprang

Jean McCaulley
Dec. 10, 19...

1523, Chri...
 under C...
1536, Lu...
 Christ...
1612, D...
1625, C...
 again...
1658, ...
 besi...
1660, ...
1716 ...
 T...
 dr...
172...
173...
Jar...

May...
 attempt of D... successful
Jan. 14, 1814, Peace of Kiel: Pomer... annexed to Denmark for Norway
1815, Pomerania and Rügen ceded to Prussia for Lauenburg
1824, Commercial treaty with England
1831, New advisory councils established
July 11, 1846, Christian VIII declares the right of the Crown to Slesvig, Holstein, &c.

1848

Jan. 20, Accession of Frederick VII; he proclaims a new constitution, uniting the duchies more closely with Denmark Jan. 28
March 23, Insurrection in the duchies: a provisional government founded
March 24, The rebels seize fortress of Rendsburg
April 9, They are defeated near Flensborg
April 23, The Danes defeated by the Prussians (helping the duchies) near Danevirke, Slesvig
Aug. 1, The North Sea blockaded by Denmark
Aug. 26, Hostilities suspended: the European Powers recommend peace

1849

March 25, Hostilities recommence
June 5, The King sanctions a liberal constitution
July 10, Armistice renewed at Malmo

1850

July 2, Separate peace with Prussia
July 4, Integrity of Denmark guaranteed by England, France, Prussia, and Sweden
July 25, Battle of Isted, and defeat of the Slesvig-Holsteiners by the Danes

...ol signed in London by the Ministers ...at Powers
... 6, Bombardment of Friedrichstadt by ...rs, and the town almost destroyed, but

1851

...lamation of the stadtholders of Slesvig- ...lacing the rights of the country under the ... of the Germanic Confederation

1852

...e integrity of the Danish Monarchy and the ...ence of Slesvig and its old union with ...guaranteed by treaty
...Austrians evacuate Holstein, &c.
...reaty of European Powers. [The succession in ...e of Sonderburg-Glücksburg settled, and the ...ty of the Danish Kingdom guaranteed. Chris- ...Duke of Augustenburg, renounced his rights ...compensation in money]

1854 to 1858

...9, 1854, The King promulgates alterations in the ...stitution relating to joint-monarchy; adopted ...t. 1, 1855
...ch 14, 1857, The sound dues abolished for a compensation
...t., 1857–62, Dissension between the Government and the duchies
...larch 27, 1858, Fortification of Copenhagen decreed

1859

Dec. 3, New ministry appointed; resigns Feb. 9; Bishop Monrad forms a ministry, Feb. 24, 1860

1860

Feb. 11, The assembly of Slesvig complain that the promise of equality of national rights in 1852 has not been kept; protest against the annexation to Denmark, March 1
May 4, The Prussian chamber of deputies receive a petition from Slesvig, and declare that they will aid the duchies; at which the Danish Government protests, May 16

1861

Jan., Correspondence ensues between the Prussian, Danish, and British Governments; the Danish Government declare for war, if German forces enter the duchies
Feb., Warlike preparations in Denmark
June, Decimal coinage adopted

1862

July 17, Agitation in favor of union of Denmark with Sweden, June; the King of Sweden visits Denmark, and is warmly received
Sept. 24, Earl Russell recommends the Government to give to Holstein and Lauenburg all that the Germanic Confederation desire for them, and to give self-government to Slesvig
Nov. 20, M. Hall, the Danish Minister, declines to accede; stating that to do so would imperil the existence of the monarchy itself

1863

March 10, Princess Alexandra of Denmark married to the Prince of Wales at Windsor
March 30, The King grants, by patent, independent rights to Holstein, but annexes Slesvig

April 17, Austria and Prussia protest against it

May, Further diplomatic correspondence

June 6, The King accepts the crown of Greece for his relative, Prince William-George

June 29, Death of the Crown Prince Frederick-Ferdinand, the King's uncle

July 9, The German diet demands annulment of the patent of March 30 (Holstein and Slesvig to be united with the same right) and threatens an army of occupation

Aug., Vain efforts for alliance with Sweden

Aug. 1, Extra levy for the army decreed

Aug. 27, The King replies that he will consider occupation to be an act of war

Sept. 29, New constitution (uniting Slesvig with Denmark) proposed in the Rigsraad

Nov. 15, Death of Frederick VII and accession of Christian IX

Nov. 16, Prince Frederick of Augustenburg claims the duchies of Slesvig and Holstein

Nov. 18, New constitution affirmed by the Rigsdag, Nov. 13; signed by King; published, Dec. 1, 2

Nov. 21 et seq., Great excitement in Holstein; many officials refuse to take oath to Christian

Nov. 26 et seq., Saxony, Bavaria, Hesse, and other German Powers resolve to support the Prince of Augustenburg

Dec., The Austrian and Prussian Ministere say that they will quit Copenhagen if the constitution of Nov. 18 is not annulled

Dec., Great excitement in Norway: proposals to support Denmark

Dec. 2, Prince Frederick's letter to the Emperor Napoleon; an ambiguous reply, Dec. 10

Dec. 19, Denmark protests against federal occupation

Dec. 21, 900 representatives of different German States meet at Frankfort, and resolve to support Prince Frederick as Duke of Slesvig and Holstein, and the inseparable union of those duchies

Dec. 24, The federal execution takes place; a Saxon regiment enters Altona; and the federal commissioners assume administrative powers Dec. 25

Dec. 24 et seq., The Danes retire from Holstein, to avoid collision with federal troops

Dec. 30, Prince Frederick enters Kiel, as Duke of Slesvig and Holstein

Dec. 31, The Danes evacuate Rendsburg

——, Ministerial crisis: Hall retires, and Bishop Monrad forms a cabinet

1864

Jan. 14, Dissension among Germans: the Austro-Prussian proposition rejected by the Diet

Jan. 16, Austria and Prussia demand abrogation of the constitution (of Nov. 18) in two days; the Danes require six weeks' time, Jan. 18

Jan. 21, The German troops under Marshal Wrangel enter Holstein

Feb. 1, The Prussians enter Slesvig, and take Eckernforde

Feb. 2, They bombard Myssunde; which is burnt, Feb. 3

Feb. 5, The Danes abandon the Danevirke to save their army; great discontent in Copenhagen, Feb. 6

Feb. 6, The Danes defeated by Wrangel at Óverson; Slesvig taken; Prince Frederick proclaimed

Feb. 7, The allies occupy Flensborg; commence their attack on Dybböl, Feb. 13

Feb. 13, The federal commissioners protest against the Prussian occupation of Altona

Feb. 18 et seq., The Prussians enter Jutland; take Kolding, Feb. 18; Danes fortify Als

Feb. 23, A conference on Danish affairs proposed by England; agreed to by allies

Feb. 24, A subscription for the wounded Danes begun in London

Feb. 26, The Rigsdag vote a firm address to the King; adjourned March 22

March 1, De Gerlach, General of the Danes

March 16, 17, The Prussians bombard and take the village of Düppel, or Dybböl, and bombard Fredericia, March 20; Danes evacuate Fredericia and retreat to Als March 28

The opening of the conference adjourned from April 12 to 20

April 18, The Prussians take the fortress of Dybböl, by assault, with much slaughter

April 25 et seq., Meetings of the conference of London: result unfavorable to Denmark

May 6 et seq., Jutland subjected to pillage for not paying a war contribution to Prussians

May 9, Agreement for an armistice for one month from May 12

——, The Danes defeat the allies in a naval battle off Helgoland

June 9, The armistice prolonged a fortnight

June 22, The conference ends

June 26, Hostilities resumed; the Prussians surprise Als; take the batteries and 2,400 prisoners, June 29

July 8–10, The Monrad Ministry resigns; Count Moltke charged to form an administration

July 9, Jutland placed under Prussian administration; Prince John of Denmark sent to negotiate at Berlin

July 11, Formation of the Bluhme Ministry

July 18, Armistice agreed to

July 26, Conference for peace at Vienna

Oct. 30, Treaty of peace signed at Vienna;—the King of Denmark resigns the duchies to the disposal of the allies, and agrees to a rectification of his frontier, and to pay a large sum of money to defray the expenses of the war

Nov. 16, Proclamation of the King to the inhabitants of the duchies, releasing them from their allegiance

Dec. 21, Project of a new constitution presented to the chambers; rejected Feb. 25, 1865

1865

Nov. 6, New Ministry formed under Count Frijsenborg; a new constitution proposed, Nov. 7; approved by the two chambers, July 19 and 27; sanctioned by the King, July 28, 1866

1866

Nov. 9, Princess Dagmar married to Prince Alexander of Russia

Nov. 12, New Rigsdag opened

1867 to 1875

The Danish West Indies, St. Thomas and St. John, proposed to be sold to the United States for 1,500,000*l.*—proclamation in the islands dated Oct. 25, 1867

Jan. 30, 1868, Proposed sale of St. Thomas to the United States approved by the assembly (not carried out)

July 28, 1869, Marriage of the Crown Prince Frederick to the Princess Louisa of Sweden

Sept. 27, 1870, Birth of a son to the Crown Prince

Oct. 6, 1873, Statue of Frederick VII, at Copenhagen, solemnly inaugurated

Dec. 4, A democratic party in the assembly (Folkething) defeat the Ministry; the King refuses to dismiss it, Dec. 6

July 14, 1874, New ministry under Fonnesbeck

March 29, 1875, The Folkething, defeating the Government on the question of fortifications, is dissolved

1876

May 15, New assembly meets; votes no confidence in the Ministry, June 12; is adjourned, June 24

Oct., Continued contest between the King and senate and the lower house

Dec., Crisis respecting the supplies

1877

April 4, The session closed without settling the budget

April 12, Provision made by the King for it in accordance with the constitution

Nov. 8, Political crisis; an armistice agreed to

1878 to 1893

Dec. 11, 1878, Marriage of Princess Thyra with the Duke of Cumberland

About May 10, 1881, The lower house dissolved for election

1881–84, Opposition of the lower house continues; legislation greatly stopped

Oct. 3, 1884, Disastrous fire at the palace of Christiansborg, Copenhagen; national gallery, parliament, royal reception rooms, &c., destroyed

May 5, 1885, Importation and possession of arms and drill prohibited

Dec. 21, The parliament condemns the restrictive press laws by great majority

Jan., 1886, M. Berg, President of the assembly, sentenced to six months' imprisonment for obstructing the police at a meeting

April 8, 1888, Amnesty granted to political prisoners on the King's 70th birthday

    The Budget rejected Oct. 16, 1885; Jan. 26, 1886; April 1, 1887; April 1, 1888; April 1, 1889; March 31, 1890; April 1, 1891—the revenue collected by royal decree, 1886–91

April 1, 1892, The King decrees a provisional budget for 1892–93; April 1, 1893, for 1893–94

June, 1893, The King and Queen visit England; present at the marriage of the Duke and Duchess of York, July 6; visit the Queen at Windsor, July 12; leave England, July 27

1894

March 30, The ministerial budget accepted by the parliament; surplus, 2,830,000 kroner

June 1, Messrs. Hunter & Erichsen, of Newcastle, v. M. Tietgen, in Copenhagen (15 years' suit); 13,000l. claimed for supplies for harbor works at Esbjerg from 1868–71; verdict for the plaintiffs reversed by the supreme court

June, The Crown Prince visits England

Aug. 7, Resignation of M. Estrup, 19 years autocratic Premier; cabinet reconstructed, Baron de Reedtz-Thott, Premier

Dec. 4, Loan of 25,000,000 kroner, at 3%, authorized

Dec. 20, Electoral district (reform) bill passed

1895

March 16, The budget passed, with a surplus

1896

March 31, Budget with a surplus, passed

July 22, Prince Charles, son of the Crown Prince, married to Princess Maud of Wales at Buckingham Palace

Oct. 12, Count Frijs-Frijsenborg (Premier, 1865–70) died, aged 79

1897

April 23, Budget, with compromise; reported

May 11, Cabinet crisis; Premier, Baron de Reedtz-Thott, resigns

May 23, New Ministry; M. Hörring, Premier

Nov. 26, Debt conversion bill passed, authorizing a 3% state loan of 72,000,000 kroner

1898

Sept. 29, The Queen dies

    See Prussia, Oct., 1898

Nov. 11, M. Bille, statesman and journalist, dies, aged 70

1899

May 31, General lockout (40,000) in the building and engineering trades; extended to other trades, Aug.; closed in favor of the employers, Sept. 5

1900

March 22, Resignation of the Hörring Cabinet

April 27, M. Sehested (conservative) forms a cabinet

Dec. 5, Committee elected to examine the taxation laws, Government majority of 1

1901

Jan. 1, Sophus Schandorph, poet and novelist, born May 8, 1837, died

May 22, Ministerial crisis, early May; M. Sehested remains in office

July 17, Cabinet resigns; Professor Deuntzer forms a radical Ministry, July 23

Sept. 1, Radical deputation from all districts received by the King

Sept. 23, 24, Great fire at Kallundborg, 30 houses burnt; estimated damage 2,000,000 kroner

Oct. 12, Bill authorizing a new state loan passed

Oct. 19, Death of Mr. C. F. Tietgen, the great merchant, "the King of the Baltic," aged 72

Oct. 24, Tercentenary of Tycho Brahe's death celebrated at Copenhagen, Prague, and Lund, in Sweden

1902

Jan. 24, Treaty for the sale of the Danish West Indies to the United States signed at Washington; rejected by the Landsthing, May 16

May 25, President Loubet visits the King

Oct. 25, Danish West Indian Company formed, Prince Waldemar, President

1903

May, Government bill, repealing existing land taxes, providing a *pro rata* property tax, an income tax, a tax on capital, and the reform of commercial assessments adopted by large majority by the Folkething

1904

Feb. 12, Arbitration treaty with Holland signed

June 10, Arbitration treaty with England to submit differences, except where vital interests or the honor of either party is involved, to the Hague court, failing ordinary diplomatic methods

1905

Jan. 5, Resignation of War Minister, and Ministers of Justice, of the Interior, of Public Instruction, and Agriculture

Jan. 11, Dr. Deuntzer fails to reconstruct his cabinet. M. Christensen summoned by the King to form a new Ministry

Jan. 17, M. Christensen, new Premier, makes a statement of his policy, which includes a Government bill giving universal suffrage in communal elections; the settlement of national defense on the basis of the neutrality of the country; and a rearrangement of the electoral districts in elections to the Folkething

Jan. 18, Order of the day introduced by Radical Party, demanding a reduction of expenditure on national defense, rejected by 74 votes to 27. Vote of confidence in the Ministry passed

March 1, Arbitration treaty between Denmark and Russia, based on the principle of the Hague convention of 1889, signed

March 31, Mr. Thygeson, a member of the Danish parliament, and probably the oldest active member of any parliament, dies, aged 99

April 1, Centenary of the birth of Hans Christian Andersen celebrated throughout Denmark

April 12, King creates two new posts, a military and a naval director, and appoints Lieutenant Colonel Seedorff, Director for Ministry of War, and Commodore Kofoed-Hansen, Director of the Ministry of Marine

April 26, Arbitration treaty between Denmark and Belgium signed at Brussels

July 31, Visit of the German Emperor to the King at Bernsdorff

Sept. 29, Death of Professor Finsen

Nov. 18, Prince Charles of Denmark accepts the crown of Norway

1906

Jan. 29, Death of King Christian IX, aged 87

Jan. 30, Succession of the Crown Prince to the throne, as King Frederick VIII, proclaimed

May 30, General election; the Government loses its absolute majority

July 18–30, Members of the Icelandic parliament visit Copenhagen as state guests, having been invited by King Frederick

Oct. 1, Parliament opened in Copenhagen by King Frederick

1907

Jan. 21, Negotiations between Denmark and Prussia result in an agreement on the so-called North Slesvig " option question" announced

July 3, Visit of the German Emperor and Empress

1908

Jan. 14, Holger Drachmann, the greatest of contemporary Danish poets, born 1846, dies

April 21, King Edward, Queen Alexandra, and Princess Victoria, arrive on an official visit

April 25, King Edward and the royal party leave Copenhagen

June 27–30, Visit of the British Channel fleet to Esbjerg

July 20–22, Visit of M. Fallières, the French President, to Copenhagen

Aug. 10, Strike of compositors, only between 30 and 40 daily papers out of 253 published

Sept. 8, Arrest of M. Alberti, ex-Minister of Justice, charged with committing huge forgeries as director of the Zealand peasants' savings bank

Sept. 12, Resignation of the Premier, M. Christensen

Oct. 7, M. Neergaard undertakes to form a ministry

1909

July 31, Resignation of the Neergaard Cabinet

Aug. 16, Count Holstein succeeds in forming a cabinet including the two former Prime Ministers, MM. Christensen and Neergaard

Oct. 22, Resignation, through a vote of no confidence, of Count Holstein

Oct. 27, New radical cabinet formed by M. Zahle

Dec. 4, Death of Princess Valdemar (Princess Amélie Françoise Hélène Marie of Orleans) born Jan. 13, 1865

1910

May 2, Visit of Mr. Roosevelt, ex-President of the United States

May 27, Resignation of the Zahle Cabinet

1911

April 12, Law enacted dealing with the control of butter export by the Government provided for certification of quality

1912

April 1, Use of metric system of weights and measures became compulsory

May 14, Death of King Frederick VIII. Succeeded by his son, Christian X

May 16, Lockout of 40,000 workmen in Copenhagen by Employers' Federation

1913

May 20, General election gave Radicals and Social Democrats 63 of 114 seats in the Chamber (Folketing)

June 12, Resignation of Berntsen Ministry

June 21, Carl Theodor Zahle, Radical leader formed Cabinet: Eric Scavenius, Foreign Affairs; Ove Rode, Interior; Peter Munch, Defense

Sept. 27, Constitution Alterations Bill passed by Chamber

Dec. 24, Death of Jakob Bronnum S. Estrup, former Prime Minister

1914

Feb. 19, Law established inspection of potatoes for export to meet American requirements

April 4, Unemployment Insurance Act passed

April 17, Advancement of Peace Treaty with the United States signed

May 6, Election Bill passed in Chamber (Folketing)

May 22, New Election Bill passed by the Landsting (senate), May 6 passed both Chambers

June 8, Election Bill defeated in Landsting

June 13, The Landsting dissolved for the first time since the Constitution of 1866 came into effect because of obstruction of Government proposal of democratic amendment to the Constitution

July 10, Election held for the Landsting gave 29 supporters of the Electoral Bill and constitutional reform, and 25 opponents

July 29, 12 conservative amendments to Election Bill and Constitutional Reform Bill rejected

Aug. 1, Royal message declared neutrality in the World War

——, The Rigsdag (Parliament) passed emergency laws

——, Mobilization of the emergency army begun

——, Stock exchange closed temporarily and finally Aug. 3

Aug. 2, Act limited withdrawals from banks

——, Act prohibited support of belligerents from Danish territory

Aug. 5, Inquiry from Germany as to whether the Government would block Danish waters with mines, which was done to prevent action by Germany

Aug. 6, Embargo prohibited the export of fodder, wheat, potatoes, and flour

Aug. 7, Committee to advise the Home Secretary appointed to regulate prices and to ensure supply of the necessities and license exports

Aug. 14, Strike of colliers ended

Aug. 28, Government took over stocks of wheat at fixed price

Sept. 10, Act provided for war risk insurance for Danish vessels

Sept. 24, Act provided for war risk insurance of cargoes

Sept. 30, Royal ordinance relieved bank from redeeming gold, cover reduced to 40%

Dec. 18–19, Meeting of the Kings of Denmark, Sweden, and Norway at Malmo to arrange for agreement on joint diplomatic and political action during the War

1915

Jan. 9, Agreement with Great Britain guaranteed embargoes in return for guarantee that ships for Danish ports would not be molested

Jan. 19, Congress of Socialists of neutral countries opened in Copenhagen which was attended by representatives from Holland, Denmark, Sweden, and Norway only

March 31, Law amended charter of the National Bank providing that reserve need be only 33% instead of 50%

April 23 and June 5, Amendment to Constitution adopted granting universal suffrage

May 10, New election law passed

June 5, New Constitution signed by the King granted full equal suffrage in elections for both Houses by men and women, at age of 35 for the Landsting, and lowered successively from 30 to 25 years for the Folketing; special electoral privileges exercised by the landlords and wealthier classes abolished

Aug. 24, Trade Agreement with Germany signed

Nov. 19, Trade Agreement with Great Britain signed

Nov. 24, Merchants and manufacturers agreed to restrict supplies to Germany

Dec. 20, Stamp tax placed on transfer of shares

Dec. 22, Act authorized loans to the poor by local districts

1916

March 21, Agreement with France signed not to re-export French merchandise to enemy countries

April 11, Act passed for reform of the judiciary separated the administrative and judicial systems, introduced oral proceedings and publicity, and trial by jury in criminal and political cases

April 17, Gold embargo introduced

June 9, Act authorized appointment of rent committees by town councils to prevent unreasonable increases in rent

July 3, Act authorized municipalities to grant rate reliefs for new houses

July 6, Accident Insurance Act made insurance of workers by employers compulsory and codified existing laws

Aug. 4, Treaty with the United States signed ceded Danish West Indies to the United States for $25,000,-000

Sept. 30, Act provided for referendum on sale of Danish West Indies to the United States

Nov. 27, Order in Council required that any advance in prices must be approved by Special Committee appointed Aug. 7, 1914

Dec. 14, Plebiscite on sale of Danish West Indies gave 283,670 votes in favor and 158,157 against

Dec. 22, Treaty with the United States for cession of West Indies ratified by Rigsdag

1917

Jan. 31, Maximum prices fixed for potatoes

Feb. 9, First rationing that of sugar after this date

March 1, Sale of alcoholic liquors temporarily suspended

April 1, Rationing of flour and bread begun

April 17, Embargo placed on gold

May 8, Conservation of national resources law passed

May 19, Maximum prices fixed for a number of commodities

Aug. 3, Grain Act prohibited sale of grain except to the Government

Sept. 29, Corporation law passed

Nov. 22, Expulsion of aliens law enacted

Nov. 28–30, Conference of Scandinavian Kings at Christiania

1918

Jan. 1, Coffee, pork, and butter rationed

April, Tea rationed

April 21, Constitution of June 5, 1915 came into effect

April 22, Elections for chamber (Folketing) at which women voted for the first time gave Government 72 seats as against an Opposition of 68: Socialists, 39; Radicals, 33; and Left, 45; and Conservatives, 23; the Landsting: 17 Conservatives, 26 Left, 13 Radicals, and 15 Socialists

July 30, Housing Act passed

Sept. 18, Trade Agreement with the United States signed

Oct. 23, Resolution of the Rigsdag stated that the question of union of Slesvig must be decided according to principles of nationality

Nov. 30, Act of Union recognized Iceland as an autonomous State united with Denmark by one King

1919

Feb. 12, Act introduced the eight-hour day in factories

Feb. 21, Danish North Slesvig delegation presented case to Peace Conference

March 1, Resignation of Zahle Cabinet

March 18, Zahle Cabinet withdrew resignation

April 1, National Loan Act provided for domestic loan of 120 million kroner

April 11, Bill passed provided for liquidation of Act of Aug. 7, 1914, which ceased to have effect on Sept. 1

May 9, New Insurance Act passed

Sept. 19, Grain Act required farmers to turn over to the State granaries all harvested cereals except what was required for sowing

Oct. 4, Land law provided for expropriation of parochial lands

Oct. 31, Food Act provided for Government regulation of supplies

Nov. 19, Commercial Agreement with Great Britain signed

Dec. 17, New Unemployment Insurance Act

1920

Jan. 1, The eight-hour day adopted by agreement of chief organizations

Jan. 15, Interallied Commission took over administration of plebiscite area of Slesvig

Feb. 10, Plebiscite in first zone (Slesvig) gave majority of votes for union with Denmark, 75,151 votes as against 25,231 for Germany

March 8, Denmark became a member of the League of Nations

March 14, Plebiscite in second zone (Slesvig) southern gave majority of votes for union with Germany, 51,000 as against 13,000 for Denmark

March 17, Law abolished the land defense and artillery of Copenhagen

March 29, The Zahle Ministry dismissed by the King because of refusal to order new elections

——, Social Democrats threatened a general strike unless Zahle reinstated

March 30, Liebe formed a non-party Cabinet

April 1–5, General strike of transport workers and seamen

April 4, Liebe Ministry resigned at request of the King

April 5, New Ministry composed chiefly of State officials appointed by Mr. Friis to formulate an electoral law and order new elections

April 11, New election law adopted based on proportional representation in the county districts

April 25, Elections a victory for the Opposition: Left, 49 seats; Conservatives, 28; Trades Party, 4; Socialists, 42; Radicals, 17

May 5, Niels Neergaard formed Left Cabinet

June 28, Insurance law passed

July 5, Treaty signed with Allied Powers and Germany as to transfer of North Slesvig

July 6, Second general election a victory for Conservatives and Liberals

July 7, North Slesvig formally transferred to Denmark

July 9, North Slesvig Reunion Act signed by the King incorporating Slesvig

Sept. 10, Amendment to Constitution provided for inclusion of North Slesvig

——, Last Grain Act passed provided for harvest of 1920–21

Sept. 21, Elections to Folketing in which people of North Slesvig took part and the voting age 25 for the first time gave the Left 52 seats

Dec. 17, Treaty with Germany signed regarding indemnity to be paid to Germany in connection with transfer of Slesvig

1921

Jan. 20, Rationing of wheat bread and flour ended

March 18, Lockout met with strike of 100,000 workers

May 17, Death of Karl Mantzius, actor

May 18, Death of Martin Nyrop, architect

June 20, Commercial *modus vivendi* with Spain established

July 2, Government informed Norway that Greenland formed part of Danish Colonial Empire

July 11, Death of Sigurd Berg, Minister of the Interior

Nov. 23, 16 new taxes proposed, income and capital levy and succession duty, customs duties, liquor tax, 10% tax on turnover of hotels and restaurants

1922

Jan. 1, New Labor Agreement between employers and employed came into effect

Feb. 22, Lockout by Danish Employers Association; compromise settlement reached April 7

May 1, Arbitration Convention of Oct. 25, 1905, with Great Britain renewed for 5 years

July 11, Agreement with Bulgaria renewed Treaty of commerce and navigation of 1909

Aug. 7, Old Age Pensions Act granting annual sum to any person 65 years of age under certain conditions replaced that of April 9, 1891

Aug. 8, Law of National Defense passed, enters recruits on conscription rolls at 17 years to receive military training between the ages of 19 and 25 for service for 8 years in the first line and 8 years in the reserve

1923

March 6, Death of Marcus Rubin, statistician

April 23, Provisional Commercial Agreement with Russia signed renewed diplomatic relations. Ratified by Parliament, June 8; constituting recognition of the Soviet Government, and followed by Agreement of June 18

May 8, Provisional Commercial Agreement with Rumania

June 30, Agreement with Austria renewed Commercial Treaty of March 4, 1887

July 18, Provisional Agreement as to commerce and navigation with Lithuania signed

Aug. 3, Commercial Agreement with Finland signed

Sept. 7, Provisional Agreement as to commerce and navigation with Estonia signed

1924

Jan. 16, Nation Bank rate raised from 6 to 7%

Jan. 31, Provisional Commercial Agreement with Czechoslovakia signed

Feb. 1, Law came into effect increasing customs duties on luxuries, fruit, silks, furs, liquors, tobacco

March 22, Treaty of commerce and navigation with Poland, Danzig, and Iceland

April 11, Elections for Folketing, a defeat for the Government: Social Democrats gained 55 seats against 45 for the Left

April 23, Theodor Stauning, Socialist, formed Cabinet: Count Moltke, Foreign Affairs; Bramsnaes, Finance; Fru Nina Bang, the first woman to hold office in a Danish Cabinet, Education; Borgbjerg, Social; Steincke, Justice

May 29, Liquor smuggling Treaty with the United States signed

June 6, Treaty of conciliation with Switzerland signed

June 24, Treaty of arbitration with the United States signed

June 27, Treaties of conciliation with Sweden, Norway, and Finland signed

July 9, Treaty with Norway signed by which Norwegians guaranteed hunting and fishing rights in East Greenland for 20 years

Oct. 8, Bill for disarmament passed first reading

Oct. 20, Treaty of commerce with Sweden signed

Nov. 3, Treaty of commerce and navigation with Latvia signed

Dec. 10, Treaty of commerce and navigation of 1843–46 with Greece prolonged by exchange of Notes

Dec. 16, Air Navigation Agreement with Poland

1925

Jan. 26, Treaty of friendship with Turkey signed

March 18, Decree gave married women absolute legal equality with husband

April 18, Further Commercial Agreement with Czechoslovakia

——, Act regulated employment of children and young persons

May 1–June 28, Combined strike and lockout ended with compromise arranged by arbitration of the Government

June 1, Commercial Bank stopped payment

July 14, Agreement signed with Great Britain regarding East Greenland

Sept. 1, Seamen's strike against wage cut

——, Treaty of friendship, commerce, and navigation with Siam signed

Nov. 5, Census gave population as 3,434,555

Nov. 18, Workmens' Compensation Agreement with Great Britain signed

1926

Jan. 14, Agreement for pacific settlement of disputes signed with Sweden

Jan. 15, Convention for pacific settlement of disputes with Norway signed

Jan. 30, Convention for pacific settlement of disputes with Finland signed

March 12, Lower House passed Disarmament Bill by vote of 75 to 71 which practically abolished the army and navy

March 22, Treaty of commerce with Turkey signed

April 23, Convention of arbitration and conciliation with Poland signed

June 1, Lieutenant Botved completed flight to Tokio

June 2, Treaty of conciliation and arbitration with Germany signed

June 4, Convention with Great Britain signed renewed for 5 years that of Oct. 25, 1905 for the pacific settlement of disputes

July 5, Treaty of arbitration with France signed replaced that of Aug., 1911

July 23, Provisional Air Agreement with the Netherlands signed

Nov. 30, Arbitration Treaty with Czechoslovakia signed

Dec. 2, Election a defeat for the Government: Liberals, 31; Socialists, 25; Conservatives, 12; Radicals, 8

Dec. 3, Resignation of Stauning Socialist Ministry

Dec. 10, T. Madsen-Mygdal, Liberal, appointed Prime Minister

Dec. 11, Convention with Lithuania for pacific settlement of disputes signed

Dec. 14, Madsen-Mygdal Cabinet assumed office: The Presidency of the Council and Ministry of Agriculture, Th. Mygdal; Foreign Affairs, L. J. Moltesen; Interior, Oluf C. Kragh; Health, V. Rubov; Justice, Svenning Rytter; Defense, S. Brorsen; Public Instruction, J. Byskov; Ecclesiastical Affairs, F. Bruun-Rasmussen; Public Works, J. P. Stensballe; Finance, N. Neergaard; Industry, Commerce, and Navigation, M. Slebsager

Dec. 18, Conciliation Convention with Estonia signed

Dec. 22, Bill passed by both Chambers reimposed on National Bank obligation to redeem its notes in gold as from Jan. 1, 1927

1927

Jan. 29, Arbitration Treaty with Estonia signed

Feb. 19, Death of Georg Morris Cohen Brandes, literary critic (85)

March 3, Treaty of arbitration and conciliation with Belgium signed

April 27, Death of Klaus Berntsen, former Premier

May 9, Treaty of conciliation with Estonia signed

Oct. 8, Customs Agreement with Germany signed

1928

Jan. 2, Treaty of commerce and navigation with Spain signed

March 14, Arbitration Treaty with Spain signed

March 25, Death of Mrs. Nina Bang, first woman member of Danish Cabinet

April 24, Election a victory for the Social Democrats

June 14, Treaty of arbitration with the United States signed

Aug. 22, Treaty of commerce and navigation with Greece signed

Sept. 12, Treaty of arbitration and commerce with Spain signed

Sept. 19, Visit of King Alfonso of Spain

Sept., Election for Landsting: Liberals, 28; Socialists, 27; Conservatives, 12; Radicals, 8

Oct. 25, Convention for assistance to nationals concluded with Finland, Norway, and Sweden

1929

March 21, Defeat of Government on budget

April 23, Parliament dissolved

April 24, Election for Folketing: Socialists, 61; Liberals, 44; Radicals, 16; Conservatives, 24; other parties, 4

April 25, Resignation of Madsen-Mygdal Ministry

April 29, Theodor Stauning formed a Cabinet: The Presidency of the Council and Ministry of Navigation and Fishing, Th. Stauning; Agriculture, K. M. Bording; Foreign Affairs, P. Munch; Interior, B. Dahlgaard; Social Affairs, K. K. Steincke; Justice, C. Th. Zahle; Defense, L. Rasmussen; Public Instruction, F. Borgbjerg; Ecclesiastical Affairs, N. P. L. Dahl; Public Works, J. F. N. Friis-Skotte; Finance, C. V. Bramsnaes; Commerce and Industry, C. N. Hauge

June 7, Passports abolished as between Denmark, Finland, Norway, and Sweden

Oct. 3, Disarmament Bill introduced provided for conversion of army and navy into a constabulary force and demolition of fortifications

Oct. 24, Suicide of H. Plum precipitated a crisis in business

1930

Feb. 28, Arbitration Treaty with Latvia signed

June 27, Treaty of friendship and arbitration signed with Finland, Sweden, and Norway

Sept. 1, Return of L. Koch exploring expedition from Greenland

Dec. 16, Sentences of 3½ years imprisonment imposed on directors involved in fraudulent dealings and failure of Harold W. Plum Companies

SOVEREIGNS

A.D.

860. Gorm, the Old

935. Harold, surnamed Blue Tooth

985. Sweyn or Svend, the Forked-beard

1014. Harold

1019. Canute II the Great, King of Denmark, Norway, and England

1035. Canute III, son (Hardicanute of England and Denmark)

1042. Magnus, surnamed the Good, of Norway

1047. Svend, or Sweyn II (Denmark only)

1077. Harold, called the Simple

1080. Canute IV

1086. Olaus IV, the Hungry

1095. Eric I, styled the Good

1103. [Interregnum]

1104. Nicholas I, killed at Slesvig 1105

1135. Eric II

1137. Eric III, the Lamb

1147. Svend, or Sweyn III, beheaded. Canute V until 1157 (civil war)

1157. Waldemar, styled the Great

1182. Canute VI

1202. Waldemar II, the Victorious

1241. Eric IV

1250. Abel: assassinated his elder brother Eric; killed in an expedition against the Frisons

1252. Christopher I, poisoned

1259. Eric V

1286. Eric VI

1320. Christopher II

1332–1340. [Interregnum]

1340. Waldemar III

1375. [Interregnum]

1376. Olaus V

1387. Margaret, styled the "Semiramis of the North," Queen of Sweden, Norway, and Denmark

1396. Margaret and Eric VII (Eric XIII of Sweden)

1412. Eric VII reigns alone; obliged to resign both crowns

1440. Christopher III, King of the three countries

1448. Christian I, Count of Oldenburg; elected King of Denmark, 1448; of Sweden, 1457; succeeded by his son

1481. John; succeeded by his son

1513. Christian II, called the Cruel, and the "Nero of the North"; he caused all the Swedish nobility to be massacred; dethroned for his tyranny in 1523; died 1559

[Sweden separated from Denmark]

DENMARK AND NORWAY

1523. Frederick I, Duke of Holstein, son of Christian I

1533–1534. [Interregnum]

1534. Christian III, son of Frederick; established the Lutheran religion; esteemed the "Father of his People"

1559. Frederick II, son of Christian III

1588. Christian IV, son

1649. Frederick III; changed the constitution from an elective to an hereditary monarchy, vested in his own family, 1660

1670. Christian V, son of Frederick III; succeeded by his son

1699. Frederick IV; leagued with the Czar Peter and the King of Poland against Charles XII of Sweden

1730. Christian VI, his son

1746. Frederick V, his son, married the Princess Louisa of England, daughter of George II

1766. Christian VII, his son

1784. Prince Frederick declared himself regent, in consequence of the mental derangement of his father

1808. Frederick VI, previously regent, now King

1814. Norway annexed to Sweden, Jan. 14

DENMARK

1839. Christian VIII (son of Frederick, brother of Christian VII)

1848. Frederick VII, son of Christian VIII, Jan. 20; born Oct. 6, 1808; separated from his first wife, Sept., 1837; from his second wife, Sept., 1846; married morganatically Louisa, Countess of Danner, Aug. 7, 1850; died Nov. 15, 1863

1863. Christian IX, son of William, Duke of Schlesvig-Holstein-Sonderburg-Glücksburg; Nov. 15, succeeded by virtue of the protocol of London, May 8, 1852, and of the law of the Danish succession, July 31, 1853. He was born April 8, 1818; married Princess Louisa of Hesse-Cassel, May 26, 1842 (born Sept. 7, 1817; died Sept. 29, 1898). [He is descended from Christian III and she from Frederick V; both from George II of England]; died Jan. 29, 1906

1906. Frederick VIII (his son), born June 3, 1843; married Princess Louisa of Sweden, July 28, 1869. Sons: Christian (heir), born Sept. 26, 1870; married Princess Alexandrine of Mecklenburg-Schwerin, 1898; Charles, born Aug. 3, 1872, married Princess Maud of Wales, 1896 (King Haakon VII of Norway, 1905)

1912. Christian X succeeded to the throne on the death of his father, May 14, 1912

DODECANESE ISLANDS

Dodecanese Islands, possession of Italy, situated near coast of Anatolia in the Ægean Sea. Under Turkish sovereignty since A.D. 1522 they were occupied by Italians during Turkish-Italian War of 1911–12. The Treaty of Ouchy, of Oct. 18, 1912, pledged evacuation by Italy as soon as the Turks had evacuated Libya. They were assigned to Greece by the London Conference of Ambassadors, Feb. 13, 1914, and Treaty of July 29, 1919 between Greece and Italy, confirmed by Treaty of Aug. 10, 1920, ceded the islands to Greece, but these treaties were denounced by Italy in 1922. The Treaty of Sèvres of Aug. 10, 1920 assigned the islands to Italy, and by the

Treaty of Lausanne, July 24, 1923, Turkey recognized Italian sovereignty.

ISLAND	AREA IN SQ. MILES	POPULATION 1927
Rhodes (Rodi)	550	45,000
Cos (Coo)	115	16,000
Patmos (Patmo)	12	2,550
Lipso (Lisso)	6	560
Kalymnos (Calino) . . .	37	24,000
Leros (Lero)	24	4,000
Nisyros (Nisiro)	15	3,160
Tilos (Piscopi)	24	1,160
Karchi (Calchi)	10	1,300
Symi (Simi)	22	7,000
Astypalæa (Stampalia) . . .	36	1,370
Karpathos (Scarpanto) . . .	109	11,500
Casos (Caso)	23	1,760
Castelrosso	3	2,740

Mario Lago, Governor.

EASTERN EMPIRE

After the death of the Emperor Jovian, in Feb., 364, the generals at Nice elected Valentinian as his successor, who, in June, made his brother Valens Emperor of the East; the final division was in 395, between the sons of Theodosius. The Eastern Empire ended with the capture of Constantinople, and death of Constantine XIII, May 29, 1453; *see* Turkey.

381 (July 9), Nestorius, the Bishop, nominated the first Patriarch of Constantinople
388, Theodosius the Great succors Valentinian II, the Western Emperor, and defeats the tyrant Maximus, at Aquileia
392, Valentinian II slain by Arbogastes the Frank, who makes Eugenius Emperor
394 (Sept. 6), Eugenius defeated and slain by Theodosius, who reunites the two Empires
395 (Jan. 17), Death of Theodosius; the Empire finally divided between his sons—Arcadius receives the east, Honorius the west
413, Constantinople walled by Theodosius II
——, Alaric the Goth begins to ravage the Empire
425, Violent religious dissensions; Theodosius II establishes schools, and revives learning
431, 449, The councils of Ephesus; of Chalcedon, 451
438, The Theodosian Code promulgated
498–520, Frequent sanguinary conflicts between the Blues and Greens, circus factions at Constantinople
529, The Justinian Code published
529–531, War with Persia; beginning of the victorious career of Belisarius, the Imperial General
532, He suppresses the "Nika" ("conquer") insurrection of the circus factions; 30,000 Greeks slain, and Constantinople burnt
533–541, Victories of Belisarius in Africa, Italy, and the East
537, Dedication of St. Sophia
542, Recalled through Justinian's jealousy; again, 548; again, 549; disgraced, 562
545, Beginning of the Turkish power in Asia
551, The Slavonians ravage Illyria
552, Narses defeats Totila and the Goths near Rome
561, Disaffection of Narses

565, Death of Belisarius, aged 84; of Justinian (83)
579 *et seq.*, Victories of Maurice and Narses in the East
594–620, Severe contests with the Avars
606, Narses burnt at Constantinople
622 (July 16), The flight (Hejira) of Mohammed from Mecca to Medina, where he establishes himself as a prophet and prince
622 *et seq.*, Victorious career of Heraclius II
627, He recovers his lost territories
632, The Saracens invade the Empire; defeat Heraclius at Aiznadin, 633; at Yermuk, 636; take Alexandria, 640; and the Greek provinces in Africa, 648
660, Constans purchases peace with them
672–77, They besiege Constantinople seven times
678, The Bulgarians establish a kingdom in Mœsia (now Bulgaria); they ravage the country up to Constantinople, 711
716, 718, The Saracens vainly invest Constantinople; defeated, 720
726, Leo III, the Isaurian, forbids the worship of images: (this leads to the Iconoclast controversy, and eventually to the separation of the eastern and western churches)
739, A great invading Arab force (90,000) defeated by Acronius
752, The Empire loses the exarchate of Italy; Dalmatia, 825; Sicily and Crete, 827
754, Destruction of images throughout the Empire decreed; image-worship restored by the Empress Irene (for which she was canonized), 787
770, The monasteries dissolved
830, Image-worship persecuted; restored, 842; forbidden at Constantinople by one council, 869; restored by another, 879
890, South Italy annexed to the Empire
928, Five emperors reigning at one time
——, Naples added to the Empire
987, 1014, Basil subdues the Bulgarians
1018, Bulgaria annexed to the Empire
1068, The Turks invade Asia Minor
1080, The Normans conquer South Italy
1097, The First Crusade; Alexis I recovers Asia
1125, The Venetians victorious over the Greeks
1152, The Hungarians repelled; peace made with the Normans in Sicily, 1156
1172, Wars with the Turks and the Venetians
1190, Cyprus lost to the Empire
1202, The Fourth Crusade begins
1203 (July 19), Revolt of Alexis against his brother Isaac; the crusaders take Constantinople, and restore Isaac and his son Alexis IV
1204 (May 9), Alexis Ducas murders Alexis IV and usurps the throne; the crusaders take Constantinople, kill Alexis, and establish the Latin Empire, under Baldwin, Count of Flanders
——, Empire of Nice founded by Theodore Lascaris
1208, Kingdom of Epirus and Ætolia established
1261 (July 25), Constantinople recovered, and the Empire reëstablished by Michael Palæologus
1299, Establishment of the Turkish Empire in Asia under Othman I
1303, The Genoese trade in the Black Sea
1340 and 1345, The Turks ravage Mysia, &c.; and settle on the coast of Thrace, 1353
1362, The Sultan Amurath takes Adrianople, and makes it his capital; and, by treaty, greatly reduces the Emperor's territories, 1373
1390, All the Greek possessions in Asia lost

1396 (Sept. 28), Sultan Bajazet defeats the Christians under Sigismund of Hungary, at Nicopolis

1400, The Emperor Manuel vainly solicits help from the western sovereigns

1401, A Turkish pasha established at Athens

1402, The Greek Empire made tributary to Timour; who subjugates the Turkish Sultan, and dismembers his empire, 1403; death of Timour, on his way to China, 1405

1403–12, Dissension amongst the Turks defers the fall of Constantinople; Mohammed I aided by the Emperor Manuel, becomes Sultan, 1413

1422, Amurath II in vain besieges Constantinople; peace made, 1425

1437–40, John Palæologus visits Rome and other places, soliciting help in vain

1448, Accession of Constantine XIII, last Emperor

1451, Accession of Mohammed II; begins the siege of Constantinople, April 6; takes it, May 29, 1453
(He granted the Christians personal security and free exercise of their religion.) *See* Turkey

EMPERORS OF THE EASTERN EMPIRE

364. Valens
379. Theodosius I, the Great
395. Arcadius, the son of Theodosius
408. Theodosius II succeeded his father
450. Marcian, a Thracian of obscure family
457. Leo I, the Thracian
474. Leo II, the Younger, died the same year
——. Zeno, called the Isaurian
491. Anastasius I, an Illyrian, of mean birth
518. Justin I, originally a private soldier
527. Justinian I, founder of the Digest
565. Justin II, nephew of Justinian
578. Tiberius II, renowned for his virtues
582. Maurice, the Cappadocian, murdered with all his children by his successor
602. Phocas, the Usurper, a centurion, whose crimes and cruelties led to his own assassination in 610
610. Heraclius, by whom Phocas was dethroned
641. (Heracleonas) Constantine III reigned a few months; poisoned by his stepmother, Martina
——. Constans II, assassinated in a bath
668. Constantine III (or IV) Pogonatus
685. Justinian II, son of the preceding; abhorred for his exactions, debaucheries, and cruelties; dethroned and mutilated by his successor
695. Leontius dethroned and mutilated by Tiberius Aspimar
698. Tiberius III Aspimar
705. Justinian II restored. Leontius and Tiberius degraded in the Hippodrome, and put to death. Justinian slain in 711
711. Philippicus-Bardanes assassinated
713. Anastasius II fled on the election of Theodosius in 716; afterwards delivered up to Leo III and put to death
716. Theodosius III
718. Leo III, the Isaurian
[In this reign (726) commences the great Iconoclastic controversy; the alternate prohibition and restoration of images involves the peace of several reigns]
741. Constantine IV (or V) Copronymus, son of the preceding; succeeded by his son
775. Leo IV
780. Constantine V (or VI) and his mother Irene

790. Constantine, alone, by the desire of the people, Irene having become unpopular
792. Irene again, jointly with her son, and afterwards alone, 797; deposed for her cruelties and murders, and exiled
802. Nicephorus I Logothetes slain
811. Stauracius reigns a few days only
——. Michael I, defeated in battle, abdicates the throne, and retires to a monastery
813. Leo V the Armenian: killed in the temple at Constantinople on Christmas-day, 820, by conspirators in the interest of his successor
820. Michael II, the Stammerer
——. Theophilus, son of Michael
842. Michael III Porphyrogenitus, and the Sot, son of the preceding; murdered by his successor
867. Basil I, the Macedonian
886. Leo VI, the Philosopher
Alexander and Constantine VI (or VII) Porphyrogenitus, brother and son of Leo, the latter only six years of age; the former dying in 912, Zoë, mother of Constantine, assumes the regency
919. Romanus Lecapenus, usurper, associates with him his sons
920. Christopher, and
928. Stephen and Constantine VII (or VIII)
[Five emperors now reign: Christopher dies, 931; Romanus exiled by his sons Constantine and Stephen, who are themselves banished the next year]
945. Constantine VII (or VIII) reigns alone; poisoned by his daughter-in-law, Theophania, 959
959. Romanus II, son of preceding, contrived his father's death; banished his mother, Helena
963. Nicephorus II Phocas, married Theophania, his predecessor's consort, who has him assassinated.
969. John I Zimisces, celebrated General; takes Basil II and Constantine VIII (or IX), sons of Romanus II, as colleagues; John dies, supposed by poison, and
976. Basil II and Constantine VIII reign; the former dies in 1025; the latter in 1028
1028. Romanus III Argyropulus poisoned by his profligate consort Zoë, who raises
1034. Michael IV, the Paphlagonian, to the throne; on his death Zoë places
1041. Michael V Calaphates, as his successor; Zoë dethrones him, has his eyes put out, and marries
1042. Constantine IX (or X) Monomachus and Zoë reign jointly; Zoë dies, 1050
1054. Theodora, widow of Constantine
1056. Michael VI Stratiotes, or Strato, deposed
1057. Isaac I Comnenus abdicates
1059. Constantine X (or XI) Ducas
1067. Eudocia, consort of the preceding, and Romanus IV Diogenes, whom she marries, reign to the prejudice of Michael, Constantine's son
1071. Michael VII Parapinaces, recovers his throne, and reigns jointly with Constantine XI (or XII)
1078. Nicephorus III dethroned by
1081. Alexis or Alexius I Comnenus, succeeded by
1118. John Comnenus (Kalos), his son, died of a wound from a poisoned arrow
1143. Manuel I Comnenus, son of John
1180. Alexis II Comnenus, son of the preceding, under the regency of the Empress Maria, his mother
1183. Andronicus I Comnenus, causes Alexis to be strangled, and seizes the throne; put to death by
1185. Isaac II Angelus-Comnenus, who is deposed, imprisoned, and deprived of his eyes by his brother

1195. Alexis III Angelus, the Tyrant, deposed, and his eyes put out; died in a monastery
1203. Isaac II again, with his son, Alexis IV; deposed
1204. Alexis V Ducas, murders Alexis IV; is killed by the crusaders

LATIN EMPERORS

1204. Baldwin I, Earl of Flanders, on the capture of Constantinople by the Latins, elected Emperor; made a prisoner by the King of Bulgaria and never heard of afterwards
1206. Henry I, his brother, dies in 1217
1216. Peter de Courtenay, his brother-in-law
1221. Robert de Courtenay, his son
1228. Baldwin II, his brother, a minor, and John de Brienne, of Jerusalem, Regent and Associate Emperor
1261. [Constantinople recovered, and the Empire of the Franks or Latins terminates]

GREEK EMPERORS AT NICE

1204. Theodore Lascaris I
1222. John Ducas Vataces
1255. Theodore Lascaris II, his son
1259. John Lascaris, and (1260) Michael VIII Palæologus

GREEK EMPERORS AT CONSTANTINOPLE

1261. Michael VIII now at Constantinople; puts out the eyes of John, and reigns alone
1282. Andronicus II Palæologus, the Elder, son of preceding; deposed by
1328. Andronicus III, the Younger, his grandson
1341. John Palæologus I under the guardianship of John Cantacuzenus; the latter proclaimed Emperor at Adrianople
1347. John Cantacuzenus abdicates
1355. John Palæologus I restored
1391. Manuel II Palæologus, his son; succeeded by his son and colleague
1425. John Palæologus II. The throne claimed by his three brothers
1448. Constantine Palæologus XII (XIII or XIV some of the other emperors being called Constantine by some writers) killed, when Constantinople was taken, May 29, 1453

ENGLAND

England (and Wales) geographically the southern part of the Island of Great Britain, became Great Britain politically by the union of the Crowns of England and Scotland May 1, 1707. The United Kingdom of Great Britain and Ireland (capital, London) comprises the British Isles and attached to the United Kingdom are the Channel Islands and Isle of Man. (*See also* Great Britain, British Empire, Ireland, Scotland and Wales). The area of England is 50,874 square miles, of Wales 7,466, of Scotland 30,405, the Isle of Man 221, Channel Islands 75, total of United Kingdom 89,041. For population *see* Great Britain.

England (from *Angles* and *lond*, land), so named, it is said, by Egbert, first King of the English, in a general council held at Winchester, 829; or by Athelstan, 925. *See* Anglo-Saxons. England was

united to Wales, 1283; to Scotland in 1603; they have had the same legislature since 1707, when the three were styled Great Britain. James I first adopted the title of King of England, Scotland, afterwards Great Britain, France, and Ireland. After the Treaty of Amiens, signed March 27, 1802, France was omitted from the royal style.

828 to 1042

828, Egbert, "King of the English"; defeats the Welsh, Danes, &c., at Hengestdune, 835
871, Alfred, King; after many vicissitudes, vanquishes the Danes, 871–896
890, He frames a code of laws; forms a militia and navy, surveys and subdivides the country, and promotes education (many statements mythical), 896
937, Athelstan's great victory over the Danes, Scots, &c., at Brunanburg
About 952, Predominance of Dunstan; he promotes monachism and the celibacy of the clergy
991, Ethelred compounds with the Danes for peace
Nov. 13, 1002, Causes their massacre
1003, Avenged by Sweyn, King of Denmark; Ethelred flees to Normandy
1014, Sweyn dies, and Ethelred returns; dies, 1016
1017, Canute, the Dane, sole monarch
1042, Edward, the Confessor, King; Saxon dynasty restored

1066

Jan. 6, Harold II crowned; defeats the Norwegians, Sept. 25; defeated and slain at Hastings by William of Normandy, Oct. 14
Dec. 25, William I crowned

1069 to 1685

1069–70, The northern counties rebel; ravaged from the Humber to the Tyne
About 1070, Introduction of the feudal system
1076, Justices of peace appointed
1085–86, Domesday book compiled
Sept. 26, 1087, William II crowned
1096, The crusades begin
Aug. 5, 1100, Henry I crowned, restores Saxon laws, &c.
1106, Defeats his brother Robert, and gains Normandy
Nov. 25, 1120, Prince William and nobles drowned
Dec. 26, 1135, Stephen crowned
Aug. 22, 1138, Civil war between the Empress Maud, Henry's daughter, and Stephen; her friends the Scots defeated at the battle of the Standard
1139, She lands in England, and is successful
March 3, 1141, Crowned at Winchester
1147, Defeated; retires to France
1153, Concludes a peace with Stephen
Dec. 19, 1154, Henry II crowned
Jan., 1164, Constitutions of Clarendon enacted
Dec. 29, 1170, Arrogance of Becket; murdered
1171, 1172, Conquest of Ireland
1176, England divided into six circuits for the administration of justice
1181, English laws digested by Glanville
Sept. 3, 1189, Richard I crowned
1191, He joins the crusades
1192, Defeats Saladin
Dec., Made prisoner by Duke of Austria, and sold to Henry VI of Germany

1194, Ransomed for about 300,000*l.*

May, 1199, John crowned

1204, Normandy lost to England

1208, England put under an interdict

June 15, 1215, Magna Charta granted. Its fundamental parts were derived from Saxon charters, continued by Henry I and his successors. On Nov. 20, 1214, the Archbishop of Canterbury and the barons met at St. Edmondsbury. On Jan. 6, 1215, they presented their demands to King John, who deferred his answer. On May 19 they were censured by the Pope. On May 24 they marched to London, and the King was compelled to yield. The charter was sealed by John at Runnymede, near Windsor, June 15, 1215

Oct. 28, 1216, Henry III crowned

1248, Charter granted to Oxford University by Henry III

1262–68, The Barons' War arose in consequence of the faithlessness of Henry III and the oppression of his favorites in 1258. The barons, headed by Simon de Montfort, Earl of Leicester, and Gilbert de Clare, Earl of Gloucester, met at Oxford in 1262, and enacted statutes to which the King objected. In 1263 their disputes were in vain referred to the decision of Louis IX of France. War broke out, and on May 14, 1264, the King's party was totally defeated at Lewes; and De Montfort became the virtual ruler of the Kingdom. The war was renewed; and at the battle of Evesham, Aug. 4, 1265, De Montfort was slain, and the barons were defeated; but they did not render their final submission till 1268

Jan., 1265, Simon de Montfort, Earl of Leicester, summoned two parliaments; one including knights of the shire, 1264 (the other first including burgesses); the first regular Parliament met

Nov. 20, 1272, Edward I crowned

1283, Wales subdued, united to England

1292, Death of Roger Bacon

1296, Scotland subdued; revolts, 1297

July 8, 1307, Edward II crowned

1308, 1315, 1325, Insurrection of the barons against his favorites

June 24, 1314, Defeated by Bruce at Bannockburn

Jan. 25, 1327, Edward III crowned

1333, Defeat of the Scots at Hallidown-hill

Aug. 26, 1346, Invades France; victorious at Crècy

1347, Takes Calais

1349, Order of the Garter instituted

Sept. 19, 1356, Victory at Poictiers

May 8, 1360, Peace of Bretigny

1362, Law pleadings in English

June 22, 1377, Richard II crowned

June 15, 1381, Insurrection of Wat Tyler, in opposition to the poll tax imposed on all persons above 15, Nov. 5, 1380. One of the collectors, acting with indecent rudeness to Wat Tyler's daughter, was struck dead by the father, June, 1381. His neighbors took arms, and in a short time almost the whole of the population of the southern and eastern counties rose, extorting freedom from their lords, and plundering. On June 12, 1381, they gathered upon Blackheath to the number of 100,000 men, and on June 14 murdered Simon of Sudbury, Archbishop of Canterbury, and Sir Robert Hales, the Royal Treasurer. The King, Richard II, invited Tyler to a parley, which took place on the 15th at Smithfield, where the latter addressed the King in a menacing manner, now and again lifting up his sword. On this the mayor, Wal-

worth, stunned Tyler with a blow of his mace, and one of the King's knights named Cavendish, dispatched him. Richard temporized with the multitude by promising a charter, and thus led them out of the city, when Sir R. Knollys and a band of knights attacked and dispersed them with much slaughter. The insurrection in Norfolk and Suffolk was subdued by the Bishop of Norwich, and 1,500 of the rebels were executed

1385, Death of Wickliffe

1385, Richard II, who succeeded his grandfather Edward III in 1377, was deposed and succeeded in 1399 by his cousin Henry IV (son of John of Gaunt, Duke of Lancaster, the fourth son of Edward III), in prejudice to the right of Roger Mortimer (grandson of Lionel, Duke of Clarence, Edward's third son), who was declared presumptive heir to the throne

Sept. 30, 1399, Henry IV crowned

Oct. 11, 1399, Order of the Bath instituted by Henry IV

1402–05, Insurrection of the Percies and the Welsh

March 21, 1413, Henry V crowned

Oct. 25, 1415, France invaded by Henry V who gains the battle of Agincourt

1420, Treaty of Troyes; the French crown gained

1429–31, Appearance of the maid of Orleans; the conquests in France lost, except Calais

Dec., 1430, Henry VI crowned at Paris

1449, Roger's grandson, Richard, Duke of York, first openly claimed the crown

June, 1450, Cade's insurrection. In May, 1450, Jack Cade, an Irishman, who assumed the name of Mortimer, laid before the royal council the complaint of the commons of Kent. He headed about 20,000 Kentish men, who armed "to punish evil ministers, and procure a redress of grievances." He defeated and slew Sir Humphry Stafford, at Sevenoaks, June 27, entered London in triumph, and beheaded the Lord Treasurer, Lord Saye, and several other persons of consequence, July 3. When the insurgents lost ground, a general pardon was proclaimed, and Cade, deserted by his followers, fled. A reward having been offered for his apprehension, he was discovered, and refusing to surrender, was slain by Alexander Iden, Sheriff of Kent, July 11

1455, Attempts at compromise failed, and the war began between the Lancastrians (who chose the red rose as their emblem) and the Yorkists (who chose the white rose), 1455–1485. It is stated that in the Wars of the Roses there perished 12 princes of the blood, 200 nobles, and 100,000 gentry and common people. The union of the roses was effected in the marriage of Henry VII with the Princess Elizabeth, daughter of Edward IV, 1486

May 23, The Lancastrians were defeated at St. Albans; the Protector Somerset was slain; a truce was made, and Richard was declared successor to Henry VI

Sept. 23, 1459, The war was renewed, and the Yorkists defeated the Lancastrians at Bloreheath

The Yorkists eventually dispersed, and the Duke was attainted

Dec. 31, 1460, He defeated his opponents at Northampton, took Henry prisoner, and was declared heir to the crown, but fell into an ambuscade near Wakefield, and was put to death

March 4, 1461, His son (Edward) continued the struggle; was installed as King Edward IV

March 29, Defeated the Lancastrians at Towton

Sept., 1470, Was deposed by Warwick, who restored Henry VI

May 4, 1471, Edward defeated the Lancastrians at Barnet, April 14, and finally at Tewkesbury

1471, Printing introduced by Caxton

April 9, 1483, Edward V accession

——, Murdered in the Tower (soon after)

June 25, Richard III deposes Edward V

1484, Valuable statutes enacted

Aug. 22, 1485, Henry VII accession; Richard defeated and slain at Bosworth Field

——, Yeomen of the guard, the first appearance of a standing army in England, instituted

1486, Henry marries Elizabeth, daughter of Edward IV

1486-87, Insurrection of Lambert Simnel quelled

1487, Court of Star-Chamber instituted

1492-98, Insurrection of Perkin Warbeck quelled

About 1502, Gardening introduced into England, principally from the Netherlands

April 2, 1502, Death of Prince Arthur

April 22, 1509, Henry VIII accession

1514, Rise of Wolsey

June 7-24, 1520, Henry VIII's interview with Francis I at Ardres ("*Field of the Cloth of Gold*")

About 1520, First map of England drawn by G. Lilly

1521, Henry VIII becomes "Defender of the Faith"

1530, Fall of Wolsey; he dies Nov. 29

Nov. 14, 1532 or January, 1533, Henry VIII marries Anne Boleyn privately; divorced from Catherine, May 23, 1533

1534, Henry VIII styled "Head of the Church"

——, The Pope's authority in England is abolished

July 6, 1535, Sir Thomas More beheaded

May 19, 1536, Queen Anne Boleyn beheaded

June 8, Articles of Religion. After much disputing, the English clergy in convocation published "Articles decreed by the king's highness" Henry VIII, who published in 1539 the "Statute of Six Articles," decreeing the acknowledgment of transubstantiation, communion in one kind, vows of chastity, private masses, celibacy of the clergy, and auricular confession. Offenders were punishable as heretics. In 1551 forty-two were prepared, and published in 1553. These were modified by the convocation, and reduced to thirty-nine in Jan., 1563; and they received the royal authority and authority of Parliament in 1571

Oct. 24, 1537, Queen Jane Seymour dies

1538, Monasteries suppressed

1539, Statute of Six Articles passed

——, Abbots of Glastonbury Reading, &c., executed

——, The first authorized edition of the Bible (Cranmer's) printed

1540, Cromwell, Lord Essex, beheaded

July 9, Anne of Cleves divorced

1542, Queen Catherine Howard beheaded

1543, The title of "King of Ireland" confirmed to the English sovereigns

July 12, Henry marries Catherine Parr

1547, Edward VI accession, Jan. 28; promotes the Reformation (Somerset, Protector)

1548, Book of Common Prayer authorized

Jan. 15, 1549, Uniformity Acts. That of 2 & 3 Edward VI ordained that the order of divine worship, drawn up by Cranmer and others, "with the aid of the Holy Ghost," should be the only one used after May 20. The penalties for refusing to use it were fine and imprisonment. This act was confirmed in 1552; repealed by Mary, 1554; and reënacted by

Elizabeth in 1559. The act of Uniformity, 14 Charles II, c. 4, was passed in 1662. It enjoined uniformity in matters of religion, and obliged all clergy to subscribe to the thirty-nine articles, and use the same form of worship, and same book of common prayer. Its enforcement on Aug. 24, 1662, termed Black Bartholomew's day, caused, it is said, upwards of 2,000 ministers to quit the church of England. This day was commemorated by dissenters in 1862. The Act of Uniformity Amendment act, whereby shortened services were authorized, and other changes made, was passed July 18, 1872. The Uniformity of Process act, which made many law changes, was passed May 23, 1832

1549, Somerset deprived of power; beheaded, 1552

1553, Mary, accession, July 6; restores popery

1554, Execution of Lady Jane Grey and her friends

——, Mary marries Philip of Spain; persecutes the Protestants

1555 and 1556, Ridley, Latimer, and Cranmer burnt

Jan. 7, 1558, Calais retaken by the French

Nov. 17, Elizabeth, accession; the church of England reëstablished

Dec. 13, 1577-Nov. 15, 1580, Circumnavigation of the globe by Sir Francis Drake

1568, Mary, Queen of Scots, lands in England; executed, Feb. 8, 1587

July, 1588, The Spanish Armada repulsed

Feb. 25, 1601, Devereux, Earl of Essex, beheaded

March 24, 1603, James I accession; union of the two crowns

Oct. 24, 1604, Styled "King of Great Britain"

Nov., 1605, The Gunpowder Plot, for springing a mine under the houses of Parliament, and destroying the King, Lords, and Commons there assembled, was discovered on Nov. 4, 1605. It was projected by Robert Catesby early in 1604, and several Roman Catholics of rank were in the plot. Guy Faux was detected in the vaults under the House of Lords, hired for the purpose, preparing the train for being fired on the next day. Catesby and Percy (of the family of Northumberland) were killed at Holbeach house, whither they had fled, Nov. 8; and Guy Faux, Sir Everard Digby, Rookwood, Winter, and others, were executed, Jan. 30, 31, 1606. Henry Garnet, a Jesuit, suffered as an accomplice, May 3 following. An anonymous letter sent to Lord Monteagle led to the discovery. It contained the following words, "Though there be no appearance of any stir, yet I say they shall receive a terrible blow this parliament, and yet they shall not see who hurts them." The vault called Guy Faux cellar, in which the conspirators lodged the barrels of gunpowder, remained till 1825, when it was converted into offices. The vaults are searched with much ceremony at the opening of each session of Parliament

1611, The present translation of the Bible completed

May, Baronets first created

Sept. 15, 1613, The Overbury murder

April 23, 1616, Shakespeare dies

May 24, 1618, Book of Sports published

Oct. 29, Raleigh beheaded

March 27, 1625, Charles I accession

April 9, 1626, Death of Lord Bacon

Aug. 23, 1628, Duke of Buckingham assassinated

1637, Hampden's trial respecting "ship money"

1641, Contest between the King and Parliament; impeachment and execution of Lord Strafford

Jan. 4, Attempted "arrest of the five members" (John Hampden, John Pym, Sir Arthur Hasilrigge, Denzil Holles, and Wm. Strode)

Feb. 15, 1641, Triennial Parliaments. An act was passed providing for the meeting of a Parliament at least once in three years. This law was broken by the Long Parliament, and was repealed in 1664. Another triennial bill, passed in 1694, was repealed by the Septennial act, 1716

Oct. 23, 1642, Civil war begins

Jan. 10, 1645, Archbishop Laud beheaded

June 14, Charles defeated at Naseby

Sept. 21, 1646, He flees to the Scotch, May 5; is given up

Jan. 30, 1649, Execution of Charles I

Sept. 3, 1651, Cromwell's victory at Worcester

Dec. 16, 1653, Oliver Cromwell, Protector of the Commonwealth

1652–57, Naval victories of Blake

Sept. 3, 1658, Richard Cromwell, Protector

May 25, 1659, Richard resigns

May 29, 1660, Charles II; monarchy reëstablished principally by General Monk

Sept. 25, Samuel Pepys records his first "cup of tea." A duty of 8d. was charged upon every gallon of tea made for sale (12 Ch. II, c. 13). Tea was brought to Europe by the Dutch, 1610. It is mentioned as having been used in England on very rare occasions prior to 1657, and sold for 6l. and even 10l. the pound. Price of inferior kinds, 1801, 4s. 2½d. the pound; in 1871, 1s. 10d.; in 1910, 1s.

1662, Act of uniformity passed; church of England restored

1665, The great plague

Oct., Five Mile Act, 17 Chas. II, c. 2, forbade Nonconformist preachers who refused to take the non-resistance oath, to come within five miles of any corporation where they had preached since the act of oblivion (unless they were traveling), under the penalty of 40l. They were relieved by Will. III in 1689

Sept., 1666, The great fire of London

Nov., 1667, Disgrace of Lord Clarendon

May, 1670, Secret treaty with France signed at Dover

Nov. 8, 1674, Death of John Milton

Aug. 12, 1678, Oates's "popish plot" creates a panic

Oct. 17, Sir Edmundbury Godfrey found murdered

1678–79, Many Roman Catholics executed

May 27, 1679, The Habeas Corpus act, for protecting English subjects against false arrest and imprisonment passed

1681, Violent reaction, many Protestants executed; London humbled

1683, Rye-House Plot, a plot (some think pretended) to secure the succession of the Duke of Monmouth to the throne in preference to the Duke of York (afterwards James II), a Roman Catholic. Some of the conspirators are said to have projected the assassination of the King, Charles II, and his brother. This design is said to have been frustrated by the King's house at Newmarket accidentally taking fire, which hastened the royal party away eight days before the plot was to take effect, March 22. The plot was discovered June 12, following. Lord William Russell on July 21, and Algernon Sidney on Dec. 7 following, suffered death for being concerned in this conspiracy. Both were illegally convicted. The name was derived from the conspirators'

place of meeting, the Rye-house at Broxbourne, Hertfordshire

Feb. 6, 1685, James II accession

Duke of Monmouth's rebellion defeated at Sedgemoor, July 6; he is beheaded, July 15

1688

June 25, Partition Act, relative to the division of property sold by direction of the court of chancery, passed

June 29, Acquittal of the seven bishops

Dec. 11, Abdication of James II

1689 to 1698

1689, Act of Settlement, for securing the succession to the British throne, to the exclusion of Roman Catholics, was passed. This name is also given to the statute by which the crown, after the death of William III and Queen Anne, without issue, was limited to Sophia, Electress of Hanover, grand-daughter of James I, and her heirs being Protestants, 1702. The Irish act of settlement, passed in 1662, was repealed in 1689

Feb. 13, William III and Mary proclaimed by the convention Parliament

April 12, Mutiny Act (1 & 2 Will. and Mary, c. 5), for the discipline, regulation, and payment of the army, &c., was passed, and has since been reënacted annually

1693, National debt begins

July 27, 1694, Bank of England incorporated

Dec. 28, Death of the Queen Regnant, Mary

1697, Peace of Ryswick

Aug. 19, 1698, Partition Treaties. The first treaty between England and Holland for regulating the Spanish succession (declaring the elector of Bavaria next heir, and ceding provinces to France) was signed

1701

March 8, 1701, Accession of Anne, second daughter of James II, wife of Prince George of Denmark

June 12, Act of Settlement regulating succession to the throne

Sept. 16, Death of James II of England and VII of Scotland in exile at St. Germain

May 4, 1702, War declared on France by the Grand Alliance including England. *See* Spanish Succession

July 24, 1704, Gibraltar taken by Sir George Rooke

Aug. 2, Victory of the Duke of Marlborough and Prince Eugene at Blenheim, a village in Bavaria on the left bank of the Danube, defeating the French and Bavarians under Marshal Tallard and the Elector of Bavaria

May 1, 1707, Union of England and Scotland under the name of Great Britain became effective. *See* Great Britain

ESTONIA

The Estonian Republic (Eesti Vabariik) is situated on the eastern shore of the Baltic Sea, south of the Gulf of Finland between 57° 27′ and 59° 42′ N. lat. and 21° 46′ and 28° 21′ long. (Greenwich), and includes the Baltic Islands Saaremaa (Oesel), Hiiumaa (Dagö), and Muhumaa (Moon). The eastern border towards Russia is formed by Lake Peipsi and the southern by the

Republic of Latvia. Total area about 18,353 square miles, population (Jan. 1, 1930) 1,114,861. Reval is the capital.

In 1721, the country, which has belonged to Sweden since the early part of the seventeenth century, was handed over by Sweden to Russia, and remained under the rule of the latter until 1917. In 1917, after the outbreak of the Russian Revolution, Estonia regained her independence, which was declared on February 24, 1918. By the Treaty of Tartu, of February 2, 1920, Soviet Russia recognized the independence of Estonia. On January 26, 1921, the Supreme Council accorded the Republic *de jure* recognition.

O. Strandman, State Head (*Riigivanem*).

1917

April 12 (March 30, O.S.), Russian Provisional Government united northern Livonia and Estonia and granted the enlarged province a Diet

July 7–8, Election for first national Diet

July 14, Diet met at Reval (Tallinn)

Oct. 12, Germans occupied Oesel Island. *See* World War

Nov. 15 (28), The Diet proclaimed independence of Russia and declared itself sovereign until a Constituent Assembly convened

Dec. 12, Baltic-German nobility invoked aid of German troops and declared separation from Russia

Dec. 17, Armistice granted Germans police power in the Baltic Provinces of Russia and forces commanded by General von der Goltz occupied the country

1918

Jan. 10 (24), Decree of Committee of Elders proclaimed Estonia an independent Republic

Jan. 13, Government made declaration of independence

Jan. 28, Baron Dellingshausen representing the nobility asked the Germans to occupy Estonia

Feb. 24, Formal declaration of independence by the Diet and a Provisional Government formed by Päts (Paez), Wilms, Poska, Larko, Kukk, and others, and the Republic proclaimed on eve of German occupation

——, Germans occupied Dorpat

Feb. 25, Germans occupied Reval

——, Provisional Government recognized by Great Britain

April 10, Estonian peasants summoned to Riga Assembly refused union with Germany as arranged by Baron Dellingshausen

April 13, Baron Dellingshausen asked for annexation of Estonia to Germany

April 21, Baron Dellingshausen received consent of the Emperor of Germany for union of Estonia with Prussia

May 3, *De facto* recognition of Diet (National Council) by Great Britain

May 13, *De facto* recognition by France

May 29, *De facto* recognition by Italy

July 1, Diet proclaimed independence and rejected aid of Germany

Aug. 27, By supplementary Agreement to Treaty of Brest-Litovsk Russia renounced sovereignty over Estonia

Nov. 11, German authorities ceded powers to the Provisional Government; K. Päts, Prime Minister and O. Strandmann, Minister of Foreign Affairs succeeding J. Poska

Nov. 12, Defense League created

Nov. 16, New national Government formed, J. Poska became Prime Minister and O. Strandmann continued as Minister of Foreign Affairs

Nov. 18, Treaty with Germany signed confirmed surrender of authority

——, Courts of law established

Nov. 19, Germans signed evacuation Agreement

Nov. 22, Soviet forces crossed the frontier near Narva

Nov. 25, Soviet forces occupied Pskov

Nov. 27, Compulsory mobilization

——, Law gave the Government control over certain lands (temporary legislation)

Nov. 28, Soviet forces took Narva

Dec. 12, British fleet commanded by Admiral Sinclair arrived at Reval bringing arms and ammunition to Estonians

Dec. 16, Soviet forces took Rakvere

Dec. 17, Decree authorized the Government to take possession of "badly managed" estates

Dec. 20, Order provided that citizens who had distinguished themselves at front should be given land expropriated by the State formerly belonging to Russian crown

Dec. 22, Soviet forces occupied Tartu

Dec. 26, British fleet captured 2 Russian destroyers and turned them over to Estonians

——, Germans evacuated Dorpat

1919

Jan. 9, Estonians took Tapa

Jan. 11, Estonians took Rakvere

Jan. 14, Estonians took Tartu (Dorpat)

Jan. 18, Estonians took Narva

Feb. 24, Announcement of General Laidoner, Commander-in-Chief that foreign troops had left Estonian territory

——, Law established Bank of Estonia

Feb. 28, Decree promised division of the large estates among soldiers and agricultural workers without land

March 15, Japan recognized the independence of Estonia

March 25, Russian tariff adopted with modifications; duties on machines, ships, raw wool, cotton and woolen goods raised three-fold, linen and clothes five-fold to meet the difference between the Russian rouble and the Estonian mark

April 1, Labor Contract Act gave Minister of Labor right to fix wages and confirm agreements between employers and employees

April 5–7, Election held for Constituent Assembly on basis of universal suffrage

April 23, Constituent Assembly met, August Rei elected president of Assembly

May 3, Amnesty law the first passed by Constituent Assembly

May 9, O. Strandmann appointed Prime Minister and J. Poska, Minister of Foreign Affairs

May 19, Constituent Assembly issued declaration of independence

May 22, Estonians reported capture of Yamburg and Koporje south of Petrograd

May 25, Estonians captured Pskov and Peterhof from the Bolsheviki

May 31, Bolsheviki withdrew from the Gulf of Riga

June 4, Provisional organic law of the Republic enacted

June 6, Baltic Landeswehr troops commanded by a German, Major Fletcher, and including a large number of Germans, advanced on and captured Venden, Latvia

June 11, Armistice declared but not kept

June 13, Fighting near Rup

June 15, Constitution adopted by Constituent Assembly

July 3, Armistice signed by Estonians and Latvians with Landeswehr

July 20, Agreement with Latvia for mutual help signed

Aug. 15, $50,000,000 loaned to the Government by the United States

Aug. 31, Peace proposals of Russia to Estonia accepted

Sept. 17, Peace negotiations with Russia begun at Pskov; no result reached

Oct. 10, Agrarian law enacted provided that all estates over 330 hectares (825 acres) should be expropriated by the Government and allotted in small holdings to soldiers and landless workers; compensation to be arranged later

Oct. 21, Constituent Assembly established a Supreme Court

Nov. 5, Customs tariff lowered

Nov. 18, J. Tonisson appointed Prime Minister, A. Berk, Minister of Foreign Affairs

Dec. 1, Dorpat University founded in 1632 reopened

Dec. 5, Peace negotiations with Russia opened at Dorpat

Dec. 31, Armistice signed with Russia

1920

Jan. 2, Seven days armistice agreement with Russians

Jan. 14, Baltic Conference at Helsingfors. *See* Finland

Feb. 2, Peace Treaty with Russia signed at Dorpat by which Russia recognized the independence of Estonia and settled boundaries; Russia agreed to pay Estonia 15,000,000 gold roubles

Feb. 19, Italy gave *de jure* recognition to Estonia

March 9, Death of Jaan Poska, Cabinet Minister

March 22, Arbitration Convention with Latvia signed and provision made for appointment of a joint commission to define frontiers

April 12, Law established a progressive income tax

April 27, Law established State monopoly of production and sale of alcohol

May 7, Law as to elementary schools published; attendance compulsory from 7 to 16

June 7, Finland gave *de jure* recognition of Estonia

June 15, Constitution adopted

July 2, Boundary with Latvia settled

July 20, Commercial Agreement with Great Britain concluded

July 30, J. Tonisson became Prime Minister, A. Burk, Minister of Foreign Affairs

Oct. 26, Antonius Piip formed a Labor Cabinet, O. Strandmann, Minister of Foreign Affairs

Nov. 28, Konstantine Päts elected head of State by the Diet

Dec. 10, Decree raised customs tariff from 30- to 120-fold because of fall of the mark

Dec. 17, Admission to the League of Nations refused because of attitude of the French and British delegates

Dec. 21, Constituent Assembly dissolved

1921

Jan. 4, The State Assembly met replacing the Constituent Assembly: Labor, 22 seats; Social Democrats including Communists, 34; Peasants Party, Christian Party, and others, 44

June 25, Päts formed new Cabinet

Jan. 26, *De jure* recognition to Estonia given by Supreme Council

May 1, Customs tariff revised, duties on articles of consumption lowered and luxuries raised 100%

July 12, Political and military Treaty with Latvia signed

——, Consular Agreement with Lithuania signed

——, Treaty of commerce and navigation with Yugoslavia signed

July 21–22, Baltic Conference at Reval of representatives of Estonia, Latvia, and Lithuania

July 28, Conference of Ministers of Foreign Affairs of border States at Helsingfors

Sept. 22, Estonia admitted to membership in League of Nations

Oct. 20, Åland Islands Convention signed

Oct. 29, Commercial Treaty with Finland signed

Nov. 1, Eight-hour day established for agricultural laborers and regulations as to work and wages

Nov. 25, Commercial Agreement with Ukrainia

Dec. 2, Emergency Housing Act for settlement of rents and sale of houses during shortage enacted

1922

Jan. 7, Commercial Treaty with France signed

Jan. 29, Treaty with Finland provided for reciprocal customs preference

March 13–17, Conference of representatives of border States at Warsaw

March 17, Political Agreement signed with Poland, Latvia, and Finland to recognize Treaties, accept arbitration, and form a defensive league. Not ratified by Finland, so never became effective

March 29, Conference at Riga of representatives of Estonia, Latvia, Poland, and Russia

May 9, Agreement with Russia concluded regarding rafting of timber

June 22, Special land law appointed regions for expropriation, Petersburg, Pleskau

June 27, Law established State flag

July 27, *De jure* recognition of Estonia by the United States

Oct. 6, Normal School Act

Oct. 10, Citizenship law enacted

Oct. 19, Commercial Agreement with Hungary

Oct. 27, Marriage law enacted

Nov. 25, Cabinet formed by I. Kukk

Dec. 2, Moscow Conference of representatives of border States on disarmament

Dec. 7, Secondary School Act

1923

Feb. 17–19, Plebiscite held resulted in favor of Bill for religious instruction in the public primary schools at the expense of the Government and Parliament which had rejected the Bill dissolved

March 7, Customs law regulated exports and imports

May 5, Election gave Agrarians a majority but increased the parties of the Right and extreme Left

June 13, M. Tonisson, president of the new Parliament, invited K. Päts to form a Cabinet

June 27, Provisional Commercial Agreement with Germany signed and as to reparations for war damage

July 7, Provisional Commercial Agreement with Sweden

Aug. 29, Coalition Cabinet formed by K. Päts, Akel, Foreign Affairs

Sept. 7, Provisional Agreement as to commerce and navigation with Denmark

Sept. 17, Declaration as to protection of minorities made

Nov. 1, Treaty of defensive alliance, and economic relations, and customs union with Latvia; frontier claims settled

Nov. 2, Defensive alliance with Lithuania signed

Nov. 8, Extradition Treaty with the United States signed

Dec. 19, New tariff duties practically unchanged but converted duties into stable value on basis of gold franc

1924

Jan. 11, Convention of consular rights with Poland signed

Feb. 16–18, Warsaw Conference. *See* Poland

March 11, Cabinet resigned

March 26, M. Akel became Prime Minister and Strandmann, Minister of Foreign Affairs

May 14, M. Strandmann became Minister of Finance and C. R. Pusta, Foreign Affairs

May 20, Labor law enacted provided regulations for protection of women and minors; children under 14 not allowed to work

June 3, Decree of Minister of Finance increased imports on wheat, coal, and tobacco up to 75%

June 14, Law passed deprived the Government of power of fixing tariff, to be changed by legislative body only

June 20, Law passed fixed Swedish gold crown (krone) equivalent to 100 Estonian marks as basis of standard gold currency to be introduced

July 22, Treaty of commerce with the Netherlands signed

Oct. 7, Pensions for municipal and government officers provided for

Nov. 27, Trial of 149 Communists ended; and sentences provided for various terms of imprisonment

Dec. 1, Unsuccessful Communist revolt against the Government; all Communist organizations closed

——, Treaty of friendship and commerce with Turkey signed

Dec. 11, Civil service law enacted

Dec. 16, J. Jaakson (Peoples' Party), appointed Prime Minister and C. R. Pusta, Minister of Foreign Affairs

1925

Jan. 8, State of siege enforced after Communist revolt in December ended

Jan. 17, Treaty of arbitration and conciliation signed with Finland, Latvia, and Poland established a permanent commission of 5, which may be increased to 7 as each contracting State may appoint an *ad hoc* member in case of dispute

Feb. 25, Law passed to grant racial minorities (Germans, Swedes, and Russians) right to form self-governing bodies organized for cultural and charitable purposes

May 9–12, Official visit of the President to Latvia

May 29, Conciliation Agreement with Sweden signed

June 16, Agrarian law provided for distribution of land by sale or on hereditary lease

June 18, University Statute

June 19, Poor Relief law enacted gave all persons in abject poverty right to relief

July 23, Heidemann, Communist, sentenced to death for conspiracy against Government

July 24, War debt to Great Britain funded at £917,000

Aug. 10, Arbitration Treaty with Germany signed

Aug. 29, Provisional Commercial Agreement with Norway signed

Sept. 14, Agreement for suppression of passport visas with Finland

Oct. 14, Commercial Agreement with Switzerland signed

Oct. 28, Debt-funding Agreement with the United States signed funding debt at $13,830,000

Nov. 1, Council for autonomy of German minorities in Estonia established, Harry Koch, President

Nov. 26, Law established metric system of weights and measures to become compulsory on Jan. 1, 1929

Dec. 1, Communist uprising at Reval suppressed, 100 persons killed

Dec. 10, Trade School Act

Dec. 15, Jaan Teemant (Peasants' Union Party) formed Cabinet, A. Piip, Minister of Foreign Affairs

——, Vocational School Act

Dec. 18, Agrarian law provided for grants of land as gift reward of services

Dec. 23, Treaty of friendship, commerce, and consular rights with the United States

1926

Jan. 18, Treaty of commerce and navigation with Great Britain signed

Feb. 26, Law provided for compulsory sale of lands of institutions and land rented in private ownership

March 5, Law passed provided compensation for lands expropriated by the State under law of Oct., 1919, except to those owners hostile to independence or who had given aid to enemy in war of liberation

March 26, Military service law provided for compulsory service for men between ages of 17 and 55

——, Land law provided for cultivation of abandoned lands

May 15–17, Elections held gave Agrarians, 25; Socialists, 24; Settlers, 14; Reformist Labor, 13; Populists, 8; Workers' Party, 6; Christian Party, 5; Minority Nationals, 5

July 23, Jaan Teemant formed new Cabinet, Akel, Minister of Foreign Affairs

Sept. 28, Treaty of commerce and navigation with Belgium

Dec. 10, Protocol signed by which the Council of the League of Nations guaranteed an international loan of £1,350,000 to facilitate creation of a national bank and place currency on gold basis

——, Law regulated industrial schools

Dec. 15, Law regulated commercial schools

Dec. 18, Conciliation Convention with Denmark signed

Dec. 21, Law provided for compulsory sale of rented lands in market towns

1927

Jan. 4, Treaty of commerce with Greece

Jan. 16, Customs Convention with Latvia concluded

Jan. 29, Arbitration Treaty with Denmark signed

Feb. 8, Consular Convention with Belgium signed

Feb. 19, Treaty of commerce and navigation with Poland

March 4, Cabinet reconstructed

March 17, Mining law enacted

April 29, A series of laws passed to come into operation Jan. 1, 1928, providing for the creation of a new currency unit, unification of the currency, termination of the privilege of note issue by the State, and reorganization of the bank of issue, the monetary unit to be the kroon, same as the Swedish gold krona

May 3, Law established statutes of Estonian Bank and the new monetary unit the kroon

May 9, Conciliation Treaty with Denmark signed

May 10, Law regarding sale of alcohol and alcoholic drinks gave the Government the right to prohibit

May 17, Agreement with Finland for suppression of passport visas

June 15, Council of the League of Nations declined to act on petition of expropriated German landlords who were not satisfied with compensation paid for lands

June 20, Commercial Treaty with Czechoslovakia signed

Aug. 4, Communist organizer killed resisting arrest by police and one policeman killed by mob

Aug. 8, Agreement with Russia signed providing method for settlement of frontier disputes

Nov. 11, A. Hellat became Minister of Foreign Affairs

Dec. 6, Law on attribution of lands to towns

Dec. 9, J. Tonisson became Prime Minister, H. Rebane, Minister of Foreign Affairs

1928

Jan. 1, Banking and currency reforms came into effect and new monetary unit the kroon

——, State Savings Bank established

Feb. 1, Commercial Treaty with Yugoslavia signed

Feb. 10, Law provided for granting of land for industrial enterprises

Feb. 11, Provisional Commercial Agreement with Bulgaria concluded

Feb. 12, Treaty of commerce and navigation with Turkey

March 25, Provisional Commercial Agreement with Latvia

July 1, Provisional Commercial Agreement with Italy

Dec. 5, New Cabinet formed by M. Rej, Socialist

Dec. 7, Provisional Commercial Agreement with Germany

Dec. 11, Treaty of commerce with Austria concluded

1929

Jan. 1, Metric system of weights and measures came into force

April 29, Treaty of commerce and navigation with Hungary replaced that of 1922

May 11–13, The elections for the Estonian State Assembly were held on May 11–13, 1929, and resulted in the return of the following parties:— Agrarians, 24; Socialists, 25; Settlers, 14; Radical Party (Tööerakond), 10; Populists, 9; Workers' Party, 6; Christian Party, 4; Minority Nationals, 5; Houseowners, 3

May 17, Commercial Treaty with Russia signed

July 1, Agreement with Finland provided for abolition of passports

July 9, Treaty of arbitration and conciliation with Czechoslovakia

July 9, New Conservative Cabinet formed by Otto Strandmann, Jaan Lattik, Minister of Foreign Affairs

Aug. 22, Commercial Agreement with Portugal signed

Aug. 27, Arbitration and Conciliation Treaties with the United States

Sept. 15, Customs duties raised, the increase on textile and leather goods amounting to from 100 to 150%

1930

March 14, Commercial Treaty with Finland signed

April 3, General Unt fatally shot by Communist assassin. Suceeded by General Jonson

April 5, Workers' Party (Communist) outlawed

April 12, Resignation of M. Kalbus on account of ill health. Succeeded by A. Andekopp, Minister of Interior and Justice since 1926

July 3, Military emergency law passed by vote of 45 to 29

FINLAND

Finland, Republic of northern Europe, lying between the Gulf of Finland and the Gulf of Bothnia, bounded on the north by Norwegian Lapland, on the east by Russia, on the south by the Gulf of Finland, and on the west by the Gulf of Bothnia and Sweden. On the southwest are the Åland Islands assigned to Finland by decision of League of Nations, June 24, 1921. The total area is 132,589 square miles excluding water area which amounts to an additional 18,397 square miles, total population according to Census of 1920, 3,634,807, estimated population, 1929, 3,634,047. The capital is Helsingfors.

Finland was conquered by the Swedes about the middle of the twelfth century who introduced Christianity. It was several times taken by the Russians and restored but finally ceded to Russia as an autonomous grand duchy in 1809 with the Åland Islands by the Treaty of Fredrikshavn. Finland declared independence of Russia Dec. 6, 1917.

Doctor Lauri Relander, President.

1891

Jan., Discontent of the Chambers and people at expected changes by the Russian Government

About March 18, Rescript of the Czar to the Governor General, assuring the people of the maintenance of their ancient rights and privileges

July, The Czar visits Finland, coolly received

Oct. 1, A new stringent press law enforced

Dec., Famine in N. W. Finland; much suffering

1897

Jan. 13, Count Heyden resigns

Jan. 25, Triennial Diet opened at Helsingfors, financial measures adopted, imperial speech read by Governor General Gontscharoff

1898

March 12, Zacharias Topelius, author and poet, born Jan. 14, 1818; died

Oct., Agitation against changes in the Constitution

Oct. 12, General Bobrikoff, Governor General, arrives

1899

Jan. 24, Diet opened with a speech from the throne

Feb. 3, Russification of Finland, revision of laws, discussion in Parliament restricted by imperial rescript issued

March, Political crisis continues

March 16–18, Deputation of over 500 Finlanders petitioning for their constitutional rights, not received by the Czar at St. Petersburg

May, Army reform to be introduced during 10 years

May, 1899–Jan. et seq., Mr. Eugene Wolff, 13 years British Vice-Consul at Viborg, resigns, owing to complaints from the Russian Government regarding his part in the political agitation, early Sept. (banished, April, 1903); similar resignations in other parts; officials from St. Petersburg appointed, Oct.; press restrictions

June 1, Diet closed by imperial edict

June, Failure of crops and floods reported

July 1, An international deputation petitioning the Czar to spare the liberties of Finland (800 eminent signatories) not received; welcomed at Helsingfors, July 2

July 2, An imperial (autocratic) rescript issued

Early Sept., M. von Plehwe, a Russian, appointed Secretary of State

1900

Jan. 27, Triennial Diet opened at Helsingfors

Feb. 14, Imperial rescript, to enforce the measures taken to solidify the Empire and Finland, issued

April, Protest against the new military law, 1899, and infringement of constitutional rights, published in England

June 26, Russian ordered to be the official language

1901

Aug. 27, Petition of the Diet regarding the present administration in Finland; rejected by the Czar, early Sept.

Sept. 30, Monster petition, 471,131 signatures, against the new army law of July 12, and other edicts issued

1902

April 18, Disturbance during a levy of recruits at Helsingfors; repressed by Cossacks

April, Emigration largely increasing

End Sept., The Senate placed under control of the Governor General, and other restrictive laws published

Oct. 18, Statue of Elias Lönnrot, patriot, unveiled at Helsingfors

1903

Feb., Several judges and governors dismissed

March 18, Famine, great distress reported

April 2, General Bobrikoff's power absolute. New rules signed by the Czar

April 27, Count Mannerheim, Baron Born, and others banished

Aug., Process of expulsion continued, 43 eminent Finlanders expelled, emigration continues

Sept. 9, Extension of repressive measures, Constitution violated, Times

Oct. 22, Finnish Senate opened in the Russian language

Dec. 17, New order of the Czar granting to two governors complete control over the elections, issued

1904

Feb. 5, Anniversary of the birthday of the celebrated Finnish poet, John Ludvig Runeberg, observed as a national day throughout Finland with great patriotic fervor

June 6, Great demonstration of working men in the Djurgarden, Helsingfors, and in other industrial centers of Finland; resolutions passed demanding the rescinding of all illegal ordinances, and the withdrawal of the dictatorial power granted to the Governor General; the recall of the exiled Finlanders, and the convening of a diet

June 16, General Brobrikoff shot at and killed by Eugen Schauman, the son of an ex-senator

Dec. 9, Diet opened: Czar's speech indicates the abolition of the special measures enacted for the suppression of resistance on the part of the people, and the limitation of the objectionable laws as a result of remonstrances made by the Senate

1906

March 28, Resignation of M. Gerhard, Governor General, reported

May 10, Finnish Senate's scheme for the reform of representation. Its principal features are: universal, equal, and direct suffrage for men and women who have completed their 24th year; women, as well as men, to be eligible as representatives; a single chamber of 200 delegates, of whom 60 will form a grand committee, devised, together with other provisions, to prevent hasty legislation; the country will be divided into 16 constituencies, one of which, in the extreme north, returns 1 member, and the others, on the average, 13 members; members to be elected by a proportional election system for 3 years; sessions to be held annually

1907

May 25, Finnish Diet opened by the Governor General, who read the Czar's speech

1908

Feb., General Bekman, commanding the 22nd army corps in Finland, appointed to succeed M. Gerhard as Governor General

1911

Feb. 4–5, Fishing village established on the ice outside Bjorko carried out to sea by breaks in the ice with 250 persons

Aug. 24, The Czar approved Bill for submission to Duma adding part of Viborg Province to Province of St. Petersburg, first step in partition of Finland

Nov. 10, Bill for equalizing rights of Russians and Finns in Finland and for increasing annual military contribution of Finland up to £800,000 passed imperial Duma

1912

Jan. 20. (7), Law accorded full rights of citizenship to Russians in temporary residence in Finland

Jan. 23 (10), Law of imperial Duma affirmed the principle of an annual indemnity in place of military service

1913

Jan. 27, District Court of St. Petersburg sentenced 23 members of Viborg Court of Appeals to 16 months imprisonment and dismissal from office for opposition to enforcement of law of Jan. 20 (7) on ground that the law had not been passed by the Finnish Diet

1916

June 22, Ordinance gave women equal rights with men to positions as teachers and professors

Oct. 26, Ordinance reformed land law

1917

March 21, Russian Provisional Government declared Finland a free and independent State in a Russian federation and abrogated all laws and imperial edicts contrary to the Constitution of Finland

March 22, Amnesty for political and religious prisoners declared by the Russian Provisional Government

April 5, Diet elected in 1916 met composed of 80% Social Democrats

April 18, Strike of metal workers union for eight-hour day and increase in wages

July 18, "Law of July 18" by which the Diet declared itself the supreme authority in all domestic affairs, taxation, and customs

July 20, The Diet announced independence of Russia

Aug. 3, Decree of Provisional Government of Russia dissolved the Diet declaring the declaration of independence illegal

Oct. 2, Elections for Diet gave coalition of bourgeois parties 102 members to 92 Socialists

Oct. 7, Finland defined as an independent republic within limits of Russia

Nov. 1, Diet met

Nov. 15, Diet declared itself vested with supreme power under the Constitution of 1772

Nov. 27, Eight-hour-day law enacted

Nov. 28, A Senate (bourgeois) of 11 members elected

Dec. 6, Declaration of independence drawn up by Diet and Senate proclaimed

1918

Jan. 2, Bolshevik Government in Russia recognized the independence of Finland

Jan. 4, Sweden recognized the independence of Finland, and Russia officially declared the political autonomy of Finland

Jan. 6, France and Germany recognized the independence of Finland

Jan. 10, Norway and Denmark recognized the independence of Finland

Jan. 28, Civil war begun between Red revolutionists and Russians and the Government, the capital seized by Reds

Jan. 29, Protest of Senate to Russia and Powers who had recognized independence against sending of arms and troops into Finland

March 1, Red Government signed Treaty of amity with Russia

March 2, Germans occupied Åland Islands at request of Finland

March 3, Treaty of Brest-Litovsk provided that Russian forces should evacuate Finland

March 7, Peace Treaty with Germany signed

April 3, German troops landed at Hango to aid General Mannerheim and his White Guards against the Bolsheviks

April 6, Bolsheviks defeated near Karis

April 13, German force of General von der Goltz took Helsingfors

April 28–29, Decisive defeat of Reds by General Mannerheim near Viborg

April 30, Germans landed at Viborg

April 30–May 2, Bolsheviks defeated by Germans in battle of Lashti-Tavastehus

May 7, Civil war ended with defeat of the Red Guards by the White Guards and Germans

May 11, Peace Treaty with Turkey signed

May 25, Ministry resigned and Prime Minister Svinhufvud became temporary Dictator

May 29, Peace Treaty with Austria-Hungary signed

June 12, Proposal of Government to the Diet that a monarchy be established

June 27, Agreement with Sweden and Germany that fortifications on Åland Islands be demolished

Oct. 8, Diet in secret session elected Prince Frederick Karl of Hesse, King of Finland; announced Oct. 9

Oct. 13, The Government asked German troops to withdraw from Finnish territory

Nov. 13, Resignation of Dictator Svinhufvud without waiting for formal deposition

Dec. 11, General Baron Karl Gustav Emil Mannerheim elected head of State

Dec. 17, Last Germans left Finland

Dec. 31, Prince Frederick Karl definitely renounced the crown

1919

March 1, Election gave Social Democrats, 80; Agrarians, 42; Coalitionists, 28; Progressives, 26; Swedish, 22; Christian Labor, 2

April, Kaarlo Castren, Prime Minister, and Dr. E. R. W. Holsti, Foreign Affairs

May 6, Independence recognized by Great Britain

May 7, Independence recognized by the United States

June 1, Anti-alcoholic liquor law came into effect

June 6, War declared on Bolshevik Russia

June 17, Constitution of the Republic adopted

July 17, Constitution proclaimed

July 25, Professor Karl J. Stahlberg elected first President of the Republic by 143 votes against 50 for General Mannerheim

1920

Jan. 14, Conference at Helsingfors attended by representatives from Estonia, Latvia, Lithuania, Poland, and Finland

Jan. 30, Amnesty Bill signed by the President provided for release of about 3,000 prisoners and restoration of civil rights to about 40,000 persons

March 15, Erich again Prime Minister

May 7, Autonomy granted to Åland Islands

June 10 and 12, Exchange of Notes with Sweden on Åland Islands

June 14, Peace Conference with Russia opened

June 19, Great Britain called attention of the League of Nations to dispute between Finland and Sweden as to the Åland Islands

June 27–July 6, First Industrial Fair held in Helsingfors

Oct. 14, Peace and Boundary Treaty of Dorpat with Russia signed provided for the cession of the Petchenga region to Finland, about 3,860 square miles of Arctic territory including an outlet to an ice free port; the autonomy of East Karelia guaranteed and neutralization of certain islands in the Baltic

Dec. 16, Finland admitted to membership in the League of Nations

1921

Feb. 14, Finnish troops withdrew from Repola and Poraiarvi to be surrendered to Russia

April 9, Coalition Government of Professor Erich resigned and was succeeded by Professor Vennola as Prime Minister with a coalition of Progressive and Agrarian parties; Dr. R. Holsti remained Minister of Foreign Affairs

June 24, Decision of the Council of the League of Nations that the Åland Islands should remain under the sovereignty of Finland (dated June 25)

July 13, Commercial Agreement with France

July 28, Conference of the Cabinet Ministers of Estonia, Latvia, Poland, and Finland at Helsingfors

Oct. 20, Convention signed provided for the neutralization and non-fortification of Åland Islands with Sweden, Germany, Denmark, Great Britain, France, Italy, Latvia, Estonia, and Poland

Oct. 29, Commercial Treaty with Estonia

1922

March 13–17, Representatives attended meeting of border States at Warsaw

March 17, Political Agreement with Latvia, Poland, and Estonia signed

April 21, Preliminary Commercial Agreement with Germany signed

May 13, Resignation of Vennola Ministry

June 1, Convention with Russia signed for maintenance of order on the frontier

June 2, "Government of Officials" Cabinet formed by Professor A. K. Cajander

July 1, Election for Diet returned 53 Social Democrats, 45 Agrarians, and 27 Communists

Sept. 20, Convention with Russia signed as to fishing and sealing in the Gulf of Finland

Oct. 14, Agrarian law enacted limited size of private estates to about 300 hectares, all in excess to be divided into small holdings to be sold to persons without land

Oct. 20, Act established presidential election by body of 300 electors chosen by general suffrage

——, Convention with Russia signed as to fishing and sealing in the Arctic Ocean

Oct. 25, Convention with Russia signed as to fishing and sealing in Lake Ladoga and as to rafting timber and maritime regulations in boundary waters

Nov. 14, Kyosti Kallio formed Cabinet

Dec. 2, Representatives attended the Moscow Disarmament Conference

1923

Jan. 1, Agrarian law, new law on conscription, and law on religious liberty came into effect

March 2–10, Economic Conference of Baltic States at Helsingfors

April 17, National Federation of Labor voted against joining Moscow International

May 1, Debt-funding Agreement with the United States signed

June 5, Provisional Agreement with Russia signed as to navigation of the Neva River

July 23, Permanent Court of International Justice declared incompetence to deal with East Karelian case

July 25, East Karelia established as an autonomous Republic of Russia

Aug. 3, Commercial Treaty with Denmark signed

Aug. 4, Communist daily newspaper suppressed and 100 leading Communists including members of Parliament arrested

Nov. 1, Provisional Commercial Agreement with the Netherlands

Nov. 10, Treaty of commerce and navigation with Poland

Dec. 14, Treaty of commerce and navigation with Great Britain

Dec. 21, Treaty of commerce and navigation with Iceland

1924

Jan. 16, Kallio Cabinet resigned

Jan. 18, Dr. A. K. Cajander formed second "Cabinet of Officials"

Jan. 19, Diet dissolved

Feb. 12, Commercial Agreement with Belgium concluded

April 1, Elections for Diet gave Social Democrats 60 seats, a gain of 7; Agrarians, 44; Union Party, 23; Communists, 18, a loss of 9

April 29, Frontier Agreement with Norway signed

May 3, Cajander Ministry resigned

June 1, Professor Lauri Ingman formed an all bourgeois coalition Cabinet

June 7, Treaty of commerce with Japan signed

June 27, Arbitration Conventions signed with Sweden and Norway and Denmark

Aug. 23, Treaty of commerce and navigation with Latvia

Oct. 22, Treaty of commerce and navigation with Italy signed

Nov. 24, Ingman Cabinet reconstructed

Nov. 24–Dec. 4, Conference of representatives of the Baltic States and Germany and Poland at Helsingfors and Protocol signed for suppression of liquor smuggling

1925

Jan. 16–17, Conference and Agreement signed as to arbitration and conciliation, communication facilities, passports, &c., by Baltic States and Poland at Helsingfors

Feb. 16, Dr. Lauri K. Relander (People's Party) declared elected President by Electoral College

March 1, President Relander inaugurated

March 14, Treaty of arbitration and conciliation with Germany signed

March 18, Ingman Ministry, defeated on electoral reform, resigned

March 21, Act provided for conciliation in collective labor disputes

March 30, Professor Antti Tulenheimo formed Cabinet in which the Union Party and Agrarian Union represented; M. Idman, Foreign Affairs, Dr. H. M. J. Relander, Finance

May 2, Commercial Agreement with the United States concluded

May 21–24, Official visit of the President to Estonia

May 29, Treaty of commerce and navigation with Hungary signed

July 16, Commercial Convention with Spain

Aug. 19, Agreement for suppression of liquor smuggling signed by Balkan and Scandinavian States

Dec. 10, Tulenheimo Ministry resigned, defeated on program of naval construction

Dec. 31, Kyosti Kallio became Prime Minister (Agrarian); M. Setala, Minister of Foreign Affairs

1926

Jan. 1, Gold standard restored

Jan. 29, Convention for pacific settlement of disputes signed with Sweden

Jan. 30, Convention for pacific settlement of disputes signed with Denmark

Feb. 3, Convention for pacific settlement of disputes signed with Norway

June 2, and Oct. 19, Provisional Commercial Agreement with Turkey signed

June 22, Provisional Commercial Agreement with Greece signed

June 26, Provisional Commercial Agreement with Germany signed

Oct. 19, Provisional Commercial Agreement with Turkey signed

Nov. 23, Kallio Ministry defeated in debate on supply of army munitions

Nov. 24, Kallio Ministry resigned

Dec. 11, Social Democratic Cabinet formed by Vaino Tanner: Dr. Vaino Voionmaa, Minister for Foreign Affairs; Dr. A. Ryoma, Finance; Rieti Itkonen, Interior; Kaarlo Heinonen, Defense; Vaino Hakkila, Justice; Dr. Julius Ailio, Education; Mauno Pekkala, Agriculture; Vaino Vuolijoki, Communications; Vaino Hupli, Commerce and Industries; Dr. Johan Helo, Social Affairs; Miss Miina Sillanpaa, Assistant Minister of Social Affairs; M. Matti Paasivuori, without Portfolio

1927

March 4, Treaty of arbitration and conciliation with Belgium signed

April 2, Cornerstone of new Parliament building laid at Helsingfors

April 11, Resignation of Hr. Itkonen, Minister of the Interior, charged with spending money in excess of amount sanctioned on the fisheries protection ship

May 17, Act conferred amnesty on persons sentenced for participation in the revolt of 1918; 1,175 persons regained civil rights

June 17, Nationality law as to loss of Finnish citizenship

June 24, Commercial Agreement with Switzerland signed

July 1-2, General election: Swedish Party, 24; Finnish Coalition, 34; Progressives, 10; Agrarians, 52; Socialists, 60; Communists, 20

Aug. 8, Commercial Treaty with Austria signed

Sept. 1, Diet met to pass budget including increased army estimates

Sept. 21, Strike of dockers in protest against the Sacco-Vanzetti executions

Oct. 14, Provisional Commercial Agreement with Turkey

Nov. 16, Treaty of conciliation and judicial settlement with Switzerland

Dec. 9, Labor Government resigned, defeated on the question of import duties on rye

Dec. 14, Trade Agreement with Sweden signed

Dec. 16, J. E. Sunila formed first entirely Agrarian Cabinet: Hj. J. Procope, Minister for Foreign Affairs; Juho Nuikkanen, Finance; Antti Aura, Interior; Jalo Lahdensuo, Defence; Torsten H. Malinen, Justice; The Rev. Antti Kukkonen, Education; Karl S. Mattsson, Agriculture; Dr. Emil Hynninen, Communications; Pekka V. Heikkinen, Commerce and Industries; Kalle A. Lohi, Social Affairs; Dr. Kalle T. Jutila, without Portfolio

1928

Feb. 28, Diet passed amendment to Prohibition Act making it more stringent as to right of search by police and other provisions

May 31, Treaty of conciliation, arbitration, and judicial settlement with Spain signed

June 7, Treaty of friendship and arbitration with the United States

July 17-Sept. 25, Trial of 50 Communists and all but 3 found guilty

Aug. 21, Treaty of arbitration and conciliation with Italy

Sept. 24, Exchange of Notes with Russia respecting settlement of frontier disputes

Oct. 6, Provisional Commercial Agreement with Lithuania

Dec. 12, Treaty of arbitration and judicial settlement with Hungary

Dec. 13, Resignation of Agrarian Cabinet of Dr. Sunila failing to obtain a vote of confidence

Dec. 22, Oskari Mantere, National Progressive, formed Cabinet, J. Procope, non-partisan, Minister of Foreign Affairs, and M. J. Relander, non-partisan, Finance

1929

April 17, Stevedores' strike ended after 10 months, increase granted and improvement in working conditions

April 19, Diet dissolved by President Relander after its rejection of Government Bill providing for adequate salaries for all classes of State employees

June 7, Passports abolished in relations with Sweden, Norway, and Denmark

July 1, Passports abolished in relations with Estonia

July 1-2, Election for Diet; Social Democrats, 59; Agrarians, 60; Finnish Coalition, 28; Socialist Labor (Communist), 23; Swedish Party, 23; Finnish Progressive Party, 7

July 31, Act regulating the employment of young persons and children in industrial work

Aug. 3, Mantere Cabinet resigned

Aug. 16, Kyosti Kallio formed all Agrarian Cabinet: J. Hj. Procope, Foreign Affairs; T. H. Reinikka, Finance; A. V. Linturi, Interior; J. Niukkanen, Defense; Professor E. Kaila, Justice; A. Kukkonen, Education; K. J. Ellila, Agriculture; J. T. Lahdensuo, Communications; P. V. Heikkinen, Commerce and Industries; H. Paavilianen, Social Affairs

Nov. 16, General strike called by Communists a failure

1930

March 14, Commercial Treaty with Estonia signed

April 28, Treaty of arbitration and conciliation with France signed

June 27, Treaty of arbitration signed with Denmark, Norway, Sweden, and Iceland

July 1, Kallio Cabinet resigned as protest against anti-Communist agitation

July 5, P. E. Svinhufvud, Union Party, formed Cabinet

——, Demonstration of 12,000 citizens at Helsingfors against continued toleration of Communist activities

July 16, Dissolution of Diet

——, Protest of Russia against deportation of Finnish Communists over the frontier into Russia

Aug. 25, Meeting of farmers in Central Finland adopted resolution to dismiss all Communist laborers and urged that their example be followed

Oct. 1-2, Elections for Diet: Social Democrats, 66; Agrarians, 59; Finnish Coalition, 42; Swedish Party, 21; Finnish Progressives, 11; Small Farmers' Party, 1; no Communists allowed as candidates

Oct. 14, Abduction of Dr. Stahlberg, former President, and his wife by extreme Fascists, the plot organized by General Kurt Wallenius, Chief of the General Staff and Colonel Kuussari

Oct. 15, Dr. Stahlberg and Mrs. Stahlberg released in Joensu after 300-mile drive in automobile toward border of Russia

Oct. 22, General Wallenius arrested

Nov. 11, Anti-Communist Bills passed prohibiting Communists from becoming members of Parliament or being nominated as candidates

Dec. 17, Government proposal for new Prohibition Bill rejected by vote of 123 to 43

Dec. 18, Wallenius and Kuussari sentenced to 3 years penal servitude for kidnapping of Dr. Stahlberg and dismissed from army; six accomplices received shorter terms

Dec. 19, Government Bill legalizing 3% beer rejected by vote of 99 to 86

FIUME

Fiume, Adriatic port, now capital of the Italian Province of Carnaro, before the War in Hungary, and claimed by both Italy and Yugoslavia at the Paris Peace Conference.

1779

April 23, Decree of Maria Theresa declared Fiume to be a separate body of the Hungarian Kingdom and a town free from all union or connection with Croatia

1915

April 26, Secret Treaty of London between Italy and Great Britain, France, and Russia assigned port of Fiume to Croatia

1918

Oct. 23, Croatian troops seized Fiume

Oct. 30, National Council declared for adherence to Italy

——, Surrender to Croats by Hungarians

Nov. 5, Italian naval force occupied Fiume and Italian troops, Nov. 15.

Nov. 17, Yugoslavs protested Italian occupation

Nov. 19, Serbian troops commanded by Colonel Maximovic entered Fiume but were persuaded by Italians to withdraw

Nov. 26, American troops entered Fiume; French and British troops added, making occupation international

Dec. 1, Conference of nationalist statesmen in Rome declared for annexation of Fiume

1919

Feb. 7, Italian territorial claims at Peace Conference included Fiume on basis of "self-determination"

April 23, President Wilson published memorandum of April 14 on Italian claims addressing the Italian people opposing grant of Fiume to Italy as the port of outlet of the commerce of Hungary, Bohemia, Rumania, and Yugoslavia to the Mediterranean

May 10, Plebiscite adopted Italian penal code and declared loyalty to Italy

June 29, Conflict between Italian and French soldiers and again July 5

July 2–3, Croat Club at Fiume wrecked by Italians in riot

July 6, French naval base at Port Baros attacked by Italians

July 8, Decision of Supreme Council to send a commission of inquiry to examine into disturbances in Fiume

Sept. 12, *Coup d'état* of Gabriele d'Annunzio who with Italian volunteer troops seized Fiume for Italy

Sept. 15, Allied international force withdrew

Dec. 9, British-French-American proposal at Peace Conference that Fiume be made a free port in a free state under sovereignty of League of Nations

1920

Jan. 14, New proposals as to Fiume of Clemenceau and Lloyd George. *See* p. 562

March 31, Independence of Fiume proclaimed by d'Annunzio

April 19–26, San Remo Conference of Allied Premiers agreed to leave negotiations to Italy and Yugoslavia

Sept. 20, D'Annunzio appointed Cabinet taking himself the office of "Chief Rector" and Minister of Foreign Affairs

Nov. 12, Treaty of Rapallo signed between Italy and Yugoslavia recognized the independence of the State of Fiume

Dec. 1, D'Annunzio declared war on Italy refusing to accept the Treaty of Rapallo

Dec. 23, General Caviglia with Italian regular troops advanced against Fiume

Dec. 27, Fiume bombed by Italian forces

Dec. 29, D'Annunzio surrendered his authority to Signor Giganti, Mayor, and the Municipal Council

Dec. 31, Pact of Abbazia signed by representatives of Fiume and the Government of Italy by which Fiume accepted the terms of the Treaty of Rapallo and provision made for occupation by Italian troops

1921

Jan. 18, D'Annunzio left for Paris and Italian troops entered the city

April 24, Election for Constituent Assembly won by autonomists headed by Riccardo Zanella, Nationalists in favor of annexation to Italy defeated, soon overthrew the Government

June 13, Royal Commissioner, Commandante Foschini, sent from Italy, took over the Government from Bellosich, Nationalist, to end strife

Oct. 5, Zanella elected President by the Constituent Assembly

1922

March 3, Fascist *coup d'état* led by Deputy Giunta overthrew the Government attacking the palace and escorting President Zanella across the frontier, the Citizens Committee of National Defense assumed the Government

March 9, Giuratti chosen head of Government

March 16, Lieutenant Cabruna seized the Government

March 17, General Giardino with Italian troops occupied Fiume, the civil administration taken over by Professor A. de Poli, Nationalist and Vice-President of the Constituent Assembly

March 26, Appeal of Zanella and 49 members of the Constituent Assembly with him in Yugoslavia to the Prime Minister of Yugoslavia to restore order in Fiume

1923

Jan. 17, General Giardino took charge of the Government

Sept. 16, The Government resigned and General Giardino placed in command as military governor by Italy

1924

Jan. 27, Treaty between Italy and Yugoslavia assigned Fiume to Italy, Port Baros and the Delta to Yugoslavia, joint administration of both ports

March 16, Fiume formally annexed to Italy

FRANCE

France, Republic of western Europe, lying between 51° 9′ and 42° 23′ N. and 4° 42′ W. and 8° E. bounded on the north by the English Channel and the Strait of Dover, on the south by the Mediterranean Sea and Spain, on the east by Belgium, Switzerland, Germany, and Italy, and on the west by the Bay of Biscay, total area 212,659 square miles as compared with 207,170 square miles before 1918, total population, 40,743,897 according to Census of 1926 and estimated as 41,130,000 in 1929, these figures including Corsica. Paris is the capital. The colonies and dependencies of France have an area given officially as about 10,255,510 square kilometers, or 3,958,626 square miles with a population of 59,474,000 as follows:

	Year of Acquisition	Area in Square Miles	Population
In Asia:—			
India	1679	196	290,460
Annam	1884	39,758	5,581,000
Cambodia	1862	67,550	2,535,000
Cochin-China . .	1861	26,476	4,118,000
Tonking . . .	1884	40,530	7,402,000
Laos	1892	82,604	855,000
Syria [1] . . .	1922	60,000	2,191,000
In Africa:—			
Algeria . . .	1830–1902	222,180	6,066,865
Tunis . . .	1881	48,300	2,159,708
Sénégal . . .	1637–1889	74,112	1,358,439
French Sudan }	1893	360,331	2,639,982
Upper Volta }		142,820	3,240,147
Guinea . . .	1843	89,436	2,220,464
Ivory Coast . .	1843	121,590	1,814,679
Dahomey . .	1893	41,302	980,000
Mauritania . .	1893	154,400	289,184
Niger . . .	1912	463,200	1,219,000
Equatorial Africa .	1884	975,635	3,130,000
Cameroon [1] . .	1919	166,489	1,878,683
Togo [1] . . .	1919	21,893	742,728
Réunion . . .	1649	970	187,000
Madagascar . .	1643–1896	241,094	3,743,642 [2]
Mayotte . . .	1843	790	12,600
Somali Coast . .	1864	5,790	86,000
In America:—			
St. Pierre and Miquelon . .	1635	93	4,030
Guadeloupe . .	1634	688	210,000
Martinique . .	1635	385	228,000
Guiana	1626	34,740	47,341
In Oceania:—			
New Caledonia and Dependencies . .	1854–1887	8,548	52,000
Tahiti, &c. . .	1841–1881	1,520	35,900

[1] Held under a mandate of the League of Nations.
[2] Including Mayotte.

A large area of Morocco is under France as a Protectorate. *See* Morocco.

Gaston Doumergue, President.

ca. 418 to 1706

About 418, The Franks settle in that part of Gaul, till late called Flanders

481, Clovis; defeats Syagrius and the Gauls at Soissons, 486; and the Alemanni at Tolbiac, near Cologne; and embraces Christianity, 496

507, He kills Alaric the Goth at the battle of Vouglé, near Poictiers, unites his conquests from the Loire to the Pyrenees, and makes Paris his capital

511, He proclaims the Salique law; and dies, leaving four sons

562–584, Frequent invasions of the Avars and Lombards

584, The mayors of the palace now assume almost sovereign authority

714, Charles Martel becomes mayor of the palace, and rules with despotic sway

720, Invasion of the Saracens; defeated by Charles Martel, near Tours, Oct. 10, 732

752, Reign of Pepin the Short

768, Charlemagne, King; conquers Saxony and Lombardy, 773–74; crowned Emperor of the West, Dec. 25, 800

876, The Normans invade Neustria; part of which is granted Rollo, as Normandy, by Charles the Simple, 911

987, Reign of Hugh Capet

996, Paris made capital of all France

1135, Letters of franchise granted to cities and towns by Louis VI

1146, Louis VII joins in the crusades

1214, Philip Augustus defeats the Germans at Bouvines

1224, Louis VIII, *Cœur de Lion*, frees his serfs

1249, Louis IX conducts an army into Palestine; takes Damietta; dies before Tunis, Aug. 25, 1270

1266, Charles of Anjou conquers Naples and Sicily

1282, His tyranny leads to the massacre called the Sicilian Vespers. *See* Sicily

1301–02, Philip the Fair's quarrels with the Pope

1307–08, Knights Templars suppressed

1314, Union of France and Navarre

Aug. 26, 1346, English invasion—Philip VI defeated at Crécy

Aug. 3, 1347, Calais taken by Edward III

1349, Dauphiny annexed to France

Sept. 19, 1356, Battle of Poictiers; King John taken (brought prisoner to England)

1407, France laid under an interdict by the Pope

Oct. 25, 1415, Battle of Agincourt, or Azincour (N. France), a village where Henry V of England, with about 9,000 men, defeated about 60,000 French on St. Crispin's day, Oct. 25, 1415. Of the French, there were, according to some accounts, 10,000 killed, including the Dukes of Alençon, Brabant, and Bar, the Archbishop of Sens, one marshal, thirteen earls, ninety-two barons, and 1,500 knights; and 14,000 prisoners, among whom were the Dukes of Orleans and Bourbon, and 7,000 barons, knights, and gentlemen. The English lost the Duke of York, the Earl of Suffolk, and about 20 others. St. Rémy asserts with more probability that the English lost 1,600 men. Henry V soon after obtained the Kingdom of France

June, 1418, Massacre of the Armagnacs by the Burgundians

1420, Henry V of England acknowledged heir to the throne

1422, Henry VI crowned at Paris; Duke of Bedford Regent

1429, Siege of Orleans raised by Joan of Arc, May 8; battle of Patay; the English defeated, June 18

May 30, 1431, Joan of Arc burnt at Rouen
England lost all her possessions (but Calais) in France, between 1434 and 1450

Dec., 1464–Oct., 1465, "League of the public good" against Louis XI by the nobles

1475, Edward IV of England invades France

1494, Charles VIII conquers Naples; loses it, 1496

1508, League of Cambray against Venice

1511, Pope Julius II forms the Holy League against France

Aug. 16, 1513, English invasion—battle of Spur

1520, Interview on the *Field of the Cloth of Gold* between Francis I and Henry VIII of England

Feb. 24, 1525, Francis I defeated and taken at Pavia

Aug. 5, 1529, Peace of Cambray

1530, Persecution of Protestants begins

1531, Royal printing press established; Robert Stephens prints his Latin Bible, 1532

1532, Brittany annexed to France

1544, League of England with the Emperor Charles V; Henry VIII invades France

June 7, 1546, Peace with England

1552, Successful defense of Metz by the Duke of Guise

1558, He takes Calais

March 1, 1562, Religious wars; massacre of Protestants at Vassy

Dec. 19, Guise defeats the Huguenots at Dreux

1563, Guise killed at siege of Orleans, Feb. 18; temporary peace of Amboise, March 19

Nov. 10, 1567, Huguenots defeated at St. Denis

1569, At Jarnac March 13; at Moncontour, Oct. 3

Aug. 24, 1572, Massacre of St. Bartholomew

1576, "Holy Catholic League" established

1588, Duke of Guise assassinated by King's order, Dec. 23; and his brother, the Cardinal, Dec. 24

1589, Henry III stabbed by Jacques Clement, a friar, Aug. 1; died Aug. 2

March 14, 1590, Henry IV defeats the League at Ivry

July 25, 1593, Henry IV becomes a Roman Catholic

Jan., 1596, The League leaders submit to him

April 13, 1598, He promulgates the edict of Nantes granting toleration to Protestants

1606–1610, Silk and other manufactures introduced by him and Sully

1608, Quebec in North America settled

May 14, 1610, Murder of Henry IV by Ravaillac

1610–14, Regency of Mary de Medici

Oct. 27, 1614, The States-General meet and complain of the management of the finances

1610, Rise of the Concinis; their fall and death, 1617

1620, Navarre annexed to France

1624, Vigorous and successful administration of Richelieu, begins with finance

Oct. 28, 1628, Rochelle taken after a long siege

Nov. 11, 1630, "Day of Dupes"; Richelieu's energy defeats the machinations of his enemies

May 30, 1631, *Gazette de France* published first by Théophraste Renaudot

1634–35, Richelieu organizes the *Académie de France*

Dec. 4, 1642, His death (aged 58)

May 14, 1643, Accession of Louis XIV, aged four years (Anne of Austria, Regent)

1643–46, Administration of Mazarin; victories of Turenne

1648, &c., Civil wars of the Fronde

1661, Death of Mazarin, March 9; Colbert, Financial Minister

1664–81, Canal of Languedoc constructed

1672, War with Holland, &c.

Aug. 10, 1678, Peace of Nimeguen

Oct. 22, 1685, Edict of Nantes revoked

——, Louis marries Madame de Maintenon

1689, &c., War with William III of England

Sept. 20, 1697, Peace of Ryswick

Sept., 1701, War of the Spanish Succession

Aug. 2, 1704, French defeated at Blenheim

May 23, 1706, At Ramillies

1713 to 1788

April 11, 1713, Peace of Utrecht (*see s.v.*)

Sept., Dissensions of Jesuits and Jansenists; the bull *Unigenitus*

Sept. 1, 1715, &c., Accession of Louis XV; stormy regency of the Duke of Orleans

1716, Law's bubble in France. John Law, of Edinburgh was made comptroller-general of the finances of France, upon the strength of a scheme for establishing a bank, and an East India and a Mississippi company, by the profits of which the national debt of France was to be paid off. The French Ministry accepted it; and in 1716, he opened a bank in his own name, under the protection of the Duke of Orleans, Regent of France, and the deluded rich subscribed for shares both in the bank and the companies. In 1718 Law's was declared a royal bank, and the shares rose to upwards of twenty-fold the original value; so that, in 1719, they were worth more than eighty times the amount of all the current specie in France. In 1720 this fabric of false credit fell to the ground, spreading ruin throughout the country. Law died in poverty at Venice in 1729

June 16, 1743, French defeated at Dettingen

1746, Successful campaign of Marshal Saxe

Oct. 18, 1748, Peace of Aix-la-Chapelle

May, 1756, Seven Years' War begun

Jan. 5, 1757, Damiens' attempt on life of Louis XV

Sept. 13, 1759, Canada lost—battle of Quebec

1762, The Jesuits banished from France, and their effects confiscated

Feb. 10, 1763, Peace of Paris; Canada ceded to England

1769, Louis XV enslaved by Madame du Barry

May 10, 1774, Death of Louis XV

May, 1775, Famine riots at Versailles

May, 1776, The Minister Turgot dismissed

Nov., Ministry of Necker

Jan. 1, 1777, *Journal of Paris* published, alleged first daily paper

1778, Louis XVI assists America to throw off its dependence on England, at first secretly

1780, Torture abolished in French judicature

1785, The diamond-necklace affair. Bœhmer, the Court Jeweler of France, offered the Queen Marie Antoinette, a diamond necklace, for 56,000*l*. The Queen desired the necklace, but feared the expense. The Countess de la Motte (of the ancient house of Valois) forged the Queen's signature, and by pretending that the Queen had an attachment for him, persuaded the Cardinal de Rohan, the Queen's Almoner, to conclude a bargain with the jeweler for the necklace for 56,000*l*. De la Motte thus obtained the necklace and made away with it. For this she was tried in 1786, and sentenced to be branded on the shoulders and imprisoned for life. She accused in vain the celebrated Italian adventurer, Cagliostro, of complicity in the affair, he being then intimate with the Cardinal. She made her escape and came to London, where she was killed by falling from a window-sill, in attempting to escape an arrest for debt.—De Rohan was tried and acquitted, April 14, 1786. The public in France at that time suspected the Queen of being a party to the fraud. Talleyrand wrote at the time, that he should not be surprised if this miserable affair overturned the throne

Feb. 22, 1787, Meeting of the assembly of notables; again Nov. 6, 1788

1789

May 5, Opening of States-General (308 ecclesiastics, 285 nobles; 621 deputies, tiers état)

June 17, The tiers état constitute themselves the National Assembly

July 13, National Guard established by Committee of Safety

July 14, The French Revolution commences with the destruction of the Bastille

Oct. 16, The National Assembly decrees that the title of the " King of France" shall be changed to that of the " King of the French"

Oct.–Dec., Emigration of nobles

Nov. 2, The property of the clergy confiscated

1790

July 14, Confederation of the *Champ de Mars;* France declared a limited monarchy; Louis XVI swears to maintain the constitution

1791

March 3, The silver plate used in the churches transferred to the mint and coined

April 2, Death of Mirabeau

June 21, The King, Queen, and royal family arrested at Varennes, in their flight

Sept. 15, Louis (a prisoner) sanctions the National Constitution

1792

April 20, War declared against the Emperor

June 18, The Jacobin club declare their sittings permanent

June 20, The multitude, bearing the red bonnet of liberty, march to the Tuileries to make demands on the King

June, First coalition against France; commencement of the great French war. *See also* French Revolution

Aug. 10, The royal Swiss Guards cut to pieces; massacre of 5,000 persons

Aug. 19, Revolutionary tribunal set up

Aug. 26, Decree of the National Assembly against the priests; 40,000 exiled

Sept. 2–5, Massacre in Paris; the prisons broken open, and 1,200 persons (100 priests) slain

Sept. 3, Murder of the Princess de Lamballe

Sept. 17, The National Convention opened

Sept. 20, Convention establishes a republic; proclaimed, Sept. 22

——, Duke of Brunswick defeated at Valmy

Nov. 19, The French people declare their fraternity with all nations who desire to be free, and offer help

Dec., Flanders conquered

Dec. 20, Decree for the perpetual banishment of the Bourbon family, those confined in the Temple excepted

1793

Jan. 19, Louis imprisoned in the Temple distinct from the Queen, and brought to trial; condemned to death, Jan. 20. Beheaded in the *Place de Louis Quinze,* Jan. 21

Jan. 21, Committee of public safety established

Feb. 1, War with England and Holland declared

March, War in La Vendée

May 31, Reign of terror—proscription of Girondists; establishment of convention, June 23

July 13, Marat stabbed by Charlotte Corday

Oct. 16, The Queen beheaded

Oct. 31, Execution of the Girondists

Nov. 6, Philip Egalité, Duke of Orleans, who had voted for the King's death, guillotined at Paris; and Madame Roland, Nov. 8

Nov. 10, Worship of goddess of reason

Nov. 24, Adoption of new Republican calendar

1794

April 5, Execution of Danton and others; of Madame Elizabeth, May 12

June 4, Robespierre, President; he and 71 others guillotined, July 28

Dec. 15, Abolition of the Revolutionary Tribunal

1795

April 5, Peace with Prussia

May 20, 21, Insurrection of the Faubourgs

June 8, Louis XVII dies in prison

Nov. 1, French directory chosen

1796–1799

1796, &c., Bonaparte's successful campaigns in Italy

May 12, 1796, Babeuf's conspiracy suppressed

May, 1797, Pichegru's conspiracy fails

July, 1798, Expedition to Syria and Egypt

April, 1799, European coalition against France

Nov. 10, Council of Five Hundred deposed by Bonaparte, who is declared First Consul

1800

June 14, He defeats the Austrians at Marengo

Dec. 24, His life attempted by the infernal machine
    The Bank of France founded by Napoleon, aided by Count Mollien

1801

July 15, Concordat between Napoleon Bonaparte and Pius VII signed reëstablished the Catholic Church and papal authority in France

Nov. 2, Metric system adopted

1802

March 25–27, Peace of Amiens (with England, Spain, and Holland) signed

April, Amnesty to the emigrants

May 19, Legion of Honor instituted

Aug. 2, Bonaparte made consul for life

1803

April 14, The Bank of France established

May 18, Declaration of war against England

1804

Feb. 15, Conspiracy of Moreau and Pichegru against Bonaparte; Pichegru found strangled in prison, April 6

March 21, Duc d'Enghien executed

May 18, France made an empire; Napoleon proclaimed Emperor; crowned by the Pope, Dec. 2

1805

May 26, He is crowned King of Italy

Aug. 5, Another coalition against France

Dec. 2, Napoleon defeats the allies at Austerlitz

1806

Oct. 14, And the Prussians at Jena

1807

Feb. 8, And the Russians at Eylau

June 25, His interview with the Czar at Tilsit; peace signed, July 7

Dec. 17, His Milan decree against British commerce

1808

March 1, New nobility of France created

May 1, Abdication of Charles IV of Spain and his son, in favor of Napoleon; insurrection in Spain, May 2

July, Commencement of the Peninsular War (*see* Spain)

1809

April, Alliance of England and Austria against France

May, Victories in Austria; Napoleon enters Vienna

Oct. 14, Peace of Vienna

Dec. 16, Divorce of the Emperor and Empress Josephine decreed by the Senate

1810

April 1, Marriage of Napoleon to Maria Louisa of Austria

July 9, Holland united to France

1811

March 20, Birth of the King of Rome (since styled Napoleon II)

1812

June 22, War with Russia declared

Sept. 7, Victory at Borodino

Oct., Disastrous retreat from Moscow; French army nearly destroyed

1813

Jan. 25, Second Concordat between Napoleon and the Pope

March, Alliance of Austria, Russia, and Prussia against France

Oct. 7, The British enter France

1814

March 31, Surrender of Paris to the allies

April 5, Abdication of Napoleon negotiated

May 3, Bourbon dynasty restored, and Louis XVIII arrives in Paris

May 4, Napoleon arrives at Elba

June 4–10, The Constitutional Charter decreed

1815

March 1, Quits Elba, and lands at Cannes

March 20, Arrives at Fontainebleau (the 100 days)

March 22, Joined by all the army

March 25, The allies sign a treaty against him

March 29, He abolishes the slave trade

June 12, Leaves Paris for the army

June 18, Defeated at Waterloo

June 20, Returns to Paris; abdicates in favor of his infant son, June 22

July 3, Intending to embark for America, he arrives at Rochefort

——, Louis XVIII enters Paris

July 15, Napoleon surrenders to Captain Maitland, of the *Bellerophon*, at Rochefort

Aug. 8, Transferred at Torbay to the *Northumberland*, and with Admiral Sir George Cockburn sails for St. Helena

Oct. 15, Arrives at St. Helena to remain for life

Dec. 7, Execution of Marshal Ney

1816

Jan. 12, The family of Bonaparte excluded for ever from France by the law of amnesty

1817

Nov. 22, Concordat with the Pope practically nullified those of 1801 and 1813

1820–1824

Feb. 13, 1820, Duke of Berry murdered

May 5, 1821, Death of Napoleon I

Sept. 16, 1824, Louis XVIII dies; Charles X, King

1827

April 30, National Guard disbanded

Nov. 4, War with Algiers; Dey's fleet defeated

Nov. 5, Seventy-six new peers created

Nov. 19, 20, Election riots at Paris; barricades; several persons killed

1828

Jan. 4, The Villèle Ministry replaced by the Martignac

Dec. 10, Béranger imprisoned for political songs

1829

Aug. 8, Polignac administration formed

1830

May 16, Chamber of Deputies dissolved

July 5, Algiers taken

July 26, The obnoxious ordinances regarding the press, and reconstruction of the Chamber of Deputies

July 27, Revolution commences with barricades

July 28–30, Conflicts in Paris between the populace (ultimately aided by the National Guard) and the army

July 31, Charles X retires to Rambouillet; flight of his ministry; he abdicates, Aug. 2

Aug. 7, The Duke of Orleans accepts the crown as Louis Philippe I

Aug. 14, The constitutional charter of July published

Aug. 17, Charles X retires to England

Dec. 21, Polignac and other ministers tried and sentenced to perpetual imprisonment

1831

Dec. 27, The abolition of the hereditary peerage decreed by both chambers; the peers (36 new peers being created) concurring by a majority of 103 to 70

1832

June 5, 6, The ABC (*abaissés*) insurrection in Paris suppressed

Sept. 18, Charles X leaves Holyrood-house for the continent

Oct. 11, Ministry of Soult, Duke of Dalmatia

1833

March 18, Bergeron and Benoit tried for an attempt on the life of Louis Philippe; acquitted

June 9, The Duchess of Berry, who has been delivered of a female child, and asserts her secret marriage with an Italian nobleman, sent to Palermo

1834

May 20, Death of Lafayette

July 15, Marshal Gerard takes office

1835

Feb. 8, M. Dupuytren dies

July 28, Fieschi attempts the King's life

[The King and his sons escaped; but Marshal Mortier, Duke of Treviso, was shot dead, many officers dangerously wounded, and upwards of forty persons killed or injured]

1836

Feb. 19, Fieschi executed

June 25, Louis Alibaud fires at the King on his way from the Tuileries; guillotined, July 11

Sept. 6, Ministry of Count Molé, *vice* M. Thiers

Oct. 29–30, Attempted insurrection at Strasbourg by Louis Napoleon (afterwards Emperor), planned, it is said, by Filain de Persigny; he is sent to America, Nov. 13

Nov. 6, Death of Charles X

Nov. 23, Prince Polignac and others set at liberty from Ham, and sent out of France

Dec. 27, Meunier fires at the King on his way to open the French chambers

1837

May 8, Amnesty for political offenses

1838

"Idées Napoléoniennes," by Prince Louis Napoleon, published

May 20, Talleyrand dies

June 28, Marshal Soult at the coronation of the Queen of England

Aug. 24, Birth of the Count of Paris

1839

Jan. 2, Death of the Duchess of Württemberg (daughter of Louis Philippe), a good sculptor

May 12, Insurrection of Barbès and Blanqui at Paris

1840

March 1, M. Thiers, Minister of Foreign Affairs

May 12, The Chambers decree the removal of Napoleon's remains from St. Helena to France

[By the permission of the British Government these were taken from the tomb at St. Helena (Oct. 15, 1840), and embarked, on the next day, on board the *Belle Poule*, French frigate, under the command of the Prince de Joinville; the vessel reached Cherbourg on November 30; and on December 15, the body was deposited in the Hôtel des Invalides. The body was finally placed in its crypt on March 31, 1861]

Aug. 6, Descent of Prince Louis Napoleon, General Montholon, and 50 followers, at Vimereux, near Boulogne; the Prince sentenced to imprisonment for life, Oct. 6

Oct. 15, Darmés fires at the King

Oct. 29, M. Guizot, Minister of Foreign Affairs

Dec. 15, Project of law for an extraordinary credit of 140,000,000 francs, for erecting the fortifications of Paris

1841

March 30, The duration of copyright to 30 years after the author's death fixed

Aug. 15, Bronze statue of Napoleon placed on the column of the Grande Armée, Boulogne

Sept. 13, Attempt to assassinate the Duke of Aumale (King's son) on return from Africa

1842

July 13, The Duke of Orleans, heir to the throne, killed by a fall from his carriage

1843

An extradition treaty with England signed

1844

May, War with Morocco; peace, Sept. 10

1846

April 16, Attempt of Lecompte to assassinate the King at Fontainebleau

May 25, Louis Napoleon escapes from Ham

July 29, The seventh attempt on the life of the King: by Joseph Henri

Oct. 10, Spanish marriages: marriage of the Queen of Spain with her cousin, and of the duc de Montpensier with the Infanta of Spain

1847

Sept. 13, Death of Marshal Oudinot (Duke of Reggio) at Paris, in his 91st year; Soult made General of France, Sept. 26

Oct. 10, Jerome Bonaparte returns to France after an exile of 32 years

Dec. 18, Death of the ex-Empress, Maria Louisa; and of Madame Adelaide, Dec. 30

Dec. 23, Surrender of Abd-el-Kader

1848

Feb. 21, The grand reform banquet at Paris prohibited

Feb. 22, Revolutionary tumult in consequence; impeachment and resignation of Guizot; barricades thrown up, the Tuileries ransacked, the prisons opened, and frightful disorders committed, Feb. 23, 24

Feb. 24, Louis Philippe abdicates in favor of his infant grandson, the Comte de Paris, who is not accepted; the royal family and ministers escape

Feb. 26, A republic proclaimed from the steps of the Hôtel de Ville

March 3, The ex-King and Queen arrive at Newhaven in England

March 4, Funeral procession in honor of the victims of the revolution

May 7, The provisional government resigns to an executive commission, elected by the National Assembly of the French Republic

[The members of this new Government were: MM. Dupont de l'Eure, Arago, Garnier-Pagès,

Marie, Lamartine, Ledru-Rollin, and Crémieux. The secretaries: Louis Blanc, Albert, Flocon, and Marrast]

May 15, The people's attack on the Assembly suppressed

May 26, Perpetual banishment of Louis Philippe and his family decreed

June 13, Election of Louis Napoleon (to the National Assembly) for the department of the Seine and three other departments

June 23, Rise of the Red Republicans: war against the troops and National Guard; more than 300 barricades thrown up, and firing continues in all parts of Paris during the night

June 24, The troops under Cavaignac and Lamoricière with immense loss, drive the insurgents from the left bank of the Seine

June 25, Paris declared in a state of siege

June 26, Faubourg du Temple carried with cannon, and the insurgents surrender

[The national losses caused by this outbreak estimated at 30,000,000 francs; 16,000 persons killed and wounded, and 8,000 prisoners were taken. The Archbishop of Paris was killed while tending the dying, June 26]

June 28, Cavaignac, President of the council

Sept. 26, Louis Napoleon takes his seat in the National Assembly

Oct. 20, Paris relieved from a state of siege which had continued four months

Nov. 12, Promulgation of the constitution of Nov. 4 in front of the Tuileries

Dec. 11, Louis Napoleon elected President of the French Republic; proclaimed, Dec. 20

[He had 5,587,759 votes; Cavaignac, 1,474,687; Ledru-Rollin, 381,026; Raspail, 37,121; Lamartine, 21,032; and Changarnier, 4,975]

1849

Jan. 29, Military demonstration to stifle an anticipated insurrection of the reds

1850

Aug. 26, Death of King Louis Philippe, at Claremont, in England

Sept. 26, Liberty of the press restricted

1851

Jan. 10, General Changarnier deprived of the command of the National Guard

Oct. 19, Death of the Duchess of Angoulême, daughter of Louis XVI, at Frohsdorf

Nov. 13, Telegraph between England and France opened

Nov. 26, Death of Marshal Soult

Dec. 2, *Coup d'état* planned by the Prince-President, Persigny, and De Morny; carried out by C. de Maupas, Minister of Police, St. Arnaud, and others; legislative assembly dissolved; universal suffrage established, and Paris declared in a state of siege; the election of a President for ten years proposed, and a second chamber or Senate

——, MM. Thiers, Changarnier, Cavaignac, Bedeau, Lamoricière, and Charres arrested, and sent to the castle of Vincennes

——, About 180 members of the Assembly, with M. Berryer at their head, attempting to meet, are arrested, and Paris is occupied by troops

Dec. 2, M. Charles Baudin, a Deputy, shot dead while protesting against the violation of the law

Dec. 3, 4, Conflicts in Paris; the troops victorious

Dec. 12, Consultative commission founded

Dec. 21, 22, Voting throughout France for the election of a President of the Republic for ten years; affirmative votes 7,473,431, negative votes 641,351

1852

Jan., Installation of the Prince-President in the Cathedral of Notre Dame; the day observed as a national holiday at Paris, and Louis Napoleon takes up his residence at the Tuilieries

Jan. 9, Generals Changarnier, Lamoricière, and others, conducted to the Belgian frontier

Jan. 10, 83 members of the legislative assembly banished; 575 persons arrested for resistance to the *coup d'état* of Dec. 2, and conveyed to Havre for transportation to Cayenne

[The inscription "*Liberty, Fraternity, Equality,*" ordered to be forthwith erased throughout France, and the old names of streets, public buildings, and places of resort to be restored. The trees of liberty are everywhere hewn down and burnt]

——, National Guard disbanded, reorganized anew, and placed under the control of the executive; the President appointing the officers

Jan. 14, New constitution published

Jan. 22, Decree obliging the Orleans family to sell all their real and personal property in France within a year

——, Second decree, annulling the settlement made by Louis Philippe upon his family previous to his accession in 1830, and annexing the property to the domain of the State

Feb. 17, The birthday of Napoleon I (Aug. 15) decreed to be the only national holiday

March 27, The departments of France released from a state of siege

March 29, Legislative chambers installed

July 1, Plot to assassinate the Prince-President discovered at Paris

Aug. 8, M. Thiers and others permitted to return to France

Sept. 13, The French Senate prays "the re-establishment of the hereditary sovereign power in the Bonaparte family"

Sept. 27, Prince-President visits Toulon; and Bordeaux, where he says "the Empire is peace" (*l'empire c'est la paix*), Oct. 7

Oct. 16, Releases Abd-el-Kader (*see* Algiers)

Oct. 19, Convokes the Senate for November to deliberate on a change of government, when a *senatus consultum* will be proposed for the ratification of the French people

Oct. 25, Protest of comte de Chambord

Nov. 4, In message to the Senate, the Prince-President announces the contemplated restoration of the Empire, and orders the people to be consulted upon this change

Nov. 21, Votes for the Empire, 7,824,189; noes, 253,145; null, 63,326

Dec. 2, The Prince-President declared Emperor; assumes the title of Napoleon III

1853

Jan. 29, His marriage with Eugénie de Montijo, Countess of Téba, at Notre Dame

Feb. 2, 4,312 political offenders pardoned
Sept., Bread riots
——, Military camp at Satory, near Paris
Oct. 2, Francis Arago, astronomer, &c., died
Nov., Attempted assassination of the Emperor—ten
persons transported for life
Nov. 20, Reconciliation of the two branches of the
Bourbons at Frohsdorf
Dec. 7, Marshal Ney's statue inaugurated exactly
38 years after his death on the spot where it occurred

1854

March 28, War declared against Russia (see Russo-
Turkish War)
Sept. 29, Death of Marshal St. Arnaud

1855

April 28, Attempted assassination of the Emperor by
Pianort; by Bellemarre, Sept. 8
May 15, Industrial exhibition at Paris opened
Nov. 24, Death of Count Molé

1856

March 16, Birth of the imperial Prince; amnesty granted
to 1,000 political prisoners
March 30, Peace with Russia signed
Oct. 6, Distress in money market

1857

Jan. 3, Sibour, Archbishop of Paris, assassinated by
Verger, a priest
June 21, 22, Elections (3,000,000 voters to elect 257
deputies): General Cavaignac elected deputy, but
declines to take the oath
July 16, Death of Béranger, poet
Aug. 6, 7, The conspirators Grilli, Bartolotti, and
Tibaldi, tried, convicted, and sentenced to transporta-
tion, &c.
Sept. 25, The Emperor meets the Emperor of Russia
at Stuttgart
Oct. 28, Death of Eugène Cavaignac (55)

1858

Jan. 4, Death of Mlle Rachel (38)
Jan. 14, Attempted assassination of the Emperor by
Orsini, Pieri, Rudio, Gomez, &c., by the explosion of
three shells (two persons killed, many wounded)
Feb. 18, Public safety bill passed—bold protest against
it by Ollivier
Feb., France divided into five military departments;
General Espinasse becomes Minister of the Interior
March 9, Republican outbreak at Chalons suppressed
March 11, "Napoleon III et l'Angleterre" published
March 13, Orsini and Pieri executed
April 12–17, Simon Bernard, tried in London as their
accomplice, acquitted
June, Espinasse retires from Ministry of the Interior
[he was killed at the battle of Magenta, June 4, 1859]
Aug. 19, Conference at Paris respecting the Danubian
principalities closes
Oct. 23, Dispute with Portugal respecting the Charles et
Georges settled
Nov. 25 Trial of comte de Montalembert
[In Oct., 1858, the comte published a pamphlet en-
titled "Un Débat sur l'Inde," eulogizing English
institutions and depreciating those of France. He
was sentenced to six months' imprisonment and a fine
of 3,000 francs, but was pardoned by the Emperor,

Dec. 2. The comte appealed against the sentence of
the court, and was again condemned; but acquitted
of a part of the charge. The sentence was once more
remitted by the Emperor (Dec. 21). In Oct., 1859,
the comte published a pamphlet entitled "Pie IX
et la France en 1849 et 1859," in which England is
severely censured for opposition to Romanism]

1859

Jan. 30, Marriage of Prince Napoleon to Princess
Clotilde of Savoy
Feb., Publication of "Napoleon III et l'Italie"
May 12, On the Austrians invading Sardinian terri-
tories, France declares war, and the French enter;
the Empress appointed Regent; the Emperor arrives
at Genoa
May 20, Victories of the allies (French and Sardinians)
at Montebello; Palestro, May 30, 31; Magenta,
June 4; Melegnano (Marignano), June 8; Napoleon
enters Milan, June 8; victory of allies at Solferino,
June 24
July 6, Armistice agreed on
July 11, Meeting of Emperors of France and Austria at
Villa Franca
July 12, Peace agreed on
July 17, Louis Napoleon returns to Paris
Aug. 8–Nov., Conference of Austrian and French
envoys at Zurich

1860

Jan., Count Walewski, the Foreign Minister, resigns;
M. Thouvenel succeeds him
Jan. 5, The Emperor announces a free trade policy;
Mr. Cobden at Paris
Jan. 23, Commercial treaty with England signed
Jan. 29, L'Univers suppressed for publishing the Pope's
letter to the Emperor
March 24, Treaty for the annexation of Savoy and Nice
signed
April 7, The press censured for attacking England
June 15–17, The Emperor meets the German sov-
ereigns at Baden
June 24, Jerome Bonaparte, the Emperor's uncle, dies
(76)
July 25, The Emperor, in a letter to Count Persigny,
disclaims hostility to England
Oct. 1, New tariff comes into operation
Nov., Public levying of Peter's pence forbidden, and
free issue of pastoral letters checked
Dec. 16, Passports for Englishmen to cease after Jan. 1,
1861

1861

Jan. 25–Feb. 15, Jerome (son of Jerome Bonaparte and
Elizabeth Paterson, American) claims his legitimate
rights; non-suited after a trial
[The marriage took place in America, on Dec. 24,
1803; but was annulled, and Jerome married the
Princess Catherine of Württemberg, Aug. 12, 1807;
their children are the Prince Napoleon and the
Princess Mathilde]
Feb. 2, Purchase of the principality of Monaco for
4,000,000 francs; announced Feb. 5
Feb. 17, Failure of Mirès, a railway banker and loan
contractor, &c.; he is arrested. Many influential
persons suspected of participating in his frauds; the
Government promises strict justice
Feb. 20, Eugène Scribe, dramatist, dies (80)

March 1, Speech of Prince Napoleon in favor of Italian unity, the English alliance, and against the Pope's temporal government

March, Strong advocacy of the temporal government of the Pope in the chambers; the French army, 687,000 men

April 11, Circular forbidding the priests to meddle with politics

May 1, Commercial treaty with Belgium

June 11, Declaration of neutrality in the American conflict

June 24, Official recognition of Kingdom of Italy

Aug. 18, Conflict between French and Swiss soldiers at Ville-la-Grande

Aug. 29, Mirès, the speculator, sentenced to five years' imprisonment

Oct. 1, Commercial treaty between France, Great Britain, and Belgium comes into operation

Oct. 6, Meeting of Emperor and King of Prussia at Compeigne; and King of Holland, Oct. 12

Oct. 27, French troops enter the valley of Dappes (Switzerland) to prevent an arrest

Oct. 31, Convention between France, Great Britain, and Spain, respecting intervention in Mexico, signed (*see* Mexico)

Nov. 14, Embarrassment in finances; Achille Fould becomes Finance Minister; with enlarged powers, Dec. 12

1862

Jan. 1, The Emperor reminds the clergy of their duty "towards Cæsar"

Jan. 7, French army lands at Vera Cruz

Jan. 20, The French masters of the Province of Bienhoa, in Annam

Feb. 24, Fould announces his finance scheme (reduction of 4½% stock to 3%, and additional taxes and stamp duties)

March 28, French victories in Cochin-China (6 provinces ceded to France)

April 16, The Spanish and British plenipotentiaries decide to quit Mexico: the French declare war against the Mexican Government (for the events, *see* Mexico)

April 21, Sentence against Mirès examined and reversed at Douai; he is released

June 3, Treaty of peace between France and Annam signed

July 5, Duke Pasquier dies (96)

Aug. 2, New commercial treaty with Prussia

Aug. 29, Camp at Chalons formed on account of Garibaldi's movements in Sicily; broken, when he is taken prisoner; great sympathy for him in France

Sept. 12, Treaty of commerce with Madagascar

Oct. 15, Drouyn de Lhuys made Foreign Minister in place of Thouvenel

Dec. 7, The Emperor inaugurates "Boulevard Prince Eugène," Paris

Dec., Great distress in the manufacturing districts through the cotton famine and the Civil War in America

1863

Jan. 17, Treaty of commerce with Italy signed

Feb. 26, Revolt in Annam suppressed

Feb. 27, Convention regulating the French and Spanish frontiers concluded

April 1, Resignation of Magne, the "speaking minister" in the Assembly

May, Persigny issues arbitrary injunctions to electors

May 8, Dissolution of the chambers

May 31–June 15, Thiers, Ollivier, Favre, and other opposition candidates elected in Paris

June 23, Changes in the Ministry—resignation of Persigny, Walewski, and Rouland

Oct. 13, Death of Billault (born 1805), "speaking minister" in legislative assembly; succeeded by Rouher, as "minister of state," Oct. 18

Nov. 4, The Emperor proposes the convocation of a European congress, and invites the sovereigns or their deputies by letter

Nov. 9, Thiers and his friends form a new opposition

Nov. 25, Invitation to the congress declined by England

1864

May 16, Convention between France, Brazil, Italy, Portugal, and Haiti, for establishing a telegraphic line between Europe and America

May 22, Death of Marshal Pelissier, Duke of Malakoff, Governor of Algeria (born 1794)

June 20, Convention between France and Japan signed by Japanese ambassadors at Paris

June 30, Convention of commerce, &c., between France and Switzerland, signed

July 16, Prince Napoleon Victor, son of Prince Napoleon Jerome and Princess Clotilde, born

Sept. 15, Convention between France and Italy respecting evacuation of Rome, &c.

Dec. 7, Garnier-Pagès and 12 others who had met at his house for election purposes convicted as members of a society "of more than 20 members"

Dec. 9, Death of the Emperor's private secretary and old friend, Mocquard

1865

Jan. 5, The clergy prohibited from reading the Popes' encyclical letter of Dec. 8 in churches; much excitement; the Archbishop of Besançon and other prelates disobey

Jan., The Prince Napoleon Jerome appointed Vice-President of the Privy Council

Jan. 19, Death of Proudhon (born 1809), who said "la propriété c'est le vol"

Feb. 1, Decree for an international exhibition of the products of agriculture and industry and of the fine arts, at Paris, on May 1, 1867

Feb. 14, Treaty with Sweden signed

March 8, The Minister Duruy's plan of compulsory education rejected by the Assembly

March 10, Death of the duc de Morny, said to be half-brother of the Emperor

March 31, "Loi des suspects" (or of public safety) suffered to expire

May 3–27, The Emperor visits Algeria

June 9, Inauguration of the statue of Napoleon I at Ajaccio, with an imprudent speech by Prince Napoleon Jerome, May 15; censured by the Emperor, May 23; the Prince resigns his offices

Aug., 1865–Feb., 1866, Protest of the United States against French intervention in Mexico—prolonged correspondence (*see* Mexico)

Sept. 2, Count Walewski nominated President of the *Corps législatif*

Sept. 11, Death of General Lamoricière

Dec. 4, Notice given of the abrogation of the extradition treaty in six months

Dec. 18, Riots of Republican students at Paris (several expelled from the Academy of Medicine)

1866

Jan. 22, Emperor opens chambers with a pacific speech

July 4, The Emperor of Austria cedes Venetia to France, and invites the Emperor's intervention with Prussia

Aug., Note to the Prussian Government desiring rectification of the French frontier to what it was in 1814; declared by Prussia to be inadmissible

Sept. 2, Resignation of M. Drouyn de Lhuys, Foreign Minister (succeeded by the Marquis de Moustier)

Sept. 16, Pacific circular of the Emperor sent to foreign courts

Oct. 18, Death of M. Thouvenel, formerly Foreign Minister

Dec. 2–12, The French troops quit Rome

Dec. 9, Publication of letter from the comte de Chambord to his adherents in favor of the Pope's temporal power dated

Dec. 11, Commercial treaty with Austria signed

1867

Jan. 19, Imperial decree announcing political reforms; interpellation in the chambers; relaxation of the restriction on the press

Jan., Ministerial changes; Rouher becomes Minister of Finance; Niel, of War, &c.

March 7, Emile Girardin fined for libel in *La Liberté*

March 18, Severe speech of Thiers on foreign policy

March 29, Resignation of Walewski, President of the Chamber; succeeded by M. Schneider, April 11

April 1, International Exhibition opened

May, Scheme for organizing the army rejected by committee

June 17–July 9, International conference at Paris respecting monetary currency

June 25, Three provinces in Annam annexed to the French Empire

July 15, Protectorate of France over Cambodia assured by treaty

July 18, Law abolishing imprisonment for debt adopted by the Senate

Aug. 15, The Emperor's letter recommending money to be expended in improving intercommunication by means of railways, canals, and roads

Aug. 18–21, Meeting of the Emperors of France and Austria at Salzburg

Oct. 30, French troops enter Rome

Nov. 3, Garibaldians defeated at Mentana

Nov. 18, Pacific and liberal speech of the Emperor on opening the Chambers

Dec. 5, During a debate in the legislative assembly, Rouher, the Minister, says, "We declare that Italy shall never seize upon Rome" (the Government supported by 238 votes to 17)

1868

Jan. 1, New army bill (allowing 100,000 men to be added to the army annually; establishing a new national guard, &c.; giving the Empire virtually an army of 1,200,000 men), passed in the *Corps législatif* (206 to 60)

Jan. 29, M. Magne announces a deficiency in the budget; and a loan for 17,600,000*l.*

Jan. 30, The army bill passes the Senate—125 to 1 (Michel Chevalier, who spoke warmly against it); becomes law, Feb. 4

June, New press law put in force; increasing facility for publishing new journals

Aug., Rochefort's weekly satirical pamphlet, "La Lan-

terne," suppressed; he and his printer condemned to fine and imprisonment, escapes to Belgium

Nov. 29, M. Berryer, the advocate (born 1790) died

Dec., Ministerial changes; Marquis de la Valette, Foreign Minister, in place of De Moustier; Forcade de la Roquette, Interior

1869

Jan. 1, The *Moniteur* replaced by the *Journal officiel*

Jan. 18, Meeting of the Assembly

Feb. 5, De Moustier dies

Feb. 28, Death of Lamartine (born Oct., 1792); of Troplong, President of the Senate, March 1

April 26, Dissolution of the legislative assembly of 1863

April 27, Difference with Belgium respecting the Luxemburg railway settled

June 11, Fierce election riots at Paris, June 9; the Emperor and Empress ride boldly through the boulevards

July 13, Message from the Emperor announcing important political changes; introducing ministerial responsibility, &c., read July 12; resignation of Ministers

July 17, New ministry: Forcade de la Roquette, Interior; La Tour d'Auvergne, Foreign; Chasseloup-Laubat, President, &c.

July 20, M. Rouher made President of the Senate

July 23, French Atlantic telegraph completely laid

Aug. 13, Marshal Niel, War Minister (66) dies

Sept. 10, New constitution promulgated

Sept. 20, Père Hyacinthe (name Loyson), popular Carmelite preacher at Paris, protests against papal infallibility and encroachments, and resigns by letter

Oct., Nov., Dec., Agitation against free trade

Nov. 22, Henri Rochefort (of "La Lanterne") elected a deputy for Paris

Dec. 27, Resignation of Ministers announced

1870

Jan. 3, New Liberal Ministry formed by Emile Ollivier, Justice; Daru, Foreign; Le Bœuf, War

Jan. 10, Victor Noir, a journalist, killed by Pierre Bonaparte during an interview at Auteuil respecting a challenge sent to M. Rochefort

Jan. 22, Great excitement among populace; prosecution of Rochefort for libel in his paper, the *Marseillaise;* he is sentenced to fine and imprisonment

Feb. 8, 9, Barricades erected in Paris, and riots after the apprehension of Rochefort, Feb. 7; soon quelled

Feb. 22, Jules Favre's attack on the Ministry in the Chamber defeated (236 to 18)

March 13, Charles, comte de Montalembert, eminent author, dies (*see* 1858)

March 21–27, Trial of Pierre Bonaparte at Tours; acquitted (but ordered to pay 1,000*l.* to Noir's family)

March 22, Emperor's letter to Ollivier, agreeing to modification of the constitution of the Senate

March 28, Senatus consultum communicated to the Senate; adopted April 20

April 10, Ministerial crisis: resignation of Daru and other Ministers opposing the proposed *plebiscite*

April 13, Ollivier Ministry reconstructed; about May 15, duc de Grammont, Foreign Minister

April 24, Proclamation of the Emperor respecting changes in the constitution

May 8, *Plebiscite* to ascertain whether the people approve of above changes,—yes, 7,527,379; no, 1,530,909

May 9, 10, Rioting and barricades in Paris; about 100 arrested, many sentenced to imprisonment, May 14

June 19, The Orleans princes address the legislative assembly, demanding their return to France, opposed by 173 to 31, July 2

July 5, 6, 7, Great excitement through the nomination of Prince Leopold of Hohenzollern Sigmaringen for the Spanish throne

July 15, The Prince Leopold withdraws from candidature; guarantees required by France from Prussia refused; France decides to declare war against Prussia; declaration signed, July 17

[For events of the war, *see* Franco-Prussian War]

July 23, The Empress appointed Regent

July 28, The Emperor joins the army

Aug. 2, The Government declare that they are only "at war with the policy of Bismarck"

Aug. 7, State of siege proclaimed in Paris after the great defeat of MacMahon at Woerth

Aug. 8, The Government appeals to France and Europe against Prussia

Aug. 9, Stormy debate in the *Corps législatif;* (M. de Kératry called on the Emperor to abdicate; M. Guyot Montpeyroux said that the army were "lions led by asses"); resignation of Ollivier and his Ministry

Aug. 10, New Ministry formed: General Cousin-Montauban comte de Palikao (distinguished in the war with China), Minister of War, chief: M. Chevreau, Interior; M. Magne, Finance; M. Clément Duvernois, Commerce and Agriculture; Admiral Rigault de Genouilly, Marine; Baron Jerome David, Public Works; Prince de la Tour d'Auvergne, Foreign Affairs; and others

——, Decree for the great augmentation of the army during the war, and appointing a "defence committee" for Paris

Aug., The Orleans princes (the duc d'Aumale, Prince de Joinville, and duc de Chartres) proffer their services in the army; declined

Aug. 14, The Government declares against any negotiations for peace

Aug. 16, Murder of M. Allain de Moneys, suspected of republicanism and Germanism, by infuriated peasants at Hautefaye, Dordogne, near Bordeaux

Aug. 17, General Trochu (Orleanist), energetic and able author of "L'Armée Française en 1867," appointed Governor of Paris; issues proclamation Aug. 18

Aug. 28, Decree of General Trochu for the expulsion from Paris of all foreigners not naturalized

Aug. 31, Death of Count Flahault de la Billarderie, Chancellor of the Legion of Honor (85)

Sept. 3, 8 P.M., Deputation from 10,000 persons call on Trochu to assume the Government; he declines

Sept. 4, 3:35 A.M. The news of the final defeat of MacMahon near Sedan, and the surrender of the Emperor and the remainder of MacMahon's army (83,000) to the King of Prussia announced by comte de Palikao to the legislative assembly! Jules Favre declares for defending France to the last gasp, attacks the imperial dynasty, and proposes concentration of all powers in the hands of General Trochu, amid profound silence

——, 3:10 P.M., On the proposition of Thiers the chamber appoints a commission of government and national defense, and orders the convocation of a constituent assembly, and adjourns

——, 4:15 P.M., Assembly invaded by the crowd, demanding a republic; most of the deputies retire. Gambetta and other liberal members of the "left"

proclaim the deposition of the imperial dynasty and the establishment of a republic

Sept. 4, Last meeting of the Senate; it declares adhesion to the Emperor

——, Proclamation of a "Government of Defense," General Trochu, President; MM. Léon Gambetta, Interior; Jules Simon, Public Instruction; Jules Favre, Foreign; Crémieux, Justice; Jules Picard, Finance; General Le Flo, War; Fourichon, Marine; Magnin, Agriculture; Dorian, Public Works; Etienne Arago, Mayor of Paris; Kératry, Police

——, Evening, An informal meeting of the Assembly held, M. Thiers, President. M. Jules Favre reports to it the formation of the provisional government; some protest; Thiers recommends moderation

——, Evening, The Empress, the comte de Palikao, and other Ministers secretly leave Paris and enter Belgium

Sept. 5, Legislative chamber dissolved; Senate abolished; regular troops and National Guard fraternize; "perfect order reigns"

——, M. Favre calls on the United States of America for moral support

——, 9:35 P.M., Napoleon arrives at Wilhelmshöhe, near Cassel

——, Henri Rochefort added to the Government

——, The red Republican flag raised at Lyons

Sept. 6, Victor Hugo and Louis Blanc arrive in Paris

——, Proffered services of the Orleans princes again declined

Sept. 7, The Imperial Prince at Hastings, joined by the Empress, Sept. 8

Sept. 8, The Republic recognized by the United States

——, The defense committee summon the King of Prussia to quit French territory

——, Decree convoking the constituent assembly, to be composed of 750 members (to be elected on Oct. 16)

——, The Republic recognized by Spain; by Switzerland, Sept. 9

Sept. 13, M. Thiers arrives in London on a mission from the Government

Sept. 16, Elections for constituent assembly ordered to take place on Oct. 2

Sept. 17, Diplomatic circular from M. Jules Favre: he admits he has no claim on Prussia for disinterestedness; urges that statesmen should hesitate to continue a war in which more than 200,000 men have already fallen; announces that a freely elected assembly is summoned, and that the Government will abide by its judgment, and that France, left to her free action, immediately asks the cessation of the war, but prefers its disasters a thousand times to dishonor. He admits that France has been wrong

Sept. 18, A government delegation at Tours under M. Crémieux, the Minister of Justice; the foreign ambassadors proceed there

About Sept. 18, Manifesto of the red Republicans signed by General Cluseret, placarded in Paris

About Sept. 19, Bronze statues of Napoleon ordered to be made into cannon

Sept. 20, Stern proclamation of Trochu respecting the cowardice of the Zouaves on Sept. 19

Sept. 23, M. Duruof in a post-balloon quits Paris with mailbags, arrives at Evreux, and reaches Tours

About Sept. 23, The *Journal officiel* replaced by the *Moniteur universel* as the organ of the Government

Sept. 24, Esquiros struggles to maintain order at Marseilles

Sept. 24, Failure of the negotiations for peace between Count Bismarck and Jules Favre; manifesto of the Government at Tours, calling on the people to rise and either disavow the Ministry or "fight to the bitter end"; the elections for the Assembly suspended

About Sept. 26, All Frenchmen between 20 and 25 years of age prohibited leaving France

Sept. 26, 27, Great enthusiasm in the provinces on the failure of the negotiations; "war to the knife" and *levée en masse* proclaimed by the prefects; efforts made to excite warlike ardor in Brittany by M. Cathelineau

About Sept. 27, The duc d'Aumale consents to become a candidate for the representative assembly, and promises submission to the *de facto* Government for defense

Sept. 28, Attempted insurrection of the red Republicans at Lyons; order restored by National Guards; General Cluseret disappears

Sept. 29–Oct. 1, The elections for the constituent assembly (753 members) ordered by the delegates at Tours to take place on Oct. 16

Sept. 30, All between 21 and 40 to be organized as a national garde mobile; all men in arms placed at the disposal of the Minister of War

Sept., The Empress and her son residing at Camdenhouse, Chislehurst, Kent

About Oct. 1, Proclamations of General Trochu for maintaining order in Paris

Oct. 1, The elections deferred till they can be carried out throughout the whole extent of the Republic, by order of the Government at Paris

Oct. 3, M. Crémieux becomes delegate Minister of War at Tours in place of Admiral Fourichon, still Minister of Marine

Oct. 5, Gustave Flourens, heading five battalions of National Guards, marches to the Hôtel de Ville and demands chassepots (not to be had)

Oct. 7, M. Gambetta escapes from Paris in a balloon; arrives at Rouen and declares for "a pact with victory or death," Oct. 8; arrives at Tours and becomes Minister of War as well as of the Interior, Oct. 9

Oct. 8, Suppression of the schools of the "brethren of the Christian doctrine" by the Republicans; much dissatisfaction

——, All Frenchmen under 60 years of age forbidden to quit France

Oct. 9, Address from the comte de Chambord, saying that his whole ambition is to found with the people a really national Government

Oct. 10, 11, Blanqui, Gustave Flourens, Ledru-Rollin, Félix Pyat, and other red Republicans defeated in their attempts to establish the Commune at Paris to supersede the Government; reconciliation effected by Rochefort, about Oct. 14

Oct. 12, Riots at Honfleur: the people oppose the embarkation of cattle to England; similar riots at St. Malo, Oct. 15

——, M. de Kératry quits Paris in a balloon; at Madrid fails in obtaining assistance from Prim, Oct. 19, 20

About Oct. 16, M. Edmond Adam, prefect of police; replacing M. de Kératry, sent on a foreign mission

Oct. 19, Marseilles disturbed by red Republicans; Esquiros still in office

Oct., Publication of the imperial correspondence seized in the Tuileries

Oct. 25, Decree for a loan of 10,000,000*l.* issued on behalf of the French Government

Oct. 26, The Imperial Guard suppressed

Oct. 28, Circular of Gambetta stigmatizing the surrender of Metz (on Oct. 27) as a crime

Oct. 30, Death of M. Baroche in Jersey

——, M. Thiers arrives in Paris with news of the surrender of Metz and the proposals for an armistice

Oct. 31, Riots in Paris: General Trochu threatened; the principal members of the defense Government imprisoned in the Hôtel de Ville; Ledru-Rollin, Victor Hugo, and Gustave Flourens, and others, established as a committee of public safety and of the Commune of Paris, under the direction of M. Picard; the National Guard releases the Government, and order is restored

——, General Boyer, replying to Gambetta, says, "We capitulated with hunger"

——, The Empress arrives at Wilhelmshöhe; interview of Bazaine with the Emperor

Nov., Etienne Arago and other mayors of Paris resign, Nov. 1; M. Jules Ferry, a member of the defense Government, becomes mayor of Paris

Nov. 1, Marshals Canrobert and Le Bœuf and many generals at Wilhelmshöhe

——, Proclamation of Gambetta calling on the army to avenge the dishonor at Metz

——, The Government proclaim a *plebiscite* in Paris on Nov. 3 to ascertain whether the people maintain the power of the Government of National Defense

Nov. 2, M. Rochefort, member of the defense Government, resigns

Nov. 3, Result of the *plebiscite:*—for the defense Government, 557,976; against, 62,638

——, Resignation of M. Esquiros at Marseilles, succeeded by M. Alphonse Gent

——, The ex-Empress returned to Chislehurst

Nov. 4, Mobilization of all able-bodied men between 20 and 40 ordered

Nov. 6, Failure of the negotiations for an armistice

——, 6, Félix Pyat and others arrested for the affair of Oct. 31

Nov. 10, Decree for melting some of the church-bells to make cannon

Dec. 10, Alexander Dumas, novelist and dramatist, dies

Dec. 11, The delegate Government removed from Tours to Bordeaux

Dec. 20, Murder of Lieutenant Arnaud at Lyons by the people for resisting them

About Dec. 23, Trial of 21 peasants for murder of M. Moneys (*see* Aug. 16); 4 condemned to death; others to imprisonment

Dec. 30, Firm proclamation of Trochu at Paris

1871

Jan. 1, Gambetta at Bordeaux declares that the Government only holds office for defense of the country; demonstration in honor of the Republic

Jan. 19, Foreigners not permitted to leave Paris by the Germans

Jan. 22, Fierce speech of Gambetta at Lille, demanding continuance of the war

Jan. 23, Disturbances at Paris suppressed by the army

Jan. 24, Resignation of Trochu; Vinoy made Governor of Paris

Jan. 28, Capitulation of Paris; armistice signed by Favre and Bismarck

Jan. 31, Disavowed by Gambetta at Bordeaux

Feb. 1, Manifesto of the duc d'Aumale in favor of a constitutional monarchy

Feb. 3, Arrival of food from London to relieve Paris

Feb. 4, The defense Government publish their reasons for capitulation (2,000,000 people in Paris with only ten days' provisions); and annul Gambetta's decree, Feb. 4; he and his Ministry resign, Feb. 5, 6

Feb. 8, Four murderers of M. Moneys (Aug. 16, 1870) executed

——, Proclamation of Napoleon III. "Betrayed by fortune," he condemns the Government of Sept. 4; states that his Government was four times confirmed in 20 years; submits to the judgment of time; saying "that a nation cannot long obey those who have no right to command"

——, General election of a National Assembly

Feb. 12, First meeting of the new National Assembly

Feb. 13, Garibaldi resigns his election; Grévy elected President by 519 out of 528, Feb. 16

Feb. 15, Supplementary armistice signed

Feb. 16, Termination of the war; the Belfort garrison (12,000) marches out with military honors

Feb. 17, "*Pact of Bordeaux*": M. Thiers made chief of the executive power, by agreement of the different parties in the Assembly; voted Feb. 18

——, Thiers Ministry: Dufaure, Justice; Jules Favre, Foreign; Picard, Interior; Jules Simon, Public Instruction; Lambrecht, Commerce; General Le Flo, War; Admiral Pothuan, Marine; De Larcy, Public Works

Feb. 18, The French Government recognized by the Great Powers of Europe

Feb. 22, 23, 24, Negotiations for peace between Thiers and Bismarck

Feb. 25, Preliminaries of a treaty of peace accepted by MM. Thiers and Favre, and 15 delegates of the National Assembly at Versailles (cession of parts of Alsace and Lorraine, including Strasbourg and Metz, and payment of five milliards of francs—200,000,-000*l.*); signed Feb. 26

March 1, Preliminaries of the treaty accepted by the Assembly (546 to 107); the fall of the Empire unanimously confirmed; and the Emperor stigmatized

——, A strong party of the National Guard seize some cannons and transport them to Montmartre and Belleville, to defend themselves against the Germans entering Paris

——, The Emperor of Germany reviews about 100,000 of his troops at Longchamp near Paris

——, About 30,000 Germans enter Paris; remain 48 hours; depart March 3

March 6, Impeachment of the defense Government demanded by the party of the left (Victor Hugo, Louis Blanc, Quinet, and others)

——, The ex-Emperor protests against his deposition

March 7–10, The army of the north and other special army corps dissolved

March 10, Meeting of National Guard in Paris quelled

——, The National Assembly vote for removal to Versailles (461–104)

March 11, *Le Vengeur* and four other violent journals suppressed in Paris by Vinoy

March 12, Blanqui, Flourens, and others condemned for insurrection of Oct. 31, 1870

March 15, Central committee of Republican confederation of National Guards (termed "the Government of the Buttes") meet; depose Vinoy and appoint Garibaldi General-in-Chief

March 18, Insurrection at Paris: the regular troops take possession of the Buttes Montmartre and Belleville, for the Assembly; the National Guard attempt to recover them; after a brief conflict the troops fraternize with the insurgents, who capture and shoot Generals Lecomte and Clément Thomas, and take possession of the Hôtel de Ville; barricades erected in Belleville and other places; General Vinoy with the gendarmerie retire across the Seine

March 19, The insurgents nominate a central committee of the National Guard, headed by Assy, a workman, which takes possession of public offices; Thiers issues a circular, enjoining obedience to the Assembly

——, The central committee order communal election in Paris; and liberate about 11,000 political prisoners in Paris, March 20

March 20, The National Assembly meet at Versailles; propose conciliatory measures; and appoint a committee to support the Government

——, Napoleon III arrives at Dover

——, The Bank of France saved by the courage of the Governor, Marquis de Plœuc, and by the forbearance of Citizen Beslay

March 21, Requisitions levied on the Paris shopkeepers

March 22, Unarmed demonstration of the Friends of Order; they are fired on by the insurgents; 10 killed, 20 wounded

——, Lullier arrested by the central committee

March 23, Admiral Saisset appointed commander of the National Guard for the Assembly

——, The 69th regiment of the line retire to Versailles

March 24, The central committee appoint some of their delegates generals

March 25, The insurgents hold central Paris; Saisset returns to Versailles

March 26, Municipal elections at Paris; 200,000 out of 500,000 vote; majority of two-thirds in favor of the insurgents

March 28, The Government of the Commune proclaimed at the Hôtel de Ville

——, Meeting of the conference for the peace at Brussels

March 29, Gustave Flourens, Blanqui, and Félix Pyat now at the head of the movement; they propose revival of the system of the Italian republics of the middle ages

——, The remission of part of the rents due by tenants ordered; the standing army to be named the National Guard

April 1, Reign of terror

April 2, Military operations commence 9 A.M.; action at Courbevoie; Flourens marches his troops to Versailles, *via* Rueil

April 3, The corps d'armée of General Bergeret at the Rond Point, near Neuilly, stopped by the artillery of Mont Valérien; exchange of shots between Fort Issy and Fort Vanves, occupied by the insurgents, and Meudon

April 4, General Duval made prisoner in the engagement at Châtillon and shot; death of Flourens at Chatou; Delescluze, Cournet, and Vermorel succeed Bergeret, Eudes, and Duval on the Executive Commission; Cluseret, Delegate of War, and Bergeret, Commandant of Paris forces

April 4, Communist insurrection at Marseilles suppressed

April 5, General Cluseret commences active operations; military service compulsory for all citizens under 40; the Archbishop of Paris arrested

April 6, Extension of action to Neuilly and Courbevoie; severe decree concerning complicity with Versailles, and arrest of hostages; Dombrowski succeeds Bergeret as commandant of Paris; the guillotine burnt on the Place Voltaire

April 8, Federals abandon Neuilly; commission of barricades created and presided over by Gailard Senior; military occupation of the railway termini by the insurgents

April 9, Insurgents repulsed in an attempt to take Châtillon; forts Vanves and Montrouge disabled; Mont Valérien shells the Avenue des Ternes; Bergeret arrested by order of the Commune

April 11, Marshal MacMahon, Commander-in-Chief for the Assembly, distributes his forces, and commences the investment of Fort Issy

April 12, Versailles batteries established on Châtillon; the Orleans railway and telegraph cut; communications of the insurgents with the south intercepted; decree ordering the fall of the column Vendôme

April 14, The redoubt of Gennevilliers taken; the troops of Versailles advance to the Château de Bécon, a post of importance; Assy at the bar of the Commune

——, The National Assembly pass the new municipal bill (419–18)

April 16, Complementary elections; organization of a court martial under the presidence of Rossel, chief officer of the staff

April 17, Capture and fortification of the Château de Bécon by the Versailles troops

April 18, Station and houses at Asnières taken by the army of Versailles

April 19, The Communists appeal to the nation

April 20, Bagneux occupied by the Versaillais; reorganization of commissions; Eudes appointed inspector-general of the southern forts; transfers his quarters from Montrouge to the palace of the Legion of Honor

April 25, The Versailles batteries at Breteuil, Brimborion, Meudon, and Moulin de Pierre trouble the federal Fort Issy, and battery between Bagneux and Châtillon shells Fort Vanves; truce at Neuilly from 9 A.M. to 5 P.M.; the inhabitants of Neuilly enter Paris by the Porte des Ternes

April 26, Capture of Les Moulineaux, outpost of the insurgents, by the troops, who strongly fortify themselves on the 27th and 28th

April 29, Cemetery and park of Issy taken by the Versaillais in the night; freemasons make a new attempt at reconciliation; the Commune levies a sum of two millions of francs from the railway companies

April 30, A flag of truce sent to Fort Issy by the Versaillais, calling upon the federals to surrender; General Eudes puts fresh troops in the fort, and takes the command; Cluseret imprisoned at Mazas by order of the Commune; Rossel appointed provisional delegate of war

May 1, The Versaillais take the station of Clamart and the Château of Issy; creation of the committee of public safety; members: Antoine Arnauld, Léo Meillet, Ranvier, Félix Pyat, Charles Gérardin; alleged massacre of Communist prisoners

May 3, Lacretelle carries the redoubt of Moulin Saquet

May 5, Colonel Rossel appointed to the direction of military affairs, defines the military quarters of Dombrowski, La Cécilia, Wroblewski, Bergeret, and Eudes

May 5, Central committee of the National Guard charged with administration of war; the Chapelle Expiatoire condemned to destruction—the materials to be sold by auction

May 6, Suppression of newspapers

May 8, Battery of Montretout (70 marine guns) opens fire; Thiers exhorts the Parisians to rise against the Commune

——, Morning; insurgents evacuate the Fort Issy; the committee of public safety renewed; members: Ranvier, Antoine Arnauld, Gambon, Eudes, Delescluze; Rossel resigns

May 10, Treaty of peace with Germany signed at Frankfort

——, Cannon from the Fort Issy taken to Versailles; decree for the demolition of M. Thiers' house; Delescluze appointed delegate of war

May 11, Thiers opposed; offers to resign; the Assembly vote confidence in him (495–10)

May 12, Troops take possession of the Convent des Oiseaux at Issy, and the Lyceum at Vanves; Aubre, the composer, dies, aged 89

May 13, Triumphal entry of the troops into Versailles with flags and cannon taken from the convent; evacuation of the village of Issy completed; Fort Vanves taken by the troops

May 14, Vigorous cannonade from the batteries of Courbevoie, Bécon, Asnières, on Levallois and Clichy, both villages evacuated; commencement of the demolition of house of M. Thiers

May 15, Report of the rearmament of Montmartre

May 16, The column Vendôme overthrown

About May 17, Stringent conscription in Paris

May 17, Secession from the Communist Government; a central club formed; a battalion of women formed

——, Silver ornaments in churches seized; explosion of a cartridge factory near the Champ de Mars; above 100 killed

May 18, The Assembly adopt the treaty of peace

May 21, Rochefort brought a prisoner to Versailles; last sitting of the Commune

——, Noon, explosion of the powder magazine of the Manège d'Etat-Major (staff riding-school); the hostages transferred from Mazas to La Roquette; Assy arrested in Paris by the Versaillais; the Assembly votes the reërection of the column Vendôme; M. Ducatel, at the risk of his life, having signaled that the way was clear, the Versailles troops enter Paris by the gates of St. Cloud and Montrouge, 2 P.M.; take possession of the south and west, and about 10,000 prisoners, after some conflicts, May 22

May 22–27, Reported results of seven days' fighting in Paris: regular troops, 877 killed, 645 wounded, 183 missing; insurgents, about 50,000 dead, 25,000 prisoners; nearly all the leaders killed or prisoners; about a fourth part of Paris destroyed

Estimated loss of property through the insurrection, 32,000,000l., April, May

May 23, Montmartre taken by Douai and Ladmirault: death of Dombrowski. Morning: Assy arrives at Versailles; execution of gendarmes and Gustave Chaudey at the prison of Sainte-Pélagie. Night: the Tuileries set on fire; Delescluze and the committee of public safety hold permanent sittings at the Hôtel de Ville

May 24, Morning: Palais Royal, Ministry of Finance, Hôtel de Ville, &c., set on fire; 1 P.M., the powder magazine at the Palais du Luxembourg blown up; the committee of public safety organize detachments of fusee-bearers; petroleum pumped into burning buildings; Raoul Rigault shot in the afternoon by the soldiers. Evening: execution in the prison of La Roquette of the Archbishop, Abbé Deguerry, President Bonjean, and 64 others hostages

May 25, The forts Montrouge, Hautes-Bruyères, Bicêtre evacuated by the insurgents; the death of Delescluze reported; executions in the Avenue d'Italie of the Pères Dominicans of Arcueil

May 26, 27, 16 priests and 38 gendarmes shot at Belleville by the insurgents; many women fighting, and casting petroleum into fires, shot

May 28, The Buttes Chaumont, the heights of Belleville, and the cemetery of Père Lachaise carried by the troops; taking of the prison of La Roquette by the marines; deliverance of 169 hostages; the investment of Belleville complete; last position captured by MacMahon; fighting ends, 5 P.M.

May 29, Federal garrison of Vincennes surrendered at discretion

——, Thiers' decree for disarming Paris and abolishing the National Guard of the Seine

May 30, Victor Hugo expelled from Belgium

——, Wholesale execution of prisoners by the Marquis de Gallifet; Paris put under martial law; about 50,000 insurgents still at large

May 31, Severe letter from Prince Napoleon Jerome to Jules Favre, dated

June 6, Changes in the Ministry; resignation (and reappointment of some) of those who had been members of the Government of Defense

June 7, Solemn funeral of Darboy, Archbishop of Paris

June 8, Abrogation of the laws of proscription by the Assembly (484–103); elections of the duc d'Aumale and the Prince de Joinville declared valid

June 12, Imposition of new taxes (463,000,000 francs) and a loan proposed by M. Pouyer Quertier

June 13, 14, General Trochu's powerful speech defending the "Government of National Defense"

June 14, Army of reserve ordered to be dissolved

About June 14, Financial measures of M. Pouyer-Quertier opposed by Dufaure and the free traders

About June 20, Theaters and public places reopened in Paris

June 22, Letter from M. Guizot to M. Grévy recommending political moderation to all parties, and maintenance of the present Government published

June 28, The loan of 2 milliards francs (80,000,000l.) decreed June 26; subscription opened, June 27; about 4 milliards subscribed for in France alone

July 2, 132 members elected for the Assembly; includes Gambetta, and a few Legitimists and Bonapartists; the rest support the Government

July 5, Letter from the comte de Chambord at Chambord, professing devotion to France, and adhesion to modern policy and liberality; but declining to give up the white flag of Henry IV; he retires to Germany to avoid all pretext for agitation

July 8, The Government said to have 500 votes in the Assembly; bill for new taxes passed (483 to 5)

About July 14, 20,000,000l., part of the indemnity, paid to the Germans

July 15, Prince Napoleon Jerome expelled from France (at Havre)

July 21, M. Devienne, President of the Court of Cassation, acquitted of blame for settling disputes relative to an imperial scandal (in Nov., 1860)

About July 23, Jules Favre, Foreign Minister, resigns; succeeded by Charles de Remusat about Aug. 3

Aug., Full compensation for losses claimed by the invaded provinces refused by Thiers, who acknowledges no debt, but proposes to act generously

Aug. 8, Trial of Communist prisoners at Paris begun

Aug. 24, Great dissensions in the Assembly between the Monarchists and Republican parties; resignation of Thiers not accepted; prolongation of his power and the sovereign and constituent authority of the Assembly voted (443 to 227) about Aug. 25.

Aug. 31, Thiers' powers prolonged, and nominated President of the French Republic by the Assembly; to continue till the Assembly shall terminate its labors (the Rivet-Vitet proposition), 491–93

Sept., French postage increased

Sept., Société de Prévoyance established to counteract the *Internationale;* becomes permanent

Sept. 2, Ferre and Lullier sentenced to death, others to transportation or imprisonment; 3 women (pétroleuses) sentenced to death for throwing petroleum on fires Sept. 5

Sept. 6, Bill for making the whole nation bear the losses of the invaded provinces adopted by the Assembly

Sept. 8, Rossel, Communist General, sentenced to death

Sept. 12, Message from Thiers to the Assembly; consideration of the budget adjourned; read Sept. 13

Sept. 14, Disarmament of the National Guard begun at Lyons, &c.

——, Bill introduced concerning treaty with Germany relating to tariff on goods from Alsace and Lorraine, and the reducing German troops in France to 50,000 men; adopted by the Assembly (533–33); the session declared closed, 2 A.M., Sept. 17

Sept., Courts martial on Communists go on

Sept. 15, "Permanent Committee" of 25 of different parties appointed by the Assembly to watch over the course of the Government during the recess (Sept. 17–Dec. 4)

——, 25,000 Communists yet to be tried; about half to be set free

About Sept. 20, Evacuation of Paris forts by the Germans begun

Sept. 21, Rochefort (of *La Lanterne* and *Le Mot d'Ordre*) sentenced to life-imprisonment

——, Difficulty in settling the Alsace and Lorraine treaty

Oct., Tranquil election of above 2,000 general councilors

Oct. 8, M. Pouyer-Quertier, the French Finance Minister, arrives at Berlin

——, M. Lambrecht, Minister of the Interior, dies suddenly; succeeded by M. Casimir Périer Oct. 10

Oct. 12 and 13, Convention for evacuation of 6 departments, and finance convention of Alsace and Lorraine signed; ratifications exchanged Oct. 21

Oct. 22, Count Benedetti publishes an apology, attacking the Prussian Government; Count Bismarck replies (in *Official Journal*) disproving his assertions

About Oct. 25, Dispute with Tunis settled

Oct. 28, Prince Napoleon resigns his seat in the council-general of Corsica; and denounces intimidation

Nov., Insurrection in Algeria ended

Nov. 18, Eight of the murderers of Generals Lecomte and Thomas condemned

Nov. 28, Rossel, Ferre, and Bourgeois, Communist leaders, shot at Satory in presence of 3,000 soldiers

Nov. 30, Gaston Crémieux executed at Marseilles

Dec. 4, Territory held by Germans put into state of siege

Dec. 7, Thiers reads his message to the Assembly; deprecates free trade, but proposes moderate protection of French manufactures

——, Sharp dispatch from Count Bismarck in reference to the acquittal of murderers of Germans at Melun and Paris

Dec. 19, After some discussion with M. Thiers, the duc d'Aumale and Prince de Joinville take their seats in the Assembly

Dec. 22, A committee of the Assembly decide against the Assembly removing to Paris

Dec. 28, Income tax proposed and negatived

1872

Jan. 7, Vautram, a Government candidate, elected deputy for Paris, and not Victor Hugo

Jan. 12, The duc de Persigny dies

Jan. 19, Long debate in the Assembly; opposition to the proposed taxes on raw materials; Government defeated (377–307)

Jan. 20, Resignation of Thiers and the Ministry opposed by the Assembly; MacMahon writes that the army will respect the orders of a majority of the Assembly, but not obey dictatorship; Thiers resumes office

About **Jan.** 22, Death of Arlès Dufour, of Lyons, St. Simonian and free trader

Jan. 22, The Government taxes voted

Jan. 23, Conviction of the assassins of Archbishop Darboy and others (on May 24, 1871), 1 to death

Jan. 29, Manifesto of the comte de Chambord; his mind unchanged; he will not become a legitimate king by revolution

Feb., Abrogation of the commercial treaties with Great Britain and Belgium determined on

Feb. 1, Sardou's play, "Rabagas," satirizing the radicals, causes much excitement

Feb. 2, Proposed return of the Assembly to Paris negatived (377–318); resignation of Casimir Périer, Minister of the Interior

Feb., League for commercial liberty formed

About **Feb.** 15, M. Rouher elected a member of the Assembly

Feb. 17, Five Communists sentenced to death for murder of the Dominicans on May 25

About **Feb.** 17, Blanqui condemned to transportation to a fortified prison

Feb., Universal subscription to pay the indemnity to the Germans begins

About **Feb.** 21, Manifesto in favor of a constitutional monarchy signed by about 280 of the "Right"

Feb. 22, Assassins of Generals Lecomte and Clément Thomas executed

About **March** 5, Janvier de la Motte, a prefect, prosecuted for forgery, &c., by Government, acquitted; M. Pouyer-Quertier, who gives evidence in his favor, resigns

March 15, The treaty of commerce with Great Britain (1860) denounced (to cease in 12 months)

March, War budget of 27,000,000*l.* (formerly 10,000,-000*l.*) proposed

April 10, Abolition of passports for British subjects announced

April 22, Law against the International Society placarded

May 12, In a letter, the ex-Emperor takes upon himself the whole responsibility of the surrender at Sedan

May 21, Rouher in the Assembly repels the duc d'Audiffret Pasquier's severe attack on the Empire

May 25, Three more condemned Communists shot

June 4, Marshal Vaillant dies

About **June** 9, Thiers threatens to resign at opposition in the chamber

June 20, Interview of delegates of the majority (the right) in the Assembly with Thiers (respecting his policy); much censured

June 26 *et seq.*, Budget for 1873; deficiency, 4,800,000*l.*; 8,000,000*l.* to be raised; Thiers advocates duty on raw materials, and opposes income tax

June 29, New convention between Germany and France respecting speedy payment of the indemnity and evacuation of territory signed

July, The majority in the Assembly propose MacMahon as President in place of Thiers

July 14, Anniversary of the destruction of the Bastille celebrated by public dinners; important moderate speech by Gambetta at Ferté-sous-Jouarre

July 25, Three Communists (murderers of hostages) executed at Satory

July 26, Announcement of a public loan of 120,000,000*l.* at 6¼ %.

July, The loan subscribed for, nearly 12 times the amount, chiefly in France

Aug. 3, Thiers' financial measures carried (taxes on raw materials, &c.); the session of the Assembly closed

Sept. 11, Meeting of Guizot and Thiers at Val Richer

Sept. 14, Arrest of Edmond About at Saverne, by the Germans, on account of a newspaper article (written Oct., 1871); released Sept. 21

Sept. 15, Three more Communist murderers shot at Satory

Sept. 22, Attempted celebration of the anniversary of the establishment of the first French Republic; banquet at Chambéry stopped

Sept., M. Thiers and the Ministry in Paris

Sept. 27, Progress of Gambetta in the south; violent speech at Grenoble against Thiers

Oct. 6, Pilgrimage of about 20,000 persons to the grotto of the Virgin Mary at Lourdes, on account of alleged miracles (the Virgin was said to have appeared to two girls, Feb. 14, 1858)

Oct. 9, The supreme council of war constituted; includes MacMahon, Canrobert, duc d'Aumale, and other eminent generals; first meeting, Thiers present

Oct. 12, Prince Napoleon and Princess Clotilde come to Paris; expelled by order of the Government (he protests)

Oct. 15, Letter from the comte de Chambord to M. de la Rochette, protesting against a republic, and asserting that France can be saved by a monarchy alone; that she is Catholic and monarchical, and cannot, therefore, perish; dated

Oct., **Nov.**, The Germans evacuate Haute Marne and other departments

Oct. 31, Banquet of monarchical party at Bordeaux

Nov. 5, New commercial treaty with Great Britain signed at London

Nov. 11, Reassembling of the National Assembly; Thiers in his message declares that the Republic is the legal Government; and that to exist it must be conservative; and proposes changes Nov. 12

Nov. 18, Fruitless attack of General Changarnier on Thiers' policy and Gambetta's speech at Grenoble; motion to pass to order of the day; majority for Government, 150 (300 did not vote)

Nov. 19, M. Kerdrel proposes a commission to consider Thiers' proposals for changes; adopted

Nov. 19, 20, Thiers threatens to resign; crisis

Nov. 26, Report of the commission read by M. Batbie, claiming the right of the Assembly to frame a constitution with a responsible Ministry; the President not to speak in the Assembly, &c.; he advocated "gouvernement de combat"

Nov. 28, Amendment proposed by Dufaure, Minister of Justice, accepting ministerial responsibility, rejected by the committee

Nov. 29, M. Thiers addresses the Assembly; declares he prefers the English to the American system; but that a monarchy in France is at present impossible; that he is faithful to the Republic; and that he wishes to render it conservative; and that he has for two years served his country with boundless devotion; Dufaure's amendment carried by 370-334 (union of Royalists with Bonapartists against the Radicals)

Nov. 30, Vote of censure on the Home Minister (Lanfranc) carried; 305-299; he resigns

Dec. 6, Agitation respecting the appointment of the commission of 30, proposed by Dufaure; it consists of 19 for the right, 11 for the Government; changes in the Ministry announced Dec. 8

Dec. 10, Manifesto of the left, proposing a dissolution of the Assembly by legal means

Dec. 14, Negatived by the Assembly (490-201)

Dec. 23, Execution of Poitevin, a traitor

Dec., Debt 748,700,000*l.* (before the war, about 460,500,000*l.*)

1873

Jan. 6, Meeting of the National Assembly

Jan. 9, Death of Napoleon III at Chislehurst

Jan. 15, Bonapartist manifesto; "the Emperor is dead, but the Empire is living and indestructible"

Jan., The "30 committee" considering Tallon's project for a constitution

Jan. 22, Three Communist murderers shot at Satory

Jan. 26, Reported recognition of the comte de Chambord as King by the Orleans princes

Feb. 2, Powerful speech of Thiers before the commission of 30 against their proposed changes

Feb. 8, The commission of 30 close their meetings

Feb., Letter of the comte de Chambord published; destroys all hopes of the fusion of the Bourbons

March 4, Debate begins on the report of the commission, which reserves the legislative rights of the present Assembly, and the adherence to the provisional state in accordance with the "pacte de Bordeaux," Feb. 27; powerful speech of Thiers in favor of this "truce of parties," adopted (475-199)

March 15, Convention for the total evacuation of the departments in Sept. on payment of indemnity, signed at Berlin

March 17, Declaration in the Assembly "that M. Thiers has deserved well of his country"

April 2, M. Grévy resigns the presidency on account of the conduct of the party of the right

May 18, Changes in the Ministry:—Casimir Périer, Interior; W. H. Waddington, of Cambridge, Public Instruction (in place of De Goulard and Jules Simon)

May 19, Meeting of the National Assembly; the Government introduce their constitutional bills, May 21; the duc de Broglie leads an attack on the Government, May 23; speech of Thiers; the Government defeated (362-348), May 24

May 24, Resignation of Thiers and his Ministry accepted (368-339); Marshal MacMahon, duc de Magenta (born, 1808) elected President of the Republic by 390 votes (the left did not vote); he accepts the office, declaring his independence of party, May 24; in his message to the Assembly he says, "The post in which you have placed me is that of a sentinel, who has to watch over the integrity of your sovereign power," May 26

May 26, The duc de Broglie chief of the new Ministry

June 3, General Ladmirault succeeds MacMahon in the command of the army of Versailles

June 11, Private circular of the Minister to prefects requesting them to sound newspapers of his department; censured in the Assembly

June 19, The Assembly (by a large majority) order the prosecution of Ranc, formerly a Communist, now deputy for Lyons

July 10, Grand review of the renovated army at Paris, and Assembly prorogued

July 24, Renewal of the Anglo-French treaty of Jan. 23, 1860 (till June 30, 1877); signed; ratified, July 29

Aug. 2, Evacuation of all the French territories by the Germans, except Verdun

Aug. 5, Fusion of the Legitimists and Orleanists, after an interview of the comte de Paris with the comte de Chambord; the latter recognized as chief

Aug. 6, Odilon-Barrot died

Aug. 15, The Imperial Prince Napoleon declares the policy of his family to be "Everything by the people for the people"

Sept. 5, Last instalment of 10,000,000*l.* of the indemnity of 200,000,000*l.* paid

Sept., About 2,700 Communists yet to be disposed of

Sept. 13, Verdun quitted by the Germans

Sept. 16, The last quitted the French territory

Sept. 19, Letter from comte de Chambord to the vicomte de Rodez-Benavent; not explicit; shows tendency to concession; says, "I want the co-operation of all, and all have need of me"

Sept. 26, Prince Napoleon Jerome joins the republican party

Sept. 29, Letter from Thiers to mayor of Nancy, censuring the fusionists, who "without the consent of France pretend to decide upon her destinies"

Sept. 30, France divided into 18 new military regions; 18 generals appointed

Oct. 6, Trial of Marshal Bazaine, late commander of the army of the Rhine in 1870, for alleged treachery and misconduct at Metz; duc d'Aumale President of the court

Oct. 6, Changes in the Ministry; duc Decazes, Foreign and Changarnier, War Minister

Oct. 9, Rouher's letter to the Bonapartists against the Monarchists

Oct. 12, M. Remusat and 3 other Republicans elected deputies

Oct. 13, Ranc condemned to death *in contumaciam*

Oct. 18, Manifesto of the Monarchists proposing restoration of the monarchy, guaranteeing all necessary liberties, &c.

Oct. 23, M. Léon Say and the left center decline negotiation with the Monarchists; who threaten abstention in the next elections, if successfully opposed

Oct. 27, Letter from the comte de Chambord to M. Chesnelong; he says, "I retract nothing, and curtail nothing of my previous declarations. I do not wish to begin a reign of reparation by an act of weakness; if enfeebled to-day, I should be powerless to-morrow; I am a necessary pilot; the only one capable of guiding the ship to port, because I have for it a mission of authority."

Oct. 30, M. Léon Say and the left center say the moment has arrived for the organization of a conservative Republic

Nov. 5, Meeting of National Assembly; message from Marshal MacMahon, requesting increased and prolonged power (ten years); this referred to a committee of 15; voted urgent (by 360 to 350)

Nov. 6, M. Buffet reëlected President

Nov. 7, Conspiracy at Autun to seize Marchioness MacMahon; offenders convicted

Nov. 13, Eight of the committee vote for prolongation of MacMahon's presidency for five years after date of meeting of the next legislature, under existing conditions till the passing of constitutional laws; the others vote for ten years' prolongation without conditions

Nov. 17, M. Laboulaye's report of the committee laid before the Assembly; MacMahon's message suggesting 7 years' prolongation of his powers

Nov. 18, Warm debate in the Assembly; majority of 68 for ministers; 7 years' power voted to Marshal MacMahon (383–317), Nov. 19; decree Nov. 20

About Nov. 20, Incognito visit of the comte de Chambord to Paris

Nov. 20, Ministry resigns; reconstituted, Nov. 26; duc de Broglie, Minister of Interior; duc Decazes, Foreign Minister

Dec. 4, Committee of 30 for constitutional changes, completed

Dec. 5, Holds its first meeting, Batbie, President

Dec. 10, Bazaine's trial ends; he is found guilty of capitulating with his army (of 170,000 men) in the open field; of negotiating dishonorably with the enemy, and surrendering a fortified place; sentence, death and degradation; commuted to 20 years' imprisonment, Dec. 12

Dec. 28, Peaceful Republican demonstration in Paris at the funeral of Victor Hugo's second son, François

1874

Jan. 8, Meeting of the Assembly; majority against the nomination of mayors bill, through the Legitimists (268–226); the Ministry resign, Jan. 9; vote of confidence in the Ministry (379 to 329), Jan. 12; the Ministers resume office, Jan. 13

Jan. 17, Vote for Ministers on the nomination of mayors bill (341–336)

Jan. 21, Nomination of mayors bill passed; many mayors replaced, Feb.

March 1, Ledru-Rollin and Lepetit elected members of the National Assembly

March 11, New electoral law presented by the committee; about 3 millions disfranchised

March 16, Demonstration at Chislehurst on Prince Louis Napoleon's coming of age (at 18); 6,000 Frenchmen present; he says that he waits the result of the 8th *plébiscite*

March 25, Gabriel Hugelmann, political spy and swindler, convicted and sentenced to 5 years' imprisonment

About March 25, Ferrand, contractor (made about 80,000*l.* during war), fined and imprisoned

March 27, Proposal of Dahirel, Legitimist, of a law enacting that on June 1 the Assembly should vote for either a monarchy or republic, negatived (330–256)

March 30, Escape of Rochefort, the Communist, from New Caledonia announced

April 4, Death of Beulé, ex-Minister

April 14, Clément Duvernois, ex-Imperial Minister, arrested for suspected fraud

May 16, The Ministry, defeated on electoral law (381–317), resigns

Announced May 21, Rochefort and other Communists arrive at San Francisco

May 22, M. Goulard failing to form a ministry, the President reappoints the former without Broglie; nominal head, General De Cissey

May 24, Bourgoing, a Bonapartist, elected for Nièvre (asserted that he was devoted to the Marshal)

——, Thiers addresses some Gironde friends; refers to the failure of his opponents; and recommends dissolution of the Assembly

June 1, Electoral bill; Assembly pass to second reading (393–318)

June 6, Bonnard, Communist, condemned for murder, Feb. 25, shot

June 8, 9, Hot disputes between Republicans and Bonapartists; left center demand the establishment of the Republic, or dissolution of the Assembly

June 10, Electoral bill; age of electors fixed at 21, not 25 (defeat of Ministry)

June 13, Gambetta having called the Bonapartists "*misérables*," is struck at a railway station by comte de Sainte Croix, June 11, who is condemned to fine and imprisonment

June 14, 15, Casimir-Périer (leader of left center) moves for recognition of the Republic; MacMahon President till Nov. 20, 1880, and revision of the constitution; voted "urgent" (345–341)

June 15, Duc de Rochefoucauld-Bisaccia's motion for restoration of the legitimate monarchy negatived; he resigns British embassy

June 19, Rochefort in London

June 29, In his order of the day, Marshal MacMahon declares that with the army he will maintain the authority of the land for the seven years

——, Casimir-Périer's motion negatived by commission of 30

June, The "fusion" between Legitimists and Orleanists ended; conflict now between Republicans and Bonapartists

July 2, Manifesto from comte de Chambord, saying, "France has need of monarchy. My birth has made me your king. . . . The Christian and French monarchy is in its very essence limited (*temperée*). It admits of the existence of two chambers: one nominated by the sovereign, the other by the nation. . . . I do not wish for those barren parliamentary struggles, whence the sovereign too frequently issues powerless and enfeebled. . . . I reject the formula of foreign importation, which all our national traditions repudiate, with its king who reigns and does not govern."—Signed, Henri V

July 4, M. Goulard, ex-Minister, dies

July 8, Debate on the manifesto; Legitimists defeated; Ministers defeated on a motion in favor of the septennate, resign (368–331); their resignation not accepted by the Marshal

July 9, He states, in a message to the Assembly, his determination to maintain the law of Nov. 20, and exhorts them to pass the constitutional laws

July 16, Reports of committee, by Ventavon (the bill proposes maintenance of the authority of the President of the Republic; ministerial responsibility; two legislative assemblies; dissolution of the Chamber of Deputies by the President; &c.), suspended

July 23, Casimir-Périer's motion for a republic rejected (375–333)

    Malleville's motion for dissolution of the Assembly rejected (374–332)

Aug. 9, Marshal Bazaine escapes from the isle of Ste. Marguerite (see Dec., 1873) 10 P.M. [His wife asserted that he descended by an old gutter by means of a knotted rope; was received into a boat by her and her nephew, Alvarez de Rul, and conveyed to the steamer *Baron Ricasola*, which landed him at Genoa]

Aug. 16, Forcade de Roquette, a Minister under the Empire, dies, aged 53

Aug. 17, MacMahon's progress in the N. W. provinces; well received

Aug. 31, Vendôme column restored

Sept. 12, Death of M. Guizot

Sept. 14, Bazaine's defense sent by him to the *New York Herald*, dated Sept. 6, published in London

Sept. 17, Trials for complicity in Bazaine's escape; Colonel Villette and others sentenced to imprisonment

Sept. 27, Thiers, at Vizille near Grenoble, in reply to an address, says, "Since you cannot establish the monarchy, establish the republic, and do it frankly and sincerely"

Sept. 29, Poirier executed at Chartres for 5 murders

Early Oct., Severe note from Spanish Government complaining of French neglect in regard to the Carlists on the Spanish frontier

Nov. 25, Clément Duvernois, ex-Imperial Minister, convicted of fraud; 2 years' imprisonment

Nov., Political parties: Extreme right. Legitimists: adherents of Henry V. Moderate right: Monarchists. Right center: Septennates, Imperialists or Bonapartists. Left center: Moderate Republicans (chief, Thiers). Left: more pronounced. Extreme left: Radicals (chief, Gambetta)

Nov., Comte de Chambord requests his friends not to vote so as to prevent or delay the restoration of the monarchy

Dec. 3, The Assembly meets; firm moderate message from MacMahon

Dec. 31, Sudden death of M. Ledru-Rollin

1875

Jan. 6, President in his message having recommended the passing a bill for constituting a Senate, motion against it passed (420 to 250); Ministers' resignation not accepted, Jan. 7

Announced Jan., Cost of the war (395,400,000*l*.)

Died Jan. 6, Emile Péreire, financier

Jan. 17, A Bonapartist elected deputy for Hautes-Pyrénées

Jan., Nine days' debate on the new army bill

Jan. 22, Stormy debate on Ventavon's bill for organizing MacMahon's powers, 1st reading passed (557 to 146)

Jan. 29, Laboulaye's amendment rejected (359–335)

Jan. 31, Wallon's amendment (the President of the Republic to be elected by absolute majority of the two chambers for 7 years, and to be eligible for reëlection; the Republic virtually established); passed 1 A.M.

Feb. 11, Duprat's amendment carried (Senate to be chosen by universal suffrage); third reading of the constitutional bill rejected (357–345); proposed dissolution of the Assembly negatived (407–266), Feb. 12; message from the Marshal disapproving of last votes, Feb. 13

Feb. 22, Senate bill (Senate to consist of 300; 225 to be elected by the departments, 75 by National Assembly)

Feb. 24, Laws passed constituting French Republic by union of moderate Monarchists and Republicans; Legitimists and Bonapartists defeated; Senate bill passed (448–244); final vote for Republic, constitutional laws passed (436–262) 5 P.M. Feb. 25, published March 1

March 10, New Ministry under Buffet constituted: Buffet, Interior; Dufaure, Justice; Léon Say, Finance; Wallon, Instruction; De Meaux, Agriculture and Commerce; Cissey, War; Decazes, Foreign; Montaignac, Marine; Caillaux, Public Works

March 15, Duc d'Audiffret Pasquier elected President of the Assembly almost unanimously

March 27, Edgar Quinet, author of "Les Jesuites," republican, died

April 23, Powerful speech of Gambetta at Belleville, defending the new constitution

May 11, Meeting of the Assembly; the Ministry propose to refer a bill to the committee of 30; defeated; part of the committee resign, May 18; new committee elected (Republican majority), May 26

June, Louis Blanc's speech against the conservative Republic, June 21; self-denying resolution of the left party (to avoid delaying the dissolution by speaking, &c.)

July 13, Election of Baron de Bourgoing, a Bonapartist, annulled by the Assembly; warm defense of his party by Rouher (on the charge of there being a central committee of Bonapartists in Paris with branches in the provinces, actively endeavoring to overthrow the Republic in 1874) July 14

July 15, Fierce debate in Assembly; Buffet defends the imperialistic prefects, and gains vote of confidence; the left not voting

Aug., H. Rochefort, after challenging Paul de Cassagnac, declines accepting the conditions of the combat at Geneva

End of Aug., Naquet, an "irreconcilable" Republican, attacks Gambetta for his moderation

Aug., Plon having lost by publishing "Julius Cæsar," by Napoleon III, sues the Emperor's executors; fails; and is adjudged to pay costs

Sept. 8, Admiral De la Roncière Noury superseded for writing a letter animadverting on the Republic (Sept. 2)

About Sept. 10, Alleged adhesion of the Orleanist Party to the Republic

Oct. 17, Important speeches; M. Thiers at Arcachon, defending his policy; advocating a conservative Republic, and censuring delay; M. Rouher at Ajaccio, advocating imperialism and universal suffrage, and asserting that the nation will not accept the Republic as a definite government

Oct. 25, Important letter of Gambetta to his friends at Lyons (in favor of the conservative Republic), said to be "too advanced for the moderate, and too moderate for the advanced"

Nov. 4, Meeting of the Assembly: duc d'Audiffret Pasquier reëlected President

Nov. 9, The Assembly virtually votes its dissolution before March 31, 1876; 6 months' residence in a commune to give right to vote, majority for ministers; the *scrutin d'arrondissement* adopted instead of *scrutin de liste* (357–326); able speech of Gambetta for the latter, Nov. 11

Nov. 17, New Catholic University opened

Dec. 9, Beginning of ballot for senators for life; duc d'Audiffret Pasquier elected; the result discloses a breach between the Legitimists and Orleanists; Government defeated

Dec. 9–21, Seventy-five senators for life (52 Republicans) elected by the Assembly

About Dec. 13, Committees on the bills relating to the press and the state of siege protest against them strongly

Dec. 23, Powerful speech of Buffet in favor of rigid press law and state of siege; much censured, but approved in a letter by MacMahon, Dec. 24

Dec. 24, Majority for Ministers (376–303)

Dec. 27, Solemn funerals of Generals Clément Thomas and Lecomte, killed by the Communists (March 18, 1871); violent recrimination in the Assembly

——, Reëlection to the Assembly declined by the duc d'Aumale; by the Prince de Joinville, Dec. 29

Dec. 29, New press law (abolishing interdiction) passed; state of siege raised except in Paris, Versailles, Lyons, and Marseilles; proposal to raise it at Paris negatived (369–279)

Dec. 31, The Assembly prorogued till March 8, 1876

Dec., Communist trials report: 9,596 convicted; 110 sentenced to death

1876

Jan. 10 *et seq.*, Ministerial crisis: difference between Buffet and Say respecting an electoral list; resignation of Say; withdrawn at MacMahon's request; the marshal issues a proclamation, countersigned by Buffet; he says, "I think that the constitution ought not to be revised before having been loyally worked. I shall fulfil to the end the mission entrusted to me," Jan. 13

Jan. 10, New Catholic University inaugurated at Paris by the Archbishop

Jan. 17, Commencement of election of senators in departments

Jan. 30, Election of senators; mostly Moderate Republicans; Thiers for Belfort nearly unanimous; Buffet and Louis Blanc rejected; Victor Hugo elected

Feb. 9, Resignation of Léon Renault, Prefect of Police, opposed to Buffet

Feb. 20–March 5, Election of deputies; great majority of Republicans; resignation of Buffet, about Feb. 22; Dufaure, chief minister, with a modified cabinet, Feb. 24

March 7, Estimated result of elections: Moderate Republicans, 270; Radicals, 60; Bonapartists, 92; Orleanists, 58; Legitimists, 36

March 8, Senate and Assembly meet; duc d'Audiffret Pasquier elected President of Senate; M. F. P. Jules Grévy, President of Assembly, March 13

About March 9, Dufaure's Ministry complete (including Decazes, Say, Waddington, de Cissey, &c.)

March 21, Amnesty bill for Communists introduced in the Senate by Victor Hugo; in the Assembly by Raspail

April 5, Proposed international exhibition, Paris, for May 1, 1878

April, Archbishop Guibert, of Paris, declines to give evidence concerning the election of comte de Mun as deputy

About April 19, Gambetta, President of budget committee for 1877

May 14, Debate on the amnesty to Communists; rejected (394–52), May 17; Victor Hugo's speech in favor of amnesty; proposal rejected almost unanimously, May 22

About May 15, Death of Ricard, popular Liberal Minister of the Interior, aged 48, May 12; succeeded by M. De Marcère, under-secretary

May 18, Funeral procession of Michelet at Paris

June 16, M. Buffet, ex-Minister, elected life-Senator

June 28, 87 Communists pardoned

July 6, Casimir-Périer dies

July 31, Nearly 2,000,000*l.* voted for public instruction

Aug. 17, 68 Communists pardoned

Aug. 22, Observatory at Puy de Dôme near Clermont inaugurated

Sept., New fortifications round Paris nearly completed

Oct. 30, The Assembly reopened; the duc Decazes' firm pacific speech, Nov. 3

Nov., Prince Napoleon Jerome becomes prominent in the Assembly

Dec. 2, Resignation of Dufaure's Ministry through defeats in the Senate, &c.

——, Pardons and commutations granted to many Communist convicts

Dec. 12, 13, New Ministry: Jules Simon, President of the Council and Minister of Interior; Martel, Justice; others remain

1877

Jan. 26, Gambetta President of the budget

Jan., Above fifty prefects, hostile to the Republic, removed

Feb. 14, General Changarnier died, aged 83

April 5, Paul de Cassagnac fined and imprisoned for libel against Chamber of Deputies in the *Pays*

May 4, M. Jules Simon compelled to yield to Gambetta in the Chamber

May 16, Peremptory letter of censure from Marshal MacMahon to Jules Simon causes him and his Ministry to resign

May 17, The duc de Broglie forms a Ministry (Royalist and imperial), De Fourtou, Interior; Cailloux, Finance; Paris, Public Works; De Meaux, Agriculture; Brunet, Public Instruction (Decazes, Foreign, and Berthaut, War, remain)

——, Gambetta's resolution in Chamber in favor of parliamentary government carried (355–154); protest of 363 Liberal deputies signed May 18

May 18, The Marshal prorogues the Chambers for a month; a firm manifesto issued by the left

About May 29, Thiers accepted as leader by the Republicans; Broglie's circular for repressing the press issued

June 8, Bonnet Duverdier, chief of municipality of Paris; arrested for speaking against the Marshal, June 1; sentenced to fine and imprisonment

June 19, Meeting of Chambers; stormy debate in second chamber, June 16; vote against Government carried (363–158)

June 21, The deputies vote the necessary supplies, but not direct taxes

June 25, The Senate votes dissolution of the Chambers (150–130) June 22; decreed

July 2, The Marshal, in an order of the day, after a review at Longchamp, says: "I appeal to the army to defend the dearest interests of the country"

July, Aug., Quarrels among Bonapartists (Rouher against Cassagnac)

About Aug. 25, Prosecution of Gambetta (and Murat, editor of the *République Française*, in which it appeared) for a speech at Lille (July 29), in which he said the Marshal must, if the elections be against him, "submit or resign" ("se soumettre ou se démettre")

Sept. 3, Thiers dies, aged 80; public funeral, no disorder, Sept. 8

Sept. 11, Gambetta and Murat convicted; sentence 3 months imprisonment and fine of 80*l.*; on appeal sentence affirmed, Sept. 22

Sept. 24, Thiers' manifesto to electors (an historical defense of the Republic and late Chamber) published

Sept., Oct., The clergy energetically support the Government

Oct. 4, Temperate manifesto of the left; of Grévy and Gambetta, Oct. 7

Oct. 11, Justificatory manifesto of the Marshal, appealing to voters

Oct. 12, Gambetta convicted for placarding his address; fine 150*l.* and 3 months' imprisonment

Oct., M. de Fourtou interferes very energetically in elections; foreign papers stopped, &c.

Oct. 14, General election; quiet and dignified; results: defeat of Bonapartist and clerical parties (of 506 official candidates about 199 elected; Republicans, 320)

Oct. 28, Final result: 325 Republicans; 112 Bonapartists; 96 Monarchists

Nov., Ministry hold office till successors appointed; M. Pouyer-Quertier fails to form a Ministry

Nov. 4, Election of departmental councils who elect Senators; majority for Republicans

Nov. 8, Census for 1876 announced; 36,905,788 (increase of 802,867 over 1872)

——, The Marshal determines not to resign; his Ministry agree to remain temporarily; announced

Nov. 10, F. P. Jules Grévy reëlected President of the Chamber of Deputies now constituted

Nov. 13, Albert Grévy's resolution for the appointment of a commission of 33 to inquire into the conduct of the Government respecting elections; carried after a warm debate (312–205), Nov. 15

Nov. 19, Debate in Senate on M. Kerdrel's motion respecting Ministers; vote in their favor indirectly reflecting on Grévy's resolution, &c. (151–129)

Nov. 20, Resignation of Ministers announced

Nov. 23, New Ministry formed under General Rochebouet, president; no member of it in the Senate or Assembly; termed "Ministry of Affairs"

Nov. 24, No confidence in the new Ministry voted in the second Chamber (323–208)

Dec. 2, Important meeting of commercial men at Paris; petition to the Marshal agreed on

Dec. 4, The Chamber refuses to discuss the budget

Dec. 7–13, The Ministry resign; negotiations with Dufaure to form a parliamentary Ministry fail; Batbie (*see* Nov. 26, 1872) also fails

Dec. 13, The Marshal submits unconditionally. A thorough Republican Ministry formed under M. Dufaure, President of the Council and Minister of

Justice; De Marcère, Interior; Waddington (Protestant), Foreign Affairs; Bardoux, Public Instruction; General Borel, War; Vice-Admiral Pothuau, Marine; Léon Say, Finance; Teisserenc de Bort, Commerce; De Freycinet, Public Works: announced; the Marshal in his message accepts the will of the country, Dec. 14

Dec. 15 *et seq.*, Restrictions of the press removed; many prefects resign and others are removed

Dec. 17, Death of General Aurelle de Paladines

Dec. 18, Budget voted; Chambers adjourn

1878

Jan., Limoges affair; General Rochebouet said to have issued orders to General de Bressoles for a military movement which he issued Dec. 12; Major Labordère denounces the orders as illegal, Dec. 13; the orders nullified by the change of Ministry, Dec. 14; De Bressoles suspended for alleged mistake; Labordère cashiered; much excitement in Paris on account of suspected preparations for a *coup d'état*

Jan. 10, 11, General Ducrot dismissed from command for suspected connection with projected *coup d'état*

Jan. 13, Committee of 18 Liberal deputies (formed in May) virtually dissolve

March, Break up of combined reactionary parties; the Ministry generally successful

May 1, International exhibition at Paris opened by the Marshal President

June 13–July 13, M. Waddington, Foreign Minister, a plenipotentiary at the Berlin Conference

Aug., Republican success in electing departmental councils

Sept. 18, Powerful speech of Gambetta at Romans (department Drôme), proposing abolition of the exemption of theological students from military service, and at Grenoble, Oct. 10

Oct. 11, Dupanloup, Bishop of Orleans, dies suddenly

Nov. 13, Energetic manifesto of united Legitimists, Orleanists, and Bonapartists against Republicans respecting election of Senators

Nov. 18, Elections of Paul de Cassagnac (Nov. 7) and M. Fourtou invalidated by the Chamber; of Decazes, Dec. 7

Nov. 25, Letter from comte de Chambord to M. de Mun maintaining his rights; published

Dec. 31, All foreign commercial treaties *denounced* in view of a new tariff

1879

Jan. 5, Elections for Senate; 64 Republican, 16 opposition

Jan. 13, Compulsory resignation of General Borel, War Minister; succeeded by General Gresley

Jan. 15, M. Martel elected President of the Senate

Jan. 16, Ministerial program: pardons to Communists; check of clerical influence upon education; dismissal of officials opposed to the Republic, &c.

Jan. 17, 2,245 Communists pardoned by decree, issued

Jan. 20, Confidence in the Ministry voted in Chamber of Deputies (223–121)

Jan. 28, Marshal MacMahon refuses to supersede military officers; resigns; F. P. Jules Grévy elected President by the Senate, and deputies united as "The National Assembly" (536 for Grévy; 99 for General Chanzy), Jan. 30

Jan. 31, Gambetta elected President of the Chamber

Feb. 1, Resignation of Dufaure; new Ministry formed

by M. Waddington; changes (*see* Nov., 1877); M. le Royer, Keeper of Seals and Justice; Jules Ferry, Public Instruction; M. Lepère, Agriculture; Admiral Jauréguiberry, Marine; Feb. 4

Feb. 21, Communist amnesty bill passed by Chamber of Deputies

March 3, Resignation of M. de Marcère, Minister of the Interior (police scandals); succeeded by M. Lepère, March 4

March 8, Impeachment of De Broglie and Rochebouet (late Ministers) recommended by a commission

March 13, Impeachment negatived by the Chamber (317–159); vote of censure passed (240–154)

March 22, Proposed return of the assemblies to Paris; congress to be appointed (315–128)

March, M. Ferry's education bills to check clerical influences, abolishing Jesuit colleges, &c.

April 8, Pardon of 252 Communists signed

April 20, Blanqui (a convict) elected for Bordeaux

May 24, Pardon of 400 Communists signed

June 1, Prince Louis Napoleon killed while reconnoitering in Zululand

June 4, Blanqui's election annulled by the Chamber (372–33); pardoned and released, June 11

June 5, Pardon of 288 more Communists signed

June 16, Violent opposition of Paul de Cassagnac; he is expelled the house for 3 days for abusing Government

June 20, Congress of Senate and Deputies vote for their return to Paris (526–249)

July 9, M. Ferry's law of superior public instruction passed by the Deputies

July 13, President Grévy's first grand military review at Longchamp

July 20, Prince Napoleon Jerome coldly accepted as chief of the Bonapartists

July 26, Comte de Chambord's letter: "With the cooperation of all honest men, and with the grace of God, I may save France, and will"

Oct. 10, Treaties of commerce with England prolonged; signed

Oct. 11, Humbert, an amnestied Communist, elected to the municipal council, Paris; imprisoned for seditious speeches, &c., Oct. 22; election annulled Nov. 4

Nov., About 60 mayors in La Vendée dismissed for celebrating comte de Chambord's birthday

Nov. 28, Michel Chevalier, political economist, dies

Dec. 2, M. Waddington demands a vote of confidence [Republican sections: left center, pure left, advanced left, extreme left]

Dec. 4, Ministerial majority (221–97); many abstainers

Dec. 11, 12, Resignation of Lepère and Le Royer, Ministers

Dec. 21, Resignation of the Waddington Ministry

Dec. 28, 29, New Ministry (more Republican left) formed by M. de Freycinet; includes Jules Ferry, Public Instruction and Lepère, Interior; not Waddington or Léon Say

1880

Jan., General Farre, new War Minister, dismisses heads of departments in War Office

Jan. 16, M. de Freycinet's moderate program

——, Death (ex-Foreign Ministers): duc de Gramont; Jules Favre, Jan. 20

Feb. 10, Death of M. Crémieux

Feb. 12, Plenary amnesty for Communists rejected by the Chambers

March 9, Debate in Senate: 7th clause of Ferry's education bill (abolishing Jesuit schools, &c.); Jules Simon speaks against it; rejected (148–129)

March 29, Decree dissolving order of Jesuits and other orders in France

About April 5, Letter from Prince Napoleon Jerome in favor of the decree; offends Bonapartists

May 15, Ministerial defeat on public meetings bill; M. Lepère resigns; M. Constans succeeds, May 18

May 20, General Martel, President of Senate, resigns; succeeded by M. Léon Say

June 19, Amnesty bill for political offenses; presented by M. de Freycinet, June 19; passed by the Chambers (333–140), June 21

June 29, Otaheite formally annexed to France

June 30, Expulsion of religious orders (much officially opposed) carried into effect with Jesuits

July 3, Amnesty bill passed for all, except incendiaries and assassins, by Senate (143–138)

July 10, The President, Grévy, grants a general amnesty; Rochefort warmly received in Paris, July 12

Aug. 1, Elections of councils-general; great majority for Republicans (anti-clerical and anti-Bonapartist)

Aug. 8–11, MM. Grévy, Gambetta, and Léon Say, witness the launching of a man-of-war at Cherbourg

Sept. 6, 15, Two important letters from Guibert, Archbishop of Paris, to the President, recommending suspension of execution of the decree of March 29 against religious orders, delivered

Sept. 19, M. de Freycinet, in a speech at Montauban, expresses disagreement with his colleagues respecting decree against religious orders; resigns

Sept. 20, New Ministry: Jules Ferry, Premier and Public Instruction; Admiral Clouet, Marine; Sadi-Carnot, Public Works; Barthélemy St. Hilaire, Foreign; other offices unchanged

Oct. 16–Nov., Carmelites and other religious orders expelled

Oct. 19, Félix Pyat, editor of the *Commune*, sentenced to imprisonment and fine for justifying regicide

Nov. 9, Meeting of the Assembly: majority against the Ministry (who resign) (200–166)

——, M. Baudry d'Asson, Deputy, excluded; refuses to retire from the Chamber; forcibly expelled, Nov. 11

Nov. 12, The Ministry withdraw their resignation on vote of confidence (240–149)

Dec., Violent attacks of Rochefort (in *l'Intransigeant*) on Gambetta; crushing replies

1881

Jan. 9, Municipal council elections strongly in favor of the Government

Jan. 26, Bill greatly freeing the press brought in

March, Projected loan of 40,000,000*l.* (public debt, about 1,200,000*l.*) immediately taken up for 30 times the amount

March 21, 22, Discussion respecting the *scrutin de liste*, advocated by Gambetta; opposed by President Grévy, who yields

March, April, Expedition to N. Africa to chastise the Kroumirs; invasion of Tunis

May 12, Treaty with the Bey signed (*see* Tunis)

May 13 *et seq.*, Excitement at Marseilles and in Italy (*see s.v.*)

May 18, M. Bardoux's bill for the *scrutin de liste* adopted by the Chamber of Deputies (243–235)

May 23, The Tunis treaty ratified by the Chamber (453–1)

May 31, Proposed revision of the constitution negatived in the Chambers

June 9, The *scrutin de liste* rejected by the Senate (148–114)

About July 31, Election addresses. M. Rouher retires from political life (virtual end of Bonapartism); Prince Napoleon Jerome advocates progress—"everything for and by the people"—about July 31; speeches of M. Gambetta at Tours, Belleville, Aug. 12, advocating revision of the constitution, Aug.; M. Jules Ferry at Nancy deprecates division about Aug. 11

Aug. 16, Negotiations for treaty of commerce broken off; announced

Aug. 18, French treaty. French Government proposes meeting of the commissioners at Paris on Aug. 22; England requests 3 months' extension of existing treaty; France declines; negotiations stopped; announced

About Aug. 18, Complications respecting Tripoli cleared up

Aug. 21, Elections; triumph of Gambetta and moderate Republicans; gain of about 44 members; hopeless minority of extremists of both kinds

Aug. 21 *et seq.*, General elections; great Republican majority; number of extremists on both sides much reduced

Sept. 19, Negotiations respecting the commercial treaty resumed (France agrees to 3 months' extension of the treaty from Nov. 8)

Oct., Capuchins and other orders relieved from their monastic vows by the Pope

Nov. 3, M. Brisson elected President of the Chamber

Nov. 9, Treaty with the Bey of Tunis confirmed by the Chamber. Vote of censure on the Ferry Ministry respecting Tunis war negatived by a great majority; the Ministry resign, Nov. 10

Nov. 12, New Ministry gazetted: M. Gambetta, Minister of Foreign Affairs and Premier; M. Cazot, Justice; M. Waldeck-Rousseau, Interior; M. Allain-Targé, Finance; General Campenon, War; M. Gougeard, Marine; M. Paul Bert, Education and Worship; M. Raynal, Public Works; M. Rouvier, Commerce and Colonies; M. Cochery, Posts and Telegraphs; M. Devès, Agriculture; and M. Proust, Arts

Nov. 15, Moderate declaration of Gambetta to the Chambers (everything to be for France)

Dec. 15, M. H. Rochefort acquitted of bitter libel against M. Roustan in *l'Intransigeant;* a virtual censure of the Tunis affair

Dec. 30, Anglo-French treaty negotiations stop; French concessions insufficient

1882

Jan. 9, Elections for senators; Republicans gain 27; now 207–93; opposition announced

Jan. 19, Much speculation; panic on the bourse; checked by resolution

The League of Patriots established to support the army by encouraging military spirit, and support M. Gambetta

Jan. 26, Defeat of the Government; rejection of the *scrutin de liste* (305–119); resignation of M. Gambetta

Jan. 30, 31, New Ministry: M. de Freycinet, President of the Council and Minister for Foreign Affairs; M. Léon Say, Finance; M. Jules Ferry, Public In-

struction; M. Goblet, Interior and Public Worship; M. Humbert, Justice; General Billot, War; Admiral Jaurgéuiberry, Marine; M. Varroy, Public Works; M. Tirard, Commerce; M. Mahy, Agriculture; M. Cochery, Posts and Telegraphs

Jan. 30, Failure of the Union Générale Company; continuance of panic

Feb. 2, Arrest of Bontoux, President, and Feder, Manager

Feb. 6, Proposed revision of constitution negatived, 287–66

——, Anglo-French treaty renewed till March 1; till May 15, Feb. 27

March, M. Tissot Ambassador at London

About March 31, New education bill passed; much government interference

April, Commercial convention with Great Britain for ten years proposed

June 1, Vote of confidence in the Government (298–70)

July 20, Crisis: confidence in the Ministry respecting Egypt voted (286–105)

July 29, Vote of credit for protection of Suez Canal negatived on motion of M. Clemenceau (416–75); resignation of Ministry

Aug. 1, The New French Ministry, composed as follows: M. Duclerc, President of the Council and Minister for Foreign Affairs; M. Tirard, Finance; M. Dèves, Justice; M. Fallières, Interior; M. Pierre Legrand, Commerce, and *ad interim* Public Works; General Billot, War; Admiral Jauréguiberry, Navy; M. Cochery, Post Office and Telegraphs; M. de Mahy, Agriculture; M. Duvaux, Public Instruction

Aug. 9, Gambetta advocates activity in foreign affairs, and abstention in domestic; Clemenceau the reverse, July–Aug.; chambers prorogued

About Aug. 17, Disturbance amongst the miners of the Saône and Loire

About Aug. 31, The Bonapartists select Prince Victor as their chief

Aug., Discovery of an organization of anarchists (alleged origin at Geneva, and Prince Krapotkine, member); tracts distributed by groups of young men throughout the country; attempted insurrection at Montceau-les-Mines suppressed. Oct. 21, Many arrested [9 convicted, Dec. 22] About Oct. 26, Place of trial changed; dynamite explosions threatened

Oct. 2, The compulsory education act comes into operation

Oct. 23, Arrest connected with an explosion at a café (one man killed); railway station held by troops, Oct. 28

Oct. 27, Disturbances at Lyons; anarchy and panic; business and amusements suspended; the town said to be held by the mob

——, Government official note promising public security

Oct. 29, Much dynamite seized

Oct., Great distress in Lyons

Nov. 8, Panic subsiding in Paris, &c.

Nov. 21, Treaty with the King of Congo negotiated by M. Brazza ratified

Nov. 23, Crown jewels (value about 100,000*l.*) stolen from the Cathedral of St. Denis

Dec. 6, Death of Louis Blanc

Dec. 20, MM. Bontoux & Feder, directors of the "Union Générale" (a financial company established in 1878, and patronized by the Legitimists, clergy, and the middle classes), sentenced to imprisonment and fines for gross frauds, which caused very great universal distress (it stopped Jan. 28)

About Dec. 21, Prince Krapotkine, anarchist, arrested

Dec. 31, Death of M. Gambetta, aged 44, after several weeks illness through an accidental wound, midnight

1883

Jan. 5, Death of General Chanzy, aged about 60

Jan. 8, Trial of Krapotkine and about 50 anarchists begun at Lyons

Jan. 13, Gambetta's remains removed and reburied at Nice

Jan. 16, Prince Napoleon publishes a manifesto against the Government; arrested

——, M. Floquet's bill for expulsion of Bourbons and Bonapartes

Jan. 19, Krapotkine sentenced to 5 years' imprisonment and fine, others to imprisonment

Jan. 20, Government bill of M. de Fallières for power to expel the same

Jan. 23, Ministerial crisis

Jan. 25, Expulsion bill adopted by committee

Jan. 28, M. Duclerc's Ministry resigned

Jan. 29, Ministry reconstituted under M. Fallières

——, M. Fabre's bill permitting princes to remain with deprival of civil rights, discussed; passed by the Chamber (343–163), Feb. 1

Feb. 9, Prince Napoleon's indictment quashed; released

Feb. 12, Expulsion bill rejected by the Senate; amendment of MM. Say and Waddington adopted (165–127); princes to be expelled only after trial

Feb. 13, Resignation of M. Fallières and Ministry

Feb. 15, M. Barbey's bill empowering the President to expel princes when dangerous, adopted by the Deputies; rejected by the Senate, Feb. 17

Feb. 21, M. Jules Ferry (opportunist) forms a Ministry (Gambettist); M. Jules Ferry, Premier and Minister of Public Instruction; M. Challemel-Lacour, Foreign Affairs; M. Waldeck-Rousseau, Interior; M. Martin Feuillé, Justice; General Thibaudin, War; M. Charles Brun, Marine; M. Tirard, Finance; M. Raynal, Public Works; M. Meline, Agriculture; M. Cochery, Posts and Telegraphs; M. Hérisson, Commerce

Feb. 24, Decree for retirement of the Orleanist princes from the army in virtue of the law of 1834 (the duc d'Aumale, the duc de Chartres, and the duc d'Alençon), approved by the Deputies (295–103)

March 6, M. Clemenceau's motion for revision of the Constitution rejected by the deputies

March 9, Open-air meeting of artisans out of work at Paris excited to violence by Louise Michel the anarchist and others; bakers' shops rifled; checked by police; many arrested, March 10

March 30, Louise Michel arrested

April 8, Death of Louis Veuillot, ultramontane, editor of l'Univers

Marshal Bazaine publishes his defense at Madrid

April 27, Conversion of Rentes bill (5 to 4½) passed

June 20, Museum of revolution established at Versailles

June 23, Louise Michel sentenced to 6 years' imprisonment, and others to different terms

Aug. 12, The inauguration of the monument (by M. Barrias erected at Courbevoie to commemorate the defense) of Paris in 1870–71

Aug. 24, Death of the comte de Chambord, aged nearly 63

Sept. 29, The King of Spain received by President Grévy at Paris; hooted by the mob

Oct. 5, General Thibaudin, Minister of War, resigns; succeeded by General Campenon, Oct. 9

Oct. 13, M. Jules Ferry declares for a Republic of "common sense," and opposition to the extreme left at Rouen; and at Havre, Oct. 14

Oct. 29, Correspondence between France and China respecting Tonquin published in Times; China firm in resisting French encroachments

Oct. 29–31; Dec. 10, 18, Debate on Tonquin; votes of confidence in Ministry (339–160)

About Nov. 17–20, M. Ferry becomes Foreign Minister on the retirement of M. Challemel-Lacour; other changes in the Ministry

Dec. 28, Government defeated on Algerian colonization (249–211)

1884

Feb. 3, Death of M. Rouher, Prime Minister of Napoleon III

Feb. 4, Industrial crisis in Paris; defeat of the Government; a committee of investigation into the condition of the working classes appointed (254–249)

Feb. 12, Proposals for loan of 14,000,000l. issued

Feb. 16, Government defeated on its seditious meetings bill

March 24, Death of François Mignet, French historian, aged about 87

May 24, Bill for revision of the Constitution (abolition of life senators, &c.) brought in by M. Jules Ferry

June, Prince Victor acknowledged chief of the Bonapartists; his father publishes painful correspondence

June et seq., Cholera prevalent in the south, &c.

July 4, Colossal statue of Liberty by Bartholdi given to the United States of America unveiled by M. Jules Ferry at Paris

July 31, Revision bill, modified by the Senate, accepted by the Deputies

Aug. 4, Congress of Senate and Deputies meet at Versailles, M. Le Royer, President

Aug. 13, The revision of the Constitution accepted by the congress, 509–172

Oct., Dec., Excitement about the price of bread at Paris and other places

Nov. 28, Credit for Tonquin war adopted by the Deputies, 282–187; by the Senate, Dec. 11

Trade Unions legalized

1885

Jan. 3, Resignation of General Campenon, War Minister; succeeded by General Lewal, Jan. 5

Jan. 25–26, Senatorial elections (67 Republicans and 20 Conservatives returned)

Feb. 5, The Chamber votes for engagement of unemployed workmen on public works

March 30, The Ferry Ministry resign in consequence of defeat in the Chamber

April 6, New Ministry formed by M. Brisson

April 7, Peace with China announced

March 27, Duty on foreign corn voted by the Senate

March 30, M. Ferry's Ministry defeated on vote of credit for Chinese war (308–161); resigns

March 31, Vote of credit for 2,000,000l.; for 6,000,000l., April 7

April 6, New Ministry: H. Brisson, President and Justice; de Freycinet, Foreign; Allain Targé, Interior; Goblet, Public Instruction and Worship; Gen-

eral Campenon, War; Admiral Galiber, Marine;
Clamageran, afterwards Sadi-Carnot, Finance; and
others

May, *Bosphore Egyptien Affair. See* Egypt

May 22, Death of Victor Hugo, poet, dramatist, and
novelist, aged.83; buried in the Panthéon, June 1

May 24, Anarchist demonstration at Père la Chaise;
many wounded by the police

June 8, *Scrutin de liste* bill passed with the Senate's
amendments

June 11, Death of Admiral Courbet

Aug., Great excitement in Paris about Olivier Pain (*see*
Sudan)

Aug. 6, Chambers prorogued; parliamentary elections,
200 Conservatives, 230 Moderates or Opportunists,
150 Radicals, Oct. 4

Oct. 6, The Ministers not reëlected resign

Oct. 29, M. de Freycinet shot at in the Place de la
Concorde

Nov. 10, Republican Party disorganized

Nov. 16, The Ministry propose retrenchment in colonial
war expenditure, and consideration of church disestablishment

Dec. 16, Report of committee on Tonquin recommends
vote of 19,000,000 francs instead of 75,000,000 proposed by Government

Dec., Great commercial depression, attributed to Government prodigality, &c.

Dec. 21–23, Vote for Government (274–270)

Dec. 28, F. P. Jules Grévy elected President for seven
years (457 for Grévy, 68 for M. Brisson)

Dec. 29, M. Brisson's Ministry resigns

1886

Jan. 7, New Ministry: M. de Freycinet, President and
Foreign Affairs; M. Demôle, Justice; M. Sarrien,
Interior; M. Goblet, Education; M. Sadi-Carnot,
Finance; General Boulanger, War; Admiral Aube,
Marine and Colonies; M. Baïhaut, Public Works;
M. Develle, Agriculture; M. Lockroy, Commerce;
M. Granet, Posts and Telegraphs

Jan. 14, Amnesty for political offenders granted

End of Jan., Riotous strike of 3,000 miners at Decaze-
ville, in Aveyron, murder of M. Watrin, Manager

About Feb. 16, New elections increase the Republican
members to 400, the Right, 184

March 17, M. Sadi-Carnot's budget; proposed new loan
of about 58,500,000*l*. (70,000,000*l*. really wanted);
the modified loan immediately subscribed for,
20,000,000*l*. passed by the Deputies, April 21

About April 1, Archbishop Guibert of Paris, in a letter
to President Grévy, protests against prohibiting
monks and nuns to teach in schools

May 27, Bills for giving discretionary power to expel
the Orleans princes and Prince Napoleon and son
from France and confiscating their property, introduced in the Chambers (M. Freycinet influenced by
M. Clemenceau); reported disagreement in the cabinet on the subject June 2, 3; bill for immediate expulsion of heads of families and heirs of dynasties
who have reigned in France passed by the Chamber
June 11; and by the Senate (137–122) June 22; promulgated; the Bonapartes quit France June 23; the
comte de Paris and family leave; at Dover he issues a
protest declaring monarchy to be the most suitable
government for France, and places himself as head
of the royalists, June 24

July 8, Death of Guibert, Archbishop of Paris

July 13, The duc d'Aumale remonstrates against the
deprivation of his rank in the army; his expulsion
from France voted; Rev. W. J. Drought, English
chaplain at Chantilly, expelled from France for delivering an address of sympathy to the Duke, Aug.

Oct. 28, Education bill permitting lay teachers only
passed by the Chamber

Dec. 3, Ministry defeated in the Chamber (by 13
majority), resigns

Dec., New Ministry: M. Goblet, President and Inte-
rior; M. Flourens, Foreign; M. Dauphin, Finance;
M. Berthelot, Public Instruction; M. Sarrien, Jus-
tice; General Boulanger, War; Admiral Aube, Marine;
M. Granet, Posts and Telegraphs; M. Lockroy,
Commerce; M. Millaud, Public Works; M. Develle,
Agriculture

1887

Jan. 22, Continued deficit; budget rejected; amended
one accepted by Government

Feb. 1, Panic on the Bourse through war rumors

March, Bill for increasing duty on foreign corn adopted
by the Chamber (318–248), March 14; by the Senate
March 25; duty on foreign cattle and meat raised

April 20, M. Schnaebell, Commissary of Police, arrested
near Pagny-sur-Moselle, territory doubtful, and sent
to Metz; charged with treason April 22; statements
contradictory; released by order of the Emperor
William, April 29

May 12–23, Sale of the crown jewels for 274,560*l*., diamonds 289,000*l*.; the diamonds distributed between
the Louvre and other museums

May 17, The Goblet Ministry defeated on the budget
bill (275–257); resigns

May, MM. Freycinet, Floquet, Devès, and Duclerc fail

May 30, M. Rouvier forms a moderate Ministry, consisting of M. Rouvier, Finances, Posts and Telegraphs; M. Flourens, Foreign Affairs; M. Mazeau,
Justice; M. Fallières, Interior; M. Spuller, Public
Instruction and Worship; M. Barbey, Marine and
Colonies; General Ferron, War; M. Dautresme, Commerce and Public Works; M. Barbe, Agriculture

——, General Boulanger, the late War Minister, issues
a monitory order to the army

June 25, Exemption of ecclesiastical students (semina-
rists) abolished in new army bill

July 9, General Boulanger warmly received in his progress to Clermont Ferrand

July 11, Radical attack on the Ministry defeated (382–
120)

Aug., General Boulanger challenges M. Ferry for remarks in a speech about July 29; seconds differ; no
result

Aug. 31, Mobilization of 17th army corps, near Tou-
louse

Sept. 14, Manifesto of the comte de Paris calling for
the reëstablishment of a constitutional monarchy by
universal suffrage as specially needful for France

Oct. 13, Military scandal; General Caffarel of the War
Office convicted by a military tribunal of dishonorable conduct in trafficking with decorations

Oct. 14, General Boulanger under arrest for thirty days
for remarks respecting the scandal

Oct. 24, Amicable conventions respecting Suez Canal
and New Hebrides signed at Paris

Oct. 25, Prince Victor Napoleon issues a Bonapartist
manifesto

Nov. 7, Trial of General Caffarel and others; discharged

Nov. 14, General Count D'Andlau and Madame Rattazzi sentenced to imprisonment and fines for trafficking in decorations

Nov., M. Wilson, son-in-law of the President, implicated; also charged with tampering with documents

Nov., The old 4½% rentes converted to 3% accepted

Nov. 19, M. Rouvier defeated in the Chamber on a motion of M. Clemenceau (317–227); the Ministry resigns; M. Grévy refuses to resign; but is compelled by the combination of opposite parties; the Rouvier Ministry retains office; on their announcing that M. Grévy defers his resignation the Chamber immediately adjourns (531–3) Dec. 1; receives M. Grévy's resignation, Dec. 2

Dec. 3, National Assembly at Versailles; congress of Senators and Deputies (833); M. Sadi-Carnot ("moderate independent") elected President (616); General Saussier, an unwilling candidate (148); (MM. Ferry and de Freycinet withdrawn)

Dec. 9, M. Goblet fails to form à Ministry; M. Fallières fails, Dec. 10

Dec. 10, Attempted assassination of M. Ferry by Aubertin, a lunatic, in the lobby of the Chamber of Deputies, a narrow escape

Dec. 13, The tribunals find no case against M. Wilson ——, New Ministry: M. Tirard, Finance and Premier; M. Flourens, Foreign Affairs; M. Fallières, Justice; M. Sarrien, Interior; M. Faye, Education and Worship; M. de Mahy, afterwards Admiral Krantz (Jan., 1888), Marine and Colonies; M. Loubet, Public Works; M. Dautresme, Commerce; M. Viette, Agriculture; General Logerot, War

1888

March 15, General Boulanger deprived of his command for insubordination in visiting Paris against orders; announced

March 26, General Boulanger tried by court of five generals; sentenced to retirement; confirmed, March 27

March 30, M. Tirard's Ministry defeated when opposing urgency for revision of constitution (268–234), resigns

April 3, M. Floquet forms a Ministry: M. Charles Floquet, President of the Council and Minister of the Interior; M. de Freycinet, War; M. Goblet, Foreign Affairs; Admiral Krantz, Marine and the Colonies; M. Peytral, Finance, Posts, and Telegraphs; M. Edouard Lockroy, Public Instruction, Fine Arts, and Worship; M. Deluns Montaud, Public Works; M. Ferrouillat, Justice; M. Pierre Legrand, Commerce and Industry; M. Viette, Agriculture

April 8, General Boulanger begins to form a party; elected deputy for the Dordogne (59,500–35,750); for the Nord (172,528–75,901), April 15

April, Rise of an anti-parliamentary party, a mixture of Conservatives, Radicals, &c.

April 19, After vote of confidence in the Ministry (379–177), it is defeated on the revision question (340–215)

April 20, A committee advises postponement of revision; riots between students and Boulangists

May 8, Great circulation of General Boulanger's (alleged) "German Invasion, no. 1"; soon fell off, May 18

May 27, Royalist banquet at the Château de Mons, near St. Etienne; powerful speech of General de Charette

June 4, General Boulanger's motion in the Chamber for

urgency in the revision of the constitution rejected (377–186)

July 6, The manifesto of the comte de Paris to the mayors of Communes against the Republic signed

July 12, General Boulanger in the Chamber demands dissolution, firmly resisted by M. Floquet; the General accuses M. Floquet of falsehood, resigns his seat, and leaves the House in great excitement; duel, General Boulanger seriously, and M. Floquet slightly, wounded, July 13; General Boulanger reported convalescent, July 20

July 17, 67,000,000 francs voted for the defense of Brest, Toulon, and Cherbourg

July 18, Session of Chambers closed

July, General Boulanger defeated in elections for Ardèche, &c.

Aug. 8, Funeral of Eudes, the Communist; rioting suppressed; no deaths

Aug., Diplomatic dispute with Italy respecting Massowah (MM. Goblet and Crispi)

Aug. 19, General Boulanger elected for the Nord, Somme, and Charente

Sept. 23, Death of Marshal Bazaine, aged 77

Oct. 2, Decree of President Carnot and M. Floquet respecting resident foreigners and immigrants; registration causes much annoyance; time prolonged to Jan. 1, 1889 on Oct. 28

Autumn, The League of the Rose formed to promote the reëstablishment of the monarchy

Oct. 15, The Chambers reopen; M. Floquet introduces a bill for the revision of the constitution, which is declared urgent; much dissatisfaction, Oct. 16 et seq.

Nov. 17, M. Numa Gilly tried for defamation against the budget committee; acquitted for want of evidence

Dec. 2, Demonstration at Paris in honor of M. Baudin, a deputy killed on the barricades Dec. 2, 1851

Dec. 28, Prado executed

1889

Jan. 27, General Boulanger elected for the department of the Seine (244,000); M. Jacques, advanced Republican (162,000)

Jan. 31, M. Floquet has majority of 62 in the Chamber

Feb. 11, Bill for replacing the *scrutin de liste* by the *scrutin d'arrondissement* carried in the Chamber (268–222); in the Senate (228–54), Feb. 13

Feb. 14, The ministerial scheme for the revision of the constitution rejected (307–218); they resign

Feb., Dissension between the Opportunists and the Radicals

Feb. 18, M. Méline fails to form an Opportunist Ministry

Feb. 21, 22, M. Tirard forms a mixed Ministry, including several ex-Premiers: M. Tirard, Premier and Minister of Commerce; M. Constans, Interior; M. Spuller, Foreign; M. de Freycinet, War; M. Rouvier, Finance; M. Thévenet, Justice; Admiral Jaurès (died March 13; succeeded by Admiral Krantz), Marine; M. Fallières, Education; M. Yves Guyot, Public Works; M. Faye, Agriculture

Feb. 28, The League of Patriots, established in 1882, becoming seditious and connected with Boulangism, suppressed by the Government; alleged number 240,000; protest about March 2; MM. Déroulède, Laguerre, and others, committee of the League, prosecuted; trial April 2; each fined 100*fr.*, April 6

Feb., Fall in the shares of the Comptoir d'Escompte de

Paris through speculations in copper; suicide of M. Denfert-Rochereau, the Manager, March 5; panic; checked by the intervention of Government and Bank of France, March 9; supported by Messrs. Rothschild and other bankers, March; reconstituted successfully, March–May

March 7, Decree of expulsion of the duc d'Aumale revoked; the duc received by M. Carnot, March 12

March 18, Manifesto of General Boulanger to the Nord against the Government

April 1, 2, He escapes to Brussels; his trial for conspiracy by the Senate proposed; issues manifesto April 5; expects expulsion; arrives in London, April 24

April 9, M. Chevreul, chemist, dies aged 102

April 12, Senate meets as high court for Boulanger trial

April 18, M. Carnot, the President, opens the "Revolution Exhibition" of relics, at Paris

May 1, Great royalist banquet at Paris

May 5, Centenary celebration of the meeting of the States-General (afterwards the Constituent Assembly) May 5, 1789—President Carnot in the presence of a grand assembly in the "Hall of Mirrors," Versailles, delivers a eulogium on the Revolution
[On his way to Versailles, the President's carriage was fired at by a semi-lunatic named Perrin—sentenced to four months' imprisonment May 28]

May 6, The Universal Exhibition opened by the President

July 7, M. Quesnay de Beaurepaire hands in the indictment against General Boulanger

July 9, New army bill reducing the term of service from five years with exemptions to three years, nominally without exemptions, passed by the Chamber

July 15, Bill prohibiting a man to be candidate for more than one place in the Chamber passed by the Senate

——, The Chamber votes 2,400,000l. for the increase of the navy (3 ironclads, &c.); the session closed

July 17, 28, Indictment against General Boulanger, charging him when director of infantry in 1882, with courting popularity by corruption, &c., and when Minister of War in 1886 with malversation of public money, and plotting against the State, with Count Dillon, H. Rochefort and other confederates; they are cited to appear before the High Court of Justice on Aug. 6; non-appearance to be followed by loss of civil rights and sequestration of property

July 28, Cantonal elections: Republicans, 752; Conservatives, 497; General Boulanger, 12

Aug. 8, The trial of General Boulanger, Count Dillon, and H. Rochefort begins

Aug. 14, Sentenced to deportation to a fortress, and payment of costs of the trial

Aug., The comte de Paris, Prince Jerome Napoleon, his son Victor, and General Boulanger set forth their claims for political power

Sept. 22 and Oct. 6, Elections of the Chamber of Deputies; decisive victory of the Government
[112 Monarchists, 62 Bonapartists, 325 Republicans, 41 Boulangists, 32 uncertain Liberals. General Boulanger's election was annulled]

Nov. 6, The Universal Exhibition closed

Nov. 12, The Boulangist demonstration easily quelled

Nov. 18, M. Floquet elected President of the Chamber

Dec. 6, Supreme naval council created by decree

Dec. 9, General Boulanger's election, and that of several Boulangists, for Montmartre, annulled by the Chamber (370–123)

1890

Jan. 20, Three Boulangist deputies expelled from the Chamber for disorderly conduct

Feb. 7, The Duke of Orleans (aged 21) comes to Paris, and offers to enter the army; arrested; sentenced to two years' imprisonment for breaking the exile law of 1886, Feb. 12; taken to Clairvaux, Feb. 25

Feb. 20, Miners' strike at St. Etienne, 2,700 out

Feb., May, War with Dahomey

March 1, Resignation of M. Constans, Minister of the Interior, succeeded by M. Léon Bourgeois

March 14, M. Tirard and his Cabinet, defeated in the Senate, resign

March, New Ministry; M. de Freycinet, Premier and War Minister; M. Rouvier, Finance; M. Constans, Interior; M. Bourgeois, Public Instruction; M. Ribot, Foreign; M. Fallières, Justice and Public Worship; M. Jules Roche, Commerce; M. Deville, Agriculture; M. Barbey, Marine; M. Guyot, Public Works

April 16–27, M. Carnot's tour in S. France, Corsica, &c.

April 27, The Boulangists totally defeated in the Paris municipal elections

May 1, 2, Strike of thousands of workmen at Croix, Roubaix, and Tourcoing, in the Nord; serious rioting suppressed by the military; strikes subsiding, May 8

May 3 et seq., Suspected anarchist plot: the Marquis de Mores, Louise Michel, and about 300 others arrested, April 28–May 2; the Marquis and others liberated

May 5, Trial of M. Secrétan and other directors of the Comptoir d'Escompte for fraud, &c., ended

May 9, Revelations respecting the affairs of the Crédit Foncier; investigation ordered by Government

May 21, General Boulanger submits to the Government; the Boulangist committee dissolves

May 28, M. Secrétan sentenced to 6 months' imprisonment and fine of 10,000 francs; the others received lesser sentences

May 29 et seq., 17 Russian Anarchists or Nihilists, engaged in the manufacture of explosives at Raincy, arrested. All discharged except 8, June 25

May, Explanations given by M. Christophle; the inspectors' report stated that the establishment had departed from its original object and gone into banking, &c., without proper precautions, but that it is stable, June 21

June 3, The Duke of Orleans pardoned and expelled from France

July 4, Trial of 8 Russian Nihilists; 6 men convicted sentenced to 3 years' imprisonment; Landesen the instigator (absent) to 5 years' imprisonment, two women acquitted July 5

Aug. 5, Anglo-French agreement signed in London. *See* Africa

Early Sept., "Les Coulisses du Boulangisme," by M. Mermeix, published by him in the *Figaro*, describing an alleged conspiracy of Royalists; causes much excitement and involves the author in several duels, in one of which he is wounded, Sept. 15

Oct., The Union for the promotion of Free Trade in Raw Materials, &c., formed in Paris

Nov. 18, Assassination of General Michael Seliverskoff, aged 69, wealthy retired Russian general and formerly a Minister of Secret Police, at the Hôtel de Bade, Paris; died, Nov. 19

Nov., The French Africa Committee formed; expeditions proposed

Nov. 28, The Government defeated in the Chambers on a financial question (303–248)

Dec., Cardinal Lavigerie and other prelates declare their adhesion to the Republic, with the approval of the Pope

Dec. 23, Mme Duc Quercy, MM. Labruyère and Grégoire sentenced to imprisonment for aiding the escape of Padlewski, the suspected murderer of General Seliverskoff (Nov. 19)

1891

Jan. 17, Vote of censure on the Ministry relative to the loan of gold by the Bank of France to the Bank of England, during the Baring crisis, negatived (419–29)

Jan. 27, The performance of Sardou's new play *Thermidor* stopped by order of the Ministry

Feb. 7, Royalist demonstration in Paris in honor of the Duke of Orleans

Feb. 18–27, The Empress Frederick visits Paris, chiefly on behalf of the Berlin International Exhibition of Fine Arts; many French works promised, afterwards withdrawn, through popular opposition, chiefly of the Boulangists and others

March 12, Financial panic in Paris, through embarrassment of the Société des Dépôts et Comptes Courants, relieved by the Bank of France and others

March 17, Death of Prince Napoleon, son of Jerome

March 18, Communication between Paris and London by telephone

May 1, Riots at Fourmies (Nord) suppressed by the military; 14 persons killed and about 40 wounded

July 18, A protectionist customs tariff adopted by the Chamber (385–111)

July 23, A French naval squadron under Admiral Gervais warmly received at Cronstadt

July 25, Visited by the Czar. The French officers received at St. Petersburg, July 28. The fleet leaves Cronstadt, Aug. 4. The fleet (*Marengo* flagship, with Admiral Gervais), 6 other vessels, and 2 torpedo boats arrive in Osborne Bay, near Portsmouth, 5:30 P.M., Aug. 19. Admiral Gervais and officers presented to Queen Victoria at Osborne, Aug. 20. Departure of the fleet, Aug. 26

Sept. 9, Death of ex-President M. Jules Grévy, aged about 84

Sept. 30, Suicide of General Boulanger in a cemetery near Brussels

Nov. 20–21, M. de Giers, the Russian Foreign Minister, visits M. Carnot, M. de Freycinet, and M. Ribot

Nov. 24, Xavier Gouthe Soulard, Archbishop of Aix, sentenced to a fine of 3,000 francs, for writing an insulting protest against a circular of M. Fallières the Minister of Public Worship, respecting pilgrimages

Dec. 3, New customs bill issued; it authorized the Government to prolong or modify the treaties expiring Feb. 15, 1892

Dec. 10, M. de Freycinet takes his seat as a member of the French Academy

Dec. 11–13, Stormy debate in the Chamber on Church and State; the Government supports the Concordat; majority for Government (243–223)

Dec. 22, Death of Mons. Freppel, Bishop of Angers, powerful champion of the French church

Dec. 26, Walter Bedwell and John S. Cooper convicted of acting as British spies in relation to the arsenal at St. Etienne; sentenced to fine and imprisonment

Dec. 26, The new tariff bill passed by the Senate

1892

Jan. 19, M. Constans, a Minister, having been attacked by M. Laur, a Boulangist deputy, strikes him as he leaves the tribune; his apology accepted by the Chamber

Jan. 26–Feb. 19, 76 French bishops accept the declaration of Cardinal Lavigerie and four other cardinals, Dec., 1890, recognizing the Republic

Feb., The new " minimum " tariff comes into operation with Great Britain and some other Powers, Feb. 1; the " maximum " tariff to be enforced in Spain, Portugal, Italy, Rumania, and the United States

Feb. 16, Encyclical of the Pope to the French Bishops enjoining submission to the Government of the Republic

Feb. 18, The De Freycinet Cabinet defeated in a debate on the Associations bill (relating to Church and State), resign

Feb. 23–26, MM. Rouvier and Bourgeois successively fail to form a Ministry

Feb. 28, New Ministry: M. Loubet, Premier and Minister of Interior; M. de Freycinet, War; M. Ribot, Foreign Affairs; M. Rouvier, Finance; M. Bourgeois, Public Instruction; M. Ricard, Justice and Public Worship; M. Cavaignac, Marine; M. Develle, Agriculture; M. Jules Roche, Commerce; M. Viette, Public Works

March 3, The Ministerial declaration accepted by the Chamber (341 to 91)

March 7, Death of Etienne Arago, statesman and dramatist (brother of the astronomer), aged 90

March 11 *et seq.*, Dynamite explosions in the Boulevard St. Germain, in Paris, attributed to the anarchists

March 15, Explosion at the Lobau barracks, buildings injured

——, Bill introduced to punish the authors of explosions with death; several arrests March 17

March 23, A bomb factory in Paris discovered; other explosions at the houses of legal officials in Rue de Clichy, 6 injured, March 27

March 30, Ravachol, otherwise Léon Léger (real name said to be Francis Königstein), a notorious anarchist, arrested in the Café Véry in the Boulevard Magenta, through the agency of Lhérot, a waiter, and M. Véry

March 31, The anti-dynamite bill passed by the Senate

April 11, The Chamber votes 300,000,000 francs for an expedition against Dahomey

About April 22, Order for the prosecution of the Archbishop of Avignon and the Bishops of Nîmes, Montpellier, Valence, and Viviers, for their concerted addresses to the Catholic electors in opposition to the State

April 22, Many anarchists arrested at Paris, Lyons, and other places, 51 in Paris, reported

April 26, 27, Trial of anarchists; Ravachol and Simon sentenced to penal servitude for life, 3 others acquitted

May, The stipends of several bishops stopped on account of their pastorals, &c.

June 9, The duc de la Rochefoucauld's declaration of submission to the Pope in matters of the faith, but not in State affairs, signed by 40 of the 70 Royalist deputies

About July 5, Government protest against the presence of Protestant missionaries in Algeria

July 11, M. Godefroy Cavaignac, Minister of Marine, resigns (censured in relation to Dahomey); succeeded by M. Burdeau

July 13, Decree signed for the Universal Exhibition May 5–Oct. 31, 1900

July 28, Faugoux and three other anarchists, sentenced to penal servitude (for 20, 10, 6, 5 years) for stealing dynamite

Aug.–Sept., Disputes between the coal-mining company at Carmaux, in the department of Tarn, and their workmen respecting the dismissal of M. Calvignac, a Socialist workman and secretary of the miners' union, who had been elected mayor, and consequently neglected his work; a general strike with much rioting ensues; great meeting at Paris to support the strike Sept. 7; strikers supported by deputies of the Chamber, Sept.; Government intervention ineffectual Oct. 11, 12

Oct. 2, Death of Ernest Renan, scholar and philosopher, aged 69

Oct. 14, Resignation of the Marquis de Solages, Manager of the Carmaux mines, reported

Oct. 18, Attack on the Government, respecting Carmaux, in the Chamber, defeated; arbitration accepted, Oct. 21; M. Loubet, the Premier, the arbitrator, decides that M. Calvignac should be reinstated as a workman with leave of absence while mayor; that all the strikers, except those in prison for violence, should be taken back, and that the Manager, M. Humblot, should be reinstated, Oct. 26; this award rejected by the miners, Oct. 26–27; work resumed by advice Nov. 3

Oct. 29, Bill regulating the labor of women and children in factories (first introduced in 1879, and much discussed), passed

Nov. 15, Abolition of duty on wine, beer, cider, and "hygienic" drinks, and an increase of the spirit duties adopted by the Chamber [bill passed, Dec. 21, 1892; by the Senate, June 26, 1893]

About Nov. 15, Death of General de Failly, aged 81

Nov. 16, Jean Pierre François, anarchist (a companion of Ravachol), in London, extradited to Paris

Nov. 18, Press bill to check anarchical publications: confidence in the Ministry voted (329–228); the bill, much softened, passed Nov. 19

Nov. 25, Prosecution of the directors of the Panama Canal Company, Ferdinand de Lesseps, Charles de Lesseps, and others for fraud and bribery opened

Nov. 26, Death of Cardinal Lavigerie, aged 67, near Algiers

Nov. 28, The Loubet Ministry, opposing the exhumation of Baron Jacques Reinach, late director of the Panama company, defeated in the Chamber (293–195), resigns

Dec. 5, The Ministry reconstituted by M. Ribot; declaration and vote of confidence (307–104), Dec. 8

Dec. 9, The Panama committee invested with judicial powers

1893

Jan. 1 et seq., Tariff war with Switzerland, see s.v.

Jan. 10, Trial of Panama Canal Company directors begun, ended Feb. 9 with sentences of 5 years imprisonment for Ferdinand and Charles de Lesseps, and 2 years for MM. Fontane, Cottu, and Eiffe

Jan. 11, Reconstruction of the Ministry by M. Ribot (M. de Freycinet not included)

Jan. 12, The new President, M. Casimir-Périer, opens the Chamber

Jan. 14, The Socialist union, started at Paris

Feb. 3, Bill to protect savings banks against political alarms, passed

Feb. 8, M. Cavaignac's motion for sustaining prosecution of official corruption, adopted by the Chamber (446(?)–3)

Feb. 9, Treaty for reciprocal trade with Canada, signed at Paris

Feb. 16, Attack on the Ministry; confidence voted (315–186)

Feb. 24, M. Jules Ferry elected President of the Senate; died, aged nearly 61, March 17

March 5, Death of H. A. Taine, philosopher and historian, aged 64

March 10, 11, Great public excitement at the disclosures; the Ministry supported by the Chamber and Senate March 13, 14

March 23, Manifesto of the comte de Paris attacking the Republic in relation to the Panama affairs

March 27, M. Challamel-Lacour elected President of the Senate

March 28, Herr Otto Brandes, a German journalist, expelled for libeling Ernest Carnot; his family insulted by a mob (for which the Government apologized)

March 30, Resignation of the Ribot Ministry through amendments to the budget

April 1, 2, M. Méline fails to form a cabinet

April 3, New Ministry: Premier and Minister of Interior, M. Dupuy; Foreign Affairs, M. Develle; Finance, M. Peytral; Commerce, M. Terrier; Education, M. Poincaré; Justice, M. Guérin; Agriculture, M. Viger; Public Works, M. Viette; War, General Lozillon; Marine, Admiral Rieunier; Colonies, M. Delcasé

June 22, M. Millevoye, a Boulangist, accuses M. Clemenceau and others of complicity in the publication in the Cocarde of forged documents alleged to have been stolen from the British Embassy; after a stormy debate, the Chamber passes to the order of the day (389–4); Norton, for forgery, sentenced to 3 years' imprisonment; Ducret to 1 year Aug. 5, 6

June, July, Dispute with Siam (see Siam)

July 2, Death of duc d Uzés, chief of an expedition in Portuguese Congo, reported

July 6, M. Henri Guy de Maupassant, eminent novelist, dies

Aug. 16 et seq., Conflicts between French and Italian salt-workers at Aigues-Montes; see Italy

End of Aug., Four French warships launched, at St. Nazaire, Nantes, Brest, Cherbourg

Aug. 20–Sept. 3, General election; for Government, 292; Socialists, 187; "Rallied" (to republicanism), 35; Monarchists, 58; M. Clemenceau and M. Floquet rejected; many Socialists, M. Réné Goblet, leader, elected for Paris

Sept. 18, The coal miners in the Pas de Calais, &c., demand increase of wages; leads to a strike of about 42,000 men

Oct. 13–29, Visit of the Russian fleet to Toulon, &c.

Oct. 17, Death of Marshal MacMahon, aged 85

Oct. 18, Death of M. Gounod, musical composer

Nov. 4, Death of M. Tirard, ex-Premier, aged 66

——, Strike ends by submission

Nov. 26, Difference between M. Carnot and the Ministry; M. Dupuy resigns, after a crisis

Dec. 3, New Ministry:—Premier and Foreign Office, M. Casimir-Périer; Finance, M. Burdeau; Interior, M. Raynal; Education and Public Worship, M. Spuller; Justice, M. Antonin Dubost; War, General Mercier; Marine, Vice-Admiral Lefevre; Public Works, M. Jonnart; Commerce, M. Marty; Agriculture, M. Viger

Dec. 5, M. Dupuy elected President of the Chamber

Dec. 9, A bomb thrown at the President in the French Chamber during the debate, by Auguste Vaillant, an anarchist, who was apprehended and confessed; many injured, order maintained

Dec. 11, A restrictive press law in relation to anarchists passed by the Chamber (413–63)

About Dec. 13, The "Rallied" agree to call themselves "Independent Republicans"

1894

Jan. 1 et seq., Nearly 2,000 domiciliary visits on anarchists in Paris and provinces; many arrests and seizure of explosives

Jan. 10, Vaillant, when sentenced to death, cried out, "Vive l'Anarchie"; executed Feb. 4

Jan. 13, Death of Wm. Henry Waddington, aged 67

Jan. 17, Bill for the conversion of the 4½ % rentes to 3½ % passed by the Senate

Jan. 27, Maurice Charnay sentenced to 6 years imprisonment for publishing "Le catéchisme du soldat," inciting to mutiny

Feb. 12, Emile Henry, an anarchist, aged 20, throws a bomb into the café of the Terminus hotel; many injured, 2 deaths

Feb. 19, Another bomb explosion in a private house; several injured, and a woman killed

Feb. 24, M. Jean Grave sentenced to 2 years' imprisonment and a fine, for writing "La société mourante" and "l'Anarchie"

Feb. 27, Duty on corn, 7f. per quintal, passed

March 15, Joseph Pauwels killed by his own bomb at the Madeleine

March 19, The establishment of a colonial ministry passed by the Senate (225–32)

March 21, M. Boulanger created Colonial Minister

April 4, An explosion of a bomb at the Café Foyot in Paris; several persons injured

April 16, Budget introduced; deficit, 139,000,000f., met by conversion of the debt, increased taxation, &c.

April 28, Emile Henry, anarchist (see above, Feb. 12) convicted; executed May 21

April 30, Navy estimates, 277,000,000f. (issued), increase, 10,000,000f.

May 23, Defeat of the Ministry in the Chamber by the Radicals in relation to the restraining of workmen on State railways from attending a congress (251–217); resigned

May 29, New Ministry: Premier, Interior, and Public Worship, M. Dupuy; Justice, M. Guérin; Finance, M. Poincaré; Education, M. J. Leygues; War, General Mercier; Marine, M. Félix Faure; Colonies, M. Delcassé; Public Works, M. Barthou; Commerce, M. Lourties; Agriculture, M. Viger; Foreign, M. Hanotaux

May 31, The Ministry declare a moderate policy

June 2, M. Casimir-Périer elected President

June 7, Discussion in the Chamber on the Anglo-Belgian Treaty

June 12, 1,900,000f. voted by the Senate for African reinforcements

June 24, President Carnot warmly received at Lyons; stabbed in his carriage on his way to the theater by Santo Caserio, 9:30 P.M.; dies at 12:45 A.M., June 25

June 27, M. Casimir-Périer, President of the Chamber, elected President of the Republic by the Senate and Chamber

July 1, M. Dupuy and his cabinet agree to remain in office; gazetted July 2

July 5, M. Burdeau elected President of the Chamber

July, 374 pardons granted by President Casimir-Périer

July 26, New anti-anarchist bill passed by the Chamber; by the Senate, July 27

July 27, Joseph Constant Meunier arrested in London; extradited to Paris, May 11; sentenced to 20 years' penal servitude for complicity in blowing up the Véry restaurant, April 25, 1892, &c.

July 30, Socialist-Radical manifesto

Aug. 3, Caserio condemned; executed Aug. 16

Aug. 11, Three anarchists sentenced to imprisonment; 22 acquitted

Aug. 30, Execution of the Abbé Bruneau at Laval for the murder of the Abbé Fricot

Sept. 8, Death of the comte de Paris

Dec. 6, 65,000,000f. voted, &c., for the Madagascar expedition (Nov. 26), by the Senate

Dec. 7, Ferdinand de Lesseps, aged 89, died

Dec. 12, Death of M. Auguste Burdeau; aged 42; President of the Chamber of Deputies

Dec. 18, M. Brisson elected President of Chamber

Dec. 23, DREYFUS CASE, 1894–1899. Captain Alfred Dreyfus arrested Oct. 15 (trial within closed doors), convicted of delivering to a foreign power in 1894 documents connected with the defense of France; sentenced to perpetual imprisonment in a fortress

1895

Jan. 14, Resignation of M. Dupuy's Ministry through an adverse vote in the Chamber

Jan. 15, Resignation of President Casimir-Périer

Jan. 17, M. Félix Faure elected President

Jan. 24, M. Bourgeois fails to form a "concentration" cabinet

Jan. 26, A Ministry formed by M. Ribot, Finance; Interior, M. Leygues; Justice, M. Trarieux; Foreign Affairs, M. Hanotaux; War, General Zurlinden; Marine, M. Combes; Public Instruction, M. Poincaré; Public Works, M. Dupuy-Dutemps; Commerce, M. André Lebon; Agriculture, M. Gadaud; Colonies, M. Chautemps

Jan. 28, The amnesty bill passed by the Chamber

——, Death of Marshal Canrobert, aged 86

Feb. 3, Return of Henri Rochefort; six years an exile

March 1, M. Hippolyte Percher, "Harry Alis," killed in a duel near Paris by M. le Chatelier, see Egypt

April 5, M. Hanotaux's moderate speech in the Senate respecting English influence in Africa

April 13, Budget amended by the Senate passed

May 11, The Abbé Paul de Broglie, a benevolent priest, brother of the duc de Broglie, murdered in Paris by Maxence Amelot, a lunatic

May 31, Public expenditure reduced by 12,000,000f.

June 18, An Egyptian committee formed, see Egypt

July 6, Duties on hygienic drinks dropped, on alcohol increased

July, Meetings of the clergy against the monastic tax declared illegal

July, Strike in the works of the Carmaux Company's glassworks' lockout, Aug. 6; works reopened to free hands, Aug. 26; arbitration refused by M. Rességuier, Director of the firm, Nov. 4; end of strike by surrender, Nov. 22

Sept. 28, M. Louis Pasteur, chemist, physicist, and biologist, born Dec. 27, 1822; died

Oct. 1, Treaty of peace with the Hovas, *see* Madagascar

Oct. 19, M. Edmond Magnier, Senator of the Var department, sentenced to one year's imprisonment for corrupt official practices

Oct. 24–26, Debate on the Carmaux strike in the Chamber; Government majority

Oct. 28, Resignation of the Ribot Ministry through a vote of censure relating to a railway scandal (311–210)

Oct., Huahine and Bolabola, two islands in the S. Pacific, annexed by France

Oct. 31, New Cabinet (Radical but pacific): Premier and Minister of Interior, M. Bourgeois; Finance, M. Doumer; Justice, M. Ricard; War, M. Cavaignac; Marine, M. Lockroy; Public Instruction, M. Combes; Public Works, M. Guyot-Dessaigne; Commerce, M. Mesureur; Colonies, M. Paul Guieysse; Foreign Affairs, M. Berthelot; Agriculture, M. Vigo

Nov. 9, A panic on the Bourse in Paris, due to speculation, averted by MM. Rothschild and others

Emile Arton, *alias* Baron, sentenced (in absence) to 20 years' penal servitude in connection with the Panama scandals, &c.; arrested in London, Nov. 16; extradition ordered, Dec. 6; sentenced to six years' imprisonment and fine, July 10, 1896; sentence quashed on technical grounds on appeal, Aug. 6; sentenced to 8 years' imprisonment, Nov. 6, 1896

Nov. 24, M. Barthélemy Saint-Hilaire, statesman, philosopher, and savant, born Aug. 19, 1805; died

Nov. 27, M. Alexandre Dumas (fils), dramatist and novelist, born July 29, 1824; died

Dec. 28, A moderate budget finally passed

1896

Jan. 16, M. Loubet elected President of the Senate

Jan. 18, M. Floquet born 1828; died

Feb. 11, The Cabinet censured by a vote of the Senate for an illegality of M. Ricard, compromise by the Chamber, Feb. 13

Feb. 12, M. Ambrose Thomas, musical composer, born Aug. 5, 1811; died

Feb. 20, Debate in the Chamber, M. Bourgeois supports M. Ricard; confidence in the Ministry (309–185) voted

Feb. 21, The Senate, by a firm declaration, maintains its rights and withdraws from the conflict

March 26, The Government income tax replacing the house tax passed by the Chamber (5 days debate) (286–270)

April 2, Resignation of M. Berthelot; duties assumed by M. Bourgeois, March 29; M. Sarrien, Minister of Interior, March 30; confidence in the foreign policy voted in the Chamber

April 3, The Senate votes no confidence in the Ministry (who determine to retain office); and refuses the vote on the Madagascar credits to the present Ministry (171–90), April 21

April 22, M. Jean Baptiste Léon Say, eminent political economist, born 1826; died; public funeral, April 23

April 23, M. Bourgeois and his Ministry resign with a protest; the Senate adopts the Madagascar credits, April 24

April 29, New Cabinet (moderate): Premier and Minister of Agriculture, M. Méline; Justice, M. Darlan; Foreign Affairs, M. Hanotaux; Interior, M. Barthou; Finance, M. Georges Cochery; War, General Billot; Marine, Admiral Besnard; Public Instruction, M. A. Rambaud (resigned), M. Darlan, Sept.; Commerce, M. Henri Boucher; Colonies, M. André Lebon; Public Works, M. Turrel

April 30, Proposed revision of the constitution rejected by the Chamber and Senate

May 19, Differences between the Duke of Orleans and the royalist committee, which disapproves of his proposed candidature for a seat in the Chamber; his letter, *Times*

May 30, Bill for the annexation of Madagascar and its dependent islands proposed by M. Hanotaux

June 8, Death of M. Jules Simon, philosopher and philanthropist, aged 82

July 14, National fête; the President fired at by a lunatic

Aug. 16, Monument to President Carnot at Châlons-sur-Marne unveiled

Aug. 19, The *Ernest Bazin*, new roller ship, launched at St. Denis

Oct. 7, Death of General Trochu, *see above*, 1870–71

Oct. 13, The King of Greece received by M. Faure

Oct. 26, Death of M. Challemel-Lacour, statesman and scholar, aged 69

Nov. 16, Colonel Picquart, urging an inquiry into the Dreyfus case, dismissed from the War Office and replaced by Colonel Henry

Dec. 10, Mme Furtado Heine, eminent philanthropist, born 1821; died

1897

Jan. 15, M. Loubet opens the Senate, with an address

Jan. 16, M. Brisson opens the Chamber of Deputies

March 15, Vote of confidence passed in the Chamber; reinforcements sent to Crete

June 5, M. Gerault Richard, Socialist, expelled from the Chamber for disorderly conduct

July 6, M. Henri Meilhac, popular dramatist, died, aged 67

Aug. 15, Duel between Prince Henry of Orleans and the Count of Turin; *see* Italy

Aug. 23, President Faure received by the Czar at Cronstadt, arrives at Peterhof; leaves, Aug. 26; returns to Paris, Aug. 31

Aug., Franco-Russian alliance confirmed

Oct. 8, The sovereigns of Belgium, Serbia, Bulgaria, and Siam, at Paris

Nov. 16, Government inquiry instituted into Dreyfus case

Dec. 1, M. Darlan, Minister of Justice, resigns, in consequence of a qualified vote of censure; succeeded by M. Millard, Dec. 2

Dec. 3, Duties on wine, beer, and cider reduced

Dec. 4, 7, Debates in the Chamber on the Dreyfus affair

Dec., Baron Mohrenheim, Russian Ambassador, resigns, succeeded by Prince Urussoff

Dec. 10, Criminal investigations bill, an important reform (passed by the Senate, Nov.), becomes law

Dec. 16, M. Alphonse Daudet, novelist, died, aged 57

1898

Jan. 11, Count Esterhazy tried by court martial for treason, Jan. 10, and acquitted (Dreyfus case)

Jan. 13, Letter *J'accuse* to the President from M. Zola

in the *Aurore*, denouncing the conviction of Captain Dreyfus on the strength of a single document which was kept secret, as illegal; and bringing charges against Generals Mercier, Billot (Minister of War), and others; and asserting the Esterhazy court martial to have knowingly acquitted a guilty man

Jan. 22, Violent scene in the Chamber on the discussion of the Dreyfus case, sitting closed

Jan. 24, Declarations of the Government against further discussion in the Chamber, adopted, 376–133

——, Herr von Bülow, Foreign Secretary, asserts in the Reichstag at Berlin, that there never had been any relations between ex-Captain Dreyfus and any German representative; Italy declares the same, Jan. 31

Jan. 29, Dr. Pean, eminent surgeon, founder of the International hospital, born, 1830, died

Feb. 7–23, M. Zola and M. Perreux (publisher of the *Aurore*), 15 days' trial, for defamation, with reference to the Esterhazy court martial (*see above*, Jan. 13); sentence, *maximum*: M. Zola, 1 year, and M. Perreux, 4 months' imprisonment, and 3,000*f.* fine each (*Times*, Feb. 24, 1898)

Feb. 24, Interpellation in the Chamber, Government largely supported; "Disciplinary measures" introduced by M. Méline; Colonel Picquart and others punished for intervention, Feb. 25

April 2, Legal proceedings respecting M. Zola; he escapes to England, July 18

April 5, Lease of a bay S.E. coast, &c., granted by China; Kwang-chan-wan occupied, April 22

April 18, M. Jules Marco, eminent geologist and explorer, died, aged 74

May 8, General elections; Government *net* majority (4); the Chamber meets June 1; M. Méline resigns June 15; M. Brisson forms a Cabinet June 28; the Chambers meet June 30

June 14, Anglo-French agreement. *See* Africa

June 15, Resignation of M. Méline's Ministry; several failures to form a cabinet; new Ministry: Premier and Minister of the Interior, M. Brisson; Foreign Affairs, M. Delcassé; Finance, M. Peytral; Justice, M. Sarrien; Education, M. Léon Bourgeois; War, M. Cavaignac; Marine, M. Lockroy; Colonies, M. Trouillot; Commerce, M. Mauruéjouls; Agriculture, M. Viger; Public Works, M. Tillaye, June 28

July 8, Abyssinian envoys, with a letter and presents to President Faure, received by him at Paris

July 13, Colonel Picquart arrested for disclosing State papers; his trial postponed, Sept. 21

Aug. 31, Lieutenant Colonel Henry, chief of the *Espionnage* department, after confessing to forgery of documents against Dreyfus, is arrested and commits suicide in prison

Sept. 3, Proposed revision of the Dreyfus case agreed to; M. Cavaignac, Minister of War, resigns; succeeded by General Zurlinden, Sept. 5; he and M. Tillaye, both against revision of the Dreyfus case, resign, succeeded by General Chanoine, War, and M. Godin, Public Works, Sept. 17; revision commission meets, Sept. 21 *et seq.*; divided in opinion, the Dreyfus case referred to the Cour de Cassation Sept. 27

Oct. 25, The Ministry, defeated by the anti-revisionists, resigns; new conciliation Ministry: Premier and Minister of Interior, M. Dupuy; Foreign, M. Delcassé; Finance, M. Peytral; War, M. de Freycinet; Marine, M. Lockroy, Oct. 31

Nov. 21, New commercial treaty with Italy signed

Dec. 1, Bill allowing aid of counsel to accused in courts martials passed the Senate (by the Chamber, June 8, 1899); one abolishing public executions, adopted by the Senate, Dec. 5

Dec. 12, Demonstration in Paris against Colonel Picquart and in honor of the army, a stormy scene in the Chamber; Chambers closed, Dec. 24

1899

Jan., "League de la Patrie Française" (anti-revision of the Dreyfus case) founded; manifesto issued, Jan. 1; *L'Union Nationale*, opposition league, started

Jan. 4, M. Edouard Hervé, journalist, founder of the *Soleil*, 1873, died, aged 64

Jan. 10, 12, The Chambers opened, M. Deschanel elected President of the Deputies; M. Loubet re-elected President in the Senate

Jan., M. Adolphe Philippe Dennery, dramatist, born June 17, 1811; bequeaths his Paris house and collections to the nation

Jan., French maritime league founded

Feb. 7, Comte de Chambrun, benefactor, founder of the "Musée Social," 1894, dies, aged 78

Feb. 10, Anarchist disorder in Paris suppressed

——, Criminal procedure bill passed by the Chamber, 332–216

Feb. 16, Sudden death of President Faure.

Feb. 18, Emile Loubet elected President of the Republic at Versailles by 483 votes against 279 for M. Méline.

Feb. 25, M. Méline elected President of the Chamber

March 3, M. Fallières of the Senate

Feb. 25–28, Domiciliary visits to royalist houses, &c.; treasonable leagues dissolved and prosecuted, March–April

March 21, Anglo-French convention signed in London, ratified, May 30

March 26, Comte de Chaudordy, diplomatist, born 1826, dies

About April 20, M. Pailleron, eminent dramatist, born Sept. 17, 1834; died

May 5, M. de Freycinet (Minister of War), after a stormy debate in the Chamber, resigns; succeeded by M. Krantz; M. Monestier taking office of Public Works, May 6

May 6, Agreement with Germany as to Bagdad Railway, and Anatolian and Smyrna-Cassaba railways

May, M. Francisque Sarcey, eminent dramatic critic, &c., born 1828, died May 16; M. Henri Becque, dramatist and journalist, born, April 9, 1837; died

May 30, 31, Major Marchand and force from Fashoda warmly received at Toulon, Marseilles, and Paris, June 1

June 4, Anti-Dreyfus demonstration at the Auteuil races; President Loubet assaulted, ringleaders arrested

June 5, Stormy debate in the Chamber; M. Largentaye, a royalist, suspended; ministerial declarations carried, 513–32

June 9, Supplementary credit of 61,600,000*f.* for coast defenses, France and colonies, voted

June 11, Difference in the Chamber respecting the conduct of the police at Longchamp; the Ministry resigns, June 12

June 13, 16, Baron F. de Christiani sentenced to 4 years' imprisonment for assaulting President Loubet at Auteuil, 7 others to fines and short imprisonment

June 19, 22, Admiral de Cuverville superseded for criticizing defects in the defenses; General de la Rocque removed from active service

June 22, New (concentration) Cabinet: Premier and Minister of Interior, M. Waldeck-Rousseau; War, General de Galliffet; Marine, M. de Lanessan; Justice, M. Monis; Foreign Affairs, M. Delcassé; Commerce, M. Millerand; Finance, M. Caillaux; Education, M. Georges Leygues; Public Works, M. Pierre Baudin; Colonies, M. Decrais; Agriculture, M. Jean Dupuy

June 26, Ministerial declaration approved in the Chamber, 263–237, and Senate, 157–25

——, General Gilletta di San Giuseppe (Italian) charged with espionage, sentenced to 5 years' imprisonment and a fine of 5,000*f*., at Nice; pardoned by President Loubet, July 9; placed on half-pay, July 16

June 27, Stormy debate in the Chamber; M. Déroulède's proposal for the revision of the constitution refused urgency, 379–70; Chamber prorogued, July 4

July 1, Victor Cherbuliez, novelist and critic, "Comte Kostia," born at Geneva, 1829; died

July 7, General Zurlinden, Military Governor of Paris, superseded by General Brugère

July–Aug., General de Pellieux removed from the command of Paris (dies, aged 58, July 15, 1900); General de Négrier dismissed from the supreme council of war for inciting to insubordination in the army, July 26; succeeded by General Pierron

Aug. 12, Pisson, tried *in camera* and condemned to 3 years' imprisonment and 500*f*. fine, for attempting to sell to foreigners documents relating to national defenses

——, M. Paul Déroulède and others arrested on a charge of plotting against the Republic; M. Jules Guérin, founder of the "Anti-Semitic league," resists arrest, and stands siege in the Rue de Chabrol, thoroughfare closed by police, Aug. 13

Aug. 20, Anarchist demonstration in Paris, rioting, 380 persons injured, 2 churches pillaged, many arrests

Sept. 20, M. Jules Guérin surrenders in the Rue de Chabrol

——, Admiral Sallandrouze de Lamornaix, born, 1840, died suddenly on board the *Formidable*

Oct. 7, Strike at the Creuzot ironworks (20 days) ends with concessions to the men, by the arbitration of M. Waldeck-Rousseau (Premier)

Oct. 30, Suppression of the embassy to the Vatican voted by the budget committee

Oct. 31 General de Galliffet's army reforms sanctioned by the Cabinet and President, *see Times*

Nov. 6, Major Esterhazy (Dreyfus Case) tried for embezzlement (sends written defense); find 500*f*. and sentenced to 3 years' imprisonment

Nov. 14, The Chamber opens; interpellations against the Government and the Minister of War; vote of confidence, ministerial "acts of republican defense" approved, 320–215, Nov. 16

1900

Jan. 9, M. Deschanel reëlected President of the Chamber, 308–221

Jan. 22, The superior and 11 monks of the Assumptionist fathers charged with belonging to an illegal association and with issuing propaganda against the Government; the community dissolved the superior and father Bailly, director of *La Croix* newspaper, and 10 others, fined, Jan. 24 [sentence confirmed by the court of appeal, March 6]

Jan., The stipends of several bishops suspended by Government

Jan. 28, Senatorial elections, Republican victory (99 seats, 92 gained by the Government); Nationalists: General Mercier and 2 others

Feb. 5, Senate meets, Feb. 1; M. Fallières reëlected President

MM. Buffet and Déroulède charged with conspiracy against the State, Nov. 9; sentenced to 10 years' banishment; M. Jules Guérin to 10 years' detention in a fortress, Jan. 4; M. Marcel Habert, banished for 5 years, Feb. 23

March 28, Death of Count Benedetti, diplomatist (ambassador in Berlin, 1864–70), aged 83

April 12, Budget (good surplus) passed, 457–32; Chambers adjourn

April 14, Paris (international) exhibition opened by President Loubet

May 22, Chamber meets, amendment opposing a revival of the Dreyfus case carried, 457–78; noisy scene in the Chamber, Government majority 47, May 28; General de Galliffet (able War Minister) in ill health resigns, succeeded by General André, May 29; amnesty bill (stopping further prosecutions connected with the Dreyfus case) passed by the Senate, June 2

July 2, M. Berthelot's vote of censure regarding military operations in S. Algeria rejected by the Chamber, 458–60

July 4, General André's firmness in maintaining discipline among the officers, supported by the Chambers; General Delanne, Chief of the Staff, and General Jamont, Generalissimo, resign; succeeded at once by General Pendezec and General Brugère

July 16, Abyssinian envoys received by President Loubet

July 28–Aug. 11, The Shah of Persia visits Paris

Sept. 3, M. de Witte, Russian Finance Minister, arrives in Paris; President Loubet invested with the Russian Order of St. Andrew

Nov. 6, 8, The Chambers meet: M. Waldeck-Rousseau (in the Deputies) announces the religious associations bill and other important measures; vote of confidence passed, 316–237

Nov. 22, Popular ovations to Mr. Kruger, ex-President of the Transvaal, at Marseilles; and Paris; received by President Loubet, Nov. 24

Nov. 29, 30, Resolutions of sympathy to Mr. Kruger passed by the Chamber and Senate

Dec. 7, The Chamber adopts a resolution, counting on the Government to repress slavery and cruelty in the colonies (Government majority, 77)

Dec. 19, Amnesty amendment bill, against a revival of the Dreyfus agitation and stopping prosecutions pending against M. Zola, Colonel Picquart and others, passed by the Chamber, 155–2, after much debate; by the Senate, Dec. 24

Dec. 22, M. Zola's letter to President Loubet in the *Aurore* protests against the amnesty bill as a denial of justice

1901

Jan. 8, 9, Chambers meet; MM. Deschanel and Fallières reëlected Presidents

Jan. 14, M. Waldeck-Rousseau's declaration that the Pope has no power to intervene in State affairs, carried by a large majority

Jan. 15, M. Arthur Desjardins, eminent jurist and international lawyer, dies, aged 65

Jan. 19, Death of the duc de Broglie, historian, and statesman, aged 80

Early Feb., Army reorganization, M. de Montebello's plan adopted by army committee

March 16, M. de Rodays, editor of the *Figaro*, wounded in a duel with Count Boni de Castellane, near Paris

March 21, M. Edmond Got, actor, dies, aged 79

March 29, The associations (21 clauses) bill (against unauthorized religious tutelage and communities) introduced Jan. 15, passed by the Chamber after long debates, 303–224

April 1, Professor François Raoult, eminent chemist, born May 10, 1830, dies

April 8–10, President Loubet visits Nice, and entertains the Italian fleet at Toulon

June 2, Eugène Manuel, Inspector-General of Education and popular poet, dies, aged 78

June 6, Count de Lur-Saluces sentenced to 5 years' banishment for treason (with extenuating circumstances)

June 14, Scene in the Chamber on Algerian affairs, M. Drumont, an anti-Semite, expelled

Middle June, Moorish mission arrives in Paris

July 1, Associations (religious) bill (amended by the Senate) passed by the Chamber, 313–149, June 28; promulgated

July–Oct. 3, 8,800 Roman Catholic religious establishments out of a total of 16,468 apply for authorization under the new associations law; the Jesuits, Passionists, Assumptionists, Benedictines, and others leave France, many for England

Aug. 9, Prince Henry of Orleans, eminent explorer, dies at Saigon, aged 34

Aug. 18, M. Edmond Audran, popular composer (*La Mascotte*, &c.), died, aged 59

Aug. 25, Sugar bounties reduced by 55% to cover 14,000,000*f.* deficit

Aug.–Sept. 3, Diplomatic rupture with Turkey. *See s.v.*

Sept. 18, President Loubet meets the Czar and Czarina off Dunkirk; naval review held; they leave Sept. 21

Oct. 10, MM. Tailhade & Grandidier sentenced to 12 and 6 months' imprisonment respectively for inciting to murder by an anarchist propaganda in the journal *Libertaire*

Oct. 22, Chambers opened; M. Basly's proposal for a minimum wage and an 8 hours' day for miners rejected, 290–245; and a motion to repeal the law against anarchists defeated, 402–132

Nov. 4, Debate on Franco-Turkish affairs, *see* Turkey, Aug.–Nov.; vote of confidence in the Ministry, 305–77

Nov., M. de Lanessan (Marine Minister) abolishes compulsory attendance at mass, and prohibits the substitution of the religious service flag for the tricolor in the navy

Nov. 11, Diplomatic relations with Turkey resumed

Nov. 14, Railway bill (10 hours' day) passed by the Chamber, 338–87

Dec. 13, M. Hervé, professor in the Sens university, dismissed for anti-military newspaper articles; debate in the Chamber, M. Leygues' speech defending the action of the authorities ordered to be placarded; M. Roger-Ballu, fine art professor, also dismissed for insulting the Government, Dec. 19

Middle Dec., Budget (amended), surplus 146,000*f.* reported

Dec. 21, 22, The 3% loan of 265,000,000*f.* in connection with the Chinese indemnity passed by the Chamber, 335–213, Nov. 28; by the Senate, 224–43,

Dec. 6; issued and subscribed about 25 times over

End Dec., M. Fouquier, brilliant journalist, died, aged 63

1902

Jan. 14, M. Paul Deschanel again reëlected President of the Chamber

Feb. 5, Miners (eight hours) bill passed by the Chamber

Feb. 6, Death of Mme Clémence Royer, eminent *savant* and essayist, aged 72

Feb. 14, Abrogation of the Falloux law, guaranteeing liberty of instruction, voted in the Chamber, 289–239

March 18, Future chambers to last 6 instead of 4 years, voted by the Chamber, 298–237

March 21, The Chamber votes an amnesty for strikers, but rejects that for anarchists

April 14, Death of Professor Alfred Cornu, eminent scientist, aged 61

April 27–May 11, Elections (Ministerial majority, 88)

May 8, Humbert-Crawford case, extensive frauds carried on for 20 years; sham litigation; proceedings finally instituted; M. and Mme Humbert escaped

May 20–25, President Loubet warmly received in Russia and Copenhagen; holds a naval review at Dunkirk, May 27; 220 convicts pardoned, or their sentences reduced, May 30

May 26, Death of M. Benjamin Constant, painter, aged 55

——, Death of Mme Durand, "Henry Greville," novelist, aged about 60

June 3, M. Waldeck-Rousseau, Premier (in need of rest) and his Ministry resign

June 6, M. Léon Bourgeois elected President of the Chamber

June 7, New Ministry: Premier and Minister of Interior and Public Worship, M. Combes; Justice, M. Vallé; Foreign, M. Delcassé; War, General André; Public Works, M. Maruéjouls; Agriculture, M. Mougeot; Finance, M. Rouvier; Marine, M. Pelletan; Education, M. Chaumié; Commerce, M. Trouillot; Colonies, M. Doumergue; Posts and Telegraphs, M. Bérard

June 10, M. Bourgeois opens the Chamber of Deputies

June 12, Government policy, unsectarianism, fiscal reforms, &c.; vote of confidence passed

——, Mme Henry, widow of Colonel Henry (Dreyfus) *v.* M. Reinach and the manager of the *Siècle*, for libel, damages for plaintiff 500*f.*

June 20, Cabinet council decides that no official is to be appointed until questioned as to politics

June 27, Debate in the Chamber on the Humbert-Crawford frauds; vote of confidence in the Government carried, 403–74; discussed in the Senate, July 10

July 4, Debate in the Chamber on the closing of Roman Catholic schools for infringing the associations law; vote of confidence in the Government carried, 333–206

July 9, 10, Conversion of the 3½% rentes into 3% bill passed by the Senate and made law; the closing of 2,500 Catholic schools denounced in the Chamber, wild uproar, July 11

July, Prince Komatsu, Japan, the Crown Prince of Siam, and Ras Makonnen, Abyssinian envoy, visit France

July 21, Protests of the episcopate against the closing of conventual schools, July; M. Combes' defense issued;

hostile demonstrations in Paris and elsewhere; M. Coppée, Lerolle, and Conti arrested, July 22, 23, 26

July 31, Colonel Picquart is awarded 20,000*f*. damages for the libel in the *Echo de Paris*

Aug. 25, Visit of the Shah of Persia; and the Khedive, Sept. 2

Aug. 26, Sir Wilfrid Laurier, Canadian Premier, received by President Loubet; entertained at a banquet (leaves Oct. 2), Sept. 1

Sept. 26, Lieutenant-Colonel de Saint Rémy arrested, Aug. 9, for refusing to assist at the closing of a conventual school as against his religious convictions, sentenced by court martial to a day's imprisonment, Sept. 5; placed on the retired list, Sept. 9; Major Le Roy Ladurie also dismissed

Sept. 29, M. Emile Zola, eminent writer and novelist (*see* Dreyfus case), found suffocated in his bedroom, from a foul chimney (Mme Zola was also unconscious, but recovered)

Sept. 30, M. Rouvier's budget approved by the Cabinet

Oct. 3, M. Combes calls on 22 bishops to renounce the employment of Lazarists and Marists

Oct. 7, Franco-Siamese treaty, ratification of frontier, signed

Oct. 8, 9, General coal strike declared (about 100,000 out); riot at St. Etienne, 2 miners killed, Oct. 11

Oct. 13–15, Boer generals visit Paris

Oct. 14, 16, Chambers meet, budget estimates, large deficits for 1902; debate on the closing of conventual schools; resolution supporting the Government passed, 329–233, Oct. 17

Oct. 18–Nov. 16, Visit of the King of Portugal, again Dec. 8–10

Oct. 20, Committee appointed by the Chamber to consider the question of separation of Church and State

Oct. 30, M. Clemenceau upholds the Government and criticizes the Concordat; resolution for the Ministry carried, 163–90

Nov. 10, Navy estimates, 306,000,000*f*., issued

Nov. 20, Colonel Picquart (charged with treason by the *Jour*) awarded 10,000*f*.

Nov. 28, Petition of 74 bishops in favor of the religious orders declared illegal, reported

Nov. 29, Two years' military service bill to come into operation 1904

About Dec. 4, Colliers' strike over, award accepted

Dec. 6, Violent scenes in the Chamber, on an interpellation *re* the escape of the Humberts (swindlers); vote of confidence carried, 338–133

Dec. 11, Strike riots at Marseilles

Dec. 20, The Humbert family arrested in Madrid

Dec. 29, And brought to Paris

Dec. 30, Report of new Panama canal company to sell concessions and property to the United States for 40,000,000 dollars and to verification of company's title adopted (Paris)

1903

Jan. 4, Senatorial elections: Government gain 13

Jan. 13, Chamber meets, M. Bourgeois reëlected President

Jan. 15, Interpellation *re* religious orders, Government acts approved, 313–211

Jan. 18, Eight hours' day extended to naval establishments

——, Death of M. de Blowitz, 30 years Paris correspondent of *The Times*, aged 78

Feb., Dispute with the Vatican concerning vacant bishopric nominations

Feb. 13, Scene in the Chamber regarding the Humbert swindle, interpellation postponed

March 6, Death of M. Gaston, Paris, scholar and writer

March 12–18, Debates on the religious orders, 54 refused authorization, Ministerial vote carried

March 14, Death of M. Ernest Legouvé, dramatist, aged 96

March 21, Motion for the suppression of the budget of public worship rejected, M. Combes' declaration *re* Church and State, approved

April 6–7, M. Jaurès in the Chamber urges the reopening of the Dreyfus case in a long speech

April 14, Socialist congress at Bordeaux, M. Millerand, *opportunist*, remains a member by majority of 20

April 15, President Loubet visits Algiers, confers honors on Admiral Curzon-Howe, and other officers of the British squadron

April 29, Government measures resisted by several bishops, and various religious associations; expulsions of religious orders continue

May 1–2, King Edward warmly welcomed, Paris *en fête*; review of troops at Vincennes; races held at Longchamp; State banquet, &c.; leaves May 4

May 17, Anti-clerical demonstrations held in various places

May 20, Debate in the Chamber on the action of the Government with regard to the religious bodies; motion for the separation of Church and State rejected, 278–247; order of the day the Government's policy, and counting on its firmness to repress the encroachments of the clergy, and the maintenance of religious liberty, adopted

May 24, "Max O'Rell," Paul Blouët, author, and Paris correspondent of the *New York Journal*, died, aged 55

June 23, Violent scene in the Chamber during a debate on the religious question: expenditure of 256,000,000*f*. on the improvement of French ports and canals approved by the Senate

July 9, President Loubet, on his return from England, sends a message to King Edward VII expressing his warm gratitude for his reception; the King in reply expressed his ardent desire that the *rapprochement* between the two countries should be lasting

Aug. 22, M. and Mme Humbert found guilty of forgery and swindling, and the Daurignacs for complicity in swindling; the Humberts sentenced to 5 years' solitary confinement, Romain Daurignac to 3 years', and Emile Daurignac to 2 years' imprisonment

Late Aug., Territory on the right bank of the Lower Senegal added to French colonial possessions, announced

Sept. 4, King of the Belgians received by M. Loubet

——, M. Combes, at Auxerre, announces that the Government proposes to introduce measures providing for an income tax for workmen's pensions, and for the separation of Church and State

Oct. 5–13, Strikes: mills and factories stopped round Lille and Armentières, troops called out, many arrests reported

Oct. 14, Anglo-French arbitration agreement signed, London

Oct. 14–18, Visit of King and Queen of Italy

Oct. 22, Chambers opened Oct. 20; resolution on M. Combes' policy against clerical and monarchist reactionaries, carried by 332 votes to 233

Oct. 28, London international and commercial association visit Paris

Oct. 30, Czar's letter to M. Loubet expressing his pleasure at the Anglo-French arbitration agreement and the *rapprochement* with Italy read at the Cabinet council

Nov. 12, Motion for a commission of inquiry as to the complicity of politicians in the Humbert frauds carried in the Chamber by 360 votes to 203

Nov. 20, Amendment to the education bill excluding members of religious bodies, whether authorized or unauthorized, from teaching, passed by the Senate, by 147 votes to 136

Nov. 27, Second revision of the Dreyfus case decided upon; commission appointed by M. Vallé, Minister of Justice, announced

Dec. 5, M. Jaurès, leader of the Socialist Party, puts forward as his program the secularization of education, the separation of Church and State, and the imposition of a general and progressive income tax

Dec. 25, Arbitration treaty with Italy signed

Dec. 31, Baron Arthur de Rothschild died Dec. 10; he bequeathed his valuable collection of paintings to the Louvre, and collection of ancient rings to the Cluny museum, reported

1904

Jan. 6, Joan d'Arc publicly declared to have passed her second stage of canonization, and acquired the title of "Venerable"

Jan. 12, Chambers reassemble: M. Henri Brisson elected President of the Chamber, M. Fallières President of the Senate

Jan. 22, Debate on the expulsion of the German Abbé Delsor from France; action of the Government supported by 295 to 243 votes

Feb. 13, New treaty with Siam signed at Paris

Feb. 20, Panic on the Bourse, the worst since 1870, heavy fall of French rentes

Feb. 22, Statement by M. Pelletan, Minister of Marine, to the naval commission of the Chamber on the resources of the French navy received with great satisfaction

Feb. 27, Arbitration treaty with Spain signed

March 5, Criminal chamber of the Court of Cassation, after lengthened inquiry, acquiesce in the application for the revision of the Dreyfus case, and orders a supplementary inquiry into the fresh facts disclosed

March 7, Chamber votes urgency for the Government bill for the suppression of teaching by religious bodies in conventual and monastic schools within the next 5 years, by 310 to 262 votes; bill passed in its entirety by 316 votes to 269, March 28

March 28, Demonstration of weavers on strike at Roubaix, charged at by mounted troops, many persons wounded

April 2, Religious emblems ordered by the Government to be removed from French law courts

April 6, Arbitration treaty with Holland signed

April 8, Anglo-French Agreement, disposing wholly or partially of outstanding questions between France and Great Britain. It consists of (1) a *convention* with regard to Newfoundland (providing for the abandonment of French rights of landing on the Newfoundland treaty shore), and W. Africa (boundaries); (2) a *déclaration* dealing with Egypt (France recognizes Great Britain's predominant position in Egypt) and Morocco (Great Britain recognizes

France's influence in Morocco); (3) a *déclaration annexe* relating to Siam, Madagascar, and the New Hebrides signed

April 24, Visit of President Loubet, accompanied by M. Delcassé, to Rome, on a return visit to the King of Italy; meet with an enthusiastic welcome in Rome; entertained by the King and Queen at the Quirinal; State banquet, April 25; military review, April 26; banquet at the French Embassy, April 27; naval review of combined French and Italian squadrons at Naples, April 28; return to France, April 29

May 4, Pope expresses his unqualified disapproval of President Loubet's visit to the King of Italy, on the ground that the President being the head of a Catholic State by this action recognizes the power which deprived the Vatican of its temporal dominions, and addresses a formal protest

May 17, Government decides the papal protest remain unanswered, regarding as offensive the tone of remonstrance expressed in a circular sent by the Pope respecting the incident to certain foreign powers

May 21, French Ambassador recalled from the Vatican; M. de Courcel left as Chargé d'Affaires to conduct the business of the Embassy; M. Nisard leaves Rome

May 27, Chamber of Deputies unanimously approves the action of the Government in its withdrawal of the French Ambassador

June 6, Navy estimates, 310,000,000f. (12,400,000l.), communicated to the Chamber, increase in the navy for forthcoming year; debate on new military bill; proposal to substitute a national militia for a permanent army rejected by 506 votes to 68; article 1, declaring every Frenchman subject to personal service; and article 2, abolishing all exemptions, adopted, June 7

June 10, Scene in the Chamber between M. Combes and M. Millerand arising from M. Combes' statement of an alleged attempt to bribe him if he would propose a bill favoring the Carthusian monks; a special committee of 33 members (Chartreux inquiry commission) appointed by the Chamber to inquire into the matter

July 4, M. Loubet at the Elysée receives a deputation from a party of British workmen who visit Paris

July 5, Military service bill, substituting two for three years' service, adopted by the Chamber by 577 votes to 43

——, Chartreux inquiry commission declare M. Combes, his son M. Edgar Combes, and others, alleged to be implicated, are absolved from all blame in connection with the Carthusian bribery affair

July 9, Arbitration treaty with Sweden and Norway signed

July 12, Report of the Chartreux inquiry commission discussed in the Chamber; motion exculpating the Prime Minister and Government carried by 370 votes to 82

July, Manager Geay, Bishop of Laval, receives orders from the Vatican to resign his see, and Manager Le Nordez, Bishop of Dijon, is commanded to abstain from fulfilling certain duties, including the ordination of priests; called upon to resign; they appeal to the Minister of Public Worship, who directs them to return to their dioceses; summoned by the Curia to Rome, and Minister orders them not to leave their dioceses

Middle July, Note addressed by Government to the Vatican requesting the withdrawal of the letters addressed to the two bishops as being inconsistent with the Concordat

July 26, Bishop of Dijon, in obedience to the papal summons, goes to Rome

July 30, Rupture of diplomatic relations between the French Government and the Vatican; French Chargé d'Affaires recalled from Rome; the papal nuncio receives an intimation from M. Delcassé that his mission no longer serves any purpose; he leaves Paris; Government publishes the principal documents relating to the conflict with the Vatican

Aug. 8, Serious fires in the arsenals of Toulon and St. Nazaire, estimated loss 2,000,000*f.* (80,000*l.*); famous Vauban docks at Toulon destroyed

Aug. 10, Death of M. Waldeck-Rousseau, Premier 1899–1902

Aug. 16, Strike of sailors at Marseilles; important companies suspend the sailing of their vessels, 176 vessels with aggregate burden of 450,000 tons idle; strike spreads to other ports; dockers decline to accept the terms of the masters; resume work, Sept. 7

Aug. 17, Inhabitants of Clermont-Ferrand prevent the expulsion of the Ursuline nuns at Ambert, the officer in command of the *gendarmerie* is beaten by the mob

Sept. 4, M. Combes speaks at Auxerre, and refers to the difference with the Vatican, declares his opinion that a concordat is no longer possible, and that the only solution is separation by mutual consent

Sept. 5, Cardinal Merry del Val notifies his acceptance of the resignation of Manager Le Nordez as Bishop of Dijon, and of Manager Geay as Bishop of Laval

Oct. 9, Colonel Rollin and Captains Dautriche, François, and Naréehal, who were set at liberty after the investigation of certain charges made against them in the Dreyfus case, rearrested

Oct. 12, Paris *Figaro* publishes a number of hitherto unpublished papers left behind by M. Waldeck-Rousseau, dealing with the associations law of 1901, the policy of the Combes Cabinet on the Church question and the Humbert affair

Oct. 14, Shipping strike ends

Oct. 22, Debate in the Chamber on the rupture with the Vatican; Premier, in a powerful speech, reviews the history of the relations between the Government and the Vatican since 1870, and declares that there had been deliberate disregard and violation on the part of the Vatican, both of the Concordat and organic articles; order of the day accepted by the Government, passed by 318 votes to 230

Oct. 28, Debate in the Chamber on the measures alleged to have been employed by M. André or his staff to remove anti-Republican and clerical partisans from the army, and the promotion and preference shown to Republican officers; General André declares his ignorance of many of the letters adduced by M. Guyot de Villeneuve during the debate; Chamber censures the methods employed, but expresses its confidence in General André, by 278 to 274 votes

Nov. 1, Arbitration treaty with the United States signed

Nov. 4, Violent assault committed on General André by M. Syveton, a nationalist deputy, during the debate in the Chamber on the charge that the Minister of War had employed a system of delation among army officers

Nov. 7, Court martial on the 4 officers accused in connection with the Dreyfus case closes, Major Rabier, military public prosecutor, states he had been au-

thorized "by superior authority" to abandon the prosecution

Nov. 10, Bill for separation of Church and State introduced in the Chamber by M. Combes, and referred to a committee

——, Chamber, by 415 votes to 141, authorizes the prosecution of M. Syveton

Nov. 12, Anglo-French agreement considered in the Chamber; action of the Government approved by 493 votes to 94; convention concerning Newfoundland and W. Africa confirmed by 457 votes to 5; ratification of the entire convention authorized by 443 votes to 105

Nov. 15, Resignation of General André, Minister of War, succeeded by M. Berteaux

Nov. 26, Chamber adopts a resolution expressing the intention of France to substitute lay schools progressively for conventual schools in the east

Nov. 28, Committee of the Chamber appointed to report on the bill introduced by the Government for the separation of Church and State reject the measure by a snap vote; committee composed of 33 members, the majority of Ministerial members absent at its sitting

——, Government scheme substituting an income tax in place of the personal or furniture tax, the door and window tax, and the duty on certain transactions in land, introduced by M. Rouvier, Minister of Finance

Dec. 2, M. Deville's bill for the separation of Church and State, identical with that of M. Combes, adopted by the committee

Dec. 4, Duel between MM. Déroulède and Jaurès at Hendaye

Dec. 7, Senate approves the Anglo-French agreement by 215 votes to 37

Dec. 8, Suicide of M. Syveton, nationalist deputy, the assailant of General André

Dec. 23, Railway collision in Paris, 13 killed, 21 injured, at the Porte de la Chapelle

Dec. 27, Circular on delation, issued by the Minister of War to the military governors of Paris and Lyons, and generals commanding army corps

1905

Jan. 2, Death of Manager Langênieux, Archbishop of Rheims, aged 81

Jan. 3, Territories of Krat and the Isle of Kochong transferred to Siam, reported; Chentabum evacuated, Jan. 8

Jan. 9, Death of Louise Michel, the "Red Virgin," revolutionist, at Paris, aged 74

Jan. 13, Debate in the Chamber on an interpellation challenging the general policy of the Ministry. M. Deschanel condemns the policy of the Cabinet; vote on the order of the day gives the Government a majority, 291 votes to 277; followed by an unseemly incident, M. Baudry d'Asson appearing with a brand new saucepan (*casserole*, slang for *mouchard*, a spy), which he hands to M. Combes; scene of violent disorder; vote of censure on M. Baudry d'Asson carried

Jan. 18, Resignation of M. Combes and his Cabinet

Middle Jan., Death of M. Félix Kuhn, President of the French Lutheran consistory, and author of a remarkable work on Luther, aged 80

Jan. 25, New Ministry formed by M. Rouvier, as Premier and Minister of Finance; M. Delcassé, Minister for Foreign Affairs

Jan. 27, M. Rouvier in the Chamber of Deputies makes a statement of the Government's policy, and enumerates various proposed reforms: 2 years' military service bill before the Senate, and other reforms to be taken up at point left by preceding Cabinet, and the commissions placed as follows: assistance to the aged and the incurable; abrogation of the Falloux law; an income tax; separation of Church and State; and a workmen's superannuation fund. Resolution proposed by M. Sarrien and accepted by the Government, "the Chamber, counting on the Government to realize by the union of all republicans, the lay, democratic, and social reforms, and rejecting every addition, passes to the order of the day," adopted by 410 votes to 107

Jan. 30, Two bomb outrages in Paris; a bomb placed in front of the house of Prince Troubetzkoi, military attaché of the Russian Embassy, and discovered before exploding; another, placed on the footpath in the Avenue de la République, explodes, 4 persons injured; Francis, an anarchist, and his mistress arrested, Jan. 31

Feb. 1, "League for the defense of the rights of Hellenism," founded in Paris

Feb. 5, Society founded in Paris, "Les Amis du Peuple Russe," having as its object the promotion of the movement towards emancipation in the Russian Empire

Feb. 10, M. Rouvier, Premier, in Chamber of Deputies, on the interpellation of M. Morlot on the ecclesiastical policy of the Ministry, demands priority for a motion that the Chamber, realizing that the attitude of the Vatican makes the separation of Church and State inevitable, and trusting that the Government will deal with the question immediately after the budget and army bill, passes to the order of the day. First part of the motion carried by 343 votes to 189, the second by 379 votes to 115, and the whole resolution by 386 votes to 111

Feb. 18, 19, Series of meetings organized all over France by the Socialists to "affirm the solidarity of French working-men with the heroic combatants of Russian liberty"; 21 meetings of protest are held at Lille, St. Etienne, Tours, Havre, and other important places

Feb. 23, M. Thomson, Minister of Marine, admits that France has lost her naval superiority over the Triple Alliance

Feb. 28, Chamber, by 450 votes to 108, calls for a new naval ship-building program

March 1, Death of M. Guillaume, sculptor

March 17, Senate's text of the 2 years' military service bill adopted by the Chamber by 519 votes to 32

March 23, Debate on the bill and proposals relative to the separation of the Church and the State begins in the Chamber

March 24, Death of M. Jules Verne

March 26, Letter, dated Woodnorton, March 25, from the Duke of Orleans, signed "Philippe," prophesying anarchy unless France seeks refuge in the monarchy, read at meeting of presidents of the royalist committees

End March, The 5 French cardinals address a letter to M. Loubet, recapitulating the principal arguments in favor of the Concordat and demand its maintenance

April 12, First article of bill for the separation of Church and State carried in the Chamber by a large majority

April 13, Death at Mentone of Prince Henry of Bourbon, aged 52, great-grandson of Charles X, and nephew of the comte de Chambord

April 15, Chamber adopts by 336 votes to 236, article 2 of the separation bill: "The republic neither recognizes, pays salaries to, nor subsidizes any form of worship"

——, Labor conflict in the Haviland porcelain works at Limoges culminates in rioting and pillage; bomb explosion in front of the house of one of the directors, April 16; conflict of strikers with dragoons and mounted gendarmes, 1 man killed, 3 wounded, April 17

April 18, Debate in the Chamber on the disturbances at Limoges; M. Etienne, Minister of the Interior, explains and defends the action of the authorities; M. Vaillant and M. Jaurès condemn the conduct of the prefect in employing troops

April 20, Attack made in the Chamber by M. Jaurès and Nationalist deputies on M. Delcassé's policy in Morocco. M. Delcassé defends the course he has pursued. M. Deschanel unfavorably criticizes M. Delcassé's attitude towards Germany, which M. Rouvier, Premier, defends in an important speech; no division taken

April 22, Crucial clause of the separation bill, dealing with the devolution of Church property, passes in the Chamber by 509 votes to 44

——, Delegation of London municipal working men visit their comrades in the service of the city of Paris, and are entertained by the Republican committee of commerce and industry

April 23, Resignation of M. Delcassé announced, April 21; urged by the Ministry to reconsider his decision, M. Delcassé withdraws his resignation

April 25, M. Loubet presides at the inauguration of the Gambetta monument at Bordeaux

April 29, King Edward VII arrives in Paris; received by President Loubet

May 8, Captain Tamburini, a retired officer and three accomplices tried for conspiracy against the existing form of government in France, a crime punishable by death under the penal code

May 30, Visit of the King of Spain; received by M. Loubet; entertained at State banquet at the Elysée

June 1, Attempt by an anarchist to assassinate King Alfonso of Spain by means of a bomb thrown under the carriage in which the King with President Loubet were driving in Paris

June 6, Resignation of M. Delcassé, Minister of Foreign Affairs, on the Moroccan question

June 16, M. Rouvier, Premier, takes the portfolio also of Foreign Minister; M. Merlou becomes Minister of Finance

June 17, Death of M. Pingard, Secretary of the French Academy, aged 78, the third and last of the family of that name who as secretaries had served the academy since 1775

June 30, U. S. squadron, under command of Rear-Admiral C. D. Sigsbee, arrives at Cherbourg to transfer to America the remains of the naval hero, Paul Jones; naval officers and special envoys, Mr. Loomis and General Porter, ex-U. S. Ambassador in Paris, fêted by French Government, July 5

July 1, M. Rouvier hands note to Prince Radolin, which declares that France no longer objects to the meeting of the proposed conference on Morocco in presence of the satisfaction which has been given her

[French and German cabinets in agreement on following points: that the integrity of the Moroccan Empire will be preserved; that the sovereignty of the Sultan will not be infringed; that all treaties and conventions concluded between Morocco and the Powers will be respected; that there will be no infringement of the Franco-English and Franco-Spanish conventions; and that special rights will be recognized for France owing to her common frontier with Morocco]

July 3, Separation bill (Church and State) passes the Chamber of Deputies by 341 votes to 233, and goes to the Senate

July 5, Prince Bülow, German Imperial Chancellor, prohibits the appearance of M. Jaurès at the Socialist mass meeting in Berlin, July 9, at which he was to have appeared, on the ground that considerations of domestic policy render his presence undesirable

July 13, Amnesty bill voted by the Senate as presented by the Government, discussed in Chamber of Deputies; as the result of the opposition of M. Lasies, Bonapartist, and heated discussion, M. Berteaux, Minister for War, while approving the bill, announces its withdrawal

July 15, British Atlantic fleet visits Brest: 8 battleships, including the flagship King Edward VII, Vice-Admiral Sir H. May, and 3 cruisers sail from Brest

July 31, Serious financial difficulties of a director of the Grand-Magasins du Printemps causes a panic among the customers who are depositors in the savings-bank department

Aug. 1, Naval estimates for 1906 provide for the votes of credits amounting to 325,037,217f. (13,000,000l.)

Aug. 7–14, Visit of the French fleet to Portsmouth

Aug. 8, Hague tribunal gives its award in the Anglo-French arbitration, deciding that as from Jan., 1902, France has not the right to authorize subjects of the Sultan of Muscat to fly the French flag

Aug. 9, Minister of Commerce nominates a commission to consider the organization of an international exhibition in Paris in 1909

End Aug., Crisis in the sugar market caused by miscalculations of speculators as to the extent of the beetroot crop of 1904; suicide of M. Ernest Cronier, through speculative losses

Sept. 13, Death of M. Goblet, ex-Premier

Sept. 16, Franco-Danish arbitration treaty signed

Sept. 28, Franco-German agreement re Morocco signed

Oct. 30, Chamber passes an amnesty bill by 541 votes to 5

Nov. 9, Ministerial crisis in consequence of the declaration of the Prime Minister that the Government could not admit the right of agents of the State to form trade unions; Premier supported by members of the Right; majority of 76; Left brings forward an interpellation; M. Berteaux, Minister of War, resigns; Government majority, 246

Nov. 10, Reconstitution of the Cabinet; M. Etienne becomes Minister of War; M. Dubief, Minister of the Interior; and M. Trouillot, Minister of Commerce

Dec. 6, Separation bill passes the Senate by 181 votes to 102

Dec. 29, M. Hervé, an anti-patriot, sentenced to 4 years' imprisonment for provocation to murder and mutiny

1906

Jan. 1, Lord Cheylesmore and other members of the municipal deputation from the city of Westminster received at the Elysée by President Loubet

Jan. 11, Conditions of the Russian loan announced in the *Temps*, the advance to be made on short term treasury notes, 266 $^2/_3$ million francs (10,666,666l.) at 5½% interest and a commission of 1%

——, M. Doumer elected President of the Chamber of Deputies, by a majority of 18 in a total vote of 556 against M. Sarrien, formerly Minister of Justice

Jan. 14, Rupture of relations between France and Venezuela

Jan. 17, M. Fallières, elected President of the Republic in succession to M. Loubet by 449 votes against 371 given to M. Doumer

Feb. 2, Chamber adopts the bill authorizing the Bank of France to raise its note issue to 5,800,000,000 francs (232,000,000l.)

Feb. 5, Sir E. A. Cornwall and members of the London County Council visit Paris

Feb. 12, Chamber adopts by 407 votes to 55 the Franco-Russian commercial convention

Feb. 24, 40 members of the British section of the Alliance-Française-Brittanique, arrive in Paris

Feb. 27, Chambers pass a bill establishing penny postage throughout France and her colonies

March 4, King Edward VII on his continental tour via Paris, entertains the President at dinner at the English Embassy

March 7, Government defeated by 267 votes to 234 on the question of the resistance to taking of Church inventories in connection with the separation law; M. Rouvier and his Ministry resign

March 12, New Ministry constituted with M. Sarrien as Premier and Minister of Justice; M. Léon Bourgeois, Foreign Affairs; M. Clemenceau, Interior; M. Poincaré, Finance; M. Etienne, War; M. Thomson, Marine; M. Briand, Public Instruction and Worship; M. Doumergue, Commerce

March 26, The Abbé Richard, Curé of the Gros-Caillou, sentenced by the correctional tribunal to eight days' imprisonment for inciting his followers to resist the taking of church inventories; and the Abbé Solange-Bodin, Curé of Palisance, fined 25frs., reported

March 27, Death of Eugène Carrière, painter

22,640 claims for a pension under the separation bill sent in to the Government by the French clergy up to April 1

April 7, Strike disorders in the Lens district

April 10, Congress of delegates from the trade unions of the Nord, Anzin, and the Pas de Calais, held at Lens, decide to again submit the claims of the miners to the companies, maintaining a minimum wage of 7f. 18c. (5s. 9d.)

April 11, Postmen's strike discussed in the Chamber, which adopts a vote of confidence in the Government by 442 votes to 74

April 17, Strikers at Liérin besiege the *gendarmerie* barracks, stone the police and troops; pillage the stalls in the market place; party of strikers from Liérin sack the house at Lens of M. Reumaux, director of the mines, April 18

April 19, Death of Professor Pierre Curie, discoverer of radium, by a street accident in Paris, aged 46

April 20, Dynamite outrages near Lens and Denain

April 23, Strike declared in different branches of the jewelry industry in Paris

April 26, Gradual resumption of work among the coal miners of the Lens and Valenciennes district reported

May 6, General election throughout the country

May 7, Work resumed in the Pas de Calais coal field

May 11, Number of strikers out of work, in consequence of the lockout in Paris, estimated at 95,000

May 14, Disturbance by Toulon strikers in building trade

May 20, Result of the elections for the Chamber of Deputies shows 246 Radicals and Socialist-Radicals; 77 Republicans of the Left; 7 Dissident Radicals; 22 Independent Socialists; 53 Unified Socialists; 64 Progressives; 117 Royalists, Bonapartists, and members of the *action libérale* and Nationalists; the old *bloc* gains 56 members, chiefly Radicals and Socialist-Radicals

June 1, New Parliament opens; M. Henri Brisson elected President of the Chamber

June 4, M. Fallières makes his first official visit as President of the Republic to the provinces

June 21, Debate in the Chamber upon the general policy of the Government; an order of the day approving the declarations of the Government, adopted by 410 votes to 87

June 26, General Hagron appointed Commander-in-Chief of the French army, in succession to General Bougère

June 29, Death of M. Albert Sorel, recipient of the Osiris prize of 100,000*fr.*, 1906, aged 64

About end June, Death of M. Jean Lorrain, littérateur and poet

July 4, Death of M. Jules Breton, painter, aged 78

July 10, Chamber, by 575 votes to 1, passes a bill, adopted by the Senate, for a weekly day of rest for employees and workmen

July 11, Amnesty bill voted by the Chamber of Deputies

July 12, Court of Cassation holds the innocence of Captain Dreyfus to be established, quashes the judgment of the Rennes court, &c.

July 13, Bill for removing the remains of M. Zola to the Panthéon adopted; the Chamber session closes

July 14, Death of M. Frantz Despagnet, international law authority

July 16, Major Dreyfus appointed to the 12th artillery regiment at Vincennes; General Picquart appointed to the command of the 10th infantry division in Paris, gazetted July 18

Aug. 2, Death of M. Edmond Rousse, of the French Academy, in his 90th year, reported

Aug. 7, Duel between Generals André and de Négrier; General André fired without hitting General de Négrier, who did not fire

Sept. 13, Mme Humbert released from prison

Oct. 19, M. Sarrien, the Premier, announces his resignation owing to ill health; thereupon, the other ministers all tendered their resignations

About Oct. 19, Death of Baron Mohrenheim, formerly Russian Ambassador to France

Oct. 20, New Franco-Swiss commercial treaty signed

Oct. 23, M. Clemenceau forms a new Ministry, with himself as Premier and Minister of the Interior; M. Pichon, Foreign Minister; M. Caillaux, Finance; M. Briand, Public Instruction and Worship; General Picquart, War; M. Thomson, Marine; M. Doumergue, Commerce; and M. Viviani, Labor and Hygiene

Nov. 9, M. Briand, Minister of Public Instruction, declares that they would apply the separation law in its entirety; that the State was bound to oppose any political intervention by the Church

About Nov. 19, Death of M. de Mahy, deputy for La Réunion, aged 76

Nov. 20, After a speech by the Premier concerning the enforcement of the separation law, a resolution of confidence in the Government was carried by 213 votes to 32

Nov. 30, Chamber decided to increase the salaries of Senators and Deputies from 360*l.* to 600*l.* per annum

Dec. 2, Death of M. Gontaut, Senator for Ardennes

Dec. 6, Act of Algeciras ratified in the Chamber

Dec. 8, The Pope forbids French Catholics to comply with the provisions of the act of 1881, governing public meetings, to which the Church in France will be subject after Dec. 11

Dec. 10, M. Brunetière, the academician and editor of the *Revue des Deux Mondes*, died, aged 56

Dec. 11, Separation Law comes into effect; Manager Montagnine expelled from France

——, Death of M. Augustin Normand, naval constructor, aged 68

Dec. 14, Death of Count Carl Lewenhaupt, aged 71, Swedish and Norwegian Minister in Paris, 1884–88, reported

Dec. 15, In the Chamber, the Minister of Public Worship explains the provisions of the new bill proposed by the Government, in consequence of the uncompromising attitude of the Vatican

Dec. 17, Expulsion of the Archbishop of Paris, under the separation law, from his official residence

Dec. 29, Supplementary worship bill adopted by the Senate, carrying it by 180 votes to 90

1907

Jan. 18, Customs returns for the year 1906 show that imports amounted to 5,229,425,000*f.* (209,177,000*l.*), and exports to 5,043,665,000*f.* (201,746,600*l.*)

Jan. 30, Notification bill passed in the Chamber

Feb. 7, Cardinal Mathieu received at the Academy on his election to the seat left vacant by the death of Cardinal Perraud

——, Death of Mme Marie Thérèse Blanc, authoress (Th. Bentzon Mme Blanc), aged 67, reported

March 11, Death of M. Casimir-Périer, President in 1894, aged 60

March 18, M. Marcelin Berthelot, an ex-Minister for Foreign Affairs, dies, aged 79

March 20, Motion of M. Jaurès adopted in the Chamber that a committee be appointed to examine the political significance of the Montagnini papers

March 26, Debate in the Chamber on the murder of Dr. Mauchamp at Marakest; the Government decides on the occupation of Udja until full reparation is obtained

April 13, The Abbé Jouin was fined 16*f.* and costs for having, in a place of public worship, incited to direct resistance to the law

April 23, Death of M. André Theuriet, member of French Academy, born 1833

April 25, President Fallières and the Minister for Foreign Affairs interview the Empress Marie of Russia at Bourget

April 29, Arrest of M. Bousquet, and MM. Lévy and Delahaye, members of the confederation of labor, for violent speeches

May 17, Glut of wine in the south causes widespread economic distress

May 26–29, Visit of Queen Alexandra

May 27–30, Visit of King Haakon and Queen Maud of Norway

May 31–June 5, Second strike in the French mercantile marine

June 9, Demonstration, attended by over 500,000 persons, in connection with the wine-producers' agitation, held at Montpellier

June 10, Franco-Japanese treaty signed in Paris

June 14, Arrival of the King and Queen of Denmark

June 19, Arrest of the mayor of Narbonne and three members of the committee of Argeliers

——, Police and troops called out to suppress riotous demonstrations in Montpellier and Narbonne; 1 person killed and a number wounded; 4 persons killed and 11 injured, June 20

June 21, Mutiny of troops at Agde owing to their removal from Béziers in connection with the wine crisis

June 22, Government bill for preventing the adulteration of wine passed by the Chamber

June 26, Surrender of M. Marcellin Albert to the authorities at Montpellier

July 20, General de Lacroix appointed generalissimo of the French army

July 24, Japanese squadron arrives at Brest

Aug. 21, Visit of the King of Siam

Sept. 6, Death of M. Sully Prudhomme, poet and academician, aged 67

Sept. 19, Franco-Canadian treaty signed

Dec. 24, M. Hervé, for libeling the army, sentenced to one year's imprisonment and a fine of 120*l.*

Dec. 31, Death of M. Guyot-Dessaigne, Minister of Justice, aged 74

1908

Jan. 28, Death of Cardinal Richard, Archbishop of Paris, aged 88

——, The Franco-American Tariff agreement signed at Washington

March 10, The Seine is 7 feet above its normal height

March 19, Bill for the removal of the remains of M. Zola to the Panthéon passed in the Chamber by 356 to 164 votes

April 2, The amnesty bill to offenders in connection with the wine-growers' agitation passes the Chamber by 432 votes to five

April 8, Devolution of Church property bill passed by the Senate

April 10, Death of Count Tornielli, Italian Ambassador in Paris, aged 71

May 24, Death of M. François Coppée, dramatist and poet, aged 66

May 25–29, President Fallières visits England

June 10, Death of M. Boissier, permanent secretary of the French Academy, b. 1823

July 12, Bill for the purchase, by the State, of the western railway of France, becomes law

July 18, President Fallières leaves Paris, for Dunkirk, on his visit to the courts of southern Europe

July 30, Labor riots occur at Villeneuve Saint Georges; troops fire on the rioters

Aug. 4, President Fallières returns to Paris

About Aug. 19, Death of M. Hector France, novelist, aged 68

Oct. 26, Death of Cardinal Mathieu, b. 1839

Nov. 8, Death of M. Victorien Sardou, b. 1831

Nov. 10, The Casablanca incident closed by Germany and France agreeing to exchange expressions of regret prior to the decision of the arbitration tribunal, announced. This incident at Casablanca took place on Sept. 25; six men of the French Foreign Legion, attempting to escape on board a German steamer, were stopped by a French guard who had orders to arrest the deserters. In the scrimmage a German clerk was said to have been struck. Germany magnified the incident into an international event of the first importance. Settled by the Hague court of arbitration, May, 1909

Dec. 2, New commercial treaty concluded with Sweden

1909

Jan. 16, Launch of the *Voltaire*, first of the new French dreadnoughts; displacement, 18,500 tons

Jan. 27, Death of M. Coquelin, *aîné*, actor, b. 1841

Feb. 8, Death of M. Catulle Mendès, poet, b. 1841

Feb. 9, Franco-German agreement concerning Morocco signed in Berlin

Feb. 16, Death of the Marquis de Noailles (Emmanuel), born 1830

March 9, Income tax bill passed by the Chamber by 406 to 166 votes

March 23, Telegraph strike ends

April 10, Disorders in Méru, many arrests

May 12, Postmen and telegraphists in Paris and the provinces strike

May 21, Acknowledged a failure by the confederation of labor

May 24, Strike of naval reservists

May 26, Mr. Carnegie's offer of 200,000*l.* to France to form a peace heroes' fund accepted

May 27, The Moorish mission to France received by President Fallières

June 11, Earthquake in the Bouches-du-Rhône; about 55 lives lost

July 8, Death of General de Galliffet, b. 1830

July 13, The Franco-Canadian commercial convention ratified by the French Chamber

July 17, President Fallières opens a new quay at Havre

July 20, Resignation of the Clemenceau Ministry in consequence of an adverse navy vote

July 24, M. Briand forms a Ministry, with himself as Premier and Minister of the Interior, retaining in addition, the portfolio of Public Worship; M. Pichon, Foreign Minister; M. Barthou, Justice; M. Cochery, Finance; and General Brun, War

July 31, President Fallières exchanges visits with the Czar and the Empress of Russia who arrive in their yacht, the *Standart*, at Cherbourg harbor

About Oct. 22, Death of General Hagron, former Commander-in-Chief of the French army, b. 1845

Dec. 6, Death of Manager Petit, Archbishop of Besançon

1910

Jan. 11, Bills introduced in Parliament to provide for State control in Catholic and other private schools

Jan. 20, The Seine began to rise and the Yonne and the Marne flooding the country and Paris and suburbs, seamen employed by Government to rescue marooned inhabitants of Grenoble and Anger

Jan. 30, Death of Professor Edouard Rod, author

Feb. 29, The Seine River reached maximum height, the greatest in 3 centuries, floods causing great damage and property loss

March 22, Old Age Pension Bill amended passed Senate, and Chamber April 1

March 24, Death of vicomte Eugène Melchior de Voguë (61) author

March 29, Act revised French tariff, the minimum scale of dues accorded to all countries granting concessions of same value as regards French articles, and a general tariff with double dues applied to all taxed articles from countries not granting reciprocal concessions. Into effect April 1

April 1, The Chamber of Deputies authorized immediate construction of 2 of the 7 battleships voted

April 3, Strike of ship's crews at Marseilles begun which stopped over-seas trade for 2 months

April 5, Old Age Pensions law enacted but was largely nullified by decision of highest court that employers not compelled to deduct workers' contribution

——, Law providing for relief of aged poor amended reduced age limit from 70 to 65

April 12, Launch at Bordeaux of the *Vergniaud*, sixth battleship of the Danton class

April 24, Elections for Parliament begun which resulted in Chamber of 19 Right, 34 Liberal Action, 76 Progressists, 73 Democratic Left, 112 Radical Left, 149 Radical Socialists, 30 Independent Socialists, 75 Unified Socialists, 20 Independents

April 27, Paulhan won the London *Daily Mail* prize for journey from London to Manchester, 298 km. in 4 hours and 12 minutes with one stop, 188 km. in one flight

May 29, Treaty with Turkey settled Tunis-Tripoli frontier

May 31, Railway strike in the district between Nice and the Rhône, behind the Côte d'Azur; 10,000 men out

June 5, Dr. Charcot arrived at Rouen, after an absence of 18 months, during which he was engaged in the exploration of the Antarctic continent

June 7, Republican Socialist platform declared for gradual transfer of industry to State operation

July 12, Arrival of King Albert of Belgium and Queen Elizabeth on visit of State

July 16, Decree created the National Office of Workers' and Peasants Pensions

Sept. 16, Flight of the dirigible "Clement-Bayard II" from Lamotte-Breuil to London, England, 242 miles at average rate of 40 miles an hour

Sept. 17, France demanded explanation and satisfaction from Turkey for alleged treaty violations in Tunis and Algiers

Sept. 23, Flight of Chavez across the Alps from Brigue to Demodossels but fatally injured attempting to land at Domdossola

Oct. 11–15, Strike of railroad employees on northern and western railroads which cost $55,000,000. Briand called out troops. Wage increase granted

Oct. 19, Agreement with Turkey for floating $30,000,000 Turkish loan

Oct. 30, Briand Ministry resigned because of withdrawal of Viviani, Minister of Labor, disagreeing with his colleagues on railroad strike suppression measures

Nov. 3, Briand reappointed Premier formed new Radical Cabinet

Nov. 6, The dirigible "Morning Post" purchased by England flew from Moisson to Farnborough, England, 230 miles in 5 hours and 30 minutes

Dec. 5, Death of Robert Philippe Louis Eugène Ferdinand d' Orleans, duc de Chartres

1911

Jan. 1, Old Age Pensions Act came into effect

Jan. 4, Institute of France declared against admission of women to membership

Jan. 13, Franco-Liberian Treaty signed as to boundary with Ivory Coast

Jan. 19, Wine growers revolt begun as protest against fraud and illegal sale of white wine as champagne, Perrier cellars sacked at Epernay and wine destroyed

Jan. 23, International Oceanographic Institute opened in Paris

Feb. 27, Briand Cabinet resigned because of accusation of Radical Socialists led by Malvy that church laws of 1901 and 1904 had not been enforced

March 2, A. E. E. Monis, Radical Republican, formed Cabinet; M. Cruppi, Foreign Affairs; Caillaux, Finance; Messimy, Colonies; Delcassé, Marine; Berteaux, War; Dumont, Public Works; Perrier, Justice; Boncourt, Labor; Pams, Agriculture

March 5, Total population 39,601,509; urban, 17,508,940; rural, 22,093,318; Paris, 2,888,110

March 10, At midnight Greenwich time became legal time in France

March 28, Several thousand wine growers at Bar-sur-Aube protested against French law which excluded Aube from delimited champagne region

April 11–14, Riots of wine growers in protest against Senate measure abolishing territorial delimitations for production of champagne

April 12, Paprier made first non-stop flight between London and Paris, 250 miles in less than 4 hours

April 26, French troops entered Fez. *See* Morocco

April 27, France notified Powers signatories of the Algeciras Convention of French intervention in Morocco as necessary to protect foreigners

May 8, Germany warned France of serious consequences which might follow French occupation of Fez

May 21, Death of Henri Maurice Berteaux (58), War Minister

June 7, Germany again warned France regarding military policy in Morocco

——, Death of Maurice Rouvier, former Premier (68)

June 23, Resignation of Monis Ministry defeated for acceptance of proportional representation

June 27, Joseph M. A. Caillaux became Prime Minister; M. Cruppi, Minister of Justice; de Selves, Foreign Affairs; Messimy, War; Delcassé, Marine; Klotz, Finance; Pams, Agriculture

July 1, German ambassador announced that his Government had sent a gunboat to Agadir to protect lives and property of Germans, and the French Foreign Minister informed that the German occupation of Agadir would last as long as the French occupied Fez. The *Panther* later replaced by the *Berlin*

July 8, Conversations begun in Berlin with view to settlement of Morocco question

July 15, Germany asked France for territorial cessions in Central Africa

July 28, Terms of Franco-Spanish *modus vivendi* as to Morocco outlined by Spanish Premier

——, General Joseph Joffre appointed Chief of General Staff

Aug. 15, End of trial of 33 persons accused in riots in April in champagne districts, 27 acquitted and 6 given prison sentences

Aug. 19, Commercial and Navigation Agreement with Japan signed

Aug. 21–22, Theft of "La Gioconda," the "Mona Lisa" of Leonardo da Vinci, from the Louvre

Aug. 26, André Jaeger-Schmidt arrived at Paris completing trip around the world in 39 days, 19 hours, and 43 minutes

Sept. 13, France rejected proposals of Germany of Sept. 10 as to settlement of Morocco dispute

Nov. 4, Franco-German Treaty signed by which Germany recognized French interests in Morocco and right of France to conduct necessary military, financial, and administrative reforms, the word "protectorate" not used in Treaty but in an official letter to French Foreign Minister, France guaranteeing freedom and equality of foreign trade and commerce

——, Congo Convention with Germany signed by which Germany gained region in Central Africa south and east of the Cameroons in excess of 100,000 square miles, France receiving territory between the Shari and Logone Rivers, part of Duck's Beak near Lake Chad

Nov. 7, The Nobel prize awarded to Mme Curie

1912

Jan. 9, Resignation of M. de Selves, Minister of Foreign Affairs

Jan. 10, Resignation of Joseph Caillaux, Prime Minister, on Treaty with Germany, and his negotiations with Germany were later the subject of a special parliamentary inquiry

——, Census gave total population as 39,604,992 including 1,152,096 foreigners; males, 19,254,444; females, 19,937,689; the population of Paris, 2,847,-229; of Lyons, 523,796; of Marseilles, 421,116; of Bordeaux, 237,767

Jan. 14, Raymond Poincaré formed Cabinet: Briand, Justice; Klotz, Finance; Léon Bourgeois, Labor; Millerand, War; Delcassé, Navy; the Premier, Foreign Affairs

Jan. 17, Seizure of French vessel, the *Carthage*, by Italy on charge of transport of airplanes to Tunis for use of Turks in Tripoli

Jan. 19, Seizure of French vessel, the *Manouba*, by Italy on charge of having Turkish officials on board

Jan. 26, France and Italy reached settlement of dispute over 2 French vessels seized

Feb. 9, Death of Charles Loyson (Father Hyacinthe), preacher (84)

Feb. 10, Franco-German Treaties on Morocco and the Congo ratified by the Senate

Feb. 12, Naval Bill carrying program of construction by 1920 of battle fleet of 28 ships and appropriation of $300,000,000 passed

Feb. 27 and July 11, Acts modified the Old Age Pension Act

March 30, Treaty of Fez signed with the Sultan of Morocco by which the French Protectorate accepted and the "special character" of Tangier recognized

April 27, General Lyautey assumed office as first French Resident General of Morocco

April, Death of Eugène Henri Brisson, former Premier

June 12, Death of Frederic Passy (90), economist and pacifist

July 12, *Scrutin de liste* Bill passed provided for election of deputies and for system of proportional representation and the department made the electoral unit

July 17, Death of Henri Poincaré, mathematician

Sept. 28, Boundary Declaration signed by France and Germany determining new frontier of French Equatorial Africa and the Cameroons and Dahomey and the Sudan with German Togo

Nov. 26, Book II of the Labor Code promulgated came into effect

Nov. 27, Franco-Spanish Treaty signed as to Morocco and Tangier

Dec. 13, Housing Act passed

Dec. 16, Order for general strike of 24 hours not complied with, so a failure

1913

Jan. 17, Raymond Poincaré received 483 votes for presidency as against Pams, receiving only 296, and resigned as Premier

Jan. 21, Briand became Premier

Jan., Millerand resigned as Minister of War because of opposition to his decision to appoint Colonel du Paty de Clam a commissioner in Territorial Army; he had been retired from army because of conduct in Dreyfus case. Succeeded by M. Etienne

Feb. 13, Arbitration Treaty with the United States signed

——, The paper franc at 5.45 to the dollar

Feb. 15, Agreement with Germany as to Berlin-Bagdad railway

Feb. 18, President Poincaré inaugurated

Feb. 27, Bill providing for military credit of £20,000,000 tabled in Chamber

March 6, Bill introduced provided for raising period of compulsory military service from 2 to 3 years

March 18, Resignation of Briand Ministry after defeat in Senate on electoral reform, proportional representation by means of the electoral quotient

March 21, Barthou Jean Louis formed a Cabinet

——, Housing Act of Dec., 1912, amended

June 10, The Senate voted for establishment of *scrutin de liste* without proportional representation

June 17, Old Age Pension Act amended

——, Law provided for relief varying from .50 to 1.50 francs or more a day to women in confinement

July 13, Non-stop flight of Letort from Paris to Berlin, 920 km. in 7 hours and 47 minutes

July 14, Law granted relief to families with numerous children, 5 francs per month for every child beyond the third

Aug. 7, Act established the period of compulsory service in the active army as 3 years increasing peace strength of army to 673,000 at increased cost of $35,000,000 in annual expenditure, and non-recurring cost of $145,000,000

Sept. 2, Adolphe Pegoud, the first to do air stunts by making the loop-the-loop

Sept. 23, Garros flew across the Mediterranean from Saint Raphael to Bizerte, over 700 km. in 7 hours and 30 minutes

Oct. 24, Law granted supplementary relief to nursing mothers

Nov. 18, The Chamber voted for electoral reform including proportional representation

Nov. 19, Strike of coal miners in north against changes made by Senate in Eight Hour Bill

Dec. 2, The Barthou Ministry overthrown on proposal of loan of £52,000,000 to meet increased expenditure on armaments

Dec. 8, Gaston Doumergue became Prime Minister

and Minister of Foreign Affairs forming a Cabinet of Socialist-Radicals; René Renoult, Interior; Bienvenu-Martin, Justice; Noulens, War; Monis, Marine; Caillaux, Finance; Viviani, Public Instruction; Malvy, Commerce; Lebrun, Colonies; Métin, Labor

Dec. 12, The "Mona Lisa" of Da Vinci discovered in Florence

Dec. 29, Vedrines and Bonnier made long distance flight record from Paris to Cairo

Dec. 31, The mercantile navy consisted of 15,824 sailing vessels, of 601,983 tons net, with crews 67,453, and 1,895 steamers of 980,433 tons and crews 18,552 plus 12,725 mechanicians and drivers

1914

Jan. 1, Public debt 33 billion francs

Jan. 19, Death of Francis de Pressensé Tour (60)

——, Death of General Picquart (59), former Minister of War and leading figure in the Dreyfus case

Jan. 28, The Chamber voted loan of 230,000,000 francs for Morocco

Jan. 30, Death of Paul Déroulède (67), poet

Feb. 11, French pilot flew over Mt. Blanc, Swiss Alps, at altitude over 16,000 feet

Feb. 15, Secret Convention with Germany signed by which Northern Anatolia and Syria recognized as spheres of French influence for purposes of railway development, and the regions traversed by the Anatolian and Bagdad railways were defined as a German sphere, the Deutsche Bank agreeing to repurchase from the Imperial Ottoman Bank all of the latter's shares and debentures of the Bagdad Railway and its subsidiary enterprises amounting to 69,400,000 francs

Feb. 25, Miners' Pension Act of 1894 amended created autonomous insurance fund

March 10, The Senate voted for scheme of electoral reform establishing the *scrutin de liste* not proportional representation

March 16, Mme Caillaux, wife of Finance Minister, shot and fatally wounded Gaston Calmette, editor of the *Figaro* because of his attacks in the paper on her husband charging that as Minister of Finance he had used his position for his own gain and in particular that he had brought pressure to bear on the judicial authorities for postponement of trial of a notorious swindler, Rochette, enabling him to abscond to Mexico

——, Joseph Caillaux resigned as Finance Minister and was succeeded by Doumergue

March 23, Law passed gave the Chamber the right to summon witnesses to appear before it

March 25, Death of Frédéric Mistral, poet

March 29, Law reformed land tax to come into effect Jan. 1, 1915 increased the *impôt de quotité* on building property to 4% and placed same tax on unimproved real estate on basis of $^4/_5$ of rental value as of valuation under law of Dec. 31, 1907

April 5, General election begun which resulted in Chamber as follows: Radical Socialists, 172; Unified Socialists, 101; Republican Socialists, 30; Liberal Action, 32; Republican Federation, 54; Democratic Left, 34; Radical Left, 66; Republican Left, 54; Republican Union, 21; Republican Right, 15; Independents, 41

May 23, Strike of postal workers in Paris

June 1, Resignation of Doumergue Ministry before Parliament reassembled according to custom

June 9, Alexandre Ribot formed Cabinet, Left and Center

June 12, Ribot Ministry fell because of support of 3-year military service law to which Radicals opposed

June 13, René Viviani assumed office as Prime Minister and Minister of Foreign Affairs; Bienvenu-Martin, Justice; Malvy, Interior; Noulens, Finance; Messimy, War; Gauthier, Marine; Augagneur, Public Instruction; René Renoult, Public Works; Gaston Thomson, Commerce and Posts and Telegraphs; Fernand David, Agriculture; Raynaud, Colonies; Colyba, Labor

June 23, Strike of postoffice employees ended

July 2, Resolution in favor of proportional representation adopted by Chamber but no action taken before adjournment

July 13, Speech of Charles Humbert in the Senate regarding poverty of France as compared with Germany in artillery and war material pointing out that Germany between 1900 and 1905 had spent £28,000,000 on her army as compared with £11,250,-000 spent by France, £37,200,000 in period between 1906 and 1910 as compared with French expenditure of £19,000,000, and £23,400,000 from 1911–13 as compared with French expenditure of £16,500,000

July 15, The Senate passed military credits for £56,-320,000

——, First general income tax enacted to take effect in 1916 affected all incomes over 5,000 francs at rate of 2% with deductions according to size of family

——, Law extended benefits of accident legislation to wood cutters in forests of area of more than 3 hectares

July 17–29, Visit of President Poincaré and Viviani to Russia

July 20, Trial of Mme Caillaux opened for the assassination of Calmette, and ended July 28 with acquittal by the jury

July 30, Decree limited withdrawals from savings banks to 50 francs a fortnight from each account

July 31, Jean Jaurès, Socialist leader, shot and killed in a Paris café by Raoul Villain, a student, instigated by extreme Royalists

——, Railroads over German frontier ceased operation

——, German Note to France asked if France would remain neutral in the event of a war between Germany and Russia

——, France informed Belgium of intention to respect Belgian neutrality

Aug. 1, Note of France to Germany stated that France would do "what her interests demand" in case of German war with her Ally

——, General mobilization ordered by President Poincaré to take effect the next day

——, Renewal of assurance to Belgium of intention to respect neutrality

Aug. 2, Declaration of state of siege which substituted military for civil control under law of Aug. 9, 1849

——, German troops invaded France. *See* World War

——, British assurance that British fleet would oppose German fleet attempting to enter the Pas-de-Calais

——, Railroads placed under military control

——, M. Doumergue appointed Minister of Foreign Affairs

Aug. 3, Germany declared war on France and France declared war on Germany

Aug. 4, Parliament assembled in extraordinary session and passed Bills for national defense

Aug. 5, Law confirmed decree of state of siege empowering the President to suspend or reimpose it

——, Decree prohibited export of milk

——, Law modified that of Dec. 14, 1879 on opening of extraordinary credits by decree while Chambers prorogued

——, Bill passed conferred French nationality on natives of Alsace-Lorraine enlisting in the army

——, Law enacted for suppression of indiscretions of the press in time of war

Aug. 9, Moratorium decree as to deposits of cash in banks, manufacturers whose establishments requisitioned for national defense excepted

Aug. 10, Diplomatic relations with Austria-Hungary severed

Aug. 10 and Sept. 8, Decree applied rules of procedure for courts martial at front to entire country

Aug. 13, Declaration of war on Austria-Hungary

Aug. 14, Rent moratorium decreed

Aug. 16, Circular regarding advances of funds to War Office contractors

Aug. 17, Decree suspended action of Councils of Revision on sentences at front

Aug. 20, Law created national unemployment fund

Aug. 26, Resignation of Premier Viviani

——, General Galliéni replaced General Michel as Military Governor of Paris

Aug. 27, Viviani formed new Cabinet, Millerand replacing Messimy as Minister of War; Delcassé, Foreign Affairs; Augagneur, Navy; Ribot, Finance; Marcel Sembat, Socialist, Public Works; Jules Guesde, Socialist, Minister without Portfolio, Briand, Justice

Aug. 28, Declaration of Socialists of patriotic duty as justification of joining of a bourgeois Government; no Socialists had been in a Cabinet since 1905

Aug. 29, Moratorium decree as to bank deposits amended, right of withdrawal reduced by amount "of the advances granted by the State" for purchase of materials and payment of wages

Sept. 2, The Government moved to Bordeaux, leaving Paris at request of General Joffre

Sept. 3, Paris Bourse closed

——, Parliament closed by decree, had been adjourned since Aug. 4

Sept. 6, Decree set up extraordinary courts martial at front

Sept. 8, Service of Civil Food Supply established

Sept. 13, Decree authorized the Treasury to issue National Defense Bonds of 3, 6, and 12 months maturity

Sept. 27, Decree prohibited trading with the enemy

Oct. 6, Death of Count Albert de Mun (73)

Oct. 13, German occupation of Lille begun which continued until November, 1918, General von Heinrich appointed Governor

Oct. 27, Circular addressed to prefects in invaded regions announced Government proposed to aid populations suffering from the war

Oct. 28, Central office created for placing unemployed and refugees

Nov. 5 and 7, France declared war against Turkey

Nov. 18, The Government returned to Paris

Dec. 4, A Service for the purchase of coal set up in the Directorate of State Railways

Dec. 7, Paris Bourse resumed operations

Dec. 20, Decree sanctioned ministerial circular of

Aug. 16 and period for repayment extended from one month to two

Dec. 22, Chamber of Deputies met in extraordinary session to vote credits and was addressed by Premier Viviani who appealed for national unity

Dec. 24, Law postponed election of Senate until the end of the War

——, Law stated the State would make good the damages done in invaded regions

Dec. 26, Law enacted provided for opening of provisional credits applicable to first 6 months of 1915 in lump sum, and authorized collection of taxes and public revenues for same period for all public expenses civil and military

Dec. 30, Income tax law of 1914 amended to increase rates, applied to every income exceeding 3,000 francs calculated on basis of one-tenth for incomes between 3,000 and 8,000 francs, three-tenths from 8,000 to 12,000 and reaching nine-tenths for incomes from 100,000 to 150,000

1915

Jan. 7, Decree prohibited sale of absinthe and the opening of new premises for the sale of alcoholic liquor, and was confirmed by Parliament Feb. 12

Jan. 12, The Chamber of Deputies opened session and remained in permanent session until the fall of 1919

Feb. 4, A Commission for evaluation for reconstruction appointed

March 15, Agricultural Labor Office opened in Paris

April 4, Law imposed sanctions for trading with the enemy

——, Law enacted to protect owners of property in territory occupied by the enemy

April 8, Law instituted decoration of the military cross

June 21, Superior Commission established to organize the import and sale of refrigerated meat

July 3, Export of gold on private account prohibited

July 10, Minimum Wage Act enacted, wages to be determined by the Labor Councils set up by Act of July 17, 1908 and Decree of May 10, 1909; wages of women in the clothing trade working at home established

July 15, Decree authorized granting advances to War Office contractors for the creation and extension of their plants

July 20, Decree provided for evaluation of war damages

July 30, The franc at 5.70 to the dollar

Aug. 17, Old Age Pension Act amended

——, Law provided for regulation of wages of mobilized workers

Aug. 31, Consultative economic committees established in each military district

Sept. 1, Government Circular restored to prefects and mayors in interior districts all normal police powers lost under state of siege law of Aug. 5, 1914

Sept. 5–9, Extreme Socialists led by Bourderon and Merrheim at meeting at Zimmerwald, Switzerland, agreed to address manifesto to the proletariat of all nations condemning the War and asking for immediate peace

Oct. 5, Subscriptions for first war "Loan of Deliverance" opened

Oct. 11, Death of Jean Henri Fabre, scientist

Oct. 13, Resignation of Delcassé from the Cabinet in protest against the Salonika expedition

Oct. 16, Declaration of state of war with Bulgaria

——, Ministry of Food Supply organized and prefects authorized to requisition wheat and flour for supply of population, and fixed prices instituted, wheat 30 francs a quintal (220 pounds)

Oct. 28, Failure of Balkan policy brought about fall of Viviani Ministry

Oct. 29, Wheat Executive Committee established

Oct. 30, Briand formed Coalition Cabinet as Prime Minister and Minister of Foreign Affairs; Viviani, Justice; Galliéni, War; Malvy, Interior; Painlevé, Public Instruction; Ribot, Finance; Lacaze, Marine; Doumergue, Colonies; Méline, Agriculture; Clémentel, Commerce; Sembat, Public Works; Métin, Labor; de Freycinet, Léon Bourgeois, Guesde and Denys Cochin, Ministers without Portfolio

Nov. 9, A Consultative Committee created by Minister of Agriculture

Nov. 15, Law prohibited export of gold bullion and gold and silver coins

Nov. 16, Law and decrees authorized issue of first war loans, a 5% perpetual *rente* adopted

Nov. 25, Subscriptions to "Victory Loan" opened which produced 13,307,811,576 francs

Dec. 3, General Joffre given supreme command of all armies except colonial and North African

Dec. 18, Act passed regarding the coöperative societies

1916

Jan. 1, Income tax law came into effect

Jan. 3, General Directorate of relations with the Press established

Jan. 27, The Chamber adopted a system of supervision by parliamentary committees for the military zone; confirmed by Senate, Aug. 2

Feb. 2 and 9, Agricultural Committees established in the Communes

Feb. 29, A Committee on Maritime Transport appointed to study questions of freight

March 2, Decree prohibited the private importation of sugar

March 16, Resignation of General Galliéni, Minister of War.   Succeeded by General Pierre Auguste Roques

April 6, Circular of General Joffre abolished the special courts martial at the front

——, National Council of Socialist Party voted against motion to ask Government for immediate discussion of peace terms and for renewal of relations with German Socialists

April 12, Export of silver bullion prohibited by law

April 13, Decree provided for creation of special service to prepare measures looking forward to construction of houses in devastated regions

April 15, Act established public dispensaries of social hygiene and provided for anti-tuberculosis measures

April 17 and 20, Laws authorized the Government to fix by decree prices of certain food stuffs and of coal

April 20–22, Laws instituted régime of requisition and fixed prices for large number of commodities

April 21, Committee on female labor appointed by Munitions Ministry

April 26, Secret Treaty with Russia signed as to their respective territorial rights in Asiatic Turkey

April 27, Law confirmed the suppression of the *cours martiales*, the extraordinary tribunals at the front and defined cases in which a civilian was amenable to court martial

April 28, Act organized more definitely the State monopoly on tobacco

April 30, Ministerial order organized a Reconstruction of Buildings Service for invaded regions

May 5, Decree enumerated certain securities that might be loaned to the State

May 6, Law authorized Government to prohibit importations and to raise tariff rates by decrees

May 9 and 16, Secret Treaty signed with Great Britain (Sykes-Picot) defining French and British spheres of influence in Turkey, France to have the Syrian coast from Tyre to Alexandretta, the Province of Cilicia and southern Armenia in full sovereignty, and zone of influence established over area including the provinces of Aleppo, Damascus, Deir, and Mosul

May 11, Decree prohibited import of goods articles of luxury

May 12, German Order of deportation in Lille granted one and one-half hours for preparation

May 18, Inter-Ministerial Committee established for restoration of devastated districts

May 27, Death of General Galliéni, "saviour of Paris"

May 29, Decree supplemented that of May 5 as to admissible securities as to those of Canada and the United States

June 6, Further decree established composition of Inter-Ministerial Committee for restoration of devastated districts

June 8, Decree following Resolution of Chamber ordered submission of sentences pronounced at the front entailing capital punishment to review of a Council of Revision

June 30, Duties raised on alcohol

July 1, New taxes imposed included heavy tax on excess profits above normal and "exceptional" war profits, 50%

July 3, Decree created a Consultative Committee on agricultural chemicals

——, The Paris Clearing House obliged to suspend its regular meetings for the first time since its establishment in 1872

July 6, Central Food Supply Committee set up

July 16, Announcement of formation of an Economic Council charged with measures as to supply and distribution to diminish the cost of living

July 29, Maximum price of wheat fixed at 33 francs the quintal to producer

Sept. 15, Second war loan authorized

Sept. 23, Decree of July 30, 1914 as to savings banks withdrawals repealed

Oct. 5, War Loan opened to subscription issued at 88¾ gave 10,082,452,965 francs

Oct. 6, Law provided for bringing uncultivated land under cultivation, and requisition of buildings and farm animals

Oct. 10, Law provided for insurance for soldiers

Oct. 30, Butter, cheese, and oil cakes added to commodities controlled by State

Nov. 25, Law completed by decree of Jan. 2, 1917 regarding the disabled of the war victims of labor accidents

Nov. 26, Ministry of Industrial Reconstruction created. Abolished Jan. 20, 1920

Dec. 5, Commission to develop yield of sugar created

Dec. 9, Death of Pierre Paul Leroy Beaulieu

Dec. 12, Armament Ministry created.   Abolished Nov. 26, 1918

——, Briand reorganized the Ministry reducing members from 22 to 10 and formed a War Cabinet of 5 members, Briand remaining Minister of Foreign

Affairs; Ribot, Finance; Admiral Lacaze, Marine; Malvy, Interior; Viviani, Justice, Public Instruction, and Labor consolidated; Clémentel, Commerce, Industry, and Agriculture consolidated as new portfolio of National Economy; Herriot, Transport and Supplies; Albert Thomas, Armaments; Doumergue, Colonies; General Lyautey, War

——, General Nivelle succeeded General Joffre in supreme command of the armies

Dec. 22, Letter from naval attaché at Rome charged Caillaux with interview with Italian Government in interests of defeatism; not given out until 1917

Dec. 23, Decision of Government to attach services of military supply to those of civil supply under direction of an Under-Secretary of State, control later transferred to a Minister

Dec. 26, General Joseph Joffre, created a Marshal of France

Dec. 30, Excise revenue tax taxed the theater, mineral waters, patent medicines, colonial foods, saccharine, chicory and substitutes for coffee, and increased tax on hygienic drinks and sugar, duty placed on prices of seats at entertainments

——, Law increased tax on incomes and placed special tax on Frenchmen of military age not serving with the armies equal to 25% of the general income tax paid

1917

Jan. 11, Circular instructed prefects to fix price of Gruyère cheese as from April 1

Jan. 12, Circular fixed prices of butter according to regions and quality ranging from 4.5 francs to 5.40 francs the kilo (2.2 pounds)

Jan. 16, Decree provided for the drawing up of wage scales in the munition factories by joint committees establishing a minimum wage; subsequently this system applied to other industries

Jan. 17, Decree made use of arbitration for settlement of disputes in factories obligatory

Jan. 25, Number of dishes served in restaurants restricted

Feb. 10, Decree prohibited the sale of new and fancy bread

Feb. 14, Russo-French secret exchange of views as to left bank of Rhine, Saar Valley, and Poland

Feb. 18, Death of Emile Auguste Carolus-Duran, artist

Feb., Price of milk in Paris fixed at 50 centimes a liter (1¾ pints)

March 1, Secret Agreement with Japan promised support of Japanese claims

——, From this date sugar cards entitled bearer to 750 grams (26½ ounces), a month with extra rations for children

March 11–17, First meeting of the *Congrès National du Livre* in Paris under presidency of Pierre Decourcelle, the inaugural meeting presided over by the President of the Republic

March 14, Resignation of General Lyautey, Minister of War, because of opposition to his war measures

March 17, Briand Ministry resigned

March 19, Alexandre Ribot formed Cabinet; Ribot, Foreign Affairs; Viviani, Justice; Painlevé, War; Lacaze, Marine; Thomas, Munitions; Thierry, Finance; Malvy, Interior; Steeg, Public Instruction; L. Bourgeois, Labor

March 20, Ministry of Supply created; after Nov. 16

a department in Ministry of Agriculture. Abolished Jan. 20, 1920

March 22, Decree and Order of Sept. 8 prohibited the import without license of foreign merchandise with a few exceptions

——, Decree created a Committee of Derogations and Prohibitions charged with determining quarterly contingents of importations for certain specified articles. Ratified by law of Jan. 20, 1919

April 14, Decree inaugurated 2 meatless days a week

April 15, War Mission to the United States headed by Viviani and including Marshal Joffre left Paris

April 19, Decree prohibited the sale and manufacture of pastry from June 1

April 29, The post of Chief of General Staff created and General Pétain appointed

May 3, Decree provided that wheaten flour be used only for making of bread

May 15, General Pétain appointed Commander-in-Chief in place of General Nivelle and General Foch made Chief of General Staff

May 28, Socialists voted to attend the proposed Congress at Stockholm

June 1, The Government refused passports to French delegates to Stockholm Congress

June 31, Act with decrees of July 4 and Sept. 5, 1918 assured the Saturday half-holiday to women in the clothing trade

July 6, Decree suspended operation of Circular of Sept. 1 of 1915 in certain cantons of the Department of Loire-Inférieure where American troops were landing to restore military control

July 13, General Petroleum Committee established

July 27, Secret Agreement with Italy concluded as to spheres of influence in Asia Minor

July 28, Inter-Ministerial Commission to aid in reconstruction of devastated regions reorganized

July 31, Decree created a cereals office in each department for purchase and distribution

——, Finance law adopted system of schedule taxes and provided that tax on doors and windows should not be levied after Jan. 1, 1918, increased income tax to 12½% enforced by decree Dec. 15. Taxes imposed on industrial and commercial profits, on agricultural exploitation profits, on public and private agreements, indemnities, salaries, pensions, annuities, non-commercial professional profits, on interest of loans, deposits, and securities. A slight tax on business turnovers. Tax on personal property, rental values and on patents abolished

Aug. 3, Law gave the State general powers to requisition supplies and fix prices

——, Oil for food requisitioned

Aug. 14, Death of Almeyra, founder of the "Bonnet Rouge" in prison on charges of treason

Aug. 25, Establishment of Associations of Chambers of Commerce in districts

Aug. 31, Malvy, Minister of the Interior, attacked in Senate by Clemenceau for allowing a number of anti-patriotic organizations to spread pacificism and defeatism, resigned, accused of complicity in "Bonnet Rouge" scandal

Sept. 3, Decree prohibited consumption of milk and cream in restaurants after 9 A.M.

Sept. 7, Ribot Cabinet resigned

Sept. 11, Death of Captain George Guyne, aviator, in flight over Flanders

Sept. 12, Ribot failed to form new Ministry because of opposition of Socialists

——, Economic Committee established to coördinate services dealing with food supply, production, and transportation

Sept. 13, Paul Painlevé formed Cabinet as Prime Minister and Minister of War; Ribot, Foreign Affairs

Sept. 22, General Directorate of relations with the Press abolished and the censorship resumed title of Press Bureau

Sept. 25, Special Committee attached to Ministry of Public Works appointed to consider "general measures" connected with reconstruction of buildings in the devastated areas

Sept. 28, Bolo Pasha, Levantine financier resident in Paris, arrested on charge of being a German agent

Oct. 1, Law imposed fine and imprisonment for second offense of anyone found in state of "manifest drunkenness"

Oct. 3, Sugar ration reduced to 500 grams a month

Oct. 4, Letter from Léon Daudet to Prime Minister read in Chamber of Deputies accusing Malvy of giving diplomatic and military information to the enemy

Oct. 23, M. Barthou appointed Minister of Foreign Affairs

Oct. 26, Law and decrees of Oct. 28 and Nov. 1, 5, and 10 authorized third war loan

Nov. 10, Central Foodstuffs Office established to facilitate provisioning of coöperative societies, municipalities, and commercial associations

Nov. 13, Resignation of Painlevé Ministry defeated by vote of 279 to 186, charged with defeatism

Nov. 16, Clemenceau became Prime Minister and Minister of War; Nail, Justice; Pichon, Foreign Affairs; Pams, Interior; Klotz, Finance; Georges Leygues, Marine; Clémentel, Commerce; Claveille, Public Works; Loucheur, Munitions; Laffere, Public Instruction; Henri Simond, Colonies; Colliard, Labor; Jonnart, Blockade; Boret, Supplies and Agriculture

——, Ministry of Blockade and Liberated Districts created

Nov. 17, Decree instituted State monopoly of cereals

——, Death of auguste Rodin, sculptor

Nov. 26, Third War loan opened brought in total of 10,209,073,212 francs

Nov. 30, Law created a State monopoly in home wheat trade, all cereals requisitioned from Jan. 1

——, Decree regulated manufacture, sale, and rationing of bread, restricted in restaurants

Dec., Office of Agricultural Reconstruction established

Dec. 8, Senator Humbert, Director of the *Journal* resigned from Senate because of charges against the *Journal* of receiving funds from Bolo Pasha

Dec. 11, Clemenceau demanded suspension of parliamentary immunity for Caillaux and 2 other members of Parliament which was voted by Senate Dec. 23

Dec. 28, Statement of war aims of France by Minister of Foreign Affairs

Dec. 30, Circular issued as to requisition of potatoes

Dec. 31, Law postponed election of Chamber of Deputies until the end of the War

——, Law made tax on war profits progressive, from 50% on so much of the taxable profits as did not exceed 100,000 francs to 80% on so much as exceeded 500,000 francs. Small stamp duty placed on retail purchases over 10 francs and an *ad valorem*

tax of 10% on purchase of goods classed as luxuries. Taxes on gifts and legacies increased

1918

Jan. 1, Law of July 31, 1917 came into effect reforming taxes

Jan. 5, Circular of Sept. 1, 1915 suspended removing Nantes district from civil jurisdiction and Atlantic coast from Bordeaux to Brest and later including the Mediterranean coast

Jan. 14, Arrest of Joseph Caillaux charged with intrigue with German Foreign Office with view to peace dating from his visit to the Argentine in 1915

Jan. 21–Aug. 6, Trial of Louis J. Malvy, former Minister of the Interior, by Senate

Feb. 1, Bread cards introduced in Paris and in all communes in June

Feb. 2, Law passed under which National Office of Disabled and Discharged Soldiers established

——, Malt placed under control of State

Feb. 4, Trial of Bolo Pasha begun before military court on charge of conspiracy to manipulate the press in interests of Germany

——, Decree empowered Office of Agricultural Reconstruction to make advances to agriculturists for the purchase of cattle, plants, and fertilizers

Feb. 10, Law passed authorized requisition of merchant marine and decree 5 days later requisitioned entire fleet

——, Law passed authorized Government to regulate or suspend by decree the production, transportation, and sale of produce serving as food for men or animals

Feb. 12, Decree fixed "type meal" to be served at restaurants for 20 francs

——, Decree restricted consumption of butter, cream, and soft cheese

——, Commissary General for Public Security established

——, Decree prohibited manufacture and sale of all confectionery

Feb. 14, Bolo Pasha sentenced by court martial to death for treasonable activities, and his associates, Porchère to 3 years' imprisonment, Cavallini to death *in contumaciam*, proved that Bolo Pasha had received funds from Germany to corrupt the French press

Feb. 14, 18, 19, and June 14, Decrees by which the Government undertook to reorganize the Ministries of Commerce, Agriculture, Labor, and Foreign Affairs

Feb. 15, Shipping requisitioned by Government

Feb. 18, Charles Humbert, former Senator and proprietor of *Le Journal* arrested charged with complicity in treasonable intrigues of Bolo Pasha

Feb. 22, Superior Coöperative Council established

Feb. 27, Treaty of Arbitration of Feb. 10, 1908 **with** the United States extended

Feb. 28, Decree submitted to review of Council of Revision sentences of perpetual imprisonment, penal servitude, and deportation pronounced at the front

March 9, Housing Act as to leases

March 14, Social Insurance law passed by which workers and employers and State contributed to insurance fund

March 18, Decree set up Consultative Commission on Rents to examine proceedings under law of March 9

March 23, Bombardment of Paris begun by long range gun from Crépy-en-Valois, a distance of 75 miles

March 26, Death of Claude A. Debussy, musical composer (55)

March 28, Act regulated night work

April 3, Law prohibited export of capital and export and import of securities

April 7, and Dec. 28, Old Age Pension Act amended

April 15, Rates for railroad transportation of goods increased 25%

April 17, Bolo Pasha executed at Vincennes

April 20, Executive Committee on Maritime Transport established

April 23, Abrogation of all commercial treaties containing the most favored nation clause

April 26, Death of M. de Marcère, last life senator

——, Meatless days increased from 2 to 3 a week (May 15–July 16)

April 29, The "Bonnet Rouge" treason trial opened of Duval, editor, Marion, Goldsky, and Landau charged with intelligence and commerce with the enemy, Joucla with intelligence with the enemy only, and Vercasson and Leymarie with complicity in commerce with the enemy

May 4, Law of 1916 amended as to cultivation and requisition of unused land

May 5, Death of Georges Ohnet, novelist and dramatist

May 13, Death of Charles Wagner, author

May 15, Conviction by court martial of Duval sentenced to death and his associates to terms of imprisonment. Shown at trial that Duval had received about £40,000 from German banker, Marx, acting for Germany in Switzerland, and that Malvy as Minister of the Interior, had granted passports for visits of Duval to Switzerland through his private secretary, Leymarie

May 28, Decree provided for census of cattle and maximum prices

May 31, National Defense short term notes issued

June 1, Food cards made obligatory

June 19, A Commissary for Franco-American war relations established

June 28, Decree established a central office for Agricultural Chemicals to assist farmers

June 29, Statistical customs duty increased and extended to postal parcels, luxury tax on wine and spirituous liquors raised, mineral waters, sugar, vinegar, chicory and coffee substitutes raised and duty on transport, license duty retailers of spirits

——, Law provided for awarding prizes in money to large families

June 30, Tax law increased tax on incomes up to 5,000 francs from 1½%, between 5,000 and 150,000 from 1½ to 16%, an increase of 1 centime per 100 francs, between 150,000 and 550,000 from 16 to 20% with increase of 1 centime per 1,000 francs

July 1, Aërial postal service started between Paris and Saint Nazaire

——, Price of eggs fixed at 3.60 francs a dozen

July 16, Public proceedings begun before the Senate sitting as High Court against Malvy, former Senator, for negligence in administration equivalent to treason

July 17, Duval executed

July 29–30, At National Council meeting of Socialist Party motion of Longuet voted for revision of war aims and peace based on terms as defined by Russian Bolsheviks

July 30, Decree regarding fourth war loan entrusting it to Loan Commission

Aug. 6, Louis J. Malvy found guilty of negligence of

duty during administration as Minister of the Interior by vote of 101 to 81 and sentenced to exile for 5 years but without civic degradation

Aug. 21, Commissariat General for motor spirit and petroleum established

Aug. 29, Decree fixed maximum prices instead of fixed prices for commodities

Sept. 19, Law and decree of Sept. 24 as to fourth war loan

Sept. 26, Alfred Dreyfus made a Lieutenant Colonel

Oct. 1, Prices of pork fixed ranging from 4.60 to 5 francs

Oct. 18, Law empowered the Minister of War to suspend execution of sentences pronounced by court martial

Oct. 20, Fourth War Loan opened for subscription, produced 22,163,222,724 francs

Oct. 29, Trial of Joseph Caillaux begun, indicted for trial before High Court of Senate as having "since the declaration of war, in 1914, 1915, 1916 and 1917, in France, and especially in Paris, and abroad sought to undermine the security of the State abroad by manœuvres, machinations, and intelligence with the enemy. . . ."

Oct., Execution of spy, Mata Hari

Nov. 11, Armistice with Germany ended the War

Nov. 18, Last German troops crossed the frontiers of France

——, General Pétain made a Marshal of France

Nov. 19, The French led by General Pétain occupied Metz, Alsace-Lorraine

Nov. 22, Act guaranteed to mobilized workers resumption of their contracts of employment

Dec. 2, Death of Edmond Rostand, poet and dramatist

Dec. 5, Alsace-Lorraine Diet convened as a National Assembly and formally announced return of French Government

Dec. 18, Customs agreement with Switzerland of 1881 denounced with other commercial treaties and request made that free zones be abolished

Dec. 24, Ministry of Blockade and Liberated Districts became Ministry of Liberated Districts

——, Scale of maximum prices for live stock published for each department

Dec. 29, Commissariat General for restoration of liberated districts established

1919

Jan. 1, The national debt was 147,472,421,289 francs of which 116,874,224,289 was internal and 30,598,-197,000 external; total fixed debt, internal, 67,738,-554,789; floating, 49,135,696,500 including National Defense bonds and advances of the Bank of France. Total fixed debt, external, 15,127,000,000; floating, 15,147,197,000

Jan. 2, Railroads restored to private ownership

Jan. 4, Decree removed restrictions as to condensed milk, eggs, rice, beans, and peas

Jan. 6, Law enacted to establish regional and departmental agricultural offices to promote improved methods of farming

Jan. 13, Address of French workers presented to President Wilson, program of minimum demands adopted by committee of the C.G.T. (Confédération Générale du Travail)

Jan. 14, Decree regulated trade in oil, nuts, and cereals in West African colonies

Jan. 18, Peace Conference formally opened in Paris. See p. 558

Jan. 20, Decree removed prohibitions on exportation of all but 140 articles of the 654 upon the tariff

Jan. 24–25, Transport strike in Paris for wage increase of 2 francs a day and shorter hours ended by Government placing the system under military control and promises of reform

Jan. 26, Captain Colet and Lieutenant Roget flew the double crossing of the Mediterranean (Merimas-Alger-Rossa) the same day

Feb. 1, Restrictions as to confectionery repealed

Feb. 3, Sugar ration increased by 50%

Feb. 4, Law enacted gave French citizenship to natives of Algeria under certain conditions

Feb. 19, Clemenceau shot and wounded by anarchist, Emile Cottin, but was able to resume work on the 28th

Feb. 21 and July 18, Laws passed Chamber granting right of employees of the State, departments, and communes, to organize with the exception of military, police, magistrates, and prefects and sub-prefects

Feb. 24, Note to Swiss Government asked revision of free zones system

March 4, Law provided for delimitation and reapportionment of landed property where boundaries obliterated

March 5, Decree released meat trade from Government control

March 8, "Revolt of the functionaries," meeting of functionaries and railroad workers which on the 13th voted to adhere to the C.G.T.

March 13, Figures of cost of living published in Le Petit Journal stated that since 1914 the price of beef, mutton, pork, and veal had increased nearly six-fold, eggs, cheese, and butter four-fold (eggs selling at 9 cents each and butter at 40 cents a pound in 1915 at this date $2 a pound)

March 14, Town-Planning law enacted

March 15, Cottin sentenced to death by military court for attempted assassination of Clemenceau

March 21, Alexandre Millerand appointed Governor of Alsace-Lorraine

March 22, Control of milk ended

March 25, Law on Collective Labor Agreements enacted

March 28, Law prohibited night work in bakeries

March 30, The jury acquitted R. Villain, confessed assassin of Jaurès

March 31–May 9, Senator Charles Humbert, Pierre Lenoir, and others brought before Third Court Martial for treason, charged with purchase of the Journal with enemy funds. Humbert and Ladoux acquitted, Detouches sentenced to 5 years in prison, and Lenoir to death

——, Figures published as to financial situation: Aug. 1, 1914 to March 31, 1919, expenses. 182,000,000,000; receipts deposited or discounted, 158,000,000,000; deficit, 24,000,000,000 francs

——, War Pensions Act amended

April 5, The General Association of Under-Agents of Posts resolved itself into a syndicate and declared for affiliation with the C.G.T.

April 17, Law enacted as to reparation for damage caused by War imposed on the State the duty of making good damages to real or personal property

April 18, Anglo-French Oil Agreement. See Iraq

——, Electoral Reform Bill including scrutin de liste and partial proportional representation passed in Chamber by vote of 287 to 138

April 20–22, National Congress of Unified Socialists met in Paris and adopted a compromise program

April 23, Eight hour day law enacted, established general principle to be followed by special legislation, extended to industrial and commercial establishments

April 24, Housing law provided regulations and provision for loans

May 1, Anarchist and Socialist riots in Paris by extremists, casualty list including 428 wounded police and nearly as many civilians, 118 arrests

May 3, National Federation of State and Commune Employees resolved to join the C.G.T.

May 5, Note from Swiss Government as to zone of Upper Savoy and reply of France of May 18

May 6, Law required all cultivators to declare to Commune officials the area of land planted in cereals

May 7, Supreme Council assigned mandate for Cameroon and Togo. See p. 560

May 13, General Union of Customs Agents resolved to become a syndicate and ask to join the C.G.T.

May 14, Decree published removed prohibitions on export of all but 19 articles on the tariff

May 20, Decree allowed importation of principal raw materials necessary to resumption of French production

——, Chamber of Deputies voted in favor of suffrage for women

May 24, Non-stop flight of Lieutenant Roget from Villacoublay to Kenitra, Morocco, 1,348 miles

June 1, Strikes on transport lines of Paris and strikes of metal workers, miners and chemical workers during the month for higher wages and shorter hours

——, Bread cards abolished

June 6, Decree repealed prohibition of importation of sugar

June 7, Casale, aviator, made new world altitude record of 31,152 feet

June 9, National Union of Secretaries and Employees of French Mayors resolved to become a syndicate and join the C.G.T.

June 14, Altitude world flight record made by Adjutant Casala of 33,136 feet, 5,610 feet higher than Mt. Everest, highest mountain in the world

June 19, July 7 and 8, Decrees removed almost all prohibitions on importations but increased tariff rates to almost prohibitive rates

June 24, Durafour Act established eight-hour day in mines

June 26, Electoral Reform Bill amended passed Senate, amendments accepted by Chamber, July 7

June 28, Peace Treaty with Germany signed at Versailles by which Alsace-Lorraine ceded to France and control of Saar coal mines and Franco-American, and Franco-British Guarantee Treaties signed by which the United States and Great Britain agreed to give military aid to France in the event of unprovoked German aggression, the Guarantees Treaties never effective because not ratified by the United States

June 29, Ministry of the Colonies reorganized and colonies re-grouped

July 1, Departments dealing with fixed prices and requisitions except wheat ended

July 8, Decree initiated the system of increasing customs duties by application of certain coefficients

July 10, Agreement with Great Britain as to Togo and Cameroons

July 12, Electoral Reform Act promulgated established the *scrutin de liste* with restricted proportional representation applied in elections that gave no party list an absolute majority

July 14, Victory parade in Paris

July 18, Resolution passed censured the economic policy of the Government since cost of living during the year had diminished by one-half in Belgium and one-quarter in England since the Armistice but had not ceased to increase in France

July 21, General strike planned for this date averted by energetic measures of the Government

July 27, Congress of Radicals and Radical Socialists in Paris proposed that measures be taken against speculators, that small salaries be exempted from the income tax, abolition of 3-year military service and gradual disarmament

Aug. 2, Act established the eight-hour day on oceangoing vessels and in shipping undertakings of all kinds for both sexes

Aug. 12, Order defined limits of devastated areas

Aug. 15, Law as to coöperative societies of reconstruction enacted

Sept. 5, Georges Gaston Quièn condemned to death by Paris court martial for betrayal of Edith Cavell to the Germans

——, The franc at 8.37 to the dollar

Sept. 7, International Labor Convention with Poland signed

Sept. 8, Anglo-French Boundary Convention readjusted frontiers in Africa. *See* p. 647

Sept. 9, Mines law enacted reorganized concession system

Sept. 10, Treaty of Peace with Austria signed at St. Germain

Sept. 15, Anglo-French Agreement as to Syria, Palestine, and Mosul

——, Congress of the C.G.T. met at Lyons; first full assembly since 1912

Sept. 21–Oct. 5, Strike of railroad workers

Sept. 24, Congress of School Teachers voted to become a syndicate and join the C.G.T.

Oct. 2, Treaty of Versailles ratified by Chamber of Deputies by vote of 372 to 52

Oct. 5, Meeting of National Socialists to organize *bloc* against Unified Socialists

Oct. 10, Decree prohibited consumption of fresh milk and cream on premises open to the public

Oct. 11, Treaty of Versailles ratified by Senate by unanimous vote

Oct. 12, Peace Treaty with Germany Bill signed by the President

——, Decree announced the War ended

Oct. 13, Censorship ended

Oct. 14, Decree for general demobilization

Oct. 15, Léon Bourgeois appointed French representative to League of Nations

——, Decree established Court of Justice

——, Decree of the President provided for certain modifications in regulations governing delivery of goods retaining those in force until Dec. 31, 1920

Oct. 17, French electoral and fiscal systems installed in Alsace-Lorraine

Oct. 20, Amnesty Act provided for full and complete amnesty for all political and military crimes committed before Oct. 17, 1919 with certain exceptions as to cases of mutiny and deserters, having to do with forest fires and war profits

Oct. 23, Profiteering Act of Aug., 1916, extended

——, Housing Act of March, 1918, extended

Oct. 24, Pierre Lenoir executed

Oct. 25, Workmen's Compensation Act extended to include industrial diseases

——, Act created Chambers of Agriculture in each department

Oct. 26, Law regulated water power system

Oct. 29, Law reorganized railroad administration

Oct. 29–Nov. 29, At first International Labor Conference in Washington Albert Thomas chosen Director General of International Labor Office

Nov. 10, Air mail service established between Paris (Bourget) and London (Hounslow)

Nov. 16, Elections begun which resulted in victory of the National *Bloc*, the party of Clemenceau and Millerand and overthrow of the Radical Socialists announced Nov. 30 as follows: Republican Left, 133; Republican Socialists, 27; Radical Socialists, 143; Unified Socialists, 68; Dissident Socialists, 6; Progressists, 133; Liberal Action, 69; Conservatives, 31 (180 Left, 216 Center, and 221 Right)

Dec. 3, Death of Pierre Auguste Renoir, artist

Dec. 8, New Chamber opened, 24 deputies from Alsace-Lorraine taking their places received with acclamations

Dec. 12, Decree regulated eight-hour day in textile industry under law of April 23

Dec. 18, M. Deschanel reëlected to the presidency of the Chamber of Deputies

1920

Jan. 8, First meeting of the Economic Labor Council set up by workers

Jan. 10, By ratification of the Treaty of Versailles France became an original member of the League of Nations

Jan. 11, Election for Senate a victory for the National Bloc: Conservatives, 28; Progressists, 31; Republican Left, 68; Radicals, 106; Republican Socialists, 5; Unified Socialists, 2

Jan. 12, Clemenceau withdrew as candidate for the presidency

Jan. 13, New Parliament officially called into existence

Jan. 14, Léon Bourgeois elected president of the Senate

Jan. 17, Paul Deschanel elected President of the Republic by vote of 734 out of 888 cast in the National Assembly at Versailles

Jan. 18, Decree established Immigration Commission

——, Resignation of Clemenceau Ministry

——, Government took possession of coal mines and other properties assigned by Treaty of Versailles in Saar

Jan. 19, Alexandre Millerand formed Cabinet as Prime Minister and Minister of Foreign Affairs; L'Hopiteau, Justice; Steeg, Interior; François Marsal, Finance; Lefèvre, War; Landry, Navy; Honnorat, Public Instruction and Fine Arts; Le Trocquer, Public Works and Transport; Ricard, Agriculture; Isaac, Commerce, Industry, Posts and Telegraphs; Sarraut, Colonies; Jourdain, Labor; Ogier, Liberated Regions; Maginot, Pensions and War Allowances; Breton, Hygiene

Feb. 3, National Labor Supply Council established by decree of the Ministry of Labor to advise the Government as to placing of French and foreign labor

Feb. 8, Socialists of the Department of the Seine voted for adherence to the Third International

Feb. 17, Decree closed confectionery and pastry shops for 2 days a week; repealed Sept. 25

——, Trial of former Premier Joseph Caillaux charged with defeatist activities and of relations with the enemy begun before High Court of the Senate

Feb. 18, President Deschanel took office

Feb. 19, Strike of railway employees on Paris, Lyons, and Mediterranean Railroad begun which developed into a general strike

Feb. 20, Poincaré appointed president of the Reparation Commission

Feb. 25, Socialist Congress at Strasbourg voted for meeting with Third International to make a platform

Feb., Strike of miners in northern coal mines due to high cost of living

Feb. 29, All railroad employees joined strikers

March 1, Railroad strike ended by Government intervention and promises of redress

March 9, Act fixed minimum pension for miners and widows of miners

March 12, Act extended the rights of industrial associations, trade unions, amending law of March 21, 1884

March 13, 400,000 persons on strike

March 21, Peace Loan opened which produced 15,730,000,000 francs

April 6, French troops occupied Frankfort and Darmstadt and Hanau and the following day Homburg claiming German violations of Treaty of Versailles

April 8, New Socialist Party founded, Paul Aubriot, President

April 23, Joseph Caillaux sentenced to imprisonment for 3 years, loss of civic rights and to reside for 5 years in zone to be selected by the Government, and to pay costs of case about 53,000 francs, found guilty of relations with enemy agents in South America, Paris, and Italy, correspondence with the enemy, giving enemy information for conduct of defeatist propaganda in France, but exonerated him from guilty intention

——, Chamber adopted amendments to law taxing business transfers

April 24, Caillaux released as he had already served 3 years in prison, and went to live in Mamers

——, San Remo Oil Agreement modified the Bérenguer-Long Agreement, the French and British Governments agreeing to support their respective nationals in securing oil concessions in certain territories including Rumania, Asia Minor, parts of the old Russian Empire, Galicia, French and British Crown Colonies, and other countries by mutual consent, Great Britain in effect assigning to France the former German interest in the Turkish Petroleum Company for exploitation of oilfields in the vilayets of Mosul and Bagdad, France to agree to special facilities for Great Britain and construction as to pipe lines and railways necessary for transportation of oil, oil transported to be free from French taxes

May 1, Dockers, seamen, and miners called out

May 3, Strike of about 20% of railroad employees. Strike leaders arrested

May 6, Strike of metal workers in Department of the Seine, and transport workers and builders

May 11, Millerand announced intention to order dissolution of the General Confederation of Labor and arrested strike leaders

May 21, Second strike of railroad employees ended and general strike by order of the General Confederation of Labor

May 23, President Deschanel fell from compartment of moving train while traveling by night to Montbrison, and was not seriously injured, but the shock made it necessary for him to take leave of absence

May 26, The prosecution of the General Confederation of Labor begun by the Government under Articles 3, 5, and 9 of law of March 25, 1884

June 4, World duration record set by Lieutenant Bossontrol and Lieutenant Bernard in flight at Etampes, 24 hours, 19 minutes, and 7 seconds

June 25, Law provided for increased customs duties and new taxes, tax on industrial and commercial profits raised from 4.5% to 8%, annual tax on agricultural products raised from 3.75% to 6%, considered as being equal to half the rental value of the land, income tax on salaries, annuities, &c., raised from 3.75% to 6%, new tax on business transfers (chiffre d'affaires) levied on all business except the selling of bread at 1%, luxury taxes 10%

July 11, Death of the Empress Eugénie, widow of Napoleon III, in Madrid, while on visit to her nephew, the Duke of Alva

July 14, French ultimatum to Faisal. *See* Syria

July 16, Spa Agreement assured France of delivery by Germany of 80% of her coal requirements

Aug. 3, Convention signed with Austria as to settlement of debts of French nationals under Article 248 of the Treaty of St. Germain

Aug. 5, Management of Crédit Agricole (coöperative banks) transferred to central body

Aug. 9, Law provided for purchase or requisition of supply of food stuffs by magistrates if necessary

Aug. 10, Treaty of Peace with Turkey recognized French mandate in Syria, protectorate in Morocco, French sphere in Cilicia

Aug. 12, Decree fixed price of quintal (220 pounds) of wheat at 100 francs, rye, 80

Sept. 7, Military Agreement with Belgium signed

Sept. 15, Resignation of President Deschanel on account of ill health

Sept. 23, Millerand elected President of the Republic by vote of 695 out of 892 votes cast

Sept. 24, Georges Leygues became Prime Minister and Minister of Foreign Affairs, the Cabinet remaining otherwise unchanged

Sept. 29, Dr. von Meyer, German Ambassador, presented credentials, first since 1914

Nov. 4, Commercial Treaty with Czechoslovakia signed

Nov. 30, Bill for reëstablishment of French embassy to the Vatican passed in Chamber by vote of 391 to 179

Dec. 10, The Nobel peace prize for 1919 awarded to Léon Bourgeois

Dec. 23, Anglo-French Convention defined boundaries between Palestine and Syria

Dec. 30, Socialists at Congress of Tours voted by 3,208 against 1,220 to unite with the Third International

1921

Jan. 1, Control of State of imports ended with certain exceptions as veto abolished

Jan. 3, Death of Jeanne Louiseau (Daniel Le Suer), author

Jan. 7, Minority Socialists met to reconstruct the United Socialist Party

Jan. 12, Leygues Ministry resigned after defeat in

Chamber as a result of the serious deficit in the revenue

Jan. 13, Court decision ordered dissolution of the General Confederation of Labor

Jan. 14, International Labor Convention with Czechoslovakia signed

Jan. 16, Aristide Briand became Prime Minister and Minister of Foreign Affairs, Paul Doumer, Finance

Jan. 18, Agreement regarding sequestration of property signed with Czechoslovakia

Jan. 31, Decree reorganized the Superior Labor Council

Feb. 1, Death of Emile Sicard (44), writer

Feb. 19, Political Agreement with Poland signed, defensive alliance and pledging economic and diplomatic coöperation

——, Generals Fayolle, Franchet d'Esperey, and Lyautey made marshals of France

March 8, French and Belgian troops occupied German towns of Düsseldorf, Duisburg, and Ruhrort because of alleged default of Germany in payment of reparations, applying sanctions for non-fulfilment of the Treaty of Versailles

March 9, Franco-Turkish Peace Treaty signed terminating hostilities along the Syrian frontier and in Cilicia and agreement as to boundary

March 22, Death of Jean Paul Laurens, painter

——, First draft of Workers' Insurance law presented in Chamber later law of 1928

March 31, Death of Gabriel Fabre, musician

April 1, Decree of the President raised tariff on German imports up to from 100 to 300%

April 12, The late General Galliéni, defender of Paris in the War, voted a marshal

April 14, The Chamber adopted 50% tariff on German importations by vote of 383 to 79

April 18, Death of Joseph Reinach (64), author

April 23, Convention regarding wines and spirits signed with Norway

May 10, Trial of Communist leaders arrested in revolutionary strike of May, 1920 begun

May 15, From this date freedom of trade in cereals and flour

May 25, Death of Justin Louis Emile Combes, former Premier

May 27, Resolution of Chamber authorized free importation of wheat

May 28, Relations with Holy See resumed after 17 years, M. Jonnart, presenting credentials as French Ambassador at the Vatican, Monseigneur Cerretti presenting credentials as Papal Nuntius in Paris, Aug. 6

June 7, Peace Treaty with Hungary ratified

June 23, Act to guarantee reëmployment of railroad men called for military service

June 28, Convention made by which the State guaranteed to railroad companies under concessions which expire at various dates from 1950 to 1960 working expenses and the interest and redemption of capital and loans

July 1, Census published gave total population including Alsace-Lorraine as of March as 39,209,518, military and naval forces of the commercial navy abroad estimated as 93,471 in addition, urban population 18,205,492, rural 21,004,026; number of foreigners 1,550,449 during year 1921; population of colonies nearly 100,000,000

July 7, The Senate voted credit of 10 million francs for relief of the unemployed

July 13, Commercial Treaty with Finland signed

——, Death of Professor Gabriel Lippmann, inventor of color photography

Aug. 1, All control by Government of cereals and flour ended, importation allowed

Aug. 7, Convention with Switzerland as to Savoy zones signed by which Switzerland agreed to transfer French customs line to the political frontier, in return for certain economic advantages rejected by Swiss plebiscite

Aug. 25, Agreement with Germany as to delivery of 3,500,000 tons of Saar coal annually

Sept. 23, Hostile demonstration in Venice against French Mission on visit to Italy

Oct. 6, Loucheur-Rathenau Agreement signed providing for direct supply of deliveries in kind from Germany

Oct. 20, Franco-Turkish Agreement signed at Angora by which the French acquired extensive commercial, mining, and political privileges in the Near East, France recognizing the Turkish Nationalist Government and agreeing to evacuate Cilicia, strip of territory along north frontier of Syria, ceded to Turkey

Oct. 29, Railway Organization law enacted created Superior Council and Committee of Management

Oct. 30, Sadi Lecointe in a Nieuport plane made world record for altitude rising to height of 11,145 meters (36,564 feet)

Nov. 22, Death of Emile Boutroux, philosopher

Nov. 25, French consulate at Naples attacked by mob

Dec. 9, Naval construction program voted provided for 3 light cruisers, 6 destroyers, 12 torpedo boats, and 12 submarines at cost of 755,000,000 francs

Dec. 16, Death of Charles Camille Saint Saens, musical composer

Dec. 25, Minority Congress of C.G.T. in Paris formed C.G.T.U.

1922

Jan. 7, Most favored nation Commercial Treaty with Estonia signed

Jan. 12, Resignation of Briand Ministry because of attacks on his foreign policy deemed too conciliatory. *See* Conferences, p. 565

Jan. 15, Raymond Poincaré formed Cabinet as Prime Minister and Minister of Foreign Affairs declaring for fulfilment by Germany of reparation obligations: Barthou, Justice and Vice-Premier; de Lasteyrie, Finance; Manoury, Interior; Maginot, War; Raiberti, Marine; Albert Sarraut, Colonies; M. L. Dior, Agriculture

Jan. 17, Decision of Council of State that civil servants representing public interests may not organize in trade unions

Jan. 30, Provisional Commercial Agreement with Portugal signed

Feb. 3, Anglo-French Convention fixed boundaries of Syria

Feb. 6, Commercial Convention with Poland signed provided for reciprocal tariff concessions and French loan to Poland

Feb. 10, Death of Paul Mounet, actor

Feb. 26, Death of Alexandre Duval, founder of the restaurants

March 2, Death of Henri Bataille, dramatist

March 11, Decree reorganized the Superior Council of Agriculture

March 24, Death of Denys Cochin, statesman

March 31, Housing Act enacted

April 6, President Millerand began tour of African colonies

April 16, Colonial Exhibition opened at Marseilles

April 28, Death of Paul Deschanel, former President

June 1, Jean V. Parmentier appointed head of Mission to the United States to confer on war debts

July 8, New Commercial Agreement with Spain signed

July 24, The mandate of France over Syria and the Lebanon and southern Cameroons and western Togo confirmed by the League of Nations Council

July 28, Commercial Agreement with Guatemala signed

Aug. 12, Expulsion of Germans from Alsace-Lorraine begun

Aug. 18, Death of Ernest Lavisse, historian

Aug. 24, General strike at Havre

Aug. 26, Troops called out to suppress rioting in strike by metal workers at Havre

Aug. 31, Germany granted a six months' moratorium by the Reparation Commission

Sept. 5, Decree revoked eight-hour day for seamen granted Aug., 1919, and serious strike followed

——, Housing Act "to encourage building of cheap and sanitary houses for persons of small means"

——, Death of Marcel Sembat, Socialist statesman

——, Lubersac-Stinnes Agreement provided for private arrangements of French property owners with German industrialists as to system of deliveries in kind and reconstruction

Sept. 7, Death of Léon Bonnat, portrait painter

Oct. 7, Convention with Czechoslovakia signed as to legal protection and assistance

Oct. 9, Strike of metal workers in Havre which had lasted 110 days ended with acceptance of employers' terms

Oct. 19, Communist Congress voted for affiliation with the Third International

Oct. 22, Announcement of resignation of General Gouraud as High Commissioner in Syria

Nov. 1, Death of Alfred Capus, dramatist

Nov. 8, The franc 16.6 to the dollar

Nov. 11–Dec. 20, Clemenceau made visit to the United States

Nov. 13, New Commercial Treaty with Italy signed

Nov. 18, Death of Marcel Proust, novelist

Nov. 21, The Senate by vote of 156 to 134 rejected Bill for woman suffrage

Dec. 8, Military Air Service organized as separate service

Dec. 15, Workmen's Compensation Act of 1898 extended to all agricultural laborers

——, Commercial Agreement with Canada signed

Dec. 16, Law as to mines regulated exploitation and concessions

1923

Jan. 10, Communist headquarters in Paris raided by police and 5 leaders, Monmousson, Masanne, Pietri, Sourdot, and Treint arrested

——, France notified Germany of decision to occupy Ruhr towns as a result of German default in coal deliveries

Jan. 11, French troops occupied Essen at 4:45 A.M.

Jan. 13, Death of Alexandre Ribot (80), former Premier

Jan. 29, Alexis Maneyrol, aviator, made world record for duration flight in glider at Vauville, 8 hours and 4 minutes

Feb. 7, Strike of 360,000 miners in Saar Basin coal district for increase in wages of 7 francs a day

Feb. 9, Miners in Moselle district joined strike

Feb. 15, Léon Bourgeois resigned as president of the Senate to give all his time to the League of Nations; succeeded by G. Doumergue Feb. 22

——, Loan of 400 million francs to Poland

Feb. 16, Law enacted providing for transfer of customs line to political frontier with Switzerland in Upper Savoy

Feb. 19, Death of Frédéric Masson, historian

Feb. 21, Strike settled with slight increase

——, Death of Théophile Delcassé, former Foreign Minister

March 1, Franco-Belgian Administration created for occupied Ruhr region which took over the direction of the railroads, a system of 3,720 miles

March 8, Death of Sarah Bernhardt, actress, in Paris

March 28, Death of General Manoury

April 1, Law enacted reducing term of compulsory military service to one and one-half years with liberal exemptions to begin at the age of 21

——, War Pensions Act amended

April 5, Law provided for agricultural instruction by motion pictures

May 6, Georges Barbot crossed the English Channel and returned in a motor glider, 38¼ miles in 61 minutes, return trip 44 minutes, Inglevert to Lympne

May 7, Letter from Monseigneur Cerretti, Papal Nuntius, presented to president of the Council a draft statute for organization of the private *associations cultuelles*; accepted by France May 13 and by Council Dec. 13

May 12, Commercial Agreement with Belgium signed; rejected by Belgian Chamber, Feb. 27, 1924

May 14, Death of Charles de Freycinet, former Premier (94)

May 21, Death of M.C.F.W. Esterhazy, who figured in the Dreyfus case, living in England under an assumed name

May 24, The Senate refused to sit as High Court for trial of Deputy Marcel Cachin and his Communist lieutenants for sedition which precipitated Cabinet crisis and resignation of Poincaré, but he was persuaded to remain in office and presently received vote of confidence of 356 to 162

May 25, Unsuccessful attempt made to assassinate monarchist, Charles Maurras, editor of *L'Action Française*

May 29, Loan of 100 million francs to Rumania

May 30, Royalists assaulted and beat 3 Republican deputies in retaliation for attack on Maurras

May 31, Agreement with Bulgaria as to private debts to French creditors

June 9, Law as to adoption of children passed

June 10, Death of Pierre Loti (Julien Viaud), writer

June 13, Case of Cachin and other Communists accused of plotting against France by taking the side of Germany in the Ruhr dismissed by judge

June 22, Commercial Convention with Austria signed

June 24, The *L'Action Française* forced to suspend publication temporarily by the calling out of its employees by labor organization in protest against management

July 7, Washington Naval Disarmament Treaty ratified by Chamber by vote of 460 to 106 and by the Senate July 11 by vote of 287–3

July 12, Loan of 300 million francs to Yugoslavia

July 13, Decrees of Aug. 10, 1899 dealing with working conditions amended

July 24, Treaty of Lausanne signed. *See* p. 567

July 27, Decree provided regulations for eight-hour day in banks

July 28, Customs Agreement with Italy signed

Aug. 2, Workmen's Compensation Act amended to include domestic servants, porters, chauffeurs, governesses, and all persons in household service

Aug. 13, Decree as to family allowances of Aug. 10, 1899, amended

Aug. 14, The armored cruiser *Duguay Trouin*, 8,000 tons, launched, first war vessel built since the War

Aug. 17, Commercial Treaty with Czechoslovakia

Aug. 29, Arbitration Treaty of Oct. 14, 1903 with Great Britain renewed by exchange of Notes

Aug. 31, Index numbers taken from receipts of railways, value of output of minerals, imports of raw materials, canal and harbor traffic stated as 102.9 (on basis of 100 in 1913) for August as compared with 91.6 in February indicating great increase of industrial activity

Sept. 30, The dirigible "Dixmude" former German L-72, largest airship in the world completed uninterrupted trip of 4,500 miles over Sahara desert and return by Sicily and Corsica in 118 hours and 41 minutes

Oct. 10, Decree as to customs frontier in Upper Savoy. *See* Nov. 10

Nov. 10, Customs line established at political frontier in Upper Savoy, abolishing free zones along Swiss frontier

Nov. 23, Industrial Agreement as to Ruhr signed. *See* p. 568

Dec. 4, Death of Maurice Barres, novelist

Dec. 18, Tangier Agreement signed with Great Britain providing for permanent neutralization. *See also* Morocco; signed by Spain, Feb. 7, 1924

——, The dirigible "Dixmude" started cruise and was last seen crossing over Tunis Dec. 21, believed to have been destroyed by storm; the body of the commander, Lieutenant de Grenedan, found by fishermen off coast of Sicily Dec. 27

Dec. 20, The number of unemployed stated as 441 as compared with 91,000 in 1921

——, Housing Act of March, 1922, extended

Dec. 24, Act to improve Old Age and Invalidity Pensions enacted for miners

Dec. 27, Law passed restricting rent advances to 100% over charges of 1914

——, Death of Alexandre Gustave Eiffel, engineer who built the Eiffel Tower

Dec. 28, Protocol with England signed defining frontiers Anglo-Egyptian Sudan and French Equatorial Africa

——, Act extended Miners' Pension and Benefit Act to persons employed in industries subsidiary to mining as well as those actually employed in mining coal

1924

Jan. 3, Act established a Chamber of Agriculture in each department

Jan. 6, The Catholic Church granted legal status by the Government with right to occupy former property as a result of acceptance by the Holy See of system of "diocesan associations"

Jan. 6, Election of Senate; only 6 members defeated for reëlection

Jan. 7, Franc at 4.91 cents on New York stock exchange

Jan. 9, Gaston Doumergue reëlected president of the Senate

Jan. 10, Boundary Protocol signed with Great Britain as to frontiers of Anglo-Egyptian Sudan and French Equatorial Africa, Wadai and Darfur

Jan. 11, Senate elected as follows: Gauche Démocratique, 157; Union Républicaine, 88; Gauche Républicaine, 30; Right, 10; Union Démocratique et Radicale, 23; Independents, 6

Jan. 12–Sept. 27, German passive resistance against French occupation. *See* Germany

Jan. 14, The franc at 4.27 cents

Jan. 18, Pope Pius XI in encyclical letter (Maximam) sanctioned statute for organization of diocesan associations in France allowing French Church to become legal owner of money required for maintenance of church and priesthood

Jan. 25, Franco-Czech Treaty of Alliance signed, pledged each to render the other military assistance in case of unprovoked aggression by third party

Feb. 3–March 24, Flight of Lieutenants Arrachart and Lemaitre to Timbuktu and return

Feb. 16, Arbitration Agreement with Spain of Feb. 26, 1904, renewed for 5 years

Feb. 21, Commercial Agreement with Greece

Feb. 22, The Chamber gave the Government authority to proceed by decrees in State Council for 4 months to reforms and simplification of administration to effect economies; passed Senate March 17

——, Bill passed in Chamber and in Senate March 17 to increase nearly all taxes by 20%, parcel post and telephone rates increased, and match monopoly run by State at a loss to be sold to private enterprise

March 10, The franc at 3.42 cents on New York stock exchange

March 22, Act prescribing the *bordereau de coupons* and *double décime* added to most direct and indirect taxes, and rates of others increased, and economy cuts during 1924 to the extent of 1 billion provided for

March 23, Death of General Robert George Nivelle

March 26, Poincaré Ministry defeated by 7 votes on adding 2,000,000 francs to a pension Bill, but Poincaré reorganized Cabinet 2 days later

March 27, Decree annexed Adélie Land, sub-Antarctic

April 1, German Recovery Act levying duty of 26% on imports came into effect

April 7, Decree instituted *ad valorem* export tax ranging from 5 to 15% on meat, preserved meat, condensed milk, cheese, fresh vegetables, fruit, &c.

April 9, Agreement with Salvador signed modified Commercial Treaty of Jan. 9, 1901

April 10, The franc at 5.96 cents

April 14, Death of Prince Roland Bonaparte, geographer

——, Statute codified all matters as to pensions of soldiers, sailors, and civil servants fixing maximum and minimum

April 15, Agreement with Germany as to deliveries of coal and coke of Nov. 23, 1923 renewed until June 15

April 17, Etienne Oehmichen made horizontal flight of 525 meters (1,772 feet) first helicopter record

April 24–June 8, Flight of Lieutenant Peltier d'Oisy and Sergeant Vesin from Paris to Tokio arriving at Calcutta May 3, 51 hours, 55 minutes

May 11, Election for Chamber resulted in defeat of the *Bloc National* and retirement of Poincaré, and victory of the *Bloc des Gauches*, the Radical Socialists the largest single group in an election in which 14 parties in the field and 2,754 candidates put up for 584 seats

May 15, Death of Baron d'Estournelle de Constant, pacifist

May 22, Decree established the Superior Consultative Committee on Commerce and Industry

May 29, Death of Paul Cambon, diplomatist

——, The Government received gift of $1,000,000 from J. D. Rockefeller for reconstruction of roof of cathedral at Rheims, reconstruction of palace at Fontainebleau

May 31, Law enacted regulated all matters dealing with aviation

June 1, Resignation of Poincaré Ministry

——, New Chamber assembled: Communists, 26; Democrats, 14; Left Radicals, 41; Left Republican Democrats, 43; Socialists, 105; Radicals and Radical Socialists, 140; Republican Socialists and French Socialists, 42; Republicans of the Left, 36; Democratic Republican Union, 103; Independents, 30

——, Law enacted applied French Civil Code and a number of laws specified to Alsace-Lorraine

June 4, Painlevé elected president of the Chamber, G. Doumergue president of Senate

June 8, Frédéric François-Marsal formed Cabinet

June 10, François-Marsal Ministry forced out

June 11, Resignation of President Millerand forced by Radicals and Socialists of the Left, Herriot refusing to form Ministry while Millerand remained President

June 13, Gaston Doumergue elected President of the Republic by 515 votes as against 309 cast for Painlevé

June 14, Edouard Herriot, Radical Socialist, appointed Premier

June 21, Act codified laws relating to labor councils

June 30, Liquor smuggling Treaty with the United States signed

July 7, Franc at 5.15 cents on the New York stock exchange

July 12, Caillaux's Bill for tax on business turnovers passed in Chamber by vote of 295 to 228

July 15, The Chamber voted Amnesty Bill which included amnesty to Joseph Caillaux, former Premier, and L. J. Malvy, former Minister of the Interior

July 16–17, World flight duration record of 37 hours, 59 minutes, and 10 seconds made by Coupet and Drouhin

July 30, The Chamber voted to reëstablish the Government monopoly on matches

Aug. 4, The franc at .0538 cents on New York stock exchange

Aug. 16, Declaration as to evacuation of Ruhr. *See* p. 568

Aug. 18, Supplementary Commercial Agreement with Czechoslovakia signed

Aug. 27, Act authorized the city of Paris to borrow 300,000,000 francs for the construction and purchase of cheap dwellings

Sept. 1, Dawes Plan for reparations from Germany came into effect. *See* p. 568. Up to this date France had received as reparations a total of 1,794 million gold marks under all heads, 8% of which was in cash

Sept. 21, Decree brought into effect imposition of duty of 26% on goods imported from Germany, to be counted as part of reparations due

Sept. 22, Announced that budget for 1925 would not contain an appropriation for Vatican Embassy

Sept. 25, Claims Convention with Mexico signed

Oct. 10, M. Callizo reached altitude in flight of 39,586 feet making world record

Oct. 13, Death of Anatole France (real name Jacques Anatole Thibault), novelist (80)

Oct. 15, Russian refugees in France presented memorandum asking for status

Oct. 24, Provisional Commercial Agreement with Belgium signed

Oct. 28, Recognition of Soviet Government of Russia, *de jure*, by Herriot Government

Oct. 29, Treaty with Lithuania signed of extradition and judicial assistance

Oct. 30, Commercial Agreement with Latvia signed

——, Compromise Agreement with Switzerland as to free zones

Nov. 1–2, Minority in C.G.T.U. formed the C.G.T.S.R. (Union Fédérative des Syndicates Autonomes)

Nov. 4, Death of Gabriel Faure, composer (79)

Nov. 18, Announcement of Premier Herriot that General Wrangel's fleet interned at Bizerta, Tunis, to be handed over to the Russian Government

——, Amnesty Bill passed by Senate granting amnesty to Caillaux and Malvy

Nov. 19, Commercial Agreement with Spain signed

Nov. 21, Successful strike of sardine packers for increase begun which ended Jan. 7, 1925

Nov. 23, State funeral at the Panthéon for Jean Jaurès

Nov. 28, Decree established the Superior Railway Council (*Conseil Superieur des Chemins de Fer*)

——, Bond issue of $100 million subscribed in the United States

Dec. 4, Arrival of Leonid Krassin, first Soviet Ambassador, in Paris

Dec. 7, Protest meeting against anti-clerical policy of the Government at Quimper, Brittany

Dec. 9, Commercial Treaty with Poland signed

Dec. 11, Bonnet made speed airplane record at 278.5 per hour

Dec. 13, M. Krassin, Russian Ambassador, presented credentials

Dec. 20, Proposal of M. Krassin that a loan to Russia be made condition of Russian recognition of French pre-War debts (those of private nationals as distinct from State amounted to £732,650,267)

1925

Jan. 1, Up to this date 74,206,000,000 francs spent by France for reconstruction. *See* July 15, *infra*

Jan. 16, Decree established a National Economic Council

Jan. 18, Death of General Charles Louis Lanrezac (72)

Jan. 24, Act amended Labor Code as to night work of women and children to agree with the International Labor Convention (1919)

Feb. 2, The Chamber voted for suppression of Embassy at Vatican by vote of 314 to 250, but agreed to special arrangement for Alsace-Lorraine, to be represented at the Vatican by a diplomatic agent

Feb. 3, Captain Lemaitre and Lieutenant Arrachard left Paris on flight for French West Africa, reached Villade Cisneros in 28 hours (2,400 miles)

Feb. 10, Catholic mass meeting at Marseilles attacked by Communists, 2 persons killed, 100 injured

Feb. 11, Death of Maitre Demange, lawyer (85), advocate for the defense in the Dreyfus case

Feb. 14, The franc at 91.925 to pound sterling

——, Treaty of commerce and navigation with Siam signed

Feb. 15, Parade of 30,000 Catholics at Rennes, demonstration against anti-religious policy of the Government

Feb. 21, Strike of telephone and telegraph operators for an increase in wages

Feb. 25, Act passed as to Employment Exchanges and Departmental Employment Offices

March 4, New Commercial Treaty with Portugal signed

March 14, Archbishop Ruch of Strasbourg called 3-day strike of school children in a number of Catholic schools as protest against setting up of certain undenominational schools

March 20, The Chamber session almost in riot over religious questions

March 28, Strike of 6,000 Alsatian miners

March 31, Decree established a three-shift system in the mercantile marine

April 2, Resignation of Clémentel, Finance Minister, after discovery that the Bank of France had issued an excess of several milliards of bank notes beyond amount permitted legally; succeeded by Anatole de Monzie April 3

April 4, New commercial *modus vivendi* with Belgium signed

April 6, Treaty of conciliation and arbitration with Switzerland replacing that of 1904

April 7, The Chamber passed Bill giving suffrage to women of 21 in provincial and cantonal elections

——, National Labor Supply Council reorganized

April 10, Herriot Ministry resigned after defeat in Senate on issue of excess number of bank notes exceeding legal limit

April 12, Agreement with China settled "gold franc" controversy, France agreed that unpaid Boxer instalments should be used for rehabilitation of Bank of China

April 13, Riffs began offensive against tribes friendly to French in Morocco. *See* Morocco

April 17, Painlevé formed Cabinet: Briand, Foreign Affairs; Caillaux, Finance

April 18, Ministry of Liberated Districts became an under-secretaryship

April 22, Herriot elected president of Chamber

April 23, Clash of Nationalists and Communists in Paris, 3 Nationalists killed

May 12, Death of General Charles M. E. Mangin, the defender of Verdun

May 26, The Government and the Opposition agreed to maintain embassy at the Vatican

June 1, Death of Lucien Guitry, actor

June 4, Death of Camille Flammarion, astronomer

June 10–13, Visit of M. Painlevé, Premier, to Morocco to confer with Marshal Lyautey on offensive of Abdel Krim

June 17–July 25, Franco-Spanish Conference in Madrid on Morocco

June 22, Agreement with Spain on coast blockade of Morocco

July 7, General Naulin appointed to command in Morocco

July 8, Agreement with Spain on land blockade of Morocco

——, The Washington Labor Convention pending since 1919 ratified by Chamber

July 9, The Chamber voted war credit of 183 million francs

July 10, Commercial Treaty with Poland signed

July 11, Miners' Pension Act amended increasing pensions

——, Agreement concluded with Germany as to commercial exchanges between Germany and the Saar

July 13, New taxes on business wages and salaries, on foreign currency transactions, and "replacement" taxes on sales by mines of coal, slaughtering of animals to replace turnover tax

——, Law enacted by which 120 francs per annum granted to every family with more than 3 children for every child under 13 beyond the third

July 15, Report on reconstruction in devastated regions published, stated that of 7,520,000 acres unfit for use in Nov., 1918, 95% had been restored by Jan. 1, 1925, of 893,792 buildings destroyed 508,-319 had been restored, of 22,900 factories 21,000 had been replaced or restored, of 5,081 schools and 3,311 churches about one-half had been replaced

July 18, Druse insurrection against French rule. *See* Syria

July 26, Act established Trade Councils (*Chambres de Métiers*)

——, Agreement with Spain signed for military coöperation in Morocco

——, Customs Agreement with Turkey signed

July 30, Strike of bank clerks in Paris for increase in salaries and recognition of union which spread to other cities, not successful

Aug. 7–9, Drouhin and Landry made airplane world record for duration and distance, 2,734 miles in 45 hours, 11 minutes, and 59 seconds without refuelling

Aug. 11, Miners' Pension Act again amended increasing pensions

Aug. 18, Marshal Pétain left for Morocco to take military command for supervision of reinforcements sent out from France

Aug. 21, Final conference with Spain at Algeciras

Aug. 26–Sept. 12, Marshal Lyautey in France to report on Morocco situation

Sept. 7, Death of René Viviani, former Premier

Sept. 11, Bank strike ended

Sept. 16, French financial Mission headed by Caillaux left for the United States to confer on debt

Sept. 21, Two-hour strike of telegraph and telephone operators

Sept. 28, Marshal Lyautey resigned as Resident General of Morocco

Sept. 29, Death of Léon Bourgeois (74), former Premier and "Spiritual Father" of the League of Nations

Sept. 30, Budget presented included expenditure of 32,500,000 francs, a deficit of about 6,000,000 on basis of receipts of 1924

Oct. 3, Caillaux Financial Mission sailed from New York after failure of negotiations on debt; American proposal of 5-year partial moratorium under which France would pay $40,000,000 representing a rate of 1% on debt for five years not accepted

Oct. 11, Theodore Steeg appointed Resident General in Morocco

Oct. 12, One-day general strike against the war in Morocco not successful

Oct. 13, Commercial Convention with Hungary signed

Oct. 14–21, Strike of sailors and longshoremen

Oct. 16 and Dec. 1, Locarno Treaties signed. *See* p. 569

Oct. 22, Commercial Agreement with Bulgaria signed

Oct. 27, Painlevé Cabinet resigned

Oct. 29, Painlevé reconstituted Cabinet without Caillaux as Minister of Finance

Oct. 30, Decision to recall General Sarrail, High Commissioner in Syria, after bombardment of Damascus Oct. 18–20 (*see* Syria); General Duport appointed in his place

Nov. 6, Henri de Jouvenel appointed High Commissioner in Syria

——, Saar Trade Agreement as to commercial exchanges signed with Germany

Nov. 7, Marshal Pétain returned to France from Morocco

Nov. 22, Painlevé Ministry defeated in Chamber on proposal to stop the payment of Government Treasury bonds resigned

Nov. 25, Death of Paul Bruat, novelist

Nov. 27, Briand formed his eighth Ministry; Louis Loucheur, Finance; Painlevé, War

Dec. 2, Death of Paul Dutasta (52), diplomatist

Dec. 3, Finance Bill passed in Chamber and in the Senate the following day, provided for increased taxes and inflation, income tax of from 12 to 20% on income derived from property, marketable securities, 9.6 to 12 from commercial and industrial property, 7.2–10% from salaries and agricultural profits

Dec. 15, Resignation of Loucheur as Finance Minister; succeeded by Paul Doumer the following day

Dec. 21, Act gave final jurisdiction to the provisional courts in disputes between employers and employed when sums less than 600 francs involved. Sum raised to 1,000 francs Nov. 20, 1926

Dec. 22, Captain Gordon Canning arrived in Paris bringing credentials from Abd-el-Krim authorizing him to ask peace terms

Dec. 23, The Appellate Court dismissed claim of Soviet Government to vessels of old Russian Corporation at Marseilles

Dec. 26, Death of Senator Jules Méline, former Premier (87)

1926

Jan. 10–12, National Congress of Socialist Party met and voted against collaboration with Radicals or affiliation with any political party

Jan. 11, Meeting of presidents of Chambers of Commerce voted approval of Doumer's financial proposals

Jan. 12, Herriot reëlected president of the Chamber of Deputies

Jan. 16, International Institute for Intellectual Coöperation inaugurated in Paris

Jan. 22, Commercial Treaty with Hungary signed

Feb., Table published showing effect of the War on economic life of France stated that of 1,363,000 killed 669,000 were farmers, 235,000 industrial workers and 159,000 in commercial enterprises, 21,000 civil service, and 40,000 members of the professions

Feb. 2, At Landerneaux, Brittany, 60,000 Breton farmers of the Catholic League protested against anti-clerical laws

Feb. 4, The Chamber of Deputies voted for income tax publicity

Feb. 12, Provisional Commercial Agreement with Germany signed

Feb. 19, Franc fell to 136.70 to the English pound

Feb. 25, Conference with Russia begun in Paris regarding financial questions, pre-War debts, &c.

Feb. 27, Doumer's Tax Bill voted by Chamber in mutilated form Feb. 16 passed Senate which replaced sales tax and duties on alcohol, coffee, and salt removed by Chamber

Feb. 28, Meeting of 60,000 Breton farmers at Landerneau to protest against anti-clerical laws

March 1, Striking building workers in clash with police

March 2, The Chamber ratified the Locarno Treaties by vote of 413 to 17

March 3, Strike of retailers, restaurant owners, café proprietors for 2 hours in Paris in protest against the excessive taxes proposed

March 6, Briand Ministry defeated on sales tax proposal of Finance Bill resigned

March 9, New Ministry reconstituted by Briand took office, Raoul Péret, Minister of Finance; Malvy, Interior

March 24, Franc fell to 139.95 to the English pound

March 26, Increased sale tax approved

March 28, Death of Louis Philippe Robert, Duke of Orléans, Pretender to throne of France, at Palermo, Sicily, Prince Jean, Duke of Guise, becoming the new Pretender

March 29, Franc at 144 to the English pound

March 31, Rental law extended leases to April 1, 1931 and rents to April 1, 1929

April 1, Strike of 6,000 Paris steel workers for raise in wages and eight-hour day

April 2, The Chamber voted an increase of 30% on imports except certain agricultural machinery, wood pulp, wheat, sugar, coffee, and cocoa, Senate April 4

April 4, Taxes increased and income tax of "householders" extended to persons living in hotels, furnished rooms, &c., and declaration of total income required

April 5, Announcement that negotiations for peace had begun with Abd-el-Krim in Morocco

April 6, Congress of Russian Emigrés in Paris chose as leader Grand Duke Nicholas, uncle of the late Czar

April 7, Declaration signed regarding Commercial Declaration of Feb. 14, 1885 with Italy

April 8, Supplementary Provisional Commercial Agreement signed

April 14, Strike of employees of the Government and railroad workers in Paris

April 16, Spain denounced Franco-Spanish Commercial Treaty of July, 1922, as from July 15 because of increase in French customs duties

April 19, Letter of General Adolph Messimy stated that he was the author of letters to Mata Hari, spy, not L. Malvy

April 20, Franc at 147.60 to the English pound

April 29, Debt-funding Agreement with the United States signed in Washington, by which France agreed to pay $6,847,674,104.17 over a period of 62 years, the annual payments varying from $30,000,-000 during the first two years to $125,000,000 in the 17th year, and remaining then at that figure until final payment, no interest to be paid for the first 5 years, then for 10 years the interest to be at rate of 1%, then for the next 10 years at 2%, the next 8 years at 2½%, the following 7 years at 3, and the remaining 22 years at 3½% (Mellon-Bérenger Agreement). Insertion of a clause making French debt payments to the United States contingent upon the receipt by France of German reparations payments finally given up by French Government

April 29, Budget Bill passed after long crisis, 37,338,389,-202 francs for expenditure revenue 37,498,739,468

May 2, Ultimatum to Riff set May 6 for acceptance of terms or resumption of hostilities

May 6, Negotiations broken off and hostilities resumed in Morocco

May 13, Speed record for seaplanes made by Lieutenant Demougeot at 126.309 per hour

May 17, Strike of Paris automobile and airplane workers for increase in pay

May 19, The franc at 36.17 to the dollar

May 21, The franc reached 30.84 to the dollar, part of the Morgan million dollar loan used for its support

May 24, A group of Alsatians met at Strasbourg and formed Home League (Heimatbund) publishing manifesto asking for complete autonomy within the French State on June 8

May 29, Commercial Agreement with Italy signed

May 30, Treaty of friendship with Turkey signed, and provision for boundary commission to be appointed according to the Franklin-Bouillon Agreement of Oct. 20, 1921

June 4, The Senate ratified the Locarno Treaties

June 10, Treaty of friendship and guarantee with Rumania signed

June 11, Lockout of longshoremen at Dunkirk, troops sent

June 14, Franc fell to 36.50 to dollar

June 14–July 10, Franco-Spanish Conference in Paris on Morocco

June 15, Fall of Briand Ministry on financial questions after resignation of Raoul Péret, Finance Minister; franc at 180 to the pound

June 18, Trade Treaty with Czechoslovakia signed

June 23, Briand formed his 10th Cabinet including Joseph Caillaux as Minister of Finance

June 26, Captain Ludovic Arrachard and Adjutant Arrachard made world record on non-stop flight from Paris to Basra, Mesopotamia, 2,675 miles in 26½ hours

June 27, Meeting of Fascist Congress at Rheims with over 700 delegates

July 2, Death of Philippe Emile Coué in Paris, practitioner of auto-suggestion

July 5, Arbitration Agreement with Denmark signed replaced that of Aug. 9, 1911

July 10, Socialist measure for capital levy defeated in Chamber by vote of 324 to 203

July 12, Debt-funding Agreement with Great Britain signed funded debt at 600 million pounds, repayment fixed by annual instalments varying as follows: for 1926–27, 4 millions; 1927–28, 6; 1928–29, 8; 1929–30, 10; 1930–31 to 1956–57, 12½, and from 1957–58 to 1987–88, 14 millions

July 13, Franco-Spanish Agreement as to Morocco signed in Paris, Abd-el-Krim banished to Réunion Island, Indian Ocean

July 14–15, Captain Girier and Lieutenant Dordilly in non-stop flight from Paris to Omsk, Siberia, 2,930 miles established world record, 29 hours flying time

July 15, Fall of franc to 42.49 on the dollar

July 17, Fall of Briand Ministry

July 18, The franc 47.17 to the dollar

July 20–21, Herriot formed interim Ministry

July 21–24, Financial panic

July 23, R. Poincaré formed Cabinet with Briand as Minister of Foreign Affairs and including former premiers Barthou, Herriot, Painlevé, and Leygues

July 26, Proposals of Soviet Russia as to pre-War debts not accepted

July 29, Commercial Agreement with Haiti signed

July 31, New tax Bill passed in Chamber increasing duty on imports, railroad, and motor transportation, taxes on foreign investments and on direct inheritance passed Senate Aug. 3

Aug. 4, The franc at 36.07 to the dollar

Aug. 5, Provisional Commercial Agreement with Germany signed

——, Bill allowing the Bank of France to purchase gold and foreign currency in the open market passed in Chamber and in Senate, Aug. 7

——, Sinking fund measure passed Chamber; passed Senate Aug. 7

Aug. 10, Change made in constitutional laws for first time since 1884 by vote of the Chamber and Senate acting as National Assembly at Versailles adopting the sinking fund measure under constitutional guarantee, fund created from the tobacco monopoly and succession duties for redemption of 49 billion francs of the floating debt

Aug. 11, Act for protection of labor promulgated regulating employment of foreign labor

Aug. 13, and Dec. 11, Decrees authorized departments and communes to levy general taxes

Aug. 14, New Commercial Agreement with Spain signed

Aug. 25, Cabinet meeting to discuss regularization of price of bread, and food prices

Aug. 31, Pay of government employees increased 12%

Sept. 3, The Minister of Justice abolished 228 out of 359 local courts, 218 prisons and 83 prefect councils, 228 clerks of court, 396 posts of magistrates

Sept. 8, Commercial Treaty with Greece signed

Sept. 10, Decree abolished 106 out of 274 subprefectures with their staffs, 360 odd councils replacing them with 23 from groups of departments, and 70 out of 87 general secretary offices suppressed in interests of economy

Sept. 25, New manifesto issued by the autonomist Home League, Alsace-Lorraine

Oct. 12, The Premier presented budget for 1927 asking for 39,960,000,000 the largest appropriation ever asked of a French legislature

Oct. 15, Decree codified income tax laws

Oct. 20, Commercial *modus vivendi* with Guatemala established

Oct. 24, Demonstration of railroad workers for enforcement of eight-hour day and better working conditions

Oct. 28–Nov. 11, Paris-Calcutta flight of M. Coste and Captain Rignot, non-stop to Jask, 3,343 miles in 32 hours world record

Oct. 30, Agreement with Germany as to sequestrated property rights and interests

Nov. 1, At Ventimeglia Italian Fascists assaulted hostel of French railroad employees because of alleged discourtesy to Fascists

Nov. 2, French police arrested 93 "tourists" at Perpignan near Spanish border leaders of Catalan conspiracy, frustrating separatist plot

Nov. 3, Colonel Francesco-Macia, leader of Catalans arrested

Nov. 4, The franc reached 29.63 to the dollar

——, Arrest at Nice of Colonel Ricciotti Garibaldi, grandson of the Liberator, on charge of being an *agent provocateur* of Italian police and connected with the Catalan conspiracy, Fascist plot to make France appear to harbor conspirators against both France and Italy; Garibaldi proved to be acting as agent of the Government and instigating anti-Fascist activities of émigrés and then betraying them to Rome

Dec. 4, Two Agreements with the Vatican signed as to religious observances in countries under French protection

Dec. 5, Death of Claude Monet, artist (86)

Dec. 7, Agreement for settlement of Greek war debt

Dec. 12, Death of Jean Richepin, author (77)

Dec. 18, Commercial Agreement with Hungary revised

Dec. 19, By provision of budget law foreigners residing in France more than 60 days required to have identity cards

Dec. 22, Agreement with Germany as to delimitation of Franco-Saar frontier

Dec. 23, Commercial Agreement with Turkey signed

1927

Jan. 16, Election for Senate of about one-third of members, slight majority of Left remained unchanged

Jan. 20, Naturalization of all foreigners temporarily suspended at request of labor leaders in interests of unemployed

Jan. 20–22, Trial of Macia, Garibaldi, and others accused of plotting on French territory against a foreign government and of illegal possession of arms, Macia and Garibaldi sentenced to 2 months in prison and fines of 100 francs and 16 other persons to short prison terms and fines

Jan. 21, Russian protest against French-Rumanian Treaty as unfriendly act of France in recognizing Rumanian possession of Bessarabia

Jan. 22, Demonstration of telephone and telegraph operators for reforms

Jan. 26, Commercial Agreement with Italy as to duties on silk

Feb. 3, Convention of Government with Bank of France

Feb. 9, Franco-Spanish Conference begun in Paris on status of Tangier

Feb. 15, France rejected proposal of President Coolidge for conference on limitation of naval armaments

March 1, Demonstration of workers in building trades against violations of eight-hour-day law

March 7, Bill providing for nationalization of all needed industry in times of war adopted by Chamber

March 10, Extradition law enacted, the first

March 12, Further Claims Convention with Mexico signed

March 16, Agreement with Peru as to military service

March 25, New proposal of Russian Soviet Government for settlement of pre-War debts, not accepted

March 31, Commercial Agreement with Germany signed

April 1, Settlement between coal miners and operators reached, wage cut reduced from 3.60 francs to 2.60, and price of coal to be reduced

——, Law giving Government sole right to import oil including gasoline became effective

April 5, Act passed under which building of 1 cruiser, 6 destroyers, 5 submarines, 1 mine-laying submarine,

and 2 dispatch vessels authorized to be built between July 1, 1927 and June 30, 1928

April 6, Briand in statement to the press suggested renunciation of war between the United States and France to take the place of the Treaty of Arbitration of 1908 about to expire

April 7, Naturalization Bill reducing requirement of 10 to 3 years passed third reading, French women marrying foreigners to retain nationality

April 9, Agreement of Bank of France and Bank of England for return of £18 million deposited in London as security for American loans accomplished April 22 raised gold reserve in Bank of France to approximately $1,000,000,000 making France second only to the United States in amount of gold reserve

April 22, Lockout in motor works at Citroen of 10,000 workers

May 8, Captain Charles Nungesser and Captain François Coli left Paris on flight to New York and were lost on the Atlantic Ocean

May 21, Charles A. Lindbergh, American aviator, the first to make flight from New York to Paris, arrived at Le Bourget field at 10 P.M. in his plane, the "Spirit of St. Louis"

June 11–12, Conflict of followers of Léon Daudet and police in Paris, Daudet condemned to prison in successful prosecution of chauffeur he had accused of the murder of his son

June 13, Daudet surrendered to the police but escaped from prison June 25 by ruse of Royalists and fled to Belgium

June 20, Draft and Pact of perpetual friendship between France and the United States, proposal to outlaw war, transmitted to the United States by Briand

July 4, Marcel Cachin, Communist leader, freed "temporarily" by Chamber, charged with inciting soldiers and sailors to revolt

July 11, Electoral Reform Bill passed Chamber and Senate July 13 returning to the *scrutin d'arrondissement*

July 25, Arrest of 8 Communists suspected of activities against the Government

Aug. 7, Management of tobacco monopoly turned over to autonomous Caisse d'Amortissement

Aug. 10, New Nationality Bill became law, promulgated on the 14th, superseding law of 1889, foreigners of 3 years residence able to be naturalized instead of 10 years residence as required previously

Aug. 17, Commercial Agreement with Germany signed

Aug. 23, Riots in Paris after execution in the United States of Sacco and Vanzetti

Sept. 8, New tariff of Sept. 6, published increased duties on American goods from 200 to 800%, increasing rates on over 400 items

Sept. 21, Proposal of Russian Government of annuity of 60 million gold francs for 61 years and reduction of loan demanded

Sept. 25, Under leadership of Dr. Roos, former German officer, the Heimatbund formally organized as Autonomist Party of Alsace-Lorraine

Sept. 30, The Government requested recall of Soviet Minister Rakovsky because of his propagandist activities

Oct. 1, Platform of the Autonomist Party of Alsace-Lorraine published in *Le Temps*, disclaimed all separatist intentions

Oct. 10, Flight of Captain Dieudonne Coste and Lieutenant Joseph Le Brix from Paris to Senegal, Africa, begun round the world trip, first hop 2,700 miles, 25 hours, 20 minutes

Oct. 14–15, Flight of Coste and Le Brix from Senegal, Africa, to Rio de Janeiro, Brazil, in 21 hours and 15 minutes

Oct. 20, Arbitration Treaty with Luxembourg signed

——, Coste and Le Brix reached Buenos Aires, Argentina, from Rio de Janeiro (Oct. 19–20)

Nov. 11, Treaty of friendship and arbitration with Yugoslavia signed

Nov. 13, Three newspapers in Alsace-Lorraine agitating for autonomy suppressed by the Government, *Die Wahrheit*, *Die Volksstimme*, and *Die Zukunft*

Nov. 15, Provisional Customs Tariff Agreement with the United States

Nov. 21, Discriminating tariff against certain American imports removed

Dec. 3, *Modus vivendi* with Italy regulated reciprocal position of nationals and corporate bodies in territory of other country

Dec. 7, Agreement with Greece for submission to arbitration Greek payment for munitions, war debt

Dec. 12, Decree signed by the President restored duties on American goods as before the Act of Sept. 6

Dec. 24, Homes of Alsatian Heimatbund leaders raided by police

Dec. 28, Reply of Secretary of State Kellogg to Note and proposal of Briand of June 20 suggested a general treaty for renunciation of war

1928

Jan. 1, Arrest of 20 persons in Alsace-Lorraine for activities in Heimatsbund

Jan. 5 and Jan. 21, Notes to the United States accepted proposal for general treaty for outlawry of war "in principle" but suggested limitation to wars of aggression and that treaty between the United States and France be negotiated immediately, and later to be expanded into a general treaty. *See also* p. 570

Jan. 21, Commercial Agreement with Switzerland signed

Jan. 29, Decree required identity cards for foreigners

Feb. 6, Arbitration Treaty with the United States signed replaced that of 1908

Feb. 17, Bill prescribing war time organization of civil population passed the Senate

Feb. 23, Commercial Agreement with Belgium signed and Agreement as to Saar customs with Germany

Feb. 26, Clash of Communists and Fascists in Paris

Feb. 28, New Tariff Bill passed Chamber

March 3, Arbitration Treaty with Sweden signed

——, Treaty with Spain signed sanctioned increased control by Spain over Tangier

March 7, Commercial Agreement with Italy signed

March 10, Treaty of arbitration and conciliation with the Netherlands signed

March 20, Civil procedure Convention with Great Britain signed

March 28, Rumanian debt Agreement signed funded at 525 million gold francs repayable in 62 annuities

——, Act reduced compulsory military service from 18 months to 1 year to begin Nov. 1, 1930

March 29, Dispute with Switzerland as to Savoy free zones submitted to the Permanent Court

March 30, Note to the United States regarding multilateral treaty for the outlawry of war

April 5, Act created a national social insurance system which came into effect Feb. 5, 1930

April 7, Agreement with the United States to submit correspondence as to treaty for renunciation of war to Great Britain, Germany, Italy, and Japan

April 14, Costes and Lebrix reached Paris from Athens ending flight around the world by way of Africa, South America, the United States, and Japan

April 18, Agreement with Yugoslavia for a loan signed

April 21, French Draft Treaty for outlawry of war published

April 22 and 29, General election for Chamber a victory for Premier Poincaré: Communists, 16; Democrats, 22; Independent Radicals, 64; Left Republican Democrats, 34; Socialists, 104; Radicals and Radical Socialists, 110; Republican Socialists and French Socialists, 46; Republicans of the Left, 94; Democratic Republican Union, 110; Conservatives, 12

April 30, Announcement of loan to be offered May 7, 5% long term notes

May 1, Trial of 15 of 22 Alsatians charged with autonomist conspiracy begun at Colmar

May 7, German opera presented in the original for the first time in Paris since 1914

May 9, Extradition and other legal Conventions with Lithuania signed

May 16, Commercial Agreement with Austria signed

——, Labor Agreement with Great Britain signed

May 24, Trial of Alsatian autonomists ended, 4 out of 15 found guilty, G. E. Ricklin, P. J. Schall, J. V. Rossé, and Abbé Joseph Fasshauer, sentenced to imprisonment for 1 year

May 27, Consular Convention with Poland signed

June 3, Provisional Commercial Agreement with Persia signed

June 24, New Monetary Act for legal stabilization of the franc adopted, the franc the monetary unit to consist of 65.5 milligrams of gold nine-tenths fine, return to gold standard fixed by decree of June 25

June 25, Official decree as to stabilization of franc

June 30, Age of children in industry raised

July 2, Commercial Agreement with Czechoslovakia signed

July 4, Labor Agreement with Belgium signed

July 6, Arbitration Treaty with Portugal signed

July 8, Supplementary Commercial Protocol with Poland signed

July 13, General Housing law enacted

July 14, American proposals as to Treaty for renunciation of war formally accepted as not in opposition to provisions of the Covenant of the League of Nations

July 19, Labor Contracts law amended

July 20, Provisional Commercial Treaty with Lithuania signed

July 25, Tangier Statute signed. *See* Morocco

Aug. 5, Communist demonstration outside Paris, more than 1,000 persons arrested

Aug. 13 and Sept. 7, Agreement with Germany signed as to readmission of residents of each country into the other

Aug. 27, Treaty for the Renunciation of War (Briand-Kellogg) the Paris Peace Pact signed in Paris by representatives of 15 nations. *See also* p. 570

——, Death of Marshal Marie Emile Fayolle

Aug. 31, The Minister of Marine denied the statement made in British Parliament on July 30 of Franco-British Naval Accord

Sept. 2, Death of Maurice Bokanowski, Minister of Commerce and Aviation, and 4 others in crash of airplane near Toul. Succeeded in Cabinet by Henri Cheron as Minister of Commerce, and by Laurent Eynac, appointed first Minister of Aviation

Sept. 14 and Oct. 13, Decrees created new Air Ministry with authority over military, naval, colonial, and commercial aviation, the authority over staff of air-squadrons carried on board men-of-war retained by Minister of the Navy

Oct. 1, Sales of sugar exempted from turnover tax and a replacement production tax came into effect

Oct. 5, Publication in press of the Anglo-French Naval Compromise

Oct. 7, Agreement with China signed which settled Nanking incident of March 24, 1927. *See* China

Oct. 23, Death of François Victor Alphonse Aulard (79), historian

Oct. 28, Royalist riot in protest at unveiling of statue by Herriot to Emile Combes, former Prime Minister, and author of legislation for separation of Church and State

Oct. 29, Death of Theodore Reinach, author

Nov. 6, Fall of Poincaré Ministry because of manifesto of Socialist-Radical Congress at Angers which obliged resignation of 4 Socialist-Radical Ministers from the Cabinet, Herriot, Sarraut, Queille, and Perrier

Nov. 11, Poincaré reconstructed Ministry without the Ministers resigned: Louis Barthou, Justice and Deputy Prime Minister; Briand, Foreign Affairs; Tardieu, Interior; Painlevé, War

Dec. 14, Minimum Wage Act extended provisions of 1915 Act to all workers, and included additional trades

Dec. 31, Arrest of 20 persons in Alsace-Lorraine charged with Heimatsbund activities

1929

Jan. 13 and 20, Autonomist candidates elected by large majorities in Haut-Rhin department, Alsace, to the 2 seats in Chamber of Deputies vacant because of refusal of the Chamber to seat Alsatian deputies Ricklin and Rossé convicted in Colmar trial in May, 1928, of autonomist conspiracy

Jan. 15, Supplementary Extradition Treaty with the United States signed

Jan. 25–28, Debate in Chamber on seating candidates from Alsace-Lorraine

March 1, The Chamber of Deputies ratified the Paris Peace Pact (Kellogg-Briand) and the Senate on the 29th

March 11, Most-favored nation Commercial Agreement with Greece signed

March 20, Death of Marshal Ferdinand Foch (77)

March 23, Death of General Maurice Sarrail (72)

March 24, All delegates, 120 persons, to Communist Congress in Paris arrested by police

March 31, Merger of the newspapers *Le Gaulois* with *Le Figaro*

April 16, Act increased old age and invalidity pensions for miners

May 1, More than 3,000 persons arrested in May Day riots

May 5, Municipal elections a victory for the Radical-Socialists

May 10, Treaty of friendship and arbitration with Persia signed

May 27, Death of Ernest Monis, former Premier

June 13–14, Trans-Atlantic flight of Armond Lotti, Jean Assolant, and René Lefevre from Old Orchard, Maine, in the monoplane "Yellow Bird" to near Comillas, Spain, 3,128 miles in 29 hours and 52 minutes, non-stop flight, storms and the presence of an American stowaway prevented their completing distance to Paris

June 22, Five documents signed with Turkey and a sixth June 29 as to Syrian frontiers, &c.

June 29, Housing Act continued rent restriction legislation as to leases of Act of March, 1918

July 8, Commercial Agreement with Switzerland signed

July 10, Treaty of friendship and arbitration with Spain signed

July 21, The Chamber ratified the War Debt Agreements, the Mellon-Bérenger as to the debt with the United States and the Churchill-Caillaux as to debt with Great Britain. Separate Resolution adopted declared that charges imposed should be covered by German reparations payments

July 26, Ratification of the War Debt Agreements by the Senate

——, Resignation of Poincaré because of ill health and the completion of his financial tasks

July 27, Cabinet formed by Aristide Briand, Foreign Minister, continued the same Ministers

Aug. 19, Order of Permanent Court of International Justice fixed May 1, 1930 as date of expiration of period within which France and Switzerland might settle between themselves the dispute as to the free zones, decision in favor of Switzerland that free zones were not suppressed and that Treaty of Versailles did not affect former treaties

Aug. 29, Most-favored-nation Commercial Treaty with Turkey signed

Aug. 30 and 31, Agreement as to evacuation of Rhineland and Final Protocol signed at Hague Conference. *See* p. 571

Sept. 1, Renewed Treaty of alliance with Poland signed

Sept. 5, Briand made plea before League of Nations Assembly for a "Federated Europe"

Sept. 23, Death of Louis Ernest Cardinal Dubois, Archbishop of Paris

Sept. 27–29, Non-stop flight to China of M. Coste and Bellonte established world record

Oct. 1, Death of Emile Antoine Bourdelle, sculptor

Oct. 22, Resignation of Briand's eleventh Cabinet following defeat by 11 votes in the Senate

Oct. 25, Edouard Daladier, Radical-Socialist, invited to form a Cabinet not successful

Oct. 30, Senator Etienne Clémentel invited to form a Cabinet not successful

Nov. 1, A. Tardieu formed Cabinet as Prime Minister and Minister of the Interior; Briand, Foreign Affairs; Henri Cheron, Finance

Nov. 4, Death of Maurice Herbette, diplomat

Nov. 18, *Le Surcouf*, launched at Cherbourg, believed to be the world's most costly and powerful submarine

Nov. 21, Franco-German negotiations as to the Saar began in Paris

Nov. 24, Death of Georges Clemenceau (88), Premier during the War, and president of the Paris Peace Conference

Dec. 15–17, Flight of Lieutenant Challe from Spain to Brazil, third flight from Europe to South America

Dec. 17, Treaty of friendship and neutrality with Turkey signed

Dec. 20, Death of Emile Loubet (91), former President

Dec. 27, The Young plan and Tardieu's Rhineland policy approved by Chamber

Dec. 30, Decree of amnesty signed by the President by which Léon Daudet pardoned and Camille Renault

Dec. 31, Agreement with Germany as to liquidation of private claims signed

1930

Jan. 2, Announcement of Minister of Commerce that first 11 months of 1929 showed deficit in trade balance of 7,529,000,000 francs

Jan. 9, France rejected proposal of Italy for naval parity between the 2 countries

Jan. 13 and 20, By-elections in Alsace-Lorraine won by autonomists

Jan. 15–July 7, Franco-German negotiations which broke down over question of French interest in mines formerly owned by States of Prussia and Bavaria in Saar Valley

Jan. 17, Debt-funding Agreement with Rumania signed in addition to that of March, 1928

Jan. 18, Agreement with Germany signed as to reparation levy on imports from Germany

Jan. 20, Debt-funding Agreement with Yugoslavia signed and with Greece as to pre-Armistice debt

Jan. 21, Debt-funding Agreement with Czechoslovakia signed

Jan. 24, Debt-funding Agreement with Poland signed

Jan. 26, General Alexander Kutiepov, leader of White Russians, kidnapped in streets of Paris; Soviet Russia denied complicity

Jan. 28, Labor Treaty with Rumania signed

Feb. 3, Franco-Turkish Treaty of friendship, conciliation, and arbitration signed

Feb. 5, The national system of social insurance (law of April 5, 1928) came into effect and registration begun of 9,000,000 workers subject to the law, all employed workers between the ages of 13 and 60 except those in specified occupations, who receive less than a given amount per year, and state employees in railways, tramways, coal mines, and public utilities already provided with protection of a similar character to that furnished by the law, and workers in Alsace-Lorraine which continued under its own system. *See also* July 1

Feb. 9, Meeting of Protestant Federation, Metropolitan Russian Church, and Grand Rabbi of French Jews passed resolution denouncing anti-religious policy of Russia

Feb. 17, Resignation of Premier Tardieu defeated on financial questions in Chamber demands of the Opposition for tax reduction

Feb. 21, Debt-funding Agreement with the United States of April, 1926, came officially into effect

——, Camille Chautemps, Radical Socialist, formed Cabinet

Feb. 24, Chautemps Ministry defeated on its first vote and France again without a Government

March 2, Tardieu formed new Cabinet: André Tardieu (Deputy), Prime Minister and Minister of the Interior; Raoul Péret, Deputy Prime Minister and Minister of Justice; Paul Reynaud, Finance; Germain-Martin, Budget; André Maginot (Deputy), War; J. L. Dumesnil, Marine; Aristide Briand (Deputy), Foreign Affairs; François Pietri (Deputy), Colonies; Pierre Marraud (Senator), Public Instruction and Fine Arts; Georges Pernot (Deputy), Public Works; P. E. Flandin (Deputy), Commerce; Fernand

David, Agriculture; Pierre Laval, Labor; Champetier de Ribes, Pensions; Laurent Eynac (Deputy), Air; Mallarmé Posts and Telegraphs; Louis Rollin (Deputy), Mercantile Marine; Desiré Ferry, Public Health

March 13, Bill passed providing for free tuition for day pupils in all State secondary schools

March 22, "Rectification" of the National Workmen's Insurance law of April, 1928, passed the Senate reduced contributions for first few years from 10 to 8%, created a special system for agriculture with contributions only approximately one-fourth of those in industry and commerce, and government subsidies, and the entire system of insurance brought under administrative control of the Ministry of Labor

March 30, Ratification of Young Plan by Chamber by vote of 527 to 38

April 5, Ratification of the Young Plan by the Senate by vote of 284 to 8

April 8, New automobile tariff adopted in Chamber raising duties on foreign cars by 10 to 60% and in Senate April 15

April 11, France with Italy agreed to halt battleship construction until 1936 thus joining the three other powers at the London Naval Conference in one part of the Treaty

April 13, The Government of Switzerland notified the Permanent Court of failure of Franco-Swiss negotiations as to Savoy free zones

April 16, Budget which should have been passed in December finally voted of 50,465,000,000 francs, the highest ever voted

April 24, Social Insurance Act as amended passed after 10 years discussion

April 28, Treaty of arbitration and conciliation with Finland signed

April 30, Amended Workmen's Insurance Act became law to go into effect July 1

May 3, President Doumergue and party of members of Parliament left France for visit to Algeria

May 12–13, Non-stop flight of Jean Mermoz from St. Louis, Senegal, to Natal, Brazil

May 16, Commercial Treaty with China as to Indo-China

May 17, Aristide Briand, Minister of Foreign Affairs, issued "Memorandum on the Organization of a Régime of European Federal Union" addressed to 26 European Governments exclusive of Russia and Turkey, plan for economic federation within the framework of the League of Nations

May 28, Death of Cardinal Lucon in Reims (87)

June 1, Speech of Premier Tardieu at Dijon said that "France to-day is in a position which frees her both from the need to fear or to boast" taken as an answer to Mussolini

June 17, 13 Annamese nationalist chiefs out of 39 sentenced to death for participation in uprising in February

June 30, Complete evacuation of Rhineland

July 1, Insurance Act of April 5, 1928 as amended April, 1930, came into effect, made contributions to insurance compulsory for all wage earners with annual income less than 15,000 francs for those who have no dependent children, but for those employed in certain industrial areas the limit is 18,000 francs raised by 2,000 francs for each of the first 2 dependent children, and becomes 17,000 and 19,000 francs, and for those employed in large industrial and metropolitan areas 20,000 and 22,000 with limit for those with 3 or more dependent children fixed at 25,000 francs a year

July 3, Decree set up a standing committee of 22 members within Superior Insurance Council divided into 4 sections to deal with the following subjects: technical and financial; administration and unemployment benefit; judicial; and medico-pharmaceutical

July 5, Strike of textile workers and iron workers in north against deductions from pay under new social insurance law

Aug. 19, Exchange of Notes with Great Britain as to boundaries between mandated territories in Africa

Sept. 1, William Randolph Hearst, American, expelled from France, because of publication in the Hearst newspapers of the secret documents regarding the Franco-British naval negotiations in 1928

Sept. 1-2, Flight of Captain Dieudonne Coste and Maurice Bellonte from Le Bourget airfield, Paris, to Curtis field, Long Island, New York, time 37 hours and 18 minutes, first non-stop flight from Paris to New York

Sept. 8, Meeting of European States, members of the League of Nations, at Geneva, to consider result of inquiry as to Briand plan for European Federation. *See also* League of Nations

Sept. 11, End of textile strike against social insurance contributions under new law on condition that bonus granted by employers approximately equal to assessments be paid on attendance (prime de présence) during preceding year rather than fidelity (prime de fidélité) which they believed would be used to penalize those who might go out on strike in any given year

Oct. 3, Decree placed Russian exports under license system to permit the Government to control quantities sold and the price

Oct. 9, France launched sixth new 10,000-ton cruiser at Brest

——, Freyssinet's Brest Bridge of 3,612-foot concrete arch spans opened, longest in the world

Oct. 15-21, Visit of President Doumergue to Morocco

Nov. 1, Army reorganization law of 1928 came into effect by which compulsory military service reduced from 18 months to 1 year beginning at age of 21, total duration of service in active army and reserve 28 years

Nov. 7, Death of Cardinal Alexis Armand Charost

Nov. 8-11, Flight of Captain Goulette and Lieutenant Lalouette from Paris to Calcutta

Nov. 24, Negotiations opened by China as to extra-territoriality

Dec. 4, Resignation of Tardieu Ministry defeated in Senate

Dec. 6, Decision of Permanent Court upheld Swiss claims as to Savoy free zones

Dec. 10, Senator Pierre Laval unsuccessful in attempt to form a Cabinet

Dec. 13, Théodore Steeg, Radical, formed Cabinet after failure of Barthou and Laval; G. Leygues, Interior; Cheron, Justice; Briand, Foreign Affairs; G. Martin, Finance; Louis Barthou, War

SOVEREIGNS OF FRANCE

MEROVINGIAN RACE

Pharamond (his existence doubtful)

428. Clodion the Hairy; his supposed son; King of the Salic Franks

447. Merovæus, or Mérovée; son-in-law of Clodion
458. Childeric; son of Mérovée
481. Clovis the Great, his son, real founder of the monarchy. His four sons divided the empire
511. Childebert; Paris
——. Clodomir; Orleans
——. Thierry; Metz; and
——. Clotaire; Soissons
534. Theodebert; Metz
548. Theodebald; succeeded in Metz
558. Clotaire I; sole ruler. Upon his death the kingdom divided between four sons: viz.
561. Charibert, ruled at Paris
——. Gontram, in Orleans and Burgundy
——. Sigebert, at Metz, and ⎫ Both assassinated by
——. Chilperic, at Soissons ⎭ Fredegond
575. Childebert II
584. Clotaire II; Soissons
596. Thierry II, son of Childebert; in Orleans
——. Theodebert II; Metz
613. Clotaire II; became sole King
628. Dagobert I the Great, son of Clotaire II; divided the kingdom between his two sons
638. Clovis II, Burgundy and Neustria
——. Sigebert II, Austrasia
656. Clotaire III, son of Clovis II
670. Childeric II; sole King; assassinated, with his Queen and his son Dagobert, in the forest of Livri
——. Thierry III; Burgundy and Neustria
674. Dagobert II, son of Sigebert, in Austrasia; assassinated 679
691. Clovis III (Pepin, mayor of the palace, rules in his name; succeeded by his brother)
695. Childebert III, the Just; Pepin supreme
711. Dagobert III, son of Childebert
715. Chilperic II, deposed by Charles Martel, mayor of the palace
717. Clotaire IV, of obscure origin, raised by Charles Martel to the throne; dies soon after; Chilperic is recalled from Aquitaine
720. Chilperic II restored; shortly afterwards dies at Noyon; succeeded by
——. Thierry IV, son of Dagobert III, surnamed *de Chelles;* died in 737. Charles Martel now reigns under the new title of " Duke of the French." *Hénault*
737. Interregnum, till the death of Charles Martel, in 741
742. Childeric III, son of Chilperic II, surnamed the Stupid. Carloman and Pepin, the sons of Charles Martel, share the Government

THE CARLOVINGIANS

752. Pepin the Short, son of Charles Martel; he is succeeded by his two sons
768. Charles the Great (Charlemagne) and Carloman; Charles crowned Emperor of the West, by Leo III, 800. Carloman reigned but three years
814. Louis I *le Débonnaire,* Emperor; dethroned, but restored to his dominions
840. Charles, surnamed the Bald, King; Emperor in 875; poisoned by Zedechias, a Jewish physician
877. Louis II, the Stammerer, son of Charles the Bald, King
879. Louis III and Carloman II; the former died in 882, and Carloman reigned alone
884. Charles III *le Gros;* a usurper, in prejudice to Charles the Simple
887. Eudes, or Hugh, Count of Paris

898. Charles III (or IV), the Simple; deposed, and died in prison in 929; he married Edgiva, daughter of Edward the Elder, of England, by whom he had a son, King Louis IV

922. Robert, brother of Eudes; crowned at Rheims; Charles killed him in battle. *Hénault*

923. Rudolf or Raoul, Duke of Burgundy; elected King, but never acknowledged by the southern provinces. *Hénault*

936. Louis IV *d'Outremer*, or Transmarine (from having been conveyed by his mother into England), son of Charles III (or IV); died by a fall from his horse

954. Lothaire, his son; reigned jointly with his father from 952, and succeeds him at 15 years of age, under the protection of Hugh the Great; poisoned

986. Louis V, the Indolent, son of Lothaire; also poisoned, it is supposed by his Queen, Blanche; last of the race of Charlemagne

THE CAPETS

987. Hugh Capet, the Great, Count of Paris, &c., eldest son of Hugh the Abbot, July 3; he seizes the crown, in prejudice to Charles of Lorraine, uncle of Louis Transmarine. From him this race of kings is called Capevingians and Capetians. He died Oct. 24

996. Robert II, surnamed the Sage; son; died lamented, July 20

1031. Henry I, son; died Aug. 29

1060. Philip I the Fair, *l'Amoureux;* son; succeeded at 8 years of age; ruled at 14; died Aug. 3

1108. Louis VI, surnamed the Lusty, or *le Gros;* son; died Aug. 1

1137. Louis VII; son; surnamed the Young, to distinguish him from his father, with whom he reigned for some years; died Sept. 18

1180. Philip II (Augustus); son; succeeds at 15; crowned at Rheims in his father's lifetime; died July 14

1223. Louis VIII, *Cœur de Lion;* son; died Nov. 8

1226. Louis IX; son; called St. Louis; ascended the throne at 15, under the guardianship of his mother, who was also regent; died in his camp before Tunis, Aug. 25

1270. Philip III, the Hardy; son; died at Perpignan, Oct. 6

1285. Philip IV, the Fair; son; King in his 17th year; died Nov. 29

1314. Louis X; son; surnamed *Hutin,* an old word for headstrong, or mutinous; died, June 5

1316. John I, posthumous son of Louis X; born Nov. 15; died Nov. 19

——. Philip V, the Long (on account of his stature); brother of Louis; died Jan. 3

1322. Charles IV, the Handsome; brother; died Jan. 31, 1328

HOUSE OF VALOIS

1328. Philip VI, de Valois, the Fortunate; grandson of Philip III; died Aug. 23

1350. John II, the Good; son; died suddenly in the Savoy in London, April 8

1364. Charles V, the Wise; son; died Sept. 16

1380. Charles VI, the Beloved; son; died Oct. 21

1422. Charles VII, the Victorious; son; died July 22

1461. Louis XI; son; able but cruel; died Aug. 30

1483. Charles VIII, the Affable; son; died April 7

1498. Louis XII, *Duke of Orleans;* the Father of his People; great-grandson of Charles V; died Jan. 1

1515. Francis I *of Angoulême;* called the Father of Letters; great-great-grandson of Charles V; died March 31

1547. Henry II; son; received a wound at a tournament at the nuptials (by proxy) of his daughter Isabella with King Philip II of Spain, accidentally inflicted by Montgomèry, a Scotch nobleman in his service, June 29; died July 10, 1559

1559. Francis II; son; married Mary Stuart, Queen of Scots; died Dec. 5

1560. Charles IX; brother; Catherine de Medicis, his mother, regent; died May 30

1574. Henry III; brother; elected King of Poland; last of the house of Valois; stabbed by Jacques Clement, a Dominican friar, Aug. 1; died Aug. 2, 1589

HOUSE OF BOURBON

1589. Henry IV, the Great, of Bourbon, King of Navarre; son-in-law of Henry II; murdered by Francis Ravaillac, May 14

1610. Louis XIII, the Just; son; died May 14

1643. Louis XIV, the Great, *Dieudonné;* son; died Sept. 1

1715. Louis XV, the Well-beloved; great-grandson; died May 10

1774. Louis XVI, his grandson; ascended the throne in his 20th year; married the Archduchess Marie Antoinette, of Austria, May, 1770; dethroned, July 14, 1789; guillotined, Jan. 21, 1793, and his Queen, Oct. 16 following

[Louis was executed Monday, January 21, 1793, at eight o'clock A.M. On the scaffold he said, "Frenchmen, I die innocent of the offences imputed to me. I pardon all my enemies, and I implore of Heaven that my beloved France——" At this instant Santerre ordered the drums to beat, and the executioners to perform their office. When the guillotine descended, the priest exclaimed: "Son of St. Louis! ascend to heaven." The bleeding head was then held up, and a few of the populace shouted, *"Vive la République!"* The body was interred in a grave that was immediately afterwards filled up with quicklime, and a strong guard was placed around until it should be consumed]

1793. Louis XVII, son of Louis XVI. He never reigned; and died in prison, supposed by poison, June 8, 1795, aged 10 years 2 months. It is believed by some that he escaped to England, and lived there some time as Augustus Meves. In 1874 a person calling himself Auguste de Bourbon claimed to be his son. In France also Albert de Bourbon, son of one Naundorff, claimed to be son of Louis XVII. At a trial in Paris, when Jules Favre was his counsel, the verdict was strongly against his claim, Feb. 27, 1874

THE FIRST REPUBLIC

1792. The National Convention (750 members), first sitting, Sept. 21

1795. The Directory (Lareveillère Lépaux, Letourneur, Rewbell, Barras, and Carnot) nominated Nov. 1; abolished, and Bonaparte, Ducos, and Siéyès appointed an executive commission, Nov., 1799

1799. The Consulate. Napoleon Bonaparte, Cambacérès, and Lebrun appointed consuls, Dec. 24. Napoleon appointed consul for 10 years, May 6, 1802; for life, Aug. 2, 1802

[Established by the Senate May 18, 1804]

1804. Napoleon (Bonaparte) I; born Aug. 15, 1769
He married
1st, Josephine, widow of Alexis, vicomte de Beau-
harnais, March 8, 1796 (who was divorced Dec. 16,
1809, and died May 29, 1814)
2nd, Maria-Louisa of Austria, April 2, 1810 (she died
Dec. 17, 1847). Son, Napoleon Joseph, Duke of
Reichstadt, born March 20, 1811; died, July 22, 1832
He renounced the thrones of France and Italy, and
accepted the isle of Elba for his retreat, April 5, 1814
Again appeared in France, March 1, 1815
Was defeated at Waterloo, June 18, 1815
Abdicated in favor of his infant son, June 22, 1815
Banished to St. Helena, where he dies, May 5, 1821.
(*See* France, 1840)

BOURBONS RESTORED

1814. Louis XVIII (*comte de Provence*), brother of
Louis XVI; born Nov. 17, 1755; married Marie-
Josephine-Louise of Savoy; entered Paris, and took
possession of the throne, May 3, 1814; obliged to flee,
March 20, 1815; returned July 8, same year; died
without issue, Sept. 16, 1824
1824. Charles X (*comte d'Artois*), his brother; born
Oct. 9, 1757; married Marie-Thérèse of Savoy; deposed July 30, 1830. He resided in Britain till 1832,
and died at Gratz, in Hungary, Nov. 6, 1836
[His grandson, Henry, duc de Bordeaux, called comte
de Chambord, son of the duc de Berry; born Sept.
29, 1820; married Princess Theresa of Modena,
Nov., 1846; no issue; styled himself Henri V. *See*
France, 1870, *et seq.*]

HOUSE OF ORLEANS. (*See* Orleans)

1830. Louis-Philippe, son of Louis-Philippe, Duke of
Orleans, called *Egalité*, descended from Philippe,
Duke of Orleans, son of Louis XIII; born Oct. 6,
1773; married Nov. 25, 1809, Maria-Amelia, daughter
of Ferdinand I (IV), King of the Two Sicilies (she
died March 24, 1866). Raised to the throne as King
of the French, Aug. 9, 1830; abdicated Feb. 24, 1848.
Died in exile, in England, Aug. 26, 1850
[Heir: Louis-Philippe, Count of Paris; born Aug. 24,
1838]

SECOND REPUBLIC, 1848

The revolution commenced in a popular insurrection
at Paris, Feb. 22, 1848. The royal family escaped by
flight to England, a provisional government was
established, monarchy abolished, and France declared a republic
Charles-Louis-Napoleon Bonaparte, elected Dec. 11,
declared by the National Assembly (Dec. 19) President of the Republic of France; and proclaimed next
day, Dec. 20; elected for ten years, Dec. 22, 1851

FRENCH EMPIRE REVIVED

[1821. Napoleon II (decreed to be so termed by Napoleon III on his accession). Napoleon, Joseph, son
of Napoleon I and Maria-Louisa, Archduchess of
Austria; born March 20, 1811; created King of Rome.
On the abdication of his father he was made Duke
of Reichstadt, in Austria; and died at the palace of
Schoenbrunn, July 22, 1832, aged 21]
1852. Napoleon III formerly President of the French
Republic, elected Emperor, Nov. 21, 22, 1852; pro-

claimed, Dec. 2, 1852; surrendered himself a prisoner
to the King of Prussia at Sedan, Sept. 2, 1870; deposed
at Paris, Sept. 4; arrives at Wilhelmshöhe, near
Cassel, Sept. 5; deposition confirmed by the National
Assembly, March 1; he protested against it, March 6,
1871; died at Chislehurst, England, Jan. 9, 1873;
buried there Jan. 15
Empress: Eugénie-Marie (a Spaniard, Countess of
Teba), born May 5, 1826; married Jan. 29, 1853
Heir: Napoleon-Eugène-Louis-Jean-Joseph, son; styled
Napoleon IV, born March 16, 1856; killed in Zulu-
land, June 1, 1879
[On Dec. 18, 1852, the succession, in default of issue
from the Emperor, was determined in favor of Prince
Jerome-Napoleon and his heirs male]

FRANCO-PRUSSIAN WAR

Franco-Prussian War, The, was caused by the
growing hostility between France and Prussia due
to the increased territory and power of Prussia
after 1866, and the failure of France to receive
territorial compensation demanded, first of the
Bavarian Palatinate and Hessian districts west
of the Rhine, and then of Belgium and Luxemburg, and finally of only Luxemburg, and also the
opposition of France to German political unity.
In his recollections of that period Bismarck writes:
"I did not doubt that a Franco-German war must
take place before the construction of a United
Germany could be realized."

The immediate cause of the war was the "Hohenzollern Incident" (*see infra,* July 4). King
William did not desire war with France and
though he refused as asked by Napoleon to forbid
Prince Leopold to accept the Spanish Crown he
privately informed him of his desire that he should
voluntarily withdraw his candidature, which
Leopold did. Napoleon through his ambassador,
Count Benedetti, asked (July 13) for the further
assurance from the King "that he would never
again permit the candidacy of the Prince for the
Spanish Crown," which William refused, saying
it was "neither right nor possible to undertake
engagements of this kind *à tout jamais.*" After
receiving confirmation of the news which Benedetti
had imparted of the formal renunciation of Leopold the King sent word to Count Benedetti
through an aide-de-camp that he had nothing
further to say. The telegraphed account of the
negotiations sent to Bismarck from Ems, with
permission to communicate the demand and refusal to the press and the embassies, was condensed by Bismarck without falsification of the
facts so that it appeared as if the negotiations had
been decisively terminated instead of referred to
Bismarck in Berlin, and gave the French people
the impression that their ambassador had been
dismissed without an audience which was regarded
as a national insult. The Germans resented the
French demand as "outrageous arrogance"

1866

In a draft treaty, secretly proposed to the Prussian Government by the French Emperor in 1866: " 1. The Emperor recognizes the acquisitions which Prussia has made in the last war; 2. The King of Prussia promises to facilitate the acquisition of Luxemburg by France; 3. The Emperor will not oppose a federal union of the northern and southern states of Germany, excluding Austria; 4. The King of Prussia, in case the Emperor should enter or conquer Belgium, will support him in arms against any opposing power; 5. They enter into an alliance offensive and defensive"

[This draft treaty Count Bismarck asserted emanated entirely from the French Emperor. The scheme had never been seriously entertained by himself]

1867

May 7–11, In March, 1867, a dispute arose through the French Emperor's proposal for purchasing Luxemburg from the King of Holland, which was strongly opposed by Prussia, as that province had formed part of the dissolved Germanic Confederation; and the affair was only settled by a conference of the representatives of the Great Powers in London, at which the perfect neutrality of Luxemburg was determined, together with the withdrawal of the Prussian garrison and the destruction of the fortifications

1870

July 4, Prince Leopold of Hohenzollern-Sigmaringen (connected with the Prussian dynasty, and brother of Charles, Prince of Rumania), consented to become a candidate for the throne of Spain

July 12, This was denounced by the French Government. Threatening speeches were made in the French Chamber by the duc de Grammont, the Foreign Minister, and eventually, after some negotiation and the intervention of Great Britain, Prince Leopold, with the consent of his sovereign, declined the proffered crown

July 13, The submission did not satisfy the French Government and nation, and the demand was made for a guarantee against the repetition of such an acceptance which was refused

July 15, War was announced by the French Emperor, with the hearty consent of the great majority of the Chambers. The Left or Republican Party opposed the war; M. Thiers and a few others only protested against it as premature

[After his surrender on Sept. 2, the Emperor told Count Bismarck that he did not desire war, but was driven into it by public opinion. He appears to have been greatly deceived as to the numerical strength of his army, and its state of preparation]

French Army, about 300,000:—1st corps, under Marshal MacMahon; 2nd corps, under General Frossard; 3rd corps, under Marshal Bazaine; 4th corps, under General Ladmirault; 5th corps, under General De Failly; 6th corps, under Marshal Canrobert; Imperial guard, under General Bourbaki; Commander-in-Chief, the Emperor; General Le Bœuf, second; succeeded by Marshal Bazaine

Prussian Army, about 640,000:—1. Northern, under General Vögel von Falckenstein, about 220,000, defending the Elbe, Hanover, &c.; 2. Right, under Prince Frederick Charles, about 180,000; 3. Center,

under Generals Von Bittenfeld and Von Steinmetz, about 80,000; 4. The left, under the Crown Prince of Prussia, about 166,000; Commander-in-Chief, King William; second, General Helmuth Karl Bernhard von Moltke (born Oct. 26, 1800; died April 24, 1891)

The North German army, at the beginning of August, consisted, firstly, of 550,000 line, with 1,200 guns and 53,000 cavalry; secondly, of 187,000 reserve, with 234 guns and 18,000 cavalry; and, thirdly, of 205,000 landwehr or militia, with 10,000 cavalry, making a grand total of 944,000 men, with 1,680 mobilized guns and 193,000 horses

To these must be added, firstly, the Bavarians, 69,000 line, with 192 guns and 14,800 horses—25,000 reserve with 2,400 horses, and 22,000 landwehr; secondly, the Würtembergers—22,000 line with 54 guns and 6,200 horses, 6,500 reserve, and 6,000 landwehr; and, thirdly, the Badenese—16,000 line with 54 guns, 4,000 reserve, and 9,600 landwehr

All the German troops taken together as under arms in Aug., 1870, 1,124,000 men

Four weeks previously, on the peace footing, they numbered only 360,000

The French generals appear to have acted greatly upon impulse. The Germans seem to have been invariably guided by a well-matured plan, their tactics mainly consisting in bringing vast masses to bear on the point where they were anxious to prevail. From Saarbrück to Sedan, Moltke appears to have left nothing to chance; and all his arrangements were ably carried out

The causes of the early ruin of the French army were: " 1, the enormous superiority of the Germans in regard to numbers; 2, the absolute unity of their command and concert of operation; 3, their superior mechanism in equipment and supplies; 4, the superior intelligence, steadiness and discipline of the soldiers; 5, superior education of the officers, and the dash and intelligence of the cavalry."—*Quarterly Review*

Estimated cost of the war to France, 395,400,000*l.*, Jan., 1875

July 15, War resolved on by the French Government; declaration delivered at Berlin, July 19

July 19, The north German Parliament meet at Berlin, and engage to support Prussia in the war

July 20, Würtemberg, Bavaria, Baden, and Hesse Darmstadt declare war against France, and send contingents to the army

July 23, War proclamation of the Emperor Napoleon, declaring that the national honor, violently excited . . . alone takes in hand the destinies of the country

——, Part of the bridge at Kehl blown up by the Prussians

July 25, Proclamation of the King that "love of the common fatherland, and the unanimous uprising of the German races, have conciliated all opinions, and dissipated all disagreements. . . . The war will procure for Germany a durable peace, and from this bloody seed will arise a harvest blessed by God— the liberty and unity of Germany"

July 27, Day of general prayer observed in Prussia

July 28, 29, The Emperor Napoleon joins the army; at Metz assumes the chief command, and issues a proclamation declaring that the war will be long and severe

July 30, Repulse of a French attack at Saarbrück
July 31, 20 Badenese enter France at Lauterburg; Mr. Winsloe killed; some captured; others escape with valuable information
——, Proclamation of the King of Prussia to his people, granting an amnesty for political offenses, and "resolving, like our forefathers, placing full trust in God, to accept the battle for the defence of the fatherland"
Aug. 1, He leaves Berlin for the army, and announces that "all Germany stands united in arms," Aug. 3
Aug. 2, The French Government announce that "they make war, not against Germany, but against Prussia, or rather against the policy of Count Bismarck"
——, The French under Fossard bombard and take Saarbrück in the presence of the Emperor and his son; the Prussians, dislodged, retire with little loss
Aug. 4, The Crown Prince crosses the Lauter, the boundary of France, and defeats the French under Frossard, storming the lines of Wissemburg and Geisberg; General Douay killed
Aug. 6, Battle of Woerth: in a desperate, long-continued battle the Crown Prince defeats Marshal MacMahon and the army of the Rhine; they retire to Saverne to cover Nancy
——, Battle of Forbach: Saarbrück recaptured, and Forbach (in France) taken by Generals Von Goeben and Von Steinmetz, after a fierce contest; all the French retreat
Aug. 7, The Germans occupy Forbach, Haguenau, and Saarguemines
Aug. 8, Marshal Bazaine appointed to the chief command of the French army at Metz (about 130,000); MacMahon has about 50,000 near Saverne; Canrobert about 50,000 near Nancy
Aug. 9, St. Avold occupied by the Germans
——, Marshal Bazaine takes command of the army at Metz
——, Phalsburg invested
Aug. 10, Strasburg invested by the Germans
——, The King of Prussia, at Saarbrück, proclaims that "he makes war against soldiers, not against French citizens"
——, Lichtenburg capitulates to the Germans
Aug. 11, MacMahon's army retreating upon the Moselle
——, The little fortress, "La Petite Pierre," evacuated
——, Communication with Strasburg cut off
Aug. 12, Nancy occupied by the Germans without resistance
——, The Bavarians pass the Vosges
Aug. 13, Marshal Bazaine made commander of the Army of the Rhine
Aug. 14, Bombardment of Strasburg begun
——, The French Government declare that "there can be, for a moment, no question of negotiation of peace"
——, Blockade of the German ports on the Baltic, from Aug. 15, announced by the French admiral
About Aug. 14, Many French volunteer sharp-shooters (francs-tireurs) take the field (not recognized as soldiers by the Germans)
Aug. 14, Toul refuses to surrender
——, The Emperor retires to Verdun
Aug. 14 to 18, Marshal Bazaine's army defeated in several long-continued sanguinary battles before Metz
    1. Battle of Courcelles (Pange or Longeville) gained by Von Steinmetz and the 1st army, Aug. 14

    2. Battle of Vionville or Mars-la-Tour, gained by Prince Frederick Charles and the 2nd army, Aug. 16
    3. Battles of Gravelotte and Rezonville, gained by the combined armies commanded by the King, Aug. 18
Aug. 16, French sortie from Strasburg repulsed; German attack on Phalsburg repulsed
——, MacMahon reaches Châlons; joined by the Emperor; his army between 130,000 and 150,000, Aug. 20
Aug. 17, The King appoints governors general of Alsace and Lorraine
Aug. 18, Energetic fortification of Paris by General Trochu, the Governor, and the "defence committee"
Up to Aug. 18, Estimated German losses: killed, wounded, and missing, 2,088 officers, 46,480 men
Aug. 19, Severe bombardment of Strasburg
About Aug. 20, MacMahon's Army of the Rhine retreats as the Prussians under the King and Crown Prince advance; Prince Frederick Charles opposed to Bazaine at Metz; [German armies in France about 500,000; the French armies about 300,000; communications between Marshals Bazaine and MacMahon very difficult]
Aug. 20, Lieutenant Harth, a Prussian spy, tried and shot at Maris
——, MacMahon raises his camp at Châlons
Aug. 21, The troops extended along the line of the Marne
——, Exportation of food prohibited
Aug. 22, Bazaine at Metz said to be completely isolated
Aug. 23, MacMahon at Rheims with his army, including the remains of the corps of Failly and Canrobert; he marches in hope of joining Bazaine; the Crown Prince and Prince of Saxony start in pursuit, Aug. 23; march upon Châlons, Aug. 24
Aug. 23–26, Strasburg suffering much by bombardment
Aug. 24, Prussian royal headquarters removed from Pont à Mousson to Bar-le-Duc (125 miles from Paris)
Aug. 25, Germans repulsed in an attack on Verdun
——, 800 French National Guards captured at St. Menehould
——, Châlons occupied by the Germans
——, Capitulation of Vitry, a small fortress
Aug. 26, Formation of three German armies of reserve in Germany, and a fourth army in the field, under the Crown Prince of Saxony, to coöperate with the Crown Prince of Prussia against Paris
——, Powerful sortie of Bazaine from Metz repulsed
——, Phalsburg heroically resisting
Aug. 27, Thionville invested by the Germans
——, Engagement at Busancy, between Vouziers and Stenay: a regiment of French chasseurs nearly annihilated
Aug. 28, Two German armies (220,000) marching on Paris
——, Continued retreat of MacMahon's army; severe fighting at Dun, Stenay, and Mouzon
——, Nicholas Schull, a German spy, shot at Metz
Aug. 29, Vrizy, between Vouziers and Attigny, stormed by the Germans
Aug. 30, MacMahon's army, about 150,000, accompanied by the Emperor, retreating northwards; part of it, under De Failly, surprised and defeated near Beaumont, between Mouzon and Moulins; several other engagements, unfavorable to the French, occurred during the day

Aug. 30, Count Bismarck-Bohlen installed Governor of Alsace at Haguenau

Aug. 31, The Germans enter Carignan; attack the French in the plain of Douzy; the French, at first successful, are defeated, and retreat to Sedan

——, A French army of old soldiers, about 100,000, are said to be forming near Lyons

Aug. 31–Sept. 1, Bazaine defeated in his endeavor to escape from Metz; after a fierce struggle, retreats into Metz

Sept. 1, Battle round Sedan: begun at 4 A.M. between Sedan and Douzy; the French at first successful; after a severe struggle and dreadful carnage, the Germans victorious; MacMahon wounded, 5:30 P.M.; General de Wimpffen refuses to accept the terms offered by the King of Prussia

Sept. 2, Capitulation of Sedan and the remainder of MacMahon's army; the Emperor surrenders to the King

——, Vigorous artillery action at Strasburg; a sortie repulsed

Sept. 4, Revolution at Paris after the declaration of the capture of MacMahon's army; proclamation of a republic (see France)

Sept. 5, Rheims occupied by the Germans and the King

Sept. 6, Jules Favre, the French Foreign Minister, in a circular to the French diplomatic representatives, says, "We will not cede either an inch of our territories or a stone of our fortresses"

Sept. 6–7, General Vinoy and a corps sent too late to aid MacMahon; retreat and arrive in Paris

Sept. 7, St. Dizier occupied by the Germans

Sept. 8, Strasburg invested by 60,000 men

——, Verdun vigorously resisting

Sept. 9, The German army, in five corps, advancing on Paris

——, Laon surrendered to save the town from destruction; by the accidental or treacherous explosion of a magazine some of the German staff and many French perish

Sept. 9–10, Messages between belligerents transmitted by Lord Lyons (at Paris) and Count Bernstorff (Prussian Minister) in London

Sept. 10, Metz, Strasburg, Thionville, Phalsburg, Toul, Bitsche, and other fortified places holding out

——, German attack on Toul repulsed

Sept. 12, Bridge at Creil over the Oise blown up

Sept. 13, Seven German corps (about 300,000 men) approaching Paris, which is said to contain 300,000 combatants

——, M. Thiers arrives in London on a mission from the Government

——, General Trochu reviews the troops in Paris; the daily guard ordered to be 70,000 Sept. 14

Sept. 14, Colmar occupied by the Germans

Sept. 15, Estimated German loss: 60,000 killed and wounded; between 20,000 and 30,000 sick; about 1,000 prisoners

About Sept. 15, French prisoners in Germany: 62 generals, 4,800 officers, 140,000 privates

Sept. 15, Siege of Paris begun; ingress and egress prohibited without a permit

——, Blockade of the Elbe and Weser non-effective

Sept. 18, Prussian headquarters at Meux (20 miles from Paris)

32 German merchant ships reported to have been captured by the French fleet up to Sept. 18

Sept. 18, 19, Vessels sunk in the Seine and Marne, and other vigorous defensive measures adopted

Sept. 19, Paris said to be completely invested; the fortifications reconnoitered by the King, who has fixed his headquarters at Baron Rothschild's château at Ferrières, near Lagny

——, Three French divisions under General Vinoy attack the Germans on the heights of Sceaux; repulsed with loss of 7 guns and 2,500 prisoners: the defeat attributed to the disorder of the Zouaves; the National Guard behave well

——, Versailles and the troops there surrender; entered by the Crown Prince of Prussia, Sept. 20

Sept. 20, Count Bismarck consents to receive Jules Favre (about Sept. 16); they meet at Château de la Haute Maison, Sept. 19; and at the King's headquarters, Ferrières, near Lagny

Sept. 21, Jules Favre reports to the Government the result of his interviews with Count Bismarck: Prussia demands the cession of the departments of the Upper and Lower Rhine and part of that of Moselle, with Metz, Château Salins, and Soissons, and would agree to an armistice in order that a French constituent assembly might meet; the French to surrender Strasburg, Toul, and Verdun (or Phalsburg according to Favre), and Mont Valérien, if the assembly meet at Paris; these terms are positively rejected by the French Government

——, General Von Steinmetz sent to Posen as Governor General; Prince Frederick Charles sole commander before Metz

Sept. 22, Sèvres surrenders

——, The blockade of German ports raised; officially announced in London

Sept. 23, The French Government issue a circular expressing readiness to consent to an equitable peace, but refusing "to cede an inch of our territory or a stone of our fortresses"

——, Three conflicts before Paris: at Drancy, Pierrefitte, and Villejuif; the two last reported favorable to the French

——, Toul surrenders after a most vigorous resistance

——, Levée en masse of men under 25 ordered by the French Government

——, Germans repulsed in conflicts before Paris; said by them to be unimportant

Sept. 23, 24, 27, Desperate ineffective sallies from Metz

Sept. 25, Verdun invested by the Germans

Sept. 26, All the departments of the Seine and Marne occupied by Germans

——, The Iron Cross given by the Crown Prince of Prussia to above 30 soldiers beneath the statue of Louis XIV at Versailles

Sept. 27, Circular of Von Thile, Prussian Foreign Minister, stating that as the ruling powers in France decline an armistice, and as no recognized Government exists in Paris (the Government de facto being removed to Tours) all communications with and from Paris can only be carried on so far as the military events may permit

——, Clermont occupied by the Germans after a brief vigorous resistance, overcome by artillery

——, Capitulation of Strasburg; formally surrendered Sept. 28

Sept. 28, Commencement of attack on Soissons

Sept. 30, Sortie of General Vinoy's army (at Paris); repulsed, after two hours' fighting, Crown Prince present; above 200 prisoners taken; General Giulham killed

Sept. 30, Above 375,000 National Guards said to be in Paris

——, Conflict near Rouen; at first favorable to the French; their loss 1,200 killed and wounded; 300 prisoners

——, Beauvais captured by the Germans

Oct. 1, Nantes occupied by the Germans

——, Surgeon-Major Wyatt writes that Paris is well provisioned, and nearly inexpugnable

M. Thiers' fruitless visit to Vienna, Sept. 23; to St. Petersburg, Sept. 27; dined with the Czar, Oct. 2

Oct. 2, The Grand Duke of Mecklenburg at Rheims appointed governor of the country conquered in addition to Alsace and Lorraine

Oct. 3, M. Favre, in the name of the diplomatic body, requests Count Bismarck to give notice before bombarding Paris, and to allow a weekly courier; the Count declines both requests, but permits the passage of open letters; reported

——, Count Bismarck in a circular corrects Favre's report of the negotiations, and accuses the French Government of keeping up the difficulties opposed to a conclusion of peace; reported

Oct. 4, Epernon and La Ferté occupied by the Germans after an engagement

Oct. 5, The King's headquarters removed to Versailles; arrival of the King, Bismarck, Moltke, and others

——, General Treskow, in command of a German army, to advance into Southern France

——, Battle at Thoury; General Reyan, with the advanced Guard of the Army of the Loire under General La Motte Rouge, defeats the Germans between Chaussy and Thoury, and captures some prisoners and cattle

Oct. 6, M. Thiers' mission to foreign courts reported to be quite abortive

——, Part of the army of Lyons, under General Dupré, defeated by the Badenese under General Von Gegenfeld, near St. Rémy; French loss, about 1,500, and 660 prisoners; German loss, about 430

Oct. 7, Great sortie from Metz; the Germans surprised; 40,000 French engaged; repulsed after severe conflicts; French loss, about 2,000; German, about 600

Oct. 8, Estimated number of French prisoners in Germany, 3,577 officers, and 123,700 men

——, Neu Breisach bombarded

——, Breton volunteers organizing by M. Cathelineau; volunteers in the west organizing by General Charette (from Rome)

——, German attack on St. Quintin vigorously repulsed

——, Long dispatch from Count Bernstorff to Carl Granville, complaining of the British supplying arms to France

——, M. Thiers again at Vienna

Oct. 9, Garibaldi arrives at Tours; enthusiastically received; reviews the National Guard at Tours

Oct. 10, Direct mediation declined by Russia, Great Britain, and Spain

——, Prussian circular to the European Powers, regretting the obstinate resistance of the French Government to peace, and foretelling the consequences—social disorganization and much starvation

——, Ablis, near Paris, burnt for alleged treachery (killing sleeping soldiers)

——, M. Gambetta escapes from Paris by a balloon, Oct. 7; in his proclamation at Tours, states that

Paris possesses 560,000 troops; that cannon are cast daily, and that women are making cartridges; he urges unanimous devoted coöperation in carrying on the war

Oct. 7, Part of the Army of the Loire defeated at Arthenay, near Orleans, by Bavarians under Von der Tann; about 2,000 prisoners taken

——, Prussian attack on Cherizy repulsed

——, French reply to Bismarck's circular on the negotiations

Up to Oct. 11, About 20 villages burnt, and 150 peasants shot for illicit warfare

Oct. 11, 3,000 National Guard mobilized at Rouen

——, Three first shots fired against Paris

——, Orleans captured by General Von der Tann after nine hours' fighting; the Army of the Loire defeated retires behind the Loire

——, Stenay captured by a sortie from the French garrison of Montmédy

Oct. 12, General Bourbaki accepts the command at Tours; General La Motte Rouge superseded in the command of the Army of the Loire by General D'Aurelle de Paladines

——, Battalions of Amazons said to be forming in Paris

——, Garibaldi appointed commander of the French irregulars

——, Epinal captured by the Germans

——, M. Arlès Dufour of Lyons appeals to the people of Great Britain for active sympathy in endeavoring to obtain peace

——, Breteuil occupied by the Germans after a sharp resistance

Oct. 13, All the Vosges district in arms; no regular army; the defiles occupied by the franc-tireurs

——, Reported successful sorties; Neu Breisach completely invested

——, Reported French success at Bagneux, near Paris—the Prussians surprised

Oct. 13, 14, St. Cloud fired on by the French and burnt

About Oct. 14, Frequent sorties from Metz

Oct. 14, Sharp fight at Ecouis; the French escape from being surrounded

——, General Boyer, Aide-de-Camp to Marshal Bazaine, arrives at Versailles and meets Count Bismarck

Oct. 16, Soissons surrenders after three weeks' investment and four days' bombardment

Oct. 17, M. Gambetta proceeds to the Army of the Vosges; General Bourbaki appointed commander of the Army of the North; General Mazière appointed to a command in the Army of the Loire

——, Montdidier attacked by the Germans: 150 mobile guards captured

——, The Emperor Napoleon declares that "there can be no prospect of peace, near or remote, on the basis of ceding to Prussia a single foot of French territory; and no government in France can attach its signature to such a treaty and remain in power a single day"

Oct. 18, 4,000 French attacked and defeated near Châteaudun after ten hours' fighting and the barricaded town stormed

——, Circular of Jules Favre, asserting that Prussia "coldly and systematically pursues her task of annihilating us. France has now no illusions left. For her it is now a question of existence. . . . We prefer our present sufferings, our perils, and our sacrifices to the consequences of the inflexible and cruel ambition of our enemy. France needed, perhaps, to pass through a supreme trial—she will issue from it transfigured"

Oct. 20, Dispatch from Earl Granville to Count Bismarck urging the negotiations for peace on terms lenient to the French

Oct. 21, Conclusive reply of Earl Granville to Count Bernstorff's charge of breach of neutrality

——, Vigorous sortie from Mont Valérien against Versailles; an engagement at Malmaison; the French retire after three hours' fighting, losing about 400 killed and wounded and 100 prisoners; German loss about 230 killed and wounded

——, Chartres occupied by the Germans under Wittich

——, Intervention of the British Government (supported by the neutral Powers) to obtain an armistice for the election of a national assembly

——, Vesoul occupied by the Germans

——, St. Quentin taken by the Germans after half-an-hour's cannonading; evacuated by them, Oct. 23

Oct. 22, Schelestadt bombarded vigorously

——, Engagement near Evreux

——, Fighting at Vouray, Cussey, &c., in the Vosges; French "Army of the East" defeated

——German attack on Châtillon le Duc repulsed by General Cambriels

Oct. 23, M. de Kératry assumes command of the army in Brittany

Oct. 24, Reported failure of the suggestions concerning an armistice, through Prussia demanding that France should consent to a cession of territory

About Oct. 24, Thiers undertakes the mission to obtain an armistice

Oct. 24, Capitulation of Schelestadt (2,400 prisoners and 120 guns taken)

Oct. 27, Marshal Bazaine surrenders Metz and his army, "conquered by famine" (See France, Oct.–Dec., 1873)

——, The French defeated near Gray (Haute Saône) by Von Werder

——, About 2,000 sick and wounded of both nations in Versailles

Oct. 28, Le Bourget, near Paris, recaptured by the French

——, A safe-conduct given to M. Thiers to enter Paris for negotiation

——, Dispatch from Count Bismarck to Earl Granville, expressing desire for the meeting of a French national assembly to consider terms of peace; but stating that overtures must come from the French

——, Badenese troops defeated near Besançon; Prussian attack on Formerie on the Oise repulsed

——, General Von Moltke created a count on his 70th birthday

Oct. 29, The Crown Prince and Prince Frederick Charles created field-marshals

——, The francs-tireurs defeated by the Würtembergers between Montereau and Nangis

——, Estimated: 856,000 Germans in France; French prisoners in Germany, 223,000

Oct. 30, Le Bourget retaken by the Germans; heavy losses on both sides; about 1,200 French prisoners

——, Proclamation of Gambetta, accusing Bazaine of treason; the war to go on

——, M. Thiers enters Paris

Oct. 31, Garibaldi defending Dôle (Jura) with about 7,500 men

——, Dijon captured after bombardment

Oct. 31 and Nov. 1, M. Thiers receives powers from the French defense Government to treat for an armistice, and has interviews with Count Bismarck

Oct.–Nov., General Bourbaki attempting to form an Army of the North, near Lille

Nov. 1, Thionville invested

Nov. 2, Letter from Marshal Bazaine repelling the charge of treason

Nov. 2, 3, The francs-tireurs dispersed in several slight engagements between Colmar and Belfort

Nov. 3, Count Bismarck offers an armistice of 25 days for the election of a French national assembly

——, Defeat of an attempted revolution in Paris: see France

Nov. 6, Failure of the negotiation, as Count Bismarck will not permit food to enter Paris during the armistice without any military equivalent; M. Thiers ordered to break off negotiation

——, Châteaudun recaptured by the French

Nov. 7, The Prussian semi-official journal says, "The French Government having refused to listen to reason the cannon will be resorted to for giving them a lesson"

——, Bombardment of Thionville

——, The King's permission for the election of a French national assembly declined by the French Government

——, Orders that no one shall enter or quit Paris

——, A Prussian column repulsed in an attack on the Army of the Loire at Marchenoir

Nov. 8, Capitulation of Verdun

——, Seven persons, captured in balloons from Paris, sent to German fortresses to be tried by court martial

——, German corps, under Manteuffel, advancing on Amiens and Rouen

Nov. 9, The Germans enter Montbeliard (Doubs)

——, The Germans, under General Von der Tann, defeated between Coulmiers and Baccon, near Orleans, retire to Thoury

Dated Nov. 9, M. Thiers' report of the unsuccessful negotiations for an armistice

Nov. 9, Reported naval victory of the Prussian steamer *Meteor* over the French steamer *Bouvet* off Havannah

Nov. 10, Continued fighting; Orleans retaken by General D'Aurelle de Paladines; French losses, 2,000; Germans about 700, and 2,000 prisoners

——, Capitulation of Neu Breisach, 5,000 prisoners and 100 guns taken

——, The French repulsed near Montbeliard on the Swiss frontier

Nov. 12, Von der Tann's army reinforced by 30,000, now 70,000, the Grand Duke of Mecklenburg commander; the Loire army about 150,000, but only 12,000 regulars

About Nov. 12, Bankers at Berlin and Frankfort arrested for dealing in French war loan

Nov. 13, Dôle, near Dijon, occupied by the Germans

Nov. 14, The armies in central France have been placed under Prince Frederick Charles and the Grand Duke of Mecklenburg

Up to Nov. 14, Eleven French towns, 3,653 guns, 155 mitrailleuses, nearly 500,000 chassepots, about 90 eagles and standards, and nearly 4,000,000*l.* in money, taken by the Germans

Nov. 15, Montmédy completely invested

——, French sorties from Mézières repulsed; from Belfort repulsed, Nov. 16

Nov. 17, The Grand Duke of Mecklenburg repulses the Army of the Loire near Dreux, which is captured by Von Treskow

Nov. 17, Successful French sortie from Mézières, 500 Germans said to be killed

Nov. 18, Germans victorious in an engagement near Châteaudun; French claim the success

Nov. 19, The National Guard at Evreux repulse a German attack

——, The German army under Prince Frederick Charles and the Grand Duke of Mecklenburg (135,000) said to be retreating towards Paris

Nov. 20, Paris engirdled with a second line of investment

——, French attempt to release La Fère repulsed with heavy loss

About Nov. 20, Several balloons from Paris captured

Nov. 21, French mobile guard defeated at Bretoncelles

Nov. 22, Bombardment of Thionville begun

——, Ham occupied by the Prussians

Nov. 24, Prince Frederick Charles takes up a position near Orleans

——, Thionville, in flames, capitulates, with about 2,000 prisoners

——, The Germans repulsed near Amiens and near Stagil

Nov. 27, La Fère surrenders, after two days' bombardment, with about 70 guns and 2,000 men

——, The Garibaldians defeated near Pasques (Côte d'Or) by Von Werder

——, The French Army of the North defeated by Manteuffel between Villers Bretonneux and Soleur, near Amiens

Nov. 28, Amiens occupied by Von Goeben after a severe engagement

——, Severe engagement near Beaune la Rolande (Loiret) between part of the Army of the Loire under D'Aurelle de Paladines and the Germans under Voigts Rhetz; Prince Frederick Charles arrives and turns the day; the French retire; heavy loss on both sides

Nov. 29–Dec. 4, Fruitless endeavors of the army in Paris and the Army of the Loire to unite

Nov. 29, Sorties from various parts of Paris repulsed with loss

Nov. 30, Great sortie of 120,000, under Generals Trochu and Ducrot, who cross the Marne; severest conflict between Champigny-sur-Marne, Brie-sur-Marne, and Villiers-sur-Marne; the French retain the taken possessions, but their advance is checked; great loss on both sides (chiefly Saxons and Würtembergers engaged)

Dec. 2, The contest resumed at Avron; the Germans retake Champigny and Brie; the French retreat

——, The Army of the Loire: Chanzy defeated by the Grand Duke of Mecklenburg at Bazoche des Hautes; near Chevilly (the French report these engagements indecisive), Dec. 3

Dec. 3, Ducrot bivouacks in the woods of Vincennes; he issues a final order of the day, referring to two days' glorious battles, Dec. 4

Dec. 4, General D'Aurelle de Paladines entrenched before Orleans; proposes to retreat; the Government opposes him, but yields; he determines to await the attack; part of his army defeated by Prince Frederick Charles, and the Grand Duke of Mecklenburg; he retreats with about 100,000 men; Orleans threatened with bombardment; surrenders at midnight

Dec. 5, The Germans said to be in pursuit of D'Aurelle de Paladines (superseded)

——, 10,000 prisoners, 77 guns, and 4 gunboats captured at Orleans

Dec. 6, Rouen occupied by Manteuffel

——, General order of the King of Prussia, "We enter on a new phase of the war . . . Every attempt to break through the investment or relieve Paris has failed"

Dec. 7, The Grand Duke of Mecklenburg attacks General Chanzy and the Army of the Loire near Beaugency; indecisive; the Germans victorious, taking about 1,100 prisoners and six guns, and occupying Beaugency (severe loss to Germans), Dec. 8

Dec. 8, General Manteuffel's army in two parts, one occupies Evreux, and marching to Cherbourg; the other marching to Havre

Dec. 9, Vigorous siege of Belfort; obstinately defended

Dec. 9, 10, Continued severe engagements between the Germans and the Army of the Loire; the defeated French retreat (7 battles in 9 days)

Early in Dec., Pamphlet (attributed to the Emperor Napoleon) published under the name of his friend, the Marquis de Gricourt, throwing the blame of the war upon the French nation

Dec. 10, Fighting along the whole line of the Army of the Loire, under General Chanzy and others Dec. 5–10; it retreats, but obstinately resists

Dec. 11, Brilliant action by De Chanzy

——, The delegate Government transferred from Tours to Bordeaux; Gambetta remains with the Army of the Loire

Dec. 12, Dieppe occupied by the Germans

——, La Fère threatened by Faidherbe, Commander of the Army of the North

——, Phalsburg surrenders, subdued by famine; commencement of bombardment of Montmédy

Dec. 13, Evreux and Blois occupied by the Germans

Dec. 14, Montmédy surrenders

——, Sharp engagement of Frèteval; which is taken and abandoned by the Germans

Dec. 18, Nuits near Dijon captured by the Badenese under Von Werder, after a severe conflict

Dec. 20, Conflict at Monnaie: about 6,000 French gardes mobiles driven back to Tours

Dec. 21, Vigorous sortie from Paris repulsed—an artillery action

——, Tours partially shelled; submits, but not occupied by Germans

Dec. 21, Six English colliers, said to have had Prussian permits, after delivering coal at Rouen, are sunk in the Seine at Duclair near Havre by the Prussians for strategic reasons

About Dec. 21, Chanzy and part of the Army of the Loire said to have reached Le Mans and joined the Bretons

Dec. 23, Seven hours' battle at Pont à Noyelles between Manteuffel and the Army of the North under Faidherbe; both claim the victory; Faidherbe retreats

Dec. 26, Explanation given by Bismarck and compensation promised

——, Chanzy, in a letter to the German commandant at Vendôme, accuses the Germans of cruelly pillaging St. Calais, and, denying his defeat, says, "We have fought you and held you in check since Dec. 4"

Dec. 27, Trochu said to be making Mont Valérien a vast citadel

——, Alleged defeat of the Germans by detachment of Chanzy's army near Montoire

Dec. 29, Mont Avron, an outlying fort near Paris, after a day's bombardment, abandoned and occupied by the Germans

1871

Jan. 1, 2, Capitulation of Mézières with 2,000 men and 106 guns

Jan. 2, 3, Severe battles near Bapaume between the Army of the North under Faidherbe and the Germans under Manteuffel and Von Goeben; victory claimed by both, the French retreat

Jan. 4, Bombardment of eastern front of Paris, and of the southern forts; forts of Issy and Vanvres silenced, Jan. 6

Jan. 5, 6, Fortress of Rocroy taken by the Germans

Jan. 6, Indecisive conflict near Dijon le Mans: between General Chanzy and Prince Frederick Charles

——, Daujoutin, S. of Belfort, stormed by Germans

Jan. 7, General Roy defeated near Jumiéges

About Jan. 7, Von Goeben in the north, Manteuffel sent to the east

Jan. 9, Capitulation of Péronne with garrison

Jan. 9, 10, Conflicts (in the east) between Von Werder and Bourbaki at Villarais, south of Vesoul

——, Bombardment of Paris, many buildings injured, and people killed: the French Government appeal to foreign powers

Jan. 11, Chanzy retreating; defeated near Le Mans by Prince Frederick Charles and the Grand Duke of Mecklenburg

Jan. 12, Prince Frederick Charles enters Le Mans; after 6 days' fighting (about 20,000 French prisoners made; German loss about 3,400)

Jan. 13, Vigorous sorties from Paris repulsed

Jan. 14, Chanzy retreating; defeated near Vosges, Jan. 15, 16

Jan. 15, 16, Indecisive conflicts between Bourbaki and Von Werder, near Belfort

Jan. 16, St. Quentin recaptured by Isnard under Faidherbe

Jan. 17, The Grand Duke of Mecklenburg enters Alençon

——, Bombardment of Longwy begun

Jan. 18, Bourbaki defeated near Belfort after three days' fighting, Jan. 15-17; retreats south

Jan. 19, Faidherbe defeated near St. Quentin; after seven hours' fighting; by Von Goeben, 4,000 prisoners taken

——, Great sortie from Paris of Trochu and 100,000 men repulsed with loss of about 1,000 dead and 5,000 wounded

——, Bourbaki hard pressed by Von Werder

Jan. 22, Armistice for two days at Paris refused

——, Bombardment of St. Denis and Cambrai

——, Faidherbe asserts that the German successes are exaggerated

Jan. 23, 24, Resignation of Trochu; Vinoy, Governor of Paris

Jan. 24, Favre opens negotiations with Bismarck

Jan. 25, Longwy capitulates; 4,000 prisoners, 200 guns

Jan. 28, Capitulation of Paris; armistice for 21 days signed by Count Bismarck and Jules Favre

Jan. 29, The forts round Paris occupied by the Germans

Jan. 30, Advance of German troops into France suspended

Jan. 30–Feb. 1, Bourbaki and his army, about 80,000, driven by Manteuffel into Switzerland near Pontarlier, about 6,000 having been captured

Up to Jan., French loss about 350,000 men, 800 guns

Feb. 1, Dijon occupied by the Germans

Feb. 16, Belfort capitulates with military honors

Feb. 22–24, Negotiations for peace between Thiers and Bismarck

Feb. 25, Preliminaries of a treaty accepted by Thiers, Favre, and 15 delegates from the National Assembly; it includes cession of parts of Lorraine, including Metz and Thionville and Alsace less Belfort; and payment of 5 milliards of francs, 200,000,000l., signed Feb. 26, accepted by the National Assembly, March 1

German loss in battles throughout the war; killed or died soon after, 17,570; died of wounds eventually 10,707; total killed and wounded 127,867

March 1–3, German troops enter Paris and remain 48 hours

March 12, They quit Versailles

March 28, Conference for peace opens at Brussels

May 10, Treaty of peace signed at Frankfort; ratified by the French National Assembly, May 18

FRENCH REVOLUTION
See also France
(1792)

April 28, Quiévrain (French repulsed)

Sept. 20, Valmy (French defeat Prussians)

Nov. 6, Jemappes (French victorious)

1793

March 18, Neerwinden (French beaten by Austrians)

May 8, St. Amand (French defeated by English)

May 23–July 28, Valenciennes (French defeated by English)

Aug. 18, Lincelles (Lake defeats French)

Sept. 7, 8, Dunkirk (Duke of York defeated)

Sept. 11, Quesnoy (reduced by Austrians)

Sept. 14, Pirmasens (Prussians defeat French)

Oct. 14, 15, 16, Wattignies (French defeat Coburg)

Dec. 19, Toulon (retaken by British)

1794

April 24, Cambray (French defeated)

April 30, Troisville, Landrecy (taken by Allies)

May 18–22, Tourcoing (Moreau defeats Allies)

May 22, Espierres (taken by Allies)

June 1, Howe's naval victory

June 26, Charleroi or Fleurus (French defeat Allies)

July 28, Misdon (Vendeans defeated)

Sept. 14, Bois-le-Duc (Duke of York defeated)

Sept. 17, Boxtel (Duke of York defeated)

Oct. 10, Maciejovice (Poles defeated)

Nov. 3, Nimeguen (French victorious) Oct. 28 (def.)

Nov. 4, Praga (Warsaw taken by Suwarrow)

1795

June 23, Bridport's victory off l'Orient, n.

July 21, Quiberon (emigrants defeated)

Sept. 20, Mannheim (taken by Pichegru)

Nov. 23, 24, Loano (French defeat Austrians)

1796

April 12, Montenotte (Bonaparte victorious)
April 22, Mondovi (Bonaparte victorious)
May 10, Lodi (Bonaparte victorious)
June 4, Altenkirchen (Austrians defeated)
July 5, Radstadt (Moreau defeats Austrians)
Aug. 3–5, Lonato and Castiglione (French defeat Austrians)
Aug. 10, Neresheim (Moreau def. Archduke Charles)
Sept. 4, Roveredo (French defeat Austrians)
Sept. 8, Bassano (French defeat Austrians)
Sept. 16, Altenkirchen (Austrians victors)
Oct. 2, Biberach (French defeat Austrians)
Nov. 14–17, Arcola (Bonaparte victorious)
Nov. 21, Castelnuovo (Bonaparte victorious)

1797

Jan. 14, 15, Rivoli (Bonaparte victorious)
Feb. 14, Cape St. Vincent, *n.* (Spaniards defeated)
March 16, Tagliamento (Bonaparte defeated Austrians)
Oct. 11, Camperdown, *n.* (Duncan defeats Dutch)

GERMAN CONFEDERATION, NORTH

German Confederation, North, established in place of the Germanic Confederation (*see s.v.*): population 1867, estimated 29,906,092. The confederation ceased on the reëstablishment of the German Empire, Jan. 1, 1871.

1866

July 16, The King of Prussia invites the States of North Germany to form a new confederation
Aug. 18, Treaty of alliance, offensive and defensive, between Prussia and the following States:—Saxe-Weimar, Oldenburg, Brunswick, Saxe-Altenburg, Saxe-Coburg-Gotha, Anhalt, two Schwarzburgs, Waldeck, the younger Reuss, two Lippes, Lübeck, Bremen, and Hamburg, signed
Aug. 21, And two Mecklenburgs
Sept. 3, And Hesse (for country north of the Maine)
Sept. 26, And the elder Reuss
Oct. 8, And Saxe-Meiningen
Oct. 21, And Saxony

1867

Feb. 24, Meeting of North German Parliament (295 deputies from the 22 States) at Berlin. *See* Germany

GERMANIC CONFEDERATION

Germanic Confederation, superseding the Confederation of the Rhine (*see s.v.*), was constituted June 8, 1815; held its first diet at Frankfort, Nov. 16, 1816, and its last, Aug. 24, 1866. *See* Germany. It comprised—

1. Austria; 2. Prussia; 3. Bavaria; 4. Saxony; 5. Hanover; 6. Würtemberg; 7. Baden; 8, 9. Hesse (Electorate and Grand Duchy); 10. Denmark (for Holstein and Lauenburg); 11. Netherlands (for Luxemburg); 12. Saxe-Weimar, Saxe-Coburg, Saxe-Meiningen, and Saxe-Altenburg; 13. Brunswick and Nassau; 14. Mecklenburg-Schwerin, and Mecklenburg-Strelitz; 15. Oldenburg, three Anhalts, and two Schwarzburgs; 16. Two Hohenzollerns, Liechtenstein, two Reuss, Schaumburg-Lippe, Lippe, and Waldeck; 17. Free cities:—Lübeck, Frankfort, Bremen, and Hamburg

1848

March 30, The Diet declares for a constituent assembly which met, May 18
July 12, The Diet remits its functions to the Archduke John, Vicar of the Empire (*see* Germany)

1851

May 30, The Diet reëstablished, meets

1863

Aug. 17, The Emperor of Austria proposes a reform of the Confederation; accepted by the Diet, Sept. 1; rejected by Prussia Sept. 22

1865

June 8, The Diet celebrates the fiftieth anniversary of its establishment

1866

June 14, Vote of the majority of the Diet supports Austria in the dispute respecting Schleswig and Holstein; Prussia announces her withdrawal from the Confederation, and its dissolution; the Diet declares itself indissoluble, continues its functions, and protests
July 14, The Diet removes to Augsburg during the war
July 26, The Confederation renounced by Austria at Nikolsburg
Aug. 24, The Diet holds its last sitting

GERMANY

Germany (*Deutches Reich*), country of central Europe, since Nov. 9, 1918 a republic, bounded on the north by the Baltic Sea and Jutland Peninsula of Denmark, north and west by the North Sea, Netherlands, Belgium, Luxemburg, and France, south by Switzerland, Austria, and Czechoslovakia, and east by Poland. East Prussia is separated from the rest of Germany by the Polish "corridor" which gives Poland access to the Baltic Sea at Gulf of Danzig, and is bordered by Poland and Lithuania. The territorial changes after the World War reduced the total area of Germany from 208,780 square miles to 181,723 square miles, and the population from 67,812,000 in 1914 to 63,178,619. Berlin is the capital. The estimated area of the German colonies renounced by Germany under the Treaty of Versailles was 1,027,820 square miles with population of 24,389 white persons, and 12,041,603 natives.

STATES OF THE EMPIRE	AREA ENGLISH SQ. MILES	POPULATION JUNE 16, 1925			POP. PER SQ. MILE 1925
		Male	Female	Total	
Prussia (excluding the Saar and including Waldeck [1])	113,036	18,531,108	19,644,881	38,175,989	338
Bavaria (excluding the Saar)	29,343	3,553,857	3,825,737	7,379,594	251
Württemberg	7,532	1,243,507	1,336,728	2,580,235	342
Baden	5,819	1,115,477	1,196,985	2,312,462	397
Saxony	5,789	2,372,091	2,620,229	4,992,320	863
Mecklenburg-Schw.	5,066	331,290	342,755	674,045	133
Thuringia	4,537	776,822	832,478	1,609,300	355
Hesse	2,970	655,964	691,315	1,347,279	454
Oldenburg.	2,480	270,223	274,949	545,172	220
Brunswick	1,418	241,606	260,269	501,875	354
Mecklenburg-Str.	1,131	54,084	56,185	110,269	98
Anhalt.	890	170,568	180,477	351,045	396
Lippe	469	78,947	84,701	163,648	349
Schaumburg-Lippe	131	23,309	24,737	48,046	367
Hamburg	160	551,473	601,050	1,152,523	7,203
Lübeck	115	61,548	66,423	127,971	1,123
Bremen	99	164,949	173,897	338,846	3,423
German Republic (excluding the Saar) . . .	180,985	30,196,823	32,213,796	62,410,619	345
Prussian Saar District [2]	574	338,000	332,000	670,000	1,167
Saarpfalz [2]	164	49,000	49,000	98,000	598
Saar District (altogether)	738	387,000	381,000	768,000	1,041
German Republic (with Saar District) [2] . . .	181,723	30,583,823	32,594,796	63,178,619	348

[1] Waldeck was absorbed by Prussia on April 1, 1929.
[2] The figures for the population of the Saar District, in which the Census of 1925 could not be taken, are estimated.

According to the Treaty of Versailles (June 28, 1919) Germany agreed to the following territorial arrangements:—(1) Alsace-Lorraine ceded to France, (2) the greater part of the Provinces of West Prussia and Posen ceded to Poland, (3) a part of Upper Silesia and of East Prussia likewise to Poland, (4) a portion of Upper Silesia to Czechoslovakia, (5) Memel to Lithuania, (6) Danzig, a Free State under the protection of the League of Nations, (7) Eupen and Malmédy to Belgium, (8) a part of Schleswig to Denmark.

Provision was made in the Treaty to settle the ultimate fate of the following areas by *plébiscite:*—

(1) The Saar Basin (after 15 years), (2) Schleswig (in two zones), (3) districts in Southern East Prussia, in West Prussia and in Upper Silesia. Results of the *plébiscites:*—Schleswig (March, 1920), northern zone for Denmark, southern zone for Germany; East and West Prussia (July, 1920) for Germany; Upper Silesia (March, 1921) for Germany. Despite the decision in Upper Silesia, 1,241 square miles, with a population of 892,537, were transferred to Poland.

An estimate of the actual areas and populations (according to the Census of 1910) lost to pre-War Germany has been made as follows: Alsace-Lor-

COLONIES, 1913	DATE OF ACQUISITION	CAPITAL	ESTIMATED AREA SQ. MILES	WHITE POPULATION	ESTIMATED NATIVE POPULATION
In Africa:—					
Togo	1884	Lome . .	33,700	368	1,031,978
Kamerun [1]	1884	Buea . . .	191,130	1,871	2,648,720
German Southwest Africa.	1884–90	Windhuk .	322,450	14,830	79,556
German East Africa	1885–90	Daressalam .	384,180	5,336	7,645,770
Total African Possessions	1884–90		931,460	22,405	11,406,024
In Asia:—					
Kiauchau	1897	Tsingtau .	200 [2]	—	168,900
In the Pacific:—					
German New Guinea:—					
Kaiser Wilhelm's Land.	1885–86		70,000		
Bismarck Archipelago	1885		20,000		
Caroline Islands	1899				
Palau or Pelew Islands.	1899	Rabaul .	560	1,427	600,000
Marianne Islands	1899		250		
Solomon Islands	1886		4,200		
Marshall Islands, &c.	1886		150		
Samoan Islands:—					
Savaii	1899	Apia .	660	557	34,579
Upolu	1899		340		
Total Pacific Possessions	1884–99		96,160	1,984	634,579
Total Foreign Dependencies	1884–99		1,027,820	24,389	12,041,603

[1] Not including the 107,270 square miles with a population of 1,000,000 conceded (1911) by France, but including the 6,450 square miles conceded by Germany to France.
[2] Exclusive of the Bay with an area of about 200 square miles.

raine, 5,607 square miles, population 1,874,014; ceded to Belgium, 400 square miles, population 60,003; ceded to Poland, 17,816 square miles, population 3,854,961; Memel, 1,026 square miles, population 141,238; Danzig, 739 square miles, population 330,630; ceded to Denmark, 1,542 square miles, population 166,348; ceded to Czecho-slovakia, 122 square miles, population 48,446; total 27,252 square miles, population, 6,475,640.

The Saar Basin, which has been placed under the government of the League of Nations for 15 years, has an area of 726 square miles and a population (1927) of 770,030.

The area of the territory occupied under the Treaty was originally about 12,528 square miles, containing about 7 million inhabitants, but by January 31, 1926, the Cologne zone, with 2,527 square miles and 2,640,798 inhabitants, had been evacuated.

The preceding table is a list of the various Colonies and regions under the protection or in-fluence of Germany before the War, the estimates (1913) given being necessarily vague. All the Colonies were governed by an Imperial Governor.

Germany (*Germania*, *Alemania*), anciently, as now, divided into independent States. The Ger-mans long withstood the attempts of the Romans to subdue them; and although that people con-quered some parts of the country, they were ex-pelled before the close of the third century. In the fifth century the Huns and other tribes prevailed over the greater portion of Germany. In the latter part of the eighth century, Charlemagne subdued the Saxons and other tribes, and was crowned Emperor at Rome, Dec. 25, 800. A list of his successors is given on another page. At the ex-tinction of his family, the Empire became elective, 911, and was subsequently obtained by members of the house of Hapsburg (from 1437 till 1804). Germany was divided into circles, 1501–12. The Confederation of the Rhine was formed July 12, 1806; the Germanic Confederation, June 8, 1815; and the North German Confederation, Aug. 18, 1866; the treaty ratified, Sept. 8, 1866.

The Empire of Germany was established Jan. 1, 1871, founded upon treaties concluded between the North German Confederation (*which see*) and, 1. the Grand Duchies of Baden and Hesse, Nov. 15, 1870; 2. the Kingdom of Bavaria, Nov. 23, 1870; 3. the Kingdom of Würtemberg, Nov. 25, 1870; ratified, Jan. 29, 1871. William I, King of Prussia, was proclaimed German Emperor at Ver-sailles, Jan. 18, 1871.

The first Chancellor of the Empire, Prince Otho von Bismarck, May, 1871; resigned March 18, 1890.

See also Prussia; Confederation of the Rhine; German Confederation, North; Germanic Con-federation; Franco-Prussian War.

Paul von Hindenburg, President.

b.c. 113, The Teutones, united with the Cymry, defeat the Romans at Noreia
b.c. 102, After varying success are defeated by Marius
b.c. 12–3, Drusus invaded Germany
a.d. 9, Battle of Teutoburg; Hermann or Arminius de-stroys the Romans under Varus
19, Hermann assassinated
238, The Franks invade Gaul
450 *et seq.*, Great irruption of Germanic tribes into Gaul
772–785, Charlemagne after a long contest subdues the Saxons, who become Christians
Dec. 25, 800, He is crowned Emperor of the West at Rome by the Pope
802, He adds a second head to the eagle, to denote that the empires of Rome and Germany are united
839–840, Louis (*le Débonnaire*) separates Germany from France
896, The Germans under Arnold take Rome
Nov. 8, 911, The German princes assert their independ-ence, and Conrad I of Franconia reigns
Electors of Germany. In the reign of Conrad I, King of Germany (912–918), the dukes and counts, from being merely officers, became gradually independent of the sovereign, and subsequently elected him. In 919 they confirmed the nomination of Henry I, Duke of Saxony, by Conrad as his successor. In the thir-teenth century seven princes (the Archbishops of Mentz, Treves, and Cologne, the King of Bohemia, the Electors of Brandenburg and Saxony, and the Elector Palatine), assumed the exclusive privilege of nominating the Emperor. *Robertson.* An eighth elector (Bavaria) was made in 1648; and a ninth (Hanover) in 1692. The number was reduced to eight in 1777 (by the Elector Palatine acquiring Bavaria) and increased to ten at the Peace of Lune-ville, in 1801. On the dissolution of the German Em-pire, the crown of Austria was made hereditary, 1804–1806.
918–934, Reign of Henry I [King], surnamed the Fowler; he vanquishes the Huns, Danes, Vandals, and Bo-hemians
962, Otho I extends his dominions, and is crowned Emperor by the Pope
978, Otho II conquers Lorraine
1041, Henry III conquers Bohemia
1073–1123, Disputes with the Pope relating to ecclesi-astical investitures
1075, Contest between Henry IV and Gregory VII (Hildebrand)
1077, Henry's humiliation at Canossa (submission to penance imposed by the Pope)
1085, He takes Rome 1084; and Gregory dies in exile at Salerno
1122, Concordat between Henry V and the Pope, fun-damental law of church
1140, The Guelph and the Ghibelline feuds begin
1147, Conrad III leads an army to the holy wars; it was destroyed by Greek treachery
1154–77, Frederick Barbarossa, Emperor, 1152; wars in Italy
1162, He destroys Milan
1180, Ruins Henry the Lion
June 10, 1190, Is drowned during the crusade in Syria
1190, Teutonic order of knighthood
About 1245, Hanseatic League established

1273, Reign of Rodolph, Count of Hapsburg, chosen by the electors

1356, The edict, called the Golden Bull, by Charles IV

1363, The Tyrol acquired

1414–16, Sigismund, King of Bohemia, elected Emperor. He betrays John Huss and Jerome of Prague, who are burned alive (*see* Bohemia)

1438, Sigismund driven from the throne, Albert V, Duke of Austria, succeeds

1439, The pragmatic sanction confining the Empire to the house of Austria

1502 to 1844

1502, 1514, 1524, Peasants' wars

1517, Era of the Reformation

April 17, 1521, Luther excommunicated by the Diet at Worms

1522–46, German Bible and liturgy published by Luther

1527, War with the Pope—the Germans storm Rome

March 13, 1529, Diet at Spires; Protestants condemned

Jan. 25, 1530, Confession of Augsburg published

Dec. 31, 1531, Protestant League of Smalcald

June 24, 1535, The anabaptists seize Munster; defeated, and John of Leyden slain, 1536

Feb. 18, 1546, Death of Luther

June 26, War with the Protestants

July 31, 1552, Who are helped by Henry II of France— Peace of religion at Passau

Oct. 25, 1555, Abdication of Charles V announced

1570, Hungary joined to the Empire

1618, The Thirty years' war begins between the evangelic union under the Elector Palatine, and the Catholic League under the Duke of Bavaria

Nov. 8, 1620, Battle of Prague, which ruined the Elector Palatine

June, 1630, Gustavus-Adolphus of Sweden invades Germany

Nov. 16, 1632, Gustavus-Adolphus, victor, killed at Lutzen

Feb. 25, 1634, Treason of Wallenstein; he is assassinated

Oct. 24, 1648, End of the Thirty years' war: treaty of Westphalia, establishing religious toleration

1674, War with France

Sept. 12, 1683, John Sobieski, King of Poland, after defeating the Turks, obliges them to raise the siege of Vienna

Sept. 20, 1697, Peace of Ryswick (with France)

Jan. 26, 1699, The peace of Carlowitz (with the Turks)

Oct. 6, 1702, War with France, &c.; Marlborough's victory at Blenheim, Aug. 13, 1704

April 11, 1713, Peace of Utrecht

1723, The Pragmatic Sanction for settling the Empire of Germany in the house of Austria, 1439. The Emperor Charles VI published the Pragmatic Sanction, whereby, in default of male issue, his daughters should succeed in preference to the daughters of his brother Joseph I, April 19, 1713; and he settled his dominions on his daughter Maria Theresa, in conformity thereto, 1723. She succeeded in Oct., 1740; but it gave rise to a war, in which most of the powers of Europe were engaged, and which lasted till 1748

Oct. 20, 1740, Francis I, Duke of Lorraine, marries the heiress of Austria, Maria Theresa (1736); she succeeds her father, and becomes Queen of Hungary

Jan. 22, 1742, The Elector of Bavaria elected Emperor as Charles VII

Sept. 15, 1745, He dies Jan. 20; Francis I, Duke of Lorraine, elected Emperor

Feb. 15, 1763, The Seven Years' War (*see s v.*) between Austria and Prussia and their respective allies begins Aug., 1756; ends with the peace of Hubertsburg

1765, Lorraine ceded to France

1772, Joseph II extends his dominions by the dismemberment of Poland; many civil reforms and liberal changes, 1782

1788, War with Turkey

Sept. 22, 1789, Victory of the Austrians and Russians at Rimnik

July 25, 1790, J. B. Basedow, educational reformer, dies

1793, The Rhenish provinces revolt

1793–1803, In the ruinous wars between Germany and France, the Emperor loses the Netherlands, all his territories west of the Rhine, and his States in Italy

1795, Francis I joins in the second partition of Poland

Feb. 9, 1801, Cessions of territory to France by the Treaty of Luneville

Aug. 11, 1804, Francis II assumes the title of Francis I, Emperor of Austria

1805, Napoleon establishes the Kingdoms of Bavaria and Würtemberg; and of Westphalia, 1807; dissolution of the German Empire; formation of the Confederation of the Rhine, July 12, 1806

Dec. 13, 1810–11, North Germany annexed to France

March, 1813, Commencement of the war of independence: the order of the *iron cross* instituted

Oct. 16–18, Final defeat of the French at Leipsic

Nov. 1, 1814 & May 25, 1815, Congress of Vienna

June 8, 1815, The Germanic Confederation (*see s.v.*) formed

1818, The Zollverein (*Customs' Union*), formed; the name given to the German commercial union, projected by Prussia 1818, and gradually joined by nearly all the German states except Austria. On Feb. 19, 1853, an important treaty of commerce and navigation, between Austria and Prussia, to last from Jan., 1854, to Dec., 1865, was signed, to which the other States of the Zollverein gave in their adhesion on April 5, 1853. In Nov., 1861, Prussia threatened to withdraw unless certain changes were made. By the treaty of July 8, 1867, between the North German Confederation and the southern states (Bavaria, Würtemberg, Baden, and Hesse), various changes were made, and by other treaties signed in Oct. these States agreed to send delegates to a customs Parliament to be held at Berlin. A session of this Parliament was opened by the King of Prussia, April 27, and closed May 23, 1868

1819, "Society for promoting the knowledge of ancient German history," founded by Stein

Sept., 1822, A German scientific association formed, "Naturforscher Vereine"

March 29, 1826, Death of J. H. Voss, poet

Sept. 7, 1830, Revolution at Brunswick (flight of the Duke)

Sept. 13, In Saxony (abdication of the King)

March 22, 1832, Death of Goethe, poet, novelist, and philosopher

Sept. 10, Railroad to Magdeburg opened

1844, Excitement about Ronge, the Catholic reformer, and the holy coat of Treves

1848

Insurrection at Vienna and throughout Germany (*see* Austria, Hungary, &c.)

March, Revolt in Schleswig and Holstein (*see* Denmark)

March 27, The King of Prussia takes the lead as an agitator, to promote the reconsolidation of the German Empire, by a proclamation

May 18, German national assembly meet at Frankfort (*see* Germanic Confederation)

July 12, Archduke John of Austria elected Vicar of the Empire

1849

March 28, The national assembly elects the King of Prussia Emperor; he declines, April 3

May 14, He recalls the Prussian members of the Assembly

May 30, The Frankfort Assembly transfers its sittings to Stuttgardt

Sept. 30, Treaty of Vienna between Austria and Prussia for the formation of a new central power for a limited time; appeal to be made to the governments of Germany

Nov. 6, Protest of Austria against the alliance of Prussia with the smaller German states

1850

Feb. 27, Treaty of Munich between Bavaria, Saxony, and Würtemberg, for a revision of the German confederation

March, Parliament meets at Erfurt

March 15, The King of Würtemberg denounces the insidious ambition of the King of Prussia

May 10, German Diet meets at Frankfort

June 20, Hesse-Cassel sends no representative to Erfurt, June 7; Hesse-Darmstadt withdraws from the Prussian League

July 19, Austria calls an assembly of the German Confederation; which meets at Frankfort, Sept. 2

Nov. 12, Austrian, Bavarian, and Prussian forces enter Hesse-Cassel

Dec. 23 to May 15, 1851, Conferences on German affairs at Dresden

1851

Max Schneckenburger, author of the song "Die Wacht am Rhein," died

May 30, Reëstablishment of the Diet of the Germanic Confederation at Frankfort

1857

Jan. 15, Conference at Nuremberg relative to a general code of commerce

1859

May and June, Great excitement in Germany at the French successes in Lombardy: warlike preparations in Bavaria, &c.

July 17, Meetings of new liberal party in Eisenach, Saxe Weimar; seven resolutions put forth recommending that the imperfect federal constitution be changed; that the German Diet be replaced by a strong central government; that a national assembly be summoned; and that Prussia be invited to take the initiative, Aug. 14

Sept., This proposal not accepted by Prussia, and warmly opposed by Hanover

Sept., The Austrian Minister, Rechberg, severely censuring the Duke of Saxe-Gotha, for a liberal speech, Sept. 4; and accusing the Prussian Government of favoring the Liberals, meets with cutting retorts

1860

Jan. 29, Death of Ernst Moritz Arndt, patriot and poet

March 24, The Federal Diet maintains the Hesse-Cassel constitution of 1852 against Prussia

Sept. 5, Meeting at Coburg in favor of German unity against French aggression

Nov., Dispute with Denmark respecting the rights of Holstein and Schleswig

1861

Aug. 23, Meeting of German national association at Heidelberg; decides to form a fleet

Sept. and Oct., Subscriptions received for fleet

1862

March 13, The national association meet at Berlin; they recommend the formation of a united federal Government with a central executive, under the leadership of Prussia

July 8–Aug. 10, Meetings of plenipotentiaries from German States on federal reform

Sept. 28, 29, Deputies from German States meet at Weimar, and declare that Germany wants formation into one federal State

1863

July 31, The Emperor of Austria invites the German sovereigns to a congress at Frankfort; King of Prussia declines, Aug. 4; nearly all the sovereigns meet, Aug. 16, 17; they approve the Austrian plan of federal reform, Sept. 1; which is rejected by Prussia, Sept. 22

Aug. 21, Congress of deputies from German States declare in favor of unity

Oct. 1, The Diet determines to have recourse to federal execution in Holstein if Denmark does not fulfill her obligations

Nov. 15, Death of Frederick VII of Denmark

Dec. 23, German troops enter Holstein for "federal execution" (*see* Denmark for events)

1864

March 10, Death of Maximilian II of Bavaria

1865

April 6, Prussia retains the duchies; discussion between Austria and Prussia; the Diet adopt the resolution of Bavaria and Saxony, requesting Austria and Prussia to give up Holstein to the Duke of Augustenburg; rejected

Aug. 14, The Gastein convention (*see* Prussia)

Oct. 1, Condemned by the Diet at Frankfort

1866

May 19, The Diet calls on Austria and Prussia to disarm

May 20, Meeting of deputies from smaller German States condemn the impending war

June 11, Austria declares that Prussia has broken the treaty by invading Holstein; the Diet adopts this by 9 votes; the Prussian representative declares the Germanic Confederation at an end, and invites the members to form a new one, excluding Austria, June 14

June 15, The Prussians enter Saxony, and the war begins

June 16, The Diet determines for war; proclaims Prince Charles of Bavaria General of the Confederation troops, June 27

[For the war and its consequences, *see* Prussia, and German Confederation, North]

Sept. 8, Treaty of alliance between Prussia and the Northern States; ratified

Oct. and Nov., Continued disputes between the Diet and Austria and Prussia respecting Schleswig-Holstein

1867

Feb. 9, Draft of new constitution for North Germany settled

Feb. 24, North German Parliament opened at Berlin by the King of Prussia; Dr. Simson elected president, March 2

April 17, The federal constitution adopted; the Parliament closed

July 1, The constitution put in action

Aug., Meeting of 50 deputies from Parliaments of Bavaria, Würtemberg, Baden, and Hesse-Darmstadt, declare necessity of union with North Germany

Sept. 9, Luxemburg evacuated by the Prussian garrison

1868

Oct., After negotiations between Bavaria, Würtemberg, and Baden, July, a South German military commission appointed

1869

June 17, Wilhelmshafen, at Hippens, bay of Jahde, Oldenburg, the first German military port, inaugurated by the King of Prussia

1870

May, Count Arnim, German representative at Rome, protests against the doctrine of papal infallibility

July 19, Count Bismarck announces the declaration of war by France, and terms it groundless and presumptuous

July 15, Bavaria, Würtemberg, Hesse-Darmstadt, and Baden, support Prussia in the war declared by France. (*See* Franco-Prussian War)

About Sept. 6, Munich, Stuttgart, and other cities, declare for union with North Germany

Sept.–Nov., Socialists declare against annexation of Alsace, &c.

Nov., Baden and Hesse-Darmstadt join the North German Confederation by treaty, about Nov. 15; also Würtemberg, Nov. 25; and Bavaria, Nov. 22; retaining certain powers in military and diplomatic affairs

Nov. 28, The Parliament vote 100,000,000 thalers to continue the war

About Dec. 4, The King of Bavaria, in a letter to the King of Saxony, proposes the King of Prussia to be nominated Emperor of Germany

Dec. 10, The Parliament in an address request the King to become Emperor (votes for, 188; against, 6)

Dec. 18, The address presented to the King in an assembly of princes by Dr. Simson

1871

Jan. 1, Reëstablishment of the German empire; William I of Prussia proclaimed Emperor at Versailles, Jan. 18

Jan. 3, Several German bankers condemned to imprisonment for subscribing to the French loan

Feb. 26, Preliminaries of peace with France signed at Versailles

March 21, First Reichstag or imperial Parliament opened at Berlin by the Emperor, 397 members

May 4, The new constitution of the Empire comes into force

May 12, Chancery of the Empire: Prince Bismarck, Chancellor

May 16, The treaty of peace ratified

April 18, Dr. Döllinger, of Munich, excommunicated for opposing the dogma of papal infallibility

June 29, Dr. Döllinger elected rector of the university at Munich

Sept. 27, The Bavarian Minister of Public Worship declares against the dogma of papal infallibility in a letter to the Archbishop of Munich

Oct. 16, The German Parliament opened by the Emperor; who expresses his conviction "that the new German Empire will be a reliable shield of peace"

About Nov. 6, Reform in the coinage: introduction of a gold coin approved by the federal council

About Nov. 26, Law forbidding the clergy to meddle with politics in the pulpit

Dec. 7, Sharp dispatch from Count Bismarck to the German Ambassador at Paris respecting the acquittal of murderers of Germans at Melun and Paris

1872

March, Ultramontane agitation against the Government; excitement amongst the Polish Romanists; Count Bismarck carries his school inspection bill against the Roman Catholic clergy

May 14, Bismarck reports to the Parliament the Pope's refusal to receive Cardinal Hohenlohe as Ambassador

June 19, Bill for the expulsion of the Jesuits passed in the German Parliament (131–93); end of session, the law published, July 5

About Sept. 6, Imperial congress: the Czar arrives at Berlin, Sept. 5; the Emperor of Austria, Sept. 6; both leave; Prince Bismarck declares the meeting to be merely an act of friendship; "prince Gortschakoff thankful that nothing was written"

Sept., Great emigration of young men to America to avoid the conscription; forbidden by government

1873

March 15, Treaty with France settling the total evacuation of the departments held by German troops on payment of the indemnity in Sept. signed

June 23, The monetary reform law passed; the Parliament closed, June 25

Sept. 5, Last payment of French war indemnity

1874

Jan. 10, Elections for the Parliament—(397 members; about two-thirds nationalist liberals; about 100 ultramontanists)

March, Constitutional struggle in the Parliament respecting the army bill

About April 10, The Government require 401,659 men (instead of 360,000) permanently:—compromise; the army to be settled for seven years

About June, German liberal association, formed against particularists and ultramontanists

Oct. 4, Count Harry Arnim, formerly Ambassador at Rome and Paris, suddenly arrested and imprisoned in Berlin: ostensibly for refusing to give up official papers; released on bail, Oct. 28

Dec. 16, Bismarck resigns the chancellorship after an adverse vote in the Parliament; on a vote of confidence (199–71) retains it, Dec. 18

1875

Jan., Important registration law for births, deaths, and marriages passed
Jan. 25, Civil marriage bill passed

1876

Jan. 1, The Imperial Bank of Germany opens
March 20, Proposal for purchase of all the railways by the Imperial Government (opposed in the south)

1877

Jan. 10, 11, Elections: liberal majority; socialist democrats elected for Berlin
March 21, Supreme court for Germany settled to be at Leipsic by Parliament
New code of laws enacted
April 8, Resignation of Bismarck as Chancellor, April 3; withdrawn
July 7, Exportation of horses forbidden

1878

May 24, 25, In consequence of the attempted assassination of the Emperor by Hödel, May 11, a stringent bill to repress socialism is brought into the Parliament, and rejected (251–57)
June 2, The Emperor fired at and wounded by Dr. Karl Edouard Nobiling, a professor of philology and socialist, at Berlin
June 4, 5, The Crown Prince authorized to direct public affairs
June 12, Death of King George of Hanover
June 13–July 13, The Berlin Conference (*see s.v.*)
July 10, Emil Heinrich Max Hödel condemned
July 30, Elections held (severe struggle)
Aug. 16, Hödel executed at Berlin
Sept. 9, New Parliament opened: national liberals, 123; 119 imperialists and conservatives; 105 center (Roman Catholics, &c.)
Sept. 10, Dr. Nobiling dies of self-inflicted wounds
Oct. 19, The repressive socialist bill passed (72 majority)
Nov., Decree for expulsion of socialists and others, issued
Dec. 5, The Emperor resumes government
Up to Dec., 174 clubs, 44 newspapers, and 157 other papers suppressed by injunctions

1879

About Jan. 9, Parliamentary discipline bill (to "muzzle" speakers); a "gagging bill" introduced
Jan., Bismarck's negotiations with the Roman curia respecting the Falk laws (*Culturkampf*) fruitless
March 7, "Gagging" bill rejected by the Parliament
About May 9, Prince Bismarck's protectionist tariff bill virtually passed
May 20, Resignation of Von Forckenbeck (liberal), President of the Parliament; election of an ultramontane, about May 22
June 30, Resignation of Falk and other Ministers; announced
July 9, Bismarck in the Parliament disclaims connection with the liberal party
July 12, The customs bill finally passed (217–117); session closed
July 14, Ministry reconstituted about

About Sept. 16, Meeting of Bismarck and Jacobini, papal nuncio, at Gastein
Oct. 1, Bismarck visits Vienna; renews friendship with Andrassy, Sept. 21–24; supreme court for all Germany, opened at Leipsic
Nov., New code of laws made in 1877 come into operation

1880

Jan., Bill for enlargement of the army (by 27,000 men), proposed
April 3, In the federal council 22 small States out-vote Prussia, Saxony, and Bavaria, respecting new stamp duties
April, Bismarck's resignation not accepted by the Emperor; the States give in
April 9, The new army bill passed (186–96)
Aug., "New liberal" party formed by secession from the reactionary "national liberals"

1881

Oct. 28, General elections; large liberal majority
Nov. 29, Bismarck says Germany is not to be ruled after English fashion
Dec. 1, He is defeated in a financial question 169–83

1882

Jan. 7, Imperial rescript against parliamentary government published
Jan. 24 *et seq.*, Violent debates in the Parliament
March 21, Bismarck's tobacco tax bill rejected by his economic council; rejected by Parliament, 276–43, June 14
Dec. 6, German colonization society constituted at Frankfort
Dec. 11, The budget rejected by the Chambers

1883

Jan. 12, Death of Prince Charles, brother of the Emperor

1884

March 26, Mr. Sargent, the obnoxious U.S. Minister, settled to be removed to St. Petersburg; declined March 27
May 10, Anti-socialist law prolonged for two years (189–157); trial of Kraszewski, Polish poet and novelist, and Captain Hentsch, ex-telegraph official at Leipsic, for high treason in military communications to Austrian, French, and other governments in 1866–71; Kraszewski sentenced to 3½ years' imprisonment [released on bail Nov., 1885]; Hentsch to 9 years' penal servitude, May 12–19
July 14, German colony founded at Cameroons, and Bimbia, west coast of Africa, by Herr Nachtigall
Oct. 28, Elections for the Parliament; number of liberals diminished, social democrats increased
Nov. 26, Bismarck defeated; votes for payment of members, 180–99; parts of May ecclesiastical laws repealed (217–93), Dec. 3
Dec., German flag said to be hoisted on N. coast of New Guinea, New Britain, and other islands
Great increase of emigration (five-fold), 1879–1884

1885

Jan. 10, "Germany does not want colonies"—Bismarck, 1871—180,000 marks voted for protection of colonies
March 2, Speech of Prince Bismarck attacking the Gladstone Cabinet

March 9, Dispute said to be settled

July 1, Lieske convicted of murder of Rumpff at Frankfort

1886

Jan. 11, Prince Bismarck's "Schnapps" (dram of spirits) monopoly bill introduced; rejected by committee March 12

Feb. 11, Sarauw sentenced to 12 years' penal servitude for high treason (giving information respecting fortresses to the French Government)

March 26, Prince Bismarck reproves Parliament for opposing Government bills

March 27, The "Schnapps" bill rejected (181–3)

March 31, Socialist law prolonged for two years

May 23, Leopold von Ranke, the historian, died (aged 90)

Dec. 3, Bill for increase of the army (41,000) for seven years brought in; much opposed by clericals, socialists, and others; adjourned to Jan., 1887, Dec. 17, 1886; amendment limiting increase to three years carried (183–154); Parliament immediately dissolved, Jan. 4, 1887

1887

Feb. 21, Elections (efforts to make the army parliamentary instead of imperial); majority for the Government

March 11, Army bill passed (227–31)

March 13, Treaty of alliance with Austria and Italy signed

April 20–22, Arrest of M. Schnæbell (*see under* France)

June 3, Foundation stone of opening lock of a canal from the Baltic to the North Sea, 61 miles long, laid at Holtenau near Kiel by the Emperor; (estimated cost 7,800,000*l.*)

June 13, Eight Alsatians, members of the "Ligue des Patriotes" formed for the reunion of Alsace-Lorraine to France (advocated by M. Déroulède, a fiery poet of "La Revanche"), tried at Leipsic for high treason; four sentenced to one to two years' imprisonment; four acquitted, June 18; Klein and Grebert sentenced to six and five years' respectively, July 8

Nov., Statement in the *Cologne Gazette* of the existence of letters, &c., purporting to come from Prince Bismarck sent to the Czar tending to create disaffection; asserted to be forged; attributed to Orleanists, especially Princess Clementine of Coburg, daughter of King Louis Philippe

Dec. 19, Cabannes sentenced to ten years' penal servitude for selling military secrets to the French Government

1888

Feb. 3, Defensive treaty with Austria against Russian or other aggression, Oct. 7, 1879; first published

Feb. 17, Herr von Puttkamer's more stringent anti-socialist bill opposed by all parties; revelations of government detectives inciting socialists to violence in Zurich: the bill committed Jan. 30, 1888; passed

March 8, Serious illness of the Emperor; Prince William (grandson) entrusted with official powers, Nov. 17, 1887; this publicly announced

March 11, The Emperor Frederick III arrives at Berlin

March 21, Rescript empowering the Crown Prince to act for the Emperor in State affairs when required

June 11, 12, The Emperor becomes much worse; dies (of cancer of the larynx), June 15

June 25, The imperial Parliament opened by the Emperor William II; many princes present; in his speech the Emperor said "I will follow the same path by which my deceased grandfather won the confidence of his allies, the love of the German people, and the goodwill of foreign countries." The house adjourns after voting a cordial address, June 26

July 5, Herr Dietz, a former railway official in Alsace-Lorraine, his wife, and Appel convicted of treason and giving railway information to the French Government; Dietz sentenced to ten years' penal servitude, his wife to four years, and Appel to ten years' confinement, July 9

July, The Emperor's visit to the Czar at Peterhof, July 19–23; visited Stockholm and Copenhagen

Oct. 3, The Emperor arrives at Vienna; at Rome, Oct. 11; at Naples, Oct. 16

Oct. 6, First railway concession in Turkey. *See* Turkey

1889

Jan. 30, The East African bill passed, granting money for the defense of German interests and the suppression of the slave trade; adopted by the federal council (*see* Africa, German East Africa), Feb. 1

The Empress Frederick and her daughters visit England, Nov. 19, 1888–Feb. 26, 1889

May, Great strike of coal miners in Westphalia

May 21–26, The King of Italy, his son, and Signor Crispi received at Berlin

May 24, Prince Bismarck's bill to compel the working class, with the assistance of the State and their employees, to provide for sickness (passed 1883), for accidents (passed 1884), for old age and infirmity, passed

July 24, 33 Silesian miners engaged in the strikes; sentenced to various terms of penal servitude (Enkel, the ringleader, to 7 years for riotous conduct)

Aug. 1, The Emperor with a fleet arrives at Spithead, and proceeds to Osborne, Aug. 2; the Emperor leaves England, Aug. 8

Aug. 12–15, The Emperor of Austria and his heir at Berlin

Sept., Prince Bismarck declines to give state support to the German colonial company in S. W. Africa

Oct. 11–13, The Czar visits Berlin

Oct., Bill for amending the socialist law of 1878, prolonging it indefinitely, introduced

Nov. 2–6, The Emperor and Empress received by Sultan at Constantinople

Nov. 12, Visits Venice

Nov. 14, The Austrian and German Emperors meet at Innsbruck

Nov. 20 *et seq.*, 91 socialists, members of a secret society, tried at Elberfeld for illegally promoting socialism; 47 acquitted, the rest sentenced to imprisonment (terms 18 months to 14 days), Dec. 30

1890

Jan. 25, The stringent anti-socialist bill rejected (169–98), the Parliament closed with a moderate speech by the Emperor

Feb. 4, Two rescripts issued by the Emperor, urgently recommending action for the improvement of the condition of the working classes, and suggesting the coöperation of France, England, Belgium, and Switzerland

Feb. 20 *et seq.*, Elections for the new Parliament, increased number of socialists elected, and destroyed the Government majority, 23, of the powerful coalition of Conservatives and National Liberals of the last 5 years

March 18, Resignation of Prince Bismarck, Chancellor of the Empire [his political maxim was said to be *Do ut des* (Grotius?)—I give that thou mayest give]

About March 20, He is succeeded by General George von Caprivi de Caprera de Montecucculi

About March 23, He declines being created Duke of Lauenburg

About April 1, Count Herbert Bismarck, Secretary for Foreign Affairs, resigns, succeeded by Baron Marschall von Biederstein

April 16, New colonial department formed, reported

April 30, About 25,000 workmen on strike in Germany reported

May 6, The new Parliament opened by the Emperor; in his speech, while professing ardent desire for peace, he required supplies for the increase of the army (18,000,000 marks)

May 12, Vote of 4,500,000 marks, and an annual subsidy of 350,000 marks, for the suppression of slavery, and protection of German interests in East Africa, proposed by General von Caprivi

June 12 *et seq.*, First German national horse show (at Berlin)

June 28, The new army bill passed

July 1, Anglo-German convention (*see Africa*) respecting East Africa, signed at Berlin

July, Newly created colonial department subjected to the Chancellor

Aug. 4–8, The Emperor visits Queen Victoria at Osborne; visits Heligoland (ceded under Anglo-German Convention of July 1), Aug. 10

Aug. 17, The Emperor visits Russia; met by the Czar at Nawa; at Peterhof; left Aug. 23

Sept. 17–20, Cordial meeting of the German Emperor and the Emperor of Austria at Rhonstock in Silesia; at Vienna, &c., Oct. 1–8

Sept. 30, The socialist (or "muzzling") law of 1878 expires; great demonstration

Oct. 12–18, International socialist congress at Halle, Prussian Saxony

Oct. 15, Establishment of a colonial council decreed

Nov. 19, Marriage of the Princess Victoria, daughter of the Empress Frederick II, to Prince Adolphus of Schaumburg-Lippe, at Berlin

Dec. 4–17, The Emperor, at a conference in Berlin, strongly advocates reform in public education

1891

April 24, Sudden death of Field-Marshal Count Helmuth von Moltke, aged 90

May 1, Prince Bismarck elected deputy for the Parliament at Geestemünde

May 9, The important Trades law amendment act passed

June 28, The Triple Alliance renewed

June 30, Tour of the Emperor and Empress; they land at Heligoland; arrive at Amsterdam (in the *Hohenzollern*), July 1; at The Hague and Rotterdam, July 3; received at Port Victoria by a British squadron; arrive at Windsor, July 4; at Buckingham palace, July 8; the Empress goes to her five sons at Felixstowe, Suffolk, July 13; the Emperor proceeds from London to Leith; embarks on the *Hohenzollern*, sails up the Forth to view the bridge, and then proceeds to the coast of Norway, July 13, 14; lands at various places, July 18 *et seq.*; at North Cape, July 21; leaves Bergen, Aug. 4; arrives at Kiel, Aug. 8; the Empress and the Princes leave Felixstowe, Aug. 6

Aug., Great rise in the price of grain, especially rye, through the prohibition of exportation by the Czar

Oct. 21, Socialist congress at Erfurt closed

About Nov. 2, Strike of journeymen printers throughout Germany for a 9 hours' day begun at Berlin

Dec., New commercial treaty with Austria, Italy, and Belgium, adopted by the Parliament

1892

Jan. 2, The printers' strike supported by above 3,000*l.* sent by English trade unions; collapse of the strike reported Jan. 15

Feb. 24 *et seq.*, The Emperor's speech at Brandenburg, in which he severely censures the opponents of his political policy, styling them "grumblers," causes great sensation among all parties

Feb. 25 *et seq.*, Rioting at Berlin, Hanover, Dantzig, and other places through distress

March 3, Several newspapers at Berlin confiscated for reprinting the *Times* leader on the Emperor's speech

March 22, Ministerial crisis in Prussia (*see s.v.*)

March 29, The Government defeated in the Parliament; the vote for an imperial corvette negatived

May–July, The Government warns its representatives abroad against Prince Bismarck's strictures on its policy

July 30, 31, Prince Bismarck visits Jena; makes defensive speeches

Aug. 1–8, The Emperor visits England

Nov. 23, The army bills introduced by Count von Caprivi

Dec. 9, Herr Ahlwardt, a member of the Chamber, anti-semitic agitator, sentenced to five months' imprisonment for libels against Löwe & Co., Jewish rifle manufacturers

Dec. 22, A new National party advocating bi-metallism, anti-semitism, colonization, &c., reported

1893

Feb., Meeting at Berlin to establish a German agrarian league to oppose the importation of foreign grain, Feb. 18; agitation throughout the empire

Feb. 15, Railway concession in Turkey. *See* Turkey

March 8, Navy estimates: increase of the navy, &c., stopped by Parliament

April 22, The Emperor and Empress present at the silver wedding of the King and Queen of Italy, Rome; they visit the Pope, April 23; received at Naples, April 27; at Lucerne, May 2; at Berlin, May 4

April 27, Official examination into Ahlwardt's anti-semitic charges; declared unfounded, April 29; he withdraws them, and is censured by vote of the committee, May 2

May 6, The Parliament finally rejects the army bills (210–162) and is dissolved

June, General election, small majority for the Government

July 8, The army bills read a first time; passed (201–185); the session closed July 15

July 29–Aug. 7, The Emperor visits Queen Victoria at Osborne

Aug. 2 *et seq.*, Russian duty on German imports raised 50%; German reprisals

Oct. 1, The army bill comes into force

Two years' service substituted for three; the peace footing of the army is fixed at 469,229 men, from October 1 to March 31, 1899, being an increase of 70,000

Dec. 1, Anti-Jesuit law of July 4, 1872; bill for its repeal introduced; passed (173–136)

Dec. 16, Degony and Delguey-Malvas arrested as French spies at Kiel, Aug. 28. Degony sentenced to 6 years', Delguey-Malvas to 4 years' imprisonment

1894

Jan. 26, Reconciliation between the Emperor and Prince Bismarck

Feb. 10, Commercial treaty with Russia for 10 years signed; comes into force March 20

July 1, Two French officers, *see above*, Dec., 1893, released by the Emperor

Aug. 6–14, The Emperor visits Queen Victoria at Osborne, &c.

Sept. 8, Death of Hermann von Helmholtz, eminent physiologist and physicist, aged 73

Oct. 18, Dedication of 132 new standards presented to the new fourth battalions by the Emperor

Oct. 26, Resignation of the Chancellor, Count von Caprivi

Oct. 29, Prince Clovis von Hohenlohe appointed Chancellor and President of the Prussian Ministry

Dec. 5, The new Parliament-House opened by the Emperor, at Berlin

1895

Jan. 27, Imperial finance (reform) bill introduced

Feb. 18, Agrarian congress meets; an address presented to the Emperor, well received

April 3, An association formed at Berlin to maintain the existing gold currency

April 30, Gustav Freytag, author of "Soll und Haben," &c., born, 1816; died

May 11, The anti-revolutionary bills rejected by the Parliament

May 13, Tobacco-taxation bill rejected

June 20, The North Sea and Baltic Canal opened by the Emperor William II

July 21, Professor Rudolf von Gneist, jurist and statesman, born, Aug. 13, 1816; died

Aug. 13, Christian Bernhard Tauchnitz, eminent publisher, born, Aug. 25, 1816; died

Oct.–Dec., Several editors of the Social Democratic press imprisoned for lèse-majesté

1896

Jan. 2, The Emperor sends congratulations to President Kruger (*see* Transvaal)

Jan. 18, Celebration of the 25th anniversary of the foundation of the German Empire, which the Emperor terms a "world empire"

Jan., New civil code for the Empire, based on the report of commissions in 1874 and 1890, submitted to Parliament

April 15, Baron von Schrader killed in a duel with Herr von Kotze, much scandal; semi-public funeral; Herr von Kotze sentenced to 2 years' imprisonment, May 18

April 20, 21, The Reichstag request the Government to endeavor to suppress duelling; again with little effect Nov.

April 28, Heinrich von Treitschke, historian and poet, born Sept. 15, 1834; died

May 15–18, Prosecution of 47 Social Democrats at Berlin; 32 acquitted and the rest fined

May 21, Mr. Stern, an American, heavily fined for resenting regulations and scale of fees on foreign

visitors; United States Government protests, but the German Government justifies the sentence reported

July 1, The new civil code (to come into force, Jan. 1, 1900) passed

Oct. 20, Baron Ehrhardt and 6 others sentenced at Dusseldorf to various terms of imprisonment for insulting a court of honor respecting duels

Nov. 11–16, Discussion in the Reichsrath respecting the so-called Bismarckian "revelations" on a Russo-German treaty of William I and the Triple Alliance; affair closed

Dec. 7, Herr Leckert and Herr von Lützow, journalists, sentenced to 18 months' imprisonment for libel against Baron Marschall, Foreign Minister, and Count von Eulenburg, Court Marshal, in connection with the report of the Czar's speech at Breslau, others fined

1897

Jan. 1, New stock and produce regulations come into force; much opposed; business transacted under the auspices of the new "Free commercial union," Jan. 2

Jan. 5, Imperial cabinet order restricting duelling in the army announced

April 7, New commercial code passed

May 20, Emergency bill declaring that associations of every kind may enter into union, and repealing all provisions to the contrary in the laws of the other States passed in the Reichstag (207–53)

July 30, Denunciation of the Anglo-German treaty of commerce (May 30, 1865) by the British Government

Sept. 3 *et seq.*, Visit of the King and Queen of Italy; received by the Emperor at Hamburg

Dec. 16, Squadron, under the command of Prince Henry, leaves Kiel for the east

Dec., New coinage completed

1898

Jan. 12, Budget presented by Dr. von Miquel

Jan. 25, Herr Johannes Trojan, editor of the comic paper, *Kladderadatsch*, sentenced to 2 months' imprisonment in a fortress for lèse-majesté

March 6, Kiao-chau treaty with China (*see* China) signed; Captain Rosendahl appointed governor at Kiao-chau, March 7; Prince Henry arrives there, June 1

March 28, Bill for the reform of military judicial procedure, civil code, and navy act passed; Reichstag closed by the Emperor, May 6

June 16–29, General elections

July 30, Death of Prince Bismarck (born, April 1, 1815)

Oct. 11, The Emperor and Empress leave Berlin for a tour in the east; received by King Humbert at Venice, Oct. 13; by the Sultan at Constantinople, Oct. 18; land at Haifa, Palestine, Oct. 25; Jaffa, Oct. 27; Jerusalem, Oct. 29; Beirut, Nov. 5; Damascus, Nov. 7; leave Beirut to visit harbors, Nov. 12; return to Potsdam, Nov. 26

Dec. 1, State entry of the Emperor and Empress into Berlin

1899

Jan. 19, Imperial bank notes forged by Gränenthal, Manager of the Imperial Printing Office (who committed suicide in prison); 483,000 marks loss made up

Feb. 6, General Count von Caprivi, Chancellor 1890–94, born, Feb. 24, 1831, died

Feb., New German Imperial 3% loan, and the new Prussian 3% consols, well taken up

March 11–16, Mr. Cecil Rhodes received by the Emperor; successful negotiations respecting the Trans-African telegraph

March 14, Ludwig Bamberger, political author (born, 1823), and Professor Heymann Steinthal, philologist and author (born, 1823), died

March 16, Army bill, amended by the budget committee, adopted

March 25, Professor Hans Delbrück fined 500 marks for censuring the Government for the expulsion of Danes from Schleswig-Holstein

May 1, Imperial penny postage (letters) to colonies and protectorates started

May 2, Dr. Martin Eduard von Simson, ex-President of the Reichstag, and of the supreme court of the Empire, &c., died, aged 88

May 6, Agreement with France as to Bagdad Railway which removed French opposition

About June 2, Death of Professor Klaus Groth (*Platt-deutsch*), poet

June 21, 22, Bill prolonging the most-favored-nation treatment to the commerce of the British Empire (except Canada), and one ratifying treaty with Spain, June 30, for the acquisition of the Caroline Islands, passed; penal servitude (labor strikes) bill rejected by a large majority in the Diet

Middle June, Dr. Quarck, socialist editor, sentenced to 4 months' imprisonment for lèse-majesté

June 27–29, Strike-riot of colliers at Herne, near Bochum, 5 deaths; troops called out

Aug. 11, The Dortmund-Ems canal opened by the Emperor at Dortmund

Sept., Demonstrations in the provinces in honor of the deposed Landräthe; *see* Prussia

Oct. 7–11, Queen of Holland and her mother visit Potsdam

Nov. 8, The Czar and Czarina visit Potsdam

Nov. 14, Reichstag meets; labor (penal servitude) bill again rejected, Nov. 20

Nov. 20, The Emperor and Empress visit Queen Victoria; return to Potsdam, Nov. 30

Dec. 11, 14, Debate in the Reichstag on the proposed increase of the navy; able speech of Herr Richter, leader of the opposition

End of 1899, *Herzog* and *Bundesrath*, German vessels, seized by English cruisers on suspicion of carrying contraband of war; some controversy ensued

1900

Jan. 7, The Emperor's speech in favor of the navy bill, Berlin

Jan. 9, Diet opened, *see* Prussia

Jan. 25, Death of the Duchess Frederick of Augustenburg, mother of the Empress

Feb. 8, Navy (increase) bill introduced

Feb. 13, Prince Henry of Prussia warmly received in Berlin after 2 years' naval duty in the Far East

April 4, Imperial loan, 15,000,000*l.*, at 3%, successful

June 10, Anti-semitic riot in Konitz, W. Prussia; "state of siege" proclaimed

June 12, Navy bill passed, 201–103; the Reichstag adjourns

July 12, Circular note on the Chinese crisis to the federated States issued, reported

Sept. 14, Treasury bonds (80,000,000 marks) placed in the United States, announced

Oct. 8, Max Harden, writer and editor, sentenced to 6 months' imprisonment for lèse-majesté; 4 other trials

Oct. 11, Foundation-stone of the Imperial "Limes" museum, in the Saalburg, near Homburg, laid by the Emperor

Oct. 16, Prince Hohenlohe, Imperial Chancellor, aged 81, resigns; succeeded by Count von Bülow, Oct. 18

Oct. 24, Baron von Richthofen appointed Foreign Secretary

Dec. 1, The Emperor declines to receive Mr. Kruger, ex-President of the Transvaal; *see* The Netherlands, Dec. 6

Dec. 2, Imperial edict, granting reforms in secondary schools, issued

Dec. 10, Count von Bülow announces German intervention in S. Africa to be impossible

Dec. 21, Failure of the "Spielhagen banks," 4 directors arrested

——, Field-Marshal Count von Blumenthal dies, aged 90

1901

Jan. 5, Grand Duke of Saxe-Weimar-Eisenach, patron of art and literature, dies, aged 86

Jan. 8, Reichstag opened by Count von Bülow; interpellation on duelling, General von Gossler's statement unsatisfactory, Jan. 15

Feb. 15, Police-Commissary Thiel sentenced to 3 years' imprisonment for taking bribes, &c.

Feb. 25–March 2, King Edward visits the Empress Frederick at Kronberg

Feb. 26, Tariff bill, introduced by Count von Bülow, early Dec.; first reading carried

March 6, The Emperor wounded in the face, while driving in Bremen, by Wieland, an epileptic

March 8, Baron von Stumm, ironmaster and a leader of the free conservatives, died

May 30–June 1, The Queen of Holland and her consort visit Berlin

June 25, Stoppage of banks at Leipzig and Dresden

Early July, Industrial crisis through speculation and overproduction

July 6, Death of Prince Hohenlohe, ex-Chancellor, aged 82

July 12, Declaration against duelling signed by 104 German nobles, issued

Aug. 5, Death of the Empress Frederick (the Princess Royal of Great Britain and Ireland), aged 60

Aug. 20, Marten, a non commissioned officer, sentenced to death by court martial for the murder of Captain von Krosigk; evidence inconclusive; great indignation at the sentence

Sept. 4, Prince Chun, Chinese Envoy, presents a letter to the Emperor from the Chinese Emperor, and expresses regret for the revolutionary events of 1900, and particularly for the death of Baron von Ketteler

Sept. 11, 12, The Czar and Emperor meet at Danzig; view the German naval manœuvers

Middle Sept., Prince Henry of Prussia made full admiral of the fleet

Oct. 23, Dr. Georg von Siemens, eminent business man and promoter of railways in Asia Minor, died, aged 62

Oct. 24, The Emperor receives Dr. Benzler, the Roman Catholic Bishop of Metz, in state

Nov., Lieutenant Blaskowitz killed by Lieutenant Hildebrand in a duel at Insterburg, forced on him by a court of honor, Nov. 4; Colonel von Reisswitz, who could have prevented the disaster, suspended by imperial order and cashiered; Lieutenant Hildebrand sentenced to 2 years' imprisonment (but released May, 1902)

Nov. 11, Dr. Leyds, Transvaal Envoy, arrives in Berlin

Middle Nov., Anti-British agitation; Mr. Chamberlain's speech at Edinburgh (Oct. 25) misinterpreted and denounced; meetings held

Nov. 22, Count Hatzfeldt, 16 years Ambassador in London, dies, aged 70

Dec. 2–12, New customs tariff bill debated

Dec. 5, Visit of the Marquis Ito from Japan

Dec. 15, Visit of the Grand Duke Michael, heir-presumptive of Russia

1902

Jan. 10, Adverse speeches by Count von Bülow and others in the Reichstag on England and the war

Jan. 11, Mr. Chamberlain's firm British speech at Birmingham effective on the continent

Jan. 17, Socialist interpellation in the Reichstag on the industrial crisis and the unemployed

Jan. 23, Imperial and Prussian 3% loans (115 and 185 million marks) subscribed 61 and 43 times over

Feb. 7, Navy estimates adopted

Feb. 23–March 11, Prince Henry of Prussia visits America

March 18, First concession for Bagdad-Berlin Railroad granted by Turkey

March 28, Prince Münster, formerly Ambassador in London and Paris, dies, aged 81

April 30, Sergeants Marten and Hickel charged with being concerned in the murder of Captain von Krosigk, in custody since early 1901, tried for the third time and acquitted; *see supra*, Aug. 20, 1901

May 7, Commercial losses in consequence of German Anglophobia, reported

May 29, Visit of the Shah and Crown Prince of Siam

June 11, Sugar bill passed; Reichstag adjourns

June 19, King Albert of Saxony, eminent Commander in the war of 1870, died, aged 74

June 24, Torpedo-boat sunk in collision with the SS. *Firsby*, off Cuxhaven, 6 deaths, Sir Edw. Birkbeck and 3 other Englishmen saved; message of sympathy from King Edward, June 28

June 28, The Triple Alliance renewed

July 18, Bank trial (8 weeks) in connection with the Spielhagen failure, Dec., 1900; Eduard Sanden and 3 other directors sentenced to various terms of imprisonment and fines; Leipzig bank trial, re failure, June, 1901; Exner and Gentsch, Managers, sentenced to 5 and 3 years' imprisonment; 6 members of the board fined, July 23

Aug. 6–8, The Emperor and the Czar meet at Reval

About Aug. 8, Rudolph von Bennigsen, statesman, died, aged 80

Aug. 11, 101st sitting of the Reichstag tariff committee, tariff bill, 946 clauses, read first time

Aug. 13, The Emperor's telegram to the Prince Regent of Bavaria, criticizing the Diet's rejection of a vote for art, severely commented on

Aug. 27–31, Visit of the King of Italy

Sept. 5, Professor Rudolf Virchow, scientist and politician, died, aged 81

Sept. 19, 20, Congress of German bankers, Frankfort; resolutions against existing Bourse laws and increased taxation, passed

Sept., New articles of war promulgated by the Emperor

Oct. 10, Congress on German colonial enterprise, Berlin

Oct. 20, Reichstag meets, Oct. 14; deadlock on the tariff bill

Nov. 8, Four Italians sentenced from 8 to 3 years' imprisonment, &c., for betrayal of military secrets to France

Nov. 8–10, The Emperor visits England

Nov. 14, New rule of procedure in the Reichstag; vote by ballot instead of roll-call adopted

Nov. 22, Death of Friedrich Alfred Krupp, aged 48

Nov. 27–29, Dec. 1, 3, Parliamentary crisis: indignation at an attempt to pass the new tariff *en bloc*, angry scenes; Herr Singer suspended, sitting adjourns, Dec. 4, 5; changes in the rule of procedure passed, 206–92, Dec. 9; tariff bill read 2nd time *en bloc*, 183–136, Dec. 11; passed Dec. 14

Dec. 15, Count von Bülow and others decorated

1903

Jan. 20, Adverse criticism on the Emperor's political speeches stopped by the President of the Reichstag, Count Ballestrem; resigns, Jan. 23; reëlected, Jan. 29

Feb. 1, Dr. Rudolph von Delbrück, eminent statesman died, aged 85

Feb. 9, Agrarian league meets in Berlin, protests against the new tariff

Feb. 22, Hugo Wolf, musician and songwriter, dies, aged 43

March 5, Revised Bagdad Railway Convention with Turkey signed

March 9, Herr Bebel, the social democratic leader, calls attention to duelling in the army, and the ill-treatment of soldiers by non-commissioned officers

March 10, Large reductions made in the budget

Early April, General order on subject of the maltreatment of private soldiers by their superiors issued

April 17, New 3% loan of 14,500,000*l.* issued

May 26, Naval Ensign Hussner degraded and sentenced to 4 years' imprisonment for fatally stabbing Hartmann, a marine

———, *Elsass*, battleship, launched at Danzig

June 16–27, General elections

June 25, Second ballots show the composition of the new Reichstag to be: clericals, 99; social democrats, 83; national liberals, 47; conservatives, 67; radical left, 25; moderate radicals, 10; other groups, 37

Aug. 12, Court at Leipzig decides that Tolstoy's pamphlet, "Thou shalt not kill," amounts to *lèse-majesté;* all unsold copies to be destroyed

Middle Aug., Trust of sugar refiners formed with reference to the situation created by the Brussels convention

End Aug., Final accounts for the financial year 1902 show a deficit of about 1,536,120*l.*

Sept. 13, Socialist congress opened at Dresden

Sept. 20, Army scandal: 50 officers, 525 non-commissioned officers, and 52 others convicted between July 8, 1902, and July 8, 1903, for ill-treatment of soldiers; Breitenbach sentenced to 8 years' imprisonment

Sept. 25, Trial at Berlin of Karl Leid and Julius Kaliski, social democrat journalists, for *lèse-majesté* and libel

Oct. 23, Death of Gustav von Moser, dramatist, aged 78

Oct. 25, Congress of non-socialist democratic workmen at Frankfort

Nov. 1, Death of Professor Mommsen, historian, aged 85

Nov. 4, 5, Meeting of the Emperor and the Czar at Wiesbaden and Darmstadt

Nov. 11, Lieutenant Bilse sentenced to 6 months' imprisonment for libelling officers in his novel, "Auf einer kleinen Garnison"

Dec. 15, Franzky, a non-commissioned officer, sentenced to 5 years' imprisonment and degradation for maltreatment of soldiers in 1,520 cases; Lieutenant Schilling to 15 months for 600 cases of a similar character

1904

Jan. 18, Count von Bülow makes a statement in the Reichstag respecting the gravity of the situation in S. W. Africa, caused by the rising of the Hereros (*see* S. W. Africa)

Jan. 26, Visit of the King of the Belgians

Feb. 19, Representatives of various political parties in the budget committee of the Riechstag express their disapproval of the military expenditure of Germany in China

Feb. 22, Ministerial statements made in Prussian Chamber with regard to the expulsion of Russian subjects from Prussia, and the activity of the Russian political police in Germany; the subject of a debate in the Reichstag Jan. 19

March 1, Debate in the Reichstag on the political activity of the Russian police in Germany

March 8, Bill passed by the Reichstag repealing paragraph 2 of the law of July 4, 1872, prohibiting Jesuits from settling in Germany, receives the assent of the federal council

March 19, Discussion in the Reichstag on the navy estimates concludes; proposals for increasing the number of officers of higher grades defeated; many reductions made; Reichstag adjourns

March 24, Cruise of the German Emperor in the *Hohenzollern*: reaches Naples; visits Capri, March 25; meets the King of Italy, March 26

March 26, Cruiser *Lübeck*, the first vessel in the German navy fitted with turbines, launched at Stettin

April 26, Reichstag adopts resolution of the budget committee recommending 2,000,000 marks (100,000*l*. be devoted to the assistance of the persons rendered necessitous by the rising in S. W. Africa

April 28, Emperor, replying to an address of welcome at Carlsruhe, said:—"That the events which were moving the world should lead to internal discords being forgotten. He hoped that peace would not be disturbed, and that the events which were enacted before their eyes would make them steel their courage, and would find Germans united if it became necessary to intervene in world-policy"

May 2, Emperor opens a bridge across the Rhine

May 9, Herr Bebel, in the Reichstag, calls attention to increasing isolation of Germany; Count Bülow vindicates the policy of the Government

June 28, King Edward VII visits the German Emperor at Kiel; King visits Hamburg

July 12, M. Witte arrives at Norderney to confer with Count von Bülow concerning the settlement of the negotiations for a new Russo-German commercial treaty; M. Witte's visit rumored to be connected with a new Russian loan

——, Arbitration treaty between Germany and Great Britain, signed

July 25, Könisberg trial of 9 Germans tried for complicity in high treason against Russia concluded; defendants acquitted of the charge of treason, but found guilty of belonging to a conspiracy or secret society for unknown purposes; proceedings very damaging to the credit of Russia; ex-Professor von Reussner, of Tomsk University, makes a scathing exposure of the internal and administrative methods of the Russian authorities

July 28, Commercial treaty with Russia signed

July 30, First-Lieutenant Withe, who figured as the villain in Lieutenant Bilse's novel, "Auf einer kleinen Garnison, sentenced to 1 year's penal servitude, and dismissal from the army and loss of civil rights for 2 years for maltreating soldiers in 17 cases and for perjury

Sept. 8, Crown Prince betrothed to Cecilia, Duchess of Mecklenburg-Schwerin

Sept. 18, Death of Prince Herbert Bismarck, ex-Secretary of State for Foreign Affairs under his distinguished father, aged 54

Sept. 26, Death of Count Ernest, Prince Regent of Lippe-Detmold; his eldest son, Count Leopold, formally assumes the regency, Sept. 27

End Sept., Estimates for the naval budget for 1905 provide for an increase of 2,000 men, raising the personnel of the navy to 40,000

Oct. 8, Commercial treaty with Rumania signed

Nov. 12, Commercial treaty with Switzerland signed

Nov. 22, Arbitration treaty with the United States signed

Nov. 29, Commercial treaty with Serbia signed

Nov. 30, Negotiations for commercial treaty with Austria-Hungary broken off, Germany's proposals not being accepted

Dec. 3, Minister of War in the Reichstag introduces the new army bill

Dec. 5, Herr Bebel attacks the foreign policy of the Government; Count Bülow in reply repudiates idea of hostility to Great Britain

1905

Jan. 10, Colliery strike in the Ruhr district of Westphalia, some 40 collieries affected, 24,000 out; some 50,000 on Jan. 11

Jan. 13, Death of Prince Charles Alexander of Lippe-Detmold

Jan. 16, Strike of miners in district between Dortmund and Essen continues to spread, 54,000 men officially stated to be out; number increased to 154,000, serious riot at the Centrum pit, Jan. 17, and to 184,000 Jan. 18

Feb. 1, Death at Düsseldorf of Professor Oswald Achenbach, well-known painter, aged 78

——, Yielding to pressure of public opinion Prussian Government announces its intention to introduce legislative measures to remedy the evils of which the miners on strike in the Ruhr district complained

Feb. 9, Death of Adolf Friedrich Menzel, painter at Berlin, aged 89

Feb. 11, About 150,000 of the strikers return to work throughout the Ruhr district, thus virtually ending the strike. Estimated cost of the miners' strike and loss to the parties concerned, 90,000,000 marks (4,500,000*l*.)

Feb. 15, Budget committee of the Imperial Reichstag discuss navy estimates. Administrator von Tirpitz, Minister of Marine, stated that the new navy bill to be introduced will probably contain proposals for the construction of battleships. Agitation of the German Navy League criticized

March 7, Treaty of commerce with Abyssinia signed at Addis Abeba

March 8, New army bill passes the first reading with considerable amendment in the budget committee

March 17, Reichstag calls for a denunciation of the Prussian and Bavarian extradition treaties with Russia; resolution carried by large majority

March 20, Estimates for German S. W. Africa presented to the Reichstag; amount, 3,080,525*l.*, including 1,255,000*l.* for increase of troops and hospitals, and 95,000*l.* for repairing railway between Swakopmund and Windhoek

Middle March, New Prussian bill for redressing the grievances of the miners published

March 22, Emperor speaks at a banquet at Bremen, after unveiling an equestrian statue of the late Emperor Frederick, and says "that the world-wide empire he had dreamt of consisted in the German Empire enjoying absolute confidence as a quiet, honourable, and peaceful neighbour. Every new German battlefield was another pledge for peace on earth. The German people were the salt of the earth, but they must be worthy of their condition"

March 29, Count von Bülow in Reichstag says that Germany, aiming at the maintenance of the open door in Morocco, intends to open direct communication with the Sultan

March 31, Emperor lands at Tangier, and holds an official reception at the German Legation, responds to an address from German residents, and holds conversations with El Menebhi and the Sultan's delegates, and informs them that he had come to assert that he would maintain the absolute equality of German economic and commercial rights, and would insist on always carrying on German affairs direct with the Sultan; Emperor arrives at Messina on board the *Hohenzollern*, April 13

April 1, Emperor on board imperial yacht arrives at Gibraltar; entertains Sir George White and other guests on board the *Hohenzollern;* arrives at Corfu, April 11

April 3, Issue of new German imperial loan of 15,-000,000*l.* at 3½%, announced in Berlin

April 6, Emperor meets the King of Italy on board the imperial yacht at Naples

June 6, Crown Prince married to the Duchess Cecilia at Berlin; Count von Bülow raised to the rank of prince

June 15, Death of Major Hermann von Wissman, African traveler and ex-Governor of German East Africa

June 17, Pan-German League passes resolution advocating increase in naval construction

July 5, Prince Bülow prohibits the appearance of M. Jaurès, the French socialist orator, at a socialist mass meeting to be held in Berlin July 9, on the ground "that considerations of domestic policy render his presence at this present juncture undesirable." Prohibition conveyed from the Imperial Chancellor to German Ambassador in Paris

July 14, Meeting of Emperor and King Oscar of Sweden at Gefle

Middle July, Intense anti-British feeling reported in Berlin

July 19, Duke Charles Edward of Saxe-Coburg and Gotha celebrates the attainment of his majority and takes the oath of accession

July 28, Fuller details of the trial of the socialist deputy Herr Kunert, sentenced, June 27, at Halle to 3 months' imprisonment for libeling the German army by accusing the German contingent on active service in China in 1900 of devastating the country, of plundering and spoiling property, and of violating women

Aug., Meeting of the Emperor and Czar on the *Hohenzollern* at Bjoerkoe

Aug. 17, General von Trotha's proclamation to the Hereros received Oct., 1904, published in Berlin, occasions much indignation

Aug. 20, Herr von Lindequest appointed Governor of German S. W. Africa

Oct. 11, Marriage of Duke Edward of Saxe-Coburg and Gotha with Princess Victoria Adelaide of Schleswig-Holstein-Sonderburg-Glücksburg

Oct. 25, Supreme court of the German Empire decides the Lippe-Detmold dynastic controversy in favor of Count Leopold, who is entitled Leopold III, Prince zur Lippe

Nov. 6, State visit of King Alfonso of Spain to the Emperor at Berlin

Dec. 1, Population of the German Empire 60,605,183, of which 29,868,096 are males and 30,737,087 are females according to the new census taken

Dec. 30, Demonstrations in favor of better relations with Great Britain reported from Hamburg and Frankfurt

1906

Jan. 1, Lieutenant-General von Moltke, nephew of the late Field-Marshal Count von Moltke, appointed Chief of the General Staff of the army in succession to General Count von Schlieffen

Jan. 6, Meeting of several thousand people held at Munich in favor of friendly relations between Germany and Great Britain

Jan. 17, Death of Baron von Richthofen, German Foreign Secretary

Jan. 21, 93 socialist meetings held in Berlin and the neighborhood in favor of electoral reform

Jan. 26, Herr von Tschirschky und Bögendorff appointed Foreign Secretary

Feb. 22, Bill granting the United States most favored nation treatment, pending negotiations for a regular treaty of commerce, carried in the Reichstag

Feb. 27, Marriage of Prince Eitel Friedrich, second son of the Emperor, with the Duchess Sophia Charlotte of Oldenburg

March 1, New tariff comes into operation

March 6, Budget committee agree to the navy bill proposals, including the building in 1906 of two large battleships and a large cruiser, and a program of six additional large cruisers; vote passed for the expenditure of 845,000*l.* for torpedo boats and submarines, March 7

March 7, Death of General Albert von Mischke

March 10, Death of Herr Eugen Richter, radical leader in the Reichstag

March 17, Death of Geheimrath Oskar Knack, director of the bureau of the German Reichstag, in his 68th year

March 24, Unanimous vote of the budget committee, reducing by 15,000,000 marks (750,000*l.*), the estimate for the maintenance of the expeditionary force in German S. W. Africa, unanimously confirmed by the Reichstag

March 28, Reichstag passes the navy bill against the votes of the socialists and radical left

April, Emperor sends a telegram thanking Count Goluchowski, who represented Austria-Hungary at the Moroccan conference, for his "unshakable support," at Algeciras, and declaring that he had been "a brilliant second on the dueling ground." Discussion in the Reichstag on

April 18, Resignation of Herr von Holstein, senior official of the Foreign Office, accepted by the Emperor

About April 22, Death of Prince Leopold of Schwarzburg-Sonderhausen

May 1, Second reading of the imperial finance reform bill, and the scheme of taxation by which the Government seek to increase the imperial revenue by about 11,000,000*l.*

May 2, Death of Prince Henry VII of Reuss

May 8, Treaty of commerce and navigation signed with Sweden

May 12, Death of Princess Frederick Charles of Prussia

May 15, Bill passed by the Reichstag for the payment of members

May 16, Visit Windsor Castle at the invitation of the King

May 26, Reichstag rejects by 143 to 119 votes the credit for the new colonial secretary's salary, and also the supplementary estimates for S. W. Africa

June 2, Emperor opens the new Tetlow canal, 24 miles in length, establishing a fresh and most important link between the eastern and western canal systems of Prussia

June 6, Death of Herr Eduard von Hartmann, philosopher, *b.* 1842

June 6–7, Visit of the Emperor William to Vienna

June 19, Emperor, speaking at Cuxhaven, refers to the marvelous development of the German mercantile marine, adding that the navy was following its footsteps, but for such development, peace was the first necessity

Aug. 15, Meeting of King Edward and the Emperor William at Cronberg

Sept. 2, Pan-German congress holds its first general meeting at Dresden

Sept. 3, Resignation of the hereditary Prince of Hohenlohe-Langenburg, acting-director of the colonial department of the Foreign Office, and appointment of Herr Bernhard Dernburg as director, reported

Sept. 13, Prince Albrecht of Prussia, Regent of the Duchy of Brunswick since 1885, dies at Kamenz, aged 69

Sept. 23, Socialistic congress held at Mannheim

Oct. 6, Publication of the memoirs of Prince Hohenlohe (third German Chancellor)

Oct. 8, Prince Hohenlohe-Schillingsfürst sharply censured by the Emperor in consequence

Oct. 15, Resignation of Prince Alexander Hohenlohe-Schillingsfürst, second son of the Chancellor, as President of upper Alsace

Nov. 12, Resignation of General von Podbielski, Prussian Minister of Agriculture, accepted by the Emperor

Nov. 14, Prince Bülow, in reply to an interpellation by Herr Basserman (nat. lib.), spoke on the relations of Germany with the various European powers, and said there was no justification for depicting the future of the Empire in gloomy colors

Nov. 19, Arrival of the King and Queen of Denmark on a visit to the Emperor

Nov. 22, Herr von Arnim-Criewen appointed to succeed General von Podbielski, reported

Nov. 28, Debate on the first reading of the supplementary estimate for S. W. Africa, Prince Bülow defends the estimate; Herr von Erzberger makes a severe attack on the colonial department, Nov. 30; Herr Bebel, socialist leader, denounces the whole colonial administration with great violence, Dec. 1

Dec. 3, Death of Prince Karl of Baden, *b.* 1832

——, In the Reichstag, Herr Rören makes charges against certain officials in Togoland

Dec. 13, Reichstag dissolved

1907

Jan. 18, Brunswick Diet pass resolution to the effect, that friendly relations between the Duchy of Brunswick and Prussia would not be impaired by the succession to the ducal throne of the second son of the Duke of Cumberland

Jan. 21, Negotiations between Denmark and Prussia, result in an agreement on the so-called North Schleswig "option question"; announced

Feb. 7, As a result of the elections, the composition of the new Reichstag is approximately as follows: the strength of parties in the old Reichstag at the dissolution, being given in brackets:—The Center, 105 (104); the Poles, 20 (16); the Alsatians, 7 (1); the Guelphs, 1 (5); the two Conservative parties, 83 (74); the National liberals, 55 (51); the three Radical sections, together with independent liberals, 51 (36); the social democrats, 43 (79); the anti-Semites including 23 deputies belonging to the Economic league, and the Agrarian league, and 6 belonging to the so-called reform party, 30 (21); one Dane (1), and one Lorrainer. *Times*

Feb. 14, Dr. Franz von Rottenburg, curator of the university of Bonn, *b.* 1845, died

Feb. 19, New Reichstag opened by the Emperor William at the Royal castle

Feb. 20, In the Reichstag, Count Stolberg-Wernigerode (C.) elected President; Dr. Paasche (N.L.) and Herr Kaempf (R.) Vice-Presidents

March 4, The Grand Dukes of Mechlenburg-Schwerin and Mechlenburg-Strelitz simultaneously announce their intention to introduce a form of constitutional government in the two grand duchies

March 7, Dr. Heinrich von Bötticher, born 1833, died

March 19, Death of General von Werder, aged 84

March 25, Professor von Bergmann, *doyen* of German surgeons, *b.* 1836, died

——, Prince Arenberg, former president of the Colonial society, *b.* 1849, died

April 25, Trial of Herr von Puttkamer, late Governor of the Cameroons, for breaches of discipline; the ex-Governor was reprimanded, fined 50*l.*, and ordered to pay the costs of the proceedings

May 6, Trial of Herr Horn, ex-Governor of Togoland, on a charge of causing the death of a native convicted of theft in 1902; sentenced to be dismissed the service with loss of one-third pension

May 18, Lockout in the Berlin building trade begun; about 45,000 men affected

May 25, Death of Baron von Roggenbach, former Foreign Minister of Baden, *b.* 1825

May 28, Duke John Albrecht of Mecklenburg-Schwerin unanimously elected by the Brunswick Diet to fill the office of Regent of the Duchy of Brunswick

May 31, Death of Karl Blind, veteran German revolutionary agitator, aged 80

June 1, New commercial agreement with the United States, announced

July 4, Death of Professor Kuno Fischer

July 21, Death of Herr Wilhelm von Kardorff, aged 79

Aug. 3–6, Meeting between the Emperor and the Czar at Swinemünde

Aug. 14, Meeting between King Edward and the Emperor William at Wilhelmshöhe

——, Death of Jn. Hy. XI Prince of Pless, *b.* 1833

Aug. 25, German Catholic congress opened at Würzburg

Sept. 14, Death of Prince Augustus of Saxe-Coburg and Gotha, *b.* 1845

Sept. 27, Death of Prince Charles Gustavus of Thurn und Taxis, age 22

Oct. 7, Herr von Tschirschky appointed Ambassador in Vienna and Herr von Schön appointed to the Foreign Office

Oct. 29, Trial of the Moltke-Harden libel action concluded; judgment for the defendant

Nov. 6, Adolph Brand, journalist, sentenced to 18 months' imprisonment for libeling Prince Bülow

Nov. 8, The Emperor and Empress leave Berlin on their way to England

Dec. 15, Death of Dowager Queen Caroline of Saxony

1908

Jan. 3, Herr Harden, for libeling Count Kuno von Moltke, sentenced to 4 months' imprisonment and to pay the costs of the trial

(Sentence quashed on appeal, May 23)

Jan. 12, Extensive social democratic demonstrations at Berlin in favor of franchise reform

Jan. 24, Labor troubles in Berlin; the central labor bureau estimates the number of unemployed at 30,000

Feb. 20, Herr Sydow succeeds Baron von Stengel at the Imperial Treasury, on the latter's retirement

Feb. 27, Polish expropriation bill passes

March 7, Launch of the *Nassau*, the first of the new large battleships for the German navy, at Wilhelmshaven

March 20, Death of Professor Edward Zeller, aged 94

——, Strike of journalists belonging to the press gallery in the Reichstag

April 2, Admiral von Tirpitz made a life member of the upper chamber by the Emperor William in recognition of his success in obtaining the enactment of the new Navy bill, which reduces the age limit for battleships

April 3, Total of the new loans issued by the Imperial and Prussian Governments this year amounts to considerably over 50,000,000*l. See Times*

April 8, Associations law passed

April 11, Launch of the armored cruiser *Blücher* from Kiel

June 2, Further railway agreement with Turkey. *See Turkey*

July 6, Death of F. M. von Loe, born 1828

Aug. 11, Meeting between the Emperor William and King Edward at Cronberg

Aug. 23, Death of Baron Speck von Sternburg, Ambassador to the United States, aged 57

Sept. 6, Pan-German congress opened in Berlin

Sept. 26, Launch of the *Rheinland*, sister ship to the *Nassau*

Oct. 22, Marriage of Prince Augustus William, fourth son of the Emperor William, with Princess Alexandra Victoria of Schleswig-Holstein-Sonderburg-Glücksburg, niece of the Empress

Nov. 10, Debate in the Reichstag on the interpellations with reference to the Kaiser's recent "revelations," begins

Nov. 20, Sir Edward Goschen, new British Ambassador in Berlin, received by the Emperor William

Nov. 30, Commercial treaty with Portugal signed

1909

Jan. 17, The Emperor William and the Czar exchange visits on their yachts off Björkö on the Finnish coast,

Feb. 9, King Edward and Queen Alexandra arrive in Berlin

——, Franco-German agreement concerning Morocco signed in Berlin

Feb. 12, King Edward and Queen Alexandra leave Berlin

March 20, Launch of the cruiser "F," the first German *Invincible*

April 20, Moltke-Harden libel case—Herr Harden found guilty of libeling Count von Moltke and fined 30*l.*

May 3, New German Imperial and Prussian loans issued—total amount 40,000,000

May 9, Herr von Holstein, for many years chief of the political department of the German Foreign Office, *b.* 1837, died

July 10, Frankfurt aëronautical exhibition opens

July 14, Prince Bülow resigns the imperial chancellorship and is succeeded by Herr von Bethmann-Hollweg

Aug. 4, The 20th Eucharistic congress opens at Cologne

Aug. 7, Meeting between the Emperor William and the Czar at lake Audorf in the Kiel canal on the Czar's return from England

Sept. 13–19, German socialist congress, the 20th congress holds its meetings at Leipzig

Sept. 25, The fifth German dreadnought or first "improved Dreadnought" named, *Helgoland*, launched at Kiel

Sept. 30, The second "improved Dreadnought" launched

Oct. 21, Death of Herr Reinhart Schmidt, formerly leader of the radical party in the Reichstag, aged 70

Nov. 27, Launch of the *Thüringen*, seventh German dreadnought, at Bremen

1910

Jan. 4, First complete flotilla of turbine torpedo-boats consisting of 11 vessels commissioned

Feb. 1, Commercial treaty with Portugal accepted by the Reichstag by a small majority

Feb. 4, Electoral Reform Bill presented, passed the Upper House April 29 but so amended that the Government withdrew the Bill, May 27

Feb. 10, Death of Count Tattenbach, Ambassador to the court of Madrid, *b.* 1846

Feb. 17–18, Rioting at Frankfurt-on-Main; collisions with the police; a policeman was stabbed in the back and a workman shot; several persons including police were more or less seriously injured

Feb. 19, Death of Count Stolberg Wernigerode, President of the Reichstag, aged 69

Feb. 22, Count Aehrenthal received by the Imperial Chancellor, Herr von Bethmann Hollweg

March 1, Count Schwerin, of Löwitz, elected President of the Reichstag

March 6, Franchise demonstrations in Berlin; serious conflict between the crowd and the police; 25 persons more or less seriously injured; 40 arrests

March 15, Reichstag agreed to introduction of Bill providing for making the Chancellor responsible to the Reichstag for acts of the Emperor

March 16, Prussian Franchise Bill passed, provided for direct voting. Clause retained as to group electors according to taxes paid but more persons, officers and educated classes, placed in first and second groups

March 30, First German battleship squadron took up permanent station at Wilhelmshaven thereby superseding Kiel as principal naval base

April 7, Launch of the cruiser *Moltke* at Hamburg

April 15, Lock-out in the German building trade begun: 4,000 men went out at Cologne, and about four-fifths of the trade in Rhenish Westphalia became idle

May 10, Mr. Roosevelt received by the Emperor William at Potsdam

——, Professor Gottlieb Planck, chief curator of the the civil code of the German Empire; died aged 85

May 24, Legislation enacted by which prices of potash almost 100% higher

May 28, Death of Robert Koch, scientist

May 30, Visit of King Albert of Belgium and the queen

June 7, American potash interests notified German mines that no deliveries of potash would be accepted which were subject to super-contingent tax

June 9, Resignation of Herr Dernburg, and appointment of Herr von Lindequist as Secretary of State for the Colonies, officially announced

——, The Minister-President, Herr von Bethmann Hollweg, replied in the lower house of the Prussian Diet to three interpellations concerning the recent encyclical of the Pope which had been much resented by Protestant Germany. He stated that he had instructed the Prussian Minister to the Vatican to make an official protest and to express the hope that the curia would counteract the injurious effects of the encyclical

June 11, Reply, signed by the Cardinal-Secretary of State, to the protest against the publication of the recent encyclical, expressed the regret of his holiness of the excitement of opinion raised, as no intention of slighting the non-Catholics of Germany or their provinces had ever entered his mind. The Prussian Minister was officially informed that the Pope had already instructed the Prussian bishops to abstain from the publication of the encyclical

June 22, Count Zeppelin inaugurated the first airship passenger service with the "Deutchland" from Friedrichshafen to Stuttgart, Mannheim, Cologne, and Düsseldorf, 300 miles

June 28, On third passenger service the "Deutchland" sprang a leak in storm and landed a wreck in the Teutoberger forest. 35 passengers landed without loss of life

June 30, Launch of the eighth German dreadnought battleship named "Oldenburg"

July 10, Death of Dr. Johann Galle, astronomer

Aug. 3, 8,000 mechanics in Hamburg shipyards went on strike demanding a 10% increase and other concessions

Aug. 19, Agreement with Russia signed as to railroads in Persia (Berlin-Bagdad)

Aug. 25, Speech of the Emperor at Königsberg in which he said "Looking on myself as God's instrument, I shall go on my way without regard to the ideas and opinions of the time" asserting again his belief in the divine right of kings

Sept. 20, Visit of the Emperor to the Emperor of Austria at Vienna

Sept. 26–30, Strike riots and conflict with police in Moabit district of Berlin because of police protection of non-union men employed during strike by firm of coal merchants

Oct. 6, Shipbuilding trades strike at Berlin ended with victory for strikers

Oct. 25, Visit of King and Queen of Belgium

Nov. 4, Meeting of the Emperor and the Tsar of Russia at Potsdam

——, Potsdam Agreement with Russia signed by which Russia withdrew objections to Berlin-Bagdad railroad in return for recognition by Germany of Russian special interests in Persia as defined by Anglo-Russian Agreement of 1907

Nov. 30, New Reichstag opened

Dec. 21, Trial of 2 English officers for espionage ended with sentence of 4 years' imprisonment

1911

Jan. 11–23, Trial of 34 persons involved in strike riots in Moabit district in Berlin in 1910 resulted in acquittal of 3 and terms of imprisonment for the others

Jan. 25, German-Swiss-Italian Agreement concluded for telephone between Berlin and Rome

Jan. 28, Constitutional and franchise Bills for Alsace-Lorraine read for the first time in the Reichstag

Jan. 30, Extradition Treaty with Great Britain signed to apply to German and British protectorates

Jan. 31, Increment tax Bill passed by Reichstag, provided for taxation of increment in value of property not due to agency of owner at rates from 10 to 30%

——, Death of Paul Singer, Socialist leader (67). Succeeded as leader of Party by Hermann Molken Nehr

March 21, Convention with Turkey as to Berlin to Bagdad railway, concessions of land from Turkey for railroad

March 27, Army Bill passed, provided for increase in men during next 5 years from 615,000 to 625,000 and increased expenditure for armament. Became law April 1

May 2, Commercial Treaty with Sweden signed

May 8, Germany warned France against occupation of Fez, Morocco

May 13, Death of Karl Baedeker, guide book publisher

May 17, Agreement with the United States concluded as to price of potash

May 26, Bill to organize Alsace-Lorraine as a constitutional province of the Empire passed by vote of 211 to 93 in third reading in Reichstag gave a considerable measure of autonomy in home affairs, established Diet of 2 Chambers

May 30, Workmens' Insurance Bill passed third reading in Reichstag combining various measures into a single law and extending sickness insurance to agricultural workers, and home workers and making a beginning of insurance for widows and orphans

June 7, Germany again warned France to respect the sovereignty of Morocco

June 10, The tenth German dreadnought the "Friedrich der Grosse" launched

June 24, Most-favored nation Commercial Treaty with Japan signed

July 1, German troops landed at Agadir, Morocco, closed port, from the "Panther" to protect German interests

——, New patent law enacted

July 4, German cruiser sent to Agadir

July 8, Conversations begun with France at Berlin with view to settlement of Morocco dispute

July 15, Germany asked for territorial cessions from France in Central Africa

July 19, Insurance law extended in application

July 21, Warning of Lloyd George to Germany in public speech as to demands on France

Aug. 3, Death of Reinhold Begas, sculptor

Aug. 5, Lockout declared against 19,000 metal workers in Leipzig and Thuringia

Aug. 19, Potsdam Agreement with Russia as to rail-roads in Persia signed

Sept. 13, German proposals of Sept. 10 for settlement as to Morocco rejected by France

Nov. 4, Two Conventions with France signed as to Morocco, the first provided for equality of nations in Morocco as to tariff and customs and Germany recognized practical protectorate of France, the second ceded part of French colonies in Congo to Germany and Germany gave part of Duck's Beak near Lake Chad between Shari and Logone Rivers

Nov. 26, Germany recalled 2 warships from Agadir

Dec. 20, Law passed, provided for old age pensions for workers and special insurance for salaried employees, in commerce and shipping, teachers, employees in theaters and orchestras and home crafts

——, Wilhelm Solf appointed Minister of Colonies

1912

Jan. 11, General elections for Reichstag. The Socialists (Social Democrats) polled 4,250,000 votes, one-third of total of 12,200,000 cast gaining 110 seats, Catholic Center Party, 90 seats; National Liberals, 44; Conservatives, 45; Free Conservatives, 13; Radicals, 41; Poles, 18, &c.

Jan. 28, The National Defense League (Wehrverein) established at Berlin under leadership of General Keim

Jan. 31, Trial of Bertrand Stewart (British) on charge of espionage. Found guilty after 4 days and sentenced to imprisonment of 3 years and 6 months

Feb. 7–May 22, Reichstag in session

Feb. 8, Federal Council adopted new Nationality Bill to render loss of German citizenship more difficult and recovery easier

——, Arrival of Lord Haldane on mission to discuss Anglo-German relations

Feb., Federal Council suspended import duties on potatoes until May on account of high prices of food

March 16, Hermann Kuhn appointed Secretary of the Treasury

March, Strike of 200,000 miners in Ruhr district

May 8, Amendment to rules of parliamentary procedure adopted

May 21, Supplementary Defense Bills passed third reading in Reichstag provided for formation of 2 new army corps to protect the Franco-German frontier and increased army in times of peace to approximately 655,000

July 4, Meeting of the Emperor with the Tsar of Russia at Baltic port

Sept. 3–7, Visit of Emperor to Zurich and Berne, Switzerland

Sept. 28, Declaration signed by Germany and France determined new frontier of French Equatorial Africa and the Cameroons and of Togo with French Dahomey and Sudan

Nov. 26, Decree of Federal Council reversed decision as to privileges restored to Jesuits

Dec. 5, Renewal of Triple Alliance

Dec. 12, Death of Prince Regent of Bavaria (91)

Dec. 20, Death of Waechter Kiderlen Waechter, Minister of Foreign Affairs

1913

Jan. 14, Herr von Jago appointed Secretary of Foreign Affairs

Jan. 30, Reichstag passed vote of censure (the first ever passed) declaring the "permission of the Imperial Chancellor for the expropriation of Polish landowners for purposes of Prussian Settlement Commission (settling of Germans on land in Polish Prussia) is at variance with the judgment of the Reichstag"

Feb. 15, Agreement with France as to Berlin-Bagdad Railroad

Feb. 19, Clericals in Reichstag introduced resolution to repeal Jesuit law of 1872

March 28, Army Bill with supplementary Finance Bills passed Bundesrat

April 18, Dr. Liebknecht accused Krupp firm of misinforming French press to stimulate militarism and of obtaining information by bribery and corruption of government officials

May 24, Marriage of Princess Victoria Luise of Prussia to Prince Ernest August of Cumberland, son of exiled Guelph, pretender to the throne of Hanover. The Tsar and King George V among those present at ceremony

June 30, Army and Finance Bill passed by Reichstag to go into effect Oct. 1 by which the total number of men in peace army raised to 870,000. The levy on property called the Wehrbeitrag (contribution to defense), provided for a special tax on income, profits, inheritance and capital. Passed by Bundesrat, July 3

July 3, Act provided that amount of gold received for war purposes, "warchest," be doubled

July 15–Aug., Strike of workers in Hamburg ship-yards against increase of hours

July 22, Imperial and state citizenship law passed

July 31–Aug. 5, Court-martial trial in Krupp case. 7 persons found guilty of surrender of secrets affecting the national defense to Krupp agents sentenced to imprisonment

Aug. 14, Death of Ferdinand August Bebel (73), founder with Liebknecht of the Social Democratic Party

Oct. 1, Death of Rudolf Diesel inventor of oil engine

Oct. 23, Trial of Maximilian Brandt former agent of Krupp firm and Otto Eccius, a director resulted in sentence of imprisonment of 4 months of Brandt, and fine of Eccius

Nov. 1, Accession of Prince Ernest Augustus to the throne of Brunswick ending regency of Johann Albrecht

Nov. 5, Otto, King of Bavaria (insane), deposed by authorization of Bill passed Oct. 30, altering the succession to the throne and Regency declared at end

Nov. 12, Accession of Ludwig III, cousin of Otto, as King of Bavaria

Dec. 4, Second vote of censure passed in Reichstag on Zabern affair

Dec. 13–17, H. Kaulen made world record for duration in balloon flight

Dec. 19, Lieutenant Forstner sentenced by court martial to 43 days' imprisonment for "assaulting and wounding and the unlawful employment of weapons" his striking and wounding a lame cobbler with his sword in Zabern, Alsace-Lorraine who he charged "jeered" at him in the street

Public debt $1,194,000,000

1914

Jan. 5–11, Trial of Colonel Reuter and Lieutenant Schad by court martial at Strassburg accused of ill treatment of civilians at Zabern, Alsace, resulted in acquittal and reversal of sentence of Lieutenant Forstner of Dec. 19, 1913

Jan. 20, Resolution of Upper Chamber of Diet of Alsace as to Zabern incident characterized action of Lieutenant Forstner as "unworthy, insulting, and provocative behavior"

Jan. 29, Resignation of Government of Alsace-Lorraine on account of decision of military court martial in Zabern affair

Feb. 8–10, Berliner made world record for distance in balloon flight, 3052.7 kil.

Feb., Resolution adopted, abolished serfdom in German East Africa by Jan. 1, 1921

Feb. 15, Secret Convention with France by which Northern Anatolia and Syria recognized as French sphere for construction of railroads and regions traversed by Anatolian and Bagdad Railways as German sphere

March 4, Death of Cardinal George Kopp

March 5, The editor of "Vorwärts" sentenced to 3 months' imprisonment for parody of the farewell of the Crown Prince to his regiment

——, Journalist, Leuss, sentenced to 6 months' imprisonment for article "Wilhelm der Letzte" in the *Welt am Montag* in which he spoke of the interference of the Crown Prince in the Zabern affair

March 8–14, "Red Week" instituted by Social Democrats

March 20, War credit of $2,500,000 authorized

March 31, Linnekogel at Johannesthal made new aëroplane height record at 20,564 feet

April 2, Death of Paul Johann Ludwig von Heyse (84), novelist and dramatist

May 2, Commercial Treaty with Turkey signed

May 4, Reichstag opened

May 20, Reichstag prorogued. Had passed laws for prevention of betrayal of military secrets, law to facilitate construction of dwellings

June 15, Anglo-German Convention settled controversy over German railroad construction in Mesopotamia (Berlin-Bagdad)

June 24, Reconstructed Kiel Canal opened by German Emperor

July 3, Announcement made that the Berlin-Bagdad Railway would terminate at Basra

July 6, The Kaiser left for cruise in northern waters (July 6–26)

July 10–14, Non-stop flight of Boehm made record at Johannesthal

July 14, Oelrich made new altitude record at Leipzig at height of 26,730 feet

July 24, Statement of Government of approval of Austrian Note to Serbia and of settlement of affair by military measures between Austria and Serbia

July 26, Emperor William returned to Berlin from northern tour

July 27, Treaty of June 14–15, initiated in London signed by Germany

July 31, Germany protested Russian mobilization and declared a state of imminence of war (kriegsgefahr-zustand) and in Note to France asked if France would remain neutral in the event of a war between Germany and Russia

Aug. 1, General mobilization of army and navy

——, Germany declared war on Russia

——, Government ordered suspension of cash payments at banks

Aug. 2, Treaty of alliance with Turkey signed

——, German Note to Belgium requested free passage of troops through Belgian territory, and began invasion of France and Luxemburg. *See* World War

——, General von Moltke appointed Chief of General Staff armies in the field

Aug. 3, Germany declared war on France and France on Germany

Aug. 4, Interview of Sir Edward Goschen, British Minister in Germany, with the Chancellor. *See* World War

——, Declaration of war on Belgium and crossing of frontier by German troops

——, Great Britain declared war on Germany. For further declarations *see* World War

——, Speech of the Kaiser declared Germany must now defend herself against the chauvinism of Russia and the malice of France

——, War expenditure of $1,250,000,000 authorized

Aug. 23, General von Hindenburg appointed to command of Eighth Army

Sept. 9, First war loan of 100 milliard marks in 5% Treasury Bills due Oct. 1, 1920 and 5% Imperial loan redeemable Oct. 1, 1924, and thereafter loans every 6 months

Sept. 18, General von Hindenburg appointed Commander-in-Chief of German Armies in Eastern field

Nov. 3, General von Falkenhayn succeeded General von Moltke as Chief of Staff

Nov. 25, Treaty with Turkey of Aug. 26, 1890 extended

Nov. 27, General von Hindenburg promoted to Field-Marshal

Dec. 2, Second war credit of $2,250,000,000 voted

1915

Jan. 3, Death of Professor Anton von Werner (74), historical painter

Jan. 21, Resignation of General von Falkenhayn as Minister of War. Succeeded by Major General von Hohenborn. General von Falkenhayn continued as Chief of Staff

Jan. 25, Government decree sequestered all stocks of corn, wheat, and flour to be taken over by War Grain Association and all private transactions in grains prohibited to take effect Feb. 1

Feb. 1, On this date all private stocks of corn, wheat, and flour confiscated at a fixed price by the Government. Municipalities ordered to lay up stores of

preserved meats, and limited bread ration fixed for the Empire. All supplies of copper, tin, aluminum, lead, antimony, and nickel reserved for military use
Feb. 27–March 19, Second war loan at 98½ at 5% interest opened to the public resulted in subscription of nearly 9,000,000 marks
March 10, Reichstag met
March 26, Federal Council authorized local authorities to prohibit sale of alcoholic spirits
March 31, Proclamation and regulations April 16 restricted production of spirituous liquors
April 1, Regulations designed to prohibit any further rise in the price of fodder promulgated and conservation of petroleum provided for
May 21, Treaty with Italy provided for mutual protection of citizens and property
June 23, Social Democratic Party issued manifesto calling on Government to open peace negotiations
June 26, The *Vorwaerts*, Berlin Socialist daily, published the appeal for peace and was suspended by the Government
July 31, Proclamation of the Emperor affirmed German innocence "Before God and history my conscience is clear. I did not want the war"
Aug. 1, University at Frankfort-on-the-Main chartered
Aug. 11, Third war loan of $1,250,000,000 authorized
Aug. 19, Reichstag convened
Sept. 4–22, Third war loan opened to subscription at 99 at 5%
Sept. 24, Trade Agreement with Denmark concluded
Dec. 9, Dr. Scheidemann introduced debate on peace terms in the Reichstag
Dec. 21, Fifth war credit of 10,000,000,000 marks voted

1916

Jan. 9, Social Democratic Party repudiated party journal *Vorwaerts* because of its pacifist tendencies
Jan. 11, The Reichstag voted for reduction of old age pensions from 70 to 65 years
Jan. 12, Dr. Karl Liebknecht, extreme pacifist, expelled from the Social Democratic Party in Reichstag
Jan. 13, The Chancellor promised the Prussian Diet electoral reform at end of War
March 4–24, Fourth war loan opened 4½% Treasury Bills. Nearly 9 milliard marks subscribed
March 16, Resignation of Admiral von Tirpitz. Succeeded by Vice-Admiral Eduard von Capelle
March 24, Herr Haase and 18 pacifists expelled from Social Democratic Party formed new pacifist Social Democratic Labor Party
May 1, Liebknecht arrested in Berlin for denouncing the War
May 22, War Food Office created headed by Herr Henri von Batocki
May, Resignation of Dr. Delbrück, Minister of the Interior. Succeeded by Dr. Helfferich. Count von Roedern became Finance Minister
June 18, Death of General H. J. L. von Moltke
June 21, Taxation of war profits law enacted
June 28, Karl Liebknecht dismissed from army and sentenced to 30 months' penal servitude for attempted high treason
July 10, The *Deutschland* submarine arrived at Baltimore, U.S. of A.
July, War Clothing Office established
Aug. 3, Decree of Bundesrat nominated an imperial commission for period of economic transition

Aug. 16, The submarine *Deutschland* returned from voyage to the United States
Aug. 23, Karl Liebknecht on appeal sentenced by court martial to 49 months' penal servitude and expulsion from army
Aug. 29, General von Falkenhayn replaced as Chief of German General Staff by Field-Marshal von Hindenburg
Oct. 7, Announcement that £530,000,000 subscribed by fifth war loan of September
Oct. 28, Speech of Herr Dittmann against principle of "preventive arrest" in the Reichstag, supported by Socialists, Radicals, and National Liberals
Oct. 30, Lieutenant-General von Stein succeeded Lieutenant-General von Hohenborn as Minister of War
Nov. 5, Declaration of Emperors of Germany and Austria agreed to form new independent Kingdom of Poland
Nov. 20, Resignation of Herr von Jagow as Minister of Foreign Affairs
Nov. 21, Dr. Zimmermann appointed Minister of Foreign Affairs
Dec. 2, Auxiliary Service Act provided for compulsory civilian service of all males between ages of 17 and 60
Dec. 26, Reply to Note of President Wilson. *See* World War

1917

Jan. 11, Note as to responsibility for continuance of War. *See* World War
Jan. 11 and Nov. 27, Agreements with Turkey signed provided for abolition of capitulations
Jan. 17, Bundesrat adopted measure prohibiting importation of all commodities except by permission of the Imperial Chancellor
Feb. 1, The Chancellor announced to the Reichstag the Government policy of unrestricted submarine warfare
March 8, Death of Count Frederick von Zeppelin
April 1, Death of Emil A. von Behring, bacteriologist
April 16–23, 200,000 workers in factories in Berlin on strike in protest against reduction of bread ration
April 18, Death of General Baron Moritz Ferdinand von Bissing
May 15, Chancellor von Bethmann-Hollweg outlined his war aims to the Reichstag
June 6, Hunger strike begun on board the *Prinzregent Luitpold* at Kiel
June 27, Letter of General Hindenburg to the Kaiser on the decline of German morale
July 6, Reichstag reassembled
July 11, Declaration of the Emperor promising franchise reform in Prussia after the War promulgated the abolition of plural suffrage which permitted the wealthy class to rule elections
July 14, Resignation of von Bethmann-Hollweg, Chancellor since 1909. Succeeded by Dr. George Michaelis; Helfferich, Vice-Chancellor and Interior; Zimmermann, Foreign Affairs; Count Roedern, Finance; Solf, Colonies; von Capelle, Marine
July 19, Peace resolution adopted in Reichstag by majority composed of Center, Progressive People's Party, and Social Democrats. Erzberger called for a peace by agreement without annexations
July 20, 140 sailors marched off the *Pillau* at Kiel because furlongs restricted for which 40 condemned by court martial 16 to death later. All but 2 reprieved

Aug. 1, 49 firemen left the *Prinzregent Luitpold* in protest against removal of movie privileges
Aug. 3, Mutiny of First Fleet
Aug. 5, Richard von Kühlmann became Minister of Foreign Affairs on resignation of Zimmermann
Sept. 11, Ludendorff opposed peace resolution at meeting of the Crown Council
Sept. 19, The Chancellor replied to Peace Note of the Pope
Oct. 12, Resignation of Admiral von Capelle
Oct. 21, Imperial Economic Office established with Freiherr von Stein at head
Oct. 28, Resignation of Chancellor Michaelis
Oct. 30, Count Georg F. von Hertling of Bavaria appointed Imperial Chancellor
Nov. 9, Statement of Kühlmann that "Germany will never give back Alsace-Lorraine"
Nov. 12–16, Zeppelin flight in unsuccessful attempt to take hospital supplies to German East Africa established new world record for distance of 4,225 miles
Nov. 28, Agreement for armistice with Russia concluded
Dec. 1, War credit of 15,000,000,000 marks passed by Reichstag
Dec. 3, Armistice Convention with Russians at Brest-Litovsk begun

1918

Jan. 24, Reply of Chancellor von Hertling in Reichstag to Lloyd George and President Wilson's war aims addresses
Jan. 28–31, Strikes in Berlin, Hamburg, Munich, and other cities
Jan. 31, Martial law declared in Berlin and Hamburg
Feb. 1, Central Powers recognized the Ukraine Republic
Feb. 9, Peace Treaty with the Ukraine signed
Feb. 18, Armistice with Russia declared ended and hostilities resumed
Feb. 25, Military Convention with Poland signed
March 3, Brest-Litovsk Treaty with Russia signed. *See* World War
March 7, Treaty with Finland signed. *See* World War
March 15, Prince Lichnowski's Denkschrift entitled "My London Mission" written in Aug., 1916, first published in Berlin
April 3, German invasion of Finland. *See* World War
April 9, Count Mirbach appointed Ambassador to Russia
April 13, Resignation of Admiral von Capelle, von Behnke appointed Minister of Marine
April 19, Resolution of "Fatherland Party" announced Belgium and Flanders must be kept by Germany "politically, militarily and economically"
April 29, Germany established a military dictatorship in the Ukraine
May 12, Preliminary Agreement with Austria concluded for military and economic alliance
May 14, Proclamation of the Emperor declared Lithuania free and independent "allied to the German Empire"
June 18, Act increased the number of deputies to the Reichstag for larger municipal and rural constituencies and proportional representation provided for election of these additional deputies
June 24, Dr. von Kühlmann in speech in Reichstag declared attainment of peace by military victory of Germany impossible
July 5, Prussian Diet passed electoral reform Bill

July 6, Assassination of Count von Mirbach, Ambassador to Russia, in Moscow by bomb
July 9, Resignation of von Kühlmann, Minister of Foreign Affairs. Succeeded by Admiral von Hintze
July 12, Speech of Count von Hertling in Reichstag referred to Belgium as "a pawn for future negotiations"
——, Prussian Upper House expelled Prince Lichnowski because of his revelations of policy in the Denkschrift
Sept. 12, Speech of the Emperor to Krupp's workmen
Sept. 29, Resignation of Count von Hertling and Admiral von Hintze
——, General Ludendorff asked Foreign Office to arrange for an immediate armistice
Oct. 3, Prince Max of Baden appointed Chancellor, and Dr. W. S. Solf, Minister of Foreign Affairs, Philip Scheidemann, Secretary of State without Portfolio, and Mathias Erzberger succeeded von Payer as Vice-Chancellor
Oct. 4, Note of Chancellor to President Wilson asked him "to take steps for restoration of peace" and to notify belligerents of this request
Oct. 5, Prince Max announced peace Note in Reichstag
Oct. 8, Reply of President Wilson. *See* World War, Oct. 8, 14, 23
Oct. 9, Major General Scheuch appointed Minister of War
Oct. 12 and 20, German Government in reply to President Wilson accepted conditions
Oct. 15, Imperial order subjected military to civil authority
Oct. 16, Federal Council accepted amended Constitution restricting right of Emperor to declare war and make treaties without consent of Federal Council and Reichstag
Oct. 21, Dr. Karl Liebknecht released from prison became leader of the Radicals now called Spartacides
Oct. 23, President Wilson replied to German Note that he would submit peace conditions to Allied and Associated Powers
Oct. 25, Prussian Upper House passed the 3 electoral reform Bills
Oct. 27, Resignation of General Ludendorff. Succeeded by General Groener
——, Peace Note to President Wilson
Oct. 28, The Emperor signed decree accepting constitutional reform demanded by the Federal Council. Published, Nov. 3
——, Mutiny of part of German fleet at Kiel begun
Oct. 29, The Kaiser left Berlin for army headquarters
Nov. 2, Notice of Bavarian Government that in case of the abdication of the Kaiser the Wittelsbach dynasty would claim reversion to throne
Nov. 3, Allied Powers agreed to armistice with Germany
——, Mutiny of crews at Kiel and Wilhelmshaven became general revolt of workers and *landwehr*
——, Letter of the Kaiser to Prince Max accepted constitutional reform
Nov. 4, First Workers' Council founded by citizens at Stuttgart
Nov. 5, Note of President Wilson announced armistice accepted. *See* World War
——, Revolution in Bavaria
Nov. 6, German delegation left Berlin for armistice conference

Nov. 6, Diplomatic relations with Russia severed because of revolutionary propaganda of representatives

——, Strike of dock laborers at Hamburg and Lübeck which spread to other cities

Nov. 7, Red Republic proclaimed in Bavaria by Kurt Eisner

——, Majority of Socialists led by Scheideman demanded of Chancellor the abdication of the Kaiser and Crown Prince on threat of resignation

Nov. 8, Socialists resigned from Reichstag and threatened to call a general strike

——, Great popular assembly at Munich and in other cities demanded abdication of the Kaiser

——, Bavarian Diet passed decree deposing the Wittelsbach dynasty and proclaimed the Bavarian Republic. Kurt Eisner chosen Prime Minister

——, Resignation of the Chancellor. Not accepted

Nov. 9, German delegation received by Marshal Foch and given terms of armistice

——, Prince Max announced the abdication of the Kaiser and became Regent; F. Ebert, Chancellor

——, Revolution in Berlin. Workmens' and Soldiers' Council assumed control, proclaimed republic

——, Saxony proclaimed a Republic

——, Abdication of the Duke of Brunswick

Nov. 10, 3,000 delegates of Workmens' and Soldiers' Council elected Council of People's Commissars; (Cabinet) Ebert, Scheidemann, Landsberg, Haase, Dittmann, and Barth

——, The Kaiser fled to Holland

——, Abdication of the King of Württemberg

Nov. 11, Armistice of 30 days begun

——, Abdication of King of Saxony

——, Abdication of Grand Dukes of Oldenburg and Mecklenburg

Nov. 12, Abdication of Prince of Reuss

——, Declaration of rights of Council of People's Commissars (Rat der Volksbeauftragten) organized at Nov. 10 meeting of Workmen's and Soldiers' Council proclaimed abolition of censorship, amnesty for all political offenses, and eight-hour day for workers, and announced constituent assembly would be elected by universal suffrage. Economic Demobilization Bureau established

Nov. 13, Abdication of Grand Duke of Saxe-Weimar and Prince of Lippe-Detmold. Republics proclaimed in Württemberg and Hesse and Prussia

Nov. 14, The Bundesrat authorized to continue its functions

——, Abdication of the Prince of Waldeck-Pyrmont and Grand Dukes of Baden and Anhalt

Nov. 15, Central Labor Chamber founded on initiative of employers and employees to establish wages and working conditions. Eight-hour day established

Nov. 16, Abdication of the King of Bavaria

——, Dr. Schacht headed a group for formation of a Democratic Party

Nov. 17, Abdication of the Grand Duke of Mecklenburg-Schwerin, and Grand Duke of Saxe-Coburg

Nov. 21, The former Crown Prince interned in Mosterland, Holland

Nov. 22 and Dec. 1, Demobilization decrees established eight-hour day

Nov. 22, Abdication of the Grand Duke of Baden and Republic proclaimed

——, Republic of Bavaria proclaimed

——, Spartacists defeated in attempt to seize police headquarters at Berlin

Nov. 22, United Workmen's and Soldiers' Councils proclaimed union of Hamburg, Bremen, Ostfriesland, and Schleswig-Holstein as the North Sea Republic

Nov. 23, Joint meeting of Council of Commissars and Executive Committee of Workmens' and Soldiers' Council agreed on their respective functions

Nov. 25, Conference of State Governments met in Berlin. Agreed that a constituent assembly should meet and that until then the "Workers' and Soldiers' Councils are the representatives of the people's will" through their Executive Committee

Nov. 26, Manifesto of Spartacists called for revolution

Nov. 28, Formal Act of abdication signed by William II of his throne as King of Prussia

Nov. 30, Electoral law promulgated by decree of Commissars of the People provided for universal, direct, and secret suffrage on basis of principle of proportional representation for a constituent assembly

Dec. 1, Formal renunciation of rights of former Crown Prince Friedrich Wilhelm of Crown of Prussia and the Imperial Crown

Dec. 3, Revolt of sailors, followers of Liebknecht

Dec. 6, Clash between Government troops and a parade of Spartacists in Berlin. 180 casualties

Dec. 11, Resignation of Dr. Solf as Minister of Foreign Affairs. Succeeded by Brockdorf-Rantzau

Dec. 12, Decree established Republican Guard, Noske, Commander

Dec. 14, Armistice renewed on same terms

Dec. 15, Peoples Party issued program

Dec. 16, National Conference of Soldiers' and Workers' Councils of all States with 450 deputies met in Berlin

Dec. 17, Resignation of General Scheuch, Minister of War

Dec. 18, Conference adopted resolution to transfer legislative and executive power to the People's Commissaries headed by Ebert

Dec. 19, Conference declared Jan. 19 date for elections for constituent assembly and adjourned the following day

Dec. 20, Council of Workers' and Soldiers' the revolutionary Parliament adjourned giving full powers to the Ebert Cabinet

Dec. 23, Revolt of Spartacists and Marines in Berlin seized Chancery. Suppressed by troops the following day. 20 Spartacists and 9 sailors killed

——, Law gave Department of Labor right to fix conditions of work and wages

——, Collective agreements between employers and employees legalized by ordinance of the People's Commissars following private agreement of Nov. 15

Dec. 24, Nationalists issued program

Dec. 25, Spartacists seized office of Socialist newspaper the *Vorwärts*

Dec. 28, Resignation of Haase, Dittmann, and Barth from Council of Commissars followed by resignation of other 3 members to Central Committee. Replaced by Social Democrats including Noske and Wessel

1919

Jan. 4, Death of Count von Hertling (76)

Jan. 5, Revolt of Spartacists in Berlin led by Liebknecht, Rosa Luxemburg, and Eichorn began civil war of 10 days

Jan. 9, Martial law declared in Berlin. Spartacist leader Ledebour arrested

Jan. 10–Feb. 4, Radicals in possession of Government in Bremen

Jan. 12, Government troops recaptured Berlin police headquarters from the Spartacists

Jan. 15, Liebknecht and Luxemburg arrested and killed by soldiers on their way to prison because of alleged attempt to escape

Jan. 17, Armistice terms extended to Feb. 17

Jan. 18, Coal Commissioner appointed

Jan. 19, Election held for national constituent assembly gave Social Democrats 165 seats; Independent Social Democrats, 22; German National People's Party, 42 (conservative); German People's Party (National-Liberal), 21; Democrats (bourgeois), 75; German Monarchists, 34; Center or Clerical Party, 90; Minor, 7

Jan. 24, Hours for farm laborers regulated on basis of eight-hour day for 4 months, and 10 and 11 for next 4 month periods

Jan. 25, Draft Constitution submitted to Staatenau-schuss or Committee of States, provisional upper House appointed to replace the Bundesrat

Feb., Spartacists attempted to seize Wilhelmshaven on North Sea, street fighting and bombardment

Feb. 6, National Assembly met at Weimar, Thuringia

Feb. 10, Provisional Constitution adopted by National Assembly

Feb. 11, Friedrich Ebert elected President and Philipp Scheidemann, Chancellor with a coalition Cabinet, Brockdorff-Rantzau, Foreign Affairs; J. Bauer, Labor; G. Noske, Defense

——, Central Council of Workers' and Soldiers' Council formally deposited power in the National Assembly

Feb. 13, Mathias Erzberger appointed Minister without Portfolio

Feb. 14–19, General strike in the Ruhr district; Sparti-cists taking control of Bochum, Hamborn, and other places

Feb. 16, Armistice renewed

Feb. 19, Reactionary revolt in Munich, Bavaria

Feb. 21, Kurt Eisner, Socialist Premier of Bavaria, assassinated by Count Arco Valley as part of plot to restore monarchy

Feb. 25, Spartacist revolt in Mannheim

Feb. 27, General strike begun in chief towns of Thu-ringia and Saxony

March 3–6, General strike in Berlin. Hundreds killed in street fighting. Spartacists seized police head-quarters which were recovered by troops

March 8, Agreement to turn over ships for transpor-tation of American and Australian soldiers, the ships on return voyage to carry cargoes of food for Ger-many

March 16, Food terms formally accepted providing for 300,000 tons of cereals and 70,000 tons of fats per month and merchant marine handed over to Allies

March 18, Ordinance regulated hours of salaried em-ployees

March 21, New Constitution of Baden promulgated abolished all privileges of birth, religion, and caste and granted universal suffrage to men and women

March 23, Socialization of industry Act passed

March 25, Food ship docked in Hamburg with 6,627 tons of white flour

April 2, Strike of 30,000 mechanics and clerks in metal industry, Berlin

April 3, Strike begun in Krupp works at Essen

April 4, New revolution in Bavaria proclaimed a Soviet Republic in Munich, April 6

April 8, Second Congress of all the Work Councils met

April 9, Strike of bank employees in Berlin

April 9–17, Revolt in Brunswick

April 14, Waldeck adopted a Constitution

April 16, General strike in Bremen

April 21, President Ebert sent troops to Munich under Minister of War Noske to put down revolt

——, Allied terms accepted by Germany

May 1, Munich recaptured by Government troops from Spartacists

——, German delegation to Peace Conference at Ver-sailles presented credentials

May 2, Resignation of Field-Marshal von Hindenburg as commander-in-chief of the army to be effective on conclusion of peace

May 6, Mandates for German colonies under League of Nations announced by Council of Three at Peace Conference

May 7, Draft Treaty of Peace presented to German delegation

May 8, Germany protested against peace terms

May 10, 11, 13, and 16, German Notes protesting terms of Treaty of Peace

May 12, National Assembly met to discuss peace terms

May 20, Brockdorff-Rantzau asked for extension of time for consideration of terms which was granted to May 29 by Council of Four

——, Statement of Cabinet refused to sign peace terms

May 29, German counter-proposals to Versailles Treaty presented

June 1, Rhineland Republic proclaimed with provi-sional Government headed by Dr. Dorton at Wies-baden, Herr von Winterstein named as President

June 3, German Armistice Commission protested to Peace Conference against French support of Rhine-land Republic

June 8, Government troops ejected heads of Rhineland Republic. Movement not supported by Rhenish people

June 16, Treaty of Peace and final reply of Allies to German counter proposals presented to German delegation

June 17, Republic of Oldenberg adopted a Constitution

June 20, Scheidemann Ministry refused to sign the Peace Treaty and resigned

June 21, German crews at Scapa Flow scuttled their fleet by order of Admiral Reuter

——, Gustav Bauer formed coalition Cabinet, Count von Brockdorff-Rantzau, Minister of Foreign Af-fairs; M. Erzeberger, Vice-Chancellor and Minister of Finance; Noske, Defense

June 22, National Assembly at Weimar voted 237 to 138 conditional acceptance of Treaty omitting Articles as to trial of war criminals and war guilt

June 23, Soldiers in Berlin burned French flags cap-tured in Franco-Prussian War

——, Unconditional acceptance of Treaty sent

June 27, Strike of railroad workers in Berlin

June 28, Treaty of Versailles signed by Germany. According to the Treaty of Versailles (June 28, 1919) Germany has agreed to the following territorial arrangements:—(1) Alsace-Lorraine ceded to France, (2) the greater part of the Provinces of West Prussia and Posen ceded to Poland, (3) a part of Eastern Silesia and of East Prussia likewise to Poland, (4) a portion of Upper Silesia to Czechoslovakia, (5) Memel to Lithuania, (6) Danzig, a Free State under the protection of the League of Nations, (7) Eupen and Malmédy to Belgium, (8) a part of Schleswig to Denmark

Provision was made in the Treaty to settle the ultimate fate of the following areas by plebiscite:— (1) The Saar Basin (after 15 years), (2) Schleswig (in two zones), (3) districts in Southern East Prussia, in West Prussia, and in Upper Silesia. Results of the plebiscites:—Schleswig (March, 1920), northern zone for Denmark, southern zone for Germany; East and West Prussia (July, 1920) for Germany; Upper Silesia (March, 1921) for Germany. Despite the decision in Upper Silesia, 1,241 square miles, with a population of 892,547, were transferred to Poland; colonies in Africa given up, and territory in China. *See also* Peace Conference

July 9, Peace Treaty ratified by National Assembly by vote of 208 to 115, 99 deputies not voting

July 10, Peace Treaty ratified by President Ebert

July 12, Five-year blockade lifted by Allies

July 18, Free State of Anhalt adopted a Constitution

July 31, New Constitution adopted and became effective Aug. 11 by executive order

——, Assembly prorogued later to assemble as provisional Reichstag

Aug. 8, Death of Professor Ernest Haeckel, scientist

——, Food riots at Chemnitz, Saxony. 50 persons killed

Aug. 11, President Ebert signed the Constitution which became immediately effective

Aug. 14, New Constitution of Bavaria adopted

Aug. 16, Bill establishing Labor Councils passed the Assembly

——, General von der Goltz recalled by Government from Latvia as requested by Allies in April. *See* p. 345

Aug. 18, Polish rising against Germans in Upper Silesia

Aug. 21, President Ebert inaugurated as President under new Constitution

Aug. 29, Rioting at Ludwigshafen (Rhineland Republic)

Sept. 2, German Government informed by Supreme Council that Article 61 of the Constitution providing for representation of Austria in Reichstag in conflict with Peace Treaty Article 80, Section 6, binding Germany to respect strictly the independence of Austria

Sept. 22, Germany nullified clause of Constitution in conflict with Treaty of Versailles by signing Protocol

Sept. 25, Constitution of Württemberg adopted

Sept. 26, Maternity Benefit Act passed

Oct. 6, Proclamation of the Government ordered immediate evacuation of Baltic Provinces by General von der Goltz

Oct. 8, Census of cities gave Berlin population of 3,803,770; Hamburg, 985,779; Cologne, 633,904; Munich, 630,711; Leipzig, 604,380; Dresden, 587,748

——, Hugo Haase fatally shot by Austrian

Oct. 23, Provisional Treaty with Poland signed

Nov. 1, Government declared every soldier in Baltic region must cross German frontier by the 11th on penalty of loss of citizenship ending occupation of Latvia

Nov. 4–15, All railroad passenger transportation suspended to relieve coal shortage

Nov. 7, Death of Hugo Haase, Socialist leader

Nov. 17, "Emergency Contribution" Act passed amounted to a partial confiscation of wealth, became law Dec. 1

Nov. 23 and Dec. 17, Decrees regulated hours of labor for industrial workers

Nov. 30, The Free State of Coburg voted by large majority to join with Bavaria

Dec. 18, The Supreme Court given jurisdiction over the war criminals indicted by the Allies in the Treaty of Versailles

Dec. 20, New Constitution adopted by Hesse

Dec. 24, Decision of 7 States of Thuringia to unite into one State

——, Sales tax law enacted

1920

Jan. 10, Treaty of Versailles came into effect with exchange of ratifications

Jan. 11, Inter-Allied Commission took over Rhineland establishing headquarters at Coblenz

Jan. 13, Demonstration of Communists before Reichstag building. Martial law proclaimed

Jan. 25, Proposal of Germany that war criminals be tried in Germany instead of before an international tribunal. Accepted by Supreme Council, Feb. 13

Jan. 26, Mark at 5.62 centimes

Feb. 3, List of persons accused of violation of laws of war under Treaty of Versailles handed to Germany

Feb. 4, Workers' Council Act placing workmen's councils under State control signed by the President

Feb. 10, Plebiscite in Schleswig gave decision in favor of union of northern zone with Denmark

Feb. 12, Regulations promulgated for engagement and dismissal of workers and salaried employees

——, Allied Commission of Control with 15,000 French troops arrived in Upper Silesia. Established at Oppeln

Feb. 24, Resignation of Minister of Finance Erzeberger under charges of Helfferich

Feb. 26, Governing Commission appointed by League of Nations under Treaty of Versailles officially assumed control over Saar Basin

March 11, Bavarian Diet adopted Bill for union of Coburg with Bavaria

——, Libel trial of Erzeberger ended. Helfferich sentenced to pay fine of 300 marks

March 13–15, Monarchical counter-revolution, the "Kapp Putsch" led by Dr. von Kapp and General von Luttwitz seized principal buildings in Berlin and set up a Government, Dr. von Kapp proclaimed Chancellor

March 14, Plebiscite in southern zone of Schleswig decided in favor of union with Germany

March 15, President Ebert established the Government at Stuttgart

March 17, Von Kapp Government forced to evacuate Berlin by general strike of trade unions and lack of support of people

——, Germany requested permission of Allies to send troops into the Ruhr district to suppress revolt

March 18, Meeting of National Assembly at Stuttgart

March 19, Spartacist (Bolshevik) risings all over Germany except in West Prussia, Bavaria, Württemberg and Leipzig

March 21, Return of Government to Berlin

March 23, Resignation of Noske and Erzberger from the Cabinet

March 26, Resignation of Bauer Cabinet. Succeeded by Dr. Hermann Müller as Chancellor

March 28, Government troops defeated Ruhr rebels near Wesel

March 31, Treaty of commerce and navigation with Sweden signed

——, All volunteer corps of army disbanded to meet demands of Allies

April 1, Transfer of all German State railroads to the central Government

——, Unified tax on income came into force

April 3, German troops entered Ruhr district to put down Sparticist revolt

April 6, French troops occupied Frankfurt and the following day Homburg and other Ruhr towns and declared martial law claiming Treaty violated by German troop advance

April 18, Note of Allied Premiers at San Remo Conference warned Germany against violations of Treaty, insisted on disarmament, and invited Germany to send representatives to an economic conference

April 19, Agreement with Russia as to repatriation of prisoners signed at Berlin

April 26, Note of Allied Premiers asked Germany to submit proposals as to reparations

April 27, New electoral law passed adopted system of proportional representation

April 28, Law passed made 4 years' course of instruction in "Foundation School" (Grundschule) compulsory

April 30, Union of Coburg with Bavaria recognized by law

——, Union of 8 small central States into one State of "Great Thuringia" recognized

May 15, Constitution adopted by Bremen

May 17, French troops withdrawn from towns of Ruhr district occupied April 6

——, Mecklenburg-Schwerin adopted a Constitution

May 20, First National Assembly under the Republic adjourned

May 29, Announcement of France that colored troops of army of occupation would be withdrawn

May 31, Protocol signed with Allied Powers as to delivery of dye stuffs

June 1, Provisional commercial Agreement with Hungary signed

June 6, General election for Reichstag gave Majority Socialists 110 seats; Independent Socialists, 80; Centrists, 67; German Nationalists, 65; German People's Party, 61; Democrats, 45; Christian Federationists, 21; Guelphists, 5; Communists, 2; and Bavarian Peasants' Party, 4

June 8, Resignation of Müller Ministry

June 25, Reichstag convened. New Ministry formed by Konstantine Fehrenbach, leader of Catholic Party

June 30, Germany declared by Reparation Commission to be in default as to coal deliveries

July 5, Treaty with Denmark signed regarding transfer of part of Schleswig to Denmark

July 5–16, German representatives attended the Spa Conference

July 9, Protocol as to disarmament signed at Spa Conference

July 11, Plebiscite in Allenstein-Marienwerder districts under Treaty of Versailles gave vote in favor of union with Germany by large majorities as against Poland

July 15, Peace Protocol with Latvia signed

July 16, Protocol as to coal deliveries signed by Germany at Spa Conference

July 17, Death of Prince Joaquim, youngest son of ex-Kaiser

July 26, Award as to districts of East Prussia and West Prussia to Germany in part

July 31, Bill passed by Reichstag abolished compulsory military service

Aug. 1, Agreement with Poland signed providing for substitution of material by Germany for that taken from Poland during World War

Aug. 2, General amnesty granted to persons involved in "Kapp Putsch" except leaders

Aug. 12, and Jan. 27, 1922, Decision of Conference of Ambassadors that under Article 97 of the Treaty of Versailles 5 villages east of the Vistula be given to Poland

Sept. 1, Commercial and financial Agreement with Austria signed

——, Death of William Wundt, psychologist

Sept. 20, Decision of League of Nations gave Belgium Eupen and Malmédy and Prussian Moresnet

Oct. 26, New Constitution adopted by Saxony

Nov. 2, Agreement with Poland regarding restitution of German ships

Nov. 6–10, Strike of electricians in Berlin ended by ordinance of President Ebert

Nov. 6 and 26, Financial and legal Agreements with Hungary signed

Nov. 9, Danzig proclaimed as a free city under protection of the League of Nations according to decision of Conference of Ambassadors of Oct. 27

Nov. 23, Protocol as to exchange of prisoners with Poland signed

Nov. 30, New Constitution of Prussia adopted

Dec. 17, Agreement as to frontiers of Saar Basin concluded by exchange of Notes with the Allied Powers

——, Convention with Denmark, indemnity regarding Schleswig

Dec. 21, Lippe adopted Constitution

Dec. 26, Announcement of Government that the army had been reduced to 100,000 as required by the Treaty of Versailles

Dec. 30, Law organized army on basis of 100,000

1921

Jan. 1, Death of Theobald von Bethmann-Hollweg, former Chancellor (64)

Jan. 7, Constitution adopted by State and Free City of Hamburg

Jan 21, Protocol signed revised Mannheim Convention of 1868 governing navigation of the Rhine

Jan. 25, Commercial Agreement with the Netherlands signed

Jan. 29, Reparation terms communicated to German delegation at Paris Conference. *See* p. 564

Feb. 3, Convention with Czechoslovakia transferred to Czechoslovakia territory in Silesia in vicinity of Hultschin

Feb. 12 and May 4, Germany protested to League of Nations regarding presence of French troops in the Saar

Feb. 19, Provisional Commercial Agreement with Bulgaria signed

March 4, Bill adopted in Reichstag provided for trial of war criminals

March 8, Allied troops occupied Dusseldorf, Duisburg, and Ruhrort because of alleged default of Germany in payment of advance of 20,000,000,000 gold marks on account as provided by Treaty of Versailles. *See also* p. 564

March 11, Constitution adopted by Thuringia

March 13, Arrest of Communists caused general strike in Halle region which was ended by proclamation of state of siege by President Ebert

March 20, Plebiscite in Upper Silesia gave a majority vote for union with Germany against Poland

March 24, Germany declared in default by Reparation Commission

April 9, Allied customs barrier drawn around Rhineland

April 11, Death of former Empress Augusta Victoria at Castle of Doorn, Holland

April 20, Germany asked mediation of the United States on reparations; refused

April 27, Reparation Commission established German liability at 132 billion gold marks. *See* p. 564

April 28, Number of members of Reichsrat settled at 66

April 30, Ultimatum to Germany of Allied Council in London

May 2–3, Polish insurrection in Upper Silesia led by Korfanty

May 4, Fehrenbach Ministry resigned

May 6, Trade Agreement with Russia signed

May 10, Dr. Julius Wirth formed coalition Cabinet

——, The Reichstag voted 221 to 175 to submit to Allied terms

May 11, Germany accepted unconditionally Allied schedule of reparations

May 20, Treaty of amity and commerce with China signed

May 21, Counter-offensive against the Poles in Upper Silesia begun

May 23–July 16, Trial of 12 "war criminals" at Leipzig. 6 persons convicted

May 28, Form of armistice with Korfanty signed by General Hoefer

June 3, Protocol signed with Saar Governing Commission regarding application of provisions of the Treaty of Versailles

June 7, Anglo-German Arbitral Tribunal held first session in London

July 1, Germany delivered treasury bonds Series A, 12,000,000,000 gold marks as due

July 2, Resolution of Congress of the United States ended state of war with Germany

July 9, Law defined the National Court of the Republic created by Constitution

Aug. 12, Question of rival claims of Germany and Poland in Upper Silesia turned over to League of Nations

Aug. 19–20, Poles in conflict with German Security Police in Upper Silesia

Aug. 25, Treaty of peace with the United States signed

——, Agreement with France as to deliveries of coal from Saar mines

Aug. 26, Assassination of Matthias Erzeberger by ex-officers of the "Kapp Putsch," Schulz and Tillessen, who escaped to Hungary

Aug. 28, Provisional commercial Agreement with Italy signed

Aug. 31, Payment of one billion gold marks reparations payment by Germany

——, Death of Field-Marshal Karl von Bülow

Sept. 4, Commercial Agreement with Latvia signed

Sept. 12, Resignation of Dr. von Kahr, reactionary Premier of Bavaria, and his chief of police

Sept. 17, Peace Treaty with the United States ratified by the Reichsrat

Sept. 21, Explosion at synthetic nitrate factory at Oppau practically destroyed the town and killed 800 persons and wounded about 2,000

Sept. 22, Count Hugo Lerchenfeld became Prime Minister in Bavaria and agreement followed with central Government by which state of siege of Bavaria raised

Sept. 27, Death of Engelbert Humperdinck, composer

Sept. 29, Allied Occupation of Dusseldorf, Duisburg, and Ruhrort ended after first reparation payment by Germany

Sept. 30, Peace Treaty with the United States ratified by the Reichstag

Oct. 1, Customs barrier around Rhineland abolished with ending of occupation

Oct. 2, Death of William, Duke of Württemberg, former King William II

Oct. 6, Loucheur-Rathenau Agreement signed at Wiesbaden between France and Germany providing for direct supply of deliveries in kind to France

——, Warrants issued for arrest of Dr. Kapp, Colonel Bauer, Major Pabst, General von Luttwitz, and other leaders of the "Kapp Putsch"

Oct. 12, Award of League of Nations gave Poland districts of Pless, Rybnik, Kattowitz, and Konigshütte in Upper Silesia. Confirmed by Conference of Ambassadors Oct. 20. Germany accepted Oct. 26

Oct. 17, Death of ex-King Ludwig of Bavaria

Oct. 21, Increase of pay of railroad workers of 15 to 20% granted

Oct. 22, Chancellor Wirth and his cabinet resigned

Oct. 26, Dr. Wirth reorganized Cabinet with G. Bauer, Vice-Chancellor and Treasury

Oct. 28, Delivery of treasury bonds Series B and C. *See* Reparations

Dec. 3, Arbitration and Conciliation Treaty with Switzerland signed

Dec. 5, Commercial Treaty with Yugoslavia signed

Dec. 6, Commercial Agreement with Portugal signed

Dec. 7, Von Jagow sentenced to 5 years' imprisonment

Dec. 10, Public statement of Chancellor Wirth denied charges of France that Germany had not disarmed

Dec. 14, German Government notified Reparation Commission that it was not able to pay instalments due Jan. 15 and Feb. 15, 1922

1922

Jan. 6, New Constitution adopted by Brunswick

Jan. 21, Strike of coal miners in the Ruhr

Jan. 26, Strike of 30,000 textile workers at Muenchen-Gladbach won 25% increase in wages

Feb. 2–8, Strike of railroad workers for increase of wages and better conditions

Feb. 5, Strike of public utility employees in Berlin stopped light, water, and trolley service

Feb. 7, Draft Agreement concluded with Reparation Commission for deliveries in kind

Feb. 24, Schaumburg-Lippe adopted Constitution

March 3, National rent law passed

March 9, Death of General von Falkenhayn

March 15, Note from Conference of Ambassadors regarding the organization of police (Sicherheitpolizei)

——, The Ruppel-Gillet Agreement signed in Berlin with France as to deliveries in kind

March 21, Notes of Reparation Commission to Germany granted conditional partial moratorium

March 25, Saar Commission published ordinance outlining a Constitution

April 1, Sales tax amended

April 8, Death of General Erich von Falkenhayn

——, Chancellor Wirth introduced the forced loan. Corporation tax amended

April 12, Agreement with Poland signed as to transfer of jurisdiction in Upper Silesia districts

April 16, Treaty of Rapallo signed with Soviet Russia established most favored nation commercial relations and mutual economic assistance. Both waived indemnities arising from the War

April 21, Germany paid 18 billion gold marks reparation

May 5, Allied Air Commission of Control disbanded

May 15, Commercial Treaty with Poland signed and Convention as to Upper Silesia

May 16, Germany paid 18 billion gold marks reparation

May 31, Note to Germany granted moratorium in reparation payments for 1922

June 2, Bemelmans-Cuntze Agreement signed as to deliveries in kind by Germany

June 12, Death of Dr. Wolfgang Kapp

June 15, Agreement signed with Poland and Inter-Allied Commission as to transfer of jurisdiction in Upper Silesia

——, Germany paid 50 million gold marks reparation

June 24, Assassination of Walter Rathenau, Minister of Foreign Affairs, by reactionary Monarchists, H. Fischer and Edwin Kern who July 18 committed suicide to escape capture by police

June 30, Decree made it a criminal offense to belong to or support monarchist organizations. Death penalty provided

July 3, Attempt at assassination of Maximilian Harden

July 9, "Government Law relating to Juvenile Welfare" passed included regulations for all official means for promotion of welfare of youth including rearing of children, assistance in education and Juvenile Courts, and coöperation of the authorities in regard to trusteeships, guardianships, &c.

July 12, Formal request of Germany for 2½ half years moratorium on reparation cash payments to Reparation Commission

July 15, Germany paid installment due on this date of reparations

July 18, Defense of the Republic Bill passed third reading in Reichstag

Aug. 4, German Government asked for moratorium of private debts as well as reparation payments

Aug. 10, Agreement with the United States signed provided for Mixed Claims Commission

Aug. 12, Expulsion of Germans from Alsace-Lorraine begun

——, Collapse of stock market. The mark fell to 3,330 to the English pound

Aug. 18, 5,575; Aug. 23, 8,750; Aug. 24, 11,000; Aug. 25, 9,000

Aug. 31, Reparation Commission granted Germany 6 months moratorium

Sept. 5, Lubersac-Stinnes Agreement with France signed by which building materials to be furnished by Germany to value of 13 billion marks to be charged to reparation account

Sept. 24, Union of German Independent Socialists and Majority Socialists to form new party

Sept. 25, Treasury Bills for Belgium paid to Reparation Commission

Oct. 3, Trial of 13 accomplices of the murderers of Rathenau begun at Supreme Court in Leipzig

Oct. 10, Mark at 13,750 to the English pound

Oct. 24, Reichstag voted to extend term of office of President Ebert to June 30, 1925

Oct. 31, Mark 20,800 to the English pound

——, Mark 20,500 to the English pound

Nov. 2, Foreign economic experts met in Berlin to evolve scheme for stabilization of the mark

Nov. 5, Ex-Emperor William married Princess Hermine of Schonaich-Carolath

Nov. 8, Mark stood at 9,000 to the dollar

Nov. 10, Workmen's Insurance and Code law amended to take effect Jan. 1, 1923

Nov. 14, Resignation of Wirth Ministry on refusal of Socialists to join coalition

——, Request of Germany for total moratorium for 3 or 4 years to Reparation Commission

Nov. 16, Wilhelm Cuno appointed Chancellor; Dr. Carl Heinze, Vice-Chancellor and Justice; von Rosenberg, Foreign Affairs; Dr. Hermes, Finance

Nov. 28–Dec. 18, Strike in the Baden aniline works

Dec. 20, Commercial Treaty with Spain of Feb. 12, 1899, extended

Dec. 26, Reparation Commission declared Germany in voluntary default on wood deliveries

1923

Jan. 3, Food riots in Berlin when 14 municipal markets closed because of strike against increased price of stalls and booths

Jan. 9, Reparation Commission declared Germany in default on deliveries of coal

Jan. 10, American troops withdrawn from Coblenz

Jan. 11, Franco-Belgian troops occupied the Ruhr Valley acting, they stated, under provision of the Treaty of Versailles which authorized the Allied Governments to take measures deemed necessary in case of voluntary default by Germany

——, Reich Coal Commission notified all mines in Ruhr that no payments would be made for transport of coal to France

——, Protest of Germany to the Government of the United States and Great Britain against French and Belgian invasion

Jan. 12, 13, Note stated German reparation deliveries in kind to France and Belgium would be suspended during occupation

Jan. 15 and 16, Riots at Bochum and Essen. French troops fired on crowds

Jan. 16, 26, Reparation Commission declared Germany in voluntary default in deliveries of coal, cattle, and timber

Jan. 20, Arrest of 6 coal magnates including Fritz Thyssen for refusal to deliver coal to France followed by strike

Jan. 24, Court martial at Mainz fined coal magnates 307,206 francs

——, Last American soldiers left the Rhineland

Jan. 30, Strike of railroad workers in occupied territory. Railroads taken over by French and Belgian troops

Feb. 10, Death of Professor Wilhelm Konrad von Röntgen, discoverer of X-ray

Feb. 13, Wesel and Emmerich occupied

Feb. 25, Territory between bridgeheads of Cologne, Coblenz, and Mainz occupied

March 10, At Buer French troops fired on crowd protesting against arrest of 2 Germans, killing 8 persons

March 16, Government issued ordinance in support of passive resistance in the Ruhr also March 20, April 17, and Aug. 11

March 31, French soldiers requisitioning automobiles at Krupps fired on crowd of workmen killing 13 and wounding 30

April 12, Large purchase of the Stinnes interests of securities believed to have started decline of the currency as reported by commission of investigation

April 28, Commercial Agreement with Poland signed

May 2 and June 7, Germany made new proposals for settlement of reparations. *See* p. 567

May 4–7, Trial by court martial of directors of Krupps on charge of obstructionist activities against army of occupation

May 8, Baron Krupp sentenced to 15 years imprisonment and fine of 100 million marks

May 11, Ferdinand Schulz, glider, established new world duration record for gliders of 8 hours and 40 minutes of flight in which he maintained an average altitude of 150 feet

May 24, Constitution adopted by Mecklenburg-Strelitz

May 29, Budget adopted by Council of the Empire showed deficit of 121,400 million marks

May 31, Mark stood at 8,000 to the dollar

June 2, Most favored nation commercial Treaty with Lithuania signed

June 3, Commercial Treaty with the Netherlands

June 4, Frontier Traffic Agreement with Poland signed

June 18, Employees of the Government demanded payment on dollar basis

July 30, The paper mark passed million to the dollar point

July 31, German press published decree respecting requisition of foreign bills of exchange and foreign securities

Aug. 11, Announcement of Government that all reparation deliveries in kind would stop. Inter-Allied Commission ordered seizure of mines in occupied area

Aug. 12, Resignation of Chancellor Cuno and Cabinet

Aug. 13, Dr. Gustav Stresemann, leader of the German People's Party, appointed Chancellor, formed coalition Cabinet of United Socialist, Clerical, People's, and Democratic parties, von Bergen, Clerical, Foreign Affairs; Sollmann, Socialist, Interior; Fuchs, Clerical, Occupied Areas; Hilferding, Socialist, Finance; Hans von Raumer, People's Party, Economics; Schmidt, Reconstruction and Vice-Chancellor, Socialist; Labor, Braun, Clerical; Radbruch, Socialist, Justice; Hans Luther, Democrat, Food Controller

Aug. 14, Gold-backed mark decreed

Aug. 15, Subscriptions to a gold loan opened

Aug. 24, Decision of Imperial Bank published instituted credits at a fixed value with design of ending speculation and profiteering in the depreciation of the mark

Aug. 25, Decree signed by President provided for raising of fund of from 300 to 500 million gold marks in cash by forcible levy if not raised by subscription

Sept. 2, Monarchist review at Nuremberg, Bavaria, before Field-Marshal Ludendorff. Many followers of Hitler marched in parade

——, Proposal that a guarantee be arranged for permanency of western frontiers

Sept. 4, Imperial Bank sold foreign bills of exchange in attempt to check the depreciation of the mark

Sept. 7, Address of Chancellor Stresemann declared Germany "wished to create the gold mark"

Sept. 15, Reichsbank raised rate of discount from 30% adopted Aug. 2, to 90%

Sept. 23, Meetings held in Wiesbaden, Bochum, and Essen declared in favor of a Rhenish-Westphalian neutral and independent republic

Sept. 25, Germany gave treasury bills due Belgium to Reparation Commission. *See also* p. 567

Sept. 26, President Ebert issued decree declaring passive resistance in the Ruhr ended canceling regulation and orders issued in its support

——, Dr. Gustav von Kahr appointed General State Commissioner in Bavaria with powers of a dictator and Cabinet Government suspended

——, A modified form of martial law declared for Germany and an officer of the national army assigned to coöperate with Dr. von Kahr at Munich in suppression of monarchist "drive"

Sept. 28, Order of Jan. 12 suspending deliveries to France and Belgium withdrawn

Oct. 3, Resignation of Stresemann Ministry

Oct. 5, Proposal of Herr Stinnes and other large industrialists to General Degoutte at Dusseldorf of plan for future coöperation and reparations payment

Oct. 6, Dr. Stresemann recalled reorganized Cabinet taking himself the portfolio of Foreign Affairs and replacing Hilferding as Finance Minister by Dr. Hans Luther

Oct. 10, Communist Government formed in Dresden

Oct. 11, The mark 19,000,000,000 to the pound sterling

Oct. 13, Constitutional amendment conferring extraordinary powers on Stresemann Government passed by Reichstag by vote of 316 to 24, 7 not voting. Bavarians and Communists in opposition

Oct. 15, Stresemann issued Renten Bank decree

Oct. 16, Estimated that 1,500,000 workers without employment and between 4 to 5 million on part time. Prices of food high, a loaf of bread weighing 1,200 grams 480,000,000 marks, a pound of potatoes 50,000,000, and a pound of margarine 900,000,000

Oct. 21 and 25, Rhenish Republic proclaimed in Aix-la-Chapelle (Aachen). Separatists supported by Belgian troops

Oct. 23, Separatists seized Wiesbaden

Oct. 24, Note of Government to Reparation Commission asked for examination of Germany's resources and capacity to pay

Oct. 26, Central Government ordered the Saxon Government at Dresden to resign

Oct. 27, Separatists set up provisional Government at Coblenz

Oct. 27–29, Central Government called on Government of Saxony to resign because of acts of Communist Ministers

Oct. 30, Law enacted provided that labor arbitration decisions should be binding

Oct. 31, Zeigner Ministry in Saxony replaced by moderate Socialist Ministry

Nov. 2, Decree terminated licenses of cartels and other combinations to control trade. A cartel court created with presiding justice appointed by the President of the Reich, and the Minister of Economics charged with supervision of all contracts and resolutions regulating the production, distribution, and sale of commodities. Went into effect Nov. 20

——, Belgian High Commissioner compelled Separatists to evacuate Aix-la-Chapelle (Aachen)

Nov. 5, Appeal signed by President Ebert and Dr. Stresemann called for unity in view of the danger of civil war

Nov. 8, Reactionary leaders in revolt against the Central Government. Adolf Hitler and General Ludendorff seized the Government at Munich, Bavaria (Beer Hall Putsch)

Nov. 9, Bavarian nationalist revolt put down by General von Lossow in command of the Reichswehr and Dr. von Kahr, Civil Commissioner. General Ludendorff captured

Nov. 11, Revolt ended with the arrest of Adolf Hitler

Nov. 12, Announcement Government of the Palatinate by Heintz Bleu and Otto Meyer

Nov. 13, The ex-Crown Prince William arrived at Oels, Silesia, from exile in Holland

Nov. 15, Renten Bank opened. Mark at 2½ billion to the dollar

Nov. 16, Announcement of the Chancellor of abandonment of policy of aiding the population in the Ruhr and Rhineland

Nov. 23, Agreement of Stinnes, Thyssen, and other industrial leaders in the Ruhr for Allied control of mines

——, Fall of Stresemann Ministry

Nov. 30, Dr. Wilhelm Marx, leader of the Center Party, appointed Chancellor, formed Cabinet of Center, German People's Party, Democrats, and Bavarian People's Party, Dr. Jarres, Vice-Chancellor and Minister of the Interior; Dr. Gustav Stresemann, Foreign Affairs; Dr. Otto Gessler, Defense; Heinrich Brauns, Labor; Dr. Hans Luther, Finance; Dr. Anton Hoefle, Posts and Telegraphs and Occupied Regions; Rudolph Oeser, Transport; Count Kanitz, Food Control; A. D. Hamm, Public Economy; Dr. Emminger, Justice

Dec. 1, Agreement for working of railroads in occupied territory signed with French and Belgians

Dec. 8, The Reichstag granted the Chancellor plenary powers until Feb. 15, 1924

——, Treaty of friendship, commerce, and consular rights with the United States signed

Dec. 15, New boundary with Belgium proclaimed by the Government

Dec. 22, Agreement as to resumption of deliveries in kind concluded with French and Belgian Governments

——, Maximum rent law limiting returns from rented property repealed to take effect Jan. 1

1924

Jan. 1, Labor courts established under Act of Oct. 30, 1923

Jan. 2, Lockout of 150,000 metal workers in Berlin

Jan. 9, Herr Heinz, "President of the Autonomous Government of the Palatinate" assassinated at Speyer

Jan. 10, Strike for shorter hours in the Ruhr and Rhineland

Jan. 31, Public buildings at Wiesbaden evacuated by Separatists

Feb. 13, "Government regulations regarding public assistance"

Feb. 26, Trial of Adolf Hitler, General Ludendorff, and 8 others begun; leaders of revolt of Nov., 1923

Feb. 28, State of siege suspended except in Bavaria

March 3, Treaty of friendship with Turkey signed provided for resuming of diplomatic relations and of commercial and consular relations

——, Raid of police on offices of Soviet Trade Delegation in Berlin

March 6, Treaty with Nicaragua extended Commercial Treaty of 1896

March 13, Reichstag dissolved

March 19, Law established the Gold Discount Bank

March 28, Lockout of 50,000 chemical workers

April 1, Hitler and Ludendorff, Dr. Weber and Colonel Kriebel each fined 200 marks and sentenced to terms of imprisonment

April 7, Gold Discount Bank actually established

April 9, Dawes Plan adopted for reparations. *See* p. 568

April 10, Death of Hugo Stinnes, industrialist (54)

April 15, New Ruhr Agreement as to reparation deliveries of coal and coke signed

April 23, Death of Karl Helferrich, economist

May 4, Elections a victory for extreme Right and Left at expense of middle parties supporting the Republic. German National People's Party gained 96 seats, the Communists 62

May 19, Liquor traffic Treaty with the United States signed

May 26, Cabinet resigned but reorganized by Marx 2 days later

June 1, Commercial Agreement with Lithuania signed

June 30, Demand of Allies for investigation of military conditions and reorganization of police force accepted

July 3, Provisional commercial Agreement with Greece signed

July 12, Commercial Agreement with Belgium signed

July 25, Commercial Treaty with Spain signed

July 29, Protocol and Agreement with Russia signed, Germany offering compensation for raid of March 3 and Soviet promising non-interference with domestic affairs of Germany

Aug. 18, Evacuation of French troops from the Ruhr begun and Belgian Aug. 22

Aug. 28, Reichstag passed law putting the Dawes Plan into effect

Aug. 29, Arbitration and Conciliation Agreement with Sweden signed

Aug. 30, Currency law to come into force Oct. 11 established currency on gold basis. Privileges of the Reichsbank renewed for 50 years

——, Railroad law passed in accordance with Dawes Plan

——, Germany signed Protocol at London Conference accepting Dawes Plan

Sept. 1, Germany made first payment of reparations under the Dawes Plan of 20,000,000 gold marks

Sept. 8, Inspection of German armaments by Inter-Allied Mission of Control begun

Sept. 9, Levying of duty on customs on line between occupied and unoccupied territory ceased

Sept. 29, Memorandum sent to Council of League of Nations giving conditions for entry into League of Nations

Sept. 30, Naval Commission of Control (Allied) dissolved

Oct. 4, Commercial Treaty with Guatemala signed

Oct. 10, Contract of loan to Germany under Dawes Plan of 800,000,000 in gold marks signed with international bankers in London

Oct. 11, Reichsbank formally reconstituted and German External Loan put it in possession of 800 million gold marks in foreign currencies

——, As a result of the adoption of the Dawes Plan the German State railways transferred to a private company, the Deutsche Reichsbahn-Gesellschaft, for management and administration

Oct. 12–15, Flight of the giant dirigible ZR-3 from Friedrichshafen on Lake Constance to Lakehurst, New Jersey, piloted by Dr. Hugo Eckener

Oct. 20, Reichstag dissolved

Nov. 15–16, At midnight railroads handed over to Germans by French and Belgians

Nov. 17–18, Evacuation of occupied Ruhr territory completed

Nov. 24–Dec. 4, Conference with Baltic States at Helsingfors. *See* Finland

Dec. 2, Treaty of commerce and navigation with Great Britain signed

Dec. 7, Election for Reichstag resulted in Socialist gains of 131 seats; Center Party, 69; German National People's Party, 110; German People's Party, 51; German Democratic Party, 32; Bavarian People's Party, 19; Communists, 45; minor parties, 36

Dec. 11, Resignation of Chancellor Marx but continued in office

1925

Jan. 5, Joint Note of Allies notified Germany that evacuation of Cologne on Jan. 10 as under Treaty would not be carried out because of failure of Germany to fulfill Treaty provisions for disarmament. *See also* p. 569

Jan. 7, Paoli Loebe, Socialist, elected president of the Reichstag

Jan. 10, Provisional commercial Agreement with Italy signed

Jan. 15, Dr. Hans Luther appointed Chancellor, first conservative-bourgeois Cabinet, and first to include a Nationalist Minister, Otto Gessler, Defense; Dr. Gustav Stresemann, Minister of Foreign Affairs; Dr. Otto von Schlieben, Finance; Martin Schiele, Justice; Karl Neuhaus, Economics; Heinrich Brauns, Labor

Jan. 18, Government decreed resumption of eight-hour law on April 1

Jan. 25, Dr. Weber and Major General Aechter acquitted of treason charges at Munich

Feb. 9, Germany proposed to Allies a Rhineland Guarantee Pact

Feb. 10, Trial of Communist organizations charged with instigating revolution begun in Leipiz, the "Cheka" case

Feb. 13, General von Ludendorff, von Greaefe, and Strasser resigned from leadership of National Party

Feb. 28, Death of President Ebert after operation for appendicitis

March 10, Dr. Walther Simons, president of the Reichsgericht (national court) named by the Reichstag as acting President of the Republic

March 13, Clash of police and Communists, 6 killed, 36 wounded

March 16, Death of Professor August von Wasserman, pathologist (59)

March 29, Election for President held but none of the 7 candidates received required majority, Dr. Jarres, Nationalist, leading

April 4, Constitution adopted by Lübeck

——, Colonial trade Agreement with Belgium signed

April 22, "Cheka" trial ended. Three Communists sentenced to death, 13 others received prison sentences

April 26, Second election held for the presidency. Field-Marshal von Hindenburg elected receiving 14,655,766 votes defeating former Chancellor Marx who received 13,751,615 votes

May 1, Agreement with England as to assessment on imports into England

May 12, Inauguration of President von Hindenburg

June 2, Inter-Allied Note presented June 4 gave 13 instances of non-fulfillment of Treaty of Versailles as to disarmament

June 4, Allied Military Control Mission reached Berlin

June 24, Council of Ambassadors presented Germany with revised schedule of restrictions on manufacture and use of aircraft

July 2, The North German Lloyd established wireless communication with both shores of the Atlantic Ocean

July 11, Agreement with France signed as to commercial relations between Germany and the Saar

July 17, Revaluation Act signed by the President, provided for revaluation of State loans at 2½% of their face value

July 27, Strike of miners in the Saar

July 31, Evacuation of French soldiers of the Ruhr ended officially and troops left Essen and Mülheim

Aug. 1, Mutual eviction of non-nationals begun under Treaty by Poland and Germany. About 15,000 German persons evicted from Poland and 12,000 Polish families from Germany

Aug. 6, Payment of reparations under the Dawes Plan ratified by the Reichstag

——, Poles not taking German nationality given 48 hours to leave Germany

Aug., Tariff Bill passed, reimposed import duties on food and increased duties on automobiles, typewriters, cash registers, and calculating machines

Aug. 7, Bill passed provided for increased internal duties especially on liquor and tobacco and for higher rates on property

Aug. 10, Treaty of arbitration with Estonia

Aug. 12, Strike of 150,000 textile workers in Saxony

Aug. 17, First regular flight on Munich-Frankfort-London air route

Aug. 19, Convention for prevention of liquor smuggling signed at Helsingfors by Germany, Denmark, Estonia, Finland, Latvia, Lithuania, Norway, Poland, and Sweden

Aug. 24, Resignation of Dr. Karl Joseph Wirth, former Chancellor from the Centrist Party

Aug. 25, Evacuation of Dusseldorf, Ruhrort, and Duisburg by French and Belgian troops completed

Sept. 1–4, Allied and German jurists met in London to consider drafts of Security Pact (Rhineland) and arbitration treaties between France and Germany and Belgium and Germany

Oct. 1, M. Coste, French aviator, fined for flying over German territory and released

Oct. 3, Customs Convention with Austria signed

Oct. 12, Commercial and consular Treaty with Russia signed

——, New tariff Bill passed, by which customs to again become important source of revenue

Oct. 16, Germany signed the Locarno Pact reaffirming the renunciation of Alsace-Lorraine and undertaking not to attempt any forcible alteration of boundaries, the boundaries between Germany and France and Belgium guaranteed by the Powers, and Germany undertook to arbitrate disputes with France, Belgium, Poland, and Czechoslovakia

Oct. 23, Germany notified Allied Powers that she had satisfied demands made in June

Oct. 25, Dr. Schiele, Minister of the Interior, Schlieben, Finance, and Neuhaus, Commerce, resigned in Cabinet crisis on Locarno Treaties

Nov. 7, Allied Note raised questions as to German general staff and the military training conducted by patriotic societies

Nov. 11, Note informed Allies of compliance with demands as to disarmament

Nov. 18, Commercial *modus vivendi* signed with Spain ended tariff war begun Nov. 8

Nov. 21, The Reichsrat approved ratification of the Locarno Treaties and authorized the Government to ask admission to the League of Nations

Nov. 26, Commercial Treaty with the Netherlands signed

Nov. 26–27, Reichstag voted for ratification of the Locarno Treaties and agreed to application for membership in League of Nations

Nov. 28, Act giving effect to Locarno Treaties signed by the President

Nov. 29, Prussia granted claims of Hohenzollerns to 250,000 acres of land, certain castles and works of art, and about $7,000,000

Dec. 1, Evacuation of British, French, and Belgian troops from Cologne zone

Dec. 5, Resignation of Luther Ministry but reorganized in January

Dec. 13, Provisional Commercial Agreement with Turkey signed

Dec. 14–17, Dr. Erich Koch (Democrat), failed to form a Cabinet

1926

Jan. 8, Social Insurance Agreement with Austria signed

Jan. 9, Agreement with Switzerland provided for mutual abolition of passports

Jan. 19, Dr. Luther completed second Cabinet, Gustav Stresemann (People's Party), Minister of Foreign Affairs; Dr. Peter Reinhold (Democrat), Finance; Wilhelm Kuelz (Democrat), Interior; Julius Curtius (People's Party), Economics

Jan. 27, Treaty with Poland signed regarding settlement of frontier disputes

Jan. 30, Evacuation of Cologne zone completed by Allied troops

Feb. 2, Death sentence imposed on 4 and terms of imprisonment on 2 of 11 ex-officers and soldiers of the "Feme" or retribution commission of the Black Reichswehr accused of participation in 25 political murders

Feb. 10, Application of Germany for admission to the League of Nations presented to League by German Consul-General at Geneva

Feb. 15–17, Visit of Sir Eric Drummond, Secretary General of League of Nations

March 16, Council of League of Nations failed to admit Germany because of opposition of Brazil. *See also* League of Nations

March 20, Commercial Treaty with Portugal signed

March 21, President Hindenburg made tour of the region freed from Allied occupation

March 26, Death of former Chancellor Constantin Fehrenbach (74)

April 4, Death of August Thyssen (84), Ruhr industrialist

April 24, Treaty of friendship and neutrality with Russia signed

May 5, Decision of Cabinet that diplomatic and consular service abroad should use the old imperial colors along with the black, red, and gold of the Republic

May 6, Proposal of confiscation of deposed princely houses without compensation rejected by Reichstag

May 11, Local option Bill rejected by Reichstag by vote of 241 to 163

May 12, Resignation of Luther Cabinet defeated on flag issue of use of imperial colors

May 14, Treaty of commerce with Sweden signed

——, Steel trust organized

May 17, Dr. Marx took office as Chancellor retaining most of the members of the Luther Cabinet

May 20, Arbitration Treaty with the Netherlands signed

May 22, Convention signed with Conference of Ambassadors as to rules for German aircraft

June 22, Resignation of Dr. Hjalmar Schacht as president of the Reichsbank and from Democratic Party on confiscation issue

June 26, Provisional Commercial Agreement with Finland signed

June 28, Commercial Treaty with Latvia signed

June 30, Referendum vote on proposal of confiscation of royal property failed of adoption because majority of qualified voters refrained from voting and the total 5 million short of required number, the vote being 542,000 against and 14,889,000 for confiscation

July 1, Unemployed estimated as 1,718,000

July 13, Agreement with Sweden concluded for mutual abolition of passports

——, Unemployment riots in Berlin

July 14, Commercial Treaty with Switzerland signed

July 24–Sept. 26, Berlin-Peking flight of Schnabel and Poldi

Aug. 30, Ernest Vierkoetter swam the English Channel in record time of 12 hours and 43 minutes

Sept. 8, Germany admitted as member of the League of Nations with permanent seat on Council

Sept. 15, Death of Rudolf C. Eucken, philosopher

Sept. 30, International steel Agreement signed with France, Belgium, and Luxembourg

Oct. 9, General Wilhelm Heye appointed Commander-in-Chief of the army succeeding General von Seeckt whose resignation was accepted after his admission that he had approved of participation of son of former Crown Prince in Reichswehr manœuvers

Oct. 15, Prussia agreed to surrender to the Kaiser 250,000 acres of land, and about $3,750,000 for compensation for estates and castles formerly owned

Oct. 20, Convention between French Office of Devastated Mines and Rhenish Westphalian Coal Syndicate for purchase of coal by French individuals

Oct. 23, Note to Reparation Commission declared inability to make deliveries in kind and asked examination of Germany's capacity to pay

Oct. 29, Treaty of commerce with Turkey signed

Nov. 6, Saar Trade Agreement with France signed

Dec. 17, Resignation of Marx Cabinet forced by Socialists. Agreed to remain in office until successor appointed

Dec. 29, Treaty of friendship, conciliation, and arbitration with Italy signed

1927

Jan. 12, Treaty of commerce and Treaty regarding right of domicile with Turkey signed

Jan. 31, Inter-Allied Military Commission on Control withdrawn; duties to be taken over by League of Nations

Feb. 1, Dr. Wilhelm Marx formed new Cabinet taking himself the portfolio of the Occupied Provinces: Dr. Gustav Stresemann (German People's Party), Minister of Foreign Affairs; Oskar Hergt (Nationalist), Justice and Vice-Chancellor; Dr. Otto Gessler (No Party), Defense; Dr. Heinrich Brauns (Center), Labor; Martin Schiele (Nationalist), Food and Agriculture; Dr. Julius Curtius (German People's Party), Economic Affairs

Feb. 19–24, Lockout of 150,000 metal workers in Saxony controversy over wages and hours. Settlement by compromise

March 26, Conviction of 4 in Black Reichswehr trial sentenced to death, and acquittal of 3

April 6, Largest budget in history passed by the Reichstag provided for expenditure of more than 8 billion marks of which less than $1/8$th reparations payments, 700,000 marks for army and navy

May 5, Edict of Berlin police dissolved the Fascist organizations in Berlin

May 10, Treaty of friendship, commerce, and navigation with Persia of June 11, 1873, denounced by Persia

July 1, Number of unemployed estimated as 493,000; a decrease during the year

July 16, Law introduced unemployment insurance to take the place of unemployment welfare which had been in existence since the end of the War

July 20, Most favored nation commercial Treaty with Japan concluded and memorandum as to importation by Japan of German dyestuffs

July 25, Resignation of Chancellor Marx from the Republican organization the Reichsbanner

July 31, Tariff law of Aug., 1925, prolonged until Jan., 1930, with an increase of the duty on sugar, potatoes, and pork

Aug. 1, Postal rates increased by an average of 50%

Aug. 3–5, World airplane record for duration made by Cornelius Edzard and Johann Risctics at Dessau in 52 hours, 22 minutes, and 31 seconds, and also world record for distance of 2,895.97 miles

Aug. 11, Gliding flight lasting 14 hours and 7 minutes made by Rossitten in East Prussia

Aug. 17, Most favored nation commercial Treaty with France signed

Aug. 31, Airplane carrying the Princess Anne Lowenstein-Wertheim, Captain Leslie Hamilton, and Lieutenant Colonel Frederick F. Minchin left Upavan, England, for trans-Atlantic flight to Canada and was not heard from after leaving the Irish coast

Sept. 18, President Hindenburg in speech at dedication of memorial of the Battle of Tannenberg repudiated German responsibility for the War

Sept. 23, Signature of option clause Permanent Court

Oct. 1, New Unemployment insurance law came into effect. Compulsory, affecting about 16 million workers

Oct. 6, Commercial Treaty with Yugoslavia signed

Oct. 11, One-day strike of subway employees of Berlin won concession for men

Oct. 17–22, Strike of 80,000 lignite miners for increase of wages settled by compulsory arbitration

Oct. 20, Note of Agent General for Reparations Gilbert on German financial policy warned of large unnecessary expenditure of Government

Oct. 30, Death of Maximilian Harden, journalist, in Switzerland

Nov. 12, Lockout of cigar makers announced for this date brought about strike protest by 40,000 workers in Hamburg, Bremen, Westphalia, and Mannheim

Nov. 21, Commercial Treaty with Panama signed

Dec. 3, Agreement for suppression of passport visas concluded with Great Britain

1928

Jan. 29, Arbitration and conciliation Treaty with Lithuania signed, 3 frontier Treaties and a Treaty regarding Memel

Feb. 21, Government declared binding award of arbitration court in strike involving 800,000 metal workers which gave increase of 60 cents weekly

Feb. 27, Death of Prince Karl Max Lichnowsky

Feb. 29, Germany ratified the signature of optional clause of Protocol of Signature of the Permanent Court of International Justice

March 12, Report of Committee of Reichstag revealed that secret funds of the Reichswehr had been used to promote numerous industries such as yacht clubs, airplane factories, film companies, and commercial undertakings not connected with national defense

March 21, Treaty of non-aggression, conciliation, and arbitration with Rumania signed

March 24, Commercial Treaty with Greece signed

March 26, Flight of the "Bremen" from Berlin to Dublin, Ireland, in 9 hours and 35 minutes

March 31, Reichstag dissolved by the President

April 7, Treaty of friendship, commerce, and navigation with Siam signed

April 12, Lockout of metal workers in Saxony

April 12–13, Flight of the "Bremen" monoplane with Baron von Hunefeld, Captain Hermann Koehl and Commandant James Fitzmaurice first east to west transatlantic flight from Dublin, Ireland. Crashed on Greenely Island, Straits of Belle Isle, near coast of Labrador, after flight of 34 hours

April 23, Labor Minister dictated settlement of demands of Ruhr miners at an 8% increase

April 28, Customs Convention with the Netherlands signed

May 1–3, Communist riot in Berlin. 24 persons killed

May 5, Arbitration Treaty with the United States signed

May 20, Elections for Reichstag gave the Social Democrats a majority receiving 153 seats; German National Party, 45; Center Party with the Bavarian People's Party, 78; Democrats, 25; Communists, 54; and minor groups, 50

June 13, Resignation of the Marx Cabinet

June 28, Cabinet formed by Dr. Hermann Mueller, Socialist; Dr. Gustav Stresemann, Foreign Affairs; Dr. Rudolf Hilferding (Socialist), Finance; General Wilhelm Groener (Non-Partisan), Defense; Dr. Karl Severing (Socialist), Interior; Theodore von Guerard (Centrist), Justice; Adam Stegerwald (Centrist), Communications and Transport; Dr. Paul Moldenhauer (People's Party), Commerce; Rudolf Wissel (Socialist), Labor; Dr. Hermann Dietrich (Democrat), Agriculture; Joseph Wirth (Centrist), Occupied Areas

July 5, Financial Agreement with Poland signed

July 5–7, World airplane duration record made by Johann Risztics and Wilhelm Zimmerman in air without refuelling 65 hours and 25 minutes

July 6, Legal Agreement with Switzerland concluded

July 31, Commercial Treaty with Lithuania signed

Aug. 17, Agreement with China signed for reciprocity in customs and similar matters

Aug. 29, Protocol signed modified arbitration and conciliation Treaty with Switzerland

Sept. 1, Commercial Treaty with the South African Union signed

Sept. 16, Agreement with Allied Powers signed for setting up commission of experts to reconsider problem of German reparations

Oct. 11–14, Flight of the "Graf Zeppelin" with Dr. Hugo Eckener carrying 20 passengers and crew of 40 from Friedrichshafen to Baltimore, New York, and Lakehurst in approximately 111 hours covering 6,300 miles

Oct. 15, Strike of textile workers in the Rhineland for increase of wages

Oct. 29–31, Return flight of the "Graf Zeppelin" from Lakehurst to Friedrichshafen in 68 hours, 56 minutes, and 64 seconds covering about 4,000 miles, completing round trip flight of Atlantic for first time in aërial history

Oct. 30, Trade and shipping Treaty with Lithuania signed

Nov. 1–Dec. 3, Lockout of metal workers in Rhineland and Westphalia as protest against adverse decision as to wage increase award of Minister of Labor

Nov. 10, Financial Agreement with Rumania signed

Nov. 21, Death of Hermann Suderman, dramatist

Nov. 30, French and Belgian troops evacuated the second German zone leaving only third zone centering at Maintz bridgehead under Allied control

Dec. 2, Agreement for government mediation reached, ended strike of Ruhr metal workers against adverse decision

Dec. 11, Speech of Chancellor Mueller in favor of Austrian-German union and demanded evacuation of Rhineland by Allies and of Saar Valley by French

Dec. 14, Financial Convention with Poland signed

Dec. 15, Question of German minorities in Upper Silesia discussed by League of Nations Council

Dec. 20, Resignation of Dr. Walter Simons, president of Federal Supreme Court and Supreme Court of Judicature in dispute with the Government over procedure

Dec. 21, Award of Dr. Carl Severing granted increase of from 1 to 6 pfennig an hour and reduced working week by 3 hours for metal workers

——, Ruling granted wage increase of 5 pfennig an hour and reduction of hours to maximum of 50 a week for shipyard workers

Dec. 24, Bill passed provided for special relief in cases of unemployment in a dozen specified trades and industries

1929

Jan. 15, Communist uprisings in various industrial centers to commemorate the deaths of Rosa Luxemburg and Karl Liebknecht

Jan. 24, Treaty with Russia signed pledging submission of all disputes to an arbitration tribunal to be constituted annually with new appointees who are to meet once a year

Feb. 6, Pact of Paris for renunciation of war ratified by Reichstag

Feb. 17, Convention of friendship and commerce with Persia signed

Feb. 18, Trotsky applied to the President of the Reichstag for permission to enter Germany, which was refused

Feb. 20, Decision of Reichstag to reduce all pensions in excess of 12,000 marks (about $3,000) to that sum

March 24–28, Non-stop flight of the dirigible "Graf Zeppelin" from Friedrichshafen to Egypt on the Palestine border 5,040 miles in 81½ hours

April 1, The Free State of Waldeck annexed to Prussia

April 20, Death of Prince Henry of Prussia, only brother of former German Emperor

April 24, Government loan of 200 million marks (about $48,000,000) negotiated with banks

May 1–5, Communist riots in which 27 persons killed and 29 seriously wounded

May 2, Police suppressed *Die Rote Fahne*, Communist publication, for 3 weeks

May 3, Strike of workers in Berlin as protest against harsh measures of the police

May 16–17, Second attempted transatlantic flight of "Graf Zeppelin." Obliged to land at Cuers, France

May 16, Arbitration Treaty with Turkey signed

May 17, Death of Lilli Lehmann, singer

May 29, Willi Neuenhofen made new world altitude record at Dessau, Germany, flying to height of 41,704 feet

June 14, State Treaty regulated relations of Prussia with the Vatican

June 27, Failure to renew Act for defense of the Republic which did not receive the necessary two-thirds majority in the Reichstag

July 6, Death of Hans Meyer, explorer

July 13, Settlement of Belgian claim arising out of seizure of Belgian marks during German occupation

July 14, Death of Hans Delbruck, historian

July 22, The new North German Lloyd steamer *Bremen* arrived in New York City from Cherbourg in 4 days, 17 hours, and 42 minutes

July 31, The "Graf Zeppelin" left Friedrichshafen commanded by Dr. Hugo Eckener arriving at Lakehurst, New Jersey, Aug. 4, with 20 passengers, a crew of 41, and a stowaway; flying time, 93 hours

Aug. 6, Death of Karl Aver, inventor of the incandescent gas mantle

Aug. 8, The "Graf Zeppelin" left Lakehurst, New Jersey, for Friedrichshafen with 22 passengers arriving Aug. 10, flying time 55 hours, 24 minutes

Aug. 15–19, The "Graf Zeppelin" made world nonstop flight distance record from Friedrichshafen to Tokio, Japan, 6,980 miles in 101 hours and 53 minutes

Aug. 23, The "Graf Zeppelin" left airport 30 miles northeast of Tokio and landed at Los Angeles on Aug. 26, and at Lakehurst, New Jersey, Aug. 29, completing a trip around the world

Aug. 30, Provisional Agreement with Poland signed as to nationality of German minority in Poland

——, International Agreement on evacuation of the Rhineland territory signed at the Hague Conference and final Protocol recording acceptance of the Young Plan for reparations. See also p. 571

Sept. 1, The "Graf Zeppelin" left Lakehurst and arrived at Friedrichshafen Sept. 4—a globe circle from there in 20 days and 4 hours

Sept. 11, Arbitration and conciliation Treaty with Luxemburg signed

Sept. 14, The British began evacuation of the third and last zone of occupied Rhineland territory

Sept. 30, Fritz von Opel succeeded in flying an airplane propelled by rockets

Oct. 3, Death of Dr. Gustav Stresemann (51), Minister of Foreign Affairs

Oct. 5, Rhineland amnesty Agreement signed

Oct. 9, Decree of Prussian Minister of the Interior ordered dissolution of the nationalist organizations of the Steel Helmets in the Rhineland, the Ruhr, and Westphalia

Oct. 15, Evacuation of Coblenz by Allied troops begun

Oct. 17, The seaplane "DO-X" in flight for nearly an hour with 169 persons, the greatest number ever carried on any aircraft

Oct. 21, Loan to Germany by Kreuger and Toll, Swedish Match Company and International Match Corporation, in return for a match monopoly in Germany, 50-year 6% loan of 500 million marks

Oct. 28, Death of Prince Bernhardt von Bülow (80) in Rome

Oct. 31, Agreement with Poland signed provided for liquidation of property and renunciation of financial claims

Nov. 2, Reichsbank lowered discount rate from 7½ to 7%

Nov. 3, Herr Augenburg, Nationalist leader, submitted Bill against the enslavement of the German people by the Young Plan

Nov. 5, Death of Prince Max von Baden, former Chancellor (62)

Nov. 7, Claims Convention with Poland signed as to liquidation of claims of German private property in Poland

Nov. 11, Dr. Julius Curtius, acting Foreign Minister since the death of Dr. Stresemann, received permanent appointment to that office

Nov. 12, Thomas Mann, novelist, received the 1929 Nobel prize for literature

Nov. 21–Dec. 20, Saar Conference in Paris. No agreement reached

Nov. 30, The Reichstag rejected Hugenburg's "Liberty Law" to nullify the Young Plan

——, The second zone of the occupied Rhineland territory (Coblenz) evacuated by French and Belgian troops

——, Commercial Treaty with Sweden signed

Dec. 6, Memorandum of Dr. Schacht, president of the Reichsbank, criticized the financial policy of the Government and failure to adopt tax and budget reform

Dec. 12, Chancellor Mueller in answer to criticism of Dr. Schacht admitted deficit at end of year of 1,700,-000,000 marks

Dec. 13, Last British troops withdrawn from Rhineland

Dec. 21, Resignation of Dr. Rudolph Hilferding, Socialist Minister of Finance, as result of discussion of the Schacht memorandum. Succeeded by Dr. Paul Moldenhauer

Dec. 22, Young Plan upheld on referendom vote on Hugenburg anti-Young "Liberty Law" Bill by absence of voters from the polls. Only about 14% of the electorate

Dec. 31, Agreement with France concluded on liquidation of private claims

1930

Jan. 2, Agreement with Great Britain as to reparations under British German Reparations Recovery Act of 1921

Jan. 15, Communist riots caused by unemployment of 2 million workers

Jan. 15–July 7, Franco-German negotiations as to Saar reached no agreement

Jan. 20, Final Protocol with creditor nations signed by Germany at The Hague adopting Young Plan for reparations

Jan. 28, Match Monopoly Bill passed third reading in Reichstag

Feb. 5, The Young Plan ratified by the Reichsrat, Fascist delegates from Thuringia and eastern Prussia dissenting

March 6, Death of Admiral Alfred von Tirpitz (80)

March 7, Dr. Hjalmar Schacht, president of the Reichsbank, resigned declaring that Germany was not able to fulfill the conditions of the Young Plan

March 11, Dr. Hans Luther, former Chancellor, elected president of the Reichsbank

——, The Reichstag ratified the Young Plan for settlement of reparation debt of Germany to the Allies and the Hague Agreements by vote of 266 to 193

March 13, President von Hindenburg signed ratification of the Young Plan also affirming separate debt Agreement with the United States

March 15, New and drastic National Defense Act adopted by Reichstag to remain in force until Dec. 31, 1932

March 17, Provisional commercial Treaty with Poland signed

March 18, President von Hindenburg signed Polish-German liquidation Agreement and other pacts

March 25, Announcement that the *Europa* had reached New York in 4 days, 17 hours, and 6 minutes

March 27, Resignation of Chancellor Mueller's coalition Government on issue of funding the national unemployment debt

March 30, Dr. Heinrich Brüning (Center) formed Cabinet, Theodore von Guerard (Center), Minister of Transport; Dr. Julius Curtius (German People's Party), Foreign Affairs; Dr. R. Moldenhauer (German People's Party), Finance; Lieutenant-General Wilhelm Groener, Defense; Hermann Robert Dietrich (German Democratic Party), Economic Affairs; Martin Schiele (Nationalist), Agriculture; Dr. Adam Stegerwald (Center), Labor; Dr. Joseph Wirth (Center), Home Affairs; Dr. George Schaetzel (Bavarian People's Party), Posts; G. R. Treviranus (People's Conservative Party), Minister without Portfolio

April 1, Scientific expedition under leadership of Professor Alfred Wegener sailed from Copenhagen to establish stations in Greenland

——, Death of Frau Cosimo Wagner, widow of the composer, and daughter of Franz Liszt

April 2, At caucus of the Nationalist Party Hugenberg's opposition policy defeated

April 8, Law passed placed further restrictions of the sale of liquor. To become effective July 1

April 12, Commercial Treaty with Austria signed

April 19, Commercial Treaty with Poland signed

April 30, Farm Relief Bill and Tax Reform Bill increasing tariff rates signed by the President

194   GERMANY   GERMANY

May 8, The Passion Play given every 10 years since 1633 opened at Oberammergau in a formal rehearsal before 5,000 invited guests

May 9, Agreement regarding Rhineland amnesty concluded with Great Britain

May 12, Most favored nation commercial Treaty with Irish Free State signed

May 17, Young Plan came into effect replacing Dawes Plan for reparations under which Germany had paid 7,993,000,000 gold marks

May 18, The "Graf Zeppelin" commanded by Captain Hugo Eckener left Friedrichshafen with 22 passengers and crew of 42 and reached Pernambuco, Brazil, from Seville, Spain (19th), after flight of 62 hours, May 22

May 20, Burgomaster Gustav Boess, Mayor of Berlin, removed from office after an investigation of corruption in the city administration

May 22, The "Graf Zeppelin" reached Pernambuco, Brazil, from Seville and May 28, left Pernambuco reaching Lakehurst, New Jersey, May 30

May 24, Clash of frontier patrol with Polish patrol at Neuhoefen, West Prussia. Casualties on both sides

May 27, Most favored nation commercial Treaty with Turkey signed

June 2, The "Graf Zeppelin" left Lakehurst arriving at Seville, Spain, and Friedrichshafen, June 6, covering 18,000 miles during trip in air 301 hours

June 10, Agreement signed (6 documents) for floating first Young Plan loan

——, Death of Professor Adolph Harnack at Heidelberg

June 11, Award of about $82,000,000 to German shipping companies for wartime seizures by the United States

June 20, Resignation of Professor Paul Moldenhauer, Minister of Finance. Succeeded by Hermann Dietrich

June 23, Agreement with the United States signed provided for payment of war claims and cost of army of occupation

June 30, Rhineland evacuated by Allied troops ending occupation

July 1, Strikes in iron and steel factories because of wage cuts

July 10, Death of General Friedrich von Bernhardi (81)

July 12, Extradition Treaty with the United States signed

July 14, Germany approved Briand plan for social and economic union of Europe but stressed admission of Soviet Russia and Turkey, demanded disarmament and modification of certain terms of the Versailles Treaty

July 16, Government Tax Bill increasing taxes passed by vote of 256 to 193. President Hindenburg acting under Article 48 of the Constitution which gives the President extraordinary power in case the safety and existence of the State are at stake signed document authorizing the Cabinet to promulgate its financial and tax laws by decree

July 18, Socialist motion for revocation of this Act carried by vote of 236 to 221. The Reichstag dissolved

July 26, Decree of Cabinet promulgated its financial program to take effect Sept. 1

Aug. 8, Speech of Chancellor Brüning referred to Germany's disadvantageous position in international structure of Europe

Aug. 8, Death of General Walter Reinhardt

Aug. 18, Captain Wolfgang von Gronau and 3 companions left Sylt Island in the North Sea, in air flight by Iceland and Greenland and Labrador to Queensport, Nova Scotia, Aug. 24, Halifax, Aug. 25, and New York City, Aug. 26; 47 hours total flying time

Aug. 25, Resignation of General Wilhelm Heye commanding the Reichswehr

Aug. 31, Death of Eduard Meyer (75), historian

Sept. 10, Election manifesto of Hitler gave party program of militant Fascists of extreme nationalism, anti-Semitism, anti-reparations, and Versailles Treaty

Sept. 12, Council of the League of Nations voted to withdraw French and Belgium troops from the Saar within 3 months

Sept. 14, General election gave the National Socialist Party (Fascist, also called Nazis) an increase from 12 to 107 seats in the Reichstag. The members are as follows: Socialists, 143; National Socialists (Hitler's Party), 107; Communists, 77; Center Party, 68; German National People's Party, 41; German People's Party, 20; Bavarian People's Party, 19; Minor Parties, 23; total, 577

Sept. 15, Death of Captain Karl Boy-Ed (58)

Sept. 25, Testifying at the trial of 3 Reichswehr officers before Supreme Court at Leipzig charged with treason Adolf Hitler leader of the National Socialists declared that the Party refused to recognize the Versailles Treaty and that a guillotine awaited the men who made the German revolution in 1918 if the Fascists ever get into power

Sept. 28, Death of Prince Leopold of Bavaria

Oct. 4, Trial of 3 officers at Leipzig ended with finding of guilty of treason and sentence of 18 months detention in fortress and dismissal from army

Oct. 6, Crash of Berlin-to-Vienna passenger plane near Dresden, Saxony. Six men and 2 women killed

Oct. 13, Reichstag opened. Nazis (Fascists) and Communists in riot in Berlin

Oct. 14, Strike of Berlin trade unions closing 276 metal factories. Nazis (Fascists) break the windows of Jewish-owned department stores on the principal streets

Oct. 29, Reichstag Committee on Foreign Relations rejected 5 motions introduced by anti-Government Parties each demanding immediate ending of Germany's reparation payments or the revision of existing commitments

Nov. 7, Germany delivered to Treasury Department of the United States bonds as to mixed claims and costs of American army of occupation

Nov. 8, Award in metal industry provided for 30% wage cut beginning Nov. 17 and an additional 5% cut from Jan. 19, 1931 for all workers 18 years of age and older and for those below 18, 3%

Nov. 16, Nazis (Fascists) gain in municipal elections

Nov. 29, Formal protest of Government to League of Nations of alleged mistreatment of German minority in Upper Silesia in connection with election of Nov. 22

Dec. 1, Decree of President von Hindenburg promulgated Government program of fiscal and economic reform. Salaries of officials beginning with the President cut 20%

Dec. 12, Last Allied troops in Germany evacuated the Saar

EMPERORS OF ROME AND KINGS OF GERMANY
CARLOVINGIAN RACE

800. Charles I, the Great, or Charlemagne
814. Louis I, *le Débonnaire*, King of France
840. Lothaire I, or Lother, son of Louis; died in a monastery at Treves, Sept., 855
855. Louis II, son of Lothaire
875. Charles II, the Bald, King of France; died 877
881. Charles III, the Fat, crowned King of Italy; deposed; succeeded by
887. Arnulf or Arnoul; crowned Emperor at Rome, 896
899. Louis III, the Blind
——. Louis IV, the Child, son of Arnulf; the last of the Carlovingian race in Germany

SAXON DYNASTY

911. Otho, Duke of Saxony; refuses the dignity on account of his age
——. Conrad I, Duke of Franconia, King
918. Henry I, the Fowler, son of Otho, Duke of Saxony, King
936. Otho I, the Great, son of Henry, crowned by Pope John XII, Feb. 2, 962, the beginning of the Holy Roman Empire
973. Otho II, the Bloody; massacred his chief nobility at an entertainment, 981; wounded by a poisoned arrow
983. Otho III, the Red, his son, yet in his minority, poisoned
1002. Henry II, Duke of Bavaria, surnamed the Holy and the Lame

HOUSE OF FRANCONIA

1024. Conrad II, surnamed the Salique
1039. Henry III, the Black, son
1056. Henry IV, son; a minor; Agnes, regent; deposed by his son and successor; Rudolph (1077) and Herman (1082) nominated by the Pope; and Conrad (1087)
1106. Henry V; married Maud or Matilda, daughter of Henry I of England
1125. Lothaire II, surnamed the Saxon

HOUSE OF HOHENSTAUFEN, OR OF SUABIA

1138. Conrad III, Duke of Franconia
1152. Frederick I, Barbarossa; drowned by his horse throwing him into River Saleph, June 10, 1190
1190. Henry VI, son, surnamed Asper, or Sharp; detained Richard I of England a prisoner; died 1197
[Interregnum and contest for the throne between Philip of Suabia and Otho of Brunswick]
1198. Philip, brother to Henry; assassinated at Bamberg by Otto of Wittelsbach
1208. Otho IV, surnamed the Superb; excommunicated and deposed; died 1218
1215. Frederick II, King of Sicily, son of Henry VI; deposed by his subjects, who elected Henry, Landgrave of Thuringia, 1246; Frederick died in 1250, naming his son Conrad his successor; but the Pope gave the imperial title to
1247. William, Earl of Holland (nominal)
1250. Conrad IV, son of Frederick
[His son, Conradin, was proclaimed King of Sicily, which was, however, surrendered to his Uncle Manfred, 1254, on whose death it was given by the Pope to Charles of Anjou in 1263. Conradin, on the invitation of the Ghibelline Party, entered Italy with a large army, was defeated at Tagliacozzo, Aug. 23,

1268, and beheaded at Naples, Oct. 29, thus ending the Hohenstaufen family]
1256. [Interregnum]
1257. Richard, Earl of Cornwall, and Alphonso, of Castile, merely nominated

HOUSES OF HAPSBURG, LUXEMBURG, BAVARIA, &c.

1273. Rudolph, Count of Hapsburg
1291. [Interregnum]
1292. Adolphus, Count of Nassau, to the exclusion of Albert, son of Rodolph; deposed; slain at the battle of Gelheim, July 2, 1298, by
1298. Albert I, Duke of Austria, Rodolph's son; killed by his nephew at Rheinfels, May 1, 1308
1308. Henry VII of Luxemburg
1313. [Interregnum]
1314. Louis IV of Bavaria, and Frederick III of Austria, son of Albert, rival emperors; Frederick died in 1330
1330. Louis reigns alone
1347. Charles IV of Luxemburg. (At Nuremberg, in 1356, the Golden Bull became the fundamental law of the German Empire)
1378. Wenceslas, King of Bohemia, son, twice imprisoned; forced to resign; but continued to reign in Bohemia
1400. Frederick III, Duke of Brunswick; assassinated immediately after his election, and seldom placed in the list of emperors
——. Rupert, Count Palatine of the Rhine; crowned at Cologne; died 1410
1410. Jossus, Marquess of Moravia; chosen by a party of the electors; died next year
——. Sigismund, King of Hungary; elected by another party, on the death of Jossus recognized by all; King of Bohemia in 1419

HOUSE OF AUSTRIA

1438. Albert II, the Great, Duke of Austria, and King of Hungary and Bohemia; died Oct. 27, 1439
1439. [Interregnum]
1440. Frederick IV (or III), surnamed the Pacific; elected Emperor Feb. 2, but not crowned until June, 1442
1493. Maximilian I, son; died in 1519. In 1477 married Mary of Burgundy
Francis I of France and Charles I of Spain became competitors for the Empire
1519. Charles V (I of Spain) son of Joan of Castile and Philip of Austria, elected; resigned both crowns, 1556; retired to a monastery, where he died Sept. 21, 1558
1556. Ferdinand I, brother; succeeded by his son
1564. Maximilian II, King of Hungary and Bohemia
1576. Rodolph II, son
1612. Matthias, brother
1619. Ferdinand II, cousin, King of Hungary
1637. Ferdinand III, son
1658. Leopold I, son
1705. Joseph I, son
1711. Charles VI, brother
1740. Maria-Theresa, daughter, Queen of Hungary and Bohemia; her right sustained by England
1742. Charles VII, Elector of Bavaria, rival emperor, whose claim was supported by France
[This competition gave rise to a general war. Charles VII died Jan., 1745]

1745. Francis I of Lorraine, Grand Duke of Tuscany, consort of Maria-Theresa

1765. Joseph II, son

1790. Leopold II, brother

1792. Francis II, son, became Emperor of Austria only, as Francis I, 1804. *See* Austria

HOUSE OF HOHENZOLLERN (*see* PRUSSIA)

1871. William I, King of Prussia, Jan. 18 (born March 22, 1797; died March 9, 1888; Empress, Augusta, born Sept. 30, 1811, died Jan. 7, 1890)

1888. Frederick (William) III "the Noble," son; born Oct. 18, 1831; died June 15, 1888 (married Princess Victoria, Princess royal of England (born Nov. 21, 1840), Jan. 25, 1858, died Aug. 5, 1901)

——. William II, son, born Jan. 27, 1859 (married Princess Auguste Victoria (born Oct. 22, 1858), Feb. 27, 1881; abdicated Nov. 9, 1918; children: 1. Prince Friedrich Wilhelm, born May 6, 1882, Crown Prince of the German Empire and of Prussia, married June 6, 1905, to Princess Cecilie, born Sept. 20, 1886, daughter of the late Friedrich Franz III, of Mecklenburg-Schwerin; offspring, Prince Wilhelm Friedrich, born July 4, 1906; Prince Ludwig Ferdinand, born November 9, 1907; Prince Hubertus, born September 30, 1909; Prince Friedrich George, born Dec. 19, 1911; and Princess Alexandrine Irene, born April 7, 1915; 2. Prince Wilhelm Eitel-Friedrich, born July 7, 1883, married, February 27, 1906, to Princess Sophie Charlotte, daughter of the Grand Duke Friedrich August of Oldenburg; 3. Prince Adalbert, born July 14, 1884, married, August 3, 1914, to Princess Adelheid of Sachsen-Muningen; 4. Prince August Wilhelm, born Jan. 29, 1887; married, October 22, 1908, to Princess Alexandra Victoria

of Schleswig-Holstein; offspring: Prince Alexander Ferdinand, born December 26, 1912; 5. Prince Oscar, born July 27, 1888, morganatically married, July 31, 1914, to Countess Ina Marie Bassewitz (Countess Ruppin); offspring: a son; 6. Prince Joachim, born Dec. 17, 1890; married, March 11, 1916, to Princess Marie Auguste of Anhalt; 7. Princess Viktoria Luise, born Sept. 13, 1892; married, May 27, 1913, to Prince Ernst August of Cumberland, Duke of Brunswick

GIBRALTAR

Gibraltar, British Crown Colony, town and fortress on rock in southwest Spain commanding the entrance to the Mediterranean, area $1^7/_8$ square miles, total population 21,372.

The Rock of Gibraltar was under the dominion of the Moors until the fifteenth century, when it was joined to the Kingdom of Granada. It was captured by the British and Dutch after a 3 days siege July 24, 1704, in the War of the Spanish Succession, and Sir George Rooke, British admiral, took possession for Great Britain, and successfully withstood siege by Spaniards 1779–83.

General Sir Alexander J. Godley, Governor.

GREAT BRITAIN

Great Britain. *See also* England, Scotland, Ireland (Northern), Wales, and British Empire.

The population was thus distributed at the census, taken June 19, 1921:—

DIVISIONS	AREA IN SQ. MILES	MALES	FEMALES	TOTAL POPULATION ON JUNE 19, 1921
England (including Monmouthshire)	50,874	16,977,647	18,703,372	35,681,019
Wales	7,466	1,097,592	1,108,088	2,205,680
Scotland	30,405	2,347,642	2,534,855	4,882,497
Isle of Man	221	27,329	32,955	60,284
Channel Islands	75	41,741	48,489	90,230
Total	89,041	20,491,951	22,427,759	42,919,710

Population at each of the four previous decennial censuses:—

DIVISIONS	1881	1891	1901	1911
England	24,613,926	27,489,228	30,813,043	34,045,290
Wales	1,360,513	1,513,297	1,714,800	2,025,202
Scotland	3,735,573	4,025,647	4,472,103	4,760,904
Isle of Man	53,558	55,608	54,752	52,016
Channel Islands	87,702	92,234	95,618	96,899
Army, Navy, and Merchant Seamen abroad	215,374	224,211	367,736	145,729
Total	30,066,646	33,400,225	37,518,052	41,126,040

George V, reigning, King and Emperor, succeeded to the crown May 6, 1910.

1707

May 1, Union of England and Scotland came into effect under the name of Great Britain

1708–1709

Feb. 25, Sir Robert Walpole, Minister of War

Oct. 23, First Parliament of Great Britain, the second

Parliament revived by proclamation. 6 Anne, C. 7, enacted that any member of House of Commons accepting any office of profit vacates his seat

Nov. 18, 1708–Sept. 28, 1710, Third Parliament of Anne, Tory majority

Oct. 27, 1709, First barrier treaty signed between England and the Netherlands providing for mutual support; annulled 1712

1710

Nov. 25, 1710–Aug. 8, 1713, Fourth Parliament of Anne

1711

Jan. 17, Mrs. Masham succeeded the Duchess of Marlborough as keeper of the privy purse

May 29, 1711, Oxford Ministry formed: Robert, Earl of Oxford (previously Right Honorable Robert Harley), Lord Treasurer; Sir Simon (afterwards Lord) Harcourt, Lord Keeper; John, Duke of Normanby and Buckingham, Lord President; John, Bishop of Bristol (afterwards London), Privy Seal; Henry St. John (afterwards Viscount Bolingbroke), and William, Lord Dartmouth, Secretaries of State; Robert Benson (afterwards Lord Bingley), Chancellor of the Exchequer

1713

Jan. 30, Second barrier treaty with the Netherlands signed

April 11, Treaty of Utrecht signed by which the Protestant succession in England recognized, and Great Britain received Nova Scotia, Newfoundland, and the Hudson Bay region from France, the island of Minorca, Gibraltar, and contract for supplying the Spanish Colonies in South America with slaves

Nov. 11, 1713–Jan. 15, 1715, Fifth Parliament of Anne

1714

June 8, Death of Sophia, Electress of Hanover

July 30, The Duke of Shrewsbury succeeded Lord Oxford, receiving the Lord Treasurer's staff on July 30, 1714, three days before the death of Queen Anne. From the reign of George I the office of Lord Treasurer has been executed by commissioners

Aug. 1, Death of Queen Anne. Accession of George I of Hanover. He succeeded, Aug. 1, 1714, by virtue of the act of settlement passed in the reign of William III, June 12, 1701, which limited the succession to his mother (as a Protestant) in the event of Queen Anne dying without issue. Royal declaration bill modifying the terms of the oath, passed the lords, Aug. 5, dropped by the commons, Aug. 8, 1901

Oct. 5, Halifax Ministry: Charles, Earl of Halifax, was appointed First Lord of the Treasury, Oct. 5, 1714. He died May 19, 1715, and was succeeded by Charles, Earl of Carlisle, on Oct. 10 following; and Robert Walpole became Premier: Charles, Earl of Halifax, First Lord of the Treasury; William, Lord Cowper, afterwards Earl, Lord Chancellor; Daniel, Earl of Nottingham, Lord President; Thomas, Earl of Wharton, Privy Seal; Edward, Earl of Oxford, Admiralty; James Stanhope, afterwards Earl Stanhope, and Charles, Viscount Townshend, Secretaries of State; Sir Richard Onslow, Chancellor of the Exchequer; Dukes of Montrose and Marlborough, Lord Berkeley, Robt. Walpole, Mr. Pulteney, &c.

1715

March 21, 1715–March 10, 1722, First Parliament of George I

Sept. 3, 1715–1716, Rising in Scotland led by Earl of Mar in favor of the son of James II, the "Old Pretender"

Oct. 11, Sir Robert Walpole became First Lord of the Treasury and Chancellor of the Exchequer

Nov. 15, Third Barrier Treaty with the Netherlands

signed by which the Low Countries were ceded to the Emperor Charles VI signed by British, Imperial, and Dutch Ministers

1716

May 7, Triennial Act of 1694 repealed and Septennial Act voted 2 Geo. I, 1716, in consequence of the allegation that "a popish faction were designing to renew the rebellion in this kingdom, and the report of an invasion from abroad," that "the then parliament should continue for seven years." This Septennial Act, entitled "an act for enlarging the continuance of parliaments" (1715 in the statutes, 4to, given as 1 Geo. I, stat. 2, c. 38), was passed May 7, 1716

1720

April 4, The South Sea Bill passed in the Lords and received royal assent during the month, by which the South Sea Company organized in 1711 and granted a monopoly of British trade with Spanish America, was allowed to take over the national debt (£51,300,000) for which privilege it paid £3,500,000, the company then offering to exchange the State annuities for stock of the company from which marvelous profits were expected. The company stock rose from 128.5 at the beginning of the year to 1,000 in July, and 5 millions of stock was sold. The name "South Sea Bubble" was given to this financial scheme, which exploded in 1720 ruining thousands of families. The estates of the directors to the value of £2,014,000 were seized. A parliamentary inquiry in Nov. revealed that the company had been dishonestly managed and that favors from the State had been purchased by gifts to Ministers, and several members of Parliament and Aislabie, the Chancellor of the Exchequer, were expelled as guilty of corruption

1721

April, Second Walpole Ministry: Sir Robert Walpole, First Lord of the Treasury; Thomas, Lord Parker, created Earl of Macclesfield, Lord Chancellor; Henry, Lord Carleton (succeeded by William, Duke of Devonshire), Lord President; Evelyn, Duke of Kingston (succeeded by Lord Trevor), Privy Seal; James, Earl of Berkeley, First Lord of the Admiralty; Charles (Viscount Townshend), and John, Lord Carteret (the latter succeeded by the Duke of Newcastle), Secretaries of State; Duke of Marlborough (succeeded by the Earl of Cadogan), Ordnance; George Treby (succeeded by Henry Pelham), Secretary-at-War; Viscount Torrington, &c.

1722

June 16, Death of the Duke of Marlborough

Oct. 9, 1722–Aug. 7, 1727, Second Parliament of George I

1725

May 18, Order of the Bath revived by George I

1727

June 11, Death of George I. Accession of George II

March 20, Death of Sir Isaac Newton

1728

Jan. 23–April 16, 1734, First Parliament of George II

1735

Jan. 14, 1735–April 28, 1741, Second Parliament of George II

1739

Oct. 19, Declaration of war on Spain (War of Jenkins Ear)

1740

Dec. 16, War of the Austrian Succession begun, England supporting Maria Theresa joined in the war, George II personally taking part in the campaigns. *See* Austrian Succession

1741

Dec. 4, 1741–June 18, 1747, Third Parliament of George II

1742

Feb., Wilmington Ministry, succeeded that of Sir Robert Walpole: Earl of Wilmington, First Lord of the Treasury; Lord Hardwicke, Lord Chancellor; Earl of Harrington, President of the Council; Earl Gower, Lord Privy Seal; Mr. Sandys, Chancellor of the Exchequer; Lord Carteret and the Duke of Newcastle, Secretaries of State; Earl of Winchilsea, First Lord of the Admiralty; Duke of Argyll, Commander of the Forces and Master-General of the Ordnance; Mr. Henry Pelham, Paymaster of the Forces

1743

June 16, George II at the victory of Dettingen

Aug. 25, Pelham Ministry: H. Pelham replaced the Earl of Wilmington as Premier. In Nov., 1744, the following Ministry was formed (termed "the broad bottom administration," because it comprehended a grand coalition of the parties). It was dissolved by the death of Mr. Pelham, March 6, 1754. Henry Pelham, First Lord of the Treasury and Chancellor of the Exchequer; Lord Hardwicke, Lord Chancellor; Duke of Dorset, President of the Council; Earl Gower, Lord Privy Seal; Duke of Newcastle and the Earl of Harrington, Secretaries of State; Duke of Montagu, Master-General of the Ordnance; Duke of Bedford, First Lord of the Admiralty; Duke of Grafton, Lord Chamberlain; Duke of Richmond, Master of the Horse; Duke of Argyll, Keeper of the Great Seal of Scotland; Marquis of Tweeddale, Secretary of State for Scotland; The Duke of Devonshire and Duke of Bolton without portfolio

1745

July 25, Charles Edward, the "Young Pretender" landed in Scotland and proclaimed his father as James VIII of Scotland and III of England

Sept. 11, The Pretender entered Edinburgh

Sept. 21, The Pretender gained the battle of Prestonpans

1746

Jan. 17, The Pretender gained the battle at Falkirk

Feb. 10, Resignation of the Pelham Ministry. Succeeded by William Pulteney

Feb. 12, Pulteney Ministry resigned, received the name of the "Short-lived" administration. The members of it were: the Earl of Bath, First Lord of the Treasury; Lord Carlisle, Lord Privy Seal; Lord Winchilsea, First Lord of the Admiralty; and Lord Granville, one of the Secretaries of State, with the seals of the other in his pocket, "to be given to whom he might choose" and Pelham returned to office

April 16, Battle of Culloden, the Pretender decisively defeated by the Duke of Cumberland, and forced to flight

1747

Nov. 10, 1747–April 8, 1754, Fourth Parliament of George II; the journals ordered printed

1748

March 5, First notice of establishment of a uniform in the British naval service in the "Jacobite's Journal" of this date

Oct., Peace of Aix-la-Chapelle ended the War of the Austrian Succession

1749

April 13, Radcliffe Library, Oxford University, opened

1751

March 20, Death of Prince Frederick Louis, son of George II and father of George III

Sept. 11, Colonel Clive took Arcot, India. *See* India

Dec. 12, Death of Viscount Bolingbroke

1754

April, Newcastle Ministry formed; resigned Nov., 1756; when the Duke of Devonshire became First Lord of the Treasury; Thomas Holles Pelham, Duke of Newcastle, First Lord of the Treasury; Henry Bilson Legge, Chancellor of the Exchequer; Earl of Holdernesse and Sir Thomas Robinson (afterwards Lord Grantham), Secretaries of State. The latter succeeded by Henry Fox (afterwards Lord Holland); Lord Anson, First Lord of the Admiralty; Earl Granville, Lord President; Lord Gower (succeeded by the Duke of Marlborough 1755), Lord Privy Seal; Earl of Hardwicke, Lord Chancellor; Duke of Grafton, Earl of Halifax, George Grenville, &c.

Nov. 14–March 21, 1761, Fifth Parliament of George II

1756–1763, Seven Years' War in which England supported Prussia against the coalition of Austria, France, Russia, Sweden, and Saxony, the war in America called the French and Indian War. *See* Seven Years' War

Nov. 16, 1756, Devonshire and Pitt Administration formed; dismissed April 5, 1757: First Lord of the Treasury, William, Duke of Devonshire; Chancellor of the Exchequer, Hon. Henry Bilson Legge; Lord President, Earl Granville (Lord Carteret); Privy Seal, Earl Gower; Secretaries of State, Earl of Holdernesse and Wm. Pitt (afterwards Earl of Chatham, the virtual Premier); George Grenville, Earl of Halifax, Dukes of Rutland and Grafton, Earl of Rochfort, Viscount Barrington, &c. The great seal in commission

1757

June, Newcastle and Pitt Ministry formed. After various changes it resigned May, 1762; Lord Bute coming into power: Thomas Holles Pelham, Duke of Newcastle, First Lord of the Treasury; William Pitt (afterwards Lord Chatham), Secretary of State for the Northern Department, and leader of the House of Commons; Earl of Holdernesse, Secretary of State for the Southern Department; Earl Granville, Lord President; Earl Temple, Privy Seal; H. B. Legge, Chancellor of the Exchequer; Duke of Devonshire, Lord Chamberlain; Duke of Rutland,

Lord Steward; Lord Anson, Admiralty; Duke of Marlborough (succeeded by Lord Ligonier), Ordnance; Sir Robert Henley, Lord Keeper of the Great Seal; Henry Fox, George Grenville, Viscount Barrington, Lord Halifax, James Grenville, &c.

1757, Conquest of India begun by Colonel Clive. *See* India

1759

Jan. 15, The British Museum opened in London

Sept. 13, Victory and death of General Wolf at Quebec. *See* Canada

Nov. 20, Defeat of the French in the naval battle of Quiberon Bay.

1760

Jan. 22, Battle of Wandewash, ended French dominion in India

Sept. 8, Surrender of Montreal and the French army. *See* Canada

Oct. 25, Death of George II. Accession of George III

1761

July 17, The Bridgewater Canal opened near Manchester, first great work of the kind in England, length 29 miles

Sept. 8, Marriage of George III to Charlotte of Mecklenburg

Oct. 5, Resignation of Pitt because of refusal of the Cabinet to declare war on Spain because of the Treaty of alliance of Spain with France (Bourbon Family Compact, Aug. 15)

——, Ministry of the Duke of Newcastle, Egremont and Bute, Secretaries of State

Nov. 3–March 12, 1768, First Parliament of George III

1762

Jan., War declared on Spain

May, Bute Ministry formed an administration, which, after various changes, resigned April 8, 1763. It was severely attacked by Junius and John Wilkes. John, Earl of Bute, First Lord of the Treasury, Sir Francis Dashwood, Chancellor of the Exchequer; Earl Grenville, President of the Council; Duke of Bedford, Privy Seal; Earl of Halifax, Admiralty; Earl of Egremont and George Granville, Secretaries of State; Lord Ligonier, Ordnance; Henry Fox, afterwards Lord Holland, Paymaster of the Forces; Viscount Barrington, Treasurer of the Navy; Lord Sandys, First Lord of Trade; Duke of Marlborough, Earl Talbot, Lord Huntingdon, Lord Anson, Lord North, &c.

1763

Feb. 10, Treaty of Paris ended the Seven Years' War between Great Britain, France, and Spain. France ceded to Great Britain, Nova Scotia, Canada, and the country east of the Mississippi as far as the Iberville, the Mississippi to be the boundary with Louisiana, Granada in the West Indies and 4 other islands, Cape Breton Island; Spain ceded Florida to Great Britain

April 8, Grenville Ministry. The first succeeded the Bute administration; and resigned in July, 1765. George Grenville, First Lord of the Treasury and Chancellor of the Exchequer; Earl Granville (succeeded by the Duke of Bedford), Lord President; Duke of Marlborough, Privy Seal; Earls of Halifax and Sandwich, Secretaries of State; Earl Gower, Lord Chamberlain; Earl of Egmont, Admiralty;

Marquis of Granby, Ordnance; Lord Holland (late Mr. Fox), Paymaster; Welbore Ellis, Secretary-at-War; Viscount Barrington, Treasurer of the Navy; Lord Hillsborough, First Lord of Trade; Lord Henley (afterwards Earl of Northington), Lord Chancellor; Duke of Rutland, Lords North, Trevor, Hyde, &c.

1765

March 2, Stamp Act passed requiring use of stamped paper for legal documents in the Colonies

June 1, Isle of Man annexed to Great Britain

Dec. 30, Death of James Frederick Edward Stuart, the "Old Pretender"

1766

March 18, The Stamp Act repealed because of effective resistance in America so that no revenue was produced

July 13, Rockingham Ministry. The first succeeded the administration of Mr. Geo. Grenville; the second succeeded that of Lord North. First Administration, July 13, 1765 to July 30, 1766: Charles, Marq. of Rockingham, First Lord of the Treasury; William Dowdeswell, Chancellor of the Exchequer; Earl of Winchilsea and Nottingham, Lord President; Duke of Newcastle, Privy Seal; Earl of Northington, Lord Chancellor; Duke of Portland, Lord Chamberlain; Duke of Rutland, Master of the Horse; Lord Talbot, Lord Steward; Henry Seymour Conway and the Duke of Grafton, Secretaries of State; Lord Egmont, Admiralty; Marquis of Granby, Ordnance; Viscount Barrington, Secretary-at-War; Viscount Howe, Treasurer of the Navy; Charles Townshend, Paymaster of the Forces; Earl of Dartmouth, First Lord of Trade; Lords Bessborough, Grantham, and Cavendish, &c.

Aug., Chatham Ministry succeeded the first Rockingham administration: after several changes it terminated Dec., 1767. Earl of Chatham, First Minister and Lord Privy Seal; Duke of Grafton, First Lord of the Treasury; Lord Camden, Lord Chancellor; Charles Townshend, Chancellor of the Exchequer; Earl of Northington, Lord President; Earl of Shelburne and General Conway, Secretaries of State; Sir Charles Saunders (succeeded by Sir Edward Hawke), Admiralty; Marquis of Granby, Ordnance; Lord Hillsborough, First Lord of Trade; Viscount Barrington, Secretary at War; Lord North and Sir George Cooke, Joint Paymasters; Viscount Howe, Treasurer of the Navy; Duke of Ancaster, Lord le Despencer, &c.

1767

Dec., Grafton Ministry succeeded that of Lord Chatham. The Duke resigned, and Lord North became Prime Minister, Jan., 1770. Augustus Henry, Duke of Grafton, First Lord of the Treasury; Frederick, Lord North, Chancellor of the Exchequer; Earl Gower, Lord President; Earl of Chatham, Lord Privy Seal; Earl of Shelburne and Viscount Weymouth, Secretaries of State; Sir Edward Hawke, First Lord of the Admiralty; Marquis of Granby, Master-General of the Ordnance; Lords Sandwich and Le Despencer, Joint Postmasters-General; Lords Hertford, Duke of Ancaster, Thomas Townshend, &c.; Lord Camden, Lord Chancellor, succeeded by Charles Yorke (created Lord Morden).

1768

May 10, 1768–Sept. 30, 1774, Second Parliament of George III; privilege as to freedom from arrest of the servants of members relinquished by the Commons (1770).

Nov. 21, 1768–Jan. 21, 1772, The Junius Letters published in the "Public Advertiser" a series of political letters signed "Junius," the published "Woddfallen" edition begins with the second, that of Jan. 21, 1769. They have been ascribed to Mr. E. Burke, Mr. William Gerard Hamilton, commonly called Single-speech Hamilton, John Wilkes, Mr. Dunning (afterwards Lord Ashburton), Serjeant Adair, the Rev. J. Rosenhagen, John Roberts, Charles Lloyd, Samuel Dyer, General Lee, the Duke of Portland, Hugh Boyd, Lord George Sackville, Earl Temple, and Sir Philip Francis. The last-named is generally considered to have been the author. Junius said, "I am the depositary of my own secret, and it shall perish with me." The work of Mr. Chabot and Hon. E. T. B. Twisleton was considered decisive of Sir Philip Francis being Junius, May, 1871. "Junius is as much unknown as ever."—*Athenæum*, Sept. 8, 1888.

1769

Feb. 4, John Wilkes expelled from the House of Commons for an alleged libel on Lord Weymouth, re-elected Feb. 16 and again expelled, and again March 16, but in the next election April 13 his opponent Colonel Luttrell was declared elected in spite of a majority vote for Wilkes

1770

Jan., North Ministry: Frederick, Lord North, First Lord of the Treasury, and Chancellor of the Exchequer; Earl Gower, Lord President; Earl of Halifax, Privy Seal; Earl of Rochford, Lord Weymouth (succeeded by Lord Sandwich) and Earl of Hillsborough, Secretaries of State; Sir Edward Hawke, Admiralty; Marquis of Granby, Ordnance; Sir Gilbert Elliot, Lord Hertford, Duke of Ancaster, Lord Carteret, &c.

1772

June 22, Decision of the Court of King's Bench in favor of Somerset, slave, claimed by master who had brought him to England, that slavery could not exist in Great Britain

1772, Royal Marriage Act, 12 Geo. III, c. 11, was passed in 1772, in consequence of the marriage of the Duke of Gloucester, the King's brother, with the widow of the Earl Waldegrave, and of the Duke of Cumberland with the widow of Colonel Horton and daughter of Lord Irnham. [By this act, none of the descendants of George II, unless of foreign birth, can marry under the age of 25, without the consent of the King; at and after that age, after twelve months' notice given to the Privy Council, they may contract such marriage, which shall be good unless both houses of parliament disapprove]

1774

March 5, Five Acts passed applying to colonies in America called by them, the "intolerable Acts," the Boston Port Bill, Regulating Act of Massachusetts, Administration of Justice Act, Quartering Act, and Quebec Act. *See also* America

Nov. 29, 1774–Sept. 1, 1780, Third Parliament of George III; reporting the debates in Parliament conceded after arrest of Miller, printer, of "London Evening Mail" for publishing reports of debates, and of Crosby, Lord Mayor of London, for granting him bail

1775

June 17, Revolt of the American Colonies. *See* America

1778

March 13, The Treaty of Alliance of France with the United States of Feb. 6 communicated to England and war with France soon followed (1778–1783)

1780

March 26, Sunday newspapers began with "The British Gazette and Sunday Monitor"

June 2–9, "No Popery" riots led by Lord George Gordon heading a mob of 40,000 persons carrying a petition to Parliament for repeal of Act which granted relief to Catholics of certain disabilities by repeal of penal laws. 210 rioters were killed and 248 wounded. Lord George was tried to high treason but was acquitted Feb. 5, 1781

Oct. 31, 1780–March 25, 1784, Fourth Parliament of George III

Dec. 30, 1780–1783, War between Great Britain and Holland for naval supremacy

1781

Oct. 19, Surrender of Cornwallis with army of 7,000 men at Yorktown. *See* United States

1782

Feb. 27, Resolution of House of Commons against the "further prosecution of offensive war on the continent of North America"

March 5, Bill passed enabling the King to make a peace or truce with America

March 20, Resignation of Lord North, Prime Minister

March 22, Second Ministry of the Marquis of Rockingham, Whig, taking office on condition that the independence of the United States should be recognized. Marquis of Rockingham, First Lord of the Treasury; Lord John Cavendish, Chancellor of the Exchequer; Lord Camden, President of the Council; Duke of Grafton, Privy Seal; Lord Thurlow, Lord Chancellor; William, Earl of Shelburne and Charles James Fox, Secretaries of State; Augustus Viscount Keppel, First Lord of the Admiralty; Duke of Richmond, Master-General of the Ordnance; Thomas Townshend, Secretary-at-War; Isaac Barré, Edmund Burke, John Dunning, &c.

April 12, Rodney and Hood defeated the French fleet in the West Indies, Admiral de Grasse taken prisoner

July 1, Death of the Marquis of Rockingham

July 2, The Earl of Shelburne formed Ministry. The Earl of Shelburne (afterwards Marquis of Lansdowne), First Lord of the Treasury; William Pitt, Chancellor of the Exchequer; Lord (afterwards Earl) Camden, President of the Council; Duke of Grafton, Privy Seal; Thomas, Lord Grantham, and Thomas Townshend (afterwards Lord Sydney), Secretaries; Viscount Keppel, Admiralty; Duke of Richmond, Ordnance; Lord Thurlow, Lord Chancellor; Henry Dundas, Isaac Barré, Sir George Yonge, &c.

Nov. 30, Preliminary Treaty with the United States signed in Paris

1783

Jan. 20, Preliminary Treaties between France and England and Spain signed and provisional Treaty with the United States held to take effect (Treaties of Paris and Versailles)

April 5, Portland Ministry, the "Coalition Ministry," of which William Henry Cavendish, Duke of Portland, as First Lord of the Treasury, was the head. It obtained the name of the "Coalition" Ministry, and included Lord North with Mr. Fox, formerly inveterate opponents. Formed April 5, 1783; dissolved by Mr. Pitt's coming into power, Dec. same year. First Administration: Duke of Portland, First Lord of the Treasury; Viscount Stormont, President of the Council; Earl of Carlisle, Privy Seal; Frederick, Lord North, and Charles James Fox, Home and Foreign Secretaries; Lord John Cavendish, Chancellor of the Exchequer; Viscount Keppel, Admiralty; Viscount Townshend, Ordnance; Lord Loughborough, Chief Commissioner of Great Seal

Sept. 3, Definitive Treaty with the United States signed in Paris, independence of the United States recognized. *See also* United States

Dec. 18, Dismissal of the Portland Ministry by the King and first Ministry of William Pitt succeeded: William Pitt, First Lord of the Treasury and Chancellor of the Exchequer; Earl Gower, Lord President; Duke of Rutland, Privy Seal; Marquis of Carmarthen and Earl Temple (immediately succeeded by Lord Sydney), Secretaries; Lord Thurlow, Lord Chancellor; Viscount Howe, Admiralty; Duke of Richmond, Ordnance; William Wyndham Grenville, Henry Dundas, &c.

1784

March 25, Parliament dissolved

May 18,–June 21, 1790, Fifth Parliament of George III

Aug. 25, First balloon ascent made in Great Britain by James Tytler at Edinburgh

Oct. 4, James Sadler made ascent from Oxford in a Montgolfière balloon

1785

Jan. 1, Mr. John Walter published the first number of the *Daily Universal Register*, price 2½d., printed on the logographic system (invented by Henry Johnson, a compositor), in which types containing syllables and words were employed instead of single letters. On Jan. 1, 1788, the paper was named the *Times*

1788

Jan. 30, Death of Charles Edward Stuart, the "Young Pretender," grandson of James II and elder son of James, the "Old Pretender," in Rome

Feb. 13, Trial of Warren Hastings begun for high crimes and misdemeanors. Among other charges was his acceptance of a present of 100,000l. from the nabob of Oude. The trial occupied 145 days, and lasted seven years and three months; commencing Feb. 13, 1788, terminating in his acquittal, April 23, 1795. Mr. Sheridan's speech on the impeachment excited great admiration

Oct. 12–Feb., 1789, Insanity of the King, placed under restraint during this period but recovered before Regency Bill framed by Mr. Pitt had been passed

1790

Nov. 26, 1790–May 20, 1796, Sixth Parliament of George III

1791

June 10, Canada Constitutional Act passed. *See also* Canada

1792

June 26, First coalition against France. *See* France and French Revolution

1794

May 16, John Horne Tooke arrested and imprisoned in the Tower accused of revolutionary activities; acquitted of high treason Nov. 22

May 23, Habeas Corpus Act suspended due to spread of revolutionary ideas

June 1, Naval victory of Lord Howe defeating the French off Brest (Battle of June 1)

1795

April 8, Marriage of the Prince of Wales to the Princess Caroline of Brunswick

Dec. 8, "Gagging Act" passed to protect the King and Government from seditious meetings

1796

May 14, Dr. Edward Jenner, discoverer of vaccination, made his first experiment, and vaccination begun Jan. 21, 1799, soon became general

Sept. 27, 1796–June 29, 1802, Seventh Parliament of George III

1797

Feb. 26, Order in Council suspended cash payments of the Bank of England making bank-notes legal tender due to run on Bank and panic due to fear of invasion from France

April–June, Naval mutinies at Spithead for redress of grievances

May 3, Bank Restriction Act enacted

July 8, Death of Edmund Burke

1798

April 20, Habeas Corpus Act again suspended

May 4–June 21, Irish rebellion. *See* Ireland

Aug. 1, Battle of the Nile, victory of Nelson

1799

April, Coalition against France

Aug. 5, Death of Admiral Lord Richard Howe

1800

May 15, Attempt of Hatfield on the life of the King

1801

Jan. 1, Legislative Union of Great Britain with Ireland under the name of the United Kingdom. Act of Union provided that Ireland should send 4 spiritual Lords, 28 temporal Peers, 100 members of Commons to the Imperial Parliament

Feb. 2, First meeting of Parliament of the United Kingdom (Imperial); clergymen prohibited from becoming members of Parliament

Feb. 3, Resignation of Pitt Ministry, succeeded by Henry Addington

April 2, Nelson's victory at Copenhagen, destruction of Danish fleet
April 19, Habeas Corpus Act again suspended
Oct. 1, Preliminary Peace of Amiens

1802

March 27, Peace of Amiens signed by which England received Trinidad and Ceylon
June 2, Health and Morals of Apprentices Act limited hours to 12 and regulated working and living conditions
Nov. 16, 1802–Oct. 24, 1806, Seventh Parliament of George III

1803

May 18, War against France under Bonaparte
July 23, Failure of Irish revolt led by Robert Emmett; captured Aug. 25 and hanged Sept. 20

1804

May 12, Second Pitt Ministry formed: William Pitt, First Lord of the Treasury; Lord Eldon, Lord Chancellor; Duke of Portland, succeeded by Lord Sidmouth (late Mr. Addington), Lord President; Earl of Westmorland, Lord Privy Seal; Lord Hawkesbury, Lord Harrowby (succeeded by Lord Mulgrave), and Earl Camden (succeeded by Viscount Castlereagh), Home, Foreign, and Colonial Secretaries; Viscount Melville (succeeded by Lord Barham), Admiralty; Duke of Montrose, Mr. Dundas, &c.; Henry Addington, First Lord of the Treasury and Chancellor of the Exchequer; Lord Eldon, Lord Chancellor; Duke of Portland, Lord President; Earl of Westmoreland, Lord Privy Seal; Lord Pelham, Home Secretary; Mr. R. B. Jenkinson (Lord Hawkesbury, 1803; and Earl of Liverpool, 1808), Foreign Secretary; Lord Hobart, Colonial Secretary; Earl St. Vincent, First Lord of Admiralty; Earl of Chatham, Ordnance; Charles Yorke, Secretary-at-War; Viscount Lewisham, Lord Auckland, &c.

1805

May 26, Third coalition against France (England, Russia, Austria, Sweden)
April 29, Lord Melville impeached charged with financial maladministration of the admiralty; acquitted June 12
Oct. 21, Victory and death of Nelson at Trafalgar

1806

Jan. 23, Death of William Pitt, Lord Grenville succeeded him as Prime Minister: Lord Grenville, First Lord of the Treasury; Lord Henry Petty (afterwards Marquis of Lansdowne), Chancellor of the Exchequer; Earl Fitzwilliam, Lord President; Viscount Sidmouth (late Mr. Addington), Privy Seal; Charles James Fox, Foreign Secretary; Earl Spencer, Home Secretary; William Windham, Colonial Secretary; Lord Erskine, Lord Chancellor; Sir Charles Grey (afterwards Viscount Howick and Earl Grey), Admiralty; Lord Minto, Board of Control; Lord Auckland, Board of Trade; Lord Moira, Master-General of the Ordnance; R. B. Sheridan, Treasurer of the Navy; Richard Fitzpatrick, &c.; Lord Ellenborough (Lord Chief Justice) had a seat in the cabinet
May 22, Inquiry ordered by the King into charges of

incontinence of Caroline, Princess of Wales; acquitted but censured for impropriety of conduct
Sept. 13, Death of Charles James Fox
Dec. 15, 1806–April 29, 1807, Eighth Parliament of George III

1807

Jan. 7, Orders in Council issued in reply to the Berlin Decrees of Napoleon
March 25, Act for abolition of the slave trade in the Dominions received the royal assent
——, Ministry of William Henry Cavendish, Duke of Portland
June 22–Sept. 24, 1812, Ninth Parliament of George III
Aug. 16, Gas lights introduced in London at Golden Lane, in Pall Mall in 1809 and between 1814 and 1820 generally throughout London
Sept. 5, Heligoland in the North Sea taken from the Danes and held; formal cession to England in 1814

1808

1808–1814, Peninsula War. *See* Spain

1809

Jan. 16, Victory and death of Sir John Moore in battle with the French at Corunna
March 18, Enforced resignation of the Duke of York as Commander-in-Chief on account of charges of financial maladministration but acquitted of bribery and reinstated in 1811
Oct. 29, Death of the Duke of Portland; Spencer Perceval succeeded as Prime Minister, First Lord of the Treasury, Chancellor of Exchequer; Lord Eldon, Lord Chancellor; Earl Camden, Lord President; Earl of Westmorland, Lord Privy Seal; Richard Ryder, Marquis of Wellesley, and Earl of Liverpool, Home, Foreign, and Colonial Secretary; Lord Mulgrave, Admiralty; Mr. Dumas and Earl Bathurst, Boards of Control and Trade; Earl of Chatham, Ordnance; Viscount Palmerston, Secretary of War, &c.; Earl Camden, Lord President; Lord Eldon, Lord Chancellor; Earl of Westmorland, Lord Privy Seal; Hon. Spencer Perceval, Lord Hawkesbury (afterwards Earl of Liverpool), Mr. Canning, and Viscount Castlereagh (afterwards Marquis of Londonderry), Home, Foreign, and Colonial Secretaries; Earl Bathurst and Mr. Dundas, Boards of Trade and Control; Lord Mulgrave, Admiralty; Earl of Chatham, Ordnance

1810

April 6, Sir Frances Burdett, reformer, committed to the Tower because of criticism of action of House in speech; riots followed
Nov. 2, Death of the Princess Amelia followed by relapse of the King into insanity which became permanent

1811

Feb. 5, The Prince of Wales appointed Regent
Nov., Luddites, organized bands of rioters so named, first appeared in Nottingham destroying machinery which had displaced handicraftsmen in the textile industry

1812

May 11, Assassination of Prime Minister Perceval by a madman in lobby of the House of Commons
June 9, The Earl of Liverpool became Prime Minister and First Lord of the Treasury: Earl of Eldon, Lord

Chancellor; Earl of Harrowby, Lord President of the Council; Earl of Westmorland, Lord Privy Seal; N. Vansittart, Chancellor of the Exchequer (succeeded by F. J. Robinson, 1823); Viscount Sidmouth, Home Secretary (succeeded by Robert Peel, 1822); Viscount Castlereagh, aft. Marquis of Londonderry, Foreign Secretary (succeeded by George Canning, 1822); Earl Bathurst, Colonial Secretary; Viscount Melville, First Lord of Admiralty; Earl of Buckinghamshire, Board of Control (succeeded by G. Canning, 1816; C. Bathurst, 1820; C. Wynne, 1822); Charles Bathurst (1813), Chancellor of Duchy of Lancaster (succeeded by N. Vansittart, Lord Bexley, 1823); Wellesley Pole, afterwards Lord Maryborough, 1815, Master of the Mint; F. J. Robinson, 1818; W. Huskisson, 1823; Board of Trade; Earl of Mulgrave, Ordnance

June 18, War declared by the United States against Great Britain because of the British Orders in Council as to blockade in wars with the French which interfered with American commerce, and of impressment of American seamen. *See* United States

1814

May 30, First Treaty of Paris signed (Peace of Paris) after abdication of Napoleon. England acquired Trinidad (Tobago), St. Lucia, Mauritius (Isle de France), Rodrigues, Seychelles, and Malta

July 25, Trial of George Stephenson's steam engine on railroad

Dec. 24, Treaty of Ghent ended the war with the United States

1815

March 1, Napoleon returned to France from Elba and the "Hundred Days" war began, Wellington and Blucher taking command of allied army in Belgium

June 18, Battle of Waterloo, defeat of the French and Napoleon, ended war

Nov. 5, Treaty signed by which Ionian Islands placed under British sovereignty

Nov. 20, Second Treaty of Paris signed

Corn law enacted in 1815 prohibited importation of wheat except at high rates of duty unless home grown wheat at 80s. a quarter

1816

Jan. 11, Sir Humphry Davy announced the principle of the safety lamp

May 2, Marriage of Princess Charlotte to Leopold of Saxe-Coburg

July 7, Death of Richard Brinsley Sheridan, dramatist

Dec. 2, Spa fields meeting in London of the "Spencean Philanthropists," riots and bloodshed

1817

March 29, Habeas Corpus Act suspended

March, Workingmen from Manchester marching to London to present their grievances, each with his blanket for sleeping at night on the roadside (the march of the blanketeers) dispersed by troops and the leaders arrested

July 22, Windham Sadler succeeded in crossing the Irish Channel in balloon

Sept. 22, Cash payments resumed

Nov. 6, Death of the Princess Charlotte

1819

Jan. 14, 1819–Feb. 29, 1820, Eleventh Parliament of George III

July 2, Factory Act approved prohibited the employment of children under 9 years of age in cotton mills

Aug. 16, Meeting on the outskirts of Manchester for parliamentary reform attended by 80,000 men, women, and children, charged by cavalry and 11 persons killed and hundreds injured, the "Peterloo massacre"

Nov. 29, Foreign Enlistment Act forbade British subjects to enter service of a foreign State without license from the King or Privy Council, and prohibited fitting out or equipping ships to be employed against any foreign Power with which the Government at peace (59 Geo. III, c. 69)

Nov. 29–Dec. 17, The "Six Acts" (Gagging Acts) introduced and enacted by Parliament to prevent seditious meetings, and prevent collection of arms and training in the use of arms, &c.

Dec. 11, Law prohibited training persons in the use of arms

Dec. 23, Factory Act approved fixed hours at 72 a week, age limit for children 9 and limited hours to 10½ for those under 18

1820

Jan. 23, Death of Edward Augustus, Duke of Kent, fourth son of George III and the father of Victoria

Jan. 29, Death of George III, and accession of George IV (Regent since 1811)

Feb. 23, Discovery of Cato Street conspiracy to assassinate the Ministry and arrest of Thistlewood and his 4 leading associates; hanged May 1

April 23, 1820–June 2, 1826, First Parliament of George IV

June 6, Queen Caroline arrived in England from the Continent

July 5, Bill of pains and penalties against the Queen introduced by Lord Liverpool

Aug. 17–Nov. 10, Trial of Queen Caroline, defended by Brougham and Denman, resulted in abandonment of the Bill

1821

May, The Bank of England resumed specie payments

July 19, Coronation of George IV, the Queen refused admission to Westminster Abbey

Aug. 7, Death of Queen Caroline

Aug. 12, Lord Londonderry (Castlereagh) mentally disordered committed suicide; succeeded by George Canning at the Foreign Office, and Sir Robert Peel as Home Secretary

1824

April 19, Death of Lord Byron (36)

June 21, Combination Act approved repealing law against combination of workmen

1825

June 22, Factory Act approved

July 6, Combination Act repealed provisions of previous Acts

Sept. 27, Stockton and Darlington Railroad opened

1825–1826, Financial panic and failure of banks

1826

March 18, Treaty of commerce and navigation with Norway and Sweden signed

Nov. 14, 1826–July 24, 1830, Second Parliament of George IV

1827

Jan. 5, Death of Frederick Augustus, Duke of York

April 30, George Canning formed Ministry after illness forced Lord Liverpool to resign: George Canning, First Lord of the Treasury and Chancellor of the Exchequer; Earl of Harrowby, President of the Council; Duke of Portland, Lord Privy Seal; Viscount Dudley, Viscount Goderich, and Mr. Sturges Bourne, Foreign, Colonial, and Home Secretaries; W. W. Wynn, President of the India Board; Wm. Huskisson, Board of Trade; Lord Palmerston, Secretary at War; Lord Bexley, Chancellor of the Duchy of Lancaster; Duke of Clarence, Lord High Admiral; Lord Lyndhurst, Lord Chancellor, &c.; Marquis of Lansdowne, without office; afterwards Home Secretary; Earl of Carlisle, Woods and Forests

June 1, Canning's Corn Bill providing for fixed duty of 1s. per quarter when price of wheat was at or below 70s. passed in the House

July 6, Treaty of London on behalf of Greece signed. *See* Greece

July 12, International Conference in London on the affairs of Greece opened

Aug. 8, Death of George Canning, the Prime Minister ——, Viscount Goderich (afterwards Earl of Ripon) became Prime Minister

1828

Jan. 8, Resignation of Goderich Ministry. Succeeded by the Duke of Wellington: Duke of Wellington, First Lord of the Treasury; Lord Lyndhurst, Lord Chancellor; Henry Goulburn, Chancellor of the Exchequer; Earl Bathurst, President of the Council; Lord Ellenborough, Privy Seal; Mr. (afterwards Sir) Robert Peel, Earl Dudley, and Mr. Wm. Huskisson, Home, Foreign, and Colonial Secretaries; Viscount Melville, Board of Control; Mr. Charles Grant, Board of Trade; Lord Palmerston, Secretary-at-War; J. C. Herries, Master of the Mint; Earl of Aberdeen, Duchy of Lancaster; Mr. Huskisson, Earl Dudley, Viscount Palmerston, and Mr. Grant quitted the Ministry, and various changes followed in May and June same year. The Earl of Aberdeen and Sir George Murray became, respectively, Foreign and Colonial Secretaries; Sir Henry Hardinge, Secretary-at-War; Mr. Vesey Fitzgerald (afterwards Lord Fitzgerald), India Board; Lord Lowther, First Commissioner of Land Revenues, &c., May and June, 1828; Mr. Arbuthnot, Mr. Vesey Fitzgerald, &c.; Viscount Goderich, First Lord of the Treasury; Duke of Portland, President of the Council; Lord Lyndhurst, Lord Chancellor; Earl of Carlisle, Lord Privy Seal; Viscount Dudley, Mr. Huskisson, and the Marquis of Lansdowne, Foreign, Colonial, and Home Secretaries; Lord Palmerston, Secretary-at-War; Mr. C. W. Wynn, President of the India Board; Mr. Charles Grant (afterwards Lord Glenelg), Board of Trade; Mr. Herries, Chancellor of the Exchequer; Mr. Tierney, Master of the Mint, &c.

Feb. 26, Lord John Russell introduced motion for the repeal of the Test and Corporation Acts, which was carried by vote of 237 to 193, and as modified passed in Lords

May 9, The Corporation and Test Repeal Act passed for the relief of dissenters from civil and religious disabilities, the necessity for receiving the sacrament of the Lord's Supper as a qualification for certain offices repealed, the declaration "on the true faith of a Christian" substituted

July 5, Daniel O'Connell elected to Parliament for Clare County, Ireland, the first Roman Catholic commoner elected since the Revolution

July 15, Corn Law Act passed. The act (called the sliding scale), whereby wheat was allowed to be imported on payment of a duty of 1l. 5s. 8d. per quarter, whenever the average price of all England was under 62s.; from 62s. to 63s., 1l. 4s. 8d.; and so gradually reduced to 1s., when the average price was 73s. and upwards, passed July 15, 1828

1829

April 13, The Catholic Emancipation Act passed in the Commons March 30 and in the Lords April 10, received the royal assent

April 28, The Duke of Norfolk took his seat in the Lords, the first Roman Catholic peer under the Emancipation Act

May 4, The first English Roman Catholic member elected to Parliament, the Earl of Surrey

May 29, Death of Sir Humphry Davy, chemist

June 19 and 24, Factory Acts made new provisions as to employment of children

Oct. 6, Trial of locomotive engines for prize offered by the Liverpool and Manchester Railroad won by Stephenson's "Rocket" with speed of 35 miles an hour

1830

Feb. 2, Lord John Russell's proposal for enfranchisement of Leeds, Birmingham, and Manchester rejected by 188 votes to 140

June 26, Death of George IV. Accession of William IV

Sept. 15, Public opening of the Liverpool and Manchester Railroad, William Huskisson accidentally killed by engine, the "Rocket." He had resigned from the Cabinet in May, 1829

Oct. 26–April 22, 1831, First Parliament of William IV

Nov. 16, Resignation of the Duke of Wellington Ministry. Earl Grey succeeded as Prime Minister; Lord Brougham, Lord Chancellor; Viscount Althorpe, Chancellor of the Exchequer; Marquis of Lansdowne, President of the Council; Earl of Durham, Privy Seal; Viscounts Melbourne, Palmerston, and Goderich, Home, Foreign, and Colonial Secretaries; Sir James Graham, Admiralty; Lord Auckland and Mr. Charles Grant (afterwards, 1830, Lord Glenelg), Boards of Trade and Control; Lord Holland, Chancellor of Duchy of Lancaster; Lord John Russell, Paymaster of the Forces; Duke of Richmond, Earl of Carlisle, Mr. Wynne, &c.; E. G. Stanley (afterwards Earl of Derby), Chief Secretary for Ireland, became Colonial Secretary, March, 1833

1831

March 1, Reform Bill introduced by Lord John Russell carried in House by majority of 1 only, for it, 302, against, 301 on second reading

April 22, Parliament dissolved by the King in person

June 14–Dec. 3, 1832, Second Parliament of William IV; Second Reform Bill introduced

June 24, Carried on second reading July 7 by majority of 136, and on third reading Sept. 22 by majority of 109; defeated in the Lords by 41 (199 to 158), Oct. 8

Aug. 1, The new London Bridge opened by the King
Sept. 27, British Association for the Advancement of Science held first meeting
Oct. 15, Factory Act approved
Dec. 6, Third Reform Bill introduced carried on second reading Dec. 17 by majority of 162

1832

March 23, Reform Bill passed third reading in Commons with majority of 116; passed in Lords April 14 with a majority of 9
May 7, Amendment to Reform Bill adverse to the Government passed in Lords, proposal that the question of enfranchisement should precede that of disenfranchisement
May 9, Resignation of the Ministry but resumed office on the King granting them full power to secure majorities by the creation of new peers
June 4, Reform Bill passed in Lords by majority of 84 (106 against 22) and received the royal assent June 7
July 17, Scotch Reform Act received royal assent
Aug. 7, Irish Reform Act received royal assent

1833

Jan. 29, 1833–Dec. 30, 1834. Third Parliament of William IV
Aug. 23, Act for the abolition of slavery throughout the British colonies, and for the promotion of industry among the manumitted slaves, and for compensation to the persons hitherto entitled to the services of such slaves by the grant from parliament of 20,000,000l. sterling, passed
Aug. 29, Shaftesbury Factory Act passed for the protection of children from 9 to 13 years of age and young persons from 13 to 18, and for the first time factory inspection authorized

1834

April, Unsuccessful strike of tailors of London for increase in wages
July 9, Resignation of Earl Grey because of differences in the Cabinet on question of extension of the Irish Coercion Bill
July 16, Viscount Melbourne formed Ministry: Viscount Melbourne, First Lord of the Treasury; Marquis of Lansdowne, Lord President; Earl Mulgrave, Privy Seal; Viscount Althorp, Chancellor of the Exchequer; Viscount Duncannon, Viscount Palmerston, and T. Spring-Rice (afterwards Lord Monteagle), Home, Foreign, and Colonial Secretaries; Lord Auckland, Admiralty; Mr. Charles Grant (afterwards Lord Glenelg), and Mr. C. P. Thomson (afterwards Lord Sydenham), Boards of Control and Trade; Lord John Russell, Paymaster of the Forces; Lord Brougham, Lord Chancellor; Sir John Hobhouse, Mr. Ellice, Marquis of Conyngham, Mr. Littleton, &c.; Lord Lyndhurst, Lord Chancellor; Earl of Rosslyn, Lord President; Lord Wharncliffe, Privy Seal; Henry Goulburn, Duke of Wellington, and Earl of Aberdeen, Home, Foreign, and Colonial Secretaries of State; Earl De Grey, First Lord of the Admiralty; Lord Ellenborough and Alexander Baring, Board of Control and Trade; Sir Edward Knatchbull, Paymaster of the Forces; J. C. Herries, Secretary of War; Sir George Murray, Master-General of the Ordnance, &c.
July 25, Death of Samuel Taylor Coleridge

Aug. 1, Slavery terminated in the British possessions; 770,280 slaves became free
Aug. 14, Poor Law Amendment Act established central control, local boards abolished
Nov. 15, Melbourne Ministry dismissed by the King, the Duke of Wellington in control of the Government until Dec. 9
Dec. 9, Sir Robert Peel formed Ministry; as First Lord of the Treasury and Chancellor of the Exchequer

1835

Feb. 15, 1835–July 17, 1837, Fourth Parliament of William IV
April 8, Resignation of the Peel Ministry after defeat in Commons
April 18, Second Melbourne Ministry: Viscount Melbourne, First Lord of the Treasury; Marquis of Lansdowne, Lord President; Viscount Duncannon, Privy Seal, and Woods and Forests (succeeded by Earl of Clarendon, Jan., 1840); T. Spring Rice, Chancellor of the Exchequer (succeeded by Francis T. Baring, Aug., 1840); Lord John Russell, Home Secretary (succeeded by Marquis of Normanby, Aug., 1839); Viscount Palmerston, Foreign Secretary; Lord Glenelg, Colonial Secretary (succeeded by Marquis of Normanby, Feb., 1839; Lord John Russell, Aug., 1839); Viscount Howick, Secretary-at-War (succeeded by T. B. Macaulay, Sept., 1839); Lord Auckland, Admiralty (succeeded by Earl of Minto, Sept., 1835)
Sept. 9, Corporation Reform Act passed

1837

June 20, Death of William IV. Accession of Queen Victoria
——, Separation of Hanover from Great Britain, Ernest Augustus, Duke of Cumberland, eldest surviving son of George III becoming King of Hanover
July 4, Liverpool and Birmingham (Grand Junction) Railroad opened
Nov. 15, 1837–June 23, 1841, First Parliament of Victoria

1838

June 28, Coronation of Queen Victoria
Sept. 17, Railroad from Liverpool to London (Great Western) opened
Sept. 18, Anti-Corn Law League for securing repeal of laws charging duty on the import of corn founded at Manchester supported by Richard Cobden, John Bright, Charles Villiers, John Benjamin Smith, first chairman
Oct. 28, The steamer "Liverpool" sailed for New York

1839

March, Opium War with China begun. *See* China

1840

Jan. 10, Penny postage begun
——, Members of Parliament gave up privilege of franking letters
Feb. 10, Marriage of Queen Victoria to her cousin Albert of Saxe-Coburg and Gotha

1841

Aug. 19, 1841–July 23, 1847, Second Parliament of Victoria
Sept. 6, 1841–June 29, 1846, Second Ministry of Sir

Robert Peel: Sir Robert Peel, First Minister; Duke of Wellington in the cabinet without office, aft. Commander-in-Chief; Lord Lyndhurst, Lord Chancellor; Lord Wharncliffe, Lord President; Duke of Buckingham, Lord Privy Seal (succeeded by Duke of Buccleuch); Sir James Graham, Earl of Aberdeen, and Lord Stanley, Home, Foreign, and Colonial Secretaries; Henry Goulburn, Chancellor of the Exchequer; Earl of Haddington, First Lord of the Admiralty; Earl of Ripon, Board of Trade (succeeded by W. E. Gladstone); Lord Ellenborough, India Board (succeeded by Lord Fitzgerald; succeeded by Earl of Ripon); Sir Henry Hardinge, Sir Edward Knatchbull, Sir George Murray, &c.
[Terminated June 29, 1846, by Sir Robert's resignation]

1842

Jan. 24, King of Prussia visited England
April 29, The act 5 Vict. c. 14, the second sliding scale act, regulating the duty on wheat, with sliding duties, also, on other articles of corn, passed
June 12, Death of Thomas Arnold, educator
Aug. 9, Asburton Treaty with the United States settled Canadian boundary with Maine
Aug. 10, Lord Ashley's Mines Act prohibited employment of women and girls in mines and collieries and made regulations for employment of boys and men
Aug. 29, Peace of Nankin ended war with China; cession of Hong-Kong of Jan. 20, 1841, to Great Britain confirmed

1844

June 6, Factory Act established the "Office of the Factory Inspectors" in London and made definite regulations as to health and hours
July 19, Charter of the Bank of England renewed

1845

June 30, Print Works Act regulated the labor of women and children in print factories
Aug. 4, Hosiery Act regulated labor in hosiery factories
Aug. 9, Silk Weavers Act approved
Oct. 9, John Henry Newman, one of leaders with Dr. Pusey of the Tractarian movement in Oxford, formally received into membership in the Roman Catholic Church

1846

Jan. 21, The "Daily News" established
March, Commercial panic
April 30, Committal of Smith O'Brien by the Commons for contempt. See Ireland
June 26, The Corn Importation Bill (introduced by Sir Robert Peel), 9 & 10 Vict. c. 22 (by which the duty on wheat was reduced to 4s. when imported at or above 53s., until Feb. 1st, 1849; after which day the duty became 1s. per quarter only, on all kinds of grain imported into the United Kingdom, at any prices), received the royal assent
July 6, Lord John Russell formed Ministry after resignation of Peel: First Lord of the Treasury, Lord John Russell; Lord Chancellor, Lord Cottenham (succeeded by Lord Truro); Lord President of the Council, Marquis of Lansdowne; Privy Seal, Earl of Minto; Chancellor of the Exchequer, Mr. (aft. Sir Charles) Wood; Foreign, Home, and Colonial Secretaries, Viscount Palmerston, Sir George Grey, and Earl Grey; Boards of Control and Trade, Sir John

Hobhouse (aft. Lord Broughton), and Earl of Clarendon (succeeded by Mr. Labouchere); Admiralty, the Earl of Auckland (succeeded by Sir Francis Thornhill Baring); Duchy of Lancaster, Lord Campbell (succeeded by the Earl of Carlisle, late Viscount Morpeth); Secretary at War, Mr. Fox Maule; Postmaster, Marquis of Clanricarde; Paymaster-General, T. B. Macaulay; Lord John Russell and his colleagues resigned their offices, Feb. 21, 1852; but were induced (after the failure of Lord Stanley's party to form an administration) to return to power, March 3 following
Aug. 26, Fatal Accidents Act provided for compensation
Dec. 15, The Hakluyt Society named for Richard Hakluyt established for the publication of rare voyages and travels
Failure of the potato crop in Ireland, famine and emigration

1847

June 8, Factory (Ten Hours) Act reduced the working hours of women and young persons to a maximum of 10 hours a day or 58 hours a week
Nov. 18–July 1, 1852, Third Parliament of Victoria

1848

April 10, Chartist demonstration in London after presentation of petition
Aug. 12, Death of George Stephenson, engineer

1849

June 26, Repeal of the navigation laws
Dec. 2, Death of Adelaide, Queen Dowager

1850

April 19, The Clayton-Bulwer Treaty with the United States provided that neither country should obtain exclusive control over proposed interoceanic canal in Central America
April 23, Death of William Wordsworth (80)
July 2, Death of Sir Robert Peel (62)
July 18, Death of the Duke of Cambridge
Aug. 5, Factory Act approved
Sept. 30, Papal Bull issued created Roman Catholic bishops in England and Dr. Nicholas Wiseman, cardinal and lord archbishop of Westminster

1851

March, Second Ministry of Lord John Russell, continuation of first: First Lord of the Treasury, Lord John Russell; President of the Council, Marquis of Lansdowne; Lord Privy Seal, Earl of Minto; Chancellor of the Exchequer, Sir Charles Wood; Home, Foreign, and Colonial Secretaries, Sir George Grey, Viscount Palmerston (succeeded by Earl Granville, Dec. 22), and Earl Grey; Lord Chancellor, Lord Truro; First Lord of the Admiralty, Sir Francis T. Baring; Board of Control, Lord Broughton; Board of Trade, Mr. Labouchere; Secretary at War, Mr. Fox Maule (aft. Lord Panmure, and Earl of Dalhousie); Postmaster-General, Marquis of Clanricarde; Paymaster-General, Earl Granville; Lord Seymour, Earl of Carlisle, &c. This Ministry resigned Feb. 21, 1852; see Derby Administration
May 1, The first "Great Exhibition" of industries of all nations opened in Hyde Park, London

July, Ecclesiastical Titles Act (Great Britain and Ireland) passed, declared Papal Bull of 1850 null and
void and imposed fine of £100 on all who should try
to carry it into effect

July 24, Laboring Classes (Lodging Houses) Act
approved

Aug. 7, Act provided for improvement of administration
of criminal justice

Aug. 14, Inspection of Coal Mines Act approved

Nov. 13, Telegraph between England and France
opened

Dec. 16, Lord Palmerston asked to resign by Lord
John Russell because of his despatch on his own
authority submitted neither to the Queen or the
Prime Minister approving the *coup d'état* of Dec. 2
in France; followed shortly by fall of the Russell
Ministry

Census gave total population as 27,511,962; England
and Wales, 17,927,609; Scotland, 2,888,742; Ireland,
6,552,385; Islands in British Seas, 143,126

1852

Feb. 26, Death of the poet, Thomas Moore

Feb. 27, Lord Derby formed Ministry: First Lord of
the Treasury, Edward, Earl of Derby; Lord Chancellor, Lord St. Leonards (previously Sir Edward
Sugden); President of the Council, Earl of Lonsdale;
Lord Privy Seal, Marquis of Salisbury; Home,
Foreign, and Colonial Secretaries, Spencer Horatio
Walpole, Earl of Malmesbury, and Sir John Paking-
ton; Chancellor of the Exchequer, Benjamin Dis-
raeli; Board of Control, John Charles Herries; Board
of Trade, Joseph Warner Henley; Postmaster-
General, Earl of Hardwicke; Secretary-at-War,
William Beresford; First Commissioner of Works
and Public Buildings, Lord John Manners; Robert
Adam Christopher, Lord Colchester, &c.

Sept. 14, Death of the Duke of Wellington (83)

Nov. 4, 1852–March 21, 1857, Fourth Parliament of
Victoria

Dec. 28, Aberdeen Ministry formed on resignation of
Earl of Derby (Dec. 17): Earl of Aberdeen, First
Lord of the Treasury; Lord Cranworth, Lord Chan-
cellor; Earl Granville, President of the Council;
Duke of Argyll, Lord Privy Seal; Lord John Russell,
Foreign Secretary; Viscount Palmerston, Home Secre-
tary; Duke of Newcastle, Colonial and War Secretary;
William Ewart Gladstone, Chancellor of Exchequer;
Sir James Graham, First Lord of the Admiralty; Sir
Charles Wood, President of the India Board; Ed-
ward Cardwell, President of Board of Trade; Hon.
Sidney Herbert, Secretary-at-War; Sir William
Molesworth, Chief Commissioner of Works; Mar-
quess of Lansdowne (without office); Viscount Can-
ning, Lord Stanley of Alderley, Right Hon. Ed-
ward Strutt, &c.

1853

Jan. 1, First issue of "Field" newspaper

June 28, An act (called Mr. FitzRoy's act) was passed
for the better regulation of metropolitan stage and
hackney carriages, and for prohibiting the use of
advertising vehicles, by which the cab fares were
reduced to 6*d.* a mile. It came into operation July 11,
and on the 27th a general strike of the London cabmen took place. Some alterations having been made
in the act, the cabs reappeared on the stands on the
30th

Aug. 29, Death of Sir Charles Napier, Admiral

Oct. 30, British and French fleets entered the Bosphorus for purposes of observation. *See also* Turkey

1854

March 12, Treaty of alliance between England, France,
and Turkey signed

March 28, Declaration of war on Russia by England
and France. *See* Crimean War

April 29, Death of the Marquis of Anglesey, Field
Marshal

June 5, Reciprocity Treaty with the United States
(Fisheries, Commerce and Navigation)

June 10, The Crystal Palace, London, opened by the
Queen

Dec. 23, Foreign Legion Act passed for formation of a
foreign legion as a contingent in the war with Russia

1855

Jan. 20, Resignation of Aberdeen Ministry charged
with mismanagement of the war. Lord Palmerston
became Prime Minister Feb. 5: First Lord of the
Treasury, Henry Viscount Palmerston; Lord Chancellor, Lord Cranworth; President of the Council,
Earl Granville; Lord Privy Seal, Duke of Argyll;
next, Earl of Harrowby; afterwards the Marquis of
Clanricarde; Secretaries—Home, Sir George Grey;
Foreign, Earl of Clarendon; Colonial, Sidney Herbert
(resigned Feb. 22); afterwards Lord J. Russell
(resigned July 13); Sir William Molesworth (died
Oct. 22, 1855); next Henry Labouchere; War, Lord
Panmure; Chancellor of the Exchequer, W. E. Glad-
stone (resigned Feb. 22); next, Sir G. Cornewall
Lewis; First Lord of the Admiralty, Sir James
Graham (resigned Feb. 22); next, Sir Charles Wood;
Board of Control, Sir Charles Wood; next, R. Vernon
Smith; Public Works, Sir Wm. Molesworth; next,
Sir B. Hall (appointed July 22, 1855); Postmaster-
General, Viscount Canning (appointed Governor-
General of India, July 4); next, Duke of Argyll;
President of the Board of Trade, Lord Stanley of
Alderley; Marquis of Lansdowne, without office;
Chancellor of the Duchy of Lancaster, Earl of Har-
rowby; next, M. T. Baines (appointed Nov. 24, 1855)

Feb. 19, Bread riots in Liverpool, 150,000 persons out
of employment through the frost

Feb. 20, Death of Joseph Hume (78) Reformer

Feb. 22, Mr. Gladstone, Sir James Graham, and Sidney
Herbert and other "Peelites" resigned on account of
Sebastopol inquiry

Feb. 23, Sebastopol Inquiry Committee named

June 29, "Daily Telegraph," London newspaper, established

July 13, Resignation of Lord John Russell from the
Cabinet

Aug. 14, Dwelling Houses (Scotland) Act, and Inspection of Coal Mines Act approved

Sept. 6, Treaty of commerce and friendship with
Switzerland signed

1856

March 30, Treaty of peace signed in Paris ending
Crimean War

Oct., War with China. *See* China

Nov., War with Persia. *See* Persia

1857

Jan. 29, The Order of the Victoria Cross instituted to
reward persons of all ranks in army and navy

March, Indian mutiny. *See* India

April 30, 1857–April 23, 1859, Fifth Parliament of Victoria

July 4, Death of Sir Henry Lawrence fatally wounded at Lucknow

Nov. 12, Commercial panic; relieved by suspension of Bank Charter Act of 1844

1858

Jan. 25, Marriage of Victoria, eldest daughter of the Queen, to Frederick, Crown Prince of Prussia

Feb. 22, Resignation of Palmerston Ministry after vote Feb. 19 defeating the Foreign Conspiracy Bill making conspiracy to murder a felony

Feb. 25, Second Ministry of the Earl of Derby: First Lord of the Treasury, Earl of Derby; Lord Chancellor, Lord Chelmsford (previously Sir F. Thesiger); Chancellor of the Exchequer, Benjamin Disraeli; Secretaries—Foreign, Earl of Malmesbury; Home, Spencer H. Walpole (resigned March, 1859), T. Sotheron Estcourt; Colonies, Lord Stanley; in June, 1858, Sir E. Bulwer Lytton; War, Col. Jonathan Peel; Presidents—of the Council, Marquis of Salisbury; of Board of Control (India), 1, Earl of Ellenborough (who resigned in May, 1858; he had sent a letter, on his own authority, censuring the proclamation of Lord Canning to the Oude insurgents; the Government hardly escaped a vote of censure); 2, in June, 1858, Lord Stanley; Board of Trade, Mr. Joseph W. Henley (resigned in March, 1859); Earl of Donoughmore; Board of Works, Lord John Manners; Lord Privy Seal, Earl of Hardwicke; First Lord of the Admiralty, Sir John S. Pakington; Postmaster, Lord Colchester; Chancellor of the Duchy of Lancaster, Duke of Montrose

June, Act abolished the property qualification for members of Parliament

July 23, Jewish Disabilities Act passed

July 26, Baron L. Rothschild, the first Jew admitted to Parliament

Aug. 2, India Bill passed, government of India assumed by the Crown, end of rule of the British East India Company

Aug. 5, Atlantic cable laid; ceased working Sept. 4

1859

Jan. 15, National Portrait Gallery, London, opened

March 31, Defeat of the Ministry on Reform Bill introduced by Mr. Disraeli

May 31, 1859–July 6, 1865, Sixth Parliament of Victoria

June 11, Resignation of the Derby Ministry

June 18, Second Palmerston Ministry assumed office: First Lord of the Treasury, Henry Viscount Palmerston; Lord High Chancellor, John Lord Campbell (died June 23, 1861); succeeded by Sir Richard Bethell, made Lord Westbury, who resigned July 4, 1865; succeeded by Lord Cranworth; Lord President of the Council, Earl Granville; Lord Privy Seal, Duke of Argyll; Secretaries—Foreign Affairs, Lord John (afterwards Earl) Russell; Colonies, Duke of Newcastle; succeeded by Edward Cardwell, April 8, 1864; Home, Sir G. Cornewall Lewis; succeeded by Sir George Grey; War, Sidney (afterwards Lord) Herbert; succeeded by Sir G. C. Lewis (died April 13, 1863), and by Earl de Grey (May 1); India, Sir Charles Wood; Chancellor of the Exchequer, Wm. Ewart Gladstone; First Lord of the Admiralty, Duke of Somerset; President of the Board of Trade, Thos.

Milner Gibson [this office was offered to Mr. R. Cobden, and declined by him]; Secretary of State for Ireland, Edward Cardwell; succeeded by Sir R. Peel (not in the cabinet); Chancellor of the Duchy of Lancaster, Sir George Grey, Bart.; succeeded by Edward Cardwell; and by Earl Clarendon, April 8, 1864; Postmaster-General, Earl of Elgin (proceeded to China in April, 1860); succeeded by Lord Stanley of Alderley, appointed Sept., 1860; Poor-law Board, T. Milner-Gibson; succeeded by Charles P. Villiers (July 9, 1860)

July, Income tax increased to provide for the defenses of the country

Dec. 28, Death of Lord Thomas Babington Macaulay (59)

Publication of Darwin's "Origin of Species"

1860

Jan. 23, Commercial Treaty with France signed

May 12, Death of Sir Charles Barry (65), architect

July 24–Oct. 20, Visit of the Prince of Wales in the United States and Canada

Aug. 6, Bleach and Dye Works Act approved, regulations for workers

Aug. 28, Regulation and Inspection of Mines Act approved

Oct. 24, Peace Treaty with China signed

Oct. 31, Death of Admiral Thomas Cochrane, Earl of Dundonald (82)

1861

March 16, Death of the Duchess of Kent (75)

April 8, Census gave total population as 20,066,224, for England and Wales; Scotland, 3,062,294; Channel Islands and Isle of Man, 143,447

May 13, Neutrality proclaimed as to Civil War in the United States

June 30, Death of Elizabeth Barrett Browning

July 27, Diplomatic relations with Brazil severed because of plunder of British ship wrecked on coast; finally referred to arbitration

Aug. 6, Lace Works Act approved, and Naval Discipline Act

Nov. 8, The "Trent Affair," seizure of Confederate commissioners Mason and Slidell from the British mail steamer "Trent" by Captain Charles Wilkes who took them to Boston

Dec. 18, Protest of Great Britain as to seizure of Mason and Slidell; declared an "affront to the British flag and a violation of international law," and their release demanded, which was granted

Dec. 23, Death of the Prince Consort

1862

April 7, Treaty with the United States signed for suppression of the African slave trade

April 11, Open Air Bleachfields Act approved

July 1, Marriage of the Princess Alice to Louis of Hesse-Darmstadt

July 29, The "Alabama," Confederate cruiser fitted out at Liverpool allowed to sail from the Mersey in spite of protests of American Minister Adams

Aug. 7, Mines Act approved

Sept. 5, Ascent in balloon of H. T. Coxwell and James Glaisher to height of 37,000 feet at Wolverhampton

Sept. 18, At this date 24 poor law unions reported 140,165 persons in the cotton districts receiving outdoor relief at cost of £7,922 a week because of the cotton famine caused by the American Civil War

Nov. 30, 458,000 persons in the cotton districts receiving poor-law relief

1863

Feb. 24, First meeting of the Anthropological Society, Dr. James Hunt, president

March 10, Marriage of the Prince of Wales to Princess Alexandra of Denmark

Dec. 24, Death of William Makepeace Thackeray (52)

1864

Jan. 11, Charing Cross Railway opened

April 3–27, Visit of Garibaldi to England

April 24–June 25, International Conference in London on the Schleswig-Holstein question; no result

April 28, Ionian Islands made over to Greece by England (English Protectorate since Nov. 5, 1815)

June 29, Bleach and Dye Works Act approved

July 25, Factory Extension Act provided for sanitary measures in factories

Oct. 29, Death of John Leech (47), caricaturist of "Punch"

1865

Feb. 15, Death of Cardinal Wiseman (Roman Catholic), 63

March 2, First message by cable from Calcutta to London

April 2, Death of Richard Cobden (61)

June 8, Henry Edward Manning (formerly an archdeacon in the English Church) consecrated (Roman Catholic) Archbishop of Westminster

June 25, Cattle plague broke out near Barnsbury

July 5, First meeting of the "Christian Mission" led by William Booth which in June, 1880, took the name Salvation Army

Oct. 18, Death of Lord Palmerston

Nov. 6, Earl Russell formed Ministry: First Lord of the Treasury, John, Earl Russell; Lord Chancellor, Robert, Lord Cranworth; Postmaster-General, John, Lord Stanley of Alderley; President of the Poorlaw Board, Chas. Pelham Villiers; Lord President of the Council, George, Earl Granville; Lord Privy Seal, George, Duke of Argyll; Chancellor of the Exchequer, Wm. E. Gladstone; Secretaries—Foreign Affairs, George, Earl of Clarendon; Colonies, Edward Cardwell; Home, Sir George Grey; War, George, Earl de Grey and Ripon, succeeded by Spencer, Marquis of Hartington, Feb., 1866; India, Sir Charles Wood, resigned (created Viscount Halifax); succeeded by Earl de Grey, Feb., 1866; First Lord of the Admiralty, Edward, Duke of Somerset; President of the Board of Trade, Thos. Milner Gibson; Chancellor of the Duchy of Lancaster, George J. Göschen; Secretary for Ireland, Chichester Fortescue

Dec. 16, Commercial treaty with Austria-Hungary signed

1866

Jan. 12, Aëronautical Society of Great Britain founded

Feb. 1, 1866–Nov. 11, 1868, Seventh Parliament of Victoria

May 10, Commercial panic in London caused by failure of Overend, Gurney and Co. Liabilities over £19,000,000

May 13, Cholera appeared in Liverpool

May 18, Labouring Classes (Dwelling Homes) Act approved

June 6, Failure of Agra and Masterman's Bank, London

June 28, Labouring Classes Lodging Houses and Dwellings (Ireland) Act approved

July 6, Third Derby Ministry formed: First Lord of the Treasury, Edward, Earl of Derby; Lord Chancellor, Frederick, Lord Chelmsford; President of Council, Richard, Duke of Buckingham; succeeded by John, Duke of Marlborough, March 8, 1867; Lord Privy Seal, James, Earl of Malmesbury; Secretaries—Home, Spencer Horatio Walpole, resigned; Gathorne Hardy, May 17, 1867;—Foreign, Edward, Lord Stanley;—Colonies, Henry, Earl of Carnarvon, resigned; Richard, Duke of Buckingham and Chandos, March 8, 1867;—War, Lieut.-Gen. Sir Jonathan Peel, resigned; Sir John Somerset Pakington, March 8, 1867;—India, Robert, Lord Cranborne, resigned; Sir Stafford Henry Northcote, March 8, 1867; Chancellor of the Exchequer, Benjamin Disraeli; First Lord of Admiralty, Sir John S. Pakington; succeeded by Henry Thomas Corry, March 8, 1867; Chief Commissioner of Works, &c., Lord John Manners; President of Board of Trade, Sir Stafford Northcote; succeeded by Charles Henry, Duke of Richmond, March, 1867; Chief Secretary for Ireland, Richard, Lord Naas (afterwards Earl of Mayo); President of Poor-law Board, Gathorne Hardy; succeeded by Wm. Reginald, Earl of Devon (not in cabinet), May 17, 1867; Horatio Spencer Walpole, without office, died 1898. The above formed the cabinet, Feb., 1868; Postmaster-General, James, Duke of Montrose; Lord Chamberlain, Orlando, Earl of Bradford

July 27, The Atlantic cable laid and communication by telegraph with America established

1867

March 29, Metropolitan Poor Act passed

April, Great strike of colliers near St. Helens begun

April 22–Oct., Strike of London West-end tailors

Aug. 12, Act passed authorized the Queen to proclaim prorogation of Parliament during the recess

Aug. 15, New Reform Bill received the royal assent; granted an additional member of Parliament to Manchester, Leeds, and Birmingham, and greatly extended the franchise

——, Factory (Extension) Act approved extended the earlier factory acts to all places where 50 or more persons employed in any manufacturing process

Aug. 21, Workshop Regulation Act approved

1868

Feb. 25, Resignation of Earl of Derby for reasons of health

Feb. 29, First Disraeli Ministry formed: First Lord of Treasury, Benjamin Disraeli; Lord Chancellor, Hugh MacCalmont, Lord Cairns; Lord President of the Council, John, Duke of Marlborough; Lord Privy Seal, James, Earl of Malmesbury; Secretaries—Home, Gathorne Hardy;—Foreign, Edward, Lord Stanley;—Colonies, Richard, Duke of Buckingham and Chandos;—War, Sir John S. Pakington;—India, Sir Stafford Henry Northcote; Chancellor of Exchequer, George Ward Hunt; First Lord of Admiralty, Henry Thomas L. Corry; Chief Commissioner of Works, Lord John Manners; President of Board of Trade, Charles Henry, Duke of Richmond; Chief Secretary for Ireland, Richard, Earl of Mayo;

made Viceroy of India, Oct.; succeeded by Col. J. Wilson Patten, Nov. 7, 1868; President of Poor-law Board, Wm. Reginald, Earl of Devon. The above formed the Cabinet; Postmaster-General, James, Duke of Montrose; Lord Great Chamberlain, Orlando, Earl of Bradford; Chancellor of Duchy of Lancaster, Col. John Wilson Patten; succeeded by Col. Ths. E. Taylor, Nov. 7, 1868; Lord Lieutenant of Ireland, James, Earl (afterwards Marquis) of Abercorn

March 31, Vote by proxy in the House of Lords abolished by standing order

April, 40,000 colliers on strike (St. Helens)

July 13, Reform Acts for Scotland and Ireland, and Parliamentary Boundaries Act passed

July 31, Labourers' Dwelling Act approved "to provide for better dwellings"

Dec. 2, Resignation of Disraeli Ministry

Dec. 9, W. E. Gladstone formed his first Cabinet: First Lord of the Treasury, Wm. Ewart Gladstone (and Chancellor of Exchequer, Aug., 1873); Lord Chancellor, Sir Wm. Page Wood, Baron Hatherley, resigned; Sir Roundell Palmer, Baron Selborne, Oct., 1872; Lord President of the Council, Geo. Fred. Samuel Robinson, Earl de Grey and Ripon (Marquis of Ripon, 1871); succeeded by Mr. Austin Bruce, made Lord Aberdare, Aug., 1873; Lord Privy Seal, John Wodehouse, Earl of Kimberley; succeeded by Viscount Halifax, July, 1870; Chancellor of the Exchequer, Robert Lowe; succeeded by Mr. Gladstone, Aug., 1873; Secretaries—Home, Henry Austin Bruce; succeeded by Mr. Lowe, Aug., 1873; Foreign, Geo. Wm. Fred. Villiers, Earl of Clarendon (died June 27, 1870); succeeded by Earl Granville; Colonies, Granville Geo. Leveson-Gower, Earl Granville; succeeded by Earl of Kimberley, July, 1870; War, Edward Cardwell; India, George Douglas Campbell, Duke of Argyll; Chancellor of Duchy of Lancaster, Frederick, Lord Dufferin, appointed Governor-General of Canada; succeeded by H. E. Childers, Aug., 1872; by John Bright, Sept., 1873; First Lord of Admiralty, Hugh Culling Eardley Childers; succeeded by G. Joachim Goschen, March 9, 1871; Chief Secretary for Ireland, Chichester S. Fortescue; succeeded by the Marquis of Hartington, Jan. 1, 1871; President of Board of Trade, John Bright; succeeded by Chichester S. Fortescue, Dec., 1870; President of Poor Law (now Local Government) Board, George Joachim Goschen; succeeded by James Stansfeld, March 9, 1871; Wm. Edward Forster, vice-president of the committee of Council on Education; admitted to the cabinet, July, 1870

Dec. 10, 1868–Jan. 26, 1874, Eighth Parliament of Victoria

1869

Jan. 14, Convention respecting the Alabama claims signed with the United States; rejected by Senate of the United States

June 24, The one shilling duty on corn repealed

July 26, Act provided for disestablishment and partial disendowment of the Irish Church to come into effect Jan. 1, 1871

——, Bankruptcy Act established new bankruptcy court

——, Act abolished imprisonment of fraudulent debtors with certain exceptions

Aug. 11, Criminal Statistics Act passed

Oct. 23, Death of the Earl of Derby (70)

1870

Jan. 21, Colliery strike at Thorncliffe near Sheffield, riots and devastation

Feb. 5, Telegraph transferred to the State

June 9, Death of Charles Dickens (59)

June 27, Death of the Earl of Clarendon (70)

July 19, Declaration of neutrality in the Franco-Prussian War

Aug. 1, Irish Land Act received royal assent

Aug. 9, Elementary Education Act approved and Arrest of Absconding Debtors Act authorized payments to support denominational schools

Aug. 9–11, Treaty with Prussia and France signed guaranteed the neutrality of Belgium

1871

Jan. 17, Conference of the Powers which had signed the Treaty of March 30, 1865, met in London, and March 13 signed Treaty abrogating the clause for the neutralization of the Black Sea

May 8, Treaty of Washington with the United States signed provided for settlement of the Alabama claims by arbitration, reference of the dispute as to the Oregon boundary to the Emperor of Germany, and for partial settlement of the fishery dispute

May 15, Land Tenure Reform League held first meeting, John Stuart Mill presiding

May 16–Oct. 6, Successful strike of engineers at Newcastle-upon-Tyne for 9-hour day

May 25, Bank Holidays Act passed

June 28, Trade Union Act approved

July 3, Army Reorganization Bill passed third reading in Commons, and was then postponed in Lords

July 13, Act disqualified bankrupt peers from sitting or voting in Parliament

July 18, Ballot Act passed

July 24, Ecclesiastical Titles Act of 1851 repealed; never in effect

Sept. 14, Decision of Geneva Arbitral Tribunal awarded over $15,000,000 to the United States as damages due from England in the case of the "Alabama" and other vessels

Nov. 1, From this date the system of purchasing commissions in the army abolished by Royal Warrant

1872

June 19–Aug. 27, Lockout and strike of builders for 9 hour day at 9d. an hour

Aug. 1, Coal Mines Regulation Act passed

Aug. 6, Arbitration (Masters and Workmen) Act passed, Corrupt Practices (Municipal Elections) Act

Aug. 10, Coal Mines Regulation Act, Metalliferous Mines Regulation Act, approved and Act passed to prevent adulteration of food and drugs

Sept. 23–Oct. 9, Strike of London journeymen bakers

Oct. 21, Decision of German Emperor in favor of the United States in Oregon boundary dispute

Nov. 5, New Commercial Treaty with France signed

1873

Jan. 9, Death of Louis Napoleon, late Emperor of the French, in Kent
Jan. 18, Death of Edward Bulwer, Lord Lytton
May 1, Death of David Livingstone in Africa
May 8, Death of John Stuart Mill
June 18–July 5, Visit of the Shah of Persia
July 12, First London board school opened at Whitechapel
July 19, Death of Samuel Wilberforce, Bishop of Winchester
Aug. 5, Agricultural Children's Act prohibited employment of children under 8 years of age and provided for the education of older children
Oct. 1, Death of Sir Edwin Landseer

1874

Feb. 17, Resignation of Gladstone Ministry
Feb. 21, Second Ministry of Benjamin Disraeli formed: First Lord of the Treasury, Benjamin Disraeli (Earl of Beaconsfield, Aug. 16, 1876), and Lord Privy Seal, Aug., 1876, to Jan., 1878; Lord Chancellor, Hugh MacCalmont, Lord Cairns; Lord President of the Council, Charles Henry, Duke of Richmond; Lord Privy Seal, James, Earl of Malmesbury; resigned, Aug. 12, 1876; Earl of Beaconsfield, Aug., 1876; Algernon, Duke of Northumberland, Feb. 4, 1878; Secretary of State for Foreign Affairs, Edward, Earl of Derby; resigned; Robert, Marquis of Salisbury, March 28, 1878; Secretary of State for India, Robert, Marquis of Salisbury; Gathorne Hardy, created Viscount Cranbrook, April 2, 1878; Secretary of State for the Colonies, Henry, Earl of Carnarvon; resigned, Jan. 24, 1878; Sir Michael Hicks-Beach, Feb. 4, 1878; Secretary of State for War, Gathorne Hardy; Col. Fred. Arthur Stanley, April 2, 1878; Chancellor of the Duchy of Lancaster, William, Earl of Devon; succeeded by Colonel John Wilson Patten, June, 1867; Lord-Lieutenant of Ireland, James, Earl (afterwards Marquis) of Abercorn
March 5, 1874–March 2, 1880, Ninth Parliament of Victoria
June 10, Bill to repeal Education Act of 1870 much objected to by dissenters because of support of denominational schools rejected by Commons
July 30, Factory Act and Hosiery Manufacture (Wages) Act approved

1875

Jan. 2–May, Strike of 50,000 miners in South Wales
Jan. 13, Gladstone resigned the leadership of the Liberals in the Commons; succeeded by the Marquis of Hartington
March 15, Archbishop Manning created a cardinal
June 29, Artizans and Labourers' Dwellings Improvement Act approved, to facilitate dwellings for the working class in large towns; Act for Scotland Aug. 2
July 19, Act relating to municipal elections amended
Aug. 11, Public Health Act consolidated all the previous sanitary and nuisance laws
Aug. 13, Conspiracy and Protection of Property Act, Employer and Workman Act as to regulation of disputes, Agricultural Holdings Act relating to compensations of landlords and tenants for improve-

ments, &c., Foreign Jurisdiction Act (Deportation), and Merchant Shipping Act of 1854 amended to give further power to the Board of Trade for stopping unseaworthy ships, approved
Oct. 11–May 11, Visit of the Prince of Wales to India
Oct. 18, Newnham College for women opened at Cambridge
Nov. 25, Announcement of purchase of Suez Canal shares from the Khedive of Egypt
Dec. 18, Strike of workmen at Erith, engineers, against piece work

1876

April 27, Act to enable her Majesty to make addition of Empress of India to royal style and title
May 1, The Queen proclaimed Empress of India
June 30, Trade Union Amendment Act approved
Aug. 15, Elementary Education Act approved
Aug. 24, Strike of 1,600 miners at Bolton against 15% reduction of wages

1877

Jan. 1, The Queen proclaimed Empress of India at Delhi

1878

Jan. 24, Resignation of Lord Carnarvon; succeeded by Sir Michael Hicks-Beach
March 28, Resignation of Lord Derby in opposition to Berlin Memorandum; Lord Salisbury succeeded as Secretary for Foreign Affairs
April 18–June 17, Strike and lockout of 120,000 cotton spinners in Lancashire because of reduction of 10% in wages
April 30, Proclamation of neutrality in Russo-Turkish War
May, Strike of 10,000 shipwrights and lockout on the Clyde, award against men
May 27, Factory and Workshops (Consolidation) Act approved
May 28, Death of Lord John Russell
May 29–June 12, Strike of 12,000 Northumberland miners
June 4, Treaty with Turkey by which Great Britain undertook to protect Turkey in Asia against Russian conquest; provided for cession of Cyprus to England for administrative purposes
July 13, Treaty of Berlin signed. See s.v.
Aug.–Oct., Public meetings respecting Turkish atrocities in Bulgaria
Aug. 15, Artizans and Labourers' Dwellings Improvement Act approved; Act for Scotland, March 15, 1880

1879

Feb. 7–Oct. 4, Strike of London engineers (18 firms) against reduction of wages

1880

April 22, Resignation of Beaconsfield (Disraeli) Ministry after election resulted in favor of the Liberals
April 28, Second Gladstone Ministry formed: First Lord of the Treasury (and Chancellor of the Exchequer till Dec. 16, 1882), Wm. Ewart Gladstone;

Lord Chancellor, Roundell Palmer, Baron Selborne; Lord President of the Council, John Poyntz, Earl Spencer; succeeded by Chichester S. Fortescue, Lord Carlingford, March 9, 1883; Lord Privy Seal, George Douglas Campbell, Duke of Argyll; resigned; succeeded by Lord Carlingford, April, 1881; Archibald Philip Primrose, Earl of Rosebery, Feb. 11, 1885; Secretaries—Home, Sir Wm. Harcourt; Foreign Affairs, George Leveson-Gower, Earl Granville; the Colonies, John Wodehouse, Earl of Kimberley, succeeded by Edward, Earl of Derby, Dec. 16, 1882; India, Spencer C. Cavendish, Marquis of Hartington, succeeded by John Wodehouse, Earl of Kimberley, Dec. 16, 1882; War, Hugh C. E. Childers, succeeded by Marquis of Hartington, Dec. 16, 1882; First Lord of the Admiralty, Thos. Geo. Baring, Earl of Northbrook; Chancellor of the Exchequer, Hugh C. E. Childers, Dec. 16, 1882; Lord-Lieutenant of Ireland, John Poyntz, Earl Spencer, May, 1882; Chancellor of Duchy of Lancaster, John Bright; resigns about July 15, 1882; Earl of Kimberley, July 25; John George Dodson (afterwards Lord Monk Bretton), Dec. 28, 1882; George O. Trevelyan, about Oct. 20, 1884; President of Local Government Board, John George Dodson, succeeded by Sir Charles Wentworth Dilke, Dec. 28, 1882; President of Board of Trade, Joseph Chamberlain; Postmaster-General, George Shaw Lefevre, entered the cabinet, Feb. 11, 1885

April 29–Nov. 18, 1885, Tenth Parliament of Victoria

May 3, Charles Bradlaugh, M.P. for Northampton, an atheist, refused to take the oath of allegiance, his affirmation refused by the Commons, and he was imprisoned because of refusal to withdraw June 23, but released by vote, June 24

May 12, John Henry Newman created a cardinal

July 1, Resolution of Mr. Gladstone that affirmation be accepted instead of an oath in certain cases carried and Mr. Bradlaugh affirmed and was admitted, July 2

Sept. 7, Act amending the burial laws permitting dissenters to have their own service or no service in churchyards received royal assent

Sept. 13, Employers' Liability Act passed provided for compensation for personal injuries suffered by workmen not their own fault

Nov. 9, Telephone communication established between Liverpool and Manchester

1881

Jan. 12–Feb. 21, Strike of 40,000 Lancashire miners

March 3, New Irish Coercion Act passed, came into effect July 14, 1882

Aug. 22, Irish Land Act passed

Nov. 25–Dec. 6, Strike of 30,000 men in the potteries ended by reference to arbitration

1882

April 9, Death of Dante Gabriel Rossetti

April 19, Death of Charles Robert Darwin

May 6, Assassination of newly appointed Chief Secretary for Ireland and Mr. Burke, Under-Secretary in the Phœnix Park, Dublin

July 11, Bombardment of forts at Alexandria (Egypt) and resignation of John Bright from the Cabinet; succeeded by Earl of Kimberley

Aug. 18, Artizans Dwelling Act approved and Parcel Post Act (advised by Rowland Hill in 1842)

1883

May 3–4, Affirmation Bill rejected by Commons

May 12–Sept. 3, Strike of 8,000 Staffordshire colliers

July 5, Strike of 8,000 Staffordshire ironworkers at reduction of wages, ended July 24

Aug. 25, Epidemic Prevention Act passed, and new Bankruptcy Act placed bankrupts assets in charge of Board of Trade, and disqualified bankrupts for election and sitting as members of the House of Commons

Sept. 27, Strike of Lancashire cotton employees against 5% reduction in wages settled

1884

Feb. 11, Mr. Bradlaugh administered the oath to himself and sat in Commons and voted, excluded, reelected Feb. 19, reëxcluded Feb. 21

Feb. 12, Vote of censure of Government for "vacillating and inconsistent policy" in Egypt and the Sudan carried in Lords by vote of 181 to 81, but defeated in Commons, Feb. 20, by vote of 311 to 262, and again in May by vote of 303 to 275

April 3, New Education code came into effect

June 13–30 The Queen v. Bradlaugh for voting without taking the oath, Queen's Bench; verdict for the Crown

Aug. 14, Municipal Elections, Corrupt and Illegal Practices Act passed

Dec. 6, Third Reform Act, Representation of the People Act, 1884, became law, provided for uniform franchise in counties and boroughs in the United Kingdom, adding about 2,000,000 voters

1885

Jan. 20, The Mersey tunnel connecting Birkenhead and Liverpool formally opened

Jan. 26, Capture of Khartum by the mahdi and death of General Gordon before relief expedition under General Wolseley reached the besieged garrison

March 16, Strike of 2,000 miners in west Cumberland

April 27, Vote of credit by Commons of £11,000,000 for war with Russia. *See* Russia; averted by agreement to arbitration by Denmark

April–May, Strike of about half the colliers in south and west Yorkshire

June 8–9, Resignation of Gladstone Ministry defeated on budget

June 24, Lord Salisbury Ministry formed: Prime Minister and Foreign Secretary, Robert Arthur Talbot Gascoigne-Cecil, Marquis of Salisbury; First Lord of the Treasury, Sir Stafford Northcote, Earl of Iddesleigh; Lord Chancellor, Sir Hardinge Giffard, Lord Halsbury; Lord President of the Council, Gathorne Gathorne-Hardy, Viscount Cranbrook; Lord Privy Seal, Dudley Ryder, Earl of Harrowby; Secretaries: Home, Sir Richard Assheton Cross; the Colonies, Col. Frederick Arthur Stanley; India, Lord Randolph Henry Spencer-Churchill; War, William Henry Smith; G. Gathorne-Hardy, Viscount Cranbrook, about Jan. 23, 1886; Scotland, Charles Henry, Duke of Richmond, about Aug. 14, 1885; First Lord of the Admiralty, Lord George Hamilton; Chancellor of the Exchequer, Sir. Michael Hicks-Beach; Lord Lieutenant of Ireland, Henry H. M.

Herbert, Earl of Carnarvon; resigned Jan., 1886; Lord Chancellor of Ireland, Edward Gibson, Lord Ashbourne; President of Board of Trade, Charles Henry Gordon-Lennox, Duke of Richmond; Edw. Stanhope, about Aug. 17, 1885; Postmaster-General, Lord John Manners; Vice-President of the Council, Edward Stanhope

June 25, Redistribution of Seats Act received royal assent; all boroughs with population under 15,000 disfranchised and merged in county districts, all towns with population under 50,000 to be represented by one member only, towns between 50,000 and 165,000 to have 2 members, system of single member districts to be universal with these exceptions and that of the city of London

July 20–Oct. 16, Strike of cotton weavers at Oldham (25,000) against 10% reduction settled by compromise

July 28, Death of Sir Moses Montefiore

Aug. 14, Purchase of Land Act (Ireland) and Housing of the Working Classes Act approved

Oct. 1, Death of the Earl of Shaftesbury

Nov., Close of engineers strike (2½ years) at Sunderland

1886

Jan.–Feb. 24, Strike of shipwrights in the Tyne and Wear

Jan. 12–June 26, Eleventh Parliament of Victoria

Jan. 13, Mr. Bradlaugh took the oath, intervention stopped by the Speaker

Jan. 27, Resignation of Salisbury Ministry defeated on amendment to the address

Feb. 12, Gladstone formed third Ministry: First Lord of the Treasury, Wm. Ewart Gladstone; Lord Chancellor, Sir Farrer Herschell, Lord Herschell; Lord President of the Council, John Poyntz, Earl Spencer; Secretaries—Home, Hugh C. E. Childers; Foreign, Archibald Philip Primrose, Earl of Rosebery; Colonial, George Leveson-Gower, Earl Granville; India, John Wodehouse, Earl of Kimberley; War, Henry Campbell-Bannerman; Chancellor of the Exchequer, Sir William George Granville Vernon-Harcourt; First Lord of the Admiralty, George Frederick Samuel Robinson, Marquis of Ripon; President of the Local Government Board, Joseph Chamberlain, succeeded by James Stansfeld, March 27, 1886; Secretary for Scotland, George Otto Trevelyan; succeeded by John William Ramsay, Earl of Dalhousie (not in the cabinet), March 27, 1886; President of the Board of Trade, Anthony John Mundella; Chief Secretary for Ireland, John Morley

April 8, Mr. Gladstone introduced Bill to "make better provision for the future government of Ireland" providing for Irish Parliament, all matters as to peace and war, foreign relations, trade, navigation, army, navy prerogatives of Crown untouched

April 16, Mr. Gladstone introduced Land Purchase Bill for Ireland

May 4, Colonial and Indian Exhibition (the first great national exhibition) opened at South Kensington by the Queen

June 7, Home Rule Bill for Ireland defeated in Commons on second reading

July 14, End of 20 weeks strike of Shropshire iron workers; employers yield

July 20, Resignation of Gladstone Ministry defeated in elections

July 26, Lord Salisbury became Prime Minister (second Ministry); and Foreign Secretary: First Lord of the Treasury and Leader of the Commons, Wm. Henry Smith, Jan. 3, 1887; died Oct. 6, 1891; Arthur J. Balfour, Nov. 9, 1891; Lord Chancellor, Hardinge Stanley Giffard, Lord Halsbury; Lord President of the Council, Gathorne Gathorne-Hardy, Viscount Cranbrook; Chancellor of the Exchequer, Lord Randolph Henry Spencer-Churchill; resigned Dec. 22, 1886; George Joachim Goschen, Jan. 3, 1887; Secretaries: Home, Henry Matthews (R.C.); Foreign, Stafford Henry Northcote, Earl of Iddesleigh (died Jan. 12, 1887); Marquis of Salisbury, Jan., 1887; the Colonies, Edward Stanhope, Sir Henry Thurstan Holland (Baron Knutsford), Feb., 1888 (Jan., 1887); India, Sir Richard Cross (Viscount Cross); War, William Henry Smith, Edward Stanhope, Jan. 6, 1887; died Dec. 21, 1893; First Lord of the Admiralty, Lord George Francis Hamilton; Lord Chancellor of Ireland, Edward Gibson, Lord Ashbourne; Chief Secretary for Ireland, Sir Michael Edward Hicks-Beach; resigns, but remains in the cabinet (retires Jan., 1888); succeeded by Arthur J. Balfour, March 5, 1887; Wm. L. Jackson, Nov. 9, 1891; Chancellor of the Duchy of Lancaster, Lord John Manners (Duke of Rutland), March 4, 1888; President of the Board of Trade, Sir Frederick Stanley (Lord Stanley of Preston); succeeded by Sir M. E. Hicks-Beach, Feb. 15, 1888; President of the Board of Agriculture, Henry Chaplin, Sept. 5, 1889

Aug. 5, 1886–June 28, 1892, Twelfth Parliament of Victoria

Sept. 11, Mr. Parnell introduced Tenants Relief Bill; rejected Sept. 21, 297 to 202

Oct. 17, Speech of John Dillon outlined "Plan of Campaign" for tenants against unjust rents. *See* Ireland

1887

Jan. 30–May 28, Strike of Northumberland miners

July 19, Crimes Act passed to check violence in Ireland; July 23, 18 counties proclaimed under the law

Aug. 8, First Offenders Act passed

Aug. 23, Second Irish Land Act passed

Sept. 12, Strike of wrought nail trade workers (15,000), South Staffordshire

Sept. 16, Coal Mines Regulation Act and Small Holdings Act approved

Dec. 3–24, Strike of 20,000 shoemakers at Northampton settled by arbitration

Dec. 19, Nordenfelt's boat submarine successfully tried at Southampton

1888

Feb. 15, Fisheries Treaty with the United States signed; rejected by Senate

March 23, Conversion of National Debt Act passed

April 15, Death of Matthew Arnold

Aug. 13, Local Government Act (England and Wales) enacted

Sept. 17, First meeting of "Special Commission" appointed to inquire into the charges against Mr. Parnell and other Irish members of Parliament

Oct. 22–31, Strike of 30,000 miners in Yorkshire and Midland counties

Dec. 24, New Employers' Liability Act passed

1889

May 31, Naval Defense Act provided for construction of 70 additional ships including 10 battleships, 42 cruisers, 18 torpedo gunboats, authorizing expenditure of £21,500,000

Aug. 15–Sept. 16, Strike of London dock laborers for increase in wages, reduction of hours and redress of other grievances joined by nearly every class of riverside workers; settled by increase of from 4d. to 6d. an hour with 8d. an hour for overtime, contract work to be changed to piece work and other concessions

Aug. 26, Arbitration Acts codified

Oct. 2, Strike of tailors in London ended with gain of reduction of hours

Dec. 12, Death of Robert Browning

1890

Feb. 5, Strike of employees of the South Metropolitan Company against bonus system begun Dec. 12, 1889 ended

Feb. 13, Report of "Special Commission" on charges against Mr. Parnell and other Irish leaders published acquitted Mr. Parnell of specific charges, the letter published in the "Times" in which Parnell approved the murder of Burke proved a forgery

March 15–20, Strike of coal miners for 10% increase settled by advance of 5%

March 29–April 29, Strike of 11,000 boot makers, London

July 1, Treaty with Germany signed fixing frontiers in Africa; Heligoland ceded to Germany. *See also* Africa

July 11, Telephone communication opened between London, Birmingham, and Liverpool, and with Manchester, Sept. 30

July 25, New Education Code Act passed

Aug. 4–8, Visit of Emperor William II

Aug. 5, Anglo-French Agreement signed as to boundaries of possessions in Africa

Aug. 7–15, Strike of railway workers, dockers, &c., at Cardiff against time-work

Aug. 11, Death of Cardinal Newman (John Henry Newman)

Aug. 18, Public Health (Amendment) Act, Small Holdings and Allotments Act, and Housing of the Working Classes Act approved

Aug. 20, Anglo-Portuguese Agreement signed as to Africa; not ratified. *See* Portugal

Sept. 24, Anglo-Italian Agreement signed as to African possessions

Oct. 4, Death of Mrs. Catherine Booth (61), Salvation Army leader

Nov. 14, Temporary panic produced by financial embarrassments of Baring Brothers

Nov. 15, O'Shea divorce case proceedings against Mr. Parnell begun in London; no defense offered, and decree pronounced Nov. 17, Mrs. O'Shea and Parnell married June 25, 1891

Dec. 6, Division of Irish Nationalist Party following divorce proceedings against Parnell, Justin M'Carthy and 44 other members organize separate body with M'Carthy as chairman

1891

Feb. 20–March 20, Strike of colliers at Durham

March 18, Telephone communication between London and Paris established

March 24, Anglo-Italian Agreement as to boundaries in Africa

March 31, Death of the Earl of Granville

April 5, Census gave population for England and Wales as 29,001,018, for Scotland 4,025,647, Ireland 4,704,750

May–Nov., Strike in building trades in London

June 11, Anglo-Portuguese Agreement as to boundaries in Africa signed

Aug. 5, Public Health (London) Act approved, Elementary Education Act (England and Wales), Land Purchase (Ireland) Act, Factory Act raised age of children from 10 to 11

Oct. 6, Death of Charles Stewart Parnell

1892

Jan. 14, Death of Cardinal Manning

Feb. 29, Convention with the United States signed as to seal fisheries Bering Sea

March 11–June 1, Strike of Durham coal miners against proposed wage reduction; settled by acceptance of 10% reduction

June 28, Shops Regulation Act regarding the employment of young persons approved

July 27, Death of Robert Lowe, Viscount Sherbrooke (80)

Aug. 1–8, Visit of the Emperor of Germany

Aug. 4–July 8, 1895, Thirteenth Parliament of Victoria

Aug. 13, Resignation of Salisbury Ministry defeated Aug. 11 by no confidence vote

Aug. 18, Gladstone became Prime Minister (fourth Ministry): First Lord of the Treasury and Lord Privy Seal, Wm. Ewart Gladstone; Lord High Chancellor, Lord Herschell; Lord President of the Council and Secretary of State for India, Earl of Kimberley; Secretaries—Home, Herbert Henry Asquith; Foreign, Archibald Philip Primrose, Earl of Rosebery; Colonial, George Frederick Samuel Robinson, Marquis of Ripon; War, Henry Campbell-Bannerman; First Lord of the Admiralty, John Poyntz, Earl Spencer; Chancellor of the Exchequer, Sir William George Granville Vernon-Harcourt; Chief Secretary for Ireland, John Morley; Secretary for Scotland, Sir George Trevelyan; President of the Board of Trade, Anthony John Mundella; President of the Local Government Board, Henry H. Fowler; First Commissioner of Works, George John Shaw-Lefevre; Chancellor of Duchy of Lancaster, James Bryce; Postmaster-General, Arnold Morley; Vice-President of the Committee of Council on Education, Arthur Acland

Oct. 6, Death of Alfred, Lord Tennyson (83), poet laureate

Nov. 7, Strike of 4,400 cotton spinners in Lancashire against 5% reduction in wages; settled March 24, 1893 by reduction of 7d. in the pound

Dec. 18, Death of Sir Richard Owen (88), naturalist

1893

Feb. 13, Gladstone introduced Home Rule Bill which gave Ireland a legislative council and a legislative assembly and representation in the Imperial Parliament; passed third reading by vote of 301 to 267, rejected in House of Lords on second reading by vote of 419 to 41

March 27, New Education Code issued

April 21, Death of Edward Henry, Earl of Derby (66)

July 24, Strike of midland coal miners against reduction in wages which extended to Wales, Yorkshire, and Scotland ended Nov. 17, with return to work at old rate of wages

Aug. 15, Award in Bering Sea Arbitration against right of the United States to seize vessels outside the three mile limit

Sept. 12, Industrial and Provident Societies Act approved

Dec. 4, Death of John Tyndall (73), scientist

1894

Jan. 1, Ship canal from Liverpool to Manchester opened formally; inaugurated by the Queen, May 21

March 3, Resignation of Gladstone

March 5, Lord Roseberry formed Ministry: First Lord of the Treasury and Lord President of the Council, Archibald Philip Primrose (Earl of Rosebery); Lord High Chancellor, Lord Herschell; Lord Privy Seal, Edward Majoribanks (Baron Tweedmouth); Chancellor of the Exchequer and Leader, Sir Wm. G. G. Vernon-Harcourt; Secretaries—Home, Herbert Henry Asquith; Foreign, Earl of Kimberley; Colonial, George F. S. Robinson (Marquis of Ripon); War, Henry Campbell-Bannerman; India, Henry H. Fowler; Chancellor of the Duchy of Lancaster, James Bryce; succeeded by Lord Tweedmouth, May 26; First Lord of the Admiralty, John Poyntz (Earl Spencer); Chief Secretary for Ireland, John Morley; Secretary for Scotland, Sir George Trevelyan; President of the Board of Trade, Anthony John Mundella; resigned about May 12, 1894; James Bryce, about May 26, 1894; President of the Local Government Board, George J. Shaw-Lefevre; Vice-President of the Committee of Council on Education, Arthur H. Dyke Acland; Postmaster-General, Arnold Morley

——, Local Government Act (England and Wales) approved

March 19, The Government announced eight-hour day for workmen in dockyards

March 29, Death of Baron James Hannen, judge

April 10, Death of Lord Bowen, judge

May 16–June 11, Strike of cabmen in London, 7,000, the union against the proprietors; settled by mediation of Mr. Asquith

July 16, Anglo-Japanese Treaty signed. *See* Japan

July 27, Outdoor Relief (Friendly Societies) Act approved

Aug. 7, Evicted Tenants (Ireland) bill carried by vote of 199 to 167; defeated in Lords, Aug. 14

Oct. 20, Death of James Anthony Froude, historian

1895

Jan. 24, Death of Lord Randolph Churchill

April 1, Second reading of Bill to terminate establishment of the Church of England in Wales and Monmouth, carried by vote of 304 to 260

June 21, The Roseberry Ministry defeated on a vote of supply resigned

June 25, Lord Salisbury formed his third Ministry: Prime Minister and Foreign Secretary, the Marquis of Salisbury; First Lord of the Treasury and Leader of the Commons, Arthur James Balfour; Lord High Chancellor, Lord Halsbury, Earl, Jan. 1, 1898; Lord

President of the Council, Spencer C. Cavendish (Duke of Devonshire); Lord Privy Seal, Richard Assheton (Viscount Cross); Chancellor of the Exchequer, Sir Michael Hicks-Beach; Secretaries: Home, Sir Matthew White Ridley; Foreign, Marquis of Salisbury; Colonial, Joseph Chamberlain; War, Marquis of Lansdowne; India, Lord George Hamilton; Chancellor of the Duchy of Lancaster, Sir Henry James, Lord James of Hereford; First Lord of the Admiralty, George J. Goschen, retired, Nov. 10, 1900; Secretary for Scotland, Alexander H. Bruce (Lord Balfour of Burleigh); President of the Board of Trade, Charles T. Ritchie; President of the Local Government Board, Henry Chaplin; Lord Lieutenant of Ireland, George Henry, Earl Cadogan; Lord Chancellor of Ireland, Lord Ashbourne; President of the Board of Agriculture, Walter Hume Long; First Commissioner of Works, Aretas Akers-Douglas

Aug. 12–Sept. 25, 1900, Fourteenth Parliament of Victoria

Dec. 8, Lord Salisbury declined proposal of the United States for arbitration of Guiana-Venezuela frontier. *See also* United States and Venezuela

Dec. 30, Jameson raid in South Africa. *See* Transvaal

1896

Jan. 20, Death of Prince Henry of Battenberg

Jan. 25, Death of Sir Frederick Leighton, artist, sculptor

Jan. 29, British Empire League held first meeting, Sir John Lubbock (Lord Avebury), chairman

Feb. 3, Arrival of Dr. Jameson and 350 officers and men from South Africa for trial; sentenced to imprisonment, July 28

——, Bering Sea Claims' Agreement with the United States

May 4, The "Daily Mail" founded, first halfpenny London morning paper

June 2, Marconi applied for patent of his invention of wireless telegraph

July 20, Agricultural Land Rating Act received royal assent, reduction of rates by half the deficiency being supplied by imperial taxation; Act for Scotland passed Aug. 14

Aug. 7, New Public Health Act passed, and Conciliation Act approved

Aug. 14, Irish Land Act passed

Oct. 6, Lord Roseberry resigned as leader of the Liberal Party through differences with Mr. Gladstone and others on the Eastern question; Lord Kimberley became leader in the Lords, Sir William Vernon Harcourt in the Commons

1897

Jan. 11, Arbitration Treaty with the United States signed; rejected by Senate of the United States

April 8, Voluntary Schools (Aid Grant) Act received royal assent

June 20, Diamond jubilee, sixtieth anniversary, of the accession of Queen Victoria celebrated

June 20–24, Conference of Colonial Premiers in London with Colonial Secretary

July 3, Unsuccessful strike of engineers for eight hour day begun, ended Jan. 24, 1898

Aug. 6, Workmen's Compensation Act approved

Oct. 6, John Rylands Memorial Library opened at Manchester

1898

March, Revised Education Code issued

April 1–Aug. 31, Strike of coal miners, South Wales, for increase in wages unsuccessful

May 19, Death of William Ewart Gladstone

June 14, Anglo-French Boundary Convention, frontiers in Africa. *See* Africa

July 1, Convention with China by which Weihaiwei leased to Great Britain

Aug. 12, Local Government (Ireland) Act amended, and Evidence in Criminal Cases Act made the regulations as to evidence uniform in all cases

Dec. 25, Imperial penny postage established between Great Britain and every other part of the British Empire except Australia and New Zealand

1899

Jan. 19, Soudan Convention signed at Cairo. *See* Egypt

March 27, First signals of wireless telegraph sent across the English Channel

March 28, Petition signed by 23,000 British subjects in South African Republic (Transvaal) setting forth grievances forwarded to the Colonial Office

May 31–June 5, Conference of President Kruger with Sir Alfred Milner with regard to franchise of British subjects living in the Transvaal; no agreement reached

July 26, New franchise law in Transvaal published and declared inadequate by Sir Alfred Milner

Aug. 9, Seats for Shop Assistants Act and Small Dwellings Acquisition Act approved, Education Act created central Board of Education for England and Wales

Oct. 9, Ultimatum from President Kruger asked for removal of troops concentrating on border and settlement of differences by reference to arbitration

Oct. 12, Boer war begun with the Transvaal and Orange Free State. *See* South African War

Oct. 14, General Sir Redvers Buller left to take command in South Africa

Oct. 17, Parliament voted £10,000,000 for war in South Africa

Nov. 20–25, Visit of the Emperor and Empress of Germany

Dec. 16, Lord Roberts appointed to command British troops in South Africa

Dec. 22, Death of the Duke of Westminster (74)

1900

Jan. 20, Death of John Ruskin and of Richard Doddridge Blackmore

March 27, War Loan Act passed providing for 35 million pounds

March 30, New Board of Education established under Education Act of 1899

May 28, Orange Free State proclaimed annexed to British Empire

June 21–July 4, Visit of the Khedive

July 9, Act constituted Commonwealth of Australia

July 30, Mines Act prohibited child labor underground, and Land Charges Act passed, Workmen's Compensation (Agriculture) Act and Railway Employment (Prevention of Accidents) Act

Aug. 6, Merchant Shipping (Liability of ship-owners and others) Act approved

Aug. 8, Education Act and Elementary Education Act passed and Housing of the Working Classes Act

Aug. 10, Death of Lord Charles Russell of Killowen, Lord Chief Justice (68)

Aug. 26, Death of General Sir John Adye (81)

Sept. 1, Annexation of South African Republic (Transvaal) to British Empire

Oct. 16, Anglo-German Treaty agreed to maintain territorial integrity of China and maintain "open door" policy

Oct. 31, Union of Free and United Presbyterians in Scotland

Nov. 12, Salisbury Cabinet reconstructed: Lord Salisbury, Prime Minister and Lord Privy Seal; First Lord of the Treasury and Leader of the Commons, Arthur James Balfour; Lord High Chancellor, Lord Halsbury; Lord President of the Council, Duke of Devonshire; Chancellor of the Exchequer, Sir Michael Hicks-Beach; Secretaries: Home, Charles T. Ritchie; Foreign, Lord Lansdowne; Colonial, Joseph Chamberlain; War, Hon. St. John Brodrick; India, Lord George Hamilton; Scotland, Lord Balfour of Burleigh; First Lord of the Admiralty, Lord Selborne; Lord Lieutenant of Ireland, George Henry, Earl Cadogan; Lord Chancellor of Ireland, Lord Ashbourne; President of the Board of Trade, Gerald Wm. Balfour; Chancellor of the Duchy of Lancaster, Lord James of Hereford; President of the Local Government Board, Walter Hume Long; President Board of Agriculture, Robt. Wm. Hanbury; First Commissioner of Works and Public Buildings, Aretas Akers-Douglas; Postmaster-General, Lord Londonderry

——, Lord Wolseley retired as Commander-in-Chief

Nov. 22, Death of Sir Arthur Sullivan, musical composer (58)

Nov. 29, Lord Roberts left South Africa to succeed Lord Wolseley as Commander-in-Chief

Dec. 3, Fifteenth Parliament of Victoria opened

1901

Jan. 22, Death of Queen Victoria (82), at Osborne, Isle of Wight. Accession of her son Edward VII

Jan. 23, Privy Council met with the King and Parliament to take the oath of allegiance to the King

Feb. 14–Jan. 8, 1906, First Parliament of Edward VII formally opened by the King

Feb. 27, Meeting of General Committee of National Liberal Federation adopted resolution deploring continuance of war in South Africa due to policy of the Government demanding unconditional surrender

April 1, Census gave total population as 37,518,052: England, 30,813,043; Wales, 1,714,800; Scotland, 4,472,103; Isle of Man, 54,752; Channel Islands, 95,618; army, navy, and merchant seamen abroad, 367,736

June 18, New Radcliffe Library opened at Oxford

June 20, Mr. Asquith in speech to a Liberal meeting in London repudiated the resolutions and opinions of the pro-Boers

July 1, Consolidated Fund Act passed third reading

Aug. 1, Royal Titles Bill amending title of the King "in recognition of his Majesty's dominions beyond the seas" passed third reading

Aug. 6, Expedition to the Antarctic sailed, Captain Robert F. Scott. *See* Antarctic

Aug. 15, Continuance of Agricultural Land Rating Act of 1896 passed

Aug. 17, Act consolidated Factory and Workshop Acts

Oct. 2, First British submarine boat launched at Barrow

Nov. 4, By proclamation under Act of Parliament of last session the words "and of the British Dominions beyond the Seas" added to title of the King, Edward VII, by the Grace of God of the United Kingdom of Great Britain and Ireland, King, Defender of the Faith, Emperor of India, and of the British Dominions beyond the Seas

Nov. 18, Interoceanic Ship Canal Treaty (Hay-Pauncefote) signed with the United States

1902

Jan. 25, Proposals of Netherlands Government for negotiation with the Boers in South Africa presented and declined Jan. 29

Jan. 30, Anglo-Japanese defensive alliance signed as to the Far East

Feb. 12, Death of Lord Dufferin (75), diplomatist

March 26, Death of Cecil Rhodes at Cape Town, South Africa. His will left bulk of his fortune to Oxford University for foundation of Rhodes scholarships

April 8, Death of Lord Kimberley (76), Liberal statesman

May 15, Treaty with Abyssinia, boundaries with Sudan and construction of railroad through Abyssinian territory

May 24, Death of Lord Pauncefote (74), diplomatist

May 31, Peace Treaty signed at Pretoria ended the South African War; losses 1,072 officers, 20,870 men; cost of war £222,974,000

June 18, Death of Samuel Butler, author (66)

June 19, Death of Lord Acton (68), educator

July 4, Duty on imported corn included in budget, 3d. per cwt. and flour 5d. per cwt.

July 11, Resignation of the Marquis of Salisbury as Prime Minister

July 12, Arthur J. Balfour succeeded as Prime Minister without changes in the Cabinet; as First Lord of the Treasury, and Lord Privy Seal; Lord High Chancellor, Earl of Halsbury; Lord President of Council, Duke of Devonshire; Secretaries: Home, Mr. Akers Douglas; Foreign, Marquis of Lansdowne; Colonial, Mr. Chamberlain; War, Mr. Brodrick; Indian, Lord George Hamilton; First Lord of the Admiralty, Earl of Selborne; Chancellor of the Exchequer, Mr. Ritchie; Lord Chancellor of Ireland, Lord Ashbourne; Chief Secretary for Ireland, Mr. George Wyndham; Secretary for Scotland, Lord Balfour of Burleigh; President of the Board of Trade, Mr. Gerald Balfour; President of the Local Government Board, Mr. Walter Long; President of the Board of Agriculture, Mr. Hanbury (died Ap. 28, aged 58). The Earl of Onslow succ. May 21; President of the Board of Education, Marquis of Londonderry; Postmaster-General, Mr. Austen Chamberlain

July 22, Labor Bureau (London) Act approved

——, Decision of Lords in Taff Vale case made it law that trade unions were legal entities capable of suing and being sued

July 31, Strict Licensing Act passed in the interests of temperance

Aug. 9, Coronation of King Edward VII and Queen Alexandra in Westminster Abbey

Aug. 17-25, Visit of the Shah of Persia

Nov. 8-20, Visit of the Emperor of Germany

Nov. 16, Death of Field Marshal Prince Edward of Saxe-Weimar (79)

Nov. 17-Dec. 8, Visit of the King of Portugal

Dec. 7, British and German ultimatum to Venezuela as to claims, and seizure of Venezuelan fleet, Dec. 9 followed, Dec. 10 by blockade of the coast. *See also* Venezuela

Dec. 18, Education Act transferred control of elementary education to local authorities and of higher education in some measure; the Councils not to insist that any form of religious belief shall or shall not be taught, voluntary (denominational) schools to receive public support

Dec. 21, Wireless telegraph messages exchanged between Canada and England

Dec. 23, Death of Dr. Temple, Archbishop of Canterbury (81)

1903

Jan. 20, Meeting of English Church Union to discuss the Education Act

Jan. 24, Treaty with the United States on Alaska boundary

Feb. 7, Death of Edna Lyall (Miss Ada Bayley), novelist

Feb. 12, Thomas Randall Davidson (1st Baron), appointed Archbishop of Canterbury

March 22, Death of Dr. Frederic William Farrar, Dean of Canterbury (71)

March 25, Death of Major-General Hector Macdonald

April 7-May 5, Visit of the King to Portugal, Italy, and France

April 28, Death of Robert W. Hanbury, President of the Board of Agriculture

April 29, London Education Bill passed third reading

May 15, Mr. Chamberlain, Colonial Secretary, in speech at Birmingham declared for closer economic union with the colonies and an imperial preferential tariff

May 23, Demonstration in Hyde Park against the London Education Bill

June 19, Death of Cardinal Vaughan (71), Archbishop of Westminster

June 22, Corn duty of 1902 repealed

June 24, Arrival of the Khedive on visit

June 30, Coal Mines Regulation Act of 1887 amended

July 6-9, Visit of President Loubet of France

July 17, Death of James Abbott McNeill Whistler (69), American painter in London

July 21, Tariff Reform League inaugurated

Aug. 4, Royal Naval College at Osborne, Isle of Wight, opened by the King

Aug. 5, Death of Phil May, caricaturist of "Punch"

Aug. 14, Irish Land Purchase Act provided for fund for advance of money for purchase of land by tenants. Evicted tenants assisted to become owners of their former holdings, Housing of the Working Classes Act, Employment of Children Act, London Education Act received royal assent

Aug. 22, Death of Lord Salisbury (73), former Prime Minister

Aug. 29, Strike of 16,000 tin plate workers in Wales which affected about 40,000 other workers

Sept. 18, Resignation of Mr. Chamberlain, Mr. Ritchie, and Lord Hamilton from the Cabinet, and Lord Balfour of Burleigh, Sept. 21, and the Duke of Devonshire, Oct. 5

Sept. 30, Death of Sir Michael Herbert, diplomatist

Oct. 5, Balfour Cabinet reconstructed: Prime Minister and First Lord of the Treasury, Mr. Balfour; Lord Chancellor, Earl of Halsbury; Lord President of the Council and President Board of Education, Marquis of Londonderry; Lord Privy Seal and President of the Board of Trade (March 11, 1905), Marquis of Salisbury; Secretaries: Home Affairs, Mr. Akers-Douglas; Foreign Affairs, Marquis of Lansdowne; War, Mr. Arnold-Forster; Colonies, Mr. Alfred Lyttleton; India, Mr. Brodrick; First Lord of the Admiralty, Earl of Selborne, succeeded by Earl Cawdor, March 4, 1905; Chancellor of the Exchequer, Mr. Austen Chamberlain; Lord Chancellor of Ireland, Lord Ashbourne; Chief Secretary for Ireland, Mr. George Wyndham; resigned, March, 1905; Mr. Walter Long, Mar. 11, 1905; Secretary for Scotland, Mr. Graham Murray, succeeded by Marquis of Linlithgow, Feb. 2, 1905; President Board of Trade, Mr. Gerald Balfour; succeeded by Marquis of Salisbury, March 11, 1905; President Local Government Board, Mr. Walter Long; succeeded by Mr. Gerald Balfour, March 11, 1905; President Board of Agriculture and Fisheries, Earl of Onslow; succeeded by Mr. Ailwyn Fellowes, March 11, 1905; Postmaster-General, Lord Stanley

Oct. 14, Treaty of Arbitration with France

Oct. 28, Death of Mrs. Booth Tucker, daughter of General Booth, Salvation Army

Nov. 2, "Daily Mirror" founded

Nov. 9, Death of Lord Rowton

Dec. 8, Death of Herbert Spencer (83), philosopher

1904

Jan. 17, Death of Sir Henry Keppel, Admiral of the fleet (94)

Feb. 1, Anglo-Italian Arbitration Treaty signed

Feb. 10, Mass meeting held in London to protest against the importation of indentured Chinese labor in the Transvaal

Feb. 17, Debate on Chinese labor question in Commons, majority for the Government 51

Feb. 18, Retirement of Lord Roberts, as office of Commander-in-Chief of the Army abolished

Feb. 22, Death of Sir Leslie Stephen (71), first editor of the "Dictionary of National Biography"

Feb. 27, Arbitration Treaty with Spain

March 17, Death of the Duke of Cambridge (84), Commander-in-Chief of the army, 1856 to 1895

March 24, Death of Sir Edwin Arnold, author of the "Light of Asia"

April 8, Anglo-French Convention (entente cordiale) by which England recognized French position in Morocco and France the position of England in Egypt, France abandoned special privileges as to fishing rights in Newfoundland under Article 13 of the Treaty of Utrecht of 1713 and received an indemnity and cession of territory in Africa, the Isles de Los, and new boundary between Senegambia and the English colony of the Gambia to give France Yarbutenda, and new boundary with Nigeria; declarations of agreement as to Siam, Madagascar, and the New Hebrides

May 10, Death of Sir Henry M. Stanley (63), explorer

July 12, Anglo-German Arbitration Treaty signed

Aug. 1, Finance Act laid additional duties on tea and tobacco

Aug. 3, British mission of Colonel Younghusband reached Lhasa

Aug. 11, Arbitration Treaty with Sweden and Norway signed

Aug. 15, Statutes approved included Prevention of Cruelty to Children Act, Shop Hours Act (Early closing), Outdoor Relief (Friendly Societies) Act, and Education Act empowering the Board of Education to administer the provisions of the act of 1902 in default of a local authority performing its duties as respects any elementary school, and Licensing Act which provided for compensation when a license was taken away on the grounds of public policy

Sept. 7, Convention with Tibet which pledged Tibet to carry out boundary agreements, open trade at 3 marts, arrange a fixed tariff, and to make no territorial, political, or commercial concessions to any foreign Powers without similar concessions to Great Britain

Sept. 10, Return of the "Discovery" from the Antarctic. See also Antarctic

Oct. 1, Death of Sir William Vernon Harcourt (76), Chancellor of the Exchequer

Oct. 22, Russian North Sea fleet fired on English fishermen at the Doggerbank under delusion as alleged that they were Japanese torpedo boats, 2 persons killed, several injured. Message of the Tsar expressed regret (Oct. 25) and promised compensation; submission of inquiry to international commission agreed to by England, Oct. 28

Nov. 11, Death of Val Prinsep, R.A. (56)

Nov. 15, Death of the Earl of Northbrook, former Viceroy of India (78)

Nov. 16, Arbitration Treaty with Switzerland signed

Nov. 29, Death of the Earl of Hardwicke, Under-Secretary for India

Dec. 17, Royal Commission appointed to inquire into the Scottish church dispute

Dec. 30, Commercial Agreement with Russia

1905

Jan. 11, First meeting of the Royal Commission on Ecclesiastical Difficulty in Scotland

——, Arbitration Treaty with Austria-Hungary signed

Feb. 15, Arbitration Treaty with the Netherlands signed

Feb. 25, International Commission of Inquiry into North Sea affair held final meeting and gave report

Feb. 26, Death of Earl of Morley (62) and Captain Middleton (58)

March 1, Resignation of Lord Milner as High Commissioner for South Africa and Governor of the Transvaal and Orange River colonies. Succeeded by Lord Selborne

March 4, Earl of Cawdor appointed First Lord of the Admiralty

March 9, Russian Government paid £65,000 in award North Sea indemnity

March 11, Cabinet changes: Mr. Walter Long appointed Chief Secretary for Ireland in succession to Mr. Wyndham, resigned; Mr. Gerald Balfour, President of the Local Government Board; Lord Salisbury, President of the Board of Trade; Mr. Ailwyn Fellowes, President of the Board of Agriculture and Fisheries, in succession to Lord Onslow (appointed chairman of committees in the House of Lords)

June 15, Marriage of Princess Margaret of Connaught to Prince Gustavus Adolphus of Sweden and Norway

June 24, Royal Commission appointed to inquire into

the allegations made in the Report of the Butler Committee in respect of the disposal of stores in the South African War

July 10–17, Visit of British fleet to Brest followed by visit of French fleet to England, August 7–14

Aug. 11, Aliens Act restricting immigration and Unemployed Workmen Act approved and Churches (Scotland) Act

Aug. 12, Anglo-Japanese Agreement signed renewed alliance for 10 years; to secure peace in the East, independence and integrity of China, equal commercial rights

Aug. 19, Resignation of Lord Curzon. *See* India

Sept. 20, Death of George Macdonald, poet and novelist (80)

Oct. 13, Death of Sir Henry Irving, actor (67). Buried in Westminster Abbey Oct. 20

Oct. 25, Arbitration Convention with Denmark signed

Oct. 31, Treaty of commerce and navigation with Rumania signed

Dec. 4, Resignation of Unionist Ministry of Mr. Balfour

Dec. 5, Liberal Ministry of Sir Henry Campbell-Bannerman succeeded: Prime Minister and First Lord of the Treasury, Sir H. Campbell-Bannerman; Lord Chancellor, Lord Loreburn; Lord President of the Council, Earl of Crewe; Lord Privy Seal, Marquess of Ripon; Secretaries: Home, Mr. Herbert Gladstone; Foreign, Sir Edward Grey; Colonial, Earl of Elgin; War, Mr. R. B. Haldane; India, Mr. John Morley (Lord Morley, 1908); Chancellor of the Exchequer, Mr. H. H. Asquith; First Lord of the Admiralty, Lord Tweedmouth; Chief Secretary for Ireland, Mr. James Bryce; Mr. Birrell, Jan. 24, 1907; Secretary for Scotland, Mr. John Sinclair; President of the Board of Trade, Mr. David Lloyd George; President of the Local Government Board, Mr. John Burns; President of the Board of Agriculture and Fisheries, Earl Carrington; President of the Board of Education, Right Hon. Reginald McKenna, *vice* Mr. Augustine Birrell; Chancellor Duchy of Lancaster, Sir Henry Fowler (Lord Wolverhampton, 1908); Postmaster-General, Mr. Sydney Buxton

1906

Jan. 8, Parliament dissolved

Jan. 9, Death of Lord Ritchie, politician, at Biarritz

Jan. 12, General election a victory for the Liberals: Liberals, 377; Labor, 53; Irish Nationalists, 83; Conservatives and Unionists, 157

Jan. 25, Resignation of Lord Justice Mathew on account of health

Feb. 2, Death of Lord Masham, inventor

Feb. 10, New battleship "Dreadnought" launched at Portsmouth by the King

Feb. 13–Jan. 10, 1910, Second Parliament of Edward VII

April 27, Treaty with China signed embodying the adhesion of China to the Tibetan Convention

July 1, Death of Sir Wilfrid Lawson (76), member of Parliament

July 13, Death of General Patrick Maxwell

July 30, Education Bill passed third reading in Commons

Aug. 1, Visit of the King and Queen of Spain

Aug. 4, Law as to laborers in Ireland enacted, Prevention of Corruption Act

Oct. 6 and 8, Newfoundland Fisheries *modus vivendi* with the United States

Oct. 20, Convention with France signed settled differences in New Hebrides

Oct. 23, Disturbance at the House of Commons by supporters of woman suffrage who were removed from outer lobby by the police

Oct. 30, Death of Lord Cranbrook (Gathorne Hardy) (93)

Nov. 9, Death of Miss Dorothea Beale (75), educator

Dec. 6, Education Bill rejected in Lords

Dec. 13, Treaty with France and Italy signed as to Abyssinia

Dec. 17, Disturbance at the House of Commons when 8 women suffragists gained access to the central lobby and tried to make speeches

Dec. 21, Workmen's Compensation Act extending the scope of compensation and covering accidents to practically all employés including domestic servants approved, Trades Dispute Act reversing the Taff Vale decision by exempting trade union funds from liability for damages caused during a strike, Education (Provision of meals for children), Census of Production Act, and Notices of Accidents Act

1907

Jan. 23, Death of Lord Field, William Ventris Field, judge (95)

Jan. 24, Augustine Birrell appointed Chief Secretary for Ireland to succeed James Bryce appointed Ambassador to the United States

Jan. 29, Death of Sir Michael Foster, physiologist

Feb. 7, Death of Lord Goschen (George Joachim Goschen), statesman

Feb. 12, Parliament opened by the King

Feb. 13, Demonstration outside House of Commons to protest against omission of all reference to the question of woman suffrage in the King's speech, 52 women and 2 men arrested

Feb. 15, Commercial Treaty with Serbia signed

Feb. 20, Death of Lord Davey (Horace Davey), judge (73)

Feb. 21, Bill to reform its constitution introduced in House of Lords

Feb. 28, Death of Sir Francis Plunkett, diplomatist

March 24, Visit of the Russian squadron under Commodore Ronsaine

April 7, Woman suffrage demonstration in Hyde Park, London, 2,000 to 3,000 persons present

April 15–May 4, Fifth Imperial and Colonial Conference held in London discussed imperial defense, naturalization, preferential trade within the Empire

April 16, Extradition Treaty with Panama signed

April 18, Death of Lord Midleton (77)

April 21, Death of Lord Haliburton, former Under-Secretary for War (74)

April 29, Death of Lord de Ros, premier baron of England (80)

May 6–31, Visit of Prince Fushimi of Japan

May 7, Councils Bill for Ireland introduced placing administration of Ireland in hands of elective body with privilege of veto by the Lord Lieutenant was rejected by a Nationalist Convention in Dublin, May 21, and withdrawn in Commons June 3

June 8–13, Visit of the King and Queen of Denmark

June 21–27, Visit of the King of Siam

Aug. 2, Act created Expeditionary Force and Territorial Army

Aug. 9, Employment of Women Act approved

Aug. 21, Married Womens Property Act of 1882 amended, and Probation of Offenders Act

Aug. 28, Small Holdings and Allotments Act provided for acquisition by local authorities of land to be divided into small holdings for sale or lease to buyers or tenants who could not otherwise be placed on it for self support

——, Deceased Wife's Sister Act approved making marriage with deceased wife's sister legal, Education Act (Administrative Provisions), Factory and Workshop Act, Public Health (Amendment) Act, Patents and Designs Act consolidating all previous laws, Ireland Evicted Tenants Act, Act to establish a Court of Criminal Appeal

Aug. 31, Convention with Russia signed by which spheres of influence of both countries in Persia signed, Russia to control the northern half commercially, and Great Britain the southern half. Great Britain made declaration that the political status of Afghanistan would not be altered, and Russia and Great Britain engaged to respect the territorial integrity of Tibet, and to refrain from interference with its internal administration. Russia recognizing the Anglo-Tibetan Treaty of 1904

Sept. 19, Convention with France signed as to commercial relations with Canada

Oct. 6, Death of Lord Brampton (Hy Hawkins), judge (90)

Oct. 17, Wireless telegraph service for the newspaper press between England and the United States begun

Nov. 1 and 7, Settlement of threatened railway strike by agreement for conciliation and arbitration by the companies and the workers as proposed by Lloyd George, president of the Board of Trade

Dec. 17, Death of Lord Kelvin (William Thomson), physicist

1908

Jan. 15, Death of Louise de la Ramée (Ouida), novelist

Jan. 18, Death of Sir J. Lawson Walton, Attorney General (55)

Jan. 20, Death of Sir Massey Lopes, former Lord of the Admiralty (89)

Jan. 28, Sir W. S. Robson appointed Attorney General and S. T. Evans Solicitor General

Feb. 3, Wireless telegraph service extended to private and business telegraph service between Montreal and London *Times*

Feb. 11, Suffragist demonstration outside the House of Commons, 50 arrests made

Feb. 24, Education Bill introduced

March 24, Death of Spencer Compton Cavendish, 8th Duke of Devonshire, statesman

April 4, Treaty of arbitration with the United States signed

April 5, Resignation of Sir Henry Campbell-Bannerman as Prime Minister for reasons of health. Succeeded by Herbert Henry Asquith: Prime Minister, Herbert Henry Asquith; Lord High Chancellor, Lord Loreburn; Lord President of the Council, Viscount Wolverhampton (Sir Hy. Fowler), G.C.S.I. (Oct. 13, 1908); Lord Privy Seal, Earl of Crewe (Oct. 9, 1908); First Lord of the Treasury, the Prime Minister; First Lord of the Admiralty, Reginald McKenna; Secretaries of State: Home Affairs, Herbert John Gladstone; Foreign Affairs, Sir Edward Grey, Bart.; Colonies, Earl of Crewe; War,

Richard Burdon Haldane; India, Viscount Morley of Blackburn; Chancellor of the Exchequer, David Lloyd George; Secretary for Scotland, John Sinclair, (Baron of the U.K., 1909, Baron Pentland of Lyth, 1909); Chief Secretary to the Lord Lieutenant of Ireland, Augustine Birrell; Postmaster-General, Sydney Buxton; Presidents of committees of the Council: Board of Trade, Spencer Winston Churchill; Local Government Board, John Burns; Board of Agriculture, Earl Carrington, K.G.; Board of Education, Walter Runciman; Chancellor of the Duchy of Lancaster, Lord Fitzmaurice (Oct. 13, 1908) (resigned and succeeded by Mr. Samuel, M.P., June, 1909); First Commissioner of Works, Lewis Vernon Harcourt

April 11, Treaty with the United States signed as to fisheries in United States and Canadian waters

April 22, Death of Sir Henry Campbell-Bannerman

April 23, Treaty to maintain the *status quo* in the North Sea signed with Denmark, France, Germany, the Netherlands, and Sweden

May 25–29, Visit of President Fallières of France

June 2, Death of General Sir Redvers Buller

June 10, Meeting of Edward VII with the Tsar at Reval

June 13, Death of Sir John Day, Judge of the High Court

——, Suffrage demonstration, 7,000 women march from the Victoria Embankment to Albert Hall, London

June 14, Death of Lord Derby (Frederick Arthur Stanley), statesman

July 21, Letters Patent declared the Falkland Islands a British dependency

July 25, Irish Universities Bill passed and received royal assent Aug. 1. *See* Ireland

Aug. 1, Small Holdings and Allotments Act (Consolidating), Old Age Pensions Act which granted pensions of from 1s. to 5s. a week to all deserving persons over 70 years of age, British subjects residents for 20 years approved

Aug. 3, Arrival of the Prince of Wales at Cowes on his return from Canada

Aug. 10, King Edward left England for Cronberg to meet the German emperor, returned Sept. 5

Sept. 3, Death of Lord Sackville (Sir Lionel Sackville Sackville-West, 2nd baron)

Oct. 1, Two cent postage rate with the United States inaugurated

Oct. 13, Woman suffrage demonstration in Parliament Square, 24 women arrested

Oct. 28, Two women suffragists chain themselves to the grille in the House of Commons of the women's gallery and make their demands on law makers below

——, Publication in London "Daily Telegraph" of interview with the German Emperor on the subject of his attitude and that of the German people toward Great Britain

Nov. 9, Death of Sir James Mathew, formerly Lord Justice of Appeal

Nov. 12, Speech of Asquith urged a strong naval policy

Nov. 16–21, Visit of the King and Queen of Sweden

Nov. 23, Speech of Lord Roberts on the defenseless condition of England

Nov. 24, Death of Lord Glenesk (Algernon Borthwick)

Nov. 25, Arrival of the King of Norway

Nov. 27, Liberal Licensing Bill rejected by the House of Lords

Nov. 28, The Court of Appeal in the Osborne case declared it to be illegal for a trade union to provide for its parliamentary representative by a compulsory levy

Dec. 4–Feb. 26, 1909, International Naval Conference in London

Dec. 7, Withdrawal of the Education Bill as unacceptable to Roman Catholics and some others

Dec. 16, Agreement signed by employers and trade unions of British shipbuilding industry for settlement of disputes

Dec. 21, White Phosphorous Matches Act prohibiting the manufacture, importation, and exportation approved, Coal Mines Regulation Act, Children's Act, and Prevention of Crime Act providing for reform measures for the young offenders and prolonged detention for the habitual criminal

1909

Jan. 1, Old Age Pension Act came into effect, first payments made at post-offices

Jan. 11, Boundary Treaty with the United States as to frontier between the United States and Canada

Feb. 8–13, Official visit of King Edward to Berlin

Feb. 18–27, Visit of 4 Basuto chiefs from Africa; received by King Edward

March 10, Treaty with Siam signed by which British extra-territorial rights in Siam modified and Kelantan, Trengannu, and Kedah ceded to Great Britain

March 15, "Daily Sketch," illustrated newspaper, founded

March 16, Russian warships visit Portsmouth

March 19, Second reading of Representation of the People Bill providing for universal suffrage including women carried by 157 votes against 122

March 30, Consolidated Fund Act (No. 20 approved)

April 10, Children's Act consolidated and amended laws for the protection of children

——, Death of Algernon Charles Swinburne, poet

April 29, The "People's Budget" introduced by Lloyd George increasing income tax and estate duty, new taxes on land, the deficit to be raised at the expense of the wealthy and well-to-do. Receipts estimated at 162,590,000l., expenditure at 162,102,000l., estimated surplus, 488,000l. Additional taxation— (1) *Land values*, 20% on unearned increments, 10% reversion duty on determination of leases over 21 years, ½d. in the l. on undeveloped land, 5% on rental value of mineral rights and way leaves. (2) *Liquor licenses.* Duties increased for licenses for sale of liquor, and clubs brought into paying license by the imposition of 6d. in the l. on purchases. (3) *Death Duties.* Duty on settled estates, raised from 1% to 2%, and legacy and succession duties increased. Gifts, *inter vivos*, liable for duty up to 3 years before death. (4) *Income-tax* was to be raised to 1s. 2d. on incomes over 3,000l., with a further super-tax of 6d. on incomes over 5,000l., on the amount exceeding 3,000l. An abatement was to be allowed on incomes under 500l. for every child under 16 years. (5) *Stamps* on transfers of real property and leaseholds, doubled. Contract notes for sale of stock, made subject to duty. (6) *Customs and excise.* Spirit duty increased by 3s. 9d. per proof gallon, and duty on beer and tobacco increased.

May 18, Death of George Meredith, novelist and poet

May 25, Indian Councils Act received royal assent providing for popular representation in legislative councils

July 1, Coal Mines Act came into effect providing that a workman should not be below ground in a mine for the purpose of his work, or going to and from his work for more than 8 hours during any consecutive 24 hours

July 9, Death of Lord Ripon (81), former Viceroy of India

July 22, and Sept. 8, Agreement with the United States as to Newfoundland Fisheries

July 25, M. Blériot starting from Baraques near Calais on his monoplane crossed the Channel landing near Dover Castle (37 minutes)

July 28–Aug. 1, Imperial Defense Conference in London formulated plan for imperial General Staff and for military colleges in the overseas dominions

Aug. 1–5, Visit of the Tsar and the Empress of Russia

Sept. 14, Congress of Empire Chambers of Commerce

Sept. 20, Labor Exchanges Act approved and South Africa Act uniting the Colonies of the Cape of Good Hope, Natal, the Transvaal, and the Orange River into a Legislative Union under one Government named Union of South Africa

Oct. 20, Local Education Authorities (Medical Treatment) Act, Workmen's Compensation (Anglo-French Convention) Act, and Trade Boards Act for "sweated" industries approved

Nov. 4, The Finance Bill (Lloyd George's People's Budget) passed in Commons on third reading by vote of 379 to 149

Nov. 6, Death of Lord Selby (William Court Gully), former Speaker of the House of Commons

Nov. 30, The Lloyd George Budget rejected by the House of Lords by vote of 350 to 75

Dec. 3, Housing and Town Planning Act approved, and Development Act, and Irish Land Act. Mr. Asquith, Prime Minister, moved in House of Commons "that the action of the House of Lords in refusing to pass into law the financial provision made by the House for the service of the year is a breach of the Constitution and a usurpation of the rights of the Commons," adopted by vote of 349 to 134

Dec. 21, "Osborne judgment" upheld decision of Court of Appeals that it was illegal for trade unions to raise money by enforced levy of contributions towards payment of salaries of members of Parliament representing them

1910

Jan. 1, Juvenile courts opened in London under Children's Act of April, 1909

Jan. 10, Parliament dissolved

Jan. 14, General election begun which resulted in slight majority for the Liberals: Liberals, 274; Unionists, 272; Labour, 41; Nationalists, 82

Jan. 30, Death of Edward Dowden

Feb. 1, Eighty Labour Exchanges under the Board of Trade opened

Feb. 15, Third Parliament of Edward VII opened

Feb. 21, Southern miners resume work after strike in coal mines

Feb. 26, Death of A. J. Butler, Dante scholar (65)

March 14, Northern coal miners resume work

April 13, Death of Sir W. Q. Orchardson, R.A.

April 14, Government Veto Bill introduced limiting the veto of the House of Lords on money bills, if the Peers withheld consent for more than one month bill to be presented for Royal Assent and become a law, and for a Bill other than a Money Bill after passage by the Commons in 3 successive sessions to be presented for Royal Assent; text issued April 29

April 27–28, Flight of Louis Paulhan from London to Manchester with only one stop won "Daily Mail" prize of £10,000

April 28, Budget passed in House of Lords

April 29, Finance Act (1909–1910) received royal assent

May 6, Death of King Edward VII after a few days illness. Succeeded by his son as George V

May 12, Death of Sir William Huggins, astronomer (86)

May 17–June 16, Visit of Theodore Roosevelt, former President of the United States; speech in Guild Hall, London, May 31, gave results of his observations of British government in Africa

May 19–31, Strike of dockers at Newport settled by reference to arbitration

May 21, Boundary Treaty with the United States signed as between Canada and the United States in Passamaquoddy Bay

May 31, Liberal League dissolved

——, Union of South Africa inaugurated

June 1, Expedition of Captain Robert F. Scott left for the Antarctic. *See* Antarctic

June 2, H.C.S. Rolls made non-stop flight from Dover to Sangatte, France, 50 miles in 90 minutes, and made return trip (first) across Channel the same day

June 11, Announcement that Sir Charles Hardinge would succeed the Earl of Minto as Viceroy of India

July 2, Death of Dr. Frederick James Furnivall, Shakespeare scholar

July 12, Second reading of Bill granting the parliamentary franchise to women possessed of property and already voting in municipal elections carried by vote of 299 to 190 and then by vote of 320 to 175 referred to a committee of the whole House

July 16, Arbitration Convention with Austria-Hungary signed

July 18, Strike on the Grand Trunk Railway

July 18–21, Strike of 10,000 employees on the Northeastern Railway not successful

Aug. 3, Children's (Amendment) Act, Small Holdings and Allotments (Amendment) Act giving compensation to tenants disturbed with a view to the creation of small holdings under the Act of 1908, and Accession Declaration Act removing clauses offensive to Roman Catholics approved

Aug. 13, Death of Florence Nightingale, hospital reformer (90)

——, Death of John Poyntz Spencer, 5th earl

Sept. 3, Shipyard lockout at Clyde and northeast coast as result of strikes

——, Robert Loraine made first crossing of Irish Channel in biplane

Sept. 7, Death of William Holman Hunt, artist (83)

——, Hague Tribunal award as to North Atlantic Coast fisheries

Oct. 1, General lockout of 150,000 workers in Lancashire cotton district, settled by reference to arbitration Oct. 17

Oct. 22, Death of Prince Francis of Teck

Nov. 4, The Earl of Crewe succeeded Lord Morley as Secretary of State for India

Nov. 8, Strike riots in the Rhondda Valley

Nov. 28, Education (Choice of Employment) Act approved. Parliament dissolved

Dec. 1, Death of Professor John E. Bickersteth, classical scholar

Dec. 3–20, Elections held gave government majority:

Liberals, 272; Labour, 42; Nationalists, 84; Unionists, 271

Dec. 18, T. O. M. Smith made flight from England to Belgium

Dec. 29, Death of Samuel Henry Butcher, classical scholar

1911

Jan. 9–14, Agreement with the United States as to North Atlantic Coast Fisheries

Jan. 17, Death of Sir Francis Galton, anthropologist (88)

Jan. 26, Death of Sir Charles Wentworth Dilke (67)

Jan. 30, Extradition Treaty with Germany signed

Feb. 6, First Parliament of George V opened by the King with Government majority of 122

Feb. 7, Agreement with the United States as to fur seals

Feb. 8, Death of Earl Cawdor (Frederick Archibald Vaughan Campbell)

Feb. 22, Veto Bill passed first reading in the House of Commons depriving the Lords of power to hold up money bills, Bills passed by the Commons in 3 successive sessions to become law over veto by Lords, and making the maximum term of Parliament 5 years

March 2, Veto Bill passed second reading in the Commons

March 15, Veto Bill passed third reading in the Commons by vote of 362 to 241 and Bill sent to House of Lords

April 3, Treaty of trade and navigation with Japan signed

April 10, Death of Sir Alfred Lyall (76)

April 11, Government of Ireland Bill introduced in the Commons

April 22, Death of John Passmore Edwards (87)

May 5, "Conciliation Bill" assimilating the parliamentary to the municipal franchise for women passed second reading in the Commons by vote of 255 to 88

May 8, Agreement with China as to opium signed

May 22, Bill for reform of the constitution of the House of Lords passed Upper House on second reading

May 23, Sixth imperial conference opened in London considered questions of imperial defense

May 29, Death of Sir William S. Gilbert, poet and dramatist (74)

June 14, Seamen's strike begun for higher wages which extended to all the principal ports

June 17, Parade of 40,000 women suffragists in London

June 22, Ceremony of coronation of King George and Queen Mary at Westminster Abbey

July 6, Claims Convention with the United States signed as to terms of submission to arbitration, some claims antedating the War of 1812

July 7, Fur Seals Convention signed abolishing pelagic seal fishing

July 7–11, Visit of the King, the Prince of Wales, and the Princess Mary to Ireland

July 12, Death of Sir Eldon Gorst

July 13, Anglo-Japanese Alliance of 1905 renewed for 10 years

——, Investiture of Edward Albert, Prince of Wales, at Carnarvon, Wales

July 16, Announcement that Lord Kitchener had been appointed British Agent and Consul-General in Egypt

July 17–21, Royal visit to Scotland

July 20, Veto Bill amended passed third reading in House of Lords

July 21, Letter of Mr. Asquith to Mr. Balfour announced that the King had assented to use the royal prerogative for creating peers in order to pass the Veto Bill in the House of Lords in form passed in the House of Commons without amendments voted by Lords

——, Government announced support of France as against Germany in Morocco

July 22, Death of Sir Percy Bunting, editor

July 28, Seamens strike officially ended

Aug. 1, Dock strike begun in London

Aug. 2, Arbitration Treaty with the United States signed

Aug. 10, Veto Bill passed in the House of Lords after threat of creation of new peers by vote of 131 to 114. Royal assent Aug. 18

——, Resolution adopted in the House of Commons by vote of 256 to 158 provided for the payment of a salary at the rate of £400 to members of House

Aug. 14, Ship-owners announced lockout in strike of dockers

Aug. 15, Strike riots in Liverpool

Aug. 17, Strike of railroad workers begun

Aug. 18, Parliament Act (Veto), Old Age Pensions (Amendment) Act and Factory and Workshop (Cotton Cloth Factories) Act received royal assent

Aug. 19, Settlement in railroad strike by intervention of Government

Sept. 5–6, T. W. Burgess swam across the English Channel from South Foreland lighthouse to Cape Grisnez in 22 hours and 35 minutes. Only previous success Captain Webb, Aug. 24–25, 1875

Sept. 9, Air mail service begun in England between Hendon and Windsor

Sept. 16–Oct. 4, Railroad workers strike in Ireland

Sept. 21, Bank of England raised its discount rate from 4 to 5%

Oct. 10, Industrial Council established under chairmanship of Sir George Askwith to deal with trade disputes

Oct. 24, Winston Churchill appointed First Lord of Admiralty

Oct. 28, Andrew Carnegie elected Lord Rector of Aberdeen University

——, Roman Catholic Church in England and Wales divided into 3 provinces with sees at Westminster, Birmingham, and Liverpool

Oct. 31–Nov. 9, Successful strike of cab drivers

Nov. 8, Mr. Balfour announced his resignation of leadership of the Unionist Party

Nov. 11, King George and Queen Mary sailed for India

Nov. 13, Andrew Bonar Law chosen leader of Unionist Party

Dec. 6, National Insurance Act providing for sickness and unemployment insurance passed third reading in the Commons

Dec. 7, Naval Prize Bill for carrying out provisions of the Declaration of London passed in Commons by majority of 47 but was later rejected in Lords

Dec. 12, Coronation Durbar in India

Dec. 14, Death of John Strange Winter (Mrs. Arthur Stannard), author

Dec. 16, National Insurance Act, Coal Mines Act, Shop Regulations Act, and Small Landowners (Scotland) Act approved

Dec. 20, Strike in cotton factories in Lancashire

Dec. 27, Lockout in cotton industry affected 126,000 workers

1912

Jan. 1, Nationalization of telephone system completed

Jan. 15, Death of Henry Du Pre Labouchere founder of "Truth" in Florence (80)

Jan. 18, Robert Falcon Scott expedition reached the South Pole

Jan. 19, Lockout in cotton industry ended by a truce pending negotiations

Jan. 29, Death of Duke of Fife (62) at Assuan, Egypt

Feb. 4, King George and Queen Mary reached England from India

Feb. 6, Death of Frederick Seebohm (78), author

Feb. 8, Lord Haldane arrived in Berlin on mission to discuss Anglo-German relations, increase of German naval and military armaments

Feb. 10, Death of Baron Joseph Lister (84), surgeon

Feb. 26, Coal strike began at Alfreton, Derbyshire

March 1, Coal strike became general

——, Militant suffragists broke plate glass windows in the Strand, Haymarket, Regent, Oxford, and Bond Streets. 124 women arrested

March 4, Suffragists broke windows in Knightsbridge and Kensington districts of London. 200 women arrested

March 5, Police raid on headquarters of Womens' Social and Political Union and arrested leaders including Mrs. Pankhurst

March 18–24, Strike of London taxicab drivers charging owners with violation of award

March 18, Naval program called for expenditure of £44,085,400 during 1912–1913 building of 4 battleships, 8 armored cruisers, 20 destroyers, and 2,000 increase in personnel

March 28, "Conciliation Bill" (suffrage) rejected in Commons by vote of 222 to 208

March 29, Death of Robert F. Scott, commander of the British Antarctic expedition and Dr. E. A. Wilson and Lieutenant H. R. Bowers on March 27 or 29 only 11 miles from depot containing supply of food. Captain L. E. G. Oates had left the others to die on March 17

——, Coal Mines (Minimum Wage) Act and Shop Hours Act approved

April 6, Coal strike declared at an end

April 11, Home Rule Bill for Ireland introduced in Parliament

——, Final end of coal strike

April 15, The White Star liner "Titanic," largest steamer afloat, on first voyage struck iceberg and sunk 2¾ hours later with loss of 1,513 of the 2,224 persons on board

——, Death of William T. Stead on the "Titanic"

April 16, Irish Home Rule Bill passed first reading in Commons 360 to 266

——, Miss Harriet Quimby the first woman to fly across the English Channel crossed from Dover to Hardelot about 40 miles in 40 minutes

——, First publication of the "Daily Herald," new Labour paper in London

April 23, Welsh Disestablishment Bill introduced

April 24, Death of Justin McCarthy (82), author

April 25, Welsh Disestablishment Bill passed first reading in Commons 331 to 253

April 27, Death of Alfred John Church (83), classical scholar

May 1–June 4, Strike of tailors for revision of wages and hours

May 9, Irish Home Rule Bill passed second reading in Commons 372 to 271

May 16, Welsh Church Disestablishment Bill passed second reading in the Commons 348 to 267

May 20, Strike of 6,000 lightermen employed in port of London

May 22, Mrs. Pankhurst and Mr. and Mrs. Pethick Lawrence convicted of conspiracy to instigate the members of the Womens Social and Political Union to damage windows

May 23, Decision of transport workers to call a general strike

June 10, General strike of transport workers begun

———, Announcement that Lord Haldane of Cloan appointed Lord Chancellor, succeeding the Earl of Loreburn resigned

June 15, New imperial Trade commission held first session

June 24, Death of Field Marshal Sir George White (76)

June 25, Death of Sir Lawrence Alma-Tadema (76), artist

July 1, Death of Harriet Quimby in crash of her monoplane

July 20, Death of Andrew Lang (68), author

July 27, Strike of dockers ended by vote of transport union

July 28, 30,000 transport workers refused to accept terms and continued strike

Aug. 13, Death of Miss Octavia Hill (74), reformer

Aug. 17, Government protested to China regarding Chinese military invasion of Tibet

Aug. 20, Death of William Booth, founder of the Salvation Army (83)

Aug. 21, Bramwell Booth became head of the Salvation Army

Sept. 28, Covenant pledging resistance to Home Rule for Ireland signed by 471,414 persons in Ulster and England. *See* Ireland

Oct. 11, The Prince of Wales went into residence as an undergraduate at Magdalen College, Oxford

Oct. 21, Militant suffragists began destruction of letters in post office boxes

Oct. 24, Death of Arthur Wellesley Peel, First Viscount

Nov. 11, Defeat of Government in Commons on proposed limitation of imperial payment to Irish exchequer

———, Royal Commission on Divorce presented report

Dec. 6–14, Strike of employees of Eastern Railway

Dec. 9, Formal protest to the United States regarding the Panama Canal Act

———, Prince Louis of Battenberg appointed First Sea Lord

Dec. 19, Vote taken in medical profession resulted in 11,309 out of total of 13,731 taken for rejection of Lloyd George's terms for medical service under the Insurance Act

Dec. 20, Resolution adopted at meeting of British Medical Association to reject Government proposal and advising the profession to decline to serve under the Insurance Act passed by 182 votes to 21

1913

Jan. 1–March 19, Strike of cab drivers against the increase in price to them of petroleum

Jan. 3, Death of James, Duke of Abercorn (74)

Jan. 16, Irish Home Rule Bill passed in Commons by vote of 267 to 257

Jan. 27, Franchise Bill withdrawn because of controversy over the suffrage amendment

Jan. 30, Home Rule Bill rejected in House of Lords by vote of 326 to 69

Jan. 31, Death of James Ludovic Lindsay, Earl of Crawford

Feb. 5, Welsh Church Disestablishment Bill passed third reading in Commons

Feb. 10, The "Terra Nova" ship of the Scott Antarctic expedition reached New Zealand bringing report that Captain Scott reached the South Pole Jan. 18, 1912, but perished with 3 companions on return journey probably March 27 or 29

Feb. 13, Welsh Church Disestablishment Bill rejected by House of Lords 252 to 51

———, Railroad Bill passed third reading in the Commons

Feb. 15–19, Successful strike of 2,000 dock laborers at Grimsby for increase in wages and other concessions

Feb. 18, New three-year agreement signed for regulation of working conditions in shipyards

Feb. 20, Death of Sir William Arrol, engineer of the Forth Bridge (73)

Feb. 23, Mrs. Pankhurst arrested publicly accepted responsibility for attempt of militant suffragists to blow up residence of Lloyd George

Feb. 26, Strike of 5,000 dyers at Bradford settled after 7 weeks. Men agreed to one years trial of piece work

Feb. 27, Death of Adam Sedgwick, zoologist (58)

March 7, Shop Act and Trade Union Act amended. Trade unions gained power to use their funds for political purposes if empowered by a general ballot

March 25, Death of Field Marshal Viscount Wolseley

March 26, Winston Churchill in House of Commons proposed international agreement for suspension of naval construction in 1914

April 3, Mrs. Emmeline Pankhurst sentenced to 3 years penal servitude for inciting malicious destruction of property

April 4, Death of Professor Edward Dowden (69)

April 14, Death of John A. R. Westlake, international jurist

April 25, Strike of tube and other metal workers in Birmingham, Wolverhampton, and Wednesbury and other towns for increase of wages

May 6, Bill extending suffrage to women of property rejected in Commons by vote to 267 to 219

May 19–28, Visit of the King and Queen to Germany to attend royal wedding

May 28, Death of Lord Avebury (Sir John Lubbock) (79)

May 30, Treaty of London signed. *See also* Turkey

May 31, Treaty of arbitration with the United States signed

June 2, Death of Alfred Austin, poet laureate (78)

June 10, Home Rule passed second reading in House of Commons

June 17, Welsh Disestablishment Bill passed second reading in Commons

July 6, Welsh Disestablishment Bill passed third reading in Commons

July 7, Agreement for increase in wages ended strike of tube and metal workers

———, Home Rule passed third reading in Commons

July 11, End of successful strike of 40,000 unskilled workers in Birmingham for minimum wage of $5.75 a week

July 15, Home Rule Bill rejected a second time in House of Lords and a third time July 22

July 16, Robert Bridges appointed poet laureate

Aug. 15, National Insurance (Amendment) Act approved

Aug. 31, Strike riots in Dublin. *See* Ireland

Oct. 15, Marriage of Prince Arthur of Connaught and the Duchess of Fife

Nov. 7, Death of Alfred Russell Wallace, scientist

Dec. 6, Proclamation of the King prohibited the importation of arms and ammunition into Ulster

Dec. 10, Strike of municipal workers at Leeds. Settled Jan. 13

1914

Jan. 8, Death of Viscount Cross (Richard Assheton Cross) former Home Secretary (90)

Jan. 21–28, Successful strike of coal porters for increase in wages

Jan. 24, Death of Sir David Gill (70), astronomer

Jan. 26, Strike in building trade in London begun against employment of non-unionists

Jan. 31–Feb. 25, Strike of elementary school teachers in Herefordshire

Feb. mid, Strike of coal miners in Yorkshire begun

Feb. 24, Arrival of the deported labor leaders from South Africa aroused great demonstration in their support

Feb. 25, Death of Sir John Tenniel, painter

March 10, Militant suffragists mutilated the famous Rokeby Velasquez "Venus with the Mirror" in the National Gallery

March 30, Announcement by Prime Minister of resignation of Colonel Seely, and Sir J. S. Ewart and his own assumption of the post of Minister of War

March 31, Death of Sir Hubert von Herkomer (64), artist

April 1, National debt of the United Kingdom £708,-000,000

April 15, Yorkshire coal miners voted to return to work

April 21–24, Visit of the King and Queen to Paris

April 24–25, Ulster volunteers landed rifles and ammunition. *See* Ireland

May 2, Death of 9th Duke of Argyll (69)

May 4, Militant suffragists slashed Sargent's portrait of Henry James in the Royal Academy exhibition

May 7, Government of Ireland (Home Rule) Bill reintroduced passed first reading in House of Commons

May 21, 57 militant suffragists arrested in attempt to force entrance to Buckingham Palace to present petition

May 23, Militant suffragists attempted to blow up viaduct of Glasgow water supply

May 25, Irish Home Rule Bill passed third time by House of Commons 351 to 274 in 3 successive sessions became law under the Parliament Act without approval of the Lords. Received royal assent Sept. 18

May 28, Death of Sir Joseph Wilson Swan, electrical chemist

June 7, Government announcement of appointment of board of inquiry ended strike of 10,000 employees of Royal Arsenal at Woolwich the week before because of employment of non-unionists

June 10, Arbitration Convention with Switzerland signed

June 11, Attempt of militant suffragists to blow up the coronation chair at Westminster Abbey

June 15, Anglo-German Treaty signed (Berlin-Bagdad Railroad)

June 28, Turkish Petroleum Company (British 75%, German 25%) obtained from Turkey exclusive rights for exploitation of oil in Mosul and Bagdad

July 2, Death of Joseph Chamberlain

July 14, House of Lords passed Bill amending Irish Home Rule Act

July 21, The King called a conference of the Prime Minister and Sir Edward Carson, Ulster leader, and John Redmond, Irish Nationalist leader to discuss possible area for exclusion from Home Rule Bill operation

July 24, Proposal of Sir Edward Grey for international conference to avert war

July 26, Proposal of conference of ambassadors in London on Serbian crisis. Accepted the following day by Russia, France, and Italy, but declined by Germany the 28th

July 28, First fleet ordered to Scapa Flow (war base)

July 30, 31, and Aug. 1, Warnings to Germany against violation of neutrality of Belgium

July 31, London stock exchange closed. Bank rate doubled (8%)

Aug. 1, Mobilization of British fleet

——, Bank rate raised to 10%, highest in history of Bank of England

——, Sir Ernest Shackleton in the "Endurance" left England for South Polar expedition

Aug. 2, British naval reserves called

——, Government assured France of assistance of British fleet in event of attack of German fleet

——, Partial moratorium decreed for 30 days, the first in English history

Aug. 3, Statement of Sir Edward Grey in House of Commons of condition of affairs in Europe and obligations of the British Government

——, Requisition of shipping authorized

——, Decision to mobilize 6 divisions

Aug. 4, Ultimatum to Germany as to neutrality of Belgium. *See also* World War

——, Mobilization of Expeditionary and Territorial forces proclaimed

——, War declared at 11 P.M. *See also* World War

——, Sir John French appointed commander-in-chief of the British army in France and Admiral Sir John Jellicoe, commander of the fleet

——, 21 known spies and 200 suspects arrested and interned

——, Proclamation extended list of articles to be treated as contraband

Aug. 5, Prime Minister Asquith announced in House of Commons that Great Britain was at war with Germany from 11 P.M., Aug. 4

——, First war credit of £100,000,000 passed and increase of army by 500,000 men authorized and of navy by 67,000

——, Aliens Restriction Act approved as to landing, residence, departure, and prohibited areas and Order required registration of aliens

——, Lord Kitchener appointed Secretary of State for War

——, Railroad system taken over by the Government

——, Proclamation prohibited trading with the German Empire

Aug. 5, First contraband proclamation as to special specified articles issued and export of food and forage prohibited

Aug. 6, London builders strike settled

——, Currency and Bank Note Act provided for issue of notes by Treasury and suspension of Bank Act if necessary

Aug. 7, First British troops arrived in France. For battles *see* World War

——, Coal Mines Act approved. Patents, Designs, and Trade Marks Act of 1907 amended authorized revocation and suspension of enemy patents

Education (Provision of Meals) Act of 1906 amended

Aug. 7, Banks closed since bank holiday of Aug. 3 opened

Aug. 8, Prices rose to 15 to 16% above normal prices of July, sugar, 80 to 90%, potatoes, 15% in large towns and 4% in small towns

——, First Defense of the Realm Act gave the Government general powers of regulation for securing public safety

Aug. 8–16, British Expeditionary Army forces landed in France

Aug. 10, "Unreasonable Withholding of Food Supplies Act" to prevent hoarding, National Insurance Act amended, Public Health (Milk and Dairies) Act passed, Criminal Justice Administration Act amended. Bankruptcy Act consolidated laws. Anglo-Persian Oil Company Act to provide money for acquisition of shares

Aug. 12, Commercial Treaty with Portugal signed

——, Regulations as to control of liquor trade issued

——, First squadrons of the British Royal Flying Corps flew from Dover to France

——, War declared on Austria-Hungary

Aug. 13, The war with Austria-Hungary proclaimed. *See* Aug. 12

Aug. 17, Prices of flour fixed

Aug. 20, British Order in Council adopted Declaration of London of Feb. 26, 1909 with modifications and revised contraband list proclaimed

Aug. 24, War Refugees central committee established

Aug. 28, Defense of the Realm Act (No. 2) extended powers of Government

Aug. 31, Intoxicating Liquor (Temporary Control) Act

Sept. 4, Prize Court opened the first since the Crimean War

Sept. 9, Proclamation prohibited trading with Austria-Hungary

Sept. 15, Advancement of Peace Treaty with the United States signed

Sept. 17, Proclamation gave Board of Trade authority to take possession of any article of commerce unreasonably withheld

Sept. 18, National Insurance Army and Navy Act approved, Trading with the Enemy Act, and Home Rule for Ireland and Welsh Church Disestablishment Acts became law but operation suspended until close of War

Sept. 21, Contraband list further extended

Oct. 23, Aliens Restriction Consolidation Order

Oct. 24, Importation of sugar prohibited

Oct. 25, Death of Sir C. Douglas, head of Imperial General Staff. Succeeded by Sir J. Wolfe Murray

Oct. 29, Revised contraband list issued. Declaration of London further modified

——, Resignation of Prince Louis Battenberg as First Sea Lord. Succeeded by Lord Fisher

Nov. 4, Island of Cyprus annexed by Great Britain abrogating Turkish sovereignty

Nov. 5, War declared against Turkey

Nov. 6, German spy Karl Lody shot in the Tower

Nov. 9, Arbitration treaties with Norway and Sweden renewed

——, Statement of war aims by Mr. Asquith

Nov. 14, Death of Lord Roberts at St. Omer of pneumonia on visit to the front

Nov. 16, First war loan offered, bonds at 3½%, $1,750,000,000

——, The Prince of Wales joined the staff of Field Marshal Sir John French in France

——, Arbitration Agreement with Portugal signed

Nov. 17, Lloyd George introduced first war budget for increase of taxation. Chief points war loan of £350,-000,000, income and super tax doubled, tax on tea and beer raised

Nov. 25, War Council constituted composed chiefly of members of the Committee of Imperial Defense to whom the Cabinet delegated the ordinary management of the war, Lloyd George, Sir Edward Grey, Lord Haldane and Lord Crewe, the Prime Minister, Lord Kitchener, and Mr. Churchil, the three latter taking the chief responsibility

Nov. 27, Defense of the Realm Consolidation Act approved, National Insurance (Army and Navy) Act amended, and Trading with the Enemy Act amended

Nov. 30–Dec. 5, Visit of the King to headquarters in France

Dec. 10, Proposal through the United States to Germany for exchange of prisoners physically incapable of further military service. Accepted by Germany Dec. 31

Dec. 16, Air raid on Hartlepool, Scarborough, and Whitby. *See* World War for air raids

Dec. 18, Announcement of British protectorate over Egypt. Sir Arthur McMahon appointed High Commissioner. *See also* Egypt

Dec. 23, Contraband list further revised

1915

Jan. 1, Price of fish showed increase of 51% in large towns and 31% in small towns, bread about 16% increase since July, tea, 14%, milk, 6%; eggs, 63%

——, New Naturalization law went into effect by which citizens in any part of the Dominion citizens of Great Britain

Jan. 3, Death of Percy Illingsworth, Liberal

Jan. 4, London stock exchange opened

Jan. 7, Interim Note sent to the United States in reply to American Government protest of Dec. 28 of search of American ships

Jan. 11, Death of Mrs. John Wood (83), comedy actress

Jan. 15, Death of Sir George Nares, Polar explorer

Jan. 19, First Zeppelin raid over Yarmouth. *See* World War

Feb. 1, Death of Major General Sir Luke O'Connor

Feb. 4, Blockade of England announced. *See* World War

——, Death of Miss Braddon (Mrs. John Maxwell), novelist (78)

——, Sir George Askwith, Sir Francis Hopwood, and Sir George Gibb appointed a Committee on Production in Engineering and Shipbuilding Establishments

Feb. 8–15, Successful strike of 4,000 Dundee jute workers secured advance of 5% in wages

Feb. 14, Unsuccessful strike of London dockers

Feb. 15, Announcement of increase in wages of railroad workers

Feb. 16, Death of Dr. Thomas K. Cheyne, Biblical scholar

Feb. 16–March 4, Unofficial strike of Clyde engineers for increase in wages. Settled by reference to arbitration

March 1, Death of Professor James Geikie, geologist

——, $1,435,000 appropriated for war purposes

March 4, Mersey coal heavers strike ended

March 14, Death of Walter Crane, artist (70)

March 16, National Insurance (Amendments Part I and II) and Injuries in War Compensation Act approved. The powers of the Government extended to regulate all factories and workshops capable of producing munitions of war

March 17, The Miners Federation in conference with the Chancellor of the Exchequer and the President of the Board of Trade asked for 20% increase in wages

March 23, The War Department empowered to requisition factories and unoccupied premises for housing war workers

March 24, Award announced of increase of 1d. an hour to Clyde engineers and 10% on piece work

March 25, Arbitration Convention with the Netherlands renewed

April 14, Announcement of Secretary of the Colonies that the Dominions would be consulted as to peace terms

May 3, Strike of employees of Woolich Arsenal for higher wages

May 7, Sinking of the "Luisitania." *See* World War

May 13, Decision of Government to intern all unnaturalized aliens and repatriate others

May 14, Strike of London County Council tramwaymen

May 15, State control of liquor trade enacted

May 17–June 4, Strike of London tramwaymen for increase of war bonus

May 22, Collision of trains on Caledonia Railroad near Gretna Green the worst disaster in history of British railroads. 157 killed, 200 injured

May 25, National coalition Cabinet announced by Prime Minister Asquith; Sir Edward Grey, Foreign Affairs; Reginald McKenna, Exchequer; Lloyd George, Munitions; Lord Kitchener, War; A. J. Balfour, Admiralty; Austen Chamberlain, India; Lord Robert Cecil, Under-Secretary Foreign Affairs; Lord Lansdowne, without Portfolio; Lord Selborne, Agriculture; A. Bonar Law, Colonies

May 27, Announcement of resignation of Winston Churchill, First Sea Lord

——, Auxiliary ship "Princess Irene" blown up in Shrerness harbor. Only 1 of crew rescued

May 28, Arthur J. Balfour appointed First Lord of Admiralty, and Sir Henry Jackson, First Sea Lord

May 31–June 1, Strike of 10,000 hosiery workers secured bonus

June 4, Act made provision to render unnecessary re-election of members of House of Commons. Continued by successive Acts

June 9, Ministry of Munitions Act established Ministry. Lloyd George made head of new office

June 10, Order in Council created Central Liquor Traffic Control Board

June 21, War loan announced for unlimited amount, 4.5% redeemable in 10 years

June 23, German spy, Müller, shot in the Tower

July 2, Munitions of War Act prohibited strikes and lockouts and provided for settlement of disputes by arbitration and gave Government complete control of munitions plants. Labor leaders had agreed to suspension of trade regulations restricting output

——, Ministry of Munitions created

——, £250,000,000 voted for war credit

July 6, Liquor control regulations for England and Wales issued for 10 areas

July 12, Voluntary registration of munitions operatives closed with enrollment of 90,000

July 13, Proclamation placed labor dispute in South Wales coal mines under the Munitions of War Act

July 14, Sir Robert Borden, Canadian Prime Minister, the first colonial to attend a Cabinet meeting

July 15, National Registration Bill passed

——, Strike of 200,000 coal miners in South Wales begun demanding wage increase

July 26, Henry James took oath of allegiance as a British citizen

July 28, 2 Scotch areas added to liquor controlled districts

July 29, Government of India Act consolidated all enactments, Milk and Dairies Act consolidated enactments, Notification of Births Act extended, Price of Coal (Limitation) Act fixed prices

Aug. 3, First of a series of Acts passed restricting production of alcoholic liquor

Aug. 15, Registration of all persons between ages of 15 and 65 not serving in the army taken

Aug. 17–18, Flight of Harry Hawker around the British Isles, 1,043 miles in 2½ days

Aug. 21, Cotton declared absolute contraband

Aug. 25–Sept. 1, Successful strike of 12,000 South Wales coal miners for increase

Aug. 26–Sept. 4, Strike of shipwrights at Govan

Aug. 28, War Loan Act

Sept. 14, More Scotch areas added to liquor controlled districts

——, Order in Council postponed putting into operation of Irish Home Rule until end of war

Sept. 15, Prime Minister Asquith in House of Commons asked for vote of credit of £250,000,000 to cover war expenses until November, the 17th war credit since the outbreak of the war

Sept. 21, Stonehenge sold by auction to C. H. E. Chubb of Salisbury for £6,600

——, Tax of 50% placed on excess profits and income tax raised 40%, and taxes raised on imports of tobacco, petrol, and patent medicine

Sept. 21–Oct. 4, Strike of 900 boiler makers at Southampton against employment of non-unionists

Sept. 24, London district added to liquor controlled area

Sept. 25, General Sir J. Wolfe Murray, Chief of Imperial General Staff, resigned and was succeeded the following day by Lieutenant General Sir A. J. Murray

Sept. 26, Death of J. Keir Hardie, Labour member of Parliament

Sept. 29, Anglo-French loan arranged in the United States of £100 million at 5% for 5 years

Oct. 12, Execution of Miss Edith Cavell. *See* World War

Oct. 13, Diplomatic relations with Bulgaria severed

Oct. 15, Proclamation of state of war with Bulgaria

Oct. 18, Resignation of Sir Edward Carson as Attorney General because of disagreement with Government Balkan policy

Oct. 21, The King on visit to army headquarters

Oct. 28, The Cabinet decided on compulsory military service

Oct. 29–30, General Joffre in London

Nov. 2, F. E. Smith succeeded Sir Edward Carson as Attorney General

Nov. 6–22, The "Globe" newspaper suspended for printing false statement as to resignation of Lord Kitchener from War Office

Nov. 11, Mr. Asquith announced creation of War Council of the Cabinet, of himself, Lloyd George, Bonar Law, and McKenna

——, Resignation of Winston Churchill from the Cabinet and retirement from politics as not included in War Council and departure as officer to the front

Nov. 30, Lord Kitchener returned from mission to eastern Mediterranean

Dec. 9, Coalition formed by Miners Federation, the National Union of Railwaymen, and the National Transport Workers Union to protect skilled labor

——, Death of Stephen Phillips, poet, dramatist

Dec. 15, General Sir Douglas Haig appointed Commander-in-Chief

Dec. 18, Proclamation called to service on Jan. 20 single men from 19 to 22

Dec. 21, Fourth million of soldiers voted by House of Commons

Dec. 23, Extension of Trading with the Enemy Act granted powers to prohibit trading with the enemy in neutral countries

——, Rent Restriction Act forbade increase above standard rents on or before Aug. 3, 1914

1916

Jan. 1, Resignation of Sir John Simon, Home Secretary because of opposition to compulsory military service

Jan. 5, Mr. Asquith introduced Compulsory Military Service Bill. Passed by vote of 403 to 105, second reading Jan. 11, third Jan. 24, 383 to 36

Jan. 11, Herbert Louis Samuel appointed Home Secretary

Jan. 27, Compulsory Military Service Act affecting all bachelors and childless widowers between ages of 18 and 41 received royal assent. Not applied to Ireland

——, Shipping Control Committee formed

Jan. 30, Death of Sir Clements Markham

Jan. 31, Price of 4 pound loaf of bread in London 9½d.

Feb. 10, Proclamation called for service all remaining groups of unmarried men

Feb. 21, War credits voted of £120 million for 1915–16, and £300 million for 1916–17

Feb. 23, Blockade Ministry created. Lord Robert Cecil appointed head

Feb. 28, Death of Henry James, novelist

Feb. 29, General statutory list of prohibited enemy firms in neutral countries published

March 4, Proclamation called married men from 25 to 32 to military service

March 7, Mr. Hughes, Prime Minister of Australia, arrived in London

March 18, Death of Reverend Stopford Brooke

March 22, General Luigi Cadorna, Commander-in-Chief of Italian army, arrived in London

March 27–June 8, Strike of 30,000 jute workers for 15% increase in wages unsuccessful

March 29–April 1, Strike of 15,000 dockers in Liverpool against award on payment for night work

March 29, Declaration of London Article 19 as to blockade rescinded

March 31, Crown Prince of Serbia arrived in London

April 4, End of Clyde shipping strike

——, Death of Sir John Gorst

April 7, New taxes placed on amusements, matches, mineral waters, sugar, cocoa, motor cars, and excess profits

April 8, Death of Wilfrid Ward, author

April 20, Unsuccessful attempt to land arms and munitions from German ship disguised as neutral merchant vessel on coast of Ireland

April 21, Sir Roger Casement arrested charged with treason in attempting to land munitions in Ireland. *See* Ireland

April 24–30, Sinn Fein rebellion in Ireland. *See* Ireland

May 1, Resignation of Sir Augustine Birrell as Secretary for Ireland

May 3, New Military Service Bill introduced by Mr. Asquith affecting all males between ages of 18 and 41. Passed third reading May 16

May 10, Baron Wimborne, Lord Lieutenant of Ireland, resigned

May 12–18, Visit of Mr. Asquith to Ireland

May 15, Sir Roger Casement charged with high treason and committed for trial

May 17, Daylight Saving Bill received royal assent

——, First Air Board formed with Lord Curzon as president

May 23, War credit of £300,000,000 voted

May 25, Military Service Act signed by the King

May 28, Air mail service established between London and Paris

May 31, The missing antarctic explorer Sir Ernest Shackleton with 5 companions arrived at Port Stanley, Falkland Islands

June 1, Coal miners received advance of 1s. 6d. per day

June 5, Death of Lord Kitchener on the H.M.S. "Hampshire" which struck a drifting mine off Orkney Islands. Only 12 survivors

June 25, Lord Selborne resigned as President of the Board of Agriculture

June 26, Trial of Sir Roger Casement begun. Convicted on the 29th and sentenced to death

June 26–July 3, Unsuccessful strike of engineers

June 30, Death of Sir Gaston Maspero, Egyptologist

July 6, Lloyd George succeeded Lord Kitchener as Secretary of State for War

July 7, Order in Council rescinded the Declaration of London

July 12, The Earl of Crawford appointed President of the Board of Agriculture

July 19, National Insurance (Extension Abroad) approved. Finance Act added excess profits tax, income tax, and duties on cocoa, coffee, chicory, sugar, molasses, tea, tobacco, petrol, table waters

July 27, Captain Charles Fryatt shot. *See* World War

July 31, Henry Duke, Unionist, appointed to succeed Mr. Birrell as Chief Secretary for Ireland

Aug. 1, Licensing system for supply of petrol came into operation

Aug. 3, Sir Roger Casement hung in London

——. Police, Factories, &c. (Miscellaneous Provisions) Act approved

——, Act restricted production of beer

Aug. 27, Munitions of War (Amending) Act approved

Sept. 3, Sir Ernest Shackleton arrived at Puenta Arenas, Chile, with 22 members of his expedition who had been marooned on Elephant Island

Sept. 6, National Insurance Part II Munition Workers Act became effective

Oct. 2, Death of Benjamin Kidd, sociologist

Oct. 16, Price of bread 10d. for 4 pound loaf

Nov. 6, Price of bread 10½d. for 4 pound loaf

Nov. 16, Order in Council gave Board of Trade power to regulate food supply and fix prices

Nov. 23, Proclamation declared gold, silver, and paper money and securities as contraband

——, Maximum and minimum prices of milk established

Nov. 27, Use of new grade of flour designed to preserve supply decreed from this date

Nov. 29, Admiral Sir David Beatty succeeded Admiral Jellicoe as Commander-in-Chief of fleet

Nov. 30–Dec. 6, Strike of 15,000 engineers at Manchester against wage award

Dec. 1, The Government took possession of the coal mines; Act Feb. 6, 1918 regularized

Dec. 4, Admiral Jellicoe appointed First Sea Lord

Dec. 5, Resignation of Lloyd George precipitated Cabinet crisis and resignation of Prime Minister Asquith, who refused request of Lloyd George for conduct of the war by committee of 4: himself, Bonar Law, Sir Edward Carson, and a Labour member. Mr. Bonar Law failed to form Cabinet

Dec. 7, Lloyd George appointed Prime Minister with War Cabinet of four, Lloyd George, Lord Curzon, Lord Milner, Mr. Henderson. Mr. Balfour became Secretary of State for Foreign Affairs succeeding Lord Grey of Fallodon; Bonar Law, Exchequer; H. A. L. Fisher, Education; R. E. Prothero, Agriculture; Lord Derby, War; Sir Edward Carson, Admiralty; Walter Long, Colonial; Dr. Addison, Munitions; Mr. Chamberlain, India; Sir F. E. Smith, Attorney General; Sir George Cave, Home; Hodge, Labor

Dec. 9, War Cabinet held first meeting

Dec. 10, Appointment of Lord Devonport as Food Controller announced

Dec. 18, National Insurance (Temporary Employment in Agriculture) Act approved

Dec. 19, Announcement of Lloyd George that Neville Chamberlain had been appointed Director General of National Service (Nov. 10)

Dec. 22, New Ministries of Food, Labor, Pensions, and Shipping Control created, Sir Joseph Maclay appointed Shipping Controller; Lord Cowdray, Air; Mr. Hodge, Labour; George Barnes, Pensions; Lord Devenport, Food

1917

Jan. 1, Railroad regulations came into force, 50% increase in fares and fewer and slower trains

——, Food Production Department established to organize an immediate increase in home production of food

——, Wool Controller appointed for the industry

——, Standard loaf of bread became compulsory

Jan. 3, Cotton weavers granted 5% increase making 10% since outbreak of War

——, Lord Cowdray appointed chairman of Air Board

Jan. 8–9, Strike of 2,000 women munitions workers at Leeds for grievances and war bonus

Jan. 9, Order regulated price of potatoes

Jan. 11, Third war loan announced at 95 at 5% for 30 years. Closed Feb. 16, brought in £1,100,312,950

Jan. 15, Death of William Frend De Morgan, novelist

Jan. 18, Bank rate reduced from 6% (since July 13, 1916) to 5½%

Jan. 19, Explosion at munitions plant at Silvertown, East London, killed 69 persons and injured 400

Jan. 24, Regulation came into force by which the Treasury was given power to requisition securities

Jan. 27, Appeal made to men between 18 and 60 to enrol for volunteer national service

Jan. 29, Death of Lord Cromer (Evelyn Baring)

Jan. 30, Youths of 18 called for service

Feb. 2, Lord Devonport, Food Controller, called on heads of families to limit rations of bread to 4 pounds weekly for each person, meat 2½ pounds, and sugar ¾ pound

Feb. 9, Conciliation and Arbitration Board for government employees appointed

——, Order prohibited private importation of sugar

Feb. 12, Votes of credit passed House of Commons for £200,000,000 for 1916–17 and £350,000,000 for 1917–18

——, Price of 4 pound loaf of bread rose to 11d.

Feb. 14, Announcement of Government that coal mines would be taken over by the Government for the war period

Feb. 16, Agreement to support Japanese territorial claims. See World War

Feb. 17, Treasury Order required owners or custodians of specified securities to deliver them up in return for an amount of compensation based on current market values

Feb. 20, Fuel Research Board appointed

Feb. 21, Order in Council required neutral ships to call at British or Allied ports under penalty of seizure

Feb. 23, Lloyd George announced plan to prohibit unnecessary and bulky imports

March 1, Coal mines and non-railway owned canals taken over by the Government

March 7, House of Commons proposed resolution calling for immediate application of Home Rule to Ireland protested by Nationalists

March 9, Announcement of maximum prices list, English bacon 150s. per cwt., Irish and Danish, 140; Australian butter, 218s. per cwt.; Argentine, 214; New Zealand, 224; English cheese, 165s., &c.

March 12, Order came into effect that bread should be sold only by weight and must be at least 12 hours old

——, General Smuts arrived from South Africa

March 13, Mines and quarries other than coal brought under government control

March 15, Loan of £40,000,000 to Rumania announced

March 19–24, Strike of 12,000 Tyneside engineers secured 2s. increase per week

March 21–April 11, Unofficial strike of Barrow engineers against cutting of time allowance on premium bonus

March 21–May 17, Imperial War Cabinet, held 14 meetings in London. Decision to hold annual conferences

March 23, Food (conditions of sale) order

March 26, 4 pound loaf of bread rose from 11d. to 1 shilling.

March 28, Coal Mines Act amended

——, Ross Dependency declared British by Letters Patent

March 28, Ministry of National Service established

——, Revised and consolidated list of prohibited imports published

March 29, Intoxicating Liquor (Output and Delivery Order) issued by Food Controller reduced quantity of wine and spirits which could be delivered 50%

March 30, Retail prices of food showed increase of 94% as compared with July, 1914

March 31, Cost of War for 1916–1917, estimated by Bonar Law as £6,000,000 per day, National Debt £3,900,000,000, and loans to Dominions and Allies £954,000,000

April 1, Wages increased in engineering, foundry, and light casting industries

April 5, Bank rate reduced to 5% from 5½

April 6, First government farm colony established at Turk Island, Yorkshire

——, Food hoarding Order prohibited acquisition of food or sale by retailers of quantities in excess of requirements of ordinary household

April 9, Wages of women munition workers raised

——, Railroad men received 3d. war bonus of 5 shillings per week making total war bonus 15 shillings per week

April 15, Public Meals Order came into force providing for weekly meatless day, 5 days without potatoes, and rationing of bread and meat which allowed 2 ounces of bread for each meal, 2 ounces of meat at breakfast, and 5 ounces at lunch and dinner for public restaurants and hotels

April 16, Wheat, Barley, and Oats (Prices) Order issued fixed maximum prices

April 18, Cakes and Pastry Order provided that no cake should contain more than 15% of sugar nor more than 30% of wheat and flour

April 21, All doctors of military age called to military service enrollment

April 22, British Mission headed by A. J. Balfour arrived in Washington

April 25, Ministry of Food announced necessity of economy in bread to enable the country to carry through until the new harvest

April 28, Wages in building trades engaged in war work raised 1d. per hour. Extended to private work, June 9

April 30, The Food Controller given authority to take over the flour mills

——, Unofficial strike of engineers in Manchester

May 2, Royal proclamation called for economy in use of grain and reduction of 25% in consumption of bread

——, Postal war bonus gave workers an increase of from 3 to 5s. a week

May 9, Vote of credit of £500,000,000 passed House of Commons

May 10–24, Unofficial strike of 16,000 engineers and munition workers

May 13–17, Motor omnibus strike in London

May 15, Compulsory meatless day at hotels ended

May 16, Proposals of Lloyd George for Ireland. See Ireland

May 24, Billeting of Civilians Act

May 29, Cheese requisition order

June 1, Resignation of Lord Devonport, Food Controller. Succeeded June 15 by Lord Rhondda

June 21–30, Strike of 2,500 Clyde riveters against wage award

June 25, New revised contraband list published

July 2, Death of Herbert Beerbohm Tree, actor

July 10, Courts (Emergency Powers) Act approved

——, Resignation of Austen Chamberlain, Secretary of State for India on the Mesopotamian Report. Succeeded by E. S. Montagu

July 17, Proclamation of the King announced change of name of British Royal House to Windsor from Saxe-Coburg-Gotha

July 19, Sir Edward Carson resigned as first Lord of the Admiralty

July 24, Vote of credits of £650,000,000 passed Commons bringing total for 1917–1918 to £1,500,000,000

July 26–Aug. 18, Successful strike of tube makers on grievances

Aug. 2, Finance Act passed

Aug. 6–11, Strike of 27,000 coal miners in Yorkshire against recruiting

Aug. 7, Parliamentary Committee of the Trades Union Congress decided to send representatives to the Stockholm Conference

Aug. 10, Food commissioners to supervise local food control committees appointed

——, British Labour Party Conference voted to send delegates to Stockholm Conference

Aug. 11, Arthur Henderson resigned from War Cabinet because of criticism of his support of the International Socialist Conference at Stockholm. Succeeded by G. N. Barnes

Aug. 13, Announcement that British, French, Italian, and American Governments would not issue passports for attendance at Stockholm Conference

Aug. 17, Declaration of policy of the Government in regard to India. See India

Aug. 18, New Ministerial appointments announced: John Hodge, Pensions; George H. Roberts, Labour; A. C. Geddes, National Service; George J. Wardle, Parliamentary Secretary to the Board of Trade

——, Decision of railroad engineers to strike on the 17th prevented by prohibition of the Government

Aug. 21, Corn Production Act turning pasture into arable land and taking possession of untenanted land approved. Minimum wage for agricultural laborers provided for and minimum prices of wheat and oats. Workmen's Compensation (War Addition) Act, Munitions of War Act approved which fixed wages in certain industries

——, Ministry of Reconstruction established

Aug. 23, Order regulated sale of sugar

Aug. 29, Order fixed prices of meat

Aug. 30, Royal Proclamation prohibited the importation of bacon, butter, hams, and lard except under Government license, and prices fixed

Aug. 31, Order fixed prices of butter

Sept. 6, Sir Eric Geddes became first Lord of the Admiralty

Sept. 7, Wage advance of Aug. 1, made compulsory for all employers in engineering and foundry industries

Sept. 8, Food Controller fixed maximum wholesale prices of milk which made the retail price in London 7d. a quart in October and 8d. a quart for the rest of the winter

——, Coal prices fixed

Sept. 13, Potato Order controlled trade and fixed prices. After Oct. 1 all potato dealers to be registered

Sept. 15, Rationing of sugar begun

Sept. 16, Wool Textiles Production Board of Control appointed

Sept. 17, Wage increase of 1s. 6d. per day to coal miners

——, Fixed prices of bread came into effect, the 4 pound loaf to be sold at not more than 9d.

Sept. 20, Sir Arthur Yapp appointed Director of Food Economy

Sept. 25, Mercantile Marine Conciliation Committee appointed

Sept. 29, Temporary maximum prices for meat fixed

Sept. 29–Oct. 1, Army and Navy pay increased

Sept. 30, Cost of War estimated as nearly £5 billion

Oct. 2, "National War Bonds" new War Loan issued at 5%

——, Proclamation forbade exports to Sweden, Norway, Denmark, and the Netherlands

Oct. 10–13, Strike of 10,000 cotton spinners

Oct. 13, War bonus of 12½% on earnings granted to engineers and molders on time work munitions

Nov. 1, Recruiting transferred from War Office to Ministry of National Service

Nov. 2, Balfour Declaration pledged British Government to "establishment in Palestine of a National Home for the Jewish people"

Nov. 5, Prices of cheese and butter fixed

——, Wages of railroad employees increased

Nov. 18, Death of General Maude of cholera in Bagdad

Nov. 19, Strike of tool makers and tool setters at Coventry on wages and recognition of shop stewards

Nov. 22, 12½% munitions bonus extended to include unskilled workers in engineering and ship building

Nov. 24, Anglo-Russian Treaty of 1859 denounced by Russia

Nov. 26–Dec. 3, 50,000 engineers and aircraft workers in Coventry on strike for recognition of shop stewards

Nov. 26, Lord Rothermere appointed President of Air Council

——, Death of Sir Leander Starr Jameson, British South African statesman

Nov. 27, Trading with the Enemy Acts extended to apply to enemy aliens interned in neutral countries

Nov. 29, Air Force Act approved established Air Force

Dec. 6, Agricultural Wages Board held first meeting

——, Commercial Agreement with Spain signed

Dec. 12, Vote of credit of £550,000,000 passed by Commons bringing total for 1917–18 to £2,450,000,000

Dec. 20, Shop stewards recognition agreement

Dec. 26, Resignation of Sir John Jellicoe as first Lord of the Admiralty. Succeeded by Sir Rosslyn Wemyss

1918

Jan. 1, Compulsory meatless day instituted and compulsory rationing of sugar at ½ pound a week

Jan. 2, Air Ministry formed

Jan. 3, Use of gasoline for motor cars limited to essential purposes

Jan. 5, Lloyd George made statement of war aims to representatives of trades unions in London. Promised "self determination" for German colonies

——, Whiskey (restriction of sales) Order, and Jan. 17, applied to rum and gin

Jan. 7, 12½ munitions bonus extended to all munition workers in metal trades

Jan. 9–10, Strike of miners at Burnley

Jan. 10, Woman suffrage clause of the Reform Bill adopted by the House of Lords

Jan. 12, Pay of army and navy increased on basis of minimum of 10s. 6d. per day

Jan. 12, Mine explosion at the Minnie Pit at Halmerend. 160 persons killed

Jan. 14, General increase of 3s. 6d. per week to all women on munitions work

Jan. 21, Resignation of Sir Edward Carson from War Cabinet

——, Food Controller ordered 2 meatless days a week in public eating places from Jan. 25 and reduced rations of fats, meat, bread, &c., from Feb. 3

Jan. 24, Lord Rhondda outlined scheme for national food distribution

Feb. 4, Declaration of Government pledged independence of Arab peoples

Feb. 6, Electoral Reform Act approved extended suffrage to 8,000,000 new voters including 6,000,000 women over 30 either local government electors or the wives of government electors. Men over 21 with 6 months residence qualified. House of Commons enlarged to 707 members, England 492 (31 more); Wales, 36 (2 more); Scotland, 74 (2 more); Ireland, 105 (2 more)

——, Military Service Act abolished automatic addition of 2 months exemption of certain men and gave Director General of National Service power to withdraw any certificates of exemption granted on occupational grounds

——, National Health Insurance Act, National Insurance (Unemployment) Act, and Coal Mines Control Agreement (Confirmation) Act approved

Feb. 10, Lord Beaverbrook appointed Minister in charge of propaganda

Feb. 14, Death of Sir Cecil Arthur Spring-Rice

Feb. 16, General Sir William Robertson resigned his position as Chief of Staff and was succeeded by General Sir Henry Wilson

Feb. 20–23, Inter-Allied Labor Conference in London. Resolution on war aims adopted

Feb. 21, Ministry of Information (Propaganda, &c.) established

Feb. 25, Compulsory rationing came into effect in London and the Home Counties for meat, butter, and margarine

Feb. 26, New constitution adopted by Labour Party provided for inclusion of every worker who labors "by hand or by brain"

March 6, Death of John Redmond, Irish leader, in London

March 28–30, The King on visit to the front in France

March 30, Dr. John Dillon elected Nationalist leader in Dublin to succeed John Redmond

April 1, Royal Flying Corps and Royal Naval Air Services united and established as separate service, the Royal Air Force

——, Restricted tramway and railway services came into force

——, Price of cheese fixed by order of Food Controller

April 2, Curfew order announced in House of Commons, March 20, came into effect rationing gas and electric lights

April 9, New Military Service Bill raising age limit to 50, introduced in the House of Commons by the Prime Minister. Passed third reading by 301 votes to 103, April 16

April 11, Compulsory rationing extended to entire country covered sugar, lard, butter, margarine, and meat

April 12, German agent arrested as he disembarked in Ireland

April 18, Military Service Bill raising general age limit to 50 approved, became law. Provided that the Act might be extended to Ireland by Order in Council

——, Arbitration Convention with Uruguay signed

April 19, Viscount Milner succeeded the Earl of Derby as War Secretary

April 25, Resignation of Lord Rothermere as Secretary of State for Air Force

April 26, Sir William Weir appointed Secretary of State for Air Force

May 16, Workmen's Compensation (Illegal Employment) Act approved

——, Food Profits Act provided penalties for sale of food above fixed price

May 17, Military Service Act called all men born in 1898 and 1899

May 18, Announcement of discovery of conspiracy with Germany to land arms in Ireland. More than 150 persons arrested chiefly Sinn Fein including Edmund de Valera, Count Plunkett, and Countess Markievicz

May 20, First minimum wage order for agricultural wages granted 30s. per week for 54 and 48 hour men over 18 and overtime at time and ¼

June 3, Arbitration Convention with the United States extended that of April, 1908

June 4, Exemptions generally withdrawn for men over 18

June 11–July 26, Second imperial War Cabinet and War Conference. Recommended full recognition of the Dominions as autonomous States and representation of Dominions in foreign affairs. Resolution affirmed right of each State to control emigration and immigration

June 14, Cabinet Committee on Home Affairs established

——, Men of 50 ordered to report for military service as required

June 17, Military service Order called men born in 1895 and 1897

June 25, Lloyd George made public statement that volunteering substituted for conscription in Ireland

June 26, House of Lords approved principle of League of Nations

June 26–28, First annual meeting of British Labour Party under new constitution of Feb. 26

June 27–July 12, Strike of 11,000 aircraft workers in London and Liverpool for recognition of shop stewards and reinstatement of chairman of shop stewards committee

July 1, Order rationed household consumption of coal, gas, and electricity

——, Embargo Order prohibited engagement of additional skilled labor without permission of the Minister of Munitions

July 3, Death of Lord Rhondda

July 6, Publication of Montagu-Chelmsford Report on Indian constitutional reforms

July 9, J. R. Clynes appointed Food Controller successor of Lord Rhondda

July 14, National rationing books introduced

July 19, Lord Robert Cecil appointed assistant Secretary of State for Foreign Affairs. Succeeded as Minister of Blockade by Sir L. Worthington Evans

July 23–29, Strike of 12,000 munition workers in Coventry, Birmingham, and Rugby against the Embargo Order of July 1

July 25–Sept. 17, Successful strike of 5,000 employees of the Coöperative Wholesale Society for wage increase

July 26, Munitions strike against the Embargo spread to Leeds

July 29, Government decree ended the unofficial munitions strikes

July 30, Finance Act passed

——, Workmen's Compensation (Silicosis) Act approved

July–Nov., Influenza epidemic

Aug. 8, Education Act (of H. A. L. Fisher) became law providing for free and compulsory education for children from ages of 5 to 14 and attendance at continuation schools to 18. Employment of children under 12 prohibited. Salaries of teachers increased. Expenses divided between local and central governments

——, Trade Boards Act, Corn Production (Amending) Act and Maternity and Child Welfare Act approved. Trading with the Enemy (Amendment) Act prohibited enemy banks from carrying on business in England for a period of years after the War

——, Complete codification of statutes on income taxes

Aug. 17–23, Successful strike of 11,000 London tramway and omnibus workers to secure increase for women workers

Aug. 18, Announcement that the Imperial War Cabinet including Prime Ministers of the Dominions to be continued and conferences held at regular intervals

Aug. 21–22, Strike of 150,000 coal miners in Yorkshire over wages

Aug. 25–28, Successful strike of tube workers in London for equal wages for women

Aug. 29, Award to women omnibus and tramway workers of the 5s. bonus which the men had received

Aug. 30–31, Strike of London police for increase in war bonus which was granted

Sept. 5, Arrest of Litvinov and other Bolsheviks in London to guarantee the safety of British subjects in Russia

Sept. 6–11, Strike of aircraft workers in Manchester for recognition of shop stewards

Sept. 7, Wages of women munition workers raised

Sept. 10, Announcement of Food Controller that the retail price of meat would be increased by 2d. per pound from Sept. 22

Sept. 16–21, Strike of cotton spinners in Yorkshire and Lancashire for increase

Sept. 18–Oct. 1, Strike of shipwrights on the Clyde for increase in wages

Sept. 19, Railroad wage settlement granted 5 shillings per week increase

Sept. 20–27, Unofficial strike of railroad workers in South Wales for increase of 10s. per week which spread to other parts of the country

Oct. 23, House of Commons voted 274 to 25 in favor of making women eligible as members

Oct. 29–Nov. 2, Strike of 13,000 wood workers in the Liverpool district

Nov. 11, Armistice signed ending War

Nov. 12, Vote of £700,000,000 by House of Commons for 1918 brought total to £2,500,000,000 and £8,742,-000,000 since outbreak of War

Nov. 20, Imperial War Cabinet met to consider terms of peace settlement

Nov. 21, Minimum Wage Regulation Act (Temporary) provided for payment of wages in force Nov. 11 for 6 months. Time later extended to Sept., 1920

——, Scotland Education Act raised school age to 15 with no exemptions below 13

——, School Teachers Superannuation Act granted pensions

Nov. 23, Resignation of Mr. Clynes as Food Controller and of Lord Robert Cecil as assistant Foreign Secretary

Nov. 25, Dissolution of Parliament after 7 years proclaimed

——, Out-of-Work-Donation granted 24s. per week to men and 20s. to women with allowance for children

Dec. 4, Demobilization of the army begun

Dec. 6, Agreement signed provided for eight hour day to railway men

Dec. 7, Over 100,000 workers in the spinning trade stopped work in Lancashire

Dec. 9, Reconstruction Department established

Dec. 14, General election. The Coalition program summed up by Lloyd George included trial of the Kaiser, recovery of entire costs of the War "shilling for shilling and ton for ton" and punishment for war criminals. The Government Coalition returned 485 members, non-Coalition 222 including 59 Labour and 73 Sinn Fein. Women voted for the first time

Dec. 18, Grant of war pensions to parents of unmarried soldiers killed in War announced

1919

Jan. 1, 47 hour week came into effect in engineering and shipbuilding trades reduction from 53 or 54

——, Naval steam yacht "Iolaire" went ashore off Stornoway, Scotland, with loss of nearly 200 seamen on holiday leave

Jan. 4, 49 hour week for surface men in coal mines went into effect

Jan. 6–March 1, Strike of 40,000 men in engineering and shipbuilding trades against one-break system and 47 hour week

Jan. 9–23, Strike of 150,000 coal miners in Yorkshire settled by promise that grievances would be considered

Jan. 10, New Cabinet announced by Lloyd George as Prime Minister and First Lord of the Treasury; A. Bonar Law, Lord Privy Seal and Leader of the House of Commons; Earl Curzon of Kedleston, Lord President of the Council and Leader of the House of Lords; A. J. Balfour, Foreign Affairs; Winston S. Churchill, War and Air; E. S. Montagu, India; Austen Chamberlain, Exchequer; H. A. L. Fisher, Education; Viscount Milner, Colonies; G. N. Barnes, Sir F. E. Smith, and Sir Eric Geddes (without Portfolio)

Jan. 12, Death of Sir Charles Wyndham, actor-manager (82)

Jan. 18, Subscription in National War bonds closed bringing in total of about £1,600,000,000

Jan. 25–Feb. 19, Strike of shipyard workers at Belfast for 44 hour week. Work resumed on 47 hour week pending settlement

Jan. 27–Feb. 11, Strike of engineers in Clyde shipyards for 40 hour week

Jan. 31, Announcement that Government would

continue control of railroads for 2 years after signing Peace treaties

Feb. 1, Eight hour day for railroad workers came into force

——, New issue of National War Bonds (4th series) at 5%

——, National debt £7,334,000,000

Feb. 3, Sir James Carmichael appointed Director General of Housing

——, Eamonn de Valera and 2 other Irish prisoners escaped from gaol in Lincoln

Feb. 3–8, Strike of railroad workers in London and South of England for 20 minute intervals for meals in the eight hour day

Feb. 4, Third (31st) Parliament of George V met

Feb. 4–10, Unsuccessful strike of London waiters for eight hour day and reform of tipping system

Feb. 10, Industrial Training Department established by Ministry of Labour for training of demobilized soldiers and civilian war workers

Feb. 12, Coal miners rejected Government proposal of 6s. per week advance and investigation of industry claiming 30% advance and 6 hour day and nationalization of coal mines

Feb. 19, Announcement price of meat to be reduced by 2d. per pound, March 1

Feb. 24, Strike of coal miners voted but postponed pending investigation by government commission which began March 4

Feb. 26, Act to constitute a Commission to inquire into conditions in the coal industry approved

Feb. 27, First extension of Out of Work Donation 20s. to men and 15s. to women per week

——, Air Navigation Act regulated navigation over the United Kingdom

——, National Industrial Conference called by Minister of Labour met

March 2, Death of Miss Fanny Coleman, comedy actress (85)

March 4, First meeting of Industrial Committee set up by National Industrial Conference

March 4–17, Hearings before Coal Commission

March 17, Official announcement that the Cabinet had decided against recognition of the police national union

March 20, Wireless telephone communication established between Ireland and Canada

——, First reports of Sankey Coal Commission presented recommended increase in wages of 2s. per day and 7 hour day until 1921, then 6 hour. Adopted by Government

March 24–29, Strike of coal miners for full demands

March 31, Coal Mines (Emergency) Act approved limited prices of coal

April 2, Increase of Rent Amendment Act approved, Rent and Mortgage Interest (War Restrictions Act, 1915) prolonged

April 4, Report of National Industrial Conference adopted recommended a 48 hour week, universal minimum wage, recognition of and negotiations between organizations of employers and employees, and unemployment maintenance

——, Death of Sir William Crookes, chemist

April 8–18, Commercial Agreement with Spain

April 16, Vote of coalminers to accept the proposals of the Sankey Commission

April 30, State subsidy and government control of prices of pig-iron terminated

May 1, Civilian flying permitted

May 6, Mandate for German East Africa given to Great Britain by Supreme Council

May 15, Body of Edith Cavell buried at Norwich, England

May 19, First attempt to fly across Atlantic from America to Europe made by Lieutenant Harry Hawker and Lieutenant K. M. Grieve from St. Johns, Newfoundland, not successful, after 15 hours forced to alight on ocean, rescued by Danish steamer

May 29, Wages (Temporary Regulation) Act approved

May 30–July 24, Strike of 5,000 hosiery workers in Leicester and Nottingham over hours and overtime

May 30, Announcement in House of Commons that pay of metropolitan police would start at £3 10s. per week; £2 a week more than before the War

June 3, Ministry of Health Act approved, and Local Government Act

June 13, Victory Loan issued at 4%

June 14, Death of Weedon Grossmith, actor (66)

June 14–15, First non-stop flight across the Atlantic from America to Europe made by Captain John Alcock and Arthur W. Brown from St. Johns, Newfoundland, to Clifden, Ireland, in 16 hours and 12 minutes

June 20, Coal Commission presented final report; recommended nationalization of mines with compensation to royalty holders

June 21–July 12, Successful strike of 450,000 cotton workers for 30% advance in wages. Gained reduction to 48 hour week

June 27–Nov., Strike of furniture trade workers for increase in wages and 44 hour week. Secured a small increase

June 28, Peace Treaty signed with Germany at Versailles and Treaty of Alliance between France, Great Britain, and the United States to render military assistance in case of unprovoked attack by Germany. Treaty of Alliance never came into force because not ratified by the United States

July 2, The dirigible "R-34," commanded by Major G. H. Scott, started on transatlantic flight from East Fortune near Edinburgh crossing to Roosevelt Field, Long Island, New York, in 4 days, 108 hours and 12 minutes in the air

——, Formal Proclamation of peace

July 8, Captain Charles Fryatt's body interred at Dover after memorial service in London

July 9, Dirigible "R-34" started from New York on return voyage reaching Pulham in 75 hours

July 12, Death of Albert Vickers (81)

July 15–Aug. 20, Unauthorized successful strike of 150,000 coal miners in Yorkshire for advance in wages

July 19, Day of national thanksgiving celebrated the peace. Victory parade in London

July 21–26, Strike of coal miners in Nottinghamshire, Derbyshire, and Lancashire on method of fixing piece work advances

July 26, Lockout declared in furnishing trades, Manchester district

July 31, House, Town Planning, &c., Act approved required local housing authorities to provide adequate homes for workers; Finance Act passed

Aug. 1, Strike of police begun for recognition of the union. Not effective

Aug. 5–Dec. 1, Visit of the Prince of Wales to Canada and the United States

Aug. 9, Secret Treaty with Persia provided for loan to Persia and practically established Protectorate

Aug. 15, National Health Insurance Act, Coal Mines Act carrying out recommendations of the Sankey Commission of 7 hour day for workers underground, Ministry of Transport Act, Checkweighing in Various Industries Act, Court Emergency Powers Amendment Act approved

Aug. 16, Death of Dr. Thomas Joseph Lawrence

Aug. 18, Increase of wages to railroad workers by Government

——, Decision of Government against nationalization of mines

Aug. 19, Forestry Act established a commission to develop afforestation and timber development

——, Profiteering Act vested Board of Trade with authority to investigate charges of profiteering and to fix minimum prices

——, Pensions Act passed, Land Settlement (Facilities) Act, Housing, Town Planning, &c. (Scotland) Act approved

Sept. 1, First regular aëroplane service from London to Paris inaugurated

Sept. 12, Announcement of evacuation of British troops from Russia

Sept. 20–Jan. 26, 1920, Strike of iron founders for increase of wages

Sept. 26–Oct. 5, National railway strike after failure of negotiations

Sept. 27, State of national emergency proclaimed

Sept. 30, Air mail service begun from London to Birmingham, Bristol, Glasgow, Manchester, and Newcastle

Oct. 2–Nov. 17, Strike of a few hundred bricklayers and joiners in steel works in Scotland for advance threw out 12,000 steel workers

Oct. 5, Railway strike settled by compromise

Oct. 7, Death of Professor Lassa Francis Lawrence Oppenheim

Oct. 10, Ratification of the Peace Treaty with Germany (Versailles)

Oct. 17, Death of Henry Irving, actor

Oct. 28, Lloyd George announced Peace Cabinet: Bonar Law, Privy Seal; A. J. Balfour, President of the Council; Mr. Chamberlain, Exchequer; Lord French, Lord-Lieutenant of Ireland; Lord Birkenhead, Lord Chancellor; Lord Curzon, Foreign Affairs; Lord Milner, Colonies; Mr. Churchill, War and Air; Mr. Montagu, India; Mr. Fisher, Education; Sir Robert Horne, Labour

Nov. 6, Bank rate raised to 6%

Nov. 12–Dec. 10, First flight from England to Australia, Ross Smith and Keith Smith

Nov. 20, Industrial Courts Act approved created a permanent Industrial Court for the settlement of disputes

Nov. 28, Lady Astor elected to the House of Commons from Plymouth, the first woman to be elected to Parliament taking her seat Dec. 1

Dec. 4–7, Strike in Army and Navy stores

Dec. 10, Captain Ross Smith arrived at Port Darwin, Australia, after 11,509 mile flight from England

Dec. 18, Sir John Alcock killed by crash of his plane in France

Dec. 19, Lord French, Lord Lieutenant of Ireland, attacked from ambush in Ireland with rifles and bombs

Dec. 23, Unemployment Insurance Act, Workmen's Compensation (War Additions) Act, Profiteering (Continuance) Act, Housing (Additional Powers) Act, Old Age Pensions Act approved. Government of India Act carried out policy of extending greater measure of self-government. Sex Disqualification Act removed disabilities on grounds of sex or marriage preventing women from exercising public functions, &c. Aliens Restriction Act continued Act of 1914 for one year

Dec. 29, Death of Sir William Osler

1920

Jan. 1, Old age pensions increased up to 10s. per week maximum

Jan. 5, Announcement that butter to be de-controlled, Feb. 1

Jan. 10, Announcement that dairy products would be de-controlled at end of month

——, Ratification of Treaty with Germany made Great Britain original member League of Nations

Jan. 15, Government offer to railroad workers of advance in wages of 38s. per week and provision for cost of living allowances with standardized rates of pay 100% over pre-war rates

Jan. 28, Resignation of George Barnes only Labour member of the Cabinet

Jan. 31, Arrest of all Sinn Fein officials in Ireland who had committed acts or expressed words of sedition, about 58 persons including 2 members of Parliament, R. C. Barton and Joseph McGrath

Feb. 4, Resignation of George Roberts, Food Controller (Labour)

Feb. 9, Decree of George V declared Jan. 20 the official date for termination of the War

Feb. 11, One day strike of taxi-cab drivers in London as protest against increase of 8d. a gallon in price of petrol

——, Labour proposal of nationalization of coal mines defeated in House of Commons by vote of 329 to 64

Feb. 12, Agreement with Russia signed as to exchange of prisoners of war

Feb. 23, Announcement of 50% increase for taxi-cabs to come into effect March 1

Feb. 25, Home Rule Bill for Ireland introduced in the House of Commons repealing Government of Ireland Act of 1914 providing for establishment of 2 Irish Parliaments, one for the 6 counties of N.E. Ulster and another for the rest of Ireland, and a Council of Ireland

March 9, Announcement that British War Loans to Allies amounted to £1,666,000,000

March 10, National Conference of coal miners voted for general strike to enforce nationalization of mines

March 11, Trade Union Congress voted against direct action to enforce the nationalization of coal mines

March 16, The Prince of Wales left England for a visit to Australia and New Zealand

March 24, Death of Mrs. Humphry Ward, novelist

March 31, Coal Mines (Emergency) Act regulated profits replaced Coal Mines Control Agreement of 1919

April 3, Sir L. Worthington Evans succeeded G. M. Barnes resigned, as Minister without Portfolio

April 10, Strike of piano workers in London which lasted 3 months

April 15, Government offer to miners of 20% increase on gross earnings

April 24, Anglo-French Agreement as to oil concluded at San Remo by which the Governments agreed to support their respective nationals in securing oil concessions in certain territories

April 25, Mandates for Palestine and Mesopotamia (Iraq) granted to Great Britain by the Supreme Council

May 7, Death of Hugh Thomson, illustrator

May 11, Convocation at Oxford University passed Statute admitting women to degrees

May 17, Express air mail service with Amsterdam opened

May 20, National Health Insurance Act approved raised contributions from 7d. to 10d. for men and to 9d. for women, and sick benefit increase to 15s. per week for men and 12s. women. Profiteering (Amendment) Act approved

May 24, Strike of railroad men in Ireland

June 1, Food prices officially stated to have increased by 155% since 1914

——, Arbitration Convention with the Netherlands of Feb. 15, 1905 renewed

June 4, Board of Trade announced end of coal rationing as from June 7

June 5, Death of Rhoda Broughton, novelist

June 7, Agreement with Russia for resumption of trade

June 10, First court since 1914 held by the King and Queen in Buckingham Palace

June 14, Railroad workers granted an increase in wages from 2s. to 3s. 6d. per week in rural areas and from 4 to 8s. in industrial areas

June 27, Provisional Agreement reached in mining industry

July 1, Note to Russian Trade Delegation stated conditions of trade agreement as to propaganda, prisoners, compensation, &c.

July 2, Rent Restriction Act providing for increase in rents approved

July 2–Sept. 16, Strike of electricians against employment of non-union foreman

July 8, Building trade strike in Scotland ended in increase in wages

——, Anglo-Japanese Alliance terminated

July 10, Death of Sir John Arbuthnot, Lord Fisher of Kilverstone, Admiral of the Fleet, in London

July 20, British mandate for former German East Africa approved by League of Nations

July 23, Kenya (East Africa) became a Crown Colony

Aug. 4, Finance Act of 1920 approved increased duties on spirits, beer and wines, and tea, additional duty on cigars, established income tax rate at 6s. and increased excess profits tax from 40 to 60%

Aug. 9, Restoration of Order in Ireland Act approved provided for suspension of trial by jury in areas where assassination and murder had become the rule and trial by court-martial. Unemployed Insurance Act approved established a general system of compulsory insurance for all persons covered by the Health Insurance Acts with certain exceptions

Aug. 10, Peace Treaty with Turkey signed

Aug. 16, Death of Sir John Norman Lockyer, astronomer

——, Mining Industry Act constituted a Department of Mines headed by a Secretary under the Board of Trade, and Old Age Pensions (Blind Persons) Act approved

Aug. 23, "No rent" strike of 1 day in Glasgow against increases under new law

Sept. 15–Oct. 16, Unsuccessful strike of 20,000 cotton spinners at Oldham

Sept. 16, Death of Egerton Castle, novelist

Sept. 25, Death of Professor Arthur Sidgwick

Sept. 30, War time legislation on control of wages ended

Oct. 5, Death of William Henry Heinemann, publisher

Oct. 7, First women undergraduates (110) admitted to membership in Oxford University

Oct. 11, The Prince of Wales arrived in London after tour of Australia and New Zealand

Oct. 14, Degrees first conferred on women at Oxford University

——, Miners voted to reject Government proposal based on advance of 1s. per day with annual output of 240,000,000

Oct. 16, Right to sequestrate property of Germans in case of default of obligations under Treaty of Versailles renounced in order to further trade relations

Oct. 18, Strike of 1,000,000 coal miners begun after failure of negotiations

Oct. 29, Emergency Powers Act approved to provide the Government with powers to deal with any wide spread emergency which might threaten the life of the community as a whole and make regulations necessary to secure the supply of food, water, fuel, light, &c.

Nov. 4, Coal strike ended with acceptance of temporary agreement of Oct. 28 which provided for advance in wages of 2s. per day until Jan. 3 and subsequent adjustments until settlement

Nov. 8, New Unemployment Insurance Act of Aug. 9 went into effect

Nov. 29, Sugar rationing in force since 1917 ended

Dec. 1, Strike of shipyard joiners and carpenters against proposed reduction of wages

Dec. 3, Shops (Early Closing) Act and Unemployment Relief Works Act approved, the latter facilitating acquisition of land by compulsory purchase

Dec. 9, Milner Mission to Egypt presented report and recommendations

Dec. 17, Mandate of Great Britain over Nauru or Pleasant Island confirmed and defined by Council of the League of Nations

Dec. 22, Strike of 45,000 miners in Rhondda Valley

Dec. 23, Dyestuffs Act prohibited importation of synthetic dyestuffs except under licenses, Agriculture Act continued Corn Production Act of 1917 with guarantee of minimum prices of wheat and oats and provided for intensification of production, Government of Ireland Act provided for 2 Parliaments one for northern and one for southern Ireland, and Council (King and 20 members from each Parliament); executive power vested in Lord Lieutenant. Other Acts approved the Employment of Women, Young Persons, and Children Act, and as to Employment of, in Lead Processes Act, Unemployment Insurance (Temporary Provisions) Amendment Act

——, Anglo-French Convention fixed boundaries between Syria and Palestine and Mesopotamia (Iraq)

1921

Jan. 3, An increase of 3s. 6d. per shift in miners wages came into effect

Jan. 6, Death of Sir Lazarus Fletcher, mineralogist, and of Reverend Alexander Whyte

Jan. 8, Lord Reading appointed Viceroy of India to succeed Lord Chelmsford

Jan. 8, Death of Dr. John Beattie Crozier, philosopher, economist

Jan. 14–19, Strike of municipal employees stopped light, power, and tramway service

Jan. 14, Unemployed estimated at 925,000; an increase of 405,000 since Nov. 26

Feb. 1, Retail prices on an average 14 points lower than on Jan. 1

Feb. 3, Building trades unions rejected Government proposal for increase of labor in industry by "dilution" through training of ex-service men

Feb. 12, Resignation of Lord Milner as Secretary of State for the Colonies. Succeeded by Winston S. Churchill, Sir L. Worthington-Evans becoming Secretary of War

Feb. 27, Anglo-Persian Agreement of Aug. 9, 1919 denounced

Feb. 28, All restrictions on sugar withdrawn

March 3, Emergency Unemployment Act approved increased unemployment payment to 20s. per week to men and 18s. to women

March 16, Trade Agreement not involving *de jure* recognition signed with Russia

March 17, Resignation of A. Bonar Law as leader of the House of Commons and Lord Privy Seal in the Cabinet. Succeeded by Austen Chamberlain

March 22, Death of Ernest William Hornung, novelist

March 24, Coal Mines Decontrol Act provided for end of Government control

——, German Recovery Act authorized the Government to impose a charge on imports from Germany to be charged on the reparations account

March 28, Death of Charles Haddon Chambers, playwright

March 31, Proclamation of "state of emergency" as Government control of coal mines ended and strike begun

——, Termination of Shipping Ministry

April 1, Termination of Ministry of Munitions

April 2, Sir Robert S. Horn succeeded Austen Chamberlain as Chancellor of the Exchequer

April 13, Sympathetic strike of transport and railroad workers voted for April 15 but withdrawn after conference on the 14th

April 16, Death of General Sir John Cowans

April 19, Coal owners published 9 proposals for settlement of dispute

April 28, Bank rate reduced from 7 to 6½%

May 2, Lord FitzAlan sworn in as Viceroy of Ireland

May 9, Arrival in England of the Crown Prince of Japan

May 10, Death of General Sir George Benjamin Wolseley

May 12, Bill for putting into effect the Treaty of Peace with Hungary approved

May 15, 15 fires ascribed to Irish Republican incendiaries broke out in London and Liverpool

May 25, Death of Admiral Sir Arthur Knyvet Wilson

May 26, Death of Rear Admiral Sir Richard Massie Blomfield

June 1, Cost of living 9 points lower than on May 1

June 3, Government proposal to coal miners of May 28 to subsidize the industry to extent of £10,000,000 to meet wage deficiency rejected by miners

June 4–24, Strike of cotton spinners affected 500,000 operatives. Provisional compromise settlement on the 15th, concessions on both sides

June 4, Announcement of Government that offer to miners would be withdrawn within 14 days

June 17, Coal miners voted to continue the strike

June 20–Aug. 5, Imperial Conference, first since the War. Dominions declared in favor of "continuous consultation" rather than federation of the Empire. Proportion of division of reparations fixed. Resolution as to citizenship of Indians. *See also* India

June 22, Labour Party rejected request of Communist Party for affiliation by vote of 4,515,000 to 224,000

——, Bank rate reduced from 6½% to 6%

June 24, Lloyd George invited de Valera and Sir James Craig to a conference in London "to explore to the utmost the possibility of a settlement"

June 27–28, Settlement reached in coal strike subject to vote of miners. Government offer of subsidy renewed and wages increased 20% above level of basic rates existing in each district on March 31 as a minimum. National and District Wages Boards to be appointed. Agreement to last until Sept., 1922

July 1, Coal strike ended with acceptance of terms by miners and work resumed on July 4

——, Subsidy voted by House of Commons. Unemployment Insurance Act No. 2 and Housing Act approved

July 4–8, State visit of the King and Queen of Belgium

July 5, New loan announced, Treasury bonds at 5½% at 97 redeemable in 1929

July 9, Order for truce to take effect July 11 between Crown forces and Irish Republicans in Ireland

July 14–21, Conference in London of Irish Republicans headed by de Valera and Lloyd George and Sir James Craig

July 20, Death of Mrs. Molesworth, author

July 21, Bank rate reduced to 5½%

July 28, National Health Insurance Act approved

July 29, Unemployed estimated at 1,803,696

Aug. 4, Finance Act approved

Aug. 5, Announcement that Government would release unconditionally all members of the Dail Eireann in prison

Aug. 6, End of shipyard strike

Aug. 15, Government control of railroads ended at midnight

——, Government offer to Ireland of full Dominion status and complete autonomy in taxation and finance announced

Aug. 17, Licensing Act established permitted hours for sale of intoxicating liquors in licensed premises and clubs

Aug. 18, Claims (pecuniary) Treaty with the United States signed

Aug. 19, Corn Production Acts repealed, War Pensions Act amended, Reorganization of Railroads Act provided for amalgamation of railroads into 4 main groups, Education Act, and Shops (Early Closing Act, 1920) amended approved. A 33% *ad valorem* tax imposed on goods from any country whose currency had depreciated to degree below English level

Aug. 25, Letter of de Valera rejected Government proposals for Ireland

Sept. 2, Death of Henry Austin Dobson, poet

Sept. 7, and Nov. 12, Note to Russia regarding Soviet propaganda in the East

Sept. 11, Death of Lord Milford Haven known until 1917 as Prince Louis of Battenberg (67)

Sept. 12, Unemployment riots in Liverpool of from 5,000 to 6,000 persons

Sept. 17, Sir Ernest Shackleton sailed from London in the "Quest" for the Antarctic

Sept. 21, Death of Sir Ernest Cassell

Oct. 4–13, Unemployment demonstrations in London, Birmingham, and Manchester

Oct. 11, Conference on Ireland with Sinn Fein leaders in London begun which lasted until December

Oct. 15, Resignation of Sir Eric Geddes as Minister of Transport

Oct. 19, Death of Peter Graham, R.A.

Oct. 26, The Prince of Wales sailed for visit to India

Oct. 30, Visit of M. Poincare to London

Nov. 3, Bank rate reduced to 5%

Nov. 7, Viscount Peel became Minister of Transport

Nov. 8, Unemployed Workers Dependents (Temporary Provisions) Act approved

Nov. 10, National Health Insurance (Prolongation of Insurance) Act approved

Nov. 12, Washington Conference. *See* p. 565

Nov. 22, Death of Henry Mayers Hyndman, Socialist

——, Treaty with Afghanistan signed

Dec. 1, Unemployed estimated at about 1,832,440

Dec. 6, Treaty with Ireland signed gave Ireland Dominion status and established the Irish Free State. Northern Ireland given the option of continuing its separate existence under the Act of 1920 subject to the award of a Boundary Commission

Dec. 13, The Four Power Pacific Treaty signed by Great Britain

Dec. 16, Treaty with Ireland ratified by Parliament

Dec. 28, Death of Sir John Hare, actor

1922

Jan. 5, Death of Sir Ernest Shackleton, Antarctic explorer, in the "Quest" off South Georgia

Jan. 12, Royal Proclamation announced amnesty to political offenders in Ireland prior to the truce of July 11

Jan. 22, Death of James Bryce, Viscount Bryce

Feb. 4, Death of Professor Sir Henry Jones

Feb. 12, Death of Sir Edward Ernest Cooper, bart. (74)

Feb. 16, Bank rate reduced to 4½%

Feb. 18–April 3, Strike in publishing trade in London

Feb. 28, End of British protectorate over Egypt announced. *See also* Egypt

——, Marriage of Princess Mary, only daughter of the King to Viscount Lascelles

March 3, Resignation of Lord Trevethin, Chief Justice. Succeeded by Sir Gordon Hewart

March 8, Publication in London of message of Lord Reading, Viceroy of India to Mr. E. S. Montagu, Secretary of State for India, appealed to British Government for revision of the Treaty of Sevres on account of Mohammedan feeling in India

March 9, Resignation of Mr. Montagu as Secretary of State for India asked for and received by Lloyd George because of publication of message from Lord Reading

March 11, Lockout of 300,000 workers in metal trades

March 14, House of Commons approved Government policy as to Egypt by vote of 202 to 70

March 27, Irish Free State Bill passed third reading in the House of Commons

March 29–May 6, Lockout in shipbuilding trades affected 80,000 men

March 30, Conference of representatives of North and South Ireland with the British Government signed Peace Agreement

March 31, Irish Free State Bill received Royal assent

April 13, Bank rate reduced to 4%

April 21, Extradition Convention of Dec. 3, 1873 with Hungary revived

May 1, Convention with Denmark and Iceland renewed Arbitration Convention of Oct. 25, 1905

May 6, Commercial Agreement with Latvia signed

May 14, Admiralty Order announced reduction of naval officers of 1,835 out of total of 9,450 as a result of Washington Conference

May 19, Committee of Privileges of the House of Lords by vote of 20 to 4 denied right of Lady Rhondda peeress in her own right to a seat in the House of Lords, a decision affecting 21 other peeresses

May 31, Act to make better provisions for further settlement in overseas Dominions

June 15, Bank rate reduced to 3½%

——, Draft Constitution of Irish Free State published

June 21, The House of Lords voted for postponement of acceptance of mandate for Palestine until modifications effected

June 22, Field Marshal Sir Henry Wilson shot and killed at his door in London by Irish assassins

July 4, House of Commons voted by majority of 257 to accept mandate for Palestine

July 5, Death of Professor Sir John Sandys

July 10, Death of Sir George Prothero, historian

July 12, Death of Admiral John Moresby (92)

July 13, Bank rate reduced to 3%

——, Great Britain paid $12,000,000 in settlement of claims of the United States Shipping Board for services of American ships during and after the War

July 20, Unemployment Insurance Act (No.2) approved

July 24, British mandate for Palestine confirmed by the League of Nations Council

Aug. 1, Balfour Note to Allied and Associated Governments as to war debts declared that "if our undoubted obligations as a debtor are to be enforced, our not less undoubted obligations as a creditor cannot be left wholly in abeyance" stating in effect that Great Britain would remit all War loans estimated at £3,400,000,000 and give up rights to German reparations if the United States would cancel the $5,000,000,000 due from Great Britain

——, Horatio Bottomley expelled from the House of Commons because of his conviction in May of fraudulent conversion of funds entrusted to him and sentence to 7 years' penal servitude

Aug. 4, National Health Insurance Act approved

Aug. 12, Unemployment Insurance Act approved

Aug. 14, Death of Viscount Northcliffe (Sir Alfred Charles William Harmsworth), journalist and statesman

Aug. 18, Death of William Henry Hudson, writer and naturalist

Sept. 10, Death of Wilfrid Scawen Blunt, poet

Sept. 15, Appeal of Lloyd George to the Dominions, to Rumania, Yugoslavia, France and Italy against Turkey without success. See Turkey and Greece

Sept. 16, Announcement of Lloyd George that England expected to maintain neutrality of Straits

Oct. 10, Treaty with Iraq (Mesopotamia) signed by which the King of Iraq undertook to be guided by advice of the British High Commissioner in all matters affecting British international and financial obligations and interests, and Great Britain undertook to secure admission of Iraq to League of Nations, which admission would end mandate

Oct. 15, Death of Rev. James Hastings, Biblical scholar

Oct. 16, Payment to the United States of $150,000,000 interest on war debt

Oct. 19, Unionist Party leaders in caucus at the Carlton Club voted to withdraw from the Coalition and go before the country at the next election as a Conservative Party. Lloyd George resigned as Prime Minister the same day

Oct. 23, A. Bonar Law elected Leader of the Unionist Party and appointed Prime Minister and First Lord of the Treasury

Oct. 25, Unionist (Conservative) Ministry of Mr. Bonar Law sworn in: Stanley Baldwin, Exchequer; Lord Curzon, Foreign; Earl Derby, War; Viscount Peel, India; Lt. Col. Amery, Admiralty; Sir Montagu Barlow, Labour

Oct. 26, Parliament dissolved

Oct. 30, At London Conference representatives of Governments of North and South Ireland signed peace declaration

Oct. 31, Anglo-Spanish Commercial Treaty signed

——, Death of Father Bernard Vaughan, Jesuit

Nov. 14, First official broadcasting begun

Nov. 15, Election for the fourth Parliament of George V a victory for the Unionist Party receiving 344 seats; Labour, 138; Liberals, 60; National Liberals, 57; Independents, 5; Coöperators, 4; Independent Unionists, 3; Nationalists, 2; Communists, 1; Sinn Fein, 1; total, 615

Nov. 27, Death of Mrs. Alice Meynell, poet

Dec. 5, Irish Free State Constitution Act approved and Act giving effect to the Treaty

Dec. 6, Proclamation of the King announced adoption of the Irish Free State Constitution

Dec. 23, Expiration of law forbidding Germans to enter England

——, Death of Sydney S. Pawling, publisher

Dec. 27, Death of Professor T. W. Rhys Davids

Dec. 31, Total national debt £7,835,000,000

1923

Jan. 7, Labor demonstrations in London and 150 provincial cities and towns in behalf of the unemployed

Jan. 9, Death of Katherine Mansfield (Mrs. John Middleton Murray) writer (33)

Jan. 14, Death of Frederic Harrison, writer (91)

Jan. 31, Government accepted terms of American Commission for funding British debt

Feb. 5, Death of George Grosvenor Thomas, artist

Feb. 7, Birth of a son to the Princess Mary (Viscountess Lascelles)

Feb. 8, Death of Bernard Bosanquet, philosopher (74)

Feb. 13, Second session of Parliament opened by the King

March 6, Death of Sir James J. Shannon, painter

March 7, Agreement with France signed

March 15, First payment on war debt to the United States of $4,128,685.74

March 22, Death of Benjamin Williams Leader (92), artist

March 25, Four Agreements with the Hejaz signed

March 27, Death of Sir James Dewar, chemist

March 29, Unemployment Insurance Act approved

March 31, Number of unemployed in England and Wales estimated as 1,348,000

April 2, Death of William Hurrell Mallock (74), writer

April 5, Death of Lord Carnarvon, 5th Earl

April 5–7, Strike of 50,000 miners in South Wales

April 8, Lockout in building trades because of refusal to accept reduction in wages. Settled in August by arbitration award without interruption of work

April 10, Government defeated on motion for the Speaker to leave the Chair

April 11 and 12, Unionist and Labour demonstrations in House of Commons

April 20, National prohibition defeated in House of Commons by vote of 236 to 14

April 26, Marriage of the Duke of York, second son of the King, to Lady Elizabeth Bowes Lyon

April 30, Protocol to Treaty of 1922 with Iraq fixed term of Treaty to end either on entry of Iraq into the League of Nations or 4 years after ratification of peace with Turkey

May 5–14, Vist of King and Queen to Italy

May 8, Note presented to Russia threatened termination of Trade Agreement unless assurance given of cessation of Bolshevik propaganda in India, Persia, and Afghanistan against Great Britain, and illegal interference with British trawlers fishing near Russian waters, and treatment of British Notes as to religious persecution

May 14, Russian reply to British Note received proposed conference to settle disputes

May 17, Increase of Rent and Mortgage Interest Restrictions (Continuance) Act approved

May 20, Resignation of Prime Minister Bonar Law on account of health

May 22, Stanley Baldwin appointed Prime Minister

May 23, Second Note from Russia offered to conclude convention granting to English citizens the right of fishing outside the three-mile limit pending settlement by conference, offered compensation for execution of Mr. Davison and for arrest of Mrs. Stan Harding, but denied propaganda in the East

——, Death of Henry Bradley, editor of the Oxford English Dictionary

May 24, Commercial Treaty with Rumania signed

May 25, Baldwin Ministry announced. Lord Robert Cecil the only new member in the Cabinet took office of Lord Privy Seal. Sir William Joynson-Hicks became Financial Secretary to the Treasury with a seat in the Cabinet and was succeeded in the Post Office by Sir L. Worthington-Evans. Sir Samuel Hoare, Air Minister, entered the Cabinet

——, Note to the State Department of the United States denied American jurisdiction over regular rations of liquor supplies of foreign vessels

——, Treaty with the Hejaz Government recognized independence of Arabs in Iraq, and Transjordan, and in Arab States of the Arabian Peninsula exclusive of Aden

May 28, Mr. Baldwin formally elected leader of the Conservative Party

May 29, Memorandum to Russia accepted Russian assurance as to the three-mile limit and some other points and enclosed a "no propaganda pledge" to be signed

May 31, Provisional Agreement for rendition of Weihaiwei to China signed

June 5, Trade Convention with Afghanistan signed

June 7, Indemnity Bill approved for compensation loss and damage of Irish loyalists, deportations, &c.

June 8, Matrimonial Causes Bill passed third reading in the House of Commons placed sexes on equality with regard to grounds for securing divorce

June 9, Death of Princess Christian, third daughter of Queen Victoria

June 11, Russian reply to British Note received amounted practically to acceptance of British terms. Reduction of personnel of legations in Afghanistan, Persia and Russian Turkhestan agreed to

June 15, Death of Maurice Henry Hewlett (62), writer

June 18, Proposal of Great Britain to the United States as to funding of War Debt. Signed June 19

June 22, Treaty of commerce and navigation with Latvia signed

July 1, Unemployed estimated as 1,191,400

July 2–Aug. 20, Unauthorized strike of dockers against reduction of wages

July 5, Bank rate raised from 3 to 4%

July 18, Matrimonial Causes Act approved

July 24, Treaty of Peace with Turkey signed

July 30, Order in Council constituted the Ross Dependency of Antarctica as under jurisdiction of New Zealand

——, Death of Sir Charles Hawtrey, actor

July 31, Housing Act approved and Act prohibiting Sale of Intoxicating Liquors to persons under 18

——, Agricultural Credits Act approved

Aug. 2, Agricultural Rates Act approved

Aug. 14, Arbitration Agreement with Italy of Feb. 1, 1904 renewed

Aug. 29, Arbitration Agreement with France of Oct. 14, 1903 renewed

Sept. 3, Exchange of Notes with Russia as to sovereignty of Wrangel Island

Sept. 5–Oct. 20, The Prince of Wales on visit to Canada

Sept. 23, Death of Viscount John Morley of Blackburn (84)

Sept. 26, Death of Colonel Aubrey Herbert, diplomatist, traveler (43)

——, Miss Margaret Bondfield elected Chairman of the General Council of Trades Union Congress, the first woman chosen for this office

Oct. 1–Nov. 8, Imperial Conference opened in London. Recommended immigration schemes and imperial preference. Recognized right of Empire Governments to make treaties with foreign powers

——, Imperial Economic Conference opened

Oct. 6, Death of Oscar Browning, writer

Oct. 22, Anglo-Franco-Spanish Conference

Oct. 30, Death of Andrew Bonar Law

——, Speech of Prime Minister Baldwin declared for protective tariff as best remedy for unemployment

Nov. 16, Workmen's Compensation Act approved

——, Parliament prorogued

Nov. 26, Treaty of commerce and navigation with Poland signed

Nov. 30, Death of James Fitzmaurice Kelly, British Spanish scholar

Dec. 6, Election reduced Conservative seats in House of Commons from 346 to 258. Labour received 191, Liberals 158, Independents 8. Of 33 women candidates 8 elected

Dec. 11, Tangier Port Convention signed with France and Spain

Dec. 14, Treaty of commerce and navigation with Finland signed

Dec. 18, Tangier Agreement with France signed provided for permanent neutralization of area of 225 square miles. Signed by Spain Feb. 7, 1924

Dec. 19, Death of Rev. Dr. Joseph Henry Jowett

Dec. 20, Montagu Norman, governor of the Bank of

England, Sir Josiah Stamp, and Reginald McKenna appointed by Reparation Commission to act on committees to investigate German finances

Dec. 28, Protocol with France signed defined frontiers Anglo-Egyptian Sudan and French Equatorial Africa

1924

Jan. 2, Death of Sabine Baring Gould, author (90)

Jan. 8, Fifth Parliament of George V (33d imperial) opened

——, Death of Arthur Clutton-Brock, essayist

Jan. 9, Death of Dr. Frederick Cornwallis Conybeare, writer

Jan. 10, Submarine L24 sunk in collision with the dreadnought *Resolution* off Portland with loss of 43 lives

——, Protocol with France signed defined frontiers of Wadai and Dafur

Jan. 20, Strike of shipyard workers at Southampton for increase in wages

Jan. 21, Labour Amendment carried in the House of Commons by vote of 328 to 256

Jan. 22, Resignation of Prime Minister Baldwin. J. Ramsay MacDonald (Labour) commissioned by the King taking office as Prime Minister and Secretary of State for Foreign Affairs, the first Labour Government: Lord Haldane, Lord Chancellor; J. R. Clynes, Privy Seal and Deputy Leader of the House of Commons; Philip Snowden, Exchequer; Arthur Henderson, Home; J. H. Thomas, Colonies; Stephen Walsh, War; Lord Olivier, India; Lord Thomson, Air; Lord Chelmsford, Admiralty; Sidney Webb, Board of Trade; John Wheatley, Health; C. P. Trevelyan, Education

Jan. 23, Treaty with the United States signed as to smuggling of intoxicating liquors

Jan. 29, Railroad workers strike against award settled after 8 days of a partial strike, a large number of enginemen remaining at work

Feb. 1, *De jure* recognition of Soviet Government of Russia by the Labour Government

Feb. 16–26, Dockers strike for increase of wages gained a shilling a day

Feb. 20, Death of Sir Henry Lucy, journalist

Feb. 21, Unemployment Insurance Act amended

March 13, Decision of Government not to proceed with construction of naval base at Singapore

March 22–31, Tram and bus strike in London ended with acceptance by men of employers' terms

March 24, Reparations (Recovery) Act imposing tax on German imports became law

March 25, Agreement with Iraq by which Great Britain to maintain troops in Iraq until 1928, train native army and appoint administrative advisers

April 2, Rejection by House of Commons by vote of 325 to 160 of capital levy proposed by Government as disastrous for employment

April 11–24, Lockout in shipbuilding trades

April 14–Aug. 8, Anglo-Russian conference as to debts, trade relations, &c.

April 15, Ratification of Treaty with Turkey of July, 1923

——, Unemployment Insurance Act No. 3 approved

April 18, Strike of shipyard workers at Southampton settled by compromise

April 21, Death of Marie Corelli (59), novelist

April 23–Nov. 1, British Empire Exhibition at Wembley

May 5, Evictions Bill passed third reading

May 12, Arrival of King and Queen of Rumania on visit

May 16, Bill for Nationalization of Mines defeated by vote of 264 to 168

May 20, Death of Sir William Edward Goschen (76)

May 22, Treaty of commerce and navigation with Austria signed

May 23–25, Visit of the King and Queen of Italy

May 29, National Health Insurance (Cost of Medical Benefit) Act approved

——, Miners accepted coal owners' terms to be effective as from May 1 gave a higher minimum wage, better treatment of the day wage men, higher wages in the more profitable coalfields and publication of more details of the costs of production

May 31–Aug. 22, Successful strike of building trades in Liverpool to maintain wages

June 5, Unauthorized strike of railway shopmen on tube railways in London which lasted several days

June 6, Death of William James, Viscount and Baron Pirrie

June 19, Death of Sir Adolphus William Ward (86), writer and educator

June 22, Visit of King and Queen of Denmark

June 30, Unemployed registered as 1,009,500

July 7, Government announced decision against Channel Tunnel scheme

July 13, Death of Alfred Marshall (81), economist

July 15, Treaty with Italy by which Great Britain ceded a part of Kenya on west bank of Juba River to Italy

Aug. 1, Act amended Insurance Acts of 1920 and 1924

Aug. 2, Conference with representatives of northern and southern Ireland as to boundary did not reach agreement

Aug. 3, Death of Joseph Conrad (Teodor Joseph Konrad Korzeniowski), author (67)

Aug. 7, Old Age Pensions Act, Housing (Financial Provisions) Act, Agricultural Wages (Regulation) Act, National Health Insurance Act approved and Finance Act

Aug. 8, General Treaty and Commercial Treaty with Russia signed by Great Britain and Northern Ireland. Subsequently repudiated by Baldwin Ministry

Aug. 21, Birth of second son to the Princess Mary, Viscountess Lascelles

Aug. 23–Oct., Prince of Wales on visit to the United States and Canada

Sept. 3, Speech of Mr. MacDonald at Geneva gave English objections to pact of mutual assistance

Sept. 20, Death of Sir Algernon Methuen, publisher

Sept. 25–Oct. 3, Conferences of the Government with Egyptian Prime Minister Zaghlul Pasha on question of control of the Sudan. British Government refused to give up control or to withdraw troops from the Suez Canal

Sept. 29, Death of Hugh Chisholm, editor

Oct. 8, Vote of censure on the Government for dropping the prosecution of editor of the Communist organ the "Workers' Weekly" (Campbell case) on Aug. 12, for article exhorting soldiers, sailors, and airmen to refuse to turn their guns on their fellow-workers either in a military or a class war, defeated by 359 to 198 votes in House of Commons

——, Liberal Amendment that a Select Committee be appointed to investigate and report on the withdrawal of prosecution of R. J. Campbell, editor of the "Workers Weekly" carried by 364 votes to 198 defeated Labour Government

Oct. 8, Parliament dissolved

Oct. 24, Irish Free State (Confirmation of Agreement) Act approved

Oct. 25, Publication of the Zinoviev letter containing instructions to British subjects by Third International at Moscow to work for overthrow of the institutions of the country. Authenticity denied by Russian representative but letter had great effect on elections

Oct. 29, Election a great Conservative victory; gained 161 seats returning to Parliament with 413 members, a majority of 211 over all other parties combined, Labour Party, 151; Liberals, 40

Oct. 31, Commercial and Navigation Agreement with Spain signed

Nov. 4, Ramsay MacDonald resigned as Prime Minister and Stanley Baldwin, Conservative, appointed

Nov. 7, Second Conservative Ministry of Stanley Baldwin took office: Austen Chamberlain, Foreign and Deputy Leader of the House; Winston Churchill, Exchequer; Lord Birkenhead, India; Lord Curzon, President of the Council and Leader of the House of Lords; Lord Eustace Percy, Education; L.C.M.S. Amery, Colonies; Sir L. Worthington Evans, War; Sir Samuel Hoare, Air; Sir William Joynson-Hicks, Home; Sir Arthur Steel-Maitland, Labour

Nov. 10, Death of Sir Archibald Geikie, geologist

Nov. 12, Death of Edmund Dene Morel

Nov. 15, Death of Edwin S. Montagu, former Secretary for India

Nov. 17, Death of Sir Maurice FitzMaurice, engineer (63)

Nov. 20, Sir Lee Stack, Sirdar of the Sudan, shot at and fatally wounded by assassins on street in Cairo

Nov. 20–March 17, First flight to India from England made by Alan J. Cobham and Air Vice-Marshall Sir Sefton Brancker, and A. B. Elliott, 17,000 miles, flying time, 220 hours

Nov. 21, Government denounced treaties with Russia negotiated by Ramsay MacDonald

Nov. 22, British ultimatum to Egypt demanded indemnity, apologies, withdrawal of Egyptian troops from the Sudan, and removal of irrigation restrictions at Gezira

Nov. 27, Government notified League of Nations it would not recognize registration of treaties between integral parts of the British Empire in reference to registration of Treaty of Dec. 6, 1921 by Ireland on July 11

Dec. 2, Treaty of commerce and navigation with Germany signed

——, Agreement for funding of Polish debt signed

——, Sixth Parliament of George V opened

Dec. 9, Announcement that construction of naval base at Singapore would be proceeded with

Dec. 12, Lithuanian debt to Great Britain paid

Dec. 20, Death of John William North, artist (83)

Dec. 28, Death of William Archer (68), author

1925

Jan. 1, Death of Sir Francis Carruthers Gould (80) caricaturist

Jan. 8, Death of Sir William Edmund Garstin, engineer

Jan. 14, Death of Henry Furniss (70), caricaturist

Jan. 21, Death of Sir Guilford Lindsey Molesworth

Feb. 2, Death of John Lane, publisher

Feb. 9, Herbert H. Asquith made Earl of Oxford and Asquith

Feb. 18, Resolution adopted by House of Commons that British married women should not lose nationality by marriage to an alien

Feb. 20, Bill to give women of 21 the vote defeated in House by vote of 220 to 153

Feb. 24, Death of Joseph Rowntree, reformer

March 12, Sir Austen Chamberlain read to Council of the League of Nations a written statement giving reasons for rejection of Geneva Protocol by Great Britain

March 17, Return of Sir Sefton Brancker and Alan Cobham, pilot, from flight of 17,000 miles to India and Burma

March 17, Counsellors of State appointed by the King to act on his behalf during his absence from the country, Prince Henry, the Archbishop of Canterbury, the Lord Chancellor and the Prime Minister

March 18, Madame Tussaud's famous collection of wax works in London destroyed by fire

March 19, King George and Queen Mary left England for a cruise in the Mediterranean

March 20, Death of Marquess Curzon of Kedleston (64)

March 28, The Prince of Wales started on 7-months' trip to British West Africa, South Africa, and South America

——, Death of General Lord Henry Seymour Rawlinson

March 30, Number of unemployed estimated as 1,194,300

April 1, Lord Balfour inaugurated Hebrew University at Jerusalem

April 9, Housing Act, and Housing Act (Scotland), Land Registration Act, Town Planning Act, and Town Planning Act (Scotland) approved

April 28, Death of Sir Eyre Crowe, Permanent Under-Secretary for Foreign Affairs

——, Return to gold standard announced. The pound sterling rose to $4.83^{7}/8 on the foreign stock exchanges from $4.73^{3}/8 and in May to $4.86

May 1, Cyprus proclaimed a Crown Colony

May 5, Gold Standard Act passed third reading in House of Commons

May 13, Death of Lord Alfred Milner

——, Arbitration Convention with Norway renewal of Aug. 11, 1904

May 14, Death of Sir Rider Haggard, novelist

May 21, Lady Astor's Bill to allow peeresses in their own right to become members of the House of Lords defeated by that body by vote of 80 to 78

May 22, Death of Field Marshal John Denton French, 1st Earl of Ypres

May 28, Rent and Mortgage Interest (Restrictions Continuation) Act approved and Northern Ireland Land Act amended

June 4, Eight of the largest unions including railroad workers, miners, shipbuilding trades, and engineers voted against formation of one alliance in case of industrial disputes

June 11, New office of Secretary of State for the Dominions announced

June 17, Death of Arthur Christopher Benson, essayist

June 27, Government notified Governments of all countries which had not begun negotiations for settlement of war debts that settlements were expected

June 30, Finance Act reduced income tax and placed new duties on silk

July 13, The Government set up a Court of Inquiry to inquire into causes of dispute in the coal-mining industry

July 15, Death of Mary Cholmondeley, novelist

July 24, Agreement for funding Estonian debt to Great Britain signed

——, Strike of 150,000 workers in the Yorkshire woolen industry against wage reduction. Settled by Government mediation after 3 weeks

July 25, Railway workers voted not to handle coal on railroads after Aug. 1 if the miners should be locked out

July 30, Commercial Treaty with Japan signed

July 31, Coal strike averted by offer of Government to subsidize the coal industry to the amount of nearly $50,000,000 for the next 9 months. Royal Commission appointed to examine conditions in industry

——, Supreme Court of Judicature (Consolidation) Act approved

Aug. 4, Adoption of Children Act approved

Aug. 7, Public Health Act, Allotments Act, Widows', Orphans', and Old Age Contributory Pensions' Act approved and Unemployment Insurance Act amended

Aug. 13, Agreement signed for funding Latvia's debt to Great Britain

Aug. 22–Nov. 29, Unofficial seamens strike in London and Southampton against reduction in wages accepted by their leaders

Aug. 26, French war debt to Great Britain settled at total of $3,100,000,000 to be paid in 62 annual instalments of £12,500,000

Aug. 29, Arbitration Agreement of 1914 with Portugal prolonged

Aug. 31, Diplomatic relations with Mexico severed in June, 1924, resumed

——, Agreement signed as to settlement of Greek debt to Great Britain

Sept. 20, Death of Sir Francis Darwin (77), botanist

Oct. 16, Locarno Treaties initialed

——, The Prince of Wales reached London after trip to Africa and South America

Oct. 19, Agreement for funding Rumanian debt to Great Britain signed

Nov. 3, Czechoslovak debt Agreement signed

Nov. 12, Submarine M1 sunk in Channel with loss of 68 men on board

Nov. 16–Feb. 17, 1926, Flight of Alan Cobham and 2 companions from London to Cairo and to Cape Town, South Africa, 8,500 miles in 94 hours

Nov. 18, Locarno Treaties ratified by House of Commons by vote of 375 to 13

Nov. 20, Death of Queen Alexandra, widow of Edward VII (81)

Nov. 25, Trial of 12 Communists arrested Oct. 12 on charge of sedition under the Mutiny Act of 1797 found guilty and 5 including Mr. Pollitt sentenced to 1 years imprisonment and the other 7 including Mr. Campbell, editor of the "Workers' Weekly" to 6 months

Nov. 29, Seamen's strike ended with acceptance by men of reduction of wages

Dec. 1, Labour vote of censure of Government for prosecution of Communists as violation of traditional British rights of freedom of speech, &c., defeated in House of Commons by vote of 322 to 133

Dec. 1, Locarno Treaties signed. *See* p. 569

Dec. 3, Irish Boundary Agreement signed by representatives of the British Government, and of Government of Northern Ireland, and the Irish Free State

Dec. 4, Rating and Valuation Bill passed third reading in Commons

Dec. 15, Legitimacy Act approved provided for legitimatization by subsequent marriage of parents

Dec. 20, Exchange of Notes with Italy as to Lake Tsana and economic spheres of interest in Abyssinia

Dec. 21, House of Commons accepted Iraq boundary award of Council of League of Nations

Dec. 22, Mining Industry (Welfare Fund) Act and Workmen's Compensation Act approved

Dec. 31, Belgian debt funded in London

1926

Jan. 1, Property Act came into effect abolishing many ancient tenures and feudal rights providing for freehold and leasehold

——, 1,439,810 persons in receipt of Poor Law relief

——, Death of Sir John Le Sage, journalist

Jan. 4, Widows and Old Age Pensions (at sixty-five) Act came into effect

Jan. 16, Death of Lord Carmichael (Thomas David Gibson Carmichael)

Jan. 18, Treaty of commerce and navigation with Estonia signed

Jan. 20, Death of Charles Montagu Doughty, explorer and poet

Jan. 21, Railway mens Union rejected wage award of National Wages Board but accepted it Jan. 25 by a small majority

Jan. 25, Resignation of Sir Alfred Mond from the Liberal Party because of his opposition to Lloyd George's land policy. Joined the Conservative Party

Jan. 26, Announcement of Government contract for erection of 2,000 steel houses to relieve housing shortage in Scotland

——, Anglo-Italian debt settlement funded debt at £270,000,000, and annual payment for 62 years of £4,500,000

Feb. 1, Unemployed persons registered 1,175,000

——, Lloyd George reëlected chairman of the Liberal Party

Feb. 18, Strike of marine wireless operators settled. Men accepted reduction

March 3, Death of Sir Sidney Lee, Shakespearean scholar and biographer

March 6, Building of the Shakespeare Memorial Theatre at Stratford-on-Avon destroyed by fire. The contents of the Library and Museum saved

March 10, Coal Commission presented report adverse to continuation of the coal subsidy and rejected miners' plan for reorganization of industry as unworkable

April 15, Coal operators gave notice of termination of existing wage agreement as of May 1

April 21, A daughter (Elizabeth Alexandra Mary) born to the Duchess of York

April 28–30, Joint conference of miners and operators with Prime Minister Baldwin. Terms not accepted by miners

April 30, Proclamation of King George of state of emergency

May 1, Strike of coal miners begun

May 4, General strike, the first in England, begun in sympathy with the coal miners which began at midnight May 3

May 12, General strike ended

May 14, Government offered subsidy of £3,000,000 to be used chiefly as wages of coal miners during period in which a national wages board should frame new agreement. Declined by miners May 20 and by coal owners May 21

May 24, Death of Thomas Erskine Holland, jurist

May, Empire Marketing Board constituted for "furthering the market" in England of Empire products

June 11, Protest to Russia by the Government against Soviet financial support of recent general strike in England

June 16, Bankruptcy (Amendment) Act and Law of Property (Amendment) Act approved

June 18, Provisional Commercial Agreement with Yugoslavia signed

June 24, Bill to enable peeresses to become members of the House of Lords again defeated in House of Lords by vote of 125 to 80

June 30, Unemployment Insurance Act approved

——, Alan J. Cobham started on flight to Australia

July 8, Coal Mines Act approved permitted for a period of 5 years 8 hours work below ground

July 12, Death of Gertrude Bell, traveler, writer, and Arabic scholar, in Bagdad

——, French war debt agreement signed, total indebtedness computed at £6,000,000 to be paid off in 62 years, £4,000,000 in 1926–27, then £6,000,000, £8,000,000, and £10,000,000 in successive years; £12,500,000 annually from 1930–31 to 1956–57, and then £14,000,000 annually until 1987–88

July 16, Treaty of commerce and navigation with Greece signed

July 23, Treaty of commerce and navigation with Hungary signed

Aug. 1, Death of Israel Zangwill, novelist

Aug. 4, Mining Industry Act approved

——, Finance Act provided for preferential customs for Empire products

Aug. 6, Gertrude Ederle of New York, the first woman to swim the English Channel, breaking previous records of time in 14 hours and 31 minutes from Griz Nez to Dover

Aug. 12, Death of Professor Sir William Ridgeway, archæologist and writer

Aug. 28, Mrs. Clemington Corson of New York swam the Channel from Griz Nez to Dover in 15 hours and 28 minutes

Aug. 30, Herr Vierkoetter (German) swam Channel in 12½ hours, fastest time

Sept. 10, Georges Michel (French), swam the Channel in 11 hours and 5 minutes, beating all previous records

Sept. 17, Norman Leslie Derham, the third Englishman to swim the Channel, made the trip in 13 hours and 56 minutes from Griz Nez to St. Margaret's Bay

Oct. 1, Alan Cobham returned from 28,000 mile airflight to Australia and back

Oct. 6, The King conferred Knight Commandership of British Empire on Alan Cobham

Oct. 7, Offer of the Prime Minister to miners to create a national arbitration tribunal to settle dispute rejected by miners

Oct. 14, Lord Oxford (Herbert Asquith) resigned leadership of Liberal Party

Oct. 14, Miners voted to continue the strike

Oct. 19, Imperial Conference (9th) met

Oct. 26, House of Commons voted to continue the Emergency Rations in mining counties

Nov. 1, Tax on betting came into operation

Nov. 13, "Surrender" terms of coal miners presented to the Government

Nov. 16–March 13, 1927, First flight from England to South Africa by A. J. Cobham

Nov. 18, Imperial Conference Report signed which recognized Dominions as autonomous members of British Commonwealth of nations

Nov. 19, Coal strike ended, miners admitting defeat recommending all district associations to open negotiations with coal owners in their respective districts

——, Imperial Conference adopted plan for reorganization of British Empire

Dec. 8, Motion of Labour Party of censure of Government conduct as to coal strike defeated by vote of 339 to 131

Dec. 15, Lead Paint (Protection against Poisoning) Act, Workmen's Compensation Act No. 2, Housing (Rural Workers') and Small Housing and Allotments Acts approved. Merchandise Mark Act required indication of origin to be given in case of certain imported goods

Dec. 18, Memorandum issued as to policy in China

Dec. 31, Agreement for settlement of War debt of Portugal signed

1927

Jan. 6, The Duke and Duchess of York left England for visit to Australia and New Zealand

Jan. 7, Wireless telephone service between London and New York inaugurated

Jan. 12, Death of Sir John Scott Keltie, geographer

Jan. 24, British troops sailed for China for protection of British residents in view of disturbances and attack on British concession at Hankow Jan. 4. *See also* China

Jan. 27, British Note to China as to future relations

Feb. 7, Death of Sir Wilfred Stokes (66), engineer

Feb. 10, Death of Sir George Greenhill, mathematician

Feb. 19, Agreement with China signed providing for retrocession of British concession at Hankow

Feb. 20 and March 2, Agreement with China signed provided for retrocession of Kuikiang

Feb. 23, Note to Russia protested against breaches of Trade Agreement of 1921 and continued propaganda of Soviet Russia. Russian reply of Feb. 26 denied charges

Feb. 24, Death of Sir Edward Marshall Hall (68), advocate

Feb. 27, Death of Sir Luke Fields, artist

March 3, Death of Henry Frowde, publisher (86)

March 13, Alan Cobham arrived at Cape Town, 16,130 miles, 1,600 hours flying time

March 18, Death of Rev. Philip Henry Wicksteed, writer

March 24, Attack of Chinese on British residents at Nanking. *See* China

March 29, Captain G. H. Wilkins with Ben Eielson, pilot, left Point Barrow in airplane to explore the Polar region north of Asia. Forced landing at 175° W. long. and 77° 45′ N. lat. Plane abandoned 83 miles from Point Barrow because of lack of gasoline

April 4, Government Bill to amend law as to trade unions and make general strike illegal introduced in House of Commons

April 5, Bill creating separate Indian Navy to be used only for the purpose of the defense of India except in grave emergency passed third reading in the House of Commons

———, Convention with Spain revised Treaty of commerce of Oct. 31, 1922

April 8, Death of Sir John Ernest Hodder-Williams, publisher

April 9, Agreement signed for settlement of Greek War debt. Total fixed at £21,444,000 to be paid in 62 annual instalments

April 11, Death of Rev. Dr. Archibald Henderson (89)

April 12, Act provided for alteration of Royal Style and Titles and Style of Parliament as necessitated by creation of the Irish Free State

April 15, Captain Wilkins and Ben Eielson reached Beechey Point on the shore of Alaska, walking from abandoned plane

May 1, Death of Lord Cowdray (W. D. Pearson)

May 2, British Note to the United States on War debts in answer to statement of Secretary Mellon of March 17

May 10, First Colonial Conference opened in London

May 11, Death of Sir Sidney Colvin, critic (81)

May 12, Raid of London police on premises of Arcos, Ltd., Russian State trading agency in London, and seized documents in search for important missing document belonging to the War Office which was not found

———, Russia protested raid

———, Treaty of commerce and navigation with Yugoslavia signed

May 16–19, State visit of President Doumergue of France

May 19, Agreement with the United States by exchange of Notes as to certain pecuniary claims arising out of the War

May 20, Treaty signed recognized the independence of Hejaz and Nejd and dependencies

May 26, Trade Agreement with Russia of 1921 canceled and existing relations with Russia suspended by the Government in view of breaches of Trade Agreement by Russia. British representatives withdrawn from Moscow and Leningrad

May 29, Captain Charles Lindbergh arrived in London from Paris after his transatlantic flight and was received by the King May 31

June 1, Death of Professor John Bagnell Bury

June 3, Death of Marquess of Lansdowne (82)

June 14, Death of Jerome K. Jerome, novelist (68)

June 20, Conference on Naval Disarmament at Geneva with the United States and Japan opened

June 27, The Duke and Duchess of York returned from visit to Australia and New Zealand

June 28, Trade Union Bill became law, making certain strikes and lockouts illegal, altered the law as to political funds of trades unions, and placed restrictions on civil servants becoming members of certain political organizations

July 4, King Fuad of Egypt and his Prime Minister Sarwat Pasha arrived in London

July 23, The Prince of Wales, the Duke of York, and Prime Minister Baldwin left England for Canada to take part in celebrations in honor of the 60th anniversary of Canada's acquisition of Dominion status

July 23, Death of General R. E. H. Dyer, and of Sir William James Ashley, economist

July 27, Death of Solomon Joseph Solomon, artist (67)

July 29, Poor Law Act, Workmen's Compensation (Transfer of Funds) Act and Trade Disputes and Trade Unions Act approved

July 31, Death of Sir Harry H. Johnston (69), pioneer of the British Empire in Africa

Aug. 9, Yugoslav War debt funded at $127,000,000

Aug. 26, Resignation of Lord Robert Cecil from the Cabinet and as British representative on League of Nations in disagreement with Government as to foreign policy and disarmament. Succeeded in Cabinet by R. McNeill (Lord Cushendun)

———, Death of John St. Loe Strachey, editor

Sept. 1, Firms in the heavy steel industry introduced a system of rebates to consumers of steel who agreed to purchase solely from British manufacturers over a stated period

Sept. 8, Trade Union Congress broke off relations with the Russian trade unions

Sept. 19, Agreement with Austria as to debt settlement

Sept. 19–22, Exchange of Notes with China provided for remission of Boxer indemnity by England

Oct. 3, Telephone service with Canada inaugurated

Nov. 2, Death of Sir William Galloway, mining engineer

Nov. 8, Appointment of a commission to inquire into and report on the Government of India under the 1919 Act. Sir John Simon appointed Chairman, Nov. 26

Nov. 16, Ramsay MacDonald moved vote of censure on the Government for neglect of its responsibilities to the mining industry

Nov. 17, Death of Charles Frederick Gurney Masterman (54), journalist and former Minister

Nov. 24, Vote of censure of Government moved by Labour Party for attitude towards peace and disarmament at Naval Conference at Geneva

Dec. 2, Death of Arnold Louis Mumm (69), publisher

Dec. 3, Agreement with Germany provided for abolition of passport visas

Dec. 14, New Treaty with Iraq signed

———, The new Church of England Prayer Book accepted by the House of Lords by vote of 241 to 88

Dec. 15, The new form of Prayer Book rejected in House of Commons by vote of 238 to 205

Dec. 22, Landlord and Tenant Act provided for compensation for improvements, Indian Church Act repealed law under which the Bishop of Calcutta as Metropolitan of India and Ceylon had been subject to "the general superintendence and revision" of the Archbishop of Canterbury, and Unemployment Insurance Act approved

1928

Jan. 6–7, Thaw and high tide caused highest water level of the Thames River ever recorded; flooded cellars of House of Lords and Tate Gallery and overflowed its banks from Greenwich to Kew

Jan. 12, First meeting of Conference of representatives of labor and employers initiated by Sir Alfred Mond

———, Death of Thomas Hardy, poet and novelist (87)

Jan. 19, The Statutory Commission on Indian Reforms headed by Sir John Simon, left London, arriving in India Feb. 3

Jan. 20, Death of Admiral Sir Edmond Slade (68),

Admiral Sir John Michael de Roebeck (66), and Sir Dyce Duckworth

Jan. 29, Death of General Douglas Haig, first Earl Haig (66)

Feb. 7–22, First solo air flight from England to Australia made by Captain Herbert J. L. Hinkler, including first non-stop flight to Rome. Actual flying time, 134 hours, distance, 12,000 miles

Feb. 8, Death of Thomas Bailey Saunders, writer (67)

Feb. 12–May 17, Solo air flight of Lady Mary Heath from Cape Town, Africa, to London

Feb. 15, Death of Lord Oxford and Asquith (Herbert Henry Asquith), 75

Feb. 19, Captain Malcolm Campbell drove a 12 cylinder automobile on the beach at Daytona, Florida, at rate of 1 mile in 16.76 seconds with the wind at rate of 214.79 miles an hour, 1 mile against the wind in 18.03 seconds (199.66 miles an hour)

Feb. 20, Agreement with Trans-Jordan recognized independence but the Enir agreed to be guided by British advice in foreign relations, management of public finances, grant of concessions to foreigners, and legislation which might affect the rights of British and foreign subjects

March 2, Death of Sir Harry Poland, criminal lawyer (98)

March 9–Jan. 16, 1929, Flight of Lady Mary Bailey to South Africa and back

March 13, Captain Walter Hinchcliffe with Hon. Elsie MacKay left England for a transatlantic flight and were not heard from again

——, Arrival in London of the Amir of Afghanistan

March 19, The House of Commons voted against demand of Labour Party for inquiry into the authenticity of the Zinoviev letter of 1924 by 326 to 132

——, Death of Sir David Ferrier (86), neurologist

March 21, Death of Edward Walter Maunder (76), astronomer

March 28, Resignation of Lord Cave, Lord Chancellor. Succeeded by Sir David Hogg who was made Lord Halisham

March 29, Death of Viscount George Cave (72), of John Keble Bell, journalist (52)

April 11, Princess Mary and her husband Viscount Lascelles arrived at Jerusalem on visit to Palestine

April 15, Captain George H. Wilkins and Lieutenant Carl B. Eielson left Point Barrow, Alaska, in plane and reached Green Harbor, Spitzbergen, April 21, in 20½ hours actual flying time after being stormbound 5 days

April 16, Death of Jane Ellen Harrison, archæologist (77)

April 19, "Oxford English Dictionary" completed

——, Death of Baron Eversley (George John Shaw Lefevre), 96

April 28, Prince Carol of Rumania arrived in England

May 8, Prince Carol asked to leave the country by the Home Secretary because of his political activities as to Rumania which he did on the 16th

May 10, A series of conventions signed with Persia. *See* Persia

May 26, Death of Edmund Gosse (78), critic and poet, and of Professor John Burnet, classical writer (64)

May 28, Death of Edward Montagu, journalist (61)

May 31, Supplementary Commercial Agreement with Spain concluded

June 13, Death of the Marquess of Lincolnshire (85), former Lord Chamberlain

June 14, The House of Commons again rejected the revised Prayer Book by vote of 226 to 220

——, Resignation of Mr. J. H. Whitley, Speaker of the House of Commons

——, Death of Mrs. Emmeline Pankhurst, pioneer of woman suffrage (69)

June 15, Captain E. A. Fitzroy elected Speaker of the House of Commons

June 28, Death of Sir John Thorneycroft, naval architect (85), and Professor Henry William C. Davis, historian (65)

July 2, Representation of the People (Equal Franchise) Act approved gave women the franchise on the same terms as men, and National Health Insurance Act approved

July 4, Second full meeting of the Mond Conference. Reports adopted

July 21, Death of Dame Ellen Terry, actress (80)

Aug. 3, Agricultural Credits Act approved enabled farmers to obtain loans on security of their stock. Clergy Pensions Act and Shops (Hours of Closing) approved

Aug. 16, Death of Sir George Otto Trevelyan, historian

Aug. 18, Miss Ivy Hawke of Surbiton swam the Channel in 19 hours and 16 minutes

Aug. 19, Death of Viscount Haldane (Richard Burdon Haldane), 72

Aug. 21, Appeal of the Prime Minister to employers for work for the unemployed in the depressed mining areas

Aug. 27, General Pact for renunciation of War signed by Great Britain

Sept. 6, Departure of the Prince of Wales and the Duke of Gloucester for hunting trip in British East Africa

Sept. 27, Admiralty announced letting of contract for naval base at Singapore

——, Announcement of Sir John Simon that 8 of the 9 British India Provinces had decided to cooperate with the Commission by providing an Indian Central Committee elected by the Provincial legislators

Oct. 16, Resignation of the Earl of Birkenhead as Secretary of State for India. Succeeded by Viscount Peel

Nov. 1, In municipal elections the Labour Party gained over 200 seats

Nov. 5, Death of Lord Carnack (Arthur Nicholson), diplomat

Nov. 11, Resignation of the Archbishop of Canterbury

Nov. 16, Sir Hubert Wilkins with Lieutenant C. B. Eielson made first flight of an airplane in Antarctic from base at Deception Island

Nov. 17, Note to Government of the United States regarding claims of Byrd expedition in Antarctic

Nov. 21, Announcement of illness of King George

Dec. 4, Dr. Cosmo Gordon Lang enthroned as Archbishop of Canterbury and Primate of all England

——, Council of State appointed to exercise certain powers during illness of the King

Dec. 11, The Prince of Wales arrived in London from East Africa on account of the illness of the King

Dec. 13, Reform of the House of Lords by reduction of members and steps taken to ensure each political party a fair representation endorsed in principle by vote of 52 to 8 a large number of peers abstaining from voting

Dec. 20, Treaty with China signed at Nanking formally recognized the Nanking Government and recognized China's tariff autonomy. The Chinese Government undertook to abolish coast trade duties, likin, and all other irregular levies as soon as possible

Dec. 20, Main exploratory flight of Sir Hubert Wilkins in the Antarctic to point about 600 miles south-west of Deception Island. Discovered that peninsula hitherto known as Graham Island really a mass of islands

1929

Jan. 7, Death of Henry Arthur Jones, dramatist (77)

Jan. 10, Second flight of Sir Hubert Wilkins in Antarctic

——, Dr. William Temple enthroned as Archbishop of York

Jan. 15, Death of Sir William Boyd Dawkins, geologist

Jan. 16, Commissioner E. J. Higgins elected General of the Salvation Army in place of General Bramwell Booth, deposed

Jan. 17, Hilton-Young Report on East and Central Africa published

Jan. 21, Naval Conference in London opened by King George

Jan. 24, Lancashire Cotton Corporation, Ltd., established to combine cotton mills and substitute coöperation for competition

Feb. 1, Flight of Sir Hubert Wilkins in the Antarctic to 73° South on 101st W. meridian

Feb. 7, Bank rate raised to 5½%

Feb. 12, Death of Lily Langtry (Lady de Bathe), actress (77)

Feb. 13, Mond-Turner plan as adopted by Mond Conference rejected by employers

——, Salvation Army Council again deposed General Bramwell Booth and elected Edward J. Higgins as his successor

Feb. 26, On this date 1,458,000 persons on official roster as unemployed

March 11, Major H. O. D. Segrave set new world record for speed in automobile at Daytona, Florida, with average speed 231.36226 miles an hour

March 13, Death of Lord Walter George Frank Phillimore, jurist (83), and of Henry Scott Tuke, artist (70)

March 25, Delegation of more than 100 business men left England for visit to Russia to investigate trade possibilities

March 27, Superannuation (Diplomatic Service) Act, Local Government Act, Pension (Governors of Dominions) Act, Factory and Workshop (Cotton Cloth Factories) Act approved. Northern Ireland Land Act amended

April 12, Death of Mrs. Flora Annie Steel (82), novelist

April 15, Mr. Churchill's fifth Budget announced import tax on tea in effect since originally imposed in the reign of Queen Elizabeth would be abolished

April 16–May 13, International Conference on Safety at Sea held in London

April 19, Death of Lord Revelstoke (John Baring), banker (65)

April 23, Meeting of employers associations with Trade Union Council in London

April 24–26, First direct non-stop flight to India from London by A. G. Jones-Williams and N. H. Jenkins made in 50 hours and 48 minutes, 4,130 miles

May 10, Government Annuities Act, Local Government (Scotland) Act, Agricultural Rates Act, Savings Bank Act, and Industrial Assurance and Friendly Societies Act approved

——, Parliament prorogued

May 21, Death of the Earl of Rosebery (Archibald Philip Primrose), 82

May 24, General Assemblies of the Church of Scotland and of the United Free Church at Edinburgh voted to unite as a national body to be known as the Church of Scotland

May 30, General election a victory for the Labour Party which gained 287 seats to Conservatives 261, Liberals 59, minor Parties 8

June 4, Baldwin Ministry resigned

June 5, Ramsay MacDonald (Labour), appointed Prime Minister

——, Death of Admiral Sir Cecil Burney (71)

June 7, Meeting of Indian Central Committee in London

June 8, Second Labour Ministry of Ramsay MacDonald took office, Mr. MacDonald, Prime Minister and First Lord of the Treasury; Philip Snowden, Exchequer; Arthur Henderson, Foreign Affairs; J. H. Thomas, Privy Seal; Sidney Webb, Dominions and Colonies; Lord Justice Sankey, Lord Chancellor; J. R. Clynes, Home; Wedgwood Benn, India; Tom Shaw, War; Lord Thomson, Air; Miss Margaret Bondfield, Labour; Noel Buxton, Agriculture; Sir C. P. Trevelyan, Education; Lord Parmoor, President of the Council; A. V. Alexander, Admiralty; W. A. Jowitt, Attorney General

June 10, Royal Proclamation reconstituted Council of State created during the illness of the King and reduced its scope of action

June 13, Lloyd George elected leader of the Liberal Party in Parliament

June 16, Death of Bramwell Booth (73), former commander-in-chief of the Salvation Army

——, Conference of Prime Minister MacDonald with American Ambassador Dawes as to naval disarmament

June 21, Death of Professor Leonard Trelawney Hobhouse (64)

June 25, Peerage conferred on Sidney Webb (Baron Passfield)

——, New Parliament met. Formally opened July 2

June 30, The Statutory Committee began joint meetings with the Indian Central Committee headed by Sir Sankarna Nair

July 2, Mr. Baldwin elected leader of the Conservative Party

July 7, Sunday Thanksgiving services held throughout Great Britain for recovery of the King from illness

July 9, First division in new Parliament resulted in a Government majority; 340 votes to 221 rejecting proposal for free trade within the Empire and a tariff on foreign goods

July 10, The "Southern Cross," Captain Charles Kingsford Smith, landed at Croydon from Rome ending flight from Australia begun June 25, 12,000 miles in 12 days, 21 hours and 18 minutes flying time

July 17, Death of Frederick St. George de Latour Booth-Tucker, Salvation Army leader

July 18, Announcement of Minister of Education that beginning April 1, 1931 the school-leaving age would be raised to 15

July 23–25, Miners' Conference adopted resolution to restore seven-hour day

July 26, Act to amend Unemployment Insurance Acts of 1920 to 29 approved

——, Irish Free State confirmation of Agreement Act approved

July 26, Colonial Development Act approved

July 27, Lockout in cotton industry to enforce reduction in wages of 12.82% came into force affecting nearly 500,000 workers

Aug. 2, An Economic Mission headed by Lord d'Abernon left England for a visit to South America to investigate the development of English trade

Aug. 9, Agreement with China settled Nanking affair of 1927

Aug. 14, Floating dock at Singapore formally opened

Aug. 15, Cotton operatives and employers consented to submit differences to arbitration

——, Death of Sir Ray Lankester (83), scientist

Aug. 19, Cotton operatives in Lancashire resumed work

Aug. 22, Award of Arbitration Board fixed reduction in wages to cotton operatives at 6¼% to come into effect Sept. 14

——, Announcement that Ministry of Transport raised to Cabinet rank

Aug. 27, Decision of Government to allow annual vacation of a week with pay to all workers in Government establishments, about 60,000 to 70,000 men and boys in workshops of Army, Navy, and Air Force

Sept. 1, Prime Minister MacDonald went to Geneva to attend Assembly of League of Nations

Sept. 7, Flying Officer Henry R. D. Waghorn won the Schneider Trophy setting world record for speed in seaplane at 328.63, later broken by Flying Officer Richard L. R. Atcherly at rate of 331.75 miles an hour

Sept. 10, Squadron Leader Augustus H. Orlebar broke world record set in the Schneider Cup seaplane race of Sept. 7 by flight at 355.8 miles an hour

Sept. 14, Death of Sir Edward Maunde Thompson, former Librarian of the British Museum (89)

Sept. 19, Optional Clause of the Statute of the Permanent Court of International Justice signed by Great Britain binding Great Britain to refer all disputes with other nations to the arbitration of the Court

Sept. 26, Increase in discount rate of the Bank of England from 5½% to 6½%, highest rate in 8 years

Sept. 28, Prime Minister MacDonald sailed for New York to discuss Anglo-American relations with President Hoover and other American public men

Sept. 29, Rain fell in London for the first time since Aug. 22, ending longest drought in 71 years

Oct. 1, Mr. Henderson and Mr. Dovgalevsky reached agreement for terms of resuming diplomatic relations with Russia; propaganda barred

Oct. 2, Moderator signed act reuniting the Church of Scotland and the United Free Church, divided since 1843

Oct. 3, Agreement with Russia signed for resumption of relations

Oct. 7, Great Britain delivered to the American, French, Italian, and Japanese Ambassadors invitations to a naval disarmament conference to be held in London in January, 1930

Oct. 9, Joint statement of Prime Minister MacDonald and President Hoover issued pledging support of the Paris Pact to outlaw war and expressing confidence in the Five Power Naval Agreement

Oct. 12, The R-101, world's largest airship, launched at Cardington

Oct. 14, Trial flight of the R-101 with crew of 38 and 14 passengers

Oct. 19, Antarctic expedition of Sir Douglas Mawson (British, Australian, and New Zealand Research Expedition) sailed from Cape Town

Oct. 22, Death of Sir Valentine Chirol, journalist

Oct. 26, Government proposals for reorganization of the coal industry of a seven and a half hour day and gradual purchase by the State of the mineral rights, and establishment of schemes to regulate the output and sale of coal submitted to miners and coal owners and rejected by both

Oct. 30, Discussion in House of Commons regarding dumping of German wheat in England. Motion for Government action defeated by 266 votes to 157

Oct. 31, Discount rate of Bank of England reduced from 6½ to 6%

——, Agreement with China signed as to retrocession of Chinkiang which took place Nov. 15

——, Nobel prize for medicine divided between Sir Frederick Gowland Hopkins and Professor Christian Eijkman of Holland for their individual discoveries connected with vitamines

Nov. 1, Return of Prime Minister MacDonald from visit to the United States and Canada

Nov. 2, Municipal elections a gain for Labour Party

Nov. 4, Government announced Commission headed by Hugh Macmillan to inquire into relations of industry and finance

——, Government announced issue of new Five per Cent Conversion Loan to provide for maturities of Treasury bonds

Nov. 5, House of Commons voted by 324 to 129 to accept Agreement signed with Russia on Oct. 3 for resumption of diplomatic relations

Nov. 6, Representatives of miners met with Government

Nov. 21, Bank rate reduced to 5½%

Nov. 27, Proposed mining legislation, agreed to by miners, submitted to coal owners

Dec. 3, Commission on electoral reform announced by the Government of 21 members nominated by Conservative, Liberal, and Labour Parties

——, Mawson Antarctic expedition left Heard Island. See Antarctic Regions

Dec. 4, The House of Lords by vote of 43 to 21 supported motion that the diplomatic recognition of the Soviet Government was undesirable

Dec. 6, Widows', Orphans', and Old Age Pensions' Act amended, made all of those whose husbands had died before Jan. 4, 1926, between the ages of 55 and 70, beneficiaries

Dec. 13, Last British troops left the Rhineland

Dec. 15, Bank rate reduced to 5%

Dec. 16, Unemployment Insurance Bill passed third reading in the House of Commons by vote of 273 to 199

Dec. 19, Flight of Sir Hubert Wilkins from south end of Neumayer Channel along the coast to Beaschochlea Bay and to Richthofen Valley

Dec. 20, Diplomatic relations with Russia formally resumed. The Prince of Wales received G. Sokolnikov, Soviet Ambassador

Dec. 29, Flight of Sir Hubert Wilkins as far as Charcot Island added some 300 miles new coast line to the Antarctic Continent

Dec. 31, First flight of Mawson Antarctic expedition from 66° 10′ S. discovered land which he named Mac Robertson Land after Dr. MacPherson Robertson of Melbourne

1930

Jan. 3, The Prince of Wales left England for tour of South Africa

Jan. 6, Death of Judge Sir Montague Shearman (72)

Jan. 13, A party from the Mawson Antarctic expedition landed on Proclamation Island reaffirming British possession

Jan. 21, Five-Power Naval Conference in London opened by King George, England, France, Italy, Japan, and the United States represented

Jan. 22, Death of Viscount Esher (Reginald Baliol Brett)

Feb. 6, Unemployment Insurance Act amended

Feb. 9, Death of Dr. George Goudie Chisholm, geographer (79)

Feb. 12, The Archbishop of Canterbury denounced anti-religious Russian policy before the convocation of the Church and called for day of prayer to be held on March 16 in behalf of those suffering from religious persecution in Russia

——, National Economic Advisory Council appointed by Premier MacDonald to advise in economic matters

Feb. 17, Lord Beaverbrook supported by Lord Rothermere issued manifesto announcing launching of a new political party, the United Empire Party with program of safeguarding and imperial preference

Feb. 27, Death of Dr. Joseph Wright, philologist

March 1, Treaty of commerce and navigation with Turkey signed

March 4, Death of David Herbert Lawrence, novelist (44)

March 6, Death of Lord Gladstone (Herbert John Gladstone), 76

March 11, Conservative amendment to delete proposal in Coal Bill allowing a levy on coal to subsidize export carried against the Government by 8 votes

March 16, Death of Edward Clodd, writer

March 19, Death of Lord Balfour (Arthur James Balfour), 81

March 20, Act consolidating enactments regarding the relief of the poor in England and Wales approved, consolidating Poor Law Act

April 2, Speech of the Archbishop of Canterbury before the House of Lords on religious persecution in Russia

April 3, The Coal Mines Act reducing hours for miners to seven and a half passed third reading in the House of Commons by vote of 277 to 234. Central and district schemes to regulate production, supply and sale, and provision made for a Commission for further reorganization of the industry

April 10-19, Captain C. D. Barnard made flight from England to South Africa

April 14, Mr. Snowden introduced budget raising income tax but revising the graduations to protect small incomes, and raising beer duty by 3s. per standard barrel. He allowed to lapse the duty of £10 on bookmakers's certificates and the safeguarding duties on lace, cutlery, gloves, and gas mantles

——, Death of Sir Edward Pollock (89), Sir Joseph West Ridgeway (85)

April 15, The Bankers' Industrial Development Company, Ltd., established with object of "receiving and considering schemes submitted by the basic industries of the country for the purpose of their rationalization, either by industries or by regions" and in case of schemes approved "providing such moneys as might seem essential" through existing agencies

April 16, Provisional Commercial Agreement with Russia signed

April 21, Death of Robert Seymour Bridges, poet laureate (85), and of David Muirhead, artist

April 22, London Naval Conference. Treaty for limitation of naval armament signed

April 25, The Prince of Wales returned to London from hunting expedition in Africa

April 26, The "Graf Zeppelin" flew over London, the first visit of a German airship since the War

May 1, Sir John Hope, agricultural expert, appointed to report on immigration land settlement and development in Palestine

May 5, Miss Amy Johnson made solo flight to Australia

May 8, Negotiations with Prime Minister of Egypt in London as to treaty ended without agreement

May 9, John Masefield appointed poet laureate to succeed the late Robert Bridges

May 11, Miss Amy Johnson in solo flight reached Karachi

May 12, Death of John Wheatley, former Minister (61)

May 15, Death of William John Locke, novelist (67)

May 20, Sir Oswald Mosley resigned from the Cabinet as protest against the "half-measures" of the Government in dealing with unemployment

May 24, Miss Amy Johnson arrived at Port Darwin, Australia, the first woman to fly alone from England to Australia covering 10,400 miles in a little less than 20 days

May 25, Death of Lord Davidson (Randall Thomas Davidson), former Archbishop of Canterbury (82)

May 28, Motion of censure of Labour Government introduced by former Prime Minister Baldwin on unemployment policy defeated, the Government securing a majority of 29

May 30, Sir James Barrie elected Chancellor of the University of Edinburgh to succeed the late Lord Balfour

June 2, Amalgamation of the "Daily Chronicle" and the "Daily News" (first edition, 1846, Charles Dickens, editor)

——, Vote of 282 to 201 in House of Commons defeated motion of Opposition to appoint a select committee to examine the London Naval Treaty

June 5, Announcement of Prime Minister in House of Commons that Government had decided against construction of tunnel under English Channel

——, Death of William Algernon Locker, journalist (66)

June 6, J. H. Thomas (Privy Seal) appointed Secretary of State for the Dominions, Lord Passfield remaining Colonial Secretary and Vernon Hartshorn taking the Privy Seal

June 9, Death of Professor Sir Thomas Walker Arnold

June 10, First volume of the Simon Commission Report on India issued

June 13, Death of Sir Henry O. D. Seagrave, motorist (33), killed as he was making a speedboat trial

June 23, Death of Sir Israel Gollancz (66), writer and editor

June 23-26, Transatlantic flight of Captain Kingsford-Smith in the "Southern Cross" from Ireland to Harbor Grace, Newfoundland, and New York completing world trip begun May 31, 1928 by flight to California, July 2-4

June 24, Second and final volume of the Statutory (Simon) Commission Report on India recommended a federation of 8 of the 9 Indian provinces with Burma to be treated separately

June 30, New Treaty with Iraq signed "on terms of complete freedom, equality, and independence" to become operative on entrance of Iraq into League of Nations in 1932

——, Motion of advocates of tunnel under Channel refusing to accept decision of Government against the project on financial and military grounds defeated by vote of 179 to 171

July 4, Manifesto signed by 14 bankers including Reginald McKenna and Walter Wigham urged the Government to place tariff on all goods imported from foreign countries and to retain an open market for Empire products

July 6, British Arctic Air Route Expedition under H. G. Watkins sailed from London for Greenland arriving July 26 on east coast

July 7, Death of Sir Arthur Conan Doyle (71), author

July 9, Labour Government escaped defeat on an amendment to Finance Bill for tax exemption of certain factory reëquipment by vote of 278 to 275, a number of Liberals abstaining from voting

July 10, British North American Act of 1930 approved

July 17, Reply of Government to Briand proposal for a European Federal Union expressed view that an exclusive and independent union might emphasize or create inter-continental rivalries and suggested adapting proposals to bring them within the framework of the League of Nations

July 21, Death of the Marquis of Dufferin and Ava, Viscountess Ednan, Sir Edward Ward, Mrs. Henrik Loeffler, and 2 pilots in crash of airplane on return trip from France at Meopham, Kent

July 24, London Naval Treaty ratified by House of Commons

July 28, Official report gave unemployed on this date as 1,257,982, 659,685 temporarily unemployed, 93,800 in casual employment making a total of 2,011,467 registered

July 29, London Naval Treaty ratified by the House of Lords

July 29–Aug. 1, Transatlantic flight of dirigible R-100 from Cardington to Montreal in 78 hours and 51 minutes

Aug. 1, Coal Mines Act, Road Traffic Act, Housing Act, Housing (Scotland) Act, and London Naval Treaty Act approved

Aug. 12, Death of General Sir Horace L. Smith-Dorrien (72)

Aug. 14–16, Return trip of the dirigible R-100 reaching Cardington in 57 hours

Aug. 20, Death of Professor Herbert Hall Turner (69), astronomer

Aug. 21, A daughter (Margaret Rose), born to the Duchess of York, who ranks fourth in line of succession to the British throne

Sept. 10, Miss Peggy Duncan of South Africa swam the Channel in 16 hours and 17 minutes

Sept. 11, Proposals as to extraterritoriality made to China. See China

Sept. 30, Death of the Earl of Birkenhead (Frederick Edwin Smith), former Lord Chancellor

Oct. 1–Nov. 14, Imperial Conference in London

Oct. 2, Negotiations opened with Russia as to pre-War debts

Oct. 5, The airship R-101 flying over France struck hill near Beauvais and was destroyed by fire. 48

of 54 passengers and crew perished including Lord Thomson, Minister for Air, Sir Sefton Brancker, Director of Civil Aviation, and Major Scott

Oct. 7, Death of Admiral Sir William Henry May (81)

Oct. 10–19, Flight of Captain Kingsford-Smith in the "Southern Cross" from England to Port Darwin, Australia

Oct. 13, Grand Council Federation of British Industries announced in favor of "combining protection of Britain's industrial interests at home with the widest possible extension of inter-Empire preference"

Oct. 14, Lord Amulree made Air Secretary

Oct. 20, Government on basis of report of Sir J. Hope Simpson published statement of policy in Palestine promising a certain measure of self-government in the near future and announced suspension of Jewish immigration and land purchase

Oct. 21, Resignation of Dr. Chaim Weizmann, president of the Jewish Agency and the Zionist Organization, and Lord Melchett as protest against British policy in Palestine

Oct. 27, London Naval Treaty ratified by Great Britain and other Powers

Nov. 1, Death of Thomas Norton Longman (81), publisher

Nov. 3, Conservative motion of censure on industrial crisis and unemployment defeated

Nov. 5, Lord Passfield, Colonial Secretary, stated that the British policy in Palestine was in no way inconsistent with the Balfour Declaration and the mandate and there was no intention of curtailing Jewish rights in Palestine

Nov. 11, Death of Bertram Lenox Simpson (Putnam Weale) in China

Nov. 12, All India Round Table Conference opened in London

Nov. 14, Imperial Conference ended

Nov. 22, Hearings begun of claims of heirs of Abdul Hamed II against the British Government begun at Constantinople. See Turkey

Nov. 27, Conservative motion of censure on the conduct of the Imperial Conference defeated by vote of 299 to 234

——, Death of Lord Melchett (Alfred Moritz Mond), 62

Nov. 30, Strike of 100,000 Scotch miners objecting to wage cuts and seven one-half hour day

Dec. 6, Manifesto of Sir Oswald Mosley with 16 other Labour members of Parliament and Mr. A. J. Cooke published called for an "emergency Cabinet" of five with dictatorial powers, protective tariff, &c.

Dec. 9, Coal Mines Reorganization Commission set up

Dec. 13, Draft highway code published by Ministry of Transport

KINGS AND QUEENS OF ENGLAND

BEFORE THE CONQUEST

827. Egbert, styled "King of England" in 828
837. Ethelwolf, his son
857. Ethelbald, his son
860. Ethelbert, brother
866. Ethelred, brother
871. Alfred the Great, brother; born 849; died Oct. 25 or 26, 900 or 901; some say 899
901. Edward the Elder, son; died 925
925. Athelstan, eldest son; died Oct. 17, 940
940. Edmund I, fifth son of Edward the Elder; died from a wound received in an affray, May 26, 946

946. Edred, brother; died 955
955. Edwy, eldest son of Edmund; died of grief in 958
957. Edgar the Peaceable, brother; died July 1, 975
975. Edward the Martyr, his son, stabbed at Corfe Castle, at the instance of his step-mother Elfrida, March 18, 979
979. Ethelred II, half-brother; retired
1013. Sweyn, proclaimed King; died Feb. 3, 1014
1014. Canute the Great, his son
——. Ethelred restored in Canute's absence; died April 24, 1016
1016. Edmund Ironside, his son, divided the Kingdom with Canute; murdered at Oxford, Nov. 30, 1016; reigned seven months
1017. Canute sole King; married Emma, widow of Ethelred; died Nov. 12, 1035
1035. Harold I, son; died March 17, 1040
1039. Hardicanute, son of Canute and Emma; died of repletion at a marriage feast, June 8, 1042
1042. Edward the Confessor, son of Ethelred and Emma; died Jan. 5, 1066
1066. Harold II, son of Earl Godwin; reigned nine months; killed near Hastings Oct. 14, 1066

THE NORMANS

The regnal dates are those given by Sir H. Nicolas. The early Norman and Plantagenet kings reckoned their reigns from the day of their coronation; the later Plantagenets from the day after the death of their predecessor. With Edward VI began the present custom of beginning the reign on the day of the death of the preceding sovereign

1066. William the Conqueror; crowned Dec. 25; died at Rouen, Sept. 9, 1087
Queen, Matilda, daughter of Baldwin, Earl of Flanders; married in 1054; died in 1083
1087. William II Rufus; reign began Sept. 26; killed by an arrow, Aug. 2, 1100
1100. Henry I Beauclerc, his brother; reign began Aug. 5; died of a surfeit, Dec. 1, 1135
Queens, Matilda, daughter of Malcolm III, King of Scotland; married Nov. 11, 1100; died May 1, 1119. 2. Adelais, daughter of Godfrey, Earl of Louvaine; married Jan. 29, 1129; died 1151

ROYAL ARMS OF ENGLAND

William I, William II, and Henry I—two lions or leopards passant
Stephen—sagittarius, the archer, one of the signs of the zodiac (traditional)
Henry II to Edward II. Three lions passant
Edward III and his successors quartered the preceding with fleurs de lys, the arms of France
Henry V used only 3 fleurs de lys
Mary I quartered the preceding with the arms of her husband Philip II of Spain

UNITED KINGDOM

James I and his successors combined the arms of England and France (1st and 4th quarter); 2nd, the lion rampant of Scotland; 3rd, the harp of Ireland. He introduced the unicorn as a supporter of the arms
George I, George II, and George III introduced the arms of Brunswick
In 1801 the arms of France were omitted. In 1816 the arms were modified through Hanover being made a kingdom

Victoria. In 1837 the arms of Hanover were omitted. The arms are now: 1st and 4th quarters, 3 lions passant for England; 2nd, lion rampant for Scotland; 3rd, harp for Ireland. Also Edward VII, 1901
1135. Stephen, Earl of Blois, nephew of Henry; reign began Dec. 26; died Oct. 25, 1154
Queen, Matilda, daughter of Eustace, Count of Boulogne; married in 1128; died May 3, 1151
[Maud, daughter of Henry I and rightful heir to the throne; born 1101; betrothed, in 1109, at eight years of age, to Henry V, Emperor of Germany, who died 1125. She married, secondly, Geoffrey Plantagenet, Earl of Anjou, 1130. Was set aside from the English succession by Stephen, 1135; landed in England and claimed the crown, 1139. Crowned, but soon after defeated at Winchester, 1141; concluded a peace with Stephen, which secured the succession to her son Henry, 1153; died 1165]

THE PLANTAGENETS

1154. Henry II, Plantagenet, grandson of Henry I and son of Maud; reign began Dec. 19; died July 6, 1189
Queen, Eleanor, the repudiated Queen of Louis VII, King of France, and heiress of Guienne and Poitou; married to Henry, 1151; died June 26, 1202; see Rosamond
1189. Richard I, Cœur de Lion, his son; reign began Sept. 3; died of a wound, April 6, 1199
Queen, Berengaria, daughter of the King of Navarre; married May 12, 1191; survived the King
1199. John, the brother of Richard; reign began May 27; died Oct. 19, 1216
Queens, Avisa, daughter of the Earl of Gloucester; married in 1189; divorced. 2. Isabella, daughter of the Count of Angoulême: she was the young and virgin wife of the Count de la Marche; married to John in 1200. Survived the King, on whose death she was remarried to the Count de la Marche
1216. Henry III, son of John; reign began Oct. 28; died Nov. 16, 1272
Queen, Eleanor, daughter of the Count de Provence; married Jan. 14, 1236; survived the King; and died in 1291, in a monastery
1272. Edward I, son of Henry, surnamed Longshanks; reign began Nov. 20; died July 7, 1307
Queens, Eleanor of Castile; married in 1253; died of a fever, on her journey to Scotland, at Grantham, in Lincolnshire, 1290. 2. Margaret, sister of the King of France; married Sept. 12, 1299; survived the King, dying in 1317
1307. Edward II, son of Edward I; reign began July 8; dethroned Jan. 20, 1327; murdered at Berkeley Castle, Sept. 21 following
[An inscription in the castle of Melazzo, Piedmont, states that he escaped from Berkeley castle, was sheltered by Pope John XXII at Avignon. After long wandering, resided secretly in this castle, 1330–33. Reported by Count Negra, Oct., 1890]
Queen, Isabella, daughter of the King of France; married in 1308. On the death, by the gibbet, of her favorite Mortimer, she was confined for the rest of her life in her own house at Risings, near Lynn, and died in 1357
1327. Edward III, his son; reign began Jan. 25; died June 21, 1377
Queen, Philippa, daughter of the Count of Hainault; married in 1326; died Aug. 15, 1369

1377. Richard II, son of Edward the Black Prince, and grandson of Edward III; reign began June 22; dethroned Sept. 29, 1399; said to have been murdered at Pomfret castle, Feb. 10, 1400

Queens, Anne of Bohemia, sister of the Emperor Wenceslaus of Germany; married in Jan., 1382; died June 7, 1394. 2. Isabella, daughter of Charles VI of France; married when only seven years old, Nov. 1, 1396. On the deposition of her husband she returned to France; married the Duke of Orleans and died Sept. 13, 1409

HOUSE OF LANCASTER

1399. Henry IV, cousin of Richard II; reign began Sept. 30; died March 20, 1413

Queens, Mary, daughter of the Earl of Hereford; she died before Henry obtained the crown, in 1394. 2. Joan of Navarre, widow of the Duke of Bretagne; married 1403; survived the King; died 1437

1413. Henry V, his son; reign began March 21; died Aug. 31, 1422

Queen, Catherine, daughter of the King of France; married May 30, 1420. She outlived Henry, and was married to Owen Tudor, grandfather of Henry VII, in 1423; died 1437

1422. Henry VI his son; reign began Sept. 1; deposed March 4, 1461; said to have been murdered by Richard, Duke of Gloucester, in the Tower, June 20, 1471

Queen, Margaret, daughter of the Duke of Anjou; married April 22, 1445; survived the King; died Aug. 25, 1481

HOUSE OF YORK

1461. Edward IV; died April 9, 1483

Queen, Elizabeth, daughter of Sir Richard Woodville, and widow of Sir John Grey, of Groby; married 1463 or 1464. Suspected of favoring the insurrection of Lambert Simnel; and closed her life in confinement June 8, 1492

1483. Edward V, his son; deposed June 25, 1483, and said to have been murdered in the Tower; reigned two months and thirteen days

——. Richard III, brother of Edward IV; began to reign June 26; slain at Bosworth Aug. 22, 1485

Queen, Anne, daughter of the Earl of Warwick, and widow of Edward, Prince of Wales, murdered 1471. She is said to have been poisoned by Richard (having died suddenly, March 16, 1485), to make way for his intended marriage with Princess Elizabeth of York

HOUSE OF TUDOR

1485. Henry VII (son of Edmund Tudor, Earl of Richmond, and Margaret, daughter of John Beaufort, Duke of Somerset, legitimated descendant of John of Gaunt, Duke of Lancaster); began to reign Aug. 22; died April 21, 1509

Queen, Elizabeth of York, Princess of England, daughter of Edward IV; married Jan. 18, 1486; died Feb. 11, 1503

1509. Henry VIII, his son; began to reign April 22; died Jan. 28, 1547

Queens, Catherine of Aragon, widow of Henry's elder brother, Arthur, Prince of Wales; married June 11, 1509; mother of Queen Mary; repudiated, and afterwards formally divorced, May 23, 1533; died Jan. 7, 1536

2. Anne Boleyn, daughter of Sir Thomas Boleyn, and maid of honor to Catherine; privately married, before Catherine was divorced, Nov. 14, 1532, or Jan., 1533; mother of Queen Elizabeth; beheaded at the Tower, May 19, 1536

3. Jane Seymour, daughter of Sir John Seymour, and maid of honor to Anne Boleyn; married May 20, 1536, the day after Anne's execution; mother of Edward VI of whom she died in childbirth, Oct. 24, 1537

4. Anne of Cleves, sister of William, Duke of Cleves; married Jan. 6, 1540; divorced July 10, 1540; died 1557

5. Catherine Howard, niece of the Duke of Norfolk; married July 28, 1540; beheaded Feb. 12, 1542

6. Catherine Par of Parr, daughter of Sir Thomas Parr, and widow of Nevill, Lord Latimer; married July 12, 1543; survived the King, after whose death she married Sir Thomas Seymour, created Lord Sudley; died Sept. 5, 1548

1547. Edward VI, son of Henry VIII (by Jane Seymour), died July 6, 1553

1553. Jane, daughter of the Duke of Suffolk, and wife of Lord Guildford Dudley; proclaimed Queen on the death of Edward; ten days afterwards returned to private life; was tried Nov. 13, 1553; beheaded Feb. 12, 1554, when but 17 years of age

——. Mary, daughter of Henry (by Catherine of Aragon), married Philip of Spain, July 25, 1554; died Nov. 17, 1558

1558. Elizabeth, daughter of Henry (by Anne Boleyn), died March 24, 1603

HOUSE OF STUART

1603. James I of England and VI of Scotland, son of Mary, Queen of Scots; died March 27, 1625

Queen, Anne, Princess of Denmark, daughter of Frederick II; married Aug. 20, 1590; died March, 1619

1625. Charles I, his son; beheaded at Whitehall, Jan. 30, 1649

Queen, Henrietta-Maria, daughter of Henry IV, King of France; married June 13, 1625; survived the King; died in France Aug. 10, 1669

1649. Commonwealth. Oliver Cromwell made Protector, Dec. 16, 1653; died Sept. 3, 1658; grant for the erection of his statue at Westminster voted by the Commons, June 14; vote withdrawn, June 17, 1895.

1658. Richard Cromwell, his son, made Protector, Sept. 4; resigned April 22, 1659

1660. Charles II, son of Charles I; died Feb. 6, 1685

Queen, Catherine of Braganza, infanta of Portugal, daughter of John IV and sister of Alfonso VI; married May 21, 1662; survived the King; returned to Portugal; died Dec. 21, 1705

1685. James II, his brother; abdicated by flight, Dec. 11, 1688; died in exile, Sept. 6, 1701

[1st Wife, Ann Hyde, daughter of Edward Hyde, Earl of Clarendon; married Sept., 1660; died 1671; mother of Queens Mary II and Anne]

Queen, Mary Beatrice, Princess of Modena, daughter of Alphonso d'Este, Duke; married Nov. 21, 1673; in 1688 retired with James to France; died at St. Germains, 1718

1689. William III, Prince of Orange, King, and Mary, Queen, daughter of James II; married Nov. 4, 1677; began their reign, Feb. 13, 1689; Mary died Dec. 28, 1694

1694. William III, died of a fall from his horse, March 8, 1702

1702. Anne, daughter of James II; married George, Prince of Denmark, July 28, 1683; succeeded to the throne, March 8, 1702; had seventeen children, all of whom died young (William, Duke of Gloucester, born July 24, 1689, died July 30, 1700); lost her husband, Oct. 28, 1708; died Aug. 1, 1714

HOUSE OF HANOVER

1714. George I, Elector of Hanover and Duke of Brunswick-Luneburg, son of Sophia, who was daughter of Elizabeth, the daughter of James I; died June 11, 1727

Queen, Sophia-Dorothea, daughter of the Duke of Zell; died in prison, Nov. 2, 1726

1727. George II, his son; died Oct. 25, 1760

Queen, Wilhelmina Carolina Dorothea, of Brandenburg Anspach; married 1705; died Nov. 20, 1737

1760. George III, grandson of George II; died Jan. 29, 1820

Queen, Charlotte Sophia, daughter of the Duke of Mecklenburg-Strelitz; married Sept. 8, 1761; died Nov. 17, 1818

1820. George IV, his son; died June 26, 1830

Queen, Caroline Amelia Augusta, daughter of the Duke of Brunswick; married April 8, 1795; died Aug. 7, 1821

1830. William IV, brother of George IV; died June 20, 1837

Queen, Adelaide Amelia Louisa Theresa Caroline, sister of the Duke of Saxe-Meiningen; married July 11, 1818; died Dec. 2, 1849

1837. Alexandrina Victoria, only daughter of Edward, Duke of Kent (fourth son of King George III), born May 24, 1819; succeeded to the throne on the decease of her uncle, William IV, June 20, 1837; crowned at Westminster, June 28, 1838; married (Feb. 10, 1840) to her cousin; died Jan. 22, 1901

Consort Francis-Albert-Augustus-Charles-Emmanuel, Duke of Saxony, Prince of Saxe-Coburg and Gotha; born Aug. 26, 1819, naturalized, Jan. 24, 1840 (ordered to be styled Prince Consort, June 25, 1857); died Dec. 14, 1861

1901. Albert-Edward (Edward VII), born Nov. 9, 1841; married Princess Alexandra of Denmark born Dec. 1, 1844) March 10, 1863. Succeeded to the throne on the death of his mother, Queen Victoria, Jan. 22, 1901; died May 6, 1910. Issue: Albert Victor, born Jan. 8, 1864; died Jan. 14, 1892; George, born June 3, 1865; married Princess Victoria Mary (May) of Teck, July 6, 1893; see Wales; Louise, born Feb. 20, 1867; married Duke of Fife, July 27, 1889; Victoria, born July 6, 1868; Maud, Nov. 26, 1869, became Queen of Norway, 1905; Alexander John, born April 6; died April 7, 1871

1910. George Frederick (George V), born June 3, 1865; created Duke of York, Earl of Inverness, and Baron Killarney, May 24, 1892; married Princess Victoria Mary (May) of Teck, July 6, 1893; takes the title of Duke of Cornwall, Jan., 1901; made Prince of Wales and Earl of Chester, Nov. 9, 1901. Issue: Edward Albert Christian, born June 23, 1894; Albert Frederick, born Dec. 14, 1895; Victoria Alexandra, born April 25, 1897; Henry William, born March 31, 1900; George, born Dec. 20, 1902; John Charles Francis, born July 12, 1905; died Jan. 18, 1919

GRECO-TURKISH WAR

1897

April 9, Bands of Greek irregulars of the "Ethnike Hetairia," a national society, cross the frontier at Krania; 12 hours' fighting near Kalambaka; Bettino and Bozovo taken by the Greeks April 10

April 12, Frontier raids by Greeks repulsed; severe conflict at Analipsis, Turks repulsed and their outposts captured, April 16–18; Turkish forts in the Ambracian Gulf destroyed; Prevesa bombarded, April 18–20; desperate battle in the Maluna pass, Hafiz Pasha (80), a hero in the Russo-Turkish War, killed; Greek blockhouses carried by assault, April 17–19; severe fighting near Arta in Epirus, Bonghazi and Fort Vigla captured by the Greeks April 19; Filippiada and Strevina burnt and abandoned by the Turks April 21

April 20–23, Greeks severely defeated at Reveni and Turnavo, on the plain of Larissa

April 21–23, Greek fleet bombards Platamona and other places in the Gulf of Salonika, 2 Turkish ships captured

April 22, 23, Severe battle at Mati on the road to Larissa, Crown Prince and Prince Nicholas present; Greeks defeated

April 23–25, Larissa, Turnova, and Reveni abandoned by the Greeks; panic and stampede of men, women, and children, about 500 or 600 killed; retreat of the Greeks to Phersala (Pharsalia), the Crown Prince the last to leave Larissa

April 24, Gen. Ricciotti Garibaldi arrives at Athens with volunteers

——, Nicopolis and other places bombarded by the Greeks, April 23, 24; the Turks recapture fort Pentepigadia, after severe fighting

April 25, Fight (7 hours) at Kumutzades; Greek flight

April 29, Greek army (30,000) at Phersala, Col. Smolenski appointed chief commander; Turks repulsed with loss by Col. Smolenski's brigade at Velestino April 30

April 30, May 1, Battle of Pentepigadia, April 28, 29; panic and flight of the Greeks

May 5, Phersala and Velestino attacked simultaneously by the Turks; Greeks outnumbered and overpowered after desperate fighting and much slaughter; retreat to Domoko

May 8, Volo occupied by Hakki Pasha; Greek force routed and Kamerina occupied by the Turks

May 9, Colonel Vassos and Greek army recalled

May 11, Mediation of the Powers accepted; armistice proposed; Cretan autonomy agreed to by Greece; submitted to Turkey, May 12; Turkish conditions: 10,000,000l. T. indemnity, annexation of Thessaly, revision of treaties affording exterritorial privileges; a cartel of extradition, to precede an armistice, presented May 15

May 12–14, Severe fighting on the Imaret Heights

May 13–15, Nicopolis and Prevesa besieged by the Greeks

May 14, Fierce battle near Gribovo

May 17, The Powers intervene, May 16; by request of the Czar, the Sultan orders suspension of hostilities

——, Desperate battle at Domoko, nearly 3,000 Turks killed; Greeks retreat; Capt. Baratassi, in command of foreign legion, killed; Domoko occupied, and the Phourka pass taken by the Turks, May 18; the Greeks fall back on Thermopylæ, May 19;

armistice: end of the war; negotiations between the Ambassadors and the Porte, at Constantinople; announced May 20

May 25, Collective note of the Powers to the Porte on the conditions of peace

May 26, The "Ethnike Hetairia" volunteers, disarmed; ordered

June 1, Greece entrusts her cause to the Powers

June 3 *et seq.*, Peace negotiations at Constantinople: the Powers resist the demands of the Porte as to the annexation of Thessaly, the capitulations, and the war indemnity

——, Armistice till the close of the negotiations, signed at Lamia

June 18, Greece protests to the Powers of the infraction of the armistice by the Turks

July 3, 8, The Powers demand the cessation of obstruction to peace negotiations

July 7, The Sultan refuses to accept the views of the Powers on the boundary question

July 18, Draft treaty of peace presented by the Porte; not accepted by the Ambassadors, July 19; an iradè promulgated accepting the frontier, with reservations, July 21. *See* Greece, Sept. 18, 1897; Turkey, Dec. 4, 1897

GREECE

Greece, Hellenic Republic established in 1924, a kingdom, 1830–1924, occupies the southern part of the Balkan Peninsula, and includes about 500 adjacent islands; bounded on the north by Albania, Yugoslavia, and Bulgaria, and by Turkey on the northeast, on the west by the Ionian Sea, and on the east by the Aegean Sea. The total area is 49,912 square miles and the population according to the census of May 15, 1928, 6,204,684.

Old Greece (before 1912) comprised continental Greece, the Peloponnesus to the south of the Gulf of Corinth, the Aegean Island of Eubœa, the Cyclades (about 220 islands, including Syra, Naxos, Andros, Tenos, Mikonos, Thermia, Seriphos, Paros, and Amorgos), the Sporades Islands (about 20), and the islands in the Ionian Sea, including Corfu, Zante, Santa Maura, and Cephalonia. Total area, 25,223 square miles.

New Greece consists of Macedonia, Western Thrace, Epirus, Crete, and the other Aegean lands. (*See also* Aegean Islands).

As a result of the Balkan Wars Greece gained 16,919 square miles of new territory, giving the country in 1914 a total area of 41,933 square miles with population estimated as 4,821,300, and acquired part of Macedonia, Epirus, Crete and a number of islands in the Aegean, occupied during the war. By the Treaty of Lausanne acquired Aegean Islands occupied during the Balkan Wars including Lemnos, Samos, Chios, and Mytilene, (but not Imbros, Tenedos and Castellorizzo, and the small Rabbit Islands), Western Thrace and the frontier of 1913 with Bulgaria, adding 3,182 square miles of territory. Athens is the capital.

The last king was George II, who was forced to leave Greece Dec. 18, 1923.

Greece, anciently termed Hellas. The name of Græcia first occurs in the writings of Aristotle (B.C. 384–322). Greece was so called from an ancient king, Græcus, and Hellas from another king, Hellen, the son of Deucalion. From Hellen's sons, Dorus and Æolus, came the Dorians and Æolians; another son Xuthus was father of Achæus and Ion, the progenitors of the Achæans and Ionians. Homer calls the inhabitants indifferently Myrmidons, Hellenes, and Achaians. They were also termed Danai, from Danaus, king of Argos, 1474 B.C. Greece anciently consisted of the peninsula of the Peloponnesus, Greece outside of the Peloponnesus, Thessaly, and the islands. The principal states of Greece were Athens, Sparta, Corinth, Thebes, Arcadia, and afterwards Macedon.

Alexander Zaimis, President.

504 B.C. TO 1815

504, Sardis burnt by the Greeks, which occasions the Persian invasion; Thrace and Macedonia conquered, 496

491, Athens and Sparta resist the demands of the King of Persia

Sept. 28, 490, The Persians defeated at Marathon

Aug., 480, Xerxes invades Greece, but is checked at Thermopylæ by Leonidas

Oct. 20, 480 B.C., Battle of Salamis. In a great sea-fight at Salamis (near Athens), Themistocles, the Greek commander, with only 310 sail, defeated the fleet of Xerxes, King of Persia, which consisted of 1,000 sail.—Near Salamis, in Cyprus, the Greeks defeated the Persian fleet, 449 B.C.; and Demetrius Polioreetes defeated the fleet of Ptolemy and his allies, 306 B.C.

Sept. 22, 479, Mardonius defeated and slain at Platæa; Persian fleet destroyed at Mycale

469, Battle of Eurymedon (end of Persian War)

459, Athens begins to tyrannize over Greece

448, The sacred war begun

435, War between Corinth and its colony, Corcyra

431–404, Leads to the Peloponnesian war

415–413, Disastrous Athenian expedition to Syracuse

400, Retreat of the 10,000 under Xenophon

399, Death of Socrates

394, The sea-fight at Cnidus

387, The peace of Antalcidas

370–360, Rise and fall of the Theban power in Greece

362, Battle of Mantinea; death of Epaminondas

353, Ambitious designs of Philip of Macedon

346, Sacred wars ended by Philip, who takes all the cities of the Phoceans

340, Athens and allies declare war against Philip; who totally defeats them at Chæronea, B.C. 338

336, Philip assassinated by Pausanias

——, Alexander, his son, subdues the Athenians, and destroys Thebes

334–331, Alexander conquers the Persian Empire; dies, 323

284–280, Greece harassed by his successors; the Ætolian and Achaian leagues revived

280, Greece invaded by the Gauls; they are defeated at Delphi, 279; and expelled, 277

200, Dissensions lead to Roman intervention

168, Macedon made a Roman province, after the defeat of the last king, Perseus, at Pydna

147–146, Greece conquered by Mummius and made a Roman province

21 B.C., Greece visited and favored by Augustus; and by Hadrian, A.D. 122–133

396, Invaded by Alaric

1146, Plundered by the Normans of Sicily

1204, Conquered by the Latins, and subdivided into small governments

1456, The Turks under Mahomet II conquer Athens and part of Greece

1466, The Venetians hold Athens and the Morea

1540, Greece mainly subject to the Turks

1687, The Morea held by Venice; till taken by the Turks, 1715

1770 *et seq.*, Great struggle for independence with Russian help; fruitless insurrection of the Suliotes, 1803

1815, Secret Society, the Hetairia, established

1821

1821, Insurrection in Moldavia and Wallachia, in which the Greeks join, suppressed

March, Proclamation of Prince Alexander to shake off the Turkish yoke; he raised the standard of the Cross against the Crescent and the war of independence began, April 6

April 23, The Greek Patriarch put to death at Constantinople

June, The Morea gained by the Greeks

Nov., Missolonghi taken by Greeks

1822

Jan. 27, Independence of Greece proclaimed

Jan., Siege of Corinth by the Turks

April 11, Bombardment of Scio; its capture; most horrible massacre recorded in modern history

July 13, The Greeks victors at Thermopylæ, &c.

July, Massacre at Cyprus

Sept. 16, Corinth taken

1823

April 10, National congress at Argos

June, Victories of Marco Botzaris; killed Aug. 10

Aug., Lord Byron lands in Greece to devote himself to its cause

1824

Feb., First Greek loan

April 19, Death of Lord Byron at Missolonghi

Aug. 16, Defeat of the Capitan Pacha, at Samos

Oct. 12, Provisional government of Greece set up

1825

Feb. 25, Ibrahim Pacha lands; takes Navarino, May 23; Tripolitza, June 30

June, The Greek fleet defeats the Capitan Pacha

July, The provisional government invite the protection of England

1826

April 23, Ibrahim Pacha takes Missolonghi by assault, after a long and heroic defense

70,000*l.* raised in Europe for the Greeks

1827

June 2, Reschid Pacha takes Athens

July 6, Treaty of London, between Great Britain, Russia, and France, on behalf of Greece, signed

Oct. 20, Egypto-Turkish fleet destroyed at Navarino

1828

Jan. 18, Count Capo d'Istria, President of Greece

Feb. 2, The Panhellenion or Grand Council of State established

Feb. 14, National bank founded

Aug. 6, Convention of the Viceroy of Egypt with Sir Edward Codrington, for the evacuation of the Morea, and delivery of captives

Oct. 6, Patras, Navarino, and Modon surrender to the French

Oct., The Turks evacuate the Morea

1829

May 16, Missolonghi surrendered to Greece

July 23, Greek National Assembly commences its sittings at Argos

Sept. 14, The Porte acknowledges the independence of Greece by the treaty of Adrianople

1830

May 21, Prince Leopold declines the sovereignty

1831

Oct. 9, Count Capo d'Istria, President of Greece, assassinated by the brother and son of Mavromichaelis, a Mainote chief whom he had imprisoned

Oct. 29, The assassins immured within close brick walls, built around them up to their chins, and supplied with food until they died

May 7, Otho of Bavaria made King of Greece by a convention signed

Sept., Colocotroni's conspiracy

1834 to 1844

June 7, 1834, Colocotroni is condemned but spared

June 1, 1835, Otho I assumes the government

1837, University at Athens established

Sept. 14, 1843, A bloodless revolution at Athens is consummated, establishing a new constitution, enforcing ministerial responsibility and national representation

March 16, 1844, The King accepts the new constitution

1850

Jan. 18, Admiral Parker, in command of the British Mediterranean fleet, blockades the harbor of the Piræus, the Greek Government having refused the payment of moneys due to British subjects, and to surrender the islands of Sapienza and Caprera

March 1, France interposes her good offices, and the blockade is discontinued

April 25, Negotiations terminate, and the blockade of Athens is renewed

June 21, Dispute with France accommodated

1854

Jan. and Feb., Insurrections against Turkey in Thessaly and Epirus, favored by the Greek court; lead to a rupture between Greece and Turkey, March 28

May 25, 26, After many remonstrances, the English and French governments send troops which arrive at the Piræus; change of Ministry ensues, and the King promises to observe a strict neutrality

1860

Oct. 18, Great Britain, France, and Russia remonstrate with the Greek Government respecting its debts

1861

March, Agitation in the Ionian isles for annexation to Greece; the parliament prorogued

July, The King retires to Bavaria

Dec. 26, Great earthquake in the Peloponnesus

1862

Jan., Leopold of Bavaria proposed as heir to the throne

Feb. 13, Military revolt begins at Nauplia

March 9, Blockade of the coast decreed

April, The insurgents demand reforms and a new succession to the throne

April 25, The royal troops enter the citadel of Nauplia; insurgents removed

June 7, Change of ministry: Colocotroni Premier

Oct. 17, Insurrection begins at Patras and Missolonghi; a provisional government, established at Athens, deposes the King, Oct. 23; he and the Queen flee; arrive at Corfu, Oct. 27; the European powers neutral; general submission to provisional government, Oct. 31

Nov. 22, Great demonstrations in favor of Prince Alfred of Great Britain, who is proclaimed King at Lamia in Phthiotis; great excitement in his favor at Athens, Nov. 23

Dec. 4, The provisional government establish universal suffrage

Dec. 22, The National Assembly meets at Athens

1863

Jan. 29, The National Assembly elects M. Balbis, President, and declares Prince Alfred King of Greece by 230,016 out of 241,202 votes, Feb. 3

Feb. 20, Military revolt of Lieut. Canaris against Bulgaris and others, who resign; a new ministry appointed under Balbis, Feb. 23

March 18, The Assembly decides to offer the crown to Prince William of Schleswig-Holstein; proclaim him as King George I, March 30

June 5, Protocol between the three protecting Powers, France, England, and Russia, signed at London, consenting to the offer of the crown on condition of the annexation of the Ionian Isles to Greece

June 6, The King of Denmark accepts from the aged Admiral Canaris the Greek crown for Prince William, whom he advises to adhere to the constitution and gain the love of his people

June 30–July 9, Military revolt at Athens suppressed

Oct. 30, The King arrives at Athens; takes the oath to the constitution, Oct. 31

1864

April 28, The Balbis ministry formed

May 28, Protocol annexing the Ionian Isles to Greece, signed by M. Zaïmis and Sir H. Storks; the Greek troops occupy Corfu, June 2; the King arrives there June 6

Aug. 7, New Ministry under Canaris formed

Sept. 5, The Assembly recognizes the debt of 1824

Oct. 19, After much delay, and a remonstrance from the king, a new constitution (with no upper-house) is passed by the Assembly, Nov. 1; and accepted by the King Nov. 28

1865

March 29, New Ministry under Coumoundouros

April 6, The anniversary of the beginning of the war of independence (April 6, 1821) kept

April 20, The King visits the eastern provinces; general tranquillity

June 9, The King opens Chamber of Deputies

Aug. 18, Death of Alexander Mavrocordato, one of the early patriots

Sept. 25, The King gives up one-third of his civil list to relieve the Treasury

Nov., An economical financial policy proposed; a new ministry formed

1865–1866

Oct., 1865–June, 1866, Brigandage prevails; frequent ministerial changes under Deligeorges, Coumoundouros, Bulgaris, and Roufos

Jan. 23, 1866, New ministry under Bulgaris and Roufos

Feb. 3, Chambers vote payments to themselves; suddenly dissolved by the King

Aug.–Dec., Great agitation in favor of the Cretan insurrection

1867

Jan., New ministry headed by Coumoundouros

April 19, Manifesto of the so-named "Greek nation," issued at Paris

April et seq., Great sympathy with the insurrection in Crete; the blockade run by Greek vessels with volunteers, arms, and provisions

Oct. 27, Marriage of the King with the Grandduchess Olga of Russia

1868

Jan. 1, New ministry under Moraïtinis; under Bulgaris, Feb.

Aug. 2, Constantine, Duke of Sparta, heir to the crown, born

Dec. 14, Greek vessel *Enosis* fires on Turkish vessels and enters port of Syra

Dec., Rupture between Turkey and Greece in consequence of Greek armed intervention in Crete (*see* Crete)

1869

Jan., After a conference of representatives of the Western Powers at Paris, their requisitions are accepted, and diplomatic relations between Turkey and Greece resumed, Feb. 26

April 19, Prince and Princess of Wales visit Athens

Nov. 7, Law authorizing the cutting the Isthmus of Corinth passed

1870

Jan. 9, New ministry under M. Zaïmis

April, Concession to cut a canal through the Isthmus of Corinth granted to a French company

April 11, Lord and Lady Muncaster and a party of English travelers seized by brigands at Oropos, near Marathon; Lord Muncaster and the ladies sent to treat; 25,000*l.* demanded as ransom, with free pardon

April 21, The brigands retreating, and surrounded by troops, kill Mr. Vyner, Mr. Lloyd, Mr. Herbert, and the Count de Boyl

May, June, Great excitement; the King shows great liberality; but many influential persons are charged with connivance at brigandage

May 23, Several brigands killed; seven captured, tried, and condemned; five executed June 20

July 19, A new ministry under M. Deligeorges

Oct. 1, Greek college opened at Bayswater, London, W.

Oct., Decree for suppression of brigandage issued

Oct. 11, Two gentlemen carried off

Dec. 22, A new ministry under M. Coumoundouros

1871

Nov. 6, Coumoundouros Ministry resigns

Nov. 8, Succeeded by Zaïmis

1872

Jan. 7, Bulgaris, Minister; resigns; Deligeorges again Minister, July 26

Autumn, The Laurium mines of lead, zinc, &c., were purchased by MM. Roux and Serpieri and a company, 1863; and worked profitably; roads being made and a village built. The mines having been heavily taxed and scoriæ claimed by the Government, loss ensued; the company's offer to sell the mines to the Government was accepted, but payment evaded by the legislature. Hence arose disputes with France and Italy, and ministerial changes in Greece

1873

Feb. 25, Speech of the King to the legislature, announcing formation of roads and other improvements. [The Laurium mines had been purchased by M. Syngros, a Greek capitalist, supported by the banks]

Dec., The university at Athens closed, through insubordination of the students

1874

Feb. 22, New cabinet under Bulgaris; resigns, April 27; resumes office, May 7

May 8, Tricoupi, Minister; dissolves May 31

1875

July-Sept., Greece neutral in regard to insurrection in the Herzegovina

Oct. 18, The Prince of Wales at Athens

About Oct. 27, New ministry under Coumoundouros

1876

April, Several ex-Ministers fined for extortion from bishops and others on appointment

July, The King and Queen traveling in England

——, Greece neutral in the Serbian war

Dec. 8, Deligeorges forms a ministry; replaced by Zaïmis and Coumoundouros, Dec. 10

1877

March 10–May 28, Deligeorges, Prime Minister; succeeded by a coalition ministry, May 29; reformed under the aged Canaris, June 3

May 29, National excitement for war allayed by the King

About July, Revival of the Theban "Sacred Band," instituted by Epaminondas (to be 1,000 instead of 300)

Sept. 14, Death of the aged Canaris; the King takes his place as President

Sept., Oct., British and Turkish Governments remonstrate with Greece for apparently arming against Turkey

1878

About Jan. 10, Death of Bulgaris, statesman

Jan. 23, New ministry under Coumoundouros

Jan. 28, Insurrection in Thessaly against Turks; 10,000 Greeks enter the country, retire at the armistice early in Feb.

March 28, 29, Insurrection struggling; battles at Macrinitza; Mr. C. Ogle, *Times* correspondent, killed by Turks (investigation led to no result), March 29

May 6, Insurrection closed through British intervention; announced

July 13, Greece disappointed by the Berlin treaty; rectification of the frontiers by the Sultan, proposed about July 24

Aug. 8, Safvet Pacha's despatch resisting the claims for Greece

Oct. 31, New ministry under Tricoupi

Nov. 7–10, Defeated in Assembly, Nov. 4; Coumoundouros forms a ministry

Nov., Recruiting law for the army (all men between 21 and 40 liable)

1879

May 26, Death of Deligeorges, late Minister

1880

Jan. 1, Recruiting law came into force

Jan. 28, Crisis; Coumoundouros remains

March 22, Tricoupis Ministry formed

June 16, Berlin conference to propose settlement of the Turkish and Greek frontiers, meets

——, The King visits England; receives freedom of London; leaves July 5

Aug. 5, Order for mobilization of the army signed

Oct. 17, The King and Queen arrive at Athens after a long European tour; national feeling warlike; Thessaly and Epirus demanded

Oct. 22, Tricoupis Ministry defeated; resigns

Oct. 25, Coumoundouros forms a ministry

Oct., 1880–May, 1881, Much discussion with negotiations respecting Greek and Turkish frontiers

1881

July 2, Convention between Turkey and Greece agreed to at Constantinople; Thessaly ceded to Greece, May 24; signed

July 6, Carried into effect; Greek flag raised in Arta

Nov. 4, The parliament dissolved by the King

1882

March 15, New ministry under Tricoupi

May 5, Cutting of the Isthmus of Corinth begun

About Aug. 26, Frontier disputes in Thessaly, between Greeks and Turks, at Navantyk, near Derbend, Bosnia

Nov. 9, Settlement

1883

March 9, Death of statesman Coumoundouros

1885

Feb. 17, Tricoupis Ministry resigns; M. Delyannis unsuccessful; M. Tricoupi resumes office, Feb. 21

April 15, Railway between Athens and Corinth opened

About April 20, Tricoupis Ministry resigns through minority in elections; Delyannis ministry formed May 1

Oct., Enthusiastic military movements consequent upon the *coup d'état* in Roumelia

Nov. 7, Vote for loan of 1,200,000*l.*

1886

About Jan. 23, Increased warlike demonstration; British intervention supported by the great powers; foreign ironclads sent to Suda bay, Crete, Jan. 30 *et seq.*

About April 14, Proposed loan of about 800,000*l.* to raise the army from 85,000 to 110,000; and calling out of reserves, April 19

April 26, Ultimatum of the Powers calling upon Greece to disarm, delivered; special intervention of the French Minister, about April 26; inadequate reply of Greece, April 30

May 7, The British, Austrian, German, and Italian Ambassadors leave Athens

May 7, 8, Greek troops sent to the front

May 8, Blockade of Greek ports notified and enforced

May 9, Resignation of M. Delyannis; M. Tricoupis declines to form a ministry, May 10; M. Papamichalopoulos also declines, May 11; provisional one formed by M. Valvis, May 12; succeeded by M. Tricoupi, May 20

May 24, The King signs a decree for disarmament, announced to the Powers, June 1

May 20, 21, Fighting at the outposts near Nezeres; the origin uncertain; about 200 killed and wounded; armistice agreed on, May 24; formal declaration of the raising of the blockade, June 7

June 17, Great electoral reform bill passed

1888

Oct. 8, King returns to Athens after a tour

1889

June 17, Marriage of the Princess Alexandra and the Archduke Paul of Russia

Oct. 27, Marriage of the Duke of Sparta and the Princess Sophie of Prussia, at Athens, in the presence of the Empress Frederick (her mother), the King and Queen of Greece (his parents); the King and Queen of Denmark, the German Emperor and Empress, the Prince and Princess of Wales, the Czarewitch of Russia, and other relatives

1890

Aug., Formation of a "Young Greek party" at Athens, leader M. Ralli

Oct. 26, Elections; great majority for the opposition

Oct. 28, M. Tricoupi resigns; M. Delyannis forms a ministry, Nov. 3; the new chamber opened by the king, Nov. 10

1891

Sept. 25, Death of the Grandduchess Paul (*see above*, 1889)

About Dec. 27, A commission exonerates M. Tricoupi from charges against him

1892

About Jan. 21, Mr. Egerton, appointed British Minister at Athens, in succession to the Hon. Sir Edmund J. Monson

Feb. 14, A fanatical mob attack and destroy the new Protestant church at the Piræus and ill-use the ministers and congregation; the riots suppressed by the military

March 1, The King, for financial reasons, dismisses M. Delyannis; a new ministry formed by M. Constantopoulo; the King is supported by the parliament, large retrenchments to be made, March 5

May 15, New chamber elected; majority for M. Tricoupi; he forms a new ministry June 22

Oct. 1 *et seq.*, Dispute respecting Greek schools in Bulgaria (*see s.v.*)

About Oct. 15, Dispute with Rumania respecting a legacy to support Greek institutions, from Constantine Zappa and his brother, residents, declared illegal by Rumania; ineffectual negotiations; diplomatic rupture

[The Rumanian courts adjudge the property to the heirs, March 16, 1893. Diplomatic relations renewed, July, 1896]

1893

May 10, Failure of attempts to procure a loan; the ministry resigns; new ministry under M. Sotiropoulos, May 14

June 11, Convention for a loan of 4,000,000*l.* at 5% from Messrs. Hambro signed

Aug. 6, The Corinth Canal opened

Nov. 11, Resignation of M. Sotiropoulos; succeeded by M. Tricoupi

Dec. 16, Bill annulling the funding loan and authorizing reduction of interest on foreign loans passed

Dec. 24, Bill for the readjustment of the Greek debt signed by the King, reported

1894

March 20, The Government financial measures passed after much discussion; the Chamber prorogued April 1

April 20–May 7, Destructive earthquakes at Thebes, Livadia, Atalanti, Chalcis, and many villages; slight shocks at Athens; 207 deaths reported; royal decree for a grant to relieve the sufferers, April 29; much assistance given by Russian and British ships, May

May, A military commission appointed to reconstruct villages, &c.; 400 deaths reported up to May 1

June, Negotiations between the Government and foreign bondholders

July 23, M. Tricoupi's proposals accepted by the French only

Sept. 20, Increase of brigandage; a judge and officer killed; a band of brigands exterminated after a flight with the military, near Lamia, reported

1895

Jan. 17, Much opposition to proposed taxation; military called out to suppress rioting

Jan. 22, Resignation of the Ministry (owing to the Crown Prince's interference to stop a conflict between the military and the people on Jan. 20)

Jan. 24, New ministry formed by M. Nikolaos Delyanni

April 29, Elections; Government majority

June 4, 21, Capture of brigands at Kravasara

June 11, M. Zaimis elected President of the Chamber; Ministry resigns; a cabinet formed by M. Theodore Delyanni

July, Great distress; opposition to currant tax

1896

March 28, Budget passed by the Chamber, 28 hours' debate

April 6, Revival of the Olympic games

April 11, Death of M. Charilaos Tricoupi (born, 1832) at Cannes

Aug. 2, Cretan refugees (9,000) arrive at the Piræus

Sept. 5, Public meeting at Athens expressing gratitude to the Powers for their intervention in Crete

Sept. 11, 15 brigands and others executed at Athens

Dec. 6, The King issues a rescript for the increase and maintenance of the army; reported

1897

Feb. 10, Flotilla under Prince George, sanctioned by parliament, sails for Crete

Feb. 11, The Government appeals to the Powers

Feb. 14, Troops depart for Crete from the Piræus

March 2, Collective identical note from the Powers received by the Government, see Crete, Feb. 23

March 3, Col. Smolenitz, War Minister, resigns, succeeded by Col. Metaxas

March 7, Concentration of troops in Thessaly

March 10, Greek army estimated (80,000, with reserves); mobilized March 15

March 29, The Crown Prince arrives and takes the command at Larissa

Turkish army under Edhem Pasha (estimated at 150,000 men)

April 5, The Powers declare that the aggressor on the Greek frontier in case of conflict shall be held responsible and derive no benefit

April 10, The Porte protests to the Powers against Greek aggression

April 17, War declared by Turkey, with immediate action

April 28, The Delyanni Ministry dismissed

April 29, 30, M. Ralli forms a cabinet; chiefly followers of the late M. Tricoupi, M. Skouloudi, Foreign Minister

Sept. 27, Peace preliminaries signed at Constantinople, Sept. 18; presented to the Government

Sept. 30, Vote of confidence in the Government rejected; Ministry resigns Oct. 1; M. Zaimis, President of the Chamber, forms a cabinet Oct. 3

Nov., Great distress and destitution amongst the refugees in Eubœa and elsewhere; much relief sent from England; reported

Nov. 24, Committee appointed to investigate the conduct of officers during the war, and the origin of the war; officers suspended Dec.

Dec. 4, Treaty of peace signed at Constantinople, passed by the Greek Chamber, Dec. 17; ratified Dec. 19

1898

Jan. 12, Draft of the law respecting the indemnity loan, 6,850,000l., &c., signed by the Foreign Minister and the delegates of the three Powers, England, France, and Russia; negotiations closed satisfactorily, Feb. 24; bill passed April 2; final payment of the war indemnity, July 10

Feb. 3, Rifaat Bey, Turkish Minister, received by the King

——, Deaths from exposure, &c., of about 20,000 peasants in Thessaly during the last 6 months

Feb. 26, King George fired at by 2 men while driving near Athens with his daughter, Princess Marie

Feb. 28, Karditzi, aged 35, member of an anti-dynastic society, formerly a soldier, gave himself up, and confessed his guilt; John Kyriakos, accomplice (22), arrested, March 1; both executed, May 9

March 9, International control (finances) bill, passed, March 7; royal assent

March 11, Famine and disease among the Cretan refugees in the Piræus; many deaths reported

May 14–June 6, Withdrawal of Turkish troops from Thessaly

May 15, International finance commission of control, Mr. (afterwards Sir Edward) Law, chairman, meets; succeeded by Mr. V. Corbett, Dec. 30

May 21, Tour of the King and Queen in the Peloponnesus; return to Athens June 5

Nov. 7–10, The cabinet resigns; reconstructed; the Chamber dissolved

Nov. 26, Settlement of Crete; see Crete

1899

Feb. 25, Death of M. Andreas Syngros, philanthropist

April 12, M. Tsamados (Tricoupist) elected President of the Chamber; the Zainsis' Ministry resigns

April 14, M. Theotokis' cabinet formed; M. Simopulos (Finance); Chamber meets, May 24

June, The Government scheme of reforms in internal administration opposed in Thebes and elsewhere

July 27, Suppression of the military police and other important reforms voted; session ends

Oct. 26, The King visits Paris

1900

March 24, Army reorganization (by foreign officers) bill passed by the Chamber

Sept. 21, The Crown Prince appointed Commander-in-Chief

Dec. 22, Navy increase bill passed by the Chamber

1901

Jan., Commercial convention with Rumania concluded

April, Failure of currant and olive crops, great distress in W. Greece

Nov. 24, Stormy debate in the Chamber; cabinet vote, 109–87; the Ministry resigns; M. Zaimis forms a cabinet; the Chamber adjourns Nov. 26

Nov. 24, 26, University at Athens held by students in riots in opposition to the translation of the Gospel into modern Greek published in 1900

1902

Feb. 7, Vote of confidence in the Ministry carried

July 23, Revival of brigandage, popular sympathy with the outlaws reported

Aug., Currant crop injured by storms and rains

Sept. 11, Exportation of arms forbidden by decree

Early Sept., Forest fires, suspected incendiarism; again at Pikermi, great damage, Oct. 9, 10

Oct. 16, The King received by M. Loubet in Paris

Nov. 30, General election, Ministry defeated

Dec. 6, New cabinet; M. Delyanni, Premier and Finance Minister, Justice ad interim

1903

Feb. 13, Prince Mavrocordato, ex-Minister, dies

Feb. 18, M. Ralli elected President of the Chamber

Feb. 20, Budget: reduction of 9,000,000 drachmas in expenditure proposed by economies in departments of the public service

Mid March, Conflict between the Ministry and the Court by introduction of army bills

April 3, Ministerial crisis, Col. Lambritis resigns

May 25, Convention granting monopoly of the currant trade for 20 years to an English syndicate, signed

June 3, International exhibition opened at Athens

June *et seq.*, Agitation over the subject of the currant monopoly

June 25, The Ministry defeated on a vote of confidence, 114–95, resigns

June 27, M. Theotokis forms a cabinet

July 13, Delyannist cabinet formed with M. Ralli as Prime Minister; vote of confidence passed by the Chamber; bill reducing the number of deputies from 234 to 198 passed

Aug. 11, Earthquake shocks in Athens and throughout Greece

Sept. 13, Popular excitement over municipal elections; riotous demonstration and fighting at Athens, 14 persons killed and wounded

Oct. 7, Prince Andrew of Greece married to Princess Alice of Battenberg, at Darmstadt, by rites of both the Lutheran and Greek churches

Nov. 27, Return of the King after his continental tour

Dec. 16, Ministerial crisis; resignation of M. Ralli, Premier; cabinet formed by M. Theotokis, Dec. 18

1904

March 5, Government scheme of military reform passes the Chamber

March 19, First section (Piræus to Skimatari) of the new railway from Piræus to Demerli, opened by the King

May 15, Immense forest fire in the district of Lamia

Oct. 16, Resignation of M. Simopulos, Minister of Finance, in consequence of a scandal connected with a state lottery; succeeded by M. Kalogeropulos

Nov. 23, Agreement with Great Britain, with modifications in favor of specified British products, of the commercial treaty of 1886, and the convention of 1900; the British protest against legislation regarding the currant tariff to be withdrawn; agreement to remain in force 5 years, signed

1905

Jan. 5, New cabinet formed by M. Delyanni; parliament dissolved

May 21, M. Delyanni, in the Chamber, advises patience and work to obtain the wishes of Crete (*see* Crete) without any violent measures, which could only be harmful; he counsels confidence in the Hellenic Government to deal with the question

June 13, M. Delyanni, Premier, assassinated by Gherakaris, a servant from a gambling house which the police had closed

June 14, M. Gounarakis, Minister of Finance, appointed by the King *interim* Premier

June 20, Cabinet reconstructed by M. Ralli, as Premier, Minister of Finance, and Foreign Affairs

Sept. 24, Diplomatic rupture with Rumania due to outrages on Greek subjects in Rumania (*see s.v.*)

1906

Feb. 12, Parliamentary crisis

March 12, Cottageracaris, who assassinated M. Delyanni in June, 1905, sentenced to death, and Mitseas, for instigation, to eight years' imprisonment

April 8, Elections result in a victory for the Government

April 17, King Edward VII and Queen Alexandra arrive at Athens to visit the King

April 21, Inauguration of the Olympic games, in the presence of King Edward, King George, and others, at Athens

Sept. 22, Murder of the Greek Metropolitan of Coyrtza at Ravista by Ylachs

Oct. 7, Railway strike ends

Nov. 22, Outrages committed by Greek bands in connivance with the Hellenic Government and Greek bishops led to strained relations between the Turkish Government and the Greek Patriarchate

Dec. 1, M. Levidis elected President of the Greek Chamber

1907

April 8–11, Visit of King Victor Emmanuel of Italy

June 20, Serious floods in Thessaly; town of Trikala submerged; 1,000 wooden houses destroyed, and 300 lives lost

Oct. 27, Population 2,643,109

Dec. 12, Marriage of Prince George with Princess Marie Bonaparte

1908

March 6, M. Askitis, first dragoman of the Greek Consulate general, murdered by an unknown man

March 11, A Bulgarian band, assisted by some Rumanians, attack the Greek convent at Kallipetra, killing the superior and a workman, and injuring another Greek workman

June 23, Visit of British warships to Phalerum

1909

July 15, Earthquake in the province of Elis; several villages destroyed and many lives lost; material loss heavy, reported

July 17, M. Theotokis, the Premier, resigns

Oct. 15, Military crisis averted by the resignation of the Princes from the army

Oct. 29, Mutiny among the junior officers of the navy; 20 officers and 300 men, led by commander Typaldos, proceed to Salamis, where they are attacked by the loyal portion of the fleet and the Government troops

1910

Jan. 2, Military League demanded that the Chamber pass 27 specified measures, and dismiss Minister of the Interior, conditions submitted to under protest by Chamber

Jan. 18, Death of M. Nicholas Delyannis, for nearly 25 years Greek Minister in Paris, born 1847

Jan. 28, Agreement of political party leaders with Military League to convoke National Assembly for revision of the Constitution on condition that the League be dissolved

Jan. 31, M. Dragonmis forms a cabinet with Colonel Zorbas, President of Military League as Minister of War succeeding Mavromichalis

Feb. 8, General amnesty to naval officers who took part in the mutiny of Oct. 29, 1909, signed

Feb. 14, Reassembling of the Greek Chamber

March 19, Rioting at Larissa; a train containing soldiers was fired on by peasants; the soldiers returned fire, killing 5 men and wounding 15

March 29, Voluntary dissolution of Military League announced

March 30, King George issued decree for revision of the Constitution

Aug. 31, National Assembly met, formally opened by King George Sept. 14

Oct. 12, Cabinet resigned

Oct. 18, Venizelos appointed Prime Minister

Oct. 23, Venizelos resigned on defeat in Chamber but persuaded to remain in office and received new vote of confidence the following day

Oct. 25, Assembly dissolved

Dec. 11, Election held for Assembly a victory for Venizelos Ministry

1911

Jan. 21, Second Revisionary National Assembly met and adopted revised Constitution of June 11

April 2, Expropriation defined by Assembly enabling Venizelos to settle land dispute in Thessaly by voluntary sales to peasants

April 16, Diplomatic relations with Rumania resumed

June 28, Bill passed by Chamber created position of Inspector General of the Army to be filled by Crown Prince by a vote of 134 to 22

Dec. 15, Cretan delegates to National Assembly arrested by international troops

1912

Jan. 1, New military law came into effect by which all male citizens made liable for military service for 35 years

Jan. 3, National Assembly dissolved

March 25, Election gave Venizelos 150 seats out of 181 in Chamber; 69 members elected to Chamber by Cretan revolutionary Assembly

April 28–June 6, Nineteen of Cretan delegates arrested and detained at Suda by H.M.S. "Minerva"

May 16/29, Secret treaty of alliance with Bulgaria concluded; and Military Convention annexed Oct. 5

Sept. 8, Mass meeting protested against conditions of Greek populations in Turkey

Oct. 1, Mobilization near Turkish frontier announced

Oct. 13, Greece joined Serbia and Bulgaria in ultimatum to Turkey

Oct. 14, Cretan representatives admitted into Greek Parliament

Oct. 17, Declaration of war on Turkey. *See* Balkan Wars

Nov. 9, Greeks entered Salonika

1913

Feb. 7, Flight of Mutusis across the Dardanelles about 112 miles

March 18, King George I shot and killed walking on the street at Salonika by Alexandre Schinas

March 19, Constantine I, the Crown Prince, proclaimed King in Athens. Took the oath, March 21

May 19/June 1, Treaty of alliance and military convention with Serbia signed

May 30, Treaty of London signed. *See* Turkey

Nov. 14, Treaty with Turkey signed by which Greece received Crete and Ægean Islands except Tenedos, Imbros, and the Dodecanese under Italian occupation

Dec. 10, Crete taken over by Greece

Dec. 17, "Florence Protocol" with Albania signed. *See* Albania

1914

Feb. 13, Collective Note of Powers to Greece regarding withdrawal of its troops from southern Albania and disposal of Ægean Islands

Feb. 21, Note to Powers promised evacuation of Epirus and asked for certain villages in Argyrocastro Valley in exchange for extension of Albanian territory along the coast and payment to Albania of 2,500,000 francs, and rectification of frontier at Koritza

June 12, Note presented to Turkey demanding cessation of persecution of Greeks in Ottoman Empire

June 13, Greece formally announced annexation of Chios and Mitylene and cession of Island of Saseno to Albania

June 18, Conciliatory answer received from Turkey as to Greek Christians in Turkey

July 31, German Emperor invited Constantine to join Germany in War

Aug. 2, Constantine's reply to the German Emperor stated that the interests of Greece demanded an absolute neutrality

Aug. 4, Second appeal from German Emperor through Greek Minister in Berlin to Greece to join Germany in the War

Aug. 7, Second Note of Constantine to Emperor William declared that Greece must remain neutral

Aug. 25/Sept. 7, Venizelos resigned because Greece would not enter war against Turkey

Aug. 31, Formal declaration of neutrality made

Nov. 22, Entente Powers offered Greece southern Albania exclusive of Valona in return for immediate aid to Serbia. Not accepted because of lack of guarantee from Rumania against an attack of Bulgaria on Greece

Dec. 6, Rumanian Government declined to guarantee Greece against attack by Germans

1915

Jan. 11, Sir Edward Grey informed Venizelos that if Greece went to aid of Serbs the Allies would be willing to guarantee her important acquisitions in Greek coastal regions of Asia Minor. Declined

Jan. 11 and 17, Memorandum of Venizelos to King Constantine suggested that Greece declare to Entente Powers that she would concede districts of Cavalla, Drama, and Sari-Samban in Macedonia to Bulgaria to gain Bulgarian support in attack on Turkey in return for concessions from the Allies in Asia Minor

Jan. 23, Semi-official request of Great Britain to Greece to aid Serbs repeated proposals of Jan. 11 through British ambassador in Greece

Jan. 24, Offer of British Government of concessions in Asia Minor in return for help to Serbia declined on the 29th

Feb. 23, British marines occupied Ægean Island of Lemnos

March 1, Proposal of Venizelos to Entente Allies offered 3 Greek divisions for Dardanelles expedition stating that this proposal was made with King Constantine's consent. Resignation of Colonel Metaxas, Acting-Chief of Staff as protest against military proposals made without consultation with military officers

March 3 and 5, Meetings of Crown Council for discussion of plans of Venizelos as a result of which King Constantine with advice also of General Staff declined adhesion to plan of Venizelos

March 6, Venizelos Ministry resigned because of refusal of the King to join the Entente Allies in the War

——, Secret Treaty of Great Britain, France, and Russia which excluded Greece from Straits.

March 7, Greece protested British occupation of Lemnos

March 10, Gounaris formed a Cabinet

March 11, Parliament dissolved by the King

March 30/April 12, Ministers of the 3 Entente Powers at Athens handed Note to Greek Government demanding military coöperation of Greece in the War offered "territorial acquisitions in the vilayet of Aidin"

April 1/14, Greek Note to Entente Allies made formal offer of intervention and assistance in war against Turkey if Allies would guarantee integrity of Grecian territory and define territorial compensations offered as well as facilities of money and war material to be given to Greece. Not answered

April 12, Refusal to allow Serb troops to use railroads

April 18/May 1, Proposal to Entente Powers that Greece enter War with her naval forces only, reserving her army for her own protection against Bulgaria

June 13 (May 31), General election a victory for the Liberal party of Venizelos which gained 186 out of 316 seats

July 25, British Government guaranteed cession of Mitylene by Turkey to Greece

Aug. 3, Ultimatum of Entente Allies to Greece asked Greece to cede Eastern Macedonia to Bulgaria. Compensations promised in region of Smyrna. *See also* Bulgaria

Aug. 16, Chamber met and Government defeated on first important measure resigned

Aug. 21, Venizelos dispatch reaffirmed obligation of Greece to defend Serbia as ally in case of attack

Aug. 22, Venizelos again Premier

Sept. 21, Venizelos asked France and Great Britain without consent of Constantine to land 150,000 men at Salonika to make good the 150,000 combatants whom Serbia was obliged to send by Treaty for joint action against Bulgaria. Accepted, Sept. 24

Sept. 23, Greek army mobilized

Oct. 1, Protest of Venizelos "as a matter of form" against arrangements being made for landing of Allied troops at Salonika

Oct. 4, Venizelos in Chamber received support of majority of 46 for support of Serbia

Oct. 5, Allied disembarcation at Salonika begun

——, King Constantine asked Venizelos to resign or modify his war policy

Oct. 6, Zaimis formed Ministry. Declared Greece not bound to assist Serbia in non-Balkan war

Oct. 12, General Sarrail, Commander-in-Chief of the expeditionary force at Salonika arrived in Greece

Oct. 16, Sir Edward Grey offered Greece the Island of Cyprus in return for entry into War on Serbia's behalf. Declined Oct. 20

Nov. 4, Zaimis Cabinet defeated because of withdrawal of support of Venizelos resigned

Nov. 7, Cabinet formed by Stephanos Skouloudis

Nov. 8, Entente loan to Greece of £1,600,000

Nov. 11, Parliament dissolved by the King

Nov. 19, Commercial blockade of Greece by Entente Allies

Nov. 20 (7, O.S.), Germany offered Greece loan of 40,000,000 marks which was accepted Nov. 22 on condition of "no political condition," signed Dec. 19, O.S.

——, Lord Kitchener as emissary of the Allies visited Athens

Dec. 10, Greece agreed to move troops out of the way and not to oppose construction of defensive works in Macedonia in answer to an ultimatum of Entente Allies of Nov. 23

Dec. 11, Government refused Entente demand of 9th for withdrawal of troops from Salonika

Dec. 19, Election gave Government a majority

Dec. 28, French squadron took possession of the Island of Castellorizio

Dec. 30, General Sarrail arrested German, Austrian, Bulgarian, and Turkish consuls and took possession of premises at Salonika because of air raid

1916

Jan. 10, French force landed at Corfu. Greeks notified that Serbian soldiers would be conveyed there

Jan. 11, King Constantine protested against occupation of Corfu as violation of international pacts (Treaties of London, Nov. 14, 1863, March 29, 1864)

Jan. 26–Feb. 8, Circular of Minister of War ordered troops in Macedonia to withdraw from frontier in case German or Bulgarian troops appeared

March 9 (April 27, O.S.), Garrison at Fort Rupel instructed to withdraw in event of foreign invasion

March, Greece formally took possession of North Epirus occupied in Nov., 1914, with consent of the Powers

April 3, Proposal of French and British Ministers to transport Serbian army from Corfu through Greece by railroad from Patras to Saloniki to avoid danger by water of submarines refused by M. Skouloudis

April 20, Another 40,000,000 marks loaned by Germany to Greece

May 8, Railroad from Papapouli to Geda (56 miles) completed joining "Old" and "New" Greece by rail

May 10, General Sarrail occupied frontier fort of Dovatepe and Greek officers advised his occupation of Fort Rupel

May 11, Proposal of Greece to allow Serbian convoys to proceed through Gulf of Corinth and the Straits of Eubœa

May 14/27, Greeks evacuated Fort Rupel. Protest to German Government made by M. Skouloudis

May 22, Germany notified Government that troops must enter Greece to ensure free passage of Rupel defile but territorial integrity would be respected

May 26, German-Bulgarian force appeared before Fort Rupel and demanded immediate evacuation

June 3, General Sarrail proclaimed state of siege at Salonika

June 6, Commercial blockade begun again by Entente Allies

June 7, Protest of M. Skouloudis against blockade as bringing starvation to the population of the Kingdom, particularly the Islands

June 14, Protest of M. Skouloudis to the United States and other neutral countries against blockade and stopping of Greek vessels by Entente Allies

June 21, Allied Note presented ultimatum to Greece demanded demobilization of army, substitution of a "business" Cabinet for the existing Ministry, dissolution of Parliament and new elections. Premier Skouloudis resigned rather than accept ultimatum

——, Alexander Zaimis took office as Premier and Minister of Foreign Affairs

June 23, France, Great Britain, and Russia assumed protection of Greece under Treaty of July 6, 1827

June 27, Constantine signed decree demobilizing army

July 3, Allied blockade raised

July 13, Destruction by fire of Forest of Tatoi surrounding royal summer palace in which King Constantine nearly perished

July 20, New Entente loan of £800,000

Aug. 17 and 18, Notes from Germany and Bulgaria notified Government of new advance into Greek territory for military reasons, repeating guarantees given at time of occupation of Fort Rupel

Aug. 26, General Moschopolous succeeded General Dusmanis as Chief of General staff

Aug. 27, Oration of Venizelos against policy of the King addressed to the King

Aug. 30, Revolutionists at Salonika seized barracks and proclaimed a Provisional Republic

Sept. 1, Anglo-French fleet seized 13 interned Austro-German ships

Sept. 2, Allied Note demanded control of posts and telegraphs which they stated were "misused." Accepted by Greece Sept. 4

Sept. 7, Germans and Austrians expelled from Athens by Entente Allies

Sept. 11, Zaimis Cabinet resigned

Sept. 14, Kavala surrendered to Bulgarians, Greek garrison interned

Sept. 16, Cabinet formed by Nikolaus Kalogeropoulos

Sept. 19, Greece formally offered to join the Entente Powers as soon as the Entente gave its support and date fixed for entrance into War when with their help her military forces had been prepared

Sept. 20, Demand for return of army corps surrendered at Kavala

Sept. 25, Venizelos and Admiral Coundouriotis left Greece escorted by a French torpedo boat for Crete and established a Provisional Government

Oct. 4, Kalogeropoulos Ministry resigned under pressure of Allies

Oct. 5, Venizelos went to Salonika, arriving Oct. 9

Oct. 8, Professor Spiridon Lambros formed a Cabinet

Oct. 10, Ultimatum of Admiral Dartige du Fournet demanded that Greece surrender to Allies all her light ships and disarm her large ships, and disarm all coast batteries except 3 to be occupied by Allies. The port of Piræus, the railroad, and the police were to be placed under Allied control

——, Venizelos headed Provisional Government at Salonika

Oct. 16, Consuls of Entente Powers recognized Provisional Government of Venizelos

Oct. 20, Agreement of Government to withdraw half of troops from Larissa

Oct. 23, M. Benazet, French Deputy, received by King Constantine, and agreement reached for cession in return for indemnity of military and naval war supplies and withdrawal of Greek troops to the Pelponneus with guarantees as to neutrality asked for by the King

Nov. 4, Venezelists from Salonika crossed Macedonian southern border and attacked loyalist troops at Ekaterini

Nov. 7, Admiral Dartige du Fournet after ultimatum of Nov. 2 demanding cession of light vessels sequestrated up to then and arsenal at Salamis, seized vessels and occupied arsenal without guarantees of the Benazet agreement

Nov. 14/27, Greece appealed to the United States and other neutral countries protesting against treatment of a neutral country by Entente Allies

Nov. 16, Admiral du Fornet demanded surrender of large part of Greek artillery claimed as "compensation" for the war material abandoned to the Germans and Bulgarians in Kavala

Nov. 16, Admiral du Fornet ordered German, Austrian, Turkish, and Bulgarian consuls to leave Greece within 3 days

Nov. 24, Ultimatum of Admiral du Fournet demanded 10 mountain batteries be delivered to him by Dec. 1 when, if not delivered, steps would be taken to enforce delivery

Nov. 25, Venizelist Provisional Government proclaimed war against Central Powers

Dec. 1, French troops landed at the Piræus to disarm garrison and take "possession of military establishments" marching on Athens fired on by Greeks. Warships fired on Athens. The King offered 6 mountain batteries to Conference of Entente Ministers which du Fournet accepted and stopped hostilities

Dec. 2, Fighting at Athens between Venizelists and supporters of the King

Dec. 8, Admiral du Fournet proclaimed renewed blockade of coast

Dec. 11, Decision of French Government to relieve Admiral du Fournet of command

Dec. 14, Ultimatum of Entente Allies demanded withdrawal of Greek army from Thessaly to the Pelponneus. Accepted by the King the following day

Dec. 17, Warrant for arrest of Venizelos charged with high treason by Government

Dec. 19, Great Britain recognized Provisional Government at Salonika

Dec. 26, Venizelos publicly anathematized by Archbishop of Athens as a "traitor"

Dec. 30, Request to Entente Allies to raise blockade

Dec. 31, Ultimatum of Entente Powers complementary to the ultimatum of the 14th which included immediate liberation of political prisoners (Venezelists) and reëstablishment of foreign control of the police, telephone and telegraph, railroads, apology to Allies, &c.

1917

Jan. 10, Greece accepted ultimatum

Jan. 24, Government made formal apology to Entente Allies

Feb. 17, Entente Powers in joint Note protest hostility of Greek press

March 16, British Legation announced arrival at Athens of 3,300 tons of wheat "intended exclusively for the prevention of deaths by starvation"

April 18, Resignation of Lambros Ministry

May 3, Zaimis again Premier and Minister of Foreign Affairs

June 8, Italy occupied Janina

June 9, Arrival of French senator, M. Jonnart, with title of High Commissioner of the Protecting Powers of Greece" sent by Entente Allies to "reëstablish the constitutional verity" of Greece

June 11, Ultimatum of M. Jonnart handed to Premier demanded abdication of King Constantine naming as his successor his second son Prince Alexander

June 12, Abdication of King Constantine in favor of Alexander. The oath administered to Alexander

June 15, Blockade of Greece raised

June 21, Venizelos arrived off Athens on board a French warship

June 24, Zaimis resigned as Premier refusing to accept Allied ultimatum to recall the Chamber of June 13, 1915, in which Venizelos had a majority and Venizelos became Premier

June 26, Venizelos constituted his Cabinet

June 27, Venizelos supported by French troops took oath of office in Athens. French troops replaced that afternoon by Cretan force

June 30, Diplomatic relations with Central Powers severed

July 2, War declared on Central Powers

July 7, M. Jonnart left Athens, recalled

Dec. 7, General Sarrail recalled

Dec. 22, General Guillaumat succeeded General Sarrail in command at Salonika

1918

Feb. 1, Mutiny of soldiers at Lamia

April 15, Greek troops on the Struma front. *See* World War

1919

Jan. 24, Fighting between Greeks and Turks in Smyrna

April 18, Treaty of amity and friendship with Jugoslavia concluded

April 29, Dodecanese Islands voted for union with Greece

May 14, Greek forces protected by Allied fleet landed at Smyrna under mandate to administer the Government. Subsequently A. Sterghiades nominated High Commissioner

July 29, Convention with Italy (Venizelos-Tittoni) by which Dodecanese Islands ceded to Greece by Italy to take effect with Treaty of Sevres

Nov. 27, Convention with Bulgaria signed respecting emigration of minorities

1920

Feb. 27, Law enacted provided for agrarian reform

March 30, Greece became original member of the League of Nations

May 6, Royal decree abolished martial law

May 14, Agreement concluded with Italy for immediate cession of lesser Dodecanese Islands and making special provisions as to Rhodes

May 31, Venizelos obtained from Parliament reëstablishment of martial law because of demonstrations in favor of Constantine

June 20, Premiers at Hythe accepted proposal of Venizelos that a Greek army supported by British and French fleets should take the offensive against the Turkish Nationalists

June 22, Greek offensive begun in Turkey

June 24, Battle with Turks at Alashehr. Greeks took the city

July 2, Greeks took Balikesri

July 8, Greek army entered Brusa

July 25, Adrianople evacuated by Tjafer Tayar surrendered to the Greeks

July, Greeks occupied Thrace

July 28, Tjafer Tayar captured

Aug. 10, Treaty of Peace with Turkey signed at Sevres gave Greece Smyrna, the Dodecanese Islands except Rhodes and Catellorizzo, Eastern Thrace, Adrianople, Gallipoli, Imbros, Tenedos. Minorities Treaty and Treaty with Italy as to sovereignty over Ægean Islands. *See also* Italy

Aug. 29, Greek troops occupied Ushaq

Sept. 7, Martial law again suspended

Sept. 9, Enfranchisement of Thrace by Venizelos to permit voting at election

Oct. 25, Death of King Alexander from bite of pet monkey. Prince Paul designated to succeed by Parliament declined on ground that until his father and elder brother had renounced their rights he could not lawfully succeed. Admiral Koundouriotes acted as regent

Nov. 14, General election a defeat for Venizelos. The Royalists gained 250 seats to 118

Nov. 15, Venizelos resigned as Premier and left the country

Nov. 16, Rallis became Premier

Nov. 17, Queen Olga made Regent in place of Admiral Koundouriotes

Dec. 2, Allied Note stated that "the restoration of King Constantine, whose disloyal conduct during the war had caused such embarrassment and loss to the Allies would be considered as a ratification by the Greek nation of the hostile acts of the King"

Dec. 5, Plebiscite voted for return of Constantine. Of 1,013,724 votes only 10,383 voted in opposition

Dec. 6, Allied Note informed the Government that Allied war credits to Greece would be stopped

Dec. 19, King Constantine and Queen Sophia arrived at Athens from Switzerland

1921

Jan. 4, King Constantine opened the Chamber of Deputies and announced that offensive campaign in Asia Minor would be continued

Jan. 5, Murder of Colonel Fatseas (Venizelist)

Jan. 13, Greek Minister received at Rome, Italy the first to recognize the Government of Constantine

Feb., Kalogeropoulos succeeded Ralli as Prime Minister

Feb. 1, Separation between the Patriarch of Constantinople and the Synod of Athens completed

Feb. 27, Marriage of the Crown Prince to the Princess Elizabeth of Rumania

March 21, Trade Union Act

March 23, New Greek offensive against Turkey begun to enforce terms of the Sevres Treaty in Asia Minor, marching to Angora under General Papoulas

March 28, Afium-Karahissar taken

March 30, Eskishehr taken

April 2, Turks recaptured Eskishehr from the Greeks

April 8, Kalogeropoulos Ministry resigned. Succeeded by Gounaris, Kalogeropoulos remained as Finance Minister

May 18, Allied High Commissioners at Constantinople announced neutrality of their governments in war between Greece and Turkey and designated neutral zone on either side of Bosphorous and the Dardanelles

June 10, Greek offensive from Brusa in the north and Oushak in the south

June 21, Great Britain invited Greeks to accept mediation of Allies. Refused June 25

July 15, Greek forces occupied Afium-Karahissar

July 16–17, Battle before Kutahia. Greeks occupied the town

July 19, Eski Shehir captured by the Greeks

Aug. 10, Supreme Council formally proclaimed neutrality of the Allied and Associated Powers in war between Greece and Turkey

Sept. 16, Greek army fell back on Eski Shehir

Sept. 25, Retreating Greeks reached Brusa-Afiun Karahissar line

Dec. 31, Great Britain authorized loan to Greece of £15,000,000 on condition that large part be used for purchase of English products

1922

Jan. 2, Congress of Metropolitans and Bishops met at Salonika and decided to consider election of Meletios Metaxalsis null and void; confirmed by Government, Feb. 8

Jan. 6, Death of Nicholas Demetracopoulos, jurist, in Vienna

Jan. 12, Metaxalsis sentenced to life seclusion in monastery for attempt to create schism in Greek Church

Jan. 20, Deportation of Greek citizens from Konieh, Anatolia, to Erzerum ordered by Mustapha Kemal

Jan. 30, Three hundred Greek civilians in Samsun put to death by Turks

Feb. 8, Greek cruiser "Naxos" captured steamer "Berkshire" carrying cargo of coal and oil to the Turks

Feb. 14, Greeks captured French steamer "Epoir" with cargo of coal and oil for Turks

March 10, Gounaris defeated in Chamber resigned but recalled reconstituted Cabinet

March 15, Italian steamer "Umbria Abbazia" seized and Turkish passengers removed

April 7, Law authorized forced internal loan of 1,600,-000,000 drachmas

April 12, Gounaris resigned

May 11, M. Stratos invited to form Cabinet

May 18, Stratos defeated on first appearance in Assembly resigned

May 23, New Ministry headed by M. Protopapadakes in which Gounaris included as Minister of Justice

May 25, General Hadzanestis appointed to succeed General Papoulas resigned as commander on Asia Minor front

June 10, Greek naval forces in Black Sea bombarded Turkish fortified cities of Samsun and Trebizond

June 19, Allied Powers offered mediation in war with Turks; declined June 25

July 16, Act provided for compulsory insurance of wage earners and salaried employees

July 29, Greece accepted ultimatum of Allies forbidding advance on Constantinople

July 30, Greek High Commission in Smyrna proclaimed autonomy of Anatolian territory occupied by the Greeks

Aug. 26, Strong Turkish offensive begun which routed the Greeks at Afium-Karahissar

Aug. 30, Capture of Afium Karahissar by the Turks

Sept. 4, Greek armies in full retreat except in Brusa section

Sept. 5, Turkish forces occupied Brusa

Sept. 7, Resignation of Ministry of M. Protopapadakes. Succeeded by Triantafilakos who was immediately succeeded by Zaimis

Sept. 8, Resignation of M. Sterghiades at Smyrna. Allies took over administration

Sept. 9, Turkish advance cavalry entered Smyrna followed by Kemal Pasha 2 days later completing defeat of Greeks and Greek occupation of Asia Minor

Sept. 13–14, Fire in Smyrna destroyed entire waterfront

Sept. 16, Appeal of Lloyd George, Prime Minister of Great Britain, for the Greeks against the Turks to France, Italy, the Balkan States, and the Dominions

Sept. 21–22, Gonatas and Plastiras took possession of Islands of Chios and Mitylene and imprisoned officers and men loyal to the King

Sept. 23, France, Great Britain, and Italy requested an armistice. M. Franklin-Bouillon sent as special emissary

Sept. 26, Venizelists led by Colonel Gonatas occupied Salonika and manifestos demanding abdication of the King, resignation of Cabinet, dissolution of Parliament and new elections scattered from airplane on Athens

Sept. 26–29, 146,700 refugees evacuated from Smyrna

Sept. 27, Abdication of King Constantine in favor of Crown Prince George. M. Krokidas became Prime Minister

Sept. 30, Constantine left Greece sailing for Palermo

Oct. 2, Greek army reorganized and mobilization ordered

Oct. 3, Allied Generals met representatives of Kemal Pasha at Mudania and arranged for armistice

Oct. 6, General Nidar appointed commander-in-chief, took command of troops in Thrace

Oct. 8, Agreement of Aug. 10, 1920 denounced by Italy on ground that it was invalidated by lapse of Peace Treaty and Anglo-Franco-Italian Agreement as to Anatolia signed at Sevres the same day

Oct. 11, Armistice between Turks and Allies signed at Mudania by which Turkey took over the administration of Constantinople, and Greece surrendered Eastern Thrace and Adrianople to the "Grand National Assembly of Turkey" pending new treaty to replace the Treaty of Sevres. Accepted by Greece Oct. 14

——, Martial law declared by Revolutionary Committee

Oct. 13, Military Convention signed by Allied Generals in Constantinople, Turks and Greeks

Oct. 15, Evacuation of Thrace begun

Oct. 26, Revolutionary Committee arrested Prince Andrew charging him with responsibility for the Asia Minor disaster

Nov. 8, Report of Revolutionary Committee condemned all anti-Venezelist Governments from 1915 to 1922 and demanded trial of all ex-Ministers on charge of treason

Nov. 9, M. Zaimis accepted invitation to form Ministry to replace S. Krokidas but later refused

Nov. 13, Trial of ex-Ministers begun

Nov. 25, Colonel Stylien Gonatas became Prime Minister

Nov. 28, Ex-Premiers Gounaris, Stratos, and Protopapadakes and former Ministers Theotokis, Baltadjis, and General Hadjianastis found guilty of treason, executed. Great Britain broke off diplomatic relations in protest

Dec. 3, Prince Andrew, brother of ex-King Constantine tried for treason, sentenced to banishment for life

Dec. 12, Revolutionary Committee changed entire personnel of the Holy Synod replacing them with Venezelists and also teaching staff of University of Athens

Dec. 28, General Panglos made commander-in-chief of Greek army

1923

Jan. 10, Provisional Commercial Agreement with Czechoslovakia signed

Jan. 11, Death of ex-King Constantine at Palermo, Sicily

Jan. 18, Expropriation of estates of ex-King Constantine decreed by Revolutionary Committee

Jan. 21, General amnesty decreed

Jan. 30, Convention with Turkey signed as to exchange of nationals

Feb. 12, Note to Turkey threatened to deport as many Turkish residents as Greeks expelled by Turks

March 4, Protest to Turkish Government against continued deportation of Greeks from Pontus district of Anatolia

March 17, Exchange of prisoners begun with Turkey

April 1, First prisoners from Turkey reached Athens

May 10, Treaty with Yugoslavia signed created Yugoslav free zone at Salonika for 50 years

May 27, Agreement with Turkey concluded by which Greece offered Turkey the town of Karagach opposite Adrianople with triangular piece of territory surrounding and Ismet Pasha withdrew demand for war indemnity from Greece

June 1, Drachmas rose on exchange from 100 to the dollar to 25

July 24, Peace of Lausanne signed between the Allies and Turkey included agreement for exchange of Greek inhabitants in Turkey for Turkish inhabitants in Greece and territorial arrangements dissipated hopes of greater Greece

——, Protocol added Minorities Clauses of Treaty of Aug. 10, 1920

Aug. 1, Demobilization begun

Aug. 19–26, General strike at Athens

Aug. 27, Murder of General Tellini (Italian) president of International Delimitation Commission and 4 members of his staff near Janina, Greece

Aug. 29, Italian ultimatum to Greece demanded death penalty for Janina murderers, apologies, salute to Italian colors and indemnity of 50,000,000 lire within 5 days

Aug. 30, Greek reply to Italy rejected certain demands

Aug. 31, Italian fleet bombarded and occupied Corfu and later Paxos, Anti-Paxos, and other islands in the vicinity

Sept. 1, Greece formally appealed to Council of the League of Nations against Italian occupation of Corfu under Article 15 of the Covenant

Sept. 5, Italy denied competence of League of Nations to deal with Corfu affair

Sept. 6, Council of League of Nations adopted plan of settlement which was forwarded to Council of Ambassadors. Reference to the Council accepted by both Italy and Greece

Sept. 7, Note of Council of Ambassadors to Greece embodied practically all the demands of Italy, the 50,000,000 lire to be deposited in Swiss bonds as surety for indemnity to be fixed by Council

Sept. 9, The Government accepted terms of Council of Ambassadors

Sept. 19, Greek war vessels saluted the Italian flag

Sept. 23, Allied Note handed over East Thrace to Turkey

Sept. 26, Conference of Ambassadors awarded 50,000,-000 lire to Italy

Sept. 27, Corfu evacuated by Italians

Sept. 29, Protocol signed as to refugees in Greece

Sept. 30, Indemnity paid to Italy

Oct. 22–25, Royalist revolt at Corinth, Chalkis, and Lamie led by General Metaxas suppressed by government troops except in the Pelopponesus

Nov. 22, Prohibitive customs tariff came into effect

Dec. 16, General election gave Venizelists a majority, 370 seats in Chamber out of 401

Dec. 17, Republican mass meetings in Athens

Dec. 18, King George II at request of Cabinet left the country. Regency of Admiral Koundouriotis established until people should decide whether they wanted a republican or monarchical form of government

Dec. 22, King George and Queen Elizabeth arrived in Rumania

1924

Jan. 2, Newly elected National Assembly convened

Jan. 4, Venizelos arrived in Athens after absence of 3 years

Jan. 5, Venizelos elected president of National Assembly

Jan. 11, Venizelos became Premier on resignation of Gonatas

Jan. 15, Great Britain formally recognized the Government resuming diplomatic relations

Jan. 29, Recognition of the Government by the United States

Feb. 4, Venizelos resigned as Premier because of ill health

Feb. 6, George Kaphandariaris assumed office as Prime Minister and Minister of Foreign Affairs and of Justice with a Cabinet of Venezelists

Feb. 21, Treaty of commerce with France signed

March 8, The Kaphandariaris Ministry defeated, resigned. Succeeded by Papanastassiou as Prime Minister and Minister of Finance and of Foreign Affairs

——, Recognition of Soviet Government of Russia

March 10, Venizelos left Greece

March 25, National Assembly passed resolutions for establishment of a republic and abolition of the dynasty to be ratified by a plebiscite

April 13, Vote of the people ratified Assembly resolution, 758,742 voting for a republic as against 325,322 for a monarchy

April 18, Republic recognized by France

April 19, Republic recognized by Belgium

April 23, Recognition of Republic by Great Britain

April 24, Recognition of Republic by Italy

April 30, Recognition of Republic by Yugoslavia

May 1, Republic proclaimed

May 18, Draft Constitution published

May 26–June 13, Strike of ship crews

June 25, Strike of navy against Captain Hadjikyriakos, Minister of Marine who resigned

July 3, Provisional commercial agreement with Germany signed

July 18, Defeat of Papanastassiou Ministry

July 24, M. Sophoulis took office as Prime Minister and Minister of Marine

July 26, Frontier incident, clash of Bulgarians and Greeks on Macedonian frontier

Aug. 6, Minorities Treaty came into effect with ratification of Treaty of Lausanne

Oct. 1, Resignation of Souphoulis Ministry

Oct. 6, A. Michalakopoulis took office as Premier

Oct. 22, Government appealed to League of Nations respecting expulsion of Greek inhabitants from Constantinople

Nov. 15, Serbo-Greek Treaty of Alliance of 1913 denounced by Yugoslavia

Nov. 17, Death of Ecumenical Patriarch Gregory VII. Constantine elected as his successor

Dec. 9, Commercial Agreement of 1852 with Sweden prolonged by exchange of notes

Dec. 18, Treaty of commerce and navigation of Feb. 22, 1843 with the Netherlands and supplementary convention of June 18–30, 1851 extended by exchange of notes

1925

Jan. 30, Turkish Government expelled the Patriarch Constantine VI from Constantinople on ground that he was an "exchangeable" Greek

Feb. 7, Note of protest to Turkey respecting expulsion of Constantine

Feb. 11, Appeal to League of Nations as to expulsion of Constantine

March 8, General railroad strike for eight hour day and against wage cuts

March 11, Decision of Permanent Court of Justice as to compulsory exchange of nationals accepted by Greece and Turkey

March 14, League Council considered Greek request as to intervention in case of expulsion of Constantine

March 22, Strike of printers in sympathy with railroad strike

April 8, Commercial most favored nation Treaty with Czechoslovakia signed

April 17, Provisional Commercial Agreement with Poland signed

April 18, Provisional Commercial Agreement with Austria signed

May 19, Patriarch Constantine VI announced his resignation

May 30, Provisional Commercial Agreement with Japan concluded

June 4, Provisional Commercial Agreement with Hungary signed

June 11, Defeat of Michalakopoulos Ministry but reconstituted by Michalakopoulos on failure of M. Kaphandaris to form Ministry

June 21, Agreement signed with Turkey as to exchange of populations and of nationals in each country respectively

June 25, Coup d'état by which General Pangalos and Admiral Hajikyriakos took possession of Athens and forced resignation of the Michalakopoulos Ministry

June 26, General Pangalos formed Cabinet with himself as Prime Minister and Admiral Hajikyriakos as Minister of Marine and of Foreign Affairs ad interim

June 28, Customs Tariff Agreement with Belgium signed

July 13, Election of Manager Basil Georgiadas, Metropolitan of Nicæa, as Greek Patriarch to be known as Basil III

Aug. 31, Agreement with Great Britain signed as to settlement of debt

Sept. 21, Treaty of conciliation and judicial settlement of disputes with Switzerland signed

Sept. 29, Admiral Koundouriotis, Provisional President, signed new Constitution

Sept. 30, New Constitution came into force. Government decree dissolved the National Assembly and new election ordered

Oct. 18, Greek zone at Salonika inaugurated

Oct. 19, Clash of Greeks and Bulgarians near Demirhassar on frontier north of Salonika

Oct. 21, Greek ultimatum to Bulgaria demanded apology, indemnity, and punishment of offenders

Oct. 22–23, Greek troops invaded Bulgaria occupying strip of territory

Oct. 23, Bulgarian Government appealed to League of Nations. The League warned Greece and Bulgaria as to obligations under Covenant

Oct. 24, Government accepted intervention of the League of Nations

Oct. 26, Ultimatum of League of Nations to Greece and Bulgaria to withdraw troops within own frontiers

Oct. 29, Commission of League of Nations appointed to investigate Greek-Bulgarian incident

Nov. 27, Greeks in Turkey at meeting renounced rights as minorities population under Treaty of Lausanne relying on protection of new Code adopted by Turkey

Dec. 14, League of Nations Council decision imposed fine on Greece of about $219,000 to be paid to Bulgaria

Dec. 15, Greece accepted decision of League of Nations "in principle"

Dec. 31, Treaty of commerce and navigation of Sept. 23, 1903 with Spain extended

1926

Jan. 3, Premier Pangalos announced military dictatorship

Jan. 4, Pangalos declared Constitution null and void

Jan. 24, Pangalos decrees provided for forced loan of 1,250,000,000 drachmas

Feb. 17, Former Premier Papanastasiou, General Kondylis and 11 ex-officers arrested and exiled to Island of Santorin charged with plotting against the Government

March 19, Resignation of President Kondouriotis

April 9, Revolt of troops at Salonika repressed

April 10, Provisional Commercial Agreement with Egypt concluded

April 11, Pangalos as only candidate at election declared himself elected President

April 18, General Pangalos inaugurated as President

April 29, Exchange of notes with Sweden extended Treaty of commerce and navigation of Oct. 27, 1852

May 12, Commercial Treaty with the Netherlands signed

May 24, President Pangalos decreed abolition of British naval mission and French military mission on ground of economy

May 27, Frontier incident in which one Bulgarian killed and one Greek soldier

June 6–Aug. 17, Conference with representatives of Yugoslavia at Athens as to Salonika problem

June 23, Customs Agreement with Russia signed

June 26, Earthquake in Island of Rhodes destroyed more than 2,000 homes

July 16, Treaty of commerce and navigation with Great Britain signed

July 19, Athanasius Eutaxis headed Cabinet

July 27, Announcement of President Pangalos that the "exiles of Naxos" his political opponents might return

Aug. 17, Treaty of alliance with Yugoslavia signed and settlement of Salonika and other problems

Aug. 22, Military coup d'état of General Kondylis overthrew Pangalos and imprisoned him. Admiral Konduriotis recalled and proclaimed President

Aug. 26, General Kondylis took office as Prime Minister pending elections

Sept. 9, Attempt of military group headed by Colonel Dertilis and Colonel Zervas to restore General Pangalos suppressed by troops

Sept. 10, Treaty of commerce with Sweden signed and Provisional Commercial Agreement with Italy and with Belgium

——, Autonomy of Mount Athos recognized by the Government

Sept. 23, Treaty with Italy signed provided for neutrality if other attacked without provocation

Sept. 24, New Constitution promulgated

Oct. 13, Conventions of commerce and navigation, consular relations and establishment and nationality signed with Albania

Oct. 15, Agrarian law enacted

Nov. 7, Election for National Assembly in which Republicans gained 145 of the 287 seats in Chamber. General Kondylis succeeded by M. Kafandaris as Premier

Nov. 24, Commercial treaty with Italy signed

Nov. 29, Provisional commercial Agreement with Switzerland signed

Dec. 1, Agreement with Turkey signed as to property of Greeks in Turkey and of Turks in Greece abandoned by refugees

Dec. 4, A. Zaimis headed coalition Cabinet of Republicans and Royalists: Premier, A. Zaimis; Minister for Foreign Affairs, M. Michalapoulos; War, General Mazarkis; Marine, M. A. Kanaris; Interior, M. Tsaldaris; National Economy, M. G. Merkouris; Agriculture, M. M. Papanastasiou; Social Insurance, M. C. Kirkos; Justice, M. C. Angelopoulos; Finance, M. Kaphandaris; Communications, General Metaxas; Education, M. A. Argyros

1927

Jan. 4, Treaty of commerce with Estonia signed

Jan. 11, Treaty of commerce with Great Britain

Jan. 26, Decision of Parliament to investigate alleged breaches of common law committed by General Pangalos, former Dictator, and 3 of his Cabinet; General Pangalos imprisoned

Feb. 25, Commercial treaty with Latvia signed

Feb. 28, Provisional commercial Agreement with Bulgaria signed

March 28, Commercial Treaty with Rumania signed

April 9, Agreement signed for funding war debt with Great Britain

June 3, Constitution ratified and President Kounduriotis, who had formally resigned to take effect after election as a protest against failure of Zaimis Cabinet to secure ratification, remained in office

June 29, Treaty of commerce and navigation with Norway

Aug. 12, Resignation of Zaimis Cabinet in dispute as to gold cover of notes issued by National Bank of Greece

Aug. 17, Cabinet reconstituted by M. Zaimis with Kaphandaris as Finance Minister, and Michalakopoulos as Minister of Foreign Affairs

Aug. 18, Conspiracy to overthrow the Government and reinstate General Pangalos discovered in Athens and 40 non-commissioned officers of garrison at Athens arrested

Aug. 26, Parliament rejected Greco-Yugoslav Treaty of Aug. 17, 1926

Sept. 11, Provisional commercial Treaty with Italy signed

Oct. 27, Agreement signed between the Government and the National Bank of Greece for establishment for new bank of issue

Oct. 30, Unsuccessful attempt on life of Admiral Kounduriotis by unemployed waiter

Nov., Agreement signed between Refugee Settlement Commission and Minister of Agriculture providing for payment of compensation to agricultural refugees for their properties abandoned to Turkey to a total not to exceed £10,300,000

Nov. 2, Treaty of commerce with Yugoslavia signed

Dec. 5, War debt to the United States funded, Greece to pay $19,659,836 over a period of 62 years with interest at 3% and Greece to borrow $12,167,000 for 20 years at 4% to be used in refugee work

Dec. 7, Agreement with France concluded by which payment for munitions to be submitted to arbitration

1928

Jan. 18, Additional Agreement with the United States as to war debt signed

Jan. 30, New international loan issued under auspices of the League of Nations for refugee settlement and stabilization

March 24, Commercial Agreement with Germany signed

April 22, Earthquake at Corinth with continued shocks in latter part of month and in June

April 25, Liquor Traffic Convention concluded with the United States

May 12, Decree stabilized the drachma at 375 to the pound sterling

May 21, Announcement of Venizelos of his return to public life as leader of the Liberal Party after 6 years of retirement resulting in resignation of nominal leader of Liberals, Finance Minister Kafandaris, from the Cabinet and 5 other members

May 30, Provisional Commercial Agreement with Spain concluded

June 11, Strike of tobacco workers begun at Kavalla which lasted 10 days and extended to other places

June 12, Chamber decided against ratification of customs convention with Russia of June 23, 1926

June 17, Part of fleet joined strike

June 28, Navigation Agreement with Hungary concluded

——, Fall of Zaimis Government

July 4, Venizelos formed Cabinet

July 10, Decree signed by President changed electoral system, each district to elect senators and deputies on majority system

July 11, Former dictator, Pangalos, released from prison

Aug. 19, Election gave 228 out of 250 seats in Chamber of Deputies to Venizelos

Aug. 20, Death of ex-Premier Stephanos Skouloudis at Athens

Sept. 23, Pact of friendship and arbitration with Italy signed

Nov. 1, Arrest in Varna, Bulgaria, of bandit, Rentzaioi, confessed murderer of General Tellini

Nov. 15, Decision on Greek debt by President of Switzerland as umpire on points as to administration of old Hellenic external loans

1929

Jan. 26, Chamber of Deputies voted investigation of alleged breach of constitutional law by Pangalos and 3 of his Ministers

Feb. 13, Paris Pact for renunciation of war adopted

Feb. 16, War debt with the United States funded at $18,125,000

March 11, Treaty of commerce and navigation with France signed

March 17, 6 Protocols with Yugoslavia signed respecting conditions in Salonika Free Zone

March 27, Pact of friendship, conciliation, and judicial settlement with Yugoslavia signed

May 10, Final settlement of war debt with the United States funded at $15,000,000

May 16, Senate revived by Premier Venizelos met for first time since 1862

——, Arrest of ex-Dictator Pangalos and 2 of his Ministers

June 3, Admiral Konduriotis formally elected President

June 7, Venizelos reconstructed Cabinet

June 8, Treaty of friendship, conciliation, and arbitration with Czechoslovakia signed

June 11, Treaty of commerce and navigation with Russia signed

June 25, Treaty of arbitration with Belgium signed

Sept. 12, Option clause of Permanent Court of International Justice signed

Sept. 29, Death of Vassilios, Patriarch of the Greek Orthodox Church (79)

Sept. 30, Treaty of friendship with China signed

Nov. 14, Announcement of creation of Ministry of Aviation

Nov. 28–29, Demonstration of students of University of Athens against the Government

Dec. 10, Resignation of President Paul Kondouriotis because of ill health

Dec. 14, Former Premier Zaimis elected Provisional President

1930

Jan. 20, Debt Agreement with France as to pre-armistice debt

Jan. 23, Treaty of friendship and arbitration with Spain signed

March 25, Celebration of 100th anniversary of liberation from Turkish rule. Participated in by Turkish Minister to Greece and his staff

April 10, Most favored nation commercial Treaty with Poland signed

May 5, Treaty of friendship and arbitration with Hungary signed

June 10, Treaty with Turkey signed as to refugees and exchange of populations

June 13, Convention with Hungary signed respecting settlement of Greek war claims

June 26, Treaty of friendship, arbitration, and conciliation with Austria signed

Oct. 27, Venizelos arrived at Angora

Oct. 30, Treaty with Turkey signed of arbitration and conciliation and Treaty of commerce and navigation and Protocol limiting naval armaments

——, General Pangalos and a large number of his followers arrested charged with plot to overthrow the Government because of objection to the treaties with Turkey

Dec. 21, Cabinet resigned

Dec. 22, Cabinet reorganized on Venizelist basis

KINGS OF GREECE

1832. Otho I, Prince of Bavaria; born, June 1, 1815; elected King, May 7, 1832; under a regency till June 1, 1835; married Nov. 22, 1836, to Maria Frederica, daughter of the Grand-Duke of Olden-

burg; deposed, Oct. 23, 1862; died in Bavaria, July 26, 1867

1863. George I (son of Christian IX of Denmark), King of the Hellenes; born Dec. 24, 1845; made King June 5, takes the oath Oct. 31, 1863; declared of age, June 27, 1863; married Grand-Duchess Olga of Russia, Oct. 27, 1867; assassinated March 18, 1913

Heir: Constantine, Duke of Sparta, born Aug. 2, 1868; married to the Princess Sophie of Prussia, Oct. 27, 1889

Issue, George, born July 19, 1890; Alexander, Aug. 1, 1893; Heléne, born May 2, 1896; Paul, Dec. 14, 1901; Irene, Feb. 14, 1904; Catherine, born May 4, 1913

1913. Constantine (Konstantinos), abdicated June 12, 1917

1917. Alexander (Alexandros), second son of Constantine; died Oct. 25, 1920

1920. Dec. 19, Constantine returned; abdicated Sept. 27, 1922

——, George II, son of Constantine; forced to abdicate Dec. 18, 1923

HAGUE CONFERENCES

1899

May 18–July 29, First Hague Peace Conference initiated by invitation of the Czar of Russia, Nicholas II, Aug. 24, Dec. 30, 1898, and Jan. 11, 1899, with object to reach an "understanding not to increase for a fixed period the present effectives of the armed military and naval forces, and at the same time not to increase the budgets pertaining thereto; and a preliminary examination of the means by which even a reduction might be effected in future in the forces and budgets above mentioned." The Conference was attended by representatives of 26 States including delegates from the United States, Japan, China, Persia, and Siam. Conventions signed for the pacific settlement of international disputes, on laws and customs of war on land, and extending the Geneva Convention of Aug. 22, 1864 for the purpose of improving the condition of wounded soldiers of armies in the field to maritime warfare (replaced by Geneva Convention of July 6, 1906). Three Declarations were adopted, prohibition of the launching of projectiles and explosives from balloons for a period of 5 years, the use of asphyxiating or poisonous gases, and of expanding or "dum-dum" bullets. The Resolutions dealt with disarmament, rights of neutrals, private property in maritime warfare, bombardment of unfortified towns, and uniformity in naval artillery. The Convention for pacific settlement of disputes established a Permanent Court of Arbitration at The Hague.

1907

June 15–Oct. 18, Second Hague Peace Conference, attended by representatives of 44 States, initiated by circular of Oct. 21, 1904 of President Roosevelt proposing calling a second conference addressed to signatories of the Acts of the first conference, but later withdrawn in order to allow the Czar of Russia to call the conference as he had called the first. The program was submitted by the Czar April 12, 1906, and the results of the conference were an amended Convention for the pacific settlement of disputes, Convention for the limitation of the employment of force for the recovery of debts due from the citizens of one country to the citizens of another, Convention relating to the opening of hostilities in war, and 10 further conventions dealing with laws of war on land and at sea, as to rights of neutral powers and persons, status of enemy merchant ships, conversion of merchant ships into warships, placing of submarine automatic mines of contact, prohibiting bombardment of undefended harbors, towns, or buildings by naval forces in times of war, adaptation of the principles of the Geneva Convention of 1906, restrictions on exercise of the right of capture in maritime war, and establishment of an international prize court, and reënactment of Declaration of 1899 as to discharge of projectiles from balloons, &c. A draft Convention recommended the creation of a Judicial Arbitration Court.

1912

Jan. 23, International Opium Convention signed at The Hague by representatives of 12 States provided for control of distribution of raw opium and gradual suppression of prepared opium, and control of manufacture, importation, exportation, and sale of morphine, cocaine, and similar drugs.

HANSE TOWNS

The Hanseatic League (from *hansa*, association), formed by port towns in Germany against the piracies of the Swedes and Danes: began about 1140; the League signed 1241. At first it consisted only of towns situate on the coasts of the Baltic Sea, but in 1370 it was composed of sixty-six cities and forty-four confederates. The League proclaimed war against Waldemar, King of Denmark, about the year 1348, and against Eric in 1428, with forty ships and 12,000 regular troops, besides seamen. On this several princes ordered the merchants of their respective kingdoms to withdraw their effects. The Thirty Years' War in Germany (1618–48) broke up the strength of the association, and in 1630 the only towns retaining the name were Lübeck, Hamburg, and Bremen. The league suffered also by the rise of the commerce of the Low Countries in the 15th century. Their privileges by treaty in England were abolished by Elizabeth in 1578.

HOLLAND. *See* Netherlands.

HUNGARY

Hungary first became an independent kingdom in 1001, became subject to Austria in 1526, and from 1867 to 1918 constituted with Austria the dual monarchy of Austria-Hungary. Charles IV renounced "participation in the conduct of State affairs" Nov. 13, 1918. A Republic was proclaimed Nov. 16, 1918, but after period of revolution the monarchy was reëstablished with Admiral Horthy as Regent, March 1 and 23 (*See infra*). The Hungarian dominions before 1920 had an area of 125,609 square miles, including Croatia and Slavonia, and the census, Dec. 31, 1910, gave population as 20,886,487. By the Treaty of Trianon signed June 4, 1920, the boundaries of the new State with Austria, Czechoslovakia, Yugoslavia, and Rumania were defined in general terms. According to the census of Dec. 31, 1930 the area of Hungary is 35,875 square miles with a population of 8,683,740. Budapest is the capital. For early history *See also* Austria-Hungary.

Nicholas Horthy de Nagybanya, Regent.

996 to 1825

996, Stephen, founder of the monarchy of Hungary, embraces and establishes Christianity and subdues the Slavs, &c., receives the title of the Apostolic King from the Pope
1061, The Poles overrun Hungary
1174, &c., Bela III introduces the Greek civilization
1222, Golden Bull of Andrew II granting personal rights
1241 *et seq.*, Ravages of the Tartars under the sons of Genghis Khan, throughout Hungary, Bohemia, and Russia
1301, Death of Andrew III, end of the Arpad dynasty
1344–82, Victories of Louis the Great in Bulgaria, Serbia, and Dalmatia
1348, He marches into Italy and avenges the murder of his brother, Andrew, King of Naples
1382, Sanguinary anarchy: Elizabeth, Queen of Louis, is drowned: and King Mary, the daughter, marries Sigismond, of Brandenburg; they govern with great severity
[The Hungarians had an aversion to the name of queen; and whenever a female succeeded to the throne, she was termed king]
1393, Sigismond's atrocious cruelties compel his subjects to invite the assistance of the Turks
Sept. 28, 1396, Battle of Nicopolis: Bajazet vanquishes Sigismond and a large army
1410, Sigismond is elected Emperor of Germany
1437, Albert of Austria succeeds to the throne of Hungary
1442–44, Victories of the great John Hunniades (reputed illegitimate son of Sigismond) over the Turks
1444, Who obtain a truce of ten years
Nov. 10, 1444, Broken by Ladislas, King of Hungary (at the Pope's instigation); he is defeated and slain, with the papal legate, at Varna
1444–53, John Hunniades escapes; becomes Regent

1456, Raises siege of Belgrade, July 14; dies Sept. 10
1526, Hungarians insult Turkish ambassadors; war ensues: Solyman II takes Buda
Aug. 29, 1526, Disastrous battle of Mohatz (Louis defeated by Turks and killed)
——, Hungary subject to Austria
June 23, 1606, Peace of Vienna, granting toleration to Protestants
Nov. 12, 1683, John Sobieski defeats the Turks in several battles, and raises the siege of Vienna
Sept. 2, 1686, The Duke of Lorraine retakes Buda
Aug. 19, 1691, Prince Louis of Baden defeats the Turks at Salenckemen
Sept. 11, 1697, Prince Eugene defeats them at Zenta
Jan. 26, 1699, Peace of Carlowitz by which Hungary secured to Austria
1722–23, Pragmatic sanction, authorizing female succession to the throne
1739, Serbia and Wallachia ceded to Turkey at the peace of Belgrade
1741, The Hungarians enthusiastically support Maria-Theresa against France and Bavaria
April 22, 1745, Treaty of peace with Bavaria signed at Fuessen, the Elector of Bavaria renouncing claim to imperial crown
1784, The Protestants permitted to have churches
1790, Independence of Hungary guaranteed
1825, The Diet meets; Hungarian Academy established

1848

Sept. 11, The people, long discontented with the Austrian rule, break out into rebellion
Sept. 28, Murder of the military governor, Count Lamberg, by a mob at Pesth; the Hungarian Diet appoint a provisional government under Kossuth and Louis Batthyany; Hungarians defeat the Ban of Croatia, Sept. 29
Dec. 8, The Diet denounces as traitors all who acknowledge the Emperor of Austria as King of Hungary
Dec. 21, The insurgents defeated by the Austrians at Szaikszo; at Mohr by the Ban Jellachich, Dec. 29

1849

Jan. 5, Buda-Pesth taken by Windischgratz
Jan. 21, Bem defeats the Austrians at Hermannstadt
Feb. 27, The Hungarians defeat the Imperialists before Gran
April 14, Hungary declares itself a free state, Kossuth supreme governor
May 1, March of the Russian army through Gallicia to assist the Austrians
June 20, The Austro-Russian troops defeat the Hungarians at Pered
July 2, 10, Battles of Acs between the Hungarians and Austrians; former retire
July 14, Hungarians defeat Jellachich
July 15, The Hungarians defeated by the Russians; Görgey retreats after three days' battle
July 16, Battle before Komorn, between the insurgents and the Austro-Russian army
July 23, Insurgents under Bem enter Moldavia; defeated by the Russians at Schässberg, July 31
Aug. 10, Utter defeat of the Hungarian army before Temesvar, by General Haynau
Aug. 13, Görgey and his army surrender to the Russians
Aug. 21, Kossuth, Andrassy, Bem, &c., escape to the

Turkish frontiers, and are placed under protection at New Orsova (*see* Turkey)
Sept. 27, Komorn surrenders to the Austrians; close of the war
Oct. 6, Louis Batthyany tried at Pesth, and shot; many other insurgent chiefs put to death at Arad
Oct. 16, Amnesty granted to the Hungarian insurgents, who return home

1850–1859

Dec. 10, 1850, Bem dies at Aleppo
Feb. 23, 1851, Count Julius Andrassy, in exile, sentenced to death, as traitor; announced
1853–5, The country remains in an unsettled state; many executions
Sept. 8, 1853, Crown of St. Stephen and royal insignia discovered and sent to Vienna
July 12, 1856, Amnesty for political offenders of 1848–9
May 4, 1857, The Emperor and Empress visit Buda
Aug.–Oct., 1859, During the Italian war in 1859, an insurrection in Hungary was in contemplation, and communications took place between Louis Napoleon and Kossuth; which circumstances it is said led the Emperor of Austria to accede to the peace of Villafranca so suddenly, and shortly afterwards to promise many reforms and to grant more liberty to the Protestants in Hungary

1860

Oct., Demand for restoration of the old constitution; reunion of the Banat and Voivodina with Hungary, &c.
Oct. 20, Restoration of old constitution promised
Dec. 13, Schmerling appointed Minister
Dec., National conference at Gran

1861

Jan., Demand for the constitution of 1848
Feb. 26, The Emperor promulgates a new liberal constitution for the Empire
March, Which does not satisfy the Hungarians
April 6, Hungarian Diet opened
April 29, Meeting of the Reichsrath at Vienna: no deputies present from Hungary or Croatia
May 8, Count Teleki (*see* Austria, 1860) found dead in his bed at Pesth
July 5, The Diet votes an address to the Emperor, desiring restoration of the old constitution
July, The military begin to levy the taxes
July 21, Imperial rescript refusing the entire independence of Hungary: the Diet protests, Aug. 20; and is dissolved, Aug. 21
Sept.–Oct., The Archbishop of Gran, the primate, indignantly protests against the act of the Imperial Government
Oct. 25, Summoned to Vienna; he stands firm
Dec., The magistrates in the comitat of Pesth resign; military government established; passive resistance of the nobility

1862

Nov. 18, Amnesty declared for political offences, and cessation of prosecutions

1865

June 6–9, The Emperor visits Buda-Pesth; well received; inauguration of a new policy; the rights of Hungary to be restored

Sept. 21, Imperial rescript, abolishing the representative constitution of the Empire, with the view of restoring independence of Hungary, &c.

Nov. 11, The Deak or moderate party demand restoration of the monarchy, with a responsible government

Dec. 14, The Emperor visits Pesth; the Diet opened; Carl Szentivanyi elected president, Dec. 20

1866

Jan. 29, Emperor and Empress arrive at Pesth

June, Hungarian legions join the Prussian army; (after the peace, they were allowed to return to their allegiance), Oct.

Oct., Prolonged political negotiations for autonomy; Deak and national party wearied, threaten to break off

Nov. 19, Hungarian Diet opened by a conciliatory rescript

Dec. 15, Deak's address in reply, demanding the restoration of the constitution, adopted by the Diet with a large majority

1867

Jan., Much opposition to the convocation of the Reichsrath

Feb. 17, Restoration of the constitution of 1848; an independent ministry appointed, headed by Count Julius Andrassy

[Andrassy carries freedom of the press, removal of Jewish disabilities, and promotes railways, &c., 1867 et seq.]

May 25, The Croats protest against incorporation with Hungary

June 8, The Emperor and Empress crowned at Buda with the ancient ceremonies

June 9, Amnesty granted for all political offences

Aug.–Sept., Discussion between the Austrians and Hungarians respecting the division of the liability for the national debt

Sept. 23, A financial convention signed by deputations

Oct., Kossuth's letter to his constituents at Waitzen, censuring Deak and the moderate party

Nov., Deak joined by Klapka and other liberals

——, The "Nazarenes," a sect resembling Quakers, become prominent

Dec. 29, Bills for financial arrangement with Austria, and for Jewish emancipation, received royal assent

1868

Feb. 27, First trial by jury of press offences; (fine and imprisonment inflicted for publishing a letter of Kossuth)

April 14, Kossuth (elected a member of the legislature) resigns by letter

May 27, A Croatian deputation accepts union with Hungary

June, Prince Napoleon Jerome's visit

Dec. 5, Dispute respecting the apportionment of the army settled

Dec. 10, The Diet of 1865 closed with an address from the Emperor

Dec. 14, Congress of Hungarian Jews opened; Joseph Eötvos Minister

1869

Jan., Powerful counter-addresses from Andrassy and Kossuth published

Feb. 9, Royal Hungarian guard organized

1870

June 9, Remains of Louis Batthyany (executed and privately buried, Oct., 1849), re-interred solemnly in the public cemetery, Pesth

July, Count Andrassy promotes the neutrality of Austria in the Franco-German War

1871

Feb. 3, Joseph Eötvos, author, patriot, and Minister, died, deeply lamented, aged 58

Nov. 14, Andrassy succeeds Count von Beust as Foreign Minister at Vienna; Count Lonyay, Hungarian Premier

1872

July, Elections; increased majority of the Deak or constitutional party; Diet opened, Sept. 4

Dec., Resignation of the Count Lonyay Ministry, Dec. 2; Szlavy forms a ministry

1873

June 24, The Fiume railway partly opened

Nov., Buda-Pesth formally constituted the capital

1874

March 20, Ministry resigns; crisis; Bitto forms a cabinet

1875

Feb. 11, Ministry resigns; coalition ministry under Baron von Wenckheim formed, Feb. 26–March 1

July, Elections; greatly in favor of Government

Oct. 20, Koloman Tisza, chief of the Ministry

1876

Jan. 28, Death of the constitutional patriot, Francis Deak

1877

Feb., Ministerial crisis; Tisza resigns; remains in office

End of Sept., Projected raid into Rumania to favor the Turks checked; censured by Klapka

1878

Oct. 4, Resignation of Szell, Finance Minister, Sept. 26; followed by that of the Tisza Ministry

Dec. 5, Tisza Ministry retained modified

1879

March 12, 13, and Dec. 12, Distressing inundation at Szegedin; great loss of life and much property

1883

About March 29, Murder of Lord Chief Justice George von Majlath von Szekhely

June, Joseph Scharf and nine other Jews tried at Nyireghyhaza for alleged murder of a Christian maid, Esther Solymosi (on April 1, 1882)

Aug. 3, Acquitted

Aug. 29–30, Violent anti-Jewish riots Pesth, Zala, Egersseg, &c., July, Aug.; martial law proclaimed

Oct. 6, Three men convicted of the murder of the Chief Justice

1884–1889

About March 13, 1884, Thirty-six Socialists arrested at Pesth; many expelled

About June 13, Liberal majority in the elections

Sept. 30, 1886, M. Tisza declares for maintenance of the Treaty of Berlin and Bulgarian independence

March 5, 1887, Increased army estimates voted

Feb., 1889, Great opposition to M. Tisza's army bill; demonstration in Buda-Pesth

1890

Feb. 18, Count Julius Andrassy dies in Istria

March 7, M. Tisza, the Premier, an earnest liberal, resigns, through opposition of his colleagues; succeeded by Count Julius Szapáry, March 13

Oct. 6, Unveiling at Arad of the national monument of the 13 generals executed Oct. 6, 1849

1891

Jan. 23, Death of Cardinal John Simor, Archbishop of Gran, primate of Hungary, who crowned the King and Queen in 1867; succeeded by Arch-Abbot Claude Vaszara, Nov. 1

1892

May 14, Currency reform bills (gold to be the basis) introduced into the Diet

About May 17, Death of General Klapka, the hero of Komorn [buried at Buda-Pesth]

Oct. 19, The currency reform bill passed, July 19; first new gold coin presented to the Emperor

Nov. 16, Resignation of Count Szapary, Nov. 9; a new cabinet formed by Dr. Wekerle

Dec. 15–March 5, 1893, Conference of the bishops, supported by the Pope, opposing obligatory civil marriages, &c., as proposed by the government

1893

March 1, Riot at Szoboszlo, near Debreczin, against market tolls; suppressed with bloodshed

March, The Ultramontane minority in the Chamber active in opposition; the Government policy supported by the municipalities

March–April, Coolness between the Government and the Vatican in relation to Italy

April 10, Attempt on the life of Cardinal Vaszary, the primate, by a former servant; the defending secretary seriously wounded

Aug. 31, The author and publisher of the pamphlet "Replica," for attacking the Government, fined and imprisoned

Oct. 7, A Pan-Rumanian agitation for a formation of a Rumanian state denounced by the Hungarian Minister

Nov. 26, A royal ordinance, superseding the Austrian court functionaries by Hungarians at Buda-Pesth, issued

1894

March 20, Louis Kossuth, born Sept. 16, 1802, in Monok, co. Zemplin; died at Turin

May 7, Trial of the Pan-Rumanian party (20 members) for illegality; sentenced to terms of imprisonment, varying from 8 months to 5 years, May 25

May 10, The civil marriage bill rejected by the Magnates

June 10, Resignation of the Wekerle Ministry, about June 1; re-constructed

June 21, The civil marriage bill passed by the Magnates

Oct. 29, The Magnates and lower house pass 3 bills granting freedom of religious worship, and recognizing the Jewish religion; Royal assent, Dec. 10

Nov. 26, M. Francis Kossuth takes the oath of allegiance to the King

Dec. 21, Resignation of Dr. Wekerle's (liberal) Ministry

1895

Jan. 16, Ministry formed by Baron Banffy; gazetted

Jan., The Ultramontane party styled the "people's party," issue a program demanding reforms, preservation of the Roman Catholic faith, free education, &c.

March, General opposition and rejection of the clause for the reception of the Jewish faith in the freedom of worship bill due to the papal allocution; operation of the law delayed, April; the house again sends the bill unchanged to the Magnates, April 28; the mutilated bill returned to the lower house May 15

May, A protest respecting the conduct of the papal nuncio, Manager Agliardi, prepared by Baron Banffy for transmission to Rome is delayed by Count Kalnoky, May 3; the two Ministers agree to the transmission of the remonstrance to the Vatican, May 5; resignation of Count Kalnoky, May 16; differences with the Vatican amicably settled

1896

April 21, Special act of parliament in commemoration of the foundation of the monarchy, passed

June 8, The Hungarian parliament occupies its new house, speech by the Emperor-King

Oct. 28, Elections; great liberal majority, Oct. 30

1897

Jan. 6, Stephen von Papay, eminent statesman, court councillor, born 1827, died

Jan. 21, Conflict between the police and miners at Temesvar, 9 persons killed; mines held by the troops; reported

May 23, Election riots, at Bosnyaizi, 14 persons killed by the troops; reported

July 30, Long conflict in the Diet respecting the jury bill; ended by compromise

Sept. 9, M. Francis Pulszky, eminent patriot and scholar, friend of Kossuth, died, aged 83

1898

Jan. 8, Bill for the provisional extension of the Ausgleich (customs and commercial treaty) with Austria, introduced by the Diet, Oct. 21; great speech of Count Albert Apponyi in favor of the bill, Dec. 17; passed by the lower house, Jan. 4, 1898; passed by the Diet

Feb., Discontent at recent special legislation ignoring the just claims of the peasantry

Feb. 13, Agrarian socialist rioting, in the Szabolcs district; 2 deaths; again 4 deaths, March 31

April 11, Loyal address to the Emperor King on the 50th anniversary of the constitution of 1848

Sept. 30, Plot against the Emperor, 3 men sentenced to various terms of imprisonment at Buda-Pesth; and 32 socialists likewise, Nov. 4

Nov., Increasing revolt, mainly agrarian, against clerical interference in secular affairs

Nov. 21, 23, Stormy scenes in parliament respecting the removal of the Hentzi monument, some arrests

Dec. 10, Organized obstruction in the Chamber; parliament prorogued; see Austria, Dec. 31, 1898 et seq.

1899

Jan., Great tumult in the Chamber of Deputies, Dec. 30 1898; prolonged crisis

Jan. 3, Duel between Baron Banffy and M. Horansky, leader of the national party, neither hurt

Feb. 24, Banffy cabinet resigns; M. Koloman Szell forms a coalition ministry; Ausgleich prolonged provisionally, March 10; conference of Premiers respecting it at Buda-Pesth successful, due to the Emperor, May 9; bills embodying the Ausgleich compromise passed by the Reichsrath, June 14; Reichsrath prorogued, July 12

1901

July 31, M. Szilagyi, eminent statesman, died

1902

Jan. 19, Agrarian riot at Also-Idecs, 10 deaths, many wounded, reported

March 23, M. Koloman Tisza, eminent statesman, born Dec. 10, 1830, died

Nov. 3, Count Apponyi, Pres. of the Reichstag, issues a manifesto against the nationality agitation

Dec. 31 The Ausgleich renewed on revised terms

1903

Feb. 17, Parliament opened, Jan. 9; army bills opposed

April, May, Demonstration against the bills, Buda-Pesth, March 7; deadlock continues

May 12, Popular excitement among peasants in Croatia; demand for financial separation for Hungary; Count Hedervary, the Banus of Croatia, restores order with troops

May 20, Violent disturbances between soldiers and peasantry in Agram; incidents provocative of discord between Austria and Italy occur at Innsbruck and Trieste

May 31–June 1, Renewed disturbances at Agram

June 16, Resignation of the Szell Ministry

June 26, Violent earthquake at Erlau, causes much damage

June 28, Count Stephen Tisza failing to construct a cabinet, Count Khuen Hedervary forms a new ministry, with himself as Premier and Minister of the Interior

Mid July, Count Pejacsevich appointed Banus of Croatia in succession to Count Hedervary

July 14, Continued disorder in Croatia, 2 dynamite explosions in Agram, reported

About July 30, Strained relations between Hungary and Austria on the subject of the sugar allotment system

Aug. 10, Resignation of Count Hedervary and cabinet

Aug. 18, Croatian riots at Zapresic in connection with the celebration of the Emperor's 73rd birthday, 3 persons killed and many wounded by gendarmes

Sept. 16, Count Hedervary formally reinstated as Premier; an order of the day, issued by the Emperor, declaring that he will hold fast to the existing common and military organization of the army, and never relinquish his rights and privileges as its head; hostile attitude of the Hungarian and the Magyar press; manifesto of conciliation to the Hungarian nation issued by the Emperor and countersigned by Count Hedervary; it is favorably received by the liberal party

Oct. 26, Resignation of Count Hedervary, Sept. 30; new cabinet formed by Count Stephen Tisza

Nov. 5, Count Tisza's program formally received by the Chamber; his speech on the Hungarian constitutional rights much commended, Nov. 18

Nov. 22, Baron Banffy, ex-Premier, appears as the leader of a new nationalist party

Nov. 26, Count Albert Apponyi and others withdraw from the liberals; continued obstruction in the Chamber, Nov. 28–Dec. 1

Dec. 4, Crisis ends; M. Kossuth and other members of the independent party oppose further obstruction; declarations exchanged by M. Kossuth and Count Tisza

1904

March 2, Government introduces bills to sanction negotiations for new commercial treaties with Germany and Italy; to found numerous Hungarian scholarships in military educational institutes, and for the organization of a royal marshal's court for Hungary

March 11, Recruits bill for 1903 passes the house

March 18, Bill of indemnity for period May–Dec., 1903, during which the Government was carried on without supply; and vote on account for 6 months of 1904, passed

March 21, Recruits bill for 1904 carried

April 18, Royal rescript instructs the Hungarian Premier to see that the remains of the "traitor" Francis Rakoczy the Second are to be brought back from Constantinople in a manner worthy of so illustrious a figure in Hungarian history

April 20, Great strike of 70,000 employees on the state railways for higher wages; Hungary isolated from railway communication with the rest of Europe

May 14, Austro-Hungarian Government presents to the delegations assembled at Budapest to consider the common estimates for 1905 an extraordinary estimate of 88,000,000 kronen (3,666,000*l.*) for the army and 75,176,000 kronen (3,112,500*l.*) for the navy

June 8, Hungarian delegation adopt the estimates of the War Minister

June 12, Count Albert Apponyi, in a speech at Jász Berény, sets forth a program for a resuscitated Hungarian national party

July 24, Increase of 2,000,000 kronen for the Hungarian civil list voted by parliament

Sept. 1, Minister for War for the dual monarchy issues a decree ordering the extension of the use of the Hungarian language in the army

Nov. 12, Premier states that new army bills would be framed on the basis of the two-years' service system, the Hungarian honved to be supplied with the artillery formations desired by the nation

Nov. 18, Count Tisza's guillotine motion creating new provisional orders carried by a large majority, amid scenes of violent opposition; royal decree closing the session produced by the Premier

Dec. 15, Opposition leaders protest against the new rules of procedure; violent disorder, sitting suspended

Parliament adjourned by royal rescript until Dec. 28

1905

Jan. 3, Disorderly scenes in the Hungarian Chamber on dissolution of Parliament by advice to the crown of Count Tisza

Jan. 4, Hungarian Diet closed with speech from the throne by Emperor-King; Count Albert Apponyi formally joins the independence party

Mid Jan., Electoral campaign assumes a violent character, many liberal candidates stoned and beaten, some dangerously wounded. Aggressors belong chiefly to the adherents of the clerical party, worked up to hostility by the inferior clergy against the supporters of the Premier

Jan. 16, Count Tisza, Premier, strongly condemns the "nationalist" movement, initiated by certain Rumanian politicians

End Jan., Defeat of Hungarian liberal party; results of elections for 403 out of 413 constituencies, show: independence or Kossuth party, 163; liberal or government party, 152; Andrassy dissentients, 23; clerical people's party, 23; Banffy or new party, 11; unattached, 10; nationality representatives including 5 Rumanians, 8; second ballots and new elections, 13

Feb. 1, Count Tisza tenders to King the resignation of himself and cabinet

Feb. 11, M. Francis Kossuth, leader of the Hungarian independence party, received by the Emperor-King in the Hofburg at Vienna, and has an audience with his Majesty on Hungarian affairs

——, Count Julius Andrassy being unable to form a Hungarian ministry, Dr. Wekerle is summoned to Vienna

Feb. 21, M. Julius Justh, a leader of the independence party, elected President of the Hungarian Chamber by 230 votes to 168

Feb. 22, Chamber adjourns until March 8, pending the formation of a new cabinet

Mid March, Hungarian crisis assumes a very formidable aspect; Emperor-King at Buda-Pesth firmly declining to make the concessions Count Julius Andrassy considers indispensable, the latter renounces the task of forming a ministry; the coalition majority adhere obstinately to all their demands; crown declines to entertain the demand for the Magyar language of command into the Hungarian part of the army, and insists that the new cabinet shall stand on the basis of the 1867 dualism

March 28, Political crisis continues; M. Kossuth and other independent deputies invited to a court banquet at the royal palace at Buda

March 29, Fresh negotiations under the auspices of M. de Szögyeny-Marich for an Andrassy ministry reported

April 3, Count Julius Andrassy receives a mandate from the King to confer with the coalition leaders on the basis of the Szögyeny-Marich compromise; Emperor-King returns to Vienna after 16 days' fruitless effort to solve the Hungarian crisis, April 5

April 7, Hungarian Chamber, by a majority of 102 votes, annuls the Lex Daniel or Tisza "guillotine" law

April 8, Death of Dr. Strossmayer, Bp. of Diakovar, Croatia, aged 90, life-long champion of the cause of the southern Slavs. Bp. Strossmayer built the magnificent cathedral at Diakovar, and practically created the modern educational system of Croatia, Slavonia, and Dalmatia, including the university of Agram and Academy of Sciences

April 13, Address to the crown laid before Hungarian Chamber, containing *inter alia* the wish for the appointment of a responsible government able and entitled to claim the support of the majority of the Chamber; parliamentary and electoral reform; fiscal and social reform; effective establishment of economic independence for Hungary with an independent customs territory and an independent system of credit; clear expression of the national character of the Hungarian army in its language and emblems; resolution of censure on the Tisza cabinet carried by large majority; April 15, Chamber adjourns until May 3

May 8, Count Tisza, acting Hungarian Premier, leaves Vienna after a fruitless attempt to persuade the crown to relieve him and his colleagues of their duties

May 24, Count Julius Andrassy, representing the coalition leaders, visits the Emperor and sets forth the Hungarian program; Emperor intimates that no further military concessions are possible; Count Andrassy proceeds to Budapest to announce the failure of his negotiations to the coalition leaders

June 12, Baron Fejervary appointed Prime Minister and Minister of Finance; M. Kristoffy, Minister of the Interior

June 17, Count Tisza and members of the outgoing cabinet received in farewell audience by the King; Baron Fejervary presents the members of his new cabinet

June 21, Lower house and House of Magnates pass votes of no confidence in the new Ministry; lower house passes a resolution pledging the country not to pay its share to the common expenditure of the dual monarchy, and calling upon counties and communes to refuse to collect taxes or to raise recruits. Royal letter read proroguing the house until Sept. 15

June 23, Baron Fejervary tenders his resignation to the King, who refuses to accept it

July 1, Hungarian coalition leaders convened by Baron Fejervary to explain the standpoint of the crown. M. Kossuth states that they will not negotiate with an unconstitutional government. Baron Fejervary declares that the crown is willing to accept the greater part of the coalition program, but as regards the Magyar language of command the King could not meet its requirements

Aug. 22, Conference held at Ischl by Ministers of Austria and Hungary, under the presidency of the Emperor-King, to consider the situation arising out of the Hungarian political crisis.

Sept. 15, Lower house reassembles; Baron Fejervary, Premier, announces that his Ministry having been unable to fulfill its mission, he was authorized by the King to say that he wished to form a ministry from among the majority on the basis of an acceptable program

Sept. 23, Emperor-King at Vienna receives the leaders of the coalition majority in the Hungarian Diet and invites them to submit proposals for the formation of a cabinet on condition that the military questions were excluded from the program. Coalition leaders, at the sovereign's request, visit Count Goluchowski, but inform him that they could not accept the proposals of the crown, and would only conduct further negotiations with a Hungarian

Sept. 24, Count Czirsky appointed by the Emperor-King to meet the coalition leaders, who have an interview with him, and return to Budapest

Oct. 1, Serious street fighting at Brünn between Czecks and Germans, 200 persons injured, some seriously

Oct. 4, Resolution, passed at a conference of the Hungarian coalition parties at Budapest, approving of the action of the coalition leaders in their interview with the Emperor-King on Sept. 23; a manifesto to the nation adopted

1906

Jan. 16, Fatal encounter between the *gendarmerie* and an excited crowd in connection with the election of a local magistrate at Bilke, in Ogocsa county; populace, displeased with the election, attempt to demolish the town hall; *gendarmerie* fire, killing 6 persons; crowd replies with firearms and kill 2 gendarmes

Jan. 24, Hungarian frontier closed to Serbian live stock and meat

Jan. 26, Interview between the King and Count Andrassy, after a year of fruitless negotiations; the Count advocates the claims of the victorious coalition, and seeks a compromise between its desires and the constitutionally guaranteed standpoint of the crown; executive committee of the coalition sit with closed doors to consider the King's message, Jan. 29–30; committee ratify a long and detailed reply to the King, Jan. 31

Feb. 2, Count Andrassy hands the reply of the coalition to the King, who defers his decision; negotiations announced to have broken down, the King being unable to agree to the conditions specified by the coalition leaders

Feb. 19, Diet dissolved; parliament building occupied by troops and police; Chamber decide unanimously to return unopened to the royal commissioner the royal letter dissolving parliament; members disperse; decree read to empty benches by a military officer

Feb. 24, Government takes repressive measures against the coalition party; M. de Rudnay, late chief of the Budapest police, appointed royal commissioner for the county of Pest and Budapest city

Feb. 27, Coalition leaders issue a manifesto in which they call upon all Hungarians to offer determined opposition to the illegal acts of the Government

March 1, Government makes a sharp reply to the coalition and to Count Andrassy's letter to his constituents

March 4, Baron Banffy, the ex-Premier, secedes from the coalition; M. de Rudnay suspends the autonomy of Pest county

March 14, Baron Fejervary reconstructs his cabinet

March 16, Official ordinance dissolving the executive committee of the coalition issued at Budapest

April 8, The King, having accepted a basis for settlement agreed upon by Baron Fejervary and the coalition leaders, the latter accept office with Dr. Wekerle as Premier; Ministers, in their first council, decide to recommend the crown to convoke parliament for May 19, and to hold the elections from April 28 to May 8; royal approval

April 18, Hungarian liberal party decide to dissolve; Count Stephen Tisza retires, reported

April 24, Death of Count Alexander of Karolyi of Fóth

May 8, Elections result in the return of 210 members of the independence party, 62 constitutional party, 24 clericals, 12 Rumanes, 8 Slovaks, 4 Serbs

May 20, Arrival of the Emperor-King in Budapest; a statue of King Stephen unveiled by him, May 21; parliament opened by the Emperor-King in the royal palace, May 22

Aug. 21, General von Krieghammer, formerly Austro-Hungarian Minister of War, died

Sept. 2, Collision between the military and the strikers from the coal mines, 175 of the latter being injured, occurred at Petroszeny

Sept. 9, Conference of Baron von Beck, the Austrian Premier, with Dr. Wekerle, the Hungarian Premier, regarding the revision of the Ausgleich with Hungary

Oct. 29, Remains of the Hungarian patriot Rakoczy finally laid to rest at Kassa amid great pomp and enthusiasm

Nov. 16, Trial of a Slovak deputy named Juriga for "incitement against the Magyar nation"; a Slovak disturbance followed

Nov. 25, The Austro-Hungarian delegates open their sittings at Budapest; the members received at the palace in the morning by the Emperor, who briefly addressed them

1907

Jan. 30, M. Polonyi, Minister of Justice, sends in his resignation to the Premier and institutes a libel suit against M. Zoltan Lengyel

Feb. 1, M. Günther, Secretary of State, appointed Minister of Justice

Oct. 8, New customs treaty with Austria signed

Oct. 27, Disturbance in a Slovak town owing to the persecution of a Slovak priest by the Hungarian authorities; the gendarmes fire on the crowd, killing 11 persons on the spot and wounding 16, of whom 5 afterwards died

1909

Sept. 25, Resignation of Dr. Wekerle

Dec. 23, Dr. de Lukacs succeeds Dr. Wekerle as Premier

1910

Jan. 4, Dr. de Lukacs formally appointed Prime Minister

Jan. 11, Dr. de Lukacs resigned as Prime Minister. Count Khuen-Hedervary appointed in his stead by Emperor Francis Joseph, de Lukacs becoming Finance Minister

Feb. 14, Count Julius Andrassy, leader of the Constitutional Party, dissolved the Party, and declared he would not oppose the Government

Feb. 15, 24 members of the Constitutional Party declared support of the Government

——, The "National Party of Work" founded as successor of the Liberal Party established in 1875 by Coloman Tisza

March 21, Scene in the Chamber provoked by the Opposition; the Premier and the Minister of Agriculture wounded by books and inkpots thrown

March 22, Parliament dissolved before its time by Count Khuen-Hedervary

May 2, Hungarian Peasants League meeting at Bonyhad passed resolution of support to any political movement aiming at securing universal, equal, and secret suffrage

May 23, Death of Baron Desiderius Banffy, former Premier (67)

June, Elections a victory for the Government which gained 255 of 413 seats

July 17, The Ban of Croatia, Baron Rauch, resigned. Dr. Tomacic succeeded

Nov., New Civil Code adopted

1911

Jan. 10, Scheme for reorganization of military and naval forces published in Buda Pesth

Jan. 13, Loan floated in Germany

July 14/27, Treaty of commerce with Serbia signed

Aug. 12–16, Pan-Slav gymnastic festival at Agram attended by 5,000 persons

Sept. 1, German language as subject of instruction became compulsory in teachers' training colleges

Nov. 3, Resignation of Albert von Berzeviczy, president of the House of Deputies, because of obstructive tactics allowed by his interpretation of rules, and Navay, vice-president, elected in his place

Nov. 7, Croatian Diet dissolved, and the elections following a defeat for the Government

Nov. 8, The Opposition declared itself ready to drop technical obstruction to the Defense Bill

1912

Jan. 22, Count Apponyi announced that the Kossuth Party would join the Government Party on conditions stated: settlement of question of flags and military emblems, German language regulations to be expunged from the military penal code, an interpretation of the law of 1888, Article 18, as calling up reserves, and certain changes in the Defense Bill

Feb. 26–27, Anti-Hungarian demonstrations in Agram, capital of Croatia

March 7, Resignation of Count Khuen-Hedervary, Premier. Not accepted

April 3, Croatian Constitution suspended and Eduard von Cuvay appointed Dictator

April 16, Count Khuen-Hedervary not having a majority to enable him to carry the Defense Bill resigned with his Cabinet

April 21, Ladislaus von Lukacs, Finance Minister, became Prime Minister

May 22, Count Tisza elected president of the Chamber

May 23, Suffrage riots at Budapest. Socialists proclaimed 4 days strike in support of manhood suffrage

June 1, Kossuth demanded increase of electorate and secret ballot

June 4, Count Tisza ordered the police to remove 60 members of the Chamber for violence in obstructing legislation and passed the Defense Bill through third reading

June 7, Opposition Deputy Julius Kovacs suspended from the House for breaches of order entered and shot at Count Tisza without wounding him and then shot himself

Oct. 30, Opposition deputies prevented from entering the Chamber by troops

Dec. 15, Death of Count Albin Czaky

Dec. 17, Death of General Görgey

1913

Jan. 28, Contingent of recruits raised by 31,300 men of whom 13,676 to be drawn from Hungary

Feb. 3, Bomb explosion in the episcopal palace of Debreczen aimed at life of Greek-Uniat Bishop Miklossy who had decided in favor of use of Magyar in the liturgy instead of Rumanian

March 8, Franchise Reform Bill adopted by Chamber doubled number of electors but by differentiation in age and property qualifications kept the exercise of the suffrage in hands of the favored classes

June 5, Lukacs Ministry overthrown

June 8, Count Tisza appointed Prime Minister

Nov. 27, Dictatorship of Croatia ended and Baron Ivan Skerlecz appointed Ban

1914

May 25, Death of Francis Kossuth, leader of the Independent Party (72)

June 28, Assassination of the Archduke Francis Ferdinand, heir presumptive to the throne. *See* Austria-Hungary

July 28, War declared on Serbia by Austria-Hungary. *See* World War and Austria-Hungary

Nov. 7, Decree authorized the wearing of the colors and emblems of the different nationalities

Nov., First war loan, 6% stock not redeemable until Nov. 1, 1920, issued at 97.5

1915

April 19, Bill passed extending the term of Parliament for another year

May, Second war loan, 6% stock not redeemable until 1921 or 5.5 redeemable 1925

Oct., Flag and coat of arms altered settlement of Hungarian grievances

Oct., Third war loan, 6% rente not redeemable before May 1, 1921

1916

Nov. 21, Death of Francis Joseph, King of Hungary, Emperor of Austria

Dec. 5, Death of Dr. Hans Richter, musical conductor

Dec. 30, Charles I, Emperor of Austria, crowned King of Hungary as Charles IV at Budapest

1917

March 23, Parliament passed Bill conferring extraordinary powers on the Government for the duration of the War

April 25, Democratic Electoral Bloc founded by the Socialists (Karolyi) and Radicals (Jaszi)

May 23, Count Tisza resigned as Prime Minister in opposition to extension of suffrage

June 15, Count Maurice Esterhazy appointed Prime Minister

July 20, Declaration of Corfu between Pasic and Trumbic by which Serb-Croat-Slovene State created

Aug. 20, Alexander Wekerle appointed Prime Minister succeeding Esterhazy resigning because of ill health

Nov. 18, Treaty with Austria prolonged Ausgleich of 1907 due to expire on Dec. 31

1918

Jan. 18–21, Serious strikes in Buda Pest

April 17, Wekerle Ministry resigned

April 24, Count Serenyi failed to form Cabinet

May 10, Dr. Wekerle formed new Cabinet

June 22, Anti-ministerial and anti-dynastic riots at Budapest

July 18, Diet rejected woman suffrage measure

Oct. 1, Czecho-Slovak and Yugo-Slav deputies in the Reichsrat declared their right to decide their own future allegiance

Oct. 10, Yugo-Slav National Council met at Zagreb

Oct. 11, Manifesto of Emperor Charles declared Croatia, Slavonia, Bosnia and Herzegovina united into one Federal State

——, Resignation of Prime Minister Wekerle

Oct. 16, Manifesto of the Emperor declared Austria a Federal State. *See* Austria

Oct. 17, Parliament adopted resolution declaring Hungary entirely independent of Austria except for the personal factor of the Crown

Oct. 25, Independence Party formed National Council under leadership of Karolyi

Oct. 29, Croatia proclaimed independence at Agram

——, Captain John Hadik appointed Prime Minister

Oct. 31, Revolution begun at Budapest. Soldiers Councils which had been formed seized Government buildings. Hadik resigned as Prime Minister and Count Michael Karolyi appointed

——, Count Stephen Tisza assassinated by revolutionists

Nov. 1, Karolyi Government ordered soldiers on all fronts to lay down their arms

Nov. 3, Armistice signed with Italy. *See* World War

Nov. 13, Karolyi and Jaszi signed separate armistice at Belgrade for Hungary

——, Rescript of King Charles announced withdrawal from public affairs in Hungary and willingness to accept form of Government adopted

Nov. 16, The National Council proclaimed Hungary a Republic with Karolyi at head pending meeting of constituent assembly

Nov. 19, Bela Kun arrived from Russia on a forged passport

Nov. 23, Electoral law adopted

Nov. 24, New Communist Party founded by Bela Kun and other returned prisoners of war from Russia

1919

Jan. 11, Karolyi elected President of the Republic by the National Council. He appointed Dionys Berinkey Prime Minister

Feb. 20, Communists led by Bela Kun attacked buildings of Socialist newspaper killing 7 police and wounding 80

Feb. 26, Division of the large landed estates among the people begun

March 21, Karolyi resigned as President turning the Government over to the Soviet Government of the Communists, Alexander Garbai, President, and Bela Kun, People's Commissary of Foreign Affairs

——, Peace Conference notified Hungary of delimitation of neutral zone between Hungary and Rumania

March 28, Declaration of war on Serbia

April 2, Electoral decree provided for local elections and establishment of workers, soldiers, and peasants councils

April 2–6, General Smuts in Budapest sent by Paris Conference to negotiate a new armistice unsuccessful

April 10, Rumanian troops took offensive against Soviet Hungary defeated the Red army and occupied line of the Theiss

April 22, Hungary declared a defensive war against Rumania

May 2, Provisional Anti-Soviet Government established by Count Julius Karolyi, half-brother of Michael, at Szeged and began counter-revolution

June 8, Allied ultimatum threatened to use extreme measures if Hungary did not refrain from further attacks on the Czechs. Bela Kun accepted and withdrew troops from Kaschau

June 13, The Government accepted decision of Supreme Council of proposed cession of territory in northern Hungary to the States of Rumania, Yugo-Slavia, and Czecho-Slovakia

June 24, Constitution adopted by National Congress of Soviets

July 1, Hungarian troops evacuated Czecho-Slovakia

July 20, Decision of Supreme Council to cede Burgenland (German West Hungary) to Austria

——, Bela Kun's Soviet troops sent against Rumanians

Aug. 1, Soviet Government threatened by advance of Rumanian troops resigned and Bela Kun fled to Vienna

Aug. 2, Social Democrats formed Cabinet headed by Julius Peidl

Aug. 4, Rumanian troops entered Budapest

Aug. 6, Police and officers of the old régime forced resignation of the Peidl Government. The Archduke Joseph took control with the title of State Governor

Aug. 15, Lovaszy formed Cabinet but was defeated

Aug. 20, Stephen Friedrich formed Cabinet

Aug. 22, Note of Supreme Council refused recognition of Habsburg Government of Archduke Joseph

Aug. 23, Archduke Joseph resigned on ultimatum from Allies

Nov. 3, Allied ultimatum to Rumania demanded evacuation of Hungary

Nov. 14, Rumanian troops left Budapest

Nov. 16, Admiral Horthy, appointed commander-in-chief by the Szeged Government, entered Budapest

Nov. 18, The Friedrich Government resigned

Nov. 23, Karl Huszar succeeded as Prime Minister, Friedrich remaining in the Cabinet as War Minister

Dec. 1, Huszar Government recognized by the Supreme Council

1920

Jan. 6, Death of Heinrich Lammasch, international jurist, and former Premier

Jan. 7, Hungarian Delegation headed by Count Apponyi arrived at Paris to receive peace terms

Jan. 15, Draft Treaty of Peace handed to delegation in Paris

Jan. 25, General election for delegates for National Assembly a victory for parties of the Right

Jan. 28, Commercial Agreement with Austria signed

Feb. 2, Formal declaration of Allies that no member of the Habsburg family would be permitted to reign in Hungary

Feb. 10, Hungarian reply to Draft Peace Treaty presented with counter-proposals

——, Election to decide contests disputed gave 68 seats to National Christian Union, 71 to Nationalist Party representing the Clericals and Agrarians and small land owners

Feb. 16, First meeting of constituent National Assembly

Feb. 25, The Rumanians evacuated Hungary after stripping the country of grain, fodder, cattle, railroad stock, motors, machinery, &c.

March 1, Admiral Horthy elected head of the State with title of Regent by National Assembly

March 10, Dr. Alexander Simonyi-Semadan succeeded Huszar Government resigned as Prime Minister, Count Paul Teleki, Foreign Affairs; Baron F. Koranyi, Finance

March 23, Admiral Horthy proclaimed Hungary a monarchy declaring the throne vacant and assumed title of Administrator of the Realm (Reichsverweser)

May 6, Allied reply to Hungarian counter-proposals as to Peace settlement

May 21, Convention signed with Russia for reciprocal repatriation of prisoners

June 1, Provisional commercial Agreement with Germany signed

June 4, Treaty of Trianon signed with Allied and Associated Powers: Transylvania ceded to Rumania and a strip in the West, the Slovak provinces to Czecho-Slovakia, the Banat to be divided between Yugo-Slavia and Rumania. Like Austria Hungary is precluded from alienating her independence except with consent of the League of Nations, army not to exceed 35,000, armaments reduced, reparations provided for, and Hungary to assume proportional amount of Austro-Hungarian national debt

June 10, Simonyi-Semadan Ministry resigned

June 20, International Federation of Trades Unions at Amsterdam declared a boycott of Hungary because of "White terror" at instance of Austrian Socialists, which was ineffective

July 20, Count Paul Teleki appointed Prime Minister

Aug. 6, Law defined powers of the Administrator of the Realm

Nov. 6 and 26, Financial and legal Agreements with Germany signed

Nov. 12, Land law enacted provided for distribution of land to be purchased from the owners of large estates by the State

Nov. 13, Peace Treaty of Trianon ratified by Parliament

Dec. 2, Contract signed with the d'Arcy Exploration Company (British) for exploitation of Hungarian oil wells

Dec. 3, Teleki Ministry resigned but recalled, reconstructed Cabinet

Dec. 14, Hegedüs, Liberal, appointed Chancellor of the Exchequer

Dec. 19, Further Commercial Agreement with Austria signed

Dec. 25, Decree of amnesty to political prisoners

Dec. 31, Population 7,980,143

1921

March 26, King Charles returned to Hungary calling on Regent to hand over power to him

April 2, National Assembly adopted resolution against restoration of King Charles

April 3, Conference of Ambassadors reaffirmed decision against restoration of Habsburgs

April 4, King Charles left Hungary returning to Switzerland

April 5, Law for defense of the social order passed

April 10, Fall of Teleki Ministry

April 14, Count Stephen Bethlen appointed Prime Minister

July 26, Treaty of Trianon came into effect

July 28, Convention with Russia signed as to exchange of prisoners of war and interned persons

Aug. 6, Inter-Allied Commission met at Oedenburg to supervise transfer of Burgenland (West Hungary) to Austria under Treaty of Trianon

Aug. 14, Baranya district proclaimed itself a Serb-Magyar Republic

Aug. 20, Province of Baranya evacuated by Yugo-Slavs at behest of Conference of Ambassadors and taken over by Hungarians as provided for in Treaty of Trianon

Aug. 25, Commercial Agreement with Czechoslovakia signed

Aug. 26, Death of Alexander Wekerle, former Premier (73)

Aug. 28, Austrian troops occupying the Burgenland under Treaty driven out by Hungarians

Aug. 29, Peace Treaty with the United States signed

Aug. 30, Minorities of the Trianon Treaty of June 4, 1920, placed under guarantee of the League of Nations

Sept. 1, Anglo-Hungarian Mixed Arbitral Tribunal established in London

Sept. 3, Commercial Agreement with Bulgaria concluded

Sept. 22, Conference of Ambassadors demanded evacuation of Burgenland by Hungarian troops

Oct. 13, Protocol signed at Venice by Hungary, Austria, and Italy provided for settlement of Burgenland dispute and plebiscite for Oedenburg district

Oct. 21, King Charles and Queen Zita landed by airplane at Oedenburg

Oct. 23, Forces of King Charles defeated by Government troops near Torbagy and Charles and Zita taken prisoners

Oct. 24, Ultimatum of Conference of Ambassadors demanded surrender of Charles

Nov. 1, Charles removed to British gunboat on the Danube

Nov. 4, Dethronement Act passed abrogated sovereign rights of Charles IV and invalidated succession of Habsburg dynasty

Dec. 3, Charles IV and Queen Zita left Hungary and were interned at Madeira

Dec. 12, Treaty of Peace with the United States ratified by National Assembly

Dec. 14–17, Plebiscite held in Oedenburg (Sopron) district declared in favor of Hungary

Dec. 21, Decision of Conference of Ambassadors allowed Hungary to retain Oedenburg (Sopron)

1922

Jan. 1, Oedenburg (Sopron) formally transferred to Hungary by Inter-Allied Commission

Jan. 23, Death of Arthur Nikisch, musical conductor, in Leipzig

Jan. 31, Law enacted reorganized army in accordance with terms of the Treaty of Trianon

Feb. 8, Provisional Commercial Treaty with Austria signed

March 1, 3% tax on business transactions imposed

April 1, Death of ex-King Charles in exile on Island of Madeira of pneumonia

April 21, Extradition Convention of Dec. 3, 1873 with Great Britain revived

May 8, Note of Reparation Commission called attention to default in deliveries of cattle

May 28 and June 2, Elections gave a Government majority

June 17, Bethlen Ministry reconstituted

June 27, Commercial Agreement with Austria signed

July 13, Schneider and Creusot (French company) began construction of port at Csepel

July 21, Leader of organization "Awakening Hungarians," Hejjas, arrested

July 27, New taxes imposed a burden on town populations

Aug. 2, Central Office of Foreign Exchange established with monopoly of buying and selling foreign money in effort to stabilize the krone

Sept. 18, Hungary admitted to membership of the League of Nations

Sept. 22, Treaty of commerce and navigation with Latvia signed

Oct. 3, Royalists met and declared Prince Otto the King of Hungary

Oct. 19, Treaty of commerce and navigation with Estonia

Oct. 20, Death of Baron Stephen Burian (71)

Dec. 19, Geza Darivary succeeded Count Banffy as Minister of Foreign Affairs

1923

Jan. 6, Visit of Chancellor Seipel (Austria) to Budapest

Jan. 10, Frontier clash at Lokoshaza with Rumanians

Jan. 16, Metropolitan Theater at Budapest blown up by members of the "Awakening Hungarians"

Jan. 22, Death of Dr. Max Simon Nordau, author

Feb. 21, Property of Count Michael Karolyi confiscated

April 10, Arbitration Treaty with Austria signed

April 20, Frontier incident at Him-Pereny, Czech soldiers killed

April 22, Government requested Reparation Commission to lift charges on assets of Hungary to leave them free as security for a foreign loan

May 23, Rehabilitation plan for Hungary approved by Reparation Commission, a committee to be sent to Hungary to investigate conditions. Answer to Note of April 22 declared that foreign loan depended on fulfillment of engagements to deliver coal and cattle and other requirements under Treaty

June 19, Leaders in conspiracy against the Government arrested

June 25, Declaration of the Lord Chief Justice that all Habsburg propaganda treasonable

July 12, Strike of printers and compositors in Budapest because of suspension of Socialist newspaper

Aug. 3, Martial law declared and leaders of striking railroad engineers arrested

Aug. 4, Strike of railroad engineers begun in July ended

Aug. 11, Decision of Government that public officials should not be permitted to be members of secret organizations

Sept. 12, National Assembly adjourned by Regent until Jan. 13, 1924

Sept. 29, League of Nations authorized plan for financial reconstruction

Oct. 17, Reparation Commission agreed to waiving certain liens on Hungarian property and invited League of Nations to frame plan for Hungary similar to that made for Austria

Nov. 7, Delegation of the League of Nations arrived at Budapest to study economic conditions

Dec. 15, Further Commercial Agreement with Austria signed

Dec. 18, Treaty of friendship with Turkey signed

Dec. 20, Council of the League of Nations adopted a plan of reconstruction for Hungary

1924

Feb. 3, Convention with Yugo-Slavia signed regarding deliveries of coal and rolling stock as reparations

Feb. 10, Frontier Agreement with Czechoslovakia signed as to Salgo-Tarjan district

Feb. 21, League of Nations plan for reconstruction of Hungary accepted by Reparation Commission

March 14, Protocols signed with Hungary by Allied Powers accepting plan for reconstruction

March 22, Commercial Agreement with Yugo-Slavia concluded

April 6, Convention with Italy signed as to legal protection of nationals

April 16, Twelve Conventions with Rumania signed provided for settlement of judicial and financial questions arising from Treaty of Trianon and including a most-favored nation commercial agreement

April 17, Reconstruction laws passed in accordance with League of Nations plan

April 25, Debt with the United States for purchase of food stuffs consolidated

May 1, Jeremiah Smith, of Boston, appointed by League of Nations as Commissioner General in charge of finances of Hungary, arrived in Budapest

May 29, Treaty of commerce and navigation with Finland

June 18, Treaties of arbitration and conciliation with Switzerland signed

June 24, New Bank of Issue opened

July 26, Two financial Conventions with Austria signed

Aug. 19, Protocol with Austria signed adjusting frontier

Aug. 24, Aërial Navigation Treaty with Austria signed

Sept. 16, Treaty of commerce and navigation with Norway signed

Sept. 30, Commercial *modus vivendi* with Belgium signed

Oct. 16, Treaty with Russia signed

Nov. 4, Provisional Commercial Agreement with Albania

Nov. 26, Agreement with the United States signed for appointment of a claims commission

Dec. 9, Commercial Convention with the Netherlands signed

1925

Jan. 12, Public Order Act limited liberty of the press and public meetings

March 26, Commercial Treaty with Poland signed

March 30, Housing law enacted to promote building

April 4, Strike of 5,000 coal miners in Tabanza begun which lasted 2 months

June 4, Provisional Commercial Agreement with Greece signed

June 17, Commercial Agreement with Spain signed

June 24, Treaty of friendship, commerce, and consular rights signed with the United States

June 29, Protocol signed by Mixed Commission completed delimitation of frontier with Rumania

July 9, Discovery of Communist plot against the Government

July 20, Provisional Commercial Agreement with Italy signed

Sept. 23, Arrests of Communists begun in Budapest and in the provinces

Oct. 13, Commercial Agreement with France

Nov. 4, Law provided for new monetary unit the "pengo" (12,500 paper crowns) to come into use Dec. 27, 1926

1926

Jan. 4, Arrest of Prince Ludwig Windisch-Graetz, and Dr. E. von Nadossy, chief of State police, charged with manufacture of counterfeit French francs who confessed later they had done so to promote Fascist and Anti-Semitic movements

Jan. 7, Archduke Albrecht resigned as president of Fascist Federation

Jan. 22, Commercial Treaty with France signed

April 9, Commercial Treaty with Austria signed

May 4–26, Trial of 24 persons in the counterfeiting case. Prince Ludwig Windisch-Graetz and Dr. von Nadossy sentenced to 4 years imprisonment and fine of 10,000 crowns, 20 other persons for 2 years to 1 month terms

June 10, Decision of League of Nations to terminate control over Hungarian finances

June 30, League of Nations control of Hungarian finances ended

July 23, Treaty of commerce and navigation with Great Britain signed

July 24 and 28, Commercial Agreement with Yugo-Slavia and 5 Conventions as to frontiers signed

Aug. 24, Sentences of Windisch-Graetz and Nadossy reaffirmed by Judge Gado

Aug. 28, Provisional Commercial Agreement with Czecho-Slovakia signed

Oct. 14, Resignation of Bethlen Ministry

Oct. 15, Bethlen Ministry reorganized: Dr. Louis Walko, Foreign Affairs; Dr. Bela Scitovszky, Interior; Dr. John Bud, Finance; John Mayer, Agriculture; Maximilian Hermann, Commerce; Count Charles Csaky, National Defense; Dr. Paul Pesthy, Justice; Count Kuno Klebelsberg, Public Instruction

Nov. 11, Bill for reëstablishment of Upper House in place of former Chamber of Magnates in abeyance since 1918 to be elected on new basis of representation passed third reading

Nov. 16, National Assembly dissolved

Nov. 21, Decision of Ministry of Finance and Commerce to place government representatives in all large industries as recommended by Dr. E. W. Kemmerer

Dec. 8–18, Elections held. Premier Bethlen won 213 out of 245 seats

Dec. 14, Commercial Treaty with France of Jan. 22 revised

Dec. 27, The new monetary unit, the pengo, came into use

Dec. 31, Estimated population 8,457,852: according to language, Hungarian (Magyar), 7,589,239, percent 89.8; German, 577,720, percent 6.8; Slovak, 147,494, percent 1.7; Rumanian, 25,089, percent .3; Ruthenian, 1,534; Croatian, 38,340, percent .5; Serbian, 16,942, percent .2; others, 61,494

1927

Jan. 8, The hereditary nobles assembled elected 38 of their number to sit in the new Upper Chamber

Jan. 10, Hungarian-Rumanian Mixed Arbitral Tribunal declared itself competent to decide on claims of Hungarian land owners as to confiscated property, &c.

Jan. 25, National Assembly met

Jan. 28, New Upper Chamber met

Feb. 16, Commercial Convention with Egypt concluded

March, Strike of 200,000 textile workers as against award wage of Court of Arbitration

March 31, Allied Military Control Commission cease to function in Hungary

April 5, Treaty of friendship, conciliation, and arbitration with Italy signed

May 21–23, Three Conventions with Italy signed as to claims and Fiume

May 31, Commercial Treaty with Czechoslovakia signed

June 21, Workmens Insurance law passed

July 25, Convention with Italy signed as to use by Hungary of port of Fiume

——, Death of Prince Alip Csernoch, primate of Hungary

Aug. 3, Workers' Sickness and Accident Insurance law passed

Nov. 8, Penal Code modified

Nov. 10, Mortgage law enacted

Nov. 30, Cardinal J. Seridi nominated as primate

1928

Jan. 1, Finding of 5 freight cars loaded with machine gun parts at St. Gotthard on frontier by customs guards shipped from factory in Verona, Italy, to Hungary under guise of machinery

——, Telephone communication opened with London

Jan. 10, Revised Penal Code came into effect

Feb. 22, Four economic and financial Conventions with Yugo-Slavia signed

March 7, Commission of investigation of St. Gotthard incident of Jan. 1 appointed by the League of Nations on petition of Czecho-Slovakia, Yugo-Slavia, and Rumania

March 26, Insurance Convention with Poland signed

April 26, Bela Kun discovered and arrested in Vienna and sentenced to prison term of 3 months on June 26

June 2, Navigation Agreement with Albania

June 13, Granting of old age pensions and unemployment insurance under new law came into effect

June 27, Count Karolyi's petition for revision of sentence of confiscation of his property rejected

June 28, Navigation Agreement with Greece concluded

July 4, Commercial Treaty with Italy signed

July 20, Government decree ordered gypsies (about 50,000) to give up nomadic life, settle in fixed abodes, speak Hungarian, and pay taxes

Sept. 5, Ministry reorganized, Dr. Alexander Wekerle becoming Minister of Finance; Dr. John Bud, Public Economy and Commerce; Dr. Tibor de Zsitvay, Justice; Julius de Gömbös, National Defense; Dr. Joseph, Social Welfare

Oct. 20, Inauguration of free port of Csepel

Oct. 23, Commercial Agreement with Lithuania signed

Nov. 3, Telephone communication with New York opened

Nov. 8, Treaty of commerce and navigation with Sweden

Nov. 30, Conciliation and Arbitration Treaty with Poland signed

Dec. 2, Commercial Treaty with Poland signed

Dec. 16, Telephone communication with Stockholm opened

Dec. 29, Additional Commercial Agreement with Spain signed

1929

Jan. 5, Treaty of conciliation, arbitration, and friendship with Turkey signed

Jan. 23, Commercial agreement with Japan

Jan. 27, Demonstration of unemployed in Budapest stopped by police

Feb. 5, Mixed Arbitration Tribunal made decision that Czecho-Slovakia must compensate Archduke Friedrich and other Hungarians for confiscation of property after conclusion of peace treaties

April 29, Treaty of commerce and navigation with Estonia revised

May 26, Speech of Premier Bethlen

June 10, Treaty of friendship, conciliation, and arbitration with Spain signed

June 11, The Little Entente formally protested against speech of Count Bethlen of May 26

June 11, Death of Count Julius Andrassy (67), former Minister and leader of the Legitimists

June 19, Ratification of Paris Pact for the renunciation of war by lower House

July 22, Arbitration Treaty with Bulgaria signed

Aug. 13, Ratification of Protocol of Permanent Court of International Justice by which Hungary accepted compulsory jurisdiction of the court

Oct. 2, Agreement with Yugoslavia signed as to frontier traffic

Oct. 9, Anti-Semitic demonstration of university students

Oct. 12, Socialists leaders Garami and Buchinger repatriated

Oct. 28, Count Michael and Countess Karolyi admitted to the United States for 6 months, order against admission rescinded by Secretary of State Stimson

1930

April 11–14, Visit of Premier Count Bethlen to Rome

April 28, International Agreements settling claims and counter-claims of Hungary and her creditors signed in Paris by representatives of France, Great Britain, Italy, Czecho-Slovakia, Rumania, Yugo-Slavia, and Hungary

April, Military court declared Count Windisch-Graetz convicted of forging of French banknotes committed no dishonorable act and was actuated "only by patriotic motives"

May 5, Treaty of arbitration and friendship with Greece signed

May 22, Archduke Albrecht renounced pretensions to throne

June 13, Convention with Greece for settlement of Greek war claims

July 1, Demonstration of monarchists swore oath of fealty to Archduke Otto

Aug. 10, In response to a letter from the ex-Empress Zita asking every adult member of the Habsburg family for declaration of allegiance to her son the Archduke Otto and pledge to support his restoration a gathering of monarchists at Budapest took oath of fealty to Otto

Aug. 19, Order of Minister of War Gömbös issued for arrest of Zita, former Empress and her son, Archduke Otto

Aug. 31, Treaty of arbitration and conciliation with Latvia signed

Sept. 1, 50,000 Budapest workmen in riots against Fascist regime of Admiral Horthy and failure of Government to provide unemployment relief, 2 persons killed and 57 seriously wounded

Nov. 20, Archduke Otto came of age on his eighteenth birthday

SOVEREIGNS

997. St. Stephen, Duke of Hungary (son of Geisa); established the Roman Catholic religion (1000), and received from the Pope the title of Apostolic King, borne by the Emperor of Austria, as King of Hungary

1038. Peter, the German; deposed

1041. Aba or Owen

1044. Peter, again: deposed; and his eyes put out

1047. Andrew I; deposed

1061. Bela I: killed by the fall of a ruinous tower

1064. Salamon, son of Andrew

1075. Geisa I, son of Bela

1077. Ladislas I, the Pious

1095. Colomon, son of Geisa

1114. Stephen II, named Thunder

1131. Bela II: had his eyes put out

1141. Geisa II: succeeded by his son

1161. Stephen III: and Stephen IV (anarchy)

1173. Bela III: succeeded by his son

1196. Emeric: succeeded by his son

1204. Ladislas II; reigned six months only

1205. Andrew II, son of Bela III

1235. Bela IV

1270. Stephen IV (or V) his son

1272. Ladislas III: killed

1290. Andrew III, surnamed the Venetian, son-in-law of Rodolph of Hapsburg, Emperor of Germany (last of the house of Arpad), died 1301

1301. Wenceslas of Bohemia, and (1305) Otho of Bavaria, who gave way to

1309. Charobert, or Charles Robert of Anjou

1342. Louis I the Great; elected King of Poland, 1370

1382. Mary, called *King* Mary, daughter of Louis

1385–6. Charles Durazzo

1387. Mary and her consort Sigismond: the latter became King of Bohemia, and was elected Emperor in 1410

1392. Sigismond alone (on the death of Mary)

1437. Albert, Duke of Austria, married Elizabeth, daughter of Sigismond, and obtains the thrones of Hungary, Bohemia, and Germany; dies suddenly

1439. Elizabeth alone: she marries

1440. Ladislav IV, King of Poland, of which Kingdom he was Ladislas VI: slain at Varna

1444. [Interregnum]

1445. John Hunniades, Regent

1458. Ladislas V, posthumous son of Albert: poisoned

——. Matthias-Corvinus, son of Hunniades

1490. Ladislas VI, King of Bohemia: the Emperor Maximilian laid claim to both kingdoms

1516. Louis II of Hungary (I of Bohemia): loses his life at the battle of Mohatz

1526. John Zapolski, Waivode of Transylvania, elected by the Hungarians, and supported by the Sultan Solyman; by treaty with Ferdinand, he founds the principality of Transylvania, 1536

——. Ferdinand I, King of Bohemia, brother to the Emperor Charles V; rival kings

1540. Ferdinand alone: elected Emperor, 1558

1563. Maximilian, son; Emperor in 1564

1572. Rodolph, son; Emperor in 1576

1608. Matthias II, brother; Emperor in 1612

1618. Ferdinand II, cousin, Emperor

1625. Ferdinand III, son; Emperor, 1637

1647. Ferdinand IV, son; died in 1654, three years before his father

1655. Leopold I, brother: Emperor, 1657

1687. Joseph I, son: emperor in 1705

1712. Charles VI (of Germany), brother, and nominal King of Spain

1741. Maria-Theresa, daughter; Empress; survived her consort, Emperor Francis I, from 1765 until 1780; *see* Germany

1780. Joseph II, son, Emperor in 1765: succeeded to Hungary on the death of his mother

1790. Leopold II, brother; Emperor; succeeded by his son

1792. Francis I, son (Francis II as Emperor of Germany): in 1804 he became Emperor of *Austria* only

1835. Ferdinand V, son: Ferdinand I as Emperor of Austria

1848. Francis-Joseph, Emperor of Austria, nephew; succeeded on the abdication of his uncle, Dec. 2, 1848; crowned King of Hungary, July 8, 1867

1916. Charles I, Emperor of Austria, crowned King of Hungary as Charles IV, Dec. 30, 1916; withdrew from government Nov. 13, 1918

ICELAND

Iceland, island in the North Atlantic Ocean 250 miles from the southeast coast of Greenland and 600 miles west of Norway, its extreme northerly points touching the Arctic circle, area 39,709 square miles, population estimated at 108,870. Reykjavik is the capital. Iceland is united with Denmark by a personal bond of union. The first settlers came from Norway in 874, and between 930 and 1264 Iceland was an independent republic. The Althing, a general assembly of the entire Island instituted in 930 under the Constitution of Ulfliot, was the oldest Parliament in the world. By the "Old Treaty" of 1263 the country recognized the rule of the King of Norway. In 1381, Iceland, together with Norway, came under the rule of the Danish Kings, but when Norway was separated from Denmark in 1814, Iceland remained under the rule of Denmark. Since Dec. 1, 1918, it has been acknowledged as a sovereign State, united with Denmark only through the identity of the Sovereign. By the Act of Union of Nov. 30, 1918, Iceland is temporarily united with Denmark in certain affairs beyond the King's person. The present Constitution is embodied in the Charter of May 18, 1920.

1871

Jan. 2, Danish Act gave Iceland wide measure of home rule, though recognized as "an inseparable part of the State of Denmark"

1874

Jan. 5, New Constitution signed by the King came into effect Aug. 1 when King Christian of Denmark visited Iceland, and the thousandth anniversary of the colonization of the Island was celebrated

1905

Aug. 28, Telegraph cable from Iceland to the Shetland Islands completed

Oct. 25, Convention of Arbitration with Great Britain signed

1915

June 19, Bill signed by King of Denmark granted suffrage to women of Iceland

1916

Jan. 19, New Constitution came into effect

Nov. 3, New election law came into effect

1918

Nov. 30, Act of Union granted autonomy under Danish Crown; foreign affairs to be under control of Den-

mark; other affairs of common import such as communications, trade, customs, navigations, mail services, &c., to be arranged by agreement or treaty

Dec. 1, New Constitution came into effect, Act of Nov. 30

1919

Oct. 6, Supreme Court established

1920

May 18, Universal suffrage adopted

1923

July 18, Provisional Treaty of commerce and navigation with Lithuania signed

Dec. 21, Treaty of commerce and navigation with Finland signed

1924

March 22, Treaty of commerce and navigation with Poland signed

Nov. 3, Treaty of commerce and navigation with Latvia signed

1926

June 4, Agreement with Great Britain renewed Convention for pacific settlement of disputes of Oct. 25, 1905

June 24, Notes with Russia granted de jure recognition of Soviet Government

1927

May 6, Lower House passed Bill to amend the Constitution as to the suffrage clauses to lower age from 35 to 25 and fix meetings of the Alting (Parliament) for alternate years

May 25, Commercial Convention with Russia concluded

1928

April 6, Commercial Convention with Austria concluded

Nov. 30, Maritime Declaration signed with Norway

1930

May 15, Arbitration Treaty with the United States signed

June 23–28, Celebration of one thousandth anniversary of the founding of the Alting, oldest parliament in history

June 27, Treaty of friendship and arbitration signed with Denmark, Sweden, Norway, and Finland

INTERNATIONAL JUSTICE, PERMANENT COURT OF

See Permanent Court.

INTERNATIONAL LABOR ORGANIZATION

The International Labor Organization consisting of a General Conference of Representatives of the Members of the League of Nations and an International Labor Office was created June 28, 1919 by Part XIII of the Treaty of Versailles, repeated as Part XIII of the Treaties of St. Germain,

Neuilly, and Trianon, and Part XII of the Treaty of Sèvres.

Harold Butler, Director.

The number of States Members of the International Labor Organization is now 56. The Organization has held nine Conferences, in 1919 at Washington, in 1920 at Genoa, and subsequently in Geneva. At these Conferences the following Draft Conventions and Recommendations have been adopted:—

1919

Oct. 29–Nov. 29, First Session (Washington) attended by delegates from 41 countries, delegates from Germany and Austria received at later sessions, Albert Thomas appointed Director General of the International Labor Office

Draft Convention limiting the hours of work in industrial undertakings to eight in the day and forty-eight in the week

Draft Convention concerning unemployment

Recommendation concerning unemployment

Recommendation concerning reciprocity of treatment of foreign workers

Draft Convention concerning the employment of women before and after childbirth

Draft Convention concerning employment of women during the night

Recommendation concerning the prevention of anthrax

Recommendation concerning the protection of women and children against lead poisoning

Recommendation concerning the establishment of Government health services

Draft Convention fixing the minimum age for admission of children to industrial employment

Draft Convention concerning the night work of young persons employed in industry

Recommendation concerning the application of the Berne Convention of 1906, on the prohibition of the use of white phosphorus in the manufacture of matches

1920

June 15–July 10, Second Session (Genoa)

Recommendation concerning the limitation of hours of work in the fishing industry

Recommendation concerning the limitation of hours of work in inland navigation

Recommendation concerning the establishment of national seamen's codes

Draft Convention fixing the minimum age for admission of children to employment at sea

Recommendation concerning unemployment insurance for seamen

Draft Convention concerning unemployment indemnity in case of loss or foundering of the ship

Draft Convention for establishing facilities for finding employment for seamen

1921

Oct. 25–Nov. 19, Third Session (Geneva)

Recommendation concerning the prevention of unemployment in agriculture

Recommendation concerning the protection, before and after childbirth, of women wage-earners in agriculture

Recommendation concerning night work of women in agriculture

Draft Convention concerning the age for admission of children to employment in agriculture

Recommendation concerning night work of children and young persons in agriculture

Recommendation concerning the development of technical agricultural education

Recommendation concerning living-in conditions of agricultural workers

Draft Convention concerning the rights of association and combination of agricultural workers

Draft Convention concerning workmen's compensation in agriculture

Recommendation concerning social insurance in agriculture

Draft Convention concerning the use of white lead in painting

Draft Convention concerning the application of the weekly rest in industrial undertakings

Recommendation concerning the application of the weekly rest in commercial establishments

Draft Convention fixing the minimum age for the admission of young persons to employment as trimmers or stokers

Draft Convention concerning the compulsory medical examination of children and young persons employed at sea

1922

Oct. 18–Nov. 3, Fourth Session (Geneva)

Recommendation concerning communication to the International Labor Office of statistical and other information regarding emigration, immigration, and the repatriation and transit of emigrants

1923

Fifth Session (Geneva)

Recommendation concerning the general principles for the organization of systems of inspection to secure the enforcement of the laws and regulations for the protection of the workers

1924

June 16–July 5, Sixth Session (Geneva)

Recommendation concerning the development of facilities for the utilization of workers' spare time

1925

May 19–June 10, Seventh Session (Geneva)

Draft Convention concerning workmen's compensation for accidents

Recommendation concerning the minimum scale of workmen's compensation

Recommendation concerning jurisdiction in disputes on workmen's compensation

Draft Convention concerning workmen's compensation for occupational diseases

Recommendation concerning workmen's compensation for occupational diseases

Draft Convention concerning equality of treatment for national and foreign workers as regards workmen's compensation for accidents

Recommendation concerning equality of treatment for national and foreign workers as regards workmen's compensation for accidents

Draft Convention concerning night work in bakeries

1926

May 26–June 5, Eighth Session (Geneva)
Draft Convention concerning the simplification of the inspection of emigrants on board ship
Recommendation concerning the protection of emigrant women and girls on board ship
June 7–24, Ninth Session (Geneva)
Draft Convention concerning seamen's articles of agreement
Draft Convention concerning the repatriation of seamen
Recommendation concerning the repatriation of masters and apprentices
Recommendation concerning the general principles for the inspection of the conditions of work of seamen

1927

May 25–June 16, Tenth Session (Geneva)
Draft Convention concerning sickness insurance for workers in industry and commerce and domestic servants
Draft Convention concerning sickness insurance for agricultural workers
Recommendation concerning the general principles of sickness insurance

1928

May 30–June 16, Eleventh Session (Geneva)
Draft Convention concerning the creation of minimum wage fixing machinery
Recommendation concerning the application of minimum wage fixing machinery

1929

May 30–June 21, Twelfth Session (Geneva)
Draft Convention concerning the marking of the weight on heavy packages transported by vessels
Draft Convention concerning the protection against accidents of workers employed in loading or unloading ships
Recommendation concerning the prevention of industrial accidents
Recommendation concerning responsibility for the protection of power-driven machinery
Recommendation concerning reciprocity as regards protection against accidents of workers employed in loading or unloading ships
Recommendation concerning the consultation of workers' and employers' organizations in the drawing up of regulations dealing with the safety of workers employed in loading or unloading ships
Oct. 10–26, Thirteenth Session (Geneva)
(No Conventions or Recommendations)

1930

June 10–28, Fourteenth Session (Geneva)
Draft Convention concerning forced or compulsory labor
Draft Convention concerning the regulation of hours of work in commerce and offices
Recommendation concerning indirect compulsion to labor
Recommendation concerning the regulation of forced or compulsory labor
Recommendation concerning the regulation of hours of work in hotels, restaurants, and similar establishments
Recommendation concerning the regulation of hours of work in theaters and other places of amusement

Recommendation concerning the regulation of hours of work in establishments for the treatment or the care of the sick, infirm, destitute, or mentally unfit
By the terms of Part XIII of the Treaty of Versailles (Art. 405) the Members of the Organization undertake, within one year at most, or in exceptional circumstances within eighteen months, from the closing of the Conference, to bring the Recommendations or Draft Conventions adopted before the authorities "within whose competence the matter lies, for the enactment of legislation or other action." On a Recommendation the Members have to inform the Secretary-General of the League of the action taken. If a Draft Convention is approved by the competent authorities, the Members undertake to deposit their formal ratification thereof with the Secretary-General and to take the necessary action to apply its provisions
The total results obtained up to the end of January, 1931, in the ratification of the Conventions may be summarized as follows:—
Ratifications deposited with the Secretary-General of the League of Nations....................421
(excluding 14 ratifications of the Berne Convention prohibiting the use of white phosphorus in the manufacture of matches, which formed the subject of a Recommendation in 1919)
Ratifications authorized by the competent authorities..26
Ratifications recommended to the competent authorities.......................................164
The Governing Body, under the control of which the International Labor Office works, is composed of twelve Government representatives, six employers' representatives, and six workers' representatives
The following are some of the International Commissions which have been set up to assist the Office in its work:
The Joint Maritime Commission
The Mixed Advisory Committee in Agriculture
The Permanent Emigration Committee
The Correspondence Committee on Industrial Hygiene
The Correspondence Committee on Social Insurance
The Committee on Native Labor
The Committee on Article 408 (Application of Conventions)
The Advisory Committee of Professional Workers
The Advisory Committee of Salaried Employees
The Unemployment Committee
The most important publications of the Office are:
The International Labor Review (monthly)
The Industrial and Labor Information (weekly)
The Official Bulletin (irregular periodicity)
Studies and Reports
Industrial Safety Survey (bi-monthly)
International Labor Directory
The Legislative Series
The Documents of the International Labor Conference
Bibliography of Industrial Hygiene
International Survey of Legal Decisions on Labor Law

IONIAN ISLANDS

Ionian Islands, a group of islands west of Greece including Corfu, Cephalonia, Zante, Santa Maura, Ithaca, Cythera (Cerigo), and Paxo, were annexed to Greece in 1864. After 1386 the islands were subject to Venice.

Oct. 17, 1797, The islands ceded to France by the treaty of Campo Formio

March 21, 1800, Formed into the republic of the seven islands under Russia and Turkey

July 7, 1807, Restored to France by treaty of Tilsit

Oct. 3–12, 1809, Taken by the English

Nov. 5, 1815, Formed into an independent state under the protection of Great Britain (Sir Thomas Maitland, Lord High Commissioner) (Treaty of Paris)

July 11, 1817, A constitution ratified

1823, A university established at Corfu

1848–49, The constitution liberalized during the government of Lord Seaton

Nov., 1858, In consequence of complaints, Mr. W. E. Gladstone went out on a commission of inquiry, &c.

Feb., 1859, Sir H. Storks, Lord High Commissioner

March, 1861, and April, 1862, The parliament declare for annexation to Greece

1864, The islands annexed to Greece, May 28; the British troops retired, June 2, and King George I arrived at Corfu (*see* Greece), June 6

IRELAND

Ireland, an island west of Great Britain and until 1921 formed with Scotland and Wales the United Kingdom of Great Britain and Ireland, with representation in the Parliament of Great Britain and was administered by the Lord Lieutenant of Ireland. By Treaty of Dec. 6, 1921, Ireland except Northern Ireland constituted the Irish Free State with dominion status. *See also* Irish Free State; Ireland, Northern.

Area 32,586 square miles; population at different census periods:—

YEAR OF CENSUS	POPULATION	POPULATION PER SQ. MILE
1801	5,395,456	166
1811	5,937,856	186
1821	6,801,827	209
1831	7,767,401	239
1841	8,175,124	251
1851	6,552,385	201
1861	5,798,564	178
1871	5,412,377	167
1881	5,174,836	159
1891	4,704,750	144
1901	4,458,775	137
1911	4,390,219	135

ca. A.D. 400–1845

Probably 4th or 5th century, Arrival of St. Patrick

About 448, Christianity established

795, The Danes and Normans, known by the name of Easterlings, or Ostmen, invade Ireland

About 798, They build Dublin and other cities

April 23, 1014, Brian Boroimhe totally defeats the Danes at Clontarf; and is killed

1103, Magnus III, King of Norway, defeated and slain during an invasion

[In the 12th century Ireland is divided into five kingdoms, viz.: Ulster, Leinster, Meath, Connaught, and Munster, besides a number of petty principalities, whose sovereigns continually warred with each other]

1155, Adrian IV permitted Henry II to invade Ireland, on condition that he compelled every Irish family to pay a carolus to the holy see, and held it as a fief of the Church

1166, Dermot MacMurrough, King of Leinster, driven from his throne for his oppression

1168, Flees to England, where he takes an oath of fidelity to Henry II, who promises to restore him

1169, Invasion of the English under Fitz-Stephen

——, Landing of Strongbow at Waterford

1171, Dermot dies

May, 1177, Henry II lands near Waterford, and receives the submission of the princes of the country, settles the government, and makes his son John lord of Ireland

1210, Invasion of King John, English laws, &c., introduced

1316, Invasion of Edward Bruce, 1315; crowned King

1318, Defeated and slain at Foughart, near Dundalk

1361, Lionel, Duke of Clarence, third son of Edward III, marries Elizabeth de Burgh, heiress of Ulster

1367, Statute of Kilkenny passed by him. It enacted among other things, "that the alliance of the English by marriage with any Irish, the nurture of infantes, and gossipred with the Irish, be deemed high treason." And again, "if anie man of English race use an Irish name, Irish apparell, or anie other guize or fashion of the Irish, his lands shall be seized, and his body imprisoned, till he shall conform to English modes and customs." Said never to have been enforced. It abolished the Brehon laws

1394, Richard II lands at Waterford with a train of nobles, 4,000 men-at-arms, and 30,000 archers; gains the affection of the people by his munificence, and confers the honor of knighthood on their chiefs

1399, Richard again lands in Ireland

1465, The sanguinary Head act passed at Trim, by the Earl of Desmond, deputy, to suppress robbery. Much slaughter is said to have ensued

——, Apparel and surname act (the Irish to dress like the English, and to adopt surnames)

Sept. 13, 1494, Sir Edward Poynings sent to punish the Anglo-Irish for supporting Perkin Warbeck; he enacts a law, subjecting the Irish parliament to the English council

1534, Great rebellion of the Fitzgeralds, or Geraldines, subdued

1542, Henry VII assumes the title of King, instead of Lord of Ireland

1547, The reformed religion embraced by some of the English settlers in the reign of Edward VI

1561, Insurrection of Shan O'Neill, Earl of Tyrone; pardoned and received in London, 1562; rebels and becomes dominant in Ulster, 1564; assassinated June 2, 1567

1569, Ireland finally divided into shires

1571, Printing in Irish characters introduced by N. Walsh, Chancellor of St. Patrick's

1573 *et seq.*, Great expedition of Walter Devereux, Earl of Essex, to put down the O'Neills, sanguinary, but unsuccessful

1580, 700 Italians, headed by Fitzmaurice, land in Kerry; they are treacherously butchered by the Earl of Ormond

1597, Hugh or Shan O'Neill, who had been brought up at the court of Elizabeth, returns to Ireland as Earl of Tyrone; revolts; defeats the English at Blackwater, Aug. 14, 1598

1599, Unsuccessful expedition of Robert, Earl of Essex

1601–02, O'Neill invites over the Spaniards, and settles them in Kinsale; defeated by the lord deputy, Mountjoy

1606, Flight of the Earls of Tyrone, Tyrconnel, and others, to join the Spaniards

1609–12, In consequence of repeated rebellions and forfeitures, 511,465 acres of land in the province of Ulster became vested in the crown, and James I, after removing the Irish from their hills and fastnesses, divides the land among such of his English and Scottish Protestant subjects as choose to settle there

1641, Ulster civil war: More and Maguire's rebellion: the Catholics said to conspire to expel the English, and massacre the Protestant settlers in Ulster, commenced on St. Ignatius' day [some doubt the massacre], Oct. 23

June 5, 1646, O'Neill defeats the English under Monroe at Benburb

Sept. 12, Massacre and capture of Drogheda by Cromwell

1649–1659, Cromwell and Ireton reduce the whole island and redivide it

March 12, 1689, Landing of James II

July, 3,000 Protestants attainted

June 14, 1690, William III lands at Carrickfergus

July 1, Battle of the Boyne; James defeated

Oct. 3, 1691, Treaty of Limerick. By the treaty it was agreed that all arms, property, and estates should be restored; all attainders annulled, and all outlawries reversed; and that no oath but that of allegiance should be required of high or low; the freedom of the Catholic religion was secured; relief from pecuniary claims incurred by hostilities was guaranteed; permission to leave the Kingdom was extended to all who desired it; and a general pardon proclaimed to all then in arms.—*Burns*. This treaty was annulled by the Irish parliament, 1695. Limerick is still called "the city of the broken treaty".

1696, Linen manufacture encouraged

1704, Popery act passed

1724, Excitement against Wood's halfpence coined by virtue of a patent, passed, 1722. Against them, Dr. Jonathan Swift, by his letters signed M. B. Drapier, published about 1723, raised such a spirit of opposition that the patent was withdrawn. Wood received a compensation, but was virtually banished the kingdom. The half-pence were assayed in England by Sir Isaac Newton, and proved to be genuine, in 1724

1760, Thurot's invasion. Thurot, an Irish commodore in the French service, became a terror to all the merchant-ships of this kingdom. He had the command of a small armament, and landed 1,000 men at Carrickfergus in Ireland, and plundered the town. He reached the Isle of Man, and was overtaken by Captain Elliot, with three frigates, who engaged his little squadron, which was taken, and the commodore killed, Feb. 28, 1760. Thurot's true name was O'Farrell. His grandfather had followed the fortunes of James II; but his mother being of a family of some dignity in France, he assumed her name.—*Burns*

1778, Indulgences granted to the Catholics by the relief bill

1779, Ireland admitted to a free trade

Henry Grattan claims independence for the Irish parliament in speeches delivered April 19, 1780, and April 16, 1782

May, 1782, The Irish parliament declared independent by an act passed in the English parliament; confirmed by another act passed 1783

June 1, 1783, Bank of Ireland established

——, Genevese refugees received in Waterford

——, Order of St. Patrick established

May 12, 1785, Fosst balloon ascent by Richard Crosbie from Dublin

1791, Society of United Irishmen founded

1795, Diamond, a hamlet, Armagh, N. Ireland, "Battle of the Diamond," Sept. 21, 1795, between the "Peepo'-day Boys" (Presbyterians) and the "Defenders" (Catholics) and many of the latter were killed. To commemorate this conflict the first Orange Lodge was formed immediately after

1799, Irish rebellion commenced May 4, 1798; cost 150,000 Irish lives, 20,000 English; gradually suppressed

Jan. 1, 1801, Legislative Union of Great Britain and Ireland

July 23, 1803, Emmett's insurrection

Jan. 5, 1817, English and Irish exchequers consolidated

Aug. 11–Sept. 16, 1821, Visit to Ireland of George IV

1823, The Catholic Association organized by Daniel O'Connell and others

Jan. 1, 1826, The currency assimilated

July 5, 1828, Daniel O'Connell is elected M.P. for Clare, but does not sit

April 13, 1829, Roman Catholic emancipation act passed

Jan. 6, 1830, Customs consolidated

1831, Dr. Whately, supporter of Irish National School system, becomes Archbishop of Dublin

Aug. 7, 1832, Irish reform act passed

July 31, 1838, Poor laws introduced: act passed

1840, "Young Ireland" party formed

1841, Population by census, 8,196,597

March 16, 1843, Great Repeal movement, led by O'Connell; meeting at Trim

——, Molly Maguire, a secret society, formed

Jan. 15, Feb. 12, 1844, O'Connell's trial (for political conspiracy), found guilty

Dec. 1, Appointment of new commissions of charitable bequests (rank of the Roman Catholic bishops recognized)

1845

July 21, Irish Banking Act passed

Sept. 23, Irish National Education Board incorporated

1846

April 30, Committal of William Smith O'Brien to the custody of the serjeant-at-arms, for contempt in not obeying an order of the House of Commons to attend a committee

Failure of the potato crop throughout Ireland; sufferers relieved by parliament

July 29, William Smith O'Brien and the "Young Ireland," or physical force party, secede from the Repeal Association

1847

Feb. 8, O'Connell's last speech in the Commons

Grants from Parliament amounting to 10,000,000*l.* to relieve the people suffering from famine and disease

May 15, Death of O'Connell at Genoa, on his way to Rome, in his 73d year

1848

April 3, Deputation from the Irish people (?)—Smith O'Brien, Meagher, O'Gorman, &c.—to Lamartine and others, members of the provisional government at Paris

April 4, Great meeting of "Young Irelanders" at Dublin

May 13, Arrest of Mitchell, editor of the *United Irishmen*

May 15–27, State trials in the Irish Queen's Bench

May 26, Mitchell found guilty and sentenced to transportation for 14 years

July 8, Arrest of Gavon Duffy, Martin, Meagher, Doheny, &c., for felonious writings, &c.

July 26, Confederate clubs prohibited

——, The Habeas Corpus act suspended

July 29, O'Brien's rebellion suppressed

Aug. 5, Arrest of Smith O'Brien at Thurles; he is conveyed to Kilmainham gaol, Dublin

Aug. 12, Arrest of Meagher, O'Donoghue, &c.

Aug. 14, Martin sentenced to transportation

Sept., Encumbered estates act passed to enable owners of land or leases in Ireland, subject to encumbrance, to apply to commissioners appointed under it to direct a sale of such property. These commissioners held their first court in Dublin, Oct. 24, 1849, and their last July 28, 1858, a new court being established under the Landed Estates act. The number of estates sold, up to 1858, was 2,380, producing twenty-two millions of pounds

Oct. 9, Smith O'Brien, Meagher, and the other confederates tried and sentenced to death

1849

Jan. 16, The Irish Court of Queen's Bench gives judgment on writs of error sued out by the prisoners convicted of high treason, and confirms the judgment of the court below

July 9, O'Brien, Meagher, McManus, and O'Donoghue transported

July 12, Orange and Catholic affray at Dolly's Brae; several lives lost

Aug. 5, Queen Victoria visits Ireland, and holds her court at Dublin Castle

Oct. 24, First court under the encumbered estates act held in Dublin

1850

Aug. 15, Queen's University in Ireland established

1851

March 30, Census taken; population, 6,574,278

May 5, Roman Catholic university originated, and large sums subscribed

May 25, Death of R. Lalor Sheil, at Florence

June 5, McManus escapes from transportation, and arrives at San Francisco, in California

July 14, The Irish Tenant League hold a meeting on the site of the battle of the Boyne

Oct. 17, First meeting of the "Catholic Defence Association"

1852

May 24, Meagher escapes from Van Diemen's Land and arrives at New York

July 3, "Tenant Right" demonstration at Warrenstown dispersed by the magistrates

July 14, Fierce religious riots at Belfast

July 22, Fatal election riot at Six-Mile Bridge

Sept. 10, Irish members of parliament found a "Religious Equality Association"

1853

June, Income tax extended to Ireland

June 9, Mitchell escapes from Hobart Town

Oct. 4, Tenant Right League conference

1856

May 3, A pardon granted to O'Brien; he shortly after returned to Ireland

1857

Sept., Religious riots at Belfast

1858

Sept., Progress of Cardinal Wiseman in Ireland

Nov., Proclamation against secret societies

Dec., Arrests of members of Phœnix Society

1859

Jan. 27, Proposed demonstration of landlords (headed by Marquis of Downshire) given up

Feb., National Gallery founded

Sept., Agitation against the Irish National School system

1860

Great emigration to America in the spring

May, June, Many Irishmen enlist in the service of the Pope; many return dissatisfied, July, The remainder taken prisoners by the Sardinians are released, and return to Dublin, where they receive an ovation, Nov.

Oct. 23, Agrarian outrages; Alderman Sheehy murdered

Dec., Attempted revival of Repeal agitation

1861

April 8, Census taken; population, 5,798,967

Dec. 13, Irish Law Court commission appointed

1862

Numerous agrarian murders: Gustav Thiebault, April 28; Francis Fitzgerald, May 16 (and others); Michael Hayes shoots Mr. John Braddell, July 30

July 20, The Catholic university founded

Sept. 17, An Orange demonstration at Belfast leads to destructive riots

Great agricultural distress; many murders and outrages, end of 1862, beginning of 1863

1863

Great emigration of able-bodied laborers

1864

Jan., Appearance of the Fenians

June 16, Death of Smith O'Brien, descendant of King Brian Boroimhe

1865

Jan. 12, Address of the "National Association" to liberate tenant capital, recover the property of the Catholic Church, &c.

Sept. 15–17, Oct. 14, Seizure of the newspaper *Irish People* and 25 Fenians

Nov. 24–25, Stephens escapes from gaol

Dec. 1, Fenian trials began at Dublin, Nov. 27; Thomas Clarke Luby convicted of treason felony; sentenced to 20 years' penal servitude

Dec., O'Leary and others convicted; O'Donovan Rossa sentenced to imprisonment for life, Dec. 13

1866

Jan., Feb., More Fenians arrested and convicted at Cork and Dublin

Jan. 11, Discovery of an arms manufactory at Dublin; the city and county proclaimed as put under the provisions of the Peace Preservation act

Feb. 17, Habeas Corpus act suspended; many Fenians flee

April, Agitation respecting Irish church; debates in parliament

July, Lord Abercorn made Lord-Lieutenant

Sept. 1, About 320 suspected Fenians remain in prison

Dec. 15, Great seizure of fire-arms

Dec., Clare and other counties proclaimed under Peace Preservation act

Dec. 28, Election riots at Dungarvan; Capt. Barthol-Kelly killed

1867

Early in 1867, Irish college of science established at Dublin

March 5-13, Another Fenian outbreak

June 24, Appointment of commission respecting Church of Ireland agreed to

Aug. 20, Chancery and Common-law Offices act passed

Oct. 30, Irish Church commission appointed, Earl Stanhope chairman

Nov., More trials of Fenians

About Dec. 12, Protest of Irish noblemen and gentlemen against Irish Church establishment signed

Dec. 23, Declaration of many Roman Catholic clergy professing loyalty, but claiming self-government for Ireland

Dec. 30, Bp. Moriarty, of Kerry, publishes a circular censuring the funeral processions for Fenians

1868

Jan. 10, Prosecution of the *Irishman* newspaper for sedition

Jan. 18, Arrest of Geo. Francis Train on his arrival from America, on suspicion of Fenianism; soon discharged (claimed 10,000*l.*)

Feb. 6, Great Protestant defense meeting at Dublin, many peers present

Feb., Habeas Corpus act suspended till March 1, 1869 (83 persons detained on suspicion)

Feb. 18, 19, Messrs. Sullivan and Pigott, convicted of seditious libels in their newspapers (the *Weekly News* and *Irishmen*), sentenced to imprisonment and fine

March, Mr. Johnston, grand master of an Orange lodge, imprisoned for infraction of Party Processions act

March 3, Train arrested for debt

March 16, Four nights' debate on Ireland in the Commons ended (Mr. Gladstone declared for disestablishment of the Irish Protestant Church)

March 19, Irish reform bill introduced into the Commons

March 30, Debate on Mr. Gladstone's proposal for a committee on his resolutions for the disestablishment of the Church (carried by 328 to 272), to early morning of April 4

April 15, Mr. Featherstonehaugh, J.P., a deputy-lieut., shot dead while returning from Dublin (he had recently raised the rent of his tenants)

April, Increased emigration to United States

May 7, Mr. Gladstone's first resolution passed in the Commons (by 330 to 265) early on May 1, second and third resolutions passed

May 14, Irish archbishops and bishops present address to the Queen at Windsor, on behalf of the Irish Church establishment

July 27, Irish Church commission recommend consolidation of dioceses and other reforms (1st report)

Dec., Earl Spencer Lord Lieutenant

1869

May 11, Mayor of Cork, for a speech eulogizing Fenians, April 27, compelled to resign

July 26, Irish Church bill introduced into the Commons, March 1; after much opposition passed

Aug. 18, Irish mixed schools denounced by Abp. Cullen; support for a Catholic university demanded in a circular dated

Sept. 10, Tenant-right agitation; a conference at Cork; county meeting at Kilkenny, Oct. 18

Nov. 25, Jeremiah O'Donovan Rossa, a Fenian convict, elected M.P. for Tipperary

1870

Jan., Feb., Many agrarian outrages

Feb. 10, O'Donovan Rossa's election annulled

About Feb. 21, Irish Church convention met

April 4, New "Irish Peace Preservation act" passed

April 29, Eight counties placed under this act

June 17, Irish Land bill, read a second time in Commons (442 against 11), 1 A.M., March 12; read second time in the Lords

July, Reported growth of a "Nationality" party among the Protestants

Aug. 1, Irish Land act passed

Sept. 1, The "Home Government Association," to include all parties, meets at Dublin

Nov., Aggressive outrages and murders

1871

Jan., Some Fenian convicts released from prison

Jan. 5, John Martin, a nationalist, elected M.P., for Meath

April 3, Census taken; population, 5,402,759

May 2, Bill for protection of life and property in Westmeath brought in (and passed June 16) on account of ribandism

July 15, Chief Constable Talbot shot, night of July 11; died

Aug. 7, Riot through attempted repression of Fenian sympathizers; several killed

Aug. 16-28, French deputation (comte de Flavigny and others) to thank the Irish for the assistance of the Irish ambulance during the war; warmly received, with seditious demonstrations against England

Sept. 20, Mr. Isaac Butt, leader of Home-rule movement, elected M.P. for Limerick

1872

Jan., The Roman Catholic bishop of Derry, the O'Donoghue, and others, declare against the movement; members in its favor elected for Galway and Kerry, Feb.

About May 27, Capt. Nolan, M.P. for Galway, unseated for intimidation by his agents; the Roman Catholic bishops and clergy severely censured by Justice Keogh in giving sentence

July 11, O'Byrne *v.* Marquis of Hartington, and others (police) for exceeding duty in suppressing a meeting in Phœnix-park, Dublin, in Aug. 1871; verdict for plaintiff, 25*l.* damages

1874

Feb. 10–14, Fathers Loftus and Quain tried for undue interference in Galway election; jury disagreed

Feb. 13, Mr. Gladstone brings into the Commons the Irish University bill (rejected and withdrawn)

Feb. 15–19, The Roman Catholic bishop of Clonfert, Dr. Duggan, tried and acquitted

May 12, Trial: O'Keeffe *v.* Carinal Cullen; begins

March 20 & July 3, Motions in favor of Home-rule defeated in parliament

1875

Feb. 16, John Mitchell (*see above*, 1848, 1853), elected M.P. for Tipperary; election declared null by the Commons; he died March 20; his friends, John Martin, M.P., died March 29; and Sir John Gray, M.P., died April 9

May 28, Peace Preservation Act renewed

Sept., Catholic synod at Maynooth; mixed education censured

Oct. 11, Riots at Callan, Mr. O'Keeffe's chapel and house attacked (28 men committed for trial)

1876

March 30, Agrarian outrage, Mr. Bridges and party fired on in daylight, the coachman killed; several wounded at Mitchelstown, Cork (Crowe convicted of murder July 25, executed Aug. 25)

May, O'Keeffe (*see above*, May, 1874) submits to Cardinal Cullen for compensation

May 16, An Irish university bill introduced by Mr. Butt (withdrawn)

1877

Aug. 14, County officers and courts act passed

——, Supreme court of judicature act for Ireland, passed

Oct. 1, Dr. Moriarty, R. C. Bp. of Kerry, patriotic, judicious, died

1878

Jan. 1, The judicature act comes into operation

May 15, Bill for reducing Irish borough suffrage to 1*l.* rejected in the Commons (232–26)

Aug. 16, Irish Sunday closing (public houses) bill, much opposed; passed

——, Irish intermediate education act passed

1879

Aug. 7, Irish volunteer bill lost

Aug. 15, Bill to abolish the Queen's University, and to establish a new university (for Roman Catholics), introduced by Lord Chancellor Cairns, June 30; carried in Commons (257–90), July 25; passed

——, Prevention of crime act passed

Sept. 11, An Irish national convention to meet at Dublin, proposed by Mr. Charles Stewart Parnell

Oct. 9, Appeal for the Irish national land league by Mr. Parnell, soliciting subscriptions to buy the land for the tenants

Nov. 19, James Bryce Killen, barrister, J. W. Daly, proprietor of "Connaught Telegraph," and Michael Davitt (ex-Fenian, on ticket-of-leave) arrested at Dublin for sedition (at anti-rent meeting at Gurteen, Sligo, Nov. 2); [prosecution lapsed]

Dec. 5, Thos. Brennan arrested for seditious speech (at Balla, on Nov. 22)

1880

Jan. 2 Mr. Parnell arrives at New York to agitate for help to relieve Ireland politically and pecuniarily

Jan. 2 *et seq.,* Riots at Carraroe, Connemara, and other places in Galway, in consequence of notices of eviction

Jan., Feb., Contributions to the famine funds arrive from Canada, Australia, India, United States, &c.

March 1, Seed supply act passed

March 15, Relief of distress (Ireland) act passed

April 19, Charter for new Irish university signed by the Queen

Aug. 3, Compensation for Disturbance bill (to check evictions, restrain landlords, and benefit tenants), 2nd reading in Commons (295–217), July 5–6; passed in Commons (303–237), July 27; rejected by the Lords (282–51)

Aug. 23, Violent speech of Mr. Dillon, M.P., at Kildare, in favor of the land league, Aug. 15; termed "wicked and cowardly" by Mr. W. E. Forster, who justifies the terms in parliament

Sept., Mr. Parnell proposes that tenant should become owner of land after paying 35 years' just rent

Oct. 7, 105 leading landowners with agents wait on the Lord-Lieutenant at Dublin, describing the terrorist state of the south and west of the country and need of protection

Oct. 16, Agrarian outrages; John Downing, a driver, killed by a shot aimed at his employer, Mr. Samuel Hutchins, near Drimoleague, Cork

Oct. 26, 27, Arrest of Timothy M. Healy, Mr. Parnell's secretary, and Mr. Walsh, for intimidation of Mr. Manning (on Oct. 16)

Nov. 3 *et seq.,* Messrs. Parnell and others arrested for conspiracy and intimidation to prevent tenants paying rent, &c. (19 counts); notices served

Nov. 11, 12, Mr. Boycott of Lough Mask farm, near Ballinrobe, Mayo, besieged; his laborers threatened; his tradesmen refuse to supply him;—his crops gathered by immigrant laborers, protected by military, &c.

Nov. 12, Mr. Henry Wheeler, land agent, murdered

Dec., Mr. W. Bence Jones of Ballinascorthy, treated like Mr. Boycott

Dec. 28, Trial of Mr. Parnell and others for conspiracy, begins

1881

Jan. 25, Jury disagree; discharged

Jan., Report of Agricultural Commission (for Ireland) issued; great distress, 1877–79; good harvest, 1880; it opposes the three F's.; recommends emigration in some districts

Jan. 24, Bill for protection of life and property (termed *coercion bill*) brought in by Mr. Forster; long debates; much obstruction; passed Commons (281–36), Feb. 25, 26; passed Lords, March 1–3; royal assent, March 3

March 1, Peace preservation bill (arms bill); introduced; passed Commons, March 11, 12; passed Lords, March 18; royal assent, March 21

March, "Clan-Na-Gael" secret society to replace Fenians said to be formed

April 7, Irish land bill ("legalized confiscation"— *Beaconsfield*) introduced into the Commons by Mr. Gladstone

May 1, Cruel outrages in different places; Dublin city proclaimed under coercion act; John Dillon, M.P. arrested [released Aug.], May 2

About May 5, Division in Irish parliamentary party; Mr. Parnell and others oppose the land bill

May 19, 20, Irish land bill read 2nd time (352-176); Mr. Parnell and about 20 retire; 3rd time (220-14), July 29

Agrarian outrages, 439, Jan.; 170, Feb.; 146, March; 296, April; 238 in three weeks, May

June 2, Riots connected with evictions at Scareff, Co. Clare; some persons killed; many injured

June, Population diminished one-ninth in ten years (by census)

July, First publication of *United Ireland*

Aug. 2, 3, Land bill in House of Lords; read 2nd time; 3rd time (with amendments), Aug. 8; the Commons reject some of the amendments, Aug. 12; the Lords resist, Aug. 13; the Commons modify the amendments, Aug. 15; the Lords yield, Aug. 16; royal assent, Aug. 22

Sept., Increased boycotting of shop-keepers and others, and much cruelty

Oct. 13, Mr. Parnell arrested on charge of inciting to intimidation and for urging non-payment of rent; put into Kilmainham gaol, Dublin

Oct. 14-16, Arrest of Messrs. Sexton, O'Kelly, J. P. Quinn, secretary of Land League, Dillon, O'Brien, and others

Oct. 15-18, Violent rioting at Dublin and Limerick; about 2,000*l.* damage; soon suppressed; more arrests

Oct. 18, More troops sent to Ireland from Chatham, &c.; manifesto of the Land League denouncing the Government, and ordering non-payment of rent

Oct. 19, This manifesto censured by Archbishop Croke

Oct. 20, First meeting of the Irish Land Commission court; addressed by Justice O'Hagan

——, The Lord Lieutenant on the responsibility of Mr. W. E. Forster proclaims the suppression of the Land League as an illegal and criminal organization

Nov., Important decisions in favor of tenants by subcommissions at Belfast, &c.

Announced Nov. 5, 2,448 persons in prison; more arrests; some released

Nov. 8, Death of Dr. M'Hale, Archbishop of Tuam, "Lion of the fold of Judah"

Nov., Continuance of agrarian murders and outrages

Nov. 30, Strike against payment of rent in Limerick; evictions ordered

Nov.-Dec., Irish Property Defense association (formed Nov., 1880) active and successful

Dec., Great increase of crime in Munster announced

About Dec. 20, An association formed to support the law

Dec. 27, Proclamation against possession of arms in Dublin, &c.

About Dec. 30, 4,439 agrarian outrages in the year

1882

Feb. 23, Committee to enquire into working of land act voted by Lords (96-53, Feb. 17), Earl Cairns, chairman

Feb. 28, Michael Davitt, convict, elected M.P. for Co. Meath, Feb. 22; annulled by the Commons

Feb. 25, Bailey, an informer against Land League, murdered at Dublin

March 9-10, Mr. Gladstone's resolution against the Lords' committee, Feb. 27; carried (303-235)

March, Continuance of murderous outrages

March 27, Archbishop M'Cabe created Cardinal

——, Mr. Forster confesses failure of government policy through influence of secret societies

April 1, 511 suspects in prison

April 10, Mr. Parnell released *en parole* for ten days

About May 2, New government policy; resignation of Mr. W. E. Forster [Mr. Forster narrowly escaped assassination several times]; release of Mr. Parnell and other suspects; Earl Spencer appointed Lord Lieutenant; release of Michael Davitt, May 6

May 6, Lord Frederick Cavendish, new Chief Secretary, and Mr. T. H. Burke, permanent under-secretary, assassinated by stabbing, by four men ("Invincibles") about 7 P.M., in Phœnix-park, Dublin; manifesto expressing abhorrence of the deed signed by C. S. Parnell, J. Dillon, and M. Davitt, May 7

May 9, Government offers 10,000*l.* reward for discovery of the murderers; Mr. G. O. Trevelyan appointed Chief Secretary

May 11, Bill for the prevention of crime in Ireland introduced by Sir W. V. Harcourt (new tribunal of three judges without jury for special occasions; powers of police increased; alien act to be revived; supervision of newspapers and of assemblies, &c.); second reading May 19-20 (383-45)

May 11 *et seq.*, Many arrests

Early May, Alleged agreement of the Government with Mr. Parnell and party, sarcastically termed the *treaty of Kilmainham*; arrears of rent bill, second reading (269-157), May 23-24

June 30-July 1, A long discussion in the Commons on the prevention of crime bill; 23 Irish members suspended

July, Mr. Parnell and home rulers withdraw; 22 arrests at Loughrea, July 4; Government defeated in an amendment checking domiciliary visits of suspected persons at night, 207-194; prevention of crime bill read third time, July 7-8; passed by the Lords, July 11; royal assent, July 12

About July 13, 17 counties proclaimed

Aug. 2, 170 suspects in custody

Aug. 16, Mr. Edmund Dwyer Gray, M.P., High Sheriff of Dublin, ex-Lord Mayor, sentenced to three months' imprisonment and a fine of 500*l.* for contempt of court in articles in *Freeman's Journal* attacking the jury on trial of Francis Hynes

Aug. 17-18, John Joyce and his wife, son, and daughter, shot dead by band of men near Maamtrasma, in Clonder district, Galway, for giving information to the police

Aug. 18, Arrears bill passed in the Commons (285-177), July 21; by the Lords, with injurious amendments (169-98), July 31; which are modified or negatived by the Commons, Aug. 8, 9; the revision accepted by the Lords, Aug. 10; royal assent, Aug. 18

About Aug. 18, 50 suspects released

End of Aug., Discontent and insubordination of the constabulary at Dublin, Cork, and especially at Limerick, settled

Sept. 1, Dismissal of some police for holding a public meeting in Dublin; all the police of the city resign;

order maintained by the military, who charge on rioters in the evening; special constables sworn in Sept. 2; resignation withdrawn penitently with respectful petition Sept. 3; 208 reinstated Sept. 6–7

Sept. 11, Execution of Francis Hynes (for murder of John Doloughty) at Limerick; of Patrick Walsh, for murder of Martin Lyden, at Galway, Sept. 22

Sept. 29, Conviction of Michael Walsh, for murder of Kavanagh, a policeman; penal servitude for life, Oct. 19

Sept. 30, Mr. E. D. Gray released

——, Expiration of coercion act; all suspects released

Oct. 17, Nationalistic conference at Dublin constitutes a new Irish National League (ultra) to obtain self-government and land-law reform, Mr. C. Parnell, president

About Nov. 13, Irish land commission report issued

Nov., The land corporation of Ireland dissolved

Nov. 21, Conviction of murderers of Joyce family; Patrick Joyce, Nov. 15; Patrick Casey, Nov. 17; Myles Joyce, Nov. 18 [all executed, Dec. 15]; Michael Casey, Thomas Joyce, John Casey, and Martin Joyce, confess; sentence commuted; Thomas Casey and Philbyn, approvers

Nov. 25, Murderous assault on detectives in Dublin; Cox killed; his murderer, Dowling, severely wounded

Nov. 27, Mr. Field, a juryman, stabbed; reward of 5,000*l.* for assassin; Dublin proclaimed under martial law, Nov. 28

Dec. 13 and 16, Patrick and Thomas Higgins convicted of murder of Haddys at Lough Mask [executed Jan. 15–17, 1883]

Dec. 20, Also Michael Flyn

Dec. 22, Sylvester Poff, James Barrett, convicted of murder, at Cork

Emigration from Ireland, 89,566 in the year

Dec., 1882–1883, Great distress in Donegal in the north-west; 3,433 agrarian outrages in the year

1883

Jan. 12, 13, Arrest in Dublin of 21 persons, suspected of conspiracy to murder

Jan. 19, Robert Farrell, approver, reveals plot for assassination of the Government

Jan. 24, M. Davitt, Thos. Healy, M.P., and P. Quinn bound over for seditious speeches; elect to be imprisoned, Feb. 6; imprisoned, Feb. 8

Feb. 3, Eight men charged with complicity in murder of Lord Frederick Cavendish and Mr. Burke

Feb. 7, Irish national league, first meeting

Feb. 17, Revelations of James Carey, approver, implicating the Land League (Thos. Brennan, sec., and P. J. Sheridan); statement respecting the Irish Invincibles; arrest of Mrs. F. Byrne, charged with transmitting arms, &c.; discharged Feb. 20

Feb. 20, Accused prisoners committed for trial

Feb. 22–23, Mr. W. E. Forster's defense in the Commons, and charges against Mr. Parnell; Mr. O'Kelly suspended for a week, for giving him the lie

Feb. 27, Arrest of Mr. Byrne at Paris; released about March 9

March 1, Flight of Patrick Egan, treasurer of the Land League, from Dublin; in New York, March 12

March 28, Twelve members of the "Patriotic Brotherhood" (established at Crossmaglen, 1881) sentenced to penal servitude for conspiracy to murder landlords

April 11–13, Phœnix-park murders; Robt. Farrell,

Jas. Carey, and others, approvers; trial of Joseph Brady, convicted; Timothy Kelly, third trial, May 7–9; Thomas Caffrey pleads guilty, May 2; Patrick Delany and Daniel Curley, April 16–18; Michael Fagan, April 25–27

May, Detection of conspiracy of the "Vigilance" murder organization at Dublin; prisoners examined

May 16 *et seq.*, James FitzHarris and others convicted of conspiracy to murder; sentenced to penal servitude

June 4, Messrs. Davitt, Healy, and Quinn released

Executed: Joseph Brady (actual murderer), May 14; Daniel Curley, May 18; Michael Fagan, May 28; Thomas Caffrey, June 2; Timothy Kelly, June 9

July 29, James Carey, the approver, shot dead by Patrick O'Donnell on board the *Melrose Castle*, near Port Elizabeth, South Africa

Aug. 25, Loans amounting to 4,600,000*l.* for public works authorized by Parliament

End of Sept., National League invade Ulster, strongly resisted by the Orangemen at Auchnacloy, Dungannon, and other places

Oct.– Dec., Mr. Trevelyan reports great diminution in agrarian outrage

Dec. 1, Patrick O'Donnell convicted

1884

March 5, A Parnellite land law amendment bill rejected by the Commons (as tending to confiscation), by 235–72

July, Aug., Serious libelous charges against Mr. Bolton, crown solicitor; subornation of witnesses, &c.

Aug. 23, Charges disproved; letter from Earl Spencer

Sept. 6, Irish National League convention at Dublin, Mr. P. O'Connor in the chair; urges revival of agitation against the Government

Oct. 17, Death of Mr. A. M. Sullivan, eminent Nationalist

Oct. 28, Maamtrasma trial impugned; their verdict supported by the Commons (219–48)

1885

Feb. 11, Death of Cardinal McCabe, pacific and loyal

About March 16, Parnellite manifesto directing Nationalist corporations to maintain an attitude of reserve during the Prince of Wales' visit in April, issued

April 21, The Irish Roman Catholic Bishops summoned to Rome; arrive; rebuked by the Pope for disloyalty, &c., in separate interviews, April 27–May 15; Bishop Nulty's pastoral, foretelling secession of Ireland from Rome; causes great displeasure; the Bishops oppose projected reforms at Maynooth, but are said to submit, announced May 19; dismissed about May 25

June, Sir William Hart-Dyke appointed Chief Secretary

July–Aug., Stoppage of the Munster bank for about 70,000*l.*; fraud disclosed; reconstituted; opened Oct. 19

Aug. 14, Lord Ashbourne's act, granting 5,000,000*l.* for the purchase of land by tenant to be paid by instalments, passed

Sept., Prevention of crime act expires; revival of boycotting and outrages

Oct., Cork defense union formed (the Earl of Bandon president) against the tyranny of the national league

Oct. 10, The Cork steam packet company threatened with boycotting by the league; the company determined on resistance

Oct. 11, Aghadoe house, Killarney (Mr. Hussey's), attacked by "moonlighters" and defended with fire-arms

Nov. 11, Manifesto of Mr. Parnell claiming "home rule," &c., published

Nov. 13, Castle farm, Molahiffe, in Kerry, attacked for arms by moonlighters; Mr. John O'Connell Curtain killed, while his sons and daughters bravely resist; one assailant killed

[S. Cassey and D. Daly convicted of burglary, &c., Dec. 21]

Irish loyal and patriotic union (southern), afterwards Irish unionist association, formed

1886

Feb. 10, The Earl of Aberdeen, as Lord Lieut., and John Morley, as Chief Secretary, sworn in

March 27, Irish loyal union report to Mr. Gladstone the systematic cruel oppression of the national league

April 8–9, Mr. Gladstone in a long speech introduces a bill "to make better provision for the future government of Ireland"; it proposes to establish a legislative body to sit in Dublin, to consist of two orders each with a veto; I. twenty-eight representative peers and seventy-five members elected for ten years; II. the present 103 Irish members, and 101 additional: the Lord-Lieutenant with a privy council to be independent of Great Britain; the new body empowered to enact laws and to impose and collect taxes, except the customs, but not to interfere with the army and navy, or foreign and colonial affairs, and not to enact any religious endowment; present legal and police arrangements to remain temporarily subject to the crown; no Irish members to sit at Westminster; read first time, April 13–14; second reading rejected (343 [250 conservatives, 93 liberals]– 313), June 7–8

April 14, The loyal and patriotic union formed May, 1885; great meeting at H.M.'s theater, London, Earl Cowper in the chair, the Marquises of Salisbury and Hartington, and many leading conservative and liberal leaders present. Resolutions condemning Mr. Gladstone's bill passed; petitions to be presented to parliament

April 16, Sale and purchase of land bill introduced by Mr. Gladstone (proposed creation of 50,000,000l. 3% stock from 1887–90)

April, 944 agrarian offenses in 1885 reported

May, Intimidation practiced by the "house league" upon owners of houses in Kerry, &c., to procure reduction of rent

June 9, 10 et seq., Riots at Belfast

June 18, Armagh and Tyrone proclaimed under peace preservation act

July 20, Dissolution of parliament; Mr. Gladstone being in a minority, resigns; Marquis of Salisbury, supported by unionists, resumes office

July 26, The Marquis of Londonderry as Lord-Lieut., and Sir Michael Hicks-Beach as Chief Secretary, appointed

Aug. 19–22, Convention of about 1,000 delegates of Irish national league of America meet at Chicago; John Fitzgerald elected president

Aug. 30, Gen. Sir Redvers Buller with civil plenary powers appointed to command in S. Ireland

Sept. 21–22, Mr. Parnell introduces tenants' relief bill, Sept. 11; rejected (297–202)

Sept. 26, Capture of moonlighters and arms at Castle-island, Kerry

Oct. 21, Plans of organization (termed *plan of campaign*) of tenantry in each estate against the landlords with stringent measures proposed (probably by Mr. John Dillon, leader of the national party, and Mr. William O'Brien) in *United Ireland*, organ of the national league (the tenant was to pay his rent to the league, and be supported by it if evicted)

Nov. 30, Sir Robert Hamilton, under secretary (said to be home ruler) resigns (Sir Redvers Buller temporary successor); Col. Turner acts in Kerry

Nov., Increased agrarian agitation

Dec. 11, Prosecution of Mr. Dillon; the Attorney-General terms the "plan of campaign" a combination of debtors to coerce creditors; Court of Queen's Bench requires Mr. Dillon to find securities for good behavior, or be imprisoned for six months, Dec. 14

Dec. 16, Messrs. Dillon, Wm. O'Brien, Matthew Harris, and Sheehy arrested whilst receiving rents on Lord Clanricarde's estate, the books and money seized

Dec. 18, Proclamation against "plan of campaign"

About Dec. 18 et seq., Rents still illegally received by several M.P.'s

Dec. 20, The seat of prosecution removed from Loughrea to Dublin

1887

Jan. 5, Chief Baron Palles, in sentencing 36 Irish rioters, censures the "dispensing power" of the executive and the abstention of the police during riots at evictions

Jan. 11, Prosecution of Mr. Dillon, five other M.P.s, and Mr. O'Brien (editor of *United Ireland*) begun at Dublin, Dec. 23; committed and bailed

Feb. 11, 12, Mr. Parnell's amendment on the address relating to Irish affairs negatived (352 [68 liberals]– 246)

March 5, Resignation of Sir M. Hicks-Beach, Chief Secretary, from ill-health; succeeded by Mr. Arthur J. Balfour

March 7 et seq., "Parnellism and crime" published in the *Times*

March 8, Riots at Youghal with bloodshed

March 10, Justice O'Brien at Kerry says: "Law is at an end. There is a state of war with authority"

April 1, Trial of Messrs. Dillon and others, Feb. 14; jury disagreeing, discharged, Feb. 24; proceedings withdrawn

May 21–24, Arrest of Father Keller (supported by Abp. Walsh) for contempt of court in refusing to give evidence (as a confessor) in a bankruptcy case, March 18; committed to prison, March 19; Father Ryan committed for same cause, March 29; released

July 19, New criminal law procedure bill introduced by Mr. Balfour, March 28; much opposition, Irish members and others retire, June 17–30; read 3rd time, July 8–9; passed by the lords, July 18; royal assent *

* Members of parliament sentenced to imprisonment under the new act. 1887. Mr. W. O'Brien, Oct. 31; Mr. E. Harrington, Dec. 1; Mr. T. Harrington, Dec. 19; Mr. Hooper, Dec. 19; Mr. Sheehy, Dec. 21 1888. Mr. J. R. Cox, Jan. 25; Mr. P. O'Brien, Feb. 8; Mr. Pyne, Feb. 15; Mr. Flyn, Feb. 25; Mr. Gilhooly, March 5; Mr. W. O'Brien, May 3, June 20;

July 19, Great meeting at Cork to resist the operation of the crimes act

July 23, Eighteen counties proclaimed under the crimes act; twelve counties partly proclaimed, together with Dublin and nine other cities

July, Monsignor Persico visits Ireland on behalf of the Pope

Aug. 23, New Irish land bill (favorable to the tenant) passed; royal assent

Aug. 25–26, The national league proclaimed as a "dangerous association" Aug. 19; Mr. Gladstone's motion for an address to the Queen against the proclamation negatived (272–194)

Sept. 4, Nationalist meeting at Ballycoree in Clare proclaimed, Aug. 31; attempted meeting dispersed

Sept. 9, Meeting in support of Mr. W. O'Brien, M.P., and Mr. Mandeville, who refuse to obey the magistrates' summons respecting speeches at Mitchelstown on Aug. 9, 10; about 150 horsemen and crowd, about 3,000, armed with bludgeons and stones; Messrs. Labouchere, Dillon, Brunner, and other M.P.'s present; the police with the government reporter (Conderon) attacked with stones and bludgeons, retreat to barracks; return reinforced; compelled to fire; Michael Lonergan and John Shinnery killed and many wounded; town quieted by military

Sept. 20, The national league in Clare and several baronies (200 branches) suppressed by proclamation

Sept. 24, Mr. O'Brien and Mr. Mandeville sentenced to three months' imprisonment

Oct. 6, The Lord Mayor of Dublin (Mr. T. D. Sullivan) charged with offense against the crimes act

Oct. 12, Verdict of coroner's jury on deaths at Mitchelstown; willful murder against County Inspector Brownrigg, Sergeants Ryder and Kirwan, and Constables Gavan, Brennan, and Doran [Verdict quashed by the Queen's Bench, Dublin, Feb. 10, 1888]

About Oct. 15, Col. Sir Joseph West Ridgeway succeeds Sir Redvers Buller as Under-Secretary for Ireland

Oct. 27, At a riotous meeting at Woodford which had been proclaimed, Mr. Wilfrid Blunt, the chairman, and others arrested, and the meeting dispersed, Oct. 23; Mr. Blunt sentenced to two months' imprisonment; appeals [Sentence confirmed, Jan. 7, 1888]

Oct. 31, Mr. W. O'Brien withdraws his appeal; after resistance sent to prison for three months; sentence confirmed against Mr. Mandeville, two months' imprisonment; removed from Cork to Tullamore gaol, King's county, Nov. 2

Nov. 22, The national league suppressed in Kerry

Nov. 27, Serious riots at Limerick through attempted meeting to inaugurate a memorial of the so-called martyrs executed at Manchester in 1867

Mr. Condon, May 27; Mr. Dillon, June 20; Mr. James O'Kelly, Aug. 10; Mr. Redmond, Sept. 26

1889. Mr. John O'Connor, Jan. 31; Mr. D. Sheehy, Feb. 1; Mr. J. R. Cox, Feb. 2; Mr. T. Condon, Feb. 7; Mr. Kilbride, Feb. 8; Mr. W. O'Brien, Feb. 19; Mr. Carew, Feb. 21; Dr. Tanner, March 7; Mr. Condon, Mr. Connor, and Dr. Tanner, May 1; Mr. Conybeare, May 3; Mr. W. O'Brien and Mr. Gilhooly, Aug. 25; Mr. Redmond, Sept. 22

1890. Messrs. Wm. and Patrick O'Brien and John Dillon, Nov. 19

1891. Mr. W. O'Brien and J. Dillon, Feb. 13–June 31

Dec. 3, Death of Dr. Daniel M'Gettigan, Roman Catholic Archbishop of Armagh

Dec. 13–15, Convention of Irish landlords in Dublin to consider their prospects and conduct, Sept. 15; require legislation

Dec. 22, Father Matthew Ryan, Roman Catholic, sentenced to one month's imprisonment for sedition

Dec. 27, Large reductions of rents ordered by the land commission

Dec.–Jan., 1888, Many arrests under the crimes act, and imprisonments

1888

Feb. 17, Mr. Parnell's amendment on the address attacking the government Irish policy moved, Feb. 13; negatived (317–229)

March 21, Mr. Parnell's land law amendment bill dealing with arrears rejected (328–243)

April 8, Attempted proclaimed meetings dispersed by the police and military at Loughrea, Ennis (by Col. Turner), and other places

April 20, The plan of campaign and boycotting condemned by the Pope on moral grounds, April 18; rescript issued

April 25, Mr. Carew's county government bill rejected (282–195)

May 17, The exchequer division affirms right of county court to increase sentences on appeal

——, Meeting of Catholic M.P.s in Dublin, who resist the Pope's interference in political affairs; of others in Phœnix Park, May 20

May, The Roman Catholic bishops accept the papal rescript

June 25–27, Mr. John Morley's motion for vote of censure of the Government for its Irish policy negatived (366–273)

July 12, The Duke of Argyll's resolution in the Lords warmly commending the Government's Irish policy accepted *nem. con.*

July 19, 20, 24, Evictions on the Vandeleur estate violently but unsuccessfully resisted

July 28, Coroner's inquiry into the death of Mr. John Mandeville (imprisoned Nov., 1887), July 19, [suicide of Dr. Ridley of Tullamore gaol, July 20, 1888] verdict—disease caused by ill-usage in prison

Aug. 13, Mr. Parnell in the House of Commons asserts the letters attributed to him in *Parnellism and Crime* to be forgeries, and the charges against him to be false, July 6; Mr. Parnell's request for a select committee to investigate the charges in the *Times* refused by the Government, July 9; Mr. W. H. Smith proposes the appointment of a royal commission of judges to examine these charges, July 12; bill read first time, July 16–17; names mentioned, Sir James Hannen, President, Mr. Justice Day, and Mr. Justice A. L. Smith; act passed

The report of the commissioners was laid before parliament, Feb. 13, 1890. The following is an abridgment of their conclusions:—I. That the respondent members of parliament collectively were not guilty of conspiring for the absolute independence of Ireland as a separate nation, but that some of them (Messrs. M. Harris, Dillon, W. O'Brien, W. Redmond, O'Connor, J. Condon, and J. J. O'Kelly), together with Mr. Davitt, established the Land League mainly for that purpose. II. That the respondents [44] did conspire to promote agrarian agitation, the non-payment of rents, and the expulsion

of the landlords (styled the English garrison).
III. That they acquitted Mr. Parnell and others of
the charge of insincerity in their denunciations of the
Phœnix Park murders, and affirmed the fac-simile
letter to be a forgery. IV. They found that the
respondents did disseminate the *Irish World* and
other newspapers, intending to incite to sedition and
other crimes. V. That the charges of incitement
to crime, except by intimidation, and of payments
for that purpose, were not proved. VI. They found
that the respondents did not denounce the system
of intimidation, though they knew its effects; and
VII. That they defended persons charged with
agrarian crime, and supported their families, but it
was not proved that they subscribed for testimonials
for, or were intimately associated with, notorious
criminals, or aided their escape by payments. VIII.
That they found that the respondents made payments to compensate persons injured in the commission of crime. IX. That the respondents did
invite and obtain the assurance and coöperation of
the Physical Force Party in America, including the
Clan-na-Gael, and did not repudiate the action of
that party
[Certain allegations against Mr. Parnell were declared
not proved]
The report adopted with thanks, by the Commons,
after 7 days' debate, March 3–11; by the Lords
(without a division), March 21, 1890. Mr. Gladstone's amendment rejected
Aug., Great diminution of crime; boycotting reduced
by three-fourths in twelve months
Aug., Mr. Parnell proceeds against the *Times* in the
Scotch courts
Nov. 14, Nonconformist ministers of Ireland present
an address to the Marquises of Salisbury and
Hartington, protesting against the separatist policy
Nov., Mr. E. Harrington fined 500*l.* for contempt of
court in his paper, the *Kerry Sentinel*
Nov., Renewal of Lord Ashbourne's act of 1885, granting 5,000,000*l.* proposed; Mr. Gladstone's amendment rejected (330–246), Nov. 20; 2nd reading car-
ried (299–224), Nov. 22; passed, Dec. 24
Dec., Verdict for Mr. Joyce against Lord Clanricarde
for libel on appeal

1889

Jan. 1, Letter from Pope to Irish people expressing
sympathy and advice and gifts to the Irish churches
Jan. 29, Mr. Wm. O'Brien, M.P., sentenced to four
months' imprisonment, Jan. 25; (escaped), arrested
at a meeting at Manchester
Feb. 3, Deputy Inspector Wm. Limerick Martin killed
while attempting to arrest Father McFadden, P.P.,
at Gweedore, Donegal
Feb. 5, The court of session, Edinburgh, dismisses Mr.
Parnell's action against the *Times* with costs
Feb. 21, Great decrease of agrarian outrages (1881,
4,439; 1888, 660) announced
April 11, Mr. Dillon, Sir Thomas Esmonde, and Mr.
Deasy, M.P.'s, Home Rule delegates to Australia,
&c., arrive at Adelaide
April, Mr. Parnell moves for a trial against the *Times*
in the exchequer division, Dublin, Feb. 11; finally
stopped
May, Liberal subscription to support Mr. Olphert of
Gweedore, Donegal, in his conflict with the national
league and the plan of campaign

May, The negotiations between Mr. T. W. Russell and
Mr. Shaw to settle the dispute fail
May 31, Mr. A. J. Balfour explains his bills for the im-
provement of Ireland (drainage of the Bann, Barrow,
and Shannon, by grants of 383,000*l.*, and the con-
struction of light railways was also proposed)
June 30, Mr. William O'Brien arrested for speech at
Clonakilty
July 10, 11, Mr. W. O'Brien and Mr. Parnell announce
the formation of a New Tenants' Defense League
July 19, The light railways bill read second time
July 29, Dr. Tanner sentenced to one month's imprison-
ment for an assault, and to three months' for contempt of court
July, The mission of Mr. Dillon and other delegates to
Australia to obtain support for home rule, reported
unsuccessful; meetings at Sydney, Melbourne, and
Brisbane, protest against them
Aug. 25, Mr. William O'Brien sentenced to two months'
imprisonment and Mr. James Gilhooly to six
weeks
Aug. 30, The Suck drainage bill and the light railways
bill passed
Sept., Father O'Dwyer and 9 parishioners sentenced to
various terms of imprisonment for intimidation and
conspiracy
Oct. 5, The Earl of Zetland sworn in as Lord-Lieutenant
Oct. 7, National league proclaimed in Dungarvan district, and in places in county Tipperary, Oct. 11
Oct. 17, Mr. Justice Gibson at Maryborough tries
persons implicated in the murder of Deputy-Inspector
Martin at Gweedore (Feb. 3). Sentences for manslaughter Wm. Coll, 10 years' penal servitude:—
pleaded guilty, Patrick Roarty and Dominick Rogers,
7 years'; Connel M'Gee, 5 years'; 3 others, 6 months'
imprisonment with hard labor; Father M'Fadden
reprimanded, Oct. 30
Oct. 28, Meeting of the Tenants' Defense Association at
Thurles
About Oct. 31, The mission of Mr. Dillon and other
M.P.'s to Australia, said to have received 27,000*l.*;
proceeds to New Zealand
Nov. 5, The tenants on the Ponsonby estate, who have
paid no rent and refused very liberal terms, appeal
against ejectment
Nov., Failure of Plan of Campaign through combination of landlords; the tenants of the Olphert estate
pay the rent due
Dec. 18, First meeting of the Landlords' convention at
Dublin

1890

Jan. 21, The Irish Democratic Labor Association started
at Cork by Michael Davitt
Jan. 24, Feb. 16, Proclamations relaxing the stringency
of the Crimes act in some counties
Feb. 14–18, Mr. Parnell's censure of the government
policy in Ireland (negatived 307–240)
Feb. 19, Mr. Joseph Gillis Biggar, M.P., eminent
Parnellite, dies suddenly
March 24, New Land Purchase bill introduced by Mr.
A. J. Balfour, read 2nd time (348–286), May 1
The new Land Purchase bill reintroduced by Mr. A. J.
Balfour, Nov. 28
April 17–20, Ponsonby estate, Cork (237 tenants), plan
of campaign adopted, Nov., 1886; evicted, 1887, 10;
1888, 3; 1889, 32; the remainder without resistances

May 25, Nationalist meeting at New Tipperary, held though proclaimed; Messrs. Dillon, W. O'Brien, J. O'Connor, and others present

July, General Viscount Wolseley appointed Commander-in-Chief in Ireland (beginning Oct., succeeding Prince Edward of Saxe-Weimar)

July 26, Thomas Walsh and two others sentenced to seven years' penal servitude for moonlight outrages

July *et seq.*, Strikes in Dublin, Belfast, and other places

Announced Aug. 7, The National League issues a circular to its branches urging exertions to obtain subscriptions, &c.

Sept. 25, Tour of Messrs. John Dillon and William O'Brien in Tipperary, &c.; arrested with three M.P.'s and seven others, on charge of conspiring to induce Mr. Smith Barry's tenants not to pay rent, and to intimidate them; bailed, Sept. 18; prosecution begun at Tipperary before Mr. J. B. Irwin and Mr. G. R. Shannon

[Mr. W. O'Brien and Mr. Dillon do not appear, Oct. 10; at Paris, Oct. 16; sail for America, Oct. 25; at New York, Nov. 2]

Nov. 12 *et seq.*, Extensive evictions on the Olphert's estate at Falcarragh

Nov. 14, The National League suppressed in townlands in Fermanagh, Monaghan, and Waterford

Nov. 15, Intervention of the Roman Catholic bishop of Raphoe, Dr. O'Donnell: Mr. Olphert requires the total abandonment of the "plan of campaign" on the estate; no agreement, Nov. 12; evictions proceed

Nov. 19, Sentences: W. O'Brien, M.P., John Dillon, M.P., Patrick O'Brien, M.P., and John Cullinane, 6 months' imprisonment; Michael O'Brien, Dalton, Patrick Mockler, and Thos. Walsh, 4 months'

Nov. 27, Mr. Balfour introduces new Land Purchase and Congested Districts bills; and a bill to relieve the congested districts by providing seed potatoes, and by the construction of railways, roads, &c., Dec. 4; royal assent given to the bills, Dec. 9

Dec., Division in the Irish Home Rule party. In consequence of the issue of the divorce suit, Capt. O'Shea, Mrs. O'Shea, and Mr. C. S. Parnell, Nov. 15–17, 1890, Mr. Parnell was requested by Mr. W. E. Gladstone and other English liberals to retire from the chairmanship of the Irish party. He declined, and issued a manifesto to the people of Ireland, giving an account of private conferences with Mr. Gladstone and Mr. John Morley, Nov. 29. The Irish Roman Catholic bishops demanded Mr. Parnell's retirement, Dec. 3. After a week's angry discussion in the Commons' committee-room No. 15, the Irish party divided; Mr. Justin M'Carthy, the vice-chairman, was elected chairman by 44 members; Mr. Parnell continuing chairman with 26 followers, Dec. 6. Manifestoes of the two parties issued, Dec. 9, 10

Dec. 9, 10, He forcibly occupies the office of *United Ireland* at Dublin; two rival editions issued, Dec. 12

Dec. 10 *et seq.*, Mr. Parnell warmly received at Dublin, Cork, &c.

Dec. 23, North Kilkenny election; Mr. Vincent Scully, Parnellite, opposed by Sir J. Pope Hennessy, anti-Parnellite; fierce conflicts; Hennessy elected

Dec., The construction of the light railways begun at Valencia; road-making begun

About Dec. 24, The anti-Parnellite newspaper named *Insuppressible*

1891

Jan. 5, The Earl of Zetland, Lord Lieutenant, and Mr. A. J. Balfour appeal to the public for assistance in the relief of the distress in the congested districts of the western coast, Jan. 3., published

Jan., Relief works actively progressing; several thousands employed—men, women, and children

Jan. 24, The *Insuppressible* stopped

Jan. 30, Mr. Shaw-Lefevre's resolution for the application of arbitration in disputes between landlord and tenant negatived (213–152)

Feb. 2, Bartholomew Sullivan executed at Tralee for the murder of Patrick Flahive (Aug. 30, 1886), who had taken an evicted farm

——, Men employed on light railways, 281; unskilled, 7,412

Feb. 11, Mr. Parnell refuses to resign his leadership; disruption of the party; Messrs. W. O'Brien and J. Dillon, after fruitless conferences with Mr. Parnell at Boulogne, come to Folkestone, are arrested and conveyed to Clonmel gaol, Feb. 13; to Galway, Feb. 19

Feb. 16–17, Mr. John Morley's resolution, condemning the Tipperary prosecutions, negatived by the Commons (320–245)

March 7, The *National Press*, anti-Parnellite paper, first published

March 10, National Federation, anti-Parnellite, inaugurated at Dublin

March 18, Great decrease of crime in the south, reported by Justice Monroe

June 13, The crimes act suspended throughout Ireland, except in Co. Clare and a few baronies

July 31, Mr. W. O'Brien and Mr. Dillon liberated from gaol; declare their opposition to Mr. Parnell

Aug. 5, Purchase of Land and Congested Districts act passed

Aug. 28, The *Freeman's Journal* proprietors determine to support the anti-Parnellites

Sept. 27, Mr. Parnell delivers an address at Greggs, Galway; dies of rheumatic fever near Brighton, Oct. 6; public Nationalist funeral at Dublin, orderly and impressive, Oct. 11

Oct., National League convention at Limerick

Nov. 9, Mr. Wm. L. Jackson becomes Chief Secretary

Nov., Relief works closed as not required

Dec. 23, Mr. J. E. Redmond, Parnellite, elected M.P. for Waterford, in opposition to Mr. Michael Davitt, the clerical candidate

1892

Jan. 2, The corporation of London, the Irish Society, and 43 London companies, summoned to appear in Dublin to answer charges respecting the management of their Irish estates

Feb. 3, 4, Landowners' convention, annual meeting

Feb. 5, Mr. Justin M'Carthy elected by the anti-Parnellites sessional chairman

Feb., Above 150 tenants on the Ponsonby estate sign agreements to purchase their holdings under the Ashbourne act

Feb. 22, Irish Education bill introduced by Mr. Wm. L. Jackson, much opposed by the Roman Catholic clergy, early March

March 2, Evicted Tenants' (relief) bill rejected by the Commons (229–174)

About March 25, The *National Press* amalgamated with the *Freeman's Journal* (litigation ensued)

April 8, Meeting of Ulster men at Belfast to form a convention to oppose Home Rule (to be on June 17)

April 28, Meeting of Irish unionist alliance at Dublin

June 13, Local Government bill introduced by Mr. Balfour, Feb. 18, read 2nd time, May 24; withdrawn

June 17, Ulster convention at Belfast in opposition to Irish Home Rule

June 23, Great unionist meetings at Dublin

June 27, The education bill passed

July, Elections: Parnellites, 9; anti-Parnellites, 72

Aug. 18, Lord Houghton appointed Lord-Lieutenant, Mr. John Morley, Chief Secretary

Sept. 13, Operation of the Crimes act in county Mayo and other formerly disturbed counties suspended, Aug. 12; in all Ireland, and the National League declared legal

About Oct. 14, Appointment of a commission to inquire into the position of evicted tenants; Sir James C. Mathew, Judge Queen's Bench, England, and others; first sitting, Nov. 7; the landlords decline to appear, Nov.

About Oct. 17, Dismissal of Col. Turner, divisional commander and magistrate in Munster

Oct. 29, Proposal by Abp. Croke respecting the Irish fund at Paris accepted by the Parnellites and anti-Parnellites

Nov. 30, Mr. Patrick Fullam, M.P. for S. Meath, unseated on account of illegal Roman Catholic clerical influence; powerful address by Mr. Justice O'Brien

Dec. 23, Mr. Michael Davitt, M.P. for N. Meath, unseated on account of Roman Catholic priestly influence

——, The Gweedore convicts (*see above*, Feb.–Oct., 1889) released

Dec. 24, Explosions at Dublin Castle, Dec. 31, 1891, and

1893

Jan. 15, Meeting at Cork, held by the mayor, demanding the release of the dynamite prisoners

Jan. 17, Meetings in Ulster, opposing home rule; Belfast and Armagh; Dungannon, Jan. 20; Omagh, Jan. 21; Derry, Jan. 23; Ballymena, Jan. 24; Newry, Jan. 25

Jan. 17 *et seq.*, Great Unionist meetings in Ulster, Belfast, &c.; Dublin, Jan. 26

Feb. 13, Mr. Gladstone introduces a new Home Rule bill ("to amend the provision for the government of Ireland"); chief features, viceroy (non-political) for a fixed term; two chambers; legislative council, 48 members to be elected by 20*l.* voters; legislative assembly, 103 members, 80 members to sit at Westminster, as now

Feb. 16, The Queen's Bench Division decide that the police authorities have no right to refuse protection to the sheriffs on duty in the night-time; appeal of the crown disallowed

Feb. 18, Bill read 1st time; 2nd time (347–304), April 21–22; committee, May 8–July 28; the bill much changed; many amendments not considered; 3rd reading, Aug. 30–Sept. 2 (301–267); Lords: read 1st time, Sept. 1–2; on 2nd reading rejected (419–41), Sept. 5, 8, 9

Feb. 21, Irish Agricultural Association; inaugural meeting at Dublin

Feb. 24, Agrarian outrages: July 1–Sept. 30, 94 (63 in Munster); Oct. 1–Dec. 31, 80, reported

Feb. 25, The Irish National League of America condemns the new home rule bill in a manifesto

Feb.–March, Fall in bank and railway stocks

——, Many meetings and petitions against the home rule bill

Feb. 27, Mr. Justice O'Brien's severe remarks at Ennis on the lawlessness of Co. Clare; warmly discussed by the Commons, March 2; by the Lords, March 3

March 8, Anti-Parnellite convention at Dublin adopts the home rule bill

March 9, Report of the Evicted Tenants commission, with recommendations, presented to the commons

——, A Parnellite convention at Dublin, Mr. John Redmond in the chair, declares for present neutrality respecting the home rule bill

About March 13 *et seq.*, Disagreement among directors of the *Freeman's Journal* company; opposition of Abp. Walsh and Mr. T. Healy

About March 14, Manifesto of Roman Catholic laity against the home rule bill, with petition to parliament

March 14, Synod of the Protestant church at Dublin; protests against the home rule bill

March 15, Great Unionist meeting of all creeds and classes in Leinster Hall, Dublin; Lord Iveagh in the chair

——, The General Assembly of the Presbyterian church of Ireland at Belfast protests against the home rule bill

March 18, The Irish Unionist Alliance appeals for funds

——, Roman Catholic Unionist Association formed at Limerick

About March 22, Protest of Society of Friends, N. Ireland, against the home rule bill

March 27, Mr. A. J. Balfour's resolution in the Commons, censuring the Irish executive for releasing convicts, negatived (319–272)

April, Roman Catholic petition against the home rule bill

April 22, Great Unionist meeting at Albert hall, London; the Duke of Abercorn in the chair; about 10,000 persons present, including 1,200 delegates from Ireland

——, The Irish delegates entertained at St. James's hall and other places; by the Marquis of Salisbury at Hatfield; about 1,600 delegates present; addresses by the Unionist leaders, April 24

April, May, Revival of moonlighting outrages in Kerry, Kilkenny, Limerick, and Clare

Aug. 12, A petition to the Queen against home rule, signed by 103,000 Irish women of all classes and creeds; presented

1895

Feb. 16, Inaugural banquet of the Irish Loyalist club in London

March 13, Boards of guardians (Ireland) bill; 2nd reading

March 14, The seed potatoes supply bill passed

April 5, Land bill, Commons read 2nd time

May 8, Bill virtually repealing the Crimes act (1887) read 2nd time in Commons

——, Irish Agricultural Organization society; first annual meeting at Dublin; the Hon. Horace Plunkett, M.P., president

July 5, Municipal franchise bill withdrawn, in the Lords

Aug., Dissension between Mr. Justin M'Carthy, Mr. Healy, and others

Nov. 14, Expulsion of Mr. T. M. Healy and 3 others from the Irish National Federation; Mr. John Dillon elected chairman, Feb. 7, 1896

1896

Feb. 17, Mr. Harrington's amendment for the release of the Irish political prisoners (dynamiters), rejected; majority, 162

March, Disputes on the Ponsonby estates, Co. Cork, and the Smith-Barry estate, Tipperary, amicably settled

——, Lord-Lieut earl. Cadogan

April 14, Mr. Gerald Balfour's Land bill rather favorably received

May, 271 agrarian offences in 1895; reported

Aug. 4, Hybrid recess committee respecting Irish affairs, formed by Mr. H. Plunkett, M.P., autumn, 1895; report issued

Aug. 14, Local taxation; act passed

——, Land law act introduced by Mr. Gerald Balfour, April 13, based on the act of 1881; passed

Sept. 1–3, "Convention of the Irish race" (organized by Mr. Dillon), 2,000 delegates from all parts of the world; Dr. O'Donnell, Roman Catholic bishop of Raphoe, president; message from the Pope read, resolutions for unity, &c., passed; appeals for unity and money support

Oct. 15, Arrest of P. J. Tynan, "No. 1," accused of the Phœnix Park murders (see above, May 6, 1882), at Boulogne, Sept. 13; extradition refused by the French Government on legal grounds, Oct. 14; released

Dec. 14, 28, Mixed political meetings at Dublin; a resolution passed affirming the excessive imperial taxation of Ireland, 2,500,000l. too much, as disclosed by the report of the Financial Relations commission, and demanding restitution for the past and reduction in future

1897

Jan. 27, 28, Irish landowners' convention meets at Dublin, the new land act (see above, Aug. 14, 1896), censured; also by tenants and landlords, March; a great meeting at Dublin, Duke of Abercorn, Lord Londonderry, Lord Dufferin, and others present, compensation, &c., demanded, April 30

March 31, In the Commons Mr. Blake moves a resolution that the report of the royal commission proves the necessity for remedial legislation, March 29, 30; negatived (317–157)

April 20, An Independent Nationalist association (Parnellites), Mr. J. Redmond, president; inaugurated

April 22, An Irish Financial reform league formed in Dublin (annual meetings)

May 21, Mr. A. J. Balfour's statement of bills proposed for the benefit of Ireland

July 9, Royal commission on the Irish land acts, chairman, Sir Edward Fry, Messrs. Robt. Vigers, George Gordon, Dr. Traill, and others, reported; sat in Dublin, Sept. 22, 1897; last sitting at Belfast, Oct. 15; Cork, Oct. 19; report issued, Feb., 1898

Aug. 6, Judicature (Ireland) acts 1877 to 1888 (amendment), bill passed

Sept. 3, Failure of the potato and other crops in Cork, Kerry, and Clare, reported

Nov. 29, Application to the High court by the Earl of Gosford for a mandamus compelling the land commission to rehear applications made by his tenants for the fixing of fair rents; discharged without costs

Dec. 16, Lord Clarina (Eyre Massey), landowner in Limerick (conservative); born, 1830, died

1898

Jan. 30, Lord Carlingford, Chief Secretary for Ireland, 1865, died

March 31, Appeal from Dublin to the British Empire for the relief of distress in the south and west of Ireland; again April 27

May 25, Sir John Gilbert, Irish historian, born 1829, died

July 5, Resolution alleging Ireland to be unfairly treated in her financial relations rejected in the Commons 286–144

Aug. 12, Mr. Gerald Balfour's Irish local government bill passed

——, Seed supply and Potato Spraying Act passed

Oct. 10, Annual Parnellite convention, Mr. J. Redmond, president, held in Dublin

1899

Jan. 9, Country tranquil and prosperous, reported

Jan. 10, Appeal commission, under the local government act, Sir John Colomb, chairman, meets

Jan. 11, Lord Cadogan appoints a commission of inquiry into the intermediate system of education; witnesses examined

Jan. 16, Local government elections begin; many ladies vote; victory of the labour party in Dublin, Cork, and Limerick

Feb. 5, The Rt. Hon. C. Talbot Redington, Vice-Chancellor of the Royal University, born 1847; died (Lord Harris elected), July

Feb. 22, The Irish landowners' convention, annual meeting, Dublin; resolution adopted to carry out the recommendations of the Fry commission

March 31, Parliamentary grant for national education, 1,097,546l., year ending

——, Irish congested districts' board; good report of sea-fisheries and development of other industries in the west, issued for year ending

April 4, A "unity conference" of Nationalist parties, except Parnellites, held in Dublin

April 12, County council elections: 546 Nationalists, 113 Unionists, announced

May 23, Lady Betty Balfour cuts the first sod of a "Balfour line" at Carndonagh, Co. Donegal

Aug. 9, Agriculture and technical instruction (Ireland) act passed

Sept. 4, Mr. Wm. Talbot Crosbie, a beneficent landowner in Kerry, dies, aged 82

Oct. 26, Mr. Michael Davitt, M.P. for S. Mayo, opposed to the government's policy in the Transvaal, &c.; resigns his seat

Nov. 8, Sir Thos. Deane, architect, dies, aged 71

Nov. 23, Irish Nationalist conference to promote unity; committee appointed to confer with the Redmondites

Nov. 27, Killarney (the Muckross estate) bought by Lord Ardilaun for about 50,000l.

Dec. 16–18, Mr. Chamberlain visits Dublin; made LL.D. of Trinity College, and warmly received

1900

Jan. 9, The Duke of Connaught appointed Commander-in-Chief; welcomed in Dublin

Feb. 10, Mr. John Redmond, M.P., chairman of the reunited Irish party, issues a manifesto

April 3, Queen Victoria, with Princess Christian and Princess Henry of Battenberg, welcomed at Kingstown; the lord mayor at Dublin presents her with the keys of the city and the civic sword, &c.

July 20, Education grant of 1,292,069*l.* voted

Aug. 8, Irish intermediate education bill and the Irish tithe-rent-charge amendment bill passed

About Aug. 22, Irish land commission's report, April 1, 1899–March 31, 1900, issued as a blue-book

Sept. 2, Nationalist demonstration in Phœnix Park, Dublin; program of the Irish National League adopted

Nov., General election; great victory of Mr. W. M. O'Brien's United Irish League

Nov. 12, Mr. George Wyndham, Chief Secretary; tours through the western districts, Nov.; and through Connemara; receives many addresses, and returns to Dublin, Feb. 8, 1901

Dec. 11, Nationalist convention at Dublin, president, Mr. J. Redmond; exclusion of Mr. T. Healy from the party, carried

Dec. 21, Mr. Vere Foster, a promoter of social and educational work and emigration, dies at Belfast, aged 81

1901

April 22, "King *v.* M'Hugh," Mr. P. A. M'Hugh, M.P., proprietor of the *Sligo Champion,* sentenced to 6 months' imprisonment for threatening jurors, Dublin

May 9, The *Irish People,* Mr. Wm. O'Brien's Dublin weekly paper, seized for a gross libel on the King

May 16, Mrs. Smyly, philanthropist, dies, aged 87

June 29, Dr. Walsh, Roman Catholic Abp. of Dublin, resigns his seat on the Board of Nat. Education

July 12, Education grant, 1,300,771*l.,* voted

Aug., Congested districts board, satisfactory reports for year ending March 31, issued

Aug. 14, Purchase of land (No. 2) bill, passed

Aug. 16, Local govmt. (Ireland) and Congested districts board (amendment) bills (grant of 66,182*l.*), passed

Aug. 19–23, Pan-Celtic congress held in Dublin

Sept. 8, Lord Morris and Killanin, late Lord Chief Justice of Ireland, died, aged 73

Oct. 2, Demonstration in support of the compulsory land sale movement held in Londonderry

Nov., The United Irish league powerful in Leitrim and the west; much intimidation

Dec., "No-rent" campaign on Lord de Freyne's and other western estates

Dec. 18–24, Four M.P.'s and other agitators for non-payment of rent, &c., sentenced to imprisonment

1902

Jan. 8, United Irish league convention held in Dublin, Mr. J. Redmond, M.P., chairman; 1,230 branches in Ireland

Jan.–March, Coercive measures of the league in the west increasing; boycotting in Sligo

April 2, Roy. commission on university education in Ireland, Lord Robertson chairman, appointed, June, 1901; first meeting, Belfast

April 10, Irish unionist alliance meets in Dublin, strong protest against the United Irish league

April 14, Mr. Jasper Tully, M.P., placed in gaol (14 days) for illegal assembly

April 16, Certain districts placed under sections 2, 3, 4, relating to boycotting, of the crimes act (1887)

April 16, 17, Agrarian outrages Co. Galway

May 17–23, Prince Henry of Prussia, with German naval squadron, visits Dublin

May 17, United Irish league's annual meeting held in Manchester

June 18, Mr. P. A. M'Hugh, M.P., sentenced to three months' imprisonment for contempt of court

June 23, Agricultural and technical instruction act, royal assent (No. 2 bill, royal assent, Dec. 18); pauper children bill passed, June 26

July 8–23, Evictions continue on Lord de Freyne's estate

July 10, Debate in the Commons on the case of ex-Sergeant Sheridan (by whose false accusations men had been imprisoned, one of whom had died, Jan.); Mr. Dillon's motion to reduce the vote for the constabulary by 500,000*l.* rejected 195–102

July 17, Lord Cadogan, Lord-Lieut. resigns

July 22, Dr. Croke, Abp. of Cashel, died, aged 78

July 23, 24, 25, Angry debates in the Commons; reduction of the vote for the Chief Secretary, rejected, 196–135; motion to remove alleged overtaxation, rejected, 168–117

July 28, Mr. W. R. Fenton, crown solicitor for Sligo, *v.* Mr. P. A. M'Hugh, M.P., proprietor of the *Sligo Champion,* for libel and conspiracy; verdict for plaintiff, 3,500*l.* damages

July 31, Public libraries (Ireland) act passed

Aug. 8, Balfour Ministry: Lord-Lieut., Earl Dudley; Lord Chancellor, Lord Ashbourne; Chief Secretary, George Wyndham

Aug. 9, Meeting of the Irish parliamentary party, city hall, Dublin

Aug. 13, 14, Evictions resumed on Lord de Freyne's Frenchpark estate

Aug. 29, The Duke of Abercorn presides at the Irish landowners' convention; resolutions carried in favor of Mr. Wyndham's land bill, the newly-formed Irish land trust, and for a royal commission of inquiry into landlords' losses

Aug. 31 *et seq.,* Crimes act extended to Dublin, Limerick, and seven counties

Sept. 1–Oct., Several Irish M.P.'s imprisoned

Sept. 5, 12, 13, Indignation meetings at the mansion house and city hall and Phœnix Park, Dublin

Sept. 9, Roy. commission on university education in Ireland (July, 1901), 3rd report issued

Sept. 25, State entry of Lord Dudley, Lord-Lieut. into Dublin

Sept. 27, 29, Samuel Harris, secretary to the (E. Limerick) United Irish league, sentenced to nine months' imprisonment for intimidation; Mr. McCarthy, editor of the *Irish People,* sentenced to two months' imprisonment for intimidation (confirmed on appeal, Dec. 20)

Oct. 3, Meeting at the mansion house, Dublin; "Nat. Defense Fund" started to resist prosecutions under the crimes act; 300*l.* subscribed

Oct. 10, Irish landowners' convention met, Dublin; motion for a conference between *representatives* of landlords and tenants, rejected (77–14)

Oct. 16, Mr. P. A. M'Hugh, M.P., sentenced to two months' imprisonment for conspiracy and intimidation

Oct. 17, United Irish league accused of tyranny, &c.

Oct. 24, Martin, Patrick, and Thos. Joyce (*see above,* Nov., 1882) released

Oct. 27, Large consignment of arms and ammunition from Birmingham, reported

Nov. 4, Mr. W. Redmond, M.P., arrested and taken to Kilmainham gaol

Nov. 13, Tallow conspiracy case (5th trial) settled by chief Baron Palles and special jury; verdict, 5,500*l.* damages for plaintiff, David O'Keeffe, small trader, who had been boycotted by the 10 defendants, members of the United Irish league

Nov., Split between the Roman Catholic hierarchy and the leaders of the United Irish league

Dec. 4, Munster assizes, Cork; the grand jury threw out the bills in the case against Major Studdert and others charged with conspiracy in connection with the purchase of remounts

Dec., The Earl of Meath appointed chancellor of the royal university

Dec. 10, Mr. Denis Kilbride, an ex-M.P., sentenced to eight months' imprisonment for inciting to murder (in a speech at a united Irish league meeting)

Dec. 18, Local government bill (No. 2), royal assent

Dec. 22, Lord Dunraven's land conference (five hrs.)

1903

Jan. 7, Lord Dunraven's land conference (Dec. 22, 1902) issues report, Jan. 3, 1903; formally received by the landlords' convention

Jan. 23, Mr. T. Harrington, M.P., reëlected for the third time Lord Mayor of Dublin

Feb. 2, Summary jurisdiction clauses of crimes act, 1887, revoked in Dublin and many other urban and rural districts, several prisoners released

Feb. 13, McTierney, auctioneer *v.* the Clareman Newspaper co., libel action (the plaintiff's trade had suffered, his horses had been maimed, and his customers' houses fired at): verdict for plaintiff with 600*l.* damages

March 11, Irish University commission's report, scheme for a Roman Catholic college in Dublin; issued

March 23, Bank holidays (Ireland) bill, constituting St. Patrick's day a bank holiday, passed

March 25, Irish land bill, first reading (commons)

April 15, Conference held to promote the establishment of a commercial and industrial institute and an international exhibition in Dublin

April 16–17, Nationalist convention on the land bill held at Dublin; special resolution for Home rule, and amendment to the bill carried

July 2, International motor-car race

July 3, Disorderly scenes at meeting of the Dublin corporation, on motion of moderate section of members to present the King with a municipal address on the occasion of his visit to Dublin; meeting broken up by disorderly crowd in the gallery of the hall

July 21, Royal visit to Ireland, the King and Queen arrive at Kingstown and Dublin; King returns to Cowes, Aug. 2

Aug. 14, Irish Land Purchase bill; royal assent

Sept. 19, Estates commissioners under the new Land act appointed

Oct. 9, Conference of Ulster tenants at Belfast to consider the new Land act

Dec. 27, Serious collision, near Wesport, between rival factions of the United Irish League

1904

Jan. 4, Lord Dunraven addresses a letter to the Dublin Press suggesting the establishment of two additional colleges at Dublin and Belfast within the university of Dublin

Jan. 5, Resignation of the Rt. Hon. H. E. Chatterton, Vice-Chancellor of Ireland, reported

Jan. 5, Mr. John Redmond speaks at Waterford, and declared that the Irish Nationalists are the only united party returning to parliament, and points out the consequent opportunity for the immediate demand for home rule

Jan. 11, Lord Rathdonnell sells his estates in County Fermanagh to his tenants, announced

Jan. 12, Special meeting of the Roman Catholic hierarchy at Maynooth to consider scheme for the solution of the university question proposed by Mr. Wyndham and Lord Dunraven, viz., the inclusion in Dublin university of Queen's College, Belfast, and of a new Roman Catholic college in Dublin

Jan. 25, Duke of Connaught presides at the inaugural dinner of the Ireland club, which has for its principal objects the development of Irish industries and resources

Jan. 29, Large meeting at the mansion house at Dublin in support of the Roman Catholic claims in regard to university education

Feb. 1, Mr. John Redmond, M.P., reëlected chairman of the Irish parliamentary party

Feb. 3, Mr. Wyndham states that the government did not intend to introduce any measure dealing with Irish university education

Feb. 19, Irish society agrees to sell their estates near Londonderry and Coleraine to their agricultural tenants, announced

April 5, Drapers' company of London announce their intention of handing over the remainder of their Irish estates in Ulster, with an addition of 2,000*l.* in stock, to a board of trustees for educational purposes

April 12, Report of the representative body of the Church of Ireland shows that the total amount of voluntary contributions received by it since the disestablishment amounts to nearly 6,000,000*l.*; total assets of the representative body on Dec. 31, 1903, 8,414,138*l.*; investment in securities, 7,776,317*l.*, yielding a return of 4*l.* 1*s.* 4*d.* %, presented

April 14, Death of Dr. Coffey, Roman Catholic Bp. of Kerry

April 17, Serious rioting at Lisburn in connection with the visit of a Belfast team of hurlers, several persons injured

April 21, Nationalist convention in Dublin adopts resolutions on home rule and the Land act

April 26, King Edward and Queen Alexandra arrive in Ireland

April 28, The King, accompanied by Queen Alexandra, lays the foundation stone of the new buildings of the Royal College of Science in Dublin

May 4, Mr. Boland's motion in the House of Commons for the repeal of the Irish Crimes act is rejected, 197 votes to 124

May 8, Monument to Michael O'Dwyer and Samuel Macalister, well-known actors in the events of 1798, unveiled at Baltinglass, Co. Wicklow

May 10, Lord Cork's tenants near Blarney, having refused an abatement of 40%, decline to pay their rents; an unsuccessful attempt is made to distrain on their cattle; majority of tenants pay their rents in full, May 12

May 11, Emigration statistics for Ireland for 1903, issued as a parliamentary paper; 40,659 emigrants left Irish ports during the year, an increase of 258 in comparison with 1902. Of the total enumerated, 39,789 were natives of Ireland

May 27, Ulster Protestant electoral union formed to

secure democratic representation in parliament; first meeting held at Belfast

June 18, Agrarian disturbances in Loughrea reported

June 22, Roman Catholic bishops adopt at their annual meeting at Maynooth an important statement on the subject of education

July 1, Very Rev. M. Fogarty, D.D., Vice-President of St. Patrick's College, Maynooth, appointed Bp. of Kallaloe, reported

July 8, Irish land bill carried, on second reading, by majority of 117

July 23, St. Patrick's Roman Catholic cathedral, Armagh, consecrated

Aug. 14, Col. Saunderson, addressing a meeting of Orangemen at Castle Saunderson, defines the attitude of the Ulster unionists to the government and Sir Anthony MacDonnell

Aug. 15, Irish land bill, to explain and amend sect. 48 of the Land act, 1903, receives royal assent

Sept. 6, Official statement of the working of the Irish Land act issued in Dublin; applications for advances for the purchase of estates exceeding 10,500,000*l.* made to the estates commissioners, who had sanctioned advances amounting to over 3,000,000*l.*

Sept. 8, Reported intention of the directory of the United Irish league to use the whole strength of the national organization to secure the reinstatement of evicted tenants announced

Sept. 23, Land Conference committee dissolved and a new organization, named the Irish Reform association, formed, with Lord Dunraven and others as a provisional organizing committee, Aug. 25; report of organizing committee of the Irish Reform association adopted

Sept. 26, Mr. Wyndham writes to *Times*, declaring without reserve or qualification that the government is opposed to the multiplication of legislative bodies within the United Kingdom

Oct. 8, Lord Dunraven addresses a letter to the *Times* defending the Irish Reform association

Dec. 7, New great seal for Ireland, approved by the King, delivered by the Lord Lieutenant to the Lord Chancellor of Ireland

1905

Feb. 4, Prince of Wales visits Dublin; returns to England

Feb. 7, First of series of meetings held in furtherance of the objects of the Irish Reform association held in Dublin; important speech by Lord Dunraven

Feb. 9, Death of the Earl of Kenmare, Viscount and Baron Castlerosse, Lord Chamberlain of the Household, 1886, aged 79

March 3, First meeting of the unionist council formed in Belfast to consolidate unionist interests in the province, held under the presidency of Col. McCalmont

March 11, Mr. Walter Long, pres. of the local government board, appointed Chief Secretary for Ireland, in succession to Mr. Wyndham, resigned

March 12, Earl of Darnley chosen a representative peer for Ireland

——, Gaelic league's, annual week of propaganda of the movement for the furtherance of the Irish language begins at Dublin; many thousands of persons assemble in St. Stephen's green at Smithfield, where speeches are delivered

March 23, Several of the Ulster unionist members declare themselves in favor of the abolition of the Irish vice-royalty

March 24, Town Tenants (Ireland) bill, to give the tenants of urban holdings in Ireland a right to compensation from their landlords for improvements adding to the value of the premises which they have occupied, passes its second reading in the House of Commons

April 1, Ulster unionist members resolve that so long as the present under-secretary, Sir A. MacDonnell, remains at Dublin castle they cannot support the Government on any issue involving confidence in the Irish administration, reported

April 13, Nationalist motion on the Irish Roman Catholic university question rejected in the House of Commons by 263 votes to 104

April 22, Death of Capt. W. H. O'Shea, formerly M.P., 1890

June 29, Commissioners of national education for Ireland issue an important circular to teachers of national schools on the subject of the display of disloyalty at a teachers' dinner at Sligo

July 4, Motion moved by Mr. J. Redmond censuring the Government for using the Crimes act in Galway, rejected by 176 votes to 136

July 8, Important regulations as to intimidation made by the Lord Lieutenant under the Land act

July 14, Manifesto from the Independent Orangemen of Ireland, signed by Mr. T. H. Sloan, M.P., Mr. R. L. Crawford, Dublin, imperial grand master, and others, calling upon Nationalists and Unionists to unite, and describing unionism as a discredited creed, issued

July 23, Parliamentary paper issued, containing the minutes of the proceedings of the commissioners of national education relating to the multiplication of small schools, and to the new rule which requires boys under 7 years of age to be educated by female teachers. Memorandum by the senior inspector to the commissioners shows that there are 2,247 mixed schools in Ireland under Roman Catholic management

July 30, Statue to the memories of the Rev. John Murphy and of John Gallagher, two of the rebels of 1798, dedicated at Tullow, Co. Carlow; monument commemorative of the rebellion of 1798 unveiled at Wexford, Aug. 6

Aug. 12, Rioting at Londonderry between nationalists and members of a Belfast party of apprentice boys taking part in the celebration of the anniversary of the relief of Derry

Aug. 20, Resolution passed at the committee of the Gaelic league sitting at Dublin, "that the Irish people should establish a Gaelic university for themselves without delay"

Aug. 25, Irish landowners' convention meets in Dublin under the presidency of the Duke of Abercorn; report submitted by the executive committee deals with the financial deadlock in the administration of the Land act of 1903

Sept. 2, Dublin corporation decide to refuse payment, except under compulsion, of their statutory contribution to the city police tax

Sept. 12, Death of the Earl of Lanesborough, a representative peer for Ireland, aged 66

Sept. 21, Board of national education which controls and administers the whole system of primary education in Ireland, confronted with two formidable agitations—a "moral" and "religious" movement directed by the Roman Catholic bishops and clergy against the joint teaching of boys and girls and the amalgamation of small schools; and another movement, professedly non-sectarian, organized by the Gaelic league to apply the resources of the state to the development of the Irish language and the other propaganda of the league; Lord Castletown proposes the boycotting of the national schools

Sept. 25, Executive of the United Irish league at Limerick pass a resolution suggesting the dissension in the nationalist ranks be settled by a personal conference between Messrs. Redmond, Dillon, Davitt, and O'Brien; Mr. Dillon and Mr. J. Redmond express their willingness to meet Mr. O'Brien

Sept. 27, Judge Adams, at the Limerick parliamentary revision, declines to entertain a claim to the franchise the application for which was in Irish

1906

Jan. 8, Mr. W. F. Bailey, one of the estate commissioners, in the course of his evidence before the arterial drainage commission, gives a sketch of the operation of the land purchase acts; under previous acts there were in 25 years 75,000 purchasers at a price of 25,000,000*l.*; under the act of 1903, there were in two years, 88,000 purchasers at a price of 33,000,-000*l.*; about one-third of the tenants of Ireland had purchased; average price paid 24.8 years' purchase; average size of the holdings purchased was 49.47 acres in Leinster, 49.16 in Munster, 24.18 in Connaught, 21 in Ulster, and 37 acres for Ireland as a whole, reported

Jan. 16, Monster demonstration against home rule or devolution at Ulster hall, Belfast

Feb. 6, Proclamation by the Lord Lieutenant and Privy Council in Ireland revokes the provisions of sections 3 and 4 of the Criminal Law and Procedure (Ireland) Act, 1887, in so far as the same have been put in force by proclamation

April 1, Number of migratory laborers from Ireland to England and Scotland during 1905 was approximately 25,000; from a gray-book issued by the Irish department of agriculture

April 3, Five of the lay assistant commissioners to the land commission, most of whom are Unionists, were dismissed and Nationalists appointed in their place

May 31, Death of Mr. Michael Davitt, ex-Nationalist, M.P., born 1846

June 1, Royal commission appointed, Sir Edward Fry, chairman, to inquire into and report on the present state of Trinity College, Dublin, and the Royal University of Dublin

July 21, Rosslare harbor and railway, which by a fast steamer connection with Fishguard in Pembrokeshire constitutes a new route between England and the south of Ireland, opened by the Lord-Lieut.

Aug. 30, New Fishguard route between England and Ireland opened

Sept. 2, Visit of the Atlantic fleet to Queenstown

Sept. 3, Mr. Bryce, M.P., Chief Secretary for Ireland, visited Port Stewart to inspect the harbor and inquire into fishermen's grievances

Sept. 8, Monument to John Mandeville and the three men who were shot at Mitchelstown by the constabulary on Sept. 3, 1887, unveiled

Oct. 9, Serious shooting outrage at Athenry

Oct. 25, Executive committee of the Irish unionist alliance, at a meeting in Dublin, passed a resolution expressing satisfaction with Mr. Balfour's explicit denial that there were any compromising letters with reference to Sir Antony MacDonnell's appointment

Nov. 13, As a result of the disorders in connection with the recent conferring of degrees at the Royal university of Ireland, Mr. F. C. O'Brien, auditor of the literary and historical society at the Roman Catholic University College in St. Stephen's-green, has been rusticated for 12 months, deprived of his post of auditor, and expelled from the literary and historical society, by the council of the College, reported

Nov. 16, Death of Mr. John R. Wigham, aged 78, inventor of the Wigham light for lighthouses

Dec. 3, Court of appeal gives judgment in the case of "King (Drury) *v.* the Corporation of Dublin," in which the town-clerk of Dublin appealed against an order of the king's bench division directing him to submit the books and accounts of the corporation to be audited by Mr. Drury, the local government board auditor; the court allowed the appeal

Dec. 7, Irish Unionist campaign against the home rule proposals of the Government formally inaugurated in Dublin

1907

Jan. 21, Final report of the Royal commission on Trinity College, Dublin, and the University of Dublin, issued as a blue-book

Jan. 24, Mr. Birrell appointed chief secretary for Ireland in the place of Mr. Bryce

——, "Union Defence League" formed with the object of resisting the new form of Separatist policy in Sir Hy. Campbell-Bannerman's Government

Jan. 25, Mr. Bryce, replying to deputations which waited upon him, makes an important statement as to the government's views upon the Irish university question

Feb. 1, A protest, signed by 11 out of the 13 prelates in the Protestant Church of Ireland against the Government's scheme for the reorganizing of Dublin University, issued

Feb. 8, Great liberal demonstration held at Belfast; address by Mr. Lloyd-George, President of the Board of Trade

Feb. 22, Serjeant Dodd, K.C., M.P., appointed Judge of the King's Bench in the High Court, announced

March 17, Great meeting in Phœnix Park to protest against the action of the French Government in reference to the question of Church administration in France

March 31–April 2, A series of conflicts between police and peasants, owing to attempts by the police to stop meetings of the United Irish league, occurred in the neighborhood of the town of Elphin, Co. Roscommon

April 3, Emigration statistics of Ireland for 1906 show that the number of emigrants leaving Irish ports was 35,918, being an increase of 4,746 over the figures for 1905. *Times*

April 17, The Irish tobacco bill, legalizing the growing of tobacco in Ireland, after being considered by the House of Commons standing committee on trade, is, after certain amendments being agreed to, ordered to be reported to the House

May 17, Irish council bill condemned at special meeting of the Dublin corporation as "an insult to the Irish people"

May 22, Mr. T. W. Russell, M.P., appointed vice-president of the department of agriculture in Ireland in succession to Sir H. Plunkett, resigned

May 24, Demonstration of Ulster Unionists to protest against the Irish council bill, Lord Londonderry presiding, held at Belfast

June 20, Meeting of the national directory, Mr. John Redmond presiding

July 10–11, Visit of King Edward and Queen Alexandra; departure for Cardiff, July 12

July 25, Belfast ironmolders' strike settled by concession to the men of an advance of a shilling a week in wages; coal strike also settled

Aug. 7, Belfast picketed by soldiers

Aug. 27, Proclamation issued by the lord-lieut. declaring the counties of Clare, Galway, Leitrim, Longford, Roscommon, and King's county to be in a state of disturbance and requiring an additional establishment of police

——, Mr. J. P. Farrell, M.P., and 14 others committed for trial on charges arising out of cattle-driving

Aug. 28, Irish land act of 1907 passed enabling Irish land commission to dispose of mineral rights

——, Irish land act (evicted tenants) received royal assent

Aug. 31, Printers employed in the Limerick newspaper offices and printing offices of the city strike work

Sept. 4, Anti-grazing agitation. The magistrates of Kells petty sessions pass a resolution drawing the attention of the executive to the cattle raiding in the county of Meath; 27 young men charged with unlawful assembly in connection with cattle-driving at Borrisokane

Nov. 9, Suicide of Lord Kilmaine, aged 64

Dec. 2, Twenty-six men, tried in Dublin in connection with cattle-driving in county Galway, bound over to appear at petty sessions; 5 others, already convicted, sentenced to 4 months' imprisonment

1908

Jan. 20, Lord Curzon elected Irish representative peer

Feb. 4, Arrest of 15 prominent United Irish Leaguers of the Callow district on a charge of riotous assembly and disturbing the peace; 11 were returned for trial to the assizes, the other 4 being discharged

Feb. 18, Ten men arrested in connection with a cattle-drive at Carraduff, county Roscommon, and remanded, on bail, to the next petty sessions

March 3, Sixteen young men arrested in connection with a cattle-drive at Borrisokane; 5 defendants sent to prison for 3 months, 10 for 2 months, and one for 1 month

March 24, Parliamentary paper showing the number of cases of boycotting, and of persons boycotted in Ireland, on certain specified dates issued; the number of cases in July, 1903, was 86, and of persons boycotted, 422. In November, 1905, the number of cases had fallen to 37, and of persons boycotted, to 162. In January, 1908, the number of cases was 149, and of persons boycotted, 536. *Times*

April 24, Release of Mr. Ginnell, M.P., who had been sentenced to 6 months' imprisonment for contempt of court, after 4 months

May 2, Thirty-five men, arrested on charge of cattle-driving at Brierfield, county Galway, ordered to give bail for their further good behavior or go to prison for 3 months. On the following day, 100 farmers

arrived from Galway to give bail, and the prisoners were set at liberty

May 13, Twenty-five men, charged with having taken part in a cattle-drive at Ballinasloe, were ordered to keep the peace for 12 months, bails being forthcoming; 29 arrests also made in the district of Gort

May 24–26, Rioting at Thurles in consequence of the purchase of the place of business of a Mr. Richard Burke, who was evicted, by a trader named Coady

Aug. 1, The Irish universities act, by which two universities were to be established at Dublin and Belfast, received royal assent

Aug. 18, Death of E. H. Ennis, assistant under-secretary for Ireland

Aug. 24, Population statistics for 1907—blue-book issued; increase of population by excess of births over deaths, 24,408; loss by emigration, 39,082; apparent decrease in the population, 14,674 during last year

Aug. 31, A return of criminal statistics for the first six months of the year issued; 418 cattle-drivers charged, 75 cases of firing; 63 complete cases and 66 partial cases of boycotting; the number of prosecutions for the foregoing offenses was 98; claims granted for malicious injuries numbered 258, and the amount of rewards reached 10,178*l*. *Times*

Sept. 16, Irish industrial conference opened in Galway

Sept. 17, Two hundred head of cattle and 400 sheep driven from five farms in county Clare, reported

Sept. 30, Serious conflict between police and people at Ennistymon, county Clare, when 44 men had been summoned for taking part in cattle-drives

Oct. 29, Cattle-driving affray in county Sligo; one of the cattle-drivers shot dead, several police injured

Nov. 28, Outrage in county Galway; police attacked

Dec. 19, Carters' strike in Dublin settled

1909

March 13, Mr. J. P. Farrell, M.P., who, on Dec. 23, 1908, was sentenced to 6 months' imprisonment in default of giving security for good behavior, on a charge of publishing boycotting reports and articles in his newspaper, was released on the ground of ill-health

March 26, Mr. William O'Brien announced his proposed retirement from political life

July 1, Tuberculosis Prevention (Ireland) Act, 1908, comes into force

Aug. 15, Serious riots at Portadown

Aug. 16, Serious rioting at Lurgan

Aug. 17, Criminal statistics for 1908—number of indictable offences for 1908, 10,266, an increase of 9% on that of 1907; vital statistics—23,295 persons lost by emigration, a number more than 15,000 less than the average for the past ten years

——, Total estimated population, 4,371,455; marriages registered, 22,734; births, 102,039; deaths, 76,891

Nov. 1, 90 head of cattle and 250 sheep were driven from a farm near Galway; 8 men taking part in the raid were arrested

Dec. 3, Irish Land Act, 1909. Provision for future purchases could be raised by the issue of a 3% stock, and the treasury could issue such stock vice cash in making advances. The congested districts board was reconstituted, the area of its work extended, and its income increased. Compulsory powers of purchase given to estate commissioners and congested districts board

1910

Feb. 19, Death of Sir Robert Holmes, for many years Treasury Remembrancer and deputy Paymaster for Ireland

Mar. 31, The "All for Ireland" league inaugurated at Cork

April 1, Emigration report for 1909: total number of emigrants from Ireland, 29,230; an increase of 5,278 over the total for 1908

May 9, Proclamation of King George at Dublin Castle in the privy council chamber and by the Ulster King of Arms at several public places in the city

May 11, King George V proclaimed in Belfast, Cork, and other cities

May 27, Serious rioting in county Cork between the O'Brienite and Nationalist factions; the police fired over the heads of the crowd

June 29, The east Kerry election declared void; Mr. E. O'Sullivan, it was found, by his agents, had been guilty of intimidation and undue influence, and was, therefore, unseated

1911

"The year 1911 was, on the whole, uneventful in Ireland. Agrarian unrest continued with sporadic cases of cattle-driving, boycotting, shooting and bomb outrages, and incendiarism . . . " "Britannica"

July 7–11, Royal visit to Dublin

Sept. 16–Oct. 4, Railroad strike

Sept. 23, Demonstration against Home Rule at Belfast. Statement of Sir Edward Carson acclaimed Ulster leader that never "under any circumstances, would they submit to Home Rule"

1912

Jan. 3, Ulster Unionist Council passed resolutions repeating resolve of Ulster Convention of 1892 to repudiate authority of Irish Parliament should it be constituted

April 23, Home Rule Bill endorsed by Nationalist Convention meeting in Dublin

Sept. 28, "Ulster Day" a Covenant signed at Belfast by northern Protestants against Home Rule pledging defense of their position of equal citizenship in the United Kingdom and use of all means necessary to defeat Home Rule Parliament in Ireland

1913

Aug., Strike of transport workers in Dublin

Aug. 26, Mr. Larkin arrested but released on bail

Aug. 31, Strike riots in Dublin caused by harangue of Mr. Larkin who had been arrested in connection with strike violence but released on bail

Sept. 13, Decision of employers for lockout threw out of work several thousand men who refused to sign pledge not to give aid to the transport workers

Sept. 25, Ulster Unionist Council organized as a Provisional Government headed by Sir Edward Carson

Sept. 27, 20,000 men of Ulster join in demonstration in Belfast against Home Rule

Nov. 25, Meeting of the Gaelic Athletic Association, the Gaelic League, and the Irish Republican Brotherhood held in Dublin to inaugurate the National Volunteers

1914

Jan. 19, Dublin transport workers strike ended

March 14, Sir Arthur Paget, general in command of troops in Ireland, ordered to send troops to guard military supplies and government property in Ulster

March 20, General Gough stationed at Curragh with 57 of his officers offered to resign rather than march against Ulster

April 24–25, Ulster volunteer troops landed cargoes of ammunition and arms at Larne, Bangor, and Donaghade

July 10, First formal meeting of Ulster Provisional Government at Belfast

July 26, "Bachelor's Walk Massacre." Troops sent to capture consignment of arms being landed at Howth near Dublin in conflict with regiment of Irish Volunteers. On return to Dublin attacked by mob the soldiers fired on the crowd killing 3 persons and wounding 38

Aug. 5, Mr. Redmond in the House of Commons announced that the Nationalist Party would support Great Britain, and National Volunteers would join Ulstermen in defense of coasts and the Government might withdraw troops from Ireland for the war; manifesto of Sinn Fein denounced Mr. Redmond's program, Sept. 25

Sept. 18, Home Rule for Ireland received royal assent but going into effect postponed until end of war

1915

May 30, Proposal of Irish Volunteers at meeting in favor of immediate insurrection defeated by casting vote of the chairman, Professor John M. Mac Neill

July 24–29, Meeting of the Gaelic League at Dundalk elected a majority of Sinn Feiners to executive committee making the League a political body in opposition to the Government

Sept. 14, Order in Council postponed the going into effect of Home Rule until end of war

1916

April 20, Unsuccessful attempt by Sir Roger Casement to have arms landed from German ships disguised as neutral merchant vessels to support Irish revolt planned

April 21, Sir Roger Casement who had landed from a German submarine arrested with 2 companions

April 24, Sinn Fein rebels seized the Post Office in Dublin, and the Four Courts and other buildings failing in attack on the Castle, P. H. Pearse, President of the Provisional Government and commander-in-chief proclaimed the Irish Republic

April 26–27, Fire destroyed the General Post Office and a large part of Sackville Street

April 27, Martial law proclaimed in Dublin. General Sir John Maxwell took command of troops

April 28, Government troops commanded by General Sir John Maxwell established complete cordon around Dublin

April 29, Pearse surrendered unconditionally as the situation of the rebels became hopeless and issued manifesto ordering other commanders to surrender to prevent further bloodshed

April 30, Thomas MacDonagh surrendered ending rebellion

May 3–4, Leaders of rebellion, P. H. Pearse, Thomas MacDonagh, Joseph Plunkett, James Connoly,

Edmund Kent, and others executed after trials by court martial

May. 6, Countess Markievicz sentenced to death which was later changed to life imprisonment

May 12–18, Visit of Mr. Asquith to Ireland

May 15, Sir Roger Casement charged with high treason and committed for trial

June 26–29, Trial of Sir Roger Casement. Sentenced to death

July 31, Henry Duke, Unionist, appointed to succeed Mr. Birrell, resigned as Chief Secretary for Ireland

Aug. 3, Sir Roger Casement hung in London

1917

Jan. 18, Official Sinn Fein organization launched in the United States

Feb. 23, 28 Sinn Fein agitators arrested and deported under Defense of the Realm Act following discovery of new German plan to land arms in Ireland

March 7, Resolution moved in House of Commons calling for immediate application of Home Rule to Ireland protested by Mr. Redmond in name of Nationalist Party

April 19, Sinn Fein Conference in Dublin called by Count Plunkett attended by delegates from elective bodies throughout the country

May 16, Lloyd George in a letter to Mr. Redmond made 2 proposals for settlement of Irish question by introduction of Bill for application of Home Rule Act of 1914 subject to amendment providing for exclusion of the counties of N.E. Ulster for a period of time or calling of a convention of Irishmen of all parties to prepare plan for Irish self-government. The second proposal accepted by Mr. Redmond representing the Nationalist Party

May 18, Count Plunkett announced Sinn Fein would not accept Lloyd George proposal for conference

June 15, Announcement of English Government that all political prisoners of the Irish rebellion of 1916 would be released

July 11, Mr. De Valera released from prison by amnesty, elected to Parliament, and became leader of Sinn Fein movement

July 25, First meeting of Convention in Dublin to discuss Irish self-government

July 28, Proclamation of the Government prohibited carrying of weapons

Aug. 14, Prominent Sinn Fein leaders arrested and sentenced to terms of imprisonment

Sept. 25, Death of Thomas Ashe in prison as a result of forcible feeding. He had been condemned to death after Easter Rebellion of 1916, released in the general amnesty, rearrested Aug. 14, and condemned Aug. 20, to one year in prison for attempt to cause disaffection among the civil population

Oct. 25–27, Sinn Fein Convention in Dublin announced adoption of Constitution for an Irish Republic: Mr. De Valera elected President; Arthur Griffith and Father Michael O'Flanagan, Vice-Presidents; Austin Stack and Darrell Figgis, Secretaries

Nov. 15–21, 102 hunger strikers released from various prisons

1918

Jan. 6, Death of Mrs. Clement Shorter (Dora Sigerson), poet

March 6, Death of John Redmond, Nationalist leader, in London. John Dillon elected to succeed him as leader of Party

March 6, 600 Sinn Feiners seized in Kiltomagh in County Mayo

April 17, The Irish Nationalists left the House of Commons in a body after defeat of an amendment to exclude Ireland from Military Service (Conscription) Bill

April 18, Anti-conscription meeting at the Mansion House, Dublin attended by Nationalist, Sinn Feinn, and Labour leaders

——, Meeting of bishops of Catholic Church prepared pledge to resist conscription

April 20, Meeting of Nationalist Party at Dublin decided to cease attendance at British Parliament and remain in Ireland to work against conscription

April 23, One day strike of members of Transport Workers Union as a protest against conscription

May 1, Edward Shortt succeeded Mr. Duke as Chief Secretary for Ireland

May 6, Announcement of appointment of Viscount French of Ypres as Viceroy succeeding Lord Wimborne

May 18, De Valera and other Sinn Fein leaders arrested

May 20, Arthur Griffith, Count Plunkett, Countess Markievicz, John Milroy, and Herbert Mellowes, and others arrested and deported to England

June 3, Proclamation of the Lord Lieutenant called for recruits and announced that in the event of a satisfactory response the Military Service Act would not be put into force in Ireland

June 25, Lloyd George made public statement that volunteering would take place of conscription

July 3, The Sinn Feinn organizations proclaimed dangerous associations under Defense of the Realm Act

July 4, The entire western sea-coast of Ireland declared a military area

Nov. 28, Joint manifesto of Lloyd George and Bonar Law on Irish question declared that separation of Ireland from the British Empire would not be considered or forcible submission of the six counties of Ulster to a Home Rule Parliament against their will

Dec. 14, General election a victory for the Sinn Fein Party, receiving 73 out of a total 105 seats, the Nationalist Party retaining only 6 seats out of 68

1919

Jan. 8, Sinn Fein party met under presidency of Count Plunkett and adopted title of Irish Republican Party

Jan. 21, First meeting of Dail Eireann (members of the Assembly for Ireland). Declaration of independence read, and subscribed to by 29 members present. Count Plunkett, Arthur Griffith, and Mr. De Valera elected "delegates to the Peace Conference"

Jan. 22, Private session of the Dail Eireann elected Mr. De Valera "President of the Irish Republic"

Jan. 28, Proclamation of S. Tipperary as a "military area" under defense of the Realm Act after murder of Constable MacConnell on the 21st

Feb. 3, De Valera and 2 other prisoners escaped from Lincoln gaol, De Valera proceeded to the United States

Feb. 23, An All-Irish Convention held in Philadelphia (U.S.) appointed delegates to the Peace Conference in Paris to present resolution asking for independence for Ireland, Frank P. Walsh, Edward F. Dunne, and Michael F. Ryan

Feb. 24, J. T. O'Kelly, Sinn Fein member of Parliament for Dublin arrived in Paris as accredited envoy of the "Provisional Government of the Irish Republic"

March 31, Westport proclaimed a military area after murder of J. C. Milling

April 6, Limerick declared a military area after murder of Constable O'Brien

April 15, Illegal drilling led to conflict with police at Kilrush, West Clare

April 20–25, Strike for increase in wages closed Dublin hotels and restaurants

April 26, Boycott of police announced by Sinn Fein

May 31, American Delegation at the Peace Conference refused request of representatives of the "Irish Republic" to ask the Conference to receive them

June 11, President Wilson received Edward F. Dunne, and Frank P. Walsh, Irish American delegation but refused to champion the cause of Irish independence at the Peace Conference

Aug. 14, British Government announced suppression of Sinn Fein societies in Clare County, Ireland

Sept. 7, Party of soldiers leaving church at Fermoy, Cork attacked by Sinn Feiners, 1 killed, 3 wounded

Sept. 12, The Dail Eireann suppressed and Sinn Fein headquarters throughout the country raided

Oct. 16, City and County of Dublin proclaimed under the Crimes Act

Nov. 13, More districts proclaimed under the Crimes Act

Nov. 19, Sessions Court at Liscarrol, Cork County burned

Nov. 24, Government announced that hunger strikers would not be released but must "if they would not take their food, take the consequences"

Nov. 26, British Government proclaimed prohibition and suppression of Sinn Fein and similar organizations throughout Ireland

Dec. 1, Murder of Detective-Sergeant Barton in Dublin

Dec. 19, Viscount French, Lord Lieutenant, attacked from ambush with rifles and bombs while motoring from the station

Dec. 31, From May 1 to end of year 18 policemen murdered

1920

Jan. 2, Sinn Fein instructions to murder policemen and soldiers published in the "Belfast Newsletter"

Jan. 31, All Sein Fein officials who had committed acts or expressed words of sedition arrested in Dublin, Limerick, and other cities

Feb. 25, Home Rule Bill for Ireland repealing Act of 1914 introduced in Parliament providing for establishment of 2 Irish Parliaments, one for the 6 counties of N.E. Ulster and another for the rest of Ireland, and a general Council of Ireland

March 20, Alderman MacCurtain, Lord Mayor of Cork killed in his house by a band of masked men

March 27, Alan Bell, resident magistrate, who had been holding a secret inquiry under the Crimes Act, taken from crowded tramcar near Dublin, and killed by band of armed men

April 2, Sir Hamar Greenwood appointed Chief Secretary for Ireland succeeding J. I. Macpherson

April 4, Hunger strike begun by 100 Irish prisoners at Mountjoy prison, Dublin

April 13, General strike in sympathy with hunger strikers in Mountjoy prison

April 14, 56 hunger strikers in Mountjoy prison released by the Government and the following day 24 more

May 4, Decision of the Dublin Corporation to formally acknowledge the authority of Dail Eireann and to give effect to its decrees

May 12–13, Burning of police barracks in many places by armed Sinn Feiners

May 15, English army of occupation arrived in Ireland, the "black and tans"

May 19, First Sinn Fein public court established to settle land disputes and for settlement of agrarian disputes

May 24, Strike of railroad men

June 12, Strike of shirt and collar makers in Belfast which lasted 2 months and was settled by compromise

June 19, Riots between Unionists and Sinn Feiners in Derry

Aug. 8, Protestants at Lisburn burned houses of Catholics after murder of Inspector Swanzy

Aug. 26–Sept. 2, Conflicts in Belfast between British troops and Irish extremists

Sept. 17, Clash of troops and Sinn Feiners near Enmiskerry

Sept. 20, Fighting at Cork and Belfast

Sept. 21, First reprisal at Balbriggan after murder of District Inspector Burke and another constable at bar in public house. The houses and shops of Sinn Fein leaders in the town burned by troops

Sept. 29, After ambush and murder of 6 constables at Rinneen, Clare County, the police in reprisal burned houses and shot 2 men

Oct. 2, Reprisals at Tubercurry after murder of 5 constables

Oct. 17, Death of Michael Fitzgerald, on hunger strike since Aug. 10 in Cork gaol

Oct. 25, Death of Terence MacSwiney, Lord Mayor of Cork, on 74th day of hunger strike in Brixton prison, Cork

Nov. 21, 14 officers killed in their houses at 9 o'clock in the morning by bands of armed men in Dublin

Nov. 30, Detachment of soldiers ambushed and 17 killed in Dublin

Dec. 18, During the year 176 policemen killed and 251 wounded by Sinn Feiners

Dec. 23, Government of Ireland Act became law. *See supra*, Feb. 25

1921

Jan. 1–April 15, 73 civilians murdered and a large number of policemen, houses burned, conflicts of soldiers and Sinn Feinners, &c.

April 9, Death of Archbishop William John Walsh

April 14, Murder of Sir Arthur Vicars by party of armed men

April 21, Announcement that Lord Edmund Talbot created Viscount Fitzalan of Derwent appointed Lord Lieutenant. Sworn in May 2

May 5, Sir James Craig, Ulster leader, accepted invitation of Mr. De Valera for conference

May 13, Announcement of nominations for the South and West of Ireland declared return of Sinn Fein candidates uncontested in 124 out of 128 constituencies, the 4 members for Dublin University only not Sinn Fein

May 14–16, War carried into "the enemy's country" by shootings and burnings in London, St. Albans, and Liverpool

May 23, Elections for Parliament of Northern Ireland resulted in winning of 40 out of 52 seats by Unionists,

6 Nationalists including Joseph Devlin, and 6 Sinn Feiners including De Valera, Arthur Griffith, and Michael Collins

May 25, The Customs House, the most beautiful building in Dublin, burned by band of armed men and all records destroyed

June 7, The Northern Parliament opened at Belfast by Viscount Fitzalan and the Government constituted, Sir James Craig, Prime Minister

June 12, Election for Senate of Parliament of Northern Ireland completed

June 22, First session of Northern Ireland Parliament opened by King George in person

June 24, Troop train carrying part of escort of the King blown up by mine

——, Letter of Lloyd George invited De Valera to conference in London

June 28, Southern Parliament formally opened. The only members of the lower House who attended the 4 members for the University of Dublin, and 15 out of 64 Senators, and Parliament was adjourned

June 30, Four members of Dail Eireann, Arthur Griffith, John McNeill, Staines, and Eamon Duggan released from Mountjoy prison by the Government to take part in conference of Irish leaders on July 4

July 4, General Smuts arrived in Dublin for conference with De Valera

July 8, De Valera accepted invitation of Lloyd George to conference

July 10, Truce signed to take effect July 11 between Crown forces and Republicans

July 14, Conference of De Valera, Arthur Griffith, Austin Stack, R. O. Barton, and Erskine Childers with Lloyd George

July 15, Conference of Lloyd George with Sir James Craig and some other members of Northern Parliament

July 20, Government terms offered the status of a Dominion to Ireland with "complete autonomy in taxation and finance," the right to "maintain her own Courts of Law and Judges" . . . her own military forces for home defense . . .

Aug. 5, Dublin Castle announced release of members of Dail Eireann from prison

Aug. 10, Letter of De Valera to Lloyd George rejected terms unless the "right to secede" was guaranteed

Aug. 13, Answer of Lloyd George to De Valera

Aug. 15, Proposals of Government of July 20 published

Aug. 16, The Dail Eireann met to consider proposals of the British Government. All members took oath to "support and defend the Irish Republic and the Government of the Irish Republic"

Aug. 21, The Dail Eireann met in secret session to agree on formal answer to British Government proposals

Aug. 25, Letter of De Valera to Lloyd George rejected terms of settlement on behalf of the Government

Aug. 26, De Valera reëlected by Dahl Eireann President and nominated new Ministry, Michael Collins, Secretary of Finance and Countess Markievicz, Secretary for Labor

Sept. 7, Lloyd George invited De Valera to conference, announcing that the British Government would not accept an Irish Republic or repudiation of allegiance to the Crown

Sept. 14, Letter of De Valera accepted invitation to conference, reaffirming independence of Ireland

Sept. 15, Lloyd George canceled invitation to conference on basis of insistence of De Valera on independence of Ireland as a sovereign State

Sept. 29, New invitation to conference to De Valera

Sept. 30, Acceptance of De Valera of invitation to conference

Oct. 11–Dec. 6, Conference of Sinn Fein delegates with Lloyd George. De Valera did not attend. Ireland represented by Arthur Griffith, Michael Collins, Robert C. Barton, G. G. Duffy, and Erskine Childers

Dec. 6, Irish peace treaty signed gave Ireland Dominion status and established the Irish Free State. Northern Ireland given the option of continuing its separate existence under the Act of 1920 subject to the award of a Boundary Commission

Dec. 8, Message of Mr. De Valera to the Irish people disavowed and disapproved the Treaty of Dec. 6

Dec. 14, The Dail Eireann met to consider treaty

Dec. 15, Proposal of President De Valera of substitute for oath of allegiance defeated in Dail Eireann

Dec. 16, Peace treaty with Ireland ratified by British Parliament. For further chronology, see Irish Free State; Ireland, Northern

IRELAND, NORTHERN

Under the Government of Ireland Act of Feb. 25, 1920 (see Ireland) as amended by the Irish Free State (Consequential Provisions) Act of 1922, a separate Parliament and executive government were established for Northern Ireland, which comprises the parliamentary counties of Antrim, Armagh, Down, Fermanagh, Londonderry, and Tyrone, and the parliamentary boroughs of Belfast (capital city) and Londonderry. The Government of Ireland Act came into effect Dec. 23, 1920, and the first Parliament was opened at Belfast by King George June 22, 1921.

A census of Northern Ireland was taken on April 18, 1926. The area and population of the country at that date were as follows:—

COUNTIES AND COUNTY BOROUGHS	AREA IN STATUTE ACRES (EXCLUSIVE OF WATER)	MALES	FEMALES	TOTAL
Antrim	702,851	92,596	99,047	191,643
Armagh	312,767	53,609	56,461	110,070
Belfast C.B.	14,797	195,539	219,612	415,151
Down	608,861	101,202	108,026	209,228
Fermanagh	417,912	30,102	27,882	57,984
Londonderry Co.	512,494	47,119	47,415	94,534
Londonderry C.B.	2,199	20,785	24,374	45,159
Tyrone	779,563	67,136	65,656	132,792
Northern Ireland	3,351,444	608,088	648,473	1,256,561

The Duke of Abercorn, Governor, appointed for 6 years from Dec. 8, 1922, and appointment extended March 23, 1928 for a further term of 6 years. The Ministry is composed as follows:— Prime Minister, Viscount Craigavon; Finance, H. M. Pollock; Home Affairs, Sir R. Dawson Bates; Labour, J. M. Andrews; Education, Viscount Charlemont; Agriculture, Sir E. M. Archdale, Bart; Commerce, J. Milne Barbour.

IRISH FREE STATE

The Irish Free State (Saorstat Eireann), comprising 26 counties and four county boroughs of Southern Ireland with the status of a British Dominion, came into existence with the ratification of the Treaty with Great Britain of Dec. 6, 1921 by the Parliament of Southern Ireland Jan. 14, 1922. The total area of the Free State according to the census of 1926 is 17,024,481 statute acres, population, 2,971,992. Dublin is the capital. *See also* Ireland.

James McNeill, Governor General.

1922

Jan. 7, Motion for ratification of treaty carried in Dail Eireann by vote of 64 to 57

Jan. 9, Resignation of De Valera as President

Jan. 10, Arthur Griffith elected President to succeed Mr. De Valera; Gavan Duffy, Minister of Foreign Affairs; Michael Collins, Finance; M. Cosgrave, Local Government

Jan. 12, King George proclaimed amnesty for political prisoners arrested prior to July 21

Jan. 14, Formal ratification of Treaty by Southern Parliament (under Home Rule Act of 1920) convened on summons of Arthur Griffith and Provisional Government constituted, Michael Collins, William Cosgrove, Eamon J. Duggan, P. J. Hogan, Finian Lynch, Joseph McGrath, Professor John McNeill, and Bryan O'Higgins, Mr. Griffith not included because of his desire to continue to act as head of the Dail Eireann

Jan. 16, Dublin Castle taken over from British Government by the Provisional Government, Irish Free State, Michael Collins, Acting Prime Minister

Jan. 17, Evacuation of British troops from Ireland begun

Feb. 8, Sinn Fein raids began on Ulster

Feb. 21, Meeting of Sinn Feinn delegates called by De Valera

March 4, Strike of transport workers

March 5, Republicans seized the Government of Limerick

March 15, New Republican society organized by De Valera "to repudiate the proposed agreement with Great Britain as humiliating to the nation and destructive of its rightful status and claims"

March 29, Republicans wrecked office of "Freemans Journal," Dublin

March 30, Irish peace treaty signed by representatives of the British Government, Northern Ireland, and of the Provisional Government of Southern Ireland

March 31, Irish Free State (Agreement) Bill received royal assent

April 24, One day strike of Labour Party against factional fighting

May 20, Agreement of Collins and De Valera

June 16, Draft Constitution for Ireland published

——, Elections a victory for the Government, 92 members in favor of the Treaty returned and 36 against

June 22, Murder of Field Marshal Sir Henry Wilson in London by 2 Irish soldiers

June 28–30, Government troops invested the Four Courts in Dublin held by Republican rebels since April 14 and Rory O'Connor captured after he had blown up the building with all records. De Valera who had joined the insurgents escaped

July 20, Tipperary town captured by Free State troops

July 21, Free State troops captured Limerick and Waterford from the Republicans

——, Fighting in Dublin

Aug. 10, Cork captured from Republicans by Free State troops. Erskine Childers and Miss Mary McSwiney, leaders, escaped capture

Aug. 12, Sudden death of Arthur Griffith (50)

Aug. 14, Rebels surprised and captured Dundalk from National troops holding it until the 16th

Aug. 22, Michael Collins, head of the Provisional Government (31), killed by attack of Republicans from ambush

Sept. 9, Meeting of the third Dahl Eireann as a Provisional Parliament of the Irish Free State. William T. Cosgrave elected President of the Irish Free State and assumed office of Minister of Finance and constituted Cabinet

——, Kenmore taken by Republicans but soon recovered

Sept. 10, Strike of postal workers

Oct. 4, The Provisional Government offered amnesty to rebels who would surrender before Oct. 15

Oct. 25, Constitution adopted by Provisional Parliament

Oct. 30, Representatives of Governments of Northern and Southern Ireland signed peace declaration at London Conference

Nov. 4, Raids in Dublin arrested Republicans including Mary McSwiney

Nov. 10, Free State troops captured Erskine Childers, chief lieutenant of De Valera

Nov. 24, Erskine Childers convicted of treason, executed

Dec. 5, Irish Free State Constitution Act received royal assent

Dec. 6, Irish Constitution came into effect by Proclamation of the King. Timothy Healy appointed first Governor General

Dec. 7, Assassination of Sean Hales, Deputy, and Patrick O'Maille, Deputy Speaker

Dec. 8, Execution of 4 rebel leaders Rory O'Connor, Liam Mellowes, Joseph McKelvey, and Richard Barrett

Dec. 11, Senate held first session

Dec. 17, Last British troops left Ireland

Dec. 18, Adaptation of Enactments Bill passed, the first Irish statute to become law in 123 years

1923

Jan. 5, James MacNeill appointed High Commissioner in London

April 10, Death of Liam Lynch, Republican leader, wounded in capture by Free State troops

April 14, Austin Stack, rebel leader, captured

May 19, Republican riot in Dublin put down by use of machine guns

Aug. 9, Legislature (Dail Eireann) dissolved

Aug. 14, De Valera captured by Free State troops and imprisoned in Dublin

Aug. 27, Elections gave Cosgrove Government 63 seats and Republicans 44, Farmers Party 15, Independents 16, Labour Party 15

Sept. 10, Irish Free State admitted to the League of Nations

Sept. 19, New Legislature met. Of the Republicans elected three-quarters were in prison and the rest prevented from taking seats by refusal to take the oath of allegiance. Mr. Cosgrove reëlected President of the Executive Council

Nov. 14, Nobel prize for literature awarded to William Butler Yeats

1924

Feb. 2, President Cosgrave and Sir James Craik met with representatives of British Government in boundary conference

March 21, Unarmed British soldiers landing near Queenstown fired on by Free State troops killing 1 and wounding 24

June 24, British Government agreed to appointment of Irish Free State Minister to the United States

July 11, Government registered Treaty with Great Britain of Dec. 6, 1921 with the League of Nations

July 16, Eamon De Valera and Austin Stack freed from prison

July 26–Aug. 3, Strike of municipal workers, Dublin

Oct. 25, De Valera arrested at Newry in Northern Ireland and escorted across the border

Nov. 19, Death of Cardinal Michael Logue in London

Dec. 19, "Freemans Journal" of Dublin ceased publication after 161 years

1925

Jan. 10, Statement of Vice-President O'Higgins that the Government is determined that the army shall be subordinated to the civil power

April 22, Income tax reduced and certain duties dropped

Sept. 17, First election for Senate

Dec. 3, Boundary agreement supplementing Treaty of Dec. 6, 1921 signed by representatives of Great Britain, Northern Ireland, and Irish Free State

1926

Feb. 3, Announcement of constitution of Free State Banking Commission, Henry Parker Willis of New York nominated as chairman

Feb. 9, Free State registered Boundary Agreement of Dec. 3, 1925 with League of Nations despite fact that British Foreign Office had notified the League that it could not recognize registration of treaties and agreements between integral parts of the British Empire

March 11, De Valera resigned the presidency of the Sinn Fein (Republican) Party

Census of Free State gave population as 2,972,802 as compared with 3,139,688 in 1911

1927

June 9, Election reduced Government majority from 57 to 46

July 10, Assassination of Kevin O'Higgins, Vice-President of the Executive Council outside his house near Dublin

July 15, Death of the Countess Constance de Markievicz

Aug. 4, Death of John Dillon (76), in London

Aug. 12, Eamon De Valera and 44 other Republican Deputies entered the Dail Eireann, taking oath of allegiance to the King

Aug. 25, Parliament dissolved

Sept. 15, General election gave Cosgrave's Party 61 and Republicans 57

Oct. 12, W. T. Cosgrave reëlected President of the Executive Council

Nov. 26, Motion of Republicans to repeal Public Safety law defeated

Dec. 2, Announcement of loan of $15,000,000 negotiated in New York City at 5% interest

Dec. 15, T. M. Healy resigned as Governor General. Succeeded by James McNeill

1928

Feb. 1, James McNeill installed as Governor General

Feb. 5, De Valera arrested attempting to enter Northern Ireland in defiance of exclusion order of Government

Feb. 8, De Valera sentenced to 30 days in prison

Feb. 22, Paris Pact for outlawing war ratified by Dail Eireann

Feb. 25, Death of William O'Brien (76), in London

March 6, De Valera released from prison

1929

July 26, Irish Free State Confirmation of Agreement Act approved

Sept. 14, Optional Clause of Permanent Court of International Justice signed

Dec. 23, Temporary most favored nation commercial Agreement with Turkey concluded by exchange of notes

Dec. 29, Most Favored Nation Treaty of commerce with Portugal signed

1930

Jan. 15, Abp. Paschal Robinson, first Papal Nuncio to Ireland in 300 years, presented credentials to Governor General McNeill

March 27, Resignation of W. T. Cosgrove as President of the Executive Council defeated on opposition to Old Age Pension Bill

April 2, William Cosgrove reëlected President by the Dail Eireann by vote of 80 to 65 defeating De Valera, Republican candidate, and O'Connell, Labour candidate

May 12, Most Favored Nation Commercial Treaty with Germany signed

Oct., The state of the parties in October, 1930, was: Cumann na nGaedheal (Government), 63; Fianna Fail, 56; Labour, 13; Farmers, 6; Independent, 11; National League, 2; Ceann Comhairle, 1; Vacancy, 1; Total, 153. The Executive Council is as follows (October, 1930): President, Liam T. MacCosgair (William T. Cosgrave); Vice-President, Minister for Finance, Posts and Telegraphs, Earnan de Blaghd (Ernest Blythe); Defense, Deasmhumhan MacGearailt (Desmond Fitzgerald); External Affairs and Industry and Commerce, Pádraig MacGiollagáin (Patrick McGilligan); Education, Sean O'Suilleabhain (John Marcus O'Sullivan); Justice, Seumas MacGearailt-O Cionnaoith (James Fitz Gerald-Kenney); Agriculture, Pádraig O hOgain (Patrick Hogan); Local Government and Public

Health, Risteard Ua Maolchatha (General Richard Mulcahy); Lands and Fisheries, Fionán O Loinsigh (Finian Lynch)

Nov. 23, Professor Michael Hayes, Speaker of Dail Eireann, shot in revival of terrorist tactics

Nov. 29, Dublin headquarters of Sinn Fein raided by police and revolutionary documents seized

ITALY

Italy, peninsula of southern Europe, constitutional monarchy, comprising Italy proper, Sicily, Sardinia, Elba, and 70 other small islands together with territory on east coast of the Adriatic acquired by Treaties of St. Germain and Rapallo. The Ægean Islands occupied by Italy in 1912 ceded by Treaties of Sevres and Lausanne. The Italian concession of Tientsin, under the agreement with China of June 7, 1902, lies on the left bank of the Hai-Ho and has an area of about half a square kilometer with a population of 5,148 (Chinese, 4,675; Italians, 60; other Europeans, 413) in 1925. For colonies *see* Africa and names of colonies: Eritrea, Libya, and Somaliland. For early history *see also* Rome, Sardinia, Sicily, Pope. The total area of kingdom according to census of 1928 is 119,710 square miles, population, 40,783,-000, population for 1930, 41,509,000. Rome is the capital.

The following figures show the increase of the population of the Kingdom of Italy.

YEAR (JAN. 1)	POPULATION	INCREASE PER CENT. PER ANNUM
1816	18,383,000	—
1872 [3]	26,801,154	0.720
1882 [3]	28,459,628	0.619
1901 [1],[3]	32,475,253	0.738
1911 [2],[3]	34,671,377	0.658
1921 [3],[4]	38,755,576	0.675
1926	40,064,000	0.741
1927	40,411,000	0.935
1928	40,783,000	0.855
1929	41,169,000	0.965
1930	41,509,000	0.940
1931	42,874,801	3.3

[1] February 10.   [2] June 10.   [3] Census Figures.   [4] December 1.

Most genealogists trace the origin of the reigning house to a German Count Berthold, who, in the eleventh century, established himself on the western slope of the Alps, between Mont Blanc and Lake Geneva. In the end of the eleventh century the Count of Savoy acquired the countries of Turin and Susa. Count Amadeus, in 1383, founded a law of primogeniture which led to the immediate acquisition of the territory of Nice. In 1416 the Counts of Savoy adopted the title of Duke; in 1418 they acquired the Principality of Piedmont; and in 1713 they obtained the island of Sicily, with the title of King. Sicily had to be exchanged, in 1720, for the isle of Sardinia, to which henceforth the royal dignity remained attached. The Genoese

territory was added at the peace of 1815. The direct male line of the House of Savoy died out with King Carlo Felice in 1831, and the crown fell to Prince Carlo Alberto, of the house of Savoy-Carignano, a branch founded by Tommaso Francesco, born in 1596, younger son of Duke Carlo Emanuele I of Savoy. King Carlo Alberto abdicated the throne March 23, 1849, in favor of his son, the late King Vittorio Emanuele II, who, by the Peace of Zürich, November 10, 1859, obtained Lombardy, with the exception of Mantua and a part of the surrounding territory. On March 11, 1860, annexation to Sardinia was voted by *plébiscites* in Parma, Modena, the Romagna, and Tuscany; on October 21, Sicily and Naples (including Benevento and Pontecorvo, part of the Papal States), and on November 4, the Marches and Umbria. The first Italian Parliament assembled in February 1861, and declared (March 17, 1861) Vittorio Emanuele King of Italy. The remaining part of the province of Mantua and Venetia were added in 1866. Finally, the remaining part of the Papal States (province of Rome), having been taken possession of by an Italian army (September 20, 1870), was annexed to the Kingdom by *plébiscite* on October 2. After the Great War—by the Treaty of Saint Germain (Sept. 10, 1919) there were annexed to the kingdom: the Venezia Tridentina, the Venezia Giulia with Zara, the islands of Cherso, Lussino, and other minor ones. Later, on January 28, 1924, Fiume was also annexed. *See also* Vatican City.

Vittorio Emanuele III, reigning King.

ca 1710 B.C. to 1849

1710, Arrival of Œnotrus from Arcadia; and of Evander; reign of Latinus, about 1240

1182, &c., Æneas the Trojan said to land in Italy, defeat and kill Turnus, marry Lavinia, daughter of King Latinus, and found Lavinium, in South Italy

974–443, Greek colonies founded

753, Romulus builds Rome

    [For subsequent history, *see* Rome]

476 A.D., Odoacer, leader of the Heruli, establishes the Kingdom of Italy

489, The Ostrogoths invade Italy, and retain it till 761

525, They are expelled by the Imperial generals Narses and Belisarius

    [*See* Kings of Italy]

568, Narses, governor of Italy, invites the Lombards from Germany; who overrun Italy, 596

662, Invasion and defeat of Constans II

697, Venice first governed by a doge

754, Pepin gives Ravenna to the Pope

Dec. 25, 800, Charlemagne invades Italy 774; overcomes the Lombards; crowned Emperor of the West at Rome by Pope Leo III

842, The Saracens invade Italy and settle at Bari

951, Invasion of Otho I; crowned Emperor, Feb. 2, 962

1000, Genoa becomes important

1016–17, The Saracens expelled by the Normans

1051, The Normans acquire Naples from the Pope

1073–85, Pope Gregory VII, Hildebrand, pretends to universal sovereignty, in which he is assisted by

Matilda, Countess of Tuscany, mistress of the greater part of Italy

About 1073, Disputes between the Popes and Emperors, relative to ecclesiastical investitures, begin (and long agitate Italy and Germany)

About 1120, Rise of the Lombard cities, who war with each other 1144

1125, The Venetians obtain many victories over the Eastern Emperors

1154–75, Frederic I (Barbarossa) interferes: his wars

About 1161, Beginning of wars of the Guelphs and Ghibelines, names given to the papal and imperial factions who destroyed the peace of Italy from the 12th to the end of the 15th century (the invasion of Charles VIII of France in 1495). The origin of the names is ascribed to the contest for the imperial crown between Conrad of Hohenstaufen, Duke of Swabia, Lord of Wiblingen (hence Ghibelin), and Henry, nephew of Welf, or Guelf, Duke of Bavaria, in 1138. The former was successful; but the popes and several Italian cities took the side of his rival. Hie Guelf and Hie Gibelin are said to have been used as war-cries in 1140, at a battle before Weinsberg, in Würtemberg, when Guelf of Bavaria was defeated by the Emperor Conrad IV, who came to help the rival Duke Leopold. The Ghibelines were almost totally expelled from Italy in 1267, when Conradin, the last of the Hohenstaufens, was beheaded by Charles of Anjou

1167, Lombard league formed

May 29, 1176, His defeat at Legnano

1183, Peace of Constance

1199, &c., Civil wars again

1236–50, Wars of Frederick II and the Lombard league

About 1251, Rise of the Medici at Florence

Feb. 26, 1266, His natural son, Manfred, King of Sicily, defeated and killed at the battle of Benevento, by Charles of Anjou

Aug. 23, 1268, Who defeats Conradin, at Tagliacozzo

1277, The Visconti rule at Milan

March 30, 1282, The Sicilian Vespers; massacre of the French, who are expelled from Sicily

1309, Clement V (Pope, 1305), fixes his residence at Avignon in France

1328, Louis Gonzaga makes himself master of Mantua, with the title of Imperial Vicar

1339, First Doge of Genoa appointed

1370, Lucca independent

1377, Rome again the seat of the Pope

1494, Charles VIII of France invades Italy, and conquers Naples, 1495; loses it in 1496

1499, Louis XII joins Venice and conquers Milan (soon lost)

1509, League of Cambray (1508) against Venice, which is despoiled of its Italian possessions

1513–22, Leo X, Pope, patron of literature and art

1515–21, Wars of Charles V and Francis I

Feb. 24, 1525, Francis defeated and prisoner at Pavia

1545, Parma and Placentia made a duchy for his family by Pope Paul III (Alexander Farnese)

1559, Peace of Cateau-Cambresis

1627–31, War of the Mantuan succession

Oct. 4, 1693, Catinat and the French defeat the Duke of Savoy at Marsaglia

1701, War of Spanish Succession commences in Italy

Sept. 7, 1706, Battle of Turin

April 11, 1713, Division of Italy at the Peace of Utrecht

1720, The Duke of Savoy becomes King of Sardinia

1745, Successful French campaign in Italy

1748, Milan, &c., obtained by the house of Austria, 1714; confirmed by Treaty of Aix-la-Chapelle

May–Dec., 1796, Italy overrun by the French

Oct. 17, 1797, Division of the Venetian states by France and Austria by the treaty of Campo Formio; Cisalpine republic founded

Feb., 1798, Pius VI deposed by Bonaparte

1799, The Russians, under Suwarrow, defeat the French at Trebia, &c.

June 14, 1800, Bonaparte crosses the Alps, May 16–20; defeats the Austrians at Marengo

Jan., 1802, The Cisalpine becomes the Italian republic (Bonaparte, president)

May 26, 1805, Napoleon crowned King of Italy

——, Eugène Beauharnais made Viceroy of Italy

Jan. 1, 1806, Austria loses her Italian possessions by the Treaty of Presburg; ratified

1814, The Kingdom ceases on the overthrow of Napoleon; the Lombardo-Venetian Kingdom established for Austria, April 7, 1815

1831–33, Formation of the young Italy party by Mazzini; insurrections

1837, Italian Association for Science first met (at Pisa)

April, 1848, Insurrection in Lombardy and Venice, March; supported by the King of Sardinia and by the Pope

1849, The King defeated at Novara, abdicates, March 23; and Lombardy reverts to Austria, May

[See Sardinia and Austria]

1859

April 26, The Austrian ultimatum, rejected by Sardinia

April 27, The Austrians cross the Ticino; and the French enter Genoa, May 3

——, Peaceful revolution at Florence; Parma, May 3; Modena, June 15

——, Provisional governments established at Florence; Parma, May; and Modena [the sovereigns retire], June 15

May 20, The Austrians defeated at Montebello; Palestro, May 30–31; Magenta, June 4; Marignano, June 8; Solferino, June 24

June 13–15, Insurrection in the Papal States; Bologna, Ferrara, &c.

June 20, Massacre of the insurgents at Perugia by the Swiss troops

July 1, The allies cross the Mincio

July 8, Armistice between Austria and France

July 11, Preliminaries of peace signed at Villafranca; Lombardy surrendered to Sardinia

July, Italy dismayed at the peace; agitation at Milan, Florence, Modena, Parma, &c.; resignation of Count Cavour as Minister

July 12, The Pope appeals to Europe against the King of Sardinia

July 19, Garibaldi exhorts the Italians to arm

July 21, Grand Duke of Tuscany abdicates

Aug. 11, Constitutional assemblies meet at Florence; and at Modena, Aug. 16

Aug. 20–Sept. 10, Tuscany, Modena, Parma, and the Romagna enter into a defensive alliance, and declare for annexation to Piedmont; fiscal restrictions between them and Piedmont abolished, Oct. 10

Oct. 5, Assassination of Col. Anviti at Parma

Oct., Garibaldi appeals to the Neapolitans; subscriptions in Italy and elsewhere to supply arms for the Italians

Nov. 5, Tuscany, &c., choose the Prince Eugène of Carignan-Savoy, as regent of central Italy; the King of Sardinia refusing his consent, the Prince declines the office, but recommends the chevalier Buoncampagni, Nov. 14

Nov. 10, Treaty of Zurich (establishing Italian confederacy, &c.), signed

Nov. 18, Garibaldi retires from Sardinian service

Dec. 7, New Sardinian constitution proclaimed

Dec. 31, The Pope condemns the pamphlet "*Le Pape et le Congrès*"

——, The Emperor Napoleon recommends the Pope to give up the legations

1860

Jan. 8, The Pope refuses and denounces the Emperor

Jan. 16, Count Cavour charged with the formation of a ministry

March 13, Annexation to Sardinia voted for (by universal suffrage) in Parma, Modena, and the Romagna; Tuscany, March 16; accepted by the King, March 18-22

April 4; May 2, Vain insurrections in Sicily

May 29, Treaty ceding Savoy and Nice to France signed, March 24; approved by the Sardinian parliament

May, The French troops retire from Italy

July 30, Garibaldi lands at Marsala in Sicily, May 11; assumes the office of dictator, May 14; defeats the Neapolitans at Calatifimi, May 15; and at Melazzo, July 20; by a convention the Neapolitans agree to evacuate Sicily (*see* Sicily)

Aug. 21, Garibaldi takes Reggio; enters Naples; King Francis retires, Sept. 7

Sept. 8, Insurrection in Papal States; the Sardinians enter, Sept. 11; defeat the papal troops at Castelfidardo, Sept. 18; take Ancona, Sept. 17-29

Oct. 4, Victor-Emmanuel takes the command of his army

Oct. 15, The Sardinians enter Kingdom of Naples; defeat Neapolitans at Isernia, Oct. 17

Oct. 21, By universal suffrage (plebiscitum), Sicily and Naples vote for annexation to Sardinia

Oct. 26, Garibaldi defeats Neapolitans at the Volturno, Oct. 1, 1860: meets Victor-Emmanuel, and says, "King of Italy!" the latter replies, "I thank you!"

Nov. 2, Capua bombarded; the Neapolitans retire; and are defeated at the Garigliano, Nov. 3

Nov. 3, &c., Siege of Gaëta commences; attack by sea prevented by the presence of the French fleet

Nov. 7, Victor-Emmanuel enters Naples at King; Garibaldi resigns the dictatorship and retires to Caprera, Nov. 9

Nov., Victor-Emmanuel receives homage from the Neapolitan clergy, &c.; gives money to encourage education; appoints a ministry, including Poerio, &c.

Nov. 16, Decree in honor of Garibaldi's army

Nov.–Dec., Reactionary movements suppressed

1861

Jan., Prince of Carignan-Savoy appointed Lieutenant of Naples

Jan. 19, The French fleet retires from Gaëta after sever bombardment it surrenders; Francis II retires to Rome, Feb. 13

Feb., Monastic establishments in Naples abolished, with compensation to the inmates; schools established

Feb. 18, Assembly of the first Italian parliament, which decrees Victor-Emmanuel king of Italy, March 17

March and April, Naples unsettled through reactionary intrigues of the papal party

March 31, Italy recognized by Great Britain

April, Order for the levy of 70,000 soldiers

——, Cavour forms a new ministry, including members from all parts of Italy

April 15, The Pope protests against the Kingdom

April 25, Altercation in parliament between Cavour and Garibaldi, April 18; reconciled

May 7, &c., Bourbonist bands defeated

May 13, Prince of Carignan resigns; San Martino appointed Lieutenant at Naples

June 6, Death of Count Cavour, aged 52

June 11, Ricasoli forms a ministry to continue Cavour's policy

June 24, The Kingdom recognized by France

July 16, San Martino resigns the government of Naples; active measures taken against the insurgents and brigands by Cialdini, his successor, appointed

Oct. 13, The Kingdom recognized by Portugal and Belgium, Oct. 1; divided into fifty-nine prefectures, &c.

Oct., Skirmishes in the south with brigands and foreign emissaries in the cause of Francis II

Nov. 2, Cialdini retires, and La Marmora becomes Lieutenant-General of Naples

Nov. 19, Brigandage still prevailing in the south, aided by the King of Naples; insurgents defeated; and many killed

Dec. 8, José Borges, a Spaniard, lands in Calabria, Sept. 15; calls on the people to rise for Francis II, Sept.; taken and shot

Dec., 1861, Jan. and Feb., 1862, The reactionist warfare continues; cruelties of the brigands lead to reprisals

1862

March 1, The Kingdom recognized by Prussia

——, Rattazzi forms an administration

March 3, Ricasoli compelled to resign by court influence

March 14, Surrender of Civatella del Tronto, the last Bourbon fortress in Sicily

March and April, Triumphant progress of Garibaldi through Italy, establishing rifle clubs

April 2, J. F. Bishop, an active English Bourbonist propagandist, captured

April 19, Conspiracy among the Neapolitan soldiers at Milan suppressed

April 28, The King received at Naples with great enthusiasm

April, The French General Guyon aids in the suppression of the Bourbonist brigands

July 3, The Kingdom recognized by Russia

July 19, Garibaldi proceeds to Sicily; at Marsala he calls for volunteers, giving as his watchword, "Rome or death!"

July 26, Calls on the Hungarians to rise

Aug. 3, The King issues a proclamation against his proceedings, as tending to rebellion

Aug. 19, Garibaldi enters Catania, and organizes a provisional government

Aug. 21, Sicily proclaimed to be in a state of siege; and put under general Cialdini, Aug. 22

Aug. 25, Garibaldi issues his last proclamation; embarks at Catania; lands at Melito, in Calabria, and marches towards Reggio; La Marmora proclaims a state of siege, Aug. 26; Garibaldi and his followers fall in with the royalists under Pallavicini, at Aspromonte, where, after a short skirmish, he is wounded and taken prisoner, Aug. 29; removed to Varignano, near Spezzia, Sept. 1

Sept. 6, J. F. Bishop sentenced to 10 years' imprisonment

Sept. 10, General Durando issues a diplomatic circular condemning Garibaldi's proceedings, yet asserting the necessity of the Italian government possessing Rome

Sept. 27, Princess Maria Pia married by proxy to the King of Portugal

Sept. 28, Garibaldi issues a rhetorical appeal to the English nation, urging its intervention for the cause of liberty

Sept., Inflammatory manifesto addressed to the people of Italy by Joseph Mazzini

Oct. 5, Amnesty granted to Garibaldi and his followers

Oct. 8, Sharp reply of M. Drouyn de Lhuys to Durando's note

Oct. 17, End of state of siege in Naples and Sicily

Nov. 1, Disorderly encounter between Italians and Austrians on the banks of the Po

Nov., Father Passaglia and 10,000 (out of 80,000) Italian priests sign a declaration against the temporal authority of the Pope

Nov. 9, Garibaldi removed to Pisa; ball extracted from his foot by Zanetti, Nov. 23

Nov. 18, Meeting of parliament; determined opposition to Rattazzi; he resigns, Nov. 30

Dec. 9, New ministry formed by Farina

Dec. 18, It declines further negotiations with France on the Roman question

1863

Jan. 17, Commercial treaty with France signed

March 24, Farina resigns; Minghetti succeeds

June 1, Grand Cavour canal for irrigation of Piedmont opened

July, Income tax bill passed

——, Tristany and other bandits captured

Aug. 6, Commercial treaty with Great Britain signed

Sept. 5, Death of Farina

Sept. 12, Several bandits captured on board the French ship *Aunis*; given up to France, July; restored to Italy

Oct., The army of Piedmont (50,000) consolidated by La Marmora and expanded into the "Army of Italy" (250,000)

Mr. (after Sir) James Hudson, British Minister, greatly assisted Cavour in the unification of Italy, 1852–63

1864

April, Garibaldi's visit to England

Sept. 15, Franco-Italian convention signed (French troops to quit Rome in two years [from Feb. 6, 1865], Florence to be the capital of Italy, &c.)

Sept. 21–22, Riots at Turin in consequence; many persons killed by the military

Sept. 24, Minghetti and his colleagues blamed; resigned; a ministry formed by La Marmora

Oct. 10, Garibaldi denounces the convention

Nov., Desperate state of the finances announced by Sella, the minister; he proposes stringent remedies

Nov. 4, Railway from Turin to Florence opened

Nov. 19, The convention approved by the Chamber of Deputies; by the Senate (after an able speech by Cialdini, Dec. 6), Dec. 9

Dec. 11, Decree for transfer of the capital published

Dec., Prince Humbert resides at Naples

——, Stated that 346 brigands had been killed in action; 453 taken in action, and 132 surrendered; about 300 remain to be tracked; many pretend to be subjects of the ex-King Francis II of Naples

1865

Feb. 3, Demonstration against the King at Turin, Jan. 30; he goes to Florence

March, Amnesty for political offences published; brigandage in the Neapolitan and Roman states increasing

April to July, Fruitless negotiations with the Pope by Vegezzi respecting the position of bishops

May 15, Mr. Moens, a British subject, seized and retained by brigands

June 12, 45 monks and others arrested at Salerno on charge of a Bourbonist conspiracy

June 18, Inauguration of a national rifle meeting at Florence; the King fires the first shot

June 19, Numerous atrocities committed by brigands; Giardullo and 8 brigands captured

June, The Kingdom recognized by Spain

Aug. 26, Mr. Moens released after a ransom of 5,000*l.* had been paid

Nov. 7, Bank of Italy established

Nov., French troops leaving Italy; general election, the moderate party predominate

Nov. 18, The new parliament meets at Florence

Dec. 13, Serious financial deficiency; heavy taxation proposed; much dissatisfaction; the Ministers resign, Dec. 21; a new Ministry formed under La Marmora, Dec. 31

1866

Jan. 15, Death of the patriot and soldier, Massimo D'Azeglio

Feb. 27, Formation of the "Consorzio Nazionale," a public subscription for reducing the national debt

March 19, Massacre of Protestants at Barletta, Naples; attributed to priests

May 12, Alliance with Prussia

June 7 *et seq.*, Volunteers numerously enlisted

June 20, War declared against Austria

——, New ministry formed under Ricasoli

——, Royal manifesto to the people

June 24, The army, headed by the King, crosses the Mincio, June 23; defeated at Custozza

July 3, Venetia ceded to France by the Emperor of Austria

July 4, Fruitless conflicts; the volunteers under Garibaldi defeated at Monte Suello

July 7, Bill for suppression of monasteries and confiscation of property passed

July 8, Cialdini crosses the Po, and enters Venetia

July 20, Naval battle near Lissa; Italians defeated by Austrians (*Rè d'Italia* and *Palestro* blown up)

July 26, The Italians beaten at Versa; the last conflict

Aug. 12, Armistice for four weeks signed

Aug. 15, Volunteers disbanded; Garibaldi retires to Caprera

Oct. 9, The Austrians retire from Peschiera; Mantua, Oct. 10; Verona, Oct. 16; Venice, Oct. 17

Oct. 11, Court constituted at Florence to try Admiral Persano for neglect of duty at battle of Lissa

——, General Menabrea pays to Count Mensdorff a sum of money, and receives the iron crown of Italy

Oct. 12, Treaty of peace with Austria signed at Vienna, Oct. 3; ratified

Oct., National loan freely subscribed

Oct. 21, Plebiscitum in Venetia; for annexation with Italy, 641,758; against, 69

Nov. 4, This result reported, and the iron crown presented to the King at Turin

Nov., The king enters Venice, Nov. 7; visits Verona, Mantua, &c.

Nov. 15, Circular of Ricasoli to the prefects, recommending industrial development and commerce, forbidding agitation, and enjoining neutrality regarding Rome

Nov. 26, Letter from Ricasoli to the clergy recommending a free church in a free state

Dec. 1, Persano committed for trial; examination begins

Dec. 15, Parliament opened by the King, who declares that "Italy is now restored to herself"

Dec., Sig. Tonello received by the Pope, Dec. 15; many bishops return to their dioceses

1867

Jan. 30, Persano acquitted of cowardice at Lissa

Jan., Government proposal for investing part of the property of the religious bodies for support of clergy ("Free Church and Ecclesiastical Liquidation bill") brought forward

——, Great reduction in the army (to 146,000) ordered

Feb. 13, Defeat of the Ministry on question of the right of public meetings in Venetia, Feb. 11; parliament dissolved

Feb. 17, Ricasoli reconstructs his Ministry

March, The Pope accepts Italian help to suppress brigandage

——, Elections give a majority for Government

April 8, Resignation of Ricasoli, April 5; a ministry formed by Rattazzi

April 15, Persano condemned; degraded and dismissed the service for disobedience, incapacity, and negligence

April 23, Treaty of commerce with Austria signed at Florence

May 1, Public funeral of the patriot Carlo Poerio

May 7-11, Italy joins in the conference at London respecting the Luxemburg question

May et seq., National financial embarrassments; the King gives up part of his civil list; proposed sale of church lands, and reduction of expenditure

May, 17,200,000l. advanced for church lands by Fould and others of Paris

Aug., Church property bill passed

Sept. 23, Garibaldi, about to enter the Roman territory with volunteers, captured by Italian Government at Sinalunga (or Asinalunga) and sent to Alessandria

Sept. 27, Sent to Caprera, escapes to Leghorn, and is sent back, Oct. 2

Sept.–Oct., Bands of Garibaldians invade Roman territories

Oct. 15, Garibaldi escapes from Caprera

Oct. 20, Embarkation of French troops at Toulon, suspended by the resignation of Rattazzi and his Ministry

Oct. 21-25, Cialdini tries to form a ministry in vain

Oct. 22, Garibaldi at Florence announces an expedition against Rome

Oct. 25, The French Minister Moustier's circular against the invasion

——, Garibaldians defeated at Viterbo

Oct. 26, 27, Enter Roman territories; defeat papal troops, and take Monte Rotondo

Oct. 26-28 et seq., Riots at Naples, Turin, Pavia, and other places suppressed

Oct. 27, Menabrea's Ministry formed; proclamation of Victor-Emmanuel against the Garibaldian invasion

Oct. 28, French army arrives at Città Vecchia; two brigades enter Rome, Oct. 30

Oct. 30, Royal Italian troops enter papal territory; Menabrea's justificatory circular; suppression of insurrectional committees in Italy

Nov. 1, De Moustier's reply

Nov. 4, Garibaldi defeated at Mentana, Nov. 3; retreats into Italy with his son; captured and sent to Varignano, gulf of Spezzia

Nov. 8, Fiery manifesto of Mazzini

Nov. 9-Dec., French proposal of a European conference on Roman question discussed

Nov. 25, Garibaldi sent to Caprera

Dec. 3, French troops left Rome for Città Vecchia

Dec. 5, Meeting of parliament; judicious firmness; an amnesty for Garibaldians proclaimed

Dec. 22, Long army debate; vote against the ministry (201 to 199); Menabrea resigns

1868

Jan. 5, His Ministry reconstituted

Jan. 21, M. Cambray Digny's financial statement: great deficit; a grist tax proposed

Feb., Exculpatory letter of La Marmora issued

——, Government financial measures announced

Feb. 20, New order of knighthood, the "Crown of Italy," constituted

April 1, Grist tax adopted after 21 days' debate

April 22, Marriage of Prince Humbert to his cousin Margherita at Turin

April, May, Frightful atrocities committed by brigands in south Italy

June, Grist tax adopted by the senate

July 30, Arrangement made for debt of the late papal provinces

Aug. 8, Government tobacco monopoly ordered to be farmed; resignation of the Ministers, Lanza and Sella

Nov. 24, Meeting of Chamber of Deputies; Garibaldi withdraws

1869

Jan. 26, Ministerial victory respecting the grist tax in the Chambers

April, Thomas, Duke of Genoa, entered a pupil at Harrow (see Spain, 1870)

Oct. 5, Circular of Menabrea against the council at Rome

Nov. 6-20, Serious illness and recovery of the King

Nov. 11, Victor-Emmanuel Ferdinand, son of Prince Humbert, born at Naples

Dec. 8, Œcumenical council at Rome opened

Dec. 13, Offered resignation of Menabrea, about Nov. 19; Cialdini and Sella unable to form a ministry, Dec. 10; Lanza and Sella succeed

1870

About March 24, Republican risings in Pavia and other places quelled

Aug. 4, Neutrality in the Franco-Prussian war announced, July 18; additional armaments ordered

Aug. 14, Mazzini arrested at Palermo and sent to Gaëta

Aug. 21–25, Fruitless mission of Prince Napoleon to obtain help for France

Aug. 29, Circular note from the government recounting the failure of all attempts to conciliate the Pope since 1860; and proposing favorable terms

Aug., French vessel *Orénoque* placed at Cività Vecchia on behalf of the Pope

Sept. 8, Respectful letter from the King to the Pope, announcing the occupation of Rome necessary to order

Sept. 12, The Italian troops enter the papal territories; occupy Viterbo and other places

Sept. 18, 19, General Bixio marches towards Rome

Sept. 20, After a short resistance, the Italians under General Cadorna enter Rome

Oct. 2, *Plébiscite* in papal territories: for union with the Kingdom of Italy (out of 167,548 voters) 133,681; against 1,507

Oct. 8, The King receives the result of the *plébiscite*

Oct. 9, Rome incorporated with Italy by royal decree, General La Marmora, Governor

Oct., Arrival of La Marmora at Rome as Viceroy; reported agitation in Nice for reunion with Italy or autonomy

Oct. 10, Amnesty to political offenders proclaimed; including Mazzini, Oct. 16

Oct. 14, Capture and death of Pilone, a great Bourbonist brigand chief

Oct. 15, Mazzini arrives at Florence

Oct. 18, Diplomatic circular announcing the occupation of Rome as the capital of Italy

Oct. 19, Roman provinces united into one, with five subprefectures

About Nov. 14, Ricasoli retires into private life

Nov. 16, Amadeus, Duke of Aosta, the King's second son, elected King by the Spanish Cortes

Dec. 5, The King declares Rome to be the capital of Italy

About Dec. 12, Bills introduced for the transfer of the capital and the preservation of the Pope's rights

Dec. 25, The Cenis tunnel completed

1871

Jan. 26, The Senate vote the transfer of the capital from Florence to Rome (94–39)

July 1, 2, The King and Ministers remove to Rome, which is inaugurated as the capital, July 3

Nov. 27, The parliament opened there by the King

Dec. 18, Telegraphic conference at Rome

1872

March 10, Joseph Mazzini dies at Pisa

Oct., Great inundations in the valley of the Po, &c., loss of life and of much property; much saved by the exertions of the military

1873

Jan. 9, Great sorrow at the death of Napoleon III

April, Bill dealing with the religious establishments at Rome introduced

About May 4, The Lanza-Sella Ministry resign; but resume office at the request of the King

May 22, Death of Alessandro Manzoni

June 5, Death of Urbano Rattazzi

June 25, Law for expulsion of Jesuits passed

June 26, Lanza and Sella resign; a ministry formed by Minghetti, July 10

1874

Jan., Academy of San Luca replaced by a new academy

Sept.–Oct., Accoltellatori (secret assassinating societies) reported in Ravenna and other places

——, About 80 secret extortioners (Camorra) in Naples seized and transported

About Oct. 8, 9, Teodali, a papal chamberlain, seized by brigands, ransomed for 2,000*l.*

Oct. 13, The *Orénoque* (French) sails from Cività Vecchia

Oct. 15, Jesuits ordered to quit their establishments

The Camorra, Maffei, and Brigantaggio (terrorist secret societies) prevalent in south Italy

Dec. 31, Garibaldi declines a sum of money (3,500*l.*) voted to him

1875

Jan. 24, He enters Rome amid great excitement, takes his seat in the Chamber of Deputies, and takes the oath to the King

Feb. 12, Accepts the sum voted and devotes it to improvement of the Tiber, &c.

June, Treaty of commerce with Great Britain, to expire June 26, 1876, announced

July–Aug., Elections of parish priests declared valid in opposition to the bishops

Aug., Synod of Italian Catholic church held at Naples

Sept. 22–25, Italian Catholic congress, blessed by the Pope, meets at Florence; scanty attendance

1876

May 8, The *Duilio*, great iron-clad, launched at Castellamare, in presence of the King

June, Discovery of a "black book" in the home-office, recording misdeeds of many officials, &c.; gives much offense

July, Italian geographical society's expedition in Africa; ill-treated at Zeila; the Khedive informed

Aug. 31, Marchese Mantegazza tried for forging the signatures of the King and Prince Humbert on bills and letters to obtain money; confessed, but refused to disclose name of associate or instigator, Aug. 18; sentence, 8 years' penal servitude

Nov. 8, Maria Vittoria, Duchess of Aosta, ex-Queen of Spain, aged 28, dies

1877

May 7, Bill for repressing clerical abuses adopted by the deputies; the Pope expresses great displeasure in his circular to foreign powers, March 21; the Bill rejected by the Senate

June 23, Religious instruction in secondary schools abolished and July 15 in elementary schools

Dec. 15, Resignation of the Ministry; Depretis reforms his Ministry (Nicotera replaced by Crispi), Dec. 16–26

Dec., Father Curci publishes "Dissidio Moderno fra la Chiesa e l' Italia," against the Pope's temporal power

1878

Jan. 5, Death of La Marmora, aged 74; death of King Victor Emmanuel II, Jan. 9; buried in the Pantheon, Rome, Jan. 17

Feb. 20, Death of Pope Pius IX, Feb. 7; election of Leo XIII

March 10, Resignation of the Depretis Ministry

March 23, Cairoli forms a liberal Ministry, Corti foreign Minister; new men

July 10, *Dandolo*, largest Italian ironclad, launched at Spezzia

About July 21, Popular discontent at the Berlin treaty; desire for acquiring Trent and Trieste; cry of "Italia irredenta!" meetings at Rome, &c.

Aug. 3, Death of Giorgio Pallavicino, Senator, patriot, friend of Cavour, aged 84

Aug. 18, David Lazzaretti, "the saint," a peasant, aged 48, founder of a religious socialistic sect in 1868, with 12 apostles, &c., and creed somewhat Protestant; proposed to erect seven hermitages; marched towards Arcidosso, in Tuscany, with between two and three thousand followers; David, clad in a half-regal, half-pontifical costume, proclaiming the Christian Republic, resisted dispersion by the police, who, when fired on, fired and killed David and one of his followers; these retired, carrying off David's body

Oct. 19, Ministerial crisis; resignation of Corti and others; of all the Cairoli Ministry, Oct. 22

Oct. 25, Sig. Cairoli reconstitutes the Ministry

Nov. 17, Attempted assassination of the King at Naples by Giovanni Passananti, an internationalist, aged 29; the King and Cairoli, the Minister, slightly wounded

Autumn, "Pietro Barsanti" Clubs (in memory of a sergeant executed for gross insubordination a few years ago) become prominent; oppose ministry

Dec. 12, The Cairoli Ministry defeated on vote of confidence (263–189), Dec. 11; resign

Dec. 19, Sig. Depretis's Ministry takes office

1879

March 7, Passanante condemned to death at Naples; to perpetual imprisonment (by the King), March 29

July 3, Government defeated on the grist Bill (251–159); resigns

July 8–12, Sig. Cairoli forms a Ministry

Nov. 12, The followers of Lazzaretti tried and acquitted

1880

Jan. 1, First publication of "*Aurora*," a papal daily newspaper, at Rome

Sept. 20, *Italia*, great ironclad, launched at Castellamare

Sept. 27, Garibaldi (and his son Menotti) resign as deputies on account of the imprisonment of his son-in-law, General Canzio, for republican manifestations; Garibaldi goes to Genoa, Oct.; Canzio released, Oct. 10

Nov. 21, Colonel John Whitehead, "Garibaldi's Englishman," dies, aged 69

1881

March 9, Death of Lanza, General Medici patriot

About Dec. 28, The Government complain of Vatican intrigues

1882

May 20, 21, Opening of St. Gothard railway from Lucerne to Milan

June 2, Death of Garibaldi at Caprera

About Oct. 28, Elections in favor of the Ministry

Nov. 22, First reform parliament opened by King Humbert

Dec. 12, Death of the Duke of Sermoneta

Dec. 20–22, Demonstrations against Austria on account of execution of Oberdank for threatening the Emperor's life

1882–87, Increased formation of workman, socialistic, and republican leagues

1883

March 17, *Lepanto*, Italian built iron-clad launched at Leghorn; the King present

April 12, Specie payments resumed

June 15, New important Treaty with Great Britain signed

1884

March 14, Death of Sig. Sella, financial Minister

April, Discussion respecting the sale of the Propaganda Property at Rome

Nov. 28, New members added to the Senate

1885

Jan. 1, Soldiers in the army, 2,113,969

——, Navy consisted of 112 vessels afloat or building

Expedition to Assab to avenge the massacre of Guiletti and Bianchi

Feb. 6, The ministry determine to assist Great Britain in the Soudan

——, Italian flag hoisted at Massowah, Abyssinia

June 18, Resignation of the Depretis Ministry on account of Mancini's foreign policy; reconstituted about June 24

1886

About May 24, Elections: Ministerial majority about 55

Dec. 10, Death of Marco Minghetti (Prime Minister in 1864 *et seq.*), aged 70

1887

Feb. 23, 24, Destructive earthquakes

March 13, Defensive Treaty of alliance with Austria-Hungary and Germany signed

July 29, Depretis dies, aged 74; M. Crispi becomes Premier, Aug.

Oct. 2, 3, Francesco Crispi visits Prince Bismarck

Oct. 25, Signor Crispi at Turin declares his policy to be thorough peace

1887–88, For war with Abyssinia, *see s.v.*

1888

Jan. 2, Duke Torlonia, Syndic of Rome, dismissed for congratulating the Pope on his jubilee

Feb., The progress of the Italian Catholic Church opposed to the papacy, reported

June, The abolition of capital punishment passed by the Chambers

Sept. 11, Marriage of the Duke of Aosta, ex-King of Spain, with his niece Princess Lœtitia, daughter of his sister Clotilde and Prince Napoleon Jerome

Oct. 11, The Emperor William II arrived at Rome; launch of the great ironclad *Re Umberto* at Castellamare, Oct. 16

1889

Aug. 8, Death of Benedetto Cairoli, aged 63, patriot and statesman, associated with Victor Emanuel, Cavour, and Garibaldi, in the unification of Italy

Sept. 13, Sig. Crispi injured by a stone thrown at him during a carriage drive by Emilio Caporali

Oct. 2, The King ratifies Treaty with Abyssinia

1890

Jan. 18, Death of the Duke of Aosta, aged 44

May 5, Ministry defeated in the Senate on a minor question; the crisis passes over, May 9 *et seq.*

May 11 *et seq.*, Democratic congress at Rome, 470 associations represented

About May 24, Riots at Conselice, in the Romagna, 3 or 4 rioters killed by the military

May, June, The Prince of Naples visits St. Petersburg, Berlin

July 14, Major Gaetani Casati returns from his expedition to Emin Pasha (*see* Africa)

Oct. 4–10, Conference at Naples, of representatives of Great Britain and Italy, respecting the limits of the territories in East Africa; Sig. Crispi and Lord Dufferin present; disagreement respecting Kassala, &c.; the Conference closes without result

1891

About March 31, Financial difficulties; opposition to reduction of the army expenditure

April 15, Treaty for the delimitation of the British and Italian spheres of influence in East Africa, signed at Rome

April, Trial of 179 persons connected with the Mala Vita conspiracy at Bari (Camorra)

June 28, The Triple Alliance renewed

July 22, Tour of the Prince of Naples; arrives in London; leaves for Bergen, &c., Aug. 15

Oct. 12, The Russian Foreign Minister, M. de Giers, meets the Marquis di Rudini, the Italian Premier, at Milan; they visit the King at Monza (no political results), Oct. 13 and 17

Oct. 14, Trial of 60 anarchists

Dec. 16, New commercial Treaty with Austria and Germany signed at Rome

1892

Feb. 7, Death of Count de Launay, Minister at Berlin successively for Sardinia and Italy for 37 years

March 24, Cipriani Palla and other anarchists sentenced to different terms of imprisonment

April 12, Difficulty with the United States settled. *See s.v.*

April 25 *et seq.*, Anarchist leaders arrested in Rome and other places; 48 arrested up to April 29; 42 arrests on April 30

May 2, Resignation of Rudini Ministry

May 15, Giolitti formed Cabinet

Sept. 8, Death of General Cialdini, Duke of Gaëta, eminent patriot and soldier, aged 81

Oct., Increase of brigandage; many arrests

Nov. 26, Death of Admiral Pacoret de Saint-Bon, chief of the navy

1893

Jan. 22, Arrest of Signor Cuciniello, manager of the Rome branch of the Bank of Naples; report of government committee presented, March 20

Feb., The Pope's jubilee at Rome

March 8, Bill to make civil marriage obligatory introduced

April 5, Harry Ogilvie, engineer, murdered at Cività Vecchia

June 13, Signor Cuciniello sentenced to 10 years' imprisonment; Signor Dalesandro, cashier, to 6 years' imprisonment, for embezzlement

Aug. 9, New bank law passed by the Senate creating national Bank of Italy

Aug. 16, Conflicts, with bloodshed, between the French and Italian salt-workers at Aigues-Mortes, on the Mediterranean littoral; lead to demonstrations

against the French at Rome, Naples, Turin, and Milan, &c.; many rioters arrested, Aug. 18–21; rioters acquitted, Dec. 30

Oct. 16, Visit of British squadron, under Adm. Sir Michael Culme-Seymour, at Taranto; at Spezzia, Oct. 23–29

Oct. 21, Death of Lord Vivian, British Ambassador, aged 59

Nov. 24, Investigations into the affairs of the banks; Signor Giolitti censured; he and his Ministry resign

Dec. 14, Crispi formed Cabinet

1894

Jan. 9, Seizure of revolutionary manifestoes in Rome

Riots in Carrara

Jan. 25, Indemnity (420,000f.) paid by France to the relatives of the Italians killed at Aigues-Mortes (*see above*, Aug. 16, 1893)

Jan. 28, Thirty thousand francs paid by the Italian Government to France to compensate the sufferers by the riots, Aug. 16, 1893, in Rome, &c.

March 8, Bomb explosion outside the Chamber of Deputies in Rome; 2 deaths

April 16, Signor Crispi applies for extraordinary powers, executive and financial, for himself, aided by a committee

May 2, Trial of Signor Talongo, ex-governor, and officials of the Banca Romana; acquitted, July 28

May, The military budget passed

June 16, Signor Crispi shot at, whilst driving, by Paolo Lega, an Anarchist; Lega sentenced to 20 years' imprisonment, July 19

June 29, The Government financial proposals adopted by the Chamber (180–74)

July 1, Signor Bandi, a newspaper director at Leghorn, who had published articles against the anarchists, assassinated (Rosolini Romiti, the murderer, sentenced to life imprisonment, and two others to 30 years, May 22, 1895)

July 4, Murders by anarchists at Pisa and Empoli

July 9, Two hundred and fifty anarchists under arrest in Rome, and about 2,208 among the prisons in other towns, reported

July 11, Anti-anarchist bill passed by the Chamber

Oct. 22, Decree issued dissolving all revolutionary socialistic societies

Nov. 16–21, Destructive earthquakes in Reggio, Calabria, and Sicily; many deaths

Dec. 10, Baron Sonnino's financial statement; deficit reduced; additional taxation proposed; well received; announced

Dec., The deputies, Giolitti (ex-Premier), Mazzino, and Martuscelli, charged with forgery of documents relating to the Banca Romana, damaging the character of Signor Crispi and others; prosecution ordered and parliament adjourned

1895

April 24, The proceedings against Sig. Giolitti quashed by the court of cassation on his appeal

May 18, Shocks of earthquake in Central Italy

June 3, Attempted assassination of Signor Ferrari, a deputy, at Rimini; died June 10

June 13, Budget introduced; retrenchment and some additional taxation required

June 25, Marriage of the Duke of Aosta and Princess Helène of Orleans at Kingston-on-Thames

Dec. 6, War in Abyssinia. *See s.v.*

Dec. 13, Documents relating to M. Giolitti presented to parliament, Nov.; case shelved by vote

1896

March 1, Battle of Adowa, Italians defeated in Abyssinia

March 5, Resignation of Crispi Ministry; succeeded by Marquis di Rudini

March 7, Socialist manifesto against the war

March 14, Decree of amnesty to political offenders

March 17, Declaration of the Marquis di Rudini in the Chamber expressing admiration of the army; negotiations for peace authorized

March 20, The African credits adopted by the Chamber; and Senate, March 25

May 9, The Government policy adopted by the Chamber (278–133)

June 5–13, Gen. Baratieri tried by court martial at Asmara for misconduct as General; acquitted

Aug. 8, The *Doelwyk*, Dutch steamer, containing arms, captured by the *Etna*, Italian cruiser, in Italian waters

Sept. 30, Treaty between France and Italy respecting Tunis signed

Oct. 22–29, Montenegrin princely family visit Rome

Oct. 24, Marriage of the Prince of Naples to Princess Helen of Montenegro in the Quirinal; general amnesty decreed

Oct. 26, Peace with Abyssinia signed, ratified Nov. 16

Nov. 30, Debate in the Chamber on the colony of Erythrea; victory of the Government on the home policy, Dec. 9; *see* Somaliland, Dec. 2, 1896

1897

March 21, General elections; the Crispi party much reduced

April 22, Attempt to stab the King while driving to the races by Pietro Acciarito, fanatic (sentenced to penal servitude for life, May 29), at Rome

Aug. 30, Commercial treaty with Abyssinia and frontier, negotiated by Major Nerazzini, accepted

Sept., Bank scandals, 20 persons convicted, at Como; appeals

Oct. 11, A popular demonstration in Rome against the scheme of taxation on incomes and personal property came into conflict with the troops, 1 death

Oct. 15, Discontent allayed by a pacific circular

Nov. 8, All proceedings against Signor Crispi stopped on his appeal

Dec. 2, Speech of Sig. Crispi desiring an impartial inquiry with regard to his relations with the bank of Naples; neutral commission of inquiry appointed, Dec. 3; no ground for impeachment, but censured politically in its report, March 19, 1898; adopted by the Chamber (207–7), March 23; Sig. Crispi resigns as Deputy, March 24; reëlected, April 17.

1898

March 6, Sig. Felice Cavallotti, radical leader, killed in a duel by Sig. F. Maccola, conservative deputy (Maccola sentenced to 13 months' imprisonment, Oct. 21; reduced to March 7, 1899)

April 27, 28, Bread riots owing to rise in prices at Bari and Faenza, buildings sacked and burnt by the mob; council of Ministers order remedies for the distressed, April 30; further rioting, conflicts with troops at Milan, Florence, Leghorn, Pisa, Pavia, and other places, 82 killed, May 3–8; price of bread reduced,

May 9; state of siege at Naples, May 10; quiet restored, Chambers prorogued May 14

June 18, Resignation of Rudini Ministry; succeeded by General Luigi Pelloux as Premier, June 29

July 23, Arbitration treaty between Italy and Argentina

Nov. 21, New commercial treaty with France

Nov. 27, Tax riot at Picerno, one death

Dec. 7, Anglo-Italian (commercial) convention, delimiting boundaries north of Erythrea, signed

1899

Jan. 31, Bill adopted, withdrawing the 1-lira and 2-lire notes, equivalent to the abolition of forced currency

Feb. 5, Anti-fiscal demonstrations in N. Italy, and a meeting at Naples

June 20, 21, Stormy scenes and socialist obstruction to the public safety bill (relative to strikes, meetings, press offenses); the bill promulgated by royal decree, June 22; violent scene, free fight in the Chamber; session closed by royal decree, June 30

Dec. 31, Amnesty to political offenders and others (*above*, May, 1898), signed

1900

Jan. 4, Gen. Mirri, Minister of War, resigns

Jan. 24, Protocol delimiting Italian and French possessions in the Red Sea littoral signed

June 18, Resignation of Pelloux Ministry; succeeded by Saracco, June 24

July 29, King Humbert fatally shot by Gaetano Bresci, an anarchist, at Monza

July 31, Many anarchists arrested; 50 arrested in Rome, Aug. 7

Aug. 3, Proclamation, moderate in tone, issued by King Victor Emmanuel III

Aug. 29, Bresci, the regicide, tried at Milan and sentenced to life imprisonment (committed suicide, May 22, 1901); Padre Volponi, Vicar of St. Sebastian, sentenced to 8 months' imprisonment for stating that regicide was sometimes justifiable

Dec. 21, Sig. Rubini resigns office; succeeded by Sig. Finali, Jan. 7, 1901

1901

Jan. 27, Sig. Verdi, the composer, dies, aged 87

Feb. 6, Fall of Saracco Ministry

Feb. 14, Zanardelli, Liberal, formed Cabinet, Giolitti, Minister of the Interior

March 1, 2, Dockers' strike at Palermo, spreads to other classes, riots suppressed by troops

Aug. 12, Francesco Crispi, a great statesman, died, aged 81

Oct. 9, The King and Queen open large electric works at Vizzola

Nov. 26, Anglo-Italian agreement relating to the frontier between Soudan and Erythrea signed

1902

Feb. 24–March 10, General railway strike averted by prompt action of the Government, armistice; concessions to the men granted, March 8

April 10, Diplomatic rupture with Switzerland, due to excesses of the anarchist press in 1901; conciliatory tone of the Swiss nat. council, April 22

June 16, New 3½% loan, total amount, 100,000,000 lire, reported

June 28, The Triple Alliance renewed

July 13–17, The King visits Russia

July 30, Dispute with Switzerland settled through Germany

——, Mafia murders trial at Bologna, Palizzolo, ex-deputy, Trapani, and Fontona sentenced to 30 years' imprisonment for the murder of Signori Miceli (July, 1892) and Notobartolo (Feb., 1893),(10 months' trial)

Aug. 7, Death of Gen. Ferrero, Italian Ambassador in London, 1895–98

Aug. 27–31, The King visits Germany

Nov. 9, Distress in the south, reforms urged by Baron Sonnino

Dec. 28, Severe earthquake shock at Syracuse

Dec. 29, 1903, Austrian Ambassador officially denounces the commercial treaty between Austria-Hungary and Italy, which therefore lapses, Dec. 31

1903

End Jan., Court of Cassation in Rome quashes sentence passed upon Palizzolo, for the murder of Signori Miceli and Notobartolo, by the assize court of Bologna; orders a new trial in Florence

Mid March, Strike of students in secondary schools in all parts of Italy in consequence of circular issued by Signor Nasi, Minister of Education, March 1, making new regulations for the final examinations

End March, Bill for construction of a powerful radiographic station on the Marconi system for communication between Italy and Argentina approved by the Senate

April 13, International congress of agriculture opened at Rome, King and Queen present

Visit of King Edward VII to Italy: Naples, April 23; Rome, April 27; visits Pope at the Vatican, April 29; leaves Rome, April 30

April 25, First stone of the new Campanile at Venice laid

May 2, German Emperor visits Rome

May 23, Army estimates passed, 125–88

July 20, Death of Pope Leo XIII

Aug. 4, Cardinal Sarto elected Pope; takes the title of Pius X

Aug. 9, Coronation of Pius X in St. Peter's

Aug. 11, Earthquake shocks at Naples, Catania, and Syracuse

Oct. 14–19, King and Queen visit Paris

Nov. 17–21, Visit of King and Queen to England

Dec. 3, Vote of confidence in the Government program passed in the Chamber, 284–117

Dec. 25, Anglo-Italian arbitration treaty signed at Rome

Dec. 26, Death of Signor Zanardelli, ex-Premier

1904

Jan. 31, Workmen's Accident Insurance law enacted

Early March, King by royal decree adds to the number of the Senate by creating 28 new senators

March 26, German Emperor visits Naples; entertains the King of Italy on board the *Hohenzollern*, Kaiser pays a return visit on the Italian cruiser *Agordat*

April 24, M. Loubet, President of the French Republic, accompanied by M. Delcassé, Premier, arrives at Rome

April 29, Departure of M. Loubet

May 2, Religious instruction to be given in schools where demanded by parents but not during class hours

May 4, Pope formally protests against the action of the president of the French republic, as head of a Catholic state, in visiting the King of Italy and thus recognizing the power that had deprived him of the papal dominions

May 7, Chamber of Deputies reassembles; after discussion resolves to refer the reports and documents of the committee of inquiry into Nasi's administration of the Ministry of Public Instruction, to be dealt with by the judicial authorities, with power to proceed against the ex-Minister

May 16, Serious agrarian riots at Cerignola, Apulia, collision with troops, 2 rioters killed, many wounded

June 11, Chamber, by a large majority, approve the program of public works for the next 4 years presented by the Minister, Signor Tedesco; it includes the construction of a railway from Cunéo to Nice, and a new direct line between Rome and Naples

July 2, Chamber of Deputies disperses for summer vacation after passing a bill for the financial relief and reform of the municipalities of Rome and Naples; a bill for the water supply of Apulia, and gives its consent to the Government for the conclusion of commercial treaties with Austria and Switzerland

July 5, Maj. Ercolessi and his wife arrested at Messina on the charge of having sold documents containing military secrets to a foreign govt.

July 13, New commercial treaty between Italy and Switzerland signed at Rome

July 23, Third trial of Signor Palizzolo and others for complicity in the murder of Commendatore Notarbartolo in Sicily ten years previously concludes at Florence with the acquittal of all the accused; trial lasted 10 months; special interest attached to the case as one of the most important trials in Italy for many years, owing to the alleged interference of the Mafia with the course of justice

July 29, *Osservatore Romano* publishes a letter from Cardinal Merry del Val, Papal Secretary of State, dissolving the general permanent committee of the association known as "The Work of the Italian Catholic Congresses and Committees" on account of discord and want of unison

Aug. 3, Wireless telegraphic communication established between Bari, on the coast of Italy, and Antivari, on the coast of Montenegro, inaugurated

Early Sept., Miners at Buggernu, Sardinia, to the number of 2,500 go out on strike in consequence of a dispute respecting the hours of labor; conflict with troops called out to maintain order, 3 miners killed and several wounded, 7 soldiers injured

Sept. 15, Birth of Humbert, Prince of Piedmont, heir to the throne

Sept. 20, Congress of free thought opened at Rome, about 4,000 members present

Sept. 21, General strike riots, due chiefly to the instigation of the Socialist party, take place in Italy during Sept.; general strike attempted throughout the country; troops called out at Genoa; serious disturbances at Venice, Turin, and Milan; reign of terror at Milan, the Labor Exchange prevents the issue of all newspapers except its own organ; reaction against the socialists, work generally resumed

Nov. 6, First ballot in the general election; loss of socialist seats in the centers of Milan, Turin, and Genoa; 294 ministerialists, 46 members of the constitutional opposition, 27 radicals, 25 socialists, 16 republicans returned; 77 elections undecided, as against 39 the previous general election

Nov. 13, Second ballot; defeat of the extreme left, which secures only 17 out of 56 contested seats; 8 radical, 5 republican, and 4 socialist seats gained; socialists in new parliament number 30, as against 33 in the last; defeated in all three colleges for which they stood at Florence; extreme left number 91 (including the socialists), losing 16 seats

Nov. 30, New parliament opened by the King; refers to its being the first parliament elected during his reign; expresses his strong faith in liberty, by which alone the problems arising from the new aspirations and new movements of social forces among all peoples of to-day could be solved; his government would continue the policy of "ample liberty within the strongly-defended limits of the law"; Signor Macora, the ministerial candidate, elected President of the Chamber by 292 votes

1905

Feb. 25, Signor Tittoni, Minister for Foreign Affairs, lays before the Chamber bill for the reorganization of Italian Southern Somaliland. Among other things, measure approves the cession to Italy on lease by Great Britain of a strip of territory on the Kismayu roadstead, Italy to have the right to land troops on the concession by notifying the fact to local British authorities, but must obtain the consent of the British Government for landing of any large body of troops intended for an expedition. Meeting of representatives of railway employés held in Rome adopt a policy of obstruction as a protest against the government railway bills

March 4, Members of the Giolitti Ministry resign, Signor Fortis requested to form a new cabinet; King, by royal decree, creates 43 new senators

Mid March, Signor Pestalozza, Italian diplomatic agent, arrives at Aden, having concluded at Illig an agreement with the Mullah, stipulating for general peace, which the Mullah promises to observe towards both Italy and Great Britain; the Mullah to reside in a territory already belonging to the Italian protectorate, and assigned to him by the agreement; the Mullah places himself under the Italian protectorate, and recognizes the right of the Italian Government to appoint a resident; free commerce, except traffic in arms and slaves, in the territory of the Mullah

March 24, Signor Fortis having renounced the formation of a new cabinet, Signor Tittoni is sent for by the King, and entrusted with the charge of presiding over an *interim* ministry composed (with the exception of Signor Giolitti) of members of the late cabinet. Vote of confidence in the new Ministry rejected in the Chamber by 281 votes to 160; second motion approving the government program announced before the last general election carried by 273 votes to 98

March 25, Signor Tittoni announces his resignation. New cabinet constituted with Signor Fortis as Premier and Minister of the Interior and Signor Tittoni as Foreign Minister; all new ministers belong to the left

April 6, Meeting of the German Emperor and King of Italy at Naples

April 15, Railway strike proclaimed by delegates of the railway associations after interview with Signor Ferraris, owing to dissatisfaction of railway employés with article 17 of the new bill, which ordains that all employés of railways (private as well as state), whatever their rank or nature of their employment, are to be considered as "public officials," and regards them as having resigned if they leave work or interfere with the regular working of the service, thus curtailing the right of employés to strike

April 17, Riot at Foggia in connection with the railway strike; collision between troops and the strikers, 4 persons killed, 10 wounded

April 18, Railway bill for the state requisition and management of the Italian railways passes first reading in Chamber of Deputies by 306 votes to 34; minority chiefly socialists

April 20, Chamber of Deputies, by 289 votes to 45, pass the government bill for the working of railways by the state, including clause 17; Senate gives its final sanction to the bill

April 22, Strike formally declared at an end, April 21; railway traffic resumed

April 29, Important meeting in Venice between Signor Tittoni and Count Goluchowski

May 4, *Hohenzollern*, with Emperor and German imperial family on board, arrives at Bari, April 28; arrives at Venice, May 2; Emperor and Empress leave Venice on their homeward journey

June 6, International congress on agriculture at general meeting concludes its labors

June 7, International Institute of Agriculture created

June 17, Debate on the navy bill: Signor Fortis, Premier, asks for the acceptance of the naval program as a proof of confidence in the Government; an order of the day in these terms passed by 272 votes to 85

June 21, Chamber, by 190 votes to 48, disapproves of the bill for increasing the expenditure on the navy

June 24, Encyclical letter, addressed by the Pope to the Italian bishops deals with the action of Roman Catholics who are Christian socialists and democrats, published

June 28, Military estimates for 1905–06, including an addition of 11,000,000 lire (440,000*l.*) to the consolidated budget, making the whole expenditure about 11½ millions for the year, passed by the Chamber

July 1, Principal railroads taken over by the Government becoming Italian State Railways

Aug. 5, Pope addresses a letter to the leaders of the Roman Catholic party of social action, expressing regret that his former encyclical letters had been misinterpreted

Sept. 8, Earthquake in Calabria

Sept. 11, Sharp shock again felt at Monteleone

Sept. 18, Further shocks of earthquake, damage done in the provinces of Catanzaro and Cosenza

Oct. 29, King lays the first stone of a new dock at Genoa

Dec. 16, Government defeated by 277 votes to 124 on the commercial *modus vivendi* with Spain

Dec. 18, Signor Fortis, Premier, and cabinet resign. Cabinet reconstructed

1906

Jan. 4, Marquis Visconti Venosta nominated first delegate at the Algeciras conference

Mid Jan., New commercial treaty with Bulgaria, taking the place of the provisional agreement of 1887, signed at Sofia

Feb. 2, Parliament reassembles, Jan. 30; defeat of the Ministry by 221 votes to 188, Feb. 1; resignation of Signor Fortis

Feb. 8, New ministry formed; Baron Sonnino Premier and Minister of the Interior

March 6, Signor Tittoni, ex-Minister for Foreign Affairs

(Dec. 18, 1905), appointed Ambassador to Gt. Britain

April 5–8, Volcanic eruptions of Vesuvius, the most violent since 1631

April 9, Postal union congress, inaugurated in Rome by the King and Queen

May 7, Labor riot in connection with the cotton weavers of Turin; conflict with the police; 9 rioters seriously wounded; collision between police and soldiers and a riotous mob at Bologna

May 10, General labor strike in Rome; strikes also in Milan, Verona, Parma, Ancona, Leghorn, and other large towns; serious disorders reported at Bologna

May 11, Fatal riots in Sardinia against dues levied in the Cagliani market

May 13, 24 of the 28 socialist deputies tender their resignation to the Chamber

May 18, Resignation of the Sonnino Ministry

May 19, Simplon tunnel opened by the King and the President of the Swiss Confederation

May 30, New ministry officially announced; Signor Giolitti, Premier and Minister of the Interior

July 4, Government bill for the conversion of the consolidated debt from 4 to 3¾% passed

Aug. 29, Marquis di San Giuliano appointed Italian Ambassador to Gt. Britain

Sept. 2, Death of Signor Guiseppe Giacosa, well-known dramatist

Oct. 7, Socialist congress opened in Rome

Dec. 18, Signor Tittoni, in an important speech in the Chamber, said that the maintenance of the Triple Alliance, and of friendship with France and Gt. Britain was the keynote of Italian policy

1907

April 17, Resignation of Signor Massimini, Minister of Finance, announced

April 18, Meeting between King Edward, Queen Alexandra, and King Victor Emmanuel at Gaeta

April 19, Signor Lacava appointed Minister of Finance

April 27, Violent eruption of Stromboli

April 30, King Edward leaves Naples on completion of his Italian visit

May 11, Stromboli and Etna both active; violent eruptions take place

July 15, Arrest of Signor Nasi in Rome

Sept. 18, Arbitration treaty signed at The Hague with Argentina

Oct. 16, Arbitration treaty with Mexico signed at The Hague

Oct. 23, Earthquake in Calabria; 186 persons killed and 85 injured

1908

Feb. 24, Signor Nasi found guilty and sentenced to 11 months' imprisonment, and debarred from holding any public office for 4½ years

March 12, Death of Edmondo de Amicis, writer

March 25, Meeting between King Victor Emmanuel and the German Emperor at Venice

April 2, Riot in Rome in connection with a funeral procession; the police, being hard pressed, fire on the crowd; 3 persons killed and 18 wounded, and about 30 policemen wounded

April 2–4, A general strike proclaimed

April 7, Navy estimates for 1908–09 amount to 6,092,-000l., more than half a million over the amount sanctioned by the law of 1905; it is proposed to lay

down two new battleships of the Dreadnought type. *Times*

April 12, Visit of Prince Bülow to Rome

April 15, Prince Bülow visits the Pope and exchanges visits with Cardinal Merry del Val

April 23, Women's congress, the first held in Italy, opened in Rome

May 23, International Institute of Agriculture opened by the King

June 9, Death of the Marquis Prinetti, formerly Minister for Foreign Affairs, b. 1848

Aug. 7, Death of the Marquis di Rudini, eminent Italian statesman, b. 1839

Nov. 1, Papal Decree recognized the Roman Curia

Dec. 28, Earthquake in Calabria and Sicily; most of the coast towns on both sides of the straits of Messina wholly or partially destroyed; Messina itself, which suffered not only from the shocks on land, but also from an earthquake wave, entirely ruined; the whole shape of the coast-line at that point altered; a rough estimate places the number of lives lost at 75,000, and the destruction of property enormous; destruction of Reggio, reported Dec. 30; number of lives lost estimated at 200,000 up to Dec. 31

1909

Jan. 30, Another severe shock, which demolished a number of walls still standing at Messina, occurred

March 12, Murder of Lieut. Petrosino, who had been instrumental in the exposure of the "Black Hand" criminal association

April 17, King Edward and Queen Alexandra arrive at Genoa

April 26, King Edward and Queen Alexandra in Sicily

April 27, Mr. Wilbur Wright concludes his experiments at Centocelle with his aëroplane

——, King Edward and the royal party at Palermo; in Naples, April 30; at Pompeii, May 3; leave Italy, May 5

April 29, Meeting between King Edward, Queen Alexandra, and the Italian sovereigns at Baïa

May 12, Meeting between the Italian sovereigns and the German Emperor and Empress at Brindisi

Oct. 23, The Czar arrives at Racconigi on a visit to King Victor Emmanuel

Dec. 2, Resignation of Giolitti Ministry on Bill proposing reforms in taxation; succeeded by Sonnino, Dec. 9

Dec. 4, Death of Signor Fortis, ex-Premier, b. 1842

1910

Jan. 19, Death of Andrea Costa (Socialist), Vice-President of Chamber of Deputies

Feb. 10, Program of Ministry announced, improvement in primary education, arrangements with steamship companies, electoral reform, encouragement of agriculture, establishment of land and labor banks, reorganization of local taxes, reduction of military service to 2 years, assistance to coöperative societies

March 21, Sonnino Ministry defeated on mercantile marine subsidy measure

March 22, Visit of von Bethmann Hollweg, German Chancellor

March 30, Luzzatti succeeded as Prime Minister, the Marquis di San Guiliano, Foreign Affairs; included Tedesco, Facta, Credaro, and Sacchi

May 28, Temporary marine measure passed Chamber, conventions to last 3 years

July 4, Schools Bill with provision for primary schools

in communes without any passed in Chamber, 267 to 43

July 5, Death of Giovanni Shiparelli, astronomer

July 17, Law passed reorganized army with general staff and 12 commanding generals, 12 army corps, &c.

——, Law established maternity insurance

Aug. 10, Riots at Bari protesting against increase in house rents

1911

March 1, Weekly paper "L'Idea Nazionale" began publication

March 7, Death of Antonio de Fogazzaro (68), novelist

March 11, Camorra trial for murder of Cuocolos on June 5, 1906, begun near Viterbo

March 18, Resignation of Luzzatti Ministry defeated on electoral reform proposed

March 29, G. Giolitti succeeded Luzzatti as Premier and Minister of the Interior; Marquis di San Guiliano, Foreign Affairs; G. Finocchiaro-Aprile, Justice; General P. Spingardi, War; Rear Admiral P. Leonardi Cattolica, Marine; F. S. Nitti, Agriculture

April 6, Ministry presented program of electoral reform, old age pensions

May 11, General Arbitration Treaty with Paraguay signed

Sept. 25, Note to Turkey demanded recognition of economic privileges of Italians in Tripoli

Sept. 28, Ultimatum presented to Turkey recited grievances of Italians in Tripoli and Cyrenaica (Barca), the state of disorder and negligence of the Turkish Government; guarantee of reforms demanded and full protection for Italian citizens and commerce

Sept. 29, Turkish answer asked statement of reforms wanted by Italy but was not accepted by Italy and war begun and declared; 3 Turkish torpedo boats sunk by Italians off Prevesa

Sept. 30, Turkish Note to the Powers asked intervention to end hostilities

Oct. 1, Italian fleet arrived off Tripoli

Oct. 3, Italian squadron bombed fortifications of Tripoli

Oct. 5, Italian force landed at Tripoli and Italian occupation begun

Oct. 16, Derna bombed and reduced by Italians

Oct. 18, Italian landing forced at Benghazi

Oct. 23 and 26, Turkish and Arab attacks on Tripoli repulsed

Nov. 5, Decree proclaimed annexation of Tripoli and Cyrenaica to Italy

Dec. 5, Decisive battle outside Tripoli

Dec. 13, Italian occupation of Tadjura 12 miles from Tripoli

Population 35,845,048

1912

Jan. 7, Italian squadron in engagement with Turks in Red Sea off Kounfiuda sunk 7 gunboats

Jan. 16, Seizure of French mail boat "Carthage" by Italians and cargo of airplanes for Turks

Jan. 18, Seizure of French mail boat "Manouba" and 29 Turks believed to be army officers taken from boat

——, Fighting between Italians and Turks at Gargaresh oasis and occupation by Italians the following day

Jan. 30, Attack of Arabs on fort at Benghazi repulsed by Italians

Feb. 5, Italian squadron bombed Hodeida on the Red Sea

Feb. 23, The Chamber adopted Bill providing for extension of sovereignty to Tripoli and creating colonial government by vote of 433 to 9, the Senate the next day

Feb. 24, Italian warships bombed Beirut and sunk Turkish gunboat and a torpedo boat

March 1, Bill converting life insurance into a State monopoly passed Chamber and became law, April 23; protested by foreign Governments

March 3, Attack on Italian position near Derna repulsed

March 6, First use of dirigible balloons in actual warfare by Italians in Tripoli

March 11, Turks and Arabs attacked Tobruk

March 14, Unsuccessful attempt of anarchist, d'Alba, to assassinate the King

March 25, Meeting of the King of Italy and the Emperor of Germany at Venice discussed peace

March 26, S. Chiesa accused by A. Luzzatto in Chamber of defrauding the State using his position to conceal terms of important contract, blows exchanged

April 8, Manifesto of 5 Catholic societies approved proposed electoral reforms

April 16, The Powers addressed Turkey proposing mediation in the war

April 16–19, Italian naval demonstration at mouth of the Dardanelles

April 23, Turkey accepted mediation of Powers making condition that sovereign rights of Turkey be maintained in Tripoli and Italians evacuate the country

——, Engagement of Italians and Turks at Bu Kemesh

——, Italians seized Turkish island of Stampalia near entrance to the Dardanelles

——, Insurance Act created National Insurance Department and made insurance a State monopoly

May 3, Award of arbitration of Canevaro claim in Peru

May 4, Italians occupied Rhodes and by mid-June, 12 Turkish Ægean islands

May 17, Surrender of Turkish garrison at Rhodes

May 29, Electoral Reform Bill passed the Chamber by vote of 284 to 62, giving suffrage to all who could read and write and to illiterates who had reached age of 30 and had performed their military service; passed by Senate end of June

June 13, Nationality law enacted

June 30, Universal adult male suffrage law approved including all citizens who could read and write and illiterates over 30 who had performed military service, number of voters raised from 3,247,722 to 8,635,148

July 8, Italians captured Misurata east of Tripoli

July 9, Verdict given in Camorra trial for murder of Cuocolo and his wife in Naples, June 5, 1906; the 6 who executed the murders and the 2 who plotted them sentenced to 30 years imprisonment and the rest to terms of from 4 to 20 years

July 19, Italian attack on the Dardanelles

Aug. 6, Zara, Tripoli, captured by Italians

Sept. 5, General Caneva recalled from Tripoli and command given to General Bagni in Tripoli and to General Bricola in Cyrenaica

Sept. 17, Italians repulsed attack of Enver Bey on Derna

Oct. 15, Preliminary Peace Treaty with Turkey signed at Ouchy

Oct. 17, Royal decree as to Tripoli and Cyrenaica protection of religion, &c.

Oct. 18, Treaty of Peace with Turkey signed at Lausanne, the Sultan retaining only spiritual authority over Tripoli and Cyrenaica, the Italians to remain in occupation of Rhodes and the Dodecanese Islands until Turkey had withdrawn all her troops from the annexed territory and fulfilled certain other conditions of the Treaty

Oct. 28, France recognized Italian possession of Tripoli and Cyrenaica

Dec. 5, Triple Alliance renewed (fifth) between Italy, Austria-Hungary, and Germany

1913

Jan. 9, Decree organized the Government of Libya (Tripolitania and Cyrenaica)

Feb. 6, Decree organized justice in Libya

April 27, Italians occupied Ghadames oasis and Captain Pavoni received oath of allegiance from chiefs. *See also* Libya

May 6, Decision of Hague Court that Italy must pay indemnity to France for steamers seized Jan., 1912

May 16, Italians defeated Turks and Arabs at Sidi Gharba near Derna

June 14, The Chamber voted $20,200,000 for completion of conquest of Libya

June 19, Arabs and Italians in battle at Ettangi

June 22, Law established invalidity insurance fund for mercantile marine

Aug. 4–8, Strike of iron workers and of tramway men in Milan

Aug. 11–15, General strike not successful

Oct. 26, Election begun which resulted in majority for Constitutional Liberals with 318 seats in Chamber: Radicals, 70; Catholics, 24; Republicans, 16; Reformist Socialists, 23; Socialists, 51; and Independent Socialists, 6; a Catholic party represented at the polls for the first time

Dec. 16, Death of Cardinal Rampolla

1914

March 3, Italian troops entered Murzuk, capital of Fezzan

March 4, Dubab, Arabia, bombed by Italian cruiser

March 9, General strike begun in Rome

March 10, Resignation of Giolitti. Succeeded by Salandra, right wing Liberal. General Grandi succeeded Spingardi as Minister of War, San Giuliano, Foreign Affairs

March 29, Meeting of the King with the German Emperor at Venice

May 5, Treaty of conciliation with the United States signed

May 6, University of Rome closed because of irredentist demonstrations of students

June 7, Riots at Ancona because anti-militarist meeting forbidden which spread to other cities and led to general strike headed by Enrico Malatesta and Benito Mussolini. Socialist demonstrations in Florence and Turin where troops fired on crowds

June 8, Commercial Treaty with Portugal signed

June 10, General Confederation of Labor ordered the general strike stopped

June 14–16, Provincial and municipal elections held, the Constitutionalists received majority in Rome, Brecia, Modena, Sienna, and Reggio, and the Socialists in Milan and Naples

July 25, Italian announcement to Austria-Hungary that in case of war occupation of Serbia Italy would reserve right to claim compensation under Article VII of the Triple Alliance; accepted by Austria, Aug. 23

July 30, The fleet mobilized and assembled at Gaeta

July 10, General Luigi Cadorna appointed Chief of General Staff on death of Pollio

Aug. 1, War profits tax in effect from this date

——, Royal Decree prohibited export of wheat, rye, oats, corn, flour, sugar, cattle, and additional list added, Aug. 6

Aug. 2, Appeal of Pope Pius for peace to the Catholics of the world

Aug. 3, Italy declared neutrality in War as not bound by terms of the Triple Alliance to take part in aggressive war

Aug. 12, Oasis and town of Ghat in Tripolitania occupied by Italians

Aug. 13, Commercial Agreement with Brazil prolonged

Aug. 20, Death of Pope Pius X

Sept. 3, Cardinal Della Chiesa elected Pope and took name of Benedict XV

——, Fleet proceeded to Taranto

Sept. 24, Italy gave notification of adherence to recognition of neutrality of Switzerland

Sept. 28, Death of Guido Fusinato, jurist

Oct. 9, Resignation of General Grandi as Minister of War. Succeeded by General Zupelli, Oct. 11

Oct. 14, Decree reduced import duties on all grains, flour, &c.

Oct. 16, Death of Marchese di San Giuliano, former Premier and Minister of Foreign Affairs

Oct. 28, Decree prohibited export of food stuffs enumerated

Oct. 31, Italians occupied Saseno Island, Albania

——, Resignation of Rubini (Treasury) over question of supply of funds to the army

Nov. 2, Resignation of Salandra Ministry and reconstruction (Nov. 5) of Ministry by Salandra as Prime Minister and Minister of the Interior; Sonnino, Foreign Affairs; Paolo Carcano, Treasury; V. Orlando, Justice; Martini, Colonies; General Zupelli, War; Admiral Mello, Marine; Vari, Agriculture; Fusinato, Education

Nov. 14, First issue of the "Popolo d'Italia" edited by Benito Mussolini

Nov. 24, Advisory Committee on embargo established

Nov. 28, Death of Marchese Visconti-Venosta, former Premier (85)

Dec. 17, Visit of Prince von Bülow to Rome in interests of Central Powers

Dec. 20, A consortium for subsidies on industrial securities established by decree with right to rediscount a percentage of its bills with the banks of issue

Dec. 25, Italian troops occupied Valona (Avlona), Albania, town and harbor

1915

Jan. 1, Population 36,120,118

Jan. 13, Earthquake totally destroyed Avezzano and Sora and other towns (Avezzano, 96% of population of 11,000 killed); 30,000 persons killed, $60,000,000 property loss

Jan. 15, Sonnino asked for rectification of boundary with Austria-Hungary

Feb. 6, Agreement with Rumania renewed

Feb. 8, Italian troops attacked Dunedjen, Libya

Feb. 12, The Government notified Austria-Hungary that any further action in the Balkans would be regarded as an unfriendly act

Feb. 18, Ghat, Libya, retaken by Italians

March 7 and 22, Decree and regulations as to making of bread, content, weight, &c.

March 14, Bill for defense of the State passed in Chamber

March 19, Death of Cardinal Antonio Agliardi

March 28, Baron Burian, Austrian, offered Italy as price of neutrality the South Tyrol including Trent

April 8, Note of Sonnino presented demands to Austria-Hungary as price of neutrality; cession of the Trentino to frontiers of Italian kingdom of 1811, eastern frontier to include Malborghetto, Plezzo, Tolmina, Gorizia, Gradisca, and Comen, and reach the sea at Nabresina, the establishment of Trieste and district as independent State, cession to Italy of Dalmatia, islands of Lissa, Lesina, Curzola, Lagosta, Cazza, and Meleda, Austria to renounce interest in Albania. *See also* World War

April 16, Austria refused to accept Italian proposals of cession of territory, and in further Notes of April 25 and 29

April 25, Treaty of arbitration with Switzerland signed

April 26, Italy signed Treaty of London with Great Britain, France, and Russia joining the Entente Allies. *See* World War; Africa

April 29, Italians in engagement at Sidra. *See* Libya

May 3, Italy denounced the Triple Alliance

May 5, Speech of G. d'Annunzio in Rome to 150,000 persons from balcony of his hotel in favor of joining in the War

May 9, Partial mobilization ordered

May 13, Resignation of Salandra as Prime Minister; not accepted

May 20, Austria-Hungary offered rectification of frontier in the Tyrol and Venetia. *See* World War

——, War Bill passed in Chamber and in the Senate the following day giving the Cabinet power to authorize war

May 21, Treaty with Germany provided for mutual protection of citizens and of property

May 22, Mobilization of troops

May 23, War declared against Austria-Hungary to take effect May 24. *See* World War

May 29, Italian troops again landed at Valona

June 3 and 6, Decrees authorized prefects to make it compulsory for farmers to loan machinery, men and animals for harvesting for reasonable compensation, and authorized Minister of Agriculture to purchase agricultural machinery to loan

July 7, Decree announced that the Government was authorized to take over any factory for production of munitions

July 16, Signor Barzilia, president of the Press Association, appointed Minister without portfolio, and Gabriel d'Annunzio as official chronicler of the War

July 25, Decree as to acquisition of Italian nationality

July 30, Appeal of the Pope to Powers for peace

Aug. 21, Italy declared war on Turkey

Aug. 22, Regulations issued for settlement of disputes in munition industry works, committees appointed

Oct. 19, Italy declared war on Bulgaria

Oct. 20, Decree created new taxes and increased others for duration of War

Nov. 7, Sinking of the "Ancona" between Sardinia and Tunis, 208 lives lost. *See* World War

Nov. 26, Lord Kitchener at Rome

Nov. 30, Italy adhered to Pact of London. *See* World War

Dec. 31, Death of Commendatore Tomasso Salvini, actor

1916

Jan. 10, Third War loan subscription opened

Jan. 11, Decree fixed maximum prices for domestic wheat and corn requisitioned and March 11 applied to private sales

——, Death of Dr. Guido Baccelli, physician and politician

Feb. 16, Declaration of Cabinet Council of free trade with Allied countries, all machinery, raw materials, and manufactured articles necessary for home industries to enter free of duty, maximum prices for sugar declared and duty reduced

Feb. 27, Death of Count Ugo Balzani, historian

Feb. 29, Requisition of German ships in Italian ports

March 11, New milling and bread regulations issued

March 31, Arrival of Mr. Asquith on official visit to Rome

April 5, Resignation of General Zupelli. Succeeded as Minister of War by General Paolo Morrone

April 17, Trade with Germany prohibited

May 16, Import of luxuries prohibited from June 4, including mineral waters, furniture, automobiles, manufactured tobacco

June 10, Resignation of Salandra Ministry defeated on budget and because of defeat of army in Trentino and on Asiago plateau

June 19, Paolo Boselli formed Cabinet: Sonnino, Foreign Affairs; General Morrone, War; Colosino, Colonies; Orlando, Interior; Carcano, Treasury; Commissary for War Service, Bissolati; Admiral Camillo Corsi, Marine; I. Bonomi, Public Works; P. Meda, Finance

July 31, Anglo-Italian Agreement as to frontier between Libya and Egypt

Aug. 2, Decree gave Minister of Agriculture powers of food control

Aug. 27, Italy declared war on Germany to take effect Aug. 28

Dec. 6, Resolution of Socialists calling for immediate peace negotiations defeated by vote of 293 to 47 in Chamber

1917

Jan. 16, General Latini defeated the rebels in Tripolitania

——, Food Commission appointed

Jan. 20, Decree authorized issue of fourth War loan; subscription opened Feb. 5 and $440,000 received

Feb. 17, Decree amended maternity insurance law, regulations June 2

March 25, National Board for Protection and Assistance of War Invalids authorized provided for reëducation

March 31, War expenses up to £730,000,000, average about £30,000,000 a month

April 17, St. Jean de Maurienne Conference by which Anatolia and Smyrna assigned to Italy in future partition of Turkish empire. *See also* World War

April 29, Workers insurance made compulsory for all auxiliary war establishments

May 6, Decree provided for settlement of disputes among agricultural workers, committees established in each district

June 3, Italy proclaimed independence of Albania under Italian protection

June, The Government refused to grant passports for the Stockholm Conference

June 17, General Gaetano Giardino appointed Minister of War and Admiral A. Triangi, Marine

June 20, Declaration of war aims made in Chamber

July 27, Secret Agreement with France as to spheres of influence in Asia Minor

Aug. 23, Act provided for compulsory insurance against accidents in agricultural work

Aug., Riots in Turin

Aug. 26, Non-stop flight of Captain Laureati from Turin to Naples and return, 920 miles

Sept. 23, Captain Laureati made non-stop flight from Turin to London

Oct. 24, Austro-German offensive begun. *See* World War

Oct. 25, Defeat and resignation of Boselli Ministry after disaster of Caporetto

Oct. 30, Orlando formed Cabinet: Sonnino, Foreign Affairs; F. Meda, Finance; Nitti, Treasury; Colosimo, Colonies; General Alfieri, War; Admiral del Buono, Marine; War Pensions and Civil Aid, Bissolati

Nov. 6, Allied Conference at Rapallo on critical military situation of Italy

Nov. 7, General Diaz succeeded General Cadorno as Commander-in-Chief

Dec. 1–Jan. 3, 1918, Maximum prices fixed for wheat, coke, and gas

Dec. 3, First day of compulsory food rationing in Rome

Dec. 10, National Institution of Ex-Soldiers founded; regulated by Decree of Jan. 16, 1919

Dec. 30, Treaties of commerce with Brazil (1900), Rumania (1906), with France (1898), with Spain (1914), with Japan (1912), with Serbia (1907), and with Switzerland (1904), prolonged

1918

Jan. 6, Regulations issued for settlement of labor disputes in munition industries

Jan. 8, In the "Fourteen Points" President Wilson made statement as to "rectification of Italian frontiers on clearly recognized national lines"

March 14, Decree issued regulations as to laborers employed in the rice fields of Novara and Pavia

April 8–10, Conference of "subject races" of Austro-Hungarian Empire in Rome

April 10, Italy signed Pact of Rome recognizing the "unity and independence of the Yugoslav nation" as of vital interest to Italy

May 15, Resignation of General Dallolio, Minister of Munitions, succeeded by G. Villa, and resignation of Bianchi, Transportation

Sept. 8, Statement of Italian Government that movement of Yugoslavs for independence and constitution of a free State corresponded to aims for which the Allies were fighting

Sept. 15, Decree authorized commercial societies to constitute mutual share fund for the benefit of employees and workmen in said industries

Oct. 17, Committee of Germans in Upper Adige presented to Signor Nitti a program for administration and partial autonomy with local Landag and militia

Oct. 24, General Diaz attacked Austrians from Asiago to the sea, beginning campaign which ended with the armistice of Nov. 4. *See* World War

Oct. 30, National Council of Fiume declared adherence to Italy

Nov. 2, Budget statement presented showed deficit of 6,271 million lire

Nov. 3, Italian troops occupied Trent and forced landing in Trieste; the fleet at Zara

Nov. 4, Armistice with Austria-Hungary ended war; Italian loss estimated as 600,000 killed and 1,000,000 wounded

——, Allied Memo used by President Wilson in reply to the German Government did not include Orlando's reservation in the discussion as to Point 9 of the Fourteen Points

Nov. 17, Decree amended Act of Jan. 31, 1904, regulating accident insurance in industry and system of unemployment insurance established with regulations Jan. 5, 1919

Nov. 18, General Pecori-Giraldi, Italian commander, published proclamation promise that the German language would be used in Upper Adige in districts where currently used as well as Italian in the administration and the schools

Nov. 19, Fiume occupied by Serbs commanded by Colonel Maximovic but was persuaded by Italians to evacuate and General Grazuli with Italian force occupied the town. French, British, and American troops joined the Italians, making the occupation international

Dec. 1, Conference of Nationalist statesmen in Rome passed resolution in favor of annexation of Fiume, Sebenico, Spalato, and other territory

Dec. 29, Resignation of Socialist Bissolati, Minister of Civil Aid and War Pensions from the Cabinet in protest against nationalist policy of Sonnino as to Yugoslav boundary

1919

Jan. 1, State of war declared at end except in Veneto

Jan. 3, President Wilson arrived in Rome, and made speeches in Rome, Genoa, Milan, and Turin, Jan. 3–6

Jan. 16, Formation of National Institute of Ex-Soldiers authorized

Jan. 17, Resignation of F. Nitti (Treasury) and other moderate Ministers opposed to Sonnino, and reorganization of Cabinet: B. Stringher succeeding Nitti; Facta, Justice; Crespi, Food Supplies; Meda, Finance; Bonomi, Public Works

Jan. 18, Italy represented at Peace Conference by Orlando, Sonnino, Salandra, Barzilai, and Salvago-Raggi

Jan. 19, New Catholic Party founded at Rome (Partito Popolare Italiano)

Jan. 19–29, Strike of railroad employees

Feb. 7, Memo of the Government to the Peace Conference based territorial claims on the Treaty of London of 1915 and demanded Fiume not mentioned in the Treaty

Feb. 9, Decree regulated contracts as to private employment

Feb. 20, Trade Agreement signed established 48 hour week in metal industry and allied trades which affected 500,000 workers

——, Italian officers supervising movements of food trains expelled from Yugoslavia

March 17, Eight hour day went into effect in textile, printing, and paper factories

March 20, Arbitration Treaty of March 28, 1908 with the United States renewed

March 23, Creation of first Fascist *"facio di combat-timento"* by Benito Mussolini in Milan. The name Fascist derived from the *Fasces* or Roman axe in a bundle of rods, symbol of Rome

March 29, Italian troops landed at Adalia near Smyrna

April 4, Agreement signed established 48 hour week in agricultural trades with provision for over time at certain seasons

April 10, Strike of 24 hours in Rome because demonstration in favor of Russian Bolsheviks prohibited

April 13, Bolshevik demonstration at Milan and riots, the office of the Socialist paper "Avanti" wrecked

April 14, Memo of President Wilson to Italian delegation at the Peace Conference claimed that situation had changed with the dissolution of the Austro-Hungarian Empire and creation of independent States on the border of Italy, that the Pact of London no longer applied to the eastern frontier. *See also* p. 560

April 21, Legislative Decree introduced compulsory old age and invalidity insurance for practically all manual workers, salaried employees and professional classes replacing voluntary insurance subsidized by the Government

April 23, President Wilson published his Memo on Italian territorial claims, addressing the Italian people

April 24, Italian delegation published reply to President Wilson and Orlando left the Peace Conference the same day, Sonnino the day following

April 29, Orlando endorsed by Chamber by vote of 382 to 40, and by Senate the next day unanimously

May 1, Agreement signed for 8 hour day and 48 hour week in Milan clothing trades

——, Orlando published statement of Italian reservation to Point 9 of the Fourteen Points

May 2, Agreement for 8 hour day and 48 hour week in sugar refining and spirits industries

May 4, Strike of tramwaymen and secondary railway workers involving 80,000 persons

May 5, Italian delegation left Rome, returning to the Peace Conference at Paris

May 17, Civil Government proclaimed in Tripoli and other political measures designed to aid in pacification of the country. *See also* Libya

June 14, Catholic Congress at Bologna voted to form Catholic party instead of coöperating with the other political parties

June 15, Decree provided for 8 hour day and 48 hour week for employees of State railroads

June 19, Orlando defeated in Chamber by vote of 279 to 78, resigned

June 20, Signor Nitti formed Ministry as Premier and Minister of the Interior; Tittoni, Foreign Affairs; Rossi, Colonies; Lieutenant-General Albricci, War; Tedesco, Finance; Rear Admiral Sechi, Marine; Schanzer, Treasury; Mortara, Justice

June 28, Treaty of Versailles signed. Under Article 119 as to territorial adjustments (not mandates) it was planned that Italy should eventually receive in Africa Jubaland from Kenya (British East Africa), Jarabaid strip from Egypt to be added to Libya, and Ghadames and Tummo districts from French Southern Algeria and French Sahara to be added to Libya

——, New delegation left for Paris Peace Conference, Tittoni, Scialoja, Marconi, and Maggiorino Ferraris

June 30, Riots at Forli against high cost of living

July 2–3, Croatian Club at Fiume wrecked by Italians

July 3, Riots in Florence, Turin, Genoa, Milan, Pisa, shops and markets looted

July 5, Riot and fighting between French and Italians in Fiume

July 6, French naval base at Port Baros attacked by Italians

July 8, Decision of Supreme Council to send commission of inquiry to Fiume on account of disturbances

July 20–21, General strike organized in sympathy with Russia not successful

July 24, Report of Commission on causes of Caporetto disaster in War presented blamed Socialist propaganda and certain generals with the result that Generals Cadorna, Porro, Capello, and Cavaciocchi were placed on the retired list

July 29, Secret Treaty with Greece signed, Italy to support Greece as to territorial claims in East and West Thrace and North Epirus, Greece to support Italian claims to mandate for Albania and possession of Valona (Avlona) and hinterland, certain claims in Asia Minor, free zone at Smyrna, and possession of Rhodes for 15 years

——, Convention signed by Venizelos and Tittoni by which 12 Dodecanese Islands to be ceded to Greece provided that Rhodes should have "a wide local autonomy," this to take effect with the subsequent Treaty of Sèvres.

Aug. 3, Riot at Trieste and offices of the Bolshevist organ "Il Lavoratore" were wrecked

Aug. 14, Nitti organized corps of plain clothes detectives and reorganized the police to deal with continuous strikes due to inflated paper currency, high freights, scarcity of goods, and general high cost of living. Wheat had risen from $1.01 per 60 pounds before the War to $2.40, and value of dollar from 5.20 lire to 13.07, freights from 3s. per 480 pounds to 17s. with the pound more than doubled in value

Aug. 31, Factory workers in Lombardy and Piedmont seized the factories

Sept. 1, Announcement that King Victor Emmanuel had relinquished claims to Crown domains for the benefit of the peasants and soldiers

Sept. 2, New Electoral Reform Act changed manner of voting from the *scrutin d'arrondissement* to the *scrutin de liste* by which the electors of a department voted for all the deputies to be elected in that department, and number of election districts changed, proportional representation adopted

——, Decree authorized temporary occupation of uncultivated land by agricultural societies for planting of cereals and vegetables; land seized by peasants

Sept. 4, Bill giving women the suffrage passed in Chamber by vote of 174 to 55

Sept. 8, Treaty with France signed by which Italy obtained rectification of Libya (Africa) boundary gaining about 40,000 square miles. *See* Libya

Sept. 10, Treaty of St. Germain with Austria signed by which Italy acquired the boundaries of the Treaty of London of 1915 on the north and northeast and in addition the Sexten Valley and the Tarvis district, the new territory including the South Tyrol (Upper Adige), the Trentino, Istria, part of Dalmatia, and most of the Adriatic Islands

Sept. 12, Coup d'état of d'Annunzio, seizure of Fiume to save it for Italy. Most of the Italian troops in Fiume and the crews of the warships in the port joined his volunteer troops; the Allied international troops withdrew. His action was disowned by the Italian Government but he was supported by a large section of public opinion

Sept. 25, Crown Council summoned by the King to consider Fiume situation

Oct. 2, The corps of *Guardie Regie* organized under orders of the Minister of the Interior consisting of cavalry and machine-gun detachments

Oct. 5–8, Socialist Congress at Bologna declared adherence to the Moscow Third International and adopted program for elections for abolition of capitalism and institution of Socialist republic modeled on Russia

Oct. 7, Royal Decree ratified the German Peace Treaty

Oct. 10 and 13, Rising of peasants of Caltanisetta, Sicily

Oct. 19, Legislative Decree reorganized employment exchange service and introduced compulsory insurance against unemployment

Nov. 11, Decree of the Pope revoked prohibition of 1886 declaring it inexpedient for Catholics to take part in politics

Nov. 12, Tittoni resigned as Minister of Foreign Affairs for reasons of health and was succeeded by Vittorio Scialoja

——, Zara on Dalmatian coast occupied by d'Annunzio

Nov. 13, Act coördinated provisions regulating emigration and legal protection of emigrants

Nov. 16, General election for Chamber of Deputies first since 1913 gave Socialists 156 seats; Popolari (Catholic), 101; Combatants, 30; no Fascists elected; figures as finally presented on December 24th were as follows: Socialists, 160; Catholics, 103; Liberal Democrats, 93; Radicals, 58; Socialist Reformists, 14; Democrats, 23; Republicans, 4; Combatants, 24; Giolittians, 5; Radical Christian Democrats, 1; Nationalists, 2; Independents, 6; Radical Socialists, 1; Independent Socialists, 1

Nov. 24, Decree-law enacted to go into effect Jan. 1, 1922, revised income taxes

Dec. 1, Parliament opened by the King; the Socialist deputies shouted "Long live socialism" and left the Chamber which was considered as insult to the King and provoked riots in which Socialists attacked

Dec. 2, General strike in Rome, Milan, and Florence

Dec. 3, Anarchists gained possession of Mantua for a few hours, freed the criminals and burned the prison, looted shops. Order restored by troops sent the following day

Dec. 9, Joint Franco-British-American Memo to Italy on frontiers. *See* p. 562

1920

Jan. 6, Note of Nitti to Lloyd George demanded fulfilment of the Treaty of London of 1915. (*See* p. 562)

Jan. 13–22, Strike of postal employees for higher wages a failure because of work of volunteers of committees of citizens

Jan. 20, Strike of railway employees, only 66,000 men going out of a total of 193,000

Jan. 29, Nitti offered concessions ending strike

Feb. 2, Legislative Decree reconstituted Administrative Council of State Railways

Feb. 20, Ordered that everyone should make statement of entire capital including foreign investments before March 31 in preparation of tax to be levied on capital, a measure finally dropped

Feb.–April, Strike of men on Lombardy secondary railroads

March 12, Nitti Ministry resigned and reconstructed Cabinet: Bonomi, War; Schanzer, Finance; Luigi Luzzatti, Treasury; Torre, Education; Scialoaja, Foreign Affairs; Admiral Sechi, Navy

March 24–April 23, Strike of metal workers at Turin ended with defeat of the strikers

March 26, Workmens' Compensation Agreement with Argentina signed

March 31, Independence of Fiume proclaimed by d'Annunzio

April 18, Royal Decree authorized national maternity fund to increase maternity benefit

April 19–26, San Remo Conference of Allied Premiers decided to leave Adriatic question to negotiations between Italy and Yugoslavia

April 20, Royal Decree organized army on peace basis

April 22 and Oct. 8, Decrees provided that prefects should deal with applications for occupation of land and should fix compensation to owners, appeal to the Minister of Agriculture allowed

May 1–3, Serious disorders at Viareggio

May 6, Decree provided for organization of traveling professorships of agriculture; regulations, June 9

——, Death of Leonida Bissolati-Bergamaschi, Socialist statesman

May 11, Nitti Ministry defeated, again resigned

May 17, Nitti reconstructed Cabinet to include Catholics: de Nava, Clerical, made Minister of Finance; Ruini, Colonies; Falcioni, Justice; Schanzer, Treasury; Rodino, War; Peano, Public Works; Micheli, Agriculture

May 20–21, Congress of unions affiliated with Federation of Metal Workers adopted program for increase in wages from 7.29 lire to 8 per day

May, Nitti legalized seizure of Mazzonis cotton mills at Luserna and Ponta Canavese by workmen

May 23, The Pope revoked veto prohibition visits of heads of Catholic States to King of Italy

May 24, Riot in Rome, students in patriotic demonstration in conflict with the police with the result that Nitti ordered arrest of all Dalmatians and Fiumani in Rome

June 3, Royal Decree created Ministry of Labor and Social Welfare

June 4, Decree of Premier Nitti reduced bread subsidy raising price to 1.50 lire per kilogram but withdrew it 5 days later because of opposition of Socialists

June 5, Albanians attacked and captured various Italian posts in Albania including that of Tepeleni

June 8–24, Strike of railwaymen at Cremona which spread to Milan and other places

June 9, Fall of Nitti Ministry after Socialist demonstration over bread policy

June 11, Italian garrison at Valona attacked by Albanians but repulsed

June 16, Giolitti formed his fifth Ministry as Prime Minister and Interior; Rossi, Colonies; F. Tedesco, Finance; F. Meda, Treasury; I. Bonomi, War; Sechi, Navy; L. Fera, Justice; A. Labriola, Labor; Sforza, Foreign Affairs

June 24, Giolitti announced that Italian troops would be withdrawn from Albania and negotiations begun. He proposed confiscation of war profits, increase of taxes, enforced cultivation of cereals

June 26, Mutiny of soldiers at Ancona instigated by anarchists by false report that regiment to be sent to Albania; 25 persons killed before order restored in town where anarchists and criminals pillaged the shops and terrorized the citizens

June 27, Financial statement of Minister of the Treasury showed deficit of one milliard for ordinary expenditure which was raised to deficit of 14 milliards by extraordinary expenditure including sale of bread below cost

June 29, Strike of tramway workers in Rome begun

July 5–16, Spa Conference raised Italian share of German indemnity to 10%

July 11, Anti-Italian demonstration at Spalato where Croatian mob killed the commander of the Italian cruiser "Puglia" and wounded other officers and sailors

July 13, Anti-Slav demonstration at Trieste and destruction of property

July 14, Strike of tramwaymen in various towns in sympathy with strike of railwaymen on secondary railroads which was ended on the 19th

July 21, Failure of general strike but Rome offices of the "Avanti" wrecked and Socialist deputies including Modigliani beaten by crowd

July 22, Italy denounced Convention with Greece as to Dodecanese

July 29, Italo-Greek Commission adjusted Adalia boundary affair

——, Electricians strike in Rome ended

Aug. 2, Agreement with Albania signed, Italy agreeing to evacuate troops from Albania, retaining only the Island of Saseno

Aug. 10, Treaty with Turkey signed at Sèvres, Italy obtaining economic priority in southern Anatolia and a concession for exploiting the Heraclea coal fields, and cession of Dodecanese Islands, Rhodes and Island of Castellorizzo. *See also* p. 564

——, Treaty with Greece signed, confirmed cession of Dodecanese Islands to Greece and provided that Rhodes should 15 years later become Greek if Great Britain should have ceded Cyprus to Greece and a plebiscite at Rhodes under auspices of the League of Nations should decide for union

Aug. 13, The Industrial Metallurgical Federation rejected demands of the workers for increase in wages

Aug. 20, Lockout declared in metal factories at Milan due to sabotage and obstructive actions of workmen at the Romeo works, and the F.I.O.M. (*Federazione italiana operai metallurgici*) ordered workmen to remain at factories in Milan to prevent lockout

Aug. 21, Meeting of Giolitti with Lloyd George at Lucerne, agreement of non-recognition of Russia

Aug. 31, General lockout throughout Italy declared by the Federation of Mechanical Industries resulting in seizure of the factories by workmen in Lombardy and Piedmont and then in other parts of the country and of other factories of chemicals and textiles

Sept. 2, Lockout declared by employers in the metal and engineering trades

——, Last Italian troops left Albania; island of Saseno retained

Sept. 3, Declaration by Federation of Italian Metal Workers urged workers to seize all factories at first sign of lockout

——, Agrarian strikes in Romagna ended when the Government requisitioned the crops to save them from destruction

Sept. 6, The General Confederation of Labor declared action of metal workers justified but refused authorization of extension of seizures of factories to other industries

Sept. 7, The National Council of Fiume resigned and d'Annunzio proclaimed the independence of the town

——, Conference of General Federation of Labor meeting at Milan and executives of Socialist Party declared for support of workers in possession of factories

Sept. 8, Employers Federation met and adopted resolution demanding evacuation of factories as first condition of negotiations

Sept. 11, Workmen took over 200 chemical plants and several textile mills

Sept. 11–14, Conference of Giolitti with Millerand at Aix-les-Bains on the general political situation

Sept. 12, National Labor Convention at Milan voted in favor of Sovietism of Italian industries, the vote 650,000 to 450,000

Sept. 13, Representatives of the Socialist Party voted for syndicalization of Italian industries by vote of 591,000 to 245,000

Sept. 15, Giolitti summoned employers and workers to meet him in conference in Turin

Sept. 19, Representatives of employers and workers in metal industry in conference with Giolitti in Rome signed agreement and a commission appointed of 6 named by each, the employers accepting participation by workers in management of factories but not domination, and increase of 15% in wages granted, the workers agreeing to evacuate the factories

Sept. 20, Conflict of citizens and Bolshevists at Bologna, shots exchanged

——, D'Annunzio at Fiume appointed Cabinet taking office of "Chief Rector" and Minister of Foreign Affairs

——, Fascists and Communists in riots at Bologna

Sept. 22, The "red guards" at factory in Turin murdered a Nationalist student and a detective and the police seized the Gilardini works

Sept. 26, Yugoslavs and Italians in conflict in plebiscite area in Carinthia

——, Metal workers by vote of 127,904 to 44,531 accepted decision of their leaders and agreed to evacuate factories

Sept. 27, Factories evacuated by workers

Sept. 30, Law enacted to prevent excessive rise in prices

Oct. 4, Work resumed in metal trade factories

Oct. 12, Socialist Congress at Reggio Emilia adopted resolution that violence should be used only as a last resort

Oct. 14, Strike organized by Communists at Bologna and other towns to protest against the "white terror" in Hungary, and all industries suspended between 3 and 5 P.M. by orders received from Moscow

——, General amnesty proclaimed for political and military crimes committed before Sept. 19, 1919

Oct. 27, Arrest of profiteers connected with National Oil Trust of Genoa in frauds against the Government

Nov. 7, Municipal elections won by anti-Socialist bloc in Turin, Milan, Genoa, Pisa, Florence, Naples, and Palermo

Nov. 8, Conference with Yugoslavs begun at Rapallo

——, Nationality Decree in Tunis affecting Italian citizens. *See* Tunis

Nov. 10, Bill for constitution of a National Council of Labor introduced in Chamber

Nov. 12, Treaty with Yugoslavia signed by which Yugoslavia and Italy recognized independence of the State of Fiume and boundary settled, Italy renounced rights based on the Treaty of London over Dalmatia, except Zara, and Yugoslavia all claims to Trieste, Gorizia, and Istria and certain adjoining districts of Carinthia and Carniola. In Istria Yugoslavia received Mt. Blegos and Assling railway triangle, Italy, Indria, Adelsberg, and entire St. Peter railroad to Fiume, and the islands of Cherso, Lussin, Lagosta and Pelagosa, Cazza, Susak to Yugoslavia

——, Agreement signed the same day by which it was settled that Porto Baros and the Delta should pass to Yugoslavia in spite of the terms of the Treaty

Nov. 21, First meeting of Bologna "Red" town council prevented by Fascisti, 2 of the members shot and the Communists forced to leave Bologna

Dec. 1, D'Annunzio declared war on Italy refusing to accept the Treaty of Rapallo

Dec. 21, Convention with Venezuela settled claims of Italian citizens

Dec. 23, General Caviglia with Italian troops advanced against Fiume

Dec. 27, Fiume bombarded by Italian troops

Dec. 29, D'Annunzio surrendered his authority to Giganti, mayor of Fiume, and the Municipal Council

Dec. 31, Pact of Abbazia signed by representatives of the Government of Italy and the City of Fiume providing for acceptance by Fiume of the Treaty of Rapallo and replacement of d'Annunzio's troops by Italian force

1921

Jan. 9, Chamber of Commerce of Turin passed resolution demanding reduction of 20% in time of workers because of falling off of export trade

Jan. 13–22, Congress of Socialists met at Leghorn and the moderate Socialists hostile to Moscow and willing to coöperate with a bourgeois Government including Turati, Treves, Buozzi, Baldisi, and d'Aragoni calling themselves *unitari* obtained 98,028 votes for the Florence resolution; the Reggio Emilia resolution of the *centristi*, 14,695; the Imola resolution of the Communists led by Bombacci, Bordiga, Misiani, and Count Gregiadci, 58,783. The Communists left the Congress moving to another building to hold meeting

Jan. 18, D'Annunzio left Fiume for Paris and Italian troops occupied Fiume

Jan. 24, Fascists burned town hall and Socialist centers at Bologna including the Chamber of Labor

Jan. 27, Communists seized Socialist paper "Il Lavoratore" making it into a Communist organ in Trieste

Feb. 2, Death of Luigi Mancinella, musician, and of Cardinal Ferrari

Feb. 6, Italy signed the Five-Power Naval Treaty at the Washington Conference limiting Italy's maximum capital ship tonnage to 175,000 tons, tonnage of individual ships to 35,000 tons, and maximum calibre of guns to 16 inches, auxiliary ships to 10,000 tons and 8-inch guns, aircraft carriers to 135,000

Feb. 11, Fascists recovered "Il Lavoratore" plant, Trieste

Feb. 27, Communist riot at Florence, a bomb thrown at patriotic procession of schoolboys killed and wounded several persons. The Fascists in retaliation wrecked offices of the Socialist organizations and killed Lavagnini, editor of a Communist newspaper, and railway agitator

Feb. 28, Fascists and Communists in riots in Palermo, Spezia, and Florence

March 1, Bread subsidy abolished by large majority vote in Chamber notwithstanding Socialist opposition

——, General strike in Venice, Giulia, and other cities

March 4, Agreement with Yugoslavia signed at Spalato for evacuation by Italians of Dalmatia

March 12, Treaty with Turkish Nationalist Government pledged diplomatic support of Italy in return for economic concessions

March 13, Commercial Treaty with Turkey signed

March 20, Workers' Accident Insurance Act of Aug., 1917 amended

March 23, Treaty of commerce with Czechoslovakia signed

——, Bomb thrown by Anarchists at Diana Theatre, Milan, killed 20 persons and injured 100

March, Elections in the Upper Adige (former South Tyrol) returned 36,574 votes for the German Peoples Party, 3,993 Socialist, and no votes for Italians

April 2, Council of Ministers signed address to the King consisting of schedule of projects of law reforms

April 3, Resignation of Meda, Minister of Finance. Succeeded by Bonomi and Rodino succeeded Bonomi as Minister of War

April 4, Announcement of intention to submit Bill charging German imports with 50% ad valorem duty

April 7, Chamber dissolved

April 9, Regulations of the Government abolished all Alpine Clubs in former South Tyrol

——, Death of Ernesto Nathan, former mayor of Rome

April 10, Paolo Boselli made a life senator

April 11, Luigi Luzzatti made a life senator

April 24, First national election for Constituent Assembly in accordance with the Treaty of Rapallo won by autonomists led by Riccardo Zanella, a defeat for the Nationalists, in Fiume

——, Procession of citizens in national costume celebrating holiday in Botzen (now Bolzano) (former South Tyrol) attacked by Fascists, one person, the schoolmaster, killed, and 50 persons wounded

May 12, Treaty of commerce with Poland

May 15, General election, the first under universal suffrage, resulted in return of 275 Liberals and Democrats, 107 Popolari, 122 Socialists, 16 Communists, 35 Fascists, 10 Nationalists, 4 Germans from Alto Adige, and 5 Slavs from Venezia Giulia

May 19, American Immigration Act limiting number of aliens on basis of census of 1900 reduced emigration from Italy

June 9, Royal Decree enacted new general customs tariff protection for iron and steel industry

June 10, Government employees on strike since third week in May returned to work

June 11, Parliament opened by the King

June 13, Enrico de Nicola reëlected president of Chamber of Deputies

——, Commandante Foschini, Royal Commissioner arrived at Fiume to take over the Government owing to strife of Autonomist and Nationalist factions, Bellosich, Nationalist, who had become head of Government after ousting Zanella, resigned

June 25, Count Sforza announced that Porto Baros had been assigned to Yugoslavia by secret Agreement of Nov. 12, 1920

June 26, Resignation of Giolitti Cabinet because of attack on foreign policy of Count Sforza and majority of only 34 for the Government on a vote of confidence

June 27, Legionaries seized Port Baros and the Delta

July 1, Fascists attacked town of Roccastrada where Socialists had received a majority of votes in the election, the mayor's house wrecked, coöperative stores and Peasants Club burned

July 5, New Cabinet announced by I. Bonomi, Prime Minister and Interior; A. Beneduce, Labor; Marchese della Torretta, Foreign Affairs; Giardini, Colonies; Rodino, Justice; Soleri, Finance; De Nava, Treasury; Bergamasco, Marine; Corbino, Education; Micheli, Public Works; Belotti, Industry and Trade; Mauri, Agriculture; Raineri, Liberated Provinces. All parties included except the extreme Right and the Socialists

July 11–12, Commercial *modus vivendi* with Switzerland concluded

Aug. 20, Communist manifesto called for general strike. Counter-manifesto of General Confederation of Labor declared against strike during unemployment crisis

Aug. 21, Law enacted provided for compulsory engagement of men disabled in the War by public and private enterprises

Aug. 23, Provisional Commercial Agreement with Poland signed

——, Decree made the American dollar the standard for international payments instead of the English pound

Aug. 28, Provisional Commercial Agreement with Germany signed

Sept. 7, Legionaries of d'Annunzio left Fiume and General Amantea assumed military command and Commander Castelli of the Government

Sept. 23, Hostile demonstration at Venice against French mission on visit at invitation of Italian Government

Sept. 24, Convention with Switzerland signed modified terms of Convention of Oct. 3, 1909 as to St. Gothard railway; further agreements May 1, 1923, May 20, 1924, and June 3, 1925

Sept. 25, Assassination of Deputy di Vagno for political reasons

Oct. 5, Zanella elected President at Fiume

Oct. 8, Convention with Brazil signed as to emigration and labor

Oct. 14, Agreement with Yugoslavia signed as to Italian fishing rights on the Dalmatian coast

Oct. 20–23, Congress of the Popolari (Catholic) Party at Venice

Nov. 4, Celebration of the ceremony for the Unknown Soldier finally held

Nov. 6, First Fascist Congress held in Rome and political party constituted; program set forth by Benito Mussolini on the 8th

Nov. 10, Communists and Socialists proclaimed general strike as protest against Fascists in Rome

Nov. 14, Strike of printers in Rome ended after 4 days of terrorism, 6 persons killed and over 100 wounded

Nov. 23, Railroad Agreement signed with Austria-Hungary, Poland, Rumania, and Yugoslavia

Nov. 25–28, Demonstration against French embassy in Rome and consulates in Turin, Naples, and other places because of report afterwards denied that M. Briand had spoken slightingly of the Italian army at the Washington Conference

Dec. 19, Provisional Commercial Agreement with Switzerland signed

Dec. 21, Agreement with Czechoslovakia as to port of Trieste

Dec. 26, Commercial Agreements with Russia and the Ukraine signed

Dec. 29, The Bank of Discount (Banca di Sconto) suspended payments with liabilities of 4 billion lire

Italian emigration to Argentina equaled that of Spain during the year

1922

Jan. 1, Unemployed 541,775

Jan. 4, Liquidating Court decreed sequestration of private fortunes of the directors of the Bank of Discount

Jan. 22, Death of Pope Benedict XV

Feb. 2, Resignation of Bonomi Ministry after Democrats joined the Opposition

Feb. 6, Cardinal Ratti, Archbishop of Milan, elected Pope (Pius XI)

Feb. 9, Bonomi returned with reconstituted Ministry but defeated in Chamber on the 17th by vote of 295 to 107 on foreign policy and alleged pro-Catholic bias

Feb. 25, Luigi Facta formed new Cabinet; Schanzer, Foreign Affairs; C. Peano, Treasury; Bertone, Finance; G. Bertini, Agriculture

Feb., Unemployed 607,000

March 3, Fascisti coup d'état led by Deputy Giunta attacked the palace at Fiume overthrowing the Government of President Zanella who took refuge in Yugoslavia and Government transferred to Citizens Committee of National Defense

March 9, Giuratti chosen head of Government at Fiume

March 15, Announcement of Premier Facta that it was the purpose of the Government to restore order impartially and arrest of 1,000 Fascists and of Communists followed

March 16, Lieutenant Cabruna declared Fiume Committee of National Defense dissolved and took possession of the city

March 17, The Italian Government ordered occupation of Fiume by Italian troops commanded by General Giardino and civil administration handed over to Professor A. de Poli, Nationalist, and Vice-President of the Constituent Assembly

March 18, Strike of longshoremen (Communist) at all ports begun which was eventually ended by Fascists

March 26, Zanella with 49 other members of the Constituent Assembly in Yugoslavia appealed to the Prime Minister of Yugoslavia to restore order in Fiume

March 30, The newspaper "Il Lavoro d'Italia" founded by Fascists at Bologna

April 6, Six Conventions respecting judicial and financial matters, including private insurance companies, signed with Austria and Extradition and Legal Convention with Czechoslovakia, and Treaty as to legal protection with Hungary

April 9, Conference with Yugoslavia opened at Santa Margherita to deal with questions left outstanding by the Treaty of Rapallo

April 10, Genoa Economic Conference opened. *See* p. 566

April 15, Commercial Treaty with Czechoslovakia renewed and Provisional Commercial Treaty with Spain concluded

April 17, 152 vessels held in ports by shipping strike

April 23, Agreement with Yugoslavia for execution of the Treaty of Rapallo

April 24, Agreement with Russia concluded, concessions for railroads, mines, and public works in Asia Minor

May 12, Commercial Agreement with Poland signed

May 24, Commercial Agreement with Russia signed; Soviet Government refused ratification June 15

——, Funeral procession of Enrico Toti, war hero, Fascist, attacked by Communists; 21 persons wounded in Rome

May 31, Commercial Treaty with Germany prolonged

May, Bologna occupied by Fascists and Socialists and Communists forced to resign

June 15, Decision of moderate Socialists to participate in the Government

July 8, The Chamber of Deputies elected Giolitti, Orlando, Nitti, and Bonomi members of Committee of Foreign Affairs

July 12, Budget statement showed deficit of 4,500,000,-000 lire

July 20, Facta Ministry defeated in Chamber on motion that the Government had not succeeded in pacification of the country

July, Viterbo, Cremona, and Alatri occupied by Fascist forces

Aug. 1, Facta reconstituted Cabinet, a coalition of Democrats and Liberals

——, General strike of all the labor unions in Rome extended to all Italy, its professed object to affirm the authority of the State against the Fascists

Aug. 3–4, Fascists attacked the Communist-Socialist Government of Milan and raised the tricolor on the town hall for the first time since 1914; Fascists and Communists in conflict in Genoa, Ancona, and other cities

Aug. 5, The general strike ended with victory of the Fascists

Aug. 8, Manifesto of Mussolini ordered demobilization of Fascists "victorious on every front against the general strike"

Aug. 21, Syndicate of railroad men joined the Fascists

Aug. 22, Military occupation of the port of Naples which had been stormed and occupied by Fascists ordered by the Government

Aug. 24, Conference with Austrian officials as to economic union because of desperate financial situation of Austria

Aug. 25, Italy declared union of Austria with the Little Entente countries would be considered a cause of war

Aug. 27, Statement of Mussolini that the Fascists wished to govern Italy and would spring up as one man for decisive battle when the hour came

Aug. 28, Commercial Treaty with Luxemburg signed

Aug. 29, Italian delegates to Austrian-Italian Conference recommended Italian coöperation and financial assistance be given to Austria

Aug. 31, 317,985 unemployed

Sept. 1, Fascist forces seized town of Terni 49 miles northeast of Rome and compelled manager of the steel works to reopen shops closed owing to dispute about wages

Sept. 25, Death of General Carlo Caneva

Sept. 29, Mussolini in speech at Udine made declaration in favor of monarchy, thereby securing a large number of supporters

Sept.–Oct., Fascists in movement to Italianize the Trentino forced retirement of German officials and closed German schools

Oct. 2, Socialist Congress opened in Rome and split

on discussion of participation or non-participation with the Government, the Left (Maximalists) headed by Serrati representing the Communists refusing to coöperate, the Right (*Unitari*) headed by Turati in favor of sharing responsibility of Government

Oct. 3, The General Confederation of Labor declared itself a non-political body breaking off alliance with Socialists

Oct. 5, Mussolini in Milan speech declared that two governments existed in Italy, "a fictitious one, run by Facta (the Premier) and a real one run by the Fascisti"

——, The maintenance of public order in Trent placed with military authorities because of Fascist activities and their seizure of city

Oct. 8, Italy denounced the Italo-Greek Treaty of Aug. 10, 1920 as to the Dodecanese Islands

——, Rules of discipline for the Fascist militia published in "La Patria"

Oct. 14, The British Government protested against denunciation of the Treaty and Italian retention of Dodecanese Islands

Oct. 22, Mussolini offered Cabinet post as Minister without portfolio which he refused

Oct. 23, Treaty of Santa Margherita signed with Yugoslavia for execution of the stipulations of Rapallo, and 3 Conventions dealing with customs and technical matters; provided that Italy should evacuate Zara occupied since Nov., 1918, and Susak and that frontier be delimited

Oct. 24, Fascist Congress summoned by Mussolini opened in Naples attended by 90,000, and Fascist Quadrumvirate formed, Michele Bianchi, general secretary, Italo Balbo, commander of armed *squadre*, and General De Bono, and Dino Grandi

Oct. 26, Mussolini announced Fascist march on Rome

Oct. 27, Facta presented the King with decree proclaiming martial law which he refused to sign and Facta Ministry resigned

——, Law as to compulsory insurance against invalidity and old age of 1919 amended

——, Fascists seized Cremona and various other Italian cities

Oct. 29, Act provided for registration of industrial organizations

Oct. 30, Mussolini invited by the King to form a Ministry

——, Fascists began peaceful occupation of Rome

Oct. 31, Mussolini announced Cabinet retaining Ministry of Foreign Affairs; Luigi Federzoni, Colonies (Nationalist); Aldo Oviglio, Justice (Fascist); A. de Stefani, Finance and Treasury ad interim (Fascist); General A. Diaz, War; Admiral Thaon di Revel, Marine; Professor Giovanni Gentile, Education (Democrat); Gabriele Carnazza, Public Works (Nationalist); Giuseppe de Capitani, Agriculture (Fascist); Teofilo Rossi, Industry and Commerce (Nationalist); Stefano Cavazzoni, Labor (Popular Party)

Nov. 2, By this date all Fascist bands had left Rome by order of Mussolini

Nov. 3, Announcement of demobilization of Fascist forces

Nov. 5, Commercial Agreement with Canada signed

Nov. 13, Treaty of commerce with France signed

Nov. 16, Mussolini addressed the Chamber announcing program of bureaucratic and financial reform, the budget to be balanced, all treaties to be respected, and later in the day addressed the Senate

Nov. 17, The Chamber voted confidence in Mussolini Government, 306 to 116

Nov. 24, Death of Baron Sidney Sonnino, former Premier and Minister of Foreign Affairs

Nov. 25, Full powers until Dec. 31, 1923 voted by Chamber to Mussolini Cabinet by 275 to 90 for adoption of reforms

Dec. 11, Fascist victory in municipal election, Milan

Dec. 16, Council of Fascisti met under presidency of Mussolini; decision made to constitute Fascist national militia

Dec. 17, Fascist riots in Turin, 22 Communist workmen killed

Dec. 21, Tangorra who had been appointed Minister of the Treasury died; De Stefani took over Treasury

——, Agreement with Czechoslovakia signed giving Czechoslovakia transit facilities through Trieste

Dec. 23, Amnesty Decree covered all civil and military crimes committed in connection with national movements or due to economic or social causes

Dec. 26, Agreement signed provided for rectification of boundary of Eritrea with the Sudan

1923

Jan. 1, Income tax charged on pay of all public officials

Jan. 14, Royal Decree created voluntary national militia (Fascist) to come into effect Feb. 1

Jan. 17, General Giardino took charge of the Government of Fiume

Jan. 23, Decree authorized the Government to retire officials and revise all appointments

Jan. 25, The General Workers Union of Turin dissolved by the Government for alleged interference with politics and Socialist activities

Jan. 27, Commercial Agreement with Switzerland signed

Jan. 31, Unemployed numbered 391,974

Railroad staff reduced from 225,000 to 170,000

Feb. 1, War begun in Tripoli. *See* Libya

Feb. 4, Law regulated permanent charitable foundations

Feb. 6, Arrest of more than 100 persons charged with activities against the Government

Feb. 7, The Chamber ratified the Washington Treaties for limitation of armaments and the Senate Feb. 16

Feb. 11 and March 8, Decrees made accident insurance compulsory for State employees

Feb. 13, Decision of Fascist Grand Council that membership in party incompatible with freemasonry

March 1, Ministries of Agriculture and Industry united as Ministry of National Economy, and Ministry of Restored Provinces abolished

March 2, Arrest of Menotti Serrati, deputy and editor of the Socialist paper "Avanti," but released the following day

March 3, Susak evacuated by Italians

March 12, Zara evacuated by Italians

March 15, Royal Decree established the principle of the eight hour day

March 16, Transfer to private enterprise of a number of government undertakings

March 17, Mussolini ordered Grand Council to prepare Bill to reform electoral system

March 24, Royal decree as to judicial system, 1 Court of Cassation, 16 appeal court districts, divided into 115 tribunal districts and these again into mandamenti each with its own magistracy (Pretura) 1,076;

4 courts of cassation, 4 courts of appeal, 57 courts of first instance and 550 petty courts abolished

March 29, Decree ratified the Washington Labor Convention but application conditional on ratification by Germany, Belgium, Great Britain, Switzerland, and France

——, Agreement with Austria as to tariff concessions signed

March 30, The ex-Khedive of Egypt, Abbas Hilmi, expelled from the country for alleged propagandist activities

April 9, Marriage of the Princess Yolanda to Count Calvi di Bergolo

April 11, Resolution of the Catholic Party Congress to support Fascism which however was referred to as a "passing phase" of Italian politics

April 23, Mussolini accepted resignation of Cavazzoni and 3 under-secretaries of Catholic Party

April 25, Movement of Right Catholics to form a separate party

April 28, Commercial Treaty with Austria signed providing for traffic of Austrian goods through Trieste

April 29, Decree provided that life insurance business should be carried on only by the National Insurance Institute and by other institutions, national and foreign, authorized by the Government

April, Royal Decree constituted the Royal Air Force as separate force under a High Commissioner for Aviation

May 2, Decree repealed duty on sugar

May 6, First bull fight held in Rome attended by 30,000 spectators

May 7–12, Visit of the King and Queen of England

May 16, Council of the Popolari (Catholic) Party voted by large majority to coöperate with the Fascist Government

May 31, Proclamation issued by official organ of Fascist Party declared war on all their enemies

——, Commercial Treaty with Germany extended

June 9, The Chamber delegated authority to the Cabinet to proceed with reform of civil, commercial, and maritime law codes

July 1, From this date all war time rent restrictions abolished

July 10, Don Luigi Sturzo, Secretary General of the Catholic Party resigned; succeeded by a triumvirate headed by Giulio Rodino

July 12 and 15, Decree issued regulations for the press empowering prefects to warn and to suspend periodicals without reference to judiciary

——, New policy of Italianization of Upper Adige (South Tyrol) announced at Botzen of 31 points including Italianization of German names of places and streets, and family names, and dissolution of German societies

July 16, Fascist bands sacked Catholic Party offices in Florence

July 20, Fascists attacked Catholic Church Clubs in Pisa

July 21, Electoral Reform Bill passed in Chamber by vote of 223 to 123. *See* Nov. 14

July 23, Press Federation passed resolution asking the Government not to enforce press regulations

July 24, Treaty of peace with Turkey signed at Lausanne confirmed territorial cessions of Treaty of Sevres

July 31, Senator Orso Mario Corbino appointed Minister of Department of National Economy

Aug. 14, Arbitration Convention with Great Britain of Feb. 1, 1904 renewed for 5 years

Aug. 23, Royal Decree abrogated legacy and succession duties in first degree of relationship and abrogated luxury taxes substituting 8% sales tax with extension of free list and increased excise on spirits and tobacco. Income tax on officials, public servants, railway operatives, &c., of Jan. 1 abrogated

Aug. 24, The Federation of Labor voted against alliance with any political party, defeating Extremist Socialists

Aug. 27, General Tellini, Italian, president of Inter-Allied Commission delimiting Greek-Albanian boundary, murdered with 4 of his staff on Greek territory near Janini; accused of unduly favoring Albanian claims

——, Resignation of Giovanni Colonna di Cesara, Minister of Posts and Telegraphs, his department merged into new Ministry of Communications

Aug. 29, Ultimatum to Greece demanded arrest and punishment of murderers of Tellini with death penalty, Greek ships to salute the Italian flag, indemnity of 50,000,000 lire, apologies by highest Greek authorities, to be accepted within 5 days

Aug. 30, Greece accepted most of the demands

Aug. 31, Second ultimatum to Greece; Corfu bombarded and occupied by Italians

——, 178,612 unemployed

——, Greece referred Italian ultimatum to League of Nations

——, Agreement that Fiume should be administered by mixed commission of Italians, Yugoslavs, and citizens of Fiume

Sept. 1, Greece appealed to League of Nations against Italian occupation of Corfu

——, Note of Conference of Ambassadors protested murder of Tellini

Sept. 2, Greece agreed to accept decision of Conference of Ambassadors

——, Reform of educational codes passed

Sept. 5, Italy denied competence of League of Nations to deal with Corfu affair

Sept. 6, Council of the League of Nations drew up plan of settlement which was accepted by the Conference of Ambassadors on the 7th

Sept. 7, Note of Conference of Ambassadors to Greece embodied practically all Italian demands and was accepted by Greece

Sept. 11, League of Nations notified that abolition of slave holding by Italian Legation in Abyssinia ordered

Sept. 16, Government of Fiume resigned and General Giardino placed in command as military Governor

Sept. 26, Award of the 50,000,000 lire to Italy

Sept. 27, Corfu evacuated by Italians

——, Massimo Rocca expelled from Fascist Party because of article attacking Fascist leaders

Sept. 28, Mussolini demanded resignation of entire executive committee of the Fascist Party supporting Rocca against their action

Sept. 30, Decree radically reformed university education, first revision since educational law of Nov. 13, 1859

Oct. 1, Decree provided that Italian be made the language of instruction in all elementary schools to be put into effect as soon as possible in communities where languages other than Italian habitually spoken; and religious instruction to be given in elementary schools

Oct. 12, At meeting of the Fascist Grand Council Mussolini reorganized party and appointed committee of 5 members headed by himself as executive authority but no decisions to be made without his consent

Oct. 15, Decree issued regulations for dock laborers

Oct. 23, Decree applied principle of exclusive use of Italian language in Upper Adige

Oct. 28, Decree provided for Italianization of public signs in Upper Adige

Oct. 31, Decree reorganized schools for industrial training

Nov. 11, Regulations issued for instruction in religion in elementary schools

Nov. 14, Electoral Bill passed changed the system of proportional representation giving to the party that received the majority of votes two-thirds of the seats in the Chamber, the proportional system to continue to apply to the minority groups

Nov. 19–26, Visit of King and Queen of Spain and of General Primo de Rivera

Nov. 30, Lake Dezzo dam near Bergamo gave way destroying 3 villages and causing the death of about 500 persons and property loss of $6,000,000

Dec. 9, France formally refused request of Italy to participate in the Tangier Conference

Dec. 10, Royal Decree dissolved Chamber

Dec. 12, Six subversive press organs suppressed

Dec. 27, Fascists flogged Deputy Amendola, one of the directors of "Il Mondo," newspaper which had opposed Fascists, on the street in Rome

Dec. 30, Royal Decree provided for abolition of current family tax and tax on rental values from Jan. 1, 1925 and new progressive surtaxes on personal incomes ranging from 1 to 10% to be imposed

——, Decree coördinated old age pensions and invalidity insurance laws

——, Decree reorganized judicial system

Dec. 31, Repeal or drastic reduction made in duties on food stuffs

——, Cabinet Council renounced full powers granted by Parliament

1924

Jan. 1, From this date kindergartens in Upper Adige Italianized

Jan. 20, Treaty of commerce and navigation with Albania signed

Jan. 27, Treaty of friendship and coöperation with Yugoslavia signed and Agreement for division of Fiume between the 2 countries, Fiume to Italy, Port Baros and the Delta to Yugoslavia, free customs zone established at Fiume and Castua, the Eneo River the boundary line, ports to be administered jointly, special facilities for Yugoslavia at Fiume

Feb. 7, Treaty of commerce with Russia signed which accorded *de jure* recognition

Feb. 20, Nicola Bonservizi, Paris correspondent of the "Popolo d'Italia," shot; assassin later sentenced to 8 years imprisonment

Feb. 28, Delimitation of new frontier with Yugoslavia completed by mixed commission

March 15, Announcement that the King had conferred the highest rank of knighthood on Gabriele d'Annunzio, his title the Principe di Montenevoso

March 16, Fiume formally annexed to Italy with official celebration attended by the King; resignation of General Giardino as head of Government and prefect appointed

March 26, Storms caused landslides which swept away the entire village of Vettica and parts of Amalfi on the Gulf of Salerno

March 27, Convention with Hungary signed as to private debts and pre-War debt

March 29, Insurance Convention with Austria signed

April 1, Armed Fascists took Count Guglielmo Salvadori, lecturer of the University of Rome from his house and beat him because of articles unfavorable to Fascism published in English periodicals (New Statesman, March 1, and Westminster Gazette, March 24)

April 3, De Nicola withdrew his name from list of candidates for Chamber of Deputies as protest against election methods in the South against opponents of Fascism

April 6, Election gave Fascists 64.25% of the total vote, 375 out of 535 seats in Chamber, the Popolari (Catholic), 40; Unitari (moderate Socialists), 25; Maximalist Socialists, 22; Communists, 17; Constitutionalists, 12; July Democrats, 11; Republicans, 7; Sardisti, 2

——, At Lugano, just inside the Swiss frontier, Swiss officials made demonstration against Italians

April 8, Swiss demonstration against Italians at Ponte Tresa

April 11, Swiss Mayor of Ponte Tresa on business visit to Varese kidnapped by local Fascists and forced to promise apology for incident of Ponte Tresa

April 14, Report of Swiss Commission of Inquiry on Ponte Tresa incident communicated to Italian Government and the matter closed by agreement the following day to punish offenders on both sides

April 21, Death of Eleonora Duse, actress, at Pittsburgh, Pennsylvania while on American tour

April 30, Extension of privileges of religious instruction, optional courses to secondary schools

May 4–14, Visit of Mussolini to the South and Sicily

May 19 and June 18, Notes approved Eritrea-Sudan boundary under Treaty of Dec., 1922

May 24, Parliament opened; attack by Matteoti, Socialist, on legality of elections begun fight between Socialists and Fascists

June 3, Treaty regarding smuggling of liquor signed with the United States

June 10, Italy notified refusal of adherence to Tangier Statute

——, Giacomo Matteoti, Socialist, Deputy from Rovigo, kidnapped and murdered by Fascists

June 12, Disappearance of Matteoti announced by Mussolini in Chamber; complicity of the Prime Minister the accusation of Opposition deputy

June 14, Warrant issued for arrest of Cesare Rossi, head of official Press Bureau, F. Filippeli, editor of the "Corriere Italiano" and Naldi, editor of the "Nuovo Paese" in Matteoti affair

June 15, Opposition deputies withdrew from the Chamber to Aventine declaring that they would not return until Matteoti affair cleared up and question of complicity of the Government

June 16, Federzoni transferred from Ministry of Colonies to Interior

June 18, Agreement with Great Britain signed for rectification of Eritrea-Sudan boundary

June 25, Mussolini announced as concession to Opposition that the militia hereafter would take oath of allegiance to the King

June 26, All workers stopped work for 10 minutes in silent tribute to Matteoti

——, The Opposition deputies met and issued manifesto against Mussolini Government, demanding disbandment of national militia and cessation of violence by Fascists

June 30, Casati succeeded Gentile as Minister of Public Instruction, Nava succeeded Corbino as Minister of National Economy, Sarrochi succeeded Carnazza as Minister of Public Works

July 1, Severe press censorship law passed

July 5, Pact of cordial collaboration signed with Czechoslovakia

July 8, Mussolini applied decree of July 12, and 15, 1923, of control and supervision of the press by the Government, prefects ordered to confiscate seditious papers

July 11, The "Voce Repubblicana" of Rome sequestered because of publication of letter of Miguel de Unamuno, exiled Spanish scholar, against the government of Spain

July 14, Treaty of commerce and navigation and railroad convention with Yugoslavia signed

July 15, Treaty with Great Britain signed provided for cession of Jubaland to Italy

——, Decree announced that any newspaper receiving 2 warnings would be suspended

July 27, All newspapers in Milan except the Mussolini organ "Popolo d'Italia" sequestered for publication of some of Cesare Rossi's alleged revelations

July 30, Meeting of 314,000 war veterans at Assissi adopted resolution in favor of reëstablishment of constitutional law

July, Royal Decree abolished all war time rent restrictions from this time

Aug. 3, Meeting of Opposition parties planned for this date in Rome forbidden "for reasons of public safety"

Aug. 9–10, Demonstration against the Government by Communists in Rome

Aug. 16, Body of Matteoti found in woods near Fiano village, 16 miles north of Rome

Sept. 4, Official Vatican organ article opposed union of Socialists and Popolari, thus supporting Mussolini Government

Sept. 12, Armando Cassalini, Fascist deputy, fatally shot by workman, Giovanni Carvi, in retaliation for death of Matteoti

Sept. 20, Arbitration Treaty with Switzerland signed

——, Mussolini appointed 53 new senators, including Facta, Puccini, Luigi Luiggi, Salvatore di Giacomo

Oct. 5–7, Congress of Liberal Party at Leghorn expressed sympathy with resolution of veterans at Assissi for restoration of law and asked that Fascist national militia be abolished

Oct. 26, Death of General Luigi Pelloux, former Premier

Oct. 28, National militia took oath of allegiance to the King after long delay

Nov. 3, Generals Cadorna and Diaz created Marshals

Nov. 4, Conflict between Fascists and members of the Italia Libera, association of dissident Fascists in Rome, and disturbances in other cities

Nov. 12, Parliament opened, Opposition Aventine deputies not in attendance, Liberals divided, group under former Premier Salandra supporting the Government and group including Giolitti and Orlando in Opposition

Nov. 13, Decree regulated contracts of employment for salaried employees

Nov. 15, Railroad Convention with Czechoslovakia signed

Nov. 29, Death of Giacomo Puccini, composer, in Brussels

Dec. 1, Circular letter directed Fascists to cease violence after publication of letter of General Italo Balbo, Chief of national militia, urging violence, and similar letters from other Fascist leaders

Dec. 10, The Chamber approved Navy Bill providing for expansion of marine defenses and appropriating 925 million lire

Dec. 20, Mussolini presented Bill to Chamber providing for reëstablishment of a single member constituency of 15 districts. Passed by vote of 307 to 33

Dec. 27, Opposition newspapers published fac-similes of memorandum prepared by Cesare Rossi in June which involved Mussolini in deeds of violence of Fascists including beating of Amendola, sacking of house of former Premier Nitti, and destruction of Catholic clubs

Dec. 31, Group of Fascisti raided newspaper "Nuovo Giornale" in Florence and burned plant

——, Houses of members of Opposition searched for firearms

——, Six newspapers in Rome and 4 in Milan sequestered for publication of letter of former Deputy Misuri protesting against domicile search

1925

Jan. 1, From this date tax on buildings not to apply to income from industrial plants, tax on moveable property substituted, land tax to vary according to amount of rent from 11.89 to 19.15%, income tax in 5 schedules, unearned from capital, partly unearned, earnings, &c.

——, Nearly one-third of foreign residents in France Italians

Jan. 3, Speech of Mussolini in Chamber in which he assumed entire responsibility for Fascist actions, "political, moral and historical responsibility" and declared that in 48 hours he would clear up the political situation

——, Salandra joined the Opposition in Chamber

Jan. 3–4, 120 branches of the "*Italia Libera*" closed, 111 suspected revolutionaries arrested, 150 cafés closed, 655 houses searched and opposition newspapers sequestered

Jan. 5, Cabinet reorganized, Mussolini retaining portfolio of Foreign Affairs; Federzoni, Interior; Alfredo Rocco, Justice; de Stefani, Finance; P. Lanza di Scalea, Colonies; General Antonino di Giorgio, War; de Revel, Marine; Pietro Fedele, Public Instruction; Giovanni Giuriati, Public Works; Cesare Nava, National Economy

Jan. 10, Provisional Commercial Agreement with Germany signed

Jan. 12, Parliament opened, Aventine Opposition not in attendance; Bill directed against secret associations (freemasons) introduced by Mussolini forbidding membership of government employees; ratified, March 8

Jan. 15, University of Naples closed because of riots between Fascist and non-Fascist students

Jan. 17, The Chamber adopted Electoral Reform Bill reviving single member constituency

Jan. 22, Royal Decree as to use of Italian language in Upper Adige

Feb. 10, Senate passed Electoral Reform Bill

Feb. 11, Decree replaced duty of 9 gold lire per quintal of 100 kilos on refined sugar

Feb. 14, The Senate passed Bill against secret societies and Electoral Reform Bill

Feb. 23, Agreement with Austria for systemization of interests in Tyrol

March 1, Revision of stock exchange rates became operative and bank rate raised from 6 to 7%

March 12, Strike of 40,000 iron and steel workers begun in Brescia

March 13, Death of Maffeo Colonna di Sciarra, 9th Prince of Carbognano and Nerola (75)

March 15, Strike extended to whole of Lombardy

March 16, First direct cable with the United States opened at Anzio, messages exchanged by King with President Coolidge

March 20, Visit of King and Queen of England

March 28, First issue of "La Dèmocratie Italienne," newspaper published in Paris, gave letter of Vico Perrone, one of chiefs of Fascist militia in which he stated that attack on Amendola of Dec., 1923, had been ordered by General de Bono with consent of Mussolini

March, Robero Farinaca appointed General Secretary of the Fascist Party

April 5, Meetings in various cities to protest against restrictions on the press, especially power given to local prefects

April 6, Riots in Rome, Trent, and other cities between Fascists and Aventine deputies

April 7, Mussolini sworn in as Minister of War succeeding General di Giorgio who resigned when his reform measures proposed were abandoned

April 8, Riots at Faenza, Fascists, and Communists, 2 Fascists killed

——, Memorandum of Filipelli involving Mussolini in kidnapping of Matteoti published in the American "Nation" and in "La Démocratie Italienne" in Paris

April 18, The bourse closed to prevent panic in effort of Government to check speculation

April 21–Nov. 7, Flight of Colonel Marquis de Pinedo and Signor Campanelli from Rome to Melbourne to Tokio and back to Rome, 36,650 miles, 350 hours flying time

April 22, Agreement with Rumania for payment of Rumanian pre-War commercial debts

May 2, Orlando resigned, withdrawing from politics

——, Aëronautical Ministry created

May 4, Resignation of General di Giorgio, Minister of War

May 5, Resignation of Admiral T. di Revel as Minister of Marine. Mussolini took over Ministry and also Air Ministry with Admiral Sirianni and General Bonzani as under-secretaries

May 7, Speech of Senator Albertini, editor of the "Corriere della Sera" against Fascist régime as violating constitutional traditions and of the incident at Reggio Calabria, suppressed in newspapers, of extraordinary demonstrations of rejoicing at rumor the Ministry had resigned

May 9, Treaty of friendship and commerce with Siam signed

May 15, Partial municipal suffrage granted to women by Bill passed in Chamber

May 19, Government Bill against secret societies aimed at freemasons passed Chamber

May 25–27, Visit of Mussolini and reconciliation with Gabriele d'Annunzio at Gardone

May 28, Grant to Government by Parliament of power to amend penal code wherein it applied to "secret associations"

May 30, Law authorized exercise of disciplinary sanctions against public officials including professors suspected of "inactive conformity," affiliation with freemasons

May 31, Marquis de Pinedo in seaplane reached Broome, West Australia. *See supra*, April 21

——, 101,000 unemployed

May, The Dopolavoro (After Work) founded, an association to provide workers and their families with physical and cultural facilities promoting hygiene, education, and art, membership card giving reductions in fares and admissions to theaters, museums, and exhibitions

June 2, J. P. Morgan Company loaned $50,000,000 to consortium of banks of issue to stabilize the lira

June 11, Announcement that Michele Terzghi, Fascist deputy, had been expelled from the Fascist Party because politics not in accord

June 12, The Senate Judicial Committee acquitted General De Bono of complicity in the kidnapping of Matteoti

June 19, The Chamber by vote of 274 to 42 passed Bill giving Government drastic powers over government employees, civil or military; to be dismissed if behavior hostile

June 20, The Pope in address at Perugia arraigned Fascists for violence against Catholics

June 24, Agreement with Austria signed for systemization of interests in Carinthia

June 27, The Senate acting as High Court acquitted General De Bono of complicity in the Matteoti kidnapping and murder

June 29, Jubaland formally transferred to Italy

July 8, Resignation of Finance Minister De Stefani and Nava, Minister of National Economy

July 9, Count Volpi appointed Finance Minister and Senator G. Belluzo, Minister of National Economy

July 20, Nettuno Conventions with Yugoslavia signed, commercial, legal, financial, status of Italians in Dalmatia and Yugoslavs in Fiume, and Commercial Agreement with Hungary

——, Deputy Amendola again attacked and beaten by Fascists

July 24, Suspended duties on corn and meal and wheat reëstablished, wheat at rate of about 5 cents a bushel

July 25, Commercial Treaty with Latvia signed

July 27, George Seldes, correspondent of the "Chicago Tribune," ordered to leave Italy, charged that his press reports were exaggerated and alarmist, representing small groups and political minorities

July 31, Anglo-Italian Agreement signed as to Libya-Egyptian frontier

Aug. 1, Royal Decree granted amnesty for political offenses except murder

——, Certain disputed dock areas in Fiume ceded to Yugoslavia

Aug. 3, Municipal election at Palermo returned Fascist candidate for mayor refusing Orlando

Aug. 7, Royal Decree allowed certain industries to exceed the eight hour day

Aug. 11, The "Giornale d'Italia" suppressed for 1 day because of approval of criticism of the Pope

Aug. 26, Oviglio, former Minister of Justice, expelled from the Fascist Party

Aug. 27, Royal Decree appointed Senator Cremonesi Governor of Rome

Aug. 30, Death of General Asclepiade Gandolfo. Succeeded as Chief of Fascist militia by General Prince Maurizio Gonzaga

——, Cabinet reorganized: Mussolini, Prime Minister, Secretary of State and Minister of Foreign Affairs; Interior, War, Marine, Aëronautics, and of Corporations; Luigi Federzoni, Colonies; Alfredo Rocco, Justice; Pietro Fedele, Public Instruction; Count Giuseppe Volpi, Finance; Giuseppe Belluzzo, National Economy; Giovanni Giuriati, Public Works; Costanzo Ciano, Communications

Aug. 31, 74,517 unemployed

Sept. 2, The lira quoted at 25 to the dollar

Sept. 9, Trial of Professor Carlo Roselli, and Ferruccio Parri charged with assisting the aged Socialist leader, Turati, to leave Italy after passport had been refused to him; sentenced to 10 months imprisonment, and at end of that time sent to Lipari Island

Sept. 17, Treaty of friendship and collaboration with Rumania signed

Sept. 19, Aventine Bloc divided, 22 Maximalist Socialist deputies resuming liberty of action

Sept. 23, Marriage of the Princess Mafalda, second daughter of the King, to Prince Philip of Hesse, nephew of the Emperor of Germany

Sept. 30, The Turin "Stampa," important newspaper, suspended on account of publication of report tending to discredit the army describing pillaging and looting of troops

Oct. 2, Pact of Palazzo Vidoni concluded between General Fascist Confederation of Industries and Confederation of Corporations, each recognizing the other as sole representative of employers and industrial workers respectively

Oct. 3, Conflict between Fascists and anti-Fascists in Florence; Luporini, Fascist leader, killed by freemasons

Oct. 7, Royal Decree extended powers of prefects and made them presidents of provincial councils

Oct. 8, The Cabinet Council decision that municipal self-government in Rome be abolished and governor be appointed by royal decree

Oct. 9, The State Prosecutor recommended release of C. Rossi, G. Marinelli, and F. Filipelli accused of instigating Matteoti kidnapping and murder

Oct. 15, Royal Decree enforced exclusive use of Italian language in courts of law and in legal procedure in Upper Adige (South Tyrol)

Oct. 16 and Dec. 1, Locarno Treaties signed

Oct. 27, The managing board of the Press Association dissolved and provision made for government control and supervision

——, Provisional Commercial Agreement with Bulgaria signed

Oct. 28, Law provided for appointment of a Governor for Rome by royal decree to be assisted by an advisory council ending municipal self-government

Oct. 28, Speech of Mussolini stated policy as "all in the State, nothing outside the State, nothing against the State"

Oct. 30, Fascist Congress attended by representatives of 30 countries

Oct. 31, Commercial Treaty with Germany

Nov. 4, Plot to assassinate Mussolini discovered of ex-Deputy Tito Zaniboni (Socialist) who was arrested with General Capello charged with complicity, both later sentenced to 30 years imprisonment

Nov. 7, Commander Francesco de Pinedo arrived in Rome after 34,000 mile flight to Tokio and return

Nov. 14, Debt Agreement with the United States signed, debt fixed at $2,042,199,466.34 of which $199,466.34 to be paid at once and the remainder funded, payment to be made during 62 years amounting at end to $2,407,000,000

——, Senate met and received Crown Prince Umberto who had reached majority (21 years) and became by law a member of the Senate

——, "Wheat battle" begun, national wheat raising contests inaugurated, prizes given

Nov. 18, Loan of $100,000,000 from J. P. Morgan Company concluded

Nov. 19, Riots in Chamber, Fascist deputies ejected Communist deputies

——, Diet of Upper Adige (former South Tyrol) voted to ask Government of Austria to protest to Rome against the action of Italian post-office in refusing to deliver mail unless addressed in Italian

Nov. 20, Bill for suppression of secret societies passed the Senate forbidding membership of government employees; promulgated Nov. 26

Nov. 21, Announcement that Senator Albertini had been forced to resign the editorship of the "Corriere della Sera," Milan

Nov. 24, Law authorized the Government to dismiss from the public service officials who committed overt acts against the State

Nov. 27, Bill suppressing local self-government in over 7,000 municipalities by substitution of government appointees as heads approved by Chamber; the medieval title of *Podesta* revived for name of heads

Nov. 28, The Chamber passed Bill providing that political refugees abroad who plot against the Government shall lose citizenship and their property be confiscated

Dec. 1, Decision of Court of Appeals that the Matteoti murder was unpremeditated and persons charged with instigation of kidnapping could not be held responsible for his death; Amerigo Dumini and 4 accomplices committed for trial for the murder

Dec. 6, Agreement with Egypt which gave Italy sovereignty over the oasis of Jaghbub and frontier which included Kufara in Cyrenaica, Italy ceding to Egypt the Ramlah wells northwest of Sollum

Dec. 8, The Senate approved the debt settlement with the United States

Dec. 10, The Chamber passed Bill granting juridical recognition to Fascist labor syndicates and employers associations as sole parties to be heard from in industrial disputes and making arbitration obligatory

——, Act as to maternity and child welfare established National Foundation for Maternity and Child Welfare with headquarters in Rome

Dec. 14 and 20, Notes with Great Britain exchanged regarding Lake Tsana and economic spheres in Abyssinia

Dec. 24, Law conferred greater powers on the Prime Minister; no motion to be laid before Chamber or Senate without his sanction

——, Law decreed that anyone insulting the head of the Government by word or deed be subject to heavy fine and imprisonment of from 6 to 30 years

Dec. 31, Law abolished freedom of the press, all journalists to be registered and each newspaper to have responsible director appointed by the Government

——, Senator Filippo Cremonesi inaugurated as Governor of Rome

1926

Jan. 2, Decree created Royal Academy of Italy modelled on French Academy to include scientists, artists, and authors

Jan. 3, Royal Decree reconstituted Association of Italian Manufacturers for the prevention of industrial accidents

Jan. 4, Death of Dowager Queen Margherita, widow of Humbert I (75)

Jan. 10, Royal Decree ordered re-Italization of family names in Upper Adige, all citizens to watch Official Gazette to see what their names to be henceforth

Jan. 16, A number of the "Aventine" deputies returned to the Chamber and were expelled

Jan. 17, Decree recoded electoral laws to come into effect July 1

Jan. 27, Anglo-Italian debt settlement reduced debt from £610,000,000 to £583,000,000, an annual sum of £4,500,000 slightly reduced at first to be paid over a period of 62 years, the first payment to be £2,000,-000 in March

——, Anti-German demonstration at Naples due to criticism in German press of treatment of Germans in Upper Adige (former South Tyrol)

Jan. 29, Anti-German demonstration in Rome

Jan. 31, Law promulgated by which citizens abroad who committed or abetted any act injurious to Italian interests, good name, or prestige to be deprived of citizenship and property confiscated (Anti-Emigré Act, adopted by Senate, Jan. 25, received royal assent, Jan. 29)

——, Law enacted making Prime Minister responsible solely to the King and empowered him to issue decrees having the force of law whenever "reasons of urgency and absolute necessity require it"

Feb. 4, Law placed communes of less than 5,000 inhabitants under a *podesta*

——, Speech of Bavarian Premier in Diet at Munich attacked Italian treatment of Germans in Upper Adige and advocated boycott of Italian goods

Feb. 6, Mussolini in Chamber denounced plan of Premier Held of Bavaria for boycott warning the German Government that unless it ceased Italy would take vigorous action, and declared that Italian laws should be applied in Upper Adige, denying violence and terrorism of Germans

Feb. 7, Italian troops occupied Jaghbub

Feb. 9, Stresemann, German Minister of Foreign Affairs, recalled promises Italy had made to respect rights of minorities in the Tyrol

Feb. 10, Mussolini in the senate replied to Stresemann and denounced German propaganda in Upper Adige

March 2, Senate acting as High Court acquitted 13 brokers of fraud in connection with failure of the Banco di Sconto in 1921

March 10, Decree established Permanent Committee for Internal Migration to encourage settlement in the south and on islands

March 11, Bill as to legal recognition of syndical associations of employers and workers passed Senate. *See* April 3

March 16–24, Trial at Chieti of 5 persons charged with murder of Matteoti in June, 1924, ended in acquittal of Giuseppe Viola and Augusto Malacria, and sentence of Amerigo Dumini, Albino Volpi, and Ameleto Poveromo as guilty of unintentional and unpremeditated murder to imprisonment of 5 years, 11 months, and 20 days, of which only 2 months and 20 days served, deducting 1 year and 9 months time already served, and 4 years remitted under amnesty

March 22, Protocol signed to Commercial Treaty with Austria

March 31, Roberto Farinacci resigned as Secretary General of Fascist Party and was succeeded by Augusto Turati

——, At Fascist Grand Council meeting Mussolini named 9 members of new Directorate

April 1, Royal Decree granted concession for railroad to the Societa Italiana di Navigazione Internal to complete road in Po Valley

——, First commercial air line established service between Trieste and Turin making stops at Venice and Pavia

April 3, Law enacted by which 13 labor syndicates received legal recognition, 6 of employers, 6 of employees, and 1 of intellectuals, and established compulsory arbitration of disputes, labor court created and strikes and lockouts prohibited (Juridical Discipline of Collective Labor Relations Act)

——, Junior society of Fascist Party called the Balilla established for enrollment of youth

April 6, Death of Giovanni Amendola, former Minister for the Colonies and leader of Aventine Opposition, at Cannes, France, due to injuries received from Fascist attacks in Dec., 1923 and July, 1925

April 7, Declaration signed with France as to commercial declaration of Feb. 14, 1885

——, Premier Mussolini shot at and wounded in the nose by the Honorable Violet Gibson, an Irish woman of unbalanced mind

April 8–17, Mussolini on visit to Tripoli, first visit of a Premier to the African colonies

April 24, Romanetti, famous bandit, killed at Ajaccio, Corsica, by the police

May 4, Insurance Convention with Czechoslovakia signed

May 6, Decree law centralization of note issue privilege in the Bank of Italy

May 9, Treaty of commerce and navigation with Siam replaced that of 1868

May 11, Decree came into effect that lawyers who carried on public activities in contradiction to interests of the Government were not to be admitted to the bar and those already members to be expelled

May 11–14, Flight of Roald Amundsen, General Nobile, and Ellsworth in Italian built airship "Norge" from Kings Bay, Spitzbergen over the North Pole which was crossed and recrossed, May 12, Teller, Alaska, reached after 71 hours in the air covering 3,000 miles

May 18, The Cabinet Council created Ministry of (trade union) Corporations

May 29, Commercial Agreement with France signed and exchange of Notes, Aug. 14 and 23

June 9, Notes of Italy and Great Britain of Dec., 1925, communicated to the League of Nations by Abyssinia. *See* Abyssinia

June 15, Royal Decree sanctioned Agreement of May 6 between the Government and the Bank of Italy, Bank of Naples, and Bank of Sicily signed June 6

——, Agreement with Rumania signed for consolidation of war debt, Italy to take over certain Rumanian oil wells

June 18, Bank of Parma closed, charged with mismanagement, and former president and other prominent bankers arrested

June 19, Extradition Treaty with Turkey signed

June 29, Decrees increased work day from 8 to 9 hours because of Italy's adverse trade balance, suspended provincial and municipal elections indefinitely, prohibited construction of private houses except cheap housing for workers, prohibited opening of new hotels, bars, cafés, cabarets, and pastry shops, restricted newspapers to 6 pages

——, Announcement that steps had been taken by employers of largest industrial plants to open canteens to sell food to employees at minimum prices

June 30, Strike of 800 workers in jute factories of Carrosio for better working conditions declared illegal under new law and workers convicted

July 1, Royal Decree issued regulations for administration of Act of April 3

——, Decree law conferred on the Banca d'Italia sole right to issue notes

July 6, Decree raised restrictions on import of seed potatoes

July 8, National Institute of Exportation established, Dr. Raffaele Pilotti, Director General

July 11, Decree established supervision by Treasury of all dealings in foreign exchange

July 22, Law abolished inviolability of tenure in the judiciary system

July 23, Royal Decree law provided for reorganization of the Banks of Naples and Sicily in connection with the note issue

Aug. 3, Decree provided for the gradual elimination of all non-Fascist public manifestations of intellectual, sporting, and charitable character

Aug. 4, Law creating Forestry Service and a number of laws covering public education among the 55 new laws approved by Cabinet

Aug. 7, Treaty of friendship, conciliation, and arbitration with Spain signed

Aug. 10, Juridical Convention with Turkey signed

Aug. 21, The school inspector at Meran announced that teaching of 3 children from different families constituted a private school and required a permit which withheld made it more difficult for Germans to give their children a German education

Aug. 26, The Prefect of Trent ordered to list all family names which could be traced to Italian origin and change them back again to Italian form

Aug. 30, Municipal elections abolished and all cities brought under the podesta system with the exception of Rome and Naples

Aug. 31, Unemployed 78,300

Sept. 2, Treaty of friendship and commerce with the Yemen State in Arabia signed

——, The lira at 130 to pound as compared with 149 on Aug. 26

Sept. 11, Attempt of anarchist, Lucetti, who had been living in France since 1923, on life of Mussolini

Sept. 11, "Order Sheet" of Fascist Party declared that France offered asylum to all who hated Fascism

Sept. 15, Treaty of commerce and navigation with Guatemala signed

Sept. 16, Treaty with Rumania signed of friendship and coöperation and agreement for loan in return for oil concessions

Sept. 25, Bill presented authorized the police to remove from Sicily all persons dangerous to the public safety beginning campaign against the Mafia society which had terrorized the island for years

Sept. 30, Meeting of Sir Austin Chamberlain and Mussolini on yacht off Leghorn to discuss international affairs

Oct. 1, Royal Decree put anti-Emigré Act in force against 15 persons

Oct. 31, Attempt of anarchist, Antea Zamboni, to shoot Mussolini at Bologna, lynched by crowd

Nov. 1, Fascist demonstration at Ventimiglia against French railroad employees in hostel

Nov. 5, General Garibaldi arrested at Nice with 4 others and taken to Paris for examination in connection with plot of Colonel Francesco Macia to free Catalonia from rule of Spain and attempt of Lucetti on life of Mussolini, charged with acting as *agent provocateur* among Italian émigrés in France

Nov. 6, Royal Decree as to public safety provided for heavy fines and imprisonment of at least 3 years for anyone attempting to leave the country without a passport if action due to political reasons, and the same for any person giving aid, deportation of any citizens acting in any way hostile to Fascism, &c.

Nov. 9, The Chamber voted that the "Aventine" deputies be deprived of their seats and for reëstablishment of the death penalty

Nov. 24, Commercial Treaty with Greece signed

Nov. 25, Defense of the Realm Act provided for death penalty for actions directed against the King or Queen or Head of the Government

Nov. 27, Treaty of friendship and arbitration with Albania signed (practically a protectorate)

Nov. 30, Unemployed 149,000

Dec. 2, Francesco Nitti, nephew of former Premier, arrested and sentenced to exile for 5 years because of acts in memory of Matteoti, attempting to place flowers at spot where body found, &c.

Dec. 6, The Cabinet approved law which came into effect by Decree, Jan. 1, 1927, by which the provincial system completely reorganized, all sub-prefectures suppressed and prefects reorganized, 14 townships abolished, and 17 new provinces created

——, Decree established annual tax on progressive scale on unmarried men between ages of 25 and 65

Dec. 8, The *Fascio littorio* declared an official emblem

Dec. 9, Supplementary Agreement with Germany as to Commercial Treaty of Dec., 1925

Dec. 11, Escape of Filippo Turati (70), Socialist leader, from Italy to France after he had been refused a passport

Dec. 15, Defense of the Realm Act came into effect

Dec. 18, Agreement with Poland for consolidation of debt

Dec. 21, Mussolini pardoned 10 of the 942 opponents of his régime who were in prison in islands of Adriatic or Mediterranean

Dec. 29, Treaty of friendship and arbitration with Germany signed

Dec. 30, Alesandro Passaleva set new record flying 119 miles an hour with load of 2,200 pounds

1927

Jan. 3, Commercial Convention with Haiti signed

Jan. 5, Publication of Mussolini's Circular to Prefects emphasizing centralization of the government and recognizing the Prefects as highest authority in the provinces

Jan. 9, Decree ordered dissolution of youth societies in competition with the Fascist organization of the Balilla in places of less than 20,000 inhabitants including the Catholic boy scouts

Jan. 13, Claims Convention with Mexico signed

Jan. 20–22, Trial of Colonel R. Garibaldi in France resulted in judgment that he had been guilty of plotting against a foreign government on French territory

Jan. 21, Decree authorized dismissal of professors in universities, colleges, and schools if not fulfilling their duties and if placing themselves in opposition to policy and aims of the Fascist Government

Jan. 26, Commercial Agreement with France signed as to duties on silk

Jan. 31, Unemployed 225,000

Jan.–March, Average of 35 business failures a day

Feb. 1, Special Military Tribunal established for trial of all cases affecting security of the State or the Fascist régime

Feb. 9, Tax on bachelors approved by the Cabinet Council

Feb. 13–June 16, Colonel Francesco de Pinedo made flight from Sardinia to Africa, South America, the United States, and return by Portugal and Spain to Italy

Feb. 21, The invitation of President Coolidge of Feb. 10 to participate in conference for limitation of armaments declined by Italy

Feb. 24, Treaty of conciliation and judicial settlement with Chile signed

Feb. 26, Colonel de Pinedo arrived at Rio de Janeiro, Brazil, on flight from Cape Verde Islands

March 8, Italy ratified the Treaty of Paris of Oct. 28, 1920, recognizing Rumanian sovereignty over Bessarabia, ratifications deposited May 23

March 17, Russia protested Italian recognition of sovereignty of Rumania over Bessarabia

March 19, The Government formally notified Great Britain, France, and Germany that it had information of military preparation of Yugoslavs for invasion of Albania

March 24–25, Attack on foreign consulates in China. *See* China

March 27, 80,000 young men who had arrived at age of 18 inducted into membership in the Fascist Party and became members of Fascist militia

March 29, Death of Luigi Luzzatti, economist and former Minister of the Treasury, of Agriculture and Commerce, and Premier (1909–11)

March 31, Unemployed 228,000

April 5, Treaty of friendship, conciliation, and arbitration with Hungary signed

——, Announcement of suppression of the Commissariat General for Emigration

April 11–22, Trial of former Socialist deputy, Tito Zaniboni, General Luigi Capello, and 7 others charged with attempted assassination of Mussolini in Nov., 1925, Zaniboni and Capello receiving sentences of imprisonment for 30 years, and the others terms of from 7 to 12 years

April 19–May 4, 689 business failures reported

April 21, The "Facist Charter of Labor" promulgated by Mussolini which asserts the right of the State to control all forces of production, acting as guardian of both labor and capital organized in legally recognized syndicates and all relations between them to be carried out by broad collective contracts. Strikes, lockouts, and sabotage prohibited, and labor courts have final authority to settle disputes. A six day week guaranteed, indemnity on discharge, but Charter does not fix hours and declares against a minimum wage

April 24, Domizio Torrigiani, head of Freemasons sentenced to banishment to islands for 5 years for anti-Fascist activities

April 26–27, Agreement concluded as to Libya-Egypt frontier

April 29, Law published in "Manchester Guardian" of this date prohibited Italian subjects from taking service with foreign governments or international public institutions of a political character without permission of the Italian Government

May 5, Decrees provided for reduction in wages of all State employees, civil and military, and decrease of freight charges on railroads, 15% on all goods for export

May 8, Commercial *modus vivendi* with Persia established

May 20, Air Navigation Agreement with Germany signed

May 21, Convention with Hungary signed settlement of questions raised by Italian annexation of Fiume

May 23, Colonel F. de Pineda left Trepassy, Newfoundland in flight reaching Horta, the Azores, May 30, and Ostia, Italy, June 16, after journey of 25,000 miles across the Atlantic and back

May 26, Mussolini in speech to Chamber declared the population must be increased by the birth rate, reduction of mortality, and restriction of emigration

June 1, Agreement with Yemen as to commercial and economic interests of Italy supplementary to that of Sept., 1926

——, Formal apology of Yugoslavia for anti-Italian demonstration at Ragusa on May 28

June 14, Decree of Cabinet Council required landlords to reduce rents and increase prohibited

June 15, Cabinet Council directed that a "notable reduction of taxation" should be made

June 20, Italian emigration regulations amended

June 21, Italian Minister to Belgium recalled as a protest against anti-Fascist position of E. Vandervelde, Belgian Minister of Foreign Affairs

July 20, Government Committee created "for corporative action in the matter of prices, costs, and wages"

July 25, Death of Matilde Serao, novelist (71)

——, Convention with Hungary gave Hungary a free zone in port of Fiume

Aug. 10, Decree provided compensation for Italian citizens abroad killed or injured in national cause and their families extending law of Dec. 24, 1925

Aug. 15, Air Navigation Convention with Spain signed

Aug. 19, Trial of Turati (in absence) Socialist leader, and 11 friends of Turati charged with aiding him to escape from Italy, 6 including Turati sentenced to 10 months each in prison, and one to longer term

Aug. 22, New criminal code published

Sept. 11, Provisional Commercial Agreement with Greece signed

Sept. 17, Italian Vice-Consul in Paris, Count Carlo Nardini, murdered in his office by Italian anarchist, Modugno

——, Treaty of friendship and arbitration and Agreement as to trade with Lithuania signed

Oct. 15, Economic census gave returns of 732,109 industrial establishments employing 4,005,812 persons and 821,666 commercial establishments employing 1,640,290 persons

Oct. 16, Treaty of friendship and arbitration with Mexico signed

Oct. 21, Ministerial Decree authorized a supplementary fare, surtax, on the express trains of the Rome-Naples-Mergelina railroad

Oct. 25, The steamer "Principessa Mafalda" sunk off Bahia, Brazil, 314 persons drowned

Oct. 27–31, Visit of Italian fleet to Tangier to remind the Powers of interests of Italy

Nov. 4, Official world record for speed for seaplanes made by Mario de Bernardi at the Lido, Venice, 297.816 miles an hour

Nov. 11, Fascist Grand Council considered proposal to abolish universal suffrage and substitute a single electorate system for election of Chamber of Deputies, and reduction in membership of Chamber

——, Treaty of friendship and alliance with Albania

Nov. 22, Treaty of defensive alliance with Albania signed

Nov. 28, Financial Convention with Spain signed

Dec. 3, *Modus vivendi* with France as to reciprocal position of nationals in either country

Dec. 13, The "Corriere degli Italian" (organ of Italian political exiles in Paris) suppressed by order of the French Minister of the Interior

Dec. 21, Mussolini announced return to gold basis and stabilization of the lira at 19 to the American dollar, 92.46 to the English pound sterling

Dec. 23, Renato Donati at Turin established a new world altitude record at 38,792 feet

Dec. 31, Unemployed 414,283

1928

Jan. 1, Fourteen free ports authorized April 5, 1925, opened in Trieste, Venice, Ancona, Bari, Brindisi, Catania, Cagliari, Fiume, Genoa, Leghorn, Messina, Naples, Palerma, and Savona

——, Discovery of machine gun parts at Szent on Austro-Hungarian frontier shipped from Verona, Italy

Jan. 3, Surrender of Sidi Rida at Cyrenaica. *See* Libya

Jan. 8, Arrival of the King and Queen of Afghanistan at Rome

Jan. 9, Extension of Agreement with Yugoslavia

Jan. 15, Announcement of foundation in Rome of a Trade Union University for the People

Jan. 25, Protocol extended Treaty of Friendship with Yugoslavia for 6 months

Feb. 1, Unemployed reached 411,785

Feb. 4, Promulgation by Mussolini of "ten commandments" to govern activities of Fascists abroad

Feb. 9, Resolution of Tyrolese Diet at Innsbruck demanded that attention of the Powers of Europe be called to treatment of German subjects of Italy

Feb. 20, Decree exempted large families from payment of certain taxes

Feb. 20, The Cabinet approved new electoral law. *See infra*, May 12

Feb. 21, Announcement that Fascist militia would be incorporated in the regular army to act as an independent unit only in case of war

Feb. 23, Treatment of Germans in Upper Adige (former South Tyrol) discussed in Parliament of Austria and resolution of sympathy adopted

Feb. 26, Royal Decree promulgated regulations for settlement of individual disputes arising in labor controversies

Feb. 29, Death of Marshal General Armando Diaz at Rome, former Commander-in-Chief

March 2, New electoral law presented to Chamber of Deputies

March 3, Mussolini in Chamber replied to Austrian criticism of treatment of German minority in Italy as not justified and internal affair only, saying "The next time I shall make acts do the speaking. . . . A self-respecting State does not tolerate such interference"

March 7, Treaty of commerce with France signed

March 16, New electoral law passed in Chamber

March 23, Publication of list of Italian demands as to Tangier administration, protection of Italian rights, and economic interests

March 29, Decree made it obligatory for workers to use official employment offices

March 30, Cabinet approved Decree prohibiting all organizations for boys except official Fascist society of the Balilla; promulgated April 9

——, World speed record for seaplane made by Major Mario de Bernardi at 318.624 miles an hour

April 12, Bomb explosion at industrial fair about to be opened by the King resulted in death of 20 and injury of 40

April 19, Arbitration Treaty with the United States

May 1, Unemployed 356,795

May 3, General Nobile left Stolp, Germany in dirigible airship "Italia" for Spitzbergen arriving May 6

May 11, Air Navigation Convention with Austria signed

May 12, The Senate passed Electoral Bill by vote of 207 to 46 with more than 100 absentees, providing for election of Chamber of Deputies providing that members be chosen by Fascist Grand Council from list of 800 candidates voted for by selected Fascists syndicates and trade unions, 350 from this list, and 50 chosen by Fascist Grand Council to represent the cultural and spiritual leaders, making list of 400 deputies, to be submitted to the voters who must accept or reject the list as a whole; universal suffrage abolished, suffrage granted to men 21 years of age and to men between ages of 18 and 21 if married or widowers with sons, who are paying a syndicate rate or taxes to amount of 100 lire or are receiving a salary or pension from any public institution; electorate reduced from about 9,500,000 to about 3,000,000 in population of 42,000,000, the 400 deputies elected for 5 years, each to receive an annual allowance of 21,000 lire

May 15–18, General Nobile in the "Italia" left Spitzbergen (Kings Bay) making flight over unexplored lands in Arctic regions between Franz Josef Land and Nicholas II Land (now Lenin Land)

May 17, Law of electoral reform

May 23, General Nobile in the "Italia" left Kings Bay,

Spitzbergen at 4.35 A.M., reaching the North Pole at 2.20 A.M., May 24

May 25, The "Italia" on return journey wrecked within 225 miles of Kings Bay, Spitzbergen. General Nobile rescued June 22 and 6 of the crew later. *See also* Arctic

May 27–30, Anti-Italian riots at Belgrade, Sebenico, and Spalato, Yugoslavia, demonstration against ratification of the Nettuno Conventions, 100 persons wounded

May 30, Treaty of arbitration, conciliation, neutrality, and judicial regulation with Turkey signed

May 31–June 2, World airplane distance record made by Major Arturo Ferrarin and Commander Carlo Del Prete in non-stop flight of 4,763 miles

June 5, Speech of Mussolini in which he reviewed the relations of Italy with the countries of the world from "China to Peru," and as to the United States made statement that "naturalized Americans of Italian origin are American citizens and therefore foreigners as far as Italy is concerned"

June 14, Legislative Decree made regulations as to safety of life at sea

June 16–17, Anti-Italian demonstrations at Sebenico and Spalato

June 18, Railroad Convention with Switzerland signed

June 22, General Nobile rescued from ice floe in Arctic sea by Swedish aviator, Captain E. Lundborg

June 29, Commercial Agreement with Persia signed

June 30, Unemployed 297,000

July 1, Provisional Commercial Agreement with Estonia signed

——, China denounced Treaty of Oct. 26, 1866 with Italy

July 3–5, Flight from Rome to Rouros, Brazil, of Major Del Prete and Major Ferrarin, 4,466 miles in 51 hours and 59 minutes

July 4, Treaty of commerce with Hungary signed reduced tariff on raw materials in both countries, Hungary given trade facilities in Fiume and Trieste

July 8, Mussolini reorganized Cabinet, Antonio Mosconi succeeded Count Volpi in Finance, and G. Belluzzo replaced P. Fedele as Minister of Public Instruction, A. Martelli becoming Minister of National Economy succeeding Belluzo

July 11, Italy notified willingness to negotiate new treaty with China

July 12, The Russian ice-breaker "Krassin" rescued 7 of wrecked "Italia" from ice floe

July 17, Death of Giovanni Giolitti, former Premier

——, Agreement as to Tangier concluded

July 24–29, Trial of 33 Communists for agitation against the Government, 16 condemned to long terms of imprisonment, 11 to terms of 1 year, and 6 acquitted

Aug. 2, Treaty of friendship and conciliation with Abyssinia signed, Abyssinia to lease a free zone at Assab, Eritrea, and provision made for construction of a road from Abyssinia to Assab

Aug. 13, Nettuno Conventions of July, 1925, ratified by Yugoslavia

Aug. 15–16, Demonstrations at Spalato against ratification of Nettuno Conventions by which Italians permitted to hold land and Italian firms to import Italian labor; Italian consulate attacked by mob of Yugoslav irredentists

Aug. 16, Death of Major Carlo Del Prete killed in crash of his plane in Brazil

Aug. 21, Treaty of arbitration and conciliation with Finland signed

Aug. 27, Italy signed Pact for outlawry of war

Aug. 30, Cesare Rossi arrested at Campione

Sept. 7, Special Military Tribunal held trial of alleged accomplices of A. Zamboni who shot at Mussolini in Oct., 1926, and his father sentenced to 30 years' imprisonment

Sept. 9, Resignation of Prince Ludovico Potenziani as Governor of Rome, Don Francesco Boncompagni, Prince of Piombino named as his successor

Sept. 19, Meeting of Fascist Grand Council approved measure incorporating itself as the national government. *See infra*, Nov. 15

Sept. 23, Treaty of friendship and arbitration with Greece signed

Oct. 5, Commercial Convention with Lithuania signed and Extradition Treaty with Cuba

Oct. 6, Aviation Treaty and Protocol with Spain signed

Oct. 23, Announcement of membership of Fascist Party as 6,814,703

Oct. 24, Agreement with Switzerland regarding frontier traffic

Nov. 5, Mt. Etna in eruption destroyed towns of Mascali, Nunziata, and Carrabba

Nov. 7, Death of Mattia Battistini, baritone

Nov. 15, Grand Council of Fascist Party given constitutional status by vote of the Senate as "supreme organ which coördinates and embraces all the activities of the régime which issued from the revolution of Oct., 1922." Passed in the Chamber, Dec. 8, received royal assent Dec. 9, promulgated Dec. 10

Nov. 26, Trial of Modugno in Paris resulted Nov. 28 in sentence of fine of 200 francs and 2 years' imprisonment for murder of Nardini Sept. 1927 of which he had already served 18 months; great indignation in Italy

Nov. 27, Treaty with China signed recognized tariff autonomy of China and abolition of extra-territorial privileges

Dec. 8, Parliament passed law providing for reclamation of tract of 5 million acres waste land over period of 14 years at expense of 8,400,000 lire

——, Law regulating position and powers of the Fascist Grand Council passed Chamber, received royal assent Dec. 9 and was promulgated Dec. 10

Dec. 21, Death of Marshal Count Luigi Cadorna, former Chief of Staff

1929

Jan. 10, Law enacted respecting compulsory sickness and social welfare insurance for seamen and airmen

Jan. 11, Official visit of Dino Grandi, Under-Secretary of Foreign Affairs, to Greece

Jan. 21, Parliament dissolved

Jan. 27, Treaty of friendship with Yugoslavia expired and was not renewed

Feb. 2, National Council of Research inaugurated

Feb. 11, Three documents signed by Mussolini and Cardinal Gasparri recreating the Papal State under name of "State of the Vatican City," (1) recognition of the Holy See and the Kingdom of Italy as separate and independent sovereignties, (2) concordat as to religious activities of the Roman Catholic Church in Italy, and (3) financial convention granting the Pope an indemnity of 750,000,000 lire and 1 billion lire in Italian State consols at 5%. Signed by the King, May 27

Feb. 28, Publication of list of 400 candidates for membership in Chamber of Deputies by Fascist Grand Council

March 3, Court of Inquiry reported that the loss of the "Italia" was due to "faulty manœuvring" and censured General Nobile for allowing himself to be rescued ahead of his crew. General Nobile resigned from the Air Service

March 11, Air Agreement with France concluded for establishment of stations at Marseilles, Tunis, and Castellorizo for use by both countries

March 21, French-Italian-Mexican Commission began conference on outstanding questions

March 24, List of 400 candidates for Chamber of Deputies submitted to voters acting as a single electoral constituency, the ballot to be voted on as a whole "yes" or "no" for the entire list, no individual names to be rejected. Approximately 90% of the qualified voters went to the polls and 8,519,559 voted "yes" and only 137,761 voted "no"

March 31, 294,000 unemployed

April 2, Meeting of Sir Austin Chamberlain at Florence

April 13, Largest submarine of navy launched at Taranto

April 20, First Italian Corporative Parliament formally opened by the King

April 21, National Council of Corporations inaugurated to "adjust disputes between the various groups in the interest of national production" composed of representatives from the 13 syndicates, from the Government, and from certain extra-syndical co-operating institutions

May 1, The legal age for marriage was reduced from 18 to 16 for boys and from 15 to 14 for girls

——, Trial of 161 members of the band of Mafia ended with conviction of 150 for crimes ranging from murder to cattle maiming

——, Official visit of Dino Grandi, Under-Secretary of Foreign Affairs to Hungary

May 13 and 25, Speeches of Mussolini in Chamber on Vatican settlement declared Church in Italy subject to the State. *See also* Pope

May 13, Legislative Decree for protection of women wage and salaried workers before and after childbirth

May 14, Bills dealing with recognition of religious marriage and regulation of ecclesiastical bodies having civil property passed

May 22, Speech of Mussolini in Chamber on foreign policy

——, Death of Rodolfo Lanciani, archæologist

May 27, Bills giving effect to the Lateran Treaties signed by the King

May 31, Protocol with Switzerland signed supplementing Commercial Treaty of Jan. 27, 1923

June 5, Open letter of the Pope criticized remarks of Mussolini before the Chamber on May 13

June 7, Ratifications exchanged of Lateran Treaties of Feb. 11

June 10, "Fundamental law" of the papal State of the Vatican City in 21 articles promulgated by the Pope

June 13, Surrender of rebel chiefs in Cyrenaica. *See* Libya

June 17, Arbitration Treaty with Norway signed

June 23, Draft of new Code of criminal procedure published, proposed abolition of jury system

June 25, Senator Cesare Maria de Vecchi presented credentials as first Italian ambassador to the Holy See

June 30, Unemployed 192,000

July 5, The Papal Nuncio presented credentials

July 8, The Catholic publication "Youthful Life" sequestered by the Government as liable to draw young Catholics away from the State and Italian institutions

——, Protest of the Government against new American tariff

July 24, Official announcement in Upper (Alto) Adige that from October all teaching must be in the Italian language and Italian language only to be used in public

July 25, First appearance of the Pope outside the Vatican to take formal possession of territory ceded by the Italian Government, the first time since the fall of the Papal States in 1870 that a Pope had left the Vatican

Aug. 3, Commercial *modus vivendi* with Turkey concluded

Aug. 8, Announcement of escape of anti-Fascists, Professor Carlo Roselli, Emilio Lussu, and Fausto Nitti from detention on Lipari Island

——, New marriage regulations under Concordat recognizing religious marriage as sufficient without civil ceremony came into effect

Aug. 21, Commercial Agreement with Finland

Aug. 27, Pact of Paris for renunciation of war signed

Sept. 5, Treaty of friendship with Persia signed

Sept. 9, Optional Clause of Statute of Permanent Court of International Justice signed

Sept. 12, Cabinet reorganized and 9 new Ministers appointed by Mussolini, 7 of them taking portfolios that he had previously held: Prime Minister, Chief of the Government, and Minister of the Interior, Signor Benito Mussolini; Foreign Affairs, Dino Grandi; War, Pietro Gazzera; Navy, Giuseppe Sirianni; Air, Italo Balbo; Public Works, Araldo di Crollalanza; Corporations, Giuseppe Bottai; National Education, Balbino Giuliano; Agriculture and Forests, Giacomo Acerbo; Colonies, General Emilio de Bono; Finance, Antonio Mosconi; Justice, Alfredo Rocco; Communications, Constanzio Ciano

Sept. 14, Announcement by Mussolini of changes in organization of the Fascist Party, the Grand Council to be reduced from 56 to about 20 into a kind of "general staff "

Sept. 20, Suppression of the Como branch of the "Azione Cattolica"

Sept. 27, Cesare Rossi sentenced to imprisonment for 30 years charged with conspiracy against the Government

Oct. 10, Royal Decree exempted large families from taxation

Oct. 16, Treaty of friendship, commerce, and navigation with Panama signed

——, Trial of 5 young men (Slavs) at Pola charged with firing on Fascists on their way to vote on March 24, resulted in sentence of the leader to death and the others to imprisonment for 30 years

Oct. 18, Anti-Italian demonstrations at Belgrade and other Yugoslav cities against execution of Slovene student at Pola; protested by Italian Government Oct. 21

Oct. 24, The Crown Prince escaped shot of assassin Fernando, anti-Fascist, in Brussels

Oct. 26, The Yugoslav Government replied to Note of Oct. 21 promising punishment of offenders

Oct. 28, Royal Academy of Italy inaugurated, Tittoni, president

Oct. 29, Revised Statute of the Fascist Party published in which it is described as "a civilian militia in the services of the nation having for its object the realization of the greatness of the Italian people"

Nov. 3, Announcement that American born children of Italian parents residing in the United States might return to Italy without fear of conscription in time of peace

Nov. 7, The Cabinet adopted Bill modifying statutes of Fascist Grand Council

Nov. 13, Mussolini addressed wheat committee urging emancipation of Italy from foreign grown wheat

Nov. 19, Conversations with France preliminary to the London Naval Conference opened in Paris

——, Text published of Bill for reform of the National Council of Corporations

Dec. 2, Italy joined Governments of Great Britain, France, and the United States in Note to Russia and China calling attention to the Pact of Paris

——, Speech of the Pope complained of Fascist censorship of Catholic newspapers

Dec. 5, Ceremonial visit of the King and Queen to the Pope

Dec. 18, The Fascist Grand Council adopted new constitution

Dec. 20, Pope Pius XI entered Italian territory to celebrate jubilee mass at Church of St. John Lateran

Dec. 22, Fascisti League of North America with headquarters at New York City disbanded

1930

Jan. 2, Royal amnesty granted for misdemeanors and military offenses which affected 400,000 persons, 6,000 convicts freed

Jan. 8, Marriage of Crown Prince Humbert (Umberto) to Princess Marie José, only daughter of the King and Queen of Belgium, in the Pauline Chapel of the Quirinal Palace in Rome

Jan. 11, Encyclical of the Pope declared education of the young preëminently the function of the Church

Jan. 20, Agreement with Germany concluded as to liquidated property, war claims

——, Financial Agreements with Rumania and Czechoslovakia signed, and with Bulgaria as to arbitration of property rights and interests

Jan. 21–April 15, Conference on Limitation of Naval Armaments in London; France and Italy failed to reach agreement as to disarmament

Feb. 3, Death of Michele Bianchi, former Cabinet Minister

Feb. 6, Treaty of friendship, conciliation, and arbitration with Austria signed

Feb. 21, Announcement that Mussolini had pardoned German speaking subjects in the Alto Adige imprisoned for political offenses

Feb. 25, Commercial Treaty with Rumania signed

Feb. 26, Death of Cardinal Rafele Merry del Val (64)

——, Tax on single men extended to Italian colonies

March 5, Death of Antonio Fradeletto, former Minister

March 10, Bomb outrage at Trieste and arrest of Yugoslavs charged with terrorism who were condemned and shot Sept. 6

March 12, Decision of Cabinet allowed free purchase and sale of foreign currencies

March 18, Fiume with Abbazia Volosca and Laurana established as a free zone

March 23, Decree abolished the octroi system by which tolls had been levied at gates of cities and towns on all produce from the country as from April 1; taxes on alcohol, meat, gas, and electric light substituted

March 25, Death of Tina di Lorenzo, actress

April 11-14, Visit of Count Bethlen of Hungary to Rome

April 27, Five naval vessels, 4 cruisers, and a submarine, launched

April 30, Decision of Cabinet Council to lay down warships totaling 42,000 tons in the year 1930 to cost about $40,000,000

May 5, The Government ratified the Hague Agreement embodying the Young Plan

May 9, Speech of Signor Grandi, Minister of Foreign Affairs, on foreign policy

May 11, Speech of Mussolini at Leghorn regarded by foreign press as menace to peace

May 17, Speech of Mussolini at Florence reaffirmed determination to carry through naval policy, declared "words are beautiful things, rifles, machine guns, ships, airplanes, and cannon are still more beautiful"

May 24, Speech of Mussolini at Milan declared that the Treaty of Versailles had given Italy a mutilated victory but it had not mutilated her heart and arm and condemned "the spirit dominating some of our neighbors" which was answered with shouts of "Down with France"

June 3, Speech of Grandi offered to suspend new naval construction if France would do the same

June 5, Courses in religious instruction made compulsory in secondary schools and program published July 10

June 27-28, Decrees of Cabinet Council to increase tax for exchange transactions to $1\frac{1}{2}$%, $25,000,000 added to war budget and increase in certain taxes, duties raised on imports, motor cars taxed from 100 to 167% giving the Italian Fiat Automobile Company a virtual monopoly

July 3, Mussolini in interview published in "Le Petit Parisien" demanded revision of "unjust" Treaty of Versailles

July 4, Speech of Grandi stated Italian claims to naval parity with France

July 7, Briand Plan for European Union rejected by Italy as based on French security rather than disarmament and as not including States not members of the League of Nations

July 9, Death of Cardinal Vincenzo Vannutelli

July 22-23, Earthquake in south central Italy from Naples on the Mediterranean to Foggia on the Adriatic centering at Bari caused death of more than 2,000 persons and great damage of property

July 24, Act introduced new penal measures with respect to emigration

July 24-25, Additional earthquake shocks in stricken area

Aug. 2, Commercial Treaty with Russia signed

Aug. 31, Italian divers discovered wreck of the "Egypt," Peninsular and Oriental liner sunk in collision in 1922 with $6,000,000 of gold and silver 400 feet beneath the surface of the Atlantic about 25 miles southwest of the Island of Ushant and 30 miles off Point du Raz

Sept. 2, Agreement with Great Britain respecting claims arising out of raids and incidents on Anglo-Italian frontier in Somaliland

Sept. 5, Execution of 4 Italian subjects of Slav origin

and sentence of 14 others to terms of imprisonment varying from 4 to 30 years by Special Military Tribunal for terrorist activities

Sept. 8, Death of Michele Scherillo, sculptor

Sept. 24, A. Turati resigned as Secretary of the Fascist Party and was succeeded by Giovanni B. Giuriati

Oct. 23, Decree provided for free importation of bananas grown in Italian colonies

Oct. 25, Marriage of the Princess Giovanna, third daughter of the King, to King Boris III of Bulgaria

Oct. 27, Speech of Mussolini at Venice declared his late speeches were intended to tear away the mask of hypocrisy from other nations and that if war was to be avoided the peace treaties must be revised, that a state of moral war against Italian Fascism existed and that preparations for material war were being made on the frontier

Oct. 30, Serious earthquake on the Adriatic coast between Ancona and Pesaro caused death of 15 persons and injury to hundreds of others

Nov. 6, Arrest of Bartelo Belotti, former Cabinet Minister, and Professor Ernesto Bellou and other prominent Liberal and Conservative leaders charged with anti-Fascist activities and conspiracy with anti-Fascists in Paris

Nov. 18, Decision of Cabinet Council announced to cut salaries of State employees from 12 to 25% as from Dec. 1 to cover deficiency

Nov. 27-29, Visit of Tevfik Rustü Bey to Rome

Nov. 28, Announcement of reduction of wages of factory workers of 8% except the lowest paid workers

——, Official announcement that Bartelo Belotti had been sentenced to 5 years' imprisonment on penal islands

Nov. 30, Unemployed 534,356

Dec. 3, Release from prison of Professor Giuseppe Rensi of the University of Genoa, charges not proven

Dec. 12, Bill approved by the Chamber of Deputies providing for discontinuance of Sept. 20 as national holiday, the anniversary of the taking of Rome in 1870, and substituting Feb. 11, the date of signing of the Lateran Treaty

Dec. 17, Fourteen seaplanes commanded by General Italo Balbo left Italy for South America arriving in Natal, Brazil on Jan. 6, 1931

Dec. 22, Special Military Tribunal sentenced Mario Vinciguerra and Renzo Rendi to 15 years' imprisonment for anti-Fascist activities, 5 others acquitted including Mrs. Adolfo de Bosis, American widow of the Italian poet, and Professor U. Gelmetti

KINGS OF ITALY

476. Odoacer, King of the Heruli, invades Italy, and becomes King, conquered and slain by

493. Theodoric, King of the Ostrogoths, an able prince. He put to death the philosophers Boëthius and Symmachus, falsely accused, about 525

526. Athalaric, his grandson, dies of the plague

534. Theodatus elected; assassinated

536. Vitiges elected

540. Theodebald (Hildibald) elected; assassinated

541. Totila, or Badiula, a great prince; killed in battle against the imperial army under Narses

552. Theias falls in battle

——, Italy subject to the Eastern Empire till

568. Alboin, King of the Lombards, with a huge mixed army, conquers Italy; poisoned by his wife Rosa-

mond, for compelling her to drink wine out of a cup formed of her father's skull

573. Cleoph; assassinated
575. Autharis; poisoned
591. Agilulph
615. Adaloald; poisoned
625. Arioald
636. Rotharis; married the widow of Arioald; published a code of laws
652. Rodoald (son); assassinated
653. Aribert I (uncle)
661. Bertharit and Godebert (sons); dethroned by
662. Grimoald, Duke of Benevento
671. Bertharit reëstablished
686. Cunibert (son)
700. Luitbert; dethroned by
701. Ragimbert
——, Aribert II (son)
712. Ansprand elected
——, Luitprand (son), a great prince, and a favorite of the church
744. Hildebrand (nephew); deposed
——, Rachis, Duke of Friuli, elected; became a monk
749. Astolph (brother)
756. Desiderius (Didier), quarreled with the Pope Adrian, who invited Charlemagne into Italy, by whom Desiderius was deposed, and an end put to the Lombard Kingdom
781. Pepin or Carloman (son of Charlemagne)
812. Bernard
820. Lothaire (son of Louis le Débonnaire)

EMPERORS

875. Charles the Bald
877. Carloman
879. Charles the Fat
888. Berenger I
889. " and Guy
894. " and Lambert
921. " and Rudolph of Burgundy
926. Hugh of Provence
945. Lothaire II
950. Berenger II and Adalbert his son; deposed in 961 by the Emperor Otho the Great, who added Italy to the German Empire

MODERN KINGS OF ITALY

1805. Napoleon I proclaimed King of Italy, March 18; crowned at Milan, May 26; abdicated, 1814
1861. Victor-Emmanuel II (of Sardinia, see s.v.), born March 14, 1820; declared King of Italy by the parliament, March 17, 1861; died Jan. 9, 1878
1878. Humbert (son), born March 14, 1844; married his cousin Margherita (born Nov. 20, 1851), April 22, 1868; assassinated, July 29, 1900
1900. Victor-Emmanuel (son), Prince of Naples, born Nov. 11, 1869; married, Helen, Princess of Montenegro, Oct. 24, 1896; Yolanda Margherita, born June 1, 1901; Mafalda, born Nov. 19, 1902; Humbert, Prince of Piedmont, heir to the throne, born Sept. 15, 1904

JAN MAYEN ISLAND

This is a bleak and desolate island between Greenland and Northern Norway and about 300 miles north of Iceland. It is 34 miles long and its greatest breadth is 9 miles. It is of volcanic origin and is mountainous, Beerenberg in the north reaching a height of 8,350 ft. It is uninhabited, but is occasionally visited by seal hunters, whalers, and fishermen. In 1921 the Norwegian Meteorological Institute established a weather forecast station there, and the decision of the Norwegian Government to annex the island was largely due to this action.

The island was discovered by Henry Hudson in 1607, and it was first named Hudson's Tutches (Touches). It was again and again rediscovered and renamed. Its present name was taken from that of a Dutch navigator of the early 17th century, whose claim to have visited the island cannot be substantiated. For the period of a year (1882–83) an Austrian station for scientific observations was maintained there. On May 8, 1929, Jan Mayen Island was officially proclaimed as incorporated in the Norwegian State, and at the same time the manager of the meteorological station on the island was invested with magisterial authority.

JUGOSLAVIA

See Yugoslavia.

LATVIA

Latvia, a Baltic Republic of northern Europe lying east and south of the Gulf of Riga with Estonia to the north, Russia to the east, Lithuania and Poland to the south, and the Baltic Sea on the west.

Latvia consists of the former Russian Province of Courland (about 10,435 square miles), four southern districts (Riga, Wenden, Wolmar, Walk) of the former Russian Province of Livonia (about 8,715 square miles) and three western districts (Dvinsk, Reshitza, Lutsin) of total of about 24,440 square miles, or, including inland lakes, about 25,000 square miles. The total length of the frontier line of Latvia is 1,040 statute miles, with a coast line of 338 statute miles.

The chief town is Riga (the capital), population (1930) 377,917.

The census taken in 1930 showed a population of 1,900,045 in Latvia, of which 1,893,877 were Latvian citizens, and 56,168 foreigners (including 21,336 persons without nationality). Of the Latvian citizens 73.42% were Letts, 12.52% Russians, 4.97% Jews, 3.68% Germans, 3.12% Poles, 1.36% Lithuanians, 0.40% Estonians, 0.45% other nationalities, and 0.08% were persons with unknown nationality

As early as the 13th century the Letts fought against the Germans (battle of Durbe, 1260), but in the long run the Germans carried the day, and the state created by the Teutonic Order under the form of a Federal Republic (consisting of Estonia, Latgale, Livonia, and Courland) lasted until 1560. Eventually, Estonia passed under the rule of Sweden, Latgale and Livonia under that of Lithuania-Poland, while Piltene and Oesel became Danish. Courland alone retained her independence under the form of a vassal duchy of Lithuania-Poland. In 1621 Livonia was annexed by Sweden, and in 1710 by Russia. In 1772, after the first partition of Poland, Latgale was assigned to Russia, and in 1795 Courland joined Russia. From this time onwards, Latvia was under Russian rule.

In 1917 Lettish public opinion expressed itself in favor of the separate existence of Latvia, and announced its view officially in the Russian Constituent Assembly in January 1918. An organization for establishing the independence of the country was formed, and on November 18, 1918, it proclaimed in Riga the sovereign Free State of Latvia, which was recognized as an independent State by most of the Powers, and was admitted to the League of Nations on September 22, 1921.

Albert Kriesis, President.

1917

Sept. 3, Germans entered Riga forcing Russians to evacuate

Sept. 21, Courland proclaimed independence of Russia and requested protection of Germany

Nov. 16, National Council met at Walk and passed resolution declaring Latvia an autonomous unit and declared against incorporation into Germany

Dec. 17, Germans granted police power in Baltic Provinces by armistice with Russia made headquarters in Mitau (Jelgava)

Dec. 27, Municipal Council of Riga announced independence of Russia and requested protection of the German Emperor

1918

Jan. 12, Declaration of independence

March 3, Treaty of Brest-Litovsk. *See* p. 550

March 8, Offer of throne of Duchy of Courland to William II

March 15, Germany proclaimed protectorate over an independent Courland

April 13, United Diet of Baltic States adopted resolution to form State within German Empire

May 22, Red rule ended by liberation of Riga

July, National Council met and proclaimed independence

Aug. 27, Supplementary Treaty of peace with Russia by which independence recognized

Nov. 11, *De facto* recognition of the National Council by Great Britain

——, Latvian Republic proclaimed, Ulmanis, Premier

Dec. 29, The Baltic Landeswehr defeated by Bolsheviks at Hintzenberg

1919

Jan. 4, Soviet forces took Riga evacuated by Germans and established a Soviet Government headed by Shtuchka

Jan. 14, British troops landed at Riga

Jan. 31, Bolsheviks took ports of Libau and Windau in Courland

Feb. 1, General von der Goltz arrived at Libau

Feb. 3, The Government persuaded by Winnig sent to Latvia as German Commissioner promised every German who would take Lettish citizenship a large grant of land by which Winnig as able to organize a force for occupation of Latvia

April 14, Landed proprietors seized the Government

April 16, German force under General von der Goltz occupied Libau overthrowing the Lettish Government

——, Lettish minister, Needra, proclaimed a Government

May 4, The Allies demanded the recall of von der Goltz

May 20, Germans again occupied Riga

May 22, Riga liberated by Baron H. Manteuffel who died leading his men

June 6, Baltic Landeswehr troops including a large number of Germans captured Venden

June 21–22, Germans commanded by General von der Goltz defeated and driven from northern Latvia in battle of Venden-Ronneburg

July 3, Armistice signed by Estonians and Latvians with Landeswehr and Germans and Lettish Provisional Government reinstated

July 14, Needra succeeded Ulmanis as Prime Minister

July 20, Agreement with Estonia signed for mutual help

Aug. 16, The German Government recalled von der Goltz

Oct. 12, General von der Goltz placed his troops in command of General Eberhardt but continued secretly to direct affairs

Oct. 16, Letts recaptured Dunamunde from German-Russians

Oct. 18, Avalov-Bermondt in coöperation with the Germans attacked Riga and held it for a few days on pretense of war against the Bolsheviks

Nov. 18, Republic proclaimed, Ulmanis again Premier

Dec. 8, Elementary and Secondary Education Act

1920

Jan. 3–24, Latvia cleared of Red armies by Lett campaign

Jan. 14, Conference at Helsingfors. *See* Finland

March 22, Arbitration Convention with Estonia signed,

April 16–17, Election for constituent assembly

May 1, Constituent Assembly met replacing Provisional Government in operation since 1918

May 27, Proclamation of independence reaffirmed

June 1, Provisional Constitution adopted. Came into effect June 30

July 15, Peace Protocol with Germany signed

Aug. 11, Peace Treaty of Riga with Russia signed, recognized independence of Latvia, and defined frontier, Latvia to receive 4,000,000 gold rubles and valuable timber concessions and statement of nonliability for Russian State debts

Aug. 21, Alfred Nagel, Secretary to Latvian Legation, Washington arrested on arrival in the United States by immigration authorities because of alleged German activities during the War and his recall asked for which was granted

Sept. 16–17, National land reform law provided for expropriation of large estates

Sept. 28, Convention with Lithuania signed for settlement of frontier controversy by arbitration commission

Oct. 12, Russo-Polish Treaty established frontiers of Latvia with Poland

1921

Jan. 26, *De jure* independence of Latvia recognized by Supreme Council of Allied Powers

Feb. 6, Independence recognized by Sweden and Denmark

Feb. 18, Law enacted provided for civil marriage

May 14, Second Frontier Convention with Lithuania signed

June 3, Ulmanis Ministry resigned

June 15, M. Meierowitz formed Cabinet

July 12, Political and military Agreement with Estonia

July 21–22, Baltic Conference at Reval

July 22, Convention with Russia regarding option of nationality signed

Aug. 3, Treaty of friendship and commerce with the Ukraine signed

Sept. 4, Commercial Treaty with Germany signed

Sept. 22, Latvia admitted to membership in the League of Nations

Oct. 20, Agreement as to Aaland Islands signed by Latvia. *See* Åland Islands

Dec. 16, Treaty with Russia signed

1922

Feb. 15, National Constitution completed by Constituent Assembly

March 13–17, Warsaw Conference. *See* Poland

March 17, Political Agreement signed with Estonia, Poland, Finland

March 24, Act regulated hours of labor

March 28, Commercial Agreement with Germany signed

March 29, Riga Conference

May 6, Commercial Agreement with Great Britain signed

May 30, Concordat with the Vatican signed

July 14, Consular Convention with Lithuania signed

July 27, Recognition of Government by the United States

Sept. 22, Commercial Agreement with Hungary signed

Oct. 7, Commercial Agreement with Czechoslovakia signed

Oct. 7–8, Elections held for first Parliament a victory for Social Democrats

Nov. 1, Bank of Latvia opened

Nov. 7, New Constitution came into effect and first Parliament (Saeima) met

Nov. 14, J. Chapste elected President. Coalition Cabinet formed headed by J. Pauluks as Prime Minister

1923

March 2–10, Economic Conference of Baltic States and Poland at Helsingfors

March 27, University Education Act

April 7, Frontier Agreement with Russia concluded

June 22, Treaty of commerce and navigation with Great Britain signed

July 7, Declaration as to protection of minorities made before Council of League of Nations

Oct. 16, Extradition Treaty with the United States signed

Nov. 1, Treaty of defensive alliance and frontiers, customs union, claims signed with Estonia

1924

Jan. 1, Use of metric system came into effect

Jan. 16, Resignation of Meierovics Cabinet. Succeeded by W. Samuels

July 2, Commercial Agreement with the Netherlands concluded

Aug. 9, Commercial Treaty with Austria signed

Aug. 14, Commercial Agreement with Norway concluded

Dec. 2, Resignation of Cabinet of W. Samuels

Dec. 4, Commercial Agreement with Switzerland concluded

Dec. 16, Coalition Cabinet formed by Hugo Celmins, Meierovics, Foreign Affairs

Dec. 22, Commercial Agreement with Sweden concluded

1925

Jan. 3, Treaty of friendship with Turkey signed

Jan. 17, Treaty of arbitration and conciliation, communication facilities signed with Estonia, Finland, Poland, and Lithuania

Feb. 23, Police raided central office of trade unions finding communistic documents, 20 persons arrested

March 17, Teachers' Pension Act

March 28, Conciliation Convention with Sweden concluded

May 1, Air mail route opened to Lithuania, Estonia, Finland, Russia

July 4, Commercial Treaty with Japan signed

July 7, Commercial Treaty with Belgium signed

July 25, Commercial Treaty with Italy signed

Aug. 13, War Debt Agreement with Great Britain signed

Aug. 22, M. Meierovics, Minister of Foreign Affairs, killed in motor accident

Oct. 5, Election for Parliament held

Nov. 6, Chaktse reëlected President by new Parliament

Dec. 14, Provisional Commercial Treaty with Lithuania signed

1926

Jan. 12, Trial of Communists at Riga, 19 charged with plot to overthrow the Government. Prison sentences imposed

Feb. 1, Provisional Commercial Agreement with the United States signed

April 28, Resignation of Ulmanis Ministry. Succeeded by A. Alberings (Peasants League) as Prime Minister and Minister of War

June 3, Dr. Kasimir Grinius elected President

July 16, Agreement with Russia providing for settlement of frontier dispute

Sept. 28, Non-Aggression Pact with Russia signed

Oct. 21, Treaty of arbitration and neutrality with Russia signed

Dec. 18, New Socialist Government came into office, Skujenieks

1927

Feb. 5, Draft Customs Convention Union with Estonia

March 14, Death of Jan Chakste, first President

April 8, Gustav M. Zemgals (Democratic Central Party) elected President

June 1, Accident Insurance law passed for workers

June 2, Trade Agreement with Russia signed

——, Nationality law passed

Oct. 10, Convention with Russia as to arbitral procedure in civil and commercial affairs signed

Oct. 15, Frontier Treaty with Lithuania signed

Dec. 13, Fall of Socialist-Popular Ministry
Dec. 22, Provisional Commercial Treaty with Poland
signed

1928

Jan. 14, Peter Juraszewski, Conservative, formed
Cabinet
April 8, Gustav Zemgalis elected President
April 20, Treaty of friendship and commerce with the
United States signed
May 28, Treaty of commerce and navigation with
Turkey signed
June 21, Legal Agreement with Sweden signed
July 24, Court martial sentenced 4 state employees
charged with spying for Russia to be hanged, 4 to
life-imprisonment, and 11 others to prison terms
Aug. 22, Attempt of Communists to bring about a
general strike because of closing of offices of extrem-
ist unions a failure
Oct. 7, Election held under French parliamentary
system resulted in defeat of the Government. More
than 2,000 persons offered as candidates by States
representing 44 political parties
Oct. 18, Treaty of commerce and navigation with Yugoslavia signed
Nov. 13, Resignation of Juraszewski Ministry
——, Attempt to assassinate President Zemgals frustrated by police
Nov. 30, Hugo Celmins, Agrarian, took office as
Premier

1929

Jan. 15, Treaty of friendship with Persia signed
Feb. 12, Treaty of commerce and navigation with
Poland signed
Sept. 10, Latvia signed Option clause of Permanent
Court
Oct. 18, Socialists called one day strike against the
Government. Not effective

1930

Jan. 14, Treaty of arbitration and conciliation with
the United States signed
Feb. 28, Treaty of arbitration and conciliation with
Denmark signed
March 4, Resignation of Albering, Minister of Agricul-
ture, because of attacks on him
April 8, Resignation of President Zemgals before com-
pletion of his term
April 9, Albert Kvesis (Kriesis) elected President
Aug. 31, Treaty of arbitration and conciliation with
Hungary signed
Nov. 24, Arbitration and conciliation Agreement with
Lithuania signed

THE LEAGUE OF NATIONS

The League of Nations is an association of States
which have pledged themselves through signing
the Covenant (i.e., the constitution of the League)
not to go to war before submitting their disputes
with each other or States not members of the
League to arbitration or enquiry and a delay of
from three to nine months. Furthermore, any
State violating this pledge is automatically in a
state of outlawry with the other States, which are
bound to sever all economic and political relations
with the defaulting member. The States Members
of the League have pledged themselves to cooperate over a wide range of economic, social,
humanitarian, and labor questions.

The League of Nations formally came into
existence on January 10, 1920, through the coming
into force at that date of the Treaty of Versailles,
the Covenant being Part I of the Peace Treaties
made with Germany, Austria, Hungary, and Bulgaria. The two official languages of the League are
English and French. The seat of the League is
Geneva, Switzerland.

The primary organs of the League are:—
1. The Council.
2. The Assembly.
3. The Secretariat.
4. The International Labor Organization.
5. The Permanent Court of International Justice (at the Hague).
Secretary-General.—Sir James Eric Drummond

1919

Jan. 25, Resolution for the creation of a League of Nations "to promote international coöperation, to
ensure the fulfilment of accepted international obligations and to provide safeguards against war"
adopted by the Peace Conference in Paris, the League
to be treated "as an integral part of the general
Treaty of Peace"
——, A Commission of 15 members appointed to work
out the details of the constitution and functions of
the League (2 members each representing the United
States, British Empire, France, Italy, and Japan, and
5 members to represent all the Powers with special
interests)
Jan. 27, Belgium, Brazil, China, Portugal, and Serbia
chosen by League of Nations Commission (5 Great
Powers) to designate one representative each for the
Commission
Feb. 14, First draft of the Covenant prepared by the
Commission (the Hurst-Miller draft of Mr. Cecil
Hurst of Great Britain and Mr. David Hunter
Miller of the United States) presented at the plenary
session of the Peace Conference by President Woodrow Wilson
April 11, Announcement that Geneva, Switzerland to
be the seat of the League
April 28, Revised and amended draft of the Covenant
presented at the plenary session of the Peace Con-
ference and accepted
June 28, Treaty of Peace with Germany signed by
the Allies at Versailles, the Covenant of the League
of Nations, Articles 1–26, Part I
——, Minorities Treaty of the Allies with Poland
placed protection of minorities in Poland under
guarantee of the League of Nations
Aug. 9, Minorities Treaty of the Allies with Rumania
placed protection of minorities in Rumania under
guarantee of the League of Nations
Sept. 10, Treaty of Peace between the Allies and
Austria included the Covenant as Part I and contained minority clauses placed under guarantee of
the League of Nations for protection of minorities

in Austria, Rumania, Czechoslovakia, and Yugo-slavia, Oct. 22, 1920

Oct. 29–Nov. 29, International Labor Conference held in Washington under auspices of the League of Nations. *See* International Labor Office

Nov. 27. Treaty of Peace between the Allies and Bulgaria included the Covenant as Part I and clauses regarding protection of minorities placed under the guarantee of the League of Nations

1920

Jan. 10, The League of Nations came legally into existence with the exchange of ratifications of the Treaty of Versailles, Sir James Eric Drummond, appointed first Secretary General by the Peace Conference named in Annex to the Covenant

Original members of the League of Nations. Signatories of the Treaty of Peace: Belgium, Bolivia, Brazil, British Empire (Canada, Australia, South Africa, New Zealand, India), China,* Cuba, Czecho-Slovakia, Ecuador, France, Greece, Guatemala, Haiti, Hejaz, Honduras, Italy, Japan, Liberia, Nicaragua, Panama, Peru, Poland, Portugal, Rumania, Serbia, Siam, Uruguay

States Invited to Accede to the Covenant: Argentine Republic, Chile, Colombia, Denmark, Netherlands, Norway, Paraguay, Persia, Salvador, Spain, Sweden, Switzerland, Venezuela. The following States became members Jan. 10, under declarations of adherence to Covenant, Argentina, July 18; Chile, Nov. 4; Persia, Nov. 21; Paraguay, Dec. 26, 1919; and Spain, Jan. 10, 1920

Jan. 16, First meeting of the Council in Paris, Leon Bourgeois presiding, Saar Basin Frontier Commission appointed

Feb. 10, The Serb-Croat-Slovene State became member of the League of Nations

Feb. 11–13, Second meeting of the Council in Paris, Advisory Committee of Jurists appointed to draft plan for a court of international justice in conformity with Article 14 of the Covenant, the 10 members citizens of countries members of the League except Elihu Root, American; Saar Basin Governing Commission appointed, and High Commissioner of Free City of Danzig, the Permanent Health Organization established, chief subjects considered an international financial conference under auspices of the League, the order of procedure of the Council, entry of Switzerland into the League, communications and transit, minorities, and health

Feb. 16, Colombia became a member of the League of Nations

March 3, Venezuela became a member of the League of Nations

March 5, Norway became a member of the League of Nations

March 8, Denmark, Switzerland, and Cuba became members of the League of Nations

March 9, Sweden became a member of the League of Nations

——, The Netherlands became a member of the League of Nations

March 13, Third meeting of the Council in Paris, discussion of campaign against typhus in Eastern Europe, and of a commission of investigation to Russia

March 17, International Commission on Communications and Transit accepted invitation of the League

* Joined the League July 16, 1920

and transformed itself into Provisional Committee of the League of Nations

March 30, Greece became original member of the League

April 8, Portugal became original member of the League of Nations

April 9–11, Fourth meeting of the Council in Paris, discussion of the status of Armenia, Council mandate refused, decision to appoint a High Commissioner for repatriation of prisoners of war, post accepted by Dr. Nansen, and a commission to examine question of chemical warfare

April 13, First meeting Permanent Health Organization

May 9, Commission to examine question of chemical warfare appointed

May 14–19, Fifth meeting of the Council in Rome, Permanent Advisory Commission on military, naval, and air matters constituted, Financial Conference at Brussels in September decided on and a Commission of Investigation to Russia, Advisory Economic Committee on Statistics, and Advisory Committee on Opium, the protest of Germany as to Eupen and Malmedy considered

June 4, Treaty of Peace between the Allies and Hungary signed at Trianon, the Covenant of the League of Nations, Part I, clauses for protection of minorities, placed under guarantee of the League of Nations

June 14–16, Sixth meeting of the Council in London, Persian appeal for intervention against aggression of Russia refused

June 16–July 24, Advisory Committee of Jurists met at The Hague and drew up draft Constitution for the Permanent Court of International Justice

June 30, Haiti became original member of the League

July 9–12, Seventh meeting of the Council in London, Aaland Islands (Jurists Commission) approved

July 15, President Wilson issued call for first meeting of the Assembly of the League of Nations at Geneva, Switzerland, on Nov. 15

July 16, China became original member of the League

July 30–Aug. 5, Eighth meeting of the Council at San Sebastian, Spain, subjects considered the protest of the Hejaz against French action in Syria, constitution of Permanent Court of International Justice (jurists' report), obligations of the League as to mandates

Aug. 3–5, First meeting at San Sebastian of Permanent Advisory Commission on naval, military, and air matters

Aug. 10, Treaty of Peace between the Allies and Turkey signed at Sèvres, the Covenant, Part I

——, Minorities Treaty of the Allies with Greece placed protection of minorities in Greece under guarantee of the League of Nations

Sept. 16–20, Ninth meeting of the Council in Paris, discussion of Polish-Lithuanian dispute over Vilna, Aaland Islands, transfer of Eupen and Malmedy to Belgium

Sept. 24–Oct. 8, International Financial Conference held in Brussels under auspices of the League attended by representatives of 39 nations

Oct. 10, First meeting of Advisory Economic Committee on Statistics

Oct. 20–28, Tenth meeting of the Council in Brussels, Permanent Mandates Commission appointed, Commission of Investigation on the Aaland Islands appointed, and Provisional Advisory Financial and Economic Committee; discussion of League obligations to as the protection of minorities, and Polish-Lithuanian controversy

Oct. 27, Headquarters of the League transferred from London to Geneva, Switzerland

Nov. 3, Honduras and Nicaragua became members League of Nations

Nov. 14–Dec. 18, Eleventh meeting of the Council at Geneva, Statute of the Permanent Court of International Justice approved with amendments, Amendments to Covenant and the Class C mandates, South West Africa, Samoa, New Guinea, Islands north of the equator in the west Pacific and the Island of Nauru, Provisional Financial Committee appointed

Nov. 15–Dec. 18, First Assembly met at Geneva, Paul Hymans of Belgium, first president, representatives of 42 Member States present except Honduras, and during the session 6 States admitted, Albania, Austria, Bulgaria, Costa Rica, Finland, Luxembourg. Six committees appointed: (1) General Procedure and Amendments, (2) Technical Organization, (3) Permanent Court of International Justice, (4) Applications for Admission, (5) Secretariat and Budget, (6) Disarmament, Mandates, and Economic Blocade. Subjects discussed Amendments to the Covenant proposal of Canada as to abrogation of Article X, organization of the Secretariat, relations between the Council and Assembly and with the technical organizations of the League, method of selection of non-permanent members of the Council, registration of treaties, relief of children in countries affected by the War, repatriation of prisoners of war, mandates, minorities, opium, traffic in women and children, reduction of armaments, motion that the Spanish language be given official status with English and French in proceedings and publications, permanent rules of procedure adopted, and organizations in charge of health, communications, and transit, economics and finance, and intellectual coöperation established, Permanent Court Statute approved

Nov. 25–Dec. 10, First meeting of the Provisional Advisory Financial and Economic Committee

1921

Feb. 21–March 3, Twelfth meeting of the Council in Paris, a Permanent Advisory Committee on Opium appointed, a Temporary Mixed Commission on Disarmament, and a Commission of Inquiry into Deportations in the Near East, a Committee on Amendments to the Covenant, Provisional Health Committee; discussion of Vilna dispute

March 10–April 20, Conference on freedom of communications and transit held under auspices of the League at Barcelona attended by representatives of 43 States, 2 Draft Conventions adopted and Declaration

May 2–5, First session of Permanent Advisory Opium Committee

May 5, Provisional Health Committee met in Paris

June 17–28, Thirteenth meeting of the Council in Geneva, decision given on Aaland Islands, consideration of Vilna dispute, Albanian frontiers, Saar Basin, Provisional Health Committee reconstituted

June 30–July 5, Conference to consider measures for suppression of traffic in women and children met in Geneva

July 16–19, First meeting of the Temporary Mixed Commission for reduction of armaments in Paris

July 25–28, First meeting of Committee on Communications and Transit

Aug. 22–28, First meeting of International Blockade Committee

Aug. 25–29, Meeting of the new Provisional Health Committee

Aug. 29–Sept. 1, Extraordinary Session of Council in Geneva on Upper Silesia boundaries

Aug. 30–Oct. 12, Fourteenth meeting of the Council in Geneva, appointment of Saar Basin Governing Commission

Sept. 5–Oct. 5, Second Assembly met at Geneva, Paul Hymans of Belgium, president, representatives of 42 out of 48 Member States present, 3 States admitted during the session, Estonia, Latvia, and Lithuania, judges of the Permanent Court of International Justice elected, subjects considered included Amendments to Articles 4, 6, 12, 13, 15, 16, and 26 of the Covenant, method of selection of non-permanent members of the Council, publicity of debates of Council, registration of treaties, economic blockade, disputes between Poland and Lithuania, the Tacna-Arica dispute between Bolivia and Chile, disputes between Yugoslavia and Albania, and Yugoslavia and Austria, status of East Galicia, status of Armenia, coördination of intellectual work, Dr. Nansen's Report on repatriation of prisoners of war, and famine in Russia, reduction of armaments, deportations in Asia Minor, allocation of expenses of League among members, Draft Convention traffic in women and children approved

Oct. 4–9, First meeting Permanent Mandates Commission

Nov. 16–19, Fifteenth meeting of the Council in Paris considered the advance of Yugoslav forces into Albania

Dec. 12–14, Health Conference on sera and serological tests

1922

Jan. 10–14, Sixteenth meeting of the Council in Geneva, subjects considered included Report of Commission on Albania, the Vilna dispute between Poland and Lithuania, the progress of German-Polish negotiations as to Upper Silesia, and Aaland Islands (guarantee obligations accepted), Permanent Advisory Committee on traffic in women and children constituted

March 8–24, Seventeenth meeting of the Council in Paris appointed a Temporary Mixed Commission on Armaments, considered subjects of Russian refugees, Warsaw Anti-Epidemic Conference (see Poland), and Saar Basin (consultative Council and examining committee constituted)

May 11–17, Eighteenth meeting of the Council in Geneva, provisional boundaries in Vilna dispute recommended, appointment of presidents of Mixed Commission and Court of Arbitration in Upper Silesia, and consideration of minorities in Upper Silesia and Poland, decision 1 member of Committee of Inquiry remain in Albania, Russian refugees considered, Committee of Intellectual Coöperation appointed

June 28, First meeting Permanent Advisory Committee on traffic in women and children

July 3–7, Meeting of Temporary Mixed Commission for reduction of armaments

July 17–24, Nineteenth meeting of the Council in London, Class A and B mandates approved: A, Mesopotamia (Iraq), Palestine, Syria; B, comprising the ex-German central African colonies, Togoland, Cameroons, Tanganyika, and Ruanda (*see also* p. 566), competence of International Labor Office referred to the Permanent Court of International Justice, discussion of reduction of armaments and marauding bands of Bulgarians

Aug. 1–5, First session of International Committee on Intellectual Coöperation

Aug. 31–Oct. 4, Twentieth to Twenty-Second meeting of the Council in Geneva increased number of members of Council selected by Assembly from 4 to 6, scheme drafted and protocols signed for Austrian reconstruction, discussion of Holy Places in Palestine, the Transjordan (Palestine) mandate, Hungarian frontier, German colonists in Poland, Albania (financial adviser) and the permanent representation on Governing Body of the International Labor Office

Sept. 4–30, Third Assembly met at Geneva, Agustin Edwards of Chile, president, representatives of 46 Member States present, Hungary admitted to membership Sept. 18. Subjects discussed included nonpermanent members of Council, protection of minorities, allocation of expenses, Vilna dispute, hostilities in the Near East. Resolution adopted as to Treaty of mutual guarantee, and draft Convention for control of private manufacture of armaments, Dr. Nansen's Report on repatriation of prisoners of war accepted

1923

Jan. 29–Feb. 3, Twenty-third meeting of the Council in Paris considered Austrian reconstruction, Hungarian-Czech and Turkish-Iraq frontiers, Vilna boundary, Greek refugees loan, question of Polish Minority Treaty referred to Permanent Court of International Justice, plan for constitution of Permanent Health Organization adopted

April 17–23, Twenty-fourth session of the Council in Geneva discussed Austrian reconstruction (long term loan), mandated territories (nationality of native inhabitants), Hungarian-Rumanian expropriation dispute, Vilna frontier dispute, Hungarian-Czech frontiers referred to Permanent Court of International Justice, and Bulgarian armaments

July 2–7, Twenty-fifth meeting of the Council in Geneva considered amendments to Covenant, Greek refugees, administration of Saar Basin, question of German colonists in Poland referred to Permanent Court of International Justice, Draft Convention Permanent Health Organization approved

July 24, Treaty of Peace of the Allies with Turkey (Lausanne) placed stipulations as to protection on non-Moslem minorities under the guarantee of the League of Nations

July 26–Aug. 2, Second session of International Committee for Intellectual Coöperation

Aug. 3–8, Temporary Mixed Commission on reduction of armaments adopted Draft Treaty of Mutual Assistance

Aug. 31–Sept. 12, International Conference for the suppression of the circulation of and traffic in obscene publications

Aug. 31–Sept. 29, Twenty-sixth meeting of the Council in Geneva, discussion of Italian occupation of Corfu, Czech-Polish boundary dispute, frontiers of British and Belgian mandated territories (Ruanda), German

colonists in Poland, Hungarian reconstruction, exchange of Greek and Turkish populations, Draft Treaty of Mutual Assistance

Sept. 3–29, Fourth Assembly, met in Geneva, Dr. Cosme de la Torriente y Peraza of Cuba, president, representatives of 49 Member States present, Abyssinia and the Irish Free State admitted to membership during the session, Report of the Opium Committee adopted, subjects considered included Italians in Corfu, election of non-permanent members of the Council, armaments, and Draft Treaty of Mutual Assistance, financial adviser to Albania appointed

Sept. 10, Provisional Financial Committee became permanent committee

Sept. 12, New Convention for suppression of obscene publications opened for signature

Sept. 24, Protocol for arbitration of commercial disputes adopted and signed

Oct. 15–Nov. 2, International Customs Conference held in Geneva on customs formalities and agreement on draft Convention for simplification of customs

Nov. 3–Dec. 13, First Conference for gradual suppression of use and preparation of opium

Nov. 15–Dec. 8, Second Conference on freedom of communications and transit in Geneva, 4 draft Conventions and Statutes adopted

Nov. 17–Dec. 16, Second Conference to consider limitation of production of export of raw opium and manufacture of morphine and other drugs

Dec. 10–20, Twenty-seventh meeting of the Council in Paris, Plan of Finance Committee for Hungarian reconstruction adopted, German colonists in Poland Memel (Commission of investigation appointed), Czech-Polish frontier (advisory opinion of Permanent Court accepted by both countries)

1924

Jan. 15–24, Special Commission of Jurists met in Geneva to consider questions of interpretation of the Covenant, Corfu, and other international questions

Feb. 4–7, Ninth meeting of Temporary Mixed Commission on reduction of armaments

Feb. 11–21, First session of Permanent Health Committee in Geneva

Feb. 14–25, Naval Conference in Rome under auspices of the League. *See* p. 568

March 6–11, and 28–29, Meetings of Preparatory Committee for the Opium Conference

March 10–15, Twenty-eighth meeting of the Council in Geneva, subjects discussed included Czech-Polish frontier, Javorzina settled, Memel (Convention accepted), Corfu, Albanian finance, Austrian and Hungarian reconstruction, Saar Basin, Dantzig, minorities, slavery, communications and transit, &c.

March 10, Salvador admitted to membership

April 1–8, Special Body of Experts on inquiry into the traffic in women and children met in first session

June 9–12, First meeting Temporary Commission to investigate slavery, Anti-Slavery Commission constituted

June 11–17, Twenty-ninth meeting of the Council in Geneva, subjects discussed included Yugoslav-Albanian frontier (St. Naoum district) Iraq frontier, Austrian and Hungarian reconstruction, German settlers in Poland, control of ex-enemy armaments, Albanian famine, Armenian, Greek, and Russian refugees, intellectual coöperation, traffic in women and children, and Saar Basin, Temporary Commission on slavery appointed

July 7–12, Tenth session of the Temporary Mixed Commission on reduction of armaments

July 9–12, First meeting of the Temporary Committee on slavery

July, Distribution by League of Nations of Draft Treaty for disarmament and security prepared by Americans, James T. Shotwell, David Hunter Miller, General Tasker Bliss, and others, which defined aggression and aggressor

Aug. 13, Amendment to Article 6 of the Covenant came into effect

Aug. 29–Oct. 3, Thirtieth meeting of the Council in Geneva, subjects discussed included Mosul question, Iraq frontier, protection of minorities, Austrian reconstruction, Greek refugees, Protocol for the pacific settlement of international disputes, Albanian frontiers and famine, Greek refugees, control of ex-enemy armaments

Sept. 1–Oct. 2, Fifth Assembly met in Geneva, Giuseppe Motta of Switzerland, president, representatives of 50 out of 54 Member States present, Argentina, Bolivia, Honduras, and Peru not represented, attendance of 7 Prime Ministers including those of Great Britain and France, and 16 Ministers of Foreign Affairs, the Dominican Republic admitted to membership. The Protocol for the pacific settlement of international disputes approved and adopted, declared aggressive war an international crime, aggression defined as refusal to arbitrate, subjects considered included amendment to Article 16 of the Covenant, status of Georgia, reconstruction of Austria and Hungary, reduction of armaments, limitation of naval armaments, codification of international law, opium, institute for unification of private law, legal assistance to the indigent, inter-municipal coöperation, health, traffic in women and children, mandates, &c. Temporary Mixed Commission to be reorganized as Commission of Coördination

Sept. 16, Amendment to Article 15 of the Covenant came into effect

Sept. 26, Amendment to Article 12 of the Covenant came into effect

Sept. 29, Santo Domingo (Dominican Republic) admitted to membership of League

Sept. 29–Oct. 4, Third session of Permanent Health Committee

Oct. 27–31, Thirty-first meeting (extraordinary) of the Council in Brussels, subjects considered included Mosul question (Iraq frontier), Greeks in Constantinople, exchange of Greek and Turkish populations

Nov. 3–Feb. 11, 1925, First Conference for gradual suppression of use and preparation of opium held in Geneva

Nov. 17–Feb. 19, 1925, Second Opium Conference held in Geneva to consider the limitation of export and production of raw opium and the manufacture of morphine and similar drugs. The United States officially represented at this conference under auspices of the League

Dec. 8–13, Thirty-second meeting of the Council in Rome, Committee for the codification of internal law appointed, and Committee for international relief of peoples overtaken by disaster, subjects considered included the settlement of the Czech-

Polish frontier, Ottoman public debt, mixed arbitral tribunals, private manufacture of arms, control of ex-enemy armaments, social insurance funds in Upper Silesia, Corfu, Report of American Commission on Memel dispute headed by Norman Davis accepted, question of Greeks in Constantinople

Dec. 24, Costa Rica notified Secretariat of withdrawal from League to take effect Jan. 1, 1927

1925

Jan. 19–Feb. 19, Second Opium Conference which had adjourned Dec. 16 resumed

Feb. 6, The American delegation headed by Stephen Porter withdrew from the Second Opium Conference on failure of American program, Chinese delegation also withdrew

Feb. 11, Agreement and Protocol signed (First Conference) dealing with opium smoking by representatives of 10 countries

Feb. 19, Opium Convention providing for more effective restriction of the production and manufacture of narcotics and establishing stricter control and supervision of the international trade signed by 10 countries (Second Conference)

March 9–14, Thirty-third meeting of the Council in Geneva to consider demand of Germany for admission to League, discussed financial position of Estonia, Austrian and Hungarian reconstruction, Greek and Armenian refugees, Protocol for the pacific settlement of disputes, and expulsion of ecumenical Patriarch from Constantinople, postal dispute between Dantzig and Poland. Report of Permanent Advisory Committee on military, naval, and air questions

April 1–8, First meeting of Committee of experts for progressive codification of international law appointed by Council Dec. 12, 1924, eleven sub-committees appointed

May 4–June 17, International Conference on the control of the international trade in arms, munitions, and implements of war in Geneva under auspices of the League of Nations, Arms Traffic Convention drawn up and opened for signature, and Protocol prohibiting use of asphyxiating and poison gases in war

May 20–27, First meeting of reconstituted Permanent Advisory Committee on traffic in women and protection of children

May 25–28, First meeting of International Relief Union

June 7–11, Thirty-fourth meeting of the Council in Geneva, subjects considered, termination of financial control in Austria and Hungary, minorities in Greece, Lithuania, and Rumania, social insurance funds in Upper Silesia, Greek refugees, expulsion of ecumenical Patriarch from Constantinople, economic inquiry in Austria, collaboration of League with Interparliamentary Conference on commerce, Polish postal service in Danzig

June 17, Arms Traffic Convention for supervision of international trade in arms and ammunition signed by representatives of 18 countries including the United States

——, Protocol prohibiting use of asphyxiating and poison gases in war signed, also each State signatory undertaking to recognize the illegality of chemical and bacteriological warfare

July 27–30, International Committee for Intellectual Coöperation, sixth session, Statute of International

Institute of Intellectual Coöperation in Paris as offered by France adopted

Sept. 2–28, Thirty-fifth meeting of the Council in Geneva, subjects considered included report on survivals of slavery in the world, Greek refugees, the disputed Mosul boundary (Commission of investigation of boundary appointed), Austrian and Hungarian financial reconstruction, protection of children and women in the Near East, Memel, Poland-Danzig dispute

Sept. 7–26, Sixth Assembly met at Geneva, Raoul Dandurand of Canada, president, representatives of 49 out of 54 Member States present, Argentina, Bolivia, Costa Rica, Honduras, and Peru not represented, subjects considered included disarmament and security, the situation in China, adoption of amendment to Article 16 of the Covenant, and interpretation of the Covenant, inter-municipal coöperation, protection and welfare of children, collaboration of the press in organization of peace and the usual reports of committees of the League on transit, health, minorities, Austrian and Hungarian reconstruction. Draft Convention for the suppression of slavery approved, the Council asked to make a preparatory study with a view to a conference for reduction and limitation of armaments

Oct. 8–Nov. 6, Conference at The Hague to consider reversal of Industrial Property Convention of 1911

Oct. 26–30, Thirty-sixth (extraordinary) meeting of the Council in Paris to deal with frontier dispute of Bulgaria and Greece in virtue of Articles 10 and 11 of the Covenant

Nov. 20–27, Conference on unification of system of gauging tonnage of vessels on inland waterways in Europe held in Paris, Convention adopted

Dec. 7–16, Thirty-seventh meeting of the Council in Geneva, subjects considered included Greco-Bulgarian frontier, Mosul question, and the Preparatory Commission for the Disarmament Conference established to include delegates from the 10 States represented on the Council and 1 each from Germany, the United States and Russia, Bulgaria, Finland, Yugoslavia, the Netherlands, Poland, and Rumania, and list of questions to be submitted to this commission agreed upon, decision given of the "Brussels line" as the northern boundary of Iraq

1926

Jan. 12–29, Second session of the Committee of experts for the progressive codification of international law in Geneva

Jan. 16, Institute of Intellectual Coöperation inaugurated in Paris

Feb. 10, Formal application of Germany for admission to membership in the League of Nations received by the Secretary General

Feb. 12, Thirty-eighth meeting of the Council in Geneva to consider the admission of Germany to the League of Nations, Assembly convened

Feb. 16–March 6, Permanent Mandates Commission met in extraordinary session in Rome to consider the report on the Syrian mandate by France

March 8–17, Seventh Assembly (extraordinary session) met at Geneva, Affonso Augusto da Costa of Portugal, president, representatives of 48 Member States present, to consider the admission of Germany, decision made to postpone the question of admission of Germany to the September meeting because of disagreement as to composition of the Council, Brazil prepared to veto the admission of Germany unless Brazil should receive a permanent seat on the Council

March 8–18, Thirty-ninth meeting of the Council in Geneva, failure to agree on composition of Council, Spain, Poland, and Brazil claiming permanent seats, Statute for Institute for unification of private law at Rome adopted, discussion of reservations of the United States to the Protocol of Permanent Court of International Justice

March 22–April 1, Meeting of Advisory Committee on protection and welfare of children

April 26–May 1, First session Preparatory Committee for Economic Conference

May 12–18, International Conference on passports

May 18–26, First meeting of the Preparatory Commission for Disarmament Conference met in Geneva, 18 countries represented including Germany and the United States, Russia invited, declined membership, Sub-Commissions appointed, A— to deal with military, naval, and air questions, and B— to deal with economic and non-military questions

May 26, First session Sub-Commission B (Disarmament)

May 28–July 6, First session Sub-Commission A (Disarmament)

June 7–10, Fortieth meeting of the Council in Geneva, considered question of composition of the Council, termination of work of Austrian and Hungarian financial reconstruction, and preparations for an international economic conference, Spain announced withdrawal from League (June 10) in opposition to reconstitution of Council, and Brazil gave preliminary notice of withdrawal (June 10) the official telegram received June 14

June 28–July 1, Joint Commission (to advise Preparatory Commission for Disarmament Conference)

July 9, Amendment to Article 4 of the Covenant as to election of non-permanent members came into effect

Aug. 2–9, Second session Sub-Commission B (Disarmament)

Sept. 1–22, Committee on American reservations to Permanent Court of International Justice adopted Final Act recommending acceptance of first 4 but not the 5th reservation

Sept. 2–7, Forty-first meeting of the Council in Geneva, the Report of the Committee appointed to consider the reorganization of the Council accepted, giving permanent seat on the Council to Germany, but non-permanent members increased to 9, Spain to be offered non-permanent seat

Sept. 6–25, Seventh Assembly met in Geneva, Momtchilo Nintchich of Yugoslavia, president, representatives of 48 Member States present out of 55, no representatives from Spain, Brazil, Argentina, Bolivia, Costa Rica, Honduras, and Peru, Germany admitted to League as permanent member of the Council Sept. 8, and Sept. 10 the German delegation headed by Dr. Gustav Stressemann took seats in the Assembly, the number of non-permanent members of Council increased to 9, Chile, Poland, and Rumania elected for 3 years, China, Colombia, and the Netherlands for 2 years, and Belgium, Czechoslovakia, and Salvador for 1 year. The formal withdrawal of Spain dated Sept. 8 received Sept. 11, resolutions adopted as to reduction of armaments, composition of Council, and financial, technical, and economic matters, Report of Committee on American reservations to Statute of Permanent Court adopted, Slavery Convention adopted and signed by representatives of 20 States

Sept. 16–29, Forty-second meeting of the Council in Geneva

Sept. 22 and 27, Second session of the Preparatory Commission for Disarmament Conference

Sept. 27–Nov. 5, Third session of Sub-Commission A (Preparatory Disarmament)

Sept. 27, Second session of Sub-Commission B (Preparatory Disarmament)

Sept. 30–Oct. 5 and Oct. 19–27, Joint Commission (to advise Preparatory Commission for Disarmament Conference)

Nov. 3–4, Meeting of Preparatory Committee International Relief Union

Nov. 15–19, Second session of the Preparatory Committee for Economic Conference

Nov. 29–30, Third session of Sub-Commission B (Preparatory Disarmament)

Dec. 6–11, Forty-third meeting of the Council in Geneva considered form of control of German armaments to be exercised by the League when Allied Commission dissolved, banks and currency reform, Estonia, financial restoration of Danzig, Bulgarian refugee settlement plan, question of jurisdiction of Danube Commission referred to the Permanent Court

1927

Jan. 17–20, Conference of health experts on protection of children met in Paris

Jan. 21, Resignation of Costa Rica from the League came into effect

Feb. 7–18, Special Committee of experts appointed by the Council to investigate the traffic in women and children met in Geneva and drew up report

March 7–12, Forty-fourth meeting of the Council in Geneva reviewed progress of social and financial reconstruction, inquiry into opium production in Persia, preparations for economic conference

March 14–April 25, Special Arms Traffic Commission met to draft Convention on the supervision of the private manufacture of arms

March 16–17, Fourth session of Sub-Commission B (Preparatory Disarmament)

March 21–April 26, Third session of the Preparatory Commission for Disarmament Conference considered Draft Conventions for limitation of armaments submitted by British and French delegations

March 22–April 2, Third session of the Committee of experts for the progressive codification of international law

April 25–May 6, Meeting of Permanent Advisory Commission for the protection and welfare of children and young people

May 4–23, International Economic Conference held in Geneva, representatives of 50 countries present including the United States and Russia

June 13–17, Forty-fifth meeting of the Council in Geneva discussed disarmament and security, results of economic conference, and adopted Report of the Committee of experts on codification of international law

July 4–12, Conference for the foundation of an International Relief Union under auspices of the League

adopted Convention and Statute establishing Union for relief of populations stricken by disaster

Aug. 23–Sept. 2, Third Conference on Communications and Transit adopted semi-autonomous constitution and 3 Conventions

Aug. 24–29, International Conference of Journalism Experts

Sept. 1–15, Forty-sixth session of the Council met in Geneva, question of foreign loan to Bulgaria considered, and transport of Polish war material through Danzig, gift of Library building from American group

Sept. 5–27, Eighth Assembly met in Geneva, Alberto Guani of Uruguay, president, representatives of 49 Member States present, no representatives from Brazil, Spain, Argentina, Bolivia, Honduras, and Peru. Cuba, Canada, and Finland elected to serve on Council for 3 years in place of Belgium, Salvador, and Czechoslovakia retiring. Resolutions adopted as to arbitration, security, and disarmament, aggressive war declared an international crime, new Advisory Economic Committee appointed and a League Educational Information Center constituted, and a Committee to coöperate in financial reform of Greece and Bulgaria

Sept. 17–28, Forty-seventh meeting of the Council in Geneva, subjects considered included Rumanian-Hungarian controversy over rights of property owners in territory transferred, work with Preparatory Disarmament Commission and a Preparatory Committee for international codification conference appointed

Oct. 17–Nov. 8, Conference for abolition of import and export prohibitions restrictions met in Geneva and drew up Convention signed by representatives of 18 countries

Nov. 30–Dec. 3, Fourth session of the Preparatory Commission for Disarmament Conference, Russia represented for the first time submitted plan proposal of complete disarmament, new Committee on arbitration and security constituted

Dec. 1–2, First meeting of Committee on arbitration and security (Preparatory Disarmament)

Dec. 5–12, Forty-eighth session of the Council met in Geneva to consider the dispute over expulsion of Polish nationals from Lithuanian territory, and questions of minorities and refugees, Consultative Economic Committee constituted

1928

Feb. 6–15, Meeting of Committee of Jurists charged with preparation for Conference on Codification of International Law

Feb. 20–March 7, Second session of Committee on arbitration and security (Preparatory Disarmament)

Feb. 23–24, Meeting of Preparatory Committee, International Relief Union

Feb. 28–March 5, Tenth session of Committee on Communications and Transit

March 5–10, Forty-ninth meeting of the Council in Geneva, subjects considered included Greek refugees, mandates reports, economic and financial questions, resolutions adopted to invite Brazil and Spain to continue participation in the League and to ask Costa Rica to reverse decision to withdraw

March 12–14, Meeting of Advisory Commission for the protection and welfare of children and young persons

March 15–24, Fifth session of the Preparatory Commission for Disarmament Conference

March 22, Announcement that Spain canceled resignation from the League of Sept. 8, 1929

April 9, Brazil declined to return to membership in League

April 11–17, Meeting of experts on banking statistics

May 14–19, First session of Economic Consultative Committee

June 4–9, Fiftieth meeting of the Council in Geneva, subjects considered included Polish-Lithuanian negotiations, St. Gotthard machine gun incident, Hungarian optants, minorities, decision that allocation of expenses of League be revised before 1930

June 12, Withdrawal of Brazil from the League became effective

June 27–July 4, Third session of the Committee on arbitration and security (Preparatory Disarmament)

July 3–5, Meeting of Committee of health experts on protection of children

July 3–11, Second Conference on abolition of import and export prohibitions and restrictions

Aug. 27–30, Second meeting of Arms Traffic Commission to draft Convention on the supervision of private manufacture of arms

Aug. 30–Sept. 8, Fifty-first meeting of the Council in Geneva approved Draft Statute of International Educational Cinematographic Institute, preparation of measures for Assembly

Sept. 3–26, Ninth Assembly met in Geneva, Herluf Zahle of Denmark, president, representatives of 50 Member States present including Spain. Spain, Persia, and Venezuela elected to succeed China, the Netherlands, and Cuba as non-permanent members of Council, Charles E. Hughes elected to succeed John Bassett Moore as judge of Permanent Court of International Justice, Resolutions adopted General Act for pacific settlement of international disputes, model treaties of non-aggression and mutual assistance and prevention of war, review of work of Council and Secretariat, reorganization of refugee services, decision that settlement of Armenian refugees in Erivan be carried out under League auspices, appointment of Commission to investigate opium in the Far East

Sept. 12–26, Fifty-second meeting of the Council in Geneva devoted to preparing Assembly discussions or measures to give effect to its decisions, Poland and Lithuania advised to settle Vilna dispute by direct negotiation

Oct. 22–31, Meeting of experts on double taxation and tax evasion

Nov. 13–17, Meeting of Permanent Committee on road traffic

Nov. 26–Dec. 14, International Conference on Economic Statistics, Convention adopted

Dec. 5–7, Third session of Arms Traffic Commission

Dec. 10–15, Fifty-third meeting of the Council in Lugano, considered the Bolivia-Paraguay dispute, appointed new committees including Committee of Jurists to examine Statute of Permanent Court

1929

Jan. 15–19, First session of Permanent Central Opium Board

Jan. 28–Feb. 6, Meeting of Committee of experts on unification of transport statistics

Jan. 28–Feb. 17, Meeting of Preparatory Committee for Conference on Codification of International Law

Feb. 25–27, Meeting of Ports and Maritime Navigation Committee in London

March 4–9, Fifty-fourth meeting of the Council in Geneva to consider minorities, mandates, Anglo-Iraq Judiciary Agreement of March 25, 1924, application and extension of 1928 Convention on economic statistics, and Commission to inquire into preparation and consumption of opium in the Far East

March 11–13, Arms Traffic Commission of experts on supervision of manufacture of war material met to consider Belgian proposal for government control of the private manufacture of arms which was rejected

March 11–14, Conference of Institutions for scientific study of international relations held in London

March 11–19, Meeting of Committee of Jurists on amendment of Statute of Court

April 9–20, International Conference for suppression of counterfeit money adopted Convention and Protocol

April 15–May 6, Sixth session of Preparatory Commission for Disarmament Conference

May 6, The Preparatory Commission for Disarmament Conference adjourned for indefinite recess during which the new American plan for naval reductions to be studied

May 6–11, Third and final session of Preparatory Committee for Conference on Codification of International Law

June 10–14, European Conference on transit cards for emigrants held in Geneva under auspices of League and Agreement adopted signed by 11 States

June 10–15, Fifty-fifth meeting of the Council in Madrid, principal question on agenda the protection of minorities, fiscal committee constituted and arrangements made for 4 international conferences, final report of Codification Committee considered, proposals of Committee of Jurists on accession of the United States to Permanent Court adopted, Report on sanitary reorganization of Greece prepared by Health Committee presented to Council

July 1–19, Fifteenth meeting of Permanent Mandates Commission at Geneva considered questions of treatment extended to persons belonging to mandated territories in countries members of the League of Nations and as to products and goods from mandated territories

July 18–20, Conference of National Committees on Intellectual Coöperation

July 22–26, Committee on Intellectual Coöperation (eleventh session) preceded by meetings of subcommittees on university relations, intellectual rights, arts and sciences, sciences and bibliography

Aug. 26–28, Meeting of Financial Committee to study question of gold

Aug. 26–29, Meeting of Special Commission on manufacture of arms

Aug. 30–Sept. 6, Fifty-sixth meeting of the Council in Geneva, preparation of discussions of Assembly, &c.

Sept. 2–25, Tenth Assembly met in Geneva, J. Gustavo Guerrero of Salvador, president, representatives of 53 out of 54 Member States present including 9 Prime Ministers and 20 Ministers of Foreign Affairs, Bolivia, Honduras, and Peru resuming attendance after absence since Second Assembly. Poland, Peru, and Yugoslavia elected non-permanent members of the Council, amendments to Articles 12 and 15 of the Covenant to include Pact of Paris for renunciation of war referred to committee, Sir Cecil Hurst and

Henri Fromageot elected to vacancies in the Permanent Court, Protocol regarding revision of the Statute of the Permanent Court, and Protocol regarding accession of the United States to Protocol of Signature adopted, 15 States including France, Great Britain, and Italy acceded to Optional Clause of Permanent Court Statute recognizing the compulsory jurisdiction of the Court in certain categories of disputes

Sept. 4–13, Conference of signatories of the Statute of the Permanent Court for adoption of the 2 Protocols

Sept. 5, Briand, French Minister of Foreign Affairs, presented plan for European Federal Union before the Assembly

Sept. 7, Cornerstone of new League Building laid in Ariana Park, Geneva

Sept. 9, Proposal of M. Briand of European Federal Union at luncheon to 27 European delegations to the Assembly

Sept. 13–25, Fifty-seventh meeting of the Council in Geneva

Oct. 24–Nov. 1, Thirtieth session of Economic Committee drew up Tariff Truce Convention

Nov. 5–Dec. 4, International Conference on the treatment of foreigners and foreign enterprises held in Paris under the auspices of the League, Protocol adopted

Dec. 5–20, Third Conference on abolition of import and export prohibitions and restrictions, the United States joined 18 other nations in signature of Protocol to bring into active operation the League Convention of Nov. 8, 1927

1930

Jan. 6–9, Meeting of Committee of Agricultural Experts

Jan. 13–16, Fifty-eighth meeting of the Council in Geneva, decision made to convoke Customs Truce Conference, and to constitute Commission to study, define, and settle claims of Jews and Moslems as to Wailing Wall in Palestine, and Commission to study relations of the Covenant to the Pact of Paris. Proposal for independence of Iraq considered and minorities in Lithuania and Upper Silesia

Jan. 20–Feb. 14, Advisory Opium Committee (thirteenth session) drafted plan for direct limitation of manufacture of narcotics

Jan. 28–Feb. 7, First session of Committee of 13 on organization of the Secretariat, International Labor Office and Registry of the Permanent Court of International Justice

Feb. 17–March 24, Conference for concerted economic action held in Geneva attended by delegates from 26 European countries and from Japan, Colombia, and Peru adopted Tariff Truce Convention, Final Act and Protocol on future negotiations

Feb. 25–March 5, Meeting of Committee for amending the Covenant Articles 12, 13, and 15 to bring it into harmony with the Paris Pact

March 13–April 12, First Conference for Codification of International Law met at The Hague, Nationality Convention adopted, no agreement reached on territorial waters or responsibility of States

April 3–5, Meeting of Committee of Experts on protection of the whaling industry

April 2–16, Meeting of Advisory Committee for protection and welfare of young persons and children

April 14–May 2, Committee of Inquiry on the work and organization of the Committee and Institute on Intellectual Coöperation

April 28–May 2, Committee on delays in ratification of Treaties concluded under auspices of the League, a questionnaire prepared for submission to Governments as to proceedings adopted, and accession

April 28–May 9, Committee on Arbitration and Security, Draft Convention adopted as to financial assistance but no agreement on a general convention

May 12–15, Fifty-ninth meeting of the Council in Geneva, reports of Committees considered, preparation for Assembly, discussion of Bolivia-Paraguay dispute, public health program for China

May 13–June 7, Conference for unification of laws on bills of exchange, promissory notes, and cheques, 3 Conventions adopted

May 22–31, Second session of the Fiscal Committee to consider questions referred to it by Conference on double taxation

June 3–21, Permanent Mandates Commission met to consider British Report on Palestine Mandate

June 10–17, Meeting of Gold Delegation

June 16–29, Second session of the Committee of 13 on organization of the Secretariat, International Labor Office, and Registry of the Permanent Court of International Justice

June 18–July 1, Eighteenth session of the Permanent Mandates Commission

July 8–12, First meeting Air Transport Coördination Committee

Aug. 14, Italian Government presented Memorandum to the Secretary General criticizing organization of the Secretariat showing that of 180 "first division" positions 40 were held by nationals of Great Britain, 13 by nationals of the British Dominions, 30 by French nationals, 12 by Italians, 11 by Germans, and less than 10 by any other nationality, the United States, not a member, having 4 nationals on the staff

Sept. 8–12, Sixtieth session of the Council in Geneva adopted Report of the Mandates Commission on Palestine, made decision to recall remaining French and Belgian soldiers from the Saar Valley, and voted to increase the number of judges of the Permanent Court of International Justice

Sept. 10–Oct. 4, Eleventh Assembly met in Geneva, Nicholas Titulesco of Rumania, president, representatives of 52 Member States present, Argentina and Honduras only not represented, Guatemala, Norway, and Irish Free State elected non-permanent members of Council to succeed Cuba, Finland, and Canada, Resolution adopted constituted a Committee on European Federation (Briand plan), Convention for financial assistance to States victims of aggression adopted and signed by representatives of 28 nations, 15 judges and 4 deputy-judges elected to Permanent Court of International Justice, Frank B. Kellogg elected to succeed Charles E. Hughes, International Refugee Office created, Resolution adopted to study the financial depression

Sept. 18–Oct. 3, Sixty-first meeting of the Council in Geneva considered disputes between certain members of the League, decision to call road traffic conference in 1931

Oct. 6–23, First Conference on the Buoyage and Lighting of Coasts held in Lisbon and adopted a series of recommendations and agreements

Oct. 27–Nov. 11, Preliminary meeting of representatives of drug-manufacturing States held in London

Nov. 6–Dec. 9, Final session of the Preparatory Commission for the Disarmament Conference held in

Geneva attended by representatives of 32 States including Russia and the United States

Nov. 17–28, Second Conference for Concerted Economic Action

Nov. 17–Dec. 9, Conference on unification of rules for river law

LIECHTENSTEIN

The Principality of Liechtenstein, lying between the Austrian Land of Vorarlberg and the Swiss cantons of St. Gallen and Graubünden, is a sovereign State consisting of the two counties of Schellenberg and Vaduz (formerly immediate fiefs of the Roman Empire). The former in 1699 and the latter in 1712 came into the possession of the house of Liechtenstein and, by diploma of January 23, 1719, granted by the Emperor Karl VI, the two lordships were constituted as the Principality of Liechtenstein. After the break-up of the Empire in 1806 the Principality was incorporated in the Rhine Confederation; from 1815 to 1866 it formed part of the German Confederation, since the break-up of which it has joined no similar union.

The Reigning Prince is Francis I, born August 28, 1853; succeeded his brother, February 11, 1929. The reigning family originated in the twelfth century, and traces its descent through free barons who in 1608 became princes of Liechtenstein. The monarchy is hereditary in the male line. The constitution, adopted in October 1921, provides for a Diet of 15 members elected for four years by direct vote on the basis of universal suffrage and proportional representation. The capital and seat of Government is Vaduz (pop. 1,715). The Principality has a High Court. Since February 1921, Liechtenstein has had the Swiss currency, and since January, 1924, it has been included in the Swiss Customs Union; the posts and telegraphs are administered by Switzerland.

Area, 65 square miles; population, of German origin (Census 1930), 10,213; Catholics, 9,492; Protestants, 253.

Dr. Joseph Hoop, Administrator.

LITHUANIA

Lithuania (Lietuva), Baltic Republic, of northern Europe, bounded on the north by Latvia, on the east and south by Poland, on the west by Poland, East Prussia, and the Baltic Sea.

Lithuania became a Grand Duchy in the early part of the thirteenth century. In 1386 the Grand Duke Jogaila embraced Christianity and married the Polish Queen Hedvig, thus becoming King of Poland. During the reign of Vytautas (Vitold) the Great (1392–1430) Lithuania reached the zenith of her power and prosperity, her frontiers extending from the Baltic to the Black Sea. After the death of Vytautas the Great, Polish influence gradually increased in Lithuania, and in 1569 the Lithuanians were forced to unite with the Poles at Lublin, the Lithuanians retaining their own treasury, laws, courts of justice, and army. Both countries elected the same king and had a common Seim (parliament).

At the end of the eighteenth century Lithuania fell under Russian rule.

In 1917 a Lithuanian Conference of 200 representatives at Vilna elected a Lithuanian State Council (Taryba) and demanded the complete independence of Lithuania. The independence of the Lithuanian State was proclaimed on February 16, 1918.

On December 20, 1922, Lithuania received *de jure* recognition by the Great Powers. Russia had already accorded that recognition in the Treaty of Peace of July 12, 1920.

The Lithuanian Government claims that Lithuania consists of: (1) the whole of the former Russian Province of Kaunas (Kovno); (2) the Province of Vilnius (Vilna), minus the districts of Disna and Vileika; (3) a part of the Province of Gardinas (Grodno), north of the Niemen River and the narrow hinterland of the city of Gardinas (Grodno) in the south; (4) the Province of Suvalki minus the southern parts of the districts of Suvalki and Augustovo; (5) part of the Province of Courland between the old German frontier and the Holy Aa (Sventoji) River by the Baltic Sea, and (6) the territory of Klaipeda (Memel).

For the northern and eastern frontier of Lithuania, see THE STATESMAN's YEAR BOOK for 1929, p. 1075.

In the south (in the region of the Province of Suvalki) the frontier with Poland has not yet been conclusively agreed upon by Lithuania and Poland. Both Lithuania and Poland lay claim to Vilna, but though the Great Powers (on March 15, 1923) recognized the *de facto* boundary between the two countries as *de jure*, and though the League of Nations has endeavored to bring about a solution of this problem, so far (March, 1930) no agreement has been reached. The southern part of Lithuania occupied by Poland has an area of about 28,000 sq. kilometers (10,808 sq. miles), with a population of 1,025,000.

The total area of Independent Lithuania (including Memel) is 55,670 sq. kilometers (21,489 sq. miles), and the population (1930 estimate) 2,340,038.

The Memel territory (area 2,443 sq. kilometers, population 146,000), which by the Treaty of Versailles was detached from Germany and placed under the control of the conference of ambassadors, was handed over to Lithuania on February 16, 1923, subject to certain conditions intended to regulate the use of the port by both Lithuania and Poland.

The Lithuanians claim that the capital of Lithuania is Vilnius (Vilna), with a population of 214,600 in 1914. Other large towns are: Kaunas (Kovno), seat of the Government, 96,535; Gardinas (Grodno), 61,600; Klaipeda (Memel), 36,633; Suvalkai (Suvalki), 31,600; Siauliai (Shavli), 22,560; and Paneveẑys (Poneviej), 20,142. Of these cities, Vilna, Grodno, and Suvalki are in possession of Poland.

Antanas Smetona, President.

1905

Dec. 6, Congress of Lithuanians convened at Vilna demanded autonomy

1914

Oct. 21–22, Lithuanian Congress met in Chicago in the United States and demanded a Lithuanian State

1915

Aug. 3–4, Lithuanian Convention at Berne, Switzerland

1916

Feb., Lithuanian Convention at Lausanne, Switzerland
March 1–5, Lithuanian Convention at The Hague, Netherlands
April 25–30, Lithuanian Convention at The Hague, Netherlands

1917

May 18, By the Kreuznach Agreement between Austria and Germany Lithuania and Courland to be reunited to Germany
Sept. 18–23, Conference of Lithuanians at Vilna elected a National Council (Taryba) of 20 members and adopted resolutions demanding independence from Russia
Dec. 11, National Council (Taryba) proclaimed independence of Lithuania

1918

Feb. 16, The Taryba made second proclamation of independence
March 23, Germany the first to recognize the independence of Lithuania
May 14, Proclamation of the Kaiser declared Lithuania an independent State in alliance with Germany and that she "will participate in the war burdens of Germany"
June 4, Taryba proclaimed monarchical Constitution and invited William of Urach, Duke of Wurtemberg to be king. He accepted
July 11, The Taryba assumed title of State Council
Aug. 31, State Council elected Duke William of Urach
Oct. 18, Provisional Constitution adopted by the Taryba
Nov. 2, State Council retracted its Act of election of Duke William leaving form of government to be decided by constituent assembly
Nov. 11, First Cabinet formed by Professor August Voldemaras
Dec. 28, Dr. Mykolas Slezevicius, Populist, formed a coalition Cabinet

1919

Jan. 5, Vilna captured by the Bolsheviks as German troops withdrew without notifying the Lithuanian authorities

Jan. 17–23, Provisional National Assembly met at Kaunas
Feb. 16, Agreement with Poland for withdrawal of German troops from Lithuania and its occupation by Polish troops
March, Conservative Ministry formed by Pranas Dovydaitis, Christian Democrat
April 4, Provisional Constitution adopted by Taryba and Antanas Smetonas elected Provisional President to replace Committee of Three and Taryba assumed duties of a provisional Parliament
April 19, Pilsudski commanding Polish troops occupied Vilna despite protests of Lithuanians in order to block one of the main routes from Russia to Poland between the Dvina and the Dnieper Rivers driving out the Bolsheviks
July 16, Act established a Labor Inspection Department
Aug. 22, Norway recognized the Lithuanian Government
Sept. 25, Great Britain recognized the *de facto* Government of Lithuania
Nov. 17, Finland recognized the *de facto* Government
Dec. 8, The Supreme Council laid down provisional eastern boundary for Poland, the "Curzon line" which left disputed Vilna area to Lithuania
Dec. 14, Last German-Russian troops evacuated Lithuania

1920

Jan. 14, Conference at Helsingfors. *See* Finland
April 14–15, Election held for constituent assembly
May 15, Elected Constituent Assembly replaced the Taryba
July 4, *De facto* Government recognized by Poland
July 12, Treaty of Riga, peace treaty with Russia signed which defined boundaries and recognized independence of Lithuania and Vilna as the capital. Debt compensated with 3,000,000 gold rubles. Valuable cessions of forest land made to Lithuania
July 14, Lithuanians moving to occupy Vilna evacuated by Poles in Russo-Polish war attacked by Poles. Bolsheviks again occupied Vilna
Aug. 24, Lithuanians took Vilna evacuated by Russians
Sept. 5, Agreement with Poland to refrain from hostilities as to the Vilna district pending settlement
Sept. 28, Boundary Arbitration Convention with Latvia signed provided for fixing of northern frontier
Oct. 7, Suwalki Agreement by which a Commission of the League of Nations fixed a neutral zone leading to the city of Vilna and along a line running about 40 miles north and south. Lithuania accepted the Truce to go into effect on Oct. 10. Poland agreed not to advance into Lithuanian territory
Oct. 9, General Zeligowski unauthorized by the Polish Government seized Vilna for Poland driving out the Lithuanians
Nov. 8, Lithuania and Poland accepted decision of the League of Nations Council of Oct. 28 that a plebiscite should be held under auspices of the League to decide sovereignty of Vilna
Nov. 29, Armistice Convention signed at Kovno with General Zeligowski

1921

Feb. 12, Recognition of Government by Latvia
March 3, Decision of Council of League of Nations to abandon Vilna plebiscite

March 21, Boundary settlement with Latvia by which Lithuania gained access to the Baltic through Polangen

April 21–June 3, Conference with representatives from Poland at Brussels as to Vilna ended with no agreement

May 14, Frontier Convention with Latvia signed

July 28, Conference with Estonia, Latvia, and Poland at Helsingfors

Sept. 2, *De jure* independence of Lithuania recognized by Denmark and Sweden

Sept. 22, Lithuania admitted as member of the League of Nations

Sept. 30, *De jure* recognition granted by Norway

Oct. 7, *De jure* recognition given by the Netherlands

Oct. 16, *De jure* recognition given by Finland

Dec. 20, Refusal of Lithuania to accept recommendations of Council of the League of Nations as to settlement regarding Vilna

1922

Jan. 8, Plebiscite held at Vilna under the auspices of the Polish General Zeligowski declared in favor of Poland. The Council of the League of Nations refused to accept unsupervised vote, and Lithuania refused recognition

Feb. 15, Land law passed provided for expropriation of the large estates

Feb. 20, Vilna Diet voted for union with Poland

April 8, Formal incorporation of Vilna with Poland

May 6, Commercial Agreement with Great Britain concluded

May 12, Declaration as to protection of minorities made before Council League of Nations

June 30, *De jure* recognition given Lithuania by the Council of Ambassadors

July 14, Consular Convention with Latvia signed

July 18, Emigration Act

July 27, *De jure* recognition given by Spain and the United States

Aug. 1, Constituent Assembly adopted permanent Constitution

Aug. 6, Constitution promulgated

Aug. 16, Law promulgated adopted new money unit the *Litas* based on the gold standard equal to about 10 cents to replace the Ost mark, Ost rouble, and German mark hitherto in circulation but now withdrawn; first issue Oct. 1

Nov. 9, Election held for first Diet (Seimas)

Dec. 2, Moscow Conference on disarmament. *See* p. 566

Dec. 20, Lithuania received *de jure* recognition by Great Britain, Italy, France, and Japan

Dec. 21, Antanas Stulgenskis elected first President

Dec. 27, Recognition given by Belgium

1923

Jan. 11, Rising in Memel, East Prussia, organized by Lithuanians which set up a temporary government which voted for annexation to Lithuania

Jan. 15, Lithuanians occupied Memel forcing French garrison to surrender and evacuate

Jan. 17, Conference of Ambassadors appointed Inter-Allied Commission to investigate the situation at Memel

Feb. 3, Allied ultimatum to Lithuania to withdraw troops from Memel

Feb. 3, Council of League of Nations recommended neutral zone for Vilna to be divided between Poland and Lithuania

Feb. 16, Conference of Ambassadors granted juridical sovereignty over Memel but constituted it an autonomous area

March 15, Conference of Ambassadors recognized the *fait accompli* and assigned Vilna district to Poland. Lithuania refused to recognize Polish possession of her historic capital

March 16, Lithuania accepted terms of Conference of Ambassadors as to Memel

April 27, Commercial Agreement with Czechoslovakia signed

July 18, Provisional Commercial Agreement with Denmark signed

Dec. 21, Treaty of commerce and navigation with Norway signed

1924

Feb. 17, Provisional Commercial Agreement with Sweden signed

March 15, Convention signed by Great Britain, France, Italy, Japan, and Lithuania which provided for transfer of Memel constituted an autonomous territory to Lithuania

May 8, Convention signed in Paris and Statute of Memel by representatives of the Allied Powers and by Lithuania May 17

June 1, Commercial Agreement with Germany signed

June 10, Provisional Commercial Agreement with the Netherlands signed

Sept. 22, Debt funding Agreement with the United States concluded

Oct. 29, Treaty of extradition and judicial assistance with France signed

Dec. 12, Debt to Great Britain paid

1925

Feb. 6, Cabinet reconstituted, V. Petrulis, Prime Minister

June 11, Conciliation Agreement with Sweden signed

May 8, Amendment to Military Conscription law passed third reading

Sept. 1, Lithuanian-Polish Conference met in Copenhagen to conclude agreement regarding rafting on the Niemen River

Sept. 20, Cabinet resigned as a result of the Lithuanian-Polish negotiations

Sept. 25, New Cabinet announced, M. Bistras, Prime Minister

Dec. 14, Provisional Commercial Treaty with Latvia signed

Dec. 23, Commercial Agreement with the United States signed

1926

Jan. 7, Government regulations promulgated for floating timber down the Niemen

Feb. 2, Provisional Commercial Agreement with the United States signed

June 6, Dr. Kazymir Grinius elected President

Sept. 28, Second Treaty of Moscow with Russia of non-aggression signed, boundaries reaffirmed

Nov. 16–17, Military coup d'etat by which Colonel Glovatsky overthrew Ministry of Slesevicius

Dec. 11, Convention for pacific settlement of disputes signed with Denmark

Dec. 17, Successful military coup d'etat under leadership of former President Antanas Smetona seized the Government and arrested President and Cabinet

Dec. 18, Resignation of President Grinius accepted by Parliament and Dr. Smetona elected President, and Augustine Valdemaras appointed Prime Minister

1927

Sept. 9, Communist uprising at Tauroggen led by former Captain Majus suppressed by troops

Sept. 17, Treaty of conciliation and judicial settlement with Italy signed and Trade Agreement

Sept. 27, Concordat with the Vatican signed

Oct. 15, Appeal of the Government to the League of Nations against treatment of Lithuanians in Vilna area by Poland

——, Frontier Treaty with Latvia signed

Nov. 21, Request of Great Britain, France, and Italy that Lithuania terminate "state of war" with Poland over Vilna maintained since 1920. Refused

Nov. 24, Russian Note to Poland and Lithuania stated that by existing treaties Russia guaranteed the independence of Lithuania

Dec. 7, Grievances of Lithuania as to Vilna presented before the Council of the League of Nations

Dec. 10, Passive "state of war" of Lithuania and Poland ended by acceptance by both of resolution adopted by Council of League of Nations declaring war ended

Dec., Poland closed Lithuanian schools in the Vilna district

1928

Jan. 29, Treaty of arbitration and conciliation with Germany signed, three frontier Agreements and Treaty as to Memel

March 30–April 2, Lithuanian-Polish Conference opened at Koenigsberg. Committees appointed to deal with subjects of communications, indemnities, &c.

May 15, New Constitution adopted which declared Vilna the capital of Lithuania

May 26, The Constitution proclaimed

July 20, Provisional Commercial Treaty with France signed

July 31, Commercial Treaty with Germany signed

Sept. 24, Provisional Commercial Agreement with Russia signed

Oct. 5, Commercial Convention with Austria signed

Oct. 23, Commercial Convention with Hungary signed

Oct. 30, Consular and judicial Agreement with Germany signed and Trade and shipping Treaty

Nov. 3–7, Lithuanian-Polish Conference in Koenigsberg renewed to form agreement for resumption of intercourse

Nov. 7, Agreement with Poland signed as to local frontier traffic

1929

Jan. 22, Lithuania ratified the Paris Pact to outlaw war

Jan. 30, Conspiracy against the Government frustrated by discovery and arrest of General Plechavitschius, head of General Staff and 18 other leaders

Jan. 31, Martial law proclaimed in Kovno

Feb. 9, Accession of Lithuania to Litvinov Peace Pact. *See* Russia

May 6, Attempted assassination of Premier Waldemaras by student failed

July 11, Protest to League of Nations against Polish aggression. Denied by Poland

Aug. 5, Dismissal of the President of the University at Kovno and entire faculty by the Minister of Education. New appointees took their places

Aug. 16, Provisional Commercial Agreement with Belgium signed

Sept. 19, Resignation of Waldemaras Cabinet

Sept. 23, Cabinet formed by Jonas Tubelis

Oct. 20, Dr. Zaunius became Minister of Foreign Affairs

Nov. 15, Dr. Zaunius stated that Government position as to Poland would remain unchanged, the final objective of Lithuanian foreign policy the recapture of Vilna, the historic capital

Nov. 23, Forced resignation of Musteikis, Minister of the Interior. Succeeded by Senator Kavetskis

Dec. 4, Kaunas District Court reversed decision of the district commander dissolving the Social Democratic Party

1930

Jan. 13, Treaty of friendship with Persia signed

Jan. 14, Communist uprising

March 8, Treaty of arbitration, conciliation, and judicial settlement with Czechoslovakia signed

May 11, M. Klimas became Minister of Foreign Affairs

May 18, Incident at Dmitrauka on Lithuanian-Polish frontier. Group of young people ordered to disperse fired on by Polish troops when they refused

May 22, Lithuania submitted complaint as to Dmitrauka incident to Council of the League of Nations

May 24, Ex-Premier Waldemaras indicted on charge of high treason because of statement that the Constitution had no authentic foundation and that the present Government was guilty of violation of the Constitution

July 24, Waldemaras deported to isolated village in the interior

Sept. 17, Treaty of friendship with Turkey signed

Nov. 24, Trade Agreement with Latvia signed

LUXEMBURG

Luxemburg, an independent Grand Duchy in Central Europe bounded by Germany, Belgium, and France, area 999 square miles, population (Dec. 31, 1929) 222,092. The capital is Luxemburg.

The early history of Luxemburg may be divided into four periods, *viz.*, from 963 to 1443, when the country was part of the Holy Roman Empire; from 1443 to 1506, the Burgundian period; from 1506 to 1714, the Spanish period; and from 1714 to 1795, the Austrian period. From 1795 to 1815 the Duchy was French. The Congress of Vienna made the Duchy into a Grand Duchy, and from 1815 to 1866 the Grand Duchy was included in the dissolved Germanic Confederation. By the Treaty of London, May 11, 1867, it was declared neutral territory, and its integrity and independence were guaranteed.

Charlotte, reigning Grand Duchess.

1815 to 1830

1815, The Grand Duchy was annexed to the Netherlands, still remaining a member of the Germanic Confederation, the capital having a Prussian garrison

1830, A portion given to the new Kingdom of Belgium

1867

March, After the dissolution of the Germanic Confederation, the Emperor Napoleon objected to the Prussian garrison, and offered to buy the Grand Duchy from the King of Holland

Sept. 9, In consequence of the opposition of Prussia, a conference of representatives of the Great Powers met in London, May 7–11, who agreed upon a treaty guaranteeing the neutrality of the province, the retirement of the Prussian garrison, and the dismantling the fortress of Luxemburg

Nov., The Prussian soldiers retired

1868

Oct. 17, Constitution now in force proclaimed

1870

Aug., The fortifications dismantled

Oct. 21, The people protest against absorption into Germany

Dec. 3, They are accused of violating neutrality, and the abrogation of the treaty is mooted by Prussia

1871

Feb., New treaty with Prussia; indemnity to be paid for breaches of neutrality; fortresses to be garrisoned by Germans

1874

Fortifications transformed to civil purposes

1889

April 10, The Duke of Nassau, on the severe illness of the King of Holland, assumed the regency of Luxemburg

May 3, The King recovers and resumes the government

1890

Nov. 6, Duke Adolph reassumed the government as regent; becomes Grand Duke on the death of the King, Nov. 23; takes the oath and opens the parliament Dec. 9

1901

Jan. 26, M. de Xivry, the Governor, assassinated at Arlon by a lunatic who afterwards shot himself

1912

Feb. 26, Marie Adelaide succeeded as Grand Duchess on the death of her father, Grand Duke William

1914

July 31, German troops barricaded the bridges over the Moselle River and took possession of the station at Trois Vierges from whence the main railroad ran through to France

Aug. 2, German invasion of Luxemburg carried out and occupation begun which lasted for the duration of the World War in violation of Treaties of 1867 and 1872

1915

Nov. 10, Chamber dissolved for the first time since 1856 because of attack on the Cabinet and the Grand Duchess by the Left

1918

Nov. 21, American troops occupied Luxemburg after the Armistice

1919

Jan. 9, Abdication of the Grand Duchess Marie Adelaide whose German affiliations made her unpopular with the majority of her subjects in favor of her sister Charlotte Adelgonde

Jan. 15, Grand Duchess Charlotte assumed the throne

May 15, Law limited powers of the sovereign, established universal suffrage with proportional representation

Sept. 28, Referendum taken declared: for the Grand Duchess Charlotte by vote of 66,811 as against 1,286; for continuance of the Nassau-Braganza dynasty under another Grand Duchess, 1,286; for another dynasty, 889; for a Republic, 16,885; voted for an economic union with France, 60,133; and for an economic union with Belgium, 22,242

Nov. 6, Grand Duchess Charlotte married Prince Felix of Bourbon-Parma

1920

Dec. 16, Luxemburg admitted to membership in League of Nations

1921

April, Cabinet appointed, Emile Reuter, Minister of State and President of Government; A. Neyens, Finance; J. Bech, Home Affairs and Public Instruction; W. Leidenbach, Justice and Public Works; Raymond de Waha, Industry and Social Welfare

July 25, Convention with Belgium signed for economic union to take effect May 1, 1922 for 50 years, customs barriers abolished, railway systems unified, and use of Belgian currency in the Grand Duchy

1922

May 28, Chamber of Deputies elected as follows: Catholics, 26; National Party, 4; Liberals, 9; Socialists, 7; Popular Party, 2

1924

April 4, Law created 5 chambers for traders and industrialists, agriculturalists, artisans, private employees, and workmen, election being by electors in these occupations over the age of 21. These chambers have right to propose Bills for submission to Chamber of Deputies and must be consulted as to laws affecting their professional interests

May 13, Railroad Convention with Belgium signed; rejected by Chamber Jan. 20, 1925

1926

July, M. Bech appointed Minister of State and President of Government; Dumont, Justice and Home Affairs; Clemang, Public Works, Trade, and Industry; Dupong, Finance and Social Welfare

RULERS

1890, Adolphus William Charles (titular Duke of Nassau), Regent, became Grand Duke Nov. 23 on death of King of Holland without a male descendant

1905, William Alexander succeeded on death of his father, Nov. 17

Feb. 26, 1912, Marie Adelaide succeeded on death of William, her father

Jan. 9, 1919, Charlotte succeeded as Grand Duchess on abdication of her sister, Marie Adelaide, married to Prince Felix of Bourbon-Parma on November 6, 1919. Offspring: Prince Jean, born January 5, 1921; Princess

Elizabeth, born December 22, 1922; Princess Marie-Adelaide, born May 21, 1924; Princess Marie-Gabrielle, born August 2, 1925; Prince Charles, born August 7, 1927; and Princess Alix, born August 24, 1929. Sisters of the Grand Duchess: Princess Marie-Adelaide, born June 14, 1894, died January 24, 1924; Princess Hilda, born February 15, 1897; Princess Antoinette, born October 7, 1899; Princess Elizabeth, born March 7, 1901; Princess Sophie, born February 14, 1902

MADEIRA

Madeira, group of islands in the Atlantic belonging to Portugal, Madeira, and Porto Santo, and 2 groups of uninhabited rocks named the Desertas and Selvagens. They are about 360 miles from Africa, and 535 from Lisbon; area 314 square miles, population 411,014 (census 1920). Madeira, the largest island and seat of the capital city, Funchal, has a length of 30 miles and extreme breadth of 12 miles. The islands were discovered in 1418 by João Gonçalvez Zarco.

MALTA

Malta, part of British Empire, group of Maltese Islands situated in the Mediterranean between Europe and Africa, including Malta, 95 square miles, Gozo, 26 square miles, Comino, 1 square mile, and the uninhabited rocks of Cominotto and Filfila, total area 122 square miles. Malta is 17.4 miles long and distant 140 miles from the mainland of Europe and 180 from Africa. Total population according to census of 1921, 224,680, civil population Dec. 31, 1929, 232,832. Valetta is the capital.

Malta was held in turn by Phœnicians, Greeks, Carthaginians, and Romans, and was conquered by Arabs in 870. From 1090 it was joined to Sicily until 1530, when it was handed over to the Knights of St. John, who ruled until dispersed by Napoleon in 1798. The Maltese rose in rebellion against the French and the Island was subsequently blockaded by the British fleet, aided by the Maltese, from 1798 to 1800. The Treaty of Amiens of Oct. 1, 1801 provided for evacuation of the British troops and the Island to be placed under guarantee and protection of a third power to be agreed upon. The Treaty of Amiens of March 27, 1802 provided for restoration of Malta to the Knights of St. John, and independence to be under guarantee and protection of Great Britain, France, Austria, Russia, Spain, and Prussia. This Article remained unexecuted and British occupation continued in violation of treaty based on failure of execution of stipulations as listed in note of Lord Hawkesbury of March 15, 1803, to the French Ambassador in London. Proposals of Great Britain of April 23 and May 7 for continuation of British occupation

for 10 years refused by the French. By the Treaty of Paris of May 30, 1814, Malta annexed to the British Crown. It is one of the most important ports of call in the world, and is the base and resort for repair and refitment of the British fleet in the Mediterranean.

Constitution granting self-government of April 14, 1921, came into effect May 16.

General Sir John Du Cane, Governor and Commander-in-Chief.

MEMEL

Memel, Lithuania, territory (area 2,443 square kilometers, 21,489 square miles, population, 2,340,038) was by the Treaty of Versailles, Article 99, detached from Germany and ceded to the Principal Allied and Associated Powers, and administered by the Conference of Ambassadors for 3 years. In Jan. 1923 Lithuanians seized Memel forcing the French garrison to surrender and evacuate (see Lithuania) and Convention of March 14, 1924 signed by Great Britain, France, Italy, Japan, and Lithuania provided for transfer of Memel, constituted as an autonomous territory, to Lithuania, and Convention and Statute of Memel signed May 8, by the Allied Powers and by Lithuania May 17.

MOLDAVIA

Moldavia (Moldavian Autonomous Socialist Soviet Republic) was formed as a separate republic on October 12, 1924, from an area of 8,288 square km. on the left bank of the Dniester River. The population on December 17, 1926, was 572,-000. The capital is Balta.

MONACO

Monaco is a small Principality on the Mediterranean, surrounded since 1860 by the French Department of Alpes Maritimes except on the side towards the sea. From 968 it belonged to the house of Grimaldi. In 1715 it passed into the female line, Louise Hippolyte, daughter of Antony I, heiress of Monaco, marrying Jacques de Goyon Matignon, Count of Thorigny, who took the name and arms of Grimaldi. Antony I died in 1731, Louise Hippolyte reigning only ten months and dying in 1732. She was succeeded by her husband under the name of Jacques I, who also succeeded Antony I, as Duc de Valentinois, and was in his turn succeeded by his son Honorius III. This Prince was dispossessed by the French Revolution in 1792, and died in 1795. In 1814 the Principality was reestablished, but placed under the protection of the Kingdom of Sardinia by the Treaty of Vienna (1815).

In 1848 Mentone and Roccabruna revolted, and declared themselves free towns; in 1861 Charles III ceded his rights over them to France, and the Principality thus became geographically an *enclave* of France, when the Sardinian garrison was withdrawn and the Protectorate came to an end.

On January 5, 1911, a Constitution was promulgated, which provides for a National Council elected by universal suffrage and *scrutin de liste*. The Government is carried out under the authority of the Prince by a Ministry assisted by a Council of State. The legislative power is exercised by the Prince and the National Council, which consists of 21 members elected for four years. On December 26, 1930, the Prince by decree dissolved the elected bodies of the Principality and suspended some of the constitutional guarantees.

The area is 149 hectares, or 370 acres. Population (census January 9, 1928), 24,927. Towns: Monaco, 2,085; La Condamine, 11,787; Monte Carlo, 11,055.

Prince Louis II, born July 12, 1870, succeeded his father, Prince Albert, June 26, 1922.

MONTENEGRO

Montenegro, former kingdom of south-eastern Europe, since Nov. 1918 united with Yugoslavia, area estimated at 5,603 square miles (3,474 square miles before the Balkan wars). Cettinje was the capital. *See also* Yugoslavia.

A leading part in the history of the country has been played by the family of Petrovitch Njegosh, descending collaterally, since the time of Danilo Petrovitch, who, being proclaimed Vladika, or Prince-Bishop, of Montenegro in 1697, liberated the country from the Turks, and, having established himself as both spiritual and temporal ruler, entered into a religious and political alliance with Russia. His successors retained the theocratic power till the death of Peter Petrovitch II (October 31, 1851), last Vladika of Montenegro, a ruler of great wisdom, as well as a widely celebrated poet. He was succeeded by his nephew, Danilo I, who abandoned the title of Vladika, together with the spiritual functions attached to it, and substituted that of Gospodar, or Prince. At the same time Danilo I, to throw off a remnant of nominal dependency upon Turkey, acknowledged by his predecessors, obtained the recognition of his new title from Russia. In 1878 the independence of Montenegro was formally recognized by Turkey and the other Signatory Powers of the Treaty of Berlin. In 1909 the limitations which the Treaty of Berlin had placed on Montenegro's complete sovereignty were removed, except the prohibition to erect fortifications at Antivari or along the Boyana.

1851 to 1874

1851, The nephew and successor of the Vladika, Peter II, declined to assume the ecclesiastical function, and declared himself a temporal prince, with the title of Danilo I; and began war with Turkey, 1852

Dec. 14, 1852, Montenegro put in a state of blockade

Feb. 25, 1853, After indecisive encounters, tranquillity restored by the influence of the arms and negotiations of Omar Pacha, the general of the Turkish army; he left the province

April 10, 1853, Blockade raised

Nov., 1858, War again broke out; the Turks defeated at Grahovo, June; peace restored

Aug. 12, 1860, The country much disturbed through the tyrannical conduct of Prince Danilo, who was shot at Cattars 12th and died (aged 35)

Nov. 8, 1860, Succeeded by his nephew Nicolas, or Nikita, (married)

April 4, 1861, An insurrection in Herzegovina; the blockade of Montenegro

Aug., 1861, Omar Pacha invaded the province with an army of 32,000 men

Sept. 8–9, 1862, Many conflicts with various success, but latterly in favor of the Turks; peace made, Turkish supremacy recognized

Oct. 20, 1874, Conflicts between Christians and Mussulmans at Podgoritza; 21 Montenegrins said to be killed by Turks

1875

Jan., Threatened war prevented by intervention of the Great Powers

May 15, Some rioters executed

Autumn and Winter, Montenegro with difficulty restrained from intervention in Herzegovina

1876 to 1895

July 2, 1876, The Prince declared war and joined the Serbians

1876–78, *See* Turkey and Russo-Turkish war

July 13, 1878, Declared independent of Turkey by treaty of San Stefano, March 3; (with new boundaries, and Antivari for a seaport) by the Berlin treaty

Feb. 7, 1879, Podgoritza surrendered by Turkey

April, 1880, After much resistance by the Albanians, and negotiation with Turkey, Gussinge surrendered

Sept. 1883, Frontier disputes with Turkey settled, Nov. 1882; the Prince well received at Constantinople

May, 1884, A constitution promised

July 3, 4, 1886, Temporary fighting between Turks and Montenegrins at Céttingé

March, 1890, About 6,360 persons emigrate to Serbia, Oct., Nov., 1889; famine continues

July, Aug., 1890, Albanian raids checked by Turks

Jan. *et seq.*, 1893, Agitation for more liberal government

March, April, 1894, Frequent raids by the Albanians, appeal to the Porte; redress promised

July, Continued emigration into Austria-Hungary of nobles opposed to the new system of government, introduced by Prince Nicolas

1895, Formation of a standing army above 36,000 men with Russian weapons

1897

Jan. 14, *O.S.*, Nieguch, the founder, from the cathedral to the mausoleum, designed by the Princess of Naples; addresses by Prince Nicholas and others

May 18, Marriage of Prince Francis Joseph of Battenberg and Princess Anna of Montenegro, celebrated
at Céttingé

1898

June 4, Successful European tour of Prince Nicholas,
returns to Céttingé

June 16, Conflicts on the frontier between Mahometans
and Christians, many killed, including women and
children; over 700 houses burnt

1899

March, National guard, under Prince Mirko, organized

Sept. 2–6, Marriage of the Crown Prince and the Duchess Militza at Céttingé, July 27; received by the
Sultan at Constantinople

Dec. 19, Prince Nicholas assumes the title "Royal
Highness" by request of his people

1902

Feb. et seq., Conflicts with Turkish troops on the frontier

1903

Jan. 6, Existing treaty of commerce between Great
Britain and Montenegro prolonged until Jan. 1, 1904,
reported

1905

Dec. 19, Constitution granted by Prince Nicholas

1906

Oct., First National Assembly met in Cettinje, the
capital, 62 of the 74 members elected by universal
suffrage

1907

April 29, Assassination of Gen. Martinovitch, governor of Podgoritza, and M. Masiwoda, chief of
police, by an ensign, who was killed

July, National Assembly dissolved

1908

Cettinje treason trial, bombs "discovered" which it
was alleged were to be used to destroy Montenegrin
royal family and also the only daughter of King
Peter of Serbia, precursor of the Agram treason trial,
and first of series of incidents which culminated in
the Sarajevo tragedy

Dec., First railroad in Montenegro opened from Antivari to Lake of Scutari

1910

Feb. 2, Commercial and shipping treaty with Gt. Britain ratified by parliament

Aug. 28 (15/28), Montenegro proclaimed a kingdom,
and Nicholas received title of King on the occasion
of the 50th anniversary of his reign

1912

Aug., Verbal Agreement with Bulgaria as to Balkan
affairs

Oct. 8, Montenegro the first of the Balkan States to
declare war on Turkey for liberation of Macedonia.
See Balkan Wars

1913

April 1, The Powers notified the King that siege of
Scutari must be raised

April 10, Formal blockade of Montenegrin coast by
squadron of European Powers

April 20, Armistice signed by all Balkan States except
Montenegro whose objective was Scutari which the
Powers had decided to include in autonomous State
of Albania

April 22, Scutari surrendered to Montenegrins

April 30, Note of Powers demanded evacuation of
Scutari by Montenegrins

May 5, Scutari evacuated by Montenegrins

July 5, Montenegro declared war on Bulgaria joining
Greece and Serbia. See Balkan Wars

Aug. 10, Treaty of Bucharest gave Montenegro a part
of the Sanjak of Novibazar including towns of Plevlye, Bielopolie, Ipek, and Jacova

Nov. 4, Treaty of Belgrade signed with Serbia adjusting frontiers

1914

July 25, Montenegro in response to Serbian Note
promised unconditional support to Serbia

July 26, Mobilization ordered

Aug. 5 (or 7), Montenegro declared war on Austria-
Hungary

Aug. 8, Diplomatic relations with Germany severed
and state of war begun

Aug. 9, Montenegro declared war on Germany

Dec. 29, Serbian Prime Minister Pachitch and General
Pechitch asked King Nicholas to make truce with
Austria which he refused to do

1915

June 26, Montenegrin troops occupied San Giovanni
de Medua, Albania

July 29, The Entente Governments warned Montenegro that her occupation of Albanian territory would
not be recognized

Oct. 15, State of war with Bulgaria proclaimed

1916

Jan. 12–20, Armistice with Austria-Hungary

Jan. 20, King Nicholas reached Italy arriving in Rome
on the 23rd

Jan. 25, Acceptance of Austrian terms by Prince Mirko

Feb. 16, The remnants of Montenegrin army arrived
at Corfu

May 20, Open letter of Prime Minister Lazar Miuskovic
to King Nicholas accused the King of treason and
resigned. Succeeded as Premier by Andrev Radovic

May 24, King Nicholas disavowed action of his son
Prince Mirko conducting negotiations with Austria-
Hungary

Aug. 6, Prime Minister Radovic submitted formal
proposal for union with Serbia. No reply made

1917

Jan. 11, Prime Minister Radovic submitted second
proposal for union with Serbia to the King and re-
question immediate decision, and resigned. Succeeded by General Martinovic

June 5, General Martinovic resigned as Prime Minister
after presenting a memorial to the King urging union
with Serbia. Succeeded by Eugene Popovic

July 20, Montenegrin Committee for National Union
formed in Switzerland signed the Pact of Corfu by
which Serbs, Croats, and Slovenes declared for a
single kingdom under house of Karageorgevitch

Oct. 1, Montenegrins in Paris declared against Radovic
and union with Serbia

Nov. 28, General election held for the Serb-Croat-Slovene Constituent Assembly

1918

Oct. 26, King Nicholas issued manifesto in favor of Yugoslav Confederation with autonomous States

Nov. 26, A "Great National Assembly" voted for union with Serbia and deposition of King Nicholas

Dec. 15 (29), King Nicholas deposed

Dec. 16, The Prince Regent accepted resolution adopted Nov. 26 and embodied assent in law passed that day. King Nicholas refused to accede

1919

April 20, Parliament declared Nicholas dethroned and for union with Yugoslavia

May 17, Great Britain canceled exequaturs of consuls to Montenegro

Dec. 30, France withdrew consular representatives from Montenegro

1920

Nov. 28, General elections for Serb-Croat-Slovene Assembly

1921

March 1, Death of King Nicholas at Antibes. The royal title fell into abeyance as Prince Danilo refused to assume it (March 7) and his nephew Michael was a minor

1923

March 16, Death of Queen Milena

VLADIKAS OR PRINCE-BISHOPS

1696–1735, Danilo

1735–1782, Sava and Vasilije

1782–1830, Peter I (St. Peter)

1830–1851, Peter II (Vladika Rade)

Danilo, Prince, 1851–1860, born May 25, 1826; shot Aug. 12, died Aug. 13, 1860

Nicholas I, Petrovitch Njegosh (Tsernagora), born October 7 (September 25), 1841; educated at Trieste and Paris; proclaimed Prince of Montenegro, as successor of his uncle, Danilo I, August 14, 1860. Assumed title of King, in virtue of a resolution passed unanimously by the National Skupshtina, Aug. 28, 1910, on the occasion of the 50th anniversary of his accession. Married, November 8, 1860, to Milena Pétrovna Vukotitch, born May 4, 1847, daughter of Peter Vukotitch, senator, and Vice-President of the Council of State; deposed Nov. 26, 1918; died March 1, 1921

Children of the King.—(1) Princess Militza, born July 26, 1866, married, August 7, 1889, to the Russian Grand Duke Peter Nikolaievitch; (2) Princess Stana, born January 4, 1868, married August 28, 1889, to George, Duke of Leuchtenberg, and after the dissolution of that marriage, married in 1907 to the Russian Grand Duke Nicolas Nicolaiévitch; (3) Prince Danilo Alexander, heir apparent, born June 29, 1871; married July 27, 1899, to Princess Jutta (Militza) daughter of the Grand-Duke of Mecklenburg Strelitz; (4) Princess Helena, born January 8, 1873, married October 24, 1896, to Victor Emanuel, now King of Italy; (5) Princess Anna, born August 18, 1874, married May 18, 1897, to Prince Francis Joseph of Battenberg; (6) Prince Mirko, born April 17, 1879, married July 12, 1902,

to Natalie Konstantinovitch, daughter of Colonel Konstantinovitch, great uncle of the late King Alexander of Serbia; offspring, Prince Michael born September 14, 1908; Prince Paul, born May 16, 1910; (7) Princess Xenia, born April 22, 1881; (8) Princess Vera, born February 22, 1887; (9) Prince Peter, born October 10, 1889

NAPLES

Naples, formerly the continental division and seat of government of the Kingdom of the Two Sicilies, began with a Greek colony named Parthenope (about 1000 B.C.), which was afterwards divided into Palæopolis (the *old*) and Neapolis (the *new* city); from the latter the present name is derived. The colony was conquered by the Romans in the Samnite war, 326 B.C. Naples, after resisting the power of the Lombards, Franks, and Germans, was subjugated by the Normans under Roger Guiscard, king of Sicily, A.D. 1131. Few countries have had so many political changes, and cruel and despotic rulers, or suffered so much by convulsions of nature, such as earthquakes, volcanic eruptions, &c. The eldest son of the King of Italy is styled Prince of Naples. It now forms part of the revived Kingdom of Italy.

493 to 1504

493, Naples conquered by Theodoric the Goth

536, The city retaken by Belisarius

543, Taken again by Totila

552, Retaken by Narses

568 or 572, Becomes a duchy subject to the Eastern Empire

593, Duchy of Naples greatly extended

1059, Robert Guiscard, the Norman, made Duke of Apulia, founds the Kingdom of Naples

1131, Naples conquered, and the Kingdom of the Two Sicilies founded by Roger Guiscard II

1194–1266, The imperial house of Hohenstaufen obtains the Kingdom by marriage, and rules

Feb. 26, 1266, The Pope appoints Charles of Anjou King, who defeats the Regent Manfred (son of Frederick II, of Germany) at Benevento (Manfred slain)

Oct. 29, 1268, Charles defeats Conradin (the last of the Hohenstaufens who had come to Naples by invitation of the Ghibellines), at Tagliacozzo, Aug. 23: Conradin beheaded

March 30, 1282, The massacre called the Sicilian Vespers

Sept. 18, 1345, Andrew of Hungary, husband of Joanna I, murdered

1349, His brother Louis, King of Hungary, invades Naples

May 22, 1382, Queen Joanna put to death

1435, Alphonso V of Arragon (called the Wise and Magnanimous) on the death of Joanna II seizes Naples

1495, Naples conquered by Charles VIII of France

1501, And by Louis XII of France and Ferdinand of Spain, who divide it

1504, Expulsion of the French

——, Naples and Sicily united to Spain

1647

June, Insurrection of Masaniello, occasioned by the extortions of the Spanish viceroys. An impost was claimed on a basket of figs, and refused by the owner, with whom the populace took part, headed by Masaniello (Thomas Aniello), a fisherman; they obtained the command of Naples, many of the nobles were slain and their palaces burnt, and the viceroy was compelled to abolish the taxes and to restore the privileges granted by Charles V to the city

July 16, Masaniello, intoxicated by his success, was slain by his own followers

Oct., Another insurrection suppressed by Don John of Austria

1648 to 1793

April, 1648, Henry II, Duke of Guise, lands, and is proclaimed King, but in a few days is taken prisoner by the Spaniards

1706, Naples conquered by Prince Eugene of Savoy, for the Emperor

1711, Discovery of Herculaneum

1734, The Spaniards by the victory at Bitonto (May 26) having made themselves masters of both kingdoms, Charles (of Bourbon), son of the King of Spain, ascends the throne, with the ancient title of King of the Two Sicilies

1738, Order of St. Januarius instituted

1759, Charles, becoming King of Spain, vacates the throne in favor of his third son, Ferdinand, agreeably to treaty

Nov. 3, 1767, Expulsion of the Jesuits

Feb. 5, 1783, Dreadful earthquake in Calabria

1793, Enrolment of the lazzaroni as pikemen or spontoneers

1799

Jan. 14, The King flees on the approach of the French republicans, who establish the Parthenopean Republic

June, Nelson appears; Naples retaken; the restored king rules tyrannically

June 29, Prince Caracciolo tried and executed by order of Nelson

Sept. 30, The Neapolitans occupy Rome

1805

July 26, Earthquake; thousands perish

Oct. 9, Treaty of neutrality between France and Naples ratified

1806

Jan. 23, Ferdinand, through perfidy, is compelled to flee to Sicily; the French enter Naples, and Joseph Bonaparte made King, Feb.

July 4, The French defeated at Maida

1808

June, Joseph Bonaparte, after beginning many reforms, abdicates for the crown of Spain

July 15, Joachim Murat made King (rules well)

1811

His first quarrel with Napoleon

1814

Jan., His alliance with Austria

Sept. 7, Death of Queen Caroline

1815

March 15, Joachim declares war against Austria

May 3, Defeated at Tolentino

May 22, He retires to France, and Corsica: he madly attempts the recovery of his throne by landing at Pizzo: seized, tried, and shot Oct. 13

June, Ferdinand, reëstablished, soon returns to tyrannical measures

Nov., 1815 to June, 1816, A plague rages in Naples

1819 to 1844

1819, Establishment of the society of the Carbonari

July 13, 1820, Successful insurrection of the Carbonari under Gen. Pépé; the King compelled to swear solemnly to a new constitution

March 7, 1821, The Austrians invade the Kingdom, at the King's instigation; General Pépé defeated

March 23, Fall of the constitutional government

Jan. 4, 1825, Death of Ferdinand (reigned 66 years)

Aug. 1828, Insurrection of the Carbonari suppressed

Nov. 8, 1830, Accession of Ferdinand II, Bomba (as faithless and tyrannical as his predecessors)

May, 1840, Dispute with England respecting the sulphur trade, 1838; settled

Jan. 17, 1844, Attilio and Emilio Bandiero, with eighteen others, attempting an insurrection in Calabria, are shot

1848

Jan. 29, Prospect of an insurrection in Naples; the King grants a new constitution with liberal ministry

May 15, Great fighting in Naples; the liberals and the national guard almost annihilated by the royal troops, aided by the lazzaroni

1849

Dec., A martial anarchy prevails; the chiefs of the liberal party arrested

1850

June, Settembrini, Poerio, Carafa, and others, after a mock trial, are condemned, and consigned to dungeons for life

1856

Oct. 28, After remonstrances with the King on his tyrannical government (May), the English and French Ambassadors are withdrawn

Dec. 8, Attempted assassination of the King by Milano

1857

June 27–July 2, Italian refugees, under Count Pisaccane, land in Calabria, are defeated, and their leader killed

Dec. 16, Earthquake in the Apennines

1858

Dec. 27, Amnesty granted to political offenders

1859

Jan., Poerio and sixty-six companions released and sent to N. America; on their way, they seize the vessel, sail to Cork, March 7; and proceed to London, March 18

May 22, Death of Ferdinand II

June, Diplomatic relations resumed with England and France

July 7, Insubordination among the Swiss troops at

Naples, many shot; Major Latour sent to Naples by the Swiss confederation July 16

1860

March 26, Many political imprisonments; the foreign ambassadors collectively address a note to the King stating the necessity for reform in his states; the Count of Syracuse recommends reform and alliance with England, April

May 11, Garibaldi lands in Sicily; defeats the Neapolitan army at Calatafimi, May 15

June 15, Revolutionary committee at Naples

June 26, Francis II proclaims an amnesty; promises a liberal ministry; adopts a tricolor flag, &c.

June 28, A liberal ministry formed; destruction of the commissariat of the police in 12 districts; state of siege proclaimed at Naples; the Queen-Mother flees to Gaeta

July 2, Francis II proclaims the reëstablishment of the constitution of 1848; the army proclaim Count de Trani King, July 10

July 20, Garibaldi defeats Neapolitans at Melazzo; enters Messina, July 21; the Neapolitans agree to evacuate Sicily, July 30

July, The King of Sardinia in vain negotiates with Francis II for alliance

Aug. 18, Garibaldi lands at Melito; takes Reggio, Aug. 21

Sept. 6, Defection in army and navy; Francis II retires to Gaeta; Garibaldi enters Naples without troops, Sept. 7

Sept., Garibaldi assumes the dictatorship, Sept. 8; gives up the Neapolitan fleet to the Sardinian Admiral Persano, Sept. 11; expels the Jesuits; establishes trial by jury; releases political prisoners

Sept. 19, He repulses the Neapolitans at Cajazzo; defeats them at the Volturno, Oct. 1

Oct. 11, The King of Sardinia enters the Kingdom of Naples, and takes command of his army, which combines with Garibaldi's

Oct. 17, Cialdini defeats the Neapolitans at Isernia; at Venafro, Oct. 18

Oct. 21, The plebiscite at Naples, &c.; almost unanimous vote for annexation to Piedmont (1,303,064 to 10,312)

Oct. 26, Garibaldi meets Victor-Emmanuel, and salutes him as King of Italy

For further events *see* Italy

SOVEREIGNS OF NAPLES AND SICILY

1131. Roger I (of Sicily, 1130), Norman
1154. William I the Bad; son
1166. William II the Good; son
1189. Tancred, natural son of Roger
1194. William III, son, succeeded by Constance, married to Henry VI of Germany
1197. Frederick II of Germany (Hohenstaufen)

1250. Conrad; son
1254. Conradin, son; but his uncle
1258. Manfred, natural son of Frederick II, seizes the government; killed at Benevento, in 1266
1266. Chas. of Anjou, brother of St. Louis, King of France.
　　　[Conradin beheaded, Oct. 29, 1268]
1282. Insurrection in Sicily

(*Separation of the Kingdoms in* 1282.)

NAPLES	SICILY
1282. Charles I of Anjou	1282. Peter I (III of Arragon)
1285. Charles II; son	1285. James I (II of Arragon)
1309. Robert the Wise; brother	1295. Frederick II
1343. Joanna (reigns with her husband, Andrew of Hungary), 1343–45; with Louis of Tarento, 1349–62; Joanna put to death (May 22, 1382) by	1337. Peter II
	1342. Louis
	1355. Frederick III
1382. Charles III, grandson of Charles II: he becomes King of Hungary; assassinated there, 1386	1376. Maria and Martin (her husband)
——. Louis I, titular, crowned	1402. Martin I
1385. Louis II, son of Louis I	1409. Martin II
1386. Ladislas of Hungary	1410. Ferdinand I
1414. Joanna II, sister, dies in 1435, and bequeaths her dominions to Regnie, of Anjou. They are acquired by	1416. Alphonso I
	1435. Alphonso I thus King of Naples and Sicily

(*Separation of Naples and Sicily in* 1458.)

NAPLES	SICILY
1458. Ferdinand I	1458. John of Arragon
1494. Alphonso II abdicates	1479. Ferdinand the Catholic of Spain
1495. Ferdinand II	
1496. Frederic II expelled by the French, 1501	

THE CROWNS UNITED

1503. Ferdinand III (King of Spain)	1621. Philip III (IV of Spain)
1516. Charles I (V of Germany)	1665. Charles II (of Spain)
1556. Philip I (II of Spain)	1700. Philip IV (V of Spain), Bourbons
1598. Philip II (III of Spain)	1707. Charles III of Austria

(Separation in 1713.)

NAPLES	SICILY
1713. Charles III of Austria	1713. Victor Amadeus of Savoy (exchanged Sicily for Sardinia, 1720)

THE TWO SICILIES

(Part of the Empire of Germany, 1720–34)

1735. Charles IV (III of Spain)	1759. Ferdinand IV, fled from Naples to Sicily, 1806

(Separation in 1806.)

NAPLES	SICILY
1806. Joseph Napoleon Bonaparte	1806–15. Ferdinand IV
1808. Joachim Murat, shot Oct. 13, 1815	

THE TWO SICILIES

1815. Ferdinand I, formerly Ferdinand IV, of Naples and Sicily	King of Naples; deposed; fled Sept. 6, 1860; died at Arco, Dec. 27, 1894
1825. Francis I	1861. Victor-Emmanuel II of Sardinia, as King of Italy March; (*see* Italy, end)
1830. Ferdinand II, Nov. 8 (termed King Bomba)	
1859. Francis II, May 22; born Jan. 16, 1836; last	

NETHERLANDS, THE

Netherlands, The, or Holland (Koninkrijk der Nederlanden), a northern European kingdom, bounded on the north and west by the North Sea, on the south by Belgium and on the east by Germany, total area 12,579 square miles, population Dec. 31, 1930, 7,935,565, the area, including the interior waters, amounted in 1929 to 13,220 square miles, and the total area, including gulfs and bays, estimated in 1920 as 15,760 square miles. Capital: The Hague. The colonial possessions of the Netherlands are situated in the East and West Indies and embrace an area of about 788,000 English square miles with total population of 51,881,862. *See* Dutch East Indies, and Dutch West Indies which include Surinam or Dutch Guiana, and Curaçao.

The royal family of the Netherlands, known as the House of Orange, descends from a German Count Walram, who lived in the eleventh century. Through the marriage of Count Engelbrecht, of the branch of Otto, Count of Nassau, with Jane of Polanen, in 1404, the family acquired the barony of Breda, and thereby became settled in the Netherlands. The alliance with another heiress, only sister of the childless Prince of Orange and Count of Châlons, brought to the house a rich province in the south of France; and a third matrimonial union, that of Prince Willem III of Orange with a daughter of King James II, led to the transfer of the crown of Great Britain to that prince. Previous to this period, the members of the family had acquired great influence in the United Provinces of the Netherlands under the name of "stadthouders," or governors. The dignity

was formally declared to be hereditary in 1747, in Willem IV; but his successor, Willem V, had to fly to England, in 1795, at the invasion of the French republican army. The family did not return till November, 1813, when the fate of the old United Provinces, released from French incorporation, was under discussion at the Congress of Vienna. After various diplomatic negotiations, the Belgian provinces, subject before the French revolution to the House of Austria, were ordered by the Congress to be joined to the Northern Netherlands, and the whole to be erected into a kingdom, with the son of the last stadthouder, Willem V, as hereditary sovereign. In consequence, the latter was proclaimed King of the Netherlands at The Hague on the 16th of March, 1815, and recognized as sovereign by all the Powers of Europe. The union thus established between the northern and southern Netherlands was dissolved by the Belgian revolution of 1830, and their political relations were not readjusted until the signing of the Treaty of London, April 19, 1839, which constituted Belgium an independent kingdom. King Willem I abdicated in 1840, bequeathing the crown to his son Willem II, who, after a reign of nine years, left it to his heir, Willem III. This king reigned 41 years, and died in 1890; in default of male heirs, he was succeeded by his only daughter Wilhelmina.

Wilhelmina Helena Pauline Maria, reigning sovereign.

1347 to 1622

1347, The parties termed Hooks (followers of Margaret, Countess of Holland) and Cod-fish (supporters of her son William, who endeavored to supplant her) create a civil war, which lasts many years

1416, Holland united to Hainault, 1299; and Brabant

1436, Annexed to Burgundy by Duke Philip, who wrests it from his niece Jaqueline, of Holland, daughter of the last count

1477, Annexed to Austria through marriage of Mary of Burgundy with Archduke Maximilian

1495, Government of Philip of Austria

1506, Of Margaret of Austria and Charles V

1555, Of Philip II

1555 *et seq.*, Philip II establishes the Inquisition; the Hollanders having zealously embraced the reformed doctrines; severe persecution; about 100,000 persons said to have perished; the Confederacy of Gueux (Beggars) formed by the nobles, 1566

Jan., 1566, Compromise of Breda presented

1572, Commencement of the revolt under William, Prince of Orange

1575, Elizabeth of England declines the offered sovereignty, but promises help

1576, The Pacification of Ghent—union of the north and south provinces

1579, The seven northern provinces contract the League of Utrecht

July 25, 1581, And declare their independence

July 10, 1584, Assassination of William of Orange

1585, The ten southern provinces conquered by the Prince of Parma

1585-7, The provinces solicit help from England and France; expedition of the Earl of Leicester; English and Dutch disagree

Sept. 22, 1586, Battle of Zutphen—Sir Philip Sidney mortally wounded

1587, Prince Maurice appointed stadtholder

1598, Death of Philip II. His son Philip III cedes the Netherlands to Albert of Austria, and the Infanta, Isabella

1599-1604, Campaigns of Maurice and Spinola

July 2, 1600, Maurice defeats the Archduke at Nieuport

April 9 (March 29), 1609, The independence of the United Provinces recognized; truce of Antwerp for twelve years

1610, Batavia in Java built

1610-19, Fierce religious dissensions between the Arminians and Gomarists

1615, The New Netherland Company under charter of Oct. 11, 1614, built a trading house and fort on Manhattan Island in America (now New York)

1616, Maurice favors the Gomarists and intrigues for royal power

1618-19, Synod of Dort; persecution of the Arminians

May 14, 1619, Execution of the illustrious Barneveldt

1622, Renewal of the war; Maurice saves Bergen-op-Zoom

1623

Feb. 17, Massacre of the English at Amboina, in the East Indies

June, New Netherland in America made a Province of the West India Company

Maurice's tyrannical government: plot against him, and sixteen persons executed

1625 to 1863

1625, His death; his brother Frederick succeeds him, and annuls the persecution

Sept. 16 and Oct. 21, 1639, Victories of Van Tromp, who takes two Spanish fleets off the downs

1648, Peace of Westphalia, the republic recognized by Europe

Nov. 29, 1652, War with England—naval actions—Blake defeats De Ruyter, Oct. 22; but is surprised by Van Tromp, who takes some English ships, and sails through the channel with a broom at his masthead

1653, Indecisive sea-fights, June 12-14; death of Van Tromp, July 31; peace follows

1659, Victorious war with Sweden

1664 (Sept. 3), Surrender of New Netherland to the English

1665, Another war with England

July 25, 1666, Indecisive sea-fights, June 1-4; victory of Monk over De Ruyter

1668, Triple alliance of England, Holland, and Sweden against France

1670, Charles II deserts Holland; joins France

1671, The French overrun Holland

1672, Desperate condition of the States—the populace massacre the De Witts—William III made Stadtholder

——, The French repelled by the sluices being opened

1673-7, Indecisive campaigns

1677, William marries Princess Mary of England

1678, Peace with France (Nimeguen)

1689, William becomes King of England

1689-96, Sanguinary war with France

Sept. 20, 1697, Peace of Ryswick signed

March 8, 1702, Death of William

——, No stadtholder appointed—administration of Heinsius

1702-13, War against France and Spain; campaigns of Marlborough

April 11, 1713, Peace of Utrecht

1743-8, Holland supports the Empress Maria-Theresa

1747, William Henry hereditary Stadtholder

Oct. 18, 1748, Peace of Aix-la-Chapelle

1781-3, War with England for naval supremacy—Holland loses colonies

1787-9, Civil wars in the Low Countries

1793, The French republicans march into Holland; the people declare in their favor

1794, Unsuccessful campaign of the Duke of York

1795, The Batavian republic established in alliance with France

Oct. 11, 1797, Battle of Camperdown, Duncan signally defeats the Dutch

Aug. 30, 1799, The Texel fleet, of twelve ships of the line, with thirteen Indiamen, surrenders to the British admiral, without firing a gun

April 26, 1805, A new constitution is given to the Batavian republic; the chief officer (R. J. Schimmelpenninck) takes the title of Grand Pensionary

June 5, 1806, Holland erected into a kingdom, and Louis Bonaparte, father of Napoleon III, declared King

July, Sept., 1800, The ill-fated Walcheren expedition

July 1, 1810, Louis abdicates

July 9, 1810, Holland united to France

Nov. 17, 1813, Restored to the house of Orange, and Belgium annexed to its dominions

Dec. 6, 1813, The Prince of Orange proclaimed sovereign Prince of the United Netherlands

1817, &c., Religious discord between Holland and the southern provinces

Aug. 25, 1830, The revolution in Belgium

July 12, 1831, Belgium separated from Holland

Aug. 3, 1831, Holland makes war against Belgium

April 19, 1839, Treaty between Holland and Belgium, signed in London

Oct. 7–10, 1840, Abdication of William I

Dec. 12, 1843, Death of the ex-King William I

July 25, 1846, Louis Bonaparte, Count de St. Leu, ex-King of Holland, dies of apoplexy at Leghorn

April 17, 1848, The King agrees to political reform, March; a new constitution granted

March 17, 1849, Death of William II

March 12, 1853, Reëstablishment of a Roman Catholic hierarchy announced

1859, General van den Bosch's scheme carried out by the society of beneficence of home colonization in east Holland for destitute persons of all sorts, started about 1815, having failed is modified; free and penal colonies constituted; (generally successful)

Aug. 6, 1862, The States-General pass a law for the abolition of slavery in the Dutch West Indies [after July 1, 1863]

May 12, 1863, Treaty for capitalizing Scheldt dues signed

July 1, 1863, Slavery ceases in the Dutch West Indies

1865

March 8, Commencement of canal to connect Amsterdam with the North Sea

March, The government undertake a canal to connect Rotterdam with the sea

July 7, Commercial treaty with France

1866

July–Aug., Correspondence with Prussia respecting the Prussian garrison in Luxemburg

Oct. 10, The lower chamber barely passes a vote of censure on the Ministry respecting government of Java, &c.; the King dissolves the Chamber

1867 to 1889

March 22, 1867, Alleged treaty with France respecting cession of Luxemburg (see s.v.)

May, 1868, The fortifications of Luxemburg razed

July 7, 1871, Cession of Dutch possessions in Guinea to Great Britain, voted

April 1, 1872, Tercentenary celebration of the commencement of Dutch independence by the capture of Briel

June 4, 1872, Death of de Thorbecke, a great statesman

April, 1873, Discussions respecting the war against the Sultan of Achin in Sumatra

Sept. 8, 1873, New port at Flushing opened by the King

Dec., 1873, Expedition against the Achinese (Sumatra) embarks

Aug., 1875, New penal code issued

Nov. 1, 1876, Canal between North sea and Amsterdam passed by a monitor (see 1865) Oct. 4; inaugurated by the King

Aug. 24, 1878, Marriage of Prince Henry, the King's brother, to Princess Marie Elizabeth of Prussia

Jan. 13, 1879, Death of Prince Henry, the King's brother, aged 58

May 9, 1882, Commercial treaty with France rejected by the chamber; the Ministry resign

March 1, 1883, Resignation of Baron van Lynden

April 22, 1883, New ministry under Dr. Heemskerk

May 12, 1883, Committee for revision of the constitution appointed

June 21, 1884, Death of the Prince of Orange

Aug. 1, 1884, The Queen appointed by a congress to be regent if necessary

April 22, 1886, Resignation of the Ministry, April 13; declined by the King

Nov. 30, 1887, The King's assent given to bill for revision of constitution, Nov. 8; the revised constitution promulgated

April 17, 1888, New ministry; Interior, Baron Mackay

1889, Continued illness of the King; the Queen nominated regent, and the Duke of Nassau regent of Luxemburg, April; the King suddenly recovers; regency deferred, April; the King resumes government, May

1890

Oct. 29, The parliament declares the King incapable of ruling; the council of state to govern

Nov. 20, The Queen appointed regent at a sitting of the two chambers, Nov. 13; takes the oath

Nov. 23, Death of King William III, accession of his daughter Wilhelmina

1891

Aug. 11, Resignation of the Ministry, July 8; new ministry formed by M. Vantienhoven, Aug. 5; he becomes foreign minister, and M. Tak van Poortvliet Premier

1892

Aug. 4, A section of the Merwede canal, from Amsterdam to the north of the Leck, opened in presence of the Queen and Queen-Regent

1894

March 9, An electoral reform bill withdrawn on an amendment being carried in the 2nd chamber

April 26, Elections; majority for the opposition

April 28, Tak Van Poortvliet's Ministry resign

May 9, New ministry; Jonkheer Roell, Premier

Aug. 25–27, Insurrection in the Dutch East Indies; the Dutch are surprised by an ambush at Tjakra-Negara, near Mataram, in the Island of Lombok; defeated with heavy loss; Gen. Van Ham, 8 officers, and 200 men killed

Aug. 30, The Dutch men-of-war bombard Mataram, Kampong, and Tanabat, reported

Sept. 4, Reinforcements arrive

Sept. 6, Arveng captured

Sept. 29, Mataram taken after severe fighting

Nov. 18, Tjakra-Negara attacked

Nov. 21, The Rajah surrenders

Nov. 26, General submission, reported

1895

May 9, The Queen and Queen-Regent visit England; left

Oct. 5, Strike of diamond-cutters in Amsterdam; riotous demonstrations

Dec. 2, Conversion of the national debt from $3\frac{1}{2}$ to 3%, bill submitted

1896

Rising in the E. Indies: desultory fighting in Sumatra, headed by the Achinese chief Toekoe Djohan; 2 forts relieved, and rebel intrenchments captured by the Dutch, April 8, 12, 1896; 4 Achinese forts evacuated by the Dutch, after heavy fighting, April 18; Tokoe Omar's capital Lampisang taken,

May; Dutch successes, and flight of rebels; Loempong bombarded, June 14; enemy routed at Blang-Bitang; Tokoe Baid rebel chief surrenders; Gen. Moulin dies, while trying to cross a morass in Atjeh, Aug.; desultory fighting, Sept.; Lieut.-Col. Van Vliet appointed Governor of Atjeh, Oct. 20; the Sultan of Pazir overthrown, and banished, Oct.; Tokoe Omar captured after a hot fight, near Poeding, much slaughter, Jan., 1897; rebels defeated with heavy loss, reported, Jan. 26; Indrapaori occupied by the Dutch, Feb. 15; Dutch successes, March, June; Kampong taken by the Dutch; deadly fight near Indrapura, Aug.; desultory fighting, Sept., 1897; expedition to Pedir attacked by Achinese, enemy repulsed, and 110 killed; June 30, 1898, the Achinese again defeated, 80 killed, near Edı; quiet restored, flight of the enemy, July 18, 1895; further resistance in Matangkoli, Oct., 1898; Tokoe Oemar surprised by an ambuscade and mortally wounded; his troops dispersed, Feb. 10, 1899; sharp fighting, many Achinese killed, early March and mid April, 1901; Dutch punitive expedition in Djambi repulsed, 7 killed, reported Nov. 23; Dutch bivouac surprised, 12 killed, enemy 24, reported, July 19, the Sultan surrendered end, Dec., 1902

Sept. 6, Suffrage extension bill passed
Dec. 23, Sugar (bounties) bill passed

1897

March 1, Claim of Capt. J. C. Carpenter, of the Costa Rica (Australian whaler), for compensation for ill-usage and imprisonment by the Dutch authorities in the Moluccas (Nov., 1891), referred to Russian arbitration, Sept., 1895; 8,550l. awarded him
July 20, New liberal cabinet: Dr. Pierson Premier and Minister of Finance

1898

March 20, C. W. M. Van de Velde, traveler, artist, and cartographer, born 1818; died
June 16, East Indian loan of 55,000,000fl. agreed to
July 4, Obligatory personal military service, bill passed
Sept. 6, Coronation of the Queen at Amsterdam
Sept. 9, Royal entry into The Hague; States-General opened by the Queen with a speech from the throne, Sept. 20

1899

Jan. 1, Imperial penny postage started
Aug. 3, The Queen reviews the Dutch fishing fleet (about 2,000) on the Zuyder Zee
Aug. 22, 23, Riots at Hilversum, martial law proclaimed, 1 death
Oct. 7, The Queen and her mother visit the German Emperor
Dec. 6, Mr. Kruger, ex-President of the Transvaal, warmly received at The Hague; by the Queen for a few minutes, Dec. 8; at Amsterdam, Dec. 19

1901

Feb. 7, Marriage of Queen Wilhelmina to Duke Henry of Mecklenburg-Schwerin at The Hague; state entry into Amsterdam, March 5, 1901; they visit Berlin, May 30–June 1
June 28, Elections: Catholic majority, mid June; the cabinet resigns
July 27, M. de Kuyper forms a ministry (3 Roman Catholic members out of 8)

1902

Jan. 11, Death of Prof. C. P. Tiele, theologian and historian, aged 70
June 12, Conventions regarding European marriage and divorce laws drawn up at The Hague, 1900; signed
Aug. 20, The Boer generals visit Mr. Kruger at Utrecht; conference held with Dr. Leyds and others at The Hague, Aug. 21
Sept. 9, Increase of nat. debt 1890–1900 owing to costly railway and canal construction; new elementary education and military laws, budget, 1902; actual deficit, about 83,000l., reported
Sept. 22, Boer generals appeal for relief funds
Dec. 2, Brussels sugar convention ratified

1903

Feb., Strikes in Amsterdam
April 6–13, Railway and dock strikes
April 11, Anti-strike bills passed
April 25, Gift of $1,500,000 by Mr. A. Carnegie for a temple of peace for the Permanent Court of Arbitration at The Hague, reported

1904

March 24, Second chamber by a majority of the clerical party, opposed by all the members of the left, pass a higher education bill, granting the private universities under certain guarantees the same privileges as those accorded to state universities
April 6, Arbitration convention with France signed
June 23, New commercial treaty with Belgium signed
July 14, First chamber by 27 votes to 22 rejects the higher education bill, on the ground that the privileges proposed should not be granted without full guarantees against the introduction of religious dogma in the teaching of private universities
Sept. 20, States-General reassemble; government announces its intention of introducing a new education bill; deficit to be met by increased tax on alcoholic liquors, and tariff revision
Oct. 19, Government decides to purchase land between Scheveningen and The Hague for the erection of the palace of peace

1905

March 8, Baron Melvil van Leyden, Minister for Foreign Affairs, resigns
March 15, Second chamber votes the bill extending to private universities the same privileges as those accorded to state institutions
March 29, Adm. Ellis, ad interim Minister for Foreign Affairs, presents to the second chamber for its approval an arbitration treaty with Gt. Britain
April, Great strike of diamond cutters at Amsterdam
April 19, M. van Weede appointed Minister for Foreign Affairs
May 17, After long debate the second chamber passes a bill modifying the law with regard to primary education; the entire left votes against the bill
May 24, Second chamber votes 700,000fl. (58,300l.) for the purchase of a site in the park of The Hague, known as Zorgvliet, for the palace of peace
May 31, Bill revising the law of secondary education by increasing the subvention in favor of confessional schools passes the first chamber
June 30, Elections for the second chamber result in the return of 25 Catholics, 15 orthodox Protestants,

8 historic Christians, 11 democratic liberals, 10 liberals of the right, 24 liberals of the left, and 7 socialists, comprising 52 anti-ministerialists and 48 ministerialists, reported

July 5, Resignation of Dr. Kuyper, Premier, and his cabinet

Aug. 9, New ministry formed: M. van Hamel, Premier and Minister of Justice; Jonheer van Swinderen, Minister for Foreign Affairs; M. Rint, Minister of the Interior

Sept. 19, Queen opens Parliament: speech from the throne describes the general condition of the country and the colonies as satisfactory; announces various legislative proposals, including a revision of the constitution removing the barriers to general suffrage; and states that an extension of the sources of revenue was necessary to meet the unavoidable increase in expenditure

1906

Sept. 22, E. Indies: Report of fighting at Bali as the outcome of the military expedition now in progress; 400 of the enemy killed in a bayonet charge; Dutch losses, 4 killed and 10 wounded

Sept. 27, Prince of Tabanan formally surrenders with all his family, and peace reported restored in the whole of Bali

1907

May 24, Senate votes a credit of 8,330*l.* for expenditure in connection with the peace conference

July 30, Foundation stone of the Carnegie palace of peace at The Hague laid by M. Nelidoff

Dec. 25, Resignation of the cabinet on rejection by the Chamber of the military estimates

1908

Jan. 8, Bill, ratifying the additional act of the sugar convention, approved by the second chamber by the States-General

1910

April 30, Ex-President Roosevelt received at Het Loo, April 29, and at The Hague

Aug. 3–16, Lockout in the cotton industry following strike which was terminated by agreement

Dec. 19, Resignation of General Cool, Minister of War. Succeeded by M. Colyin

1911

May 17, Gambling Act passed prohibited betting by bookmakers and totalizator

June 28, Strike of seamen on 20 out of 35 liners in ports

July 11, Seamens strike ended with agreement for increase of 5s. per month

July 26, Dockers strike ended

1912

April 27, Poor Relief Act passed created Commission and local councils

May 7, Vice-Admiral Wentholt, Minister of Marine, defeated on policy resigned

June 1–4, State visit of the Queen and Prince Henry to Paris

1913

June 17 and 25, Elections held, a defeat for Clericals

June 21, Coast Defense Bill passed Chamber (Second Chamber May 6)

Aug. 28, Dedication of Palace of Peace inaugurated; representatives of 42 States present

Aug. 29, Dr. W. P. A. Cort van der Linden appointed Prime Minister and Minister of the Interior

Sept. 16, Parliament opened by the Queen

Sept. 27, Dr. J. Louden appointed Minister of Foreign Affairs

1914

Jan. 29, Academy of International Law founded at The Hague

June 25, Decision of Hague Court in favor of the Netherlands in case of the boundary with Portugal Island of Timor

July 29, Amsterdam stock exchange closed

——, Bank rate raised to 4.5%

July 30, Proclamation of neutrality in World War

Aug. 1–4, Mobilization

Aug. 1, Bank rate raised to 6%

——, Export of hay and straw prohibited

——, Bank rate raised to 6%

Aug. 3, Royal decree prohibited export of legumes

——, Act authorized the Government to suspend the redemption of bank notes amending charter of the Netherlands Bank

Aug. 4, Neutrality reaffirmed

Aug. 10, Royal National Relief Committee created to maintain activity in industry, agriculture, and horticulture

Aug. 20, Bank rate reduced to 5%

Sept. 4, Act placed the stock exchange under control of the Minister of Trade and later under Minister of Finance

Sept. 7, Export of sugar prohibited; later arrangement permitted export under permits up to 60%

Sept. 19, General Dutch Credit Bank founded

Sept. 24, Royal decree prohibited the export of linseed

Oct. 15, Decree prohibited export of potatoes

Oct. 26, Royal decree prohibited the export of cheese

Oct. 29, Royal decree prohibited the export of butter

Nov. 23, Netherlands Overseas Trust Company created, a committee of business men of highest integrity to supervise all imports

Dec. 23, Loan Act provided for issue of a voluntary loan of 275 million guilders in 5% bonds

——, Export of live cattle and pigs prohibited

Dec. 31, Population 6,339,727

1915

Feb. 9, Stock exchange reopened

Feb. 20, Decree prohibited export of meat to European countries except under special regulations

Feb. 24, Export of fodder, beets, turnips, carrots, and cabbages prohibited

March 4, Export of live sheep prohibited

March 19, The Government protested against blockade policy of the Entente

March 25, Arbitration Convention of Feb. 15, 1905 with Great Britain renewed

April 1, A Central Bureau established to regulate exports

April 22, Suspension of sea traffic with Great Britain

May 1, Sea traffic with Great Britain resumed

May 8, Marine War Risk Act passed provided for insurance of persons on ships

June 3, Act of British Parliament as to consignment of exports to Holland to the Netherlands Overseas Trust Company

Aug. 1, Export of horses prohibited

Aug. 23, Decree sanctioned weekly export of breeding cattle

Oct. 14, Decree placed export of eggs under supervision

Dec. 4, Schroeder, editor of the "Telegraaf" arrested for publication of articles favorable to the Entente Allies oh charge of endangering the neutrality of the country. Acquitted Dec. 14

Dec. 7, Agreement concluded between the Netherlands Overseas Trust and the French Government

1916

Jan. 7, Arrangements made with Great Britain for rationing the country

Jan. 13–14, Floods in which the Zuider Zee dikes gave way and a large part of northern Holland inundated

Feb. 3, Treub, Minister of Finance resigned

Feb. 8, Dr. Anton van Gijn appointed Minister of Finance

March 16, The Dutch steamer "Tubantia" torpedoed

March 17, Loan Act provided for domestic loan of 125 million guilders at 4.5%

March 18, Law prohibited the sale, hire, or transfer of ships without permission of the Minister of Commerce

——, The "Palembang" bound for Java sunk by German torpedo

June 21, Tax on war profits enacted retroactive to Aug. 1, 1914

June 30, Further Agreement of the Netherlands Overseas Trust with Great Britain for rationing Holland

Sept. 19, Government plan for unemployment insurance set up

Dec. 16, Third loan enacted of 125 million guilders at 4%

1917

Feb. 7, Invitation of the United States to sever diplomatic relations with Germany declined

Feb. 9, War Molestation Insurance Act of 1915 came into effect providing for insurance of vessels

Feb. 10, Law enacted gave Government authority to commandeer ships

Feb. 22, 7 Dutch merchant vessels torpedoed in North Sea by German submarine, and 4 sunk

Feb. 26, Dutch ships requisitioned by Great Britain

March 26, Rent Restriction Act appointed commissions to fix rents and limit unreasonable rises in every community

Oct. 15, Law established the Netherlands Export Company to grant export permits

Dec. 12, Electoral Reform Act established universal suffrage and proportional representation for citizens of both sexes not under 25

Dec. 15, Fourth Loan Act provided for loan of 500 million guilders at 4.5%

Dec. 29, First train of British prisoners arrived from Germany

1918

Jan. 4, Agreement to permit requisition of Dutch ships by Entente Allies with certain conditions

Feb. 4, General strike of 24 hours against the Government

March 18, Agreement as to requisition of Dutch ships by Allies

March 20, Dutch ships in ports of the United States requisitioned

March 25, Tenants Eviction Act passed to prevent evictions without reason

April 11–12, Food riots quelled by troops

April 20, Agricultural Laborers' Act gave opportunity to farmers to buy cattle or rent unoccupied lands

May 9, Joint Trade Committee of Entente Powers formed in the Netherlands

June 17, Housing Emergency Act enabled the Crown to require building of dwellings where needed

July 2, Advisory Commission for economic information abroad created

July 3, General election gave gains to Conservatives and Labor followed by resignation of the van der Linden Cabinet

July 26, Act regulated use of vans and boats as dwellings

Aug. 30, Jonkheer Ruys de Beerenbrouck headed a Cabinet formed by Dr. Nolens, Roman Catholic leader, Dr. H. A. van Karnebeek, Minister of Foreign Affairs

Sept. 12, Cabinet reconstructed

Nov. 10, Arrival of William, ex-Emperor of Germany taking refuge in Holland. He established residence at Amerongen and in defiance of demand of Allies for his extradition for trial was allowed to remain

Dec. 19, Loan for 350 million guilders at 5% enacted

Dec. 25, Decree established 2 new departments, Education and Labor

1919

Jan. 20, Revolt planned by Communists frustrated

July 28, Anti-Revolution Act passed directed against bolshevism defined offenses

Aug. 9, Electoral Reform Act provided for direct election of Second Chamber by citizens of both sexes not under 23

Sept. 25, Last of Dutch requisitioned ships restored

Oct. 4, Decree issued general administrative regulations for constitution of Superior Labor Council

Nov. 1, General labor law enacted; prohibited labor of children under 14

——, Royal National Relief Committee liquidated

Nov. 4, Voluntary Old Age Pension Act passed

Dec. 31, Population 6,841,155

1920

Jan. 13, Agreement with Belgium to appoint committee to settle questions in dispute as to the Scheldt and Ghent-Terneuzen Canal

Jan. 16, Supreme Council asked surrender of the ex-Emperor of Germany for trial

Jan. 23, Surrender of the ex-Emperor refused

Feb. 24–April 28, General strike of dockers paralyzed industry

March 9, The Netherlands became member of League of Nations

May 3, Note to Belgium claimed exclusive sovereignty over the Wielingen Channel

May 15, The German Emperor took up residence in new home at Doorn

May 17, Passenger and mail air service established between Amsterdam and London

May 26, Belgians broke off negotiations

June 1, Arbitration Convention with Great Britain of Feb. 15, 1905 renewed

Dec. 31, Population 6,865,314

1921

Jan. 1, New Elementary Education Act came into effect (6–13 years)

Jan. 25, Commercial Agreement with Germany signed

Feb. 9, Workmen's Compensation Convention with Belgium signed

Feb. 19, Rental Act passed to prevent houses from being left vacant supplementing Housing Act by providing for expropriation of houses to meet shortage

June 24, Commercial *modus vivendi* with Spain established

July 1, Djambi Oil Bill passed providing for exploitation of oil fields in Dutch East Indies

Sept. 21, Papal Legation reëstablished

Dec. 1, Extradition Convention of Nov. 24, 1880 with Austria revived

1922

Jan. 6, New Commercial Agreement with Spain concluded

March 9, Commercial Agreement with Bulgaria by exchange of notes

May 19, Old Age Pension Act of 1919 amended

May 20, Labor Act of 1919 amended

July 22, Cabinet resigned but postponed action

Sept. 11, Cabinet reconstructed

Dec. 19, Provisional Commercial Agreement with Rumania signed

Dec. 31, 9.1 workers out of employment as compared with 6% at close of 1921 and about 12 million florins paid out as unemployment doles

1923

Jan. 11, Trade unfavorably affected by Ruhr occupation

Jan. 20, Commercial Agreement with Czechoslovakia signed

June 3, Commercial Agreement with Germany signed

July 16, Death of Louis Couperus, novelist

Aug. 22, Provisional Commercial Agreement with Portugal replaced that of July 5, 1894

Sept. 5, Commercial Treaty with Austria concluded

Oct. 26, Naval Bill providing for increase of fleet defeated in second Chamber

Nov. 1, Provisional Commercial Agreement with Finland concluded

Nov. 12, The former Crown Prince of Germany left Holland for Germany

1924

Feb. 13, Arbitration Convention with the United States extended that of May 2, 1908

June 10, Provisional Commercial Agreement with Lithuania signed

July 2, Commercial Agreement with Latvia signed

July 22, Commercial Agreement with Estonia signed

July 26–Sept. 11, Flight from Amsterdam to Tokio of Lieutenant Van Weerden Podman and Van den Bracke, and Van der Hoop

Aug. 16, Treaty of friendship and conciliation with Turkey signed

Aug. 21, Liquor Smuggling Convention with the United States signed

Oct. 1–Nov. 24, Pioneer flight of I. Van der Hoop from Amsterdam to Batavia, Java, 9,300 miles in 27 days of flying

Nov. 20, Dutch currency at par in New York for the first time since May, 1919

Dec. 9, Commercial Convention with Hungary signed

Dec. 18, Treaty of commerce and navigation with Greece of Feb. 22, 1843 and supplementary Convention of June 18–30, 1851 extended by exchange of Notes

1925

Jan. 23, Agreement with the United States to arbitrate dispute as to sovereignty of Palmas Island

April 3, Treaty with Belgium signed to replace Treaty of April 19, 1839 as to administration of the Scheldt, free navigation established

April 27, Death of Louis Bouwmeester (82), actor

June 8, Treaty of friendship, commerce, and navigation with Siam signed

July 2, Elections gave Catholics 32 seats in Chamber and Social Democratic Labor Party 24 out of total of 100, losses to Government Coalition

July 6, Beerenbrouck Ministry defeated in election, resigned, and was succeeded by Colÿn, leader of the Calvinist Anti-Revolutionary Party who formed a Coalition Cabinet

July 12, Arbitration Convention with Great Britain signed

Nov. 11, Resignation of the Catholic Ministers in Cabinet because of passage of Bill to abolish diplomatic representation at the Vatican introduced in 1921

Nov. 14, Colÿn Cabinet resigned

Nov. 24, Marchant, Radical leader, invited to form Cabinet not successful

Nov. 26, Commercial Agreement with Germany signed

Dec. 12, Conciliation Treaty with Switzerland signed

1926

Jan. 22, Dr. de Visser, leader of Christian Historicals, failed to form a Cabinet

Jan. 25, First provincial council inaugurated that of West Java

March 3, Dr. J. Limburg failed to form Cabinet

March 4, Dr. J. de Geer, Christian Historical, formed a Cabinet ending crisis since November, van Karnebeek, Minister of Foreign Affairs

May 12, Commercial Treaty with Greece signed

May 20, Arbitration Treaty with Germany signed

May 22, Treaty with France, and Great Britain, ended neutrality of Belgium and prohibition against Antwerp being a military port

June 3 and Aug. 4, Customs Agreement with Austria concluded by exchange of Notes

July 23, Provisional Air Navigation Agreement with Denmark concluded

Aug. 4, Customs Agreement with Austria concluded

Aug. 11, Provisional Commercial Agreement with Turkey signed

Nov. 11, Treaty with Belgium of April 3, 1925 ratified by Second Chamber

Nov. 13, Communist revolt in Batavia, West Java, and other towns of the East Indies

1927

March 24, Treaty with Belgium of April 3, 1925 regarding free navigation of the Scheldt rejected by the first chamber (Senate) by 33 votes against 17

March 30, Jonkheer F. Belaerts van Blokland appointed Minister of Foreign Affairs

April 30, Princess Juliana attained political majority and became a member of the Council of State under the Constitution

May 21, Treaty of conciliation with Sweden signed

June 2, Queen Wilhelmina and the Princess Juliana broadcasted to the East Indies inaugurating successful radio-telephone conversation

July 20, Communist uprising in Java and the East Indies finally quelled

Oct. 27, The Meuse-Waal Canal formally opened

1928

Feb. 4, Death of Hendrik Antoon, physicist

Feb. 13, Customs Agreement with Germany concluded

March 10, Treaty of arbitration and conciliation with France

March 30, Treaty with Great Britain signed for delimitation of frontier in Borneo

April 4, Decision of Max Huber, arbitrator, gave the Island of Las Palmas to the Netherlands

April 28, Customs Convention with Germany signed

May 12, Accident Insurance Act of June, 1921 amended

June 24, Commercial Treaty with Portugal signed

July 25, Commercial Treaty with Turkey signed

Oct. 27, Treaty of arbitration and conciliation with Siam signed

Dec. 19, Tariff-Autonomy Treaty with China signed

Dec. 27, Treaty of arbitration and conciliation with Spain signed

1929

Feb. 12, Fire destroyed the Town Hall at Leyden built in 595

Feb. 27, Arbitration Treaty with the United States renewed that of May 2, 1908

July 3, Elections gave Catholic Party 16 seats, Anti-Revolutionists, 6; Protestant Party, 7; Liberty Union, 6; Democrats, 4; Social Democrats, 11; Second Chamber, Catholics, 30; Social Democrats, 24; Anti-Revolutionists, 12; Christian Historicals, 11; Liberty Union, 8; Democrats, 7; other parties, 8

——, Resignation of de Geer Cabinet

Aug. 10, Dr. J. M. Ruys de Beerenbrouck formed a Cabinet: President of the Council of Ministers, Minister of the Interior and of Agriculture, Dr. Ch. J. M. Ruys de Beerenbrouck, appointed August 10, 1929; Foreign Affairs, Dr. F. Beelaerts van Blokland, appointed March 30, 1927; Finance, Dr. D. J. de Geer, appointed March 8, 1926; Justice, Dr. J. Donner, appointed March 8, 1926; Colonies, S. de Graaf, appointed August 10, 1926; Defense, Dr. L. N. Deckers, appointed August 10, 1929; Public Works (Waterstaat), Dr. P. J. Reymer, appointed August 10, 1929; Labor, Commerce, and Industry, Dr. J. Th. Verschuur, appointed August 10, 1929; Instruction, Science, and Arts, Dr. J. Terpstra, appointed August 10, 1929

Sept. 14, Arbitration and Conciliation Treaty with Czechoslovakia signed

Nov. 15, Central Bank lowered discount rate from 5 to 4.5%

1930

Jan. 13, Arbitration Treaty with the United States signed

Jan. 22, Treaty of arbitration, conciliation, and judicial settlement with Rumania signed

March 12, Treaty of friendship with Persia signed

April 12, Treaty of arbitration, conciliation, and judicial settlement with Poland signed

April 29, The world's largest lock at point where the North Sea Channel cuts across North Holland opened by Queen Wilhelmina enabling the largest steamers to reach Amsterdam

PRINCES OF ORANGE, STADTHOLDERS

1502. Philibert de Chalons

1530. René de Nassau, his nephew

1544. William of Nassau, styled the Great, cousin to René, recovers the principality of Orange in 1559 Nominated stadtholder, 1579; killed by an assassin hired by Philip II of Spain, July 10, 1584

1584. Philip William, his son; stolen away from the university of Louvain; the Dutch would never suffer him to reside in their provinces: died 1618

1618. Maurice, the renowned general; became stadtholder in 1584; he was a younger son of William by a second marriage

1625. Frederick Henry (brother), stadtholder

1647. William II, stadtholder: married Mary, daughter of Charles I of England, by whom he had a son, who succeeded in 1672

1650–72. John De Witt, Grand Pensioner; no stadtholder

1660. William-Henry: stadtholder in 1672; married Mary, eldest daughter of James II of England, 1677

1702–47. No stadtholder

1702. John-William, nephew of William III, loses the Principality of Orange, which is annexed to France

1747. William-Henry becomes hereditary stadtholder; married Princess Anne of England: succeeded by his son

1751. William IV; retired on the invasion of the French in 1795; died in 1806

1795. [Holland and Belgium united to the French republic]

KINGS AND QUEEN

1806. Louis Bonaparte made King of Holland by his brother Napoleon, June 5, 1806; abdicated, July 1, 1810

1810. [Holland again united to France]

1813. House of Orange restored. William-Frederick, Prince of Orange (born 1772), proclaimed Dec. 6, 1813; took the oath of fidelity as sovereign prince, March 30, 1814; assumed the style of King of the Netherlands, March 16, 1815; formally abdicated in favor of his son, Oct. 7, 1840; died Dec. 12, 1843

1840. William II, born Dec. 6, 1792; succeeded on his father's abdication; died March 17, 1849, succeeded by

1849. William III, son; born Feb. 19, 1817; married Sophia of Würtemberg, June 18, 1839. (She died, June 3, 1877.) Issue: William, Prince of Orange, born Sept. 4, 1840; died June 11, 1879; Alexander (philosopher), born Aug. 25, 1851; died June 21, 1884. Married Emma of Waldeck-Pyrmont, Jan. 7, 1879; issue: Wilhelmina, born Aug. 31, 1880. The King died Nov. 23, 1890

1890. Wilhelmina (the Queen-Mother Regent), daughter; crowned, Sept. 6, 1898; married Duke Henry of Mecklenburg-Schwerin, Feb. 7, 1901

Juliana, Princess, *b.* April 30, 1909

NORWAY

Norway, kingdom of northern Europe, occupying the western part of the Scandinavian peninsula, bounded on the east by Sweden except in the extreme north where the frontier marches with that of Finland giving Norway in the north a narrow fringe of country on the Arctic Ocean farthest north of any other part of Europe, boundaries on the north, northwest, and west, the Arctic Ocean, Atlantic Ocean, and North Sea respectively, with the Skagerak on the south and southeast. The average width of the country is about 60 miles, the extreme width, about 260 miles, length about 1,100 miles. The total area is 125,086 miles, total population, 2,890,000. Oslo (Christiania) is the capital. Dependencies of Norway are Spitsbergen, Bear Island and adjacent islands, Jan Mayen Island and Bouvet Island.

Norway, until the seventeenth century, was governed by petty rulers. About 630, Olaf Trætelia, of the race of Odin termed Ynglings or youths, expelled from Sweden, established a colony in Vermeland, the nucleus of a monarchy, founded by his descendant, Halfdan III the Black, a great warrior and legislator, whose memory was long revered. Union with Sweden, existing since 1814, dissolved Oct. 16, 1905.

By the Treaty of January 14, 1814, Norway was ceded to the King of Sweden by the King of Denmark, but the Norwegian people declared themselves independent and elected Prince Christian Frederick of Denmark as their King. The foreign Powers refused to recognize this election, and on August 14 a convention was made proclaiming the independence of Norway in union with Sweden. This was followed on November 4 by the election of Karl XIII as King of Norway. Norway declared this union dissolved, June 7, 1905, and after some months' negotiation, a mutual agreement for the repeal of the union was signed, October 26, 1905. The throne of Norway was offered to a prince of the reigning house of Sweden, but declined, and, after a *plébescite*, Prince Carl of Denmark was formally elected King. In November, 1907, a treaty guaranteeing the integrity of Norwegian territory was signed at Christiania (Oslo) by the representatives of Norway, Great Britain, France, Germany, and Russia, and on January 8, 1908, received the unanimous approval of the Storthing. The Treaty was denounced January 8, 1924.

Haakon VII, reigning King.

630 to 1624

640, Olaf Trætelia, 630; slain by his subjects
640, Halfdan I; Eystein I, 700; Halfdan II, 730; Gudrod 784; Olaf Geirstade and Halfdan III, 824
863, Halfdan recovers his inheritance from his brother, whom he subdues, together with the neighboring chiefs, 840; accidentally drowned
865, The chiefs regain their power during the youth of his son, Harald Härfager
934, He defeats his enemies at Hafsfiord, 872; dies
Eric I (the Bloody Axe), his son, a tyrant, expelled, and succeeded by

940, Hakon (the Good); he endeavors in vain to establish Christianity; dies 963
963, Harald II, Graafeld, son of Eric, succeeds
977, Killed in battle with Harald of Denmark
995, Hakon Jarl, made governor of several provinces; becomes King, 977; his licentiousness leads to his ruin; deposed by Olaf I, Trygvæson; and slain by his slave
998, Olaf I, 995; establishes Christianity by force and cruelty
1000, Defeated and slain, during an expedition against Pomerania, by the Kings of Denmark and Sweden, who divide Norway between them
1012, Olaf II, the Saint lands in Norway
1015, Defeats his enemies and becomes King
1018–21, Fiercely zealous in the diffusion of Christianity
1028–9, Successful invasion of Canute, who becomes King
1030, Olaf expelled; returns and is killed in battle
1035, Sweyn, at the death of Canute, succeeds as King of Norway, but is expelled in favor of Magnus I, bastard son of Olaf II
1047, Magnus becomes King of Denmark, 1042; dies
——, Harald Hardrada, King of Norway
Sept. 25, 1066, Invades England; defeated and slain by Harald II at Stamford-bridge
——, Olaf III and Magnus II (sons), kings; Olaf alone (pacific), 1069–1093
1070, Olaf III founds Bergen
1093, Magnus III (Barefoot), son of Olaf
1096, Invades the Orkneys and Scotland
1103, Killed in Ireland
——, Sigurd I, Eystein II, and Olaf IV (sons)
1107–10, Sigurd visits the Holy Land as a warrior pilgrim
1130, Becomes sole king, 1122; dies
——, Magnus IV (his son) and Harald IV
1134, Magnus dethroned
1136, Harald IV murdered; succeeded by his sons, Sigurd II, &c.; civil war rages
1136–62, Numerous competitors for the crown; civil war; Inge I, Eystein III, Hakon III, Magnus V
1152, Nicolas Breakspear (afterwards Pope Adrian IV), the papal legate, arrives, reconciles the brothers, and founds the Archbishopric of Trondhjem
1162, Magnus V alone
1184, Rise of Sverre, an able adventurer, who becomes King; Magnus defeated; drowned
1202, Sverre rules vigorously; dies
——, Hakon, his son, King; Guthrum, 1204; Inge II, 1205
1207, Hakon IV, bastard son of Sverre
1263, Unsuccessfully invades Scotland, where he dies
1280, Magnus VI, his son (the legislator), dies
1286, Eric II, the priest-hater, marries Margaret of Scotland; their daughter, the Maid of Norway, becomes heiress to the crown of Scotland
1299–1319, Hakon V, his brother, King
Decline of Norwegian prosperity
1319–43, Magnus VII (III of Sweden), King
1343–80, Hakon VI
1380–87, Olaf V of Norway (II of Denmark)
1389, Norway united with Denmark and Sweden under Margaret
1397, At an assembly at Calmar the three states are formally united
1450, Sweden and Norway separated from Denmark, 1448; reunited

1523, Denmark and Norway separated from Sweden

1624, Christiania, the modern capital, built by Christian IV

1670 to 1811

1670–1699, The laws revised and codified by Charles V of Denmark

1716, Charles XII of Sweden compelled to raise the siege of Frederikshald and retire from the country by Peder Tordenskjold who destroyed the Swedish fleet at anchor in strait of Dynekil

1717–1718, Further invasions of Charles XII of Sweden

1788, Repeal of law that grain should be imported into Norway only from Denmark

1811, University of Christiania (now Oslo) founded

1814

Jan. 14, Norway given to Sweden by the treaty of Kiel; Pomerania and Rugen annexed to Denmark

May 17, The Norwegians declare their independence

July 16, The Swedish troops enter Norway

Oct. 10, Charles Frederic, Duke of Holstein, elected King of Norway; abdicates

Nov. 4, Charles XIII of Sweden proclaimed King by the National Diet (Storthing) assembled at Christiania; he accepted the constitution of May 17 which declares Norway a free, independent, indivisible, and inalienable state, united to Sweden

1821 to 1882

1821, Nobility abolished

1847, The national order of St. Olaf instituted by King Oscar I

July 18, 1872, Millennial festival of the establishment of the Kingdom, kept

July 17, 1873, The King Oscar II crowned at Trondhjem

1881, Disputes between the Storthing and the Crown respecting constitutional changes

Oct., 1882, Elections; liberal majority claiming Norwegian constitutional rights; many republicans

1883

Jan., Liberal leader, Sóren Jaabœk (violent), Mr. Sverdrup (moderate)

Feb., Opening of the Storthing, firm resistance of the Crown Ministers

March 9, Who are threatened with impeachment; which is adopted, April 23

Impeachment of the Minister, Christian Selmer, and his 10 colleagues, for advising the King to veto the bill for ministerial responsibility

Oct. 22, Trial of Selmer began

1884

Feb. 27, Selmer found guilty by the supreme council of Norway; sentenced to dismissal from public service, and payment of expenses of prosecution

March 12, M. Selmer resigns his post, the King accedes, but maintains his power of veto

March 19, The Crown Prince of Sweden appointed Viceroy of Norway

March 20–April 1, Trial and conviction of M. Kjerulf and other Ministers

April 3, New ministry formed (Councillor Schweigaard and M. Carl Lövenskjold, and others)

June 6, Resigns; M. Johan Sverdrup forms a liberal ministry, June 26

1889

July 12, Resignation of the Sverdrup Ministry, July 2; succeeded by Emil Stang

About Sept. 9, Death of Christian A. Selmer

1890

July 1 *et seq.*, Visit of the German Emperor at Christiania

1891

Feb. 23, Resignation of the Stang Ministry, in consequence of a vote in the parliament demanding greater independence for Norway in political policy, tending to separation from Sweden

March 5, M. Steen, the liberal leader, forms a cabinet

1892

June 10, Norway desires autonomy in foreign affairs; opposed by Sweden, Feb.; adopted by the Storthing

1893

March 17, Continued demand for autonomy in foreign affairs, Feb.; the Storthing ignores the conciliatory overtures of Sweden, March, and claims separate foreign consular establishment

April 17, King Oscar visits Christiania; on his refusal to consent to autonomy in foreign affairs the Steen Ministry resigns and the Storthing adjourns, April 23, 24; new ministry formed by M. Emil Stang, May 2; censured by vote (63–51), May 6

June 21, The Storthing votes the partial substitution of the Norwegian flag for that of the Union

1895

Jan. 31, Resignation of the Ministry; negotiations between the King and the Storthing, Feb.; no result, the old Ministry retains office, May 25

June 19, M. Bonnevie declines to form a ministry

Oct. 14, A coalition ministry formed by M. Hagerup, Premier

1898

Feb. 17, Resignation of the Hagerup Ministry, Feb. 12, new ministry formed by M. Steen

March 7, Report of the Norwegian committee on the union with Sweden, presented to parliament

May 16, International fisheries exhibition opened at Bergen; and festival (1st) of Norwegian music, conducted by Dr. Edvard Grieg; June 26–July 2

Oct., Joint commission to promote a *modus vivendi* with Sweden, fails

Nov. 12, New state loan of 20,000,000 kroner at 3½%, redeemable in 20 years, announced

Dec., The King refuses to sanction a purely Norwegian flag

1899

Sept. 1–3, New Norwegian national theater in Christiania opened by the King; three days' dramatic festival ovations to Ibsen, Björnson, and Grieg

Oct. 23, State loan, 30,000,000 kroner, authorized by the Storthing

1901

Aug. 12, Great fire in Farsund, over 1,200 persons homeless

1902

Jan. 11, State loan of 35,000,000 kroner at 3½% for 60 years, concluded with a Scandinavian banking syndicate

April 20, M. Steen's Ministry resigns, April 16; one formed by M. Blehr

Sept. 28, Captain Sverdrup and the *Fram* N. Pole expedition welcomed in Christiania

Oct. 13, Storthing opened, army reorganization proposed

1903

Jan., Storthing adopts, by 81 to 32, president's resolution for the establishment of a separate Norwegian consular system

Oct. 21–22, Blehr Ministry resigns, Prof. Hagerup forms coalition cabinet

1904

Jan. 23, Great fire at Aalesund, major part of the town destroyed, about 10,000 persons homeless

Negotiations between the Norwegian and Swedish Governments for the settlement of separate consulates carried on during the year

1905

Feb. 2, Prolonged negotiations on the consular question reach a deadlock, the Storthing refusing to take into consideration the Swedish proposal that the separate consuls for Norway, whom it was proposed to appoint, should be subordinate to the Minister for Foreign Affairs, who was a member of the Swedish cabinet, the demand of Norway being that Norwegian consuls should be subordinate only to Norwegian authority

March 1, The Premier, M. Hagerup, and his Ministry resign, on the ground that their proposal to renew negotiations with Sweden on the basis that the conditions of union should be revised, with an amicable dissolution of the union if the negotiations were futile, was not approved by the Storthing

March 10, M. Michelsen forms a new cabinet on the basis of the constitution of a separate Norwegian consular service, with or without the consent of Sweden

April 6, Crown Prince, at a mixed council, proposes fresh negotiations on the basis of full equality of Norway and Sweden, and providing for a joint Minister for Foreign Affairs, and a separate consular service for each country

April 13, M. Boström, Swedish Premier, resigns, April 9; succeeded by M. Ramstedt

April 25, Swedish Riksdag accepts the Crown Prince's proposals; the Norwegian Ministry refuse to enter into further negotiations until a Norwegian consular service had been established, and that there should be separate Norwegian and Swedish Ministers for Foreign Affairs

May 19, Storthing passes a bill establishing a separate consular service for Norway, to come into force April 1, 1906

May 26, King Oscar resumes government

May 27, The King refuses to sanction the consular bill; M. Michelsen and his cabinet resign; King refuses to accept resignation

June 7, Storthing passes a resolution authorizing the Ministry to remain in office, and to assume sovereign power, thereby deposing King Oscar II, who is invited to permit a prince of his house (Bernadotte) to accept election as King of Norway; the union between Norway and Sweden, based on the common monarchy, is thus dissolved

June 9, New Norwegian flag, with the mark of union omitted, hoisted with great ceremony on the old citadel of Christiania; Swedish council decides not to recognize the provisional government established in Norway

June 21, Bill introduced in the Swedish Riksdag for negotiations with the Norwegian Storthing for the dissolution and the settlement of the future relations between Sweden and Norway

July 25, Proposals of the Swedish Government referred to a special committee, which reports that the consent of Sweden to separation should not be withheld, provided an opportunity were given to the Norwegians to declare their will, either by the election of a new storthing or by a referendum, and that Norway should make representations to Sweden for the repeal of the union

July 27, Resignation of the Swedish Ministry on the rejection of its proposals by the Riksdag; M. Lundeberg forms a coalition ministry; Riksdag unanimously adopts the proposals of the special committee

July 28, Storthing adopts the proposal of Sweden for a referendum

Aug. 13, Referendum takes place, 368,200 votes recorded for the dissolution of the union, 184 votes against; 84.9% of the total number of the electors voted

Aug. 24, Storthing passes resolutions requesting the Swedish Government to coöperate in effecting a dissolution, and authorizes the government to enter into negotiations with Sweden, Aug. 22; Swedish Government acquiesces

Aug. 31, Conference between four delegates representing each country opened at Karlstad

Agreement by the conference, after difficulties respecting the proposed demolition of fortresses along the boundary between Sweden and Norway had been adjusted. The agreement provides for the reference of all differences between Norway and Sweden to The Hague Court of Arbitration, except those affecting independence, integrity, and vital interests, not settled by direct diplomatic negotiations; the establishment of a neutral zone on either side of the frontier, involving the demolition of certain new fortifications by Norway within the zone; the preservation of the grazing rights of nomad Laplanders; freedom from taxation of transit traffic; the security of vested rights in waterways; the agreement to be subject to the sanction of the Riksdag and Storthing

Oct. 9, Karlstad convention sanctioned by the Storthing by 101 votes to 16; and by both chambers of the Riksdag Oct. 13

Oct. 16, Swedish Riksdag passes bill for dissolving the act of union, and recognizing the independence of Norway

Oct. 25, King Oscar, having declined the offer of the Norwegian throne to a member of his house, the Storthing, by 87 votes to 29, adopts the proposal of the government that Prince Charles of Denmark should be asked to accept election, subject to the approval of the Norwegian people by referendum

Oct. 27, King Oscar addresses to the Norwegian Storthing a letter announcing his renunciation of the throne of Norway, and his recognition of Norway as a separate state

Nov. 10, Dr. Fritjof Nansen designated Norwegian Minister to Great Britain

Nov. 17, Referendum results in 259,563 votes being given in favor of the proposal, and 69,264 against

Nov. 18, Prince Charles unanimously elected King of
Norway by the Storthing, met in special session
——, Prince Charles of Denmark accepts election as
King of Norway, and adopts the title of Haakon
VII, his son to take the name of Olaf
Nov. 20, Deputation from the Storthing wait on King
Christian of Denmark, and receives his consent to
the election of Prince Charles
Nov. 25, King Haakon VII and Queen Maud make
their formal entry into Christiania, and are enthusi-
astically welcomed; the King takes the oath of
fidelity to the constitution before the Storthing, the
chief officials of the Church and State, in the hall of
the Storthing, Nov. 27

1906

Feb. 1, M. Knudsen, Minister of Public Worship re-
signs
May 23, Death of Henrik Ibsen
June 22, Coronation of King Haakon VII and Queen
Maud in Trondhjem Cathedral
July 8, The German Emperor visits King Haakon at
Trondhjem
Oct. 22, The Storthing at Christiania opened by King
Haakon

1907

June 14, The Storthing rejects a bill for universal suffrage for women, but adopts a measure granting
citizenship and the franchise to women under the
same conditions now existing under municipal
elections
Nov. 2, New treaty, providing for the integrity of Norway, signed at Christiania by the representatives of
Great Britain, France, Germany, Russia, and
Norway

1908

Jan. 13, King Haakon, at the opening of the Storthing,
refers to the treaty for the integrity of Norway
Jan. 18, The Norwegian integrity treaty unanimously
approved by the Storthing
March 14, Resignation of the cabinet accepted by King
Haakon; M. Gunnar Knudsen charged with the
formation of a new cabinet
March 19, New Cabinet settled, with M. Knudsen
Premier and Minister of Finance
April 28–May 3, King Edward VII, Queen Alexandra,
and Princess Victoria pay an official visit to Norway
June 19–25, Visit of the British Channel fleet to Chris-
tiania
July 20, Meeting between King Haakon and the Em-
peror William at Bergen
July 31, Visit of M. Fallières to Christiania
Oct. 23, Maritime boundary dispute with Sweden
settled by the Hague tribunal; Skjötte Grund
awarded to Norway

1910

Jan. 26, The Storthing opened by King Haakon
Jan. 27, Resignation of M. Knudsen, the Premier
Feb. 1, New Ministry formed by M. Konow
April 26, Death of Bjornstjerne Bjornson, poet (79)
June 7, Law abolished property qualification for women
for communal elections
July 25, Law provided for religious instruction in
secondary schools

1911

Feb. 1, W. Konow became Prime Minister; J. Irgens,
Foreign Affairs; A. Berge, Finance
Feb. 24, Measure passed abolished special rights of
Russian fishermen in Finmarken
March 3, Amendment to Constitution provided for
submission of diplomatic matters and certain other
questions of military command to a Committee of
the Odelsting constituted of 9 members
March 17, Miss Anna Rogstad, vice-deputy, took the
place of Jens Bratlie, president of the Chamber, for
2 weeks during his absence
April 28, 5,694,160 kroner granted for naval estimates,
100,000 kroner less than proposed by Military
Committee
Aug. 18, Bill passed admitted women to membership
in the Cabinet
——, Act established accident insurance for seamen
——, Tax law enacted, and as amended June 28, 1912,
repealed that of April 15, 1882
Dec. 14, Discovery of the South Pole by Roald Amund-
sen

1912

Feb. 16, Resignation of Prime Minister Wollert Konow
Feb. 19, General J. K. M. Bratlie, Conservative, formed
a Cabinet
March 7, Announcement of discovery of South Pole
by Roald Amundsen on Dec. 14, 1911
June 21, Highway law passed to come into effect July 1,
1913, revised and consolidated legislation, and Law
for the use of Motor Vehicles
July 6, Storthing appropriated $5,000,000 for naval
purposes
Oct. 21 and Nov. 4, General election a victory for the
Left
Dec. 23, Neutrality Agreement with Denmark signed

1913

Jan. 23, Storthing opened by the King
Jan. 24, Bratlie Ministry resigned
Jan. 29, Gunnar Knudsen, Liberal, formed Cabinet;
M. Ihlen, Foreign Affairs
June 11, Law granted vote to women without regard
to amount of income tax paid
June 26, Royal veto abolished
July 28, Eight hour day for workers in the Navy passed
Nov. 12, Election a victory for the Left

1914

May 6–11, General strike against introduction of Bill
to make strikes illegal and arbitration compulsory
July 4, Act authorized appointment of a Defense Com-
mission
July 6, New tax on incomes exceeding 4,000 kroner
(£222) and capital exceeding 100,000 kroner (£5,555)
July 29, Peace Entente with Sweden formed; affirmed
by Notes Aug. 8
Aug. 1, Neutrality declared in war between Austria-
Hungary and Serbia
——, Norges Bank raised rate from 5 to 6%
Aug. 2, Navy mobilized
——, Limitation placed on amount of bread which
could be sold
Aug. 3, Panic in which the shops were stormed to buy
food
Aug. 4, General declaration of neutrality

Aug. 4, Central Food Commission established to regulate imports and sales of food stuffs; the export of grain, flour, potatoes, coal, coke prohibited; the use of grain and potatoes for production of beer and liquors prohibited; temporary prohibition of sale of liquor

——, Gold payment suspended and general moratorium established for one month

Aug. 5, Royal decree ordered establishment of local food councils in all communes

——, Moratorium law enacted

Aug. 7, The steamer "Tysla" with cargo of zinc and lead struck mine at entrance to the Scheldt and sunk with loss of 3 men

Aug. 8, War Insurance established for the merchant fleet

——, Resignation of War Minister Keilhart. Succeeded by General Holtfodt

——, Declaration of neutrality by Denmark, Norway, and Sweden

Aug. 14, Decree restricted importation of alcoholic liquors

Aug. 18, Prohibition of sale of liquor repealed

——, Law passed authorized fixing of maximum prices for coal and food stuffs

Aug. 21, Law established compulsory mutual insurance of vessels

Sept. 8, The Norwegian Goods War Insurance Company, private joint-stock company, established

Sept. 26, Government authorized to negotiate loan of £600,000 at 7% in London to pay for 2 warships under construction in English shipyards; these ships not delivered because requisitioned by England

Sept. 26–Oct. 4, 11 Norwegian vessels sunk between Norway and Archangel with insured value of 11,000,000 krone

Dec. 18, Meeting of Kings of Norway, Sweden, and Denmark at Malmo where joint action as to a number of diplomatic and political matters agreed upon

1915

Feb. 3, Sailing vessel "Semantha" with cargo of wheat sunk

Feb. 23, Steamer "Regen" with cargo of coal struck mine and sank

Aug. 6, Act created Labor Courts for settlement of disputes between employers and employees, and Industrial Sickness and Insurance Act passed

Aug. 13, Workmen's Compensation Act passed

Sept. 18, Act for protection of industrial workers passed

Oct. 11, Women voted for the first time

Dec. 19, Arrival of Henry Ford in "peace ship" from the United States; remained 3 days

1916

Jan. 1, Laws for the protection of children adopted April, 1915, came into effect

——, Labor Courts under law of 1915 opened

March 8, From this date the Bank of Norway again obliged to redeem its bills with gold

March 9–11, Conference of the Kings of Norway, Denmark, and Sweden at Copenhagen agreed on mutual support of neutral rights

April 8, Constitutional amendment adopted declared women eligible to the Cabinet (Council of State)

April 10, Law fixed status of children born out of wedlock

April 15, Embargo on gold

June 7–15, General strike involving 200,000 workers

June 9, Compulsory arbitration of labor law again passed and renewed until 1921

June 28, Department of Trade, Sea Transport, Industry and Fisheries established

July 21, Vessels forbidden to sail to foreign countries without approval of the Government, and compensation increased for marine accidents

July 22, Strike of miners settled under new Arbitration Act

Aug. 5, Agreement by which Great Britain agreed to purchase all fish and fish oil not required for consumption of Norway

Sept. 19–20, Conference of the Kings of Norway, Sweden, and Denmark in Christiania

Oct. 13, Ordinance forbade belligerent submarines to traverse Norwegian waters except in emergency and then on the surface and flying national flag

1917

Jan. 23, Commercial Agreement with Germany concluded by exchange of Notes

Feb. 1, Norway prohibited use of her territorial waters to all foreign submarines

Feb. 14, Scandinavian Governments united in protest against German submarine warfare

May 25, Housing law enacted

June 28, Decree prohibited spirituous liquors of more than 12%

Aug., Agreement with the United States for supply of rye and wheat

Nov. 28–30, Meeting of Scandinavian Kings at Christiania

1918

Jan. 13, Complete rationing of sugar, coffee, and corn and meal

March 22, Law decreed mobilization of persons for farm work and expropriation of land for farming by municipalities

March 30, Arbitration Treaty with the United States renewed that of April 4, 1908

April 30, Trade Agreement with the United States

May 3, Agreement with the United States by which Norway to be furnished with supplies not needed by Allies and for restriction of Norwegian exports to Germany

June 26–28, Conference of Scandinavian Cabinet Ministers at Copenhagen

July 17, Law regulated price of food stuffs and authorized Government to fix prices

Sept. 16–18, Visit of King Haakon to Stockholm

Oct. 22, General election: Radicals, 52; Conservatives, 35; Liberals, 16; Socialists, 18; Labor Democrats, 3; Agrarian Union, 2

Dec. 12 and 13, Norwegian Legation withdrawn from Russia

1919

April 12, Norwegian section of Scandinavian Society "Norden" (the North) established

May 26–28, Conference of Scandinavian Cabinet Ministers at Stockholm discussed common social legislation and League of Nations

July 11, Act established eight hour day on Norwegian ships to come into effect Jan. 1

Aug. 1, Act established a State Fisheries Bank to finance Norwegian fisheries

Sept. 25, Sovereignty over Spitzbergen granted to Norway by decision of the Supreme Council

Oct. 6, National plebiscite decided by vote of 436,269 to 284,402 to prohibit all traffic in whiskey, brandy, and other distilled liquors

Dec. 1, Municipal elections a victory for the Conservatives

1920

Feb. 1–4, Conference of Scandinavian Cabinet Ministers at Christiania

Feb. 9, Treaty signed by the United States, Great Britain, France, Denmark, Italy, Japan, Norway, the Netherlands, and Sweden recognized the sovereignty of Norway over Spitsbergen

Feb. 11, Railroad between Kongsberg and Hjuksebo opened the first section of trunk-line between Christiania and Stavanger

March 5, Norway became a member of the League of Nations

April 1, Compulsory industrial arbitration law of 1915 expired

Aug. 28–30, Conference of Scandinavian Cabinet Ministers at Copenhagen

Sept. 5, First commercial fair ever held in the North opened at Christiania

Oct. 14, Commercial *modus vivendi* with Portugal arranged

Dec. 1, Strike of railway workers begun which ended in 17 days with unconditional capitulation of strikers

Dec. 10, Act established accident insurance for fishermen

1921

Feb. 10, Death of George Francis Hagerup (68)

April 23, Convention with France as to wines and spirits signed

May 8, Strike of crews of coastal vessels against reduction in wages which was joined later by transport workers and dockers

June, Resignation of the Cabinet, defeated on the prohibition question

June 22, Otto Albert Blehr appointed Prime Minister

June 30, Treaty with the United States signed settlement of claims arising out of the War

Sept. 2, Preliminary trade Agreement with Russia signed

Sept. 16, Law prohibited importation and sale of spirits and wine of more than 14%

Sept. 17, The Dovre railroad officially opened by the King at Hjerkinn, highest point of the line 3,334 feet above sea level (Domaas to Trondhjem)

Sept. 18, Serious railroad collision near Trondhjem in which Thomas Heftye and 5 other prominent persons killed and 13 injured

Oct. 2, Memorial tablet presented by Great Britain on the fortress at Bergen unveiled in honor of Norwegian seamen lost in the War (1,200 men and 831 ships)

Nov. 4, Note to Denmark refused recognition of Danish claims in Greenland

Dec. 1–12, Strike of railway employees

1922

Jan. 23, Death of Stefan Sinding, sculptor

Feb. 12, Spanish-Norwegian Maritime Treaty terminated as a result of trade war on account of Norwegian prohibition policy

March 31, New Act as to compulsory arbitration of labor disputes promulgated

May 5, Death of Carl Lumholtz, explorer and ethnologist, in the United States

May 6, Provisional Commercial Treaty with Spain signed

Aug. 21, Death of Jorgen Lovland, statesman

Oct. 13, Decision of Permanent Court of Arbitration at The Hague awarded Norway $12,239,652.47 in compensation for ships requisitioned during the World War by the United States

Oct. 17, Commercial Treaty with Spain signed

Nov. 26, System of industrial shop councils established by the Government in all establishments employing 50 or more persons

1923

Feb. 26, Award of Oct. 13, 1922 paid by the United States

March 2, Resignation of Blehr Ministry

March 5, Otto Halvorsen formed Cabinet

March 16, Radical proposal that compulsory arbitration in labor disputes due to expire on April 1 should be continued defeated

April 1, Law gave State a monopoly over importation and sale of unprohibited alcoholic liquors

April 11, Commercial Treaty with Portugal signed

April 27, Treaty (wine and fish) with Portugal signed

May 23, Death of Prime Minister Halvorsen

May 30, Abraham Berge, Finance Minister, appointed Prime Minister

June 5, Visit of King Haakon to Holland

June 13, Conflict of Government and Church over appointment of Liberal to See of Trondhjem

June 17–July 11, Strike of 14,000 workers in paper industry

July 9, Announcement that dispute with Denmark over Greenland settled and negotiators appointed to discuss respective rights Aug. 21

Sept. 7, Commercial Treaty with Yugoslavia signed renewing that of March 9, 1909 with Serbia

Oct. 30, Commercial Agreement with Czechoslovakia signed

Nov. 26, Arbitration Treaty with the United States renewed that of April 4, 1908

Dec. 21, Treaty of commerce and navigation with Lithuania signed

1924

Jan. 17, Strike of dockers

Feb. 13, Note to Russia recognized Soviet Government

Feb. 21–May 27, Lockout in building, textile, tobacco, shoe, and other trades settled by acceptance of arbitration of the Government

April 29, Frontier Agreement with Finland signed

May 24, Liquor Traffic Convention with the United States signed

June 20, Agreement with Austria for maintenance of certain former treaties

June 27, Conciliation Agreements with Denmark, Sweden, and Finland signed

July 9, Treaty with Denmark gave Denmark hunting and fishing rights in East Greenland

July 16, Government Bill for abolishing prohibition defeated by Odelsting

July 23, Berge Cabinet resigned, defeated on repeal of prohibition. Succeeded by J. L. Mowinckel

Aug. 14, Commercial Agreement with Latvia concluded

Sept. 16, Commercial and navigation Agreement with Hungary signed

Oct. 1, Treaty of commerce with Rumania signed

Oct. 2, Commercial Agreement with Bulgaria signed

Oct. 20, Election gave Conservatives a majority: Conservatives, 54; Radicals, 34; Agrarians, 22; Labor, 24; Socialists, 8; Communists, 6

Dec. 3, Provisional Commercial Agreement with Austria signed

1925

Jan. 1, Christiania resumed former name of Oslo

Feb. 13, Mrs. Helga A. Karlsen took seat in Storthing as substitute for Mr. Transmael granted leave

March 31, Captain Roald Amundsen and Lieutenant Lincoln Ellsworth (American) left Oslo for Tromsoe to make airplane flight to the North Pole

April 1, Tax of 10% on all food consumed in restaurants came into effect

May 2, Treaty of friendship with Turkey signed

May 13, Agreement with Great Britain renewed Arbitration Convention of Aug. 11, 1904

May 21, Amundsen-Ellsworth expedition in 2 airships flew north from Kings Bay, the N-24 (Ellsworth) plane wrecked, and the N-25 (Amundsen) ran out of gasoline 150 miles from objective

June 1, $30,000,000 5½% loan for 40 years floated in New York City

June 28, Death of Christian Michelsen, former Premier (69)

Aug. 14, Norway formally assumed sovereignty over Spitsbergen under Treaty of Feb. 9, 1920 and changed name to Svalbard

Aug. 21, Conciliation Treaty with Switzerland signed

Aug. 29, Provisional Commercial Agreement with Estonia

Oct. 14, Death of O. O. Lian, labor union leader

Oct. 23, Arbitration Convention with Sweden of Oct. 26, 1905 renewed

Dec. 15, Treaty of commerce and navigation with Russia signed

1926

Jan. 15, Convention for pacific settlement of disputes with Denmark signed

Feb. 3, Convention for pacific settlement of disputes with Finland signed

Feb. 6, Agreement with Austria modified Commercial Agreement of Dec. 3, 1924

Feb. 28, Mowinckel Cabinet defeated on the budget

March 4, Resignation of Mowinckel Cabinet

March 5, I. Lykke, Conservative, formed Cabinet: Prime Minister and Minister for Foreign Affairs, I. Lykke; Education and Ecclesiastical Affairs, W. C. Magelsen; Justice K. Öyen; Agriculture, O. L. Baeroe; Public Works, A. Venger; Social Affairs, P. A. Morell; Finance, F. L. Konow; Defense, I. E. Christensen; Commerce and Industry, D. Robertson

April 24, Strike of 30,000 men against reduction of wages

May 11–14, Amundsen-Ellsworth-Nobile expedition in the "Norge" airship left Spitsbergen, Kings Bay, and flew across the North Pole May 12, thence across the unexplored Arctic basin to Point Barrow, Alaska, and landed at Teller, Alaska on the 14th

May 31, Preliminary agreement of employers and workers signed and ratified

June 9, Workers accepting a 17% reduction instead of 25% proposed

July 1, Sickness Insurance Act consolidated

July 14, Odelsting voted impeachment of former Prime Minister Abraham Berge charged with placing 20,000,000 krone in the Bank of Commerce without knowledge or consent of the Storthing in May, 1923

July 16, Treaty of friendship, commerce, and navigation with Siam signed

Oct. 4, Trial of A. Berge and 6 members of his Cabinet charged with secret unconstitutional support of the Bank of Commerce begun

Oct. 13, Provisional Commercial Agreement with Turkey concluded

Oct. 15, Krone advanced to $.2328 highest since October, 1919

Oct. 18. Plebiscite vote gave a majority against continuance of prohibition after 12 years' trial: vote 531,425 against and 421,292 for

Oct. 20, Krone advanced to $.2659

Dec. 22, Treaty of commerce and navigation with Poland signed

1927

Jan. 25, Disarmament proposal of Labor Parties rejected by Storthing

March 25, Abraham Berge and his colleagues acquitted by highest court

April 4, Bill passed repealed prohibition and reintroduced system of local option

April 11, Commercial Agreement with Spain concluded

May 5, New law passed by which arbitration in labor disputes made compulsory

July 13, Death of Otto Blehr, former Prime Minister

Oct. 17, General election a victory for Labor Party: Labor Party, 59; Conservatives, 31; Liberals, 31; Communists, 3; Farmers Party, 26

Dec. 1, Bouvet Island, whaling station, South Atlantic occupied

1928

Jan. 17, British Colonial Office announced lease of Bouvet Island to Norwegian firm

Jan. 18, Norway announced annexation of Bouvet Island

Jan. 20, Resignation of Lykke Ministry

Jan. 26, Christopher Hornsrud (Harnarud), Labor, formed a Cabinet

Feb. 10, First Labor Government of Hornsrud forced to resign

Feb. 13, J. L. Mowinckel appointed Prime Minister and Minister for Foreign Affairs; Education and Ecclesiastical Affairs, S. M. Hasund; Justice, H. M. Evjenth; Agriculture, H. J. Aarstad; Public Works, O. M. Mjelde; Social Affairs, T. Værland; Finance, P. Lund; Defense, T. Anderssen-Rysst; Commerce and Industry, L. Oftedal

1928

Feb. 27, The Storthing authorized the Government to contract for a loan in the United States

March 7, A $30,000,000 5% loan floated in New York City

March 15, Celebration of Ibsen centenary

May 1, Gold standard reintroduced

June 18, Roald Amundsen left Tromose in French seaplane in attempt to rescue members of Nobile expedition to North Pole and was not heard from again

Oct. 25, Convention for assistance to nationals concluded with Sweden and Finland

Nov. 12, Tariff autonomy Treaty with China signed

Nov. 20, British Government renounced claim to Bouvet Island in the South Atlantic in favor of Norway

Dec. 19, Protest made against decree of Russian Soviet Government of April 15, 1926 as to sovereignty over Arctic Islands

Dec. 27, Arbitration and conciliation Treaty with Spain signed

1929

Feb. 2, Peter Island in South Atlantic annexed by Norway as a whaling station

March 21, Marriage of the Crown Prince Olav to Princess Martha of Sweden, niece of King Gustav

April 10, Association for naval preparedness inaugurated

May 8, Annexation of Jan Mayen Island in the Arctic Ocean between Spitsbergen and Greenland used as whaling station

June 7, Passports abolished between Norway, Sweden, Denmark, and Finland

June 10, Chamber passed Bill changing name of city of Trondhjem to Nidaros to take effect Jan. 1, 1930

June 11, Protest of 20,000 citizens of Trondhjem against change of name

June 17, Arbitration Treaty with Italy signed

June 18, Riots in Bergen against proposed legislation to change name of city to Björgvik

Aug. 1, Law providing for compulsory arbitration of labor disputes expired

Sept. 9, Treaty of arbitration with Czechoslovakia

Oct. 16, Treaty of friendship, commerce, and navigation with Panama signed

Dec. 7, Commander Ruser-Larsen on the "Norwegia" from point in Antarctic at 64° 21′ S. and 53° 14′ E. made first airplane flight in Antarctic 40 miles south

Dec. 9, Arbitration Treaty with Poland signed

1930

Jan. 14, Flight of Commander Ruser-Larsen along west coast of Enderby Land naming Ice Bay in 68° S. and 50° E.

Feb. 18, Commander Ruser-Larsen on flight of exploration discovered and named Seal Bay and Cape Norwegia in 71° 1.5

Feb. 20, Ruser-Larsen named land discovered between Seal Bay and Coats Land the Crown Princess Martha Land

April 14, Death of Sigurd Ibsen, statesman (71)

May 8, Treaty of friendship and commerce with Persia

May 13, Death of Dr. Fridtjov Nansen at Oslo (68), explorer and statesman

June 6, Storthing dissolved

June 6, Law reorganized normal schools and courses of study issued Nov. 29

July 26, Treaty of arbitration, conciliation, and judicial settlement with Portugal signed

June 27, Treaty of friendship and arbitration signed with Sweden, Denmark, Finland, and Iceland

Aug. 6, Scientific exploring expedition headed by Dr. Gunnar Horn found bodies of Solomon August Andree and Knut Kraenkel who on July 11, 1897 had flown from Dane's Island, Spitsbergen in balloon, planning to drift across the North Pole

Oct. 1, Treaty of arbitration and conciliation with Austria signed

Oct. 20, Election held: Labor Party, 47; Conservatives and Moderate Liberals, 44; Liberals, 34; Farmers Party, 25

Nov. 1, Treaty with the United States signed governing military service for persons liable because of so-called dual nationality

Nov. 18–19, Exchange of Notes with Great Britain recognition of sovereignty of Norway over Jan Mayen Island

Nov. 26, Death of Captain Otto Sverdrup, explorer

The following is a list of the Sovereigns of Norway since the year 1204, with the date of their accession:

Inge Baardsson	1204
Haakon Haakonsson	1217
Magnus Lagaboter	1263
Erik Magnusson	1280
Haakon V Magnusson	1299
Magnus Eriksson	1319
Haakon VI Magnusson	1355
Olav Haakonsson	1381
Margreta	1388
Erik af Pommern	1389
Kristofer af Bayern	1442
Karl Knutsson	1449
Same Sovereigns as in Denmark	1450–1814
Kristian Fredrik	1814
Same Sovereigns as in Sweden	1814–1905

Haakon VII, born August 3, 1872; the second son, Carl, of Frederik VIII, King of Denmark, elected King of Norway by the Storthing, November 18, 1905; accepted the crown through his grandfather, the late King Christian of Denmark, November 18, 1905; landed in Norway November 25, 1905; married, July 22, 1896, to Princess Maud, born November 26, 1869, the third daughter of the late Edward VII, King of Great Britain and Ireland.

Son.—Prince Olaf, Crown Prince, born July 2, 1903, married on March 21, 1929, to Princess Märtha of Sweden. Offspring: Princess Ragnhild Alexandra, born June 9, 1930.

According to the Constitution, Norway is a constitutional and hereditary monarchy. The royal succession is in direct male line in the order of primogeniture. In default of male heirs the King may propose a successor to the Storthing, but this assembly has the right to nominate another, if it does not agree with the proposal.

PERMANENT COURT OF ARBITRATION. THE HAGUE TRIBUNAL

The Permanent Court of Arbitration was established under the Act of July 29, 1899, signed (and subsequently ratified) on the part of 24 Powers organized by its Administrative Council, April 9, 1901. Under Protocol of June 14, 1907, for the accession of non-signatory Powers, the number of Powers represented in the Court has been largely increased. The purpose is to facilitate arbitration for international disputes which it has been impossible to settle by diplomacy. The Court is competent for all arbitration cases unless the parties agree to constitute a special tribunal, and its jurisdiction may be extended to disputes to which one or both of the parties are non-signatory Powers, if the parties so agree. When the signatory Powers desire to have recourse to the Permanent Court for the settlement of a dispute, the arbitrators called upon to form the competent tribunal for the purpose must be chosen from the general list of members of the Court. If the parties disagree on the composition of this tribunal, its members must be appointed in accordance with the course prescribed in the Act.

The Court has an International Bureau under the direction and control of a Permanent Administrative Council composed of the diplomatic representatives of the Signatory Powers accredited to The Hague, and of the Netherlands Minister for Foreign Affairs, who acts as President.

The Permanent Court consists of persons of known competency in questions of International Law, of whom four at the most are selected by each of the Signatory Powers; each appointment is for six years and may be renewed.

PERMANENT COURT OF INTER-
NATIONAL JUSTICE

The Permanent Court of International Justice of the League of Nations was organized under Article 14 of the Covenant, which reads as follows:

The Council shall formulate and submit to the Members of the League for adoption plans for the establishment of a Permanent Court of International Justice. The Court shall be competent to hear and determine any dispute of an international character which the parties thereto submit to it. The Court may also give an advisory opinion upon any dispute or question referred to it by the Council or by the Assembly.

The Statute constituting the Court was adopted by the League in 1920, and a Protocol of Signature by which the signatory powers declared their acceptance of the Statute. The Court is open to every nation of the world under conditions laid down by the Council of the League in May 1922, which require a declaration accepting the jurisdiction of the Court in accordance with the terms of the Covenant, and with the Statute and Rules of the Court, and undertaking to carry out its decisions in good faith, and not to have recourse to war against a state complying therewith. Provision is made that any signatory power may accept compulsory jurisdiction by signing the Optional Clause attached to Protocol of Signature.

The Court meets at the World Court Palace at The Hague, and holds one regular annual session beginning June 15, with additional extraordinary sessions when necessary. The judges are elected by the Assembly and the Council of the League of Nations from a list of eligible candidates nominated by the members of the Permanent Court of Arbitration, at The Hague, established by the Hague Conferences of 1899 and 1907. The membership of the Court was increased to 15 in 1930. The list of judges Jan. 1, 1930, is as follows:

Frank B. Kellogg, United States; Antonio Sanchez de Bustamente, Cuba; J. Gustavo Guerrero, El Salvador; Mineichiro Adatchi, Japan; Rafael Altimara y Crevea, Spain; Dionisio Anzilotti, Italy; Willem Van Eysinga, Holland; Henri Fromageot, France; Sir Cecil Hurst, Great Britain; Demetre Negulesco, Rumania; Baron Rokin Jaequemyns, Belgium; Count Michael Rostworski, Poland; Walther Schucking, Germany; Wang Chung-Hui, China; and Francisco Jose Urrutia, Colombia.

Frank B. Kellogg had on Sept. 17 been elected to the seat vacated by Charles E. Hughes on his appointment as Chief Justice of the United States Supreme Court and took his seat Oct. 23.

The Registrar of the Court (since 1922) is M. Ake Hammarskjold, Counselor of Legations of H. M. the King of Sweden

1920

Feb. 13, The Council of the League of Nations in accordance with Article 14 of the Covenant charged to formulate and submit plans for the establishment of a permanent court of international justice appointed an Advisory Committee of Jurists to draft plan

June 16–July 24, Meeting of Advisory Committee of Jurists including members from Great Britain, France, Belgium, Holland, Norway, Italy, Japan, Brazil, and the United States (Elihu Root) met at The Hague and drafted and adopted Statute for Court which was submitted to the Council Aug. 5

Oct. 27, Statute of the Court as amended by Committee approved by the Council

Dec. 13, The Statute constituting the Court and Optional Clause as to compulsory jurisdiction adopted by the Assembly of the League of Nations

Dec. 14, Statute of the Court and Optional Clause adopted by the Council

Dec. 16, Protocol of Signature, Statute, and Optional Clause opened for signature

1921

Sept. 2, The League Council announced that the Statute of the Court had been ratified by a majority of the members of the League of Nations and was consequently in force

Sept. 14–16, Judges of the Court elected by Assembly and Council of the League of Nations, 11 judges and 4 deputy-judges, the judges respectively citizens of France, Great Britain, Spain, Denmark, the Netherlands, Switzerland, Italy, Japan, Brazil, Cuba, and the United States (John Bassett Moore), the deputy-judges citizens of Norway, Rumania, Yugoslavia, and China

1922

Jan. 30–March 24, Preliminary session of the Court at The Hague, Judge C. J. Loder (Holland) elected president; Judge C. A. Weiss (France) vice-president; Ake Hammarskjold (Norway) registrar, and rules of procedure adopted

Feb. 15, The Permanent Court of International Justice formally opened

May 12, Resolution of the Council of the League of Nations defined admission to the Court providing that the Court should be open to States not members of the League of Nations or mentioned in the Annex to the Covenant

June 15–Aug. 15, First ordinary session of the Court for transaction of judicial business

1926

Sept. 1–23, Conference of signatories of the Protocol of the Court of Dec. 16, 1920 drew up Draft Protocol to meet the American reservations as of Resolution of the United States Senate of Jan. 27

1929

March 11–19, Jurists Committee in session, invited to examine Statute of Court with view to introduce amendments; Elihu Root a member of this committee

Sept. 4–12, Conference of States signatories of Statute discussed and agreed on amendments to be made in Statute and adherence of the United States

Sept. 14, Protocol for signature for revised Statute opened for signature and Protocol for adhesion of the United States

Sept. 19, Optional Clause of Permanent Court, agreement to accept compulsory jurisdiction of the Court signed by 7 States, Great Britain, New Zealand, South Africa, India, France, Czechoslovakia, and Peru

Dec. 1, The Optional Clause came into effect as signed by 20 States

Dec. 9, The United States signed Protocol of Signature of Dec. 16, 1920, and Protocol for revision of Statute of Sept. 14, 1929, and Protocol for adherence of the United States

1930

Sept. 9, Council of the League of Nations voted to increase court membership from 11 to 15

Sept. 25, Second election of judges and deputy-judges

POLAND

Poland, State of east-central Europe, reconstituted in 1918 as a republic, and including "Congress Poland" (*i.e.*, Poland as delimited and handed over to Russia by the Congress of Vienna, 1815), Galicia, the former Prussian Poland, Upper Silesia, and a part of the Vilna (Wilno) territory. Poland was an independent State until the end of the eighteenth century when by the three partitions of 1772, 1793, and 1795 the "Polish Commonwealth" was divided between Prussia, Russia, and Austria. In 1807 Napoleon formed part of the former "Commonwealth" into a semi-independent State under the title of the Duchy of Warsaw, but in 1815 the Congress of Vienna constituted the so-called Congress kingdom out of central Poland —about three-fourths of the territory of Napoleon's Grand Duchy—under the Emperor of Russia as King of Poland, and constituted Cracow as an independent republic which it remained until

1835, when it was annexed by Austria, despite a guarantee of neutrality by Prussia, Austria, and Russia. At the outbreak of the War in 1914 only Austrian Poland enjoyed autonomous government. During the war Russian Poland was invaded and by the end of 1915 the whole country was occupied by Austro-German forces. On Nov. 9, 1918 the independence of Poland was proclaimed, and was recognized by the Treaty of Versailles, June 28, 1919, and the same Treaty fixed the western frontier with Germany from the Baltic Sea to Upper Silesia, definitely determined after plebiscite in Upper Silesia and the territory east of the Vistula. The eastern frontier with Russia was determined by the Treaty of Riga, March 18, 1921, and the frontiers with Lithuania, Czechoslovakia, and Rumania by decisions of the Council of Ambassadors of March 15, 1923, and the boundary with Czechoslovakia as to the Duchy of Teschen, and in the Spitz and Orava regions by a decision of the Council of Ambassadors of July 28, 1920.

The total area is 149,958 square miles with a total population of 30,737,448 (Jan. 1, 1930). Warsaw is the capital.

Ignace Moscicki, President.

Ca. 842 to 1830

About 842, Piastus, a peasant, is elected to the ducal dignity

[Piastus is said to have lived to the age of 120, and his reign to have been so prosperous that succeeding native sovereigns were called Piasts.]

About 992, Introduction of Christianity

1080, Boleslas II murders St. Stanislaus, the Bishop of Cracow, with his own hands, 1079; his kingdom laid under an interdict by the Pope, and his subjects absolved of their allegiance

1081, He flies to Hungary for shelter; but is refused it by order of Gregory VII, and at length kills himself or dies in a monastery

1241, Tartar invasion

1296, Premislas assassinated

1370, Louis of Hungary elected King

1444, Ladislas VI defeated and slain by the Turks at Varna

1410; 1447, War against the Teutonic knights

1498, The Wallachian invaders carry off 100,000 Poles, and sell them to the Turks as slaves

1531, The Wallachians defeated

1548, Reign of Sigismund II

1569, Lithuania incorporated with Poland

1575, Stephen forms a militia composed of Cossacks, on whom he bestows the Ukraine

1654 *et seq.*, Poland conquered by the Swedes and Russians

1660, Recovered its independence

Jan. 30, 1667, Peace of Andrussov with Russia concluded

1668, Abdication of John Casimir

1683, Victories of John Sobieski over the Turks at Vienna

1724, Many Protestants killed after an affray at Thorn

1770, Stanislaus abolishes torture

1770, A pestilence destroys 250,000 persons

1772, Civil war so weakened the Kingdom that it fell an easy prey to Russia, Austria, and Prussia

Feb. 17, 1772, The first partition treaty

Sept. 18, 1772, The public partition treaty, Aug. 5; acted on

May 3, 1791, A new constitution granted by the King

1792, The Russians, &c., on various pretexts enter Poland

1793, Second partition treaty signed

March, 1794, Insurrection under Kosciusko

Oct. 10, 1794, After many successes he is defeated by the Russians at Maciejovice and taken prisoner

Nov. 9, 1794, Warsaw and Praga sacked by Suwarrow

1795, Courland is annexed to Russia

Nov. 25, 1795, Stanislaus resigns his crown at Grodno; final partition of his Kingdom

Dec. 25, 1796, Kosciusko set at liberty

May 30, 1797, He arrives in London

1797 *et seq.*, The Poles enter the French army and greatly help to gain their victories

Feb. 12, 1798, Stanislaus dies at St. Petersburg

1806-7, Napoleon I enters Warsaw; his army wintered in Poland

July 7, 1807, The Poles neglected by the treaty of Tilsit. *See* Prussia

June, 1812, General diet at Warsaw

April 30, 1815, The central provinces (the duchy of Warsaw, between 1807 and 1813) made the Kingdom of Poland under Alexander of Russia

Nov. 27, 1815, New constitution granted and Cracow declared to be a free republic

Sept., 1820, Polish Diet opened

Nov. 29, 1830, A revolution at Warsaw; the army declare in favor of the people

1831

Jan. 25, The Diet declares the throne vacant

Feb. 19, 20, Battle of Grochow, near Praga; the Russians lose 7,000 men; the Poles, who keep the field, 2,000

March 31, Battle of Wawz (Polish victory)

April 3, Insurrection in Wilna and Volhynia

April 6, Russians defeated at Zelicho; Seidlece, April 10; at Ostrolenka, May 26

June 19, Battle of Wilna; Poles defeated

July 14, Battle of Minsk

Sept. 8, Warsaw taken by Russians

Oct. 5, The insurrection suppressed

1832 to 1847

Feb. 26, 1832, Ukase issued by the Emperor Nicholas, decreeing that the Kingdom of Poland shall henceforth form an integral part of the Russian Empire

Feb. 22-27, 1846, Attempted revolution in Austrian Poland

Nov. 16, 1846, The courts of Austria, Russia, and Prussia revoke the treaty of 1815, which constituted Cracow a free republic, and it is declared Austrian territory

[This annexation was protested against by England, France, Sweden, and Turkey]

May, 1847, The Kingdom of Poland declared a Russian province

1861

Feb. 27, Six members of the Royal Agricultural society killed by the military

March 1-7, Great excitement at their funeral; many citizens put on mourning; an address to the Emperor Alexander signed by 60,000 persons; mild conduct of Prince Gortschakoff, the governor

March 17, Mukhanoff, curator of Poland, who had written a circular exciting the peasantry against their lords, quits Warsaw

April 7, The government promises reforms and the re-establishment of Poland as a separate kingdom; yet abolishes the Agricultural society

April 8, Great meeting in consequence; which is dispersed by the military (now 32,000 strong); above 100 are killed and wounded

April, Great agitation in the rural districts; the Russian officials quit Lublin; General Chruleff marches thither

May, 80,000 soldiers in Poland; reign of terror in Warsaw

July 15, Death of Prince Adam Czartoryski at Paris, aged 91

Oppressive regulations issued respecting dress

Oct., Fresh disturbances; Warsaw put in a state of siege

Oct. 17, Military arrests in churches in Warsaw; they are closed by the priests

Oct. 25, General Gerstenzweig, the military governor, assassinated

Dec. 18, Bialobzeski, Catholic Archbishop of Warsaw, arrested, Nov. 19; tried and condemned to death as a rebel for closing the churches [he died shortly after]

1862

Feb. 15, The new Archbishop Felinski exhorts the Poles to submission

April 29, Rigor of the government relaxed; amnesty granted to 89 convicted political prisoners

Aug. 21, The Grand-Duke Constantine appointed governor, May 28; his life is attempted by Jaroszynsky, July 3, who is executed

Sept., Count Zamoyski, an eminent loyal Pole, exiled for presenting to the government the report of a meeting of nobles at Warsaw

Nov. 9, Telkner, the chief of the secret police, found murdered

1863

Jan. 14, Severe military conscription without notice

Jan. 22, Insurrection in the night; at Warsaw

Jan. 24, Many Russians murdered; Poland put in a state of siege

Feb. 2, The Polish provisional government issues its first proclamation

Feb. 23, Louis Mieroslawski announces himself as head of the Poles, Feb. 19; his band defeated and dispersed

March 19, Marian Langiewicz declared dictator of Poland, March 10; after several defeats he enters the Austrian territory, and imprisoned

March and April, The insurrection becomes general, and is supported by the landed proprietors, Feb.; successful guerilla warfare

March, The secret central committee assumes the supreme command

April 12, The Tsar offers an amnesty to all who lay down arms before May 13; rejected

April 26, &c., European intervention on behalf of Poland, April 17, &c.; firmly replied to by the Tsar

May 9, The secret committee (as a provisional government) levies taxes, May 3, and forbids payment of taxes to Russia

June 12, 80,000*l.* taken from the Russian treasury at Warsaw for the provisional government; the Poles claim the Poland of 1772, June 26

June, Fruitless intervention of European powers; sanguinary rule of Mouravieff at Wilna

July 1, Unsuccessful invasion of Volhynia by the Poles, under Wysocki and Horodycki; Felinski, the Roman Catholic Archbishop of Warsaw, banished, July; many captured priests and nobles executed Aug.

Sept., Earl Russell decides against armed intervention, Aug.: negotiation ceases

Oct., Many eminent Poles executed; Wm. Alger, an Englishman, shot at Warsaw for making grenades; the Hotel de Ville fired, Oct. 9

Oct. 27, Mourning forbidden to be worn for the Poles at Warsaw; 41 ladies arrested at night, Nov. 3

Dec. 28, The Abbé Machiewicz, a warlike priest, venerated as a martyr, hanged

1864

Jan.–April, The insurrection gradually dying out

Aug. 5, Romuald Traugott, once a Russian colonel, head of the Polish provisional government, since Oct., 1863, and five others, hanged

Sept. 11, Decree for reorganizing education at Warsaw, founding a university, &c.

Sept. 21, The secret provisional government, after stating that 50,000 men had been slain, and 100,000 exiled to Siberia, still calls on the Poles to begin a "national war"

Nov., Many Roman Catholic convents closed for participating in the insurrection

1865

Feb., The ex-dictator Langiewicz released by the Austrians and sent to Switzerland [he died May, 1887]

May 23, The Abbé Stanislas Bizoski and his lieutenant captured and executed

Dec. 22, Estates of suspected sympathizers with rebels ordered to be sold

1866

Jan. 9, Church property appropriated by the government; the clergy to be paid by the state

Feb. 17, Military government ceases, and state of siege partially raised

Oct., Count Goluchowski, a Pole, made governor of Gallicia

Nov., Insurrection of Polish exiles in Siberia, soon suppressed, July; many executed

1867

Jan. 5, Decree abolishing all political distinctions of Poland as a kingdom promulgated

May 31, Amnesty to political offenders proclaimed

1868

Jan., Poland designated the "Vistula province" in a ukase

Feb. 29, Its separate internal government abolished, and complete union with the Empire effected

April, The distinct financial departments of Poland abolished

July, The Polish language interdicted in public places

1872 to 1894

March, 1872, Conciliatory policy towards the Poles in Russia and Austria proposed

Jan. 18, 1873, Count Berg, the last Lieutenant-General for Poland, dies

June, 1876, Polish language prohibited in courts of law and public offices in Russian Poland

Sept. 8–27, 1884, The Tsar and Tsarina visit Warsaw (great precautions)

Oct.–Nov., 1885, About 34,700 Poles expelled from Prussia

Feb., 1886, Movement for denationalizing Poland

April 23, 1889, Count Ladislaw Platu, active in the revolutions of 1830 and 1863, dies in Switzerland (aged 83)

May, 1889, Conciliatory measures towards Polish landowners proposed

July 4, 1890, The body of Adam Mickiewiez, the great Polish poet (1798–1855), brought from France, re-interred at Cracow

May 3, 1891, Centenary of the Polish constitution of 1791, celebrated in Austrian Poland

1892, The Emperor William II appoints a Polish archbishop of Posen, 1891, and otherwise favors the Poles

Nov. 26, 1894, Polish deputation warmly received by the Tsar Nicholas II; pardon granted to political prisoners of 1863, by manifesto

1897

Jan. 17, Increased toleration of the Roman Catholics; Gen. Gourko, the Governor-General of Warsaw, resigns (died Jan. 24, 1891); succeeded by Count Shuvaloff, Dec. 20, 1894; succeeded by Prince Imeribinsky

Aug. 2, Adam Asnyk, eminent poet, born 1838, died

Aug. 31, The Tsar and Tsarina at Warsaw; grand review at Bielostok, Sept. 7

1899 to 1906

Mid Sept., 1899, Petition for the instruction of Polish youth in their native language, history, &c., granted

April, 1902, Roman Catholic Archbishop of Vilna deprived of his office for opposing the government on the language question

Dec., 1903, Gen. Tchertkoff, Governor-Gen., removed for maladministration. *See under* Russia, 1904–10

Jan. 27, 1906, Twenty-eight teachers dismissed by the authorities for refusing to teach the Russian language, all schools reported closed

Nov. 24, Death of Mgr. Stablewski, Roman Catholic Abp. of Posen

1914

Aug. 6, On the day Austria declared war on Russia Joseph Pilsudski led his Polish force organized in 1905 as "Organization of Combat" (Zwiazek Walki Czynnej) and later legalized with Austrian permission as the "Union of Societies of Riflemen" (Zwiazek Towarzystow Strzeleckich) across the frontier against Russia

Aug. 12, Pilsudski's "Legion" liberated the town of Kielce

Aug. 14, Proclamation of the Grand Duke Nicholas, Commander-in-Chief of the Russian armies, to the Poles promised reconstruction of unified Poland as autonomous kingdom

Aug. 16, Followers of Pilsudski united with other groups of Poles forming a "Supreme National Committee" at Cracow, Professor Wladyslaw Leopold Jaworski, president

Aug. 27, The Archduke Frederick, Commander-in-Chief of armies of Austria-Hungary directed that 2 Polish Legions be formed for duration of the War

Sept. 2, Lemberg (Lwaw) occupied by Russians

Nov. 15, First brigade of Polish Legions formed under command of Pilsudski

Nov. 25, Polish National Committee (known as the K.N.P.) organized at Warsaw under the leadership of Dmowski favoring coöperation with Russia

1915

April 3, Russian Imperial Ukase granted municipal self-government

June 22, Lemberg recaptured by Austro-German forces

June 24, Russo-Polish Committee formed at Petrograd

Aug. 1, Full autonomy promised to Poland by Russian Government

Aug. 5, Germans occupied Warsaw

Aug. 10, Polish law courts established at Warsaw

Sept. 10, Polish law courts suppressed by Germans

Dec. 2, Conference of Dr. Vernon Kellogg sent by Herbert Hoover with representatives of the German General Staff as to distribution of food for relief of Poland

Dec. 14, Convention between Germany and Austria signed at Teschen provided for division of Russian Poland. A German Government under von Beseler established in Warsaw, and under von Kuk in Lublin

Dec. 22, Hoover in letter to Sir Edward Grey, Foreign Secretary, placed proposal for relief of Poland before the British Government

1916

Jan. 1, Day appointed by President Wilson for giving aid "to the stricken people"

July 4, National Council of the Kingdom formed by the Poles

July 25, Pilsudski withdrew his troops from the front and resigned his command as protest because nothing done toward formation of Polish kingdom of Congress Poland and Galicia. Accepted Aug. 27

July 26–29, Final refusal of British and German Governments to agree on Hoover plan for relief of Poland

Aug. 12, Secret German-Austrian Protocol signed providing for establishment of an independent hereditary kingdom of Poland, no Polish territories of Germany or Austria (Poznan (Posen) West Prussia, Galicia, &c.) to be added to the new kingdom. Frontier to be changed in favor of Germany

Sept. 20, The Polish Legions made an auxiliary corps of the Austro-Hungarian army not recognized as a Polish army of a Polish Government as requested by Council of Colonels of the Legions

Nov. 5, Joint rescript of German and Austrian Emperors announced creation of an independent kingdom of Poland

Nov. 16, Death of Henryk Sienkiewicz, novelist, at Vevey, Switzerland

Nov. 26, Central Powers placed credits at service of a Polish State Council appointed.

Dec. 25, The Tsar in address to his armies reaffirmed promise of a united autonomous Poland

1917

Jan. 12, Statement of Allies in reply to Note of President Wilson of Dec. 18, 1916 that "the intentions of his Majesty the Emperor of Russia regarding the Poles have been clearly indicated in the proclamation which he just addressed to his armies"

Jan. 15, Polish Council of State met under German auspices, Pilsudski included as chairman of the Military Commission

Jan. 18, Prince Vaoclaw von Niemoyovski appointed Viceroy of Poland by the German Emperor

Jan. 22, Speech of President Wilson favored "a united, independent, and autonomous Poland"

Jan. 30, Council of State adopted a Constitution

March 30, Declaration of the Russian Provisional Government in favor of "the creation of an independent Polish State in all territories where the Polish people constitute a majority of the population as a certain guarantee of durable peace in the remodeled Europe of the future"

April 4, Union of Polish Falcons (Sokols) Societies at meeting in Pittsburgh voted to form an "army of Kosciuszko . . . to fight by the side of the United States for the liberty and independence of Poland"

April 10, Polish Legions transferred to German control by Austria-Hungary

May 17–18, By the Kreuznach Agreement Austria-Hungary renounced her interest in the kingdom of Poland to be attached to Germany

May 30, Polish representatives in the Austrian Reichsrat declared for an independent and united Poland with control of the lower Vistula and Danzig to give access to the sea

June 4, Government of France authorized forming of a Polish army in France made up of Polish volunteers in French army and Polish prisoners of war

June 8, Agreement signed by Emperors of Austria and Germany by which Polish military forces to be controled by Germany

July 2, Pilsudski resigned from the Council of State in protest against German authorities

July 9, The Polish Legions refused to take the oath required by the authorities of occupation

July 21, General Joseph Pilsudski arrested and imprisoned at Magdeburg by German authorities

Aug. 7, Proposal of the Entente Allies to Austria provided for cession of Poland as it existed before the partition of 1772 to Austria

Aug. 15, Polish National Committee formed in November, 1914 at Warsaw established headquarters in Paris with Dmowski as president and Paderewski as delegate in the United States

Aug. 25, Resignation of members of the Council of State

Sept. 1, Germans turned courts over to Polish authorities

Sept. 12, Proclamation of the Central Powers announced appointment of a Regency Council for Poland with a reorganized Council of State and a "responsible" ministry

Sept. 20, Poles in the United States established a military commission to organize army of Poles not affected by United States compulsory service law

Oct. 12, Recruiting of Polish-American army begun

Oct. 15, Regency Council appointed took office, Mgr. Kokowski, Archbishop of Warsaw, Prince Z. Lubomirski, and J. Ostrowski

Oct. 15, Polish Supreme National Council (Cracow) dissolved

Oct. 19, Polish National Committee in Paris recognized by the Allies

Nov. 17, Professor Jan Kucharzewski appointed first Prime Minister

Dec. 8, Kucharzewski formed the first Cabinet

1918

Jan. 5, Lloyd George declared for an independent Poland

Jan. 8, President Wilson in address to Congress enumerated "Fourteen Points" as an American program of world peace, the thirteenth reaffirming his declaration of Jan. 22, 1917 for an independent Poland with access to the sea

Feb. 9, Treaty of Central Powers with the Ukraine ceded Chelm to the Ukraine

Feb. 11, Resignation of Ministry of Kucharzewski in Warsaw

Feb. 15, General Haller escaped to Russia with his brigade

Feb. 25, General Dowbor-Musnicki forced to sign "convention of neutrality" with the Germans

March 20, France recognized the Polish National Committee as political head of Polish army being organized in France

April 5, New Cabinet formed by Steczkowski

May 6, Haller's brigade in engagement with the Germans at Kaniow

June 3, Allied Supreme Council made establishment of a united and independent Poland with access to the sea a war aim

June 22, New Council of State opened in Warsaw

July 13, General Haller took command of Polish army in action on Western front

Oct. 4, Ukrainians with aid of Germans attacked Poles in Galicia which Poland had announced as annexed to Poland and recaptured Lemberg and other cities

Oct. 7, Poles in the German Reichstag declared for an independent Poland

Oct. 8, Manifesto of Regency Council at Warsaw announced dissolution of the Council of State appointed under German authority

Oct. 12, The Regency Council took over administration of the territory previously controlled by Germans at Warsaw

——, Polish National Army recognized by Great Britain

Oct. 15, Austrian Government at Lublin agreed to turn over administration of the eastern districts to the Poles

Oct. 19, Ukrainian National Council assumed control of East Galicia

Oct. 22, Joseph Swierzynski formed National Democratic anti-German Cabinet

Oct. 26, The Mid-European Union organized in the United States of nationalities "wholly or partly subject to alien dominion" met in convention in Independence Hall, Philadelphia under presidency of Professor Masaryk and adopted resolutions for united action

Oct. 28, Polish deputies in Austrian Reichsrat organized a commission in Cracow to take over government of Galicia

Oct. 30, Austrians surrendered authority in Lemberg which was taken over by a force of Ukrainians

Oct. 31, Cracow occupied by Polish troops

Nov. 1, State of war with the Ukraine proclaimed and fighting for control of Lemberg which lasted 3 weeks

Nov. 2, Joseph Pilsudski released from German prison

Nov. 3, Republic declared at Warsaw

Nov. 4, Recognition by the United States of the Polish army as autonomous and co-belligerent

Nov. 5, Central Committee of Poles and Czechs took over administration of Teschen

Nov. 7, I. Daszynski formed a Socialist Government at Lublin and demanded resignation of the Regency

Nov. 8, Warsaw Government notified Austria that Galicia had been incorporated in Poland

Nov. 10, Pilsudski arrived in Warsaw

——, Regency Council declared German occupation ended and disarmed German soldiers. German Governor General von Beseler left Warsaw

Nov. 9, Poles withdrew from Mid-European Union

Nov. 12, Regency Council appointed Polish officials to executive positions in Warsaw and granted supreme military authority to Pilsudski

Nov. 14, Resignation of Regency Council. Pilsudski became head of the State

Nov. 15, Pilsudski invited Daszynski who had recognized his authority to form a Cabinet

Nov. 16, Pilsudski declared the independence of Poland

Nov. 18, Resolution of Senator Lodge in American Senate adopted by which the Senate joined with the President in his statement as to independence of Poland and its access to the sea in Point 13 of the Fourteen Points

——, Pozzanians refusing to acknowledge the Warsaw Government elected delegates to a Supreme Popular Council

Nov. 19, J. Moraczewski (Socialist) formed Cabinet after failure of Daszynski

Nov. 21, Poles in Lemberg reinforced by troops expeled Ukrainians

Nov. 23, Polish occupation of Lemberg

Nov. 26, Decree made eight hour day working compulsory

Nov. 28, Electoral law passed granting universal suffrage to residents over 21

Dec. 3, Supreme Popular Council at Poznan (Posen) established an executive committee

Dec. 4, Ultimatum to Germany demanded withdrawal of troops from Poland

Dec. 9, Diplomatic relations with Russia severed

Dec. 15, Diplomatic relations with Germany severed

Dec. 18, Act regulating hours of labor passed

Dec. 22, Hoover sent the first American food mission to Warsaw

Dec. 25, Paderewski landed at Danzig and proceeded to Poznan (Posen) where he received a great popular ovation

Dec. 27–28, Polish force commanded by General Dowbor-Musnicki gained control of territory of Poznania legally still part of Prussia

1919

Jan. 1, Paderewski arrived in Warsaw. Received with demonstrations of enthusiasm and also in Cracow

Jan. 4, American Food Mission arrived at Warsaw, Dr. Vernon Kellogg, Colonel William R. Grove

Jan. 4–5, Conservatives and Liberals led by Prince Eustache Sapieha made unsuccessful attempt to seize the Government

Jan. 5, Bolsheviks captured Vilna

Jan. 11, The Poles relieved Lemberg

Jan. 16, Resignation of the Moraczewski Cabinet

Jan. 17, Paderewski took office as Prime Minister with a coalition Cabinet

Jan. 18, Paderewski and Dmowski received as representatives at the Paris Peace Conference

Jan. 22, Decision of Allies to send a political and military mission to Poland

Jan. 23, Evacuation of East Silesia by Polish troops demanded by Allies

Jan. 24, Warning of Supreme Council that territory taken by force will prejudice claims of aggressors

Jan. 24–28, Czechs successful in fighting with Poles in Galicia

Jan. 26, Polish Government recognized by the United States

——, Elections held for first Polish Diet (Seyma) in Congress Poland and Western Galicia

——, Czechs captured Oldenburg

Jan. 28, Polish Nationalists seized Pozan (Posen)

Jan. 29, Question of frontiers of Poland presented by Dmowski to Supreme Council at the Peace Conference and inter-allied Mission appointed to go to Poland and make report

Jan. 31, Supreme Council appointed a commission to investigate Teschen question in dispute between Poles and Czechs

Feb. 5, Armistice with Czechoslovaks

Feb. 10, Constituent Diet opened at Warsaw

Feb. 12, Commission on Polish Affairs (Polish Liaison Committee) established in Paris to receive reports of the Mission to Poland for the Supreme Council

——, Allied Mission arrived at Warsaw

Feb. 17, First American ships with food for Poland arrived at Danzig. 14,000 tons of American food reached Poland during this month

Feb. 20, The Diet confirmed Pilsudski as Chief of State and Paderewski as Prime Minister and adopted a temporary Constitution

Feb. 21, Germans renewed hostilities with the Poles in Posen

Feb. 24, Hostilities between Poles and Ukrainians in eastern Galicia ended on request of Supreme Council but truce broken 4 days later

——, France officially recognized Poland

Feb. 26, Supreme Council instructed the Commission on Polish Affairs to report on boundaries of the Polish State

Feb. 27, Great Britain officially recognized Poland

March 1, Ukrainians denounced truce with Poles and the following day resumed attack on Lemberg

March 12, First Report of Commission on Polish Affairs on Polish-German boundary recommended that Danzig and entire length of the Danzig-Mlawa-Warsaw be given to Poland, a plebiscite in Allenstein region of East Prussia, and regions in Upper Silesia with Polish majorities be ceded to Poland

March 13, Recognition of Poland by Finland

March 15, Recognition of Poland by Switzerland

March 19, Supreme Council again asked Poles and Ukrainians to cease hostilities. Conference on March 27, failed to reach agreement

March 21, Recognition of Poland by Belgium

March 28, Note to the German Government of General Nadant for Marshal Foch asked permission for passage of Polish troops of General Haller through Danzig on their return from France to Poland. Not granted because of German belief that the troops would seize Danzig for Poland

April 4, German proposal to transport Haller's troops through Coblentz, Stettin, and Konigsberg accepted

April 19, Pilsudski drove Bolsheviks out and occupied Vilna

April 28, Hoover placed in charge of coal production in Poland

May 3, Draft Constitution presented by Wojciechowski, Minister of the Interior

May 8, Offensive opened in East Galicia against Russians and Ukrainians

May 12, Draft Armistice Convention prepared in Paris submitted to Poles and Ukrainians. Accepted by Ukrainians but not by General Pilsudski

May 13–26, Fighting between Poles and Ukrainians

May 13, Resignation of Paderewski as Prime Minister not accepted

May 18, Clash with Czechs in Teschen

May 19, The Ukrainians asked for an armistice

——, Compulsory sickness insurance law for workers enacted

June 7, Recognition of Poland by Spain

June 25, The Supreme Council authorized Poles to remain in occupation of East Galicia as far as the Zbrucz River

June 28, Treaty of Versailles signed by Poland and Minorities Treaty with the Principal Allied and Associated Powers by which Poland guaranteed the rights of minorities in Poland free exercise of religion and equality in civil and political rights and right to use their own language

July 10, Land Reform law passed providing for expropriation of large estates

July 13, Mission headed by Henry Morgenthau appointed in June by President Wilson to investigate alleged pogroms against the Jews arrived in Warsaw

July 16, Colonel Gilchrist ordered to report to Hoover for typhus relief in Poland

July 17, American technical and food advisers for Poland appointed

July 22, Grodno captured

July 27, Provisional line for boundary with Lithuania fixed by Supreme Council, the Foch line, northwest of Vilna

Aug. 8, Poles captured Minsk

Aug. 18, Polish rising in Upper Silesia

Sept. 10, Treaty of St. Germain with Austria signed and Minorities Treaty

Sept. 27, Decision of Supreme Council to hold a plebiscite for Duchy of Teschen including the territories of Spisz (Zips) and Orava (Arva) in dispute between Poland and Czechoslovakia

Oct. 23, Provisional Treaty with Germany signed, main feature coal deliveries

Nov. 4, Constitution revised resubmitted to Diet

Nov. 20, Mandate over East Galicia given to Poland for 25 years by Supreme Council at end of which time a plebiscite should be held. This arrangement not satisfactory to Poland and decision reversed Dec. 22

Dec. 7, Resignation of Paderewski as Prime Minister

Dec. 8, The Curzon line established by Supreme Council as eastern boundary left Vilna outside Poland

Dec. 13, L. Skulski appointed Prime Minister

Dec. 22, First Russian proposal for peace negotiations. Not answered

1920

Jan. 4, Polish troops captured Dvinsk

Jan. 5, Town of Jitomir captured in advance on Kiev

Jan. 14, Conference at Helsingfors with Baltic States
Jan. 18, Polish troops occupied German fortress city of Thorn
Jan. 29, Second Russian Note proposed peace negotiations
Jan. 30, Commission to supervise plebiscite arrived in Teschen
Feb. 13, Minorities Treaty of June 28, 1919 placed under guardianship of League of Nations
March 7–11, Conflict with Czechs in Teschen
March 17, Commercial Convention with Austria signed
March 21, Peace terms issued by Russia
March 27, Polish Note to Russia demanded boundary of 1772, the status of the territory west of this line to be decided by plebiscite. Asked war indemnity
April 23, Agreement with Ukrainian General Petlura by which Ukrainian claim to East Galicia abandoned and Poles to aid Ukrainian Nationalists against the Bolsheviks
April 25, Polish offensive against Bolsheviks for liberation of the Ukraine begun
April 27, Poles attacked the Bolsheviks south of the Pripet Marches
May 3, Fastov 40 miles from Kiev captured by Poles
May 7, Polish occupation of Kiev
May 18, Bolshevik counter-attack between Dnieper and Dvina Rivers
——, Riot and strike in Teschen. Plebiscite abandoned
May 19, Compulsory Workmen's Insurance law passed
June 4, Public education law passed
June 11, Bolsheviks recaptured Kiev and Polish retreat begun
June 15, Bolsheviks again occupied Vilna
——, Diet passed Agrarian Reform Bill
June 23, L. Grabski appointed Prime Minister and Minister of Finance. E. Sapieha succeeded S. Patek as Minister of Foreign Affairs
June 25, General Weygand's military mission reached Warsaw
June 28, Conference of Ambassadors decided on partition of Teschen
July 4, Polish line broken by attacks of Soviet forces
July 10, Appeal of Poland of July 6 to Spa Conference for assistance against Russia refused
July 11, Plebiscite in Allenstein and Marienwerder resulted in favor of union with East Prussia
——, Minsk taken by Bolsheviks
July 12, Sarny taken by Bolsheviks
July 13, Law organized higher education
July 15, Bolsheviks occupied Vilna evacuated by the Poles
——, Land law provided for expropriation of large estates. Not put into effect
July 16, Law passed provided for establishment of land offices
July 21, Russians occupied Grodno
July 22, Russians entered Galicia
July 23, Poland asked Russia for an armistice. Refused Aug. 3
July 24, V. Witos, Peasant leader, appointed Prime Minister, formed coalition Cabinet
July 27, Russians took Pinsk
July 28, Conference of Ambassadors announced boundary line for Teschen (Spisz and Orava) as between Poland and Czecho-Slovakia
July 30, Entente Note to Russia regarding armistice with Poles

Aug. 3, Russians occupied Brest-Litovsk and established a Polish Soviet Government
Aug. 8, Russians evacuated Przasnysz and Vladimir-Volhynsk
Aug. 10, "Certain Frontiers Treaty" signed at Sevres by which the Allied and Associated Powers ceded West Galicia to Poland
——, Note of American Secretary of State Colby to Russia and Poland reaffirmed interest of the United States in Polish independence and territorial integrity
Aug. 12, Russians took Pultusk 30 miles from Warsaw
Aug. 13, Russians occupied Sierock 20 miles from Warsaw
Aug. 14, Russians took Soldau in Polish West Prussia and reached Okuniev 12 miles from Warsaw
Aug. 14–Sept. 29, Polish counter-offensive under General Weygand successful
Aug. 16–29, Armistice Conference with Russians at Minsk
Aug. 21, Second Note of Secretary Colby criticized Polish advance into Russia
——, Poles occupied Brest-Litovsk
Aug. 24, Lithuanians occupied Vilna evacuated by Russians
Sept. 13, Poles took Kovel
Sept. 16, Poles took Lutsk (Luck)
Sept. 21, Armistice Conference with Russians renewed at Riga
Sept. 27, Poles in pursuit of retreating Russians took Grodno
Oct. 7, Suwalki Agreement drafted by League of Nations, truce to go into effect Oct. 10 as to Vilna. *See* Lithuania
Oct. 9, Coup d'etat of General Zeligowski without authority of the Government seized Vilna for Poland driving out the Lithuanians
Oct. 12, Preliminary Peace Treaty with Russia signed at Riga
Oct. 21, Resolution to create an upper House (Senate) passed the Diet
Nov. 8, Decision that plebiscite should be held in Vilna under auspices of the League of Nations accepted
Nov. 9, Convention with the City of Danzig signed
Nov. 14, Peace Conference met
Nov. 29, Armistice Convention signed with Lithuanians by General Zeligowski
Dec. 17, Law passed provided for grants of land to ex-soldiers

1921

Jan. 1, Poland agreed to proposal of the Council of the League of Nations for a plebiscite in Central Lithuania
Jan. 8, Supplementary Commercial Convention with Austria signed
Feb. 19, Treaty of alliance, political and defensive, with France signed
March 3, Treaty of offensive and defensive alliance with Rumania signed
March 17, Constitution adopted
March 18, Peace Treaty with Russia signed at Riga gave Poland territory east of the Curzon line but less than the frontier of 1772
March 20, Plebiscite in Upper Silesia resulted in favor of Germany
April 21–June 3, Polish-Lithuanian Conference on Vilna ended without agreement

May 4, Polish forces led by Adalbert Korfanty overran Upper Silesia

June 1, New Constitution came into effect

July 1, Commercial Treaty with Rumania concluded

July 28, Conference at Helsingfors. *See* Finland

Aug. 12, Supreme Council referred question of Upper Silesia to Council of the League of Nations

Aug. 23, Provisional Commercial Agreement with Italy signed

Sept. 10, Fall of Witos Cabinet

Sept. 19, A. Ponikowski formed Cabinet

Oct. 8, Supplementary Agreement with Russia signed

Oct. 12, Decision of League of Nations on the partition of Upper Silesia

Oct. 20, Commercial Treaty with Czechoslovakia signed

Oct. 24, Convention regulating relations with Free City of Danzig signed

Nov. 6, Treaty with Czecho-Slovakia signed, each nation guaranteeing benevolent neutrality in case of attack

1922

Jan. 8, Plebiscite at Vilna declared in favor of Poland

Feb. 6, Commercial Treaty with France signed provided for reciprocal tariff concessions and French loan

Feb. 20, Vilna Diet voted for union with Poland

Feb. 28, The Sejm voted to continue the children's relief work after withdrawal of American Food Mission (A.R.A.)

March 10, Ponikowski Cabinet reconstituted

March 13-17, Warsaw Conference attended by representatives of Finland, Estonia, Latvia, and Poland

March 17, Treaty for the establishment of an enduring peace provided for neutrality in case of attack and recognition of peace treaties concluded. Signed by Poland, Finland, Estonia, and Latvia

March 20-28, Anti-Epidemic Conference held at Warsaw in collaboration with Health Section of League of Nations attended by representatives of 27 States

March 24, Formal vote of Diet for annexation of Vilna

March 29, Conference at Riga of representatives of Estonia, Latvia, Russia, and Poland discussed economic rehabilitation, disarmament, &c.

April 18, Formal Act of incorporation of Vilna in Poland

May 12, Commercial Treaty with Italy signed

May 15, Convention as to Upper Silesia signed

June 6, Resignation of the Ponikowski Cabinet

June 26, Commercial Treaty with Switzerland signed

June 28, Arthur Sliwinski formed a Cabinet

July 4, The Government pledged itself to return all Polish-Americans of General Haller's army still in Poland to the United States

July 7, Resignation of Sliwinski Cabinet

July 29, Electoral law passed

July 31, Professor J. Nowak formed Cabinet

Sept. 25, Commercial Treaty with Austria signed

Sept. 26, General law established local governing bodies in the provinces

Oct. 20, Commercial Treaty with Czecho-Slovakia signed

Oct. 23, Commercial Treaty with Yugo-Slavia signed

Nov. 5 and 12, Elections held for the Diet under new Constitution gave the Right parties a majority in Sejm Nov. 5

Nov. 12, Elections for the Senate, 49 Conservatives in total membership of 111

Nov. 28, President Pilsudski formally convoked the Senate and Sejm as new National Assembly

Dec. 2-11, Moscow Conference of Disarmament attended by Poland

Dec. 7, Commercial Treaty with Japan signed

Dec. 9, Gabriel Narutowicz, Radical Peasant Party, elected President by the National Assembly defeating Count Maurice Zamoyski, candidate of the Right. Pilsudski had declined to be a candidate

Dec. 11, President Narutowicz inaugurated and assumed office Dec. 16

Dec. 16, L. Sikorski succeeded Nowak as Premier, A. Skrzynski, Minister Foreign Affairs

Dec. 18, President Narutowicz assassinated by young writer probably as a result of the violence of the press campaign

Dec. 20, Stanislas Wojciechowski elected President by the Assembly

Dec. 30, Commercial Treaty with Belgium and Luxemburg signed

1923

Feb. 20, Delimitation Commission gave decision on Polish-Lithuanian boundary giving Vilna to Poland

March 15, Conference of Ambassadors laid down frontier between Poland and Lithuania assigning Vilna district to Poland

April 5, Recognition by the United States of the frontiers of Poland as established by the Treaty of Riga

April 15, Decree of Prime Minister ordered expulsion of Ukrainian refugees

April 28, Commercial Agreement with Germany signed

May 26, Resignation of Sikorski Ministry

May 28, Vincent Witos formed a coalition Cabinet

June 4, Frontier Traffic Agreement with Germany signed

June 24, Visit of King Ferdinand and Queen Marie of Rumania to Warsaw

July 6, Workmen's Social Insurance Act passed

July 7, Anti-Jewish riots in Vilna district

July 23, Treaty of friendship and juridical convention with Turkey signed

——, Agreement provided for 67% increase in wages ended textile strike

——, Diplomatic and Consular Convention with Yugoslavia

Aug. 11, Property Tax Act passed by the Sejm

Nov. 10, Commercial Treaty with Finland signed

Nov. 13, Arbitration Agreement with Austria signed

Nov. 26, Treaty of commerce and navigation with Great Britain signed

Dec. 6, Stabilization of Taxes Act passed

Dec. 15, Resignation of Witos Ministry

Dec. 19, L. Grabski formed a non-parliamentary Cabinet of experts

1924

Jan. 11, Emergency Powers Act gave Premier Grabski powers for financial reform

Jan. 23, Decree of the President introduced the new national currency, the zloty

Feb. 16-18, Economic Conference at Warsaw of representatives of Finland, Latvia, Estonia, and Poland

March 10, Loan of Italian banks to Poland

March 22, Commercial Treaty with Denmark and Iceland signed

April 1, Bank of Poland became bank of issue, the Polish State Loan Bank liquidated

April 28, Polish State Loan Bank abolished

May 1, New currency on gold basis with the zloty as unit of exchange equivalent to gold franc put into circulation

May 10, Note of Russia protested against treatment by Poland of border nationalities in distribution of land, press censorship, closing of churches in violation of Treaty of Riga

May 16, Protocol with Czechoslovakia as to Javorina signed

May 23, Compulsory military service law included all citizens between ages of 21 and 40

May 30, Commercial Treaty with the Netherlands signed

———, Commercial Treaty with Czechoslovakia signed

July 10, 3 laws dealing with minorities passed permitted parallel use of Lithuanian, White Russian, and Ukrainian languages in administration and courts and schools in certain districts

July 18, Compulsory Unemployment Insurance Act passed

Aug. 3, Town of Stolbce attacked by Bolshevik raiders

Oct. 20, Commercial Treaty with Sweden signed

Nov. 15, Poland's debt to the United States funded

Nov. 24–Dec. 4, Conference of Baltic States at Helsingfors. *See* Finland

Dec. 2, Treaty of commerce and navigation with Sweden signed

Dec. 10, Poland's debt to Great Britain funded

1925

Jan. 5, Poland put up Polish letter boxes in Free City of Danzig

Jan. 17, Treaty of arbitration and conciliation with Estonia, Finland, and Latvia

Jan. 31, Commercial Agreement with Spain signed

Feb. 4, Senate ratified debt Agreement with the United States

Feb. 10, Treaty of commerce with the United States signed

———, Concordat with the Vatican signed

March 7, Arbitration and Conciliation Agreement with Switzerland signed

March 9, Establishment of postal and telegraph communication with Russia

March 15, Treaty of friendship and commerce with Persia signed

March, $35,000,000 Polish loan floated in the United States

March 25, Commercial Treaty with Hungary signed

April 3, Death of Jean de Reszke, tenor, in Nice

April 17, Provisional Commercial Agreement with Greece signed

April 23, Arbitration Treaty with Czecho-Slovakia signed

April 30, Treaty of commerce and navigation with Bulgaria signed

May 16, Advisory opinion of Permanent Court of Justice in favor of Poland regarding establishment of Polish postal service in Danzig

May 28, Resignation of M. Thugutt, Deputy Premier

June 15, Upper Silesia coal agreement with Germany expired. German-Polish economic war begun

July 4, Polish-Jewish Declarations for better understanding and protection of Jewish minority

July 10, Commercial Treaty with France signed

July 18, Railway communication Agreement with Russia concluded

July, Expulsion of Polish and German optants

Aug. 3, Agreement with Russia signed for settlement of frontier conflicts

Sept. 1, Lithuanian-Polish Conference concluded agreements as to rafting on the Niemen River

Nov. 3, Arbitration Treaty with Sweden signed

Nov. 13, Resignation of the Grabski Ministry defeated on financial policy

Nov. 20, A. Skrzynski took office as Prime Minister

Dec. 5, Death of Ladislas Reymont, novelist

Dec. 19, Dr. E. W. Kemmerer engaged as financial adviser sailed from the United States

Dec. 28, New land law passed provided for distribution of 200,000 hectares a year for 10 years parcelling out the large estates

Dec. 30, Extradition Treaty with France signed

1926

Jan. 31, Polish-Soviet Chamber of Commerce established in Warsaw

March 26, New Treaty of alliance with Rumania signed

April 16, Arbitration Convention with Austria signed

April 21, Resignation of Count Alexander Skrzynski as Prime Minister. Accepted May 5

April 23, Treaty of arbitration and conciliation with Denmark signed

May 10, V. Witos leader of Peasant Party formed new Cabinet

May 12–14, Coup d'etat of General Pilsudski seized the Government and forced resignation of the Witos Cabinet. Loyal troops fighting to uphold the Government of President Wojciechowski defeated by Pilsudski forces

May 15, Resignation of the President and Premier Witos, Casimir Bartel adherent of Pilsudski became Premier with Cabinet of experts, Pilsudski, Minister of Military Affairs; A. Zaleski, Foreign Affairs; C. Karner, Finance

May 31, Pilsudski elected President by the National Assembly but he declined the office

June 1, Professor Ignace Moscicki elected President. Assumed office June 4

July 31, Bill modifying the Constitution and increasing the power of the President passed the Senate

Aug. 5, Constitutional Reform law promulgated

Aug. 11, $10,000,000 debt to Federal Reserve Bank of America paid

Aug. 26, Government announced completion of "Legal Council" of 26 members empowered to pass judgment on every bill submitted to Parliament

Aug. 27–Sept. 25, Warsaw-Tokio flight of Captain Orlinski and Colonel Kubiak

Sept., Report of Professor E. W. Kemmerer presented recommending financial reform, stabilization of the zloty, flotation of a foreign loan of about 10 to 15 million dollars, increase of capitalization of Bank of Poland, certain restrictions on agricultural and industrial obligations to be held by the bank, specific measures for equalization of taxation, no further issue of uncovered paper and some other important improvements of banking system, fiscal control, budget law, customs administration, &c. Professor

Kemmerer called attention to the fact that the army called for 36.5% of total budget expense

Sept. 15, Treaty of friendship and arbitration with Yugoslavia signed

Sept. 30, The Sejm refused to vote the budget. The Bartel Cabinet resigned

Oct. 2, General Pilsudski took office as Prime Minister with Casimir Bartel as deputy Prime Minister; August Zaleski, Foreign Affairs; Gabriel Czechowicz, Finance

Dec. 18, Agreement for consolidation of debt to Italy concluded

Dec. 22, Treaty of commerce and navigation with Norway

1927

Feb. 19, Treaty of commerce and navigation with Estonia

March 19, Treaty of friendship and commerce with Persia signed

March 25, Marshal Pilsudski adjourned the Sejm

——, Consular Convention with Turkey signed

June 7, Russian Minister Voikov shot and fatally wounded in railroad station at Warsaw by Boris Korenko, Russian monarchist student

June 15–16, Trial of Korenko. Sentenced to life imprisonment

July 5, Commercial Agreement with Switzerland signed

July 6, Preliminary loan of $15,000,000 negotiated with American bankers

Oct. 5, Poles arrested 20 Lithuanians in Vilna and closed 43 schools as a protest against alleged harsh treatment of Poles in Lithuania

Oct. 13, Government decree formally inaugurated program of stabilization and financial reform as to budget, banking, State loans, liquidation of the floating debt, establishment of a Treasury reserve under control of Financial Adviser, Charles S. Dewey, American, appointed Adviser. The zloty fixed at gold value of 11.22 cents and new currency issued

Oct. 18, $72,000,000 stabilization loan floated of which $47,000,000 taken in New York

Oct. 20, Pilsudski dissolved Parliament

Oct. 31, Parliament met to consider budget

Nov. 3–28, Parliament dissolved

Nov. 14, Debt funding settlement with the United States, total debt $178,560,000 to be paid over a term of 61 years

Nov. 28, Sejm dissolved

——, Note of Government to the Powers disclaimed intention of aggression towards Lithuania

Nov. 29, Warrants for arrest for 54 Deputies issued

Dec. 10, Poland accepted resolution of the Council of the League of Nations declaring "state of war" of Lithuania and Poland ended

Dec. 22, Provisional Commercial Treaty with Latvia signed

1928

Jan. 3, Exchange of political prisoners with Russia

Feb. 10, Concordat with the Vatican signed

March 4 and 11, Elections held gave Government 128 out of 446 members of the Lower House, and 53 of 110 in Upper House

March 27, Marshal Pilsudski opened the Sejm

March 30–April 2, Polish-Lithuanian Conference at Koenigsberg. Committees appointed to deal with communications, indemnities, and other subjects

April 14, New Treaty of friendship and commerce with Persia signed

May 4, Official of the Russian Legation at Warsaw shot

May 5, Protest of Russia as to shooting

May 19, Treaty of friendship and commerce with China signed

June 27, Pilsudski resigned as Premier. Succeeded by Vice Premier Bartel

July 5, Financial Agreement with Germany signed

Aug. 5, Major Idzikowski and Major Kubala in the sesquiplane "The Marshal Pilsudski" left Le-Bourget, France, for New York. Rescued 60 miles off Cape Finisterre

Aug. 16, Arbitration and Conciliation Treaty with the United States signed

Aug. 18, Legal Convention with Switzerland signed

Oct. 4–22, Strike of textile workers at Lodz gained 5% increase in wages

Oct. 25, Treaty of arbitration and conciliation with Belgium signed

Nov. 3–7, Koenigsberg Conference with Lithuania renewed as to renewal of intercourse. No agreement reached

Nov. 30, Conciliation and Arbitration Agreement with Hungary signed

Dec. 2, Commercial Agreement with Hungary signed

Dec. 5, Arbitration Convention with Spain signed

Dec. 14, Financial Convention with Germany signed

1929

Jan. 1, Bartel Cabinet sworn in

Feb. 21, Project for new Constitution published by leaders of the "Capital Party"

March 4, Report of Charles S. Dewey, American financial Adviser published

March 8, Resignation of Finance Minister Czerchowicz. Succeeded by M. Grodyrski *pro tem*

April 3, Resignation of Bartel Cabinet

April 14, Cabinet formed by Major Casimir Switalski, former Minister of Education, adherent of Pilsudski

June 29, Trial of former Finance Minister Gabriel Czerchowicz charged with spending money in excess of budget without approval of Parliament. No verdict

July 12, Polish airmen Major Kasimir Kubala and Leon Idzikowski left Paris for flight to New York. Crashed at the Azores July 13, Idzikowski killed

Sept. 1, Treaty of alliance with France renewed

Sept. 4, General Protocol and economical and technical Agreements with Rumania signed

Sept. 18, Treaty of commerce with China signed

Oct. 24, Arbitration and conciliation Treaty with Rumania signed

Oct. 30, Railroad Agreements with Rumania signed

Oct. 31, Marshal Pilsudski with 90 army officers invaded Parliament on day of opening and prevented opening

——, Agreement with Germany signed provided for cessation and liquidation of property and renunciation of financial claims

Dec. 5, Parliament opened

Dec. 6, The Sejm voted no confidence in the Switalski Government

Dec. 7, Switalski Ministry resigned. Succeeded by C. Bartel

——, Frontier Traffic Agreement with Rumania signed

Dec. 31, Treaty of arbitration and conciliation with Bulgaria signed

1930

Jan. 20, Agreement with Austria signed as to pre-War debts

March 14, Bartel Cabinet resigned

March 17, Provisional Commercial Treaty with Germany signed

March 29, Colonel Walery Slawek became Prime Minister; Military Affairs, Joseph Pilsudski; Foreign Affairs, August Zaleski; Finance, Ignacy Matuszewski; Justice, M. Car; Interior, Henryk Jozewski; Commerce and Industry, Eugène Kwiatkowski; Agriculture, Dr. Leon Janta-Polczyński; Agrarian Reforms, Witold Staniewicz; Communications, Alphonso Kühn; Labor and Social Affairs, Aleksander Prystor; Public Works, Dr. Maksymiljan Matakiewicz; Education, Dr. Slawomir Czerwinski; Posts and Telegraphs, Ing Ignacy Boerner

March 30, Parliament prorogued

April 10, Most favored nation commercial Treaty with Greece signed

April 12, Treaty of arbitration with the Netherlands

April 19, Commercial Treaty with Germany signed

May 23, The Sejm summoned by the President but adjourned 2 hours before due to meet

June 20, Senators and Deputies representing Left and Peasant Party and 5,000,000 voters organized new anti-government bloc and demanded resignation of the Government

June 29, 20,000 persons representing 6 political parties met at Cracow to organize against the dictatorship of Pilsudski

Aug. 9–12, Visit of President Moszicki to Talinn (Reval) capital of Estonia

Aug. 23, Resignation of Colonel Walery Slawek as Premier

Aug. 25, Marshal Pilsudski assumed office as Prime Minister and Minister of War. A number of other Cabinet posts filled by military men

Aug. 30, Parliament dissolved by decree of the President and new elections ordered

Sept. 10, Pilsudski ordered arrest of 19 ex-Deputies of the Opposition, including Witos and Kiernik, imprisoned for alleged civil or political offenses in conspiracy against the State

Sept. 13, Decree forbade all open air political meetings

Sept. 14, Opposition Bloc held meeting. 100 participants arrested

Sept. 26, M. Korfanty, Silesian national leader, arrested

Oct. 31, Armed forces invaded the Sejm at opening

Nov. 16 and 23, Elections for Parliament held gave the Government a majority in favor of Pilsudski dictatorship, 75 out of 111 seats in Senate, and 249 out of 444 in Sejm (Lower House) defeating fascists and farmer-laborites

Nov. 28, Pilsudski Cabinet resigned. Succeeded as Premier by Colonel Walery Slawek

Dec. 5, Slawek Cabinet sworn in

Dec. 9, New Parliament opened

Dec. 29, Professor Bartel took office as Premier; Military Affairs, Joseph Pilsudski; Foreign Affairs, August Zaleski; Finance, Ignacy Matuszewski; Justice, M. Dutkiewicz; Interior, General S. Skladowski; Commerce and Industry, Eugène Kwiatkowski; Agriculture, Dr. Leon Janta-Polczyń-ski; Agrarian Reforms, Witold Staniewicz; Communications, Alphonso Kühn; Labor and Social Affairs, Aleksander Prystor; Public Works, Dr. Maksymiljan Matakiewicz; Education, Dr. Slawomir Czerwinski; Posts and Telegraphs, Ing Ignacy Boerner

DUKES AND KINGS OF POLAND

842. Piastus, Duke

861. Ziemovitus, his son

892. Lesko or Lescus IV

913. Ziemomislas, son of Lesco

964. Miecislas I, becomes Christian

992. Boleslas I, surnamed the Lion-hearted; obtained the title of King from the Emperor Otho III Miecislas II

1034. Richense or Richsa, his consort, regent: driven from the government

1037. [Anarchy]

1041. Casimir I, her son, surnamed the Pacific; he had retired to a monastery, but was invited to the throne

1058. Boleslas II, styled the Intrepid

1081. Ladislas I, called the Careless, Duke

1102. Boleslas III, surnamed Wry-mouth

1138. Ladislas, son of the preceding

1146. Boleslas IV, the Curled

1173. Miecislas III, the Old; deposed

1177. Casimir II, surnamed the Just

1194. Lesko V, the White: abdicated

1200. Miecislas III; restored

1202. Ladislas III; retired

1206. Lesko V; restored; assassinated: succeeded by his son, an infant

1227. Boleslas V, surnamed the Chaste

1279. Lesko VI, surnamed the Black

1289. [Horrid anarchy]

1295. Premislas, styled King of Poland, governs wisely: assassinated

1296. Ladislas I (IV), the Short: deposed

1300. Wenceslas, King of Bohemia, abandons Poland

1304. Ladislas IV, the Short

1333. Casimir III, the Great: encourages the arts, and amends the law: killed by a fall from his horse

1370. Louis, king of Hungary, elected King

1382. Maria; and 1384, Hedwige (daughters of Louis), and her consort, Jagello, Duke of Lithuania, by the style of Ladislas V

1399. Ladislas II (V), alone: annexed Lithuania

1434. Ladislas III (VI), son; succeeded as King of Hungary, 1440

1445. [Interregnum]

——. Casimir IV

1492. John (Albert) I, son

1501. Alexander, Prince of Livonia, his brother

1506. Sigismund I, brother; obtained the surname of the Great

1548. Sigismund II, Augustus, son (last of the Jagellon dynasty); a splendid reign: added Livonia to his kingdom: died 1572. Interregnum

ELECTED MONARCHS

1573. Henry de Valois, Duke of Anjou, brother to the King of France; he afterwards succeeded to the French throne

1575. Stephen Bathori, Prince of Transylvania: established the Cossacks as a militia

1586. [Interregnum]

1587. Sigismund III, son of the King of Sweden, to the

exclusion of Maximilian of Austria, elected by the nobles

1632. Ladislas IV (VII), Vasa, son of Sigismund III; succeeded by his brother

1648. John II, or Casimir V; abdicated 1668, and retired to France, where he died a monk, in 1672

1668. [Interregnum]

1669. Michael-Koributh-Wiesnowiski: in this reign the Cossacks join the Turks, and ravage Poland

1674. John III, Sobieski; the last independent king illustrious for victories over the Cossacks, Turks, and Tartars

1697. [Interregnum]

——. Frederick-Augustus I, son of John-George, Elector of Saxony; and Elector in 1694; deprived of his crown

1704. Stanislas I (Leczinski): forced to retire from his kingdom in 1709

1709. Frederick-Augustus I again

1733. Frederick-Augustus II, son of the preceding sovereign

1763. [Interregnum]

1764. Stanislas II, Augustus Poniatowski, resigned his sovereignty, Nov. 25, 1795; died at St. Petersburg, a state prisoner, Feb. 12, 1798

POPE

Pope (from the Greek *Pappas* and *Papa*, a father or grandfather), considered by Romanists to be the visible chief of the church, the vicar of Jesus Christ, and the successor of St. Peter. He styles himself "servant of the servants of God." The title pope was formerly given to all bishops. It was first adopted by Hyginus, 139; and Pope Boniface III induced Phocas, Emperor of the East, to confine it to the prelates of Rome, 606.

Pope. *See also* Rome; Vatican City

BISHOPS AND POPES OF ROME

(the names in italics were antipopes):

42 to 1877

42. St. Peter: (said to have been the first bishop of Rome, and to have been crucified, head downwards, in 66)

St. Clement (Clemens Romanus); according to Tertullian

66. St. Linus: * martyred?

78. St. Cletus, or Anacletus? martyred

91. St. Clement II: abdicated?

100. St. Evaristus: martyred; multiplied churches

109. St. Alexander: martyred

119. St. Sixtus I: martyred?

127. St. Telesphorus: martyred

139. St. Hyginus: condemns Gnostics; called himself Pope

142. St. Pius: martyred

157. St. Anicetus

* St. Linus is frequently set down as the immediate successor of St. Peter; but Tertullian maintains that it was St. Clement. In the first century neither the dates nor order of succession of bishops are reconcilable by even the best authorities. Some assert that there were two or three bishops of Rome at the same time.

168. St. Soterus: martyred under Marcus Antoninus

177. St. Eleutherius: opposed the Valentinians

193. St. Victor I: martyred under Severus

202. St. Zephyrinus: claimed to be Peter's successor

219. St. Calixtus: martyred

222. [The chair vacant]

223. St. Urban I: beheaded

230. St. Pontianus: banished by the Emperor Maximin

235. St. Anterus: [martyred]

236. St. Fabian: martyred under Decius, 250

250. [The chair vacant]

251. St. Cornelius: died

252. St. Lucius: martyred 252. *Novatianus:* (denied restoration to the repentant lapsed)

253. St. Stephen I: martyred in the persecution of Valerian

257. St. Sixtus II (his coadjutor): martyred three days before his disciple St. Laurence, in the persecution of Valerian, 258

258. [The chair vacant]

259. St. Dionysius: opposed the heresy of Sabellius

269. St. Felix I died in prison

275. St. Eutychianus

283. St. Caius: a relative of the Emperor Diocletian

296. St. Marcellinus: said to have lapsed under a severe persecution?; canonised.

304. [The chair vacant]

308. St. Marcellus: banished from Rome by the Emperor Maxentius

310. St. Eusebius: died the same year

311. St. Miltiades or Melchiades: coadjutor to Eusebius

314. St. Silvester: commencement of temporal power by gifts of Constantine

336. St. Marcus: died the next year

337. St. Julius I: of great piety and learning; maintained the cause of St. Athanasius

352. Liberius: banished

355. *Felix II*, antipope: placed in the chair by Constans, during the exile of Liberius, on whose return he was driven from it with ignominy

[The Emperor would have the two popes reign together; but the people cried out, "*One God, one Christ, and one bishop!*"]

358. Liberius again: abdicated

——. *Felix* became Pope

359. Liberius again: martyred 365

366. St. Damasus: opposed the Arians: St. Jerome, his secretary, corrected Latin Bible

367. *Ursinus:* expelled by Valentinian

384. Siricius: combated heretics

398. St. Anastasius: proscribed works of Origen

402. St. Innocent I: condemned Pelagians

417. St. Zozimus: ditto

418. St. Boniface I: maintained by the Emperor Honorius, against *Eulalius*

422. St. Celestine I: sent missions to Ireland

432. Sixtus III: opposed Nestorius and Eutyches

440. St. Leo I the Great: zealous; restrained Alaric; an able writer

461. St. Hilary: rich, liberal

468. St. Simplicius: wise, prudent

483. St. Felix III: opposed Emperor Zeno respecting the Henoticon

492. St. Gelasius: opposed heresy; fixed the canon of Scriptures; compiled the mass

496. St. Anastasius II: congratulated Clovis

498. Symmachus: zealous against the Henoticon

——. *Laurentius:* antipope

514. Hormisdas: opposed Eutychians
523. John I: sent to Constantinople by Theodoric; tolerant
526. Felix IV: introduced extreme unction as a sacrament
530. Boniface II—*Dioscorus*
533. John II: called Mercurius
535. Agapetus: converted Justinian
536. St. Silverius: son of Pope Hormisdas, who had been married; the Empress Theodora procured his banishment into Lycia (where he died of hunger), and made Vigilius Pope
537. Vigilius: banished, but restored
555. Pelagius I: an ecclesiastical reformer
560. John III: great ornamenter of churches
573. [The see vacant]
574. Benedict I, surnamed Bonosus
578. Pelagius II; died of the plague
590. St. Gregory the Great: revised the liturgy; sent Augustin to convert the Anglo-Saxons
604. Sabinianus: said to have introduced church bells
606 or 607. Boniface III: died in a few months
607 or 608. Boniface IV
614 or 615. St. Deusdedit
617 or 618. Boniface V
625. Honorius I: interested in British churches
639. [The see vacant]
640. Severinus: condemned Monothelites
—. John IV: condemned Monothelites
642. Theodorus I: condemned Monothelites
649. Martin I: condemned Monothelites
654. Eugenius I: liberal
657. Vitalianus: favored education in England
672. Adeodatus, the gift of God
676. Domnus I: ornamented churches
678. St. Agathon: tribute to the Emperor ceased
682. St. Leo II: instituted holy water; favored music
683. [The see vacant]
684. Benedict II
685. John V: learned and moderate
686. Conon—*Theodore* and *Pascal*
687. Sergius: "governed wisely"
701. John VI: redeemed captives; firm and wise
705. John VII: moderate
708. Sisinnius: died 20 days after election
—. Constantine: wise and gentle; visited Constantinople; custom of kissing the Pope's toe introduced
715. St. Gregory II: sent Boniface to convert Germans
731. Gregory III, independent; first sent nuncios to foreign powers
741. St. Zacharias, a Greek
752. Stephen II elected: died before consecration
—. Stephen II or III: temporal power of the Church of Rome commenced
757. Paul I: moderate and pious
767. *Constantine Theophylactus:* killed by Lombards
768. Stephen III or IV: literary
772. Adrian I: sanctioned images; caused money to be coined with his name 780
795. Leo III: crowned Charlemagne, 800; granted indulgences for the pardon of sin about 800
816. Stephen IV or V
817. Pascal I: ascetic, and built churches
824. Eugenius II: "father of the afflicted"—*Zozimus*
827. Valentinus
—. Gregory IV; pious and learned
844. Sergius II: the first Pope who changed his name

on his election; some contend that it was Sergius I 687, and others John XII 956
847. Leo IV: defeated the Saracens
855. Pope Joan's election fabulous
—. Benedict III.—*Anastasius*
858. Nicholas I, the Great: conversion of Bulgarians
867. Adrian II: eminent for sanctity
872. John VIII: crowned 3 emperors
882. Marinus or Martin II: condemned Photius
884. Adrian III: ditto
885. Stephen V or VI: very charitable
891. Formosus: political—*Sergius*
896. Boniface VI: deposed
897. Stephen VI or VII: vicious; dishonored the corpse of Pope Formosus; strangled by the people
—. Romanus—*Sergius*
898. Theodorus II: governed 22 days
—. John IX
900. Benedict IV: "a great pope"
903. Leo V: expelled: died in prison
—. Christopher
[Several popes made by the infamous Marozia]
904. Sergius III: disgraced by his vices
911. Anastasius III
913. Landonius, or Lando
914. John X: stifled by Guy, Duke of Tuscany
928. Leo VI: considered an intruder
929. Stephen VII or VIII
931. John XI: son of Marozia; imprisoned in the castle of St. Angelo, where he died
936. Leo VII: great for zeal and piety
939. Stephen VIII or IX: "of ferocious character"
942. Marinus II or Martin III: charitable
946. Agapetus II: of holy life; moderate
956. John XII, the infamous: deposed for adultery and cruelty; and murdered
963. *Leo VIII:* an honor to the chair
964. Benedict V: chosen on the death of John XII, but opposed by Leo VIII, who was supported by the Emperor Otho: died at Hamburg
965. John XIII, elected by the authority of the Emperor against the popular will
972. Benedict VI: murdered in prison
974. Domnus II— *Boniface VII*
975. Benedict VII
984. John XIV: imprisoned by *Boniface VII*
—. John XV: died before consecration
985. John XVI: loved gain
996. Gregory V—*John XVII:* expelled by the Emperor, and barbarously used
999. Silvester II (Gerbert): learned and scientific; said to have introduced the Arabic numerals, and invented clocks
1003. John XVII: legitimate pope, died same year
—. John XVIII abdicated
1009. Sergius IV (original name "Bocca di Porco," Pig's Snout)
1012. Benedict VIII: supported by the Emperor against *Gregory*
1024. John XIX: Romanus, a layman, elected Pope and immediately ordained, taking the name of John
1033. Benedict IX; became Pope, by purchase, at 12 years of age; expelled for vices
1044. *Sylvester III:* 3 months
—. Gregory VI: deposed—*Sylvester;* and *John XX* [The Emperor very influential]
1046. Clement II died the next year (*Clemens Romanus,* the first Clement)

1047. *Benedict IX* again: again deposed
1048. Damasus II: died soon after
——. St. Leo IX: a reformer of simony and incontinence. The first Pope who kept an army, 1054
1054. [The throne vacant one year]
1055. Victor II: a reformer
1057. Stephen IX or X
1058. *Benedict X;* expelled
——. Nicholas II: increased the temporal power
1061. Alexander II: raised the papal power—*Honorius II*
1073. St. Gregory VII (Hildebrand): vigorous reformer; opposed the Emperor Henry IV respecting investitures; and excommunicated him, 1076; obliged him to stand three days, in the depth of winter, barefooted at the gate of the castle of Canossa, to implore his pardon, 1077; the Pope's authority fixed in England, 1079; died, in exile, 1085
1080. *Clement III* (Guibert)
1085. [The throne vacant one year]
1086. Victor III (Didier): learned
1088. Urban II; crusades commenced
1099. Pascal II (Ranieri): Tuscany given to the Papacy by the Countess Matilda
1118. Gelasius II: retired to a monastery—*Gregory VIII*
1119. Calixtus II: settled investiture question
1124. Honorius II
1130. Innocent II: condemned heresies: held 2nd Lateran council—*Anacletus II*
1138. *Victor IV*
1143. Celestine II: ruled 5 months
1144. Lucius II: killed by accident in a popular commotion
1145. Eugenius III: ascetic
1153. Anastasius IV
1154. Adrian IV, or Nicholas Brakespeare, the only Englishman elected Pope: born at Abbot's Langley, near St. Alban's; Frederick I prostrated himself before him, kissed his foot, held his stirrup, and led the white palfrey on which he rode; appeals from English tribunals to the Pope introduced (*Viner*), 19 Stephen
1159. Alexander III: learned; canonized Thomas à Becket; resisted Frederick I; 1159, *Victor V;* 1164, *Pascal III;* 1168, Calistus III; 1178, *Innocent III*
1181. Lucius III—The cardinals acquire power
1185. Urban III: opposed Frederick I
1187. Gregory VIII: ruled only 2 months
——. Clement III: proclaimed 3rd crusade
1191. Celestine III: kicked the Emperor Henry VI's crown off his head while kneeling, to show his prerogative of making and unmaking kings
1198. Innocent III (Lothario Conti): endeavored to free Rome from foreign influence; excommunicated John of England; preached crusade against the Albigenses, 1204; John, King of England, did homage to the Pope's legate for his dominions, and bound himself and his successors to an annual payment May 15, 1213
1216. Honorius III: learned and pious; the Pope collected the tenths of the whole Kingdom of England 1226
1227. Gregory IX: preached a new crusade; collected decretals
1241. Celestine IV: died 18 days after his election
[The throne vacant 1 year and 7 months]
1243. Innocent IV: opposed Frederick II: gave the red hat to cardinals

1254. Alexander IV: established inquisition in France
1261. Urban IV: instituted feast of "Corpus Christi"
1265. Clement IV, an enlightened Frenchman, previously legate to England; discouraged the crusades
1268. [The throne vacant 2 years and 9 months]
1271. Gregory X: held a council at Lyons to reconcile the churches of the east and west
1276. Innocent V: died shortly after
——. Adrian V: legate to England in 1254; died 36 days after election
——. Vicedominus: died the next day
——. John XX or XXI: died in 8 months
1277. Nicholas III: died in 1280
1281. Martin IV, French: supported Charles of Anjou
1285. Honorius IV: supported the French
1288. Nicholas IV: endeavored to stir up a new crusade
1292. [The throne vacant 2 years and 3 months]
1294. St. Celestine V: ascetic; resigned
——. Boniface VIII: proclaimed that "God had set him over kings and kingdoms:" imprisoned his predecessor; quarreled with Philip of France; laid France and Denmark under interdict
1303. Benedict XI: a pious and liberal pontiff: said to have been poisoned
1304. [The throne vacant 11 months]
1305. Clement V (Bertrand de Got): governed by Philip of France; removed the papal seat from Rome to Avignon, 1309
1314. [The throne vacant 2 years and 4 months]
1316. John XXII
1334. Benedict XII (*Nicholas V* at Rome)
1342. Clement VI: learned
1352. Innocent VI: favored Rienzi
1362. Urban V: charitable; a patron of learning; the Pope's demands on England refused by parliament 1363
1370. Gregory XI: protector of learning; restored the papal chair to Rome; proscribed Wickliffe's doctrines

SCHISM—1378–1447

1378. Urban VI: so severe and cruel that the cardinals chose Robert of Geneva, as
——. *Clement VII*
1389. Boniface IX
1394. *Benedict* (called *XIII*) at Avignon
1404. Innocent VII: died in 1406
1406. *Gregory XII*, Angelo Corario
1409. Alexander V: died, supposed by poison
1410. John XXIII: deposed
1417. Martin V, Otho Colonna
1424. *Clement VIII:* resigned 1429
1431. Eugenius IV, Gabriel Condolmera: deposed by the council of Basil, and Amadeus of Savoy chosen as *Felix V*, in 1439, who resigned 1449
1447. Nicholas V: learned; proposed crusade against Turks
1455. Calixtus III, Alfonso Borgia: courageous
1458. Pius II, Æneas Silvius Piccolomini: learned
1464. Paul II, Pietro Barbo: preached a crusade
1471. Sixtus IV: tried to rouse Europe against the Turks
1484. Innocent VIII
1492. Alexander VI, Roderic Borgia: after the discovery of America, Pope Alexander VI granted to the Portuguese all the countries to the east, and to the Spanish all the countries to the west, of Cape Non, Africa, they might conquer, 1493; poisoned at a feast by drinking of a bowl he had prepared for another

1503. Pius III, Francisco Piccolomini: 21 days pope
——. Julius II, Julian della Rovere: martial; began St. Peter's
1513. Leo X, Giovanni de' Medici: his grant of indulgences for crime led to the Reformation; patron of learning and art
1522. Adrian VI: just, learned, frugal
1523. Clement VII, Giulio de' Medici: refused to divorce Catherine of Aragon, and denounced the marriage of Henry VIII with Anne Boleyn; appeals to Rome from England abolished (*Viner*), 1533
1534. Paul III, Alexander Farnese: approved the Jesuits; the words "Lord Pope" struck out of all English books 1541
1550. Julius III, Giovanni M. Giocchi
1555. Marcellus II: died soon after his election
——. Paul IV, John Peter Caraffa. He would not acknowledge Elizabeth Queen of England; instituted "the Index" and leagued with France against Spain.
1559. Pius IV, Cardinal de' Medici: founded Vatican press
1566. St. Pius V, Michael Ghisleri: pious; energetic
1572. Gregory XIII, Buoncampagno: great civilian and canonist: reformed the calendar
1585. Sixtus V, Felix Peretti: an able governor; excom. Henry III and Henry IV of France
1590. Urban VII: died 12 days after election
——. Gregory XIV, Nicholas Sfrondrate
1591. Innocent IX: died in two months
1592. Clement VIII, Hippolito Aldobrandini: learned and just; published the Vulgate
1605. Leo XI: died same month
——. Paul V, Camille Borghese; quarreled with Venice
1621. Gregory XV, Alexander Ludovisio: founded the Propaganda
1623. Urban VIII, Maffei Barberini: condemned Jansenism
1644. Innocent X, John Baptist Panfili: ditto
1655. Alexander VII, Fabio Chigi: favored literature
1667. Clement IX, Giulio Rispogliosi: governed wisely
1670. Clement X, Emilio Altieri
1676. Innocent XI, Odescalchi: condemned Gallicanism and Quietism
1689. Alexander VIII, Ottoboni, Oct. 6; helped Leopold against Turks
1691. Innocent XII, Antonio Pignatelli: July 12; condemned Fénelon
1700. Clement XI, John Francis Albani: Nov. 23; issued the bull Unigenitus
1721. Innocent XIII, Michael Angelo Conti: the eighth of his family; May 8; pensioned Jas. Ed. Stuart
1724. Benedict XIII, Orsini May 29; favored J. E. Stuart
1730. Clement XII, Orsini: July 12; restored San Marino (republic)
1740. Benedict XIV, Lambertini: Aug. 17; learned, amiable
1758. Clement XIII, Chas. Rezzonico: Avignon lost
1769. Clement XIV, Ganganelli: May 19; suppressed the Jesuits; abolished kissing the Pope's toe and other ceremonies 1773
1775. Pius VI, Angelo Braschi, Feb. 15: dethroned by Bonaparte; expelled from Rome, and deposed in Feb. 1798; died at Valence, Aug. 29, 1799
1800. Pius VII, Barnabo Chiaramonte: elected March 13; agrees to a concordat with France, July 15, 1801; crowns Napoleon, Dec. 2, 1804; excommunicates him, June 10, 1809; imprisoned, July 6, 1809; re-

stored in 1814; died, Aug. 20, 1823. (He restored the Jesuits, 1814)
1823. Leo XII, Annibale della Genga, Sept. 28
1829. Pius VIII, Francis Xavier Castiglioni, March 31
1831. Gregory XVI, Mauro Capellari, Feb. 2: died June 1, 1846
1846. Pius IX, Giovanni Maria Mastaï-Ferretti (born May 13, 1792): elected, June 16. *See* Rome, 1846–71
1848. His diplomatic relations with Great Britain authorized by parliament
[Act repealed, 1875]
1860–65. His powers in France greatly checked
1869. The "Latæ Sententiæ," regarding excommunication and limiting absolution, signed, Oct. 12; issued, Dec.
1870. The Pope opens a general council (Dec. 8, 1869), which propounds the doctrine of papal infallibility and list of anathemas (*see* Councils), Feb.; deprived of the remains of his temporal power (*see* Rome), Dec.
1872. Performs no Easter solemnities March 31; in his allocution complains of the persecution of the church in Italy, Germany, and Spain, Dec. 23
1873. Letter from the Pope to the Emperor of Germany complaining of his persecuting the bishops, and asserting his authority over all baptized persons, Aug. 7; the Emperor replies in justification, and asserts that there is no mediator between God and man but Jesus Christ, Sept. 3; encyclical letter of the Pope on wrongs of the Church, Nov. 21; he appoints 12 new cardinals, Dec. 22
1874. The papal nuncio expelled from Switzerland; protests by letter, Jan. 17; a bull (said to be forged), altering mode of electing a pope, &c., dated May 28, 1873; appears, Jan.; in his allocution, the Pope exhorts the faithful to patience, and forbids priests meddling with politics, Dec. 21
1875, The Pope reappears at St. Peter's, after four years' seclusion, Feb. 9; he dedicates the universal church to "the sacred heart," June 16; his nuncio issues a circular against religious toleration in Spain, Sept.; allocution; new cardinals announced, Sept. 17
1876. Death of his cardinal-secretary, Antonelli, Nov. 6; succeeded by Simeoni, about Nov. 15
1877. Creates 11 new cardinals, and issues a warm allocution against the Italian government, March 12; and circular to foreign powers, on account of the bill to repress clerical abuses, March 21; creates 3 cardinals, June 22; 2 cardinals, &c., Dec. 28; died Feb. 7, 1878

1878

Feb. 20, Leo XIII, Gioachino Pecci (born March 2, 1810); elected
March 4, Reduces his guards: holds a consistory, with an allocution; revives Roman Catholic hierarchy in Scotland
March 5, Makes his secretary of state Cardinal Franchi; Cardinal Nina, Aug.
April 25, Publishes encyclical endorsing policy of predecessor, but moderate
Dec. 28, Issues an encyclical letter condemning communism, socialism, and nihilism, as results of the Reformation; dated

1879

May 12, Appoints 10 cardinals (including J. H. Newman)

Early in Aug., Issues encyclical against modern false philosophy; recommends Thomas Aquinas

1880

Feb. 18, Issues encyclical on marriage, as a sacrament, and against divorce; published

Aug. 20, Delivers an allocution censuring the government of Belgium and praising the bishops

Oct. 13, Cardinal Nina, secretary, resigns for bad health; Cardinal Jacobini successor, Nov. 17; he resigned Dec. 1886 (died Feb. 28, 1887)

1881

May 15, Proclaims an extra jubilee for the distressed Church

July, Issues an encyclical letter, asserting that all government is of divine origin, and that wars are consequences of the Reformation

Dec. 8, Canonizes De Rossi and three others

1882

Encyclical letter against heresy, socialism, &c.

1883

May 11, Circular to Irish bishops enjoining abstinence from disaffection to the government

June 23, Letter to President Grévy censuring the republican warfare against religion

Aug. 8, Courteous, firm answer delivered

Sept., Letter from the Pope defending the papacy, and recommending the study of ecclesiastical history

Oct. 7, The Pope addresses 20,000 pilgrims in St. Peter's, and recognizes Italian unity

Dec. 18, Visited by the Crown Prince of Germany

1884

Feb. 11, Encyclical letter to French bishops, commending early French devotion to religion, and exhorting the bishops to redouble their vigilance in regard to heresy and infidelity

Nov. 10, Allocution, 8 cardinals and many bishops created

1885

April, The Pope's messenger, Father Giulianelli, well received by the Emperor of China

1886

Feb. 1, Letter from the Pope to the Emperor of China; reply agreeing to receive a papal agent to protect Roman Catholic missionaries, July

July 30, The Pope declared it inexpedient for Catholics to vote or become candidates for elections in Italy

Nov. 6, Encyclical letter condemning liberalism, &c.

1887

March, Monsignor Rampolla becomes Pontifical Secretary of State

May 23, Allocution

June 15, Letter from the Pope asserting his territorial rights

The Pope's jubilee (on being ordained priest, Dec. 31, 1837)

1888

Jan. 1 and 5, The Pope's grand jubilee; masses at St. Peter's: present 48 cardinals, 238 archbishops and bishops, and about 30,000 persons; the Pope's speech demanding the independence of the Church,

Jan. 3; the Pope condemns the plan of campaign and boycotting on moral grounds, announced April 27

Oct. 12, The Emperor William II visits the Pope

Nov. 10, Address of English Roman Catholic bishops to the Pope protesting against Italian repressive legislation respecting his temporal power

1889

Oct. 20–Nov., The Pope receives French pilgrims

1890

Jan. 16, The Pope's encyclical letter on the moral duties of Catholics now much neglected, issued, Jan. 6, published

April 7, Negotiations respecting the Roman Catholics in Malta, between the British Government and the Pope, carried on by Sir John Lintorn Simmons, concluded; he leaves Rome

1891

May 15, Encyclical concerning socialism and the Labor question issued

1892

Feb. 16, Encyclical to the French bishops enjoining on all good Catholics entire submission to the government of the republic; obedience enforced by a brief, dated May 3

1893

Feb., The Pope celebrates his episcopal jubilee; about 50,000 pilgrims of various nations present in and about St. Peter's; mass celebrated by the Pope amid great enthusiasm

1894

June 20, Encyclical to all princes and nations from the Pope, praying that all Christian nations may be brought into the unity of the Roman Church; the Pope presides at conferences with some Eastern patriarchs to consider the reunion of the dissident Eastern churches with the Church of Rome, Oct. 24 *et seq.*; partial agreement at a final meeting, Nov. 8

1895

March 21, Allocution against the Hungarian civil marriage law, reported; "Apostolic letter to the English people," earnestly appealing for reunion with the Catholic Church, April 14

Nov. 29, Papal consistory: creation of 9 new cardinals, and 24 Italian bishops

1896

June 30, Encyclical advocating Christian unity

Sept. 13, Apostolic letter confirming the decision of Paul IV in 1555 and other Popes against the validity of the Anglican orders

1898

Feb., "A vindication of the bull" by the Roman Catholic cardinal, archbishops and bishops of Westminster, published; the English archbishops' firm reply, March 12. Encyclical to Italy, Aug.

1899

Jan. 22, Encyclical to Cardinal Gibbons and the American Catholics, condemning "Americanism" and the doctrines of the Paulists

May 11, The bull, proclaiming the universal jubilee of 1900, read

May 20, The Pope presides over the commission on the union of the churches; *see* France, June 15, 1899

Sept. 16, Papal encyclical *re* the Dreyfus case, vague and discursive, published

Dec. 14, Papal consistory and allocution

Dec. 24, The holy year 1900 inaugurated by the opening of the "holy door" of St. Peter's

1900

April 19, Preconisation of bishops and allocution

Sept. 29, Oct. 13, Nov. 15, Dec. 24, The Pope gives his blessing to multitudes at St. Peter's

Nov. 1, Encyclical to the Roman prelates, stating that multitudes have flocked to the "threshold of the apostles," relying upon the indulgence offered by the church at the close of this century

Dec. 17, Allocution against his continued loss of temporal power; closes the "holy door," Dec. 24

1901

April 15, Allocution bewailing the hostilities against the Church in various parts of Europe, and the French religious associations bill; 12 cardinals created

Aug., Commission of biblical exegesis appointed

1902

March 3, The Pope's pontifical jubilee

May 28, Encyclical to the Roman Catholic hierarchy "On the most holy eucharist"

June 9, Papal consistory: creation of 3 new cardinals and several bishops; allocution deploring the attempt to dechristianize Rome and Italy by heresy, Protestantism, &c.

Dec. 25, The Pope at his Christmas reception of the cardinals delivers a discourse in favor of the Christian democratic movement, and signifies his approval of clergy taking part in it

1903

April 29, The Pope receives King Edward VII at the Vatican; and the German Emperor, May 3

June 22, Papal consistory: 7 new cardinals created

July 20, Death of Pope Leo XIII, aged 93; temporarily interred in St. Peter's, July 25

Aug. 4, Pius X., Giuseppe Sarto (born June 2, 1835), elected Pope

Aug. 29, Declares his intention to support the King of Spain, reported

Oct. 3, Papal encyclical, dwelling on recent election, and declaring aim to be the restoration of all things in Jesus Christ, and to be in all things the minister of God, published

Nov. 1, Fire at the Vatican in rooms over the famous library

Nov. 9, Papal consistory: Mgr. Callagari and Mgr. Merry del Val (new Papal Secretary of State) created cardinals; allocution on the temporal power of the papacy, declaring continuance in the policy of his predecessors in protesting against the injury done to the pontificate by depriving it of its necessary liberty. He (the Pope) would bear his part in politics whenever they were inseparable from Catholic morality

——, Interview of M. Henri des Houx with the Pope, reported in Paris *Matin*

Nov. 12, Papal consistory (public): 5 cardinals (3 created by Leo XIII) invested with their hats; pallium conferred on Dr. Bourne, new Abp. of Westminster

1904

Nov. 14, Papal consistory; allocution on the situation of the Catholic Church in France; the Pope complains of the hostility there shown towards religion; repudiates as a calumny the charge that the Holy See had not respected the Concordat, and declares that it was the French Government which had failed to respect it; he now felt bound to enter a public protest against the violation of the rights of the church and the dignity of the Holy See

1905

March 27, Papal consistory; no new cardinals created; allocution deploring the plan for the separation of Church and State in France

Dec. 11, Secret consistory; Pope announces his intention to create 4 new Cardinals; expresses his sorrow that owing to the sad condition of the Church in Catholic countries he had no good tidings to give his Cardinals, though he found some consolation in the progress made in other countries which were not Catholic

1906

Feb. 18, Encyclical condemning the French separation law issued

Feb. 21, Secret consistory, at which the Pope nominated Bishops to 23 vacant sees (19 in France)

Aug. 14, Encyclical, dealing with the French separation law, and decreeing that religious worship associations cannot be formed without violation of the rights of the Church, issued

Sept. 23, Agreement between Spain and the Vatican on the subject of the proposed associations law, on a basis similar to that of the concordat of 1905, was reached

Nov. 26, Visit of the King of the Hellenes to the Pope

Dec. 3, The Pope receives in audience Cardinal Kopp, Prince Bishop of Breslau, and informs him that while thoroughly sympathizing with the Poles, the Holy See could not espouse their cause against Germany

Dec. 21, The Pope issues a note of protest against the violation of its archives in Paris, and the expulsion of Mgr. Montagnini

1907

Jan. 11, Encyclical letter issued explaining the attitude of the Holy See towards the separation law and refuting certain charges brought against it by the French Government

April 15, Consistory held at the Vatican, seven new cardinals created: five Italians, one Belgian, one Spaniard; Pope Pius X delivers an allocution in which he condemns the conduct of the French Government in arbitrarily breaking the Concordat, violently despoiling the Church, and violating every public and private law

July 17, Decree of the Holy Office, containing a syllabus of 65 modern errors against the faith, published in Rome

Sept. 16, Encyclical on moderism issued by Pope Pius X

Oct. 22, Father Tyrrell excommunicated by the Pope on account of two articles published by him in *The Times* in reference to the Pope's last encyclical

1908

April 15, The Pope receives Prince Bülow

July 6, Pontifical decree for the reform of the organization and working of the different congregations issued by the Vatican

Sept. 18, Jubilee of the Pope's first mass

Oct. 24, Archbishop Bourne received by the Pope

Nov. 16, Pontifical mass in St. Peter's celebrated by the Pope; missions from all the principal Catholic countries present; 36 cardinals, 400 archbishops and bishops, 50,000 of the public

1909

April 18, Ceremony of the beatification of Joan of Arc held in St. Peter's

May 20, Canonization of Joseph Oriol and Clement Hofbauer completed

Nov. 16, Pope Pius X celebrated his episcopal jubilee

1910

Jan. 8, Death of Cardinal Francesco Satolli

May 28, An encyclical letter published by Pope Pius X recalling the memory of Saint Charles Borromeo, of whose canonization the third centenary would occur on Nov. 1, issued. The Pope compared Saint Charles' catholic reform as opposed to the heretical reform of Luther

June 11, Reply signed by the Cardinal Secretary of State to the protest against the publication of the encyclical in Germany, expressed the regret of his Holiness at the excitement of opinion raised, as no intention of slighting the non-Catholics of Germany or their princes had ever entered his mind. The Prussian Minister was officially informed that the Pope had already instructed the Prussian bishops to abstain from the publication of the encyclical

Sept. 8, Encyclical *motu proprio* entitled "Sacrorum Antistitum" imposed anti-modernist oath on all the clergy

1911

May 21, Encyclical *jamdudum* against anti-religious measures of Portugal refused recognition of lay corporations and forbade clergy to accept pensions from the Government

1913

Dec. 16, Death of Cardinal Rampolla

1914

July 15, Decree of the Pope condemned syndicalist unions

Aug. 2, Circular of appeal for peace addressed by the Pope to the Catholics of the world

Aug. 20, Death of Pope Pius X

Aug. 31, Conclave of cardinals met

Sept. 3, Cardinal Giacomo della Chiesa, Archbishop of Bologna, elected Pope, taking title of Benedict XV

1915

March 19, Death of Cardinal Antonio Agliardi

July 30, Pope Benedict XV issued appeal for peace to the heads of the belligerent Governments

1916

Dec. 28, Monaco resumed relations with the Holy See after interruption of 4 years

1917

May 27, A new "Codex Juris Canonici" promulgated by papal bull to go into effect May 19, 1918

Aug. 1, Second appeal of Pope Benedict XV for peace addressed to heads of the belligerent States proposed submission of international disputes to arbitration

1918

March 17, Beatification of Oliver Plunkett, Archbishop of Armagh, Ireland, executed at Tyburn in 1861

1919

March 23, Death of Cardinal Francesco di Paola Cassetta

Nov. 11, Death of Cardinal Felix von Hartmann, Archbishop of Cologne

——, Decree of 1886 prohibiting Catholics from taking part in politics in Italy revoked

Dec. 15, Seven new cardinals created

Dec. 18, Death of Joseph Mary Cos y Macho, Archbishop of Valladolid

1920

May 16, Ceremony of canonization of Joan of Arc

May 23, Encyclical of Pope authorized Catholic heads of States to visit the King of Italy revoking former prohibition

Aug. 1, Encyclical *motu proprio* issued warning against dangers threatening modern society

1921

Jan. 28, Encyclical of the Pope addressed to bishops urged world peace and Christian reconciliation

Feb. 2, Death of Cardinal Ferrari

March 7, Announcement of creation of 6 cardinals, Dennis J. Dougherty succeeded Cardinal John Farley of New York, deceased

1922

Jan. 22, Death of Pope Benedict XV

Feb. 6, Cardinal Achille Ratti, Archbishop of Milan, elected Pope taking name of Pius XI

May 30, Concordat with Latvia concluded

Dec. 11, Announcement of creation of 8 cardinals

Dec. 23, Encyclical *ubi arcano* issued

1923

Jan. 26, Encyclical *rerum omnium* on death of St. Francis de Sales

Feb. 5, Death of Cardinal Giuseppe Prisco

Feb. 11, Beatification of St. Thérèse of Lisieux

Feb. 14, Death of Cardinal Bartholomeo Bacilieri

May 7, Letter of Papal Nuncio Cerretti presenting draft statute for organization of the private *associations cultuelles* of France; accepted by France, May 13

May 18, Formal visit to the Vatican of the King and Queen of England

May 19, Beatification of Cardinal Robert Bellarmine

May 23, Creation of 2 Cardinals, Luigi Sincero, Assessor of the Consistorial Congregation, and Giovanni Nasalli, Archbishop of Bologna

June 2, Death of Cardinal Juan Soldevilla y Romero

June 29, Encyclical *studiorum ducem* on sixth centenary of canonization of St. Thomas Aquinas

July 27, Death of Cardinal Nicolo Marini

Aug. 10, Death of Cardinal Augustin Richelmy

Nov. 19, Visit of the King and Queen of Spain

Dec. 20, Creation of 2 Cardinals, Evaristo Lucidi, Papal Auditor, and Arelio Galli, Secretary of the Segnatura

1924

Jan. 18, Pope Pius XI in encyclical letter *maximam gravissimam* consented to establishment of diocesan associations which would allow the Church in France to become legal owner of money required for maintenance of church and clergy

May 29, The Pope proclaimed Holy Year for 1925 to begin Dec. 24 at midnight

1925

Feb. 10, Concordat with Poland signed

March 30, Two Spanish cardinals created

May 17, Canonization of French nun, St. Thérèse of Lisieux

June 20, The Pope in address arraigned Fascists in Italy for violence towards Catholics

Dec. 14, The creation of 4 cardinals announced

1926

Jan. 13, Death of Cardinal Mercier

Feb. 14, Death of Cardinal Dalbor

Feb. 27, Death of Cardinal Sili

Feb. 28, Encyclical *rerum ecclesiæ* on Catholic missions

——, Death of Cardinal Cagliero

June 21, Two cardinals created

Aug. 1, Pope Pius XI called on Catholics all over the world to pray for the deliverance of the Catholics of Mexico from persecution

Sept. 23, Death of Cardinal Touchet

Nov. 18, Encyclical *iniquis afflictisque* on persecution of Catholics in Mexico

Dec. 20, Allocution of the Pope condemned Fascist idea which "makes the State an end unto itself," and condemned persecution of Catholics in Mexico

——, Creation of 2 cardinals making the number 67: 37 Italians, 30 non-Italians

1927

Feb. 16, Death of Cardinal Ranuzzi

May 10, Concordat with Rumania signed

June 20, Two cardinals created

July 25, Death of Cardinal John Czernoch, Primate of Hungary

Aug. 25, Death of Cardinal Reig y Casanova, Primate of Spain

Sept. 27, Concordat with Lithuania signed

Oct. 22, Death of Cardinal Patrick O'Donnell, Primate of Ireland

Nov. 12, Death of Cardinal Lualdi

Nov. 26, Death of Cardinal John Bonzano

Dec. 19, Creation of 5 cardinals

1928

Jan. 6, Encyclical *mortalium animos* on promotion of religious unity

Feb. 2, Diplomatic Treaty with Czechoslovakia signed

Feb. 26, The Pope in lenten address and again Aug. 15 scored the immodesty of the dress of women

May 2, The French Minister presented credentials

June 30, Death of Cardinal John Tacci and Cardinal Gaetano de Lai

Aug. 1, Message of the Pope to Chinese Catholic bishops on end of Civil War

Oct. 24, Death of Cardinal Francia Nava

1929

Feb. 7, Cardinal Gasparri informed members of the diplomatic corps summoned by him that an agreement with Italy had been concluded

Feb. 8, Protest of Pope Pius against persecution of religion by the Russian Soviet Government

Feb. 11, Papal State recreated under name of "State of the Vatican City." Three documents signed (1) Treaty recognizing the Holy See as an independent sovereignty, (2) Concordat as to religious activities of the Roman Catholic Church in Italy, and (3) Financial Convention which granted the Pope an indemnity of 750,000,000 lire and 1,000,000,000 in Italian State consols at 5%. Signed by the King May 27

Feb. 12, The Pope appeared on balcony of St. Peter's and gave pontifical blessing *urbi et orbi* to some 100,000 persons gathered in the square

March 9, The entire diplomatic corps, 70 persons representing 35 countries, received by the Pope

May 13 and 25, Mussolini spoke in Parliament on the accord with the Vatican declaring the Church to be neither sovereign nor free but "a sovereign State within the Kingdom of Italy"

May 27, The King signed the Bills giving effect to the Lateran Treaty, the Concordat, and Financial Convention

May 30, Letter of the Pope to Cardinal Gasparri answered speeches of Mussolini saying "There are face to face, if not two States, most certainly two sovereignties, in the full significance of that word, each perfect in every sense in its own sphere, which sphere is necessarily determined by the end which each pursues . . . the objective dignity of the ends pursued determines no less objectively and necessarily the absolute superiority of the Church"

June 5, Open Letter of the Pope criticized Mussolini's speech before the Chamber declaring the Catholic Church subject to the State as "heretical interpretation" of the Accord

June 7, Ratifications of the Accord of Feb. 11 exchanged

June 10, Fundamental law of Vatican City came into effect

1929

June 25, Italian Minister, Senator Cesare Maria de Vecchi, presented credentials to the Holy See

July 5, The Papal Nuncio presented credentials to Italian Government

July 25, First appearance of the Pope outside the Vatican to take formal possession of territory ceded by Italian Government, the first time since the fall of the Papal States in 1870 that a Pope had left the Vatican

Dec. 2, Speech of the Pope condemned curb on Catholic newspapers by Fascists

Dec. 5, The King and Queen of Italy paid official visit to the Pope

Dec. 16 and 19, Number of cardinals increased

Dec. 19, Encyclical urged laity to greater activity in apostolic work

Dec. 20, Pope Pius XI entered Italian territory to celebrate jubilee mass at Church of St. John the Lateran

1930

Jan. 11, Papal encyclical on education declared education preëminently the function of the Church

Feb. 8, Letter of the Pope to Vicar General of Rome condemned policy of Russian Soviet Government and asked entire Christian world to join him in prayer on March 19 for cessation of Bolshevik persecution of churches

Feb. 10, Resignation of Cardinal Pietro Gasparri as Papal Secretary of State, succeeded by Cardinal Pacelli

Feb. 26, Death of Cardinal Merry del Val (64)

July 9, Death of Cardinal Vincenzo Vannutelli

PORTUGAL

Portugal, republic, occupying one-fifth of the Iberian peninsula, bounded on south and west by the Atlantic Ocean and on the land side, north and east, by Spain. Portugal has been an independent State since the 12th century and until the revolution of 1910 a monarchy, the last king being Manoel II. (*See infra*, p. 411.) The total area is 35,490 square miles and total population 6,698,345. Lisbon is the capital.

Portugal was the ancient Lusitania. The present name is derived from Porto Callo, the original appellation of Oporto. After a nine years' struggle, under Viriathes, a brave able leader, the Lusitanians submitted to the Roman arms about 137 B.C. Portugal underwent the same changes as Spain on the fall of the Roman Empire.

General Antonio Oscar de Fragoso Carmona, President.

472 to 1809

472, Settlement of the Alains and Visigoths here

713, Conquered by the Moors

900, The kings of Asturias subdue some Saracen chiefs, and Alfonso III establishes bishops

1095, The Moor, conquered by Alfonso VI the Valiant, of Castile, assisted by many other princes and volunteers; Henry of Besançon (a relative of the Duke of Burgundy and King of France), very eminent; Alfonso bestowed upon him Theresa, his natural daughter, and Portugal as her marriage portion, which he was to hold of him as Count

July 25, 1139, Alfonso Henriquez defeats five Moorish kings, and proclaimed King

Oct. 25, 1147, Assisted by a fleet of Crusaders on their way to the Holy Land, he takes Lisbon from the Moors

1189, Part of Algarve taken from the Moors by Sancho I

1279, Reign of Dionysius I or Denis, father of his country, who builds 44 cities or towns in Portugal

1279 and 1325, Military orders of Christ and St. James instituted

1355, Iñes de Castro murdered

Aug. 14, 1385, John I of Portugal defeated John I of Castile at Aljubarrota and secured his country's independence

1415, John I, surnamed the Great, carries his arms into Africa

1419–30, Maritime discoveries

1420, Madeira and the Canaries seized

About 1433, Lisbon made the capital

1460, Prince Henry, the Navigator, dies

Nov. 20, 1497, Passage to the East Indies by the Cape of Good Hope discovered by Vasco da Gama

1499, Discovery of the Brazils

April, 1500, Brazil discovered by Cabral

About 1520, Camoens, author of the *Lusiad*, born

1526, The Inquisition established

Aug. 4, 1578, African expedition; King Sebastian defeated and slain in the battle of Alcazar

June 24, 1580, Battle of Alcantra; the kingdom seized by Philip II of Spain

1602–20, The Dutch seize the Portuguese settlements in India

Dec., 1640, The Portuguese throw off the yoke, and place John, Duke of Braganza, on the throne

1665, The Portuguese defeat the Spaniards at Villa Viciosa; war ended by the treaty of Lisbon, 1668

1703, Methuen treaty for regulating the commerce between Great Britain and Portugal, made Dec. 27. It greatly favored the importation of port wine into this country by lowering the duty, to the discouragement of French wines. It was abrogated in 1834

Nov. 1, 1755, The great earthquake destroys Lisbon

1758, Joseph I narrowly escapes death by assassins [Some of the first families were tortured to death; their very names being forbidden to be mentioned; the innocence of many was soon afterwards made manifest; the Jesuits were also expelled]

June 6, 1760, Joseph, having no son, obtains a dispensation from the Pope to enable his daughter and brother to intermarry, which took place

1762 and 1763, The Spaniards and French invade Portugal, which is saved by the English

1777, John, Prince of Brazil, marries his aunt, Maria Francesca

1792, Regency of John (afterwards King), owing to the lunacy of Queen Maria

June 6, 1801, War with Spain, March 3; peace

1807, Treaty between France and Spain for the partition of Portugal, Oct.; French invasion; Junot arrives at Lisbon, Nov. 27; the court sail for Brazil, Nov. 29

1808, Rise of the Portuguese; several times defeated, June and July; arrival of Wellington at Oporto, July; he defeats Junot at Vimiera, Aug. 21; convention of Cintra confirmed Aug. 30

March 29, 1809, Oporto taken by Soult

1810

Aug. 27, Almeida taken by Massena

Sept. 27, Massena defeated at Busaco

Oct., Wellington secures the lines of Torres Vedras

1811 to 1825

May 5, 1811, Massena defeated at Fuentes de Onoro; retreats

1814, Portugal cedes Guiana to France

1815, Union of Portugal and Brazil

Aug. 29, 1820, Revolution begins in Oporto

Oct. 1, 1820, Constitutional junta established

July 4, 1821, Return of the court

Oct. 12, 1822, Independence of Brazil; *see* Brazil

June 5, 1823, The King modifies the constitution

May 1–9, 1824, Disturbances at Lisbon; Miguel departs

Aug. 29, 1825, Treaty with Brazil

1826

March 10, Death of John VI

April 26, Dom Pedro grants a constitutional charter, and confirms the regency

May 2, He relinquishes the throne in favor of his daughter, Donna Maria da Gloria

Oct. 4, Miguel takes oath of fealty at Vienna

Oct. 6, Marquis of Chaves' insurrection at Lisbon in favor of Dom Miguel

Oct. 29, Dom Miguel and Donna Maria betrothed

Dec. 17, Portugal solicits the assistance of Great Britain, Dec. 3; departure of the first British auxiliary troops for Portugal

1827

Dec. 7, Bank of Lisbon stops payment

1828

Feb. 22, Dom Miguel made Regent; takes the oath

April 28, The British armament quits Portugal, foreign ministers withdraw May 3

June 13, Sir John Doyle, a partisan of Donna Maria, arrested

July 4, Dom Miguel assumes the title of King

Aug. 24, His troops take Madeira

Sept. 7, Release of Sir John Doyle

1829

Aug. 11, Miguel's expedition against Terceira defeated

1830

March, Duke of Palmella appointed Regent

1831

June 16, Dom Pedro arrives in England

Aug. 21, Insurrection in Portugal in favor of the Queen; more than 300 lives lost

1832

Feb. 9, Dom Pedro's expedition sails from Belle-isle; at Terceira proclaims himself regent, April 2; takes Oporto July 8

Sept. 19, The Miguelites attack Oporto, and are defeated with considerable loss on both sides

1833

April 9, Mount Cavello taken

July 5, Admiral Napier takes Dom Miguel's squadron off Cape St. Vincent

July 24, Lisbon evacuated by the Duke of Cadaval; the Queen proclaimed; enters Lisbon, Sept. 22

1834

May 26, After various conflicts Dom Miguel capitulates to the Pedroites, and Santarem surrenders; Dom Miguel embarks at Evora for Genoa, May 31

Sept. 24, Dom Pedro dies

1835

March 28, Prince Augustus (Duke of Leuchtenberg) Prince Consort; married, Dec. 1, 1834; dies

1836

April 9, The Queen marries Ferdinand of Saxe-Coburg

Aug. 9 and Nov. 8, Revolution at Lisbon

1837

Aug. 18, The Duke of Terceira attempts to restore Dom Pedro's charter

Sept. 18, He and Saldanha fail, and embark for England

1846

April 20, The northern province in a state of insurrection about this time

Oct. 31, The Duke of Palmella resigns

——, Action at Evora, the Queen's troops defeat the insurgent forces

——, British squadron under Admiral Parker arrives in the Tagus, at the Queen's request

Nov. 26, Palmella banished

Dec. 22, Marquis of Saldanha defeats Count Bomfinn at Torres Vedras

1847

Jan. 7, The insurgents enter Oporto

May 21, London conference: England, France, and Spain determine to assist the Queen of Portugal to terminate the civil war

June 11, Submission of Sá da Bandeira

June 26, A Spanish force enters Oporto, and the junta capitulates

1850

June 22, An American squadron in the Tagus to enforce claims against the Portuguese

1851

April 10, Military insurrection, headed by the Duke of Saldanha, who, being outstripped in his march on Santarem by the King of Portugal, flees northward

April 24, Oporto declares for the Duke, who had left the city for Vigo to embark for England; but is called back by the insurgents

April 29, Saldanha's entry into Oporto

May 16, The conde de Thomar, Prime Minister, resigns; arrives in England

May 23, Saldanha, Prime Minister

Sept. 24, Dom Miguel marries the Princess Adelaide of Lowenstein-Rosenberg

1852 to 1863

July 18, 1852, Revision of the charter by the Cortes sanctioned by the Queen; the Prince Royal takes the oath to the constitution

Nov. 15, 1853, Death of the Queen Maria II

Dec. 19, 1853, King-Consort recognized as Regent

Dec. 30, 1854, The slaves on royal domains freed

Sept. 16, 1855, Inauguration of the King

June 5, 1856, Resignation of Saldanha Ministry

Oct. 26, 1856, First Portuguese railway (from Lisbon to Santarem) opened

Nov. 29, 1857, The French emigrant ship for negroes, *Charles-et-Georges*, seized

Oct. 23, 1858, Anger of the French Government; its ultimatum sent, Oct. 13; and ships of war to the Tagus; the vessel restored

Nov. 11, 1861, Death of the King, Pedro V; succeeded by his brother the Duke of Oporto

Dec. 29, 1861, Death of John, the King's brother

Jan. 3, 1862, The law of succession altered in favor of the King's sisters

Oct. 6, 1862, The King married to Princess Maria Pia of Savoy by proxy, at Lisbon

Sept. 28, 1863, Birth of Dom Carlos, heir to the throne

1864

April 2, Death of the Duke of Palmella

June 1, Free-trade measures introduced

Sept. 29, Frontier treaty with Spain concluded

1865

March 27, U.S. vessels *Niagara* and *Sacramento* in the Tagus fired on, through suspicion of their sailing after the confederate vessel *Stonewall*; the difficulty with the U.S. government arranged, April 7

May, Constitutional privileges granted to the colonies

1866

Jan. 20, General Prim enters Portugal; ordered to depart Feb. 17

Nov. 14, Death of Dom Miguel, the ex-King

Dec. 11, The King and Queen of Spain visit Lisbon

1869 to 1886

Dec., 1869, Violent opposition of Saldanha; ordered back to Paris as ambassador there; he resigns

Jan., 1870, Cortes dissolved

May 19, 1870, Saldanha heads a military insurrection; seizes the royal palace; forms a new ministry

June 13, 1872, Great fire at Lisbon

About Aug. 26, 1872, Conspiracy against the government; officers in the army arrested

May 26, 1874, Death of Joaquim A. Aguiar

About Aug. 19–24, 1876, Financial crisis: banks of Oporto and Portugal suspend payment; confidence soon returns

Nov. 21, 1876, Death of the Duke de Saldanha (buried in state at Lisbon)

March 21–26, 1881, Discussion in the Chambers on treaty with Great Britain respecting Lourenço Marques, E. coast of Africa; ministry resigns

Oct. 8, 1881, The Kings of Portugal and Spain open a new railway between Lisbon and Madrid

End of Feb., 1883, Reform bill introduced abolishing hereditary peerage

Dec. 15, 1885, Death of the King Consort Ferdinand aged 69

Feb. 19, 1886, The de Mello Ministry resigns, succeeded by that of Senhor José de Castro

1889

About May 30, Strike and riots at Oporto

June *et seq.*, Dispute respecting the Delagoa railway

Oct. 19, Death of King Luis I; funeral Oct. 26

Nov., Dec., British remonstrances on Portuguese encroachments in East Africa

Dec. 28, The King Carlos inaugurated

1890

Jan. 5, Lord Salisbury demands the immediate recall of the Portuguese forces from places in Africa under British protection or influence

Jan. 6–8, Sen. Barros Gomes accedes, under conditions; delays. Ultimatum from Lord Salisbury requiring immediate submission, threatening suspension of diplomatic relations; the Council of State accede to all the British demands, under protest, Jan. 11, 12

Jan. 13–16, Excitement in Lisbon and the provinces against the British, promptly suppressed; about 63 arrests; the de Castro Ministry resigns; Sen. Serpa Pimental forms a cabinet; Sen. Hintze Ribeiro, Foreign Minister Jan. 14

April 7, Decrees respecting public meetings, liberty of the press, judicial reforms, &c., issued

April 19, The new Cortes opened by the King; friendly relations with Great Britain, reported

Aug. 20, Anglo-Portuguese agreement respecting Africa, settled in London

Sept. 17, Resignation of Sen. Serpa Pimental Ministry

Oct. 15, Gen. Chrysostomo d'Abreue-Sousa forms a ministry, Oct. 13, opposed to the proposed convention; Cortes closed

Nov. 1, East Africa: Capt. Paiva and the Bihé expedition resisted on the river Caquiema; fighting with the natives, with great loss

Nov. 14, A *modus vivendi* agreed on for six months; the agreement of Aug. 20 withdrawn; the *status quo ante* maintained, Nov. 10; signed

1891

Jan. 15 and Feb. 12, Military expedition for the defense of Manica, sails from Lisbon

Jan. 19, Arrival of Col. Paiva d'Andrade, complaining of the conduct of the British in Manica

Jan. 31, Military revolt at Oporto

March 19, Loan of 10,000,000*l.* on the tobacco monopoly voted

May 11, Financial crisis; decree authorizing the suspension of payments by the banks; the Bank of Portugal suspends cash payments for 60 days

May 14, Treaty extending the *modus vivendi* for one month, signed

June 11, New Anglo-Portuguese convention signed (afterwards ratified). *See* Africa

July 20–Aug. 20, Monetary crisis; sovereigns sold at a high price; traffic in silver coin

1892

Jan. 14, Expiration of the treaty of Goa

Jan. 20–Feb. 23, The Minister of Finance reports great deficiency in the revenue and great increase of debt, and proposes large reductions in the expenditure and increase of taxation; accepted by the King, who proposes to largely reduce his civil list, and by the Cortes

1894

Feb. 17, Dispute between France and Portugal respecting railway arrangements

March 15, Delimitation of Manicaland (Mozambique) to be submitted to arbitration, reported

March 27, Agreement arrived at

1895

March 8, The poet João de Deus decorated by the King, at Lisbon, with much honor

March 30, The Chamber dissolved by decree; electoral reform; number of deputies reduced from 170–120

Aug. 24, Death of Sen. Oliveira-Martins, historian, born 1845; Minister of Finance in 1892

Sept. 9, Sen. Carlos Lobo d'Avila, able Minister for Foreign Affairs, aged 34, died

Sept. 26, Reform of the House of Peers: 90 life members nominated by decree

1896

Jan. 11, João de Deus, popular poet, born 1830; died

1897 to 1905

April 12, 1897, Oceanographic exhibition, showing the results of the King's own scientific researches, opened by the King

June 4, 1898, Bill for the conversion of the external debt passed, April 29; Cortes closed

Nov. 15, 1898, Death of Sen. Henriques B. Gomes, ex-Minister for Foreign Affairs

Aug. 1899–Feb., 1900, Plague at Oporto

Feb. 7, 1901, The King visits England to attend the funeral of Queen Victoria, Jan. 30–Feb. 4; receives a deputation of the Evangelical alliance and promises toleration to all Protestants in his dominions

March, 1901, Some religious associations dissolved by Government (decree published April 20)

May 10, 1902, Bill for the conversion of the external debt adopted by the Chamber, April 26; and the Peers

April 2–7, 1903, King Edward VII visits Lisbon

Aug. 9, 1903, Earthquake shocks

Oct. 3, 1904, Treaty between Portugal and Holland with reference to the delimitation of the Dutch-Portuguese frontier in Timor Island, signed at The Hague

1905, Arbitration treaty with Great Britain

1906

Jan. 1, Cabinet reconstructed under Senhor Luciano de Castro

Feb. 1, The Cortes opened by the King

May 17, Resignation of the Government; new cabinet formed by Senhor Franco

June 1 and Sept. 29, The Cortes opened by King Carlos

1907

June 6, Decree dissolving the Lisbon municipal council, and substituting an administrative commission, published

Aug. 8, Warrants issued for arrest, on charge of sedition, of 21 leaders in riots which occurred on June 18

Aug. 22, Bomb explosion in Lisbon; 30 republicans arrested

1908

Jan. 1, Administrative commissions substituted for municipal and parochial boards

Jan. 28, Serious collisions between police and armed crowds in Lisbon; one policeman killed and six injured

Feb. 1, King Carlos and the Crown Prince assassinated while driving through Lisbon; the Infante Manuel also wounded

Feb. 2, Don Manoel takes the oath as King

——, The Franco Cabinet tenders its resignation, and Vice-Admiral Ferreira do Amaral is entrusted with the formation of a coalition ministry

Feb. 6, The Council of Ministers obtain the King's signature to decrees annulling Senhor Franco's measures for controlling the press and providing summary procedure for political offenses

Feb. 10, Decree pardoning the sailors, who took part in the mutiny of 1906, settled by King Manuel

Feb. 27, The council revokes the decrees adding 38,000l. to the civil list

April 4, Results of the elections are as follows: Regeneradors, 62; progressists, 59; independents, 17; nationalists, 2; republicans, 5; Fransquistas, 3; dissident progressists, 7

April 8, Disturbances during the elections lead to the arrest of about 600 persons; two soldiers were killed

April 29, The Cortes opened by King Manoel

Dec. 25, Ministerial crisis; Senhor Campos Henriques, late Minister of Justice, forms a coalition cabinet

1909

March 30, Senhor Campos Henriques resigns

April 7, New cabinet formed with Senhor Sebastiao

Telles as Premier and Minister of War and Senhor Branco as Minister of Finance

April 23, Violent shock of earthquake in Lisbon; the villages of Benevente and Samora destroyed; 46 persons killed and 38 injured

May 13, Senhor Wenceslau de Lima succeeds in forming a new ministry on a non-party basis

July 17, End of the Oporto tramway strike

Nov. 30, Commercial and shipping treaty with Germany and Portugal signed

Dec. 4, King Manoel returned to Lisbon after his visit to England

Dec. 22, New ministry formed; Senhor Beiras President and Senhor Villaca Foreign Minister

Dec. 23–24, Severe floods; railway communication almost suspended; losses estimated at 1,000,000l.

1910

Jan. 4, The Douro rose over 60 ft.; several large wine lodges and their contents were utterly destroyed by water; 10 steamships, 11 tugs, 24 sailing ships, and 700 lighters were wrecked. Private letter to *The Times*

June 26, New Cabinet with Senhor Teixeira Souza as Premier and Minister of the Interior. 7th Ministry in 18 months

Sept. 23, King Manoel opened the new Parliament elected in August, 89 Ministerialists, 41 Royalist Opposition, and 14 Republican Opposition

Oct. 3, Murder of distinguished Republican physician, Dr. Miguel Bombarda

——, Revolt of the 14th regiment began the revolution

Oct. 4, Citizens and soldiers joined Republican force of Lieutenant Machado Santos and the King fled from the palace, boarded the royal yacht at Ericeira, and proceeded to Gibraltar and from there later to England

Oct. 5, The Republic proclaimed and a provisional Government established with Dr. Theophilo Braga, President; Dr. Antonio J. de Almeida, Home Affairs; Dr. Affonzo Costa, Justice; Colonel Correa Barreto, War; Dr. A. A. Gomes, Marine; Dr. Bernardino Machado, Foreign Affairs; Dr. Basilio Telles, Finance

Oct. 7, Amnesty proclaimed

Oct. 8, Decree expelled religious orders, closing convents and confiscating their property, reviving the laws of 1759, 1767, and 1834 against the Jesuits

Oct. 12, Recognition of Republic by Switzerland

Oct. 15, The Council of State and House of Peers abolished

Oct. 22, Decree prohibited teaching of religion in the primary schools

Oct. 29, Decree provided for liberty of the press by ordaining that press offenses should be tried before a jury

Oct. 30, João Franco, former Dictator, arrested but later released on bail

Nov. 4, Divorce law included as grounds for divorce insanity, desertion, a long term of imprisonment, inveterate gambling, and mutual consent

——, Expulsion of Jesuits completed

Dec. 7, Right to strike conceded at 24 hours' notice

Dec. 11, Recognition of Republic by diplomatic representatives of the United States, Germany, Russia, Sweden, and Norway

1911

Jan. 8, Mobs in Lisbon wrecked offices of 3 monarchist newspapers; troops restored order

Jan. 10–14, Strike of 7,000 railroad workers for shorter hours successful

March 8, The Bishop of Oporto removed from his see with pension of £240

March 15, Dr. Antonio J. de Almeida appointed Prime Minister

——, Electoral decree conferred franchise on all citizens 21 with certain exceptions

March 21, Encyclical Jamdudum of the Pope deplored the anti-religious acts which were specifically enumerated

March 29, Primary education made compulsory

April 20, Decree for separation of Church and State, the Roman Catholic religion ceasing to be that of the State which recognized all creeds as of equal authority

May 22, Decree established new monetary system, unit the gold escudo (4s. 5d.)

May 28, Elections for Assembly held returned Government candidates, no Royalists offering themselves

May 30, Greenwich time officially adopted to take effect Jan. 1

June 19, Constituent Assembly met and passed resolution declaring the monarchy abolished and the Braganza dynasty banished from Portugal

July 5, Death of Queen Maria Pia in Italy

Aug. 2, Demonstration against Parliament

Aug. 20, New Constitution adopted provided for 2 Chambers, a National Council elected for 3 years by direct suffrage, and Upper Chamber elected by the municipal councils to be renewed half at a time every 3 years, president elected by both Chambers for 4 years and not to be reëlected

Aug. 24, The first President elected under the Constitution, Dr. Manuel de Arriaga defeating the Radical candidate Dr. Bernardino Machado

——, First Constitutional Cabinet, Dr. João Chagas, Prime Minister and Minister of Home Affairs; Dr. Augusto de Vasconcellos, Foreign Affairs; Dr. Duarte Leite, Finance; General Pimenta de Castro, War; Dr. Sidonio Paes, Public Works

Sept. 11, The Republic recognized by the Powers

Sept. 29, Royalist revolt in Oporto

Oct. 3, Captain Paiva Couceiro with royalist force of about 1,000 crossed the frontier and took town of Vinhaes but evacuated it Oct. 6 and within a fortnight withdrew from the country

Oct. 22, Spain disarmed 400 Portuguese royalists on the border

Nov. 8, Chagas Ministry resigned and was succeeded by Dr. Augusto de Vasconcellos as Premier

Nov. 11, Dr. Vasconcellos assumed office as Prime Minister and Minister of Foreign Affairs; A. Macieira, Finance

1912

Jan. 29, General strike in Lisbon; the city placed under martial law and over 1,000 syndicalists arrested

Feb. 6, Meeting of King Manoel and Dom Miguel, the Pretender, at Dover, at which the latter renounced claims to throne

May 3, Royalists raided customs post at Monaco and then returned to Spain

June 4, Vasconcellos Ministry resigned

June 16, Coalition Cabinet formed by Dr. Duarte Leite as Prime Minister and Minister of the Interior; Vasconcellos, Foreign Affairs

July 7, Captain Couceiro again invaded Portugal and

attacked Valenca and Chaves without success and retired to Spain within a week

1913

Jan. 6, Duarte Leite Ministry resigned

Jan. 10, Dr. Affonzo Costa became Premier

April 26, Radical republican and syndicalist revolt suppressed

June 14, Treaty with Great Britain regulated the opium monopoly in Macao and Hong-Kong

July 10, Portuguese Legation at the Vatican suppressed

July 20–21, Bomb outrages

Sept. 4, Manoel, former King, married to Princess Augustine Victoria of Hohenzollern

Sept. 11, Decree limited number of students admitted to lyceums of Lisbon, Oporto, and Coimbra

Oct. 21, Royalist plot discovered and many arrests made

1914

Jan. 24, Costa Ministry resigned

Feb. 8, Dr. Bernardino Machado appointed Prime Minister and Minister of Foreign Affairs

Feb. 22, Amnesty Bill passed both Chambers affecting about 1,300 prisoners and 1,500 exiles including Couceira

Feb. 24, Strike of railway workers

June 8, Treaty of commerce with Italy signed

June 20, Machado resigned but was reappointed and formed a non-party Cabinet

June 25, Hague Court decision sustained the Netherlands as to boundary of Timor

Aug. 7, Parliament summoned in special session proclaimed loyalty to the British alliance

Aug. 12, Treaty of commerce with Great Britain signed

Aug. 15, Administrative and financial autonomy given to Portuguese colonies

Aug. 23, Intention to coöperate with Great Britain announced

Oct. 14, Decree regulated native labor in the colonies

Oct. 19, Revolt suppressed

Nov. 16, Treaty of arbitration with Great Britain signed

Nov. 23, Parliament voted to join Entente Allies in World War as ally of Great Britain by Treaty

Dec. 4, Expeditionary force left for Angola, Africa

Dec. 5, Machado Ministry resigned

Dec. 11, Dom Victor Hugo de Azevedo Coutinho became Premier forming a Democratic Cabinet

1915

Jan. 11, Constitution modified so that Lisbon (proportional system) should receive 20 deputies instead of 10, Oporto, 10, and other constituencies between 1 and 4 each

Jan. 15, Meeting of Ministers and ex-Ministers summoned by President Arriaga in "move to restore unity"

Jan. 19, Deputation of officers of Lisbon garrison hostile to the Government including many royalists intercepted and 60 officers arrested

Jan. 23, Official Note of the President declared his intention to receive deputation on which the Ministry resigned

Jan. 28, General Pimenta de Castro formed Cabinet, and the royalist neutralist Freire d'Andrade became Minister of Foreign Affairs

March 5, Protocol signed with Great Britain defined boundary Angola and Rhodesia

May 14, Revolt of Democrats and marines overthrew the Castro Dictatorship

May 15, Castro resigned and was arrested the following day and deported to the Azores and later took refuge in Germany

——, Dr. João Chagas appointed Prime Minister by the revolutionary committee

May 16, Chagas shot and wounded on the train going to Lisbon by Senator João de Freitas who was killed

May 24, Chagas resigned as Prime Minister and was succeeded by Dr. Jose de Castro

May 27, President Arriaga resigned as from May 29

May 29, Dr. Theophilo Braga elected President *ad interim*

June 13, Election gave Democrats a large majority

June 16, Castro Ministry resigned and was reconstituted

July 30, Strike of olive workers

Aug. 6, Dr. Bernardino Machado Guimares elected President

Sept. 13, Strike of brass workers

Sept. 22, Oct. 26 and 30, Strike of coal miners

Oct. 5, President Machado Guimares assumed office

Nov. 11, Strike of dockers at Lisbon

Nov. 12, Resignation of Ferreira, Minister of the Interior, in dispute with the Prime Minister followed in a few days by resignation of the entire Cabinet

Nov. 15, 18, 19–20, Students in riots

Nov. 27, Strike of market gardeners

Nov. 29, Strike of seamstresses

——, Dr. Affonzo Costa formed Cabinet chiefly of Democrats

1916

Feb. 23, German ships in Portuguese ports requisitioned

March 9, Germany declared war on Portugal

March 15, National Ministry formed by Dr. Almeida: Premier and Minister for the Colonies, Dr. Almeida; Interior, Vacant; Justice, Mesquita de Curvalho; Finance, Dr. Affonso Costa; Public Works, Antonio Maria Silva; War, Nortom de Mattos; Marine, Victor Hugo Azevedo Coutinho; Education, Joaquim Pedro Martins; Foreign Affairs, Augusto Soares; Labor, Fernandez Costa

——, Austria-Hungary declared war on Portugal. *See* World War

Dec. 13, Revolt led by Machado Santos, leader of the independents in Parliament, suppressed

1917

Jan. 17, General Fernando Tamagnini de Alorn appointed commander of Expeditionary Force

Feb. 3, First contingent of Portuguese troops landed in France

March 5, Death of Dr. Manuel de Arriaga, first President

April 20, Almeida Ministry resigned and was succeeded by Dr. Affonso Costa as Prime Minister April 24

Sept. 13, Martial law proclaimed on account of general strike

June 17, Portuguese troops in action on West front

Dec. 5, Revolt against Costa and the Democrats at Lisbon led by Major Sidonio Paes

Dec. 7, General Norton de Mattos and Captain Leotte do Rego escaped to a British ship, and Dr. Costa and

Dr. Soares and President Machado arrested by successful revolutionists

Dec. 9, Decree dissolved Parliament

Dec. 12, Major Sidonio Paes became Prime Minister and Minister for War and Foreign Affairs

Dec. 15, President Machado escorted to the frontier

Dec. 22, Decree annulled banishment of priests

Dec. 28, Major Paes became provisional President

1918

Jan. 8, Revolt of sailors at Lisbon suppressed

March 9, Ministry of Agriculture created

March 11, Decree established universal suffrage for all citizens over 21

April 26, Decree permitted sailors and soldiers on active service to vote

April 28, Election held for Parliament and for President, Major Paes elected

May 9, Major Paes proclaimed President

May 15, Cabinet formed. (No Prime Minister. Functions exercised until Dec. 23 by Secretary of the Interior)

May 16, J. de Souza Barboza appointed Secretary of the Interior

July 14 and Sept. 8, Decrees remodeled secondary education

July 20, Declaration of renunciation by Portugal of capitulatory rights in Spanish Morocco

Dec. 11, Revolt in Lisbon

Dec. 14, President Paes shot at railroad station by Jose Julio da Costa and died in a few minutes

Dec. 16, Admiral Joao de Canto e Castro Silva Antunes was elected provisional President

Dec. 24, New Cabinet formed with Tamagnini Barboza, Premier and Minister of the Interior; A. Neves, Foreign Affairs; and Reimao, Finance

1919

Jan. 19, Royalist revolt declared the monarchy restored in Oporto, Braga, and Viseu, Captain Paiva Couceiro becoming Regent and acting as Prime Minister and Minister of Finance

Jan. 23, Monarchist revolt in garrison at Lisbon suppressed

Jan. 27, Jose Relvas became Premier

Feb. 14, Royalist revolt defeated by citizens of Oporto

March 30, Dr. Domingo Pereira became Premier

May 6, A part of German East Africa, the so-called Kionga triangle, given to Portugal by decree of the Supreme Council

May 7, Law established the eight hour day

June 26, Resignation of the Pereira Cabinet

June 28, Colonel Sa Cardoso (Democrat) became Premier

Aug. 5, Dr. Antonio Jose de Almeida elected President

Sept. 23, Portugal acknowledged as sovereign over part of German East Africa known as the "Kionga triangle" under the Treaty of Versailles and decision of Supreme Council of May 6

1920

Jan. 7, Fernandez Costa became Premier

Jan. 10–May 26, Banking Consortium

Feb. 4, Decree totally prohibited a large number of imports

Feb. 19, The President given the right to dissolve Parliament after consulting a special council appointed for the purpose

March 6, A. M. da Silva formed Cabinet succeeding Pereira but resigned immediately, overthrown on policy to use coercion to end strikes, and was succeeded by A. de Castro

March 12, Colonel A. M. Baptista formed a Cabinet

March 28, Striking postal and telegraph employees given 48 hours to return to work or be discharged

April, Papal Nuncio to Portugal appointed

April 8, Portugal became original member of the League of Nations

June 6, Death of Prime Minister Baptista. Succeeded by Dr. Ramos Preto

June 28, da Silva again Premier

July 19, Antonio Granjo (Liberal) became Premier

Sept. 5, By award of Hague Court of Arbitration Portugal to pay £21,800 to Great Britain and £80,000 to France as compensation for Church property confiscated in 1911

Oct. 1, Railroad workers began strike which lasted 70 days

Oct. 14, Commercial *modus vivendi* with Norway replaced Treaty of Dec. 31, 1895

Nov. 20, Granja Cabinet resigned

Nov. 29, Lieutenant-Colonel Liberato Pinto formed a Cabinet

1921

Feb. 12, Pinto Ministry resigned

Feb. 24, Bernardino Machado appointed Prime Minister and formed a Coalition Cabinet of Democrats, Reconstituents, Dissidents, and Popular Party

May 20, Lisbon garrison demanded the resignation of the Machado Government

May 23, Dr. Barros Queiroz, Liberal, formed Cabinet and Parliament dissolved

July 10, Elections held gave Government 74 seats and Democrats, 51

Aug. 26, B. Queiroz resigned as Prime Minister

Aug. 29, Antonio Granjo became Prime Minister

Oct. 19, Revolt forced resignation of Premier Granjo who was shot along with Admiral Machado dos Santos, Carlos da Maia and other prominent persons; Manuel Coelho appointed Prime Minister

Oct. 31, Resignation of Manuel Coelho, Prime Minister.

Nov. 4, Maia Pinto appointed Prime Minister

Dec. 6, Commercial Agreements with Germany signed

Dec. 13, Captain Cunha Leal formed Cabinet

1922

Jan. 29, Election gave Democrats 73 seats

Jan. 31, Resignation of Cunha Leal, Premier

Feb. 5, Antonio Maria da Silva appointed Prime Minister

Feb. 18, Revolt during which the Government took refuge in the fortress of Caxias

March 30, Flight of Captains Gago Coutinho and Sacadura Cabral begun from Lisbon to Brazil. Reached Rio de Janeiro June 17, first flight from Europe to South America, 6,000 miles, 62½ hours

April 17, Agreement signed in Paris by which Dom Miguel renounced succession in favor of Dom Duarte Nuno

Aug. 7–10, General strike in Lisbon against increased price of bread

Oct. 24, Death of Antonio Candido Ribeiro da Costa (70)

Nov. 27, Silva Cabinet resigned and was reconstructed

Dec. 11, Commercial Treaty with Czechoslovakia signed

1923

Jan., Cabinet reconstructed

April 11, Treaty of commerce with Norway signed

April 27, Treaty (wine and fish) with Norway signed

April 28, Provisional Commercial Agreement with Germany signed

July 21 and Dec. 18, Provisional Commercial Agreements with Austria signed

Aug. 6, Teixeira Gomez elected President

Aug. 22, Provisional Commercial Agreement with the Netherlands signed

Aug. 24, General strike unsuccessful

Sept. 5, Arbitration Treaty with the United States renewed that of April 6, 1908

Oct. 5, Inauguration of President Gomez

Nov. 6, Dr. Affonso Costa made unsuccessful attempt to form a Cabinet

Nov. 15, Dr. Ginestal Machado formed Cabinet succeeding Da Silva

Dec. 10, Revolt led by João Manuel Carvalho, former Minister of Marine, to overthrow the Machado Government fired on the city; repelled by Government troops the following day

Dec. 13, The Machado Ministry resigned and was succeeded by Colonel Alvaro de Castro

1924

Jan. 28, Death of Dr. Theophilo Braga, first President

Feb. and May, Strikes of postal workers

March, Strike of civil servants

June 26, Fall of De Castro Cabinet

July 6, Dr. Rodrigues Gaspar, Democrat, formed Cabinet

July 7, Conflict of police with soldiers of the guard, 7 persons killed and 20 injured

Aug. 11, Radical and Communist revolt

Aug. 27, Commercial Agreement with the Netherlands

Aug. 28, Attack on the garrison of the Castle of St. George repelled

Sept. 12, Attack on the Customs House repelled

Nov. 19, Resignation of Gaspar Ministry

Nov. 22, Dr. Jose Domingues dos Santos, Left Democrat, formed Cabinet

1925

Feb. 11, Cabinet defeated resigned

Feb. 15, Victorino Guimaraes (Democrat) became Prime Minister and Minister of Finance

March 5, Unsuccessful attack of revolutionists on military headquarters

April 18–19, Unsuccessful military revolt led by Captain Filomeno de Camara and Lieutenant Colonel Raul Esteves

June 26, Guimaraes Ministry resigned defeated on budget

June 29, Antonio da Silva formed Cabinet

July 17, Resignation of da Silva Ministry defeated in Parliament and finally July 20

July 18–19, Revolt suppressed

Aug. 2, D. Pereira formed Cabinet

Aug. 14, Treaty of commerce and navigation with Spain and of commerce with Siam

Aug. 29, Agreement with Great Britain extended Arbitration Agreement of 1914

Nov. 8, Election held gave Democrats 84 seats in Chamber, Nationalists 23, others 53; Senate, 41 Democrats, 9 Nationalists, others 20
Dec. 10, Resignation of President Gomez on account of ill-health
Dec. 12, Domingos Pereira Ministry resigned
Dec. 16, Dr. Bernardino Machado elected President
——, Antonio da Silva appointed Prime Minister

1926

Feb. 2, Military uprising led by Major Laoerda Almeida at Vendas Novas and in Lisbon suppressed and leaders deported
March 20, Commercial Treaty with Germany signed
May 12, Convent of Santa Clara built in 1150 destroyed by fire
May 28, Military revolt led by General Gomes da Costa and Commander Mendes Cabeçadas against alleged corruption and inefficiency of the Government
May 29, Cabinet resigned
June 1, The President deposed by the revolutionists and General Cabeçadas became Acting President and Premier with General Gomes da Costa as Minister of War
June 17, General Gomes da Costa led revolt and succeeded General Cabeçadas
June 20, Cabinet headed by da Costa established
July 9, Revolt led by General Carmona deposed Gomes da Costa who was deported; Prime Minister, General Antonio Oscar de Fragoso Carmona; Minister of the Interior, Adriano da Costa Macedo (January, 1927); Foreign Affairs, Antonio Maria de Bettencourt Rodrigues; Finance, General João José Sinel de Cordes; Justice, Manuel Rodrigues, Junior; War, Abilio Augusto Valdez de Passos e Sousa; Marine, Commander Jayme Afreixo; Colonies, João Bello; Instruction, Alfredo de Magalhães; Commerce and Communications, Julio Cesar de Carvalho Teixeira; Agriculture, Felisberto Alves Pedrosa
Aug. 15, First electric railroad opened between Lisbon and Cascaes
Aug. 25, Agreement with Spain for abolition of passport visas
Sept. 11, Military revolt at Chaves suppressed
Nov. 29, General Antonio Oscar de Fragoso Carmona appointed Acting President succeeding Gomes da Costa who was deported to the Azores
Dec. 31, War debt with Great Britain funded at £5,500,000 to be paid before Dec. 31, 1927

1927

Jan. 6, Provisional Commercial Agreement with Belgium signed
Feb. 3, Revolt of Communists supported by part of army led by General Souza Diaz broke out at Oporto and spread to Lisbon
Feb. 13, Revolt suppressed by Government troops commanded by Colonel Passos, Minister of War, "the bloodiest revolution since October, 1910"
March 2, Flight of Major Sarmento Beires from Lisbon and March 16 from the Bissagos Islands of Portuguese Guinea to Fernando do Noronha, Brazil
July 9, Treaty of arbitration and conciliation with Belgium signed

July 19–22, Convention with Belgium as to Belgian Congo and Angola
Aug. 11, Convention with Spain delimited respective rights in falls of the Douro River
——, New office of vice-president of the Council created, Colonel Passos e Sousa appointed
Aug. 12–13, Revolt of military group in Lisbon suppressed
Aug. 26, Cabinet reconstructed

1928

Jan. 18, Treaty of conciliation and arbitration with Spain signed
March 25, General Antonio Oscar de Fragoso Carmona, sole candidate for the presidency, elected by 750,000 votes legalizing his dictatorship
April 18, Colonel Vicente de Freitas appointed Prime Minister
June 24, Treaty of commerce with the Netherlands signed
June 28, Flight of Captain F. T. Harlon in monoplane from Lisbon to Azores, 1,000 miles in 11 hours
July 20, Military revolt in Lisbon against the Carmona Government suppressed
July 26, Treaty of arbitration, conciliation and judicial settlement with Norway signed
Sept. 11, New Mozambique Convention with South Africa signed
Oct. 17, Treaty of arbitration with Switzerland signed
Nov. 7, Freitas Ministry resigned and was reconstructed

1929

March 1, Treaty of arbitration with the United States signed
July 4, Freitas Ministry resigned
July 8, General Ivens Ferraz became Prime Minister
Aug. 22, Commercial Agreement with Estonia signed
Oct. 31, Death of Dr. Antonio Jose Almeida, former President
Nov. 1, Death of Jose Relvas, former Prime Minister
Nov. 10, Cabinet Council granted amnesty to 68 officers banished to the Azores for participation in revolt against dictatorship in 1927 including General Sacardozo, Colonel Costa Pinto, and Colonel Helder Ribeiro
Dec. 17, Death of General Gomes da Costa, former dictator

1930

Jan. 10, Resignation of Cabinet of General Ivens Ferraz
Jan. 20, New Cabinet formed by General Domingos de Oliveira: Interior, Dr. Antonio Lopes Matheus; Commerce and Communications, Dr. Antunes Guimaraes; Foreign Affairs, Commander Fernando Augusto Branco; Marine, Commander Magalhaes Correia; Justice, Dr. Lopes de Fonseca; War, Colonel Joao Namorado de Aguiar; Agriculture, Lieutenant Colonel Linhares de Lima; Finance, Dr. Antonio de Oliveira Salazar; Education, Dr. Gustavo Ramos; Colonies, Brigadier Eduardo Marques
May 6, Alves dos Reis and his accomplices found guilty of issue of forged notes and sentenced to terms of imprisoned
July 4, Arrest of Colonel Joao Almeida, monarchist, and other leaders thwarted plot to overthrow the Government

1095. Henry, Count or Earl of Portugal
1112. Alfonso, his son, and Theresa
1128. Alfonso, count of Portugal, alone
1139. Alfonso I declared King, having obtained a signal victory over a prodigious army of Moors on the plains of Ourique
1185. Sancho I, son of Alfonso
1212. Alfonso II, surnamed Crassus, or the Fat
1223. Sancho II, or the Idle: deposed
1248. Alfonso III
1279. Denis or Dionysius, the father of his country
1325. Alfonso IV, the Brave
1357. Peter, the Severe
1367. Ferdinand I, son
1385. John I, the Bastard and the Great; natural brother; married Philippa, daughter of John of Gaunt, Duke of Lancaster
1433. Edward or Duarte
1438. Alfonso V, the African
1481. John II, the Great and the Perfect
1495. Emmanuel, the Fortunate; cousin
1521. John III, son; admitted the Inquisition, 1536, and the Jesuits, 1540
1557. Sebastian; drowned after the great battle of Alcazarquivir, in Africa, Aug. 4, 1578
1578. Henry, the Cardinal, son of Emmanuel; great uncle
1580. Anthony, Prior of Crato, son of Emmanuel; deposed by Philip II of Spain, who united Portugal to his other dominions
1580. Philip II ⎫
1598. Philip III ⎬ kings of Spain
1621. Philip IV ⎭
1640. John IV, Duke of Braganza; dispossessed the Spaniards in a bloodless revolution, and was proclaimed King, Dec. 1
1656. Alfonso VI; deposed in 1667, and his brother Peter made regent
1683. Peter II, brother
1706. John V, son
1750. Joseph Emmanuel; son. The daughter and successor of this prince married his brother, by dispensation from the Pope, and they ascended the throne, as
    Maria I and Peter III jointly
    Maria I alone: this princess afterwards falls into a state of melancholy and derangement; dies, 1816
1792. Regency—John, son (afterwards King); declared Regent, 1791
1816. John VI, previously Regent. He had withdrawn in 1807, owing to the French invasion of Portugal, to his Brazilian dominions; but the discontent of his subjects obliged him to return in 1821; died in 1826
1826. Peter IV (Dom Pedro), son; making his election of the Empire of Brazil, abdicated the throne of Portugal in favor of
——. Maria II (da Gloria); daughter; seven years of age
1828. Dom Miguel, brother to Peter IV, usurped the crown, which he retained, amid civil contentions, until 1833
1833. Maria II restored; declared in Sept., 1834 to be of age; married Augustus, Duke of Leuchtenberg, 1835; 2nd, Ferdinand of Saxe-Coburg, April 9, 1836 (who died, Dec. 15, 1885); died, Nov. 15, 1853

1853. Peter V (Dom Pedro), son; born Sept. 16, 1837; died, Nov. 11, 1861
1861. Luis I, brother; born Oct. 31, 1838; married Maria Pia, daughter of Victor Emmanuel, King of Italy (born Oct. 16, 1847), Oct. 6, 1862; a judicious reformer; died, Oct. 19, 1889
1889. Dom Carlos (son), born Sept. 28, 1863; married Marie Amélie, daughter of the comte de Paris, May 22, 1886; assassinated Feb. 1, 1908
    Heir: Louis Philippe, born March 21, 1887; assassinated Feb. 1, 1908
1908. Manoel II (son) born 1889; deposed 1910

PRUSSIA

Prussia, largest and most important State of the German Republic, proclaimed a republic Nov. 13, 1918, occupies almost the whole of northern Germany, area as of census of 1925 113,129 square miles, population 38,175,989. Berlin is the capital. As a result of the Treaty of Versailles Prussia lost territory to extent of 21,646 square miles and a population of 4,601,621. A Constitution was adopted Nov. 30, 1920. A Constituent National Assembly met March 14, 1919 providing for a Diet (Landtag) and State Council (Staatsrat), the Diet electing the Premier, and the Premier appointing other members of the Cabinet which is invested with the powers of the former King.

On May 20, 1928, the elections were held for a Parliament, and resulted in the return of the following parties: Social Democrats, 137; Center (Catholics), 71; German National Party, 82; National Socialists, 6; German People's Party, 40; Democrats, 21; Communists, 56; Economic Party, 21; German Hanoverians, 4; Farmers' Party, 8; German Race Party, 2; People's Right Party, 2. Total, 450.

The Cabinet appointed on April 4, 1925, was composed as follows: Prime Minister, Otto Braun (Socialist); Minister of National Welfare, H. Hirtsiefer (Center); Justice, Dr. Hermann Schmidt (Center), appointed March 6, 1927; Commerce, Dr. Schreiber (Democrat); Interior, Karl Severing (Socialist), reappointed October 22, 1930; Finance, Dr. Höpker Aschoff (Democrat); Education, Adolf Grimme (Socialist), appointed January 30, 1930; Agriculture, Domains, and Forests, H. Steiger (Center).

The Kings of Prussia (Bo-Russia) traced their origin to Count Thassilo, of Zollern in Swabia, one of the generals of Charles the Great. His successor, Count Friedrich I, built the family castle of Hohenzollern, near the Danube, in the year 980. A subsequent Zollern, or Hohenzollern, Friedrich III, was elevated to the rank of a Prince of the Holy Roman Empire in 1273, and received the Burggraviate of Nuremberg in fief; and his great-grandson, Friedrich VI, was invested by King Sigmund, in 1415, with the Margraviate of Brandenburg, and obtained the rank of Elector in 1417. A century after, in 1511, the Teutonic Knights, owners of the large province of Prussia, on the Baltic, elected Margrave Albrecht, a younger son of the family of Hohenzollern, to the post of Grand-Master, and he, turning Protestant, declared himself hereditary duke. The early extinction of the male line of Albrecht brought the province of Prussia by inheritance to the electors of Brandenburg in 1618, who likewise adopted Protestantism. In the seventeenth century, the Hohenzollern territories became greatly enlarged by Friedrich Wilhelm, "the Great Elector," under whose fostering care arose the first standing army in central Europe. The Great Elector, after a reign extending from 1640 to 1688, left a country of one and a half million inhabitants, a vast treasure, and 38,000 well-drilled troops to his son, Friedrich I, who put the kingly crown on his head at Königsberg on January 18, 1701. His successor Friedrich Wilhelm I, after adding part of Pomerania to the possessions of the house, left his son and successor Friedrich II, called "the Great," a State of 47,770 square miles, with two and a half millions of inhabitants. Friedrich II added Silesia, an area of 14,200 square miles; this, and the large territory gained in the first partition of Poland, increased Prussia to 74,340 square miles, with more than five and a half million inhabitants. Under the reign of Friedrich's successor, Friedrich Wilhelm II, the State was enlarged by the acquisition of the principalities of Anspach and Baireuth, as well as the vast territory acquired in another partition of Poland, which raised its area to nearly 100,000 square miles with about nine millions of souls. Under Friedrich Wilhelm III, nearly one-half of this State and population was taken by Napoleon; but the Congress of Vienna not only restored the loss, but added part of the Kingdom of Saxony, the Rhineland, much of Westphalia, and Swedish Pomerania.

ca. 997 to 1806

About 997, St. Adalbert arrives in Prussia to preach Christianity, and is slain

1018, Boleslas of Poland revenges his death by dreadful ravages

About 1061, The Prussians resist the Poles, and renounce Christianity

1163, Berlin built by a colony from the Netherlands, in the reign of Albert the Bear

1225, The Teutonic Knights returning from the holy wars, undertake the conquest and conversion of Prussia

1231, Thorn founded by them

1283, Prussia subjugated by the Teutonic Knights

1286, Königsberg, lately built, made the capital

Largely re-peopled by German colonists 12-13th century

1415, Frederick IV of Nuremberg (the founder of the reigning family) obtains by purchase from Sigismund, Emperor of Germany, the Margraviate of Brandenburg

1446, Casimir IV of Poland assists the natives against the oppression of the Teutonic Knights

1466, Successful rebellion against the Knights consummated by the Treaty of Thorn

1525, Albert of Brandenburg, Grand Master of the Teutonic Order, seizes its territories, renounces the Roman Catholic religion, embraces Lutheranism, and is acknowledged Duke of East Prussia, to be held as a fief of Poland

1544, University of Königsberg founded by Duke Albert

1608, John Sigismond created Elector of Brandenburg and Duke of Prussia

1648, The principality of Halberstadt and the bishopric of Minden transferred to the house of Brandenburg

1657, Poland obliged to acknowledge Prussia as an independent state, under Frederick William, surnamed the Great Elector

1660, Order of Concord instituted by Christian Ernest, Elector of Brandenburg and Duke of Prussia, to commemorate the part he had taken in restoring peace to Europe

Jan. 18, 1701, Frederick III in an assembly of the states, puts a crown upon his own head and upon the head of his consort; is proclaimed King of Prussia by the name of Frederick I, and institutes the Order of the Black Eagle

1702, Gueldres taken from the Dutch

1707, Frederick I seizes Neufchâtel or Neunburg, and purchases Tecklenburg

1712, The principality of Meurs added to Prussia

1740, Frederick II the Great, King, who made the Prussian monarchy rank among the first Powers of Europe

1741, Breslau ceded to Prussia

1742, Silesia, Glatz, &c., ceded

May 22, 1744, Treaty with France and Sweden which led to war with Austria

1756–63, "Seven years' war." See s.v.

1757, Frederick II, victor at Prague, May 6; defeated at Kolin, June 18; victor at Rosbach, Nov. 5

Oct., 1760, General Lacy, with an Austrian and Russian army, marches to Berlin; the city is laid under contribution, &c.; magazines destroyed

Feb. 15, 1763, Peace of Hubertsburg (ends "Seven Years' War"); Silesia gained by Prussia

1772, Prussia shares in the first partition of Poland

Aug. 17, 1786, Frederick the Great dies

1792, Frederick William II invades France

1793, Joins the coalition against France

1801 and 1806, The Prussians seize Hanover

1806

Oct. 6, Prussia joins the allies of England against France

Oct. 14, Fatal battles of Jena and Auerstadt

[Nearly all the monarchy subdued]

Nov. 20, Berlin decree promulgated

1807

July 9, Peace of Tilsit (on the Niemen), on which river, on a raft, the Emperors of France and Russia met, June 25. By a treaty concluded between France and Russia, signed July 7, Napoleon restored to the Prussian monarch one-half of his territories, and Russia recognized the Confederation of the Rhine, and the elevation of Napoleon's three brothers,

Joseph, Louis, and Jerome, to the thrones of Naples, Holland, and Westphalia

Formation of the Tugendband, a patriotic society (promoted by Von Stein)

1808 to 1844

Nov. 5, 1808, Convention of Berlin

1809–13, Schaunhorst secretly restores the army by the system of reserves; forming a nation of soldiers

March 17, 1813, The people rise to expel the French from Germany at the King's appeal, and form the "landwehr" or militia

April 11, 1814, Treaty of Paris

June 6, 1814, The King visits England

1817, Ministry of education established

Aug. 1, 1819, Congress of Carlsbad

Sept. 12, 1819, Blücher dies in Silesia, aged 77

[From this time Prussia pursued a peaceful and undisturbed policy until 1848]

1840, Government disputes with Roman Catholic clergy begin, through ultramontanism of the Radziwill family since 1830

July 26, 1844, Serious attempt made on the life of the King, by an assassin named Tesch, who fired two shots at him

1848

March 18, Insurrection in Berlin

Nov. 12, Berlin declared in a state of siege

Nov. 29, The constituent assembly meets in Brandenburg castle

Dec. 5, This assembly dissolved; the King issues a new constitution

1849

March 28, The German National Assembly elect the King of Prussia "hereditary Emperor of the Germans"

April 3, The King declines the imperial crown

May 10, The Kingdom put under martial law

June 23, The Prussians enter Carlsruhe

July 10, Armistice between Prussia and Denmark

Sept. 8, Bavaria declared for an imperial constitution with the King of Prussia at its head

Sept. 30, Treaty between Prussia and Austria

Nov. 12, Austria protests against the alliance of Prussia with the minor states of Germany

Dec. 6, Prince Charles Anthony Hohenzollern-Sigmaringen, Minister, resigns

1850

Jan. 31, New constitution; the King takes the oath required by it, Feb. 6

Feb. 25, Hanover withdraws from the alliance

Feb. 27, Treaty signed at Munich between Austria, Bavaria, Saxony, and Würtemberg to maintain the German union

March 15, Würtemberg denounces the insidious ambition of the King of Prussia, and announces a league between Würtemberg, Bavaria, and Saxony, under the sanction of Austria

May 22, Attempt to assassinate the King

June 30, Hesse-Darmstadt withdraws from the Prussian league

July 2, Treaty of peace with Denmark

July 12, A congress of deputies from the states included in the Prussian Zollverein at Cassel

Aug. 25, Prussia refuses to join the restricted Diet of Frankfort

Sept. 21, The Prussian Government addresses a despatch to the Cabinet of Vienna, resolving to uphold the constitution in Hesse-Cassel

Nov. 7, Decree, calling out the whole Prussian army, 223,000 infantry, 38,000 cavalry, and 29,000 artillery, with 1,080 field-pieces

Nov. 9, The Prussian troops in Hesse occupy the military road in that electorate

Nov. 14, The Prussian forces withdraw from the Grand Duchy of Baden

Nov. 26, General Radowitz, late Foreign Minister, visits Queen Victoria at Windsor

Nov. 29, Convention of Olmutz for the pacification of Germany

Dec. 5, The Prussian troops commence their retreat from Hesse-Cassel

Dec. 28, Prince Schwartzenberg visits the King

1851

May 18, The King visits the Czar of Russia

May 31, The King and Czar leave Warsaw for Olmutz to meet the Emperor of Austria

1852

Jan. 12, The King revives the council of state as it existed before the revolution of 1848

June 7, Customs' union with Austria repudiated

1853

Feb. 19, But agrees to a commercial treaty

April, Democratic plot at Berlin detected

Dec. 25, Death of Radowitz

1854

March and April, Vacillation of the Government upon the Eastern question

April 7, Agrees to a protocol for preservation of the integrity of Turkey, which is signed at Vienna

Sept. 6 and Oct., Declares neutrality in the war

1855 to 1857

Feb., 1855, Excluded from the conferences at Vienna

Nov., 1856 to May, 1857, Disputes with Switzerland. *See* Switzerland

Oct. 23, 1857, Illness of the King, the Prince of Prussia appointed Regent

1858

Jan., Chevalier Bunsen ennobled

Jan. 25, Prince Frederick William of Prussia married to the Princess Royal of England

Oct. 7, Prince of Prussia permanent Regent

Nov., Resignation of Manteuffel Ministry; succeeded by that of Prince Hohenzollern-Sigmaringen (liberal): elections favor the new government

1859

May and June, Italian war—Prussia declares its neutrality, but arms to protect Germany

1860

June 15–17, The Regent and several German sovereigns meet the Emperor of the French at Baden

Nov., Disclosures respecting the oppressive system of Prussian police; Stieber, the director, prosecuted and censured, but not punished

1861

Jan. 2, Death of Frederick William IV. Accession of William I

Feb. 6, Meeting of the Chambers: on the motion for the address, M. von Vincke carries an amendment in favor of Italian Unity and "a firm alliance with England"

Sept. 23, Attempted assassination of the King by Becker, a Leipsic student, July 14; who is sentenced to 20 years' imprisonment

Oct. 6–8, The King meets the Emperor Napoleon at Compiègne

Oct. 18, The King and Queen crowned at Königsberg; he declares that he will reign by the "Grace of God"

1862

March 6, The Chamber of Representatives oppose the Government in regard to the length of military service; and resolve on discussing the items of the budget; the Ministry resigns; the King dissolves the Chambers, March 11

Sept. 11–16, Severe discussion on military expenditure; the Chamber reduces the vote for the maintenance of the army from 200,000 to 135,000 men

Sept. 23, Van der Heydt resigns; succeeded as Premier by the Count Bismarck Schönhausen; who informs the Chamber that the budget is deferred till 1863; Chamber protests, Sept. 30

Oct. 11, The Chamber of Peers passes the budget without the amendments of the Chamber of Representatives; which (by 237 against 2) resolves that the act is contrary to the constitution

Oct. 13, The King closes the session (65th) saying, "The budget for the year 1862, as decreed by the Chamber of Representatives, having been rejected by the Chamber of Peers on the ground of insufficiency, the Government is under the necessity of controlling the public affairs outside the constitution"

Nov., Agitation in favor of the constitution proceeding; passive resistance adopted; several liberal papers suppressed

1863

Jan. 14, The Chambers reassemble; unconciliatory address from the King; bold reply of the deputies; adopted Jan. 23

May, Violent dissension between the deputies and the Ministry

May 22, The Chamber of Deputies address the King on their relation with the Ministry, and the state of the country; the King replies, that his ministers possess his confidence, and adjourns the session May 27

The King resolves to govern without a Parliament

June 1, The press severely restricted; the Crown Prince in a speech disavows participation in the recent acts of the Ministry, June 5; and censures them in a letter to the King, July 6; reconciled to the King, Sept. 8

Dec., A motion in favor of maintaining the rights of the Duchies of Schleswig and Holstein, carried Dec. 2; but the Chamber obstinately refused its assent to it or to defray the expenses of war

1864

Jan., Chambers dissolved

[For the events of the war, *see* Denmark]

Aug. 1, Preliminaries for peace with Denmark

Oct. 30, Peace with Denmark signed

1865

Jan. 14, The opening of the Chambers; revival of the constitutional agitation for control over the army budget, Jan. 16

June 17, The deputies having rejected the budget, the bills for reorganizing the army and increasing the fleet, and meeting the expense of the war with Denmark, the Chamber is prorogued; the Government will rule without it

July 5, The King at Carlsbad issues a despotic decree appropriating and disposing of the revenue

July 24, A political dinner of the liberal deputies prohibited at Cologne, and forcibly prevented at Oberlahnstein, in Nassau

Aug. 14, Convention of Gastein (Austria to have the temporary government of Holstein, and Prussia that of Sleswig; the establishment of a German fleet was proposed, with Kiel as a Federal harbor, held by Prussia; Lauenburg was absolutely ceded to Prussia, and the King was to pay Austria as a compensation 2,500,000 Danish dollars), signed

Aug. 16, Navigation treaty with Great Britain

Sept. 15, The King takes possession of Lauenburg, purchased from Austria with his own money

Nov., Bismarck visits Napoleon at Biarritz

1866

Jan. 15, The Chambers opened with a supercilious speech from Bismarck

Feb. 22, The opposing Chamber prorogued

March 11, Decree asserting Prussian jurisdiction over Holstein

March 24, Prussian circular calling on German states to decide whether they will support Austria or Prussia (they profess neutrality)

March 27, Prussia prepares for war

——, Treaty between Prussia and Italy, said to have been concluded

April, The French Government professes neutrality

April 7, Austria demands the demobilization of the Prussian army; Bismarck proposes a German parliament, April 9

May 7, Attempt to assassinate Bismarck

May, Recriminatory correspondence between Mensdorff and Bismarck, calling for disarmament

——, Alliance with Italy

About June 2, Nearly all the northern states join Prussia

June 7, The Prussians enter Holstein; Austrians retire

June 14, Meeting of the Federal Diet at Frankfort; the demobilization of the Prussian army proposed by Austria; voted for by Bavaria, Saxony, Hanover, Hesse-Cassel, Nassau, and others; Prussia declares the Germanic Confederation to be dissolved

June, Prince Alexander of Hesse appointed to command the Federal army

June 15, The Prussians declare war against Hanover and Saxony

June 16–20, The Prussians occupy Hanover and Hesse-Cassel, Saxony, and Nassau

June 17, Justificatory manifestoes issued by Austria and Prussia

June 18, The Austrian northern army enters Silesia; joined by the Saxons about June 19

June 23, Prince Frederick Charles and the First Army,

and the Army of the Elbe enter Bohemia; victorious in severe engagements at Liebenau, Türnau, and Podoll, June 26; Hühnewasser, June 27; München-grätz, June 28; Gitschin, June 29

June 22, The Crown Prince and the Second Army (of Silesia) enter Bohemia; repulsed at Trautenau, June 27; victorious at Soor and Trautenau, June 28; Königinhof, June 29

June 27, The left column of the Crown Prince's army defeat the Austrians at Nachod; Skalicz, June 28; Schweinschädel, June 29

——, Fruitless victory of the Hanoverians at Lan-gensalza; they capitulate to the Prussians, June 29

June 30, Communications opened between the two armies

July 1, The command assumed by the King

July 3, Battle of Königgrätz, or Sadowa; total defeat of the Austrians under Benedek

July 8, Benedek superseded by Albrecht

Campaign of the army under Vögel von Falkenstein against the army of the Confederation under Princes Charles of Bavaria and Alexander of Hesse; Prussian victories at Wiesenthal and Dermbach, July 4; Hammelburg and Kissingen, July 10

July 10, Advance of the united armies under the King; cavalry skirmish at Saar; Austrians retire

July 12, Prince Frederick Charles enters Brünn, capital of Moravia

Campaign on the Maine: Prussian victories at Laufach, July 13, and Aschaffenburg, July 14

July 13, The members of the German Diet retire from Frankfort to Augsburg

July 15, Austrians defeated at Tobitschau

July 16, Frankfort occupied by Falkenstein

July 18, The Prussians occupy Wiesbaden; victorious at Tauberbischofsheim, Hochhausen, Werbach, July 24; Neubrunn, Helmstadt, Gerscheim, July 25; Würz-burg, July 28; armistice granted, July 30

July 22, Severe fight at Blumenau stopped by the news of an armistice

July 23–Aug. 1, Franconia occupied by the Prussian army of reserve, under the Grand-Duke of Mecklen-burg-Schwerin; armistices granted, Aug. 1–3

July 26, Preliminaries of peace signed at Nikolsburg

July 31, The army reviewed by the King fifteen miles from Vienna; begin their return home, Aug. 1

Aug. 4, The Diet at Augsburg recognized the dissolu-tion of the Germanic Confederation

Aug. 18, Bohemia and Moravia cleared

Aug. 22, The treaty of peace signed at Prague

Aug. 29, Meeting of special committee of the Chamber of Deputies; cost of the war stated, 88,000,000 dollars

Peace with Wurtemberg concluded, Aug. 13; with Baden, Aug. 17; with Bavaria, Aug. 22; with Hesse-Darmstadt (ceding Hesse-Cassel, Hesse-Homburg, &c.) Sept. 3

Aug., Formation of the North German Confederation (see Germany)

Sept. 8, Indemnity bill for the Ministry passed

Sept. 20, Entry of the army into Berlin

——, Decree for the annexation of Hanover, Electoral Hesse, Nassau, and Frankfort

Oct. 6, Possession taken of Hanover: of Hesse, Nassau, and Frankfort, Oct. 8

Oct. 21, Treaty of peace with Saxony

Oct. 23, Electoral law for new German parliament promulgated at Berlin

Nov. 12, Prussian Chambers reassemble

1867

Jan. 24, Schleswig and Holstein incorporated with Prussia by decree; promulgated

April 17, North German parliament meet at Berlin, Feb. 24; adopt a federal constitution; closed

April 29, Prussian Chambers opened by the King

May 7–11, Luxemburg question settled by a conference at London (see Luxemburg)

May 8, They accept the North German constitution (sacrificing Prussian civil rights to German unity)

June 24, The Prussian Chambers approve North Ger-man constitution; closed by the King

1868

Feb. 22, Treaty with the United States respecting naturalization of aliens signed at Berlin

March, Much of the King of Hanover's property sequestrated, on account of his maintaining a Hano-verian legion, &c.

April 22, Count Bismarck defeated in the North Ger-man parliament; his bill withdrawn

April 27–May 23, Customs' parliament at Berlin

Sept. 26–29, Workmen's congress at Berlin, to promote centralization

1869

Feb. 15, The property of the King of Hanover seques-trated for his opposition

Oct. 21, The parliament meet, Oct. 6; rejects the proposal for disarmament

1870

About July 5, Prince Leopold, of Hohenzollern-Sig-maringen, consents to become candidate for the throne of Spain

July 12, In consequence of the virulent opposition of the French government he, with the King's consent, relinquishes the candidature

July 15, The French Government requiring guarantees from the King against the future, the King repulses and declines to receive the French Minister, Ben-edetti, July 13; and issues a circular to his representa-tives at foreign courts

——, The Emperor of the French declares for war

July 19, The North German parliament meet, and vote to support Prussia

Aug. 3, Proclamation of the King, granting "amnesty for political offences," and "accepting the battle for the defence of the fatherland," July 31; and to the army, undertaking the command of the whole army

For the events of the war see Franco-Prussian War

Order of the "Iron Cross" (distributed in the war of 1813) revived; given to the Crown Prince for his victory at Wissembourg on Aug. 4

End of Aug., Prussian bishops protest against infalli-bility of the Pope

Sept. 6, Munich, Stuttgardt, and other southern cities, demand union with North Germany

Early in Sept., M. Jacoby arrested at Königsberg by Von Falckenstein for speaking against the annexation of Alsace and Lorraine

About Oct. 26, Jacoby and other liberals released by royal decree (Jacoby died March 7, 1877)

Nov., Election of new parliament; opened with speech promising internal reforms, Dec. 14; aristocratic address from the peers congratulating the King as nominated Emperor (see Germany), Dec. 21

1871

Jan. 18, The King proclaimed Emperor of Germany at Versailles

March 17, The Emperor arrives at Berlin

March 21, The new imperial Diet opened at Berlin

March 22, Bismarck created a prince

June 16, Triumphal entry of the German army into Berlin; inauguration of the statue of Frederick William III

July 5, The bishop of Ermeland excommunicates Dr. Wollner for denying the Pope's infallibility

Aug. 2, Convocation of the evangelical church at Berlin

1872

Jan. 17, Von Mühler, Minister of Public Instruction, ultra-conservative, forced to resign

Feb. 8–10, Clerical interference with schools opposed in the parliament

About May, The new "national conservative party" formed

July 5, Law for expulsion of the Jesuits, published

Government disputes with the Roman Catholic clergy supporting papal infallibility; the Bishop of Ermeland's salary ordered to be suspended, from Oct. 1

Oct. 31, The Government defeated in the House of Peers on the district administrations bill (145–18) (the bill would deprive the peers of power in the provinces by granting representatives to the peasants in the local assemblies)

Dec. 7, The principle of the reform bill passed by the Peers (114–87)

Dec. 18, Bismarck resigns the presidency; continues the foreign department; announced

Dec., Count Roon to be chairman of the Ministry

1873

Feb., Declaration of the Roman Catholic archbishops of Cologne and Posen against proposed legislation on church affairs

March 12, Subjection of the Church to the State affirmed by the legislature

May 11, Laws introduced by M. Falk, Minister of Public Worship, establishing a royal tribunal of ecclesiastical affairs, in opposition to the authority of the Pope, Jan. 9; passed

About Aug., The Emperor recognizes the "old Catholic" bishop, Reinkens

Sept. 3, Letter from the Pope to the Emperor complaining of the ecclesiastical prosecutions, and asserting his authority over all baptized persons, Aug. 7; the Emperor replies justifying them, and asserting that there is no mediator between God and man but Jesus Christ

Oct., Archbishop Ledochowski of Posen fined for threatening to excommunicate a professor; and Archbishop Melchers fined for instituting priests without government permission

Nov. 3, The Pope (by letter) encourages Archbishop Ledochowski to resist

Dec. 3, Government defeated in attempt to restrict the press

Dec., A new oath of implicit obedience to the State proposed for clergy; civil marriage bill

1874

Feb. 3, Archbishop Ledochowski imprisoned; deprived, April 15

May, New ecclesiastical laws, restraining authority of bishops, with punishment for disobedience, promulgated

June 14, Van der Heydt, statesman (see 1862), dies

July 10, Martin, Bishop of Paderborn, resists the ecclesiastical laws

July 13, Bismarck wounded by Kullmann, a fanatical cooper, near Kissingen

July 21, Catholic associations in Berlin closed

Sept. 21, Bishop of Paderborn, summoned to resign, refuses Sept. 7; imprisoned for sedition

Oct. 4, Arrest of Count Harry Arnim and confinement in Berlin for refusing to give up documents sent to him as Ambassador; for illness released on bail, Oct. 28; again arrested, Nov. 12

Oct. 30, Kullman sentenced to 14 years' imprisonment

Dec. 9, Arnim's trial; convicted of making away with ecclesio-political documents; acquitted of other charges; 3 months' imprisonment, Dec. 19

1875

Jan., Catholic bishops and priests imprisoned for infraction of ecclesiastical laws

Jan. 5, Deprivation of the Bishop of Paderborn

Jan. 25, Civil marriage adopted by the parliament

Feb. 5, Encyclical of the Pope to the bishops encouraging firmness, protested against by the Roman Catholic deputies of parliament

March 4, Exportation of horses prohibited

March 16, Clerical control over parish funds taken away; bill for depriving the Roman Catholic clergy of state aid brought in

April 9, Prussian bishops at Fulda appeal to the Emperor against ecclesiastical legislation, April 2; rebuked for not submitting to the law

May 10–13, Visit of the Czar to Berlin; war panic in Europe; diplomatic intervention of Great Britain leads to assurances of peace about May 24

May 26, Bismarck abolishes the semi-official press

June, George von Vincke, an eminent constitutional statesman, dies

June 15, Count Arnim's new trial; verdict, confirming sentence, Oct. 20

Aug., Partial submission of the bishops

Oct. 6, Förster, Prince-Bishop of Breslau, sentenced to deprivation

Letter from count Arnim rebutting accusations in the Times of Nov. 19

Nov., He is to be prosecuted for treason in a pamphlet entitled "Pro Nihilo," published at Zurich

1876

Feb. 3, Archbishop Ledochowski released from prison (proceeds to Rome)

1877

May 11, 12, Berlin Conference on Eastern question (Emperor of Russia, Prince Gortschakoff, and Count Andrassy)

Sept., Count Eulenburg's policy as Minister of Interior displeases Prince Bismarck; the Count's resignation not accepted; he is granted six months' absence

1878

Feb. 19, Prince Bismarck, in the German parliament, asserts strict neutrality and non-interference with Russia in the Eastern question

May 11, Hödel (called Lehman), a socialist, fires at the Emperor and misses, at Berlin
June–Sept., The Emperor wounded by shots by Dr. Nobiling, June 2; gradually recovered
Aug. 16, Hödel executed at Berlin

1879

Jan., Count Arnim publishes "Quid faciamus nos?"
March 13, Marriage of Princess Louise Margaret of Prussia to the Duke of Connaught

1880

Feb. 24, Letter from the Pope to Melchers, Abp. of Cologne, recommending submission of names of priests to the government, dated
June 28, Ecclesiastical laws (Falk) amendment bill, promoted by Prince Bismarck; much discussed, May; passed (maimed; 206–202)

1881

Jan., Anti-Semitic league very active; much opposed by the Prince Imperial and others
About Feb. 19, Count Eulenburg, resigns through offense of Prince Bismarck
Feb. 27, Prince William, grandson of the Emperor and of Queen Victoria, married to Princess Augusta Victoria of Schleswig-Holstein
May 19, Death of Count Arnim at Nice
Aug. 14 et seq., Dr. Felix Korum nominated Bishop of Treves, at Rome; approved by Bismarck

1882

Jan. 18, Revenue surplus announced
March 21, Bismarck's tobacco bill rejected by his economic council

1883

June 5, Prospect of reconciliation with the Vatican; amendments of the ecclesiastical laws of May, 1873, introduced
July 2, Bill passed; Diet closed

1884

June 18, Revival of the Prussian Council of State, the Crown Prince President, royal family members

1885

Jan. 15, Death of Prince Frederick Charles, the "Red Prince" aged 57
June 2, Prince Charles Anthony Hohenzollern-Sigmaringen, dies aged 73
June 17, General Manteuffel dies aged 76
Oct. 8, Prof. Graff acquitted of perjury, 9 days' trial

1886

April 7, Prince Bismarck puts forth his plan for Germanizing Posen by purchasing Polish estates to be settled by Germans; 5,000,000l. to be raised for the purpose, Feb.; finally passed
April 13, Bill for greatly amending the ecclesiastical laws (see May, 1873) passed
May 14, Political meetings without permission prohibited by decree
About Aug. 11, Convention signed between Prussia and the Vatican

1887

March, Prince Bismarck introduces Church and State bill, softening Falck laws

1888

March 9, Death of Emperor William I; succeeded by his son Frederick III
Early April, Prince Bismarck opposes the project of a marriage between Prince Alexander of Battenberg and Princess Victoria of Prussia; favored by the Emperor and Empress; he withdraws his resignation and the project deferred
May 24, Marriage of Prince Henry of Prussia and Princess Irene of Hesse
June 15, Death of Emperor Frederick III; succeeded by his son William II
Sept., Publication in the Deutsche Rundschau (Oct.) of alleged extracts from the diary of the Emperor Frederick III, when Crown Prince asserting that it was he who suggested the unity of Germany and the Empire, with other statements; said by Prince Bismarck at first to be apocryphal and afterwards to be notes falsified and colored
Sept. 29, Dr. Geffcken arrested at Hamburg
Sept., A part of the Prince's diary published in the Kieler Zeitung
Dec. 16, The Kölnische Zeitung accuses the British Ambassador at St. Petersburg (Sir Robert B. D. Morier) when chargé d'affaires at Darmstadt, of giving information to Marshal Bazaine of the movements of the Prussian army in 1870. Sir Robert writes to Count Herbert Bismarck repelling the charge (and sends a letter from the Marshal to himself to the same effect), Dec. 19; Sir Robert publishes the correspondence in the Times, Jan. 4; much discussion ensues, Jan., 1889

1889

Jan. 7, Death of the Empress Augusta
——, Dr. Geffcken acquitted of criminal intents
Jan. 16, Prince Bismarck publishes the indictment and evidence

1890

Feb. 14–28, The Emperor-King convokes the Council of State respecting the working-classes, see Germany; delivers an address; propositions considered
March 18, Prince Bismarck resigns the offices of Premier and Foreign Minister; succeeded by Gen. George von Caprivi, about March 20

1891

April 24, Death of Count Moltke, see Germany

1892

Jan. 30, Much discussion on the primary education bill, which enacts, that in all schools some form of Christianity should be taught, to counteract socialism; read first time
March 22, Ministerial crisis in relation to the education bill; Count Caprivi resigns the premiership, but remains Foreign Minister and Chancellor of the Empire
March 24, Count Botho von Eulenburg becomes Premier
About March 28, The Government withdraws the education bill
May, Certain privileges of the nobility abolished with compensation

1893

July 3, Important communal taxation bill, introduced by Dr. Miguel, passed
Oct. 31–Nov. 7, Elections for the Diet (lower house), little changed from that of 1888

1894

Oct. 26, Resignation of count Eulenburg, President of the Council; succeeded by Prince Clovis von Hohenlohe; Herr von Köller, Minister of the Interior, Oct. 29

1897

Law of association (amended) (a government) bill passed by the Diet, June 30; rejected by the lower house, July 24; Diet closed, May 18, 1898

1898

Oct., Expulsion of Danes and non-Prussians from Schleswig and elsewhere

1899

July 10, Herr Heinrich von Achenbach, chief president of the province of Brandenburg, 1879, dies, aged 69

Aug. 29, Diet meets; Government defeated on the Rhine-Elbe canal bill, Aug. 16, 19; crisis; the Emperor holds a council, Aug. 23; royal message, moderate and conciliatory, Diet closed

Sept. 1, Landräthe and other officials placed on the retired list for opposing the canal bill

Sept. 4, Baron von der Recke (Interior) and Dr. Bosse (Education) resign; Baron von Rheinbaben and Herr Studt, conservatives, appointed

1900

Jan. 9, Diet meets, speech from the throne read by Prince Hohenlohe, reintroduction of the Rhine-Elbe canal bill, announced

Dec. 2, Imperial edict granting reforms in the higher schools, English to be compulsory

1901

May 3, Crisis; agrarian victory, the canal bill given up; joint sitting of the two houses; Diet closed; Dr. von Miguel (finance) and other ministers resign

May 30, Count William Bismarck, chief president of East Prussia, dies, aged 48

Nov. 19, Frau Piasecka sentenced to 2½ years' and 22 others to various terms of imprisonment for disturbances at the Wreschen school in Posen, owing to the children being punished for refusing to receive religious instruction in German

Early Dec., Anti-German agitation

Dec. 10, Interpellation introduced by Prince Radziwill in the Diet

Dec. 15, Meeting of Polish women at Lemberg; resolution to boycott German goods, papers, and schools, carried

Mid. Dec., Religious instruction in German abandoned at Wreschen

1902

Jan. 8, Diet meets; financial depression reported

Feb. 23–March 11, Visit of Prince Henry of Prussia to the United States

June 5, Germanization of the Slav peoples urged by the Emperor

June, Polish (German) settlement bill passed

Aug. 17, Polish demonstration against ministerial Polish policy, Berlin

Nov. 2, New State college for arts and music at Charlottenburg opened by the Emperor

1903

Jan. 19, Count von Bulow defends his Polish policy

Nov. 12, Elections for the Chamber

1905

Feb. 8, Prussian canal bill, for construction of a network of inland waterways to unite the Rhine and Weser, and establish a branch communication as far as Hanover, *via* Bückeberg; included in bill is the construction of a ship canal from Berlin to Stettin, in addition to the junction of the Weichsel and Oder, and the canalization of the Oder. Government authorized to incur expenditure of 334,575,000 marks (16,728,750*l*.) for execution of this scheme. Second reading passes Diet by majority of 123 votes (Feb. 7); bill read third time

Feb. 15, Upper house of the Prussian Diet adopts the bill for the purchase by the State of the Hibernia coal-fields

1906

March 24, Death of the Duchess of Mecklenburg, formerly Princess Alexandrine of Prussia

May 12, Death of the Princess Friedrich Karl of Prussia, mother of the Duchess of Connaught

Oct. 26, Serious situation in Prussian Poland, arising from the resistance of the Poles to the government order that religious instruction in schools is to be given in the German language, reported

(*See* Germany for subsequent dates)

MARGRAVES, ELECTORS, DUKES, AND KINGS

MARGRAVES OR ELECTORS OF BRANDENBURG

1134. Albert I, the Bear, first elector of Brandenburg
1170. Otho I
1184. Otho II
1206. Albert II
1221. John I and Otho III
1266. John II
1282. Otho IV
1309. Waldemar
1319. Henry I the Young
1320. [Interregnum]
1323. Louis I of Bavaria
1352. Louis II, the Roman
1365. Otho V, the Sluggard
1373. Wenceslas, of Luxemburg
1378. Sigismund, of Luxemburg
1388. Jossus, the Bearded
1411. Sigismund, again Emperor
1415. Frederick I of Nuremberg (of the house of HOHENZOLLERN)
1440. Frederick II, surnamed Ironside
1470. Albert III, surnamed the German Achilles
1476. John III, his son; as Margrave; styled the Cicero of Germany
1486. John III as Elector
1499. Joachim I, son of John
1535. Joachim II, poisoned by a Jew
1571. John George
1598. Joachim Frederick
1608. John Sigismund

DUKES OF PRUSSIA

1618. John Sigsmund
1619. George William
1640. Frederick William, his son, the "Great Elector"
1688. Frederick III, son of the preceding; crowned King, Jan. 18. 1701

1701. Frederick I; King; died
1713. Frederick William I, son of Frederick I
1740. Frederick II (or Frederick III; styled the Great), son; made Prussia a military power
1786. Frederick William II, nephew of the preceding
1797. Frederick William III (he had to contend against the might of Napoleon, and after extraordinary vicissitudes he aided England in his overthrow), died June 7, 1840
1840. Frederick William IV, son; born Oct. 15, 1795; died Jan. 2, 1861
1861. William I, brother (born, March 22, 1797); proclaimed Emperor of Germany at Versailles, Jan. 18, 1871); married Princess Augusta of Saxe-Weimar, June 11, 1829; golden wedding kept, June 11, 1879; died March 9, 1888; she died Jan. 7, 1890
1888. Frederick III (William) son, "the noble"; born Oct. 18, 1831; (married Victoria, princess-royal of England, Jan. 25, 1858); died June 15, 1888
——. William II, son; born Jan. 27, 1859 (married Princess Augusta Victoria of Schleswig-Holstein, Feb. 27, 1881); issue, 6 sons, 1 daughter; brother, Henry, born Aug. 14, 1862 (married Princess Irene of Hesse, May 24, 1888); abdicated Nov. 9, 1918
Heir: William; born May 6, 1882 (married Cecile, Duchess of Mecklenburg-Schwerin, June 6, 1905).
See also Germany

RHODES
See Dodecanese Islands

ROME

Rome. The foundation of the city, by Romulus, was laid on April 20th, according to Varro, in the year 3961 of the Julian period (753 years before the birth of Christ, and in the fourth year of the sixth Olympiad. Other dates given: Cato, 751; Polybius, 750; Fabius Pictor, 747; Cincius, 728 B.C.). The Romans conquered nearly the whole of the then known world. In the time of Julius Cæsar, the Empire was bounded by the Euphrates, Taurus, and Armenia on the east; by Æthiopia on the south; by the Danube on the north; and by the Atlantic on the west.

The early history of Rome is legendary, and the dates purely conjectural.

753 B.C. to 1846

B.C. 753, Foundation of the city by Romulus
750, The Romans seize on the Sabine women at a public spectacle, and detain them for wives
747, Rome taken by the Sabines; the Sabines incorporated with the Romans as one nation
716, Romulus said to have been murdered by senators
710, Numa Pompilius elected King, 715; institutes the priesthood, the augurs, and vestals
About 667, The Romans and the Albans contesting for superiority, agreed to choose three champions on each part to decide it. The three Horatii, Roman knights, overcame the three Curiatii, Albans, and united Alba to Rome
665, War with the Fidenates; the city of Alba destroyed

About 627, Ostia, at the mouth of the Tiber, built
615, The capitol founded
566, The first census of the Roman state taken
550, Political institutions of Servius Tullius
509, Tarquinius II and his family expelled for tyranny and licentiousness, royalty abolished: the Patricians establish an aristocratical commonwealth
——, Junius Brutus and Tarquinius Collatinus first prætors or consuls; first alliance of the Romans with Carthage
501, First dictator Titus Lartius
496, The Latins and the Tarquins declare war against the republic, 501; defeated at lake Regillus
494, Secession of the Plebeians to the sacred mount; establishment of tribunes of the Plebeians
491, Wars with the Æquians and Volscians; exploits and exile of Coriolanus; he besieges Rome, but retires at the intercession of his mother and wife
486–5, First agrarian law passed by Spurius Cassius; he is put to death by Patricians
477, Wars with Veii and the Etruscans, indecisive, 475, 465; slaughter of the patriotic Fabii
472, 466, 463, and 451, Destructive pestilences
458, Victory of Cincinnatus over the Æquians by stratagem, liberating the Roman army
456, The Aventine mount allotted solely to the Plebeians
448, The appointment and fall of the Decemvirs, 451–
448. The Decemvirs were tried, Appius Claudius and Spurius Oppius died in prison, others were banished
447, Great defeat of the Sabines
445, The Canuleian law passed, permitting marriages between Patricians and Plebeians
444, Military tribunes first created
443, Office of censor instituted
437, The Veientes defeated, and their king Tolumnius slain
436, Spurius Mœlius, a benefactor during famine, judicially murdered by the Patricians
434, War with the Etruscans
428, Æqui and Volsci defeated by Tubertus, dictator
421, Two more quæstors appointed
409, Three quæstors are chosen from the Plebeians for the first time
396, Veii taken by Camillus after ten years' siege
391, Banishment of Camillus
390, Great victory of the Gauls near the Allia, July 16; they sack Rome, which is deserted, but are repulsed in an attack on the Capitol, which they blockade; they accept a ransom, and retire
389, Proposed removal of the state, to Veii, rejected
[Rome gradually rebuilt amid great distress and wars with neighboring states]
384, M. Manlius executed as a traitor
365, Passing of the Licinian laws; one consul is to be a Plebeian (much resisted)
365–342, War with the Etruscans, ended by a truce; war with the Latins; league renewed
362, Marcus Curtius leaps into the gulf which had opened in the forum
360, The Gauls defeated in Italy
348, Treaty with Carthage to repress Greek piracy
343–340, First Samnite war, indecisive
341, Mutiny in the army in Campania, and rise of the commons in Rome; peace restored by concessions and the general abolition of the debts caused by the Gaulish invasion
339, The Publilian law passed, equalizing the Plebeians with the Patricians in political rights

326 *et seq.*, The second Samnite war, a severe struggle; the Roman army, entrapped in the Caudine Forks, 321; victories of L. Papirius Cursor; the Samnites and their allies submit, 304

312–308, Appius Claudius Cæcus, censor, favors the lower classes; with the public money makes the road from Rome to Capua, termed the "Appian way," and erects the first aqueduct

311, War with Etruria; victories of Q. Fabius Maximus at the Vadimonian lake, &c.; the Etrurians and Umbrians submit, 309

304–302, Conquest of the Æquians, Marsians, &c.

300, Third Samnite war

300 *et seq.*, Great distress of the Plebeians, through war, pestilence, and famine

295, Coalition of the Samnites, Etruscans, and Gauls (not continuous) against Rome; nine campaigns, with many conflicts and alternate invasions; great Roman victory at Sentinum

293, Census: 262,322 Roman citizens

290, The Samnites subdued after desperate struggles, 294–291; their general, C. Pontius, put to death at Rome

——, Conquest of the Sabines by M. Curius Dentatus

286, Secession of the people to the Janiculum; the Hortensian laws passed

283, The Etruscans defeated at the Vadimonian lake

281, The Tarentines form a coalition against Rome, and invite Pyrrhus, King of Epirus, to join them; he defeats the Romans at Pandosia, 280; and at Asculum, 279; defeated by them at Beneventum, 275

265, Subjugation of Tarentum, Samnium, Bruttium, and their allies, 272–265; Rome supreme in Italy

264–241, First Punic war

260, First Roman fleet built

238 *et seq.*, Corsica and Sardinia annexed

235, Temple of Janus closed

225, Invasion of the Gauls; beaten by the consuls

218–201, Second Punic war; Rome saved by the adhesion of 18 colonies, by the free-will offerings of gold, silver, and money by the Senate and people, and by the defeat of Hasdrubal at the Metaurus, 207

213 and 200, The Macedonian wars with Philip begin; his defeat at Cynoscephalæ, 197

212, Syracuse taken by Marcellus

185, Death of Scipio Africanus the elder

171, Third Macedonian war begins; Perseus beaten at Pydna; Macedon annexed, 168

161, Philosophers and rhetoricians banished from Rome

149, Third Punic war begins

146, Corinth and Carthage destroyed by the Romans

153–133, Celtiberian and Numantine war in Spain

133, Attalus III of Pergamos bequeaths his kingdom and riches to the Romans

132, The Servile war in Sicily

——, Two Plebeian consuls chosen

121, Agrarian disturbances: Gracchus slain

112–106, The Jugurthine war

108–63, The Mithridatic war

102, The Ambrones defeated by Marius

90–88, The Social war

87, Rome besieged by four armies (*viz.*: those of Marius, Cinna, Carbo, and Sertorius) and taken

82, Sylla defeats Marius: becomes dictator; sanguinary proscriptions: abdicates, 79

74, Bithynia bequeathed to the Romans by King Nicomedes

73–71, Revolt of Spartacus and the slaves

65, Syria conquered by Pompey

63, The Catiline conspiracy suppressed by Cicero

60, The first triumvirate: Cæsar, Pompey, and Crassus

58, Cæsar's campaigns in Gaul; in Britain, 55

58–50, Gaul conquered and made a province

53, Crassus killed by the Parthians

50, War between Cæsar and Pompey

48, Pompey defeated at Pharsalia

47, Cæsar defeats Pharnaces at Zela; and writes home "Veni, vidi, vici"

46, Cato kills himself at Utica; Cæsar dictator for ten years

March 15, 44, Cæsar killed in the senate-house

43, Second triumvirate: Octavius, Antony, and Lepidus

——, Cicero killed, proscribed by Antony

42, Battle of Philippi; Brutus and Cassius defeated

36, Lepidus ejected from the triumvirate; war between Octavius and Antony, 32; Antony defeated totally at Actium, Sept. 2, 31

27, Octavius Emperor, as Augustus Cæsar

The Empire now at peace with all the world; the temple of Janus shut; Jesus Christ born

A.D. 9, Varus defeated by Hermann and the Germans

——, Ovid banished to Tomi

18, Death of Ovid and Livy

26, Tiberius retires to Caprea; tyranny of Sejanus

48, A census being taken by Claudius, the Emperor and censor, the inhabitants of Rome are stated to amount to 6,944,000.—[It is now considered that the population of Rome within the walls was under a million]

50, Caractacus brought in chains to Rome

62, St. Paul arrives in bonds at Rome

64, Nero burns Rome to the ground and charges the crime upon the Christians

65, Seneca, Lucan, &c., put to death

67, Peter and Paul said to be put to death

Sept. 8, 70, Jerusalem leveled to the ground by Titus

75, Coliseum founded by Vespasian

86, The Dacian war begins (continues 15 years)

102, Pliny, junior, proconsul in Bithynia, sends Trajan his celebrated account of the Christians

106, Trajan's expedition into the East against the Parthians, &c.; subdues Dacia

114, Trajan's column erected at Rome

121, Adrian resides in Britain, and builds the wall

188, The capitol destroyed by lightning

196, Byzantium taken; its walls razed

222, The Goths are paid tribute

[The Goths, Vandals, Alani, Suevi, and other Northern nations attack the empire]

248, Pompey's amphitheater burnt

250, Invasion of the Goths

262, Pestilence throughout the empire

269, Great victory over the Goths obtained by Claudius II; 320,000 slain

270, Dacia relinquished to the Goths

273, Palmyra conquered, and Longinus put to death

284, The era of Martyrs, or of Diocletian

287, The Franks settle in Gaul. *Fréret*

306, Constantius dies at York

308, Four emperors reign at one time

312, Constantine the Great, places the cross on his banners, and begins to favor the Christians

Sept. 18, 323, Constantine defeats Licinius, at Chrysopolis, and reigns alone

——, He tolerates the Christian faith

324, Puts his son Crispus to death

325, Constantine convokes the first general council of Christians at Nice

330, The seat of empire removed from Rome to Byzantium, 321; dedicated by Constantine

——, Constantine orders the heathen temples to be destroyed

334, Revolt of 300,000 Sarmatian slaves suppressed

337, Death of Constantine, soon after being baptized

360, The army under Julian proclaims him Emperor

361, Julian, who had been educated for the priesthood, and had frequently officiated, abjures Christianity, and reopens the heathen temples, becoming the pagan pontiff

363, Julian killed in battle in Persia; Christianity restored by Jovian

364, The Empire divided into Eastern and Western by Valentinian and Valens, brothers: the former has the Western portion, or Rome

(See Western and Eastern Empires; and Italy)

404, Rome placed under the exarchate of Ravenna

Aug. 24, 410, Taken by Alaric

July 15, 455, Taken and pillaged by Genseric

476, Odoacer takes Rome, and becomes King of Italy

536, Rome recovered for Justinian by Belisarius

546, Retaken by Totila the Goth; recovered by Belisarius, 547; seized by Totila, 549

553, Recovered by Narses, and annexed to the eastern empire; and the Senate abolished

About 600, Rome at her lowest state

About 728, Rome independent under the Popes

755, Pepin of France compels Astolphus, King of the Lombards, to cede Ravenna and other places to the Holy Church

774, Confirmed and added to by Charlemagne

Dec. 25, 800, Charlemagne crowned Emperor of the West by the Pope at Rome

896, Rome taken by Arnulf and the Germans

Feb. 2, 962, Otho I crowned at Rome

March, 1084, The Emperor Henry IV takes Rome

1155, Arnold of Brescia, endeavoring to reform Church and State and to establish a senate, is put to death as a heretic

1309, The Pope removes to Avignon

1347, Nicola di Rienzi, tribune of the people, establishes a republic, May 20; is compelled to abdicate, Dec. 15

1354, Returns; made senator, Aug. 1; assassinated, Oct. 8

1377, Papal court returns to Rome

About 1377, Rise of the families, Colonna, Orsini, &c.

1503–13, Julius II conquers the Romagna, Bologna, and Perugia

May 6, 1527, It is captured by the constable de Bourbon, who is slain

1597, Ferrara annexed

Nov. 18, 1626, St. Peter's dedicated

Aug. 16, 1773, Expulsion of the Jesuits

16th to 18th century, Harassed by the French, German, and Spanish factions

1796, The French invasion; the Legations incorporated with the Cisalpine republic

March 20, 1798, The French proclaim the Roman republic

Nov., 1799, Recovered for the Pope by the Neapolitans

1800, Retaken by the French; restored to Pius VII, July, 1801

May, 1808, Annexed by Napoleon to the Kingdom of Italy, and declared second city of the Empire

Jan. 23, 1814, Restored to the Pope, who returns

Aug. 7, He reëstablishes the Inquisition and the Jesuits

1831, The "Young Italy" party established by Joseph Mazzini; temporary insurrections at Bologna suppressed by Austrian aid

June 16, 1846, Election of Pius IX

1848

The Romans desire to join the King of Sardinia against the Austrians; the Pope hesitates; the Antonelli Ministry retires; and the Mamiani Ministry is formed

Nov. 15, Count Rossi, Minister of Justice of the pontifical government, assassinated on the staircase of the Chamber of Deputies at Rome

Nov. 16, Insurrection at Rome, the populace demand a democratic ministry and the proclamation of Italian nationality; the Pope (Pius IX) hesitates, the Romans surround the palace, and a conflict ensues. The Pope accepts a popular ministry (Cardinal Palma, the Pope's secretary, shot in this conflict)

Nov. 20, A free constitution published

Nov. 24, The Pope escapes in disguise to Gaëta

Nov. 27, M. de Corcelles leaves Paris for Rome, a French armed expedition having preceded him, to afford protection to the Pope

Nov. 28, Protest of the Pope against the acts of the provisional government

1849

Feb. 5, A constituent assembly meets at Rome

Feb. 8, The Roman National Assembly divests the Pope of all temporal power, and adopts the republican form of government

Feb., Mazzini, Armellini, and Saffi appointed triumvirs

Feb. 18, The Pope appeals to the Catholic powers

April 26, Civita Vecchia occupied by the French force under Marshal Oudinot

April 30, A French force repulsed with loss

May 19, Engagement between Romans and Neapolitans; former capture 60 men and 400 muskets

——, The Roman assembly refuses to receive the French as allies

June 3, The French under Marshal Oudinot commence an attack on Rome

June 30, After a brave resistance, the Romans capitulate to the French army

July 4, The Roman assembly dissolved

——, An officer from Oudinot's camp arrives at Gaëta, to present the Pope with the keys of Rome

July 15, The reëstablishment of the Pope's authority proclaimed at Rome

Aug. 3, Oudinot issues a general order stating that the Pope (or his representative) now repossesses the administration of affairs, but public security in the pontifical dominions remains under the special guarantee of the French army

Sept. 4, The Pope arrives at Portici on a visit to the King of Naples

1850

April, He arrives at Rome; Cardinal Antonelli becomes Foreign Minister

Sept. 24, He issues the bull establishing a Roman Catholic hierarchy in England

1855

Aug. 18, Important concordat with Austria

1857

May–Sept., The Pope visits his dominions

1859

June, Insurrection in the Romagna, at Bologna, and Ferrara

July 12, The Pope appeals to Europe for help against Sardinia

Aug. 20, The Legations form a defensive alliance with Tuscany, Parma, and Modena

Aug. 26, The Queen of Spain engages to send troops to Rome, if the French retire

Sept. 7, The assembly at Bologna vote annexation to Piedmont; the King engages to support their cause before the great Powers, Sept. 15; the Pope annuls the acts of the assembly at Bologna; and announces the punishment due to those who attack the Holy See, Sept. 26; and dismisses the Sardinian chargé d'affaires at Rome, Oct. 1

Dec. 24, The Romagna, Modena, and Parma formed into a province, to be called Æmilia

1860

Jan. 27, March 20, The Sardinian Government annul the Tuscan and Lombard concordats

March 19, Riots at Rome suppressed by the police

March 26, The Pope excommunicates all concerned in the rebellion in his states

March, General Lamoricière takes command of the papal army; which is reorganized, and increased by volunteers from Ireland, &c., May

May 19, Tuscan volunteers enter the Papal States and are repulsed

July, Irish volunteers are severely treated for insubordination; many dismissed

Aug., The papal army estimated at 20,000

Sept. 8, Insurrection in the Marches; Fossembrone subdued by the papal troops; the people appeal to the Sardinian government, whose troops enter the Papal States, Sept. 11

Sept. 12, Pesaro taken; and Perugia, including General Schmidt and 1600 prisoners, Sept. 14

Sept. 17, Ancona besieged by sea and land

Sept. 28, Severe allocution of the Pope against France and Sardinia; he appeals to Europe for help

Sept. 29, Cialdini defeats Lamoricière at Castel-Fidardo, Sept. 18; and takes Ancona

Oct., Additional French troops sent to Rome

Nov., The Marches vote for annexation to Sardinia

——, Subscriptions raised for the Pope in various countries; the formal collection forbidden in France and Belgium; permitted in England

Dec., Monastic establishments suppressed in the Legations; the monks pensioned; educational institutions founded

Dec. 21, The French Emperor advises the Pope to give up his revolted provinces

1861

March, Publication of Rome et les Evêques, Jan. 6; and of La France, Rome et l'Italie, Feb. 15; great excitement, and strong advocacy of the Pope's temporal government (attacked by Prince Napoleon) in the French Chambers

March 27, Cavour claims Rome as capital of Italy

May 10, Petition to the Emperor Napoleon to withdraw French troops from Rome

June, The Emperor of France declines a union with Austria and Spain for the maintenance of the Pope's temporal power

June 9, The Pope declares a severe allocution against the Italians

1862

July 19, Garibaldi calls for volunteers, taking as his watchword, "Rome or death!"

Nov., Railway between Rome and Naples completed; its opening opposed by the papal government

Nov. 11, Earl Russell's offer to the Pope of a residence at Malta, Oct. 25; declined

1863

March 5, Antonelli's resignation of his office not accepted

1864

Sept. 15, Convention between France and Italy: French troops to quit Rome within two years

1865

April 21 to June 23, Fruitless negotiations between the Pope and the King of Italy (by Vegezzi); mutual concessions proposed

Sept. 25, Pope's severe allocution against secret societies (Freemasons, Fenians, &c.)

Oct. 20, Merode, the papal Minister of War, dismissed

Nov., A part of the French troops leave the papal dominions

1866

Dec., 1865–Jan., 1866, Rupture with Russia

Sept. 24, A Franco-pontifical legion (1,200 men) formed at Antibes, arrives; blessed by the Pope

Dec. 6, The Pope's blessing given to French troops, who all quit Rome, Dec. 2–12

Dec. 13, Rome tranquil

Dec. 31, Law prohibiting Protestant worship except at embassies in Rome enforced

1867

April, Negotiation with Italy fruitless; the Italian councillor Tonello quits Rome

June 26, 599 bishops and thousands of priests present at the Pope's allocution; and canonization of 25 martyrs, June 29

July 8, The Pope receives an album and address from 100 cities of Italy

Sept. 23, Garibaldi arrested at Sinalunga, near the Roman frontier

Oct., Irruption of Garibaldians in Viterbo—conflicts with various results; reported appeal of Antonelli for help from the great Powers

Oct. 22, Zouave barracks at Rome blown up

——, Attempt at insurrection in Rome; state of siege proclaimed; Garibaldi within 20 miles of Rome, Oct. 24; takes Monte Rotondo, Oct. 26

Oct. 30, French brigades enter Rome

Nov. 1, Italian troops cross the frontier, Oct. 30; occupy several posts

Nov. 3, Garibaldians defeated by the papal and French troops at Mentana

Nov., Italian troops retire from the Papal States

Dec., The Roman committee of insurrection issue a narrative, and state that their watchword is "Try again and do better"

——, The papal army increased to about 15,000

Dec. 19, The Pope's short allocution (thanking and blessing the French Government)

1868

March 13, Nine cardinals made

May 15, Sudden death of Cardinal Andrea

June 22, The Pope, in his allocution, censures the Austrian new civil marriage law

July 30, Arrangement respecting the papal debt made with Italy

Nov. 24, Monti and Tognetti (for complicity in the explosion of the Zouave barracks, Oct. 22, 1867), executed

1869

Sept. 4, The Pope declares, in a letter to Archbishop Manning, that no discussions on disputed points can take place at the council

Dec. 8, The council opened, see Council XXI

1870

April 11, British and American bishops protest against discussing the dogma of papal infallibility in the council; the discussion begins May 14

May, Count Arnim, on behalf of the North German Confederation, protests against the dogma

July 18, Papal infallibility adopted by the council and promulgated (533 for; 2 against; many retire); the council adjourns to Nov. 11

Aug. 8, Rome completely evacuated by French troops in consequence of the war; 8 mortars and 15,000 shells said to be ceded to the Pope; the troops sent from Civita Vecchia, Aug. 21

Sept. 8, Conciliatory letter from Victor Emmanuel to the Pope

About Sept. 10, Agitation in the papal provinces; the Italian troops invited to enter

Sept. 11, The Pope refuses terms offered him by the King of Italy (sovereignty of the Leonine city and retention of his income)

Sept. 14, Skirmish with papal Zouaves

About Sept. 15, The Italians occupy Civita Vecchia without resistance

Sept. 17, Gen. Cadorna crosses the Tiber at Casale; sends flags of truce to Gen. Kanzler, commander of the Zouaves, who refuses to surrender; Baron Arnim in vain negotiates between them

Sept. 19, Letter from the Pope to Gen. Kanzler directing that a merely formal defense be made at Rome, and that bloodshed be avoided

Sept. 20, After a brief resistance from the foreign papal troops, stopped by order of the Pope, the Italian troops under Cadorna make a breach and enter Rome [Reported Italian loss, about 22 killed, 117 wounded; papal troops, 55 killed and wounded]

Sept. 21, Cardinal Antonelli issues a diplomatic protest against the Italian occupation of Rome

Sept. 22, The papal troops surrender arms; about 8,500 foreigners march out with honors of war; the native troops retained

——, About 10,000 persons assemble in the Coliseum, choose 44 names for a provisional government (giunta)

Sept. 26, Protest of the Pope

Sept. 28, Castle of St. Angelo occupied by Italian troops at the Pope's request

Sept. 29, Circular letter from the Pope to the cardinals complaining of the invasion and of his loss of liberty, and interference with his post bag

Sept. 30, A giunta of 14 selected from the 44 names chosen; approved by Cadorna

Sept. 30, General Masi in command of Rome and the provinces; S.P.Q.R. appears on the proclamations

Oct. 2, Plebiscite: out of 167,548 votes, 133,681 for union with the kingdom of Italy; 1,507 against; the remainder did not vote

Oct. 4, Cardinal Antonelli issues a protest

——, Pope said to have accepted 50,000 crowns (his monthly civil list) from Italian Government

Oct. 8, The result of the plebiscite sent to the King; Rome and its provinces incorporated with the kingdom by royal decree, Oct. 9

Oct. 11, General La Marmora enters Rome as viceroy; he proclaims that the Pope shall be guaranteed in his sovereign powers as head of the Church

Oct. 19, The Roman provinces united into one by decree

Nov. 10, Antonelli protests against the occupation of the Quirinal by the King

About Dec. 12, Bill introduced into the Italian parliament respecting the transfer of the seat of government to Rome in about six months, and the preservation of the spiritual and temporal sovereignty of the Pope

1871

May 15, Law guaranteeing to the Pope full personal liberty and honors, a revenue of 3,225,000 livres, &c., May 13; rejected by the Pope in his allocution

July 2, 3, The Italian Government remove to Rome

Oct. 27, Allocution of the Pope, appointing some Italian bishops; still rejecting guarantees

Nov. 21, Grand reception of the King

Nov. 27, He opens the parliament, saying, "The work to which we have consecrated our life is completed"

For further events, see Italy

KINGS OF ROME
(Dates conjectural)

B.C.

735. Romulus; murdered by the senators

[Titus Tatius, King of the Sabines, had removed to Rome in 747, and ruled jointly with Romulus six years]

716. [Interregnum]

715. Numa Pompilius, son-in-law of Tatius the Sabine, elected; died at the age of 82

673. Tullus Hostilius; murdered by his successor, by whom his palace was set on fire; his family perished in the flames

640. Ancus Martius, grandson of Numa

616. Tarquinius Priscus; son of Demaratus, a Corinthian emigrant, chosen King

578. Servius Tullius, a manumitted slave; married the King's daughter; and succeeded by the united suffrages of the army and the people

534. Tarquinius Superbus, grandson of Tarquinius Priscus; assassinates his father-in-law, and usurps the throne

510. [The rape of Lucretia, by Sextus, son of Tarquin, and consequent insurrection, leads to the abolition of royalty and the establishment of the consulate]

REPUBLIC

510–82. First period. From the expulsion of Tarquin to the dictatorship of Sylla

2–27. Second period. From Sylla to Augustus

48. Caius Julius Cæsar; perpetual dictator; assassinated, March 15, 44 B.C.

31. Octavianus Cæsar

EMPERORS

A.D.
27. Augustus Imperator, died Aug. 19, A.D. 14
14. Tiberius (Claudius Nero)
37. Caius Caligula: murdered by a tribune
41. Claudius I (Tiberius Drusus): poisoned by his wife Agrippina, to make way for
54. Claudius Nero; deposed; kills himself, 68
68. Servius Sulpicius Galba; slain by the prætorians
69. M. Salvius Otho; stabbed himself
—. Aulus Vitellius; deposed by Vespasian, and put to death
—. Titus Flavius Vespasian
79. Titus (Vespasian), his son
81. Titus Flavius Domitian, brother of Titus; last of the twelve Cæsars; assassinated
96. Cocceius Nerva
98. Trajan M. Ulpius (Crinitus)
117. Adrian or Hadrian (Publius Ælius)
138. Antonius Titus, surnamed Pius
161. Marcus Aurelius (a philosopher) and Lucius Verus, his son-in-law; the latter died in 169
180. Commodus (L. Aurelius Antoninus), son of Marcus Aurelius; poisoned by his favorite mistress, Martia
193. Publius Helvius-Pertinax; put to death by the prætorian band
[Four emperors now start up: Didianus Julianus, at Rome; Pescennius Niger, in Syria; Lucius Septimius Severus, in Pannonia; and Clodius Albinus, in Britain]
—. Lucius Septimius Severus; died at York in Britain, in 211; succeeded by his sons
211. M. Aurelius Caracalla and Septimius Geta. Geta murdered by Caracalla, 212; who is slain by his successor
217. M. Opilius Macrinus, prefect of the guards; beheaded in a mutiny
218. Heliogabalus (M. Aurelius Antoninus), a youth; put to death for his enormities
222. Alexander Severus; assassinated by some soldiers corrupted by Maximinus
235. Caius Julius Verus Maximinus; assassinated in his tent before the walls of Aquileia
237. M. Antonius Gordianus, and his son; the latter having been killed in a battle with the partisans of Maximinus, the father strangled himself in a fit of despair, at Carthage, in his 80th year
238. Balbinus and Pupienus; put to death
—. Gordian III, grandson of the elder Gordian, in his 16th year; assassinated by the guards, at the instigation of his successor
244. Philip the Arabian; assassinated by his own soldiers; his son Philip was murdered at the same time, in his mother's arms
249. Metius Decius; he perished with his two sons, and their army, in an engagement with the Goths
251. Gallus Hostilius, and his son Volusianus; both slain by the soldiery
253. Æmilianus; put to death after a reign of only four months
—. Valerianus, and his son Gallienus; the first was taken prisoner by Sapor, King of Persia, and flayed alive
260. Gallienus reigned alone
[About this time thirty pretenders to imperial power arise in different parts of the Empire; of these Cyriades is the first, but he is slain]

268. Claudius II (Gallienus having been assassinated by the officers of the guard) succeeds; dies of the plague
270. Quintillus, his brother, elected at Rome by the Senate and troops; Aurelian by the army in Illyricum. Quintillus, despairing of success against his rival, who was marching against him, opened his veins and bled himself to death
—. Aurelianus; assassinated by his soldiers on his march against Persia, in Jan., 275
275. [Interregnum of about nine months]
—. Tacitus, elected Oct. 25; died at Tarsus in Cilicia, April 13, 276
276. Florianus, his brother; his title not recognized by the Senate
—. M. Aurelius Probus; assassinated by his troops at Sirmium
282. M. Aurelius Carus; killed at Ctesiphon by lightning; succeeded by his sons
283. Carinus and Numerianus; both assassinated, after transient reigns
284. Diocletian; who associated as his colleague in the government
286. Maximianus Hercules; the two Emperors resign in favor of
305. Constantius I Chlorus and Galerius Maximianus; the first died at York, in Britain, in 306, and the troops saluted as Emperor his son
306. Constantine, afterwards styled the Great; whilst at Rome the prætorian band proclaimed
—. Maxentius, son of Maximianus Hercules. Besides these were
306. Maximianus Hercules, who endeavored to recover his abdicated power
—. Flavius Valerius Severus, murdered by the last-named pretender; and
307. Flavius Valerianus Licinius, the brother-in-law of Constantine
[Of these, Maximianus Hercules was strangled in Gaul, in 310; Galerius Maximianus died wretchedly in 311; Maxentius was drowned in the Tiber in 312; and Licinius was put to death by order of Constantine in 324]
323. Constantine the Great now reigned alone; died on Whitsunday, May 22, 337

337. { Constantine II / Constans / Constantius II } Sons of Constantine; divided the empire between them; the first was slain in 340, and the second murdered in 350, when the third became sole emperor

360. Julian, the Apostate, so called for abjuring Christianity, having been educated for the priesthood; mortally wounded in a battle with the Persians, 363
363. Jovian; reigned eight months; found dead in his bed, supposed to have died from the fumes of charcoal
364. Valentinian and Valens
375. Valens with Gratian and Valentinian II
379. Theodosius I, &c.
392. Theodosius alone
395. The Roman Empire divided; *see* Eastern Empire, Western Empire, Popes, and Italy

RUMANIA

Rumania, kingdom of southeastern Europe with coast line on the Black Sea, bounded on the north by Hungary, Czechoslovakia, Poland and the

Ukraine (Russia), on the east by the Ukraine and the Black Sea, on the south by Bulgaria and Yugoslavia, and on the west by Yugoslavia and Hungary. By the Treaty of Bucharest (1913) Bulgaria ceded to Rumania 2,969 square miles of territory formed into the departments of Durostor and Caliacra, with population of 273,090, increasing the total area of Rumania from 50,720 square miles to 53,489 square miles. The population of the 1912 census was 7,234,919 which was increased by accession of territory to 7,508,009. As a result of the Treaties of Peace of 1919, Rumania was increased by the addition of the Dobrudja, Bessarabia, Bukovina, the Banat and Transylvania; total area 122,282 square miles, total population 18,025,037. Bucharest is the capital.

Carol II, reigning King. *See also infra.*

1812 to 1888

1812, Part of Moldavia ceded to Russia

1829, The provinces having participated in the Greek insurrection in 1821, were severely treated by the Turks; but by the treaty of Adrianople were placed under the protection of Russia

June, 1840, The Porte appointed as hospodars Prince Stirbey for Wallachia, and Prince Ghika for Moldavia

July 2, 1853, They retire from their governments when the Russians enter Moldavia. *See* Russo-Turkish War

Sept., 1854, The Russians quit the provinces and the Austrians enter; March, 1857

Aug. 19, 1858, The government of the principalities finally settled at the Paris conference: (there were to be two hospodars, elected by elective assemblages, and the suzerainty of Turkey was to be preserved)

1859, Alexander Couza elected Hospodar of Moldavia, Jan. 17; of Wallachia, Feb. 5

Sept. 6, 1859, The election acknowledged by the allies

Dec. 23, 1861, The definitive union of the provinces of Wallachia and Moldavia (capitals, Bucharest and Jassy) (under the name of Rumania) proclaimed and acknowledged by the Porte

June 20, 1862, M. Catargi, the president of the Council of Ministers, assassinated as he was leaving the Chamber of Deputies

Feb. 5, 1862, The united chambers of the two principalities meet at Bucharest

May 28, 1864, *Coup d'état* of Prince Couza against the aristocrats; a plébiscite for a new constitution, May 2; which is adopted

Aug., 1864, Law passed enabling peasants to hold land

1865, Revolt at Bucharest suppressed, Aug. 15; amnesty, Sept. 11

Feb. 22, 1865, Revolution at Bucharest; forced abdication of Prince Couza; and provisional government established

1866, The offered crown declined by the Count of Flanders, Feb.; Prince Charles of Hohenzollern-Sigmaringen elected Hospodar by plébiscite, April 20; enthusiastically received at Bucharest, May 22; sworn to observe the constitution, July 12

Oct. 24, 1866, Recognized hereditary hospodar by the Sultan, and received at Constantinople

Nov., 1867, Rumania unsettled; "nationality" projects

July–Aug., 1871, The legislature proposes to repudiate the just claims of the German shareholders in the

Rumanian railways; the Prince assents reluctantly; Bismarck appeals to the Porte, which declines to interfere

Nov., 1871, Peace between the Prince and Chambers

Oct., 1874, Austria, Germany, and Russia inform Turkey that they claim the right to conclude separate treaties with Rumania; the Sultan objects

1877, Convention with Russia, giving permission to cross Rumania, signed April 16; Russians enter Moldavia, April 24

May 21, 1877, The Senate vote a declaration of independence and war with Turkey

The Rumanians actively engaged before Plevna.
See Russo-Turkish War, 1877

July 13, 1878, Rumania declared independent by treaties of San Stefano (March 3) and of Berlin (losing the part of Bessarabia acquired in 1856, in exchange for the Dobrudscha)

May 23, 1881, The Prince and Princess crowned

Sept. 3, 1885, Rumanian troops seize territory in Silistria

March 25–27, 1888, Riotous meeting at Bucharest suppressed with loss of life

April 24, 1888, Insurrection in the country towns and agricultural districts; increase reported; military called out; Bucharest threatened; revolt said to be encouraged by Russian emissaries April 16; decrease

1892

June 2, Prince Ferdinand betrothed to the Princess Marie of Edinburgh; received in London, June 21; the King invited by Queen Victoria, arrives with his brother, June 27; at Windsor, June 29; leaves England, July 4

About Oct. 15, Dispute with Greece respecting the Zappa bequest, *see* Greece

Dec., Treaty of commerce with Great Britain adopted

1893

Jan. 10, Marriage of Prince Ferdinand and Princess Marie of Edinburgh at Sigmaringen, near the Danube; the prince and princess received at Bucharest, Feb. 4

1894 to 1899

May 17, 1894, New Sulina canal, opened by King Charles

Oct. 28, 1896, Foundation stone of the new harbor laid by the King, at Constanza

Nov. 28, 30, 1896, Riots in Bucharest against the deposition of the Metropolitan Gennadius

Nov. 2, 1897, New university at Jassy opened

Dec. 5, 1897, Anti-Semitic riots in Bukharest and Galatz; shops plundered, &c.

Feb. 5, 1899, Agrarian rising suppressed by troops at Krajova

1900

Jan.–July 19, Great exodus of Jews due to restrictive legislation and persecution

Aug. 4, Several political murders by Bulgarian revolutionists: Prof. Michaileano shot dead in Bukharest

Aug., Strained relations between Bulgaria and Rumania, owing to the Macedonian agitation

Oct., Many Bulgarians expelled from the country

Nine prisoners convicted of the murder of Kiril Fitofski and Prof. Michaileano and plotting against the life of King Charles; Dimitrof and Ilief the actual assassins

1902

June, State anti-semitism, steady emigration of Jews; again, Sept.–Oct.

Sept. 17, American circular note, protesting against the treatment of Rumanian Jews as an international wrong, and as a breach of Article 44, Berlin treaty, 1878; British note of enquiry as to the action of the signatory powers

1904

Oct. 8, New commercial treaty with Germany

1905

May 23, Ultimatum to the Porte demanding redress for the ill-treatment and arrest of two Kutzo-Vlach (Rumanian) school inspectors in Yunina, and the full recognition of the Kutzo-Vlach communities on an equality with Greeks and Bulgarians. Iradé issued by the Sultan officially recognizing the Kutzo-Vlach element in Macedonia

Sept. 24, Diplomatic relations between Rumania and Greece broken off, due to the strained relations between the two governments, caused by the proceedings of bands of Greeks in Macedonia, who attempted the forcible conversion of the Vlach communities, and counter remonstrances of the treatment of Greeks in Rumania

Oct. 5, Rumanian government denounces the Greco-Bulgarian commercial treaty of 1900

Nov. 1, Commercial treaty, included the most-favored-nation clause, concluded with Great Britain, signed

1906

Feb. 16, Greek residents, including M. Chrisovelonis, a wealthy banker, expelled from Rumania for complicity in the proceedings of a society named "Hellenismos"

March 27, Rioting in Bukarest, conflict between the police and public, 250 of the latter and 150 of the former, injured

June 12, Rupture of diplomatic relations with Greece

Aug. 10 and Oct. 13, Further expulsion of Greeks ordered

1907

March 18, Spread of an agrarian movement in N. Moldavia reported; town of Botuchani plundered by 2,000 peasants; urgency bill passed by both houses of parliament authorizing the government to concentrate reserve troops for a fortnight, or longer if necessary

March 20, Continued violent peasant riots at Vaslui and Jassy; sharp encounters between the rioters and the troops reported

March 25–26, Minor state of siege proclaimed at Bukarest; town of Alexandria under martial law

March 28, Destruction to property reported enormous; the Government demands from the Chambers authority to proclaim a state of siege throughout the country, which is accorded unanimously

April 2, Revolt reported practically at an end

Apr. 9, Government manifesto to Rumanian citizens published

1908

March 3, Degradation of 60 soldiers, who mutinied and killed one of their officers during last year's peasant rising, and were sentenced to long terms of penal servitude, takes place at Bukarest

1911

Jan. 10, New Cabinet under presidency of M. Carp, Conservative

Jan. 23, Chamber dissolved

March 1, Election a victory for Conservative Government

June, Diplomatic relations with Greece broken off in 1905 resumed

1912

April 10, Resignation of Carp Ministry, Majorescu succeeding as Premier. This Ministry refused to join the Balkan League

1913

May 7, Agreement with Bulgaria, signed May 15, by which Bulgaria ceded Silistria and strip of territory to Rumania

July 3, Rumania mobilized (*see also* Balkan Wars)

July 10, Rumania declared war on Bulgaria and invaded Bulgaria

July 12, Rumanian force occupied Silistria

July 31, Armistice with Bulgaria signed

Aug. 10, Rumania signed Treaty of Bucharest by which districts of Bazargic and Durostor, of which Silistria, the chief town, ceded to Rumania by Bulgaria. *See also* Balkan Wars

Sept. 13, Decree placed army on peace footing

1914

Jan. 14, Cabinet appointed headed by J. J. C. Bratianu: E. Porumbaro, Foreign Affairs; E. Costinesco, Finance; V. Mortzun, Interior; A. Radovici, Commerce and Industry

March 27, Visit of Crown Prince to St. Petersburg

June 14, Visit of Tsar of Russia and his family

Aug. 2, Bessarabia offered to Rumania by the Central Powers as inducement to join in War

Aug. 4, Crown Council adopted resolution declaring neutrality in War

Sept. 19, Secret Agreement with Russia for mutual support

Sept. 23, Treaty with Italy signed for common action

Oct. 10, Death of King Charles. Succeeded by his nephew Prince Ferdinand of Hohenzollern-Sigmaringen

Oct. 11, Ferdinand I took oath at Bucharest

Dec. 6, Rumania refused to support Greece against Turkey

1915

Jan. 11, Loan of £5,000,000 with Great Britain concluded

Jan. 25, Rumania declined proposal of Entente Allies that she join Greece in support of Serbia

Feb. 6, Agreement with Italy of Sept., 1914 renewed

Oct. 15, Rumania refused to give aid to Serbia

1916

March 2, Death of Dowager Queen Elizabeth (Carmen Sylva)

April 7, Treaty with Germany signed provided for purchase of grain by Central Powers and free exchange of domestic products

July 1, Russian ultimatum to Rumania which forced country into War

Aug. 17, Secret Treaty with Rumania signed by Italy, France, Great Britain, and Russia by which Rumania to receive the Banat, Transylvania as far as the Tisza, Bukovina as far as the Pruth

Aug. 27, Rumania declared war on Austria-Hungary and began invasion of Transylvania. *See* World War

Dec. 1, The Government moved to Jassy

Dec. 6, German army entered Bucharest

1917

Jan. 2, Bratianu reconstructed Cabinet

March 9, Loan of £40,000,000 from Great Britain

May, Direct and universal suffrage introduced

July 14, Agrarian law passed for expropriation of large estates to be paid for in State bonds allowing the proprietors to keep 500 hectares at most

Nov. 3, Meeting of Bessarabians in Kishinev declared for autonomy

Dec. 6, Rumania obliged to suspend hostilities

Dec. 9, Truce of Foscani signed with the Central Powers. *See* World War

Dec. 15, Independence of Moldavian Republic (Bessarabia) proclaimed in Kishinev and Rumania asked to send troops for defense against Russia

1918

Jan. 13, Campaign to rid Bessarabia of Bolshevist bands begun

Jan. 28, Russia severed diplomatic relations because of Rumanian activities in Bessarabia

Feb. 6, German ultimatum to Rumania

Feb. 9, Bratianu resigned as Prime Minister rather than sign Peace Treaty. Succeeded by General Averescu

Feb. 23, German and Austro-Hungarian peace delegates arrived at Bucharest

March 5, Preliminary Peace Treaty with Central Powers signed

March 9, Agreement with Russia for withdrawal of Rumanian troops from Bessarabia

March 12, Averescu Cabinet resigned

March 20, Alexander Marghiloman appointed Premier

March 27/April 9, Bessarabia voted for political union with Rumania with certain conditions. Not accepted by Russia

April 10, Rumanians signed Pact of Rome. *See* Yugoslavia

April 23, Government of Russia protested against union of Bessarabia with Rumania

May 7, Final Peace Treaty with the Central Powers signed at Bucharest, the southern part of the Dobrudja going to Bulgaria, certain Carinthian Passes to Austria-Hungary, and northern Dobrudja to Central Powers in common

Nov. 8, General Coanda appointed Prime Minister by the King who repealed all laws of the Marghiloman Ministry and decreed compulsory universal suffrage

Nov. 10, Rumania reëntered War invading Transylvania and ordering German-Austrian General Mackensen to evacuate the country

Nov. 25, Parliament dissolved

Nov. 27, The National Council of Bessarabia held last session voting for unconditional union with Rumania

Nov. 28, General Assembly of Bukovina voted for union with Rumania

Nov. 30, Government reëstablished at Bucharest

Dec. 1, National Assembly at Alba-Julia declared for union of Transylvania and the Banat with Rumania

Dec. 2, Rumanian Government constituted at Sibiu headed by Dr. Julius Maniu

Dec. 3, Triumphal reëntry of the King into Bucharest

Dec. 14, Bratianu appointed Prime Minister and Minister of Foreign Affairs

——, Law passed ordered expropriation of more estates in Rumania and in Bessarabia regulations promulgated, Dec. 21

Dec. 27, Proclamation of the King of annexation of Rumanian provinces of Austria-Hungary

Dec. 31, Decree law established Central Bureau of Coöperation and of the Sale of Expropriated Lands under Ministry of Agriculture

1919

Jan. 10, Royal decree announced annexation of Transylvania

Jan. 21, Act of union of Transylvania with Rumania of Dec. 1 ratified by assembly of the "Saxons of Transylvania"

March 21, Neutral zone between Hungary and Rumania delimited by Peace Conference

March 24, Rumanians defeated Bolsheviks near the Dniester River

April 21–May 8, Rumanian advance into Hungary

May 2, Rumanian troops in Hungary crossed the Theiss River at Szolnok and Tisza-Polgar

——, Russian ultimatum demanded evacuation of Bessarabia

May 8, Allied ultimatum stopped Rumanian advance into Hungary

May 18, Russia declared state of war with Rumania

May 28, All Jews emancipated by royal decree henceforth to enjoy all rights of citizenship

June 13, Supreme Council announced boundaries with Czechoslovakia

July 20, Forces of Bela Kun from Hungary began new advance against Rumanians

July 28, Island of Ada Kaleh in Danube River formerly administered by Turkey assigned by Supreme Council to Rumania

Aug. 4, Rumanians occupied Budapest

Aug. 6, Rumanian ultimatum to Hungary demanded 30% of harvest, farm animals, tools, 50% of rolling stock and equipment for army of 300,000

——, Note of Allies demanded withdrawal of Rumanian troops from Hungary

Sept. 10, Rumania refused to sign Peace Treaty with Austria and Minorities Treaty. The Treaty of St. Germain confirmed Rumanian possession of Bukovina

——, Bratianu Cabinet resigned. Succeeded by General Arthur Vaitoianu

Sept. 11, Arrival of Sir George Clerk, British Minister, acting as envoy of Supreme Council

Oct. 3, Elections gave majority to the Peasant Party and the Nationalist Democrats

Nov. 1, Rumania notified Supreme Council of annexation of Bessarabia

Nov. 7, Further Note of Supreme Council demanded evacuation of Hungary

Nov. 14, Rumanian troops evacuated Budapest

Nov. 27, Peace Treaty with Bulgaria signed gave Rumania the frontier of Aug. 1, 1914

Dec. 2, Vaida Voivod became Prime Minister

Dec. 3, Ultimatum of Supreme Council demanded the Treaties be signed or diplomatic relations would be suspended

Dec. 9, Rumania signed the Peace Treaties with Austria and Bulgaria and the Minorities Treaty

1920

Feb. 25, Rumanian troops withdrawn from Hungary

March 2, Armistice with Russia signed and hostilities suspended

March 15, S. Pop, Acting Premier in absence of Dr. Vaida Voivod in Paris

March 19, General Averescu became Premier supported by the "League of the People"

March 29, Act organizing Ministry of Labor and Social Welfare

June 4, Peace Treaty with Hungary signed gave Transylvania to Rumania and divided the Banat between Rumania and Yugoslavia

June 6, Elections gave People's Party (Averescu) 212 seats in Chamber out of 365

June 21, Take Jonescu became Minister of Foreign Affairs

Aug. 10, Treaty of Frontiers signed with Great Britain, France, Italy, and Japan

Aug. 14, Commercial Treaty with Austria signed

Sept. 4, Act passed for settlement of industrial disputes

Sept. 14, Rumania became member of the League of Nations

Oct. 28, Treaty signed by Great Britain, France, Italy, and Japan recognized sovereignty of Rumania over Bessarabia

Dec. 8, Bomb in Senate killed Bishop Radu and mortally wounded M. Grecianu, Minister of Justice

1921

Feb. 27, Marriage of the Princess Elizabeth to the Crown Prince of Greece

March 3, Defensive alliance against Russia signed with Poland and Hungary

March 10, Marriage of Crown Prince Carol and the Princess Helen of Greece

April 23, Convention of alliance with Czechoslovakia signed and Commercial Treaty

June 7, Convention of alliance with Yugoslavia signed

June 8, Agreement signed with Yugoslavia for Mixed Commission to delimit frontier in the Banat of Temesvar

July 1, Commercial Treaty with Poland signed

Aug. 30, Minorities Treaty of Dec. 9, 1919 placed under guarantee of the League of Nations

Sept. 30, Commercial Treaty with Austria signed

Oct. 25, Birth of Crown Prince Michael (Mihai)

Nov. 24, Convention delimiting frontiers signed with Yugoslavia

Dec. 17, Resignation of Averescu Cabinet

Dec. 19, Take Jonescu formed Cabinet

1922

Jan. 19, J. J. Bratianu appointed Prime Minister; General Vaitoiano, Interior; Jon Duca, Foreign Affairs; Vintiliano Bratiano, Finance; G. Marzesco, Labor

April 14, Great Britain ratified Bessarabian Treaty of Oct. 28, 1920

June 8, Marriage of Princess Marie to King Alexander of Yugoslavia

June 21, Death of Take Jonescu, former Premier

June 28, Railroad Convention with Bulgaria signed

July 3, Railroad Convention with Yugoslavia signed

Oct. 14, Agreement with Czechoslovakia as to separation of records formerly belonging to Austria-Hungary

Oct. 15, Coronation of King Ferdinand and Queen Marie as monarchs of greater Rumania

Oct. 25, Commercial Agreement with Belgium signed

Nov. 11 and Dec. 18, Commercial Agreements with Sweden signed

Dec. 18 and 19, Provisional Commercial Agreements with the Netherlands signed

Dec. 22, Gold marks deposited by Rumania in Reichsbank in Berlin before the War refunded by Germany

1923

Jan. 10, Frontier clash at Lokoshaza with Hungarians

Feb. 13, Most favored nation Commercial Agreement with Sweden signed

March 27, New Constitution passed by Parliament

March 28, Constitution promulgated

April 30, Commercial *modus vivendi* with Spain concluded

May 7, Convention of alliance and defensive military Treaty renewed with Czechoslovakia

May 8, Provisional Commercial Agreement with Denmark

May 24, Commercial Agreement with Great Britain signed

July 7, Defensive Alliance with Yugoslavia renewed

Oct. 18, Discovery of Fascist plot to assassinate four of the Cabinet

Nov. 19, Frontier Convention with Bulgaria signed

Nov. 24, Protocol signed with Yugoslavia for regulation of frontiers in Banat of Temesvar

Dec. 26, The universities of Bucharest, Jassy, and Klausenburg under police and military protection because of anti-Semitic riots

1924

Feb. 5, Commercial Agreement with Austria signed

Feb. 25, Nationality law passed

March 23–April 2, Conference with representatives of Russia which broke down on question of Bessarabia

March 31, Students attacked the Economic Institute at Bucharest wounding about 100 Jews

April 15, Martial law declared in all university towns because of attacks on Jewish students

April 16, Commercial Convention with Hungary signed and other Conventions providing for settlement of judicial and financial questions arising from the Treaty of Trianon

April 30, France ratified Bessarabian Treaty of Oct. 28, 1920

July 4, New mining law promulgated, foreign companies given 10 years to transfer up to 55% of their stock to Rumanian nationals

July 29, Eight Conventions with Austria signed providing for settlement of judicial and financial questions arising out of the Treaty of St. Germain

Oct. 1, Gregorian calendar substituted for the Justinian

———, Commercial Treaty with Norway signed

Oct. 11, Moldavian autonomous Republic created on left bank of the Dniester

1925

Jan. 25, Maniu, president of the National party appealed to all parties except Liberals to unite to overthrow the Government

Jan. 27, Fusion of National and Democratic parties

Feb. 17, Juridical Convention with Austria signed

April 16, Convention signed with Czechoslovakia as to frontier communications and property rights

April 22, Agreement with Italy signed for payment of pre-War debts

May 7, Convention of Extradition and judicial assistance with Czechoslovakia signed

May 9–11, Conference of the Little Entente States at Bucharest

May 17, Demonstration of meeting of 15,000 persons against the Liberal Government

June 3, Transit Convention with Yugoslavia signed

June 29, Protocol signed with Hungary completed delimitation of frontier

Sept. 1, Twenty-eight members of Committee of Red Unions arrested at Bucharest

Sept. 15, Bolshevik raid on Tatar-Bunar, Bessarabia repelled by troops

Oct. 7, Decision of Cabinet to reduce export taxes on grain because of collapse of grain market

Oct. 19, Debt funding Agreement signed with Great Britain

Nov. 1, Mgr. Miron Cristea enthroned as first patriarch of the Orthodox Church of Rumania

Dec. 1, War debt with the United States funded at $44,591,000 payments spread over period of 62 years with interest at 3% for 10 years and 3½ thereafter

Dec. 2, End of trial of communists; 85 out of 279 convicted and sentenced

Dec. 28, Crown Prince Carol renounced right of succession to the throne from Venice after leaving the country

1926

Jan. 4, Parliament passed Succession Act accepting renunciation of Prince Carol and recognizing his four year old son Prince Michael as heir to the throne and providing for a Council of Regency

Jan. 11, Provisional Council of Regency appointed, the Patriarch Miron Cristea, the president of the Supreme Court of Appeal, and Prince Nicholas, second son of the King

Jan. 24, Death of Michael Pherekydi, president of Senate

Feb. 3, Treaty of arbitration and conciliation with Switzerland signed

Feb. 26, Commercial Agreement with Switzerland signed

——, Commercial Agreement with the United States by exchange of Notes

March 16, Bucharest University closed because of strike of students against admission of Jews

March 18, Parliament ratified debt funding Agreement with the United States, total $44,590,000

March 25, New electoral law passed provided that any party which received 40% of the total votes cast should receive half of the seats in Chamber

March 26, New Treaty of alliance with Poland signed

March 27, Resignation of Bratianu Cabinet. Parliament dissolved

March 30, Alexander Averescu became Prime Minister; Interior, M. Goga; Foreign Affairs, M. Mitilineu; Agriculture, M. Garoflid; Public Instruction, I. Petrovici; Finance, General Averescu (March, 1927); Labor, M. Trancu Jasi; Public Worship, M. Goldis; Justice, M. Cudalbu; Industry and Commerce, M. Berlescu; State for Bessarabia, M. Nita; State for Bukovina, M. Popovici; War, General Mircescu; Communications, General Valeanu; Public Health and Social Welfare, M. Lupas; Public Works, M. C. Meissner

May 25, Elections gave Government 286 seats in Lower House; Coalition, 77; Liberals, 15; Christian League, 91

June 10, Treaty of friendship and non-aggression with France signed and an Arbitration Convention

June 13, Little Entente Treaties renewed

June 15, Agreement with Italy signed for funding Rumanian War debt, and for supply of Italian capital for development of Rumanian oil wells

Sept. 16, Treaty of friendship and arbitration with Italy signed and agreement for loan of 200 million lire from Italy in return for oil concessions

——, Nationalist and Peasant Parties united forming a bloc

——, Treaty of friendship with Albania signed

Oct. 3, Queen Marie with the Princess Ileana and Prince Nicholas left for a visit to the United States. Returned Dec. 4

Nov. 30, Letter of King Ferdinand to Premier Averescu affirmed his intention to uphold the dynastic settlement of the law of Jan. 4

1927

Jan. 10, Rumanian-Hungarian Mixed Arbitration Tribunal declared competence to decide on claims of land owners whose property was practically confiscated under agrarian laws

Feb. 1, National Peasant Party asked for repeal of Succession Act of Jan. 4, 1926

March 8, Treaty with Italy signed recognizing sovereignty of Rumania over Bessarabia making Treaty of Oct. 28, 1920 effective

April 11, Labor Inspection Service established

May 23, Italy deposited ratifications of Bessarabian Treaty of Oct. 28, 1920

May 28, Commercial Agreement with Spain signed

June 4, Averescu Ministry resigned

June 6, Prince Barbu Stirbey formed a temporary Coalition Cabinet

June 21, Fall of Stirbey Ministry, J. Bratianu becoming Prime Minister and Minister of Foreign Affairs

July 7, Election under new electoral law gave Government 70% of vote

July 20, Death of King Ferdinand

July 21, Michael I proclaimed King with Regency Council to act during his minority composed of Prince Nicholas, the Patriarch Miron, and M. Buzdugan, president of the Court of Appeal

Oct. 25, Manoilescu, Under-Secretary of Finance, arrested on train on his return from Paris bringing letters from Prince Carol to political leaders suggesting his return

Nov. 2, Cabinet reconstituted: Prime Minister and Finance, M. Vintila Bratianu; Foreign Affairs, M. N. Titulescu; Interior, M. I. G. Duca; Agriculture, M. C. Argetoianu; Public Instruction, Dr. C. Angelescu; Public Worship, M. A. Lapedatu; Justice, M. I. Nistor; Public Health and Social Welfare, M. I. Inculetz; Labor, Dr. N. Lupu; Communications, M. C. D. Dimitriu; War, General P. Anghelescu; Industry and Commerce, M. L. Mrazec

Nov. 14, Manoilescu acquitted of charge of conspiracy against the State

Nov. 19, Agreement with Austria as to debt settlement

Nov. 24, Death of Premier Jon Bratianu. Vintila Bratiano, brother of Jon, appointed Prime Minister by the Regency

Dec. 8, Anti-Semitic riots of students at Oradea Mare, Cluj, and Bucharest

Dec. 13, Court martial proceedings begun against university students arrested in anti-Semitic riots

1928

Jan. 17, Additional Agreement as to debt settlement signed with Austria

March 18, 60,000 peasants camped in the streets of the capital asking for dismissal of the Bratianu Ministry

March 21, Treaty of non-aggression and arbitration with Germany signed

March 28, Debt Agreement with France signed

May 6, Meeting of the National Peasant Party at Alba Julia representing the Opposition demanded representative government, local autonomy, and economic reform

May 8, Prince Carol in England asked to leave the country charged with plots to obtain throne of Rumania and using England as a base

June 21, Court at Bucharest gave Princess Helen a divorce from Prince Carol

July 26, Two rival parliaments met in Bucharest, the Parliament summoned by the Regency and a Parliament called by Julius Maniu, leader of Peasant Party

Nov. 3, Liberal Cabinet of Bratianu resigned

Nov. 9, Julius Maniu appointed Prime Minister

Nov. 10, Parliament dissolved

——, Financial Agreement with Germany signed

Nov. 11, Cabinet appointed: Prime Minister, Dr. Julius Maniu; Foreign Affairs, Professor George Mironescu; Interior, Dr. Alexander Vayda-Voevod; Agriculture, M. Ion Mihalache; Education, Professor Costakescu; Finance, M. M. Popovici; Justice, M. Nizescu; Public Health and Social Welfare, M. Sever Dan; Labor, M. Raducanu; Public Works and Communications, M. Halippa (*pro tem.*); War, General Cikoski; Industry and Commerce, M. Mirto; Fine Arts, Dr. Aurel Vlad; The Banat, M. Bocu; The Bukovina, M. Saveanu

Dec. 11, Supplementary Commercial Convention with Germany signed

Dec. 12, First free elections held gave National Peasant Party 333 seats in Lower House: Social Democrats, 8; German Party, 7; Liberals, 13; Magyars, 16; other parties, 10

Dec. 22, New Parliament opened

1929

Feb. 9, Russian Protocol to Pact of Paris for renunciation of war signed with Poland

Feb. 11, Loan of $101,000,000 signed at Bank of France arranged with 14 countries to stabilize the currency and for rehabilitation of country

March 1, Police arrested 200 persons at meeting of Communists

March 21, Treaties of arbitration and conciliation with the United States signed

March 28, New law passed as to oil rights and mining concessions

April 7, Communists and police in clash. Arrests made

May 21, Little Entente Treaties of alliance renewed (Czechoslovakia, Yugoslavia, and Rumania)

May 26 and 29, Concordat with the Vatican ratified

June 11, Commercial Treaty with Turkey signed

July 8, Colonel Auguste Stoica with others arrested charged with Fascist plot to overthrow the Government

Aug. 1, Protective tariff law passed reduced general level of duties

Aug. 6, Battle of striking miners in Lupeni, Transylvania with the police

Sept. 4, General Protocol and economic and technical Agreements with Poland signed

Sept. 21, Twenty-six of 40 persons arrested on July 8 acquitted, the others given light sentences

Oct. 5, Attempted assassination of Vaida Voivod, Minister of the Interior, by Communist youth, Goldenberg

Oct. 7, Death of G. V. Buzdugan, Chief Justice, and member of Council of Regency

Oct. 9, Constantin Saratzeanu elected Regent succeeding M. Buzdugan. The opposition of Premier Maniu prevented proposal of Queen Marie as candidate

Oct. 24, Arbitration and conciliation Treaty with Poland signed

Oct. 30, Two railroad Agreements with Poland signed

Nov. 11, March of 30,000 peasants celebrated anniversary of assumption of office of Prime Minister Maniu, leader of National Peasant Party

Dec. 7, Frontier traffic Agreement with Poland signed

Dec. 14–17, Election for Senate elected members gave National Peasant Party 131, Liberals 3, Magyars 9, Independents 1; in addition to 22 ex-officio senators

1930

Jan. 8, Contract signed with firm of engineers of New York City for construction of more than 50,000 houses and official buildings at expense of over $100,000,000 over period of from 15 to 20 years

Jan. 17, Debt funding Agreement with France signed

Feb. 6, Municipal elections a victory for the National Peasant Party

June 6, Prince Carol landed at Bucharest from military aëroplane. Met by Prince Nicholas. His return sponsored by the Peasant Party headed by Maniu and opposed by the aristocratic Liberals headed by V. Bratianu

June 7, Maniu Ministry resigned. Succeeded by M. Mironescu

June 8, Act of Parliament repealed Act of Jan., 1926 by which Carol was excluded from succession and proclaimed Carol King

June 9, Carol formally assumed kingship as Carol II

June 11, Maniu formed new Ministry

June 12, Carol II signed decree making his wife Helen, "Queen of Rumania"

June 27, Commercial Treaty with Czechoslovakia

July 8, Treaty of arbitration, conciliation, and judicial settlement with Belgium

July 21, Dr. Constantine Angelescu, Minister of the Interior, shot and wounded at Bucharest by student assassin

Aug. 6, Commercial Agreement with Great Britain signed

Aug. 20, Provisional Commercial Agreement with the United States signed

Aug. 29, Commercial Treaty with France signed

Oct. 6, Resignation of Premier Maniu because of ill health

Oct. 10, George Mironescu formed Cabinet (National Peasant Party)

Dec. 1, Students in anti-Semitic riots at Galatz

Dec. 23, Death of Vintila Bratianu, last of Bratianu "dynasty" called uncrowned kings of Rumania
Dec. 28, Liberal Party elected M. Duca as leader of Party to succeed Bratianu

PRINCES AND KING OF RUMANIA

1859. Alexander Couza; abdicated 1866
1881, Carol I, *b.* April 20, 1839, son of late Prince Karl of Hohenzollern-Sigmaringen. Proclaimed king March 26, 1881; married Nov. 15, 1869, to Princess Elizabeth von Wied, *b.* Dec. 29, 1843

In the event of the king remaining childless, the succession to the throne was settled by art. 83 of the Constitution, upon his elder brother, Prince Leopold of Hohenzollern-Sigmaringen, who renounced his rights in favor of his son, Prince Wilhelm, the act having been registered by the Senate in Oct., 1880. Prince Wilhelm renounced his rights to the throne on Nov. 22, 1888, in favor of his brother, Prince Ferdinand, *b.* Aug. 24, 1865, who by a decree of the king, dated March 18, 1889, was created "Prince of Rumania." Married Princess Marie, daughter of the Duke of Saxe-Coburg and Gotha, Jan. 10, 1893. Offspring: Carol, *b.* Oct. 15, 1893; Elizabeth *b.* Oct. 11, 1894; Marie, *b.* Jan. 8, 1900; Nicholas, *b.* Aug. 18, 1903; and Illana, *b.* Jan. 5, 1909

1930, Carol II, born Oct. 16, 1893, son of King Ferdinand and Queen Marie, married March 10, 1921, Princess Helen, daughter of the late Constantine, King of the Helenes (this marriage was dissolved June 21, 1928, when the Princess received the title of Princess of Rumania). On Dec. 28, 1925, Prince Carol renounced his right of succession to the Throne; this was confirmed by Act of Parliament on Jan. 4, 1926, when his son, Prince Mihai, was declared Heir to the Throne. On March 24, Prince Carol assumed the name of Carol Caraiman. On June 7, 1930, he returned to Rumania and was proclaimed King in virtue of an Act of Parliament on June 8, 1930

Son of the King, Prince Mihai (Michael), born Oct. 25, 1921, proclaimed King in virtue of his father's renunciation of the succession on the death of his grandfather, King Ferdinand, July 20, 1927, under a Regency. Ceased to be King on his father's accession, June 8, 1930, when he received the title of Prince of Alba Julia

RUSSIA

Russia, Union of Socialist Soviet Republics, occupies eastern Europe and nearly half of the continent. The Union includes also Siberia, and other regions in Asia (*see also* Russia in Asia, p. 890). The former Russian Empire had total area of 8,764,586 square miles, European Russia, 1,867,737 square miles as compared with 8,241,921 square miles (1927), the diminution in territory due to separation of Finland after the revolution of 1917, and establishment of separate States of Estonia, Latvia, Lithuania, and Poland, the cession of Kars to Turkey, and occupation of Bessarabia by Rumania.

The population of January 1, 1914, was estimated as follows by the Central Statistical Committee on the basis of the census of 1897 and the yearly increase of the population. ("Statesman's Year-Book, 1916.")

European Russia	128,864,300
Poland	12,247,600
Caucasus	12,921,700
Siberia	10,000,700
Central Asian Provinces	11,103,500
Finland	3,241,000
Total Russian Empire	178,378,800

The total area of the Soviet Union in 1927 was given as 21,352,572 sq. kilometers, or 8,241,991 square miles, with a population of 147,013,609, made up as follows (capitals in brackets):—

CONSTITUENT REPUBLICS OF THE UNION	AREA IN SQ. MILES (JAN. 1, 1927)	TOTAL POPULATION (DEC. 17, 1926)	URBAN POPULATION (DEC. 17, 1926)	RURAL POPULATION (DEC. 17, 1926)
R.S.F.S.R. (Moscow)	7,626,717	100,857,985	17,440,478	83,417,507
White Russia (Minsk)	48,751	4,983,884	848,557	4,135,327
Ukraine (Kharkov)	174,201	29,020,304	5,374,047	23,646,257
Transcaucasia (Tiflis)	71,255	5,850,692	1,407,469	4,443,223
Turkmenistan (Polterask)	189,603	1,030,549	126,557	903,992
Uzbekistan (Tashkent)	74,786	4,442,795	1,059,960	3,382,835
Tajikistan (Stalinabad)	56,608	827,400	40,200	787,200
Total in U.S.S.R.	8,241,921	147,013,609	26,297,268	120,716,341

In Transcaucasia, Georgia has 2,660,963 inhabitants; Armenia, 876,557; and Azerbaijan, 2,313,172.
On April 1, 1929, the total population of the U.S.S.R. was estimated as follows—urban, 29,-300,000; rural, 125,500,000; total, 154,800,000.

The R.S.F.S.R. contains 11 autonomous Republics and 12 autonomous regions. The Ukraine contains 1 autonomous Republic (Moldavia). The 11 autonomous Republics of the R.S.F.S.R. are shown as follows (the capitals are in brackets):—

AUTONOMOUS REPUBLICS

Bashkir (Ufa), March 24, 1919	Crimean (Simferopol), October 18, 1921	German Republic on the Volga (Pokrovsk), July 19, 1923
Tartar (Kazan), May 27, 1920	Yakutsk (Yakutsk), April 20, 1922	Buriat-Mongol (Verkhnendinsk), June 4, 1923
Kirghiz (Frunze), February, 1926	Karelian (Petrosavodsk), July 27, 1923	
Dagestan (Makhach-Kala), Jan. 20, 1921	Chuvash (Cheboksara), April 21, 1925	Kazak (Kzyl-Ozda), October 14, 1924

On March 12, 1917, a revolution broke out in Russia as a result of which the Emperor Nicholas II abdicated March 15. A Provisional Government set up by the Duma under Prince George E. Lvov, who was succeeded by Alexander Kerensky Aug. 6, was overthrown Nov. 7 when the Military Revolutionary Committee of the Petrograd Soviet seized the Government.

The Constitution of the new State was adopted at the fifth All-Russian Congress of Soviets, on July 10, 1918, and additions or alterations were made at subsequent Soviet Congresses (December, 1920–23). On December 30, 1922, delegates from the four principal Soviet Republics met at Moscow and concluded a Treaty of Union, setting up a Union of Socialist Soviet Republics, covering Russia (R.S.F.S.R.), Ukraine (U.S.S.R.), White Russia (W.R.S.S.R.), and the Transcaucasian Federation (T.S.F.S.R.). In September, 1924, the Uzbek S.S.R. and the Turcoman S.S.R. were formed and joined the union. On December 5, 1929, the seventh Republic, that of Tajikistan was formed. The Constitution of the Union was ratified by the Second Union Congress of Soviets, which met in January and February, 1924.

The Government of the Union consists of a Union Central Executive Committee and a Union Council of People's Commissaries. The former is elected by the Union Congress of Soviets, the supreme authority of the Union, and between Congresses is the sovereign legislative, administrative, and judicial authority of the Union. It is convened three times a year, and consists of two chambers—the Union Council, consisting of 450 members elected on the principle of proportional representation of the six constituent Republics, and the Council of Nationalities of 135 members, elected on the basis of 5 members for every independent and autonomous republic, and 1 member for every autonomous region. All legislation must be adopted by both chambers. The Presidium, or Standing Committee, which transacts current business, is composed of 27 members, 9 from each chamber and 9 elected at a joint meeting.

Chairmen of the Union Central Executive Committee: MM. Kalinin (R.S.F.S.R.), Petrovsky (Ukraine), Cherviakov (White Russia), Musabekov (Transcaucasia), Aitakov (Turcoman S.S. Republic), Faizula-Khodzhaev (Uzbek S.S. Republic).

376 to 1809

A.D. 376, Russia invaded by the Huns
862, Ruric the Norman or Varangian, arrives at Novgorod (or New City), and becomes Grand Duke [anniversary kept Sept. 20, 1862]
907, Oleg successfully invades the Greek Empire
About 955, Baptism of Olga, widow of Duke Igor, at Constantinople
988, Vladimir the Great marries Anne, sister of the Emperor Basil II, and is baptized

About 1223, The Golden Horde of Tartars conquer a large part of Russia
1237, The Grand Duke Jurie killed in battle
1241, Alexander Newski defeats the invading Danes
1242, The Tartars establish the empire of the Khan of Kaptschak, and exercise great influence in Russia
1252, He is made Grand Duke of Russia by the Tartars
1300, Moscow made the capital
1383, Tartar war, 1380; Moscow burnt
1395, Tamerlane invades Russia, but retires
1462, Accession of Ivan III the Great—able and despotic, founds the present monarchy
1475, Ivan introduces fire-arms and cannon into Russia
1479, Great invasion of the Tartars; consternation of Ivan
1481, His general Svenigorod annihilates their power
1506–23, War with Poland
1553, The English "Russian company" established
1554, Richard Chancellor sent to open the trade
——, Discovery of Siberia
1568, The royal body-guard (the Strelitz) established
1579, Ivan solicits the hand of Queen Elizabeth of England
1598, Murder of Feodor I, last of the race of Ruric, which had governed Russia for 700 years
1606, The imposition of Demetrius. Otrefief, a monk, pretended to be Demetrius the son of Ivan, Czar of Muscovy, whom the usurper Boris had put to death; he maintained that another child had been substituted in his place: he was supported by Poland; his success led the Russians to invite him to the throne, and deliver into his hands, Feodor, the reigning Czar, and all his family: his imposition discovered he was assassinated in his palace, 1606. Matins of Moscow, May 29
1613, Michael Fedorovitz, of the house of Romanoff, ascends the throne
1617, Finland ceded to Sweden
1654, Russian victories in Poland
1671, Subjugation of the Cossacks
1682, Reign of Ivan and Peter I or the Great
1689, Peter sole sovereign
1697, He visits Holland and England, and works in the dockyard at Deptford
1698, Recalled by a conspiracy of the Strelitz, which he cruelly revenges; 2,000 tortured and slain; he beheads many with his own hand
1700, The Russians begin their new year from Jan. 1 (but retain the old style)
Nov. 30, 1700, War with Sweden; Peter totally defeated by Charles XII at Narva
May 27, 1703, Peter founds St. Petersburg as a new capital
1704, The Strelitz abolished
July 8, 1709, Charles XII totally defeated by Peter at Pultowa, and flees to Turkey
——, 14,000 Swedish prisoners sent to Siberia
1711, War with Turkey: Peter and his army cross the Pruth, and are surrounded by the Turks; they escape by the energy of the Empress Catherine, who obtains a truce July 21
April 16, 1712, Peace of Constantinople ended war
1715, Esthonia, Livonia, and a large part of Finland added to the Empire
——, Peter visits Germany, Holland, and France
1718, The Jesuits expelled
——, Conspiracy and mysterious death of Prince Alexis

1730, Peter II (last of the Romanoffs deposed, and the crown given to Anne of Courland

1741, Elizabeth, daughter of Peter I, reigns, in prejudice of Ivan VI, an infant, who is imprisoned for life

1762, Peter III, dethroned and murdered, succeeded by Catherine his wife

1764, Ivan VI, the rightful heir, till now immured, put to death

July 10, 1774, Treaty of Kutschouc Kainardji; independence of the Crimea and freedom of Black sea

1769–84, Successful invasions of the Crimea

1775, Rebellion of the Cossacks, 1774; suppressed

1795, Dismemberment of Poland; commenced by Catherine (see Poland), 1772; completed

1796, Catherine gives her subjects a new code of laws; abolishes torture in punishing criminals; and dies

——, Unsuccessful war with Persia

1798, Russian treaty with Austria and England

1799, Suwarrow, with an army joins the Austrians, and checks the French in Italy

March 24, 1801, Mental derangement of Paul, 1800; murdered

May, 1801, Alexander I, makes peace with England

April 11, 1805, He joins the coalition against France

Dec. 2, 1805, Allies defeated at Austerlitz

July 7, 1807, Treaty of Tilsit with France

Sept. 26, 1809, Russians defeated by the Turks, near Silistria

1812

June 22, War with France

Aug. 17, The Russians defeated at Smolensko; and at the Borodino, Sept. 7

Oct. 15, Moscow burnt by the Russians, Sept. 14; retreat of the French begins

1813 to 1825

Oct., 1813, Alexander present at the battle of Leipsic; entered Paris, March, 1814

1815, Forms the Holy Alliance

Jan. 26, 1822, The Grand Duke Constantine renounces the right of succession

1825, Death of Alexander, Dec. 1; Pestal's conspiracy against Nicholas I; insurrection of troops at Moscow; suppressed, Dec. 26–29

1826

Sept. 3, Nicholas crowned at Moscow

Sept. 4, Treaty with Turkey by which Russia secured the navigation of the Black Sea, recognition of the Danubian principalities, &c.

Sept. 28, War against Persia

1828 to 1849

Feb. 22, 1828, Peace between Russia and Persia

April 26, 1828, War between Russia and the Ottoman Porte declared (see Turkey)

Sept. 14, 1829, Peace of Adrianople

Nov. 29, 1830, The war for the independence of Poland against Russia (see Poland)

Jan., 1840, Failure of the expedition against Khiva

July 15, 1840, Treaty of London (see Syria)

[For the participation of Russia in the Hungarian war of 1848–9, see Hungary]

Nov. 5, 1849, Russia demands the expulsion of the Hungarian and Polish refugees from Turkey (see Turkey)

1850

Jan., They are sent to Konieh, in Asia Minor

Jan. 6, Conspiracy against the Emperor detected

Feb., Harbor of Sebastopol completed

Aug., The Emperor decrees seven men in each thousand of the population of Western Russia to be enrolled in the army, giving a total increase of 180,000 soldiers

1851

St. Petersburg and Moscow railway begun

1852

May 8, The Czar visits Vienna

1853

Feb., Concentrates forces on frontiers of Turkey

March, Origin of the Russo-Turkish war (see s.v.)

Sept. 24, Conference between the Emperors of Russia and Austria at Olmutz

Oct. 2, And King of Prussia at Warsaw

1854

Feb., Interview of Mr. J. Sturge and other Quakers with the Czar to obtain peace

March 5, Northern provinces in a state of siege

April 23, The Czar's manifesto; he will combat only for the faith and Christianity

1855

March 2, Death of the Czar Nicholas, and accession of Alexander II; no change of policy

Nov. 3, Most extensive levy ordered by the Czar (at Nicolaieff)

Nov. 10, He visits his army at Sebastopol

1856

Feb. 1, Death of Prince Ivan Paskiewitsch, aged 74

March 30, Treaty of Peace at Paris

April 29, Alexander Gortschakoff, Foreign Minister and Chancellor

May 27, Amnesty granted to the Poles; five political offenders, &c.

Sept. 2, Manifesto on account of the English and French interference in the affairs of Naples

——, St. Petersburg and Warsaw railway begun by government, 1851; ceded to Great Russian railway company (about 335 miles, the half completed)

Sept. 7, Alexander II crowned at Moscow

1858

July 2, Partial emancipation of the serfs on the imperial domains

Aug., A Russian naval station established at Villa Franca, on the Mediterranean, creates some political excitement

1859

Jan. 12, New commercial treaty with Great Britain

May 27, Russia reproves the warlike movements of the German Confederation during the Italian war

1860

Feb. 13, The Czar protests against the recognition of the sovereignty of peoples

Oct. 20–25, Fruitless meetings of Emperors of Russia, Austria, and Regent of Prussia at Warsaw

1861

March 3, Decree for the total emancipation of the serfs (23,000,000) throughout the Empire in two years (Feb. 19)

Feb.–April, Demonstrations and repression in Poland. *See* Poland

May and June, Disturbances in South Russia, caused by an impostor asserting himself to be a descendant of Peter III

May 14, Death of Prince Michael Gortschakoff, Governor of Poland

Oct. 6–9, Student riots at the University of St. Petersburg, which is closed: reopened, Oct. 24

Nov., The nobles sign a petition for a political constitution

1862

Jan. 26, Increased privileges granted to the Jews

March 20, Death of Nesselrode, the Chancellor of the Empire

June, Alarming increase of fires at St. Petersburg and Moscow; the government suppresses various educational institutions

Sept. 20, 1,000th anniversary of the foundation of the Russian monarchy at Novgorod, celebrated

Oct. 14, Reorganization of the departments of justice decreed; juries to be employed in trials, &c.

Nov. 26, Trade tax bill introduced, admitting foreigners to merchants' guilds, &c.

1863

Jan. 22–24, Insurrection in Poland
[For events, *see* Poland]

March 3, Termination of serfdom

1864

Jan. 13, Provincial institutions established throughout Russia

March 31, Great victory over the Oubykhs in the Caucasus; emigration of the Caucasian tribes into Turkey, April; submission of the Aïbgas; the war declared to be at an end, June 2

Sept. 28, The Czarevitch betrothed to the Princess Dagmar of Denmark

Dec., Serfdom abolished in the Trans-Caucasian provinces: new judicial system promulgated

1865

Jan. 24, Russian nobles request the Emperor to establish two houses of representatives [declined]

Feb. 14, New province, "Turkestan," in central Asia, created

April 24, The Czarevitch Nicholas dies at Nice

1866

Jan. and Feb., Rupture with the Pope on account of Russian severity to Polish clergy

Aug. 8, Inauguration of trial by jury in Russia

Sept. 15, Karakozow attempts to assassinate the Czar, April 16; after long investigation into the origin of the plot, he is executed

Nov., War with Bokhara; conflicts with varying results; Russians advance in May *et seq.*; ended

Nov. 9, Marriage of Prince Alexander, heir to the crown, to Princess Dagmar of Denmark

Nov. 11, Emancipation of many state serfs in Poland

1867

Jan. 1, Three decrees for abolishing the remains of Polish nationality

May 5, Congress of Slavonian deputies at Moscow

May 15, Russian America sold to the United States for 7,000,000 dollars, by treaty, March 13; ratified

May 29, Amnesty in favor of the Poles

June 6, The Czar escapes assassination by Berezowski, a Pole

July 7, Decree for the use of the Russian language in the Baltic provinces

Aug. 2, A Romanist college to replace the authority of the Pope, established at St. Petersburg

1868

Feb. 29, The separate interior government in Poland suppressed

May 26, Samarcand taken by Kaufmann

July, Polish language interdicted in public places in Poland

1869

Jan. 13, The *Government Messenger*, official journal, published at St. Petersburg

1870

Jan., Socialist secret conspiracy among the students, headed by Sergius Netschajew, detected; the informer assassinated

July, Russia neutral in the Franco-Prussian war

Sept. 27, Fruitless visit of M. Thiers at St. Petersburg on behalf of the French Government

Oct. 31, Diplomatic circular of Prince Gortschakoff, Foreign Minister, repudiating the clauses of the treaty of March 30, 1856, respecting the Black Sea; received by Earl Granville, Nov. 9, who replies, maintaining the force of the treaty, Nov. 10

Nov. 16, Vigorous protest of British and Austrian Governments

About Nov. 16, Decree for forming military reserves

Nov. 20, Conciliatory despatch from Prince Gortschakoff to Earl Granville, agreeing to a conference for revision of the treaty of 1856

Nov. 28, Firm courteous despatch from Earl Granville, consenting to a conference which shall "assemble without any foregone conclusion"

Dec. 7, The other Powers agree to a conference

1871

Jan., Reorganization of the army ordered

Jan. 17, The conference meets in London

March 13, The Black Sea clauses abrogated (The conference met in London Jan. 17, 1871, and a treaty was signed by which the neutralization of the sea was abrogated; but it was agreed by a special protocol, that no nation shall liberate itself from the obligations of a treaty without the consent of the others who signed it), by treaty, signed

About April, Schamyl, the Circassian chief, dies

Nov., Telegraph between St. Petersburg and Nagasaki, Japan, completed

1872

June 11, 200th anniversary of the birth of Peter the Great, May 30, 1672 (O.S.), solemnly observed by the court and nation

Autumn, Great Russian Encyclopædia undertaken by Prof. Beresina

Dec., Reconnoitering expedition to Khiva; defeat of Gen. Markosoff announced

1873

Jan. 13, Diplomatic visit of Count Schouvaloff to London respecting this; Russian concessions reported satisfactory

March, Expeditions against Khiva start

June 10, Khiva surrenders; a rebellion suppressed, July

Dec., New treaty with Bokhara, published

1874

Jan. 23, Marriage of the Grand Duchess Marie with the Duke of Edinburgh

Feb. 13, Visit of the Emperor of Austria at St. Petersburg; the Czar in proposing his health, says, "In the friendship which binds us and also the Emperor William and the Queen Victoria, I see a most sure guarantee of peace," Feb. 15

1875

Sept. 4–Oct., War with Khokand

Nov., Commercial panic through failure of Dr. Strousberg, a German railway speculator, at Moscow, Prague, and Berlin

1876

Jan. 29, Baltic provinces (formerly a provincial federation with a governor), incorporated with the Empire under the Ministry of the Interior, on the death of the Governor Bagration

Feb. 29, Khokand, formally annexed (as Ferghana)

April, Prosecution of a sect "White Doves"

Nov. 10, The Czar, in an address at Moscow, says that if sufficient guarantees are not given by Turkey, he will act independently

Nov. 14, Dr. Strousberg and others tried for fraud, &c., Nov.; he is sentenced to banishment

About Nov. 14, Enthusiasm for Bulgarians; partial mobilization of the army ordered

Nov. 19, Internal loan of 10 million roubles

1877

April 24, Great enthusiasm for Bulgarians; war declared, and begun

See Turkey; and Russo-Turkish War, 1877

About Oct. 31, Great trial of Nihilists for revolutionary propagandism, begun

Nov. 12, Russian loan of 15,000,000*l.* at 5%

Dec., Ill-feeling against Bulgarians

1878

About Feb. 9, Nihilist trial ended; about 160 sentenced to hard labor; about 90 acquitted

March 3, Treaty of peace with Turkey signed at San Stefano; Europe dissatisfied

June, Public depression: feeling against Bulgarians; desire to get quit of the Eastern question

June 13, Conference at Berlin (*see s.v.*) meets June 13; treaty signed

Aug., General Kaufmann's advance on the Oxus to occupy Balkh; reported

Aug. 5, Nihilists tried and condemned at Odessa

Aug. 16, General disaffection to the government; General De Mesentzoff, Chief of Police, assassinated in the street in St. Petersburg

Aug. 29, 30, 31, New 5% loan (300,000,000 roubles) issued on bonds

End of Aug., Ukase decreeing state offenses to be punished by military law

Dec., Students at a college in St. Petersburg present an address to the Czarevitch complaining of grievances, Dec. 11; they are attacked and punished by the police and cossacks, Dec. 12; they issue an address soon after

1879

Feb. 21 or 22, Prince Demetrius Krapotkine, Governor, assassinated

April 14, Attempted assassination of the Czar by Alexander Solovieff, with a revolver

April, The poll tax abolished by ukase

April 17, Ukase establishing martial law in the provinces of St. Petersburg, Moscow, Kieff, Odessa, and Warsaw, dated

June 9, Solovieff condemned, June 7; executed

May–Aug., Executions of Nihilists at Kieff and Odessa

About Aug. 13, Gen. Lazareff, commander of expedition against the Tekké Turkomans, dies at Tchat

Aug. 28 (O.S.), Sept. 9, Gen. Lomakine succeeds in command; severe battle at Geok Tepe or Dengli Tepè; Russians said to be victorious, yet retreat with heavy loss

Sept. 25, Tergukasoff succeeds Lomakine in command

Nov. 27, 28, Leon Mirsky condemned to death for attempted assassination of Gen. Drentelen

Dec. 1, Attempted assassination of the Czar, by undermining railway train near Moscow

Dec. 4, Proclamation of the executive revolutionary committee justifying the attempted assassination on Dec. 1.

Dec. 12, Plot to blow up the Winter Palace, St. Petersburg, discovered

1880

Feb. 17, Explosion in a guard-room filled with dynamite and gun-cotton under the dining-room of the Winter Palace, St. Petersburg; the Czar and family escape through being a little late for dinner; 11 soldiers killed; 47 wounded

About Feb. 20, Hartmann, owner of a house near the explosion, arrested at Paris

Feb. 24, Panic at St. Petersburg; ukase issued; appointing supreme executive commission, Gen. Loris Melikoff, president, with extensive powers

March, Extradition of Hartmann requested by Russia; declined

March 2, Twenty-fifth anniversary of the Czar's accession celebrated at St. Petersburg

About March 6, Hartmann expelled from France; goes to England; Prince Orloff, Ambassador, quits France

May, Nihilist trials at St. Petersburg; sentences to death and imprisonment (Dr. Weimar and others); commuted

June 3, Death of the Empress after a long illness

About Aug. 7, 21 extreme Nihilists convicted at Kieff (capital sentences remitted)

Aug. 18, Ukase of Feb. 24 superseded; Melikoff, who had governed well, appointed Minister of the Interior, with charge of the police

Oct. 25 *et seq.*, Count Loris Melikoff's scheme for administrative reform sanctioned by the Czar; announced Oct. 3; put into action

Nov. 10, Great Nihilist trial at St. Petersburg for assassinations, explosion at Winter Palace, &c.; sentences, Kviatofski and 4 others condemned to death: 8 men and 3 women to imprisonment

Nov. 16, Kviatofski and Priessnakoff hanged

Dec. 24, Gen. Skobeleff's expedition into Central Asia

1881

Jan. 14, Severe conflicts with the Tekké Turkomans

Jan. 24, Geok Tepé besieged; taken

March 13, 2 P.M., Assassination of the Czar Alexander II by explosion of a bomb; assassin himself killed; Risakoff seized

March 16, Circular of the new Czar Alexander III to foreign powers; he will aim at moral and material development of Russia, and a pacific foreign policy

March 22, Manifesto from the Nihilist executive committee to the Czar offering peace, if an amnesty with a legislative assembly to be elected by universal suffrage, free press, &c., be granted

March 23, Sophie Peroffskaja, and other Nihilists, arrested

About March 31, A representative council for St. Petersburg elected

April 8, 9, Trial of Risakoff, Sophie Peroffskaja, Jelaboff, Jessie Heljmann, Kibaichick, and Michailoff, all condemned to death

April 9, The Tekkés submit; maraudings cease; object of Skobeleff's expedition accomplished

April 15, Risakoff and others hanged; Heljmann (*enceinte*) reprieved

About May 4, Changes in ministerial offices; tendency to reduce autocracy of the Czar announced

Early May, Ukase supplementary to that of Feb. 19, 1861, for emancipating serfs, remitting payments to many peasant proprietors; announced

May 11, Reactionary proclamations in favor of autocracy (April 29); resignation of count Loris Melikoff and other liberal ministers May 13

May 23, General Ignatieff, chief minister, issues manifesto, declaring for suppression of rebellion, and promising reforms; manifesto from Nihilists offering peace if reforms be granted

Dec. 22, Treaty with Persia signed

1882

March, Nihilist trials at St. Petersburg; 10 sentenced to death, Feb. 28; commuted to penal servitude (except Suchanoff, to be shot)

April 3, Gen. Strelnikoff, public prosecutor, assassinated at Odessa by two students, March 30; executed

About April 9, Retirement of the Chancellor and Foreign Minister, Gortschakoff (his policy war-like); succeeded by his assistant De Giers

About April 15, Mine discovered under Moscow Cathedral; 80 workmen arrested

May 16, General Kaufmann died, aged 64

Beginning June, Decree for the gradual abolition of the poll tax (imposed by Peter the Great)

About June 12, Ignatieff resigns; succeeded by Count Tolstoy

July 7, Death of General Scobeleff, hero of Plevna

——, Revival of the Russian navy determined on

1883

March 11, Death of Prince Gortschakoff, aged 85

About March 20, Arrest of 200 persons at St. Petersburg

April 19, Trial of Nihilists at St. Petersburg

May 27, The Emperor and Empress crowned with great ceremony at Moscow

May 27, Patriotic and pacific manifesto, and amnesty; and popular festival June 2

June 8, Poll tax abolished for the poorest, reduced for others (Jan. 1, 1884)

Night of Dec. 28–29, Lieut. Sudeikin, chief of secret police, and his nephew, M. Sadovsky, assassinated at St. Petersburg

1884

Jan. 9, 37 students at Moscow arrested announced

Jan. 25, Loyal address of the nobles to the Czar, advocating union of nobles and peasantry

Feb. 14, Surrender of Merv to Russia, effected by General Komaroff, announced

May 6, Convention with Persia for cession of Sarakhs (threatening to Afghanistan), reported

May 18, The majority of the Czarevitch (aged 16) declared

July 1, Death of General Todleben, born 1818

Sept.–Oct., The letters of "Stepniak" and others expose the cruel, dishonest, and unscrupulous conduct of government officials in prohibiting the diffusion of knowledge and literature; proposed united opposition of the nobility and peasantry

Oct. 11, 14 Nihilists (including 6 officers and 3 women, one, Mary F. Figner) convicted by secret court martial; 8 sentenced to death at St. Petersburg; two men executed, Oct. 18

1885

Feb., Mission of M. Lessar, engineer-diplomatist to London respecting central Asian boundaries

Feb., Ship canal from St. Petersburg to Cronstadt completed; opened May 27

Feb., Russians advance to about 90 miles from Herat, and hold Zulfikar pass

March 1, Three courses before them: to retire; to remain and negotiate; to make war

(It was mainly through the remonstrances of General Lumsden a collision was avoided)

March 16 or 17, Arrangement that no further advance on the "debated or debatable ground" be made by Russians or Afghans (since termed a "solemn covenant")

May 4 *et seq.*, British Government announce agreement to arbitration (by Denmark)

The Russian General Komaroff, near the Kushk and Murghab rivers, commands the Afghans to retire; on their refusal, attacks them at Aktapa, near Penjdeh; defeats them with much slaughter, and captures this important strategical position with artillery and stores; many Afghans perish in the retreat through exposure March 30, 53 Russians killed and wounded; (Sir Peter Lumsden reports the attack on the Afghans to have been unprovoked April 14)

May, British Government statement: new agreement with Russia; arbitration respecting fight on March 30 accepted May 4; Denmark accepts work of arbitration

May 30, Agreement on delimitation settled by Earl Granville and Earl of Kimberley, with MM. de Staal and Lessar; approval reported

Sept. 10, The Afghan boundary question settled

1886

April, Discovery of plot against the Czar; arrest of military officers and others

July, Russia violates Treaty of Berlin by declaring Batoum not to be a free port

Sept.–Dec., Russian interference in Bulgaria (*see s.v.*)

1887

March, Plot against the Czar; students with dynamite and other explosives, detected March 13; 200 arrested

May 16, Three plotters executed March 31; seven political offenders sentenced to death, the rest to various terms of imprisonment, May 1; more arrests about May 18; five executed

May 18, Prince Nicholas, the Czarevitch, made chief Ataman (Hetman) of all the Cossacks at Novo-Tcherkask

Nov., Statement in the *Cologne Gazette* of the existence of forged letters purporting to come from Prince Bismarck (*see* Germany)

Dec., Baron Hirsch's present of 2,000,000*l.* for the establishment of primary Jewish schools in Russia, accepted by the Czar; the money to be paid into the bank of England, trustees, Barons Rothschild and Henry de Worms, announced Nov.; said to be premature

Nov.–Dec., Movement of troops on the Galacian border causes excitement in Berlin and Vienna

Dec. 15, *Invalide Russe*, a government organ, declares that Russia desires peace but is prepared for war

Nov.–Dec., The stringent restrictions on the studies of the universities lead to much insubordination among the students, and severe punishment; the universities of Moscow, St. Petersburg, Odessa, and many other academical institutions closed; undergraduate class in a state of rebellion

1888

Feb., Moscow and other universities re-opened

Feb.–March, For Prince Ferdinand's position (*see* Bulgaria)

March, The highest courts of law decide against the claim of Prince Hohenlohe to inherit the vast Wittgenstein estates in Lithuania, as a foreigner (in accordance with the ukase, March 14, 1887)

May, Attempted assassination of the Czar by Lieut. Timofeieff (mad?)

July 27, Ninth centenary of the introduction of Christianity celebrated at Kieff

May, Central Asian (or Transcaspian) railway opened; promoted by General Anhenkoff

Oct. 29, Near Borki station in S. Russia, the engine of the imperial train (with the Czar) ran off the line with four carriages (weak rails); 21 persons killed, the Czar slightly injured

Dec., Agreement for 20,000,000*l.* loan signed at St. Petersburg, Nov. 18; chiefly taken up by the French

1889

Feb., The grand council disapproves of the administrative changes proposed by Count Tolstoi substituting centralization for local self-government which, however, are approved by the Czar (1888); the *Zemstro*, established about 1864, being virtually abolished

——, Loan of 700,000,000 francs concluded with the Rothschilds and other bankers for the conversion of 5% loans into 4%

——, Captain Atchinoff, with a company of S. Cossacks (145 men with muskets and guns, also priests, women and children), evading French and Italian cruisers, landed at Tadjourah, in the bay of Obock, near the French settlement, on the Red Sea, on Jan. 18, professing to combine missionary and commercial enterprize in Abyssinia. He took possession of a fort at Sagallo, and hoisted the Russian flag. After useless negotiation, the French Admiral Olry on Feb. 18 bombarded the fort, killing 6 Russians; the party then surrendered and were eventually conveyed to Russia. The French Government virtually apologized for the precipitate conduct of the Admiral

May 18, The Czarevitch, aged 21, appointed to military and political office

July, Aug., M. Dournovo, Minister of the Interior, continues Count Tolstoy's reactionary policy

1890

Jan. 11, Capt. Solotouchine, chief of the Moscow secret police, assassinated by a female Nihilist, who commits suicide

Feb., Ukase for a conversion loan of 90,000,000 roubles, taken up, especially in France

——, Count Tolstoy's administrative changes carried into effect, together with increased Russification of the German provinces and Finland

Feb., March, Strong demonstrations of students of Moscow, St. Petersburg, Kieff, Charkoff, and other universities and schools, demanding changes; many arrests and police supervision

March 31, The Czar releases about 60 imprisoned soldiers. The man chosen to assassinate the Czar by lot, commits suicide, leaving a letter incriminating associates; many arrests, reported

April, The Czar threatened (by letter, signed Maria Tshebrikova, a popular writer on education, &c.), for continuing to suppress liberty, March 5; she is arrested, about March 10; transported to the Caucasus

April 7, Inquiry by special commission; some students expelled and others set at liberty, at St. Petersburg, &c.; order restored

July, Revival of severe edict against the Jews reported

Nov., A monster literary protest against the persecution of the Jews in preparation, headed by Count Leo Tolstoy; publication forbidden by the government

Dec. 24, Gregory Petrovitch Danilesky, historian and novelist, dies

1891

End of Feb., Arrest of Dedajeff, charged with the murder of Col. Sudeikin in 1883 (*see above*), and other Nihilists, at Kostroma

April, New law for the legitimatizing of bastards promulgated

July, Count Tolstoy's administrative changes relative to the peasantry effected at St. Petersburg and other provinces

About Aug. 11, Failure of crops; exportation of grain (especially rye) forbidden (from Aug. 27); relief works ordered and grants of money

Aug. 16, The Czarevitch returns to Moscow

[He visited Vienna, Nov. 6; at Athens, Nov. 12; at Cairo, Nov. 23; at Bombay, Dec. 23, 1890; received by the Viceroy at Calcutta, Jan. 26–28, 1891; at Madras, Feb. 6; Ceylon, Feb. 13; Bankok, Siam, March 26; in China, Japan, April, May; at Otsu, in Japan, he was wounded by a fanatical officer in a theater, May 11, 1891; Siberia, June, July, 1891.]

Aug., Disputes with Great Britain respecting the Pamir ridge.

About Sept. 2 *et seq.*, Great distress through famine in certain districts of the Volga and other places

Sept. 27, Ivan Alexandrovitch Gontcharoff, novelist, aged 80, dies

Oct., New 3% loan for 500,000,000 francs (for railways) negotiated in Paris, about Sept. 17; opposed in Berlin, about Sept. 28; taken up well

——, In order to relieve famine, the Czar forbids all state balls and festivities; great economy adopted by all classes

——, The famine very severe in the central and eastern provinces

Nov. 22, Decree issued prohibiting the exportation of wheat and all its products

Dec., The Czarevitch appointed president of a committee to deal with the effects of the famine by means of private charity, the Ministry, the Holy Synod, and others, Dec. 5; public relief works established

1892

Jan. 24, The Grand Duke Constantine (brother of the Czar, Alexander II), sometime Viceroy of Poland, removed on suspicion of favoring the Poles, 1886; dies, aged 64

March 21 *et seq.*, Stoppage of the (Baron) Günzburg bank of St. Petersburg and Paris, March 15 *et seq.*; liquidation arranged, reported

March 25, Russian Jewish emigrants prohibited from entering Germany

April 4, Large supplies of American wheat, flour, and provisions transmitted for the relief of the famine by the citizens of Philadelphia

Society of Friends famine fund: 35,989*l.* received up to May 1.

June 13, About 125,370,500 roubles expended in relief of the suffers by famine, Dec. 1891–May, 1892; reported

June 21, Removal of the restrictions on the exportation of grain, except rye; of rye, Aug. 23

Nov. 12, Tour of the Czarevitch in Greece, &c.; he is received by the Emperor at Vienna; arrives at the Caucasus, about Nov. 14

Autumn, "Darkest Russia," a periodical respecting persecution, published throughout the world

Nov. 4–Dec. 3, Trial of 154 rioters against cholera regulations (at Saratoff, &c., July 10); 23 sentenced to death, 56 to imprisonment

Dec. 30, 1892, Cholera rioters at Tashkend, in July; 20 at Astrakhan sentenced to death; others to imprisonment; severe sentences mitigated Jan., Feb., 1893

1893

Jan. 28, The Czarevitch warmly received at Berlin

About Feb. 1, Rescript of the Czar for expediting the construction of the Siberian railway

March 10, New internal loan, 100 millions of roubles, at 4½% for 81 years

Aug., Tariff war; duties on German imports raised; German reprisals; mutual injury

Oct. 13, A Russian squadron (5 vessels) under Admiral Avellan arrive at Toulon

Oct. 29, The squadron leaves Toulon

Nov. 9, Death of M. Tschaikowsky, musical composer

1894

Jan. 3, Religious persecution in Lithuania

Feb. 10, Commercial treaty with Germany for 10 years, signed; comes into force March 20

May, Conversion of the 5% loans continued

Decree of the Czar depriving his ministers and other officials of the power of appointing or dismissing their subordinates; and reëstablishing an imperial committee of control, subject to himself; to commence Nov. 13

Sept. 29, Kwiatkowski, an officer, sentenced at Kieff to penal servitude for life for stealing official documents, and 26 others to varying terms of penal servitude; reported

Sept. 30, Serious illness of the Czar; he leaves for the Crimea, with the Czarina and family

Oct. 22, The Princess Alix of Hesse is betrothed to the Czarevitch; received by the Czar

Nov. 1, Death of the Czar, Alexander III, at Livadia, aged 49

——, Accession of Nicholas II

Nov. 9, The Czar assures foreign powers, in a circular, of his adherence to his father's pacific policy

Nov. 20, Death of Anton Rubinstein, aged 65, pianist and composer, at Peterhof

Nov. 26, Marriage of the Czar to Princess Alix (Alexandra) of Hesse, at St. Petersburg

——, Imperial manifesto of clemency relating to political offenses, debts to the crown, &c.

Dec. 13, New loan of 100,000,000 roubles at 3½% (issued at 94½%, redeemable at par in 81 years), Dec. 6; thoroughly taken up

1895

Jan. 26, Death of M. de Giers, aged 74, Minister of Foreign Affairs; at St. Petersburg

Jan. 29, 30, The Czar, to the representatives of 120,-000,000 of his subjects of all classes, who came to offer their congratulations and homage, declares his intention to maintain the principle of autocracy as firmly as did his father

Feb., Delimitation of the Russo-Persian frontier, settled by commission

March 19, Prince Lobanof appointed Foreign Minister

March 24, Colonel Gregorieff sentenced to 8 years' penal servitude, in Siberia, for selling plans to the Austrian Government; 4 others exiled to Siberia

March, Agreement with Great Britain respecting the Pamirs

June, Russia guarantees a loan of 16,000,000*l.* for China

July, A Russian mission to Abyssinia returns with an embassy and presents to the Czar from the Negus, June 29; diplomatic relations proposed

Nov., Increased development of the volunteer fleet for commerce, transport of troops and emigrants to the far East

Dec., Capt. Roberofsky returns from a successful scientific expedition into Chinese Central Asia with rich collections

Dec. 23, Serge M. K. Stepniak (Kravchinsky), author of "Underground Russia," &c., killed on the railway at Chiswick

1896

May 26, The Czar enters Moscow with a grand procession, May 21; coronation of the Emperor and Empress in the Cathedral of the Assumption

May 27, M. Witte appointed Secretary of State

June, At a special fête on the Khodinsky plain, Moscow, an imperial dole of food, &c., was to be distributed; the crowds became uncontrollable, a great panic ensued, 1,429 persons were crushed to death and 644 injured, May 30; immediate relief (40,000*l.*) for the sufferers was ordered by the Czar; large public subscriptions

June 9, Pan-Russian exhibition opened at Nijni-Novgorod by M. Witte

July 4, The Czar and Czarina enter St. Petersburg

Aug. 25, The Czar and Czarina start on a foreign tour: at Vienna, Aug. 27; Kieff, Sept. 2; Breslau, Sept. 5; Kiel, Sept. 8; Copenhagen, Sept. 9–20; at Balmoral Sept. 22; at Portsmouth, Oct. 4; Cherbourg, Oct. 5; Paris, Oct. 6; exchange visits of the Czar and the German Emperor at Wiesbaden; leaves Oct. 29; at St. Petersburg, Oct. 31

Sept. 2, Several dragoon officers degraded for coercing soldiers to violence against the Jews in Podolia, whereby 5 Jews were killed, and buildings looted and burnt

Dec. 29, Imperial edict issued sanctioning the formation of the Eastern Chinese railway company, shareholders to be exclusively Russians and Chinese; line to be completed, 1,280 miles, in 6 ys., Dec. 23; subscription for shares largely over-subscribed

1897

Jan. 11, Count Muravieff appointed foreign minister

Jan., Currency reform; resumption of specie payments, gold coins of 15 and 7½ roubles substituted for silver

March 20, Apollon Nickolaievitch Maikoff, eminent poet, died, aged 75

Aug. 7–13, Visit of the German Emperor and Empress to St. Petersburg

Aug. 17, M. Nossiloff announces the discovery of a direct waterway between Siberia and Europe, and his exploration of the Yalmal peninsula

Aug. 23, Pres. Faure received by the Czar at Cronstadt, arrives at Peterhof; leaves Aug. 26

Sept. 30, Railway from Moscow to Archangel completed

Nov. 26, New currency established on a gold basis

1898

Jan., The sale of spirituous liquors made a state monopoly

Feb., April, Agricultural distress and famine in the interior and S.E.

March 3, Russia demands from China 99 yrs. lease over Port Arthur and Ta-lien-wan; 25 yrs. lease of these ports, granted; railway concessions, March 23; China to retain sovereign rights, agreement signed; Chinese garrisons withdrawn, Russian troops landed, March 28; Adm. Stark appointed commandant, July

March 10, The disbursement of 90,000,000 roubles (7 yrs.) for warships ordered

March 20, Death of Admiral Popoff, aged 77, inventor of 3 circular ironclads

March 23, Naval officers (100) charged with bribery and corruption at Sebastopol, arrested, 5 commit suicide

April, Ta-lien-wan declared open to commerce

April 12, Perovnoff (privy councillor) and his daughter (20) sentenced to life exile in Siberia; 5 others to lighter sentences for high treason, at St. Petersburg

April 25, Russo-Japanese convention respecting Corea, signed

June, Relaxation of the tariff of 1891 (favorable to England)

Aug. 17, Death of Gen. Tchernaieff

Aug. 24, Circular of Count Muravieff on behalf of the Czar proposing a conference of the Powers for the preservation of general peace by disarmament; sympathetic replies, Sept.–Oct.

[Second circular to European cabinets, Jan. 11, 1899]

Aug., Famine through bad harvests

Dec., Labor strikes and riots frequent throughout the country

1899

Jan.–May, Severe famine in the central and S.E. provinces; the Czar gives 3,000,000, the Czarina 50,000 roubles; great mortality in Kazan; over 15,000 deaths in Samara

Mid. Jan., General Annenkoff, born 1835, constructed the Transcaspian military railway; died Feb. *et seq.*, Russification of Finland. *See* Finland

May 9, Severe measures against foreign as well as Russian Jews

July 10, The Czarevitch, Grand Duke George, born May 9, 1871, dies suddenly at Abbas Tuman, in the Caucasus

Aug. 4, M. Delcassé, French Foreign Minister, received by Count Muravieff; by the Czar, Aug. 6; leaves Aug. 9

Aug., Measure passed imposing (1 to 3 yrs.) military service on rebellious students, reported

Aug., Educational system for the aristocracy, largely at government expense, established

Nov. 8, The Czar and Czarina visit the German Emperor at Potsdam

1900

Feb. 17, Trial of 43 officers and officials in Russian navy for bribery and corruption, at Sebastopol; 16 persons acquitted, 26 found guilty, April 3

May 19, Ukase announcing the final redemption of the debt of the imperial exchequer to the state bank to the amount of 50,000,000 roubles

June 25, Mobilization of the E. Siberian army corps for China, ordered

July 3, Imperial ukase, largely abolishing banishment to Siberia, issued

July 19, Visit of the Shah of Persia, July 17; grand review at St. Petersburg

July 22, Imperial ukase, reserves called out

Aug. 4, Import duties of the common tariff increased from 50 to 100%

Aug. 5, Anti-Jewish riots in Odessa and other districts, reported

Oct. 13, Thibetan envoy received by the Czar

Dec. 15, Count Tolstoi writes to the Czar appealing against religious persecutions

1901

Feb. *et seq.*, Famine due to failure of crops, population of 24 millions affected; government relief organized

Feb., M. Witte increases the duties on imports from the U.S.A.

Feb.–March, Student disturbances in St. Petersburg and all the chief towns, many arrests

Feb. 27, M. Bogoliepoff, Minister of Public Instruction, mortally wounded by Peter Karpovich (sentenced to 20 years' imprisonment, March 30), in St. Petersburg

March 15, Count Tolstoi appeals to the Czar and Government on the situation in Russia

March 17, Students' demonstration in St. Petersburg ends in serious rioting, 700 arrests

March 19 and April 9, Count Tolstoi excommunicated for his opinions, see *Times*

April 7, The Czar's rescript to Gen. Vannovsky, new Minister of Public Instruction, orders revision and reform in the present system, reported

April 9, M. Lagovski sentenced to six years' imprisonment for attempting the life of the Procurator of the Holy Synod (March 22)

May 20, Centenary of the Council of the Empire celebrated, the Czarevitch appointed a member

May 20, Strike riots in St. Petersburg and elsewhere; again in St. Petersburg, June 14

June, The Czar intervenes; students pardoned

July 6, Thibetan mission received by the Czar

Aug. 5, Moorish mission received by the Czar

Aug. 23, State of siege in the province of Moscow continued, reported

Sept. 2–10, The Czar and Czarina visit the King of Denmark; the Czar meets the German Emperor at Danzig, views the naval manœuvres, Sept. 11, 12; visit France, Sept. 18

Sept. 24, Many bank and factory failures in S. Russia during the summer, reported

Dec. 11–14, Student disorders, university at Kharkoff closed

Mid Dec., About 20 cities and towns placed under state of siege

1902

Jan. 13, Budget for 1902, about 144,000,000 roubles deficit, issued

Feb. 1, American note protests against Russian aggression in Manchuria

Feb. 15, Riots at Kieff and other university towns

Feb. 20–March 11, University of St. Petersburg closed owing to disorders; further disturbances, repressed by the troops and police, March 16; riots and disorders in Moscow, Feb. 22 and March 2; 567 students and others convicted of riot and political disaffection imprisoned (from 3 to 6 months, 95 banished to Siberia), March 25

April 3, New Russian 4% loan subscribed over 100 times in Germany, Holland, and Russia

April 17, M. Sipiaguine, Minister of the Interior, a reactionist, assassinated at St. Petersburg by Palmascheff (executed May 16), April 15; state funeral, the Czar present; M. de Plehve appointed Minister of the Interior

April, Increasing distress and poverty due to bad harvests and oppressive taxation, great economic and agricultural depression over the country

Spring, The Zemstvos, local institutions, forbidden to collect rural statistics in S. Russia

Mid April, Rioting in Poltava and Kharkoff, many estates plundered (compensation granted by decree, May 27)

April, Great unrest in central and S. Russia; much incendiarism

May 5, Martial law proclaimed in Poltava

May 18, Revolutionary outbreak at Saratoff suppressed by troops

May 20, Pres. Loubet visits the Czar; grand review of troops at St. Petersburg, May 21, 22

June 13, Lieut.-Col. Grimm, for selling army secrets to a foreign power, sentenced to 12 years' imprisonment and life banishment to Siberia

End June, Grave disturbances in Ekaterinoslaff, factories and farms sacked

July 13–17, The King of Italy visits the Czar

Aug. 6–8, Czar and German Emperor meet at Reval

Aug. 11, Prince Obolenski, the governor, wounded by Katchoor, a peasant (death sentence commuted, Nov.) at Kharkoff; M. Bessonoff, chief of police, also wounded

Early Aug., The students imprisoned at Smolensk freed by the Czar's orders

Sept. 26, The Czar pardons 62 exiles in Siberia; and 58, Dec. 19

Dec., Labor troubles in the south, conflict with troops, 4 deaths, 102 arrests, Nov. 24, 30; great distress, continued arrests

1903

About Jan. 5, Special university commission of inquiry issue their report as to reforms, &c.

Jan. 16–24, Visit of the German Crown Prince

Feb. 20, Lieut.-Col. Shavroff, chief of the Cronstadt police, sentenced to 2 years' imprisonment, and degraded for forgery

March 11, Manifesto from the Czar, favoring religious freedom, reform of peasant taxation

March 28, Labor disturbances at Slatoust, workmen's delegates imprisoned, crowd fired on, 34 killed, about 200 wounded, by order of M. Bogdanovitch, Governor of Ufa; reported

April 8, Factory riot near Nishni-Novgorod, mob fired on, many killed and wounded

April 19, 20, Kishineff atrocities, S. Russia, houses and shops of the Jews sacked and pillaged, 45 Jews killed, 84 seriously wounded, 500 crippled and injured, 10,000 rendered destitute

[Gen. von Raahen the governor, the chief of the police, and other officials who had allowed the mob free play, dismissed, May–July, great agitation abroad; M. de Plehve, Minister of Interior, much censured, the *Bessarabetz* and other anti-Semitic journals also held responsible for the outrages]

April 30, Loan of 72,000,000 roubles, 94½, at 4%, for landowners raised

May 19, Gen. Bogdanovitch, the Governor, assassinated at Ufa

June 3, M. de Plehve issues a circular against the teaching of revolutionary doctrines

June 8, Anti-Semitic disturbances at Berestechko

June 15, Jewish meeting at Lodz attacked by the police, 10 killed, many seriously injured

Mid July, Reform of district police ordered

July 28, M. Kurino, Japanese Minister at St. Petersburg, is instructed by his government "to approach the Russian Government in a spirit of conciliation and frankness with a view to the conclusion of an understanding" on the subject of the Russian occupation of Manchuria and Japan's influence in Korea

July–Aug., Agitation and unrest all over the Empire, May *et seq.*; general strikes in the south, riots at Baku, Odessa, Kieff, and elsewhere, trains wrecked, oil wells set on fire, and various other acts of outrage; murderous assaults on Prince Urussoff in Tchernigoff, and on Prince Gagarin, his wife, and Prince Sherbatoff in Riazan, reported; conflicts with the troops resulting in great loss of life, Aug. 5–7

Aug. 12, Imperial viceroyalty appointed in the "Far East," by ukase issued

Aug. 20, Disturbances at Ekaterinoslav, mob fired on, many killed

Mid Aug., Gloomy economic condition of the country; manufactures generally stagnant, reported

Aug. 29, Ministerial changes: M. Witte appointed president of the committee of ministers and members of the Imperial Council, M. Pleske, Minister of Finance

Sept. 14–15, Anti-Semitic riots at Gomel, terrible excesses and loss of life; houses wrecked; Moghileff and suburbs placed under siege, Sept. 26

Sept. 30, Czar and Czarina visit Emperor of Austria

Oct. 3, Russian Minister at Tokio submits Russia's counter-proposals to the Japanese Government, including the recognition by Japan of Manchuria and its littoral as in all respects outside her sphere of interest

Oct. 8, Three socialists sentenced to death, 2 exiled, and 7 imprisoned in connection with a strike demonstration at Rostoff, reported

Mid Oct., New law of expulsion of foreigners issued by imperial decree; special commission under the presidency of the Czar appointed to consider affairs in the "Far East"

Oct. 22, Russian substituted for Swedish at the opening of the Finish Senate

Oct. 27, Murderous attack on Prince Galitzin, Gov.-General of the Caucasus

Oct. 30, Japanese Government replies to Russian note, rejecting Russia's proposals respecting Manchuria, and proposes other amendments

Oct.–mid Nov., Disturbances of a revolutionary character in S. Russia

Nov. 4, 5, Meeting of the Czar and German Emperor

Nov. 12, M. Metlenko, chief of the police, fired at and slightly wounded in a public street in Bialystok (Grodno)

Dec. 1, M. Kurino, Japanese Minister, instructed to inform the Russian Government that the Japanese Government regarded the delay in sending a reply to the Japanese communication of Oct. 30 with grave concern

Dec. 11, Russian reply communicated to Japan

Dec. 21, Kishineff massacres (April 19, 20) trial began, Nov. 19; Gretschin and Marosjuk, indicted for murder, sentenced to 7 and 5 years' penal servitude, 22 others to periods of 1 to 2 years, and 1 to 6 months' imprisonment, 12 persons acquitted, and 48 civil actions brought against the accused dismissed, reported

Dec. 21, Japanese Government replies to Russian communication that the exclusion of Manchuria from the negotiation nullified it entirely

Nov.–end Dec., Serious disturbances among the students of the universities

Dec., 1903–Jan., 1904, Strained relations with Japan; negotiations continued, war preparations

1904

Jan. 6, Russia's reply to Japanese note of Dec. 21; Russia proposes the insertion in the agreement between the two countries of an article by which Japan would recognize Manchuria and its littoral as outside its sphere of influence, while Russia within the limits of Manchuria would not impede Japan or other powers in the enjoyment of rights and privileges acquired under existing treaties with China

Jan. 13, Baron Komura, Japanese Minister for Foreign Affairs, sends to M. Kurino the final proposals of the Japanese Government to the Russian Government (see Russo-Japanese War)

Jan. 14, Czar holds a reception of the diplomatic body in St. Petersburg, and, addressing the Japanese Minister, expresses his unshaken hope that a settlement satisfactory to both nations would be arranged

Jan. 21, Attempted assassination of Baron Korff, Governor of Lomzha; and of Prince Scherchelidze, chief of the police, Kars, Jan. 22

Jan. 23, 26, 28, 30, Urgent representations by the Japanese Government to St. Petersburg for an early reply to the proposals of Japan

Preparations for war made by Russia by the transportation of large numbers of troops over the Siberian railway, and the strengthening of the fleet in the Far East during January

Feb. 6, M. Kurino notifies to Count Lamsdorff that the Japanese Government had decided, in view of the delay of the Russian Government in connection with the negotiations, and the naval and military activity displayed by Russia, to terminate the negotiations and recall the Japanese Minister and his staff from St. Petersburg

Feb. 8, 9, Russian fleet at Port Arthur attacked by the Japanese fleet under Adm. Togo
[See Russo-Japanese War]

Feb. 13, Issue of 50,000,000 roubles (5,000,000l.) of credit notes secured by gold

Feb. 19, Government abolishes censorship on all foreign news despatches

Feb. 23, Students at the high schools and the universities object to the loyal addresses to the Czar drawn up by the professors in regard to the war; high school for women closed

March 7, Scientific expedition, organized by the Russian Ministry of Finance, under the direction of M. Kournakoff, mining engineer, with the object of exploring the auriferous districts near the source of the White Nile, starts for Abyssinia

March 10, Trial of 7 persons, one a female student, before the military tribunal in St. Petersburg, charged with being the authors, accomplices, or instigators of the chief nihilist crimes of recent years, concludes; Dr. Herschuny, Lieut. Grigorieff, and Melnikoff, a student, condemned to death, 3 others to 4 years' penal servitude, the female student to 3 months' imprisonment; Dr. Herschuny and Melnikoff executed in the Schlüsselburg, March 11

March 11, Judgment delivered in the cases of Russnak and 53 other persons tried on charges connected with the anti-Jewish riots at Kishineff; Russnak and another, Bordian, found guilty of murder, others receive various terms of imprisonment for complicity, 36 acquitted; civil claims presented by the Jews rejected

March 19, Official circular, addressed to governors of provinces and towns and the chiefs of police, recommends a more lenient disposition towards the Jews, issued

March, Scholastic disturbances in St. Petersburg and at Kieff; serious disturbances at Tver in connection with labor strikes; vigorous labor agitation reported from Kharkoff; manifesto clandestinely circulated in Russia, signed by the executive committees of several different parties representing an amalgamation of oppressed nationalities, the Polish socialist party, the Lithuanian social democratic party, and the white Ruthenian revolutionary groups denouncing the war; another manifesto issued by the central committee of the social democratic party, affirming that "the wealth of the Russian *bourgeoisie* is created by the impoverishment and ruin of the Russian workmen, and to increase this wealth the workmen must now shed their blood in order that the Russian *bourgeoisie* may be able to oppress and exploit the Chinese and Corean workmen without let or hindrance," and demanding the calling of a constituent national assembly; a manifesto in similar terms issued by the socialist revolutionary party

Early April, Report issued by M. Muravieff, Minister of Justice, shows that the number of political prisoners exiled to Siberia by "administrative order" without trial increased from 158 in 1894 to 1,988 in 1903; persons actually arrested for supposed political offenses numbered 919 in 1894 and 5,590 in 1903; prosecutions authorized by personal order of the Czar were 56 in 1894 and 1,522 in 1903

April 13, Explosion at the Hôtel du Nord, Moscow, caused by an infernal machine filled with melinite; Kazanoff, the perpetrator of the outrage, a revolutionist, killed; 20 arrests made

Early May, Revolutionists made an attempt to destroy the arsenal at Kronstadt by setting it on fire. M. de Plehve, Minister of the Interior, refuses to confirm the election of M. Shipoff, a moderate reformer, as president of the Moscow provincial zemstvo

May 30, M. de Plehve proposes to the council of the Empire an important project for the repeal of the law under which Jews are forbidden to reside within 50 versts (35 miles) of the frontier, as a step in the execution of the Czar's ukase of Feb. 26, 1903, promising freedom of conscience to his subjects

June 16, Gen. Bobrikoff, Governor-General of Finland, fatally wounded by a pistol-shot while entering the Senate at Helsingfors, fired by Eugen Schumann, son of an ex-Senator; Czar present at the funeral at the Sergiyeff monastery, St. Petersburg, June 21

July, Lieut.-Gen. Prince Obolensky appointed Governor-General of Finland

July 17, M. Andreieff, vice-governor of the government of Elizabetpol, assassinated at Agdshakent

July 28, M. de Plehve, Minister of the Interior, assassinated by a bomb thrown under his carriage at St. Petersburg

——, Gen. Schumann, father of Eugen Schumann, the assassin of Gen. Bobrikoff, secretly deported to Russia and incarcerated in the fortress of St. Peter and St. Paul in St. Petersburg

About Aug. 1, 1,000 persons stated to be arrested as a consequence of the assassination of M. de Plehve, July 30; the Czar, Dowager-Empress, and all the Grand Dukes present at the funeral in St. Petersburg, July 31; M. Durnovo, Senator and assistant to N. de Plehve, appointed minister of the interior *ad interim*

Aug. 12, Birth of the Czarevitch Alexis

Aug. 24, Czar's manifesto on the occasion of the birth of the Czarevitch announces a general amnesty for political offenses, the abolition of corporal punishment in certain cases, and remission of fines and arrears of payment; the Czarevitch christened in the church of the Peterhof Palace

Early Sept., Imperial ukase, amending the provisions relating to the residential rights of the Jews, issued

Sept. 4, 5, Anti-Jewish disturbances at Smiela, over 100 houses, 150 shops, 2 Jewish schools, and 2 synagogues demolished; great library founded by the wife of Dr. Stern entirely destroyed

Sept., Prince Sviatopolk-Mirski appointed Minister of the Interior

Oct. 14, Political trial before the Senate, the supreme court of appeal, of M. A. V. Milaskerski, a member of the council of the Saratoff zemstvo, remarkable for the fact that it was conducted publicly instead of *in camerâ*, hitherto the case in trials of a political character

Oct. 19, Serious riot among workmen at Odessa

Oct. 23, Disturbances at Kieff during the mobilization of the reserves; at Radomsk, reservists come into conflict with the regular troops, many wounded, crowd parades the streets singing Polish national songs, Nov. 7

Oct. 25, Russian Baltic fleet fires on North Sea trawlers, Oct. 21; strong British protest to Russian government (*see* England)

Nov. 13, Disturbances in Warsaw, collision with police and troops, 6 persons killed, 21 wounded

Nov. 25, Mutinous rioting of sailors, marines, and firemen on the vessels of the Black Sea fleet, at Sevastopol

Early Dec., Resolution passed by 32 out of the 34 presidents of the Russian zemstvos, divided into 12 articles, demanding the establishment of official responsibility, civil, and criminal; personal liberty, religious, civil, and political, under the protection of the law; equality of all citizens; emancipation of the peasantry from administrative tutelage; the conversion of the zemstvos and municipalities into a popular representative institution, and the creation of a separate elective body to coöperate in the government of the state

Dec. 11, Popular demonstration in St. Petersburg against the Government; great crowd of university students and others assemble in the Nevsky Prospect; cries raised "Down with the autocracy! Stop the war!"—crowd charged by mounted gendarmes; many arrests

Dec. 13, Sasanoff, the murderer of M. de Plehve, sentenced to penal servitude for life (remitted subsequently to 14 years)

Dec. 25, Manifesto issued by the Czar, insisting on the immutability of the fundamental laws of the Empire, the amelioration of the condition of the peasants, the safeguarding of the law in its full force as the most important pillar of the throne of the autocratic Empire, the enlarging of the scope of local and municipal institutions, unification of judicial procedure throughout the Empire, state insurance for workmen, revision of exceptional laws for criminal repression, revision of the laws dealing with heterodox and non-Christian confessions, and removal of restrictions on worship, revision of ordinances limiting the rights of foreigners and natives in certain territories, removal of unnecessary press restrictions

Dec. 30, Moscow and Tchernigoff zemstvos adjourn *sine die* after recording their opinion that the Czar's manifesto did not respond to the aspirations of the Russian people

1905

[The year 1905 was a year of great unrest in Russia. From end to end of the land there were scenes of violent disorder and bloodshed. The details of the principal events are recorded below, but in addition to those set out there were many other very serious riots]

Jan. 1, Prince Troubetskoi, president of the Moscow zemstvo, addresses a letter to the Minister of the Interior, declaring in outspoken language that Russia is almost on the verge of revolution, which can only be averted if the Czar allows freedom of utterance

Jan. 2, Fall of Port Arthur (*see* Russo-Japanese War) Great consternation and depression in Russia on receipt of the news

Jan. 8, Sixty oil towers stated to be burnt since Jan. 6, making about 100 since the beginning of the fires in the Baku district, reported

Internal situation of the Empire stated to be growing worse; Prince Sviatopolk-Mirski, Minister of the Interior, tenders his resignation; congress of natural science teachers at Kieff closed by order of the curator of the educational district; attempt made at Moscow to assassinate Gen. Trepoff, ex-chief of police, Jan. 15; congress on criminal law at Kieff passes a resolution in favor of representative government, Jan. 17

Jan. 16–18, General strike of workmen (over 100,000) at the Putiloff Neva shipbuilding and other works in St. Petersburg

Jan. 19, Bullet fired through a window in the winter palace, after the Czar had performed the annual ceremony of blessing the waters of the Neva; officially stated that a cannon used to fire a salute had inadvertently been loaded with shrapnel

Jan. 21, A party of strikers, led by Father Gapon, a priest prominent in organizing the strike movement, send to the Minister of the Interior, urging that the Czar should meet his people in front of the winter palace, St. Petersburg, on Jan. 22

Jan. 22, Czar remains at Tsarskoe Selo: the strikers, unarmed, moving to the palace square to present a petition, are confronted by troops, who fire upon the people; Cossacks charge the crowd; large numbers, including women and children, are killed and wounded; official numbers, 96 killed, 333 wounded, actual numbers stated to be 4,600 killed and wounded; numerous shops pillaged

Jan. 23, Street fighting renewed: Cossacks disperse a number of workmen and wound many

Jan. 24, Crowd, estimated at 20,000 to 30,000 strikers, starting from Kolpino in the direction of Tsarskoe Selo with a petition to the Czar, is met by a regiment of infantry and half a field battery from the garrison at Tsarskoe Selo; a conflict ensues, many of the workmen killed and wounded in the fight and retreat; Gen. Trepoff, ex-Minister of Police at Moscow, appointed Gov.-Gen. of St. Petersburg with plenary powers

Jan. 25, Strikers ordered by official notice to resume work within 24 hours; strike in Moscow extends to all the factories, involving 30,000 men

Jan. 26, Many prominent liberals, including Maxim Gorki, arrested

Jan. 27–30, Great disturbance in Poland; martial law proclaimed in several districts; strike riots in Lodz and Warsaw, 800 killed and injured by the soldiery

Jan. 28, Situation in St. Petersburg reported to be again practically normal

Feb. 1, Czar receives a deputation of 34 workmen representing the employés of the factories in St.

Petersburg; the Czar rebukes them and their comrades for their action in the recent disturbances, and promises that measures shall be taken to ameliorate the condition of the workmen

Feb. 3, Disorders break out at the gymnasium at Kielce; students of the upper classes demand that the Polish language shall be the medium of instruction, that only Polish masters shall be appointed, and that the regulations prohibiting admission of Jewish pupils be abolished, reported

Feb. 4, Traffic between Sosnowice and Olkusk, on the Vistula railway, suspended owing to strike of employés at Strshemenshizy

——, General strike, including the workmen employed on the Transcaucasian railway, causing the suspension of traffic on the Manchurian railways; railmen cease work, Feb. 5; dockers and miners at Pomti go on strike, Feb. 6

Feb. 7, Carmen at Batoum strike; 800 workmen force their way into Samtredi station and compel all officials and telegraphists, under pain of death, to leave it; they compel the shopkeepers of Samtredi to close their shops, Feb. 4; strike spreads, business at a standstill, scarcity of food, traffic in the streets carried on with difficulty

Feb. 9, Sanguinary encounter between troops and strikers at the German Catherine colliery, Sosnowice, 33 persons killed and many wounded; collision between the strikers and troops at Lodz, 30 deaths, numbers injured, Feb. 10; troops and crowds in conflict, 42 killed, and over 200 persons, including some women and children, injured, Feb. 12

Feb. 10, Strike movement at St. Petersburg resumed; majority of the men at the Putiloff factories go out; their example is followed by many workers at other factories; situation in Poland reported very grave; serious collisions between strikers and troops at Sosnowice and Lodz

Feb. 11, General strike resumed again at Warsaw; work suspended in all the factories

——, Imperial decree orders the formation of a committee, under the presidency of Senator Chidlovski, to ascertain immediately the causes of discontent among the workmen in St. Petersburg and the district, and to devise measures to prevent such discontent in the future

Feb. 11–13, Committee of Ministers decide that the supervision of industrial life should remain in the care of the Ministry of Finance; the committee also decide to instruct the Minister of Finance to frame a scheme for the improvement of the lot of working men, and the solution of outstanding industrial questions

Feb. 17, Grand Duke Serge, uncle of the Czar, assassinated in Moscow by a bomb thrown under his carriage

Feb. 17, 30,000 workmen strike in St. Petersburg

Feb. 18, Czar reported to desire the assembling of the zemski sobor (national assembly), to meet on the anniversary of the emancipation of the serfs, March 4

Feb. 21, Widespread disorders in connection with the strikes, and other dissatisfied elements in various parts of Russia and Poland; strikes on railways spread; traffic on the Moscow Rybinsk-Windau railway paralyzed; telegraph operators of the Moscow-Riazan railway strike work; continued disturbances at Lodz, and the districts of Sosnowice and Dombrovo

Feb. 22, Fierce fights between Armenians and Tartars at Batoum; Tartars let loose on the Armenians, many Armenians killed; terrible murders in Baku reported

Feb. 24, Abolition of the censorship of the press decided by the ministerial council, its place being taken by a committee on press offenses, to be punished by the courts instead of arbitrarily

Feb. 27, Maxim Gorki released from prison

March 1, Arbitration treaty between Russia and Denmark, signed

March 3, Manifesto issued by the Czar

March 4, Increase in number of strikers in St. Petersburg, 83 factories, 51,604 men idle; 2 boilers exploded at the Putiloff works, many lives lost, March 6

March 6, Bands of ruffians terrorize the inhabitants of Warsaw; anarchy reported to be reigning at Samara, police authorities passive in the face of appalling outrages; battle between the ruffians and inhabitants

March 7, Chidlovski commission having failed in its object owing to the refusal of the workmen to elect representatives, and disunion between the various branches of the administration, closed by command of the Czar

March 8, Men of the Baltic naval dockyard go on strike as a protest against the arrest of 4 of their comrades

March 12, Destruction of government property in Central and South Russia; 3 of the largest sugar refineries in the province of Kieff burnt to the ground, including one belonging to the Grand Duke Michael Alexandrovitch, brother of the Czar, reported

March 13, Peasant rising in the provinces; landlords murdered, houses, factories, sugar refineries burnt and pillaged; 9 proprietors brutally slaughtered in the province of Kurst; mob of 8,000 peasants surround a country seat in Vitebsk, maltreat the inmates and sack the residence; unrest of peasants stated to be rapidly increasing and extending in area; movement directed against landlords and the officials

March 13, Bomb explosion in a room in the Hotel Bristol, St. Petersburg, occupied by a man alleged to be a British subject, but believed to be a native of the Baltic provinces; man blown to pieces; numerous arrests made; violent explosion in the Theatresquare, Moscow, March 13

March 14, Estate of the late Grand Duke Serge, in the Dmitroff district of the government of Orel, pillaged

——, Rescript appointing Count Dashkoff Viceroy to pacify the Caucasus; reaffirms the Czar's intention to reorganize the Empire

March 20, M. Mjasojadoff, Governor Viborg, shot at and wounded by Matti Reinikka, a young man, who is arrested

Mid March, Peasants' insurrectionary movement assumes extraordinary proportions; forest-dwelling peasants and boatmen of the Volga march against the bourgeoisie and the nobility, laying waste their lands and carrying off their cattle; columns of insurgents in the southern provinces; secret police of Moscow reported to have discovered an organization acting in conjunction with the Russian revolutionary committee, with headquarters in London, store of infernal machines, explosives, &c., found with documents relating to the plot to assassinate the Grand Duke Serge

March 26, Constitutional agitation in Finland reported to be spreading

March 27, Bomb thrown into the carriage of Baron Nolken, chief of the Warsaw police, who is seriously wounded

Mid-end March, Continuous reports of agrarian outrages; reign of terror in the Caucasus, chiefly at Batoum, Erivan and Kars

March 29, Manifesto by the Czar suspends the military law of July 21, 1901, on condition that the diet of Finland pay annually 10,000,000 marks to the Russian exchequer for military purposes; irremovability of the judges established

Early April, General demand for the convocation of a national assembly; M. Buliguine, Minister of the Interior, announces the task of preparing such a measure exceeds his strength; repressive measures in active operation in all parts of the empire, except Finland; revolt among the Letts; sanguinary affrays at Riga; agrarian disturbances at Tula

April 13, Special commission appointed by the Czar to avert the danger of the agrarian movement

April 17, Imperial rescript to the Governor-General of Irkutsk ordains an extension of the zemstvo system to Siberia

April 18, Trial of Ivan Koliaeff on the charge of assassinating the Grand Duke Serge opens before the Senate at Moscow

April 29, Decision of the Council of Ministers, after consideration of the situation created by the interruption of work in the secondary schools caused by the disorders, to hold no examinations in schools where the work had been interrupted, to suspend any class-promotion of students, to close all auxiliary establishments for students, with other drastic measures, confirmed by the Czar

April 30, Decree conceding liberty of worship to the Old Believers, and abolishing the religious disabilities of members of the Roman Catholic and other religious communities and Mahomedans, promulgated

May 1, Conflicts in Warsaw between troops and workmen, 62 persons killed; 75,000 men reported to be on strike at Lodz

May 8, Second congress of the zemstvoists opens at Moscow, May 5: papers read on the scheme for a national representative assembly; congress unanimously vote universal suffrage as the basis for the election of a constituent assembly

May 13, Vice-Ad. Nazimoff shot by his orderly

May 14, Great demonstration of workmen in St. Petersburg; many demonstrators roughly handled by the Cossacks

May 16, Committee of Ministers draw up a scheme for granting increased facilities to the peasants for acquiring leases of crown lands with an area of 250,000,000 acres; imperial edict issued modifying the restrictive decrees in regard to the 9 western governments of Russia; granting concessions to the Poles; committee of Ministers decide to permit all Jewish artizans to reside in any part of the country

——, Maj.-Gen. Sokolovsky, Governor of the Province of Ufa, fired at and seriously wounded

Mid May, Extensive agrarian movement reported from the province of Minsk; peasants of several communes in the district of Borisoff partition the lands of the nobles and plough them

May 24, Prince Nakashidze, Governor of Baku, killed by a bomb

——, Jewish disturbances in Warsaw, 8 killed, 100 wounded

May 27–28, Destruction of the Russian Baltic fleet at Tsu Shima (*see* Russo-Japanese War)

June 4, News of defeat of the Russian fleet renews the agitation in favor of peace; many public bodies declare in favor of stopping the war; ukase published appointing Gen. Trepoff Gov.-Gen. of St. Petersburg, Assistant-Minister of the Interior and Chief of the Police, with full powers "in all matters connected with crime and the protection of the public safety." M. Buliguine, Minister of the Interior, resigns (his resignation not accepted until Aug. 24)

June 6, Congress of zemstvoists appointed to assemble in Moscow, prohibited meeting; members assemble privately, and adopt a resolution demanding the immediate convocation of a national assembly

June 9, Czar informs a deputation from the zemstvos and dumas, who present an address urging reforms, that it was his irrevocable will to call the National Assembly, which would establish, as of old, the union between Russia and the Czar

June 22, Massacres reported in Transcaucasia; indiscriminate slaughter, in which Armenians, Tartars, Persians, and Kurds all engage, combatants stated to number 30,000; in the district of Sharukhan, in the province of Erivan, 37,000 insurgents sack and burn 4 Armenian villages; terrible atrocities committed at Nakhitchevan, in the province of Erivan, the Armenians in that district stated to be completely ruined, their houses demolished and burnt down, cattle carried off, crops destroyed, churches and schools sacked, holy images torn down and broken; at Djagrakh women stated to have been outraged before the eyes of their husbands and sons, and other atrocities committed, reported

About June 23, Abolition of the committee of the Far East decreed

June 23, Grave outbreak in Poland; fierce fighting at Lodz; street barricades defended by thousands of armed workmen against the troops; city in darkness; 561 persons stated to be killed and 1,000 wounded in the disturbances; barricades erected in Warsaw

June 27, Mutiny on board the Russian battleship *Kniaz Potemkin*, belonging to the Black Sea squadron, and commanded by Capt. Golikoff. The *Kniaz Potemkin* leaves Sevastopol June 25 for Trendovo bay for firing practice; crew refuse to eat the meat provided on account of its bad quality; the shooting of one of the sailors by the second officer enrages the crew, who fire upon their officers, killing Capt. Golikoff and all the officers except 5; committee of 20 sailors organized who take command of the ship

June 28, *Kniaz Potemkin* arrives at Odessa; the sailors carry the body of their dead comrade ashore amid scenes of great excitement, and subsequently take an active part in the revolutionary outbreak in Odessa, and engage in conflict with the Cossacks; strikers make common cause with the mutineers, granaries and shipping in the harbor fired, quays burned, conflicts with military, 6,000 persons killed

——, Sailors of the imperial navy in barracks at Liban revolt and wreck the barracks, sack the storehouses, and attack their officers' quarters; in a conflict with troops sent to suppress the revolt, 20 sailors are killed

June 29, Agrarian riots extend over almost the whole of the province of Kherson; many estates abandoned by their owners, who flee to Elisabetgrad; similar conditions prevail in the province of Ekaterinoslaff, reported

June 30, Black Sea squadron, under Adm. Krieger, arrives at Odessa for the purpose of compelling the crew of the *Kniaz Potemkin* to surrender; crew refuses, and is joined by the sailors of the *Georgei Pobiedonosets*; Adm. Krieger returns to Sevastopol

——, General strike and threatened dissatisfaction among the sailors at Kronstadt; workmen at the arms factory at Kolpino, near St. Petersburg, mutiny and seize arms

——, Decision of the war board to abolish the separate military administration of Finland, and incorporate the troops in that country into a 22nd army corps, announced

July 2, Immense fires at Warsaw

July 2, *Kniaz Potemkin* arrives and anchors at the Rumanian port of Constanza; leaves July 3, and proceeds to Theodosia (Crimea), demanding supplies, and threatening to bombard the town if molested, July 5

July 3, Mutinous battleship *Georgei Pobiedonosets* surrenders to the authorities at Odessa; Black Sea fleet stated to be practically out of existence, the men being sent ashore and the engines disabled

——, Labor agitation, extending to all the ports of the Baltic, breaks out among the dockers of St. Petersburg; serious disturbances reported

——, Battalion of reservists, numbering 1,038 men, at Bialystok, become insubordinate and strike, refusing to accept the food served out to them, July 2; riotous disturbances among the reservists at Kieff

——, Gen. Sakharoff, Minister of War, resigns, to be succeeded by Gen. Ridiger, chief secretary at the War Office, announced

July 4, Czar receives a deputation opposing peace, and asking an elective assembly; in reply the Czar refers to "the great work" he had projected for the welfare of his people

July 8, Serious outbreak among the men of the 14th and 15th naval battalions stationed in the Krinkovski barracks, St. Petersburg

——, Crew of the *Kniaz Potemkin* surrender to Rumanian authorities at Constauza; vessel handed to Russian authorities, July 9

July 10, Strike of shoemakers and butchers at Warsaw assumes a serious aspect; workmen adopt terrorist methods; conflict with infantry, several strikers killed and wounded

July 11, Count Shuvaloff assassinated

July 19–22, Congress of zemstvos and dumas meet at Moscow, about 250 accredited delegates present; constitutional program and an appeal to the people adopted

July 23, Czar sails from Peterhof in the *Pole Star* for Borgo in the Gulf of Finland, where he meets the German Emperor

July 23, Rioting at Nijni Novgorod; town in the hands of thousands of ruffians; many outrages perpetrated; 60 persons killed

July 25, 4,000 workmen of the Warsaw ironworks, and 5,000 from the Dombrowa steelworks go on strike; the Pargolvo gardens, St. Petersburg, sacked by peasants and ruffians; desperate fight with the police many injured

——, Authorities at Odessa arrest and expel numbers of lawyers, doctors, and journalists, and others belonging to the party of the "intelligents"; renewed disturbances reported in the country districts round the city; Armenians and Tartars in collision at Tiflis

Aug. 1, Grand council of Ministers, under presidency of the Czar, meets at Peterhof, to reconsider the Buliguine scheme for a national assembly before its final promulgation; and decides that only the opinions of the majority of the proposed national assembly shall go to the Council of the Empire as an upper house, while in case of disagreement between the two houses the views of the majority of both shall be referred to the Czar, Aug. 6

Aug. 10, Peace conference meets at Portsmouth, U.S. (*see* Russo-Japanese War)

Aug. 15, Peasants' union demand universal suffrage, legislative powers for the proposed national assembly, with control of finance and administration, free education, and the distribution among the peasants of land belonging to religious corporations and the state

Aug. 19, Czar issues a manifesto announcing that he has granted a constitution to Russia; the main features of the Gosondarstvennaia Duma (state council) were to be " the preliminary study of legislative proposals, which, according to the fundamental, were to be submitted to the supreme autocratic authority by the council of the Empire; its competence extended to departmental and national budgets and railways, and it was also to have limited powers of interpellating ministers; on an average one deputy for 250,000 inhabitants

Aug. 21, General strike threatened in Poland as a manifestation of discontent with the way in which the Polish population are treated in the constitution; employés in all the factories in Warsaw, Lodz, and Pabianice, and the staffs of several railways go on strike

Aug. 25, Whole of the Government of Warsaw placed under martial law

Sept. 3, Shah of Persia arrives at Peterhof, Sept. 2; gala dinner given in his honor in the grand palace of St. Petersburg; the Czar proposes the health of his guest

——, Grand Duke Michael Nikolaievitch appointed honorary president of the Council of the Empire, and Count Solsky president

Sept. 4, Moscow zemstvo meets in a private house to discuss its attitude towards the Duma; police enter the room by order of the new Governor-General, M. Durnovo, and oblige the meeting to break up under threat of force, Sept. 3; members meet again under police supervision

Sept. 5, Peace between Russia and Japan signed by M. Witte and Baron Komura at Portsmouth, New Hampshire (U.S.)

Sept. 6, Terrible scenes at Shusha; fierce fighting between Tartars and Armenians; Armenian commercial quarter a mass of smoking ruins, whole streets destroyed; damage estimated at 500,000*l.*; 250 killed, reported

Sept. 7, State of serious revolution prevails in the Caucasus; serious fighting and destruction of property and outrages at Baku; over 1,000 persons killed and several thousands wounded, chiefly Tartars, Armenians, and Persians; 500 oil mills reported to be burning in the Baku district; naphtha store-houses ablaze

——, Sir Chas. Hardinge, British Ambassador, in view of the urgent requests to afford protection to the lives and property of British subjects in the Baku districts communicates with the Russian Government

Sept. 7, First sitting of the ministerial committee to deal with the relief of the famine-stricken provinces recommend the treasury to grant 4,000,000*l.* for the purchase of cereals

Sept. 9, Renewed rioting and anarchy at Baku; Mr. Willan and 3 other Englishmen cut off and besieged at Balakhany, near Baku, are rescued by the gallant efforts of Mr. Urquhart, formerly British vice-consul at Baku, with a small escort of cavalry lent by the governor

Sept. 10, Mr. Urquhart appointed British vice-consul at Baku

——, Destruction of the oil industry in the Baku district stated to be complete; 3,000 out of a total of 3,600 wells ruined; losses estimated to amount from 40,-000,000 to 50,000,000 roubles (4,000,000*l.* to 5,000,-000*l.*)

——, Many Armenian villages in the Zangezursk district completely destroyed and hundreds of people killed; wholesale rising of the Tartar population joined by 4,000 armed Kurds from the Persian bank of the Arax; reported

Sept. 11, Cossacks massacre a number of persons while holding a meeting in a hall at Tiflis

——, Secret dépôt of arms discovered on a barren island in the Gulf of Bothnia, Finland, Sept. 10; mysterious steamer laden with explosives, and flying the American flag, but with its name obliterated, blown up off Helsingfors, reported

Sept. 12, Tartar bands in the Zangezur and Djebrail districts proclaim a holy war; Armenians without distinction of age or sex massacred; many thousands of Tartar horsemen cross the Perso-Russian frontier and join the insurgents

Mid Sept., Russian papers publish details showing that during April and May, 1905, attempts were made on the lives of 116 officials; in 42 cases the victims, including one governor, were killed on the spot; 62 attempts resulted in the wounding of the official attacked; 12 attempts were unsuccessful

Sept. 16, Czar orders a conference to report on the Baku disorders

Sept. 20, Central prison at Riga stormed by a revolutionary crowd, who release 2 political prisoners

Sept. 21, Explosion near the Governor's residence at Vasa, near Helsingfors

Sept. 22, Further repressive measures against Finland reported to be in execution, several thousand troops despatched from St. Petersburg to various parts of the country

——, Gov.-Gen. of Warsaw issues an order to the army, stating that the military must act with vigor, without fearing responsibility or troubling themselves as to whether their action will cause superfluous victims

Sept. 24, Conference of leading Armenians and Tartars at Baku for the purpose of restoring, sign a regular peace

Sept. 25, The zemstvo congress, the first political congress representing the whole Russian Empire, assembles at a private residence in Moscow; nearly 300 delegates attend with the consent of the Government; resolution adopted, that "though the Government scheme for the Duma was imperfect, it was none the less necessary to utilize it in order to win civic rights and liberties"

——, Bomb outrage at Kovno; M. Ivanoff, chief of police, and 6 other persons wounded

Sept. 29, M. Witte arrives in St. Petersburg and meets with an enthusiastic reception, Sept. 28; Czar raises M. Witte to the rank of a Count

Sept. 30, Imperial decree issued directing arrangements to be made immediately in regard to the elections in the state Duma

Oct. 12, Col. von Eitmann, chief of the police at Krasnoyarsk, Eastern Siberia, assassinated

Oct. 14, Peace treaty between Russia and Japan signed by the Czar and the Mikado (*see* Russo-Japanese War)

Oct. 16, Dismissal of the Grand Duke Cyril from all his appointments and his exclusion from Russia gazetted in St. Petersburg on account of his clandestine marriage with his cousin, the divorced wife of the Grand Duke of Hesse

Oct. 21, Organized strike on all the Russian railways to force the Government to concede the political demands of the strikers, who are supported by the workmen in the principal industries

Oct. 23, Moscow and St. Petersburg cut off from railway communication with the rest of Russia

Oct. 24, Railway delegates' congress in St. Petersburg send a deputation to Count Witte with an address demanding political guarantees for freedom and the convocation of a constituent assembly elected by universal suffrage

——, Disorders in connection with workmen and students at Kharkoff; barricades thrown up; archives of the courts of justice torn up; armorers' shops pillaged; university transformed by 3,000 rioters into a fortress; precincts of the university placed under martial law; besieged and surrounded by troops; surrender on conditions

Oct. 26, Over 1,000,000 men out on strike; famine threatened in many cities, gas and electric light cut off, shops plundered, disorder in many places, but generally an attitude of passive revolt

Oct. 27, State of war proclaimed at Kharkoff

——, Moscow in darkness owing to the strike

Oct. 28, No newspapers published in St. Petersburg owing to a strike of compositors

——, Rapid spread of the strike movement in Odessa, all trades and professions join

Oct. 29, City forms a committee of public defense; crowds of workmen led by students seize the tramcars and erect barricades: Cossacks fire upon the crowd, killing and wounding many

——, Streets in St. Petersburg in darkness; squads of infantry patrol the streets; nation in passive revolt; Government incapable of enforcing authority

——, Council of Ministers assembles at Peterhof; court stated to be in revolt against the Czar, who vacillates between announcing a constitution with Count Witte as Premier, and the proclamation of a dictatorship under Count Alexis Ignatieff

Oct. 30, Moscow isolated; price of provisions reaches an alarming figure

——, Strike movement throughout the country extends; condition of Riga and Reval growing worse; all the Caucasian railways and the Transcaspian lines cease working

——, State of revolution at Lodz; shops closed; crowds tearing down the Russian flag are dispersed by the soldiers; city completely isolated

——, Czar signs a constitution at Peterhof conceding civic freedom, an extended suffrage, a legislative

duma, and ministerial responsibility. Count Witte appointed Prime Minister

Oct. 31, The new constitution received with mingled feelings on the part of the people; the liberals generally regard it with great disfavor on account of its half-hearted recognition of their demands, and as a confession on the part of the Czar that he has failed to recognize what the people required until the whole country had been thrown into turmoil; enormous demonstration in the Nevsky Prospekt, St. Petersburg; social democrats issue a manifesto declaring that the people must continue the strikes, organize a militia, and demand an amnesty: in Moscow imperial manifesto enthusiastically received by the public; strikers in that city resume work on hearing the news

——, Fatal rioting in Poland; *employés* of the Warsaw-Vienna railway decide not to return to work until the Government settles the question of the use of Polish in the railway service, and proclaims an amnesty for political prisoners and self-government for Russian Poland

——, General strike continues at Lodz; collision between strikers and troops, several people killed and wounded

——, Publication of the Czar's manifesto received with great enthusiasm in Odessa and in Kieff

——, Strike ends on the Moscow-St. Petersburg, Moscow-Kazan and Moscow-Archangel railways, the three great lines of northern Russia

——, Mass meeting of citizens in Odessa attacked by Cossacks, 37 persons killed, 81 wounded

Nov. 1, Imperial ukase issued, by which the Council of Ministers is reorganized

——, In Warsaw, a serious collision between the troops and a crowd, who demand the release of political prisoners; many killed and wounded

——, General strike breaks out in Helsingfors and in all the provincial towns of Finland, chiefly to emphasize the demands of the Finns for the restitution of their constitutional rights, Oct. 31; strike continues, no troops or police visible, order maintained by a citizen militia; Senate resigns in a body; Russian dictatorship stated to be withdrawn

——, Fighting between processions of "patriots" and revolutionaries in the streets of Moscow

——, Anarchy in Odessa, town in the hands of ruffians, who fraternize with the police and march through the principal streets carrying flags, portraits of the Czar and ikons, and singing national hymns; rioters loot many houses and shops; population in a state of panic, many killed and injured in the disorder

Nov. 2–4, Anarchy and terrible massacres in Odessa by mobs incited against the Jews and reformers by reactionaries and officials; marauders pillage shops chiefly in the Jewish quarter; horrible atrocities perpetrated upon the Jews, men, women, and children; 600 families rendered homeless; 964 killed; police and troops remain inactive; British and other embassies make representations to the Government regarding the safety of residents of their nationalities

Nov. 3, Amnesty for offenses committed up to Oct. 30 proclaimed by imperial manifesto and giving a pardon to certain classes of political criminals, and a reduction of sentences to others

——, Horrible massacre of Jews at Kishineff; outrages on Jews at Sevastopol, Rostoff-on-Don, and Elisabetgrad; numbers killed and injured, reported

Nov. 4, Imperial ukase cancelling the obnoxious decrees of recent years, and restoring the Finnish constitution, issued

[The strike in Finland had assumed the form of a complete disregard of the Russian authorities; in many places the police were disarmed, and the troops agreed not to fire unless the people took the offensive; order was maintained by the people themselves)

Nov. 7, The *Russkoe Slovo* reports from Tomsk that over 1,000 Jews and Christians have been burnt to death or massacred by the troops and mob instigated by the police; official outrages at Irkutsk so incense the inhabitants that they form a committee of public safety

——, Serious mutiny of sailors at Kronstadt; wild firing from forts and ships; some quarters of the town set on fire; wholesale plundering; mutiny suppressed, with heavy loss to the mutineers, after great destruction of property, Nov. 9

Nov. 9, Numerous resignations in the cabinet of Count Witte

Nov. 13, Official *communiqué* published, declaring that the Polish revolutionary organizations were plotting for the restoration of the Kingdom of Poland, and stating that martial law had consequently been proclaimed in that province, since the Government would not tolerate attacks on the integrity of the Empire; and that so long as the troubles in the Vistula districts continue, those districts will receive none of the benefits resulting from the recent manifestoes

Nov. 15, Great mutiny of malcontent reservists at Vladivostok; state of war declared; mutineers set fire to the town and plunder it; the greater part of the town and port burnt; 300 rioters, chiefly sailors and artillerymen, killed and wounded

——, Central labor committee decrees another general strike as a protest against coercion in Poland and the court-martial on the mutinous sailors at Kronstadt; strike takes place

——, Continued rioting, pillage and attacks on Jews in Southern Russia: 70 Jews killed and 120 injured at Kishineff; 52 killed, 65 wounded, at Simferopol; mob at Ismail burn alive 11 Jews; village of Kalarasch devastated and burnt, 59 Jews perish in the flames; rioting breaks out among the peasants of Volokolamsk in the Moscow province; they surround the property of Prince Schakovsky, who is thus their prisoner; massacres and pillage of Jews in the provinces of Kherson and Ekaterinoslaff, and in other places, reported

Nov. 17, Imperial manifesto issued dealing with the agrarian question, and making certain considerable concessions to the peasants by the remission of land redemption dues and the increase of facilities for the purchase of land through the peasants' bank, involving a sacrifice of annual revenue to the government of about 7,000,000*l.*

Nov. 24, Organized political revolt of the naval and military forces and workmen at Sevastopol; mutineers capture the city; Adm. Pisarevsky is shot; railway station taken possession of by the sailors, who stop the traffic

Nov. 28, Battle between loyal troops and mutineers at Sevastopol; rebels shell the city; government forces storm the batteries held by the mutineers; the rebel ships sunk or severely damaged; the rising suppressed

Nov. 30, Constitutional senate appointed in Finland

Dec. 1, Great riots in Kieff and Nikolaieff; fighting between workmen and troops, many casualties, martial law proclaimed at Kieff

Dec. 5, Proclamation abolishing martial law in Poland issued

Dec. 9, Strike of postal and telegraph employés as a protest against an order forbidding them to form a union, Nov. 30; telegraphic communication with Russia almost entirely closed; demands of the strikers rejected by the Government

Dec. 12, An imperial ukase places the Baltic Provinces, where terrible disorder prevails, under the almost unlimited authority of the Governor-General, reported

Dec. 15, Revolution extends in the Baltic provinces; Riga in open revolt; railway and telegraphic communication stopped; many public buildings in flames; general panic; Mitau, Libau, and Reval also stated to be in the hands of the revolutionaries

Dec. 17, Congress in Warsaw of 1,400 peasants, representing all the rural communes in the Kingdom of Poland, pass resolutions in favor of autonomy, the establishment of a diet in Warsaw, and the use of the Polish language in schools, courts of law, and government offices

Dec. 20, A general strike begins in Moscow; 125,000 men out on strike in St. Petersburg, Dec. 22

Dec. 28, District of Odessa placed under martial law

Dec. 31, Serious revolutionary movement in Moscow, arrest of a body of revolutionaries followed by furious fighting in the streets; artillery fire upon the people, killing hundreds, Dec. 23; fighting continued, total of killed and wounded among the revolutionaries stated to be 15,000, Dec. 26; fighting ceases, all members of the local social revolutionary committee arrested

1906

Jan. 1, Strikers resume work in St. Petersburg

Jan. 3, Railway bridge blown up on the Dombrovo line, near the station of Jastrzomb, by revolutionists

Jan. 12, French banks agree to place 10,666,666*l.* in short term Russian treasury notes, reported

Jan. 22, Anniversary of "Red Sunday" celebrated at St. Petersburg

——, Mutinous sailors invade the arms store and seize a number of rifles and a quantity of ammunition at Vladivostock

Feb. 3, Official returns of foreign trade over the European frontiers in 1905 show—exports, 99,200,000; and imports, 52,300,000*l.*; reported

Feb. 10, Bomb outrage in Warsaw and St. Petersburg

March 5, Imperial manifesto issued announcing various changes in the constitution of the Duma as promulgated on Oct. 30, 1905

March 19, Lieut. Schmidt, leader of the Black Sea mutiny, and 3 sailors shot at Otchakoff

March 20, Moscow bank raided by a band of armed men, who steal 85,000*l.*

April 1, Elections for the Duma in St. Petersburg result in a sweeping victory for the constitutional democrats (the constitutional democrats and their allies secure 300 seats out of 371)

April 26, Total amount of new loan stated to be 80,-000,000*l.*, issued at 88 and bearing interest at 5%; 48,000,000*l.* reserved for Paris market, and 12,000,-000*l.* for London, to be issued

May 2, Resignation of Count Witte announced

May 6, M. Goremykin appointed successor to Count Witte

May 8, Count Ignatieff assassinated at Kieff

May 10, Professor Muromtseff elected president by 426 votes

May 11, New Council of the Empire opened; M. Isvolsky succeeds Count Lamsdorff as Foreign Minister

May 14, Bomb outrage in Warsaw; Police Captain Constantinoff blown to pieces, and 7 persons severely wounded

May 16, The Duma, in its address in reply to the speech from the throne, demands "freedom, equality and amnesty"

May 26, The Premier reads to the Duma a ministerial declaration rejecting the proposed solution of the agrarian problem, ignoring the demand for an amnesty, and declaring ministerial responsibility to be outside the Duma's competency; the Duma replies almost unanimously that the ministry are not fit to remain in office

June 14, Christians attack the Jewish quarter at Bialystok, and massacre the inhabitants, hundreds killed and wounded

June 19, Mutinies among army troops and sailors at Cronstadt and Sevastopol

June 21 and 22, Remarkable speech of Prince Urusof in the Duma regarding the organization of the pogrom movement

June 24, Chief of the police at Pietrokoff, Poland, assassinated

June 28, Imperial order transforms the first batt. of the Preobrazkensky life-guard regiment into a special infantry battalion, and its privileges withdrawn

July 2, Bill for the abolition of capital punishment passed rapidly through all its stages in the Duma

July 10, Court martial acquits Admiral Roszhdestvensky on the charge concerning the surrender of the torpedo-boat *Biedovy* to the Japanese

July 21, The Czar issues a ukase dissolving the Duma and ordering the convocation of a new duma on March 5, 1907

——, Another ukase replaces M. Goremykin, Premier, by M. Stolypin, Minister of the Interior

July 22, Manifesto issued signed by 181 deputies out of a total number of 478, who meet in Finland, stating that in consequence of the violation of the constitution by the government, citizens should not pay taxes, sanction loans, or furnish a single soldier

July 24, Military outbreak at Brest-Litovsk; disturbances at Odessa, cossacks and hooligans plunder the houses of Jews

July 30, Mutiny in the fortress of Sveaborg; 500 men killed and wounded

Aug. 2, General Markgrafsky, chief of gendarmerie at Warsaw, assassinated

Aug. 3, General strike begun in St. Petersburg

——, Governor of Samara killed by a bomb

Aug. 11, Manifesto issued by the Octobrist leaders insisting on the establishment of a constitutional monarchy with ministerial responsibility and complete abandonment of the old régime

Aug. 15, Sanguinary encounters between revolutionists and police and troops at Warsaw

Aug. 18, Determined attempt made on the life of the Governor-General of Warsaw, who sustained concussion of the brain

Aug. 22, Disbandment of the Finnish Red Guard begun

Aug. 25, Desperate attempt on the life of M. Stolypin at his house near St. Petersburg; 30 persons killed, and 20 seriously injured; M. Stolypin unhurt; 3 of the assassins killed and 1 arrested

Aug. 26, General Minn shot by a woman

Sept. 9, Great massacre at Siedlce; about 400 persons either killed or wounded by the soldiers

Sept. 10, Township of Kwareli, in the Caucasus, almost entirely destroyed by an avalanche; about 250 persons perished

Sept. 15, Death of General Trepoff at Peterhof

Sept. 21, Sir A. Nicolson conveys to the Russian Government the proposal of the British Government, that the whole case of the sinking of the Br. steamer *Knight Commander*, during the Russo-Japanese war, should be referred to the Hague Court of Arbitration

Oct. 1, 23 peasants beaten to death and 130 severely injured by Cossacks at Kherson

Oct. 13, Retirement of Gen. Stössel on ground of ill-health

Oct. 21, Imperial ukase instructing the Senate to amend the laws relating to peasants, as to remove nearly all the restrictions left untouched by the emancipation of 1861, or imposed by subsequent reactionary legislation, signed Oct. 18, published

Oct. 25, Council of Ministers decide to reduce the rate of interest on loans made by the peasants' bank to 4½%; reduction in revenue to be made good by the treasury, announced

Oct. 28, Daring outrages and robberies daily reported from the provinces, chief of secret police at Sevastopol murdered, Oct 27; murderer caught and shot

Oct. 30, Ukase removing all restrictions on the Old Believers, who number about 15 millions, promulgated

Nov. 16, Serious mutiny at Odessa prison reported

Nov. 26, Further terrorist attacks reported from Warsaw

Nov. 27, 35 prisoners, including 9 notorious criminals, escape from the prison at Vladimir, after tying up the governor of the prison, 2 of his subordinates, and all the inspectors

End Nov., Scandal arising out of the grain contract and implicating M. Gourko, Assistant-Minister of the Interior, reported

Dec. 6, Resignation of M. Gourko, Assistant-Minister of the Interior, reported

Dec. 14, Imperial ukase, published in St. Petersburg, bore for the first time the ministerial countersign

Dec. 29, General Kuropatkin's book on the Russo-Japanese war confiscated by the Government

1907

Jan. 15, Conference on famine relief held at the Winter palace under the presidency of M. Stolypin; amount of relief needed estimated at 17,000,000*l.*

Jan. 19, Report of the commission appointed to investigate the Gourko-Lidwall scandal recommends the trial of M. Gourko and M. Litvinoff for criminal acts committed in their official capacity; the commission distinctly absolves M. Gourko of peculation, ascribing his misdeeds merely to "overweening self-confidence"

Jan. 25, The Government gives orders for the immediate evacuation of N. Manchuria, although the date fixed for evacuation was April 15, announced

Jan. 31, M. Victor Grün, chief of the secret police at Warsaw, shot by a band of terrorists

Feb. 1, The exigencies of famine relief call for a loan of

5,000,000*l.*, which the Government proposes to raise by the issue of internal rentes, announced

Feb. 10, Government issues an internal loan of 7,500,-000*l.*, chiefly for famine relief purposes

Feb. 15, Condition of the people in the province of Ufa reported desperate owing to the famine; children and old people only receiving relief

Feb. 16, Great distress reported from Poland; owing to the lock-out in the largest factories, 25,000 families reported starving

Feb. 20, Several outrages on foreign residents reported from Odessa; foreign consuls appeal to their ambassadors, reported

Feb. 22, Terrorist outrage reported from Warsaw, where an armed band robbed a post office and shot a number of officials

Feb. 26, Attempt to blow up a train conveying the Grand Duke Nicholas Nicolaievitch from Tsarskoe Selo to St. Petersburg

March 5, New duma opened; M. Golovin, constitutional democrat of Moscow, elected president by 356 votes to 102

March 15–16, Voting in Finland under the new system of universal adult suffrage, more than half the electors being women, took place

March 19, M. Stolypin makes a ministerial statement to the Duma; he declared that the country must be transformed into a constitutional state, and proceeded to enumerate the laws already promulgated or in course of preparation for this purpose

March 27, Professor Jollos, editor of the *Russkiya Viedomosti*, murdered in Moscow by a hired assassin belonging to the Union of the Russian people

April 11, Scene in the duma caused by irregular proceedings on the part of M. Purishkevitch vice-pres. of the Union of the Russian people, who was ultimately excluded from the sitting

April 23, M. Golovin, president of the Duma, received in audience by the Czar

May 1, Serious strikes reported from Warsaw and Lodz

May 17, Terrorist outrages reported from Lodz, Warsaw, and elsewhere; during an attack on a mail van, at Lodz, 1 Cossack and 21 civilians killed

May 24, 1,750,000*l.* voted by the Duma to defray the cost of government famine relief

June 16, Duma dissolved by imperial ukase; elections fixed for Sept. 14; meeting of new Duma for Nov. 14; new electoral law reducing the peasant electorate promulgated

June 17, Military mutiny at Kieff

June 26, A band of terrorists attack a treasury van, containing 34,000*l.*, in the center of Tiflis, throwing eight bombs; several persons killed, robbers escape with the money

July 30, Russo-Japanese convention, maintaining the integrity of China, signed in St. Petersburg

July 31–Aug. 1, Strike riots at Lodz; 30 persons killed or wounded

Aug. 1, The Czar sails for Swinemünde

Aug. 3–6, Meeting between the German Emperor and the Czar at Swinemünde

Aug. 29, Judgment pronounced on the persons accused of plotting against the Czar: 3 sentenced to be hanged, 9 to penal servitude, and some, including 4 women, banished in Siberia

Aug. 31, Anglo-Russian agreement signed

Sept. 9, Commercial and fishery agreements with Japan, signed in St. Petersburg July 28; ratified

Oct. 30, Naval mutiny at Vladivostok

Nov. 7, M. Gourko, charged in connection with the recent grain scandals, sentenced to be dismissed from his office and deprived the right of holding any state or public appointment for 3 years

Nov. 14, Third Duma opened

Dec. 3, Visit of Mr. Taft

1908

Feb. 16, M. Gerhard, Governor-General of Finland, is "relieved" of his post and is succeeded by General Bekmann

Feb. 20, Trial of the officers concerned in the loss of Port Arthur concluded; General Stössel condemned to death, without loss of rights or of his honor; General Fock reprimanded and Generals Reuss and Smirnoff acquitted; in view of General Stössel's personal bravery, the court recommends the commutation of that officer's sentence to ten years' imprisonment in a fortress

(Death sentence commuted March 17)

——, Arrest of 35 terrorists, some of them being women, in various parts of St. Petersburg; seven condemned to death, including two women, Feb. 28

Mid-March, Executions and death sentences in Russia average from ten to seven daily

April 4, The Czar dissolves the Finnish Diet; new elections to be held July 1

April 8, The Tokio embassy bill adopted by the Council of the Empire

April 24, Extensive floods reported from various parts of central Russia

May 3, Grand-Duchess Marie married Prince William of Sweden

May 8–12, Serious prison mutinies reported from Ekaterinoslaff and Likhvin; in Ekaterinoslaff 29 prisoners were killed and 28 wounded

May 13, Another prison outbreak reported at Simferopol

May 14, Three executions took place in St. Petersburg, and 21 death sentences were pronounced

June 9, King Edward and the Czar meet at Reval

June 10, The Czar appointed an Admiral of the British fleet

July 1, Mine explosion at Jusovka, more than 200 men killed

July 27, Meeting between M. Fallières and the Czar at Reval

Sept. 6, Appeal of the Holy Synod to the faithful, enjoining true believers to abstain from celebrating Count Tolstoi's 80th birthday, read in all the churches of Russia

Outbreak of cholera in St. Petersburg early in Sept.; total since the outbreak 7,796 cases, 3,188 deaths up to Oct. 30

Dec. 9, 17 executions take place, and 37 death sentences pronounced, establishing a record

1909

Feb. 17, Death of the Grand Duke Vladimir, *b.* 1847 (son of Alex. II)

March 21, Russo-British Chamber of Commerce; first meeting held in St. Petersburg

April 19, Russo-Bulgarian agreement, protocol signed. *See* Bulgaria

July 15, The King and Queen of Denmark welcomed by the Czar at Kronstadt

Outbreak of cholera in St. Petersburg; total number

of cases recorded in the Governments of St. Petersburg, Archangel, and Wologda 3,409, of which 1,253
proved fatal from the beginning of June to July 18

Dec. 2, Vital statistics—increase of population, 2,695,-
142; death rate, 27.8 per 1,000; birth rate, 46.3 per
1,000; total population of the Empire on Jan. 1,
1908, 156,250,000. *Times*

Dec. 22, Colonel Karpoff, chief of the St. Petersburg
secret police, killed by an infernal machine

1910

Jan. 23–24, Religious riots between Sunnis and Shiahs
in Bokhara

Jan. 25, Execution of Petroff, alias Voskresensky, for
the murder of Col. Karpoff

Feb. 2, It was stated in the Duma that there were 1,959
death sentences and 825 executions in 1908, and
543 executions in 1909 by order of courts-martial

——, Resolution of Duma favored abolition of system
of exiling by administrative decree persons whose
conduct was regarded as a menace to the State

Feb. 18, French parliamentary deputation arrives in
St. Petersburg

Feb. 19, Received by the Czar

Feb. 23, King Ferdinand of Bulgaria, with the Queen,
arrives at Tsarskoe Selo on a visit to the Czar

Feb. 25, Debate on the budget opens in the Duma; for
the first time in 22 years there was no deficit

March 3, King Ferdinand leaves St. Petersburg

March 9, M. Tchaikovsky, charged with being concerned in the socialist revolutionary movement, was
acquitted; Mme Breshkowskaya was found guilty
and sentenced to exile in Siberia

March 17, Resignation of Homiakov, president of the
Duma, on ground of opposition of members and defiance of his authority and absence of government
members

March 22, King Peter of Servia arrives on a visit to the
Czar

During recent years (1900–1910) there have been
many assassinations by revolutionaries. Governors
of districts, chief constables, and high officials were
the principal sufferers

March 21, Guchkov, Octobrist leader, elected president
of the Duma

March 28, Bill as to Finland laid before Duma provided
that Finnish legislation on which the Grand Duchy
not alone concerned should be transferred to Russian
legislature and asserted right to alter the Finnish
constitution

April 2, Duma adopted proposal for construction of
airship fleet

April 20, The Duma rejected credit for construction
of battleships which had been voted by the Council
of the Empire in 1909

May 18, Duel of M. Guchkov, president of the Duma,
and Count Urvarov. Both sentenced to terms of
imprisonment

May 22, Expulsion of Jews from Kiev by soldiers begun

May 30, Duma passed Stolypin's Bill to create zemstvos
and establish separate classes of voters according to
nationality in western or Polish provinces. Provided for numerical preponderance of Russians over
Poles and excluded Jews from all participation.
Peasants restricted to one-third representation

June 10, Legislative Act for Finland passed third
reading in the Duma

June 25, Baron Ungern-Sternberg arrested charged

with giving secret documents and military information to Austrians

June 27, Council of the Empire passed the "Anti-Polish
Bill"

——, Agrarian reform law passed

June 30, Imperial edict promulgated legislative Act for
Finland; the Finnish Diet to enact legislation only
in matters the exclusive concern of Finland, all other
matters to be the work of the Russian Duma and
Imperial Council which might also amend and change
matters of internal administration

July 4, Convention signed with Japan an agreement to
guarantee the *status quo* in Manchuria in joint opposition to American (Knox) proposal that China should
purchase the Manchurian railroads which should be
neutralized

July 4–15, 1,121 Jews warned to leave Russia and 497
expelled without warning

Aug. 6, Official statement placed number of deaths
from cholera during the week at 8,679

Aug. 19, Agreement with Germany as to railroads in
Persia

Oct. 8, Finnish Diet dissolved by imperial decree and
new elections ordered

Oct. 22, Ukase against German immigration into the
3 western frontier provinces

Oct. 28, Duma reassembled and Guchkov who had
resigned to serve his term of imprisonment reëlected
president

Nov. 4, Visit of Czar to the German Emperor at Potsdam

Nov. 10, Baron Sternberg sentenced to 4 years hard
labor for betrayal of military secrets to Austria

Nov. 20, Death of Count Leo Tolstoi, author, at
Astapova

1911

Jan. 23, Meetings of students except for scientific purposes forbidden

March 17, Rejection by Council of the Empire of
Stolypin's Zemstvo Bill giving restricted self-government to western or Polish provinces establishing
separate classes of voters according to nationality

March 20, Resignation of Premier Stolypin but recalled on his own terms, prorogation of Duma for
3 days, and proclamation of Zemstvo measure by
imperial ukase during suspension as permitted by
emergency clause of the Constitution, and suspension from the Duma of Trepov and Durnovo, opposition members

——, Copyright law enacted

March 25, Imperial ukase passed Zemstvo Bill during
3 day suspension of Duma

——, Andrew Yushinsky, Christian boy, murdered
and Mendel Beiliss, Jew, accused of ritual murder

May 10, Duma passed resolution of censure of promulgation of Zemstvo Bill under emergency clause

May 27, Third Duma prorogued

June 20, Russo-Japanese Agreement settling all claims
arising out of the war

July 7, Treaty signed with Great Britain, Japan, and
the United States prohibiting pelagic sealing

Aug. 19, Agreement with Germany signed as to railroads in Persia (Berlin-Bagdad) at Pottsdam

Aug. 24, The Czar approved Bill for submission to
Duma the addition of part of Viborg province to that
of St. Petersburg, first step in partition of Finland

Sept. 14, Premier Peter A. Stolypin fatally shot at

theater in Kiev in the presence of the Czar by a Jew, Mordka Bogrov, said to be agent of the secret service police

Sept. 15, Russians made their first landing on Wrangel Island on hydrographic expedition

Sept. 18, Death of Stolypin

Sept. 22, Kokovosoff, Minister of Finance, appointed Prime Minister

Sept. 25, Bogrov executed

Nov. 10, Bill for equalizing rights of Russians and Finns in Grand Duchy of Finland passed and for increase of Finland's annual military contribution up to £800,000

Dec. 15, Extradition law passed, extradition heretofore dependent on treaty arrangements

Dec. 17, President Taft abrogated Russian Treaty because of treatment of American Jews in Russia

Dec. 27, Nationalists introduced Bill providing that no American Jews should be admitted into Russia

1912

Jan., Russian troops advanced into Persia occupying provinces of Azerbaijan and northeast part of Khorasan province

Jan. 20 (7), Law enacted gave Russians rights of Finnish citizens in Finland

Jan. 23 (10), Law enacted affirmed principle of annual indemnity in place of military service in Finland. *See also* Finland

April 4/17, Striking miners in gold mines at Lena, Siberia, asked for decent conditions and regular payment of wages

April 22, Troops fired on striking miners killing 190 and wounding 210

June 19, Naval Bill passed provided for expenditure of 502,000,000 roubles' building of 4 armored cruisers and 8 small cruisers, 36 destroyers, 18 submarines, and enlargement of docks between 1912 and 1917

June 21, Third Duma prorogued

June 23, Law reorganized military service

——, Law made provision for workmen in sickness, medical attention and allowance

——, Accident insurance law passed

June 28, Law extended general juridical system to entire peasant population. Land captains to be replaced by justices of the peace

——, Law abolished judicial powers of the country chiefs

July 4, Meeting of Czar with German Emperor and Foreign Ministers at Baltic port

Aug. 5, New Recruiting law signed to go into effect Dec. 14. Age placed at 20 instead of 21

Sept. 12, Duma dissolved

Oct., Election for new Duma a victory for the reactionary Right and defeat of Center Party

Nov. 3, Treaty of alliance with Mongolia signed. Agreement of Russia to support autonomy in return for concessions

Nov. 28, Fourth Duma opened, Right, 60; Nationalists or moderate Right, 125; Octobrists, 90; Opposition groups, 160

1913

Jan. 27, St. Petersburg District Court sentenced 23 members of Viborg Court of Appeals to 16 months imprisonment and dismissal from office for opposition to enforcement of Russian law of 1912 as to rights of Russians in Finland on ground that law had not been passed by Finnish Diet

May 30, Agreement with China as to Mongolia

July 8, Military budget passed by Duma in secret session extended term of service of infantry from 3 years to 3¼ years. Duma prorogued to October

Oct. 8–Nov. 10, Trial of Mendel Beiliss, Jew, at Kiev on charge of ritual murder of Christian boy ended in acquittal after 2 years imprisonment

Oct. 27, Agreement with Turkey signed regarding government of Armenia and railroad concessions

Oct. 28, Duma reassembled

Nov. 5, Russo-Chinese declaration signed recognized autonomy of Outer Mongolia under suzerainty of China

Nov. 14, Marakov apologized for attack on Ministry in previous session ending "Cabinet strike" and non-attendance

Dec. 20, Duma adjourned until Jan. 27 by imperial ukase

Public debt $4,538,000,000

1914

Feb. 11, Resignation of Premier Kokovosoff

Feb. 12 (Jan. 30), Goremykin appointed Prime Minister

May 1, Strikes at St. Petersburg and other cities

May 14, Duma rejected budget

June 9–11, Industrial riots

July 13, Rasputin stabbed in his house near Tobolsk by a woman

July 17–18, Prohibition of sale of intoxicating liquors during mobilization

July 21–25, Protest strikes in St. Petersburg and other cities following suppression of strike of workers in the Baku oil fields by troops

July 23–26, Armed conflicts of strikers and police in St. Petersburg, streets barricaded. Ended by war crisis

July 26, St. Petersburg placed under martial law and strike ended

1915

Feb. 9, Formal opening of the Duma

Feb. 11, Budget enacted calling for expenditure of over $1,500,000,000

Feb. 28, Customs tariff increased

March 4, Telegram to the Entente Governments claimed Constantinople for Russia. Accepted by Great Britain March 12, France April 12

March 12, Death of Count Witte (66)

March 31, Act confirmed imperial ukase of March 4 creating Ministry of Transport

April 3, Imperial ukase granted municipal self-government to Polish towns

April 24, Second Domestic Loan of 1,000,000 rubles at 5½%

May 25, Russo-Chinese-Mongolian Treaty signed guaranteed autonomy of Outer Mongolia under suzerainty of China

June 9–11, Industrial riots. 113 German houses pillaged and destroyed and 500 other houses

June 25, Resignation of General Sukhomlinov as Minister of War. Succeeded by General Polianov

Aug. 1, Duma reassembled voted unanimously to prosecute the war until Russia was victorious

Aug. 6, Council of the Empire opened

Aug. 15, Special Councils of National Defense, Transport, Fuel, and Food Supply constituted

Sept. 5, The Czar took command of the army, General Alexiev made Chief of Staff removing Grand Duke Nicholas from the command

Sept. 8, Grand Duke Nicholas given command of army in the Caucasus

Sept. 16, Imperial ukase suspended Duma to Nov. 14

Oct. 5, Diplomatic relations with Bulgaria severed

Oct. 10, Resignation of Prince Cherbatov, Minister of the Interior. Succeeded by M. Khvostov

Nov. 5, General Gregoriev, former commander at Kovno sentenced to 15 years hard labor for insufficient defense of Kovno

1916

Feb. 1, Premier Goremykin retired

Feb. 3, Boris Stürmer, ultra-Conservative appointed Prime Minister

Feb. 22, Duma opened by the Czar for the first time in person

March 24, Debate in Duma on alleged persecution of Jews ended in tumult in which Conservative Party left the hall

March 28, Russo-Chinese Agreement signed whereby Russia received permission to construct railroad between Blagoveshschensk and Harbin and Tsitsikar in Manchuria

March 29, Resignation of General Polivanov as Minister of War. Succeeded by General Shuvaiev

——, Cabinet: Ministry of the Imperial House and Imperial Domains, General W. Freedericksz, aide-de-camp of the Emperor, appointed 1898; Foreign Affairs, Actual State Councillor Sazonoff, appointed 1910; War, General Shuvayeff, appointed March, 1916; Navy, Admiral Grigorovich, appointed 1911; Interior, Actual Privy Councillor Stürmer, appointed March, 1916; Public Instruction, Actual State Councillor Count Ignatieff, appointed February, 1915; Finance, Actual State Councillor Bark, appointed January 30 (February 12), 1914; Justice, State Councillor A. A. Khvostoff, appointed 1915; Agriculture, Actual State Councillor Naumoff, appointed 1915; Ways of Communications, General A. Trepoff, appointed 1915; Commerce and Industry, Actual State Councillor Prince Shakhovskoy, appointed March, 1915; Department of General Control, Actual Privy Councillor Kharitonoff, appointed 1907; Holy Synod, Actual State Councillor Volzhin, appointed 1915; General Direction of State Studs, General Stakhovitch

April 24, Budget approved by the Czar included income tax applying to all incomes of 850 rubles and over and a large appropriation for education

April 26, The Secret Treaty of France and Russia (Sazonov-Paleologue) for partition of Asiatic Turkey, Russia to have full sovereignty over the vilayets of Trebizond, Erzerum, Bitilis, and Van

July 2, Duma passed Bill conferring on peasants the same civil rights as enjoyed by other classes

July 3, Secret Treaty with Japan as to interests in China signed mutual

——, Duma suspended until Nov. 14

July 16, Death of Professor Elias Metchnikov

July 23, Sazonov resigned as Minister of Foreign Affairs. Stürmer took portfolio

Aug. 17, Announcement by J. P. Morgan and Company of loan of $250,000,000 to Russia for 2 years at 5%

Sept. 4, Russia informed Allied Powers of incorporation

in Russian Empire of islands off the coast of Fridtjov Nansen Land formerly Franz Josef Land

Sept. 23, The Czar approved plan for establishment of Ministry of Public Health

Oct. 4, Premier Stürmer ordered all meetings of the All-Russian Union of Zemstvos, the Union of Municipalities, and War Industries Committee and other popular organizations to be held only under police surveillance

Nov. 15, Grand Duke Nicholas in interview with the Czar gave him summary of situation in Russia and the harm done by Rasputin and the Empress and forces in employ of Germany

Nov. 18, Duma opened

Nov. 24, Count Stürmer dismissed as Prime Minister and Alexander Trepov appointed to succeed him

Nov., Second foreign Loan of $300,000,000 at 5½%

Dec. 8, Railroad from Murmansk to Petrograd declared open

Dec. 14, Appointment of Pokrovsky as Minister of Foreign Affairs

Dec. 15, Duma voted to reject German peace proposals

Dec. 30, Assassination of the monk, Rasputin, in house of Prince Felix Yussupov

1917

Jan. 1, New income tax became effective

——, Body of Rasputin found in the Neva River

——, Number of Credit Coöperative Societies 16,500, Consumers' Coöperative Societies 20,000

Jan. 9, Resignation of Trepov as Prime Minister. Succeeded by Prince Nikolai Golitzin. Count Ignatiev, Minister of Public Instruction resigned

Jan. 17, General Bieliaev appointed Minister of War replacing General Shuvaiev

Jan. 19, Imperial ukase postponed convening of Duma and Imperial Council

Jan., Strikes of 244,000 men during this month

Feb. 1, Conference of Entente Allies in Petrograd

Feb. 7, 100,000 men went on strike in Petrograd and 25,000 in Moscow as a demonstration in favor of the Social Democrats

Feb. 27 (14 O.S.), Duma opened

Feb. 11–12, Twenty labor leaders arrested and Central Committee on War Production accused of revolutionary activities

March 5, Secret Agreement by which Russia to support claims of Japan

March 8, Bread riots in Petrograd and conflicts of strikers and police. Red flags appeared

——, The Czar left for military headquarters

March 10, Conflict of strikers and police. 50 persons killed or wounded in Petrograd

——, Mutiny of Volynsky regiment in Petrograd

March 11 (Feb. 26, O.S.), Strikes in munitions factories. Garrison at Petrograd joined revolt

——, 2 imperial ukases suspended Duma and Council of the Empire and strikers ordered to return to work

——, Proclamation dated March 10 (Feb. 25, O.S.) forbade street meetings

——, Secret exchange of views with France as to left bank of Rhine, Saar Valley, and Poland

March 12, Duma met defying Czar's decree of dissolution. Provisional committee elected headed by Rodzianko in attempt to control and lead the revolution

——, Petrograd Soviet of Workers and Soldiers Deputies organized at 7 P.M.

March 13, Telegram of members of the Council of the Empire to the Czar urged convening of Duma and a new Cabinet

——, Proclamation of the Executive Committee of the Duma taking over the Government

——, First proclamation of the Petrograd Soviet

——, The Czar left Mogilev for Tsarskoe-Selo

——, Battle in Petrograd continued. Winter Palace taken by the revolutionists

March 14, Proclamation of Duma announced a Provisional Government headed by Prince George E. Lvov

——, Moscow and other cities declared for the Provisional Government

——, The Czar's train stopped at Pskov and the Czar placed under arrest

——, "Order Number 1" issued by Soviet organized as "Council of Workmen's and Soldier's Delegates" declaring army under committees of soldiers responsible to the Soviet destroyed organization and discipline in the army

——, Grand Duke Cyril Vladimirovitch declared adherence to the Duma

March 15, The Czar signed abdication for himself and his son in favor of the Grand Duke Michael. The Czar permitted to return to army headquarters

——, Coalition Cabinet appointed by Duma: Prince Lvov, Prime Minister and Minister of the Interior; Milukov, Foreign Affairs; A. Kerensky, Justice; Professor Manuilov, Public Instruction; A. J. Guchkov, War and Navy; Ichingarev, Agriculture; Tereschtenko, Finance; N. V. Nekrasov, Communications; Godnev, Controller of State

March 16, Grand Duke Michael refused to accept supreme power unless authorized by a constituent assembly and plebiscite

——, Manifesto of Provisional Government granted general amnesty, granted freedom of speech and press, and association and summoned constituent assembly

March 18, Foreign Minister Milukov addressed representatives of Allies in capital assuring them that Russia "would fight by their side against the common enemy until the end"

——, New oath of allegiance taken by the army

——, Meeting of Holy Synod at St. Petersburg accepted the revolution

March 19, Work resumed at factories

March 21, Government restored the Constitution of Finland declaring it a free and independent State in Russian federation

——, Government ordered the ex-Czar and Czarina imprisoned at Tsarskoe Selo

March 22, Provisional Government recognized by the United States, Great Britain, France, Italy, Rumania, and Switzerland

March 24, General M. V. Alexiev made commander-in-chief of the Russian armies

March 25, Government proclamation granted absolute equality to Jews as to political, economic, educational, and military rights

——, Capital punishment abolished

March 27, The grand dukes and royal princes renounced their hereditary rights

——, At mass meeting the Petrograd Soviet issued proclamation to peoples of the world calling for "concerted and decisive action in favor of peace"

March 30, Provisional Government proclaimed the independence of Poland

March 30, Provisional Government confiscated all imperial lands and lands of monasteries

March 31, Food prices fixed at from 20 to 50% lower prices

April 1, Exiles from Siberia arrived in Petrograd including Catharina Breshkovskaya and Marie Spiridonovar. Great reception given to them

April 2, Provisional Government repealed all laws abridging religious freedom

April 9, Manifesto of the Government signed by Prince Lvov declared object to establish a durable peace on the basis of rights of nations to decide their own destiny

April 11, Grain monopoly instituted by the Provisional Government

April 12, Decree proclaimed autonomy for Estonia

April 13, All-Russia Conference of Workers' and Soldiers' Delegates, first national congress of Soviets met at Petrograd

——, Arrival of Lenin and other Russian radicals from Switzerland at Stockholm on their way to Russia

April 21, Proclamation of the Provisional Government declared that historic rights of Cossacks to lands could not be violated

April 25, Freedom of assemblage and association granted by law enacted

April 27, Right to inheritance abolished

May 1, Note to Miliukov to Allies declared that no separate peace would be made with Germany. Published May 3 and protested by Council of Workers' and Soldiers' Delegates

May 3, First demonstration against the Provisional Government under slogan "Down with Miliukov"

May 4, Meeting of Executive Committee of Council of Workers' and Soldiers' Delegates with representatives of the Provisional Government. Government agreed to send another Note to Allies reaffirming declaration of April 9 disregarding the Miliukov Note of May 1

May 5, Council of Workers' and Soldiers' Delegates adopted vote of confidence in the Provisional Government by a small majority

May 9, Council of Workers' and Soldiers' Delegates voted to call an international peace conference to meet in a neutral country. Stockholm selected as place of meeting

——, Act abolished deportation to Siberia

May 13, General Kornilov commanding Petrograd garrison resigned because of interference of Council of Workers' and Soldiers' Delegates with his orders

May 14, First All-Russian Moslem Conference held at Moscow, Council established

——, Resignation of Guchkov, Minister of War, Conservative

May 15, German Chancellor offered an immediate and separate peace

May 16, Lvov formed new Cabinet with Kerensky as Minister of War and Terestschenko as Minister of Foreign Affairs replacing Miliukov forced to resign

May 19, Reorganized Cabinet declared against separate peace and declared war aim peace "without annexations or indemnities"

May 20, Prince Lvov appealed to soldiers to break armistice they had established at the front

May 22, Kerensky, Minister of War, issued order known as "Declaration of Soldiers' Rights" which confirmed "Order Number 1" of the Petrograd Soviet disorganizing army

May 24, Rising of peasants against large land owners and Germans

May 25, Law created new democratic system of local self-government

May 30, Soviets announced International Conference at Stockholm and asked for restatement of war aims of Allies

May 31, Austrian Emperor repeated German peace offer of May 15

June 1, Kronstadt Committee of Workers' and Soldiers' Delegates repudiated the Provisional Government and assumed control of the fortress

June 2, Grand Duke Nicholas arrested at Tiflis on charge of plotting against the Government

June 4, General Brussilov succeeded General Alexiev as commander-in-chief

June 6, Election for municipal and district councils held with universal suffrage

——, 140 factories in Petrograd placed on a six hour day basis

June 7, Kronstadt rebels recognized the Provisional Government

June 8, Meeting of representatives of commercial and banking institutions declared for a separate peace

June 9, Provisional Government refused German offer of unlimited armistice

June 13, American Mission and American Railroad Commission arrived at Petrograd

June 14, Women admitted to the bar

June 16, All-Russian Congress of Workers' and Soldiers' Delegates met at Petrograd

June 21, Woman's regiment, "The Command of Death" reviewed by Kerensky at Petrograd

——, Mutiny of Black Sea fleet at Sevastopol

June 22, Universal suffrage extended to the zemstvo elections

June 26, Manifesto of the Ukraine Rada declared it would manage its own affairs

June 29, Law increased progressive income tax to 30% on incomes over $200,000

June 30, General Kaledin elected Hetman of the Don Cossacks

July 3, Act gave coöperative societies legal status; incorporation required

July 9, Administration of State railroads handed over to committees of the employees by order of Minister of Communications

July 16–18, Bolshevik rising against the Government suppressed by cavalry and troops from the front. Trotsky and other leaders arrested. Lenin fled to Finland

July 19, Regiments under Bolshevist influence in East Galicia left trenches and refused to obey commands

July 20, Kerensky became acting Premier on resignation of Prince Lvov

——, Finnish Diet announced independence. See Finland

July 25, Death penalty for treason and mutiny in the army restored

Aug. 1, General Brussilov appointed by Kerensky replaced Kornilov as commander-in-chief of the Russian armies

Aug. 3, Resignation of N. Terestschenko, Minister of Foreign Affairs

Aug. 6, Alexander Kerensky became Prime Minister and Minister of War

Aug. 7, Kerensky announced new coalition Cabinet

Aug. 8, Restrictions removed as to Roman Catholic Church and liberty granted to Jesuit order

Aug. 15, The Czar and family removed from Tsarskoe Selo to Tobolsk, Siberia

Aug. 26, "Extraordinary National" Council at Moscow representative of all important political groups opened by Kerensky to consider the state of the nation and make plans for permanent government

——, General strike of radicals

Sept. 3, Germans entered Riga. See Latvia

Sept. 5, Grand Dukes Michael and Paul arrested

Sept. 8, General Kornilov dismissed headed revolt against the Provisional Government and began march on Petrograd

Sept. 9, Kerensky ordered Kornilov to surrender his command

Sept. 10, Kerensky assumed dictatorship

Sept. 12, Kornilov advance on Petrograd, occupied Gotchina 30 miles from the capital

——, Kerensky assumed supreme command of the army and appointed General Alexiev chief of the General staff

Sept. 14, General Kornilov forced to surrender to Provisional Government

Sept. 15, Manifesto of Kerensky proclaimed the Russian Republican State. The Provisional Government reconstructed in form of a directorate of five headed by Kerensky

Sept. 20, Transcaucasian Republic proclaimed

Sept. 26, General W. A. Soukhomlinov, former Minister of War, placed on trial Aug. 23, on charge of having withheld ammunition and supplies from the army and betrayed military information to the enemy, sentenced to imprisonment for life at hard labor

Sept. 27, Democratic Congress called by the Council of Workers' and Soldiers' Delegates assembled at Petrograd

Oct. 8, Kerensky named coalition Cabinet ignoring request of Democratic Congress to take part in reorganization of the Government

Oct. 18, Municipal elections held returned a majority of moderate Socialists

Oct. 20, Pre-Parliament met at Petrograd

Oct. 21, Duma dissolved. General elections to be held Nov. 25

——, Peace terms proposed by Council of Workers' and Soldiers' Delegates; no annexations and no indemnities

Oct. 23, Bolshevik Central Committee agreed on seizure of power

Oct. 29, Decree as to eight hour day law

Nov. 1, Statement of Kerensky to press declared Russia exhausted and Allies must bear burden of the War

Nov. 3/16, Declaration of rights of people

Nov. 7, Second All-Russian Congress of Soviets met, Kamenev, Bolshevik chosen president

——, Bolshevik minority headed by Lenin seized the Government taking all members of the Provisional Government prisoners except Kerensky who escaped proceeding to the front to bring back troops to quell the revolution

Nov. 8, Council of Peoples' Commissars with Lenin at head elected by Congress of Soviets declared itself highest military authority for defense of the capital; Trotsky named "Commissary of the people for Foreign Affairs," Krylenko of War, Rykov for Internal Affairs, Stalin of Nationalities, Lunacharsky of Education

Nov. 8, Decree of Bolshevik Government announced adoption of peace without annexation or indemnities
——, Decree of Lenin of nationalization abolished private ownership of land
Nov. 9, Kerensky joined General Krasnov commanding 1,500 Cossacks at Gatchina
Nov. 11, Eight hour working day established
Nov. 13, Bolsheviks defeated Kerensky forces near Tsarskoe Selo
Nov. 14, General Krasnov taken prisoner and released on parole
Nov. 15, Kerensky fled from Russia
Nov. 16, Decree instituted land committees for each rural district to be elected by people
Nov. 20, Government order to army headquarters to propose cessation of hostilities to the enemy
——, The Ukrainian Rada proclaimed a separate State to be part of the Federal Republic of Russia
——, The German Emperor announced he would not treat with the Bolshevik Government
Nov. 21, General Dukhonin, commander-in-chief, deposed because of his refusal to offer armistice to "all nations allied and hostile" and Ensign Krylenko appointed in his place
Nov. 22, Note of Trotsky to Allied ambassadors in Petrograd proposed "immediate armistice on all fronts and the immediate opening of peace negotiations"
Nov. 23, Decree abolished classes and titles
Nov. 24, Resignation of Alexander Kerensky as Prime Minister
——, Publication of secret documents in diplomatic archives begun by Trotsky
Nov. 25, Election of delegates to constituent assembly resulted in return of a majority of Socialists, 420; Bolsheviks, 225; Mohammedans, 60; Cossacks, 25; Maximalists, 25; Constitutional Democrats, 24; Jews, 4
Nov. 26, Proclamation abolishing all class privileges declared all persons "citizens of the Russian Republic"
Nov. 27, Decree instituted Soviets of Workmens' Control in factories
Nov. 28, General armistice on all fronts proposed by Lenin. Accepted by Germany
Nov. 29, Law established Insurance Council
Nov. 30, Constitution adopted by Congress
Dec. 1, Bolshevik Government sent representatives through the German lines to discuss peace
Dec. 2, Act reaffirmed Dec. 21, proclaimed independence of Union of the Caucasus
Dec. 3, First negotiations at Brest-Litovsk with the Central Powers. Bolshevik peace terms submitted
Dec. 5, General Dukhonin killed by being thrown from a railroad train
Dec. 6, Finland proclaimed independence. *See also* Finland
——, Hostilities suspended and truce with Central Powers came into effect the following day
Dec. 9, Cossack revolt against Bolshevik Government headed by Generals Kaledine and Kornilov in Ural and Don regions
Dec. 11, Lithuania proclaimed independence. *See also* Lithuania
Dec. 12, Constituent Assembly convening in Petrograd dispersed by Bolsheviks and delegates arrested
Dec. 14, Decree closed all private banks, all banks merged in a People's Bank

Dec. 15, Armistice between Russia and the Central Powers signed at Brest-Litovsk to continue until Jan. 14
——, Independence of Moldavian Republic proclaimed
Dec. 17, Announcement that property of the Russian Church would be confiscated. Religious instruction in schools abolished
Dec. 18, Decree declared that only civil marriages would be recognized and established divorce regulations
——, Decree constituted Supreme Soviet (Council) of National Economy. Workers committees in factories placed under general guidance of this body
——, Decree created a special Commissariat for local government
Dec. 20, Order of Lenin created Revolutionary Tribunal (Cheka) for suppression of counter-revolution which began the "red terror," Felix Dzerzhinsky, head
Dec. 22, Peace negotiations with Central Powers begun at Brest-Litovsk
Dec. 23, Ukrainia adopted Constitution
——, Secret Anglo-French Convention defined proposed zones of influence in southern Russia
Dec. 24, Decree recognized Soviets of Workmens, Soldiers, and Peasants Deputies as organs of local government. Commissariat issued instructions as to organization
Dec. 27, Decree nationalized banks. *See supra* Dec. 14 O.S.
Dec. 28, Brest-Litovsk negotiations broken off
Dec. 29, Institute of Insurance Soviets created to initiate compulsory insurance of workers
Dec. 30, Period of foreign intervention begun with arrival of Japanese warships at Vladivostok

1918

Jan. 4, Independence of Finland officially recognized
Jan. 5, Institute of Local Soviets of National Economy created subject to authority of Supreme Council
Jan. 10, Republic of the Don declared independence, General Kaledin, President
Jan. 18, Constituent Assembly opened in Petrograd, Tchernov elected President
Jan. 19, Decree dissolved the Constituent Assembly as "unduly bourgeois." Closed by soldiers
Jan. 23/Feb. 4 Decree announced separation of Church and State
——, Proclamation protested German peace terms
Jan. 26, Third Congress of Councils of Workers and Soldiers Delegates met in Petrograd
Jan. 28, The Ukraine proclaimed an independent republic
Jan. 30, Decree created Committee on prices with wide powers
Jan. 31, Decree for replacement of Julian by Gregorian calendar. Feb. 1 became Feb. 14
Feb. 4, General Alexiev commanding Don Cossacks marched on Moscow
Feb. 8, Official proclamation of Decree of Jan. 28, repudiated Russian national debts
——, Non-Soviet Government established at Tomsk, Siberia
Feb. 9, The Ukraine signed separate peace with the Central Powers at Brest-Litovsk. Boundary defined
Feb. 10, Proclamation announced war with Germany ended and ordered demobilization of army without signing an "annexationist treaty"

Feb. 13, Cossacks defeated by Bolsheviks. General Kaledin, Hetman, committed suicide

Feb. 18, Armistice expired and Germans resumed hostilities crossing the Dvina bridge entering Dvinsk. The Germans declared statement of Feb. 10 equivalent to denouncement of truce of Dec. 15. *See also* World War for battles

——, Bolsheviks captured Kiev, Ukrainian capital

Feb. 19, Proclamation of Lenin protested German advance and announced the Treaty with the Central Powers would be signed

——, Decree nationalized land, farm buildings, machinery, and livestock

Feb. 22, New volunteer army under General Kornilov invaded Kuban district to support Cossacks

Feb. 23, Turkish army began offensive in the Caucasus driving Russian army in rout

——, Germany offered new and more drastic peace terms

Feb. 24, Turks took Trebizond

——, Peoples Commissaries decided to accept new terms of Central Powers

Feb. 26, Allied diplomats left Petrograd as Germans approached going to Yologda

Feb. 28, Patriarch Tikhon issued appeal against the Soviet régime which caused street fighting.

March 2, Kiev occupied by German and Ukrainian troops driving out Bolsheviks

——, "Extraordinary" tax in kind introduced

March 3, Treaty of Brest-Litovsk signed with Central Powers. Reduced Russia to practically the size of the medieval Grand Duchy of Moscow (Hayes)

March 8, Trotsky resigned as Commissar of Foreign Affairs but remained in the Cabinet as Commissar of Military and Naval Affairs. Tchitcherin appointed in charge of foreign affairs

March 9, Announced that capital is to be transferred to Moscow

March 13, Germans took Odessa

March 14–16, Fourth Congress of Soviets met at Moscow

March 16, Soviet Congress ratified the Treaty of Brest-Litovsk

March 17, Turks took Batum

March 20, Germans in possession of all Ukraine west of the Dnieper. Held Zhitomir, Kiev, Nikolayev, and Odessa

March 27, General Kornilov succeeded in joining Kuban forces but failed in attack on Ekaterinburg, Bolshevik center

April 3, Germans took Ekaterinburg

April 5, Japanese and British landed troops at Vladivostok

April 11, Bessarabia voted to join Rumania

April 13, General Kornilov killed by shell. General Denikin succeeded him as commander-in-chief of anti-Bolshevik forces

April 22, Trans-Caucasia declared independence (Armenia, Azerbaijan, and Georgia)

April 23, Government protested the union of Bessarabia with Rumania

April 26, Protest of Government to Germany of invasion and violation of the Treaty of Brest-Litovsk

April 27, Private rights of inheritance abolished

April 29, Military dictatorship established by Germans in the Ukraine

April 30, The Czar and Czarina brought to Ekaterinburg

May 4, Armistice signed with the Ukraine

May 11, Cossacks elected General Krasnov Hetman of the Don Cossacks

May 14, Decree provided regulations for control of grain

May 23, General Semenov and General Kolchak established an independent government in eastern Siberia beyond Lake Baikal

May 24, Bolsheviks defeated Turco-German force in Kars district of Transylvania

May 26, Georgia (Caucasus) proclaimed independence

——, Czechs began operations against Bolsheviks in Volga region and Siberia

——, Trans Caucasian Federal Government dissolved into 3 independent republics of Armenia, Georgia, and Azerbaijan

May 28, Azerbaijan and Armenia declared independent Republics

May 29, Announcement of new Cossack Government headed by General Krasnov

June 4, Don Cossacks declared independence

June 6, Ultimatum of Germany demanded return of remainder of Black Sea fleet to Sebastopol as condition of cession of hostilities. Accepted by Lenin

June 11, Decree regarding organization of poor peasants and supply to them of grain, and agricultural implements began class war in villages

June 12, Truce signed with the Ukraine at Kiev provided for cessation of war and negotiations for peace

June 17, Ukraine severed diplomatic relations with Rumania

June 23, British landed at Murmansk

June 28, Decree announced nationalization of industry affected about 2,000 enterprises

June 30, The Czechs defeated the Bolsheviks at Irkutsk and Vladivostok

July 4, Fifth All-Russian Congress of Soviets met

——, Czechs organized a provisional government of Siberia at Vladivostok

July 6, Count von Mirbach, German ambassador to Russia, assassinated by bomb at Moscow

July 10, General Horvat formed new government at Vladivostok

——, New Constitution of the Socialist Federated Soviet Republics (RSFSR) adopted by Congress of Soviets

July 15, British and French marines and soldiers landed at Murmansk and Kola

July 16, Ex-Czar Nicholas II and his family murdered at Ekaterinburg by the Bolshevik Ural Regional Council

July 23, Independence of Siberia proclaimed by government organized with a capital at Omsk under Vologodsky. Irkutsk and Vladivostok joined

July 25, Soviet decree made purchase, sale or possession of precious metals in bullion or gold punishable by imprisonment of not less than 10 years and the confiscation of entire property of the offender

——, Allied diplomats removed from Vologda to Archangel

July 26, National Congress in Turkestan declared that country a republic in alliance with Russia instead of a province

——, Czechs captured Ekaterinburg

July 29, Czechs occupied Shmakova

——, State of war declared with Great Britain and her Allies

July 30, Field Marshal von Eichorn, German commander in the Ukraine and his adjutant Captain von Dressler killed by bomb

Aug. 2, French and British troops landed at Archangel and instituted Government of Russian Northern Territory

Aug. 3, Statement of American intentions for which troops employed, to guard military stores and give such aid as was acceptable to the Russian people without interference in internal affairs

Aug. 4, Instructions of Commissariat of Food as to confiscation of grain by armed units

Aug. 6, Declaration of the British Government to Russian people of non-interference with Russian politics

Aug. 7, Treaty of the Ukraine with the Don Republic established boundary

Aug. 8, Decree published established right of everyone of age of 16 to enter universities without examination

Aug. 9, French marines landed at Vladivostok

Aug. 10, French and British consuls in Moscow arrested in retaliation for attack on Bolsheviks at Archangel

Aug. 24, General Horvat at Vladivostok proclaimed himself dictator

——, Battle of Dukhovskaya in eastern Siberia. Bolsheviks defeated by Allies

Aug. 27, Supplementary Treaty of peace with Central Powers

Aug. 29, Decree ordered arrest of all French and British nationals between ages of 18 and 40 for anti-Bolshevik activities

——, Decree announced treaties relating to partition of Poland void

Aug. 30, Attempt of Dora Kaplan to assassinate Lenin led to arrest and massacre of hundreds of the intellectual class

Aug. 31, Russian attack on British embassy. Captain Francis Crombie, naval attaché, killed

Sept. 4, Dora Kaplan executed at Moscow

——, American troops landed at Murmansk. Obozerskaya occupied by Allies

Sept. 8, Government of the North of Nikolai Tschaikovsky overthrown by reactionaries headed by army officer Chaplin

——, Announcement of agreement with Great Britain by which British and French diplomatic prisoners be exchanged for Russians in London

Sept. 8–23, Conference of anti-Soviet Russians at Ufa organized a provisional Government, the "Directorate of Five" for government of Siberia with Nicholas D. Avksentiev at head

Sept. 18, Japanese troops captured Blagoveschensk and took large number of Austrian and German prisoners and quantities of ammunition and supplies, 326 railroad passenger cars, 55 river steamers

Sept. 26, Proclamation of Lenin ended massacre of intellectuals

Oct. 1, Primary and secondary schools placed under Commissariat of Education and called Uniform Labor School, tuition charges abolished

Oct. 5, Decree established autonomy of universities, lecturers became professors after 3 years

Oct. 8, Death of General Alexeiev

Oct. 13, Decree abolished tax on capital

Oct. 18, Government of Northern Russia reëstablished after peremptory demand of Allies

Oct. 19, German Volga Labor Commune established an autonomous region

——, Ukrainian National Council assumed control in eastern Galicia

Oct. 30, Decree abolished all land taxes

Nov. 1, State of war with the Ukraine declared by Poland

Nov. 6, Sixth Congress of Soviets met

Nov. 7, Appeal of President Asksentiev of Siberia to President Wilson for recognition from the United States and Allies

Nov. 15, Revolt of General Petlura against Ukraine Government

Nov. 17, Allied force commanded by General Thompson (British) entered Baku invited by Government of Azerbaijan

Nov. 18, Coup d'état of Admiral Kolchak overthrew Omsk "Directorate of Five" and proclaimed himself dictator of Siberian Government

Nov. 26, Russian Black Sea fleet surrendered to Allies

Nov. 30, Russian-American force captured Korpagarskoi 200 miles southeast of Archangel after fight with Bolsheviks

Dec. 18, French troops occupied Odessa

Dec. 20, Kiev occupied by Petlura's revolutionary forces

Dec. 23, Constitution for independent Ukraine adopted by the Rada

Dec. 24, Perm, eastern Russia occupied by Kolchak forces

Dec. 29, Decree abolished the industrial tax

Dec. 30, Birsk taken by Kolchak forces

1919

Jan. 1, White Russian Soviet Socialist Republic formed including former provinces of Minsk, Vitepsk, Mogilov, and parts of Grodo and Gomel

Jan. 4, Ukrainian Republic of the West (Austrian) formed union with Russian Ukraine each preserving its own government but under supreme authority of Directory headed by Petlura

Jan. 9, General Denikin took Alexandrovsk Grushevsky in the Caucasus

Jan. 12, Tchicherin, Commissar of Foreign Affairs, asked American State Department to open peace negotiations

Jan. 14, Denikin defeated Bolsheviks on the River Kuma in Caucasus

Jan. 16, Allies defeated Bolsheviks in fight for Merv

Jan. 19–25, Bolshevik attack of Archangel front at Shenkursk 180 miles south of Archangel forced Allies to withdraw

Jan. 20, Ufa, Siberia taken by the Bolsheviks

——, Ruthenians recognized supreme authority of Ukraine Rada

Jan. 25, Orenburg taken by Bolsheviks

Jan. 27, Bolsheviks occupied Ekaterinburg

Jan. 28, Vladikavkez captured from Soviet forces by General Denikin

——, Soviet Government of the Ukraine established at Kharkov

——, Russian Grand Dukes executed by order of the Revolutionary Tribunal

Jan. 29, Allies again withdrew on Archangel front

Jan. 30, Kolchak Government announced Cabinet

Jan. 31, Ports of Libau and Windau in Courland taken by Soviet forces

Feb. 3, Soviet forces took Kiev

Feb. 3–9, Denikin forces routed Soviet forces in northern Caucasus

Feb. 4, Constitution of the White Russian Socialist Soviet Republic promulgated

Feb. 6, Government accepted invitation of Paris Peace Conference to hold a conference at Prinkipo on sea of Marmora

Feb. 12, Ukrainians defeated Soviet forces near Kiev

Feb. 14, Statute of Socialist Land Settlement issued, step toward collectivization

Feb. 16, Ukrainians resumed hostilities against the Poles occupying oil fields near Lemberg, Galicia. *See also* Poland

Feb. 19, Decree abolished tax rates on town property

March 1, Ukrainians denounced truce with Poles of Feb. 24

March 2, Ukrainians attacked Lemberg

——, Bolsheviks captured Vevsievskawa in northern Russia

March 2–6, First Congress of Third International at Moscow founded by Lenin as successor of First International of Marx

March 7, Soviet forces bombed American position on the Vaga River from airplane

March 13, The French proclaimed authority in Odessa region

March 14, Constitution of independent Ukraine promulgated

——, Ufa captured by Kolchak forces

March 15–April 20, Soviet forces advanced in southern Russia forcing Denikin to retreat to bases on Black Sea

March 16–17, Americans and White Russians in battle with Soviet forces defending base at Obzerskaya

March 23, Bashkir (Ufa) autonomous Republic established

March 25, American engineers arrived at Murmansk

March 28, and April 8, American railroad troops arrived at Murmansk

March 31, Soviet forces repulsed in attack on Archangel front

April 5, Attack of Soviet forces on Archangel front again repulsed

April 6, Franco-Grecian army defeated by Soviet forces near Odessa

April 8, Allies evacuated Odessa which was occupied by Soviet forces

April 12, Soviet forces occupied Yalta (Crimea)

April 13, Decree ordered registration of shares and bonds

April 17, Allies captured Vajmosalma, northern Russia

April 18, Allies occupied Bolshie Ojerki

May 2, Attack of Soviet forces repulsed on Archangel front

——, Ultimatum to Rumania demanded evacuation of Bessarabia

May 8–15, Denikin successful in engagements in South

May 10, Soviet forces repulsed on Archangel front

May 18, State of war declared to exist with Rumania

May 19, Ukrainian National Council asked Poles for an armistice

May 20, Allies in the North captured Lumbushki, Ostreche, and Kolodari

June 1, Decree of Central Executive Committee ratified union of the Russian, Ukrainian, Latvian, Lithuanian, and White Russian Republics

June 6, Declaration of war against Russia by Finland

June 9, Ufa recaptured by Soviet forces

June 12, Conditional recognition of Kolchak Government as government of Russia by Allied Powers (Council of Four)

June 27, Bolsheviks abandon Kharkov

July 14, Soviet forces capture Ekaterinburg. Announce Kolchak decisively defeated in Urals

July 30, General Denikin in new offensive on Kharkov-Poltava front

Aug. 2, Allies destroyed Bolshevist flotilla on Lake Onega in the North

——, General Denikin captured Poltava

Aug. 5, Allied Black Sea fleet bombed Ochakov and Stanislavov

Aug. 10, Soviet forces defeated by Anglo-Russian force on the Dvina River near Barok

Aug. 18, Naval engagement of British squadron with Soviet fleet in Gulf of Finland sunk 2 Russian battleships and bombarded Kronstadt

——, Japanese troops commanded by General Otani landed at Vladivostok

——, Official announcement that Odessa occupied by General Denikin's forces driving out the Bolsheviki

Aug. 24, Soviet forces defeated by Allies near Krasfesky

Aug. 27, Soviet force captured Pskov

Sept. 2, Kiev occupied by troops of General Denikin

Sept. 6, Soviet forces took Tobolsk

Sept. 30, Allied evacuation of Archangel completed

Oct. 8, Denikin troops captured Voronezh and Grafskia

Oct. 12, Evacuation of northern Russia completed as last British troops left Murmansk

——, Koloshova captured from the Bolsheviks

Oct. 13, Pskov captured from Bolsheviks

Oct. 14, General Denikin captured Orel within 200 miles of Moscow

Oct. 19, General Yudenitch reached outskirts of Petrograd

Oct. 20, General Denikin recaptured Kiev

Oct. 21, General Denikin victorious on Volga front

Oct. 26–27, General Yudenitch in engagement with Soviet forces near Petrograd

Oct. 30, Tax in kind on agriculturalists who had surplus introduced

Nov. 5, Retreat of armies of General Yudenitch and Admiral Kolchak

Nov. 14, Omsk the capital of Kolchak Government taken by Soviet forces

Nov. 17, Seat of Siberian Kolchak Government transferred to Irkutsk

Dec. 5, Seventh Congress of Soviets met

Dec. 13, Poltava captured by Soviet forces from General Denikin

Dec. 17, Soviet forces recaptured Kiev. General Kolchak resigned command of army in Siberia to General Semenov, Cossack leader

1920

Jan. 3, Armistice with Estonia became effective

——, Soviet forces crossed the Volga and stormed town of Tsaritsyn attacking Denikin's right wing

Jan. 5, Soviet forces commanded by General Budenny captured Taganrog Denikin's headquarters on Sea of Azov

Jan. 7, Novo-Tcherksk capital of the Don Cossacks taken by Soviet forces

Jan. 8, Battle of Krasnoyarsk. Kolchak's army defeated by Soviet forces and Krasnoyarsk taken

Jan. 10, Rostov taken by Soviet forces

Jan. 16, Supreme Council announced that exchange of goods with Russia would be permitted through the coöperative organizations raising the economic blockade

Jan. 17, Decree of Council of People's Commissars abolished capital punishment

——, April 3, American forces withdrawn from Siberia

Jan. 20, General Semenov proclaimed himself ruler of Siberia

Jan. 26, General Denikin's armies holding line from Don to the Caucasus forced to retreat

Jan. 27, Decree ordered fusion of all coöperative societies under control of the Consumers' Union, Credit Coöperative Societies abolished

Jan. 29, General Yudenitch arrested

Jan. 30–31, "White" Russian government of General Rozanov at Vladivostok overthrown by Bolsheviks

Jan., Decree abolished the People's Bank

Feb. 1, Russian Central Coöperatives authorized to enter into commercial relations with firms in other countries

Feb. 2, Treaty of Dorpat signed recognized independence of Estonia and defined boundaries with Estonia. Reciprocal commercial advantages arranged for

Feb. 7, Admiral Kolchak and his premier Pepelaiev executed at Irkutsk after their surrender to Bolsheviks by General Janin commanding Czech army

Feb. 8, Soviet forces reached Odessa

Feb. 11, Agreement signed with Great Britain for repatriation of prisoners of war

Feb. 20, Soviet forces entered Archangel

——, Treaty of Dorpat with Estonia recognized independence

Feb. 21, Code of laws for regulation of labor enacted, first article made all citizens between ages of 16 and 50 subject to compulsory labor

Feb. 23, Revolt at Kronstadt

Feb. 24, Peace proposals made to the United States, Japan, and other Powers

Feb. 29, Russian attack forced surrender of Japanese garrison at Nikolaesvska, Siberia. 140 survivors imprisoned

March 27, Novo-Rossisk Denikin's last base taken by Soviet forces. Denikin resigned command succeeded by General Wrangel

April 2, Demands of Japanese to Partisan Government at Vladivostok. Agreed to under protest, April 29

April 5, Japanese troops attacked Vladivostok because of alleged firing of Russians on Japanese troops

April 6, Far Eastern Republic proclaimed by constituent convention at Verkhte-Udinsk on southern end of Lake Baikal, Alexander Krasnoschekov, President

April 8, General Denikin who had fled to Constantinople took ship for England

April 16, Declaration of Soviet Government of refusal to recognize debts of the Czarist Government or industrial contracts of the Czar's regime

April 22, The name of Petrograd changed to Leningrad

April 28, Soviet forces entered Baku, Azerbaijan and established a Soviet Government

April 29, Agreement with France for exchange of war prisoners

May 7, Poles occupied Kiev

May 14, Japanese troops landed at Decastri marching to relieve Japanese garrison at Nikolaevska, Siberia

May 16, Far Eastern Republic with capital Chita recognized by Soviet Government

May 24, Capital punishment reintroduced

May 27, Decree established the Tartar Republic as an autonomous republic of the Russian Socialist Federated Soviet Republic

May 27, Nikolaevska burned by the brigand Tripitzin and Japanese prisoners massacred

June 6, Wrangel troops occupied lands on north shore of Sea of Azov

June 7, General Wrangel promulgated an agrarian law vesting the land in the peasants

June 8, East Karelia established as autonomous republic

June 14, Wrangel forces occupied Berdiansk

June 24, Chuvash district created an autonomous region

July 4, Japanese occupied northern Sakhalin in retaliation for the Nikolaevska incident

July 8, Trade embargo against Russia raised by the United States

July 12, Treaty of Moscow recognized independence of Lithuania, defined boundaries and recognized Vilna as the capital

July 15, Meeting of Third International at Moscow

——, Vilna evacuated by the Poles occupied by Soviet forces

Aug. 11, General Wrangel's "South Russian Government" recognized by France

——, Treaty with Latvia signed at Riga recognized independence of Latvia and defined frontiers

Aug. 16–29, Armistice conference with Poles at Minsk

Aug. 17–26, Japanese troops withdrawn from eastern Transbaikalia and main line of the Chinese Eastern Railroad as far as Harbin

Aug. 26, The Khirgiz autonomous Republic established

Sept. 21, Armistice Conference with Poles renewed at Riga

Sept. 30, Treaty of alliance signed and affirmation of independence of Khorezm Soviet Socialist Republic (Khiva)

——, Military and economic Treaty with Azerbaijan signed

Oct. 12, Preliminary Peace Treaty with Poland signed recognized independence of Poland and adjusted boundaries. *See also* Poland

——, Soviet forces reached the Sea of Azov

Oct. 14, Peace Treaty of Dorpat signed with Finland. Boundaries defined. *See also* Finland

Oct. 17, Decree allowed possession of gold, silver, platinum, foreign exchange, &c., but subject to compulsory delivery to State at price fixed by Commissariat of Finance

Oct. 20, Semenov driven from Chita by troops of Far Eastern Republic

Oct. 28, Treaty signed with Rumania by Great Britain, France, Italy, and Japan assigned Bessarabia to Rumania

Nov. 1, Soviet forces attacked Wrangel on entire front forcing his retreat into Crimea

Nov. 4, Votyak, Kalmuck, and Mariusk established autonomous governments

Nov. 11, General Wrangel defeated at Isthmus of Perekop in Crimea by Soviet army

Nov. 14, General Wrangel and army took refuge on French warships as Soviet forces reached Sebastopol and proceeded to Constantinople

Nov. 19, Petlura's capital Kamenetz-Podolsk captured by Soviet forces

Nov. 20, Chechenskai established as an autonomous republic

Nov. 23, Decree issued regulating the granting of concessions to foreign capitalists to restore Russian industry

Nov. 29, Decree of Supreme Council of National

Economy nationalized all industrial enterprises employing more than 5 workers if possessing mechanical power and more than 10 if not

Dec. 3, Moscow People's Coöperative bank nationalized

Dec. 14, Agrarian law promulgated, peasants to cultivate given area and deliver to State all produce above that necessary for support of family

Dec. 15, Agreement with Far Eastern Republic signed at Moscow, and at Chita Dec. 30

Dec. 21–28, Eighth All-Russian Congress of Soviets met

Dec. 28, Treaty with the Ukraine signed provided for economic alliance and mutual recognition of independence

Dec. 30, Decree of All-Russian Congress to reduce army by one-half by 1921

1921

Jan. 1, The purchasing power of the paper ruble 1/26,539 part of pre-war level

Jan. 16, Commercial and military Treaty with White Russia signed

Jan. 20, Daghestan and Gorski established as autonomous republics

Jan. 27, Japan and China signed agreement for coöperation against Russia in Siberia

——, Independence of Georgia recognized by England, France, Italy, and Japan

Feb. 8, Death of Prince Peter A. Kropotkin in England

Feb. 12, Constitutional Convention met at Chita

Feb. 23, Rebellion of sailors at Kronstadt began general revolt against the dictatorship of the Commissaries

Feb. 25, Soviet Government established in Georgia by Bolsheviks

Feb. 26, Strike of government workers joined the Kronstadt revolt

——, Treaty with Persia signed by which Persia gave *de jure* recognition to the Soviet Government

Feb. 28, Treaty with Afghanistan signed at Kabul recognized independence of Bokhara and Khiva, granted yearly subsidy to Afghanistan, provided for establishment of 5 Russian consulates

March 2, Treaty with Persia by which all advances and loans to Persia cancelled

March 4, Agreement concluded affirmed the independence of the Bokhara People's Soviet Republic

March 16, Trade Agreement with Great Britain signed which gave Soviet Government *de facto* recognition

——, Treaty with Turkey signed by which Turkey engaged to cede Batum back to Georgia

——, Treaty signed by the Ukraine with Poland

March 17, First Lenin decree inaugurating NEP (New Economic Policy) replaced commandeering of surplus of farmers by "sole agricultural tax" introduced March 21

——, Kronstadt surrendered to Soviet troops

March 18, Peace Treaty with Poland signed at Riga

March 19, Ultimatum to Turkey demanded evacuation of Batum

March 21, Agrarian law prohibited redistribution of land for 9 years

March 29, Law enacted allowed sale of surplus grain and potatoes

——, Law on the tax in kind adopted

April 2, Armenia proclaimed a Soviet Republic

April 7, Supplies sent to Tambov and other districts affected by revolt which ended revolt

——, "New Economic Policy" (NEP) decree giving workers a certain amount of their produce as part of their wages, ordered freedom of buying and selling with money

April 11, Turkestan constituted an autonomous Republic

April 26, Constitutional Convention at Chita adopted a constitution

April 29, Permanent Government of the Far Eastern Republic elected

May 6, Trade Agreement with Germany signed

——, Statement of Lenin "we cannot prevent the progress of capitalism but we can try to develop it into Russian State capitalism"

May 21, Commercial and military Treaty with Georgia signed

May 26–27, Semenov's "partisans" overthrew Government at Vladivostok

May 31, Anti-Bolshevik Government established at Vladivostok headed by Merkulov

June 19–July 20, Congress of the Third International met at Moscow

July 5, Decree legalized certain farms of private industry, "the leased" industry

July 12, Decree applied the new economic policy to minor industries, handicraft workers and coöperative societies

July 26, Industrial tax introduced

Aug. 9, New Economic Policy (NEP) confirmed by decree permitted freedom of trade within the country, sanctioned overtime and piece work payment for workers, made private business legal and possible, and offered encouragement to foreign capitalists and concessionaires

Aug. 15–17, Conference of Red Cross Societies in Geneva appointed Dr. Nansen and Herbert Hoover head of Russian relief administration

Aug. 20, Agreement concluded by the Government with American Relief Administration

Aug. 26–April 16, Russo-Japanese Conference of Darien to arrange for evacuation of Japanese troops. Japan made demands on Far Eastern Republic which were not acceptable and no agreement resulted

Aug. 27, Agreement as to relief credits signed in Moscow with Dr. Nansen

Sept. 1, Kabarda-Balkarskaua region established as autonomous

Sept. 2, Trade Agreement with Norway signed

Sept. 14, Japanese troops evacuated Habarovsk (Khabarovsk)

Sept. 20, Baron Ungern captured, shot

Sept. 27, Tchitcherin denied anti-British propaganda in Persia, Afghanistan and Central Asia

Oct. 1, Number of leased factories 600

Oct. 12, Decree established the State Bank of the U.S.S.R.

Oct. 13, Treaty with Turkey signed restored Batum to Russia and left Kars, Ardahan, and Artvin in Turkey

Oct. 18, Crimean autonomous Republic established

Oct. 19, Speech of Lenin at Moscow on new economic policy stated that capitalism would be made subject to State

Oct. 28, Note of Soviet Government to Powers as to recognition of debts

Nov. 3, Decree introduced new paper money

Nov. 5, Treaty of friendship signed with Mongolia

Nov. 10, Chita made capital of the Far Eastern Republic

Nov. 15, State Bank at Moscow opened. Granted monopoly of purchase and sale of foreign money and precious metals

Nov. 15 and Dec. 19, Decrees regulated social insurance for wage earners

Dec. 3, Vladivostok recognized the Chita Government

Dec. 7, Treaty with Austria resumed political and commercial relations

Dec. 14, Decree against émigrés deprived certain categories of persons located abroad of rights of citizenship

Dec. 16, Treaty with Latvia signed

Dec. 22, The White Government of Merklulov took Habarovsk

Dec. 23–Jan. 4, Ninth All-Russian Soviet Congress met at Moscow

Dec. 26, Commercial Agreement with Italy signed

Public debt $22,774,000,000

1922

Jan. 2, The Ukraine signed Treaty with Turkey which recognized the independence of the Ukraine

Jan. 2, 12, and Feb. 9, Decrees established rates of contribution of workers to insurance

Jan. 12, Karachaevo-Cheress region established as an autonomous government

Jan. 21, Government accepted invitation to attend Genoa Conference

Jan. 25, Dagestan (Makhach-Kala) established as an autonomous Republic

Feb. 11, General tax on citizens introduced

Feb. 17, Treaty of economic alliance with the Far Eastern Republic signed

Feb., Troops of the Far Eastern Republic recaptured Habarovsk

March 12, Georgia, Armenia, and Azerbaijan formed a Trans-Caucasian Federation establishing the Trans-Caucasian Soviet Socialist Republic

March, Duties placed on industrial alcohol, salt, petroleum, beer, and mineral waters

April 4, Decree repealed compulsory delivery clause to State of precious metals or foreign exchange but monopoly of State Bank on purchase and sale of coin and foreign exchange continued

April 10–May 19, Genoa Conference the first to include representatives of the Soviet Government. No agreement resulted

April 16, Peace Treaty with Germany signed at Rapallo included most favored nation commercial provisions and for mutual economic assistance. De jure recognition given by Germany to the Soviet Government

April 27, Yakutsk autonomous Republic established

May 10, Agreement with the Vatican signed

May 11, Statement of Tchicherin that Russia would accept liability for payment of pre-war public debts provided damages caused to Russia by Allied intervention and blockade be recognized

May 17, Resignation of Patriarch Tikhon charged with anti-Government activities

May 22, Law of succession reintroduced in that the sum of 10,000 gold rubles rights of inheritance established for family if incapable of working

May, Taxes imposed on beet sugar, tea, coffee, and substitutes

May, A tax in kind established by which peasants permitted to pay in specified commodities the graduated taxes imposed. The unit chosen was a pood (36 pounds) of rye grain

June 1, Oiratsk region established as autonomous

——, Convention with Finland signed for maintenance of order on the frontier

June 5, Trade Agreement with Czechoslovakia signed

June 7, Trial of 36 persons for counter revolutionary activities; 15 sentenced to death the following day

June 15–July 19, Conference of 29 nations' representatives at The Hague to discuss recognition of Russia's pre-war debts and restitution of nationalized property in Russia formerly belonging to foreigners

July 27, Adigeevsko-Cherkess region established as an autonomous government

——, Decree allowed State and coöperative institutions to take gold or precious metals in coin in payment, but immediate deposit thereof must be made to their accounts in the State Bank

Sept. 1, Price index 5,600,000

——, Number of leased factories and works 6,220 and leased mills 6,500

Sept. 4–25, Russo-Japanese Conference at Chang-Chun. Russia asked for recognition and evacuation of northern Sakhalin which Japan refused until indemnity for Nikolaevsk massacre. No agreement reached

Sept. 30, Conscription introduced

Oct. 25, Last contingent of Japanese troops left Vladivostok, completing the evacuation of the mainland. Occupied by troops of the Far Eastern Republic

Oct. 30, Codification of land laws

Nov. 9, Order brought new Labor Code into operation

Nov. 11, Inheritance tax established

Nov. 14, National Assembly of the Far Eastern Republic voted dissolution and union with the Russian Socialist Federated Republic

Nov. 16, Decree established graduated income and property taxes

Nov. 19, Formal annexation of Far Eastern Republic

Nov. 23, Decree promulgated regulations for granting foreign concessions

Nov. 25, Law enacted as to marriage, families, and guardianship

Dec. 2–12, Moscow Disarmament Conference of representatives of Finland, Estonia, Latvia, Lithuania, Poland, and Russia. No agreement as to disarmament reached

Dec. 11, Decree authorized State Bank to issue new money unit the "chervonets" (10-ruble units)

Dec. 26, Decree revived the Savings Banks

Dec. 30, Declaration and Treaty of Union of Socialist Soviet Republics covering Russia (R.S.F.S.R.), Ukraine (U.S.S.R.), White Russia (W.R.S.S.R.), and the Transcaucasian Federation (T.S.F.S.R.), Armenia, Georgia, and Azerbaijan at Union Congress (first)

1923

Jan. 29, Decree abolished monopoly of the State Bank on purchase and sale of foreign money

——, Important oil and gas concessions in North Sakhalin granted to Sinclair Oil Company (American)

March 23, Decree defined duties of Supreme Court

March 26, Archbishop Cieplak (Roman Catholic) sentenced to 10 years imprisonment which was later commuted to banishment because of anti-Government activities

March 31, Mgr. Butchkaivitch, Vicar General, Roman Catholic Church, convicted of opposition to the Soviet Government, executed

April 7, Frontier Agreement with Latvia concluded

April 10, Decree placed basic industries and combines in a system of state trusts chartered "on a commercial basis with the aim of acquiring profits"

April 23, Trade Agreement with Denmark concluded which provided for recognition of the Soviet Government as *de facto*

April 29, All Russian Church Conclave opened in Moscow

May 3, All Russian Church Conclave unfrocked Patriarch Tikhon and expelled him from the Church as a traitor

May 9, British Foreign Office demanded cessation of anti-British propaganda in the East and non-interference with British fishing outside three mile limit

May 10, Decree established the "Single Agricultural Tax." Money payments gradually substituted for commodity payments

——, Agreement signed with Catholic Mission in Russia granted religious liberty and protection

——, M. Vorovski, Russian observer at Lausanne Conference, assassinated by Russian émigré, Conradi, former officer in Wrangel and Denikin armies

May 15, Soviet Note to Swiss Government regarding assassination of Vorovski

May 19, Swiss Government denied responsibility for assassination of Vorovski

May 24 and 28 and Aug. 21, Soviet Government protested against Canadian occupation of Wrangel Island

June 11, Note of reply to England practically accepted British terms

June 15, Note to France protested sale of ships which General Wrangel had transferred to France

June 30, Beveiato-Mongolia (Verklinendinsk) established as an autonomous Republic

July 1, Boycott of Swiss goods declared by the Government on account of the Vorovski affair

July 6, New Constitution of the Union of Socialist Soviet Republics adopted by approval of the Central Executive Committee

July 14, Central Executive Committee approved laws for creation of a Federal State Bank, a Central Commission for granting concessions and a Council of Labor and National Defense

July 25, Karelian autonomous Republic established

Aug. 14, Straits Convention signed by Russia at Constantinople

Aug. 30, The British Government consented to receive C. G. Rakovsky as the official agent of the Union of the Soviet Republics in Great Britain

Sept. 3, Exchange of Notes with Great Britain as to sovereignty of Wrangel Island

Sept. 12, Buryat-Mongol autonomous republic established

Oct., Price index 550,000,000

Oct. 10, First International Peasant Conference opened at Moscow with delegates from 40 countries including the United States, Mexico, and Argentina

Nov. 2, Over 1,000 delegates of local soviets at Moscow voted to call the new republic "The Union of Soviet Socialist Republics"

Nov. 12, Rent tax introduced

Nov. 16, Conradi acquitted of murder of Vorovski

Dec. 18, American Secretary of State Hughes rejected overtures of Tchicherin negotiations as to renewal of diplomatic relations unless decrees as to nationalization of property and repudiation of debts canceled

Dec. 19, German Republic on Volga (Pokrovsk) established

1924

Jan., Second customs tariff of Soviet Union made average ad valorem rates 22 to 24%

Jan. 21, Death of Lenin near Moscow made Central Committee of Communist Party (Kamenev, Zinoviev, and Stalin) rulers of Russia. Rykov elected to succeed Lenin as President of the Council of Peoples Commissaries

Jan., Second Union Congress met

Feb. 1, British Labour Government gave *de jure* recognition to Russia

Feb. 7, Commercial Treaty with Italy signed by which Italy gave *de jure* recognition

Feb. 13, Recognition of the Soviet Government by Norway

Feb. 15, Soviet paper ruble abolished as on this date and the "chervonets" of State Bank made the standard currency

Feb. 20, Recognition of the Soviet Government by Austria

March 8, Recognition of the Soviet Government by Greece

March 10, Announcement that Soviet paper currency would be redeemed in chervonets

March 14, Preliminary Agreement with China signed

March 15, Commercial Agreement with Sweden signed which gave *de jure* recognition to the Soviet Government

May 31, Agreement with China settled questions in dispute as to Chinese Eastern Railway in Manchuria, included recognition of Soviet Government by China and Chinese control and joint management of railway, Russia renounced indemnity

June 18, Recognition of the Soviet Government by Denmark

July 3, Commercial Agreement with Persia signed

July 20, The Soviet ice breaker "Red October" landed on Wrangel Island and raised Soviet flag removing Alaskan trappers and 13 Esquimos left by the Canadian expedition as trespassers

July 29, Protocol with Germany signed, non-interference with German internal affairs promised

Aug. 4, Recognition of the Soviet Government by Mexico

Aug. 8, General Treaty and Commercial Treaty with Great Britain signed

Aug. 11, Commercial Treaty with Persia signed

Aug. 28, Insurrection in Georgia against Soviet rule

Sept. 16, Treaty with Hungary signed for resumption of normal diplomatic relations

Sept. 20 and 30, Treaties with China. *See* China and Mongolia

Oct. 11, Moldavian Republic established

Oct. 24, Uzbek and Turkoman Socialist Republics formed from Bokhara, Khorezm, and part of Turkestan and admitted into the Soviet Union

Oct. 28, De jure recognition of Soviet Government given by the Herriot Government of France

Nov. 6, Soviet Government notified the Powers of its claim to islands north of Siberia

Dec. 27, Death of Leon Bakst (58), theatrical designer

1925

Jan. 15, Trotsky relieved of duties as chairman of Revolutionary War Council by Central Executive Committee

Jan. 21, Treaty with Japan signed by which Japan recognized Government of Russia and diplomatic and consular relations established. Japan agreed to withdraw troops from north Sakhalin

Jan. 24, Death of General Kuropatkin (77)

Jan. 30, Michael Frunse succeeded Trotsky dismissed as Commissary of War

Feb. 9, All non-Communist members of factory committees arrested in strike in central Urals. The following day 9 strike leaders shot

Feb. 20, All-Bokharan Congress of Soviets formally announced the creation of the Socialist Republic of Uzbekistan

Feb., Turkoman Soviet Socialist Republic formed

March 8, Death of Prince Lyov, former President of the Provisional Government (65) in France

March 24, Sinclair oil concession on Saghalien declared void by Moscow court on ground of delay in development

April 4, Japanese evacuated northern Sakhalien

April 7, Death of Patriarch Tikhon

April 18, Provisional regulations on hired labor in agriculture issued

April 21, Chuvash (Cheboksara) autonomous Republic established

——, Regulations for renting land issued benefiting peasants

April 30, Government concession made to British Lena Gold Fields Corporation for 50 years in which American interests had 50% share

May 1, Soviet Federal Parliament met at Tiflis, Georgia

May 7, Trotsky returned from exile in the Caucasus

May 11, Revised Constitution adopted

May 12, Soviet Union Constitution formally ratified by Soviet Congress

May 13, Trotsky elected member of Cabinet

May 15, Protocol with Japan signed completed transfer of northern Sakhalien to Russia

May 16, Full diplomatic relations with Japan resumed

May 30, Kazakskaia (Kzyl-Ozda) established as autonomous Republic

Aug. 3, Treaty with Poland signed for settlement of frontier conflicts. *See* Poland, March 9 and July 18

Aug. 30, Trial of 66 officials for misappropriation of army stores. 9 received death sentence

Sept. 23, New Conscription law introduced for entire Union of Soviet Socialist Republics provided that all "working" elements of population should serve in army from 19 to 40, other classes to serve as "working battalions" or pay a military tax

Oct. 4, Prohibition repealed and the distilling of 40% vodka became a government monopoly

Oct. 12, Commercial and consular Treaty with Germany signed

Oct. 31, Death of Frunse who succeeded Trotsky as Commissary of War. K. Voroshilov appointed to office

Nov. 19, Decree of Central Executive Committee merged the Foreign Trade Monopoly with Department of Internal Trade to form the Commissariat of Foreign and Internal Trade. Tsurupa appointed head

Nov. 30, Agreement with Japan as to oil fields of Sakhalin

Dec. 15, Treaty of commerce and navigation with Norway signed

Dec. 17, Three year Guarantee Pact with Turkey signed of mutual neutrality and conciliation

Dec. 18–31, Fourteenth Conference of the Communist Party

1926

Jan. 2, Political Bureau increased from 7 to 9 members, L. Trotsky, Voroshilov, G. S. Zinoviev, Molotov, J. Stalin, Kalenin, N. Bucharin, A. I. Rykov, and Tomsky. Kamenev removed from offices as President of the Council of Labor and Defense and Vice-President of the Council of People's Commissaries and appointed Commissary of Internal and Foreign Trade. Rykov took over presidency of the Council of People's Commissaries and of Council of Labor and Defense

Jan. 6, 400,000 acres in the Don district assigned by Government for a Jewish colony

Jan. 15, Soviet Government accepted invitation to be represented on Preparatory Commission for Disarmament Conference

Jan. 21, Ultimatum to Peking and Mukden Governments demanded cessation of military interference with operations of the South Manchurian railway

Feb. 2, Death of General Sukhomlinov (78), Minister of war, 1909–1915, in Brandenburg, Germany

Feb. 12, New trademark law enacted

March 2, 70 of 96 Soviet judges on trial at Kharkov received prison sentences charged with incompetency, bribery, and corruption

March 17, Death of General Alexei A. Brusilov. Succeeded by S. S. Kamenev as head of army

——, New statutes of the Communist International adopted

March 25, Nicholas Komarov replaced Zinoviev as head of Leningrad (Petrograd) Soviet

April 6, Russian refugees in Paris elected Grand Duke Nicholas, cousin of the late Czar, as monarchist leader

April 15, Decree of Central Executive Committee declared all lands and islands discovered or to be discovered between Arctic coast of Russia and North Pole in section between meridians of 168° 49′ 30″ West and 32° 4′ 35″ East not acknowledged by Soviet Government to be foreign territory belonging to Russia

April 24, Treaty of friendship with Germany signed

May 9, Zinoviev made a speech against the Central Committee before a non-party meeting

May 25, Simon Petlura, Ukrainian, assassinated in Paris

June 23, Customs Agreement with Greece signed

July 16, Frontier Agreement with Latvia signed

July 18, Super tax introduced

July 20, Death of Felix E. Dzerzhinsky, chairman of the Supreme Economic Council

July 24, Gregory Zinoviev expelled from Political Bureau of the Communist Party and Rudsutak appointed in his place

Aug., Colony of 9 Russians and 51 Chukchis established on Wrangel Island

Aug. 23, Recognition of Soviet Government by Uruguay

Aug. 31, Treaty of friendship, neutrality, and non-aggression with Afghanistan

Sept. 28, Non-Aggression Treaty with Lithuania signed. Boundaries reaffirmed

Oct. 1, Meeting of 100 workmen in Moscow addressed by members of the Opposition, Trotsky, Zinoviev, Radek, Pjatakov, Smilga, and Sapronov. Meetings criticizing the policy of the Central Committee also held in Leningrad

Oct. 16, Trotsky, Kamenev, Zinoviev, and other leaders of the Opposition signed agreement to dissolve their minority organization and abandon attacks on Central Committee

Oct. 21, Treaty of arbitration and neutrality with Latvia signed

Oct. 23, Trotsky, Kamenev, and Zinoviev expelled from Political Bureau

Nov. 19, Kalinin announced formation of "Agrokustbank" to help Jewish settlers in the Crimea finance their agriculture and handicraft

Nov. 22, Trotsky removed from chairmanship of the Scientific and Technical Department of the Supreme Economic Council

Nov. 22–Dec. 16, Meeting of the Executive Committee of the Communist International in Moscow

Nov. 23, Gregory Zinoviev resigned as President of the Third International

Nov. 24, Death of Leonid Krassin, Minister to Great Britain, in London

Nov. 26, Announcement that heaviest possible taxes to be levied on private business

Nov., Kirghiz (Pishpek) established as an autonomous Republic

Dec. 2, Trotsky removed as head of the Dnieper Ostrov Hydroelectric Power Works

1927

Jan. 1, Metric system of weights and measures established

Jan. 21, Note protested Franco-Rumanian Treaty recognition by France of Rumanian sovereignty over Bessarabia

Feb. 11, Third customs tariff issued by the Soviet Union approved average ad valorem rates from 29 to 33%

Feb. 23, Note from British Government protested against breaches of Trade Agreement of 1921 and of undertaking to abstain from propaganda

March 3, Death of M. P. Artzbashev, novelist

March 11, Treaty of commerce and navigation with Turkey signed

April 15, Agreement with Switzerland signed adjusted controversy over the assassination of Vorovski at Lausanne Conference in 1923

May 12, Premises of Arcos Ltd. (Russian) in London raided by British police in search for confidential War Office document

May 12 and 17, Protest to Great Britain of raid of premises of Arcos Ltd.

May 26, British Note announced severance of diplomatic relations with Russia and termination of Trade Agreement of March 16, 1921

June 2, Trade Agreement with Latvia signed

Aug. 10, Central Executive Committee and Central Control Committee of the Communist Party reprimanded Trotsky and Zinoviev

Sept. 9, The 1927–1928 Economic Plan published

Sept. 30, Expulsion of Vuyovich and Leon Trotsky from the executive body of the Communist International

Oct. 1, Trade Agreement and Neutrality and Mutual Non-Aggression Pact with Persia signed

Oct. 10, Convention with Latvia as to arbitral procedure in civil and commercial matters signed

Oct. 14, All judicial functions as to nomadic natives handed over to local governments

Oct. 23, Trotsky and Zinoviev expelled from the Central Committee

Nov. 30, Commission of industrial engineers and mining experts left Moscow to study American industrial methods arriving in New York Dec. 14

Dec. 2, Fifteenth Congress of Communist Party convened; first since December, 1925

Dec. 17, Treaty of neutrality and friendship of December, 1925, with Turkey renewed

Dec. 25, Death at Nice of Sergiei D. Sazonov, Czarist Minister of Foreign Affairs

Dec. 27, Communist Party expelled Kamenev, Radek, Piatakov, Rakovsky, Smilga, Smirnov, and other Opposition leaders

1928

Jan. 3, Thirty members of the Opposition including Trotsky banished to the provinces and others "invited" to take up residence outside Moscow

——, Exchange of political prisoners with Poland

Jan. 16, Trotsky left Moscow for Vernye in Kirghiz Kazak Republic in Central Asia

Jan. 23, Fisheries Convention with Japan signed

April 11–23, Session of Central Executive Committee of Union of Soviet Republics

April 19, New peasant tax law enacted by which the poorest peasants (about 35%) paid no tax, the kulaks (about 12%) to pay 62% of entire tax

April 25, Death of Baron Peter Wrangel in Brussels

May 18–July 6, Sixty-three officials of the Donetz mining industry on trial for sabotage and alleged bribery by former owners of mines in Paris. Of 11 who received death sentences 6 were later commuted. 34 sentenced to imprisonment. 3 Germans included were released and deported

May 31, Frontier Traffic Convention with Persia signed

——, Liquor Traffic Convention with the United States signed

June 5, Disbandment of Pan-Soviet Congress of Collective Agriculturalists by the Government because of demands for a relaxation of State control

July 17–Sept. 2, Sixth Congress of the Third International held in Moscow

July 28, Soviet flag raised on southern shore of Hooker Island and at Cape Flora, Franz Josef Land

Aug. 6, Four Treaties with Turkey signed respecting frontier pasture rights and communications, inspection of cattle and settlement of disputes

Aug. 29, Regulations published governing conciliation, arbitration, and court procedure for dealing with labor disputes

Aug. 31, Russia declared adherence to the Paris Pact for renunciation of war

Sept. 24, Provisional Commercial Agreement with Lithuania signed

Oct. 1, Five Year Plan, scheme of economic activities setting goal of increase of production in industry announced

Oct. 13, Death of Marie, Dowager Empress of Russia, widow of Czar Alexander III

Nov. 7, Agreement with Poland signed regarding local frontier traffic

Dec. 3–17, Central Executive Committee of the Union met in Moscow

Dec. 15, Law as to division and utilization of land adopted by the Central Executive Committee

Dec. 29, Note of M. Litvinov to Poland with draft Protocol proposed to make Paris Pact for renunciation of war immediately effective in Russia, Poland, and Lithuania

1929

Jan. 2, Decree instituted 7 hour day for industrial, transport, and communal enterprises

Jan. 5, Death of Grand Duke Nicholas at Antibes

Jan. 18, Order for expulsion of Trotsky from the Soviet Union signed and put into effect 3 days later on account of his "anti-Soviet activities." From Turkestan he went to Constantinople

Jan. 23, 150 supporters of Trotsky arrested on conspiracy charges

Jan. 24, Pact with Germany signed pledging submission of all disputes to joint commission

Feb. 9, Peace Pact signed at Moscow with Poland, Rumania, Estonia, and Latvia to come into effect April 2 for putting into effect the Pact of Paris of Aug. 27, 1928

March 15, Bread ration cards introduced into Moscow

March 28, Announcement that professional and technical education must devote special attention to anti-religious activity

March 29, Delegation of 84 British business men arrived at Moscow to discuss Anglo-Soviet trade

April 8, Decree restricted religious organizations to purely religious work

——, Anti-religious laws codified by decree into law of 68 articles

April 25–29, Conference of All Union Communist Party met at Moscow and adopted economic five-year plan

May 17, Commercial Treaty with Estonia signed

May 27, Police raids on Russian consulates at Manchoulu, Harbin, Tsitsihar

June 11, Provisional most favored nation commercial Treaty with Greece signed

June 28, The village soviets empowered to decide what amount of grain each peasant must sell to the State, kulaks not permitted to participate in soviets

July 10, Chinese Eastern Railroad telephone and telegraph lines seized by Chinese and Russian officials and employees deported

July 11, Speech of E. Yaroslavsky stating that 60 to 70 million of laboring class remained actively religious

July 13, Russian ultimatum to China as to Chinese Eastern Railway demanded conference

July 17, Second Note to China broke off diplomatic relations

July 18, Recall of consular representatives in China

July 19, Note of American Secretary of State Stimson reminded Government of obligations under Paris Pact as to war

July 22, French offer of mediation of dispute with China refused

July 25, Clash with Chinese near Manchuli

Aug. 19, Death of Serge Diaghilev, opera and ballet producer, in Venice

Aug. 23–Nov. 1, Flight of monoplane "Land of the Soviets," pilot S. A. Shestakov, from Moscow to New York over Siberia and Alaska reaching Seward, Alaska, on Sept. 27. Actual flying time to New York 141 hours and 33 minutes, 12,883 miles

Sept. 7, Decree gave dictatorial authority to factory managers destroying the authority of the labor unions

Sept. 24, Decree established "continuous working week" of 4 days with 1 of rest

Oct. 1, Conference of British Secretary of Foreign Affairs Henderson and Russian Minister to Paris Dovgalevsky, agreed to resume diplomatic relations

Oct. 13, "Land of the Soviets" reached Seattle proceeding to Vancouver on the 17th, Oakland, 19th, Salt Lake City the 22d, Chicago the 24th, and Curtiss Air Port, Long Island, Nov. 1

Oct. 16, New Soviet autonomous Republic of Tajikistan proclaimed

Nov. 15, The Right Opposition of Bucharin, Rykov and Tomsky capitulated to ultimatum of Stalin declaring adhesion to Government

Nov. 17, Nikolai Bucharin expelled from Political Bureau of the Central Committee of the Communist Party for lack of support of the Five Year Plan

——, Soviet troops began advance into Manchuria along line of Chinese Eastern Railroad

Nov. 22, Decree proclaimed that Soviet citizens resident abroad who refused to return to Russia when summoned by the Government were guilty of treason. Law made retroactive

Nov. 28, Note of American Secretary of State Stimson to Powers asked for joint diplomatic intervention to maintain Paris Pact as between Russia and China in Manchuria

Dec. 2, Note of Governments of the United States, France, Great Britain, and Italy called attention to Pact of Paris

Dec. 3, Preliminary Protocol with China signed

——, Litinov, Commissar of Foreign Affairs, protested Stimson Note as outside interference in Russian affairs

Dec. 17, Russo-Turkish Neutrality Pact of 1925 renewed

Dec. 22, Agreement with China signed restored *status quo* of Chinese Eastern Railroad and Soviet consulates in Manchuria

Dec. 27, Speech of Stalin at Union Conference of Communist Agrarians declared "The destruction of the kulaks in the regions where wholesale collectivization is being carried out . . . is part of the scheme for development of the collective policy . . . the kulaks must go. . . . We cannot permit them to enter the collectives because they are sworn enemies of the collectives"

1930

Jan. 20, On this date there were 59,400 collective farms in the U.S.S.R.

Jan. 25, Agreement with Germany signed

Feb. 1, Decree ordered suspension of laws and regulations as to renting of land and hiring of labor in regions of collectivization

Feb. 2, Decree authorized confiscation of property of kulaks

Feb. 8, Protest of the Pope against Soviet anti-religious policy

Feb. 12, Protest of the Archbishop of Canterbury against Soviet anti-religious policy

March 1, Number of collective farms increased to 110,200

March 2, Model articles of association of agricultural artels published

——, Article of Stalin published in the press entitled "Intoxicated by Success" pronounced against forcible methods of collectivization and nationalization and for modification of economic policy subsequently embodied in decrees

March 14, Central Committee of Communist Party adopted resolutions in accord with Stalin's new economic policy

March 15, Decrees abrogated suppression of kulaks by administrative measures and cessation of religious persecution

March 16, Protest of Bishop Manning of New York against Soviet anti-religious policy

April 7, Decree published regulations for labor penal camps established

April 8, Soviet decree as to religious associations

April 12, Decree as to factory management reduced pressure of politics stipulating that executives be chosen according to merit without regard for party affiliations and that political party committees should cease to interfere with industry

April 16, Provisional Commercial Agreement with Great Britain signed

April 23, Decree of Soviet Government that all non-voters (priests, private traders, ex-aristocrats, &c.) are entitled to homes, food, rations, medical aid, and schooling. Self-supporting persons over 23 will not share in any parental disfranchisement

April 28, Opening of Turksib Railroad (1,700 miles) connecting with Central Railroad at Aris, Uzbekistan and with Tran-Siberian at Novesibirsk

April 29, Note to Poland charged attempt to induce war after discovery of bomb in Soviet Legation at Warsaw on April 26. Note of Poland of explanation accepted May 1

June 1, Russian Academy of Science voted to rename archipelago of Franz Joseph Land, Fridtjof Nansen Land

June 13, Decree on citizenship in U.S.R.R. adopted

June 24, Speech of Stalin: "Collectivization, the fight with the kulaks, the fight with the enemies of Socialist construction, anti-religious propaganda, &c., is the inevitable right of the workmen and peasants of the U.S.S.R., a right fixed by our Constitution. We must and shall uphold the Constitution of the U.S.S.R., with full consistency" (Pravda, No. 177, June 29, 1930)

June 26–July 13, Sixteenth Communist Party Conference held in Moscow

July 21, Litinov succeeded Chicherin as Commissar for Foreign Affairs

July 23, Siberia divided into 3 districts; Western, Eastern, and District on the Pacific

Aug. 2, Commercial Treaty with Italy signed

Aug. 26, Decree of Court of Arbitration in Lena Goldfields case that Russia should pay £13,000,000. Russia refused to accept decision

Sept. 25, 48 alleged counter-revolutionaries shot, former officers and industrialists

Oct. 2, Negotiations with Great Britain opened as to pre-war debts

Oct. 3, Decree regulated social insurance for persons working on peasant farms

Oct. 9, Decree provided for immediate despatch of all unemployed to work and cessation of unemployment benefit because of labor shortage

Oct. 11, Arrest of 8 technical experts, Professor Ramsin, Kuprianov, Laritchev, Tarnovsky, Fedotov, Otchkind, and Sitnin, Kalinnikov charged with counter-revolutionary plot and naming Sir Henry Deterding of England, ex-Premier Poincare and Foreign Minister Briand of France and Colonel Lawrence (Lawrence of Arabia) as implicated along with a number

of foreign capitalists to overthrow the Soviet Government

Oct. 11, Negotiations with China resumed

Nov. 25–Dec. 7, Trial of Professor L. K. Ramsin and colleagues in Moscow who pleaded guilty to charges of conspiracy. 5 engineers sentenced to death and 3 to 10 years' imprisonment

Dec. 8, Sentences of death imposed on 5 engineers commuted to ten-years' imprisonment and the ten-year sentences imposed on 3 others reduced to eight

Dec. 16, Second Conference with China as to Chinese Eastern Railroad begun Dec. 4, broke up without result

Dec. 19, Rykov removed as President of the Council of Peoples Commissaries and other posts. Succeeded by Molotov as head of Soviet State. Stalin succeeded as Chairman of the Council of Labor and Defense and Mikhail Tomski became Vice-President of the Supreme Economic Council

Dec. 22, Decree reorganized food services and Government took over the management of restaurants and boardinghouses stating that food services had not been sufficiently efficient as agencies of class war for which 48 officials recently shot and that "ultimate object" to "abolish domestic preparation of meals"

SOVEREIGNS OF RUSSIA

DUKES OF KIOW OR KIEF

850? Ruric
879. Oleg
913. Igor I
945. Olga, widow; regent
955. Swiatoslaw I—victorious
973. Jaropalk I
980. Vladimir, Wladimir, the Great
1015. Swiatopalk
1018. Jaraslaw, or Jaroslaf I
1054. Isiaslaw I
1073. Swiatoslaw II
1078. Wsewolod I
1093. Swiatopalk II
1113. Vladimir II
1125. Mitislaw
1132. Jaropalk II
1138. ⎰ Wiatschelaw
1139. ⎱ Wsewolod II
1146. ⎰ Isialaw II and Igor II
1153. ⎱ Rostislaw
1149. Jurie or George I; the city of Moscow was built by this duke

GRAND-DUKES AT WLADIMIR

1157. ⎰ Andrew I until 1175; first grand-duke
1175. ⎱ Michael I
1177. Wsewolod III
1213. ⎰ Jurie or George II
1217–18. ⎱ Constantine
1238. Jaraslaw II; succeeded by his son
1245. Alexander-Nevski or Newski, the Saint
1263. Jaraslaw III
1270. Vasali or Basil I
1275. Dmitri or Demetrius
1281. Andrew II
1294. Daniel-Alexandrovitz
1303. Jurie or George III; deposed
1305. Michael III
1320. Vasali or Basil II

1325. Jurie or George III; restored
1327. Alexander II
[The dates are doubtful, owing to the difficulty that occurs at every step in early Russian annals]

GRAND-DUKES OF MOSCOW

1328. Ivan or John I
1340. Simeon, the Proud
1353. Ivan or John II
1359. Demetrius II, prince of Susdal
1362. Demetrius III, Donskoi
1389. Vasali or Basil III, Temnoi
1425. Vasali or Basil IV

CZARS OF MUSCOVY

1462. Ivan (Basilovitz) or John III: took the title of Czar, 1482
1505. Vasali or Basil V obtained the title of Emperor from Maximilian I
1533. Ivan IV the Terrible; a tyrant
1584. Feodor or Theodor I; and his son, Demetrius, murdered by his successor
1598. Boris-Godonof, who usurped the throne
1605. Feodor II, murdered
1606. Demetrius, the Impostor, a young Polish monk; pretended to be the murdered Prince Demetrius; put to death
——. Vasali-Chouiski, or Zouinski
1610. Ladislaus of Poland; retired 1613
1613. Michael-Feodorovitz, of the house of Romanoff, descended from the Czar Ivan-Basilovitz
1645. Alexis, son; styled the father of his country
1676. Feodor or Theodor II
1682. { Ivan V and
       { Peter I, brothers of the preceding

EMPERORS AND EMPRESSES

1689. Peter I, the Great, alone; took the title of Emperor, Oct. 22, 1721; founded St. Petersburg
1725. Catherine I, his widow; at first the wife of a Swedish dragoon, said to have been killed on the day of marriage
1727. Peter II, son of Alexis-Petrovitz, and grandson of Peter the Great; deposed
1730. Anne, Duchess of Courland, daughter of the Czar Ivan
1740. Ivan VI, an infant, grand-nephew to Peter the Great; immured in a dungeon for 18 years, murdered in 1764
1741. Elizabeth, daughter of Peter the Great, reigned during Ivan's captivity
1762. Peter III, son of Anne and of Charles-Frederick, duke of Holstein-Gottorp: deposed, and died soon after, supposed to have been murdered
——. Catherine II, his consort: a great sovereign; extended the Russian territories on all sides; died Nov. 17, 1796
1796. Paul, her son, murdered, March 24, 1801
1801. Alexander I, son (who, after many adverse battles, and a forced alliance with France, at length aided in the overthrow of Napoleon Bonaparte), died Dec. 1, 1825
1825. Nicholas I, brother; died March 2, 1855
1855. Alexander II, son, born April 29, 1818; married April 28, 1841, Mary Princess of Hesse (she died June 3, 1880); said to have married (morganatic) Princess Dolgorouki, July 19 (31); marriage an-

nounced, Oct., 1880; assassinated at St. Petersburg, 2 P.M., March 13, 1881
1881. Alexander III, born March 10, 1845; married Mary (formerly Dagmar), Princess of Denmark (born Nov. 26, 1847), Nov. 9, 1866; died Nov. 1, 1894
1894. Nicholas II (termed Educator), son, born May 18, 1868; married Alexandra (formerly Alix), Princess of Hesse (born, June 6, 1872), Nov. 26, 1894, executed with his family, July 16, 1918. Grand Duchess Olga Nicolaevna, born Nov. 15, 1895. Tatiana, born June 10, 1897; Marie, born June 26, 1899; Anastasia, born June 18, 1901. Grand Duke Alexis Nicholaievitch (Czarevitch), born July 30 (Aug. 12), 1904

RUSSO-TURKISH WAR, 1853

Russo-Turkish War.—The Russian and French governments having each taken a side in the dispute between the Greek and Latin churches as to the exclusive possession of the Holy Places in Palestine, the Porte advised the formation of a mixed commission, which decided in favor of the Greeks, and a firman was promulgated accordingly, March 9, 1853: to this decision the French acceded.

1853

March 22–May 18, The Russians make further claims, and Prince Menschikoff (who arrived at Constantinople Feb. 28, 1853), by various notes (between March 22 and May 18), demands that a convention should be signed by the Sultan granting to the Czar such a protectorate over the Greek Christians in Turkey, as the Sultan considered inimical to his own authority
May 21, Menschikoff's ultimatum rejected; he quits Constantinople
June 6, The Sultan issues a hatti-scherif confirming all the rights and privileges of the Greek Christians, and appeals to his allies
June 13, The English and French fleets anchor in Besika Bay
July 2, The Russians, under Gen. Luders, cross the Pruth and enter Moldavia
July 16, Circular of Count Nesselrode in justification, July 2; Lord Clarendon's reply
July 31, The conference of representatives of England, France, Austria, and Prussia meet at Vienna, agree to a note; accepted by the Czar, Aug. 10; the Sultan requires modifications, Aug. 19; which the Czar rejects, Sept. 7
Sept. 14, Two English and two French ships enter the Dardanelles
Oct. 5, The Sultan declares war against Russia
Oct. 23, The Turkish fortress at Isaktocha fires on a Russian flotilla (the first act of war)
Oct. 28–Nov. 3, The Turks occupy Kalafat
Nov. 1, Russia declares war against Turkey
Nov. 2, English and French fleets enter Bosphorus
Nov. 4, Russians defeated at Oltenitza
Nov. 14, 18, 26, Turks (in Asia) defeated at Bayandur, Atskur, and Achaltzik
Nov. 30, Turkish fleet destroyed at Sinope
Dec. 5, Collective note from the four Powers asking what terms the Porte will negotiate for peace

1854

Dec. 31, 1853–Jan. 9, Contests at Kalafat

Jan. 4, At the request of the Porte (Dec. 5), the allied fleets enter the Black Sea

Jan. 6, Russians defeated at Citate

Jan. 13, Reply of the Porte to the note of Dec. 5, containing four points as bases of negotiation: *viz.*, 1. The promptest possible evacuation of the principalities. 2. Revision of the treaties. 3. Maintenance of religious privileges to the communities of all confessions. 4. A definitive settlement of the convention respecting the Holy Places (dated Dec. 31),—approved by the four Powers

Jan. 16, Vienna conferences close

Jan. 28–31, Kalafat invested by the Russians

Feb. 9, Proposal in a letter from the Emperor of the French to the Czar (Jan. 29) declined

Feb. 15, Turkish flotilla at Rustchuk destroyed by the Russians under Schilders

Feb. 27, Ultimatum of England and France sent to St. Petersburg

March 11, Baltic fleet sails, under Sir C. Napier

March 12, Treaty between England, France, and Turkey

March 19, The Czar "did not judge it suitable to give an answer"

March 23, 24, Russians under Gortschakoff pass the Danube and occupy the Dobrudscha; severe conflicts; the Turks retire

March 28, France and England declare war against Russia

——, Rupture between Turkey and Greece

March 31, Gen. Canrobert and French troops arrive at Gallipoli, followed by the English

April 8, English vessel *Furious*, with a flag of truce, fired on at Odessa

April 10, Four Powers sign a protocol at Vienna guaranteeing the integrity of Turkey

——, Russians defeated at Kostelli

——, Offensive and defensive alliance between England and France

April 19–21, Russians, under Gen. Schilders, assault Kalafat; repulsed; the blockade raised

April 20, Treaty between Austria and Prussia

April 22, Bombardment of Odessa by allied fleet

May 12, The *Tiger* steamer run aground near Odessa, captured by the Russians

May 13, Russians defeated at Turtukai

May 17, Siege of Silistria begun

May 29, Allied armies disembark at Varna

May 30, Russians defeated by the Turks at Karakai

June 1, The Danube blockaded by allied fleets

June 5, Russians repulsed at Silistria; Paskiewitsch and many officers wounded

June 16, Turks defeated at Ozurgheti (in Asia)

June 18–26, Severe conflict before Silistria; the siege raised

June 26, 27, Batteries at the Sulina mouths destroyed by Capt. Parker

July 7, Russians defeated at Giurgevo

July 8, Captain Parker killed

July 15, 10,000 French troops embark at Boulogne for the Baltic

July 29, 30, Turks defeated at Bayazid in Armenia; and near Kars, Aug. 5

Aug. 16, Surrender of Bomarsund

[In July and August the allied armies and fleets in the east suffered severely from cholera]

Aug. 28, The Russians defeated in Georgia

Aug.–Sept. 20, They evacuate the principalities

Sept. 6, By virtue of a treaty with Turkey (June 14) the Austrians enter Bucharest

Sept. 14, Allies sail from Varna, Sept. 3, and land at Old Fort, near Eupatoria

Sept. 19, Skirmish at the Bulganac

Sept. 20, Battle of the Alma

Sept. 23, Russians sink part of their fleet at Sebastopol

Sept. 26, Allies occupy Balaklava

Sept. 29, Death of Marshal St. Arnaud, General Canrobert appointed his successor, Nov. 24

Oct. 17, Siege of Sebastopol commenced

Oct. 25, Battle of Balaklava

Oct. 26, Sortie from Sebastopol repulsed by Generals Evans and Bosquet

Nov. 5, Russian attack at Inkerman; defeated

Nov. 6, Miss Florence Nightingale and nurses arrive at Scutari

Nov. 13–16, Great tempest in the Black Sea, loss of the *Prince* and store vessels

Dec. 2, Treaty of alliance between England, France, Austria, and Prussia—a commission to meet at Vienna; signed

1855

Jan. 5, Omar Pacha arrives in the Crimea (followed by the Turkish army from Varna)

Jan. 26, Sardinia joins England and France

Feb. 17, Russians defeated by the Turks at Eupatoria

March 2, Death of Emperor Nicholas; accession of Alexander II (no change of policy)

March 22, Sortie from the Malakhoff tower

April 19, Capture of Russian rifle-pits

May 8, Arrival of Sardinian contingent

May 16, Resignation of Gen. Canrobert, succeeded by Gen. Pelissier

May 24–June 3, Expedition into the sea of Azov (under Sir E. Lyons and Sir G. Brown); destruction of Kertch and large amount of stores

June 3, Taganrog bombarded

June 5, Massacre of an English boat's crew with flag of truce at Hango

——, Russians evacuate Anapa

June 6, 7, The White Works and Mamelon Vert taken

June 18, Unsuccessful attack on the Malakhoff tower and Redan

June 28, Death of Lord Raglan; succeeded by General Simpson

July 15, Russians invest Kars in Armenia, defended by Gen. Williams

Aug. 9, Bombardment of Sweaborg

Aug. 16, Defeat of the Russians at the Tchernaya

Aug. 18, Ambuscade on the glacis of the Malakhoff taken; Russian sortie repulsed

Sept. 8, &c., The French take the Malakhoff by assault; the English assault the Redan without success; the Russians retire from Sebastopol to the North Forts, and the Allies enter the city; the Russians destroy remainder of their fleet

Sept. 29, The Russians assaulting Kars are defeated with great loss

——, Russian cavalry defeated (50 killed, 105 prisoners) at Koughil, by the French

Nov. 6, Defeat of the Russians, and passage of the Ingour by the Turks under Omar Pacha

Nov. 14, Sir Wm. Codrington takes the command in place of Gen. Simpson

Nov. 15, Explosion of 100,000 pounds of powder in the French siege-train at Inkerman, loss of life

Nov. 26, Capitulation of Kars to Gen. Mouravieff, after a gallant defense by Gen. Williams

Nov. 27, Death of Admiral Bruat

Dec. 12, Proposals of peace from Austria, with the consent of the Allies, sent to St. Petersburg

1856

Jan. 2, Center dock at Sebastopol blown up by the English

Feb. 1, Protocol signed accepting the Austrian propositions as a basis of negotiations for peace

——, Destruction of Sebastopol docks

Feb. 25, Peace conferences open at Paris, an armistice till March 31 agreed on

Feb. 29, Suspension of hostilities

March 30, Treaty of peace concluded at Paris

July 9,* The Crimea evacuated

RUSSO-TURKISH WAR, 1877

Russo-Turkish War, 1877. For the insurrections, Serbian war, and the negotiations, *see* Turkey.

1877

April 23, The Czar addresses the army near Kischeneff, saying that "he has done everything in his power to avoid war, and patience is exhausted"; the Russian Embassy quits Constantinople

April 24, War declared; the Russians enter the Turkish dominions in Rumania and Armenia

April 25, The Sultan protests against the war, and refers to his reforms

April 26, Russians defeated at Tchuruk Sou

April 29, 30, The Russians, under the Grand Duke Michael and Loris Melikoff, advance into Armenia, defeat Turks and occupy Bayazid (deserted)

May 1, The Earl of Derby replies to the Russian circular; he refers to the treaty of 1856 as broken; asserts that Russia has separated herself from European concert; the British Government gives neither concurrence nor approval to the war

May 3, The Turks blockade the Black Sea

May 4, Russians defeated in attacking Batoum

May 11, The *Lufti-Djelil*, Turkish monitor, with 300 men, blown up near Ibraila, or Braila, on the Danube (said to be by Russian shells)

May 14, Sukhum Khaleh, Russian fortress in the Caucasus, captured by Turks

May 17, Ardahan, near Kars, stormed by Melikoff

May 26, Explosion of Turkish monitor *Dar-Matoin*, with torpedoes

June 3, Kars invested by Russians

June 12–20, Turks successful in Montenegro

June 16, Turks defeated at Tahir, or Taghir, Armenia

* The English lost: killed in action and died of wounds, about 3,500; died of cholera, 4,244; of other diseases, nearly 16,000; total loss nearly 24,000 (including 270 officers); 2,873 were disabled. The war added to the national debt 41,041,000*l*. The French lost about 63,500 men; the Russians about half a million.

June 20, Turks victors at Zewin Dooz, Eshek-Khalian, Delibaba; Russians retreating

June 22, Russians cross Lower Danube by bridges at Galatz and Braila; 6 hours' conflict ensues; Turks retire; Russians occupy Matchin, June 23, and Hirsova, June 25, 26

June 27, The Grand Duke Nicholas crosses the Danube at Simnitza by 208 pontoons, and enters Bulgaria; the Turks retire after severe conflicts; 289 Russians said to be killed

June 30, The Simnitza bridge destroyed, about

About July 5, Biela, Bulgaria, taken by Russians

July 6, Plevna, Bulgaria, occupied by Russians

July 6, 7, Tirnova, ancient capital of Bulgaria, captured by Russians under Gen. Gourko

July 12, Bayazid reoccupied by Turks

July 13, Russians compelled to retire from Kars by Mukhtar Pasha

July, The invasion of Armenia considered a failure

July 13, Gourko crosses the Balkans and enters Roumelia; several skirmishes, July 14, 15, 20

July 15, 16, Nicopolis (Nikopol) surrenders; capture of 2 pashas, 6,000 men, 2 monitors, and 40 guns

July, The Turkish commander Abdul-Kerim replaced by Mehemet Ali (Jules Détroit, of French extraction); Russians retreating

July 19, 20, Russians severely defeated; Plevna retaken by Osman Pasha; Russians again defeated, July 30, 31

About July 21, Suleiman Pasha brought from Montenegro to the Schipka Passes

July 26 or 28, Aziz Pasha (able and popular) killed in a rash conflict at Esirje, near Rasgrad

July, Hostilities revive in Montenegro; the Turkish fortress Niksich besieged

——, Severe conflicts between Russians and Suleiman Pasha; the Turks eventually victors: Eski Saghra and Yeni Sagra; Kezanlik and Kalofer, July 30 *et seq.*

Aug. 9, The Rumanian army joins the Russians

About Aug. 11, Russians under Gourko expelled from Roumelia; retreat to Schipka Passes

Aug. 14, Russians defeated at Kara Silar, near Osman Bazar; in the valley of the Lom, by Mehemet Ali, about Aug. 22–24

Aug. 20–27, Desperate fruitless attempts of Suleiman Pasha to gain the Schipka Pass held by Gourko and Radetzky; great slaughter

Aug. 21, Russians in the Schipka Passes relieved

Aug. 24, 25, Russians defeated by Mukhtar Pasha at Kurukdara, between Kars and Alexandropol

Aug. 30, Severe twelve hours' battle in valley of the Lom, near Szedina; Karahassankoi taken and retaken six times; Russians (under the Czarevitch) retire in good order

Sept. 3, Lovatz or Luftcha (important) captured by Prince Imeritinsky and Russians

Sept. 4–6, Further successes of Mehemet Ali on the Lom at Katzelevo, Ablava, &c.

Sept. 7–10, Sanguinary conflicts at Plevna, greatly strengthened by Osman Pasha; artillery duel

Sept. 11, 12, Fierce assault by Russians and Rumanians; they gain the strong Gravitza redoubt (with others, which are retaken); the Czar present; Russian loss about 20,000

Sept. 17, Fort St. Nicholas in Schipka Pass taken by Suleiman Pasha and quickly lost

Sept. 21, Mehemet Ali repulsed in his attack on position at Tchercovna, fifteen miles from Biela

Sept. 22, Siege of Plevna; Chefket Pasha enters with reinforcements after several skirmishes

About Sept. 27, 30, Battles of the Yagni; severe conflicts; Russians repulsed near Ardahan, Asia

Russian losses killed, wounded, and missing, 47,400 reported up to Sept. 20

About Sept. 25, Mehemet Ali retires to Kara Lom

Sept. 28, Gen. Todleben made chief of staff before Plevna

Oct. 2, 3, Mehemet Ali replaced by Suleiman Pasha; Raouf Pasha sent to Schipka

Oct. 2–4, Battles near Kars; army of Grand Duke Michael attacks Turks under Mukhtar Pasha; severely defeated

Oct. 8, Turkish monitor in the Danube exploded by torpedoes

Oct. 9, Relief received by Turks at Plevna

Oct. 14, 15, Battle of Aladia Dagh before Kars; Russians, under Grand Duke Michael, and Generals Loris Melikoff, Lazareff, and Heimann, totally defeat Ahmed Mukhtar, taking 10,000 prisoners

Oct. 19–20, Gravitza battery, near Plevna, captured by Rumanians, is quickly retaken

Oct. 24, Battle at Gornij Dubnik, near Plevna; Russians under Gourko said to be victorious

Oct. 28, Battle of Sofia Road, near Plevna; Turkish position at Teliche captured

Nov. 4, Mukhtar Pasha defeated by Heimann and Tergukasoff at Deve-Boyun, Armenia

Nov. 9, Russians severely defeated at Azizi, before Erzeroum, by Mukhtar Pasha

Early in Nov., Change in Turkish generals: Suleiman ordered to command the army of Roumelia, replaced by Azli Pasha; Mehemet Ali organizes army to relieve Plevna

Nov. 12, Russian attack on Plevna repulsed

Nov. 15, Turks thrice repulsed near Plevna

Nov. 17–18, Kars taken by storm; the Russians climbed steep rocks; fierce conflict from 8 P.M. to 8 A.M.; 300 guns and 10,000 prisoners taken; about 5,000 Turks killed and wounded; Russian loss about 2,500; the Grand-Duke Michael present

Nov., Plevna said to be thoroughly invested (30 miles round, with 120,000 men)

Nov. 24, Entrepol (fortified) taken by Russians

Nov. 30, Indecisive fighting in the valley of the Lom between the Czarevitch and Mehemet Ali

Dec. 4, Turks capture Elena with prisoners

Dec. 10, Osman Pasha endeavors to break out of Plevna, about 7 P.M., Dec. 9; unconditional surrender; 30,000 prisoners

Dec. 12, The Serbians declare war against Turkey; cross the frontier and capture villages, Dec. 15 et seq.

——, Turkish circular note to the great Powers, requesting mediation; merely acknowledged, action declined about Dec. 12

About Dec. 19, Suleiman made General of the army of Roumelia; and Todleben of that of Rustchuk

About Dec. 20, Suleiman retires on the quadrilateral; visits Constantinople; armies concentrating near Adrianople

About Dec. 24, Erzeroum, Armenia, nearly invested; brave resistance by Mukhtar Pasha

Dec. 26–31, The Sultan requests mediation of England; the British Government only convey to Russia the Sultan's desire to make peace; Russia declines mediation

Dec. 31, Gourko crosses the Balkans and advances on Sofia; Turks defeated

1878

Jan. 1, Col. Baker gallantly protects the retreating Turkish army, defeating the Russians

Jan. 3, Sofia taken by Russians after an engagement

Jan. 6, 7, Serbians defeated; Kurschumli reoccupied by Turks

About Jan. 10, Nisch taken by the Serbians; Antivari by the Montenegrines

Jan. 11, Gen. Radetzky crosses the Balkans; the Trojan pass taken about Jan. 9; the Turkish army (about 32,000) and cannon taken by Skobeleff and Radetzky, after conflicts, Jan. 8, 9, 10; Gourko advances towards Adrianople

Jan. 16, 17, Gourko advances toward Philippopolis; totally defeats Suleiman Pasha, who retreats to the sea, losing many prisoners

About Jan. 16–18, Russians advance successfully; Turkish envoys proceed to treat for peace

Jan. 29, Serbians occupy nearly all Old Serbia

Jan. 31, Armistice signed at Adrianople

Feb., Russian losses announced 89,879 men

Feb. 13, Part of British fleet ordered to Constantinople to protect British life and property, Feb. 8; enters Dardanelles

March 17, Treaty of peace signed at San Stefano, March 3; ratified at St. Petersburg

The war lasted 322 days, April 12, 1877, to March 3, 1878

June 13, Conference at Berlin, meets; treaty signed (see Berlin), July 13; ratified Aug. 3

1879

Feb. 8, Definitive treaty of peace with Turkey signed at Constantinople

Estimated cost of the war to Russia, 120,000,000l.

SAMOS

An island off the coast of Asia Minor, forming a principality under the sovereignty of Turkey, under the guarantee of France, Great Britain, and Russia, December 11, 1832.

In November, 1912, the island was seized by the Greeks and has since then been governed by them. The question of the Ægean Islands has not yet been settled, and therefore Samos is still under Greek rule. Population in 1928, 70,947.

SAN MARINO

San Marino, Republic included in the area of northeastern Italy, situated in the Appenines near the Adriatic coast, claims to be the oldest independent State in Europe, area, 38 square miles, population (December, 1928), 13,013. A treaty of friendship with Italy was concluded, June 28, 1907, revised in 1908 and in 1914. The legislative power is vested in the Grand Council of 60 members elected by popular vote, two of whom are appointed every 6 months to act as Regents.

SARDINIA

Sardinia, an island in the Mediterranean, successively possessed by the Phœnicians, Greeks, Carthaginians (about 500 B.C.), Romans (238), Vandals (A.D. 456), Saracens (720–40), Genoese (1022), Pisans (1165), Aragonese (1352), and Spaniards. From settlers belonging to these various nations the present inhabitants derive their origin. Victor Amadeus, Duke of Savoy, acquired Sardinia in 1720, with the title of King; *see* Savoy. The King of Sardinia was recognized as King of Italy by his parliament in Feb., 1861; *see* Italy.

1708 to 1847

1708, Conquered by the English naval forces, under Sir John Leake and Gen. Stanhope
1714, Ceded to the Emperor Charles VI
Aug. 22, 1717, Recovery by the Spaniards
1720, Ceded to the Duke of Savoy with the title of King, as an equivalent for Sicily
1730, Victor-Amadeus abdicates in favor of his son
1732, Attempting to recover his throne, he is taken, and dies in prison
1792, The court kept at Turin, till Piedmont is overrun by the French
June 4, 1802, Charles-Emmanuel resigns to his brother, Duke of Aosta
1798–1814, The King resides in Sardinia
May 26, 1805, Piedmont annexed to Italy
Dec., 1814, Piedmont restored to its sovereign, with Genoa added
1837, King Charles-Albert promulgates a new code
1847, Cavour establishes the newspaper "Il Risorgimento" ("the Revival")

1848

March 23, The King grants a constitution, and openly espouses the cause of Italian regeneration against Austria
May 30, Defeats the Austrians at Goito; and takes Peschiera
June 28, Incorporation of Lombardy with Sardinia, and Venice, July 4
July 26, Sardinian army defeated by Radetzky
Aug. 5, Sardinians at Milan capitulate to Radetzky

1849

March 12, Hostilities resumed
March 21, Radetzky defeats a division of the Sardinians, and occupies Mortara
March 23, Complete defeat of the Sardinians by the Austrians at Novara
——, Charles-Albert abdicates in favor of his son, Victor-Emmanuel
March 25, The Austrians occupy Novara, &c.
July 28, Death of Charles-Albert, at Oporto
Aug. 6, Treaty of Milan between Austria and Sardinia, signed

1850

April 9, Adoption of the Siccardi law, which abolishes ecclesiastical jurisdictions
May 4, Arrest of the bishop of Turin
June 2, He is released from the citadel

1851

Cavour, Minister of Foreign Affairs

1855

March 2, Bill for suppression of convents and support of clergy by the state passed
April 10, Convention with England and France signed; a contingent of 15,000 troops to be supplied against Russia
May 8, 10,000 troops under General La Marmora arrive in the Crimea
Aug. 16, Who distinguish themselves in the battle of the Tchernaya

1856

April 16, Important note on Italy from Count Cavour to England
Rupture with Austria; subsequent war (*see* Austria, 1857 *et seq.*)

1857

June, Cavour declares in favor of free trade

1859

Jan. 30, Prince Napoleon Jerome marries Princess Clotilde (*see* Italy)
July 11, Preliminaries of peace signed at Villa Franca; Count Cavour resigns, July 13; Rattazzi administration formed, July 19
Oct. 20, The Emperor Napoleon's letter to Victor-Emmanuel advocating the formation of an Italian confederation: the latter declares it to be impracticable, and maintains his engagements with the Italians
Nov., Treaty of peace signed at Zurich
Nov. 18, Garibaldi retires into private life
[For the disputes, and war with Austria, and the events of 1859–61, *see* Austria, France, Rome, Sicily, and Naples]

1860

Jan. 16, Count Cavour returns to office
Feb. 25, Annexation of Savoy and Nice proposed by the French Government; the Sardinian Government refer it to the vote of the people
Feb. 29, The Sardinian Government refers the question of annexation of Tuscany, &c., to the vote of the people
March 18–20, Annexation to Sardinia voted almost unanimously by Æmilia, March 14; by Tuscany, March 16; accepted by Victor-Emmanuel
March 24, Savoy and Nice ceded to France
April 2, New Sardinian parliament opens
April 15, Annexation to France almost unanimously voted for by Nice; by Savoy, April 22
May 18, The Government professes disapproval of Garibaldi's expedition to Sicily. *See* Sicily
May 29, The Chambers ratify treaty of cession of Savoy and Nice
Sept. 11, The Sardinian troops enter the papal territories (*see* Italy and Rome)
Oct. 15, Victor-Emmanuel enters the Kingdom of Naples
Oct. 21, Naples and Sicily vote for annexation to Sardinia

KINGS OF SARDINIA. *See* Savoy

1720. Victor-Amadeus I, King (as Duke II); resigned, in 1730, in favor of his son; died in 1732

1730. Charles-Emmanuel I (III of Savoy), son
1773. Victor-Amadeus II, son
1796. Charles-Emmanuel II, son; resigned his crown in favor of his brother
1802. Victor-Emmanuel I, brother; June 4
1805. [Sardinia merged in the Kingdom of Italy, of which the Emperor Napoleon was crowned King, May 26, 1805]
1814. Victor-Emmanuel restored; resigned in March, 1821; and died in 1824
1821. Charles-Felix
1831. Charles-Albert; abdicated in favor of his son, March 23, 1849. Died at Oporto, July 28, 1849
1849. Victor-Emmanuel II, son; born March 14, 1820; died, Jan. 9, 1878
[From this point the Kings of Sardinia became Kings of united Italy. *See* Italy]

SAVOY

Savoy, the ancient *Sapaudia* or *Sabaudia*, formerly a province in N. Italy, east of Piedmont. It became a Roman province about 118 B.C. The Alemanni seized it in A.D. 395, and the Franks in 490. It shared the revolutions of Switzerland till about 1048, when Conrad, Emperor of Germany, gave it to Humbert, with the title of Count. Count Thomas acquired Piedmont in the 13th century. Amadeus, Count of Savoy, having entered his dominions, solicited Sigismund to erect them into a duchy, which he did at Cambray, Feb. 19, 1416. Victor-Amadeus, Duke of Savoy, obtained the Kingdom of Sicily from Spain, by a treaty, in 1713, but afterwards exchanged it with the Emperor for the island of Sardinia, with the title of King, 1720. The French subdued Savoy in 1792, and made it a department of France, under the name of Mont Blanc, in 1800. It was restored to the King of Sardinia in 1814; but with Nice annexed to France in 1860, in accordance with a vote by universal suffrage, April 23, 1860.

DUKES OF SAVOY

1391. Count Amadeus VIII is made Duke in 1416; he was named Pope, as Felix V. He abdicated as Duke of Savoy, 1439; renounced the tiara, 1449; died in 1451
1439. Louis
1465. Amadeus IX
1472. Philibert I
1482. Charles I
1489. Charles II
1496. Philip II
1497. Philibert II
1504. Charles III
1553. Emmanuel-Philibert
1580. Charles-Emmanuel I
1630. Victor-Amadeus I
1637. Francis-Hyacinthe
1638. Charles-Emmanuel II
1675. Victor-Amadeus II became King of Sicily, 1713; exchanged for Sardinia in 1720

SCOTLAND

Scotland, division of the United Kingdom of Great Britain, north of England, separated from England by the Solway Firth and the Cheviot Hills, area, 29,796 square miles, greatest length, 274 miles, and greatest breadth, 154 miles, population: 4,882,497 (census 1921); as estimated June 30, 1930, 4,879,700. Before the union Edinburgh was the capital.

In ancient times Scotland was known to the Romans, who subdued the Scots and Picts, as Caledonia.

838 to 1558

838–843, Kenneth II, King of the Scots, subdued the Picts and Caledonians and established one kingdom
937, Constantine III defeated in battle at Brunanburh by Athelstan of England
1018, Malcolm II defeated the Northumbrians at the Battle of Carham, near Coldstream
1040, The Danes driven out of Scotland
——, Duncan I is murdered by his kinsman Macbeth, by whom the crown is seized
1054, Malcolm III, aided by Edward the Confessor, defeats the usurper at Dunsinane; Macbeth killed by Macduff, 1056 or 1057
1080, The Saxon-English language introduced into Scotland by fugitives from England escaping from the Normans
1093, Siege of Alnwick: Malcolm III killed
1124–53, Reign of David I, a legislator
1263, Scotland invaded by Hacho, King of Norway, with 160 ships and 20,000 men; the invaders are defeated by Alexander III, who now recovers the Western Isles
Oct. 7, 1290, Death of Margaret of Norway, heiress to the throne
Nov., 1292, John Balliol and Robert Bruce contend for the throne, 1291; Edward I of England, as umpire, decides in favor of John
1293, John Balliol, King of Scotland, appears to a summons, and defends his own cause in Westminster hall against the Earl of Fife
1296, Edward, wishing to annex Scotland to England, dethrones John, ravages the country, destroys the muniments of Scottish history, and seizes the prophetic stone
1297, William Wallace defeats the English at Cambus Kenneth, and expels them; is defeated at Falkirk, July 22, 1298; taken by the English, and executed at Smithfield, Aug. 23, 1305
1306, Robert Bruce, crowned; he defeats the English, 1307; and takes Inverness, 1313; defeats the English at Bannockburn, June 24, 1314
Aug. 11, 1332, Edward Balliol gains the throne for a little time by his victory at Dupplin; and by the victory at Halidon-hill, July 19, 1333
1346, David II taken prisoner at the battle of Durham (and detained in captivity 11 years)
Aug. 10, 1388, Battle of Chevy Chase, between Hotspur Percy and Earl Douglas
April 3, 1401, Murder of Duke of Rothesay, heir of Robert III, by starvation
Sept. 14, 1402, The Scots defeated at Homildon-hill
March 30, 1406, James I captured by the English near Flamborough head on his passage to France

1411, St. Andrews University founded by Bishop Wardlaw

1494, University of Aberdeen founded

Sept. 9, 1513, James IV invades England, slain at Flodden Field, and his army cut to pieces

1528, James V banishes the Douglases

1532, He establishes the court of session

1540, Order of St. Andrew, or the Thistle, is revived

Dec. 14, Mary, the Queen of Scots, born Dec. 7; succeeds her father, James V, who dies

May 29, 1546, The Regent, Cardinal Beaton, persecutes the reformers, 1539, 1546; he is assassinated at St. Andrews

Sept. 10, 1547, The Scots defeated at Pinkie

April, 1558, Mary marries the Dauphin of France

1560

Aug. 24, The parliament abolishes the jurisdiction of the Pope in Scotland

Dec., Francis II dies, leaving Mary a widow

The Reformation in Scotland, by John Knox, and others, during the minority of Mary, between 1550 & 1560

1561 to 1566

Aug. 21, 1561, Mary, after an absence of thirteen years, arrives at Leith from France

1562, Upon an inquisition, which was officially taken, by order of Queen Elizabeth, only 58 Scotsmen were found in London. *Stow*

July 29, 1565, Mary marries her cousin, Henry Stuart, Lord Darnley

March 9, 1566, David Rizzio, her confidential secretary, murdered by Darnley in her presence

1567

Feb. 10, Lord Darnley blown up by gunpowder in his house (Mary accused of conniving at his death)

May 15, James Hepburn, Earl of Bothwell, carries off the Queen, who marries him

June 15, Mary made prisoner at Carberry hill by her nobles

July 22, Resigns her crown to her infant son James VI; the Earl of Murray appointed Regent

1568 to 1604

May 16, 1568, Mary escapes from prison, and collects a large army, which is defeated by the Regent Murray, at the battle of Langside, May 13; enters England

Jan. 23, 1570, The Regent Murray murdered

July 12, The Earl of Lennox appointed Regent

Sept., 1571, The Earl of Lennox murdered, Sept. 4; the Earl of Mar chosen Regent

Nov. 24, 1572, Death of the reformer John Knox

1582, The University of Edinburgh founded

———, The raid of Ruthven

Feb. 8, 1587, Mary having taken refuge in England, May 16, 1568, is, after a long captivity, beheaded at Fotheringay castle

Aug. 5, 1600, Gowrie's conspiracy fails

March 24, 1603, Union of the crown of Scotland with that of England by the accession of James VI

Oct. 24, 1604, James proclaimed "King of Great Britain, France, and Ireland." *See* Great Britain

SERB–CROAT–SLOVENE STATE
See Yugoslavia

SERBIA

Serbia, former Balkan Kingdom of south-eastern Europe, now incorporated in Yugoslavia. (*See also* Yugoslavia.) The frontiers were established by the Berlin Treaty of July 13, 1878, which established independence from Turkey, and the Treaty of Bucarest of Aug. 10, 1913, by which Serbia gained 15,241 square miles of new territory, including 1,795 square miles of Salonica, 3,473 square miles of Monastir (Bitolj), and 9,973 square miles of Kossovo, making total area 33,891 square miles, as compared with 18,650 square miles as stated in census of 1910, population, 4,547,992, according to census of 1910, 2,911,701 in Old Serbia and 1,636,291 in New Serbia. The capital of Serbia was Belgrade.

1159 to 1875

1159 *et seq.*, Stephen Nemanya, a Serbian chief, founds the Racian dynasty, under whom the country progressed

1336–56, Stephen Dushan subdues Bulgaria, &c., and aims at resisting the Turks

1371, The Serbians, weakened by dissensions, defeated by the Turks

June 15, 1389, The Sultan Amurath I defeated the combined Christian army of Serbians, Hungarians, Albanians, &c., and was himself killed by a wounded Serbian soldier in the plain of Cossova, or Kossova

1459 *et seq.*, Serbia, subdued by the Sultan Mahomet II, is rigorously ruled; ceded to Austria, 1718; regained by Turkey, 1739

1788–90, The Serbians aid Austria by free companies

1806, Again rebel, and capture Belgrade

1807–11, Kara George, founder of Serbian dynasty, chosen leader, 1801; aided by the Russians, establishes a government

1814, The Turks break a treaty, and Kara George flees

March, 1815, Their governor, Milosch, rebels

1817, Kara George, returning, is assassinated

Aug. 15, 1829, Alexander Milosch I Obrenovitch recognized as hereditary prince by the Sultan

June 13, 1839, Milosch becoming despotic, made to abdicate, and a new constitution established

Sept. 14, 1842, His son and successor Milan soon dies, whose brother Michael also retires; Alexander, son of Kara George, chosen Prince

Dec. 23, 1858, Alexander becoming unpopular, made to abdicate by the national party; Alexander Milosch reëlected Prince

July 13, 1860, Plot against Milosch frustrated, July 11; the Serbian assembly meets

Sept. 26, Milosch dies; succeeded by his son Michael Obrenovitch (born Sept. 4, 1825)

March, 1861, Rising movement to render Serbia independent of Turkey

June 19, 1862, Disputes between the Serbians and the Turkish garrison at Belgrade, which lead to bloodshed; the city bombarded, June 15; submits, June 17; the Turkish Pacha dismissed

Oct. 7, A conference of the representatives of the

great Powers at Constantinople, Aug.; the Porte agrees to liberal concessions to the Serbians, which their Prince accepts

Oct. 5, 1866, Serbians demand withdrawal of Turkish garrisons from Belgrade and other fortresses

March 30, 1867, Which are evacuated, March; Prince Michael, at Constantinople, thanks the Sultan

June 10, 1868, Prince Michael assassinated in Belgrade

July 28, Milan IV, grand-nephew of Prince Michael, chosen his successor, June 22; 14 of the murderers were executed

1869, Constitution affirming the hereditary rights of the Obrenovitch family

May, 1871, Prince Karageorgevitch accused of complicity with murder; acquitted

Aug. 22, 1872, The regents surrender the government to Prince Milan at Belgrade

1875, Excitement through insurrection in Herzegovina, new ministry hostile to Turkey, formed about Aug. 31; resign; announced Oct. 4; peace ministry formed Oct. 9

1876

July, Ristitch, Premier, opposed to Turkey

July 1, See Turkey, for the war declared

Sept. 16, Milan proclaimed King by Tchernayeff and the army at Deligrad; not approved

1877

March 4, Peace with Turkey ratified

[Serbian losses in the war, about 8,000 killed, 20,000 wounded]

Dec. 14, 15, Serbians again declare war and enter Turkey (see Russo-Turkish war)

Dec. 22, Sultan deposes Prince Milan

1878

March 3, Serbia declared independent, with new frontiers, by treaty of San Stefano; and of Berlin, July 13

Aug. 22, Proclamation of peace and national independence at Belgrade

About Oct. 15, The Ministry remodeled by Ristitch

1880

Oct. 25, Resignation of Ristitch (virtual dictator)

1882

March 6, Milan proclaimed King by Assembly

[Married Natalie Keschko (born 1859), Oct. 17, 1875]

Oct. 23, Escaped assassination by Mad. Markovitch

1883

Nov. 5–10, New military organization leads to insurrection in S.E. Serbia; soon suppressed

About Nov. 10, Insurgents defeated

Nov. 13, General tranquillity reported

Dec. 18 rebel leaders executed, about Nov. 19; many others reprieved

1884

June, Rebels enter Bulgaria; disputes with that country ensue; prospect of war

About Nov. 10, Dispute settled by arrangement

1885

Oct., Military movements consequent upon the coup d'état in Roumelia

Nov. 13, Declaration of war against Bulgaria

Nov. 14–24, Invasion

1886

Feb. 11, Royal decree calling out the army

March 3, Peace between Serbia and Bulgaria signed at Bucharest

1888

July 18, The King demands a divorce from the Queen for disagreements; he favors Austria, she Russia; she refused the deed of terms offered; she gives up the Crown Prince and goes to Paris

Oct., Queen Natalie protests against the divorce Aug. 20 & Oct. 30; the divorce decreed by the metropolitan Theodosius, Abp. of Belgrade (authority questionable)

Oct. 24, A royal commission recommends universal suffrage, all electors eligible to the Skuptschina, independence of the church, all religions free and protected, liberty of the press, &c.

Nov. 28, Elections of the chambers annulled by the King as not free

Dec. 16, New elections give majority to the radicals, headed by M. Ristitch, against the progressists under M. Christitch, the Minister

Dec. 30, The Skuptschina opened

1889

Jan. 1, The King informs a deputation desiring changes in the proposed constitution that the deputies must accept it unaltered; otherwise he will set it aside and rule absolutely

Jan. 3, The new constitution passed (494–73), Jan. 2; the session closed

March 6, Abdication of the King; his son Alexander proclaimed; liberal regency, M. Ristitch, Gen. Bolimarkovitch, and Gen. Protitch; radical cabinet headed by M. Taushanovitch

June 27, The Serbians celebrate with mourning the quincentenary of the battle of Cossova

July 2, The King founds a monument in memory of the slain. The King was anointed by the metropolitan Michael in the church of Zitcha, near Kraljevo

Oct. 13, Queen Natalie arrives at Belgrade, Sept. 29; interview with her son

1890

April 19, King Milan agrees to live out of Serbia, till his son's majority, about April 14; he arrives at Vienna

About May 10, Queen Natalie requested by the Government to leave the country, refuses; attempted expulsion stopped by students and people; 2 persons killed and several wounded by the troops, May 18. The Queen forcibly conveyed to Semlin in Hungary, early May 19

July 1, The Serbian vice-consul at Pristina, M. Marinkovite, assassinated. The arrested assassins confess and are tried; the excessive demands of the Serbian government refused by Turkey; the affair arranged about July 28

Nov. 18, King Milan resigns definitely all his military and political rights, reported

Dec. 8 et seq., Queen Natalie agitates to annul her isolation from her son; her memorandum (Nov. 22) to the parliament dismissed

1893

Jan. 19, Reconciliation of King Milan and Queen Natalie at Biarritz announced

April 14, Coup d'état: King Alexander, after a banquet,

and appealing to the army, April 13, proclaims his majority and dismisses the regents and their ministry, and appoints a radical ministry (Dr. Dokitsch, Premier); the parliament dissolved; popular rejoicing

June 16, The new parliament opened by the King; he takes the oath of the constitution

July 19, The impeachment of the Avakumovitch Cabinet agreed to by the parliament

Sept. 8, Resignation of Dr. Dokitsch, the Premier

Oct. 15, Reconciliation of the King and the liberal party; public demonstration

1894

Jan. 21, Resignation of the Gruitch Ministry on the arrival of King Milan, invited by his son

Jan. 26, Amnesty to political offenders granted

——, Trial of M. Avakumovitch and his former colleagues; began Dec. 21; suspended

March 18, King Milan's divorce annulled by the episcopal synod, reported

May 21, *Coup d'état:* the King suspends the constitution of 1888 and reëstablishes that of June 29, 1869; despotic changes; the press restricted, &c.; M. Nicolas Christitch, President of the Council of State

1895

Jan. 12, M. Ranko Taisitch and 3 others sentenced to 3 years' and M. Czebinatz to 2 years' imprisonment for treason; pardoned, July

May 10, Return of Queen Natalie to Belgrade; warmly received

May 12, A pension of 12,000*l.* per annum voted to King Milan

1897

July, Many Albanian raids, 204 notes in 3 yrs. addressed to the Porte, on the subject

1898

Jan. 6, The ex-King Milan appointed commander-in-chief of the army

1899

Jan. 26, Note to the Porte regarding the Albanian outrages in Kossovo, Oct. 31, 1898; claims disallowed by the Porte

June 14–16, Albanian raids: Turkish troops engaged near Vrania, much bloodshed

July 9–Oct. 2, The ex-King Milan shot at in Belgrade by Payitch, alias Knezevitch, a fanatic, July 6 (wholesale arrests followed); loyal demonstration in honor of the King and ex-King, July 8; martial law proclaimed

July 21, 22, Betrothal of the King to Mdme. Draga Maschin (unpopular); ex-King Milan, commander-in-chief, resigns (afterwards banished)

Early Aug., Regulations for frontier service agreed to by a mixed commission

Aug. 5, King Alexander married Madame Draga

——, Political amnesty to radicals announced

Sept. 8–25, State trial; Knezevitch and 27 others charged with high treason (M. Angjelitch commits suicide in his cell, Sept. 8); 22 found guilty; Knezevitch and Rankl Tisitch (who escaped) sentenced to death, 10 others to 20 years' penal servitude, the rest to various terms of imprisonment (M. Pasitch, radical leader, afterwards pardoned); Knezevitch (reaffirming the absolute innocence of 10 of the condemned) shot in public, Sept. 25; the trial regarded unjust,

the prisoners' defense having been entirely ignored; *see Times,* Sept. 26

Sept. 27, M. Vesnitch, an able lawyer, Professor Paolovitch (without evidence), and 2 others accused of *lèse majesté,* sentenced from 2 to 8 years' penal servitude

Dec. 12, M. Genchitch, ex-Minister, sentenced to 7 years' imprisonment for *lèse majesté*

1901

Feb. 11, Death of ex-King Milan at Vienna, aged 47

April 19, New liberal Constitution promulgated; fuller civil liberties restored

June, Frequent Albanian affrays on the frontier

Sept. 4, Supreme council of war (for 3 years) ordered, reported

1902

March 5, Alavantich, a Serbian agitator, is mortally wounded in a revolutionary attempt at Shabatz

Aug. 26, 31, Commercial agreements with Russia

1903

April 6, Political riots in Belgrade, 18 killed

April 7, *Coup d'état* Chamber dissolved, laws annulled, liberal constitution of 1901 restored

June 10–11, Military *coup d'état* and revolution raised by the radicals at Belgrade; Col. Maschin, the Queen's brother-in-law, Col. Misitch and a band of officers, forced their way into the palace (Col. Naumovitch killed by the explosion of a bomb, which he himself had thrown at one of the doors) and massacred King Alexander and Queen Draga, Gen. Petrovitch, 2 aides-de-camp, many of the guards and others who tried to defend them; Gen. Markovitch, Premier, Gen. Pavlovitch (War Minister), 2 other ministers, (Nimkode alleged heir to the throne), Nikola Lungevica, the Queen's brothers, and 17 others, murdered, and about 10 wounded in the town at night

June 11, Provisional government formed, M. Avakumovitch, Premier, Col. Maschin, Board of Works

June 12, The King and Queen buried at dawn

June 15, Parliament meets, Prince Peter Karageorgevitch elected King

——, The new King by proclamation asserts "that he will be faithful to the traditions of his ancestors, and that all that has passed will be buried in oblivion"

June 16, Thanksgiving service at Belgrade, the Metropolitan thanked, and praised the army for its recent action

June 17, The liberal constitution of 1889 adopted

June 23, Sir G. Bonham, British Minister, recalled

June 25, King Peter enthusiastically received, Russian and Austrian the only foreign ministers present, June 24; he takes the oath of the constitution, and holds a review of troops, the provisional ministry retained

June 28, Political amnesty and perpetual indemnity for acts of treason up to the present time, issued

June 30, King Edward VII's reply to the King's message concludes, "Whilst expressing my sincere desire that your reign may bring to the people entrusted to your charge the blessings of peace and prosperity, I hope that your Majesty will succeed in restoring the good repute of your country upon which recent events have left so regrettable a stain"

Sept. 17, Rumors of unrest and conspiracies, Col. Misitch removed from the War Ministry

Sept. 19, Continued unrest reported, the army divided between the "old conspirators" (assassins of the King and Queen) still in power, and the "new conspirators"

Oct. 7, The Skupshtina opened by the King: he requests it to work in earnest for the advancement of the country

Oct. 10, Six officers sentenced to 13 months' imprisonment for conspiring against officers connected with the murder of the late King and Queen

Early Oct., Gen. Maschin, who took a prominent part in the assassination of King Alexander and Queen Draga, appointed to the command of the Belgrade-Danube division, reported

1904

Feb. 3, Cabinet resigns (reconstructed after some delay, Gen. Gruitch again Premier)

April 1, Various officers implicated in the assassination of King Alexander and Queen Draga promoted; Col. Maschin appointed chief of the general staff; chief conspirator, Col. Popovitch, removed from the position of aide-de-camp-general of the King to the command of the Belgrade-Danube division; posts about the person of the King given to non-conspirators

Sept. 21, Coronation of King Peter, at Belgrade; Mgr. Innocent, Archbp. of Belgrade, conducts the service at the cathedral; the King places the crown upon his head himself; reception at the palace, ministers and envoys of various countries present letters from their monarchs; Great Britain is unrepresented

Dec. 7, Gen. Gruitch reconstructs his Cabinet

Dec. 10, New ministry, composed of members of the moderate radical party, with M. Pashitch as Premier and Minister for Foreign Affairs, formed

1905

May 22, Resignation of M. Pashitch and cabinet

May 28, M. Stojanovitch forms a new ministry, composed of members of the extreme radical party

Aug. 8, Reconstruction of the Cabinet after the general election in July, M. Stojanovitch remaining Premier

Nov. 21, Contract for a new loan, 70,000,000 dinars, for railway construction, war material, and other purposes, signed by Dr. Markovitch, Minister for Finance

1906

Jan. 5, Serbo-Bulgarian convention, aiming at the establishment of a customs' union to come into force March 1, 1906, and end March 1, 1917, reported

Feb. 19, M. Vladan Georgevitch, formerly Prime Minister of Serbia, sentenced in Belgrade to 6 months' imprisonment on the charge of having acted injuriously to the interests of Serbia in revealing state secrets

March 14, Resignation of the Stojanovitch Cabinet, March 7; Ministry reconstructed under Gen. Gruitch, as Premier and Minister for War

May 1, New cabinet formed, with M. Pasitch as Premier and Foreign Minister

May 30, Ukase issued by the King placing the principal regicides on the retired list

June 13, Dr. Militchevitch appointed Serbian Minister in London

Aug. 20, Mr. Whitehead, new British Minister to Serbia, received by King Peter

Dec. 26, Loan and armament bills accepted by the Shupshtina and signed by the King

1907

Feb. 15, Anglo-Serbian commercial treaty signed

April 2, Death of M. Kalievitch, a former Premier and Minister for Foreign Affairs in the revolutionary cabinet, announced

June 8, Resignation of the Ministry

June 12, All the Ministers reoccupy their former posts, with the exception of M. Protitch, Minister of the Interior; M. Pashitch, Prime Minister and Minister for Foreign Affairs

1908

July 6, Cabinet crisis; new cabinet formed, with M. Pera Velimirovitch as Premier

July 13, Death of M. Militchevitch, Serbian minister in London, b. 1869

July 20, New cabinet formed, with M. Velimirovitch again as Premier

Sept. 1, The Austro-Serbian commercial treaty came into force

1909

March 25, The Crown Prince addressed a letter to the Prime Minister announcing his resolve to surrender his right of succession to the throne; and King Peter declared his second son, Alexander, heir to the throne, March 27

Nov. 25, Visit of King Ferdinand of Bulgaria to Belgrade

1910

March 22, King Peter arrived at Tsarskoe Selo on a visit to the Czar; and in Constantinople, April 3

April 20, Floods in the town of Kragujevatz; 12 deaths reported

1911

July 8, New Cabinet formed by Dr. Milovanovic, Radical

1912

Feb. 29/March 13, Political Treaty of alliance with Bulgaria with secret annex providing for partition of Macedonia. *See also* Bulgaria. Serbia to receive territory north and west of the Shar Mountains

June 19, Military Convention with Bulgaria signed by which Bulgaria undertook to send military aid to Serbia in event of war, and Serbia to Bulgaria respectively

July 1, Death of Prime Minister Milovanovic. Succeeded by Trifkovic as Prime Minister with Pasic as Minister of Foreign Affairs

Sept. 12, Pasic became Premier with Radical Cabinet

Sept. 28, On eve of Balkan War Bulgaria notified Serbia that only one division instead of three could be sent to aid of Serbians in Macedonia contrary to Convention of June 19

Sept. 30–Oct. 1, Mobilization against Turkey

Oct. 13, Note to Turkey. *See* Balkan Wars

Oct. 17, War declared on Turkey. *See* Balkan Wars

Dec. 16, Serbia represented at the Peace Conference in London by Novakovic, former Premier

1913

May 6, Serbs evacuated Durazzo

May 19/June 1, Offensive and defensive alliance with Greece against Bulgaria concluded for 10 years

May 28, Serbia demanded revision of Treaty of 1912
with Bulgaria
May 30, Treaty of Peace signed in London. *See* Balkan
Wars. The creation of Albanian State shut Serbia
out from the Adriatic
July 8, Serbia declared war on Bulgaria formally
Aug. 10, Treaty of Peace signed after Second Balkan
War gave Serbia Macedonia west of the Vardar, and
Istib (Stip), and Kocana (Kotchana) and Rado-
vishta
Aug. 19, Note of Powers demanded withdrawal of
Serbian troops from Albania
Sept. 22, Albanians captured Dibra which Serbians
recovered and invaded Albania
Oct. 25, Serbian troops withdrawn from Albania after
ultimatum of Oct. 18 from Austria-Hungary
Nov. 4, Treaty with Montenegro signed by which
Montenegro received Metoya and the Sandjak of
Novi Bazar

1914

March 4, Opposition withdrew from the Chamber as a
protest against action of Government in budget
matters which was declared unconstitutional
March 14, Final Treaty of Peace with Turkey signed
June 2, Pasic Ministry resigned. Reinstated June 11
June 15, Parliament dissolved and general election or-
dered. The order canceled after outbreak of war
and former Parliament convened of 142 Radicals and
Progressives, 22 Nationalists, and 2 Socialists
June 24, King Peter appointed his son Crown Prince
Alexander as Regent because of ill health
June 28, Murder of Archduke Francis Ferdinand, and
his morganatic wife at Sarajevo, Bosnia, by a student,
Gavrio Prinzip, shot as they rode in a carriage from
the City Hall. An attempt earlier in the day by
Medeljko Kaprinovic, a printer, as they drove to
the City Hall, by throwing a bomb had failed. The
assassins had been in Belgrade and had received
bombs and pistols from Serbian officials, Majors
Ciganovic and Tankosic
July 23, Austrian ultimatum to Serbia. *See* World War
——, Major Tankosic arrested
July 24, Note to Russia asked for diplomatic aid
July 25, Serbian reply not accepted by Austria-Hun-
gary as satisfactory and diplomatic relations severed
——, Mobilization of Serbia and Government trans-
ferred to Nish
——, Government asked Greece if it could count on
armed support of Greece in case of attack under
Treaty of alliance and received assurance from
Venizelos that Greece would support Serbia against
Bulgarian attack
July 28, Austria-Hungary declared war on Serbia. *See*
World War
Aug. 1, Parliament met and endorsed action of the
Government
Aug. 6, Serbia declared war on Germany
Oct. 28, Prinzip and 23 accomplices found guilty of
treason and conspiracy to murder the Archduke
Ferdinand; Prinzip and 3 others hung, 3 sentenced to
imprisonment for 20 years, and 7 to shorter terms
Dec. 2, Serbia declared war on Turkey
Dec. 5, Cabinet resigned
Dec. 13, N. P. Pasic resumed office with a Coalition
Cabinet as Prime Minister and Minister for Foreign
Affairs; Finance, M. Mintenititch; Interior, M.
Liouba Jovanovitch; War, Colonel Boyovitch;

Public Instruction, M. Davidovitch; Commerce,
Agriculture and Industry, M. Voislav Marinovitch;
Public Works, M. Drachkovitch; Justice, M. Djurit-
chitch

1915

Jan. 11 and 23, Proposals of Great Britain that Greece
aid Serbia. *See* Greece
May 7, British Minister of Foreign Affairs gave pledge
to Serbian Government as to eventual conditional
cession of Bosnia, and on Aug. 30 as to eventual
freedom and self-determination of Bosnia. *See also*
World War, Nov. 2
July 25, Government established at Nish
Aug. 21, Venizelos reaffirmed obligation of Greece to
aid Serbia in case of attack
Oct. 12, Greece declared against military aid to Serbia
Oct. 15, Rumanian Government refused to aid Serbia
Oct. 16, Serbia declared war on Bulgaria
Oct. 19, Government left Nish and was established at
Prisrend
Dec. 3, Government established at Scutari
Dec. 15, King Peter arrived at Brindisi, Italy

1916

Jan. 1–15, King Peter at Salonica
Jan. 15, Government established at Brindisi, Italy
——, First Serbian troops arrived in Corfu
Feb. 9, Government established at Corfu where Serbs
were transported by Allies after final retreat across
mountains of Albania and Montenegro to the
Adriatic. Conquered Serbia administered by Austria-
Hungary and Bulgaria
April 3, Greek Government refused overland passage
for Serbian troops to Salonika
April 15, First Serbian troops arrived at Salonika from
Corfu
May 7, Government established at Salonika
July 25, Serbian troops in action on the Salonika front
Dec. 15, Arrest of Colonel Dragutin Dimitrievic on
charge of conspiring to deliver the Serb front to the
enemy

1917

Jan. 26, Establishment of a Serbian Legation in the
United States. M. L. Michailovic received by the
President
Jan., Conspiracy trial in Salonika which ended in sen-
tence of death of 9 Serbian officers including Colonel
Dimitrievic, head of the "Black Hand" and author
and organizer of Sarajevo conspiracy and charged
with plot against life of Prince Alexander
May 17, Death of Marshal (Voivoda) Putnik, chief of
army retired, at Nice
June, Dimitrievic shot
June 24, Pasic formed new Cabinet
July 20, Pact of Corfu signed. *See* Yugoslavia

1918

Feb. 28, Pasic Cabinet resigned
Sept. 30, Bulgarians agreed to evacuate Serbian terri-
tory
Nov. 3, Government reoccupied Belgrade
Nov. 6, King Peter reëntered the capital
Nov. 12, Serbs occupied Temesvar
Nov. 17, Pasic formed Coalition Cabinet
Nov. 23, Act of union of Serbia and Montenegro
Nov. 24, The United Serb-Croat-Slovene State pro-
claimed

Dec. 1, Prince Alexander accepted regency over the new Serb-Croat-Slovene State. *See also* Yugoslavia for further events in Serbia

Dec. 29, Protic formed Cabinet

HEREDITARY PRINCES

1829. Milosch (Obrenovitch) I, recognized by Turkey, Aug. 15, 1833; abdicates June 13, 1839

1839. Michael II, son; dies 1840

1840. Michael III, brother; abdicates 1842

1842. Alexander (Karageorgevitch), son of Kara George; chosen, Sept. 14; deposed, Dec. 23, 1858; died May 3, 1885; his son, Peter, b. 1844

1858. Milosch (Obrenovitch), reëlected, Dec. 23; dies, 1860

1860. Michael III, son; succeeds, Sept. 26; assassinated, June 10, 1868

1868. Milan (Obrenovitch) IV, grand-nephew, born, Aug. 22, 1854; married to Natalie Keschko, Oct. 17, 1875; again proclaimed, July 2, 1868; he abdicated March 6, 1889; died, Feb. 11, 1901

1889. Alexander, son, born Aug. 14, 1876; married Mme. Draga, *née* Lungevica, Aug. 5, 1900; both assassinated, June 10, 1903

1903. Peter I (Karageorgevitch), born 1846; married Princess Zorka of Montenegro, Aug., 1883 (died 1890); elected King, June 15, 1903; crowned Sept. 21, 1904; died, Aug. 16, 1921

Heir: Prince George, born 1887; surrenders his right of succession, March 25, and his brother, Alexander, born Dec. 4, 1888, nominated heir, March 27, 1909

1914. June 24, Alexander, Prince Regent. *See* Yugoslavia

SEVEN YEARS' WAR

Seven Years' War, The (1756–1763), arose from the fear of the continental powers of the aggression of Frederick II, the Great, of Prussia, and the desire of Maria Theresa, of Austria, to regain the province of Silesia, which resulted in alliance of Austria with Russia and Saxony. Prussia gained England as an ally, and France already at war with England in the colonies joined the coalition Maria Theresa was forming against Frederick, and Sweden the following year, and Spain renewed the family compact with France, Aug. 15, 1761. Without waiting for a declaration of war against him Frederick began hostilities by invading Saxony and captured Dresden (Aug. 1756). The war was fought in North America and India and Africa as well. For the "French and Indian War," *see* America. The war ended with the Treaty of Hubertsburg, Feb. 15, 1763, and restoration of the *status quo*, Prussia confirmed in the possession of Silesia, and in America and India by the Treaty of Paris, signed Nov. 3, 1762.

SEVEN YEARS' WAR, 1756–63

1757

May 6, Prague (Frederick defeats Allies)
June 18, Kollin (Frederick defeated)
June 23, Plassey (Clive's victory)

Aug. 13, Norkitten (Russians defeated)
Nov. 5, Rosbach (Frederick defeats French)
Nov. 22, Breslau (Austrians victors)
Dec. 5, Lissa (Frederick defeats Austrians)

1758

June 23, Creveldt (Ferdinand defeats French)
Aug. 25, 26, Zorndorff (Frederick defeats Russians)
Oct. 14, Hochkirchen (Austrians defeat Prussians)

1759

April 13, Bergen (French defeat Allies)
July 23, Zullichau (Russians defeat Prussians)
July 24, Niagara (English take Fort)
Aug. 1, Minden (Ferdinand defeats French)
Aug. 12, Cunnersdorf (Russians defeat Prussians)
Sept. 13, Quebec (Wolfe, victor, killed)

1760

Jan. 22, Wandewash (Coote defeats Lally)
June 23, Landshut, Silesia (Prussians defeated)
July 31, Warburg (Ferdinand defeats French)
Aug. 15, Pfaffendorf (Frederick defeats Austrians)
Oct. 15, 16, Kloster Campen (English and Germans with French, indecisive)
Nov. 3, Torgau (Frederick defeats Austrians)

1761

July 15, Kirchdenkern (Allies defeat French)

1762

May 16, Schweidnitz (Frederick II defeats Austrians)
Aug. 30, Johannisberg (French defeat Prussians)
Oct. 29, Freiberg (Prussians defeat Austrians)

SICILY

Sicily (anciently Trinacria, three-cornered). The early inhabitants were the Sicani, or Siculi, a people of Spain, and Etruscans, who came from Italy. The Phœnicians and Greeks settled some colonies here (735–582). In modern times its government has frequently been united with and separated from that of Naples (*see s.v.*); the two now form part of the Kingdom of Italy.

735 B.C. to 1820

About B.C. 735, Naxos built by the Greeks from Eubœa

734, Syracuse founded by Archias from Corinth

730 *et seq.*, Leontini and other cities founded

579, Agrigentum founded by a Dorian colony; ruled by Phalaris, about 563

480, Gelon, tyrant of Gela, becomes supreme at Syracuse; the Carthaginians enter Sicily to found colonies, but are severely defeated by Gelon, at Himera

478, Gelon succeeded by his brother Hiero

453, Syracuse becomes predominant in Sicily

415, Great Athenian expedition under Nicias; defeated by the aid of Gylippus, the Lacedemonian, 413

412, An excellent code of laws established by Diocles

406, Dionysius the elder, able and ambitious, becomes captain-general at Syracuse; subdues the aristocracy, becomes tyrant, and gradually supreme in Sicily, 405; makes successful war with the Italian Greeks; declares war against Carthage, 397

395, Syracuse closely besieged by the Carthaginians; their army is crippled by a pestilence; their fleet destroyed by Dionysius; a treaty made

393, War renewed; peace made 392

387, Dionysius plants colonies in Italy; dies, 367

367, His dissolute son, Dionysius II, succeeds him; receives Plato and other philosophers; he is dethroned by Dion, his banished relative, who becomes ruler, 356

353, Dion rules severely and becomes unpopular; is assassinated by Calippus

346, Dionysius II (tyrant at Socri 10 years) recovers his authority at Syracuse; rules till his expulsion by Timoleon with a small Corinthian army, and retires to Corinth, 343

343 *et seq.*, Timoleon restores the republic, deposes the other Sicilian tyrants, and becomes supreme; totally defeats the Carthaginians at the Crimisus, 339; rules Sicily till his death, 337

317, Agathocles overthrows the republic with bloodshed, and becomes "autocrat," and afterwards king; defeated by the Carthaginians at the Himera, 310; he invades Africa, gains victories over the Carthaginians, but is compelled to return to Sicily by revolts, 307; dies, 289

278, Political dissensions; Pyrrhus, King of Epirus, enters Sicily, and defeats the Carthaginians; retires, 276

270, Hiero II made King of Syracuse; makes war with the Romans, is defeated, and makes peace, 263

264, The first Punic war begins

216, Hiero II dies

214, Hieronymus, his grandson, succeeds, 216; renounces the alliance with Rome; and is assassinated

214, The Roman consul, Marcellus, invades Sicily, and besieges Syracuse, which is vigorously defended by the aid of Archimedes; it is taken, when Archimedes is slain, 212

210, Sicily becomes a Roman province

135, 134, 132, The Servile wars; much slaughter

73–71, Tyrannical government of Verres (for which he was accused by Cicero)

42, Sicily held by Sextus Pompeius, son of the great Pompey; defeated; expelled, 36; killed, 35

* * * * * *

A.D. 440, Invaded by the Vandals; by the Goths, 493; taken for the Greek emperors by Belisarius, 536

832–78, Conquered by the Saracens and held

1038, Greatly recovered by the Greek Emperor by the aid of Normans

1058, The Greeks and Arabs driven out by a Norman prince, Roger I, son of Tancred; who takes the title of Count of Sicily, 1061–1090

1131, Roger II, son of the above named, unites Sicily with Naples, and is crowned King of the Two Sicilies

1266, Charles of Anjou, brother of St. Louis, King of France, conquers Naples and Sicily, deposes the Norman princes, and makes himself King

1282, Sicilian Vespers, the term given to the massacre of the French (who had conquered Sicily, 1266), commenced at Palermo, March 30

On Easter Monday conspirators assembled at Palermo; and while the French were engaged in festivities, a Sicilian bride passed by with her train. One Drochet, a Frenchman, used her rudely, under pretence of searching for arms. A young Sicilian stabbed him with his own sword; and a tumult ensuing, 200 French were instantly murdered. The

populace ran through the city, crying out, "Let the French die!" and, without distinction of rank, age, or sex slaughtered about 8,000 persons

1282, Sicily seized by a fleet sent by the kings of Aragon; Naples remains to the house of Anjou

1435, Alphonso, King of Aragon, takes possession of Naples

1501, The Kingdom of Naples and Sicily united to the Spanish monarchy under Ferdinand the Catholic

1713, Victor, Duke of Savoy, by the treaty of Utrecht, made King of Sicily

1720, Which he gives up to the Emperor Charles VI, and becomes King of Sardinia

1734, Charles, son of the King of Spain, becomes King of the Two Sicilies

1759, The throne of Spain becoming vacant, Charles, who is heir, vacates the throne of the Two Sicilies, in favor of his third son Ferdinand, agreeably to treaty

1783, Earthquake at Messina, in Sicily, which destroys 40,000 persons

1806, The French conquer Naples (*see s.v.*); Ferdinand IV retires to Sicily

1812, New constitution granted, under British auspices

1815, The French expelled; Kingdom of Two Sicilies reëstablished; Ferdinand returns to Naples; abolishes the constitution

1820, Revolution at Palermo suppressed

1848

Jan. 12, The great towns in Sicily rise and demand the constitution; a provisional government proclaimed

Jan. 29, The King nominates his brother, the Count of Aquila, Viceroy, Jan. 17; promises a new constitution

July 11, The Sicilian parliament decrees the exclusion of the Bourbon family, April 13; and invites the duke of Genoa to the throne

Sept. 7, Messina bombarded and taken by the Neapolitans

1849

April 6, Catania taken by assault; Syracuse surrenders April 23; and Palermo, May 14

1860

April 4 *et seq.*, Insurrections suppressed at Palermo, Messina, and Catania; the rebels retire into the interior April 21 *et seq.*

May 5, Garibaldi and his followers (2,200 men) embark at Genoa; and land at Marsala, May 11; he abandons his ships; and assumes the dictatorship in the name of the King of Sardinia, May 14

May 15, He defeats the royal troops at Calatafimi; storms Palermo, May 27; which is bombarded by the royal fleet, May 28; an armistice agreed to May 31

June, A provisional government formed at Palermo; which is evacuated by the Neapolitans, June 6

July 20, 21, Garibaldi defeats the Neapolitans at Melazzo

July 30, Convention signed, by which the Neapolitans agree to evacuate Sicily (retaining the citadel of Messina)

Aug. 3, New Sicilian constitution proclaimed

Aug. 21, Garibaldi embarks for Calabria (*see* Naples)

Sept., Professor Saffi (late of Oxford), a short time dictator

Oct. 21, The Sicilians by universal suffrage vote for annexation to Sardinia (432,054 against 667)

Dec. 1, Victor-Emmanuel visits Sicily

1861

March 13, Citadel of Messina blockaded, Feb. 28; surrenders to General Cialdini

1862

May, King Victor-Emmanuel warmly received at Messina

July 19, Imprudent speeches of Garibaldi at Marsala; he enters Catania, and establishes a provisional government, Aug. 19; embarks for Italy Aug. 24

Sicily placed under blockade; removed in Sept.; tranquil, Oct.

1866 to 1892

Sept. 21–26, 1866, Insurrection in Palermo, attributed to the priests and brigands, Sept. 16; suppressed with bloodshed by Italian troops

Aug., 1872, Revival of brigandage and murder

Sept. 1874, Martial law established in some places

Nov. 1874, Aliano, a brigand, tried at Potenza, for numerous murders, and other crimes

About Oct. 2, 1875, Capraro, brigand, killed during capture

Nov. 1876, Mr. Forester Rose carried off by brigands, Nov. 3; ransomed for about 4,000l.

June 1, 1877, Leone and other brigands shot

About Nov. 6, 1877 Five chief brigands surrender

Sept. 26–Oct. 9, 1892, Increase of brigandage by secret societies; many arrests

1893

Oct. 23, Despatch of troops to suppress brigandage; nearly a state of siege, reported

Dec., Violent rioting, with bloodshed at Palermo; rioting in Trapani against the *octroi* dues; reinforcements sent, Dec. 30; destructive rioting, with bloodshed, at different places; Gen. Morra di Lavriano invested with full powers to establish order, Jan. 2, 1894

1894

Jan. 4, State of siege in Sicily proclaimed at Palermo

Jan., The rising attributed to misgovernment and oppression by the municipal authorities

May 30, Signor de Felice Giuffrida (deputy) sentenced to 18 years, and 7 others to various terms of imprisonment, for connection with rioting (*see above*)

Sept. 25, Order restored, reported

Nov. 16, Destructive earthquakes, with loss of life, at Messinia, &c.

1895

March 23, Severe shock in Catania; many persons buried by the fall of a church

Dec. 29, Military rule ended in Sicily after 2 years

1896

April 6, Administration committed to a Royal Commission with headquarters at Palermo

1898

Jan. 10, Jubilee celebration of the Sicilian revolution (1848)

1902 to 1910

Oct. 13, 1902, Fatal riot at Giarratana

April 21, 22, 1903, Visit of King Edward VII

Sept 12, 1905 and Dec. 1908, Earthquake shock felt at Messina, connected with the earthquake in Calabria (*see* Italy)

March 23, 1910, Eruption of Mount Etna

For further events *See* Italy

SPAIN

Spain (the ancient Iberia and Hispania), kingdom in southwestern Europe occupying about four-fifths of the Iberian peninsula, surrounding Portugal on its land side, and bounded on the northeast by France from which it is separated by the Pyrenees, otherwise bounded by the Atlantic Ocean and the Mediterranean Sea connected by the Strait of Gibraltar. Spain also includes the Balearic Islands, the Canary Islands, and Ceuta on the Moroccan coast opposite Gibraltar. The rock of Gibraltar belongs to Great Britain (*see s.v.*). The total area is 190,050 square miles, but including the Balearic and Canary Islands, the total area is 196,607 square miles, the total population as estimated Dec. 31, 1929, 22,760,854. Madrid is the capital. The area of the Canary Islands is 2,810 square miles, population, 503,151, the area of the Balearic Islands, 1,935 square miles, population, 352,926. The population of Ceuta (39,510) is included in that of Cadiz. Besides Ceuta, Spain has on the African coast the Alhucema Isles (population, 322), the Chafarinas (320), Melilla (61,985), Peñon de la Gomera (398), Rio de Oro (253), and Nador (3,247), and exercises a protectorate over part of north-west Morocco, including the Tangier zone (*see* Morocco).

The area and population of the colonial possessions of Spain are approximately as follows:—

COLONIAL POSSESSIONS	AREA: ENGLISH SQ. MILES	POPULATION
Possessions in Africa:		
Rio de Oro and Adrar . .	109,200	495
Ifni	965	20,000
Spanish Guinea . . .	10,036	140,000
Fernando Po, Annobon, Corisco, Great Elobey, Little Elobey	795	23,846
Spanish Morocco	7,700	600,000
Total, Africa	128,696	784,341

Alfonso XIII, reigning King, 1902–1931. A Republic was proclaimed April 14, 1931.

360 B.C. to 1580

B.C. 360, The Carthaginians, enriched by the mines of Spain (480 B.C. *et seq.*), form settlements

242, New Carthage (Carthagena) founded by Hasdrubal

238–233, Hamilcar extends their dominions in Spain

221, At his death, Hannibal, his son, takes the command; prepares for war, 220; takes Saguntum, 219; crosses the Alps, and enters Italy, 218

212, The Romans carry the war into Spain; two Scipios defeated and slain by Hasdrubal

207, Pub. Cornelius Scipio Africanus takes New Carthage, 210 or 209; drives the Carthaginians out of Spain

153–133, Celtiberian and Numantine war

145, Viriathus, general of the Celtiberians and Lusitanians, subdued all West Spain; makes peace with the consul Fabius Servilianus, 142; assassinated by order of the Romans, 140

72, Insurrection of Sertorius, 78; subdued by Pompey, and assassinated

67, Julius Cæsar quells an insurrection in Spain

60–50, Pompey governs Spain

48–47, Revolt through the rapacity of Crassus

38, Era of Spain: conquest by Augustus begun, Jan. 1

A.D. 409, The Vandals, Alani, and Suevi, wrest Spain from the Romans

414, Adolphus founds the Kingdom of the Visigoths

429, The Vandals pass over to Africa

452, Theodoric I vanquishes the Suevi

466, Assassinated by his brother Euric, who becomes master of all Spain

587, Recared I expels the Franks

Till 601, He abjures Arianism, and rules ably

672–677, Wamba's wise administration; he prepared a fleet for defense against the Saracens

709, The Arabs invited into Spain against King Roderic

711, His defeat and death at Xeres

——, Establishment of the Saracens at Cordova

712–13, Victorious progress of Musa and Tarik

718, Emirs rule at Cordova; Pelayo, of Gothic blood, rules in Asturias and Leon

733, The Saracens defeated at Tours by Charles Martel

755, Abderahman the first king at Cordova

777–78, Invasion of Charlemagne

873, Sancho Iñigo, Count of Navarre, &c.

1026, Sancho of Navarre becomes King of Castile

1035, The Kingdom of Aragon commenced under Ramirez I

1037, Leon and Asturias united to Castile

1095, Portugal taken from the Saracens by Henry of Besançon (see Portugal)

1091 et seq., The Saracens, beset on all sides by the Christians, call in the aid of the Moors from Africa, who seize the dominions they came to protect, and subdue the Saracens

1094–1144, Dynasty of the Almoravides at Cordova

About 1099, Exploits of the Cid Rodrigo; dies

1144, The Moors defeated in several battles by Alfonso of Leon

1144–1225, Dynasty of the Almohades at Cordova

1233–48, Cordova, Toledo, Seville, &c., taken by Ferdinand of Castile and Leon

1238, The Kingdom of Granada begun by the Moors, last refuge from the power of the Christians

1274, The crown of Navarre passes to the royal family of France

1327, 200,000 Moors arrive to assist the King of Granada

1340, They are defeated at Tarifa by Alfonso XI of Castile with great slaughter

1350, Reign of Pedro the Cruel

1363, His alliance with Edward the Black Prince

1369, Defeated at Montiel and treacherously slain

1479, Ferdinand II of Aragon marries Isabella of Castile, Oct. 18, 1469; and nearly the whole Christian dominions of Spain are united in one monarchy

1480–84, Establishment of the Inquisition

1492–98, Persecution of the Jews

1492, Granada taken after a two years' siege; and the power of the Moors is extirpated by Ferdinand

——, Jews expelled

April 17, Columbus is sent to explore the western ocean

1499–1502, Mahometans persecuted and expelled

May 20, 1506, Death of Columbus

1512, Ferdinand conquers great part of Navarre

1516, Accession of the house of Austria to the throne of Spain; Charles I of Spain

1517, Able administration of Ximenes; ungratefully used, 1516; his death

1519, Charles elected Emperor of Germany

1520–21, Insurrection in Castile

July 25, 1554, Philip of Spain marries Mary of England

1556, Charles abdicates and retires from the world

Aug. 10, 1557, War with France; victory at St. Quentin

1561, Philip II commences persecution of Protestants

1563, The Escurial begun building

1570, Revolt of the Moriscoes, 1567; suppressed

Oct. 7, 1571, Naval victory of Lepanto over the Turks

1580, Portugal united to Spain by conquest

1587

Armada, the Invincible, collected and equipped by Philip II, King of Spain, for the subjugation of England. It consisted of 130 ships (besides caravels), 3,165 cannon, 8,050 sailors, 2,088 galley-slaves, 18,973 soldiers, 1,382 volunteers (noblemen, gentlemen, and their attendants), and 150 monks, with Martin Alarco, vicar of the Inquisition,—the whole under the command of the Duke of Medina-Sidonia

Dec., The English fleet, 80 vessels, under Lord Charles Howard, Sir Francis Drake, and Sir John Hawkins, ready for sea, and three armies on land

1588

May 19, The Armada sailed from Lisbon; soon after dispersed by a storm

July 19, Re-collected, entered the Channel off Cornwall

July 21–27, Suffered in a series of engagements (the sharpest on July 25)

July 28, Dispersed by fire-ships sent into the midst

July 29, Many vessels sunk or taken by the English

Aug. and Sept., The remainder retreat northward to Spain, suffering much loss by severe storms

Computed Spanish loss—35 ships; 13,000 men

1598 to 1806

1598–1610, Philip III banishes the Moors (900,000)

1598–1618, Ministry of the Duke of Lerma

1621–43, Ministry of Olivarez

1640, Philip IV loses Portugal

1700, Death of Charles II, last of the house of Austria; accession of Philip V of the house of Bourbon

1701–13, War of the Succession

1704, Gibraltar taken by the English

1713, Siege of Barcelona

1720, Cardinal Alberoni reëstablished the authority of the King, and raised Spain to the rank of a first power, 1715–20; ordered to quit Spain

1735, Charles, son of Philip V, conquers Naples

1759, Charles III, King of the Two Sicilies, succeeds to the crown of Spain

1762–63, War with England; and 1796

Feb. 14, 1797, Battle of Cape St. Vincent

Oct., 1804, Spanish treasure-ships, valued at 3,000,000 dollars, seized by the English

Oct. 21, 1805, Battle of Trafalgar. A great naval victory was gained by the British, under Nelson, over the combined fleets of France and Spain, commanded by Admiral Villeneuve and two Spanish admirals. The enemy's force was eighteen French and fifteen Spanish vessels, all of the line: that of the British, twenty-seven ships. After a protracted fight, Villeneuve and the other admirals were taken, and nineteen of their ships captured, sunk, or destroyed. Nelson was killed, and Admiral Collingwood succeeded to the command. Nelson's ship was the *Victory*; and his last signal was, "England expects every man will do his duty"

1806, Sway of Godoy, prince of the peace

1807

The French enter Spain; a Spanish army sent to the Baltic

July 25, Conspiracy of the Prince of Asturias against his father

Oct. 27, Treaty of Fontainebleau

1808

March, The French take Madrid

March 19, Abdication of Charles IV in favor of Ferdinand; and at Bayonne, in favor of his "friend and ally" Napoleon, when Ferdinand relinquished the crown May 1

May 2, Revolution: the French massacred at Madrid

May 3, The province of Asturias rises *en masse*

May 25, Napoleon assembles the notables at Bayonne

July 12, Joseph Bonaparte enters Madrid as King of Spain; retires July 29

Aug. 21, Battle of Vimiera; French defeated

Sept., Supreme junta installed

Dec. 2, Madrid taken by French; Joseph restored

Dec. 4, Napoleon enters Madrid

Dec. 5, The royal family of Spain imprisoned in the palace of Chambery in Savoy

1809

Jan. 16, The French defeated at Corunna; take Ferrol, Jan. 27; Saragossa, Feb. 21; Oporto, Feb. 29; Cordova and Seville, Nov.; Gerona, Dec. 12

1810

July 10, Ney takes Ciudad Rodrigo

Sept. 24, The Spanish Cortes meet

1811

May 5, Wellington defeats Massena at Fuentes de Onoro

May 16, Soult defeated at Albuera

1812

Jan. 19, Wellington takes Ciudad Rodrigo, defeats Marmont at Salamanca, July 22

May 8, Constitution of the Cortes (Democratic)

1813

June 21, He occupies Madrid, and totally defeats the French at Vittoria; defeats Soult in the Pyrenees, July 28; takes St. Sebastian, Aug. 31; and enters France, Oct. 8

1814 to 1820

May 14, 1814, Ferdinand VII restored

1817, Slave trade abolished for a compensation

Jan., 1820, Spanish revolution begun by Riego

March 8, Ferdinand swears to the constitution of the Cortes

1823

March, The Cortes remove the King to Seville, and thence to Cadiz

June 25, The French enter Spain; invest Cadiz

Aug. 31, Battle of the Trocadero

Oct., Despotism resumed

Nov. 7, Riego put to death

1828 to 1832

Sept. 21, 1828, The French evacuate Cadiz

Feb. 24, 1829, Cadiz made a free port

1830, Salique law abolished, March 29; Carlist and Christina parties formed

Oct. 25, 1832, Queen of Spain appointed Regent during the King's indisposition; change in the Ministry

1833

April 29, Don Carlos declares himself legitimate successor to the King

Sept. 29, Death of Ferdinand VII; his Queen assumes the title of Governing Queen until Isabella II, her infant daughter, attains her majority

Constitution termed "Estatuto Real" granted by advice of Martinez de la Rosa

Oct. 27, The royalist volunteers disarmed at Madrid

Dec. 28, Queen Christina marries Ferdinand Muñoz (afterwards Duke of Rianzarés)

1834

April 22, The quadruple treaty establishes the right of Isabella to the throne

July 10, Don Carlos suddenly appears in Spain

Aug. 30, The peers vote his exclusion

1835

June, Mendizabal, Prime Minister; Mina and Espartero commanded the royalists; the rebel leader, Zumalacarregui, killed near Bilbao

Sir De Lacy Evans and others raise a British legion for the Queen of Spain

1836

Oct. 1, They defeat the Carlists at St. Sebastian

Dec. 25, Espartero gains the battle of Bilbao

1837

May 17, General Evans takes Irun

Constituent Cortes proclaimed

Dissolution of the monasteries

1839

Aug. 31, The Carlists under Maroto desert Don Carlos and conclude a treaty of peace with Espartero, at Vergara

Sept. 13, Don Carlos seeks refuge in France

1840

May 28, Surrender of Morello

July 7, Cabrera, the Carlist general, unable to maintain the war, enters France

Aug. 25, The British auxiliaries evacuate St. Sebastian and Passages

Sept. 1, Revolutionary movement at Madrid: the authorities triumphant

Sept. 9, Dismissal of the Ministry, and dissolution of the Cortes

Oct. 3, Espartero, Minister, makes his triumphal entry into Madrid

Oct. 5, The Queen Regent appoints a new ministry, who are nominated by Espartero; she abdicates and leaves the Kingdom; returns to France, Oct. 12

Dec. 29, Espartero expels the papal nuncio

1841

April 12, The Spanish Cortes declare Espartero regent during the Queen's minority

July 19, Queen Christina's protest

Oct. 2, Insurrection in favor of Christina commenced at Pampeluna by General O'Donnell and Concha

Oct. 7, Don Diego Leon attacks the palace at Madrid; his followers repulsed; he is shot at Madrid, Oct. 15

Oct. 21, Zurbano captures Bilbao

——, Rodil, constitutional general, enters Vittoria

——, Montes de Oca shot

——, General O'Donnell takes refuge in the French territory

Oct. 26, Espartero decrees the suspension of Queen Christina's pension

Oct. 29, Fueros of the Basque provinces abolished

Nov. 9, Borio and Gobernado, implicated in the Christina plot, put to death at Madrid

Nov. 23, Espartero enters Madrid

1842

Nov. 15, An insurrection at Barcelona; the national guard joins the populace, Nov. 13; battle in the streets between the national guard and the troops: the latter lose 500 in killed and wounded, and retreat to the citadel

Nov. 26, Barcelona blockaded; Espartero arrives before it, Nov. 29; its bombardment and surrender, Dec. 3, 4

1843

June 11, The revolutionary junta is reëstablished at Barcelona

[Corunna, Seville, Burgos, Santiago, and numerous other towns, shortly afterwards "pronounce" against the Regent Espartero]

July 15, Arrival of General Narvaez at Madrid, which surrenders

July 21, Espartero bombards Seville

July 27, The siege is raised

[The revolution is completely successful, and Espartero flees to Cadiz]

Aug. 16, Espartero deprived of his titles and rank; he arrives in London Aug. 23

Nov. 8, Isabella II, 13 years old, is declared by the Cortes to be of age; Narvaez (friend of the Queen-Mother), Lieutenant-General

1844

March 23, The Queen-Mother returns to Spain

Nov. 12, Zurbano's insurrection; he is shot Jan. 21, 1845

1845

May 18, Don Carlos relinquishes his right to the crown in favor of his son

England removed from "favored nation" clause (Treaty of Utrecht, 1713)

1846

Sept. 14, Escape of Don Carlos from France

Oct. 10, Marriage of the Queen to her cousin, Don Francisco d'Assiz, Duke of Cadiz, and marriage also

of the Infanta Louisa (she died Feb. 1, 1897) to the duc de Montpensier

[The Spanish marriages disturb the friendly relations of the French and English Governments]

1847

May 4, Two shots fired at the Queen by La Riva

June 23, He suffers "death by the cord"

Sept. 3, Espartero restored

1848

May 17, Sir Henry Lytton Bulwer, British envoy, ordered to quit Spain in 48 hours

1850

April 18, Diplomatic relations with England restored

July 12, The Queen of Spain delivered of a male child, which lives but ten minutes

1850, 1851, The American expeditions under Lopez against Cuba (see Cuba and the United States)

1851

Feb. 2, The Infante Don Henrique permitted to return to Spain

Feb. 9, Madrid-Aranjuez railway opened

Aug. 1, Law respecting the public debt (which has since excluded Spain from the European money-markets)

Oct. 4, Death of Godoy, prince of the peace

Dec. 20, The Queen gives birth to a princess

1852

Feb. 2, Attempt made on the life of the Queen; she is slightly wounded by the dagger of Merino, a Franciscan

Sept. 23, Gen. Castaños, Duke of Baylen, renowned in the French war, dies, aged 95

1853

Jan., Narvaez exiled to Vienna

Sept., Ministerial changes—Lersundi forms a cabinet, April 11; resigns: Sartorius' cabinet

1854

Jan. 5, Birth and death of a princess

Jan. 17, General O'Donnell, Concha, and others banished

June 28, Military insurrection, under O'Donnell, near Madrid

July 1–17, The movement headed by Espartero; Barcelona and Madrid pronounce against the Government; barricades in Madrid

July 19, Triumph of the insurrection: resignation of the Ministry; the Queen sends for Espartero

July 31, Peace restored: the degraded generals reinstated, &c.; Espartero forms an administration

Aug. 28, The Queen Mother impeached; she quits Spain

1855

Jan. 13, New constitution of the Cortes

Feb., The Cortes vote that all power proceeds from the people; they permit liberty of belief, but not of worship

March 10, Don Carlos dies

1856

April 6, Insurrection of Valencia

July 15–16, Resignation of Espartero; new cabinet formed, headed by Marshal O'Donnell; insurrection in Madrid, July 14; O'Donnell and the government troops subdue the insurgents

July 15–23, Insurrection at Barcelona and Saragossa quelled by O'Donnell, as dictator

Oct. 12, O'Donnell compelled to resign; Narvaez becomes Minister

1857

Jan. 14, Isturitz, minister; O'Donnell, Minister, July 1

Feb. 1, Espartero resigns as senator

June and July, Insurrection in Andalusia; quickly suppressed; cruel military executions; 98 insurgents shot (24 at Seville)

Nov. 28, Birth of the Prince Royal

1858

Sept. 20, Cessation of state of siege at Barcelona, &c.

Dec. 1, Joint French and Spanish expedition against Cochin China announced

1859

Nov.–Dec., War with Morocco. *See* Morocco

1860

Jan. 1, O'Donnell commands the army in Africa; battle at Castillejos; a Spanish "Balaklava" charge

Feb. 4, The Moors defeated near Tetuan, which surrenders and at Guad-el-ras, March 23

March 26, Treaty of peace signed; 400,000,000 reals to be paid by Moors

April 19, General Ortega, Governor of the Balearic Isles, lands near Tortosa, in Valencia, with 3,000 men, and proclaims the comte de Montemolin King, as Charles VI; Ortega shot

April 23, The comte de Montemolin and his brother Ferdinand arrested at Tortosa, April 21; renounce their claim to the throne

June 5, Their brother Juan asserts his right; and they, when at Cologne, annul their renunciation, June 28

1861

Jan. 14, The comte de Montemolin and his wife die at Trieste

May 19, The annexation of St. Domingo to Spain ratified; slavery not to be reëstablished

Dec. 8, Intervention in Mexico (*see* Mexico)

1862

Oct. 14, José Alhama and Manuel Matamoras, Protestant propagandists, sentenced to 10 years' imprisonment

1863

Jan. 8, Don Juan de Bourbon renounces his right to the throne

Feb. 26, Resignation of the Premier, Marshal O'Donnell; Marquis de Miraflores Minister, March 4

Sept. 1, Insurrection in St. Domingo; war ensues

1864

April, Rupture with Peru. *See* Peru

Aug. 13, General Prim exiled for conspiracy

Sept., Narvaez forms a cabinet

Sept. 26, Queen Christina returns to Spain

Dec. 14–18, English Government recognizes the insurrection at St. Domingo; Narvaez advises abandonment of the contest; the Queen refuses; the Ministry resign; but resume office

1865

Jan. 27, Peace with Peru

Feb. 20, The Queen orders the sale of crown lands, giving up three-fourths to the nation

May 5, Decree relinquishing St. Domingo

June 10, Suppression of a conspiracy at Valencia to reunite Spain and Portugal

June 22, Resignation of Narvaez, June 19; O'Donnell forms a liberal cabinet

July 25, Dispute with Chili; M. Tavira's settlement (May 20) disavowed by the Government

Sept. 18, Admiral Pareja, at Valparaiso, insults the Chilian Government; which declares war, Sept. 29; Pareja declares a blockade, Sept. 24

Nov. 26, The Chilian Captain Williams captures the Spanish vessel *Covadonga* (Pareja commits suicide)

Dec. 27, New Cortes elected; the great Progresista party still abstains from action in public affairs; Queen opens Cortes

1866

Jan. 3, Military insurrection at Aranjuez, headed by Gen. Prim; martial law in Madrid, Jan. 4; Concha and Zabala march against rebels, Jan. 4, &c.; riots at Barcelona, Jan. 9, 10; state of siege in New Castile, Catalonia, and Aragon, Jan. 6–12

Jan. 15, *Queen Victoria*, British sloop, seized by a guarda-costa

Jan. 20, Prim enters Portugal and lays down arms

May 2, Admiral Mendez bombards Valparaiso, destroying much property, March 31; he is repulsed at Callao with loss

June 15, The Queen declares the campaign in the Pacific ended

June 22, Great military revolt in favor of Prim at Madrid; about 1,200 men, headed by non-commissioned officers, with cannon, quelled summarily by Marshals O'Donnell and Narvaez, with much bloodshed; 200 prisoners shot; 21 sergeants shot; (Sen. Castelar escaped to France), June 26

June 23, Military revolts at Barcelona and at various other places

July, Resignation of O'Donnell as minister, succeeded by Narvaez and Bravo

Aug.–Sept., Freedom of the press abolished, and writers transported to the colonies

Aug. 21–22, British screw steamer *Tornado*, Com. E. Collier, seized by Spaniards (charged with aiding Chili), and carried to Cadiz

Oct. 3, Reëstablishment of tranquillity at Madrid

——, Public instruction placed under the clergy

——, Reform of the municipal institutions decreed on account of revolutionary proceedings

Nov., Crew of *Tornado* detained as prisoners, Oct. 31, the case referred to law

Dec. 30, The queen dismissed the Cortes (and imprisoned many deputies for petitioning against it)

1867

Jan., O'Donnell and his colleagues residing in Paris

Feb. 8, Decision in *Tornado* case—the ship a prize and the crew prisoners of war, Dec. 18, 1866; Lord Stanley protests against the proceedings

Feb. 16, Decree for making secret publication of journals and pamphlets penal

Feb., The *Tornado* prisoners released

April 21, *Queen Victoria* sloop declared by Spain to have been wrongfully seized

April 25, Amnesty to revolters of June 1866

May 1, Son of Duchess of Montpensier born

About Aug. 15, Attempted insurrection in different parts (attributed to Prim) failed

Nov. 5, Death of Marshal O'Donnell, Duke of Tetuan

1868

Jan. 22, An armament bill adopted by the Chamber of Deputies

April 23, Death of Marshal Narvaez, Duke of Valencia, aged 67

May 13, Marriage of Princess Isabella, the Queen's eldest daughter, to the Count of Girgenti, brother of ex-King of Naples

June 2, Law enacted abolishing normal schools and subjecting education to the priests

July 6, Duke and Duchess of Montpensier exiled

About July 10, Marshal Serrano, General Dolce, and others exiled

Sept. 18, Insurrection begins in the fleet; joined by the garrison and city of Cadiz, Sept. 19; accepted by nearly all Spain, Sept. 19–30

Sept. 19, Prim arrives at Cadiz, Sept. 17; announces a provisional government

Sept. 19, 20, The Ministers resign; José Concha becomes president of the council, Sept. 22; Bravo Murillo and his colleagues flee to Bayonne, Sept. 23

[Royalist leaders: José Concha, Marquis de Havaña, Manuel Concha, Marquis de Duero, at Madrid; the Marquis de Pezuela at Barcelona; Eusebio de Calonge in the north; Pavia y Lacy, Marquis de Novaliches in Andalusia]

Sept. 28, Novaliches, the royalist general, defeated at Alcolea by Serrano, Sept. 27; surrenders

Sept. 29, 30, The Queen flies to Bayonne and thence to Pau, and protests

Sept. 29, The deposition of the Queen declared

Oct. 3, Don Juan, son of Don Carlos, renounces his hereditary rights in favor of his son, Carlos

——, Serrano enters Madrid; Serrano, Prim, and Olozaga constitute a provisional government, Oct. 5

About Oct. 12, 13, The education law of June 2 annulled; the Jesuits and other religious orders suppressed; the laws expelling the Jews abrogated; freedom of religious worship decreed

Oct. 20, All the local juntas dissolved by manifesto of the provisional government

Oct. 26, Manifesto of the government declaring for universal suffrage, and free press and education

About Nov. 6, Prim created a marshal

Nov. 6, The Queen arrives at Paris

Nov. 14, The joint electoral committee at Madrid declare in favor of a limited monarchy

Nov. 18, Decree for formation of a citizen force of the Volunteers of Freedom

About Nov. 25, Loan of 20,000,000l. proposed by Figueras, Minister of Finance; 4,000,000l. said to be undertaken by Rothschilds

Dec. 5, Insurrection against the provisional government breaks out at Cadiz; murderous conflicts, Dec. 6; the city invested; surrenders; entry of General Caballero de Roda, general of the army of Andalusia, Dec. 12

Dec. 31, Violent insurrection at Malaga suppressed with much slaughter

1869

Jan. 23, The Spanish envoy at Rome not received

Jan. 24, Gutierez de Castro, civil governor of Burgos, murdered in the cathedral

Feb. 13, Meeting of the Cortes, Feb. 11; Rivero elected president

Feb. 25, 26, The provisional government resigns; Serrano reappointed head of the government with same ministry

March 28, Spanish Protestant religious service at Madrid

April, Insurrection in Cuba fomented by Americans

May 21, The Cortes vote for a monarchy (214 to 71)

June 6, The new constitution promulgated

June 18, Marshal Serrano elected Regent by the Cortes, June 15; sworn

About June 18, New ministry under Prim

July–Aug., Carlist risings in La Mancha and at Ciudad Real, suppressed

About Sept. 18, United States' overtures respecting Cuba indignantly rejected

Sept., Republican risings at Tarragona, Barcelona, and other places, suppressed with bloodshed; republicans defeated near Reus, Oct. 4; Saragossa cannonaded, Oct. 8; Valencia surrendered, Oct. 16; tranquillity generally restored, Oct. 20

Nov. 23, General Dulce dies

1870

Jan. 4, Resignation of Prim and the Ministry on the Italian Government opposing the nomination of the Duke of Genoa as King of Spain

Jan. 10, Prim resumes office with Topete and Rivero

April 12, The duc de Montpensier kills Don Enrique de Bourbon, brother of the ex-King, in a duel, March 12; tried and fined

May, The offered crown declined by Espartero

May 28, Bill for gradual abolition of slavery in the colonies presented to the Cortes

June, Two Englishmen of Gibraltar seized by brigands; ransomed for 5,200l.; brigands afterwards attacked by the Spanish civil guard; several of them killed, and part of the ransom recovered

——, Rojo Arias carries a resolution requiring an absolute majority in the Cortes for any proposed sovereign (179 out of 356); this excludes all present candidates

June 25, Isabella II, abdicates in favor of her son Alfonso

July 12, Prince Leopold of Hohenzollern-Sigmaringen nominated King, accepted by the Regent and Ministry, July 6; this justified by the Government in a circular, July 7; on the strong opposition of France he resigns

Aug. 10, Amnesty for all political offences since, Sept. 29, 1868 published

Aug. 28, Irruption of Carlists into Navarre, Aug. 27; defeated

——, The Basque provinces put into a state of siege

Oct. 4, Claret, the ex-Queen's confessor, dies

Oct. 20, Amadeus, Duke of Aosta (born May 30, 1845), accepts the candidature for the crown

Nov. 16, Elected by the Cortes by 191 votes: (63 for a republic; 27 for the duc de Montpensier)

Nov. 17, Proclaimed King

Nov. 21, The ex-Queen, on behalf of her son Alfonso, protests against the election

Dec. 4, The duke accepts the crown from a deputation of the Cortes at Florence

Dec. 25, Stormy session in the Cortes respecting arrangements for the new King, Dec. 19; Rivero, the president, resigns

Dec. 28, Prim fired at and wounded in his carriage by six men, who escaped; Topete rejoins the Ministry; vote of confidence in it

Dec. 30, Prim dies in the evening (aged 56); the King received by Topete at Cartagena

1871

Jan. 2, The King enters Madrid and takes the oath

Jan. 5, New ministry under Serrano

April 3, New Cortes opened

April 4, Olozaga elected president of the Cortes

May, The *Tornado* difficulty settled (Aug.–Nov., 1866), compensation to be paid by the Spanish Government

Sept. 30, The King visits the provinces; welcomed by Espartero at Logroño

Oct. 1, Cortes opened; Sagasta elected president in opposition to Rivero (123–113), Oct. 3; the Zorrilla Ministry resigns, Oct. 4; Malcampo forms a ministry, Oct. 5

Nov. 27, Angulo, the Finance Minister, proposes to tax the foreign national creditors 18%

——, Suicide of the Count of Girgenti

Dec. 21, Ministry formed under Sagasta

1872

Jan., Espartero, made Prince of Vergara

About April 20, Insurrection of Carlists incited by priests in Navarre, Leon, &c.; manifesto of Don Carlos, Duke of Madrid; Diaz de Rada, his general

April 25, Navarre, &c., in state of siege

May 4, Marshal Serrano enters Navarre with an army; Don Carlos, calling himself Carlos VII, crosses the frontiers near Véra, and takes the command, Rada retiring, May 2; totally defeated at Oroquieta

May 21, The Carlists surrender by hundreds

May 22, Resignation of the Sagasta Ministry

About May 22, Band of Carlists defeated near Gerona

May 25, New ministry (supported by Serrano), Adm. Topete president

——, Serrano offers amnesty to Carlists who surrender; it is accepted, May 27; he is censured, but exonerated by the Cortes, June 8; he assumes the presidency of the Ministry, June 4

June 12, Carlism increases; the Ministry propose martial law; the King opposes it; the Ministry resign

June 14, Ruiz Zorrilla (who had just retired from political life) becomes president of a new ministry

June, Letter of the duc de Montpensier advocating the rights of Prince Alfonso, April 17; published

July 16, Don Carlos calls on Catalonia, Arragon, and Valencia, to rise, promising to restore their ancient liberties

July 18–19, Attempted assassination of the King and Queen by about 15 men; one assassin killed, two taken; a little after midnight

Oct. 13, Republican rising at Ferrol; town captured by the Captain-General of Galicia

Oct. 17, The insurgents disperse or surrender; about 500 prisoners

End of Oct., Impeachment of the Sagasta Ministry for financial corruption proposed in the Cortes; much agitation

Nov., Gen. Hidalgo appointed to a military command; the artillery officers resigned: punished

Dec. 24, Bill for abolition of slavery in Porto Rico, for compensation, brought into congress

1873

Feb. 11, King Amadeus' message to the Cortes, announcing his abdication; he states that he sees Spain in a continual struggle, the era of peace more distant; he sought for remedies within the law, and did not find them; his efforts were sterile. The two chambers combine as the sovereign Cortes of Spain, and vote for a republic (126–32)

Feb. 12, Reported success of the Carlists; agitation for the duc de Montpensier among the Orleanists in France

Feb. 13, King Amadeus arrives at Libson

Feb. 22, 23, Carlists; hold part of Catalonia; demonstrations in favor of a federal republic

Feb. 27, Powerful circular to European powers from Castelar, foreign minister

March 22, Appointment of a permanent committee of the Cortes

March 23, Slavery in Porto Rico abolished

March 25, Proclamation of the Government calling for volunteers against the Carlists

April 23, The Carlists beaten in several encounters; Don Alfonso de Bourbon reënters France

April 26, The old "monarchical volunteers" take possession of the bull-ring at Madrid; are disarmed and dispersed by the government troops; the "permanent committee" dissolved by the Government, which assumes supreme power

April 29, Serrano and Sagasta leave Spain

April 29, 30–May 4, More defeats of the Carlists

June, The Intransigentes or Irreconcilables (extreme republicans) very powerful

June 7, Carlists besieging Irun

June 9, The federal republic voted by the Cortes (210–2) and proclaimed, June 8; Pi y Margall, president of a new ministry, rejected; Figueras and his ministry resume office

June 11, Ministerial crisis renewed, June 10; Pi y Margall becomes minister; Figueras quits Spain

June 26, Carlists defeat Castañon near Murieta

June 29, Cadiz, Seville, Malaga, and Valencia very insubordinate

July 1, The Intransigentes withdraw from the Cortes

July 11, Defeat and death of Calvinety by Carlists; insurrection at Alcoy, promoted by Internationalists; the mayor and others killed, announced

July 13, Don Carlos (as Carlos VII) enters Spain, "to save the country"

July 17, 18, Fighting at Igualada, Catalonia

Four prevailing parties:—1. The government, highly democratic; 2. The Intransigentes, or irreconcilables: extremely democratic; 3. The International, or communists; 4. The legitimists, Carlists

July 18, Murcia and Valencia proclaim themselves federal cantons

——, Pi y Margall compelled to resign; Salmeron forms a ministry opposed to the Intransigentes

July 19, Igualada taken by the Carlists

July 26, Troops attack Valencia; it surrenders, Aug. 8

July 31, Don Carlos enters Biscay

——, Insurgents repulsed in their attack on Almeria; beaten in fights at Seville, July 28–30; Gen. Pavia warmly received

Aug., Carlists hold chief of N. Spain

Aug. 1, Bombardment of Malaga stopped by the British and German admirals

Aug. 4, Cadiz surrenders to him

Aug., New constitution printed, July 27, discussed [118 Articles; includes separation of Church and State; free religious worship; nobility abolished; 15 states in and near peninsula; 2 in the Antilles; Cortes (senate and congress) to have legislative power; one deputy to 50,000 souls; Cortes to be renewed in 2 years; members to be paid; executive: president and ministry; president elected for 4 years]

Aug. 10, Reported total defeat of the insurgents at Chinchilla, while marching on Madrid

Aug. 13, The *Deerhound*, English yacht, conveying stores to Carlists, seized by the Spaniards, 11½ miles off Biarritz; crew imprisoned, and captain sent to Ferrol

Aug. 21, Carlists defeat republicans at Arrichulegui, near Renteria, many killed

Aug. 22, Cartagena, held by Intransigentes, besieged

Aug. 25, They take Estella

Aug. 26, Castelar elected president of the Cortes

Sept. 1, Capt. Werner, of German ship, *Friedrich Karl*, captures *Almanza* and *Vittoria*, Spanish ironclads, held by rebels, gives them up to Adm. Yelverton, who prepares for action against Intransigentes, claiming them, and sends them to Gibraltar unmolested

Sept. 7, 8, Castelar heads a ministry; proposes calling out 150,000 men, to end the war

Sept. 9, Salmeron elected president of the Cortes

Sept. 12, Ferdinand Muñoz, Duke of Rianzarès, husband of Queen Christina, dies at Havre

Sept. 15, Castelar made virtually dictator

About Sept. 18, The *Deerhound* and crew given up; announced

Sept. 18, Speech of Castelar, the Cortes to be closed Jan. 2, 1874

Sept. 19, Carlist attack on Tolosa repulsed by Loma

About Sept. 26, The Carlist Merendon killed

Sept. 26, The *Vittoria* and *Almanza* given up to the Spanish Government

Sept. 27, Carlists in Navarre defeated by Moriones

Sept. 28, The Intransigentes' ironclads, *Mendez Nuñez* and *Numancia*, bombarding Alicante, repulsed

Oct. 6, Battle at Maneru, near Puenta de la Reyna, in Navarre, between republicans, under Moriones, and Carlists, under Ollo; both claim a victory; advantage with Carlists

About Oct. 8, Carlists said to be repulsed at La Junquera, in Catalonia

Oct. 11, Battle of Escombrera bay; the Intransigentes' ships attempt to break blockade of Cartagena; repulsed by Admiral Lobo

Oct. 18, Collision of the Intransigentes' vessels *Numancia* and *Fernando del Catolico*, the latter sunk and 66 drowned

Oct. 21, Unsuccessful sortie at Cartagena

Oct. 22, Lobo declines to fight, and retires, pursued by the Intransigentes, Oct. 13; justifies himself at Madrid

Oct. 25, Tristany, with 2,500 Carlists, defeated by Salamanca

Nov. 3, Death of Rios Rosas, statesman

Nov., The *Murillo* captured; condemned to be sold by the British court of admiralty

Nov. 7, 8, 9, Indecisive conflicts at Monte Jurre and Monjardin, victories claimed by Carlists

Nov. 26 *et seq.*, Cartagena bombarded

Dec. 13, Lopez Dominguez becomes commander before Cartagena

Dec. 30, *Tetuan*, insurgent vessel, at Cartagena, blew up (? purposely)

1874

Jan. 3, Pronunciamento:—Meeting of the Cortes; speech of Castelar; vote of confidence in him lost by 20; he resigns; Salmeron attempts to form a ministry, Jan. 2, 3; Pavia, Captain-General of Madrid, forcibly dissolves the Cortes

Jan. 4, Marshal Serrano made president of a new ministry, including Topete

——, Insurrection at Saragossa, suppressed

Jan. 12, 13, Insurrection at Barcelona quelled

Jan. 12, Cartagena captured by Lopez Dominguez

——, *Numancia* ironclad, with Intransigentes' leaders and convicts, escapes; they land at Mers el Kebir, near Oran, on the African coast; are interned by the French

Jan. 31, Blockade of the coast of Spain announced

Feb. 25, The Carlists besiege Bilbao. Moriones defeated at Somorrostro

Feb. 28, Marshal Serrano resigns presidency of the Ministry, and becomes chief of the Executive, succeeded by Zabala; Serrano proceeds to Bilbao

March 2, The blockade of the coast (Jan. 31) raised

About March 8, Serrano assumes command

March 25, 26, 27, Three days' conflict at Somorrostro, near Bilbao; the Carlists defeated, but retain their positions (about 2,000 killed and wounded on both sides)

March 28, Armistice for three days

About April 8, General Manuel da Concha joins Serrano at Santander

May 2, After several days' conflict, Carlists retreat; Marshal Concha enters Bilbao

May 6, A battle at Prats de Llusanés, indecisive

May 13, New ministry formed under Zabala

May 20, Carlists repulsed at Ramales

About June 6, Carlists defeated at Gondesa

June 25–27, Republicans repulsed before Estella

June 27, Concha killed (succeeded by Zabala)

June and July, Carlists accused of butchering prisoners

July, Carlists hold Navarre, Guipuscoa, Biscay, and Alara

July 13, The Carlists capture Cuenca (about 80 miles from Madrid)

July 17, Massacre of 86 republican prisoners by Carlists under Saballo at Valfogona

About July 18, All Spain placed under martial law; levy of 125,000 men

Aug. 3, The Government appeals to the French Government respecting French assistance to Carlists; justificatory reply

Aug. 4, The British Mediterranean squadron under Admiral Drummond sails from Malta for Barcelona

Aug. 6, Don Carlos appeals to the chief powers not to intervene; justifies Dorregaray's severities, and the execution of Schmidt

Aug. 13, Duty of 5d. a ton on imported iron granted to Bilbao for repairs

About Aug. 14, Serrano's government recognized by Great Britain, Germany, France, and other powers (not by Russia)

Aug., 185 prisoners of war at Olot said to be shot by Carlists

Aug.–Sept., Puycerda besieged by Carlists

Sept. 4, Zabala resigns; ministry formed under Sagasta

About Sept. 5, Carlists fire on German gunboats *Nautilus* and *Albatross* near San Sebastian; the Germans fire shells into the town

About Sept. 6, Lopez Dominguez said to have defeated Carlists five times, and relieved Puycerda

Sept. 6, Carlists fire on German and Austrian Ambassadors on the road to Madrid

About Sept. 9, Carlists defeated by Lopez Pinto near Mora; by Moriones at Barasoam near Tafalla, about Sept. 25

Oct., The ruthless Carlist General Dorregaray retires to Bayonne; said to have been superseded by Mendiri

——, Pavia superseded by Jovellar in Valencia

Early in Oct., Note sent to French Government complaining of neglect respecting the Carlists on the frontiers

Oct. 11, Carlists said to have been defeated at Fortuna, in Murcia; and at Villa Fortuna, Oct. 30

Nov. 4, Carlists bombard Irun; repulsed, Nov. 10

Nov., Serrano commander of the army in the north

Dec. 29, The army at Murviedro pronounces in favor of Alfonso; he is proclaimed King by Gen. Martinez Campos; recognized by the other armies and the navy, Dec. 30; proclaimed by Gen. Primo da Rivera at Madrid; Antonio Canovas del Castillo head of a royal ministry, Dec. 31

1875

Jan. 1, The President Marshal Serrano withdraws to France

Jan. 6, Proclamation of Carlos against Alfonso

Jan. 14, Alfonso XII recognized throughout Spain; enters Madrid

Jan., Orders of knighthood reëstablished; payments to clergy to be renewed

——, Increased barbarities of the Carlists reported

Feb., Serrano returns to Madrid

Feb. 3, Carlists defeat royalists at Lucar

Feb. 9, Carlists retreat from Pampeluna; entered by the King, Feb. 6; he exchanges decorations with Espartero at Logroño

Feb., Resignation of Generals Moriones, Loma, and Blanco; Concha sent for from Cuba

March 11, Cabrera, an old Carlist general (*see* 1840) publishes an address, declaring for Alfonso XII

March, April, Several professors seized and exiled for liberal opinions

About May 9, Aguirre, Carlist general, joins the royalists

About June 7, Jovellar, commander of royal army

July, Vigorous action of the government troops; Carlists expelled from Castile

July 31, Carlists defeated by Quesada and others

Aug. 26, Strong citadel at Urgel surrendered by Carlists to Campos, after a gallant defense; the Bishop and the brave General Lizarraga captured

Sept. 11, 12, Resignation of "conciliation ministry"; liberal cabinet headed by General Jovellar

Sept., Dorregaray said to be nominated to the chief command; declaration from Don Carlos stating that his mission is "to quell the revolution, and that it will die"

Oct. 11, Bombardment of San Sebastian, Sept. 28–Oct. 2; resumed

Early in Oct., The Government declare the civil war at an end, and purpose summoning the Cortes to assist the King in reorganizing the country

Oct., Reported defection of Mendiri from the Carlists, and trial of Dorregaray and Caballi for misconduct; and Carlist successes

Oct., Nov., Reported interference of United States respecting Cuba

Nov. 9, Letter from Don Carlos to the King proposing a truce, and offering help if war occurs with the United States (not answered)

Nov., Formation of a new constitutional party under Sagasta

Nov. 27, Ministry reconstructed under Canovas del Castillo

1876

Jan., Cortes elected, 364 nominal ministerialists out of 406

Feb. 15, Cortes opened by the King

Feb., Carlists defeated at Estella, Vera, and Tolosa, by Quesada and Moriones

Feb. 18, The King assumes command; Estella surrenders to Primo da Rivera: severe loss

Feb. 24–26, Many Carlists submit or flee into France

March 4, Don Carlos with General Lizarraga and five battalions surrender to the Governor of Bayonne, at St. Jean Pied de Port, Feb. 27; he lands with some officers at Folkestone, and proceeds to London

March 20, Triumphal entry of Alfonso XII into Madrid

March 28, Draft of new constitution submitted to the Cortes

April, The Pope opposes moderate religious toleration in Art. II of the constitution

About May 27, Outbreaks in the Basque provinces reported; martial law

About July 21, Long debate in the Cortes; the constitution passed; proclaimed, June 30; Cortes adjourns

July 31, Queen Isabella received by the King at Santander; declares that "her share in public affairs is at an end"

Sept., Repression of public worship of Protestants by authority

1877

Feb. 1, State of siege in Old Castile raised

Treaty favored nation clause in regard to England abrogated

End of Dec., The ex-Queen, after visiting her son, disapproves of his proposed marriage, and associates with Don Carlos in Paris, who is privately forbidden to remain, and goes to England; she is forbidden to return to Spain; her pension stopped

1878

Jan. 23, The King married to his cousin Mercedes, daughter of the duc de Montpensier

Feb. 21, End of the insurrection in Cuba announced

June 26, Death of Queen Mercedes, deeply lamented

Aug. 21, Death of the Queen Dowager Christina

Oct. 25, The King fired at (not injured) by Juan Oliva Moncasi, a member of the International Society, aged 23

1879

Jan. 4, Moncasi executed

Jan. 8, Espartero, Duque de Victoria, dies

March 3, Castillo Ministry (1874) resigns; Marshal Campos forms a ministry

Nov. 29, The King married to the Archduchess Maria Christina of Austria

Dec. 9, Resignation of the Campos Ministry; Canovas del Castillo forms a cabinet

Dec. 30, Attempted assassination of the King and Queen by Francisco Otero y Gonzalez by shooting

1880

Feb. 18, Promulgation of law for gradually abolishing slavery in Cuba

April 14, Otero executed

1881

Feb. 9, Resignation of Ministry; Sagasta forms a ministry (liberal), Feb. 8; the Chambers adjourned

May 23, Calderon centenary, Madrid, begins

June, Permission said to be given to about 60,000 Russian Jews to come to Spain

July 17, Don Carlos expelled from France for expressing sympathy with legitimists (goes to London)

Oct. 8, The Kings of Spain and Portugal open a new railway between Madrid and Lisbon

Dec. 10, Consolidation of the National debt (60,000,-000*l.*) proposed, Sept.; law published

Great agitation against the free trade policy of the Minister Camacho, in Catalonia, &c.

1882

April 22, Treaty with France passed by Cortes

Dec. 4, Gen. Maceo and five Cuban insurgent leaders surrendered at Gibraltar to the Spaniards (they had escaped from Cadiz, Aug. 20); they petition Queen Victoria to ask for their release; application made for inquiry; Gen. Baynes, Colonial Secretary at Gibraltar, and Mr. Blair, the chief inspector of police, dismissed for exceeding their authority, announced

1883

Jan. 8, New cabinet formed by Sagasta

March 4, A secret society, entitled the "Black Hand (Mano Negra)," reported; arrests, Feb. 28; total suppression reported

Aug. 4, 5, 6, Temporary republican military insurrection at Badajoz, said to be planned by Ruiz Zorrilla; on the approach of troops, mutineers enter Portugal, and are disarmed

Oct. 11–13, Resignation of Sagasta and his Ministry; succeeded by Posada Herrera and others

Dec. 1, Treaty for new commercial tariff signed

1884

Jan., Treaty with England condemned by the Council of State; free traders indignant

Jan. 18, Ministry resigned; Canovas del Castillo (conservative) forms a ministry

About March 17, Suspected military insurrection; about 25 persons arrested; 7 of 15 condemned; Black Hand conspirators garrotted at Xeres, June 14; Commander Fernandez and Lieut. Telles shot as rebels, June 28

April 26, Fall of the Alcudia railway bridge near Badajoz, great loss of life (said to be 90); believed to be due to criminal work of republicans

Aug. 15, Last section of the Great Asturian railway opened by the King

Dec. 25–31, Much sufferings by earthquakes

1885

Feb. 6, Protocol restoring Great Britain to position of most "favored nation" in regard to commerce

(lost since 1845); wine duties modified; signed at Madrid, Dec. 21, 1884; gazetted

May 18, Commercial treaty with England ratified by the Deputies, March 11; by the Senate, March 28; by the King, April 1; failure of negotiations announced

About Sept. 26, Riots at Madrid through the Germans occupying Yap, a Caroline isle; the German legation attacked, Sept. 4, 5; quiet restored, Sept. 6; Spanish note of apology sent to Berlin about Sept. 26; mediation of the Pope accepted

About Nov. 4, 5, Attempted military insurrection at Cartagena, Nov. 1; suppressed

Nov. 25, Death of King Alfonso XII; resignation of Canovas del Castillo; ministry formed by Señor Sagasta, Nov. 26, 27

Nov. 26, Death of Marshal Serrano

1886

Jan. 6, Manifesto of the Spanish bishops to their dioceses, declaring the distinction to be observed between religion and politics, and the submission of the Church to any lawful form of government, monarchical or republican

Jan. 10, 11, 50 soldiers at Cartagena mutiny; most escape to a ship; General Fajardo wounded; dies Jan. 27; ringleader of mutiny shot, March 3

Jan., Suspected intrigue of Zorrilla

About Feb. 27, The Duke of Seville sentenced to eight years' imprisonment, &c., for insulting, &c., the Queen Regent

April 19, Assassination of the Bishop of Madrid

Aug. 15, The commercial treaty with England (till 1892) again accepted by the Cortes, May; ratified, July 24; comes into operation

May 17, King Alfonso XIII born

May 20, Don Carlos protests against recognition of Alfonso XIII

Oct., Revolt of 300 of Madrid garrison under Brigadier Villacampa; unsupported, quickly suppressed; three officers killed, Sept. 19; capital punishment of insurgents commuted

1887

Dec. 1, Opening of the Cortes; the infant King enthroned; speech of the Queen Regent

1888

Feb. 4, 5, Rioting at the Rio Tinto mines suppressed with bloodshed

Feb. 27, Trial by jury introduced by the Senate

March 4, Ruiz Zorrilla's revolutionary manifesto issued, demanding a *plébiscite* for the form of national government

June 14, Señor Sagasta forms a new ministry

Sept. 8, The "Pearl," submarine torpedo boat, launched

Oct. 20, Republican outbreak at Saragossa against conservatives; Señor Canovas del Castillo attacked; outbreak at Seville, Nov. 7; outbreak at Madrid, Nov. 11

Dec. 10, Resignation of the Ministry, Dec. 9; reconstituted by Señor Sagasta

1889

Jan. 23, Amnesty to political offenders and mutinous soldiers decreed

May 29, Trial by jury first put in force (at Madrid)

July 14, Victory of Señor Sagasta over Señor Canovas del Castillo and the combined conservatives and dissentient liberals, reported

Sept. 29, Dispute with Morocco settled. *See* Morocco

1890

Jan. 20, Resignation of the Ministry, Jan. 3; Señor Sagasta forms a slightly modified cabinet

Feb. 7, Death of the duc de Montpensier, Feb. 4; buried in the Escurial

Feb. 27, The Duke of Seville, who had escaped from prison (*see above*, 1886), pardoned by the Queen Regent

March 30, Strike of about 40,000 workmen in Barcelona and other parts of Catalonia

May 1 *et seq.*, Barcelona placed under martial law; the anarchists and socialists opposed by the people; tranquillity restored, May 5 *et seq.*

July 5 *et seq.*, Señ. Antonio Canovas del Castillo (Castelár) forms a coalition ministry

July 15 *et seq.*, Strikes of workmen in Catalonia

1891

Jan. 14, Death of Señ. Alonzo Martinez, eminent statesman

Sept. 18, Above 100,000 persons homeless through floods of the Amarguillo, Tagus, Guadalquivir, and other rivers; palaces and country houses open to receive sufferers, reported

Nov. 22, Resignation of the Ministry, Nov. 21; reconstituted by Señ. Canovas del Castillo

Dec. 28, Decree for new loan of 250,000,000 pesetas, at 4%, Dec. 18; opened

1892

Jan. 9, Anarchist attack on Xeres suppressed with bloodshed; 4 rioters sentenced to death, others to imprisonment, Feb. 4; executed, Feb. 10

Feb. 1, Rupture with France through the new commercial tariff

April 4, Alleged discovery of a plot to blow up the Chamber of Deputies, the palace, and other places; Jean Marie Delboche, a Frenchman, and Manuel Ferriera, a Portuguese, arrested with documents; 13 anarchists arrested at their club, April 5; Philip Munoz, an Anarchist chief, arrested, April 10; released, April 24

April 16 *et seq.*, Explosions or attempts at Barcelona and other places, arrests made

May 28, A commercial *modus vivendi* with France signed by the Queen

Oct. 12, Celebration of the fourth centenary of the sailing of Columbus from Palos, near Huelva, Aug. 3, 1492; ships from all nations present, Aug. 3; grand banquet at Huelva, Aug. 4; national holiday

Oct. 12 *et seq.*, National celebration of the discovery of America, especially at Huelva; the Queen Regent, the King, and Foreign Dignitaries present; historical exhibition at Madrid, Oct. 30

Dec. 2, Resignation of the Minister of the Interior and all the civil authorities at Madrid, Nov. 30; reappointments made

Dec. 5, Trial of anarchists: 18 sentenced to imprisonment, 29 acquitted

Dec. 10, Resignation of Señ. Canovas del Castillo, Dec. 7; succeeded by Señ. Sagasta as Prime Minister

1893

Jan. 24, José Zorilla, poet and dramatist, died, aged 75

May 12, The Government defeats the republicans in the Chamber (after sitting nearly 60 hours)

June 20, Explosion at the house of Señ. Canovas del Castillo; 1 man killed

About July 28, Retirement of Señ. Canovas del Castillo (Castelár) from political life

Sept., Anarchist movements in Catalonia; dynamite explosions in Barcelona; Pallas, a leader, who threw a bomb amongst a group of officers, executed Oct. 6

Oct. 2, Fighting with the Moors at Melilla. *See* Morocco

About Nov. 7, Depression of the finances; national subscriptions to support the war with the Moors

Nov. 7, Destructive bomb explosion (by Anarchists) at Barcelona

1894

Feb. 23, Close of dispute with Morocco. *See* Morocco

March 8, Resignation of the Cabinet; reconstituted under Señ. Sagasta, March 12; legislation against anarchism, April 4

April 28, The marriage of Don Carlos, Duke of Madrid, to Princess Maria Bertha of Rohan, celebrated at Prague

April, May, Anarchists' trial and execution (Barcelona)

Sept. 23, Señor Cabrera consecrated first bishop of the reformed church

Nov. 4, Resignation of Señ. Sagasta and cabinet, Oct. 30; reconstituted by him

1895

The *Resumen*, Madrid newspaper, accuses military officers of want of zeal in the royal cause

March 16–17, The offices of the *Resumen* and others attacked by officers and the staff ill-treated

——, Debate in the Cortes, which favors the officers; resignation of the Sagasta Cabinet

March 23, Señ. Canovas del Castillo (conservative) forms a cabinet

April 16, Marshal Martinez Campos appointed commander in Cuba; arrives there

June 3, Attempted assassination of Gen. Primo de Rivera, Capt.-Gen. of Madrid, by Capt. Clavijo

June 5, Capt. Clavijo shot

June 12, A loan of about 24,000,000*l.* authorized by the Senate

June 13, Ruiz Zorrilla, the republican leader, died

July 2, Count Casa Valencia appointed Ambassador at London

Nov. 5, Death of Capt.-Gen. Concha, Marquis de Habaña, eminent statesman, aged 87

1896

Feb. 28 *et seq.*, Much resentment against the United States (*see s.v.*) for the resolutions of the Senate, relating to Cuba

March 4, Duke of Tetuan appointed Foreign Minister

March 7, Señ. Canovas del Castillo defends his policy, and declines American intervention

May 11, The Chambers opened by the Queen-Regent, reforms in Cuba promised

Aug. 11, Budget presented, large deficit for 1895–96, June 20; ordinary budget adopted

Aug. 21, Reported conspiracy for the independence of Philippines, 25 arrests at Madrid

1897

Feb. 4, Cuban reform bill drawn up by Señ. Canovas, signed by the Queen-Regent (*see* Cuba)

May 8, Royal decree authorizing a war loan for Cuba and the Philippines

May 21, The United States Senate recognize the Cubans as belligerents

May 22, Budget statement: new loan proposed

June 2, Deadlock: the Canovas Ministry resigns; but agree to remain in office June 6

Aug. 8, Señ. Canovas del Castillo assassinated at Santa Agueda, by Michele A. Golli (to avenge the Barcelona anarchists); state funeral at Madrid, Aug. 13; Golli executed Aug. 20

Aug. 9, Gen. Azcarraga appointed Premier (same policy); the cabinet resigns Sept. 29

Oct. 4, Señ. Sagasta forms a ministry

1898

Feb. 24, Scarcity of food in the provinces, high price of wheat, bread riots in Salamanca

March 31, United States proposals respecting Cuba: Spain to proclaim an armistice till Oct. to relieve the starvation and distress, and the United States to assist; Spain agrees to an armistice if asked for by the Cubans, April 1

April 9, Mediation of the Pope, April 6; an armistice granted on the recommendation of the 6 Powers. *See* United States, April 11–13, 1898

April 14, The council rejects United States intervention; note issued to the Powers protesting against the resolution of U.S. Congress, April 20

April 21, The Cortes opened with a firm speech by the Queen-Regent, the King present; U.S. ultimatum sent, April 20; diplomatic relations broken off; Gen. Woodford leaves Madrid

April 22, Spanish reserve (30,000) called out

[For details of war *see* United States]

May 3, Riots at Valencia, Talavera, and elsewhere owing to the price of bread, state of siege proclaimed; corn duties reduced May 5

May 5, Riots at Murcia, the law courts pillaged and burnt, prisoners in the gaol set free; state of siege in Catalonia, Badajos, Alicante, Lináres, and other places, with loss of life, May 8–10

May 10, 12, War expenditure bill passed by the Chamber and Senate, after a hot debate

May 16, Resignation of the Ministry, Señ. Sagasta commissioned to reconstruct the Cabinet

May 31, Bill passed to prevent the exportation of silver

June 1, Bank panic, arrangements for a loan of 1,000,-000,000 pesetas at 4%

June, Serious mining agitation in Catalonia, over 17,000 men out of work

July 11, The Government opens an issue of 5% treasury bonds

July 15, Decree suspending the constitutional guarantees (martial law) proclaimed

Sept. 5, The Cortes meets; peace protocol adopted, Sept. 13; the Cortes prorogued, Sept. 14

1899

Jan. 6, Col. San Martin, who surrendered Puerto Rico to the Americans, sentenced to life imprisonment

Jan. 7, Colonial Ministry abolished

Feb. 28, Stormy debates in the Cortes on the government policy and conduct of the late war, Feb. 20–25; the Ministry resigns

March 5, 6, New cabinet, Señ. Silvela, Premier and Foreign Minister; the Cortes suspended

March 17, Peace treaty with U.S. ratified, Cortes dissolved

May 14, Financial decree against existing abuses

May 25, Don Emilio Castelar, leader of the republican party, born 1832, died

June 2, The Cortes opened by the Queen-Regent; the Carolinas, Pelews, Marianne, and Ladrones ceded to Germany for 837,500*l.*, announced

June 17, Budget, 1899–1900; suspension of the sinking fund, reduction of interest on bonds, increased taxation proposed; 5% loan of 300,000,000 pesetas to be issued

July 1, Anti-budget riots in Barcelona and Badalona, 4 deaths reported

July 13, The Queen-Regent gives up another 2,000,000 pesetas of her civil list

July 28, Bill for reorganizing internal debts passed by the Chamber

Sept. 4, Catholic congress at Burgos; recent prescriptions of the Vatican resisted

Sept. 13, Martial law decreed throughout Vizcaya, due to increase of Separatism

Sept. 18, Card. Cascajares and the Bps. issue a statement demanding Catholic ascendancy in education and civil affairs

Sept., Clearance of goods through the customs stopped to non-payers of the new industrial tax at Barcelona

Sept. 22, Adm. Montojo, who surrendered to the Americans at Cavite, dismissed from the service by court-martial

Sept. 30, Ministerial crisis regarding military expenditure; Gen. Polavieja resigns; succeeded by Gen. Azcarraga

1900

March 26, Conversion of debt bill signed by the Queen-Regent

April 18, Cabinet reconstructed; Señ. Silvela, Premier and Minister of Marine; Marquis of Aguilar Campo, Foreign Minister

June 6, New consolidation loan subscribed for 25½ times over, announced

Sept. 23, Death of Marshal Martinez de Campos

Oct. 21, Gen. Weyler appointed Capt.-Gen. of Madrid; Señ. Silvela, Premier, resigns; Gen. Azcarraga forms a cabinet Oct. 22

Nov. 7, The Cagayan and Sibutu islands ceded to the U.S. for 100,000 dols.; convention signed at Washington

1901

Feb. 14, Mercedes, Princess of the Asturias, married to Prince Carlos of Bourbon, son of the Count de Caserta, at Madrid

Feb. 19, Anti-Jesuit rioting (due to a law case) in Madrid, spreads to other towns; monasteries, &c., attacked, Feb. 7–13; the case is decided against the Jesuits

March 6, Cabinet resigns, Feb. 26; Señ. Sagasta forms one; Gen. Weyler, War; Duke of Almodovar, Foreign; Señ. Moret, Interior

Sept. 19, Decree ordering the registration of religious associations issued

1902

Feb. 17–20, General strike in Barcelona and neighboring towns; conflicts with troops; over 40 deaths; bill suspending the constitutional guarantees passed by the Senate; martial law proclaimed in Zaragoza and Tarragona

March 13, Bill for the reconstruction of the Bank of Spain fails; the Ministry resigns

March 18, Señ. Sagasta reconstructs the Cabinet

May 12, The Queen-Regent, after over 16 years' noble constitutional rule, bids farewell to her Ministers (her letter published May 18)

May 17, Alfonso XIII enthroned as a constitutional ruler in Madrid

——, Anarchist plot discovered; 6 arrested

May 27, Señ. Canalejas (agriculture) and other Ministers later resign

May 30, Cortes suspended by royal decree

June 1, Labor troubles; rioting at Badajoz; martial law

June 20, Total religious communities in Spain, 2,586 for women, with 40,188 members; 529 for men, with 10,745 members; announced

June 23, New 5% loan of 338,400,000 pesetas issued June 5; well taken up, 16 times over

July 1, Decree for the regulation of non-official instruction signed by the King

Nov. 11–14, Cabinet crisis: Señ. Sagasta forms a ministry

Nov. 17, Arrests of Carlists at Barcelona

Dec. 2, Señ. Sagasta resigns on a hostile division in the Chamber

Dec. 6, Señ. Silvela, conservative, forms a cabinet; Señ. Abarzuza, Foreign; Señ. Villaverde, Finance; Señ. Maura, Interior; Gen. Linares, War

1903

Jan. 5, Señ. Sagasta, liberal leader, died, aged 75

Jan. 10, The Duke of Sotomayor shot at by a delusionist in Madrid

Feb., Strikes in Barcelona begin Dec. 30, and Reus

Feb. 9, Duke of Tetuan, ex-Minister (Foreign), dies

Oct. 11, Fatal rioting at Bilbao between a religious procession and an anti-clerical crowd; 1 killed, 47 injured

Mid Oct., Great strike of 40,000 miners and others at Bilbao; dynamite outrages, several killed, many injured; state of siege proclaimed

Dec. 1, Formation of a democratic liberal party, under the leadership of Señors Montero, Rios, Canalejas, and Gen. Weyler, reported

Dec. 5, Resignation of Ministry under Señor Villaverde, Dec. 3; new cabinet (ultra conservative), Señor Maura, Premier; Señor San Pedro, Minister for Foreign Affairs

1904

Jan. 4, Great strike at Barcelona among the shipping hands, 4,000 men leave work; strike extends to Alicante, Valencia, and other ports

Mid Jan., Appointment by the government of Mgr. Nozaleda, formerly Archbishop of Manila, to the bishopric of Valencia, who was accused of lack of patriotism when the United States took over the Philippines after the battle of Cavite, leads to an outburst of popular feeling and criticism of the conduct of the war with America

Feb. 27, Arbitration treaties with England and France signed

March 15, German Emperor visits King Alfonso at Vigo; review of the Spanish fleet in Vigo bay

April 8, Spanish interests in Morocco admitted by Great Britain and France under the Anglo-French agreement, signed

April 9, Ex-Queen Isabella dies, aged 68

April 26, Attempted assassination of Señor Maura by Artal, an anarchist

April–May, King Alfonso makes a tour throughout Spain, visiting Barcelona and other towns, the Balearic islands and Seville

Oct. 3, Franco-Spanish convention, supplementary to the Anglo-French agreement of April 8, settling the respective spheres of influence of the two countries in Morocco, concluded

Dec. 14, Resignation of Señor Maura and his Cabinet on the question of military reform

1905

Jan. 27, Gen. Azcarraga forms a new cabinet, himself as Premier; resigns, and is succeeded by Señor Villaverde

May 27, King leaves Madrid for Paris on a visit to the President of the French Republic

May 29, Death of Señor Silvela, ex-Premier

June 1, Anarchist attempt on the King by means of a bomb thrown under the carriage in which the King and President Loubet were driving in Paris

June 4, King Alfonso attends a military review at Vincennes; leaves for England, June 5

June 11, Leaves London, June 10, and arrives at San Sebastian

June 20, Defeat of Señor Villaverde's administration in the Cortes, Señor Maura, supported by a number of conservative deputies, opposing the Government; resignation of Señor Villaverde

June 23, Señor Rios forms a liberal cabinet

Oct. 23, Visit of M. Loubet to King Alfonso at Madrid; present at review of troops, Oct. 24

Oct. 30, Señor Rios reconstructs his Cabinet

Dec. 1, Resignation of Señor Rios and Cabinet

Dec. 4, Señor Moret, ex-Minister of the Interior, forms a new ministry, himself as Premier; Señor Romanones, Minister of the Interior; Duke of Almodovar, Minister for Foreign Affairs; Señor Salvador, Minister of Finance

Dec. 6, King Alfonso visits the German Emperor at Berlin

Dec. 24, Attempted assassination of Cardinal Casañas at Barcelona, by an anarchist, José Salascomas, who committed suicide

1906

Jan. 12, Marriage of the Infanta Maria Theresa, sister of the King, with Prince Ferdinand of Bavaria in Madrid

Early March, Death of Señor Romero Robledo, statesman, born 1838

March 7, Princess Ena of Battenberg abjures the Protestant faith, and is received into the Roman Catholic Church at San Sebastian

March 9, Betrothal of King Alfonso to Princess Ena of Battenberg announced

April 4, Death of General Blanco, born 1832

April 7, King Alfonso arrives at Cadiz on his return from the Canary Islands

May 21, Señor Moret and his colleagues resign; King requests Señor Moret to remain in office and to reconstruct the Ministry

May 31, Marriage of King Alfonso with the Princess Ena of Battenberg at Madrid

——, Attempted assassination of the King by a bomb thrown near to the carriage in which the King and Queen were riding; 23 persons killed, 99 injured by the explosion

June 16, Death of the Duke of Almodovar, Minister of Foreign Affairs in two of the cabinets of Señor Sagasta, aged 54

July 5, Resignation of the Moret Ministry

July 6, New cabinet formed under General Lopez Dominguez, Premier and Minister of War

Aug. 22, Strike of federated workmen at Bilbao; strikers, who had a collision with the troops, numbered 30,000

Aug. 28, Royal decree published revising the legal formalities to be observed in civil marriages

Sept. 14, Marquis Emilio Ojeda appointed Spanish Ambassador to the Vatican

Sept. 23, Agreement between the Spanish Government and the Vatican on the subject of the proposed associations law, on a basis similar to that of the concordat signed last year, reported arranged

Oct. 23, Budget bill for 1907 shows an estimated surplus of 1,570,000*l.*; it makes provision for the gradual abolition of the octroi duties; submitted to the Chamber

Oct. 31, Death of Count de Cheste, oldest Spanish marshal, aged 97

Nov. 19, Commercial bill with Switzerland passed the Senate and receives the King's sanction

Nov. 28, Resignation of the Ministry

Dec. 3, Señor Moret forms a new liberal cabinet, Nov. 29; which resigns

Dec. 4, A new liberal concentration cabinet, with the Marquis de la Vega de Armijo as Premier, sworn in

1907

Jan. 24, Resignation of the liberal cabinet

Jan. 25, Señor Maura forms a conservative administration

Feb. 5, Royal decree published in Madrid suspending trial by jury of crimes committed with explosives in the provinces of Barcelona and Gerona

March 1, Royal command published abrogating the decree of Aug. 1906 which authorized civil marriages without a declaration relative to the religion of the contracting parties

March 31, The Cortes dissolved by royal decree

April 8, King Alfonso meets King Edward and Queen Alexandra at Cartagena

April 18, Attempt to assassinate Señor Salmeron, in Barcelona

April 21, Elections to the lower house of the Cortes, throughout Spain, took place

May 10, Heir born to the Spanish throne

May 13, Cortes opened by the King

June 12, Of the six persons charged with complicity in the anarchist attempt on the King and Queen on May 31, 1906, three were convicted and sentenced to nine years' imprisonment

Sept. 16, Suicide of the Marquis de Vallecirato, aide-de-camp to Don Carlos

1908

Jan. 6, Visit of M. Pichon, French Minister for Foreign Affairs, to Madrid

Feb. 27, National Institute created to administer system of social insurance and grant old age pensions

March 9, King Alfonso leaves Madrid for Barcelona

April 14, Trial of anarchists at Barcelona; 3 sentenced to death, 4 others to terms of imprisonment, 2 acquitted

May 7, King Alfonso, in commemoration of the anniversary of the birth of the Prince of the Asturias, signs the pardon of the 3 men undergoing sentences of imprisonment in connection with the attempted assassination of the King and Queen on May 31, 1906

June 9, Law made education obligatory

June 13, Death of the Marquis de la Vega de Armijo

Aug. 8, Voting made compulsory for all males over 25, voters must be registered and residents of municipal district at least 2 years

1909

Feb. 14, King Alfonso returns to Madrid from his visit to King Manuel of Portugal

Feb. 25, Death of Cardinal Sancha, primate of Spain, born 1838

April 3, Death of Admiral Cervera, born 1839

May 22, King Alfonso opens the exhibition at Valencia

July 9, Fighting between the garrison of Melilla and Moorish tribesmen, who attacked Spanish laborers in the mines of the Riff country, of whom 4 were killed; of the men comprising the garrison, 4 were killed and 25 wounded

July 18, The hostile tribesmen attack the Spanish headquarters; Spanish losses, 15 killed and 22 wounded

——, Death of the pretender, Don Carlos

July 23, Moors numbering 16,000 make an attack on the Spanish positions at Melilla; the Spanish casualties numbered 300, and the Moors left 300 dead on the field

July 26, New Spanish fleet; King Alfonso present at the laying down of the first warship

——, Martial law proclaimed at Barcelona in consequence of meetings of protest against the campaign in Melilla, where also a general strike was proclaimed

July 27, Great fight with the tribesmen (censorship stringent); supposed to have been many officers and 1,000 men killed and 1,500 men wounded; 2,000 tribesmen killed

July 28, Further fighting; 220 Spaniards killed, including General Pintos

——, Further serious rioting at Barcelona; the constitutional guarantees suspended over all Spain

July 31, Sanguinary conflicts incessant in the streets of Barcelona; a committee of public safety formed by 9,000 revolutionaries; the movement in Catalonia, nominally one of protest against operations in Morocco, is really an insurrectionary rising against the Government

A report from Barcelona states that during the revolutionary movement there 36 convents were burned, 100 persons were killed and 1,000 wounded; 400 prisoners were in the fortress of Montjuich on Aug. 3

El-Arba occupied by a column which left Melilla on Aug. 24

Sept. 6, Operations at Suk El-Arba; the Riffs lose 45 killed and 100 wounded

Sept. 27, The Kasbah of Zeluan, an important Riff position, occupied by the Spanish troops

——, The constitutional guarantees restored, except in Barcelona and Gerona

Sept. 29, Mount Gurugu occupied

Oct. 11, During a reconnoissance from Zeluan, the Moors made an attack; Gen. Diaz Vicario, three other officers, and 14 men killed, and about 180 men wounded

Oct. 13, Señor Ferrer, condemned as having been the instigator of the riots in Barcelona, executed

Oct. 21, Resignation of Señor Maura; Señor Moret, liberal leader, entrusted with the formation of a new cabinet

Nov. 8, The constitutional guarantees restored in Barcelona and Gerona

——, Meeting between King Alfonso and King Manuel of Portugal in Madrid

Nov. 12, King Manuel leaves Madrid

Nov. 19, Conference between the Riff delegates and General Marina

1910

Feb. 8, Former decrees, dealing with the lay schools, abrogated by a royal decree. These schools are defined as ones in which no religion is obliged to be taught. Those which were closed by executive order, without any offense, being charged to be reopened

Feb. 9, Señor Moret resigns and Señor Canalejas (democrat) forms a new cabinet

Feb. 21, General amnesty, condoning all offenses against public order, with certain exceptions, approved by the Council of Ministers, Feb. 17; signed by King Alfonso

Feb. 27, Anti-clerical riots at Bilbao

April 14, Cortes dissolved

May 8 and 22, Elections gave Liberals a majority; official returns of the elections show the following results: Ministerialists, 226; Conservatives, 108; Republicans, 39; Carlists, 8; Catalanists, 7; Integrists, 3; Catholics, 2; Independents, 3; Socialist, 1

May 23, Bomb outrage in Madrid; suicide of the criminal

June 11, Royal order published granting the dissident religious establishments the right to show external signs of their belief on the walls of their churches and in their notices

June 15, King Alfonso, at the opening of the Cortes, announced that a measure to deal with the excessive multiplicity of religious orders was included in the program of the Government

June, A campaign of protest against the Government's policy in regard to the religious congregations vigorously maintained

June 16, Royal speech at opening of Cortes declared there would be a check on growth of religious orders

June 28, Bomb explosion in Barcelona; 8 persons injured, one fatally

July 3, Anti-clerical demonstrations in Madrid and other cities

July 7, Act prohibited further religious orders from entering Spain pending negotiations with Vatican

July 11, Protest of the Vatican to Spanish Government in matter of action against religious orders

July 29, Ambassador to Vatican recalled

Aug. 23, Liberals and Clericals in fight in suburbs of Barcelona

Sept. 1, Strike riots at Bilbao suppressed by troops

Sept. 21, Strike settled, working day limited to 9½ hours

Dec. 23, "Padlock" Bill passed prohibited entrance into the country of any new religious congregations for 2 years

1911

Jan. 12, Agreement with Sultan of Morocco signed settlement of disputes in regions under control of Spain

March 10, Announcement of Premier that negotiations with Vatican had broken down

March 31, Resignation of Canalejas Ministry after debate on the Ferrer controversy

April 3, Canalejas reconstituted Cabinet

April 6, Ferrer debate in Cortes ended with victory for Government 179 votes to 23

April 10, Uprising in Province of Malaga at Canillas de Aceituna. Republic proclaimed

April 11, Death of Martinez Campos, president of the Supreme Court

April 25, Law enacted placed a tax on profits

May 13, Spanish troops occupied Zain near Zeluan, Morocco to end brigandage and civil wars

May 15, New military law passed

May 16, Treaty of amity with Japan signed

May 20, Decree that after July 1 the octroi would be abolished and replaced by taxes on wealthy classes

June 9, Spanish troops landed at Larache, Morocco and took possession

Aug. 1–2, Mutiny on warship "Numancia" off Tangier. Republic proclaimed

Aug., Strike of dockers at Bilbao followed by strikes of railroad employees, miners, house painters which became general and revolutionary

Sept. 19, Royal decree suspended constitutional guarantees of personal liberty because of riots of strikers

Sept. 22, Announcement of Premier that strike had ended

Oct. 7, Spanish troops from Melilla occupied Zebuya in Morocco after 10 hour battle with Riff tribesmen

Oct. 21, Royal decree reëstablished constitutional guarantees

Oct. 22, 400 Portuguese royalists disarmed on border

1912

Jan. 24, Resignation of Cabinet not accepted

March 12, Canalejas Ministry reconstructed

May 1, Cortes reopened

May 25–Oct. 7, General strike of railroad employees in Andalusia

Sept., Railroad strike in Catalonia and decision for general strike Oct. 8 unless wages and conditions improved

Oct. 3, Demand of railroad employees for minimum wage presented

Oct. 7, Strike settled by intervention of Government

Nov. 12, Premier José Canalejas assassinated by anarchist, Pardinas, who then committed suicide

Nov. 14, Count Romanones became Prime Minister

Nov. 27, Treaty with France signed regarding Morocco in which Spanish zones defined

Dec. 25, Finance Act published

Dec. 31, Resignation of Romanones Cabinet but withdrawn and Cabinet reconstituted; S. Alba, Foreign Affairs; J. Navarro Reverter, Finance

1913

Jan., Maura with 92 deputies withdrew from Cortes as demonstration against Romanones which however had no effect and they returned

Jan. 14, Conference held by the King with S. Azcarate, Socialist leader, on social reform and education

Feb. 5, Formal relations with the Vatican resumed

April 13, Attack of Catalonian anarchist, S. Alegre, on King failed

April 27, Rising of radical Republicans led by General Fausto Guedes suppressed

May 4, Resignation of Cabinet but persuaded by King to remain in office

May 7–9, Visit of King Alfonso to Paris

May 31, Resignation of Romanones Cabinet but again reconstituted

June 21–22, Labor uprising in Barcelona which spread to all Catalonia protest against Spanish policy in Morocco

Oct. 17, Strike of 20,000 copper miners in Huelva district

Oct. 20, Bureau of Moroccan Affairs established by royal decree

Oct. 25, Romanones defeated in Cortes on Regional Decentralization Bill, resigned

Oct. 27, New Ministry formed by Señor Dato

Nov. 9, Election for municipal councils a victory for Conservatives

Dec. 18, Provisional decree gave effect to principle of regional decentralization, allowing municipalities and provinces to voluntarily group into regional associations for administrative purposes

Dec. 31, Cortes dissolved

1914

Jan. 4, Decree summoned electors to choose members of Cortes

Jan., Rio Tinto strike for increase in wages begun in April 1913 settled by arbitration

Feb. 19, Royal order provided for workmen's compensation for government workers

Feb. 25, General strike in Valencia against increase in municipal taxes suppressed by troops

March 8, Election for Chamber a victory for Conservatives. Maurist Conservatives won 10 seats; Jaimists, 16; Dato Conservatives, 235; Lerroux Radicals, 4; Romanones Liberals, 80; Prieto Liberals, 30; Reformist Republicans, 12; Republican Socialists, 21

March 22, Election for Senate. Conservatives won 92 seats; Liberals, 51; Democrats, 9; Republicans, 7

April 2, Cortes met

May 12, Death of Don Eugenio Montero Rios (82), former Premier

June 22, Strike in shipping industry which had lasted a fortnight ended with victory for strikers

Aug. 7, Declaration of neutrality in European War

1915

Feb. 2, Neutrality in War reaffirmed

Dec. 6, Resignation of Dato Cabinet on debate on military reform

Dec. 9, Count Alvaro de Romanones formed new Cabinet

Dec. 23, Royal decree dissolved the Cortes

1916

March 12, Post Office Savings Banks created under law of June 4, 1909 opened

April 9, Election a victory for the Liberal Ministry

May 1, Cabinet constituted: President of the Council, Conde de Romanones; Minister of Foreign Affairs, Don Amalio Gimeno; Justice and Worship, Don Antonio Barroso; War, Don Agustin Luque; Marine, Don Augusto Miranda; Finance, Don Santiago

Alba; Interior, Don Ruiz Jimenez; Public Instruction, Don Julio Burrell; Public Works, Don Rafael Gasset

July 9, Arbitration Treaty with Argentina signed

July 17–18, General strike

Sept. 16, Death of Jose Echegary, author

Nov. 6, Royal decree announced regulations as to naturalization

1917

Jan. 9, Resignation of Romanones Ministry because of opposition of Parliament to financial measures. Asked by the King to remain in office

March 6, Cortes met

March 27, Debate on Ferrer trial begun in Cortes

April 19, Resignation of Romanones Cabinet accepted. Succeeded by Ministry of Marquis (Manuel Garcia Prieto) Ahucemas

June 1, Ultimatum of army group demanded resignation of Prieto

June 9, Prieto Ministry resigned

June 11, Eduardo Dato, Liberal-Conservative, formed Cabinet

June 27, Martial law proclaimed

July 5, Demand of 20 senators and deputies in Barcelona that the Chamber be called as a constituent assembly to consider Catalonian demand for home rule. Refused

Aug. 10, Strike of railroad employees in the North

Aug. 13, General revolutionary strike proclaimed. Martial law proclaimed because of rioting

Oct. 18, Decree terminated suspension of constitutional guarantees

Oct. 27, Resignation of Dato Ministry. Succeeded by Alhucemas as Prime Minister

Dec. 6, Commercial Agreement with Great Britain signed

1918

Feb. 24, General election held a victory of Moderate-Conservatives and Liberals and a defeat for extremists

March 9, Resignation of Alhucemas Cabinet

March 22, Antonio Maura formed Cabinet, a coalition of Conservatives and Liberals, Alhucemas, Minister of the Interior; Dato, Minister of Foreign Affairs

April 8–18, New Commercial Agreement with Great Britain

June 29, Law enacted reorganized army

July 1, Law established continuous rest period of 12 hours in each week in mercantile establishments

July 7, A stringent espionage law on account of German political intrigues passed

Oct. 8, Maura Ministry reorganized

Oct. 9, Resignation of Alba from the Cabinet

Nov. 6, Resignation of Maura Cabinet

Nov. 9, New Cabinet formed by the Marquis de Alhucemas; Alba, Minister of Finance; Romanones, Minister of Foreign Affairs

Dec. 3, Romanones succeeded as Prime Minister

1919

Jan. 21, Parliament reopened. The Prime Minister obtained a majority for his proposal to submit the question of Catalonian autonomy to an extra-parliamentary commission

Jan. 24, Meeting of Catalonian Union at Barcelona drew up program for home rule

Jan. 28, Debate in Parliament on Catalonian question

and extra-parliamentary commission appointed which later reported a moderate plan for home rule which was rejected by the Catalonians

Feb. 24, Count Romanones resigned but persuaded to remain in office

——, Strike of telephone officials in Barcelona began general strike

Feb. 27, Suspension of Cortes. Martial law proclaimed in province of Lerida, Catalonia

March 7, Decree provided penalties for hoarding of food stuffs

March 11, Decree established improved system of compulsory old age pensions

March 24, General strike declared in Barcelona

March 25, Martial law proclaimed throughout Spain

April 3 and Aug. 21, Royal decree established eight hour working day, effective Oct. 1

April 14, Romanones Liberal Ministry resigned

May 2, Cabinet formed by Maura, ultra-Conservative

May, Ex-Empress Zita of Austria-Hungary took up residence in Spain

June 1, Election for Chamber of Deputies a Conservative victory. Conservatives gained 233 seats; Liberals, 110; Reformists, 12; Regionalists (Catalonian), 15; Carlists, 5; Independents, 6

July, Resignation of Maura Cabinet. Succeeded by S. Toca

Oct. 14, Royal decree issued regulations for compulsory insurance for seamen

Nov. 3, General lockout begun by employers at Barcelona

Nov. 12, Lockout ended by agreement

Nov. 27, Workmen's Compensation Convention signed with Argentina

Dec. 6, Cabinet resigned

Dec. 11, Allende Salazar became head of a coalition Cabinet

1920

Jan. 4, Death of Benito Perez-Galdos, novelist

Jan. 10, Spain became an original member of the League of Nations

April 28, Salazar Cabinet resigned. Dato formed new Ministry

July 9, Rural Bank established agency of National Catholic Agricultural Confederation

Aug. 30, Resignation of Dato Cabinet. Reorganized 2 days later

1921

Jan. 12, Steamer "Santa Isabel" shipwrecked near Salvora Island; 800 lives lost

Feb., Visit of the King and Queen of Belgium

March 8, Assassination of Prime Minister Eduardo Dato

March 13, Cabinet formed by Allende Salazar after failure of Maura

May 12, Death of Countess Emilia Pardo-Bazan, novelist and suffragist

May 19, New tariff became effective

June 20, Commercial modus vivendi with Sweden and with Denmark established

July 21, Defeat of Spanish troops at Anual, Morocco. General Silvestre killed and 3 colonels

Aug. 10, Resignation of Allende-Salazar Ministry

Aug. 13, Maura became Prime Minister

Nov. 19, Commercial Agreement with Czechoslovakia signed

1922

Jan. 3, General Weyler resigned as Chief of General Staff

Jan. 6, Exchange of Notes established commercial agreement with the Netherlands

Jan. 11, Resignation of Maura Ministry because the King refused to sign a decree for the dissolution of the Cortes

Jan. 16, Maura Cabinet resumed office

Feb. 12, Maritime Treaty with Norway signed

Feb. 23–24, Commercial agreement with Bulgaria by exchange of Notes

March 7, Maura Cabinet resigned

March 8, Cabinet formed by Sanchez Guerra

March 23, Arbitration Treaty with Uruguay signed

April 15, Provisional Commercial Agreement with Italy concluded

May 6, Provisional Commercial Agreement with Norway signed

May 11, New Commercial Agreement with Switzerland signed

May 15, Strike of ironworkers in Bilbao against reduction of wages

July 8, Commercial Agreement with France signed

Aug. 20, Defeat of Spanish troops at Tifarauin, Morocco, by Abdul Krim

Sept. 25, Submission of Chief El Raisuli ended war in western Morocco

Oct. 31, Commercial Treaty with Great Britain signed

Nov. 14, Decree promulgated ordered the dissolution of the military juntas or committees of army officers

Dec. 5, Resignation of the Guerra Cabinet

Dec. 7, New Cabinet formed by Alhucemas, Liberal

Dec. 20, Commercial Treaty of Feb. 12, 1899 with Germany prolonged

Dec. 26, Civil commissioner replaced military commissioner in Morocco

1923

Jan. 3, Villaneuva appointed High Commissioner of Morocco but illness prevented him from taking office

Jan. 29, Release of Spanish prisoners at Anual, Morocco, after 18 months captivity

Feb. 10, Silvela appointed High Commissioner for Morocco

March 14, Death of Allende Salazar, former Premier

April 4, Resignation of Pedregal, Minister of Finance

April 6, Cortes dissolved and new elections ordered

April 25 and 30, Commercial modus vivendi with Rumania concluded

April 29, Election held a victory for the Government

April 30, Commercial modus vivendi with Rumania signed

June 4, Murder of Archbishop Soldevila at Saragossa

June 13, Senate Committee appointed to investigate Spanish reverses in Morocco reported in favor of impeachment of General Berenguer, June 29

July 12, End of strike of transport workers at Barcelona which had lasted 10 weeks

July 24, Parliament adjourned to Oct. 1

Aug. 23, Mutiny of troops assembled at Malaga for transportation to Melilla, Morocco

Aug. 25, Royal decree regarding intervention of public authorities in strikes and lockouts

Aug. 27, The battleship "Espana" stranded on the rocks off Cape Tres Farcas

Sept. 1, Resignation of Ministers of Finance and Public Works

Sept. 12, Separatist movement begun in Barcelona by mutiny of garrison

Sept. 13, Military coup d'état of General Ferdinando Primo Rivera took Barcelona

Sept. 14, Resignation of Alhucemas Ministry forced by Rivera

Sept. 15, Military Directorate formed with Rivera, President, for government of the country

——, Martial law proclaimed

Sept. 16, Parliament dissolved by decree

Sept. 21, Jury trial suspended by decree signed by the King and new censorship provisions went into effect

Nov. 15, Further Commercial Agreement with Italy signed

Dec. 6, Commercial *modus vivendi* with Japan concluded

1924

Jan. 6, Liberal leader, Marquis Cortina, banished

Jan. 31, Superior Council of Railways appointed by Royal order

Feb. 7, Tangier Convention signed provided for permanent neutralization of zone

Feb. 9, Agreement with Great Britain extended Arbitration Agreement of Feb. 27, 1904

Feb. 20, Senor Sariano, Republican, exiled

Feb. 25, Trial of General Marquis Cavalcanti for disaster of Tizza in Sept., 1921, ended in acquittal

Feb. 26, Don Miguel de Unamuno, Republican, banished

April 1, Municipal statute came into force granting wide measure of local autonomy

May 12, Visit of Don Alfonso and family to Barcelona

June 8, Visit of King and Queen of Italy to Madrid

June 16, Trial of General Berenguer for responsibility disaster at Annual, Morocco. His name struck off the active list. Case of General Navarro for surrender of Monte Arruit withdrawn

June 30, General rising of tribes in Morocco

July 1, Agreement with Great Britain concluded as to standing of British companies in Spain

July 4, Royal decree modified dictatorial powers of Rivera

July 25, Commercial Treaty with Germany signed

Aug. 1, Commercial *modus vivendi* with Germany came into effect

Aug. 12, New Railroad Statute enacted

Aug. 28, New National Telephone Company established

Sept. 27, Treaty of friendship with Turkey signed

Oct. 4, Decree for suppression of gambling promulgated

Oct. 16, Marquis de Estella assumed office as High Commissioner and Commander-in-Chief in Morocco, Admiral Magaz becoming Acting President of the Directory

Nov. 6, Raid across the frontier at St. Jean de Luz and affair at Barcelona

Nov. 19–28, Visit of King and General Rivera to Italy. Political *rapprochement*

Dec. 12, Commercial *modus vivendi* with Belgium signed

Dec. 18, Supreme Court found Blanco Ibanez guilty of lese-majesty for denouncing the King and the military directorate in pamphlet

1925

Jan. 2, Spanish troops completed evacuation of 4,000 square miles of territory in Morocco

Jan. 31, Commercial Agreement with Poland concluded

Feb. 3, Commercial *modus vivendi* with Austria concluded

Feb. 13, Death of General Daban, one of the 5 members of Provisional Directory

March 19, Death of Dr. Lago y Gonzales, archbishop

March 20, New Provincial Statute signed by the King

April 4, The King opened irrigation works bringing 60,000 acres in province of Alicante under cultivation

May 4, Commercial Agreement with Sweden signed

May 17, Decree suspended martial law

June 17–July 25, Conferences with France regarding Morocco in Madrid

June 17, Commercial Agreement with Hungary concluded

July 1, Court of Minors established for trial of cases of delinquency of boys and girls from 9 to 18 years

July 7, Government Board of Agriculture Credits established under the Department of the Interior to make loans to farmers and breeders

July 16, Commercial Agreements with Czechoslovakia and Finland signed

July 26, Agreement with France for military and naval coöperation in Morocco signed

Aug. 21, Final conference with France at Algeciras

Nov. 8, Tariff war with Germany went into effect because of embargo on Spanish grapes

Nov. 18, *Modus vivendi* with Germany signed ended tariff war

Dec. 3, Military Directorate ended with resignation of Primo de Rivera as head. Rivera immediately appointed Prime Minister by the King and mixed civil and military cabinet created

Dec. 9, Death of Pablo Iglesias, editor, president of Socialist Party (75)

Dec. 13, Death of Antonio Maura y Montaner (66), former Prime Minister

Dec. 31, Treaty of commerce and navigation of Sept. 23, 1903, with Greece extended

1926

Jan. 9, Judicial Convention with Switzerland signed

Jan. 22–30, Flight of Commander Raimon Franco from Palos by Las Palmas and the Cape Verde Islands to Brazil, 8th crossing of the Atlantic in airship

Feb. 10, Liquor smuggling Treaty with the United States signed

March 10, Spain announced intention to resign from League of Nations

March 25, Royal decree regulating military status of emigrants enabled several hundred thousand Spaniards in America to resume native citizenship

March 28, Naval program authorized

April 5, Return of Commandante Franco. Given reception by the King at Seville and royal and national honors

April 20, Treaty with Switzerland signed for conciliation and judicial settlement of disputes

May 7, Final offensive against Abd-el-Krim begun by French and Spanish troops in Morocco

May 10, Tax of 10 pesetas to 100 kg. levied on all oil from ground nut and sesame seeds. Imports of seeds limited and later prohibited

June 9, Decree published forbade army officers to refuse promotion by merit

June 23, Arrest of 30 persons including Dr. Maranon, General Aguilera, and Captain General Weyler who had signed a manifesto in conspiracy against the Government

July 6, Minimum price of wheat fixed. Importation of wheat prohibited

July 9, Decree issued for protection of national industries

——, Decree instituted "extraordinary" budget for public works for 10 years of 3,538,000,000 pesetas

July 13, Franco-Spanish Agreement regarding Morocco signed

July 31, Attack of anarchist on Rivera at Barcelona

Aug. 7, Treaty of friendship, conciliation, and arbitration with Italy signed

Aug. 15, Statement of Primo de Rivera that it was unjust that the Tangier zone surrounded by Spanish protectorate in Morocco should be excluded from it

Aug. 23, Labor Code promulgated

Aug. 25, Note to signers of Algeciras Act asked for incorporation of Tangier in Spanish zone or under Spanish mandate

Sept. 4, Mutiny of artillery corps stationed at Segovia, Valladolid, and Pamplona against Primo de Rivera

Sept. 5–8, Martial law established throughout the country

Sept. 11, Resignation of Spain from the League of Nations dated Sept. 8 received by Secretary General

Sept. 11–13, Plebiscite vote upheld the dictatorship of Primo de Rivera

Sept. 17, Note to Great Britain and France renounced demand that Tangier be included in Spanish zone

Oct., Decree established Silk Commission to encourage silk worm culture

Nov. 2, 93 "Tourists" including Colonel Macia (Nov. 4), leader of conspiracy to start revolt in Catalonia, arrested by the French police at Perpignan near frontier, frustrating plot of invasion

Nov. 4, Decree prohibited establishment of any new industrial undertakings or extension of existing works without consent of a Government committee

Dec. 11, Royal order established Orange Committee to encourage industry

Dec. 25, The "Atlantida" air squadron reached Fernando Po

Dec. 31, Pardon of artillery officers involved in revolt of September

1927

Jan. 1, Martial law suspended

Jan. 7, Royal order provided for inspection of oranges prior to shipment

Jan. 18, Royal order published measure for encouragement of poultry farming

——, Note reaffirmed claim of Spain to Tangier

Jan. 28, The cruiser "Blas de Lezo" sent to Chinese waters in support of western policy in China, first Spanish flag in Far East for many years

Feb. 9, International Conference on Tangier begun in Paris

Feb. 18, Royal order published provided for grant of credits to small growers against crops of wheat, oil, wine, rice, and wool

Feb. 20, Resignation of Minister of Foreign Affairs in dispute with Rivera over policy in Morocco. Primo de Rivera took over the portfolio of Foreign Affairs

Feb. 26, Resignation of Minister of Education

April 5, Convention with Great Britain revised commercial Treaty of Oct. 31, 1922

April 11, Commercial Agreement with Norway concluded

May 28, Commercial Agreement with Rumania concluded

May 31, Official announcement of convocation in autumn of consultative assembly to prepare for return of more constitutional form of government

June, Raisin Committee founded for encouragement of grape industry

June 7, Decree provided that companies in which Spanish nationals held 60% capital should be exempt from taxation for one year and thereafter pay only 25% the second year, and 50% the third year, of normal taxes

June 28, Decree established petroleum industry as a government monopoly

July 10, Spanish Morocco again "pacified" with aid of French troops and end of campaign officially proclaimed

July 15, Treaty of commerce with Cuba signed

July 19, Treaty of conciliation, arbitration, and judicial settlement with Belgium

Aug. 11, Convention with Portugal delimited respective rights in falls of the Douro River

Sept. 12, Royal decree convoked National Assembly to meet Oct. 10

Oct. 2, Revolutionary plot discovered and 200 persons arrested

Oct. 10, National Assembly (advisory) met

Nov. 27, Commercial Convention with the United States signed

Nov. 28, Financial Convention with Italy signed

1928

Jan. 2, Treaty of commerce and navigation with Denmark signed

Jan. 18, Treaty of conciliation and arbitration with Portugal

Jan. 28, Death of Blasco Ibanez, novelist, in exile in Mentone, France

March 3, Agreement with France signed gave Spain increased control over Tangier

March 9, Consortium of lead producers established

——, Council of the League of Nations invited Spain to reconsider resignation from League of Nations of Sept. 8, 1926

March 14, Treaty of arbitration with Denmark signed

March 22, Announcement that resignation from the League of Nations withdrawn

April 26, Treaty of arbitration and judicial settlement with Sweden signed

May 7, Decree law authorized credits on wines at 5% interest up to 60% of value

May 28, Agreement with Sweden revised commercial Treaty of May 4, 1925

May 30, Provisional Commercial Agreement with Greece signed

May 31, Treaty of arbitration and conciliation with Finland

——, Supplementary Commercial Agreement with Great Britain concluded

June 11, Arbitration and Conciliation Agreement with Austria signed

July 18, New railroad through the Pyrenees opened

July 25, Protocol revising Statute of Tangier signed

Sept. 13, Plot to overthrow the dictator discovered in Barcelona

Sept. 18, Juan de la Cierva made first long distance flight in autogiro across the Channel from London to Paris at average speed of 90 miles an hour, crossing the Channel in 20 minutes, landing at St. Inglevert and proceeding to Paris

Nov. 3, Reorganization of Cabinet announced suppression of Ministry of Foreign Affairs, duties added to office of Prime Minister

Nov. 16, Arbitration Convention with Czechoslovakia signed

Dec. 13, Commercial Agreement with Czechoslovakia signed

Dec. 15, Commercial *modus vivendi* with Belgium signed

Dec. 27, Tariff autonomy and extra-Territorial Treaty with China signed

——, Treaty of arbitration and conciliation with Denmark signed

Dec. 29, Additional Commercial Convention with Hungary signed

Dec. 31, Commercial *modus vivendi* with Switzerland signed

1929

Jan. 29, Revolt of artillery garrisons at Ciudad Real

Feb. 6, Death of Dowager Queen Maria Cristina

Feb. 19, Royal decree disbanded entire artillery corps

Feb. 27, Segovia Artillery Academy closed

March 9, Strike of students at Madrid because of closing of Artillery Academy

March 17, University of Madrid closed by royal decree until Oct., 1930, because of rioting of students and later other universities

March 22, Legislative decree introduced compulsory maternity insurance for workers

March 24–25, Non-stop trans-Atlantic flight of Captains Ignacio Jiminez and Francisco Iglesias from Seville to Bahia, Brazil, 4,200 miles in 43 hours and 48 minutes

April 17, University at Oviedo closed

April 22, University at Barcelona closed

May 9, International fair at Seville opened in presence of King and Prime Minister and other notables

May 24, Trial by court martial of 40 artillery officers involved in Ciudad Real revolt in January

May 29, All universities reopened

June 10, Treaty of friendship, arbitration, and conciliation with Hungary signed

July 5, Proposed new Constitution submitted to National Assembly. Power of Cortes curtailed

July 10, Treaty with France signed provided for arbitration of commercial disputes

Sept. 12, Treaty of commerce and arbitration with Denmark signed

Sept. 27, Commercial Treaty with Yugoslavia signed

Oct. 25, Court martial trial of Jose Sanchez Guerra, former Premier, and his son resulted in acquittal on charge of inciting revolt in January

Nov. 24, Release of Sanchez Guerra on parole pending trial before highest military court

Dec. 4, 10 year loan of $49,000,000 (350,000,000 pesetas) at 6% signed by the King

Dec. 7, Amnesty granted to numerous military offenders including Castro Girona former Captain General involved in Guerra revolt, but Guerra not pardoned

Dec. 13, Announcement of dictator that no national election would be held in 1930 as had been expected

Dec. 15–16, Flight of Major Larre-Borges (French) and Lieutenant Challe (Uruguayan) from Seville to Montevideo. Crashed unharmed in a Brazilian jungle, their flight the third non-stop flight from Europe to South America

Dec. 19, Supreme Court removed 3 death sentences of officers involved in Ciudad Real. Colonel Paz and others received prison terms

1930

Jan. 20, Minister of Finance compelled to resign because his program had not prevented continued fall of the peseta

Jan. 23, Treaty of friendship and arbitration with Greece signed

Jan. 28, Resignation of General Primo de Rivera as Prime Minister, dictator since 1923

Jan. 30, General D'Amaso Berenguer took office as Prime Minister and Minister of War, the Duke of Alba, Minister of Education

Feb. 6, Amnesty signed by the King released hundreds of political prisoners

Feb. 7, University students at Seville demanded retirement of municipal administration because appointed by Rivera

Feb. 9, Return of Professor Miguel de Unamuno, exiled rector of the University of Salamanca

Feb. 12, Procession of workers to the palace demanding work

Feb. 13, Food riots in Madrid

Feb. 15, Royal decree abolished the National Assembly created by Rivera; the county councils restored and new civil governors appointed in provinces

——, Decree of King made promotion in the army the result of seniority

Feb. 21, Order of Council of Ministers suspended importation of wheat

Feb. 22, Great demonstration of welcome to student leader, Antonio Maria Sbert, returned from exile

Feb. 23, Ministry of State (Foreign Affairs), reëstablished and Duke of Alba appointed to office

Feb. 27, Public speech of Guerra attack on king. Riots and clash with police

March 1, Peseta closed at 40.16 to the English pound

March 13, Royal decree reëstablished juridical rights

March 16, Death of General Primo de Rivera (60) in Paris

March 30, Arbitration, conciliation, and judicial settlement Treaty with Yugoslavia signed

April 13, Speech of Alcala Zamora, Liberal leader, denounced the monarchy and declared for a republic

April 28, Arbitration and Conciliation Agreement with Turkey signed

May 1, Professor Unamuno reappointed to Chair of Greek at Salamanca University

May 4, Police called to break up riots after speech by Professor Unamuno denouncing the monarchy and demanding establishment of a republic

May 5, Demonstrations of university students against the Government continued. In Madrid 2 persons killed and 40 injured in riots

May 7, Valladolid University closed because of riots of students, Seville University the next day

May 30, Riots at San Sebastian

June 22, Conference of the King in Paris with Santiago Alba, former Liberal Minister, who had left the country at beginning of Rivera dictatorship

June 23, General strike proclaimed at Seville

June 24, Speech of Marcelino Domingo in favor of revolution

July 22, Tariff rates on luxuries notably automobiles raised, and duties in general, already the highest in Europe, raised

Aug. 5, Announcement of Prime Minister that press censorship would be removed before October

Aug. 19, Resignation of Minister of Finance on account of fall of the peseta. Succeeded by Julio Wais, Minister of Economy, and Luis Rodriguez Viguera appointed Minister of Economy

Sept. 18, The newspapers appeared uncensored for first time in 7 years

Sept. 23, Monster Republican meeting at Madrid

Sept. 28, 20,000 Republicans denounce King Alfonso and cheer Liberal speakers at Madrid bull ring

Oct. 11, World airplane speed record made by Carlos de Haya Gonzales and Cipriano Rodriques Diaz for 2,000 kilometers at 136.967 miles an hour

Oct. 14, Peseta dropped from 10.15 to 10.25 to the dollar and 2 days later to 10.50 to the dollar

Oct. 20, Death of General Valeriano Weyler (92)

Nov. 14, Clash between workers in building trades and police in Madrid and general strike begun which spread to other cities

Nov. 17, Strike riots in Barcelona

Dec. 12–13, Mutiny of garrison at Jaca near the French border imprisoned its officers in the fort and declared for a republic. Suppressed by government troops

Dec. 14, Captains Galan and Garcia Hernandez leaders of Jaca revolt court-martialed and shot, and 4 other officers condemned to life imprisonment

Dec. 15, Mutiny of air force led by Major Ramon Francia at Cuatro Vientos near Madrid suppressed by government troops. Major Ramon Francia escaped to Portugal

——, Martial law proclaimed throughout Spain

SOVEREIGNS OF SPAIN

GOTHIC SOVEREIGNS

411. Ataulfo; murdered by his soldiers
415. Sigerico; reigned a few days only
——. Valia, or Wallia
420. Theodoric I; killed in a battle, which he gained, against Attila
451. Thorismund, or Torrismund; assassinated
452. Theodoric II; assassinated
466. Euric, the first monarch of all Spain
483. Alaric II; killed in battle
506. Gesalric; his bastard son
511. Amalric, or Amalaric; legitimate son of Alaric
531. Theudis, or Theodat; assassinated by a madman
548. Theudisela, or Theodisele; murdered
549. Agila; taken prisoner, and put to death
554. Atanagildo
567. Liuva, or Levua I
568. Leuvigildo; associated on the throne with Liuva, in 568; and sole king in 572
586. Recaredo I
601. Liuva II; assassinated
603. Vitericus; also murdered
610. Gundemar
612. Sisibut, or Sisebuth, or Sisebert
621. Recaredo II
——. Suintila; dethroned
631. Sisenando
636. Chintella
640. Tulga, or Tulca
642. Cindasuinto; died in 652
649. Recesuinto; associated; in 653 became sole king
672. Vamba, or Wamba; dethroned, and died in a monastery
680. Ervigius, or Ervigio

687. Egica, or Egiza
698. Vitiza, or Witiza, associated; in 701 sole king
711. Rodrigo, or Roderic; slain in battle
[Six independent Suevic kings reigned 409–469; and two Vandalic kings: Gunderic, 409–425; his successor Genseric with his whole nation passed over to Africa]

MAHOMETAN SPAIN

CORDOVA

Emirs. The first, Abdelasis: the last, Yussuf-el-Tehri: A.D. 714–755

Kings. The first, Abderahman I; the last, Abu Ali; 755–1238

GRANADA

Kings. The first, Mohammed I; the last, Abdalla; 1238–1492

CHRISTIAN SPAIN

KINGS OF ASTURIAS AND LEON

718. Pelagius, or Pelayo; overthrew the Moors, and checked their conquests
737. Favila; killed in hunting
739. Alfonso the Catholic
757. Froila; murdered his brother Samaran, in revenge for which he was murdered by his brother, and successor
768. Aurelius or Aurelio
774. Mauregato, the Usurper
788. Veremundo (Bermuda) I
791. Alfonso II, the Chaste
842. Ramiro I: he put 70,000 Saracens to the sword in one battle. Rabbe
850. Ordoño I
866. Alfonso III, surnamed the Great; relinquished his crown to his son
910. Garcias
914. Ordoño II
923. Froila II
925. Alfonso IV, the Monk; abdicated
930. Ramiro II, killed in battle
950. Ordoño III
955. Ordoño IV
956. Sancho I, the Fat; poisoned with an apple
967. Ramiro III
983. Veremundo II (Bermuda), the Gouty
999. Alfonso V; killed in a siege
1027. Veremundo III (Bermuda); killed

KINGS OF NAVARRE

873. Sancho Iñigo. Count
885. Garcia I, King
905. Sancho Garcias; a renowned warrior
924. Garcias II, surnamed the Trembler
970. Sancho III, surnamed the Great (King of Castile through his wife)
1035. Garcias III
1054. Sancho III
1076. Sancho IV, Ramirez, King of Aragon
1094. Peter of Aragon
1104. Alfonso I, of Aragon
1134. Garcias IV, Ramirez
1150. Sancho V, surnamed the Wise
1194. Sancho VI, surnamed the Infirm
1234. Theobald I, Count of Champagne
1253. Theobald II
1270. Henry Crassus
1274. Joanna; married to Philip the Fair of France, 1285

1305. Louis Hutin, of France
1316. John; lived but a few days
——. Philip V, the Long, of France
1322. Charles I, the IV of France
1328. Joanna II, and Philip, Count d'Evreux
1343. Joanna alone
1349. Charles II, or the Bad
1387. Charles III, or the Noble
1425. Blanche and her husband John II, afterwards King of Aragon
1479. Eleanor
——. Francis Phœbus de Foix
1483. Catherine and John d'Albret
1512. Navarre conquered by Ferdinand the Catholic, and united with Castile

KINGS OF LEON AND CASTILE

1035. Ferdinand the Great
1065. Sancho II, the Strong, son of Ferdinand; Alfonso in Leon and Asturias, and Garcias in Galicia
1072. Alfonso VI, the Valiant, King of Leon
1109. Uraca and Alfonso VII
1126. Alfonso VII, Raymond
1157. Sancho III, surnamed the Beloved
1158. Alfonso VIII, the Noble
[Leon is separated from Castile under Ferdinand II, 1157–88]
1188. Alfonso IX, of Leon
1214. Henry I
1217. Ferdinand III, the Saint and the Holy. By him Leon and Castile were permanently united
1252. Alfonso X, the Wise (the Alphonsine Tables were drawn up under his direction)
1284. Sancho IV, the Great and the Brave
1295. Ferdinand IV
1312. Alfonso XI
1350. Peter the Cruel: deposed; reinstated by Edward the Black Prince of England; slain by his natural brother and successor
1369. Henry II, the Gracious; poisoned by a monk
1379. John I: he united Biscay to Castile
1390. Henry III, the Sickly
1406. John II, son of Henry
1454. Henry IV, the Impotent
1474. Isabella, sister (had married Ferdinand of Aragon, Oct. 18, 1469)
1504. Joanna (daughter of Ferdinand and Isabella) and Philip I of Austria. On her mother's death Joanna succeeded, jointly with her husband Philip; but Philip dying in 1506, and Joanna becoming imbecile, her father Ferdinand continued the reign; and thus perpetuated the union of Castile with Aragon

KINGS OF ARAGON

1035. Ramiro I
1065. Sancho Ramirez (IV of Navarre)
1094. Peter of Navarre
1104. Alfonso I, the Warrior, King of Navarre
1134. Ramiro II, the Monk
1137. Petronilla, and Raymond, Count of Barcelona
1163. Alfonso II
1196. Peter II
1213. James I; succeeded by his son
1276. Peter III; conquered Sicily in 1282. *See* Sicily
1285. Alfonso III, the Beneficent
1291. James II, surnamed the Just
1327. Alfonso IV

1336. Peter IV, the Ceremonious
1387. John I
1395. Martin
1410. [Interregnum]
1412. Ferdinand the Just, King of Sicily
1416. Alfonso V, the Wise
1458. John II, King of Navarre, brother of Alfonso; died 1479
1479. Ferdinand II, the Catholic, the next heir; by marriage with Isabella of Castile (styled the Catholic Kings), the Kingdoms were united

SPAIN

1512. Ferdinand V (of Castile), the Catholic; having conquered Granada and Navarre, became King of all Spain
1516. Charles I, grandson, son of Joanna of Castile and Philip of Austria (Emperor of Germany, as Charles V, in 1519); resigned both crowns, and retired to a monastery
1556. Philip II, son, King of Naples and Sicily; a merciless bigot; married Mary of Portugal, 1543; Mary of England, 1554; and Isabella of France, 1559
1598. Philip III, son, drove the Moors from Granada and the adjacent provinces
1621. Philip IV, son: wars with the Dutch and French; lost Portugal in 1640
1665. Charles II, son; last of the Austrian line; nominated, by will, as his successor
1700. Philip V, Duke of Anjou, grandson of Louis XIV of France: hence arose the "war of the Succession," terminated by the Treaty of Utrecht in 1713; resigned
1724. Louis I, son; reigned only a few months
——. Philip V again
1746. Ferdinand VI, the Wise, son; liberal and beneficent
1759. Charles III, brother, King of the Two Sicilies, which he gave to his third son, Ferdinand
1788. Charles IV, son; the influence of Godoy, prince of the peace, reached to almost royal authority in this reign; Charles abdicated in favor of his son in 1808, and died in 1819
1808. Ferdinand VII, whom Napoleon of France also forced to resign
——. Joseph Bonaparte, brother of Napoleon; forced to abdicate
1814. Ferdinand VII restored; married Maria Christina of Naples, Dec. 11, 1829; died Sept. 29, 1833; succeeded by
1833. Isabella II, daughter (born Oct. 10, 1830); declared of age, Nov. 8, 1843; married her cousin, Don Francis d'Assisi, Oct. 10, 1846 (born May 13, 1822; died April 17, 1902); deposed Sept. 30, 1868; separated from her husband, March, 1870; and abdicated, June 25, 1870, in favor of her son, Alfonso, Prince of Asturias (born, Nov. 28, 1857). Visits Queen Victoria at Windsor, May 20; leaves England May 29, 1890
1870. Amadeo I (Duke of Aosta, son of Victor-Emanuel II, King of Italy); born May 30, 1845; married Maria Victoria of Pozzo della Cisterna, May 30, 1867; accepted the crown offered him by the Cortes, Dec. 4, 1870; abdicated Feb. 11, 1873; died Jan. 18, 1890
Republic founded, Feb. 11, 1873. Very unsettled, 1873–74

KINGS

1874. Alfonso XII, son of Isabella II (born Nov. 28, 1857); proclaimed Dec. 30, 1874; married 1st, his cousin Mercedes, daughter of the duc de Montpensier (born June 24, 1860), Jan. 23, 1878; she died June 26, 1878; and Archduchess Maria Christina of Austria (born July 21, 1858), Nov. 29, 1879. He died Nov. 25, 1885

1885. Maria Mercedes Isabella (Princess of Asturias), born Sept. 11, 1880; replaced by her brother; married Prince Carlos of Bourbon (born 1870), Feb. 14, 1901; son, Alfonso, born Nov. 30, 1901

1886. Alfonso (Leon, &c.) XIII, born May 17; formally enthroned May 17, 1902; married Princess Victoria Eugénie of Battenberg (born Oct. 24, 1887); deposed 1931. Heir, Alfonso, Prince of the Asturias, born May 10, 1907; Prince Jaimé, born June 23, 1908; Princess Beatrice Maria, born June 22, 1909

CARLIST LEGITIMIST PRETENDERS
(*See* above 1833 *et seq.*)

Carlos V, brother of Ferdinand VII, born March 29, 1788; died March 10, 1855

Carlos VI, his son (Conde de Montemolin), died Jan. 14, 1861

Carlos VII (son of Don Juan, brother of Carlos VI, who renounced his right, Jan. 8, 1863); born, March 30, 1848; *see* above 1873–76

SPANISH SUCCESSION, WAR OF THE

Spanish Succession, War of the (1701–1713), general European war after the death of Charles II of Spain without an heir, caused by refusal of Louis XIV to accept the settlement of the "Partition Treaties" of 1698 and 1700, France, Germany, Bavaria, and Savoy claiming succession. Begun by the Grand Alliance of which England and Holland were the most important members when the fortresses in the Spanish Netherlands were given to the French, and ended with the Treaties of Utrecht, signed April 11 (March 31 O.S.), 1713, and the Treaty of Rastatt between Austria and France, signed March 7, 1714.

SPITSBERGEN

Spitsbergen (Svalbard) in possession of Norway, an Arctic archipelago situated between 10° and 35° longitude east of Greenwich and between 74° and 81° latitude north. The distance from Norway to Bear Island is 240 miles, and to Spitsbergen (South Cape) 360 miles.

It is claimed that in all probability the archipelago was discovered by Norwegians in 1194 and rediscovered by the Dutch navigator Barents in 1596. The English explorer Henry Hudson visited Spitsbergen in 1607. In the seventeenth century a very lucrative whale-hunting was started and for some time there were Dutch, British, and Norwegian claims to sovereignty and quarrels about the hunting-places. But when in the eighteenth

century the whale-hunting ended, the question of the sovereignty of Spitsbergen lost its actuality, and it was not until the beginning of this century that the question was again raised, owing to the discovery and exploitation of rich coalfields. It was settled by a Treaty, signed on February 9, 1920, at Paris, in which Norway's sovereignty over the archipelago was recognized. On August 14, 1925, the archipelago was officially taken possession of by Norway.

Total area about 25,000 square miles. The chief islands are West Spitsbergen or Mainland, North East Land (about half the former), Prince Charles Foreland, Edge Island, Barents Land, King Karl's Land, Hope Island, and Bear Island. The climate is essentially arctic, tempered by the Gulf Stream.

SWEDEN

Sweden, kingdom of northern Europe occupying the eastern and larger part of the Scandinavian peninsula, bounded on the west by Norway and the Kattegat, and on the east by Finland (Lapland) and the Baltic Sea, the length about 990 miles and the average width of the country 190 miles with extreme width about 250 miles, total area 173,356 square miles, population 6,141,571. Stockholm is the capital.

Gustav V, reigning King. For a period of union with Norway *see* Norway.

40 B.C. to 1792

B.C. 40, The mythical hero Odin said to arrive in the north, and died

His son Skiold reigns

About A.D. 1000, The Skioldungs reign till Olaf the infant is baptized, and introduces Christianity

1260, Stockholm founded

1279, Magnus Laduläs establishes a regular form of government

1319, The Crown of Sweden, which had been hereditary, is made elective; and Magnus, surnamed Smæk, or the Foolish, King of Norway, is elected

1361, Waldemar lays Gothland waste

1363, Albert of Mecklenburg reigns

1397, Treaty or union of Calmar, by which Sweden is united to Denmark and Norway, under Margaret

1476, University of Upsala founded

1520, Christian II of Denmark, "the Nero of the North," massacres the Swedish nobility

1521, The Swedes delivered from the Danish yoke by the valor of Gustavus Vasa

1523, Gustavus Vasa raised to the throne

1527, He introduces Lutheranism and religious liberty

1544, Makes the crown hereditary

1628, Gustavus Adolphus heads the Protestant cause in Germany

1648, Rugen ceded to Sweden by the Emperor

June 16, 1654, Abdication of Christina

1655, Charles X overruns Poland

1666, University of Lund founded

Charles XII, "the Madman of the North," begins his reign; he makes himself absolute; abolishes the Senate, 1699; and defeats the Russians at Narva, Nov. 30, 1700

July 8, 1709, Battle of Pultowa, where Charles is defeated by the Czar of Russia

1713, He escapes to Bender, where, after three years' protection, he is made a prisoner by the Turks

Dec. 11, 1718, He is restored; and after ruinous wars, and fighting numerous battles, is killed at the siege of Fredericshald

1719, Queen Ulrica abolishes despotism

Nov., 1719, Bremen and Verden ceded to Hanover

1741, Royal Academy founded by Linnæus

1756, Conspiracy of Counts of Brahe and Horne, who are beheaded

1770, The Hats and Caps (French and Russian parties), 1738–57; put down by Gustavus III

1772, Despotism reëstablished

——, Order of the Sword instituted

1792, Assassination of Gustavus III by Count Ankerström, at a ball, March 16; he expired March 29

1806

March 13, Gustavus IV dethroned and the government assumed by his uncle, the Duke of Sudermania (Charles XIII)

June 7, Representative constitution established

Sept. 17, Sweden cedes Finland to Russia

1810

Aug. 21, Marshal Bernadotte, the Prince of Ponte Corvo (one of Bonaparte's generals), chosen the Crown Prince of Sweden

Nov. 12, Gustavus IV arrived in London

1812

Jan. 9, Swedish Pomerania seized by Napoleon

July 12, Alliance with England

1813 to 1863

March 13, 1813, Sweden joins the Grand Alliance against Napoleon

1814, Norway is ceded to Sweden by the treaty of Kiel, Jan. 14; carried into effect, Nov.

Feb. 5, 1818, Bernadotte King, as Charles John XIV

May 19, 1826, Treaty of navigation between Great Britain and Sweden

Mar. 8, 1844, Death of Charles John; his son Oscar I, King

Nov. 21, 1855, Alliance with England and France

Oct., 1857, Banishment decreed against Catholic converts from Lutheranism

Dec. 17, 1859, Demonstration in favor of Italy

May, 1860, Increased religious toleration

June 14, 1862, Treaty of commerce with Italy, signed

April, 1863, Demonstration in favor of Poland

1864

Jan. 1, Inauguration of free trade

Jan. 22, Sweden protests against the occupation of Sleswig by the Allies

Dec., Foundation of a "National Scandinavian Society" at Stockholm to obtain by legal means a confederation of the three kingdoms for military and foreign affairs, reserving independent interior administration

Dec. 4–8, New Constitution passed by the Chambers

1866 to 1869

Feb., 1866, Commercial Treaty with France approved

Oct.–Dec., 1867, Severe famine in North Sweden

July 28, 1869, Princess Louisa was married to Frederic, Crown Prince of Denmark

1870

July 27, Prince Oscar visits England

Aug. 4, Neutrality in the Franco-Prussian war was proclaimed

Oct., Reorganization of the army proposed, Aug.; negatived

1872 to 1888

Sept. 18, 1872, Death of King Charles XV

Jan. 20, 1873, The Diet opened by King Oscar II

May 12, 1873, The King and Queen crowned

May 11, 1875, Ministry under Baron de Geer

March 19, 1884, The Crown Prince made Viceroy of Norway

Sept. 23, 1885, Nordenfelt's submarine boat exhibited in presence of officers sent by all the Great Powers

March 15, 1888, Prince Oscar married to Miss Munck at Bournemouth, England; his mother present

1892

Feb., Norway agitates for autonomy in foreign affairs; opposed by Sweden

Oct. 22 et seq., Extraordinary session of the Diet to consider the national defenses

Nov. 27, Bills for the reorganization of the army adopted by the legislature

1893 to 1897

Sept. 5–7, 1893, The 300th anniversary of the Swedish reformation celebrated at Upsala, the King present

March 1, 1894, Revision of the Constitution of the two Chambers

Dec. 5, 1895, The King receives the committee of Union, and deprecates change

Jan. 18, 1896, The King in opening parliament, maintains the union with Norway, announces a large surplus of revenue, provision for national defense proposed

Jan. 9, 1897, Karl Herman Satherberg, poet and physician, born 1812, died

1898

March 7, Report of the Swedish committee on the Union, to Parliament

Spring, Swedish Arctic (scientific) expedition, under Dr. A. G. Nathorst, to explore the regions between Spitzbergen and Franz Josef Land, starts

1900

Mid Sept., M. Boström, Premier, resigns, succeeded by Admiral von Otter

Oct. 17, Illness of the King, the Crown Prince Regent; the King resumes his office, Jan. 21, 1901

1901

Oct. 16, Dr. Otto Nordenskjöld's South Polar expedition leaves

1902

July 5, Ministry resigns; M. Boström forms one

1903

Jan. 27, The council meets; in consequence of the continued ill-health of the King, the Crown Prince assumes the regency

Aug. 17, Expedition for the relief of Dr. Nordenskjöld's South Polar expedition, under command of Capt. Glyden, of the Swedish navy, leaves Stockholm on board the *Frithjof*

1905

Jan. 18, Riksdag opened. Arbitration treaties with France, Great Britain, Belgium, Russia, and Switzerland announced to have been concluded. A Bill for extending the franchise in elections to the Second Chamber to be submitted to the Riksdag

Feb. 8, King Oscar, through illness, hands over the government to the Crown Prince

April 13, M. Boström, Premier, resigns, April 9; he is succeeded by M. Ramstedt

June 15, Marriage of Prince Gustavus Adolphus with the Princess Margaret of Connaught

June 27, In the Riksdag the government proposals for negotiations with Norway referred to a special committee

Aug. 2, Coalition ministry under M. Lundeberg formed, after the resignation of the Ramstedt administration, to carry through the negotiations for the dissolution between Sweden and Norway

Aug. 7, King Oscar, owing to the necessity for rest, hands over the government to the Crown Prince

Aug. 31–Sept. 24, Conference at Karlstad

Oct. 13, Riksdag sanctions the Karlstad agreement

Oct. 16, Bills repealing the union between Sweden and Norway passed by the Riksdag; Norway recognized as an independent state

Oct. 26, Final formalities for the dissolution of the Union between Sweden and Norway completed

Oct. 27, King Oscar addresses a letter to the Norwegian Storthing, announcing his renunciation of the throne of Norway and his recognition of Norway as a separate state

Oct. 29, Resignation of M. Lundeberg and Cabinet

Nov. 9, New liberal ministry formed by M. Staaf

1906

Jan. 5, Ministerial Council resolve that the general staffs of the army and navy be called upon to elaborate a plan for increasing the effective forces of the army and navy

Feb. 24, Count Wrangel, Swedish Minister at St. Petersburg, appointed Swedish representative in London, Feb. 21; reform Bill for the extension of the franchise, promised in the speech from the throne, brought forward by the Ministry in both houses, practically establishing universal suffrage in place of the existing restricted franchise

May 29, King Oscar having refused to dissolve the lower chamber of the Riksdag on account of the opposing votes of the two Chambers on the suffrage bill, the Ministry resigns, May 25; new Cabinet, Commodore Lindman, Premier, sworn in

May 30, Commercial treaty and tariff Convention with Germany voted in both houses by large majorities

Sept. 11, Visit of King Frederick of Denmark

Dec. 14, In consequence of King Oscar's illness, the Crown Prince assumes the regency

1907

Jan. 16, Riksdag opens with a speech from the throne by the Crown Prince, acting as Regent

Feb. 21, Death of M. Boström, chancellor of the university and formerly Premier, announced

May 13, Reform Bill, establishing universal suffrage and proportional representation, passed by both houses of the Riksdag

July 29, Anti-alcohol Congress opened in Stockholm by Prince Gustavus Adolphus

Dec. 4, The Crown Prince appointed Regent during illness of King Oscar

Dec. 8, Death of King Oscar II; the Crown Prince, on succeeding to the throne, takes the name of Gustav V

1908

March 4, Agreement with Germany establishing direct railway transport between the two countries by a combined service of powerful ferry-boats between Trelleborg and Sassnitz, ratified

April 7, The remains of Emanuel Swedenborg conveyed at night to the Swedish warship awaiting them in Dartmouth harbor

April 26–27, King Edward, Queen Alexandra and Princess Victoria pay an official visit to Stockholm

May 3, Prince William marries the Grand Duchess Marie of Russia

July 2, Treaty of friendship and commerce with China signed

July 24, Visit of President Fallières to Stockholm

Aug. 3, Visit of the German Emperor and Empress to Stockholm

Dec. 2, New commercial Treaty with France concluded

1909

Feb. 10, Both Chambers of the Riksdag pass, by large majorities, the Bill establishing universal suffrage and proportional representation

June 26–28, Visit of the Czar and Czarina to the King and Queen of Sweden

June 26, General Beckman murdered by a young man who immediately afterwards committed suicide

Aug. 2, Lock-out declared by the Masters' federation; 80,000 workmen affected

Aug. 4, General strike proclaimed by the Swedish labor federation comes into full operation; workmen on strike number 250,000, of whom 30,000 are in Stockholm; the general strike ends, Sept. 4

Oct. 23, Maritime boundary dispute with Norway settled by the Hague tribunal; the Grisbadarna islands allotted to Sweden

1910

Feb. 7, Sudden death in Brixton Prison, London, of Dr. Martin Ekenberg, the Swedish scientist, who had been committed for extradition to Sweden, on a charge of attempting murder by means of bombs sent through the post

Feb. 8, The Crown Prince appointed Regent during the illness of King Gustav

May 7–9, Visit of ex-President Roosevelt to Stockholm

June 2, The Riksdag accepted in principle Government proposal for tax on income and capital

June 7, Municipal Suffrage Bill extending the suffrage to women approved

July 4, Royal decree promulgated new customs tariff to come into effect Dec. 1, 1911

Dec. 6, Defense Committee of investigation appointed in Sept., 1907 resigned in disagreement as to estimate of defense expenditure required

Dec. 31, Census gave population as 5,522,403

1911

Jan. 17, Riksdag opened by King Gustav

March 17, Act provided for construction of a hydro-electric power station at Alkarleby

May 2, New Treaty of commerce and navigation with Germany signed

May 23, Act provided for construction of a State railroad from Veilijarvi in Lapland to Karnugi on the Swedish-Finnish frontier and from Karnugi to Matarengi

Sept. 27, Election conducted for the first time under system of proportional representation resulted in defeat of Conservatives and gains to Liberals; Liberals, 101; Social Democrats, 64; Right (Conservatives), 65

Sept. 30, Resignation of Lindman Conservative Cabinet

Oct. 7, Karl Staaf appointed Prime Minister formed Liberal Cabinet; Count Albert Ehrensvard, Minister of Foreign Affairs; Alfred Petersson, Agriculture

Oct. 19, Premier Staaf dissolved Chamber

Nov. 30, Election for Upper Chamber a gain for Liberals and Social Democrats; vote: Liberals, 51; Social Democrats, 12; Conservatives, 87

Dec. 1, Substitution of specific duties for *ad valorem* in a number of cases, a single tariff instead of maximum and minimum tariffs, and authorized the Government to retaliate for discrimination against Swedish products

———, Law provided for contribution of the State to sick funds

1912

April 2, Government introduced Bill to grant suffrage to women which was not carried

May 14, Death of Johann August Strindberg, novelist, dramatist (72)

June 29, Law as to State contributions to sick funds amended

Dec. 1, Keel for battleship laid, money raised by voluntary subscription on refusal of Government to appropriate funds

Dec. 6, Royal decree added maternity benefits to State contributions to sick funds

Dec. 23, Neutrality Agreement with Denmark and Norway signed

1913

March 13, Alteration of sugar duty passed the Riksdag

May 21, Labor Pension Bill passed

June 28, Arbitration Treaty with the United States renewed that of May 2, 1908

Dec. 30, Death of Dowager Queen Sophie, widow of Oscar II

1914

Feb. 6, Procession of 30,000 peasants arrived at Stockholm to present to the King request for provision for adequate defense of the country because of Russian military preparations

Feb. 10, Resignation of Staaf Ministry

Feb. 13, K. H. L. Hammarskjöld appointed Prime Minister, Minister of State (Premier); Foreign Affairs, K. A. Wallenberg; Justice, B. F. E. Hasselrot; Interior, H. O. F. von Sydow; Finance, A. F. Vennersten; Marine, D. Broström; Education and Ecclesiastical Affairs, K. G. Westman; Agriculture, Baron J. G. Beck-Friis; War, Col. B. B. E. Mörcke; Ministers without Portfolio, S. J. Stenberg, S. N. Linnér

Feb. 16, Cabinet announced

March 5, Riksdag dissolved to obtain popular mandate on national defense

March 27–April 7, Elections gave Conservatives 86 seats; Socialists, 73; Liberals, 71

May 23, Defense Bill introduced provided for construction of 8 battleships, 16 destroyers and other craft

June 13, Bill introduced imposed special tax on income and capital for national defense

July 3, Regulations enacted for religious instructions in schools

July 29, Peace Entente with Sweden formed, affirmed by Notes Aug. 8 declaring neutrality in World War

Aug. 4, Mobilization

Aug. 5, Moratorium established

Aug. 17, War Insurance Commission established to provide insurance for shipping

Sept. 17, National Defense Act established compulsory military service

Sept., Election for Second Chamber: Conservatives, 86; Socialists, 87; Liberals, 557; for First Chamber (Senate): Socialists, 14; Liberals, 47; Conservatives, 89

Oct. 9, Defense tax imposed, and government control over goods in time of war

Oct. 24, Army and Navy Discipline Act repealed law of 1881

Nov. 12, Norway, Sweden, and Denmark agreed on identical Notes protesting against destruction of neutral commerce and shipping to Great Britain, France, Russia, and Germany

Nov. 25, Export of gold prohibited

Dec. 18, Meeting of Kings of Sweden, Norway, and Denmark at Malmo at invitation of King Gustav agreed on joint diplomatic action during the War

Dec. 31, Census gave population as 5,679,607: 2,777,447 males; 2,902,160 females

1915

Sept. 20, Announcement of 5 leading banks that loan of 40,000,000 kroner would be granted to Germany in return for imports of coal

Sept. 23–30, Election for Second Chamber gave majority to Social Democrats

Nov. 12, Law enacted as to marriage and divorce modernized system

Nov. 29, Ordinance prohibited entrance of belligerent submarine in Swedish territorial waters except in emergency of weather in which case submarines ordered to remain on the surface and fly national flag

Dec. 15, Royal ordinance established government monopoly of tobacco

1916

Feb. 8, Law temporarily suspended free coinage of gold

March 9–11, Conference of the Kings of Norway, Denmark, and Sweden at Copenhagen agreed on mutual support of neutral rights

June 17, Workmen's Accident Insurance Act passed

July 19, Decree of Government instructed ships to fire on belligerent submarines passing through Swedish waters unless submarine complied with conditions laid down Nov. 29, 1915

Sept. 19–20, Conference of Scandinavian Kings at Christiania

Oct., Cards issued for rationing of sugar

Dec. 6, Law enacted gave insurance societies which provided for maternity benefits a State subsidy

Dec. 19, Flour rationed

1917

Jan., Bread cards first issued

Feb. 14, Scandinavian States refused to recognize the German blockade

March 1, Hammarskjold Ministry resigned

March 30, Carl Schwartz formed Moderate Conservative Cabinet; Admiral A. Lindman, Minister of Foreign Affairs

April 21, Several thousand workmen gathered before Parliament demanding that export of food stuffs cease

June 14, Laws adopted as to children born in wedlock, born out of wedlock and adopted

July 31, Socialist Conference at Stockholm

Aug. 13, Announcement that Allies would not issue passports for Socialist Conference planned to be held in Stockholm which was not held

Sept., Elections gave Conservatives, 59; Liberals, 62; Social Democrats, 86; Farmers Party, 12; and Left Socialists, 11

Oct. 2, Schwartz Ministry resigned

Oct. 19, Professor Nils Eden, Liberal, formed Liberal-Social-Democratic Cabinet: J. Hellner, Foreign Affairs; H. Branting, Finance

Nov., 56,000 workmen employed at wood cutting by the Fuel Commission to make up deficiency of fuel due to non-importation of coal and coke from England and wood cards issued to households

Nov. 28–30, Conference of Scandinavian Kings at Christiania

Dec. 25–29, Plebiscite at Aaland Islands voted for reunion with Sweden

1918

Feb., Modus vivendi with Great Britain established by which Sweden enabled to import about 75,000 tons of maize, feeding-stuffs, raw phosphate, mineral oils, and coffee

April–Nov., Rationing of wool and woolen goods begun and cotton yarn

May 29, Commercial and tonnage Treaty signed with Great Britain, France, Italy, and the United States by which Sweden enabled to import in larger quantities in return for placing a part of her commercial fleet at the disposal of the Allies

June 20, Law prohibited sailing of Swedish ships to foreign ports without a special license and Import Regulations Board constituted

June 26–28, Conference of Scandinavian Cabinet Ministers at Copenhagen

Dec. 8, Diplomatic relations with Soviet Government of Russia severed

Dec. 17, Eden program of reform adopted including provision that voting privileges should be the same for all adult males in communal elections and that the provision for forfeiture of right to vote on failure to pay taxes should be repealed, and that property qualifications for voting in general elections be abolished by the next Riksdag

1919

Jan. 25, Representatives of Russian Government expelled because of treatment of Swedes in Russia and disputes as to Swedish property in Russia

March 1, Fuel Commission dissolved and rationing ended

April 1, Import Regulation Board dissolved

May 26, Women given full suffrage by Parliament

May 26–28, Conference of Scandinavian Cabinet Ministers at Stockholm

June, International Socialist Congress at Stockholm

Aug. 1, Rationing of sugar ceased and during the month bread cards ceased

Oct. 17, Act established the eight hour day

1920

Jan. 1, New eight hour law became effective

Feb. 1–4, Conference of Scandinavian Cabinet Ministers at Christiania

March 4, Accession to membership of League of Nations voted

March 6, Eden Ministry resigned, defeated on question of communal taxes

March 9, Sweden became a member of the League of Nations

March 10, Hjalmar Branting formed new Cabinet entirely Socialists: Baron Palmstierna, Minister of Foreign Affairs; F. W. Thorssen continued as Finance Minister

March 31 and May 2, Treaty of commerce and navigation with Germany prolonged by exchange of Notes

April 17, New liberal marriage law passed by both Chambers, gave wife property rights, and secured equality for women as to divorce, divorce desired by both parties made valid by registration of both before a judge

May 1, Death of Crown Princess Margaret, wife of Prince Gustav

May 10, Exchange of Notes with Finland provided for maintenance of Russo-Swedish Declaration of July 3, 1917 as to floating timber on rivers

May 28, Law as to arbitration of labor disputes superseded that of 1906

Aug. 28–30, Conference of Scandinavian Cabinet Ministers at Copenhagen

Sept., General election a defeat for the Government

Oct. 22, Branting Ministry resigned

Oct. 29, Baron Louis de Geer formed Cabinet

1921

Feb. 23, Oskar F. von Sydow formed Cabinet succeeding the de Geer Ministry resigned

April 14, Treaty of commerce with Bulgaria signed

May 10, Commission appointed by League of Nations to decide controversy as to sovereignty over Aaland Islands

June 20, Commercial modus vivendi established with Spain

June 25, Council of League of Nations assigned Aaland Islands to Finland

Oct. 13, Hjalmar Branting succeeded von Sydow as Prime Minister and Minister of Foreign Affairs

Dec. 10, Nobel peace prize awarded to Branting

1922

March 18, Conference at Stockholm of representatives of countries neutral during the War

May 19, End of lumber mills lock out

Aug. 27, Plebiscite on prohibition; vote 930,655 against prohibition and 901,053 for it

Nov. 11 and Dec. 18, Commercial Agreement with Rumania concluded

Nov. 22, Death of Christine Nilsson, singer

Dec. 18 and 19, Provisional Commercial Agreement with the Netherlands

1923

Jan. 29, Lockout over wages in paper and pulp industry affected 30,000 workers

Feb. 13, Most favored nation commercial Agreement with Rumania concluded

April 6, Fall of Branting Ministry on question of unemployment doles

April 20, Ernest Trygger (Conservative) formed Cabinet

July 7, Trade Agreement with Estonia

Nov. 3, Marriage of Crown Prince Gustav to Lady Louise Mountbatten, great-granddaughter of Queen Victoria

1924

Feb. 17, Provisional Commercial Agreement with Lithuania concluded

March 15, Commercial Agreement with Russia signed gave *de jure* recognition of the Soviet Government

March 20, Provisional Commercial Agreement with Switzerland concluded

May 31, Treaty of friendship with Turkey signed

June 2, Treaty of conciliation with Switzerland signed

June 24, Treaty of arbitration with the United States signed

June 27, Treaty of conciliation with Norway signed and with Denmark

Aug. 29, Arbitration and Conciliation Agreement with Germany signed

Sept. 22, General election a defeat for the Government

Oct. 14, Trygger Ministry resigned

Oct. 18, Branting formed his third Ministry with Professor Osten Unden as Minister of Foreign Affairs

Oct. 20, Treaty of commerce with Denmark

Nov. 9, Arbitration Convention of Aug., 1904, with Great Britain renewed

Nov. 10, Agreement with Austria renewed Treaty of commerce and navigation of Nov. 3, 1873

Dec. 2, Treaty of commerce and navigation with Poland signed

Dec. 9, Commercial Agreement with Greece of 1852 prolonged by exchange of Notes

Dec. 22, Commercial Agreement with Latvia signed

1925

Jan. 25, Rickard Sandler appointed Prime Minister because of ill health of Branting

Feb. 24, Death of Hjalmar Branting, former Socialist Prime Minister

March 16–26, General lockout

March 28, Conciliation Convention with Latvia

April 8, Strike of seamen over control of employment exchanges

May 4, New Commercial Agreement with Spain

May 5, Death of Frederich Wilhelm Thorsson, former Cabinet Minister (60)

May 8, Ernest Wigforss appointed Minister of Finance

May 26, Army reduced to about 10,000 and military expenditure reduced

May 29, Conciliation Agreement with Estonia

June 11, Conciliation Agreement with Lithuania signed

Aug. 14, Treaty of commerce and navigation with Czechoslovakia

Oct. 23, Arbitration Convention of Oct. 26, 1905 with Norway renewed

Nov. 3, Treaty of arbitration and conciliation with Poland signed

Nov. 25, Commercial Treaty with Turkey

1926

Jan. 2, Treaty of conciliation and arbitration with Czechoslovakia

Jan. 14, Agreement for pacific settlement of disputes with Denmark

Jan. 29, Convention for pacific settlement of disputes with Finland

April 24, Death of Ellen Key, author (76)

April 29, Treaty of commerce and navigation with Greece of Oct. 27, 1852 extended

April 30, Treaty of arbitration and conciliation with Belgium

May 14, Treaty of commerce and navigation with Germany

May 15, Treaty of commerce with Turkey

May 21, Bills for workmen's insurance, sickness, and maternity benefit rejected by Riksdag

May 28, Arbitration Convention with Austria signed

June 1, Resignation of Sandler Ministry

June 7, Carl G. Ekman, Liberal, formed Cabinet: Minister of State (Premier), Carl Gustaf Ekman; Foreign Affairs, Eliel Löfgren; Justice, Johan Thyrén; Defense, Gustav Rosén; Social Affairs, Yakob Pettersson; Communications, Carl Meurling; Finance, Ernst Lyberg (Sept. 30); Education and Ecclesiastical Affairs, John Almkvist; Agriculture, Paul Hellström; Commerce, Felix Hamrin; Ministers without Portfolio, Sigurd Ribbing and Natanael Gärde

Sept. 10, Treaties of commerce with Greece and with Italy signed

Nov. 4, Marriage of the Princess Astrid, niece of the King, to Crown Prince Leopold at Stockholm

1927

Feb. 24, Commercial Agreement with Turkey

May 21, Treaty of conciliation with the Netherlands

Oct. 2, Death of Svante Arrhenius, chemist

Dec. 14, Trade Agreement with Finland signed

1928

Jan. 2, Lockout in wood pulp industry, and of miners in central district in wage dispute

March 3, Arbitration Treaty with France

April 26, Treaty of arbitration, conciliation, and judicial settlement with Spain

May 22, One day strike at Stockholm against new compulsory arbitration legislation

May 28, Revision of Commercial Agreement of May 4, 1925 with Spain

June 22, Act established Labor Court for compulsory arbitration of disputes

Aug. 9, End of strike of miners settled by compulsory arbitration

Sept. 26, Resignation of Ekman Ministry

Oct. 2, Admiral Arvid Lindman (Conservative) formed Cabinet: Minister of Foreign Affairs, Ernst Trygger; Justice, Georg Bissmark; Defense, Harald Malmberg; Social Affairs, Sven Lübeck; Communications, Theodor Borell; Finance, Adolf Dahl; Education and Ecclesiastical Affairs, Claes Lindskog; Agriculture, J. B. Johansson; Commerce, Vilhelm Lundvik; Ministers without Portfolio, August Beskow and Nils Vult von Steijern

Oct. 27, Treaty of arbitration with the United States

Nov. 8, Most favored nation commercial Agreement with Hungary

Dec. 22, Collective agreement between employers and workmen signed which affected 234,000 workers in shipyards, building trades, electric industries, paper mills, lumber industry, and iron and steel works

1929

Jan. 1, Court for Agreement established to act on cases in dispute between employers and employees

March 21, Marriage of Crown Prince Olaf of Norway to Princess Martha, niece of King Gustav

May 10, Most favored nation Treaty of commerce with Persia

May 12, Plebiscite defeated proposed legislation for local option on sale of hard liquor

June 7, Finance Minister Wohlin dismissed, charged with irregularities in connection with recent bank failures

——, Passports abolished in relations with Denmark, Finland, and Norway

Sept. 11, Treaty of commerce with Turkey

Nov. 7, Strike of saw mill workers for increase of wages averted by arbitration

Nov. 30, Treaty of commerce with Germany

1930

March 6, Communist uprising in capital

March 8, Both Houses rejected proposal of Government for increased protection for beet sugar

March 16, Recommendation of Commission that tithes be abolished and clergy be placed on State pay roll on a par with civil servants

April 4, Death of Queen Victoria in Rome

June 2, Resignation of Lindman Ministry, defeated on proposal for increased agricultural imports duties

June 7, Karl Gustav Ekman, leader of the People's Party formed Cabinet: Prime Minister and Minister of Defense, C. G. Ekman; Foreign Affairs, S. G. F. Ramel; Justice, J. N. Garde; Social Affairs, A. S. E. Larsso; Communications, O. Jeppsson; Finance, F. T. Hamrin; Education and Ecclesiastical Affairs, N. S. Stadener; Agriculture, B. H. von Stockenström; Commerce, D. Hansen; Ministers without Portfolio, R. H. F. Gyllensward, A. E. V. Holmback, and A. W. Rundqvist (December 12, 1930)

June 27, Treaty of friendship and arbitration with Norway, Denmark, Finland, and Iceland

Aug. 6, Norwegian scientific expedition headed by Dr. Gunnar Horn found bodies of Salomon Auguste Andree, Swedish balloonist and explorer, and Nils Strindberg on White Island (Hvitvoen) who perished in attempt to fly across the North Pole in 1897

Sept. 15, Death of Victor Nielsen, aviator

Nov. 27, Nobel peace prize awarded to Nathan Soederblom, Archbishop of Upsala and Primate of Sweden

Dec. 5, National Socialist Party (Fascist) held first meeting

KINGS OF SWEDEN (previously Kings of Upsal)

1001. Olaf Schotkonung is styled King, 1015
1026. Edmund Colbrenner
1051. Edmund Slemme
1056. Stenkill
1066. Halstan
1090. Ingo I, the Good
1112. Philip
1118. Ingo II
1129. Swerker or Suerche I
1155. St. Eric IX
1161. Charles VII; made prisoner by his successor
1167. Canute, son of Eric I

1199. Swerker or Suerche II; killed in battle
1210. Eric X
1216. John I
1222. Eric XI, the Stammerer
1250. Birger Jarl, Regent
——. Waldemar I
1275. Magnus I Ladulæs
1290. Birger II
1319. Magnus II Smæk; dethroned
1350. Eric XII
1359. Magnus restored; deposed 1363
1363. Albert of Mecklenburg: his tyranny causes a revolt of his subjects, who invite Margaret of Denmark to the throne
1389. Margaret, Queen of Sweden and Norway, now also of Denmark, and Eric XIII
1397. [Union of Calmar, by which the three kingdoms are united under one sovereign]
1412. Eric XIII governs alone; deposed
1440. Christopher III
1448. Charles VIII Canuteson, King of Sweden only
1457. Christian
1471. [Interregnum] Sten Sture, Protector
1483. John II (I of Denmark)
1502. [Interregnum]
1503. Swante Sture, Protector
1512. Sten Sture, Protector
1520. Christiern, or Christian II, of Denmark, styled the "Nero of the North"; deposed for his cruelties
1523. Gustavus I Vasa; by whose valor the Swedes are delivered from the Danish yoke
1560. Eric XIV, son; dethroned and slain by
1569. John III, brother, deposed; died 1577
1592. Sigismund, King of Poland, son; disputes for the succession continued the whole of this reign
1604. Charles IX, brother of John III
1611. Gustavus II Adolphus, the Great, son; fell at the battle of Lutzen, Nov. 16, 1632
1633. Christina, daughter of Gustavus. Resigned the crown to her cousin, June 16, 1654; died at Rome in 1689
1654. Charles X Gustavus, son of John Casimir, Count Palatine of the Rhine
1660. Charles XI, son; the arts and sciences flourished in this reign
1697. Charles XII, son; styled the "Alexander" and the "Madman of the North"; killed at Frederickshall, Dec. 11, 1718
1718. Ulrica Eleanora, sister, and her consort, Frederick I, Landgrave of Hesse Cassel. Ulrica relinquishes the crown, and in
1741. Frederick reigned alone
1751. Adolphus Frederick of Holstein Gottorp, descended from the family of Vasa
1771. Gustavus III Adolphus, son; assassinated by Count Ankarström at a masked ball, March 16; died March 29, 1792
1792. Gustavus IV Adolphus, son; dethroned and the government assumed by his uncle, the Duke of Sudermania
1809. Charles XIII, Duke of Sudermania
[Treaty of Kiel (1814), by which Norway falls under the sovereignty of Sweden]
1818. Charles (John) XIV Bernadotte, the French Prince of Ponte Corvo; died March 8, 1844
1844. Oscar I, son; born July 4, 1799; died July 8, 1859
1859. Charles XV, son; born May 3, 1826; died Sept. 18, 1872; a poet; brave and impulsive; much beloved

1872. Oscar II, brother; born Jan. 21, 1829; married Princess Sophia of Nassau, June 6, 1857

1907, Gustav V, son, born June 16, 1858. Succeeded to the throne on the death of his father, Oscar II, December 8, 1907. Married, Sept. 20, 1881, to Princess Victoria, born August 7, 1862, died April 4, 1930, daughter of Friedrich, Grand Duke of Baden

SWITZERLAND

Switzerland, republic of south-central Europe, bounded on the north by Germany, on the east by Austria and Liechtenstein, south-east and south by Italy, and south-west, west, and north-west by France, mountainous country with average elevation greater than any other country in Europe, and containing the three river valleys of the Rhone, Rhine, and Aar. The total area is 15,940 square miles, and total population, 4,066,400. Bern is the capital.

Switzerland was in ancient times inhabited by the Helvetii. The country was colonized by the Romans after Cæsar's victory over the Helvetii in their invasion of Gaul, 58 B.C., and the people were gradually combined with the Romans and partook of the fortunes of their empire. The canton Schweitz has given name to the whole confederacy.

Dr. Jean Musy, President of the Confederation.

SWISS CONFEDERATION OF 1815

Uri, 1307	first con-	Schaffhausen
Schweitz	federa-	Appenzell
Unterwalden	tion.	St. Gall
Zurich		Glaris
Berne		Zug
Lucerne		Freiburg
Solothurn		Tessins
Basle		Pays de Vaud
Grisons		Valais
Aargau		Neufchatel
Thurgau		Geneva

909 to 1802

909, Helvetia ravaged by the Huns
1032, Becomes subject to Germany
1179, Friburg built by Berthold IV
1191, Berne built
1291, Aug. 1, The men of Uri, Unterwalden, and Schwytz made a solemn defensive league and covenant forever against the Austrians; this is regarded as the foundation of the Swiss Confederation; said to have been confirmed Nov. 17, 1307, by the leaders, Werner Stauffacher (of Schwytz), Walter Fürst (Uri), and Arnold von Melchthal (Unterwalden), determined to free their country from a foreign yoke
1306, Tyranny of Gesler, heroism of William Tell, and revolt (demonstrated to be mythical), dated
Nov. 4, 1307, Confederation against Austria; declaration of Swiss independence
1315, Form of government made perpetual
Nov. 15, Leopold of Austria defeated at Morgarten
1332, Lucerne joins the confederacy

1350, The canton of Zurich joins and becomes head of the league
1351, Berne, Glaris, and Zug join
1353, 8 cantons form a perpetual league
July 9, 1386, Leopold II of Austria defeated and slain at Sempach
1389, The Austrians defeated at Näfels, April 9, 1388; make peace
1396 to 1419, The Grisons league. Caddee, or League of God's House, the league of independence in Switzerland, formed by the Grisons to resist domestic tyranny
1424, Second league of the Grisons
1436, The third league of the Grisons
Aug. 26, 1444, Battle of St. Jacobs on the Birs, near Basle (1,600 Swiss resist 30,000 French, and are all killed, the enemy losing 10,000)
1476, The Swiss defeat Charles the Bold at Granson, March 5; and at Morat, June 22
Jan. 5, 1477, And aid the Duke of Lorraine at Nancy, where Charles is slain
1480, Swiss soldiers first enter into the pay of France, under Louis XI
1481, Fribourg and Soleure join; confederation formed
1499, Maximilian I, Emperor, acknowledges Swiss independence
1501, Schaffhausen and Basle join the union
1513, Confederation of 13 cantons
June 6, The Swiss invade Milan and defeat the French at Novara
Sept. 13, 14, 1515, Defeated by them at Marignano
1516, The Swiss Confederacy acknowledged by France and other powers
1519, The Reformation begins at Basle; the bishop compelled to retire
Oct. 12, 1531, The Reformation adopted by some cantons; battle of Cappel, Zwingli killed and reformers defeated
1544, The Grison leagues join the Swiss Confederacy as allies
1597, Appenzel joins the other cantons
1602, Charles Emanuel of Savoy attempts Geneva by surprise, scales the walls, and penetrates the town, but in the end is defeated
[This circumstance gave rise to an annual festival commemorative of their escape from tyranny]
1648, Independence of Switzerland recognized by the Treaty of Westphalia
Aug., 1712, Peace of Aargau, end of religious war
[From this period until the French revolution the cantons enjoyed tranquillity, disturbed only by the changes arising out of their various constitutions]
May 25, 1777, Alliance with France
1781, Strife in Geneva, between the aristocratic and democratic parties; France interferes
1782, 1,000 fugitive Genevese seek an asylum in Ireland
1792, Swiss Guards ordered to quit France
1798, Helvetic confederation dissolved; its subjugation by France
——, Helvetian republic formed
1799–1802, Switzerland the seat of war

1802

May 12, The number of cantons increased to 19; the federal government restored; and a landamman appointed by France
July 13, Uri, Schweitz, and Underwald separate from the republic

1811 to 1844

Aug. 24, 1811, Switzerland joins France with 6,000 men

1814, The Allies entered Switzerland in the spring

1815, The number of cantons increased to 22, and the independence and neutrality of Switzerland secured by the Treaty of Vienna

1830, Law to make education independent of the clergy

1839, Revision of the constitution of the cantons

1840–44, Leads to dissensions between the Catholics and Protestants

1846

Dispute about the convents of Aargau, 1844; to put education into the hands of the Jesuits, &c.; opposition of the protestant cantons

Lucerne, Uri, Schweitz, Unterwalden, Freiburg, Zug, and Valais (Roman Catholic cantons), form a separate league (Sonderbund) to support education by the Jesuits, &c.

Oct. 7, Insurrection at Geneva against Jesuit teaching; a temporary provisional government established

1847

July 20, The Diet declares the Sonderbund illegal, and dissolves it; the seven cantons protest, July 22; the Diet orders the expulsion of the Jesuits, Sept. 3; communal assemblies held to resist it, Sept. 26, Oct. 3, 10; appeal to arms, Oct. 21

Nov. 29, The Diet prepares to repress the Sonderbund, Nov. 4; Friburg surrenders, Nov. 14; civil war; the Sonderbund defeated by Gen. H. Dufour, near Lucerne, Nov. 23; end of the Sonderbund; it submits to the expulsion of the Jesuits, and the secularization of monastic property

1848 to 1857

Sept. 12, 1848, New federal constitution

June 11, 1857, Dispute about Neufchâtel. War threatened by the King of Prussia, and great energy and determination manifested by the Swiss. On the intervention of the English and French Governments, a treaty was signed by which the King of Prussia virtually renounced his claims, on receiving a pecuniary compensation, which he eventually gave up. He retains the title of Prince of Neufchâtel, without any political rights

1859

March 14, Declaration of neutrality in the coming Italian war

July and Aug., Mutiny and punishment of the Swiss mercenary troops at Naples; the Confederation forbid foreign enlistment

1860

March 15, Swiss Government protests against the annexation of Savoy to France

March 30, 150 Swiss attempt to enter Savoy; stopped by Genevese Government

July 30, The Government forbid the Swiss to enlist in foreign service without permission

July, Proposed European congress to preserve Swiss neutrality put off

1861

May 3, Glarus destroyed by fire

Nov. 5, French troops occupy Vallée des Dappes, Oct. 28; the Swiss announce the violation of their territory

1862 to 1869

Dec. 8, 1862, Treaty of France settles the question of the Vallée des Dappes by mutual cession of territory; no military works to be constructed on territory ceded; signed

Oct. 23, 1865, Revision of the constitution; deliberations begin

Jan. 14, 1866, Nearly all the revised articles of the federal constitution rejected by the vote of the Swiss burgesses

Sept. 9–12, 1867, International peace and liberty congress, at Geneva; at Berne, Sept. 22–26, 1868

April 18, 1869, New constitution adopted by Zurich

1871

Feb. 1, The French army under Clinchant (84,000), crosses the frontiers and is disarmed

Mar. 9–12, The French soldiers interned at Zurich, and oppose German demonstrations

Nov. 6, Extraordinary session of the federal assembly to revise the constitution

1872

May 12, Plebiscite respecting a new constitution, reorganizing the army, and promoting uniform education, &c., rejected by majority of 4,967 out of 509,921

Aug. 8, M. Favre engaged to construct a tunnel through St. Gothard in 8 years, for 2,000,000*l.*

1873

Jan. 16, The papal nuncio, Mermillod, expelled

1874

April 19, Revised federal constitution voted (321,870 for, 177,800 against)

June, Swiss National Catholic Church constituted

Sept. 5, 19 Catholic priests deprived for refusal to take constitutional oath

Oct. 9, International postal congress at Berne, Sept. 15; protocol signed

1875 to 1888

May 23, 1875, Civil marriage law and registration adopted by universal suffrage (212,854–204,700)

March 16, 1878, Continued deficit in revenue, announced

Nov. 6, 1878, Death of James Fazy, eminent statesman

Jan. 19, 1879, National voting for St. Gothard, railway and tunnel (161,000 majority)

May 20, 21, 1882, Opening of St. Gothard railway from Milan to Lucerne

Jan. *et seq.*, 1884, Invasion of the salvation army, autumn, 1883, much resisted at Berne, Geneva, &c.

April 7, 1884, The watch-tool making village, Vallorbes, almost destroyed by fire

April 23, 1885, Village of Mulligan, Aargau, destroyed by fire

July 5, 1886, Fifth centenary of the battle of Sempach (July 9, 1386), celebrated

Dec. 13, 1888, Mr. Hertenstein, the President at Berne, died after a surgical operation, Nov. 30; Vice-President Bernard Hammer elected President

1889

June, The German Government protests against the expulsion of its police officer, Wohlgemuth, from Switzerland, May; the great Powers protest against the asylum given to political criminals; the Swiss propose new legal measures, June; the Swiss Government repels the charge, but prepares legal measures for redress

July 14, The Swiss Government in a reply note to Berlin, stands firm

July 23, Loan for 25,000,000 francs, to supply new arms for the federal troops, subscribed for by Berne alone, reported

1890

Sept. 12–14, Insurrection at Ticino

1891

Oct. 25, Meiringen, canton of Berne, totally burnt; 2 deaths, about 2,000 persons homeless

Dec. 7, Bill for giving effect to the popular vote of July, affirming the right of the people to take the initiative in constitutional reforms, considered by the national council

1892

Jan. 28, The commercial treaties with Germany and Austria-Hungary adopted by the states council

1893

Jan. 1, Rejection of the Franco-Swiss convention by France; duties on French goods increased

Oct. 29, Extreme socialists defeated in elections

Dec. 21, A state loan of 20,000,000f. authorized

1894

Oct. 30, Decree for a referendum respecting representation of Switzerland abroad

1895

June 25, A Frano-Swiss liberal commercial agreement signed

July 18, Carl Schenk, 6 times president of the confederation, death by an accident

1896

Aug. 11, Railway traffic suspended through floods

1898

July, Traveling from Basle to London (595 miles) accomplished in 14 hrs., 35 mins.

Sept., Expulsion of anarchists

Nov., Unification of civil and penal codes accepted by a referendum

Dec. 31, Switzerland admitted by America as a favored nation

1899

Feb. 24, M. Welti (6 times President) died, aged 73

April 3, M. Guyer-Zeller, banker, died

1900

Nov. 4, The "double initiative," viz., the election by proportional representation of members of the national council and the election of the federal council by the people, rejected by the nation

1902

April 1, New palace of the Swiss parliament begun, 1894; opened

June 7, Museum of war and peace founded by the late M. de Bloch at Lucerne, opened

July 30, Rupture with Italy (see s.v.), April 10; relations resumed

Aug. 26, The King of Italy received by the President at Göschenen

Aug., Dr. Largin, chief judge of the Berne court, killed on the Nadelhorn, about Aug. 15; many fatal Alpine accidents, reported

Dec. 24, Bomb explosion at entrance to Geneva Cathedral, Machetto, an Italian, arrested

1903

Mid. Sept., Swiss Government give one year's notice to terminate the commercial treaty, dated April 19, 1892, between Switzerland and Italy, but is prepared to negotiate a new treaty

Early Oct., Subvention for construction of the projected Jura tunnel for a line between Soleure and Münster agreed to by grand council of Berne; also agreement between federal council and the Simplon tunnel company

Dec. 16, M. Comtesse, radical, elected President

1904

July 14, Death of ex-President Krüger at Clarens

Dec. 14, M. Ruchet elected President for 1905

1905

Jan. 2–3, Intense cold throughout Switzerland, 20° below 0° cent. The lowest readings marked since records were first kept; Rhone frozen over, stopping electric generating station at St. Maurice

Feb. 24, Simplon tunnel pierced

June, Arbitration treaties with Great Britain, Belgium, Italy, Austria-Hungary, France, Sweden, and Norway, ratified by the federal council

1906

May 19, Simplon tunnel opened by the King of Italy and the President of the Republic

June 15, Arrest of 60 Russian students of both sexes, chiefly anarchists

Aug. 18, New mountain electric line, from Yevnayaz to Chatelard and Chamonix, opened

Oct. 20, Franco-Swiss commercial treaty, signed

1907

Feb. 18, Count Julius Bylandt, of The Hague, killed on the Cresta ice toboggan run, owing to a plank being left on the course

Mar. 25, Strike disturbances at Vevey; workmen maltreated

April 2, Strike ended; men resume work

April 12, New army bill, making important changes in the organization and training of the federal army, passed in both houses of the federal assembly at Berne, by overwhelming majorities

Sept. 8, British military commission, to study the Swiss army system, arrives at Basel

H. Ernest Brenner elected President for 1908

1908

April 7, The Swiss national council decides to prohibit completely the sale and manufacture of absinthe on Swiss territory

Dec. 17, Dr. Deucher elected President of the Swiss Confederation for 1909

1909

July 2, The 400th anniversary of the birth of Calvin; celebrations begun at Geneva

Dec., M. Comtesse elected President for 1910

1910

Jan. 1–Dec. 31, Robert Comtesse, President, Marc Emile Ruchet, Vice-President

Jan. 25, Law promulgated reorganized the Federal Military Department

June 15, Serious floods begun lasting through the month and amounting to a national disaster, the amount of water unprecedented since 1867

July 24, Airship passenger service inaugurated at Lucerne

Oct. 23, The question of proportional representation defeated by vote of 262,066 to 238,928

Dec. 1, Census of population gave 3,741,971 inhabitants, of whom 552,011 were foreigners, 219,530 Germans, 63,695 French, 202,809 Italians, 4,118 English, 37,641 Austrians, 2,363 Hungarians, and 8,457 Russians

1911

Jan. 1–Dec. 31, Marc Emile Ruchet, President, Louis Forrer, Vice-President

March 31, The piercing of the Loetschberg tunnel completed between Kandersteg and the Rhone Valley

June 13, Bill for compulsory insurance against sickness and accident passed both Houses; referendum vote provided for

Oct. 29, Election for National Council gave Radicals 113 of 189 seats

1912

Jan. 1–Dec. 31, Dr. Louis Forrer, President, E. Müller, Vice-President

Jan. 1, New Civil Code superseding 25 cantonal codes came into effect

Feb. 4, Referendum vote by which the Compulsory Insurance Bill of June, 1911 ratified by vote of 285,037 against 238,694

Sept. 3–7, Visit of the Emperor of Germany to Zurich and Berne

1913

Jan. 1–Dec. 31, E. Müller, President, Dr. A. Hoffmann, Vice-President

April 4, St. Gotthard Agreement with Italy of Oct. 13, 1909 ratified by the National Council

May 4, Constitutional Amendment passed gave Government authority to take measures as to infectious diseases

May 14, Oskar Bidar made airplane flight over Bernese Alps from Berne to Sion in 1 hour and 44 minutes

June 28, Formal opening of the Loetschberg tunnel

Nov. 3, Treaty of arbitration with the United States extended that of Feb. 29, 1908

1914

Jan. 1–Dec. 31, Dr. A. Hoffmann, President, Giuseppe Motta, Vice-President

May 15, National Exhibition opened at Berne

June 10, Arbitration Convention with Great Britain of Nov. 16, 1904 renewed

June 18, Factory law enacted

July 7, Visit of the King of Belgium

Aug. 1, Mobilization ordered

Aug. 2, Export of food stuffs, hay, fodder, &c., prohibited

Aug. 3, Parliament gave executive unlimited powers

——, Colonel Ulrich Wille named commander-in-chief and Colonel Sprecher von Bernegg as chief of the General Staff

Aug. 4, Neutrality in World War proclaimed and Note to Germany declared that any attempt to violate neutrality would be repelled by armed force

Aug. 27, The grinding of "full flour" sanctioned

1915

Jan. 1–Dec. 31, G. Motta, President, C. Decoppet, Vice-President

Jan. 9, Provisional monopoly of corn ordered and the entire harvest requisitioned

April 15, War tax placed on all fortunes over £400 and incomes over £100 voted and carried by referendum vote, June 6

April 25, Treaty of arbitration with Italy signed

May 5, Economic Agreement with Italy

June 28, Flour sent to suffering population of Luxemburg

Sept. 22, Society to regulate imports established by the Federal Council

Sept. 25, The Government issued circular warning against undesirable immigration

Oct. 11, The *Societe suisse de Surveillance economique* founded to regulate the circulation and employment of goods in the interest of the Entente Powers and another organization the *Treuhandstelle* for commerce with the Central Powers

1916

Jan. 1–Dec. 31, Camille Decoppet, President, Edmund Schulthess, Vice-President

Jan. 15, Colonels Egli and von Wattenwyl arrested charged with violation of Swiss neutrality by communications to German and Austrian military attaches. Acquitted Feb. 29

Feb. 21, Arrangement made as to exchange of severely wounded German and French prisoners passing through Switzerland

Sept. 2, Economic Agreement by which Germany to release 253,000 tons of coal and iron and steel required in exchange for milk, meat, &c.

Dec. 23, Note of Federal Council to belligerents' proposals for peace

1917

Jan. 1–Dec. 31, Edmund Schulthess, President, F. L. Calonder, Vice-President

Feb. 12, Two meatless days a week ordered and sale of fresh baked bread prohibited

March 1, Cards issued for rationing of rice and sugar

March 7, Decree prohibited purchase of supply of provisions sufficient for more than 3 months

April, Maximum price for a liter of milk (1¾ pint) fixed at 33 centimes (about 7 cents)

April 14, Declaration of neutrality in war between Germany and the United States

May 13, Constitutional amendment provided for introduction of stamp tax on securities

Aug., Central Bureau for supply of milk established

Aug. 10, Central Bureau for the provision of bread established

Aug. 20, Agreement with Germany by which 200,000 tons of coal to be exported and 19,000 tons of iron and steel per month

Aug. 30, Agreement with France and Italy for export of wood from Switzerland

Sept. 29, Economic Agreement with France

Dec. 5, Agreement with the United States by which the United States to supply 240,000 tons of breadstuffs until the next harvest

1918

Jan. 1–Dec. 31, Felix L. Calonder, President, Dr. Edward Müller, Vice-President

Jan. 1, The daily allowance of bread per person $^3/_5$ of a liter

Jan., A Central Bureau for Fat established to ensure provisioning for food

March 1, Train service reduced by one-third

——, Fat and butter cards issued, 12 ounces of fat and about 5 ounces of butter a month per person

March 20, Economic Agreement with Great Britain

April 24, Agreement with Germany that free passage be given for cargoes bound for Switzerland

May 15, New Economic Agreement with Germany

June 2, Referendum vote rejected permanent income tax

July 12, Decree authorized cantons to take special measures to prevent political meetings

July 19, New Economic Agreement with France

Aug. 1, Swiss Financial Association established at Lucerne to execute financial arrangements

Sept. 13, Swiss Provision Department established

Oct. 13, Referendum vote adopted proportional representation in election of National Council

Nov., State railroads raised tariff for goods by about 80%

Nov. 12, General strike of revolutionary Socialists which broke down after 48 hours and the 48 signers of the "Olten Appeal" arrested

Dec. 1, Passenger travel on steam railroads prohibited on Sundays and holidays

Dec. 4, 10 trucks of flour and 9 of rice sent to Innsbruck to relieve starving Austrians

Dec. 8, Diplomatic relations with Russia severed

1919

Jan. 1–Dec. 31, Gustav Ador, President, G. Motta, Vice-President

Jan. 22, Economic Agreement with the United States

Feb. 2–9, International Socialist Conference at Berne

Feb. 15, Decree required land owners and renters to cultivate additional land in order to increase the production of food stuffs

March 20, Credit arrangement with Great Britain

March 24, Arrival of ex-Emperor Charles of Austria with his family to take up residence

March 25, New Agreement with France signed as to supply of coal and facilities for the transportation of goods, Switzerland to deliver cattle for breeding, chocolate, watches, embroideries. &c., and new credits arranged

April 11, Announcement that Geneva had been decided on as seat of League of Nations

April 28, The "black lists" were abolished and certificates of nationality and limitation of imports

May 4, Referendum vote approved renewal of war tax to provide for payment of war debt

May 11, Plebiscite in Voralberg voted for union with Switzerland, 45,000 for and 11,000 against

May 27, Law decreed that census should be taken July 1 of land cultivated and crops of vegetables and cereals

June 3, Bolshevik riots in Zurich

June 27, Forty-eight hour week established for factory workers

June 28, Treaty of Versailles recognized the neutrality of Switzerland

July 19, New Agreement with France by which Switzerland received a credit of about £1,250,000

Oct. 26, Election for the National Council reduced Radical majority from 102 to 60 in Assembly of 189 members

Oct. 29, Decree as to unemployment insurance replaced previous laws

Nov., Treaty with Italy provided for imports of oil cakes and hay in return for breeding cattle

Nov. 19, Resolution of Parliament in favor of joining the League of Nations

1920

Jan. 1–Dec. 31, Giuseppe Motta, President, E. Schulthess, Vice-President

Jan., Eight hour day adopted in factories

Feb. 13, Council of the League of Nations adopted a resolution recognizing the perpetual neutrality of Switzerland and guaranteeing the inviolability of her territory

March 5, Resolution recommending accession to League of Nations adopted subject to ratification by plebiscite

March 6, Commercial Agreement with Czechoslovakia signed

March 8, Switzerland became a member of the League of Nations

March 21, Referendum vote resulted in favor of abolition of gambling

April 8, Act regulated work on railroads, 8 hour day average over 14 day period

May 16, Referendum vote on accession to the League of Nations resulted in favor by vote of 415,819 to 323,225 against

Oct. 8, Resolution adopted established Federal Labor Office

Nov. 10, Treaties with Liechtenstein as to posts, telegraph, and telephone

Dec. 1, Census gave population as 3,880,320, number of foreign residents 402,385

1921

Jan. 1–Dec. 31, E. Schulthess, President, R. Haab, Vice-President

Jan. 8, New Tariff Act

Feb. 12, The Government refused request of French Government of Dec. 21, 1920 to allow international troops passage through Switzerland en route to Vilna

Aug. 7, Convention with France as to free tariff zones (Savoy) by which the customs line to be retired to the political frontier in return for certain economic advantages

Dec. 3, Treaty of arbitration with Germany signed

Dec. 10, Nobel peace prize awarded to Christian Large, Secretary General of the Inter-Parliamentary Bureau

Dec. 19, Provisional Customs Agreement with Italy signed

1922

Jan. 1–Dec. 31, Dr. Robert Haab, President, Charles Scheurer, Vice-President

Feb. 28, The number of unemployed reached a maximum of 146,302

March 17, Death of Heinrich Sutter, mathematician

March 18, Representatives from Switzerland attended the Stockholm Conference

May 11, New Commercial Agreement with Spain signed

June 26, Commercial Agreement with Poland signed
Sept. 24, Referendum vote rejected Lex Haberlin or Bill against revolutionary tendencies
Sept. 27, Death of Philippe Godet, historian
Dec. 3, Referendum vote rejected, Federal capital levy proposed
Dec. 25, Death of Emil Frey, former President

1923

Jan. 1–Dec. 31, Charles Scheurer, President, Ernest Chuard, Vice-President
Jan. 23, Number of unemployed about 100,000
Jan. 27, Provisional Commercial Agreement with Italy signed
Feb. 13, Commercial Agreement with Rumania signed
Feb. 18, Convention of 1921 with France for abolition of the Savoy economic zones rejected by popular plebiscite
March 29, Customs Union with Liechtenstein
——, 500,000 francs appropriated by the Government to aid unemployed workmen to emigrate to Canada
May 10, V. V. Vorovsky, official Russian representative at Lausanne Conference, assassinated by Maurice Conradi, who had lived in Russia and suffered at hands of the Soviet régime
June 3, Proposal to give the State a monopoly of alcoholic liquor rejected by popular vote of 452,772 to 259,741
July 1, Boycott of Swiss goods by Russia because of Vorovsky murder
Oct. 10, Death of Paul Robert, painter
Oct. 12, Note from French Government announced that French customs line would be established at Swiss frontier, Nov. 20
Nov. 5, Trial of Conradi and of M. Polunin as accomplice for the murder of Vorovsky resulted in acquittal, Nov. 16
Nov. 10, French customs line transferred to political frontier eliminating the free zone of Upper Savoy

1924

Jan. 1–Dec. 31, Dr. Ernest Chuard, President, Dr. Jean M. Musy, Vice-President
Feb. 15, Death of Heinrich Kundert, president of the national bank (69)
Feb. 17, Plebiscite on increase of working hours from 48 to 52 hours a week defeated by majority of 116,000 votes
June 2, Conciliation Treaty with Sweden signed
June 6, Conciliation Treaty with Denmark signed
June 18, Treaties of conciliation and arbitration with Hungary signed
Aug. 5, Police of Schaffhausen dispersed Communist mob attacking police station
Aug. 22, Tariff Agreement concluded with Bulgaria
Sept. 20, Treaty of friendship, conciliation, and compulsory arbitration with Italy
Oct. 11, Arbitration Treaty with Austria signed
Oct. 23, Arbitration Treaty with Brazil signed
Oct. 30, Arbitration Agreement with France signed a compromise as to Savoy zones
Nov. 19, Treaty with Austria provided for straightening the Rhine River
Nov. 7, Arbitration Treaty with Argentina signed
Dec. 4, Commercial Agreement with Latvia signed
Dec. 26, Arbitration Treaty with Japan signed
Dec. 29, Death of Carl F. G. Spitteler, poet

1925

Jan. 1–Dec. 31, Dr. Jean M. Musy, President, Heinrich Haeberlin, Vice-President
Feb. 13, Treaty of conciliation and arbitration with Belgium
March 7, Treaty of conciliation and arbitration with Poland
March 18, National Council accepted proposal to refer dispute as to free zones to arbitration
April 6, Treaty of arbitration and conciliation with France
Aug. 21, Treaty of conciliation with Norway
Sept. 19, Treaty of friendship with Turkey
Sept. 21, Treaty of conciliation and judicial settlement of disputes with Greece
Oct. 14, Commercial Agreement with Estonia
Oct. 24–25, Elections for Parliament returned 59 Radicals, 42 Catholics, 49 Social Democrats, 31 Agrarians, 7 Liberal Conservatives, 10 minor parties
Dec. 6, Constitutional amendment adopting principle of old age insurance ratified by popular vote
Dec. 7, Celebration of 400th anniversary of Treaty of alliance and mutual citizenship of cities of Berne, Freiburg, and Lausanne
Dec. 12, Treaty of conciliation with the Netherlands
Dec. 17, National Council reëlected and President and Vice-President

1926

Jan. 1–Dec. 31, Heinrich Haeberlin, President, and G. Motta, Vice-President
Jan. 6, Commercial Treaty with Austria signed
Jan. 9, Judicial Convention with Spain signed
Feb. 3, Treaty of arbitration and conciliation with Rumania signed
April 17, Provisional Commercial Agreement with Turkey
April 20, Treaty of conciliation and judicial settlement of disputes with Spain concluded
May 18, Customs Convention with Austria
July 14, Treaty of commerce with Germany signed
Nov. 29, Provisional Commercial Agreement with Greece signed
Dec. 8, New article of Constitution intended to create a corn monopoly rejected by popular vote

1927

Jan. 1–Dec. 31, Giuseppe Motta, President, Edmund Schulthess, Vice-President
Jan. 24, Russia declined invitation to economic conference at Geneva on account of murder of Vorovski on Swiss territory in 1923
Feb. 5, Treaty of arbitration and conciliation with Belgium
Feb. 16, Commercial Treaty with Czechoslovakia
March 2, Commercial Treaty with Finland
April 15, Agreement with Russia signed adjusted controversy over assassination of Vorovski
May 4, Treaty of commerce with Turkey
May 15, Automobile Act rejected by popular vote
June 13, New military code of penal law adopted replacing that of 1851
June 24, Provisional Commercial Treaty with Finland signed
June 30, Act codified existing laws respecting federal employees; strikes prohibited
July 5, Commercial Agreement with Poland signed

Sept. 30, Constitutional amendment allowed acquisition of Swiss citizenship

Nov. 16, Treaty of conciliation and judicial settlement with Finland

Dec. 24, Government refused request of Soviet Government of Russia to establish a permanent official bureau in Geneva to keep in touch with work of the League of Nations

1928

Jan. 1–Dec. 31, Edmund Schulthess, President, Dr. Robert Haab, Vice-President

Jan. 1, New military penal code came into effect

Jan. 21, Commercial Treaty with France signed

March 31, Death of Gustav Ador, former President

June 9, Provisional Commercial Agreement with Egypt

June 30, Resolution of the Federal Council fixed termination of corn monopoly for this date

Aug. 18, Legal Convention with Poland signed

Aug. 29, Protocol with Germany signed modified Treaty of arbitration and conciliation

Sept. 9, Demonstration of Peasants Party at Berne in agrarian crisis

Sept. 24, Federal Council refused to grant request of Swiss women for right of suffrage

Oct. 24, Frontier Traffic Agreement with Italy signed

Oct. 27–28, Elections for Federal Assembly returned 58 Radicals, 46 Catholics, 50 Social Democrats, 31 Agrarians, 6 Liberal Conservatives, other parties 7

Dec. 5, Convention of arbitration with Spain

Dec. 11, Treaty of arbitration and conciliation with Turkey signed

Dec. 31, Commercial *modus vivendi* with Spain signed

1929

Jan. 1–Dec. 31, Robert Haab, President, Charles Scheurer, Vice-President

March 24, Anti-Fascist riots by Communists at Basle

March 28, Agreement with Germany signed for regulation of the Rhine between Strassburg and Istein

June 20, Most favored nation Commercial Agreement with Albania signed

July 8, Commercial Agreement with France signed

Aug. 19, Order of the Permanent Court of International Justice fixed May 1, 1930 as date of expiration of period within which France and Switzerland might settle between themselves the régime of free zones

Aug. 26, Commercial Agreement with Belgium signed

Sept. 20, Treaty of friendship and arbitration with Czechoslovakia signed

1930

Jan. 1–Dec. 31, Jean Marie Musy, President, Dr. H. Haeberlin, Vice-President

April 6, Prohibition referendum placed heavy tax on all alcohol, brandies, and similar liquors, with the exception that the people have the right to distil their own liquor solely for their own consumption without taxation. Neither light wines nor beer taxed or interfered with. The vote stood 487,340 to 314,316

April 13, The Government notified the Permanent Court of International Justice of failure of Franco-Swiss negotiations respecting the Savoy free zones

May 12, International Bank constituted at Basel

Dec. 1, Census gave population as 4,067,305

TURKEY IN EUROPE

Turkey, in Europe, is a district of about 8,819 square miles extending north from the Sea of Marmora to Bulgaria, and divided from Greece chiefly by the Maritsa River though a part of Turkish (West) Thrace extends west of the river in the neighborhood of Adrianople. The cities of Constantinople (Istanbul) and Adrianople are included in European Turkey. *See* Turkey, p. 905.

TREATIES OF UTRECHT

Utrecht, Treaties of, signed April 11 (March 31 O.S.), 1713, confirmed the disunion of the Crowns of France and Spain, recognized the Protestant succession in England, Philip V recognized as King of Spain and the Spanish Colonies; Austria received the Spanish Netherlands, Naples, and Milan, England received from France Nova Scotia, Newfoundland, and the Hudson Bay region, the island of Minorca, and Gibraltar, and contract for supplying the Spanish Colonies with slaves, Savoy received Sicily, Lille restored to France, the fortifications of Dunkirk to be demolished.

UKRAINE

The Ukrainian Soviet Socialist Republic was proclaimed on December 27, 1917, that is, soon after the Soviet Revolution of November 7, 1917, and was finally established in December, 1919. In December, 1920, the Ukrainian Soviet Socialist Republic concluded a military and economic alliance with the Russian Socialist Federal Soviet Republic and the following united People's Commissariats were formed:—For military and naval affairs, the Supreme Economic Council, Foreign Trade, Finance, Labor, Transport and Posts and Telegraphs.

On July 6, 1923, the Ukrainian Socialist Soviet Republic formed, together with the other Soviet Socialist Republics in Russia, the Union of Soviet Socialist Republics.

The Ukrainian S.S.R. covers an area of 451,731 sq. kilometers (166,368 sq. miles), i.e., 2.3% of the whole Soviet Union, and includes the Autonomous Moldavian Republic.

The population on December 17, 1926, was 29,020,304, of whom 5,374,000 were urban and 23,646,000 rural.

The principal towns are the capital, Kharkov (population 417,186), Kiev (513,789), Odessa (420,888), Dnepropetrovsk (233,801), Stalingrad (148,370), and Nikolaev (104,945). In accordance with the Government decision to erect fourteen Socialist towns in the Donetz basin, the construction of the first town, to be known as "Gorlowka," was commenced in April, 1930. The total cost of construction of these towns will amount to 634 million roubles.

VATICAN CITY

Vatican City, State of the, created Feb. 11, 1929, by treaties signed by Italy and the Vatican, recreating the Papal State. On that day there was signed (1) a Political Treaty, which recognized the full and independent sovereignty of the Holy See in the city of the Vatican; (2) a Concordat, to regulate the condition of religion and of the Church in Italy; and (3) a Financial Convention, in accordance with which the Holy See shall receive 750,-000,000 lire in cash and 1,000,000,000 lire in Italian 5% State bonds. This sum is to be a definitive settlement of all the financial claims of the Holy See against Italy in consequence of the loss of its temporal power in 1870. The treaties were ratified and the sum of 750,000,000 lire paid on June 7, 1929.

The Pope exercises the Sovereignty and has full legal, executive, and judicial powers. A Governor, directly and exclusively responsible to the Pope, exercises executive powers. The Judicial power is delegated to a tribunal in first instance, to the *Sacra Romana Rota* in appeal and to the Supreme Tribunal of the *Segnatura*, which is the ultimate authority where there is an appeal.

In its diplomatic relations with foreign countries, Città del Vaticano is represented by the Segreteria di Stato del Sommo Pontefice.

The area of the Vatican City is 44 hectares (108.7 acres). It includes the Piazza di San Pietro (St. Peter's Square), which is to remain normally open to the public and subject to the powers of the Italian police. It is to have its own railway station, postal facilities, and radio. The official journal is the *Acta Apostolicæ Sedis.* Thirteen buildings in Rome, although outside the Vatican City, enjoy extra-territorial rights. The census of the population of the Vatican City on December 17, 1929, showed 528 inhabitants, originally of the following nationalities: Italian, 389; Swiss, 113; French, 11; German, 5; Spanish, 2; U.S.A., 1; Belgian, 1; Norwegian, 1; Austrian, 1; Dutch, 1; Abyssinian, 1; Native-born, 2. There were 230 foreigners resident in the Vatican City.

Supreme Pontiff. Pius XI (Achilles Ratti), born at Desio, May 31, 1857; Archbishop of Milan and Cardinal, June 13, 1921; elected Supreme Pontiff, as successor of Benedict XV, February 6, 1922.

See also Pope; Rome.

WALES

Wales, principality of Great Britain, 12 counties on west coast of England between Irish Sea on the north, and Bristol Channel on the south, total area 4,780,470 square miles, population 4,882,497, census 1921.

Wales, Cambria, Cymru, the land of the Cymry, called by the Romans *Britannia Secunda.* Welsh and Wales are corruptions of Teutonic epithets applied to foreigners, especially Gauls. After the Roman emperor Honorius gave up Britain, Vortigern was elected king of South Britain. He invited over the Saxons to defend his country against the Picts and Scots; but the Saxons perfidiously sent for reinforcements, consisting of Saxons, Danes, and Angles, by which they made themselves masters of South Britain. Many of the Britons retired to Wales, and defended themselves against the Saxons, in their inaccessible mountains, about 447. In this state Wales remained unconquered till Henry II subdued South Wales in 1157; and in 1282 Edward I entirely reduced the whole country, an end being put to its independence by the death of Llewelyn, the last prince. The statute of Wales, enacted at Rhuddlan, March 19, 1284 (or March, 1283), alleges that—"Divine Providence has now removed all obstacles, and transferred wholly and entirely to the king's dominion the land of Wales and its inhabitants, heretofore subject unto him in feudal right." The ancient laws were to be preserved in civil causes; but the law of inheritance was to be changed, and the English criminal law to be put in force. *Annals of England.* In 1284 the queen gave birth to a son at Caernarvon, whom Edward styled Prince of Wales, now title of the heir to the crown of Great Britain. Wales was united and incorporated with England by act of parliament, 1536.

(Early dates uncertain)

SOVEREIGNS OF WALES

630. Cadwallawn, King of Gwynedd
634. Cadwaladr, his son
661. Idwal, son
728. Rhodri, or Roderic; heroic defender
755. Cynan and Howel, sons; incessant war
818. Mervyn, son-in-law; and Essyllt (wife)
844. Roderic the Great, son

PRINCES OF GWYNEDD OR NORTH WALES AND FREQUENTLY OF ALL WALES

877. Anarawd, son of Roderic
915. Idwal Voel
943. Howel Da the Good, Prince of all Wales
948. Iefan and Iago; sons of Idwal
972. Howel ap Iefan, the Bad
984. Cadwallon, brother
985. Meredith ap Owen ap Howel Da
992. Idwal ap Meyric ap Idwal Voel: able, brave
998. Aedan, a usurper
1015. Llewelyn ap Sitsyllt, good sovereign
1023. Iago ap Idwal ap Meyric
1039. Griffith ap Llewelyn ap Sitsyllt; killed
1067. Bleddyn
1073. Trahaern ap Caradoc

1079. Griffith ap Cynan; able; warlike; generous
1137. Owain Gwynedd; energetic, successful warrior
1169. Howel, son
——. David ap Owain Gwynedd, brother; married sister of Henry II
1194. Llewelyn, the Great
1240. David ap Llewelyn
1246. Llewelyn ap Griffith, last Prince of the Blood; slain after battle, Dec. 11, 1282

ENGLISH PRINCES OF WALES *

1284. Edward Plantagenet (afterwards King Edward II), son of Edward I, born in Caernarvon Castle on April 25, 1284. It is asserted that immediately after his birth he was presented by his father to the Welsh chieftains as their future sovereign, the King holding up the royal infant in his arms, and saying, in the Welsh language, "*Eich Dyn*," literally in English, "This is your man," but signifying, "This is your countryman and King." *See, however*, "*Ich Dien*"
1301. Edward of Carnarvon made Prince of Wales and Earl of Chester
1343. Edward the Black Prince
1376. Richard, his son (afterwards Richard II)
1399. Henry (afterwards Henry V), son of Henry IV
1454. Edward, son of Henry VI; slain at Tewkesbury, May 4, 1471
1471. Edward (aft. Edward V), son of Edward IV
1483. Edward, son of Richard III; died in 1484
1489. Arthur, son of Henry VII; died in 1502
1503. Henry, his brother (afterwards Henry VIII)
Edward, his son (afterwards Edward VI) was Duke of Cornwall, and not Prince of Wales
1610. Henry Frederic, son of James I; died Nov. 6, 1612
1616. Charles, his brother (afterwards Charles I)
Charles, his son (afterwards Charles II), never created Prince of Wales
1714. George Augustus (afterwards George II)
1729. Frederic Lewis, his son; died March 20, 1751
1751. George, his son (afterwards George III)
1762. George, his son (afterwards George IV): born Aug. 12
1841. Albert Edward, son of Queen Victoria (afterwards Edward VII): born Nov. 9; baptized, King of Prussia a sponsor, Jan. 15, 1842
1901. George Frederick Ernest Albert, son of Edward VII (afterwards George V)
1910. Edward Albert Christian George Andrew Patrick David, son of George V

WESTERN EMPIRE

Western Empire. The Roman empire was divided into Eastern and Western by Diocletian in 296; but was reunited under Constans in 340.

* Wales, Princess of. This title was held, some authors say, during the early period of her life, by the Princess Mary of England, eldest daughter of Henry VIII, and afterwards Queen Mary I. She was created, they state, by her father James I., in order to conciliate the Welsh people and keep alive the name, and was the only Princess of Wales in her own right; a rank she enjoyed until the birth of a son to Henry, who was afterwards Edward VI, born in 1537. This is denied by Banks

It was again divided into Eastern and Western by Valentinian and Valens, the former having the Western portion or Rome, 364; *see* Eastern Empire, Italy, and Rome.

EMPERORS

364. Valentinian, son of Gratian, takes the Western, and his brother Valens the Eastern empire
367. Gratian, a youth, son of Valentinian, made a colleague in the government by his father
375. Valentinian II, another son, also very young, is, on the death of his father, associated with Gratian, who is assassinated by his general, Andragathius, in 383. Valentinian murdered by one of his officers, Arbogastes, in 392
392. Eugenius, a usurper, assumes the imperial dignity; he and Arbogastes are defeated by
394. Theodosius the Great, who becomes sole emperor [Andragathius threw himself into the sea, and Arbogastes died by his own hand]
395. Honorius, son of Theodosius, reigns, on his father's death, in the West, and his brother Arcadius in the East. Honorius dies in 423
423. Usurpation of John, the Notary, defeated and slain near Ravenna
425. Valentinian III, son of the Empress Placidia, daughter of Theodosius the Great: murdered at the instance of his successor
455. Maximus: he marries Eudoxia, widow of Valentinian, who, to avenge the death of her first husband and the guilt of her second, invites the African Vandals into Italy, and Rome is sacked. Maximus stoned to death
——. Marcus Mæcilius Avitus; forced to resign, and dies in his flight towards the Alps
457. Julius Valerius Majorianus; murdered at the instance of his Minister, Ricimer, who raises
461. Libius Severus to the throne, but holds the supreme power; Severus poisoned by Ricimer
465. [Interregnum. Ricimer retains the authority, without assuming the title of emperor]
467. Anthemius, chosen by the joint suffrages of the senate and army; murdered by Ricimer, who dies soon after
472. Flavius-Anicius Olybrius: slain by the Goths soon after his accession
473. Glycerius: forced to abdicate by his successor
474. Julius Nepos: deposed by his general, Orestes, and retires to Salonæ
475. Romulus (called Augustulus, or Little Augustus), son of Orestes. Orestes is slain, and the Emperor deposed by
476. Odoacer, King of the Heruli: takes Rome, assumes the style of King of Italy, and completes the fall of the Western Empire
See Italy, Rome, and Germany

WHITE RUSSIA

The White Russian Soviet Socialist Republic was formed on January 1, 1919. At present, its territory covers 126,790 sq. kilometers (48,940 sq. miles), and includes the former provinces of Minsk, Vitepsk, Mogilov, and a section of the Grodno provinces as well as the Gomel province.

The most important towns of White Russia are Minsk, Vitepsk, and Gomel. In 1926, the population of White Russia was 4,983,884, of whom 82.2% were White Russians, 3.4% Russians and Ukrainians, 10.6% Jews, 2.0% Poles, and 1.1% others. About 16% of the population live in towns. White Russia forms one of the constituent Republics of the U.S.S.R. Its constitution is similar to that of the R.S.F.S.R.

WORLD WAR
1914

June 28, Assassination of Archduke Franz Ferdinand, heir to the throne of the monarchy of Austria-Hungary and his wife the Duchess of Hohenberg at Sarajevo, the capital of Bosnia by a Bosnian student, Gavrio Prinzip. Political conspiracy which inspired plot against the Archduke alleged by Austria to have been aided by Serbia

July 6, The Kaiser in reply to Austrian note presented July 5 stated that Austria could count on "the complete support of Germany" in regard to Serbia

July 14, Council of ministers of Austria-Hungary decided to take action against Serbia

July 19, Serbian ultimatum drawn up at joint Austro-Hungarian ministerial conference (Speech of Count Tisza, Lower House, Oct. 24, 1918)

July 23, Austria presented ultimatum (48 hours) to Serbia making demands which it was impossible for Serbia to accept and remain an independent state, Serbia charged with failure to fulfil promises of Declaration of March 31, 1909, Serbian officers accused of planning the Sarajevo murders of June 28

July 24, Serbian note to Russia asked her ally for diplomatic aid

——, Russia advised Serbia to accept Austrian conditions as far as possible

——, Russia asked Austria to extend time of ultimatum to Serbia to allow diplomatic action of the Powers stating that she could not remain indifferent to an Austro-Serbian conflict. Great Britain also protested the time limit

——, Statement of German Government to Powers of approval of Austrian note to Serbia and of settlement of affair by military measures between Austria and Serbia exclusively

——, Proposal of Sir Edward Grey of international conference to avert war

July 25, Serbian reply to Austrian ultimatum accepted all demands of Austria except two which violated the rights of a sovereign state which it asked might be submitted to the Hague Tribunal

——, Russia began partial mobilization

——, Austrian ambassador made answer to Serbian note that the reply was not satisfactory and that he was leaving Belgrade severing diplomatic relations

——, Serbia ordered general mobilization

——, Austria ordered partial mobilization against Serbia

——, Serbia moved seat of capital from Belgrade to Kragouyevatz as Austria concentrated troops on the Danube opposite Belgrade

July 26, Great Britain (Sir Edward Grey) proposed conference of ambassadors in London of England, Russia, France, Germany, and Italy on Serbian crisis

July 26, Montenegro ordered mobilization

July 27, Russia, France, and Italy accepted British proposal for conference

——, Germany declined to enter conference which would impair Austria's freedom of action

July 28, Austria-Hungary declared war on Serbia by an open telegram

——, England ordered the first fleet to Scapa Flow (war base)

July 29, Austria began bombardment of Belgrade. Serbians had destroyed the bridge across the Danube

——, Russia ordered partial mobilization in the south against Austria

——, Belgium announced that as a precautionary measure the army would be placed on a strengthened peace footing

——, Bulgaria made declaration of neutrality

——, British ambassador in Berlin asked to give assurance of England's neutrality in event of a European war

——, International Socialist Congress at Brussels declared against the War

July 30, Sir Edward Grey refused to entertain proposal of neutrality made by Germany July 29

——, The Netherlands declared neutrality

——, Russia ordered general mobilization, which was proclaimed on the 31st

July 31, Austria ordered general mobilization for the Empire

——, German note to France asked if in the event of a war between Germany and Russia France would remain neutral

——, Germany declared a state of imminence of war (Kriegsgefahr)

——, German ultimatum to Russia requiring demobilization to begin within 12 hours

Aug. 1, Reply of France to German note of July 31 that "France will do what her interests demand"

——, General mobilization of French army and navy ordered

——, General mobilization of German army and navy ordered

——, Complete mobilization of British fleet ordered

——, Germany declared war on Russia

——, Denmark declared neutrality

——, Treaty with Germany signed by Turkey, an alliance against Russia

——, Norway declared neutrality

——, German submarines assembled off Heligoland, and fleet in Jade anchorage

——, Hostilities begun on Polish frontier

Aug. 2, German note to Belgium demanded free passage of troops through Belgian territory, a friendly neutrality, warning that in case of opposition it would be necessary for Germany to consider Belgium an enemy

——, British naval reserves called

——, Great Britain assured France of assistance of British fleet in the event of attack by German fleet on French coast or shipping

——, German troops entered the Duchy of Luxemburg by bridges of Wasserbillig and Remich a violation of neutrality guaranteed by Treaty of London of 1867

——, German invasion of France near Longwy and near Sirey-sur-Vezouze and separate invasions at about 20 frontier posts, e.g., Joncherey, Suarce, Reppe, and others

Aug. 2, Rumania promised Bessarabia by Germany and Austria if it will join the Central Powers

——, Libau bombarded by German cruiser "Augsburg"

——, Turkey signed secret treaty with the Central Powers but declared her neutrality

——, General Von Moltke appointed commander-in-chief of general staff of German field armies

Aug. 3, Germany declared war on France and France on Germany

——, German prize code of 1909 published, recognized right to destroy neutral vessels for breach of blockade, carrying contraband, unneutral service, &c.

——, Belgium replied to German ultimatum that to accept infringement of neutrality would be to accept violation of law and sacrifice the honor of the nation, and that Belgium would repel any attack made

——, Appeal of King of Belgium to King George of Great Britain to safeguard the neutrality of Belgium

——, Statement of condition of affairs in Europe and obligations of the British Government by Sir Edward Grey in House of Commons

——, Italy declared neutrality

——, Greece in council agreed on neutrality as long as Bulgaria and Turkey remained neutral

——, Great Britain made decision to mobilize 6 divisions

——, Grand Duke Nicholas appointed commander-in-chief of Russian armies

Aug. 4, German warships the "Goeben" and "Breslau" bombard Algerian coast towns

——, German troops crossed the Belgian frontier and the Meuse River near Lixhe marching to enter France at Maubege. Demanded of the governor the surrender of Liège and Liège forts commanding the railways

——, Meeting of special advisory council in Rumania declared for neutrality

——, Note from Switzerland to Germany declared neutrality and that any attempt to violate neutrality would be repelled by armed force

——, Sir Edward Goschen, British Ambassador in Germany, asked if Imperial Government would refrain from violation of neutrality of Belgium and notified that refusal would lead to demand of his passports. Interview of Sir Edward Goschen with the Chancellor in which Bethmann-Hollweg referred to the Belgian guarantee as a "scrap of paper"

——, Great Britain declared war on Germany at 11 P.M. and ordered the mobilization of the Expeditionary and Territorial forces

——, Sir John French appointed Commander-in-Chief of British army in France, Admiral Sir John Jellicoe Commander of fleet

——, Germany declared war on Belgium

——, Second proclamation of neutrality of the Netherlands

——, President Wilson declared the neutrality of the United States in war between Austria-Hungary and Serbia, Germany and Russia, and Germany and France

——, Japan declared her desire to remain neutral

——, Rumania declared neutrality

——, Brazil published decree of neutrality

Aug. 4–5, First recorded hostile act the passage of 2 German airships over Brussels during the night

Aug. 5, President Wilson proclaimed neutrality as to war of Great Britain and Germany

——, Cuba proclaimed neutrality

Aug. 5, As a signatory of the Hague Convention President Wilson offered mediation in interests of peace to all belligerent Powers

——, Proclamation of British Government named special articles to be treated as contraband

——, German attack on Liège repulsed by Belgians commanded by General Leman checking German advance

——, British cruiser "Amphion" sunk, the German "Konigin Luise" laying mines in the English Channel

——, German cables in the Atlantic from Emden to Vigo and the Azores cut by the British

——, Uruguay declared neutrality

——, Mexico declared neutrality

——, Argentina declared neutrality

——, Montenegro declared war on Austria-Hungary

——, Russian army of General Samsonov advanced into East Prussia on both sides of the railway from Mlawa by Soldau to Allenstein

Aug. 6, Austria declared war on Russia

——, Serbia declared war on Germany

——, China declared neutrality

——, The "Amphibion" struck mine in Channel and sank with loss of 1 officer and 130 men

——, The "Emden," small German cruiser under orders to destroy enemy commerce began spectacular career by capture of Russian vessel near Quelport Island in Pacific waters

——, Belgians continue to repel German attack on Liège but 2 forts lost

Aug. 6–7, Bonga and Senga, enemy posts in the Cameroons captured by French force. *See also* Cameroons

Aug. 7, President Wilson declared neutrality in war between Austria-Hungary and Russia

——, Spain declared neutrality

——, Action between H.M.S. "Gloucester" and the "Goeben" and "Breslau" off the coast of Greece

——, Russian troops commanded by Rennenkampf crossed the frontier into East Prussia at Suwalki and Wirballen

——, French troops under General Pau invaded Alsace and captured Altkirch

——, Germans enter town of Liège but are repulsed from forts with heavy loss. General Leman ordered evacuation of army

——, Haiti proclaimed neutrality

——, First British troops arrived in France

——, Norwegian steamer "Tysla" with cargo of zinc sunk by mine at entrance of the Scheldt

Aug. 8, Montenegro severed diplomatic relations with Germany

——, Venezuela announced neutrality

——, German wireless station at Dar-es-Salaam in German East Africa destroyed by British force. *See also* Tanganyika

——, Switzerland proclaimed neutrality

——, Lome, Togoland occupied by British. *See also* Togoland

——, German army commanded by General Ludendorff occupied Liège

——, Belgians repulsed Germans attacking Dinant

——, French army occupied Mulhausen, Alsace

Aug. 9, Montenegro declared war on Germany

——, Fall of Forts Barchon and Evegnée (Liège)

——, German Government through the Dutch Government asked King Albert to cease hostile opposition to passage of German troops through Belgium

——, The "Birmingham" sank one German submarine

making attack on British squadron. The second submarine escaped

Aug. 9, Austria declared war on Montenegro

Aug. 10, Austrian troops commanded by General Danki crossed the Polish frontier, captured Krasnik and forced the Russians under General Ivanov to retreat across the Bug River

——, Germans evacuated Swakopmund and Luderitz Bay, German Southwest Africa

——, France and Austria severed diplomatic relations

——, Liberia proclaimed neutrality

——, Montenegrins occupied Scutari

Aug. 11, The "Goeben" and "Breslau" escaped from pursuit of British fleet to Dardanelles and are purchased by Turkey

——, French forced to evacuate Mulhausen

——, Capt. F. L. Bryant from the Gold Coast landed at Lome, Togoland. *See also* Togoland

——, Herbertshöhe, German New Guinea captured without opposition

——, French government issued a revised contraband list

——, The Austrians commanded by General Dankl began invasion of Poland

——, French force in Lorraine defeated and driven across the frontier

Aug. 11–12, Austrian invasion of Serbia begun during night

Aug. 12, German army repulsed by Belgians in attempt to cross the Gette River at Haelen

——, Fort Pontisse fell (Liège)

——, The Austrian army crossed the Save and the Drina into Serbia taking Loznitza (Lesnica) and Shabatz

——, Serbs and Montenegrins invade Bosnia

——, Wireless station on Island of Yap in the Pacific destroyed by British naval force

——, Great Britain declared war on Austria

——, Decree of neutrality of Guatemala

Aug. 13, France declared war on Austria-Hungary

——, The United States proclaimed neutrality in war between Great Britain and Austria-Hungary

——, Fort Embourg fell after bombardment of 26 hours (Liège) also Chaudfontaine and Nameche

——, Egypt severed diplomatic relations with Germany

——, Colombia declared neutrality as to ports

——, General Ruszky with Russian army captured Sokol, Galicia

Aug. 14, Fall of Forts Boncelles, Liers, and Fleron (Liège)

——, The United States proclaimed neutrality in war between France and Austria-Hungary

——, Proclamation of Grand Duke Nicholas promised reconstruction and autonomy to the "Kingdom of Poland"

Aug. 14–20, Battle of Morhange, and Battle of Sarrebourg (Lorraine)

Aug. 14–Sept. 12, Battle of Lorraine

Aug. 15, Ultimatum of Japan to Germany demanded the withdrawal of German warships from the Far East and delivery to custody of Japan of leased territory of Kiao-chau, China before Sept. 15. 8 days allowed for reply. No reply received

——, Forts Loncin and Lantin fell (Liège). General Leman picked up unconscious at Fort Loncin and made a prisoner

——, Germans occupy Taveta, British East Africa, menacing capital at Nairobi

Aug. 15, Battle fought at Dinant. French repulse Germans

Aug. 16, Austrians captured Krupanj threatening the Valjevo-Osecina road behind the Serbian positions

——, Von François attacked near Insterburg, by Russians advancing into East Prussia and forced to retreat

——, Fort Flemalle fell (Liège)

——, Belgians forced Germans to retreat after battle at Enghezee

——, The Government and royal family left Brussels for Antwerp

——, Franco-British fleet entered the Adriatic, Austrian cruiser "Zenta" sunk

Aug. 17–21, Battles of the Jadar and the Tser, Serbs defeated the Austrians and forced them to flight

Aug. 17, Seat of Belgian government established at Antwerp

——, Austrian cruiser sunk in Adriatic by Allied fleet

——, Declaration of neutrality of Ecuador

Aug. 18, Generals Ruzsky and Brusiloff began advance against Austria invading Galicia by attack on the army of Von Auffenberg

——, The United States proclaimed neutrality in war between Belgium and Germany

——, Serbians secured important position of Kosaningrad

——, Germans drove Belgians from Tirlemont

——, Fort Hollogne fell (Liège)

——, French army commanded by General Castelnau occupied Saarburg, Lorraine

Aug. 18–19, Battle of the Gette River (Belgian front) Belgians retreat

Aug. 19, Germans occupied Louvain after battle with Belgian army, and Aerschot which was burned and inhabitants massacred

——, French recaptured Mulhausen, Alsace

Aug. 19–20, Battle of Gawaiten-Gumbinnen (East Prussia) General Rennenkampf (Russian) defeated Germans in battle

Aug. 20, British Order in Council revised contraband list and declared adherence to the Declaration of London in principle

——, Von Kluck with 40,000 Germans entered Brussels. The Belgian army fell back to Antwerp

——, End of Battle of Morhange-Sarburg. The Germans forced the French army of General Castelnau to retreat across frontier from Lorraine

——, General Pau reoccupied Mulhausen, Alsace, together with Altkirch and Munster but Alsace army dissolved and sent to other fronts

——, Longwy invested by Germans

Aug. 21, Ghent occupied by Germans

——, Bombardment of Namur, Belgium, commanding the passages over Meuse and Sambre begun by Germans

——, Allenstein, East Prussia, occupied by Russians

——, Germans attacked General Lanrezac and gained the crossing of the Sambre

——, Germans crossed the frontier into Union of South Africa and occupied a position near Nakab

Aug. 21–24, Battle of Charleroi in which General Lanrezac forced by Germans to retreat from line between the Meuse and the Sambre

Aug. 22, Russians occupied Brody

——, Germans took Charleroi

——, Paul von Hindenburg appointed commander-in-chief of VIII German army in the East against the Russians with Ludendorff as chief of staff

Aug. 22, First fight in air between German and British machines over Maubeuge

——, Austria-Hungary declared war on Belgium

Aug. 22–24, French defeated in Battles of the Ardennes

Aug. 23–24, Battle of Mons of Sir John French with Von Kluck in which British forced to evacuate Mons

Aug. 23, Germans entered Namur. Belgians retreat on Antwerp

——, Germany severed diplomatic relations with Japan

——, Japan declared state of war with Germany

——, Belgian force from Antwerp drove the Germans from Malines

Aug. 23–25, Battle of Krasnik (Poland) in which the Austrians commanded by General Dankl defeated the Russians

——, Dinant, Belgium, captured by Germans and destroyed. Inhabitants deported to Germany

Aug. 23–31, Battle of Tannenberg, Russian defeat

Aug. 24, End of Battle of Charleroi and Battle of the Ardennes, General Lanrezac began retreat

——, British General French began march of retreat to the Marne from Mons, and General Lanzerac's French army from Charleroi region

——, Germans took Lunèville, France

——, Lille declared an open town and evacuated

——, Russians occupied Insterburg, East Prussia

——, Franco-British squadron in Adriatic bombard Cattaro

——, The United States proclaimed neutrality in war between Japan and Germany

——, Shabalz, Serbia, evacuated by the Austrians. Invasion of Serbia ended

——, Germans took Tournai and Dinant, Belgium

——, Germans from Belgium crossed the frontier into France

Aug. 24–26, First Belgian sortie from Antwerp

Aug. 25, Tepe in the Cameroons (German South-West Africa) occupied by British, Chad frontier crossed by French forces. *See also* Cameroons

——, End of first Battle of Krasnik (Poland) an Austrian victory

——, First use of aircraft patrol by Britons in retreat from Mons

——, Decree of French Government announced adoption of Declaration of London during War

——, Germans in Louvain set fires in several parts of the town and fired the University with its celebrated library

——, Mulhausen occupied by Germans

——, Shabatz reoccupied by Serbians

——, Last two forts at Namur surrendered to Germans

——, Battle at Landrecies. Germans attacking British right forced retreat of General Smith-Dorrien

——, Allenstein occupied by Russian General Samsonov

——, Japan declared state of war with Austria-Hungary

Aug. 25–27, Battle of Malines (Belgian front)

Aug. 25–28, Battle of the Meuse (West front)

Aug. 25–Sept. 3, Battle of the Mortagne (West front) Vosges

Aug. 26, British in engagement with Germans at Le Cateau. General Smith-Dorien

——, More fires started by Germans in Louvain

——, Kamina, Togo, surrendered unconditionally to Captain Bryant who entered the town the following day

——, German armed merchant cruiser "Kaiser Wilhelm der Grosse" sunk off the Rio de Oro

Aug. 26, German cruiser "Magdeburg" sunk by Russian squadron off the Aaland Islands

——, Noyon, Cambrai and Douai, French towns, occupied by Germans

——, Fortress of Longwy, France, captured by Germans

Aug. 26–29, Attack on the Russian outposts of General Samsonov in East Prussia at Uzdowo and at Rothfliess by Germans commanded by General Hindenburg and General Ludendorff forced disastrous retreat of Russians (Battle of Tannenberg)

Aug. 26–30, First Battle of Lemberg. Russians advancing in Galicia defeated the Austrians under Generals Dankl and Von Auffenburg

Aug. 26–Sept. 2, Battle of Zamosc-Komarow, Russians and Austrians in battle about Zloczow

Aug. 27, Sack of Louvain begun

——, Tarnopol, Galicia, taken by Russian General Brussilov, evacuated by Germans on the 23rd

——, Bombardment of Maubeuge begun by Germans

——, Blockade of Kiachow Bay declared by the Japanese

——, First British attack on Mora in the Cameroons unsuccessful

——, Battle of Tannenberg continued resulted in annihilation of 2 Russian corps and reduction of 3 to half their numbers

——, Tilsit, East Prussia, occupied by Russians

——, General Brussilov took Halicz, Galicia

——, Lille, Mezières, Valenciennes and other towns of northern France occupied by Germans

——, British marines landed at Ostend

——, Austria announced severance of diplomatic relations with Japan. Neither country made declaration of war at any time

——, The United States proclaimed neutrality in war between Japan and Austria-Hungary

Aug. 28, German and British fleets in battle off Heligoland, a British victory

——, Austrian declaration of war received by Belgian government

Aug. 28–30, Battle of Guise. General Lanrezac led French advance across the Oise toward St. Quentin and made a stand which checked the German progress

Aug. 29, British in retreat took position on south bank of the Oise between La Fère and Noyon

——, Archibourg, German South-West Africa, occupied by Allies

——, Kronstadt, Transylvania, occupied by Rumanians

Aug. 29–30, Austrians defeated in battle with Russians on the Gnila Lipa, retreated to Lemberg

——, British reverse at Garua, Cameroons

——, German Samoa taken by a force from New Zealand commanded by Colonel Robert Logan. Apia surrendered

Aug. 30, Laon, La Fère and Roye, French towns, occupied by Germans

——, Nsanalsong, German South-West Africa, occupied by Allies

——, The French evacuate Amiens which is occupied by the Germans the next day

——, Germans occupied Montmédy

——, Bombs dropped on Paris from German æroplane, first air raid

Aug. 30–31, General von Hindenburg enveloped and practically annihilated the Russian army of the Narew near Tannenberg

Aug. 31, Convention between Great Britain and France defined spheres of influence in Togo

——, Greece declared neutrality

Sept. 1, British force from India reached Mombassa, East Africa. General J. Stewart took command in East Africa

——, Soissons and Craonne taken by Germans

——, The United States proclaimed neutrality in war between Belgium and Austria-Hungary

Sept. 1-2, Russians defeated Austrian army of General Von Auffenburg near Lemberg, Galicia, driving Austrians west and north on second line of defenses dominated by fortress of Przsmysl and Jaroslav

Sept. 2, Austrian invasion of Poland checked outside Lublin

——, Von Kluck's army began crossing the Marne

——, French government moved to Bordeaux

——, Japanese under Lieutenant General Kamio landed at Lungkow, Shantung Peninsula

Sept. 3, Italian steamer "Loredoro" held up by the "Emden" off Calcutta

——, Lemberg, capital of Galicia, evacuated by retreating Austrian General Dankl occupied by Russians, and also Halicz

Sept. 4, German troops as near Paris as Montmirail

——, Von Goltz took Mlawa, Poland

——, German government published list of contraband

——, Germans occupied Termonde at junction of the Dendre with the Scheldt but expelled by British

——, Russians began attack on Austrian army of General Dankl

Sept. 4-12, Battle of the Grand Couronné (Nancy) attack of the Crown Prince which failed with great loss

Sept. 5, The Germans took Reims and Pont-à-Mousson, north of Nancy

——, Declaration of Great Britain, France and Russia, the Triple Entente, signed in London, agreed not to make a separate peace

——, Lille evacuated by Germans

——, Austrians beaten by Russians at Tomashov, Poland

——, British cruiser "Pathfinder" sunk by German submarine off St. Alban's Head

——, Retreat from Mons and from the Ardennes ended

——, A division of Von Kluck's army reached Claye 10 miles from Paris (British official chronology)

——, Order of the day issued by General Joffre which stopped the retreat of French armies from Belgium and the Ardennes towards the Marne preparatory to Allied attack: "A body of troops which cannot advance must at all costs keep the ground it has acquired and be shot down rather than retreat"

Sept. 5-9, Germans crossed into northern Rhodesia and attacked Abercorn

Sept. 5-10, Battle of the Ourcq (West front)

Sept. 5-12, Battle of the Masurian Lakes in which General von Hindenburg defeated and dispersed the Russian Army of the Niemen commanded by General Rennenkamp (East front)

Sept. 6, Indian troops marched from Mombassa, East Africa, and defeated German force sent to destroy railroad bridge at Tsavo

——, Germans took Johannisburg and Nikolaiken approaching Masurian Lakes

Sept. 6-10, General Ivanov began battle of Rawa-Russka defeating Austrians under General Dankl in Galicia

Sept. 6-10, First Battle of the Marne in which the Germans were forced back to the Aisne by Allied offensive in a series of battles along entire West front

Sept. 6-12, Russian offensive from Vistula to Upper Danube successful. Battle of Grodek

Sept. 7, Germans with 40,000 men captured fortress of Maubeuge, France

——, Germans took Bialla and Arys (Masurian Lakes)

——, British cable station at Fanning Island destroyed by German cruiser "Nurnberg"

Sept. 8, Austrians began second invasion of Serbia

Sept. 8-11, Second Battle of Lemberg. Great Russian victory. Armies of the Archduke Joseph, and Dankl routed

Sept. 8-17, Battle of the Drina (Serbia)

Sept. 9, Turkey declared the capitulations abolished

——, Russians abandoned Augustovo

——, Russians in possession of Dukla Pass

——, End of the Battle of the Marne. The Germans began retreat to the Aisne River (Sept. 9, French date; Sept. 10, British and German dates)

——, General François attacked Russians at Soltmahnen inflicting severe defeat (Battle of the Masurian Lakes)

——, Serbians occupied Dech. Montenegrins invaded Bosnia

——, Germans repulsed in attack on Karonga in British Nyasaland

Sept. 9-13, Second Belgian sortie from Antwerp

Sept. 10, Serbians occupied Semlin and Hermannstadt, Hungary

——, Austrians beaten at Krasnik by Russians

——, Germans evacuated Pont-à-Mousson north of Nancy (West front). Occupied by French

——, Germans occupied Kisi, East Africa

Sept. 10-14, The "Emden" sank 5 British steamers in the Bay of Bengal

Sept. 11, Retreating Germans cross the Aisne and formed new entrenched line

——, Insterburg, East Prussia, evacuated by retreating Russians

——, Australian troops occupied Herbertshöhe, capital of the Bismarck Archipelago and Solomon Islands

Sept. 12, Australian troops occupied Rabaul and New Britain Island of German New Guinea

——, Battle of the Masurian Lakes ended in defeat of Russians forced to retire from East Prussia

——, Allied pursuit of German army retreating from the Battle of the Marne checked at the Aisne River

——, Austrians in retreat before the Russians reached the San River

——, Orsova, Hungary, occupied by Rumanians

—— Germans evacuated Luneville, northern France. St. Mihiel salient occupied by Germans

——, Wireless station on Nauru Island in the Pacific destroyed by British naval force

Sept. 12-15, Battle of the Aisne on the West front. Allied advance

Sept. 13, Fort de Troyon on the Meuse south of Verdun repulsed German assault

——, Military occupation proclaimed at Rabaul, seat of government of German New Guinea

——, Germans checked by Russian stand at the Niemen River

——, Soissons and Amiens reoccupied by the French

——, Capture of railroad station of Kiaochau by Japanese

Sept. 14, Grodek captured by Russians (East front)

Sept. 14, Russians forced Austrians to retreat from the San River to the line of the Dunajec

——, Germans evacuated Reims. Occupied by the Allies the following day

——, Resignation of General von Moltke as Chief German General Staff. Succeeded by General von Falkenhayn

——, The "Carmania" sank the German "Cap Trafalgar" off Trinada Island

Sept. 15, General De La Rey, rebel leader, South Africa, shot by a police patrol on his way to join insurgent camp

——, Russians took Czernowitz, Bukowina

——, Hindenburg pursuing Russians in retreat from East Prussia invaded Russia in district of Suaki

——, Serbs forced Austrians to retreat across the Drina ending second invasion of their country

——, Reims occupied by the Allies

——, General Beyers in South Africa resigned in protest against plan to invade German Southwest Africa

——, Montenegrins and Serbians invaded Bosnia and occupied Vishegrad

Sept. 16, Longido, East Africa, occupied by Germans

Sept. 17, Formal surrender of German New Guinea made to Australian force

Sept. 18, General von Hindenburg appointed Commander-in-Chief of German armies East front

——, Bombardment of fortress of Przemysl, Galicia, by Russians. Defended by General Kusmanek

——, Bombardment of Reims, France, begun by the Germans

Sept. 19, Lüderitzbucht, South-West Africa occupied by troops from Union of South Africa under Colonel Beves

——, Secret agreement between Russia and Rumania for mutual support

——, British and French Governments guarantee the integrity of Belgian colonies

——, Force from the Union of South Africa entered German South West Africa

——, Cattaro, Montenegro bombarded by French squadron

——, Reims cathedral bombarded and badly damaged

——, German attack threatening the Paris-Verdun railway stopped by General Sarrail

Sept. 20, French force captured Kuseri in the Cameroons

——, Bavarians gained foothold on left bank of Meuse, a wedge in West Front which they held until dislodged by American attack in 1918

——, The "Königsberg" appeared off Zanzibar and destroyed the "Pegasus"

Sept. 21, French forces recapture Noyon

——, Jaroslav taken by Russians

——, Hindenburg's army reached the Niemen

——, British proclamation added to list of contraband

——, German troops in New Guinea surrendered

——, Unsuccessful attack on Longido, East Africa, reoccupied by Germans

Sept. 22–26, First Battle of Picardy

Sept. 22, Von Spee with German cruiser in the Pacific bombarded Papeete, Tahiti and sunk French gunboat

——, The "Emden" off Madras opened fire on large oil tanks of the Burma Oil Company causing damage of over $100,000 in a few minutes

Sept. 22, Serbians invade Bosnia a second time moving on Serajevo

——, British air raid on Zeppelin sheds at Düsseldorf and Cologne

——, Lieutenant Weddigen in submarine U9 sank the English 12,000 ton armored cruisers "Aboukir," "Hogue," and "Cressy" in one hour with loss of 1,400 men in North Sea near Hook of Holland

Sept. 23, Germans occupied St. Mihiel on the Meuse

——, Investment of Przemysl by Russians completed, the railroad from Przemysl to Cracow taken

——, British force landed at Laoshan Bay to join Japanese army before Tsing-tao

Sept. 24, Serbs entered Shabatz

Sept. 24–25, Australians take possession of Kaiser Wilhelm's Land (New Guinea)

Sept. 24–Oct. 8, Invasion of Hungary by Russians

Sept. 25, Noyon retaken by Germans

——, General Rennenkampf in retreat made stand at Niemen River

——, Mexico made second declaration of neutrality

Sept., 25–29, Battel of Albert, German offensive on West Front, between Noyon and the Somme

——, Battle of the Niemen begun by German attack (East front)

Sept. 26, First Indian troops landed at Marseilles

——, Gen. Lukin, British South African force surrendered after battle at Sandfontein, Southwest Africa to German commander Colonel von Heydebreck

——, Austrians retreating from San River reached line of the Dunajec. Russians occupied Rzeszov on Cracow railway

——, Baupaume, France occupied by Germans

Sept. 26–27, Duala in the Cameroons surrendered to an Anglo-French force after attack

——, Bombs dropped on Paris from German aëroplane

Sept. 27–28, Germans last attempt to cross Niemen River failed and retreat begun

Sept. 27–Oct. 12, First Battle of Artois

Sept. 28, Germans bombarded and occupied Malines, Belgium

——, Bombardment of Antwerp begun

——, Germans withdraw from Prince Heinrich Hill after severe battle with the Japanese

——, Battle of the Aisne ended in trench warfare

——, Krosno and Dukla and Uzok, Carpathian passes seized by Russians

——, Investment of Tsing-tao completed by Anglo-Japanese force and siege begun

Sept. 29, Battle of Albert ended with repulse of Germans

——, Russians occupied Dembica advancing toward Cracow

Sept. 29–30, Battle of Guise (West front)

Sept. 30, French reënter Arras and reoccupy Lille

——, Battle extended north around Roye and Arras (West front) with German effort to break Allied line

Oct. 1, Turkey closed the Dardanelles

——, Russians recaptured Augustowo, Poland and began 9 days battle with retreating Germans

Oct. 2, Termonde, Belgium taken by Germans

Oct. 3, End of retreat of Austro-Hungarian forces in Galicia after Battle of Lemberg

——, First Austro-German invasion of Poland for capture of Warsaw

——, Germans took Ypres and attacked from Varennes to Verdun

Oct. 3, British troops arrived at Antwerp

——, Maramaros-Sziget in northern Hungary taken by Russians

Oct. 4, Lens, Comines, and Bailleul, northern France occupied by Germans in rapid advance toward coast

——, Austro-Hungarian counter-offensive against Russians begun in Galicia

Oct. 5, Germans forced line of the Nethe at Duffel (Belgian front)

——, First aërial battle in which Frantz with a Voisin biplane compelled the enemy to descent

——, Hindenburg's army shifted around the frontier of Silesia, began advance on Warsaw

Oct. 5, Japanese seized German railroad at Shantung

Oct. 6, Russians retreat along entire front in Poland and Galicia

——, Germans captured Lierre, Belgium

Oct. 6–8, Bombardment of Arras by Germans

Oct. 7, Maramos-Sziget recaptured by Austrians

——, Belgian government moved from Antwerp to Ostend and evacuation of troops from Antwerp begun

——, Japanese occupied Jaluit, seat of government of the Marshall Islands, and Yap

Oct. 8, Russians retreat over Carpathian passes from northern Hungary

——, Lodz, Poland, occupied by advancing Germans

——, British air raid on Zeppelin shed at Cologne and Düsseldorf

——, Capture of Prince Heinrich Hill (Tzing-tau)

Oct. 9, Przemsyl relieved by Austrians, Siege of Przemysl raised by Russian army of General Radko-Dimitriev as Austrians reached the San

——, End of Battle of Augustowo, a Russian victory

——, The Germans entered Antwerp

——, Armentières taken by Germans

Oct. 9–19, Battle of Warsaw, first German offensive

Oct. 9–20, Battle of Ivangorod

Oct. 10, Bombardment of Lille begun

——, Capitulation of Antwerp signed by the governor

——, General attack of Japanese and British at Tsing-tao begun

Oct. 10–Nov. 2, Battle of La Bassée begun with British attack

Oct. 11, Battle of Ypres-Armentières begun as General Gough in engagement with German cavalry north of the Bethune-Aire Canal

——, Air raid on Paris. Cathedral of Notre Dame hit

——, Vermelles 4 miles south of La Bassée canal taken by Germans

Oct. 12, Germans entered Lille and remained until Oct. 1918

——, Air raid on Paris

——, Martial law declared in South Africa as rebellion begun. Colonel S. G. Maritz in Cape Colony joined Germans. *See* South Africa

——, Ghent occupied by Germans

Oct. 12–Nov. 2, Battle of Messines, Flanders

Oct. 13, Capitulation of Lille

——, Allies dispersed Germans and occupied Ypres

——, Belgian government moved from Ostend to Havre, France

Oct. 13–Nov. 2, Battle of Armentières (West front)

——, Battle of Chyrow, Galicia

Oct. 14, First Canadian troops arrived at Plymouth, England

——, British recapture Bailleul

——, Yabasi (Cameroons) occupied by Allied forces

Oct. 15, Germans occupied Zeebrugge and Ostend

Oct. 15, South African rebels defeated at Ratedrai

——, Battle for Warsaw along line of Vistula

Oct. 16, German army within 7 miles of Warsaw

——, Allies recaptured Armentières, Aubers, and Neuve Chapelle

Oct. 16–Nov. 10, Battle of the Yser begun with attack on Belgian army front from Nieuport to Dixmude in German drive to capture Dunkirk and Calais as basis for attack on England

Oct. 17, British cruiser "Undaunted" sunk 4 German destroyers off Holland

——, Japanese cruiser sunk in Kiao-Chau Bay

——, Russian troops arrived at Warsaw for defense

——, German island of Kaewieng occupied by Australians

——, Air raid over Paris

——, German submarine raid on Scapa Flow

Oct. 18, Admiral Von Spee left Easter Island with 5 cruisers for coast of Chile

——, German attack on Nieuport repulsed, attempt to break through Allied line to Channel ports

——, Germans took Roulers, Belgium

——, British submarine E3 torpedoed in North Sea by U27

——, Grand fleet withdrew from Scapa Flow

Oct. 19–Nov. 22, First Battle of Ypres on front from Bixschoote to Armentières in the south

——, Allied advance to Roulers, Belgium

Oct. 20, Russians took offensive around Warsaw driving Germans back

——, Russian War Office announced capture of the outer forts of Przemysl

——, Germans began attack on Arras

Oct. 21, Germans began retreat from Warsaw

——, Mariannas, Marshall Islands taken by British and Japanese

Oct. 21–22, Germans gained possession of bridge near Tervaete to cross Yser

Oct. 21–24, Battle of Langemarck, Flanders

Oct. 22, Committee for Belgian Relief formed in London

——, Germans crossed the Yser to left bank at Tervaete

——, 10-day battle begun as Germans try to break Allied line between Bethune and La Bassée

——, Czernowitz, Bukowina, occupied by Austrians

——, Hindenburg's army retired from the Vistula

——, Provisions as to list of free goods in Declaration of London denounced by France and Great Britain

——, American circular note to belligerent governments insisted on preservation of existing rules of war

Oct. 23, British Indian troops arrived at Bahrein Islands, Persian Gulf

Oct. 23–24, 14 assaults made by Germans during the night on Dixmude repulsed

Oct. 24, Battle around Arras at its height

——, Rebel General De Wet seized Heilbron (New Free State)

Oct. 26, General Smuts defeated the South African leader Maritz

——, Edea (Cameroons) occupied by French forces

——, German invasion of Portuguese colony at Angola

Oct. 27, French liner "Admiral Ganteaume" sunk without warning by submarine in the Channel off Cape Griznis

——, British dreadnought "Audacious" sunk by mine off north-east coast of Ireland

——, General Botha defeated and dispersed rebel forces of General Beyers near Rustenburg, Transvaal

——, Belgians opened the Nieuport sluices letting the

sea flood the country in front of their line on the Yser

Oct. 27, Russian victory in Poland along line Petrokov-Radow

Oct. 28, Czernowitz, Bukowina, recaptured by Russians

——, The German cruiser "Emden" sank Russian cruiser "Jemtchug" and French destroyer "Mousquet" in harbor of Penang

——, Russians recapture Lodz, Poland

——, Austrians defeated in Galicia at Sambor

Oct. 29, The "Goeben" and other Turkish warships bombarded Odessa and Thedosia and sank a Russian destroyer

——, War declared on Entente Powers by Turkey

——, British Order in Council modified Declaration of London

——, Lord Fisher succeeded Prince Louis of Battenberg as First Lord of the British Admiralty

——, Germans took Ramscapelle

——, Great Britain issued revised contraband list

Oct. 29–31, Battle of Gheluvelt. German attack attempt to break Allied line south-east of Ypres

Oct. 30, Russian ambassador declared state of war existed and left Constantinople. French and British ambassadors ask for passports

——, Russians captured Stanislau, Galicia

——, Serbians retreated from the line of the Drina

Oct. 31, Crisis of Battle of Yser. British line broken and Gheluvelt taken by Germans but recovered by part of the Worcestershire regiment. Belgians opened the dykes and the floods forced Germans to retreat across the Yser

——, Lord Kitchener sent conditional guarantee of independence of Arabia to Sherif at Mecca

——, Bombardment of Tsing-Tao begun by Japanese and British forces

——, General Aitken succeeded General Stewart in command in East Africa

Nov. 1, In naval battle off Coronel, Chile, between Admiral Von Spee with 5 cruisers and Admiral Sir Christopher Craddock with 3 cruisers, two of the British cruisers sunk by victorious Germans

——, Germans take Messines (Battle of Ypres)

——, Turks bombarded Sevastopol

——, Martial law proclaimed in Egypt

——, Mackensen attacked Russians checking pursuit after Battle of Warsaw

——, Persia made declaration of neutrality

Nov. 2, Fighting near La Bassée on West front

——, British declared the entire North Sea a military area and warned neutral shipping of the blockade

——, Russia made formal declaration of war on Turkey

——, Serbia declared "state of war" with Turkey

——, Announcement of Government of India that Holy Places in Arabia and Mesopotamia should be immune from attack

——, Russians began new invasion of East Prussia

——, End of Battle of Chyrow (Galicia)

Nov. 2–5, British made unsuccessful attack on Tanga, East Africa

Nov. 3, The Grand fleet ordered back to Scapa Flow

——, Russia declared war on Turkey

——, German warships shelled Yarmouth and Lowestoft on English coast

——, British attack on Longido repulsed

——, British fleet bombarded outer forts of the Dardanelles

Nov. 3, Austrian armies in Galicia retreat

——, The "Karlsruhe" blew up at sea. Had captured 17 ships

Nov. 4, British and Indians repulsed in attack on Tanga, East Africa, reëmbarked and returned to Mombassa the following day. Failure of General Stewart's attack on Longido

——, German cruiser "Yorck" sunk by mine in Wilhelshafen harbor

——, Great Britain announced annexation of Cyprus

Nov. 5, Russians reoccupied Jaroslav, Galicia

——, Great Britain and France declared war on Turkey

——, Germans repulsed at Le Quesnoy-en-Santerre (Roye)

——, Montenegrins defeated invasion by Albanians

Nov. 6, German island of Nauru occupied by Australians

——, Keupri-Keui, Armenia, taken by Russians

——, British submarine entered the straits of the Dardanelles, first warship to enter, proceeding about 2 miles

——, German attack repelled (Ypres)

——, Turkey severed diplomatic relations with Belgium

——, The United States proclaimed neutrality in war between Great Britain and Turkey

——, French government published revised list of contraband

Nov. 7, French notification of declaration of war on Turkey published in Official Journal

——, British General Delamain formed entrenched camp opposite Abadan, Mesopotamia

——, Tsing-tao surrendered to Japanese and British. Formal transfer Nov. 10

——, France abrogated decree of Aug. 25, 1914 adopting Declaration of London

Nov. 8, Russians entered Prussia at Eydtkuhnen and Stallüponen

——, De Wet defeated Union forces under General Cronje at Doornberg

——, Third Austrian invasion of Serbia begun towards Nish, Shabats, and Valyevo

Nov. 9, The German cruiser "Emden" landed at South Keeling Harbor, Cocos Islands and destroyed radio and cable stations. Captured by the "Sydney," Australian cruiser and burned

——, Statement of British war aims by Asquith

——, Convention of Great Britain and France relating to prizes captured

Nov. 10, Germans captured Dixmude and forced French to withdraw to the west of the Yser. End of the Battle of the Yser

——, Second siege of Przemsyl begun

Nov. 11, Advance of General Mackensen preliminary to the Battle of Lodz which stopped the intended Russian invasion of Silesia

——, Attack of Prussian Guard repulsed by British on Menin Road (Battle of Ypres)

——, Memel occupied by Russians (approximate date British official chronology)

——, Russians in Galicia threatened both Thorn and Cracow

——, Holy War against the Entente Allies declared by Sheikh ul Islam

Nov. 12, General Botha routed rebel force under De Wet in Orange Free State

Nov. 13, Russians captured position near Koprukeni and Erzerum in Caucasus but compelled to withdraw

Nov. 14, Keupri-Keui retaken by Turks

Nov. 14, Death of Lord Roberts in France from pneumonia

Nov. 15, Holy War proclaimed in Constantinople

——, Colonel Celliers defeated General Beyers at Bulfonstein

Nov. 15–Dec. 2, Battle of Cracow. Second Russian offensive in Galicia

Nov. 15–Dec. 12, Second invasion of Hungary by Russians

Nov. 16–Dec. 15, Second German offensive against Warsaw. Battle of Lodz

Nov. 17, The British occupied Longido, East Africa, evacuated by Germans

——, Russian squadron bombarded Trebizond

——, German fleet bombarded Libau

Nov. 18, Russians defeated at Soldau, East Prussia

——, Russian battleships in engagement with Turks in Black Sea damaged the "Goeben"

——, French government returned to Paris

Nov. 19, Valievo, Serbia taken by Austrians

Nov. 21, Skirmish near Suez Canal

——, British air raid on Zeppelin sheds at Friedrichshafen, Germany

Nov. 22, Russians occupied Keupri-Keui

——, End of Battle of Ypres

——, Basra, Iraq occupied by British and Indian troops

Nov. 23, Germans attacked Indian troops at Festubert (West front)

——, Hindenburg pierced Russian line near Lodz and captured 90,000 prisoners

——, Portugal passed resolution authorizing military intervention as ally of Great Britain

——, Turkey made formal declaration of war against Allies

Nov. 24, Russian line near Lodz restored by arrival of reinforcements

Nov. 25, Shaffer's force broke through Russian encircling troops after capture of Brzeziny on Nov. 24

Nov. 26, British battleship "Bulwark" blown up off Sheerness

——, French government issued revised list of contraband

Nov. 28, Russians recaptured Dukla Pass in the Carpathians

——, Turks with 200 Bedouins advanced toward Suez Canal

Nov. 29, Serbs evacuated Belgrade

Nov. 30–Dec. 17, Battle of Lowicz-Sanniki, Poland

Dec. 1, Rebel General Christian De Wet captured at Waterburg about 100 miles west of Mafeking

——, Russian army commanded by General Ivanov in West Galicia reached Wielicza, 5 miles south of Cracow

Dec. 1–15, Battle of Limanova-Lapanow, Austrian offensive in Galicia

Dec. 2, Russians occupied Bartfeld, Hungary

——, Serbia declared war against Turkey

——, Austrians occupied Belgrade, Serbia

Dec. 3–6, Battle of the Kolubara River (Serbia)

Dec. 3–8, Battle of the Ridges in Serbia in which the Serbs Generals Putnik and Mischitch defeated the Austrians recapturing the Suvobor Mountain positions

Dec. 4, Battle of Limanova-Lapanow (East front)

Dec. 4–8, First action at Kurna (Qurna), Mesopotamia

Dec. 6, Lodz evacuated by Russians and occupied by Germans

——, Austrians in flight from Serbia

Dec. 7, Hindenburg began 3 weeks' battle in second unsuccessful struggle for Warsaw

——, The French took Vermelles in effort to break through German lines

——, Bombardment of forts of Cracow by the Russians

Dec. 8, Admiral Sturdee in battle with German fleet of Von Spee off Falkland Islands sunk all but one of the 5 German cruisers

——, General Beyers in effort to escape capture by South African Union force jumped into the Vaal and was drowned south of Bothaville

——, Russian army under Radko Dmitriev fought indecisive battle close to Cracow

——, Austrian counter-offensive in North Hungary begun. Bartfeld (Bartfa) retaken

Dec. 9, Kurna at junction of the Tigris and Euphrates surrendered to British force

——, Serbs reoccupied Valievo

——, Rumanian declaration declined to support Greece against Turkey

Dec. 10, Nkongsamba (Cameroons) surrendered to Allies

——, Austrians defeated by Russians near Cracow

Dec. 12, Austrians recaptured Dukla pass

——, Russians forced to retreat from before Cracow, and last troops retreated through Carpathian passes, ending invasion of Hungary

Dec. 13, British submarine commanded by Lieutenant Holbrook proceeded through mine field up the Dardanelles and sunk the Turkish battleship "Messudieh"

——, French force occupied Mara and Lake Chad region. Cameroons, except garrison at Mora, cleared of enemy

Dec. 14, British note to American government in defense of blockade policy

——, Ypres again attacked by Germans

Dec. 14–24, Fighting in Flanders begun with Allied attack on Wytschaete

Dec. 15, End of Battle of Lodz

——, End of 3rd Austrian invasion of Serbia. Serbs occupied Belgrade. 28,000 Austrian prisoners taken

——, Allied advance across Yser Canal from Nieuport towards Lombartzyde

Dec. 16, Russians end retreat making stand on the Bzura-Ravka-Pilitza line southwest of Warsaw

——, German cruisers bombarded Scarborough, Hartlepool, and Whitby on the English coast

——, Announcement of Japan that German islands in the Pacific would not be given up

Dec. 17, Turkish offensive begun in the Caucasus. Keupri-Keui recovered

Dec. 18, British protectorate declared over Egypt

——, The Kings of Norway, Sweden, and Denmark met in conference at Malmo, Sweden, and arranged for common action during the war

——, Battle of the Rawka-Bzura begun (East front). Ended in trench warfare

Dec. 20, German advance into Poland checked by the Russians at the Bzura River 30 miles from Warsaw

Dec. 20–21, Defense of Givenchy by Indians and British

Dec. 20–30, Battle of Perthes (Battle of Champagne)

Dec. 20–March 17, First Battle of Champagne. French attacked on front of 20 miles east of Reims

Dec. 21, First raid on England near Dover by German aëroplanes

Dec. 23, Proclamation of British government added to list of articles to be treated as contraband
——, Russians forced to raise siege of Cracow
Dec. 24, Second aëroplane raid over Dover, England
——, British bombarded German airsheds at Brussels
——, French success at Perthes-les-Hurlus (Champagne)
——, Germans invaded Portuguese colony of Angola, South West Africa
Dec. 25, Pastoral letter of Cardinal Mercier to be read in churches of Belgium on January 3
——, Walfish Bay reoccupied by British troops, South West Africa
——, British naval and air raid on Cuxhaven, German port
——, Italians occupied Valona (Avlona), Albanian port
Dec. 26, Note of Secretary Bryan to Great Britain protested against seizure and detention of American vessels
Dec. 27, Russians reoccupied Carpathian passes
Dec. 28, Village of St. Georges recaptured by French and Belgians (West front)
——, End of second Battle of Warsaw, failure for Germans
——, End of organized rebellion in South Africa
Dec. 29, British note to the United States defended policy at sea
——, American note to Great Britain protested detention of ships
Dec. 29–Jan. 2, Battle of Sarikamish in the Caucasus
Dec. 30, Raid by German aëroplanes on Dunkirk
Dec. 31–Jan. 7, Trench warfare in Champagne

1915

Jan. 1, British battleship "Formidable" sunk in the Channel by German submarine U24, 600 lives lost
——, Turks occupied Ardahan, fortified Russian town in the Caucasus
Jan. 2, Grand Duke Nicholas asked Great Britain to make a demonstration against Turkey to relieve Russian army in the Caucasus
——, Jassin, East Africa, occupied by British Indian force. See also Cameroons
——, End of Battle of Sarikamish, Transcaucasia. Turks defeated by Russians
——, Major General Sir Charles Dobell took Chang (Dschang), Cameroons, and destroyed German fort
Jan. 3, Arrest of Cardinal Mercier because of pastoral letter. See Belgium
——, French Government publish revised contraband list
——, Ardahan, Turkey, reoccupied by Russians
Jan. 3–4, French capture village of Steinbach, Upper Alsace
Jan. 5, German attack on Edea (Cameroons) repulsed by French garrison
——, Tabriz, Persia, evacuated by Russians and taken by Turks
Jan. 6, Russians in Bukowina captured Kimpolung and reached Hungarian frontier
——, The "Dacia," German steamer interned in the United States, sold to American citizen, Mr. Breitung
Jan. 7, British provisional reply to American note of Dec. 26, protesting treatment of American commerce
Jan. 8–13, Battle of Kara Urgan begun in the Caucasus between Russians and Turks
——, Tabriz, north Persia, occupied by Turks
Jan. 8–14, Battle of Soissons, French offensive in the

Aisne sector begun with capture of German outposts of Hill 132. (Variously called Second Battle of Perthes and also Action of Crouy) Germans gained bridgehead of Aisne
Jan. 9, The French recapture Steinbach, Alsace
——, German port of Shirati on Lake Victoria, East Africa, taken
Jan. 10, Dunkirk bombed by German aëroplanes, and east coast of England raided
——, British occupied Mafia Island off German East Africa
——, French gained possession of Hill 132 and front line of trenches north of Soissons
Jan. 11, Rumania negotiated loan in Great Britain for £5,000,000
Jan. 11–12, Aisne River rose and carried away most of bridges behind French lines near Soissons
Jan. 13, Battle of Kara Urgan ended with defeat of Turks
Jan. 14, End of Battle of Soissons. French forced back from north bank of the Aisne northeast of Soissons and lost over 5,000 prisoners
——, Memel on the Baltic occupied by Germans
——, British occupied Swakopmund, German South-West Africa
——, Russian advance in north Poland on lower Vistula in direction of German fortress of Thorn
Jan. 15, First action at Givenchy (West front)
——, Italian and Rumanian governments made secret agreement for mutual support
——, Russians defeated Turks for third time in the Caucasus near Kara Urgan
Jan. 16, Russians occupied Kirlibaba Pass in the Carpathians leading westward into Hungary
Jan. 19, British force compelled to surrender at Jassin, East Africa
——, First serious German airship raid over England attacked Yarmouth, Kings Lynn, and other towns in Norfolk county
Jan. 20, Russians occupied Sierpiecon on River Skrwa
Jan. 21, Germans captured the Hartmannswillerkopf near German frontier in Alsace. Fighting for this position continued during February and March
Jan. 22, Fleet of 12 airships raided Dunkirk. Before June 30, 25 raids
——, German armies advance in Bukowina and recapture Kirlibaba
Jan. 23, Austrian attack on Carpathian passes from Dukla to Kirlibaba which continued for 5 weeks
Jan. 24, Greek government offered concessions in Asia Minor by Entente Allies in return for help to Serbs
——, South African rebels under Maritz and Kemp defeated by Colonel Van Deventer at Upington
——, Battle of Dogger Bank. German cruiser "Blücher" sunk in engagement of English and German fleets in the North Sea
Jan. 25, Germans repulsed with heavy loss in attack on British positions at Givenchy near La Bassée, and French east of Ypres
Jan. 26, Russian counter-offensive begun against Austrians in Battles of the Carpathians
——, Turks led by Germans began advance across the Sinai Peninsula towards the Suez Canal
Jan. 27, French recapture the Hartmannswillerkopf and repulsed German attack in the Argonne
Jan. 28, The "William P. Frye," American vessel, sunk in the Atlantic by the "Prince Eitel Friedrich"

Jan. 28, Russian torpedo boats bombarded Trebizond and Riza, Black Sea ports

Jan. 29, Greek government refused to intervene on behalf of Serbs

Jan. 30, Russians took Tabriz, Persia

Jan. 31, Air raid over midland counties of England, the industrial centers

——, Idrisi Arab forces occupied Farasan Island in the Red Sea

Feb. 1, British order forbade neutral fishing vessels to use British ports

Feb. 1–5, Third Battle of Perthes on West front, German offensive in Battle of Champagne

Feb. 3, Agreement between Great Britain and Belgium as to delimitation of Uganda and Congo territory

——, Bulgarian government negotiated a loan of £3,000,000 in Germany

——, Lieut.-Colonel Kemp, the last rebel leader with his Boer forces, surrendered to British

——, Austrians evacuate Tarnow, Galicia

——, Russians defeated Germans near Bolimov, Poland, in attempted break through Russian lines

Feb. 3–4, Turks defeated in attack near Suez Canal at Tussum and Serapeum

Feb. 4, German decree declared waters around British Isles a war zone from and after Feb. 18, and announced destruction of every enemy vessel without regard to safety of crew or passengers

——, Announcement of British Foreign Office that in view of Berlin decree the British fleet ordered to treat cargoes of grain and flour for Germany as contraband

Feb. 4–22, Battle of Masuria (East front) freed East Prussia from Russians

Feb. 6, Berlin decree of Jan. 26 modified as to imported food supplies

——, The Cunard steamer "Lusitania" flew American flag for protection against submarine attack in passage through war zone to Liverpool

——, Germans recapture Kimpolung, Bukowina

——, British made successful attack south of the La Bassée Canal

Feb. 6–15, Trench warfare on West front

Feb. 7, British Foreign Office issued a memo a justification of use of neutral flag by belligerents

——, German advance against Russians along line Tilsit-Johannisburg who make good their retreat behind the Bohr River (Battles of the Masurian Lakes)

Feb. 9, American steamer "Wilhelmina" with cargo of foodstuffs entered Falmouth, England, harbor. Cargo seized for prize court

Feb. 10, American note to Germany stated that the government of the United States would hold the Imperial German government to a strict accountability for acts on the sea. Note to Great Britain protested use of neutral flags by British vessels

——, Note of German government to neutral nations states that armed merchantmen would be regarded as belligerents

Feb. 11, The "Dacia" with cargo of cotton sailed from the United States for Bremen

——, General Botha arrived at Swakopmund to take command in South West Africa

Feb. 11–12, British air raid on Bruges, Zeebrugge, and Ostend districts

Feb. 13, Germans captured Russian positions before Lyck

Feb. 14, Austrian squadron bombarded Antivari, Montenegro

Feb. 14–15, Germans attacked British at St. Eloi

Feb. 15, First Canadian division reached France. Billeted in area to east of Hazebrouch

——, The Germans captured Bielsk and Plock, Poland. Austrians captured Nadworna, Bukowina

Feb. 16, Oyem (Cameroons) occupied by French force

——, British proclamation extended prohibition of "trading with the enemy"

——, German note to United States refused to give up submarine warfare

——, British air raid on Ostend, Ghistelles, and Zeebrugge

——, Austrians recapture Kolomea

Feb. 16–19, Fourth Battle of Perthes (Champagne), French advance on sector northwest of Perthes to strongly fortified farm of Beauséjour, about 4 miles, and captured German trenches along a front of about 2 miles

Feb. 17, Czernowitz, capital of Bukowina, occupied by Austro-Hungarians

——, Retreating Russians evacuated Augustowo

——, Germans reoccupied Memel on the Baltic

——, Indian troops defended position at St. Eloi

Feb. 17–21, French offensive, first action of Les Espargnes (West front), effort to force the Germans out of the St. Mihiel salient

Feb. 17–March 6, First action of Vauquois (West front) in Argonne resulted in capture of fortified post of Vauquois south of Varennes

Feb. 18, German proclamation of war zone about British Isles went into effect, the submarine blockade

Feb. 19, Stanislau, Galicia, captured by Austrians

——, Anglo-French fleet began bombardment of forts at entrance to the Dardanelles

——, Norwegian steamer "Belridge" torpedoed without warning, reached port

——, American steamer "Evelyn" sunk by mine off Borkum Island

Feb. 20, Liquid fire first used by Germans against French in the Argonne

Feb. 21–March 20, Winter Battle of Champagne on the West front begun with second action of Les Espargnes

Feb. 22, General Mackenzie took Garub, Southwest Africa

Feb. 22–27, First Battle of Przasnysz, north Poland (East front)

Feb. 23, American steamer "Carib" sunk by mine in North Sea

——, Lemnos (Ægean) occupied by British marines, occupation protested by Greece

Feb. 25, Bombardment of outer forts of Dardanelles renewed and entrance to Straits cleared

——, Announcement of Great Britain of blockade of German East Africa as from the 28th

Feb. 26, The Russians occupied Przasnyz

Feb. 27, American vessel "Dacia" with cargo of cotton consigned to Bremen, seized by French warship

——, End of Battle of Przasnyz, Russian victory

Feb. 28, Canadians attacked enemy trenches near St. Eloi

March 1, British blockade of German East Africa begun

——, German offensive in North-West Poland stopped on Plotsk-Raciaz line after severe battle, Feb. 16–18

——, Great Britain and France signed declaration to prevent trade by or with Germany

March 4, Russians recaptured Stanislau, Galicia

March 4, Russian memorandum to Great Britain and France claimed Constantinople and listed other territory to be held by Russia in event of victorious war

March 4–6, Warships attacked forts of the Dardanelles

March 5–9, Smyrna bombarded by British squadron

——, Venezelos offered Greek fleet to Entente Allies for attack on Gallipoli

March 6, Venizelos resigned as Premier of Greece on refusal of the King to assent to his war policy

March 10, The "Prinz Eitel Friedrich," German cruiser arrived at Newport News and announced sinking of American vessel "William P. Frye." Interned

March 10–13, Capture of Neuve Chapelle by British (Battle of Neuve Chapelle) commanded by Sir Douglas Haig and Sir Horace Smith-Dorrien

March 11, British Order in Council proclaimed extension of list of "absolute contraband"

——, New German offensive near Przasnyz, Poland

——, British regulations as to "continuous voyage" imposed on shippers of goods to Holland and Scandinavian countries burden of proof that goods not destined for Germany on peril of confiscation

March 12, British Government accepted claim of Russia to Constantinople under certain conditions

——, General Sir Ian Hamilton appointed Commander-in-Chief of Mediterranean Expeditionary Force

March 13, End of Battle of Neuve Chapelle. British victory

——, Swedish vessel "Hana" first neutral vessel to be sunk by German submarine

March 13–15, German offensive in Poland checked by Russian counter-offensive near Augustovo Woods and Przasnyz

March 14, The German cruiser "Dresden" which had escaped after Battle of the Falkland Islands sunk off Island of Juan Fernandez by British fleet

March 14–15, Battle of St. Eloi. German bombardment of British lines 4 miles southeast of Ypres

March 15, British Order in Council prohibited all traffic to and from Germany

——, Russians defeat Austrians in counter-offensive near Smolnik in Carpathians

March 17, End of first Battle of Champagne

——, Sir Ian Hamilton arrived at Tenedos

March 18, Air raid on Calais, France by Germans

——, Sortie ordered by General Von Kusmanek from Przemysl a failure

——, Memel, East Prussia recaptured by Russians

——, Anglo-French fleet attack on Turkish forts and effort to pass through the Dardanelles Straits a costly failure in loss of men and ships (Battle of the Narrows). The British battleships "Ocean" and "Irresistible" lost, and French battleship "Bouvet"

——, Agreement between Great Britain and Americans that cotton should be contraband

——, General Sir J. E. Nixon appointed Commander-in-Chief in Mesopotamia

March 19, Dutch Government protested blockade policy of Entente

——, Sortie of Austrians from Przemysl a failure

March 20, Great Britain, France, and Russia signed secret agreement by which Russia was to receive Constantinople and the Straits and Great Britain the neutral zone of Persia (Cocks)

——, British guarantee Island of Lemnos to Greece

——, General Botha defeated Germans in engagement at Pforteberg, South Africa

March 20–April 20, Battle of the Carpathians, Russian offensive attempted to break through Austrian lines

March 21, Germans recapture Memel

——, Airship raid on Calais and Paris

March 22, French Prize Court declared seizure of the "Dacia" valid

——, Turkish attack near Suez Canal defeated

——, Surrender of the Austrian fortress of Przemysl in Galicia besieged by Russians since Nov. 12

March 25, Dutch ship "Medea" sunk by German submarine after visit and search

March 27, The French captured the Heights of Hartmanns-Weilerkopf, Alsace

March 28, The "Falaba," British passenger ship, sunk by German submarine in St. George's Channel; 111 persons lost their lives

——, Libau bombed by German warships

March 29, Agreement of Great Britain with Americans that rubber should be exported only to Great Britain

March 30, Entente Allies offered Aiden Vilayet (Asia Minor) to Greece (Cocks)

April 1, Anus Hasur, German Southwest Africa, taken by General Mackenzie

April 3–23, Battle of the Woevre (West front) French action for reduction of St. Mihiel salient

April 5–9, Third action of les Epargnes (West front). French capture crests of les Epargnes

April 7, Kalkfontein, German South West Africa occupied

April 8, Deportation and massacre of Armenians begun by order of Turkish Government

——, Italy presented demands to Austria-Hungary for cession of territory as price of neutrality: extension of boundary in Trentino, new boundary on the Isonzo, special provision for Trieste, cession of certain islands off the coast of Dalmatia, abandonment by Austria of claims in Albania, recognition of Italian possession of Ægean Islands occupied, and Valona

April 9, Arrival of Sir John Nixon at Basra to take command in Mesopotamia

April 10, The "Prinz Eitel Friedrich" formally interned at Newport News, U.S.A.

April 12, Smyrna offered to Greece by Entente Nations in return for aid against Turkey. Offer declined

——, French Government accepted Russia's claim to Constantinople

——, Advance on Yaunde (Cameroons) begun

April 12–14, Battle of Shaiba, Mesopotamia. Turks routed

April 13, Russians capture heights near Uzsok Pass in Carpathians

April 16, 25, and 29, Austria refused demands of Italy as to cession of territory

April 17–22, British offensive on West front. Hill 60, 3 miles southeast of Ypres captured

——, Austrian offensive towards Stryj, East Galicia a failure

April 18, First affair at Hafiz Kor (northwest frontier of India)

April 20, South African Union forces defeated Germans north of Keetmanshoop; Mandera (Cameroons) taken by Anglo-French force

——, Armenian revolt begun at Van

April 21–26, German-Austrian attacks in Uzsok Valley repulsed

April 22, First release of poison (chlorine) gas by Germans (Ypres)

April 22–23, Battle of Gravenstafel Ridge (Ypres)

April 22–May 5, Belgians in action of Steenstraet

April 22–May 25, Second Battle of Ypres. First poison gas attack by Germans made 4 mile breach in Allied line

April 23, British blockade of German West Africa (Cameroons) begun

April 24–May 4, Battle of St. Julien (Ypres) second gas attack

April 24, French and Belgians recaptured Lizerne. Germans took St. Julien

April 25, Landing of Allied armies at the Dardanelles begun at Cape Helles and Anzac on the Gallipoli peninsula under fire of Turks

——, Severe fighting near Stryj, East Galicia

——, Germans recapture the Hartmannswillerkopf

April 26, German raider "Kronprinz Wilhelm" interned at Newport News, Virginia

——, Italy signed secret treaty with Allies in London fixing conditions under which Italy would join Entente Allies in war. Cession of territory included southern Tyrol up to the Brenner Pass, Gorizia, Trieste, Istria, northern Dalmatia, Valona, and certain islands. *See also* Turkey for territory in Asia Minor concessions, and war indemnity arranged for

——, German Baltic offensive begun with advance towards Shavli (Baltic)

——, Main French corps disembarked at Gallipoli

April 28, Great Austro-German offensive begun between the Dunajec and Biala Rivers in West Galicia by Von Mackensen which drove Russians back

——, German aëroplane dropped 3 bombs on American steamer "Cushing" in the North Sea

——, Idrisi Arabs concluded treaty with British Government to fight the Turks

April 28–May 2, First Battle of Krithia, Allied advance up Gallipoli

April 30, Shavli, Baltic provinces, occupied by Germans

May 1, Battle of Delman (North Persia)

——, Notice sent by German Ambassador published in American newspapers warning travellers of danger of sailing in war zone on ships of Great Britain or her Allies

——, American oil tankship "Gulflight" torpedoed by German submarine off the Scilly Islands

May 1–5, Battle of Gorlice (Gorlitz)-Tarnow (East front) Austro-German offensive in the Carpathians in western Galicia

May 2, General Mackensen occupied Gorlitz. Russians in retreat to the Wisloka

May 2–3, Attack of Australians and New Zealanders on Monash Gully (Saari Bair) unsuccessful

May 3, Italy denounced the Triple Alliance

——, Austrian army of Archduke Joseph Ferdinand took Tarnow

May 4, Germans recaptured Hill 60 and villages east of Ypres

May 5, South African force commanded by General Botha occupied Karibib

——, Germans repulsed at Mitau (Jelgava) south of Riga

May 6–8, Second Battle of Krithia. Anglo-French attack unsuccessful in Gallipoli

May 7, Retreating Russians dislodged from position on the eastern bank of the Wisloka

——, Serbia given guarantee by Sir Edward Grey of cession of Bosnia and Herzegovina

——, Libau on the Baltic permanently occupied by Germans

May 7, The British mailship "Lusitania" of the Cunard line sailing from New York torpedoed without warning by German submarine off Kinsale Head on the Irish coast. Of 1,918 persons aboard, 1,153 were drowned including 114 Americans

May 8–13, Battle of Frezenberg Ridge (West front), Ypres

May 8, British destroyer "Maiori" sunk off Belgium by mine

——, Attack on Krithi unsuccessful

May 9, Portugal declared war on Germany

——, Unsuccessful British attack on Aubers Ridge (Neuve Chapelle)

——, Italians capture Monfalcone, Austrian torpedo craft base

——, Germans defeated at Krakinow (Baltic Province)

May 9–June 18, Second Battle of Artois. French offensive on West front between Lens and Arras. British attacked toward Aubers Ridge and Festubert region

May 10, Naval convention between Great Britain, France, and Italy

——, French took cemetery Neuville St. Vaast and part of Carency (Arras)

May 11, Russians forced Germans to evacuate Shavli (Lithuania)

——, Capture of Eseka. *See* Cameroons

May 12, Austro-German advance in Galicia continued

——, Bryce commission published report of investigation of German atrocities in Belgium

——, Windhoek, capital of German South West Africa captured by General Botha

——, French took Carency and summit of Notre Dame de Lorette with fort (Artois)

May 13, H.M.S. "Goliath" sunk by Turkish destroyer in the Dardanelles

——, First Lusitania note from American Government to German Government

May 14, Retreating Russians pursued by German army made stand on line of the San River

——, Germans occupied Jaroslav, Galicia

May 15–25, British break German lines in Battle of Festubert (West front)

May 15–June 18, French offensive against trenches of the "Labyrinthe," and Neuville, St. Vaast, and Souchez

May 16, Entente Allies offered Kavala to Bulgaria (Cocks)

May 16–23, Great Battle of the San began with Russian counter-offensive in Galicia

May 17, Germans and Austrians forced crossing of the San River

May 19, Van, Armenia, taken by Russians relieving Armenian garrison

May 19–21, Defense of Anzac by Australians and New Zealanders against Turkish attack (Gallipoli)

May 20, Austria offered Italy concessions in South Tirol, the west bank of the Isonzo as far as population Italian, Trieste to be a free imperial city and recognition of Italian sovereignty in Valona, Austrian disinterest in Albania

May 21, Russian force landed at Enzeli, West Persia

May 23, Italy formally declared war on Austria, to take effect May 24

May 24, Germany severed diplomatic relations with Italy

——, The United States proclaimed neutrality in war between Italy and Austria-Hungary

May 24, Italians entered Austrian territory on all fronts driving Austrians back to their fortified lines. Austrian naval attack on Adriatic coast

May 24–25, Battle of Bellewaarde Ridge (West front), Ypres

May 24–June 11, Battles of Przemsyl and Stryji (East front), Galicia

May 25, End of Battle of Festubert, Battle of Bellewaarde Ridge and Battle of Ypres (West front)

——, Loss of British warship "Triumph" in the Dardanelles

——, German aëroplane raid on Kent and Folkestone, England; 290 casualties

——, American steamship "Nebraskan" torpedoed by German submarine off north coast of Scotland

May 26, British hospital ship "Dover Castle" sunk by submarine

——, Italy declared blockade of coasts of Austria-Hungary, and Albania on May 30

May 27, Italians captured frontier town of Ala on the Adige

——, British battleship "Majestic" torpedoed in the Dardanelles

May 28, Russians capture Urumiah, Persia

May 29, Italians formally occupied Valona, Albania

May 30, Italian air raid on Pola arsenal on Adriatic

——, Italians captured Cortina in Venetian Alps

——, British at Sphinxhaven gain command of Lake Nyasa, Central Africa

May 31, Sugar factory Souchez taken by French (Artois)

——, Siege of Garua, Cameroons begun by British

——, Airship raid over London

——, Turks dispersed in action north of Kurna, Mesopotamia

——, Statement of British Ambassador Spring Rice that the "Lusitania" was not carrying any guns and had never done so

June 1, The French captured trenches at Souchez

——, Stryj, railroad center Galicia captured by Germans

——, Great Britain declared blockade of coast of Asia Minor

June 2, Brazil revoked neutrality and seized German ships in Brazilian waters

——, Germans capture Hooge chateau (West front)

June 3, General Townshend advancing up the Tigris occupied Amarah (Imara)

——, Przemsyl Galicia recaptured by Austro-German forces

——, First meeting of Allied Conference on Economics of the War met in Paris

——, The British captured trenches at Givenchy

——, San Marino declared war on Austria-Hungary

June 4, Third Battle of Krithia, Anglo-French offensive in Gallipoli a failure

June 5, Naval engagement in the Baltic between Russians and Germans

June 6–16, French in action near Quennevières (West front) between Oisne and Aisne Rivers gained ground

June 7, German airship LZ.37 destroyed near Ghent by Lieutenant Warneford attacking from aëroplane

——, Vaux fell (Verdun)

——, First meeting of the Dardanelles Committee of the British Cabinet

——, German army of General Linsingen crossed the Dniester at Zydaczow

June 7–10, French took Neuville and the trenches of the "Labyrinthe"

June 7–13, French successful in action between Hébuterne and Serre (West front)

June 8, Stanislau recaptured by Austrians

——, Resignation of American Secretary of State, William Jennings Bryan on account of note on Lusitania crisis drawn up by President Wilson

June 8–10, Russians attacked and defeated Germans, in region of Zurdawno, driving them back across Dniester

June 9, Monfalcone taken by Italians

——, Second Lusitania note of American government to German government demanded disavowal of destruction of Lusitania and pledge that attacks on unresisting non-combatants should cease. Reparation for victims of disaster

June 10, Garua, in the Cameroons, surrendered to Allied force of Sir Charles Dobell

June 11, End of Battle of Przemsyl (East front). Russians forced to retreat

June 12–13, Austro-Germans attacked Russians on front of 40 miles from Piskorovice on the San to the vicinity of Mosciska and broke Russian front southeast of Jaroslau

June 13, French repulsed at Souchez but successful southeast of Hebuterne (West front)

June 14, Mosciska taken by Germans

June 14–15, Turks made unsuccessful attack on Perim, Arabia

June 15, German zeppelins bombarded northeast coast of England. French airmen bombarded Karlsruhe

June 15–16, Second action of Givenchy (West front)

June 15–27, Battle of Festubert, British offensive (West front)

June 16, British advance west of Hooge and east of Festubert, French north of Arras (West front)

June 17–22, Third Battle of Lemberg (East front)

June 18, End of second Battle of Artois. Results indecisive in both Artois and Champagne

——, End of Second Battle of Artois

June 19, Battle of Grodnek (East front). Mackensen forced Russians to retreat from Grodnek position west of Lemberg

——, Advance on Otavifonstein begun in South West Africa

June 20–July 14, German offensive in Argonne

June 21, Austro-Germans captured Rawa-Ruska after fierce battle, forcing Russians to retreat to last of positions before Lemberg

June 22, Lemberg, capital of Galicia, reoccupied by Austrian General Bohm-Ermolli

June 24, French and Belgians captured Lomie, Cameroons

June 25, General Stewart defeated Germans and occupied Bukoba, Lake Victoria, East Africa

June 26, British advance up the Euphrates begun

June 27, Austrians recapture Halicz and turn Russian line

June 28–29, Battle of the Gnila Lipa (East front)

June 28–July 2, Battle of the Gully Ravine (Gallipoli)

June 29–July 7, First Battle of the Isonzo. Italian offensive against Austrians led by General Cadorna directed against Gorizia

July 1, General Botha occupied Otavi, South West Africa

July 1–7, Second Battle of Krasnik, Austro-German offensive in Poland

July 2, Battle for possession of Carso Plateau begun on Italian front in Julien Alps

——, Russian and Germans in naval battle in the Baltic Sea

July 4, Italians made successful air raid on arsenal and shipyards at Trieste

——, Durazzo, Albania, occupied by Serbians

July 5, Lahej, South Arabia, taken by Turks

July 6, Russians defeated Austrian army of the Archduke Joseph Ferdinand advancing on Lyublin from Krasnik

July 7, End of First Battle of the Isonzo, failure to force Austrian defenses

——, Italian cruiser "Amalfi" sunk by Austrian submarine in Adriatic

——, Italy proclaimed blockade of Austrian and Albanian coasts

July 9, General Botha received surrender of enemy forces of German South West Africa at Grootfonstein

July 11, The "Königsberg" sunk in the Rufiji River, German East Africa, by British

July 12, Italian airships bombed arsenal at Pola on Adriatic

——, The French repulsed German attack on the "Labyrinth," North Arras

——, British residency at Bushire, Persia, attacked by Tangistani tribesmen

July 13, Great Austrian offensive begun on East front with Battle of the Narew and Bobr. For separate actions see Great Britain. Committee on Imperial Defense in Official History of the War

July 14, Germans captured town of Przasnyz, North Poland

July 16, Austrians attacked Russians on the Krasnik-Lublin road

July 17, Durazzo, Albania, evacuated by Serbs at request of Italian government

——, Bulgaria signed treaty of alliance with Central Powers at Sofia. Territory ceded to Bulgaria included Albania

July 18, Windau taken by Germans. Russians retreat to Vistula

——, Prussian and Russian Guards in indecisive engagement (Battle of Brest Litovsk)

——, Italian cruiser "Giuseppe Garibaldi" sunk by Austrian submarine off Cattaro

——, Russians defeated at Krasnotow, Poland

——, German submarine shelled towns in Cumberland county, England, near Whitehaven

July 18–Aug. 10, Second Battle of the Isonzo

July 19, Action of Hooge crater (West front)

July 20–21, Second Battle of Ivangorod (East front)

July 21, Russian offensive forced enemy from right bank of upper Bug River

——, Ivangorod, Poland, invested by Germans

July 22, Bukoba on Lake Victoria, Nyanza in East Africa, captured by British force

——, Italians captured crest of San Michele dominating the Doberdo plateau

July 23–26, Battle of the Narew and Bobr (East front)

July 24, German attack in the Argonne ended

July 25, Government of Serbia moved to Nish

——, Colonel Morrisson occupied Dume, Cameroons

——, British in Mesopotamia captured An Nasiriya on the Euphrates

——, British government guaranteed cession of Mitylene to Greece

July 25, American steamship "Leelanaw" sunk by German submarine off Scotland

July 26, Pelagosa Island in the Adriatic occupied by Italians

——, Germans repulsed at Shlok (Riga front)

——, Italians successful in engagement on Carseau Plateau, captured Monte Sei Busi

July 29, Mackensen broke through Russian line between Lublin and Chelm (East front)

July 30, Pope Benedict sent appeal for peace to belligerent governments

——, Second action at Hooge (West front), Germans captured 500 yards of British trenches using flame projectors

——, Russians evacuated Lublin, Poland

July 31, Russians evacuated Cholm, Poland

Aug. 1, Constantinople harbor raided by British submarine

——, Mitau, Russia, taken by Germans

Aug. 3, Reply of Entente Powers to Bulgarian Note of June 14 (Texts not published)

Aug. 4, Warsaw and Ivangorod taken by Austro-Germans

——, Van, Armenia, occupied by Turks

——, Russians evacuated Deblin, Poland

Aug. 5, Libau on Courland coast bombed and captured by Germans

Aug. 6, General Sarrail appointed Commander-in-Chief in Near East

Aug. 6–7, Turkish position, Table Top and Beauchops Hill, taken by New Zealanders

Aug. 6–10, Battle of Sari Bair (Gallipoli), Australian attack on Lone Pine

Aug. 6–21, Battles of Suvla Bay. Landing of troops at Gallipoli

Aug. 8, New Zealanders stormed Chunuk Bair; driven off Aug. 10 by Turks

——, Bushire, Persia, occupied by British force

Aug. 8–21, German naval attack in Gulf of Riga

Aug. 9, British regain trenches lost July 30 at Hooge chateau

——, Prime Minister Radoslavoff declared that Bulgaria would enter the War if she received Serbian Macedonia, Greek Macedonia east of the Struma, and the Rumanian acquisitions in Silistria

Aug. 10, End of Second Battle of the Isonzo

——, Russian and German fleets in engagement at entrance south channel of Gulf of Riga

Aug. 14, British transport "Royal Edward" sunk by enemy submarine in the Ægean

Aug. 15, Entente Allies made conditional offer of territory to Serbia

Aug. 16, Russian and German fleets in engagement in both channels Gulf of Riga

Aug. 17, Kovno captured by Germans and Russian line of the Niemen broken. Railroad between Bialystok and Brest-Litovsk cut

Aug. 19, Steamer "Arabic" sunk by German submarine off Fastnett. British submarine torpedoed German cruiser "Moltke" in the Baltic

Aug. 20, Fortress of Novo Georgievsk captured by Germans (East front)

——, Russian victory in Gulf of Riga. Capture and destruction of 4 barges of German troops making attempt to land at Pernau

Aug. 21, Italy declared war on Turkey

——, Germans evacuated Gulf of Riga

Aug. 21, Battle of Scimitar Hill, Gallipoli, last great action on this front

——, Great Britain and France declare cotton absolute contraband

Aug. 22, Russians abandon Osowiec, north Poland, stormed by Germans

Aug. 23, Kovel, 40 miles southeast of Brest-Litovsk, occupied by Germans

Aug. 25, Germans captured fortress of Brest-Litovsk

——, Rhodesians occupied Morogoro, East Africa

Aug. 26, Bialystok, Poland, taken by Austro-Germans

Aug. 27, Battle of Zlota-Lipa (East front), Austrian victory in Eastern Galicia

——, Olita on the Niemen evacuated by Russians

Aug. 30, British foreign minister, Sir Edward Grey, gave conditional guarantee of freedom and self determination to Bosnia, Herzegovina, South Dalmatia, Slavonia, and Croatia

Aug. 31, Lutsk fortress, Poland, captured by Serbians (Austro-Germans)

——, Durazzo, Albania, again occupied by Italians

Sept. 1, German government announced acceptance of limitations on submarine warfare demanded by the United States

——, Ruad Island off coast of Syria occupied by the French

Sept. 2, Austrians defeated by Russians near Lemberg in Galicia

Sept. 3, Germans occupied fortress of Grodno, Poland, evacuated by Russians

——, Lemberg evacuated by retreating Austrians, occupied by Russians

Sept. 5, The Tsar assumed supreme command of the Russian armies. General Alexiev made chief of Russian general staff

Sept. 5–14, Battle of the Masurian Lakes (East front)

Sept. 6, French aëroplanes raided Saarbrucken, Prussia

——, Bulgaria signed military convention with Central Powers arrangement for concerted invasion of Serbia

Sept. 7–16, Battle of Tarnopol (East front), Galicia. Russian victory

Sept. 8, Allied attack on Mora, Cameroons

——, The Grand Duke Nicholas transferred to command of Russian armies in the Caucasus

——, The American government requested recall of Dr. Dumba, Austrian ambassador

Sept. 9–Oct. 2, Battle of Vilna (East front) forced Russian retreat

Sept. 9–Nov. 1, Battle of Dvinsk (East front)

Sept. 9, Turco-Bulgarian Convention signed at Demotika

——, Bushire, Persia, attacked by tribesmen

Sept. 11, General Austrian retreat before Russians in Galicia to San River

Sept. 13, Air raid on east coast of England

Sept. 14, Serbs gained pass of Garniceyo breaking through enemy front

Sept. 15, General Nixon drove Turks from position on right bank of the Tigris

Sept. 16, Pinsk, Poland, taken by Austro-Germans

——, End of Battle of Tarnopol

Sept. 18, Germans occupied Vilna

Sept. 18–30, Russian counter-attacks in Volhynia and Galicia

Sept. 19, Tabora, East Africa, occupied by Belgian force

Sept. 21, Venizelos asked for guarantee of 150,000 French and British troops as condition of Greece entering war

Sept. 21, Bulgaria mobilized

Sept. 22, Dede Agatch Agreement between Turkey and Bulgaria altered boundary in favor of Bulgaria

——, Second advance on Yaunde, Cameroons, begun

——, French aëroplane raid on Stuttgart as reprisal

Sept. 23, Russians recapture fortress of Lutsk, Poland

Sept. 25–27, Germans repulsed by Russians in attack on Dvinsk

Sept. 25–Oct. 8, Battle of Loos, British offensive

Sept. 25–Oct. 15, Third Battle of Artois in Battle of Champagne, French offensive

Sept. 25–Nov. 6, Second Battle of Champagne (West front)

Sept. 28, Vimy Ridge, western slopes, and part of Givenchy wood captured by French (West front)

——, British defeated Turks in Battle of Kut-el-Amara, forcing their retreat during night on Bagdad

——, Russians abandon Lutsk

——, Austrian ambassador recalled from the United States

Sept. 29, British General Townshend reoccupied Kut-el-Amara

——, French capture Hohenzollern redoubt (West front)

Oct. 1, German line included all Poland, Courland, the Russian governments of Grodno and Kovno, and parts of Minsk and Volhynia (McPherson)

Oct. 2, Battle of Vilna ended

Oct. 3, Germans captured the Hohenzollern Redoubt (West front)

——, Battle of the Lakes south of Dvinsk (East front)

Oct. 3–5, French and British troops began to disembark at Salonika for passage to Serbia. Greek promise of aid to Serbia repudiated by King Constantine

Oct. 4, Ultimatum of Entente Powers to Bulgaria demanded break with Teutonic Powers

Oct. 5, Russia severed diplomatic relations with Bulgaria

Oct. 6, Austro-German armies began third invasion of Serbia

——, French captured village of Tahure, Champagne, in new offensive

Oct. 7, Austro-German armies crossed the Save and the Danube

——, End of second Battle of Champagne

——, Birjand, East Persia, occupied by British

Oct. 8, End of Battle of Loos with German counter-attack of one day repulsed

——, New Greek government announced armed neutrality

Oct. 9, Wum Biagas (Cameroons) recaptured by British force

——, Belgrade evacuated by Serbs, occupied by Austro-Germans

Oct. 10, Greeks refused aid to Serbia rejecting treaty of 1912

Oct. 11, Sir Ian Hamilton, general in command of the British land forces at Gallipoli, recalled

——, Hostilities begun by Bulgarians across Serbian frontier

——, Renewed French offensive in Artois

Oct. 12, Edith Cavell, English nurse in Brussels, shot by Germans after court martial, for harboring and aiding Allied soldiers to escape

Oct. 13, British recaptured main trenches of Hohenzollern redoubt

——, Air raid over east coast of England and London, 200 casualties

——, General Sarrail arrived at Salonika

Oct. 14, Bulgaria declared war on Serbia

——, French troops from Salonika going to aid Serbs in engagement with Bulgarians at Strumitsa station

Oct. 15, Rumania refused to aid Serbia

——, End of third Battle of Artois

——, Great Britain declared war on Bulgaria

——, Vranje, Serbia, taken by Bulgarians

——, General Sir Charles Monroe appointed to succeed General Hamilton at Gallipoli

——, Montenegro declared "state of war" with Bulgaria

Oct. 16, Serbia and France declared war on Bulgaria

——, Allies announced blockade of the Ægean coast

——, Summit of Hartmannsweilerkopf recaptured by French

Oct. 17, French and Serbs defeated Bulgarians at Strumitsa

Oct. 18, The Bulgarians cut the Salonika Railroad at Vrania, advancing in Serbia

Oct. 18–Nov. 3, Third Battle of Isonzo

Oct. 19, Italy and Russia declared war on Bulgaria

——, Japan declared adherence to Pact of London

Oct. 19–27, Fighting near Mitau (Riga front)

Oct. 20, Sir Ian Hamilton relieved by Sir Charles Monroe

——, British proclamation of modification of the Declaration of London abandonment of Art. 57

Oct. 21, American note to Great Britain protested restraints on neutral trade

——, Second engagement at Strumitsa station, Bulgaria

——, Veles, Serbia, taken by Bulgarians

——, Dede Agatch, Bulgaria, bombarded by Allied squadron

Oct. 22, Bulgarians captured Uskub, Serbia, cutting off Serbian line of retreat to Salonika

——, Shabatch, Serbia, taken by Austrians, and Kumanovo by Bulgarians

Oct. 23, French and Bulgarian troops in engagement at Rabro

——, France declared modification of the Declaration of London

——, British submarine sunk German cruiser "Prinz Adelbert" in the Baltic

Oct. 24, End of Battle of Langemark

——, First action of Krivolak, Macedonia

——, French carried German work La Courtrine (Champagne)

Oct. 25, Sende (Cameroons) captured by French force

Oct. 27, Bulgarians capture Zayechar, Knyatevats, and heights northwest of Pirot

Oct. 28, Cruiser "Argyll" wrecked off east coast of Scotland

Oct. 29, Bulgarians recovered Veles. French took Strumitsa Station

Oct. 30, Battle of Siemilko, East Africa, begun

——, The French repulsed the Bulgarians at Krivolak (Vardar River)

——, Third Allied attack on Mora, Cameroons

Nov. 1, End of Battle of Dvinsk

——, Kraguyevatz, chief Serbian arsenal, captured by Germans

Nov. 2, Mr. Asquith proclaimed independence of Serbia an essential object of the war

——, Russians occupied Kasvin, West Persia

Nov. 3, General Sarrail from Salonika began offensive northward to aid Serbian retreat

——, End of third Battle of Isonzo

Nov. 5, Germans repulsed in Riga district

Nov. 5, Nish, Serbia, captured by Bulgarians

——, End of successful Austro-German offensive against Russia

Nov. 5–8, Battle of Kachanik Pass, Serbia

Nov. 6, End of second Battle of Champagne

——, German position on Banyo Mountain (Cameroons) taken by British

——, Sollum, West Egypt, attacked by German submarine

——, P. and O. steamer "Arabia" sunk by submarine off Island of Cerigo

Nov. 7, Italian steamer "Ancona" sunk in Mediterranean by Austrian submarine. 200 lives lost. German cruiser "Undine" sunk by British submarine

——, Austro-Germans reached Kraguyevatz commanded by Von Gallwitz and forced passage of Morava River at Kralyevo, Serbia

Nov. 10–Dec. 10, Fourth Battle of the Isonzo

Nov. 11, British advance on Bagdad begun

——, The United States proclaimed neutrality in war between the Allies and Bulgaria

Nov. 12, Russians took Hamadan, Persia

Nov. 14, The Senussi begun hostilities by attack on Sollum, Egypt

Nov. 14 and 27, German attacks on the trenches of the "Labyrinth," North Arras, repulsed by French

Nov. 16, Babuna Pass and Prileb, Serbia, taken by Bulgarians

Nov. 17, British hospital ship "Anglia" sunk by mine in the Channel. 80 lives lost

Nov. 20, Novibazar taken by Austrians

——, Russians took Kum, Persia

Nov. 20–25, Serbians made last stand against Austrians on plain of Kosovo Polje

Nov. 22–24, Battle of Ctesiphon, Mesopotamia. General Townshend captured Ctesiphon, only 18 miles from Bagdad

Nov. 23, Entente note to Greece asked permission for defeated Anglo-French Vardar Army to establish themselves at Salonika, guaranteed eventual restoration of occupied Greek territory

——, Sollum evacuated and British begun operations against the Senussi

——, Rovereto (Trentino) taken by Italians

——, Mitrovitza and Prishtina, Serbia, taken by Austro-Germans. Serbian government left Prizren for Scutari

Nov. 24, Greece consented to occupation of Salonika

——, German Field Marshal Von der Goltz took command of Turkish army in Mesopotamia

Nov. 25, Sir William Birdwood appointed commander-in-chief of Mediterranean Expeditionary Force

Nov. 26, General Townshend began retreat from Ctesiphon to Kut-el-Amara

Nov. 28, German official announcement of end of campaign in Balkans

Nov. 30, Italy declared adherence to Pact of London

——, Declaration of Great Britain, Russia, France, Italy, and Japan engaging not to conclude peace separately

——, Serbs began retreat through Albania

Dec. 1, Prizren, Serbia, taken by Bulgarians

Dec. 2, Krivolak on the Varder evacuated by French, Greek frontier

——, Monastir, Serbia, evacuated by Serbs, and occupied by Bulgarians on the 5th

Dec. 3, Serbian government established at Scutari

——, General Joffre placed in command of all French armies

Dec. 3–12, Battle of the Vardar. Anglo-French force pushed back into Greek territory

Dec. 4, American government requested recall of German attaches, Captains Boy-Ed and Von-Papen

Dec. 5, Austrian submarine torpedoed American tank steamer "Petrolite"

Dec. 5–6, Action of Demir Kapu on Vardar River. Bulgarians repulsed. French retreat from Serbia

Dec. 6, Economic blockade of Greece by Entente

Dec. 7, Kut-el-Amara invested by Turks

——, Bulgarians occupied Djakova, Serbia, Austrians occupied Ipek

Dec. 7–8, Action of Kosturino, Bulgaria

Dec. 8, Bulgarians occupied Okhrida, Serbia

——, Evacuation of Gallipoli peninsula by Allied forces at Suvla and Anzac begun

Dec. 9, Retreat of Allied troops from Vardar region

——, General Castelnau placed in command of French armies in France

——, Entente Allies demanded withdrawal of Greek troops from Salonika

Dec. 10, Captains Boy-Ed and Von Papen formally recalled in compliance with wishes of United States government

——, Fourth Battle of the Isonzo ended

Dec. 11, Greek government refused to withdraw troops from Salonika

——, Doiran and Gevgeli, Serbia, taken by Bulgarians

Dec. 11–13, British in engagement with the Senussi at Wad Senab

Dec. 13, Blockade of Greece by Entente relaxed

Dec. 14, Hamadan, West Persia, occupied by Russians

——, Convention between Germany and Austria provided for partition of Russian Poland

Dec. 15, Quasi-i-Shirin, West Persia, occupied by Turks

——, Last Anglo-French troops withdrew from Macedonia retreating into Greek territory

——, Poland severed diplomatic relations with Germany

Dec. 17, Retirement of Sir John French from command of British army in France

——, German cruiser "Bremen" sunk by British submarine

Dec. 19, Sir Douglas Haig succeeded Sir John French in supreme command of British army in France

——, 44 air duels fought on this day (F. H. Sykes)

Dec. 20, Durazzo, Albania, occupied by Italians

——, Evacuation of Suvla and Anzac completed

Dec. 21, Japanese steamer "Yasaka Maru" sunk by submarine in the Mediterranean near Port Said. All passengers and crew escape

Dec. 23, British naval operations on Lake Tanganyika begun

Dec. 24, Russian offensive against the Bukovina begun

Dec. 24–25, Turks attacked Kut-el-Amara

Dec. 25, Kangavar, West Persia, occupied by Russians

——, British in engagement with the Senussi at Majid

——, Bombardment of fort at Kut-el-Amara begun

Dec. 26, German gunboat "Kingani" captured by British on Lake Tanganyika by gunboats dragged across Belgian Congo forests by Commander G. Spicer Simson

——, German raider "Moewe" sailed from Bremen

Dec. 28, Evacuation of the entire Gallipoli peninsula positions ordered

Dec. 29, Austrian naval raid on Durazzo

Dec. 30, British passenger steamer "Persia" sunk by submarine without warning in Mediterranean

1916

Jan. 1, Yaunde (Cameroons) taken by British force

Jan. 1–17, Russian offensive on the Strypa and the Styr, Galicia, of General Lechitski against Bukowina

Jan. 2, Russians renew offensive in eastern Poland

——, Heavy fighting northeast of Czernowitz

Jan. 4, First attempt to relieve Kut-el-Amara garrison made by British force advancing from Ali Gharbi

Jan. 5, Austrian offensive in Montenegro begun

Jan. 6, Battleship "King Edward VII" sunk by mine off north coast of Scotland

Jan. 6–8, Action of Sheikh Sa'ad, Mesopotamia. Turks defeated by British advancing to Kut-el-Amara

Jan. 7–8, Evacuation of Cape Helles, last position on Gallipoli peninsula by Anglo-French forces

Jan. 9, German offensive in Champagne

Jan. 10, Austrians capture Mount Lovtchen, Montenegro, after 3 days bombardment of fleet

Jan. 11, Russians begin general offensive in the Caucasus

——, French troops occupy the Greek Island of Corfu

Jan. 12–20, Armistice between Austria-Hungary and Montenegro

Jan. 13, Kirmanshah, West Persia, occupied by Turks

——, Austrian troops occupied Cettinje, capital of Montenegro

——, Greek government refused consent to Allied occupation of Corfu

——, The Turks defeated on the Tigris at Orah

Jan. 13–14, Action of the Wadi, Mesopotamia

Jan. 14, Lieutenant General Sir Percy Lake appointed to command in Mesopotamia

Jan. 15, End of unsuccessful Russian offensive against Bukowina

——, Serbian government established at Brindisi, Italy. Serbian troops began landing at Corfu Island

——, British liner "Appam" captured by the German cruiser "Moewe" off the Canary Islands

Jan. 16, General Sarrail took command at Salonika

——, General Sussky commanded Russians in battle in the Caucasus. Turks retreated on Erzerum

Jan. 17, Keupri-Keui, Armenia, recaptured by Russians

Jan. 18, Allied warships bombarded Bulgarian port of Dede Agatch

——, Circular note of President Wilson to belligerents as to disarmament of merchant ships and rules of submarine warfare

Jan. 20, Rumania opened negotiations with Russia regarding military assistance

——, Russians occupied Sultanabad, Persia

Jan. 21, Attempt to relieve Kut-el-Amara a failure. Action of Hanna

Jan. 22, Austrians occupied Montenegrin seaports of Antivari and Dulcigno

——, Rumanian negotiations with Russia for military assistance

——, General Malleson occupied Serengeti forcing enemy evacuation of Kasigau (East Africa)

Jan. 23, Austrians took Scutari, Albania, and Podgorica, Montenegro

——, Action at Halazin, British against the Senussi, commanded by German and Turkish officers

Jan. 24–25, Germans attacked Nieuport (West front)

Jan. 25, Montenegro accepted Austrian terms

Jan. 26, American note protested against "black list" policy adopted by Great Britain Dec. 23

Jan. 27, Bombardment of German troops on Belgian coast from the sea

Jan. 28, American note to Great Britain protested search of mails

Jan. 29, Enemy airships raided Paris

Jan. 31, Airship raid on east coast of England and midland counties. 183 casualties

——, General Sir Horace Smith obliged to give up command because of illness. Succeeded by General Jan Smuts

Feb. 1, The British steamer "Appam" captured by the "Moewe" arrived at Newport News under German prize crew

Feb. 2, Elbasan, Albania, taken by Bulgarians

——, First trial of armored motor cars named "tanks" to ensure secrecy during experimental stages

Feb. 3–5, Action against the Senussi at the Siwa Oasis

Feb. 8, Great Britain asked Japan for naval assistance in western hemisphere

——, French cruiser "Admiral Charner" sunk by submarine off Syrian coast

——, Russians reached west bank of the Dniester

Feb. 9, German gunboat "Hedwig von Wissman" sunk by British on Lake Tanganyika

——, Serbian government established at Corfu

Feb. 10, German note to American government announced that from March 1 armed enemy merchant ships would be treated as belligerents and attacked without warning

——, British minesweepers off Dogger Bank raided by Germans

Feb. 11, H.M.S. "Arethusa" sunk by mine in North Sea

Feb. 12, Russians began action against Erzerum, Asia Minor

Feb. 12–14, German attack repulsed at Hooge and Sanctuary Wood but successful at The Bluff on north bank of Ypres-Comines canal

Feb. 15–March 17, Fifth Battle of the Isonzo

Feb. 16, Entente Powers jointly pledged themselves to continue hostilities until Belgium should be restored to independence

——, Army of the Grand Duke Nicholas after battle with the Turks occupied Erzerum, strongest fortified city in Asiatic Turkey defended by Field Marshal von der Goltz

Feb. 17, Berat, Albania, taken by Austrians

——, Island of Chios in Ægean occupied by Allies

——, German troops crossed the border from the Cameroons into Spanish territory for internment

Feb. 18, Surrender of garrison of Mora to General Sir Charles Dobell completed Allied conquest of Cameroons

——, Mush, Armenia, taken by Russians

Feb. 19, General Smuts arrived in Mombassa, East Africa, to take command

Feb. 19–20, Bombardment begun by Germans of unprecedented intensity on secondary fortifications north of Verdun

Feb. 21, German attack on Verdun under general command of the Crown Prince begun with bombardment on front of 25 miles from the Bois d'Avocourt to Etain piercing the French line at Haumont Wood

Feb. 22–23, Brabant evacuated by Allies (Verdun)

Feb. 23, Germans took Caures

——, At request of Great Britain Portugal seized German and Austrian ships lying in Portuguese harbors

Feb. 24, The French lost Hill 344 and Fosse wood. Evacuated villages of Ormes and Samogneux (Verdun) and Bezonvaux stormed

Feb. 25, Germans occupied Fort Douamont (Verdun) evacuated by French

Feb. 26, Kirmanshah, West Persia, occupied by Russians

——, General Petain launched counter-offensive at Verdun around fort and village of Douamont checking German advance

——, British force advancing to reoccupy Es Sollum defeated Senussi at Agagya

Feb. 27, Austrians occupied Durazzo evacuated by Italians

——, French transport "Provence" sunk by submarine in Mediterranean. About 700 survivors of 4,000 on board

Feb. 28, The British reached Aziziyeh halfway to Bagdad

Feb. 29, British blockade of Cameroons raised

——, Action between German cruiser "Greif" and British cruiser "Alcantara" in North Sea. Both vessels sunk

March 1, Italian defeat at Adua

——, "Unlimited" submarine campaign begun by Germany

March 2, Russians in Armenia capture Bitlis

——, German attack on front from Douamont southward to Vaux

March 3, Agreement between Great Britain and France as to administration of Cameroons

——, French evacuated Malancourt

March 4, Russians landed at Atna for advance on Trebizond

——, The German commerce raider "Moewe" effected a safe return to Wilhelmshafen with 199 prisoners, booty of $1,000,000 marks in gold after capture of 16 vessels and laying mines

March 5, Advance on Kilimanjaro, East Africa, begun by General Smuts

March 6, Germans attacked on both sides of the Meuse (Verdun). Hill de l'Oie captured and Forges

March 8, Second unsuccessful attempt made to relieve General Townshend at Kut-el-Amara by attack at Dujailah Redoubt and Ess Sin

March 9, Germany declared war on Portugal

March 10, Germans captured the Bois de Cumières (Verdun)

——, British advance from Nahud into Darfur (Sudan)

——, Taveta, East Africa, occupied by General Smuts

March 11, Scandinavian Governments renewed declarations of neutrality

March 11–12, Action of Latema Nek, East Africa. Von Lettow made retreat, escaping encirclement

March 12, Karind in West Persia taken by Russian General Baratov

March 13, New Moshi, East Africa, taken by British

March 14, Germans captured Hill 265 southern crest of Mort Homme (Verdun)

——, Sollum on west coast of Egypt reoccupied by Allied force from Arabs who had held it since Nov., 1915

March 15, Austria declared war on Portugal

March 16, Von Tirpitz, German admiral, conductor of submarine campaign resigned. Succeeded by Admiral von Capelle

——, French repulsed 5 successive attacks on fort at Vaux

——, Loss of Dutch steamer "Tubantia," passenger ship torpedoed

March 17, End of fifth Battle of the Isonzo

March 18, The "Palembang" bound for Java sunk by German torpedo

March 18–April 30, Battle of Lake Naroch (White Russia). Russian offensive a disastrous failure

March 21, Russians victorious in battle on Dniester River

——, Battle with Von Lettow, Kahe Station, East Africa taken, ending Kilimanjaro operations

——, General E. S. Sheppard in indecisive engagement with Germans northern East Africa

March 24, The British passenger steamer "Sussex" torpedoed in Channel

March 27, British captured 2 lines of German trenches of German salient at St. Eloi (Ypres)

March 27–28, First general war council of Entente Allies held in Paris

March 28, Declaration of unity made by Powers in Paris conference

——, Germans attack on Haucourt-Malancourt front repulsed by French

March 30, Russian hospital ship "Portugal" sunk by submarine in Black Sea

——, Germans repulsed at Douamont fort

March 31, German air raid on east coast of England. 112 casualties

——, French evacuate and Germans occupied village of Malancourt, France

April 1, Germans renewed assault on Douamont fort and took part of village of Vaux

April 1–22, Third unsuccessful attempt to relieve Allied garrison at Kut-el-Amara

April 3, French recaptured Vaux (Verdun)

——, Note of Great Britain and France reply to protest of the United States against censorship and detention of neutral mails

April 3–20, Battle of St. Eloi (West front). British success

April 4, General Brussilov appointed to command on southern East front of Volhynia and Galicia

April 6, British preliminary attack Sanna-i-Yat a failure (Mesopotamia)

——, Germans captured Haucourt village (Verdun)

April 7, Renewal of Battle of Lake Naroch south of Dvinsk

——, General Van Deventer defeated Germans at Ufiome, East Africa

April 8, French evacuated Béthincourt village. Occupied by Germans (Verdun)

April 9, British attack on Turkish position at Sanna-i-Yat a failure (Mesopotamia)

April 9–11, Great German offensive at Verdun with no significant results from line west of Meuse

April 11, German assault on Douamont-Vaux failed

——, Kionga, East Africa, taken by Portuguese

——, General Van Deventer defeated Germans at Umbulu, East Africa

April 12, Germans repulsed by Russians near Dvinsk

——, British success at Kothershein, East Africa

April 14, Constantinople and Adrianople bombarded by British naval aëroplanes

——, End of first Battle of Lake Naroch

——, British success at Salanga, East Africa

April 15, Serbian army headquarters established at Salonika

——, British occupied Kharga oasis

April 17, Germans repulsed west of Douamont

——, Italians took Col di Lana

——, Italian decree prohibited trading with Germany

April 17, Russians captured Trebizond on Black Sea

April 17–18, Action of Bait Aissa, Mesopotamia

April 17–30, Battle of Lake Naroch (East front) a Russian victory

April 18, American note to Germany regarding "Sussex" threatened to sever diplomatic relations unless outrages at sea stopped

——, Airship raid on England

——, German attack on Poivre Ridge (Verdun) repulsed

——, Russian Grand Duke Nicholas captured important port of Trebizond on the Black Sea

April 19, Germans repulsed in attacks at Les Epargnes, captured position north of Langemarck and 2 craters at St. Eloi

——, Kondoa Irangi, German East Africa, taken by Allied General Van Deventer

——, Field Marshall Von der Goltz assassinated by Albanian officer

April 20, French counter-attack on east bank of Meuse (Verdun)

——, The "Aud," German transport, attempting to land arms on Irish coast sunk by crew to avoid capture. Sir Roger Casement, landing from submarine, captured

April 22, Third British attack on Sanna-i-Yat unsuccessful

April 23, Turks made unsuccessful attack on post of Dudweidar and on village of Katia near Suez Canal. British evacuated Katia

April 24, Irish rebels seized Dublin and issued proclamation declaring establishment of republic with Padraic Pearse as president

——, British river vessel "Julnar" lost in attempt to relieve Kut-el-Amara

April 25, Lowestoft and Yarmouth, England, bombarded by German cruisers

April 26, French and Russian governments concluded agreement for future division of Asiatic Turkey

April 27, British battleship "Russell" sunk by mine near Malta

——, British took Moghara oasis

April 28, Germans regain all ground lost at Lake Naroch (Second Battle of Lake Naroch)

April 29, Provisional President of Irish republic ordered surrender to prevent useless slaughter

——, General Townshend surrendered Kut-el-Amara to Turks

——, Italians capture Adamello crest above glacier gaining position on flank of Austrian lines in the Giudicaria valley

——, The Havre declaration guaranteed the territorial integrity of the Belgian Congo

April 30, End of Irish rebellion

May 2, Germans agreed to British proposal for transference of prisoners of war to Switzerland

May 3, German attack on Hill 304 (West front, Verdun) began new offensive for Mort Homme and Avocourt Wood

——, Three Irish rebel leaders executed

——, Belgians occupied Shunzugu, East Africa

May 4, German note to the United States promised that ships should not be sunk without warning but refused to abandon submarine warfare

May 5, Italians repulsed Austrians at Zugna Torta (Trentino)

May 6, Belgians took Kigali, East Africa

May 7, Quasr-i-Shirin, West Persia taken by Russians

May 7, Serbian government established at Salonika

May 9, French successful northwest of Thiaumont

May 9 and 16, Great Britain and France agreed as to eventual partition of Asia Minor (Sykes-Picot agreement) French zone in Syria, British zone in Mesopotamia, and Palestine to be an international zone

May 10, German note admitted torpedoing of the "Sussex" and offered indemnity to injured Americans

——, German attack on Kondoa Irangi repulsed (East Africa)

——, French successful at Mort Homme and Hill 287

May 11, Germans take British trenches northeast of Vermelles (La Bassée)

May 14–June 3, Austrian offensive in the Trentino against Italians, the Battle of Asiago

May 15, Austrians forced Italian retreat south of Rovereto

——, Blockade of Hejaz coast established

——, Khanaquin, northeast of Bagdad taken by Russians and Rowanduz, North Mesopotamia

May 16, Austrians and Italians in battle on Zugna ridge

——, Great Britain and France agree as to claims in Turkish territory (Sykes-Picot agreement). *See* May 9

May 18, Italians evacuated Zugna Torta (Trentino) retiring to line Coni Zugna over Pasubio *massif* and north of the Val Posina across the Sette Communi plateau to the Val Sugana

May 20, German successful attack on crest of Mort Homme, Hill 295 (Verdun)

May 21, French recapture Haudromont quarries east of Meuse

——, Germans make successful attack on British position on Vimy Ridge

——, Austrians capture Armenterra ridge (Trentino), and take summit of Mort Homme from the French

May 22, Forces of the Sultan of Dafur defeated at Beringia, Sudan

——, French attack on Douamont fort successful

May 23, Italians retreat between Astico and Brenta

——, El Fasher, capital of Dafur, occupied by Allied Sudan troops

May 23–25, German assault on Thiaumont-Douamont front and Cumières (Verdun)

May 24, Mama Khatun, Armenia, taken by Russians

May 25, Austrians took Bettale on the Posina and the height of Cimone dominating Arsiero

——, Germans take Cumières and storm Fort Douamont

——, British advance from North Rhodesia and Nyasaland into German East Africa begun

May 26, American note to British government protested search of mails

——, Greek commander forced to surrender Fort Rupel commanding Struma gate to Macedonian Plain to Bulgarians. Evacuated by Greeks May 27

May 26–30, Austrian fighting for pass of Buolo (Trentino)

May 27, Austrians stormed Monte Moschicce north of Asiago

——, New Langenberg, German East Africa taken

May 28, Lieut.-General Sir Julian Byng succeeded Sir E. A. Alderson as commander of Canadian corps

May 29, German final attack on Hill 304 repulsed (Verdun)

May 30, Pass of Buole attacked by Austrians (Trentino) took the peak of Pria Fora

May 31, Austrians occupied Asiago and Arsiero, Italy

May 31–June 1, Battle of Jutland, naval battle in North Sea between British and Germans

June 1, Turkish offensive in Armenia begun

June 1–2, Austrians attack from Posina to Astico (Trentino)

June 1–3, Kozin, Demidovka, and Kolki taken by Russians advancing on Kovel, General Lechitski occupied Sniatyn advancing on Czernowitz

June 2, Germans attacked on front from Mount Sorrel to Hooge carrying all of front line except extreme left at Hooge (Battle of Mount Sorrel)

June 3, Allies assumed administration of Salonika and proclaimed martial law

——, General Cadorna announced that Austrians had been checked in the Trentino

June 4, Russians commanded by General Lechitski attacked the Austrians on the Okna-Dobronovstse line and crossed the Dniester

June 4–16, Austrian attacks on Ciove last Italian position south of the Posina repulsed

June 4–Aug. 11, General Brusilov launched successful Russian offensive on front from the Pripet to the Pruth (Battles of Lutsk)

June 5, Austrians repulsed on Asiago plateau

——, British cruiser "Hampshire" off Orkney Islands sunk by mine. Lord Kitchener and his staff drowned

——, Arab revolt against Turkey begun by Sherif of Mecca

——, Turkish offensive in West Persia begun. Khanaquin evacuated by Russians

——, German attack which carried Hooge position (Battle of Mount Sorrel)

June 6, Russians advancing from Rovno captured fortress of Lutsk, Volhynia

——, "Pacific blockade" of Greece by Entente Allies begun

——, Arabs repulsed in attack on Turkish garrison at Medina

June 7, Austrians repulsed south and west of Asiago

——, Vaux Fort stormed by Germans and Thiaumont farm. French date generally accepted. German date June 2

——, The Sherif of Mecca proclaimed independence

June 8, Russians commanded by General Sakharoff crossed Sereth River in eastern Galicia and captured Buczacz on the Strypa

——, Bismarckburg (Kasanga), East Africa, taken by British

June 9, Jidda, Arabia captured by Arab Allies

——, Capture of Island of Ukerewe, north of Mwanza, East Africa by Allies

——, Russians occupied fortress of Dubno, Volhynia and Rojitche on railroad line

June 9–10, German attack on Kondoa Irangi repulsed (East Central Africa)

June 10, Turkish garrison at Mecca surrendered to the Sherif

June 11, Austro-Hungarians defeated by Russians at Dobronovtse

June 11–30, Battle of the Strypa. Russians commanded by General Scherbatcheff advanced in Galicia

June 12, Kirman, East Africa occupied by British

June 13, General Smuts took Wilhelmstal, German East Africa

——, Belgians took Kitega, German East Africa

——, British General Edward Northey took Old Langenburg (Lumbira) at head of Lake Nyassa

June 13, Successful counter-attack of Canadians recaptured ground on original front (Battle of Mount Sorrel)

——, Russians repulsed at Baranovichi reach the Stokhod River

——, Russians advancing on Kovel took Kozin, Demidovka, and Kolki. General Lechitski advancing on Czernowitz took Sniatyn, East Galicia

June 14–17, Entente Powers Economic Conference met in Paris

June 15, Korogwe taken by Allies completing conquest of Usambara region, East Africa

June 15–17, Italians on Monte Pau, southern edge of the Setti Communi, repulsed Austrian attacks

June 16, British and French abandon Declaration of London. *See also* July 8

June 16–20, Germans under Lisingen counter-attacked Russians in defense of Kovel

June 16–July 7, Italian offensive on Trentino front, Asiago plateau

June 17, Russian General Lechitski reoccupied Czernowitz, Bukowina

June 19, German attack on Hill 321, Thiaumont and Fleury begun

——, Handeni, German East Africa, taken

June 20, Qasr-i-Shirin, West Persia, taken by Turks

June 21, Germans take Hills 321 and 320 but are checked at Les Epargnes

——, Allied note to Greece demanded demobilization and change of government. Accepted the next day and "pacific blockade" suspended

——, Radautz, Bukowina taken by Russians

June 23, Kimpolung, Bukowina, on Rumanian border taken by Russians

——, Fort Thiaumont (Verdun) finally stormed by Germans

——, The steamer "Brussels" captured by Germans, Captain Charles Fryatt

June 24, Fleury captured by Germans (West front) Verdun

——, Greek government ordered demobilization

——, Austro-Hungarians driven out of the Bukowina

——, General Van Deventer resumed offensive and by end of July in possession of railroad from Kilimantinde to Kikombo (100 miles)

June 25, Austrians began retreat on Trentino front evacuating Asiago

June 27, Italians recaptured Posina and Arsiero

——, Belgian force reached Lake Victoria Nyanza, East Africa, in advance on Tabora

June 28, Turks in possession of West Persia

June 29, Russian General Lechitski occupied Kolomea on the Pruth

——, Sir Roger Casement convicted of high treason and sentenced to death for conspiracy with Germany

June 30, Fort Thiaumont (Verdun) recaptured by French

July 1, Kirmanshah, West Persia, retaken by Turks

——, Montauban taken by British (Somme) the villages of Dompierre, Becquincourt, and Bussu south of the Somme by the French

——, Russian ultimatum to Rumania which forced that country into the War

July 1–13, Battle of Albert (Somme)

July 1–Nov. 17, Battles of the Somme, Anglo-French offensive (West front)

July 2, British took Fricourt and the French Curlu, Frise, and Herbécourt (Somme)

July 2–9, First Battle of Baranovichi (East front). Russian offensive of General Evert

July 3, French captured Feuillieres, Flaucourt, and Assevilliers getting within 3 miles of Péronne. British took La Boiselle and part of Ovillers (Somme)

——, Secret Russo-Japanese treaty as to policy and interests in Far East

——, French broke into German second line taking a number of villages beyond the Somme

July 4, Second Russian advance of General Lesh in the Ukraine across the Styr at Kolki and Rafaloka. Austrians retreated toward Stokhod River

——, French took Belloy-en-Santerre in German third line

July 7, Tanga, East Africa, occupied by Allied force

——, End of Italian counter-offensive in Trentino

——, Turks recaptured Erzingan, Armenia

——, Russians reached the Stokhod where Austrian line held

——, Germans in East Galicia retired behind the Zlota Lipa River

——, British gain part of Leipzig redoubt in engagement east of Contalmaison

July 8, Turks recaptured Mush and Bitlis, Armenia

——, Russians broke through enemy line north of Lusk and captured Delatyn

——, British Order in Council denounced the Declaration of London. France also rescinded the Declaration

July 9, French took Biaches and high ground called La Maisonette and advanced along Bray-Péronne road

——, German submarine "Deutschland" arrived at Norfolk, Virginia, U.S.A.

July 10–Aug. 9, Second Battle of Barnaovichi (East front), Russian offensive in Poland

July 11, German attack from Vaux to Souville east of the Meuse (Verdun)

——, Contalmaison captured by Allies

——, Seaham, Durham coast of England shelled by German submarine

July 12, Russians in Armenia captured Mamakhatun

——, British captured Mametz wood (West front)

July 14, British capture Longueval and Bazentin le Petit and Trones wood (Somme) in new offensive attack

——, Mwanza on Lake Victoria Nyanza taken by British

July 14–17, Battle of Bazentin Ridge (Somme). The French captured German second line

July 15–16, Russian attack at Shklin of General Sakharoff southwest of Lutsk drove Austrians across the Lipa

July 15–Sept. 3, Battle of Delville Wood (Somme) British advance

July 17, French repulsed attack of Germans on La Maisonette and at Biaches. British took Ovillers and Waterlot farm

July 18, "Black list" of 85 American firms published by Great Britain under Act of Dec. 23, 1915

July 19, Turks began action against Suez Canal from Oghratina

July 19–20, Battle of Fromelles (West front)

July 20–22, Russian army of General Sakharoff defeated Germans on the Lipa River southwest of Lutsk salient

July 23, Pangani, East Africa taken by Allies

July 23–Sept. 3, Battle of Pozières Ridge (Somme)

July 24, General Northey defeated the Germans at Malangali, East Africa

July 25, Erzinjan, Armenia taken by Russians

July 26, Pozières village taken by British, Australians, and New Zealanders

——, American note protested British "black list"

July 27, Captain Charles Fryatt, commander of British merchant vessel, shot after German court martial at Zeebrugge, Belgium for attempt to ram submarine attacking his ship on March 20, 1915

——, Yenbo, port of Medina, surrendered to Arab force

——, Meia, German East Africa taken by General Smuts' forces

July 28, Russians took Brody, Galicia

——, Belgians under Olsen occupied Kigoma, East Africa

——, Longueval taken by British and entire Delville Wood. French gain west of Thiaumont (Verdun)

July 28–Aug. 17, Battle of Kowel (East front)

July 29, British occupied Dodoma, East Africa

July 30, Forces of General Smuts reached Kikombo, German East Africa completing occupation of 100 miles of Central Railroad

July 31, Kilimatinde, German East Africa taken and Saranda

Aug. 1, Sadani, East Africa occupied by Allies

Aug. 2, Italian dreadnought "Leonardo da Vinci" sunk by explosion in harbor of Taranto

Aug. 2–21, General Sarrail took offensive in Battle of Doiran (South Serbia)

Aug. 3, Ujiji, Lake Tanganyika occupied by Belgians

——, Sir Roger Casement hanged in London

Aug. 4, German attack on Thiaumont repulsed. British take trenches on German second line north of Pozières

Aug. 4–5, Battle of Rumani (Sinai). Turks defeated in attack on British positions near Katia

Aug. 4–6, Russians successful in battle on Sereth River

Aug. 5, British advance through Nguru Hills, German East Africa begun

Aug. 6–17, Sixth Battle of Isonzo, Italian offensive with Gorizia as objective

Aug. 7, Russian army of General Lechitski won battle south of the Dniester River

Aug. 8, Delatyn and the Carpathian pass of Jablonitsa taken by Russians

Aug. 9, Gorizia occupied by Italians

——, Germans recaptured Thiaumont fort

Aug. 10, Russians occupied Stanislau

——, Hamadan, West Persia occupied by Turks

Aug. 11, Mpwapwa, German East Africa occupied

Aug. 12, Russians crossed Zlota Lipa and occupied Mariampol

——, Turks evacuated Bir-el-Abd Sinai after battle

——, Declaration of neutrality of Guatemala

Aug. 15, Bagamoyo, German East Africa occupied

——, Mush and Bitlis, Armenia captured by Turks

——, Anglo-French-Serb advance up Vardar Valley against Monastir

Aug. 16, Date of the Lichnowsky memoir "My London Mission," published early in 1918

——, French captured German trenches near Belloy-en-Santerre

——, British in engagement at Dakawa on the Wami River, East Africa

Aug. 17, Austria announced capitulation of Montenegro

——, End of Battle of Gorizia (Sixth Battle of the Isonzo)

Aug 17, Rumania concluded secret treaty of alliance with the Entente Allies

——, End of offensive of General Brusilov (Battles of Lutsk or Luck)

——, Bulgarians invaded Greek territory by way of the Struma Valley

Aug. 18, Fleury reoccupied by French colonial regiment from Morocco and held in face of assaults

——, British advanced from Pozières to the Somme

Aug. 18–25, Successful Russian counter-offensive in Armenia

Aug. 19, British cruisers "Falmouth" and "Nottingham" sunk in North Sea by submarine

——, Engagement at Msagara, East Africa and British took Lupembe

Aug. 20, Austrian-Montenegrin negotiations broken off

Aug. 21, Declaration of neutrality of Peru

Aug. 22, Kilosa, German East Africa occupied

Aug. 23, Battle of Rayat, Armenia

Aug. 24, Mush and Bitlis, Armenia recaptured by Russians

——, Mlali, East Africa occupied by South African Union forces

——, Heavy fighting for Thiepval Ridge. French captured Maurepas village

Aug. 26, Mrogoro, seat of government, German East Africa taken by General Smuts and enemy driven from Uleia

Aug. 27, Italy declared war on Germany to take effect Aug. 28

——, Rumania declared war on Austria-Hungary

Aug. 28, Italy in state of war with Germany

——, Rumanians began invasion of Transylvania

——, Germany declared war on Rumania

——, General F. S. Maude succeeded General Sir P. H. Lake in command in Mesopotamia

Aug. 28–29, Russian advance in the Carpathians (Galicia)

Aug. 29, General Hindenburg superseded General Falkenhayn demoted as German chief of General staff

——, Rumanians took Brasov and Kronstadt, Transylvania

——, Iringa, German East Africa occupied. Portuguese occupied Bay of Menasi

Aug. 30, Turkey declared war against Rumania

——, Rumania severed diplomatic relations with Bulgaria

Aug. 31, End of Battle of Verdun (West front)

Sept. 1, Rumanians took Sibiu, Transylvania

——, Bulgaria declared war against Rumania

——, Great Britain and Russia agree on division of territory in Turkish Asia Minor (Sykes-Picot agreement)

Sept. 2, German ships in Piraeus, Greece seized by Entente force

——, Raid of 14 airships on London. 170 casualties

——, Germans and Bulgarians invaded the Dobrudja district of Rumania

Sept. 3, Russian victory of General Brussilov on the Zlota Lipa River. German line broken at Brzezany

——, British defeated attack of Prussian guard at Thiepval and took Ginchy and Guillement. French took Le Forst village and Clery-sur-Somme

——, Dar-es-Salaam, German East Africa surrendered to British

Sept. 3–6, Battle of Guillemont (Somme), Allied offensive

Sept. 6, Tutrakan, Rumania taken by Bulgarians after 4 days' battle

Sept. 7, Kilwa, German East Africa taken

——, Halicz on the Dniester taken by Russians

Sept. 8, Orsova, Hungary occupied by Rumanians

Sept. 9, The British took Ginchy (Somme). Irish regiment

Sept. 10, Germans and Bulgarians took Silistria, in the Dobrudja evacuated by Rumanians

——, Kidodi, German East Africa taken

Sept. 11, Russian army of General Lechitski took Mount Kapul 50,000 feet above the Kirlibaba Pass

Sept. 12, A Greek army corps surrendered to Germans at Kavala and was interned

Sept. 13, Bouchavesnes east of Baupaume-Peronne Road taken by French, and trenches at L'Abbe Wood farm southeast of Combles

——, Mikindani, German East Africa taken

Sept. 14, Germany declared war on Rumania

——, Forts of Kavala, Greek Macedonia, taken by Bulgarians

Sept. 14–18, Seventh Battle of the Isonzo

Sept. 15, Kissaki, East Africa, taken with stores by British

Sept. 15–22, Battle of Flers-Courcelette (Somme). Tanks used for the first time in Allied attack

Sept. 16, Russians in successful battle on Zlota Lipa

——, Lindi, German East Africa occupied

——, The *Oberste Kriegsleitung* signed by Germany and Austria, giving Germany supreme command

Sept. 17, Kilwa Kissiwani, German East Africa taken

Sept. 18, End of seventh Battle of the Isonzo

——, French capture Deniecourt (Somme) and British the quadrilateral between Bourleaux Wood and Ginchy

Sept. 19, Belgian force occupied Tabora, German East Africa

Sept. 20, Provisional government of Albania moved from Naples to Salonika

Sept. 20 and Oct. 25, Portuguese troops crossed into German East Africa

Sept. 22, Turkish garrison at Taif (Hejaz) surrendered to Arabs

Sept. 22–25, Heavy fighting for Thiepval Ridge

Sept. 23, Airship raid on east coast of England and London

Sept. 24, French made air raid on Krupp works at Essen

Sept. 25–28, Battle of Morval (Somme)

Sept. 25–Oct. 31, German offensive towards Dvinsk and Riga repulsed

Sept. 26, Thiepval village on Ancre taken by Allies

Sept. 26–28, Battle of Thiepval Ridge (Somme). British take Thiepval Ridge on the 26th. Combles taken by French

Sept. 26–29, Battle of Sibiu. Vulcan pass taken by Germans

Sept. 28, Bulgarians occupied Giurevo on the Danube

——, British took Kut-el-Amara

——, British took Schwaben Redoubt on Thiepval Plateau except small part north of Thiepval (Somme)

Sept. 29, Sibiu, Transylvania, retaken by Austro-Hungarians

——, M. Venezelos established a provisional government to aid Allies in Crete in opposition to Athens

Oct. 1–18, Battle of Transloy Ridges (Somme)

Oct. 1–Nov. 11, Battle of Ancre Heights (Somme)

Oct. 3, General Von Bissing, German military governor of Belgium issued decree subjecting to forced labor outside Belgium all able-bodied Belgians unemployed

——, Allies took Yenikeiu on left bank of the Struma

Oct. 4–23, Austro-German offensive in Rumania

Oct. 5–Dec. 11, Battle of the Cerna and Monastir (Serbia)

Oct. 7, British capture Le Sars village on Albert-Bapaume Road

——, German submarine U53 arrived at Newport, Rhode Island

Oct. 7–9, Battle of Brasov (Transylvania). City retaken by Austro-Germans

Oct. 8, Orsova in Hungary captured by Rumanians

——, German submarine U53 destroyed 5 ships off Newport, Rhode Island

Oct. 9–12, Eighth Battle of the Isonzo. Italian offensive in the Carso region

Oct. 10, Entente note to Greece demanded surrender of Greek fleet. Accepted

Oct. 11, Italians took Austrian second line on Carso plateau

Oct. 13, Franco-British squadron of 40 machines made successful air raid on Mauser rifle factory at Oberndorf on the Neckar

Oct. 17–22, Battle of the Dakhla Oasis with the Senussi (West Egypt)

Oct. 19, Germans defeated south of New Iringa, East Africa

Oct. 20, Mackensen led German attack on entire line in Dobruja

Oct. 21, Germans under Kraut defeated at Mkapira, East Africa

Oct. 22, Constanza, Rumanian port on Black Sea taken by Germans and Bulgarians (British official chronology, Aston, Oct. 25, Ploetz and Gleichen, Oct. 23)

Oct. 24–Nov. 19, Between these dates 50,000 Belgians deported to Germany. By December 100,000

Oct. 24–Dec. 18, General Nivelle launched first offensive battle of Verdun. Fort Douamont recaptured

Oct. 25, Cernavoda, Rumania taken by Austro-Germans

——, General Falkenhayn captured Vulcan Pass

Oct. 26, Deportation begun in district of Mons, Belgium

Oct. 26–27, German destroyer raid in Dover Straits

Oct. 27, Serbs gained in Cherna region

Oct. 28, Circular issued by Governor Von Bissing for execution of deportations

——, British hospital ship "Galeka" sunk by mine off Havre

——, American steamship "Lanao" sunk by German submarine off Portugal

Oct. 29, Sherif of Mecca proclaimed King of the Arabs

Oct. 31–Nov. 4, Ninth Battle of the Isonzo

Nov. 1, Fort Vaux (Verdun) evacuated by Germans and occupied by French Nov. 3

——, The German submarine "Deutschland" arrived at New London, Connecticut, on second voyage to America

——, Rumanians regain Vulcan Pass

Nov. 4, End of ninth Battle of the Isonzo

Nov. 5, Attack of General Nivelle (Verdun) captured Vaux and Damloup villages

Nov. 6, Forces of the Sultan of Dafur defeated near Gyuba (Darfur) and Sultan killed

Nov. 7, American steamship "Columbian" sunk by German submarine off Spain

Nov. 11, End of Battle of Ancre Heights

Nov. 12, Shiraz, South Persia, occupied by British

——, Malangali, East Africa, besieged by the Germans since the 8th, relieved

——, French took Salissel (Somme)

Nov. 13–18, Battle of the Ancre River (Somme). Beaumont-Hamel stormed by British forces

Nov. 15, Hafiz Kar affair on northwest frontier of India

——, German advance in pursuit of Rumanians captured Targu Jiu

Nov. 15–Jan. 9, 1917, British advance in Sinai

Nov. 16–17, Battle of Targau-Jiu, Rumania. Germans began reconquest of Transylvania and Wallachia

Nov. 17, German attack on Lupembe, East Africa, unsuccessful

Nov. 18, Munich bombed by French aviator de Beauchamp

——, End of Battles of the Somme. Allies advance front beyond the Thiepval Ridge and north and west of Grandcourt

Nov. 19, Monastir captured by the French (Serbian Macedonia)

——, Entente note to Greece demanded surrender of military material and dismissal of ministers of the Central Powers. Refused

Nov. 21, British hospital ship "Britannic" sunk by mine in Ægean

——, German army of von Falkenhayn entered Crajova evacuated by Rumanians

Nov. 22, Orsova, Hungary recaptured by Austro-Germans

Nov. 23, British hospital ship "Braemar Castle" hit by mine or torpedoed in Ægean

——, German army under Mackensen crossed the Danube at Izlaz and Simnitza

——, Venezelos government declared war against Germany and Bulgaria

Nov. 26, German raider "Moewe" sailed from Kiel on second cruise

——, Second German naval raid on Lowestoft, England

——, French battleship "Suffren" sunk by submarine in Bay of Biscay

Nov. 27, Airship raid on east coast of England

——, Germans took Alexandria, Rumania

——, Wheat Executive Agreement signed by Great Britain, France, and Italy for united control and purchase

Nov. 28, Daylight raid on London by single German aëroplane

——, Bulgarians occupied Giurgevo on Danube

Nov. 29, Sir David Beatty succeeded Admiral Jellicoe as commander-in-chief of British fleet

Nov. 30, Allied troops landed at the Piraeus, Athens

Dec. 1, Allied troops fired on by Greek troops at Athens as they disembarked

——, German raider "Wolff" left Germany

Dec. 2, Allies declared blockade of Greece

Dec. 3, Funchal, Madeira, shelled by German submarine

Dec. 4, British steamer "Caledonia" sunk in Mediterranean

Dec. 6, Ipek, Montenegro taken by Austrians

——, Germans occupied Bucharest, Rumania

Dec. 7, French regained trenches lost on Hill 304 (West front)

——, Rumanian force of Colonel Anastasiu surrendered at Caracaliu

Dec. 8, Blockade of Greece by Entente Powers begun

Dec. 11, Italian battleship "Regina Margherita" sunk by mine

——, Entente note to Greece asked for complete demobilization

Dec. 12, General Nivelle succeeded Foch in chief command of armies in France

——, The German Imperial Government with the assent of its Allies sent notes to the Entente Powers suggesting negotiations for peace but mentioning no terms

Dec. 13, Anglo-Indian force begun operations for recapture of Kut-el-Amara

Dec. 14, Hamadan, West Persia occupied by Russians

——, Entente note to Greece demanded withdrawal of Greek army from Thessaly. Accepted

Dec. 15–16, French General Mangin in successful offensive, Battle of Louvemont (Verdun) east of the Meuse

Dec. 18, End of first offensive Battle of Verdun

——, President Wilson addressed circular note to the belligerents suggesting negotiations for peace and asking statement of terms

Dec. 19, British government recognized the Venizelos government of Greece

Dec. 21, British force occupied El Arish (Sinai) evacuated by Turks

——, Battle of Rimnicul-Sarat in Rumania

Dec. 25–28, Van Deventer and Northey in engagement with Germans in the Mahenge district, East Africa

Dec. 26, Central Powers and Turkey sent note to President Wilson suggesting meeting of delegates in neutral country. No peace terms stated

——, Austro-German offensive on the Trotus front begun

——, General Joffre created marshal of France

Dec. 27, French battleship "Gaulois" sunk by submarine in Mediterranean

——, Convention between Great Britain and France as to administration of Togo

Dec. 30, Bulgarian note to President Wilson in answer to American note of 18th accepted peace proposals

——, Entente Powers reply to German peace proposals of Dec. 12 dismissed offer as "empty and insincere"

1917

Jan. 1, General Smuts began new offensive against von Lettow in East Africa

Jan. 3, Focsani and Macen, Rumania, taken by Germans

——, Portuguese troops landed in France

Jan. 3–4, Engagement with Germans at Beho Beho, East Africa, in which F. C. Selous, explorer, killed

Jan. 4, Russian battleship "Peresvyet" sunk by mine off Port Said

Jan. 5, Braila, Rumania taken by Germans

——, General Cobbe began operations to clear the Khadairi Bend of Tigris

Jan. 6, Last Russian and Rumanian troops evacuated the Dobrudja

Jan. 7, End of Austro-German offensive (East front)

Jan. 8, Foscani, Rumania, lost

Jan. 9–24, Battle of Kut

Jan. 9, Engagement at Rafah, Sinai. Rafah taken, Sir Philip Chetwode defeated Turks clearing Egyptian province of enemy

——, British battleship "Cornwallis" torpedoed in Mediterranean

Jan. 10, Statement of Allied War aims in reply to

American note of Dec. 18. Note to President Wilson in which they stated war aims included "compensation and equitable indemnities for harm suffered," "restoration of Belgium, Serbia and Montenegro with the compensation due them" and the "evacuation of the invaded territories in France, in Russia, and in Rumania with just reparation" and liberation of Czechoslovaks and Slavs

Jan. 10, German memo on treatment of armed merchant ships

Jan. 11, Settlement Treaty signed at Berlin between Germany and Turkey

——, Note of Central Powers addressed to Neutral Powers repudiated responsibility for continuation of war

——, British advanced on Beaumont-Hamel spur

Jan. 17, Japanese battleship "Tsukuba" sunk by internal explosion

Jan. 19, General Cobbe successful in clearing Khadairi Bend on Tigris in operations against Kut-el-Amara

Jan. 20, General Smuts left East Africa to attend Imperial Conference in London; succeeded by General Hoskins

——, German minister in Mexico instructed by his government to negotiate an alliance between Mexico and Japan against the United States in event of war

Jan. 23, British destroyer "Simoom" sunk in engagement with German torpedo boat flotilla

——, German attacks between Aa and Tirul marshes forced Russians back

Jan. 24, Wejd, Arabia surrendered to Arab force

——, Formal apology of Greek government for affair of Dec. 1 to Allies

Jan. 25, German assault made gains at Hill 304 (Verdun)

Jan. 26, Raid by German destroyers on Southwold, England

Jan. 31, German government announced "unrestricted submarine warfare" to begin Feb. 1

Feb. 1, Russian line broken near Haliz but recovered

——, Unrestricted submarine warfare begun by Germany

——, Norway forbade all submarines to use Norwegian waters

Feb. 3, The United States severed diplomatic relations with Germany

Feb. 3–5, Engagements at Siwa Oasis, West Egypt. Senussi (Sidi Ahmed) defeated

——, Important German line of defense on Beaumont-Hamel spur captured by British

Feb. 7, Grandcourt occupied and Baillescourt farm carried by British

——, The British ship "California" with American passengers sunk off the coast of Ireland without warning

Feb. 8, End of British campaign against the Senussi in Egypt and the Sudan in final engagement

Feb. 10, German air raid on Dunkirk, Amiens, and Nancy

Feb. 10–11, British attack on enemy position Beaucourt Valley begun with attack on Serre Hill

Feb. 13, Scandinavian countries issue joint protest against German submarine warfare

Feb. 14, Scandinavian countries declared non-recognition of German blockade

Feb. 15, Great Britain announced that restoration of Alsace-Lorraine to France was one object of Great Britain in War

Feb. 16, Agreement of British Government to support Japanese claims to Pacific Islands and German rights in Shantung

Feb. 17, Note of Entente Powers protested hostility of Greek press

——, British began advance north and south of the Ancre River, forcing Germans to retreat

Feb. 17–24, British attack on Turkish positions at Sanna-i-Yat, Mesopotamia, successful

Feb. 21, Americans entered the line near Luneville

——, British Order-in-Council required neutral ships to call at British or Allied ports under penalty of seizure

Feb. 21–March 31, Germans withdraw to Hindenburg line from Ancre River salient which was occupied by British

Feb. 22, German submarine torpedoed 7 Dutch merchant vessels in the North Sea, sinking 4

Feb. 23, Kut reoccupied by British force

Feb. 24, German retreat on the Ancre begun

——, British force entered Kut-el-Amara unopposed, the Turks in retreat pursued by cavalry

Feb. 25, The villages of Warlencourt-Eaucourt, Pys, Miraumont, famous dovecot at Beauregard and important position of Serre taken by Allies (West front)

——, British merchant ship "Laconia" sunk by German submarine

——, German destroyer raid on Margate and Broadstairs

Feb. 26, President Wilson asked Congress for permission to arm merchant ships

Feb. 27, Statement of President Wilson that he considered the sinking of the "Laconia" an "overt act" against the United States

Feb. 28, Publication of German plan to induce Japan and Mexico to join in war against the United States

March 2, Hamadan, West Persia, recaptured by Russians

March 3, French entered Roye (River Ancre)

March 5, Russians occupied Kangaver, Persia

March 10, British took Irles, west of Peronne

March 10–19, Allied offensive in Monastir area

March 11, General Maude occupied Bagdad

——, Russians took Kirmanshah, Persia

——, Secret agreement of France and Russia as to left bank of Rhine, Saar Valley, and Poland (Cocks)

——, Village of Monchy-le-Preux taken by Allies, key position of country between Scarpe and Sensée

March 12, Revolution begun in Russia. *See* Russia

——, British advanced on Doiran fort

——, American Congress passed measure to arm merchant ships

March 13, German army began retreat from the Somme

March 14, China severed diplomatic relations with Germany

——, Action of Mushaidiya, Mesopotamia

March 15, Abdication of Tsar of Russia signed

——, General Alexieff officially commander-in-chief of Russian armies

March 16, Mutiny in Russian Baltic fleet

——, German raider "Leopard" sunk in North Sea by H.M.S. "Achilles"

——, German retreat to Siegfried line begun

March 17, Allied attack captured Roye, Baupaume, and Chaulnes (Somme)

Karind, West Persia, occupied by Russians

March 18, Air raid on Ramsgate and Broadstairs and Nesle, England

March 18, Péronne and Noyon occupied by Allies

March 19, Allies occupied Feludja on the Euphrates

——, French battleship "Danton" sunk in Mediterranean by submarine

March 21, American tank steamer "Healdton" sunk by German submarine off Holland. 20 lives lost

——, British captured Beaumetz-les-Cambrai

——, The "Asturias," British hospital ship, sunk by submarine off Start Point

March 23, French gain favorable positions south of St. Quentin

March 24, General M. V. Alexiev took command of Russian armies

March 25, Russians took Qasri-i-Shirin, West Persia

March 26–27, Turks repulsed British, First Battle of Gaza, Gaza the "natural gate" to Palestine

March 30, British hospital ship "Gloucester Castle" attacked by submarine in Channel, but towed into port

March 31, Secret proposals of Emperor Charles of Austria to French President addressed to Prince Sixtus of Bourbon with view to peace

April 1, Armed American steamer "Aztec" torpedoed by submarine near Brest. 28 lives lost

April 3, H.M.S. "Jason" sunk by mine off west coast of Scotland

——, German attack west of St. Quentin failed

——, Germans successful in battle on the Stokhod (Volhynia). Took 10,000 Russian prisoners

April 4, Khanaqin, northeast of Bagdad, taken by Russians

——, British captured Monchey-le-Preux

April 5, German retreat to Hindenburg line completed

April 6, The United States declared war on Germany

——, German and Austrian vessels in American ports seized

April 7, Cuba and Panama declared war on Germany

April 8, Diplomatic relations with the United States severed by Austria-Hungary

April 9, 14 Austrian vessels in American ports seized

——, American Admiral Sims arrived in England

——, Russian declaration in favor of self determination of peoples

——, Canadians capture Vimy Ridge

April 9–14, First Battle of Scarpe River, France

April 9–May 17, Battle of Arras (West front) opened with Battle of Vimy Ridge

April 10, British hospital ship "Salta" sunk by submarine off Havre

——, Hill 145 taken by Allies and capture of Vimy Ridge completed by Canadians

——, Bulgaria severed diplomatic relations with the United States

April 11, Argentine made statement of "benevolent neutrality" toward the United States in war

——, Chile declared neutrality in war between the United States and Germany

——, Brazil severed diplomatic relations with Germany

——, Attack on Monchy-le-Preux repelled by British

April 12, The British pierced the Hindenburg line at Arras

April 13, Bolivia severed diplomatic relations with Germany

April 14, End of Battles of Scarpe and Vimy Ridge

April 16–20, Second Battle of the Aisne, French offensive (West front) between Soissons and Reims

April 17, St. Jean de Maurienne agreement between Great Britain, France, and Italy by which Italy

agreed to Sykes-Picot territorial arrangements and received compensation in Alexandretta, Haifa, and Akka

April 17–19, Second Battle of Gaza (Palestine), British attack unsuccessful

April 17–20, Battle of "The Hills" (Champagne) ended French unsuccessful offensive

April 18, Nicaragua severed diplomatic relations with Germany

April 19, First shot of American gun in the War from the American steamer "Mongolia" repulsed submarine attack

April 20, Turkey severed diplomatic relations with the United States

——, Second German destroyer raid in Dover Straits

——, End of French offensive with end of Battles of the Aisne and "The Hills"

April 21–22, Action at Istabulat, Mesopotamia

April 23–24, Second Battle of the Scarpe (Arras)

April 24, Samarra, Mesopotamia, taken by British General Maude, northern railhead of uncompleted Berlin to Bagdad railway, 60 miles from Bagdad

April 24–May 9, Battle of Doiran (Salonika campaign) Doiran fort taken

April 26, German destroyer raid on Ramsgate, England

April 27, Guatemala severed relations with Germany

April 28, American tank steamship "Vacuum" sunk by German submarine off Scotland. 24 lives lost

April 28–29, Battle of Arleux, France. Arleux taken by Canadians

April 29, General Petain became chief of General Staff in Paris

April 30, Mush, Armenia, occupied by Turks

May 2–4, Third Battle of Scarpe (Arras)

May 2–17, Battle of Bullecourt (Arras)

May 3, First squadron of American destroyers commanded by Admiral Sims reached Queenstown, Ireland

——, British take Fresnoy and Australians break through Hindenburg switch at Quéant

May 4, Craonne (Aisne) retaken by French

May 4–5, French attack along Chemin-des-Dames north of the Aisne capture crest of Craonne Ridge including Chemin des Dames

May 5–22, Battle of the Vardar (Macedonia)

May 7, Night air raid on London

May 8, British evacuated Fresnoy (Arras) which was occupied by Germans

——, Liberia severed diplomatic relations with Germany

May 9–10, Fighting at Kharkwasta, northwest frontier of India

May 10, Major-General John J. Pershing appointed to command American Expeditionary Force in France

May 11–13, German attack around Craonne repulsed and north of Reims and in Maisons de Champagne

May 12, British vessels bombard Zeebrugge

May 12–June 8, Tenth Battle of the Isonzo. Italians advanced from Gorizia and Plava toward Biansizza plateau

May 13, British took Rœux after 2 days battle

May 14–15, Italians crossed the Isonzo north of Canal between Loga and Bodrez, making surprise attack

May 15, General Pétain replaced General Nivelle as commander-in-chief of the French armies, General Foch becoming Chief of Staff

May 17, Honduras severed diplomatic relations with Germany

May 17, End of Battle of Bullecourt. Australians carried salient near Bullecourt (West front) and the village

May 19, Russian provisional government issued declaration repudiating separate peace

——, Nicaragua severed diplomatic relations with Germany

May 19–22, Austrians attacked on the Val Sugana on Asiago plateau, valley of Adige, Pasubio bulwarks and west of Lake Garda

May 20, Serbian government transferred from Corfu to Salonika

May 22, End of the Battle of the Vardar

May 23–27, Great Italian offensive from Kostanjevica to the sea. Successful on the Carso

May 25, Great aëroplane raid on Kent and Folkestone, England, 150 casualties

May 26, British hospital ship "Dover Castle" sunk by submarine in the Mediterranean

——, John J. Pershing appointed commander-in-chief of American forces in France by formal letter and instructed to proceed with staff to Paris

May 29, General Van Deventer succeeded to command in East Africa

May 30, American ship "Silver Shell" in successful engagement with German submarine

June 2, Brazil revoked her neutrality as between the United States and Germany and seized German ships

June 3, 5 German attacks on Chemin des Dames repulsed

——, Great Austrian offensive on the Carso plateau

June 4, General Brusilov became Russian commander-in-chief

June 5, General Brusilov launched great offensive in Galicia

——, Air raid on Sheerness and British naval establishments at Medway. 157 killed and 432 injured

——, Italians forced back south of Jamiano

June 7–14, Battle of Messines, British offensive in Flanders captured Messines-Wytschaete ridge and towns. Messines Village captured the first day by New Zealanders

June 8, End of tenth Battle of the Isonzo

——, Italians occupied Janina, Greece

June 9, General Pershing, commander of American Expeditionary Force, arrived in London on his way to France

——, Russia refused armistice offered by Germany

June 10, Italians gained Agnello Pass and Austrian positions on Monte Ortigara

June 11, San Domingo severed diplomatic relations with Germany

——, Entente Powers demanded abdication of King Constantine of Greece

June 12, Allied forces occupied Corintha and Larissa, Greece

——, Abdication of King Constantine in favor of his second son Alexander

June 13, General Pershing arrived in France

——, Air raid on London

June 14, Schooner "A. B. Johnson," American, captured by German raider "Seeadler" in Pacific Ocean and burned

June 14–27, Heavy fighting on Aisne, in Champagne, on Arras-Cambrai front, Trentino, &c.

June 15, Announcement of Italian premier in Chamber of Deputies that Germany had asked for separate peace

June 16, American schooner "Winslow" captured by German raider "Wolf" in Pacific Ocean and burned and sunk

——, American tanker "John D. Archbold" sunk off France by German submarine

June 17, Portuguese troops first in action on West front

——, Germans captured French trenches near Hurtebise

——, Haiti severed diplomatic relations with Germany

June 19, General Currie appointed to command of Canadian troops in France, Sir Julian Byng taking command of Third Army

June 19–24, Fighting in Shafur Valley on frontier of India

June 20, Italians attacked on Asiago plateau and gained Monte Ortigaro

June 21, Mutiny of crews of Russian Black Sea fleet at Sebastopol

June 24, French successful in attack east of Vauzaillon. British advance near Lens

June 25, First American troops arrived in France

——, French made successful attack taking spur the "Finger" northwest of Hurtebise

June 27, French cruiser "Kleber" sunk by mine off Brest

——, General Hindenburg's letter to Kaiser on decline of *morale* of nation

June 27 and 30, Venizelos, premier of Greece, severed diplomatic relations with Central Powers, Bulgaria, and Turkey

June 28, General Allenby took command in Egypt, succeeding General Murray

——, Brazil revoked decree of neutrality as to Allied Powers

June 28–29, German attack won to Col de Pommerieux east and west of Hill 304 in Verdun region

June 30, Germans attacked at Mort Homme and Chemins des Dames

June 30–July 6, Battles of Brzezany, Koniuchy, and Zloczow (East front)

July 1, Russian offensive begun toward Lemberg in Galicia on 50 mile front

July 2, Greece, government of Alexander, declared war on Germany and Bulgaria, Turkey and Austria

——, First regular convoy of merchant ships sailed from Hampton Roads, Virginia

July 3–9, German attack on 12 mile front from Malmaison to woods of Chevreux north of Craonne (Aisne)

July 4, German submarine attack on United States transports defeated. Ponta Delgada in Azores shelled by German submarine

July 6, Aqaba, (Akaba), Arabia, taken by Arab troops

July 7, French made gains at Cerny, north of Aisne and Verdun

——, Aëroplane raid on Margate and London. 250 casualties

July 8, American schooner "Manila" captured by German raider "Seeadler" in Pacific Ocean and blown up with dynamite

——, Austrian front broken west of Stanislau by General Kornilov

——, Russian withdrawal from West Prussia begun

July 9, American bark "Beluya" captured by German raider "Wolf" in Pacific Ocean and sunk by gunfire. 14 prisoners, including 2 women passengers taken

July 10, American steamship "Kansan" torpedoed and sunk without warning by enemy submarine off Kerdonis Point, France

July 10, American steamer "Hildegarde" sunk by German submarine off Start Point, England

——, Halicz taken by Russians

July 10–11, German counter-offensive took Nieuport bridgehead

July 11, Russians captured Kalusz, Galicia

July 11–14, British attacked Ramadi, Mesopotamia

July 12, American merchant ship "Grace" sunk by German submarine in the Mediterranean

July 13, American schooner "Encore" captured and burned in Pacific by German raider "Wolf"

July 14, German attack on Chemin des Dames ridge made gains west of Cerny

——, Austrian attack east of Gorizia repulsed

July 18–28, Battle of East Galicia. Russians defeated and disorganized by German counter-offensive

July 19, "Majority resolution" in German Reichstag declared for a peace with no annexations or indemnities

——, American armored cruiser "San Diego" sunk by submarine or mine 10 miles south of Fire Island, New York

——, Action at Narungombe, East Africa, Germans forced to retreat to Mahungo

——, German attack on Nieuport sector repulsed

——, German success in Galicia due to desertion of Russian regiments under Bolshevik influence

July 21, Germans in suburbs of Tarnopol

July 22, German attack (West front)

——, Siam declared war on Germany and Austria

July 22–Aug. 1, Battle of Maraseti in Rumania, first phase

July 23, Halicz captured by Germans

——, Russian retreat in Galicia continued

July 24, Austrians captured Tarnopol and Stanislau

——, French recovered positions on Casemale Plateau lost July 19

July 26–29, Rumanians commanded by General Avarescu attacked Austrian position in the Susitza Valley, forcing Austrians to retreat south to Putna Valley

July 27, American steamer "Carmelia" captured and sunk by submarine in English Channel, and the "John Hays Hammond" off Ireland

——, France and Italy agreed on spheres of influence in Asia Minor

——, Allied force crossed Yser canal and occupied enemy trenches east and north of Boesinghe

July 30, Zaleszcyzyki, Galicia, recaptured by Austro-Germans

July 31–Nov. 10, Third Battle of Ypres. Allied offensive begun with Battle of Pilckem Ridge. British take Sanctuary Wood

Aug. 1, General Kornilov replaced General Brusilov as commander-in-chief of Russian armies

——, The Pope addressed a second peace note to the belligerent governments

Aug. 2, German raider "Seeadler" wrecked on Mopelia Island in the Pacific

——, End of Battle of Pilckem Ridge (Ypres)

Aug. 3, Austro-Germans occupied Czernowitz evacuated by Russians retreating from province of Bukowina

——, Mutiny in German fleet at Wilhelmshaven

——, St. Julien (Ypres) reoccupied by British

Aug. 4, Liberia declared war on Germany. Published Aug. 7

——, Offer of Norway and Holland to place shipping at disposal of Allies in return for food supplies

Aug. 4, The Standard Oil steamer "O. B. Jennings" sunk 70 miles off the Virginia coast

Aug. 5, The steamer "Stanley M. Seaman" from Boston sunk by submarine off Cape Hatteras

Aug. 6, American steamer "Campania" sunk by German submarine in the Bay of Biscay, 6 men taken prisoners

——, British schooner "Gladys M. Holt" sunk by submarine off New York

Aug. 6–Sept. 3, Battle of Maraseti, Rumania, second phase. Russians defeated by Mackensen

Aug. 7, American merchant ship "Christiane" bombed and sunk by German submarine off the Azores

Aug. 8, Swedish steamship "Sydland" torpedoed 100 miles south-east of Nantucket Island

Aug. 11, German attack on Moronvilliers

Aug. 12, The "Somerstad" Norwegian freighter torpedoed 25 miles south of Fire Island

Aug. 12–13, Rumanian advance from Ocna in Trotus Valley

Aug. 14, China declared war on Germany and Austria

Aug. 15, German advance in Focsani region, Rumania, and Russians and Rumanians retreat toward Sereth River

Aug. 15–25, Battle of Lens. British offensive. Canadians captured Hill 70

Aug. 16–18, Battle of Langemarck (Ypres) successful Allied offensive

Aug. 17–Sept. 12, Eleventh Battle of the Isonzo. Italians crossed Isonzo at many points north of Goritzia and made advance on Bainsizza plateau

Aug. 20–Dec. 15, General Pétain launched French offensive on Verdun front carrying enemy defenses north of Verdun. Held Avocourt Wood, Mort Homme, and Hill 240

Aug. 21, French take Samogneux (Verdun) and northern slope of Hill 344

——, Canadian troops on Lens front took German trenches southwest and west of town

Aug. 22, German advance on Riga begun across the Dvina about 25 miles above city

——, Daylight aëroplane raid on Kent coast of England

Aug. 24, French took Hill 304 and the Bois Camard

——, Italians capture Monte Santo north and east of Gorizia

Aug. 25, French progress north of Hill 304 (West front)

Aug. 26, Bainsizza Plateau almost entirely in possession of Italians

Aug. 27, President Wilson replied to Pope's peace note of Aug. 1 giving reasons for rejection of overtures

Aug. 28, French positions almost completely restored to those before great attack of Feb., 1916

Aug. 29, General Von Hindenburg succeeded General Von Falkenhayn as chief of General Staff German field armies

Aug. 30, German attack on British south east of Lens failed

Sept. 1–5, Battle of Riga

Sept. 2, Air raid on England by moonlight

Sept. 3, Russians forced to evacuate Riga. Occupied by Germans

Sept. 4, German submarine shelled Scarborough, Yorkshire. Air raid on London

——, Italians took fortified position of San Gabriele

——, First Americans killed in France by bombs

dropped on U.S. Army Base Hospital No. 5 at Dannes-Camiers

Sept. 7, Atlantic transport "Minnehaha" sunk off Ireland by submarine. 48 lives lost

Sept. 8, General Kornilov dismissed, marched on Petrograd

——, French attack took Chaume Wood and high ground commanding wood of Caures

Sept. 12, End of eleventh Battle of the Isonzo

——, Count Karl von Luxburg, German chargé, handed his passports by Argentine government

Sept. 14, Italians recaptured Monte San Gabriele peak after 2 weeks battle

Sept. 15, Russian republic proclaimed

Sept. 16, French air raids on Stuttgart, Sarrbruken, and other German cities

Sept. 19, German chancellor's reply to peace note from the Pope

——, Mutiny of crews of Russian Black Sea fleet at Sebastopol

Sept. 20, Austrian emperor replied to peace note from the Pope

Sept. 20–25, Battle of the Menin Road Ridge (Ypres), successful Allied offensive

Sept. 21, Costa Rica severed diplomatic relations with Germany

——, International Sugar Committee established by England, France, Italy, the United States, and Canada

Sept. 21–22, Germans took Jacobstadt on the Baltic

Sept. 24, Air raid on London

Sept. 24–25, German attacks north of Verdun repulsed

Sept. 26–Oct. 3, Battle of Polygon Wood (Ypres). Allied successful offensive

Sept. 28, Mahungo, East Africa, captured from Germans

Sept. 28–29, British successful in attack on Ramadie (Iraq)

Sept. 29, Italian success on Bainsizza plateau

Oct. 2, British cruiser "Drake" sunk by submarine in North Channel

Oct. 4, Battle of Broodseinde (Ypres). Crest of Passchendæle ridge taken by Allies

Oct. 5, Peru severed diplomatic relations with Germany

Oct. 6, Major-General Pershing made a general

——, General Gouraud crossed the Aisne at several points, forcing German retreat

Oct. 7, Uruguay severed diplomatic relations with Germany

——, Belgians occupied Mahenge, East Africa

Oct. 8, Belgians attacked at Mahenge, East Africa, forcing retreat of Tafel attempting to join von Lettow

Oct. 9, Battle of Pœlcapelle (Ypres). Allied offensive

Oct. 11, British hospital ship "Goorhka" damaged by mine off Malta

——, American merchant ship "Lewis Luckenbach" torpedoed and sunk by German submarine off north-west coast of France

Oct. 12, German conquest of Baltic Islands begun with capture of Osel Island

Oct. 12–26, First Battle of Passchendæle (Ypres). British offensive in Flanders

Oct. 15, U.S. destroyer "Cassin" torpedoed by submarine off south coast of Ireland

Oct. 16, Russian battleship "Salva" sunk in Gulf of Riga

Oct. 16–19, Action at Nyangao (East Africa) the Battle of Mahiwa

Oct. 17, Scandinavian vessels escorting convoy sunk by German submarine

——, Troopship "Antilles" sunk returning to the United States

Oct. 18, Germans occupied Moon and Dago Islands at entrance of Gulf of Riga

Oct. 19, Airship raid on London

——, American merchant ship "J. L. Luckenbach" shelled by German submarines. Made port badly damaged

Oct. 21, Turkish attack on Petra, Arabia, repulsed

——, Americans entered the line at the Toul sector

Oct. 23, American troops in first action (West front)

——, French and Belgians crossed the Yser opposite Knockehœk, capturing Aschoop, Kippe, and Merckem

Oct. 23–Nov. 1, Battle of Malmaison. French offensive which gained the Chemin des Dames ridge and Malmaison Fort

Oct. 24–Dec. 26, Austro-German offensive in Julian Alps, the twelfth battle of the Isonzo. Germans crossed the Isonzo at Tomlino and Plezzo. Forced Italians to retreat to Piave (Battle of Caporetto). Gains of 2½ years lost by Italians

Oct. 26, Brazil declared war against Germany

Oct. 26–Nov. 10, Second Battle of Passchendæle (Ypres). British and Canadians attacked on front from the Ypres-Roulers Railway to the Pœlcappelle-Westroosebeke road

Oct. 27–Nov. 7, General Allenby successful in third Battle of Gaza

Oct. 28, American transport "Finland" torpedoed off France

Oct. 28–29, Gorizia, Cividale, Cormons, and Udine retaken by Austro-Germans, and Italians retreat toward the Tagliamenco River

——, French and Belgians completed capture of the Merckem peninsula (Flanders)

Oct. 31, Beersheba, Palestine, stormed by British General Allenby

Nov. 1, End of Battle of Malmaison

Nov. 1–4, Austro-Germans pursued retreating Italians across the Tagliamento River

Nov. 2, Germans retreated from positions on Chemin des Dames

——, British naval raid in the Cattegat

Nov. 3, Americans in trench fighting for first time

Nov. 5, U.S.S. "Aleedo" sunk by submarine off France

Nov. 6, British capture Sheria position (Palestine)

——, British occupy Tilkrit, Mesopotamia

——, Passchendæle captured by Canadians

——, Allied conference at Rapallo, Italy, on critical situation in Italy

Nov. 7, End of third successful Battle of Gaza. Gaza captured

——, General Diaz made commander-in-chief of Italian armies, replacing General Cadorna

——, Italians retreat from the Tagliamento to tne Livenza

Nov. 8, Vittorio, Veneto, taken by Austro-Germans

——, Coup d'état in Russia. Bolsheviks seize government

——, Action at Huj with Turks (Palestine front)

Nov. 9, British occupied Ascalon, Palestine

——, Italian army on line behind the Piave River

——, Austrians recaptured Asiago

Nov. 10, Second Battle of Passchendæle (Ypres)

Nov. 11, Austro-Germans reached the Piave and fighting continued on the Asiago, Piave, until Dec. 26

Nov. 13, The Turks driven from Katrah (Cedron) and El Mughar, Palestine

——, Austro-Germans crossed the Piave at the Zenson bend near Venice

Nov. 14, Italians made stand on the Piave

——, Junction station Jerusalem to Damascus railroad occupied by British

——, Chiwata, East Africa, taken by British

Nov. 15–18, Von Lettow made stand on the Lukuledi River, East Africa

Nov. 16, Austrians won bridge-head at Fogare and carried Monte Prassolan east of the Brenta

——, Jaffa, port of Jerusalem, occupied by British forces

Nov. 17, Action of British and German cruisers off Heligoland

——, Austrians won Quero on the Piave

Nov. 17–24, Battle of Nebi Samwill (the ancient Mizpah), Palestine

Nov. 18, Death of British General Maude of cholera at Bagdad. Succeeded by Lieut. General Sir W. R. Marshall

——, American bark "John A. Kirby" captured and sunk with bombs by German raider "Wolf" in the Pacific

——, Austrian-German advance halted at heights of Tomba, Fenera, and Grappa by Italians

Nov. 19, American destroyer, "Chauncey" sunk in collision with British steamer "Rose" off Gibraltar. 21 lives lost

Nov. 20, Marcoing, Masnières, Graincourt, La Vacquerie Ribecourt and Havrincourt captured by British (Cambrai)

——, General Dukhonin, commander-in-chief of the Russians, ordered to offer armistice to "all nations allied and hostile"

Nov. 20–Dec. 3, Battle of Cambrai. Offensive of General Haig (West front) broke Hindenburg line. American troops in this battle

Nov. 21, British force reached Nebi Samwill

——, Flesquières, Anneux, and Cantaig captured by British (Cambrai)

——, General Dukhonin dismissed because of his refusal to offer armistice and Ensign Krylenko made commander-in-chief of Russian army

Nov. 21–25, German Zeppelin L59 in flight from Yambol, Bulgaria, to latitude of Khartum turned back without landing, in attempt to carry supplies to von Lettow in East Africa

Nov. 22, Turks counter-offensive at Nebi Samwill

——, Germans drove British from village of Fontaine-Notre Dame, nearest approach to Cambrai

——, Publication of Entente Secret Treaties begun by Trotsky

Nov. 23–29, Heavy fighting at Bourlon Wood

Nov. 25, German General von Lettow-Vorbeck in retreat from East Africa defeated Portuguese in battle at Ngomano (Portuguese East Africa)

——, Turks counter-attacks begun in defense of Jerusalem

——, French made successful attack east of Meuse and north of Verdun

Nov. 27, Fontaine-Notre Dame captured by British

Nov. 28, German force under Captain Tafel surrendered to the British in Mwiti Valley, German East Africa

——, Germans agreed to armistice with Russia

Nov. 29–30, Turks attacked Beit'Ur el Foka in Palestine offensive, the Nebi Samwill ridge, and temporarily broke British line northeast of Jaffa

Nov. 30, Germans commanded by General von der Marwitz successful at first in counter-attack at Cambrai. American engineers took part in this action

——, Austria-Hungary accepted Bolshevik proposals for negotiation of armistice

Dec. 1, Germans occupied Gonnelieu, France. British evacuated Bourlon Wood

——, Announcement of Great Britain that campaign in German East Africa concluded. Last German troops interned in Portuguese territory

——, Permanent Allied Supreme War Council established. First meeting at Versailles

Dec. 1–7, British evacuated Masnières-Crevecœur salient, giving up about half of territory originally gained

Dec. 2–8, Hostilities suspended between Russian and German armies

Dec. 3, Germans took La Vacquerie (Cambrai)

——, First session of delegates to armistice convention at Brest-Litovsk

Dec. 4–5, General Byng withdrew his lines from about one-third of ground gained (Battle of Cambrai)

Dec. 5, Austro-German attack drove Italians from main position on the Asiago Plateau

Dec. 6, U.S.S. "Jacob Jones," destroyer, torpedoed and sunk by German submarine off English coast

——, American squadron joined Allied fleet

——, Rumanians obliged to suspend hostilities

Dec. 7, Resolution of Congress signed by President Wilson declared state of war with Austria-Hungary

——, Ecuador severed diplomatic relations with Germany

Dec. 8, Attack made on Jerusalem

Dec. 9, Jerusalem surrendered to the British

——, Truce of Focsani signed between Rumania and the Central Powers and hostilities ceased the following day

Dec. 9–10, Italian naval raid on Trieste. Austrian battleship "Wien" sunk

Dec. 10, Panama declared war against Austria

Dec. 11, Sir Edmund Allenby made formal entry into Jerusalem by the Jaffa Gate

Dec. 12, Austrian attack between the Brenta and the Piave failed to turn Italian line on Piave

——, Funchal, Madeira, shelled by German submarine

——, Scandinavian convoy attacked by German destroyers which sunk the H.M.S. "Partridge"

Dec. 14, French cruiser "Chateau Renault" sunk by submarine

Dec. 15, End of second Allied offensive battle at Verdun

Dec. 15–Jan. 17, Armistice between Russia and Central Powers signed for 28 days as from Dec. 17

Dec. 16, Cuba declared war on Austria-Hungary

Dec. 17, Written assurance given by British government to King of the Hejaz of future independence of Arabs

Dec. 19, Czechoslovak army organized in France recognized by French Government as "autonomous army"

Dec. 20–21, Italian counter attack at Monte Asolone

Dec. 21–22, Battle of Jaffa (Palestine)

Dec. 22, Peace negotiations begun at Brest-Litovsk

——, General Guillaumat succeeded General Sarrail in command at Salonika

Dec. 23, Secret Anglo-French Convention assigned zones of influence in southern Russia

Dec. 24, British air raid on Mannehim on the Rhine

Dec. 26, American pilots of the Lafayette Escadrille transferred from the French to the American service

Dec. 26–30, Jerusalem successfully defended against Turkish attack

Dec. 27, Admiral Sir Rosslyn Wemyss appointed First Sea Lord, Great Britain

——, U.S.S. "Santee" torpedoed off Queenstown, Ireland. Made port

Dec. 28, French Minister of Foreign Affairs announced war aims of France

Dec. 30, French division west of Piave took trenches east of Monte Tomba

1918

Jan. 4, British hospital ship "Rewa" sunk by submarine in the Bristol Channel

Jan. 5, Lloyd George, Prime Minister of Great Britain, in speech to trade union delegates outlined British war aims

Jan. 8, Qasr-i-Shirin, West Persia, occupied by British

——, President Wilson in message to Congress outlined an American peace program of "Fourteen Points"

Jan. 14, German destroyer raid on Yarmouth, England

Jan. 15, Americans relieved the French in sector northwest of Toul

Jan. 20, The German-Turkish cruiser "Breslau" sunk by mine at entrance of Dardanelles and the "Goeben" damaged and beached in action with British warships; the "Goeben" refloated on the 27th

Jan. 22, First meeting of Allied Naval Council in London

Jan. 24, Reply of Central Powers to Lloyd George and Wilson by Chancellor von Hertling in address to the Reichstag, and Count von Czernin in address to the Austrian delegations in the Reichsrath

Jan. 27, Turkish flotilla in Dead Sea taken at El Mezraa by Arab Camel Corps

Jan. 28, Spanish steamer "Giralda" torpedoed by German submarine

——, Soviet Russia severed diplomatic relations with Rumania

Jan. 28–29, Air raids on Kent, Sussex, and London

Jan. 30, Air raid on Paris

Feb. 5, British transport "Tuscania" carrying American troops to Europe sunk by submarine off Ireland

Feb. 6, German ultimatum to Rumania

Feb. 9, Peace signed between Central Powers, Bulgaria, Turkey, and the Ukraine Rada, and boundaries defined in supplementary treaty

Feb. 10, Bolshevik government of Russia announced end of war with Central Powers, Bulgaria, and Turkey, but that Russia would not sign formal peace treaty

Feb. 15–16, German destroyer raid on Dover

Feb. 16–17, Air raids on Kent, Sussex, and London

Feb. 17, British force under Dunsterville arrived at Enzeli, Persia, from Bagdad

Feb. 18, End of armistice. Germans resumed hostilities against Russia. Dvinsk occupied

Feb. 19, Russian Bolshevik government announced peace treaty with Germany would be signed

——, General Sir H. H. Wilson appointed Chief of British Imperial General Staff succeeding General Sir W. Robertson resigned

Feb. 21, Jericho taken by General Allenby. Turks retreated beyond the Jordan

Feb. 23, Americans with French in Chemin des Dames sector

Feb. 24, Trebizond taken by Turks in offensive in Caucasus, driving out Russians

——, Dorpat, Estonia, occupied by Germans

Feb. 25, Military convention signed at Bobruisk between Germany and Poland

——, Reval, Pskov, and Pernau on the Baltic taken by Germans

——, Kirmanshah, Persia occupied by the British

Feb. 26, "Glenarth Castle," hospital ship sunk by submarine in Bristol Channel

——, Air raid on Venice

——, American naval tug "Cherokee" foundered and sunk off Maryland

March 1, German attack on Moronvilliers Heights

——, Treaty of amity signed between Bolshevik Russian government and Finland (Red) Republic

March 2, Kiev, capital of Ukraine, occupied by Germans

——, Germans landed in Aaland Islands at request of Finnish government (British official chronology). March 3, Aston, March 6, Gleichen

March 3, Treaty of Brest-Litovsk signed made peace between Russia and Central Powers, Bulgaria, and Turkey. Promises of evacuation. Reduced Russian Empire to practically the size of the medieval Grand Duchy of Moscow (Hayes)

March 4, Narva, Estonia, occupied by Germans

March 4–5, American "Rainbow Division" repulsed German attack near Badonvilliers on the Lorraine front

March 5, Rumania signed preliminary peace treaty with the Central Powers at Buftea

March 7, Allied note asked for use of Dutch ships in Entente ports. Accepted March 18

——, Peace signed at Berlin between Germany and Finland

——, Aëroplane raid on London, England; 60 civilians and 2 soldiers casualties

March 8, Air raid on Paris

——, Americans went into trenches near Verdun

March 9, Hit, Mesopotamia, taken by British

——, Peace treaty signed by Rumania with Russia

——, Peace treaty signed between Turkey, Armenia, and Georgia

March 10, "Guildford Castle," British hospital ship sunk by submarine in Bristol Channel

——, War Dep't announced that American troops were in trenches in Lorraine, Alsace, Champagne, and near Chemin des Dames

March 11, First meeting of Allied Maritime Transport Council

——, Air raid on Naples

——, American troops entered German trenches at Toul

March 12, Erzerum retaken by Turks

March 13, Germans occupied Odessa

March 13–14, German air raid on Durham, England

March 14, Congress of Soviets met at Moscow to ratify Brest-Litovsk Treaty

March 15, Prince Lichnowsky's memorandum published

——, Germany proclaimed protectorate over an independent Kurland (Courland)

March 16, Hamadan, West Persia, evacuated by Russians

March 17, Nicolaiev, South Russia, occupied by Germans

——, Italian air raid on Metz

March 18, Allies denounced Treaties of Brest-Litovsk

March 20, Allied Blockade Committee established

March 21, Dutch ships in American and British ports requisitioned

——, Action in North Sea between Allied and German destroyer flotillas

March 21–23, Battle of St. Quentin

March 21–April 6, Great German offensive (West front) begun with Battles of St. Quentin, Noyon, Picardy (First Battles of the Somme of 1918). American engineers in action

March 21–April 9, Second Battle of Picardy

March 22, British line of defense broken through west of St. Quentin

March 23, Italian air raid on Metz

——, Germans reached the line of the Somme

——, Bombardment of Paris begun by long range gun from Crépy-en-Valois, a distance of 75 miles

March 24–25, First Battle of Bapaume. Bapaume and Péronne taken by Germans

——, First action of Es Salt, Palestine

March 25, German airships raided Naples

——, Noyon taken by Germans

March 26, Germans took Albert, Bray, Chaulnes, Roye

——, Allied conference at Doullens appointed General Foch in supreme command to "coördinate" operations of Allied armies; Supreme Council constituted

March 26–27, Action of Khan Baghdada, Mesopotamia

——, Battle of Rosières (Somme). German offensive

March 27, Montdidier, important railroad junction taken by Germans (West front)

——, First British attack on Amman, Palestine

March 28, Ana, Iraq, taken by British (Mesopotamia)

——, First Battle of Arras. Great German attack north and south of Scarpe River defeated with heavy loss

——, General Pershing tendered entire American force to General Foch giving up plan of building up a distinctive American force in Lorraine. Formal memorandum signed April 3

March 28–29, Hamel taken by Germans (Somme)

March 29, Poltava (South Russia) captured by Germans

——, Church wrecked in Paris by bombardment of long range gun, the "Big Bertha," on Good Friday

March 31, British air raid on Mainz, Stuttgart, Coblenz, and Freiburg

April 1, Enzeli, Persia, evacuated by Russians

April 3, Germans landed at Hangö, in southern Finland. British submarines at Helsingfors destroyed to avoid capture

——, Ekaterinoslav, southern Russia, occupied by Germans

——, Memorandum of Pershing. *See* March 28

April 4, Battle of the River Avre. German attack on French front took Hamel and Vaire wood

——, British at Festubert hold line against attack

——, Sarikamish in Russian Caucasus taken by Turks

April 5, Van, Armenia, occupied by Turks

——, Battle of the Ancre brought to end first Battles of the Somme

——, Japanese and British landed at Vladivostock

April 6–9, Germans advanced from Chauny to the Oise-Aisne Canal

April 8, Kharkov, southern Russia, occupied by Germans

April 9, End of Battles of Picardy and Noyon

——, Neuve Chapelle taken by Germans

April 9–11, Battle of Estaires, France

April 9–29, Battle of the Lys, German attack on British-Portuguese line in West Flanders between Lens and Ypres

April 10, Estaires, France, taken by Germans

——, Greeks occupied Seres and Demir Hissar

——, German submarine bombarded Monrovia, Liberia

——, Agreement between Italy and the Yugo-Slavs (Pact of Rome)

April 10–11, Battle of Messines (West front)

April 11, U.S.S. "Lakemoor," cargo vessel, torpedoed and sunk by German submarine off Scotland. 46 lives lost

——, Germans took Messines-Wytschaete Ridge and outskirts of Armentières and Merville

April 12, Air raid on Paris

——, "Backs to the wall," Order of the Day of Sir Douglas Haig to British army

——, Airship raid over England

April 12–15, Battle of Hazebrouck (Lys)

April 13, German force in East Africa reached the Chambezi River, Rhodesia

——, Germans occupied Helsingfors, Finland

April 13–15, Battle of Bailleul (Lys)

April 14, Neuve Eglise village taken by Germans

——, General Foch made commander-in-chief of Allied armies in France

April 15, Batum, Georgia, taken by Turks

——, British naval raid on the Cattegat

——, Bailleul taken by Germans

April 16, Passchendæle reoccupied by Germans

——, Wytschaele taken by Germans

April 17–19, First Battle of Kemmel Ridge (Lys). German attack repulsed

April 18, Airship raid on England

——, Battle of Bethune (Lys). German attack repulsed

April 19, German forces entered the Crimea

April 20–21, German attack on two-mile front west from the Bois de Remieres near Seicheprey, taking the town. (Americans in this action)

April 22–23, Blocking raid of British naval force on Zeebrugge and Ostend sunk 2 ships in canal entrance at Zeebrugge

April 23, Guatemala declared war on Germany

April 24–25, Action of Villers-Bretonneux (Somme)

April 25–26, Second Battle of Kemmel Ridge. Successful German attack captured village and hill

April 26, American troops first in active sector on Picardy front, Montdidier salient

April 27, Kars, Georgia taken by Turks

——, First contingent of Italian troops arrived at West front

April 28–29, First Division of Americans occupied sector near Breteuil, northwest of Montdidier

April 29, Battle of the Scherpenberg ended Battles of the Lys (West front)

April 30, Germans landed at Viborg, southern Finland

April 30–May 4, Second action of Es Salt, Palestine

May 1, Germans occupied Sebastopol and captured part of Russia Black Sea fleet

May 4, Second action of Es Salt, Palestine, ended

——, Armistice signed at Korenevo between Russia and the Ukraine

May 5, Greeks took strong Bulgarian position known as the Srka di Legen and over 2,000 prisoners west of the Vardar River

May 7, Kirkuk, Mesopotamia, taken by British

——, Treaty between Rumania and Central Powers

signed at Bucharest supplementing agreement of March 5 provided for indemnity from Rumania and cession of territory

May 8, Nicaragua declared war on Germany and Austria-Hungary

——, Rostov, southern Russia captured by Germans

May 9–10, British blocking raid on Ostend sunk H.M.S. "Vindictive" across harbor

May 11, Peace signed between Finland and Turkey at Berlin

May 12, Meeting of German and Austrian Emperors at German military headquarters at Spa

——, Austro-Hungarian-German military treaty signed

May 14, Italian naval raid on Pola, Austrian Adriatic base

May 15, German submarine raid on St. Kilda, Hebrides

May 18, Alexandropol, Georgia taken by Turks

——, First British retaliatory air raid on German towns by daylight on Cologne

——, U.S.S. "William Rockefeller" sunk by enemy submarine in North Sea

May 19, German air raid on Etaples hospitals caused heavy casualties

——, German night aëroplane raid on Kent, Sussex, and London. 49 killed and 177 wounded

May 19 and 23, Agreement of China and Japan to coöperate in action against Germans and Bolsheviks

May 23, Costa Rica declared war on Germany

May 24, Kirkuk, Mesopotamia evacuated by British

——, General F. C. Poole landed at Murmansk to organize northern Russian Expeditionary Force

May 26, Czechs began operations against the Bolsheviki in Volga region and Siberia

May 26–28, Turkish invasion of Transcaucasia

May 27, Chemin des Dames captured by Germans

——, Craonne retaken by Germans

May 27–28, German center crossed the Vesle

May 27–June 6, Third Battle of the Aisne. German offensive launched against the Chemin des Dames ridge between Soissons and Reims. (French front)

May 28, First American military success the capture of the village of Cantigny in Picardy by First Division commanded by General Robert Bullard held in face of 3 counter-attacks

——, Germans crossed the Aisne

May 29, Peace Treaty between Austria-Hungary and Finland signed at Vienna

May 29–30, Germans took Soissons and Fère-en-Tardenois

May 30, First American troops arrived in Italy

May 31, The German advance reached the Marne. (Battle of the Aisne)

——, Third American Division (Dickman). Machine gunners on motors reached Chateau-Thierry and went at once into action

——, Dormans, France captured by Germans

——, Chateau-Thierry and Neilly-St. Front taken by Germans

——, The American transport "President Lincoln" torpedoed by submarine off France on return voyage. Of 715 on board 3 officers and 23 men lost with ship. One officer taken prisoner

May 31–June 1, Americans and French in action against Germans on front of 10 miles from Chateau Thierry to Dormans

June 1, Third American Division took position from Chateau Thierry eastward to Jaulgonne on south bank of Marne

June 1, Second American Division deployed across the Chateau Thierry Paris road near Lucy-le-Bocage to check German advance on Paris

June 1–2, Battle on the River Ourcq (West front)

June 2, American Second Division made effective counter-attack before Veuilly de Poterie

——, American merchant ships "Isabel B. Wiley," "Winneconne," "Jacob M. Haskell," "Texel," "Edward H. Cole," and the "Carolina" sunk by German submarine U-151 off Virginia and New Jersey coast

June 3, American schooner "Sam C. Mengel" sunk by the U-151 off Virginia coast

——, Declaration of British, French, and Italian Governments supported the national aspirations of the Poles, Czecho-Slovaks, and Yugo-Slavs

June 4, Germans took Chateau Thierry

——, British marines landed at Pechenga, northern Russia

June 6, End of Battle of the Aisne

——, Americans took Bouresches

——, Dutch hospital ship "Königin Regentes" sunk by mine or torpedo

June 7, Kem, in northern Russia occupied by Allied force

——, British regained Bligny

——, Omsk, Siberia occupied by Czecho-Slovaks

——, French and Americans captured Veuilly-la-Poterie and Vinly west of Chateau Thierry

June 8, German troops landed at Poti, Georgia

——, Georgia and Armenia signed peace treaty with Germany

June 9, Armistice concluded between Ukraine and Bolshevik Government of Russia

June 9–14, Battle of the Matz. Germans attacked on front between Noyon and Montdidier

June 10, Austrian battleship "Suzent Istvan" sunk by Italian motor launch off Bermuda Island

——, American Second Division attacked in Belleau Wood. Held Hill 204 in advance

June 11, Czech troops reached Irkutsk

——, French attack from Rubescourt to St. Maur checked German advance

——, Americans dropped bombs on railroad station at Dommary-Barancourt northwest of Metz in first raid

June 11–12, Americans captured Belleau Wood north of Chateau-Thierry

June 12, Tiflis, Georgia occupied by Germans

June 13, German attack against Belleau Wood and Bouresches

June 14, Turks took Tabriz, Persia

June 15–24, Austrian offensive on the Piave from the Astico to the Adriatic

June 16, Austrians crossed the Piave

June 17, Air raid on Kent, England

June 18, Russian battleship "Svobodnaya" sunk in Black Sea by crew to avoid capture

——, French repulsed German attacks on Reims front

——, Italian counter-attack checked Austrian offensive

June 19, On Asiago Plateau the French captured Mts. Bertigo and Pennar, the Italians Mt. Costalunga

June 23, Austrians began retreat across the Piave

——, British landed at Murmansk

June 24, Americans began attack which resulted in complete possession of Belleau Wood

June 27, British hospital ship "Llandovery Castle" sunk by submarine off Irish coast

June 29, United States declared that Slavs should be freed from rule of Germany and Austria-Hungary

June 29–30, British force seized railroad between Murmansk and Suroki

June 30, First contingent of American troops arrived in Italy

——, Treaty between Czecho-Slovaks (Bohemia) and Italy signed

July 1, American transport "Covington" torpedoed off France

——, Americans captured village of Vaux in Marne Valley

July 1–3, Affair at Nyamkura, Portuguese East Africa. Germans reached point near Quelimane

July 4, Australians and Americans recapture Hamel and Hamel and Vaire woods

July 6, French and Italian offensive in Albania begun

——, Italian counter-attack drove enemy from section between old and new deltas of the Piave from Santa Dona de Piave south to the sea

July 10, Berat, Albania taken by Italians

July 11, U.S.S. "Westover" sunk off France by submarine

July 12, Japanese battleship "Kawachi" sunk by internal explosion

——, Haiti declared war on Germany

July 13, Irkutsk, Siberia occupied by Czecho-Slovaks

July 14, Kazan, eastern Russia occupied by Czecho-Slovaks

July 15, Americans repulsed German attack at Vaux

——, Germans passed the Marne at points between Chateau-Thierry and Dormons in advance toward Paris

July 15–18, Fourth Battle of Champagne, German offensive east and west of Reims checked by French and Americans. 85,000 Americans in this battle

July 16, French and Americans recovered St. Agnan and La Chapelle-Monthodon

——, Vierzy and Missy-aux-Bois captured by Americans

July 18–Aug. 7, Second Battle of the Marne. General Foch launched successful offensive against western side of Chateau-Thierry salient from Belleau to Fontenoy

July 18, Americans with Moroccan Division pierced the Marne salient below Soissons. Americans captured Torcy, Givre, and Belleau and station of Bouresches and assisted in capture of Noroy, Hautevesnes, Courchamps, and Chevillon

July 19, American cruiser "San Diego" sunk by mine off Fire Island, N.Y.

——, British seaplanes bombed Zeppelin sheds at Tondern, Schleswig

——, French and Americans took Priey and farm of La Grenouillières

——, Honduras declared war on Germany

July 19–20, Failure of French attack on Hill 193

July 20, German air raid on England unsuccessful

——, British defense of Resht, northern Persia

——, Germans retreat across the Marne

July 21, French recaptured Château-Thierry and Americans entered Barbillon wood

——, Americans took Berzy-le-Sec and Mont St. Pere

July 22, Dormans, France recaptured by French

——, Jaulgonne and Trugny taken by Americans

——, Allied offensive in Albania checked

July 23, Americans took Mont l'Evèque Wood from the Germans

July 23–Aug. 2, Battle of Soissonais and Ourcq (West front)

July 25, French recaptured Main de Messignes east of Reims

——, Americans captured Le Charmel but were withdrawn during the night. Germans retreated to Ourcq River

——, General Henri Berthelot drove Germans from southern half of forest of Fère and from Oulchy north of Ourcq River

July 27, Germans in full retreat north of the Marne

July 28, Fère-en-Tardenois occupied by Allies (de Goutte) and German advance checked (West front)

——, American troops landed in Italy (hospital unit)

——, Americans crossed the Ourcq and captured villages of Sergy and Seringes on the 29th. Ronchères captured. Gains not held

July 28–29, Australians captured Meteren and Merris

July 29, Czechs occupied Shmakova and captured Ekaterinburg

July 30, Americans captured the Bois des Grimpettes

July 31, Americans captured Cierges and Hill 230, and recaptured Seringes-et-Nesles

Aug. 1, Allies captured the defenses of Archangel

——, Germans withdrew during the night to the Vesle River, about ten miles

Aug. 2, British air raid on Stuttgart and Coblenz railroad stations

——, General Mangin drove the Germans 5 miles beyond the Crise and to the north his troops retook Soissons

——, The Americans took Coulonges and pushed on to Fismes, the last of the German bases in the salient under attack

——, Allied troops occupied Archangel by request of citizens

Aug. 3, Official announcement by governments of Japan and the United States of adoption of plan for joint intervention in Siberia

——, The Allied line at the Vesle River (West front)

——, British ambulance transport "Warilda" sunk by submarine

——, British troops landed at Vladivostok

Aug. 4, American troops landed at Vladivostok

——, Baku on Caspian sea occupied by British to defend against Turks

——, Allied troops on right bank of the Vesle River (West front)

——, Americans stormed Fismes (West front)

Aug. 5, Air raid on England

Aug. 6, General Foch made a Marshal of France

——, Declaration of British government to Russian people of lack of intention to interfere with Russian politics

Aug. 7, End of second Battle of the Marne

——, French cruiser "Dupetit Thomas" sunk by submarine in Atlantic

Aug. 8, Greeks occupied Drama

Aug. 8–11, Battle of Amiens. General Haig's surprise offensive eastward from Amiens led by General Rawlinson on German lines between Montdidier and Albert

Aug. 8–15, Battle of Montdidier. French offensive led by General Debeney towards Moreuil and Montdidier

Aug. 9, British and Americans captured the Morlancourt-Chipilly Ridge north of the Somme

——, Greeks occupied Kavalla

Aug. 10, Organization of first American army under General Pershing

Aug. 10, Montdidier taken by the French

Aug. 11, General Byng attacked toward Bapaume

——, Japanese force landed at Vladivostok

Aug. 13, The Czecho-Slovaks declared war on Germany

——, Great Britain recognized Czecho-Slovaks as allied nation

——, American tank steamer "Frederick R. Kellogg" torpedoed by submarine 10 miles off Barnegat, New Jersey

Aug. 14, Germans began retreat from Ancre River evacuating Beaumont-Hamel, Serre, Pusieux, and Bucquoi. French capture Ribécourt

Aug. 15, The "Westbridge" American cargo carrier torpedoed by submarine reached a French port

——, Last bombardment of Paris by long range gun

——, French complete capture of Lassigny Massif. British cross Ancre and advance between Beaucourt and Puisieux

Aug. 15–16, American troops from the Philippines arrived at Vladivostok

Aug. 17, Infantry of American Fifth Division took Frapelle village

Aug. 17–29, Second Battle of Noyon (West front)

Aug. 18, British advance in Flanders begun with action of Outtersteene ridge

——, British took Combles

——, Japanese force landed at Vladivostok

Aug. 19, Merville taken by Allies (Lys)

——, Fresnières captured by the French

Aug. 21, The French occupied Lassigny

Aug. 21–Sept. 3, Second Battles of the Somme begun with Battle of Albert and Battle of Baupaume. Allied offensive

Aug. 22, Albert recaptured by British

——, Austrian counter-offensive in Albania

Aug. 23, End of Battle of Albert

Aug. 23–24, Battle of Dukhovskaya, East Siberia. Bolsheviks defeated by Allied force

Aug. 24, Bray taken by Australians (Somme)

——, Allied force defeated enemy at Krasfesky, Siberia

——, British advanced from the Somme to Neuville Citasse. Bray, Miraumont, Pys, Biefvillers, and other towns taken by the Australians and the Thiepval Ridge

Aug. 26, Beaucourt captured by Americans

——, Americans reached Bazoches

——, Berat, Albania taken by Austrians

——, Defense of Baku against Turkish attack

——, Monchey-le-Preux taken by Canadians

Aug. 26–Sept. 3, Second Battle of Arras began with Battle of the Scarpe (Aug. 26–30)

Aug. 27, Roye taken by the French and Toeux and Trones wood by British

——, Bolshevik government of Russia concluded a supplementary treaty of peace with Germany

Aug. 28, Chaulnes and Nesle taken by the French

Aug. 29, Noyon evacuated by Germans, taken by French

——, Baupaume retaken by British New Zealanders

——, French army began attack to force retirement of enemy from the Vesle and Aisne Rivers

Aug. 30, Sector from Port-sur-Seille (east of the Moselle River) to Watronviller (north of Les Esparges) 42 miles in extent including the St. Mihiel salient turned over to command of General Pershing

——, End of Battle of the Scarpe

——, Bailleul occupied by Allies

——, Juvigny taken by the Americans

Aug. 31, Australians took Mount St. Quentin

——, Germans evacuated Mount Kemmel position (West front), occupied by British

Aug. 31–Sept. 3, Second Battle of Baupaume

Sept. 1, Péronne taken by Australians

——, British attack Bulgarians in Vardar Valley

Sept. 2, Italian contingent landed at Murmansk

Sept. 2–3, Germans fell back to line of the Canal du Nord from Péronne to Hermies (Flanders)

——, Battle of the Drocourt-Quéant line in which the British and Canadians broke through enemy line south of the Scarpe

Sept. 3, End of second Battles of the Sommes and second Battle of Arras, and second Battle of Baupaume

——, Lens evacuated by Germans and presently occupied by British

——, United States recognized Czecho-Slovakia National Council as belligerent government

Sept. 4, Obozoerskaya, northern Russia occupied by Allies

——, American contingent landed at Murmansk

Sept. 4–5, French attacked between Aisne and Ailette

Sept. 5, American transport "Mount Vernon" torpedoed off France

——, Czechs seized Novo Nikolaievsk, Siberia

——, Khabarovsk, eastern Siberia important enemy base taken by Japanese

Sept. 6, French troops occupied Ham Tugny, and Chauny

Sept. 7, American Seventy-Seventh Division drove enemy from La Cendiere Farm and passed the Aisne Canal

Sept. 8, French troops reached line of the Crozat Canal in pursuit of retreating Germans

Sept. 9, British transport "Missanabie" sunk by submarine off Irish coast

——, Franco-American attack begun in Argonne

——, British captured Ginchy, and trenches in advance northeast of Pozières. French take trenches before Douamont

Sept. 10, Hindenburg recommended peace measures to Austrian emperor

Sept. 11, Ukhtinskaya (Murman fort) taken by Allies

Sept. 12–13, Battle of St. Mihiel. Successful American offensive reduced the St. Mihiel salient (14 American divisions and 3 French)

Sept. 12, Americans occupied Thiaucourt

——, British recognized autonomy of Polish national army as cobelligerent

——, British steamer "Galway Castle" torpedoed and sunk with loss of 189 lives

Sept. 12–14, Action of Chamova (Archangel front)

Sept. 12–Oct. 9, Battles of the Hindenburg line, British offensive began with Battle of Havrincourt and Epéhy

Sept. 14, German Government made peace offer to Belgium

——, British evacuated Baku

——, General advance along entire line (West front) American army established itself on front of Manheulles, Fresnes, Pintheville, St. Hilaire, Doncourt, northeast of Woel, south end of the Etang de Lachaussee, Vandieres and across the Moselle at Champney

Sept. 15, Turks occupied Baku

——, Austrian Government note to belligerent governments suggested "unofficial" peace conference, and Note to President Wilson and all neutrals

Sept. 15–16, Battle of the Drobropolje (Battle of the Moglenitza) successful Allied offensive in Macedonia. Serbs and French attacked Bulgarian positions from Sokol to Vetrenik breaking Bulgarian line

Sept. 16, U.S.S. "Buena Ventura" cargo vessel sunk by German submarine off Spain

——, German aëroplane raid on Paris

——, H.M.S. "Glatton" sunk by "explosion" in Dover harbor

——, President Wilson rejected Austrian suggestion of Sept. 15

Sept. 17, Holnon wood and village of Maissemy taken by Allies

——, Americans gained points at Ronvaux, Manheulles, Pintheville, Haumont, Hattonchatel and north of Vandieres consolidating their line between the Meuse Heights and the Moselle River

Sept. 18, Battle of Epéhy. British advance northwest of St. Quentin

——, Blagovyeschensk, Siberia taken by Japanese; 2,000 Austrian and German troops captured

Sept. 18–24, Battle of Monastir-Doiran on Balkan front. Anglo-Greeks commanded by General Milne attacked Bulgarians north and south of Lake Doiran

Sept. 18–Oct. 31, Battles of Megiddo, final offensive in Palestine against Turks, the Battle of Sharon and the Battle of Nablus (British Official Chronicle)

Sept. 19, End of Battle of Doiran

Sept. 19–30, Battle of Samaria

Sept. 20, Nazareth and Beisan, Palestine occupied by British

Sept. 21, Belgians took the towns of Zarren, Staden, and Morslede (Flanders)

——, Bulgarian troops west of the Vardar began retreat

Sept. 22, Americans took over entire front from the Moselle River via Verdun to include the Argonne Forest at La Harazée

——, Serbs reached the Vardar at Demir-Kapu, Krivolak, and Gradsko cutting line of communication of 1st Bulgarian and 11th German armies

——, Vendeuil taken by French

——, Bulgarian troops between the Vardar and Lake Doiran began retreat

——, Doiran occupied by British

Sept. 23, Haifa, Es Salt, and Acre, Palestine occupied by British

——, Prilep, southern Serbia taken by French

——, The French reached the Oise 3 miles north of La Fère and advanced line east of St. Quentin canal

Sept. 24 and 27, Bulgaria asked Allied headquarters for armistice

Sept. 25, Gercourt captured by Americans

——, Hejaz railroad cut by Arab Allies

——, Italy recognized independence of Yugoslav State

——, Capture of Samakh (Palestine offensive)

Sept. 26, Charpentry taken by Americans and French

——, Serbs entered Ishtip (Stip)

——, First American Army launched attack northwest of Verdun on front of 20 miles and penetrated an average depth of 7 miles. Septarges captured

——, Strumica, Salonica taken by British, Stip (Ishtip) by the Serbs

——, Strumitsa, Bulgaria, taken by British

——, American steamer "Tampa" on convoy service torpedoed off English coast. 118 lives lost

Sept. 26–Oct. 15, French and American Battle of the Champagne and Argonne (Meuse-Argonne)

Sept. 27, Canadians took Bourlon Wood

——, Montfaucon, Nantillos, Charpentry, and Apremont taken by Americans

——, Americans fighting at Guillemont farm and Quennemont farm gained ground on the Knoll, outposts of Hindenburg line

——, Canal du Nord stormed by Allies

——, Battle of Cambrai and the Hindenburg line begun by British

Sept. 28, British took Fontaine-Notre Dame

——, British captured Kortewilde, Zandvoorde, Kruiseecke, and Becelaere, and Belgians, Zonnebeke, Poelcapelle, and Schaap Baillie and cleared enemy from Houthulst Forest (Flanders)

——, The French took Chaulnes and reached the Somme

——, Americans captured Baulny, Epinonville, and Dannevoux

——, Messines and Wytschaete retaken by British

Sept. 28–Oct. 1, Battle of the Flanders ridges

Sept. 28–Oct. 2, Battle of Ypres and Dixmude

Sept. 28–Oct. 5, Battle of Cambrai and the Hindenburg line

Sept. 29, The British Empire army with 2 American divisions, under Major General Read pierced the Hindenburg line between Cambrai and St. Quentin

——, Armistice with Bulgaria signed with Allies at Salonika

——, Uskub, Salonika taken by French cavalry

——, Passchendaele retaken by Allied force

——, Dixmude recaptured by Belgians

——, Gesnes taken by Americans

——, American attack captured ridge of Bellicourt tunnel (St. Quentin Canal), a German shelter, and part of the Hindenburg line and took Bellicourt

Sept. 29–Oct. 2, Battle of St. Quentin Canal

Sept. 30, Bulgaria accepted Entente terms and surrendered

——, Roulers taken by Belgians and British completed occupation of the Passchendaele Ridge

——, The Knoll, Hindenburg line taken by Americans

——, The steamer "Ticonderoga" sunk by submarine off American coast. 113 lives lost

——, Hindenburg line pierced to average depth of 7 miles on front of 25 miles. 36,500 prisoners reported by General Haig

——, Canadian contingent landed at Archangel

Oct. 1, Berat, Albania taken by Italians

——, Damascus occupied by British and Arabs

Oct. 2, End of Battle of St. Quentin Canal. St. Quentin taken by French. Germans retired to line north and south of the La Bassée Canal

——, Durazzo bombarded by British and Italian warships

——, British occupied Le Catelet

Oct. 2–7, Machine gun company under Major Charles S. Whittlesey, the "lost battalion" cut off in ravine at Charlevau Mill until rescued

Oct. 3, Battle of Beaurevoir line

——, Armentières recovered by British

——, French-American attack on German position took the Blanc Mont-Médeah Ridge Farm

Oct. 4, Notes from Germany and Austria asked President Wilson "to take steps for restoration of peace" and to notify belligerents of this request

——, American army transport "Herman Frasch" sunk by collision

Oct. 4, Japanese liner "Hirano Maru" sunk off Irish coast by submarine. 29 out of 320 on board saved

——, American attack west of Meuse on Kriemhilde line defenses which captured Hill 240 north of Exermont and villages of Gesnes, Fleville, La Farge, and others

Oct. 5, Allied force crossed the Scheldt Canal and occupied the Hindenburg Line east of it, evacuated by General von der Marwitz

——, American First Division captured Arietal Farm, Sixth Division repulsed raid on Sondernach

——, Vranje, Serbia retaken by Serbs

Oct. 6, Sidon, Syria occupied by British

Oct. 6–7, Americans crossed the Aire River and attacked the Argonne heights about Cornay

Oct. 6–12, Second Battle of Le Cateau

Oct. 7, Elbasan, Albania taken by Italians

——, Beirut, Syria evacuated by Germans, occupied by French troops

——, Americans captured Chatel-Chehery and Hill 180, and Mazenghien

——, British take Fresnoy, and Berry-au-Bac

——, Biache St. Vaast and Oppy captured by British

Oct. 8, President Wilson in reply to note of Central Powers demanded evacuation of occupied territory as first condition of an armistice

——, Consenvoye, Brancourt, and Prémont taken by French and Americans, Serain, Villers, Outreaux and finally Malincourt by British, St. Etienne by British and Americans

Oct. 8–9, Battle of Cambrai brought Battles of the Hindenburg line to close. Cambrai evacuated by Germans

Oct. 9, Cambrai occupied by British

——, Americans occupied Busigny and Becquigny establishing their line across railroad from Metz through Mexieres and Hirson to Valenciennes and Lille

——, Americans took Fleville, partially cleared Bois de Cunel and took Madeleine farm

——, American destroyer "Chauncey" sunk in collision

Oct. 10, Andigny captured by Americans

——, Battle of Flanders Ridges ended

——, British took Le Cateau

——, Irish mail boat "Leinster" sunk by submarine. 480 lives lost

——, Pristina, Serbia retaken by French

——, Argonne forest cleared of enemy by Americans

Oct. 11, Nish, Serbia retaken by Allies

——, Prizren, Serbia retaken by French

Oct. 12, Second American Army organized under command of Major General R. L. Bullard, line from the Moselle to Fresnes-en-Woevre. First Army under command of Major General Liggett, line from Fesnes-en-Woevre to the Argonne Forest inclusive

——, Vouziers captured by British

——, Craonne reoccupied by the French

——, German government note to President Wilson accepted conditions

Oct. 13, La Fère and Laon occupied by French

——, Tripoli, Syria occupied by Allies

Oct. 14, Durazzo, Albania, Novi Bazar, and Ipek, Montenegro retaken by Italians

——, French and American attack renewed. Chemin des Dames Ridge recaptured. Americans captured stronghold of Côte Dame Marie breaking Hindenburg line (Edward B. Winans) town of Romagne and St. Juvin

Oct. 14, Roulers recaptured by Allies

——, President Wilson's reply to German note imposed further conditions as essential for armistice

——, Belgians gained another 5 miles in offensive on Lys River from Comines to Dixmude

——, Appeal of Turkey for armistice, addressed to President Wilson delivered at Washington

Oct. 14–19, Battle of Courtrai (West front)

Oct. 15, Menin captured by Allies

——, British cavalry in Homs, Syria

——, End of Battle of Champagne and Argonne

Oct. 16, Courtrai taken by British

——, Germans evacuated Lille

——, Americans entered Grand Pré, northern bank of Aire River after 3 day attack

——, Dunkirk shelled by long range guns

Oct. 17, Americans took Molain and St. Martin Rivière, Côte de Châtillon, Bandival Farm and hamlet of Arbre and Guernon west of Grand Pré

——, Ostend, Lille, and Douai occupied by Allies

Oct. 17–25, Battle of the Selle begun by British and American attack south of Le Cateau

Oct. 18, President Wilson replied to Austro-Hungarian note

Oct. 19, Belgian troops occupied Bruges and Zeebrugge

——, End of Battle of Courtrai

Oct. 20, Mont St. Père captured

——, Entire Belgian coast evacuated by Germans

——, Reply of German government to President Wilson's third note

Oct. 21, Fifth and Third Divisions, Americans, took Hill 297 and Bois des Rappes

——, Submarine campaign suspended by German Government

Oct. 22, British occupied Valenciennes

——, Affair at Imrad near Aden, Arabia

Oct. 23, British began advance on Mosul, Mesopotamia

——, British attacked on Valenciennes-Le Cateau front

——, President Wilson replied to German note and agreed to submit matter to Allied and Associated Governments

——, American troops captured ridge of the Bois d'Etrayes and Hill 361, and Bantheville

Oct. 24, Kriemhilde Line pierced on 3 mile front at Landres-et-St. Georges

Oct. 24–Nov. 4, Battle of Vittoria-Veneto, Italian offensive begun by General Diaz against Austrians between the Brenta and Piave rivers around the Asiago Plateau and Monte Grappa

Oct. 25, End of Battle of the Selle

Oct. 26, British occupied Aleppo, Syria, Suria, and Kirkuk, Mesopotamia

Oct. 27, Resignation of General Ludendorff

——, Fourth German peace note addressed to President Wilson

——, Austrian Government asked Italy for armistice

——, Italians broke line east of Piave

——, Americans took Belle-Joyeuse north of Grand Pré evacuated by Germans

——, Second note from Austria-Hungary asked President Wilson for immediate armistice

Oct. 28, General advance on Italian front drove Austrians back

——, Plan of German naval officers to make attack frustrated by sailors who put out fires of ships

Oct. 28–30, Battle of Shargquat (Mesopotamia)

Oct. 29, San Giovanni de Medua, Albania taken by Italians

——, American regiment arrived at Treviso, Italy

Oct. 30, Aincreville captured by Americans

——, Turkey signed armistice with Allies to go into effect the following day

——, Fiume, Croatia surrendered by Hungarian authorities to Croats

Oct. 30–31, Representatives of Allied governments met in Paris and, in session adjourned to Versailles, drew up armistice terms

Oct. 31, Americans with French army in Flanders took Cruyshautem Ridge

——, Scutari, Albania taken by Italians

——, Hostilities with Turks ended, armistice coming into effect at noon

——, Austrian emperor made over fleet to Yugo-Slav Council

Nov. 1, Americans and French advanced between the Meuse and the Aisne in Argonne to Bois de la Folie and captured heights of Barricourt and Andevanne. Americans captured Clery-le-Grand north of Brieulles and Imecourt, Ancreville, Doulcon, Andevanne, Landres, and St. Georges

——, Allied force reached Gavere on the Scheldt

——, Serbs occupied Belgrade

——, Germans attacked Fife, Rhodesia

——, Austrian battleship "Viribus Unitis" sunk in Pola harbor

Nov. 1–2, Battle of Valenciennes

Nov. 2, British warships "Surada" and "Murcia" sunk by submarine in Mediterranean

——, Americans occupied Busancy, and Briquenay Tailly, Doulcon, Villers-devant-Dun, and Thenorgues

——, Audenarde (Flanders) captured by Americans

Nov. 2–3, Americans forced crossing of the Escaut River and established a bridgehead (Flanders)

Nov. 3, Valenciennes occupied by Canadians

——, Trieste, Trent, and Udine occupied by Italians

——, Armistice with Austria signed at Belgrade with General Franchet d'Esperey

——, Allied governments agreed on armistice with Germany and peace on basis of President Wilson's Fourteen Points

——, Mutiny of German crews begun at Kiel and spread to other naval bases

——, German force from East Africa reached Chambezi River, Rhodesia

——, Americans captured Barricourt, Germont and Verrières, and Laneuville on west bank of Meuse and made effective crossing of Meuse establishing bridge-heads south of Dunsur-Meuse, reaching Authe, Châtillon-sur-Bar, Fosse, and Nouart

Nov. 4, Mosul occupied by British

——, Antivari occupied by Italians

——, Americans captured Vaux-en-Dieulet and Sommauthe, Beaufort, and les Petites Armoises

——, Landrecies occupied by Allies

——, End of Battle of Vittoria-Veneto. Italian victory

——, Hostilities with Austria-Hungary ceased

——, The United States recognized the Polish army as autonomous and cobelligerent

Nov. 4–5, Second Battle of Guise

Nov. 4–11, Battle of the Sambre. General Haig attacked on 30 mile front from near Valenciennes to beyond Sambre-Oise Canal. French and Americans pressed enemy between Sambre and Meuse

Nov. 5, Americans crossed the Meuse near Brieulles and Clery le Petit

——, Americans captured Milly, and established line south to Bois de Châtillon. Cesse occupied

——, General retreat of Germans begun from the Escaut to the Meuse

——, Further naval mutinies of Germans at Kiel

——, Italian naval division entered Pola

——, Italians occupied Fiume

——, American note to German government stated that Allied governments would agree to an armistice and that Marshal Foch was authorized to receive delegates and communicate terms

Nov. 6, British advanced toward Mons, Maubeuge, and the Avesnes

——, Rethel and Vervin between the Oise and the Aisne taken by the French

——, German delegates left Berlin for armistice conference

——, Sedan taken by Americans and French and occupied by French Division

Nov. 7, Borne de Cornouille captured by Americans, and Flabas, Raucourt, Haracourt, and Autrecourt taken, and Murvaux, Fontaine, and Vilosnes-sur-Meuse

——, Third Army of the United States created under Major General Joseph T. Dickman

Nov. 8, Joint declaration of Great Britain and France as to future of Syria and Mesopotamia

Nov. 8–9, British occupied Maubeuge

Nov. 9, German delegates received by General Foch in the Compiègne Forest near Réthonde and given terms under which armistice would be granted

——, British took Tournai

——, Americans took Manheulles, Moranville, and Abacourt. Grimacourt taken but evacuated

——, Prince Maximilian announced the adbication of the Kaiser

——, Alexandretta, Syria occupied by Allies

——, British battleship "Britannica" sunk by submarine in Atlantic off Gibraltar

——, French took Hirson

——, Kasama, Rhodesia captured by Germans

Nov. 10, French and Americans captured Chaumont-devant-Damvillers, and Ville-devant-Chaumont. Marcheville taken but not held. Americans took Jametz and cleared Forêt de Woevre

——, Mézières retaken by French

——, Rumania announced reëntry into War

——, Ghent reoccupied by Belgians

——, The Kaiser and the Crown Prince fled to Holland

Nov. 11, Americans occupied Stenay, Pouilly-sur-Meuse and Autreville, and Baalon. American line on the 11th: First Army from Fresnes-en-Woevre to Pont Maugis, Second Army from Port-sur-Seille to Fresnes-en-Woevre

——, American troopship "Ophir" destroyed by explosion

——, Canadians took Mons

——, Germans signed the armistice terms at 5.15 A.M. Hostilities on West front ceased at 11 A.M.

Nov. 12, Abdication of Emperor Charles of Austria

——, Allied fleet entered the Dardanelles

Nov. 13, Separate armistice granted to Hungary

——, Allied ultimatum ordered German fleet to meet Allies off Firth of Fourth at 5 A.M. Nov. 18

Nov. 14, Hostilities in East Africa ended

Nov. 16, Allied armies began march into Germany

Nov. 17, Mulhausen occupied by the French, Baku by British

——, Yugo-Slavs protested Italian occupation of Fiume

Nov. 18, Allied governments issued note refusing to recognize the Russo-German peace treaty

——, Last German troops recrossed the frontier of France

——, Brussels reoccupied by Belgians

——, Poles occupied Lemberg

——, Italian troops joined naval division at Fiume

——, Death of General Maude. Succeeded in command by Lieutenant General Sir W. R. Marshall

Nov. 19, Metz occupied by French

——, Antwerp reoccupied by Belgians

——, General Philippe Pétain made a Marshal of France

Nov. 20, First surrendered submarines arrived at Harwich

Nov. 21, American soldiers commanded by General Dickman entered Luxemburg. Received welcome from citizens

——, Surrender of German High Seas fleet to Admiral Beatty at Rosyth before internment in the Orkneys at Scapa Flow

——, Namur occupied by British

Nov. 23, Lemberg taken by Poles

Nov. 25, Strasbourg occupied by French

——, German force in East Africa commanded by General von Lettow surrendered to Allies at Abercorn, Rhodesia

Nov. 26, American troops entered Fiume

——, Russian Black Sea fleet surrendered to Allies

——, Last German troops recrossed the Belgian frontier

Nov. 30, Russian American force captured Korpagarskoi 200 miles southeast of Archangel after fight with Bolsheviki

Dec. 1, British and American troops crossed the German frontier. American troops occupied Trèves

Dec. 6, Cologne entered by British troops

——, American troops entered Mayence

Dec. 8, Coblenz occupied by American force

Dec. 9, Lahej, Arabia reoccupied by British

Dec. 12, British troops crossed the Rhine at Cologne

Dec. 13, Trier Conference. Negotiations begun for return of confiscated property of Allied nationals

Dec. 14, Armistice on West Front prolonged to Jan. 17

Dec. 15, Poland severed diplomatic relations with Germany

Dec. 16, Armistice of Nov. 11 revised and renewed

——, Marshal Mackensen and his army surrendered to Hungarian force near Budapest

Dec. 27, Batum, Georgia occupied by British

COST

Total direct cost, $180,500,000,000, indirect cost, $151,612,552,000, total $331,612,552,000

Known dead, 9,998,771

Seriously wounded, 6,295,512

Otherwise wounded, 14,002,039

Missing or prisoners, 5,983,600

1919

Jan. 3, Food Council headed by Herbert Hoover appointed to administer relief to the liberated and enemy countries. Allied Relief Missions sent to Poland, Serbia, Rumania, Turkey, Czechoslovakia, Hungary, Austria, Trieste, and later to the Baltic Provinces and Southern Russia

Jan. 9, Announcement of constitution of the Supreme Council of the Peace Conference composed of 2 representatives each from Great Britain, France, Italy, the United States, and Japan, the five "Powers with general interests"

Jan. 12, Meeting of the Supreme War Council in Paris attended by Mr. Wilson, Mr. Lansing, M. Clemenceau, M. Pichon, Mr. Lloyd George, Mr. Balfour, Signor Orlando, and Baron Sonnino and first formal meeting of the Supreme Council, decision taken that only the representatives of the five chief Allied and Associated Powers should be entitled to attend all meetings of the Conference, that other members should be summoned to attendance only when their special interests were involved in the discussion, all belligerents and all Powers who had severed diplomatic relations with Germany entitled to attend at the plenary sessions

Jan. 16, Germany signed revised and renewed armistice agreement extending the time for one month

Jan. 18, Opening session of the Peace Conference in Paris, Georges Clemenceau, Prime Minister of France, elected president, the following countries represented: British Empire, United States, France, Italy, Japan (5 members each); Belgium, Brazil, and Serbia (3 members each); China, Greece, the Hejaz, Poland, Portugal, Rumania, Siam, and Czechoslovakia (2 members each); Cuba, Guatemala, Haiti, Honduras, Liberia, Nicaragua, Panama, Bolivia, Ecuador, Peru, and Uruguay (1 member each). Rules of procedure adopted, Secretariat appointed, and a Drafting Committee. Because of opposition of Italy Yugoslavs not recognized except as representing Serbia

Jan. 22, Decision of Supreme Council to invite Russia to a conference at Prinkipo (Prince's Island in the Sea of Marmora) and to send a Mission to Poland

Jan. 24, Supreme Council issued warning that taking of territory by force would prejudice claims of aggressors

——, Commission on Control of Production of War Material in Germany appointed

——, Territorial Claims of the British Dominions presented before Supreme Council

Jan. 25, Second plenary session of the Peace Conference, Resolution moved by President Wilson for the creation of a League of Nations as an integral part of the Peace Treaty adopted, and Commission appointed to draft constitution. *See also* League of Nations. Certain minor Powers including Belgium and Canada protested against powers assumed by the Five. Commissions appointed; League of Nations, Woodrow Wilson, president; International Labor Legislation, Samuel Gompers, president; Responsibilities for the War, and Guarantees, Robert Lansing, president, with 3 sub-committees on criminal acts, responsibilities for the war, and responsibilities for the violations of the laws of war; Reparation for Damages, L. L. Klotz, president, with 3 sub-committees; International Control of Ports, Waterways, and Railways, Signor Crespi, president, with 2 sub-committees; Committee on German Materials of War and Disarmament, Committee on Financial Questions, E. S. Montagu, president, with 5 sub-committees; Committee on Economic Questions, M. Clementel, president

Jan. 27, Japan presented claims for German rights and holdings in Shantung and for Islands in the Pacific before the Supreme Council (Council of Ten)

——, Economic Drafting Commission appointed

Jan. 28, China represented by Wellington Koo presented claims before the Supreme Council

——, France presented claims to the Cameroons and Togo to the Supreme Council

Jan. 29, Commission of Polish Affairs constituted and Inter-Allied Commission sent to Poland

Jan. 30, Mandates system later incorporated in Article 22 of the Covenant of the League of Nations adopted by the Supreme Council

Jan. 31, Commission on Teschen appointed and Inter-Allied Mission sent to Teschen

Jan. 31, and Feb. 18, Serb-Croat-Slovene claims presented before Supreme Council

Feb. 1, Rumanian delegation presented territorial claims before Supreme Council

Feb. 1 and 18, Commission on Rumania and Yugoslavia constituted, André Tardieu appointed head

Feb. 3, Teschen Agreement signed

Feb. 3–4, Claims of Greece for Smyrna zone presented by Venizelos and Politis before Supreme Council

Feb. 5, Territorial claims of Czechoslovakia presented and Commission on Czechoslovakia constituted, Jules Cambon, president

——, The Russian Soviet Government accepted invitation to attend conference of all Russian factions with representatives of the Allies at Prinkipo

Feb. 6, Arab claims presented by Emir Faisal to the Supreme Council for an independent Hejaz

——, Agreement with Germany as to food supplies

Feb. 7, Territorial claims of Italy presented before Supreme Council

——, Special Commission on German Materials of War and Disarmament appointed

Feb. 8, Supreme Economic Council constituted to consider economic questions. Sections: Food and Relief, Herbert Hoover, president; Finance, Norman H. Davis, president; Means of Communication, H. O. Mance, president; Raw Materials, M. Loucheur; Superior Blockade Council, Vance McCormick; Shipping, K. Cooke; Urgent Business, Bernard M. Baruch, president

Feb. 10, Committee on Armistice with Germany appointed, Marshal Foch, president

Feb. 11, Belgian claims presented to Supreme Council

Feb. 12, Inter-Allied Military and Naval Committee appointed, Marshal Foch, president

——, Permanent Committee on Polish Affairs constituted, Jules Cambon, president

Feb. 13, Central Syrian Committee and Dr. Howard Bliss presented Syrian claims to the Supreme Council

——, Japanese "Racial Equality Clause" for insertion in Covenant presented by Baron Makino at meeting of League of Nations Commission

Feb. 14, Third plenary session of the Peace Conference, the Covenant (Draft Constitution for the League of Nations prepared by David Hunter Miller, American, and Cecil Hurst, British) presented with Report of Commission of the League of Nations

Feb. 15, Blockade of the Dardanelles raised by the Supreme Economic Council

——, Claims of the Druses presented to Supreme Council

Feb. 16, Armistice with Germany renewed

Feb. 18, Statement of Yugoslav territorial claims before the Supreme Council

Feb. 19, Attempted assassination of Clemenceau who was shot and wounded by young Anarchist

Feb. 21, Territorial claims of Denmark presented to Supreme Council and Commission on Belgian and Danish Affairs appointed, André Tardieu, president

Feb. 24, Albanian claims presented and Commission on Greek and Albanian Affairs appointed, Jules Cambon, president

Feb. 26, Armenian claims presented to Supreme Council

Feb. 27, Central Commission on Territorial Questions appointed

——, Zionist claims presented for national home for Jews in Palestine

Feb. 28, Announcement that Prinkipo Conference with Russians would not be held

March 5, Claims of Montenegro presented to Supreme Council

March 6, Negotiations with Germany at Spa on food relief terminated by Allied Delegation because of refusal of Germany to surrender ships without guarantee of food supplies

March 12, Air Commission appointed. Colonel Dhe, president

——, Lord Allenby presented views as to Syria and Arabia before Supreme Council

March 14, Brussels Agreement under which Germany supplied with foodstuffs

——, Defensive Treaties offered by Great Britain and the United States to France pledging their countries to come to aid of France in case of unprovoked attack by Germany in lieu of proposals for "Rhineland Republic" on left bank of the Rhine detached from Germany, and prolonged Allied military occupation

March 16, New armistice agreement with Germany provided for sending of food to Germany. *See also* Germany

March 19, Note to Hungary delimited neutral zone between Hungary and Rumania. *See also* April 1

——, Supreme War Council ordered Poles and Ruthenians to cease hostilities

——, Indian Delegation presented claims for Turkey to full sovereignty over Constantinople and Thrace and in Asia Minor and asked to have Holy places of Islam placed under control of Turkey

March 20–21, Discussion of the Covenant of the League of Nations with representatives of the neutral States

March 21, Navigation of the Danube opened

March 25, Announcement of reduction of Council of Ten to Council of Four (Supreme Council) President Wilson, and Premiers Lloyd George, Clemenceau, and Orlando

March 26, Allied Note to Germany asked passage of Polish troops of General Haller from France through Danzig which was refused

March 28, Morocco Commission appointed, M. De Peretti de la Roca, president

April 1–8, Passage of Polish troops of General Haller through Danzig to Poland

April 1, Saar Valley Commission appointed, André Tardieu, president

——, The Council of Four sent General Smuts to Hungary to investigate armistice problems and acceptance of Allied military line by Communist Government

April 7, Deadlock in discussion of French claims to the Saar. President Wilson ordered the "George Washington" and consulted with the American Delegation as to withdrawal from the Conference

April 9, Decision to place Saar Valley under the administration of the League of Nations for 15 years, France renouncing claims for annexation, but as compensation for the destruction of the coal mines in the North of France France to have the exclusive rights of the coal mines in the Saar Basin in full ownership during this period, the ultimate status of the region to be decided by a plebiscite

——, The Council of Four signed document indicting the former Kaiser and directing his trial for violations of international morality and sanctity of treaties

April 11, Fourth plenary session of the Peace Conference, the International Labor Legislation Commission Report presented outlining the organization, powers, and procedure of a Labor Conference (international labor parliament), and a Labor Office (bureau of experts), the original members of the League of Nations to be the original members of the Conference

——, Commission of the League of Nations adopted amendment to the Covenant recognizing Monroe doctrine but rejected the racial equality amendment proposed by the Japanese for a clause declaring all members of the League without respect of race or color to be equal (vote of 11 out of 17 in favor but failed because not unanimous)

April 14, The Germans invited to come to Paris on April 25

——, Memorandum of President Wilson to Italian Delegation opposed Italian claim to Fiume or any part of the coastline south of Fiume, but accepted the northern frontier of the secret Treaty of London of 1915 and Italian claim to Lisa and Valona, the "Wilson line" giving Trieste, Pola, and the greater half of the Istrian Peninsula to Italy

April 22, Alsace Lorraine Commission appointed, André Tardieu, president

——, Japanese claims presented to Supreme Council

April 23, President Wilson published statement as to Fiume, an appeal to the Italian people, to renounce claims to Fiume and Dalmatia

——, The Supreme War Council called for an end of German interference in the local affairs of the Baltic Provinces and asked for recall of General von der Goltz

April 24, Reply of Premier Orlando to President Wilson on Fiume and withdrawal of Italian Delegation from the Peace Conference because of the Wilson statement as to Fiume

April 25, Chinese proposals as to Shantung presented

——, First German delegates arrived at Versailles

April 28, Fifth plenary session of the Peace Conference, the revised and amended Draft of Covenant of the League of Nations presented by President Wilson and adopted, and resolution appointing Sir James Eric Drummond first Secretary General of the League, and a committee of nine to prepare plans for the organization of the League and for first meeting of the Assembly, and adoption of the International Labor Organization Convention

April 29, Arrival of Count von Brockdorff-Rantzau, head of the German Delegation

April 30, Japanese claim to German rights and holdings in Shantung conceded under verbal promise of eventual restoration to China

May 1, Commission for protection of minorities in "new" and other States appointed, M. Berthelot, president

May 4, The Supreme Council (Council of Three; President Wilson, and Premiers Clemenceau and Lloyd George) sent formal invitation to Italy to return to the Conference

May 6, Sixth (private) session of the Peace Conference approved the Draft Treaty of Peace with Germany

——, Italian Delegation returned to the Peace Conference

——, Protest of Chinese Delegation against the Shantung clauses of the German Treaty

——, The Council of Three decided to allow the Greeks to occupy Smyrna

May 7, Seventh (plenary) session of the Peace Conference, Draft Treaty of Peace handed to the German Delegation headed by Count von Brockdorff-Rantzau at the Trianon Palace, Versailles and 15 days allowed for consideration of Treaty, the time later extended to May 29

——, Announcement of Class B and C mandates by the Supreme Council, dated May 6. German East Africa assigned to Great Britain, German South West Africa to the Union of South Africa, Nauru Island to the British Empire, German Islands in the Pacific north of the Equator to Japan except Nauru and German Samoa, German Samoa to New Zealand, German New Guinea (Kaiser Wilhelmsland) together with the Bismarck Archipelago (New Britain, New Ireland, &c.) and the northern Solomon Islands to Australia, Togo and the Cameroons to France and Great Britain who were to make joint recommendations as to their future

May 8, German Delegation protested peace terms, first Note followed by others May 10, 11 and 13, 16, 19, each dealing with one topic, the League of Nations, the Labor Charter, bargaining in German territories, Sarre Basin, prisoners of war, &c., which were referred to 13 committees each of which was specially responsible for one section of the Treaty and interim replies returned to the Germans

May 14, Austrian Delegation headed by Dr. Renner arrived at St. Germain-en-Laye

May 15, Greeks occupied Smyrna. See also p. 263

May 26, Supreme Council offered support, munitions, and supplies to Russian Government of Admiral Kolchak at Omsk on certain conditions which were accepted June 7

——, Request of Sweden that Aaland Islands be permitted to decide by plebiscite whether they desired to belong to Sweden or Finland

May 27, Draft Minorities Treaty presented to Poland by Allies

May 29, Allies offered Italy the Brenner frontier far in advance of line of Treaty of 1915

——, German counter-proposals for Treaty presented included offer to pay a sum not exceeding 100 milliards of gold marks partly in gold and mainly in commodities and services and claimed right of appeal from the assessment of the Reparation Committee to a neutral arbitrator, 20 milliards to be paid by May 1, 1926, credit to be allowed for war material surrendered to Allies under conditions of the Armistice, and for railways and property ceded with Alsace-Lorraine and the German colonies, fixed annual supplies of coal offered to France in lieu of Saar Valley, plebiscite asked for in Alsace-Lorraine, the question of the colonies to be referred to arbitration, Danzig, Memel, and Konigsberg to be free ports under German sovereignty, immediate admission to the League of Nations, withdrawal of armies of occupation within 6 months after signing of Treaty

May 29, Seventh plenary session of the Peace Conference received incomplete Draft Austrian Peace Treaty, the military, financial, and reparation terms and part of political terms not ready for submission

May 30, The "Tardieu Compromise" proposal to create a buffer State of Fiume (not Susak) with hinterland up to and including the St. Peter railway under League of Nations refused by Yugoslavia

May 31, Allied Note to Germany regarding German troops in Baltic Provinces

June 2, Incomplete Draft Austrian Peace Treaty handed to Dr. Renner, head of Austrian Delegation

——, The Banat claimed by Rumania, divided between Rumania and Yugoslavia

June 3, Germany protested to Peace Conference regarding French support of independent Rhineland Republic. *See also* Germany

June 8, Note from Allies to Bela Kun asked that Hungarians cease offensive against Czechoslovakia and invited him to Paris. He replied the following day denying offensive and accepting invitation

June 10, Austrian Delegation protested peace terms

June 16, Final Reply of Allies to German counterproposals to Draft Treaty required acceptance or rejection of Treaty within 5 days, made concessions, admission to the League of Nations promised at an early date, a plebiscite in Upper Silesia, some slight changes in the Polish frontier

June 17, Treaty handed to German Delegation

June 20, The Supreme Council authorized Marshal Foch to prepare for advance of troops into Germany if Treaty not accepted by 7 P.M. on the 23rd

June 21, The entire $350,000,000 fleet of German warships interned at Scapa Flow were sunk by their commanders acting under command of Admiral Reuter

June 22, The German Assembly at Weimar voted to accept the Treaty with certain conditions

——, The Supreme Council refused to accept German reservations to Treaty on war criminals and war guilt

June 23, Germany announced agreement to sign the Treaty, unconditional acceptance

June 24, The Supreme Council granted Belgium priority in German reparations up to $500,000,000

June 27, China announced that the Chinese Delegation would not sign the Peace Treaty because of Shantung clauses

June 28, Ninth plenary session of the Peace Conference, Treaty of Peace with Germany signed at Versailles by Germany and the Allies except China, the Covenant of the League of Nations included as Part I, the Labor Convention creating an annual International Labor Conference and International Labor Office, Part XIII, Germany ceded Alsace-Lorraine to France, Prussian Moresnet, Eupen, and Malmédy to Belgium with provision of plebiscite in Malmédy, Memel to the Allies, parts of Posen and West Prussia to Poland, plebiscite provided for in Upper Silesia and part of East Prussia to decide as to sovereignty of Germany or Poland, Danzig to be a

free international city, plebiscite in North and Central Schleswig to decide as to sovereignty of Germany or Denmark, Saar Basin in control of international commission with possession of the coal mines by France for 15 years with plebiscite at end of this period to decide sovereignty, all overseas colonies and protectorates surrendered to be administered in general under mandate system by countries specified, all special rights and privileges in China, Siam, Liberia, Morocco, Egypt, and Turkey surrendered, the complete independence of Belgium, Czechoslovakia, and German Austria to be recognized, Treaties of Brest-Litovsk and Bucharest denounced, German army to be reduced to 100,000 men and officers by March 1920, General Staff to be abolished, conscription abolished, district 30 miles east of the Rhine to be demilitarized, Navy to be limited as specified and no military air service or submarines permitted, fortifications of Heligoland to be dismantled and no German fortifications to be built in the Baltic region, sum of reparations to be stated by Allies on May 1, 1921 by Reparation Commission appointed, payments in kind to be made specified, Allied occupation of left bank of the Rhine, and bridgeheads at Cologne, Coblenz, and Mainz to end in 15 years if Germany meeting her international obligations

June 28, Defensive Treaties with France signed by the United States and Great Britain undertaking to give military assistance to France in case of unprovoked aggression by Germany never became effective because of non-ratification of the United States

——, Minorities Treaty between the Allies and Poland signed by which Poland agreed to respect the civil and political rights of racial and religious minorities in Poland. Placed under guarantee of the League of Nations, Feb. 13, 1920

——, Agreement as to military occupation of the Rhineland signed by the United States, Belgium, the British Empire, France, and Germany

July 2, Agreement for administration of Nauru Island by Great Britain, Australia, and New Zealand

July 10, Austrian Delegation presented counterproposals to Treaty

July 20, Second Draft Treaty presented to Austrian Delegation

——, Decision to cede the Burgenland, West Hungary to Austria

July 26, Bulgarian Delegation headed by M. Theodoroff, Prime Minister, arrived in Paris

Aug. 6, Austrian Delegation submitted observations and counter-proposals to Treaty

Aug. 21, Agreement of Great Britain and Belgium of May 30 as to mandate of Ruanda and Urundi to Belgium accepted by the Supreme Council and division of Togo and the Cameroons between France and Great Britain

Aug. 29, Protocol as to deliveries of coal signed by Germany at Versailles

Sept. 2, Ultimatum to Germany demanded withdrawal from German Constitution of Article 61 as to admission of Austrian deputies to German Imperial Council as in conflict with the Treaty of Versailles. Accepted by Germany

——, Reply of Supreme Council to Austrian Note of Aug. 6 on the Treaty and delivery of revised terms, the railroad junction of Radkersburg returned to Austria

Sept. 6, Austrian National Assembly accepted terms of Treaty

Sept. 10, Treaty of Peace with Austria signed at St. Germain by Austria and the Allies, Rumania and Yugoslavia refusing to sign, included the Covenant and Labor Convention, Austria ceded to Italy the Trentino and Upper Adige (South Tirol), Istria, a part of Dalmatia and a number of Adriatic Islands, a plebiscite in the Klagenfurt Basin of Carinthia which in 1920 decided in favor of Austria, the independence of Hungary, Czechoslovakia, Poland, and Yugoslavia recognized, Austria to "abstain from any act which might compromise her independence," clauses for the protection of racial and religious minorities included which were later placed under guarantee of the League of Nations, army reduced to 30,000, conscription prohibited and no military or naval aircraft to be maintained, navy limited to 3 patrol boats on the Danube, surrender of "war criminals" provided for, reparations to be fixed by Reparation Commission, a "reasonable sum" to be paid before May 1, 1921, all transferred territories liable for share of pre-war Austrian debt, Austria guaranteed free access by railway to the Adriatic

——, Minorities Treaty between the Allies and Czechoslovakia signed

——, Conventions regarding liquor traffic in Africa signed and control of international traffic in arms and munitions

Sept. 12, Gabriele D'Annunzio at head of volunteer army without authorization of the Italian Government seized Fiume

Sept. 15, Anglo-French Agreement as to Syria. *See* Syria

Sept. 19, Draft Treaty presented to Bulgarian Delegation

Sept. 27, Decision of Supreme Council for plebiscite in (former Austrian) Teschen, later abandoned. *See* Poland, and in Zips and Orava in dispute between Poland and Czechoslovakia

——, Allied Note to Germany demanded immediate withdrawal of German troops from Baltic Provinces

Oct. 24, Bulgarian observations on the Peace Treaty presented to Supreme Council protested terms of territorial settlement, against abolition of conscription and asked for immediate entrance into League of Nations

——, General Degoutte succeeded General Fayolle in command of Allied Army of Occupation

Oct. 29–Nov. 29, First International Labor Conference held in Washington. *See also* International Labor Organization

Nov. 3, Reply of the Supreme Council to Bulgarian Note of Oct. 24 made no notable concessions but promised early admittance to the League of Nations

Nov. 13, New Bulgarian Government of Stambolisky accepted terms of Treaty

Nov. 19, The Treaty of Peace with Germany failed of ratification by the Senate of the United States

Nov., Last meeting of Supreme Economic Council in Rome

Nov. 27, Treaty of Peace with Bulgaria signed at Neuilly-sur-Seine by Bulgaria and the Allies, Rumania and Yugoslavia refusing to sign, included the Covenant of the League of Nations and the Labor Convention, Thrace ceded to Allied and Associated Powers and Bulgaria guaranteed outlets for trade on the Ægean Sea, independence of Yugoslavia rec-

ognized and certain districts transferred to Yugoslavia including the town of Strumitza, reparations set at 2,250,000,000 gold francs by half-yearly instalments for period of 37 years, maximum size of army to be 20,000 officers and men raised by voluntary enlistment but police customs officials, forest guards armed with rifles allowed up to 13,000, limitation of navy to 4 torpedo-boats and 6 motorboats, no air forces or submarines allowed, provision made for payment of reparations in kind including 50,000 tons of coal a year for 5 years to Yugoslavia. *See also* Bulgaria

Dec. 5, Yugoslavia signed Treaties of Peace with Austria and Bulgaria and the Minorities Treaty

Dec. 8, Allied ultimatum to Germany as to reparation for ships sunk at Scapa Flow

Dec. 9, Rumania signed Treaties of Peace with Austria and Bulgaria and Minorities Treaty

——, Supreme Council (British, French, and American proposal) proposed creation of buffer State of Fiume and frontier on basis of slight modification of the so-called "Wilson Line" (*see* April 14), but Albona to Italy, a special régime in Zara, the rest of Dalmatia to Yugoslavia, Valona (Avlona) in full sovereignty to Italy, an Italian mandate in Albania, and the Adriatic Islands of Pelagossa, Lissa, Lussin, and Unie to Italy

1920

Jan. 6, Italian Note (Nitti to Lloyd George) demanded fulfilment of the Treaty of London of 1915

Jan. 7, Hungarian delegation headed by Count Apponyi arrived in Paris

Jan. 8, Yugoslav Note protested mandate of Italy for Albania and claimed Scutari and territory north of the Drin (Drim) River in case of revision of boundaries

Jan. 8–16, Meeting of Supreme Council (Great Britain, France, and Italy) to discuss Fiume, war criminals, and trade with Russia

Jan. 9, Joint memorandum of Clemenceau and Lloyd George to Italians declared in favor of Treaty of London

Jan. 10, Final ceremony of ratification of Peace Treaty with Germany by Allies and Germany, Protocols signed, and Germany signed Protocol agreeing to reparation for ships sunk at Scapa Flow. With ratification of Treaty of Versailles the League of Nations and the mandate system came into effect

Jan. 14, Revised proposals of Clemenceau and Lloyd George as to Adriatic called for independent State of Fiume under the League of Nations, the "January compromise," Susak to Yugoslavia and St. Peter railway, Zara to be independent under the League, Albania to be under Italian mandate, Lussin, Lissa, Cherso, and Lagosta to go to Italy

——, Conference at Helsingfors of representatives of Finland, Estonia, Latvia, Lithuania, and Poland to discuss preservation of independence, policy towards Russia, &c.

Jan. 15, Draft Peace Treaty presented to Hungarians

Jan. 16, Note of Supreme Council to the Netherlands asked for surrender of the ex-Emperor of Germany for trial

——, Announcement of Supreme Council that Russian blockade would be raised and trade relations resumed

——, First meeting of the Council of the League of Nations. *See* League of Nations

Jan. 20 and 28, The January compromise proposal rejected by Yugoslavs

Jan. 20, Ultimatum of France and Great Britain to Yugoslavs demanded acceptance of proposals of Jan. 14 within 4 days, otherwise Great Britain and France would authorize the execution of the Treaty of London leaving Fiume to Yugoslavia (as not mentioned in the Treaty) but all northern Dalmatia to Italy. This settlement prevented by protest from the United States against change of terms of settlement without participation of the United States (Jan. 19) followed by Notes of President Wilson of Feb. 10, 25, and March 6

Jan. 21, Clemenceau resigned from Supreme Council and Supreme Council and Peace Conference closed, unsettled questions to be dealt with by Conference of Premiers and Conference of Ambassadors

Jan. 22, Recognition of Armenian Republic of Erivan by Allied Powers as a *de facto* Government

Jan. 23, The Government of the Netherlands refused to surrender the ex-Kaiser under the Dutch Constitution and the traditional rights of asylum

Jan. 24, Reparation Commission organized, M. Jonnart, French delegate, elected president

Jan. 25, German proposal that war criminals be tried by German Federal Court at Leipzig accepted

Jan. 26, First meeting of the Conference of Ambassadors succeeding the Supreme Council in interpretation and supervision of the execution of the Treaties

Feb. 10, Memorandum of President Wilson objecting to compromise settlement as to Fiume differing from that agreed upon on Dec. 9, 1919

Feb. 12, Hungarian counter-proposals to Treaty presented asked that the Szeklers of East Transylvania be left under Hungarian sovereignty according to principle of self-determination, and that no territories be transferred without a plebiscite or better protection of Hungarian minorities

Feb. 12–23, Inter-Allied Conference in London (Great Britain, France, Italy, and Greece) for discussion of Fiume and Near East, and drafting of Turkish Treaty

Feb. 14, Second Allied Note to the Netherlands asked for internment of the ex-Emperor of Germany which was granted March 5 and accepted March 31 instead of surrender

Feb. 16, Announcement of London Conference that Constantinople would remain the capital of the Ottoman Empire

Feb. 18, Germany notified that the Allies would consent to reduction of army to 200,000 by April 10 and to 100,000 by July 10 instead of March 31 as required by Treaty of Versailles

Feb. 20, Raymond Poincaré appointed president of the Reparation Commission

March 6, Note of President Wilson agreed with France and Great Britain to leave determination of frontier in Fiume to settlement by Italy and Yugoslavia

April 19–26, Inter-Allied Conference at San Remo (Great Britain, France, Italy, Belgium, Japan, and Greece) discussed German disarmament, the Near East, Russia and Adriatic, the Peace Treaty with Turkey, and allocation of Class A mandates. Decision to leave Adriatic question in negotiation between Yugoslavia and Italy

April 25, The San Remo Conference granted mandate for Palestine and Iraq to Great Britain and mandate for Syria and the Lebanon to France

April 26, Note of Allied Premiers to Germany asked for proposals as to reparations

May 5, Announcement of acceptance of mandates by Great Britain and France

May 6, Turkish Delegation arrived in Paris to receive Treaty from Allied Powers

——, Reply of Allies to Hungarian Note on the Treaty of Feb. 12 declared that the League of Nations would be free to make minor rectifications of frontiers if recommended by frontier commissions

May 11, Draft Treaty handed to Turkish Delegation representing the Constantinople Government

May 14–16, Inter-Allied Conference at Lympne, Franco-British Committee set up to consider methods of payment of reparations by Germany

May 15–17, Conference of France and Great Britain (Lloyd George and Millerand) at Hythe, England, to arrange program for Spa Conference

June 4, Treaty of Peace with Hungary signed at Trianon by Hungary and the Allies, Transylvania ceded to Rumania and a strip in the West, the Banat divided between Rumania and Yugoslavia, Croatia to Yugoslavia, Slovak provinces to Czechoslovakia, army not to exceed 35,000, reparations to be fixed by Reparation Commission, Hungary to assume share of Austro-Hungarian national debt

June 19–20, Inter-Allied Conference (Great Britain, France, and Greece) at Hythe, discussion of Turkish offensive, approved war against Turkish Nationalists by Greeks

June 21–22, Inter-Allied Conference at Boulogne attended by representatives of Great Britain, France, Italy, Belgium, Greece, and Japan discussed reparations and disarmament

June 30, Reparation Commission declared Germany in default in coal deliveries

July 2–3, Inter-Allied Financial Conference at Brussels on reparations agreed tentatively that German indemnity should be $30,000,000,000 payable annually; $750,000,000 for the first five years and $1,250,000,000 annually thereafter

July 5–16, Inter-Allied Conference at Spa of Premiers of Great Britain, France, Japan, Italy, Belgium, Poland with German delegation, and Portugal represented, German scheme for reparations submitted, Germany signed Protocol of Disarmament (July 9) agreeing to dissolve the *Sicherheitswehr* and *Einwohnerswehr*, surrender concealed arms, and observe military clauses of the Treaty of Versailles, Spa Protocol signed by Allies apportioned reparations: France, 52%; British Empire, 22%; Italy, 10%; Belgium, 8%; Japan and Portugal, .75 of 1% each; 6.5% to the others (Greece, Rumania, Yugoslavia). Germany signed Protocol as to deliveries of coal. Allied assistance to Poland against Russia refused

July 16, Ratification of the Treaty of St. Germain with Austria in Paris

——, Coal Protocol with Germany signed at Spa

July 19, Allied ultimatum to Turkey demanded signing of Treaty within 10 days

Aug. 8, Conference at Hythe (Great Britain and France) discussed Russo-Polish war (*see* Poland), and adopted program of non-military assistance to Poland if negotiations between the 2 countries failed

Aug. 10, Treaty of Peace with Turkey signed by Turkey and Allies at Sèvres, Smyrna to remain under Turkish sovereignty but to be administered by Greece, Thrace outside the zone of the Straits,

Imbros, Tenedos, Lemnos, Samothrace, Mytilene, Chios, Samos and Nikaria, the Ægean Islands of Rhodes, Stampalia, Calki, Scarpanto, Casos, Pscopis, Misiros, Calymnos, Leros, Patmos, Lipsos, Sini, Cos and Castellorizzo ceded to Italy, the Dardanelles and the Bosphorous internationalized, the British mandate in Palestine, Mesopotamia (Iraq), and Transjordan, the French mandate in Syria recognized and ultimate independence of these States, the French protectorate in Morocco, Tunis, the annexation of Cyprus by Great Britain. Turkey renounced rights over Egypt and recognized the British protectorate, the independence of the Hejaz and Armenia, claims of Allies for reparation waived, but Turkey to pay costs of army of occupation, clauses for protection of minorities included

Aug. 10, Greece signed Minorities Treaty with the Allies

——, Armenia signed Minorities Treaty with the Allies

——, Treaty of frontiers signed by the Allies at Sèvres with Poland, Rumania, Czechoslovakia, and Yugoslavia

Aug. 14, First Little Entente Treaty, Alliance between Czechoslovakia and Yugoslavia for mutual support against Hungarian aggression

Sept. 24–Oct. 8, International Financial Conference at Brussels

Nov. 12, Treaty of Rapallo between Italy and Yugoslavia signed fixed boundaries in the Adriatic region, Fiume to be an independent city, Italy renouncing claim to Dalmatia except Zara, and Adriatic Islands except Cherso, Lussin, Lagosta, Cazza, Pelagosa, Istrian boundary redrawn

Dec. 1, Permanent Mandates Commission of the League of Nations constituted

Dec. 9, Drafts of Class C mandates received by the Secretary General of the League of Nations

Dec. 16–22, Second Brussels Conference of Allied and German economic experts on reparations

Dec. 17, Class C mandates approved by the League of Nations Council assigning German South West Africa to Union of South Africa, German New Guinea (Kaiserwilhelmsland) the Bismarck Archipelago, part of the Solomon and other former German South Pacific Islands to Australia, former German Samoa to New Zealand, Nauru to the British Empire, Yap, the Marianne (Ladrone), Pelew, Caroline, and other former German North Pacific Islands to Japan

1921

Jan. 24–30, Inter-Allied Conference in Paris (Great Britain, France, Italy, Belgium, and Japan) discussed disarmament, Near East and Austrian affairs, and reparations. Resolution adopted that Germany should pay beginning May 1, 2 milliard gold marks for 2 years, 3 milliards for the next 3 years, 4 milliards for the next 3 years, 5 milliards for the next 3 years, and then 6 milliards for 31 years, and a second series of annual payments for 42 years equal to 12% of value of German exports. Notes to Germany as to disarmament and coal deliveries

Feb. 21–March 14, Inter-Allied Conference in London (Great Britain, France, Italy, Belgium, Japan, Greece, Turkey, and Germany) delegations from Greece and the two rival governments, Constantinople and Angora, in Turkey to discuss revision of the Treaty of Sèvres, and discussion of reparations, Germany proposed 1,500 million pounds over 30 years with credit for 1,000 millions already paid

March 7, Decision of London Conference as to "sanctions" if Paris proposals not accepted by Germany

March 8, French troops occupied Düsseldorf, Duisburg, and Ruhrort because of alleged default of Germany in payment of advance of 20 milliard gold marks on account as provided in the Treaty of Versailles

March 14, Germany claimed to have liquidated the 20 milliard gold marks required under the Treaty of Versailles, Article 235, to be paid by May 1, 1921

March 15, The Reparation Commission demanded payment of 1 milliard gold marks by March 23 and 12 milliard by May 1

March 24, Germany declared to be in default by the Reparation Commission

April 6–June 1, General Conference of Succession States of Austro-Hungarian Empire at Rome

April 9, In accordance with decision of Allies of March 7 as to "sanctions" on Allied customs cordon drawn around the Rhineland which was not raised until Oct. 1

April 20, Germany asked mediation of the United States as to reparations; refused

April 23, Rumania joined the Little Entente Alliance

April 23–25, Briand and Lloyd George met at Lympne and agreed on sanctions to be applied to Germany if terms not complied with

April 24, German proposal for reparations submitted to the Government of the United States of total of 50 milliard gold marks and assumption of part of Allied indebtedness to the United States

April 27, The Reparation Commission established total liabilities of Germany at 132 billion gold marks (6,600 million sterling) exclusive of Belgian War debt of 4 billion gold marks, three series of A, B, and C bonds to be issued covering this amount, A 600 million pounds, B 1,900 million, and the balance C to be issued at later date to be determined by Commission

April 29–May 5, Inter-Allied Conference in London to discuss reparations (Great Britain, France, Belgium, Italy, Japan, and Germany). Report of Reparations Commission of April 27 adopted and the "London schedule" of payments sent to German Government May 5

May 3, Reparation Commission notified Allied Governments of further default on the part of Germany

May 5, Allied ultimatum to Germany demanded acceptance of "London schedule" on penalty of occupation of the Ruhr by May 12

May 11, Germany accepted Allied terms of "London schedule" for payment of reparations and other conditions

June 19, Inter-Allied Conference in Paris (Great Britain, France, and Italy) on the Near East

July 1, Germany delivered treasury bonds series A, 12,000,000,000 gold marks as due under London schedule

July 8, Reparation Commission agreed on postponement for 1 year of reparation payments from Bulgaria

July 23, Convention for internationalization of the Danube signed in Paris by Austria, Belgium, Bulgaria, Czechoslovakia, France, Germany, Great Britain, Greece, Hungary, Italy, Rumania, and Yugoslavia

July 25–28, Conference of the Foreign Ministers of Finland, Estonia, Latvia and Poland at Helsingfors to discuss common economic and other problems

Aug. 8–13, Inter-Allied Conference in Paris (Great Britain, France, Belgium, Italy, and Japan) for discussion of disarmament problems, war criminals, Near East, and Upper Silesia

Aug. 24, Treaty of peace and friendly relations between Austria and the United States ending state of war

Aug. 25, Treaty of peace and friendly relations between Germany and the United States signed ending state of war

——, Agreement of France and Germany for delivery of Saar coal, 3,500,000 tons annually to Germany

Aug. 29, Treaty of peace and friendly relations between Hungary and the United States signed ending state of war

Aug. 31, Germany completed payment of 1,000,000,000 gold marks covering cash instalments due July 15 and Oct. 15 under the London schedule

Sept. 12–20, Economic Conference at Riga of representatives of Finland, Latvia, Estonia, and Poland

Sept. 21, The "sanctions" are canceled as of Sept. 30, except that occupation of Dusseldorf, Duisburg, and Ruhrort continued and British Recovery Act still in effect

Oct. 1, Customs barrier of Rhineland abolished with ending of sanctions

Oct. 6, Loucheur-Rathenau Agreement between France and Germany signed providing for direct supply of deliveries in kind to France from Germany

Oct. 15–Nov. 25, Conference of Succession States at Portorosa

Oct. 20, Convention providing for neutralization and non-fortification of the Aaland Islands signed at Geneva by representatives of Finland, Sweden, Germany, Denmark, Estonia, France, Great Britain, Italy, Latvia, and Poland

Oct. 28, Germany delivered treasury bonds series B 38,000,000,000 gold marks and series C 82,000,-000,000 gold marks

Nov. 12–Feb. 6, 1922, Washington Conference on Disarmament, delegates from the United States, British Empire, France, Italy, Japan, China, the Netherlands, Belgium, and Portugal

Nov. 15, Germany's first quarterly instalment of 300,000,000 gold marks payment of 26% of the value of German exports as required under London schedule covered by payments in kind prior to this date

Dec. 13, Four Power Pacific Treaty signed at Washington Conference by the United States, Great Britain, France, and Japan, agreement to respect insular possessions in the Pacific, all disputes on Pacific questions to be settled by conference; Anglo-Japanese Alliance terminated

Dec. 14, German Government notified Reparation Commission that it was not able to pay more than 200 million gold marks on instalments due Jan. 15 and Feb. 15, 1922

Dec. 18–22, Conference in London of France and Great Britain on reparations, security, and reconstruction

1922

Jan. 6–13, Inter-Allied Conference at Cannes (Great Britain, France, Belgium, Italy, Japan, and Germany) to discuss reparations. Resolution adopted to call conference on reconstruction at Genoa and outline agenda adopted

Jan. 13, Germany granted provisional postponement of instalments on reparations due in Jan. and Feb.

Jan. 27, Resolution adopted at the Washington Dis-

armament Conference created a commission of 10 jurists, 2 each from the United States, Great Britain, France, Italy, and Japan to consider and report on the rules of international law respecting new agencies of warfare

Jan. 28, Germany offered to pay 720 million gold marks annually with 1,450,000,000 by deliveries in kind, agreeing to balance the budget, stabilize the currency, and prevent exports of capital, and asked for reduction of Treaty payment to an amount within her capacity to pay

Feb. 4, Shantung Treaty signed at the Washington Conference by China and Japan provided for return of Kiao-chau by Japan to China and the Shantung railway to be bought by China

Feb. 6, Five Power Treaty for limitation of naval armaments signed at the Washington Conference by the United States, Great Britain, France, Italy, and Japan; 68 capital ships to be scrapped or converted, total capital ship replacement for Great Britain not to exceed 525,000 tons, for the United States 525,000 tons, for Japan 315,000 tons, and for France and Italy, each 175,000 tons. Maximum tonnage of individual ships to be restricted to 35,000 tons; maximum caliber of guns to 16 inches, &c.; limitation of tonnage and armaments of aircraft carriers; no restrictions agreed upon as to submarines and aircraft

——, Treaty on Chinese integrity, the "open door" signed at the Washington Conference by the United States, Great Britain, France, Italy, the Netherlands, Belgium, Portugal, Japan, and China, on principles and policies to be followed regarding China

——, Nine Power Treaty on the Chinese Customs Tariff signed at the Washington Conference by the United States, Great Britain, France, Belgium, the Netherlands, Italy, Portugal, Japan, and China, provided for revision of the tariff to make it equivalent to 5% *ad valorem* instead of 3.5%, and for eventual abolition of the likin (internal customs), and authorized levy of a special surtax of 2.5% on Chinese imports

——, Treaty embodying Resolutions adopted at the Washington Conference regulating submarines in time of war, and prohibiting and outlawing the use of "asphyxiating, poisonous or other gases, and all other analogous liquids, materials or devices" signed by the United States, Great Britain, France, Italy, and Japan. Never became effective

Feb. 7, Draft Agreement signed by Germany with the Reparation Commission for procedure as to deliveries in kind

Feb. 15, The Permanent Court of International Justice opened at The Hague. *See* Permanent Court

Feb. 16–April 6, Conference of Succession States of the Austro-Hungarian Empire held in Rome and 12 Agreements signed April 6 as to administrative, financial, economic, and other matters

Feb. 20–24, Conference of the Little Entente States at Bucharest

Feb. 22, Convention for internationalization of the Elbe instituting Statute signed by Belgium, Czechoslovakia, France, Germany, Great Britain, and Italy

Feb. 25, Conference of Lloyd George and Poincaré at Boulogne on the agenda for the Genoa Conference

March 9–12, Conference of the Little Entente States at Belgrade

March 13–17, Warsaw Conference of representatives of Finland, Estonia, Latvia, and Poland, agreement severally to recognize Treaties with Russia, agreement for arbitration in cases of dispute and formation of a defensive league and neutrality in case of attack on any of the signatory States

March 15, The Ruppel-Gillet Agreement signed in Berlin between France and Germany as to deliveries in kind

March 18, Conference at Stockholm of Neutrals in War (Denmark, Switzerland, Spain, Sweden) on common economic questions

March 21, The Reparation Commission in 2 Notes to Germany announced details of conditional partial moratorium and asked for 720 million gold marks for annual payment and 1,450 million in kind, Germany to impose her new taxation at once or be exposed to the "sanctions" of the London Agreement

March 22–26, Inter-Allied Conference in Paris (Great Britain, France, and Italy) reached agreement for revision of Sèvres Treaty

April 3, The Reparation Commission fixed Bulgarian reparation payments for 1922 and 1923

April 10–May 19, Economic Conference at Genoa at which 34 nations represented including Germany and Russia and the British Dominions to discuss reconstruction of Europe and renewal of relations with Russia. No agreement reached because of insistence of Belgium and France on recognition by Soviet Government of pre-war debts and restoration of foreign owned property. Announcement of Treaty signed by Germany and Russia April 16, mutual renunciation of reparations and resumption of consular and diplomatic relations

April 18, Allied Note to Germany protested the Treaty of Rapallo

April 21, Germany paid 18,000,000 gold marks reparation payment in accordance with decision of March 21

May 16, Germany paid 18,000,000 gold marks reparation payment in accordance with decision of March 21

May 17, Lord Balfour before the Supreme Council of the League of Nations defined mandates as "a self-imposed limitation by the conquerors on the sovereignty which they obtained over conquered nations"

May 31, Note to Germany announced granting of moratorium for 1922

June 2, Bemelmans-Cuntze Agreement (Reparation Commission and German Government) signed established procedure for deliveries in kind from Germany

June 8, Conference of the Little Entente States at Belgrade

June 15, Germany paid 50,000,000 gold marks reparations under agreement March 21

June 15–July 19, Conference at The Hague at which 29 nations represented including Germany and Russia on relations with Russia for the purpose of effecting an agreement whereby the Soviet Government would recognize pre-war debts and restitution of foreign owned nationalized property

June 26–July 20, Conference of experts at The Hague on relations with Russia of questions remitted to it from its agenda by the Genoa Conference

June 30, New Danube Statute ratified created European Commission of the Danube, representatives from Great Britain, France, Italy, and Rumania, granted jurisdiction over the River from its mouth to Braila

July 5, Arrangement for issue of certificates of identity to Russian refugees signed at Geneva

July 12, Germany presented formal request to Repara-

tion Commission for moratorium on cash payments for 2 years and 6 months

July 15, Germany paid 32,110,000 gold marks of the 50,000,000 due on this date in accordance with decision of March 21, the other 17,800,000 having been credited July 11 on interest and payments in kind

July 20 (meeting of July 17–24), Ratification of the Class A mandates by the Council of the League of Nations, Mesopotamia (Iraq), by Great Britain not included as arrangements made by Great Britain and Iraq by Treaty, Palestine and Transjordan to Great Britain, Syria and The Lebanon to France, the B mandates of Great Britain for northern Cameroons, western Togo, and East Africa now Tanganyika Territory, of France for southern Cameroons, eastern Togo, and of Belgium for Ruanda and Urandi

July 21, Bulgarian Government notified of expiration of time limit for payment of reparations and payment of 112 million gold marks asked for

July 27, Bulgarian Government declared inability to pay reparations and asked for 3 years moratorium

Aug. 1, Balfour Note to countries owing war debts to Great Britain offered to remit debts and German reparations to Great Britain if this policy were adopted as an international agreement. *See also* Great Britain

Aug. 4, Germany asked for moratorium for private debts as well as reparations

Aug. 7–14, Inter-Allied Conference in London (Great Britain, France, Italy, and Belgium) on reparations and war debts failed to reach agreement

Aug. 25–28, Conference of the Little Entente States and Poland at Prague

Aug. 31, Germany granted a six months moratorium by Reparation Commission

Sept. 8, Economic Conference at Reval (Finland, Estonia, Latvia, Poland)

Sept. 15, Appeal of Lloyd George to the Dominions, to Rumania, Yugoslavia, France, and Italy against Turkey. *See* Turkey, Greece

Sept. 29, Note of Conference of Ambassadors to German Government regarding non-compliance with military clauses of the Treaty

Oct. 8–9, Conference at Reval to discuss Russian proposals for Treaty of non-aggression (Finland, Estonia, Latvia, Poland)

Nov. 14, Germany made request to Reparation Commission for total moratorium for 3 or 4 years, and for definitive fixing of German liabilities

Nov. 20–Feb. 4, 1923, First Lausanne Conference between the Turkish Government (Angora) and Great Britain, France, Italy, Japan, Greece, Bulgaria, and Yugoslavia, the United States represented by an observer, no agreement reached as Turks refused to accept Allied peace terms presented

Dec. 2–12, Disarmament Conference at Moscow attended by representatives of Finland, Estonia, Latvia, Lithuania, Poland, and Russia, no agreement reached

Dec. 9–11, Inter-Allied Conference in London (Great Britain, France, and Italy) to discuss reparations. Germany submitted reparations proposals which were not accepted

Dec. 26, The Reparation Commission declared Germany in voluntary default as to delivery of timber

1923

Jan. 2–4, Inter-Allied Conference in Paris (Great Britain, France, Belgium, and Italy) to discuss reparations, British plan proposed ending the London schedule and substituting a new series of bonds with 4 year moratorium as to interest and an opportunity for an amortization loan of about 30 billion gold marks, French plan proposed a 2 year moratorium, cancellation of Series C bonds as a set-off to Inter-Allied debts and guarantees in Germany amounting to 1,000,000,000 gold marks annually. Italian plan also presented. No agreement reached

Jan. 7, Germany asked for investigation of Germany's capacity to pay by impartial body

Jan. 9, The Reparation Commission declared Germany in voluntary default on coal deliveries

Jan. 11, Franco-Belgian troops occupied the Ruhr Valley, Germany, acting, they stated, under provisions of the Treaty of Versailles which authorized the Allied Governments to take measures they deemed necessary in case of voluntary default by Germany

——, Protest of Germany to the United States and Great Britain against the French and Belgian invasion

Jan. 12, German Note protested against occupation and announced payment in kind of reparations suspended during period of occupation to France and Belgium

Jan. 16, The Reparation Commission declared Germany in voluntary default in deliveries of coal and cattle

Jan. 26, The Reparation Commission declared Germany in general default

Jan. 31, Draft Treaty presented to Turks by Allied Powers at Lausanne Conference

March 5–8, Economic Conference at Helsingfors (Finland, Estonia, Latvia, Poland)

March 6, The Turkish National Assembly rejected the Lausanne Treaty

March 9, Turkish counter-proposals of March 8 handed to the Allied High Commissioner in Constantinople and observations on Lausanne Treaty

March 12 and April 13–14, Franco-Belgian Conference in Brussels as to Ruhr policy

March 21, Agreement of Reparation Commission with Bulgaria signed as to payments by Bulgaria

March 21–27, Inter-Allied Conference in London considered Turkish proposals of March 8

April 23, Second Lausanne Conference opened, Allied Powers and Turkey

May 2, Germany made new proposals to Allies for settlement of reparations, the total amount to be reduced to 30,000,000,000 gold marks to be raised by international loans and paid in 3 instalments: 20,000,000,000, July 1, 1927; 5,000,000,000, July 1, 1929; 5,000,000,000, July 1, 1931; payments contingent on returns from the loans and in case of failure the matter to be referred to an international non-partisan commission

May 6, France and Belgium rejected German proposals of May 2

May 12, Italy rejected German proposals of May 2 asking for more concise guarantees and larger reparation sum total

May 13, Great Britain rejected German proposals of May 2

May 15, Japan rejected German proposals of May 2

May 25, Wadsworth Agreement of Allied Powers with the United States as to payment of costs of American army of occupation

June 7, New German offer submitted based on recom-

mendations of American Secretary of State, Charles E. Hughes, in speech in Dec., 1922, that a non-partisan and independent body should meet and name a fair figure for reparations, declared Germany would accept the decision of an impartial international body as to amount and method of reparation payments, and as security for an international loan of 10,000,-000,000 gold marks at 5% offered the German railway system, and real estate, and specified customs receipts, with moratorium for 4 years

June 8, Declaration of the Prime Minister of France that no offer would be considered unless passive resistance in the Ruhr ended

July 9–11, Disarmament Conference at Riga (Finland, Estonia, Latvia, Poland)

July 20, Draft Note as reply to German proposals sent by British Government to French, Belgian, Italian, and Japanese ambassadors in London for approval stated that no guarantees would be accepted unless a provision were made for some form of international control of German finances, and expert international commission proposed as suggested by Mr. Hughes to advise the Allied Governments and Reparation Commission as to Germany's capacity to pay and methods of payment and economic guarantees, rejected by France and Belgium

July 24, Lausanne Conference ended and Treaty of Peace between the Allied Powers and Turkey signed replacing Treaty of Sèvres and ending Græco-Turkish war, Turkey ceded the Hejaz, Palestine, Mesopotamia (Iraq), Syria, the Dodecanese Islands, Cyprus, Egypt, and Tripoli, and received Smyrna, Turkish Armenia, Cicilia, Anatolia, Adalia, Constantinople, Gallipoli, Adrianople, and Eastern Thrace, reparations abolished, provision for protection of non-Moslem minorities, exchange of Greek and Turkish populations, Straits to be demilitarized, recognition of abolition of the capitulations

——, Protocol as to Minorities Treaty of Aug. 10, 1920 between the Allies and Greece which now came into effect

July 28–29, Conference of the Little Entente States at Sinai

Aug. 6, Separate Peace Treaty between the United States and Turkey signed

Aug. 11, Note of German Government declared that all deliveries in kind would stop

Aug. 12, Statement of British Government declared definite disagreement with policy of France and Belgium in the Ruhr

Sept. 25, Germany paid Reparation Commission treasury bills for 96,000,000 gold marks to be paid to Belgium, the balance of 4,000,000 being credited in merchandise

Sept. 26, Decree of President Ebert declared passive resistance in the Ruhr ended

Sept. 28, German order of Jan. 12 suspending deliveries in kind to France and Belgium canceled

Oct. 5, Report of Reparation Commission stated that the amount paid by Germany to June 30 was 8,213,-670,000 gold marks of which 3,250,000,000 were in merchandise, 1,900,000,000 in cash, and the remainder in shipping, cables, credits for the mines of the Saar Valley, and ceded territory

Oct. 12, British Note to the United States asked for coöperation in inquiry as to reparations which was accepted

Oct. 24, Note of German Government to the Reparation Commission asked for examination of Germany's capacity to pay and resources

Nov. 23, Industrial leaders in the Ruhr signed the M.I.C.U.M. (Mission Interallie pour le Control des Usines et des Mines) for Allied control of factories and coal mines

Nov. 30, Reparation Commission made decision to appoint 2 committees of experts to inquire into (1) means of balancing the German budget and stabilizing the currency, and (2) to determine Germany's wealth abroad, exported capital and of bringing it back to Germany

Dec. 1, Agreement for working of railways in occupied territory signed by French, Belgians, and Germans

Dec. 20, Montagu Norman, governor of the Bank of England, Sir Josiah Stamp, economist, and Reginald McKenna, former Chancellor of the Exchequer, appointed by Reparation Commission to act as British experts on committees investigating German finances

Dec. 22, Agreement as to resumption of deliveries in kind concluded between French, Belgian, and German Governments

1924

Jan. 10–12, Conference of the Little Entente States at Belgrade

Jan. 14, First meeting of First Committee of Experts to investigate German budget and currency met in Paris, Charles G. Dawes, American, chairman, other members Owen D. Young, American, R. M. Kindersley and J. C. Stamp, English, J. Parmentier and Edgar Allix, French, Alberto Pirelli and Federico Flora, Italian, and E. Francqui and Maurice Houtard, Belgian

Jan. 21, First meeting of Second Committee of Experts on export of German capital met in Paris, Reginald McKenna, English, chairman, other members Henry M. Robinson, American, André Laurent-Atthalin, French, Mario Alberti, Italian, Albert E. Jannssen, Belgian

Feb. 14–25, Conference of Naval experts in Rome held under auspices of the League of Nations to consider limitation of naval armaments and application of the Washington Conference Treaties to non-signatory States

Feb. 16–19, Economic Conference at Warsaw (Finland, Estonia, Latvia, Poland)

March 6, Agreement as to resumption of deliveries in kind between Germany and Yugoslavia signed

April 9, The First Committee of Experts (the Dawes Committee) presented Report to the Reparation Commission, made recommendations as to payment by Germany on basis of sliding scale beginning with 1,000,000,000 for the first year and reaching 2,500,-000,000 gold marks the fifth year (standard year) the increase thereafter to be determined by an "Index of Prosperity" based on comparative statistics of public revenues, exports, imports, population, &c., the charges to be defrayed from taxation, railways, and industrial debentures, a foreign gold loan of 800 million gold marks to be raised to act as gold reserve and to finance the internal payment for the treaty in 1924 and 1925, a bank of issue to be set up to stabilize the currency, and international commission of control, France and Belgium to relinquish economic control of the occupied territory. No total of reparation fixed or period of time for annual payments

April 9, The Second Committee of Experts (the McKenna Committee) presented Report to the Reparation Commission, estimated that 6,750,000,000 gold marks had been exported from Germany to avoid payment of reparations

April 16, The German Government accepted the "Dawes Plan"

April 17, Circular Note of the Reparation Commission to Allied Powers recommended acceptance of Reports

May 19, Economic Conference at Kovno (Estonia, Latvia, Lithuania)

July 3, Publication of "A Practical Plan for Disarmament," the "American Plan" drawn up by committee of private citizens, Dr. J. T. Shotwell, D. H. Miller, and others

July 11–12, Conference of the Little Entente States at Belgrade

July 16–Aug. 16, Conference of Allied Premiers in London on reparations adopted Dawes Plan

Aug. 5, Chancellor Marx of Germany and G. Stresemann joined the Allied Reparation Conference

Aug. 16, Declaration of French and Belgian Governments agreement to evacuate Germany within a year after Dawes Plan went into effect

Aug. 27–29, Conference of the Little Entente States at Ljubljana

Aug. 30, Protocol and 4 Agreements signed by Allied Powers and Germany as to carrying out of Dawes Plan of April 9, Owen D. Young appointed Agent General of Reparation Payments *ad interim*

Sept. 1, Germany made first reparation payment under the Dawes Plan of 20,000,000 gold marks

Sept. 3, Seymour Parker Gilbert, former Assistant Secretary of the Treasury of the United States appointed Agent General for Reparations Payments

Sept. 9, Customs line between occupied and unoccupied Germany removed

Oct. 2, Protocol for the Pacific Settlement of International Disputes adopted by Fifth Assembly of the League of Nations and opened for signature

Oct. 6–7, Wiesbaden Agreement as to deliveries to France by Germany for reconstruction

Oct. 10, Contract for loan to Germany under Dawes Plan of 800,000,000 gold marks signed in London by British, Belgian, and American bankers and German financial delegates

Oct. 27–Dec. 23, Inter-Allied Conference of financial experts in Paris to consider questions relating to German reparation payments

Oct. 28, The M.I.C.U.M. abolished

Oct. 31, S. P. Gilbert assumed duties as Agent General for Reparations Payments

Nov. 3–Feb. 11, First Opium Conference held in Geneva. *See* League of Nations

Nov. 17–Feb. 19, Second Opium Conference held in Geneva. *See* League of Nations

Nov. 22, Protocol signed in Paris amendment to Paragraph 13 of Annex 2 to Part 8 of the Treaty of Versailles (unanimity of Reparation Commission)

Dec. 27, Decision of Conference of Ambassadors in Paris that evacuation of bridgehead at Cologne on Jan. 10 impossible as Germany had not fulfilled the disarmament clauses of the Treaty of Versailles

1925

Jan. 5, Joint Note of Allies notified Germany that the Cologne bridgehead would not be evacuated on

Jan. 10 as provided for in the Treaty of Versailles

Jan. 7, Germany protested against Allied contention that Germany had failed to fulfill terms of disarmament clauses of the Treaty of Versailles

Jan. 7–14, Conference of Allied Finance Ministers in Paris to discuss distribution of annuities to be paid by Germany under Dawes Plan. Attended by representative from the United States

Jan. 14, International Financial Agreement signed in Paris by Belgium, France, Great Britain, Italy, Japan, Greece, Portugal, Rumania, Yugoslavia, Czechoslovakia, Brazil, and the United States determined apportionment of reparation receipts under Dawes Plan

Jan. 16–17, Conference at Helsingfors (Finland, Estonia, Latvia, Poland) reached agreements as to arbitration, communications, passports, &c.

Feb. 9, German Note to Allies proposed Rhineland Mutual Guarantee Pact

Feb. 11 and 19, International Opium Conventions signed. See League of Nations

Feb. 18, Report of Inter-Allied Military Control Commission on German disarmament delivered to Marshal Foch

May 4–June 17, International Conference on the control of traffic in arms at Geneva and Arms Traffic Convention and Protocol prohibiting use of poison gases adopted and opened for signature

May 9–11, Conference of the Little Entente States in Bucharest

June 2, Allied Note to Germany gave 13 instances of failure to fulfill the disarmament requirements of the Treaty of Versailles

June 30–July 15, First session of the Institute of Pacific Relations in Honolulu

Aug. 19, Convention for repression of liquor smuggling signed at Helsingfors by Germany, Denmark, Estonia, Finland, Latvia, Lithuania, Norway, Poland, and Sweden and Russia

Aug. 25, Dusseldorf, Duisburg, and Ruhrort evacuated by Allied troops

Sept. 1, German payments under Dawes Plan (first year) totaled 1,000.5 million gold marks

Sept. 1–4, Committee of Allied and German jurists met in London to consider drafts of Security Pacts and Arbitration Treaties between France and Germany, and Belgium and Germany

Sept. 21, Agreement signed in Paris regulation of amounts to be allocated for armies of occupation costs out of second Dawes annuity

Oct. 5–16, International Security Pact Conference at Locarno, Switzerland, reaching agreement as to " the means for preserving their respective nations from the scourge of war and for the providing for the peaceful settlement of disputes of every nature which might eventually arise between them "

Oct. 8–Nov. 6, Conference at The Hague to revise Industrial Property Convention

Oct. 16, The following Treaties were initialed at Locarno for submission to the respective governments for ratification: Treaty between Germany, Belgium, France, Great Britain, and Italy (The Security Pact), Arbitration Convention between Germany and Belgium, Arbitration Convention between Germany and France, Arbitration Convention between Germany and Poland, and Arbitration Convention between Germany and Czechoslovakia, Collective Note

of Allies to Germany regarding Article 16 of the Covenant, Treaty of Guarantee between France and Czechoslovakia, Treaty of Guarantee between France and Poland, and Final Protocol

Oct. 23, German Note notified Allies that Germany had complied with demands for disarmament made in June

Nov. 14, Decision of Conference of Ambassadors that evacuation of Cologne bridgehead should begin Dec. 1

Dec. 1, Locarno Treaties (see Oct. 16) formally signed in London by which Germany, Belgium, France, Great Britain, and Italy mutually guaranteed peace in Western Europe, and Germany undertook to arbitrate in disputes with France, Belgium, Poland, and Czechoslovakia

1926

Jan. 6, Air Conference begun in Paris (France, Great Britain, Italy, Belgium, Japan, and Germany)

Jan. 16, International Institute for Intellectual Co-operation dedicated in Paris

Jan. 19, The Senate of the United States rejected the Lausanne Treaty of July, 1923

Jan. 31, Inter-Allied Military Control Commission terminated work in Germany, supervision of disarmament provisions of the Treaty of Versailles transferred to League of Nations

March 19, The Labor Ministers of Belgium, France, Germany, Great Britain, and Italy in London signed agreement for 48 hour week

May 22, Convention signed by Allied Powers and Germany, rules regarding German aircraft

June 14, Foreign Ministers of the Little Entente States renewed their defensive alliance for 3 years

Sept. 1, Second annual payment by Germany of reparations under the Dawes Plan announced of 1,060.2 million gold marks

Sept. 14, Locarno Treaties of Oct. 16 and Dec. 1, 1925, came into effect

Sept. 25, Slavery Convention adopted at meeting of Assembly of the League of Nations and signed by representatives of 20 States

Sept. 30, International Steel Agreement signed by Germany, France, Belgium, and Luxembourg created European steel trust to limit production and restrict competition

Oct. 19, Publication of "Tariff Manifesto" signed by representatives of banking and commerce of 15 countries including the United States, an appeal to Europe to level barriers created by tariffs, special licenses, and other prohibitions and restraints of trade

Oct. 23, German Note to Reparation Commission declared inability to make deliveries in kind and asked examination of Germany's capacity to pay

Dec. 11, Foreign Ministers of Great Britain, France, Belgium, Italy, and Japan reached decision that formal control over German armaments should be exercised by the League of Nations after Jan. 31, 1927, when Inter-Allied Commission withdrawn

1927

Jan. 13, Agreement signed by Allied and Associated Powers regulated amounts to be allocated for armies of occupation, Military Commission of Control, and Rhineland High Commission out of Dawes annuities

Jan. 31, Inter-Allied Military Commission of Control withdrawn from Germany

April 6, Briand, Foreign Minister of France, in statement to the press suggested renunciation of war between the United States and France to take the place of the Treaty of Arbitration of 1908, about to expire

May 4–23, International Economic Conference at Geneva under auspices of the League of Nations

May 13–15, Conference of the Foreign Ministers of the Little Entente States at Joachimstahl

May 20–21, Solo airplane flight of Captain Charles A. Lindbergh from New York to Paris in first non-stop flight in the "Spirit of St. Louis." *See also* United States

June 20, Draft and Pact of perpetual friendship between France and the United States, proposal to outlaw war transmitted to the United States by M. Briand, Foreign Minister of France

June 20–Aug. 4, Three Power Naval Conference called by President Coolidge held in Geneva (Great Britain, Japan, and the United States) to discuss limitation by treaty of cruisers, destroyers, and submarines which were not covered by the Washington Treaty of Feb., 1922. Failed to agree on question of cruisers. France and Italy represented by observers

July 15–28, Second meeting of the Institute of Pacific Relations at Honolulu

Sept. 1, Germany paid 1,670.8 million gold marks under Dawes Plan for reparations

Sept. 6, Germany notified that Allied Army of Occupation would be reduced from 70,000 to 60,000

Oct. 17–Nov. 8, Conference at Geneva under auspices of the League of Nations for abolition of import and export restrictions, Convention signed Nov. 8 by representatives of 18 countries

Oct. 20, Note to German Government of Mr. Gilbert, Agent General of Reparations, called attention to large unnecessary expenses of the Government and unsound financial policies

Dec. 28, Note from Secretary of State Kellogg to France suggested a universal Treaty instead of a bilateral Treaty between France and the United States for the renunciation of war

1928

Jan. 5, French Note to Secretary Kellogg limited renunciation of war to wars of aggression. *See also* France

Jan. 11, American reply noted that the original Treaty proposed "provided unequivocally for the renunciation by the high contracting parties of all war as an instrument of national policy"

Jan. 21, French Note called attention to obligations of France under the Covenant under which certain wars were not only legitimate but obligatory, and to Resolution of the Assembly of League of Nations "that the action to be condemned as an international crime is aggressive war"

March 20–July 17, Conference of France, Spain, Great Britain, and Italy agreed on international status of Tangier

April 7, Agreement of France and the United States to submit correspondence as to Treaty for renunciation of war to Great Britain, Germany, Italy, and Japan

April 13, American Note to signatories of the Locarno Treaties enclosed Draft Treaty for universal renunciation of war

April 21, French Draft Treaty for outlawry of war published

May 7–June 2, Conference for the protection of literary and artistic works held in Rome

June 7, Report of Mr. Gilbert, Agent General of Reparations, urged final determination of Germany's reparation liabilities by mutual agreement

June 20–22, Conference of the Little Entente States at Bucharest

June 30, Arrangement signed at Geneva further defining legal status of Russian refugees

July 25, Tangier Statute revision of and modification of Statute proposed by Conference signed by representatives of Great Britain, France, Spain, and Italy

Aug. 27, Treaty for the Renunciation of War (Briand-Kellogg Peace Pact) as an instrument of national policy in their relations with one another, signed at Paris by the United States, France, Great Britain, Germany, Italy, Japan, Irish Free State, Canada, Australia, New Zealand, South Africa, India, Belgium, Czechoslovakia, and Poland

——, The United States sent invitations to other nations to adhere to the Pact

Aug. 29–31, Conference on European Minorities held at Geneva under auspices of the League of Nations

Aug. 31, Under Dawes Plan Germany had paid 7,970,-000,000 gold marks at this date

Sept. 5, Franco-German negotiations as to evacuation of the Rhineland begun at Geneva joined by Great Britain, Italy, Japan, and Belgium during the week

Sept. 16, Agreement as to evacuation of the Rhineland and for a Commission of experts to reconsider the question of German reparations signed by France, Great Britain, Italy, Belgium, and Japan

Sept. 26, General Act for Pacific Settlement of International Disputes adopted by Ninth Assembly of the League of Nations

Oct. 19, Meeting of Mr. Churchill and M. Poincaré with Mr. Gilbert agreed on revision of reparations on basis of Balfour Note of Aug. 1, 1922

Nov. 26–Dec. 14, International Conference on economic statistics held at Geneva under auspices of the League of Nations and Convention and Final Act adopted and signed

Dec. 12–14, International Conference on Civil Aëronautics held in Washington

1929

Jan. 19, Reparation Commission appointed committee of experts to draw up proposals for a complete and final settlement of the reparation problem: Emile Francqui, and Camille Gutt, Belgian, Sir Josiah Stamp and Lord Revelstoke, British, Emile Moreau and Jean Parmentier, French, Dr. Hjalmar Schacht and Dr. A. Voegler, German, Dr. Alberto Pirelli and Fulvio Suvich, Italian, Kengo Mori and Takashi, Japanese, and Owen D. Young and J. P. Morgan, American

Feb. 9, Preliminary meeting of Committee of Experts (Reparations)

——, Litvinov Protocol, Eastern Pact for Renunciation of War, signed at Moscow by Russia, Poland, Rumania, Estonia, Latvia, to come into effect April 2

Feb. 11, First regular meeting of the Committee of Experts (Reparations), in Paris, Owen D. Young, American, elected president

——, Recreation of the Papal State as State of the Vatican City. *See* Italy

March 2, The Paris Peace Pact (Briand-Kellogg) for Renunciation of War came into effect with deposit of ratifications

March 11–14, Conference of Institutions for Scientific Study of International Relations in London

April 12, Committee of Experts (Reparations) reached agreement upon revised amount of payment of reparations which Germany should be asked to pay, 37 annuities rising from £92,500,000 to £122,500,000, 20 further annuities of £85,000,000 and 1 of £45,000,000, capital value of £1,950,000,000 for Inter-Allied debts, service of Dawes Plan, cost of American Army of Occupation, and reparations proper

April 13, Memorandum containing Allied proposals for reparations handed to Dr. Schacht, head of German Delegation in Paris

April 16–May 13, International Conference on Safety of Life at Sea, Convention adopted

April 17, Dr. Schacht submitted counter proposals to Committee of Experts, an annuity of £82,500,000 for 37 years, with present capital value of £1,300,000,000

April 19, Death of Lord Revelstoke in Paris, succeeded on Committee of Experts by the Alternate, Sir Charles Addis

April 22, Speech of Hugh S. Gibson, American Ambassador to Belgium, representing the United States at Preparatory Commission for Disarmament Conference, that the United States would agree to any reduction of naval armaments provided no category of vessels was left unrestricted

May 4, Tentative Agreement reached by Committee of Experts for German reparations for annuities averaging £103,000,000 for 37 years and from the 38th to 58th, the year Germany to be responsible for meeting Inter-Allied debts at rate of £85,000,000 for 20 years and £45,000,000 for 59th year, present capital value £1,800,000,000

May 21, Draft proposals formulated for revision of Spa percentages as to Great Britain

——, The Little Entente Treaties of Alliance renewed after Conference of Foreign Ministers at Belgrade (Czechoslovakia, Yugoslavia, Rumania)

May 29, Agreement of Committee of Experts, German Delegation and Allies, as to reparations to be paid by Germany

June 7, Committee of Experts (Reparations) adjourned after signing Report, a series of recommendations for permanent settlement of reparations to be submitted to Governments for approval; substitution of the Young Plan for the Dawes Plan, Germany to pay 37 annuities of 1,988.8 million reichsmarks beginning Sept. 1, and rising from 1,707.9 in 1930 to 2,428.8 in 1966, followed by annual payments averaging slightly over 1,500,000,000 reichsmarks for 22 years thereafter from 1966 to 1988 beginning at 1,607.7 and ending at 897.8 million reichsmarks, provided for a Bank for International Settlement, to take the place of existing agencies for reparations collection and distribution, deliveries in kind to be continued for a time but reduced, 750 million reichsmarks the first year declining to 300 million the tenth year

July 24, The Paris Peace Pact (Briand-Kellogg) proclaimed ratified by 46 countries in formal ceremony at Washington

Aug. 6–31, Conference of Allied Governments at The Hague to consider the Young Plan of June 7 on German reparations and the evacuation of the Rhineland, reached agreement adopting the Young Plan in principle and revision of distribution of reparations among the creditor nations, share of

Great Britain of the unconditional annuities increased and fixed the date of evacuation of the Rhineland as June 1, 1930, the non-postponeable annuities of Young Plan increased from 660 million reichsmarks to 700 million at insistence of Great Britain to be paid no matter what the state of foreign exchange

Aug. 30, Agreement signed at the Hague Conference on evacuation of the Rhineland

Aug. 31, Final Protocol signed at the Hague Conference recording acceptance of modified Young Plan and 4 Annexes as to finance, deliveries in kind, provisions for transition period before ratification of Young Plan, and costs of Army of Occupation in Rhineland by France, Belgium, Great Britain, Italy, Japan, and Germany

Sept. 5 and 9, Proposals of M. Briand for European Federation before League of Nations

Sept. 16, Three Committees appointed by the Hague Conference to deal with financial liquidation of reparations in kind, ceded property, liberation debts, and Eastern European reparations, began meetings in Paris

Oct. 3, Organization Committee for the Bank for International Settlement met under temporary chairmanship of Dr. Hjalmer Schacht and elected Jackson E. Reynolds, American, chairman

Oct. 28–Nov. 9, Third Conference of the Institute of Pacific Relations at Kyoto

Nov. 13, Statutes, Charter, and Trust Deed for Bank for International Settlement signed by representatives of Great Britain, France, Germany, Italy, Japan, and the United States

Nov. 21–Dec. 20, Saar Conference between France and Germany in Paris did not reach agreement

Dec. 10, Committee of Jurists met at Brussels to draft texts for second Hague Conference

1930

Jan. 3–20, Second Hague Conference at which 14 Agreements approved and signed providing for definite settlement of the reparation payments of the German Government as to amount and period of time, constitution of the Bank for International Settlement, settlement of the reparation liabilities of Austria, Hungary, and Bulgaria and for the consolidation or cancellation of the so-called "liberation" debts of Czechoslovakia, Yugoslavia, Poland, and Rumania

Jan. 20, Final Protocol adopting revised Young Plan for reparations signed at The Hague by representatives of 15 nations and 3 British Dominions including Great Britain, France, Belgium, Italy, and Japan, and Germany, and Agreement with Germany with 12 Annexes, Convention with Switzerland respecting the Bank for International Settlement including Statutes for the Bank, Arrangement relating to the "Concurrent Memorandum" of the Report of June 7, 1929, that Germany shall have benefit of any relief which any of the Powers enumerated receive in respect of its net outward payments on account of War Debts under certain conditions, Exchange of Notes respecting the Agreement between Germany and the United States, Agreement as to the financial mobilization of the German annuities, Exchange of Notes concerning the tariffs of the German Railway Company, Statement of German and Belgian Governments as to satisfactory Agreement of July 13, 1929, settling controversy as to marks, Provision for transition period before ratification of Young Plan, Agreement between the Creditor Powers (of Germany), Reparation Agreements with Austria, Bulgaria, Hungary, and Czechoslovakia and the Creditor Powers, Arrangement between the Creditor Powers as to State properties ceded by Austria, Hungary, and Bulgaria, the Liberation Debts, and the distribution of non-German reparations

Jan. 21–April 22, Conference on limitation of naval armaments in London (Great Britain, France, Italy, Japan, and the United States)

Feb. 5–April 28, Committee on Eastern-European Reparations met in Paris and adopted Agreement April 28

Feb. 17–March 24, Conference for concerted economic action at Geneva. *See* League of Nations

Feb. 19–March 6, London Naval Conference adjourned because France without a Government to act

March 13–April 12, International Conference on Codification of International Law met at The Hague, Nationality Convention adopted

April 10, At London Naval Conference agreement reached by the United States, England, and Japan covering all classes of ships

April 22, First meeting of Board of Directors of the Bank for International Settlement at Basle, Switzerland, Gates W. McGarrah (American) elected chairman, Pierre Quesnay, general manager

——, Treaty for the limitation of naval armaments signed by Great Britain, France, Italy, the United States, and Japan, Part III signed by the United States, Great Britain, and Japan only limited construction of cruisers, destroyers, aircraft carriers, and submarines

May 17, The Reparation Commission formally dissolved as Young Plan came into effect. Under the Dawes Plan Germany had paid aggregate of 7,993,000,000 gold marks (about £400 million)

——, Memorandum of French Government submitted Briand plan for the organization of a system of European Federal Union to 26 Governments of Europe

May 20, 124,000 shares of capital stock of Bank for International Settlement subscribed for in 10 countries, authorized capitalization of about $100,000,000

June 10, Agreements signed (6 documents) by representatives of 9 countries for issuance of first Young Plan Loan to Germany of $300,000,000

June 21–24, Agrarian Conference at Bucharest (Hungary, Czechoslovakia, and Yugoslavia)

June 23, Separate Agreement between Germany and the United States signed as to reparations and costs of American Army of Occupation

June 25–27, Meeting of the Little Entente States at Strbske Pleso, Czechoslovakia

Aug. 9, Agreement signed at Berlin by producers of natural and synthetic nitrates of all countries except the United States dealing mainly with price fixing to be in effect for 1 year

Aug. 28–30, Agrarian Conference at Warsaw (Bulgaria, Czechoslovakia, Estonia, Hungary, Yugoslavia, Latvia, Poland, and Rumania)

Sept. 12, The Council of the League of Nations ordered withdrawal of Allied soldiers from the Saar Basin

Oct. 5–12, First Balkan Conference at Athens (Albania, Bulgaria, Greece, Yugoslavia, Rumania, and Turkey)

Oct. 18–21, Further Agrarian Conference at Bucharest reached decision to appoint a permanent commission

Oct. 27, Ratifications of the London Naval Treaty of April 22 deposited in London

Nov. 6–Dec. 9, Final session of the Preparatory Disarmament Commission. *See* League of Nations

Nov. 7, The German Minister in Washington delivered to Treasury Department of the United States bonds of German Government in final liquidation as to Mixed Claims and costs of Army of Occupation

Nov. 11–12, Further Agrarian Conference at Belgrade

Dec. 4–16, International Sugar Conference met at Brussels and reached agreement as to limitation representing 9 of the chief sugar producing countries

Dec. 18–22, Conference at Oslo (Belgium, Luxembourg, Denmark, Sweden, Norway, Netherlands) adopted and signed Convention and Protocol as to tariff

YUGOSLAVIA

Yugoslavia, kingdom of southern Europe, constituted and proclaimed Dec. 1, 1918, as Kingdom of the Serbs, Croats, and Slovenes, the union with Serbia of Slav, Croat, and Slovene provinces of the former Austria-Hungary, and of Montenegro in March, 1921, including Bosnia and Herzegovina, Dalmatia except Zara, Croatia-Slavonia without Fiume, and the Voyvodina or Duchy, comprising the north-east part of the Kingdom north of the Danube and Drave rivers including the territories of the Banat, Baranya, Batchka, and Srem. The coast line on the Adriatic extends from the Fiumara River to the Bojana River which forms the boundary with Albania, and on the land side Yugoslavia has frontiers with Italy, Austria, Hungary, Rumania, Bulgaria, and Greece. The name of the State was changed Oct. 3, 1929, to Kingdom of Yugoslavia. The estimated population on Jan. 1, 1929, was 13,290,000. Belgrade is the capital.

According to the census taken January 31, 1921, the area and population of Yugoslavia are shown as follows:—

	AREA IN SQ. MILES	MALES	FEMALES	TOTAL	PER SQ. MILE
North Serbia	19,286	1,273,167	1,381,911	2,655,078	137.6
South Serbia	17,651	734,164	740,396	1,474,560	83.5
Montenegro	3,733	99,622	100,235	199,857	53.5
Bosnia and the Herzegovina	19,768	965,894	924,035	1,889,929	95.5
Dalmatia	4,916	309,012	312,417	621,429	126.4
Croatia and Slavonia, Medyumurye, and the island of Krk (Veglia) and the community of Kastav	16,920	1,334,543	1,405,050	2,739,593	161.9
Slovenia	6,253	503,645	552,819	1,056,464	168.9
The Voyvodina	7,607	673,500	706,913	1,380,413	181.4
Total	96,134	5,893,547	6,123,776	12,017,323	125.0

Alexander I, reigning King, born December 17, 1888, son of King Peter I of Serbia and Princess Zorka, daughter of the late Nicholas I, King of Montenegro; married on June 8, 1922, to Princess Marie, born January 9, 1899, daughter of King Ferdinand I of Rumania; Prince Regent from June 24, 1914 to August 16, 1921, when his father died.

Sons of the King.—Prince Peter, born September 6, 1923; Prince Tomislav, born January 19, 1928; Prince Andrey, born June 28, 1929.

For history of the dynasty, *see* Serbia.

April 30, A Yugoslav Committee formed in Paris by leaders who had reached foreign soil before the outbreak of the War including Dr. Trumbic, Mr. Supilo, Dr. Hinkovic, Ivan Mestrovic, the Slovene deputies Gregorin and Trinajstic, Vasiljevic, Stojanovic and Srskic; the Bosnian-Serb deputies, Marjanovic, and Banjanin, and prominent leaders in the United States and South America as the scientist, Pupin, and the shipping magnate Baburica

Aug. 30, Conditional guarantee of self-determination to certain provinces. *See* World War

1917

Jan. 10, Entente Note to President Wilson stated liberation of Slavs from foreign dominion a war aim

May 30, A "Yugoslav Parliamentary Club" formed by Serb, Croat and Slovene deputies in Austria which demanded "the union of all the Yugoslav territories of the monarchy in an independent state organism . . . under the sceptre of the Habsburg-Lorraine dynasty"

July 20, The "Pact of Corfu" signed by Pasic, Prime Minister of Serbia representing the Serbs, and Dr. Trumbic, president of the Yugoslav Committee, affirming the Serbs, Croats and Slovenes a single nation with right of self-determination

1918

Jan. 31, Memorandum of Yugoslav Club to Brest-Litovsk Conference demanding self-determination for nationalities

March 7, Agreement signed in London between representatives of the Yugoslav Committee and Committee of Italian deputies and senators as basis of cooperation published as "Pact of Rome" at Congress of subject "oppressed" nationalities in Rome, April 10

April 8–10, Congress of Nationalities at Rome, subject nationalities of the Austro-Hungarian Empire. Pact of Rome adopted April 10 by which Italy recognized "unity and independence of the Yugoslav nation" as of vital interest to Italy

May 16, Congress of subject nationalities held at Prague

May 29, Statement of Secretary of State Lansing that the national aspirations of the Czechs and Yugoslavs had sympathy of the United States

June 3, Declaration of Prime Ministers of Great Britain, France and Italy declared support of the national aspirations of the Czechoslovaks and Yugoslavs

June 28, Statement of the President of the United

States that "all branches of the Slav race should be completely freed from German and Austrian rule"

Aug. 17, Slovenes formed a National Council at Laibach (Ljubljana) the seat of which was later transferred to Zagreb (Agram)

Sept. 24, Charter signed at Agram

Sept. 25, Italy recognized independence of the Yugoslavs

Oct. 5, National Council at Laibach extended to include representatives of all parties of Yugoslavs as a "United" National Council

Oct. 10, National Council moved from Laibach to Zagreb (Agram)

Oct. 11, Manifesto of the Emperor of Austria of union of Croatia, Slavonia, Bosnia and Herzegovina in one State

Oct. 16, Manifesto of the Emperor of Federal State of Austria. *See* Austria

Oct. 18, Note of President Wilson to Austria recognized national aspirations of Yugoslavs and Czechoslavs

Oct. 19, National Council at Zagreb named itself as the highest political authority of Serbs, Croats and Slovenes united in single State

Oct. 21, National Council at Zagreb adopted a Constitution

Oct. 23, Croat troops occupied Fiume

Oct. 28, Military command at Zagreb surrendered to the National Council

Oct. 29, Croatians declared Dalmatia, Croatia and Slavonia with Fiume a single State independent of Austria-Hungary

Oct. 31, The Emperor of Austria surrendered fleet to the Yugoslav National Council recognizing the new Serb-Croat-Slovene State

Nov. 3, Yugoslav Republic proclaimed at Zagreb, Joseph Pogaonik, first President

Nov. 7, Congress of Yugoslavs at Geneva, Switzerland signed the Declaration of Geneva of the new State

Nov. 12, Armistice allowed Serbs to occupy Temesvar and most of the Banat

Nov. 16–19, Congress at Laibach (Ljubljana) formed Slovene National Council headed by Father Korosec

Nov. 17, The National Council protested against the occupation of Fiume on Nov. 5 by Italians

Nov. 23, Act of Union with Serbia and Montenegro proclaimed by the National Council at Zagreb and Prince Alexander of Serbia invited to assume the regency of the new State

Nov. 24, The united Serb-Croat-Slovene State proclaimed

Nov. 26, National Assembly of Montenegro proclaimed deposition of King Nicholas and his dynasty and union with the Serb-Croat-Slovene State

Dec. 1, Alexander accepted the Regency over the new State of the Yugoslavs

Dec. 4, The National Council proclaimed the Kingdom of the Serbs, Croats and Slovenes

Dec. 16, The National Council and the Skupshtina in joint session as an Assembly passed an Act ratifying Proclamation of Dec. 4

Dec. 29, First Cabinet formed, Stoyan Protic, Prime Minister and Father Korosec, Vice-Prime Minister, Trumbic, Minister of Foreign Affairs. Pasic appointed chief delegate to the Peace Conference at Paris, with Trumbic, Vesnic, and Zolger, members of Delegation

1919

Feb. 1, Agrarian law passed

Feb. 7, The Serb-Croat-Slovene State formally recognized by the United States

Feb. 11, Yugoslav Delegation at Peace Conference proposed submission of the Adriatic dispute with Italy to the arbitration of President Wilson. Declined by Italy March 3

April 16, Yugoslav Delegation proposed settlement of frontiers with Italy to a plebiscite

April 18, Treaty of amity and friendship with Greece concluded

April 23, Manifesto of President Wilson addressed to the Italian nation repudiating Treaty of London, and appealing as to Fiume

May 1, Serb-Croat-Slovene State officially recognized by the Peace Conference

May 28, Yugoslavs began hostilities against the Austrians in Carinthia

June 2, Serb-Croat-Slovene State formally recognized by Great Britain

June 6, Serb-Croat-Slovene State recognized by France

——, Armistice with Austria became effective

June 13, Decision of Peace Conference divided Banat between Yugoslavia and Rumania

June 28, Peace Treaty with Germany gave full recognition to Serb-Croat-Slovene State

Aug. 2, Resignation of Prime Minister Protic (Protitch) leader of Radicals. Succeeded by Davidovic, Democrat

Aug. 13, Yugoslavs occupied Austrian territory east of the Mur River allotted to them by Peace Conference

Sept. 10, Peace Treaty with Austria signed at St. Germain recognized independence of Yugoslavia. Yugoslavs refused to sign Treaty and Minorities Treaty

Sept. 12, Seizure of Fiume by D'Annunzio. *See* Italy

Sept. 23, Trau, Dalmatia occupied by Italians but recovered by American naval force and restored to Yugoslavia

Nov. 27, By the Peace Treaty with Bulgaria signed at Neuilly Bulgaria surrendered to Yugoslavia the Strumnica salient, the district of Kocana and the Bregalnica and the town and district of Tsaribrod. Provision made for delivery of 50,000 tons of coal for 5 years

Dec. 5, Yugoslavia signed Treaties of Peace with Austria and Bulgaria

1920

Feb. 6, Commercial Convention with Austria signed

April 1, Diplomatic relations with Germany resumed

April 20, Act of union with Montenegro

May 1, The Prince Regent ratified the German, Austrian, Bulgarian and Minorities treaties

May, Cabinet reconstructed under Vesnic

May 11, Negotiations of Trumbic with Nitti (Italy) on Adriatic question a failure

June 4, Peace Treaty with Hungary gave Croatia to Yugoslavia and part of the Banat

June 27, Provisional Commercial Agreement with Austria signed

July 20, Vesnic Ministry resigned and Vesnic reconstituted Cabinet

Aug. 10, Treaty of frontiers signed with Great Britain, France, Italy and Japan

Aug. 14, Alliance of Aug. 1922 with Czechoslovakia renewed

Oct. 10, Plebiscite in Klagenfurt region (Carinthia) gave decision by vote of 221,852 as against 15,096 for remaining under sovereignty of Austria

Oct. 14, Yugoslav troops occupied part of Klagenfurt district but withdrawn after ultimatum of Conference of Ambassadors

Oct. 18, Commercial Agreement with Czechoslovakia

Nov. 12, Treaty of Rapallo signed with Italy fixed Yugoslav-Italian boundary in the Adriatic, Italy renouncing claim to Dalmatia except Zara, and the Adriatic Islands except Cherso, Lussin, Lagosta, Cazza, Pelagosa, &c., Fiume to be a Free State

Nov. 28, Election held for Constituent Assembly to draft Constitution. No party secured a majority, the Radicals and Democrats being almost exactly balanced

——, Elections held in Croatia a victory for Stephen Radic, peasant leader and leader of Opposition in Yugoslav Parliament

Nov. 29, Minorities Treaty of Sept. 10, 1919 placed under guarantee of the League of Nations

1921

Jan. 1, Constitution adopted by Assembly

Jan. 2, Coalition Cabinet of Radicals and Democrats with Nikola Pasic as Premier assumed office

March 1, Death of ex-King Nicholas of Montenegro

May 28, Death of Dr. Vesnic, former Premier

June 7, Defensive alliance with Rumania signed (Little Entente Treaty)

June 8, Agreement with Rumania signed for delimitation by Mixed Commission of frontier in Banat of Temesvar

June 28, Alexander, Prince Regent, on Kosovo Day took oath to the new Constitution. An attack on his life made at instigation of Communists, bomb thrown at carriage

——, The official name adopted for the State, the Kingdom of the Serbs, Croats and Slovenes "abbreviated S.H.S. the popular name 'Yugoslavia' adopted by Permanent Committee on Geographical Names for British Official Use" and for unofficial use by the United States Geographic Board

July 2, Defensive alliance with Rumania against Hungary and Bulgaria

July 12, Treaty of commerce and navigation with Estonia

July 21, Draskovic, Minister of the Interior, assassinated by Bosnian Communist

July 31, Laws for "the Defence of the State" passed

Aug. 14, Baranya proclaimed a Serb-Magyar Republic. Decision of Conference of Ambassadors of Aug. 17 against this arrangement

——, Defensive alliance and Military Convention with Czechoslovakia signed

Aug. 16, Death of King Peter. Succeeded by his son Prince Regent Alexander as Alexander I

Aug. 20, Province of Baranya evacuated by Yugoslavs and taken over by Hungarians as provided for in the Treaty of Trianon

Nov. 6, King Alexander I swore to the Constitution and received full royal rights

Nov. 8, Death of Pavol Orszagh, Slovak poet

Nov. 14, Acceptance of frontiers of Albania and agreement to withdraw troops

Dec. 5, Commercial Treaty with Germany signed

1922

Feb. 28, Workers Protection Act promulgated

May 14, Workers Insurance Act promulgated

June 8, Marriage of King Alexander to Princess Marie, second daughter of the King of Rumania

June 21, New electoral law passed

June 22, Exchange of Notes established commercial relations with the United States

July 12, Commercial Treaty of June 1920 with Austria extended indefinitely

Aug. 31, Alliance with Czechoslovakia renewed and extended for 5 years

Sept. 15, Commercial Agreement with Czechoslovakia signed

Oct. 23, Commercial Agreement with Poland signed

——, Santa Margherita Agreement with Italy and 3 technical Conventions to provide for execution of the stipulations of the Treaty of Rapallo ended dispute on Dalmatian questions

Dec. 4, Fall of Pasic Ministry

Dec. 6, Final Boundary Protocol signed with Bulgaria

Dec. 16, Pasic reconstituted Cabinet

1923

Feb. 24, Protocol with Austria signed regarding abolition of sequestration property of Austrian subjects in Yugoslavia and of Yugoslav subjects in Austria

March 1–23, Serbo-Bulgarian Commission met and settled frontier disputes

March 7, Judicial Convention with Czechoslovakia signed

March 18, Election for first Parliament gave the Radicals (Government) 128 seats, the Democrats 54, Slovenian Catholics 24, Bosnian Moslems 18, Serbian Agrarians 11, Pan-Germans 9, Croatian Party 68

April 5, Further Commercial Agreement with Yugoslavia

April 6, Government asked Conference of Ambassadors to revise decision assigning Monastery of St. Naun to Albania

May 10, Agreement with Greece signed created Yugoslav free zone at Salonika for 50 years

July 7, Defensive alliance with Rumania to prevent Hungarian or Bulgarian attempts against the Treaties extended for 3 years

July 19, Military law passed established 18 months as period of service

July 23, Diplomatic and consular Convention with Poland signed

Aug. 24, Death of Milan Ogrizovic, Croat poet

Sept. 6, Birth of Prince Peter

Sept. 7, Commercial Treaty of March 9, 1909 with Norway renewed

Nov. 16, Treaty of commerce and navigation with Japan signed

Nov. 22, Six Conventions regarding frontiers signed with Austria

Nov. 24, Protocol with Rumania signed as to regulations at frontier in the Banat of Temesvar

Dec. 2, Free zone at Salonica obtained

1924

Jan. 27, Treaty of friendship with Italy signed, the "Pact of Rome" and Agreement by which Fiume to be annexed to Italy, and Porto Barros to Yugoslavia

Feb. 3, Reparation Agreement with Hungary provided for delivery by Hungary of coal and rolling stock

March 6, Agreement with Germany signed as to resumption of deliveries in kind

March 22, Commercial Agreement with Hungary signed

March 24, Pasic Ministry reorganized

April 12, Pasic Coalition Cabinet resigned

May 21, Coalition Cabinet reinstated

July 14, Treaty of commerce and navigation and Railroad Agreements with Italy signed

July 18, Resignation of Pasic Ministry who lost majority when deputies of Radic instructed to abandon abstention entered Parliament

July 24, Liouba Davidovic assumed office as Premier

Oct. 15, Davidovic Ministry resigned

Nov. 5, Pasic formed Cabinet, the "Pasic-Pribicevic" Ministry

Nov. 15, Serbo-Greek Treaty of alliance of 1913 denounced

Dec. 24, Executive Act outlawed the Croatian Peasant Party as Bolshevist and imprisoned Stefan Radic and 5 other leaders

1925

Jan. 21, Preliminary trial of Radic and 5 other Croat Republicans

Feb. 8, Elections held for Parliament gave Radicals (Government) 140 seats; Independent Democrats, 22; Democrats, 37; Croatian Agrarians (Radic Party), 67; Serb Agrarians, 5; Mahomedans, 15; Catholic People's Party, 20; and 4 members of other parties

March 6, Yugoslav zone at Salonika formally turned over by Greece

March 7, Parliament met

April 30, Resignation of Pasic-Pribicevic Cabinet but immediately reappointed

June 3, Transit Convention with Rumania signed

July 16, Cabinet resigned

July 18, Radic freed from prison after recognition of the Constitution, dynasty and army, and the other 5 Croats

July 19, Pasic-Radic Cabinet sworn in

July 20, Nettuno Agreements with Italy signed as to Fiume, Zara, Dalmatia, economic concessions to Italy

Aug. 1, Agreement with Italy signed ceded dock areas in dispute in Fiume to Yugoslavia

Aug. 6, Decision of Conference of Ambassadors reversed decision of Dec. 6, 1922 and assigned Monastery of Sveti Naun to Yugoslavia

Sept. 3, Commercial Agreement with Austria signed

Oct. 28, Treaty of peace and friendship with Turkey signed

Nov. 8, Italian Government offered apology for Italian attack on Yugoslav consulate at Trieste

Nov. 18, Stefan Radic became Minister of Public Instruction

1926

Jan. 21, Arrest of 200 Communists charged with plot to overthrow the Government

April 1, Resignation of Stefan Radic from the Cabinet with 4 other Croatians

April 4, Pasic Cabinet losing support of Radic forced to resign

April 8, Nikola Uzunovic (Ouzenovic), Radical, formed Cabinet

May 3, Debt funding Agreement with the United States signed

May 15, Cabinet resigned in debate on corruption but reorganized
June 13, Little Entente Treaties of alliance renewed for 3 years
June 18, Provisional Commercial Agreement with Great Britain signed
June 22, Treaty of commerce and navigation with Albania
July 28, Commercial Agreement with Hungary signed
Aug. 17, Treaty of alliance with Greece signed and settlement of Salonika and other matters in dispute
Sept. 15, Treaty of friendship and arbitration with Poland signed
Sept. 17 and Dec. 16, Provisional Commercial Agreements with Belgium signed
Oct. 27, Murder of General Kovachevic by Bulgarian band. Frontier with Bulgaria closed
Dec. 6, Resignation of Dr. Nincic, Minister of Foreign Affairs, on publication of the Italo-Albanian Treaty
Dec. 7, Cabinet resigned
Dec. 10, Death of Nicola P. Pasic, Premier. Ouzounovic succeeded him as Prime Minister

1927

Jan. 28, Ouzounovic Cabinet forced to resign
Feb. 1, Ouzounovic formed new Cabinet; Prime Minister, M. Ouzounovic; Minister of Finance, M. Bogdan Markovic; Foreign Affairs, M. Ninko Peric; Interior, M. Boja Maximovic; Justice, M. Srchkitch; Public Worship, M. Trifounovic; Posts and Telegraphs, M. Vuitchic; Education, M. Vukitchevic; Public Health, M. Slavko Miletic; Forests and Mines, M. Krsta Miletic; Agrarian Reform and Commerce (ad interim), M. Simonovic; Unification of Laws, M. Vassa Yovanovic; Agriculture, M. Coulovets; Public Works, M. Cernets; Social Affairs, M. Hodjar; War, General Hadjic; Communications, General Milosavlievic
Feb. 7, Bulgarian frontier opened to traffic
April 10, Cabinet of Velya Vukitchevic (Radical) took office
May 12, Treaty of commerce and navigation with Great Britain signed
June 5, Diplomatic relations with Albania severed following arrest of official of the Yugoslav Legation in Tirana on charge of espionage
June 8, Customs Agreement with Austria signed
July 3, Settlement of break with Albania proposed by League of Nations accepted
Aug. 8, Agreement with Great Britain signed for funding and payment of Yugoslav relief debt to Great Britain, Australia and certain States of Europe
Aug. 9, Agreement with Great Britain settled War debt funded at £32,800,000
Sept. 11, Elections held for National Assembly gave Government a majority
Oct. 6, Commercial Treaty with Germany signed
Nov. 11, Treaty of friendship and arbitration with France signed

1928

Feb. 1, Treaty of commerce with Estonia signed
Feb. 8, Cabinet resigned
Feb. 22, Four economic and financial Conventions with Hungary signed
Feb. 23, Vukitchevic formed third Cabinet: Prime Minister, M. Velja Vukitchevic; Minister of Finance, M. Bogdan Markovic; Foreign Affairs, M. Vojislav

Marinkovic; The Interior, Father Anton Korosec; Justice, Milorai Vuitchic; Public Worship, Milan Simonovic; Posts and Telegraphs, M. Vlajko Kotic; Public Health, Velimir Popovic; Forests and Mines, M. Aleksanolar Mijovic; Agrarian Reform, Vladimir Andvic; the Unification of Laws, Ilia Shumenkovic; Agriculture, M. Svetszar Stankovic; Public Works, Petar Markovic; Social Affairs, Chedo Radovic; War, General Stevan Hadjic; Communications, General Svetislav Milosaoljevic; Commerce and Industry, Mehmed Spaho; Education, Dr. Milan Groll
May 27–30, Anti-Italian riots at Belgrade, Sebenico and Spalato demonstration ratification of Nettuno Conventions
June 16–17, Anti-Italian riots at Sebenico and Spalato
June 20, Stefan Radic mortally wounded, Pavle Radic and another Croat deputy, George Basaric, killed by shots of a Montenegrin Radical deputy on floor of Parliament in fight over the Nettuno Agreement with Italy opposed by Radic. Croat deputies withdrew from Parliament
July 4, Vukitchevic Ministry resigned. Cabinet reconstructed under Father Korosec, Slovene Clerical leader
July 9, Supplementary Commercial Agreement with Austria signed
July 27, Cabinet of Father Korosec formally approved by the King
Aug. 1, Croats in Zagreb demanded a reorganization of the Government on a Federal basis setting up a Parliament of their own
Aug. 8, Death of Stefan Radic, Leader of Croat Peasant Party
Aug. 13, Nettuno Agreements with Italy ratified of July 1925 and Belgrade Conventions of July 1924
Aug. 15, Demonstration at Spalato against ratification of the Nettuno Conventions, houses of Italian consuls attacked and consulates
Aug. 22, The Government promised indemnity and punishment in answer to Italian protests of raids
Sept. 19, Protocol signed with Czechoslovakia prolonging the Treaty alliance
Sept. 21, Law of nationality signed, promulgated Nov. 1
Oct. 18, Treaty of commerce and navigation with Latvia signed
Nov. 1, Treaty with Greece signed giving Yugoslavia commercial facilities in Salonika
Dec. 30, Korosec Ministry resigned forced out because of its "mailed fist" policies in Croatia

1929

Jan. 4, Macek and Pribicevic, Croat leaders, received by the King, presented claims for full autonomy for the Croats
Jan. 6, Manifesto of the King established a dictatorship and appointed General Pera Zivkovic Prime Minister with a Cabinet formed of representatives from all the different provinces. Proclamation announced the dissolution of Parliament and suspension of the Constitution. Special edition of the Official Gazette published 4 new laws as to the dictatorship establishing the King as sole source of power
Jan. 7, Cabinet appointed: Prime Minister and Minister of the Interior, General Petar Zivkovic; Deputy Prime Minister, N. Ouzounovic; Minister of the Presidency of the Council, Dr. Milan Srchkitch; For-

eign Affairs, Dr. Vojislav Marinkovic; Transport and Communications, Lazar Radivoyevic; Defense, General Dragomir Stoyanovic (April 6, 1931); Finance, Stanko Shverlyuga; Commerce and Industry, Zhuray Demetrovic; Education, Boha Maximovic; Justice and Public Worship, Mita Lyotic; Social Affairs and Health, Dr. N. Preka; Mines and Forests, Dr. D. Sernetch; Posts and Telegraphs, Dr. K. Kumanudi; Agriculture and Agrarian Reform, Dr. S. Shibenik; without Portfolio, Dr M. Drinkovic and Dr. M. Neudorfer

Jan. 9, All public assemblies prohibited

Jan. 13, Four newspapers suppressed, the *Budapest Peter Lloyd*, the *Berliner Tageblatt*, and 2 Turkish papers

Jan. 19, Decree of the King reorganized and unified the judicial system

Jan. 21, Croat Peasant Party officially dissolved, headquarters closed by the police and records confiscated

Jan. 24, The Radical, Independent Democrat, Serbian Peasant, and Socialist Parties officially dissolved

Jan. 27, Two decrees promulgated, one established new Penal Code, the other greatly increased the powers of the Prime Minister

——, Five year Treaty of friendship with Italy expired

Feb. 14, Elective municipal boards abolished and mayors and municipal parish counselors appointed by the King

Feb. 16, Penal Procedure Code promulgated

Feb. 17, Decree of the King constituted a Supreme Legislative Council of 17 nominated members (11 Serbs, 4 Croats, 2 Slovenes)

March 1, Decree imposed new and heavy penalties for offenders against laws of Jan. 6 for protection of the State

March 17, Six Conventions signed with Greece as to Salonika free zone

March 22, Decree of the King ordered use of Latin alphabet to replace the Cyrillic characters

——, Assassination of Toni Schlegel, Croat leader, supporter of the dictatorship

March 27, Pact of friendship, conciliation, and judicial settlement with Greece signed

April 1, The number of members of the Cabinet reduced from 17 to 12

April 12, General Pesic retired as Chief of General Staff and General Milovanovic appointed

——, Thirty-seven generals placed on half pay

April 24, Dr. Ante Pavelic charged with high treason condemned to death

May 20, Internment of Svetozar Pribitcevic, Croat leader

May 22, Arrest of Croat leader Dr. Vladka Machek

May 27–June 7, Trial of Punica Racic for murder of Stefan Radic and other deputies. Sentenced to 60 years imprisonment

June 12, Commercial Treaty with Greece signed

June 27, Dr. Milovan Zanic, Croat ex-deputy, sentenced to 6 months in prison for propaganda against the dictatorship

Aug. 25, Koshutic former Cabinet Minister and Secretary of the Croat Party escaped to Italy disguised as a seaman, and 3 days later Dr. Anton Trumbic Croat leader, reached Vienna

Sept 27, Commercial Treaty with Spain signed

Oct. 2, Agreement as to frontier traffic signed with Hungary

Oct. 3, King Alexander announced change of name of the State from the Kingdom of the Serbs, Croats, and Slovenes to Kingdom of Yugoslavia, and division of the country into 9 banats (counties)

Oct. 16 and 18, Anti-Italian demonstrations at Belgrade and other cities because of execution of Slav student at Pola. *See* Italy

Nov. 11, The bans or governors of banats appointed by the King assumed duties

Dec. 4, National sokols societies for gymnastic training abolished

Dec. 27, Arrest of Dr. Vladko Matcek, Croat leader

Dec. 31, Professor Jacob Jelatic and Colonel W. Begiric and 8 other Croats arrested charged with outrages and bomb plots

1930

Jan. 20, Debt funding Agreement with France signed

Feb. 2, A tablet unveiled to Princip the assassin of the Austrian Archduke Ferdinand in 1914

Feb. 14, Agreement with Bulgaria signed as to maintenance of order on frontier

Feb. 17, Convention with Bulgaria signed to regulate administration of border populations

March 15 and 20, Protest to Bulgarian Government regarding border raids

March 25, Arbitration, conciliation, and judicial settlement Conventions with Belgium

March 30, Arbitration, conciliation, and judicial settlement Treaty with Spain signed

April 6, Death of Patriarch Dimitrije

April 12, Varnava (Barnabas) elected Patriarch

April 24–June 14, Trial of Dr. Macek, Croat leader, and 23 other Croats, charged with sedition and terrorist activities. Acquitted with 8 others

May 9, Zivkovic Cabinet reconstituted, 2 Croats added, Dr. Stanko Schipenik, Minister of Agriculture, and Nikola Preka, Minister of Social Welfare

May 15, Statement of Minister of Foreign Affairs to press at Geneva regarding aggression of Bulgarian Macedonian bandits against Yugoslavia amounting practically to war

May 27, Death of Morco Trifkovic

June 14, Nine Croats on trial for treason found guilty, Dr. Matchek acquitted

July 18, National Defense law promulgated

Dec. 16, Decree imposed graduated tax based on income tax on bachelors ranging from 50% of income tax for those between 30 and 35 to 10% for those between 50 and 60; certain classes exempted

AFRICA

Africa is one of the five continents second only to Asia in size (area about 11,500,-000 square miles) separated from Europe by the Mediterranean Sea and from Asia by the Red Sea and Gulf of Aden, and connected with Asia by the Isthmus of Suez making it a peninsula bounded on the north by the Mediterranean Sea, on the west by the Atlantic Ocean, on the south by the Indian Ocean and the east by the Indian Ocean and the Red Sea. The greater part of Africa lies within the tropics and includes the great desert of Sahara (area 3,500,000 square miles).

Its greatest length from north to south is 5,000 miles, and its breadth from Cape Verde to Ras Hafoon is 4,650 miles. The name Africa was given by the Romans to their Carthage colonies but both Greek and Roman writers refer to the continent as Libya.

POLITICAL DIVISIONS

Independent countries. *See* Abyssinia, Egypt, Liberia, Union of South Africa, and Morocco, a large part of which is under France as a Protectorate.

Mandated territories. Former German colonies ceded under the Treaty of Versailles June 28, 1919, assigned as mandates by Allied Supreme Council May 7, 1919, confirmed by the Council of the League of Nations Dec. 17, 1920.

British: Tanganyika Territory (former German East Africa), South West Africa under Union of South Africa, British Cameroon, and British Togoland.

French: French Cameroon and French Togoland.

Belgian: Ruanda and Urundi (formerly in German East Africa).

Colonies and Protectorates. *British:* Anglo-Egyptian Sudan, Ascension Island, Ashanti, Basutoland, Bechuanaland, Gambia, Gold Coast, Kenya Colony and Protectorate, Mauritius and Dependencies, Nigeria, Northern Rhodesia, Northern Territories (Gold Coast), Nyasaland, Saint Helena, Seychelles, Sierra Leone, Somaliland, Southern Rhodesia, Swaziland, Uganda, Zanzibar, and Pemba.

French: Algeria, Circle of Dakar and Dependencies, Dahomey, Equatorial Africa (French Congo), French Guinea, French Morocco, French Somaliland, French Sudan, French West Africa and the Sahara Desert, Ivory Coast, Madagascar, Mauritania, Mayotte and the Comoro Islands, Niger, Reunion, Senegal, Tunis, and Upper Volta.

Belgian: Belgian Congo (formerly Congo Free State).

Italian: Eritrea, Italian Libya (Tripolitania and Cyrenaica), and Italian Somaliland.

Portuguese: Cape Verde Islands, Angola, Mozambique, Portuguese Guinea, S. Tomè and Principe (Saint Thomas and Prince's) Islands, the Azores and Madeira Islands considered for administrative purposes part of Portugal.

Spanish: Spanish Morocco and Ifni (in Morocco), Spanish Guinea, Rio de Oro and Adrar, and Islands of Fernando Po, Annobon, Little Elobey, Great Elobey and Corisco, the Canary Islands considered for administrative purposes part of Spain.

146 B.C. to 709

146 B.C., Carthage subdued by the Romans; other provinces gained by Pompey, 82

A.D. 296, Revolts subdued by Diocletian; by Theodosius, 373

429–35, North Africa conquered by the Vandals under Genseric; reconquered by Belisarius, 533–55

637–709, The Saracens subdue the north of Africa

1415

July 25, Expedition of Prince Henry of Portugal sailed for Morocco and took Ceuta after battle, the first of a series of conquests and voyages of exploration in Africa

1434

Gil Eannes, Portuguese, rounded Cape Bojador

1442

The first African slaves brought to Europe by the Portuguese

1443

Cape Blanco doubled and Rio de Oro reached by Antonio Gonsalvez (Gonçalves)

1445

The mouth of the Senegal River entered by Dinis Diaz

1446

Sierra Leone discovered by Alvaro Fernandes
Bolama Island (Bulama) discovered by Dinis Diaz

1448

Prince Henry began fort on Arguin Bay, south of Cape Blanco

1455

Cadamosto ascended the Senegal River and the Gambia

1462

Pedro da Cintra discovered the coast of Sierra Leone

1482

Jan., Fort established by Portuguese on Guinea Coast, Sao Jorge da Mina (Elmina)
Diogo Cão erected pillar at Cape Cross, South West Africa

1485

Diogo Cão or Cam discovered the mouth of the Congo River and erected a pillar on what is now Sharks Point to take possession of the territory for Portugal

1494

June 7, Treaty of Tordesillas, demarcation of lands of Portugal and Spain, excluded Spain from Africa

1497

Nov. 19, Vasco da Gama doubled Cape of Good Hope discovering the passage to India

1500

Pedro Alvares Cabral, Portuguese, the first European to visit East Africa (Kilwa)

1505

Fort established at Kilwa, East Africa, by Portuguese and conquest of Zanzibar and the coast from the Arabs begun

1562

April 6, Expedition of Jan van Riebeek for the Dutch East India Company reached Table Bay and made first permanent settlement in South Africa
Voyage of Sir John Hawkins to Guinea for slaves which he sold in Hispaniola

1578

Portuguese colony founded on west coast, St. Paul de Loanda, capital

1595

First trading on the west coast by the Dutch

1626

First French settlement at St. Louis. *See* Senegal

1638

The Dutch established a post on Arguin Island

1680

German expedition to Togoland. *See* Togoland

1698

The Portuguese expelled from Zanzibar and the east coast by Arabs

1699

Missionary party accompanied by Dr. C. Poncet made journey from Cairo through Dongola and Sennar across the Blue Nile to Gondar, Abyssinia

1723

Captain Stubbs sailed up the Gambia for the English Royal African Company

1736

Moravian mission established on the Gold Coast

1768

June, James Bruce, the "Abyssinian traveller," set out in June, 1768, to discover the source of the Nile. Proceeding first to Cairo, he navigated the Nile to Syene, thence crossed the desert to the Red Sea, and, arriving at Jedda, passed some months in Arabia Felix, and after various detentions reached Gondar, the capital of Abyssinia, in Feb., 1770. On Nov. 14, 1770, he obtained a sight of the sources of the Blue Nile. He returned to England in 1773, and died April 27, 1794

1787

May, Establishment of colony at Sierra Leone. *See* Sierra Leone

1788

June, African Association, for promoting the exploration of central Africa, was formed in June, 1788, principally by Sir Joseph Banks; and under its auspices many additions were made to African geography by Ledyard, Park, Burckhardt, Hornemann, &c. It merged into the Royal Geographical Society, July, 1831

1794

Feb. 4 and April 11, French Decrees suppressed slavery in French territories

1795

May 22, Mungo Park sailed under patronage of English African Society to trace the source of the Niger River and returned, Dec. 22, 1797. He reached the Gambia, June 21, 1795 and ascended the river for 200 miles to British trading station of Pisania. On Dec. 2 he started to explore the unknown interior, proceeding across the upper Senegal basin into region of Kaarta, and July 21, 1796, reached the Niger at Segu and followed the river down stream 80 miles to Silla. On return journey he traveled along the Niger to Bamako tracing the course of the river. Reached Pisania, June 10, 1797

1797

John Browne, the first European to reach the Oasis of Siwa on southern edge of Cyrenaica

1798

July 2, Napoleon Bonaparte landed 40,000 troops at Alexandria, Egypt
July 3, Journey of the Portuguese, Dr. Francisco de Lacerda, from the lower Zambesi to Tete and from there to Lake Mweru (Moero), reaching Cazembe country in October, where he died

1802

1802–1811, First recorded crossing of Africa from Angola to Tete on the Zambezi by Portuguese traders, Pedro Baptista and A. José

1805

Jan. 21, Mungo Park sailed on second voyage to Africa, the expedition reaching the Niger River the middle of

August. Nov. 19 with the surviving members he started from Segu to explore the unknown interior and reached Yauri where at the Bussa rapids the boat struck rock and was attacked by natives and all drowned trying to escape but one native

1807

African Institution founded in London for the abolition of the slave trade

March 25, British Parliament abolished the slave trade to take effect from May 1

1812

1812–1814, J. L. Burckhardt, Swiss Orientalist, ascended the Nile to Korosko and traveled across the desert through Nubia to Berber, and Shendi to the Red Sea, and made pilgrimage to Mecca disguised as a Mohammedan

1815

March 29, Decree of Napoleon Bonaparte abolished slavery in French territory; confirmed by Louis XVIII, Jan. 8, 1817 and law of April 15, 1818

1816

July 6, Captain J. K. Tuckey sent by the British Admiralty reached the Congo River and ascending the river reached Isangila but sickness broke out and the commander and 16 other Europeans died

1818

Discovery of the sources of the Gambia by Gaspard Mollien proceeding from St. Louis, Senegal by way of the Senegal and Bondu

1819–1823

Frédéric Caillaud explored the Nile as far as Khartum and the Blue Nile to Fazog

1820

March 9, Establishment of the Liberia Colony of American negroes. *See* Liberia

1820–1822, Egyptian military expedition under Ismail Pasha, accompanied by the French scientist, Frédéric Cailliaud, ascended the Nile to the confluence of the White and Blue Niles and founded the city of Khartum and proceeded up the Blue Nile to Fazokl

1822

1822–1825, Expedition of Walter Oudney, Dixon Denham, and Hugh Clapperton reached Lake Chad from Tripoli in 1823, the first white men, and explored the Central Sudan from Lake Chad to the Niger River. (Death of Dr. Oudney, Jan. 12, 1824)

1825

July 16, Alexander Gordon Laing left Tripoli and started across the Sahara desert, reaching the Tuat territory in Jan., 1826 and Timbuktu Aug. 18, the first European. Was murdered Sept. 26 after he left Timbuktu

Dec. 7, Hugh Clapperton accompanied by Richard Lander left Badagry in the Bight of Benin and started overland for the Niger, crossed the Niger at Bussa, Jan., 1826 and July 20 arrived at Kano. He died at Sokoto, April 13, 1827

1827

Adolfe Linant de Bellefonds ascended the White Nile to 13° 6′ North Lat. for the African Association, 150 miles beyond Khartum

April 19, René Caillé started journey from Kakony, now Boké, Rio Nunez, French Guinea, and by boat from Jenné reached Timbuktu, April 20, 1828, and Fez, Aug. 12

1830

March 22, Richard and John Lander led expedition overland from Badagry, reaching the Niger River in July at Bussa and in canoe descended the river from Yauri (60 miles above Bussa) demonstrating that its outlet, reached Aug., 1832, was in the Bight of Benim

May, French Conquest of Algiers. *See* Algeria

1832

July, Expedition organized by Macgregor Laird and headed by Richard Lander went up the Niger to the confluence of the Benue (Shary)

1834

Feb. 2, Richard Lander mortally wounded by natives

1836

Exploration of Captain Sir James E. Alexander in South West Africa

1840

Jan. 28, Expedition commanded by Selim Bimbashi from Egypt ascended White Nile to point at 6° 30′ N.

Dec. 8, David Livingstone, the great missionary-explorer, sailed from England for Bechualand to mission established by Robert Moffat 20 years earlier

1841

Aug. 20, The great Niger expedition, Captain H. D. Trotter in command, to start a colony in Central Africa (for which Parliament voted 60,000*l*.), consisting of the *Albert, Wilberforce,* and *Soudan* steamships, commenced the ascent of the Niger, Aug. 20, 1841; when they reached Iddah, fever broke out among the crews, and they were successively obliged to return, the *Albert* having ascended the river to Egga, 320 miles from the sea, Sept. 28. The expedition was relinquished owing to disease, heat, and hardships, and all the vessels had cast anchor at Clarence Cove, Fernando Po, Oct. 17

Ferdinand Werne traveled up the Nile to Gondoroko and made map of Nile from Khartum to Gondoroko

1845

James Richardson explored the Sahara desert

1848

May 11, Mr. Rebmann, missionary, saw Mt. Kilimanjaro in the distance

1849

Aug. 1, Dr. Livingstone reached Lake Ngami (the first European) across the Kalahari desert

Dec. 3, Discovery of Mt. Kenya by Dr. Lewis Krapf

1850

March, Expedition of James Richardson accompanied by Dr. Heinrich Barth and Dr. Overweg left Tripoli to explore Central Africa. Richardson died March 4,

1851 and Overweg Sept. 27, 1852. Dr. Barth crossed the country from Lake Chad to the Niger River, crossed the Benue at its junction with the Faro arriving at Say, June 20, 1853 and arrived at Timbuktu, Sept. 7, 1853. He visited Bornu, Kano, Nupe, Sokoto, and Gando

F. Gallon and K. J. Anderson made unsuccessful attempt to reach Lake Ngami from Walvis (Walfish Bay), explored South West Africa (1850–52)

Expedition of Leopold Panet from St. Louis, Senegal attempted to reach Timbuktu, murdered on way to Morocco

1851

March 13, Barth crossed the frontier into Bornu and entered Kuka, April 2

April, Livingstone started again for the country of the Makololo, proceeding to the Chobe (Kwando) tributary of the Zambezi and in June discovered the Zambezi at town of Sesheke, returning to Cape Town in April, 1852

1852

June 8, Livingstone left Cape Town, arriving at Kuruman in August and left there Nov. 20 for the Makololo country

Dec. 20–Feb., 1853, Journey of Sir George Cathcart into Basutoland

1853

Jan. 30, Barth left Zinder and journeyed to Katsena, leaving there March 21 for Wurna where he arrived Feb. 4 and remained several weeks, making visit to Sokoto, and from there on May 17 proceeded to Gando and thence to the Niger at Say

May 23, Livingstone reached Linyante, Makololo capital on the Chobe River, and in June ascended the river, returning in September

July 17–Sept. 23, Richard Burton, disguised as a native, made the pilgrimage from Egypt to Jambu and El-Medina and thence to Mecca

Sept. 7, Barth, the third European to enter Timbuktu

Nov. 11, Livingstone left Linyante, ascended the Liba and reached Lake Dilolo Feb. 20, 1854 and on May 31 the western coast at St. Paul de Loanda

K. J. Anderson reached Lake Ngami and about 60 miles to the north of the Lake

Journey of Silva Porto from Benguela to the mouth of the Rovuma

Nov., John Petherick descended the Bahr-el-Ghazal from Khartum

1854

May 20, Expedition sent by the English Government, equipped by Macgregor Laird and headed by John Beecroft (after death of Beecroft by Dr. William Baikie) sailed from England to explore the Benue River in the "Pleiad." They arrived at the Nun mouth of the Niger July 12, and began ascent of river Aug. 7, and by end of September reached point 200 miles above Dagbo, adding 40 miles to chart of Benue River; turned back by hostility of natives and unable to get to Yola, reached Fernando Po, Nov. 7 and England in Feb.

Sept. 20, Livingstone left Loanda, reaching Lake Dilolo June 13, 1855 and Linyante in September

Oct. 17, Barth reached Kano and Kuka in mid-Dec. where he met Church and Macguire

Oct. 18, John H. Speke started to join Burton at Berbera but obliged to return without finding Burton

who had journeyed alone to Harrar, Somaliland, the first white man to reach there

1855

Jan. 21, Edward Vogel who had been sent from England to relieve Barth left Kuka for Yakoba (Bautshi) and Adamawa and was murdered by natives in April of the next year at Wara, the capital of the Wadai

March 21, John H. Speke started to join Richard F. Burton in Somaliland, arriving at Berbera, April 3; attacked by the Somali Speke and Burton were wounded and Lieutenant Stroyan killed

May 4, Dr. Barth and Church of the Vogel expedition left Kuka on homeward journey arriving in London, Sept. 6

Oct., Paul Du Chaillu sailed from New York for African west coast commissioned by the Academy of Sciences at Philadelphia to explore the delta of the Ogowé River, and spent nearly 4 years exploring tributaries of the estuary of the Gaboon and deltaic arms of the Ogowé, studied the Fan Fan tribe

Nov. 3, Livingstone left Linyante with purpose to follow the Zambezi to its mouth, arriving at Sesheke on the 13th and on the 17th discovered the Victoria Falls which he named after Queen Victoria

Exploring expeditions and conquest of Senegal hinterland by French Governor Faidherbe. *See* Senegal

1856

Jan. 14, Livingstone reached the confluence of the Loangwa and the Zambezi and Zumbo on the 15th, the Portuguese settlement of Tete March 2, descended Zambezi to the Mazaro and overland to Kwa Kwa River, descending the stream reaching Quelimane on the 22th at the coast, and Dec. 12 arrived in England after an absence of 16 years

Dec. 21, Richard Burton and John Speke reached Zanzibar from Bombay

1857

July, Expedition commanded by Dr. Baikie with Lieutenant John Glover entered the Niger and established 3 trading stations at Abo, Onitsha, and Gbebe (Laird's Town) named for Macgregor Laird, under contract with the Admiralty (Jan. 1) to place a steamer on the river for trade and passengers in return for annual subsidy

Nov. 7, Richard Burton and John H. Speke arrived at Kazé from Zanzibar

1858

Feb. 14, Burton and Speke discovered Lake Tanganyika, arriving at Ujiji, the first Europeans

Feb., Dr. Livingstone appointed Consul at Quilimane (Quelimane) and commander of expedition to explore east and central Africa

March 10, Livingstone expedition sailed from England reaching the mouth of the Zambezi May 14 and ascending the river from the Kongone mouth in steam launch reaching Tete Sept. 8, and from there explored the river, especially the Kebrabasa rapids

June 30, Laird's steamer the "Sunbeam" reached the Niger and the "Rainbow" in Sept.

July 9, Speke left Kaze and on Aug. 3 discovered Lake Victoria Nyanza, which he recognized as the head reservoir of the White Nile and named after the Queen of England

1859

Sept. 16, Livingstone arrived at the southern shore of Lake Nyasa, the first white men to see the lake

K. J. Andersson reached and explored the Okovango River

1860

March–June, Expedition of Major Vincent from Mauretania explored Adrar

April 27, J. H. Speke with J. A. Grant left England to explore Lake Victoria Nyanza and prove his assertion that the lake was a source of the Nile, which was not believed by Burton, reaching Zanzibar in September

May 15, Livingstone started up the Zambezi reaching Sesheke, Aug. 18, returned to Tete, Nov. 23

Dec. 23, Expedition of Lieutenant Mage reached the Bakar country, Mauretania, and Mata, Jan. 22, 1861

Miani and Antinori traveled along banks of the Bahr-el-Ghazal and Dur into Nile Valley

Expedition of Von der Decken from Mombassa on eastern coast to Mount Kilimanjaro

1861

Jan. 24, Speke and Grant reached Kazé from Zanzibar and the Victoria Nyanza in October

Feb., The "Universities Mission to east central Africa," consisting of Charles F. Mackenzie, bishop of central Africa, and six clergymen and others, started Dec., 1860, and arrived at the Zambesi, in Feb., 1861. All died from privations and disease except two, who returned in 1864. The bishop died Jan. 31, 1862; succeeded by Dr. Tozer

March 11, Cession of Obok to France (Somaliland)

——, Livingstone ascended the Rovuma River for 30 miles and then with the missionaries up the Shiré to Chibisa's

March 21, Sir Samuel Baker arrived at Cairo and made preliminary exploring expedition into Abyssinia of the Nile tributaries arriving at Khartum, June 11, 1862

March, Richard Burton, appointed Consul at Fernando, Po explored Cameroon mountains

Sept. 2, Livingstone sailed into Lake Nyasa exploring the western coast

F. G. Rohlfs, German explorer, entered the Sahara desert from Morocco disguised as a Mussulman and traveled to the Wad Draa, the second European (R. Caillé, the first) to visit Tafilet (1861–1862)

Nov., Speke and Grant arrived at Karague (Karagwe) Tanganyika

Thomas Baines joined Chapman expedition making journey from Walvis Bay to Lake Ngami and Victoria Falls

1862

Jan. 9, Alexandrine P. F. Tinné, Dutch heiress, left Cairo with her mother and her aunt and from Khartum ascended the White Nile to a point above Gondokoro and explored a part of the Sobat

Jan. 16, Speke and Grant discovered and crossed the Kagera River and arrived at palace of King Mtesa of Uganda, Feb. 19

April 27, Death of Mrs. David Livingstone from fever at Shupanga

July 21, Speke reached the Nile at Urondog and July 28 reached and named Ripon Falls where the Nile issued from the lake, and started down stream July 31, was obliged to abandon the river in August

because of the hostility of the natives, but followed course of the Nile as far as possible

Aug. 6, Livingstone made second ascent of the Rovuma River in the "Lady Nyasa," about 156 miles

Nov. 19, Speke and Grant reached Karuma Falls and Dec. 3 De Bono's ivory post

Dec. 18, Sir Samuel Baker started up the Nile reaching Gondokoro, Feb. 2

1863

Jan. 13, Speke and Grant reached Paira and traveling down the right bank of the Nile arrived at Gondoroko, Feb. 15

Feb. 2, Sir Samuel Baker reached Gondoroko and on the arrival of Speke and Grant obtained from them information and maps which led to his discovery of Lake Albert Nyanza

Feb.– July, 1864, Miss Tinné's expedition left Khartum for the Bahr-el-Ghazal (Gazelle River) reaching the limit of navigation, March 10 made overland journey across the Bahr Jur and southwest to Jebel Kosango and into Nyam Nyam country

March 26, Sir Samuel Baker and his wife left Gondoroko following the route of Speke and Grant to Unyoro and then journeyed west

Aug. 6, Paul Du Chaillu sailed from England arriving at mouth of the Ogowé, Sept. 6, returning in 1865 with additional knowledge of the geography of West Africa, traveled from Gabun to the Kombo River, discovered pigmy tribe

Nov. 25–May 6, 1866, Expedition of Lieutenant Mage and Lieutenant Quintin explored the Niger country. *See* Sudan, French

Official mission of Richard Burton to the King of Dahomey (1863–1864)

1864

March 14, Sir Samuel White Baker discovered Lake Albert Nyanza and paddled up the lake to the Nile and up the Nile to Murchison's Falls, thence overland to Karuma Rapids and back to Gondokoro, arriving in Khartum, May 5, 1865

March, Rohlfs started from Tangier and again visited Tafilet, and journeyed across the desert to the oasis of Tuat never before visited by European, returning by Ghadames to Tripoli

July 23, Livingstone arrived in England

Sept. 15, Death of Captain Speke who accidentally shot himself when out hunting

Nov. 30, Death of Dr. W. B. Baikie at Sierra Leone

1865

March 24, David Livingstone appointed British Consul for Central Africa

Aug. 13, Livingstone left London for India on his way to Africa and arrived off the Rovuma River, March 22, 1866

Aug., Baron K. K. von der Decken killed by natives on Juba River, Somaliland.

Rohlfs on mission to the King of Bornu and to territory north of the Mandara Mountains (1865–1867), crossed the desert from Murzuk, Fezzan, to Bornu, proceeded to the Benue River and sailed down it and the Niger

1866

April 4, Livingstone started for the interior to Lake Nyasa (Aug. 8) and crossed the Loangwa, Dec. 14, and from there traveled toward Lake Tanganyika over unexplored country, sighting the lake, April 1, 1867

1867

April 25, Lieutenant Aymis began exploration of the Ogowé River

July 25, Expedition of Edward Young sent from England to find Livingstone, reported killed by natives, reached the Zambezi and ascended the Shiré River, returning then to England with evidence that Livingstone was alive and in the interior

Nov. 8, Livingstone reached Lake Moero (Mweru) first seen by Lacerda and visited Lake Mofwa and the Lualaba

1868

July 18, Livingstone discovered Lake Bangweulu

Dec., Dr. G. Schweinfurth, botanist, journeyed from Khartum to Bahr-el Ghazal and Nian Nian country and discovered the Welle River (1868–1871)

1869

Jan., Miss Tinné started from Tripoli for Lake Chad and the upper Nile and was murdered on the route from Murzuk to Ghat by Tuaregs

Feb., Gustav Nachtigal left Tripoli for Murzuk and thence to Tibesti Highlands

Feb. 14, Livingstone arrived at Lake Tanganyika and at Ujiji, March 14, left Ujiji, July 17 and again crossed the Lake, traveling northwest to Luabala River

Nov. 16, Suez Canal formally opened

1870

Exploration of Lake Chad and Bornu by Gustav Nachtigal (1870–74)

Sept. 4, F. C. Selous landed at Algo Bay and began hunting trips in the Zambezi basin which he continued until 1893, *Geog. Jour.*, April, 1893

Dec. 1, Sir Samuel Baker started from Khartum and arrived at Gondokoro, April 15, 1871, commissioned to suppress the slave trade in upper Nile region and open up the country for commerce and civilization, appointed Governor General by the Khedive of Egypt

1871

Jan. 6, Henry M. Stanley, sent by James Gordon Bennett, proprietor of the New York "Herald" to find Livingstone, reached Zanzibar and began journey into the interior, March 21, and Oct. 28 found Livingstone at Ujiji on Lake Tanganyika

March 29, Livingstone reached the Lualaba River at Nyangwe and Ujiji on Lake Tanganyika, Oct. 23, to find that stores sent him had been taken by Arabs

Dec. 27, Livingstone and Stanley left Ujiji and proceeded to Unyanyembe arriving Feb. 18, 1872, explored the north end of Lake Tanganyika and proved that the Rusizi runs into and not out of it

1872

March 14, Stanley left Livingstone at Unyamwezi, bringing away his diary and other documents and returned to Zanzibar and England

May 14, Baker at Masindi declared Unyoro under the protection of Egypt

Aug. 15, Livingstone started for Lake Bangweulu, reached April 29 and Lake Tanganyika, Oct. 14, and from there proceeded to Kalongosi River

Nov. 20, Sir H. E. Bartle Frere sailed to negotiate treaty with the Sultan of Zanzibar for the suppression of the slave trade and with him the expedition of Lieutenant Verney Lovett Cameron to search for Livingstone

Scientific expedition of Reinhold Buchholz on Guinea coast (1872–1875)

1873

Feb., Dr. Emil Holub made first journey in Africa into southern Bechualand and in Nov. a second in which he traveled as far as Shoshong

March 8–May 24, Exploration of the Ogowé River valley by Alfred Marsh and the Marquis de Compiègne

April 4, Livingstone reached the jungle region east of Lake Bangweulu and crossed the Chambezi River in northern Rhodesia, so ill that he soon had to be carried on a litter

April 30, Livingstone reached Chitambo's village on the Lulimala River in the Ilala country on the south shore of Lake Bangweulu where he died May 1, the last entry in his journal, April 27; buried in Westminster Abbey April 18, 1874

Lieutenant W. Grandy sent from England for relief of Livingstone proceeded from Ambriz on west coast to point on Congo below the cataracts, the expedition recalled before he could ascend the river (April, 1874)

Scientific expedition of Güssfeldt to Loango coast

Dec., G. Rohlfs left Cairo for the Libyan Desert and from Siout to Oasis of Farafrah, and Oasis of Dachel, and explored the Behar bela Nea, empty river bed

1874

Jan. 16–Feb. 20, G. Rohlfs visited Siwa in the desert from Dakla, 1,486 miles in 68½ days marching

April 20, Colonel Charles Chaillé-Long, an American in the service of the Government of Egypt, on mission to the King of Uganda, left Gondokoro, reached the capital June 19, visited Lake Victoria Nyanza July 14, reached the Nile, July 28 and followed it from the Ripon Falls to the Karuma Rapids and Aug. 11 discovered Lake Kioga which he named Lake Ibrahim, name changed by Great Britain later

May 14, Cameron left Ujiji following Livingstone's route by Lake Tanganyika, whose outflow to the Lualaba he discovered, proceeded to Nyangwe and thence south to Kikemba and the western Lualaba and to Bihé and reached Benguela on the Atlantic coast, Portuguese settlement, Nov. 4 having crossed Africa from sea to sea

Nov. 11, Henry M. Stanley, on second journey, left Zanzibar with 2 white companions, spending 3 years crossing the continent, circumnavigated the Victoria Nyanza, visited Uganda where he persuaded the King to receive British missionaries, discovered Lake Dweru, and descended the Congo River to its mouth reached Aug. 12, 1877, starting from Nyangwe on the Luabala, a journey to be compared with La Salle's descent of the Mississippi

1875

Jan., George Grenfell, missionary traveler, arrived in Africa with Alfred Saker, and began exploration of rivers inland from the Cameroons traversing the lower course of the Sanaga as far as Edea on his first expedition

March 8, Stanley began circumnavigation of Lake Victoria Nyanza

March, Journey of Dr. E. Holub begun into Barotse country north of the Zambezi (1875–1876)

Oct. 20, Count de Brazza arrived at Gabun (*see* French Equatorial Africa) and began exploration of the Ogowé River and discovered the Alima and Lefini rivers, branches of the Congo

Expedition of Dr. Pogge in Congo basin, crossing from the west coast to Muata Yamvo's kingdom beyond the Lulua River in Belgian Congo

M. J. Bonnat explored the hinterland of the Gold Coast, and the Volta River basin

1876

June 11–July 28, Stanley made voyage of circumnavigation of Lake Tanganyika

Aug. 9, Stanley reached Boma

Sept. 12, International Association for the Exploration and Civilization of Africa founded. *See* Belgian Congo

1877

Oct. 21, H. M. Stanley reached Cape Town and London, Jan. 22, 1878; published his "Through the Dark Continent," May, 1878

Nov. 12, Serpa Pinto from Benguela on the west coast started across the continent, proceeding to the Zambezi, tracing part of the Kwando River, traversing east Bechualand, arriving at Durban, Natal, April 14, 1879

Brito Capello and Roberto Ivens, Portuguese expedition for exploration of the hinterland of Angola, journeyed from the valley of the Cunene River to the valley of the Kwanza, thence to the Kwango, explored the Yacca Territory, and disproved existence of Lake Aquilunda which had appeared on maps since the seventeenth century

Dr. Wilhelm Junker in the Sudan followed the Khor-Baraka from Suakin by Tokar to Kassala

1878

March 12, British occupation of Walvis Bay proclaimed

Nov. 14, Expedition of A. Keith Johnston left England under auspices of the Royal Geographical Society to explore East Africa, reached Zanzibar Jan. 5, 1879

Nov. 25, Belgian National Committee of the International Association founded. *See* Belgian Congo

Expedition of G. Rohlfs to oasis of Kufra from Tripoli

Dr. R. W. Felkin ascended the Nile from Suakin to Uganda

1879

Feb. 8–June 1, 1880, Expedition of Captain Joseph S. Gallieni from St. Louis, Senegal, to Segu on the Niger

May 19, A. K. Johnston expedition started from Zanzibar and after death of Johnston, June 28, was headed by Joseph Thomson, reaching Lake Tanganyika, Nov. 3

Aug. 14, Henry M. Stanley, in service of the Belgian National Committee, began ascent of the Congo River from its mouth, establishing stations in country which became the Belgian Congo, remaining in the region until June, 1884, mapping area of 900,000 square miles

Sept. 29, Proclamation declared the Transvaal British Territory. *See* Transvaal

Dec. 24, Gætani Casati sailed from Italy for Africa, reached Khartum in May, 1880, and joined Romolo Gessi in service of Egypt in the Sudan and joined Enim Pasha in April, 1883

Dec. 27, Count Savorgnan de Brazza sailed from Liverpool to establish French posts on the Congo

Dr. Buchner crossed the country from Loanda to Muata Yamvo's kingdom at Kawende (Belgian Congo)

Sources of the Niger River discovered by French expedition of Zweifel and Moustier in hills near Nelia, about 200 miles east of Freetown, Sierra Leone

G. Schaudt explored the Moroccan Sahara (1879–1882)

1880

Feb., Dr. Wilhelm Junker reached Meshra er Rek and started into the interior (Bahr-el Ghazal)

March 1, Joseph Thomson, turned back by mutiny, discovered Lake Leopold (Rukwa or Hikwa) on return journey (March); reached coast, July 1, had explored unknown country between Lake Nyassa and Lake Tanganyika

July, H. O. Lenz reached Timbuktu from Morocco and then proceeded to Senegamia on Atlantic coast

Nov. 7, De Brazza and Stanley met on Congo River at Isangila. For settlement of Congo basin *see* Belgian Congo *and* French Equatorial Africa

Tanganyika explored by the German expedition of Böhm, Kaiser, and Reichard

Expedition of P. Matteucci, and Pellegrino crossed the continent from east to west from Suakin by Khartum, El Obeid, Darfur, Lake Chad to mouth of the Niger (1880–1881)

Expedition of Paul Pogge and Hermann von Wissmann crossed the continent from west to east, passing through unknown country beyond Mutata Yanvo's kingdom (Belgian Congo) to Upper Congo at Nyangwe, then to Lake Tanganyika to Ujii and Tabora to coast (1880–1883)

Expedition of Edward Robert Flegel up the Benue and Upper Niger rivers, reaching Gomba up the Niger and visiting Sokoto

Böhm, Kaiser, and Reichard began exploration of country between Zanzibar and the eastern edge of Congo basin (Tanganyika)

1881

Oct., French occupation of Tunis. *See* Tunis

Revolt of the Mahdi. *See* Sudan

Settlement of the Niger country by National African Company. *See* Nigeria

1882

Aug. 18, E. W. R. Flegel discovered the source of the Benue River near Ngaundere in Adamawa after traversing the entire southern basin of the Niger

Dec. 6, German Colonial Society founded at Frankfort

Dec. 10, Joseph Thomson sailed from England under auspices of the Royal Geographical Society commissioned to report as to caravan route through the Masai country

Victor Giraud journeyed from Dar-es-Salaam to north end of Lake Nyasa and to Lake Bangweulu of which he made the first accurate map (1882–1884)

Dr. Junker traced course of the Ubangi to near its confluence with the Bomu, showing that it belonged to the Congo system

Sir Harry Johnston made journey from Angola to the Congo River

1883

Jan. 3, Administration of Egypt by England begun with Lord Granville's circular despatch. *See also* Egypt

Feb. 1, General Gallieni reached Bammako

March 15, Joseph Thomson left coast from Mombassa, reaching Taveta May 5 and ascended Mount Kilimanjaro, proceeded north to Rift Valley through the Masai country, discovered and named the Aberdare Mountains, discovered Lake Baringo and proceeded west and southwest to northern shore of Lake Victoria Nyanza, which he reached Dec. 10

——, Italian occupation of Somaliland begun. *See* Somaliland

April 3, German Colonial Society founded in Berlin by Karl Peters and others

April 9, German occupation of South West Africa begun. *See* South West Africa

April 25, Count de Brazza reached Gabun on third expedition to Africa and began exploration and survey of region from Franceville on the Upper Ogowé northward to Lake Chad (1883–1885)

June–April, 1884, Scientific expedition of Henry Drummond in lake district, Lake Nyasa and Tanganyika

Aug. 9, Death of Dr. Moffatt, missionary (87)

F. L. and W. D. James journeyed from Berbera to the Webi Shebeli Somaliland

Foureau led expedition to Hassi Messegnem in Sahara desert

De Foucauld in disguise crossed and recrossed the Atlas Mountains

Antonio Cardoza explored the district between Save River and Buzi

1884

Jan., Dr. Junker joined Emin Pasha at Lado, ending his exploration of the Nile-Congo watershed, after establishment of identity of the Welle with the Ubangi River, prevented by Mahdi uprising from further investigation

Jan. 28, G. Grenfell started to survey the Congo River up to the Equator, passed mouth of the Kwa and visited Bolobo, Lukolea and Ireby, at confluence of the Ubangi with the Congo

Feb. 2, British Protectorate declared over Basutoland

Feb. 14, Treaty between Portugal and Great Britain by which Great Britain recognized Portuguese claim to both banks of the Congo. (*See also* Angola.) Not ratified because of protests of the Powers

Feb. 26, Treaty between Great Britain and Portugal recognizing freedom of navigation of Congo and Zambezi Rivers

March 28, New German Colonization Society founded

May 1, First Protectorate Treaty signed by Great Britain with Chiefs of Somaliland, and May 3 with Chiefs of Bechuanaland

July 5, Germany signed Protectorate Treaty with the King of Togo

July 7, George Grenfell started voyage in the "Peace" up Kwa, Kwango, and Kasai rivers

July 12, Protectorate declared by Germany over Cameroons (Kamerun)

Aug. 7, German flag raised at Angra Pequena (Southwest Africa)

Aug. 15, German Protectorate proclaimed over coasts of Namaqualand and Damaraland (South West Africa)

Sept. 8, German Protectorate over coast of South West Africa except Walvis Bay (annexed by Great Britain in 1878) notified to Great Britain and to the Powers Oct. 15

Oct. 13, Grenfell expedition discovered the Ruki or Black River, then ascended the Itimbiri or Rubi River, visited Tipu Tipu, arrived at Stanley Falls Dec. 24, and ascended the Ubangi for 200 miles to Grenfell Falls

Oct. 18, German Protectorate declared over Great Namaqualand

Nov. 15–Feb. 26, 1885, International Conference on African Affairs held in Berlin recognized position of British on the Lower and French on the Upper Niger

Nov. 19, Dr. Karl Peters signed first Treaty with native chiefs in East Africa

Nov., H. H. Johnston on scientific expedition ascended Mt. Kilimanjaro 16,200 feet from the summit of Kibo (East Africa)

Dec. 8, F. L. and W. D. James, and G. P. V. Aylmer left Aden for Berbera and penetrated Somali country hitherto unknown as far as the Webi-Shebeli (Somaliland) and Barri, 350 miles from Berbera

Dec. 18, Notification of British occupation of St. Lucia Bay

Portuguese Government expedition headed by Major Carvalho from Loanda to Muata Yanvo kingdom, explored territory between the Kwanza and the Kasai (1884–1888)

Journey of Walter M. Kerr through Mashonaland and Matabeleland

German expedition headed by H. von Wissmann journeyed from Loanda to Malange, and returning descended the Kasai River, largest southern tributary of the Congo, solving important geographical problem, proving that it united with the Kwango and other tributaries before joining the main river (1884–1885)

Dr. Schinz made journey from Walvis Bay to the Cunene River

Capello and Ivens explored Southern Angola and Northern Rhodesia, crossing continent from Mossamedes to mouth of the Zambezi (1884–1885)

1885

Jan. 9, Spain declared protectorate over Rio de Oro

Jan. 26, Capture of Khartum and death of Gordon. *See* Sudan

Jan. 27, Great Britain proclaimed Protectorate over Bechualand

Feb. 14, Convention of Portugal with the International Association of the Congo as to African affairs. *See* Belgian Congo *and* Angola

Feb. 26, Berlin Act signed by the International Conference provided for freedom of trade in the basin of the Congo, abolished the slave trade in Congo basin, decreed free navigation of Congo and Niger Rivers, and decreed that any Power annexing African territory must give notice to the Powers

——, Constitution of the Congo Free State

Feb. 27, German East Africa Company founded

March 15, Joseph Thomson left Akassa, proceeding up the Niger to Rabba (April 7), and then inland to Sokoto (May 21), Wurnu (May 23), Gandu (June 7), and made treaties with the chiefs for the National African Company (British)

June 5, British Protectorate of Niger coast proclaimed

Aug. 2, G. Grenfell on third voyage in the "Peace"

explored the Lulongo, Maringa, and Busira (Juapa) rivers, ascended Ubangi to Zongo Falls

Sept., Expedition of J. T. Last under auspices of the Royal Geographical Society to Zanzibar

1886

Jan. 1, J. Barelli left Tadjura, beginning journey in Abyssinia, reaching farthest south at Mt. Bobbé

Jan. 2, Dr. Wilhelm Junker left Emin Pasha, crossed Albert Nyanza Lake, and in June reached the capital of Uganda, and proceeded across Victoria Nyanza to Tabora, and there joined caravan of trader, Tippo Tip, and reached the coast safely in Dec.

Feb. 24, G. Grenfell, with von Wissmann, ascended the Kasai River, the Sankuru, Luebo, and Lulua rivers

April 19, Protocol of ratification of the Berlin Act

April 23, British Protectorate over Sokotra Island proclaimed

June, Emil Holub crossed the Zambezi west of Victoria Falls and explored the unknown country between the Zambezi and the Kafue

July 10, Royal Niger Company (former National African Company) received a royal charter and was authorized to administer Niger territory

Sept. 11, Death of Flegel at Brass at mouth of the Niger

Sept. 30, G. Grenfell made fifth voyage up the Kwa and Mfini rivers to Lake Leopold II

Oct., Von Wissman journeyed from Luluaburg (Belgian Congo) to the Zambezi

Dec., Grenfell made sixth voyage up the Kwango River to Kingunji rapids

Expedition of A. van Gèle explored the Ubangi River and established identity of the Welle (Uele) River of Schweinfurth and Junker with the Ubangi (1886–1889)

German expedition of Dr. Zintgraff opened up routes from Duala in the Cameroons to Adamawa

G. A. Krause explored the Volta River on Togo frontier and reached the bend of the Niger country (French Sudan)

1887

Jan. 21, Henry M. Stanley left England at head of relief expedition to find Emin Pasha (Eduard Schnitzler), Governor of equatorial province of the Sudan, isolated at Wadelai after fall of Khartum and Mahdist rising 1881–1885

Jan. 23–Oct. 26, 1888, Samuel Teleki and Lieutenant Ludwig von Höhnel journeyed into the Masai country, discovered the Basso Norok now known as Lake Rudolf, March, 1888, and Lake Stefanie

Feb. 25, Stanley left Zanzibar for mouth of the Congo

May 2, Treich-Laplène on mission to Kong left Assinie, Ivory Coast

June 15, Stanley, working up the Congo River, reached Yambuya on the lower Aruwimi, where he left Major E. M. Barttelot and J. S. Jameson, starting himself on the 28th for Lake Albert Nyanza through jungle forest from which they emerged after 160 days of twilight Dec. 5, and reached Albert Nyanza Dec. 13, opening communication with Emin Pasha

July 1–March 20, 1889, Expedition of Captain Louis Gustave Binger from Senegal to the Ivory Coast leaving Bamaku on the Niger July 1. *See* Sudan, French

——, Expedition of Lieutenant Caron by water on the Niger from Bamako to Timbuktu

1888

Feb. 11, Great Britain gained protectorate over Matabeleland and Mashonaland by Treaty with Chief Lobengula

Feb. 20, Captain Binger, the first European to reach Kong, Ivory Coast

March 6, Discovery of Lake Rudolf by Teleki

March 17, Expedition of Joseph Thomson started to explore the Atlas Mountains of Morocco

Aug. 12, Expedition of Paul Crampel from Lastourville on the Ogowé toward Lake Chad, and discovery of the Djah (N'Tem) River, exploring country between the Ogowé and Likuala (1888–89)

Expedition of Kundt, Tappenbeck, and Weissbaum to Yaunde

Baron von Steinäcker explored Damaraland and made first accurate maps of region

Aug. 17, Stanley returning to discover the reason for non-appearance of rear guard found near Yambuya that Barttelot had been murdered

Sept. 3, British East African Association received charter

Dec. 10, Captain Trivier left Loango, crossing Africa, reaching Quelimane Dec. 1, 1880, shortest time crossing to date

Dec. 17–June, 1889, Dr. Zintgraff made journey from the Benue River to Adamawa

1889

April–Dec. 5, Stanley expedition, with Emin Pasha, marched from Lake Albert Nyanza to the east coast, discovering the Ruwenzori (Mountains of the Moon) and tracing the Semliki River to its source in Lake Edward, which he discovered and named after Albert Edward afterwards Edward VII

May 20, Notification of Italian Protectorate over Oppia

Aug., Sir Harry Johnston arrived at the Shiré River, explored region between Lakes Nyasa and Tanganyika, discovered south end of Lake Rukwa

Oct. 6, Hans Meyer (second attempt) reached summit of Mt. Kilimanjaro

Oct. 22, German Protectorate over East Africa proclaimed

Oct. 29, British South Africa Company chartered, included among members Cecil J. Rhodes, to settle the immense area lying between Lower and Central Zambesi on the north, and the Transvaal border on the south

Oct., Discovery of the navigability of the Chinde mouth of the Zambezi by D. J. Rankin

Nov. 15, Brussels Conference to put an end to African slavery opened

Nov. 19, Italian Protectorate over part of east coast proclaimed and Dec. 9 over Aussa (Danakils)

Dec. 21, Captain F. D. Lugard started from Mombassa on 6 months journey, establishing posts in Uganda and going as far as Ukamba, Kenya

Kurt Morgen explored upper Sanaga River (1889–1891) and region between Jaunde and the river

Expedition of Sir F. J. Jackson and E. Gedge from Mombassa to Uganda, opening new route to Lake Victoria Nyanza (1889–1890)

J. R. W. Piggott traveled from Malindi to the Tana River at Golanti, exploring upper river

1890

March 4, British East Africa Company received concessions on coast. *See* Kenya

April 21, F. L. James killed by elephant

July 1, Anglo-German Agreement of 1890 determined the boundaries of the British and German proposed territories in East Africa; the protectorate of Zanzibar, Witu, Somaliland or Vitu, was given up to Great Britain; Heligoland was ceded to Germany; signed at Berlin by Sir Edward Malet and Sir Henry Percy Anderson for England; by Gen. von Caprivi and Dr. Krauel for Germany, July 1; ratified by an act of parliament which received the royal assent, Aug. 4, 1890

July 2, Brussels Act for abolition of slave trade signed by the Powers

Aug. 5, Anglo-French Agreement respecting Africa signed by the Marquis of Salisbury and M. Waddington, French ambassador in London, Aug. 5, 1890. By this agreement the British protectorate over Zanzibar and the French protectorate over Madagascar are recognized, and the delimitation of territories in Africa, subject to the influence of France, was to be settled by two commissioners at Paris

——, British Protectorate of Zanzibar declared

——, French Protectorate of Madagascar declared

Aug. 10, Expedition of Paul Crampel to Lake Chad. *See* French Equatorial Africa

Aug. 20, Anglo-Portuguese Agreement delimiting the territories subject to the influence of Great Britain and Portugal in East Africa; the text of the agreement was settled in London Aug. 20 and published in the *Times*. The free navigation of the Zambezi, and uninterrupted communication between British territories ensured, Aug. 26, 1890. Portugal gives up all claim to Zambezi and Nyasaland. The agreement was annulled, and a *modus vivendi* agreed to, Nov. 14, 1890. A new modified treaty, signed at Lisbon, June 11, 1891, and afterwards ratified

Aug. 23, Joseph Thomson left Kotakota, Nyasaland, arriving at the Kwa River Sept. 21

Sept. 24, Anglo-Italian Agreement respecting Africa. Sir Evelyn Baring and Gen. Sir Francis Grenfell received at Rome by Sig. Crispi, Sept. 24, 1890. Meeting of the conference at Naples, Lord Dufferin and Sig. Crispi present; no result, Oct. 4–10, 1890. Treaty for the delimitation of the British and Italian spheres of influence in East Africa; signed at Rome, April 15, 1891

Oct. 10, Lieutenant Mizon started journey toward Lake Chad from the Nun mouth of the Niger, reaching Yola on the Upper Benue, Aug. 20, 1891. *See also* French Equatorial Africa

Nov. 4, Notification of British Protectorate of Zanzibar and Nov. 19 of Witu

Dec., Major P. L. Monteil left Senegal on journey to Lake Chad, arriving at Segu Aug. 19, 1891, and by Sokoto and Kano reached Lake Chad in March, 1892, and Tripoli, Dec. 10

——, P. le Marinel started from Lusambo on the Sankuru, following the Lubi branch for about 100 miles, and then proceeding east to Bunkeia

E. Cholet explored the Sangha River, northern tributary of the Congo

H. G. Fleck traversed the little known country of the western Kalahri Desert

Captain J. Becker made journey from the Aruwimi to the Welle River, exploring the country between the 2 rivers (1890–1891)

Sir Alfred Sharpe made journey from the Shiré Highlands to Lake Nyasa, to the Langwa River, Lake Tanganyika, and Lake Mweru (1890–1891)

1891

Jan. 4, Expedition of Paul Crampel left Bangui for unknown country and reached Baguirmi and El-Kouti and Crampel was killed by natives May 25

March 24 and April 15, Treaties between Great Britain and Italy defined spheres of influence

May 14, British Protectorate of Nyasaland notified

May 18, M. A. Delcommune made journey from the lower Lomani to Lake Kasale (Aug. 27) and Bunkeia (Oct. 16) to the Katanga and Lualaba rivers and returned by Lake Tanganyika

May, F. Stuhlmann with Emin Pasha crossed Tanganyika to Lake Albert Nyanza and proceeded to region west of Lake (1890–1891)

June 11, Anglo-Portuguese Treaty defined boundaries. *See also* Nyasaland, Angola, and Mozambique

June 26, Treaty between Great Britain and France as to Niger region

June 28, Jean Dybowski began journey to the Shari River, accompanied by Behagle, Clozel, and others, returning from Yola to the mouth of the Niger, March 23, 1893

July 4, Captain W. G. Stairs left Bagamoyo, crossing Tanganyika to Lake Tanganyika, and across lake to Mrumbi, reaching Bunkeia Dec. 14

Oct. 26, Formal notification of French Protectorate of Ivory Coast

Nov., F. Stuhlmann began return journey from Undusuma to Semliki River, to Bukoba on Lake Victoria Nyanza (Jan. 15, 1892). Emin Pasha turned toward west coast and was murdered by natives just before reaching the Congo at Kinena

Dec. 15, Journey of Lieutenant P. Mizon from Yola on the Benue River to Ngaundéré, French Equitorial Africa

F. G. Dundas navigated the Juba River, North East Africa, for 400 miles

H. H. von Behr explored the region between the Rovuma and the Rufiji rivers in Tanganyika

Dr. O. Baumann made journey from Tanga on eastern coast to region between Kilimanjaro and Victoria Nyanza where he discovered Lakes Manyara and Eiassi, explored head-streams of the Kagera (1891–1893)

Italian expeditions of Captain Baudi di Vesme from Berbera to the Webbe River, of Robecchi from Mogdishu into Somali country

Lieutenant Chaltin explored the Lulu River and country between the Aruwimi and the Welle Makua Rivers in Belgian Congo

1892

Jan. 2, Captain Bia reached Lake Kabele, Belgian Congo, from Lusambo, and Jan. 30 arrived at Bunkeia

Jan. 11, Binger expedition landed at Assinie, Ivory Coast, reaching Bonduku April 29, explored hinterland of Ivory Coast and southern Sudan (French) between Bonduku and Kong, traveling 1,200 miles

Feb. 25, Delcommune began descent of Upper Lualaba River but forced to give up and proceed by land and returned to Bunkeia June 8

March, Captain Monteil reached Lake Chad from Senegal (*see supra*, Dec., 1890) and traveled across the Sahara, reaching Tripoli Dec. 10

March 21, Discovery of Lake Eiassa by Dr. Oscar Baumann

April 24, Casimir Maistre began journey from Congo River to the Ubangi River, began voyage on river, June 9, proceeded to the Shari, and reached Ibi on the Benue River, March 6, 1893

May 7, Lease at Chinde by Portugal to Great Britain and of land on Lake Nyasa to Portugal by Great Britain

Aug. 12, Treaty between Italy and Zanzibar by which Benadir ports leased to Italy

Sept. 18, William Astor Chanler with Lieutenant von Höhnel left coast of Witu, Kenya Colony, with caravan, proceeded to Tana River, marched along left bank to Subaki, traced source of MacKenzie River, and found Lake Lorian to be a swamp flooded during rainy season, visited Mt. Kenya and Jombine mountains, returned to Mombassa, Feb., 1894

Oct. 23, Emin Pasha murdered by natives

Dec. 3, Proclamation of French Protectorate of Dahomey

Dec. 26–Feb. 15, 1893, Journey of M. Ponel from Batouri to Ngaundéré.

V Bottego made journey from Berbera to Upper Juba River, tracing it to source

Journey of Sir Alfred Sharpe to Lake Tanganyika and Lake Mweru from Nyasaland and up the Luapula to the Johnston Falls

Lieutenant Kurt Morgen from Banjo reached the Benue at Ibi

G. Méry from Algeria reached Temassinin in the Sahara

1893

Jan. 1–Oct. 22, Mission of Sir Gerald Portal to Uganda

July 11, Baron von Uechtriz and Dr. S. Passarge left Akassa for the Benue River, arrived at Yola Aug. 30, Oct. 13 at Garua; Passarge began geological investigation of country south of Yola, the Benue from Garua to Bubandjika

July 12, Anglo-French Boundary Agreement as to Gold Coast with Ivory Coast and French Sudan

Oct., Count von Götzen started inland from Pangani north of Zanzibar, discovered Lake Umburri and first European to cross Ruanda

Nov. 15, Anglo-German Boundary Agreement as to Gulf of Guinea, Yola, Lake Chad

Dec. 30, Death of Sir Samuel Baker (72)

J. W. Gregory explored the Rift Valley between Lakes Naivasha and Baringo in northern Kenya, and ascended Mt. Kenya to height of 16,000 feet

Baron von Schele explored the region between Rufiji and Rovuma rivers, Tanganyika

Scientific expedition of Neumann to southern Uganda (1893–1895)

Scientific expedition of Scott Elliott reached Ruwenzori through Uganda, returning by Tanganyika and Nyasa

1894

March 15, Franco-German Boundary Agreement, Cameroons, French Congo, Lake Chad

March 26, Death of Captain Lovett Cameron, explorer, companion of Burton and others

May 12, Agreement of Great Britain and the Congo Free State as to boundaries

June 18, British Protectorate over Uganda announced

Aug. 14, Boundary Agreement of France and the Congo Free State

Aug. 24, F. J. Clozel began journey from post at Berberati, northeast of Bania, and proceeded to explore the Congo-Shari divide. *See also* French Equatorial Africa

Oct. 20, Notification of British Protectorate over Borgu

Dec. 8, Count von Götzen completed journey across the continent from Tanganyika to the mouth of the Congo, discovered Lake Kivu in Belgian Congo

Dr. Donaldson-Smith from Berbera made journey to Lake Rudolf

R. Dorsey Mohun and Dr. Hinde explored Upper Congo River to its junction with the Lukuga and a short distance up the Lukuga

E. A. Foa crossed the continent from Zanzibar to the Congo, covering some new ground between Lake Tanganyika and the Congo above Nyangwe

1895

Feb. 13, French expedition of Commander Toutée up the Niger (*see* French Sudan) reached Tibi Farca opposite Zinder June 12

June 11, Notification of British Protectorate over Tongaland

July 27, Emile Gentil left Loango and traveled up the Congo and Ubangi rivers toward Lake Chad, carrying boat, the "Léon Blot"

Aug. 2, Death of Joseph Thomson

Dec. 29, Jameson raid. *See* Transvaal

V. Bottego revisited the Juba River and investigated the rivers north of Lake Rudolf, traced the Omo to Lake Rudolf, and discovered Lake Regina Margherita

Hanolet, exploring the Shari basin, penetrated to about Lat. 9° N.

A. St. H. Gibbon explored the eastern tributaries of the Zambezi (1895–96)

1896

Jan. 23, Lieutenant Hourst left Kabara, port of Timbuktu, in 3 boats, proceeding down the Niger River making a survey to its mouth, reaching Gao March 4, left Say Sept. 15, and left the River at Warri, reaching Porto Novo, Dahomey Nov. 1

March 1, Battle of Adowa, Italians defeated by Abyssinians. *See* Abyssinia

June 2, Death of Gerhard Rohlfs, explorer

July 23, Major Marchand's expedition lands at Loango, July 23, 1896, reaches Loudima, Sept. 27; defeats the rebels, and arrives at Brazzaville, Nov. 8; ascends the Congo, and up the M'Bornu to Mehreh, March 1 –Sept. 12, 1897; crossed the bush and reaches Fashoda, July 10, 1898; left Fashoda, Dec. 11; ascended the Sobat river; crossed Abyssinia to Adis-Abeba, March 10, 1899; reaching Jibuti, mid May, 1899. *See also* French Equatorial Africa and Sudan, Anglo-Egyptian

Aug. 6, French law declared Madagascar a French Colony

Aug. 31, British Protectorate proclaimed over territory adjacent to Sierra Leone

Sept. 5, H. S. Cavendish started from Berbera on the Gulf of Aden and made journey through Somaliland to Juba River and around Lake Rudolf

Oct. 26, Treaty signed by Italy and Abyssinia, peace and frontiers

P. Weatherley surveyed Lake Bangweulu

C. W. Hobley made circuit of Mt. Elgon, north-east of Lake Victoria Nyanza

Passarge made geological investigation of Lake Ngami and region to northwest

E. Stache explored the region between the Kasai and the Sankuru

A. Kaiser explored Rift Valley between Lakes Manyara and Naivasha

1897

Jan. 1, Journey of Lieutenant Bretennet up the Niger. *See* Sudan, French

Feb. 1, French missions united at Tibga (Tibja), completing occupation of about 100,000 square kilometers of territory. *See also* Sudan, French

March 20, Death of Antoine d'Abbadie, explorer of Abyssinia (1837–1848)

July 23, Franco-German Boundary Treaty defined frontiers of Dahomey, Sudan, and Togoland

Sept., Lieutenant von Carnap left Yaunde in the Cameroons, proceeded to Matadi, and made journey down the Sangha River to Congo River, for first time effecting direct communication by land from the Cameroons to the Congo

Nov. 1, Gentil expedition descending the Shari reached Lake Chad. *See also* French Equatorial Africa

Bonchamps coöperating with Marchand reached head of Sobat River and then returned to Abyssinia

1898

Jan., Captain M. S. Wellby explored chain of lakes in south-east Abyssinia (1898–1899). *See also* Abyssinia

Jan. 28, Death of Captain Roberto Ivens, explorer

May, Major A. St. H. Gibbons left England, returning to complete exploration of the Zambezi tributaries, explored Marotseland, discovered source of the Middle Zambezi and returned by Lakes Mweru, Tanganyika, Kivu, Edward, and Albert to Uganda and reached Omdurman, Anglo-Egyptian Sudan, Aug. 20, 1900

April 9, H. Weld Blundell began journey from Abyssinia to the Nile (1898–1899)

June 14, Anglo-French Treaty delimited boundaries and spheres of influence east and west of the Niger

July 10, Major Marchand reached Fashoda. *See supra* July 23, 1896

Sept. 2, Battle of Omdurman and capture of Khartum by Kitchener. *See* Sudan, Anglo-Egyptian

Sept. 27, Foureau-Lamy mission left Biskra, Algeria, to cross the Sahara desert to Lake Chad, proceeding through Ain Taiba, Temassinin, Agades to Zinder (Nov. 2) and thence to the Lake, Feb. 2, 1900, meeting Gentil mission April 11 at Manjafl

Oct.–Feb., 1900, E. S. Grogan made first journey the length of the continent from Cape Town to Cairo, Mr. A. H. Sharpe, his companion, turning east in Uganda proceeded to the coast at Mombassa

Major Austin surveyed the west shore of Lake Rudolf. *See also* Abyssinia, 1899–1900

Lieutenant von Carnap from Yaunde in the Cameroons traveled to Kunde, reaching the Congo River by the Sangha

Dr. Cureau crossed from the Mbonui to Dem Ziber in the Bahr-el-Ghazal region

Captain C. F. Close and F. F. R. Boileau surveyed the region between Lakes Tanganyika and Nyasa

1899

Jan. 19, Agreement of Great Britain and Egypt for administration of the Sudan

March 21, Anglo-French Declaration as to spheres of influence in Central Africa and Sudan, France withdrawing from the Nile Valley

June 8, International Convention on liquor traffic in Africa

Aug. 1, Dr. A. Donaldson-Smith started from Berbera, reached the Shebeli, Sept. 8 and Godi, 400 miles from Berbera, Sept. 11, Lake Rudolf Dec. 10, and the Nile at Fort Berkeley in March, 1900, from there taking boat to Cairo

Aug., Scientific expedition of J. Moore explored the lakes, Nyasa and Tanganyika (1899–1900)

Oct. 12, Boer war begun. *See* South African War

Oct. 22, Joalland-Meynier mission reached Lake Chad

Dec.–Feb., 1900, M. Flamand explored oasis of Tibikelt south of Algeria and took possession for France

Dr. Baum explored southern Angola, proceeding inland from Mossamedes

M. Julien explored the Unangi Valley to north of middle course of the river and to the west of the Mbonui

C. W. Gynn and H. H. Austin surveyed frontiers of Abyssinia (1899–1901)

Grendon mission explored the region between the Ogowé and the Congo, continuing the work of De Brazza and Mizon

Hostains and Captain d'Ollone explored the hinterland of the Ivory Coast and French Guinea, ascending the Cavally basin to Beyla, and thence to Konakry (1899–1900)

M. S. Wellby journeyed to Lake Rudolf by the Omo River and explored part of the course of the Sobat

J. J. Harrison made journey from Zeila to Lake Stefanie (1899–1900)

1900

Jan. 10, First train reached Khartum from Cairo

Jan. 12–June, 1901, Journey of Oscar Neumann and Baron von Erlanger from Zeila to Khartum chiefly through unknown country. Baron von Erlanger made zoölogical investigations in southern Abyssinia traveling from Zeila to Harrar and to Galla region and the Sobat making a map of the route

Feb. 2, Foureau-Lamy mission arrived at Lake Chad

April 22, French conquest of the Lake Chad kingdoms. *See* French Equatorial Africa

May 19, International Convention for preservation of wild animals in Africa from 20° N. to the Zambezi and north of German South West Africa

May 24, Proclamation of annexation of Orange Free State by Great Britain

June 6, Paul Blanchard arrived at Atar, capital of Adrar, Mauretania

June 27, Franco-Spanish Boundary Convention defined possessions in West Africa

Sept. 1, Proclamation of annexation of South African Republic (Transvaal) by Great Britain

Dec. 28, Death of Serpa Pinto, Portuguese explorer

Belgian expedition of Captain C. le Maire explored upper Zambezi and the Congo-Zambezi divide on scientific mission to Katanga

Dr. Kandt finished surveys in Lake Kivu region and Dr. Kölshutter scientific surveys of German East Africa, Dècle of region west of Lake Victoria between the Upper Kagera and the lake

1901

Jan., Captain Loefler from Carnot on the Sangha made journey to Lake Chad through the valley of the Logone, tributary of the Shari, which he explored

Jan. 12, Anglo-Portuguese Boundary Convention ceded land on Lake Nyasa to Portugal

Feb. 23, Anglo-German Boundary Convention defined Nyasa-Tanganyika frontiers

Sept. 26, Ashanti formally annexed by Great Britain

Captain E. Lenfant navigated the Bussa rapids on the Niger River

Vicomte R. du Bourg de Bozas explored region between Harrar and northern end of Lake Rudolf and between Lake Rudolf and the Nile at Nimule (1901–1903)

1902

Feb. 21, Death of Dr. Emil Holub, Austrian explorer

Feb. 22, Major P. H. G. Powell-Cotton began journey from Mombassa through northern Uganda

March 26, Death of Cecil Rhodes

——, German expedition headed by Colonel Pavel left Garua on Upper Benue and reached Lake Chad May 3

May, Agreement signed for extension of Cape to Cairo Railroad to Lake Kasala from northern boundary of Rhodesia

May 31, Peace Treaty signed, ending South African War

Colonel Destenave completed first survey of Lake Chad and Lower Shari

July 17, M. A. Chevalier started from Brazzaville on voyage up Congo and Ubangi to Bangui and proceeded to the Shari River, reaching its sources and exploring practically unknown country to southwest of Darfur

July, Captain Lenfant sailed from France on mission to examine possible routes to Lake Chad by way of the Benue and Kebbi rivers instead of by the Congo and Niger, reached Garua on the Benue, Aug. 26, ascended the Kebbi and discovered Lata Falls, and continued up river to point of its issue from Tuburi

Nov. 2, Archibald Butter and Philip Maud left Adis Ababa and journeyed to Lake Rudolf and Lake Baringo, making survey of Galla-Somali uplands between Lake Rudolf and the Upper Juba, Lake Stefanie reached for the third time by Europeans

Journey of Lieutenant Cottenest from In Salah to Ideles, in Ahaggar and Guilo-Lohain in Sahara

Captain Loefler explored the Logone, tributary of the Shari, from the south-west

Dec. 12, Anglo-German Convention as to boundaries Yola-Lake Chad

1903

June 12, Captain Boyd Cunninghame started from Kakonda, traveled to Chisambe, to Kissalonga and Kwanza Rivers and south-west to Cunene

Aug. 4, Captain Lenfant began ascent of the Benue from Lokoja, after voyage up the Lower Niger, thence to Yola, to Garua (Aug. 26) to Kebbi and Logone rivers to Lake Chad, proving that at certain months of the year there is an almost continuous water communication between the Atlantic and Lake Chad, returning Oct. 29 down the Logone reaching Fort Lamy, Nov. 4

Herrero rebellion in German South West Africa

Lapérine made journey from Tuat to In Sise in the Sahara

1904

Jan. 13, A. St. H. Gibbons landed at Mombassa and proceeded to Guas Ngishu plateau, East Africa

Feb. 27, Expedition of Captain Boyd Alexander left England beginning 3 year exploration across Africa

from the Niger to the Nile, arriving at Lokoja on March 24, survey of rivers of Northern Nigeria, and the country between the Benue and Lake Chad, and showed that Lake Chad was not a continuous sheet of water but 2 larger lakes joined by a series of small lakes. Reached Port Sudan on return journey Jan. 14, 1907

March 14, Colonel Lapérine made journey from Tidikelt to Adrar, the first European to cross this part of the desert, meeting there Theveniaut who had made the journey from Timbuktu

April 8, Anglo-French Boundary Convention, Isles de Los ceded to France. *See also* Egypt, Morocco

June 12, Colonel W. H. Broun left Fort Hall, making journey to the Lorain swamp

July 6, C. W. Hobley started journey of exploration of region between Lakes Nakuro and Baringo and the western Laikipia

July, Journey of Dr. F. Uhlig and Dr. F. Jaeger, ascent of Mt. Kilimanjaro, visit to Lake Mweru and Lake Victoria Nyanza and Lake Natron

——, V. Dickens explored south-east Mashonaland and corrected map as to the rivers in that region

Nov. 2, Major Powell-Cotton left London for Khartum, crossing Africa from Mombassa by way of Lake Rudolf to White Nile, exploring region between the Zambezi and the Nile

1905

Jan. 13, Anglo-Italian Agreement, lease to Italy of land near Kismayu

——, Cession of Benadir ports to Italy. *See* Somaliland, Italian

March 5, Peace Agreement with the Mullah ended war. *See* Somaliland

March 31, Visit of German Emperor to Tangier. *See* Morocco

May 12, M. E. F. Gautier started from Tuat on journey from Algeria to the Niger, reaching Gao on the Niger Oct. 5 from Adrar

H. Weld Blundell surveyed the Blue Nile from Addis Abeba to about 35° E., continuing work he began in 1899

Captain Flye Sainte-Marie began exploration of the desert west of Tuat

1906

Jan. 16, Algeciras Conference

Jan. 18, Successful ascent of secondary ridges of Ruwenzori Mountains by Grauer, Tegart, and Maddox

April 7, General Act as to Morocco of Algeciras Conference. *See* Morocco

July 1, Death of George Grenfell, explorer, at Basoko

July 9, Colonel Lapérine at Tuat on Sahara expedition

Nov. 3, International Convention as to liquor traffic in Africa

Dec. 6, Boundary Convention between Abyssinia and Great Britain. *See* Abyssinia

Dec. 23, Submission of Bondelwarts and Hottentots to Germans

Captain Arnaud crossed the Sahara from Algeria to Dahomey, covered over 3,000 miles of which 750 were over new country

H. Vischer crossed the desert from Tripoli to Bornu, the first Englishman of modern times to make the journey

The Duke of the Abruzzi ascended the Ruwenzori, reaching twin summits (16,800 feet) which he named

Margherita and Alexander, and made first detailed map of mountains

1907

Jan., Baron von Stein, starting from Yaunde in Cameroons, explored the Upper Sanaga and little known country between the Sanaga and Wuri

Jan.–Feb., 1908, Captain Tilho explored Lake Chad region from the Niger to lake (Anglo-French Boundary Commission)

June 9, Scientific expedition of the Duke of Mecklenburg arrived at Bukoba, on west coast of Lake Victoria Nyanza, visited Lake Kivu, Lake Albert Edward, and the Semlike valley

July, Captain Aylmer left Kibwezi and explored the country south of the Tana River to the Tiva River

Sept., Expedition of Professor Kurt Hassert and Professor Thorbeck to Kamerun Mountain and to north-east

Nov. 28, Annexation Treaty concluded between Belgium and the Congo Free State

1908

March, Major Bright and Captain Jack began delimitation of Uganda boundary

July 30, Major Gwynn began journey from Dire Daua into southern Abyssinia delimiting boundary, returning, May 10, 1909, the main caravan having traveled over 2,000 miles and some of the detachments over 3,000 miles

Nov. 4, Belgium assumed sovereignty over Congo State

Nov. 20, H. K. W. Kumm left Lokoja and made journey from Hausaland to Egypt

Dec. 23, Belgium and France renewed arrangement of Feb. 5, 1895 as to French right of preëmption, Belgian Congo

Dr. Pöch reached Oas, German South West Africa, taking anthropological measurements of natives

1909

Feb., Captain W. C. Macfie began survey of Uganda, first accurate topographical survey of large block of country of tropical Africa (14,000 square miles)

Cortier and Niéger made surveys in north and central Sahara desert including the Tazili plateau, Ahaggar and Air, including much new country

April 23, Theodore Roosevelt sailed for Africa on scientific expedition under auspices of the Smithsonian Institution, proceeding inland from Mombassa and returning from Gondokoro Feb., 1910, bringing back 11,000 specimens of African fauna and variegated flora

Dec. 12, Boyd Alexander expedition left England, planning to cross from Cameroons to Khartum, proceeded from Fort Lamy on the Shari reaching Abesher, capital of Wadi, March 4, March 28 at Dar Tama, and April 2 Alexander killed by natives at village of Nieri

G. F. Archer explored region in north of Kenya

1910

March 1, George Montandon left Addis Ababa for the south-west, proceeding to the Wosho River making scientific investigation of Gimirra country

May 31, Union of South Africa inaugurated

July 9, Second expedition of the Duke of Mecklenburg

left Germany for Africa to explore boundary between the Cameroons and French Equatorial Africa

Nov.–Dec., 1911, Count René Le Mare crossed west Sahara from Algiers to Timbuktu and return

1911

Feb. 27, The expedition of the Duke of Mecklenburg divided into 3 parties, the first to Lake Chad and south to Bagirmi country, the second to the southern Cameroons, and the third to Upper Ubangi and Upper Nile

May, Hans Meyer returned to East Africa and proceeded to Bukoba and to Lake Kivu and explored the Kirunga group of volcanoes

July 1, Second Morocco crisis, German warship sent to Morocco. *See* Morocco

Sept.–May, 1914, Anglo-Belgian Boundary Commission delimited boundary

Sept. 29, Italian invasion and conquest of Tripoli and Cyrenaica. *See* Libya

Nov. 6, G. F. Archer and Colonel Thesiger started from Serenli, Somaliland, for Lake Rudolf exploring country south-west of the lake

Captain E. M. Jack explored region north-east of Lake Kivu and west of Lake Victoria Nyanza, and Mfumbiro range of volcanoes

Captain Strümpel surveyed last unknown stretch of Benue River

Captain H. D. Pearson in upper Nile basin explored head streams of the Pibor, western branch of the Sobat

1912

Jan. 17–Nov. 18, French expedition headed by Captain J. Nieger made preliminary survey for Trans-Sahara railroad to connect South Algeria with Lake Chad district and central valley of the Niger

March 30, Protectorate Treaty with France signed by the Sultan of Morocco

March, C. Christy reached Iturbi River and explored country to south and Semliki rift

March–Jan., 1914, Expedition of Jacques de Rohan Jabot in southern Angola, in Cunene basin and on borders of the Zambezi River

June, Jean Tilho appointed to command in Kanem made investigations between 1912 and 1917 of possible connection between basins of the Nile and Lake Chad, and made journeys to Tibesti, Erdi Borku, and Ennedi

Oct.–March, Anglo-German Boundary Commission delimited Kamerun-Nigeria frontier between Yola and Cross River

Oct. 15, Treaty of Lausanne signed by Italy and Turkey established Italian sovereignty in Tripoli and Cyrenaica. *See also* Libya

Nov., I. N. Dracopoli proceeded from Mombassa to Jubaland and investigated the Lorian Swamp, the first white man to penetrate west of 41° 30′. He discovered that in wet seasons water flows from the swamp to the Indian Ocean (1912–1913)

Nov. 27, Spanish zones in Morocco defined in Convention between France and Spain

R. H. Leeke explored country between Bahr-el-Jebel and Lake Rudolf

First ascent of second highest peak of Kilimanjaro, Mt. Mawenzi, by Eduard Oehler and F. Klute

Sir Alfred Sharp and M. Elphinstone explored little known districts west of Lake Kivu (1912–1913)

1913

Captain R. Walker showed that the Luapula did not issue from Lake Bangweulu but was a direct continuation of the Chambezi

Captain Augiéras began series of journeys to the southwest of Tuat

1914

Feb. 1, Railroad from Dar-es-Salaam to Lake Tanganyika at Kigoma completed, 777 miles, making it possible to reach the lake in 2 days from the seacoast, the trip by caravan taking 42 days

Aug. 23, Germany asked the United States to ask the Powers to observe neutrality of the Congo Basin according to Congo Act which would have included one-third of the Cameroons, and all of German East Africa. Reply of the United States Oct. 7 after Germany had taken the initiative in hostilities. For Africa in the War *see* World War, and names of country divisions

Dec. 18, British Protectorate over Egypt proclaimed

1915

March, The first railway and steamer route across Africa completed by opening of railroad from Kabalo to Albertville

April 26, By Article XIII of the Treaty of London, Great Britain, France, and Russia agreed that in the event of extension of French and British colonial possessions in Africa, Italy to receive compensation by rectification of boundaries in Eritrea, Somaliland, and Libya

June 12, Captain Frank J. Magee and Lieutenant J. R. Lee left England with boats to launch on Lake Tanganyika, which were dragged across the forests of the Belgian Congo and launched on lake, Dec. 23, and in engagement Dec. 26 captured the German gunboat "Kingani"

June 25, All railroad east to west route effected by completion of Prieska to Kalkfontein connection

July 15, Proclamation announced annexation of German South West Africa to the Union of South Africa for customs purposes

Major Cuthbert Christy made 10 months journey along the Congo-Nile divide where it forms frontier of Anglo-Egyptian Sudan

1915–1917

Surveys made of Libyan Desert by Dr. John Ball, Captain C. H. Williams, and Captain A. S. Lindsay

1918

May, The Cape to Cairo Railroad completed to Bukama on the Lualaba in Belgian Congo making it possible by the Congo and Tanganyika systems to travel alternately by train and steamer from the Cape to Cairo with only 2 breaks comprising about 300 miles, the southern from Tabora to Mwanza, and the northern from Nimule to Rejaf along banks of an unnavigable part of the Upper Nile

1919

May 7, The Supreme Council of the Peace Conference made preliminary division of former German territories assigned as mandates. *See* p. 560

June 28, By Treaty of Versailles Germany renounced African colonies

Sept. 8, Anglo-French Boundary Convention settled frontier of Darfur and Wadai in dispute since 1899

Sept. 10, Convention of St. Germain-en-Laye revised Act of Berlin of Feb. 26, 1885 and General Act and Declaration of Brussels of July 2, 1890

——, Liquor Traffic Convention signed by the United States, British Empire, France, Belgium, Italy, Japan, and Portugal, prohibition of importation of liquor and manufacture in African territory

——, International Convention for control of trade in arms and ammunition

1920

Feb., First attempt to cross Africa in aëroplane made by Dr. P. Chalmers Mitchell, the machine crashing, Feb. 27 at Tabora a little over half-way over from Cairo

Feb. 22–March 20, First successful flight from Cairo to Cape Town made by Colonel Sir H. A. van Ryneveld, and Major Sir C. J. Brand of the South African forces, using 3 machines, flying time 72 hours and 40 minutes

Feb.–March, Major Vulleman and a companion flew from Algiers across the Sahara to the Niger at Gao, and from there to Dakar

Oct. 29, Captain Augiéras left Algiers for Dakar

Dec. 5, Major Lauzanne started journey to Sahara from Atar, Mauretania

Dec. 17, Mandate for former German South West Africa to Union of South Africa approved by the Council of the League of Nations

Dec. 25, Expedition of Captain Augiéras from Algeria met in mid-desert at El Mzereb the expedition of Major Lauzanne which had started from Atar in Mauretania

French expedition headed by Courtot crossed the Sahara from north to south by motor to Lake Chad, route east of the Hoggar, Tunis, Fort Polignac, Djanet-Djado, Bilma, Lake Chad

1921

Jan. 14, Mrs. Rosita Forbes and Hassanein Bey reached Kufra in the Libyan Desert from Cyrenaica, Mrs. Forbes disguised as a Mohammedan woman, the oasis visited only once before by Europeans, G. Rohlfs and Anton Stecker in 1879, returning through Jaghbub and Siwa to Alexandria crossing some unknown country

Cape to Cairo aërial mail route established

Nov. 18, French mission for delimitation of boundary of Sudan and French Equatorial Africa arrived at El Fasher, M. Grossard at head, Colonel Pearson head of English mission

Journey of M. Bruneau de Laborie across the Sahara, and through Dahomey to Kano, Nigeria, northern Cameroons and to Fort Archambault to investigate economic possibilities of the Lake Chad region, returning from Abeshr north of Lake Chad to Zinder and across the Sahara to Algiers by way of Air and Ahaggar

1922

April, F. R. Rodd left Kano for Air in Sahara Desert

July 20, Mandates for former German colonies approved by Council of the League of Nations. *See* p. 566

Dec.–March, 1923, Scientific Italian expedition of Corni, Calciati, and Bracciani explored northern Eritrea especially less known districts between Gash and Setit rivers

Dec. 17, French expedition headed by M. Haardt started from Tuggurt across the Sahara Desert in 5 Citroen motor cars with caterpillar attachments proceeding to Wargla and Insalah and reaching the Niger River, Jan. 4, and Timbuktu, Jan. 7, reaching Tuggurt on return journey, March 6, 1923

Dec. 26, Anglo-Italian Treaty rectification of boundaries of Eritrea and Sudan

1923

Jan. 2, Hassanein Bey started from Sollum to make second journey to the Kufra Oasis and to the Sudan beyond traveling to Siwa and Jaghbub and Jalo reaching Kufra (Kufara), April 1, and from there he crossed unexplored desert from Furawiya, Darfur (July 2) by Erdi hills and uncharted oases of Arkenu and Owenat, and returning to Egypt through El Fasher to El Obeid and the railroad from there to Khartum, arriving in Cairo, Aug. 1

Jan., Bruneau de Labordie left Duala for French Cameroons traveling by motor to Yaunde and by canoe to Fort Lamy, and up the Shari by boat to Fort Archambault, and thence to Abeshr and by caravan (camels) to Faya, Borku (Sept. 11), to Kufra and Jaghbub, arriving at Port Said, Jan. 2, 1924

Feb. 16, The tomb of Tutankh-Amen opened by Howard Carter in Egypt

March 1, Prince Kemal el Din Hussein accompanied by John Ball started motor trip from Kharga to Kufra over Rohlfs' itinerary

May, Colonel J. C. B. Statham started journey from Mossamedes to Victoria Falls

July, Marseilles-Algiers Air route opened by way of Barcelona and Palma bringing Marseilles within 10 hours of Algiers as against 30 hours by ship

Dec. 2, Prince Kemal el Din Hussein accompanied by John Ball started motor trip from Cairo to Baharia, Farafra, and Dakhla

Italian expedition of Major V. Tedesco-Zammarano examined lower course of the Webbe River, and expedition of Corni to study anthropology and natural history of Eritrea

French scientific expeditions sent during the year to ascertain the resources of the French possessions were Balzac (Tunisian ornithology), Babault (Saharian fauna), Brassard and Owenart-Daryur, boundary surveys

Dec. 18, Tangier Statute adopted. *See* Morocco

Dec. 28, Protocol defined frontiers of French Equatorial Africa and the Anglo-Egyptian Sudan

1924

Jan. 4, Edmond Tranin reached Lake Chad from Konakry, French Guinea, by way of Jibuti and Bamako

Jan. 10, Protocol defined frontier of Wadai and Darfur

July 15, Anglo-Italian Treaty by which Juba River and a strip on British side of river ceded to Italy

Oct. 28, French expedition headed by Haardt and Audouin-Dubreuil in 8 Citroen-Kegresse caterpillar motor cars left Colomb-Bechar and traveled to Lake Chad, Dec. 16, reaching Mao Kanem, Dec. 20 and Fort Lamy 8 days later (149 hours for journey)

Nov., First crossing of Africa from north to south by motor by Captain Delingette accompanied by his wife from Oran to Cape Town (Nov.–July 4)

Dec.–Jan. 17, 1925, Prince Kemal accompanied by

John Ball on motor trip to Tarfoui, and Ouenat Mountain

1925

Jan. 3, Haardt and Audouin-Dubreuil motor expedition proceeded to Bangui reached Jan. 11

April, T. A. Leach made journey to Selima Oasis

Sept. 19, Death of Georg Schweinfurth, explorer, in Berlin

Dec. 6, Anglo-Italian Convention by which Jaghbub (Jarabub) Oasis included in Cyrenaica

Dec. 26–Feb. 23, 1926, Prince Kemal and John Ball made motor trip in Libyan Desert from Kharga to Dakla and Ouenat Mountain

1926

May 15, Harvard University African expedition headed by Dr. Richard P. Strong left New York to make study of tropical diseases in Belgian Congo and medical survey of Liberia (1926–1927)

Sept. 25, International Slavery Convention signed at Geneva by representatives of 20 States

Oct.–March, 1927, Scientific investigation of Tibesti by Commander Rottier

Nov. 17, Death of Carl Akeley in Central Africa on his fifth journey for the American Museum of National History

1927

May, F. R. Rodd began second journey to Air and west to Tuareg country from Kalsen, Nigeria, and then west to Timbuktu and the Niger

Oct. 28, W. B. K. Shaw and D. Newbold left El Obeid and explored Libyan Desert west of the Nile in Dongola and Halfa provinces

Nov. 14–March, 1928, Journey by motor of Augiéras and Draper from Silet, Algeria, to the Sahara and Timbuktu and then Dakar

1928

March 28, L. M. Nesbitt from Addis Ababa made journey from south to north in Danakil country

June 20, Captain B. E. H. Clifford made motor journey from Mahalapye through the Kalahari Desert

July 25, Protocol revising Tangier Statute signed by representatives of Spain, France, Great Britain, and Italy

1929

Jan. 26–April 6, French mission headed by Prince Sixte de Bourbon made journey across the Sahara from Algiers to Lake Chad, opening motor route

March 13, Journey of Captain Crofton and Owen Tweedy across Nile-Congo divide by motor from Rejaf to Lake Chad, to Kano, Gao on Niger and to Algiers

Dec., Journey of Comte Lagarde from Djibuti to Khartum reached, Jan. 31

1930

Expedition of Major Bagnold in motor cars covered 3,100 miles of desert in search of lost Oasis of Zerzura which was not found

ABYSSINIA

The ancient Empire of Abyssinia, or Ethiopia, includes the former kingdoms of Tigré, in the northeast; Amhara and Gojjam, in the center, and

Shoa in the south; besides many other smaller and formerly independent or quasi-independent dependencies, together with the modern acquisitions to the south, Harrar, and the Galla, Shankalla, and Dankali territories. The following are the principal provinces into which the country is divided: Harrar, Wollo, Gurage, Kaffa, Gore, Sayu, Benishangul, Wogera, Southern Tigré, Adowa and Aksun, Sokota, Lasta, Goffa, Nekemti (Lekempti) and the Western Galla countries, Sellale, Wollaga, Gimira, Sidamo, Arussi, Borana, Gojjam, Gondar, Jimma. The whole area is 350,000 sq. miles.

No reliable figures of population exist, but recent estimates indicate a figure of about 10,000,000. The Abyssinians, properly so called, number rather less than 3 millions, and inhabit the provinces of Tigré, Amhara, Gojjam, and Shoa (in part), covering an area of over one-third of the whole country. They are Christians, and are of Hamitic origin, semiticized by waves of Semitic invasion from Arabia and adulterated by intermarriage with Negro and other conquered races. The Gallas, some of whom are Christian, some Moslem, and some Pagan, comprise more than two-thirds of the entire population, and are a pastoral and agricultural people of Hamitic origin. Ogaden, Issa, and other Somalis inhabit Harrar, the Somaliland plateau, and the southeast. The Danakil are Mohammedans, and are still somewhat turbulent. There are also Negroes (in the southwest), and the Falashas (of Jewish religion), in the northeast center with a growing number of foreigners (Indians, Arabs, Armenians, Europeans) in the towns.

There are few towns in Abyssinia in our sense of the word—Addis Ababa, Dire Dawa, and Harrar being the most important. Addis Ababa, the capital, has 60,000 to 70,000 inhabitants with a foreign population of several thousands, of whom the majority are British Indian and British Arab subjects, Greeks, and Armenians. Dire Dawa contains about 30,000 people, of whom about 300 are Europeans, and the old walled city of Harar has a population of about 40,000, with about 100 foreigners, mostly Indians and Arabs. Other important towns, politically or commercially, are: Debra Markos, capital of Gojjam, 5,000; Gondar, capital of Amhara, 3,000; Adua, capital of Tigré, 5,000; Axum, ancient capital of Ethiopia, 5,000; Antalo, former capital of Tigré, 1,000; Ankober, former capital of Shoa, 2,000; Debra-Tabor and Makallé; Gore, Saiyu, Nekemti, Sameré, 3,000–4,000, and Sokoto, 1,500, important trading centers. Gambeila, in Western Abyssinia, is a trading station leased to the Sudan Government.

Its ancient history is very uncertain. The Kingdom of the Axumitæ (its chief town Axum) flourished in the 1st and 2nd centuries after Christ. Christianity was introduced about 329 by Frumentius, consecrated Bishop of Abyssinia by St. Athanasius. Between 470 and 480 monasteries were established. In 522 Caleb, King of Abyssinia, at the request of the Emperor Justinian, conquered Yemen. The Ethiopians possessed at that time the richest part of Arabia, traded to India, and were in constant communication with Greece. In the 7th century the Mohammedans expelled them from Arabia, and by the conquest of Egypt cut them off from the civilized world. About 960, Judith, a Jewish princess, murdered a great part of the royal family, and reigned forty years. The young King escaped: and the royal house was restored in 1268 in the person of his descendant Icon Amlac. In the middle ages it was said to be ruled by Prester John, or Prete Janni. The Portuguese missions, commenced in the 15th century, after much struggling against opposition, were expelled about 1633. The encroachments of the Gallas and intestine disorders soon after broke up the empire into petty governments. From the visits of James Bruce, 1768–73; Henry Salt, 1809–10; Edward Rüppell, 1834–37; Major Harris, 1841; Mansfield Parkyns, 1844–47, much information respecting Abyssinia has been gained. Several expeditions into Abyssinia have been organized by the French Government. The brothers Antoine and Arnauld Abbadie visited the country 1837–45. Abyssinia was divided into four provinces. In 1847, Ras Ali was ruler of Amhara; Ras Ubie of Tigré and Samien; and Sahela Selassie of Shoa. The ruler of Abyssinia is termed *Negus*, a title dating from the 13th century.

After the overthrow of the Emperor Theodore by the British in 1868, the suzerain power passed to Prince Kassai of Tigré, who assumed the old title of Negusa Nagast ("King of Kings"), and was crowned in 1872 as John II, Emperor of Ethiopia. After the death of this potentate in 1889, Menelik II, King of Shoa (born 1844), became the supreme ruler of Abyssinia. Menelik died in December, 1913, and was succeeded by Lij Yasu, born in 1896, son of his second daughter, Waizeru Shoaragga and Ras Mikael, the chief of the Wollo Gallas.

On September 27, 1916, Lij Yasu was deposed by public proclamation, and Zauditu, another daughter of Menelik, was nominated Empress and "Queen of Kings of Ethiopia," and Ras Taffari son of Ras Makonnen, and great-nephew of Menelik, proclaimed heir to the throne.

Emperor.—Haile Silassie I, born July 17, 1891; crowned King (Negus) on October 7, 1928, and proclaimed Emperor, after the death of the Empress Zauditu, on April 3, 1930. Married Waizeru Menen in 1912, and has 2 sons and 3 daughters. On January 25, 1931, the eldest son, Asfaou Wosan was proclaimed Crown Prince and heir to the throne.

1841

Nov. 16, Treaty of commerce with the King of Shoa concluded by Great Britain

1849

Nov. 2, Treaty of friendship between Great Britain and Ras Ali, ruler of Amhara, concluded

1855

Feb. 11, Ras Ali deposed by his son-in-law Theodore, who is crowned, and takes the title of Negus, or King of Kings

Protestant missionaries received, replacing Roman Catholics

1860 to 1862

1860, Walter Plowden (who had joined the party of Theodore) killed by rebels, Feb.; his friend Bell killed soon after, when avenging him; Theodore overcomes the rebels and massacres about 150 prisoners as a sacrifice to their manes

Feb. 9, 1862, Captain C. D. Cameron appointed to succeed Consul Plowden; arrived at Massowah; goes to Abyssinia, May; received by Theodore, Oct. 7; is sent away with a letter for Queen Victoria, desiring alliance against the Turks; which arrived, Feb. 12, 1863

1863

June, It is decided that this letter is not to be answered; Cameron, ordered by Earl Russell to remain at Massowah, returns to Abyssinia

Oct., Rev. H. Stern, missionary, beaten and imprisoned for alleged intrusion upon Theodore

1864

Jan. 3, Cameron, and all British subjects and missionaries, imprisoned for pretended insults; report of imprisonment reached London, May 7; prisoners sent to Magdala, and chained like criminals, Nov.

July 24, Mr. Hormuzd Rassam, a Chaldee Christian, first assistant British political resident at Aden, sent on mission to Abyssinia; arrives at Massowah; Lieut. Prideaux and Dr. Blanc appointed to accompany him

1865

Aug. 12, Mr. Rassam having negotiated without effect for a year, Mr. Gifford Palgrave is appointed by Earl Russell to go to Abyssinia, July; but is stopped on the intelligence that Theodore has invited Rassam to come to him

1866

Jan. 28, Mr. Rassam, Lieut. Prideaux, and Dr. Blanc arrive at Matemma from Massowah, Nov. 21, 1865; and are well received by Theodore

About April 13, Prisoners released, March 12; all seized and imprisoned

1867

April 16, Lord Stanley's ultimatum to Theodore, demanding release of the captives in three months (not received), sent

May, Mr. Flad received by the King, and made to join his family in prison

Sept. 9, A formal letter from the British Government sent to Theodore (never arrived)

Sept. 14, Preparations for war; Sir Robert Napier appointed commander of an expedition; pioneer force sails from Bombay

Oct. 21, Advanced brigade (3,500) sail from Bombay, Oct. 7, 8; land at Zoulla

Oct. 26, Napier's proclamation issued in Abyssinia

Nov. 11, Captives at Magdala reported well

Nov. 19, The British parliament meets; the Queen's speech announces the war; 2,000,000*l.* voted, Nov. 26, 27

Nov. 25, Report that the Gallas have joined the revolt against Theodore

1868

Third ultimatum sent by Sir R. Napier; intercepted by a rebel chief and given to Mr. Rassam, who suppressed it as likely to endanger the lives of the captives

Jan. 4, Arrival of Sir R. Napier at Annesley Bay

March 29, The captives relieved of their chains

April 2, Sir R. Napier arrives below Magdala

April 9, Theodore massacres about 300 native prisoners

April 10, Battle of Arogee; Theodore's troops attack the British first brigade; defeated with much slaughter

April 11, Theodore requests Mr. Rassam to mediate; Lieut. Prideaux sent to Sir R. Napier, returns with a letter; Theodore receives it indignantly, and sends an insulting reply

April 12, Theodore sends a letter of apology offering a present of cattle; Mr. Rassam understanding this present to have been accepted, tells the King's agents; the European artisans and families sent to the British camp

April 13, Part of the Abyssinian troops mutiny; Magdala bombarded and stormed; Theodore kills himself

April 17, Magdala burnt to the ground

May 10, Death of Theodore's queen

May 28, Henry Dufton of the "Intelligence department" shot by Shosho robbers

June 2, Immediate return of the troops;—all had embarked

June 21, Troops arrive at Plymouth; Sir R. Napier at Dover, July 2

July 14, Theodore's son Alamayoú, aged 7, arrives at Plymouth; presented to Queen Victoria, July 16

1871

June 21, War between Gobazye, King of Amhara and Kassa, King of Tigré; Kassa victor

July 11, Gobazye beaten and taken prisoner

Nov. 21, Kassa proposes to be crowned Emperor and Negus of all Abyssinia; punishes the Catholic missionaries for partisanship; and forms alliance with Egypt, July

1872 to 1887

Jan. 12, 1872, Kassa crowned at Axum as Johanni II

1873–74, Said to be ruling tyrannically

Oct. 16, 1875, War with Egypt; the Khedive's troops enter Abyssinia; the natives retire, but surprise and defeat the Egyptians at Kherad Iska (a massacre), and at Gonda Gouddi (a desperate fight)

Feb. 17–19, 1876, Abyssinians defeated in three days' conflict

Middle of June, 1877, King Johanni totally defeats Menelek, King of Shoa

Oct., 1879, Col. Gordon concludes peace; Abyssinia to have a port

Nov. 14, Prince Alamayoú dies at Leeds, buried at Windsor

May 21, 1883, Treaty with Italy opened trade route between Assab Bay and Shoa

June 3, 1884, Treaty with Great Britain and Egypt, Bogos restored to Abyssinia, suppression of slave trade

For disputes with Italy *see* Eritrea

Dec. 10–16, 1887, Mr. Portal and a mission from Queen Victoria to mediate between Italy and Abyssinia received by the King, after much delay; without effect

1888

Feb. 1, The Italians march to Saati to form a camp, announced

Feb. 6, Abyssinians defeated in a skirmish

March 4, Slight beginning of actual hostilities; slight firing near Saati, March 28; the Negus, through deficiency in commissariat, &c., sues for peace; two chiefs sent to General San Marzano, March 29

April 2, The Negus refuses the terms and retires

April 13 *et seq.*, The Italian troops return to Italy

Dec., Rebellion of Menelek, King of Shoa, against King John

1889

March 12, The Negus is stated to have been defeated in his attack on the dervishes, March 10; and to have been attacked and killed by them

May 2, Treaty of friendship and commerce with Italy, adjusted boundaries and provided that negotiations with foreign Powers should be made through the Italian Government; Italian notification of the Powers of conduct of foreign relations, Oct. 12

Oct. 1, Additional Convention to Treaty of Uccialli signed with Italy recognized Menelik as Emperor and guaranteed loan to Abyssinia of 4,000,000 lire to be contracted with Italian bank under guarantee of Italian Government which was negotiated by a further Convention on Oct. 26

Nov. 3, Menelik crowned Negus of Abyssinia

Nov.–Dec., Ras Mangascia and other opponents of Menelek defeated

1890

Jan. 27, Gen. Orero, on behalf of Menelek, marches on Adua, and is warmly received

March 17, Submission of Degiac Mangascia; he meets Count Antonelli at Adowa, May 16

1891

Feb. 9, Rupture with Italy on interpretation of the Treaty of May 2, 1889

March 24, Great Britain recognized Italian Protectorate over Abyssinia

March, Count Antonelli visits the Negus in relation to the treaty; Count leaves, Feb. 11; the Negus writes to King Humbert

Sept. 29, The chief Debeb defeated and killed by the chiefs Mangascia and Ras Alula

1893

Feb. 11, and March 9, 1894, and Nov. 5, 1896, Concessions for building railroad from Jibuti to Addis Ababa granted by Menelik

1894

July 17, Capture of Kassala by Italians and Adowa, Dec. 28. *See* Eritrea for war

1895

Sept. 17, Proclamation of the Negus called on his subjects to resist the Italian invasion

Dec. 7–8, Defeat of the Italians in battle and retreat. *See* Eritrea

1896

March 1, Italians defeated by Abyssinians at the Battle of Adowa

Oct. 26, Treaty of Adis Ababa with Italy signed, independence of Abyssinia recognized

1897

Feb., Death of Ras Alula, Chief and General

March 20, Treaty with France relative to frontier of French coastal zone

March, Italian expedition under Captain Bottego attacked by Abyssinians in the Gabo district and the Captain and 66 men killed

May 14, Treaty with Great Britain, frontiers with British Somaliland, and suppression of slave trade and Note of June 4

June 24, Commercial Treaty with Italy signed

July 28, Commercial Treaty with Great Britain signed

1898

April, Abyssinian expedition with French officers started with plan to occupy right bank of White Nile between Sobat and Fashoda, reached June 22, but retired without effecting junction with Marchand. *See* Sudan

1899

Jan. 11, Ras Makunen (ruler of Tigré) is defeated by Ras Mangascia

Feb., Ras Mangasha taken prisoner

Mid April, The Marchand mission welcomed at Adis Abeba

June, Concession granted to Leontiev (Russian) for exploitation of district northeast of Lake Rudolf

Capt. Wellby explores the mountain districts of Kambat, Walamo, and Gamo (10,500 ft. alt.), lakes Rudolf and Gallop, and discovers two sources of the river Sobat, &c., Jan.–July [died of his wounds in the S. African war, Aug. 5, 1900]

Sept., Capt. Bulatovich crosses the region S. of Kaffa and W. of the Omo, and discovers a chain of mountains, reported

Dec. 25, Concessions granted to English and to French company in Beni Shangul country and Wallega country respectively, to search for gold

1900

March 19, Mahdist bands beaten by Ethiopians in Ogaden

July 10, Italian frontier, the Mareb-Belesa-Muna line, settled, March, 1899; treaty signed

1901

July 17, Successful expedition against the Mad Mullah; *see* Somaliland

Sept. 6, Major Austin's Anglo-Abyssinian frontier expedition to delimit boundary between Lake Rudolf and the Sobat, Oct. *et seq.*, 1899, returned, Oct., 1900, left Omdurman December, surveyed and mapped country between Nasser and the north of Lake Rudolf (45 Sudanese died), reached Mombasa

1902

Feb. 6, Railroad Convention with France signed

March 18, Exchange of Notes with Great Britain as to waters of Blue Nile and Lake Tana

May 15, Boundary of the British Sudan fixed, agreement signed and Great Britain agreed to construct railroad from Uganda to Sudan through Abyssinia, and leased territory on the Baro River for a commercial station

——, S. W. boundary of Eritrea settled, protocol signed

Sept. 9, Ras Makunen, Emperor's envoy, visits England, June 23–July; France, mid July; received by the King, made K.C.M.G., London, Aug. 8; returns to Zibuti

1903

Jan. 1, Railroad from French Somaliland reached Diredawa, formally opened by Menelik, Jan. 27

May 4, Troops coöperate with British against Mad Mullah; dervishes defeated, 300 killed

May 5, Party of exploration of S. Abyssinian frontier, under Mr. A. E. Butler, reached Lake Rudolf, having accomplished its purpose

Mid Oct., Emperor Menelek prohibits the slave trade, reported

Dec. 27, Commercial Treaty with the United States

1905

March 7, Commercial Treaty with Germany signed

March 21, Commercial Treaty with Austria-Hungary signed

March, Menelik granted charter to National Bank of Egypt for the establishment of a State bank in Abyssinia

1906

April 22, Mariam, an Abyssinian outlaw, raids several Soudanese villages in Soudan territory about 60 miles S. E. of Kedaref; 101 of the villagers killed, 41 men and 133 women seized and carried into Abyssinia, large number of cattle driven off, reported

May 22, Rebels defeated and Mariam killed, reported

July 4, Terms of an international agreement, relative to Abyssinia, finally settled, subject to the subsequent approval of the French and Italian Governments between Sir Edward Grey (England), M. Cambon (France), and Signor Tittoni (Italy). Maintenance of the *status quo* in Abyssinia to be guaranteed, protection of foreign interests or the lives and property of strangers; equality of the commercial rights of all countries to be recognized; the Ethiopian railway concession from Jibutil to Adis Abeba to be recognized, the company to remain French but to be reorganized and one British and one Italian director to be added to the board of direction

Sept. 6, Commercial Treaty with Belgium signed

Nov. 13, Death of Ras Mangascia, son of the late King John of Abyssinia, and rival to the Emperor Menelek

Dec. 13, The international agreement for preserving the integrity of Abyssinia signed in London

1907

Oct. 26, Decree issued by the Emperor Menelek announcing the formation of a cabinet on European lines

Nov. 2, Decree issued by the Emperor Menelek enjoining compulsory education on all male children over the age of 12

Dec. 6, Boundary Convention with Great Britain settled frontier with Uganda and East Africa, defining frontier from Dolo to the Sudan

About Dec. 12, 2,000 Abyssinians make an incursion into the regions of Baidoa, Revai, and Buracaba, plundering caravans, and killing or taking prisoners a number of merchants. The Italian *chargé d'affaires* at Adis Abeba was instructed to address, to the Emperor Menelek, a formal protest

1908

Jan. 10, New Treaty of amity and commerce with France signed

Jan. 17, Statement of Menelek that raid into Lugh district contrary to his orders

Jan. 30, Menelek granted railroad concession to new French company. *See* French Somaliland

May 16, Convention with Italy signed as to boundary and additional territory ceded to Italy including Lugh for 3 million lire

June 19, Official announcement to Powers that Menelek had appointed his grandson, Lij Yasu, son of his second daughter and Ras Mikael, Chief of the Wollo Gallas, his heir

July, First meeting of Council of Ministers constituted by the Emperor, of Justice, Finance, Commerce, War, and Foreign Affairs

Oct. 27, Public designation of Lij Yasu (born 1896) as his successor by Menelek and Ras Tesamma as Regent because of illness which incapacitated him as ruler

1909

April 13 and May 12, Treaties with Great Britain regulated import duties

Oct. 9, Victory of Ras Abata over Dejazmach Abraha in revolt at Kworam in Tigre

1910

March 10, Shoan Chiefs accused Ras Tesamma of allowing the Empress to usurp power and insisted on her complete withdrawal from Government, all her appointments canceled and the army she had gathered for her support disbanded

1911

April 10, Death of Ras Tesamma

May 15, Prince Lij Yasu proclaimed Emperor

1913

Dec. 12, Death of Menelek

1914

Feb. 24, Battle of Dejazmach Gabra Selassye with Ras Sebhat who had invaded his province in Tigre, Ras Sebhat and his 2 sons killed

March 3, Gabra Selassye defeated in battle by Ras Seyum Mangasha, sent to restore order at Maiken, and put to flight

June 1, Mikael, father of Lij Yasu, crowned Negus of Wollo Galla and Tigre

1916

April, Lij Yasu acknowledged overlordship of Turkish Sultan as Caliph sending to Turkish Consul General at Harrar an Abyssinian flag bearing the crescent, and openly adhered to Moslem religion, thereby antagonizing his subjects by his abandonment of the Christian national church

Sept. 27, Lij Yasu deposed as Emperor by head of the Abyssinian Church by public proclamation on the ground of apostasy. His aunt, Zauditu (Judith) proclaimed Empress and "Queen of Kings of Ethiopia," and Ras Taffari, son of Ras Makonnen, and great-nephew of Menelek, proclaimed heir to the throne with the title of Prince

Oct. 8, Lij Yasu fled from Harrar, a Moslem center, where he had received the news of his deposition, and proceeded to the Danakil country after publicly renouncing Islam

Oct. 9, Harrar occupied by the Shoans (Government troops) and 400 Somalis killed

Oct. 17, Ras Mikael defeated in engagement with Shoans under Ras Lul Seged

Oct. 19, Ras Mikael surrounded and defeated Shoans in battle in which 12,000 men killed including Ras Lul Seged

Oct. 22, Shoans under the Ras of Gondar (Waldo Giorgis) defeated force Mikael had left to guard his northern frontier at Wollo Galla

Oct. 27, Battle at Shano in which Mikael defeated and taken prisoner

1917

The Jibuti railroad reached Akaki from French Somaliland

Feb. 11, Zauditu crowned Empress

Dec., The town of Magdala where Lij Yasu had taken refuge surrendered but Li Yasu escaped capture

1918

Feb. 11, Death of Taitu, former Empress, wife of Menelek

May 21, Railroad completed to Addis Abbaba

Oct., Lij Yasu appealed to Turks in Arabia to help him, and organized raids against the Jibuti railway

1921

Jan., Lij Yasu captured by troops of the Government in the province of Tigré

1922

Feb. 18, Commercial Convention with Greece signed

1923

June, Decree revived ancient law making slave trading punishable by death; domestic slavery recognized

Sept. 28, Abyssinia admitted to membership in the League of Nations after adhering to Convention of St. Germain-en-Laye and Acts as to control of arms traffic and slavery in Africa

1924

Ras Tafari made visit of 5 months in Europe

1925

Dec. 14 and 20, Exchange of Notes of Great Britain and Italy as to economic spheres of influence in Abyssinia

1926

June 9, Notes communicated Anglo-Italian Notes relating to Abyssinia to Ras Tafari

June 19, Ras Tafari sent British and Italian Notes to League of Nations with protest against agreement made without consultation of the Abyssinian Government

Aug. 3, Note of British Government to the League stated that there was no intention of exerting economic pressure on Abyssinia

Aug. 7, Italian Note to League disclaimed intention to exert economic pressure upon Abyssinia

Sept. 30, Commercial Treaty with the Netherlands signed

1927

Aug. 14, British memorandum presented request for construction of dam at outlet of Lake Tsana

Nov. 7, Statement of Abyssinian representative that no contract had been signed with American company to construct dam across the Blue Nile and that Great Britain and the Sudan would be consulted as provided by Treaty

1928

Aug. 2, Treaty of friendship and arbitration with Italy signed and Agreement by which Italy agreed to lease to Abyssinia for nominal sum for 130 years land near port of Assab in Eritrea for seaport

Oct. 7, Regent Ras Tafari crowned King

1929

Jan. 26, Treaties of arbitration and conciliation with the United States signed

1930

March 1, Conclusion of contract with J. G. White Engineering Corporation of New York for construction of dam at outlet of Lake Tsana to impound waters of the Blue Nile

March 5, Announcement of Agreement with the Sudan Government as to construction of dam

March 31, Revolt of conservatives and clericals led by Ras Gugsa Wali against progressive policy of the King crushed in decisive battle

April 2, Death of Empress Zauditu, co-ruler, and descendant of line claiming descent from King Solomon and the Queen of Sheba

April 3, Ras Tafari proclaimed Emperor

Aug. 21, Arms Traffic Convention signed with France, Great Britain, and Italy

Sept. 27, Everett Colson, American, appointed financial adviser of Government

Nov. 2, Ras Tafari crowned Emperor under name Haile Silassi I

ADRAR

See Mauretania

ALGERIA

Algeria, dependency of France in North Africa, bounded on the north by the Mediterranean, east by Tunisia, west by Morocco, and south by Italian Libya and French West Africa, organized in 2 divisions, Northern (80,117 square miles), and Southern (767,435 square miles).

Population, according to Department and Territories (census of March 7, 1927):—

NORTHERN ALGERIA (DEPARTMENTS)	POPULATION	SOUTHERN ALGERIA (TERRITORIES)	POPULATION
Algiers	1,866,714	Ain Sefra	173,832
Oran	1,380,801	Ghardaia	119,940
Constantine	2,273,756	Touggourt	212,783
		Saharan Oases	35,670
Total	5,521,271	Total	542,225

Grand Total 6,063,496

	CIVILIAN POPULATION			MILITARY POPULATION			GRAND TOTAL
	European	Native	Total	European	Native	Total	
Northern Territory	828,580	4,615,781	5,444,361	34,476	42,434	76,910	5,521,271
Southern Territory	4,779	532,091	536,870	2,535	2,820	5,355	542,225
Grand Total	833,359	5,147,872	5,981,231	37,011	45,254	82,265	6,063,496

In 1926, of the total European population of 833,359, the French numbered 549,146 and the naturalized French, 108,495; Spaniards, 135,032; Italians, 28,594; Maltese, 3,985; other foreigners, 8,107; total foreigners, 175,718.

The chief towns with population in 1926 were: Algiers, 226,218; Oran, 150,301; Constantine, 93,733; Bona, 51,895; Sidibel-Abbes, 43,148; Philippeville, 29,242; Mascara, 28,033; Tlemçen, 26,758; Sétif, 26,677; Mostaganem, 26,355; Blida, 24,758; Bougie, 15,941; Tizi Ouzon, 2,944.

Algeria in ancient times was conquered by the Carthaginians, the Romans, the Vandals, the Byzantines, Arabs, Turks, and finally by the French.

Jules Carde, Governor General

935 to 1684

About 935, The town Algiers founded by the Arabs near the site of Icosium

1509, Becoming the seat of the Barbary pirates, captured by Ferdinand of Spain; retaken by Horuc Barbarossa, and made the capital of a state; governed by a dey, nominally subject to Turkey, 1516. Barbarossa was defeated and slain by the Spaniards, 1518

1541, The Emperor Charles V loses a fine fleet and army in an expedition against Algiers

1655, Algiers terrified into pacific measures by Blake; by Du Quesne 1683–84

1816

Aug. 27, For continued piracy, the city successfully bombarded by the British fleet under Lord Exmouth

Aug. 28, Treaty of peace with Great Britain and declaration of Dey of abolition of Christian slavery

1827

April 30, The Dey Hussein at Algiers struck the French consul with a fly whisk in dispute in connection with wheat supplied to the directoire by 2 French Jews which led to demand for apologies and French blockade (1827–1830)

1830

May 25, French army sailed from Toulon for conquest of Algiers

July 5, Algiers surrendered to a French armament under Bourmont and Duperré, after severe conflicts; the Dey deposed, and the barbarian government wholly overthrown

1832

Nov. 21, The Arab chief Abd-el-Kader preaches a holy war, becomes powerful, and attacks the French, at first successfully

1834

He is recognized as Emir of Mascara, by treaty with the French

May 20, The French ministry announce their intention to retain Algiers permanently

July 22, Decree appointed French Governor General, M. Bourmont appointed

1835 to 1836

1835–36, War renewed

Dec. 5, 1835, The French take Mascara

Dec. 8, 1836, Marshal Clausel defeats the Arabs in two battles, and enters Mascara

1837

May 30, Abd-el-Kader, thoroughly defeated, recognizes the French supremacy and Treaty signed July 5, partition of territory, the Dey to have administration of interior regions

Oct. 13, Gen. Damremont killed in taking Constantina

1839 to 1842

Dec., 1839, French defeated

Dec., 1840, Marshal Bugeaud appointed Governor General and began conquest of the country with large army

Feb., 1842, Algeria annexed to France, and the Emir declared a rebel

1844

Aug. 14, He is defeated by Bugeaud at Isly

Sept. 1, Order established Department for Native Affairs and Arab Bureau

Sept. 10 and March 18, 1845, Statement of boundary with Morocco

1845 to 1850

June 18, 1845, 500 Arabs in a cave at Khartani refuse to surrender; suffocated by smoke, said to have been ordered by General Pelissier

Dec. 23, 1847, After a long struggle Abd-el-Kader surrenders to Lamoricière

Dec., Duc d'Aumale, Governor

1850, Revolt subdued

1851

Jan. 11, Algeria included in French customs system

An insurrection of the Kabyles subdued by the French, after several sharp engagements

1852 to 1859

1852, Abd-el-Kader, a prisoner in France, freed by Louis Napoleon

1857, Another insurrection suppressed

1858, The government entrusted (for a short time) to Prince Napoleon

Oct. 31 and Nov. 6, 1859, The Arab tribes attack the French; defeated

1860

Sept., Algiers visited by Napoleon III

Nov. 24, Marshal Pelissier, Duke of Malakhoff, appointed Governor-General of Algeria

1863

Feb., The Emperor promises a constitution securing the rights of the Arabs, saying: "I am as much Emperor of the Arabs as of the French"

April 23, Senatorial decree gave tribes ownership of the lands they occupied

1864

May, Insurrection of the Arabs; submission, June

Sept. 8, Death of Marshal Pelissier, May 22; MacMahon, Duke of Magenta, succeeds him (1864–67)

Oct. 2, Fresh revolts; insurgents defeated by Jolivet

1865

May 3–27, The Emperor well received during his visit

July 14, Natives declared French subjects and facilities given for acquisition of French citizenship

Nov., The Emperor publishes his letter on the policy of France in Algeria (July 20)

1869

Feb. 2, 4,000 Arabs defeated by Col. Sounis

1870

July, Resignation of Marshal MacMahon

Aug. 15, Algeria proclaimed in a state of siege

1871

June 24, State of siege raised

Admiral de Gueydon appointed Governor General

1878

Gen. Chanzy (1873–79) accused of governing despotically; his resignation not accepted by Marshal MacMahon, July; replaced by Albert Grévy

1879

June, 1879, An insurrection soon quelled

1881

April, Dispute with Tunis; outrages of the savage tribes, Kroumirs, &c. (see Tunis)

July 13, Arab insurrection, headed by Bou Ameema, June; he is said to be defeated, and a fugitive

Aug., Bou Ameema defeated by the French, July 13th; said to be preparing for a fresh revolt; three French columns advancing against him, Aug.; indecisive skirmishes

Aug. 26, Allotment of Algerian affairs to the various Ministries of France, powers of Governor reduced; order revoked

About Aug. 26, Insurrection dreaded; troops sent from France

Nov., Resignation of the governor, A. Grévy (died July 11, 1899)

Dec., M. Tirman appointed

1882

April, Topographical expedition attacked, 40 said to be killed

Dec., The province Mzab annexed to Algeria, announced

1883 to 1889

June 13, 1883, Submission of insurgents announced

June 26, 1889, Naturalization Act

1891

March 5, The Chamber of Deputies, Paris, direct the appointment to inquire respecting Algerian political affairs

March, Resignation of M. Louis Tirman (dies July, 1899), ten years governor; succeeded by M. Jules Cambon, arrived May 11

1896

May 10 and Dec. 31, France reorganized government; decentralization completed by order of Aug. 23, 1898 establishing present system of government

1897

Oct. 31, M. Lépine appointed Governor-Gen. arrives

Dec. 28, Severe famine, M. Lépine appeals for help, 120,000 francs granted

1898

Jan. 23–24, Serious riots in connection with the Dreyfus case (see France, 1894 and 1898), against the Jews, 2 deaths, and shops, &c., pillaged; over 78 persons sentenced to various terms of imprisonment, Jan. 26; order restored, Jan. 28; 58 Anti-Semites pardoned June 13

July 27, M. Leferrière appointed Governor-Gen. reported

Aug. 23, Government reorganized, powers of Governor defined and Superior Council reorganized, and new Assembly established with chiefly elected members

Nov. 12, Anti-Jewish rioting in Tunis; M. Max Regis, anti-Semite mayor, suspended, Dec. 12; M. Pujade (mayor) and municipality suspended for anti-Semitic agitation, he dies, Feb. 5; fatal rioting Feb. 9, 1899

1899

Sept. 20–22, Anti-Semitic demonstrations by M. Max Regis, some fighting

1900

April 5–May, Military operations in S. Algeria, Insalah occupied by the French, Dec. 28; natives routed at Inrhar, March 19, 1900; the oases of Twab, Tidikelt, and Gurara and the district of Igli occupied

Aug. 28, Sept. 7, Further fighting with Berbers near Timmimum, French loss, 17 killed

Dec. 19, Superior Council and Assembly given right of voting the budget, subject to supervision

1901

Feb. 18, Berbers routed at Timmimum, Capt. Guisard and 9 others killed

April 28, Marguerite, a village, sacked by Arabs, reported

May, M. Jounart appointed Gov.-Gen., Oct. 5, 1900; resigns

July 20, Convention with Morocco, signed in Paris

Oct. 6, M. Paul Revoil, new governor, arrives

1902

Jan. 14, M. Max Regis imprisoned for 3 years

May 31, Expedition against the Tuaregs

Oct. 13, Morocco frontier question settled

Nov. 17, Earthquake shocks at Oran and Oned Marsa

Dec. 24, Southern Territory created administrative unit

1903

April 11, M. Revoil, Gov.-Gen., resigns

April 15, Pres. Loubet well received

May, M. Jonnart, Governor General (1903–1911)

July, Organized system of women medical doctors for the Zenanas; dispensary opened at Algiers, other establishments in progress, reported

Sept. 5, French convoy attacked by brigands at El Mungar; 37 killed, 47 wounded, Captain Vauchez mortally

1904

Sept. 13, Decree established modes of transfer of land, system of open sale to colonists, sale at fixed price at public office, sale by auction under public control, and sale by private treaty and free concession

1905

Aug. 14, Southern Territory reorganized

1906

March 4, Census gave population as 5,231,850 (including military forces)

1908

Dec. 13, Mutiny of foreign legion

Frontier disturbances. *See* Morocco

1911

March 22, M. Lutaud appointed Governor General (1911–1918)

Census gave total population as 5,492,569 of whom 752,043 were Europeans including 558,572 French, 134,746 Spaniards resident chiefly of Oran, and 36,661 Italians resident in region of Constantine

1912

Feb. 3, Native conscription instituted

1914

Aug. 4, German warships bombarded Philippeville and Bona without warning

1916

Sept. 25, Suleiman el Baruni appointed Turkish Governor General. *See* Tripoli

1918

Jan. 29, M. Jonnart appointed Governor General for the third time

Nov. 30, Arab taxes abolished, ending all inequalities and privileges in taxes

Dec. 1, Decree imposed special taxes on land, industrial, commercial, and agricultural profits

In World War (1914–1918) Algeria furnished 173,000 fighting men, and 119,000 workers, and losses in killed and missing were 25,000

1919

Feb. 4, Law granted French citizenship to natives above the age of 25 and monogamous, who served in the War, who are proprietors or farmers, who can read or write or hold a French decoration

Sept. 12, Franco-Italian Boundary Accord by which Algeria ceded territory from the territory of Oases

ANGOLA

Angola, Portuguese West Africa, with a coast line of about 1,000 miles, and bounded by French Congo (Equatorial Africa), Belgian Congo, Union of South Africa, and the former German Southwest Africa. The area is 1,259,252 square km. (486,071 square miles).

In 1482 Diogo Cam discovered the Congo River and the coast of Angola in voyages of the 3 following years. A mission sent from Portugal under Gonçalo de Sousa brought the first missionaries in 1490, and the King was converted. Paulo Diaz was sent as the first Governor in 1559, and in 1574 he founded Loanda. The colony has belonged to the Portuguese since 1575, with the exception of the years 1641 to 1648, when it was held by the Dutch. From September 1, 1928, the new capital has been established at Huambo, now called New Lisbon (Nova Lisbôa). It is under a High Commissioner, who resides at Luanda, and is vested with large powers. By the Charter of October 15, 1926, it is divided into 8 administrative districts and 1 Intenderia: Luanda, Benguela, Congo, Cubango, Huila, Lunda, Malanje, Moxico, and Intendencia do Zaire e Cabinda. The important towns are S. Paulo de Loanda, Cabinda, Ambriz, Novo Redondo, Benguella, Mossâmedes, and Porto Alexandre. The indigenous population numbered 2,481,956 on December 31, 1926 (1,197,099 males and 1,284,857 females), and is now estimated to include 40,000 Europeans, of whom 90% are Portuguese.

José Dionisio Carneiro de Sousa e Faro, Governor General.

1884

Feb. 26, Agreement by which Great Britain recognized both banks of the Congo as Portuguese territory at the coast between 5° 12′ and 8° S. Lat. and in interior as far as Noki

1885

Feb. 14, Convention of Portugal with the International Association of the Congo by which the Portuguese claim to the "Kabinda enclave" was recognized, and of the southern bank of the Congo as far as Noki

1886

May 12, Boundary Convention of France and Portugal settled frontiers with French Congo (French Equatorial Africa)

Dec. 30, Convention between Germany and Portugal settled frontiers with South West Africa; boundaries protested by Great Britain Aug. 13, 1887

1890

Aug. 20, Convention with Great Britain fixed frontier; not ratified

Nov. 14, Treaty with Great Britain signed included boundaries of Convention of Aug. 20

1891

May 25, Treaty of Portugal with International Association of the Congo altered boundaries dividing the country of Luanda between the 2 countries

June 11, Anglo-Portuguese Treaty included Barotse Kingdom and Manica in British sphere and fixed frontier with British South Africa

1894

March 24, Declaration of boundary made by Belgian Congo and Portugal accepting report of delimitation commissions in the Lunda region

1897

Count Almoster, with a small force, massacred by natives near Humbe, reported December 23

1898

Native attacks on fort Humbe repulsed with loss, reported Feb. 3

Aug. 30, Secret Anglo-German Agreement as to division of Portuguese colonies

1902

Revolt suppressed, 4 native chiefs and 13 others arrested at Bailundu, reported, May 29; natives repulsed at Bailundu, July 13, 14; further successes, Aug. 20, 28; Sept. 6

1905

May 30, Award delivered by King of Italy as arbitrator as to Barotse boundary in dispute with Great Britain

1907

Jan. 30, Award as to Manica boundary in dispute with Great Britain

Aug. 27, Portuguese victory over 7,000 Cuamatas at Musile

1910

Nov. 23, The Minister of Foreign Affairs stated to British Anti-Slavery Society that assurance had been given that the new Portuguese Government would abolish abuses in Angola in the supplying of labor to the cocoa plantations

1913

Native Affairs Department created

1914

Aug. 15, Measure of autonomy granted by Portugal

1915

March 5, Protocol signed defined frontier with Rhodesia, and exchange of Notes Nov. 3, 1925

1926

June 22 and July 1, Agreement signed as to boundary with Union of South Africa (Kunene River)

Oct. 15, Charter divided the country into 12 administrative districts

Sept. 3, Decree coördinated ordinances in force as to liberty of the press

1927

June 27, Regulations as to liberty of the press issued

July 21, Railroad Convention with Belgian Congo signed

July 22, Convention between Portugal and Belgium provided for exchange of territory, 480 square miles in southwest of Belgian Congo of area known as the Dilolo Boot ceded to Angola, and 1 square mile near Matadi ceded by Angola to Belgian Congo, needed for Matadi-Stanley railroad

1928

July 1, As from this date the escudo superseded by new monetary unit, the "angolar"

Dec. 16, Decree provided native labor code

1929

Feb. 6, Decree established political, civil, and criminal statute for natives and non-natives

May 15, Public education organized

May 25, Income tax imposed

June 10, Formal opening of railroad at Luao, Portuguese section of Katanga-Lobito railroad

Oct. 29, Decree established Supreme Technical Board of Agriculture

1930

Nov. 6, Vocational Guidance Bureau established in Loanda

ANNOBON

See Guinea, Spanish

ASCENSION

Ascension, British island of volcanic origin, of 34 square miles area, in the South Atlantic, 700 miles northwest of St. Helena to which it is annexed.

ASHANTI

Ashanti, British Colony in West Africa, annexed under Orders in Council of Sept. 26, 1901, the Governor of the Gold Coast being appointed Governor. *See also* Gold Coast. The area is 24,560 square miles and the population (census, 1921) was 407,000; Europeans (1921), 400. Kumasi, the chief town, has about 25,000 inhabitants.

1824

Jan. 21, Sir Charles M'Carthy, Governor of the Gold Coast, espousing the cause of the Fantees, killed in battle with the Ashantis at Essamako; Kwado (Osai Tutu Kwado), Ashanti King, also killed—the skull of Sir Charles used as a royal drinking cup by his successors

1826

Aug. 7, Ashantis defeated by Colonel Purdon at Dodowa near Acre

1831

April 27, Treaty of peace and commerce with the Ashantis concluded by British, the independence of the Fantees recognized

1873

Jan. 22, Ashanti force crossed the Prah, advancing toward the coast

April 5, Ashantis began war, offended by British occupation of Elmina ceded by the Dutch under Treaty of Feb. 25, 1871, attacking the Fantees, Allies of British

June 13, Ashantis defeated

June 14, British bombarded Elmina for favoring Ashantis

Sept. 12, Sir Garnet Wolseley, appointed Governor of West African Colonies, sailed with troops, arrived at Cape Coast Castle, Oct. 2 and met an assembly of friendly chiefs, Oct. 4

Oct. 14, Ashantees defeated in a conflict in the bush, at Essaman, near Elmina; villages burnt; again at Escabeo, near Dunquah, by Col. Festing, Oct. 27

Oct. 31, Dispatch from Sir Garnet Wolseley, declaring native allies worthless, and more British troops needed

Nov. 5, 6, Indecisive conflict at Dunquah; Lieut. Eardley Wilmot killed, Nov. 3; Ashantees' attack on Abrakampra totally defeated; their camp taken; disorderly retreat

Nov. 27, Col. Wood's indecisive attack at Faisorah

Dec. 15, The Ashantees said to be retreating in disorder

Dec. 27, Sir Garnet Wolseley marches towards the Prah

1874

Jan., King Koffee Kalcalli pretends to accept the terms offered; releases captives; prepares for battle

Jan. 29, Skirmish at Borborassie; Captain Nicol killed

Jan. 31, Ashantees defeated by Sir Garnet Wolseley at Amoaful

Feb. 1, Bocquah captured by Sir A. Alison

Feb. 2, Ashantee attack at Fommanah repulsed

Feb. 4, The King takes command: defeated at Ordahsa

——, Sir Garnet Wolseley enters Coomassie

Feb. 6, The King not acceding to proposals, his palace and city burnt

Feb. 13, The British retreat; a treaty of peace (terms: perpetual peace; indemnity of 50,000 oz. of gold; supremacy over Adansi and other tribes renounced; free trade guaranteed; human sacrifices to be prohibited) signed

——, The King fearing attack from Capt. Glover, sends first instalment of gold (1,000 oz.)

Feb. 19, Sir Garnet Wolseley enters Cape Coast Castle; sails; arrives at Portsmouth, March 21

1876

Sept., The deposed King Koffee Kalcalli, said to be defeated in his attack on his brother, King Mensah

1881

April, The King demands surrender of a fugitive prince by the Governor of Cape Coast Castle, Jan. 18; no result; professes desire of peace

June 30, The King sends the golden axe to the Queen, who receives it at Windsor Castle

1883

June 28, Deposition of King Mensah and desire of British protection announced

Aug. 3 and 5, Fighting at Coomassie between partisans of King Mensah and the ex-King, Koffee Kalcalli

Aug., King Bugay requests British intervention

Aug. 31, Koffee Kalcalli's partisans totally defeated, announced

Aug.–Nov., He and Mensah prisoners

Dec., Massacre of Koffee's adherents

1884 to 1893

Aug.–Dec., 1884, Death of the King, and Koffee Kalcalli; civil war reported

Nov. 21, 1893, Troubles in the country; Col. Sir Francis Scott sent to protect the British settlement; arrives at Abetifi, reported

1894

Feb. *et seq.*, Accused of promoting slave trade, human sacrifices, attacking friendly tribes, and obstructing commerce, all contrary to treaties, British negotiations fruitless

April, Expedition successful, reported

June 11, Prempeh the young King of Coomassie installed

1895

April, The King protests against a British protectorate

——, The King's envoys not received at the colonial office

Oct., Ultimatum sent to the King

Nov.–Dec., Native kings support the British

Dec. 13, Expedition under Col. Sir Francis Scott, including Prince Henry of Battenberg, Prince Christian Victor, son of Prince Christian, and 30 officers, leaves England, Nov. 23 *et seq.*; arrives at Cape Coast Castle

Dec. 25, Bridge over the river Prah completed, reported

1896

Jan. 5, The road to Coomassie cleared by the withdrawal of the Ashanti pickets at Essian Kwanta

Jan. 9, Major Ferguson dies of fever at Prahsu

Jan. 11, Bekwai and Abodom placed under British protection by treaty signed by the kings at Essian Kwanta

Jan. 17–18, Coomassie occupied unopposed by Sir Francis Scott

Grand palaver; John and Albert Ansah, envoys, returned from England, act as interpreters; the King, reminded of his offenses by Governor Maxwell, accedes to all the British demands, including the payment of 50,000 oz. of gold for the expenses of the expedition; unable to pay, he is arrested with his relatives (2 war-chiefs, and the Kings of Mampon, Ejesu, and Ofesu, secured as hostages); John and Albert Ansah arrested for alleged forgery, &c.; Jan. 20, released May 20

Jan. 20, Prince Henry of Battenberg dies of African fever on board H.M.S. *Blonde*

Jan. 28, Capt. Donald Stewart appointed British resident with a detachment of troops at Coomassie; Jan. 22 (Major C. B. Pigott temporary acting resident)

Feb. 4, King Prempeh and prisoners arrive at Cape Coast Castle, embark for Elmina

Feb. 25, Mr. Maxwell on his tour north of Coomassie received with great enthusiasm at Insuta, Feb. 3, 1896, treaties concluded with 7 tribes; Mr. (aft. Sir) Wm. Maxwell returns to Cape Coast Castle (see Gold Coast)

May, British improvements at Coomassie

Aug. 27, British Protectorate declared

Nov. 9, Col. Pigott relieved at Coomassie by Capt. Donald Stewart, Nov.; country quiet and trade reviving, reported

1900

March 25, Sir Fred. and Lady Hodgson arrived at Coomassie, he holds a palaver of kings and chiefs, March 28, 1900; Capt. Armitage's small force sent in quest of the "Golden stool," symbol of royalty, is attacked by Ashantees, March 31

Mid April, Fort Coomassie closely invested by rebels, April 6; Capt. Middlemist and about 50 men charge through into Coomassie

April 29, Rebels defeated round Coomassie, April 23, 25; Capt. Aplix's force arrives after 2 days' hard fighting

April–May, Great suffering, 30 and 40 deaths per day in the fort; great loss inflicted on the rebels, May 2; Maj. Morris with 230 men arrives, May 15; the loyal Bekwais after much fighting burn Abodom, May 24; Hausa quarters destroyed at Coomassie, Capts. Maguire and Slater and others killed, May 29

June 6, Carter and Hall rout the enemy at Bekwai; Capt. Wilson and 6 men killed

June 23, Flight of Sir Fred. and Lady Hodgson with 600 men under Maj. Morris and 1,000 non-combatants (Capts. Bishop and Ralph with 115 men left behind); they break through the rebels, capturing a stockade, Capts. Leggett and Marshall being mortally wounded, and after much fighting reach Ekwanta, June 26; cross the river Ofin, June 30, and arrive at Accra after great suffering and many deaths, July 11

July 3, Col. Burroughs is repulsed at Kokofu, Lieut. Brownlie and 5 men killed

July 15, Relief of Coomassie by Col. Willcocks after a rapid march with his black troops and severe fighting; leaves Capt. Eden there in command and returns with the remainder of the sick and starving garrison to Bekwai, July 17; Morland and Mellis destroy a rebel camp at Kokofu, 30 killed, July 22

July 30, Beddoes routs the rebels at Formera

Aug. 7, Coomassie reinforced by Burroughs, camp and stockades destroyed; Lieut. Greer and 5 others killed

Aug., Opoku defeated and camp destroyed

Aug. 29, 31, Col. Brake destroys Ojesu, a fetish town; Lieut. Burton and Capt. Benson killed

Sept. 1, 22, Continued fighting, villages destroyed

Oct. 4, Sir J. Willcocks totally defeats about 4,000 rebels at Obassa, Sept. 30; enemy pursued and completely dispersed, reported

Nov. 14, Rebel chief of Odumasi captured

1901

March 14, 15, Major Nathan (aft. Sir), governor, receives the kings and chiefs of Ashanti at Coomassie

April 21, Mutiny in a native regiment at Coomassie, early April, deserters captured, some shot, 128 surrender, reported

Sept. 26, Ashanti formally annexed by Great Britain to the Crown and placed under the administration of the Gold Coast

1903

Oct. 1, Railway 180 miles from Sekondi to Coomassie opened

1906

Feb. 9, Suggested abolition of caravan tolls in connection with trade and goods produce, owing to deplorable state of affairs in Ashanti through famine, &c., reported

Oct. 22, Order in Council readjusted and defined boundaries with Gold Coast

1921

The hidden Golden Stool found. See Gold Coast

1924

Return of Prempeh. See Gold Coast

BASUTOLAND

Basutoland, British South Africa, an elevated but rugged plateau, forms an irregular parallelogram on the north-east of the Cape of Good Hope Province. The provinces of the Orange Free State, Natal, and the Cape of Good Hope form its boundaries. Area, 11,716 square miles. The territory, which is well watered and has a fine climate, is stated to be the best grain-producing country in South Africa, and the abundant grass enables the Basutos to rear large herds of cattle.

Basutoland has been under the authority of the Crown since Feb. 2, 1884, and is governed by a Resident Commissioner under the direction of the High Commissioner for South Africa, the latter possessing the legislative authority which is exercised by proclamation. The country is divided into seven districts, namely: Maseru, Leribe, Mohale's Hoek, Berea, Mafeteng, Quthing, and Qacha's Nek. Each of the districts is subdivided into wards, mostly presided over by hereditary chiefs allied to the Moshesh family.

According to the census of 1921 the population numbered 495,937 natives, 1,603 Europeans, 172 Asiatics, and 1,069 colored. European settlement is in general prohibited, and is more or less limited to the few engaged in trade, Government, and missionary work. Maseru, the capital and largest town, has a population of 1,890 natives and 399 Europeans.

John C. R. Sturrock, Resident Commissioner.

1843

Oct. 5 and Dec. 13, General George Napier, Governor of Cape Colony, concluded Treaty with Moshesh, Chief of the Basutos, creating Basutoland, native state under British protection, boundaries defined

1867

July 17–Jan. 28, War with Orange Free State and victory of Boers over Moshesh. *See* Orange Free State

1868

March 12, British Proclamation declared Basutoland annexed to the Crown in order to save Basutoland from the Free State

1869

Feb. 12, Convention of Great Britain with the Orange Free State defined frontier

1871

Aug. 11, Act of Government of Cape Colony declared annexation of Basutoland and boundaries defined, but disannexed in 1883 because of rebellion of natives, the "Gun War" of 1880–1881

1876

Oct. 16, Announcement of increase of hut tax from 10s. to 20s. a year and call for surrender of arms

1879

Nov. 20, Moiroso, a warlike chief, entrenches himself on a mountain and makes predatory sallies, Feb. *et seq.*; his stronghold captured and himself killed during the fight

Dec. 22, The Basutos ordered to give up their arms; many resist; Letsi, Molappo, and others who surrender, attacked by Masupha and others, June, July, who make war on the colonist forces, Sept. 13, 1880

1880

Sept. 21, Lerothodi defeated in attack on Mafeteng by Col. Carrington

Oct. 19, Mafeteng, besieged, relieved by Col. Clarke after a severe conflict

Oct. 22, Lerothodi's village stormed

Oct. 31, Moletsane's stronghold stormed by Colonel Clarke

Nov. 12, Mr. Hope, magistrate, and others treacherously murdered by Umhlonhlo, Oct.; who is defeated by Mr. Hawthorn; announced

Dec. 21, Umhlonhlo totally defeated by Baker

1881

Jan. 6, 14, Victories of Col. Carrington

Feb. 18–26, Armistice granted

March 26, Hostilities resumed; indecisive; Col. Carrington wounded

April 6, Proclamation repealed application of Disarmament Act to Basutoland

About April 16, Basutos severely defeated

May, Peace concluded

Sept. 10, The chief Masupha submits

1882

Oct., Again troublesome

Autumn, Gen. Gordon appointed to settle difficulties, resigns through disagreement with the Cape Government, announced

Dec., Peace restored

1883

Feb., Self-government granted

May, Much fighting among chiefs; subsides

June, The British agree to resume the government as a crown colony under conditions

July 27, The Cape Parliament assents

Dec. 8, The Basuto chiefs accept conditions at a great meeting; Masupha stands aloof, announced

1884

Feb. 2, Order in Council proclaimed exercise of direct authority of Great Britain over Basutoland

March 15–16, Jonathan defeats Joel with great slaughter

March 18, Basutoland officially disannexed from Cape Colony

March 23, Battles between Khetisa, Masupha, and Lerothodi

1887 to 1890

Basutoland reported quiet and prosperous

1898

Jan. 7, Masupha (died, July, 1899) refuses to give up his son Moiketsi (for assault and gaol-breaking in the Orange Free State); Lerothodi, the paramount chief, captures Thaba Besigo

Feb. 1, Moiketsi given up to Lerothodi, Jan. 18; Masupha surrenders, Jan. 31; is banished and fined; Moiketsi sentenced to over a year's imprisonment

1899 to 1910

Oct. 24, 1899, Lerothodi and his chiefs pledge loyalty to Queen Victoria, Sir Godfrey Lagden present

July 17, 1902, Joel Molapo, a minor chief, sentenced to a year's imprisonment for treason, &c.

Sept. 19, 1905, Letsie inaugurated as paramount chief of Basutoland

Feb. 24, 1906, Lord Selborne, high commissioner, and Lady Selborne arrived at Maseru

Feb. 18, 1909, Four Basuto chiefs received by King Edward; they had come to England with a petition from their paramount chief with regard to the status of their country in view of the proposed union of South Africa

1910

March 31, Proclamation of the Government placed the native National Pitso or Council, tribal gathering, on a permanent basis, the Resident Commissioner being the only European member

BECHUANALAND

Bechuanaland, South Africa, includes the Bechuanaland Protectorate and British Bechuanaland, the latter, the region between the Orange and Molopo rivers, was included in Cape Colony in 1895 (*see s.v.*). The Bechuanaland Protectorate comprises the territory lying between the Molopo River on the south and the Zambezi on the north, and extending from the Transvaal Province and Matabeleland on the east to South-West Africa. Area about 275,000 square miles; population, according to the census of 1921, 152,983, of whom 1,743 were Europeans. The most important tribes are the Bamangwato (35,000), under the Chief Tshekedi (acting as regent during the minority of Seretse, the son of Sekgoma, who died in November, 1925) whose capital is Serowe (population 17,000), 40 miles west of the railway line at Palapye Road; the Bakhatla (11,000), under Chief Molefi Pilane; the Bakwena (13,000), under Sebele II; the Bangwaketse (18,000), under chief Bathoeñ, the eldest son of the late chief Gaseitsiwe; the Batawana, under Mathibe; and the Bamalete (4,500), under Seboko Mokgosi, who assumed the Chieftainship on July 9, 1917. In 1885, the territory was declared to be within the British sphere; in 1889 it was included in the sphere of the British South Africa Company, but was never administered by the company; in 1890 a Resident Commissioner was appointed, and in 1895, on the annexation of the Crown Colony of British Bechuanaland to the Cape of Good Hope, new arrangements were made for the administration of the Protectorate, and special agreements were made in view of the extension of the railway northwards from Mafeking. Each of the chiefs rules his own people as formerly, under the protection of the King, who is represented by a Resident Commissioner, acting under the High Commissioner. The headquarters of the Administration are in Mafeking, in the Cape Province, where there is a reserve for Imperial purposes, with ample buildings.

Lieutenant-Colonel R. M. Daniel, Resident Commissioner.

1878

The Bechuanas invade Griqualand West, and are repulsed, and part of their territory subdued by British volunteers

1882

July 26, Peace concluded between warring chiefs through mediation of Transvaal authorities, land allotted to G. J. Van Niekirk

1883

Aug. 7, Van Niekirk proclaimed an independent republic in Stellaland

1884

April 12, Rev. John Mackenzie (an active missionary) appointed British resident
May 3, May 20, and May 22, British protectorate treaties signed with native chiefs
July 30, Compelled to resign by the Dutch party
Aug. 20, Replaced by Mr. Cecil Rhodes
Sept. 10, The Boer filibusters seize and annex the territory of Montsioa, under British protection; compelled to retire
Oct., Sir Charles Warren made special commissioner
Nov., Military expedition against Dutch freebooters
Dec., (Stellaland and Goshen republics), who accept allotments of land, announced, Nov. 27; this policy of the Cape Government strongly disapproved by colony

1885

Jan. 27 and Sept. 30, British Protectorate proclaimed
Jan. 29, Sir Charles Warren meets President Krüger, Jan 24 and comes to an agreement
Feb. 24, Military government established by Sir C. Warren, announced
July 8, Arrest of Mr. Van Niekirk, President of Stella-

land Republic, and others, on charge of murder of Mr. Honey, an Englishman, in 1883. Announced March 24, 1885; released about May 27. Sir C. Warren thanks the volunteers
Sept. 29, The Governor of Cape Colony appointed Governor and Judge (afterwards Sir S.) Shippard nominated administrator; Sir C. Warren after great success recalled

1889

April 30, Proposals of the British South African Company (Cecil Rhodes) for creation of a company to develop the Bechuanaland Protectorate submitted to the British Government

1891

May 9, Order in Council defined boundaries and reorganized the Government
June 10, Laws in force in Cape Colony declared in force

1895

June 11, A proposal to annex it to Cape Colony was negatived, autumn, 1888; adopted
Oct. 3, Order in Council annexed Bechuanaland to Colony of the Cape of Good Hope
Nov. 6, Bechuanaland made a protectorate
Nov. 19, Mr. F. J. Newton appointed resident commissioner; announced
Nov. 23, Khama and 2 other chiefs received at the Colonial office by Mr. Chamberlain, Sept. 11; visited Birmingham and other places, Sept., Oct.; received presents from Queen Victoria, at Windsor, Nov. 20, left England
Difficulties with the S. Africa company settled by Mr. Chamberlain; imperial government granted

1896

Feb. 6, Montsioa and Ikanning withdrawn from the British S. Africa company and placed under the high commissioner; Mr. Surmon appointed assistant-commissioner; announced
Dec. 23, Native rising through the killing of diseased cattle, at Pokwani; expedition sent under Major Peakman; reported
Dec. 29, Pokwani, Galishwe's stronghold, taken by Mr. Robinson and natives routed, Dec. 27; many natives captured, rising quelled

1897

Jan. 5, Mr. Robinson, a trader, murdered on the Mashowing river; the Batlaros tribe in revolt; reported; further raid reported, Jan. 8
Jan. 16, Rebels totally defeated, 40 killed in the Takoon district; reported
Feb. 18, Capt. Wood and a small patrol surprised by rebels in Langeberg; Lieut. Hopkins and Private Venn killed, rebel loss heavy; reported
April 30, Gamasep, Lukas Jantje's village, captured and burnt, Lieut. Harris killed, April 6; other kraals burnt by Col. Dalgety's column, announced, April 10; further fighting, reported
May 9, Toto's stronghold captured by Col. Dalgety, 3 privates killed
June 3, Rebels repulsed with loss at Gamasep
June 30, Reinforcements sent to Langeberg; several skirmishes reported, July 25; decisive victory over the rebels, at Langeberg, July 30 and Aug. 1; many surrenders, Aug. 2

Dec. 21, Major Goold-Adams appointed resident-commissioner; reported

1901

Jan., Ralph Champneys Williams, resident-commissioner

1904

May 16, Lands abandoned by certain chiefs declared Crown lands

1906

April 14, Visit of Lord Selborne, High Commissioner, who received a warm welcome from a large gathering of natives

1907

June 1, Gold found and the Madibi fields proclaimed public diggings

1910

Jan. 10, By Order in Council lands in the Protectorate vested in the High Commissioner (except Taiti district) and declared Crown lands under Ordinance of May 16 except native reserves and the 41 Barolong farms held by members of the Barolong tribe by certificates of issue of Chief Montisioa of March 28, 1895

1914

Oct. 18, Railroad from Prieska, Cape Colony, to Upington completed

1923

Feb. 2, Death of Khama, Chief of the Bamangwato (93) at Serowe

1929

Jan. 4, Proclamation amended laws as to dairies and dairy produce and made provision for government control of the industry
June 29, Proclamation established land agricultural loan fund

BELGIAN CONGO

Belgian Congo, Colony of Central Africa, formerly the Congo Free State, occupies the larger part of the basin of the Congo River and a small part of the basin of the Upper Nile, bounded on the west by Angola and by the Atlantic for a coast line of 25 miles only extending north from the mouth of the Congo, on the north by French Equatorial Africa and the Anglo-Egyptian Sudan, on the east by Uganda, Tanganyika, and Northern Rhodesia, and on the south by Northern Rhodesia and Angola, area estimated at 918,000,000 square miles. Population of Bantu origin 8,700,000, the white population on Jan. 1, 1930 numbered 25,679. Leopoldville is the capital. The districts of Ruanda and Urundi (former German East Africa) ceded to Belgium as mandatory of the League of Nations united administratively with the Congo, area 20,550 square miles.

Lieutenant General Tilkens, Governor General.

1485

Discovery of the Congo River by Diogo Cam, Portuguese, largest of African rivers and exceeded in size among rivers of the world by the Amazon only, length fully 3,000 miles

1816

July 6, Captain J. K. Tuckey sent by the British Admiralty reached the Congo River and pushed up stream as far as Isangila beyond lowest series of rapids

1868

July 18, David Livingstone traced the course of the Chambezi to Lake Bangweulu

1873

Expedition of Lieutenant W. Grandy sent from England to relief of David Livingstone reached point on the Congo below the cataracts

1876

Sept. 12, International Congress of Geographical Experts met in Brussels and founded the International Association for the Exploration and Civilization of Africa, an international commission with headquarters at Brussels and national committees in various countries
Oct., H. M. Stanley reached Nyangwe and proceeded to navigate the Lualaba River and descended the Congo reaching its mouth Aug. 12, 1877

1878

Nov. 25, Stanley met King Leopold and members of the International Association at Brussels, and the Comité d'Etudes du Haut-Congo was formed, regarded as national committee of the International Association, and Stanley in its service accepted offer of King Leopold to establish a chain of stations on the banks of the Congo River and conclude treaties with the chiefs

1879

Aug. 14, Stanley expedition began the ascent of the Congo River from its mouth

1880

Jan. 24, The first station on the Congo established by Stanley at Vivi, the limit of navigation on the lower Congo
Oct. 1, De Brazza by treaty with chiefs established claim of France to Congo region

1882

King Leopold changed the name of the Comité d'etudes du Haut Congo to the International Association of the Congo

1883

April 24, Treaty with native chiefs ceded land from Congo River to Leopoldville

1884

Feb. 26, Anglo-Portuguese Convention recognized Portuguese claims to coast line on both banks of the mouth of the Congo between 5° 12' and 8° South Lat. with an interior limit at Nokki, on south bank of the Congo below Vivi
April 9, The International Association, Colonel Strauch, president, announced that 30 stations had been established
April 22, The United States the first to recognize the

International Association of the Congo as a federal state by Convention signed on this date

April 23, Colonel Strauch (Belgian) concluded agreement with France giving France the right of preemption (first right to purchase) should the Association sell its territory

June 26, Lord Granville announced that he abandoned Treaty of Feb. 26

June, Sir Francis de Winton appointed Administrator General of Congo Territories

Nov. 8, German Agreement recognized International Association of the Congo

Nov. 15–Feb. 26, International Conference in Berlin on West African affairs. The Independent State of the Congo founded at but not by this Conference, and by the international treaties enumerated of recognition and boundaries

Dec. 16, Great Britain recognized the independence of the International Association

Dec. 19, Italy recognized independence

Dec. 24, Austria-Hungary recognized the International Association

Dec. 27, International Association recognized by the Netherlands

1885

Jan. 7, Spain recognized independence

Feb. 5, France and Russia recognized independence of the International Association of the Congo

Feb. 10, Sweden and Norway recognized independence

Feb. 14, Portugal recognized independence of the International Association

Feb. 23, Denmark and Belgium recognized the International Association

Feb. 26, General Act of the Berlin Conference signed, dealing with freedom of trade in the basin of the Congo, the slave trade, neutrality of territories in the basin of the Congo, free navigation of the Congo, navigation of the Niger, and rules for future occupation of African coasts as to notification by Powers of annexation or protectorate

April, King Leopold with sanction of Belgian Legislature formally assumed sovereignty over the Independent State of the Congo.

July 1, Leopold proclaimed sovereign at Bomba by Colonel (later Sir) Francis de Winton, who as first Governor General had succeeded Stanley and Sir Frederic Goldsmid as Administrator

——, The new State proclaimed at Banana on the Congo

Aug. 1, Circular letter of Leopold to the Powers declared perpetual neutrality of the "Independent State of the Congo" and stated the frontiers claimed

Oct. 30, Decree of Leopold proclaimed sovereignty

Nov. 22, Boundary Protocol with France as to boundary with French Equatorial Africa

1886

March 26, Decree organized local government defining powers of Administrator General made Governor General in April 1887

April 19, Conference at Berlin (which met 1884–85), ratifying the recognition of the Congo State by the Powers

1887

April 29, Further Boundary Protocol with France

1889

April 16, Decree of Leopold created Superior council

Aug. 2, Will of King Leopold of this date made Belgium heir to sovereign rights of Congo State

About Aug. 12, The state appeals to Belgium for an annual subsidy of 1,500,000 francs for ten years

Oct. 17, Decree of King Leopold that merchants in the Congo State should limit commercial operations in rubber to bartering with the natives

Dec. 18, Supreme council of the Congo State, King Leopold president, held its first sitting at Brussels

1890

July, The Belgian government agree to lend to the Congo State 5,000,000 francs at once, and 2,000,000 francs annually for the next 10 years, without interest; the bill passed by the Chamber, July 11, by the Senate, July 30

July 3, Treaty with Belgium by which Belgium to have right of annexation after 10 years

Aug. 1, Territories declared inalienable

1891

April 15, Katanga Company formed in Brussels to develop Katanga native kingdom near head stream of the Congo in Central Africa and settlement formed in Feb. 1892

May 25, Boundary Agreement with Portugal

Sept. 21, Secret decree of King Leopold ordered officials to "take urgent and necessary measures to preserve the fruits of the domain to the State" in particular rubber and ivory

Dec. 15, Government order forbade natives to hunt elephants unless they brought tusks to State officers (Bangala)

1892

Feb. 14, Order forbade natives to collect rubber unless they brought it to the State officers (Yokoma)

May 8, Order forbade natives to collect ivory or rubber unless they brought it to State officers (Basankusu)

About May 15, Rising of the Arabs in the Upper Congo, and massacre of Europeans, anti-slavery agents, &c., including M. Hodister, an able officer of the Katanga company

Aug. 26, Major de Wahis appointed governor

About Aug. 25, Exploring expedition of M. Van den Kerckhoven, a Belgian, with above 1,000 men, which started in 1891, reported arrival at Wadelai

Sept., The killing of M. de Poumayrac in debatable land causes a territory dispute between France and Belgium; the Congo State declines responsibility; arbitration proposed and deferred, July, Aug.; the French demand indemnity and evacuation of the land, Aug. 7; the death of M. Poumayrac and some of his party, attributed to indiscreet dealings with the natives

Nov. 22, Lieut. Dhanis severely defeats the slave traders under Sefu, son of Tippoo Tib, and takes many prisoners

Dec. 5, Decree exacted forced labor from the natives by tax in kind and in labor by levy on chiefs and delegated to concessionary companies the right to enforce these taxes

1893

Jan., Expedition under Lieut. Dhanis against the Arabs of Munie Moharra

Feb., Expedition for the relief of Capt. Jacques [reported safe, Oct. 25, 1892], engaged in the suppression of the slave trade, organized in Brussels

Feb. 26, The Arabs defeated by Lieut. Chaltin; 80 slaves released, reported

March, Successful expedition of M. Delcommune up the Lukuga to the Congo; important discoveries, about Sept. 29, 1892 *et seq.*, reported

——, Capt. Bia, who started on an expedition, Dec. 19, 1891, from Lupongo in the Lomami valley, after exploring Lakes Mweru and Bangeweolo, died, Aug. 30, 1892; reported

March 4, Nyangwe taken by Capt., aft. Baron, Dhanis

March, April, Gradual suppression of the Arab slave-traders, and subjection of the country to the Congo Free State

March 30, The Ponthier expedition leaves Antwerp, March 6; reached Boma

July, M. van den Kerckhoven killed, reported May 5, succeeded by Capt. Delanghe, reported

Oct. 25, Defeat of Rumaliza at Kassango by Baron Dhanis with heavy loss, Oct. 20; Capt. Ponthier dies of his wounds

Nov. 16, Said ben Abadi, the murderer of Emin Pasha, taken and shot, reported

Nov. 17, Sefu killed in battle

Nov. 28, A new district constructed on the Upper Congo, the capital to be Nyangwe, reported

Dec. 4, First section of the Congo railway (24 m.) opened

Dec., Gov. Gen. in Boma, M. Wahis

1894

March, Rumaliza defeated by Baron Dhanis and Lieut. Lothaire, Jan. 14, reported

March 18, An attack of the Mahdists on Mundu, Upper Nile, repulsed by Capt. Delanghe; Capt. Bonvalet and M. Devos killed

March 24, Belgian-Portuguese declaration of boundary

May 12, Anglo-Belgian treaty settling the boundaries of the Congo State and the British possessions, signed at Brussels

June 22, A dispute with Germany settled by compromise

June 23, Capt. Jacques, leader of the Anti-slavery committee, warmly welcomed in Brussels

Aug. 14, Agreement with France signed by which the Mbomu River recognized by France as northern frontier, and Leopold renounced all rights west of 30° E. and north of a line to the Nile along 5° 30′ N.

Oct. 11, Baron Dhanis, commander of the expedition to Katanga, warmly received at Antwerp

1895

Annexation of the Congo State to Belgium proposed at Brussels

Jan. 9, Treaty of cession of the Congo Free State to Belgium; submitted to Chamber Feb. 13 but withdrawn

June 27, The debt of the state adopted by Belgium

Aug., Excitement respecting Capt. Lothaire's execution of Mr. Stokes, ivory dealer, after a court-martial (Jan. 1), charged with selling arms, &c.

Sept., Capt. Lothaire summoned to give explanations to Col. Wahis, Governor-Gen. of the Congo

Nov. 14, 150,000 francs paid as indemnity to the British government for Mr. Stokes' family; 100,000 francs to the German Government; announced

Dec. 2, Zemio, on the Mbomu river, occupied by the French; reported

1896

May 15, Arrival of Maj. Lothaire at Boma, March 27; his trial begun, April 25; acquitted, on the ground that Stokes was inciting to civil war by allying himself with Kibonge, a native chief, and placing himself at the head of an armed troop, April 27; Mr. Arthur, British Consul at Boma, appeals against the finding of the court

May 21, A native educational military colony established and declared successful; pacification of the river tribes and others; reported

June 5, Maj. Lothaire arrives at Brussels: second trial there, Aug. 3; acquitted, Aug. 6 (resigns, announced Aug. 6, 1897)

June 19, Royal warrant withdrawing the proposal of annexation of the State read in the Chamber, Brussels

July 22, First half of the Congo railway inaugurated

Sept. 2, Successful expedition of Baron Dhanis in the Upper Nile; Lado occupied, and an alliance concluded with the natives; reported

Sept. 4, Baron Dhanis appointed Governor-Gen.

Sept. 20, A European committee for protection of natives appointed by the Belgian Government, with regulations; reported

Nov. 11, Mutinous native troops defeated at Kohoa, in Munsa, by Capt. Michaux

1897

Feb. 17, Capt. Chaltin totally defeats the Mahdists and occupies Rejaf; Lieut. Bardlea killed

March 4, Mutiny of native troops at Ndirfa, commander Leroi and other officers killed; reported

April 2, Sir Charles Dilke called attention of British Parliament to ill-treatment of the natives in the Belgian Congo

June 17, Frequent raids; British fort on Salt lake destroyed

July, Lado captured by Capt. Chaltin; reported

July 15, Lieut. Henry totally defeats the Batetela rebels near Lake Albert Nyanza

Sept., Baron Dhanis' Batetela soldiers mutiny on their way to put down the rebellion; Lieut. Julien and two officers killed; mutiny suppressed and the country subjugated, reported

1898

March 23, Rebels totally defeated by Lieut. Dorme

End of April, Lieut. Chargois' column attacked by mutineers on Lake Tanganyika, and compelled to retreat, the enemy finally routed and 25 killed

June, Prosperity reported, May; a loan to meet expenses for public works concluded by the King at Brussels

June 3, 4, Dervish attack on Rejaf repulsed, MM. Desneux and Bartholi killed

June 17, Lieut. Glorie defeats the Batatelas at Givese

July 7, Lieut. Dubois' expedition of 100 men to occupy Lake Rivu, surprised by rebels and 31 killed, he himself deserted afterwards by his men and killed; reported

Nov. 4, The Batatelas defeat the Belgians, 3 officers and 200 men killed at Sungula; Kabambaré captured, 5 whites killed, Nov. 14; Kabambaré reoccupied by the troops after severe fighting, Dec. 31: rebels defeated by Baron Dhanis, Feb. 1899

1899

Feb., The Budjas defeated by Maj. Lothaire, reported
May, Capt. Maurice Bell, in an expedition against the Aruwimis, killed by cannibals, Jan.; 100 natives killed by a punitive expedition and many made prisoners
July 20, Baron Dhanis defeats the rebels near Sungula, much bloodshed; rebels again defeated, Oct. 8–12

1900

Early 1900, Alleged atrocities by the Zappo Zaps, villages burnt and natives massacred, reported
March 4, Lieut. Weylants and M. Rabe massacred by the Budjas near Zambeta
April 4, Explorations in Katanga, down the Kasai to lake Dilolo, under Lieut. Lemaire, reported
April 10, Provisional agreement between Germany and the Congo State regarding territory near Lake Kivu, signed at Brussels
April 19, Revolt at Chinkakassa, fort seized by mutineers, April 17; but recaptured by the Boma troops, rebels fled
Oct., Batatela mutiny ended, mutineers surrender
Nov., Much slaughter of natives, villages burnt, for refusing to work rubber
Dec. 21, Colonel Bartels, Governor-General

1901

Feb., Lacroix and Mathys sentenced to 15 and 12 years' imprisonment for murdering natives in Katanga, Nov.; confirmed
Mid-Feb., Rebellion in Kassai, Jan., suppressed
Mid-July, Native rising in the Welle district, April; revolt quelled
Nov., Batatelas severely defeated

1902

April 22, 25, Concession reported to be obtained for a railway between the northern borders of Rhodesia across the Congo territory to Lake Kasali,—*Times*
July 1, Taxes on religious, charitable, and scientific institutions lowered, by decree

1903

May 20, Debate in the British House of Commons on the administration of the Congo territory, and illtreatment of the natives; correspondence of British government with Belgium respecting the question; blue book published
Sept. 19, Reply of Leopold to Powers denies charges of cruelty to natives. *See* Belgium

1904

March 15, Reply of the Free State to the charges of forced labor, slavery, and cruelty by officials of the Congo, formulated in the report of Mr. Casement, British Consul, denies the truth of the allegations, but admits isolated cases of cruelty
March 23, Three non-Belgian inspectors-general appointed
April 19, Impartial and searching inquiry into the allegations promised by the State; British Government expresses its satisfaction
May 10, Sir Henry M. Stanley, whose explorations on the Congo in connection with the Belgian Government led to the foundation of the international association of the Congo, 1878, dies, aged 63

June 6, British Government proposes a special commission of inquiry
July 23, Commission of 3 appointed to inquire fully into the condition of the natives of the Congo
Aug. 7, Fifty Swedish sub-officers appointed for service in the Congo State
Sept. 14, Official instructions to commissioners published, stating that formal orders had been issued to all officials and agents in the Free State to give their unreserved aid and coöperation
Nov. 7, Commission arrives at Boma

1905

Jan. 31, Many tribes in French Congo in open revolt; Capt. Mechat, in district of Ibenga, with 100 men, attacked by 30,000 natives, village of Bissako stormed and taken by the rebels; in district of Uguai 20,000 Pahouins surround a military post, burn the factory, and massacre a white sergeant and 10 Senegalese, reported
March 12, Members of the Congo commission of inquiry leave Boma Feb. 21; arrive at Southampton on their return home
Mid-May, Construction of the great lakes railway reported to be rapidly progressing
July 3, King of the Belgians, at official celebration of the 75th anniversary of Belgian independence, when laying the stone of a new colonial institute near Brussels, built and maintained at the expense of the Congo Free State, says: "If I have created the Congo Free State, and, as you remind me, have supplemented its budget from my private purse, it is because I desired that the new state should serve the cause of civilization as well as our own interests "
July 6, Congo reform association addresses the British Foreign Office with regard to the great injustice to which native witnesses in atrocity cases are subjected by being compelled to leave their homes for long periods to attend the court at Boma; Foreign Office in reply states that the British Minister at Brussels has been instructed to ascertain from the Congo Government if such trials cannot be held at Basankusu in the Abir concession, where a resident judge has been appointed
Oct. 31, Report of Commission of Inquiry on the Congo published condemned Belgian administration as cruel oppression of the natives

1906

Jan. 8, Congo reform association hold a meeting at the City Temple, London, "to protest against the atrocities on the Congo"
May 9, Anglo-Belgian Convention giving Leopold the Lado Enclave during his lifetime cancelled Treaty May 12, 1894. *See* also Belgium
June 3, Decree signed by Leopold provided for certain changes in administration recognized "lands occupied by natives"; regarded as inadequate
June 29, Mr. Stannard, English missionary, charged with libeling a Major in the state service, sentenced by the court of Coquilhatville to pay a fine of 40*l*. and 1 franc damages
July 1, Death of the Rev. George Grenfell, explorer and missionary on the Congo for 26 years
Sept. 30, Rumored massacre of Commandant Moll in the district of Shanga. Com. Bruneel left with 150 men to restore order, reported
Oct. 22, Mr. Thomas Ryan, American financier, signed

a convention with the Congo State, on behalf of an American rubber company, which secures him the right of making certain experiments in a given district adjoining Stanley Falls; no cession of any territory, reported

Nov. 15, Convention concluded between the Congo State and a Belgian company for the construction of a railway from Leopoldville to Katanga, reported

Nov. 21, The Brussels *Indépéndence Belge*, in an article on Sir E. Grey's reply to the deputation which waited on him with respect to the administration of the Congo State, took strong exception to the attitude of the British Foreign Secretary

Nov. 28, Debate on administration of Congo State begun in Belgian Chamber

——, Treaty of cession between Belgium and the Congo Free State concluded; text published Dec. 6, 1907

1908

March 5, Act provided for suppression of Crown Domain and financial compensation to King Leopold

March 27, British Memorandum regarding taxation and currency in Congo Free State presented reforms expected

April 7 and 16, American Memorandum to Belgium expressed hopes and expectations of administrative reforms in Congo State

Aug. 20, Belgian Chamber adopted Treaty of Nov. 28, 1907 and Act of March 5, 1908, Senate Sept. 9

Oct. 18, Law made gold and silver money current in Belgium also current in the Congo

——, Law for Government of the Congo State passed by Belgian Legislature

Oct. 20, Act of Belgian Parliament promulgated completed annexation of Congo Free State

Nov. 15, The Congo Free State became the Belgian Congo annexed to Belgium, control by Colonial Minister responsible to Belgian Parliament

1909

Jan. 6, Decree authorized impressment of 2,595 natives for work on Grand Lacs Railroad

Jan. 11, Bank of Belgian Congo constituted

Feb. 24, Statement in British Parliament that "oppression of the natives was still going on just as before the annexation"

March 15, Decree established current coins of 20, 10, and 5 centimes and copper coins of 2 and 1 centimes special to the Colony

April 3, Prince Albert started from London for visit to Congo arriving at Bomba in August after walk of 1,500 miles through the forests

June 11, Note of Secretary Root stated that the United States would be gratified by assurance that Belgian Government would consider itself bound to discharge obligations assumed by Independent State of the Congo in the Brussels Convention of July 2, 1890, and withheld recognition of the annexation awaiting assurance of reforms

Oct. 28, Program of reforms to be introduced in Belgian Congo announced in Belgian Chamber

1910

Jan. 29, Announcement that forced labor on Congo railroads abandoned

March 22, Decree provided for gradual reforms and establishment of free trade for natives

March 31, German Congo Reform League formed in Hanover

May 2, Decree on "chefferies" basis of native tax administration

——, Decree abolished labor tax and provided that taxes should be paid exclusively in money within the limits of 5 to 12 francs to be fixed for each district

May 14, Protocol on Congo frontier signed by representatives of Great Britain and Belgium at Brussels gave Belgium the western shores of Albert Nyanza

June 16, The Lado Enclave transferred to the Anglo-Egyptian Sudan

July 1, Congo reforms into effect, reduction of taxes, payment of taxes in money, appointment of native officials, restriction of obligatory labor, suppression of polygamy

——, The districts of the Lower Congo, Stanley Pool, Ubangi, Bangala, Kwango, the Kasai, the Katanga, Aruwimi, the southern part of the Eastern Province, and the banks of the Congo River as far as Stanleyville opened to free trade

Aug. 11, Boundary Protocol between Belgium and Germany fixed frontiers with German East Africa

Aug. 17, Decree regulated native labor contracts and recruitment

——, Law introduced the metric system

1911

May 4, Boundary Agreement between Great Britain and Belgium fixed frontier with Uganda

June 25, Boundary Protocol between Belgium and Germany fixed frontier

July 1, District of the Crown (*Domaine de la Couronne*) made a free trade district

July 7, Arrangement made and renewed Oct. 10, 1927, by which the Banque de Congo Belge was authorized to issue notes payable to bearer

1912

Feb. 6, Ordinance regarding tax of natives reduced tax in certain regions (under law of Oct. 18, 1908 and decree of May 2, 1910)

May, M. Fuchs became Governor General succeeding Baron Wahis

July 1, Freedom of trade extended to the whole of the Colony

1913

Jan. 31, From this date liquor traffic suppressed throughout the Colony

May 29, British Government recognized the Belgian annexation of the Congo

1914

Feb. 3, Boundary Agreement between Great Britain and Belgium fixed frontier with British East Africa (Kenya) from Mt. Sabinio to Congo-Nile watershed

July, Division of the Congo into 4 provinces, 22 districts, and 176 territories in decentralization of administration policy, and Colonial office staff in Brussels reduced

1915

March, Railroad from Kabulo to Lake Tanganyıka completed

1916

Aug. 20, Decree prohibited payment of natives in anything but money. M. Henry became Governor General

1917

Feb. 20, Ordinance obliged natives to cultivate food stuffs

1918

May, The Cape to Cairo Railroad reached Bukama on the Lualaba

1919

May 30, Anglo-Belgian Agreement signed by which Belgium received mandated area northwest of East Africa of States of Ruanda and Urundi, part of the region conquered by Belgian-Congo troops in the World War

1920

Dec. 28, Royal Decree by which currency given to special moneys of inferior metal, in pieces of 1 franc and 50 centimes nominal value

1921

Jan., Maurice Lippens, Governor of East Flanders, appointed Governor General

Aug. 21, Law authorized the Minister of the Colonies to proceed with the execution of large projects of public works, railroads, roads, &c.

Sept. 12, The prophet, Kimbangu and his followers arrested and Oct. 3 sentenced to death for sedition, which was commuted to imprisonment for terms of from 2 to 20 years

1922

March 16, Decree provided that no labor contract might be valid for more than 3 years

July, Law limited powers of Colonial Office in Brussels to general supervision, and powers of vice-governors enlarged

1923

Resignation of Governor General Lippens. Succeeded by M. Rutten

July 1, Royal Decree constituted Leopoldville the capital

Aug. 3, Anglo-Belgian Boundary Protocol signed which enlarged Ruanda-Urundi by about 2,400 square miles of territory in the northwestern part of Tanganyika; approved by the League of Nations on Aug. 31

1925

Aug. 21, Law enacted by Belgian Government on administration of Ruanda-Urundi

Sept. 9, Bill passed and promulgated Sept. 28 made Ruanda-Urundi a part of the Belgian Congo

Dec. 1, Decree increased the poll tax on male adult natives, maximum to be not more than 50 francs

Dec. 9, Decree placed native itinerant traders under government control

1926

March 27, Decree regulated native jurisdiction recognizing 3 types of native courts

1927

June 6, Ordinance placed tax on cattle of from 1 to 5 francs

June 21, Income tax laws coördinated

Sept. 11, Convention was signed between Belgium and Portugal by which the former ceded to the latter territory in the extreme south-west portion of the Belgian Congo, having an area of 3,500 square kilometers (480 square miles), in return for a cession by Portugal of an area in the estuary of the Congo, near Matadi, of three square kilometers. Belgium further undertook to commence the construction of a railway to link up with the Portuguese railway (the Lobito Bay-Katanga line)

Nov. 12, Importation of alcoholic liquors prohibited

Dec. 22, Decree amended July 12, 1928 modified income tax

Dec. 27, Lieutenant General Tilkens appointed Governor General

1928

Jan. 13, Decree created National Committee of Kivu

June, Visit of King Albert for opening of the completed Bas Congo-Katanga Railroad, 695 miles in length, connecting Katanga with Leopoldville by the Kasai River

CAMEROON, FRENCH

Cameroon, French, former German Colony of Kamerun (*See also* Cameroons) administered under mandate confirmed by the League of Nations July 22, 1920. The part of the territory assigned to France by Supreme Council May 6, 1919 as defined by Agreement with Great Britain of July 10, 1919 includes 166,489 square miles excluding the 107,270 square miles ceded to Germany in 1911 which is now included in French Equatorial Africa, population (1928) 1,900,000 including 2,009 Europeans of whom 1,633 were French. A Decree of March 23, 1921 constituted French Cameroon as autonomous territory both administratively and financially. The seat of government is Yaoundé.

M. Marchand, Commissioner.

1916

March 4, Franco-British Agreement as to respective spheres of influence in the occupied territory

April 7, and May 14, Decree and Arret organized the government, General Aymerich, at head

April 29, Program of education announced

Sept. 5, Decree established civil government

Nov. 22, Sale of alcoholic spirits to natives prohibited

Dec. 30, Arret fixed capitation and other taxes

1917

Jan. 12, Decree reorganized European justice put into effect by Arret of Feb. 23; announced that native justice would be regulated by orders of Commissioner

Feb. 16 and July 20, Charges for native porters fixed

April 19, Laws in force in Equatorial Africa declared in force

April 21, Announced that native tribunals of German administration would be retained

June 30, Arret fixed civil status of natives

July 8, Decree attached the territory to Equatorial Africa

Sept. 8, Decree regulated education

1919

May 6, Mandate over the territory assigned by the Supreme Council to France and Great Britain

July 10, Agreement of France and Great Britain defined boundaries of mandates

Sept. 12, Sale of wine and beer to natives in limited amounts permitted

Sept. 13, Tax imposed on women (the number of wives a sign of wealth) capitation tax fixed at 10 francs

1920

May 1 and Sept. 10, The import and sale of arms and munitions prohibited in accordance with Convention of St. Germain-en-Laye of Sept. 17, 1919

June 21, Railroad administration organized

June 23, Decree of April 14 promulgated created Council of Administration

Aug. 7, Customs régime of Congo Basin Convention applied

——, Decree made applicable as of Equatorial Africa rights of *d'entree* and *sortie*

Aug. 8, Tribunal of first degree instituted at Duala

Aug. 11, Land law published in *Journal Officiel*

Oct. 1, Regulations for private education issued

Oct. 7, Capitation tax for natives fixed at 10 francs and 5 for women without children

Oct. 23, Decree applied the mining regulations of Equatorial Africa; modified March 5, 1921

1921

March 5, Decree and Arret of April 28 applied law of Equatorial Africa as to petroleum

March 23, Decree granted political and financial autonomy; amended Feb. 21 and Sept. 18, 1925

April 13, Decree regulated administration of native justice and established *"tribunals de races"* in each district, promulgated May 26, Arret July 1

May 10, Régime of customs of Equatorial Africa declared in force

July 22, Chamber of Commerce, Industry and Agriculture established

July 25, Arret organized public education

Sept. 15, Regulations as to land (*domain privè*) and forests and Decree of Jan. 12, 1922, promulgated March 22

1922

July 9 and Aug. 4, Decree and regulations as to labor

July 10 and Oct. 6, Decree and regulations as to expropriation of public lands

July 20, Mandate confirmed by League of Nations

Nov. 2 and Dec. 16, Decree and Arret prohibited importation of opium and similar drugs, amended Oct. 9, 1926

Nov. 23, Arret fixed rights and charges (money) for natives in courts

Dec. 26 and Oct. 11, 1928, Decree and Arret regulated marriage of natives

Dec. 26, Regulations issued as to recruiting of labor

1923

Oct. 27, Decree instituted tax on Europeans

1924

May 22, Decree promulgated July 12 extended to Cameroon the laws and decrees of French Equatorial Africa before Jan. 1, 1924

Oct. 30, Decree issued as to assignment of land taxes

Dec. 31, Arret as to military service of natives

1925

Sept. 14, Decree regulated immigration and emigration

1926

June 5, Chamber of Commerce and Industry established at Duala

Oct. 30, Decree fixed conditions of admission and stay of foreigners and French nationals

1927

April 13, Decree reorganized Council of Administration, defining powers

June 30, Decree reorganized native justice

July 15, Decree organized European justice

1928

April 13, Law as to customs régime enacted

May 20, Decree regulated mining concessions, regulations April 20, 1930

Nov. 3, Decree reorganized composition of Administrative Council

Nov. 17, Arret made compulsory cards of identity for native workers

1929

Sept. 12, Arret established registration for native workers in commerce

1930

Jan. 13, Decree regulated the sale, trade, and export of produce

April 16, Decree as to hunting replaced earlier law of Aug. 16, 1916, arret of Aug. 13, 1921

June 24, Office of Public Works instituted, including railroads

July 6, Decree fixed conditions of trade, sale, and export of rubber and palm oils

July 15, Decree as to marriage of natives replaced earlier laws

Sept. 19, Arret bringing into effect Decree of June 13, 1929 as to exploitation and concessions in forests

Nov. 7, Decree announced requirements for acquisition of French citizenship

CAMEROONS

The Cameroons, lying between British Nigeria and the French Congo, extends from the coast north-eastwards to the southern shore of Lake Chad. It was captured from the Germans in February, 1916, and is now divided between the British and French under a Declaration signed at London July 10, 1919.

The Cameroons were discovered by the Portuguese navigator Fernando Po at the end of the 15th century, the name Cameroons derived from Portuguese name for the Duala estuary, the Rio dos Camaroes or Shrimp River.

1845

Alfred Saker of the English Baptist Missionary Society obtained cession of land for site of a mission station on Island of Fernando Po

1858

Saker established settlement on Ambas Bay which he named Victoria

1860

Woermann, Hamburg merchant, established first German trade factory in the estuary

1882

Dec. 6, German Colonial Society founded at Frankfort (*Kolonial Verein*)

1883

April 3, The *Gesellschaft für Deutsche Kolonisation* founded by Karl Peters and others in Berlin

1884

April 17, Dr. Gustav Nachtigal appointed Consul to West Africa by Bismarck

July 12, Dr. Gustav Nachtigal, German, raised German flag on coast and proclaimed a protectorate

July 15, Treaty with King Bell and other chiefs signed, placing Belltown, Aquatown, Didotown under German flag 5 days before the arrival of the British Consul, E. H. Hewett with mission to annex the country to Great Britain

July 19, British protectorate over Ambas Bay including Victoria settlement declared

July 26, French gunboat arrived with plans of annexation

Oct. 15, Germany gave official notice of the Protectorate

1885

April 29–May 7, Anglo-German exchange of notes as to spheres of influence in Gulf of Guinea, recognition by Great Britain of German Protectorate of Kamerun, the British missionary settlement at Victoria reserved to Great Britain but in March, 1887 ceded to Germany

July, Von Soden appointed first Governor

Dec. 24, Franco-German Boundary Convention, France ceding Great Batanga and some islands in exchange for Konakri, renouncing rights over Little Popo and Porto Seguro, and recognition of German Protectorate

1886

July 27, Anglo-German Boundary Convention defined frontiers up to Yola

1887

March 28, Great Britain ceded Ambas Bay including Victoria missionary settlement to Germany

Nov. 19, Union of the 2 German colonial societies into the *Deutsche Kolonial Gesellschaft*

1889

A German expedition in 1889 left the Cameroons under the command of Lieut. Morgan with 250 men, to investigate the inland district of the Niger tributaries; after suffering many privations and troubles with the men, and losing over 100 men, Lieut. Morgan and his party were brought from the Benue river to Akassa by an agent of the royal Niger company, reported March 20, 1891

1890

July 1, Anglo-German Boundary Convention fixed frontier with Nigeria

1891

Von Zimmerer became Governor. Recalled in 1883 and Kleist appointed Deputy

1892

May 16, Order established tribunals for native justice

1893

Nov. 15, Anglo-German Boundary Convention

Bali station abandoned with other interior posts

Dec. 15, Mutiny of 60 Dahomey soldiers, assisted by 40 women; the women flogged by order of Herr Kleist; the rising suppressed by the crew of the *Hyæna* and others, Dec. 21; Herr Kleist is recalled to Berlin, April; tried, censured, but acquitted, Oct. 16, 1894; a higher court sentenced him to expulsion from the public service. &c., April, 1895

1894

March 15, Franco-German Boundary Convention fixed boundary with French Equatorial Africa

March 20, Major Leutwein appointed chief commander in S. W. Africa; Major von François commander of the troops, reported

Aug. 27, Hendrik Witboi's stronghold stormed; he surrenders unconditionally; reported Sept. 14

1895

Feb. 17, Buea captured by the Germans after slaughter of the natives, reported

June 7, Bakoko tribes defeated: Jaunde occupied without resistance, reported

July 25, German law forbade the sale and ownership of slaves

Von Puttkamer, Governor (1895–1907)

1896

Jan., Native outbreak suppressed

April 5, Two engagements near Gobabis, natives repulsed, with loss, by Capt. Estorff

April 18, 19, Capt. Estorff defeats the Hottentots and Hereros, near Gobabis

June 15, Imperial decree regulated lands and acquisition of land from natives

June 19, The insurrection of Hottentots suppressed by Major Leutwein; reported

June, A large tract of land acquired by the Germans

1898 to 1900

May, 1898, Rebellion in the south, repressed

Aug. 25, 1899, Capt. Kamptz captures the native usurper in the Tibati country

Sept. 21–26, 1899, Rebel raids into Kribi, Batanga, repulsed after some days' fighting; English and other factories looted by the Bulis, native rising, reported, Nov. 14; 2 Germans murdered, reported, Jan. 14; punitive expedition sent, officers wounded, reported, March 23, 1900

1902

Feb. 21, German law for West Africa declared all children of domestic slaves to be half free and their children entirely free

May 2, Shores of Lake Chad first reached by German troops

July 9, Military operations in Adamawa, chiefs submit, reported

Nov. 21, Imperial order introduced registration system for land

Dec. 12, Anglo-German Boundary Agreement

1904

Jan. 12–13, Rising of the Hereros; they surround Okahandja, destroy a railway bridge at Osona, 3 miles east of Okahandja, and interrupt telegraphic communication with Windhoek. Reinforcements, 56 reservists, with 2 officers, sent by Germans to Okahandja, progress stopped at Waldau station, which is attacked by the Hereros

Jan. 17, Attempts to relieve Windhoek unsuccessful, 5 bands of Hereros marching on Windhoek; patrols sent towards Okahandja driven back, attempts to relieve garrison fail with heavy loss

Jan. 18, Count von Bülow states in the German Reichstag that the insurrection in a few days had spread to the district traversed by the railway from Swakopmund, on the coast, to Windhoek in the interior, and most thickly inhabited by German colonists; the fruits of the industry and perseverance of ten years were destroyed in the region of the insurrection; a large section of the settlers had lost their property, their homes, their land, and their cattle; Windhoek, the capital of the colony, was reported in danger. Preparations were being made to dispatch 500 men with 6 machine guns, and a detachment of railway troops, to arrive at Swakopmund on Feb. 8

Jan. 27, Attempts by Germans to maintain communication with Karibib fail, railway being destroyed near Waldau, 16 persons reported murdered by Hereros, 70 missing; unrest among the natives of German S. W. Africa stated to be extending to the north of the colony towards Grootfontein and the concessions of the Otavi mining company, reported

Jan. 28, Windhoek and Okahandja relieved

Feb. 6, Telegraphic communication between Windhoek and Swakopmund reëstablished; 2 German officials stated to have been murdered at Waterburg on Jan. 14, list of killed amounts to 91, and 200 missing; German force capture Omaruru after fierce fighting, 230 newly-arrived troops sent to its relief from the natives besieging it, Feb. 4; second contingent of the German S. W. African expeditionary force, 400 strong, sails from Hamburg

Feb. 11, Count Pückler in charge of the post of Ossidinge killed while fighting with the natives at Basso, punitive expedition dispatched; Lieut. Winkler surprises the insurgents at Ausis, E. of Windhoek, several of the enemy killed and large number of cattle captured by the Germans

Feb. 25, Column under Maj. von Estorff engages a large and stubborn force of Hereros at Otuehinanaka, E. of Omaruru, and carry the enemy's position, 1 officer killed, 3 wounded, 5 men wounded, 26 Hereros killed, including 2 chiefs and a headman

Losses sustained by German settlers and military forces at the hands of Hereros: 39 killed in action, 65 murdered, 46 wounded, 63 missing up to Feb. 28

March 4, Captain Puder, with company of riflemen of the naval battalion, defeat the Hereros S. of Kleinbarmen, 5 Germans killed, 1 wounded

March 13, Insurgents surprise Maj. von Glasenapp, commander of the marines division and his staff, at Owikokorero; German loss 7 officers and 19 men killed

March 24, Owikokorero occupied by Maj. von Glasenapp

April 2, Sharp engagement between Maj. von Glase-

napp's column and natives near Okaharui; German loss, 1 officer and 31 men killed, 1 officer and 15 men wounded, enemy's loss 92

April 11, Col. Leutwein, the Governor, with force 1,000 strong, successfully attacks the main body of the Hereros near Onganyira; 80 Hereros killed, 2 officers and 2 troopers killed

May 24, Engagement at Otymoasu between German troops under Maj. von Estorff and Hereros, who are put to flight

June 11, Lieut.-Gen. von Trotha, with 80 officers and 600 non-commissioned officers and men, arrive at Swakopmund

Early Aug., 100 Hereros, attacking German troops near Okateitei, are repulsed and 50 killed

Aug. 15, Lieut-Gen von Trotha, with 4,000 to 5,000 men, begins a simultaneous advance on the strongly-entrenched position of the Hereros at Waterberg, resulting in its capture and the dispersal of the enemy with heavy loss, chiefs Banyo and Mutate reported slain; German loss 5 officers and 19 men killed, 5 officers and 52 men wounded, Aug. 11, 12; further severe defeat

Oct. 3, Hottentot chief Hendrik Witboi sends a declaration of war

Oct. 6, Col. Leutwein reports rising of the Witbois, who inhabit Gideon, an important German post in S. of the colony, who have left the town with the intention of taking the field against the Germans; Koes, a station attacked by the Witbois

Dec. 5, Infantry company attacked near Naris by 250 Hottentots, enemy driven from their position, Hendrik Witboi and followers pursued by Col. Deimling

Dec. 15, The Veldschoenträger rise, and are dispersed by Maj. von Lengerke near Koes

Dec. 23, Lieut. Ritter takes by surprise the rebellious North Bethanians, Kamadamas, and Witbois, and completely disperses them from an entrenched position on the Hudub, S. of Aub., 1,000 head of cattle and several thousand sheep captured

1905

Jan. 1, Severe and indecisive engagement between a German column, 3 field companies and 1 battery of artillery, and a body of 500 to 600 Hottentots, near Stamprietfontein, 4 German officers and 15 men killed, 5 officers and 40 men wounded, Hottentot loss estimated 80 killed

Jan. 2–4, Maj. Meister engages force of 1,000 Hereros, and after 50 hours' fighting captures Grossnabas

Jan. 3, Col. Deimling successfully engages the enemy at Haruchas, s. of Gochas, at Gochas, Jan. 5, and at Urikuribis, Jan. 7

Mid. Jan., Zacharias Zerua, the leader of the Hereros at Otyimbingue, 69 miles west of Windhoek, surrenders to Maj. Estorff at Ovinaua

Jan. 12, 39 officers and 286 men killed, 15 officers and 247 men died of typhoid. To date, troops in the Protectorate number 10,400, including 700 wounded and invalids; 2,730 men on way out to seat of war, reported

Jan. 19, Submission of William Maharero, leader of the well-armed Okahandja tribe, reported

Early Feb., Sharp encounter between detachment under Lieut. Eymael and several Herero bands, 200 miles N. of Dabis; insurgents flee, leaving 62 dead

April 17, Capt. Welck, commanding the station garrison at the Waterberg, breaks up a large Herero kraal on the Osondjache hill, it having refused voluntarily to surrender

April 27, German patrol loses Lieut. von Bulow, its commanding officer, and 2 troopers killed; 1 officer and 4 troopers wounded in an engagement with Hottentots near Huams

May 8, German force engages unsuccessfully 300 Hottentots, Capt. von Rappard and 6 men wounded

May 12, 16, and 18, Series of successful skirmishes with the Hottentots

May 19, German force defeats and disperses a band of 150 insurgent Hottentots under the leadership of Hendrik Marengo and Hans Hendrik, Captain of the Veldtschoentrager

June 2, Hottentots reported to have captured Warmbad; after seizing the ammunition and stores, they evacuate the place and capture Kalkfontein

June 6, Successful fight of Capt. von Erckert's company in the Karib Gamtoab district; surprise one of the enemy's kraals, some 30 natives killed, 250 head of cattle and 40 horses and asses captured, June 14; Major von Kamptz, marching with Capt. Siebert's detachment along the Karib, comes on the whole of Marengo's band, who offer a desperate resistance, German troops reinforced by Capt. von Erckert's detachment, and after 14 hours' severe fighting capture the enemy's position; loss to Germans 15 killed, 3 missing, 25 wounded, including Major von Kamptz, June 17

June 26, Marengo, the rebel leader, attacks Capt. Siebert at Amoas in the Karas mountains, defeats the Germans with heavy loss and captures their ammunition and supplies, reported

Early July, Major von Kamptz ambushed by Petrus Christian, at Karriesberg, 15 Germans killed, 26 wounded

Mid July, Estimate of loss of life and cost to Germany of the S.W. African war: 1,100 Germans killed, 512 men wounded in action; estimated cost 250,000,000 marks (12,500,000l.) to

Dec. 29, Number of Hottentot prisoners in German hands on Dec. 24 amounted to 1,100, including 390 men with 192 rifles, reported

1906

Jan. 5, Big drive by the Germans 30 miles S.W. of Aries; several Hottentots killed, including Morenga's brother

Jan. 11, Total number of the enemy who had been made prisoners, or who had surrendered voluntarily, was 12,190 consisting of 10,024 Hereros and 2,166 Hottentots, and including in all, 3,005 men, reported

Feb. 3, Surrender of Hendrik Witbois' son Isaac and 21 of his followers

Feb. 20, Cornelius, the most dangerous of the Hottentot chiefs after Morenga, offers surrender, reported

March 19, Anglo-Germany Boundary Convention delineated the boundary from Yola to the coast. Accepted by both Governments, March 11, 1913

April 10, Total losses of the German troops from the beginning of the insurrection officially stated to be 1,226 killed and 73 wounded, besides 1,200 invalided home and 800 sick in the colony, reported

May 16, Morenga, with several followers, captured at Reimfastmaak in Cape Colony

Nov. 17, Colonel von Deimling reports from Keetman-

shoop that on Nov. 1 a Hottentot band surprised a German force, killing 5 and wounding 3 men

Dec. 21, Herr von Lindequist, Governor of German S. W. Africa, arrived in London for the purpose of negotiating with the British Government on various frontier questions, reported

Dec. 25, Surrender of the Bondelzwarts reported

1907

March 3, Simon Copper, leader of the Franzmann Hottentots, surrenders

April 3, Simon Copper takes refuge with his tribe in the Kalahari district; pursuit begun by Major Pierer, reported

April 25, Trial of former Governor von Puttkamer. *See* Germany

Aug. 14, Hottentot chief Morenga reported in British territory

Sept. 22, Death of Morenga in a fight with British force reported

T. Seitz, Governor (1907–10)

1908

March 16, Reports of heavy fighting in the Kalahari Desert against the native chief Simon Copper received

Dec. 28, 50 Hottentots raid some cattle posts and murder 2 Europeans; 7 soldiers and civilians sent in pursuit were shot down; reported

1909

Feb. 21, Imperial order recognized Duala custom of recognition of children of house slaves as half free but decreed that the children of "half-freed" should be free and in same order prohibited debt bondage

1910

April 25, Imperial Ordinance published organized education

O. Gleim, Governor (1910–1912)

1911

Nov. 4, Franco-German Treaty by which Germany recognized the French Protectorate in Morocco in return for cession of 107,200 square miles of French Equatorial Africa added to Kamerun; 6,450 square miles of Kamerun in the Lake Chad region ceded to France

1912

K. Ebermeier, Governor (1912–1914)

1913

Jan. 1, The Government expropriated land at the mouth of the Wurri River moving 4 native villages in spite of the opposition of the tribes

March 11, Anglo-German Boundary Convention settled the frontier with Nigeria between the Cross River and Yola

Native capitation tax raised from 6 marks to 10

1914

Aug. 6-7, French troops of General Aymerich from Equatorial Africa began hostilities by capture of Bonga and Singa on the Ubangi

Aug. 25, British troops under Colonel P. Maclear crossed the frontier from Nigeria from Yola and occupied Tepe

Aug. 27, British troops from Nigeria under Captain Fox made unsuccessful attack on Mora

Aug. 29–30, British troops under Colonel Maclear attacked Garua but forced to retreat by counter-attack of Germans. Colonel Maclear killed

Aug. 31, The French occupied Wesso

Sept. 6, British at Nsanakang attacked by Germans and forced to surrender

Sept. 20, Capture of Kuseri by French under Colonel Largeau

Sept. 27, Capture of Duala by General Sir C. Dobell

Oct. 6, British captured Yapoma and occupied Susa on the 8th

Oct. 14, British captured Yabasi

Oct. 17, French and Belgians captured Nola and the following day occupied Carnot

Oct. 26, The French commanded by Colonel Mayer occupied Edea and Kopongo 20 miles into the interior

Oct. 30–31, and Nov. 4–5, Unsuccessful attacks on German garrison at Mora

Nov. 15, Capture of Buea by Colonel Gorges

Dec. 2, Commandant Mathieu occupied Kribi

Dec. 9, French and Belgians occupied Baturi, Molundu on the 19th and Bertua on the 29th

Dec. 10, Nkongsamba, terminus of Northern Railway, surrendered by Germans and occupied by Colonel Gorges

Dec. 11, Colonel Gorges occupied Bare capturing about 40 Germans and many stores and 2 aëroplanes in packing cases, the first to reach West Africa

Dec. 12, French occupied Mara and Lake Chad region except Mora cleared of enemy

1915

Jan. 2, General Gorges captured Chang (Dschang) withdrawing on the 7th after destroying the fortifications

Jan. 5, Germans made unsuccessful attacks on Kopongo and Edea

Jan. 15, Junction of French and British forces opposite Garua

Jan. 30, French and Belgians occupied Yukaduma

Feb. 16, Oyem evacuated by Germans occupied by French

April 10, General Dobell began advance on Yaunde, German headquarters, from Edea

April 14, Engagements of forces in Yaunde advance at Ngwe and Kele Rivers

April 29, German attack on Gurin

May 4, Enemy post at Wum Biagas carried by Commandant Mechet, and Sende on the 6th

May 11, Recapture of Eseka by Commandant Mechet

June 10, Garua on the Benue River taken by General Cunliffe

June 24, French and Belgians commanded by General Aymerich captured Lomie

June 28–29, Capture of Ngaundere by General Cunliffe 300 miles northeast of Yaunde

July 19, Occupation of Tingere by British and French forces

July 22, French and Belgians under Colonel Morrison captured Bertua

July 25, Dume occupied by French and Abong Mbang on the 29th

Sept. 7–8, Unsuccessful attack on Mora

Oct. 9, Recapture of Wum Biagas by British and Gold Coast troops

Oct. 30, Capture of Eseka

Nov. 6, Capture of Banyo Mt. position

1916

Jan. 1, Colonel E. H. Gorges occupied Yaunde, unopposed, evacuated by Colonel Zimmermann, the Germans making for Spanish Guinea which they reached about Jan. 20

Jan. 19, Occupation of Ebolowa

Feb. 15, Occupation of Banyassa

Feb. 18, Mora garrison commanded by German Captain von Raben surrendered to Allies, after blockade of 18 months, ending campaign

March 4, Franco-British Agreement as to spheres of influence in the Cameroons

CAMEROONS, BRITISH

The British portion is a strip, area about 31,000 square miles and population estimated at 660,000, stretching from the sea along the Nigerian frontier to Lake Chad. Bantu negroes live near the coast, Sudan negroes inland. The country is administered under a mandate which contains provisions directed against slavery, forced labor (except for essential public services), and abuses of the traffic in arms and spirituous liquors. The northern part is attached to the Provinces of Bornu and Yola in Nigeria, and the southern part, known as the Cameroons Province, to the Southern Provinces of Nigeria. There are Government schools at Victoria.

1916

March 23, Sir F. Lugard, Governor of Nigeria, empowered to administer the British occupied territory in the Cameroons

June 10, Proclamation applied laws of Nigeria to the Cameroons, Native Courts Ordinance, 1914, Native Authority Ordinance (1916), &c.

Sept. 20, Proclamation applied criminal code of Nigeria to Cameroons

Nov. 15, Proclamation prohibited importation of trade spirits

1917

Dec. 20, Forestry law proclaimed

Dec. 27, Proclamation for control of traffic in arms, not to be imported without consent of Resident and importation of trade spirits

1918

Crown Lands ordinance provided for 4 types of leases agricultural, building, railroads, and native occupation

1919

May 6, Supreme Council assigned Cameroons to French and British administration

July 10, Anglo-French Agreement provided for boundaries of spheres of influence in new agreement

Sept. 20, Proclamation made criminal code of Nigeria applicable which prohibited all transactions in slaves

1920

July 3, Proclamation prohibited trade in injurious spirits and possession and importation, reaffirming Proclamation of Dec., 1917

1921

Nov. 1, Proclamation applied customs tariff of Nigeria of 1916 to the Cameroons

Dec. 21, Native courts reorganized to take effect from Jan. 1, 1922, reduced from 11 to 6

1922

April 1, A native treasury set up in each of 4 divisions

July 20, Mandate confirmed by the League of Nations

1923

Feb. 16, Proclamation applied Nigeria Drugs and Poisons Ordinance to the Cameroons, prohibiting importation of opium and similar drugs

June 26, British Cameroons Order in Council applied to the Cameroons the Nigeria Protectorate Order in Council and the Nigeria (Legislative Council) Order in Council

Oct. 22, Death of Waziri Abba Haji Bashir at Bornu

1924

Feb. 28, A large number of Nigerian laws came into effect from this date, Labor Charter, Arms Ordinance, Slavery Abolition, Restrictive Liquor, Native Courts, &c.

May 12, School at Dikwa formally opened by Sheikh

1925

No. 1 British Cameroons Administration Ordinance enacted

1926

May, New Nigerian Education Ordinance became law

1927

British Cameroons Administration (Ordinance) amended to provide for extension of native rights, land laws, &c.

CANARY ISLANDS

Canary Islands, Spanish archipelago in the Atlantic Ocean off the northwest coast of Africa, forming a province of Spain. The principal islands are Teneriffe, Grand Canary, Palma, Hierro or Ferro, Landzarote, Gomera, and Fuerteventura; the other six are small and uninhabited, Graciosa, Rocca, Allegranza, Santa Clara, Inferno, and Lobos. The islands were known in ancient times and are mentioned by Pliny. They were rediscovered in 1334 by a French vessel driven ashore in a storm, and in 1402 Jean de Bethencourt, a Norman, took possession, landing on Lanzarote. Islands sold by his nephew to the envoy of Queen Catherine of Castile, and then resold by him to Prince Henry, the Navigator. The Portuguese claims were resigned in favor of Spain by the Treaty of Alcaçova in 1479 between Portugal and Castile. Palma was conquered by the Spaniards in 1491 and Teneriffe in 1495. The area of the islands is 2,810 square miles, and population 503,151. Santa Cruz on Teneriffe is the capital.

CAPE OF GOOD HOPE

Cape of Good Hope, Province of the, one of the four constituent provinces of the Union of South Africa, formerly known as Cape Colony, occupying the southern end of Africa, was originally founded by the Dutch in the year 1652. Britain took possession of it in 1795 but evacuated it in 1803. A British force again took possession in 1806 and the Colony has remained a British Possession since that date. It was formally ceded to Great Britain by the Convention of London, August 13, 1814. Letters Patent issued in 1850 declared that in the Colony there should be a Parliament which should consist of the Governor, a Legislative Council, and a House of Assembly. On May 31, 1910, the Colony was merged in the Union of South Africa, thereafter forming an original province of the Union.

Cape Town is the seat of the Provincial Administration.

	AREA IN SQ. MILES	1921			1926
		European	Non-European	Total	European
Colony Proper	260,185	635,651	1,183,077	1,818,728	690,079
East Griqualand	6,602	6,245	258,582	264,827	7,065
Tembuland	3,339	4,627	230,361	234,988	4,693
Transkei	2,504	2,292	195,803	198,095	2,477
Pondoland	3,906	1,512	263,392	264,904	1,823

J. H. Conrache, Administrator.

1487

The Cape of Good Hope named by John II of Portugal was discovered by the Portuguese Bartholomew de Diaz

1497

Nov. 19, The Cape doubled and passage to India discovered by Vasco da Gama

1652

April 7, Dutch expedition sent by the East India Company of 3 ships under command of Jan van Riebeek landed at Table Bay and erected fort in Cape Town

1666

Jan. 2, The present Castle founded by Zacharias Wagenar (May 6, 1662–Sept. 27, 1666) who succeeded van Riebeek

Sept. 27, Cornelis van Quaelberg, Governor (to June 18, 1668)

1679–1699

Simon van der Stel, Commander and then Governor, called the "second founder of the Cape"

1688

Huguenots driven from France by revocation of the Edict of Nantes, joined the Dutch settlement

1699–1707

Adriaan van der Stel, son of Simon, Governor

1751–1771

Ryk Tulbach, the last great Dutch Governor, and "halcyon" period of rule of the Dutch East India Company

1795 to 1834

Sept. 16, 1795, Colony taken by the English under Admiral Elphinstone and General Clarke
March 27, 1802, Restored at the peace of Amiens
Jan. 19, 1806, Taken by Sir D. Baird and Sir H. Popham
Aug. 13, 1814, Finally ceded to England under Treaty of Paris, May 30, 1814. Lord Charles Somerset, first regular British Governor
1819, The Kaffirs, headed by Mokanna, a prophet, attack Grahamstown; repulsed with much slaughter; again defeated, 1828, 1831, 1834
March, 1820, British emigrants arrive
Oct., 1834, The Kaffirs make irruptions on the British settlements, and ravage Grahamstown
Dec. 11, Treaty with Griqua chief, Nicholas Waterboer

1835

May 10, Proclamation extended the boundary east to right bank of Kei River
June 16, Proclamation and Order in Council of annexation, boundary extended
Sept. 17, Treaty by which Gaika, Tslambie territory, annexed

1846 to 1849

Oct. 10, 1846, The Governor appointed High Commissioner
1847, Bishopric of Cape Town founded; Dr. Robert Gray, first bishop
Sept. 4, 1848, Order in Council making Cape Colony a penal settlement
May 19, 1849, The inhabitants successfully resist the attempt to make the cape a penal colony

1850

Dec. 31, The Kaffirs rise; Sir Harry Smith, the governor, proclaims martial law, and orders the inhabitants to rise *en masse* to defend the frontier

1851

March, Territories north of Great Orange river placed under British authority, Feb. 3, 1848; annexed as the Orange river territory
Nov. 6, Disastrous operations against the Kaffirs in the Waterkloeff follow; Colonel Fordyce and several officers and men of the 74th regiment killed

1852

Feb. 26, Wreck of the *Birkenhead* with reinforcements from England
Dec. 20, The hostilities of the Kaffirs having assumed all the features of regular warfare, the Governor-General, Cathcart, attacked and defeated them

1853

March 9, The conditions offered by Cathcart accepted, and peace restored
July 1, The constitution granted to the colony promulgated, dated May 23, 1850
Aug., General Prætorius, chief of the Transvaal republic, died

1854

April 10, The British jurisdiction over the Orange river territory abandoned, Feb. 23; a free state was formed
July 1, The first Parliament meets at Cape Town

1856

Aug., The Kaffirs much excited by a prophet named Umhla-kaza; by the exertions of Sir George Grey, the governor, tranquillity maintained

1860 to 1865

About Dec., 1860, The first railway from Cape Town, about 58 miles long, opened
1863–65, Disputes between bishops of Cape Town and Natal

1870

March 11, Death of Moshesh, an eminent chief of the Basutos, friendly to the British
Dec. 31, Sir Henry Barkly took office as Governor

1871

March, Energy of Sir Henry Barkly (governor), in repressing aggressions of the President of the Orange River Territory
Oct. 27, Colony of Griqualand West, annexed Aug. 15, constituted
Nov. 17, The British flag erected amidst the diamond fields with great acclamation

1873

Sept. 11, Macomo, an eminent Kaffir chief, died
Nov., Dec., Insurrection of Langalibalele, a chief, suppressed (*see* Natal)

1875

Nov. 11, South African Confederation proposed by Earl of Carnarvon; opposed by Mr. Molteno and his cabinet, May; long debate commenced on it in the Cape parliament
Nov., Earl of Carnarvon, in a dispatch, proposes that the conference on the confederation shall be transferred to England, Oct. 22; much resented
Nov. 26, Earl of Carnarvon's dispatch expressing earnest desire for the confederation, and proposing a meeting of delegates in London, their decision not to be conclusive, Nov. 15; parliament prorogued

1876

Aug. 5, Conference of delegates in London began; Earl of Carnarvon, not Mr. Molteno, present

1877

March 31, Sir Henry Bartle Edward Frere took office as Governor
April 12, Transvaal republic (*see s.v.*) annexed
Aug. 8, Royal charter granted to University of Cape of Good Hope created by Act of Parliament in 1873

Sept., Troublesome disputes between tribes (Fingoes and Galekas); lead to war

Oct., Sir Bartle Frere, the governor general, with officers and volunteers, proceeds to the spot; Kreli defeated by Commandant Griffith, his kraal burnt, Oct. 9; deposed and his lands annexed

Dec. 2, Galekas defeated and expelled

About Dec. 30, Rise of the Gaikas under Sandilli, an old chief (who after education relapsed into barbarism)

1878

Jan., Cetywayo, King of the Zulus, troublesome; Sir B. Frere requests help; 90th regiment and a battery of artillery sent from England

March–May, British advance; rebels defeated, Jan. 24, 26; at Quintana, Feb. 7, by Gen. Thesiger (about 400 Kaffirs killed; Sandilli escapes), March 18, 19; again (Capt. Donovan, Lieut. Ward, and Capt. Shawe killed), about March 21; continued fighting, sometimes severe

March 12, Commander Dyer took possession of Walvis (Walfish Bay) and 300 square miles adjacent for Great Britain

April, Mr. Molteno's ministry dismissed; one formed by Mr. J. Gordon Sprigg, about Feb. 12; reported successful

June, Sandilli and other chiefs reported dead; his sons captured

July 2, Kaffir war ended; amnesty to surrendering rebels announced

Aug. 1, Thanksgiving day for restoration of peace

Sept., Tini Macomo and Gangubele condemned to death as traitors; reprieved

All Kaffraria to the frontiers of Natal included within the bounds of Cape Colony

For the war, *see also* Basuto Land, Transvaal, and Zululand

1879

Jan. 12, Zulu war begins (*see* Zululand)

Dec., Insurrection in the Transvaal (*see s.v.*)

Dec. 25, Telegraphic communication with Great Britain completed

1880

About June 24, Government proposition for conference of delegates to promote federation, rejected by the assembly

June, War with Basutos

Aug. 2, Recall of Sir Bartle Frere, Aug. 1; announced in parliament

Opinions [as to his policy and that of the home government greatly differed]

Aug. 21, Sir Hercules G. R. Robinson appointed Governor and Lord High Commissioner for South Africa

1881

Jan. 22, Sir Hercules G. R. Robinson assumed office as Governor

May 6, 7, Resignation of Mr. Sprigg's Ministry, through narrow escape of vote of censure; succeeded by Mr. Scanlen and Mr. Molteno

1882

May 1, Bill making use of Dutch language optional in both Houses of the Legislature passed third reading

1883 to 1884

Settled difficulty with Transvaal (*see s.v.*)

1884

May 7, Ministry defeated, resigns; Mr. Upington, new minister

Oct., They agree to support the imperial government in repressing the Boer filibusters

1885

July 14, Annexation of Tembuland

July 25, Annexation of Walfish Bay

Nov. 28, Railway to Kimberley opened

The houses of Parliament opened

1886

About Nov. 25, New ministry; Sir J. Gordon Sprigg Prime Minister

Dec. 9, The Pondos invade Xesibeland, Oct. 20; peace announced

1887

Oct., New registration act disfranchising many natives passed; much opposed Aug.–Sept.; supported by the home government

Nov. 1, Rode Valley annexed

1888

Feb. 18, Conference of delegates from Cape Colony, Natal, and the Orange Free State held at Cape Town; a customs union and railway extension proposed; a movement towards S. African federation; conference closed

1889

Dec. 13, Sir H. Brougham Loch appointed governor and high commissioner for South Africa about June 22, 1889; arrives

1890

July 10, Defeat of the ministry on the great railway schemes about July 5; resignation of Sir J. Gordon Sprigg

July 17, New ministry formed by Mr. Cecil John Rhodes, founder of the British South Africa company

Oct. 16, Failure of the Cape of Good Hope bank after long run on it; much alarm throughout the colony, Sept. 24; reported deficiency, 464,000*l.*

1891

March 6, Sir Henry Loch and Mr. Rhodes visit London to discuss South African affairs with the government, Feb. 2–27. Results reported

1892

March 10, Sir H. B. Loch opens the junction railway between Cape Colony and the Free State

1893

Feb., A new franchise act opposed by the colored population (1892), not vetoed by the Queen

May 4, Mr. Cecil Rhodes returns from a visit to England, March 8; he resigns; reconstructs his ministry, including Sir J. Gordon Sprigg

June 22, Vote disapproving Mr. Cecil Rhodes' continuance as premier and a director of the S. Africa company, rejected (57–2)

1894

Jan. 3, Mr. Cecil Rhodes arrives at Cape Town after

his tour through Mashonaland and Matabeleland, reports the conquest of Matabeleland
Sept. 25, Annexation of Pondoland

1895

Feb. 2, Mr. Cecil Rhodes made Privy Councillor
Feb., Sir Hercules Robinson appointed to succeed Sir Henry Loch
March 31, Sir Charles Mills, Agent-General for the Colony, 1882, *et seq.*, born in 1825, died
April 25, Wm. Lippert, formerly manager of the Union bank of Cape Town, sentenced to 7 years' penal servitude for forgeries on the bank amounting to 200,000*l.*
June 11, Tongaland annexed
June 11, Aug. 1 and Nov. 11, British Bechuanaland annexed by the assembly

1896

Jan. 6, Mr. Cecil Rhodes accused of complicity with Dr. Jameson's action; *see* Transvaal, Jan., 1896; resigns, Jan. 6; succeeded by Sir John Gordon Sprigg
Feb. 10, Mr. Cecil Rhodes arrives in London, Feb. 4; interview with Mr. Chamberlain, Feb. 6; leaves for Rhodesia
May 1, Parliament opened
Aug. 31, Sir H. Robinson leaves for England, May 20; created Baron Rosmead, July (1896); returns to Cape Town
Sept. 22, Petition for the reinstatement of Mr. Cecil Rhodes, 13,000 signatures, transmitted to Mr. Chamberlain

1897

Jan. 6, Mr. Cecil Rhodes warmly received at Cape Town; Dec. 30; sails for England
Feb. 15, Lord Rosmead resigns, succeeded by Sir Alfred Milner; announced
March 29, Great meeting in favor of Mr. Cecil Rhodes, and against the evidence of Mr. Schreiner at the S. Africa committee, London
April 20, Mr. Rhodes arrives at Cape Town
April 21, Lord Rosmead leaves for England
Aug. 30–Sept. 26, Colonial tour of Sir Alfred Milner
Dec. 16, Sir J. Gordon Sprigg (in London) authorized by the Cape Parliament, offers Mr. Goschen, First Lord of the Admiralty, to present the cost of a 1st class battleship, as a contribution from Cape Colony, July 10; proposed to take the form of the payment of the yearly interest (abt. 25,000*l.*); announced
Dec. 30, Sigcau, the Pondo chief, claims 1,500*l.* from the Government as damages for false imprisonment; announced

1898

Jan., Legislative council dissolved
Feb. 11, Galishwe, rebel chief, captured by Capt. Denison; Aug. 30, 1897; sentenced to 10 years' imprisonment
March 3, The Graaf Reinet-Middelburg railway, opened by Sir A. Milner
April 12, The Customs union conference opened at Cape Town
April 20, Telegraphic communication established between Cape Town and Blantyre
Oct. 14, Parliament opened May 20; Mr. Schreiner's motion of want of confidence voted, June 22–23; Parliament prorogued, June 28; opened by Sir A. Milner, Oct. 10; Mr. Schreiner's vote of want of

confidence carried, 39–37, Oct. 11; (Ministry resigns) new one under Mr. Schreiner
Oct. 24, Death of General Sir W. Goodenough, commander-in-chief; succeeded by general Butler, who arrives at Cape Town, Nov. 30
Dec. 7, Redistribution act, 16 new seats; total, 95 members, passed
Dec. 9, Imperial navy contribution bill (30,000*l.* annually) passed without debate

1899

Jan. 3, Customs union convention comes into operation
June, The Swellendam railway opened by Sir A. Milner, April 12; he leaves Cape Town for Natal (*see s.v.*), May 29; returns, his Transvaal policy, "equality all round," warmly supported
July 14, Parliament opened, with Queen's speech
July 18, Demonstration to Mr. Rhodes on his return to Cape Town
Sept. 6, General Sir F. Forestier-Walker arrives to take command of troops
Oct. 31, General Sir Redvers Buller arrived at Cape Town (*see* South African War)
Oct. 30, Loyal meeting of Mahomedans at Cape Town
Nov. 23, Sir A. Milner's proclamation of equality to British and Dutch alike, issued

1900

Jan. 10, Field-Marshal Lord Roberts and Lord Kitchener arrive at Cape Town
Feb. 15, Great rejoicings at the relief of Kimberley (*see* South African War); the surrender of general Cronje, Feb. 27, and the relief of Ladysmith, Feb. 28
March 16, Public meeting of Irishmen, loyal message to the Queen
March 27, Sir George White received at Cape Town
April 23, Many Cape rebels sentenced to various terms of imprisonment
May 28, Annexation of the Orange Free State proclaimed at Cape Town
June 18, Ministerial crisis, disruption of the Bond party, Mr. Schreiner, Premier, upholds the policy of Sir A. Milner and home government, June 11, 12; he resigns, June 13; Sir J. Gordon Sprigg forms a (progressive) cabinet, Mr. Rose-Innes, Att.-Gen.; Mr. Graham, Col. Sec.
Aug. 23, Letters found at Pretoria and Bloemfontein, written by leading South Africans in Cape Colony and English M.P.'s to Boer officials, published as a parliamentary paper
Sept. 3, The annexation of the Transvaal announced in the House of Assembly
Sept. 7–12, General Baden-Powell arrives at Cape Town
Sept. 28, Treason bill read third time in the house of assembly, 46–37, Sept. 21, and the legislative council, 12–8
Oct. 2, Transvaal concessions commission began work in South Africa, end of Aug.; meets at Cape Town (*see* Transvaal, June and Nov., 1901)
Oct. 10, 13, South African league congress opened with a speech by Mr. Rhodes, president
Oct. 23, 24, General Buller arrives at Cape Town
Dec. 12, Afrikander congress at Worcester; resolutions against the war and demanding the independence of the Boer republics carried, Dec. 6; presented to Sir A. Milner

Dec. 21, Lord Kitchener issued order for gathering non-combatant population in "concentration camps"
Boer raids. *See* South African War

1901

Jan. 1, Proclamation calling for volunteers (loyal response), issued

March 6, Sir Walter F. Hely-Hutchinson appointed governor, Jan.; arrives

April 19, 22, Mr. Malan, editor of *Ons Land*, and two others sentenced to 6 months, and Mr. Cartwright, editor of the *South African News*, to a year's imprisonment for seditious libel

May 24, Sir A. Milner leaves for Pretoria, Feb. 28; returns to Cape Town, presented with an address of confidence (over 10,000 signatures), leaves for England, May 4–8; made a peer (Lord Milner of St. James' and Cape Town)

July 4, South African constabulary formed, reported successful

Aug. 27, Lord Milner returns to Cape Town

Oct. 9, Martial law extended through the Colony

Dec. 18, Mr. Marais charged with violating certain regulations in the Paarl district under martial law, and imprisoned, Aug.; his claim to be tried by a civil tribunal rejected by the supreme court, and again by the judicial committee of the privy council, London

1902

Feb., Mass meeting at Cape Town, the mayor, chairman, to protest against Continental and pro-Boer slanders on British troops in South Africa; another by Germans, Feb. 10

March 26, Mr. Cecil Rhodes, born July 5, 1853; died; laid in state, impressive funeral ceremonies at Cape Town (*see* Rhodesia), April 3

June 2, Sir J. Gordon Sprigg opposes the suspension of the constitution

June 6, 21, 23 and July 4, 5, Meetings in favor of the suspension of the constitution

June 11, Proclamation calling on rebels to surrender before July 10, issued

July 5, Petition for the temporary suspension of the Cape constitution, signed by 42 members of the Cape parliament and over 34,000 others, negatived by Mr. Chamberlain, but the speedy summoning of the legislature agreed to, in order to pass the necessary legislation

July 16, Ex-pres. and Mrs. Steyn leave for England

July 30, Generals Louis Botha, Delarey, and De Wet well received, July 23–29; sail for Europe

Aug. 1, Sir W. Hely-Hutchinson opens the new railway at Caledon

Aug. 13, The first *train de luxe* from Bulawayo reaches Cape Town in 74 hours

Aug. 20, Split in the progressives; Dr. Smartt elected leader

Aug. 28, Dr. Jameson denounces the proposed colonial commission of inquiry into martial law

Sept. 2, Conference of Dutch loyalists at Paarl, Aug.; petition of grievances presented

Aug.–Sept., Breach between Sir Gordon Sprigg and the progressives

Sept. 11, Indemnity bills passed

Sept. 12, Royal commission (Lord Alverstone, Mr. Justice Bigham, and others) reviews martial law sentences at Cape Town, Aug. 26 *et seq.*; leaves for the north

Sept. 17, Martial law repealed; peace preservation Act proclaimed

1903

Cape Town branch of progressive association formed

Feb. 10, Mr. Chamberlain at Cape Town; receives deputations from S. African league, and other bodies; receives deputation of loyal Dutchmen of Cape Colony, headed by Sir Henry Juta, Feb. 23; leaves Cape Town for England, Feb. 24

April 30, Bond congress opened at Somerset East

May 1, Passes resolution urging a colonial commission of inquiry into the administration of martial law. Revision of the constitution of the Bond agreed to. Mr. Theron elected president

Late June, Bill authorizing expenditure of over 2,000,-000*l.* on new railways introduced in Cape assembly

——, Appointment of members of legislative council of the Transvaal and Orange River Colonies announced

July 30, Customs amendment and tariff preferential treatment for British imports passed

Aug. 20–22, Congress of Progressive Associations at Cape Town; resolutions carried recognizing the services of Lord Milner and Mr. Chamberlain; Dr. Jameson elected president

Sept. 2, Ministry defeated on a motion concerning an enquiry into martial law, fines and compensation claims, Aug. 25; deadlock; Parliament dissolved

Mid Nov., Legislative council elections result in the return of progressives by a majority of one

Nov. 30, Great distress among immigrants

Dec. 15, Lord Milner returns from England

Dec. 19, Mass meeting to protest against the introduction of Chinese labor in the Transvaal

1904

Early Feb., Elections for the House of Assembly: progressive party secure a majority of 5

Feb. 18, Sir Gordon Sprigg, Premier, resigns

Feb. 21, Dr. Jameson forms a new ministry, himself Premier, with the charge of native affairs

March 2, Bond Congress opens at Stellenbosch

March 4, Parliament opens; Governor in his speech announces bills dealing with representative Chinese immigration and repeal of the Peace Preservation act

——, Additional representation bill introduced in the Assembly providing 12 new seats in the House of Assembly and 3 in the Legislative Council; after much obstruction, the Bond members' bill passes the second reading by 42 votes to 34, March 29; and its third reading by 49 votes to 43, April 18

Early April, Chief justice of Cape Colony decides, in the case of a Jewish alien, that the Crown may, by the exercise of its prerogative, prohibit the entry of aliens into British territory, and that the Colonial immigration law does not interfere with, and does not limit the power of, the common law

April 21, Legislative Council pass the additional representation bill

May 4, Proposes an excise duty on spirits and beer and a graduated income tax

May 13, Dr. Jameson announces the pardon of all rebels except one guilty of murder

May 23, Government defeated in House of Assembly by 43 votes to 33 on a motion for the reduction of the estimates

Early July, Elections for the extra seats created by the

Additional Representation act; 11 progressives returned

Dec. 5, Dr. Jameson, speaking at Grahamstown, states that he is in favor of the taxation of the profits on diamonds; he declares his entire adhesion to Mr. Chamberlain's fiscal policy

1905

Mid Jan., Education bill introducing compulsory education of children of European parentage between the ages of 7 and 14; establishes school boards in place of the old committees, one-third of the members of the board to be government nominees, one-third elected by the local governing body, and one-third elected by parents, published

End Jan., Report of the Bloemfontein conference of South African attorney-generals proposes a federal appeal court for civil and criminal actions, the minimum amount in the former being 100*l.*; power of appeal to the privy council to be retained, 2,000*l.* being the minimum amount on which an appeal can be made, issued

Feb. 8, Report of the S. African native affairs commission issued

March 1, Resignation of Viscount Milner, the Earl of Selborne appointed his successor

March 10, Cape Parliament opened by Sir W. Hely-Hutchinson; release of all rebels promised; estimates of expenditure for 1905–6 show a decrease of 1,600,-000*l.*, as compared with 1904–5

March 29, Death of Sir David Tennant, Agent-General of Cape Colony, 1896–1902 and for 30 years member of the Legislative Assembly, Cape Colony, and Speaker 1874–96

April 5, Mr. Marlan's motion in the House of Assembly in favor of compulsory proficiency in Dutch in the Cape civil service rejected by 51 votes to 44. Question referred to the civil service commission

May 10, Labor clauses of the Glen Grey act, the subject of controversy since their proposal by the late Mr. Rhodes, repealed

May 11, Select committee on the estimates recommends a further retrenchment of 127,320*l.*

May 30, Third session of the inter-colonial council, opened by Sir Arthur Lawley at Pretoria

June 3, Government defeated on a motion by Mr. Sauer to modify the customs unions tariffs, so as to give more reasonable protection to products of the soil and colonial manufactures; amendments reserving the right to impose duties on imports in excess of the convention duties and the favoring of colonial products carried against the Government

June 5, Debate in the House of Assembly on the railway bill; the schedule providing for the construction of a line between Aliwal North and Ladybrand rejected by 40 votes to 30

June 6, Legislative Council agrees by 10 votes to 8 to the adoption of the railway conference proposals, which were defeated in the House of Assembly
——, Loan bill for 662,000*l.* read second time, May 29, passes the House of Assembly

Aug. 15, British Association meets at Cape Town

1906

Jan. 9, Arrival at Cape Town of the Duke and Duchess of Connaught and Princess Patricia

May 16, Capture of the Hottentot chief, Morenga

May 25, Parliament opened: Governor, in his speech, announces compensation for war losses and an amnesty for rebels among the measures for the session, which would be devoted to irrigation and other needed reforms

June 18, Customs Union bill passes its final stages in the Legislative Council

June 19, The treasurer announces that Lord Selborne would convene a conference on bounties by individual colonies after the union was settled; council accepts the convention by 14 votes to 11, but adds a rider expressing the regret that it included the principle of preference

June 27, The West-Ridgeway committee of inquiry leaves Cape Town for England

July 16, Death of Mr. Alfred Beit (*b.* 1853)

Aug. 6–8, Disturbances among the colored population of Cape Town

Aug. 14, Amnesty bill passed by the House of Assembly

Oct. 26, Meeting held by the British Indians of Cape Town protesting against the Asiatic legislation of the colony

Nov. 10, Ferreira and several other Boers, recently employed in German S.W. Africa, entered Cape Colony and endeavored to organize a rebellion. The Dutch leaders in Cape Town are supporting the Government, reported

Nov. 14, General Botha describes the raiders as mere filibusters, and offers his personal services to the Government

Nov. 16, Ferreira and his followers captured by a force of Cape mounted rifles and others

Nov. 20, Lord Selborne issues memorandum on the railway rate dispute

Nov. 21, The imperial union congress met at Grahamstown

Nov. 27, Preliminary examination of Ferreira and his fellow-raiders begun at Upington

1907

Jan. 31, The Transkeian native council resolves to contribute 10,000*l.* in five instalments for the establishment of an inter-state native college, and to offer a free site for the college, reported

Feb. 4, Government scheme for State advances to farmers for agricultural purposes promulgated

Feb. 20, Trial of Ferreira and four other raiders concluded at Kimberley; all sentenced to death, two being recommended to mercy

March 7, Great depression reported from the colony; passages to England, of men on the relief works, paid by the Government

March 13, Death sentences on the Ferreira raiders commuted; Ferreira and two of his companions to be imprisoned for life, and the other two prisoners for 15 years

March 27, General Botha arrives at Cape Town on his way to England for the colonial conference

May 9, As a result of the prevailing depression, 700 Australians, half of them being from the Transvaal, are repatriated by the Australian Government; they sail from Cape Town

May 28, General Botha arrives at Cape Town on his return from the Imperial conference

Aug. 29, Government measure, imposing a profit tax of 10% on diamond and copper mining companies earning above 50,000*l.* per annum, passed by the House of Assembly

Sept. 22, Death of Morenga, Hottentot chief, in a fight with a British force

1908

Jan. 31, Dr. Jameson resigns the premiership

Feb. 1, Mr. T. X. Merriman forms a ministry

April 6, Results of the elections to the Assembly—Ministerialists, 69; Unionists, 33; and Independents, 5

April 10, The Tariff Commission reports in favor of a moderate increase of duties

June 19, Parliament opened by the Governor

Oct. 12–Feb. 3, 1909, Constitutional Convention met at Cape Town, delegates including Dr. Jameson, Chief Justice de Villiers, ex-President Steyn, Sir George Farrer, Sir Percy Fitzpatrick, F. T. Moor, J. C. Smuts, Generals Herzog and de Wet, Louis Botha, A. Fisher and drew up "Draft Act" providing for incorporation of the colonies of the Transvaal, Orange River, Natal, and Cape of Good Hope into the South African Union on equal basis

Nov. 5–12, Visit of a British cruiser squadron to Cape Town

Dec. 17, The Rt. Rev. Dr. Carter, Bishop of Pretoria, elected Archbishop of Cape Town

1909

April 16, Draft Act of Union passes the House of Assembly, April 15; and the Legislative Council

May 3–11, Second Constitutional Convention held at Bloemfontein, Orange River Colony and approved Draft Act for Union

Sept. 20, The Draft Act Bill taken to England by a select committee and introduced into Parliament, became law

Oct. 16, Death of J. H. Hofmeyer

1910

April 24–27, Formation of South African Party (Nationalist Party) led by Botha and Herzog

May 17, Arrival of Lord and Lady Gladstone at Cape Town

May 19, Lord Gladstone sworn in as High Commissioner

May 23–24, Formation of Progressives or Unionist Party

May 31, Union of South Africa inaugurated. *See* South Africa, Union of

CAPE VERDE ISLANDS

Cape Verde Islands, archipelago belonging to Portugal, off the west African coast, discovered in 1456 by the Venetian Cadamosto in the service of Prince Henry, the Navigator.

The Cape Verde Islands consist of ten islands and four islets which are administered by a Governor, whose seat is at Praia, the capital. The islands are divided into two groups, named Barlavento (windward) and Sotavento (leeward). The former is constituted by the islands of S. Vicente, S. Antaõ, S. Nicolau, Santa Luzia, Sal and Bõa Vista, and the small islands named Branco and Raso. The latter is constituted by the islands of São Tiago, Maio, Fogo, and Brava, and the

small islands named Rei and Rombo. S. Vicente is a coaling station which supplies all navigation to South America. The total area is 3,929 square kilometers (1,475 square miles). The population according to the census of 1928, is 150,160 (67,427 males and 82,733 females), including Europeans and foreigners.

COMORO ISLANDS

Comoro Islands, group of volcanic islands in the Indian Ocean belonging to France, situated at northern entrance of the Mozambique Channel between Madagascar and the continent of Africa. Mayotte was ceded to France by Treaty with the Sultan of March 25, 1841. The archipelago includes Mayotte, Anjouan, Grande Comore, and Moheli. Before 1912, Anjouan, Moheli, and Grande Comore were only under French protection; Mayotte alone being a colony. But by a law of July 25, 1912, and a decree of February 23, 1914, the whole archipelago has become a colony, attached to the general government of Madagascar, of which it forms a twenty-first province, the Province de "Mayotte et Dépendances."

In 1925, the combined population was 119,305, including 804 Europeans.

The island of Mayotte (140 square miles) had a population (1925) of 12,674.

CORISCO ISLAND.

See Guinea, Spanish

DAHOMEY

Dahomey, French West Africa stretches from the coast between Togoland on the west and the British possessions of Lagos and Nigeria on the east, and is bounded on the northeast by the river Niger and on the north and northwest by the colony of the Upper Volta, northwards to the French Military Territories. France obtained a footing on the coast in 1851, and gradually extended her power until in 1894 the whole kingdom of Dahomey was annexed. The colony has only about 70 miles of coast, but opens out northwards into a wide hinterland. The area is about 41,302 square miles, and the population, according to the latest census of 1929, 1,080,447, including 1,093 Europeans. The seat of government is Porto Novo (the chief business center), which has about 23,614 inhabitants.

1838

April 4, the Portuguese declared claim to Whydah on the coast in view of rights of discovery; same region claimed by France

1851

July 1, The French (Bouët–Willaumez) concluded

treaty with King of Dahomey at Abomey, of commerce and amity

1852

Jan. 1, Dahomey coast blockaded by British in operations to suppress the slave trade. Raised June 15 after Anti-Slave Trade Treaty signed by King Feb. 13

1863

Feb. 25, Protectorate Treaty over Porto Novo and French settlement

1868

May 19, Cession of Kotonu to France by the King Glégle; confirmed by new Treaty of April 19, 1878
Dec. 23, Admiral Laffont lowered the French flag at Porto Novo abandoning the Protectorate

1879

Feb. 4, Consular Agent established at Porto Novo

1882

April 14, Protectorate reëstablished by the French over Porto Novo and Resident installed, made effective April 2, 1883
Oct. 12, Decree placed Dahomey under administration of Senegal

1883

July 19, Protectorate declared over Porto Seguro and Grand Popo and Little Popo in view of earlier treaties

1885

May 10, The King attacks Lagos, kills many and takes about 1,000 prisoners
June 10, Treaty by which France acquired protectorate over the Ouatchis
By Treaty of Aug. 5 Dahomey placed under the protectorate of Portugal at the request of the King
Dec. 24, Franco-German Convention by which Porto Seguro and Little Popo ceded to Germany (Togoland)

1886

Jan. 21, Portuguese proclaimed Protectorate over Dahomey at request of the King of Dahomey
Aug. 4, Decree placed Kotonu and Porto Novo under administration of French Guinea

1887

Dec. 22, Portugal withdrew claim to coast

1888

Jan. 2, Boundary *modus vivendi* as to frontier with Lagos

1889

Aug. 1, Decree reorganized the government
Aug. 10, Anglo-French Boundary Agreement; Great Britain withdrew claim to Kotonu
Dec. 1, Victor Ballot named Resident Gulf of Benin, appointed Oct. 12 to succeed Dr. Tautain, took office

1890

Jan. 3, Senagalese troops landed at Kotonu
Feb. 18–19, More troops from Senegal commanded by Lieutenant Colonel Terrillon arrived at Kotonu and occupation proclaimed

Feb. 23, Hostile demonstration of natives suppressed and their village burned
Feb. 24, Dahomeyans returned in large numbers and attacked troops
March 1, Dahomey warriors defeated by French at Zogbo (Zebo) on Kake Denham
March 4, Dahomey troops again attacked Kotonu
April 24, Lieutenant Colonel Klipfel occupied and fortified Porto Novo
The King in a letter to President Carnot justifies his retention of French merchants at Whydah for meddling with politics, received about April 28
April 29, 30, Whydah bombarded by the French vessel *Kerguelin*; Commander Fournier demands the surrender of 13 Frenchmen, in prison since Feb., May 3; they are surrendered, and Dahomeyan prisoners released May 5
May 12, The new King Behanzin installed; he writes to President Carnot desiring a just peace
Oct. 3, Peace concluded and the King of Dahomey agreed to recognize French Protectorate over Porto Novo and Kotonu in return for annual payment

1891

Dec. 17, Decree placed settlements Gulf of Benin under a lieutenant-governor and M. Ballot named first Lieutenant-Governor

1892

March 26, The Dahomey troops attacked 3 villages beginning hostilities
April 11, The King's continued aggressions and threats lead to war, April; the French Chamber votes 300,000,000 francs for an expedition to protect Porto Novo and Kotonou, and avenge injuries
April 20, French reinforcements from Senegal arrive at Kotonou
May 23, Porto Novo and Kotonou besieged, reported
May 28, Col. Dodds (aft. Gen.), commander of the French expedition, arrives at Kotonou; Whydah occupied by 4,000 French troops, June 11; the coast blockaded June 16; several villages bombarded; about July 5; the coast bombarded, Aug. 9 *et seq.*, Taku captured, Aug. 20; Katagu taken, Aug. 24; reinforcements from France arrive, Aug. 24; about 4,000 Dahomeyans defeated with heavy loss in an attack on Gen. Dodds' column at Dogba; French loss slight; Commandant Faurax killed, Sept. 17 or 19; Dahomeyans again defeated Oct. 4, 19
Sept. 30, An attack of 4,000 Dahomeyans defeated with severe loss, by Gen. Dodds, reported
Oct. 4, The Dahomeyans, commanded by King Behanzin, routed near Poguessa; Capt. Falamine, Lieut. Amelot, and 7 French killed
Oct. 13–15, Sabovi occupied by the French without resistance, Oct. 10; successful advance of Gen. Dodds, with loss on both sides
Oct. 20, 21, 26, The Dahomeyans defeated with great loss
Nov. 2, The fortress of Muates taken; the Dahomeyan army disperse after 4 hours' fighting, Nov. 3; Cana and Dioxoue taken Nov. 4
Nov. 7, French loss during the campaign, 215 men, reported
Nov. 16, King Behanzin proposes inadmissible terms of peace, about Nov. 15; he burns palaces, &c., and retires
Nov. 18, Gen. Dodds occupies Abomey, Nov. 17, and

proclaims the deposition of Behanzin; the chiefs and people submit

Nov. 27, Gen. Dodds at Porto Novo

Dec. 3–6, Whydah and other towns occupied, and French Protectorate established by decree of Dec. 3

Dec. 19, Blockade of the coast raised

1893

About Jan. 9, Behanzin on the Mahi with 2,000 men

May 2, King Behanzin issues to all nations a justificatory manifesto, March 2; proffers submission to France under conditions reported

June, Message from King Behanzin to President Carnot charging the French with treachery

Aug. 31. Gen. Dodds and 400 officers at Kotonou

Oct. 27 *et seq.*, Advance successfully into the interior

Nov. 12, Flight of Behanzin and submission of the chiefs; Gen. Dodds arrives at Youneton

——, Behanzin's envoys at Paris not received by Pres. Carnot

Dec. 4, The Dahomeyans defeated at Badagha

1894

Jan. 15, Gouthili chosen as King of Allada, and recognized by Gen. Dodds and the chiefs at Goho

Jan. 25, Behanzin surrenders unconditionally; sent to Martinique, Feb.; arrives March 30

Feb. 22, M. Ballot appointed civil governor

June 22, The coast territory made a French colony

1895

Jan. 8, The Kotonou canal, between Porto Novo and Godomey, constructed by native labor, opened

Aug. 8, Successful explorations by Lieut. Baud, treaties signed with chiefs, reported

1896

Oct. 12, Report delimited boundary between Lagos and Dahomey

1897

July 23, Convention for the delimitation of the French and German possessions in the *Hinterland*, signed at Paris

1898

June 14, Anglo-French Boundary Agreement, boundary with Lagos carried to the Niger River

1899

Sept. 21, The Franco-German boundary commission opposed, natives defeated with heavy loss near Lama, reported

Oct. 17, Decree attached Dahomey to Government General of West Africa

1900

June 5, Behanzin's brother made King of Abomey, afterwards deposed and imprisoned at Porto Novo, reported

1904

May 30, The Alake of Abeokuta visits England, and is received by King Edward VII at Buckingham Palace

1906

July 7, The son of Behanzin, the ex-King of Dahomey, who with his father, had been, for the last 12 years,

the ward of the republic in Algeria, attempted to commit suicide

Oct. 19, Boundary Convention determined the course of the Anglo-French boundary from the Gulf of Guinea to the Niger

Dec. 10, Death of Behanzin in exile, reported

1911

The French deposed the Dahomey ruler they had set up at Abomey in 1900, for intrigue against French rule, and the whole country made the Colony of Dahomey and its dependencies

1912

Sept. 28, Further definition of the boundary with Togoland

1914

Feb. 16, Delimitation of frontier from coast to Okpara River accepted, the Togoland frontier, by Franco-German Convention

Aug. 3, Proposal of Germans for neutrality during War not considered

1919

May 21, Decree established Councils of Notables (local assemblies)

1923

Aug. 16, Chamber of Commerce established at Kotonu

1924

March 22, Decree regulated native justice

May 1, West African ordinances for education and land ordinance applied to Dahomey

1925

Oct. 22, Decree regulated the employment of natives followed by arret of the Governor General of March 29, 1926, and arret of the Lieutenant Governor of Dahomey of Sept. 17, 1926, and April 11, 17, and Aug. 18, 1927

1928

Aug. 20, Decree regulated Crown lands

1929

June 28, Decree provided for control of labor of natives and of their emigration

Aug. 29, Circular of the Lieutenant Governor issued regulations for recruiting of labor

Sept. 3, Regulations for control of labor of domestic servants enacted, and payment

Sept. 27, Native Labor Service created

1930

June 1, Railroad opened connecting the capital, Dakka, with port of Kotonu (22 miles)

Dec. 19, Decree reorganized native administration

EGYPT

Egypt was originally part of the Turkish Empire. On December 18, 1914, a British Protectorate over Egypt was declared, and the next day a Proclamation was issued deposing 'Abbâs Hilmi, lately Khedive of Egypt, and conferring the title of Sultan of Egypt upon Hussein Kamil, eldest living prince of the family of Muhammad Ali. The British Protectorate was recognized by France, Russia, Belgium, Serbia, Greece, Portugal, and the United States of America. Sultan Hussein Hamil died in 1917, and was succeeded by his brother. The protectorate terminated on February 28, 1922, and the Sultan was proclaimed King on March 15, 1922.

The total area of Egypt proper, including the Libyan Desert, the region between the Nile and the Red Sea, and the Sinai Peninsula is about 383,000 square miles; but the cultivated and settled area, that is, the Nile Valley, Delta, and Oases covers only about 13,600 square miles.

The growth of the general population of the country is exhibited by the following figures:

1846 (Census)	. . . .	4,476,440
1882 (Census)	. . . .	6,831,131
1897 (Census)	. . . .	9,734,405
1907 (Census)	. . . .	11,287,359
1917 (Census)	. . . .	12,750,918
1927 (Census)	. . . .	14,213,364

The principal towns, with their populations, according to the census of 1927, are: Cairo, 1,064,567; Alexandria, 573,063; Port Said, 100,899; Tanta, 90,016; Mansura, 63,676; Asyût, 57,136; Faiyûm, 52,863; Zagazig, 52,839; Damanhûr, 51,709; Mehall el Kubra, 45,642; Minya, 44,323.

FUAD I (AHMED FUAD) KING
5000 B.C. TO 332 B.C.

The following table of Dynasties, including the more important kings, is derived from various sources, the names and dates vary. B. stands for Brugsch, and M. for Mariette

I. Thinite (from This, near Abydus) M. 5004; B. 4400 B.C.
Mena or Menes; first known king and law-giver, founder of Memphis. M. 5004; B. 4455. His tomb and remains, &c., discovered at N'gada by M. de Morgan in the spring of 1897, and placed in the museum at Gizeh. Tola or Athothis—Ouenephes I, conjectured to have built the Steppe pyramid of Sakkárah
II. Memphite. M. 4751; B. 4133
Kakaoo or Kaiechos. The worship of Apis the bull established at Memphis. B. 4100
III. Memphite (monumental history properly begins). M. 4449; B. 3966
Seneferoo—soldier, architect and patron of literature and art
IV. Memphite. M. 4235; B. 3733
Shoofoo or Khufa, the Cheops of Herodotus, built the great pyramid of Gêezeh. M. 4235; B. 3733. The great limestone rock at the foot of the Libyan mountains was converted into a man-headed lion, termed by the Greeks Sphinx. Khafra built the second Gîzeh pyramid. B. 3666. Menkaura (Mycerinus III). B. 3633. High state of civilization and art, and the vast cemetery of Memphis erected. The book or ritual of the dead (papyri) found in tombs
V. Memphite. M. 3951; B. 3566
Raencoser. B. 3433. Katkara. B. 3366. Unas truncated pyramid near Sakkárah built. B. 3333

VI. Memphite (history nearly a blank to the 11th dynasty). M. 3703; B. 3300
Pepi I—powerful—long reign. B. 3233. Romantic story of queen Nitocris in Herodotus
VII. Memphite. B. 3100
Petty kings
VIII. Memphite
IX. Heracleopolite. M. 3358
X. Heracleopolite. M. 3249
XI. Theban. M. 3064
Sankhkara, expedition to Ophir and Punt (S. Arabia?). B. 2500
XII. Theban (Egypt very prosperous). B. 2466
Amenemhat I. M. 3064; B. 2466
Osirtasen I (obelisk of On or Heliopolis erected)
Osirtasen II (memorial temple discovered in 1889)
Osirtasen III, important national works, excavated the lake Moeris and made the labyrinth and the Nilometer. B. 2300
XIII. Theban. M. 2851; B. 2233
Sebekhotep, name of several kings
XIV. Xoite. M. 2398
XV. Hyksos or Shepherd kings. M. 2214
Invaders from Asia take Memphis and settle in Lower Egypt
XVI. Hyksos or Shepherd kings
XVII. Hyksos or Shepherd kings
Nub—arrival of Joseph. B. 1750
Dynasties XIII–XVII history very obscure; probably Theban kings reigned in southern, while the Hyksos reigned in Lower Egypt
XVIII. Theban. M. 1703; B. 1700
Achmes I conquers the Hyksos. M. 1703; B. 1700. Amenhotep I. B. 1666. Thothmes I. B. 1633. Thothmes II and Hatasoo, sister. B. 1600. Thothmes III, great king, victor in western Asia, &c., his exploits recorded in his temple at Karnak. B. 1600. Amenhotep II. B. 1566. Thothmes IV. B. 1533. Amenhotep III victorious in Ethiopia; the Colossi or vocal Memnon bear his name. B. 1500. Amenhotep IV introduced Semetic worship. Two or three heretical successors. Haremhebi or Horus restores the old worship. See Thebes, 1898
XIX. Theban. M. 1462; B. 1400
Rameses I. M. 1462; B. 1400. Seti or Sethos (Menetah I) victorious in Asia; made first canal from the Red sea to the Nile; many monuments of him at Karnak, &c. B. 1333. Rameses II son, the legendary Sesostris, took Salem, conquered Ethiopia, and set up a fleet, his epoch about 1322. Maneptah son, probably the Pharaoh of the Exodus, 1300; Seli II and two or three unimportant kings
XX. Theban. M. 1288; B. 1200
Rameses III (Rhampsinitus of Herodotus) victorious, cultivated navigation and commerce. M. 1288; B. 1200. Inglorious line of kings named Rameses
XXI. Tanite. M. 1110; B. 1100
History obscure—Hirhor, high priest of Amen, probably first of priest kings—Assyrian governors
XXII. Bubasite. M. 980; B. 966. Shashank or Sheshonk I, Shishak, 1 Kings XIV, 25–28
XXIII. Tanite probably only three petty kings. M. 810; B. 766
XXIV. Saite. M. 721; B. 733
Bocchoris (Bokenranef), taken prisoner by Sabaco, King of Ethiopia, and burnt alive. During the last three dynasties, the Ethiopians appear to have ruled in the south

XXV. Karnak. Ethiopian. M. 715; B. 700

Shabat or Sabaco. M. 715; B. 700. Takaraka or Tirhakah (2 *Kings* XIX, 9). B. 693. Egypt frequently invaded by the Assyrians; subdued and divided into 12 governments

XXVI. Saite. M. 665; B. 666

Psammetichus I (Greek), one of the governors under the Assyrians, restored the monarchy and revived art. M. 665; B. 666. Necho II son, attempted the construction of a canal across the Isthmus of Suez, defeated Josiah King of Judah at Megiddo (II *Kings* xxiii, 29); defeated by Nebuchadnezzar at Carchemish, 612. Psammetichus II; inglorious. B. 596. Uahbra or Hophra (*Jer*. xliv, 30) son; went to help Zedekiah, but deserted him. B. 591. Apries loses the conquests and is strangled by Amasis, who has a long prosperous reign and increased intercourse with the Greeks. B. 572. Psammetichus III son (defeated by Cambyses, son of Cyrus, King of Persia). B. 528.

XXVII. Persian. M. 527; B. 527

Cambyses, conquers Egypt; his army perished in an expedition against Ethiopia. M. 527; B. 527. Darius I Hystaspes, greatly favored Egypt, 521. Xerxes I severe (Egyptian revolt) subdued), 486. Artaxerxes I Longimanus (another revolt), 465. Darius II Nothos, 424. Egypt regained its independence by Armyrtæus, 424

XXVIII. Saite. M. 406

Armyrtæus, 406

XXIX. Mendesian. M. 399; B. 399

Nepherches and Achoris maintain Greek alliance

XXX. Sebennyte. M. 378; B. 378

Nectanebes I. Nectanebes II conquered by Artaxerxes Ochus, King of Persia

XXXI. Persia 340

Darius III. Codomanus—defeated by Alexander the Great and killed

332, Alexander conquered Egypt and founded Alexandria

323 B.C. to 30 B.C.

323, The empire divided, 323. One of Alexander's generals, Ptolemy I (the son of Lagus) Soter became King of Egypt

285, Ptolemy II Philadelphus (with his father); alone [the museum of Alexandria founded; the Septuagint version of the Hebrew Scriptures made; the Pharos completed], 283–247

269, Ambassadors first sent to Rome

247, Ptolemy III Euergetes; overruns Syria, and returns laden with spoils, 246

Nov. 222, Ptolemy IV Philopator

217, Battle of Raphia; Ptolemy defeats Antiochus, King of Syria

Nov. 205, Ptolemy V Epiphanes

200, Embassy to Rome

Oct. 181, Ptolemy VI Philometor

Nov. 146, At the death of Philometor, his brother Physcon (Ptolemy VII Euergetes) marries his queen, and on the day of his nuptials murders the infant son of Philometor in its mother's arms

130, His subjects, wearied by his cruelties and crimes, compel him to flee

128, He defeats the Egyptians and recovers his throne; dies, 117

117, Ptolemy VIII, Soter II, and Cleopatra his mother

107, Alexander I and Cleopatra

89, Ptolemy VIII restored

82, Revolt in Upper Egypt; Thebes destroyed after a siege of three years (*Diod. Siculus*)

81, Alexander II and Cleopatra I

80, Ptolemy IX Auletes

58, Berenice and Tryphæna

51, Auletes restored, 55; leaves his kingdom to Ptolemy and Cleopatra

47, During a civil war between Ptolemy and Cleopatra II, Alexandria is besieged by Cæsar, and the library nearly destroyed by fire (*Blair*)

46, Cæsar defeats the King, who, in crossing the Nile, is drowned; and the younger Ptolemy and Cleopatra reign

43, Cleopatra poisons her brother, and reigns alone

41, She appears before Marc Antony, to answer for this crime; he follows her into Egypt

36, Cleopatra in Syria

31, Antony defeated by Octavius Cæsar at the battle of Actium (*Blair*), Sept. 2

30, Octavius enters Egypt; Antony and Cleopatra kill themselves; and the kingdom becomes a Roman province, Sept.

122 A.D. to 1859

122, Egypt visited by Adrian; by Severus, 200

305, Monarchism begun in Egypt by Antony

389, Destruction of the temple and worship of Serapis

616, Egypt conquered by Chosroes II of Persia

June, 638, Invasion of the Saracens under Amrou

Dec. 22, 640, Conquest of Alexandria

969, Cairo founded by the Saracens

1163–91, Conquest by the Turks

1250, Government of the Mamelukes established

1567, Selim I, Emperor of the Turks, conquers Egypt

1798–99, It is governed by beys till a great part of the country is conquered by the French, under Bonaparte

1801, The invaders dispossessed by the British, and the Turkish Government restored

March 1, 1811, Mehemet Ali massacres the Mamelukes, and obtains the supreme power

1820, Formation of the Mahmoud canal, connecting Alexandria with the Nile

1831, Mehemet Pasha revolts and invades Syria

1832, His son Ibrahim takes Acre, May 27; overruns Syria; defeats the Turks at Konieh, Dec. 21

1833, He advances on Constantinople, which is entered by Russian auxiliaries, April 3; war ends with convention of Kutayah, May 4

1839, Mehemet again revolts, claiming hereditary power; Ibrahim defeats the Turks at Nezib, June 24

1840, England, Austria, Russia, and Prussia undertake to expel Ibrahim from Syria; Napier bombards Beyrout, Oct. 10; Acre taken by the British and Austrian fleets, under Sir R. Stopford, Nov. 3; the Egyptians quit Syria, Nov. 21, *et seq.*

July 15, 1841, Peace restored by treaty; Mehemet made hereditary Viceroy of Egypt, but deprived of Syria

Nov. 10, 1848, Ibrahim Pacha dies

April 25, 1859, The Suez canal begun

1861

April 19, Commercial treaty with Great Britain signed

May 27, Hereditary succession and right of coining money granted; but tribute raised from 400,000*l.* to 750,000*l.*

Nov. 1, Malta and Alexandria telegraph opened

1863 to 1865

April 7, 1863, Sultan of Turkey visits Egypt
May, 1864, At the demand of the Sultan, the Viceroy
sends troops to repress the insurgents in Arabia
Aug. 15, 1865, Opening of part of the Suez canal

1866

May 21, Direct succession to the Viceroyalty granted
by the Porte
Nov. 27, Egyptian legislative chamber opened with a
speech from the Viceroy

1867

June 9, Viceroy designated "sovereign" by the Sultan

1869

May 10, Sir Samuel Baker appointed sole commander
of a military expedition to suppress the slave-trade
up the Nile, with absolute authority over the country
south of Gondokoro (for four years from April 1,
1869)
Nov. 16, The inauguration of the Suez canal
Dec., The differences between the Sultan and himself
respecting prerogatives arranged, the Viceroy giving
up the power of imposing taxes and of contracting
loans

1870

Aug. 11, Many delays and impediments; Sir Samuel
Baker proceeds to explore White Nile

1871

April 15, Arrives at Gondokoro; names it Ismailia, and
officially annexes it to Egypt, May 26
July–Sept., War with the warlike and treacherous Baris
of Belinian; beats them in several engagements
Oct., Supported by his model corps, "the forty thieves,"
he quells disaffection and mutiny in his troops
Nov. 3, Sends vessels with women, children, and sick,
to Khartoum
Nov. 19, Makes peace with the Baris, and returns to
Gondokoro

1872

March 6, Arrives at the African Paradise, Faliko; meets
there his enemy, Abou Saoud, the slave-dealer; at
Masindi, in Unyoro, April 25
June 8, Received by Kabba Rega, the young King, who
attempts to poison Baker's party, and attacks them
in the night; he is defeated, and Masindi burnt
June 25, The Khedive (Viceroy) visits the Sultan; Constantinople rejoices
July 18, Baker marches to Foweera; received by Raongi,
enemy of Kabba Rega; returns to Faliko, and suppresses an insurrection of slave-dealers, probably incited by Abou Saoud, Aug. 2
Dec. 31, Slave-trade apparently subdued; "peace and
prospect of prosperity"

1873

June 8, The Sultan, by a firman, renders the Khedive
practically independent; (he must not coin money,
make treaties, or build ironclads)
Oct., First Egyptian budget produced; asserted revenue,
10,166,000l.; expenditure, 9,040,000l.
Oct. 9, Baker returns to Gondokoro, April 1; receives
honors from the Khedive at Cairo, Aug. 25; arrives
in London

Col. Gordon appointed his successor; Abou Saoud his
subordinate

1875

Spring, Mr. Acton and Mr. Pennell employed to arrange
finances of Egypt
June 28, International court of justice opened by the
Khedive
Oct. 16, Egyptian expedition into Abyssinia surprised
and defeated with much slaughter
Nov., The Khedive's shares of Suez canal purchased by
the British Government; announced
Dec., Rt. Hon. Stephen Cave sent on special mission to
Egypt
1875–77, War with Abyssinia (*see s.v.*)

1876

Jan. 1, New (Gregorian) style adopted; mixed courts
opened
Jan. 4, Resignation of Nubar Pasha, able Minister of
Commerce, announced
April 4, Mr. Cave's report—(refers to waste and ex-
travagance; great works undertaken with insufficient
means; loss by adventurers; military expenditure;
and necessity for intervention of superior power
to restore credit and restrain expenditure); sent
March 13; published in *Times*
May 14 and 25, The Khedive decrees consolidation of
his debt, 91,000,000l., at 7%, and a sinking fund,
May 7; decrees signed
July, Decisions of the international law court not accepted by the Government; the court closed by M.
Haakman; he is superseded
Nov. 18, Mr. Goschen with M. Joubert (on behalf of
the Khedive's creditors), arrive at Cairo, Oct. 14;
their scheme accepted (debt of about 91,000,000l. to
be reduced to about 59,000,000l., interest of 7% to
be reduced to about 6%); agreement signed about
Nov. 10 announced (termed since, "Goschen decree")
Nov., Ismail Sadyk, autocratic Finance Minister, suspected of conspiracy; resigns insolently; seized and
banished
Nov. 28, Mr. Goschen's report approved by a meeting
in London

1877

Feb., Col. Gordon, after successful administration, re-
turns to England
Oct., Peace with Abyssinia negotiated by Col. Gordon,
June; terms accepted

1878

March, Bad report respecting Egyptian finances, Feb.;
commission appointed
May 12, Confidence restored by decree for payment of
official salaries
Aug. 15, Nubar Pasha again Minister
Aug., The Khedive accepts the terms of the commission;
he and his family give up landed property to the state
Sept., Mr. Rivers Wilson appointed Finance Minister;
and M. de Blignières, Minister of Works, soon after

1879

Feb. 18, Attacks on them and Nubar Pasha by discontented officers at Cairo dispersed
Feb. 19, Nubar Pasha resigns
Feb., Definitive peace between the Khedive and Abyssinia, announced

March 5, Prince Tewfik, President of the Council, and Nubar Pasha, Foreign Minister, about

April 6, Mr. Rivers Wilson and M. de Blignières remonstrate with the Khedive

April 7, He puts forth a new financial scheme; Tewfik Pasha, Mr. Rivers Wilson, and M. de Blignières, dismissed; new ministry under Cherif Pasha formed about

May 5, Col. Gordon's lieutenant, Gessi (Nov., 1878), completely defeats the rebel slave-dealers in the Sudan, Central Africa

——, England and France in a note require the appointment of European ministers

June 20, England, France, Germany, Austria, and Italy, recommend the Khedive to abdicate, about

June 22, He refers to the Sultan, who declines to interfere, the Khedive offers to pay his debts in full

June 26, The Khedive deposed by the Sultan, Prince Tewfik, his son, proclaimed his successor

Aug. 8, Tewfik succeeds as Khedive

Sept. 4, Mr. Baring and M. de Blignières appointed comptrollers-general

Oct., Col. Gordon negotiating with Abyssinia to prevent war, reported successful

1880

Jan., He resigns governorship of the Soudan, Oct., 1879; accepted

End of June, Peace with Abyssinia announced

July 17, International committee on the debt appointed, April 4; issue a report, on which is based a law of liquidation in 99 articles, approved by the Khedive

1881

Feb. 1–11, Military revolt (for pay) at Cairo vigorously checked by Mr. E. Malet (British Minister, 1879) and Baron de Ring

End of July, Decree for abolition of slavery

July, Insurrection in the Sudan

About Aug. 11, British pacific interference

Sept. 9, Ahmed Arabi Bey and about 4,000 soldiers surround the Khedive's palace, demanding increased pay—agreed to; Cherif Pasha made Minister

Sept. 11–13, Negotiations of Cherif and the consuls with the troops succeed; tranquillity restored

Oct. 7, Envoys from the Sultan received by the Khedive

Oct. 18, Jealousy of England and France, the envoys leave Cairo

Nov. 4, Important letter from Earl Granville to Sir Edwd. Malet

1882

Jan., Arabi Bey appointed under-secretary of war

About Jan. 7, English and French note in support of the Khedive

Jan. 27, Deputies demand entire control of the ministry, about Jan. 19; deadlock

Feb. 3 et seq., Resignation of Cherif Pasha, Feb. 2; new ministry under Mahmoud Pasha

About April 10, Alleged conspiracy of Circassian officers to assassinate Arabi Pasha

May 9, 43 persons convicted of conspiracy to kill Arabi Pasha, and dethrone the Khedive; exiled April 28; sentence confirmed by Khedive

May 9–13, Political crisis continues; the Khedive firm; Ministry submits, about May 16; English and French squadron arrive at Alexandria, May 20; Arabi Pasha refuses to resign, May 23; ultimatum of English and

French consuls; Arabi Pasha to retire; Khedive's authority to be restored, &c., May 25

May, Ministry resigns; Cherif Pasha appointed, the officers resist; Arabi Pasha reinstated, May 27–28; anarchy; Europeans quitting the country, May 29; 6,000 Egyptian soldiers said to be massacred, June

June 8, Dervish Pasha and others sent to Cairo by the Sultan, June 4; well received at Cairo

June 11, Commencement of a rebellion; riots at Alexandria; Arabs attack Europeans; quelled by Egyptian troops, with great loss of life (about 60 Europeans killed), town deserted

June 15, 16, Panic at Cairo and Alexandria

About 37,000 Europeans in Egypt

June, Ragheb Pasha forms a ministry

June 19, The Powers agree to a conference at Constantinople; Turkey objects

June 24, Conference opened

June, Great emigration from Alexandria to Malta

June 29, 30,000 Arabs said to be starving at Alexandria

About July 4, The English and French admirals protest against the fortifying of Alexandria

About July 6, British subjects warned to quit Egypt

July 9, Bombardment of forts of Alexandria threatened by Adm. Sir Beauchamp Seymour, if works threatening the British fleet are not stopped

July 11, Bombardment begun by the *Alexandra*, 7.5 A.M.; vessels engaged: *Monarch, Invincible, Penelope, Téméraire,* and *Inflexible; gunboats, Condor, Cygnet, Bittern, Decoy,* &c., very effective; forts Mexs, Marabout, &c., silenced; 10 sailors from *Invincible* land and spike guns of fort Mexs; object of bombardment fully obtained; the bombardment ceases 5.30 P.M. Egyptians fought well; heavy loss in forts and part of the town, British loss, 6 killed, including Lieut. Jackson of the *Inflexible,* and 28 wounded

About July 12, Defiant letter of Arabi Pasha to Mr. Gladstone, July 2, received

——, 1,000 marines sent from Malta to Alexandria

July 12, Gaining time by a flag of truce, Arabi Pasha and part of his army abandon Alexandria and retreat into the interior; he releases convicts, who with the Arab mob plunder and set fire to the city, and massacre, it is said, many Christians

July 12, 13, The Khedive escapes assassination, and gains over part of Arabi Pasha's army

July 13, Conflagration increasing (about a mile long); about 800 marines land to maintain order as police

——, European portion entirely destroyed

July 15, Fire dying out; order restored; foreign marines enter city

About July 16, The Khedive at his palace Ras-el-Tin guarded by British marines; degrades Arabi Pasha from his offices; sends for Cherif Pasha, Riaz Pasha, and others

July 17, About 5,000 soldiers land at Alexandria

July 18, Identical note from the six Powers inviting the Porte to intervene to support the Khedive and restore order

——, Arabi Pasha with his army intrenched at Kafr-Douar

About July 20–21, Arabi Pasha attempts to cut off water supply; denounces the Khedive, and calls on the people

July 23, Proclamation of the Khedive declaring Arabia rebel, &c.; reported anarchy at Cairo

July 24, Skirmish with the Arabs by Sir A. Alison; he takes about 60 prisoners, and holds Ramleh

About July 24, Arabi proclaims a Jihad or holy war, said to have 30,000 men

July 24, British troops landed at Alexandria

About July 25, Troops sent to Egypt from England and India

July 31, Withdrawal of French fleet ordered

Aug. 3, Town of Suez occupied by British marines

Aug. 5, Reconnaissance; sharp skirmish near Mahmoudieh canal; Gen. Sir A. Alison commanding; British success; Lieut. Howard Vyse and 3 others killed; 30 wounded; Egyptian loss 300

Aug. 14, The conference agrees to the international protection of the Suez canal

Sir Garnet Wolseley lands at Alexandria and assumes the command; the Khedive gives up power to the British commanders to establish order

Aug. 20, Troops, &c., under Gen. Willis embark and occupy Port Said, Ismailia, and Kantara; thus command the canal, Aug. 19-20; skirmishes near Mahmoudieh canal, Sir Evelyn Wood successful; the enemy shelled out of Nefiche

——, Total British force in Egypt, 31,468 men of all ranks

——, Chaloux-el-Terraba captured by sailors, &c., great Egyptian loss

——, Successful skirmishes; Gen. Hamley, &c., from Ramleh; Capt. Hastings and Maj. Kelsey repel Egyptians, who suffer heavy loss; Sir G. Wolseley's proclamation to the Arabs, Aug. 21

Aug. 21, Arrival of Gen. Macpherson with the Indian troops at Suez

Aug. 24, Advance from Ismailia of two squadrons of household cavalry, with two guns, and detachment of 19th hussars, mounted infantry, &c., on Nefiche met by above 10,000 Egyptians with much artillery

Aug. 25, Cavalry and artillery engagement; enemy routed; capture of 5 Krupp guns, and train of ammunition and provisions, Egyptian camps at Tel-el-Mahuta and Mahsameh occupied; British loss, 6 killed, 30 wounded

Aug. 26, Kassassin occupied by Gen. Graham with above 2,000 infantry

Aug. 27, Mustapha Fehmy, Arabi Pasha's second in command, captured while reconnoitering (sent to the Khedive)

Aug. 28, Gen. Graham at Kassassin vigorously attacked by 13,000 Egyptians; signals for assistance, rendered by Gen. Drury Lowe with household cavalry; brilliant charge and capture of 11 guns (afterwards lost), rout of the enemy; disorderly flight; British loss, 7 killed, 70 wounded

Aug. 29, Military convention with Turkey about to be signed

About Aug. 31, Arabi Pasha strengthening his intrenchments near Tel-el-Kebir

Arabi Pasha's estimated forces: infantry, 44,600; cavalry, 1,802; guns, 143; Bedouins 30,500

Sept. 9, Vigorous attack on the British camp at Kassassin repelled with severe loss, 4 guns taken, 6 British killed

Sept. 13, Capture of Tel-el-Kebir; total defeat of the Egyptians; flight of Arabi Pasha; surrender of Zagazig with railway trains, &c.

Sept. 14, The British enter Cairo; Arabi Pasha and his officers surrender unconditionally; about 10,000 Egyptian soldiers lay down their arms

Sept. 15, Sir Garnet Wolseley and British troops enter Cairo; warmly received

Sept. 16, 17, Surrender of Kafr Douar; about 500 Egyptians march to Damietta

Sept. 17, The Khedive dissolves the Egyptian army

Sept. 19, Surrender of Aboukir, Sept. 17; reëstablishment of the Khedive's authority

——, Valentine Baker Pasha nominated commander of a new Egyptian army (10,900)

Sept. 21, Abd-el-Al holding Damietta with about 7,000 men; British expedition sent against him, Sept. 22; he surrenders to Sir Evelyn Wood, Sept. 23

Sept. 25, Triumphal entry of the Khedive into Cairo

Sept. 30, 18,000 British troops "march past" the Khedive at the Abdin palace

——, 12,000 British to remain in Egypt, Sir A. Alison commander

Oct. 24, An amnesty of officers signed by the Khedive

Oct. 25, The prophet said to hold all the country south of Khartoum

Nov. 9, Anglo-French control abolished

Nov., Trial of Arabi Pasha; secret examination of witnesses (his defense supported by Mr. Wilfrid Blunt)

About Dec. 1, General amnesty and release of political prisoners

Dec. 3, Pleads guilty of rebellion; sentence of death commuted to banishment for life

Dec. 7, Mahoud and other rebel leaders sentenced to banishment

Dec. 7, 8, Riaz Pasha resigns; succeeded by Nubar Pasha

Dec. 9, Arabi Pasha and others to be sent to Ceylon

Dec. 22, Sir Evelyn Wood, appointed commander of the new Egyptian army, arrives at Cairo

About Dec. 30, Nine of the murderers of Professor Palmer and others captured

1883

Jan. 10, Arabi and others sailed for Ceylon, Dec. 27; arrived

Jan. 11, End of the dual control

Jan. 11 et seq., British circular to the Powers laid before the Porte, &c. (the Suez Canal to be free, with restrictions in time of war; formation of Egyptian army, &c.)

Jan. 24, Sir Auckland Colvin appointed financial adviser

About Jan. 27, All the Powers accept proposals except France and Turkey

March 20, Lord Dufferin's report on reorganization of Egypt published

May 1, Constitution signed by the Khedive, April 30; promulgated

May, Major Evelyn Baring nominated resident

June 9, Suleiman Sami convicted of the firing, massacre, and plundering at Alexandria (June 11, 1882), hanged

June, Greatly improved condition of the country

June 28, The ex-Khedive Ismail in London

Aug., British force reduced to 6,763

Sept. 24, Council of state nominated

About Oct. 10, The Khedive grants a general amnesty

Oct. 30, New council of state opened by Cherif Pasha

Nov., Departure of part of the British troops countermanded on account of the destruction of Gen. Hicks' army (Sudan)

1884

Jan. 6, The British government require a limitation of the line of defense in regard to the Sudan

About Jan. 7, Cherif Pasha and his ministry resign; Nubar Pasha (an Armenian Christian) becomes Minister

About Jan. 30, Loan of 950,000*l.* to the Khedive by Messrs. Rothschild

March 20, Disorder in the government and finances reported

British army: total killed, 255; July, 1882, to March

April 6, Resignation of Nubar Pasha in opposition to Mr. Clifford Lloyd; both remain in office, April 11

May, Conference of the Powers, respecting Egyptian finance proposed by England accepted by Germany, Austria, Russia, Italy, France, and Turkey

——, Need of loan of 8,000,000*l.* to meet several years' deficits, indemnification for damages at Alexandria (3,950,000*l.*), civil and Sudan war expenses, &c.

June 28, Conference of six great Powers on Egyptian affairs meets

Aug. 2, Conference adjourns, without result, *sine die*

Aug. 5, Credit for 300,000*l.* voted to assist Gen. Gordon

Sept. 9, Lord Northbrook, as high commissioner, and Lord Wolseley as commander-in-chief, sail Aug. 31, arrive at Cairo

Sept. 20, Suspension of the international law of liquidation in regard to the sinking fund, from Sept. 18 to Oct. 25 decreed, with consent of Lord Northbrook

Oct., France, Germany, Austria, Russia, and Italy protest, Sept. 25 *et seq.*, but tacitly acquiesce

Oct. 24, Egyptian army reduced to 4,000 men, announced

Oct. 28, Lord Northbrook leaves Egypt

Nov., British force in Egypt and Sudan, about 16,000 men

Dec., Action of the *caisse* (commission) of the public debt against the Egyptian Government for suspension of the sinking fund; the court condemns it to refund, Dec. 9; the Khedive appeals

1884–85, Great improvements in irrigation, conducted by Col. Scott Moncrieff

1885

Jan. 24, Reply of France and other powers to the British proposals respecting the financial condition of Egypt, Jan. 17; English reply

About Feb. 15, Prince Hassan, brother of the Khedive, appointed high commissioner in the Sudan

March 27–28, Egyptian financial scheme; convention agreed to by the Powers signed, March 18 [reduction of interest on debt, loan of 9,000,000*l.* on international guarantee, &c.]; adopted by the Commons on Mr. Gladstone's resolution (294–246)

About April 1, Gen. Grenfell succeeds Sir E. Wood as Commander-in-Chief

April 9, *Bosphore Egyptien*, a Cairo newspaper, suppressed by decree, Feb. 29, 1884; carried into effect, for publication of a proclamation of the Madhi; the French Government much offended by the manner of suppression; the dispute settled by British intervention, announced, April 28, 1885; paper reappears, May 20, 1885; stopped, Sept. 5

July 6, Sir F. Stephenson, Commander-in-Chief of British army

Aug. 16, Payment of indemnity begins

About Sept. 12, Telegraph system freed from Eastern company, through Mr. Floyer

Oct. 24, Turkish convention with Sir H. D. Wolff on Egyptian affairs; departure of the British deferred till their work be accomplished, signed

Nov., High commissioners, Ghazi-Mukhtar Pasha and Sir H. D. Wolff

Dec. 1, British forces in Egypt, exclusive of Indians and Egyptians, 14,000

1886

March, Discovery of petroleum at Jebel Zeit on the Red Sea; probable success reported about April 24

June, Ismail Pasha claims 5,000,000*l.* arrears of annual payments for surrendered estates

1887

Jan., Reduction of the British army begins

Feb., Improvement in the state of the country reported

Feb. 9 (?), Neutralization of Egypt and defense of the Suez Canal proposed to the Sultan by Sir H. Drummond Wolff

May 28, Anglo-Turkish convention respecting Egypt signed at Constantinople (British troops to leave in three years: Turkish troops to intervene or British to return; Suez canal to be neutral, etc.); ratified by Queen Victoria, June; not ratified by the Sultan; Sir H. D. Wolff leaves Constantinople, July 15

Nov. 17, Sudden death of General Valentine Baker Pasha, aged 62

Dec., Major Dormer appointed commander of the British army

——, Ismail Pasha permitted to reside at Constantinople

1888

Jan., General prosperity of the country; surplus in the budget

——, The exorbitant claims of the ex-Khedive on the Egyptian Government reduced and liberally settled by the influence of Sir Edgar Vincent and Mr. Marriott, Q.C., the Judge Advocate General; he receives 100,000*l.* with much land

March 22, Death of Prince Hassan

May, Mr. Limperopoulos's claim for 2,910*l.* (Egyptian) on Gordon bonds said to have been issued at Khartoum, disallowed

June 8, Nubar Pasha dismissed; Riaz Pasha succeeds (Sudan)

June 13, The Caisse de la Dette (general reserve fund) established

1889

June 27 *et seq.*, Sir Edgar Vincent's proposal to convert the Egyptian preference debt of 22,000,000*l.* at 5% to a loan at 4% not accepted by the French Government, unless a time be fixed for the evacuation of Egypt by the British

Sept., Sir Edgar Vincent resigns the office of financial adviser to the Khedive, Aug. 21; succeeded by Mr. Elwin Palmer, director-general of accounts

Nov. 1, The Prince of Wales and Prince George received by the Khedive at Cairo; leave Egypt, Nov. 5

Nov. 18, Mr. Palmer's budget, surplus 150,000*l.* after reduced taxation, announced

1888–89, The Equatorial province lost by the retirement of Emin Pasha, through the mutiny of his officers

Dec. 17, Abolition of forced labor (*corvée*) of the peasantry (fellaheen), a tax proposed to the general assembly, Dec. 15, bill passed

1890

Jan., Negotiations with France respecting the conversion scheme (*see* June, 1889), again fails

Jan. 1, New commercial treaty with Great Britain (signed Oct. 29, 1889) from

Jan. 28, National accounts for 1889, declared surplus 196,000*l.*

May 7, The French Government assents to the conversion of the preference debt, under conditions which are accepted by the Egyptians, reported

May 21, The first settlement was effected at Paris by Tigrane Pasha, Mr. Elwin Palmer, and M. Ribot; the assent of the other great Powers reported June 2, the Khedive's decree authorizing the conversion issued, June 7

July 3, Mr. Justice Scott's plan for the decentralization of justice and creation of local courts, adopted by decree reported

Aug. 17, The corvée tax for 1890 not to be collected

1891

Feb. 2, Much needed judicial reforms recommended by Mr. Justice Scott, of Bombay, Jan., opposed by a commission

Feb. 8, Return of the Khedive from a successful five weeks' tour (during which he visited Wady-Halfa); Cairo illuminated

Feb. 11, Sir Evelyn Baring recommends to the Khedive the nomination of Mr. Justice Scott as judicial adviser and president of a judicial committee of three (one Italian and one Egyptian) for the supervision of the local tribunals, about

Feb. 16, The Khedive assents; officially announced

Feb. 20, The judicial changes disapproved by France, about

March 1, Count d'Aubigny, the French Minister, recalled, and disgraced, leaves

May 12, Resignation of Riaz Pasha, the Premier, for ill-health

May 13, New ministry under Mustapha Fehmy Pasha (influence of the Khedive increased)

June, Sir Colin Moncrieff reports the beneficial results of the great improvements in irrigation, March 5, published

End of Nov., Great increase in the crops of cotton and cereals, and in railway receipts; large surplus revenue; proposed reduction of taxation

1892

Jan. 7, Sudden death of the Khedive Tewfik

Jan. 16, His eldest son, Abbas, recognized by the Porte, Jan. 8; state reception at Cairo

About Jan. 28, Reduction of the salt tax, 40%, ordered

April 14, Arrival of Ahmed Eyoub Pasha at Cairo with the Sultan's firman for the investiture of the Khedive April 4; the reading delayed through proposed changes relating to Mount Sinai, which are settled satisfactorily through British influence; the firman read in public

May 5, New railway bridge over the Nile, opened by the Khedive

Sir Evelyn Baring created a peer (Baron Cromer)

1893

Jan. 15, The Khedive suddenly dismisses the Premier, Mustapha Pasha Fehmy and his colleagues, supporters of the English reforms, and nominates Fakhri Pasha and others, anti-reformers; Lord Cromer, for the British government protests, Jan. 17; the Khedive expresses regret, and proposes the appointment of Riaz Pasha and others, which is accepted by Lord Cromer, Jan. 18

Jan. 22, Popular agitation; the British army of occupation (about 3,000 under Major-Gen. Walker) increased; end of the crisis, Jan. 27

Feb. 5, The Khedive opens the railway extension to Girgeh

Dec. 2, The Khedive opens the steam tramway connecting Ismailia and Port Said (50 miles)

1894

April 14–16, Resignation of Riaz Pasha; new ministry formed by Nubar Pasha

April 22, The first national exhibition of art and industry, at Alexandria, opened by the Khedive

May 26, A strike of coal porters at Port Said, May 21, closed

June 3, The construction of a Nile reservoir at Assuan, ordered by the Khedive and his council; Sir Benjamin Baker appointed technical adviser, Dec. 10

June 21, Tour of the Khedive; Nubar Pasha appointed regent

June 25, The Khedive arrives at Constantinople; honored by the Sultan, July; visits Italy and Switzerland, July; at The Hague, Aug. 8

Sept. 9, Death of Prof. Heinrich Karl Brugsch Pasha, Egyptologist; born 1827

Oct. 28, Important reforms in the civil administration introduced by Lord Cromer; Mr. J. L. Gorst, influential adviser

1895

Feb. 1, Gen. Sir H. H. Kitchener starts for Wady Halfa on a tour of inspection; reported

Feb., Intrigues against the Nubar Pasha Ministry; serious disorders at Alexandria

Feb. 19, Contract of marriage with Ikbal Hanem signed by the Khedive

Feb. 22, A decree creating a special tribunal to deal with offenses against the British issued

Feb. 24, Fall of 25% in the value of the cotton crop, &c.

Feb. 25, Agreement with the Khedive and Lord Cromer

Feb. 27, The Khedive reviews the army of occupation at Cairo

March 2, Death of Ismail Pasha, ex-Khedive at Constantinople

March 19–21, Slatin Bey, an Austrian, 12 years prisoner of the Mahdi, escapes; warmly received at Cairo; made Pasha

Nov. 11, Resignation of Nubar Pasha, Premier and reformer

Nov. 21, New Anglo-Egyptian Anti-Slavery Convention ratified by the Khedive

1896

March 19, Advance of 9,000 troops commanded by Sir H. H. Kitchener up the Nile to Dongola to check the dervishes and relieve Kasala. *See* Sudan

May 15, The Beit-el-Mal (native court) abolished and other reforms made

Nov. 22, Important legal reforms passed by the Council

1897

Oct. 7, Sir Francis Grenfell takes command of the army of occupation, Cairo

Dec., Reform of the native penal Code

1898

Feb. 20, Contract (5 years) concluded with John Aird and Company for the construction of dams across the Nile at Assuan and Assuit

July 11, Sir Elwin Palmer appointed governor of the National Bank of Egypt

1899

Jan. 14, Death of Nubar Pasha, former Premier, in Paris

Jan. 19, Sudan Convention signed at Cairo

Feb. 12, Foundation stone of the Nile reservoir dam at Assuan laid by the Duke of Connaught

March 21, Anglo-French agreement concluded by which the Bahr-el-Ghazal and Darfur are recognized as being reserved to Great Britain, France retaining Wadai Bagirmi and Kannem; mutual equality of commercial treatment conceded from the Nile to lake Chad, between 5th and 15th parallels of latitude, giving France trade rights on the Nile

May, Decree signed reforming the Court of Appeal

June 3, Reform of the Grand Cadi's Court; Mahomet Abdul, progressive and capable, appointed grand mufti

July 17, International commission of judicial reform, 1898, *see Times*

End Oct., Sir J. G. Rogers, head of the sanitary department, successful in suppressing the plague in Egypt, resigns, and is succeeded by Pinching Bey

Nov. 17, The Khedive unveils statue of Ferdinand de Lesseps at Port Said

Dec. 12, Sudan declared open to all comers; railway from Khartoum to Cairo completed

1900

Jan. 30, Mixed tribunals prolonged 5 years; decree signed

June 27–July 4, The Khedive visits England

1901

Sept. 30, Arabi Pasha released (exiled 1882), May; returns a staunch friend to Britain, reported

Dec. 9, The Khedive's tour; views the great Nile dam at Assuan

1902

April 24, Saadeddin Pasha, Governor of Gharbieh, charged with torturing natives, accused of stealing, dismissed from service, April 13, 14; other officials punished

Nov. 8, Gordon memorial college at Khartum opened

Dec. 8, Mr. Chamberlain received by the Khedive

Dec. 10, Nile dam at Assuan completed July 31; opened by Duke of Connaught

1903

March 7, Zifteh barrage between Cairo and the sea opened

June 24–July 3, The Khedive visits London

1904

Jan. 1, Sir John Gorst's note on the budget for 1904, states that the receipts are estimated at E. 11,500,000*l.*, and the expenditure, including payments to the sinking fund of the loan, to conversion and reserve fund, E. 11,400,000*l.*; real surplus will amount to E. 927,000*l.*; large appropriations proposed for reduction of land tax and irrigation works, reported

April 8, Anglo-French agreement recognizing Great Britain's predominant position in Egypt, signed

July 30, Aly Dinar, Sultan of Darfur, reported to be actively coöperating with the Sudan government in suppressing the slave trade within his province

Dec. 20, Death of Menshawi Pasha, one of the wealthiest landowners in Egypt

1905

Jan. 31, Khedive signs decree prolonging the existence and functions of the international tribunals in Egypt for a further term of five years

Early March, Success of expedition under Maj. Boulnois, of the Egyptian army, sent to punish the cannibal Niam-Niams of the upper Nile; Sultan of Yambie captured, and subsequently died of his wounds; country pacified, reported

April 17, Khedive publishes in Cairo a decree admitting English as a judicial language in the mixed tribunals

June 15, The Khedive visits England

Sept. 6–Oct. 8, *Chatham* ss. sinks in the Suez canal and blocks the traffic

Dec. 24, Commercial treaty signed between the Italian and Egyptian Governments, reported

1906

Jan. 27, The Nile-Red sea railway from Port Sudan to the Atbara junction opened by Lord Cromer

Jan. 28, Death of Sir Elwin M. Palmer, governor of the National Bank of Egypt

Feb. 20, Death of Baker Pasha, about

Mar. 8, The Karima-Abu Hamed railway, which opens the Dongola province to the Red sea, opened by Sir R. Wingate

Mar. 22, Tabah claimed by the Porte as an integral part of the Ottoman Empire

April 2, Ottoman commissioners decide that Tabah is in Turkish territory

About April 26, Death of M. Félix Saurès, Egyptian financier, in his 64th year

May 1, Lord Cromer's annual report issued by the foreign office as a blue-book; in it he sets forth the proposals for dealing with the question of the capitulations, and for providing effective legislative machinery with the necessary safeguards for the protection of the interests of foreigners in Egypt

May 3, British ultimatum to the Sultan to withdraw his troops from the Sinai peninsula

May 12, Turkish garrison withdrawn from Tabah

June 12, O'Connell Bey, Governor of Kordofan, attacks the rebels at Jebel Elliri, inflicting a loss of 350 killed and 100 taken prisoners

June 13, Attack on five British officers at Denshawi, near Tanta; Captain Bull killed

June 28, For the attack on the British officers, four natives were sentenced to death, two to penal servitude for life, and others to varying terms of imprisonment

Aug. 18, Death of the Egyptian prince, Ibrahim Mohammed, as the result of a motor-car accident

Sept. 25, Sultan agrees to a straight line of demarcation from Akabah to Rafah, and the Turkish force stationed at Kuseimeh was withdrawn

Oct. 1, The agreement signed in Cairo

1907

March 3, National assembly in Cairo carries resolutions demanding the creation of a municipality for Cairo and the use of Arabic as the sole means of instruction in all government schools

March 21, Council of ministers decide to raise the Assuan dam so as to raise the level of the water by 23 ft., thus enabling a million more acres of land to be irrigated; estimated cost of the work, 1,500,000*l.*

April 11, Resignation of Lord Cromer published; Sir Eldon Gorst appointed to succeed him

April 24, Arrival of Sir Eldon and Lady Gorst in Cairo

May, Census returns show population of Egypt to be 11,206,359, an increase of nearly 1,500,000 since 1897

Dec. 30, New pass. into Alexandria harbor, 35 ft. deep and 600 ft. wide, and costing E. 100,000*l.*, formally opened

1908

Feb. 6, The Rodah bridges opened

Feb. 10, Mustapha Kamel, leader of the nationalist party, dies in Cairo

April 23, Death of Kassim Bey Amin, judge of the native court of appeal, aged 44. *Times*

Nov. 12, New ministry formed with Boutros Pasha as Premier and Minister for Foreign Affairs

1909

Feb. 9, New Nile barrage opened at Esneh by the Khedive

May 14, Death of M. Raphael Suarès, born 1846, financier, at Alexandria, about

1910

Jan. 24, The Khedive, on his return from Mecca, reaches Alexandria, and Cairo, Jan. 25

Feb. 20, Boutros Pasha Ghali, Prime Minister, fatally shot by a Nationalist student, Ibrahim Wardani, and died the following day

Feb. 22, Mohammed Said Bey formed Cabinet

March 28, Theodore Roosevelt delivered an address at the University in Cairo

June 14, Assize courts given jurisdiction in press cases

June 28, Ibrahim Wardani, condemned May 13, executed

1911

March 6, Coptic Congress met at Assiut

April 29, Mussulman Congress met

June 17, Death of Riaz Pasha, statesman

July 12, Death of Sir Eldon Gorst, British Consul General

July 16, Lord Kitchener appointed Consul General to succeed Sir Eldon Gorst

1912

Jan. 26, New Cathedral at Khartoum dedicated by the Bishop of London

April 10, Mahomed Farid Bey, Nationalist leader, sentenced in absence to imprisonment for one year at hard labor for seditious speech

July 2, Three Nationalists arrested charged with conspiracy against the life of the Khedive and sentenced Aug. 13 to prison terms

July, System of popular justice administered by village "cantonal" courts introduced

Dec. 4, "Five Fedans" law passed by which small holdings up to 5 fedans (about 5.15 acres) were exempted from distraint from debt

1913

July 21, New organic and electoral laws replaced the law of May 1, 1883, the Legislative Council and General Assembly abolished and a new body called the Legislative Assembly constituted with right to initiate legislation

Oct. 26, Elections for the new Legislative Assembly begun which resulted in membership of 49 landowners, 2 lawyers, 3 clericals, and 1 engineer, Zaghlul Pasha elected vice-president

Nov. 20, Ministries of Pious Foundations and of Agriculture constituted

1914

Jan. 22–June 17, First session of Assembly

April 3, Resignation of Cabinet of Mohammed Said Bey

April 5, Hussein Rushdi Pasha formed Cabinet

July 25, Unsuccessful attempt to assassinate the Khedive by student

Aug. 6, Decree of the Khedive placed Egypt in "state of war"

Sept. 10, German and Austrian representatives expelled

Oct. 1, Enemy subjects ordered to register and those of military age deported to Malta

Nov. 1, General Sir John Maxwell appointed General Officer (British) in command, proclaimed martial law

Nov. 6, State of war with Turkey proclaimed

Dec. 18, Egypt proclaimed a British Protectorate; Lieutenant Colonel Sir Henry MacMahon appointed High Commissioner

Dec. 19, Khedive Abbas Hilmi deposed and Prince Hussein Kamil Pasha proclaimed Sultan

1915

Jan. 9, Sir H. McMahon appointed High Commissioner, arrived in Egypt

April 8, Attempt to assassinate the Sultan by fanatical Mohammedan who declared him a traitor to the Khalif

July 9, Second attempt to assassinate the Sultan by a Mohammedan fanatic

1916

Jan. 19, Ministry of Hussein Rushdi Pasha as constituted: Premier and Minister of the Interior, Hussein Rushdi Pasha; Public Works and War, Ismail Sirri Pasha; Education, Adli Yeghen Pasha; Finance, Yûsuf Wahba Pasha; Pious Foundations, Ibrahim Fathi Pasha; Justice, Abd el Khâlek Sarwât Pasha; Agriculture, Ahmed Hilmi Pasha

March 19, General Sir Archibald Murray appointed to command in Egypt succeeding General Sir John Maxwell

Oct. 18, Decree made the monetary unit the gold Egyptian pound of 100 piastres and new coinage replaced the monogram of the Sultan of Turkey by that of the Sultan of Egypt

Oct. 27, Decree postponed meeting of Legislative Assembly and elections because of state of war

1917

Jan. 1, General Sir Reginald Wingate succeeded as High Commissioner

Jan. 9, Last Turkish troops driven back across frontier

June 28, General Sir Edmund Allenby took command of Egyptian Expeditionary Army

Oct. 9, Death of Sultan Hussein Kamil. Succeeded by his brother Ahmed Fuad

1919

March 3, Committee of 12 headed by Zaghlul Pasha presented petition to the Sultan declaring the nullity of the protectorate

March 8, Zaghlul Pasha and 3 other Nationalist leaders, Ismail Sidky Pasha, Mohammed Mahmud Pasha, and Hamad-el-Bassel Pasha arrested and the following day deported to Malta

March 9–11, Riots in Cairo

March 12, Rioting spread to other parts of the country especially at Tanta and the Delta provinces and attacks on British citizens and soldiers

March 21, General Allenby appointed Special High Commissioner during absence of Sir R. Wingate in London arrived in Egypt on the 25th

April 9, Rushdi Pasha reconstituted Cabinet with Adli Pasha as Minister of the Interior

April 21, Rushdi Pasha, Prime Minister, resigned finally

May 21, New Cabinet formed by Mahomed Said Pasha

May 24, King Fuad married Princess Nazli

Aug., Conciliation Board established for settlement of labor disputes

Oct. 17, Field Marshal Viscount Allenby appointed High Commissioner for Egypt and the Sudan

Nov. 28, Yusef Wahba Pasha became Prime Minister on resignation of Mahomed Said Pasha after protest against the Milner Mission

Dec. 7, Lord Milner's Mission arrived in Egypt "to inquire into the causes of the recent disorders, and to report on the existing situation in the country and the form of constitution which, under the protectorate, will be best . . ."

1920

Feb. 11, Son and heir born to the Sultan (Prince Faruk)

March 6, Milner Mission left Egypt

March 10, Legislative Assembly adopted resolution declaring independence

April, Price of cotton in Liverpool 84.50d.

May 19, Resignation of Premier Wahba Pasha because of ill health. Succeeded by Tewfiq Nessim Pasha

June 7–Nov. 9, Negotiations of delegation headed by Zaghlul Pasha with the Milner Mission in London

Aug. 10, By Treaty of Sèvres Turkey renounced all rights over Egypt and recognized the Protectorate

Sept. 4, Agreement signed by Great Britain and Greece for suppression of the capitulations in Egypt

Nov. 13–14, Strike of students in Cairo

Dec. 9, Report of Milner Mission presented; published Feb. 18, 1921

———, British-Portuguese Agreement signed for suppression of the capitulations in Egypt

1921

March 15, New Coalition Cabinet formed by Adly Yeghen Pasha

April 5, Zaghlul Pasha returned to Egypt and took position of hostility to the new Government which he declared unrepresentative

April 22, British-Norwegian Agreement signed for abolition of the capitulations

April, Price of cotton in Liverpool only 17.75d.

May 20–22, Anti-European riots in Cairo and Alexandria, 68 Egyptians and 19 Europeans killed and 162 Egyptians and 66 Europeans, chiefly Greeks, wounded

July 8, British-Swedish Agreement signed for abolition of the capitulations

July 12–Nov. 20, Conference in London with British Government of delegation headed by Adli Pasha

July 14, British-Danish Agreement signed for abolition of the capitulations

Aug. 10, Agreement with Belgium signed modified the Treaty of commerce and navigation of June 24, 1891

Nov. 10, Draft Convention presented to Egyptian delegation in London by Lord Curzon; rejected by delegation Nov. 15

Nov. 20, Delegation left England after negotiations broke down on the military issue as to British troops in Egypt

Dec. 22, Zaghlul Pasha arrested and deported with 5 of his followers

1922

Jan. 23, Manifesto of the Nationalist Party called for passive resistance

Jan. 24, Signers of the Nationalist manifesto arrested

Jan. 29, Announcement of British Government that Great Britain was ready to end the Protectorate and recognize Egypt on certain conditions

Feb. 22, Lord Allenby returned to Egypt from London after a month's absence

Feb. 28, British protectorate over Egypt terminated by declaration of the Government of recognition of independence of Egypt as an independent sovereign State with reservations as to foreign affairs and the Sudan

March 1, Sarwat Pasha formed new Cabinet

March 15, The Sultan proclaimed King as Fuad I

April 13, Rescript of King Fuad declared the throne hereditary in dynasty of Mehemet Ali in direct male line by primogeniture, the ex-Khedive Abbas Hilmi expressly excluded

April 26, New Government recognized by the United States but on condition that the capitulations should not be abolished

May 9, Decree issued prohibited the import and export of opium, cocaine, hashish, and morphine except by special license

Aug. 14, Seven supporters of Zaghlul condemned by British military court to death for sedition; later, sentences commuted to penal servitude for 7 years and fine

Sept. 5, Decree exiled deposed Khedive Abbas Hilmi and confiscated his property

Nov. 29, Discovery of tomb of Tutankhamen by Howard Carter and Lord Carnarvon

Nov. 30, Sarwat Ministry resigned and was succeeded by Tewfik Nessim Pasha

1923

Feb. 4, Agreement of Prime Minister with Lord Allenby that 2 clauses of the draft Constitution declaring Egyptian sovereignty over the Sudan should be removed

Feb. 5, Tewik Nessim Pasha forced to resign because of Agreement of Feb. 4 relinquishing Egyptian claim to the Sudan

Feb. 16, The sepulchral chamber of Tutankhamen opened

March 5, Leading members of party of Zaghlul arrested and extreme Nationalist newspapers suspended

March 15, New Ministry formed by Yehia Ibrahim Pasha

April 4, Zaghlul released from prison at Gibraltar where he had been confined since August, 1922 on ground of ill health

April 19, Constitution signed by King Fuad and promulgated

April 30, Electoral law signed gave vote to every Egyptian but did not define what constituted an Egyptian

May 2, 15 Egyptians arrested because of outrages against British

May 12, Provisional Commercial Agreement with Persia concluded

May 31, Censorship over public speech set up by the Government

June 1, Release of followers of Zaghlul deported in 1921

July 5, Proclamation issued abolished British martial law in force since 1914, replaced by Egyptian Statute

——, Act of indemnity concluded with British Government

Sept. 27, Elections a victory for the followers of Zaghlul Pasha

Dec. 28, Anglo-French Agreement signed settled boundary between the Anglo-Egyptian Sudan and French Equatorial Africa

1924

Jan. 17, Resignation of Cabinet of Yehia Pasha

Jan. 28, Zaghlul Pasha appointed Prime Minister

March 6, Official opening of the tomb of Tutankhamen by the Government

March 15, First Parliament of independent Egypt opened by King Fuad

June 24–25, Anti-British demonstrations and riots at Khartoum and Omdurman in the Sudan

Aug. 9–10, Demonstration against British by the cadets of the Khartoum Military School

Aug. 9–11, Riots of Egyptian soldiers at Atbara and Port Sudan

Aug. 16, Note protested British action in Sudan

Sept. 25–Oct. 3, Conferences of Zaghlul Pasha with Ramsay MacDonald in London ended without agreement

Nov. 19, Sir Lee Stack, Governor General of the Sudan and Sirdar of the Egyptian army was shot driving through Cairo and died the following day

Nov. 22, British Government ultimatum to Egypt demanded apology, prosecution of assassins of Sir Lee Stack, indemnity of £500,000, suppression of political demonstrations and withdrawal from the Sudan within 24 hours of all Egyptian officers and purely Egyptian units of the Egyptian army, and withdrawal of opposition to British protection of foreign interests

Nov. 23, Egyptian Government accepted demands except those regarding the Sudan, and protection of foreign interests

Nov. 24, Evacuation of Egyptian units of Sudan army begun and fine paid in view of British action in the Sudan and occupation of the customs at Alexandria by a British force

——, Resignation of Ministry of Zaghlul Pasha

Nov. 25, Cabinet formed by Ahmed Pasha Ziwar

Nov. 27–28, British troops suppressed mutiny of Sudanese troops at Khartoum

Nov. 29, British terms as to protection of foreign interests accepted

——, Sudanese regiments surrendered to British at Khartoum

Dec. 2, British troops withdrawn from custom house at Alexandria

Dec. 22, Parliament dissolved

Dec. 23, Zaghlul Pasha removed from Cairo because of his political activities

Dec. 24, Riots at Gizeh and conflict with troops

1925

Jan. 17, New defense force in Sudan announced by Governor General

Feb. 12, Export of wheat, maize, milled barley, and flour prohibited

Feb. 26, Lord Allenby resigned as High Commissioner and was succeeded by Sir George Lloyd

March 12, Election for Parliament a victory for the anti-British party of Zaghlul Pasha

March 23, Parliament met, elected Zaghlul president of Chamber and was dissolved the same day by the Prime Minister

May 8, The Blue Nile dam at Makwar completed

Aug. 23, Seven persons condemned as murderers of Sir Lee Stack executed at Cairo

Oct. 21, Sir George Lloyd, British High Commissioner, landed at Port Said

Dec. 6, Agreement signed with Italy provided for rectification of frontier between Egypt and Cyrenaica by which the oasis of Jaghbub included in Cyrenaica, Egypt receiving the Ramlah wells north-west of Sollum

——, Riot in Cairo, 5 killed, 4 wounded

Dec. 8, Government announced new electoral law

Dec. 20, Law prohibited planting of more than one-third of arable land with cotton in the year 1926

1926

Jan. 21, The Sennar dam officially opened at Makwar, Sudan

April 10, Provisional Commercial Agreement with Greece

April 17, Provisional Commercial Agreement with Turkey

April 27, John D. Rockefeller, Jr. withdrew offer of $10,000,000 for museum

May 13–19, Caliphate Congress at Cairo unable to agree on candidate for Caliph

May 22, Election for Parliament a defeat for the Government

May 23, Hussein Pasha Rushdi made president of the Senate

June 6, Adly Pasha formed Coalition Cabinet

June 10, Parliament assembled

July 17, Resignation of Sir Geoffrey Archer as Governor General of the Sudan

Oct. 28, Decree limited area of arable land for cultivation of cotton to one third

Oct. 31, Announcement that Sir John Loader Maffey appointed Governor-General of the Sudan

Nov. 9, Treaty with Italy fixed frontier near Sollum and Jarabub (Egypt and Cyrenaica)

Nov. 18, Parliament met and speech from the throne asked ratification of loan of $20,000,000 to cotton cultivators

Dec. 8, Law passed limiting cotton acreage for 3 years to one-third of every plantation

Dec. 21, Port Fuad on Red Sea opposite Port Said opened

1927

Jan., International Cotton Spinners' Congress held at Cairo to consider the decline in quantity and quality of exports of Egyptian cotton

Feb. 16, Commercial Convention with Hungary signed

April 18, Abdul Khalik Pasha Sarwat appointed Prime Minister on resignation of Adly Yeghen Pasha forced out by the Wafdists (Zaghlul Nationalists)

May 23, Committee of Parliament published report on army budget recommending large increase and in personnel of army and suppression of credits for the Sirdarate

May 30, Note of British High Commissioner protested report; accepted June 14

June 29, Anglo-Turkish Mixed Arbitration Tribunal declared itself incompetent to act on claims of damages against British Government by ex-Khedive Abbas Hilmi

July 4–26, King Fuad in Great Britain on state visit

July 18, Draft Treaty with England presented by Sarwat Pasha

Aug. 23, Death of Nationalist leader, Zaghlul Pasha (74)

Sept. 14, Meeting of the Wafd Party elected Mustapha Nahas Pasha to succeed Zaghlul as leader

Oct. 30–Nov. 8, Conferences of Sarwat Pasha with British Government in London

Nov. 17, Parliament opened

1928

Jan. 16, New bridge across the Blue Nile between Khartoum and Omdurman opened

March 4, Note of Prime Minister notified Great Britain that the draft Treaty of alliance did not protect the independence of Egypt and was not acceptable

——, Resignation of Sarwat Cabinet but consented to remain in office until new Cabinet appointed

——, British Note presented objection to Public Assemblies Bill before the Egyptian Parliament

March 7, Draft Treaty of alliance published by the British Government

March 8, Student demonstrations against British in Cairo and Assiut

March 13, Death of Hussein Rushdi Pasha, former Premier

March 16, Mustapha Nahas Pasha, leader of Wafd or Nationalist Party formed Cabinet: Prime Minister and Minister of Interior, Mustapha Nahas Pasha; Foreign Affairs, Wassif Ghaly Pasha; Justice, Ahmed Khashaba Pasha; Agriculture, Mohammed Safwat Pasha; Finance, Mohammed Mahmoud Pasha; Wakfs, Mohammed Naguib El Gharably Pasha; Education, Aly El Chamsy Pasha; War, Gaafar Wali Pasha; Communications, William Makram Ebeid Bey; Public Works, Ibrahim Fahmy Bey

March 30, Note of Hahas Pasha to British Government declared British Note of March 4 a departure from the rules of diplomatic intervention

April 4, British Note declared that as negotiations for Treaty had broken down relations with Egypt had returned to *status quo ante*

April 29, British ultimatum demanded withdrawal of Public Assemblies Bill as an abuse of the protection of life and property in Egypt

April 30, Decision to withdraw the Public Assemblies Bill; reply to Great Britain presented May 1

May 2, British warships en route from Malta to Egypt changed course

June 9, Provisional Commercial Agreement with Switzerland concluded

June 13, Provisional Commercial Agreement with the Levant States under French mandate

June 19, Resignation from Cabinet of Gaafar Wali Pasha, Minister of War, succeeding resignation of Mohammed Mahmoud Pasha, Minister of Finance

June 21, Provisional Commercial Agreement with Palestine signed

June 24, Photographs of documents published in Cairo seriously compromised Nahas

June 25, King Fuad dismissed Nahas Pasha, Premier, and invited Mohammed Mahmoud Pasha (Liberal) to form a Cabinet

June 28, Mohammed Mahmoud Pasha dissolved the Chamber for 1 month

July 19, Both Houses of Parliament dissolved for 3 years and the Constitution suspended for 3 years by royal decree

July 28, Members of Parliament met and protested against their suspension as unconstitutional

Sept. 11, Arrival of the Prince of Wales in Cairo

Sept. 22, Death of Abdul Khalik Sarwat Pasha, former Premier

1929

Feb. 16, Announcement that new customs tariff would be put into effect in one year and foreign governments notified that all existing commercial treaties would be terminated

March 8–May 11, Egyptian Minister of Foreign Affairs in England for conferences with British Government

March 10, Decree promulgated nationality law

March 17, Agreement signed with Great Britain regarding the Ottoman loan of 1855 and other financial questions

March 21, Royal decree provided punishment for anyone instigating any hostility or demonstration against the Government

May 7, Agreement as to Nile waters concluded with Great Britain based on report of Commission appointed Jan. 26, 1925 and presenting report March 21, 1926

May 9–15, Series of meetings of Wafd Party refused to approve Nile Waters Agreement signed with Great Britain May 7

May 30, King Fuad left Egypt for visit to Europe arriving in London July 20

July 24, Resignation of Lord Lloyd, British High Commissioner, announced

Aug. 3, Treaty of friendship with Turkey

Aug. 8, Sir Percy Lyham Loraine appointed British High Commissioner for Egypt and the Sudan

Aug. 23, King Fuad and Mohammed Mahmoud Pasha arrived in Egypt

Aug. 27, Treaty of conciliation and friendship with the United States signed

Sept. 2, Sir Percy Loraine, British High Commissioner, arrived in Cairo

Oct. 2, Resignation of Mohammed Mahmoud Pasha, Prime Minister

Oct. 4, Adly Pasha Yeghen appointed Prime Minister

Oct. 31, King Fuad decreed restoration of the Constitution

Dec. 21, Elections held gave Wafdists, 187; Ittihadists, 3; Nationalists, 4; Independents, 20

1930

Jan. 1, Mustapha Pasha Nahas formed Cabinet as Prime Minister and Minister of Interior; Foreign Affairs, Wassef Pasha Ghali; War, Hassan Pasha Hassib; Justice, Neguib Pasha Gharabli; Agriculture, Mohamed Pasha Safwat; Public Works, Osman Pasha Moharram; Finance, Makram Effendi Ebeid; Wakfs, Mahmud Bey Bassiuni; Education, Baha-ed-din Bey Barakat; Communications, Mahmud Fahmy Effendi Nekrashi

Jan. 11, Parliament opened

Feb. 16, New customs tariff with high protective duties came into effect

March 19, Commercial Agreement with Japan signed

March 27–May 8, Negotiations for Anglo-Egyptian Treaty in London
April 17, British Draft Treaty handed to Nahas Pasha
May 8, Anglo-Egyptian negotiations broke down because of demands of Egyptian delegation for greater concessions in the Sudan
May 26, Provisional Commercial Agreement with the United States
June 17, Resignation of Nahas Pasha Cabinet because King Fuad refused approval of Bills
June 21, Ismail Pasha Sidky took office as Prime Minister and Minister of Interior; Foreign Affairs, Abdel Fattah Pasha Yehia; War and Marine, Mohamed Tewfik Pasha Rifaa; Justice, Aly Pasha Maher; Agriculture, Hafez Pasha Hassan; Public Works, Ibrahim Pasha Fahmy; Wakfs, Mohamed Halim Jasa Pasha; Education, Murad Sid Ahmed Pasha; Communications, Tewfik Pasha Doss
——, Royal decree prorogued Parliament for one month
June 23, Senators and Deputies held meeting of protest
June 26, Wafd National Congress met and resolved to start a non-coöperation movement and adopted resolution of lack of confidence in Sidky Ministry
July 1, Riots at Bilbeis
July 8, Riots at Mansurah
July 12, Royal decree ordered closure of session of Parliament
July 15, Wafdist riots in Alexandria, 15 Egyptian civilians and a policeman killed and 400 injured
July 16, Two British battleships ordered to Alexandria
July 21, Riots in Cairo and Port Said; 6 killed and 250 wounded in Cairo
July 24, Import duties on wheat, flour, and sugar increased
July 26, Wafd non-coöperation movement begun; refused to pay taxes
Aug. 28, The Cabinet ordered all land rents reduced one-fifth for one year beginning Sept. 1
Sept. 29, King Fuad opened the "Petroleum Basin"
Oct. 22, New Constitution and electoral law promulgated
Nov. 25, Wafd and Liberal joint commissions set up to boycott elections
Nov. 26, Welfare centers and night schools opened in Cairo and Alexandria by American Near East Foundation
Dec. 8, The "Peoples' Party" (Ash Sha'b) founded by Sidqi Pasha

KHEDIVES OR HEREDITARY VICEROYS
(nearly independent)

1806. Mehemet Ali Pasha; abdicated Sept., 1848; dies Aug. 2, 1849
1848. Ibrahim (adopted son), Sept.; dies Nov. 9 or 10, 1848. Abbas (his son), Nov. 10; dies July 14, 1854.
1854. Saïd (brother), July 14; dies Jan. 18, 1863.
1863. Ismaïl (nephew), Jan. 18 (born Dec. 31, 1830); deposed by the Sultan at the request of England, France, and other Powers, June 26, 1879; died March 2, 1895
1879. Mechmet Tewfik, born Nov., 1852; proclaimed June 26, invested Aug. 14; died Jan. 7, 1892
1892. Abbas Hilmi, born July 14, 1874; heir, Abdul Mouneim Bey, born Feb. 20, 1899, deposed Dec. 19, 1914
1914. Hussein Kamil, son of Ismail; died Oct. 9, 1917
1917. Ahmed Fuad, brother of Hussein Kamil; took title of King (Fuad I) March 15, 1922

ELOBEY

Elobey, Great and Little, Spanish islands. *See* Guinea, Spanish

ERITREA

Eritrea, Italian Colony on the Red Sea with inland boundaries with the Anglo-Egyptian Sudan, Abyssinia and French Somaliland, extending from Cape Kasar on the coast to Cape Dumeirah on the Strait of Bab-el-Mandeb, about 670 miles. The total area is 45,754 square miles, and the whole population is estimated at 402,793, exclusive of 4,681 Europeans, of whom 4,283 are Italian (exclusive of the military forces) and 398 of other nationalities. Massawah has (1923) 12,275 inhabitants, of whom 350 are European, mainly Italian. The seat of the Government is Asmara, a modern town 7,765 feet above the sea-level, with 18,500 inhabitants (3,500 European).

The Italian possessions on the Red Sea are constituted as the Colony of Eritrea, with the management of its own finances and an autonomous administration in 7 commissariats, as follows:

COMMISSARIAT	AREA IN SQ. MILES	TOTAL NATIVE POPULATION (CENSUS 1921)	CAPITAL
Hamasien . . .	1,165	60,234	Asmara
Acchelé Guzai .	3,505	62,169	Adi Caieh
Serae	3,317	69,311	Adi Ugri
Barca, Gasc, and Setit	18,299	85,506	Agordat
Cheren . . .	8,836	73,737	Cheren
Massawah . . .	5,109	47,910	Massawah
Assab	5,523	3,926	Assab
	45,754	402,793	

From August 1, 1929, the Commissariats of Hamasien, Acchelé Guzai, and Serae were united into the single Regional Commissariat of the Uplands, with Asmara as the capital; and the Commissariats of Barca, Gasc, and Setit and of Cheren into the Regional Commissariat of Western Lowlands, with the capital at Agordat. The Regional Commissariat of Massawah, with somewhat modified boundaries, has changed its name to that of Regional Commissariat of Eastern Lowlands with the capital at Massawah as before. The Commissariat of Assab has been changed to the seat of the Southern Dancalia, with capital at Assab.

In the Italian dependencies the central government is represented by a civil governor, who is nominated by the King and is under the direction of the Minister for the Colonies.

Riccardo Astuto dei Duchi di Lucchesi. Governor.

1865

Massawah (Massowah) and the adjacent coast under the control of the Egyptians

1869

Nov. 15, The Rubattino Company (Italian) acquired territory in the Bay of Assab near the Strait of Bab-el-Mandeb from the Sultan of Assab, and further concessions March 11, 1870, Dec. 30, 1879, May 15 and Nov. 5, 1880

1880

Sept. 20, Protectorate Treaty signed by the Sultan of Raheita with the Rubattino Company

1882

March 10, All rights of the Rubattino Company transferred to the Italian Government by the Company
July 5, Assab declared an Italian Colony

1883

March 15, Cession to Italy of Ablis (Aussa)

1885

Feb. 3 and 10, Proclamation of Italian occupation of Massowah
Feb. 6, The Italian flag hoisted beside the Egyptian at Massowah with consent of England
Aug., Italian occupation extended as far as Saati of posts formerly garrisoned by Egyptians
Sept. 23, The Abyssinians under Ras Aloula severely defeat the Arabs at Kufeit near Amadib
Dec. 2, Government of Massowah assumed by the Italians

1887

Jan. 18 *et seq.*, Abyssinians attack Massowah and Italian outposts, but suffer loss and retire
Jan. 25–26, About 500 Italians proceeding with supplies to Sahati cut off by Abyssinians under Ras Aloula at Dagoli, near Massowah
March 11, Negotiations with Ras Aloula with respect to release of prisoners
March 27–28, Skirmishes between Italians and Deber tribe
May 2, Proclamation issued declaring that a state of war exists in Massowah, with blockade of ports
Sept., Major Savoiroux made a prisoner, April; released
Oct. 18, The chief Kantibay submits to Italy
Nov. 8, General Asinari reached Massawa and reoccupied abandoned positions restoring Italian prestige

1888

April 2, Abyssinians withdraw without attacking Saati
June 1, Italians levied municipal tax on householders in Massowah
July, Italy notifies to the Powers that it has annexed Massowah
Aug. 1, Italian flag raised at Zulla
Aug. 3, Protectorate proclaimed at Zulla
Aug., Severe defeat of Italians at Sanganeiti on the borders through native treachery; four Italian officers killed

1889

June 2, Keren occupied and annexed by the Italians
Aug. 4, Gen. Baldissera occupies Asmara
Dec. 9, Treaty with Sultan of the Danakils, recognition

of Italian possession of coast, superceding treaties of March 15, 1883, July 7 and Aug. 10, 1887

1890

Jan. 1, Italian possessions on Red Sea united as Colony
June 29, About 1,000 dervishes severely defeated after the incursion into Italian-protected country; captives and booty rescued, reported
July 1, Gen. Gandolfi, new governor, announces the termination of military rule, in the Italian possessions on the Red Sea (named Eritrea, Feb. 1)

1891

April 15, Boundary Protocol of Great Britain and Italy as to frontier with the Sudan

1893

Dec. 20, Severe defeat of about 10,000 dervishes by the Italian troops under Col. Arimondi at Fort Agordat; about 4,000 dervishes killed, also Ghen Daref and 4 emirs, reported

1894

July 17, The dervishes, after a murderous raid, pursued by Italians under Col. Baratieri, Gov.-Gen., who captures Kassala by assault
Dec. 20, Batagos, an Abyssinian chief, defeated and killed at Halai by Major Toselli, reported
Dec. 28, Italians occupied Adowa

1895

Jan. 3, Italians not strong enough to hold Adowa and Baratieri retired
Jan. 13, 14, Gen. Baratieri defeats the Abyssinians under Ras Mangascia at Coatit
Jan. 17, Another victory at Senafa, reported
March 25, Adigrat occupied by the Italians
Oct. 9, The heights of Debra carried by assault, and Antalo occupied by Gen. Baratieri, after a rapid march
Dec. 8, Major Toselli's column (about 2,450) surprised and defeated by 15,000 Shoans at Amba Alagi, Major Toselli and 3 Lieuts. killed, after a heroic defense, great slaughter on both sides; Capts. Botrero and Pagella with the scattered troops retreat to Adera, and join Gen. Arimondi

1896

Jan. 7–11, Shoans repulsed with heavy loss at Makaleh, by Lieut.-Col. Galliano
Jan. 30, The Italians largely outnumbered, after a gallant resistance and great suffering, evacuate Fort Agordat with honors of war, Jan. 23; and arrive at Adigrat
Feb. 16, Shoans defeated, and the Pass of Seeta captured; again defeated by Col. Stevani at Maimara, Feb. 26
Feb. 29, March 1, The battle of Adowa: Italians under Gen. Baratieri severely defeated by the Shoans; Gen. Dabormida and Prince Chigi killed at the head of their men (the brigade fought heroically all day); Gen. Baratieri, incapable through weakness, retired; Gen. Arimondi (fate unknown) and 150 officers killed; estimated Italian loss, 7,000, and 2,000 natives; Gen. Albertoni, Cols. Nava and Galliano (mortally wounded), 48 officers, and 1,500 men prisoners; Shoan loss, 4,000
March 2, Fort Adigrat, provisioned for a month under

Major Prestinari, surrounded by Shoans; the garrison relieved, May 5; evacuated by the Italians, reported May 18

March 4, Gen. Baldissera assumes the command in Massowah; Gen. Baratieri arrives there greatly prostrated, March 11

March 13, Negotiations for peace opened

March 8 and 18, Dervishes repulsed with heavy loss near Kassala; again by Col. Stevani at Mt. Mocram; forts captured at Tucruf, April 2

April 7, Dervish retreat from Kassala

May 13 *et seq.*, Negotiations between Gen. Baldissera and Ras Mangascia and other chiefs for release of prisoners, May 8; many released

May 18, Ambra Debra captured in a night attack by Lieut. Sapelli, flight of enemy

May 26, The Italians strongly entrenched at Dongollo and other places, the Abyssinians retreating

June 5-13, Gen. Baratieri tried by court martial at Asmara, and acquitted

Oct. 26, Treaty of peace signed (*see* Abyssinia)

Nov. 6, 1,300 Italian prisoners reported in Abyssinia

1897

Jan., Advance of (5,000 or 6,000) dervishes on Agordat, Tucular occupied

Jan. 22, General Vigano arrived at Agordat, concentration of troops, and defense organized

Feb. 1, Retreat of the Dervishes to Amdarab

Dec. 25, Cession of fort at Kassala by Italians to Egyptians

1898

Dec. 7, Anglo-Italian Boundary Convention settled frontier with Anglo-Egyptian Sudan from Red Sea to Baraka

1899

June 1, Anglo-Italian Boundary Convention settled frontier with Anglo-Egyptian Sudan from Baraka to Sabderat

1900

Jan. 24, Franco-Italian Boundary Protocol for the delimitation of possessions on coast of Red Sea and Gulf of Aden signed and July 10, 1901 fixed frontiers with French Somaliland

July 10, Treaty of Italy with Abyssinia signed settled frontiers

1901

April 16, Anglo-Italian Boundary Convention settled frontier with Anglo-Egyptian Sudan from Sabderat to Todluc

Nov. 22, Declaration of Great Britain and Italy as to boundary from Abu Gamal to the Setit, and May 15, 1902 of Great Britain, Italy, and Abyssinia which placed territory of the Kanama tribe on the north bank of the Setit in Eritrea, and description, Feb. 18, 1903

1904

Jan. 19, Anglo-Italian Boundary Convention settled frontier with the Sudan at Carora

July 18, Law promulgated to encourage production of wheat permitted free import into Italy up to 2,000, tons

1906

July, Commercial Treaty with Abyssinia signed

1907

Dec. 18-19, Frontier with Sudan fixed as to Marks, Jebel Injaha, and Ras Casar

1908

May 16, Boundary Convention between Italy and Abyssinia finally settled Danakil frontier

1909

Dec. 30, Royal Decree empowered Governor General to contract loan of 17 million lire with Bank of Italy for railroad construction

1911

Dec. 6, Railroad opened from Massowah to Asmara

1915

April, Italian law provided that cattle and meat from Eritrea should receive preferential treatment, Italian customs

1922

Dec. 26, Anglo-Italian Treaty signed, rectification of boundary with Sudan

1924

May 19 and June 18, Anglo-Italian exchange of Notes on Eritrea-Sudan frontier

1925

June 15, Anglo-Italian Agreement as to utilization of waters of Gash River for irrigation

1928

Aug. 2, Agreement with Abyssinia for cession of free zone at port of Assah and construction of a road from there to Addis Ababa

1929

Jan. 4, Order of the Governor General established a commission to study agricultural problems of the country

1930

Oct. 11, Regulations of the Governor established tax on unmarried men for Italian citizens resident

FERNANDO PO

Fernando Po, Spanish island off west coast of Africa about 20 miles from the mainland in the Bight of Biafra in 3° 12' N. and 8° 48' E., the largest island in the Gulf of Guinea; area, 810 square miles; population, 20,873. The island was discovered at close of 15th century by Portuguese navigator for whom it was named. *See also* Guinea, Spanish.

FRENCH EQUATORIAL AFRICA

French Equatorial Africa (French Congo).

The French Congo extends along the Atlantic coast between Cameroon and the territories of the Belgian Congo, with the exception of the

Spanish territory on the coast from the Muni river on 1° N. lat. to Cameroon, and inland to the meridian of 11° 20' E. of Greenwich, and the Kabinda region, which is Portuguese. Inland it is bounded by the Congo and Ubangi rivers and stretches northwards to the Bahr-el-Ghazal and Lake Chad. French acquisition began on the Gabun river in 1841; Libreville was founded in 1849; Cape Lopez was gained in 1862, and the French possessions extended along the coast for about 200 miles. Since then the territories have been increased by exploration and military occupation and their limits have been defined in a series of international conventions. The boundary between French Equatorial Africa and the Anglo-Egyptian Sudan was fixed by a protocol signed on February 28, 1924.

By decree of January 15, 1910, the French Congo was divided into three circumscriptions which form three colonies, viz.: the Gabun Colony (capital Libreville), the Middle Congo Colony (capital Brazzaville), and the Ubangi-Shari Colony (capital Bangui). The Chad Territory, which was formerly a dependency of the Ubangi-Shari Colony, was, by decree issued on March 17, 1920, made a separate colony. It extends from Lake Chad across the Eastern Sudan and includes Wadai. Capital, Fort Lamy.

By decrees issued on January 15, 1910, the name of the French Congo was changed into French Equatorial Africa, which extends over the Gabun, the Middle Congo, the Ubangi-Shari, and Chad Colonies.

The area is about 912,049 square miles, containing a population which at the 1926 census numbered 3,127,707; the Europeans numbered 2,502.

COLONY	AREA IN SQ. MILES	MEN	WOMEN	BOYS	GIRLS	TOTAL
Gabun	104,320	126,840	161,388	51,524	49,147	388,899
Middle Congo	172,411	212,035	261,447	118,862	106,409	698,753
Ubangi-Shari	236,363	350,800	377,594	174,349	163,701	1,066,444
Chad	398,955	331,011	317,259	166,491	158,850	973,611
Total	912,049	1,020,686	1,117,688	511,226	478,097	3,127,707

The Colonies have each a Lieutenant-Governor; they all have financial and administrative autonomy, and each has an administrative council; the Lieutenant-Governors are under the Governor-General of French Equatorial Africa, having his headquarters at Brazzaville, who is assisted by a Secretary-General and a Council of Government.

R. Antonetti, Governor General.

1839

Feb. 9, Captain Bouët-Willaumetz by Treaty with King Denis of Gabun obtained for France land on the left (south) bank of the Gabun River

1842

March 18, Treaty with King Louis signed by which territory on right (north) bank of the Gabun River ceded to France

1843

April 27, Treaty by which village of Quabens ceded to France

June 11, Official occupation of territory and establishment of Fort d'Aumale

1844

March 28, April 1, 22, July 6 and 7, Further treaties with chiefs of Gabun territory

1845

Sept. 4, and Oct. 19, Further treaties with the chiefs of the Gabun estuary

1849

Libreville founded by the French with negroes freed from a captured slave ship

1852

Sept. 18, Treaty with chiefs north of the Gabun estuary

at Cape Esterias by which they recognized French Protectorate

1855

April, Treaty by which the Island of Great Elobey (ceded to Spain in 1846) recognized French Protectorate

1857–1859

Exploration of the Gabun estuary and the Ogowé River by Paul Du Chaillu

1860

Aug. 4, Decree established Government of Ivory Coast and Gabun at Gabun

1863–1865

Second expedition of Du Chaillu to south of the Ogowé River

1867

April 25, Lieutenant de Vaisseau Aymès began exploration of the Ogowé River and made Treaty with King Rakenga (Rénoqué) of the Irengas, May 10

1869

Sept. 11, Decree established court at Libreville, appeal to be before court at St. Louis, Senegal

1870

Dr. Gustav Nachtigal from Tripoli reached Lake Chad

1873

March 8–May 24, Exploration of the Ogowé basin by Alfred Marsh and the Marquis de Compiègne

1875

Aug. 10, Count Savorgnan de Brazza left Paris, arrived at Gabun, Oct. 20, and with Dr. Noel Ballay explored the Ogowé River and discovered the Alima and the Lefini Rivers, branches of the Congo, regaining the coast, Nov., 1878

1879

Dec. 27, De Brazza left Liverpool on second expedition instructed to go to the Congo River and arrived at Gabun early in 1880, ascended the Ogowé and founded Franceville in June on upper waters of that river and Brazzaville (N'tamo) opposite the Belgian post of Stanley Pool on the Congo

1880

Sept. 10, De Brazza concluded Treaty with Makoko, chief of the Bateke tribe, placing his country under French protection. Act of taking possession signed Oct. 3. Ratified by the Parliament of France, Nov. 20, 1882

Nov. 7, De Brazza met Stanley at Isangila

1881

Jan. 24, Decree placed administration of Gabun and coast settlements under naval commander

1882

June 7, De Brazza returned to France after exploration of the hinterland of the Gabun

1883

March 21, De Brazza left France on third expedition to Africa reaching Gabun April 25, having been appointed Feb. 5 Commissioner of the Government to West Africa with powers of a colonial Governor and authorized to make treaties with native chiefs

April 9, Primary schools established

Dec. 16, Government reorganized, Gabun separated from Ivory Coast

1884

April 23, Exchange of Notes by which France secured right of preëmption over Congo Free State

1885

Feb. 5, Treaty of France with Belgium settled frontiers of French and Belgian Congo

Feb. 26, Berlin Act provided for free navigation of the Congo River

Oct. 18, De Brazza arrived at Libreville and delegated his powers to M. Pradier, Governor of Gabun, returning to France after exploring and surveying some 4,000 kilometers from Franceville on the Upper Ogowé (Ogoove) northward to Lake Chad

Nov. 22, Boundary Convention with Belgium fixed frontier in region of Manyanga with Congo Free State

Dec. 24, Boundary Convention with Germany fixed frontier with Cameroons

1886

April 27, Decree gave De Brazza the title Commissioner General of the Government of the French Congo, with a lieutenant governor, Noel Ballay, appointed for Gabun at Libreville

May 12, Boundary Convention with Portugal fixed frontier with Angola

June 29, Decree gave the 2 colonies of Gabun and French Congo autonomy under De Brazza, Commissioner General

1887

April 29, Franco-Belgian Boundary Convention by

which France received the Ubangi River as boundary

1888

Aug. 12, Paul Crampel left Lastourville for the north towards Lake Chad returning by the coast in September, discovered the Djah River but forced to retreat by attacks of natives

Dec. 11, Decree reunited Gabun and French Congo under one government

1889

Jan. 3, Post at Bangui, extreme point of French occupation, attacked by natives and M. Musy killed

Feb. 27, Decree of De Brazza created a board composed of heads of posts and stations and others to develop agriculture and trade

1890

Aug. 5, Anglo-French Boundary Convention fixed boundary by line drawn from Say on the Niger due east to Lake Chad

Aug. 10, Paul Crampel arrived at Brazzaville from France and started for the Ubangi River and the hinterland to establish connection for the Colony with Lake Chad, reaching the Ubangi Sept. 25 at Bangui last French post; murdered on journey toward the Lake

Oct. 10, Lieutenant Mizon embarked at Nun mouth of the Niger to journey up the Niger and the Benue, perhaps to Lake Chad, and explore Sanga and Congo regions, and in spite of the opposition of the British officials of the Royal Niger Company reached Yola on Upper Benue, Aug. 20, 1891

Nov. 18, *Comité de l'Afrique française* established

Dec., Captain Monteil on journey from St. Louis, Senegal, left Segu, Aug. 19, 1891, and by Sokoto and Kano reached Lake Chad, March, 1892 and Tripoli across the desert, Dec. 10

1891

March 5, Mission of Alfred Fourneau to explore Sanga region established Wesso

April 30, Decree established Government General and gave name French Congo to the country

May 22, Monteil placed Liptako in Upper Volta under Protectorate

May 25, Paul Crampel who had reached the Baguirmi country (6° N. Lat.) and El-Kouti killed by the Senussi

Aug. 14, Treaty settled boundary with Congo Free State

Aug. 19, Monteil returned to the Niger at Say after exploration of the bend of the Niger, hitherto unexplored country

Nov. 22, Jean Dybowski mission attacked Senussi camp killing a large number and dispersing the remainder to avenge the death of Crampel

Dec. 15, Mizon left Yola and proceeded to Ngaundéré where he arrived, Jan. 29, 1892

1892

March, Captain Monteil reached Lake Chad from Senegal by way of Sokoto, Kano, and Bornu

April 24, Mission of Casimir Maistre left for the Ubangi, began voyage June 9 and reached Ibi on the Benue River, March 6, 1893

Dec. 10, Captain Monteil reached Tripoli from Lake Chad

Dec. 26, Ponel mission left post of Batouri and arrived at Ngaundéré, Feb. 15, 1893

1893

Jan. 29, Maistre returned to Yola on the Benue River from the Adamaua country (Cameroons)

June 10, Mission of Captain Monteil, appointed High Commissioner of the Ubangi, left France to establish posts on the Ubangi, Captain Decazes and Captain Julien in charge of divisions

Oct. 30 and Nov. 17, Concessions granted to M. Daumas in Fernand Vaz and upper Ogowé regions. Not made public

1894

Feb. 4, Franco-German Boundary Agreement as to Cameroon frontier to Lake Chad

March 15, Franco-German Boundary Convention recognized French claim to Baguirmi with access to Lake Chad from the south

March 20, Agreement with Belgium to settle differences by negotiation

May 12, Anglo-French Boundary Convention

July 13, Decree placed Upper Ubangi under commander

Aug. 14, Delimitation of boundary Treaty with the Congo Free State defined southern frontier as the Bomu and Ubangi rivers

Aug. 24, F. J. Clozel mission started from post of Berberati, northeast of Bania

Sept. 25, Clozel established post he named Carnot on the Ekela-Sanga River and proceeded by the Lobay and Bali Rivers to the Oua branch of the Bahr-Sara, a tributary, through the Chari to Lake Chad

Oct. 20, Victor Liotard appointed Commissioner in Upper Ubangi (Haut-Oubangi)

1895

June 17, Verbal proposals of M. Hanotaux, French Minister of Foreign Affairs, to Captain Marchand to occupy Fashoda and left bank of the Nile. Postponed

July 27, Mission of Emile Gentil left Loango and proceeded up the Congo, and Ubangi Rivers toward Lake Chad, bringing boat, the "Léon Blot"

1896

June 26, Commandant Marchand sailed from Marseilles for the Congo, instructed to occupy Fashoda

July 16, The Minister of the Colonies created a Commission of Concessions

July 26, Marchand mission left Loango with 8 officers and 120 men who explored the Ubangi region and proceeded to the Bahr-el-Ghazal country occupying Fort Desaix on the Jur River in 1897

1897

Jan., Captain Clochette left Djibuti to occupy right bank of the Nile for Abyssinia and effect junction with Marchand mission to Fashoda which he did not accomplish

June 8, Gentil mission established Fort Crampel on the Gribingui River

Sept. 17, Gentil Mission arrived at Bousso (Fort Bretonnet) Baguirmi country

Sept. 28, Court of Appeals created at Libreville

Nov. 1, Gentil mission reached Lake Chad, descending the Shari River in the boat, the "Léon Blot," where he remained 2 years establishing French authority

1898

Jan. 2, De Brazza recalled to France

April 9, Organization of judicial system

June 4, The Marchand mission left Fort Desaix, proceeding to the Nile River

June 14, Anglo-French Boundary Agreement

July 10, Marchand mission occupied Fashoda on the Nile

Aug. 25, Marchand repulsed attack of Dervishes

Sept. 9, Marchand sent letter to Kitchener notifying him of French occupation of Bahr-el-Ghazal and the Shillucks country from the confluence of the Bahr-el-Jebel along left bank of White Nile to Fashoda

Sept. 19, Anglo-Egyptian expedition of Lord Kitchener arrived at Fashoda and protested the French invasion, demanding immediate withdrawal of Marchand who replied that he was acting under orders of the Government and could not leave until he was officially ordered to do so. Kitchener left Colonel Jackson at Fashoda, the Egyptian flag flying on Egyptian fort 500 meters from the French flag

Sept. 27, Mission of Fernand Foureau left Biskra, Algeria, to cross the Sahara to Lake Chad

Oct. 23, Foureau-Lamy mission left Sedrata, Algeria, for Lake Chad

Nov. 4, Decision of French Government to evacuate Fashoda and Marchand instructed to withdraw from Fashoda by the Sobat River in Abyssinia

1899

Jan. 2, Voulet-Chanoine mission to Lake Chad left Say

Jan., E. Gentil appointed Commissioner in Ubangi-Shari district

Feb. 8, French decree regulating public lands according to French law, unoccupied lands property of the State

Feb.–June, Mission Fourneau-Fondère explored basin of the Ivindo and region north of the Ogowé

March 21, Anglo-French Boundary Treaty by which France recognized British possession of Nile Valley, Bahr-el-Ghazal and Darfur, Wadai (Ouadai) with the oases of Tibesti and Borku to France

March 27, Ferdinand de Béhagle arrived at Dikoa and was taken prisoner by Rabah

March 28, French decrees instituted concessions and promulgated regulations as to lands, land taxes, and forests and applied Torrens system in French Congo. By July concessions had been granted to 40 companies of 650,000 square kilometers

May 24, Native lands of concessions defined as only areas necessary for growing of food stuffs

July 14, Colonel Klobb sent to inquire into reported cruelty to the natives of the Voulet-Chanoine mission, overtook them near Zinder on the Niger and was fired on by them, Colonel Klobb and 6 men killed. Voulet and Chanoine later killed by their native troops. The mission became the Joalland-Meynier mission

July 17, Lieutenant de Bretonnet, mission to Lake Chad, attacked and killed by forces of Rabah at Togbao

Sept. 9, Further Decree as to forest lands

Oct. 15, Death of F. de Béhagle, ordered killed by Rabah

Oct. 22, The Joalland-Meynier mission reached Lake Chad

Oct. 28, Attack of the French on Rabah at Kouno

1900

Feb. 2, Foureau-Lamy mission arrived at Lake Chad from Zinder (Nov. 2, 1899) and united with the Joalland-Meynier mission

April 5, Regulations for concessions of 10,000 hectares and below issued

April 21, Gentil marched from Fort Archambault and the 3 missions joined forces at Kousseri, one from Algeria, one from the Sudan, and one from the Congo

April 22, Major Lamy with combined forces attacked and defeated Rabah at Lakhta, who was killed as was Major Lamy

May 24, The campaign ended and armies began return march founding a post on the Chari named Fort Lamy

June 27, Franco-Spanish Boundary Convention as to Rio Muni (Spanish Guinea)

Sept. 5, Decree established the Military Territory and Protectorate of the Chad

Sept., The French Court at Loango upheld the concession companies taking possession of the English factories, long established in the country, declaring that the land did not belong to the natives and they therefore could not alienate the land

1901

Jan. 25, Franco-Portuguese Boundary Convention

Feb. 2, Campaign against Fadr-el-Allah, sheik of Bornu, son of Rabah

May 31, Captain Robillot entered Dikoa, evacuated by Fadr-el-Allah

Aug. 23, Captain Dangerville defeated Fadr-el-Allah who was killed in battle at Gujba where he had fled into British territory

Oct. 31, Treaty of commerce with Congo Free State

Nov. 9, Captain Millot killed in attack of Senussi near Kanem

1902

Feb. 15, Law provided for protection of public health

June 1 and Dec. 3, The post Bir Alali (Fort Pradié) attacked by Tuaregs

July 5, Decree divided the territory into Lower Congo and Gabun, and Chad

1903

March 17, Decree regulated native justice

May 11, French Decree regulated labor contracts

July 2, Emigration of natives regulated

Dec. 29, Decree divided the Congo into 4 autonomous districts, Gabun, Middle Congo, Ubangi-Shari, and Chad

1904

April 8, Anglo-French Boundary Convention fixed boundary from the Niger to Lake Chad, modified Convention of June 14, 1898 in favor of France

1905

Feb., De Brazza accepted mission to investigate charges of cruelty to natives of Congo officials

Sept. 14, Death of Count Savorgnan de Brazza at Dakar, Senegal, on his return journey to France

1906

Feb. 11, A Secretary General appointed and decrees reorganized administration and judiciary and native tribunals organized

Feb. 22, Decree revised system of administration in effort to eliminate abuse of natives and protect them from the concession companies

1908

April 18, Franco-German Boundary Convention settled boundary with the Cameroons

June 26, Decree changed title of Commissioner General to Governor General

Sept. 8, French Decree as to concession companies

Dec. 23, Franco-Belgian Boundary Convention defined frontiers

1909

March 12, The Middle Congo placed under a lieutenant governor

June 2, D'Abéché (Wadai) taken by the French

Sept. 30, The Governor General abolished the rubber tax in favor of payment of capitation and other native taxes in money to prevent abuse of natives by concession companies

Nov. 27, Battle near Ziguei, Lieutenant Moutot, severely wounded, forced to retreat

1910

Jan., French force massacred during night in surprise attack L'Ouadi Kadja Wadai

Jan. 15, Decree divided French Congo into 3 circumscriptions, the Gabun with capital at Libreville, the Middle Congo with capital at Brazzaville, and the Ubangi-Shari with capital at Bangui, and the name changed to French Equatorial Africa. Councils of Administration established in each division

April 2, Lieutenant Boyd Alexander, British explorer, murdered by the natives in Wadai

May 12 and 31, Decrees reorganized native justice

June 13, Agreement signed by 11 concession companies with French Government

June 20, Decree by which a number of concession companies agreed to surrender concessions granted in 1899 in return for 10,000 hectares full property and rights of gathering rubber on original concessions for 10 years

Oct. 6, Local decree regulating land concessions

Nov., Lieutenant Colonel Moll commanding at Wadai repulsed attack of 5,000 natives south of Drigele, Colonel Moll killed

1911

March and June, Revolts in Wadai region

April 4, Decree organized educational system establishing 2 degrees of primary instruction and professional tuition

Nov. 4, Treaty with Germany signed by which France ceded about 107,270 square miles of the Colony lying directly south and east of the Cameroons to Germany in return for German recognition of the French Protectorate in Morocco; the region between Shari and the Logoné rivers (area 6,450 miles) and Lat. 10° N. transferred to France

1912

Sept. 28, Agreement between France and Germany signed fixed exact boundaries under Treaty of Nov. 4, 1911

Oct. 3 and 5, Decree created the 3 communes of Libreville, Brazzaville, and Bangui

1913

March 10, Inspection of education organized

April 16, Decree organized Court of Appeal at Brazzaville, and tribunals of first degree at Brazzaville, Libreville, and Bangui

Nov. 26–27, Colonel Largeau in engagement in Borkou district

Dec. 3, The French occupied Faya

1914

Aug. 6, French force from Equatorial Africa captured Bonga and the following day, Singa. *See* Cameroons

1915

Feb. 18, Colonial Council of Hygiene established at Brazzaville

1916

April 12, Territory of Chad which had been dependency of Ubangi-Shari separated and placed directly under the Governor General

Aug. 1, Decree as to concession companies

1917

Oct. 30, Decree placed Office of Public Works under control of an Inspector General

1918

March 13, Decrees as to land of March, 1899, amended

June 1, Société de la Kotto gave up concession in return for 6,000 hectares of land in full ownership

1919

June 28, The Treaty of Versailles returned to Equatorial Africa the territory ceded to Germany by Treaty of Nov. 4, 1911

Sept. 8, Anglo-French Convention readjusted frontier with Anglo-Egyptian Sudan and final delimitation in Protocol of Jan. 10, 1924 confirmed by British and French declarations of Jan. 21

1920

March 17, The Chad Territory constituted a Colony

Dec. 19, Decrees as to land amended

Dec. 28, Arret organized private education of natives

The Derde Chaffai of Tibesti accepted French protection

1921

Feb. 6, New railroad begun to connect Brazzaville with the Atlantic Ocean at Pointe-Noire

1922

May 4, Decree issued regulations for labor

Sept. 2, Decree regulated liquor traffic

1923

Dec. 28, Protocol defined frontier with Anglo-Egyptian Sudan

1924

Jan. 10, Protocol defined frontier of Wadai and Darfur

Jan. 21, Exchange of Notes of France and Great Britain fixed boundary demarcation under Treaty of June 14, 1898 and Treaty of Sept. 8, 1919

1925

Jan. 7, Order reorganized system of labor dues

April 30, Central Council of Administration reorganized, powers defined

May 8, Circular reorganized education in the Colony

June 9, Land laws amended

1926

July 8, Decree organized mines, exploitation, taxes, concessions, &c.

Sept. 13, Decree regulated indentures of apprentices

——, Arret established system as to rural concessions of 10,000 hectares and less; amended Oct. 18, 1928

Nov. 30, Arret established in each colony an advisory council for natives

1927

April 27, Decree reorganized native justice; amended May 16, 1928 and Jan. 18, 1930

July 31, Mining regulations promulgated

1928

April 13, Law gave Gabun customs autonomy

May 14, Decree made law of May 31 as to aviation applicable to Equatorial Africa

July 18, Decree and Arret of Nov. 20, established taxes

Aug. 17 and Dec. 27, European education reorganized

1929

May 4, Declaration of exclusive right of Colony to search for minerals in the territory of the Colony

May 31, Frontier between Chad (Tschad) and Ubangi-Shari altered

June 5, Decree regulated land taxes

1930

July 21, Decree and Arret of Sept. 8 reorganized judicial system, created a Grand Jury and gave added powers to Court of Appeals

Tibesti attached to Equatorial Africa

FRENCH WEST AFRICA

French West Africa comprises the following colonies:—(1) Senegal, (2) French Guinea, (3) the Ivory Coast, (4) Dahomey, (5) French Sudan, (6) Upper Volta, (7) Mauritania, (8) Niger, and (9) Circle of Dakar and Dependencies. *See also* names of Colonies.

COLONY	AREA (IN SQUARE MILES)	POPULATION 1926			
		Europeans		Native Races	TOTAL
		French	Foreign		
Senegal	74,112	3,057	1,593	1,313,637	1,318,287
Guinea	89,436	1,135	1,127	2,093,726	2,095,988
Ivory Coast	121,590	1,410	204	1,722,931	1,724,545
Dahomey	41,302	737	147	978,725	979,609
French Sudan	360,331	1,453	366	2,633,163	2,634,982
Upper Volta	142,820	388	37	3,259,722	3,240,147
Mauritania	347,400	178	101	288,905	289,184
Niger	463,200	253	7	1,218,457	1,218,717
Dakar and Dependencies	—	2,488	718	36,946	40,152
Total	1,440,191	11,099	4,300	13,526,212	13,541,611

Of the French population, 7,207 were men, 2,578 women, and 1,314 children; while of the foreign population, 2,466 were men, 939 women, and 895 children.

The principal tribes are the Ouolofs in Senegal (about 500,000, mostly Moslems); the Mandingos in the Sudan (about 5 million people); the Mossi in the Upper Volta (about 2 millions), and the Kroumen on the Ivory Coast.

M. J. Brévie, Governor General.

1889

Aug. 10, Anglo-French Convention settled boundaries on west coast of Africa

1892

Jan. 11, Law established customs for West African colonies

July, Expedition of M. Maistre and 5 others; after many difficulties arrives near the mouth of the Niger, March 26, 1893; treaties signed with the Garua and Sarra countries, reported, Nov., 1893

1895

June 16, Decree created the Government General of West Africa with capital at Dakar in Senegal, M. Chaudie, Governor General (1895–1900). Each Colony retained full autonomy

1896

Sept. 27–Oct. 17, The Ivory Coast separated from West African Government

1897

Jan. 15, Lieut. Voulet concludes treaties with the chiefs of the Nabas, Gurunsi, and Sati; reported

——, Lieut. Hourst and members of the expedition from Timbuktu down the Niger (in 1896), received in Paris

March 25, Successful operations of two missions: the "Guma" district placed under French protection, contact established between Dahomey and the French Sudan; announced

July 23, Franco-German convention, settling the Niger frontier

Aug. 4, A French column takes possession of Say, on the Middle Niger; reported

Aug. 21, Treacherous attack on a detachment, by Samory's bands; 2 officers and others killed

Dec. 5, Bontuku occupied by the French, by arrangement with the British

1898

June 14, Anglo-French Boundary Convention fixed boundaries from the Niger to Lake Chad

1899

March 21, Declaration of territory which enabled France to link up her West African possessions

Oct. 17, The Sudan constituted a separate Colony. *See* Sudan

1900

June 27, Convention between France and Spain fixed boundaries (Rio de Oro) Sebkha d'Idjil in Sahara added to French West Africa

M. Ballay, Governor General (1900–1902)

1901

June 29, Decree established Bank of West Africa (formerly Bank of Senegal)

1902

Jan. 31, Ernest Roume appointed Governor General (1902–1908)

Oct. 1, Decree reconstituted government, the central government had an independent budget and was relieved of direction of administration of Senegal

1903

July 5, Law provided for loan from France of 65,000,000 francs for refunding loans

Nov. 10, Decree created Court of Appeals and established native courts; regulations issued April 25, 1905

Nov. 4, Sanitary inspection instituted

1904

April 8, Anglo-French Boundary Convention by which Yarbatenda on the Gambia ceded to France, and the Los Islands which were attached to West African Government July 4, 1905

Oct. 18, Decree reconstituted government, budget of Federal Government relieved of last local charges making it exclusively for federal purposes; Upper Senegal-Niger Colony made part of West African Government

Oct. 23, Decree established government ownership for lands without owners, "vacant" lands, and consolidated land laws

1906

May 29, Anglo-French Boundary Treaty settled frontier east of the Niger

July 24, Decree provided for registration of property in lands under Torrens system

Oct. 19, Anglo-French Boundary Treaty determined the boundary from the Gulf of Guinea to the Niger

1907

Jan. 22, Law provided for loan from France of 100,-000,000 francs for construction of ports, railways, hospitals, telegraph lines

Sept. 18, Boundary Convention with Liberia

1908

Feb. 18, William Merland-Ponty appointed Governor (1908–1915)

Feb. 25, Anglo-French Boundary settled frontier east of the Niger

1910

Feb. 18, Law provided for loan from France of 14,-000,000 francs for railroad

June 22, Extension of civil government to Timbuktu and other territories on right bank of the Niger, parts of Gao, Tillabery and Djerma (Sudan)

1911

Jan. 1, Decree established mixed communes

June 26, Regulations as to recruitment of native labor

Sept. 7, Decree separated the military Territory of the Niger from Upper Senegal and Niger, placed under administrator to take effect Jan. 1, 1912 as part of Government of West Africa

1912

June 1, Decree reorganized medical service

Aug. 16, Decree reorganized system of justice for natives establishing separate courts, and defining natives subject to native jurisdiction

1913

Aug. 26, Decree organized agricultural education
Aug. 27, Sanitary Inspection Service became Inspector General of Sanitation and Medicine
Dec. 23, Law provided for loan from France of 167,-000,000 francs to execute a general system of public works such as railways and ports

1914

March 9, Decree defining natives subject to jurisdiction of native courts instead of French of Aug. 16, 1912, modified because of protests of natives

1915

April 26 and Oct. 9, Decree provided for enlistment of natives in Sengalese corps. *See* Senegal
June 13, Death of Governor Merland-Ponty. Succeeded by M. Clozel (1915–1917)

1916

July 23, Decree made natives of the 4 communes of Senegal full French citizens
Sept. 29, Law extended conscription to descendants of natives outside communes of Senegal, recognizing natives as French citizens
Tibesti in Central Sahara reoccupied by the French and attached to Government of French West Africa

1917

March 15, Decree reorganized Chamber of Commerce, made effective by arret of Dec. 30, 1920
Oct. 20, Arret reorganized medical service
Joost Van Vollenhoven, Governor (1917–1918)

1918

Jan. 14, French decree authorized universal conscription in West Africa
——, Decree established School of Medicine at Dakka for native auxiliary doctors
June 14, Decree by which natives who had received the croix de guerre or military cross became citizens by renouncing their personal status; only 14 soldiers took advantage of this
June 18, Governor Van Vollenhoven killed in action at front. Succeeded by M. Angoulvant (1918–1919)
Nov. 1, Decree reorganized education
Nov. 21, Decree reorganized animal service (*zootechnique*)
Dec. 20, Decree established Bamako and Kayes as mixed communes

1919

Jan. 14, French Decree regulated trade in oil nuts, and cereals in West Africa
Feb. 1, From this date importation of trade spirits prohibited
March 1, Decree created new Colony of Upper Volta
July 4, Decree regulated provident societies
July 30, French decree made natives liable to conscription for term of 3 years
Sept. 8, Anglo-French Convention fixed Tibesti and Wadai frontier, the right of France recognized to all territory west of the Nile basin, which practically includes the whole of the Sahara (exclusive of the

Libyan Desert), and the State of Wadai. The French Sahara may be roughly estimated at about 1½ million square miles.
Dec. 29, Mopti made a mixed commune
M. Merlin, Governor (1919–1923)

1920

Dec. 4, Decree reorganized administration. Name of Upper-Senegal-Niger Colony changed to French Sudan. *See also* Senegal, Niger
Dec. 31, Decree established agricultural service

1921

Jan. 1, Mauretania became a Colony with Lieutenant Governor at head

1922

Feb. 14, Decree provided regulations for private education, chiefly the mission (religious) schools
July 20, French mandates over Togoland and Cameroons ratified by the League of Nations
Oct. 1, Savings Bank of West Africa established by Decree of July 22, 1920, opened at Dakar
Oct. 13, Colony of the Niger formed. *See s.v.*

1923

Jan. 1, Timbuktu made a "Civilian Territory"
Feb. 20, M. Carde appointed Governor General
April 1, Term of military service reduced to 18 months
July 23, First Congress of Tropical Medicine in West Africa held at St. Paul de Loanda
July 27, Cabinet constituted (Services Généraux du Gouvernement) directors of departments

1924

Jan. 1, The railroad from Thiès to Kayes completed
Jan. 10, Anglo-French Convention fixed frontiers, Great Britain recognizing the right of France to all territory west of the Nile basin, including practically all of the Sahara (exclusive of the Libyan Desert); area of French Sahara about 1½ million square miles
March 22, Decree reorganized native justice, tribunals of first and second degree established
May 1, Decree of the Governor General reorganized education
May 31, Law regulated aërial navigation
Oct. 21 and Nov. 27, Decrees formed Dakar and its suburbs into a special autonomous territory called *circumscription de Dakar et Dependances* with budget of its own
Oct. 22, Decree regulated the exploitation of mines
Nov. 16, Decree organized French justice

1925

March 7, School Committee established
March 30, Decree reorganized Council and a series of decrees gave natives a part in affairs
Oct. 8, Land registration Decree of July 24, 1906 modified
Oct. 22, Decree and arret of March 29, 1926, regulated native labor, labor contracts not to be longer than 2 years

1926

May 23, Decree and regulations of Feb. 25, 1927 established agricultural credit for natives (*caisses de credit agricole mutual*)

1927

Jan. 13, Decree reorganized native justice
Jan. 22, Decree created region of Say in the Sudan
Feb. 25, Order of the Governor General established a Workmen's Dwelling Office
May 1, Regulations as to medical assistance to natives issued
May 6, Decree established permanent Public Works Service
Oct. 5, Arret promulgated Decree of Sept. 27 as to protection of public health

1928

April 13, Law and Decree of July 2 established tariff
May 13, Order of the Governor General provided for control of emigration and immigration of natives in Dakar
Dec. 26, Decree transferred circle of Say and part of circle of Dori from the Colony of Upper Volta to the Colony of the Niger
Sept. 29, Decree regulating public lands (*domaine public*)

1929

April 29, Meteorological Service created to study climate, economic geography, &c. of French West Africa
Sept. 12, Decree established naval bases
Nov. 27, New Decree as to mixed communes
Dec. 26, Office of Agricultural Produce and Credit established

1930

June 23, Order established a permanent supervision of Mutual Agricultural Credit
July 17, Decree reorganized French justice amending Decree of Nov. 16, 1924
July 28, Geological Service established

GAMBIA

Gambia, British West Africa, consists of a narrow strip of territory along both sides of the lower reaches of the Gambia River from the coast.

Gambia was discovered by the early Portuguese navigators, but they made no settlement. During the seventeenth century various companies of merchants obtained trading charters and established a settlement on the river, which, from 1807, was controlled from Sierra Leone; in 1843 it was made an independent Crown Colony; on Feb. 19, 1866 formed part of the West African Settlements, but Nov. 28, 1888, it again became a separate Crown Colony. It is administered under a Governor with an Executive and a nominated Legislative Council containing an unofficial element. With the exception of the Island of St. Mary, on which Bathurst, the capital, first British settlement stands, the whole Colony is administered on the Protectorate system. Since 1901 both banks of the Gambia have been under direct British control up to the Anglo-French boundary.

Area of Colony proper 4 square miles, population 10,000. Herbert R. Palmer, Governor

1783 to 1807

Sept. 3, 1783, Recognized by the Treaty of Versailles, as British, France guaranteeing to Great Britain the possession of Fort James (Albreda) and the Gambia River
1786–1857, French at Albreda
1807, Put under the Government of Sierra Leone

1826

June 15, Cession of Gambia River district by native chiefs

1829

Lieutenant Colonel Alexander Findlay appointed first Lieutenant Governor of "the settlement of Bathurst and its dependencies in the Gambia"

1857 to 1889

March 7, 1857, Convention by which the French ceded Albreda, giving British the full control of the river
Dec. 22, 1888, Gambia separated from Sierra Leone and made an independent colony
Aug. 10, 1889, By Anglo-French Treaty a ten-kilometer strip on either side of the river inland to Yarbatenda ceded to Great Britain

1892

About Jan. 7, Chief town, Bathurst, founded 1816. Some villages of a marauding chief punished for agressions
May 11, Toniataba destroyed after a battle; Capt. A. S. Roberts killed, April 28; successful British expedition, reported

1894

Feb. 23, An expedition of 200 men of the naval brigade under Capt. Gamble, from H.M.S. *Raleigh* and others, against Fodi-Silah, a slave-raiding chief, destroy 2 villages; a division is surprised by an ambush while returning to their boats, and 15 men, including Lieuts. W. H. Arnold, Francis W. Hervey, sub-Lieut. Francis W. Meister, are killed at Medina Creek
Feb. 26, An attack of about 2,000 natives repulsed by Lieut.-Col. Corbet and about 100 men of the West India regiment, on the British Combo river
March 1, Reinforcements arrive at Bathurst, commanded by Major S. G. Fairtlough (he died at Sierra Leone, May, 1894)
March 21, Busamballa occupied by the West India column under Major Madden, an attack of the natives repulsed, March 3; continued fighting, enemy's loss reported heavy, March 6; Birkama taken after a hot fight, March 7; Gonjur bombarded by Rear-Admiral Bedford, March 7; Fodi-Silah's force broken, reported March 10; he surrendered to the French in Senegal, March 11 (died Sept. 19, 1894); peace restored, reported
Dec. 27, Ordinance abolished slave trade in territory adjacent to Colony

1901

Jan. 11, Messrs. Sitwell and Silva and 6 constables killed at Sannkandi, June, 1900; Anglo-French punitive operations; Col. Brake captures Dumbutu, 6 chiefs, and 200 men
Jan. 16, 17, Sallikeni burnt; 6 ringleaders captured
March 23, Medina taken by the French; the hostile chief Fodi Kabba and 150 others killed

1902

Successful punitive expedition against the Yolahs, May

1904

April 8, By Anglo-French Convention Yarbatenda was ceded to France

1906

April 3, Ordinance abolished slave trade in the Protectorate

GOLD COAST

Gold Coast, West Africa, British Colony on the Guinea Coast with coast line of 370 miles, bounded on the west by the Ivory Coast and east by Togoland, on the north by Ashanti and the Northern Territories, named Gold Coast because of the quantities of grains of gold mixed with the sands of the rivers. The British mandated territory of Togoland is attached to the Gold Coast for administrative purposes. (*See also* Togoland and Ashanti.) The area of the Colony, Ashanti, and Protectorate is about 80,000 square miles, the Colony, 23,490 square miles, Ashanti, 24,560, and Northern Territories, 30,600, British mandated territory of Togoland, 13,040 square miles; population, census 1921, 2,078,043; Europeans, 2,165. Chief towns: Accra (the capital), 38,000; Sekondi, 10,000; Cape Coast, 15,000; Keta, 10,000; Winneba, 7,000; Saltpond, 6,500; Koforidua, 5,500.

Sir Alexander Ransford Slater, Governor.

The Gold Coast first became known through Portuguese navigators in the fourteenth century. In the reign of Edward I English navigators voyaged to the coast as a center of the slave trade, and in the seventeenth century French, Portuguese, Dutch, English, Brandenburgers, Swedes, and Danes occupied territory

1482

A fort built at Elmina by Diogo d'Azambuja sent by John of Portugal, the first permanent European settlement. Captured by Dutch in 1637

1618

First British settlements on the coast by the "Company of Adventurers of London trading in Africa"

1642

Feb. 1, First treaties for purchase of land made by the Dutch with native chiefs

1664

Captain Robert Holmes seized Cape Coast Castle, the strongest fort on the coast after Elmina (built by the Swedes in 1652) from the Dutch, and made it the capital of the English settlements on the coast

1821

Forts transferred from African Company of Merchants to administration of Sierra Leone

1824

Jan. 21, Sir Charles M'Carthy, Governor, killed in battle with the Ashantis. *See* Ashanti

1826

Aug. 7, Decisive defeat of the Ashantis by the British at Dodowa near Accra

1831

April 29, Treaty of peace and commerce with the Ashantis by which the Ashantis acknowledged the Prah as their southern boundary, concluded by George Maclean who had been made Administrator by the merchant settlers

1843

The Colonial Office took over control of the forts

1844

March 6, Agreement with native chiefs defined British jurisdiction

1850

Jan. 13/24, The Gold Coast separated from Sierra Leone and made a separate Colony with Governor and Legislative Council

Feb. 1, Denmark ceded forts at Quetta, Nongo, and Adda to English

Aug. 17, Convention with Denmark by which Denmark ceded all forts and property and rights on the coast to England for £10,000

1866

Feb. 19, The Gold Coast reunited with Sierra Leone

1871

Feb. 25, Treaty with the Netherlands by which all Dutch forts and towns made over to Great Britain in exchange for recognition of Dutch claims in the Far East

April 6, Formal entry of English into Elmina

1873

April 5, Ashanti war begun. *See* Ashanti

1874

Feb. 13, Peace Treaty signed with the Ashantis

July 24, New Charter separated the Gold Coast from Sierra Leone

July 25, Captain George C. Strahan appointed Governor of the Gold Coast Colony

Nov. 23, Slave dealing abolished by Ordinance No. 2 of 1874 and all children born after Nov. 5 declared free

1886

Jan. 13, New Charter divided Gold Coast into 2 separate Colonies of Lagos and Gold Coast

July 14, Anglo-German Boundary Agreement defined frontier with Togoland

1887

May 9, The chiefs of Aquamoo acknowledged British Protectorate

1889

Aug. 10, Anglo-French Boundary Convention defined frontier with Ivory Coast

1890

July 1, Anglo-German Boundary Convention fixed boundary with Togoland

1891

June 26, Anglo-French Boundary Convention

1893

July 12, Further Anglo-French Boundary Convention

1894

Feb. 24, Anglo-German Convention established customs union. Terminated by Germany April 30, 1904

1897

Jan. 1, Bank of British West Africa established at Accra

1898

April 19, Punitive expedition, under Lieut.-Col. Northcott and others; enemy driven off, and their town occupied

April 25, Appeal to government against the house-tax at Accra

June 14, Anglo-French Boundary Convention settled frontier with Ivory Coast from 9th parallel to 11th parallel along Black Volta River and along 11th parallel to Franco-German boundary of 1897 leaving Dagati, Wa, and South Grunshi in British sphere

1899

March, Col. H. P. Northcott's Gambaga expedition very successful, British post established, order restored; Col. Northcott appointed administrator of the Northern Territories, Aug.; killed at Modder river (*see* S. African War), Nov. 28

Nov. 8, Frontier in the Hinterland of German Togoland, agreed to, announced

Nov. 14, Agreement with Germany provided for partition of the neutral zone and Salaga and Mamprusi assigned to Great Britain

1900

March 25, Governor Hodgson at Kumasi (Coomassie) demanded of the Ashantis the "Golden Stool," symbol of royalty of the Ashantis, which brought on a war with the Ashantis. *See* Ashanti

June 23–July 10, Retreat of Sir Frederick and Lady Hodgson and part of garrison from Kumasi to the coast

Aug. 6, Sir Fred. Hodgson entertains the loyal kings and chiefs of Ashanti who escaped with him from Kumasi

1901

April 17, Railroad begun in 1898 from Sekondi reached Tarkwa

Sept. 26, Order in Council annexing Ashanti appointed the Governor of the Gold Coast Governor of Ashanti, and Northern Territories declared a British Protectorate, completed by Administrative Ordinance of Jan. 1, 1902

——, Anglo-German Boundary Convention provided for a delimitation commission. Report of commission accepted, June 2, 1904

1903

Feb. 1, April 23, and May 11, Anglo-French Agreements defined boundary of the Gold Coast and the Ivory

Coast from Nugua to 9th parallel finally accepted by exchange of Notes of May 11 and 15, 1905 and May 24 and July 19, 1906

Oct. 1, Sekondi-Kumasi railroad reached Kumasi

1906

Oct. 22, Boundary with Ashanti and Northern Territories defined

1907

Jan. 1, The Protectorate given staff of Civil District and Assistant District Commissioners replacing semimilitary administration

1908

Jan.–March, Outbreak of the plague

1909

Jan., First sod of railroad from Accra to Akwapim turned by Sir John Rodger

1910

May 14, Sekondi seaport declared infected with yellow fever

Aug. 26, Native Jurisdiction Act replaced that of No. 5, 1883

Aug. 27, Railroad from Accra to Nsawam opened

1911

Jan. 11, Tarkwa-Prestea-Broomassie railroad branch opened

1912

March 19, British Letters Patent appointed Deputy Governor

1914

July 31, Mobilization begun

Aug. 5, Acting Governor von Doering of Togoland proposed neutrality for Gold Coast and Togoland which was refused

Aug. 6, Ultimatum to Togoland demanded surrender

Aug. 8, Lome, Togoland, evacuated by Germans, occupied by Gold Coast troops commanded by Captain Barker

Aug. 12, French and English force landed at Lome, commanded by Lieutenant Colonel Bryant

Aug. 22, Attack on enemy at Chra village failed to carry position but evacuated during the night by Germans who retired to Kamina

Aug. 24–25, The wireless station at Kamina blown up by the Germans

Aug. 26, Surrender of von Doering to Lieutenant Colonel Bryant giving the Allies control of southern Togoland

1916

July 6, Gold Coast regiment left Accra for service in the Cameroons

Sept. 20, Letters Patent reorganized the Government, Executive, and Legislative Councils reconstituted, proclaimed Sept. 23, into effect Sept. 25

Sept. 25, First session of enlarged Legislative Council including 6 representatives for natives

1917

Feb. 24, Barclay's Bank opened bank at Accra

June 1, Railroad from Koforidua to Tafo opened

1919

Feb., Discovery of diamonds in the region about Abomo Su

1920

Dec. 31, Spirituous liquors Ordinance enacted to give better effect to the Convention of St. Germain-en-Laye of Sept. 10, 1919

1921

Feb. 21, Regulations for employment Ordinance enacted

Chapter 107 of laws, the Roads Ordinance, provided for compulsory labor

The hidden Golden Stool discovered by road workers and certain Ashanti chiefs stripped it of gold which they began to sell. They were apprehended and handed over to the Ashantis for punishment, and death penalty imposed, later changed to banishment by the Government

1923

March 17, Customs Ordinance provided for management and regulation of customs

1924

Prempeh, Ashanti chief in exile for 28 years, allowed to return as a private citizen

1925

March 17, Immigration Restriction Ordinance enacted

April 8, Order in Council and royal instructions of May 23 reconstituted Legislative Council and provincial Councils

April 9–14, Visit of the Prince of Wales

May 10–20, Visit of the Princess Marie Louise

Dec. 30, Education Ordinance repealed and amended previous laws, into effect Jan. 1, 1927

1926

April 1, Import tax of 5s. per horse and 4s. per head of cattle and 6s. per goat or sheep imposed

Aug. 30, Meeting of new Legislative Council (15 official members, 14 un-official members including 5 Europeans and 9 Africans)

Prempeh restored as Paramount Chief of the Kumasi tribe

1927

Jan. 1, New system of primary education introduced

Jan. 28, Formal opening of the Prince of Wales School and College at Achimota by the Governor-General

March 29, Ordinance for protection of forests and establishment of forest reserves promulgated

May 3, Native Administrative Bill introduced in Legislative Council to consolidate laws as to native administration and jurisdiction recognized for the first time the Oman Councils consisting of the Paramount Chief, head chiefs, linguists, and elders to have jurisdiction as a tribunal of first instance "to determine all causes and matters civil or criminal arising from within the State whenever such causes or matters are governed by the Native Customary Law" of the State, with appeal to the Provincial Council which consists of all the Paramount Chiefs of the Province, the Provincial Council having final decision as to lands. Became law April 22

July 30, Death of Dr. Kivegyir Aggrey, a Fanti, vice-principal of Achimota College

Sept. 28, Ordinance established Defense Force and Territorial Force

Nov. 16, Visit of King George and Queen Mary

Dec. 3, Ordinance established Board of Education, Director of Education

1928

Jan. 12, Visit of the Prince of Wales

April 3, Takoradi harbor formally opened

April 28, Arbitration Ordinance provided for reference and submission of disputes to arbitration and agreements out of court

Nov. 9, Ordinance provided for care and reformation of children

1930

May 26, Code of criminal law promulgated

July 17, Native Administration Ordinance amended as to warrants for arrest and procedure in courts protecting native rights

GUINEA, FRENCH

French Guinea, West Africa, lies on the Atlantic coast between Portuguese Guinea and the British Colony of Sierra Leone, and borders on Senegal, French Sudan, and Ivory Coast, area about 89,436 square miles, population in 1929, 2,220,267, including 1,496 Europeans chiefly French. Konakry is the capital.

1827

April 19, René Caillé started his journey to Timbuktu from Kakundi on the Rio Nunez

1842

Jan. 10 and Dec. 6, Convention with chiefs of the Landoumans for freedom of trade

1845

April 17, Convention with the Chief of the Mellacorée (Melakori)

May 27, Convention with the Nalus (Rio Nunez)

1849

April 5, Treaty by which the villages of the Rio Nunez placed under French protection

1859

April 21, Treaty with native chiefs of the Rio Pongo by which lands ceded including the present Circle of Boffa

1865

Nov. 28, Treaty with Youra, King of Nalous by which region of Victoria ceded

1876

Feb. 15, Protectorate Treaty with John Cotty, King of Rio Pongo region

1877

Sept. 13, and Oct. 24, Protectorate and annexation Treaties signed with chiefs in Futa region

1880

Jan. 20, Treaty with chiefs in region of Dubreka established French protectorate

1881

July 14, Treaty by which the Almany of Futa Jallon placed his country under French protectorate

1882

June 28, Agreement with Great Britain as to boundary with Sierra Leone, basin of the Melakori to France

Oct. 12, Decree organized territory of *Rivières du Sud* under Senegal but with a lieutenant governor, Dr. Bayol

1885

Dec. 24, Treaty with Germany by which Germany renounced claim to Konakri and recognized French claim to Melakori

1886

May 12, Boundary Convention with Portugal and French protectorate recognized

June 16 and Aug. 4, Decrees placed Ivory Coast and Dahomey under *Rivières du Sud*

1887

May 8, Konakri, now the capital, occupied, and Futa Jallon finally reduced and new Treaty signed March 30, 1888

1889

Aug. 1, Decree gave Rivières du Sud practically autonomous government under Senegal

Aug. 10, Anglo-French Boundary Convention defined frontiers and recognition of French protectorate over Futa Jallon

1891

June 26, Anglo-French Boundary Convention

Dec. 17, Decree gave entire autonomy detaching region from Senegal, M. Ballay named Governor of *Rivières du Sud*

1892

Dec. 8, Boundary Convention with Sierra Leone

1893

March 10, Name changed to French Guinea

1895

Jan. 21, Anglo-French Boundary Convention replaced that of June 26, 1891

June 16, Farrana annexed

1896

April 17, New Protectorate Treaty with the Almany

1901

Nov. 3, Timbo occupied

Dec. 2, Arret organized education in Colony

1904

April 8, Anglo-French Boundary Convention by which the Los Islands ceded by Great Britain to France

Oct. 18, French Guinea became part of the Government of West Africa

1907

Sept. 1, Program for regional schools for boys published in Official Gazette

Sept. 9, Normal School and School for apprentices established at Konakri

Sept. 18, New Boundary Agreement with Liberia

1911

Jan., Railroad from Konakri on the coast to Kourassa on the Niger opened

Jan. 3, Final Boundary Agreement with Liberia

July 6, Anglo-French Boundary Convention of 1904 modified by exchange of Notes

1913

Sept. 4, New Anglo-French Boundary Convention settled frontier with Sierra Leone

1914

March 22, Decree established tribunes of first and second degree, native justice

Aug., The railroad reached Kankan

GUINEA, PORTUGUESE

Portuguese Guinea, on the coast of Senegambia, is bounded by the limits fixed by the convention of May 12, 1886, with France, and is entirely enclosed on the land side by French possessions. It includes the adjacent archipelago of Bijagoz, with the island of Bolama, in which the capital of the same name is situated. Area is 36,125 square km. (22,000 square miles). Population (1928), 343,961. In 1446 Bolama Island (Bulama) discovered by Dinis Dias. The coast was granted to Cape Verde Islands who founded "factories" at Cacheu in 1462, and the district became center of slave trade in 17th and 18th centuries. In April 21, 1870 award of President Grant decision in favor of Portuguese ownership of the Island of Bolama (Bulama) claimed by England; Portugal took possession Oct. 1.

GUINEA, SPANISH

Spanish Guinea or the Muni River Settlements. The Spanish territory on the Gulf of Guinea extends from the Muni to the Campo river and the Cameroons, its eastern boundary being on the meridian of 11° 20′ E. of Greenwich. The capital is Santa Isabel, in the Island of Fernando Po, with a population of 8,345. The principal mountain is known as the Pico de Santa Isabel, or Clarence Peak (9,185 feet). The island is considered one of the most fertile spots on the West Coast of Africa. The other possessions of Spain in the Gulf of Guinea comprise the Islands of Annobon (7½ square miles), Little Elobey (22 acres), Great Elobey (¾ square mile), and Corisco (5½ square miles), and the district of Rio Muni on the mainland (9,470 square miles), the principal town of which is Bata. The coast region is low and marshy and contains vast forests. The vegetation is luxuriant and at places along the coast there are Spanish, French, and English factories. But there are no harbors and the rivers are all inaccessible to vessels. The population of Fernando Po is

20,873. There are about 250 to 300 Europeans in the island, about 30 of these being British. The population of Little Elobey is 222. Great Elobey is covered with bush; its population is 123. Corisco has a population of 1,438 and Annobon of 1,204, while the population of Rio Muni territory is estimated at 130 whites and 89,000 natives. All the colonies are under the control of a Governor-General, resident at Santa Isabel. A Sub-Governor is appointed to the district of Bata and another to the district of Elobey, which includes the Islands of Corisco and Annobon.

The Island of Fernando Po was discovered by a Portuguese of that name in 1471, Annobon Jan. 1, 1472, and March 1, 1778 both islands were ceded by Portugal to Spain, Act of cession, Oct. 24. The Spanish Protectorate proclaimed over coast and islands Jan. 9, 1885, and the boundaries in Treaty with France of June 27, 1900.

1829

Occupation of Island of Fernando Po by British Slave Trade Commissioners which continued until 1833

1830

Oct. 28, British recognized Spanish sovereignty over Island of Fernando Po

1843

March 15, Captain Don Juan de Lerena sent out as Royal Commissioner appointed English Resident to be Spanish Governor and took Corisco and the Elobey Islands under Spanish protection, annexing them in 1846 and extending protection to the mainland

1900

June 27, Boundary Treaty settled frontier with French Equatorial Africa

1913

July 27, Native labor Ordinance provided for compulsory labor for unemployed with no means of subsistence and regulations for protection of native labor

INFI

See Morocco

IVORY COAST

Ivory Coast, French West Africa, lies between Liberia and the British Gold Coast Colony, and has frontiers with French Guinea, French Sudan, and the Upper Volta Colony, area about 121,976 square miles, population 1,724,545; Europeans 1,614. The coast was visited by merchants from Dieppe in 1364 to 1365, and a French mission was founded at Assini in 1701 which was abandoned in 1704.

Books of travel give earlier names for the Ivory Coast, Tooth Coast and Coast of the Five and Six Stripes after a cotton fabric favored by the natives.

1842–1843

Captain Bouët-Willaumez obtained treaties (Feb. 19, 1842, Grand Bassam, July 4, 1843, Assinie) from the native chiefs under which posts were established at Assini and Grand Bassam and Dabu governed by residents responsible to Senegal

1860

Aug. 4, Decree for administration of trade settlements from Gabun

1883

Dec. 16, Establishments Gulf of Guinea divided into 2 administrations, Gabun and Ivory Coast

1886

April 16, The Ivory Coast separated from Gabun and attached to Senegal

1888

Nov. 13, Treaty signed with the King of Bonduku by mission of Captain L. G. Binger which placed Bonduku under French protectorate

1889

Jan. 10, Protectorate Treaty signed with the King of Kong by Captain Binger

Aug. 1, Decree gave Ivory Coast financial and administrative autonomy

Aug. 10, Anglo-French Boundary Convention fixed frontier with Gold Coast to 9° N. Lat.

Oct. 12, M. Treich-Lapléne appointed Administrator

1891

Oct. 26, Formal notice given under the Berlin Act of French Protectorate from Lahu to the Kavalli River on the coast

Dec. 10, France gave notice of further protectorate treaties with chiefs

1892

Dec. 8, Boundary Agreement with Liberia

1893

March 10, French Colony constituted, Captain Binger, the first Governor

July 12, Further Boundary Agreement with the Gold Coast

1894

Sept. 8, Post of Kodiokofi established by Captain Marchand

1895

June 16, The Ivory Coast became part of Government General of West Africa

1896

Sept. 27, Ivory Coast separated from West Africa, given autonomy

1898

June 14, Anglo-French Boundary Convention extended boundary from 9° to 11° N. Lat. France kept Bona, Lobi, Moshi

July 2, Post of Assikasso relieved after siege of 63 days in native revolt

1899

Oct. 17, Northern boundary fixed on division of middle Niger territories by which Kong region including

Blairsville High School Library
Blairsville, Pennsylvania

Odienne, Tombugu, Bandama, Dabakala, and Groumanie included in Ivory Coast Colony and the Colony again attached to Government General of West Africa

1903

Feb. 1, April 23, and May 11, Agreement defined boundary with Gold Coast

1904

Oct. 18, Federation decree by which the Ivory Coast became part of the Government General of West Africa

1905

May 11–15, Frontier with Gold Coast defined

1907

Sept. 18, Boundary Agreement with Liberia

1911

Jan. 13, Frontier towards Liberia under Agreement of 1907 defined

1924

March 24, Native judicial system organized
Nov. 16, Decree organized French judicial system

1925

Oct. 22, Decree and arret of March 29, 1926, and March 16, 1927 regulated employment and labor of natives
Nov. 28, Decree instituted Chamber of Agriculture and Industry

1926

Nov. 15, Local decree created Labor Office

KENYA COLONY

Kenya Colony and Protectorate (British East Africa) extends, on the Indian Ocean, from the Umba River to Dick's Head, and inland as far as Lake Victoria and Uganda. The Protectorate consists of the mainland dominions of the Sultan of Zanzibar, viz., a coastal strip of territory ten miles wide, to the northern branch of the Tana River; also Kau, Kipini, and the Island of Lamu, and all adjacent islands between Rivers Umba and Tana, these territories having been leased to Great Britain in 1895 for an annual rent of 10,000*l.* The colony and protectorate were formerly known as the East Africa Protectorate. The territory has an area of 224,960 square miles; population in 1929 estimated at 3,003,158, including 16,663 Europeans, 39,504 Asiatics, and 12,504 Arabs.

Brigadier General Sir Joseph A. Byrne, Governor and Commander-in-Chief.

1886

Oct. 29/Nov. 8, First Anglo-German Boundary Agreement as to East Africa

1887

May 24, British obtained concession of 50 year lease of ten-mile strip of coast from the Umba on the south to Kipini at mouth of Tana River on the north

1889

Sept. 1, The Imperial British East Africa Company, supported by Mr. Wm. Mackenzie, Lord Brassey, Gen. Donald Stewart, Mr. Burdett-Coutts, and others, Sir Wm. Mackinnon, chairman; charter Sept. 3, 1888; large territories having been conceded to Mr. W. Mackenzie by the Sultan of Zanzibar; concession signed, Oct. 9, 1888; confirmed
Dec. 26, The Sultan of Zanzibar surrenders all control over the British East Africa Company's territory for an annual payment of 26,000 dollars; reported

1890

Jan. 1, At Rabai mission station 10 miles inland from Mombassa 1,442 slaves freed on payment of £3,500 by the British East Africa Company
March 4, The British East Africa Company received concession from the Sultan on the coast between Kipini and Mruti and some islands and places on the Benadir coast
May, Sir Francis de Winton appointed administrator of the company's territories; arrives at Zanzibar and proceeds to Mombasa, the chief station, Lamu, &c.
May 4, All slaves in the territory declared free by Mr. Mackenzie about
July, Mr. George S. Mackenzie, administrator of the territory, returns to England
July 1, Anglo-German Convention settled boundaries in East Africa. *See* Africa
July 25, First general meeting of the company, London; report and statement of accounts read
Aug. 26, Inauguration of the railway between Mombasa and Victoria Nyanza
Nov. 19, British Protectorate declared over Witu and coast between Tana and Juba Rivers

1891

Feb., Resignation of Sir Francis de Winton
March 24, Protocol for the delimitation of the British and Italian spheres of influence in East Africa, signed at Rome
Sept., General Mathews, H.M.'s commissioner, arrives at Zanzibar
——, Proposed withdrawal of representative from Uganda; serious consequences apprehended; great need of a railway from coastline to Victoria Nyanza
1891–92, Treaty of the company with the King of Uganda (*see s.v.*)

1892

Feb., Sir Gerald H. Portal appointed commissioner and consul-general in British East Africa. He and Mr. E. J. L. Berkeley, the administrator, suppress a revolt in Witu, April
June 10, Witu tranquillized by Mr. Berkeley; the ex-Sultan submits, reported
——, The company's new courts of justice at Mombasa opened by Judge Cracknall

1893

Feb. 5, Disaffection of the Somalis suppressed with bloodshed, reported
March 31, Uganda evacuated by the company
May 29, Meeting of the company in London; illness and resignation of Sir William Mackinnon; he died June 22
July 25, Anglo-German Boundary Convention as to

frontier with Tanganyika to Kilimanjaro from Indian Ocean

July 31, Evacuation of Witu by the company and Imperial Protectorate administration declared; the deposed Sultan Fumo Omari resists the British occupation, his stronghold stormed and captured, reported, Aug. 13; Jongeni stormed by Mr. R. Rodd, Aug.; the Somalis at Kismayu revolt; part of the garrison desert, Mr. Hamilton, superintendent, killed in an attack, Aug. 11; the mutiny suppressed by Lieut. Lewes and Count Lovatelli (Italian traveler), Aug. 18–23, 1893

1894

June 30, The rioters and murderers of Mr. Hamilton tried at Mombasa and punished

1895

Jan., Commissioner and Consul-Gen. Sir A. H. Hardinge

March 20, Famine through drought and locusts, reported

March 27, At a meeting of directors in London, arbitration having been refused, they resolve to accept 250,000*l.* in return for the surrender of their charter, concessions, and assets, with some exceptions, and to request compensation for expenses connected with holding Uganda; adopted April 11; 50,000*l.* voted to the company, with 30,000*l.* for administration of territory, June 13; a resolution for the winding-up of the company, &c., passed July 24, confirmed Oct. 30, 1895. [The territory made a Protectorate June 15, 1895.]

July 1, Formal transfer of territory to the Crown between the coast and Naivasha in interior

Aug. 12, Expedition of Admiral Rawson and Sir Wm. Matthews against M'bruck bin Rashed, leaves Mombasa; his stronghold taken at M'wele, Aug. 17; his camp burnt, Oct. 2, 1895

Oct., Punitive expedition against Hamis Kombo, an ally of Rashed, at Mpwapwa; Capt. Lawrence killed in a skirmish near Gazi; Mpwapwa captured

Dec. 14, Agreement with Sultan of Zanzibar for administration of his mainland dominions

1896

Feb. 29, Ali bin Abdullah a powerful Arab, sentenced to 7 yrs. imprisonment and a fine of 5,000 rupees for cruelty to slaves; reported

April 22, An expedition sent from Mombasa against the rebel chief M'Baruk Aziz; March 15–22, he and 1,000 followers surrendered to Major von Wissmann in German territory; reported

May 27, Notice brought Land Acquisition Act of India of 1894 into effect in East Africa

Aug. 31, The name East African Protectorate officially adopted, and boundaries defined

1897

Jan. 10, Land regulations adopted

July 9, British judicial system introduced by order in council

Dec. 29, New land regulations provided for authorization by Commissioner of certificates of 99 year leases for occupation

1898

May 19, Order in Council by which the silver rupee of India ordered to be the standard coin from Jan. 1, 1899

June, Punitive expedition under Mr. Jenner against the Ogaden Somalis in Jubaland, some fighting, chiefs surrender, Aug. 21, 1898

1899

March 5, Col. Macdonald's successful expedition returns to Mombasa (*see* Uganda)

March–Aug., Famine in several provinces, great mortality

Sept. 12, 13, Mt. Kenya, over 17,000 ft. high, first ascended by Mr. H. J. Mackinder

Nov. 16, Mr. Jenner, commissioner, murdered by the Ogaden Somalis in Jubaland; the Ogaden Sultan taken prisoner and Aff-Madu occupied by the British

1901

Oct. 23, Hut tax imposed published in the Gazette Nov. 15, not to exceed 2 rupees a year

Dec. 19, The Uganda Railroad completed to Lake Victoria Nyanza

1902

Feb. 17, Regulations as to native porters and labor prescribed rates of pay and making of contracts

March 2, Hut tax increased to 3 rupees a year

March 5, Ordinance by which Kisumu and Naivasha provinces of Uganda added to East African Protectorate

April 12, Mining regulations published

Sept. 27, First Crown Lands Ordinance repealed earlier land legislation, provided for leasehold not exceeding 1,000 acres for period of 99 years, rents from 3 to 12 cents per acre a year

Dec. 2, The S.S. "Winifred" launched on Lake Victoria Nyanza

Dec. 12, Native Courts Amendment Ordinance

1904

June 20, Sir D. W. Stewart succeeded Sir Charles Eliot as Commissioner

1905

April 1, Control of Protectorate transferred from the British Foreign Office to the Colonial Office

1906

March 17, Statue of Queen Victoria presented to town of Nairobi by an Indian merchant, unveiled by the Duke of Connaught

Aug. 5, Immigration Restriction Act passed

Oct. 4, F. J. Jackson appointed Lieutenant-Governor

Oct. 22, Order in Council constituted Executive and Legislative Councils

Nov. 9, The Protectorate placed under the control of a Governor and Commander-in-Chief by Order in Council

1907

June 3, Exchange of Notes settled frontier with Mozambique

Dec. 6, Boundary Agreement with Abyssinia

1909

June 29, Sir Percy Girouard appointed Governor and Commander-in-Chief

Dec. 11, Ordinance made provision for removal of native political offenders from one part of the Protectorate to another

1910

March 21, Master and Servant Ordinance for protection of labor regulated employment of natives, recruiting contracts, &c.

April 24, Collective Punishment Ordinance (No. 4 of 1909) came into effect allowing imposition of fine by a magistrate on all the natives of any village, community, tribe, &c., if guilty of collusion with or harboring criminals, or failure to restore stolen property

Aug. 27, The Masai tribe informed the Government that they would leave Laikipia only under compulsion, giving up their lands to Europeans

1911

April 4, Treaty with Masai by which they agreed to evacuate Laikipia

Sept., Deportation of Galbraith Cole, pioneer settler, by order of British Colonial Secretary, after he had killed a Kikuyu native caught stealing sheep, and had been acquitted by a Nairobi jury

1912

Feb. 17, Master and Servant Ordinance amended

May 21, The Masai ordered to remove to southern area refused to go, but were finally forced to make the move, and the last out by March, 1913

July 8/15, Boundary Agreement with Italian Somaliland

July, Resignation of Sir Percy Girouard. Succeeded by Sir H. C. Belfield as Governor in October

Oct. 16, Native Authority Ordinance enacted

1913

June 26, Stock and Produce Theft Ordinance (No. 8 of 1913) came into effect by which the court in addition to any other punishment authorized by law might sentence a convicted native to fine to be not less than 10 times the value of stock or produce stolen, and in case of non-payment a warrant to be issued to levy fine by sale of any property of native or his tribe

July 1, Control of the Protectorate transferred from the Foreign Office to the Colonial Office, the Governor of East Africa Protectorate to be High Commissioner for Zanzibar, local affairs under a British Resident who took over functions of first Minister

Dec., Expedition against the hostile Merehan tribe in Jubaland

1914

Jan. 21, Two Orders in Council provided for administration of Protectorate, a Council established

Feb. 3, Boundary Agreement with Belgian Congo, Mt. Sabinio to Congo-Nile watershed

Aug. 15, German force under General von Lettow-Vorbeck seized Taveta. For military operations in East Africa, see World War. 3,145 Europeans served in the War and 9,643 natives recruited and 201,431 carriers and porters

1915

May 18, Crown Lands Ordinance (No. 12 of 1915) came into effect, provided for leases of 999 years at rents of 20 cents an acre to be revised in 1945 and every 30 years thereafter, the right of the Governor to veto transfers of land from members of one race to members of another established

Sept. 13, Ordinance provided for registration of persons in the Protectorate

1916

April 25, Railroad from Voi to Taveta carried through Latema Neck and joined to Tanga railway at Kahne in Tanganyika

1918

March 11, Immigration Restriction Act amended, further defining prohibited immigrants

Dec. 31, Master and Servant Ordinance amended

1919

July 22, Major General E. Northey, Governor. Ordinance enlarged the Legislative Council to consist of 11 elected representatives of the European community, 2 representing the Indian population and 1 the Arabs, and a sufficient number of official members to give a majority

——, Immigration Restriction Ordinance amended to keep out convicts, &c.

Oct. 20, Registration of titles Ordinance provided system of registration, an adaptation of Torrens system

Oct. 23, Labor Circular No. 1 as to native labor required for non-native farms and other private undertakings asked provincial and district commissioners to exercise every possible lawful influence to get labor, recommended that list be kept of those chiefs who had been helpful and those who had not

Oct., Master and Servant Ordinance amended

1920

Feb. 11, Native Authority Amendment Ordinance provided for compulsory paid labor of not more than 60 days for porters for tours for government service, work on roads and railroads

March 31, Value of rupee in East Africa fixed at 2 shillings as published in the official Gazette

May 21, Order of Lord Milner that arrangements be made for election of 2 Indian members to the Legislative Council, the principle of race segregation to be adhered to in resident areas and in commerce but no restriction to be made on Indian immigration

June 16, The rupee fell below 2 shillings

July 23, Order in Council of June 11 came into effect by which the territories outside the mainland dominions of the Sultan of Zanzibar were recognized as a Crown Colony, annexed to the Crown, the Sultan's mainland dominions to be styled the Protectorate of Kenya

July 28, Labor Circular No. 1 of Oct. 23, 1919 canceled in application to women and children by order Secretary

Aug. 13, Order in Council as to administration under Order in Council of June 11

Sept. 11, Royal instructions reconstituted the Executive Council

Sept. 22, The rupee fell to 1s. 10d.

Nov. 29, Income tax Ordinance passed

1921

Jan. 1, Scheme of administration providing for separate control of native and settled areas came into operation

Feb. 2, The rupee reached 1s. 5d.

June 27, Order in Council defined boundaries of Colony and Protectorate

Sept. 5, Winston Churchill notified Administration that officials of the Government were to take no part in recruiting voluntary labor for private enterprises, reversing the policy of his predecessor in the Colonial Office

1922

Feb. 11, Constitutional Amendment provided for 4 nominated instead of 2 elected Indian members on Legislative Council

March 14, Native riot on arrest of Harry Thuku suppressed by troops

May 25, Income tax of 1920 repealed

Dec. 30, Amendment to Native Authority Ordinance replaced Ordinance of 1920, compulsory labor assigned to be on specified work and with approval of the Secretary of State

1923

Dec. 31, Customs Tariff Ordinance provided for a uniform tariff for Kenya, Uganda, and Tanganyika, free trade between the 3, specific duties on imports of certain classes ranging between 10 and 50% of their value, and *ad valorem* duties on other imports generally between 10 and 30%, entire abolition of export duties

1924

Jan. 4, Ordinance made provision for 5 elected Indian members and 1 Arab member for the Legislative Council

July 15, Anglo-Italian Treaty by which Juba River and a strip from 50 to 100 miles wide on the British side of the River ceded to Italy, cession taking place June 29, 1925 after ratification of the Treaty

Sept. 26, Native Authority Amendment Ordinance invested native councils with statutory powers in matters affecting purely local native administration affairs, management of communal matters such as lands, forests, veterinary service, health, education, agriculture, trade and labor recruiting, roads

Dec. 16, Kenya and Uganda (Transport) Order in Council enacted to come into effect Feb. 3, 1926 established office of High Commissioner for Transport for Kenya and Uganda to control transport and for a Kenya and Uganda Railway Advisory Council

1926

Sept. 18, Immigration Restriction Ordinance enacted

Sept. 28, Native Lands Trust Ordinance amended to enable Governor in Council to declare any of the Crown lands native reserves

1927

March 1, New Bankruptcy Ordinance came into effect

March 28, Royal instructions provided that if at any time the number of Indian elected members of Legislative Council was less than 5 the vacancies might be filled by the appointment of nominated Indian unofficial members, the ex-officio members to be the members of the Executive Council, with the General Manager of the Kenya and Uganda Railway, Commissioner of Lands, Directors of Public Works, and Commissioner of Customs

Aug. 1, New Civil Procedure Ordinance came into effect

Oct. 22, Native Liquor Amendment Ordinance enacted

Nov. 1, Railroad from Thika-Nyeri branch to Naro Moru opened

Nov. 7, Employment of Natives Ordinance

1928

Jan. 11, The Tororo-Mbulamuti-Jinja extension of the Kenya and Uganda Railroad opened

July 2, Ordinance provided for organization of the European inhabitants of the Colony into a defense force

July 7, Royal instructions reconstituted Executive Council

Sept. 28, Arrival of the Prince of Wales at Mombassa and at Nairobi, Oct. 1

Oct. 8, Ordinance amended Local Municipal Government law and Local Government (District Councils) Ordinance extending powers of local government in municipalities and settled areas, the Local Government (Rating) Ordinance enabling local authorities to impose and collect rates

Dec. 31, Ordinance Public Health (Division of Lands) established Board

1929

Jan. 18, Report of Hilton-Young Commission published in England on closer union of dependencies in East and Central Africa

Feb. 23, Order provided for conservation, control, and distribution of food stuffs during the year

May 10–June 12, Visit of V. S. Srinivasa Sastri appointed by the Government of India to help Indians in East Africa express views on questions arising out of the Hilton-Young Report

July 8, Non-Native Poll-tax Ordinance amended

——, Crown Lands (Amendment) Ordinance empowered Government to declare land jointly occupied by Arabs and native tribe to be a communal reserve

July 15, Registration of domestic servants Ordinance

1930

April 17, Ordinance consolidated laws as to customs tariff

May 13, Native Lands and Trust Ordinance created a central board to provide for reservation of land and management and control

May 26, Ordinance established Penal Code and May 28 Code of criminal procedure

May 31, The Governor authorized to make loans to farmers

Aug. 11, Native Authority (Amendment) Ordinance authorized establishment of communal councils

Sept. 3, Native liquor Ordinance consolidated and amended laws regulating native liquor

——, Native Tribunals Ordinance provided for constitution and jurisdiction of native tribunals, appeals to be through native courts of appeals and district commissioner

Sept. 15, Railroad extension from Naro Moru to Nanyuke opened

KERGUELEN ISLAND

Kerguélen Island, French possession, about 2,000 miles southeast of Madagascar in about 50° S. Lat. and 70° E. Long. was discovered by French navigator, Joseph de Kerguélen-Trémarec Feb. 13, 1772, was annexed to France in Jan. 1893 and became a dependency of Madagascar in Nov. 1924.

LAGOS

Lagos (Southern Nigeria), West Africa, now a part of the British Colony of Nigeria. *See also* Nigeria. Named by the Portuguese because of the many lagoons and lakes along the coast.

1851

Dec. 28, British squadron under Commodore Bruce landed on Lagos Island after sharp fight with King Kosoko, in operations against the slave trade and in support of settlement of British traders at Badagry 40 miles west of Lagos, and reinstated Akitoye, the rightful king, who agreed to abolish the slave trade and human sacrifice and signed Treaty in 1852

1852

March 1, Akitoye signed Treaty granting lands to missionary society

1861

Aug. 6, King Docemo, son and successor of Akitoye, signed Treaty ceding his lands to the British and occupation proclaimed

1863

June 27, 29, July 4, July 7, Protectorate Treaties over Addo, Pocrah, Okeodan, respectively and cession of Badagry

1866

Feb. 19, Lagos united with Sierra Leone

1874

July 24, Lagos separated from Sierra Leone and with the Gold Coast made a separate administration in political dependence on the Gold Coast

1885

June 5, Notification of British Protectorate. *See also* Nigeria

1886

Jan. 13, Lagos made a separate Colony

1887

Oct. 18, Notification of British Protectorate
Dec. 29, British Order in Council proclaimed jurisdiction over adjacent territory

1889

Aug. 10, Anglo-French Boundary Agreement settled frontiers with Dahomey, completed by report of Delimitation Commission, Oct. 12, 1896

1892

Jan. 21, Treaty with the King of Jebu securing freedom of roads, signed at Lagos by delegates
April, The Jebus and Egbas threaten Lagos and the Gold Coast; checked by the arrival of troops under Major Madden and Col. Scott; the Jebus repulsed in their attack on Col. Scott's expedition and their villages taken, May 12 *et seq.*
May 17–20, Total defeat of the Jebus, surrender of the King, Jebu Ode occupied, army dispersed

1893

Jan. 12, Abeokuta, the Egba capital, visited by Sir G. T. Carter, reported

Aug. 15, Informal treaty with the Egbas, about Feb. 3; confirmed

1894

Aug. 4, Treaty of the governor with the chiefs at Jebu Remo to abolish human sacrifice, slave dealing, &c.

1895

June, Destructive effects of the increased importation of cheap spirituous liquors, reported
Nov. 12, Native rising in the Hinterland, Capt. Bower defeats the King of Yoruba, and bombards Oyo; the King murdered, about Nov. 20; 2,000 Ilorins attack the British, and are repulsed, March 31, 1896; defeated again with loss at Odo Otin, April; totally defeated, their chief Adamu killed, early March, 1897

1896

Oct. 12, Boundary with Dahomey settled

1897

Aug. 21, Great loyal meeting of chiefs and natives
Oct. 15, Various posts on the N.W. frontier occupied by the British; the French retire to Boussa: a British force mistaken for French is attacked by Baribas, who are repulsed (about 300 killed) by Capt. Homfrey, reported
Nov., French encroachments: Saki and Hassi in Yoruba occupied by them; they retire on the arrival of a British force; Ilesha and Bere occupied by the British, Dec. 29

1898

Feb. 9, The French advance to Borea, and order the Haussa officer to haul down the British flag, demand refused; the French retired
Feb. 28, Lt.-col. M'Callum receives the envoys of the Kings of Borgu and Yoruba at Saki; settlement of the feud; treaties made; he is well received at Ilesha by the King and chiefs of Bariba; Wori Yaro made King of Borgu, March 9; arrives at Okuma, March 11
March, Col. Allan holds a palaver with the King and chiefs and hoists the British flag at Bode, treaties signed; reported
May, Kishi (*Hinterland*) evacuated by the French, occupied by the British
Aug. 28, An expeditionary force from Lagos, under major Arnold, attacks and destroys Siama in Forcados to punish native piracy, &c.
Oct. 10, The French evacuate Boussa and occupy Bona and Lobi, reported

1899

April 21, 22, Capt. Denton opens the railway from Lagos to Abbeokuta; a durbah held, &c.
Dec. 27, Order in Council fixed limits

1901

April 1, Proclamation made slave dealing a penal offense
Dec. 14, Sir Wm. MacGregor opens the Lagos-Ibadan railway, amid great rejoicings, March 5; a branch from Aro to Abbeokuta

1906

Feb. 16, Administration of the S. Nigeria Protectorate placed under that of the colony of Lagos; the name of Lagos changed to that of Colony of Southern Nigeria by order in Council dated

1914

Jan. 1, The Colony and Protectorate of Southern Nigeria (Lagos and Southern Nigeria) amalgamated with the Protectorate of Northern Nigeria to form the Colony and Protectorate of Nigeria under a Governor, Lagos, the seat of the Central Government. *See* Nigeria

LIBERIA

Liberia (Republic) had its origin in the efforts of several American philanthropic societies to make permanent provision for freed American slaves by establishing them in a colony on the West African coast. In 1822 a settlement was formed on the west coast of Africa near the spot where Monrovia now stands. On July 26, 1847, the State was constituted as the Free and Independent Republic of Liberia. The new State was first recognized by Great Britain and France, and ultimately by other Powers. The Constitution of the Republic is on the model of that of the United States. Liberia has about 350 miles of coast line, extending from the British Colony of Sierra Leone, on the west, to the French colony of the Ivory Coast on the east, and it stretches inland to a distance, in some places, of about 200 miles. The boundaries were determined by the Anglo-Liberian agreement of Nov. 11, 1885, and the Franco-Liberian agreements of Dec. 8, 1892 and 1907–10. Jan. 21, 1911 an agreement was concluded between the British and Liberian Governments transferring the territory of Kanre Lahun to Sierra Leone in exchange for a strip of undeveloped territory of about the same area on the south side of Morro River, which now becomes the boundary.

The total area is about 43,000 square miles. The total population is estimated at 2,000,000 to 2,500,000, all of the African race. Since the organization of the frontier force the Government has obtained complete control of Northern Liberia and of the Kroo countries in Southern Liberia. The indigenous natives belong in the main to six principal stocks: (1) the Mandingos (Muhammadan), (2) the Gissi; (3) the Gola, (4) the Kpwesi, (5) the Kru negroes and their allies, and (6) the Greboes. The Kru tribes are mostly Pagan. The number of Americo-Liberians is estimated at about 15,000. About 60,000 of the coast negroes may be considered civilized There is a British negro colony of about 500, and there are about 150 Europeans and Americans. The coast region is divided into counties, Bassa, Sino, Maryland, and Grand Cape Mount, each under a Government superintendent, and Montserrado, subdivided into 2 districts, each under a superintendent. Monrovia, the capital, has, including Krutown, an estimated population of 10,000, and is administered as a Federal District by a Municipal Board appointed by the President. The independence of Liberia was proclaimed,

Aug. 24, 1847; recognized by Europe in 1848, by America, in 1862. Presidents: J. J. Roberts, an able statesman, 1847; Daniel B. Warner, elected 1864; James Spriggs Payne, installed Jan. 6, 1868; E. J. Roy, president, Jan., 1870, was deposed, Oct., 1871; escaped from prison; drowned, Feb., 1872. J. J. Roberts reëlected Jan., 1872 and 1874; died Feb. 25; J. Spriggs Payne, elected June 3, 1876; A. W. Gardner, 1878; A. J. Russell, 1883; H. R. W. Johnson, Jan. 7, 1884; J. J. Cheesman, Jan. 4, 1892; died Nov. 11. Wm. David Coleman, Nov. 13, 1896 (resigns Dec. 11); G. W. Gibson, Dec. 20, 1900; A. Barclay elected, 1903, and reëlected till 1908 in 1905, again reëlected May, 1907, till Jan., 1911.

Charles D. B. King, President.

1820

Feb. 6, The *Mayflower* with the first negro colonists from America left New York arriving at Sierra Leone March 9, and proceeded to Sherbro Islands where natives had promised to sell land but had reconsidered and now refused. Colonists returned to Sierra Leone

1821

March 28, Party of new emigrants reached Freetown in the ship "Nautilus"

Dec. 15, Representatives of the Government of the United States negotiated purchase of strip of coast land 130 miles long and 40 miles broad at Cape Mesurado which they named Monrovia in honor of President Monroe

1824

Aug. 15, The Colony named Liberia, the capital, Monrovia

1847

July 26, Independent Republic of Liberia constituted

1848

Jan. 3, Joseph J. Roberts inaugurated first President

Nov. 21, Treaty of friendship and commerce with Great Britain

1857

Feb. 19, Annexation of Maryland

1862

June 3, Liberia recognized by the United States

1875 to 1893

Sept. 17, 1875, The aborigines defeated at Cape Palmas

March, 1876, Peace concluded

Feb., 1880, Kingdom of Medina annexed

Feb. 23, 1893, War with cape Palmas native chiefs at Rock Town; the Liberians defeated about

1894

Jan. 21, Limitation convention respecting the French territories, signed at Paris, Dec. 8, 1892, ratified at Monrovia, reported

Feb., French encroachments on the territory

Aug. 10, Limitation treaty signed

1895

Oct., Several ports blockaded for tribal disturbances

1896

Nov., Col. Cardew, governor of Sierra Leone, in H.M.S. *Alecto*, arrives at Monrovia, to protect British subjects, Oct. 28; indemnity paid

1897

Feb., Native towns burnt by Liberian troops
July 5, Treaty of extradition with France, signed

1898

June 5, Sub-Lieut. Baily Forelière and M. Pauly, French explorers, murdered at Zoulon, N. Liberia, reported

1899

Feb. 2, Chief Kafra invades British territory, is defeated, and 4 towns captured, reported
Aug. 23, Big town raided by the Gebroes, reported

1904

Conference held at Monrovia, at which all the important chiefs sign a declaration of peace

1907

May 7, Arthur Barclay reëlected President
Sept. 18, Frontier Agreement with France signed as to Ivory Coast and French Guinea
Second foreign loan negotiated in London

1908

Jan. 25, Commission appointed to visit the United States, received by the Secretary of State in Washington May 26, asked for assistance of the United States to maintain a peaceful and orderly government

1909

Jan. 15, German vessel fired on by Liberian gunboat
Feb. 4, Apology of Government to Germany
April 13 and May 12, Agreement with Great Britain as to import duties
April 23, Commission from the United States, W. Morgan Shuster, Dr. George Sale, and Emmet J. Scott, proceeded to Monrovia to investigate the condition of the country

1910

March 20, The U.S.S. "Birmingham" sailed for Liberia to give aid to Liberia in revolt of natives
March 25, Report of Commission to Liberia presented to Congress of the United States recommended aid to Liberia in reforming finances and refunding its debt, settlement of boundary disputes, organizing a police force, and by guarantee of independence
July 9, Dr. R. F. Falkner appointed financial adviser to Liberia sailed from the United States

1911

Jan. 3, Final boundary settlement with French Guinea
Jan. 13, Boundary Convention with France defined frontier with the Ivory Coast. France obtaining cession of some 2,000 square miles which Liberia had claimed but not been able to administer
Jan. 21, Boundary Convention with Great Britain settled frontier with Sierra Leone, a part of the Kissi country (district of Kanre Lahun) transferred to Sierra Leone in exchange for territory between the Mano and Morro Rivers and money payment

1912

Jan. 1, Daniel Howard inaugurated President
March 12, Agreement signed in London for rehabilitation of finances of Liberia by American, German, French, and British bankers
June, International loan of $1,700,000 raised, bonds payable in New York, bonds issued for period of 40 years and for this period the control of the finances arranged by the United States, customs duties, rubber tax &c. pledged for security, an American Receiver-General appointed, a frontier police force to be organized by officers of the United States army to control the Kru tribes
Nov. 12, German ultimatum and gunboat sent for protection of German subjects in native disturbances

1913

April 10, Agreement with France made regulations for navigation of the Mano River

1914

June 27, Treaty of Commerce with the United States signed
Aug. 10, Liberia declared neutrality in the European war

1915

Oct. 29, Agreement with British Bank of West Africa as to loan
Nov. 8, Arrival of U.S.S. "Chester," and R. P. Clarke appointed with B. W. Payne (Liberian) to aid in settlement of dispute with the Krus
Dec. 16, The "Chester" sailed for Sinoe and landed frontier force on coast

1916

Feb. 4, Depositary Agreement with the British Bank of West Africa

1917

Feb. 21, Supplementary Agreement with British Bank of West Africa
April 4, Note from the United States protested failure to reform administration and finances
May 8, Liberia severed diplomatic relations with Germany
June 19–26, Exchange of Notes with Great Britain settled frontier with Sierra Leone from the Makona River at Moa in the north to the Magowi River in the south
Aug. 4, Joint Resolution of Congress published Aug. 7 declared war with Germany

1918

April 10, Monrovia bombarded by German submarine and the steamer "President Howard" sunk, submarine driven away by British warship
Sept., American loan to Liberia concluded under authorization of Liberian Loan Act of Sept. 24

1919

May 6, C. D. B. King elected President
June 28, Abyssinia a signatory of the Treaty of Versailles

1920

June 15, Agreement provided for an American loan
June 30, Liberia declared adherence to League of Nations as an original member of Jan. 10

1921

Oct. 21, Agreement for loan of $5,000,000 at 5% signed with the United States; not ratified by United States Senate

1924

June 19, Agreement with the Barclay Firestone Rubber Plantation Company (American) approved by Act of Liberian Legislature Jan. 13, 1925

1925

Jan. 14, Act defined rules of the road for motor cars

Sept. 16, Three Agreements signed with the Firestone Rubber Company in the United States providing for lease of 1,000,000 acres of land for rubber plantations for 99 years and arrangement for loan of $5,000,000 at 7%

1926

Jan. 10, The Legislature ratified the Firestone Agreement

Feb. 10, Arbitration Treaty with the United States signed

Nov. 18, Firestone Agreement and loan approved by Legislature

1927

July 1, The Firestone Agreement went into effect

July 26, Entire war debt to the United States paid

1928

Feb. 14, Act abolished practice of recruiting and shipping of natives for service outside Liberia

1930

March 8, Arrival of Dr. Charles S. Johnson (American) and Dr. C. Christy (League of Nations appointment) to investigate conditions as to slavery

May 19, The Government deposited ratifications of Slavery Convention of 1926

Sept. 8, Report of Commission declared slavery as defined under Convention of 1926 existed, forced labor for roads &c.

Oct. 23, The Government officially informed the League of Nations that all domestic slaves of native tribes had been declared free

LIBYA

Libya, Italian Colony on the north coast of Africa, between Tunis on the west and Egypt on the east, comprising the former Tripolitania and Cyrenaica. Tripolitania commonly called Tripoli was originally a Phœnician Colony, Cyrenaica was founded by the Greeks (631 B.C.) and became an Egyptian and then a Roman province, both Tripoli and Cyrenaica becoming Turkish provinces in 1578. In 1714 Ahmed Pasha Karamanli achieved independence for the Arabs of Tripoli which lasted until 1835, when the last Karamanli was deposed by the Turks. The Barbary coast was the center of piracy from the fourteenth until the early part of the nineteenth century, the Beys submitting to the demands of the Powers in 1819. The Congress of Vienna of 1815 took up the question of the pirates and gave to England the task of liberation of the Christian slaves. For war with the United States, see s.v. 1801–1805, and 1815. Tripoli was annexed by Italy after war with Turkey Nov. 5, 1911 by decree which was ratified by Chamber Feb. 23, 1912.

The area of Tripoli is estimated at about 900,000 square kilometers. According to a census taken on December 1, 1921, there were about 550,000 natives and 20,716 Europeans (18,093 Italians). It is estimated that of the total population, 203,000 are Arabs, 135,000 Berbers, 172,000 Arab-Berbers, and about 40,000 Jews. Of the Mussulman population the negroes of various races form about 35%. Arabic is more generally spoken than written, and both Italian and Arabic are the official languages. The principal towns of Tripolitania are on the coast: Tripoli with about 60,000 inhabitants, Misurata with 14,000, and Homs with 5,000; other important centers are at Azizia, Zuara, and Zavia on the west coast, Sirte on the east coast, and Gariàn, Jefren, Giado, and Nalut on the highland. Inland are the caravan halting places, Ghadames, Sinauen, Mizda, Murzûk, and Ghat. The area of Cyrenaica is estimated at about 75,340 square miles, and with the hinterland (zone of Cufra) 285,640 square miles. According to a census taken in 1929, there were 135,000 Mohammedans, 4,000 Jews, and 10,000 Europeans, making a total of 149,000. The principal town is Benghazi with 33,794 inhabitants in December, 1929.

The oasis of Jarabub, on the eastern border of Cyrenaica, was ceded by Egypt to Italy, and Italian troops occupied it on February 7, 1926. On the other hand, the frontier in the neighborhood of Sollum on the sea was rectified in favor of Egypt.

Marshall Pietro Badoglio, Governor.

1899

March 21, Anglo-French Boundary Convention determined the boundaries of the Wadai and the hinterland of the Vilayet of Tripoli

1900

Dec. 14, French and English declarations as to Tripoli

1910

May 19, Boundary Convention with France and change in territory made by French-Ottoman Commission, Nov. 1

1911

Sept. 25, Italian Note to Turkey demanded recognition of Italian economic privileges in Tripoli

Sept. 28, Italian ultimatum to Turkey gave 48 hours for guarantee that reforms would be introduced in the government of Tripoli and full protection to Italian citizens and commerce with threat of military occupation of Tripoli and Cyrenaica

Sept. 29, War declared on Turkey by Italy

Oct. 1, The Italian fleet arrived off Tripoli

Oct. 3, Tripoli bombarded by Italian fleet

Oct. 5, Surrender of Tripoli, Italian occupation begun at city of Tripoli and Tobruk in Cyrenaica

Oct. 7, Admiral Borea Ricci d'Olmo landed, appointed first Italian Governor

Oct. 16, Derma bombarded by Italians and landing made on the 18th

Oct. 19, Italian blockade of coast of Cyrenaica withdrawn to west of 25° 1' Long.; Benghazi taken by Italians

Oct. 21, Homs occupied by Italians

Oct. 23 and 26, Attack of Arab and Turkish force, attempt to retake Tripoli, unsuccessful

Nov. 5, Italian royal decree published in Gazette announced annexation of Tripoli and Cyrenaica

Nov. 9, British official statement that Egyptian Government regarded the Jaghbub oasis as belonging to Egypt

Dec. 5, Decisive battle outside of Tripoli which gave Italians possession of the country

Dec. 21, Statement of British Foreign Office that in 1904 both Turkish and Italian governments had been informed that the frontier with Egypt was to the west of Sollum

1912

Jan. 18, Fighting at Gargaresh Oasis with Turks; occupied by Italians, Jan. 20

Jan. 27, Russia issued circular urging the Powers of Europe to take joint action in the interests of peace

Jan. 30, Attack of Bedouins on fort at Bengazi repulsed

Feb. 23, Italian Chamber provided for extension of Italian sovereignty to Tripoli and creation of special colonial government

Feb. 24, Beirut bombarded by Italians

March 3, Attack on Italian position at Derna repulsed

March 6, First use of dirigible balloons in actual war made by the Italians in Tripoli

April 23, Engagement at Bu Kemmesh, Italians and Turks

Aug. 6, Zuara, Tripoli, captured by Italians

Sept. 17, Italians repulsed attack of Enver Bey on Derna

Oct. 15, Preliminary Treaty of peace signed between Italy and Turkey at Ouchy

Oct. 16, Turkish Decree as to autonomy of Cyrenaica and Tripoli

Oct. 18, Italo-Turkish Peace Treaty signed at Lausanne ceded Tripoli to Italy, though in text no mention made of transference as by Ottoman law the Sultan is forbidden to dispose of territory, but the evacuation of military forces, and military and civil officials in Tripoli and Cyrenaica provided for, and territory understood to have passed into Italian possession in spite of the will of the Sultan of Turkey. Firman of the Sultan to the inhabitants granted them full autonomy

Oct. 28, France recognized Italian possession of Tripoli and Cyrenaica, most favored treatment of nationals of the 2 countries in Morocco and Libya

Dec. 10, Turkish troops left Tripoli

1913

Jan. 9, Italian Decree organized 2 separate governments for Tripoli and Cyrenaica

Jan., Italians began advance into interior of Tripoli through Misna, and Socna south to the Fezzan, and Murzuk which was captured March 13, and through Zintan, Fessato, and Nalut to the frontier of Tunis and south to Ghadames

Feb. 6, Decree provided for administration of justice

April 27, Italian force commanded by Captain Pavoni

entered Ghadames and administered the oath of allegiance to a large number of sheiks

May 16, Italians in severe engagement with Arabs and Turks near Derna at Sidi Gharba

1914

March 3, The Italians commanded by Colonel Miani entered Murzuk, the capital of Fezzan

May 29, Agreement of France and Italy of most favored treatment of nationals in Libya and Tunis respectively

Aug. 12, Italians occupied Ghat, the oasis and town, junction of 3 important caravan routes

Sept., The Fezzani rose in revolt attacking Italian garrisons between Murzuk and the coast and by Nov. forced evacuation of Murzuk by Italians, and the garrisons at Ghat and Ghadames withdrew into French territory

Dec. 8, The Sultan's representative in Tripoli proclaimed a Holy War

1915

Feb. 8, Italian troops attacked at Du-medjem about 50 miles from coast dispersed Arabs after day's battle

Feb. 18, Colonel Giannani retook Ghat after hard fighting

April 29, Italians in engagement near Sidra in which the native troops mutinied and went over to the enemy causing Italian Colonel Miani to lose 800 men killed or wounded

May 23, Italy's declaration of war on Austria-Hungary caused general uprising of natives and forced Italians to evacuate posts in the interior and withdraw to coast; serious revolt at Sirte

July 15, General Ameglio, Governor of Cyrenaica, named also Governor of Tripoli

July 19, Ghadames garrison withdrew to French territory completing evacuation of interior

Nov. 14, Hostilities with the Senussi begun by Senussi attack on West Sollum, Egypt. *See* World War

1916

July 31, Anglo-Italian Agreement as to war against the Senussi, and consideration of the Libyan-Egyptian boundary deferred

Aug., Italians reoccupied coast town of Zuara

Sept. 25, Suleiman el Baruni, Berber Chief, landed at Misurata with firman from the Sultan of Turkey appointing him Governor General of the vilayets of Tripoli, Tunis, and Algiers, and was joined by Ramadhan el Shtewi established a "Republic of Tripoli" at Misurata which became a German submarine base

Nov., Sidi Ahmed given title of "Viceroy of Africa"

1917

Jan. 16, The Italians commanded by General Latini defeated Suleiman el Baruni in engagement

Feb. 3–5, The British defeated Sidi Ahmed in Egypt which weakened Senussi prestige in Tripoli

March 28, The French adhered to Italo-British Agreement of July 31, 1916 for war with the Senussi

April 14, The Sidi Idris, Senussi tribe, made submission to and agreement with the British and Italians

1918

April, Prince Osman Fuad, sent by the Turkish Government, arrived at Misurata by submarine, but did not succeed in composing the quarrels and rivalries of the Senussi tribes

1919

April 24, Armistice signed with Arab chiefs

May 17, Civil government proclaimed in Tripolitania, Decree divided the country into 2 independent districts, Tripolitania and Cyrenaica under Minister of Colonies, with respective capitals at Tripoli and Bengazi

June 1, Italian citizenship decreed for the natives, "complete local citizenship" and elective assembly announced

June 12, Italian flag raised at 'Azizya to proclaim peace and Italian sovereignty

July 1, Constitution announced for Tripolitania

Aug., Vittorio Menzinger appointed Governor to carry out new policies

Sept. 8, Accord fixed boundary of Tibesti, frontier altered from west of Ghadames to south of Tummo in curve including Ghat

Nov. 2, Constitution announced for Cyrenaica

1920

July, Luigi Mercatelli succeeded as Governor

Aug. 10, In Treaty of Sèvres Turkey renounced rights reserved in Treaty of Lausanne of 1912 of having a representative in Tripoli, his name mentioned in public prayers, &c.

Oct. 25, Convention of Regima with the Senussi by which Sidi Idriss acknowledged as Emir and administration of Kufra, Jarabub (also spelled Jaghbub, Jarabaib, Djarboub, &c.) were given to him

1921

April 30, Parliament inaugurated at Benghazi, Cyrenaica

Aug., Giuseppe Volpi became Governor

Sept., Visit of Crown Prince Humbert

1922

May 22, General Badoglio began offensive against Arabs

1923

Feb. 27, Misurata reoccupied by Italian force

1924

Feb. 11, Oases of Ghadames reoccupied

Nov. 23, Italians occupied Sirte completing conquest of Tripolitania

1925

March 5, Armed clash with Bedouins at Jarabub oasis not yet given to Italy as promised in 1919

July, Resignation of Governor Volpi. Succeeded by General de Bono

Dec. 6, Anglo-Italian Agreement as to Libya-Egypt frontier, cession of Jarabub oasis

1926

Feb. 7, Italian troops occupied oasis of Jarabub ceded by Egypt

1927

Feb. 20, Royal Decree and law of July 7 authorized import into Italy of products of Tripoli and Cyrenaica free of duty

March 9, Cabinet of Italy approved organic law revoking self-government granted in 1919

April 26–27, Agreements signed as to Libya-Egypt frontier

June 18, Decree granted bonus for each house constructed for owner

1928

Jan. 3, Surrender of Mohammed Rida el Mahdi, Senussi chief in Cyrenaica

Feb. 14–19, Enemy defeated at Waddam ending revolt in southern Tripoli

Feb. 27, Oasis of Zella 300 miles southwest of Benghazi captured

April 12, Successful engagement with rebel tribes in hinterland of Cyrenaica

Aug. 16, Close of successful campaign against rebel tribes in Cyrenaica

1929

Jan. 24, Government of Tripoli and Cyrenaica combined as 2 districts

June 13, Submission of rebel chiefs in Cyrenaica

1930

Jan. 7, Italian Decree law of Oct. 10, 1929 as to exemption of large families from taxation extended to Tripoli

Jan. 24, Murzuk reoccupied by Italians, advance of 300 kilos Jan. 6–24

Feb. 24, Ghat reoccupied, advance of 450 kilos, Jan. 25–Feb. 24

Feb. 26, Announcement that Italians had completed occupation of Fezzan to include the entire hinterland

Dec. 9, By occupation of Brach oasis and subjugation of 3 tribes in the district Italians controlled the country inland nearly 400 miles from the coast

MADAGASCAR

Madagascar, French Colony, island in the Indian Ocean, is situated to the south-east coast of Africa, from which it is separated by the Mozambique Channel, the least distance between island and continent being 240 miles; its length is 980 miles; greatest breadth, 360 miles, and it has a coast line of over 3,000 miles. The area is estimated at 241,094 square miles. According to the last census (1926) the population (including that of the Mayotte and Comoro islands) was 3,621,342 (15.0 per sq. mile), of whom 3,591,943 were Malagasy, 18,040 were French and 11,359 foreigners, including Europeans and others. The populations of the chief towns were, in 1926, the capital, Antanànarìvo, in the center of the island, 70,847 (3,648 French and 601 foreigners); Tamatave, 15,022; Fianarantsoa, 11,156; Antsirabe, 19,130; Majunga, 16,570; Diégo Suarez, 8,604; Tulear, 7,780; Mananjary, 12,013; Saint-Marie, 8,127; Nosy-Be, 14,022. The principal ports are Tamatave, on the east coast, Majungà on the north-west coast, Diégo Suarez in the north, and Tulear in the south-west.

In 1896, Diégo-Suarez (a French colony from 1885), the island of Noss Bé (area 130 sq. miles) on the west coast, and the island of Ste. Marie on the east coast (area 64 sq. miles), and in 1914 the Comoro Islands, were placed under the authority of the Governor-General of Madagascar. By decree of Nov. 11, 1924 the islands of St. Paul, Amsterdam, and Kerguélen made dependencies of Madagascar.

The last native sovereign of Madagascar, Rànavàlona III (born 1861, died 1916), succeeded in 1883. The French having claimed a portion of the north-west coast as having been transferred to them by local chiefs, hostilities were carried on in 1882–84 against the Hovas, who refused to recognize the cession. In 1885 peace was made, Diégo Suarez having been surrendered to France. A French Resident General was received at the capital, and the foreign relations of the country were claimed to be regulated by France. The Native Government having refused to carry out the clauses of the treaty of 1885, a French expedition was despatched in May, 1895, to enforce the claims of France, and on October 1, the capital having been occupied, a treaty was signed whereby the Queen recognized and accepted the protectorate. By a unilateral convention made in January, 1896, Madagascar became a French possession, and by law promulgated August 6, 1896, the island and its dependencies were declared a French colony.

Leon Cayla, Governor General, appointed February 10, 1930.

1548 to 1669

1548, Portuguese settlement; destroyed by the French one, 1642, on arrival of a French governor, 1669

1750

July 30, Cession of Island of Sainte Marie to the French; possession retaken Oct. 15, 1818

1774

The French attempted to settle at Antongel-bay

1786

May 23, Count Benyowski supreme in the island, Oct., 1775, killed in an encounter with the French

1810–1811

Their establishment at Fort Dauphin fell into the hands of the English with Bourbon and Mauritius

1818

Nov. 4, The French reoccupied Port of Tintingue and region between Cape Bellone and the Azaphe River
The settlements ceded to King Radàma, on his giving up the slave trade

1819

Aug. 1, The French reoccupied Fort Dauphin

1828

Radàma I, King 1810, who favored Europeans and encouraged Christianity, died

1835

A reactionary policy under his energetic queen Rànavàlona, 1828. The English missionaries who came in 1820 obliged to depart

1840

July 14, Cession to France of territory on west coast and of Islands of Nossi Bé and Nossi Comba, possession taken Feb. 3, 1841

1841

March 5, Cession to France of Ankara and dependent Islands, and of Nossi-Mitsion (Ankara)

1845

June, The application of the native laws to the European settlers occasioned an unsuccessful attack on the town of Tamatave, by a united expedition from the English at the Mauritius, and the French from the isle of Bourbon

1846 et seq.

All amicable intercourse ceases, the native Christians suffer persecution

1855

Oct. 19, The French defeated in an attack on the island

1857

June, Conspiracy against the Queen frustrated

1859

Feb. 26, Convention by which Chiefs on West Coast accepted French Protectorate, Mahafales, Aug. 10, the Sakalavas of the Féhéréna Province, Aug. 19

1861

Aug. 23, The Queen dies; succeeded by her son, Radàma II, a Christian

1862

Sept. 12, Treaty with Great Britain and France signed

1863

May, A revolution; the King and his ministers assassinated; the Queen Rasohérina proclaimed sovereign
Nov., Disputes with the French

1866

July 5, Treaty with Great Britain; Christians to be tolerated, &c., June 27, 1865; ratified

1868

April 1, The Queen died in March; her cousin, Rànavàlona II, succeeded as Queen
Aug. 8, Treaty of friendship and commerce with France signed

1872

Dec., Dr. Henry Rowley was consecrated Bishop of Madagascar; Dr. R. Kestell-Cornish, 1874

1873 to 1879

1873, African slavery prohibited; and June, 1877
1879 et seq., Disputes with the French begin respecting land given to Laborde, a missionary, reclaimed by the Hovas; aggressive insolent conduct of French consuls, Cassas, Meyer, and Baudais

1882

July, Aug., The French claim protectorate of part of N.W. Madagascar, by virtue of a treaty made with rebel chiefs, 1840–41; on appeal the British Government correspond with the French ministry

Oct., Native embassy to France objecting to French protectorate, &c.

Nov., The French Government unyielding; the envoys come to London; received by Earl Granville, Dec. 2, by the Queen Dec. 12

1883

Feb., Friendly modification of the treaty of 1868 with England

Feb. 23, Arrival of French war vessels in Madagascar

March 14, Treaty with the United States ratified

May 15, Treaty with Germany

May 24, Admiral Pierre bombards and seizes the custom-house at Majunga; Adm. Pierre bombards Tamatave, unresisting, June 11, captures it, June 13

June 13, French ultimatum, offered and rejected

Adm. Pierre reports repulse of two night-attacks on June 22 and July 5

July, The Queen Rànavàlona II dies about July 13; succeeded by her niece Rànavàlona III

Aug., Tenoarivo destroyed; state of siege at Tamatave; Adm. Pierre orders the British consul T. C. Pakenham (ill) to quit within 24 hours, who dies, June 22. Mr. Shaw, missionary, arrested; Capt. Johnson of H.M.S. *Dryad* insulted; the British Government demands explanations, July 12, satisfaction ordered to be given

Aug. 7, Release of Mr. Shaw about

Sept. 6, The Hovas retake French posts, except Majunga, announced

Sept. 10, Adm. Pierre dies

Sept. 27, Mr. Shaw at Exeter Hall, describes his arrest, false charges against him, cruel usage, and abrupt release

Sept., Great mortality among French troops

Oct. 29, 1,000*l*. awarded to Mr. Shaw, and apology made to the British Government by the French

Nov., Much British property destroyed

1884

Jan., French demand raised, by M. Baudais

March 27, The French chambers vote to support French honor in Madagascar (450–32)

June 27, French attack on the Hova camp repulsed

Aug., Two blue-books published by the Hova government giving the history of the disputes with the French, 1879–84

Aug., Desultory warfare and negotiations reported, French settlements in progress at Majunga, &c.; the Hovas prepare for war

Sept. 22, The French bombard Mahanoro

Nov., Mr. T. Wilkinson, missionary and trader, expelled from Antananarivo for newspaper correspondence

Dec. 2, The Hovas severely defeated

Dec. 6–11, The French take forts after sharp conflict

1885

Jan., Seven French ships of war at Tamatave, the Hovas retreating inland

June 13–Aug. 17, Negotiations for peace fail; French protectorate rejected

July–Aug., French chambers vote for maintaining of *status quo*

Sept. 10, Unsuccessful French attack on the Malagasy position near Tamatave

Sept. 28, Another conflict (undecisive) announced

Dec. 17, Treaty signed conceding partial French control on foreign affairs; 400,000*l*. as compensation for local injuries, &c., by the agency of Adm. Miot; ratified by French Senate, March 13, 1886

1886

M. le Myre de Vilers, first French resident, April

1887 to 1890

Jan. 25, 1887, Tamatave evacuated by the French, reoccupied by the natives

Oct., 1889, Prosperity of the island reported

Aug. 5, 1890, French protectorate recognized by Great Britain

1891

Jan. 9, Massacre of about 200 complaining natives, by the governor of Belanona, reported

March 24, The governor and his brother tried and executed, reported

March 28, Insurrection in the Comoro Islands (near Madagascar), ruled by Arab chiefs under French protection; massacres and exactions. Prince Salim refuses to negotiate with Dr. Ormières, the French resident, reported

April 3, The residents take refuge in the ships; slaves hold the town in Johanna Island, reported

Oct. 30, Murder of Dr. Beziat, chief of the French medical staff, reported

1893

Aug., M. Georges Muller, French explorer, shot by brigands near Mandritsara

Dec. 24, Conflicts between the French and the Hovas, reported

1894

July-Aug., Exploring expedition of Prince Henri d'Orleans and M. de Grandmaison

Oct. 3, Partial blockade of the ports by the French, reported

Nov. 2, Arrival of M. le Myre de Vilers at Tamatave; his ultimatum rejected by the Hova government, reported, Nov. 5; diplomatic rupture, Nov. 10; Tamatave deserted by the Hovas, Nov. 14

Dec. 10, Tamatave occupied by the French

——, The Queen accepts the conditions of the French

Dec. 25, Murder of Mr. Sornay, a British subject

Dec. 28, Defeat of the Hovas at Farafatra

1895

Jan. 16, Majunga bombarded and occupied by the French

Jan. 20, M. le Myre de Vilers, dissatisfied with the Queen's concessions, leaves, Dec. 27, 1894; arrives at Marseilles

Feb. 14, Nossi-Vey, island, S.W. coast, taken by the French

April 3, Gen. Metzinger storms Miadane, the Hovas fled

April 20, Mr. Waller, formerly U.S. consul at Tamatave, imprisoned by French for aiding the Hovas; U.S. government protests; he arrives at Marseilles (released, March 19, 1896)

April 21, The French occupy Ambommarine after severe fighting, reported

April 25, Murder of M. Grève, naturalist, by the Hovas, reported

May 2, Marovoay stormed by Gen. Metzinger; much slaughter; flight of the Hovas

May 6, Gen. Duchesne, commander-in-chief, arrives at Majunga

May 19 *et seq.*, Defeat of the Hovas; successful advance of the French, reported

May 21, Great mortality amongst the French from fever, reported

July 12, Mevatanana occupied without resistance

July 22, Bridge over the Betsiboka completed; 300 ft. long

Aug.–Sept., Capture of Andriba by Gen. Duchesne, Aug. 22; slow advance of the French; the Hova government apparently incapable of preparing for defense or surrender; many French soldiers invalided and dying

Sept. 15, The Hovas defeated with great loss at Tsinainondry by Gen. Duchesne

Sept. 30, Antananarivo, the capital, bombarded and captured by Gen. Duchesne; flight of the Queen and court; treaty of peace ratified by the Queen, Oct. 1; she accepts the French protectorate, and is reinstated; the Prime Minister arrested, Oct. 4; Gen. Metzinger appointed governor, Oct. 10

Oct. 10, Hova works at Farafatra captured

Nov. 6, The Queen holds an assembly, announcing the peace

Nov. 23, Rebels defeated with much loss

Nov., Estimated French loss during the campaign by disease, 3,500

Dec. 1, M. Laroche appointed resident-general

Dec. 11, Administrative Council established

Dec. 28 and June 6, 1896, Native justice organized

1896

Jan., Tribal risings against the Hovas

April, Skirmishes with the French

May, Several pioneer explorers murdered by brigands

About June 4, Antsirabo burnt by rebels, 3 days' siege of the Norwegian mission raised by M. Allez, rebel loss 200

Aug. 6, Madagascar made a French Colony

Sept. 27, Slavery abolished

Sept. 28, M. Laroche recalled; Gen. Gallieni appointed Governor-Gen. and commander-in-chief, arrives

Oct 5, and Nov. 11, Circulars of the Governor General organized education in the Colony

Oct. 30, Prince Ratsimananga (the Queen's uncle) and the ex-Governor of Tamatave, tried and executed for rebellion at Antananarivo

1897

Feb. 28, The Queen deposed by General Gallieni

March 7, The Queen exiled to Réunion (later leaves for Algeria)

Abt. June 10, Two French Protestant missionaries massacred in Ankaratra

Oct., Skirmish on the Tsiribihina, 3 officers and others killed

1898

Mid Jan., Siege raised at Imerina and Betsiloe

Feb. 22, Natives repulsed with loss by the French at Ambiky

July 9, Lord Salisbury protests against the abolition of the rights of British commerce

Nov., Mutiny of soldiers, Andjia plundered; they are disarmed and sent back to Diego Suares

Nov., Concessions demanded by Mr. Waller (*see above*), Feb., 1895; refused by the French

Nov. 24, Decree reorganized native justice, tribunals of first and second degree established and Court of Appeals

1899

June 24, 25, Rising at Ikongo, rebel position captured

1901

Jan. 1, System of forced labor in the public service abolished

Oct.–mid Nov., Successful operations against rebels in the south

1904

April 8, In Anglo-French Treaty Great Britain withdrew protests against French customs régime

1908

April 9, Decree attached Mayotte and Comoro Islands to Madagascar

1926

Jan. 13, Decree reorganized native administration

1928

July 11, Decree reorganized education

MAURETANIA

Mauretania, French Colony in West Africa north of Senegal, bounded on the west by the Atlantic Ocean and the Spanish Colony of Rio de Oro, on the east by the French Sudan, boundaries to the north towards the Sahara indefinite. The name of the ancient Roman colony of north-west Africa was revived for official designation of the country.

Mauritania, formed into a Protectorate in May, 1903, converted into a special "Civilian Territory" in October, 1904, became a Colony on January 1, 1921, with a Lieutenant-Governor at its head. It consists of the districts of Trarza, Brakna, Gorgol, Assaba, Guidimaka, Adrar, Levrier Bay, and Tagant, with a total area of 347,400 square miles. The native population numbers 296,516, mostly Moorish Mussulmans. European population about 300.

1717

Jan. 15, André Brue made Treaty with Eli Chandara which confirmed the French in the possession of Portendik (Njeil) on the coast

1773

May 5, Treaty with chiefs of Arguin Island ceding Portendik

1828

Explorations of René Caille

MAURETANIA

1837

Nov. 1, Treaty of Governor Faidherbe of Senegal with Bakar, king of Idouaichs (Maures)

1860

Dec. 9, The Mage mission left Bakel and arrived in country of Bakar on the 23d, and Jan. 22, 1861 at Matam

1900

June 6, Mission of Paul Blanchet reached Atar, the capital of Adrar (T-Marr) and was kept a prisoner until ransomed

June 27, Boundary Treaty between France and Spain, the Sebkha d'Idjil added

1902

Dec. 12, Coppolani sent to establish French authority among the Maures (Traza, Brakna, Adrar) arrived at Dagana and began negotiations with Ahmet Saloum who accepted French suzerainty

1903

May 12, Decree organized the Protectorate of Mauretania

June, Coppolani received submission of chief at Brakna and established post at Aleg

1904

Oct. 18, Mauretania organized into a Civil Territory and Brakna occupied

Nov. 26, Coppolani appointed Commissioner

Dec. 18, Decree placed Mauretania under Government of French West Africa

1905

Feb. 24, Coppolani arrived at Ksar-el-Bakar and April 2 at Tidjika

Feb. 25, Boundary with Senegal fixed

May 12, Coppolani assassinated by a native at Tidjika Oases. Succeeded as Commissioner by Lieutenant Colonel Montané-Capdeboscq

1906

Oct. 24, Captain Tissot ordered to evacuate the country by Moulai Idris and defeated in battle at Tidjika

1908

March 16–Dec. 6, In this period the French attacked 125 times by natives, 142 killed including 8 officers

Dec.–Oct., 1909, Campaign of Colonel Goureaud for occupation of Adrar

1909

Jan. 9, Expedition of Colonel Gouraud captured Atar, chief center of Adrar

Aug. 15, Natives defeated in engagement at Turine, 2,000 camels captured by French

1910

Jan. 1, Lieutenant Colonel Patey appointed Commissioner of Mauretania

1912

Nov. 27, Boundary Convention of France and Spain fixed frontier

1918

Jan. 14, Decree organized native justice

1919

Jan. 22, Submission of chiefs to the French

Aug. 9, Colonel Gaden named Commissioner

1920

Dec. 4, Decree made Mauretania a Colony to take effect Jan. 1, 1921, with a Lieutenant Governor at the head and Council of Administration

1924

March 22, Decree established courts of first and second degree for native justice

MAURITIUS

Mauritius, British Colony, island in the Indian Ocean 500 miles east of Madagascar, has an area of about 720 square miles, population including dependencies 8,394, (census 1921) 385,074. The estimated population at the end of 1928 was 404,802. The dependencies are Rodrigues, island with area of 42 square miles, 18 miles long by 7 miles broad, about 350 miles east of Mauritius; and Diego Garcia, the most important of the Oil Islands Group, 12½ miles along, and 6¼ miles wide, with 445 inhabitants (census of 1921).

The Lesser Dependencies are Diego Garcia, Six Islands, Peros Banhos, Solomon Islands, Agalega, St. Brandon Group, Trois Freres. The nearest island is 230 miles from Mauritius, and the most remote about 1,200 miles. Total population of the lesser dependencies, census 1921, 1,810 (1,038 males, 772 females).

Mauritius was discovered by the Portuguese early in the 16th century, but the Dutch were the first settlers. In 1710 they abandoned the island and it was occupied by the French under the name of Isle de France. The British occupied the island in 1810, and it was formally ceded to Great Britain by the Treaty of Paris of 1814.

W. E. Francis, Governor.

MAYOTTE

See Comoro Islands

MOROCCO

Morocco (Moghreb-el-Aksa, *i.e.*, The Farthest West). The Empire of Morocco is in principle an absolute monarchy, in which the Sultan exercises supreme civil and religious authority; the latter in his capacity of Emir-el-Muminin or Commander of the Faithful. The majority of his subjects are Sunni Moslems of the Malekite school, the teachings of which formerly constituted the common law of Morocco. The country is now, however, divided into three Zones, in each of which a different system of government prevails as the outcome of the Protectorate Treaty concluded between

France and the Sultan at Fez on March 30, 1912, the subsequent Convention between France and Spain of November 27, 1912, and the Convention between Great Britain, France, and Spain of December 18, 1923 (modified July 25, 1928), providing for a special Statute in the Tangier Zone.

The French Zone comprises the whole of Morocco (except the Ifni enclave and the Cape Juby area) from the Atlantic to the Algerian frontier, and from the confines of the Sahara to the boundary of the Spanish Zone as agreed to in 1912. The Franco-Spanish boundary has not been fully delimited. It follows a generally eastern direction from a point on the Atlantic about 16 miles south of Larache to the river Moulouya, which completes the boundary to the Mediterranean. The Spanish Zone comprises the area between this line and the sea, with the exception of the small territory around Tangier which is included in the international zone.

Ifni was ceded to Spain by Morocco in 1860. By the Franco-Spanish agreement of 1912 it extends along the West Coast of Morocco to the north of Wadi Draa, from Wad Nun on the south to Wad Bu Sedra on the north, and a distance of 15 miles inland from the coast. The occupation is purely nominal. Area, 965 square miles, population, 20,000. There are several small harbors and villages; the population is engaged in fishing. The southern and eastern boundaries of Morocco being largely indeterminate, no exact estimate can be made of the total area, but it may be estimated as follows:—

French Zone approximately 200,000 square miles.
Spanish Zone   "   18,300   "   "
Tangier Zone   "   225   "   "
                         ─────────
            Total   218,525

A census of the French Zone taken in March, 1926, puts the population at 4,016,882 native Moslems, 107,552 native Jews, and 104,712 foreigners; total 4,229,146. That of the Spanish Zone may be put at something under 1,000,000, and that of the Tangier Zone at about 80,000.

The introduction of Islam into Morocco about the end of the 7th century was followed by an exceedingly confused period, to the latter part of which belongs the great Arab influx of the 11th century known as the Hilalian invasion. This period witnessed the rise and fall of various Arab and Berber dynasties, notably the Idrissids, under whom Fez was founded or refounded early in the 9th century, and the Almoravids, the first of whom, Youssef Ben Tashfin, founded Marrakesh in 1062, and later extended his power over the north of Morocco and into Spain. His dynasty was followed by the Almohads (12th and 13th centuries), and the Merinids (13th to 16th centuries), whose decline led up to the establishment of the Sherifian

dynasties, the Saadians (16th and 17th centuries) and the Alaouis. The latter claim descent from Ali, the son-in-law of the Prophet, through the Filali Sherifs of Tafilelt. The present Sultan is the 18th of this dynasty.

Ceuta, captured by King John I of Portugal in 1415 came into possession of Spain in 1580, limits defined by treaties between Spain and Morocco of Aug. 25, 1844 confirmed Oct. 7, May 6, 1845, and April 26, 1860 which greatly enlarged limits; boundary with Algeria fixed by Treaty of Sept. 10, 1844. Melilla was conquered by Spain in 1470 and boundaries established by treaties of Aug. 24, 1859, April 26, 1860, Oct. 30, 1861, and June 26, 1862.

Sidi Mohammed, Sultan.

1578

Aug. 4, Invasion of Sebastian of Portugal, who perishes with his army at the battle of Alcazar

1683

Tangiers acquired by England, 1662; given up

1786

June 28 and July 15, Treaty of peace and friendship with the United States signed and again Sept. 16, 1836

1844

Aug. 6, The Moors attack the French in Algeria at the instigation of Abd-el-Kader; the Prince de Joinville bombards Tangiers, and Mogador, Aug. 16
Aug. 14, Marshal Bugeaud defeats the Moors at the river Isly, and acquires the title of Duke
Sept. 10, Peace between France and Morocco

1859

Oct. 22, The Spaniards, who possess several places on the coast of Morocco (Ceuta, Penon de Velez, &c.), having suffered much annoyance by Moorish pirates, declare war. *See* Spain

1860

June–Aug., A Moorish ambassador (the first since the time of Charles II) in London

1861

Oct. 24, The British government gave a guarantee for a loan of 426,000*l.* to the Sultan to meet his engagements with Spain

1873

Dec., Insurrection of a pretender, Elkadin ben Abderahman, suppressed

1877

Aug., Prince Sidi Shereef visits Britain

1880

July 3, Convention of Madrid signed by the Powers European and the United States for protection in Morocco, "open door" established

1884

Jan., The Grand Shereef of Wazan marries an English wife; liberates his slaves, &c.; persecuted, becomes a French subject

1888

June 25, The rebel tribes of Benin Guild district defeated after a severe engagement

1890

Sept. 26, The sultan defeats rebel tribes, and beheads 80 prisoners, reported Aug. 20; further defeats of the rebels reported

1892

About Jan. 5, Hostility of the Kabyles and other tribes to the governor; two British war-vessels arrive off Tangier; 3 foreign vessels arrive, Jan. 13

Jan. 22, Tranquillity restored by the Sultan dismissing the governor, and appointing a successor

July 22 et seq., The British Minister's (Sir C. Euan Smith), negotiations for a commercial treaty fail; the mission withdraws to Tangier

Oct. 26, Rebellion of 1,200 Angherites, or Anjerites, headed by Hmam, a desperate fanatic (chiefly against the governor), near Tangier, about July 27; the Angherites defeated after severe fighting; they sue for peace, Sept. 4; a new governor appointed, Sept. 13; peace proclaimed, Sept. 16; agreement signed

Dec. 5, A French mission, under Count d'Aubigny, arrives at Fez, Oct. 4; departs, having obtained some concessions

1893

Feb. 24, Reappearance of Ould Hmam in Anghera; fresh outrages, about Jan. 22, he is captured and taken to Tangier, reported

July 9, The mountaineers enter Wazan, and are subdued with much slaughter, reported Feb. 20, again

Oct. 2, About 7,000 Moors (Riff tribe) attack Fort Guaraich, near Ceuta, held by 300 Spanish troops, severe fighting, the Moors repulsed

Oct. 21, The Moors driven from their entrenchments

Nov. 9, The Spaniards repulsed, Oct. 27; General Margallo killed, his body and cannon recovered, Spanish loss 22 killed and 81 wounded, Oct. 28; General Macias appointed to the command, Oct. 29; skirmishes, Nov. 3; the Sultan condemns the action of the tribesmen and threatens punishment, reported

Nov., Reinforcements sent from Spain

Nov. 28, Marshal Campos takes the command

Dec. 7, Terms of peace proposed by Marshal Campos to the tribes

Dec. 27, Moorish concessions, two chiefs surrendered

1894

About Feb. 3, Arrival of Moorish troops at Melilla, to punish the Riff tribes, &c.

June 11, Death of Sultan Muley Hassan, June 7; son, Muley Abdul Aziz, succeeds

1895

Feb., Spanish claims acceded to (792,000l.), March 10, 1894; treaty completed

April 20, British mission warmly received at Fez by the Sultan, Oct. 29, 1894; retires successful

Nov. 7–11, Arab rebellion, Saffi attacked, severe fighting

1898

Jan. et seq., The Sultan marches with about 60,000 men to awe the Riffians and disaffected districts, Sept. 16; rebels defeated at Tadla, Oct., 1897; rebels and prisoners treated with great cruelty

July 2, Trial of Mr. Gray and the crew of the British steamer Tourmaline for alleged attempt to smuggle arms into Sus, begins at Tangier, June 14; all sentenced to short terms of imprisonment

[Major Spilsbury tried and acquitted at Gibraltar, April 19, 1899]

1899

Jan. 3, Indemnity paid to the Portuguese and Italian Governments for Riffian piracy (1898)

Dec., 1898–March 22, Tribal fighting on the frontier, great slaughter

April 28, Kaid Gilooli's troops attack Sus and loot European property; estimated loss, 20,000l., reported

1900

May 13, Sid Ahmed Ben Musa, Grand Vizier and stern ruler, dies

June 9, The Moorish Government protests against French encroachments upon Twat and Igli as a violation of the frontier treaty of 1845 (see Algeria 1900), and asks for arbitration

June 28, Great excitement at Fez owing to the French occupation of the Twat oases; M. Marcos Essagin murdered by the mob

Aug. 20, The Powers appealed to

1901

July 20, A modus vivendi with France regarding the Algerian frontier settled as to regulation of trade and police

Sept., Free trade between the coast towns (due to Lord Lansdowne) instituted

1902

Nov. 3, Rebels, under Omar Zarhuni "Bu Hamara," pretender to the throne, defeated near Tesa

Dec. 9, Several skirmishes: the Sultan is defeated at Tesa, Nov. 29; the pretender holds Tesa and surrounding districts

Dec. 22, Rout of the Sultan's army, 17 guns captured, near Tesa

1903

Jan. 4, The Sultan holds Fez, Dec. 23; many tribes return and swear fealty, reported

Jan. 19, Feb. 14, 15, Skirmishing in the Fez district, many rebels killed and captured

Jan. 27, French loan of 7,500,000 francs

April 3, The Sultan's brother, Mulai Mohammed, proclaimed Sultan by the Riff tribes

April 13, Fort Trajana captured by the rebels

May 7, Defeat of the Sultan's troops at Zelwan

May 16, Tetuan attacked, suburbs destroyed, May 11; fort of Tesa captured, villages pillaged and burnt; Teutan relieved, reported

May 26, Heavy loss of Sultan's troops near Rebat

June 8, Zenaga bombarded by the French

July 7, Tesa recovered from rebels by El Menebhi

July 21, Rebel villages near Tangier burnt by the Sultan's troops

Aug. 13, Severe fighting, Aug. 6, 7; the rebel forces under Mulai Mohammed routed at Meknessa; other successes by Sultan's troops, reported

Aug. 28, Troops defeated with loss near Tesa, reported

Sept. 18, Sultan orders all Europeans except the consuls to leave Fez

Early Oct., Pourparlers between England and France

respecting the guarantee of the *status quo* in Morocco, by agreement with the other powers, leaving the solution of affairs to France, interrupted by British ministerial crisis; no agreement arrived at by the Powers, reported

Oct. 12, Troops commanded by the Sultan in person, severely repulsed by the rebels

Oct. 28, Sultan abandons his expedition against the rebels, which has proved a failure, Sultan returning to Fez; the road to Fez blocked by the rebels; general state of anarchy, reported

Dec. 1, Outrages on the Jews by government troops on reoccupation of Tesa, reported

1904

April 8, The tranquillity of the country, giving assistance with a view to its financial and military reform, entrusted to France by the Anglo-French agreement

May, French Government successful in arranging an amalgamation of the rival French syndicates offering a loan to the Sultan

May 18, Mr. Perdicaris, an American citizen and a wealthy resident of Tangier, and his stepson, Mr. Vorley, a British subject, carried off by the brigand Raisuli from the suburbs of Tangier

May, American and British men-of-war sent to Tangier to enforce the demands of the two governments for the release of the captives

June 24, Raisuli offers to release his prisoners on condition that he should receive a ransom of 11,000*l.*, and that the Sultan should dismiss the governor of Tangier, and release all Raisuli's tribesmen in prison. Sultan having agreed to these terms, the governor is dismissed by royal edict, June 8; the captives released

July 31, Confiscation by the Sultan of the property of the ex-Minister of War, El Menebhi, a British protected subject

Aug. 1, British demand for the return of El Menebhi's property made to the Sultan

Aug. 3, Moorish guards fire on a boat's crew of sailors from a French warship at Tangier

Aug. 15, Moorish Government refuses to recognize El Menebhi as a protected British subject. British cruiser *Minerva* arrives at Tangier

Sept. 23, Military posts established by the French on the undefined frontier of southern Morocco

Oct. 3, Treaty between France and Spain in regard to Mocecco, a sphere of influence on the Riff littoral, including Tetuan and Tangier, conceded to Spain, that country agreeing not to extend her fortifications on the N. Atlantic, nor to cede her Moorish territory to any other power than France, signed

Mid Dec., Daily outrages by brigands reported to be occurring under the very flags of the foreign legations at Tangier; Sultan notifies officially to the respective legations his intention to dismiss all the foreign officers and non-commissioned officers attached to the Moorish court and army, including Sir Harry Maclean, Major Ogilvy, and 2 British non-commissioned officers

Dec. 24, French minister recalls the French military mission and residents from Fez; British consul and all British subjects also recalled

Dec. 25, Extortions of the governor of Tangier stated to be driving the local tribes to Raisuli for the settlement of their affairs; Raisuli appoints a sheikh over a district extending to the walls of Tangier

1905

Early Jan., Case of El Menebhi reported to be settled on satisfactory terms. Sultan intimates his desire to accept the advice and assistance of France; French mission to proceed to Fez

Jan. 6, Serious defeat of the Sultan's troops by the pretender near Ujda, reported

Mid March, Return of the French Minister from Fez in consequence of the failure of the negotiations. Sultan demands an explanation of French aggressions in Twat and Figig

March 29, Count von Bülow, Imperial Chancellor, in the German Reichstag, says that Germany, aiming at the maintenance of an open door in Morocco, intended to open communication with Sultan

——, Sir Harry Maclean appointed to the supreme command of the Tangier troops; Raisuli appointed governor of the local tribes

March 31, Visit of the German Emperor to Tangier; he informs the Sultan's representatives that he would maintain the absolute equality of German economic and commercial rights, and would insist on always carrying on her affairs direct with the Sultan

April 9, Sanguinary encounter between the troops of the Maghzen and Bu Amama, the capture of Ujda being the pretender's object; government troops in a critical situation are saved by the intervention of the frontier section of the French military mission, who sweep back the rebels

April, Sultan stated to be desirous that Germany should send a special mission to Fez to negotiate a new treaty of commerce and discuss the best means of procuring a European convention and international guarantees for the integrity of Morocco

April 14, Discussion of details and working of the reforms included in M. Saint-René Taillandier's program progressing rapidly; attitude of the maghzen reported satisfactory

Mid April, Punitive force of government troops attack the Sahal district, and burn villages, and take many prisoners

May 2, French cableship *Charente* completes the laying of the cable from Cadiz to Tangier, provided for by the Franco-Spanish convention

——, German mission leaves Tangier for Fez; German Minister states that he has no proposals to submit to the Sultan for a commercial convention

May 13, The maghzen declined all the proposals of the French mission on the ground that they are incompatible with existing international treaties; the maghzen only consents to the formation of a special force of 2,000 Moorish soldiers, under French military instructors, for the defence of the frontier, dated

May 20, British mission leaves for Fez

——, Count von Tattenbach informs the maghzen that German financiers would be prepared to grant a considerable loan to Morocco at a very low rate of interest, reported

May 28, Sultan definitely signs the rejection of the French demands, and states that the assembly of Moorish notables declare that they will allow no reform to be carried out by any one foreign power unless such reforms have been previously discussed by an international conference at Tangier

June 3, Sultan's invitation, dated May 30, to the European representatives to hold a conference, delivered at the foreign legations

June 6, Mr. Lowther, British Minister, enters Fez, and meets with a very cordial reception, May 31; is received in private audience by the Sultan, and hands the Sultan a number of presents, including a sword of honor

June, Mr. Daniel Madden, an Englishman living at Mazagan, acting as Austrian and Danish vice-consul, murdered by the Moors

June 8, Mr. Lowther presents Great Britain's reply to the Sultan's invitation to take part in a conference, giving a categorical refusal

[Germany notified her acceptance; Austria accepted, with the proviso that such acceptance depended upon the action of the other great powers; the United States declined to take part unless Great Britain also agreed; France refused.]

Early June, Sultan grants a concession to a German firm for the construction of a port at Tangier

July 9, Battle between the Sultan's troops and those of the pretender near Ujda; rebel forces put to flight

July 10, Franco-German *pourparlers* as to the proposed conference, after passing an acute stage, result in an agreement between the two governments on the subject; announcement to this effect made by M. Rouvier in the French Chamber

Aug. 2, A second French note, giving details of the French program for the conference, handed to the German Ambassador in Paris

Aug. 5, Memorandum presented to Prince Radolin sets forth the program of police and financial reforms which France regards as necessary for Morocco

Aug. 26, German reply to French draft program of the conference handed by M. Rouvier to the German Ambassador in Paris

Mid Sept., Representatives of the Powers at Tangier demand that steps shall be taken by the government to ensure the security of Europeans living in that town and its suburbs

Sept. 28, Franco-German agreement signed: text of draft program of the proposed conference consists of 4 clauses; clause I relates to police organization, to be settled outside the frontier regions by international agreement, and within those regions by France and Morocco exclusively; clause II suggests financial reform by means of a state bank; clause III proposes investigation as to a better result of taxation, and the creation of new revenues; clause IV lays down the principles that the maghzen should engage not to pledge any of the public services for the benefit of private interests, and that public works shall be tendered for without distinction of nationality

Oct. 4, Contract for a German advance of 10,000,000 marks (500,000*l.*) signed by the maghzen

Oct. 16, H.M. torpedo-boat destroyer *Cherwell* fired upon by Moors from the coast between Ceuta and Ceres

Oct. 17, Capt. J. E. Crowther and Lieut. E. A. S. Hatton of the marines, H.M. battleship *Victorious*, captured by Anjera tribesmen, relatives of the famous brigand Valiente, on their way to Ceuta. Special couriers sent by Mohammed el Torres, the Sultan's representative for foreign affairs, to open negotiations with their captors. Brigands demand the release of Valiente, imprisoned by order of the Spanish Government, as the condition of the release of the two officers

Oct. 26, The British officers released by the Anjera brigands in exchange for the chief Valiente

Oct., French and German Ministers present identical notes regarding the program of the proposed conference to the Sultan and maghzen, which the Sultan accepts

1906

Jan. 16, International conference meets at Algeciras, the Duke of Almodovar, representative of Spain, elected president; conference reaches an agreement on all points, including the police and bank questions· international agreement signed, April 7

April 19, A number of Raisuli's followers stormed an burned the house of an Anjera tribesman in Tangic

May, Anti-foreign riots at Sud-Oranais, Tafilet, an Mogador and murder of M. Charbonnier in Tangier for which Moorish Government accepted full responsibility

June 3, Signor Malmusi, with the Italian mission, bearing the protocol of the Algeciras conference, arrives at Fez

June 18, Sultan signs the protocol, by which he accepts and ratifies in its entirety the general acts of the Algeciras conference

Aug. 15, Arrival of the French northern squadron at Tangier

Sept. 7, Raid of the Berber chief Anflus on the city of Mogador, reported

Sept. 18, Followers of Maclain, a fanatical sorcerer from the Sahara, looted a French store, wounded several Europeans, and attempted to incite the inhabitants against Christians

Oct. 20, Arzila, a walled town on the Atlantic coast, about 25 miles from Tangier, captured by the mountain tribesmen of Beni Arros

Oct. 26, At the request of the Sultan's representative for foreign affairs, Raisuli restores order in Arzila, and establishes himself at the governor's house

Oct. 27, Defeat of the pretender's troops reported from Melilla

Oct. 29, Anjera tribesmen, taking advantage of Raisuli's absence at Arzila, pillage villages on the east side of Tangier

Nov. 5, Arrival of the French cruiser *Jeanne d'Arc* and the Spanish cruiser *Princesa de Asturias*

——, Bluejackets of the French cruiser *Galilée* assaulted by Moorish boatmen on their arrival at Tangier

Nov. 13, Raisuli returns to his stronghold and leaves Arzila to itself

Nov. 24, Note sent by the European representatives at Tangier to the Moorish Foreign Minister at Fez, protesting against Raisuli's actions, and demanding that an end be put to the existing state of affairs at Tangier

Dec. 8, Arrival of the French squadron under Admiral Touchard

Dec. 10, Raisuli threatens a Christian massacre

Dec. 12, Spanish warships arrive off Tangier

Dec. 27, Raisuli deposed

1907

Jan. 5–6, Raisuli's stronghold attacked by the Shereefian troops; Zinat and other villages found completely deserted; escape of Raisuli to the mountains

Jan. 23, The French and Spanish squadrons sail from Tangier, each leaving a guardship

Feb. 23, The European representatives at Tangier address to the maghzen two collective notes, one calling attention to the state of anarchy which exists at Mogador, and the other pointing out that certain reforms, stipulated by the Algeciras act, have not yet been applied

March 14, Col. Müller, chosen by the Swiss Government to take control of the Franco-Spanish police, arrives at Tangier

March 19, Assassination of Dr. Mauchamp, a French doctor, residing at Marakesh, by a fanatical crowd

March 29, French expeditionary force from Oran occupies Udja (Oudjda)

May 5, *Coup d'État* at Marakesh; Mulai Hafid, brother of the Sultan and Viceroy of S. Morocco, proclaimed Sultan and accepted by the townspeople and surrounding tribes; reported

May 16, All European residents, including the British consular agent, leave Marakesh and arrive safely at the coast

July 3, Sir H. Maclean captured by Raisuli, reported

July 31, Anti-European outbreak; 5 Frenchmen, 2 Spaniards, and an Italian massacred at Casablanca

Aug. 4, Bombardment of Casablanca; number of Moors killed, 200

Aug. 18, Tribal attack on Casablanca

Aug. 21, Reinforcements despatched to Gen. Drude from Oran

Aug. 25, Proclamation of Mulai Hafid as Sultan in Marrakesh

Aug. 28, Sharp attack on a French patrol by Arabs

Sept. 3, Engagement with the Arabs; 3 officers and 8 men killed, 17 wounded; number of Arabs engaged, 8,000

Sept. 21, General Drude disperses some hundreds of Arabs concentrated at Sid Ibrahim; French losses, 2 killed, 8 wounded

Nov. 24, Defeat of Mulai Hafid; Shereefian troops occupy Mazagan, reported

Nov. 24–25, Frontier fighting between the French troops and the Beni Snassen tribe, who numbered 10,000 men; 8 French and about 1,200 Beni Snassen killed

1908

Jan. 1, Capture of the Kasbah of Mediuna by the French forces at Casablanca

Jan. 4, Mulai Hafid unanimously proclaimed Sultan at Fez

Jan. 27, Abdul Aziz releases his brother Mulai Mohammed, after 14 years' imprisonment, and nominates him to the command of such army as exists at Robat

Feb. 2, Serious engagement between a French column and a body of tribesmen near Bu Reshid; the Moors are repulsed with loss of 500 dead, but the French lose 8 killed and 50 wounded, reported

Feb. 6, Kaid Sir Harry Maclean is brought to the house of the British *chargé d'affaires* at Tangier at midnight

——, General d'Amade reports an attack on the camp at El Mekki by those of the Shawai tribes who are still unsubdued; the French casualties were 3 killed and 24 wounded

Feb. 14, Mar Chica occupied by a Spanish force

Feb. 18, Further serious fighting between the tribesmen and the French in the vicinity of Settat, and also south-east of Fedallah; in both engagements the Moors are repelled with heavy loss

Feb. 28, France decides to send reinforcements to Morocco, comprising some 4,000 men, from the garrisons of Algeria and Tunis

Feb. 29, General d'Amade reports a severe action with large bodies of the M'Draka tribe; the enemy were repulsed and pursued, sustaining considerable loss; the French losses were 13 killed and 36 wounded

March 9, General d'Amade reports the rout of two hostile Moorish tribes with heavy loss

March 11, Mulai Hafid asks for an armistice

March 25, Crew of a French trawler, 20 in number, captured by the Moors near Cape Juby, March 18, and rescued by Lord Mountmorres by means of a trick

March 29, Severe engagement with a body of hostile tribesmen, who suddenly attack a detachment of French cavalry; the French lose 8 killed and 12 wounded, reported

April 7, Settat occupied by General d'Amade

April 16, Attack on the French camp by a Moorish harka, numbering about 2,000, on the Algero-Moroccan frontier; the Moors were completely routed, leaving 125 killed; the French lost 19 killed and about 100 wounded

May 13, The policing of the Algero-Moroccan frontier taken over by the French Government; the new Shereefian police, trained by French and Spanish officers, enter on their duties

May 13–14, General Vigy routs, with considerable loss, a gathering of hostile tribesmen in the neighborhood of Bu Denib, on the Algerian frontier; the French casualties include 10 men and 3 officers killed, and 65 wounded

June 18, Mulai Hafid proclaimed Sultan at Tetuan

Aug. 23, Abdul Aziz completely defeated near Marakesh

Sept. 3, Note of German Emperor to the Powers announced intention of recognizing Mulai-el-Hafid as Sultan

Sept. 9, Mogador tendered allegiance to Mulai-el-Hafid

Sept. 14, Joint Note of France and Spain recommended recognition of Mulai-el-Hafid provided that he would recognize the Act of Algeciras, and existing treaties, assume State debts, and disavow Holy War proclaimed against Europeans

——, Note of Mulai-el-Hafid asked for recognition from the European Powers and offered to recognize Act of Algeciras and other treaties

Sept. 25, Six soldiers of the French Foreign Legation, deserters, including 3 Germans took refuge with German consul, and were forcibly taken from his protection by French troops. Germany protested and the dispute referred to the Court of Arbitration at The Hague, Nov. 24

Nov. 19, Note of the Powers presented to Mulai-el-Hafid omitted clause as to Holy War from the terms proposed

Dec. 17, Official recognition of Mulai-el-Hafid as Sultan

1909

Feb. 9, Franco-German Agreement signed by which Germany conceded "the special political interests of France" in Morocco, France promised to respect the integrity of the Sheerefian empire and to "safeguard the principle of economic equality"

April 17, Shereefian troops defeated by the Beni Mtir

May 22, Decision of Hague Court in Casablanca affair that German consul was in error to try to embark deserters not of German nationality on German steamer, and the French should have accepted the *de facto* protection of the deserters by German Consulate

June 2, Proposal of Germany that in future all concessions in Morocco should be reserved to certain French and German groups of financiers not accepted by France

June 15, Defeat of the Sultan's forces by those of the Pretender, Bu Hamora

June 17, Death of Mulai Mohammed, brother of the Sultan

June 26, Sultan's forces in engagement with those of the Pretender

Aug. 14, Submission to the Sultan by the French of plan providing for withdrawal of French troops, establishment of frontier police, liquidation of the Moroccan debt, and payment of French claims, modified by Notes of Dec. 15, 21, and 25

Aug. 25, Capture of Bu Hamora reported

1910

Feb. 18, Ultimatum presented to the Sultan demanding definite answer and acceptance of terms within 48 hours

March 4, Treaty between France and the Sultan signed, France agreeing to evacuate the Chaouia and Oudjda districts as soon as the Moroccan Government could replace them with a force trained by French military mission, the French to retain the "territory of the Doui-Menia and the Oulad-Djerir, who have accepted the jurisdiction of the general government of Algeria," and the post, Berguent, as necessary for protection of Algerian frontier, financial matters arranged

June 23, Fighting between Moors and French troops in district of Tedla

Nov. 16, Convention with Spain signed as to Spanish administration in the Riff country and the Ceuta district, and finances, officially approved by the Sultan, Dec. 23

1911

Jan. 12, Agreement with Spain for settlement of disputes

Jan. 14, French force and its commander Lieutenant Marchand massacred by Arabs

April 2, Berber tribes attacked and besieged Fez

April 26, French and native troops commanded by Major Bremond entered Fez

May 13, Spanish troops occupied Zain near Zeluan to end civil war and banditry

May 21, General Moinier with French troops occupied Fez ending investment by tribesmen of the Sultan

June 8, Surrender of Mulai el Zin to siege of French and Moroccans at Mekinez

June 9, Spanish squadron landed troops at Larache and occupied Alcazar

July 1, Germany advised France of dispatch of warship "Panther" to Agadir to protect German interests

July 4, The German cruiser "Berlin" joined the "Panther" at Agadir

Oct. 7, Spanish troops from Melilla occupied Zebuya after 10 hour battle with Riff tribesmen

Nov. 4, Franco-German Treaty by which Germany recognized French protectorate over Morocco and economic equality reaffirmed

Nov. 26, German warships recalled from Agadir

1912

March 30, Treaty of Fez signed established French Protectorate, and recognized the "special character" of Tangier, administrative reforms established

April 17, Revolt at Fez in which 13 French officers killed, 40 soldiers, and 9 civilians started by mutiny against regulations holding back part of pay of soldiers and police for rations

May 24, General Lyautey assumed office as Resident General of French Protectorate

May 26, Attack of tribesmen on Fez

Aug. 11, Mulai Hafid abdicated in favor of his brother Mulai Yusef

Aug. 16, Hamed el Hiba, new Pretender, occupied Marakesh but was not supported by the people and fled on approach of French troops

Aug. 18, Mulai Yusef proclaimed Sultan

Sept. 7, Colonel Mangin entered Marakesh after defeat of El Hiba

Nov. 27, France and Spain signed Treaty as to Tangier and Spanish zones in Morocco revising boundaries and making arrangements as to customs, railroads

1913

Jan. 13, General Brulard captured the Kasbah of Anflous on punitive expedition

Feb. 11, Spanish force commanded by General Alfau defeated Moors near Ceuta

Feb. 22–23, French post of Oued Zem attacked by Tadlas

April 7, Colonel Mangin defeated the Tadlas and entered their Kabash

April 19, Mulai El-Mehdi appointed Khalifa of the Spanish Zone

June 9–10, Colonel Mangin captured the Kabash of the Kribas

June 24, Battle at Ben Karich

July 11, Moors defeated by Spanish force near Ceuta

1914

Jan. 15–22, Russia renounced capitulations, Spain and Luxemburg, Feb. 27, Greece, May 8–21, Portugal, March 9, and other Powers in 1915 and 1916

May 8, Capture of important strategic position of Taza by French army

June, Fortress of Khenifra in the Zayan district taken by French

July 27–28, Orders for withdrawal of French regular troops for service in France

Aug. 5 and 13, Capitulation regulations abolished as to Germany and Austria-Hungary

Dec. 24, French Protectorate in Morocco recognized by Great Britain

1915–1916

Revolt of tribes around Taza and the Zayan and fighting along the Wad Waghra led by Abd el Malek and Abd es Salam and Moha u Said

1916

May, Raisuli agreed to recognize the Khalifa as the representative of the Sultan

Oct., German submarine U20 failed in attempt to land rifles at mouth of the Wad Nun

Dec. 12, General Gouraud became French Resident General ad interim while General Lyautey a member of the Briand War Cabinet

1917

March 24, El Hiba in the Sus decisively defeated at Wijan by French forces

April 7, Marshal Lyautey appointed for second term as Resident General of the French Protectorate

May 29, General Lyautey returned to Morocco

1919

Jan. 25, General Berenguer succeeded General Jordana as Spanish High Commissioner

June 28, By Treaty of Versailles Germany renounced all rights in Morocco including those of Treaty of Algeciras of 1906 and Treaty of Nov. 4, 1911

July 5, Raisuli proclaimed an outlaw by the Khalifa

July 11–13, Raisuli attacked Spanish troops in Wad Ras region near Tangier. The Spanish lost about 300 killed and 1,000 wounded

Oct. 5. Raisuli driven from entrenched position at Fondak of Ain Jedida

1920

Oct. 14, Sheshuan occupied by Spanish force

Oct. 21, Attack of Jibala tribes failed to recover Sheshuan but Spaniards lost 11 officers and 120 men in the battle

1921

Jan. 15, Anual occupied by Spanish troops commanded by General Silvestre

May 15, Inauguration of new French town of Meknes

May 30, Rifi attack and mutiny of native police force at Abaran, the Spanish officers massacred

June 1, General Silvestre occupied Mount Araban and established Spanish post

June 14, French operations against the Beni-Warain successfully concluded

July 18, Military post at Igerriben attacked by Rifi and Spanish forced to retreat leaving arms and ammunition

July 21, Fortified post of Anual attacked and captured by forces of Abd el Krim, Colonel Silvestre and his staff remaining to end of evacuation either killed or committed suicide

Aug. 1, Fez-Taza railroad connecting Morocco and Algeria opened

Aug. 5, Spanish garrisons at Nador and Zeluan surrendered to Rifis and were massacred

Aug. 11, Spanish garrison at Monte Arruit forced to surrender, General Navarro taken prisoner with a few others, the rest massacred

Aug. 16, Spanish General Sanjurjo captured Sidi Amaran

Aug. 20–27, Spanish warships bombarded the coast between Cape Tres Forcas and Alhucemas

Aug. 23, Rifis defeated by Spanish force at Melilla

Sept. 12, General Berenguer began advance against Rifis

Sept. 17, Spanish took town of Nadar

Sept. 29, Spanish and Rifis in engagement at Melilla

Oct. 14, Positions on Gurugu range taken by Spaniards

Oct. 21–Nov. 19, Attacks of Abd el Krim forces on line between Tatwan and Shifshawan

Oct. 24, Spanish reoccupied Monte Arruit

Nov. 8, Nationality Decrees of French Government declared as French citizens children of European origin born to parents who had themselves been born in Morocco; not applied to Italians. Protested by British and referred on appeal to League of Nations to Permanent Court (Oct. 3, 1922)

Nov. 22, General Sanjurjo occupied Rasmedura

Dec. 10, Council of Native Policy established

1922

Feb. 10, Company of Railroads of Morocco constituted

April 5, President Millerand of France arrived at Casa Blanca on visit

April 10, Spanish air raid on coast

May 12, Spanish occupied Tazarut evacuated by Raisuli

July 10, Resignation of General Berenguer, Spanish High Commissioner. Succeeded by General Ricardo Burguete

Aug. 20, Defeat of Spanish troops by Abd el Krim at Tifarauin

Sept. 28, Submission of Mulai Ahmed el Raisuli ended revolt against Spaniards in western Morocco

Oct. 6, Passenger and air mail service inaugurated between Casa Blanca and Oran

Dec. 26, Civilian Protectorate established in Spanish Morocco, a Civil Commissioner taking the place of the Military Commissioner

1923

Jan. 29, Spanish prisoners taken after fall of Anual and Monte Arruit in 1921 released including General Navarro; 274 of the 570 survived. Ransom of nearly £150,000 paid to Abd el Krim

Feb. 7, Tangier Convention signed provided for permanent neutralization of zone

Feb. 10, Don Luis Silvela appointed Spanish High Commissioner

April 5, Railroad from Rabat to Petitjean opened

June 4, Spanish force defeated Rifis at Tizziaza near Melilla

July 15, Ultimatum to Abd el Krim from Spanish Secretary General as to peace terms

July 17–Oct. 7, Conference on Tangier in London of representatives of Great Britain, France, and Spain

July 24, Reply of Abd el Krim to Spanish Note of July 15 refused to reopen negotiations except on basis of recognition of the independence of the Rif

Aug. 16, Rifis attacked Spanish at Melilla

Aug. 20, Spanish forces ambushed near Tdargo

——, General Sanjurjo appointed Commander-in-Chief succeeding General Martinez Anido resigned at Melilla

Sept., Railroad from Casa Blanca to Wadzem opened

Oct. 27, Conference of representatives of Great Britain, France, and Spain in Paris opened to discuss status of Tangier

Dec. 11, Tangier Port Convention signed by Great Britain, France, and Spain

Dec. 18, Convention signed by Great Britain, France, and by Spain with reservations and finally Feb. 7, 1924 provided for permanent neutralization of Tangier

1924

Feb., Rifis began to attack on the Melilla front near Tizi Azza and Dar el Midar

May 7, The Wad Lau Spanish posts attacked by Rifis

May 26, French garrison at Fez attacked

July, Arrival of General Primo de Rivera at Tetuan, Spanish capital

Aug. 24, Spanish troops stormed enemy positions on hills above Wad Lau Valley

Sept. 1, Battle near Tetuan

Sept. 8, General Primo de Rivera again in Tetuan ordered evacuation of all interior posts outlying

Sept. 23, Advance to relieve garrison at Sheshuan begun from Tetuan and Laraiche, 40,000 troops in 4 columns commanded by Colonels Ovilo, Castro Girona, and Generals Serrano and Frederico Berenguer

Sept. 30, General Serrano entered Sheshuan

Oct. 15, Resignation of General Aizpuru, Spanish High Commissioner. General Primo de Rivera (President of the Spanish Directory) took over the office

Nov. 15, All the Wad Lau posts evacuated by Spanish troops

Nov. 16, Colonel Carrasco relieved the Spanish post at Meshra

Nov. 17, Evacuation of Sheshuan begun by Spanish forces

Nov. 18, Rear guard retiring from Sheshuan attacked, General Serrano killed, General F. Berenguer wounded, and over 1,000 casualties

Dec. 11, Last Spanish troops left Sok el-Arba half way between Sheshuan and Tetuan under heavy attack by Rifis

Dec. 12, Spanish post of Alcazar-Seguir on Straits of Gibraltar captured

——, Colonel Villegas killed and 450 Spanish casualties on last day of retirement

Dec. 13, Spanish forces reached Ben Karich and Tetuan behind permanent line from Tetuan to the east of Alcazar

1925

Jan. 25, Investment of Raisuli's stronghold at Tazrut by Abd el Krim forces commanded by Ahmedo Heriro and attack begun the following day

Jan. 27, Tazrut taken and Raisuli made a prisoner and taken to the Rif near Alhucemas where he died in April

Jan. 30, Spanish forces recaptured Alcazar Soreir on the Straits of Gibraltar

April 13, Abd el Krim began offensive against French by attack on the "Zawia" of the Derkawi Shereef at Amjat, "buffer tribe"

April 25–28, Rifis attacked entire French front

May 2, General Colombat advancing from Tafrant to relief of Biban in engagement with Rifis near French post of Aoudur

May 13, General Colombat stormed the Rifi trenches and relieved Biban, Dar Remich, and Mjala

May 15, Post of Alouai besieged for 3 weeks relieved by French troops

May 19, Biban again relieved

May 20, The French blockhouse of Bu Azzun rushed by enemy and Amzez, Ain Leuh, and Taunat assaulted

May 25, French forces increased to 50,000

May 25, 26, and 27, Attacks of Rifis on Biban repulsed. Further French posts evacuated

May 26, Anizer and Ain Leuh evacuated by the French

June 1, New Statute for Tangier zone came into effect according to Treaty of Dec. 18, 1923 providing for international jurisdiction

June 4, Taunat attacked by Rifis

June 6, Astar and Sker evacuated by the French

June 10–13, Visit of M. Painlevé, French Premier

June 16, The Rifi forces driven back across the Wergha River

June 20, Rifi and Jibala tribes attacked in upper valley of the Wad Leben

June 22, France and Spain agree on joint blockade of coast

June 23–25, Rifi offensive in the Taza district repulsed by French with loss

June 27, Si Mahammed, brother of Abd el Krim, attacking French posts of Ain Maatof and Bu Halima and a convoy of military cars on the Tissa-Fez road driven back

July 2, The Sultan celebrated the Islamic feast of Eid el-Kebir at Fez which Abd el Krim had declared that he himself would celebrate

July 5–7, The post of Bab Taza on the upper Leben taken and retaken by the French in heavy fighting

July 7, General Naulin appointed to command of army of French Protectorate, succeeding General Daugan

——, Rifi attacked in region of Fez

July 8, France and Spain agree on land blockade

July 12, Rifis and Jibala repulsed in attack on Kla es-Sless

July 17, The road between the French camp at Ain Aicha cut and the camp attacked and the Zawia of Mulai Bushta in Fishtala was destroyed

July 19, New Rifi offensive along line from Kla es-Sless to upper valley of the Leben

July 20, The camp at Ain Aicha relieved by French force

July 21, General Naulin took over the command of French army which in August numbered 150,000

July 26, Agreement signed in Madrid for French and Spanish military coöperation in Morocco

July 28, Conference of Marshal Petain and General Primo de Rivera at Tetuan

July 29, Fez-Taza railroad torn up near station of Sidi Abdullah

July 30, The French post of Ain bu Aissa destroyed by enemy shell bursting in its magazine

Aug. 2, Colonel Freydenberg stormed enemy position on hill of Asjen on the Wazzan front

Aug. 7, French took important Riff position of Jibel Amergu

Aug. 14 and 16, France and Spain respectively published peace terms offered Abd el Krim in mid July

Aug. 19, French army commanded by General Boichut occupied territory of the Tsul on East front

Aug. 23, Marshal Petain took command of military operations in Morocco

Sept. 2, Franco-Spanish offensive begun bombardment of coast to the south and east of Alhucemas

Sept. 5, Spanish Post of Nator captured by Rifis

Sept. 6, Abd el Krim invited General Primo de Rivera to send representatives to discuss terms of peace

Sept. 8, Spanish force made successful landing at western point of Alhucemas Bay at Cebadilla

Sept. 9, Franco-Spanish offensive opened

Sept. 11, French troops advanced on 37 mile front between Ain Aicha and Fez el-Bali

Sept. 11–12, Enemy attack on Spanish lines at Alhucemas Bay repulsed

Sept. 13, The post of Kudia Taher relieved by Spanish force after 10 days of attack

Sept. 15, The last enemy positions on Biban taken by the French and the entire mountain which the Rifis had held since June occupied

Sept. 23, Spanish advance took hills surrounding Alhucemas with loss of about 700 men

Sept. 24, Resignation of Marshal Lyautey as Resident General of the French Protectorate

Oct. 1, Spanish troops occupied Ajdir, Abd el Krim's capital

Oct. 10, Franco-Spanish forces advancing from Tizi Uzli and from the Melilla zone respectively met at Sidi bu Rokbar and proceeded to occupy the lands of the Gznaia and Metalsa tribes

Oct. 11, Theodore Steeg appointed Resident General of the French Protectorate

Nov., Mulai Hassan succeeded his father who had died 2 years before as Khalifa of the Spanish zone

——, General Sunjurgo became High Commissioner of Spanish Morocco

Nov. 7, Marshal Petain returned to France

1926

April 5, Announcement that negotiations had begun between representatives of Abd el Krim and representatives of the French and Spanish Governments for a conference at request of Abd el Krim

April 11, Conditions of peace offered included recognition of the Sultan by the Rifis, release of French and Spanish prisoners, disarmament of Rifi tribes and exile of Abd el Krim, the Rif to be autonomous under existing treaties

April 18, Preliminary meeting of French, Spanish, and Rifi delegates at French Camp Bertaux. New terms presented of release of prisoners as a preliminary to conference and advance of French and Spanish troops not accepted by Rifis and later withdrawn

April 26, Peace Conference opened at Ujda

May 6, Peace Conference ended without agreement

May 7, Franco-Spanish offensive against Abd el Krim begun

May 19, Jibel Rokdi and Jibel Zineb occupied by Franco-Spanish advance

May 23, Targuist, Abd el Krim's headquarters, taken by Spanish force, abandoned by Abd el Krim, who retired to Snada and asked for new conference with view to peace

May 25, Abd el Krim sent letter to Colonel Corap nearest French commander announcing his surrender and that the prisoners would be released

May 26, The prisoners crossed the French lines

May 27, Abd el Krim reached Targuist and made formal surrender, ending war in the Rif

July 13, Franco-Spanish Agreement as to Morocco signed in Paris

Aug. 28, Abd el Krim left Casablanca for Reunion Island chosen by French and Spanish Governments as his place of exile

Oct. 3, Decree of the President of France placed army in French Protectorate under control of the Resident General for all purposes except actual operations

Nov. 7, Ahmedo Heriro, leader of Jibala tribes, after surrender of Abd el Krim and the rifis, killed in battle with Spaniards in the Beni Idir district

1927

Feb. 9, Franco-Spanish negotiations on the status of Tangier opened in Paris

July 10, Occupation of Spanish zone completed and end of campaign proclaimed

Oct. 27–31, Visit of Italian naval squadron to Tangier

Nov. 17, Death of Mulai Yusef, Sultan

Nov. 18, Mulai Mohammed succeeded his father as Sultan

1928

March 3, Franco-Spanish Agreement signed in Paris as to application of Statute of 1923 as to Tangier gave Spain increased control

July 25, Protocol revising Tangier Statute signed by representatives of Spain, France, Great Britain, and Italy

1929

Jan. 2, Lucien Saint appointed French Resident General succeeding M. Steeg, resigned. Arrived at Casablanca, Feb. 21

Jan. 18, New Statute of Tangier came into effect

May 10, French post of El Bagi 100 miles south of Fez repelled attack of tribesmen

June 8, French column ambushed and 81 men lost

June 9, French post of Aiy Yakoub invested by tribesmen

June 12, French troops in battle with tribesmen in Atlas Mountains

1930

Jan. 1, Port of Agadir declared opened to international trade

Oct. 16–21, State visit of President Doumergue of France to the Sultan

SULTANS

1822. Muley Abderahman

1859. Sidi Muley Mohammed, Sept., died Sept., 1873

1873. Muley Hassan (son), proclaimed Sept. 25; died June 7, 1894

1894. Muley Abdul Aziz (son, born 1879), proclaimed, June 11

1908. Mulai Hafid, brother, Jan.–1912

1912. Mulai Yusef

Sidi Mohammed, third son of Mulai Yusef (reigned 1912–1927), was proclaimed Sultan on November 18, 1927, on the death of his father

MOZAMBIQUE

Mozambique, Portuguese East Africa, is separated from British Central and South Africa by the limits of the arrangement between Great Britain and Portugal in June, 1891. It is separated from Tanganyika Territory, according to agreements of October and December, 1886, and July, 1890, by a line running from Cape Delgado at 10° 40′ S. lat. till it meets the course of the Rovuma, which it follows to the point of its confluence with the 'Msinje, the boundary thence to Lake Nyasa being the parallel of latitude of this point. In accordance with the Treaty of Versailles the Peace Conference on September 23, 1919, allotted to Portugal "as the original and rightful owner" the territory south of the Rovuma, known as the "Kionga Triangle" (formerly part of German East Africa).

Portuguese East Africa, with an area of 428,132 square miles, comprises three distinct entities: (1) the Province of Mozambique, administered by the State (295,000 square miles), (2) the territory under the Companhia de Moçambique (59,840 square miles), and (3) the territory under the Companhia do Nyasa (73,292 square miles). The first is divided into 5 districts: Lourenço Marques, Inhambane, Quelimane, Tete and Mozambique, each with its own governor.

The district of Cabo Delgade and Nyassa was formed from the former territories of the Nyassa

Company (Companhia do Niassa) when its contract expired Oct. 27, 1929. The population of the Colony in 1930 was 3,514,602, including 17,842 Europeans. Lourenço Marques, the capital, has population of 37,311 (1928–29).

Colonel José Cabral, Governor General.

1498 to 1752

Jan. 11, 1498, Vasco da Gama arrived at Delagoa Bay; on the 25th he reached mouth of the Zambesi and March 1 or 2 was at Mozambique on voyage to India. In 1502 he visited Sofala and a companion, Antonio de Campo, discovered Delagoa Bay and entered the Espirito Santo River. In 1500 Alvares Cabral visited the coast. A fleet of 6 ships under Pedro da Nhaya left Portugal to make settlement at Sofala, arriving in September, 1505. A fort erected at Mozambique in 1507. Francisco Barreto, made Captain General in 1569, made unsuccesful attempt to conquer the "country of the gold mines" in the interior. In 1752 the territory was constituted a separate administration separated from Goa

1817

July 28, Formal statement of Portuguese jurisdiction over territory between Delagoa Bay and Lourenço Marques in Treaty with Great Britain

1869

Jan. 13, Anglo-Portuguese Boundary Convention referred claim to Island of Bulama and certain part of territory on coast to arbitration of the President of the United States; decided in favor of Portugal by President Grant April 21, 1870

1875

July 24, Decision of the President of France as arbitrator in favor of Portugal in territory disputed by Portugal and Great Britain

1883

Dec. 14, Concession granted by Portuguese Government for railroad from Delagoa Bay to Transval territory

1886

Dec. 30, Declaration of frontiers as to German East Africa according to agreements of October and December

Dec., Native revolt suppressed

1887

Feb. 16–March, War with the Sultan of Zanzibar because of territorial disputes, Tungi stormed by the Portuguese

March 2–4, Native uprising suppressed

1888–1889

Expeditions of Major Serpa Pinto into Nyasaland and Rhodesia. See Nyasaland

June 26, 1889, Railroad concession canceled and confiscated by Portuguese Government; protest of Governments of Great Britain and the United States

Oct., Discovery of the Chinde mouth of the Zambesi

Nov. 7, The Portuguese exploring expedition under Lieut. Cordon; he receives the allegiance of several tribes; the limits of the districts sanctioned by royal decree, and the province named Zumbo

1890

Jan. 10, British ultimatum to Portugal demanded withdrawal of Portuguese expedition of Pinto from hinterland

April 28, Railroad completed to Transvaal from Delagoa Bay

Aug. 2, Lieut. Azevedo Continho in the *Shiré* seizes the *James Stevenson*, belonging to the British African Lakes Company, at Chimoro, and sends the crew to Quilimane for trial, reported July 31; he is censured by the Government

1891

Jan., Mr. (aft. Sir) H. H. Johnston, British consul at Mozambique, nominated consul-general for the Portuguese East Africa territories

June 11, Anglo-Portuguese Treaty defined frontiers in East and Central Africa, Portugal receiving both banks of the Zambezi to a point 10 miles west of Zumbo, the Rovuma River recognized as northern boundary, stipulations as to customs, railways, roads, telegraphs, &c. Annex granted lease of land at Chinde to Great Britain and land on Lake Nyasa to Portugal, lease signed May 7, 1892 in Lisbon

July 30, A Portuguese royal charter granted to a company in Mozambique, Feb. 11; modified

1893

May 31–June 5, Agreement with Great Britain as to spheres of influence north of the Zambezi

Aug. 30–Sept. 1, Exchange of Notes between Portugal and Germany settled boundary with German East Africa

Oct. 9, Kaffir rising against the hut tax

1895

Feb. 2, Treacherous attack on the Portuguese camp at Maraqueen; Lieut. Antonio and many others killed

Feb. 6, The rebels routed and kraals destroyed on the Incomati river, reported

March 21, Kaffirs defeated with heavy loss near Maraqueen

May 24, Defeat of the rebels; end of the revolt, reported

July 8, Railroad from Delagoa Bay to Pretoria opened

Sept. 8, Natives defeated at Mague (300 killed)

Nov. 5, Gungunhana's army defeated with great slaughter, by Col. Galhardo, near Lake Coolera

Nov. 11, Manjacaze taken, submission of tribes

1896

Jan. 4, Gungunhana, and his son Godide, captured by Capt. Mousinho, at Chaimite, reported

Jan. 9, Two German warships in Delagoa bay, withdrawn, Feb.

Jan. 20, Anglo-Portuguese Agreement as to spheres of influence north of the Zambezi

Feb. 25, The Portuguese Government grant 450*l.* to the English at Catembe, for losses during the native rising, announced

March 13, Gungunhana, his son Godide, 2 indunas, &c., arrive as prisoners in Lisbon

1897

Jan. 30, Award of arbitrator as to Manica boundary in dispute with Great Britain

April 5, Natives repulsed in an attack on Portuguese troops under Major Mousinho Albuquerque, Gov.-

Gen., Oct. 19, 1896; martial law, Nov. 5, 1896; campaign ended, commercial transit opened to Macuane in the interior, reported

May 29, Expedition against the Namarallos, reaches Monte Pao, reported successful, March 8, 1897; chiefs submit, reported

Aug. 3, Rising in Gazaland, against the hut-tax, rebels defeated, May 29; rebellion crushed

Oct. 2, Boundary Agreement with Great Britain as to British Amatongaland

1898

Jan. 19, Major M. D'Albuquerque, Governor-Gen.; trouble with the natives on the Limpopo, soldiers captured, reported

1899

Mid Aug., A Portuguese expedition against Mataka; routs the natives

Aug. 30, Secret Anglo-German Agreement, division of Portuguese colonies

Oct. 6, Thousands of refugees from the Transvaal arrive, reported

Nov. 24, Portuguese troops return, after suppressing a rising on the Sabi river

1900

Jan. 8, Law revived enforcing passports on all leaving Portuguese territory, reported

1901

Jan. 12, Agreement with Great Britain as to concession by Great Britain of a tract of land on Lake Nyasa in lieu of Leopard Bay concession of June 11, 1891

May 19, Fire at the government offices, some destroyed

Dec., *Modus vivendi* settled between Portugal and Great Britain, *re* the harbor

1902

March 18, Severe encounter with slave-dealers, 50 killed, 162 captured, 12 dhows seized, 700 slaves released, reported

July, 3, 4, British military stores, estimated value 500,000*l.*, burnt down

Aug. 11–14, Lord Milner warmly received

1903

Jan. 29, Royal regulations confirmed authority of central committee in control of recruitment of native labor and emigration in coöperation with native chiefs

1906

Sept. 15, Boundary Agreement as to frontier with British Nyasaland

1907

May 23, Decree as to administration of the Colony granted partial autonomy

June 3, Boundary Agreement with Great Britain from parallel 18° 30' south to the Limpopo

1909

April 1, Convention with the Transvaal as to natives, commerce, and customs

1911

May 13, Regulations of 1903 for control of recruitment of native labor revised

Nov., Agreement signed as to boundary on Shiré and Ruo Rivers with Nyasaland

1914

Aug. 15, Partial autonomy granted by Portugal

Oct., Decree authorized the Government to place natives not otherwise employed at disposal of colonists or merchants

1917

Nov. 25, German force commanded by General von Lettow-Vorbeck from East Africa crossed frontier and defeated the Portuguese at Ngomano

1918

March 16, Land law regulated granting of concessions

1919

Sept. 23, In accordance with the Treaty of Versailles the "Kionga Triangle" part of German East Africa allotted to Portugal

1922

July 1, The Trans-Zambezia Railroad, 175 miles in length, from Dondo, on the Beira Junction Railway, to Murraça, on the southern bank of the Zambezi, opened for traffic

Sept. 1, Since this date escudo currency used

Oct. 9, Law of May 23, 1907 amended as to administration of the Colony

1923

March 31, Labor Convention with the Transvaal renewed

1926

Oct. 23, Decree abolished compulsory private labor except when indispensable for the public good

1927

Oct. 6, Exchange of Notes by which report of delimitation commissions as to boundary with Union of South Africa accepted by both Governments

1928

Feb. 13, Railroad opened linked 2 sections, the Bas Congo-Katanga railway through Beira connected from Cape Town and Beira to Matadi

Sept. 11, New Convention with Transvaal replaced that of 1909 as to labor, &c.

Dec. 8, Code of native labor promulgated

1929

Feb. 6, Political, civil, and criminal statute promulgated for Colony

1930

April 12 and May 17, Legislative Decree and Regulations issued provided for primary code of education, and organization of native education, regulations for vocational schools for female natives, &c.

April 23, Legislative Decree promulgated an administrative code for the Colony

Aug. 23, Act prohibited preparation or manufacture of alcoholic spirits

NATAL

Natal, a province of the Union of South Africa annexed to Cape Colony in 1844, area (including

Zululand, 10,427 square miles) 35,284 square miles with a seacoast of 360 miles, the seat of the provincial government, Pietermaritzburg, population in 1921 1,429,398, natives 1,139,804, Asiatics 141,649, population of Durban, Europeans 58,085, other 93,557, total 151,642. The census of the European population of Durban in 1926 was 70,883, and of Pietermaritzburg 19,748. Vasco da Gama sighted the bluff at entrance to Durban harbor on Dec. 25, 1497 and named the country Terra Natalis.

1824

Aug. 7, Francis George Farwell with other merchants of Cape Town formed into a trading company, obtained a treaty from Chaka ceding land which included the port and harbor of Natal, and Aug. 27 raised British flag and declared the country British territory

1828

Sept., Chaka murdered by his brother Dingaan who appointed Henry Francis Fynn, who had succeeded James S. King as head of settlement after deaths of Farwell and King, his representative as "great chief of the Natal Kafirs"

1835

Town of Durban laid out named after Sir Benjamin d'Urban, Governor of Cape Colony
May 6, Treaty of Captain Allen Gardiner, missionary, with the Zulus

1837

Oct., First emigrant Boers led by Peter Retief reached Natal

1838

Feb. 4, Dingaan signed Treaty with the Boers making cession of land from the Tugela to the Umzimvubu. In a few days Dingaan treacherously killed Retief and all his party
Feb. 17, Zulus attacked advance parties of Boers near present village of Weenen (Weeping) named in commemoration of the massacre
April 11, Boers aided by English in attempt to avenge their companions defeated by superior numbers of Zulus and again on April 17. Durban then destroyed
Nov., Andries Pretorius arrived in Natal and was elected commandant general by the Boers
Dec. 4, Port Natal occupied by British troops who remained until Dec. 24, 1839 sent from Capetown to prevent Boer settlement on the coast
Dec. 16, Dingaan defeated by the Boers in decisive battle since commemorated as Dingaan's Day

1839

March, Pietermaritzburg founded, named after Pieter Retief and Gerrit Maritz, Boer leaders
Sept., Panda, half-brother of Dingaan, led rebellion against Dingaan and asked for assistance from the Boers who agreed to support him

1840

Jan. 30, Dingaan defeated in battle and forced to flight and was murdered soon after
Feb. 10, Panda named chief of the Zulus by Mr. Pretorius in formal ceremony and accepted vassalage to Boer Government
Town of Weenen founded by Boers

1842

May 4, British force commanded by Captain T. C. Smith sent by Sir George Napier from Cape Colony reached Durban and closed port to Boers
May 23, Captain Smith attacked Boers assembled by Pretorius in camp at Kongela; repulsed with loss of 19 men and 31 wounded
May 24, Dick King started from Durban and rode 600 miles to Graham's Town to get reinforcements for British arriving on the ninth day
May 31, The Boers invested the British camp
June 26, Two British vessels arrived bringing troops commanded by Colonel A. J. Cloete
July 15, The Volksraad submitted to Colonel Cloete

1843

May 12, Natal made a British Colony
Aug. 8, The Volksraad agreed to terms proposed by Colonel Cloete but the great majority of the Boers moved north of the Val River
Oct. 5, Treaty with Panda, Zulu chief, by which territory in St. Lucia ceded

1844

May 31, Natal annexed to Cape Colony
Aug. 21, Boundaries defined

1847

March 2, Legislative Council established

1854

Dr. John William Colenso appointed Bishop of Natal arrived

1856

July 12, Natal constituted a separate Colony with Legislative Council of 16 members, 12 elected and 4 nominated by the Crown

1858

Feb. 3, Order in Council defined boundaries proclaimed June 5

1860

First Indian coolies arrived under indenture and were allowed to settle in the country on expiration of labor contracts

1863

Dec. 9, Nomans land annexed

1864

April 16, Bishop Colenso deposed by Bishop of Capetown because of views in book published in 1862 on the Pentateuch
April 27, Letters Patent placed Bantu locations under a Commission

1865

March 21, Privy Council declared deposition of Bishop Colenso by a colonial bishop null and void

1867

May 24, R. W. Keate became Lieutenant Governor

1869

Jan. 25, Party in opposition to Bishop Colenso, charged with unsound doctrinal views, consecrated Dr. W. K. Macrorie bishop in his stead

1870

Feb. 19, Decision of Lieutenant-Governor Keate fixed boundary with Orange Free State

1872

July 19, Anthony Musgrave, Lieutenant Governor

1873

April 30–July 22, Lieutenant Colonel T. Milles acted as Administrator on resignation of Mr. Musgrave

July 22, Sir Benjamin Chilley Campbell Pine took office as Lieutenant Governor

Nov., Rebellion of Langalibalele, Bantu chief of Hlubis, refusing to register their guns as required by law

Dec. 11, Langalibalele and his body-guard of 84 hemmed in by troops surrendered

1874

Feb. 9, Langalibalele sentenced by special court to banishment later changed to imprisonment

1875

April 1–Sept. 3, Sir Garnet Joseph Wolseley, Administrator

May 31, Constitutional Bill reducing powers of the Legislative Council passed third reading

Sept. 3, Sir Henry Ernest Bulwer assumed office as Lieutenant Governor

Dec. 10, Protectorate Treaty with chief of Amaquatis Act 26 created Native High Court

1876

Jan. 1, First sod of railroad from Durban to Maritzburg turned by Sir Henry Bulwer

1877

Nov. 15, Educational law enacted

1878

Feb. 9, Railroad opened from Durban to Pinetown

1879

June 28–April 27, 1880, Sir G. J. Wolseley, Governor

1880

July 2, Sir George Pomeroy Colley took office as Governor

1881

Feb. 27, Governor Colley killed at Battle of Majuba Hill

Dec. 1, Legislative Council voted that return of Cetywayo to Zululand would be against the best interests of the native tribes and imperil the peace of South Africa

1882

March 6–Oct. 23, 1885, Sir Henry Ernest Bulwer, Governor

Dec. 22, J. W. Shepstone appointed Resident Commissioner to the native reserves

1883

June 20, Death of Bishop Colenso

1884

Jan. 5, J. W. Shepstone appointed judge of Native High Court

Dec. 18, Annexation of St. Lucia Bay notified

1886

Oct. 27, The legislative council offers to undertake the administration of Zululand at the cost of the colony to check the encroaching Boers Oct. 22; sanction refused by the British government announced

1887

May 19, Royal Commission for government of Zululand by Government of Natal

Sept. 18, New law as to native justice

1890

June 26, The council vote for a free and responsible government

1891

Feb. 3, The bill for a new constitution voted

April 30, Parliament opened

Aug. 8, Constitutional bill passed

July 13, Railway to Orange Free State opened

1893

June 23, Death of Sir Theophilus Shepstone

July 4, Responsible government deferred by the legislative council, about Oct. 7, 1892; approved by the council, March 1, 1893; bill passed by the council, May 11, proclaimed

Oct. 27, A ministry formed, Sir John Robinson, Premier, Oct. 10; parliament opened by the Governor, Oct. 19; prorogued

1897

Jan., Strong resistance to the immigration of Indians at Durban, reported

Oct. 5, Sir J. Robinson resigns; new ministry formed by the Hon. H. Escombe, Att.-Gen. Feb. 13; resigns, succeeded by Mr. Henry Binns (Knt. 1898, died June, 1899)

Dec. 1, Letters Patent for annexation of Zululand

1899

June 10, New ministry, Col. Hime, Premier

July 1, Loyal meetings sympathizing with the Uitlanders, *see* Transvaal

Sept., Preparations for war, reserves called out

Oct. 7, Sir George White appointed commander of British forces in Natal; arrives

Oct. 10, Boers concentrated on the frontier, Sept.; invade Natal; *see* S. African War

1902

May 12, Annexation (territory) bill (Vryheid reunited to Zululand; Utrecht and part of the Wakkerstroom district added to Natal) passed

Oct. 4, Martial law repealed; certain restrictions

Dec. 30, Mr. Chamberlain in a great speech at Pietermaritzburg, urged the necessity of imperial as well as colonial union

1903

Aug. 17, New ministry, Mr. Sutton, Premier

1904

Jan., Legislative assembly rejects by 30 votes to 2 a motion opposing the introduction of Chinese into the Transvaal

Oct. 20, Lord Roberts arrives at Ladysmith on his visit to the S. African battlefields

Early Nov., Reconstruction of the Ministry; Mr. L'Estrange, Colonial Secretary; Mr. Maydon, Minister of Railways and Harbours; and Mr. Leuchars, Minister of Public Works and Secretary for Native Affairs

1905

April 17, Treasurer announces in the legislative assembly additional taxation, including a poll-tax of 1*l.* on every man of legal age, and a death duty from 1 to 5%, to meet 200,000*l.* of the total deficit for the current year, estimated at 450,000*l.*

May, Resignation of Sir G. M. Sutton, Premier; coalition cabinet formed with Mr. Smythe, Premier and Colonial Secretary; Mr. Hyslop, Treasurer

June, Report of the delimitation commission issued; it condemns 4/5 ths of Zululand as unfit for European habitation, while the balance is densely populated. Commissioners pay a tribute to native loyalty, and deprecate any change in the policy of upholding the tribal system

Aug. 9, Legislative council reject the government bill imposing house and land taxes and death duties, except the last; legislative assembly pass the poll-tax bill; assembly prorogued

Sept. 13, Lord Selborne, the new high commissioner, arrives at Pietermaritzburg

1906

Jan. 10, Death of Dr. Green, dean of Maritzburg, aged 84

Feb. 8, Collision between 14 Natal police and a party of armed Zulus near Pietermaritzburg, owing to the friction occasioned by the collection of the poll-tax, one officer and a police-trooper killed

Feb. 10, Martial law proclaimed in Natal; a force of 350 men leave Pietermaritzburg for the scene of the disturbance

Feb. 17, Col. Mackenzie's force, 800 strong, arrives at Springval, S. Natal; 2 natives concerned in the attack on the police, court-martialed and shot; several others captured or killed by Mocli's natives; a number of armed natives assemble at Verulam, but dispersed at their chief's orders

Feb. 23, Native unrest continues, a battery of field artillery with detachments of mounted rifles and light infantry mobilized

Feb. 26, Six more natives implicated in the affray at Richmond, captured Feb. 25; Chief Mskofeli arrives in Col. Mackenzie's camp, Ixopo, and pays the poll-tax for his tribe

March 8, Opening of the inter-colonial customs conference at Pietermaritzburg, Lord Selborne presiding

March 10, Chief Mskofeli pays the fine of cattle imposed upon him; Col. Leuchars at a parade of the field force at Mapumulo, announced to the natives assembled that a fine of 1,200 cattle and 3,500 sheep and goats had been imposed on Gobizembe and his tribe

March 17, Dutch farmers resolve to establish a congress

March 28, Mr. Smythe, Premier, states that 12 natives implicated in the murder of sub-inspector Hurt, of the Natal police, had been sentenced to death by court-martial at Richmond, and that these sentences had been confirmed

March 29, Natal Ministry resigns, in consequence of the action of the imperial government in suspending the execution of 12 natives condemned for participation in the murder of a police inspector

April 2, Judicial committee of the privy council reject a petition on behalf of the 12 natives sentenced to death at Natal, for special leave to appeal against the sentence

——, Imperial government decides to leave the matter to the Natal Ministry, which resumes office; culprits shot

April 3, Bambaata, a chief in the Greytown district, who was deposed by the Natal Government and fled with part of his tribe, returned to his kraal and put to death; the regent appointed in his stead

April 5, Greytown rebels attack a portion of the field force operating against them; 5 men of the force, including Inspector Dimmick, wounded; field force at Impanza forced to abandon its laager and retire on Greytown after heavy fighting

April 7–8, Bambaata, after having his kraals shelled by Col. Leuchars, escaped into Zululand

April 17, Natal Government offers 500*l.* for the capture of Bambaata; 23 natives suspected of having been concerned in the Bambaata rebellion sent to Pietermaritzburg to be tried by court-martial; white inhabitants at Melmoth and Eshowe go into laager, reported

April 19, Dinizulu offers to send an impi to capture Bambaata

April 20, Mr. Smythe, Premier, in a speech, defends the action taken up by the Natal Government towards the home government during the recent crisis, and totally rejects the suggestion that imperial troops should be requisitioned to assist in suppressing the rebellion

April 23, Bambaata stated to have fled with 300 followers from Nkandhla in the direction of Natal

May 3, Colonial legislature opened in Pietermaritzburg

May 5, Col. Mansel's vanguard attacked by about 200 Zulus; 60 Zulus and 3 British killed

May 10, Natal government decides to raise an infantry corps of 800 men for special service during the native rebellion, under the command of Lt.-Col. Dick, the men to be recruited, partly in Natal, and partly in the Transvaal, reported

——, Suspected chief, Kula, with 6 of his indunas, brought in by a patrol, May 9; and conveyed to Pietermaritzburg

May 15, Col. Mackenzie destroys the principal kraals of the rebel chiefs Sigananda and Noma; 500 rebels driven out of N'Tingwe, reported

——, Ministerial crisis in connection with the unoccupied land-tax bill; Mr. Smythe, Premier, moves the adjournment of the House

May 31, Umvoti field force dislodges a party of rebels in the state valley, killing 21, May 30; Col. Mackenzie promoted to the supreme command of all the forces

June 1, Proffered assistance of Silwane, most powerful chief in Natal, accepted by the Government; surrender of Sigananda's induna, Mpikwa, with 2 of his headmen and 70 other rebels

June 3, Fighting between Royston's horse and the rebels, 5 British killed and 4 severely wounded

June 9, Severe fighting in the neighborhood of the Mome rebels' stronghold, Sigananda's chief induna and 200 rebels killed

June 18, 350 rebels killed in engagement with Col. Mackenzie, June 10; death of Bambaata, June 10; surrender of Sigananda and his son, June 13; surrender of about 275 natives, and demobilization of troops begun

July 2, 600 native rebels killed near Noodsberg by Natal forces under Col. Mackenzie engaged in the "great drive"

July 3, Victory followed up by the simultaneous attack by 4 columns of Mesini's impi; heavy fighting, Mesini's kraals burnt, 350 rebels killed

July 12, Surrender of Mesini and Ndhlovukatimuni

July 23, Official statement of Sigananda's death given; his age was 104 years

Aug. 22, Native chief Sikikuku found guilty of high treason, Aug. 14; death sentences on Mesini and Ndhlovukatimuni passed July 17, commuted to penal servitude for life

Sept. 18, Judge Beaumont's report acquitted Royston's horse of the charges of cruelty brought against them by the Bishop of Zululand

Sept. 29, Proclamation published at Pietermaritzburg announced the establishment of a customs reciprocity between Natal and Australia

Oct. 2, Martial law formally withdrawn and the indemnity act published

Oct. 13, Zulu chiefs Tilorko and Sikikuku sentenced to 10 years' hard labor and fined 500 head of cattle each

Nov. 13, Parliament opened in Pietermaritzburg; fresh taxation announced

Nov. 15, Bill for the abolition of the poll-tax, as well as a bill restricting the issue of trade licenses to persons possessing the franchise, rejected by the Legislative Assembly

Nov. 28, Resignation of the Ministry, Nov. 22; new ministry formed, with Mr. Moor as Premier and Minister of Native Affairs

Dec. 16, Death of Mr. A. J. Crawford, president of the Natal Legislative Council

Dec. 21, Mr. Moor, the Premier, resigns office on the ground that he is concerned in a government contract

Dec. 29, Deposed Zulu chief Gobizembe reported dead

1907

June 1, 25 noted native rebels, sentenced to expatriation, depart for St. Helena

Aug. 25, Murder of Sitsistheli, a loyal chief, at Nkandhla, by a Kolwa native

Oct. 3, Parliament prorogued

1908

June 17, Parliament opened by the Governor

July 22, Natal indemnity act passed

July 31, Dinizulu committed for trial charged with treason, sedition, inciting to murder, and other offenses

Oct. 12, Convention of the South African Union opens at Durban

Nov. 11, Cakijana, convicted of overt acts of rebellion in conjunction with Bambaata, was sentenced to 7 years' hard labor

1909

March 30, At Greytown, Dinizulu, found guilty of harboring rebels and members of Bambaata's family, was sentenced to 4 years' imprisonment, to date from his arrest 15 months ago, and to a fine of 100l.

April 21, The draft act of union, with the assembly's amendments, passed by the legislative council

April 26–May 8, Strike of railwaymen

Sept. 20, The South African union bill receives royal assent (see South Africa)

1910

April 22, Release of the Zulu chief Cakijana

May 31, Natal entered the Union of South Africa

NIGER

Niger, Colony of French West Africa, was formed by a decree of October 13, 1922. Estimated area, 404,914 square miles; population (1929), 1,441,413 (324 Europeans). It was originally a Military Territory of the French Sudan (Upper Senegal and Niger) (1912) by decree of Sept. 7, 1911 effective Jan. 1; on Dec. 4, 1920, it was placed under civil administration. The country is composed of a zone in the north, which is largely desolate country; a central strip which is wooded; and the southern zone, richly wooded and abounding in cattle. By a decree dated December 28, 1926, the circle of Say and part of the circle of Dori were transferred from the Colony of Upper-Volta to the Colony of the Niger, the new districts comprising 119,946 inhabitants. Zinder is the capital.

NIGERIA

Nigeria Colony and Protectorate in British West Africa, formed in 1914 by union of the two Protectorates of Northern and Southern Nigeria. See also Lagos and Oil Rivers. The British mandated territory of Cameroon is attached to Nigeria for administrative purposes. Nigeria is situated on the shore of the Gulf of Guinea and extends inland to the borders of the Sahara, is bounded on the west by the French Colony of Dahomey, on the north and northwest by the French Military Territory of the Niger, and on the east by Cameroon, area approximately 335,700 square miles, population 18,966,574, including about 5,200 Europeans (Northern Provinces: 275,724 square miles, 10,783,303 population, Southern Provinces: 89,627 square miles, 8,183,271 population). Lagos is the capital.

Sir Donald C. Cameron, Governor.

1879

All British interests on the Niger River amalgamated into the United African Company headed by Sir George Taubman Goldie

1881

The United African Company enlarged and changed name to National African Company. The company's territories were constituted by the combination of various settlements and by treaties with petty chiefs and especially by the Treaty of Nikki concluded by Captain Lugard placing Kishi

(Oct. 13) and Busa (Nov. 10), 1894, under British protection

1884

Nov. 15–Feb. 26, 1885, Berlin Conference recognized British position as only Europeans on the lower Niger (National African Company)

1885

Feb. 26, Berlin Act provided for free navigation of the Niger River for merchant ships of all nations and for transportation of passengers and goods

April 29/May 7, Exchange of Notes with Germany agreed to define British and German spheres of influence in the Gulf of Guinea

May 16/June 16, Further exchange of Notes with Germany provided that customs duties in Gulf of Guinea should be restricted to sums necessary for administration and in matters affecting persons and property there should be no differential treatment of British or German subjects

June 5, Notification of British Protectorate over the Niger districts, on the coast from Lagos to the Rio del Rey; inland over both banks of the Niger from its confluence with the Benue River to the sea, together with territories watered by the latter up to Ibi

Nov. 12, Treaty of Boussa (Busa)

1886

July 10, Royal charter granted to National African Company and name changed to Royal Niger Company, Lord Aberdare, Governor, and Sir George T. Goldie, Vice-Governor. 37 treaties with native chiefs listed

July 27, Anglo-German Boundary Agreement defined frontiers with Cameroon up to Yola River

1887

Oct. 18, Formal announcement of British Protectorate extending to all territory in basin of the Niger River and its affluents

Dec. 29, Lagos Protectorate order in Council proclaimed British jurisdiction over territory adjacent to Lagos

1890

Jan. 20, Treaty signed at Busa

April 30, Notice of the Governor and Council of fine and imprisonment in case of illicit slave traffic

July 1, Anglo-German Boundary Agreement as to the Rio del Rey in dispute

July 29, Prohibition of trade with natives in spirituous liquors

Aug. 5, Anglo-French Boundary Declaration which left Sokoto within sphere of the Company, and settled line from Say on the Upper Niger to Barua, Lake Chad

1891

Dec. 31, Death of Samuel Adjai Crowther, native African, first Bishop of the Niger Territory

1893

April 14, Anglo-German Boundary Agreement as to Gulf of Guinea (Rio del Rey)

May 13, Oil Rivers Protectorate made the Niger Coast Protectorate

Nov. 15, Anglo-German Boundary Agreement as to

line from Old Calabar or Cross River to Yola River, to Benue River and to Lake Chad

1894

April 10, The Royal Niger Company submitted revised list of 306 treaties with native chiefs to the Secretary of State

July 2, Treaty with King of Mossi

Sept. 25, Capture of stronghold of Chief Nana in Benin ended conflicts

Oct. 13, Treaty of Kishi

Oct. 26, Surrender of Nana; sentenced to life imprisonment in December

Nov. 10, Treaty of Nikki signed with King of Nikki renewing Protectorate in view of French advances in Borgu

1895

Jan. 1, British Protectorate over Borgu including Busa (Boussa) and Nikki formally announced to the French. *See also* June 5, 1884

Jan. 27, Repressive measures of the company lead to native risings at Brass

Feb. 13, French occupation of Busa. *See* French Sudan

Feb. 15, Akassa looted, Jan. 28; Mr. Wyse and other prisoners killed; Sir Claude Macdonald holds Brass; reinforcements arriving, reported

Feb. 20–25, Adm. Bedford takes Sacrifice island, Nimbi, and Fishtown, defeats and punishes the Brass chiefs; Lieut. Geo. J. Taylor and 2 seamen killed

Feb. 25, Death of Lord Aberdare. Succeeded as Governor of the Company by Sir George T. Goldie

April 25, Dispute ended; Brass reopened to trade

1896

Jan. 15, Anglo-French Boundary Convention as to territory to the west of the Lower Niger region (Dahomey)

1897

Jan. 5, Mission to Benin killed from ambush, Consul General Phillips and 6 other Europeans and over 200 native carriers

Jan. 27, Bida, capital of the Fulah States of Nupé, taken by assault in expedition against slave raiding

Feb. 5, Treaty of peace signed with new Emir of Nupé

Feb. 11, Punitive expedition to Benin commanded by Lieutenant Colonel Bruce Hamilton and flotilla under Rear Admiral Rawson captured Gwato, and Ologbo the following day

Feb. 13, French expedition from Dahomey occupied Busa. *See also* Sudan, French

Feb. 18, Benin City taken and the territory placed under British protection, A. H. Turner appointed Resident

Feb. 23, Treaty signed with the Emir of Lafiagi and other emirs send submission

March 5, Submission of the Patanis at Abutshi

June 9, Second expedition under Lieutenants Carrol and Fitzgerald defeated the fugitive King of Benin who surrendered with about 3,000 of his men Aug. 7

Nov. 17, Kiffi, stronghold of Prince Arku, rebel slave raider, taken by Major Arnold

Nov. 30, Nikki occupied by the French

1898

Jan., The Sultan of Sokoto accepts terms of the British alliance

Feb. 17, Durbar held by Mr. Wallace, Agent-General made terms of peace with Ibouzas

June 14, Anglo-French Boundary Convention which preserved to the British the country of the lower Niger basin and provided for lease of 2 pieces of land to the French Government on the Niger

June 21, Expedition against slave raiders took Lapai and Argeyes on the 24th

Oct. 4, Busa (evacuated by the French) and Ilo occupied by British according to Treaty

Oct.–Nov., Revolt in the Assaba hinterland against interference with sacrificial rites and severe fighting

Nov. 13–16, Further operations against rebellious tribes in the hinterland of Benin

Dec. 3–25, Assaba district subdued and submission of King Ibo

1899

Feb. 4–March 15, Successful expedition of Major Carter and Captain R. Gabbett to suppress fetishism in the Kwo Ibibio country

April 20–June, Punitive expedition under Major Carter leaves Benin City April 20; Ologbosheri's town and himself captured by Capt. Gabbett after heavy fighting, Lieut. Uniacke killed, April 24; the chief charged with the massacre of Europeans and natives (Jan., 1897), is hanged, June 28, 1899; his son Okoro given up by the natives

July 13, Punitive expedition captured Chief of Suntai and his town

Aug. 9, Order in Council announced taking over of the territory from the Company

Aug. 23, Lord Scarborough succeeded Sir G. Goldie as head of the Company. Government terms accepted

Oct. 13, Successful punitive expedition to the Binue

Dec. 28, Notice of revocation of charter of the Royal Niger Company

1900

Jan. 1, British protectorate: Upper and Lower Nigeria and Lagos; Col. (aft. Sir Frederick) Lugard proclaimed High Commissioner in N. Nigeria; Sir R. D. Moor, High Commissioner in S. Nigeria

Jan. 8, 10, Capt. Carroll, with a telegraph construction staff, under Lieut. McClintock, N.E. of Lokoja, attacked by the Munshis tribes; enemy routed, 80 killed; enemy again defeated and Ibi captured, Jan. 15

Feb. 21, Natives again routed by Lieut. Monck-Mason and 150 men on the Gurara, N. of Lokoja

March 5, Punitive expedition under Lieut.-Col. Lowry-Cole against the Munshis; much fighting, 5 British killed, reported

March 23, Further fighting on the Gurara, enemy's camp destroyed, reported

May 9, The Pagan stronghold at Lemo, N. Nigeria, stormed and burnt by Col. Lowry-Cole, many natives killed

Ordinance No. 1, Native Lands Acquisition Ordinance forbade sale of land without consent of Governor

Nov. 26, David Carnegie killed near Lokoja

1901

Jan. 19–Feb. 17, Punitive expedition under Col. Kemball; Kantagora and Bida, in N. Nigeria, captured

March 20–May, Operations in S. Nigeria under Maj. Heneker; towns captured

March 31, Proclamation made slave dealing a penal offense. All children born after this date free

June 21, Capt. Keyes (26), in command of Ilo, on the French frontier, treacherously murdered in Argungu by 3 French traders; in some after fighting 2 of his party and 12 others were killed

Aug., Negotiations with Fadr-Allah, Rabah's son, concluded; he was afterwards attacked and killed by the French, at Godiba, Sept.

Sept. 8, Punitive expedition under Lieut.-Col. Morland against the Emir of Adamawa; Yola captured, the Emir fled, Sept. 2; his brother Bobo Amadu installed as Emir by Mr. Wallace

About Nov. 15, The Aros attack Obagu and massacre the natives; their position at Enyong creek, Cross river, shelled and occupied by the British under Col. Montanaro, Nov. 28; enemy again defeated, Nov. 30; rapid progress, enemy's strong resistance successfully repulsed, Dec. 2, 5, 6, 8; Bendi taken after 3 days' fighting, Dec. 16; Oror taken, the Aros defeated, 6 chiefs surrender, Dec. 24–31

1902

Jan. 2, 11, Col. Festing captures Oloks; 25 chiefs and others captured

Jan. 25, 29, Stubborn resistance, enemy's loss severe; a stronghold of the Igas captured; enemy defeated in Ngwa country, Feb. 12, 19; many towns submit; campaign closed, March 23, 1902

Feb., Sir Fred. Lugard reports British occupation of 9 provinces, chiefly on the Niger and the Binue

——, Gombe, Gujba, and Bautshi occupied by Col. Morland without opposition; Mr. C. L. Temple installed as resident at Bautshi

June, Col. Morland's expedition to lake Chad very successful; British posts established, reported

Sept., Slave trade abolished in Long Ju-Ju; fetish destroyed, cash currency introduced in the Aro country, S. Nigeria, &c., reported

Oct. 4, Capt. Moloney, resident at Keffi, murdered by a native chief in N. Nigeria

Nov. 17, Successful Ju-Ju expedition (to stop human sacrifices, against Oma Nabad, 7 natives rescued, 4 chiefs killed)

Dec. 5, The Emir of Kano, N. Nigeria, makes hostile preparations against the British, reported

Dec. 10, The Opobo chief, in S. Nigeria, surrenders; successful expedition, reported

End Dec., Sir F. Lugard decides upon active operations against the Emir of Kano, said to be the greatest military chief in Hausaland, in consequence of his increased hostility in affording protection to the murderer of Capt. Moloney, British resident at Keffi

Dec. 12, Anglo-German Boundary Convention

1903

Jan. 2, Emir of Kano flees to Sokoto, reported

Jan. 12, British force of 37 officers and 1,050 men under the command of Col. Morland concentrate at Zaria, the nearest port to Kano

Mid Jan., Mixed British and German commission to demarcate at boundaries laid down by the Anglo-German agreement of 1893; frontier to be fixed from southern shore of lake Chad to Zola, reported

Jan. 27, Two companies 600 strong of Lagos batt. of W. Africa frontier force leave Lagos for expedition against Emir of Kano

Feb. 3, Capture of Kano by Col. Morland, 300 natives killed, 2 British officers, and 12 men wounded

Feb. 16, Gen. Kemball leaves Kano for Sokoto, the great Fulah capital

March 15, Sokoto occupied after some fighting, the Sultan and chief having fled

[British supremacy completed over 500,000 sq. mi., with a population of about 20,000,000]

May 16, The ex-Sultan of Sokoto, joined by a large number, who had fled N.E. of Bantshi, pursued by Capt. Sword's column to Burmi on the Dongola river; but want of guns causes failure of the attempt to capture the town; after severe fighting Capt. Sword retreats with the loss of 4 killed and 60 wounded, enemy's loss much greater

May 20, Lease to French Government of land at junction of Doko with the Niger and at mouth of Forcados River

May 21, New Sultan chosen by Council of Elders installed by British

July 27, Capt. Sword reaches Bantshi May 23, the ex-Sultan begins negotiations, but is only promised his life if he submits; Burmi again attacked by a force of 40 British and 500 native troops, and completely destroyed after desperate fighting, in which the ex-Sultan Ataibihu, most of his emirs, and about 700 natives were killed, the British loss being Maj. Marsh and 10 others killed, 3 officers and 69 men wounded

Aug. 24, Anglo-German boundary commission under Lt.-Col. Jackson, completes survey of districts S. of lake Chad, reported

Sept., Revolt among the Eket tribes (S. Nigeria)

Oct. 12, Expedition under Maj. Mackenzie successful; N'doite, King of Agoi, and people, surrender

Early Nov., Mr. W. Egerton appointed commissioner

Nov., Escort of 50 men, Southern Nigerian regiment, under Lieut. A. Moore, proceeding to N'doto, a town on the N.W. boundary of S. Nigeria, escorting Mr. Raikes, the district commissioner, on a peaceful mission to the natives, is attacked by the warlike tribesmen; Lieut. Moore suffers defeat, with loss of nearly half the escort, and is compelled to retire to friendly territory and await reinforcements

1904

Early Jan., Large force, under Capt. J. G. Hogg, dispatched to punish the tribes concerned, and succeeds

Mid Jan., Capt. D. S. P. O'Riordan and Lieut. Cecil Amyatt-Burney, assist.-supt. of police, killed, and the greater part of escort (15 soldiers and 37 police) cut up, while on their way from Dekina, the chief post of the Bassa province, N. Nigeria, on a patrol among the Okpoto tribe

Jan. 19, Serious anti-European rising breaks out in S. Nigeria, the work of a native secret society known as the Ekumeku, or the "Silent Ones," which had been insufficiently dealt with in 1902; murders committed and property destroyed in friendly towns, mission stations at various places looted and destroyed by fire; Capt. Hogg, with his force, marches to suppress the rising, saves Assaba, which is threatened, and marches to the relief of Mr. Crawford, divisional commissioner who had gone to Issele-Uku with a small escort to relieve the mission station there and is hemmed in; attack on Akuku made by the troops; after severe fighting the rebels are dispersed

End Jan., Akuku, Onitshaolona, and the surrounding country subdued, after hard fighting, by the troops; many of the Hausas and carriers killed; Lieut. Vickery, R.A., wounded

Feb. 14, Force joined by reinforcements of 1 gun and 100 rifles, under Capt. H. P. Gordon; clearing of the country between Idumoge, Obubuku, and Oboru-Uku proceeded with; much resistance at the last town; reconnaissance, under Capt. Wallis and Lieut. Halfpenny, retire after severe fighting and heavy loss

Feb. 15, Oboru-Uku, the stronghold of the Ekumekus, attacked by the whole force and captured; 17 casualties

Feb. 24, Anglo-German Boundary Protocol signed (Yola-Lake Chad)

March 14, Rebellion in S. Nigeria quelled, whole of the ringleaders, and chief men captured or surrender themselves; Ekumeku society practically suppressed, reported

April 8, Anglo-French Boundary Agreement signed modified that of June 14, 1898, in favor of France

Early May, Column 250 strong, under Maj. Trinchard, one of three sent to pacify the country lying between the Niger and Cross rivers, encounter natives of the Ohoho country about 80 miles up the Emo river beyond Egwanga, who are defeated after stubborn resistance, losing 200 killed and wounded

Mid May, Emir of Kano, with an escort of 300 cavalry and 400 footmen, pays a state visit to Sir Frederick Lugard, the high commissioner of Northern Nigeria, at headquarters at Zungeru

June 6, The land telegraph connecting Lagos with Forcados, Southern Nigeria, is to be completed and shortly opened for traffic; Old Calabar, the headquarters of the Southern Nigeria Government, also connected by telegraph, the first message received in Liverpool

Aug., Mr. A. Egerton, High Commissioner of S. Nigeria, appointed also Governor of Lagos

Oct., Mr. Sayer, British commissioner, with friendly chief accompanying him, attacked while proceeding on a peaceful mission to open a trading market in the interior

Mid Dec., Sir F. Lugard's report on N. Nigeria for the past year states that order in the Sokoto province has been restored; favorable reports from Gando and Argungu; population increasing in Bornu; successful progress in checking the slave trade, and slave raiding stopped; local trade in the protectorate flourishing; total revenue for 1902–3, 357,000*l.*; expenditure, 389,391*l.*

December, Important extension of telegraphs to be made in S. Nigeria; expedition in the hinterland of Onitsha, on the left bank of the Niger, opposite Asaba, composed of 200 infantry under the command of Maj. Moorhouse, starts up the Anambara creek to safeguard the interests of the trading firms of Onitsha; punitive expedition under Capt. Carleton, 150 strong, despatched from Degama, near Bonny, completes its operations during December, against the town, which had attacked Mr. Sayer, reported, Jan. 2, 1905

1905

Early April, Emir of Hadeija, the last great hostile emir in N. Nigeria, tenders his submission, and asks that a resident may be sent to his capital; Capt. Phillips sent as resident, reported

June 21, Liner *Akabo*, leaving Foscades river May 28, arrives at Liverpool, bringing news of severe fighting in S. Nigeria; portion of the force under Capt. Barrow and Capt. Byrne, acting as an escort to the district commissioner to Oweti to collect fines, ambushed at Akataka, near Afikpo, 4 native soldiers killed, remainder fall back on Afikpo

Aug. 1, Trouble breaks out in N. Nigeria with Hadeija, the last of the important emirates of the protectorate to come under direct administration, reported

Oct. 17, Fighting in the Kwale country in S. Nigeria, Mr. J. Davidson, the district commissioner, and Lieuts. P. S. Vassall, and C. A. L. Irvine, reported

Oct. 26, Annual report of the S. Nigerian protectorate issued by the colonial office states trade is increasing, the first telegraph opened, roads opened up, forestry department now fully organized, schools established, civil force established in place of the military, mineralogical and geological surveys, and sanitary improvements making progress

1906

Proclamation (no. 11) prohibited sale of any native land to any person without written consent of Governor

Feb. 16, Order in council places the administration of the S. Nigeria Protectorate under that of the colony of Lagos and changing the name of that colony to that of the colony of Southern Nigeria

Feb. 26, Rising of fanatics in Sokoto; 3 British officers and 25 natives reported killed, Feb. 20; the mahdi reported dead from his wounds

March 12, Rebels in N. Nigeria crushed at Sokoto; operations against the Munshi tribe reported successful

March 19, Hostility of the Emir of Hadeija; expedition to be sent against him, reported

——, Anglo-German Boundary Agreement as to frontier with Cameroons. Accepted March 11, 1913

March 31, Expedition despatched from Lokoja by Sir Fredk. Lugard, the High Commissioner, against the Munshis, who, in Jan., 1906, rose on the mid-Binue and sacked the Niger company's station at Abinsi, stopped by order of the home government after it had proceeded up the Binue, and reached the enemy's country, reported

April 4, Sir Fredk. Lugard reports that the chiefs of the Sokoto and Gando provinces had behaved with great loyalty during the recent disturbances except the Emir of Gando, who had been deposed for complicity with the rebels; a leader of the rebels who had killed 2 French officers, executed after trial by the Sultan of Sokoto and a native court

May 1, Letters patent constituting the colony of S. Nigeria proclaimed at Lagos

May 3, British punitive expedition under Col. Lowry Cole, gains a decisive victory over the Hadeija people; the Emir captured

May 29, Anglo-French Boundary Convention as to frontier east of the Niger

June 20, Mr. James Jamieson Thorburn, Colonial Secretary of S. Nigeria, appointed Lieutenant-Governor of the Colony, announced

July 1, Return of Capt. R. Ommanney, and Capt. G. F. Evans, to England, on completion of the telegraphic longitude work for which they were sent to N. Nigeria previous autumn

Sept. 11, Sir F. Lugard resigns his position as High Commissioner for N. Nigeria, to take effect from

Sept. 22, News received in the neighborhood of Yola of two of the protectorate police being killed and eaten by the pagan tribes living near the Binue; a punitive force was sent and reported at Zungeru

Oct. 19, Definition of boundaries of Southern Nigeria and Lagos

——, Anglo-French Boundary Agreement on entire frontier from Gulf of Guinea to the Niger

1907

Jan. 17, Sir E. P. Girouard appointed High Commissioner of N. Nigeria

1908

Feb. 25, Anglo-French boundaries east of the Niger defined

Aug. 27, Extension of the S. Nigerian government railway to Horin, 245 miles from the coast terminus, opened

1909

Feb. 9, New Nile barrage at Esneh opened by the Khedive

May 6, Lieut. Vansenen, assistant resident in N. Nigeria, while marching to a Guari town with 3 Europeans and 35 native police to instal a chief, was ambushed, and he, the chief, and 11 police, were killed

Sept. 14, Death of Sir Ralph Moor, formerly High Commissioner of S. Nigeria, in London

1910

Feb. 19, Anglo-French Boundary Protocol signed

March 1, Sir Henry Hesketh Bell, appointed Governor of northern Nigeria, Sept. 28, 1909; makes his entry into Kano, being escorted by 14,000 mounted men

May 24, 500 Arabs attacked a detachment of the French native auxiliary troops at Daffa, in the region north of Lake Chad; the Arabs left 100 dead and 37 wounded on the field; the French lost 10 killed and 19 wounded

June 27, The Southern Nigerian government reports the successful conclusion of operations against the members of the secret society known as the "Silent Ones," whose chief with 200 followers surrendered. *Times*

Land and Native Rights Proclamation and Act (no. 9) declared lands other than Crown to be native lands under control of the Government to be administered for the benefit of the natives

1912

July 20, Anglo-French Boundary Convention settled frontier under Treaty of Oct. 19, 1906, from Gulf of Guinea to the Niger on portion to Okpara River

1913

Jan. 1, New Governor General held Durbar at Kano which was attended by practically all of the chiefs of the Protectorate—from the great Mohammedan Emirs to the petty chiefs of pagan hill tribes—with their retinues estimated as 20,000 horsemen and 40,000 foot

March 11, Anglo-German Boundary Convention defined frontiers between Nigeria and the Cameroons, and from Yola to the sea

Nov. 29, Letters Patent, and Order in Council of Nov. 22, to come into effect Jan. 1, the Colony and Protectorate of Southern Nigeria and the Colony and Protectorate of Northern Nigeria were amalgated and formed into the Colony and Protectorate of Nigeria, the boundaries were defined, and an advisory and deliberative body known as the Nigerian Council was established

1914

Jan. 1, Amalgamation of Northern and Southern Nigeria came into effect

——, Sir Frederick Lugard, the first Governor General

Feb. 18, Exchange of Notes by which Great Britain and France defined western limits of boundary

Aug. 25, Four Nigerian columns crossed frontier into Cameroons. *See* Cameroons and World War

Sept. 16, New Treaty with King Alake of Abeokuta replaced that of Jan. 18, 1893, Egba ceded and made a Province with a Resident

Native Courts Ordinance enacted (no. 7 of 1914, and chap. 5 of laws) established 4 classes of courts

1915

Benin reëstablished as a kingdom and made the Benin province of Southern Nigeria with a Resident, and the son of Overami, who had died in exile in 1914, recognized as *oba*

Sept. 1, Eastern Railroad opened to Udi coalfields

1916

Feb. 28, Land and Native Rights Ordinance recognized administration of native chiefs

March 23, The Governor of Nigeria empowered to administer that part of the Cameroons occupied by the British

June, Duty of £2 per bushel on export of palm kernels to foreign countries imposed

Aug. 31, Ordinance declared legal status of slavery abolished in the Protectorate

Nov. 15–17, General Cunliffe with Nigerian troops left for service in East Africa, arriving at Dar-es-Salaam, Dec. 10

Dec., Education Ordinance became law

1917

Aug. 30, Native Lands and Acquisition Act provided that no person not a native could acquire land without approval of the Governor

Oct. 4, Master and Servant Ordinance enacted

Native Revenue Ordinance (no. 1) applied to Northern Province established taxes, Liquor and Arms Ordinances enacted

1918

May 2, Crown Lands Ordinance enacted

1919

Aug. 8, Sir Hugh Clifford arrived at Lagos, succeeding Sir F. Lugard as Governor General

1922

Nov. 21, Nigeria (Legislative Council) Order in Council created a Legislative Council consisting of the Governor, the members of the Executive Council, and other official members (total official membership not to exceed 30), 3 members elected by the ratepayers of Lagos, 1 member by the ratepayers of Calabar, 4 members selected respectively by the Chamber of Commerce of Lagos, Port Harcourt and Kano, and the local Chamber of Mines; 2 members to represent respectively banking and shipping interests, and 8 members to represent African interests in those parts of the Colony and Southern Provinces which do not return elected representatives; Royal instructions to the Governor, Dec. 9

1923

Roads and Rivers Ordinance provided for compulsory labor (chap. 107)

Sept. 20, First election for unofficial members of the Legislative Council held in Lagos and Calabar

Oct. 31, New Legislative Council opened by the Governor

1924

Feb. 24, Abolition of slavery Ordinance in effect from this date

Land Registration Ordinance enacted (no. 36)

1925

July 12, Eastern Railroad to Kafanchan opened by the Governor

1926

Profiteering Rent Repeal Ordinance (no. 2) repealed chap. 92 of laws, emergency legislation enacted during the World War

1927

April 27, Ordinance regulated the import, export, manufacture, sale, and use of opium and similar drugs

Sept. 3, Ordinance regulated levy and collection of income tax for every adult citizen from April 1, 1928, to begin with incomes between £30 and 50

Sept. 30, Anti-tax demonstration in Warri Province, riots in which police fired on the crowd, finally suppressed by troops

1928

Feb. 17, Royal Instructions to the Governor amended Nigeria Protectorate Order in Council of Nov., 1922

May 16, Nigeria (Legislative Order in Council) of Nov., 1922, amended

Dec. 5, Ordinance provided for establishment of European reserve defense force

Dec. 19, Lagos Town Planning Ordinance provided for improvement and development of towns

1929

Feb. 7, Labor Code enacted

Oct. 17, Land and Native Rights Ordinance amended as to principles to be observed in fixing and revising rents

NORTHERN RHODESIA

See also Rhodesia.

By an Order in Council, dated May 4, 1911, the two provinces of North-eastern and North-western Rhodesia were amalgamated under the title of Northern Rhodesia, the amalgamation taking effect as from August 17, 1911. The limits of the territory, as defined by the Order in Council, are "the parts of Africa bounded by Southern Rhodesia, German South-West Africa (now South-West Africa), Portuguese West Africa, the Congo Free State (now the Belgian Congo), German East Africa (now Tanganyika Territory), Nyasaland, and Portuguese East Africa."

An Administrator was appointed by the British South Africa Company with the approval of the Secretary of State, and had, for consultative purposes, an Advisory Council of five members, chosen by the white settlers.

By an Order in Council dated February 20, 1924, the office of Governor was created, an Executive Council constituted and provision made for the institution of a Legislative Council. This latter Council is composed of five *ex-officio* members, who also constitute the Executive Council, four nominated official members and five elected unofficial members. On April 1, 1924, the British South Africa Company was relieved of the administration of the Territory by the Crown, from which date the Order in Council of February 20, 1924, took effect.

Northern Rhodesia has an area of 287,950 square miles, and consists for the most part of high plateau country, covered with thin forest. Much of the country is suitable for farming and contains areas carrying good arable and grazing land. The permanent European population in December, 1925, was 4,624. The native population on December 31, 1925, was 1,140,642. Livingstone is the capital.

Sir James Crawford Maxwell, Governor, appointed Aug. 31, 1927.

1921

Feb. 25, Gazette published poll tax, not to exceed £1, fixed at 10s. with an additional 10s. for each wife after the first; this tax provided half of the revenue

1928

March 22, Order in Council set aside Crown lands for native reserves, regulations, Oct. 12

NORTHERN TERRITORIES

Northern Territories, British Colony in West Africa, lying to the north of the parallel of 8° N. lat., bounded on the west and north by the French possessions and on the east by Togoland, were placed under British protection Sept. 26, 1901. They are administered, under the Governor, by a Chief Commissioner and 21 Political officers. The country is divided into two provinces Northern and Southern, with headquarters at Tamale in the Southern Province, 237 miles north of Kumasi. Population (1921), 527,914; Europeans (1921), 49. Chief towns, Tamale, 4,000; Navrengo, 15,000. Area of the Protectorate, 35,000 square miles; Mandated Territory is about 10,000 square miles in addition.

NYASALAND

Nyasaland Protectorate, until 1907 (British Central Africa) lies along the southern and western shores of Lake Nyasa and extends towards the Zambezi, the country settled by English missionaries and Scotch settlers after discovery of Lake Nyasa by David Livingstone in 1859. Area 37,596 square miles, population Dec. 31, 1929, 1,936 Europeans (mostly in the Shiré Highlands), 1,117

Asiatics, and 1,356,945 natives. Zomba is the capital.

Sir T. S. W. Thomas, Governor and Commander-in-Chief.

1878

African Lakes Company of Scotch merchants formed to open to navigation and trade the rivers and lakes of Central Africa to which the Zambezi is the approach, James Stevenson, chairman

1883

Captain Foot appointed to Blantyre

1884

Feb. 26, Anglo-Portuguese Treaty recognized freedom of navigation of the Congo and Zambezi rivers and declared claims of Portugal on the Shiré should not extend beyond the confluence of the Ruo with that river

1886

May 12, Treaty of Portugal with France fixing boundaries secured recognition of Portuguese claim to territories lying between Angola and Mozambique, the entire basin of the Zambezi, Matabeleland, and districts of Lake Nyasa up to the latitude of the Rovuma River

Dec. 30, Boundary Treaty of Portugal with Germany also secured recognition of Portuguese territorial claims

1887

Aug. 2, Lord Salisbury formally protested against Portuguese claims as not founded on occupation and including countries in which there were British settlements

1888

Portuguese expedition under Antonio Cardoso sent into Nyasaland reached the south shore of the Lake

1889

Second armed Portuguese expedition under Major Serpa Pinto into Rhodesia and Nyasaland

Sept. 21, British Protectorate declared over Shiré Heights

Oct., Discovery of the Chinde mouth of the Zambezi of great benefit to Nyasa

Oct. 22, Sir H. H. Johnston concluded peace Treaty with Mlazi (Nkonde country)

1890

Jan. 10, Lord Salisbury sent ultimatum to Portugal demanding immediate withdrawal of Major Serpa Pinto

March 8, The Portuguese evacuated disputed territory

July 1, Anglo-German Treaty settled respective spheres in the Nyasa region

Aug. 20, Anglo-Portuguese Treaty signed but not ratified

Nov. 14, *Modus vivendi* with Portugal signed pending new treaty

1891

Feb. 1, H. H. Johnston appointed Commissioner and Consul General of British Central Africa

May 14, British protectorate over the Nyasaland districts formally proclaimed

June 11, Anglo-Portuguese Treaty settled spheres and provided for British concession at Chinde where goods might be landed and trans-shipped and for Portuguese concession in British sphere on west shore of Lake Nyasa

Oct.–Nov., Commissioner Johnston and Captain Cecil Maguire attack Arab slave-dealers and release slaves

Dec. 15–17, Capt. Maguire, with 30 sepoys, releases a number of slaves in a caravan and burns dhows in presence of a large party of enemies, but is killed while swimming to his ship; Dr. Boyce and Mr. M'Ewan are treacherously killed when about to treat for a truce

1892

Jan., Makanjira, and two other chiefs, slave-dealers, predominant

April, The Arabs surprise Fort Johnston and capture a gun; Mr. H. H. Johnston has only 70 sepoys and two gunboats on the Shiré; reported

About April 4, Mr. H. H. Johnston reports the pacification of the district

May 7, Lease of Chinde concession signed

1893

Feb. 22, Name of Protectorate changed to British Central African Protectorate

African Lakes Company merged into British South African Company

Nov. 15, Anglo-German Boundary Treaty settled frontier with German East Africa (Tanganyika)

1894

Jan. 12, Commissioner Johnston, reinforced with 2 gunboats, &c., captures Makanjira's positions; releases many slaves, and founds Fort Maguire on Lake Nyasa, reported; arrives in England, reports the defeat of Makanjira, general submission of chiefs, by Maj. C. A. Edwards at Fort Maguire, and peace made in Nyasaland, 4 June, 1894; returns, May, 1895

July, Death of Jumbe, Arab Sultan, on W. coast of Lake Nyasa, a friend of the British

Nov. 20, Municipal powers given to Blantyre, the capital; reported

1895

July 28, Mr. H. Johnston returns to Zomba from his tour of inspection

Sept. 3, Successful N.W. expedition of Mr. Codrington; treaties with several chiefs; reported

Oct. 28, Zarafi slave-trading chief completely defeated by a British expedition under Major C. A. Edwards, his town occupied, and many slaves released; expedition returns to Zomba, Nov. 17; North Nyasa Arabs severely defeated after 3 days fighting, Dec. 1–3, 1895

Dec. 4, Mlozi, a slave-raiding chief, tried by native chiefs under commissioner Johnston, condemned and hanged

Dec. 19, Telegraphic communication opened, message to the Queen, and her reply sent

1896

John S. Brabant, Commissioner during absence of H. H. Johnston

Jan. 25, Great victories over Mwasi and other slave-dealing chiefs, by Lieut. Alston and Capt. F. T. Stewart on the west of Lake Nyasa; British forts

erected; power of the slave-trade completely broken; total of slaves released, 1,184; reported

Sept. 30, Lieut. Alston captures Katuri, a cruel Yao chief, releases many slaves, and burns his town, other Yao chiefs submit to the British; reported

Oct. 12, Serious attacks on the S.-W. frontier, by the Angoni-Zulus under Chikusi, villages raided and people massacred; Mr. Sharpe, acting-commissioner at Blantyre, sends 3 columns under Capts. Stewart, Manning, and Lieut. Alston. [Lieut. Alston died of fever; reported, May 8, 1897.]

——, North Charterland exploration company; Lieut.-Col. R. Gardner Warton successfully occupies Mpseni's country in Central Africa, north of the Zambezi, and establishes friendly relations with this chief; reported, *Times*

Oct. 21, The rising in S. Nyasaland suppressed, and Chikusi captured, tried, and hanged; Odete's stronghold carried by assault by Capt. Manning, and Odete exiled, Oct. 10, 1896

1897

Aug. 9, 10, Punitive expedition under Capt. W. H. Manning against the Angurus for raids, &c., S.-E. Lake Shirwa, Serumba's town and he himself taken

Aug. 16, Expedition under Major Macdonald into the interior organized at Kikuyu

1898

Jan., Raids and revolt of the Angoni Zulus; repressed by a strong force under Col. Manning, about 20 natives killed, and the impi broken up; Mr. Carl Wiese and party relieved, Jan. 18; successful campaign against Mpseni, he surrenders, Feb. 9

Nov. 11, Delimitation of boundary with Tanganyika

1901

Feb. 23, Anglo-German Boundary Agreement settled boundary between Lake Nyasa and Tanganyika

Dec. 31, Native hut tax of 12s. each hut in proclaimed districts declared replaced the hut tax published in Gazette Aug. 20, 1894, 6s. only if native has worked for 1 month of current year in employment of a European

1902

May 11, British Order in Council, and Sept. 7, 1907, provided for administration under Colonial Office by the Governor and Commander-in-Chief, assisted by an Executive and a Legislative Council, both consisting of nominated members, the Governor having right of veto

1904

April 1, Administration transferred from the Foreign Office to the Colonial Office

Nov. 30, Native Land Ordinance (native locations) authorized the Government to set aside one tenth of any undeveloped lands as native reserves

1906

Sept. 15, Boundary Treaty settled frontier with Portuguese East Africa

1907

July 6, Name changed to Nyasaland Protectorate

Sept. 4, Order in Council made the Commissioner, Sir Alfred Sharp, Governor and Commander-in-Chief and constituted an Executive and Legislative Council both consisting of nominated members, the Governor having right of veto

1908

March 31, First passenger train arrived at Blantyre on the Shiré Highlands railroad completed from Port Herald on the Lower Shiré

1910

March 1, Employment of natives Ordinance regulated contracts and apprenticeship, recruitment prohibited to prevent natives from going to the Rand where they died in great numbers

Nov. 12, Ordinance provided for compulsory registration of documents including land leases

1911

Feb., Sir W. H. Manning succeeded Sir Alfred Sharpe as Governor

March 9, Land Tax Ordinance provided for tax on all except Crown lands to come into effect April 1, 1912

July 24, Ordinance organized the Kings African Rifles

Aug. 31, Native hut tax Ordinance enacted, tax not to exceed 12s. a year

Nov., Agreement signed as to boundary on Shiré and Ruo Rivers with Portuguese East Africa

Census gave population as 969,183 natives, Europeans 766, Asiatics 481

1912

Nov. 8, Crown Lands Ordinance regulated method of disposal of lands

1913

Sir George Smith appointed Governor

1914

Aug. 13, The one German boat on Lake Nyasa disabled by Commander Rhoades gave command of the lake

Sept. 9, German attack on Karonga repulsed, the only German invasion during War

1915

Jan. 23, Native revolt led by John Chilembwe, negro teacher and preacher, begun by attack and murder of 3 men, Europeans, including Mr. Livingstone, a descendant of the explorer, his wife and children carried off

Feb. 3, Chilembwe in flight from volunteer British and native force was killed by native police at Mlanje station which ended the rising for independence

Railroad from Port Herald on the Shiré to Ghindi on the north bank of the Zambezi completed (61 miles)

1917

Sept. 20, Native Rents (Private estates) Ordinance prohibited the natives from giving service in lieu of rent, and limited rents to amount fixed by Governor in Council to remedy abuses relating to natives living on European private estates

1920

March, Census of Europeans gave number as 1,015; Asiatics, 481; the natives estimated in 1919 as 1,216,000

1921

March 31, Hut tax imposed at rate of 6s. per hut with additional 6s. for every wife after the first, and an alternative poll tax for natives not liable to hut tax

April, Export duties on cotton, tea, and tobacco removed because of fall in prices and financial panic in latter part of 1920

1922

April, Railroad from Murraça on the Zambezi to the port of Beira, Portuguese East Africa opened (175) miles establishing direct communication between Blantyre and Beira

1927

May 23, Education Ordinance enacted. Grant of £4,000 to the missionary societies conducting the schools under the Ordinance

1928

Oct. 10 and 13, New Private Estates Ordinance (Native Rents) established a District Rent Board

1929

April, New customs tariff introduced protective duties on coffee, ghee, rice, soap and tea, cigo, and all produce and manufactured articles a general advance ad valorem to 17%

1930

April 11, New Education Ordinance enacted

OIL RIVERS

Oil Rivers Protectorate, now incorporated in the Colony of Nigeria, the coast region of Nigeria between Lagos and the Cameroons, the so-called Oil Rivers being the Benin, Escravos, Warri (Forcados), Brass, St. Nicholas, St. Barbara, St. Bartholomew, Sombrero, New Calabar, Bonny, Andoni (St. Antonio), Opobo, Kwo Ibo, Akpayafe, Kwa, and Cross, the last four flowing into the Old Calabar before reaching the sea. Proclamation of British Protectorate June 5, 1885. Notification of British Protectorate over Niger districts, coast and interior published in the London Gazette. Aug. 1, 1891, Major Sir Claude Maxwell MacDonald appointed British Commissioner and Consul General, and May 13, 1893, name changed to Niger Coast Protectorate. *See* Nigeria.

ORANGE FREE STATE

Orange Free State, one of the four constituent provinces of the Union of South Africa, bounded on the south by the Orange River.

The Orange River was first crossed by Europeans about the middle of the eighteenth century. Between 1810 and 1820, settlements were made in the southern parts of the Orange Free State, and the Great Trek greatly augmented the number of settlers during and after 1836. In 1848, Sir Harry Smith proclaimed the whole territory between the Orange and Vaal Rivers as a British Possession and established what was called the Orange River Sovereignty. Great dissatisfaction was caused by this step, as well as by the native policy of the British Government. In 1854, by the Convention of Bloemfontein, British Sovereignty was withdrawn and the independence of the country was recognized.

During the first five years of its existence the Orange Free State was much harassed by incessant raids by, and fighting with, the Basutos. These were at length conquered. The British Government then stepped in and arranged matters much to the dissatisfaction of the conquering party. By the Treaty of Aliwal North, only a part of the territory of the Basutos was incorporated in the Orange Free State.

On account of the Treaty between the Orange Free State and South African Republic, the former State took a prominent part in the South African War (1899–1902), and was annexed on May 28, 1900, as the Orange River Colony. After peace was declared Crown Colony Government was established and continued until 1907, when responsible government was introduced. On May 31, 1910, the Orange River Colony was merged in the Union of South Africa as the Province of the Orange Free State.

The seat of provincial government is at Bloemfontein.

The area of the Province is 49,647 square miles; it is divided into 27 districts. The census population has varied as follows:

Census Year	All Races			White		Colored	
	Total	Males	Females	Males	Females	Males	Females
1880	133,518	70,150	63,368	31,906	29,116	38,244	34,252
1890	207,503	108,362	99,141	40,571	37,145	67,791	61,996
1904	387,315	210,095	177,220	81,571	61,108	128,524	116,112
1911	528,174	277,518	250,656	94,488	80,701	183,030	169,955
1918	—	—	—	93,969	87,709		
1921	628,827	321,373	307,454	97,776	90,780	223,597	216,674
1926	—	—	—	103,830	98,361		

The capital, Bloemfontein, had, in 1921, 19,367 white inhabitants, and 19,667 natives and other colored persons; total, 39,034. The 1926 preliminary unaudited Census figures for the European population are 22,577.

1834

First settled by Dutch farmers from Cape Colony

1836

First settlers of the Great Trek of Boers from Cape Colony to escape from British sovereignty led by A. H. Potgieter who purchased land between the Vet and Vaal rivers from Makwana, chief of Bataung tribe of Bechuanas

1837

Jan. 17, Zulu Chief Mosilikatze defeated by Boers and driven northward and the settlers founded Winburg named to commemorate the victory and Piet Retief elected Governor and Commandant-General

1843

Dec. 13, Treaty with Moshesh, chief of Basutos, by which his lands placed under British protectorate

1845

May 2, Agreement of Governor of Cape Colony with Griqua chief, Adam Kok III, by which his lands on which Boers had settled placed under British sovereignty

1848

Feb. 3, Proclamation of Sir Harry Smith, Governor of Cape Colony, declared British sovereignty over the region between the Orange and Val Rivers up to the Drakensburg as the Orange River Territory, Major H. D. Warden, appointed British Resident, head of the Government, established at Bloemfontein

Aug. 29, Sir Harry Smith defeated the Boers led by Pretorius who had resisted British authority and ousted the British Resident

1849

Oct. 1, Treaty with Mosesh, chief of the Basutos, established boundary known as the "Warden line"

1851

March 22, Letters Patent established the Orange River Territory

June 30, Major Donovan drawn into war with Molitsane, one of the Basuto chiefs subordinate to Moshesh defeated at Viervoet

Aug. 25, Petition of citizens at Winburg asked Pretorius (outlawed by British Government) to come from beyond the Vaal to their assistance

Sept. 3, Peace Treaty with Moshesh signed at Thaba Bosigo

1852

Jan. 17, Sand River Convention signed with the Transvaal by Commission from Cape Colony recognizing independence of Transvaal to secure their friendship and prevent alliance with Moshesh. Approved by British Secretary of State for the Colonies June 24

June 21, Assembly convened at Bloemfontein voted in favor of remaining under British authority and asked for assistance against Moshesh

June 24, Boundary Convention with African Republic (Transvaal)

July 23, Henry Green succeeded Major Warden as British Resident

Dec. 14, Ultimatum to Moshesh demanded cession of cattle and observance of boundaries

Dec. 20, Indecisive battle fought with Moshesh by forces commanded by Sir George Cathcart, Governor of Cape Colony at Berea and acceptance of peace proposals of Moshesh

1853

April 6, Sir G. R. Clark appointed Special Commissioner to arrange for withdrawal of British dominion, and arrived at Bloemfontein Aug. 8

Sept. 5, Elected Assembly met at Bloemfontein (76 Dutch and 19 English according to proportion of the 2 nationalities) and appointed committee to petition for continuance of British rule

1854

Jan. 30, Royal Proclamation "abandoned and renounced dominion" over Orange River

Feb. 23, Convention with Great Britain recognized independence

March 28, Constitutional Convention met at Bloemfontein

April 10, Constitution of the Republic proclaimed, J. H. Hoffman, first President

April 15, Ordinance established the Dutch language

1855

Feb., Jacobus Nicolaas Boshof elected President succeeding Mr. Hoffman forced to resign

Oct., Sir George Grey, Governor of Cape Colony, arranged conference between Moshesh and President Boshof in effort to preserve peace and Agreement signed by Moshesh which he kept for a few weeks

1857

Jan., Armed raid of Pretorius from the Transvaal not successful

June 1, Peace Treaty with the Transvaal signed, each State recognizing the independence of the other

1858

Feb., Armed bands of Basutos seized Free State farms and destroyed buildings and orchards

March 19, Declaration of war against Moshesh who refused redress of grievances and unsuccessful campaign against the Basutos

Sept. 29, Treaty of Peace signed with Moshesh at Aliwal North and cession of territory by the Free State

Nov. 19, Proposal of Sir George Grey for union of Cape Colony, Natal, and the Orange Free State which was not approved by Imperial Government

1859

Feb., Resignation of President Boshof not accepted

June 25, Final resignation of President Boshof, E. R. Snyman appointed Acting President

Oct. 8, District of Bethulie ceded by Chief Lepui

Dec. 15, J. J. Venter elected President

1860

Feb. 8, Marthinus Wessel Pretorius, son of Commandant General Andries Pretorius, elected President, obtaining leave of absence from the Transvaal where he was President

1861

Dec. 26, Treaty with Adam Kok by which he ceded his lands to the Free State for £4,000 and removed to East Griqualand, this cession becoming the District of Philippolis

1862

June 19, Bloemfontein Bank established

1863

April 15, Resignation of President Pretorius

June 20, J. J. Venter became Acting President

Nov. 5, Jan Hendrik Brand elected President

1864

Feb. 2, President Brand assumed office

Oct. 28, Decision of Sir Philip Wodehouse in conference with representatives of the Free State and Moshesh in favor of Free State boundary as laid down by Sir Harry Smith

1865

June 9, Declaration of war on Moshesh to enforce award

1866

March 4, Molapo, second son of Moshesh, asked for peace terms which were accepted

March 16, Peace Treaty with Molapo and annexation of his lands

April 3, Peace Treaty and Boundary Agreement with Moshesh at Thaba Bosigo

May 23, Ordinance for control of Molapo tribe

1867

July 17, War declared on Moshesh to enforce terms of Treaty

Sept. 25, Makwais Mountain stronghold taken by Free State force commanded by Commander Pansegrow and other victories followed by which all Basuto positions except Thaba Bosigo taken ending 30 years war with the Basutos

1868

March 12, Proclamation declared Basutoland annexed to the British Crown after petition by the defeated Moshesh considered violation of the Treaty of 1854 by the Free State

1869

Feb. 12, Boundary Convention with Great Britain defined boundary with Basutoland the Caledon River from its source to Jammerberg Drift and from there eastward to Kornet Spruit

1870

Feb. 19, Decision of Lieutenant Governor Keate fixed boundary with Natal in favor of the Free State

1871

Oct. 27, Territory claimed by Nicholas Waterboer, Griqua, administered by the Free State since 1854, in which diamonds had been found, ceded by him to Great Britain, proclaimed British territory (West Griqualand)

Oct. 17, Award of Lieutenant Governor Keate gave Nicholas Waterboer territory claimed by him west of Platberg on the Vaal and to Bantu tribes the country west of the Makwasi Spruit

Dec. 19, Protest of Free State against award and subsequent proceedings

1874

May 5, President Brand entered on third term of office

Dec. 24, Convention signed with Cape Colony for construction of bridges over the Orange River

1876

May 6, President Brand presented claims in England for restitution of lands east of the Vaal River and north of Vetberg line pronounced by British court as never in possession of Waterboer or the Griquas

July 13, Boundary Convention with Great Britain settled frontier with West Griqualand and agreement for compensation of £90,000 as compensation for territory taken in 1871 not restored

1877

May 23, Resolution of the Volksraad expressed regret at British annexation of the Transvaal against wishes of the majority of the citizens and the Government

June 27, National Bank established

1879

Feb. 14, Bridge across the Orange River opened at Bethulie

1880

July 17, President Brand supported Tsepinare to succeed Moroko, Chief of Barolong, designated by Moroko before his death as his successor as against Samuel, eldest son of Moroko

1884

May 9, President Brand entered on his fifth term of office

July 10, Samuel attacked and killed Tsepinare, in attack on Thaba Ntshu

July 12, President Brand, invited by Baralongs refusing to recognize Samuel as their chief, proclaimed Thaba Ntshu annexed to the Free State as District of Moroka

1888

July 14, Death of President Brand

1889

Jan. 11, Frederick William Reitz, Chief Justice, elected President

1892

June 29, Award settled southwest boundary

1893

Nov. 27, President Reitz reëlected

1895

Nov. 17, President Reitz resigned

1896

Feb. 21, Judge Martinus Theunis Steyn elected President

1898

Oct. 5, Closer union with the Transvaal adopted

1899

Jan. 31, Railway from Bloemfontein to Heilbron opened

April 4, The raad opened; federation with the Transvaal rejected, until the abrogation of article iv of the 1884 convention (*i.e.* British suzerainty) be obtained

May 31–June 5, Conference at Bloemfontein between Sir A. Milner and Presidents Kruger and Steyn; negotiations fail

June 23, The raad votes 53,977*l.* for war purposes

July 2–4, Conference between Messrs. Hofmeyr, Herholdt (Cape Ministers), and Pres. Steyn, Mr. Fischer, and others; proposals inadequate

Sept. 21, Raad opened with a defiant speech by Pres. Steyn

Sept. 27, Resolution adopted by the Volksraad and communicated to the British High Commissioner by President Steyn that the Government should continue efforts for peaceful settlement of differences between the South African Republic and Great Britain, but declared that "if a war is now begun or occasioned by Her Majesty's Government against South African Republic, this would morally be a war against the whole white population of South Africa" and that the Free State would observe its obligations arising out of political alliance with the South African Republic

Oct. 11, 12, Pres. Steyn espouses the cause of the Transvaal, Oct. 10; British government denounced and martial law proclaimed

Oct. 11, State of war existed. *See* South African War

1900

March 13, Bloemfontein occupied by Lord Roberts receiving formal surrender of city, the Free State Government retiring to Kroonstad

April 4, Raad opened at Kroonstadt by Pres. Steyn, April 2; adjourns sine die

April 20, Major-Gen. Pretyman appointed military gov. of the Free State

May 9, The British occupied Kroonstad putting Free State Government to flight

May 21, The State formally annexed to the British Empire, under the name of "Orange River Colony," proclaimed May 24 by Lord Roberts

June 11, Counter Proclamation of President Steyn from Reitz declared annexation null and void

1901

Jan., Sir A. Milner, High Commissioner of S. Africa, appointed Governor (made a peer May 24), and Major Hamilton Goold-Adams, Lieut.-Gov.

Jan.–Dec., Civil administration appointed; industries and education reëstablished, country progressing

Nov. 22, Land settlements begun; several returned yeomanry occupy government farms in Thaba Nchu district, reported

1902

June 23, Lord Milner sworn in as Governor of the Colony at Bloemfontein)

Nov. 5, Vote of 8,000,000*l.* for the Colony and the Transvaal, passed the Commons

Nov. 19, Martial law repealed

1903

Jan. 6, Rev. H. Duplessis, minister of the Dutch Reformed Church at Lindley, forced to resign owing to the systematic boycott of his congregation on account of his British sympathies, appointed by the Government inspector of schools in the Transvaal

Jan. 14, Legislative council (enlarged) opened

Feb. 6, Mr. Chamberlain arrived at Bloemfontein, Feb. 3; he receives a deputation headed by Gen. Christian De Wet and Boer delegates who present a petition setting forth alleged grievances

Feb. 16, Law providing for naturalization of aliens passed

March 10–23, Intercolonial conference at Bloemfontein,

Lord Milner, president; Customs Union Convention, preferential treatment of British imports signed

June 15, Intercolonial Council for the affairs of the Orange River Colony and the Transvaal established

Nov. 26, Legislative council opened; Sir H. Goold-Adams referred to the drought, the severest in the colony since 1862, and the labor difficulty, which had affected railway construction; finances of the colony most satisfactory, large surplus over the estimates, which would be partly devoted to paying the contribution of 80,000*l.* toward the inter-colonial deficits

1904

Dec. 2, 3, Congress of Orange Colony Boers held at Brandfort; resolutions passed demanding a full statement regarding the distribution and administration of compensation funds; demands formulated with reference to the Dutch language, education, repatriation, the constabulary, relief camps, and responsible government

1905

Jan. 12, Legislative council opened by Sir H. Goold-Adams, who stated that the agricultural prospects of the colony were unsatisfactory; financial position of the colony generally satisfactory

Early Feb., Report of the industrial commission recommends bonuses should be paid in some cases for 3, and others 5 years, on wool, leather, preserved cement, tobacco, and pottery raised or produced in the colony, and that assistance should be given to the basket-making industry. The establishment of an industrial board for Orange River Colony is recommended

March 1, Railway connecting Bethlehem and Harrismith opened by Sir H. Goold-Adams

——, Viscount Milner resigns his office as High Commissioner in S. Africa and Administrator of the Transvaal and Orange River colonies; succeeded by the Earl of Selborne

End March, Sir H. Goold-Adams, at a banquet at Ladybrand, announces that the government grant of 3,000,000*l.* would be paid at an early date, the distribution being *pro rata* on the claims assessed

May 20, Lord Selborne is sworn in at Bloemfontein as Governor of the Colony

Mid June, Representative deputation received by Lord Selborne at Wimburg states that nothing short of responsible government would satisfy the people of the colony

July 19, 20, Boer congress opens at Bloemfontein; ex-President Steyn, unable to be present, writes affirming that self-government on the lines of the constitution of Cape Colony had been promised by the treaty of Vereeniging; reply of the Imperial Government to the resolutions passed by the Brandfort congress held Dec. 2 and 3, 1904, presented to the congress; the government entirely denies that its pledges have not been fulfilled, and that while English will be the official language of the colony, the use of Dutch will be duly recognized by the authorities; resolution passed to form a union with the object of obtaining responsible government; the congress passes resolutions welcoming Lord Selborne, and pleasure at Mr. Steyn's return

1906

May 3, The Orangia Unie Congress opened in Bloemfontein

1907

June 5, New Constitution granted

July 1, Formal promulgation of the new constitution at Bloemfontein

Nov. 20, First elections under the new constitution result in 30 seats for the Orangie Unie; constitutional party, 4; independent candidates, 4

Nov. 25, New ministry announced: Mr. Fischer, Premier and Colonial Secretary; Gen. Hertzog, Att.-Gen. and Director of Education; Dr. Ramsbottom, Treasurer; Mr. Wessels, Minister of Public Works; Gen. de Wet, Minister of Agriculture

Dec. 18, First parliament under the new constitution assembles at Bloemfontein

1908

April 8, The Bloemfontein-Kimberley railway opened by the Governor

April 18, New education act, establishing an educational system similar to that which obtained under the old Free State, gazetted

Sept. 20, The South Africa bill received royal assent (*see* South Africa)

1910

March 30, Education crisis, resignation of Mr. Gunn, director of education

May 31, Entered Union of South Africa as Orange Free State Province. *See* South Africa, Union of

PRINCIPE (PRINCE'S ISLAND)

See St. Tomé (St. Thomas)

RÉUNION

Réunion (or Bourbon), about 420 miles east of Madagascar, has belonged to France since 1643. It is administered by a Governor assisted by a Privy Council, and an elective Council-General, and is represented in the French Parliament by a Senator and two Deputies. It has an area of 970 square miles and population (1926) of 186,637, of whom 180,694 were French; there were also 628 British Indians, 1,963 natives of Madagascar, 411 Africans, 1,626 Chinese. The chief towns are: St. Denis, with 23,390 inhabitants in 1926; St. Pierre, 20,479; St. Paul, 21,643; St. Louis, 15,867. The towns are under the French municipal law.

RHODESIA

Rhodesia, named after Cecil Rhodes, includes the whole of the region extending from the Transvaal Province northwards to the borders of the Belgian Congo and Tanganyika Territory, bounded on the east by Portuguese East Africa, Nyasaland, and the Tanganyika Territory, and on the west by the Belgian Congo, Portuguese West Africa, and Bechuanaland. The region south of the Zambezi (Matabeleland and Mashonaland) is called Southern Rhodesia; that north of the Zambezi is known as Northern Rhodesia, formed in 1911 of the former provinces of Northeastern and Northwestern Rhodesia. Southern Rhodesia has an area of 149,000 square miles with estimated population of 1,032,703 in 1929 of whom 981,140 are natives. Northern Rhodesia has an area of 287,950 square miles, the permanent European population in December, 1928, computed at 7,536, the native population on December 31, 1927, was estimated at 1,261,972, Sir Cecil Rodwell, Governor of Southern Rhodesia, Sir James Crawford Maxwell, Governor of Northern Rhodesia. For Northern Rhodesia, *see also* p. 689.

1872

Nov. 25, Frederick C. Selous made first visit to Mashonaland

1888

Feb. 11, Lobengula, chief of the Matabeles made Treaty with J. S. Moffat, the British Resident at Bulawayo, which placed all the Matabele dominions under British protection. For claims of Portuguese, *see* Nyasaland, 1886

Oct. 30, Treaty with Chief Lobengula giving mining rights in Matabeleland and Mashonaland

1889

March 2, A deputation of two head men from him was received by Queen Victoria, requesting protection against a syndicate, to which he had inconsiderately conceded lands. The concession was afterwards legally withdrawn

Oct. 29, Royal charter of incorporation granted to the British South Africa Company, by which large administrative powers in the region (afterwards called Rhodesia) north of Cape Colony, were conferred

Nov. 21, The Marquis of Salisbury protests against the assumption of Zumbo by the Portuguese, referring to the agreement of Great Britain with Lobengula, ruler of Mashona and Makalakaland, of Feb. 11, 1888, and also to British agreements with other tribes (referred to by Consul Johnston, Aug. 26, and by Consul Buchanan, Sept. 30

Nov. 29, Senhor de Barros Gomes, Portuguese Foreign Minister, in his reply sustains the claims of Portugal, based on discoveries and consequent effective occupation of the territories in question for centuries, relics of which still remain

Dec. 5, Major Serpa Pinto, with about 4,000 men with cannon, forms a camp in the Makololo country, quarrels with the natives, conquers them, and calls on the British settlers to submit to Portugal, reported by Bishop C. A. Smythies

Dec. 17, Lord Salisbury telegraphs to the Portuguese Government in relation to Major Serpa Pinto's action, that they should not permit any such attacks on British settlements, or on any other settlement under British protection

Dec. 20, Sen. Barros Gomes, in his reply, justifies the actions of Major Serpa Pinto, by referring to the disturbed state of the country

Dec. 26, Lord Salisbury, in a dispatch, declines to recognize the claims of Portugal as antiquated, and unsupported by action in modern times

1890

Jan. 6, A peremptory note sent by Lord Salisbury, requiring immediate withdrawal of Major Serpa Pinto delivered

Jan. 8, Sen. Barros Gomes' reply being deemed unsatisfactory, Lord Salisbury requests that matters in dispute be referred to a conference of the Powers, in accordance with the Treaty of Berlin

Jan. 10, Lord Salisbury, by telegram, requires to know that explicit instructions have been sent from Mozambique for the immediate withdrawal of Portuguese forces from the territories in question; Sen. Barros Gomes informs the British Minister, Mr. Petre, that such instructions had been sent Jan. 9. Lord Salisbury, having learned from Consul Churchill at Mozambique, that Major Serpa Pinto's forces still occupied his positions, and treated Nyasaland as a conquered country, directs Mr. Petre to require acceptance of the British demands before 10 P.M., Jan. 11; if not accepted he is to order H.M.S. *Enchantress*, at Vigo, to enter the Tagus

Jan. 12, The Council of State decide to yield under protest, reserving all Portuguese rights

Jan. 29, The Imperial Mission conveying Queen Victoria's letter to Lobengula, recommending the British South Africa chartered company, favorably received by him at Buluwayo, the Matabele capital

Feb., British South Africa Co.'s surveying expedition under Mr. Selous, starts

March 8, The Portuguese evacuate the disputed territory in the Shiré district, reported

June 11, Telegraph lines rapidly constructed

June 28, Expedition of the South Africa company into Mashonaland under Lieut.-Col. E. G. Pennefather, broke camp on the Matcloutsie River and reached and founded Fort Salisbury a distance of 400 miles on Sept. 12

July 1, Anglo-German Boundary Convention

Sept. 14, Part of the Manica country ceded to the company by the Chief Umtasa, by treaty

Oct. 1, The force disbands to occupy the land granted them Oct. 1

Oct. 8, H.M. gunboats, the *Herald* and *Musquito*, enter the Zambezi, with stores

Oct. 10, Mr. Colquhoun, administrator of the company, assumes government at Fort Salisbury

Oct. 17, H.M.S. *Redbreast*, man-of-war, leaves Zanzibar, Sept. 3, amid many difficulties and some Portuguese opposition, with other vessels, proceeds up the Zambezi, reaches Zumbo, and returns to Zanzibar

Nov. 14, The Anglo-Portuguese agreement of Aug. 20 withdrawn, and a *modus vivendi* agreed on

Nov. 15, Col. Paiva d'Andrade and the Baron de Rezendi, with Gouveia, a half-breed native chief, and about 300 followers, seize Umtasa's kraal at Massi Kesse, and replace the British by the Portuguese flag, Nov. 8; Major Forbes, with the company's police, retakes the kraal, restores the British flag, and temporarily imprisons the Portuguese officers; Gouveia, with his men, flee

Dec. 19, The South Africa company ordered by the British to withdraw from Manica

Dec. 31, Gungunhama, nominal King of Manica, said to have replaced the Portuguese flag by the English, reported

Dec. *et seq.*, Gold discovered in Mashonaland

1891

Feb. 3, Deed of settlement authorized exploration and colonization of the country between the Limpopo and Zambezi rivers by the British South African Company

April 23, The British steamer, *Norseman*, containing Sir John Willoughby and party, with the imperial British mail for Mashonaland, stopped by the Portuguese at Port Beira, in the Pungwé river, although the prescribed duty of 3% on the stores had been offered, according to the *modus vivendi*; the British flag replaced by the Portuguese. Two steam launches seized, and the crews imprisoned, reported by Sir John at Delagoa bay, April 20; on the remonstrance of Lord Salisbury the Portuguese Government declares the Pungwé river open to British subjects; three of H.M.'s ships sent to the Pungwé, announced

April 30, Massi Kessi evacuated by the British by government orders, reported

May, Gungunhama, King of Gazaland, sends an embassy to Queen Victoria, soliciting alliance; received at Windsor, July 10

May 9 and July 30, Orders in Council amended Charter

May 11, Portuguese attack on the company's police post, W. of Massi Kesse, repulsed

June 10, Laws of Cape Colony of this date declared in force

June 11, Anglo-Portuguese Treaty settled boundaries

Sept. 10, Dr. Starr Jameson succeeded Mr. Colquhoun as Administrator

Oct. 16, Mr. Cecil Rhodes, commissioner, arrives at Fort Salisbury

Nov. 17, Treaty with Lobengula secured by E. A. Lippert gave the Company right to lease farms and land and levy taxes and rents for 100 years

Dec. 22, First annual meeting of the British South Africa company

1893

July 9 *et seq.*, Murderous raids of Matabeles on the Mashonas; invasion on British settlement near Fort Victoria, unauthorized by Lobengula; repulsed with slaughter; Dr. Jameson, administrator at Fort Victoria, and Mr. C. J. Rhodes, prepare for war; angry message from Lobengula, reported Aug. 1; intervention of Sir H. B. Loch, Aug.; Aug. 14, Secret "Victoria Agreement" signed by Sir Starr Jameson offering lands, gold, and "loot" to those who will enlist for invasion of Matabeleland to seize lands from Lobengula and the Matabeles; the chartered company directed to avoid aggression, Sept. 7; reinforcements and volunteers from Cape Colony sent by the company to fort Victoria, against which 2 impis (native contingents) are advancing, Sept. 21; Capt. White's defensive force fired at by a Matabele impi, about Oct. 1; the company's troops well armed, 500 men at Forts Salisbury, Victoria, and Charter, Oct. 3; an attack on the Bechuanaland border police (Major Goold Adams, commander) by the Matabele on the Shasi River, near Macloutsie, Oct. 5; the company's forces advancing to Matabele border; a free hand given to Dr. Jameson, Oct. 7; junction of all the forces, joined by volunteers from Cape Town regiments, Oct. 16; Major Forbes commander; skirmish at Intaba Zimbi (the iron mountain), Oct. 15; 22 Matabele killed; Capt. Campbell wounded, died Oct 16; two envoys from Lobengula shot by mistake

at Tati, about Oct. 23; Lobengula's army (about 5,000 strong) severely repulsed, with heavy loss, near the Shangani river, Oct. 24–26 [British loss, Walters, Burnett, Capt. Gwinydd Williams, and others]. British advance on Bulawayo attacked by Lobengula's picked regiments; the enemy defeated, with heavy loss, by deadly fire of Maxim guns, near the M'Bembezu river; British loss, 3, Nov. 1, 1893.

Nov. 4, Major Forbes and Dr. Jameson occupy Bulawayo

Nov. 9, Lobengula retreats towards Zambezi; ultimatum sent to Lobengula

Nov. 14, Major Forbes starts in pursuit of Lobengula, sends forward Major Allan Wilson, Dec. 3, who is encountered by an ambush and cut off from the main force, Dec. 4

Dec. 4, Major Allan Wilson and all his party killed, after severe fighting; Capts. Fitzgerald, Judd, H. Greenfield, Kirton, H. J. Borrow; lieuts. G. Hughes and Hofmeyer, and 22 others, died singing "God save the Queen," reported, Jan. 3, 6, 1894

Dec. 15, Major Forbes' advance attacked by the Matabele, and checked by the rising of the Shangani river, retreats; arrives at Inyati

1894

Submission of the Matabele

Jan., Mr. A. R. Colquhoun 1st administrator of Mashonaland

Jan. 14, Submission of Matabele chiefs

Feb. 9, Death of Lobengula by fever, Jan. 23, 40 m. S. of the Zambezi; most of his army surrenders, reported

Feb. 27, Settlement of the country proceeding

March 5, The officers and men of the Bechuanaland police exonerated from blame by the Government respecting the shooting of Lobengula's envoys at Tati in Oct., 1893, reported

Some anonymous charges of cruelty made against the officers and men of the company's forces engaged in the war, which appeared in *Truth*, Feb. 15, 1894, a paper published in London by Mr. Labouchere, M.P., and which he justified in the *Times*, Feb. 21 and March 2, were repelled, especially by the African explorer, Mr. F. C. Selous, in the *Times*, Feb. 19, and in a lecture at the Royal colonial institute, March 13, 1894

March, Temporary government; the administrator, a council of three, and a judge nominated by the company, with the assent of the secretary for the colonies

April 6, Col. Rhodes at Buluwayo

April 25, Settlements in Matabeleland (named Rhodesia) open to claimants

May 29, Daniels and Wilson, of the Bechuanaland police, having suppressed a message of submission from Lobengula to Major Forbes and appropriated a present of 1,000*l.*, thereby causing the deaths of Major Wilson and his party, were tried at Buluwayo, and sentenced to 14 years' penal servitude

July 18, Matabele Order in Council amended Charter

July, Dr. Jameson and the company's officers exonerated by a government commission of inquiry

Oct. 16, Dr. Jameson appointed administrator for the British S. Africa company; superseded, Jan. 5, 1896, *see* Transvaal, 1895

Nov. 13, Three of Lobengula's sons arrive at Cape Town, to be educated at Mr. Cecil Rhodes' expense

Nov. 24, Agreement between the British Government

and the company relating to administration north of the Zambezi, signed

1895

May 3, Proclamation gave name of Rhodesia to the territories of the British South Africa Company (*i.e.*, Southern Rhodesia)

July 26, Rhodesia Chamber of Mines formed, formally incorporated, Nov. 22, 1901

1896

Feb. 4, Mr. Cecil Rhodes after the troubles in the Transvaal, visits London; returns to Salisbury

March 20, Revolt of the Matabele, joined by many of the native police in the Insega and Filibusi districts and Matoppo hills; massacre of 8 whites, including inspectors Bentley and Jackson

March 27, The Hon. Maurice Gifford's force repulses large body of natives

——, Commissioners Graham, Handley, and 6 others attacked and killed, after a desperate fight with 300 natives at Inyati

March 29, Salisbury, Bulawayo, and other places fortified; relief parties sent out; Mr. M. Gifford returns to Bulawayo after relieving Shangani and defeating the natives; Mr. Cecil Rhodes and Col. Plumer arrive at Salisbury, March 30

March 31, Capt. Macfarlane repulses the natives at Queen's Reef, and returns to Bulawayo

April 1, Olimo, instigator of the rebellion, styles himself King of the Matabele

April 2, Earl Grey appointed administrator of Rhodesia

April 4–8, The Hon. Maurice Gifford repulses a large body of rebels in the Shiloh district, 5 engagements in 4 days, Mr. Gifford severely wounded; British loss, 3, Matabele loss, about 200; Gifford's party relieved by Capt. Macfarlane

April 10, Capt. Brand's patrol attacked by 1,500 rebels on the Tuli road

April 14–May 2, Mr. Duncan, acting-administrator at Bulawayo, establishes 7 forts in the Mangwe Pass with 400 men

April 22, Natives severely defeated by Mr. Duncan and Capt. Napier on the Umgusa river; repulsed again, after a desperate fight, by Capt. Macfarlane and Mr. Duncan, 500 killed, April 25

April 28, Earl Grey arrives at Bulawayo

May 1, Mr. Cecil Rhodes and the Salisbury column repulse an attack, near Gwelo

May 14, Rebels routed at Thabas Induna, by Col. Napier

May 15, Col. Sir Richard Martin, deputy-commissioner, arrives with reinforcements, at Bulawayo

May 24, 25, 26, Rebels defeated near Bulawayo and near the Umgusa river, with great loss

June 6, Rebels defeated, with heavy loss, by Col. Spreckley and Lieut.-Col. Beal's column on the Gwelo road; the Makalaka driven from the hills, by Capt. Gibbs, June 9

June 21, Martial law proclaimed at Salisbury, rising of the Mashonas

June 22, Escort from the Mazoe district attacked, Messrs. Blakiston and Routledge and 7 men killed; after a long fight, reported

——, Mr. Graham, native commissioner, and 3 others found murdered at Inyati; mission station at Ingwengwesi river destroyed; severe fighting with the Mashonas, on the Umfuli

June 24, Lieut. Bremner, the Meyers, and others mur-

dered; the whole Ayrshire party killed on their way to Salisbury; M'Limo, the prophet, killed in the Matoppos; Fort Charter surrounded, 14 herdboys killed, reported

June 26, Resignation of the Hon. Cecil J. Rhodes and Mr. Beit as directors (May 3), accepted by the company in London

July 5, The enemy surprised and defeated at Thabas-I-Mhamba, about 150 killed, 500 women and children, and much cattle, captured; British loss 8, and 2 mortally wounded

Aug. 5, Matabele (5 impis) defeated by Col. Plumer's force, at Secombo's stronghold in the Matoppos; heroic conduct of Capt. Beresford's party, Capt. Llewellyn, and the Cape "boys," under Lieut. H. Howard; rebel loss, about 300; British, Major F. Kershaw, Lieut. H. F. Hervey, and 5 other officers killed

Aug. 8, Col. Alderson captures Makoni's kraal; Capt. Alfred E. Haynes and 3 troopers killed, rebel loss, 200

Aug. 9, Terms of surrender proclaimed

Aug. 11, Capt. M'Callum murdered by Mashonas at Matelimi (June 25); 101 murders in Mashonaland up to

Aug. 14, Select committee of the Commons on the administration of the British S. Africa company and the "Jameson Raid": chairman, Mr. W. L. Jackson, Sir Richard Webster, Sir H. Campbell-Bannerman, Mr. Chamberlain, Sir M. Hicks-Beach, Sir Wm. Harcourt, Mr. Labouchere, and others, appointed, Aug. 11; 1st meeting

Aug. 19, Marandella's kraal and others destroyed; W. B. Joliffe killed

Aug. 21, Mr. Cecil Rhodes, Dr. Sauer, and Mr. J. Colenbrander unarmed, meet Secombo and other chiefs, who surrender unconditionally

Sept. 4, Makoni, rebel chief, captured near Umtali by Lieut. Richat; tried by court-martial, and shot, by order of Major Watts, Sept. 7; Major Watts arrested, Sept. 9; exonerated on inquiry, Sept. 30

Sept. 12, Major Ridley captures 2 chiefs and 60 natives

Sept. 13, Aweenya, rebel chief, convicted of atrocities, &c., shot

Mid Sept., Major Tennant captures Simbanoatu, after much slaughter; 2 chiefs and 425 men surrender; Major Jenner defeats Mtigeza (who surrenders) near Fort Charter, strongholds captured

Sept. 20, Gen. Sir Frederick Carrington, Mr. Rhodes, and others hold an indaba with Babyan and other chiefs; terms accepted

Sept. 21, Judge Vintcent holds a meeting with the Mazoe chiefs, terms agreed to

Sept. 30, Mazoe and district cleared of rebels

Oct., Lieut. H. G. Morris and W. A. Smith, killed

Oct. 13, Earl Grey, Mr. Rhodes, and others hold a final meeting with chiefs in the Matoppos, peaceful settlement

Oct., Major Alderson takes Chena's kraal, after a hot fight; 180 natives surrender in the Somnabula forest to Capt. Robinson and Mr. Driver

Oct. 22, Gatze's kraal taken, Major F. S. Evans, Capt. Edw. Finucane, and trooper Earnshaw killed

Oct. 30, Lieut.-Col. Baden-Powell captures 8 kraals, Oct. 16, 28; Dango's burnt, after a fight

Nov. 6, Meeting of the British S. Africa company in London; the capital over a million, in hand (Feb., 1895), exhausted; issue of 500,000 2*l.* shares authorized

Nov. 20, Col. Paget disperses rebels on the Thaba In-
simba hills, and returns to Gwelo

1897

Jan. 5, Change of government announced to 85 Matabele chiefs by the Hon. A. Lawley in the name of
Earl Grey, at Bulawayo; 12 districts to be under
paid chiefs and native commissioners

Mid Jan., Major Gosling captures Seka's kraal on his
refusing to surrender his guns

[The select committee of inquiry of the Commons on
the Transvaal Raid (Aug. 14, 1896), reappointed,
Jan. 30, 1897; evidence of Mr. Cecil Rhodes, Feb. 16–
March 5, also of Sir Graham Bower and Mr. Wm. P.
Schreiner, March 12, 26; Dr. Jameson, March 26;
Col. Frank Rhodes, March 29; Sir John Willoughby,
April 2, he declined to answer certain questions,
April 6; Dr. Jameson recalled, explanations given
by him and Sir John Willoughby, April 9; Dr. Harris,
April 30; the Duke of Abercorn and the Duke of Fife
expressed their total ignorance of any raid, May 12;
Mr. Chas. Leonard, May 14; Miss Flora Shaw, correspondent of the Times, May 25 (again July 2); Mr.
Chamberlain, June 1; Lord Selborne, June 4. Report
presented to parliament, July 15. Conclusions: Discontent in Johannesburg previous to raid owing to
grievances of the Uitlanders, Mr. Cecil Rhodes involved in grave breaches of duty, in his course of
action. The imperial and colonial governments, the
directors of the S. Africa company, with the exception
of Mr. Beit and Mr. Maguire, exonerated from complicity in the raid. Mr. P. Stanhope's vote of censure
on the report of the committee on Mr. Rhodes, and
on the Chartered company, rejected in the Commons, 304–77, July 26, 1897.]

April 23, The Prospectors' association repudiate the
reports of the pacification of the country, and appeal
for imperial aid

May 23–26, Marandella's kraals captured

June 18, Mr. Cecil Rhodes returns to Bulawayo; holds
an indaba of Matabele chiefs, June 23; Earl Grey
arrives, June 28

July 7, 10, Severe fighting on the Unyami; 600 rebels
and 40 guns captured, 111 rebels surrender, July 13;
desultory fighting near Fort Charter, district cleared,
3 British killed, July 15; Sir Richard Martin assumes
command, July 20; a kraal taken, 4 British killed;
600 prisoners liberated and located in Cherimba,
July 24

July 22, 24, Dr. Jameson welcomed at Bulawayo, and
Fort Salisbury

Oct. 29, Surrender of all the Mashona chiefs

Nov. 4, Railway from Vryburg to Bulawayo opened by
Sir A. Milner at Bulawayo

Col. Rivett Carnac appointed deputy-commissioner
during the absence of Sir R. Martin

Dec. 1, First public telephone at Bulawayo

Dec. 5, William Henry Milton succeeded Earl Grey as
Administrator of Mashonaland and Senior Administrator of Southern Rhodesia; Captain A. Lawley
appointed Administrator of Matabeleland

Authority of British South Africa Company extended
over Northern Rhodesia

1898

Feb. 25, Mr. Chamberlain's scheme for the reconstitution of the S. Africa company, issued; Times

April 21, British S. Africa co.'s 2 yrs. report, ended

March 31, 1897, 360,000l. compensation to settlers
for losses during the native rising; surplus over expenditure, 59,650l. for 1895–6; expenditure during
the rebellion, 2,266,976l., Times, April 14, 1898; increase of capital, 1,500,000l.; Mr. Rhodes (arrived
in London, April 2), reëlected director, his scheme of
administration approved, report adopted at a meeting, London

May 6, Meeting in London of the security holders of
the Bechuanaland railway co., Mr. Cecil Rhodes in
the chair; the railway from Vryburg to Bulawayo,
600 miles, cost 2,000,000l.; supplemental trust deed
approved, May 6; debate in the commons, defence
of the Chartered company by Mr. Chamberlain

Oct. 20, Southern Rhodesia Order in Council defined
boundaries

1899

Jan. 25, Growth of the gold industry and rapid development of the country, reported

May 3, Mr. Cecil Rhodes's negotiations in Berlin re
the Trans-Atlantic telegraph, successful, Mar. 11–16;
he raises nearly 10,000,000l. in a few weeks, Times

May 15, Legislative council (S. Rhodesia) first meets at
Salisbury

May 31, First train (E. Coast line) enters Salisbury,
May 1; first sod of the northern extension railway
cut at Bulawayo

Aug. 1, Rhodesia entered into Customs Agreement
with Cape Colony

Oct. 27, Expedition against Kazembe, a cruel chief; he
flees into the Congo Free State

N. E. Rhodesia (administrator, Mr. Codrington), constituted in

1900

Sept., Protectorate proclaimed over Marotseland under
the title N.W. Rhodesia; Major Coryndon appointed
administrator

Autumn, Sir M. J. Clarke, resident commissioner

1901

Dec. 20, W. H. Milton appointed Administrator of
Southern Rhodesia

1902

Mar. 26, Death of Mr. Cecil Rhodes, aged 48, at Cape
Town; great demonstrations of grief and homage
during the funeral ceremonies and along the route
from Cape Town to the Matoppos, where he was
buried (according to his own wish) in the hill which
he called the "view of the world," April 10

[By his will, dated July 1, 1899, he practically bequeathed his immense fortune and possessions (about
6,000,000l.) to the public service, viz., his landed
property near Bulawayo and at Inyanga, near Salisbury, to his trustees, Lord Rosebery, Lord Grey,
Lord Milner, Mr. A. Beit, Dr. Jameson, Mr. L.
Michell, and Mr. B. F. Hawksley, to cultivate, for
the instruction of the people of Rhodesia; 100,000l.
to Oriel college, Oxford, nearly 52,000l. per annum
for scholarships, viz., to be created at Oxford university, 60 colonial of 300l. each a year, 24 for S. Africa,
36 for Australasia and the North American and
W. Indian colonies, and 2 for each of the 50 states
or territories of the U.S.N.A.; also 15 of the value
of 250l. per annum for German students, to be nominated by the German emperor. His residence, De
Groote Schuur (i.e., the Great Granary, or Barn),
near Cape Town, with contents, and all his land

under Table Mountain, he left to the Federal government of S. Africa (when constituted), the house for the prime minister, and the other lands for public purposes, with an income of 1,000*l.* a year for maintenance; also 4,000*l.* per annum to be invested as a Matoppos and Bulawayo fund; and 2,000*l.* a year to be called the Inyanga fund, &c. Mr. G. R. Parkin, author of "The Great Dominion," principal of the Upper Canada college of Toronto, appointed by the trustees to prepare a scheme *re* the Colonial and American scholarships, reported Aug. 13, 1902]

July 1, Proclamation established regulations for native administration

Oct. 6, Cape to Cairo railway, line from Bulawayo to Salisbury, *via* Gwelo, 300 miles, completed

Nov. 6, Sir W. H. Milton, administrator, opens the legislative council

1903

Feb. 17, An order in council amending the provisions of the Southern Rhodesia Order in Council, 1898, published. Legislative council to consist of the administrator, the resident commissioner, with 7 nominated and 7 elected members

Dec. 30, New Education law repealed that of 1899, a Director of Education established

1905

Jan. 1, Post Office Savings Bank established

April 1, Great Victoria Falls bridge over the Zambezi on the Cape to Cairo railway, stated to be the highest bridge in the world, 2,875 ft. above the sea level, 650 ft. in length, linked up

April 13, British S. Africa co. receive cablegram of gold production in S. Rhodesia for March amounting to 34,927 ozs., the highest on record

Sept. 12, Visit of the members of the British association to the Victoria Falls; Prof. G. H. Darwin, president of the association, formally opens the new Victoria Falls railway bridge

Nov. 9, Leading American and continental experts stated to report favorably on a proposal to transmit electric power from the Victoria Falls to the Rand

1906

July, Death of Alfred Beit

Sept. 1, Railroad from Bulawayo extended in Northern Rhodesia to Broken Hill Mine, 375 miles from Victoria Falls opened

1908

June 29, Question of ownership of unalienated land raised by Charles Coghlan in Legislative Council and resolution asked Imperial Government to consider the questions in dispute between the settlers and the Company

1909

Imperial Act provided for voluntary entry of Rhodesia into the Union of South Africa at expiration of charter of the Company

Dec. 11, Railroad crossed the Congo frontier, distance of 132 miles from Broken Hill

1910

Oct. 3, Native Administration regulations amended

1911

May 4, Order in Council gave the elected members a majority of seats in the Legislative Council, provision made for safeguarding interests of the Company

July 19, Native Schools Ordinance published provided for grants in aid and inspection

Aug. 17, Amalgamation of North-East and North-West Rhodesia in the Protectorate of Northern Rhodesia, Lawrence Wallace appointed Administrator

1913

Jan. 3, Death of the Duke of Abercorn, president of the British South Africa Company. Sir Starr (Dr.) Jameson appointed to succeed him as president

July, An elective advisory Council established in Northern Rhodesia

1914

April 17, Resolution of Legislative Council affirmed that the unalienated land of Southern Rhodesia was public land and not the property of the Company

July 10, Native Labor Contracts Ordinance published

July 14, Order in Council referred question of unalienated land to the Privy Council

Aug. 4, Declaration of war on Germany by Great Britain

——, Rhodesian land case brought before Judicial Committee of the Privy Council

Sept. 5–9, German force in attack on Abercorn, Northern Rhodesia

Oct. 29, Expiration of term of charter (25 years) of the British South Africa Company but renewed by the Imperial Government for a further 10 years in accordance with vote of Legislative Council (Rhodesia) in March, but subject to right of people of Rhodesia to obtain responsible Government earlier on certain conditions. Elected members of Legislative Council increased to 12

Nov. 1, Drummond Chaplin appointed Administrator of Southern Rhodesia on resignation of Sir W. H. Milton

Nov. 14, First Rhodesian regiment left Salisbury for Bloemfontein where it remained until the end of the rebellion in the Union

Dec. 25, First Rhodesian regiment arrived at Walvis Bay for service in South West Africa

1915

Jan. 14, First Rhodesian regiment occupied and garrisoned Swakopmund, German South West Africa

March 9, Second Rhodesian regiment commanded by Lieutenant Colonel Capell left Salisbury for service in East Africa

March 13, Supplemental Charter granted which conceded right to establish responsible Government at earlier date than the original terms if desired

July 26–Aug. 3, Attack of Germans at Saisi about 25 miles from Abercorn

July 27, Death of Major Gordon Forbes, member of Legislative Council, in France

Aug. 7, Death of Captain D. E. Brodie in France

1916

May 1, First Rhodesian Native regiment formed in Salisbury and July 18 left for East Africa, Lieutenant Colonel A. J. Tomlinson, commander

Sept. 22, Native Administration regulations amended

1917

Feb. 7, Second Rhodesian Native regiment formed and

Sept. 16 left for East Africa, Major S. N. G. Jackson, commander

Aug. 29, Death of Earl Grey

Sept. 11, Second Rhodesian regiment left Salisbury for France

Nov. 26, Death of Sir Starr Jameson, P. L. Gell succeeding him as chairman of the Board of directors of the Company

1918

Feb. 15, Lands assigned as native reserves

April 16, Death of Sir John Willoughby, second in command of "Pioneer Column" settlers of Rhodesia

July 29, Decision of Judicial Committee of the Privy Council that the unalienated land the property of the Crown

Nov. 1, Germans under General von Lettow Vorbeck entered Northern Rhodesia and attacked Fife, Nov. 1–2

Nov. 11, End of War. 6,859 Rhodesians (Europeans) were in active service and 2,721 natives served in East Africa and 40,732 carriers, 152,000 other carriers in war service in Northern Rhodesia, 1,340 natives served in Kings African Rifles and 250 in Rhodesian native regiments

Nov. 21, British South Africa Company claimed from the Crown £7,569,435 in re deficits in administration expenditure paid by the Company

Nov. 25, Surrender of Germans at Abercorn

1919

Feb. 10, Death of George Pauling

March 10, Death of Justice Hopley

1920

Jan. 15, Cave Commission Report advocated award to the British South Africa Company £4,435,225, less value of lands and other interests appropriated or alienated but plus the sums the Company would be entitled to for public works and buildings taken over by succeeding government, estimated at £8,000,000

April 30, Election of Legislative Council resulted in election of 12 supporting immediate responsible government and 1 favoring responsible government under the Crown

May 12–17, Debate resulted in approval of responsible government by 12 to 5 in the Legislative Council

Nov. 9, Order in Council defined lands known as Native Reserves assigned April 23, June 25, and July 2 as 21,594,957 acres and vested reserves in High Commissioner

1921

March 7, Second Committee headed by Lord Buxton appointed, made report April 12, recommending plan for responsible government be drawn up and submitted to electors and that the control of the natives and of the unalienated land be retained by the High Commissioner

July 31, Official memorandum published gave terms Union Government prepared to recommend to Parliament for the admission of Southern Rhodesia

Nov. 13, Death of Sir Douglas Fox

Nov. 22, Death of H. Wilson Fox

1922

Oct. 27, Draft Letters Patent for responsible government and the terms of admission to the South African

Union placed before the electors with result that 8,774 voted for responsible government, and 5,989 for joining the Union, a majority of 2,785 in favor of the former chiefly because of unwillingness of the colonists to be exposed to the race difficulties of the Union

1923

Feb. 27, Announcement of British Government that home rule would be granted

July 13, Proposal of the British Government for settlement of claims of the British South Africa Company offered £3,750,000, the Company to retain mineral rights under its concessions in Northern Rhodesia, and retain a half interest for 40 years in the net proceeds of the disposal of lands in North-Western Rhodesia. Accepted by shareholders of the Company July 24, and approved by the House of Commons, July 25

July 28, Last session of the Legislative Council

Sept. 12, On the 23rd anniversary of the occupation of Mashonaland the territory was formally annexed to the British Dominions with the title Colony of Southern Rhodesia to take effect Oct. 1

Oct. 1, Letters Patent granted responsible government under a Constitution which provided for a Legislature consisting of a Legislative Council and a Legislative Assembly of 30 members

——, Lieutenant-Colonel Sir John Robert Chancellor, assumed office as Governor and Commander-in-Chief, Sir Drummond Chaplin retiring from post of Administrator of Southern Rhodesia

1924

April 29, First general election held

May 30, First session of the Assembly opened, prorogued, Aug. 2

June, Cabinet formed by Sir C. P. J. Coghlan

Sept. 16, Native Administration regulations amended provided for removal of natives to reserves and compulsory return of natives who have moved from one district to another, came into effect Sept. 26

Sept. 26, Native Tax Amendment Act came into effect

Oct. 20, Customs Agreement with the Union of South Africa signed

Dec., Plague of locusts cost the Colony £18,000

1925

Feb. 13, Draft scheme published regarding formation of a Progressive Party

April 18, Death of Rochfort Maguire, president of the British South Africa Company

May 29, Native Reserves Augmentation Act assigned additional land to native reserves

June 29–July 10, Visit of the Prince of Wales to Southern Rhodesia

Sept. 1, First internal loan issued, £1,000,000 at 5%

1926

Feb. 7, Railroad Act established Commission to control rates; into effect, Feb. 24

May 21, Labor Fees Repealing Act abolished fees payable for natives employed in mines under tax imposed in 1906

Nov. 22, Sir E. Montagu announced acceptance of leadership of Opposition

Dec. 4, Act for regulation of employment of native

juveniles requires certificates for employment of children under 14

Dec. 20, Legislative Assembly ratified Agreement whereby all railroads of Northern and Southern Rhodesia, Bechualand, and Mozambique became one transportation system

Dec. 24, Defense Act promulgated provided for compulsory military training of all males between the ages of 19 and 23

1927

April 29, Sir W. Hoy appointed chairman of the Railroad Commission

May 3, Death of "Matabele" Thompson

June 14, Formal inaugural of the Progressive Party with Sir Ernest Montagu at head, first public meeting, June 30

Aug. 5, Native Affairs Act made provision for control and administration of natives

Aug. 28, Death of Sir Charles Coghlan, Prime Minister

Sept. 2, H. U. Moffat became Prime Minister

Oct. 1, Formation of Territorial Active Force

1928

Feb. 9, Death of Major W. J. Boggie, pioneer settler

July 24, Strike of one day of railroad workers at Umtali

July 27, New Electoral law promulgated extended the franchise to all British subjects by birth or naturalization not under 21 years of age, who have resided in the Colony for at least 6 months, subject to certain other qualifications as to occupancy of houses and other buildings, ownership of a mining location, the receipt of income, wages, or salary at rate of not less than £100 a year, natives to acquire the franchise on the same conditions as Europeans

Oct. 11, Sir Ernest Montagu retired from politics and was succeeded as leader of the Progressive Party by Captain Bertin

Nov. 23, Sir Cecil Hunter Rodwell arrived succeeding Sir J. R. Chancellor as Governor and Commander-in-Chief

RIO DE ORO

Rio de Oro, Spanish possession on northwest coast of Africa. Rio de Oro and Adrar stretch from the Wadi Draa 29° N. and 11° 4' W. to Cape Blanco 20° 46' N. and 17° 3' W. Politically there are three zones: (1) Colony of Rio de Oro, 26° N. to 20° 46' N., an area of 65,500 square miles; (2) the Protectorate, between 27° 40' N. and 26° N. bordered on the East by 8° 40' W., an area of 34,700 square miles; (3) the occupied territory, between 27° 40' N. and the Wadi Draa, an area of about 9,000 square miles, settled by various treaties, 1900 to 1912. The Colonies are under the governorship of the Canary Islands, with a subgovernor resident at Rio de Oro. The capital of this Colony is Villa Cisneros. There is no town called Rio de Oro, the name being applied to the arm of the sea and the Colony generally.

The coast was explored by Portuguese navigators Affonso Gonçalves Baldaya and Gil Eannes in 1433 and 1444 and settlement made on Arguin Island which later became possession of France. Fort of Santa Cruz de Mar Pequeña was estab-

lished by the Spaniards north of Cape Bojador in 1476. Jan. 9, 1885 Spain declared a protectorate over the coast from Cape Bojador to Cape Blanco and factory built on Rio de Oro Territory. An expedition under Cervera and Quiroga explored the interior toward Adrar (T-Marr) in 1886.

1887

April 6, The Rio de Oro Protectorate placed under administration of the Governor General of the Canary Islands

1900

June 27, Convention between France and Spain delimited boundary

1904

Oct. 3, Treaty between France and Spain by which Spanish protectorate recognized in region north of the Colony

1912

Nov. 27, Treaty between France and Spain fixed southern boundary of Morocco at the Wad Draa River; ratified at Madrid, April 2, 1913

1916

Spanish force stationed at Cape Juby

RIO MUNI

See Guinea, Spanish

SAINT HELENA

Saint Helena, island of volcanic origin, British possession in Atlantic Ocean, 1,200 miles from the west coast of Africa; area, 47 square miles; population (1921 census), 3,747; estimated civil population in 1929, 3,846. Jamestown is the capital. The island was discovered May 21, 1502, by the Portuguese, Juan de Nova Castella, on return voyage from India, and named by him. Thomas Cavendish visited the island in June, 1588, on his voyage around the world. The island was in possession of the Dutch from 1645 to 1651, and was then taken by the East India Company who were confirmed in their possession by a charter from Charles II dated April 3, 1661, and a second charter of Dec. 16, 1673, and was brought under direct administration of the Crown April 22, 1834. In October, 1815, Napoleon Bonaparte was brought to the island and lodged at Longwood, where he died in May, 1821. In 1922 Ascension Island was made a dependency.

SAINT MARIE

Saint Marie, island on the east coast of Madagascar, French possession and dependency of Madagascar, area 64 square miles.

SAINT PAUL

Saint Paul, volcanic island, French possession and dependency of Madagascar, in Indian Ocean 60 miles south of Amsterdam Island, area 2¾ square miles.

SAINT TOMÉ

Saint Tomé (St. Thomas) and Principe (Prince) islands, Portuguese province, about 125 miles off the coast of Africa in the Gulf of Guinea, were discovered in 1471 by Portuguese navigators João de Santarem and Pero de Escobar; area 320 square miles. According to the census of 1921 the population of the two islands was 59,055; 52,150 in S. Tomé and 6,905 in Principe.

SENEGAL

Senegal, Colony of French West Africa (see s.v.) total area 74,112 square miles; total population in 1926 estimated at 1,318,287; capital, St. Louis.

1626

First French settlement in West Africa by the *Compagnie Normande*, association of merchants of Dieppe and Rouen, at St. Louis on the Senegal River

1633

Jan. 25, Association of merchants of Rouen and Dieppe obtained privileges of trade for 10 years

1638

Feb. 5, The Dutch established a fort on Arguin Island

1658

St. Louis founded

1664

May 28, French settlements assigned to Colbert's West India Company

1672

April 9, Royal edict forced sale of establishments of West India Company to new company which in June, 1679, took title Compagnie d'Afrique and obtained exclusive trading privileges from Cap Blanc to Cap Bonne-Espérance

1677

Nov. 1, Admiral Jean d'Estrées made conquest of Gorée Island, Rufisque, Portudal and Joâl from the Dutch, possession confirmed by Treaty of Nijmwegwn in Aug., 1678

1684

Sept. 12 and Jan. 6, 1685, Royal decrees defined concessions of Company of Senegal which had succeeded to West African concession as from Cap Blanc to Sierra Leone

1687

Expedition of the Great Elector of Brandenburg occupied Arguin Island

1696

March, New Royal Company of Senegal received charter

1697

André Brue, Governor until 1724

1701

April 18, War of French and English in Africa begun with English attack on Gorée

1709

July 30, New Company of Senegal received charter

1717

July 29, Cession of Portendic on the coast to the French by the Maures which was confirmed by Treaty, Jan. 15, 1727

1718

Dec. 15, The Compagnie des Indes bought all rights and privileges of the Company of Senegal; confirmed by Council of State, Jan. 10, 1719

1724

Feb. 20, The French seized the Dutch fort on Arguin Island

1758

April 30, The English seized Senegal and Dec., Gorée held until 1763

1765

June 5, Treaty with Damel of Cayor by which land ceded to the French along the coast between St. Louis and Dakar (Gorée)

1783

Sept. 3, Treaty of Peace between England and France recognized French possession of Senegal

1789

Jan. 29, The duc de Lauzun took forcible possession of St. Louis

1794

Feb. 4 and April 11, Decree suppressing slavery

1800

April 5, Gorée Island captured by the English

1809

July 14, The English seized St. Louis

1814

May 30, Treaty of Paris restored to France all settlements on West African coast in possession of France on Jan. 1, 1792

1817

Jan. 25, Colonel Schmaltz reëstablished French possession of Senegal

1819

May 8, Treaty of Wallo with chiefs of cession of lands and creation of post of Dagana
May 28, Decree closed colony to foreign trade

1822

Jan. 7, Royal ordinance established courts
Custom house established at Gorée

1827

March 24 and April 1, Land ceded by native chiefs and post of Carabane established

1831

March 4, Law prohibited slave trade

1833

April 24, Law promulgated as to government

1840

Sept. 7, Royal ordinance established Governor and Council

1843

Feb. 5–Dec. 8, Commandant Bouët-Willaumez, Administrator

1845

Aug. 23, Treaty ceded Bondu, and of Oct. 19, Gabun

1848

April 27, Decree abolishing slavery

1854

Dec. 16, L. L. C. Faidherbe appointed Governor, and began war on El Hadj Omar

1855

Sept. 12, Treaty of alliance with Diouka Sambala and authorization for construction of fort at Médine, now French Sudan, for defense against Moslems
Bank of Senegal founded

1856

Annexation of country of Walo (Oualo) by General Faidherbe, Governor

1857

March 7, Convention by which Albreda on the Gambia River ceded to the English
April 20–June 15, Attack on Fort Médine by Arabs led by Omar al-Haji repulsed by Paul Holle
May 25, The French took possession of Dakar

1858

Aug. 18, Treaty ceded Bambouk

1861

Feb. 1, Treaty by which Cayor ceded to the French, renewed Feb. 2, 1862, and Dec. 4, 1863, followed by other treaties, conquest not completed until 1886

1863–1866

Nov. 25–May 6, 1866, Exploration of the Niger country by Lieutenants Mage and Quintin and making of treaties with the natives and construction of posts
July 14–July 12, 1865, L. L. L. C. Faidherbe again Governor

1869

Dec. 29, Decree created Chamber of Commerce in St. Louis and in Gorée

1871

Jan. 12, Treaty by which Lat Dior, Damel, renounced claim to Cap Vert territory

Colony of Senegal elected one deputy to Parliament of France
Colonel Brière de l'Isle, Governor (1876–1881)

1877

Oct. 24, Protectorate Treaty over Fouta

1879

Feb. 4, Decree established General Council of 20 members

1882

Oct. 12, Decree created Lieutenant Governor in addition to Governor

1885

July 6, Railroad from Dakar to St. Louis opened
Oct. 26, Lat Dior killed and Le Cayor finally annexed

1886

Jan. 10, 11, and 13, Protectorate Treaties signed with chiefs of Borokoné, Bondu, and Bambuk respectively
May 12, Franco-Portuguese Convention fixed frontiers with Portuguese Guinea

1887

Nov. 30, Notification of occupation of the Alcatras Islands
St. Louis, Dakar, Gorée, and Rufisque made communes and inhabitants citizens without distinction of race or color

1889

Aug. 10, Anglo-French Convention fixed frontiers with Gambia

1891

June 9, Boundary Convention delimited frontiers with Gambia
Sept. 15, Treaties with native chiefs and cession of territory

1893

Fodé Kaba, chief of Fogny (Casamance) accepted French protectorate for his lands

1895

May 11, Senegal divided into 8 circles
June 16, Decree constituted the General Government of French West Africa

1903

Nov. 24, Primary, commercial, and professional schools established

1904

Feb. 13, Decree divided the Colony into 2 divisions, Colony and Protectorate
April 8, Anglo-French Boundary Convention by which Senegal acquired a port (Yarbatenda)
Oct. 16, Decree made Senegal part of the Government General of West Africa, Federal system established much opposed in Senegal

1905

April, Submarine cable between Brest and Dakar completed

1910

Jan. 11, Decree of Jan. 5 promulgated regulations for elections

June 29, Decree gave legal existence to native provident societies

1914

Diagne, first native to be elected as deputy to represent the Colony in the French Chamber of Deputies, and again in 1919 and 1924

1915

April 26, Decree authorized enlistment of natives in Sengalese Corps

Oct. 19, Law made natives liable to conscription under law of 1905

1916

Sept. 29, Law extended conscription to descendants of natives outside the 4 communes recognizing them as French citizens

1919

June 20, *La Lycée Faidherbe* established at St. Louis by Decree and Order of Nov. 6, 1920

Aug. 24, Order of the Lieutenant Governor put into execution Decree of May 21 which established native councils of notables

1920

Dec. 4, Decree of President of the French Republic established *Conseil Prive* and *Conseil Colonial*, councils to assist the Governor in Senegal

1924

Oct. 21 and Nov. 27, Decrees made Dakar an autonomous territory under the Governor General of West Africa

1925

June 25, New Convention with Lebou Chiefs signed as to lands

Sept. 27, Order as to regulations for public works and the sale of lands in the towns

1927

May 13, Order issued regulations consolidating previous regulations as to land concessions and sales

1928

May 13, Order of the Governor General provided for control of emigration and immigration of natives in Dakar Circle

1930

Jan. 13, French presidential Decree reorganized the Colonial Council (*Conseil Colonial*), promulgated, Jan. 27

May 31, Order reorganized Chamber of Commerce

SEYCHELLES

Seychelles and its Dependencies consist of 101 islands and islets with a total estimated area of 156 square miles. The principal island is Mahé (55 square miles), smaller islands of the group being Praslin, Silhouette, La Digue, Curieuse, and Félicité. Among dependent islands are the Amirantes, Alphonse Island, Bijoutier Island, St. François, St. Pierre, the Cosmoledo Group, Astove Island, Assumption Island, the Aldabra Islands, Providence Island, Coetivy, Farquhar Islands, and Flat Island.

The islands were first colonized by the French in the middle of the eighteenth century, the object being to establish plantations of spices to compete with the lucrative Dutch monopoly. They were captured by the English in 1794 and incorporated as a dependency of Mauritius in 1810. In 1888 the office of Administrator was created, an Executive Council of 2 *ex-officio* members and 1 nominated member was appointed, with a Legislative Council of 3 official and 3 unofficial members, the Administrator being president of both Councils and having an original and casting vote in the Legislative Council. In 1897 the Administrator was given full powers as Governor, and in November, 1903, he was raised to the rank of Governor.

The population at December 31, 1926, was estimated to be 26,397; census of April 24, 1921, 24,523 (11,974 males and 12,549 females). The capital is Victoria.

Mr. de Symons M. G. Honey, Governor and Commander-in-Chief, January, 1928.

SIERRA LEONE

Sierra Leone, British West Africa Colony and Protectorate, lies between French Guinea on the north and the Republic of Liberia on the east and southeast. Sierra Leone proper consists of a peninsula about 26 miles long, and 12 miles broad, with an area of about 260 square miles, terminating in Cape Sierra Leone. The Colony of Sierra Leone extends from the Scarcies River on the north, to the border of Liberia on the south, 180 miles. It extends inland to a distance varying from 8 to 20 miles and includes the Yellaboi and other islands towards the north, as well as Sherbro and several smaller islands to the south, but the Isles de Los were ceded to France under the Convention of 1904.

First explorers the expedition of Hanno the Carthaginian, 60 ships containing 30,000 women and men colonists who founded towns along the West African coast and reached the "Western Horn" identified as Sierra Leone by Sir Richard Burton. In 1462 Pedro da Cintra, Portuguese, discovered the coast. Sir John Hawkins came to the coast in 1562 and took 300 negroes from Tagrin to sell as slaves in Hispaniola, and Sir Francis Drake reprovisioned there July 22–24, 1579. Trading companies formed at end of the fifteenth century by Dutch and English, one to Thomas Gregory in May, 1592, and in 1651 the Company of Adventurers of London trading to Africa were granted exclusive rights on each side of the Sherboro River, and in 1663 Charles II granted charter to the Company of Royal Adventurers into Africa which established forts and factories and engaged in slave trade, which were attacked by the Dutch under Admiral de Ruyter in 1664.

Population (census 1921) 85,163, including 1,161

Europeans. Freetown is the capital. Sir J. A. Byrne, Governor.

1786

Proposal of Dr. Henry Smeatham of plan to found settlement for negroes, slaves who had found asylum in England from the West Indies and the United States

1787

Feb. 22, First negro settlers sailed from Portsmouth in charge of Captain B. Thomson and arrived in Sierra Leone May 9 and landed May 14, having purchased land from King Tom

1788

Aug. 22, First grant of land from Frenchman's Bay to Gambia Island by King Tom confirmed by King Naimbanna, chief of Sierra Leone

1791

July, A charter granted to the Sierra Leone Company founded by Granville Sharp and others for trading and to help the colonists

1792

March, A company of freed slaves brought from Nova Scotia by Lieutenant John Clarkson arrived, founded Freetown and in August came under the protection of the Sierra Leone Company

1794

Sept. 28–Oct. 13, Freetown captured and sacked by the French at war with England

1799

July 5, New charter made the settlement an independent colony empowered to appoint a Governor and Council

1801

Nov. 18, Natives, the Temnes, led by 2 Nova Scotian colonists who had been in revolt the previous year, attacked Fort Thornton and were repulsed with loss to settlers of 10 persons and 42 wounded including Governor Dawes, and after a few days Governor Dawes led attack of reprisal into native territory burning towns

1802

April 11, Second attack of the Temnes on the Freetown settlement defeated

1807

July 10, Treaty of Peace and Alliance between the Governor, Mr. Ludlam, and King Firama and King Tom, Temne chiefs, by which their lands ceded

1808

Jan. 1, Sierra Leone became a Crown Colony by Act of British Parliament of Aug. 8, 1807
July 21, T. P. Thomson, first Governor appointed by the Crown, arrived and took office July 27

1811

April, Census of Freetown gave population of 1917 including 28 Europeans

1814

July 9, Population of the Colony 5,520 increased largely by negro slaves, rescued from slave ships captured, who were landed at Sierra Leone

1818

July 6, Treaty by which Isles de Los ceded to Great Britain by Bago

1820

July 21, Banana Islands ceded to Great Britain by Treaty with native chiefs

1821

May 7, The African Company terminated by Act of Parliament and all property transferred to the Crown
Oct. 17, Royal charter constituted Colony and its Dependencies, the Governor having title Governor-in-Chief of the West African Settlements

1822

Jan. 1, Census gave population of the Colony as 15,081 (128 Europeans) exclusive of troops

1824

Jan. 21, Governor Sir Charles MacCarthy killed in battle with the Ashantis

1825

Sept. 24, Turner's Peninsula ceded to Great Britain
Dec. 12, Bacca Lokkoh (Port Lokko) ceded to Great Britain

1826

March 7, Death of Major General Sir Charles Turner, Governor

1829

Aug., Ordinance authorized raising military force and the following year white troops were removed

1850

Jan. 13, Letters Patent separated the Gold Coast from Sierra Leone as a separate Government

1852

Dec. 26, Arrival of Dr. Vidal, first Bishop of Sierra Leone, at Freetown

1862

Feb. 1, Quiah (Koya) country annexed

1863

May 27, New Charter created an Executive Council

1866

Feb. 19, New Charter united Sierra Leone, Gambia, Gold Coast, and Lagos under one Government with capital in Sierra Leone

1874

July 24, New Charter separated the Gold Coast and Lagos from Sierra Leone
Dec. 17, Sierra Leone and Gambia united under one Governor with separate Legislative Councils as the "West Africa Settlements"

1882

June 28, First Anglo-French Boundary Convention gave the French the Mellacouri River basin and the

English the Scarcies as western boundary of the Colony

1885

Nov. 11, Liberia recognized the Mano River as the boundary

1887

Nov. 21, Robarrie, the stronghold of the insurgent Yonnie tribe, captured by Sir Francis De Winton King captured and the rebellion suppressed

1888

Nov. 28, The Gambia territory isolated and made an independent colony

1889

Feb. 14, Largoh, capital of the chief Mackiah captured by the British under Governor Hay; 700 prisoners liberated; announced

1890

Jan. 15, Frontier police force constituted

Oct., In accordance with an agreement with the French government, Aug. 10, 1889, a commission was appointed for the delimitation of the British and French possessions in West Africa

1891

May, British expedition sent to punish aggressions in; fighting at Tambi; the British retreat; Tambi taken and destroyed, April 7, 1894

June 26, Boundary Convention with France further defined frontier with French Guinea

1893

Dec. 23, A British expedition, under Col. A. B. Ellis, against the Sofas, a marauding tribe, are mistaken for the Sofas by a French force, under Lieut. Maritz, at Waima, on the British border, and attacked; British loss: Capt. Lendy, Lieuts. Liston and Wroughton, Serg.-Major Carraher, and 2 privates; French loss: Lieut. Maritz and 10 Sengalese; many wounded [The collision attributed to the false statements of Korona, a chief, who was afterwards executed; the British awarded 9,000l. by arbitration 1902]

Dec. 29, Sub-inspector Taylor, at Tungea, with a detachment of frontier police and some natives, defeat a body of about 4,000 Sofas; 50 killed, 150 taken prisoners

1894

Jan. 2, The Sofas, after a destructive raid, severely defeated by Col. A. B. Ellis at Bagwema

Jan. 29, Capture of Kerra-Yemma and rescue of 673 slaves

Feb. 3, Another conflict between the British and French (native police) on the borders of Sierra Leone; several killed

1895

Jan. 21, Anglo-French Treaty settled frontier with French Guinea

Aug. 24, Order in Council, British Protectorate established over territory of districts including Karene, Ronietta, Bandajuma, Panguma, and Koinadugu adjacent

1896

Aug. 31 and Sept. 16, Order in Council and Ordinance for administration of Protectorate

Sept., "Human Leopard" society (men clothed in leopard skins) vow to kill people to be eaten; efforts made for its suppression; 3 men hanged, July, 1895; 5 men hanged

1898

Feb., Serious rising of the natives due to suppression of slavery and hut tax

March, Conflicts between the natives and frontier police under Major Tarbet at Karene, Lieut. F. E. Yeld mortally wounded; Quiah burnt by Capt. Moore

March 26, Serious fighting: Ekuta and Tabira occupied by the British

April, Desultory fighting round Port Lokko, the Rev. W. J. Humphrey killed; Sorie Bunkey, the King, killed by Bai Bureh, rebel chief

May, Rising spreading in the S.E., Benda in ruins; Mr. Hughes, native commissioner, and over 200 inhabitants, massacred by the Mendis; 5 American missionaries massacred at Rotifunk; 2 others at Taiama

May, British warships and reinforcements sent to Freetown, rebels repulsed at Kwellu by Capt. Fairtlough, 3 chiefs arrested; Col. Woodgate returns to Freetown, after successful operations against the rebels in Karene, May 13; H.M.S. Fox returns to Freetown, after burning several villages, May 14

June 13, Rotifunk occupied by Col. Woodgate's punitive expedition (about 100 men) after desperate fights with hordes of Mendis, who were finally driven off with great loss, June 1; Bompeh, their stronghold, taken by Lieut.-Col. Cunningham and Lieut. Russell; enemy's loss heavy

June 18, Col. Marshall's punitive operations in the Karene and Kwellu districts successful

July 12, The expeditionary force returns to Freetown after destroying 4 towns in the Bompeh and Shengeh districts

July 18, Sir David Patrick Chalmers appointed royal commissioner to inquire into the rising (computed loss of life about 1,000); arrives (leaves Nov. 22)

July 21, Rebels repulsed with loss at Songo Town

Sept., The Mendis repeatedly defeated, the chiefs sue for peace, Aug. 10; King of the Upper Mendis captured

Nov. 14, Further operations against Bai Bureh, Oct.; he is captured by Capt. Goodwin (brought to Freetown with 4 other ringleaders, Feb. 25, 1899)

Dec., Lahai, rebel chief, and followers surrender to Capt. Robertson at Karene (Bai Forkey captured, Jan., 1899)

1899

Jan. 12, Judge Bonner tries 240 prisoners at Kwellu and elsewhere for murder during the rising (Aug.); 151 sentenced to death, about half commuted; he returns to England

Dec., 1898–March 1, Col. Woodgate's expedition to explore unknown country and overawe the Mendi and Kissi tribes, very successful; the Kissi chiefs submit after some days' continuous fighting, British loss slight

May 1, The Sierra Leone railway (32 mi. to Songo town) opened by Major Nathan, acting governor

July 26, Sir David Chalmers issued his report condemning the hut tax, &c.

Aug. 10, Major Ronald Ross, head of the Liverpool malaria research expedition, arrives; discovers the Anopheles malarial mosquito in stagnant pools, &c.; grubs killed by kerosene oil; leaves end Sept.

1901

Dec. 4, Protectorate Ordinance for administration divided into North, Central, and Southern Provinces each in charge of a Commissioner

1902

April, Anti-malaria work in Freetown very successful, reported

May 9, Concessions Ordinance as to native lands

1903

June 26, Protectorate Courts Ordinance established jurisdiction of chiefs

1904

April 8, The Los islands (pop. 1,422) transferred from Sierra Leone, and made part of French Guinea, by the Anglo-French agreement

1905

July 24, Protectorate Native Law Ordinance provided for improvement of financial relations between settlers and natives and created combined courts for settlement of disputes between settlers and natives, land tenure and leases to non-natives, and land transfers

July 31, Railroad from Sierra Leone to Bauma opened (200 miles)

Aug., Railway from Freetown, *via* Songotown, Rotifunk, Morjamba, and Bo to Balima, 222 miles, completed

1907

March 26, Centenary of the abolition of the slave trade celebrated

1910

Dec. 15, Arrival of the Duke and Duchess of Connaught and the Princess Patricia at Freetown

1911

Jan. 21, Boundary Convention with Liberia secured a part of the Kissi country in exchange for territory between the Mano and Morro Rivers

July 6, Anglo-French Boundary Convention settled frontier with French Guinea, modified Sept. 4, 1913

1913

March 7, Order in Council as to administration of Protectorate

March 12, Palm Oil Concession Ordinance regulating right to erect mills, &c.

April 10, Agreement with Liberia provided for regulations for navigation of the Mano River

May 15, Special Court sentenced members of native society the Human Leopards, for murders committed in 1912, death for 9, imprisonment for life for 2, and 8 to terms of imprisonment varying from 1 to 14 years

Sept. 4, New Boundary Agreement as to frontier with French New Guinea

1914

July 30, Mobilization orders received

Aug. 22, Sierra Leone troops under Lieutenant Colonel J. G. F. Newstead embarked for Togoland and after a fortnight proceeded to the German Cameroons for service

1915

Feb. 3, Troops attacked enemy position at Hartmann's Farm, Cameroons

Feb. 27, Troops coöperated with West African Regiment in attack on Mbureku

March 4, Attack on enemy position at Stoebel's Farm, Colonel Newstead mortally wounded

1916

Jan. 1, Troops took part in campaign and capture of Yaunde (Jaunde)

Jan. 15, Sir Edward Merewether, retiring Governor, captured with a number of Sierra Leone officials on the "Appam," ocean liner taken by the German cruiser "Moewe"

1917

April 22, 3,500 men sailed from Freetown for service in East African campaign as carriers

June 19–26, Exchange of Notes as to boundary with Liberia

1918

Laws, Chap. 134, Native Produce Ordinance provided penalties for adulteration of palm kernels

1919

July 15, Strike of railway employees because of nonpayment of bonus which lasted about a week, and anti-Syrian riots and looting of shops by natives because of belief Syrians holding quantities of rice during shortage, which were suppressed by troops, and the strike followed by strike of employees of public works

1921

Nov. 24, Census gave population of Colony as 85,163, of the Protectorate as 1,456,148

1922

Aug. 5, Concessions Ordinance (Palm Oil) amended, grants for palm cultivation exempted from Ordinance regulations

1924

Jan. 16, Orders in Council replaced that of March 7, 1913 for administration of Protectorate and Letters Patent of Jan. 28, made changes in Legislative Council

Sept. 11, Native Produce (Standardization and Grading) Ordinance passed respecting palm kernels

Sept. 20, Legislative Council consisting of the members of the Executive Council with 4 nominated unofficial members ended

Oct. 28, Elections held for new Legislative Council

Nov. 25, New Legislative Council opened by the Governor as president, consisting of the 5 senior members of the Executive Council, 7 nominated unofficial members and of these 3 to be Paramount Chiefs of the Protectorate, 1 representing general European interests, 1 European representing the Chamber of Commerce interests, and 2 representing African interests

C. 167, Laws declared slaves brought into Protectorate free and provided that slaves could redeem themselves by payment of sum not to exceed £4

1925

Jan. 1, Education laws consolidated

1926

Jan.–Feb., Strike of railroad employees against examinations for grades of service for promotions and increases in salary

April 14, Protectorate Amendment Order declared slavery abolished

1927

July, Supreme Court decision that a slave owner had the "right to use reasonable force to re-take a runaway slave"

Sept. 22, Ordinance abolished slavery in the Protectorate to come into effect Jan. 1, 1928

1929

Dec. 21, New Education Ordinance came into effect with complete code for all colonial schools

SOMALILAND, BRITISH

Somaliland, British, Protectorate in East Africa, extending along the Gulf of Aden from Lahadu, west of Zeyla, to Bandar Ziyada 49° E. long. After 1884, when Egyptian control ceased, the territory was administered by the Government of India, but was taken over by the Foreign Office on October 1, 1898, and was transferred to the Colonial Office on April 1, 1905. Berbera is the capital.

Sir H. B. Kittermaster, Governor and Commander-in-Chief.

1840

Aug. 19, Treaty with Sultan of Tajura by which land ceded to Great Britain, the Island of Mussa (Musha)

Aug. 27, Cession of Island of Bab to Great Britain

Sept. 3, Treaty by which Island of Aubad (Eftat) ceded to Great Britain

1870

Ismail I, Khedive of Egypt, acquired from Turkey the Somali coast from Berbera to Zeyla

1874–1875

Egyptian occupation of Tajura, Berbera and Bulhar and Harrar in hinterland

1877

Sept. 7, Agreement of Great Britain and Egypt by which Egyptian sovereignty over Somali coast recognized

1884

May 1, July 14, Dec. 11, Dec. 26, Protectorate Treaties signed with native chiefs by British over Mijjertayn, Habr-Awal, Gadabursi, and Habr-Toljaalo

Egyptian troops withdrawn from coast

1885

Jan. 13, Further Protectorate Treaty signed and Feb. 1 and March 15, 1886

1887

July 20, Notification of British Protectorate from Ras Jibuti to Bunder Ziadeh

1888

Feb. 2–9, Exchange of Notes defined British and French spheres, British jurisdiction over Mussa (Musha) and Bab Islands relinquished

1889

Dec. 13, British Order in Council provided for administration of Protectorate

1890

July 1, Anglo-German Boundary Agreement by which Germany recognized Protectorate

1894

May 5, Agreement with Italy defined spheres of influence

May, Successful expedition of Dr. Donaldson Smith (American), through new country

1896

Nov. 26, Sig. Cecchi, Italian consul-gen., 7 officers, 6 Italians, and 18 Askaris (with a caravan) massacred by Wadans, on the Benadir coast

Dec. 2, Gezira bombarded by an Italian gunboat

Dec. 5, Prisoners, guilty of the massacre, shot

1897

Feb. 25, Wadan villages destroyed

April 23, 50 Somalis killed by Italian force

May 14–June 4, Exchange of Notes defined boundary with Abyssinia

1899

Sept. 1, Letter received from the "Mad" Mullah, Mohammed bin Abdullah, who had proclaimed himself Mahdi in answer to demand of British Consul General for restitution of cattle to tribes, British allies, taken in raids, amounted to declaration of war, and was so received

Oct. 7, Somaliland Order in Council provided for administration of Protectorate; amended in 1903, 1904, and 1906

1900

June, Dr. Donaldson Smith explores new regions and returns with valuable collections

Mid June, Mullah's power increasing; raids frequent

Nov. 16, Mr. Jenner, inspector, attacked and murdered by Ogadens, and his escort cut up

1901

Feb. 16, Punitive expedition against Ogaden Somalis; Col. Ternan occupies Aff Madu, Feb. 5; enemy routed

——, Sharp fighting, Lieut.-Col. Maitland and 17 others killed at Sannasa, 150 of the enemy killed

1902

May–July, Successful British and Abyssinian expedition; the Mad Mullah is defeated and put to flight by Col. Swayne and Capt. MacNeill at Moyo, May 30, and at Somali, June 3, 4, and finally routed at Fardiddih, July 17; the Mullah again active, fresh operations successful; Col. Cobbe defeats the enemy in the Nogal valley, 150 killed, large captures of camels and sheep, July, again Aug. 8–Sept. 3, 1902; again attacked in thick bush at Erego, Capts. Phillips, Angus, and 99 men killed, enemy finally repulsed and 62 killed, Oct. 6 (Lieut.-Col. Cobbe made

V.C. for great bravery in this action, Jan. 20, 1903); British reach Bohotle safely, reported Oct. 22; fresh expedition decided on; Col. Swayne in ill-health leaves, Gen. Manning arrives at Burao, Nov. 14; coöperation of the Italians, the Obbia-Mudug route agreed to, Dec. 16

1903

End Jan., Yusuf Ali, sultan of Obbia, captured

March 3, 4, Galkayn and Damot occupied, enemy driven off Lasakante, 15 killed, 16 captured; Galadi occupied March 30; successful operations in the south, heavy loss of the enemy, April 2, 5

April 15, The Abyssinians inflict severe defeat on the Dervishes at Burhilli; 300 killed

April 18, 19, British reverse: Col. Cobbe's reconnoitering column left Galadi April 10; a patrol was attacked near Gumburru, Capt. Chichester killed, enemy repulsed, April 16; Capt. Olivey's patrol of Col. Cobbe's flying column was attacked on all sides by overwhelming numbers near Gumburru; Lt.-Col. Plunket sent in support; the British force fought with heroic courage until the last, only 40 (34 of whom were wounded) escaped; 9 officers, 48 Sikhs and about 171 British were killed; the Mullah's loss about 2,000, April 17; Col. Cobbe relieved by Gen. Manning

April 22, 23, Force under Gen. Gough attacked at Daratoleh, Capts. Bruce and Godfrey and 13 men killed; enemy's loss about 150

May 31, The Abyssinians under Gen. Gabriz surprise and rout the Mullah's force, 1,000 killed

June 24, The Ogaden Somalis defeated by the Abyssinians, reported; Mullah's retreat, end of June

July 15, Maj.-Gen. Sir C. Egerton takes command

Oct. 15, Illig shelled by Italian cruiser *Lombardia*

Nov. 25, Galadi reoccupied after a forced march, 100 miles from Bohotle

Dec. 7, Mullah's force defeated with heavy loss by Somalis at Damot, reported

Dec. 13, Italian war vessel *Galileo* bombards Durbo

Dec. 19, Col. Kenna surprises 2,000 dervishes at Jidballi, 80 killed, 100 wounded

1904

Jan. 11, British, under Gen. Egerton, attack force of some 5,000 dervishes at Jidballi, 1,000 of whom are killed; many prisoners taken, 3 British officers killed, and 9 wounded

Jan. 17, Gen. Kenna surprises some Karias of Aligheri, near Eilinaade; 50 of the enemy killed, and 3,000 camels and many sheep captured

April 21, Capture of Illig from the dervish garrison by a joint naval and military British force

June, Expeditionary force under Gen. Egerton withdrawn, with the exception of two native mounted infantry companies, left as a temporary garrison; Col. Swayne assumes full civil and military control over the protectorate, and begins the organization of the tribes for their self-defense

1906

Jan. 8, Order in Council reorganized administration

May 8, Captain H. E. Cordeaux, of the Indian army, appointed commissioner and commander-in-chief of the Somaliland Protectorate, reported

1908

Sept. 21, The Mullah attacks some friendlies, killing

many women and children; defeated with heavy loss by a British force; British losses, 1 killed, 4 injured, reported

1909

Nov. 12, Decision of Government received to withdraw forces from the interior and concentrate on the coast

1910

Jan., Col. Sir W. Manning appointed commissioner and commander-in-chief

March 20, General Manning announces that the withdrawal of the troops from British Somaliland is to commence

April 3, The Somali Mullah slaughters 800 of the friendly natives, and captures their stock; the friendlies reported to be fleeing towards the coast

1911

July, Horace A. Byatt, Acting Administrator, appointed Commissioner

Nov., The Dervishes made successful attack on the Dolbahanta, tribe friendly to the British, holding former government outpost at Bohotle

1912

Jan. Dervish attack on the Dolbahanta repulsed at Eil Dab

Dec. 4, Camel Constabulary organized left Berbera and formed camp at Mandera

1913

Jan., The Mullah moved from the vicinity of Gerrowei making his headquarters at Tale where fortress was constructed

April 8, The Commissioner received letter from the Mullah asking for a personal interview

April 24, Terms sent by the Commissioner received by the Mullah, the envoys put in chains

Aug. 9, A Camel Constabulary force commanded by R. C. Corfield engaged dervishes at Dul Madoba, though ordered to avoid any action, and was killed and his force made difficult retreat to Burao

1914

March 12–13, Dervishes made night surprise attack on Berbera

May, Geoffrey Archer made Commissioner

Nov. 20 and 23, Major T. A. Cubitt defeated the dervishes at Shimber Berris and captured their forts which were demolished

1915

Feb. 3–4, Major Cubitt again defeated the dervishes who had reoccupied Shimber Berris

Dec. 24, Anglo-Italian Agreement to appoint a mixed commission on Jubaland

1916

May 16, Las Khorai surrounded by dervishes relieved

1917

March 1 and Oct. 8, Dervishes defeated at Endow Pass

1919

Sept., The Mullah moved from Tale to Jidballi establishing his own headquarters in the Medishe hills

Oct., Title of the Commissioner changed to Governor
Dec. 30, Landing at Berbera of 36 officers and 189 of other ranks

1920

Jan. 21, First aërial attack on Medishe camp of the Mullah followed by attacks on Jan. 22 and 23 by Captain R. Gordon

——, Somali Camel Corps commanded by Lieutenant Colonel Ismay arrived at Eil Afweina and constructed a post

Jan. 23, The Kings African Rifles commanded by Lieutenant Colonel G. H. Summers in charge of operations against the Dervishes reached Baron fort attacking the dervishes, the fort occupied on the third day

Jan. 27, Troops arrived before the Jidal fort and began attack. Dervishes evacuated fort during the night

Jan. 28, The Jidal fort occupied. The Mullah began flight south

Feb. 2–3, The Mullah entered the Tale fortress

Feb. 9–10, The British captured Tale and most of the followers of the Mullah who escaped with his eldest son, a brother and a few followers

Feb. 17, Governor Archer offered immunity to the Mullah on surrender

Nov. 23, Death of the Mullah probably from influenza

SOMALILAND, FRENCH

The colony of the Somali Coast lies between the Italian Colony of Eritrea and British Somaliland. On the north it is bounded by Cape Doumeirah, which separates it from the Italian possessions; on the south by a line drawn from the wells of Hadou to Gueldessa, which separates it from the British possessions; the inland boundary towards Abyssinia being, by convention of March 20, 1897, at a distance of 90 kilometers (about 56 miles) from the coast. The territory has an area of about 5,790 square miles, and the population was estimated in 1928 at 85,778, including Europeans. Jibuti is the capital. It is administered by a Governor, assisted by an Administrative Council.

French scientific missions explored the country, Combes and Tamisier (1835–37), Ferret, Gallinier, and Roger (1839–42), Antoine and Arnauld d'Abbadie (1836), and Rochet d'Héricourt in 1842 obtained a political and commercial treaty from the Sultan of Sahlé Salassié

1858

First settlement by the French in Obok after voyage of Henri Lambert, French consular agent at Aden to Zeila and Bay of Tajura

1859

June 4, Henri Lambert murdered near Musha Islands as he embarked for Zeila

Oct. 13, Mission of Captain Russell sent by Napoleon III to the coast

1862

March 11, Treaty signed with Sultan of Tajura and other Danakil chiefs by which Obok ceded to France with adjoining country

1884

April 9, Treaty with Sultan of Gobad under which he placed his foreign relations under French control

June 24, Decree established French colony

July, M. Lagarde arrived at Obok with troops and first effective occupation made

Sept. 21, Treaty with Sultan of Tajura by which Tajura territory ceded to French on coast

Oct. 18 and Dec. 14, Treaties by which land on coast ceded to France (Gulf of Tajura) Ras-Ali, Sagallo, and Gubbed Kharab and lands between Adaeli and Ambado

1885

Jan. 2, The Sultan of Gobad accepted French Protectorate

Feb. 11, Notification of annexation by France of Danakil and Somali coasts

March 26, Chiefs of Issa accepted French Protectorate

Aug. 12, French law established Colony of Obok and Protectorate of Tajura and adjacent territory

Dec. 1, Local decree as to concessions of land granted for 30 years

1887

Sept. 2, Decree established justice of the peace with extensive powers

1888

Feb. 2–9, Anglo-French Boundary Agreement as to Gulf of Tajura region, spheres defined

1891

Jan. 24, Ministerial decree established regulations as to concessions

1893

Feb. 11, Concession granted for construction of railroad from Jibuti (Djibuti) to Addis Ababa

1894

March 9 and Nov. 5, 1896, Menelik of Abyssinia granted concessions for the railroad to Abyssinia by Convention and law respectively

Sept. 4, Courts established

1896

May, Seat of Government transferred to Jibuti
The Colony of Obok received name of French Somaliland

1897

March 20, Boundary Convention with Abyssinia

1898

Aug. 28, Decree established a Council of Administration
Oct., Work begun on the railroad

1899

Oct. 11, Council of Administration reorganized
Nov. 13 and Dec. 29, Local decrees issued as to concessions

1900

Jan. 24, Boundary Convention with Italy

Aug. 18, Decree established customs duties as to trade with Abyssinia

Aug. 20, First section of railroad opened to frontier of Abyssinia

1901

Feb. 1, Decree established a custom house at Djibouti

——, School of the Brothers of Saint Gabriel opened at Djibouti, primary grade, children admitted free of charge without distinction of race

July 10, Further Boundary Convention with Italy

1902

Feb. 6, Convention with Abyssinian Railroad Company signed

——, The Government agreed to annual sum subsidy to railroad company

1903

Jan. 1, Railroad reached Diredawa, Abyssinia

1906

July 6 and Dec. 13, Agreement as to railroads in Abyssinia by France, England, and Italy, France continuing to control the railroad to Addis Ababa

1908

Jan. 30, Abyssinian railroad concession of 1894 to M. Ilg transferred to Dr. Vitalien, the new concession approved by Government of France Dec. 8

SOMALILAND, ITALIAN

Somaliland, Italian Colony, has an area of about 190,000 sq. miles and a population of about 1,200,-000 (1,000 Italians). It extends along the east coast of Africa from British Somaliland to Dik's Head in Kenya Colony. The inland boundaries are determined under the Treaty of May 6, 1908, between Italy and Abyssinia, by a line (only partially demarcated) from the confluence of the Ganale with the Daua, thence to Bender Ziada (45th parallel) on the Gulf of Aden following an irregular line which runs at a mean distance of 180 miles from the coast through Jet, Ato, El Gorum, Bur Lelmis, Bur Gumburn, Bur Burdubo, and Bur Galambaladi to Bender Ziada. As a result of the Treaty of 1915 and the Colonial rearrangements consequent on the war, Britain has ceded Italy territories on the right bank of the Juba with the port of Kismayu (Chisimaio). This district is incorporated in Somalia and forms one of its provinces. It has an area of 35,000 sq. miles and an estimated population of 100,000.

Italian Somaliland comprises (I) The territories of Northern Somalia, viz.: (1) The territory of the Mijertins, from Bender Ziade, the most northerly point belonging to Italy on the Gulf of Aden, to Cape Gabà on the Indian Ocean (8° 13′ N. lat.); (2) the territory of the Nogal, from Cape Gaba to Cape Garad (6° 47′ N. lat.), formerly occupied by the Mad Mullah; (3) the territory of Obbia, from Cape Garad to the northern boundary of the Colony of Benadir, determined by a line which ends at the sea near the wells of El Gabobe (about 4° 30′ N. lat.). (II) Southern Somalia, formerly called "Benadir," which extends from 4° 30′ N. lat. to Ras Chiamboni (Dik's Head). Mogadiscio (population 28,000, of whom 800 are Europeans), capital of the Colony, with its territory, has been placed under the direct dependence of the Governor.

De Guido Corni, Governor.

1889

March 2 and May 20, Protectorate declared over Obbia (Oppia)

Aug. 3, Treaty with the Sultan of Zanzibar by which Italy acquired coast from beyond Cape Gardafui to Kismayu

Nov. 19, Italian notification to the Powers of Protectorate over Benadir coast

1890

April 8, Concession of the Sultan of Zanzibar to British East Africa Company of administration of ports Kismayu and of Benadir ports of Brava, Meurka, Magadisho, and Warsheikh transferred to Italy

1891

March 24, Protocol between Italy and Great Britain defined spheres of influence on the coast

April 15, Anglo-Italian Boundary Convention signed as to spheres of influence inland; Great Britain agreed to Italian occupation of Kassala

1892

Aug. 12, The Sultan of Zanzibar leased Benadir ports to Italy for 50 years on payment of 160,000 rupees a year, and additional Article Sept. 1, 1896

1893

May 15, The Italian Government leased administration of Benadir ports to the Filonardi Company

1894

May 5, Further Agreement of Italy with Great Britain defining spheres of influence

1898

May 25, Convention by which the Italian Government ceded the Benadir coast to Milanese Commercial Society

1905

Jan. 13, The Sultan of Zanzibar ceded sovereign rights as to ports of Benadir to Italy for payment of £144,000

——, Anglo-Italian Agreement, lease of land to Italy near Kismayu

March 5, Peace Agreement with the Mullah (Sheikh Mohammed-ben-Abdullah) and territory assigned to him and his followers in the Italian sphere of influence; adhered to by Great Britain March 24, and further Agreement March 19, 1907

March 16, Italian Government assumed direction of affairs of the Milanese Company

July 28, Italian flag raised and Royal Commissioner for southern Somaliland appointed

1908

April 5, Laws for administration promulgated, constitution of Somaliland under Civil Governor

May 16, Boundary Convention with Abyssinia signed

by Italy as to frontier and additional territory ceded to Italy including Lugh

1910

July, Southern Somaliland constituted as a Crown Colony

1911

July 8–15, Boundary with British East Africa fixed at mouth of Juba River

1915

Dec. 24, Anglo-Italian Agreement for regulation of Juba River and division of islands in the River

1924

July 15, Anglo-Italian Treaty by which Juba River and a strip from 50 to 100 miles wide on the British side of the River ceded to Italy, cession taking place June 29, 1925 after ratification of Treaty

1929

Jan. 23, Ordinance regulated export and imports, agriculture, manufactures, transport

April 18, Royal Ordinance established a property tax

1930

Sept. 17, Regulations issued for extension to Colony of Italian Ordinance of April 10, 1929 exempting head of large families from taxation

SOUTH AFRICA, UNION OF

The Union of South Africa is constituted under the South Africa Act, 1909 (9 Edw. 7, Ch. 9), passed by the Parliament of the United Kingdom on September 20, 1909. Under the terms of that Act the self-governing Colonies of the Cape of Good Hope, Natal, the Transvaal, and the Orange River Colony were united on May 31, 1910, in a legislative union under one Government under the name of the Union of South Africa, these Colonies becoming original provinces of the Union under the names of the Cape of Good Hope, Natal, the Transvaal, and the Orange Free State respectively. There is a Governor-General, and an Executive Council in charge of the Departments of State.

The total area of the Union is 471,917 square miles divided between the Provinces as follows:— Cape of Good Hope, 276,536; Natal, 35,284; Transvaal, 110,450; Orange Free State, 49,647.

The census taken in 1904 in each of the four Colonies was the first simultaneous census taken in South Africa. In 1911 the first Union census was taken.

		ALL RACES			EUROPEAN		NON-EUROPEAN	
YEAR		Total	European	Non-European	Males	Females	Males	Females
1904	. . . . . .	5,175,824	1,116,806	4,059,018	635,117	481,689	2,047,118	2,011,900
1911	. . . . . .	5,973,394	1,276,242	4,697,152	685,164	591,078	2,384,228	2,312,924
1918	. . . . . .	—	1,421,781	—	728,866	692,915	—	—
1921	. . . . . .	6,928,580	1,519,488	5,409,092	782,035	737,453	2,754,957	2,654,135
1926	. . . . . .	—	1,676,660	—	856,918	819,742	—	—

Of the non-European population in 1921, 4,697,813 were Bantu, 165,731 Asiatic, and 545,548 of other races.

The increase in the total population, 1911–21, was: Union, 15.99%; Cape, 8.49%; Natal, 19.71%; Transvaal, 23.81%; O.F.S., 10.06%. The increase in the European population in the Union, 1911–21, was 19.06%, and in other races 15.16%. The proportion of Europeans to the total population in 1921 was 21.03%.

Pretoria is the seat of government of the Union, and Cape Town is the seat of Legislature.

Earl of Clarendon, Governor-General and Commander-in-Chief, appointed January, 1931.

1910

April 24–27, Formation of South African (Nationalist) Party, pro-Boer, led by Botha and Herzog

May 23–24, Unionist or Progressive Party formed at meeting of 150 delegates

May 31, Union of South Africa inaugurated, Lord Gladstone took oath of office as Governor General, and General Botha as Prime Minister and Minister of Agriculture; General Smuts, Interior; General Herzog, Justice; Mr. Hull, Finance; Mr. Sauer, Railways; Mr. Malan, Education; Mr. Fischer, Lands; Mr. Burton, Native Affairs; Mr. Moor, Commerce

and Industry; Mr. Graaf, Public Works; Dr. Gubbins, without portfolio

July 17, Groote Schuur taken over by the Union Government to be the official residence of General Botha, Prime Minister, in Cape Town

Aug. 1, Immigration Regulation Act

Sept. 15, First general election for Parliament gave a majority for the "South African" party of General Botha, though General Botha himself was defeated in Pretoria (East), Nationalists, 67; Unionists, 37; Labor, 4; Independents, 13

Nov. 4, First Parliament opened by the Duke of Connaught

Dec. 23, Act provided for naturalization of aliens

1911

Feb. 4, Death of General Piet A. Cronje, Boer General (75)

April 15, Mines and Works consolidated laws

April 20, Native Labor Regulation Act signed

April 24, General Herzog's educational policy adopted in Orange Free State, Transvaal, and Cape, providing for instruction in schools in both Dutch and English

April 25, Miners' Pthisis Act provided compensation for persons who had contracted the disease

May 7, Official census of population gave total population as 5,973,394, including 1,276,242 Europeans and 4,697,152 non-Europeans

1912

April, Sir Starr Jameson (Dr. Jameson) resigned leadership of the Unionist Party, the Opposition, and was succeeded by Sir Thomas Smartt

May 27, Irrigation Act consolidated all provincial statutes

June 8, Land Settlement Act provided for allotment of Crown lands

June 13, Defense Act increased expenditure from £320,000 a year to £500,000

June 22, Miners' Pthisis Act amended and Land and Agricultural Bank Act passed

June 24, Public Service and Railway and Harbor Service Acts provided for pensions for employees

June 25, General Herzog became Minister of Native Affairs

Nov. 21, Motion to commit the Unionist Party to policy of segregation of natives defeated in party congress by vote of 91 to 7

Dec. 12, Colonel Leuchers, Minister of Public Works resigned as a protest against General Herzog's "anti-British and anti-imperial" speeches

Dec. 15, General Botha resigned because of refusal of General Herzog to resign

Dec. 20, Cabinet reconstituted by General Botha without General Herzog

1913

Feb. 4, Death of Sir John Sprigg (82) four times Prime Minister of Cape Colony

April 1, South African Permanent Force of Mounted Riflemen established

May 17, Financial Relations Act passed which was extended in 1917 and 1920

May–June, Strike of white miners at the New Kleinfontein mine over hours

June 14, Immigration Regulation Act restricted entry of Asiatics by use of ministerial certificate, and restricted Asiatics to the province in which they were resident

June 16, Native Land Act provided restrictions for purchase and lease of land by natives prohibiting the further acquisition of land

July 4, General strike of miners called and serious riots in Johannesburg

July 5, Temporary settlement of strike by General Botha pending hearings by the Government on grievances, and reinstatement of men at the New Kleinfontein mine

July 6, Further rioting. In all 20 persons killed and 250 injured

July 24, Death of J. W. Sauer member of Cabinet

July 31, Miners voted against calling a general strike

Nov. 6, Gandhi arrested and sentenced to 9 months in prison, marching at head of some 2,700 Indians to assert right of Indians to move from one province to another, from Natal to the Transvaal

Nov. 27, 9 Indians killed in clash of police and Indians in Natal

Nov. 30, At conference of the South African party at Cape Town General de Wet's proposal to make ex-President Steyn "leader of the party outside Parliament, with power to nominate the Prime Minister" defeated, and a large number left the party

Dec. 10, Commission of Inquiry appointed on strike of Indians in Natal

1914

Jan., New Nationalist party formed under leadership of General Hertzog of secessionists from the South African party

Jan. 7, Strike of employees on government railroads due to policy of retrenchment and a general strike declared for Jan. 14

Jan. 13, Martial law proclaimed as general strike begun and 20,000 troops mobilized and concentrated on the Rand

Jan. 21, Strike ended

Jan. 24, Death of David Gill, astronomer

Jan. 27, Ten prominent labor leaders concerned in strike charged with revolutionary conspiracy and arrested and secretly deported

May 14, Sydney Buxton appointed Governor General to succeed Lord Gladstone and created a viscount

June 20, Workmens' Wage Protection Act

June 30, Smuts-Gandhi agreement by exchange of letter as to Indians, General Smuts, Minister of the Interior, and in charge of legislation affecting Indians, gave assurance that existing laws would be administered "in a just manner and with due regard to vested rights"

July 1, Workmens' Compensation Act to take effect Jan. 1, 1915

——, Indian Relief Act made provision for redress of certain grievances and disabilities, repealed £3 tax and directed that the sole wife of a polygamous marriage should be admitted and the marriage registered as monogamous

July 20, Farewell letter of Gandhi to Indians urged them to continue agitation for removal of disabilities, as he left for India considering his mission in Africa ended

Aug. 7, Great Britain declared war on Germany

——, Telegram of the Imperial Government stated that the seizure of ports of German S. W. Africa which would give command of Luderitzbucht, Swakopmund, and the wireless stations there would be "a great and urgent imperial service"

Aug. 10, General Botha replied to Imperial Government that the expedition into German S. W. Africa would be undertaken

Aug. 21, German force from South West Africa crossed the frontier into Union near Nakab

Sept. 8, Lord Buxton assumed office as Governor General

Sept. 9, Special War session of Parliament opened to which General Botha submitted resolution authorizing expedition into German S. W. Africa which was denounced by General Hertzog and Dutch Nationalists but passed the House by a large majority Sept. 10 and the Senate Sept. 14

Sept. 14, Protection of Currency Act passed

Sept. 15, Resignation of General Beyers of post as commander-general of Union Forces because of disapproval of expedition against Germans in South West Africa. General Botha announced that he would take command of forces and personally command expedition

——, General De La Rey on his way to Pretoria to join rebels planning to restore the Dutch Republic, revolt scheduled to begin the next morning, was shot and killed by patrol guard when his car challenged and no answer given. The revolution delayed by loss of this leader

Sept. 21, Manifesto of General Beyers denouncing the Government of Sept. 15 published

Sept. 25, Resignation of Lieutenant-Colonel Solomon

G. Maritz refusing to take part in the expedition into German S. W. Africa. He was later proved to have been in treasonable relations with the Germans before the War began

Oct. 9, Maritz crossed the frontier after disarming machine gun section under British officers and surrendered 60 loyal officers and men of his force of 600 to the Germans

Oct. 11, Appeal of the Government to ex-President Steyn to use his influence against treason in the Free State and Transvaal

Oct. 12, Martial law declared by the Union Government

Oct. 13, Meeting of leaders of the rebellion at Kopjes, Orange Free State

Oct. 14, Meeting of Beyers and De Wet at Pretoria

Oct. 15, Rebels defeated at Ratedrai

Oct. 18, Railroad from Prieska to Upington, Bechualand, opened

Oct. 22, At meeting in Kopjes the Dutch in Orange Free State and Transvaal declared for General De Wet and General Beyers in rebellion

Oct. 23, General De Wet seized Heilbron, Orange Free State

——, Steyn in response to second appeal from the Government began to make efforts to restrain leaders of rebellion in conferences which led to no result

Oct. 24, Maritz defeated by Colonel Coen Brits at Kakamas and forced to take refuge in German territory

Oct. 27, General Botha defeated General Beyers at Commissie Drift, south of Rustenberg

Oct. 29, General De Wet looted Vrede in the Free State

Nov. 7, Beyers defeated in engagement at Gruis Drift on the Vet River and 400 rebels taken prisoners

Nov. 8, Government troops under Commandant Cronje defeated by De Wet who seized town of Winburg the following day

Nov. 12, General Botha defeated De Wet's main army at Mushroom Valley 18 miles southeast of Winburg in Free State

Nov. 17, General Smuts informed Mr. Steyn that unconditional surrender on the lenient terms offered by the Government was demanded in refusing to allow conference with De Wet who had previously refused to go to see Steyn

Dec. 1, General De Wet captured at Waterburg about 100 miles west of Mafeking by Colonel Brits while trying to reach German territory

Dec. 8, General Beyers defeated by Union troops in the Hoopstad district reached the Vaal River near Zand Spruit and was drowned attempting to escape pursuing forces by crossing the river

Dec. 16, Rebel commander, Fourie, defeated, surrendered and was tried by court martial and shot, Dec. 20

Dec. 21, Expeditionary force under Colonel Skinner left Cape Town for Walvis Bay which had been taken by Germans and landed and occupied it Dec. 25

Dec. 31, Defense Act enforced to permit conscription

1915

Jan. 24, Rebels under Maritz and Kemp repulsed in attack on Upington, Bechuanaland

Feb. 3, Surrender of Major Kemp with 600 of his men including "the prophet," Van Rensburg, who had incited Dutch farmers to sedition with his visions, to Colonel J. L. Van Deventer at Upington; Maritz

withdrew to German S. W. Africa and eventually went to Spain

Feb. 26, Germans driven from position taken at Nakab by Colonel Van Deventer

April 11, General Smuts arrived at Kalkfontein, German South West Africa, and took command of army. For campaign in German East Africa see World War

May 12, Windhoek, capital of German South West Africa, surrendered to General Botha

June 21, De Wet, rebel leader, convicted of treason and sentenced to fine of £2,000 and imprisonment for 6 years

July 1, General Botha occupied Otavi, German South West Africa

July 9, General Botha received surrender of enemy forces of German South West Africa at Grootfontein

July 15, Proclamation announced assimilation of former German South West Africa to Union of South Africa for customs purposes, General P. S. Beves appointed military governor

July 22, Arrival of General Botha at Cape Town after victorious campaign

Aug. 23, Parliament dissolved

Oct. 20, General election held gave (Botha's) the South African party 54 seats in the House out of a total of 130, the Nationalists (Herzog), 27; the Unionists (mainly British), 40; Labor, 3; Independents, 6

Oct. 28, E. H. L. Gorges appointed Administrator of the South West Africa Protectorate on departure of General Beves

Nov. 19, Second Parliament of the Union opened by Lord Buxton, Governor General

Dec. 20, General De Wet and 118 other political prisoners released on undertaking to abstain from political agitation

1916

April 7, Patent Act consolidated the laws of the various provinces

April 27, Three universities established, the South African College incorporated as the University of Cape Town, Victoria College became Stellenbosch University, and University of the Cape of Good Hope became the University of South Africa

June 9, War Pensions Act

June 10, Trading with the Enemy Act

Nov. 28, Death of Marthinus Steyn, former President of the Orange Free State

1917

Jan. 14, Death of Boer General Benjamin J. Viljoen at La Mesa, New Mexico

Jan. 20, General Van Deventer succeeded General Smuts in command in E. Africa

May 29, Workmens Compensation Act amended

June 18, House passed resolution condemning the republican propaganda of the Nationalists by 72 votes to 21

June 26, Land Settlement Act amended

Nov. 26, Death of Sir Leander Starr Jameson (Dr. Jameson) in England

British Government took over the South African wool clip paying a price 55% in excess of pre-War price of 1913–14

1918

March 22, Permanent Cost of Living Commission established

April 2, University legislation of 1916 came into effect

April 13, Seditious speech of General Hertzog demanded separation from the British Empire

April 21, Lord Buxton, Governor General, warned Nationalists against republican propaganda

May 5, Census of European population gave total as 1,421,781

May 7, Miners' Phthisis Act amended

May 8, Factories Act placed working conditions under supervision of the Government, and Regulation of Wages, and Apprentices Act established wage boards and regulated work of women and minors in specified trades

June, A 23% rise in cost of living reported

June 11–July 26, General Smuts and the Hon. H. Burton attended the Imperial Conference in England. A reciprocity resolution accepted for the Dominions affirmed right of members of the British Commonwealth to control composition of its population by means of restriction on immigration from any of the other communities

Aug.–Dec., Epidemic of influenza; estimated total of mortality, 11,726, white; 127,745, colored

Nov. 14, Armistice with Germany signed; surrender of General von Lettow-Vorbeck ended hostilities in East Africa

Dec. 16, General Botha arrived in London to represent the Union at Peace Conference

1919

Jan. 30, War losses published, 6,800 killed of whom 4,630 died in Europe, 11,500 South Africans wounded or gassed

Feb. 20, At Loyalist meeting at Cape Town Sir N. F. de Waal declared a large section of the Dutch were in accord with the British element and determined to maintain the Union

March, End of general strike at Johannesburg

April 18, Nationalist Delegation headed by General Hertzog arrived in England and presented petition to British Government asking independence for South Africa

May 7, Supreme Council assigned mandate for German South West Africa to the Union

June 21, Asiatics Land and Trading Act confirmed right of Indians in land for trading purposes which they then held but prevented further acquisition of land by Indians through private companies, the number registered having increased from 3 in 1913 to 370 in 1919 with a total capital of £479,000

——, Native Reserve Location Act for Cape of Good Hope Province enacted

June 28, Death of William Philip Schreiner, former High Commissioner

——, Treaty of peace with Germany signed by Generals Botha and Smuts for the Union

Aug. 27, Death of General Louis Botha, Prime Minister

Sept. 3, General J. C. Smuts formed Cabinet

Sept. 8, Law gave effect to Union of South Africa mandate for former German South West Africa

Oct. 10 and 16, At Nationalist Conference at Bloemfontein General Hertzog postponed revolution but declared all laws of Imperial Parliament for South Africa should be declared null and void, only Union legislation legal

1920

Feb. 6, Proclamation dissolved the House

Feb., Strike of natives begun on Rand for wages and

better conditions which involved 42,000 laborers and was believed to have been partly organized by the Third International

March 10, General election gave South African Party, 40; Unionist, 25; Nationalists, 45; Labour, 21; Independents, 3

March 19, Third Parliament opened

May 29, Constitution of Supreme Court

June 19, Rents Act to fix and reduce rents for one year made permanent in 1921

July 28, Native Affairs Act provided commissions and councils and set aside areas for the exclusive occupation of the natives in which they had greater opportunity than before of obtaining local self-government

Aug. 5, Prince Arthur of Connaught appointed Governor General

——, Profiteering Act signed

Aug. 16, Housing Act authorized borrowing money from the State for local loans

——, Currency and Banking Act passed to come into effect Dec. 17

Oct. 23, Riot at Port Elizabeth when Europeans fired on native strikers who attacked court house in attempt to release their leader, Masabalala, arrested and refused bail, 20 persons killed and 40 injured

Oct. 31, Term of first Senate expired

Nov. 20, Prince Arthur of Connaught assumed office as Prime Minister

Nov. 27, The Unionists joined the South African Party

Dec. 11, Death of Olive Schreiner (Mrs. Conwright Schreiner) author

Dec. 17, The mandate of the Union over former German South West Africa as assigned by the Supreme Council approved by Council of the League of Nations (South West Africa Protectorate. *See* p. 564)

Dec. 31, House dissolved

1921

Feb. 8, Election an overwhelming victory for General Smuts and the new South African Party over the Nationalists (Hertzog); South Africans, 76 seats; Nationalists, 47; Labor, 10; Independents, 1; the Senate, Ministerialists, 25, Nationalists, 13; Labor, 2

Feb. 21, Arrival of Field Marshal Earl Haig at Cape Town to inaugurate the first congress of the League of Comrades of the Great War

March 10, Cabinet reconstituted, General Jan C. Smuts, Prime Minister; Henry Burton, Finance; Patrick Duncan, Interior

March 11, Fourth Parliament opened

May 24, Native gathering of religious fanatics calling themselves Israelites led by one named Enoch refused to disperse at Bulhoeck, and were fired on and 150 killed

June 20, General Smuts, Sir Thomas Smartt, and Colonel H. Mentz represented the Union at Imperial Conference in England, South Africa refused to adopt resolution affirming rights of Indians to citizenship in Dominions be recognized

June 30, South African Reserve Bank opened at Pretoria

July 5, Juveniles Act provided for boards for supervision of all matters of employment and general welfare of persons under 17

Census gave total population as 6,928,580 including 1,519,488 Europeans and 5,409,092 non-Europeans of whom 4,697,813 were Bantu, and 165,731 Asiatic

1922

Jan. 8, General strike of miners due to 5 shilling wage cut proposed

Feb. 3, Death of General Christian De Wet at Bloemfontein

March 8, Government troops called against revolutionary strikers, 188 persons killed and more than 500 wounded

March 10, Martial law declared

March 11–13, Strikers in control of suburbs of Johannesburg finally defeated after 4 days fighting by Government troops

March 19, Several unions acting independently of the federation declared strike ended and resumed work

July 5, Defense Act amended, reorganization of permanent force

July 17, Apprenticeship Act passed to come into force Jan. 1, 1923

July 19, Defense Act amended to provide for taking over buildings and land by the Government for purposes of defense

Oct. 4, University of the Witwatersrand established March 1 opened

Oct. 27, Referendum vote in Rhodesia declared against union with South Africa

1923

May 21, Aviation Act to consolidate regulations and encourage aviation passed to go into effect July 1, 1924

June 14, Ordinance of Natal provided for restriction of sale of borough and township lands in order to prevent purchase or lease by Indians

July 9, Opposition parties met and voted "no confidence" in General Smuts and demanded a separate portfolio for native affairs

July 27, The Vaal barrage opened

Sept. 12, South Rhodesia formally annexed to the British Crown. *See* Rhodesia

Nov. 21, The Earl of Athlone appointed Governor General

1924

Jan. 21, The Earl of Athlone assumed office as Governor General

Feb. 20, Order in Council announced that Northern Rhodesia would be taken over by the British Government as a protectorate from April 1. *See* Northern Rhodesia

March 4, Industrial Conciliation Bill passed third reading, provided for industrial councils for the settlement of disputes

May 9, Proclamation dissolved the House and ended discussion of Class Areas Bill to give the Government power to enforce segregation of Asiatics in urban areas

June 17, Election a defeat for the Smuts Government: Nationalists, 63 seats; South African Party, 53; Labor, 18; Independent, 1

June 23, Resignation of General Smuts as Premier

June 30, General J. M. B. Hertzog appointed Prime Minister formed Cabinet: Dr. D. F. Malan, Interior; N. C. Havenga, Finance; F. H. P. Creswell, Defense and Labor; F. W. Beyers, Mines and Industries; General J. C. G. Kemp, Agriculture; the Prime Minister retaining the Ministry of Native Affairs

July 25, Labor Department constituted

——, Fifth Parliament opened

Dec. 25, Natal Municipal Ordinance and that of April 30, 1925, deprived Indians of municipal franchise

1925

Feb., Nationality and Flag Bill introduced authorizing the Government to choose design for a Union of South Africa flag

April 20, Riot of 4,000 natives at Bloemfontein, Orange Free State

April 30, Arrival of the Prince of Wales on visit to South Africa

May 18, Return to the gold standard

June 25, "Color Bar" Bill passed third reading in the Assembly by vote of 44 to 31

July 7, "Color Bar" Bill to prohibit native Africans and Asiatics from employment in certain categories of skilled labor in factories and mines rejected by Senate

July 21, Land Act amended

——, Nationality and Flag Bill withdrawn by the Government

July 25, Wage Act provided Wage Board for the Union

July 27, Act passed gave the Government the control of the production and sale of diamonds

——, Act granted a constitution to South West Africa

——, New Tariff Act makes provision for preference for British products, and reciprocal most favored foreign nation agreements

——, Native Tax and Development Act provided that every adult male pay tax of £1 and local tax of 10s. per hut

Aug. 28, Durban seamen joined the British strike

Sept. 1, Branch of Central Reserve Bank established at Johannesburg and further branches at Cape Town, Durban, Port Elizabeth, and East London by the end of the year

Oct. 12, Shipping strike officially ended

Dec. 26, Indian National Congress at Cawnpore at suggestion of Mr. Gandhi passed resolution assuring South African Indians of their support

1926

Jan. 22, The Governor General opening Parliament (3rd sess. 5th) appealed for "the greatest possible measure of national unity and coöperation" in relations with the native races

Feb. 4, General Hertzog reintroduced "Color Bar" Bill (Mines and Works Amendment)

Feb. 12, Union Wage Board constituted, F. A. W. Lucas, Chairman

Feb. 18, Alan Cobham completed 8,000 mile flight from London to Cape Town

March 17, "Color Bar" Bill rejected by Senate

April 23, Announcement of Government of agreement with India for Conference and postponement of action on Areas Reservation and Immigration Bill

May 4, The House passed the "Color Bar" Bill restricting certain occupations to white persons by vote of 83 to 67

May 19, Government proposal of adoption of flag for the Union as designed by Professor Walker

June 22, Agreement with Portugal signed as to frontier between Angola and South West Africa

Aug. 30, Union deputation headed by Mr. Beyers sailed for India

Dec. 17–Jan. 11, 1927, Conference at Cape Town of delegation from India with the Government to discuss problems of Indian population and especially the Class Areas Bill reintroduced by the Government in 1926 session of Parliament and the Immigration Bill amendment proposed. Recommendations adopted approved by both Governments provided for assisted emigration for Indians to India or other countries where Western standards are not required, the Union Government recognizing that Indians domiciled in the Union and prepared to conform to Western standards of living should be enabled to do so, and the Class Areas and Immigration and Registration Bill to be dropped

1927

Feb. 15, Provincial elections held a victory for the South African Party

Feb. 21, Round Table Conference of Union with Great Britain and India to consider proposal to segregate and repatriate Indians in Union of South Africa agreed on voluntary repatriation at Government expense

March 4, The rush for Grosfontein diamond field participated in by 25,000 runners

March 26, Land Survey Act passed to come into force Jan. 1, 1929

June 1, Department of External Affairs constituted

June 17, Work Colonies Act provided for establishment of colonies for prisoners to come into effect March 1, 1929

June 23, Nationality and Flag Bill passed by the Assembly

June 29, Nationality and Flag Bill vetoed by Senate

July 29, Immigrations Regulations Act amended by the Immigration and Indian Relief (Further Provisions) Act, and Native Administration Act consolidated systems of native administration, native laws and customs recognized in special courts

Oct. 24, Flag controversy settled by agreement of General Hertzog representing the Nationalists and General Smuts representing the South African Party to use the Union Jack in the new national flag

Nov. 11, Nationality and Flag Act passed

1928

Feb. 12–May 17, Solo flight of Lady Mary Heath from Cape Town to Cairo and to England

March 22, Land Settlement Act amended

March 29, Assembly voted acceptance of report of Imperial Conference of 1926

June 1, Riots at unfurling of new Union flag

June 5, Old Age Pensions Act made universal

July 8, National Council of Labor Party at Durban expelled Colonel Creswell

July 13, Liquor Control Act consolidated liquor laws in 4 provinces

Sept. 1, Commercial Treaty with Germany signed

Sept. 11, New Mozambique Convention with Portugal signed as to regulation of native labor, commerce, customs, &c., replacing that of April 2, 1909

Oct. 17, Treaties of arbitration signed with Portugal and Switzerland

Nov. 6, Nationalist-Labor Cabinet of General Hertzog reconstituted omitting W. B. Madely, Minister of Posts and Telegraphs and Public Works who had refused to resign, and H. W. Sampson appointed

1929

Feb. 4, Settlement of 327 Dutch Boer families from Angola in South West Africa arranged

Feb. 25, Natives Representation Bill which provided that the natives of Cape Province be enrolled separately as voters to be represented by 5 white Europeans in House, &c., was rejected by Assembly

April 1, First work colony for prisoners inaugurated at Nuuwberg

April 30, Parliament dissolved

June 12, Election a victory for Premier Hertzog and the Nationalist Party accentuating the division between the English-speaking coast and the Dutch-speaking (Nationalist) interior, and postponing citizenship for black natives; Nationalists, 78 seats; South African Party, 61; Creswellite Labor, 5; Labor (National Council), 3; Independent, 1

June 14, New Cabinet sworn in, General Hertzog, Prime Minister and External Affairs; O. Pirow, Justice; Dr. D. F. Malan, Interior, Public Health and Education; F. H. P. Creswell, Defense and Labor; N. C. Havenga, Finance; A. P. J. Fourie, Mines and Industries; C. W. Malan, Railways and Harbors; P. G. W. Grobler, Lands; H. W. Sampson, Posts, Telegraphs, and Public Works; E. G. Jansen, Native Affairs

July 19, Sixth Parliament opened

Aug. 19, Senate dissolved

Aug. 31, Alfred Beit Road and Rail Bridge over the Limpopo River connecting the Union with Southern Rhodesia opened

Sept. 6, Elections for Senate returned 17 Nationalists (Government) and 15 South African Party, 8 additional members to be nominated by the Governor General in Council, of whom 4 selected to represent the native population

Nov. 5, Union entered into direct diplomatic relations with the United States

1930

March 4, Alien Quota Act restricted to 50 a year immigrants from any country except 12 Nordic nations of Europe, the British Commonwealth, and the United States

March 21, Commission of Enquiry into economic and social conditions of the natives appointed

May 19, Women's Enfranchisement Act extended the Parliamentary and Provincial franchise to all white women

May 22, The Assembly adopted resolution reaffirming the right of the Union of South Africa or any other British Dominion to secede from the British Empire

May 28, Union Wage Act amended

June 20, New Customs Agreement with North and South Rhodesia published

Oct., World's deepest workings on Village Deep (gold mining) 7,638 feet

Dec. 1, General Hertzog arrived at Cape Town from England and attendance at the Imperial Conference and 2 days later made statement that "No State knows greater freedom" than Union of South Africa

Dec. 3, The Earl of Clarendon appointed Governor General and assumed office Jan. 26, 1931

Dec. 10, Speech of General Hertzog denounced republicanism

SOUTH AFRICAN WAR
(Boer Republics)

For the origin of this war, *see* Transvaal, 1876 *et seq.*

1899

Oct. 11, Boer ultimatum, demanding arbitration, withdrawal of troops from the frontier, compliance within

48 hours demanded, Oct. 9, 1899; rejected by Gt. Britain

Oct. 11, Gen. Sir George White arrives at Ladysmith

Oct. 12, General advance of Boers, Oct. 11; they invade Natal at Laing's Nek and Van Reenen's pass

——, Armored train under Capt. Nesbit captured by Boers at Kraaipan

Oct. 13, Mafeking invested: Boers repulsed; sorties under Col. Baden-Powell, 2 British killed

Oct. 15, Newcastle occupied by the Boers

Oct. 15 et seq., Siege of Kimberley: garrison, 500 Lancashires and about 3,000 colonials, under Col. Kekewich, aided by Mr. Cecil Rhodes; successful sorties

Oct. 19, 20, Boers occupy Vryburg and Klipdam (under cover of the white flag)

Oct. 20, Battle of Glencoe or Dundee: Boers under Comm. Lucas Meyer storm the British camp; Talana hill captured by the King's Royal Rifles and the Irish Fusiliers, Boers routed and 6 guns taken; Gen. Sir Wm. Penn Symons mortally wounded (died Oct. 23), Cols. Sherston and Gunning, 6 officers killed; total casualties, 432; Boer casualties estimated, 500

Oct. 21, Battle of Elandslaagte: Gens. French and Ian Hamilton rout the Boers under Ben Viljoen, their guns, camp, and position taken; Col. Scott-Chisholme and 4 officers killed; total casualties, 223; Boer loss, Gen. Koch mortally wounded, 208 killed and wounded, 188 prisoners taken

Oct. 22, A party of 18th Hussars under Col. Möller, in pursuit of the Boers after the battle, was captured and taken to Pretoria

Oct. 22–26, Yule joins White at Ladysmith after a hard march

Oct. 23 et seq., Mafeking bombarded; Boers repulsed

Oct. 24, Rietfontein: White routs the O.F.S. Boers, Col. Wilford and 11 men killed; total British casualties, 111

——, Sortie from Kimberley; Comm. Botha and others killed; British loss, 3

Oct. 26, Plumer engages the Boers near Tuli

Oct. 30, Lombard's Kop or Farquhar's Farm: position captured and Boers put to flight; Major Myers (eminent art collector) killed

——, Nicholson's Nek disaster: attempt to turn the Boers' position failed through a stampede of the battery mules, with the guns, &c.; after desperate fighting, Col. Carleton and 870 Gloucesters and Artillery surrendered

[British casualties in these 2 actions, 1,227. Gen. White nobly took all the blame for last affair]

Oct. 27–31, Brilliant sorties from Mafeking; Capt. Pechell, Lieut. Marsham, and 10 others killed; Boer loss heavy

Oct. 31, Gen. Sir Redvers Buller lands at Cape Town

Nov. 1, Cape Colony invaded by Boers

Nov. 2, Ladysmith isolated and bombarded: Capt. Lambton's naval guns used effectively on Boer camp; Lieut. F. G. Egerton, of H.M.S. Powerful, mortally wounded

——, British garrison evacuates Colenso, retires on Estcourt

Nov. 6, Successful cavalry action by Brocklehurst outside Ladysmith, near Dewdrop

Nov. 7, Brilliant sortie from Mafeking

Nov. 9, General attack on Ladysmith repulsed; Boer casualties over 800

Nov. 14, Free Staters occupy Aliwal North

Nov. 15, Boers capture an armored train near Chieveley; Mr. Winston Churchill, war correspondent Morning Post (he escaped from Pretoria, Dec. 12), and over 100 British captured or missing

Nov. 18, 23, Gen. Hildyard repulses the Boers at Ulundi and near Estcourt

Nov. 23, Belmont: Lord Methuen, advancing to relieve Kimberley, attacks the Boers under Gen. Cronje and drives them with heavy loss from their positions (grand charge of the Guards); British casualties, 270 (53 killed)

Nov. 25, Enslin or Graspan: Methuen defeats the Boers with heavy loss; Commander Ethelston, R.N., killed; total British casualties, 185

——, Gen. Sir Redvers Buller arrives at Natal

Nov. 28, Modder River: Methuen attacks 11,000 Boers under Cronje and forces them to quit their positions after 10 or 16 hours' fierce fighting; Cols. Northcott and Stopford, 2 officers and 66 men, killed; total casualties, 461; Boer loss unknown, 70 captured

——, Gallant sortie from Kimberley, Boer redoubts rushed, and 23 British killed

Dec. 3–8, Col. Plumer's column invades the Transvaal

Dec. 8, Successful sorties from Ladysmith under Sir A. Hunter; Gun hill surprised, 2 guns destroyed and 1 taken; Surprise hill captured and gun destroyed by 2nd Rifle Brigade, bayonet charge, 28 Boers and 12 British killed, Dec. 10

Dec. 10, Stormberg reverse: Gatacre (misled by guides) attacks position by night, after a hard march, and is driven back; complete disaster averted by the artillery; 31 killed, about 500 captured; total casualties, 702

Dec. 10, 11, Magersfontein: Methuen's attack on the Boer lines repulsed with loss; grand courage shown by the Black Watch, Gordons, Yorks, and artillery under a terrific fire; Major-Gen. Wauchope, Lord Winchester, Lieut.-Cols. Downman, Coode, 19 officers, and 167 men killed, total casualties, 395; Boer loss estimated over 700

Dec. 15, Colenso, Natal: Buller's advance from Chieveley on the Boer lines repulsed; attempt to cross the Tugela fails, 12 guns lost, Lieut. F. Roberts, V.C. (Lord Roberts' only surviving son), mortally wounded in trying to save the guns; 6 officers and 134 men killed; total casualties, 1,100

Dec. 23, Lord Roberts appointed Commander-in-Chief in S. Africa (Lord Kitchener as Chief of Staff); leaves Southampton

Dec. 24, Col. Dalgety occupies Dordrecht

Dec. 26, Attack on Game Tree fort; sortie from Mafeking repulsed, Capts. Sandford and Vernon, Lieut. Paton, and 21 killed

1900

Jan. 1, Col. Pilcher, with colonials and regulars, captures Boer camp at Sunnyside, many killed and 48 taken prisoners

Jan. 1 et seq., Mafeking bombarded, the hospital and women's laager shelled with loss

Jan. 2, British garrison surrenders at Kuruman after sharp resistance

Jan. 6, Ladysmith: Boer attack repulsed; "a soldier's battle," Cæsar's Camp and Wagon hill attacked, British intrenchments 3 times taken and again retaken, enemy finally driven off after 17 hours' fighting by bayonet charge of the Devons under Col. Park, and great gallantry displayed by the Imperial

Light Horse (Boer casualties estimated 1,700, over 200 killed); British loss, Lord Ava (Lord Dufferin's son) mortally wounded, Lieut.-Col. Dick-Cunyngham, 13 officers, and 164 men killed; total casualties, 453

Jan. 6, Suffolk regiment attacks a hill at Colesberg at dawn, but are overcome by treachery; Lieut.-Col. Watson, 7 officers, and 33 men killed, over 100 captured

Jan. 10, Lords Roberts and Kitchener arrive at Cape Town

——, Buller again advances towards Ladysmith; Dundonald surprises the Boers and occupies Zwart Kop

Jan. 11, Dundonald seizes Potgeiter's Drift on the Tugela

Jan. 13, Buller again retires on his lines

Jan. 16–18, British under Lyttelton and Warren cross the Tugela

Jan. 20, Clery's force captures ridge after ridge near Venter's spruit

Jan. 20, 21, Warren attacks Boers on Tabamyama, Capt. Hensley mortally wounded, Major Childe, and 16 others killed and missing

Jan. 24, 25, Spion Kop captured by Buller's forces, Jan. 23, 24; found untenable, being exposed to a raking shell fire, and evacuated, Major-Gen. Sir Edw. Woodgate mortally wounded (died March 24), Col. Buchanan Riddell killed; total casualties, 595; Boer loss about 53 killed

[British loss, Spion Kop, &c., 30 officers, 276 men killed; total casualties, 1,437, Jan. 17–24; Spion Kop dispatches issued, see *Times*, April 18, 1902]

Jan. 26, 27, Buller's force retires across the Tugela

Feb. 2–4, Hector Macdonald (Knt. 1901), with Highland brigade, marches from Modder River and occupies Koodoesberg (died March 25, 1903)

Feb. 6, 7, Buller again crosses the Tugela; Vaal Krantz captured, Feb. 5; but evacuated after severe fighting, and the army again withdrawn

Feb. 12, Boers attack Rensburg; Lieut.-Col. Coningham mortally wounded, about 28 killed

——, Operations for the relief of Kimberley commence; Col. Hannay marches to Ramdam from Orange River

Feb. 13, French leaves Modder River, Feb. 11, and by rapid marches seizes Dekiel's Drift, Riet River, Capt. Majendie mortally wounded, Feb. 12; crosses the Modder at Klip's and Rondeval Drifts, 5 laagers captured, Boers fled

Feb. 14, Buller moves from Chieveley and captures Hussar hill

Feb. 15, Jacobsdal captured by the City Imp. Volunteers and others; Lord Roberts enters Orange Free State

——, Relief of Kimberley (total casualties during the siege since Oct. 15, 1899, 163; from other causes, 1,694): French with cavalry division marches rapidly from Klip Drift, joins Col. Kekewich, drives the Boers out of Alexandersfontein and the district, and enters Kimberley

——, Cronje evacuates Magersfontein and Spytfontein and retreats towards Paardeberg

Feb. 16, 17, Kelly-Kenny pursues Cronje's army (10,000) *via* Modder towards Bloemfontein, constant rearguard action; 2 laagers captured by Knox at Koodoosrand Drift

Feb. 18, Paardeberg: Kelly-Kenny's and Colvile's divisions under Lord Kitchener attack Cronje at Woolvekraal Drift, desperate fighting, cordon round the Boers completed by the Welsh regiment seizing the

drift; Major Day mortally wounded, British casualties over 1,100; armistice 24 hours granted to Cronje

Feb. 18, Buller advances steadily; Dundonald captures Cingolo hill, Feb. 17; Monte Christo won by Lyttelton and Hildyard's brigades; Colenso reoccupied

Feb. 19, Hlangwane hill taken

Feb. 20, Lord Roberts reaches Paardeberg, revokes armistice, issues a proclamation promising protection to the Free Staters if they cease hostilities, Feb. 19; enemy repulsed with loss, about 50 captured; Cronje asks for 24 hours' armistice and is told to surrender; he refuses, and his camp is heavily bombarded

Feb. 21, Buller's 5th division crosses the Tugela, Boers driven back

——, Cronje refuses Lord Roberts's offer of safe-conduct for the women and children and medical aid

Feb. 22, Buller advances again, Grobler's Kloof boldly taken by the Dublin Fusiliers

Feb. 24, Capt. R. de Montmorency, V.C. and Lieut.-Col. Hoskier and others killed in a reconnaissance on Stormberg

Feb. 25, 26, Col. Sandbach finds a new passage of the Tugela; Buller's army crosses

Feb. 27, Pieter's Hill: Railway and Terrace hills; Tugela Heights: the Boer main positions between the Tugela and Ladysmith carried by Hildyard and Warren, 60 Boers captured; British loss: Lieut.-Col. McCarthy O'Leary, Maj. Lewis, Capt. Sykes, and many others killed

——, Cronje surrenders unconditionally at Paardeberg, (the anniversary of Majuba); the British had drawn in closer each night, and a heavy bombardment had been kept up; at 3 A.M. the Canadians, backed by the Gordons and Shropshires, rushed the enemy's trenches, thus "clinching matters," for at 6 A.M. they surrendered; total Boer prisoners 4,000 (including 1,150 Free Staters) and 46 officers

[British loss at Paardeburg, 18 officers, 245 men killed; total casualties, 1,440, Feb. 16–27]

Feb. 19–27, Buller, *en route* to Ladysmith, drives back Louis Botha's forces, severe fighting; British loss: 22 officers, 241 men killed; total casualties, 1,782

Feb. 28, Relief of Ladysmith (besieged since Nov. 2, 1899; total casualties, 805): Lord Dundonald, with Natal Carbineers and Imperial Horse, entered first, Buller arriving later; reported complete defeat of the Boers and district clear to the south

March 1, Buller advances to Nelthorpe

March 2, 3, French shells and checks Boer advance near Osfontein, O.F.S.

March 5, Stormberg occupied by Gatacre

March 7, Lord Roberts routs Delarey

March 10, Driefontein: Boers defeated by Lord Roberts, 102 killed and about 20 captured; British loss: Col. Umphelby mortally wounded, 4 officers and 58 men killed, 4 mortally wounded

March 11, Lord Roberts protests against the Boers' gross abuse of the white flag witnessed by himself at Driefontein

——, Peace overtures made by the Boer president, March 5; rejected by Lord Salisbury

March 12, French seizes the hills and railway commanding Bloemfontein; Maj. Hunter-Weston, with 10 men, gets through the Boer lines, cuts the telegraph, and blows up the railway N. of the town; Pres. Steyn escapes

March 13, Lord Roberts enters Bloemfontein: Boers retreat to Kroonstad

March 15, Proclamation issued at Bloemfontein; surrender of arms ordered

March 16, Methuen, advancing towards Mafeking, seizes the ferry at Warrenton

——, Plumer, after advancing to Lobatsi, is forced to retire to Crocodile Pools

March 16–18, Boers repulsed at Fourteen Streams by Drummond and Peakman's column

March 24, Mr. Fraser, member of the late Free State Government, appointed administrator of the Free State, announced

March 27, Gen. "Piet" Joubert dies at Pretoria

March 28, Methuen, at Warrenton, opposed by a large force of Boers, artillery duel, March 21–27; he is recalled to Kimberley

——, Sir George White leaves for England

March 29, Karee Siding, near Brandfort: Boers defeated and their position seized by Tucker; British loss, 20 men and 1 officer killed

March 30, Broadwood, hard pressed by Comm. Olivier and about 10,000 Boers at Thabanchu, retires to Bloemfontein waterworks

March 30, 31, Sanna's Post or Koorn Spruit; De Wet attacks Broadwood; 2 batteries of R.H.A. and a large convoy were entrapped at Waterval Drift; 6 guns lost; total casualties, 350; Boer loss unknown

April 3, 4, Reddersburg, S. of Bloemfontein: a detachment of Irish Rifles and mounted infantry surrounded and captured when all their ammunition was gone; total casualties, 440

April 5, Clements arrives at Bloemfontein

——, Methuen surrounds the Boers near Boshof and takes 51 prisoners; Col. De Villebois-Mareuil and 7 Boers killed

April 7, 9, Col. Dalgety and Cape Mounted Rifles isolated near Wepener; heavily engaged

April 21, Rundle engages the Boers and seizes their position near Dewetsdorp

April 22, 23, Pole-Carew seizes Leeuw Kop

April 23, Ian Hamilton reoccupies Bloemfontein waterworks

April 24, Pole-Carew reaches Roode Kop

April 24, 25, Ian Hamilton outflanks the enemy and drives them off the Waterworks and their position at Israel's Poort

April 25, Wepener relieved by Brabant and Hart, cooperating with Rundle; Louis Botha retreats North

May 1, Ian Hamilton and Smith-Dorrien defeat strong Boer force at Houtnek (a day's halt ordered, men having fought 7 out of 10 days)

May 2, Lord Roberts begs Mafeking to hold out until May 18, announced

May 3, Brandfort captured by Pole-Carew

May 5, Lord Roberts advances: Hutton turns the enemy's right and crosses the Vet river, great gallantry of colonials; a maxim and 25 men captured

May 6, Winburg surrenders to Hamilton

May 7, Hunter defeats the Boers at Fourteen Streams

May 10, Boer white flag treachery: Capt. Elworthy killed, 2 officers and 21 men entrapped, near Kroonstad

——, Lord Roberts crosses the Zand river; Boers in full retreat

May 12, Lord Roberts enters Kroonstad without resistance; Pres. Steyn flies to Heilbron, which he proclaims his new capital

——, Mafeking: Boers repulsed, Comm. Eloff and 108 Boers captured

May 13, Col. Mahon, with Mafeking relief column, defeats the Boers at Koodoosrand

May 9–14, Buller drives the Boers from the Biggarsberg, after a hard march over a waterless country

May 14, Boer white flag treachery near Kroonstad; officer wounded, 2 men killed

May 15, Buller occupies Dundee and Glencoe; Boer rout complete

May 16, Hunter enters the Transvaal and occupies Christiania

May 14–16, Mahon marches rapidly from Barkly West and joins Plumer; they drive the Boers from their western positions, and by an action at Malopo river the advance to Mafeking is secured

May 17, Ian Hamilton occupies Lindley, slight resistance

May 17, 18, Relief of Mafeking, gallantly defended by Maj.-Gen. R. Baden-Powell and all under him since Oct. 13, 1899; siege raised; Mahon, with a flying column, enters the town 4 A.M.

May 20, Bethune's mounted infantry ambushed near Vryheid; 66 casualties

May 22, Ian Hamilton occupies Heilbron after several actions with retreating enemy

May 24, Hunter occupies Vryburg after forced march

May 26–27, French crosses the Vaal at Parys and pushes on towards Johannesburg; Rundle occupies Senekal

May 27, Lord Roberts occupies Vereeniging

——, Utrecht surrenders to Hildyard

May 28, Buller, sweeping eastwards, drives back the enemy; reaches Newcastle

May 28, Annexation of the Orange Free State, under the name of Orange River Colony, proclaimed at Bloemfontein

May 29, Senekal: Rundle severely defeats the Boers; 38 British killed

——, Sir H. Colvile's force reaches Heilbron from Ventersburg, after hard fighting

——, British advance to Johannesburg: Lord Roberts arrives at Germiston; Boers defeated and their positions carried by the Gordon Highlanders and City Imp. Volunteers, under French and Ian Hamilton, near Roodepoort

——, Comm. Botha, 100 men, and Creuzot gun captured at Doornkop

May 30, Pres. Kruger flees from Pretoria to Watervalboven

——, Lord Roberts grants 24 hours' armistice to Comm. Krause at Johannesburg

May 31, British flag hoisted at Johannesburg

May 27–31, Col. Spragge, with Imp. Yeomanry (Irish), after a brave defense, captured by De Wet at Lindley; British casualties, 78

June 1, 2, Methuen defeats the Boers at Lindley

June 4, Lord Roberts marches north, June 3; routs the Boers at Six Miles Spruit and bivouacs outside Pretoria

June 5, Pretoria entered; British flag hoisted

June 6, Buller advances in Natal; Talbot Coke seizes Van Wyk hill

June 6, 7, British reverse: 4th Derbyshires and Imp. Yeomanry surrounded at Roodeval by De Wet; Lieut.-Col. Baird-Douglas and 35 killed, 5 officers and 111 wounded, the rest captured

June 8, 9, Botha's Pass captured by Hildyard; Buller's army through the Drakensberg

June 11, Methuen routs De Wet at the Rhenoster and seizes railway

June 10, 11, 12, Gans Vlei and Almond's Nek forced by Buller's forces; heavy Boer losses; Langs Nek and Majuba evacuated

June 11, Gen. Villiers (French) mortally wounded and Comm. Olivier killed at Rooikrantz, announced

June 11, 12, French, Ian Hamilton, and Pole-Carew attack Botha at Eerste Fabrieken; hard fight on Diamond Hill, E. of Pretoria, Boers routed; the Earl of Airlie, Maj. Fortescue, Lieut. the Hon. Chas. Cavendish, and others killed; great gallantry of the C.I.V.'s (Lieut. Alt and 2 men killed) and troops

June 12, Kelly-Kenny defeats the Boers at Honing Spruit

——, Buller enters the Transvaal, occupies Volksrust

June 13, Wakkerstroom surrenders to Lyttelton

June 9–15, Hunter occupies Klerksdorp; Comm. Andreas Cronje surrenders

June 15, Baden-Powell occupies Rustenburg; Comm. Steyn and 2 officers captured

——, Lord Roberts's offer of 5 days' armistice, June 12, declined by Gen. Louis Botha

June 19, Methuen defeats De Wet at Heilbron

——, Hutton's M.I. capture 2 guns near Pretoria

June 20, Railway restored from Pretoria to Cape Town

——, De Villiers' commando surrenders to Warren in Cape Colony

June 23, Ian Hamilton occupies Heidelberg after slight resistance

June 24, Clements drives the enemy N. of the Zand

About July 2, Andries Wessels, head of the *Afrikander Bond*, captured by Methuen, near Paardekraal

July 3, 4, Paget defeats the Boers near Leeuwkop, and pursues them towards Bethlehem; flight of ex-Pres. Steyn

July 4, Roberts and Buller join at Vlakfontein; railway to Natal clear

July 7, Bethlehem captured by Clements and Paget; British casualties about 100

Early July, Guerilla warfare adopted by the Boers

July 8–10, Free State government officials surrender at Heilbron

July 11, Uitvals Nek: surrender Scots Greys and Lincolns; 3 officers and 16 men killed; total casualties, 255; Boer loss also heavy

——, Mahon captures Boer positions near Rietfontein

July 11, 12, Lord Roberts repulses the enemy in 2 actions near Eerste Fabricken

July 19, Boers break through British cordon between Bethlehem and Ficksburg, July 17; overtaken and dispersed by Col. Little

July 21, Methuen routs the Boers at Oliphant's Nek, relieves Rustenburg, and joins Baden-Powell

July 23, Hunter seizes a kopje S. of Bethlehem and forces Retief's Nek at dusk

——, Lord Roberts's general advance begins

July 24, Boers driven back; Vredefort reached

July 26, Boers twice repulsed at Vlaklaagte

July 29, 30, Gen. Prinsloo and over 3,000 Boers surrender (De Wet escaped) to Hunter at Naauwpoort, in Brandwater Basin

Aug., Collapse of Boer resistance in the Caledon valley and Basuto border

Aug. 2, Ian Hamilton drives the Boers off the Magaliesberg

Aug. 7, Bergendal Farm: here Botha's force checked for 24 hours the combined efforts of Buller, French, and Pole-Carew, but was finally routed on the arrival of Lord Roberts

Aug. 9, 10, Boer Plot in Pretoria to seize Lord Roberts discovered; 15 arrests

Aug. 12, 182 men surrender to Clery

Aug. 16, Elands River garrison of 300 Australians under Col. Hore besieged by Delarey since July 28 (17 killed), relieved by Kitchener

Aug. 17, Ian Hamilton captures 2 Krupp guns at Oliphant's Nek

Aug. 21, Baden-Powell attacks Comm. Grobler's rearguard E. of Pienaar's river, Lieut.-Col. Spreckley and 4 men killed; Boer loss heavy

——, Buller reaches Van Wyk's Vlei after sharp fighting

Aug. 22, Baden-Powell rescues 100 British and captures 25 Boers near Warmbaths

Aug. 23, Buller opposed at Geluk's farm; Liverpool regiment cut off, 10 killed and 32 missing

Aug. 25, Boer Plot to kidnap Lord Roberts. Hans Cordua found guilty, Aug. 21, and executed

——, Lord Roberts joins Buller at Belfast

Aug. 26, Boers defeated at Winburg by Ridley and Bruce Hamilton; Gen. Olivier and his 3 sons captured by Queenstown volunteers

Aug. 26, 27, Dalmanutha, sharp fighting

Aug. 27, Bergendal, N. Transvaal, captured by Buller from Louis Botha; Boer general and 19 men taken, about 20 killed; British officer and 13 men killed

Aug. 28, Machadodorp captured by Buller; Botha retreats to the hills

Aug. 29, Lord Roberts takes Waterval Boven

Aug. 30, French releases British prisoners at Nooitgedacht

Sept. 1 *et seq.*, Transvaal republic annexed to Gt. Britain by Lord Roberts; proclamation issued

Sept. 4, 5, Ladybrand garrison hard pressed; relieved by Bruce Hamilton

Sept. 6, 7, Lydenburg taken by Buller

Sept. 8, 9, Buller captures the Mauchberg

Sept. 11, Kruger and others fly to Lorenzo Marques

——, Transvaal placed under martial law

——, Hart captures many Boers and reoccupies Potchefstroom

Sept. 13, Barberton occupied by French, over 100 Boers captured; 74 British released

——, Macdonald routs the enemy near Tapel Kop, Vet river

——, Roberts calls on burghers to surrender; proclamation issued

Sept. 15, Boer peace delegates at The Hague issue an appeal to the powers for intervention

Sept., Over 400 foreigners under suspect deported

Sept. 17 *et seq.*, Lord Roberts occupies Nelspruit; further successes

Sept. 23, Gen. Pienaar and 3,000 Boers surrender to the Portuguese, and are sent to Delagoa bay

Sept. 24, 25, Komati Poort; Portuguese frontier, occupied by the Guards with slight opposition

Sept. 27, 28, Buller seizes Pilgrim's hill after a night march; Boers fled

Oct. 1, Gen. Maxwell appointed administrator of the Transvaal

Oct. 2, Baden-Powell assumes command of the Transvaal and Orange river police

Oct. 5–9, Col. de Lisle drives De Wet out of Orange River Colony, N. of the Vaal

Oct. 13, Mahon's column heavily attacked at Dalmanutha, 3 officers and 8 men killed

Oct. 14, Settle enters Bloemhof and captures 50 Boers

Oct. 20, Kruger leaves Lorenzo Marques for Europe in the *Gelderland*, Dutch cruiser

Oct. 21–23, Paget captures 65 Boers and 25,000 cattle near Pienaars river

Oct. 24, Buller leaves Cape Town for England

Oct. 18–24, Plucky defense of the little garrison under Lieut. Tonkin at Philippolis until relieved by Kelly-Kenny

Oct. 24, 25, Barton captures 2 guns and scatters De Wet's force with loss

Oct. 25, South African Boer Republic formally annexed and styled Transvaal Colony

Oct. 27, Knox inflicts heavy loss on De Wet at Rensburg

Oct. 29, Prince Christian Victor of Schleswig-Holstein, an able soldier, aged 33, dies of enteric, at Pretoria; much liked and lamented

Nov. 5, De Wet and Steyn severely defeated by Cols. Le Gallais and De Lisle near Bothaville, 8 guns and 100 Boers captured; Col. Le Gallais, Major Legge, and 10 men killed

Nov. 6, 7, Smith-Dorrien drives the enemy near Belfast east of Komati river; Gen. Fourie and Comm. Prinsloo killed

Nov. 17–23, De Wet captures Dewetsdorp

Nov. 18, Clements defeats Delarey at Baberspan

Nov. 29, Lord Kitchener takes supreme command

Dec. 2, 3, Knox sharply engages De Wet east of Slick Spruit

Dec. 3, Lord Roberts's farewell army order testifies to the courage, endurance, and humanity of the troops

Dec. 5–8, De Wet's attempt on Cape Colony defeated by Knox

Dec. 11, Vryheid fiercely attacked; Botha retreats with heavy loss

Dec. 11, 12, Knox drives De Wet in a running fight north of Helvetia

——, Lord Roberts leaves Cape Town for England

Dec. 13, Delarey and Beyers attack Clements before daybreak at Nooitgedacht; British outpost seized; Clements retires on Commando Nek; Lieut.-Col. Legge, 4 officers and 9 men killed, about 500 captured; Boer loss heavy

Dec. 14, De Wet and Steyn, after being twice repulsed and 2 guns seized, escaped

Dec. 16–19, Herzog and Kritzinger invade Cape Colony

Dec. 19, 20, French and Clements rout the Boers at Thorndale and drive them from the Magaliesberg; about 130 killed

Dec. 26, 27, Lord Kitchener's offer of protection to the burghers on surrender well received at Pretoria

Dec. 26, 28, De Wet fails to get back into Cape Colony; raiders driven back

Dec. 29, Helvetia: Boers capture gun and garrison, 11 British killed

1901

Jan. 1, Colonial defense force called out in Cape Colony

Jan. 4, Bruce-Hamilton relieves Bultfontein after 2 months' siege

Jan. 6, Disaster to the Imperial Light Horse after a gallant charge, 18 killed and 6 mortally wounded

Early Jan., Burgher peace committee at Pretoria issue earnest appeals to the Boers to surrender

Jan. 7, 8, Boer night attacks on Belfast, Dalmanutha, Machadodorp, repulsed after fierce fighting and much loss along the Delagoa railway, British officer and 20 men killed

Jan. *et seq.*, Guerilla warfare continues

Jan. 17, 18, Col. Grey routs Delarey

Jan. 28, Ermelo occupied, and Smith-Dorrien defeats Louis Botha at Bothwell, Gen. Spruit and many Boers killed; 23 British killed

Jan. 28, 29, French (Knt. May, 1901) drives Beyers from posts covering the Wilge river valley; and Knox hotly engaged De Wet on the Tabaksberg

Feb. 5, Mr. Piet De Wet, president of the Boer peace committee at Bloemfontein, urges his brother, Gen. De Wet, to surrender, Jan. 11

Feb. 11–22, Botha's attempt on Natal fails; French inflicts heavy loss on the enemy; Luneburg and other places occupied

Feb. 12, 13, De Wet again enters Cape Colony, Feb. 10; Plumer repulses him at Philipstown

Feb. 23–28, De Wet, hotly pursued, is driven out of Cape Colony; recrosses Orange river between Sand Drift and Colesberg, having lost guns, stock, 200 prisoners and many killed

Feb. 27, 28, Peace conference between Lord Kitchener and Gen. Botha at Middelburg

March 9, Mr. Boyd and 4 others shot by Delarey's orders at Wolmaranstad

March 11, Boers capture a train near Wilge river, Transvaal, and murder 10 unarmed natives

March 15, 16, Lord Kitchener's offers of peace and amnesty, March 7, rejected by Botha

Mid March, Philip Botha killed at Doomberg

March 22, 23, Ventersdorp: Babington routs Delarey; 3 guns and 6 maxims captured

April 5, French's operations very successful; 11 guns, many men and stock, &c., captured in S.E. district, reported

April 6, Zekoe river fight in Cape Colony; British (about 100) surrounded, 4 killed, 13 wounded, 25 escaped

April 8, Pietersburg captured by Plumer; Bosman Kop and 16 men, &c., seized by Byng

April 14, Klerksdorp; Rawlinson captures a laager and 2 guns

April, Sir Bindon Blood takes command in E. Transvaal; train wrecking stopped

——, The Tantesberg and Bothasberg cleared; 1,081 Boers taken or surrendered

May 22, Zeerust relieved by Methuen after several months' siege

May 29, Vlakfontein: Dixon (K.C.B., June 26, 1902) defeats Delarey, 41 Boers left dead on the field; 6 British officers and 51 men killed, 5 mortally wounded

May 31, Laager at Pienaar's river rushed by Kitchener's Scouts, 27 Boers killed, 86 wounded; 5 British killed and 21 wounded

June 6, Jamestown, Cape Colony, taken by Kritzinger, June 2; one of his forces is routed near Roodenek

——, Elliot defeats De Wet at Graspan, near Reitz, convoy and 45 Boers captured (Lieut. Mair and 2 others shot in cold blood by the Boers)

About June 10, Comm. Van Rensburg and force surrender at Pietersburg

June 12, Disaster to Victorians (350), 18 killed, 42 wounded, 2 guns lost at Wilmansrust, Transvaal

Mid June, Boers defeated with heavy loss near Zeerust; at Orange Pan, July 19

July 5, Kruger telegraphs to Botha, in reply to inquiries, to continue fighting

July 8–15, French very successful; drives Scheepers' commando out of the Camdeboos

July 12, Broadwood captures 29 officials of the late

Orange Free State; ex-Pres. Steyn escaped, but his papers were seized, at Reitz

July 30, W. Kitchener captures gun and 32 men from Viljoen near Middelburg

July 31, Many laagers captured in July; Comm. H. Steyn killed at Ficksburg

Aug. 1, Lord Kitchener reports shooting of unarmed natives by Boers

Aug. 7, Jas. Madhaila, native constable (unarmed), shot by Boers at Steytleville

Aug. 8, Comm. de Villiers and 2 field cornets surrender at Warmbaths

Aug. 13, Gorringe routs Kritzinger's commandos near Steynsburg, 2 leaders mortally wounded and about 20 killed

Aug. 15, Proclamation, calling on the Boers to surrender before Sept. 15 under pain of banishment and confiscation of property, issued

Aug., French's operations in Cape Colony result in expulsion of Kritzinger and disorganization of other commandos

Aug. 29, 30, Methuen, Cols. Hickie and Williams clear district between Taungs and Mafeking, Krugersdorp and Magaliesberg regions, reported

Aug. 31, Train wrecked and fired by Boers near Waterval, Lieut.-Col. Vandeleur, 13 men and 3 others killed, 25 wounded

Aug., Concentration camps: 35,000 Boers and 74,589 women and children

Sept. 1–5, Methuen operates successfully in Great Maries valley, Gen. Lemmer and 19 Boers killed, 44 prisoners and stock seized

Early Sept., Trains wrecked and looted by Boers in Cape Colony

Sept. 5, Lotter's commando near Petersburg, Cape Colony, captured by Col. Scobell, 19 Boers killed; Lotter and Breedt and 102 prisoners taken

Sept. 10, Scheepers' commando routed at Laingsburg by Col. Crabze, Van de Merwe killed, Du Plessis and 37 Boers captured

[Boer leaders encouraged by pro-Boer speakers and press, reported, Sept.]

Sept. 17, Blood River Poort, near Utrecht: Maj. Gough's force trapped by Botha, Capt. Mildmay, Lieuts. Blewiit, Lambton, and 31 killed, 25 wounded

——, Lancers (17th) surprised at Elands River Poort by Smuts' commando, Lieuts. R. Brinsley Sheridan, Morritt, and 24 killed, 33 wounded, 3 mortally; enemy, in khaki, also suffered heavily

Sept. 20, Lovat's Scouts rushed by Kritzinger, who fails to cross the Orange river, Lieut.-Col. and Capt. Murray and 16 killed; 20 Boers captured

Sept. 25, Capt. R. Miers murdered by Boers bearing a white flag at Riversdraai

Sept. 25, 26, Forts Itala and Prospect, on the Zulu border, bravely defended by Maj. Chapman and Capt. Rowley; Botha's army defeated and Natal saved from invasion; 19 hours' heavy fighting, estimated Boer loss, 128 killed, 270 wounded; British loss, Lieut. Kane and 11 others killed, many wounded

Sept. 29, 30, Moedwill: Delarey and Kemp's attack on Kekewich defeated, heavy loss on both sides; 1 British officer and 46 killed, 26 officers and 124 (some mortally) wounded

Sept.–Dec., Blockhouse system reported successful; concentration of Boer forces prevented

Early Oct., Guerilla warfare, many engagements

Oct. 8, Martial law extended in Cape Colony

Oct. 11, Comm. Lotter convicted of murder, &c., executed

——, French captures Comm. Scheepers

Oct. 14, Sir H. Rawlinson captures Meyer's transport, Boer loss 20

Oct. 17, Many death sentences commuted: J. S. Kruger and Lieut. Breda executed

Oct. 24, Badfontein blockhouse line attacked by Viljoen; Kemp repulsed by Von Donop's column, near Marico river, 40 Boers left dead, Comm. Ouisterhuysen mortally wounded; 2 British officers and 26 men killed, 55 wounded

Oct. 30, 31, Brakenlaagte: here Botha's force, about 1,000, attacked Col. Benson's column, charging close under cover of violent rain and hail; Benson, Lieut.-Col. E. Guinness, Maj. F. E. Murray, Capts. Thorold, Eyre, and 56 others killed; 16 officers and 149 wounded; about 44 Boers killed, many wounded (Boers charged with cruel and brutal treatment of the wounded); the fight lasted till the arrival of Col. Barter's relief column, when the Boers retired, early Nov. 1

Nov. 1, Kekewich captures Van Albert's laager

Nov. 11, Dutoit's laager at Doornhoek captured

Nov. 19, Plot discovered in Johannesburg to betray the town to Delarey, 20 arrests

Nov., Gens. Celliers and Andries Cronje form a volunteer burgher corps on the British side

Nov. 26, Knox's column capture Comm. Joubert

Dec. 3, 4, Hon. Col. A. Wools-Sampson (K.C.B., June 26, 1902) captures a laager in Ermelo district

Dec. 4, Dawkins captures part of Beyer's laager near Nylstrom

Dec. 7, National Scouts corps established

Dec. 11, Extension of blockhouse lines

Dec. 12, Bruce Hamilton's columns, after a rapid march, capture nearly the whole Bethel commando, Dec. 10; also Piet Viljoen's at Witkranz, 16 killed, 70 taken prisoners, gun recaptured

Dec. 14, 15, Comm. Badenhorst and 14 captured at Sterkfontein

Dec. 16, Comm. Kritzinger (wounded) and others captured near Hanover road

——, Comm. Haasbroek killed

Dec. 18, Dartnell repulses De Wet with loss near Landberg

Dec. 19, Allenby captures Staats Artillerie under Pretorius

Dec. 20, Tafelkop, O.R.C.: Col. Damant's force surprised, repels a fierce attack of Wessels, over 27 Boers killed; 2 British officers and about 30 killed, 23 wounded [Boers charged with cruelty]

Dec. 25, Tweefontein disaster: Col. Firman's camp on a hill slope rushed from the other side by De Wet with about 1,200 men (about 2 A.M.), Maj. Williams, 5 officers, and 51 men killed, 88 wounded; Boer loss about 30 killed and 50 wounded

Dec. 29–Jan. 2, 1902, Bruce Hamilton, operating E. of Ermelo, captures 105 Boers, also General Erasmus

1902

Jan. 3, 4, Onverwacht: Plumer drives the Boers from their positions, Gen. Opperman killed; Maj. Vallentin and 7 killed, 37 (2 mortally) wounded

Jan. 11, Liebenberg, Boer leader, executed for the murder of Lieut. Neumeyer, Aliwal North

Jan. 16 and Feb. 5, Court-martials held at Pietersburg (resulting from evidence collected by the court of inquiry, held first Oct. 16, 1901); 4 Australian officers of the Bushveldt Carbineers (an irregular colonial corps recruited in N. Transvaal) tried and "found guilty as principal or accessories in 12 Boer murders" during Aug., 1901; Lieuts. P. J. Handcock and H. H. Morant executed, Feb. 26, 27 [Lieut. G. R. Witton sentenced to life imprisonment, Lieut. H. Picton found guilty of manslaughter and cashiered, *Times*, April 5, 1902]

Jan. 18, Comm. Scheepers, convicted of murder, &c., executed at Graaf Reinet

Jan. 25, Gen. Ben Viljoen captured near Lydenburg

Jan. 30, 31, Laager captured by Price, Comm. Vanzyl killed at Klaarfontein; Marais, rebel leader, captured near Laingsburg

Feb. 4, Dutch government's proposals for negotiations with the Boers, Jan. 25; declined by the British government, Jan. 29; correspondence issued

Feb. 5, 6, Successful British operations in the Liebenberg Vlei district, O.R.C.: Byng defeats Comm. Wessels, 3 guns taken, 72 Boers captured, Feb. 3; Maj. Leader captures Comm. Alberts and 130 men from Delarey, near Krugersdorp, Feb. 4; British lines close round the Boers; De Wet and a few others break through the Lindley-Kroonstad blockhouse lines

Feb. 12, Klip River, S. of Johannesburg: Mounted Infantry lose 11 killed, 45 wounded

Feb. 16, 17, Col. Edw. Locke Elliot (K.C.B., June 26) engages De Wet at Trommel, 10 Boers captured

Feb. 17, Judge Kock captured in Cape Colony

Feb. 18, Klipdam: disaster to Scots Greys, 2 killed, Maj. Fielden and Capt. Ussher mortally wounded, 46 captured, afterwards released

Feb. 20, Col. Park surprises Trichardt's commando, 164 captured at Nooitgedacht, no British casualties

Feb. 21, Christian Botha, Natal rebel, sentenced to 10 years' imprisonment

Feb. 22, Mackenzie captures Hans Grobelaar's force near Lake Chrissie

Feb. 23, Klerksdorp: Von Donop's convoy, under Col. Anderson, captured by Delarey near Wolmaranstad, 5 officers, 48 men killed

Feb. 27, Successful movement against De Wet in the Harrismith district began about Feb. 16; the enemy's efforts to break through the British lines by night at Langverwacht, near Bothasberg (De Wet escaped, Feb. 24), defeated by the gallantry of the New Zealanders, who lost 27 killed, 41 wounded (out of 84); total Boer casualties, 819, Feb. 25; on the last day of the operations, Comm. Truther, being hemmed in between the Wilge river and Natal frontier, was granted an hour's armistice, and 600 surrendered

March 7, Klip Drift or Tweebosch: Lord Methuen's force, moving in 2 parties, was charged and routed by Delarey, Kemp, Cellier, and 4 other leaders with about 1,500 men; gallant stand made by Northumbrians and Lancastrians, Lieuts. Nesham and Venning and their men were all shot down beside their guns; 4 British officers and 64 men killed, 10 officers and 111 men wounded; Lord Methuen wounded, captured by the Boers (but afterwards released and taken to Klerksdorp, March 13)

March 9–15, Successful "drive" in the West against De Wet, 190 Boers captured

March 15, Bruce Hamilton captures Gen. Emmett

March 23, Mr. Schalk Burger and other members of the "Boer government," with flag of truce, arrive

at Pretoria, to treat, and then leave for Kroonstad to consult with the other leaders

March 23–25, Combined movement against Delarey; W. Kitchener recaptures Methuen's 5 guns, 8 Boers killed, 165 prisoners

March 30, Railway disaster near Barberton, 42 soldiers and 3 others killed, 38 injured

March 31, Brakspruit or Boschbult, Hart's River: Delarey, Kemp, and 4 other leaders repulsed on all sides by Cols. Keir and Cookson, great gallantry of the troops; the Canadians (21) under Lieut. Bruce Carruthers held their position bravely, the Lieut. and 5 men killed and 12 wounded; total British loss, 27 killed, 149 wounded

April 1, Boschman's Kop, near Leeuwkop: severe action fought here by the Queen's Bays under Lieut.-Col. Fanshawe; on the arrival of Col. Lawley with reinforcements the Boers retreated with loss; 13 British killed, 5 officers and 59 wounded

April 3, Comm. Erasmus killed near Boshof

April 8, Colenbrander captures Beyers' laager and over 100 Boers near Pietersburg

April 9, Mr. Steyn, Gens. Delarey and De Wet join the peace delegates at Klerksdorp

April 11, Rooiwal: here Kekewich's column severely repulsed Kemp and Vermaas; Comm. Potgieter and 43 Boers killed, and 39 and 2 guns captured

April 16, Bloemfontein-Sanna's Post railway extension opened

April 17–20, Maj.-Gen. Bruce Hamilton's (K.C.B., June 26) eastern move successful

April 18–24, Boer peace delegates at Pretoria, April 12; consult the commandos

April 30, Vryheid and Utrecht districts added to Natal; announced

May 6, John Potgieter's force raids and burns Sikobobo's kraals, 3 natives burnt alive; the Zulus forthwith attacked him at Holkrantz; 56 Boers and 52 Zulus killed

May 7, Ookiep, Cape Colony, invested by rebels, May 1; relieved by Col. Cooper

——, Operations in O.R. colony successful, 321 prisoners brought in

May 7–13, Ian Hamilton's drive on the Bechuanaland blockhouse line very successful, Van Zyl's convoy captured and many prisoners

May 16 and 25, Jack Hindon, train-wrecker, and his force surrender at Balmoral

May 18, Peace conference, May 15, 16; Louis Botha, De Wet, Delarey, Smuts, and Hertzog leave Vereeniging to confer with Lords Milner and Kitchener in Pretoria

May 20, Visaye, with 50 men, surrenders at Balmoral

May 21, Lord Lovat captures Fouché's laager at Stapleford

May 27, Comm. Malan, mortally wounded, captured at Ripon Road, Cape Colony

May 28, 29, British Government's final answer received at Pretoria; Boer delegates return to Vereeniging

May 31, British terms: unconditional surrender, imperial grant of 3,000,000*l.* and loans for Boer repatriation, &c.; no death penalty on rebels; Dutch language to be used in law courts when necessary; accepted and signed by the Boers before Lords Milner and Kitchener at Pretoria

June 2, Lord Kitchener congratulated the Boers on the good fight they had made; welcomed them as citizens of the British Empire

June 4, Thanks of the King and parliament to the army and navy, colonials, Indian force, volunteers, &c.; grant of 50,000*l.* to Lord Kitchener (Visct., June 26), who had dealt with 90 mobile Boer columns over an area larger than the European states; carried, 380-44

June 23, Lord Kitchener sailed for England, leaving Lieut.-Gen. Lyttelton in command

July 8, Total Boer force during the war about 75,000; about 3,700 killed or mortally wounded; about 32,000 prisoners of war, 700 of whom died, announced ——, Boer archives delivered up to the British at Pilgrim's Rest, reported

Total Boer surrenders: 21,256 (Transvaal, 11,166; O.R.C., 6,455; Cape Colony, 3,635)

Cost of the war: 222,974,000*l.* up to end of financial year

Total British force in S. Africa, 9,940, Aug. 1, 1899; total sent there up to May 31, 1902, 396,021; from home, 337,219; India, 18,534; Colonies, 30,238; raised in S. Africa, 52,414; grand total, 448,345; killed in action, 5,744; wounded, 22,829; died of wounds or disease in S. Africa, 16,168. Returned to England, sound, 68,531; invalided, about 75,430; to India, 10,134; to Colonies, regulars, 3,967; colonials, 12,294; total, 170,356; report issued, Sept. 4

Aug. 9, Royal commission (Lord Alverstone, Mr. Justice Bigham, and Sir John Ardagh) to inquire into the sentences passed by martial law during the war, left for S. Africa; 794 cases tried, Aug. 26-Oct. 8; 119 prisoners released, many sentences reduced; report signed, Oct. 28; issued, Dec. 2

Sept. 25, The Boer generals visit Europe and issue an appeal for the "General Boer Relief Fund" (Mr. H. Phipps, of U.S.N.A., gives 20,586*l.* 14*s.* 5*d.*, Sept. 20); press

1903

Jan. 7, Boer meeting held at Pretoria to hear the report of the generals on their tour; total amount collected in Europe, 105,000*l.*

Aug. 25, Royal commission of inquiry into the conduct of the war up to the occupation of Pretoria; Adm. Sir John Hopkins, Sir Henry Norman, Sir George Goldie, Lord Elgin, chairman, and others; holds many meetings, Oct. 7 *et seq.*, 1902; sittings resumed Feb. 7. Report issued

1905

Jan., Committee (Sir W. Butler, chairman) appointed to inquire into alleged errors or malpractices of certain contractors who supplied stores for the army during the S.A. war appointed

July 11, War Stores Commission act, 1905, introduced June 28; royal assent

SOUTH-WEST AFRICA

The country was annexed by Germany in 1884, but was surrendered to the Forces of the Union of South Africa on July 9, 1915, at Khorab. It is now administered by the Union under a Mandate from the League of Nations, dated December 17, 1920. The laws of the Union, subject to local modifications, if required, may be applied to the country and are gradually being introduced.

Bounded on the north by Portuguese West Africa, on the west by the Atlantic Ocean, on the south and southern portion of the eastern boundary by the Cape Province of the Union, and on the remainder of the eastern boundary by the Bechuanaland Protectorate.

The total area of the country including the Caprivi Zipfel is 322,394 square miles; that of Walvis Bay, administered by S.W.A., 374 square miles.

The European population according to the figures of the 1926 Census amounts to 24,115. The Native population is estimated at 237,701. As large areas of the country, particularly along the coast and in the north, are uncivilized, it has been impossible to procure precise figures. In particular it has been difficult to estimate the numbers of the Bushmen, who still exist in considerable numbers in the north-eastern portion of the country.

The principal native races are the Ovambos, Hereros, Bergdamaras or Klipkaffirs, Hottentots, and Bushmen.

A. J. Werth, Administrator.

1482

The Portuguese, Diogo Cão, discovered this coast, and a stone column was erected at Cape Cross, which has been taken to Germany and is now in the Kiel Museum

1685

A Dutch expedition from Cape Colony reached Namaqualand

1842

First permanent settlement at Bethany by the Barmen Rhine Mission, mission posts of London Missionary Society who had had missionaries in the country since 1805 transferred to Germans about 1840

1863

War between the Hereros and Namaquas begun

1867

Twelve islands off Angra Pequena on coast of Damaraland (Plum-pudding, Roast-beef, Hollam's Bird, Mercury, Ichaboe, Seal, Penguin, Halifax, Long, Possession, Albatross, and Mona) which had valuable guano deposits were annexed by Great Britain, and added to Cape Colony in 1874

1868

The Rhenish missionaries seeking protection against the Hereros of Damaraland asked for annexation to Great Britain, which was refused though the appeal was supported by Bismarck

1876

The Government of Cape Colony sent W. Coates Palgrave as "Special Commissioner to the tribes north of the Orange," and treaties were concluded by him which placed the entire region up to Portuguese Angola under British control; the British Government refused to approve these treaties

1878

March 12, Walvis Bay, the only good harbor on the

coast, and adjacent strip of territory (about 300 square miles), annexed by Great Britain

1880

Nov. 4, Bismarck asked the British Government for protection of German missionaries during native wars which had broken out again in Namaqualand

Nov. 29, The British Government replied that they could not "accept responsibility for anything occurring outside of British territory, which includes only Whale Bay (Walvis Bay) and its immediate region"

1883

Feb. 4, Note of Bismarck to Great Britain asked if the British exercised any authority over the Angra Pequena region

Feb. 7, Count Herbert Bismarck asked if England would afford protection to Bremen merchant, Lüderitz, who was about to establish a factory for trade on the coast

Feh. 23, Reply of Great Britain asked for precise location of factory

April 9, Heinrich Vogelsang, agent of F. A. E. Lüderitz, sent to take possession of Angra Pequena, made treaty with Hottentot chief, Joseph Friedrichs, for about 150 square miles of additional territory

Aug., Lüderitz negotiated for purchase of entire tract from the Orange River to Lat. 26° S. for $3,000 and 60 guns

Sept. 10, Memorandum of German Chargé d'Affaires in London presented, stated purchase of Lüderitz, and asked as to British claims in that region

Nov. 16, German Government again asked for definite statement from Great Britain as to sovereignty in Angra Pequena Bay region

Nov. 21, Lord Granville replied to German Government inquiries that sovereignty of Great Britain had been proclaimed only over Walvis Bay and islands near Angra Pequena Bay, but that "any claim to sovereignty or jurisdiction by a foreign power between the southern point of Portuguese jurisdiction at Lat. 18° and the frontier of Cape Colony would infringe their legitimate rights"

Dec. 31, Bismarck sent Note to Great Britain asking by what right or title England could claim sovereignty over a territory formerly considered independent

1884

Feb. 3 and May 7, Telegrams to the Cape Government asked if the Colony would accept "responsibility and cost" of extending British jurisdiction to Angra Pequena, and on May 29, Sir H. Robinson replied that the Ministry would recommend the Cape Parliament to take this step

April 24, Bismarck instructed the imperial Consul-General at Cape Town to declare officially that Lüderitz and his establishments were under the protection of the German Government

June 4, The German Ambassador called on Lord Granville and informed him that Bismarck could not recognize the right of Cape Colony to annex Angra Pequena

July 14, The Foreign Office announced it would not contest German claim to a protectorate over Angra Pequena

July 16, Bill for annexation of the land north of Angra Pequena passed in Parliament of Cape Colony

Aug. 7, The German warship "Elizabeth" took possession of entire region between the Orange River and Lat. 26° S.

Aug. 15 (or 16), German proclamation announced protectorate over coasts of Namaqualand and Damaraland

Sept. 8, Germany notified Great Britain of protectorate over the coast between the Orange River and Cape Frio except Walvis Bay

Oct. 15, German official notification to the Powers of protectorate

Oct. 18, German protectorate declared over Great Namaqualand

1885

April 13, German South-West Africa Company acquired rights over territory from Lüderitz for the sum of 500,000 marks and was confirmed in rights of sovereignty

Sept. 2, Treaty with Red Nation in Namaqualand signed by Germans establishing protectorate

Sept. 15, Treaty with the Bastards by which they accepted German protectorate over Rehoboth

Oct. 21, Treaty with the Herreros of Damaraland by which they accepted German protectorate

1886

Dec. 30, German-Portuguese Boundary Treaty defined boundary with Portuguese Angola

Imperial Commissioner, Dr. Goering, sent to take charge of the interior

1888

First rising of the Herreros against German rule

Dr. Goering assumed control over entire region, the political rule of Company ending

1890

July 1, Anglo-German Treaty defined boundaries

1892

Sept. 14, Protectorate declared over "unclaimed district lying between Herrero and Ovamboland"

1893

April 12, Captain François, with German force, took stronghold of Hendrik Witboi, Hottentot leader in revolt

1894

Theodor von Leutwein appointed Governor (1894–1905)

1897

July 5–Aug. 10, Hottentot uprising suppressed with great loss

1898

Swakopmund harbor founded

1902

Railroad from Swakopmund to Windhuk completed

Feb. 21, Law declared all children of domestic slaves to be half free and their children entirely free

1903

Oct., Rising of the Bondelzwart Hottentots against German rule and loss of their grazing lands, which developed into a prolonged native war led by Willem Christian, Chief, who, summoned to appear before local official on trivial charge, resisted arrest, and

German Lieutenant Jobst and party attempting to seize him killed

1904

Jan. 11, The Hereros began war by murder of a number of German farmers and their families

Jan. 27, Peace concluded with Bondelzwarts led by Christian

Aug., General von Trotha with troops from Germany stormed the Herero stronghold, but the main body of the enemy escaped and kept up guerilla warfare

Oct., Hendrik Witboi, Hottentot chief who had made peace with the Germans in 1894, joined the war with other Hottentot tribes, because of cruelties of von Trotha, his "extermination" order of Oct. 20 against the Hereros, and the recall of von Leutwein to Germany, succeeded by von Trotha as Governor

1905

Jan. 12, Statement of Director of the Colonial Department in the Reichstag that 11,000 German troops had been employed against the Hereros and Witbois and that the campaign of 1904 had cost 42,000,000 marks, the military estimate for 1905 being 60,000,000 marks

Aug. 8, German imperial Ordinance regulated mining

Nov., Von Lindequist succeeded von Trotha recalled, as Governor

——, Death of Hendrik Witboi, but the struggle continued by Hottentot chiefs in spite of amnesty offered by von Lindequist until 1908

1906

The Germans had 19,000 men in the field in war

Dec. 23, The Bondelzwarts signed Treaty of submission with Germans, no cession of territory

1908

June 20, August Stauch arrived at Swakomund to register diamonds discovered in April in Kolmanskop near Luderitz Bay by native

1910

Dr. T. Seitz appointed Governor

1911

May 23, Walvis Bay boundary arbitration award

1914

Sept. 19, Troops from the Union of South Africa commanded by Colonel Beves occupied Luderitz Bay. For campaign see South Africa and World War

1915

June 25, Important railway connection with Union of South Africa completed, Prieska-Kalfontein

July 9, Surrender of German forces to General Botha

July 15, General P. S. Beves appointed military Governor. Proclamation announced assimilation of German South-West Africa to the Union of South Africa as a Protectorate

Oct. 30, E. H. L. Gorges appointed Administrator to the South-West Africa Protectorate assumed office

1917

March 5, Proclamation signed made provisions for control and treatment of natives employed on mines and other large works

1919

May 7, Supreme Council assigned mandate for former German South-West Africa to the Union of South Africa

June 21, Native Reserve Act of Union Parliament confirmed natives in possession of their lands

July, Willem Christian, Hottentot chief, returned to Bondelwartz Reserve, and was arrested by the police by a ruse, but subsequently released by authorities

Sept. 8, Act of Union Parliament gave effect to mandate

Dec. 12, Proclamation amended German mining ordinance of Aug. 8, 1905 for control of mines which remained the mining law with subsequent amendments

Dec. 31, South-West African police replaced military constabulary

1920

Jan. 1, Roman Dutch law superseded German common law under Proclamation No. 21 of 1919

Jan. 6, High Court established

Jan. 15, Proclamation No. 6 provided penalties, fines, and imprisonment for sale of liquor to natives

March 5, Proclamation applied Union land settlement law and law of Transvaal

March 25, Draft Treaty with the King of England submitted by the Rehoboth Bastards (Dutch-Hottentot half-breeds), proposals for local government

July 17, Proclamation established law as to contracts and relations, the Masters and Servants Act of 1917 amended

Oct. 1, Gysbert Hofmeyer succeeded Sir E. H. L. Gorges as Administrator

Dec. 15, Proclamation established Arbitration Board to settle problems of debts and currency

Dec. 17, Terms of mandate approved by League of Nations Council

1921

Jan. 1, Martial law withdrawn by repeal

——, New Land Bank established, branch of Union Bank

Jan. 3, Proclamation established an Advisory Council of 6 members selected by the Administrator and representing farming, commercial, mining, wage-earning, and native interests

Jan. 5, Diamond Board established with 3 members representing the producers and 2 the Administration to control the production and marketing of diamonds

Feb. 1, A dog tax imposed by the Administration which proved to be prohibitive to the natives and occasioned great hardship

Feb. 2, First meeting of Advisory Council

July 7, Act of Union Parliament provided that South-West Africa should be regarded as part of the Union for purposes of customs and excise duties

Aug. 13, Regulations made purchasing of branding irons (30s. each) compulsory, the Bondelzwarts not allowed to keep possession of theirs which were held by the police

Nov. 19, General education code established a Department of Education

Dec. 20, Act of Union Parliament provided that the part of the territory known as Caprivi Zipfel should by reason of its geographical position and lack of communications be administered as if it were part of the Bechualand Protectorate

Dec. 31, Debts Settlement Board established

1922

Feb. 15, Native Administration Proclamation made regulations as to natives, native reserves, passes, &c.

Feb. 22, Dog tax reduced 50%

April 28, Abraham Morris made unauthorized return to the Bondelzwarts Reservation

May 8, Arrest of Abraham Morris resisted

May 26, Military operations against the Bondelzwarts started because of refusal to surrender Morris and 4 of his companions

May 29, Final attack enveloping and use of airplanes forced surrender of Bondelzwarts

June 3, Engagement in which Morris was killed

June 7, Surrender of J. Christian who with other Bondelzwarts leaders were convicted and sentenced to imprisonment

July 14, Union Parliament Act provided that Walvis Bay be part of territory for judicial purposes

July 19, South-West Africa Affairs Act provided for jurisdiction of High Court and circuit courts at Swakopmund

July 22, General Smuts appointed a commission to inquire into the Bondelzwarts rebellion

1923

March 19, Report of South African Union Commission on Bondelzwarts rebellion

July 4, Master and Servant Act amended

Aug. 17, Agreement signed put in operation by Proclamation of Administration of Oct. 2 application of laws of South-West Africa to Rehoboth territory

1924

Jan. 11, Proclamation reduced dog tax by one-half again, reduced to one-fourth of original tax of Feb., 1921

Jan., The Raad of Rehoboth Bastards prevented from holding election by opposition which in April declared it deposed and held irregular election electing a Raad and a Parlements Raad (the new Raad)

March 28, Police in conflict with crowd prevented from arrest of Rehoboths charged with violation of cattle branding regulation

May 12, Jacobus Christian in letter accepted terms of Administration as condition for his release from prison

June 16, Election for Raad reëlected the old Raad as arranged for by Administration, election of April set aside by Proclamation of May 5

Sept. 15, By Union law coming into effect German nationals became British subjects unless within 6 months from date they declared otherwise. About 250 declared against naturalization and 2,900 naturalized under the law

Oct. 29, Immigration Board of Appeal constituted

Nov. 3, The Prime Minister held conference with members of old and new Raads each claiming jurisdiction

——, The old Rehoboth Raad submitted petition to Permanent Mandates Commission of the League of Nations

Nov. 15, Workmen's Compensation law promulgated repealed German law of June 7, 1871, and Aug. 18, 1896

Dec. 1, Letter of new Raad to local magistrate practically a declaration of independence

Dec. 4, Letter of old Raad appealed to Administration for protection

Dec. 16, Proclamation dismissing the Raad came into effect transferred its powers to magistrate

Dec. 31, Natives (Urban Areas) proclamation amended that of 1923

1925

Jan. 12, 13, and 14, The Rehoboths held elections for Raad in defiance of the Administration

March 19, Martial law established in Rehoboth district but withdrawn May 8

April 5, Rehoboth village surrounded at daybreak and resistance prevented, arms surrendered

July 27, South-West Africa Constitutional Act passed in Union Parliament giving South-West Africa a Constitution which came into effect Aug. 5, providing for an Executive Committee, an Advisory Council, and Legislative Assembly

1926

March 31, Retirement of Administrator G. R. Hofmeyr

April 1, A. J. Wert succeeded as Administrator

May 25, Election for first Legislative Assembly, 7 out of 12 elective seats gained by South Africans of German origin

Nov. 26, Petition of Rehoboths to Permanent Mandates Commission

1927

June 20, Act of Union Parliament slightly amended the Constitution to take effect April 1, 1928

1928

July 4, Proclamation in 6 chapters dealt with native administration as to control, reserves, courts, native commissions, &c.

1929

July 3, Election for Legislative Assembly, only 4 members of German party returned

1930

Jan. 1, Native Administration Proclamation of 1928 brought into operation except part relating to marriages and succession

March 8, Regulations governing courts of native commissioners promulgated as to civil procedure

May 1, As from this date immigration restricted of persons not from countries named as follows: Austria, Belgium, Denmark, France, Germany, Holland, Italy, Norway, Portugal, Spain, Sweden, Switzerland, and the United States, and only 50 of these persons allowed to enter during calendar year. For others written approval must be obtained

During this year the worst drought within the memory of the oldest European residents caused loss of crops and death of cattle

SUDAN, ANGLO-EGYPTIAN

Sudan, Anglo-Egyptian, African territory extending southward from the frontier of Egypt to Uganda and the Belgian Congo and extending from the Red Sea to the confines of Wadai in Central Africa, area about 1,008,100 square miles, population in 1929 estimated at 5,579,776, Khartoum, the capital. The Sudan is the chief source of the world's supply of gum arabic and ivory though chief export is cotton. On June 12, 1821, Badi, King of Sennar, declared his submission to Egypt to Ismail, the son of Mehemet Ali. A permanent Egyptian camp established at Khartoum from which grew the city which was made the Egyptian capital in 1830. *See also* Egypt.

Sir John L. Maffey, Governor General.

1881

July, Insurrection headed by Sheik Mahomed Ahmed of Dongola, declaring himself to be a prophet (Mahdi foretold by Moslem prophets)

Winter, Defeated; retires up the Blue Nile

1882

June 14, Surrounds and massacres 6,000 Egyptians under Yussuf Pasha; occupies Shala, July; defeated at Bara, Aug. 19; at Duem, Aug. 28; repulsed at Obeid, Sept. 8, 14; defeats Egyptians, Sept. 15–Oct. 24; rebels defeated at Bara, Nov. 4; Col. Stewart at Khartoum, Dec. 16

1883

Jan. 5, The Mahdi captures Bara and Obeid; he is repulsed, Feb. 23–26

April 29, Col. Hicks Pasha with an army starts for the Kordofan; arrives at Berber, March 1; defeats the Mahdi with great loss

About May 14, The Mahdi defeated at Khartoum

Nov. 3–5, Battle of El-Obeid, or Kashgal; Col. Hicks decoyed into a defile; about 11,000 men attacked by overwhelming multitudes, they form squares and resist till nearly all are killed, including Col. Hicks, Col. Farquhar, and other European officers; the Mahdi gains arms and ammunition

Nov. 6, Surprise and defeat of Egyptian detachment at Tokar, near Suakin; about 150 killed

Nov., Egyptian force concentrated at Khartoum under Col. Coetlogon

About Nov. 23, General rising throughout the country; the British Government sends gunboats to defend Suakin and Red Sea ports; attack on Suakin forts, Nov. 26–Dec. 1; about 720 Egyptians surrounded and 682 killed (asserted), Dec. 2

About Dec. 26, Khartoum garrison strengthened

1884

Jan. 18, General (Chinese) Gordon sent to the Sudan (to report), starts Jan. 19; appointed governor-general of the Sudan, Jan. 25

Nov., 1883–Jan., Sinkat closely besieged

Feb. 8, Tokar besieged by rebels; surrenders, Feb. 21; Baker Pasha with 3,500 men defeated near Tokar, loses about 2,250 men (demoralized), with the remnant retreats to Trinkitat, Feb. 4; received by H.M.S. *Ranger*, Feb. 5, 6; reinforcements ordered to be sent to Adm. Hewett at Suakin, Feb. 6; Suakin in state of siege; Adm. Hewett in full command, Feb. 7–9; desperate sortie of the garrison, headed by Tewfik Bey, from Sinkat, all killed; women and children prisoners, town taken

Feb. 18, General Gordon arrives at Berber, Feb. 11; received as a deliverer at Khartoum; proclaims the Mahdi Sultan of Kordofan; remission of half the taxes, and non-interference with the slave trade, releases prisoners, remits debts

Feb., Restoration of the former Sultanate of Darfour proposed; Kassala besieged by Osman Digna

Feb. 25, The Black troops at Suakin mutiny and disperse; announced

Feb. 29, Battle of El-Teb, near where Baker Pasha was defeated, Feb. 4. After fruitless attempt at negotiation, Gen. Gerald Graham, with about 4,000 men (consisting of 10th and 19th Hussars, Gordon Highlanders, the Black Watch, Lancashire and Yorkshire battalions, and Marines), at 11 A.M., advanced on the rebels, about 12,000, who, after a most desperate, heroic resistance, were totally defeated with the loss of about 2,000 men, at 2.30 P.M.; the British loss was five officers and 24 men killed, and 142 wounded

March 1, Tokar surrendered, the garrison fled

March 3, Osman Digna at Tamanieb

About March 10, Osman Digna rejects British proposals, and proclaims death to infidels

March 13, Battle of Tamanieb. The British advance to capture Osman Digna's camp at Tamasi, near El-Teb, 7.20 A.M.; the British were massed in oblong squares, one square broken into by a violent onslaught of hidden Arabs, who creep under and capture the Gatling and other guns, desperate hand-to-hand conflict; the British driven back; no panic; Col. Wood with 700 cavalry charges the Arabs in flank, and drives them back, the infantry rally and recover the guns, the other square perfectly successful; the camp taken, 12.30 P. M. The British loss, killed, 6 officers and 86 men, 111 wounded, and 19 missing; 2,000 of the enemy killed. The Black Watch and Naval Brigade suffered much

About March 15, Gordon defeats rebels

March 16, Through cowardice and treachery Gordon's troops (1,500) defeated by about 60 rebels with great slaughter

March 23, Hassan and Said Pashas, Turko-Egyptian Generals, tried and shot

——, The Mahdi rejects Gordon's offers

March 27, Osman Digna's villages burnt

March 29, March to Berber reported safe

March 30, Gordon contending with the rebels, with varying success; Kassala closely besieged

April, Khartoum said to be closely invested; the rebels frequently defeated

April 8, General Gordon, Col. Stewart, and Mr. Power, the only British there

April 19, Shendy closely besieged; 51 fugitives from it killed by Arabs; announced

April 20, Berber said to be closely invested

April 26, Reported evacuation of Berber; troops withdrawn to Korosko; announced

April, The whole country in insurrection; Egyptian troops joining the Mahdi

The Government declining to send help, Gordon writes to Sir Evelyn Baring, "I shall hold on here as long as I can, and if I can suppress the rebellion, I will do so. If I cannot, I shall retire to the equator "

April, May, Gordon said to have been opposed by Government in all his propositions

May 27, 28, 31, June 2, 4, 10, Fruitless attacks on Suakin checked by Marines

May 28, Highly successful sally from Khartoum; Major Chermside made governor of Suakin; refugees from Korosko arrive at Assouan; reported rise of another Mahdi

June 10, Fall of Berber on May 20 announced
June 29–30, Rebels defeated at Debbeh
July 12, Assouan occupied by the British
July 22, Gordon dominant at Khartoum
Aug. 2, Continued desertion of Egyptian troops, announced July; Gordon reports Khartoum and Sennaar holding out
Aug. 12, Gen. Gordon repulses severe attack, Aug. 10; defeats rebels
Aug., Osman Digna frequently defeated
Aug. 23 et seq., Preparation for the expedition to relieve Khartoum, Gen. Earle commander; British troops arrive at Wady Halfa
Sept.–Oct., The expedition to ascend the Nile in about 800 flat-bottomed boats, navigated by Canadian Indians (voyageurs); Sarras
Sept., Telegrams from Gordon requiring assistance
About Sept. 17, Friendly tribes defeat rebels, and relieve Suakin
Sept. 20, Victories of Gordon on July 24 and Aug. 30, and siege of Khartoum raised, reported
Sept. 24, Lord John Hay with fleet at Alexandria
Oct. 6, Shendy taken
About Oct. 6, Col. J. D. Stewart, with Mr. Power and M. Herbin, and about 40 men in a steamer, wrecked near Wady Garna, fifth cataract; land; massacred by Arabs offering guidance; announced
Nov. 1, Gordon returns to Khartoum; announced
Nov. 4, Gordon reports all well at Khartoum
Dec. 3, Two hours' attack of the rebels on Suakin without effect; rebels defeated with loss, Dec. 8
Dec. 26, Successful sally of the garrison of Kassala
Dec. 28, Forward movement of the army
Dec., Rapid marches of Gen. Sir Herbert Stewart

1885

Jan., Successful march in the desert
Jan. 17, Battle of Abu Klea. At Abu Klea wells, 120 miles from Khartoum, Gen. Stewart, with 1,500 men, defeats 10,000 Arabs, who retire after a fierce conflict, leaving about 800 dead. The British lose 9 officers (including Col. Fred. A. Burnaby) and 65 men killed, with 85 wounded
Jan. 18, Gen. Stewart wounded by hidden sharpshooters; Sir Charles Wilson takes command
Jan. 19, At Gubat, near Metammeh, fierce Arab onset repulsed with very heavy loss
——, Gen. Gordon writes Dec. 29: "Khartoum is all right; could hold out for a year" received
Jan. 24, Communications opened with Khartoum
Jan., Gen. Stewart succeeded by Sir Redvers Buller
Early Jan. 26, Surrender of Khartoum; Gordon and his faithful followers killed
Feb. 2, Reconnaissances of Gen. Fremantle; heavy Arab loss, about Jan. 30; Handoub captured and burnt by a party which is intercepted by Arabs, and lose 12 men
Feb. 6, The Italian flag hoisted beside Egyptian at Massowah. See Eritrea
Feb. 9, Sir Charles Wilson and party, within 800 yards of Khartoum, fired upon; retreats; his steamer is wrecked by treachery of Arab pilots; lands on an island; is rescued from peril by the daring courage of Lord Charles Beresford in face of batteries; arrives at Korti
Feb. 10, Victory at Kirbekan: the Arabs on a ridge, surrounded by Gen. Earle's column (the Black Watch and Staffordshire regiments), many killed;

Gen. Earle and Lieut.-Cols. Eyre and Coveney, and nine others killed; Gen. Brackenbury takes the command
Feb. 13–15, Gen. Buller retreats from Gubat
Feb., Railway between Suakin and Berber ordered to be constructed
Feb. 17, Near Abu-Klea, Arabs demoralized by skillful feat of Major Wardrop, who takes the heights after much skirmishing; Arabs flee
Feb. 19–21, Gen. Gerald Graham, with Coldstream and Grenadier Guards, start for the Sudan
Feb. 22, Rebels attack Kassala garrison
March 4, Successful sally from Kassala announced
About March 16, Gen. Graham calls on Osman Digna to surrender, to avoid bloodshed
March 20, Battle of Hasheen: Graham, with part of his army, starts at daybreak; several of Osman Digna's positions on the hills taken after conflicts: about 21 British killed
March 22, Gen. McNeil's brigade attacked by about 4,500 Arabs, about 6 miles from Suakin; they are repulsed with heavy loss (about 1,500), after a severe fight; British loss about 100 killed
About March 28, Fever at Korti; evacuated
March 24, Arab attacks repulsed by the Guards
March 26, The last Egyptian troops leave Suakin
March 29, Zebehr Pasha arrested at request of Lord Wolseley, March 14; sent to Gibraltar
[Released under conditions, Aug. 3, 1887]
March 29, 30, New South Wales contingent arrives at Suakin
April 2, 3, Graham advances; finds Tamai deserted; burns it and returns to Suakin
April, The railway to Berber constructing under military protection
April 8, Handoub (deserted) occupied by the British
May 5–6, Takool burnt and cattle captured
May 17 et seq., General Graham with British troops, and the Indian (part) and New South Wales contingents, quit Suakin
May 22, Handoub evacuated by the British; occupied by the Arabs, many of whom join Osman Digna, June 15
June 15, Dongola evacuated
June 15, 16, Repulse of attack on Kassala, about 3,000 of the rebels killed
June, Death of the Mahdi by smallpox, reported
June 20, 21, or 22; succeeded by his kinsman Khalifa Abdullah El Taashi
July 30, Kassala captured by Dervishes
Aug. 16, Sennaar surprised and taken
Aug. 19, Rebels defeated near Suakin
Aug., Major Chermside sent to relieve Kassala
Dec. 12, Attack of 3,000 Arabs on Mograkeh
Dec. 30, 6,000 Arabs defeated at Giniss, near Kosheh, 3½ hours' fight; about 600 Arabs killed

1886

Feb. 11, Attack on Suakin repulsed
March, Sir C. Warren appointed governor at Suakin, about Jan. 16; Gen. Dixon left in command
April, Country south of Wady Halfa abandoned by the Egyptians, announced
May 8, General Watson nominated governor of the Red Sea territories about April 14; arrives
May 16, British evacuation of Suakin completed
Aug., Major Kitchener succeeds General Watson
Oct. 7, By judicious advice of Gen. Watson and Col. Kitchener, the Arabs combine to overthrow Osman

Digna; after serious losses he quits his stronghold at Tamai, which is captured

Nov., Emin Bey (Austrian physician), an associate of Gen. Gordon, holds Wadelai as governor of Equatorial Africa since 1878, with black troops; news brought by Dr. Junker

1887

Jan. 21, Expedition of Mr. H. M. Stanley on behalf of the Emin Pasha committee, with a small armament with able volunteer officers, starts from London

April 29, Col. Chermside, with the Egyptians, defeats the Dervishes at Sarras, near Wady Halfa, after stubborn resistance; about 190 killed

Aug. 29, Great defeat of the Dervishes

Oct. 27, Arab attack on Wady Halfa repulsed, Oct. 25; reinforcements sent

Dec. 29, Osman Digna defeated with great loss by the friendly tribes

1888

Jan. 17, His camp at Handoub captured and his followers dispersed; they return and retake the camp; the friendly tribes forced to retreat, Col. Kitchener and Major McMurdo wounded

March 4, A band of Dervishes dispersed after fierce conflict near Suakin, Col. Tapp killed

July 20, Defeat of the Dervishes near Wady Halfa

Midnight, Aug. 27, The Dervishes severely defeated in an attack on Fort Khormoussa

Sept. 13, Lt.-Col. H. Smith succeeds Col. Kitchener as gov.-general and commandant at Suakin

Sept. 22, Oct., Continued investment of Suakin by Arabs (Dervishes) with guns, &c.; severe night attacks; reinforcements ordered

Nov. 5, General Grenfell with reinforcements arrives at Suakin

Nov., Defeat of the nominal Mahdi by the Sultan of Wadai's people; Gen. Grenfell reconnoiters; the enemy very strong; the Madhi afterwards captures Wadai, and the Sultan flees

Dec. 20, The enemy's redoubts stormed by the black brigade under Gen. Grenfell; great slaughter, slight British loss; total flight of the enemy with loss of about 400

1889

Feb. 11, Handoub abandoned and burnt

Feb. 26, Dr. Carl Peters, with 100 soldiers, &c., starts to relieve Emin Pasha

April 19, The Dervishes repulsed with loss after their attack on Haliab; again repulsed, April 29, 30; again repulsed, June 2

July 2, Colonel Wodehouse, with three Egyptian black battalions, &c., defeats about 3,500 Dervishes at Arguin near Wady Halfa; they lose about 500; Egyptian loss about 70

July 8, The Dervishes repulsed with the loss of about 100 men, July 4; they break up their camp, July 7; which is occupied by the British

About July 14, Dervish deserters come in; prisoners sent to Cairo; their loss estimated to be since July 1, 2,500 killed and wounded

July 17, Gen. Grenfell summons Wad-el-N'jumi to surrender; the messenger beaten

July 21–31, Frequent skirmishes; many killed

Aug. 3, Battle of Toski; after seven hours' hard fighting about 3,000 Dervishes are defeated by Gen. Sir Francis Grenfell. Wad-el-N'jumi with his principal

emirs, and about half his army are killed, the other half are either wounded or fugitives; the repeated desperate charges of the Dervishes are chiefly repulsed by the 20th Hussars and the Egyptian cavalry, who pursue them till they are utterly routed and their arms and standards captured. The British loss 17 killed (1 English, 16 Egyptians); wounded, 131; above 1,000 Dervishes prisoners and wounded

Aug. 7, The Egyptian troops occupy Matuka; the British ordered to return to Cairo

1890

March 31 *et seq.*, Emin Pasha, after a long illness, arrives at Zanzibar, March 2; accepts the offers of Major Wissmann, enters the German service, and proceeds with a military expedition to Victoria Nyanza

[For his connection with Capt. Casati, *see* Italy, July 14, 1890]

July, The Khalifa Abdullahi reported supreme in the south

Oct., Osman Digna's forces broken up by desertion, reported

Dec. 19, Emin Pasha, in good health at Tabora, Aug.; his letter received at Brunswick, about Nov. 25; he establishes German stations on the shores of lake Victoria Nyanza, reported Dec. 7; recalled to the coast, reported

1891

Jan. 27, A raid of the Dervishes on Suakin; they are pursued and defeated; after a sharp engagement, the governor-general takes possession of Handoub, Jan. 28; several Dervish leaders captured, peace restored, about Feb. 4

Feb. 17, Col. Holled Smith, governor-general of the Red Sea littoral, conducts an expedition of 2,000 Soudanese and Egyptian troops, aided by friendly Arabs; El Teb occupied and fortified

Feb. 19, Col. H. Smith, with brigade of Egyptian troops, advances at daybreak from El Teb against Tokar, strongly held by Osman Digna with 2,000 Dervishes; after a desperate fight of one and a half hours, Tokar is occupied; all the principal emirs and about 700 Dervishes killed; Osman Digna fled south with 30 horsemen. Our loss—Capt. Barrow, and 15 Egyptian soldiers killed

Feb. 23, The Red Sea littoral reported clear of rebels; the sheikhs solicit and obtain pardon, general rejoicing, reported

Dec. 21, Father Ohrwalder and two Roman Catholic sisters, long prisoners in the Mahdi's camp, Omdurman, Khartoum, escape, Nov. 29, and arrive at Cairo

1892

Oct., Osman Digna encamped near Suakin with about 300 followers; retires to Amet, Nov. 2; a raid on Tokar repulsed, reported, Nov. 24

Dec. 31 and Jan. 1, 1893, Two dervish attacks at Gemai and Sarras near Wady Halfa, repulsed

1893

Jan. 2, Sharp engagement at Ambigol Wells, heavy loss on both sides

April 8, Osman Digna, with a band moving about Suakin, Jan., Feb., defeated after a raid

1895

Dec. 10, Dervish raid near Wady Halfa

1896

March 12, Lord Cromer (Egypt) received notice of decision of British Government to reoccupy Dongola in the Sudan

March 20, British advance up the Nile to check the Dervishes and to reconquer territory up to Dongola; Akasheh occupied without resistance

April 8, 11, Osman Digna repulsed with loss at Erkowit; again by Col. Fenwick and Major Sidney near Tokar, April 15

May 1, Dervishes severely repulsed near Akasheh

May 4, Murat wells occupied by the British after a march of 120 miles in 65 hours, 117° in the shade

Apr.–June, Akasheh fortified, railways constructed

June 7, The Dervishes defeated at Ferkeh

June 8, Suarda occupied, Dervish camp captured, road clear to Dongola

Aug. 2, Cholera at Kosheh; 244 deaths among the troops between Assuan and Suarda up to

Aug. 23, 25, Advance of the army; Absarat occupied, Aug. 25; 7 steamers successfully pass the cataracts and arrive at Kosheh

Sept. 19, Fereig occupied, Sept. 14; Kubudeh: Sept. 18; Kerman occupied unresisted; a strong Dervish fort at Hafir bombarded by 3 Egyptian gunboats under commander Colville, and heavy fire of Maxims from the opposite banks; a Dervish gunboat sunk and the fort evacuated

Sept. 21, Dongola found undefended; grain and stores seized by the British, Sept. 20; the gunboat *Abu Klea*, under Lieut. Beatty, bombards and dismantles the fort and works

Sept. 22, 23, Dongola occupied with little resistance, the Dervishes retreat into the desert; all the guns and stores captured; about 200 Dervishes killed, 900 prisoners taken

Oct., Col. Hunter left in command of the frontier; Dongola settled and clear of Dervishes

Oct., Rebel sheikhs tender submission to the Government

1897

Jan. 15, Osman Digna appointed governor of Berber, "Emir of Emirs," by the Khalifa, summons 25,000 Dervishes to rise

March, The Arabs defeat the Dervishes, and recapture women and cattle

July 1, Dervishes defeat the Jaalin, 2,000 killed; Metammeh occupied, and massacres by the Dervishes

July 13, Dervishes defeated by Egyptians, north of Dongola, June 1; advance of Sir H. Kitchener and the army to Merawi

Aug. 7, Abu-Hamed held by 1,000 Dervishes, captured, after severe fighting, by Major-Gen. Hunter's column, Major H. M. Sidney, Lieut. Fitzclarence, and others killed; Emir Mahomed Zein, Dervish commander, and 50 others captured

Sept. 7–13, Berber evacuated by the Dervishes; occupied by the Anglo-Egyptian troops

Oct. 2, All the E. Soudan tribes renounce Mahdism

Nov., Railway from Abu-Hamed to Wady-Halfa completed

Dec., Fashoda occupied by the French

1898

Jan. 13, Es-Sofiyeh Mugatta captured from the Dervishes by Col. Parsons' Kassala troops

Feb. 25–March 10, Strong position of Anglo-Egyptian troops, from Berber to the Atbara; march across the desert from Abu Dis to Berber

March 21, Dervishes driven from Shebaliya island by Major Sitwell, 38 killed, March 14; repulsed again at Adarama, 42 killed, March 18; Dervish cavalry repulsed with loss by Anglo-Egyptian cavalry, near Ras el Hudi

March 26, Shendy attacked, and forts destroyed by Major Hickman and Capt. Keppel, 160 Baggara killed, 645 slaves freed, cattle, &c., captured

April 8, Battle of the Atbara, brilliant victory: rout of the Dervish army (16,000), Mahmud (Dervish general) captured, flight of Osman Digna; British loss, Capt. Urquhart and Major Napier, Capts. Findlay and Baillie, Lieut. P. A. Gore, and 21 men killed: 18 Egyptian officers, and 51 men killed; Dervishes, 3,000 (many emirs) killed; 2,000 surrendered, 10 guns, and over 100 flags, &c., taken: Dervish camp rushed

April 13, Triumphant entry of the army into Berber

June 14, Frontier Convention with France

July, Khalifa's army concentrated at Omdurman

Aug. 31–Sept. 1, Advance of the Anglo-Egyptian force and the flotilla of gunboats up the Nile

Sept. 2, The battle of Omdurman (5:30 A.M.–11:50 A.M.); total defeat of the Dervishes (50,000), after desperate resistance, and flight of the Khalifa Abdullahi; 28 killed; 334 wounded, some mortally. Dervish loss, 10,800, and about 400 killed in the town, between 3,000 and 4,000 prisoners; about 150 European prisoners released Sept. 3

Sept. 4, The British and Egyptian flags hoisted on the palace at Khartoum

Sept. 19, Hostilities over, more surrenders, Sept. 8; Sir H. Kitchener finds Major Marchand and a French force at Fashoda, who refuse to retire without orders from their government; Sir H. Kitchener establishes garrisons at Fashoda and Sobat, and returns to Omdurman, Sept. 24

Sept. 22, Col. Parsons defeats the Dervishes (500 killed) and captures Gedarif, their last stronghold, after a desperate fight; Ahmed Fedil, Dervish leader, defeated again, Sept. 28; his army broken up and followers surrender Oct. 23 *et seq.*

Oct. 27, Major-Gen. Sir H. Kitchener (Lord Kitchener of Khartoum), arrives in London

About Nov. 18, The khalifa defeated near Sherkela

Dec. 26, Col. Lewis defeats Ahmed Fedil near Roseires, on the Nile; 500 Dervishes killed and 1,500 taken prisoners

1899

Jan. 5, Lord Cromer addresses sheikhs at Omdurman, promises religious freedom, &c.

Jan. 19, Anglo-Egyptian convention signed at Cairo established joint sovereignty of the two States throughout the Sudan

Jan. 21, Lord Kitchener appointed Gov.-General of the Sudan

March 21, Agreement of France and Great Britain completed Convention of June 14, 1898, as to frontiers

May 19, Total expenditure for military operations in the Sudan charged on the public revenues of the United Kingdom, 1883–97, 7,890,112*l.*, announced

June, Majors Maxse and Capper explore the Sobat river and its tributary the Pibor

Aug. 26, The Atbara bridge opened by Lord Kitchener

Nov. 24, Sir Francis Reginald Wingate's Anglo-Egyptian

force defeats Ahmed Fedil (about 2,400 men) at Abu Adil (White Nile); 400 Dervishes killed, many captured, reported, Nov. 23; the Khalifa Abdullahi overtaken, defeated, and killed, "disdaining surrender," at Om Debrikat; Ahmed Fedil, 4 chief emirs, and many others died with him; 1,000 Dervishes killed and wounded, and 9,400 prisoners, including women and children; Egyptian loss slight

Dec., Egyptian Government grants 10,000*l.*, to cut the *sudd* of the White Nile

Dec. 23, Sir Francis Wingate appointed Sirdar succeeding Lord Kitchener

1900

Jan. 10, The first through train from Cairo reached Khartoum

1901

End June, The Bahr-el-Ghazal occupied by an Anglo-Egyptian force

Dec., 1900–Aug. 26, Major Austin's survey expedition from Omdurman to Mombasa underwent much suffering, Soudanese died

Dec. 2, 3, The Khedive welcomed at Berber and Khartoum; witnesses a sham fight at Omdurman; holds a review at Khartoum and opens the new mosque; leaves Dec. 5–7

1902

May 15, Agreement with Abyssinia *re* boundary signed

Nov. 8, Gordon Memorial college opened

1903

Jan., Lord Cromer visits stations as far as Gondokoro abt. 500 miles south of Khartoum

Dec. 8, Successful expedition under Col. Mahon in El Obeid against the new Mahdi, Mahomed El Amin, who was captured and hanged

1904

Mid April, As the result of an important agreement signed at Cairo between the Sudan government and Mr. Leigh Hunt, of New York, work is commenced which is expected to have great influence on the development of the Sudan and in the cotton industry, a large tract of territory having been purchased from the government at the mouth of the Atbara river, on the new railway route between Berber and Suakim, reported

1905

Oct. 15, Railway 312 miles in length, from Port Sudan, 30 miles N. of Suakim, to the mouth of the Atbara river, 20 miles S. of Berber, to join the existing line to Khartoum, in course of construction; work reported to be proceeding satisfactorily July; trial train gets through to Suakim

Nov. 26, Sudan government announces the creation of a new Sudan province, to be named the Mongolo province, with an initial subsidy of 5,994*l.*E.; Suakim governorship to be known in future as the Red Sea governorship; a new administration to deal with sanitary questions and matters of public health in the Sudan in course of establishment under the title of the Provincial Administrative Service, reported

1906

May 9, Anglo-Belgian Agreement fixed Nile frontier with the Sudan, the Lado Enclave granted to Leopold only for his life time, to revert at his death to the Sudan

June 6, Garrison of Talodi attacked by a local tribe; 40 Egyptians killed, troops dispatched from El Obeid, Bara, and Shendi, reported

1908

May 1, Dervishes, numbering about 150, murder Mr. Scott-Moncrieff, deputy-inspector of the Blue Nile province, and an Egyptian police commandant, in a village near Kamlin. Dickenson Bey, who started after the band with a small force, was wounded after a sharp action; the British loss was 10 killed, and the enemy left 35 dead

May 23, Abd-el-Kader Habuba, leader of the band, captured by villagers and handed to the authorities, May 5; executed, May 17; 20 persons who were implicated were condemned to imprisonment for life

1909

April 1, The port and harbor of Port Sudan inaugurated by the Khedive

1910

Jan., A Governor-General's Council created to assist the Governor-General in the discharge of his executive and legislative powers, all ordinances, laws, and regulations to be made by the Governor General in Council

June 16, The Lado Enclave transferred from Belgian Congo to the Sudan Government, reverting on death of King Leopold, and was made part of the Mongalla province

1911

Nov. 1, The railroad from Khartoum reached Sennar

Dec. 2, The railroad reached El Obeid connecting the city with Khartoum

1914

Nov. 15, Attack of the Senussi on Sollum, West Egypt, began hostilities. *See* World War

1916

May 22, Major P. V. Kelly commanding Egyptian troops, defeated Ali Dinar at Beringa near El Fasher, the capital of Darfur

Nov. 6, Ali Dinar, Sultan of Darfur, killed in action. The Province of Darfur annexed to the Sudan

1919

Sept. 8, Anglo-French Convention settled frontier of Darfur and Wadai. *See also* French Equatorial Africa

Nov.–Dec., Serious revolt of the Dinkas in Mongalla province during which the Governor, Major C. H. Stigand, and Major R. F. White killed

1920

May 4, Defeat and surrender of the Dinkas

1924

Feb. 28, Anglo-French Boundary Treaty, frontier with French Equatorial Africa

Nov. 19, Sir Lee Stack, Governor General of the Sudan, shot while driving in Cairo and died the following day

Nov. 22, British Government ultimatum to Egypt. *See* Egypt

Nov. 24, Evacuation of Egyptian units of Sudan army begun as required by the British Government

Nov. 27–28, British troops suppressed mutiny of Sudanese troops at Khartoum

1925

Jan., Sir Geoffrey Archer became Governor General, but not Sirdar of Egyptian army

May 8, The Blue Nile dam at Makwar completed

1926

Jan. 21, Sennar dam formally opened at Makwar

July 17, Resignation of Sir Geoffrey Archer, Governor General, because of ill health

Oct. 31, Sir John Loader Maffey appointed Governor General

1928

Jan. 16, New bridge across the Blue Nile between Khartoum and Omdurman opened

1929

May 7, Agreement of Great Britain and Egypt as to Nile waters and coöperation between the Egyptian and Sudanese irrigation services

SUDAN, FRENCH

Sudan, French, colony of French West Africa, was formed in 1904, from the Territories of Senegambia and the Niger, less the Senegal Protectorate, which was restored to Senegal. Its old name of Upper Senegal-Niger was changed to French Sudan by decree of December 4, 1920.

The Colony is bounded on the north by the Algerian sphere; on the west by Mauritania, the Falémé river, and the frontier of French Guinea; on the south by the frontiers of the Ivory Coast, and the Upper Volta, and on the east by the Colony of the Niger. It therefore includes the valley of the Upper Senegal, about two-thirds of the course of the Niger, much of the country enclosed in the great Bend, and a large part of the Sahara to the Algerian sphere of influence. The area is 360,331 square miles, with a population of about 2,634,982 in 1926. Bamaku is the capital.

At the same time that this Colony was formed the Military Territories, which now form an integral part of it, were broken up. The Second Military Territory, which included nearly all the country within the Bend, was handed over to the Military administration, and the First (Timbuktu) incorporated in Upper Senegal-Niger, was administered by a colonel under the authority of the Lieutenant-Governor. Since January 1, 1923, however, the region of Timbuktu has been converted into a "Civilian Territory," presided over by a chief administrator under the authority of the Lieutenant-Governor. The Third (Zinder-Chad) Territory has been constituted an autonomous unit. In 1919 the greater part of the southern portion in the bend of the Niger was created a separate Colony in the name of the Upper Volta (Haute Volta).

1855

Sept. 13, Treaty with Diouka Sambala gave permission for fort, constructed at Médine by Governor of Senegal for defense against Arabs in Upper Senegal country, which was completed early in 1856

1857

April 20–July 18, Siege of Médine by Arabs led by Omar al-Haji and heroic defense by Paul Holle

1863

Nov. 25, French mission to the Niger country of Lieutenant E. Mage and Dr. Quintin sent by Governor Faidherbe of Senegal to join Upper Senegal and Upper Niger reached Kita Jan. 18, 1864

1864

Feb. 28 to May 5, 1866, French mission of Mage and Quintin forcibly held at Segu, capital of Ahmadu, a son of Omar al-Haji

1866

March 28, Boundary Treaty with Ahmadu

1879

Feb. 8, Expedition of Captain Joseph S. Gallieni from St. Louis to Segu (June 1, 1880) to investigate route for a railway

1880

Sept. 6, Decree created the Upper Senegal a separate autonomous territory separated from Senegal, seat of government at Médine

1881

Jan. 1, Lieutenant Colonel Bergnis-Desbordes assumed office as head of Government

Jan. 17, Post established at Kita

March 21, Ahmadu signed Treaty by which French protectorate established on left bank of the Niger (Treaty of Nango)

Nov. 13, Parliament of France voted funds for railway from Médine to Bafulabé

1883

Feb. 1, Post established at Bamako, first fort in the Sudan, on the Niger River by Lieutenant Colonel Borgnis-Desbordes

1885

Feb. 26, Berlin Conference recognized French position on Upper Niger

1886

March 28, Boundary Treaty signed by Chief Samory after defeat by the French

May 12, Boundary Treaty with Portugal established frontier with Portuguese Guinea

Dec. 1, General Gallieni established school at Kayes

Dec. 20, General Gallieni made Governor (1866–88)

1887

March 23, General Gallieni compelled Samory to surrender left bank of the Tinkiss and left bank of the Niger from the junction of the Tinkiss to Bamako and sign Treaty (March 25) placing his country under protection of France

May 12, Ahmadu, opponent of the French, signed Treaty of Gouri placing his country in Upper Niger basin under French protection

July 1, Captain Louis Gustave Binger left Bamaku on the Niger for Sikasso and reached Kong on the Ivory Coast Feb. 20, then visited Bobo-Diulasso, went into the Mossi country, explored the Gourounsi region and Dagomba, Kintampo, returned to Kong Jan. 5, 1889, and from there reached Grand Bassam March 20, 1889

Sept. 5, Protectorate Treaty with Chief Mobendjelle signed, one of 5 treaties linking the Upper Niger with the coast

1888

Feb. 20, Protectorate Treaty with Chief of Kong

Oct. 18, Protectorate Treaty with Chiefs Mindong and Kaleton signed

1889

Feb. 21, Treaty with Chief Samory signed, the Niger to form boundary for his kingdom

Aug. 10, Further Treaty with Samory

——, Anglo-French Boundary Convention

Creation of a post at Niamina

1890

Jan. 20, Anglo-French Treaty signed at Busa

Feb. 19, Order of Colonel Archinard establishing schools

April 6, Colonel Archinard, commander of the Sudan, took Segu in war with Ahmadu

June 16, Koniakari taken by Archinard

Aug. 5, Anglo-French Boundary Convention fixed frontier by line east from Say to Lake Chad, Sokoto included in British sphere

Aug. 18, Decree reorganized government

1891

Jan. 1, Nioro, the capital of Kaarta, taken by Archinard

Feb. 24, Diéna taken by the French

May 22, Monteil placed Liptako in Upper Volta under Protectorate

June 26, Anglo-French Boundary Convention settled frontier with Gold Coast

1892

Jan.–March, Expedition of Colonel Humbert and Lieutenant Colonel Combes against Samory successful, Kankan and Bissandougou taken

Jan. 11, Lieutenant Binger landed at Assinie on journey of exploration of south Sudan. *See also* Africa

Aug. 27, Decree gave French Sudan autonomous government

Nov. 12, Colonel Archinard appointed Governor of the Sudan

1893

April 12, Dienne (Jenné) taken by Colonel Archinard

April 28, Bandiagara taken by the French

Nov. 21, Decree replaced military with civil government, M. Grodet, Governor

Dec. 16, Lieutenant (de Vaisseau) Boiteux occupied Timbuktu

Dec. 28, French flotilla on the Upper Niger at Kabara attacked by Tuaregs and Ensign Aube and others killed

1894

Jan. 6, Colonel Bonnier entered Timbuktu with 2 gunboats

Jan. 14–15, Colonel Bonnier's flying column attacked by Tuaregs near Timbuktu and Colonel Bonnier, 10 Europeans, and 70 natives killed

Jan. 24, Colonel Joffre in battle with the Tuaregs at Niafunké

Feb. 12, Colonel Joffre entered Timbuktu

Nov. 26, Protectorate Treaty with King of Nikki (Borgu)

1895

Jan. 25, Lieutenant Baud exploring hinterland of Dahomey arrived at Say

Feb. 13, Commander Toutée from Porto Novo on the Gulf of Guinea proceeded up the Niger to Badjibo and built Fort Arenberg on the right bank, the occupation protested by British Royal Niger Company and eventually he was ordered to withdraw from this position. He ascended the river to Tibi-Farca opposite Zinder

May 18, Treaty with King of Yalenga

June 16, Sudan became part of the Government General of West Africa, an autonomous colony, under Governor General Chaudié of Senegal, and a Lieutenant-Governor appointed, General de Trentinian (1895–99)

July 3, Protectorate Treaty over Busa signed

Aug. 20, School at Kayes reorganized (School of sons of chiefs)

1896

Jan. 23, Lieutenant Hourst left Timbuktu in aluminum boat and descended the Niger to Zinder, Say, and Boussa (Busa) reaching Porto Novo Nov. 1, 1896

April 7, Hourst mission reached Say

Sept. 1, Voulet occupied Ougadougou, Upper Volta

Sept. 19, Voulet-Chanoine mission to Lake Chad (*see* French Equatorial Africa) secured protectorate treaties over Gourounsi and Mossi

Nov., Mission of Captains Baud and Vermeesch left Porto Novo

1897

Jan. 1, Lieutenant Bretennet, commissioned to make permanent connection between Dahomey and the Sudan, left Dahomey proceeding to the Niger through Borgu, established posts at Bori, Saore, Bouay, and Kandi reaching the Niger Jan. 25 at Ilo

Jan. 20, Voulet at Ougadougou concluded protectorate Treaty over Moussi country

Feb. 1, Mission of Baud and Vermeesch effected junction with Voulet and Chanoine at Tibga (Tibja), the two missions completing occupation of about 100,000 square kilometers of territory

Feb. 13, Lieutenant Bretennet occupied Busa, assumed title of French Resident of the Middle Niger, and M. Carron made French Resident at Busa

Feb. 20, Commandant Destenave reached Ougádougou and installed a French Resident

July 23, Boundary Treaty with Germany settled Togoland frontier

Nov., Nikki occupied by the French. *See also* Nigeria

1898

April 11, Lieutenant Cazemajou arrived at Zinder, capital of Ahmadu

May 1, Colonel Audeou occupied Sikasso, capital of Kenedugu, on punitive expedition, King Babema killed
May 5, Lieutenant Cazemajou killed by natives at command of Ahmadu
June 14, Anglo-French Boundary Treaty settled disputes in Niger region (Nikki-Busa)
June 28, Foureau-Lamy mission placed Air under French protection
Sept. 9, Lieutenant Woelfel defeated the Sofas at Cavally
Sept. 29, Samory defeated on the Cavalla to the north of Liberia, taken prisoner and deported to the Gabun where he died in 1900

1899

Jan. 1, Colonel Klobb reached Gao and established fort
March 21, The 2 oases of the Tibesti and Borku included in the kingdom of the Ouadi (Wadai) ceded to France by the Anglo-French Boundary Convention
July 14, Colonel Klobb killed near Zinder by Voulet-Chanoine mission to Lake Chad. *See* French Equatorial Africa
July 29, Lieutenant Pallier defeated troops of the Emir and entered Zinder the following day where post was established named Fort Cazemajou
Oct. 17, Decree constituted the Sudan as the Territory of Upper Senegal and Niger under the Governor of Senegal and ceded territory to other colonies adjoining

1900

June 2, Death of Chief Samory, prisoner of the French
July 25, Decree created new military Territory of the Niger with headquarters at Zinder

1902

Oct. 1, Decree created the Territory of the Niger and of Senegambia
Oct. 15, Decree created a Council of Administration

1903

Jan. 23, Firhoun, chief of the Oulmidden (Tuareg) submitted to Colonel Dagneaud at Gao
Sept. 29, Post of Gouré established

1904

Oct. 18, Decree established the Colony as Upper Senegal-Niger under lieutenant-governor as part of Government General of West Africa

1905

Feb. 4, Lieutenant Ayasse established a post at Bilmar to guard caravan route from Tibesti to Fezzan.

1908

June 10, Colonel Laverdure received submission of revolting Tuaregs (Oulmidden) at Banéi after defeating them in battle

1910

June 22, Extension of civil government to Timbuktu and other territories on right bank of Niger

1911

Sept. 7, Zinder detached from Upper Senegal-Niger and made Military Territory of the Niger

1914

Oct., Siege of Timbuktu region by Firhoun leading Touaregs (Oulmidden)
Nov. 3, Captain Ferron captured Firhoun and took him a prisoner to Gao Nov. 20 deposing him in favor of his brother Zohor

1915

Jan. 15, Firhoun and 5 others received sentences of imprisonment which were later remitted for inciting revolt

1916

Feb. 13–14, Firhoun again led revolt attacking Menaka March 13 and 28
May 9, Firhoun defeated in battle by Captain Loyer and his army put to flight, Zohor killed
June 25, Firhoun killed and was succeeded by Akorakor
Sept. 1, Submission of Akorakor and other chiefs to the French

1917

March, Agades, capital of Air, besieged since Dec., relieved

1919

March 1, Decree divided the Colony of Upper Senegal-Niger and created new colony of the Upper Volta (Haute Volta)

1920

Dec. 4, The Colony of Upper Senegal-Niger given the name of the French Sudan. *See* French West Africa

SWAZILAND

Swaziland, British Protectorate, lies at the south-eastern corner of the Transvaal. On June 25, 1903, an Order in Council was issued conferring on the Governor of the Transvaal authority over Swaziland, and by Order in Council of December 1, 1906, this authority was transferred to the High Commissioner for South Africa.

The present seat of the administration is at Mbabane; altitude 3,800 feet.

Area, 6,704 square miles. Population, census 1921: 112,838 (Europeans, 2,235).

T. Ainsworth Dickson, Resident Commissioner.

1881

Aug. 3, Independence of the Swazi recognized by the Boers and again Feb. 27, 1884

1889

Oct. 6, Great disorders through the weakness of the king, Umbandeni; influenced successively by opposing white factions, English and Boers; the King dies
Oct. 8, To settle the government of the country, Sir Francis de Winton was appointed British commissioner, sailed; Boer commissioners were appointed about Oct. 21
About Oct. 23, Boon, eldest son of Umbandeni, elected king; Mr. Shepstone appointed to take charge of European affairs
Dec. 11, Sir Francis de Winton and the Transvaal commissioners meet 100 head-men of the Swazis; results: the independence of the nation to be pre-

served; the accession of the King recognized; the Queen-Mother to be regent during his minority; Mr. Shepstone to be adviser; the commissioners to govern the whites during their stay, to be succeeded by 3 delegates; a legal tribunal to be appointed to inquire respecting concessions of land to the whites

Dec., The Queen-Regent (by Mr. Shepstone) proclaims submission to the commissioners, about Dec. 16; the commissioners appoint 3 delegates (British, Boer, and Swazi) to help the Queen, pending the decision of the British and Transvaal governments, and leave

1890

March 12, At a conference with President Krüger at Blignauts Pont, it was agreed to defer the settlement for four months

Aug. 2, Independence of the Swazis reaffirmed by a convention; a joint administration over the white settlers to be established with other conditions; signed by President Krüger; ratified by the Volksraad, Aug. 8

1893

April 18–20, Conference of commissioners, Sir H. B. Loch and President Krüger at Colesberg; Sir H. B. Loch arrives at Pretoria June 3

Aug. 8, Convention of 1890 prolonged

Nov. 13, Convention transferring Swaziland to the Transvaal Government, signed at Pretoria

1894

April 13, Renewed political complications, the Queen-Regent refuses to sign the convention, reported

June 29, New convention agreed to, dual control extended for 6 months

Oct. 27, A deputation of 6 indunas (chiefs) from the Queen, desiring a British protectorate for their country, accompanied by Mr. J. Stuart and Mr. Hulett, arrive at Plymouth; interview with the Marquis of Ripon, Oct. 31; visit Queen Victoria, Nov. 15; leave Southampton Nov. 17

Nov. 27, British residents and others oppose annexation to the Transvaal

Dec. 10, Conference between Sir Henry Loch and President Krüger in the Transvaal, Dec. 7; a new convention signed

Dec. 15, Sir Henry Loch delivers Queen Victoria's message to the envoys

1895

Feb. 13, The Transvaal Volksraad adopt the new convention without the consent of Swaziland

Feb. 19, Mr. T. Krogh appointed administrator; the government taken over Feb. 21

March 16, King Bunu installed as chief captain

Dec., Financial agreement between the King and the Transvaal Government

1898

June 21, The Transvaal volunteer force, with an advance guard, crosses the border on the King disobeying an ultimatum summoning him to appear at Bremersdorp to answer for the murder of the head induna; fails to obey the summons, July 5; an indaba held at Bremersdorp, Commissioner Krogh president, Gen. Joubert and the British consul present, the Queen to stand in Bunu's place as chief of the Swazi nation, July 14

Oct. 5, Protocol of the convention, "a wise and satisfactory settlement," signed

1899

Nov., King Bunu fined 500l. for allowing acts of rapine, he dies later

1900

April, The Queen-Regent appoints Isitoso, her son, King; reported

1904

Oct. 3, Proclamation providing for the establishment of magistrates' circuit courts to apply Transvaal laws in Swaziland. Civil cases between natives to continue to be settled according to native custom; published at Pretoria

1906

Sept. 15–17, Important indaba held, when Lord Selborne, High Commissioner, explained the administration to the natives

1907

Oct. 10, Government proclamation, defining proportionate areas to be allotted to Europeans and natives, promulgated at Mbabane

1908

Feb. 29, Creation of a force of Swaziland police, gazetted

TANGANYIKA

Tanganyika Territory (former German East Africa) administered under mandate by Great Britain since 1920. The Territory extends from the Umba River on the north to the Rovuma River on the south, the coast-line being about 500 miles in length, and includes the adjacent islands. The northern boundary runs approximately northwest to Lake Victoria at the intersection of the first parallel of southern latitude with the eastern shore (Mohuru Point). The boundary on the west follows the Kagera River (the eastern frontier of Ruanda), thence the eastern boundary of Urundi to Lake Tanganyika. The western boundary then follows the middle of Lake Tanganyika to its southern end at Kasanga (formerly Bismarckburg), whence it goes south-east to the northern end of Lake Nyasa. Rather less than half-way down the lake the boundary turns east and joins the Rovuma River, whose course it follows to the sea. The total area is about 373,500 square miles. Dar-es-Salaam is the capital, population, 25,000.

The native population consists mostly of tribes of mixed Bantu race, and was enumerated (April, 1921) at 4,107,000. Asiatics numbered 14,991 (Indians 9,411, Goans 798, Arabs 4,782), and Europeans 2,447. In 1926 the European population was estimated at 4,330 and the native population at 4,319,000.

Sir D. C. Cameron, Governor.

1882

Dec. 6, German Colonial Society founded at Frankfort

1884

April 3, *Die Gesellschaft für Deutsche Kolonisation* founded in Berlin by Karl Peters and others

Oct. 1, Bismarck appointed Dr. Rohlfs Consul for East Africa

Nov. 4, Dr. Carl Peters goes to Africa as chief agent for the committee for German colonization, concludes treaties with 10 sultans; the German flag hoisted

Nov. 19. First Treaty signed

1885

Feb. 17, Protectorate Treaty signed as to territory from the Umba to the Rovuma River

Feb. 27, The German East African Company, mainly founded by Dr. Peters, at Berlin, chartered

March 6, Germany gave notification of Protectorate Treaties signed of Nov. 26 (Nguru), Nov. 29, Dec. 2, 1884; and May 16, 17, 25, June 8, 13, 19, 21, July 3, in 1885

Aug. 14, The Sultan yielded to German squadron and acknowledged German protectorate over Usagora and Witu

Sept., Dar-es-Salaam granted to the Germans as a naval station by the Sultan

1886

March, April, Settlements founded in the valley of the Kingani

Aug. 19, Treaty with the sultan of Zanzibar comes into force

Oct. 29/Nov. 1, Anglo-German Agreement. *See* Africa

Dec. 30, Declaration of boundary with Portugal

1887

April, Dr. Peters, with a party of 23 engineers, medical men, &c., leaves Germany as the agent of the German Emin Pasha Relief Society

Nov. 19, The Deutsche Kolonial Gesellschaft founded, amalgamation of societies

1888

April 28, The Germans obtained a 50 year lease for occupation of the coast from the Sultan of Zanzibar

Aug. 16, German East African Association took over administration of the coast causing an Arab uprising

Sept. 23, The Germans attack Bagamoyo and kill natives

Oct., Collapse of the German settlement, attributed to the Arab slave-dealers; reported

1889

Jan. 30, The East African Bill passed by the Parliament, granting money for the defense of German interests, and the suppression of the slave trade

March 6, The Germans defeat the Arabs at Bagamoyo

March 31, Capt., after Major, Wissmann, appointed imperial commissioner in East Africa, Feb. 21 (dissension with Dr. Peters)

April 5, The German flag hoisted at the consulate; Capt. Wissmann assumes the command

March, April, Dr. Peters organizing his Emin Relief Expedition; men and camels engaged

May, Capt. Wissmann, aided by 200 German sailors, defeats Bushiri, an Arab slave-dealer, with little loss; Bushiri loses 80 killed and 20 prisoners, his camp destroyed

July 8, Capt. Wissmann captures Pangani

Oct. 22, German Protectorate over Witu proclaimed

Oct. 31, Adm. Freemantle seizes the steamship *Neera*, belonging to the Emin Relief Expedition at Lamu, and takes it to Zanzibar, June; Dr. Peters remonstrates, June 29; after a trial the ship is released, the owners paying costs, Aug. 6; Dr. Peters directed by his committee to proceed no farther

About Nov. 8, Differences between the Sultan of Zanzibar and the Germans respecting territory

Dec. 5, Major Wissmann receives Mr. H. M. Stanley, Emin Pasha, and party at Bagamoyo

Dec. 16, After fights, Bushiri captured and hanged

1890

Jan. 5, Major Wissmann, after severe fighting, captures Bwana Heri's fortified position near Saadani

About Jan. 18, Arab tribes come to Bagamoyo and submit

Feb. 16, Bwana Heri holds a considerable force against Major Wissmann, reported

March 2, Emin Pasha, after a long illness, occasioned by a fall from a window at Bagamoyo, Dec. 5, 1889, arrives at Zanzibar; accepts the offers of Major Wissmann, enters the German service, and proceeds with a military expedition to Victoria Nyanza, March 31 *et seq.*, 1890

May 4, Major Wissmann occupies Kilwa without resistance; also Mikindani, May 14; letter from Dr. Peters dated Kapte in Kamassia, Jan. 16, stating that he was 340 English miles from Wadelia in good health, received May, 1890

May 26, Major Wissmann leaves for Germany, Lieut. Schmidt left in command

May, German forces: 207 officers, military and naval; 1,200 Soudanese, 380 Zulus, 120 Askaris, a number of Soumalis as police, a medical staff and sanitary officers; a fleet of 4 steamers, besides whale-boats; reported

May 28, A letter from Dr. Peters dated Rubaga in Uganda, March 2, received; another dated Ukumi in Ussukuma, April 13, received May 30, 1890

June 24, The German Parliament votes 4,850,000 marks for East African service

June 27, Mahomed Bin Cassim and three companions were hanged at Bagamoyo, after trial for murder of a German merchant about 8 years previously

July 1, Anglo-German convention, signed at Berlin by the Emperor. Germany withdrew from Witu

July 18, Dr. Peters and party arrive at Zanzibar about July 10, telegraphs to his company

[His treaty with the King of Uganda invalid; he is accused of living by raids on the natives]

July 31, Advance of Emin Pasha, severe fighting with the Masai in Ugogo, reported

Aug. 25, Dr. Carl Peters arrives in Berlin

Oct. 28, The German East Africa Company cedes all its territorial rights to the Imperial Government

About Dec. 5, The Emperor contributes 3,000 marks toward the building of the steamer *Wissmann*, to be placed on Lake Victoria Nyanza

Dec. 15, The Emin Pasha Relief Committee dissolves itself

Dec. 19, Emin Pasha (refractory) recalled to the coast by Major von Wissmann, imperial commissary, reported

1891

Jan. 1, The German Imperial flag hoisted at Bagamoyo; Major von Wissmann established there, Jan. 26

Feb., Baron von Soden appointed Governor of German East Africa, Dr. Carl Peters his commissary

March 6, Major von Wissmann severely punishes the Kishobo tribe for robbery, reported

April 14, Returns to Bagamoyo March 15, recalled for rest, reported

Aug. 17, The German expeditionary colonial troops under Lieut. von Zelewski attacked by the natives (about 3,000) S. of the Ruaha river, the lieut. and other officers killed, 10 Europeans, and about 300 native members of the expedition massacred near the station Mpwapwa, Kondora; large capture of arms and ammunition

Sept. 4, Law forbade sale and ownership of slaves

About Oct. 1, Captain Ruediger, appointed acting-governor of German East Africa

Oct., Movements of Emin Pasha about Albert Nyanza, repudiated by the German Government, July; resignation of Major von Wissmann

Dec. 12, Revolt of the Wadigoes against taxation; the Germans under Captain Krenzler defeated; defeated again Dec. 19

1892

Jan., Baron von Soden pursues a peaceful policy in opposition to Major von Wissman

Feb., He meets Lieut. C. S. Smith and Dr. Peters, joint commissioners for the delimitation of the territories at Wanga

March 5, The German parliament votes 2,500,000 marks for German interests in E. Africa and the suppression of the slave trade

May, Dr. Kayser sent to E. Africa to examine the state of the colony

——, Emin Pasha's geographical expedition starts from Kahura, March 22, with Dr. Stuhlmann; suffers by want of provisions, &c., Dec., 1891; expedition divides, Emin ill, left behind by Dr. Stuhlmann, who goes to the German station on Lake Victoria, Feb. 15, reported

July 29, An expedition defeated by the natives in Moshi territory, near Kilima Njaro, Baron von Bülow, Lieut. Wolfram, and 30 men killed, June 10 et seq., the station at Kilima Njaro abandoned, reported, June 30; re-occupied without fighting

Aug. 1, Dr. Stuhlmann at Bagamoyo

Oct. 6, Collision of Germans with the Wahehes near Kilossa, Lieut. Brüning and 4 soldiers killed

Dec., Tranquillity restored

1893

March, Explorations of Dr. Oscar Baumann, 1892; discovers Lake Eiassi, &c., near Victoria Nyanza, reported

April, Baron von Soden commended by the government, March 2, resigns

May, Emin Pasha murdered near Wadelai, about Oct. 20, 1892; reported

July 25, Anglo-German Boundary Agreement, frontier with Kenya

Aug. 12, Sultan Meli's camp stormed on Kilima-Njaro by Freiherr von Schele

Sept. 21, Baron von Schele appointed governor of German East Africa

Oct. 24, Sultan Meli submits to the Germans, reported

1894

July, German flag hoisted at Kionga, Portugal objects; but afterwards yields, Sept. 10

Aug. 30–Sept. 1, Exchange of Notes settled boundary with Mozambique

Oct. 30–Nov., Successful campaign of Baron von Schele against the Wahehe, Kuirenga destroyed

1895

Feb., Severe famine, through drought and locusts, Nov. to Jan.; relief measures undertaken, reported

April, Major von Wissmann appointed governor; returns home, June, 1896; succeeded by Major-Gen. Liebert, Dec., 1896

Nov. 26, Imperial decree declared all vacant lands (Herrenloses) Crown lands, approval of Governor required for transfers of land by natives

1896

March 13, Dr. Peters, governor of Lake Tanganyika, &c., charged in the diet at Berlin with great inhumanity to the natives while acting as imperial commissioner, in Africa; judicial inquiry ordered, March 16; dismissed the service and fined April 24, 1897, appeal dismissed Nov., 1897

July 18, German law created protectorate troops

Oct. 19, Two missionaries murdered by natives of Meru in the Kilima-Njaro district

Oct. 30–Nov. 6, Punitive expedition from Mochi very successful, natives sue for peace; reported Feb. 3, 1897

Nov., House and hut tax established

Nov. 9, Friedrich Schröder, agent, sentenced to 5 yrs. imprisonment for cruelty to the natives

Dec. 4, Ordinance provided for reserving lands for natives

1898

Sept. 7, Suicide of the sultan of Quawa to avoid capture; end of the Wahehe rising, reported

1899

Oct. 28, Agreement re the Trans-African telegraph from Cape Town to Cairo, signed at Berlin, March 15, ratified

1900

Jan. 12, Great mortality from famine, plague, and leprosy prevalent, reported

April 29, Land Commission appointed to set aside native reserves

Dec., General von Liebert, governor, succeeded by Count von Götzen

1901

Feb. 23, Anglo-German Boundary Agreement settled frontier with Nyasa

March 12, Sentence of death on Prince Prosper Arenberg for murder of a native commuted to 15 years' imprisonment

1902

Nov. 21, Land laws consolidated

1904

Dec. 24, German law declared all children of domestic slaves born after Dec. 31, 1905, to be free

1905

Feb. 9, First soil of Central railroad turned by Prince Adalbert of Prussia

June 16, Death of Major von Wissmann, former Governor

Aug., Murder of Bishop Spiers and 4 missionaries by natives brought about conflict with the Wangonis of Zulu race

1906

Feb. 2, Native rising suppressed

March 14, Permission given for importation of Chinese for employment in railroad construction

June, Rising of natives in the Kilima-Njaro district

Aug. 2, Germans captured insurgent camp and cattle and take 179 prisoners and the majority of the Wangoni chiefs surrendered with the exception of the Sultan who escaped

1907

Sept. 9, The Central Railroad from Dar-es-Salaam completed to Morogoro

1910

April, Murder of Catholic missionary Father Loupias by rebel chief Lukarra

1911

Dec. 1, *Handels Bank* for East Africa opened at Tanga

1912

Feb. 26, The railroad from Dar-es-Salaam reached Tabora

1913

Jan. 21, Mining Ordinance regulated exploitation and concessions

Oct. 13, Circular of the Governor recommended pig breeding as effective means of combating Mohammedanism

1914

Feb. 1, Railroad from Dar-es-Salaam on the coast reached Kigoma on Lake Tanganyika (788 miles)

Aug. 8, British cruisers "Astraea" and "Pegasus" appeared before Dar-es-Salaam from Zanzibar and obtained practical surrender from Governor von Schnee, but were unable to leave a garrison; the wireless station destroyed

Aug. 9, The vessel "Moewe" blown up by Germans

Nov. 4, Von Lettow defeated British offensive of Nov. 2–5 at Tanga. *See also* World War

1915

Jan. 17, British and Indian force compelled to surrender at Jassin

March 6, British vessel "Winifred" defeated and disabled German vessel "Muanza" on Lake Victoria Nyanza

1916

Feb. 19, General Smuts arrived from Union of South Africa beginning successful campaign in German East Africa. *See* World War

Sept. 10, Customs station established at Tanga and the port opened by British

Oct. 9, British Proclamation provided for administration of justice

Oct. 10, Port of Dar-es-Salaam opened

Oct. 19, The Standard Bank of the Union of South Africa and the National Bank of India opened branches in Tanga

Nov. 27, The National Bank of South Africa opened a branch at Tanga

Dec. 1, Branch banks opened in Dar-es-Salaam

Dec. 2, Ports of Mwanza and Bukoba on Lake Victoria opened

1917

Jan. 1, Provisional civil administration established for the northern district

May 26, Enemy property vested in a Custodian appointed in March

June 1, Civil postal service opened

1918

March 1, Area under civil administration extended

June 1, Civil administration assumed control of telegraphs in northern district

1919

Jan. 1, Dar-es-Salaam placed under civil administration

Jan. 31, Sir H. A. Byatt appointed Administrator of occupied German East Africa

March 1, Civil administration assumed control of telegraphs for entire territory

May 7, The Supreme Council assigned German East Africa to mandate of Great Britain

May 30, Agreement of Great Britain and Belgium, cession of Ruanda-Urundi to Belgium

June 28, German Peace Treaty signed at Versailles by which Germany relinquished colonies

1920

Jan. 10, Ratification of Treaty of Versailles and coming into effect of mandates. The name Tanganyika given to territory

April 26, Order in Council provided for British currency

July 22, Tanganyika Order in Council provided for administration by a Governor and nominated Council, the name Tanganyika first used in this document

Aug. 5, Sir H. A. Byatt appointed Governor and Commander

Sept. 25, The Tanganyika Order in Council of July 22 proclaimed in Dar-es-Salaam

Sept., Education Department with a Director established

Dec. 14, Ordinance established native courts

1921

March 22, Districts administered by Belgium formally transferred

1922

Jan. 1, Ordinance as to metallic currency came into effect establishing the East African shilling as the standard coin

June 9, Hut and poll tax established

June 16, Ordinance abolished slavery

Dec. 1, Ordinance for suppression of witchcraft

1923

Jan. 25–26, Land Ordinance declared all lands public lands under control of the Governor but validity of land titles acquired before the date of the Ordinance not affected

Jan. 31, Credit to Natives (Restriction) Ordinance gave effect to provisions of mandate as to usury

April 1, New Ordinance as to taxation of 1922 came into effect, taxes on profits, trade, licenses, livestock, house tax, hut and poll tax (in general 6s. a hut)

——, Arms and Ammunition Ordinance came into

effect to make more effective the Convention of St. Germain of Sept. 10, 1919

April 20, Ordinance provided for registration of titles of land and laws as to registration of documents consolidated

July 24, Native Liquor Ordinance provided regulations for sale, manufacture, and consumption in towns

July 27, Intoxicating Liquors Ordinance regulated sale and manufacture for non-natives

Aug. 3, Anglo-Belgian Boundary Convention as to Ruanda-Urundi

Aug. 24, Native Authority Ordinance consolidated powers of native chiefs repealing Ordinance of 1921

Nov. 23, Master and Native Servant Ordinance provided for protection of natives

Dec. 31, The Lukira sub-district handed over to Belgian Government and frontier with Belgian Congo formally ratified

1924

Jan. 1, The Master and Native Servant Ordinance came into effect

——, New railroad tariff and traffic regulations came into effect giving reduced rates on long hauls

Oct. 24, Immigration Regulation Ordinance issued to come into effect Jan. 1, 1925

1925

April 1, Hut and poll tax increased from 6 to 10s. except in certain districts and in Bukoba raised from 9 to 12s.

Oct. 5–12, Educational Conference at Dar-es-Salaam under chairmanship of Director of Education Rivers Smith

1926

March 19, Tanganyika Order in Council established Legislative Council

Aug. 25, Ordinance empowered the Governor to acquire lands for public purposes

Sept. 24, Native Authority Ordinance replaced that of 1923

Oct. 1, Legislative Council constituted, 13 official members and 10 non-official members

1927

March 31, Education Ordinance provided for assistance to Africans who do not attend the Government schools, came into effect Jan. 1, 1928

April 1, Trades Licensing Ordinance came into effect repealing earlier laws

April 26, Hut and poll tax abolished in townships, the house tax to replace the charges

1928

Jan. 27, Ordinance provided for establishment and management of markets; amended Dec. 27

——, Amendment to Land Ordinance

Jan. 31, Ordinance provided for a Reserve of officers former Kings African Rifles

——, Hut and poll tax amended to provide penalties for defaulters

June 22, Ordinance for registration and licensing of land surveyors

June 25, Ordinance for protection of the diamond industry

June 27, Ordinance provided for the registration of newspapers

June 29, Coffee industry (registration and improvement) Ordinance provided for registration of coffee planted by dealers

Aug. 15, Branch of Central Railroad from Tabora to Mwanza on Lake Victoria opened (238 miles)

Dec. 4, Locust invasion in the north and in Tanga Province

Dec. 27, Ordinance provided for control of public ferries

——, Ordinance provided for suppression of gambling houses and cock fights

——, Ordinance to provide for the punishment of witchcraft

1929

April 12, Native Courts Ordinance enacted

Aug. 1, New Mining Ordinance amended earlier law

Dec. 13, The Northern Railroad extended from Moshi to Arushaope

1930

Feb. 20, Ordinance provided for tax of 30 shillings a year on non-natives to make provision for non-native education

Feb. 27, Ordinance established penal code and code of criminal law

April 25, Hut and poll tax law amended as to penalties

TOGOLAND

Togoland, between the Gold Coast Colony on the west and French Dahomey on the east, was surrendered unconditionally by the Germans to British and French forces in August, 1914. On September 30th, 1920, the country was divided between France and Britain in accordance with the Franco-British declaration of July 10th, 1919. The boundary between the two spheres extends from the north-west corner in a general direction south-east and south, terminating not far from the port of Lome, but so that no part of the British sphere reaches the coast. Map in the STATESMAN's YEAR BOOK 1920. The area allotted to Great Britain is approximately 12,600 square miles, and for administrative purposes it is attached to adjacent provinces of the Gold Coast Colony and Northern Territories. The population, according to the 1921 census, is 188,265 (including 20 non-Africans, of whom 15 are Europeans). The Mandate was approved by the League of Nations on July 20, 1922. Of the total area of 33,700 square miles, the French have obtained about two-thirds, 21,893 square miles, the boundary running from the north-east in a generally south-east and south direction to Lome, in such a manner that no part of the coast is included in the British sphere. Lome is the seat of the administration. The total population of the whole of Togo is estimated at 747,000 natives, with a European population of 545.

1680

German expedition sent out by the Elector of Brandenburg headed by Dutch Captain Blonck concluded treaties with 3 chiefs at Cape Three Points (present Gold Coast)

Possession taken 1683 and fort built

1687

Brandenburg settlers established at Arguin Island off the coast of the present French West Africa south of Cape Blanco; sold to the French in 1721

1840

German mission founded

1884

Jan. 30, German war ship arrived off Little Popo and proceeded along the coast collecting native hostages and obtaining petitions from native chiefs for German protection

July 5, German mission, Dr. Nachtigal, proclaimed Treaty with King of Togo placing his country under German sovereignty and German flag raised at Lome

Sept. 5, Small independent State of Porto-Seguro placed under German flag

1885

Dec. 24, Boundary Agreement with French Dahomey, defined Feb. 1, 1887, French recognition of German Protectorate

1886

July 14, Anglo-German Convention fixed boundary with Gold Coast

1888

March, Further Anglo-German Boundary Agreement established neutral zone

1889

June 2, Foundation of Bismarcksburg by Woolf

1890

May 7, Post at Misahöhe founded

July 1, Anglo-German Boundary Treaty (Heligoland) settled boundary with Gold Coast

1894

Station founded at Kete Krachi

1897

July 23, Boundary Convention with France as to eastern boundary and hinterland extended boundary to 11° N. Lat.

1899

Nov. 14, Anglo-German Boundary Convention (Samoa Treaty) established neutral zone on both sides of the Volta River

1901

Sept. 26–Dec. 2, Anglo-German Convention modified boundary with Gold Coast, recognized by exchange of Notes of June 25, 1904

1904

June 25, Notes exchanged between Germany and Great Britain defined boundary with Gold Coast to the North of the 9th Parallel of North Latitude

1914

Aug. 5, Acting Governor von Doering made proposals of neutrality to Gold Coast

Aug. 6, Ultimatum from Government of Gold Coast demanded surrender

Aug. 8, Lome, evacuated by Germans, occupied by Captain Barker with force from the Gold Coast

Aug. 12, French and English force commanded by Lieutenant Colonel Bryant landed at Lome

Aug. 22, British and French attack on German position at Chra village failed to carry position which was evacuated during the night by Germans retiring to Kamina

Aug. 24–25, Wireless station at Kamina blown up by the Germans

Aug. 26, Surrender of Germans to Lieutenant Colonel Bryant

Aug. 31, Franco-British Agreement defined provisional zones

1916

Dec. 27, Franco-British Agreement for administration of occupied territory

1919

May 6, Supreme Council assigned Togoland to France and Great Britain

June 28, Treaty of Versailles signed, Germany renounced colonies

July 10, Franco-British Agreement, division of territory left Lome to Great Britain which was not satisfactory to the French, altered Sept. 30, 1920

TOGOLAND, BRITISH

Togoland, British, administered by the Governor of the Gold Coast under Order in Council of Oct. 11, 1923 amended April 1, 1924. The area allotted to Great Britain of the former German Colony is approximately 12,600 square miles, the population according to the census of 1921 is 188,265, including 20 non-Africans of whom 15 are Europeans. The Mandate was confirmed by the League of Nations, July 20, 1922.

TOGOLAND, FRENCH

Togoland (Togo) French, the former German Colony, lies between the Gold Coast Colony on the west and French Dahomey on the east. It was surrendered unconditionally by the Germans to British and French forces in August, 1914, and is now divided between the French and British. The Mandate was approved by the League of Nations on July 20, 1922. Of the total area of 33,700 square miles, the French have obtained about two-thirds, 21,893 square miles, the boundary running from the north-east in a generally south-east and south direction to Lomé, in such a manner that no part of the coast is included in the British sphere. Lomé (population about 8,000 natives) is the seat of the administration. The total population of the whole of Togo is estimated at 730,027 natives, with a European population of 477.

M. Marchand, Commissioner.

1915

Feb., The occupied territory organized by the Governor General of French West Africa with headquarters at Anecho

1916

Aug. 21, Decree attached Togo to French West Africa
Sept. 4, Governor General commissioned to govern the territory under the Minister of the Colonies

1920

Sept. 30, Convention between France and Great Britain signed by which Lomé and the seacoast assigned to France in exchange for enlargement of British territory in the interior

1922

July 20, Mandate confirmed by the League of Nations
Dec. 23, Decree established registration system for land

1926

Aug. 24, Decree introduced new system of native land titles

1927

May 16, Education organized

1930

Nov. 7, Decree announced requirements for acquisition of French citizenship

TRANSVAAL

Transvaal, one of the four constituent provinces of the Union of South Africa. The area of the Province is 110,450 square miles, divided into 34 districts. The following table shows the population at each of the last six censuses:—

Census Year	All Races			European		Colored	
	Total	Males	Females	Males	Females	Males	Females
1890	—	—	—	66,498	52,630	—	—
1904	1,269,951	702,569	567,382	178,244	119,033	524,325	448,349
1911	1,686,212	971,555	714,657	236,913	183,649	734,642	531,008
1918	—	—	—	260,840	238,507	—	—
1921	2,087,636	1,159,430	928,206	284,388	259,097	875,042	669,109
1926	—	—	—	313,773	294,849	—	—

The largest towns had in 1926 a European population as follows:—Johannesburg, 170,741; Pretoria, 54,326; Germiston, 16,545; Benoni, 14,899; Krugersdorp, 14,524; Boksburg, 12,144; Potchefstroom, 9,336; and Roodepoort-Maraisburg, 7,217.

1835

The first party of Boers of the Great Trek from Cape Colony to escape British rule to cross the Vaal River were 98 persons led by Louis Triechard and Jan van Rensburg, Rensburg's party soon murdered by the natives, but the others reached the coast in 1838

1837

Jan. 17, Second party of Boers led by Andries Hendrik Potgieter reached the southern military kral of the Zulu chief, Mosilikatze, at Mosega, near present town of Zeerust and defeated him in battle (*see* Orange Free State)
Nov., Second defeat of Mosilikatze who fled to region known as Matabeleland

1838

Nov., First permanent white settlement north of the Vaal made by Potgieter and others, claiming the lands of the defeated Mosilikatze, the town of Potchefstroom on the banks of the Mooi River

1844

April 9, Constitution adopted

1848

Jan., Pretorius left Natal on establishment of British authority and settled in the Magalisberg north of the Vaal River
July 20, Pretorius at request of Boers of Winburg occupied Bloemfontein, Orange Free State, to lead Boers in war against the British

Aug. 29, Defeat of Boers by Sir Harry Smith at Boomplaats. *See* Orange Free State. A reward of £2,000 offered by the British for capture of Pretorius who retreated beyond the Vaal River

1849

May 23, Agreement for a single Volksraad over the 4 districts of Potchefstroom, Lydenburg, Zoutpansberg, and Rustenburg

1852

Jan. 17, Sand River Convention signed by Pretorius with the British in the Orange River Sovereignty by which the independence of the communities north of the Vaal River recognized
March 16, The Volksraad ratified the Sand River Convention
June 24, Boundary Convention with the Orange River Sovereignty
Aug., Punitive raid into land of the Bechuana against chief who had looted Boer cattle

1853

March, Death of A. H. Potgieter, leader, rival of Pretorius. Succeeded by his eldest son as commandant at Zoutpansburg
July 23, Death of Andries Pretorius at Magalisberg. Succeeded by his son, Marthinius Pretorius, as commandant general of Potchefstroom and Rustenburg

1855

Pretoria town and district founded named after Pretorius

1856

Apprentice law provided penalties for traffic in apprentices practiced, virtual slavery
Dec. 16, Representatives of the districts of Potchefstroom, Rustenburg, and Pretoria met in special assembly and adopted a constitution for a central

government, a national flag for the South African Republic

Dec. 17, Meeting of the old Volksraad repudiated the Potchefstroom constitution of Pretorius and Paul Kruger and established the Republic of Lydenburg of the districts of Lydenburg, Utrecht, and Zoutpansburg

1857

Jan. 6, Marthinius Pretorius inaugurated first President of the South African Republic formally constituted

Jan., Armed raid into Orange Free State to force union with the South African Republic of Pretorius and Kruger failed

June 1, Peace Treaty with the Orange Free State signed, each recognizing the independence of the other

1858

Jan., Zoutpansburg joined the South African Republic

1860

Feb. 6, M. Pretorius receiving leave of absence as President took office as President of the Orange Free State and remained in office until April 15, 1863

April 4, Union of Lydenburg and Utrecht with the South African Republic signed at Pretoria

1863

Oct., Election of W. J. C. van Rensburg as President resulted in armed resistance by Pretorius party to "disputed election" and new election followed at which Pretorius again elected

1864

May 10, Pretorius assumed office as President

1868

April 29, Proclamation of President Pretorius declared boundary on the west and north included Bechuanaland, following the discovery of gold at Tati

1869

July 29, Boundary Treaty with Portugal defined frontier with Mozambique

1871

Oct. 17, Award of Lieutenant Governor Keate of Natal gave Nicholas Waterboer, Griqua, territory claimed by him west of Platberg on the Vaal cutting off from the South African Republic a part of the district of Marico on which were farms of the first European settlers, the entire districts of Bloemhof and part of district of Potchefstroom as well as land occupied by Barolong and Batlapin tribes

Oct. 27, British Proclamation declared annexation of territory ceded to Waterboer by the award as West Griqualand, territory in which diamonds had been found

Nov. 25, Proclamation and protest of the South African Republic against the award which led to fall of Pretorius Government

1872

July 1, Thomas F. Burgers, clergyman and member of prominent family at the Cape Colony, took office as President

1876

July, Burgers defeated in war against the Kaffir chief, Sekukuni (Secocoeni) of the Bapedi tribe

1877

Jan. 22, Sir Theophilus Shepstone reached Pretoria, appointed by Lord Carnarvon Special Commissioner to the Transvaal, to inquire into "grievous disturbances" and authorized to annex the territory if "necessary, in order to secure the peace and safety of our said colonies, and of our subjects elsewhere"

April 12, Proclamation of Sir Theophilus Shepstone declared annexation of the Transvaal by Great Britain

May 30, Sir Theophilus Shepstone sworn in as Administrator

May–Dec., Mission of Boers headed by Paul Kruger to England to protest annexation

1878

April, Second mission of Boer delegation to England with petition

Sept. 11, Boundary award fixed frontiers with Zulus

1879

Jan. 10, Mass meeting of Boers appointed committee to work for reversal of Act of British annexation

Jan. 22, Defeat of Lord Chelmsford's troops by Cetywayo, Zulu chief. *See* Zululand

March 4, William Owen Lanyon made Administrator of the Transvaal

April 12, Revolt of Boers near Pretoria but serious outbreak averted by conference of Sir Bartle Frere with Pretorius, Kruger, and Joubert

Sept. 29, Sir Garnet Wolseley took oath as Governor and reaffirmed annexation

Nov. 8, Letters Patent established Executive Council and Legislative Council also constituted

Nov. 28, Stronghold of Sekukuni captured by Colonel Murray

Dec. 2, Surrender of Sekukuni

Dec. 16, Meeting of Boers at Luipards Vlei resolved to take up arms for their independence in 1880 and sent declaration of rights to Sir Garnet Wolseley who replied by having M. Pretorius and Eduard Bok arrested as chairman and secretary of the meeting

1880

March 10, Nominated Legislative Council met

July 2, Major General Sir George P. Colley succeeded Wolseley as Governor

Nov. 11, Seizure of ox wagon of Piet Bezuidenhout, "passive resister" in default of taxes caused open revolt of Boers

Dec. 13, Republic proclaimed by Boers at Paardekral

Dec. 16, On Dingaan's Day the Boers proclaimed the Republic at Heidelberg, Kruger, Pretorius, and Joubert made a Provisional Government

Dec. 20, A party of Boers stop at Bronker's Spruit about 250 British troops of the 94th regiment, who resist; some killed or wounded; others disarmed and dismissed

Dec. 27 *et seq.*, Potchefstrom seized by Boers, who retire when the place is shelled; Col. Bellairs besieged in it

Dec. 29, Capt. J. M. Elliot said to be treacherously killed while fording the Vaal

Dec. 30, The South Africa Republic proclaimed by a triumvirate; Kruger, Joubert, and Pretorius

1881

Jan. 28, Gen. Colley's attack on Laing's Nek, a pass,

repulsed with heavy loss; Col. Bonar Millet Deane, Majors Ruscombe Poole and Wm. Hunt Hingestion killed

Feb. 8, Severe conflict on the Ingogo river; the British 12 hours under fire; repulsed

——, Sir G. P. Colley informed that British Government had (Jan. 26) notified the Government at Cape Town that they were ready to negotiate with the Boers

Feb. 17, Sir Evelyn Wood arrives with reinforcements and joins Gen. Colley

Feb. 21, Dispatch from Sir G. P. Colley to General Kruger stated that the British Government would appoint a commission with large powers if the Boers would stop armed resistance, which was not received by Kruger until Feb. 28, and his reply accepting offer not received by Sir Evelyn Wood who succeeded Colley until March 7

About Feb. 22, The Orange Free State proclaim neutrality and mediation

Feb. 26–27, On Saturday night, Feb. 26, 1881, above 600 men under Sir George P. Colley marching from the camp at Mount Prospect, ascended Majuba hill overlooking Laing's Nek, where the Boers were encamped, to surprise them. The attack of the Boers began 10.30 A.M. of the 27th. Fierce conflicts ensued; eventually overwhelmed by numbers and deadly fire, the British were routed and fled. Sir George Colley fell with his face to the enemy. Boer loss unknown, some say only one man. About 350 British engaged. Loss: killed, 3 officers and about 82 men; many wounded, 122 prisoners, and some missing

Feb. 28, Gen. Sir F. Roberts sent to Africa

March 24, Armistice proposed by the Boers; accepted for March 6–14; armistice extended, March 14; Boers agree to British terms, March 21, 22; peace proclaimed

April, Potchefstrom surrenders with honors of war, March 21; given up as occupied by mistake

April 5, Treaty of Pretoria signed and Commissioners to carry out treaty of peace appointed; agree to convention ceding virtually all the territory to "The Transvaal State" on August 8, subject to suzerainty of Britain and a British resident; with debt of about 420,867l., &c.; independence of the Swazies guaranteed; signed by Royal commissioners and Martin W. Pretorius and Peter J. Joubert (Kruger not present), Aug. 3; effected, Aug. 8

Oct. 25, Meeting of the Volksraad, Sept. 21; treaty confirmed

Nov., Mr. G. Hudson appointed first British resident

About Dec. 28, Departure of the British troops

1882

Feb., Fighting with the natives

July 10, Law required residence of from 2 to 4 years for franchise

Aug., Secocoeni killed by a rival chief

Oct., War with the insubordinate chief Mapoch

Nov. 16–17, Fighting with the natives who are repulsed, under their chief Mapoch

1883

Jan. 2, Natives defeated and Boschberg taken

Feb. 26, Native stronghold of Vlugtkraal taken

April 8, and July 9 and 10, Surrender of chiefs ended war

April 16, Paul Kruger elected President

May 8, President Kruger inaugurated

July 8, Mampuru who had killed Sikukuni delivered to the Boers as prisoner by Njabel

July 10, Surrender of Chief Njabel with 8,000 of his people

July 26, Peace concluded between Bechualand chiefs though mediation of Transvaal authorities

Aug. 7, Bechualand proclaimed an independent republic by G. J. van Nierkerk

Nov. 7, Transvaal delegation headed by President Paul Kruger received in London by Lord Derby

Dec. 22, Definite proposals submitted to the government

1884

Feb. 27, Amended boundary lines accepted, Feb. 2; convention signed, the republic to be styled the "South Africa Republic" under British suzerainty

Aug. 8, The convention adopted by the Transvaal Assembly

Oct., The filibustering settlers of Goshen and Stellaland break the convention; seize and annex Montsioa's lands in Bechuanaland; sanctioned by a proclamation; withdrawn on remonstrance

Oct. 14, Sir H. Robinson's ultimatum from Cape Town requiring protection of the frontiers

1885

June 1, Law enacted by which Asiatics cannot obtain burgher rights or own property except in designated districts

Dec. 2, Short war with the natives, refusing to pay taxes; Mamusa taken; battle

1887

Johannesburg founded through the development of gold mining; inhabitants chiefly English

1888

July 30, Law No. 10 made Dutch the official language

1889

About March 13, Defensive treaty with the Orange Free State

1890

March 4, Visit of President Kruger to Johannesburg, resisted by a violent crowd

About Aug. 4, He signs the agreement for Swaziland

Dec., Gen. Joubert entertained in London

1891

About July 2, About 100 Boers prevented by the police from crossing the Limpopo

1893

April 12, Paul Kruger reëlected President, 7,881; Gen. Joubert, 7,009; M. Kotze, 76; reported

Nov. 3, Extradition Treaty with Portugal signed and not submitted to the Queen's approval

1894

June 20, Malaboch's stronghold in Zoutpansberg stormed by the Transvaal forces; reported

June 26, Sir Henry B. Loch, the high commissioner, visits Pretoria to obtain redress of the grievances of British and foreign residents

June 28, British subjects exempted from military service by the Transvaal government

July 14, Mass meeting at Johannesburg demanded franchise should be extended to all aliens
Aug. 13, Destructive revolt of the Kaffirs (Zoutpansberg district), reported
Aug. 18, Malaboch and 200 followers imprisoned at Pretoria
Aug. 29, The Kaffirs defeated; sue for peace
Sept. 13, The chiefs surrender; reported

1895

Feb. 13, The Swaziland convention passed by the Volksraad; *see* Swaziland
June 11, British Protectorate over Tongoland blocked Boer road to the sea
——, Rebellion in Zoutpansberg suppressed
July 8, The Delagoa railway opened at Pretoria
Nov. 8, Protest of the British Government at the closing of the Vaal River drifts as contrary to the convention of London, Nov. 4; agreed to
Dec. 16, Increased opposition to the despotic government of Pres. Kruger; Mr. Esselen, State Attorney, Mr. Christian Joubert, and other officials resign; the Uitlanders (settlers) demand a voice in public affairs, &c., reported
Dec. 30, Dr. Jameson having received an appeal for help from the Uitlanders in Johannesburg, crosses the frontier with a force from Pitsani Pitlogo, Dec. 29; Col. Grey and others start from Mafeking, with about 460 men (volunteers) of the British S. Africa company's troops
——, Sir Hercules Robinson telegraphs to Dr. Jameson to retire
Dec. 31, Mr. Chamberlain and Sir H. Robinson intervene to stop hostilities

1896

Jan. 1, Dr. Jameson's party defeated by the Boers near Krugersdorp
Jan. 2, They surrender conditionally, after another fight at Vlakfontein, Jan. 2; British loss, 21 killed, 46 wounded; 9 officers and 550 men prisoners at Pretoria
Jan. 2, Johannesburg surrenders unconditionally, on the advice of the British Government
Jan. 5, The German Emperor congratulates Pres. Kruger, Jan. 2; who replies gratefully
Jan. 6, Some of the Reform committee at Johannesburg arrested
Jan. 7, Dr. Jameson and other prisoners handed over to Sir H. Robinson
Jan. 9, The British South Africa company in London request a judicial inquiry relating to Dr. Jameson's entry into the Transvaal (Dec. 29)
——, General amnesty (with exceptions) at Johannesburg
Jan. 10, Between 50 and 60 members of the Reform committee of the Uitlanders, Col. Rhodes, Sir Drummond Dunbar, Mr. Lionel Phillips, and others, arrested, and sent to Pretoria
Jan. 21, Dr. Jameson and his party (350 officers and men) sail from Durban; arrive in London, Feb. 25; charged, after examination, before Sir John Bridge at Bow St., Feb. 25 *et seq.*; Leander Starr (Dr.) Jameson and 5 others were committed, and bailed, June 15; trial at bar, before Lord Chief Justice Russell, Mr. Baron Pollock, and Mr. Justice Hawkins: counsel for the crown, Attorney-Gen. Sir R. Webster, Sol.-Gen. Sir R. B. Finlay, and others: for Dr. Jame-

son and defendants, Sir Edward Clarke, and others; South Africa Republic represented by Mr. Cohen, and others; verdict, guilty of offenses under the Foreign enlistment act: appeal for new trial declined by defendants; sentences: imprisonment without hard labor: Dr. Jameson, 15 months [ill; released, Dec. 2, 1896]; Sir John Willoughby, 10 months; Major Robt. White, 7 months; Col. Henry White, Col. Grey, and Major Coventry, 5 months: July 20–28, 1896. Major Coventry, ill, released, Aug. 22, 1896; the 5 officers permitted to retire from the army 8 officers unconvicted, reprimanded, and return to duty, reported, Sept. 15, 1896
Feb. 4, Pres. Krüger invited to London
Feb. 25, Preliminary trial of the Reform leaders begins at Pretoria, Feb. 3; confiscation of property adjudged
March 17, Offensive and defensive alliance concluded with the Orange Free State
April 24, Friendly but firm dispatch from Mr. Chamberlain to the President, insisting on redress of Uitlanders' grievances, April 1; Pres. Krüger defers his visit for the present
April 24–28, Trial of the Reform leaders: they plead guilty of high treason, sentence of death passed on Mr. Lionel Phillips, Mr. Hays Hammond, George P. Farrar, and Col. Frank Rhodes (commuted to imprisonment and banishment)
[59 principal men of the Rand, sentenced to 2 yrs. imprisonment, 3 yrs. banishment, and heavy fines, April 28, 1896]
May 11, Resignation of Sir Jacobus de Wet, British agent in Pretoria
May 12, Dr. Jameson and Major Robt. White write to the *Times* emphatically denying the receipt of any message from Mr. Cecil Rhodes directing them to move to Johannesburg
May 16, Mr. Grey, one of the reform committee, became insane and commits suicide in prison; 9 released and shorter sentences on the others, May 20; 45 released under conditions, May 30
June 11, The executive decide to release the reform leaders on payment of 25,000*l.* each, or in default 15 years' banishment; fines paid; Col. Rhodes, not accepting conditions, banished
Aug. 4, Bill for the education of Uitlanders' children passed by the Volksraad
Sept. 24, Restrictive Press Act passed
Sept. 26, Aliens (dangerous) expulsion bill passed empowered the President and Executive Council to expel any alien from the State who was considered in any way a danger to the public peace
Nov. 26, Aliens immigration restriction law passed (comes into operation, Jan. 1, 1897), required all foreigners to have passports showing they possessed means of support or were in a position to obtain such by work
Dec. 1, Mr. Wm. Conyngham Greene appointed British agent at Pretoria, Aug.; arrives

1897

Jan. 22, Pres. Krüger opens the new railway from Krugersdorp to Potchefstroom
Feb., The Government extended full franchise to 862 Uitlanders who had supported it in Jameson raid
March 19, Indemnity claimed for the Jameson raid, 677,938*l.* 3*s.* 3*d.*, "moral or intellectual damage, 1,000,000*l.*," total, 1,677,938*l.* 3*s.* 3*d.*

March 26 *et seq.*, Dr. Jameson examined by the S. Africa committee (*see* Rhodesia)

April *et seq.*, Construction of forts round Pretoria

May 7, Alien immigration bill repealed

June, Defensive alliance with the Orange Free State

June 22, Messrs. Sampson and Davies, Uitlander reformers, who refused pardon, not accepting conditions, released on Jubilee day

1898

Feb. 10, Presidential election, candidates: Mr. Krüger, Gen. Joubert, and Mr. Burger, 4 days' poll, closed, Jan. 22; Mr. Krüger reëlected, majority, 9,005, announced

Feb. 16, Chief Justice Kotze dismissed from office (unconstitutional); succeeded by State-Attorney Gregorowski

May 24, The government's reply to Mr. Chamberlain's dispatch of Oct. 16, 1897, to the effect that it cannot recognize British suzerainty since the convention of 1884, but that it will abide by the stipulations of that convention, and reaffirms its right to arbitration, published

June 13, Aliens expulsion amendment bill passed

Nov., Mr. Kotze, ex-chief justice, allowed to practice as advocate

Nov. 16, Punitive expedition under Gen. Joubert against Mpefu, Kaffir chief, in the Zoutpansberg district, much fighting, Oct. 21; Magato's mountain captured

Nov. 19, Resolution notified coolies and other Asiatics that they must take up residence in the "locations" by July 1, 1899

Dec. 30, Mpefu captured by the Chartered company's force and sent to Bulawayo, reported

1899

Jan. 14, Stormy British meeting at Johannesburg to protest against the arrest of Messrs. Webb and Dodd, of the S. African league; the British vice-consul refuses to appear at the trial, prisoners discharged, April 14

March 24, A petition to Queen Victoria signed by 23,000 Uitlanders, stating their grievances (the franchise, dynamite monopoly, &c.) forwarded by Sir A. Milner, April 3 (over 40,000 signatures, July)

April, Mr. Chamberlain declares the dynamite monopoly to be a breach of the convention

April *et seq.*, Much intimidation of Uitlanders

May 30–June 5, Bloemfontein conference: Sir A. Milner's franchise proposals rejected by Pres. Kruger; negotiations fail

May 31, Gen. Joubert opens Pietersburg railway

June 14, Pres. Kruger's franchise proposals adopted by the Raad

June 19 *et seq.*, Exodus of miners begins

July 3, Dispatches on the suzerainty of Great Britain, published at Pretoria

July 6, Ministers from the Cape and Orange Free State confer with Pres. Kruger on Sir A. Milner's franchise proposals at Pretoria, July 5, 6; secret session of the Raad

July 13, The British Government adhere to Sir A. Milner's minimum franchise scheme

July 26, Draft franchise law, 7 years' prospective and retrospective franchise to Uitlanders, passed by the Raad, July 11; ratified

July 27, Blue-book, with dispatches, Sir A. Milner declares the new franchise law inadequate, issued

July 31, Mr. Chamberlain proposes a joint inquiry into the new law; Mr. Conyngham Greene asks the Transvaal government to appoint delegates, Aug. 2; rejected; Pres. Kruger proposes a five years' retrospective franchise, 10 members from the goldfields, renunciation of British suzerainty, and international arbitration, Aug. 19

Aug. 28, Mr. Chamberlain proposes an inquiry by the British agent, and insists on the terms of the conventions 1881 and 1884

Aug., Crisis, business suspended at Johannesburg

Aug. 31, Military preparations amongst the Boers; ammunition for the Transvaal stopped at Delagoa bay; released

Sept. 2, The Transvaal withdraws its proposal of a 5 years' and returns to the 7 years' franchise

Sept., Boer troops gathered on the frontiers

Sept. 17, Urgent British dispatch, demands 5 years' franchise, a quarter representation for the goldfields, and equality of Dutch and English in the Volksraad, Sept. 8; Boer reply, negative

Sept. 22, Two firm dispatches from Mr. Chamberlain maintaining the terms of previous dispatches, and announcing that the imperial government would now formulate its own proposals

Oct. 2 *et seq.*, Boer troops (about 30,000) mobilized

Oct. 2, Exodus of Uitlanders; mail train from Natal stopped by Government order, passengers sent back at Volksrust, Sept. 30; another stopped and 800,000*l.* worth of gold confiscated

Oct. 11, Boer Ultimatum presented by Mr. Reitz (Secretary of State) to Mr. C. Greene, at Pretoria, demanding arbitration; withdrawal of British troops on the border, &c., Oct. 9; due compliance to be intimated by 5 P.M., Oct. 11; British reply states that these demands are such as are impossible to be discussed

——, Martial law proclaimed at Pretoria

Oct. 12, War proclaimed in Johannesburg, Boer manifesto issued to the Afrikanders

1900

Feb. 8, The Robinson bank at Johannesburg seized by Boer officials; cash and securities restored and bank reopened, Feb. 25

March 27, Death of Gen. Piet Joubert, aged 66

March 29, The Rand mines closed and all British expelled from the republic

April 19–May 2, The Boer peace mission received at The Hague; at Washington, May 18; neutral policy to be maintained, announced, May 21; at Paris, July 7

April 24, Commandant Prinsloo sentenced to 9 months' imprisonment for treason

——, Begbie's foundry, under the management of the Creuzot firm, wrecked by explosion at Johannesburg, 30 deaths and 54 injured, many arrests; Mr. Begbie, jun., and 3 others acquitted, charges withdrawn by the state prosecutor, May 24

May 14, Rev. Adrian Hofmeyr imprisoned 7 months without trial for speeches in favor of the progressives; released at Pretoria

Sept. 10, Proclamation of the Executive Council of the Boer Government announced leave of absence of President Kruger to go to Europe to plead cause of the Republic, S. W. Burger, Vice-President, to be Acting-President

Oct. 25, Transvaal annexed to Great Britain; proclamation issued by Lord Roberts, Sept. 1; formal annexation took place

Oct., Transvaal concessions commission (the Hon. A. Lyttleton, Mr. A. M. Ashmore, and Mr. R. K. Loveday) met in S. Africa, end of Aug.; public sittings at Pretoria during

1901

March 4, Sir A. Milner, High Commissioner for S. Africa, appointed governor of the Transvaal, Jan. 4, 1901; arrives at Pretoria

April 10, Civil jurisdiction reëstablished in Pretoria and 4 chief towns

May 8, Municipal government in Johannesburg

July 20, Mrs. Kruger dies at Pretoria, aged 67

Sept. 30, Mr. Broeksma, ex-public prosecutor (tried and sentenced to death for treachery and treason, Sept. 13–29), shot at Johannesburg

Nov. 9, S. African Compensation Commission, Mr. Milvain, chairman (Sir John Ardagh and others for the imperial government); long negotiations: total foreign claims, 1,631; amount claimed, 1,116,450*l.*; amount awarded, 106,950*l.*; Holland claimed, 706,355*l.*; amount awarded, 37,500*l.*; sittings closed in London

Nov. 22, Werneck, a surrendered burgher, convicted of high treason, &c., shot at Johannesburg

Nov. 26, The British return to the owners 23,000 oz. of gold commandeered by the late Boer government and found in the Pretoria mint

Nov. 27, A commission appointed to inquire into the working of the Gold Law; Sir Richard Solomon, chairman

Nov. 30, Proclamations issued prohibiting betting houses and abolishing various laws of the late republic relating to the franchise, &c.

Dec. 11, Regulations controlling native labor; flogging, forced labor, &c., strictly forbidden

Dec. 17, Johannesburg stock exchange reopened

1902

March 19, Military governorship of Pretoria relinquished by Sir J. Maxwell

April 3, First general meeting of the chamber of mines since the war; estimated loss due to the war, over 6,000,000*l.*

May 10, Transvaal high court in the new palace of justice at Pretoria opened

June 9, New mining tax, 10% on net produce, issued

June 21, Lord Milner installed governor of the Transvaal and commander-in-chief at Pretoria

Early July, Sir Percy Girouard appointed railway commissioner, line to be styled Central S. African railway

Aug. 4, Advocates Smuts, Jacobs, and De Wet (of the staff of the late government) admitted into the supreme court, reported

——, Gens. Botha, De Wet, and Delarey announced their intention to start a Boer fund abroad (*see* end of S. African War)

Aug. 31, Sir Arthur Lawley appointed Lieut.-Gov.; arrives

Oct. 8, Customs tariff revised

Nov. 5, Grant of 8,000,000*l.* for the Transvaal and Orange River colony voted in the Commons

June–Nov., 70,000 persons repatriated

Nov. 19, Martial law withdrawn

Nov. 21, Land department established

Mid Dec., Coal struck, 30 ft. thick, at Grootvlei

1903

Jan. 13, Mr. Chamberlain's successful tour to promote reconciliation and unity; the Vereeniging treaty to be kept, Jan. 8; at Johannesburg: Transvaal war contribution, 30,000,000*l.*, to be raised in 3 years, agreed to by the mine leaders; an imperial loan of 35,000,000*l.* for the new colonies guaranteed

End Jan., Ordinance issued empowering municipality of Johannesburg to raise loans

May 20, Intercolonial council "to advise the high commissioner and governor on the financial administration of the South African railways and the employment of their revenue, the expenditure on the South African constabulary, certain official expenditure of the two colonies which is placed by the order under the administration of the council, and any other common expenditure which may from time to time be placed under its authority by the legislative councils of the two colonies with the consent of secretary of state;" established

Nov. 19, Report of the native labor commission signed; majority find that there is an immense insufficiency of native labor

Dec. 7, Legislative council opened

Dec. 30, Motion in the legislative council by Sir Geo. Farrar to import unskilled colored laborers, carried by 22 votes to 4

——, Legislative council approves Asiatic labor, and decides to ask the government to introduce a labor ordinance providing for the importation of indentured colored workmen

1904

Jan. 6, Draft ordinance to regulate the introduction into the Transvaal of unskilled non-European laborers, published by the government

Jan. 25, Petition in favor of Chinese labor, with 45,000 signatures of white males over 16 years of age, presented to the legislative council

Feb. 10, Ordinance passed by the legislative council

Feb. 12, Letter published, with the signatures of Messrs. Botha, Delarey, Smuts, Kruger, and other Boer leaders, sent to the Colonial Secretary by their request, objecting that the question of the introduction of Chinese labor into the Transvaal had not been submitted for popular sanction, and stating that the majority of the Boers were opposed to the ordinance

March 1, An extraordinary session of the inter-colonial council opened at Johannesburg by Lord Milner to consider the financial position of the two colonies in view of the decrease in the revenue derived from the railways due to the want of unskilled labor for the mines; Lord Milner stated that out of a guaranteed loan of 35,000,000*l.* only 30,000,000*l.* had been raised, and in consequence of the inability to raise the 5,000,000*l.* expenditure must be restricted; the council decide to reduce the expenditure on new railway lines, and effect other economies

March 11, Imperial government states that it would not disallow the labor ordinance

May 13, Convention of the Chinese Minister respecting Chinese labor signed in London

June 14, Inter-colonial council resolve that an auditor with extensive powers and a treasurer responsible to the council only in respect of inter-colonial funds be appointed for the better financial control of the railways

June 17, Resignation of Sir P. Girouard, commissioner of railways

June 22, First contingent of Chinese laborers arrives on the Rand

July 14, Death of ex-President Krüger, aged 78, at Clarens, Switzerland

Aug. 16, Colonial Secretary, replying to the legislative council, states "that the imperial government, while ready to sanction legislation similar to that in force in Cape Colony and Natal, were unable to sanction legislation which would interfere with the existing rights of Asiatics as regards trading"

Sept. 30, Mr. Alfred Beit presents the Frankenwald estate, 12½ miles N.E. of Johannesburg, to the government for the purpose of furthering the cause of education in the Transvaal

Nov. 10, National convention on the question of Asiatic traders meets in Pretoria, 160 delegates present, representing each municipality in the Transvaal, resolution carried recommending that Asiatic immigration be prohibited except under the terms of the Foreign Labor Importation act

Nov. 16, Inter-colonial council ratifies agreements for the construction of new lines, 339 miles in length: Bethlehem to Kroonstadt, Bethlehem to Modderpoort, Ladybrand to Modderpoort, and Aliwal North to Wepener; other lines, 218 miles in length: Pretoria to Rustenburg and Krugerdorp to Mafeking, sanctioned, Nov. 17

Dec. 16, Funeral of Mr. Kruger at Pretoria

Dec. 31, 21,462 Chinese coolies imported

1905

Jan. 14, Responsible government association to advocate the immediate grant of self-government to the Transvaal, formed (Mr. E. P. Solomon, chairman)

Jan. 29, Het Volk, a Boer political organization, Gen. Botha chairman, demanding full responsible government, and opposing the principles of one vote one value, periodical redistribution and equal electoral districts inaugurated

April 2, Lord Milner leaves for England

April 19, Responsible government association and Het Volk agree to a common political course of action, the basis of the union being, "loyalty to the imperial connection, that the Boers should not oppose Chinese labor for 5 years, that the franchise should be exclusively white, that the one vote one value principle be accepted, that the Dutch language should be permitted in parliament, and local control of education under departmental safeguards"

April 25, The terms of the letters patent, dated March 31, constituting the Transvaal Constitution, published. In effect the Constitution creates a legislative assembly of 30 to 35 elected members, and 6 to 9 official members. All white male British subjects over 21 years of age may be registered as voters, including all ex-burghers on the last burgher roll of the South African Republic; occupiers for 6 months of premises of the annual value of 10l., or freehold value of 100l.; employees in receipt of an income of not less than 100l. per annum. Provision is made for the creation of single-member constituencies, and the constitution of electoral districts on the basis of the number of voters in a district, not of population; no person to be registered or vote in more than one district; biennial registration of voters; redistribu-

tion to take place every 4 years; 80,406 voters on the register, Sept., 1905

April 29, Lord Selborne, appointed governor of the Transvaal and Orange River colonies, in succession to Lord Milner, sails for South Africa

May 17, Gen. Botha addresses the Het Volk at Johannesburg, and counsels conciliation

May 23, Lord Selborne arrives at Pretoria

July 4, Deputation of the Het Volk waits on Lord Selborne with a petition against various points in the working of the new Transvaal Constitution

July 5, Gen. Botha, at a congress of the Het Volk, condemns the new constitution

Sept. 4, Public attention attracted to desertions from the mines and crimes committed by Chinese deserters, Aug.–Sept.; Attorney-General states that 46,895 Chinese coolies have been imported; number of convictions 2,543

Sept. 21, Death of Col. Frank Rhodes

Oct. 10, Nine Chinese coolies attempt to raid a homestead in the Krugersdorp district, but were repulsed, 1 shot dead

Oct. 18, 65 Chinese arrested, under the new regulations, as the ringleaders of a band of 450 coolies of bad characters, reported

Oct., Boer committee appointed to inquire into the conditions obtaining in German S.W. Africa, return to Pretoria, and issue their report, which is adverse to emigration to that part

Oct. 23, Joint meeting of the responsible government association, Het Volk, and the labor party, held at Germiston

Oct. 24, Chinese coolies at the Jumper's Deep mine refuse to work until two of their number, who had been arrested for an infringement of the mining regulations, were released; 40 coolies arrested, 20 of these afterwards sentenced, some to 2, others to 3 months' hard labor; coolies return to work

Early Nov., Organized secret society among the Chinese named the "Red Door," its object being the committal of crime, discovered; authorities repatriating the ringleaders

End Dec., Lord Selborne makes a recommendation to the home government that the Transvaal constitution should be so far amended as to admit of an increase in the number of constituencies from 35 to 50 or 60, the legislative assembly to comprise at least 50 members

1906

Feb. 7, Duke of Connaught meets in audience the native chiefs and their followers, numbering 400

March 3, Round table conference of representatives of the progressive and responsible government parties and of Het Volk held at Pretoria on the subject of the constitution

March 22, Sir H. Campbell-Bannerman announces that the committee to go to S. Africa, and to advise the government concerning the new constitution for the Transvaal and the Orange River colony, will be Sir West Ridgeway, chairman, Lord Sandhurst, Sir F. Hopwood, and Col. Johnson

Aug. 11, 200 Chinese applied for repatriation under the first notice of the new order and 370 under the second, up to

Sept. 11, New party called the Transvaal national association formed in Johannesburg

Sept. 12, Asiatic amendment ordinance, regarding the

registration of Asiatics who had not passed the educational test, and the Pensions ordinance, passed by the legislative council

Nov. 9, Government statistics show that the whites employed on the producing mines on the Rand numbered, in Aug., 14,927, or 47% more than in May, 1904; in the non-producing mines there were employed 1,985 whites, a decrease since May, 1904, of 13%; published

Nov. 17, Faction fight at Amos Matibi's kraal, Nov. 14; 200 natives arrested

Dec. 8, Total number of Chinese in the Transvaal on Nov. 30, 53,004

Dec. 12, New constitution of Dec. 6 published as a parliamentary paper

1907

Jan. 7, Deputation of the railway employés' labor organizations wait upon Lord Selborne asking for a withdrawal of the railway circular prohibiting railway employés from participating actively in electioneering; Lord Selborne held out no hope of the suspension or repeal of the circular; labor mass meeting held in Johannesburg to protest against Lord Selborne's action, and a resolution, appealing to Lord Elgin, passed

Jan. 12, Lord Selborne takes the oath as Governor and Commander-in-Chief of the Transvaal

Jan. 14, Resignation of Sir Richard Solomon, Transvaal Attorney-General, reported

Feb. 9, Nomination of candidates for the parliamentary elections

Feb. 20, Elections to the first legislative assembly under the new Constitution took place throughout the Transvaal

Feb. 26, The final result of the elections is as follows:— Het Volk, 37; Progressives, 21; Nationalists, 6; Labor Party, 3; Independents, 2

March 4, Composition of the new Cabinet: General Botha, Premier and Minister of Agriculture; Mr. Smuts, Colonial Secretary; Mr. J. de Villiers, Attorney-General and Minister of Mines; Mr. Hull, Treasurer; Mr. Rissik, Lands and Native Affairs; Mr. E. Solomon, Public Works; announced

March 11, General Botha, speaking at a banquet given in honor of the new ministry, said that British interests would be absolutely safe in the hands of the new cabinet

March 16, Gen. Botha to receive a salary of 4,000l. a year as Premier, and the other Ministers 3,000l. a year each, announced

March 18, Mr. Crawford, chairman of the national bank, gazetted president of the upper house

March 21, New Parliament opened; speech from the throne delivered by Lord Selborne; Gen. Beyers elected speaker

March 22, Asiatic Registration Bill passed by the Legislative Council

May 2, Sir Richard Solomon appointed Agent-General of the Transvaal in England by Gen. Botha

May 3, Rand labor commission, to inquire into the subject of white and native labor in the Rand mines, appointment gazetted

May 7, Strike of Rand miners

May 24, Strike demonstration at Crœsus mine dispersed by cavalry

May 30, Welcome to Gen. Botha on his return from England

June 14, Parliament opened; Gen. Botha announces the decision not to reënact the labor ordinance, but to send the Chinese home immediately on the expiration of their contracts

July 27, The strike declared finished; the Government induces the mine-owners to reëngage most of the men on the old terms

Oct. 1, Education law enacted

Dec. 27, Imperial assent to the Immigrants Restriction Act gazetted

1908

Jan. 10, Fourteen leaders of the passive resistance movement in the Asiatic controversy, including Mr. Gandhi, committed to prison under the Registration Act

Jan. 31, The whole of the Asiatics imprisoned for disregard of the Registration Ordinance released

Feb. 4, Boycott of Asiatic traders and employers of Asiatics inaugurated

Feb. 10, The registration office in Johannesburg reopened for voluntary registration; Mr. Gandhi and other leaders attend

May 9, The Transvaal Civil Service bill issued

Aug. 28, Four leading Natal Indians, who refused to comply with orders to leave the Transvaal, deported to the Natal border

Aug. 31, Total number of Chinese on the Rand, 17,006

Oct. 2, 67 Indians, arrested as prohibited immigrants, sent to prison for two months

1909

Jan. 21, Riot at the Village Deep mine between Chinese coolies and the police; six Chinamen were shot dead and 15 wounded

April 1, Convention for the regulation of the railway traffic and of the recruiting of native labor in the Portuguese territories signed

1910

Feb. 28, The last batch of Chinese laborers leaves the Rand for home

April 18, Lord and Lady Selborne leave Pretoria

May 31, Union day celebrated

See South Africa

TRIPOLI

See Libya.

TRISTAN DA CUNHA

Tristan da Cunha, British possession, a small group of islands in the Atlantic, half-way between the Cape and S. America, in 37° 6' S. lat. 12° 1' W. long. Besides Tristan da Cunha and Gough's Island, there are Inaccessible and Nightingale Islands, the former two and the latter one mile long, and a number of rocks. Tristan consists of an extinct volcano rising to a height of 8,000 feet, with a circumference at its base of 21 miles. The habitable area is a small plateau on the north-west side of about 12 square miles, 100 feet above sea-level. The islands were discovered by the Portuguese navigator, Admiral Tristão da Cunha, were formally annexed to Cape Colony, Aug. 14, 1816.

In 1880 the population numbered 109, declining to 52 in 1893, since when it has increased to 130 (1925).

TUNIS

Tunis (Afrikiya.) The present boundaries are: on the north and east the Mediterranean Sea, on the west the Algerian province of Constantine, and on the south the great desert of the Sahara and Libya. Area about 48,300 English square miles, including that portion of the Sahara which is to the east of the Djerid, extending towards Gadamés.

According to the census held on April 20, 1926, the total European population was 173,281, composed of 71,020 French (exclusive of the army of occupation and of the navy), 89,216 Italians, 8,396 Maltese, 517 Spaniards, 646 Greeks, and 3,486 other foreigners. The total native population was 1,986,427, of whom 1,932,184 were Arabs and Bedouins, and 54,243 Jews. Grand total was 2,159,708.

The capital, the city of Tunis, had, in 1926, a population of 185,996, of whom 106,860 were Moslems, and 24,131 Jews, besides 27,922 French, 44,076 Italians, 4,994 Maltese, and 1,763 other Europeans. By means of the channel, which was opened in 1893, Tunis is directly accessible to ocean-going vessels. Other towns are Bizerta with 20,593 inhabitants (6,738 Europeans); Sousse with 21,298; Sfax with 27,723; Kaisouan, the Holy City of the Moslems, with 18,527 natives exclusively; Ferryville with 4,462 (4,155 Europeans), and Tindja, 1,500 inhabitants.

Tunis stands nearly on the site of Carthage. Tunis was besieged by Louis IX of France, who died near it Aug. 25, 1270. It remained under African kings till taken by Barbarossa, for Solyman the Magnificent, 1531. Barbarossa was expelled by the Emperor Charles V, when 10,000 Christian slaves were set at liberty, June, 1535. The country was recovered by the Turks under Selim II, 1575. The Bey of Tunis was first appointed in 1574; Tunis was reduced by Admiral Blake, on the bey refusing to deliver up the British captives, 1655. The Hussein dynasty was founded 1705. In July, 1856, the Bey agreed to make constitutional reforms. He died Sept. 22, 1859; and his brother and successor Mohamed-es-Sadok took the oath of fidelity to the constitution. He died, and was succeeded by his brother Sidi Ali, Oct. 28, 1882; died, June 11, 1902; succeeded by his son Mohamed; succeeded by Mohamed en Nasir, 1906.

Sidi Ahmed Bey, born 1858 succeeded his cousin, Sidi Mohamed el Habib Bey, February 11, 1929.

The reigning family of Tunis, occupants of the throne since 1705, descend from Hussein ben Ali, commonly believed to be a native of the Isle of Crete, who made himself master of the country, acknowledging, however, the suzerainty of the Sultan of Turkey.

After the French invasion of the country in the spring of 1881, the treaty of Kasr-es-Said (May 12, 1881), confirmed by convention signed June 8, 1883, placed Tunis under the protectorate of France. The government is carried on under the direction of the French Foreign Office, which has a special department for Tunisian affairs, under the control of a French Minister Resident-General, who is also Minister of Foreign Affairs, and a ministry of 11 heads of departments, 8 of the ministers being French and 3 Tunisian. The country is divided into 19 districts (contrôles civils), and 6 military circles; the district governors (contrôleurs) are French; the subordinate officials (Caids, Kahias, and Sheiks) are Native. French tribunals administer justice between subjects of European powers, and also between them and natives; there are Native courts for cases between natives (tribunals at Ouzara and Charaã). In 1914, the Tunisian penal law was codified. French administration in Tunis has been confirmed by conventions with all the European Powers regulating the status and the conditions of trade of their respective citizens within the Regency.

M. Manceron, French Resident-General, appointed January 2, 1929

1864 to 1879

May, 1864, Insurrection, April 18; ships of war sent to protect Europeans

Oct. 25, 1871, Tunis decreed to be an integral part of the Turkish Empire

July 19, 1875, Commercial treaty with Great Britain

Jan., 1879, A dispute with France settled by submission of the Bey

1880

The Bey, embarrassed by debt (5,000,000*l.*), places his finances in hands of an international commission

Aug., Disputes between France and Italy respecting railway concessions

1881

March, Dispute with France; predatory incursions of the Kroumirs, nomadic shepherd tribes, on Algerian territory: the Bey appeals to Turkey, April 11; and the Great Powers, April 27: military expedition sent from France; lands in Tabarka, bombards fortress, and occupies Bizerta, April 30

Early May, The Kroumirs said to be enclosed by the French; the Bey's army retreats

May 11, The French approach Tunis, alleging the object to be to restrain warlike tribes and protect their frontier

May 12, Treaty with France signed; it assures to France the right to occupy the positions which the French military authorities might deem necessary for the maintenance of order and the security of the frontier and the coast, and to send a resident minister to the capital. The French Government guarantees to the Bey the security of his person, his states, and his dynasty, and the maintenance of existing treaties with the European powers; while the Bey undertakes not to conclude any international convention without a previous understanding with the French Government, and to prevent the introduction of arms into Algeria through Tunis. The financial system of the regency to be regulated by France in concert with the Bey

May 16, The Sultan of Turkey protests against the treaty

June, M. Roustan, the consul, appointed French resident minister (said to be virtual ruler, replacing Bey), French army returning home

June 30, Insurrection at Sfax, revolt of great Chief Ali Ben Khalifa

July 16, Sfax bombarded by the French, July 5 *et seq.*; captured after severe conflict

July 31, Europeans attacked, nearly all flee to ships, alleged massacres

About Aug. 15, Collapse of Bey's authority

Sept. 8, Asserted conflict at Hammamet, the French repulsed, Aug. 31; the French retreating

Sept. 9, Arrival of 2,000 French troops at Goletta

About Sept. 13, General Sabattier with troops at Zaghouan surrounded by Arabs

About Sept. 25, Alleged defeat of the Bey's troops under Ali Bey; 4 hours' conflict

Sept. 26, 28,000 men sent to Tunis announced

About Oct. 4 *et seq.*, Ali Bey's army surrounded

Oct. 8, Union of the French and Ali Bey's army

Oct. 10, Tunis occupied by the French

Oct. 13, Gen. Sabattier defeats the Arabs; six hours' conflict; 800 killed, French loss slight

1882

Feb., Paul Cambon appointed Resident General

Oct., Death of Mohammed VI, Bey. Succeeded by his brother Ali IV

1883

Feb. 4, Office of Secretary General created

March 27, French law provided for establishment of French courts in the principal cities with Decree of the Bey May 5, which gave the courts jurisdiction over all foreigners who gave up their extraterritoriality

June 8, Convention of Marsa with the Bey by which France took over the Tunis debt, and the Bey agreed to permit such administrative, judicial, and financial reforms as the French considered advisable

Dec. 31, British consular jurisdiction given up

1884

Nov. 10, Decree gave the Resident General power to approve in the name of the Government of France all decrees rendered by the Bey

1886

M. Massicault, Resident General

1891

Jan. 23, First meeting of Council (consultative)

1892

Nov. 18, M. Rouvier, Resident General

1894

Sept., R. Millet, Resident General

1896

Feb. 22, Council (consultative) enlarged by the addition of native members

Sept. 28, Treaty between France and Italy and Tunis signed of commerce and navigation, consular rights and extradition, the nationality of Italians and their descendants in Tunis to be governed by Italian law

Nov. 6, Railroad between Tunis and Susa completed

1900

April 1, Decree established the *Conseil Supérior de l'Assistance Publique*

Nov., M. Benoit, Resident General

1901

April 7, M. S. Pichon, Resident General

1902

April 6, Law gave Tunis control of its railroads

May 11, Death of Bey of Tunis, Mahomed el Hadi Pacha, Sidi Mahomed El-Hajd succeeded

1905

Jan. 2, Decree provided for election by direct and universal suffrage of members of the Consultative Council

1906

April 27, Native unrest; French colonists murdered

May 11, Death of Sidi Mohamed el Hadi Bey

May 12, Sidi Mohamed Ben Nasr Bey succeeded his cousin

Dec. 27, Gabriel Alapetite succeeded M. Pichon as Resident General (1906–1918)

1907

Feb. 2, Decree added 16 natives (including 1 Jew) to the "Conférence Consultative" composed of 12 members each from the commercial, financial, and other French organizations in Tunis

Nov. 1, Plague reported

1908

Dec. 22, Decree instituted appeal before the Civil Tribunal as to decision of the Commissions of Revision of the electorate

1910

April 27, Decree established a "Conseil Supérieur du Gouvernement" consisting of the members of the ministry, the heads of the public service, and 3 representatives from each section of the "Conférence," the native and French representatives sitting separately

May 18, Decree established Committee for improvement of the Emile Loubet School

May 19, Convention with Turkey as to frontiers signed

1911

April, Visit of President Fallières of the French Republic

June 18, Decree added land available for colonists

July 12, Decree established a Consultative Committee on Colonization

Nov. 27, French Sahara police occupied oasis of Djanet claimed also by Turkey

Population according to census consisted of 1,739,744 natives, 11,300 Maltese, and 50,477 Jews

1914

Jan. 24, Decree with that of June 18, 1911 added 40,000 hectares to land available to colonists

Penal law codified

May 29, Franco-Italian Agreement as to status of their nationals in Tunis and Libya respectively, most favored treatment

1918

In the World War Tunis assisted France with a total of 62,000 men, 3,000 volunteers in addition to the regular army, of whom 10,500 were killed

Etienne Flandin succeeded M. Alapetite as Resident General

1919

Sept. 12, Franco-Italian Agreement signed as to their nationals, equal taxation, equal status in schools, &c., for Italians

1920

March, Nationalists adopted program of 9 demands, asking for a deliberative Assembly elected by universal suffrage, complete financial control, a government responsible to the Assembly, elective municipal councils, liberty of press, &c.

March 22, Decree introduced proportional representation for election of the members of the "Conférence Consultative"

Aug. 10, In Treaty of Sèvres Turkey renounced rights over Tunis

Nov. 24, Lucien Saint appointed Resident General

1921

Jan. 21, The nine demands presented to new Resident General Lucien Saint on his arrival

March 6, Census gave population as 1,938,920 natives, including 1,891,280 (Arabs and Bedouins, and 47,640 Jews), 156,170 Europeans (84,819 Italians, 54,477 Jews)

April 24, New Ministry of Justice created

Nov. 8, Nationality decree naturalized as French citizens (not Tunisians) children of European origin born to parents who had themselves been born in Tunisia; not applied to Italians. Protested by British

1922

April 4, Political crisis. The Bey offered his resignation because publication of his interview with the Resident General on political situation was misquoted and the Resident General refused to make statement

April 27, Arrival of President Millerand on visit

July 10, Sidi Mohamed el Habib Bey succeeded to the throne on death of his cousin

July 13, Decrees divided the country into 5 "regions" based on the cities of Bizerta, Tunis, LeKef, Soussa, and Sfax, and instituted a regional council in each, composed of 10 native and 11 French members and a council in each Kaidat, composed of natives elected by and from those named by the notables of the Sheikats and any French residents named by the Resident General, and a Grand Council replaced the Conférence Consultative

July 14, The office of Secretary General abolished and its functions divided between a General Division of the Interior and a Division of Justice

The three orders of councils meet to discuss economic questions and are prohibited from discussion of political questions

Aug. 21, Oct. 28, 30, and 31, Arrêté made provisions for elections to the regional and Kaidat councils and the Grand Council

Oct. 3, Council of the League of Nations appealed to by Great Britain referred question of nationality in Tunis to Permanent Court

Nov. 25, Decree defined composition and functions of the Grand Council and provided for an Arbitral Council of 5 natives and 5 French elected by the respective sections to decide questions in dispute, and in case of the controversy failing to be settled representatives of the Government are added, the final decision being given by 14 French and 8 natives

Dec. 11, First meeting of the Grand Council rejected income, business, and certain other taxes proposed by the Government, and substituted a tax on vehicles, and higher taxes on spirits, coffee, sugar, and tea

1923

Feb. 7, Decision of Permanent Court of International Justice that matter of nationality in Tunisia was within the jurisdiction of France and League of Nations had jurisdiction

May 24, Agreement of France and Great Britain as to nationality in Tunis, children born in Tunis of British parents themselves born in Tunis permitted to elect to retain British nationality, but the same privilege not to be extended to their children and succeeding generations

Dec. 20, French law offered French nationality to Moslem and Jewish Tunisians possessing certain qualifications

1925

Feb. 26, Consultative Committee appointed to study political questions in Tunisia held first meeting; no representatives of French colonists or natives on the committee

March 21, Political demonstration of native political parties

1926

Nov. 10, 13 decrees issued dealing with recommendations of the Commission as to reforms in administration, as to numbers of staffs, salaries, &c., the Resident General to be assisted by a Civil Cabinet and and a Military Cabinet

Population census gave total population as 2,159,708, of whom 1,932,184 are Moslems, 54,243 Jews, and 173,281 Europeans including 71,020 French of whom 33,272 are Tunisian-born, 82,216 Italians including 50,395 Tunisian-born, 8,396 Maltese and 4,649 other Europeans; Tunis, the chief city has population of 185,996 (106,860 natives and 79,150 Europeans)

1929

Jan. 2, M. Manceron appointed Resident General

Feb. 11, Death of Sidi Mohammed el Habib Bey. Succeeded by his cousin Sidi Ahmed Bey

UGANDA

The territories now comprised within this Protectorate came under British influence in 1890, and a portion of them was for a time administered by the Imperial British East African Company. In 1894 a British Protectorate was declared over the Kingdom of Uganda and some of the adjoining territories. The present limits are approximately as follows:—On the north, the Uganda-Sudan boundary; on the east, a line drawn from Mt. Zulia on the Sudan boundary along the Turkana escarpment over the top of Mt. Elgon, and along the west boundary of the Colony of Kenya to the eastern shores of Lake Victoria; on the south by Tanganyika Territory (late German East Africa); and on the west by the eastern boundary of the Belgian Congo. Within these boundaries lie part of the Victoria Nyanza, part of Lake Edward, the whole of Lake George, half of Lake Albert, the whole of Lake Kioga, the whole of Lake Salisbury, and the course of the Nile from its exit from Lake Victoria to Nimule, where the Egyptian Sudan commences. Total area 94,204 square miles, including 15,017 square miles of water.

The total population of Uganda (December, 1929) was estimated at 3,410,857, composed as follows: Native, 3,396,323; Asiatic, 12,539; European, 1,995. Entebbe is the capital.

Sir W. F. Gowers, Governor General.

1884

Oct. 10, The King Mtesa, friendly to Grant, Stanley, and other travelers and missionaries, dies

1885

Oct. 29, His son M'wanga, kills Bishop Hannington, for advancing by a new route, about

1888

Sept., Revolution with bloodshed; M'wanga deposed and replaced by his brother Kawewa (Oct.), whose attempts to revive his father's policy are frustrated by the Arab slave-dealers; much persecution ensues; the Europeans flee and their settlements are destroyed Nov., 1888. King Kawewa resists the Arabs, and is expelled, they set up his brother Kalema; civil war, Nov.

1889

Oct. 11, M'wanga severely defeats the Arabs, Oct. 4, and reëstablishes his power

1890

March 5, M'wanga professes himself a Christian, and appoints Catholic officials, reported

April 14 and Dec. 26, He places Uganda under the influence of the British East African company, by treaty with Mr. Jackson

July 1, Uganda placed within the sphere of British influence by the Anglo-German treaty

Dec. 31, Capt. (aft. Sir) F. D. Lugard and Capt. W. H. Williams lent by the British war-office to assist the company; they arrive

1891

Jan., They strenuously endeavor to maintain peace between the French Catholics and British Protestant missionaries and their converts; they hold Kampala, a fortified station near Mengo; Capt. Lugard constructs and garrisons several forts in the country; about 1,450 Soudanese placed there (about 450 being

soldiers), who afterwards, under Selim Bey, join Capt. Lugard

1892

Jan. 20, Revival of religious feuds and outrages; a Protestant murdered in the street; Capt. Lugard demands redress, the King refuses it, and threatens him and his party; fruitless negotiations; other murders of Protestants; the Catholics arm and attack Kampala, and are repulsed with severe loss by Capt. Williams, who is compelled to use Maxim guns, Jan. 24; the Catholic houses wrecked; Bishop Hirth and the priests taken to Kampala, Jan. 24; the King, with 300 of the Catholic party, flees to the isle of Burenguge, where he is joined by the Bishop; the isle is taken by Capt. Williams, with bloodshed; the King and Bishop flee to Sesse, Jan. 30

March 30, Second Treaty signed with British by M'wanga. Not ratified

June, July, Letters received from Bishop Hirth by the French Government, accusing the British of outrages, and claiming compensation; the British Government promises investigation

June 16, King M'wanga and the native Christians in Uganda petition against British evacuation

July 27, The King rejoins the Protestants; the company predominant, reported

Oct. 3, The Imperial East Africa company accepts the offered support of the government in postponing the evacuation of Uganda from Dec. 31, 1892, to March 31, 1893

Dec. 13, Capt. Lugard's reply to French charges

Dec. 31, Bishop Hannington's remains found and interred in the new church, Bishop Tucker present

1893

Jan. 1, British commission, headed by Sir Gerald Portal, starts for Uganda *via* Mombasa; he arrives at Mengo, March 17, and is received by the King, March 20; engages the Soudanese troops and leaves Capt. Macdonald in command at Kampala, early April

May 15, The Imperial East Africa company evacuates Uganda, March 31; the company's officers and stores taken over by government

May 29, Final Treaty with M'wanga

June 17 *et seq.*, Insurrection of Mahomedans, joined by Selim Bey; the Catholics and Protestants united under Capt. Macdonald defeat and expel the insurgents from Uganda

Aug., Selim Bey dies in exile

Nov. 4, Col. Covile (administratr.) arrives in Uganda

Dec. 13, Kabarega, King of Unyoro, an aggressive slave raider, severely defeated about

1894

Jan. 25, Death of Sir Gerald Portal

Feb. 4, Wadelai taken by Major Owen; he leaves for Mombasa March 24; in London, June 4

April 12, Lord Rosebery announces a future British protectorate

Aug. 13, Kabarega's forces annihilated, reported

Aug. 24, E. L. Berkeley (from Zanzibar) appointed Commissioner of Uganda, &c., about May 11; arrives at Kampala

Aug. 27, The protectorate formally announced, June 18; published in London Gazette on the 19th; proclaimed at Mengo

End Sept., Kabarega's assault on Fort Hoima repulsed by Capt. Thurston and garrison

Nov. 26, Slaughter of a government caravan party (1,200) in the Eldoma ravine by the Masai; Mr. Andrew Dick killed

1896

June 30, Unyoro made a British protectorate
July 3, Protectorate extended over Usoga
Aug. 14, Uganda railway act passed

1897

July 10, Land Regulation Ordinance promulgated
July 20, Revolt in the Buddu district; King M'wanga defeated by Major Ternan at Kiango, July 24; again at Marongo, July 28; Mr. Grant's force attacked, rebels driven off, Aug. 23; M'wanga surrenders to the Germans, about Aug. 26
Sept. 23, Soudanese troops (Nubians) refuse to go with an expedition, under Major Macdonald, to explore and delimit the boundary near the Italian sphere fixed by treaty (1891); mutiny ensues
Oct. 19, Fort Lubwas, in Usoga, betrayed by the Soudanese garrison to the mutineers, Oct. 17; Major A. B. Thruston, Mr. N. Wilson, and Mr. W. Scott massacred by them, Oct. 19; the fort besieged by Major Macdonald's forces, Oct. 18; heavy fighting, Lieut. Fielding and 15 others killed, enemy's loss severe
Nov., Chowa, infant son of M'wanga, made King with a regency at Mengo
Nov. 10, Severe 10 hours' fight, heavy losses
Dec. 11, Several engagements, Lieut. Macdonald and the Rev. Geo. L. Pilkington, killed

1898

Jan. 19, M'wanga escapes from the Germans and attacks Koki, missions, &c., burnt, Jan.; his force routed by Major Macdonald in Ankoli
Feb. 23, The mutineers escape from fort Lubwas, Jan. 15, and cross the Nile, Feb.; overtaken by Major Macdonald and Capt. Harrison, their stockades at Kabagambi, Lake Kioga, captured after severe fighting, Capt. Maloney killed, British loss 15, rebels' loss about 55, survivors dispersed
March, Revolt in Unyoro; the ex-King M'wanga ravaging the west of Uganda, churches burnt, &c.
April 11, Mr. Berkeley, British commissioner, enters Kampala fort with great ceremony, country settling down
Mid-May, New railway (100 miles) opened
May 30, Major Macdonald reports 280 killed (30 Europeans) 1,300 rebels in 7 months' fighting
Aug. 4, Soudanese rebels totally defeated at Mruli by Lieut.-Col. Martyr, 40 killed, 34 taken prisoners
Dec. 6, Lieut. Hannyngton's party attacked at Kisiliza, 13 British and 100 rebels killed, Oct. 10, 1898; further fighting, 7 British killed, early Nov.; Bilal (Major Thurston's murderer) killed in action, mutineers dispersed by Cole's force

1899

March, Major Martyr's expedition down the Nile; Wadelai and other posts occupied as far as Rejaf, Sept., 1898; Fort Berkely, the last built by the expedition, early 1899; further progress stopped by sudd (river swamps)
March 5, Col. Macdonald's E. African expedition, to explore unknown country N. of Uganda, starts, May 3, 1898 (divided into 3 columns); Capt. Kirkpatrick and 7 men treacherously murdered at Nakwai

by natives, who are afterwards routed by Col. Macdonald, Nov., 1898; Major Austin's and Lieut. Hanbury-Tracy's columns, after adventurous marches with good results, join Col. Macdonald, and all return to Mombasa
April 9, Col. Evatt's force defeats and captures Kabarega and M'Wanga in Unyoro
July 8, The Macupa railway bridge, between Mombasa and the mainland, opened
July, Mr. Berkely resigns; Sir H. H. Johnston appointed special commissioner

1900

March 10, General Treaty with Great Britain signed by the Regents for the King of Uganda and by the leading chiefs by which system of Government outlined, land tenure, taxation, justice, military service, &c.
June 25, Uganda railway act passed
Aug., Caravans attacked and telegraphs cut by natives in the Nandi district
Oct., Dr. J. Sherlock and 10 natives killed in action, Oct. 13; the tribes submit
Dec., Sir H. Johnston tours through the Toru and Nkole districts and the western districts; ascends mount Ruwenzori (probably the highest in Africa) to 14,800 ft. alt., May et seq., reported

1901

June, Operations against the raiding Suk and Turkana tribes conducted
Aug. 24, Maj. Delmé-Radcliffe's operations against raiding Lango tribes, some Soudanese mutineers, May; successfully completed
Oct. 23, Mr. Kühlewindt explores unknown country north of Satuka; journeys from Mombasa to Khartoum in 10 months, reported
Dec. 20, Uganda railway, 584 miles, completed, to Lake Victoria Nyanza; estim. cost, 5,550,000l.

1902

Jan. 17, Notice that Uganda within zone in which alcoholic liquors prohibited by Brussels Act
April 1, Eastern Province annexed to the E. Africa Protectorate (Naivasha and Kisumu) by Ordinance of March 5
Aug. 8, The Katikiro (Prime Minister) of Uganda received by the King, London
Aug. 11, Uganda Order in Council enacted Constitution and created High Court

1903

March 2, Crown Lands Ordinance
May 8, M'wanga, ex-King of Uganda died

1904

June 16, Tax Collection Ordinance
Sept. 23, Poll tax agreement

1905

Nov. 15, Native Courts Ordinance

1906

Early Jan., Sentence of death pronounced by the Uganda court on the two Waganda chiefs accused of the murder of Mr. Galt, sub-commissioner of Uganda, on May 19, 1905, quashed by the court of appeal at Mombasa; the prisoners released, reported

Feb. 3, Land Transfer Ordinance, no land to be transferred from native to non-native without consent Government

1907

Oct. 18, H. J. Bell appointed governor of Uganda

1908

May, Severe famine through failure of the crops; 4,000 deaths reported; 'ꞓe government feeds 50,000 natives
June 5, Land Transfer law enacted
June 12, Registration of Land Titles Ordinance

1909

Feb. 15, Order in Council established Court of Appeals
June 5, New Poll Tax Agreement
Aug. 11, Native Courts Ordinance of 1905 amended
Nov. 17, Report of Sir Hesketh Bell stated that measures adopted for prevention of sleeping sickness had reduced deaths in 1908 to 3,662 (1898–1906, 200,000 deaths in Buganda and Busoga)

1910

Jan., Captain H. E. S. Cordeaux appointed Governor and Commander-in-Chief

1911

March, Sir Frederick John Jackson appointed Governor and Commander-in-Chief

1912

Jan. 1, The Busoga railway 61 miles long from Jinja on Lake Victoria to the first navigable point on the Nile at Namasagali opened
Jan., Formal transfer to Uganda of district of Kigezi (2,056 square miles) former German East Africa and western shores of Albert Nyanza with adjacent strip of territory to the Belgian Congo from Uganda

1914

April, Agreement transferred northernmost part of protectorate east of the Nile to the Sudan Government and Uganda received from the Sudan some 4,000 square miles west of the Nile and north of Albert Nyanza
Aug. 5, Mobilization of natives ordered
Aug. 8, Daudi Chaw, the King of Buganda, attained his majority
Aug. 11, Ordinance provided for calling the Reserves out for active service
Aug. 16, First 1,000 native carriers left for service in East Africa

1915

March 31, The population 2,927,429, natives 2,923,031, Asiatics 3,560, Europeans 903
June 1, Railroad from Port Bell to Kampala opened for traffic

1918

Feb., Sir R. F. Coryndon succeeded as Governor
During the War 60,000 natives recruited for carriers, 100,000 "job porters" and 10,000 African soldiers

1920

April 12, Poll tax of 15 shillings enacted and regulations Nov. 30 for collection of hut and poll tax, exemptions, penalties, &c.

June 5, Royal instructions reconstituted Executive and Legislative Councils
Aug. 24, Agreement as to land tax by which every native of Buganda with land of 5 acres paid 20 shillings

1921

March 23, First session of new Legislative Council to which various sections of the community nominated members. The Indians declined to send a representative

1923

May 15, Native Authority (Amendment) Ordinance
Nov. 30, Master and Servant Ordinance

1926

Dec. 31, Population 3,136,946, natives 3,123,581, Asiatics 11,613, Europeans 1,752

1927

Jan. 1, New Cotton (Tax) Ordinance came into effect calculating tax on sliding scale according to closing price of Liverpool Cotton Exchange on Dec. 14, 15, or 16, tax for 1927 was 2 cents on the pound of lint
Feb. 21, Death of Sir Apolo Kagwa, Prime Minister of Buganda, and Regent 1900 to 1914
Oct. 8, Kenya and Uganda Railway Ordinance provided regulations for control and management of railroad and steamship service
Dec. 19, Ordinance provided for development and regulation of education and established an Advisory Council for native education

1928

Jan. 1, Native laws came into effect in Buganda by which rents and dues payable by native tenants to native landlords were limited and stabilized and the customary right to free labor of natives on public works regulated
Jan. 11, Railroad from Kenya to Uganda completed and opened to Jinja which enabled the cotton crop to be sent direct to Mombasa
Sept.–October, Visit of the Prince of Wales
Dec. 4, Ordinance for control of arms and ammunition
——, Ordinance to provide for and regulate supply of water to the public

1930

March 27, Code of criminal law and of procedure promulgated
March 29, Ordinance established public markets
Sept. 29, Regulations published as to employment of children between 12 and 14 in factories and workshops under license

UPPER VOLTA

Upper Volta, colony of French West Africa, was formed by a decree of March 1, 1919, from the southern section of the Upper Senegal Niger. It lies within the bend of the Niger. By a decree of December 28, 1926, the circle of Say and the eastern part of the circle of Dori were detached from the colony and added to the colony of the Niger.

The eastern boundary, therefore, follows an irregular line through the villages Yatakala, Bossé,

Tangou, and Botou; its southern boundary is formed by the river Mekrou and the northern boundary of Dahomey, Togoland, the Gold Coast, and the Ivory Coast; thence the boundary runs in a northeasterly direction from the river Bagoë to the Niger, about 16° N., below Ansongo. It embraces the circles of Gaoua, Bobo-Dioulasso, Dédougou, Ouagadougou, Ouahigouya, Teukodogo, Kaya, Koudougo, Fada, and Batiá. Area about 142,000 square miles, and native population 3,091,462 (census 1928), with 450 Europeans. The administrative center is Ouagadougou (population 10,000); other towns are Bobo-Dioulasso (10,000), Dedougou (3,000), and Ouahigouya (6,000). Administratively, it is on the same footing as the other Colonies of French West Africa.

ZANZIBAR

Zanzibar, a Sultanate and British Protectorate in East Africa, the sultanate reduced to the islands of Zanzibar and Pemba and adjacent islets and the nominal sovereignty of the coast strip 10 miles deep, the Kenya Protectorate.

The island of Zanzibar is situated in 6° S. latitude, and is separated from the mainland by a channel 22½ miles across at its narrowest part. It is the largest coralline island on the African coast, being 53 miles long by 24 broad, and having an area of 640 square miles. To the north-east, at a distance of some 25 miles, lies the Island of Pemba in 5° S. latitude, 42 miles long by 14 broad, having an area of 380 square miles. The population of Zanzibar according to the census of 1924 was 128,099, and for Pemba 88,691. The Islands supply provide the bulk of the world's supply of cloves. The ancient Zenj empire comprising Zanzibar and the eastern coast with capital at Kilwa began to decline with the appearance of the Portuguese at the close of the fifteenth century. Pedro Alvares Cabral, the Portuguese navigator, was the first European to visit Kilwa on his way to India in 1500. The Portuguese occupied Kilwa in 1505 and Zanzibar. In 1698 the Portuguese were expelled, Zanzibar, Pemba, Mombassa, and Kilwa becoming dependencies of the Inmans of Muscat, and in 1832 Sayyid Said of Muscat made Zanzibar the capital of his dominions. At the death of Said in 1856 his African dominions fell to his son Majid, and from this time Zanzibar separated from Muscat, confirmed by award of Lord Canning, Governor General of India. In 1862 March 10 Declaration of Great Britain and France recognized the independence of Zanzibar. Barghash Seyyid became Sultan on Oct. 7, 1870 on the death of his brother. The present Sultan is Seyyid Khalifa bin Harub.

1873

June 5, The Sultan signed Treaty with Great Britain

prohibiting export of slaves and closing public slave markets

1876

Jan. 15 and April 18, Proclamations of the Sultan abolishing slavery and slave trade

1885

April 27, Sultan Barghash protested to German Government against treaties made in East Africa acquiring districts over which he claimed jurisdiction, obliged to withdraw protest and accept German ultimatum Aug. 11

1886

Oct. 29 & Nov. 1, Treaty with Germany comes into force, Aug. 19, 1886. The sultan's rights recognized by Anglo-German treaty

Nov. 8, The Sultan adhered to the West African settlement of Jan. 7, 1885, prohibiting the slave trade

1887

Feb.–March, Rupture with Portugal respecting non-cession of territories (see Mozambique)

May 24, Cession territory to British East Africa company

1888

March 26, Seyyid Barghash died; succeeded by his brother Seyyid Khalifah

April 28, Fifty year lease of strip of coast to Germans. See Tanganyika

June 6, Dispute with Italy respecting cession of territories by the late Sultan

Oct. 9, Territories ceded to the British East Africa company; treaty signed

Oct. 17, Lieut. Cooper captures a dhow but is killed

Dec. 7, The coast blockaded by Germany and England, Dec. 2; the Germans make war on the chiefs, who burn Bagamoyo and retire

1889

Jan. 11–13, The Arab slave dealers attack some German stations and carry off the freed slaves; eight missionaries killed

Jan. 21, Mr. Brooks and 26 others, missionaries, murdered near Saadani

July 19, 20, Meeting of the Sultan's bodyguard stopped by the intervention of Mr. Portal and Gen. Mathews

Sept. 1, The Sultan signs a concession of territory to the British East Africa company

Oct. 1, The blockade on the coast abandoned after

Oct., Ordered that all native children born in Zanzibar after Jan. 1, 1890, to be free subjects of the Sultan

Oct. 25, The Marquis of Salisbury receives the two envoys from Zanzibar; received by Queen Victoria at Balmoral Oct. 29

Nov. 14, Gerald Portal leaves Africa

Dec. 6, Mr. Stanley and party arrive at Zanzibar

Dec. 26, The Sultan surrenders all control over the British East Africa company's territory for an annual payment, reported

1890

Feb. 16, Expedition from Aden to Harrar under Gen. Hogg, to chastise the Eesa tribe for a murderous raid on Bulhar, Somaliland, on Jan. 11, reported successful, with some loss

Feb. 17, Death of the Sultan, Seyyid Khalifah, by apoplexy, succeeded by his brother, Seyyid Ali

June 18, The protectorate of Zanzibar, Witu, &c., assumed by Great Britain with the consent of the Sultan, in conformity with the Anglo-German convention, announced

July 1, Anglo-German Boundary Agreement. (*See* Africa) recognized British protectorate and German claims to Witu withdrawn

Aug. 1, Decree of the Sultan against slavery; the sale, purchase, or exchange of slaves strictly prohibited; slaves of persons dying without lawful heirs, declared free; slaves not to be disposable by will, &c.

Sept. 14, Herr Küntzel and a party of Germans in Witu, or Witu, disarmed by the Sultan

Sept. 15, Küntzel's conduct leads to the massacre by the natives of all the party except Menschel

Oct. 23, Redress demanded by the British and Germans; the Sultan of Witu refuses to surrender the criminals

Oct. 25, 26, An expedition under Captain Curzen-Howe and Commander M'Quhae; certain evacuated villages on the coast burnt; Adm. Fremantle at Kipini; the Admiral, with nearly 1,000 men, advances on Witu

Oct. 27, Witu captured and destroyed, the enemy disperse; there were 13 British wounded; the success of the expedition was mainly attributed to Capt. Curzon-Howe, the chief of the staff

Nov. 4, British Protectorate over Zanzibar formally proclaimed

1891

Jan. 14, Death of the deposed Sultan of Witu

Jan. 26, Sir C. B. Euan-Smith makes terms with the Witu chiefs; a younger brother of the late Sultan elected successor, announced; peace and amnesty proclaimed about Jan. 29

March 6, Sir C. B. Euan-Smith leaves for Europe (succeeded by Gerald Portal)

July 20, Tipoo Tib at Zanzibar, received by the Sultan

Dec. 20, Import duties, except on alcohol and dangerous objects, abolished

1892

Feb. 1, Zanzibar declared a free port

Nov. 9, The international bureau, for the suppression of the slave trade, first meeting at Zanzibar; Sir Gerald Portal, president

Sir Gerald Portal sent to Uganda (*see s.v.*)

About Dec. 12, Mr. Rennell Rodd, deputy

1893

March 5, Death of the Sultan; succeeded by Said Hamed bin Thwain, grand-nephew, proclaimed by Mr. Rodd; the King's son set aside

April 10, May 2, Rescue of 60 children from an Arab dhow, with French colors, by *Philomel*, an English cruiser, reported

July 12, The Benadir ports and territories conceded to Italy for 3 years

Nov. 22, Capt. Filouardi starts an Italian trading company, headquarters at Magadoxo, reported

1894

Feb., Death of Sir Gerald Portal, consul-general, Jan. 25; succeeded by Mr. Arthur Henry Hardinge

1895

July 1, British E. Africa company's territory transferred to the British Government under the jurisdiction of Mr. (aft. Sir) A. Hardinge

Dec. 14, Agreement of the Sultan for British administration of the Sultan's dominions on the mainland and the adjacent islands except Zanzibar and Pemba

1896

May, Four slavers captured by H.M.S. *Barossa*, and the persons implicated imprisoned

Aug. 25, Death of the Sultan, aged about 40; Said Khalid, his cousin, at once takes possession of the palace, and proclaims himself Sultan

Aug. 27, British ultimatum, sent by Rear-Adm. Rawson, 7 A.M., bombardment began, 9 A.M.; firing ceased, 9.40 A.M.; Sultan's corvette, *Glasgow*, sunk; usurper Khalid surrenders to the German consul; enemy's loss heavy; the late Sultan's brother, Said Hamud bin Mahomed, proclaimed Sultan; looting, &c., in the town suppressed by the British

Sept., The Sultan in full accord with the British; the military, financial, and executive departments placed under their control

Oct. 2, The usurper, Said Khalid, taken on board the German sloop, *Seeadler*

1897

April 6, Slavery abolished, with compensation, by the Sultan's decree

July 9, British judicial system introduced, by orders in council

1899

Sept. 15, New 5% duty on imports, with a few exceptions

1901

Oct. 11, Gen. Sir Lloyd Wm. Mathews, Prime Minister and Treasurer, dies, aged 51

1902

July 18, Death of the Sultan Hamud, aged 51

July 20, Seyyid Ali, aged 18, proclaimed Sultan; Mr. Rogers, regent

1906

Sept. 19, Strike of native troops and police for an increase of pay

Sept. 20, Disaffection among native troops

1908

July, Wireless telegraphy installed between the islands of Pemba and Zanzibar

1909

Aug. 4–Oct. 8, Sultan visits London, April 30, 1906; Oct. 9, 1907; July, 1908; and again

1911

Dec. 9, Seyyid Khalifa bin Harub succeeded as Sultan on abdication of his brother-in-law Ali bin Hamoud bin Mahomed and was installed on the 16th

1912

Aug. 23, Decree of the Sultan regulating native liquor, limited to 3% alcohol

1913

July 1, Control of the Protectorate transferred from the Foreign Office to the Colonial Office, the Governor of the East Africa Protectorate becoming High Commissioner for Zanzibar, local affairs under a

British Resident who took over functions of first Minister

1914

Jan. 21, Two Orders in Council as to British jurisdiction in Zanzibar and administration of Protectorate, a Council established

Aug. 5, The Sultan proclaimed alliance with Great Britain and war with Germany

Aug. 13, The Sultan declared war on Austria-Hungary

Sept. 20, The British cruiser "Pegasus," at anchor in Zanzibar waters undergoing repairs, sunk by the German cruiser "Königsberg"

Nov. 5, The Sultan declared war on Turkey

1915

Oct. 18, The Sultan declared war on Bulgaria

1925

Sept. 5, The post of British High Commissioner abolished and duties transferred to British Resident

1926

Jan. 15, Decree of the Sultan providing for establishment of Executive and Legislative Councils

March 2, First meeting of Executive Council presided over by Sultan

March 5, First meeting of Legislative Council inaugurated by the Sultan presided over by the British Resident, has 3 ex-officio official members and 5 others, and 6 unofficial members representing various communities

1927

Oct. 28, Decree raised import duties from 10 to 15% ad valorem

ZULULAND

Zululand, South-east Africa, ceded to Great Britain Oct. 5, 1843, capital, Eshowe; near the British colony, Natal, to which it has been annexed Dec. 1, 1897.

1812 to 1876

About 1812, Godongwana, a chief (termed Dingiswayo, "the Wanderer," from his early life), began a military organization by forming a celibate army; killed in battle and succeeded by Chaka, styled King

May 6, 1835, Chaka assassinated; succeeded by his brother Dingaan, crafty, treacherous, and cruel; at first friendly with the British at Natal (*see s.v.*); made treaty with Capt. Allen Gardiner

1838, Massacres Retief, 70 Boers, and their servants (who had recovered his stolen cattle), Feb. 2, and about 600 afterwards; defeats the British and Dutch in several encounters; but is severely beaten by Andries Pretorius, Dec.

1840 *et seq.*, Dingaan again defeated; killed by one of his chiefs; succeeded by his brother Umpanda

Oct., 1872, Cetywayo (pronounced Ketchwáyo), his eldest son, kills his brothers; succeeds at his father's death; organizes still further his army, named by Frere "the celibate man-slaying war-machine"

Sept. 1, 1873, Recognized on behalf of the British by Mr. Shepstone; crowned

1876, Opposes missionaries; organizes armed resistance to the British

1878

Jan., Sir Bartle Frere, governor of the Cape, requests help from England; 90th regiment and a battery sent

Dec., Cetywayo refuses to give up leaders of a raid on British territory (in July); and tenders a fine; Sir Bartle Frere demands, as an ultimatum, their surrender within 30 days

1879

Jan. 12, The time (extended) having elapsed, Jan. 11, the British, under Lord Chelmsford, cross the Tugela and enter Zululand

Jan. 21, Col. Pearson defeats the Zulus and advances to Echowe (which he fortifies)

Jan. 22, British camp at Isandula or Isandlwana, about 10 miles from Rorke's Drift (on the Tugela), surprised and attacked by about 15,000 Zulus; 5 companies of the 24th regiment, and many natives killed, with Cols. Durnford and Pulleine, and other officers; total loss about 837; 2,000 Zulus killed; (Lieuts. Melville and Coghill perished while preserving the colors)

——, Rorke's Drift severely attacked; successfully defended by Lieuts. Chard and Bromhead

Jan. 24, Zulus attack Inkanyana; defeated by Col. Evelyn Wood

Feb. 19 *et seq.*, Reinforcements from England

Feb. 27, Prince Louis Napoleon requesting to join the British, permitted to go as a guest; sails

March 11, Arrival of the *Tamar* with 800 men, &c., at Pietermaritzburg

March 12, British convoy near Itombi river cut to pieces by Zulus; Capt. Moriarty killed

March 18, Cetywayo's brother Oham, with 600 men, joins the British; announced

March 29, Col. Evelyn Wood attacks the Zulus on the Zlobani mountains; suffers much loss, March 28; gains victory at Kambula

——, British advance to relieve Echowe

April 2, Zulus defeated at Ginghilovo

April 2, 3, Col. Pearson marches out of Echowe

May, Sir Garnet Wolseley appointed commander-in-chief, Governor of Natal, &c., sails for the Cape

May 27, British total loss; 1,186 killed; 86 died of disease; announced

May, Cetywayo said to have suppressed an insurrection, and retired to his kraal at Ulundi

June 1, Reconnoitring party, under Capt. J. Brenton Carey, on Imbabani, near the Mozani river, surprised; Prince Louis Napoleon (acting as commander) killed

June 12, Ultimatum sent to Cetywayo, requiring total submission; time expired

June 23, Sir G. Wolseley arrives at the Cape

June 28 or 29, Sir Garnet Wolseley sworn in as high commissioner at Pietermaritzburg

July 4, Cetywayo totally defeated at Ulundi

July 12 *et seq.*, Sir G. Wolseley receives chiefs

July 15, Lord Chelmsford resigns

Aug. 22, Sentence upon Capt. Carey, respecting death of Prince Napoleon, quashed

Aug. 28, Cetywayo captured by Major R. Marter

Sept. 1, Meeting of Sir G. Wolseley with Zulu chiefs; settlement by treaty; Zululand to be divided into 13 independent districts; John Dunn to be a chief;

lands reserved for the British; British residents in each district (to be eyes and ears); celibate military system abolished; no arms to be imported; ancient laws and liberties retained; [John Dunn, 20 years in Zululand; conformed to Zulu ways]
Sept. 15, Cetywayo arrives at Cape Town

1881

July 11, His petition for restitution declined
July 30, John Dunn subdues a revolting chief
Cost of Zulu war, 4,922,141*l.*
Sept., Sir Evelyn Wood visits Zululand
Dec., The country reported quiet by John Dunn

1882

Aug. 3, Cetywayo arrives in London
Aug. 9, Visited Mr. Gladstone; received by the Queen, Aug. 14; by the Prince of Wales Aug. 16
Sept. 1, His restoration to part of his kingdom with restrictions, proposed by the British Government Aug.; sails from Southampton
Dec. 29, Changes made in the territories previous to Cetywayo's return, announced

1883

Jan. 29, Cetywayo's restoration accepted; proclaimed at Ulundi
April 25, Struggle between Cetywayo and chiefs
May 16, Cetywayo defeated by Oham and others
June, Mr. Fynn, British resident, resigns
July 21, Cetywayo is attacked at Ulundi, by Usibepu, July 20; and captured
Aug. 16, Great battle; Usibepu defeated by Cetywayo's supporters, announced
Aug. 20, Cetywayo demands a British enquiry
About Oct. 15, Cetywayo surrenders to Mr. Osborn, and is taken to Durban; at Ekowe Nov. 5
Nov., Defeats of Usibepu by other chiefs

1884

Jan. 27, 28, Flight, and recapture of Cetywayo
About Jan. 31, Zibedu defeats Usutus
Feb. 8, Cetywayo dies of heart disease
May 21, Dinizulu, son of Cetywayo, crowned king by the Boers; grants an amnesty, and promises fidelity to the British
June 14, Usibepu, severely defeated by the Boers and Usutus, flees, announced
Aug., A Boer republic established; Joubert, president
Dec. 18, British flag hoisted at St. Lucia's bay

1886

Jan., Quietness in Zululand reported
Nov., Proposed annexation of Zululand to Natal declined, Oct.; British protectorate over the Zulu territories planned by government
Nov. 4, Agreement with the Boer republic

1887

June 21, Annexation of Zululand as a British possession; the governor to rule by proclamation, May 14; proclaimed at Durban
Nov. 5, Troubles with Dinizulu announced; his uncle Undabuko and others submit to Sir Arthur Havelock, announced Nov. 7; military preparations; Dinizulu submits, Nov. 13; Usibepu reinstated in his lands Nov. 15

1888

June 2, The chiefs attacked by the police and military for stealing cattle
——, Zulu rebels under Ishingana defeated after a severe conflict
July 11, Rebellion of Dinizulu announced
Aug. 1, Somkeli, the rebel chief, surrenders
Aug. 29, Dinizulu and about 1,000 rebels with cattle enters into the Transvaal territory, Aug. 10; revolt ended; reported
Sept., Dinizulu surrenders conditionally to the Transvaal government
Sept. 27, Surrender of Undabuko, Sept. 19; his trial began
Nov. 12, Ishingana, rebel chief, surrenders
Nov. 15, Trial of Undabuko and Somkeli for treason, began
Nov., Dinizulu surrenders to the British
Nov. 22, Somhlolo sentenced to five years' hard labor for high treason

1889

April 27, Dinizulu sentenced to ten years', Undabuko to 15 years', and Ishingana to 12 years' imprisonment

1890

Jan. 15, Douglas M'Kenzie, appointed Bishop of Zululand in 1880, dies, announced
Feb. 7, Dinizulu, Undabuko, and others, transported to St. Helena

1895

April 23, Tongaland annexed
Aug. 6, Death of John Dunn, announced

1897

Dec. 1, Province of Zululand annexed to Natal
Dec. 27, Amaputaland Protectorate, created June 11, 1895, annexed to Zululand

1903

Jan. 27, Northern Districts, so-called, territory (consisting of the Magisterial Divisions of Vryheid, Utrecht, Paulpietersburg, and Babanango, annexed to Natal
See Natal
Jan., Rev. Wilmot Vyvyan appointed Bishop of Zululand on translation of Dr. Carter to diocese of Pretoria
End Jan., Col. Mills's report on fight between Boers and Zulus at Holkrantz (*see* S. African war, May 6, 1902) exonerates the Zulus, published
Early Feb., Engineer's report on the scheme for a harbor in Zululand condemns St. Lucia Bay, and recommends Umlatoosi again
Sept. 17, Zulu railway extension opened at Hlabisa

1906

April 7-8, Bambaata, a chief in the Greytown district, who had been deposed by the Natal government, revolted and fled into Zululand; two Zulu chiefs, Siganandi and N'Dubi, refuse to coöperate in his pursuit, April 17; 200 Zulus attack Colonel Mansel's vanguard, 60 Zulus and 3 British killed, May 5; surrender of Siganada's induna Mpikwa with two of his headsmen and 70 other rebels, June 1; surrender of Siganada and his son, June 13; official statement of Siganada's death given, July 23; Zulu chiefs

Tilonko and Sikikuku found guilty of high treason and sentenced to 10 years' hard labor and fined 500 head of cattle each, Oct. 13; Gobizembi, deposed Zulu chief, reported dead Dec. 29

1908

Feb. 1, Sir M. Nathan, governor of Natal, leaves Pieter-maritzburg for a tour through Zululand

Feb. 3, Free pardon to the rank and file concerned in the rebellion of 1906, announced

See South African War

1909

March, Dinizulu sentenced to 4 years' imprisonment for harboring rebels. Released by General Botha in 1910. He died in 1913 on his farm in the Transvaal

ASIA

Asia is the largest of the continents with an area of 17,200,000 square miles, contained entirely in the northeast hemisphere extending from within the Arctic circle nearly to the Equator at Singapore at end of Malay Peninsula 1.5° N. The greatest length from north to south is 5,300 miles, and from east to west to Cape Baba on the Mediterranean 6,820 miles. Asia contains about one-third of the dry land and one-twelfth of the entire surface of the globe. Except for the continent of Europe on the northwest Asia is surrounded by water, the Arctic Ocean on the north, the Pacific on the east, and the Indian Ocean on the south. The Suez Canal separates Asia from Africa, and the Bering Strait from North America. Mt. Everest in the Himalayas is the highest mountain in the world, 29,141 feet above sea level, and the lowest part of the Dead Sea in Palestine is 1,293 feet below sea level. Russia and Great Britain control about two-fifths of Asia. The independent States are Afghanistan, China, Japan, Persia, Siam, and certain states of Arabia freed from Turkey after the World War. Palestine, Trans-Jordan, Iraq, and Syria are mandated territories.

ADEN

Aden and the Aden (British) Protectorate form a peninsula on the Yemen coast of Arabia near the entrance to the Red Sea 100 miles east of the Straits of Bab-el-Mandeb, including the peninsula of Little Aden, and settlement and town of Shaikh Othman on the mainland with the villages of Imad and Hiswa. The Settlement also includes the island of Perim at entrance to the Red Sea and the island of Sokotra off the coast of Africa and the Kuria Muria Islands off the coast of Arabia are also attached to Aden. The area of Aden and Little Aden is 75 square miles, Aden proper 21 square miles, population 43,106, Little Aden, area 15 square miles, population 565, coast strip area (Shaik Othman) 39 square miles, population 10,754. The Aden Protectorate to the north and northeast has an area of about 9,000 square miles and population of over 100,000. The area of Perim is 5 square miles, population 2,000; of Sokotra 1,382 square miles, population about 12,000; the Kuria Muria Islands, five in number, off the southeast coast of Arabia, were ceded by the Inman of Muskat in 1854 for the purpose of landing the Red Sea telegraph cable, total area 28 square miles, Hallania, the largest being 22 square miles. Aden, after being a trade center under its native kings, became subject in succession to the Abyssinians, the Persians, and the early Caliphs. In 1538 it was captured by the Turks Solyman the Magnificent, but a successful revolt again restored its freedom, but recaptured by the Turks in 1551 and held until 1630, subsequently held by one Arab chief after another. In January 1839 Aden was attacked and taken by British ships, and annexed to British India. Little Aden was secured by purchase in 1868. The frontiers were demarcated by British-Ottoman Conventions of April, 1905, and 1914. The coastal strip between the 2 peninsulas was secured by purchases in 1882 and 1888. The Settlement forms part of British India and is subject to the Government of Bombay. By an Order in Council, August 15, 1929, the superintendence, direction, and control of the military government of Aden and its dependencies are transferred from the Viceroy of India to the Resident and Commander-in-Chief at Aden.

Lieut.-Colonel Sir Stewart Symes, Resident and Commander-in-Chief.

AFGHANISTAN

Afghanistan, country of Asia lying between parallels 29° and 38.20° N. Lat., and 61° and 72° E. Long. (Wákhán). The extreme breadth from north-east to south-west is about 700 miles; its length from the Herát frontier to the Kháibar Pass about 600 miles; area given variously as about 245,000 or 270,000 square miles. It is bounded on the north by Turkmenistan, on the west by Persia, and on the east and south by British India (Kashmir, Punjaub, Baluchistan). The population according to the latest estimate is about eleven millions. The government is, since 1922, a constitutional monarchy, the title of King replacing that of Amir in 1926.

Nadir Khan, reigning King, called to the throne Oct. 16, 1929

1200 to 1838

1200–1290, Early Afghan conquests in India

About 1221, Conquests of Genghis Khan, and by Tamerlane, 1398

1525, Baber conquered Cabul

On his death Afghanistan divided between Persia and Hindostan

1738, The Afghans revolt in 1720; invade Persia and take Ispahan; repulsed by Nadir Shah in 1728, who subdues the whole of the country

1747–73, On his assassination, one of his officers, Ahmed Shah, an Afghan, made Afghanistan independent, and reigned prosperously

1793, Timur Shah (son), succeeds, 1773; rules cruelly; dies leaving 23 sons

1800, Zeman becomes Ameer, 1793; cripples the power of the sirdars; blinded and dethroned

1816, Mahmud Shah, son, Ameer 1800; deposed for his brother, Suja Shah, 1803; Mahmud restored, Futtih Khan the vizier predominant, 1809; Futtih blinded; Mahmud flees from Cabul and becomes ruler at Herat

1826, Impotent rulers at Kabul; Dost Mohammed Khan becomes ameer

1838, He is dethroned by the British, and sent to Calcutta; Suja Shah restored

1841

Nov. 2, British occupation of Kabul causes great discontent; insurrection; Sir Alexander Burnes and 23 others killed

Dec. 23, Akbar Khan, son of Dost Mohammed, head of the rebels; invites Sir Wm. Macnaghten to meet, and assassinates him and others

1842

Jan. 6–13, The British army retires from Kabul, and is destroyed by the Ghilzais in the Khyber pass; of 3,849 soldiers, and about 12,000 camp followers, only Dr. Brydone and four or five natives escaped massacre

Oct. 12, Sir George Pollock forces the Khyber pass; defeats Akbar Khan at Tezeen; captures Kabul and releases Lady Sale and others, Sept. 16; destroys the great bazaar; retires

Dost Mohammed becomes Ameer

1863

Sept., He dies leaving 16 sons; appointing as his successor Shere Ali, the third son, June 9; who is much opposed by his brothers, especially by Ufzul, the eldest son (and his son Abdul-Rahman, or Abdur-Rahman), Azim, Ameen, and Shureef; yet is recognized by them

1864

June 2, Unsuccessful insurrection of Ufzul and Azim; Azim flees to British territories, May 16; Ufzul reconciled to Shere Ali

Aug., Insurrection of Abdul-Rahman; Ufzul imprisoned

Nov. 14, Shere Ali enters Kabul

1865

June 14, Azim and his confederates defeated at Kujhboz, near Khelat-i-Ghilzye, by Shere Ali (whose gallant son is killed), June 6; he enters Candahar

1866

March 2, Azim joins his nephew Abdul-Rahman; defection of Mahomed Rufeek from Ibrahim (Shere Ali's son) weakly ruling Kabul; it surrenders to Azim

May 10, Shere Ali rouses himself from his grief; raises an army; some of his treacherous friends return to him; he is defeated at Sheikhabad, and flees to Candahar

May et seq., Ufzul (sensual and easy), and Azim (cruel and tyrannical) rule at Kabul

1867

Jan., Azim and Abdul-Rahman defeat Shere Ali at Kujhbaz, Jan. 17; he flees to Candahar: shut out, flees to Herat held by his son, Yakoob

Sept. 17, His army again defeated and his general and brother, Fyz Mahommed, killed

Oct., Ufzul dies; Azim sole ruler at Kabul

1868

March, He quarrels with Abdul-Rahman; who leaves him, and refuses to help him

April, Yakoob defeats Azim's troops, and enters Candahar

Sept. 8, Azim leaves Kabul, July; his army dissolves by desertion; Shere Ali enters Kabul

Nov.–Dec., Sir John Lawrence helps Shere Ali with arms and money, the attempts of Abdul-Rahman repulsed

1869

Jan., Shere Ali totally defeats him and Azim (who dies soon after)

March 27 et seq., Shere Ali honorably received at Umballah by the Viceroy, the Earl of Mayo, and receives a subsidy

1870

June, The limits of his territories defined, about

May 6, His son, Yakoob, rebels; captures Herat

1871

June, Feramoz Khan, his father's general, assassinated

Sept., Yakoob reconciled to his father through Lord Mayo, July; made governor of Herat; soon rebels

Oct., Uslum, murderer of Feramoz, killed in prison

1873

Dec., Shere Ali agrees to new boundaries, and receives another British subsidy, Oct.; nominates his youngest son, Abdoola Jan, his successor, to the great dissatisfaction of his older son Yakoob

1874

About Dec., Yakoob Khan, imprisoned by his father

1877

1877–78, Shere Ali refusing to allow a British Resident, the subsidy withheld; he raises an army, and is said to promote disaffection to the British

1878

Aug. 17, Death of the heir Abdoola Jan

Aug., Stolietoff, a Russian envoy, favorably received at

Kabul, June; a treaty signed; Russia to be the guardian of the Ameer

Sept., The Nawab Gholam Hussein Khan sent as envoy to the Ameer with letters from the Viceroy (Aug. 16 and 24), Aug. 30; dismissed with presents; intercourse with the British declined

Sept. 21, A mission with military escort under Sir Neville B. Chamberlain, commander of the Madras army, starts from Peshawur

Oct. 28, At Ali Musjid, a fort in the Khyber pass, Major Cavagnari and an advance party are threatened with attack if they proceed, Sept. 22; they retire to Peshawur, Sept. 23, 24; Gholam Hussein sent with an ultimatum (answer required before Nov. 20)

About Nov. 16, British army formed in three divisions: at Quettah, Peshawur, and Kuram (34,730 natives, 12,740 Europeans)

Nov. 21, No answer received from the Ameer; the army advances

Nov. 22, Ali Musjid shelled and occupied by the British; 21 guns taken; Major Birch and Lieut. Fitzgerald and about 35 men killed

Nov. 23, Occupation of Dakka and Pisheen; of Kuram fort Nov. 25

Dec. 1, Kuddum burnt to punish marauding hillmen

Dec. 2, Gen. Roberts victorious at Peiwar pass

Dec. 20, The British occupy Jellalabad

Dec., Shere Ali flees from Cabul to Balkh, Dec. 13; Yakoob Khan assumes command; the Russian mission withdraws

Dec. 26, Gen. Roberts proclaims annexation of Kuram district, &c.

1879

Jan. 7, He enters the Khoost territory Jan. 3; defeats the Mangals near Matoon

——, Candahar abandoned, Jan. 6; entered by General Stewart unopposed

Jan., Wali Mahomed, a relative of Shere Ali, joins the British

Feb. 16, The Alizais defeated in an attack

Feb. 20, Death of Shere Ali, the Ameer (announced)

March 31, About 46 of the 10th hussars drowned by current while crossing the Kabul river, 10 P.M.

April 2, Gen. Gough, with the 10th hussars and others, defeats about 5,000 Khugianis near Futtehabad; gallant Major Wigram Batty killed

May 9, Yakoob Khan, son of the late Ameer, arrives at Gandamak to negotiate, May 8; recognized as Ameer

June 8, Treaty of peace signed at Gandamak; (the British to occupy Khyber pass, and the Kuram and Pisheen valleys; to have a Resident at Kabul; and to pay an annual subsidy of 60,000*l.* per ann.), May 26; ratified May 30; the British troops retire

July 24, Sir Louis Cavagnari and escort honorably received in Kabul

Sept. 3, 4, Several regiments of Afghan soldiers arrive in Kabul from Herat; about Aug. 13 aided by the populace they besiege the British residents, who after a brave resistance are massacred (including Sir L. Cavagnari, Mr. Jenkyns, his secretary, Lieut. Hamilton, and Dr. Ambrose Kelly), with about 26 native cavalry and 50 infantry; a few natives escape

Sept. 5, Mutiny at Herat; military and civil governors killed

Sept. 6 *et seq.*, Gen. Roberts marches towards Kabul

Sept. 19, Repulse of an attack on Baker's entrenchments at Shutargardan

Sept. 22, A British convoy attacked by Mongols, near Shutargardan; 8 sepoys and 15 muleteers killed; mules taken

Sept. 27, Gen. Baker reaches Kushi Sept. 24; receives the Ameer Yakoob and his son, his General Daoud, and suite

Sept. 29, Gen. Roberts arrives at Kabul, Sept. 28; occupies Dakka

Oct. 2, Attack on British camp at Shutargardan repulsed

Oct. 6, Battle of Char-asiab; severe conflict with Afghans before Kabul; Captain Young, Dr. Duncan, Lieut. Fergusson, and about 70 killed and wounded

Oct. 8–9, The enemy decamps; about 98 guns abandoned; pursued by cavalry; small parties only overtaken

Oct. 11, Gen. Roberts visits the abandoned Bala Hissar; enters Kabul, Oct. 12; Jellalabad occupied by Gough

Oct. 14, Gen. Roberts, proclamation; heavy fine; martial law; Gen. Hills to be military governor, with Gholab Hussein Khan

Oct. 16, Great explosions (supposed treacherous) in the Bala Hissar; destruction of much arms and ammunition; Capt. Shafto and about 20 others missing

Oct. 19, Abdication of Yakoob Khan announced

Oct. 20–24, 5 prisoners (mollahs and others) hanged as murderers of Major Cavagnari and others

Oct. 24, Sahib Jan, a freebooter, with a strong force of Taraki Ghilzais, defeated and killed by General Hughes at Shahjui, near Candahar

Oct. 30, Proclamation of Gen. Roberts announcing British occupation of Kabul, &c.

Nov. 6, Junction of columns of Generals Macpherson and Bright at Katasang

Oct., Nov., 163 Afghan mutineers, &c., tried; 87 executed as murderers; 76 released

Dec., Combination of tribes under Mohammed Jan Wardak

Dec. 11–14, Continued severe fighting, with heavy loss on both sides

Dec. 14, Gen. Roberts concentrates his forces in the Sherpur cantonments

About Dec. 17, Musa Khan, son of Yakoob, said to be proclaimed Ameer

Dec. 18, 19, Gen. Gough at Jugdulluk attacked; retreats into the fort, Dec. 16; indecisive conflicts

Dec. 23, The Afghans (25,000) defeated with great loss near Sherpur cantonments, by Gens. Roberts and Gough

Dec. 26, Kabul left by the enemy, Dec. 24; the city and Bala Hissar reoccupied by the British

Dec. 28, The enemy dispersed

Dec. 29, Attack of Afghan chiefs on Col. Norman repulsed at Jugdulluk

1880

About Jan. 6, Gen. Roberts proclaims an amnesty with few exceptions; the hill tribes generally subdued

About Jan. 10, Ghuznee seized and held for Musa Khan as the new ameer, by Mohammed Jan

Jan. 15, Mohmands and other tribes defeated in an attack near Daka

Feb. 6, Correspondence with Russia; papers found in Kabul (to be kept secret)

March 21, Musa Khan and chiefs at Ghuznee submit

About April 3, Mohammed Jan defeated and killed, fighting with Hazaris

April 16, A camp at Duwai attacked by Pathans; garrison killed

April, Shere Ali, cousin of the late Ameer, made Wali or Governor of Candahar by the British

April 19, Gen. Sir Donald Stewart defeats a furious attack of Ghilzais at Ahmad Khel; again near Ghuznee April 23

April 25, Col. Jenkins, at Char-asiab, attacked by 4,000 Logaris; resists till reinforced by Gen. Macpherson; totally defeats them

May 2, Sir D. Stewart takes chief command at Kabul

May 19, 22, Alleged defeats of Safis and Ghazis near Jellalabad

July 1, Gen. Burrows (with about 2,400 men) sent from Bombay towards Candahar

About July 14, The troops of the inefficient wali of Candahar, Shere Ali, revolt and join Ayoob Khan

July 17, Gen. Burrows at Maiwand, near Kusck-i-Nakhud

July 22, Abdul-Rahman, or Abdur-Rahman, born 1845 (see above, 1863 et seq.), recognized as Ameer at Kabul by the British (previously an exile at Samarcand), and proclaimed

July 27, Ayoob Khan (son of the late Ameer, Shere Ali), Governor of Herat, marches upon Candahar with about 20,000 men and 20 guns; defeats the attack of Gen. Burrows after severe conflicts; heavy loss on both sides; many officers of 66th regiment killed

July 28, Candahar citadel held by British with about 4,000 men

Aug. 9, Ayoob encamped at Kokaran

——, Gen. Sir F. Roberts with about 10,000 men, &c., marches from Kabul to relieve Candahar

Aug. 11, Sir D. Stewart, with all the troops, after an interview with the Ameer Abdur-Rahman, withdraws from Kabul

Aug. 16, Attack of Pathans (hill tribes) on the post at Kaeh Amadan firmly beaten off by sepoys; 80 Pathans killed

——, Ineffectual sortie from Candahar, under Gen. Primrose, against Deh Kwajee village, with heavy loss on both sides; Gen. Brooke, Col. Newport, Majors Vandaleur and French, Capt. Cruickshank, Lieut. Marsh, and Rev. Mr. Gordon, and 180 men killed

About Aug. 30, Ayoob Khan's army (strengthened by Ghilzais) about 20,000, about Aug. 25; he retires from Candahar

Sept. 1, Gen. Roberts arrives at Candahar, Aug. 31; declines Ayoob's terms; defeats and disperses his army at Mazra near the Argandab; and captures his camp at Baba Wali Kotal

Oct. 10, Ayoob Khan arrives in Herat; reported

Nov., Tranquillity at Kabul, announced

Dec., Shere Ali, Wali of Candahar, resigns and retires to India

1881

Aug., Alleged expenses of the war, 1878–80, 23,494,480*l*., of which 5,000,000*l*. paid by British exchequer

Feb. 9, 10, Russian correspondence with the Ameer Shere Ali in 1878, published; explained by Russia as relating to probable war in the east

May, June, Prospect of war between Ayoob Khan of Herat and Abdur-Rahman of Kabul

June 3 & 11, Conflicts between partisans of the Ameer and Ayoob Khan; the latter defeated

July 30, Ayoob Khan defeats the Ameer's army under Gholam-Hyder at Karez-i-atta, July 26; enters Candahar

Aug. 6, Gholam Hyder holding Kelat i-Ghilzai; receives reinforcements from Kabul Aug. 21

About Sept. 8, Ayoob prepares to march; the Ameer's troops at Kelat-i-Ghilzai; rejects Ayoob's proposals, Sept. 1–4; marches to Candahar

Sept. 22, Ayoob, defeated at Old Candahar chiefly through desertion of his troops, flees to Herat

Sept. 30, The Ameer enters Candahar

Oct., His army under Abdul-Kudus Khan twice defeats Ayoob's adherents; again Oct. 2

Oct. 4, Enters Herat

——, Ayoob flees to Persia

Oct., Abdur-Rahman now virtual ruler of all Afghanistan

1882

Feb., Afzul Khan chosen by the Ameer as British resident in Kabul

1883

About April 27, The Ameer defeats the Shinwarris

About June 21, Peace made

July 21, Indian government grants subsidy to the Ameer: accepted

Aug. 24, Slight insurrection of the Ghilzais under Mollah Mushki Alum, announced

1884

Aug., The proposal of an Afghan frontier commission accepted by the Ameer

Oct., Dec. Gen. Sir Peter Lumsden with staff proceeds, and successful progress reported

1885

April 8, Penjdeh assured to Afghanistan by Lord Auckland, 1840; Russian advances resisted up to Nov. 1884. The Ameer visits Lord Dufferin, the Viceroy, at Rawul Pindi April 2–12, who declares at a grand dunbar, England and Afghanistan will stand side by side

June 6, Sir Peter Lumsden arrives in London

July, Difference between England and Russia respecting the Zulfikar Pass

——, Strong Russian garrison at Askabad

Aug. 22, The Russians relinquish Zulfikar Pass, announced

Sept. 10, Anglo-Russian Protocol, closing the dispute, signed in London

Oct. 28, Construction of Quetta Railway begun Sept. 1879; stopped Oct. 1880; resumed April 1884. Lower Bolan Railway joining India opened

1886

Feb. 13, Penjdeh given up to Russia, July, 1885, entered

July, Joint Commission appointed; First boundary pillar formally erected Nov. 12, 1885; the last, many perils and privations endured

Sept. 6, Joint Commission dissolved

Oct. 15, Sir Joseph West Ridgeway, chief, and the Commission received at Kabul

Nov., Rising against taxation (treasure seized in transit) about Oct. 30; rebellion said to be repressed

1887

April 19, The Ameer's troops defeated by the Ghilzais, announced; again at Khelat-i-Ghilzai, announced April 25

July 20, Meetings of Afghan Frontier Commission at St. Petersburg; temporarily closed May 12; resumed July 6; question settled

June 9, Mutiny of Ghilzais at Herat, suppressed with much bloodshed

June 13 & 16, General Gholam reported that he defeated the Ghilzais

July 8, The Ameer proclaims peace, amnesty, and remission of taxes for two years, announced

July 13, Taimar Shah chief of the Herat mutineers, executed at Kabul

July 15, Great defeat of the rebels at Mashakai, announced

July 26, Reported conflicting accounts of victory of Gholam Hyder Khan at Kotaldab

Aug. 29, Rebellion said to have collapsed Aug. 21; several tribes return home

Aug. 31, Severe fighting at Mashakai between the Ameer's troops and the insurgents

Early Sept., Escape of Ayoob Khan from Teheran, Aug. 14; enters Afghanistan with a few followers and is driven out

Sept. 7, Fighting near Mukur; rebel leader, Jalander Khan, captured

Sept.–Oct., Reported fighting with varying success

Nov. 9, Ayoob Khan surrenders at Meshed to the Indian Government, announced

Nov. 13, Southern Afghanistan quiet, announced

Nov. 15, Reported conflict between Ameer's troops and the insurgents, 60 killed

Dec. 10, Amnesty proclamation issued by the Ameer

1888

May 9, Conflict between Afghans and Turcomans, Afghans victorious

Aug., Revolt of Ishak Khan, Governor of Afghan Turkestan; defeated at Tash Kurgan Sept. 29, 1888; at Mazari Sherif Sept. 30; Ishak Khan a fugitive in Russian territory

Dec. 26, The Ameer narrowly escapes assassination

1889

Feb. 3, The Ameer's troops under Gholam Hyder defeat the Shinwarris

Feb. 20, Gholam Hyder Khan, made Governor-General

1890

Aug., Abdur-Rahman (two years absent) returns to Cabul with strengthened power

1891

Sept. Oct., Disputes with the Russians respecting the Pamir frontier

1892

Feb., Mr. T. Salter Pyne, engineer-in-chief to the Ameer (5½ years), reports great progress in arts and manufactures, many English being employed

May, June, The Ameer's encroachments on the Hazaras (checked by the Indian Government) lead to frequent conflicts, and insurrection of other tribes; the ameer unsuccessful. Rebels join the Hazara tribes, July

Aug., The Indian government proposes to send to the Ameer a deputation headed by Lord Roberts; he approves, but defers receiving it, about Aug. 7; the Ameer's army about 40,000 reported

Aug. 22, The Governor of Candahar and his troops repulsed by the Hazaras, reported

Sept., Oct., The Ameer's troops capture Kamsin from the rebels, reported Aug. 30; the war continues with varying results

Oct. 2, The Ameer's troops occupy Oruzghan, reported

Oct. 25, Death of Abdul Kudus Khan, the Ameer's general, reported

1893

March 16, Amicable dispatches from the Ameer to the Viceroy brought by Mr. Pyne, reported

Sept. 12, Boundary disputes with Russia settled by Capt. Yates, reported

Sept. 20, The British mission under Sir Henry Mortimer Durand and Maj. Elles cordially received at Dakka by Gen. Gholam Haidar; at Jellalabad, Sept. 23, at Kabul, with much honor, Oct. 2; cordial interview of three hours with the Ameer, Oct. 10; agreement signed, Nov. 12; friendly speech of the Ameer at a durbah, Nov. 13; Sir Henry Mortimer Durand and his party leave Kabul, Nov. 15

1894

Nov. 3, Frontier warfare, *see* India

1895

April 13, The Afghan boundary commission complete their work, agreement signed by Mr. Udney and Ghola Haidar Khan; ratified by the Ameer, July

May 24, The Shahzada Nasrulla Khan, second son of the Ameer, arrives in London; he leaves England for Paris, Sept. 3 [returns to Kabul, Feb., 1896]

Nov. 4, Lieut.-Col. Mahomed Akram Khan, British agent in Kabul, and his son killed by a messenger, the murderer killed; reported

Dec. 20, The Ameer attacks the Kafirs in the Verno valley

1896

Jan. 19, The Bashgol valley dominated, the chiefs submit; reported

1897

Aug. 25, The Ameer swears loyalty to the British Government at a durbar; reported; again Oct. 5

1900

June–July, Cholera epidemic; government houses closed; 4,500 deaths in Kabul

Aug., Army reserve and reforms started; reported

1901

Oct. 1, Death of the Ameer, a great ruler and a firm ally of the British; aged 61

Oct. 3, Habibullah, his son (born 1872), proclaimed Ameer; declares his intention to maintain the boundaries, and remain in alliance with Gt. Britain

Oct. 16, Proclamation issued; reducing the taxes and land revenue and raising the pay of the army, reported

Oct., Release of tribal prisoners

1902

March 29, The Hadda Mullah received by the Ameer

1903

Feb. 10, Ameer divorces all his wives except four, forbids his subjects to have more, reported

Feb. 12, British Commission under Maj. McMahon to settle Persia-Afghan frontier dispute, arrives at the Helmand river

April, Col. Yate detained as prisoner for crossing the border

Oct. 25, 36 sepoys charged with inciting to rebellion put to death, at Kabul, reported

1904

Jan. 26, Advices from Kabul report the removal from office of Mohammed Umar Khan by the Ameer, his brother, and his confinement as a state prisoner

Oct., Ameer declines repeated invitations from Lord Curzon for a meeting in India but sends his son, Sirdar Inayatulla Khan, to meet the Viceroy on his return to India

Nov. 27, By agreement with the Ameer, a British mission, with Louis Dane, the Indian Foreign Secretary, as its head, to discuss questions between the governments, leaves Peshawar for Kabul

Delimitation of the Indo-Afghan boundary adjoining the Mohmand, commenced in 1904

1905

June 20, Ameer starts on a prolonged tour through Afghanistan, reported

See India, 1905

1906

Jan. 29, The Ameer reaches Jalalabad with an escort of 9,000 troops to hold a tribal durbar

April 29, Death of Sir Thomas Acquin Martin, Agent-Gen.

Dec. 3, Visit of the Ameer to India—see India, 1907. The Ameer leaves Kabul on the first stage of his journey

1907

March 9, Arrival of the Ameer at Jalalabad on return from his visit to India

March 21, The Ameer takes steps to develop the coalfield at Ghorband, 40 miles n. of Kabul

Aug. 31, Anglo-Russian Treaty by which Great Britain undertook to neither annex nor occupy any Afghan territory, and Russia agreed to conduct political relations through the British Government

1909

March 21, Plot to murder the Ameer and certain members of his family discovered; several hundred persons, implicated in the plot, arrested at Jalalabad

April 11–27, The Khaibar Pass closed to caravan traffic

April 16, The Ameer starts on a tour of his kingdom; Inayatulla Khan, his eldest son, to act during his absence

1919

Feb. 20, Amir Habibulla Khan murdered in camp while touring in the district of Lamaghan. His brother Nasrulla Khan proclaimed himself Amir at Jalabad but Amanulla Khan, third son of Habibulla, was proclaimed Amir, and Nasrulla submitted, and charged with complicity in the murder, was imprisoned for life

March 3, Letter of Amir Amanulla Khan to Government of India declared friendship to the British Government

April, The Amir proclaimed external independence as well as internal for Afghanistan

——, A mission headed by General Wali Mohammed Khan sent to Moscow to institute relations with the Soviet Government

May 2, A holy war begun by the Amir to free India from the British rule

May 3, The Khyber rifles escorting a caravan turned back at the Afghan border by armed pickets

May 5, Afghan troops occupied the heights commanding Landi Kotal

May 13, British troops from the Khyber commanded by General Fowler advanced into Afghanistan and occupied Dakka

May 27, British took Afghan fortress of Spin Baldak

May 28, The Amir asked for terms of peace

June 2, Amir informed that armistice would be granted on terms which included the withdrawal of Afghan troops from within 20 miles of the British front

June 3, Hostilities ceased with regular troops but guerilla warfare of tribesmen continued

June 11, Armistice signed

July 25–Aug. 8, Peace Conference at Rawalpindi, India

Aug. 8, Treaty of peace signed, the privilege of importing arms and munitions from India withdrawn and British subsidy enjoyed by former Amirs ended, the British boundary demarcation in the Khyber region to be accepted, and the Indo-Afghan frontier as otherwise accepted by the late Amir to be recognized

Aug. 14, Fort of Spin Baldak evacuated by the British

Sept. 13, Dakka evacuated by British after demarcation of Khyber boundary completed

1920

April 14–July 24, Afghan mission to India in accordance with arrangements of Treaty of Aug. 8, 1919 in conference with British delegation at Mussoorie

1921

Feb. 28, Treaty with Russia signed provided for a subsidy from Russia, the establishment of 5 Russian consulates in the country, and the independence of Bokhara and Khiva

March 1, Treaty with Turkey signed of friendship and offensive and defensive alliance

June 5, Son and heir born to the Amir

June 18, First code of criminal procedure promulgated by the Amir

June 22, Treaty with Persia signed regarding diplomatic and consular relations

Nov. 22, Treaty with Great Britain signed by which Great Britain recognized the complete independence of Afghanistan, import of arms by way of India permitted, and boundaries reaffirmed, no Russian consulate to be established on Indian frontier

1923

Feb. 26, Commercial Agreement with Belgium signed

June 5, Trade Convention with Great Britain granted transportation and customs advantages to the Afghans

Sept. 7, Treaty of friendship and neutrality with Persia signed

Dec., Murder of several English men and women by bandits

1924

Jan. 13, "Kohat" bandits and murderers arrested

July 27, Sentence of death pronounced on Italian, Piperno, for shooting Afghan policeman

1925

May 25, 60 Khost rebels shot including the "Lame Mullah"

June 2, Italian engineer, Piperno, executed at Kabul on sentence of July, 1924, which had been remitted by payment of "blood money"

June 12, Formal protest of Italian Government demanded apology and indemnity for execution of Piperno which was accepted

1926

March 3, Treaty of friendship and commerce with Germany signed

March, New currency introduced

June 10, The Amir adopted the title of King

Aug. 31, Treaty of friendship, neutrality, and mutual non-aggression with Russia signed

1927

Nov. 3, Treaties of friendship with Poland and Turkey signed

Nov. 28, Treaty of friendship and security with Persia signed

1928

Jan. 8, The King and Queen of Afghanistan arrived in Rome beginning tour of Europe, visiting Italy, France, Belgium, Poland, Germany, England, Turkey, Persia, and Russia

Feb. 16, Treaty of friendship with Latvia signed

Feb. 17, Treaty of friendship with Switzerland signed

April 4, Treaty of friendship with Japan signed

May 25, Treaty of friendship with Turkey signed

June 7, Treaty of friendship with Egypt signed

June 15, Supplementary Treaty with Persia signed

July 1, The King and Queen arrived at Kabul from visit to Europe

Oct. 30, Chief Kadi and 3 other mullahs arrested for preaching against the reforms introduced by the King in dress, education, &c.

Nov. 22, Serious revolt begun against reforms, Jalabad attacked

Dec. 14, Kabul attacked by the rebels but driven back Dec. 26–27

Dec. 23–Feb. 25, 1929, 580 persons transported by British airships into India in evacuation of foreigners from Kabul

1929

Jan. 7, Proclamation of the King canceled the reforms and introduction of conscription

Jan. 14, King Amanulla forced to abdicate in favor of his elder brother Inayatulla

Jan. 17, Kabul taken by Bacha-i-Saquao who forced Inayatulla to abdicate and proclaimed himself ruler as Amir Habibulla Ghazi

Jan. 29, Amanulla withdrew his abdication and with Turkish assistance organized an army at Kandahar

March 26, Amanulla took the field against Amir Habibulla

March 31, From this date by Decree of Nov., 1928, western dress compulsory for visitors to capital

April 19, Amanulla defeated in battle south of Ghazni

May 4, Forces of Habibulla captured Herat

May 9, Nadir Khan supporting Amanulla defeated at Baraki

May 23, Amanulla and his wife and brother left the country proceeding to India

May 31, Forces of Habibulla captured Kandahar

June 25, Habibulla took Gardez

Aug. 22, Nadir Khan recaptured Gardez

Sept. 15, Habibulla defeated the brother of Nadir Khan in battle at Gamdamal

Oct. 6, Army of Nadir Khan defeated Habibulla's troops outside Kabul

Oct. 10, Nadir Khan's army occupied Kabul

Oct. 16, Nadhir Khan proclaimed King

Nov. 2, Habibulla Ghazi, usurper, and his chief officers captured and executed

Nov. 15, Nadir Khan recognized by Great Britain as lawful ruler of Afghanistan

1930

May 6, Notes exchanged with Great Britain as to treaty relations

Dec. 6, Treaty of friendship with Estonia

Dec. 9, Treaty of friendship with Lithuania

ANDAMAN ISLANDS

The Andaman Islands, British possession, under the government of India lie in the Bay of Bengal, 120 miles from Cape Negrais in Burma, the nearest point of the mainland. Five large islands closely grouped together are called the Great Andaman, and to the south is the island of Little Andaman. There are some 200 islets, the two principal groups being the Ritchie Archipelago and the Labyrinth Islands. The total area is 2,508 square miles. The Great Andaman group is about 219 miles long and, at the widest, 32 miles broad. The aborigines, 786 (414 males and 372 females) in 1921, live in small groups over the islands; some are savages of a low Negrito type. The total population of the Andaman Islands in 1921 was 17,814 (15,551 males and 2,263 females).

ANNAM

Annam, French Protectorate, the eastern coastal belt of the peninsula of French Indo-China, bounded on the north by Tonking, east and southeast by the China Sea, southwest by Cochin China, and west by Cambodia and Laos, area about 39,758 square miles with population of 5,399,674 including 3,220 Europeans. King Bao-Dai succeeded to the throne on Nov. 6, 1925, a Regency Council to govern during his minority. French intervention began as early as 1787 and was terminated by Treaty of Aug. 25, 1883 by which French Protectorate accepted, confirmed and extended by Treaty of June 6, 1884. By Treaties of May 11, 1884, April 4 and June 9, 1885, with France China recognized the Treaties with Annam. The French Resident General at

Hué, the capital (population 60,611), is the adviser of the King and virtual ruler.

ARABIA

Arabia, a peninsula in southwestern Asia, bounded on the west by the Red Sea, on the south by the Gulf of Aden and the Indian Ocean, on the east by the Gulf of Oman and the Persian Gulf, and on the north by the mandated territories of Iraq (Mesopotamia) and Trans-Jordan (Palestine). The area is estimated at 1,000,000 square miles, and the population at about 7 million and divided as estimated as follows: Yemen and Asir, 3,000,000; Hejaz, 1,000,000; Oman and Hadhramaut, 1,000,000; Nejd, Hasa, and the desert, 2,000,000. Aden is a British Protectorate. *See s.v.*

The Kingdom of Hejaz and Nejd is under the rule of Abdul Aziz II ibn Saud, G.C.I.E., who on January 8, 1926, was proclaimed king in Mecca under the style King of the Hejaz and Sultan (in 1927 changed to King) of Nejd and its dependencies. On May 20, 1927, a treaty was signed at Jedda between Great Britain and Ibn Saud, by which the former recognized the complete independence of the dominions of the latter. The chief administrative divisions or districts of the Kingdom of Nejd are: (1) Hasa; (2) Aridh including Riyadh; (3) Wadi Dawasir; (4) Aflaj; (5) Kharj; (6) Sudair; (7) Mahmal; (8) Washm; (9) Qasim; (10) Jabal Shammar including Haïl; (11) Jauf; and (12) numerous scattered oasis groups such as Khurma, Turaba, Ranya, and Khaibar, each of which is administered independently by a local Amir. The total population is estimated at about 3,000,000. Towns with a population exceeding 10,000 inhabitants are: (1) Hufuf; (2) Mubarraz; (3) Riyadh; (4) Shaqra; (5) Anaiza; (6) Buraida; (7) Haïl; (8) Jauf; (9) Sakaka; and (10) Hauta. Of these Hufuf has a population of about 30,000, but none of the others exceed 20,000.

The Hadramaut is a considerable tract of fertile valleys lying to the East of the Aden Protectorate. The greater part of it owes allegiance to the Qa'aiti dynasty, whose representative is the present Sultan of Makalla. A rival dynasty, the Kathiri, rules a number of towns and villages inland. The whole area is loosely under British protection and control.

The State of Kuwait is situated on the northwestern coast of the Persian Gulf. The reigning dynasty was founded by Subah abu Abdullah, who ruled from 1756 to 1762. The Sheikh is subsidized by the British Government, which maintains a Political Agent at his Court. The present Sheikh, Ahmed ibn Jabir al Subah (b. 1885), succeeded his uncle, the 9th Sheikh Salim ibn Mubarak, on February 23, 1921. Although His Highness has two sons by his first marriage—Abdullah (b. 1905) and Mohamed (b. 1909)—and

one by his present consort, the daughter of the late Sheikh Salim ibn Mubarak Jabir (b. June 29, 1926)—the Heir Presumptive according to the Koweiti rule of succession is the Sheikh's uncle, Hamad ibn Mubarak (b. 1894), who has a son Mubarak.

Estimated population, 50,000, to which an indeterminate number of Bedouins must be added.

Oman.—An independent State, in South-eastern Arabia, extending along the southern shore of the gulf of that name from the entrance into the Persian Gulf to the extreme eastern point of Arabia, and thence S.W. as far as Ras Sajir, lat. 16° 8″ N. The coast line is nearly 1,000 miles long. Inland Oman is bounded on the S.W. by the great desert. Area, 82,000 square miles; population, estimated at 500,000, chiefly Arabs, but there is a strong infusion of negro blood, especially along the coast. The towns of Muscat and Matrah hardly contain an Arab, being inhabited almost entirely by Baluchis and Negroes. The capital, Muscat, and the adjacent town of Matrah have together about 20,000 inhabitants.

Muscat was occupied by the Portuguese from 1508 to the middle of the seventeenth century. After various vicissitudes it was recovered in the eighteenth century by Ahmed bin Sa'id, of Yemenite origin, who was elected Imam in 1741, and whose family has since ruled, though under the title of Sultans for the last three generations.

The present Sultan is H.H. Seyyid Taimur bin Feisal bin Turki, C.S.I., eldest son of H.H. the late Seyydi Feisal bin Turki, who succeeded his father October 5, 1913.

Yemen.—The Yemen may be divided as follows: Aden; the Aden Protectorate; and the domains of Imam Yahya b. Muhammad b. Hamid ed Din.

The Zaidi Imam Yahya, whose capital is Sana' (Lat. 15° 20′ N., Long. 44° 12′ E.), has a domain of some 75,000 square miles with a population of two to three millions. His territories include the area recently abandoned by the Turks, and so march with the Anglo-Turkish boundary drawn in 1902–04. In a northerly direction his influence extends to Nejran (Lat. 17° 30′ N., Long. 44° 15′ E.) of the Yam, whose tenets are those of the sect of Ismailiya or Fatimiya, and their chief is the Da'i Ali Mohsin Al Shibami, of the house of the Makarima, whose descent is from Ismail b. Jafar Alsadiq, the offspring of Al Husein, the second son of the fourth Caliph Ali. The same tenets are professed by the inhabitants of Haraz near Menakha. To the north of San'a are the Imamic large towns of Amran, Tawila, Al Khamr, Al Suda, Sada (Lat. 16° 47′ N., Long. 43° 43′ E.), Quflat Al Udhr, and also the region of Al Jauf, Upper, Middle, and Lower, with their capitals respectively at Al Matamma, Al Hazm, and Al Ghail, where live the "Shawaf," clansmen of the influential Bakil tribe, all of which tracts, watered by the River Kharid, own the Imam's suzerainty. To south of Al Jauf, and to east by north of Sana' at a distance of six days' journey, lies the district of Marib, or Saba, whose ruler pays homage to Imam Yahya. Other large towns in the Yemen are Taizz (alt. 4,600 ft.), Ibb (6,275 ft.), Yerim (8,600 ft.), Dhamar (7,650 ft.). The altitude of Sana' is 7,260 ft. The highest mountain is Nabi Shuaib (11,000 ft.). Sumara, Kinan, Takar, and many others are all over 9,000 feet altitude.

The population of Sana', a walled city with eight gates, is between 20,000 and 25,000.

The terms *Petræa* (stony), *Felix* (happy), and *Deserta* are said to have been applied to divisions of Arabia by Ptolemy, about A.D. 140. The Arabs claim descent from Ishmael, the eldest son of Abraham, born 1910 B.C. (*Gen.* xvi). Arabia was unsuccessfully invaded by Gallus, the Roman governor of Egypt, 24 B.C. The Abyssinians conquered part of Arabia Felix, and retained it 76 years. In A.D. 622, the Arabians, under the name of Saracens, followers of Mahomet (born at Mecca, 570), their general and prophet, commenced their course of conquest. Arabia was conquered by the Ottomans 1518–39. The Arabs greatly favored literature and the sciences, especially mathematics, astronomy, and chemistry. The Koran was written in Arabic (622–632). The Bible was printed in Arabic in 1671.

1873

Nov., The aggression of the Turks on the South Arabs excited jealousy in England, and was checked by the Sultan

1882

Jan. 5–Feb. 7, Insurrection in Yemen or Arabia Felix

Jan., Egyptian commission for preservation of Arab monuments appointed

1883

March 17, Revolts in Yemen, announced

1884

Sept., Conflicts reported

1891

June–Oct., Several revolts against the Turkish Government suppressed

1892

May–July, Rebellion headed by Iman Ahmed Eddin, Jan.; reinforcements sent, successful

Sept. 7, Iman Ahmed Eddin, killed; the rebellion quelled, and the province Yemen pacified by the Turkish governor, reported

1898

June 14, Insurrection in Yemen; the Turks defeated by the Imam of Sana in three engagements, Nov., 1895; another spreading, Abdullah Pasha ordered to take the command

Nov. 30, Insurgents routed in Shanel, Turkish loss heavy

1899

April, Turkish atrocities, continued fighting

June, Abdullah Pasha forced to retire on Sana

1901

April 12, Ibn Raschid, ex-King of Nejd, defeats Mabaroukh, the conqueror of Nejd, with great slaughter, reported

Aug. 24, Turks attempt to land troops at Koweyt, foiled by the captain of H.M.S. *Perseus*

1902

Oct. 20, Abdullah pasha made vali, Yemen

Dec., Ibn Raschid defeats the Wahabis

1904

May, Fights between the chief of the Wahabis and Ibn Raschid, who is supplied with arms by the Turkish authorities

Rising in Yemen, 1904–05, *see* Turkey

1906

Oct. 11, Severe fighting between Turkish troops and tribesmen in the Azir district reported

1908

July 25, Hamud Ibn Rashid (Emir of Haïl) assassinated, by his people (reported)

Aug. 31, Hedjaz Railroad completed to Medina

1912

Colony of Artawiya founded by Ibn Saud as part of the Akhwan movement, Wahhabi religious revival or reform, and the first of similar agricultural colonies which in 1927 numbered 73, constituting a permanent territorial army

1913

April 13, Ibn Saud took Hafuk, the last Turkish garrison in Eastern Arabia, and annexed the Hasa province on the Persian Gulf, the conquest recognized

1914

May 15, Treaty of friendship between Ibd Saud and Turkey signed

Oct. 31, Message of Lord Kitchener to Sherif Abdullah asked Arab guarantee that no internal intervention take place in Arabia in return for guarantee from Great Britain of independence and rights and protection from foreign aggression

Nov. 2, The Government of India announcement that Holy Places in Arabia and Mesopotamia should be immune from attack; France and Russia joined in this declaration

Nov. 3, Great Britain gave assurance to the Sheik of Koweit of recognition of Koweit as an independent principality under British protection in agreement of alliance

Nov. 22, Agreement of alliance of Great Britain with the Sheik of Mohammera

Captain W. H. I. Shakespear became British representative with Ibn Saud at Nejd

1915

Jan. 11, Arab tribes of Oman repulsed in attack on capital of Muscat

Jan. 24, Ibn Saud taking the field for the British was defeated by Ibn Rashid supporting the Turks in battle at Jarrab. Captain Shakespear killed in action

Feb. 3, Speech of the Viceroy of ·India promised assembly of notables of Basra (Iraq) liberation from Turkish rule

April 30, Treaty of friendship between Great Britain and the Idrisi Sayyid of Sabia by which Great Britain guaranteed the latter's independence and seacoast from attack

July 14, Letter of the Sherif Hussein of Mecca to Sir Henry McMahon, British High Commissioner in Egypt, proposing coöperation with Great Britain and asking for recognition of independence of Arab countries, giving boundaries which included Syria

Aug. 30, First letter of Sir Henry McMahon to Sherif Hussein reaffirmed Lord Kitchener's pledges as to an independent Arabia but alluded to discussion of boundaries as premature

Sept. 9, Sherif Hussein asked for definite statement from British as to boundaries

Oct. 24, Letter of Sir Henry McMahon to Sherif Hussein gave assurance of British recognition of boundaries of Arab State as proposed with the exception of "the districts of Mersina and Alexandretta and portions of Syria lying to the west of the districts of Damascus, Homs, Hama and Aleppo" not purely Arab, as Great Britain free to act without detriment to the interests of her ally, France

Nov. 5, Letter of Sherif Hussein accepted exclusion of Mersina and Adana from the Arab kingdom but claimed the provinces of Aleppo and Beirut and seacoast as Arab provinces and in allusion to Christian Arabs claimed indirectly the Lebanon, but agreed to leave disputed points for future settlement, and the area under British occupation to temporary British administration

Dec. 13, Letter of Sir Henry McMahon in reply asked for more time to examine proposals as to Aleppo and Beirut

Dec. 26, Treaty of friendship between Great Britain and Abdul Aziz Ibn Saud of Nejd and Al Hasa

1916

Jan. 1, Sherif Hussein accepted British alliance and promised Arab support

May 9 and 16, Sykes-Picot Agreement of France and Great Britain. *See* World War

May 15, Blockade by Entente Allies in support of revolt begun

June 5, Hussein began hostilities against the Turks. *See* World War

June 7, Hussein declared independence of Turkey

June 27, Hussein, Sherif of Mecca, proclaimed new State of Arabia

July 29, Official communique published in Egypt affirmed the policy of Great Britain that the Holy Places should remain under independent Moslem rule and authority and secure from aggression

Oct. 29, Hussein proclaimed King of the Arabs at Mecca

Nov. 3, Treaty between Sheik El-Katr and Great Britain

Nov. 4, Hussein crowned King of the Arabs

Nov. 6, The Governments of Great Britain, France, and Russia recognized Hussein as head of the Arab peoples and *de facto* King of the Hejaz

Nov. 11, Recognition of the Kingdom of Arabia independent of Turkey asked of the Powers

Dec. 26, Treaty of Great Britain with Ibn Saud recognized him as an independent ruler

1917

Jan. 22, Great Britain recognized the Farson Islands as part of the Idrisi domain

May 19, King Hussein in conversation with Sir Mark Sykes and M. Picot admitted the necessity of European advisers in Syria and Mesopotamia but objected to advisers having any executive authority

May 20, King Hussein promised coöperation with France in Syria and with England in Mesopotamia and asked help from Great Britain to gain recognition from his enemy Ibn Saud of his position as leader of the Arab movement

Nov. 2, Balfour declaration as to Palestine. *See* Palestine

Dec. 17, Written assurance to King Hussein of the future independence of the Arab people given by the British Government

1918

Jan. 4, Great Britain notified Hussein that Palestine must have special régime and renewed pledges as to freedom of Arab people

Jan. 8, President Wilson in Point XII of the Fourteen Points declared that the nationalities under Turkish rule should be assured opportunity of autonomous development

Feb. 4, Great Britain reaffirmed pledges of freeing Arab peoples to King Hussein

Oct. 30, Armistice with Turkey. *See* World War

Nov. 8, Anglo-French declaration renewed promises of enfranchisement of peoples oppressed so long by the Turks and establishment of governments and national governments deriving their authority from the initiative and free choice of the indigenous populations

1919

Jan. 13, Medina capitulated to the King of the Hejaz

Jan. 19, With Colonel Lawrence as interpreter Emir Faisal made public statement in Paris of Arab desire to form independent State and appealed to America "as the most powerful protector of the freedom of man" for aid

Feb. 6, Emir Faisal presented Arab claims at the Peace Conference

March, Lord Curzon adjudicated the oasis of Khurma in dispute between Ibn Saud and King Hussein to Hussein and informed Ibn Saud of this decision warning him to accept British award

May, The Hejaz forces under Abdullah, second son of King Hussein, advancing to take possession of Khurma, attacked and defeated in battle at Turaba which was annexed by Ibn Saud

1920

Jan. 7, Agreement for the creation of an Arab State and Emir Faisal acknowledged the French mandate for Syria

Feb. 11, Commercial Treaty between Great Britain and Muscat renewed that of 1891

April 25, Supreme Council assigned mandate for Syria to France and for Iraq and Palestine to Great Britain. *See* Palestine, Syria, Iraq

Aug. 10, In Treaty of Sèvres Turkey recognized the independence of the Hejaz

Ibn Saud troops captured and annexed the province of Asir and its capital, Abha

1921

Jan. 31, Hudaydah evacuated by British troops and occupied by Idrisi Sayyid of Sabya (Yemen)

Sept., Capture of town of Hali the capital of Jabal Shammar by forces of Ibn Saud

Nov. 2, Muhammad ibn Talal surrendered the fort of Hail after 2 months' siege ending the rule of the Rashids, and Ibn Saud annexed the Amirate

1922

May 5, Treaty of Muhammara between Nejd and Kuwait defined boundaries arranged by Sir Percy Cox, repudiated by Ibn Saud as too favorable to Iraq

July, Ibn Saud captured the Jauf district from the Shalan dynasty

Dec. 2, Protocols of Uqair amending Treaty of Muhammara accepted by Ibn Saud established frontiers

1923

Dec. 17–April 12, 1924, Conference with Ibn Saud on tribal raids reached no agreement

1924

March 6, King Hussein proclaimed Caliph by Arabian Mohammedans of Hejaz, Iraq, and Transjordan three days after Assembly in Turkey had abolished the Caliphate

Aug. 29, The Wahabis attacked Taif, the summer capital of the Hejaz, which deserted by the Kings eldest son, Ali, then in residence, surrendered to the forces of Ibn Saud Sept. 5

Oct. 3, Hussein forced to abdicate by his subjects in favor of his son, Ali, who evacuated Mecca about the middle of the month moving his capital to Jidda

Oct. 13, The Wahabi forces occupied Mecca

Dec. 5, Ibn Saud arrived at Mecca in the garments of a pilgrim and performed the customary rites in the Great Mosque

1925

Jan. 6, The Wahabi army began the siege of Jidda which lasted until June when siege was raised

Nov. 1–2, The Treaty of Bahra and the Treaty of Hadda signed between Iraq and Nejd by Ibn Saud and Sir Gilbert Clayton settled tribal relations and defined boundary with Transjordan

Nov. 2, Agreement of Ibn Saud with Great Britain fixed Nejd-Transjordan frontier

Dec. 5, Medina surrendered to the Wahabis

Dec. 19, King Ali abdicated after arrangement for armistice with Ibn Saud and the Wahabis entered Jidda, Ali proceeding to Iraq

Dec. 23, Ibn Saud entered Jidda to receive submission of the town

1926

Jan. 8, Ibn Saud proclaimed King of Hejaz and Sultan of Nejd at Mecca

June 7, Congress of Islam at Mecca called by Ibn Saud

Aug. 29, King Ibn Saud published a constitution for the Hejaz

Sept. 2, Treaty of friendship and commerce between the Yemen and Italy

Oct. 21, Treaty signed at Mecca between Ibn Saud and the Idrisi which made the principality of Asir a protectorate under Ibn Saud

1927

Feb., Ibn Saud changed his title to King of the Hejaz and Nejd and its dependencies

Feb. 11, Treaty of Muscat with Great Britain of March 19, 1891, commerce and friendship renewed

May 20, Treaty with Great Britain signed by which the "complete and absolute independence of the Hejaz, Nejd and dependencies" recognized and coöperation in suppression of the slave trade announced, superseding Treaty of Dec. 26, 1915

June 1, Agreement of Italy with the Yemen superseded that of Sept. 2, 1926

1928

Jan. 22, A new silver currency of *riyals* introduced to take the place of the Turkish currency, 10 *riyals* equal to £1

Feb. 9, Yemenite raiders captured 2 Arab sheiks in treaty relations with Great Britain, and after 48 hours warning British aircraft bombed the town of Kataba until end of March when the kidnapped sheiks were returned

May 8–22, and Aug. 1–7, Conference of Ibn Saud with Sir Gilbert Clayton

Nov. 1, Treaty of friendship between the Yemen and Russia signed

1929

Jan. 21, Wahabis fired on 2 automobiles in which a party of Americans including Charles R. Crane were traveling to Koweit. *See* Iraq

March 31, Raids in Iraq and Transjordan by tribesmen during March and battle with rebels in which insurgent leader Feisal ed-Dowish was wounded and captured and Ibn Hithlain killed

April 26, Treaty of friendship with Germany signed

Aug. 3, Treaty of friendship between Nejd-Hejaz and Turkey signed

Aug. 24, Treaty of friendship between Nejd-Hejaz and Persia signed

Sept., Expedition of Ibn Saud against Sheik Feisal ed-Dowlish who had been pardoned and again in rebellion

1930

Feb. 24, Treaty of arbitration and friendship signed by King Faisal of Iraq and King Ibn Saud of Hejaz and Nejd on board British warship in Persian Gulf

ARMENIA

Armenia, a Socialist Soviet Republic created in April, 1921, and with Azerbaijan and Georgia united in 1922 to form the Transcaucasian Socialist Federated Soviet Republic, bounded on the north by Georgia, west and southwest, Turkey, southwest, Nakhichevan, south, the Araxes River and east, Azerbaijan, area 11,945 square miles, population (1926) 876,557.

The original inhabitants of Armenia called themselves Khaldini or Khaldians from the name of their god, Khaldi, and are assumed to have been a non-Aryan people (about 1500 B.C.) who were conquered about 710 B.C. by an Indo-European people. The name Armeniya or Arminia first appears in the Behistun inscription of Darius Hystaspes (521 B.C.). After forming part of the Assyrian, Median, and Persian empires, Armenia became subject to the Greek kings of Syria after the defeat of Antiochus the Great 190 B.C. The Romans established the kingdoms of Armenia, Major and Minor. In A.D. 303 King Tirdat established Christianity as the State religion.

186 B.C to 1889

B.C. 186, City of Artaxarta built
165, Antiochus Epiphanes invades Armenia
95, Tigranes the Great reigns in Armenia Major
83, Becomes King of Syria, and assumes the title of "King of Kings"
66, Defeated by Lucullus, 69; he lays his crown at the feet of Pompey
54, His son, Artavasdes, reigns; he assists Pompey against Julius Cæsar, 48; and the Parthians against Marc Antony, 36
34, Antony subdues, and sends him loaded with silver chains to Egypt
33, Artaxias, his son, made king by the Parthians
20, Deposed by the Romans, who enthrone Tigranes II
A.D. 15, Armenia subjected to Parthia
18, Reconquered by Germanicus, grandson of Augustus
58, After many changes Tiridates is made king by the Romans
115, The Parthian conquerors of Armenia are expelled by Trajan
199, Severus makes Volagarses king of part of Armenia
Christianity introduced, between A.D. 100–300
232, Armenia added to the Persian Empire
298, Tiridates obtains the throne through Diocletian, 286; is expelled by Narses, 294; restored by Galerius
342, On his death, Armenia becomes subject to Persia; is made neutral by Rome and Persia, 384; who divide it by treaty, 443
577–687, Armenia conquered and reconquered by the Greek and Persian sovereigns
693–1065, And by the Greek emperors and Mahometans
1235, Overrun by the Mongols; by Timour, 1383; by the Turks, 1516; by the Persians, 1534; by the Turks, 1583
1330, The Armenian church reconciled to Rome, about
1375, Leon VI, last King of Armenia, taken prisoner by the Saracens; released: he dies at Paris, 1393
1604, Shah Abbas, of Persia, surrenders Armenia to the Turks, but transports 22,000 Armenian families into his own states
1828, Armenia overrun by the Russians
July 9, 1829, Surrender of Erzeroum
(See Syria and Russo-Turkish Wars)
July 13, 1878, By the Berlin treaty, Kars, Ardahan, and Batoum were ceded to Russia, with other changes
Aug., 1889, The Turkish Government charged with oppression and cruelty

1890

Sept., Oct., Moussa Bey, a Kurdish chief, tried at Constantinople for alleged cruelties, Nov. 23; acquitted (a new trial refused), Dec. 2 et seq., 1889; eventually exiled to Medina
June 27, Riotous conflicts between Armenians and Mussulmans at Erzeroum, 9 persons killed, reported

July 27, The Armenians in Constantinople attack their Patriarch, Achikian, in a church during service, riot suppressed by the military with loss of life; many arrested Aug., and punished, Oct.; the Patriarch resigns, July 31; the chief rioter sentenced to death, others to imprisonment, Aug. 16
Nov. 2, Armed band of Armenians on the Turco-Russian frontier dispersed by the Turks and Russians, reported
Dec. 28, Friendly negotiations with the Porte; loyal address to the Sultan, and gracious reply; the Patriarch withdraws his resignation

1891

Jan. 17 et seq., He is received by the Sultan, who announces a general amnesty, with great release of prisoners
Jan. 25, The central committee for reforms, issue a proclamation against the Turkish government, about

1892

Nov. 18, Death of Archbishop Chorène Nar Bey Lusignan. Succeeded by Mgr. Khrimian, anointed as Supreme Patriarch, Oct. 8, 1893

1893

June 20, Seventeen Christians condemned to death at Angora as alleged revolutionaries; alleged unfair trial, British intervention, sentences of death confirmed in 5 cases

1894

April 12, The Patriarch resigned
Aug. 25, Massacre of Armenians begun by Kurds and Turkish soldiers, and villages in Sasum burned

1895

Jan. 8, Mgr. Izmarlian enthroned as Patriarch at Kum-Kapu
April 23, Meeting in Constantinople of Commission appointed by the Sultan to consider reforms in Armenia
May 11, Scheme of Armenian reform drawn up by the British, French, and Russian ambassadors presented to the Sultan; terms: appointment of a high commissioner, general amnesty and release of prisoners, political reforms, &c.
Sept. 30, Armenian demonstration at Constantinople provoked riot
Oct. 13–Nov. 30, Massacre of Armenians in the provinces by Kurds, Circassians, and Turkish soldiers, about 25,000 killed
Oct. 20, Decree of the Sultan promulgated ordering the reforms proposed

1896

Aug. 4, Forced resignation of Patriarch Izmirlian
Aug. 26, Attack on the Ottoman Bank at Constantinople caused massacre of Armenians by organized mob of Turks, 6,000 killed
Nov. 11, Execution of reforms ordered
Nov. 18, Malachias Ormanian, Bishop of Armash elected Patriarch
Dec. 22, General amnesty covered all Mohammedans and most of the Armenians

1897

March 19–20, Massacre of 100 Armenians at Tokat;

the embassies demand redress and send consuls to attend Turkish inquiry

1899

Oct. 11, Decree issued granted certain reforms, 54 Armenians pardoned and death sentences of 24 commuted to life imprisonment

1903

Aug. 11 and 15, Villages pillaged by Kurds, panic in Mush and Sasun

Dec. 26, Armed Armenian bands of revolutionaries from Persia and Russia in conflict with Turks

1904

April 25–May 29, Massacre of Armenians at Sasun, Gueligouzan, Talvorik, and other villages

June 6, Protest of British, French, and Russian ambassadors and demand of cessation of destruction of Armenian villages

1909

April 14, Moslems and Armenians in conflict at Adana; several Armenians killed, martial law proclaimed

April 15, Massacre of Armenians at seaport of Mersina

April 18, A large part of the town of Adana burned, 1,000 to 2,000 persons killed in the town, and 5,000 in the vilayet

April 21, H.M.S. "Diana" landed 50 marines at Alexandretta, and the German warship "Loreley" arrived

April 25, Hajin reported burned; massacre at Latakia

April 27, New outbreak at Adana, looting and burning

1915

April 8, Deportation and massacre of Armenians begun which continued through the year

April 15, 500 young Armenian men at Akantz summoned to hear proclamation and then shot; this procedure repeated in about 80 Armenian villages in districts north of Lake Van, and in 3 days about 24,000 murdered (Morgenthau)

April 20, Successful self-defense of the Armenians in Van

Aug. 10, Anatolia College (Armenian) with more than 400 students deported and all the men killed

1916

American Armenian Relief Committee reported number of Armenians killed as between 600,000 and 850,000

1917

Sept. 20, Armenia with Georgia and Azerbaijan established the Republic of Trans-Caucasia and formed a Provisional Government

1918

March 3, Treaty of Brest-Litovsk; Russia ceded districts of Batum and Kars to Turkey

April 13, Armenia and Georgia rejected cession of land under Brest-Litovsk Treaty

May 26, Dissolution of Trans-Caucasian Republic

May 28, Armenia declared independence

June 4, Armenia signed peace Treaty with Turkey

Aug. 10, Peace Agreement with the Soviet Russians signed at Tiflis

1920

Jan. 22, Allied Governments gave *de facto* recognition of the Armenian Republic of Erivan

Jan. 26, Recognition of the Armenian Republic by the United States

March 12, Mandate for Armenia offered by Supreme Council to League of Nations

April 9–10, The League of Nations declined to accept mandate for Armenia

April 23, Formal recognition by the United States of the *de facto* Government

April 25, Armenian mandate offered to the United States by Allied Premiers at San Remo

June 1, The Senate of the United States rejected request of President Wilson that mandate for Armenia be accepted by the United States

Aug. 10, Armenians forced by Russian invasion to sign Treaty with Russia and signed Treaty of Sèvres, recognition of independence by Turkey the frontier in the vilayets of Erzerum, Trebizond, Van, and Bitlis with Turkey to be submitted to arbitration of the President of the United States; Minorities Treaty signed

Oct. 13, Russian ultimatum demanded recognition of territorial terms of Brest-Litovsk Treaty

Oct. 15, Turkish invasion

Oct. 21, Turks took Kars, chief fortress in Armenian territory

Nov. 7, Armistice with Turkey asked for by Armenians

Nov. 22, Decision of President Wilson as to boundaries transmitted to Supreme Council

Dec. 2, Soviet Armenian Republic proclaimed

Dec. 3, Turco-Armenian Peace Treaty signed, Kars and Ardahan ceded to Turkey, Armenia reduced to district of Erivan and Lake Gokcha

Dec. 16, Request of the Government for admission to the League of Nations refused on the ground that there was not an established Government in Armenia

1921

Feb. 18, Dashnakzagan party seized Erivan but by April 2 put to flight and the Soviet Government reëstablished

April 2, Republic proclaimed

April 21, Turks evacuated Armenia

Oct. 13, Treaty of Kars; Turkey recognized Armenia

1922

March 12, Armenia, Azerbaijan and Georgia established Trans-Caucasian Soviet Socialist Republic

AZERBAIJAN

Azerbaijan Socialist Soviet Republic of Russia, part of the Trans-Caucasian Republic, bordering on the Caspian Sea and Persia, area 32,686 square miles, population (1926) 2,313,172, population of Baku, the capital, 452,000. Azerbaijan includes the Nakhichevan S.S.R. and the Nagorni Karabakh Autonomous Region.

1917

Sept. 20, The Russian "Governments" of Baku and Elisavetopol united to form the republic of Azerbaijan and in Council at Tiflis joined Armenia and Georgia in establishment of the Trans-Caucasian Republic

1918

May 26, The Trans-Caucasian Federal Republic was

dissolved and Azerbaijan proclaimed independence May 28

Aug. 4, British force under Colonel Dunsterville occupied Baku to prevent Turkish and German occupation

Sept. 14, British force compelled by Turks to evacuate Baku which was occupied by Turks

Oct. 30, Armistice signed ensured evacuation of Turks

Nov. 11, Armistice ensured evacuation by Germans

Nov. 17, British force from Mesopotamia occupied Baku

1920

April 28, Russian Soviet army occupied Baku, and local Bolsheviks deposed the Government and established a Government in alliance with Moscow

May 7, Treaty of friendship with Georgia signed

Sept. 30, Treaty of alliance, military and economic, with Soviet Russia signed

1921

Oct. 13, Treaty with Turkey signed

1922

March 12, Union with Armenia and Georgia as the Transcaucasian S.S.S.R.

BAHRAIN ISLANDS

Bahrain Islands, archipelago in the Persian Gulf 20 miles off al Hasa on the Arabian coast, British dependency, Bahrain, the largest island is 27 miles long and 10 miles wide. Other islands are Maharaq, 4 miles long and one-half mile wide, Sitra, 3 miles long and 1 mile wide, Nebi Saleh, about 2 miles in circumference, and several uninhabited islets. The total population is estimated at about 120,000. *See also* Arabia.

CAMBODIA

Cambodia, French Protectorate in Indo-China, bounded on the south by Cochin China, on the east by Annam, on the north by Laos and Siam, on the west by Siam, and on the south-west by the Gulf of Siam.

Area, 67,550 square miles; population according to the census of 1929: 2,611,349, of whom 2,004 were Europeans (including the military forces), 156,277 Chinese, 2,234,055 Cambodians, Sino-Cambodians, Malayans, and Laotians, and 219,013 of various races.

By Treaty of Aug. 11, 1863, King Norodom accepted the protection of the French, confirmed by Treaty of June 17, 1884 which extended French influence. By Treaty with Siam of July 15, 1867 the French Protectorate was recognized, and Treaties of Oct. 3, 1893, Feb. 13, 1904, and March 23, 1907 made boundary changes (*see* Siam). In

1904 King Norodom was succeeded by his brother Sisowath, and the present King Monivong succeeded his late father, Sisowath, on Aug. 9, 1927.

CEYLON

Ceylon, the ancient Taprobane (Tamraparni, the island of "dusky leaves"), is an island in the Indian Ocean, by the south of India, area 25,332 square miles; population estimated Dec. 31, 1929, as 5,479,000.

The authentic history of Ceylon begins in the sixth century B.C., when an invasion of Hindus from Northern India established the Sinhalese dynasty. As a result of many generations of warfare the northern districts were occupied by Tamils from South India, and the population of these districts is almost wholly Tamil, and mainly Hindu in religion.

In 1505 the Portuguese formed settlements on the west and south, which were taken from them about the middle of the next century by the Dutch. In 1796 the British Government annexed the foreign settlements to the Presidency of Madras; in 1802 Ceylon was ceded to England by the Peace of Amiens, separated from India and formed into a Crown colony.

The Maldive Islands, 400 miles southwest, are a dependency of Ceylon.

The Constitution is embodied in Order in Council dated Dec. 19, 1923, and amended March 21, 1924.

Sir Graeme Thomson, Governor.

CHANDERNAGOR

Chandernagor (Chandargnagar) French Colony in India, province of Bengal, situated on the right bank of the Hugli River, 20 miles above Calcutta, area 3 square miles, population 27,393, settled by the French in 1688, captured by the English in 1757, restored in 1763, taken again in 1794, and restored in 1816.

CHINA

China, Republic in eastern Asia, the Pacific Ocean, the eastern boundary, Siberia on the north, India and French Indo-China on the south, and Central Asiatic Russia on the west. *See also* Manchuria, Mongolia, Sinkiang, and Tibet.

The table on page 779 gives a statement of the area and population of the Chinese Republic according to the estimate of the Post Office in 1923.

Peking (now called Peiping), the capital of China until 1928, has a population of 811,138 according to the 1926 census of the Municipal

THE 18 PROVINCES OF CHINA PROPER	AREA: ENGLISH SQUARE MILES	POPULATION (ESTIMATED)	CAPITAL
Chihli	115,800	34,186,711	Peiping
Shantung	55,970	30,803,245	Tsi-nan
Shansi	81,940	11,080,827	Tai-yuan
Honan	69,830	30,831,909	K'ai-fêng
Kiangsu	38,600	33,786,064	Chinkiang
Anhui	54,810	19,832,665	Anking
Kiangsi	69,480	24,466,800	Nanch'ang
Chêkiang	36,670	22,043,300	Hangchow
Fukien	46,320	13,157,791	Foochow
Hupeh	71,410	27,167,244	Wuchang
Hunan	83,380	28,443,279	Ch'angsha
Shensi	75,270	9,465,558	Sian
Kansu	125,450	5,927,997	Lanchow
Szechwan	218,480	49,782,810	Ch'êngtu
Kwangtung	99,970	37,167,701	Canton
Kwangsi	77,200	12,258,335	Kueliñ
Kweichow	67,160	11,114,951	Kuei-yang
Yünnan	146,680	9,839,180	Yünnan
Total	1,534,420	411,356,367	
New Dominion:—			
Sinkiang	550,340	2,519,579	Urumchi (Tihwafu)
Manchuria	—	—	
Liaoning	} 363,610	} 22,083,434	Shenyang
Kirin			Kirin
Heilungkiang			Tsitsihar Heilung (Hsien)
		24,603,013	
Dependencies:—			
Mongolia	1,367,600	1,800,000	Urga
Tibet	463,200	2,000,000	Lhasa
Grand Total	4,279,170	439,759,380	

Bureau. According to the Census of the Metropolitan Police Administration, taken in 1927, the population of Peking and its suburbs is close on 1,297,718 (779,704 males and 518,014 females). The population of the treaty ports is given as follows for 1929 by the Chinese Maritime Customs: Aigun, 36,800; Harbin, 252,988; Hunchun, 37,535; Lungchingtsun, 6,313; Antung, 93,781; Darien, 220,588; Newchwang, 106,242; Chinwangtao, 19,100; Tientsin, 1,388,747; Lungkow, 9,409; Chefoo, 119,305; Tsingtao, 350,464; Chungking, 635,000; Wanhsien, 207,837; Changsha, 606,972; Yochow, 4,200; Ichang, 112,309; Shasi, 95,843; Hankow, 777,993 (including Wuchang and Hanyang); Kiukiang, 43,987; Wuhu, 130,706; Nanking, 522,696; Chinkiang, 153,613; Shanghai (including neighboring districts), 2,674,447 (the International Settlement at Shanghai has a total of 1,007,868 inhabitants, of which 971,397 are Chinese and 36,471 foreigners); Soochow, 260,000; Hangchow, 426,916; Ningpo, 212,518; Wenchow, 678,376; Santuao, 9,000; Foochow, 388,164; Amoy, 196,717; Swatow, 141,063; Canton, 812,241; Kongmoon, 94,598; Samshui, 9,050; Kiungchow, 45,751; Pakhoi, 34,600; Wuchow, 77,353; Nanning, 73,412; Lungchow, 14,731; Mengtsz, 38,562; Szemao, 10,000; Tengyueh, 19,000. In addition, there are also a number of other places open to international trade; these are called commercial ports or marts, and were opened at the instance of the Chinese Government. Nanking is the present capital.

According to the estimate of the Customs authorities, in 1929 the total number of foreigners resident in China was 356,233, made up as follows:—

American	6,966
Austrian	218
Belgian	739
Brazilian	11
British	11,612
Czechoslovak	585
Danish	635
Dutch	734
Finnish	38
French	6,704
German	3,092
Italian	638
Japanese	245,634
Mexican	10
Norwegian	274
Polish	1,505
Portuguese	2,353
Russian	73,476
Spanish	292
Swedish	201
Swiss	457
Other Countries	59
Total	356,233

On February 12, 1912, China, one of the oldest of Monarchies, became a Republic.

The Chinese Imperial family was of Manchu origin, dating from 1644, and was styled Ta Ch'ing Ch'ao ("Great Pure Dynasty"). The last Emperor, P'u-yi, was the tenth of the line; but the official genealogy is carried back six generations earlier than the real founder, and P'u-yi's will be the sixteenth name in the canonized series of Ta Ch'ing Emperors. He was born on February 11, 1906, succeeded his uncle the Emperor Kuang-Hsü on November 14, 1908, and abdicated on

February 12, 1912. On December 1, 1923, he was married. He retained the title of Emperor of the Manchu Imperial House up to November 5, 1924 (when it was abolished), together with other rights of preferential treatment secured under the Abdication Agreement, making P'u-y'i an ordinary citizen of the republic.

CHINESE EMPERORS

1627. Chwang-lei.
1643. Shun-che (first of the Tsing dynasty).
1662. Kang-hi, an able sovereign; consolidated the empire, compiled a great Chinese dictionary.
1723. Yung-ching.
1736. Keen-lung, warlike; fond of art; greatly embellished Pekin.
1795. Kea-king.
1820. Taou-Kwang.
1850. Hieng-fung, Feb. 25.
1861. Kietsiang (altered to Toung-chi) Aug. 21; born April 27, 1856; married Oct. 16, 1872; died Jan. 12, 1875.
1875. Tsai T'ien (altered to Kwang-Hsu), aged 4, Jan. 12; married Feb. 21, 1889.

[China was ruled by two empresses (Tsze An and Tsze Chi), 1861–1881; and by one (Tsze Chi, born 1834), a powerful woman, 1881; died Nov. 15, 1908.]

1887. The Emperor nominally assumed the government, Feb. 7; died Nov. 14, 1908.
1908. Pu Yi (assumes the name of Hsuan Tung) *b.* Feb. 8, 1906, succeeded Nov. 14, 1908.

The present Government at Nanking (March, 1929) is a Committee Government, representing broadly the "Kuomintang," or Nationalist party. According to the "Organic law of the Nationalist Government of the Republic of China" which the Kuomintang promulgated on October 4, 1928, the Nationalist Government is to be composed of five *Yuan* (Councils)—Executive, Legislative, Judicial, Examination, and Control. There shall be a President and from 12 to 16 State Councilors of the National Government, from whom Presidents and Vice-Presidents of the five Councils shall be appointed.

The early condition of China was tribal, which gradually merged into a vast feudal system, nominally ruled by many contemporaneous dynasties, dated from 2205 B.C. The King of Ts'in put down all other rulers and assumed the title of Hwang Tî, or Emperor, declaring that "as there is but one sun in the sky, there should be but one ruler in the nation." 221 B.C.

Principal dynasties: Han, 206 B.C.–220 A.D.; T'ang, 618–906; Sung, 960–1279; Yüan, the Mongol, 1280–1367; the Ming, 1368–1643; the Ch'ing, or Ts'ing, Manchû Tartar, 1643 to the present date. *Legge.*

Chiang Kai-shek, President and Chairman of the State Council.

551 B.C. to 1760

B.C., 551–479 Supposed age of Confucius (Kungfutze), the philosopher
211, Stupendous wall of China completed
202, Literature and the art of printing encouraged
129, Battle between Phraates and the Scythians; the Chinese aided the latter, and ravaged the coasts of the Caspian: their first appearance in history (*Lenglet*)
15, The religion of Laot-se begun
About 68–81 A.D., A form of Buddhism, or the religion of Fŏ, introduced
420, Nankin becomes the capital
449, The atheistical philosopher, San-Shin, flourishes
635, The Nestorian Christians permitted to preach
845, They are proscribed and extirpated
China ravaged by Tartars, 9th to 11th centuries
1260, Seat of government transferred to Pekin
1275, Marco Polo introduces missionaries
About 1275, Kublai Khan establishes the Yuen or Mongol dynasty
1368, Ming dynasty
About 1400, Canal, called the Yu Ho, completed
1517, Europeans first arrive at Canton
1536, Macao is granted to the Portuguese
1575, Jesuit missionaries are sent from Rome
1616–43, The country is conquered by the eastern or Manchu Tartars, who establish the present reigning Tsing dynasty
1660, Tea brought to England
1662, An earthquake throughout China, buries 300,000 persons at Pekin alone
1678, Galdan, a prince of Jangaria, conquers Kashgaria and becomes supreme in Central Asia; checked by Kang-hi, 1689; totally defeated, 1695
1680, Commerce with East India Company begins
1692, Jesuit missionaries preach
1719–27, Commercial relations with Russia
1724–32, The Jesuits expelled
1731, Another general earthquake destroys 100,000 persons at Pekin, and 80,000 in a suburb
1755 *et seq.*, Successful war in Central Asia; Davatsi and his opponent Amursana, subdued by Keen-lung; Kashgar, Khokand, the Khirgez, &c., annexed, 1760

1793

Sept. 14, Earl Macartney's embassy arrives at Pekin; his reception by the Emperor
[This embassy threw light on the empire; it appeared to be divided into 15 provinces, containing 4,402 walled cities; the population of the whole was given at 333,000,000: its annual revenues at 66,000,000*l.*; and the army, including the Tartars, 1,000,000 of infantry and 800,000 cavalry; the religion Pagan, and the government absolute. Learning, and the arts and sciences, were encouraged, and ethics studied]
Oct. 7, He is ordered to depart

1812

Edict against Christianity
Chinese rule in Central Asia weakened

1816

Feb. 8, Lord Amherst's embassy; he leaves England

[His lordship failed in the objects of his mission, having refused to make the prostration of the *kotou*, lest he should thereby compromise the majesty of England]

1834

April 22, Exclusive rights of the East India Co. cease

April 25, Free-trade ships sail for England

July 15, Lord Napier arrives at Macao to superintend British commerce

Sept. 5, Affair between the natives and two British ships of war; several Chinese killed

Oct. 11, Lord Napier dies, and is succeeded by Mr. (afterwards Sir John) Davis

Nov., Opium dispute begins; the trade prohibited by the Emperor

1835

Jan. 31, Chinese seize the *Argyle* and crew

Feb. 23, Opium burnt at Canton by Chinese

1836 to 1838

Dec. 14, 1836, Captain Elliot, chief British commissioner

March, 1837, A British commissioner settled at Canton

July 12, 1838, Admiral Maitland arrives at Macao

1839

March 24, Commissioner Lin orders seizure of opium, March 18; British and other residents forbidden to leave Canton, March 19: the factories surrounded and outrages committed

March 27, Captain Elliot requires British subjects to surrender to him all opium, promising them full value of it; half of it is given up as contraband to the Chinese, April 20; the remainder (20,283 chests) surrendered, May 21; Captain Elliot and the British merchants leave Canton, May 24; the opium destroyed by the Chinese, June 3

July 7, Affair between the British and American seamen and the Chinese; a native killed

Aug. 23, Hong-Kong taken

Aug. 26, The British boat *Black Joke* attacked, and the crew murdered, Aug. 24; the British merchants retire from Macao

Sept. 4, Affair at Kow-lung between British boats and Chinese junks

Nov. 3, Attack by 28 armed junks on the British frigates *Volage* and *Hyacinth:* several junks blown up

Dec. 6, The British trade with China ceases, by an edict of the Emperor, and the last servant of the company leaves this day

1840

Jan. 5, Edict of the Emperor interdicting all trade and intercourse with England for ever

May 2, The *Hellas* ship attacked by armed junks; blockade of Canton by a British fleet, by orders from Sir Gordon Bremer, June 28; the *Blonde* with a flag of truce fired on at Amoy, July; Ting-hai, in Chusan, surrenders, July 5; blockade established along the Chinese coast, July 10; Mr. Staunton carried off to Canton, Aug. 6

Aug. 11, Captain Elliot, on board a British steam-ship, enters the Peiho river, near Pekin

Sept. 16, Lin finally degraded; Keshin appointed imperial commissioner; Capt. Elliot's truce with him, Nov. 6

Nov. 20, British plenipotentiaries off Macao

Nov. 29, Admiral Elliot's resignation announced

Dec. 12, Mr. Staunton released

1841

Jan. 6, Negotiations cease, owing to breach of faith on the part of the Chinese Emperor

Jan. 7, Chuen-pe and Tae-coc-tow, and 173 guns (some sent to England) captured

Jan. 20, Hong-Kong ceded by Keshin to Great Britain, and 6,000,000 dollars agreed to be paid within ten days to the British authorities

Jan. 26, Hong-Kong taken possession of

Feb. 25, The Emperor rejects Keshin's treaty, Feb. 11; hostilities resumed, Feb. 23; Chusan evacuated, Feb. 24; rewards proclaimed at Canton for the bodies of Englishmen, dead or alive: 50,000 dollars to be given for chiefs

Feb. 26, Bogue forts taken by Sir G. Bremer; Admiral Kwan killed; 459 guns captured

March 1, The British squadron proceeds to Canton; Sir H. Gough takes command of the army, March 2; hostilities again suspended, March 3; and resumed, March 6; Keshin degraded by the Emperor, March 12

March 18, Flotilla of boats destroyed, Canton threatened, the foreign factories seized, and 461 guns taken by the British forces

April 14, New commissioners from Pekin arrived at Canton

May 1, *Hong Kong Gazette* first published

May 17, Capt. Elliot prepares to attack Canton

May 25, Heights behind Canton taken

May 31, The city ransomed for 6,000,000 dollars; 5,000,000 paid down; hostilities cease

July 16, British forces withdrawn, June 1; and British trade reopened

Aug. 10, Arrival at Macao of Sir Henry Pottinger, who, as plenipotentiary, proclaims the objects of his mission; Capt. Elliot superseded

Aug. 27, Amoy taken, and 296 guns destroyed

Sept. 14, The Bogue forts destroyed

Oct. 1, Ting-hae taken, 136 guns captured, and Chusan reoccupied by the British; they take Chin-hae, Oct. 10; Ning-po, Oct. 13; Yu-yaou, Tsze-kee, and Foong-hua, Dec. 28

1842

March 10, Chinese attack Ning-po and Chin-hae, and are repulsed with great loss; 8,000 Chinese are routed near Tze-kee, March 15

May 18, Cha-pou attacked; defenses destroyed

June 13, The British squadron enters the river Kiang; capture of Woosung and of 230 guns and stores, June 16; Shang-hae taken, June 19

July 20, The British armament anchors near the "Golden Isle"; Chin-Keang taken; the Tartar general and many of the garrison commit suicide, July 21; the advanced ships reach Nankin, Aug. 4; the whole fleet arrives, and the disembarkation commences, Aug. 9; Keying arrives at Nankin, with full powers to treat for peace, Aug. 12

Aug. 29, Treaty of peace signed before Nankin, on board the *Cornwallis* by Sir Henry Pottinger for England, and Keying Elepoo and Neu-Kien on the part of the Chinese Emperor—[Conditions: lasting peace and friendship between the two empires; China to pay 21,000,000 of dollars; Canton, Amoy, Foochoofoo, Ningpo, and Shang-hai to be thrown open to the British, and consuls to reside at these cities; Hong-Kong to be ceded in perpetuity to England, &c.; Chusan and Ku-lang-su to be held by the British until the provisions are fulfilled]

1843

July 22, The ratification signed by Queen Victoria and the Emperor formally exchanged
July 27, Canton opened to the British

1844 to 1848

Feb. 16, 1844, Appointment of Mr. Davis in place of Sir Henry Pottinger
April 5, 1847, Bogue forts captured by the British
Oct., 1848, Hong-Kong and the neighborhood visited by a violent typhoon; immense damage done to the shipping; upwards of 1,000 boat-dwellers on the Canton river drowned

1850

March 4, H.M. steam-ship *Medea* destroys 13 pirate junks in the Chinese seas
Aug., Rebellion breaks out in Quang-si

1851

March, Appearance of the pretender, Tien-teh

1852

June 19, Defeat of Leu, the imperial commissioner, and destruction of half the army

1853

March and April, Successful progress of the rebels; the Emperor applies to the Europeans for help, without success
March 19, 20, The rebels take Nankin; Amoy, May 19; Shang-hae, Sept. 7

1854

Aug.–Nov., And besiege Canton without success

1855

The scanty accounts are unfavorable to the rebels, the imperialists having retaken Shang-hae, Amoy, and many important places

1856

Oct. 8, Outrage on the British lorcha *Arrow*, in Canton river
Oct. 23, After vain negotiations with Commissioner Yeh, Canton forts attacked and taken
A Chinese fleet destroyed and Canton bombarded
Nov. 6, Imperialists defeated, quit Shang-hae
Nov. 21–23, The Americans revenge an attack by capturing three forts
Nov. 25, Rebels take Kuriking
Dec., Other forts taken by the British
Dec. 14, The Chinese burn European factories
Dec. 30, And murder the crew of the *Thistle*
The Mahometans of Panthay, in Yunan, become independent during Tae-ping rebellion

1857

March, Troops arrive from Madras and England; and Lord Elgin appointed envoy
May, No change on either side: Yeh said to be straitened for money; the imperialists seem to be gaining ground upon the rebels
June 1, Total destruction of the Chinese fleet by Commodore Elliot, May 25, 27; and Sir M. Seymour and Commodore Keppel
Aug., Blockade of Canton
Sept. 25, Stagnation in the war—Lord Elgin departs to Calcutta, with assistance to the English against the Sepoys, July 16; returns to Hong-Kong
Oct. 19, Gen. Ashburnham departs for India, and Gen. Straubenzee assumes the command

1858

Jan. 5, Canton bombarded and taken by English and French, Dec. 28, 29, 1857; who enter it
Jan., Yeh sent a prisoner to Calcutta
May 20, The allies proceed towards Pekin, and take the Pei-ho forts
——, The expedition arrives at Tien-tsin
June 26, 28, 29, Negotiations commence, June 5; treaty of peace signed at Tien-tsin by Lord Elgin, Baron Gros, and Keying (who signed the treaty of 1842)— [Ambassadors to be at both courts; freedom of trade; toleration of Christianity; expenses of war to be paid by China; a revised tariff; term I (barbarian) to be no longer applied to Europeans]
Aug. 28, Lord Elgin visits Japan, and concludes an important treaty with the Emperor
Aug. and Sept., The British destroy about 130 piratical junks in the Chinese seas

1859

Jan., Lord Elgin proceeds up the Yang-tse-Kiang to Nankin; returns to England, May
June 25, Mr. Bruce, the British envoy, on his way to Pekin, is stopped in the river Pei-ho (or Tien-tsin); Admiral Hope attempting to force a passage, is repulsed with the loss of 81 killed, and about 390 wounded
July 29, The American envoy Ward arrives at Pekin, and refusing to submit to degrading ceremonies, does not see the Emperor
Oct., The English and French prepare an expedition against China
Nov. 24, Commercial treaty with America

1860

June 29, Lord Elgin and Baron Gros sail for China, April 26; wrecked near Point de Galle, Ceylon, May 23; arrive at Shang-hae
Aug. 12, The war begins: the British commanded by Sir Hope Grant, the French by General Montauban. The Chinese defeated in a skirmish near the Pei-ho
Aug. 21, The allies repulse the Taeping rebels attacking Shang-hae, Aug. 18–20; and take the Taku forts, losing 500 killed and wounded; the Tartar general San-ko-lin-sin retreats
Sept. 18 and 21, After vain negotiations, the allies advance towards Pekin; they defeat the Chinese at Chang-kia-wan and Pa-li-chiau
Sept. 21, Consul Parkes, Captains Anderson and Brabazon, Mr. de Norman, Mr. Bowlby (the *Times* correspondent), and 14 others (Europeans and Sikhs) advance to Tung-chow, to arrange conditions for a meeting of the ministers, and are captured by San-ko-lin-sin; Capt. Brabazon and abbé de Luc beheaded, and said to be thrown into the canal; others carried into Pekin
Oct. 8–11, The allies march towards Pekin; the French ravage the Emperor's summer palace, Oct. 6; Mr. Parkes, Mr. Loch, and others, restored alive, Oct. 8;

Capt. Anderson, Mr. De Norman, and others die of ill-usage

Oct. 15, Pekin invested; surrenders, Oct. 12; severe proclamation of Sir Hope Grant

Oct. 24, Convention signed in Pekin by Lord Elgin and the Prince Kung, by which the treaty of Tientsin is ratified; apology made for the attack at Pei-ho (June 25, 1859); a large indemnity to be paid immediately, and compensation in money given to the families of the murdered prisoners, &c.; Kowloon ceded in exchange for Chusan, and the treaty and convention to be proclaimed throughout the empire

Nov. 5, Allies quit Pekin

Nov. 14, Treaty between Russia and China—the former obtaining free trade, territories, &c.

Nov. 30, First installment of indemnity paid

1861

Jan. 5, Part of the allied troops settled at Tien-tsin; consulate established

Feb., Adm. Hope examines Yang-tse-Kiang, &c.

March, English and French embassies established at Pekin

Aug. 21, The Emperor Heinfung dies

Oct. 21, Canton restored to the Chinese

Dec. 13, Ministerial crisis; several ministers put to death, Nov.; Kung appointed regent

Dec., Advance of the rebels; they seize and desolate Ning-po and Hang-chow

1862

Jan., They advance on Shang-hae, which is placed under protection of the English and French, and fortified

April, Rebels defeated in two engagements

May 10, English and French assist the government against the rebels—Ning-po retaken

May 17, French admiral Protet killed in an attack on rebels

July, Captain Sherard Osborne permitted by the British government to organize a small fleet of gunboats to aid the imperialists to establish order

Oct., Imperialists gain ground, take Kah-sing, &c.

Tungani (Mahometan) revolt in Central Asia; massacre of Buddhists

1863

Jan. 14, Commercial treaty with Prussia ratified

Oct., The Imperialists under Col. Charles Gordon defeat the Taepings under Burgevine, &c.

Dec. 4, 5, Gordon captures Sowchow (after a severe attack, Nov. 27, 28); the rebel chiefs treacherously butchered by the Chinese

Dec. 31, Capt. Osborne came to China; but retired in consequence of the Chinese Government departing from its engagements

1864

Jan. to April, Gordon's successes continue

March 23, Repulsed; he takes Chang-chow-foo

July 18, He takes Nankin (a heap of ruins); Hun-seutseun, the Tien-wang, the rebel emperor, commits suicide by eating gold leaf, June 30; Chang-wang and Kan-wang, the rebel generals, are "cut into a thousand pieces"

1865

Jan., Great mortality among British troops at Kowloon

Jan.–March, The Taepings hold Ming-chow; the Mahometan rebellion (Douganese) progressing in Honan

May 23, Taepings evacuate Ming-chow

June, Rebellion in the north advancing

July, A rebellion of the Nien-fei in the north; Pekin in danger

——, The Chinese general San-ko-lin-sin defeated and slain; his son more successful

Nov. 7, Prince Kung chief of the regency again

Nov. 26, Sir Rutherford Alcock, ambassador at Pekin

1866

Jan. 14, Chinese newspaper "Messenger of the Flying Dragon," appears in London

March 13, Great victory over the Nien-fei announced at Canton

June, Chinese commissioners visit London

July, Rivalry of two great political chiefs in China, Li Hung Chang and Tsen-kwo-fan

1867

Dec., Reported victory of the Nien-fei over the imperialists

Mahomed Yakoob Beg defeats the Tungani, becomes supreme in Kashgar, 1866; is recognized by Europe

1868

July 4, Chinese embassy (Mr. Anson Burlinghame, Chin Kang, and Sun Chia Su) received by President Johnson at Washington, June 5; they sign a treaty

Oct., The rebels seize Ningpo

Nov. 14, The people at Yang-chow, incited by the "literati" (learned classes) destroy the Protestant mission-houses, Aug. 22: redress not obtained; a British squadron proceeds to Nankin, Nov. 8; the Viceroy Li Hung Chang is superseded, and the British demands acceded to

1869

Jan. 24, Chinese embassy received by the Emperor at Paris

Oct. 24, Supplementary convention to the treaty of Tien-tsin (June, 1858) for additional commercial freedom, signed

1870

May, Successful rebellion of Mahometans in north-west provinces reported

June 21, Cruel massacre of the French consul at Tientsin, Roman Catholic priests, sisters of Mercy (22 persons), besides many native converts, and above 30 children in the orphanage, by a mob, with, it is said, the complicity of the authorities: the missionaries were accused of kidnapping children

July, Increased hatred of the people to foreigners at Tien-tsin; lukewarm proceedings of the Government against the murderers

About Aug. 22, Ma, a viceroy of Nankin, favorable to Europeans, assassinated

Sept. 21, Chapels destroyed at Fatshan

Sept. 26, The French ultimatum refused; the murderers of the nuns unpunished; Chinese warlike preparations reported

Oct., Judicious mandate from the mandarin Tsengkwo-fan, exculpating the missionaries, and condemning their massacre

Oct. 26, 16 coolies beheaded, Sept. 15, and 23 exiled; indemnity to the sufferers by the outrage ordered; reported

Nov. 3, End of the difficulty announced

1871

Aug., Chung-how, an envoy, arrives in London

Autumn, Memorial addressed to the Chinese Government by Mr. Hart, inspector of customs, recommending changes in civil and military administration

Oct. 16, The young Emperor married

Nov. 23, Received at Paris; apologizes for Tien-tsin massacres, and reports redress

Russia annexes Kuldja

Dec., Wm. Armstrong Russell consecrated Anglican Bishop of North China

1873

Feb. 23, The Emperor's majority; he assumes the government

Feb., Talifoo, capital of the insurgent Panthay Mahometans, captured; thousands massacred

June 29, Foreign ministers for the first time received by the Emperor

1874

July–Aug., Dispute with Japan, see Formosa; settled by treaty, Oct. 31

Aug. 22, The *Spark* sails from Canton to Macao; Capt. Brady and Mr. Mundy, and a foreign crew and passengers; pirates, who came on board secretly, kill captain and others, and carry off booty, while on voyage; the wounded crew manage to reach Macao

1875

Jan. 12, Death of the Emperor

Feb. 4, Proclamation of his successor, Tsai-tien, son of Chun, 7th son of Taou-Twang (nephew of Kung)

March 12, Exploring expedition under Col. Horace Browne to open a passage from Burmah into S.W. China, Dec., 1874; Mr. Margary and 5 Chinese going before, killed at Manwyne, Feb. 21; Col. Browne and his troops repulse an attack by Chinese, but retreat to Rangoon, Feb. 22; some of the party missing

Sept., Through negotiations of Mr. Wade, the Chinese Government promise due reparation; announced

Oct. 11, Edict permitting intercourse between chiefs of departments and foreign ministers, about Oct. 4; enjoining proper treatment of foreigners

Oct. 18, Telegram from Mr. Wade; he has obtained necessary guarantees, satisfaction for the murder of Mr. Margary, and concessions for foreign trade

1876

May 5, Gen. Lee-see-ta-hee ordered for trial, Feb. 11; Margary's murderers said to be executed

June 30, First railway in China, from Shang-hae to Oussoon (Woosung), (11 miles); trial trip, March 16 (at first opposed); publicly opened

June, Mr. Grosvenor and others, sent to inquire respecting the murder of Mr. Margary, arrive at the place and report the proposed punishment of the murderers

Sept. 17, Chee-foo convention between Sir Thos. Wade and Li Hung Chang; difficulties in the negotiations removed (the government agree to compensation to Mr. Margary's family; removal of commercial grievances; opening of four ports; proper official intercourse; said to be signed, Sept. 13; ratified

Nov. 6, War against the Tungani; Manas captured; great massacre of rebels

1877

Jan. 21, Accredited Chinese envoy (Quo-ta-Zhan) lands at Southampton

Feb. 1, Decree of equal rights to Chinese Christians

April 1, Four more Chinese ports opened

Aug., Opium smoking interdicted after 3 years; announced

About Nov., Quo-ta-Zhan (or Kuo-ta-Jên) first accredited minister at London; Liu-ta-Jên at Berlin

Dec., The railway from Shang-hae bought to be stopped, Oct. 31; resumed

——, Yakoob Beg of Kashgaria totally defeated by the Chinese general, Tso-tsung-tang; is assassinated, May; Kashgar and other towns captured; end of war

1878

Aug. 30, Destruction of mission property at Wu-shih-shan by a fanatical mob, unrestrained by the mandarins

The Shang-hae railway plant removed to Formosa

Chinese immigrants virtually excluded from Australia by a poll-tax

Oct., Rebellion in Kwang-si, announced

Dec., Chung-How, ambassador at St. Petersburg, demands the surrender of Kuli Beg, a fugitive from Kashgar, and restitution of the territory

1879

Jan., Rebellion in Hainan, in Canton province; Li-Yang-tsai, who invades Annam, claims the throne by descent; reported

March 20, Marquis Tsêng, the new Chinese ambassador, arrives in London, Feb. 28; presents his credentials to the Queen

About June, Treaty with Russia, who agrees to evacuate the Kuldja territory, China to pay an indemnity

Dec. 2, Li-Yang-tsai, rebel chief, captured; announced

1880

Spring, 1880, Chung-How, the late Chinese Ambassador at St. Petersburg, imprisoned and the Treaty disavowed

April, Thomas, Duke of Genoa, sails up the Yang-tse-Kiang in an Italian vessel

May, Chinese from Kashgar said to invade Russian territory

June, Prospect of war; Col. Gordon goes to China from Bombay

July, Li Hung Chang, governor of metropolitan provinces, fortifies approaches to the capital, June; visited by Col. Gordon

July 15, Chung-How released; proposed war with Russia given up; announced

1881

Aug. 19, Peace with Russia, who makes concessions negotiated by Marquis Tsêng; Treaty signed

1883

Sept., Complication with France respecting Tonking (see Tonking)

Nov., China issues a circular claiming Annam as a dependency

1884

April 11 et seq., *Coup d'état* at Pekin effected by Prince Chun, father of the reigning Emperor, who becomes dictator; Prince Kung, and the Viceroy Li Hung Chang, deposed

May 2, The Marquis Tsêng recalled from Paris, announced

About May 8, Replaced by Li-Fong-Pao

May 11, Treaty with France, signed by Capt. Fournier and Li Hung Chang, at Tientsin; French protectorate of Annam and Tonking recognized; three southern provinces opened to commerce

The Chinese break the treaty by attacking the French marching to occupy Langson (*see* Tonking)

July, The French demand evacuation of the Tonking frontier forts, and 10,000,000*l.* indemnity

——, The war party at Pekin oppose the Empress and Li Hung Chang the Viceroy

July 30, The frontier towns to be surrendered, the indemnity refused, announced

Aug., China offers reduced indemnity

Aug. 5, 6, Kelung in Formosa bombarded and forts destroyed by alleged treachery by Adm. Lespès

Aug. 10, Adm. Courbet at Foochow

Aug., Negotiations at Shanghai

Aug. 17, France declines mediation of the Powers; France issues a circular to the Powers

Aug. 19, Indemnity claimed by France, reduced to 3,000,000*l.*; refused by China

Aug. 21, The French Ambassador, Semallé, leaves Pekin; war ensues

Aug. 26–28, Adm. Courbet with his fleet sails up the Min river unattacked; destroys the Chinese fleet with much slaughter, Aug. 23; bombards the arsenal at Foochow, and dismantles the forts; destroys the forts and batteries, &c., at Mingan and Kinpai; French killed, about 7; Chinese said to be about 1,000

Aug. 28, Li Hung Chang deprived of his highest offices

Sept. 6, Chinese declaration of war, in a manifesto to the people, announced

Sept. 18, H.M. gun-boat *Zephyr* fired on by mistake, Sept. 6; Chinese apologize

Sept. 16, Chinese said to be defeated at Kinpai Pass

Sept., Europeans, at Shanghai and other places, protest against the war

Sept. 24, Li Hung Chang reappointed Viceroy about

Oct. 1, Adm. Courbet captures Kelung; Adm. Lespès bombards Tamsui, Oct. 2 *et seq.*; lands; retires Oct. 8

Oct. 8, Kelung occupied by French; little resistance

Oct. 23, N. and W. Formosa blockaded

Nov. 12, 1,000 Chinese defeated near Tamsui, Nov. 2; repulsed in attack on Kelung, announced

Dec. 10, Fruitless mediation of Earl Granville with Marquis Tsêng, announced

Dec. 13, Reported Chinese defeat near Kelung

1885

Jan. 23, Foreign Enlistment Act proclaimed at Hong Kong

Jan. 25, French attack near Kelung, Chinese works carried

Jan. 31, Chinese defeated with much loss

Feb. 15, Two Chinese junks sunk by French torpedoes

March 2, Bombardment of Chin-hae, at the mouth of the Yung-Kiang river

March 2–3, Siege of Tuyen Quan, much slaughter

March 4–12, Several forts at Kelung captured; sanguinary conflicts

March 30–31, Pescadores Islands captured

About April 6, Preliminaries of peace, through intervention of Sir Robt. Hart, signed at Pekin; treaty signed June 9; ratified, Nov. 28

June 23, Sir Robert Hart, British Ambassador, resigns about Aug. 31

June 23, Formosa evacuated about

July, The Emperor agrees to receive a papal agent to protect Roman Catholic missionaries

About Aug., Introduction of railways authorized— new policy

Aug., Disputes with Japan settled; reported

Sept. 4, Death of Tso Tsung-Tang, a great statesman and guardian of the King

1886

April 7, Sir John Walsham, British Minister

April 28, Liu-shin-fun, ambassador for Great Britain, arrives

July 14, M. Agliardi appointed Internuncio

July 24, Convention with many concessions by the British Government respecting the Burmese frontiers and trade signed at Pekin

About Sept. 15, The scheme suspended by the Pope through French opposition

Nov., The French consent to the transfer of the Cathedral from its contiguity with the palace

——, The Chinese annul the French protectorate over all Christians

Nov. 21, Decanville railway successfully opened

1887

Jan., General proclamations for protection of Christian missionaries and converts, excluding foreign protection

Feb. 7, The Emperor, aged 16, assumes the government

Aug. 25, Convention between Great Britain and China, respecting Burma and Tibet, signed July 24, and ratified

Aug., Commercial treaty with France, 1886; signed and ratified

Sept., Chinese fleet of five ironclads (three constructed in Britain) at Spithead; sail for China under Admiral Lang with others lent by the Admiralty

Oct., Reported convention of Li Hung Chang, the Viceroy, with Count Mitkiewicz and an American syndicate for introduction of railways, telegraphs, telephones, &c., and a loan, Aug.; repudiated by the Chinese Government

Sept.–Oct., Overflow of the Hoang Ho, or Yellow River, causing immense destruction; about 1,500 populous villages destroyed, and the important city Chuhsien Chen narrowly escaped with loss of suburbs; millions of persons said to have perished; famine imminent; the government active in providing relief

1888

March 14, Treaty with United States to allow Chinese immigration for 20 years with some exceptions (lawful marriage and children, property worth 1,000 dollars, &c.) signed; China refuses the ratification, Sept.

July 27, The Empress-Mother announces her resignation of the administration of government, which is to be assumed by the Emperor

Middle Oct., The Chinese Exclusion Act vigorously carried out at San Francisco, and at other places

Nov., Railway from Tientsin to Taku opened

Dec., Conventions with Italy and Germany for them to protect their missionaries, announced

Dec. 8, New Roman Catholic cathedral at Pekin consecrated

1889

Jan., Great famine in consequence of inundations of the Yangtsze and Yellow River valleys announced

Feb. 4, 5, Riots at Chin-Kiang, the British consulate and foreigners' houses burnt

Feb. 25, Marriage of the Emperor

June 4, Hsieh Ta Jên appointed Minister for London, Paris, Brussels, and Rome, announced

June 27, Luchow, in the province of Szechuen, destroyed by fire, about 1,200 persons perish

July 26, The Yellow River bursts its banks at Shantung, and inundates the country, and countless lives are lost, reported

Aug. 30, Great inundations in North China through typhoons; about 5,000 persons perish, reported

Aug., The construction of a trunk railway from Pekin to Hankow, 700 miles, proposed

Sept. 9, Insurrection in the province of Fuhkien; suppressed; 100 insurgents killed; announced

Dec., The project postponed through opposition

——, Insurrection in the Amour district of Manchuria; reported success of the rebels; they seize the town Lan-pei-tuan; imperialists defeated in battles; announced

1890

March 31, Convention for the opening of the Chung-King to commerce signed at Pekin

Oct. 16, Great floods at Pekin, Tungchow, and Tientsin; business stopped, Aug. 3; renewal of the Yellow River inundations early Sept.; also in the provinces Shantung and Chihli; great loss of life and prospect of famine reported

Dec., Massacre of many native Christians at Jong-tuytsin and other places by a fanatical society reported

Dec. 12, An imperial decree, granting audience of the Emperor to representatives of foreign powers issued

Death of Prince Chung, father of the emperor, reported

1891

May 12, 13, Anti-European riots at Wuhu; much destruction; British consulate wrecked; the consul and his wife escape; quiet restored by force

June 15, Increased popular anti-foreign agitation throughout China, June; the diplomatic body appeal to the Government; the Emperor issues a decree for the protection of foreigners and punishment of aggressors, about

Aug. 18, Continued persecution of foreigners; the imperial decree ineffectual; the diplomatic body press the Government, about

The Kolao Hui, a secret society, strongly opposed to foreigners and Christianity, active, summer

Sept. 11, The American mission at Ishang destroyed

Sept. 15, The outrages against foreigners increase; the diplomatic body report to their respective governments, about

Sept. 21, Great Britain, France, Germany, and the United States, N.A., unite for the common support of their people against Chinese violence, reported

Oct. 23, Compensation paid to the sufferers in Wuhu by the Viceroy, about

Oct. 23, British squadron and other vessels at Nagasaki and other ports, about

Nov. 11, A *modus vivendi* with the Chinese authorities arranged by the European ministers, reported

Nov. 28, 29, Insurrection in Mongolia and N. China against foreigners and native Christians; reported massacres, Nov.; suppressed by Government troops after battles, with much slaughter

Dec. 7, Agreement of the Hunan societies against Europeans, &c., published at Shanghai, about

Dec., Memorials of the Viceroys of Nanking and Hukuang (attributing the anti-foreign outrages to baseless rumors circulated by conspirators) issued

——, The Government pays indemnities amounting to 100,000*l.* to Christian missions and others, and punishes Chinese officials and offenders

——, Mr. Christopher Gardner, British consul, and Dr. Griffith John, missionary, assert that the anti-foreign outbreaks originated with the local mandarins, aided by Chanhan (or Chou Han), an eminent Hunan scholar and writer of offensive placards, &c., reported

1892

Jan. 3, The rebels in the north, headed by Li Hung, defeated by Yulu, reported

March 4, Mr. Nicholas R. O'Conor appointed British Minister at Pekin, about

April, Chanhan, the agitator, ordered to be arrested, March 25; not arrested; the right of audience by the Emperor requested by the foreign ministers, rejected, early

Early May, Bill for the stringent exclusion of Chinese immigrants from the United States, passed by Congress

June 14, Renewed outrages on European missionaries, April 27, reported

Sept. 23, Great inundation by the Yellow River; 12 towns said to be destroyed; reported

Dec. 13, Mr. O'Conor, British Minister, received informally by the Emperor

Dec., The ancestors of Sir Halliday Macartney raised to mandarins, reported

1893

March 8, Famine in N. Shen-si reported

May 5, The Chinese exclusion (immigration) act in the United States comes into effect; (107,475 in the States)

June 29, Kung Chao-quan appointed Minister at St. James's reported

Nov. 2, Chinese exclusion amended bill passed by the U.S. Senate

1894

May 31, Insurrection in Manchuria reported

June 14, Gen. Ting sent to suppress the rising, and to redress grievances, reported June 4; rebellion subsides

July, War with Japan, *see* Korea

Aug., Treaty between China and U.S. ratified

Sept. 15, Murderous outrages on missionaries; murder of the Rev. James Wylie, Presbyterian, by soldiers at Liao-Yang; the murderers beheaded and officers degraded, reported

Oct., Prince Kung returns to power, announced

Oct. 15, Imperial edict for the protection of foreigners and missionaries

Nov. 4, Li Hung Chang (Minister) superseded by Prince Kung with enlarged powers

Dec. 10, Rebellion at Wu-hu; Admiral Fremantle proceeds there, reported

Dec. 13, Prince Kung appointed president of the grand council, virtually dictator; Li Hung Chang returns to power

1895

March 22, Risings in S.W. Kwang-tung, government troops repulsed, reported

May 8, Treaty of peace with Japan, concluded; see Korea, April 17; ratifications exchanged

May 29, 31, Foreign mission houses at Chengtu and Szechuan destroyed by rioters; missionaries safe

June 25, Treaty with France respecting boundaries, commerce, &c., signed at Pekin

July 4, Loan of 400,000,000f. 4% guaranteed by Russia, signed at Pekin, at St. Petersburg, July 6

Aug. 1, Massacre of British missionaries (the Rev. R. W. Stewart, 8 ladies, and 2 children) at Whasang, near Ku-cheng by a fanatical sect called Vegetarians

Aug. 7, British and American missions attacked, hospitals destroyed at Fatshan

Aug. 17, The British Government demands immediate redress

Aug., Japan demands an indemnity for giving up the Liao-tong peninsula; evacuations to begin on first payment, Aug.; supplementary treaty signed Nov. 8

Aug., The Chinese Government acting with the foreign consuls; arrests and punishes criminals; reported

Aug., Additional outrages reported; 10 members of the Vegetarian society and others convicted about Aug. 28; 7 criminals executed at Kucheng, Sept. 17

Sept. 22, Insurrection of the Dungans, Chinese troops defeated near Su-chau, Gen. Soui beheaded; reported

Sept. 30, British ultimatum demanding the degradation of the Viceroy of Szu-chuan and others, Sept. 28; accepted by China

Oct. 15, The Viceroy of Fo-kien agrees to the trial and punishment of those convicted in the Ku-cheng massacres, owing to the arrival of the British admiral; reported

Oct. 30, China agrees to pay compensation to Germany for the plundering of a mission station at Swatau; an agreement concluded at Shanghai for a crown concession to Germany at Han-kau, Oct. 6; and at Tien-tsin; reported

Oct. 31, Lan-chau-fu, capital of Kansu, captured by Mahomedans; reported

Nov., Li Hung Chang charged with orders to suppress the insurrection; mutiny of troops at Kiu-kiang Khiang

1896

Jan., Sir C. M. Macdonald appointed British envoy and Minister at Pekin; arrives, April 22

March 24, Anglo-German loan for 16,000,000l. at 5% signed at Pekin

March 30, Sir Robert Hart appointed superintendent of posts and telegraphs; reported

April 2, China enters the postal union

——, M. Gérard, French Minister, recalled

May 4, Li Hung Chang, Grand Secretary, received by the Czar at St. Petersburg; travels in Germany—Berlin (honored), Essen, &c., visits Prince Bismarck, June 25; at The Hague, July 4; Brussels, July 8; Paris, July 13; London and other cities, Aug. 1–21; received by the Marquis of Salisbury, Aug. 4; received and decorated by the Queen at Osborne, Aug. 5; arrives at New York, Aug. 28, received by Pres. Cleve-

land, Aug. 29; Canada: Toronto, Sept. 7; leaves Victoria, Sept. 16; Yokohama, Sept. 27; Pekin, Oct. 20; appointed Minister for Foreign Affairs, Oct. 26

May 8, Second payment of war indemnity to Japan at the Bank of England (4,400,506l.)

May 25, Mahomedan rebellion: a town in Kansu captured by the Dungans; reported

Sept., Reparation granted for the injuries done to French missionaries, at Kwei-chau, since 1886

Nov. 24, Ministers appointed in London, Washington, Berlin, and St. Petersburg; announced

Dec. 29, Chinese Eastern, or Russian Manchurian railway; see Russia

1897

Jan. 10, Baron von Wahlborn appointed first Austro-Hungarian Minister at Pekin; announced

May 26, Chang Yin-huan, special envoy, arrives in England

May, Prince Oukhtomsky's mission to Pekin; well received

May 27, New Russian bank opened at Pekin

May 30, Sheng Ta-jên, director of railways; contract for the construction of the Han-Kau railway signed with a Belgian syndicate

June 4, The West river opened to foreign trade

Nov. 14, Reparation demanded by Germany for the recent murder of 2 German missionaries; troops landed at Kiao-chau bay: the Chinese retired; indemnity, 200,000 taels (about 35,000l.), &c., refused; Nov. 29 [Kiao-chau, ceded to Germany, with adjacent territory, 99 yrs. lease; Jan. 5: ratified; Jan. 24, 1898]

Dec. 18, Russian fleet, arrives at Kinchau, near Port Arthur, with China's approval

1898

Jan. 3, Li Hung Chang recalled to power

Jan., Feb., Negotiations with Gt. Britain and Russia, respecting loans, fail

Feb. 9, Japan claims payment of the indemnity (11,008,-857l. paid by the Bank of England on behalf of China, May 7)

Feb. 20, Inland waters to be opened to British and other steamers, with regulations, in June

——, Père Favier (30 years resident) consecrated as Bishop at Pekin

March 3, Chinese loan of 16,000,000l. at 4½% between Hong-kong and other banks; ratified

March 6, German-Chinese agreement relating to privileges in Shan-tung, signed

Four ports opened to trade, April; see Russia, England, and France, 1898

May 9, Serious riots at Sha-shi, Japanese consulate and other offices, &c., destroyed; indemnity, &c., paid, July 12

May 13, The Yangtsze trade regulations, drawn up by Sir Robert Hart, agreed to

May, Successful steam navigation of the Yangtsze rapids (750 miles) by Mr. Little

May 15–18, Prince Henry and the German squadron visits Kiaochau, May 5; received by the Emperor and Empress at Pekin

May 29, Death of Prince Kung, aged 68

May 30, Wei-hai-wei, occupied by the British, May 30; convention signed, July 1

June 7, Indemnity and concessions granted to France for the murder of Père Berthollet

June 9, Convention signed at Pekin leasing extension of boundaries to Hong-kong

June 10, Rebellion in Kwang-tung; a magistrate and his wife killed; reported

June 15, Concession for Grand-central railway from Hankau to Pekin secured by Franco-Belgian syndicate; reported

June 21, Contract signed at Pekin, authorizing the Anglo-Italian syndicate to work coal and iron mines in Honan, &c., for 60 years

June 23, Typhoon at Port Arthur, 130 Chinese sailors drowned; reported

July 18, Riots in Shanghai concerning the sale by the French local authorities of the Ning-po guild cemetery, French marines and police fire on the mob, 14 natives killed, July 16; provisional agreement, quiet restored

Aug. 12, Contract for Russian loan for the Pekin Hankau railway ratified

Aug. 19, Black Flag rising in Kwang-si; British consul at Wu-chau telegraphs for gunboats, June 28; a magistrate and many officials killed; nine towns captured, and troops defeated near Wu-chau, reported July 12; further conflicts reported

Sept. 7, Li Hung Chang dismissed from the Tsung-li-Yamên by decree

Sept., American and French missions attacked at Ho-chau, 50 miles from Chung-king; reported [indemnity paid to the United States, Jan., 1899]

Sept. 20, The Marquis Ito visits Pekin, received by the Emperor

Sept. 22, *Coup d'état*, regency of the Empress restored, reactionary policy, flight of Kang-Yu-Wei, reformer (saved by British consuls, and conveyed to Hong-kong)

Sept. 28, Six members of the reform party executed

Oct. 7, Violent insults to Europeans, Oct. 1; foreign escorts arrive at Pekin

Oct. 10, Reformers in office dismissed

Oct. 16, Lord Charles Beresford, on a commercial mission, arrives at Pekin; well received at Chinese ports; returns to Hong-kong, advocates the "open door," Jan. 3, 1899

Oct. 20, French missionary and converts massacred at Paklung; indemnity demanded by France

Oct. 23, 24, Military outrages on Englishmen near Pekin, railway work stopped; Chinese troops removed, Nov. 15–27

Early Nov., Yellow River floods in Shan-tung, villages destroyed; Li Hung Chang sent to concert preventive measures, Nov. 30 [his report issued, end of March, 1899]

Nov. 4, Mr. W. S. Fleming, British missionary, murdered at Pang-hai (2 murderers executed and 3 officials degraded, Jan., 1899; further reparation demanded, June, July)

Mid-Nov., Chinese force (1,000) enrolled under British officers at Wei-hai-wei

Nov. 24, M. de Giers, new Russian Minister, arrives

Dec., Anti-Christian riot in Hu-pei, French priest killed

Dec. 27, Rebels defeated at Sah-chiao-tsang

Dec. 30, Edict initiating administrative reforms issued

1899

Jan., Tseng-ho, governor of Hu-pei, in favor of reforms, degraded

——, Insurrection in An-hui

Jan., Hu Yu Fen, director of northern railways, dismissed; Sir Claude Macdonald insists on an investigation, Jan. 31; Hu Yu Fen is acquitted, March 7

Feb., Russian troops (1,300) at Port Arthur and neighborhood; fight between Russians and Chinese at Ta-lien-wan, many Chinese killed, reported, Feb. 19

——, 2,800 miles of railway granted to British investors

March 14, Sig. Martino, Italian Minister, demands a naval station at Sammun bay, &c., Feb. 28; refused, March 3; ultimatum presented to China, rejected, March 11, 12; Sig. Martino recalled, and his action disavowed by his Government

March, Yu Hsien, founder of the anti-foreign and anti-Christian sect, the "Boxers," made governor of Shantung

April, Boundary of territory leased by Russia near Port Arthur settled, mid March; anti-foreign disturbances by the Boxers (Red Fist) and the Big Knife societies, in Shantung, March; German punitive expedition, villages burnt, Yi-chau occupied

April 28, Anglo-Russian agreement with regard to railway extension in Manchuria and the Yang-tsze-kiang, &c., signed at St. Petersburg

May 18, Anglo-German Tien-tsin–Chin-kiang railway loan, 7,400,000*l.* (5%), ratified at Pekin

June 20, Extension of the cosmopolitan settlement at Shanghai, agreed to (ratified Dec.)

June 22, French consulate and other houses at Mong-tsze destroyed in a riot

June 23–26, German railway works raided (June 18) near Kiaochau, troops sent, 17 Chinese killed

June, Two Russian engineers and 10 Cossacks killed by brigands in Niu-chwang

July, Burmo-Chinese boundary completed

July 12, Imperial edict against the malpractices of revenue officials issued

Aug. 13, Ta-lien-wan declared a free port

Mid Aug., Fight between Chinese troops and brigands at Cokton on the West River, many killed

Early Sept., Russian province of Kwang-tung placed under a gov.-gen.

Mid-Oct., Yano Fumio, Japanese Minister at Pekin, recalled

Nov. 15–18, Two French naval officers massacred near Montao; villages seized by Adm. Courregolles; the Chinese repulsed with loss

Nov., Indemnity demanded by M. Pichon [paid Jan. 16, 1900]

——, Li Hung Chang appointed Minister of Commerce, and Viceroy of Canton, Dec.

1900

Jan. 11, Rev. Mr. Brooks massacred by rioters in Shan-tung, officials degraded and 2 of the murderers beheaded, by edict issued Jan. 5, 1900; another edict, evasive as to the suppression of the "Boxers" and other anti-Christian societies, issued

Jan. 24, *Coup d'état* by the Empress-Dowager, edict issued, naming Po Ching (14), son of Prince Tuan, the heir-designate

Jan. 27, Foreign ministers demand the suppression of the Boxers and other hostile secret societies

Feb.–March, Negotiations, edicts issued without effect

March 4, Boundary convention of Kwang-chau-wan, 99 years' lease to France, ratified, reported

Mid-March, Extension of the French settlement in Shanghai

March, The "open door" in China for the world's commerce successfully promoted by Mr. Hay, U.S.A. Secretary of State

May 5, 6, Treacherous attacks on the Wei-hai-wei boundary commission repulsed by Chinese under Col. Bower and Capt. Watson

Mid May, Massacre of native Christians by Boxers between Pao-ting-fu and Pekin

May 20–30, Emphatic protests *re* the Boxer movement from the legations to the Yamên

May 21, Troops sent to the disturbed areas; 6 leaders arrested in Pekin

May 27, Insurrection spreads; railway property, &c., destroyed; Chinese employés killed

May 28, Feng-tai railway station burnt by the Boxers; refugees arrive at Pekin

May 29, Evasive edict, practically encouraging the Boxers, issued

May 31, Foreign marine guards (340; 75 British), arrive at the Pekin legation

——, Pao-ting-fu refugees attacked by Boxers, 4 killed and many missing

June 2, Mr. Norman and Mr. Robinson, missionaries, and 5 converts murdered at Yung-ching

June 3–5, German and Austrian guards arrive in Pekin

June 4, Huang-tsun station burnt, employés killed by the Boxers

June 5, Foreign reinforcements land at Tien-tsin

June 6, Railway communication stopped at Pekin, anti-foreign movement still spreading, another evasive edict issued

June 7, 8, Massacres and destruction of railway and mission stations spreading from Pekin district to other provinces

June 9, Imperial edict decreeing a massacre of foreigners, issued (changed into a protective edict by 3 members of the Tsung-li-Yamên, who were afterwards cruelly executed, Aug. 14)

June 10, The Tsung-li-Yamên reorganized under Prince Tuan and 3 Manchus

June 11, Adm. Sir Edw. Seymour's force defeats the Boxers at Lang-fang

——, M. Sugiyama, Japanese chancellor, murdered by Chinese troops in Pekin

June 13, 14, Massacre of native converts and foreign employés in Pekin, buildings burnt

June 14, 18, Adm. Seymour repels the enemy at Lang-fang

June 17, Disbandment of troops in the Taku forts demanded by allies, June 16; the forts open fire on allied fleets, but are captured

——, Tien-tsin foreign settlement fiercely attacked

June 18, Stern message from France to the Viceroy of Yunnan, respecting the safety of the missions there

June 19, Mr. James Watts carries dispatches from Tien-tsin to Ta-ku

——, Foreign legations ordered to quit Pekin

June 20, Baron von Ketteler murdered by Chinese troops in Pekin, the legations besieged (*see below*)

June 22 or 23, The Dowager-Empress and Prince Tuan issue anti-foreign decrees

June 23, Seymour captures arsenal near Tien-tsin, June 22; Chinese driven back, Capt. Beyts killed

——, Tien-tsin foreign garrison hard pressed, June 21; relieved by allies after hard fighting

June 26, Seymour returns to Tien-tsin

——, Edict issued at Pekin virtually declares war on all foreigners, and their expulsion ordered

June 27, Arsenal N.E. of Tien-tsin captured by the allies

June 28 and July 9, Massacre of about 54 missionaries, men, women, and children, at Tai-ynen-fu in Shan-si, by Yu-Hsien, the governor's orders

June 29, Insurrection spreads to Manchuria in the north and Shantung in the south, slaughter of Chinese near Tien-tsin, reported

——, Imperial edict disclaims responsibility for the fighting and throws all blame on the Europeans

——, Adm. Seymour's advance to Pekin checked, retires to Tien-tsin

July 3, Joint proclamation by the Nankin and Wuchang viceroys, generally satisfactory, issued

July 3, 4, Chinese attack on foreign settlements of Tien-tsin repulsed

July, Anarchy in Manchuria, missions destroyed, Bishop Guillon, Roman Catholic, and others, burned alive in the cathedral of Mukden

——, Edict from Pekin ordering the extermination of foreigners, issued

July 5, British Government announces that it will hold the authorities in Pekin responsible for injuries to foreigners

July 6, Li Hung Chang maintains order in Canton, frequent executions of robbers and pirates, reported

——, Coöperation of the Powers, Japan allowed a free hand, about

July 8, British Government assures the Viceroy of Nankin of support in quelling disorder in the Yang-tsze region

July 11, Fierce fighting at Tien-tsin, July 6; the allies seize an arsenal, about 386 Chinese killed, July 9; Chinese attack on the railway station repelled with heavy loss

July 13, 14, Tien-tsin, native city and forts, captured, a fort and 48 guns seized by the Japanese

[Allies casualties about 800; 26 British of the naval contingent alone killed and 149 wounded during the 4 weeks' fighting]

July 16, Fighting on the Russian frontier of the Amur, Blagovestschensk bombarded

July 18, Li Hung Chang confers with the governor in Hong-kong

——, 19, Russians rout the Chinese on the Amur

July 19, 21, The Emperor appeals in vain for mediation to France, Germany, America, and Japan

July 19–26, Severe fighting at Niu-Chwang

July 20, Capt. Watts-Jones and 10 or 12 Europeans murdered at Kwei-hua-cheng by the governor's order

July 21, Li Hung Chang arrives at Shanghai

——, Further massacres of missionaries and others in Shan-si at Pao-ting-fu, Chu-Chau, and other places in the north

July 23, British successes near Wei-hai-wei, reported

July 28, Gen. Zakharoff captures San-sung in Manchuria

July 29, 31, Two progressive Yamên ministers beheaded in Pekin by the Empress's order, and the exiled Chang-Yin-Huan, G.C.M.G., executed in Kashgaria

Aug. 3, 4, The Russians seize Hailar, Harbin relieved, Chinese defeated at Blagovestschensk, Sakhalin, and Niuchwang captured

Aug. 6, Allies advance to Pekin, Japanese victory, Chinese driven out of Pei-tsang, many killed, Aug. 4, 5; Yang-tsun captured

Aug., Frequent executions of pirates in Canton

Aug. 9, Bengal lancers charge Tartar cavalry at Ho-si-pou with success

——, British troops land at Shanghai

Aug. 12, Allies occupy Tung-chau, enemy fled

Aug. 14, Emperor, Empress, and court flee from Pekin after ordering the execution of 5 pro-foreign members of the Yamên

——, Russians seize both banks of the Amur, massacre of about 4,800 Chinese by Gribsky and his Cossacks at Blagovestschensk

[Siege of the Pekin Legations begins; total guards: 18 officers, 389 men; the British legation filled with refugees; outposts fiercely attacked; Prof. J. Huberty and others killed, June 20; Sir Claude Macdonald takes command at the British legation, the Hanlin academy burnt by Chinese, June 22; the Japanese repulse a fierce attack, many Chinese killed, June 24; combined attack of Boxers and troops repulsed with severe loss, June 27; brilliant sortie, many Chinese killed, July 3; Captain Strouts killed, July 16; armistice concluded, but siege continued, July 17; the allies relieve the legations after a rapid march and much fighting, General Gaselee and his Sikhs arrive first, followed by the Americans, amid the wildest joy, 3 p.m., Aug. 14 (total casualties during the siege, about 67 killed, 120 wounded, and 5 other deaths)

Aug. 17, Pei-Tang Roman Catholic bishopric, in Pekin, nobly defended by Mgr. Favier, 133 priests, and 42 French and Italian marines, with about 3,000 refugees, June 20, till relieved by the Japanese and allies. [Total deaths during the siege, 400]

——, Imperial city entered, palace gates held by allies

——, Forbidden city closely guarded by allies

Aug. 19, Boxers defeated near Tien-tsin, 300 killed, 64 captured

Aug. 20, British force defeats Chinese and Boxers in the park, Pekin

Aug. 21, Sir Robert Hart resumes his office in Pekin

Aug. 22, Li Hung Chang's peace overtures rejected by the Powers

——, The allies forbid looting, and call on the Chinese to return; they march through the Forbidden city and occupy the imperial palace, Aug. 28

Aug. 24–29, Continued Russian successes in Manchuria

Aug., Wholesale massacres of missionaries and native converts at Fu-chau-fu, Aug. 15, and many other places

Aug. 30, Four Boxer leaders executed at Tien-tsin

Early Sept., Boxers routed round Pekin

——. British troops occupy Feng-tai, near Pekin

Sept. 11, Liang-hsiang, S.W. of Pekin, stormed by German marines and Bengal lancers, 500 Boxers killed

Sept. 13, 20 Germans killed in an encounter with Boxers near Pekin

Mid Sept., Boxers routed, and over 200 killed by Americans and Bengal lancers, at Mo-tao

Sept. 14, Total allies in Pekin, 62,000 (22,000 Russians, 19,000 Japanese, and 5,000 British)

——, Accident to British party while destroying gunpowder at Tung-chau, 16 deaths and 22 wounded

Sept. 17, Boxers defeated at Pa-ta-chu

Mid-Sept., Ti-lin occupied by the allies and afterwards burnt

Sept. 18, Russians occupy the Manchurian frontier and 6 towns, columns penetrating the interior, much slaughter, reported

Sept. 20, 21, Pei-tang and Lutai captured with heavy losses by the allies

Sept. 21, Anti-Christian riots in the south, converts slaughtered, reported

Sept. 21, Punitive expeditions of the allies against the Boxers, reported effective

Sept. 24, Kirin, a rich town in Manchuria, occupied by the Russians; An-shan-jan captured, Sept. 26

Sept. 25, Boxers routed by the British, 15 m. S. of Pekin

Sept. 26, Degradation and punishment of Prince Tuan and 4 others, ordered by imperial edict (reported a forgery, Oct. 15)

Sept. 27, Count von Waldersee appointed commander-in-chief of the allies, Aug.; arrives at Tien-tsin

Sept. 29, Shan-hai-kwan forts surrender to the British

——, Russian garrison in Pekin reduced

Oct. 1, The German Emperor, in reply to the Emperor Kwang-su's message, states that he cannot regard the murder of Baron von Ketteler as expiated by certain ceremonies, refers to the massacres of missionaries, and insists on full reparation for the crimes committed and punishment of the guilty officials

——, Mukden taken by the Russians

Oct. 3, Summer palace looted by the Russians, Sept.; occupied by the British and Italians

Oct. 4, French note, demanding punishment of the chief culprits, prohibition of the import of arms, indemnities for states, societies, or persons, establishment of permanent legation guards at Pekin, dismantlement of the Taku forts, and military occupation of certain points between Tien-tsin and Taku (accepted as the basis of negotiations), issued

Oct. 8, Pekin-Tien-tsin railway held by the British; Russian claim to left bank of river at Tien-tsin disputed

——, The Czar announces that no part of China shall be annexed by Russia

Oct. 10, Conference of ministers in Pekin: Chinese proposals pronounced inadequate, Oct. 8; punishment of guilty officials, payment of an indemnity, dismantling of Taku and other forts, abolition of the Tsung-li-Yamên and appointment of one minister for foreign affairs, provision for rational intercourse with the emperor, &c., agreed to as a basis of negotiations

Oct. 14, Chinese camp, 3 officers and 200 men, captured in Manchuria

Mid Oct., Anti-dynastic rebellion in S. China, reported

Oct., Reactionary Manchus appointed to high posts in Yang-tsze districts

Oct. 15–21, Allies (4,000, under Gens. Campbell and Bailloud) enter Pao-ting-fu

Oct. 16, Anglo-German agreement—chief points: the "open door" and the integrity of China to be maintained

Oct. 24, Death of Kang Yi, instigator of the Boxer movement and chief secretary of state, confirmed

Oct. 25, Rebels victorious in Kwai-sin, much slaughter, reported

Oct., Punitive expeditions by the allies, villages destroyed

242 missionaries (mainly British), with their wives and children, murdered during the Boxer rising in 1900

Oct. 27, The governor and 13 headmen beheaded at Pao-ting-fu for the murder of missionaries and others; city bastions and temple destroyed

Oct. 31, Boxers defeated near Shun-i-hsien

Oct.–Nov., Russian excesses, indiscriminate slaughter, 5,000 Chinese thrown into the Amur

Nov. 2, Fatal explosion at Nankin, the Yamên destroyed, reported

Nov. 2, 3, Kunan-sien captured by an Italo-German column

Nov. 6, Explosion at Tiu-lin, 5 soldiers and many Chinese killed

Nov. 13, Illusory punishments on guilty princes and officials decreed

Nov., China resumes the civil government of Manchuria under Russian protection

Nov. 14, The Emperor writes to the German Emperor owning that punishment of the guilty officials would be just

Nov. 18, Count Yorck's column occupies Kalgan, Chinese flee [he died Nov. 25]

Mid-Nov., Yu-chang, Governor of Hu-pei (Oct.), dismissed through Sir E. Satow, and one friendly to foreigners appointed

Nov. 19, Anti-Christian riots in Kwang-si, reported

——, Boxers defeated in several small actions, and the Ming tombs occupied, reported

Nov. 28, Che-kiang, Governor, to whom was due the Chu-chau massacre of 20 missionaries (9 British) and others, dismissed

Nov. 29, The astronomical instruments, erected over 2 centuries ago by the Jesuits, seized by the Germans

Nov.–Dec., Russians exterminate brigands and Chinese troops in Manchuria

Dec. 19, Districts round Pekin placed under the allies

——, Yu-Hsien, ex-Governor of Shan-si, executed

Dec. 22, Gen. Bailloud defeats Boxers and Chinese, many killed, near Pei-chau, town burnt

Dec. 27, Joint note, after long negotiations, demanding China's compliance to "12 irrevocable conditions," preliminary to the withdrawal of the allies from Pekin and provinces, signed by the ministers in Pekin, Dec. 20; presented, Dec. 22; accepted by the Emperor in his decree

Dec. 28, German operations in Chi-li, indiscriminate punishment, Dec. 5–15; much criticized

Dec. 31, En-hai, the murderer of Baron von. Ketteler, executed in Pekin

——, Russian *de facto* protectorate over Feng-tien and Mukden; Manchuria-Russo-Chinese agreement signed, about

1901

Jan. 3–5, Germans defeat the Boxers in Chi-li, about 200 killed

Jan. 6, Col. Tulloch's punitive expedition to Kao-li-ying successful, returns to Pekin

Jan. 17, Peace protocol signed at Pekin, Jan. 14; ratified by the Emperor

Jan., New judicial system, under Chinese, instituted by the allies in Pekin

——, The Russians hand over the Shan-hai-kwan-Pekin railway to the Germans

Jan. 24, Kwei-chau rebels defeated by Chinese

Jan., Russian operations against the Hungus in Manchuria

Jan. 30, Imperial government reform decree, issued

——, Explosion at Shan-hai-kwan, 40 Japanese killed, reported

Feb. 1, Edict suppressing anti-foreign societies, under penalty of death

Feb. 13, 21, Prince Tuan sentenced to life-imprisonment, Duke Lan and Gen. Tung-fuh-siang banished, Prince Chuang and 2 others ordered to commit suicide, and 2 others to be executed, by edicts

Feb. 16, 8 Boxer leaders executed at Han-kau

Feb. 21, Germans rout the Chinese W. of Pao-ting-fu

Feb. 26, Chi-hsiu and Hsu-Cheng-yu executed

Feb. 21–28, N. China railway restored to the British

March 22, 23, Anglo-Russian dispute over a railway siding at Tien-tsin, March 15; British reinforcements arrive, matter referred to arbitration

March 23, Rev. J. Stonehouse murdered by Chinese near Lo-fa, on the Tien-tsin line, about

April 5, Manchurian convention, opposed by the Powers and rejected by the Emperor, end of March; withdrawn by Russia

April 23, The Privy Council replaced by a "general board of state affairs," by edict

About April 23, Sharp fighting near Ching-wang-tao, Maj. Browning and a sepoy killed; enemy defeated by the allies near Shan-hai-kwan

April 23, 24, Chinese routed by Germans at the Great Wall

April 26, British capture 16 Krupp guns, &c., reported

April, Famine in Shan-si spreading, great mortality

——, German raids on the borders of Shan-si

May 1, The Viceroy of Canton abolishes the privileges of the Manchus

——, Fresh fighting in Manchuria, reported

May 19, M. Beau succeeds M. Pichon as French Minister

May 21, Six out of the 11 chief criminals reported to have met their death; punishments demanded by all the Powers, Russia excepted, in 107 cases

May 22, Boxers dispersed, 110 killed near Pao-ting-fu, reported

May *et seq.*, Departure of foreign troops

June 3, Count von Waldersee leaves Pekin for Germany

June 4, Great fire in the Forbidden city at Pekin

June 24, "Allied villagers" new anti-foreign movement spreading, reported

July 1, Chinese government partially resumed in the British section of Pekin

July 13, New Russian concession at Tien-tsin opened

July 14, General Gaselee leaves Pekin

July 15–24, Destructive floods in the Yang-tsze districts, June 1; many deaths (over 10,000,000 homeless)

July 28, Sixtieth ministerial meeting in Pekin; Chinese indemnity of 450,000,000 taels at 4% finally agreed upon, July 26; notified to Chinese envoys

Aug. 19, Edict forbidding examinations in all cities where foreigners were massacred or cruelly treated

Mid-Aug., British famine relief mission leaves Pekin for Shan-si

Sir E. Satow demands the punishment of the authors of the Chu-chan massacre, when Mr. and Mrs. Thompson, their children, Miss Desmond, and 5 other English missionaries, Wu, a Chinese magistrate, and 31 others, were barbarously killed, about July 21, 1900 [4 high officials banished, 15 others executed, 9 banished and 7 imprisoned, reported, Sept. 13]

Sept., Prince Chun's mission received at Potsdam (*see* Germany), Sept. 4, 1901; Chinese envoy sent to Japan

Sept. 7, Peace protocol with China signed by the 11 foreign ministers, Aug. 15; by Prince Ching and envoys

——, Missionary work and reform encouraged by the Viceroys of Shan-si, Shan-tung, and Yang-tsze, reported

Sept. 14, The summer palace occupied by the British

and Italians, Oct. 12, 1900; transferred to the Chinese

Sept. 17, The Japanese and Americans hand over the Forbidden city to the Chinese; the evacuation of Pekin completed

Sept. 23, Total German losses during the expedition to China, 676, including deaths from disease, reported; French casualties, 433, 61 killed, Oct.

Oct. 5, The Basel mission at Piang-tong, N.E. Kwang-tung, burnt by Triad rebels, end Sept.; rebels routed near Swatau with great slaughter by Gen. Wu, Oct. 1; another station destroyed in the Hsing-ning district, reported

Oct., The Chinese maintain peace and order in Pekin, N. China, and railways, mines, &c., active

Nov. 1, Welsh barracks burnt at Tien-tsin, 2 deaths

Nov. 5, Yang-tsze valley reported peaceful and prosperous

Nov. 8, Death of Li Hung Chang, diplomatist, friend of Russia, aged about 78, Nov. 7; succeeded by Yuan Shih-kai, as governor of Chi-li

Nov. 30, Imperial edicts favoring reorganization and reforms issued; Pu Chun, heir-apparent, disinherited but styled Duke

Mid Dec., Sir Robert Hart appointed one of the guardians of the heir-apparent

——, Rising in N. Chi-li suppressed, daily executions of rebels in Pekin

Dec. 20, Impressive funeral to the Christians massacred in 1900, and public atonement made by the officials of Tung-chau and 50 villages

1902

Jan., Two missionaries and 3 converts murdered in Kan-su, Dec.; officials degraded by edict issued Dec. 31; Tung-fuh-siang ordered to be beheaded

Jan. 7, The imperial court returns to Pekin; the Dowager-Empress again supreme

Jan. 14, Edicts protecting missionaries and native Christians, and ordering punishment of officials complicated in the Boxer movement, issued

Jan. 16, A French priest and 2 converts murdered in Kwang-tung

Jan.–Feb., Conflicts in Manchuria between Russians and Tunguses

Feb. 1, Foreign ministers received at court, Jan. 22; the ladies received by the Dowager-Empress, who expressed regrets for late events, and desire for progress

——, Marriage between Chinese and Manchus legalized; the custom of foot-binding deprecated by edicts

——, United States of America note protesting against Russian encroachments in Manchuria

Feb. 2, Yung-lu appointed first grand secretary by edict

Feb. 8, European professors dismissed from the Imperial university

Feb. 10, German mission in Kwang-tung destroyed by Chinese, reported

Feb. 11, Anglo-Japanese agreement, maintaining the status quo, the "open door" policy, independence and territorial integrity of China and Korea, signed in London, Jan. 30, issued

Feb. 24, Sir Robt. Hart and Mgr. Favier received in court

March 12, 13, Marshal Su defeats the rebels at Lang-chau, Kwang-si; 2 French officers murdered on the frontier, reported

March 19, Franco-Russian joint declaration, the integrity of China to be maintained

March 25, Edict issued degrading 2 magistrates in consequence of a rebellion and murder of 14 converts in S. Honan

March 26, Chinese attack on a Russian post in Kwan-tung, Manchuria, defeated

March 29, Riots at Ta-ming-fu in Chi-li, many killed, reported

April 8, 9, Manchurian convention revised, the status quo to be maintained, Russia to withdraw gradually in 18 months, signed and ratified

Early April, Kwang-si rebels severely defeated

April 12, Russian force inflicts terrible loss on a robber band on the Mukden frontier, reported

April 29, N. China railway restored to China, agreement signed by Sir E. Satow, Yuan Shih-kai, and Hu Yu-fen

April 30, Imperial postal service gradually supersedes private agencies, reported

May 2, Anti-indemnity riots at Ching-ting-fu, French missionary murdered, reported

May 5, Rebels totally defeated by the troops at Nanning

May 12, Export duty on tea reduced, to about ½d. per lb. (5%), reported

About May 30, Chou-fu, treasurer of Chi-li appointed governor of Shan-tung

June 6, Grand Duke Cyril (Russian) received with highest honors at Pekin

June 12, Sir Ernest Satow agrees to a pro rata reduction of the final indemnity claims to about 2%, reported

June 15, Anglo-French syndicate secures a mining concession (60 years) in Yun-nan

June 20, Russia withdraws from the Tien-tsin foreign government, announced

June 22, Kai Chi, Chinese cruiser, blown up by an explosion in the powder-magazine near Nankin, 150 lives lost

June 23, 27, Boxer movement in Sze-chuan, Methodist chapel destroyed, 10 converts killed; English and American missions at Tien-ku-chao destroyed, and a missionary killed, reported

June 30, Yuan Shih-kai's plan for the reorganization of Manchuria, published

July 19, Chinese accept the conditions for the restoration of Tien-tsin

July 29, Chang Chih-tung, viceroy of Wun-chang, appointed imperial commissioner of trade, about

——, Tariff revision completed by China, Great Britain, and 8 powers

End July, Order restored in Sze-chuan, over 300 rioters killed; rebel leader in S. Chi-li captured and executed

Early Aug., The Viceroy of Sze-chuan deposed

Aug. 12, Rebels defeated with great slaughter in Sze-chuan

Aug. 15, Tien-tsin transferred to the Chinese

——, Rev. H. R. Lowis and Rev. J. R. Bruce murdered by rioters at Cheu-chau, in Hu-nan (Lin-Hann-Yu, a mandarin, executed Nov. 17)

Aug. 16, Protocol tariff signed by the British and 6 other powers

Sept. 5, Sir James Mackay's (G.C.M.G. Nov. 9) British treaty, abolishing likin dues on all goods, native or foreign, and substituting other import and export duties, &c., signed after long negotiations

1903

Jan. 3, Evacuation of Shanghai completed by departure of last detachment of German troops

Jan. 7, Shanghai Taotai makes half-year's indemnity payments on a silver basis. Foreign ministers, except U.S. representative, sign joint note that protocol adopted by the bankers' commission provides for payment of the indemnity in gold: failure to fulfil obligation must entail grave consequences

Early Jan., Telegraphic returns from treaty ports show customs revenue for 1902 over 30,000,000 taels, as compared with 25,500,000 taels in 1901. Total of Shanghai 10,000,000 taels

——, Agreement for construction of a railway from Shanghai to Nankin, in substitution for the preliminary contract of May, 1898, concluded with government by British and Chinese corporation

Jan. 18, Memorial arch erected at Pekin by Chinese Government as atonement for murder of Baron von Ketteler in 1900, formally dedicated by Prince Chun in presence of Baron Goltz and large number of foreigners and natives

April 23, Russia presents 7 demands as conditions for carrying out the Manchurian Convention, and the evacuation of Niu-chwang and the two southern provinces of Manchuria. Chief provisions: No new treaty ports to be opened in Manchuria, and no new foreign consuls permitted; all customs revenues to be paid into Russo-Chinese bank; no portion of Manchuria to be alienated to any other power; none but Russians to be employed in any administrative capacity, civil or military, in Manchuria; reported

April 29, Demand rejected by China

June 11, Imperial decree sanctioning construction of the Shanghai-Nankin railway; to be completed in 5 years from date of signing final contract

June 12, Settlement of a Chinese customs at Dalny, on the Russian frontier of leased territory

——, Negotiations with Japan for revision of commercial treaty, in consequence of the insistence of Japan on clause in treaty opening Mukden, Ta-ku-shen, and other Manchurian centers to foreign trade, announced

Mid-June, Report of U.S. consul at Niu-chwang on trade of Manchuria in 1902. Increase of foreign imports for last 10 years from 100 to 500%, reached highest point in 1902; total import and export trade about 8,000,000*l*.

June 22, Secret agreement between China and Russia regarding Manchuria, reported

June 28, Ratification of Mackay treaty announced on way to Pekin

Mid-July, Wang Chi-chung, the notorious governor of Kwangsi, Marshal Su, and other high officials of that province, removed by imperial decree

End July, Negotiations for opening the ports desired by Japan and U.S. reported to be successful

July 28, Ratifications of Anglo-Chinese commercial treaty exchanged

July 31, Chinese journalist and reformer, Shen Chien, beaten to death by order of government

Aug. 7, Protest of British Government

Aug. 12, Russian viceroy appointed for the Amur and Kwan-tung territories, ukase issued

Aug. 13, Chinese troops defeated at Hevei-chan, reported

Sept., Messrs. Claude Russell and Hicks-Beach suc-

cessfully explore 100 miles east of the Khingan mts. in E. Mongolia, July–Sept.

Sept. 7, Chinese board of commerce created by edict

Oct. 8, Commercial treaties signed with the United States and Japan

——, Russia fails to evacuate Manchuria according to agreement on appointed date

Nov. 5, M. Lassar, Russian Minister, demands the appointment of a Russian resident at Mukden, reported

Nov. 12, Canton-Fatshan branch of the Canton-Hankau railway (joint American and Belgian undertaking) opened

Nov. 13, Fight between Russian and Chinese imperial troops near Shan-hai-Kwan, reported

Dec. 5, Army amalgamation on a national basis ordered; Yuan Shih-Kai, viceroy of Chi-li appointed head of the army and navy, reported

Dec. 8, Russian defeat of the Chunchuses on the Lian river, Manchuria; 200 killed, reported

Dec. 16, Shanghai sedition case; 6 Chinese journalists arrested end of June for seditious writings in the *Supao;* their surrender to Pekin refused by the British legation after protracted negotiations; tried at Shanghai, Dec. 3; 4 released, 2 convicted, sentence deferred

Mid Dec., Chang-yi, director of Northern railways, degraded for selling the Kai-ping mines

1904

Early Jan., Japanese Government in view of a possible conflict with Russia instructs M. Uchida, Japanese Minister at Pekin, to advise China to observe neutrality should hostilities break out

Jan. 13, Commercial Treaty by which United States consuls may be sent to Mukden and Antung in Manchuria, signed by the Emperor, ratified by telegraph, and consuls appointed by the U.S. Government. Commercial treaty with Japan for opening the foreign trade and settlement of two treaty ports, Mukden and Ta-tung-Ku in Manchuria, ratified

Mid Jan., To strengthen the Wai-wu-pu, government appoints as one of its ministers, Wu Ting-fang, formerly Minister at Washington

Feb. 12, Secretary Hay's note in reference to the neutralization of China made public. It expresses the earnest desire of the U.S. Government that the neutrality of China, and in all practicable ways, her administrative entity shall be respected by both belligerents, and that the area of hostilities shall be localized as much as possible. Imperial edict published in Pekin proclaiming the neutrality of China

Feb. 13, Chinese Minister at Tokio intimates to the Japanese Foreign Minister the intention of China to observe neutrality in the war

Mid Feb., Japanese Government in reply state that in all parts of Chinese territory, except the regions occupied by Russia, Japan will respect the neutrality of China so long as it is respected by Russia

Feb. 22, German Shan-tung railway from Tsing-tau to Tsi-nan-fu, 388 kilometers, reported to be near completion; first construction train runs to Tsi-na-fu East

March 3, Russian consul at Shanghai informs the Taotai that as the result of instructions received from Pekin, he is prepared to arrange for the disarmament of the gunboat *Manjur*

March 25, Totai informs the Japanese consul that the

Russian Government has finally agreed to complete the disarmament of the *Manjur*

March 26, Trade returns of the maritime customs for 1903, show development of the import of cotton fabrics from Japan, and a serious falling off of these from Great Britain and America; exports of tea show continued increase, issued

April 3, Sir Robert Hart's scheme for the reorganization of the financial and military resources of China, upon which the high provincial authorities were instructed to memorialize the throne, published in the native press

Mid April, Prince Su dismissed, Na-tung appointed his successor in office

May 6, Ministers of the Powers in Pekin act unitedly in recommending the Chinese Government to maintain strict neutrality during the Russo-Japanese war

May 8, Washington despatch states that the Russian Ambassador, Count Cassini, acting on instructions from his Government, appeals to the U.S. as a friendly neutral power to use her influence with China towards preserving neutrality

May 12, Anglo-Chinese labor convention containing regulations for the importation of Chinese laborers into the Transvaal, and their control there, signed

May 16, Sharp fighting between Russians and Chunchuses near Liu-yang and Port Adams, reported

Early June, Sir John Lister-Kaye, representing a London syndicate, signs at Pekin the final contract, sanctioned by imperial decree, whereby a concession is granted to work the iron and copper mines in the Tung-ting district of the province of Hu-nan, reported

July 2, Chang-sha, in Hu-nan, opened as a treaty port

Early July, Official commencement of work on the Shanghai-Nankin railway, arranged for June 30, postponed on difficulties raised by Shêng-Ta-jin; British Minister intimates to that official that the British Government cannot view with equanimity any further manifestation of hostility to British interests

July 18, Edict ordering an inquiry into the methods of collecting the land tax, published

July 19, Roman Catholic Bishop Verhaeghen, his brother, and another Belgian missionary murdered in Hu-pei

July 28, Dowager-Empress publicly recognizes the medical work of the Protestant missions by contributing through the British Minister 10,000 taels (1,450*l.*) towards the Lockhart medical college in course of construction, reported

End July, Extension of the rebellion in province of Kwang-si, reported

Aug. 2, 2,000 coolies sail from Tien-tsin for Durban

Aug. 20, Japanese Government state their attitude with regard to the seizure of the *Reshitelni* at Chifu, and declares their position on the question of Chinese neutrality

End Aug., Revival of Boxerism reported from Taning-fu in province of Chi-li

Sept. 2, French Government demands the punishment of the culprits, and degradation of officials concerned in the murder of the Belgian missionaries

Sept. 15, Fracas between Italian and Chinese soldiers in Pekin

Mid Sept., U.S. Minister at Pekin states that China promises definitely that American or British shall have the preference if foreign capital is required for the extension of the Han-Kau railway to Ching-Kung

Sept. 26, M. Lassar reported to be negotiating for the purchase of the Trans-Manchurian railway by a Chinese company

Mid Oct., Large body of rebels defeated at Lo-cheng-hosien by Chinese troops; Boxer movement reported to be spreading

Early Nov., Deposed Dalai Lama enters Chinese territory; officials sent to escort him to Urga and place him in a monastery

Nov. 11, Treaty with Portugal, on lines of the treaties with Great Britain, and the United States and Japan; deals with Macao and its commercial rights and protection, improves facilities for the prevention of contraband opium trade; contract signed for construction of a railway from Macao to Sung-shin by a Chino-Portuguese syndicate

——, Proposals made by China for the settlement of the vexed question whether the international indemnity of 1901 should be regarded as a gold or silver debt

Dec. 1, Foreign ministers jointly protest against the levying of additional transit dues by Chinese authorities as being contrary to treaty

1905

Jan. 1, Peking-Han-Kau railway reported finished as far as the Yellow River, total length, 600 kilometers

Jan. 29, German efforts to establish in the province of Shan-tung a supreme control similar to the Russians in Manchuria, reported

Feb. 3, Final contract signed in Pekin by Chao Erh-tsun, president of the board of revenue, Mr. E. G. Hillier, G.M.G., agent of the Hong-Kong and Shanghai Bank, and Herr Cordes, agent of the Deutsh Asiatische bank, for a Chinese government gold loan (1,000,000*l.* issued at 91, 5%, redeemable in 20 years, secured by the *likin* revenues of the Shan-si province) to be devoted to the payment of the balance required for converting the Boxer indemnity into gold

Early Feb., New council formed composed of high officials from the various government departments which will discuss matters of importance to the Empire, including foreign affairs. Council will only hold discussions when commanded to do so by the throne, its consultations being conducted by correspondence, reported

March 1, Tang Shao-yi, special envoy for the settlement of the Thibetan question, appointed Chinese Minister to Gt. Britain

Early April, Death of Mgr. Favier, aged 68, Apostolic Vicar of Pekin, an eminent champion of French interests in China for 40 years

April 15, Draft of new Chino-German commercial treaty completed at Shanghai sent to Pekin for consideration

April 16, Shanghai correspondent of *Times* states no single important clause of the Mackay treaty is yet effective since its ratification by China, July 28, 1903, and that the provincial officials are encouraged by the government in flagrant violations of its provisions

April 24, M. Pokotiloff, one of the directors of the Russo-Chinese bank, appointed Russian Minister at Pekin in succession to the late M. Lassar

——, Decree issued summarizing criminal proceedings, and abolishing the cruel punishment of slicing to death and the punishment of a family for the fault of an individual: decree issued in response to a memorial from Wy-ting-Fang, formerly Minister at Washington and a barrister-at-law of Lincoln's Inn

Early May, Tseng-chi, Tartar general of Mukden, highest Chinese official in Manchuria, retires, and is succeeded by Chao Erh-tsun, president of the board of revenue and one of the most enlightened officials in China

May 10, Large meeting of Chinese merchants held at Shanghai protest vigorously against the Chinese-American exclusion treaty: they unanimously decide to boycott American goods until the treaty is modified

May 23, Convention signed at the Wai-wu-pu between China and Great Britain renewing art. 16 of the Burma convention of 1894, respecting a junction between the Burma and Chinese telegraph lines

June 11, First locomotive drawing an inspection train crosses the Yellow River bridge on the Pekin-Han-Kau railway line (to be opened in Nov., 1905)

June 14, M. Pokotiloff, new Russian Minister to China, calls on the Dalai Lama at Urga with present from the Czar

June 19, 600 students representing 26 colleges hold meetings in the native city at Tientsin in connection with the anti-American movement and pass a resolution in favor of a boycott on American goods, and the encouragement of Chinese manufactures

July 2, All the Powers sign note accepting China's proposal that the Boxer indemnity should be a gold instead of a silver debt

July 3, Chinese merchants of Selangor unanimously resolve to boycott American manufactures; boycott adopted by all the Chinese in the Straits Settlements

July 18, Four high Chinese officials have been ordered to proceed to Japan, Europe, and America, to investigate the systems of constitutional governments (after the manner of the commission of Prince Iwakura subsequent to the restoration in Japan); one other object of the mission believed to be an endeavor to induce the Powers to call an international conference on Far Eastern affairs, reported

July 19, Officials of the province of An-hui hold a great meeting, at which they decide to construct railways throughout the whole territory under their jurisdiction, reported

Aug. 1, Boycott on American goods started

Early Sept., Imperial edict issued with reference to the boycott and the U.S. Government

Sept. 24, Explosion of a bomb thrown into the carriage of the reform commissioners when leaving Pekin, kills 4 and injures 20 other persons

1906

Jan. 3, Maritime customs revenue for 1905 exceeds that of 1904 by about 3½ million taels (500,000l.), an increase of over 10%, reported

Jan. 12, Text of the Manchurian convention, concluded on Dec. 22, 1905, published in the Times

Early Feb., English and Roman Catholic missions at Chang-pu, 30 miles from Amoy, destroyed by a Boxer mob; estimated damage, 10,000l.

Feb. 13, Opening ceremony of the Lockhart medical college at Pekin

Feb. 22, Rioting and murder of missionaries at Nan-chang-fu

Mar. 12, Kwang-si, rebel leader, together with three men, implicated in the attack on the house of Dr. Beattie, the American missionary, at Fati in Feb.: beheaded

Mar. 22, The Comet, a launch belonging to the Standard Oil Company, plundered by Chinese pirates

April 10, Disturbances in Southern Ho-nan and Western Shan-tung, caused by the "big knife" society, a kind of relic of the Boxer movement; bandits stated to number 12,000; troops sent to quell the movement, reported

April 27, Treaty with England, embodying the adhesion of China to the Tibetan convention, signed

May 7, Customs revenue for 1905 was 5,281,280l., an increase of 767,262 over the receipts of 1904, previously the largest on record

June 1, Mukden opened as a free port

June 8, Death of Sir Haliday Macartney, for nearly 30 years British secretary and adviser to the Chinese legation in London, b. 1833

June 19, Two British subjects killed near Amoy, reported

July 13, The Rev. Dr. Macdonald, British missionary, killed by pirates in an attack on the steamer, Sainam, 50 miles from Wuchau; a British gunboat despatched to the scene of the outrage

July 16, Two sections of the Shanghai-Nanking railway, extending 91 miles, opened

Aug. 10, A British launch attacked near Wu-Chau by pirates, who killed one man, wounded three others, and carried off about 75l. and a chest of opium

Sept. 10, Sir John Jordan, the new British Minister, arrives in Peking

Sept. 18, Typhoon at Hong-Kong; a fleet of 600 junks swept away and 10,000 lives lost; the Rt. Rev. Jos. Chas. Hoare, D.D., Bishop of Victoria, Hong-Kong, b. 1851, was drowned

Sept. 20, Edict, abolishing the use of opium within 10 years, issued

Sept. 30, First section of the railway from Peking to Kalgan formally opened

Oct. 11, Prince Fushimi, the first Japanese prince who has officially visited Peking, arrived on a visit to the Chinese court

Nov. 3, Mr. Pless, an Englishman, murdered in Peking

Nov. 4, Severe famine reported in the province of Kiangsu; about 10 millions people on the brink of starvation

Nov. 6, Imperial edict, making important changes in the high offices of the central administration in Peking, the most important of which is the creation of a new board of communications to control the telegraphs, steamship lines, railways, and postal service, issued

Nov. 10, Negotiations concerning the Canton-Kau-lung railway concluded by an agreement signed by the representatives of the Wai-wu-pu and of the British and Chinese corporation for the issue of a loan of 1,500,000l. for the construction of a line from the frontier of Kau-lung to Canton, a distance of 102 miles

Nov. 22, Regulations for enforcing the abolition of the use of opium received the imperial sanction, Nov. 21; officially submitted to the British Minister

Dec. 1, Administration of Niu-chwang handed over by Japan

Dec. 12, Disturbances in the province of Hu-nan reported as serious. The rebels, whose object is anti-dynastic, are reported several thousand strong and well armed; 2,000 foreign-drilled troops despatched against them by the Viceroy, Chang-chih-ting

Dec. 18, Officially announced, that by agreement with Russia, China will open, as international places of residence and trade, Kwang-cheng-tsze, Kirin,

Kharbin, Tsitsihar, and Manchuria; to take effect Jan. 14, 1907

Dec. 23, Revenue of China during the past year reported to be the largest on record

1907

Jan. 3, Famine reported prevailing in the Tsing-kiang-pu, Su-chien, Yaowan, and Hsu-chau district; relief work begun

Jan. 8, Total maritime customs collected for 1906 amounts to about 6,000,000*l.*—the highest amount ever received, reported

Jan. 28, The China Society, Caxton-hall, Westminster, for the encouragement of the study of Chinese language, literature, history and folklore, and other Chinese matters. Inaugural meeting

Feb., Ratification, by imperial edict, of the agreement for the construction of the Canton-Kau-lung railway, signed in Nov., 1906; China thereby undertakes to carry out the work with British capital and British engineers

April 23, Li Chin-fang, the adopted son of Li Hung-chang, appointed Chinese Minister in London

May 10, Maritime customs trade report for 1906 shows that Great Britain's share of the export trade was 19.42%, and of the imports 47.34%

May 27, Outbreak in Wong-kong; all military and civil officials murdered and the yamêns burnt, reported

May 30, Rebels defeated by provincial troops, losing over 100 men; capture of the leader reported

May 31, Insurrection 40 miles south of Amoy; 30,000 men reported in revolt

June 1, Severe encounter between imperial troops and rebels near Amoy; 700 casualties reported

June 17, Dismissal of Chu Hung-chi, president of the Ministry of Foreign Affairs, who is succeeded by Lu Hai-huan

Sept. 27, Outbreak of boxerism in the south of Kiang-si; several converts and an Italian priest murdered

1908

Jan. 13, Contract for the Tien-tsin-Yang-tsze main line of railway signed by the Chinese Government and the representatives of the Deutsche-Asiatische Bank and of the British and Chinese corporation, control being entirely vested in the Chinese Government with European advisory engineers and auditors

Jan. 28, Sir R. Bredon appointed acting inspector-general of maritime customs

April 14, Disastrous floods at Han-kau, at the junction of the Han-kiang and Yang-tsze-kiang; 2,000 persons drowned and 700 junks sunk or wrecked. *Times*

May 16, The Ya-lu forestry agreement with Japan signed

June 6, Sir Walter Hillier appointed British adviser to the Chinese Government

June 22, Disastrous floods in the Fu and West rivers; enormous destruction of crops and other property reported

July 2, Treaty of friendship and commerce with Sweden signed (Sweden refuses to ratify, Dec. 4)

Aug. 13, Mutiny of 1,000 soldiers at Konghau

Sept. 28, Reception of the Dalai Lama in Peking

Oct. 29, The Russian Government notifies its intention of withdrawing the Legation guard from Peking and the Russian troops from Tientsin

Oct. 30–Nov. 5, Visit of the United States battleship fleet to Amoy

Nov. 1, Serious riots in Hong-Kong organized by the Chinese who had been promoting the anti-Japanese boycott

Nov. 14, Death of the Emperor Kwang-Hsu; Prince Chun appointed regent during the minority of Pu Yi

Nov. 15, Death of the Empress Dowager Tsze-Chi

Dec. 2, Enthronement of Pu Yi

Dec. 3, An imperial decree reaffirms a previous decree announcing the convocation of a parliament and the proclamation of a constitution nine years hence

1909

Jan 2, Removal of Yuan Shih-kai from office

Jan. 12, Telegraphic convention with Japan, signed on Oct. 12, 1908, and supplementary agreement signed Nov. 7, 1908, ratified

Feb. 8, Chen-pi, president of the board of communications, cashiered for corruption

Sept. 4, The Manchurian convention, settling the railway dispute with Japan, and the Korean boundary agreement, signed

Oct. 14, The new provincial assemblies meet in accordance with the regulations established by the imperial decrees of Oct. 19, 1907 and July 22, 1908, for the first time

1910

Jan. 7, Collision at Tonking between a band of 150 deserters from the Chinese army and French troops, many Chinese killed and wounded and one French officer killed and two wounded, reported

Jan. 21, Japan and Russia declined to agree to proposal of American Secretary of State Knox of Dec., 1909, of neutralization of Manchurian railways

Jan. 30, Imperial decree denied petition of representatives of provincial assemblies for immediate establishment of a Parliament

Jan. 31, Imperial rescript abolished slavery. Published Feb. 19

Feb. 9, Postal Convention with Japan signed

Feb. 22, Lhasa, Tibet, occupied to compel Dalai Lama to govern in accord with orders from Peking. The Dalai Lama fled to India

Feb. 25, Edict published in Peking deposed the Dalai Lama

March 16, Foundation stone for new Hong-Kong University laid by Sir F. Lugard

April 14, At Changsha in Hunan a "corner" in rice started riots first directed against Government offices and schools and later on all foreign establishments. The Japanese Consulate and most of the foreign business houses and 6 out of 9 missionary stations burned

May 24, Decree commanded that the unit of national currency should be the yuan or dollar and temporary standard silver

——, Hankow-Szechuan Railroad Loan signed by American, French, German, and English bankers

July 4, Convention of Japan and Russia as to Manchuria. *See* Manchuria

July 21, China approved the Russo-Japanese Convention of July 4 as to Manchuria

Oct. 3, First National Assembly met in Peking. Opened by the Regent who declared that this was the first step towards granting a Constitution and that though the Assembly had not powers of legislation it could recommend legislation

Nov. 4, Imperial edict announced that Parliament of an Upper and Lower House would be convoked in 1913 2 years earlier than promised

Nov. 30, Resolution of radicals in the Assembly asked that the Grand Council be made responsible to the Assembly. Rejected by Regent Dec. 18

Dec. 4, Opening of foreign Chinese loan of $25,000,000 for development of navy

Dec. 26, Edict ordered preparation by Constitutional Bureau of a constitutional program

1911

Jan. 2, Yuan Shih-Kai ordered into exile by Regent Prince Chun

Jan. 11, National Assembly dissolved

April 15, $50,000,000 loan Agreement for reform of the currency system and development of Manchuria signed at Peking with group of bankers of the United States, Great Britain, France, and Germany

April 27, Revolutionary rising in Canton led by Huang Hsing. The "seventy-two heroes of Hoang Hoa Kang" lost their lives

May 8, Revolt in Szechuan Province

——, Imperial edict abolished the Grand Council, Grand Secretariat, and Commission of Constitutional Reform and substituted a Cabinet of 13 members and a Privy Council. Prince Cheng appointed Prime Minister, and Natung and Hsu-Schilchang as Vice-Ministers

——, Agreement signed with Great Britain provided for gradual extinction of Chinese production and importation of opium

May 9, Imperial edict ordered all railroads under construction or projected taken over by the Government

May 20, Second loan Agreement with international bankers for $30,000,000 for construction of Szechuan Railroad in Hunan and Hupei provinces

May 28, Postal service transferred from Customs to Ministry of Communications under Yu-Chuan-pu and Li Cheng-fang; T. Piry, administrative head

Aug. 4, 18, and Sept. 4, Meetings of shareholders of provincial company for building Szechuan Railroad asked reimbursement from the Government

Aug. 24, Strike of students begun in Chengtu

Sept. 5, Great floods in Yangtze-Kiang Valley caused loss of life and property

Sept. 7, Revolt in Szechuan Province

Sept. 9, Armed mob representing provincial shareholders of Szechuan Railroad surrendered arms and were then massacred, resulting in insurrection of the Szechuan Province

Sept. 20, Death of Sir Robert Hart, Inspector General of Imperial Maritime Customs since Nov. 30, 1863

Sept. 21, Troops relieved besieged city of Cheng-Tu

Oct. 3, National Assembly opened

Oct. 9, Explosion of bomb in house in Russian concession in Hankow led to discovery of headquarters of revolt planned

Oct. 10, Revolt begun at Wuchang (Hankow) led by General Li Yuan-hung

Oct. 12, The Hu Peh provincial Assembly seceded from Chinese Imperial Government. Rebels occupied Hankow and Hanyang

Oct. 14, Yuan Shih-Kai recalled from exile and appointed viceroy of Hunan and Hupeh provinces, which appointment he accepted Oct. 18 to put down revolt

Oct. 18, Indecisive engagement with rebels near Hankow. General Yinchang (Yen Tchang), Minister of War, sent with troops to southern provinces

Oct. 20, Hankow retaken by rebels, Shansi joined the revolution

Oct. 22, Second session of National Assembly convened at Peking. Demand renewed for real legislative power

Oct. 24, Sian-Fu and Kin-Kiang captured by rebels

Oct. 25, Sir Francis Aglen appointed Inspector General of Customs

Oct. 26, Impeachment and dismissal of Sheng-Hsuan-Huai, Minister of Communications, political rival of Yuan

Oct. 27, Rebels proclaimed republic with General Li Yuan-hung president and commander-in-chief

Oct. 28, General Yin Chang, Minister of War, instructed to turn over forces to Yuan Shih-Kai made military dictator

Oct. 29, Government forces recaptured Hankow

Oct. 30, Imperial edict issued provided for immediate promulgation of Constitution

——, Yunnan joined the revolution

Oct. 31, Kiansi joined the revolution

Nov. 1, Prince Cheng resigned with Cabinet and Yuan Shih-Kai appointed Premier and Generalissimo with powers of a dictator

Nov. 2, Constitution adopted by Assembly of 19 fundamental principles of government

Nov. 3, Convention of rebels meeting at Shanghai, later Hankow, and then Nanking drafted articles for provisional government. General Li Yuan-hung elected chief executive

——, Shanghai taken by rebels

Nov. 4, Imperial edict accepted Constitution and appointed Yuan Premier

——, Kweichow joined the revolution

Nov. 5, Rebels occupied Suchow; Chekiang joined the revolution

Nov. 6, Rebels at Shanghai formed Cabinet, Wu Ting Fang, Minister of Foreign Affairs

Nov. 7, Yuan elected Premier by the Assembly

——, Kwangsi joined the revolution

Nov. 8, Canton and Foo-Chow surrendered to rebels

Nov. 9, Kwangtung and Fukien joined the revolution

Nov. 10, Manchu forces massacred persons at Nanking suspected as rebels

——, Foreign consuls issued proclamation declaring that consuls of Treaty Powers had appointed 3 Chinese magistrates for Mixed Court to act with "foreign assessors" appointed by consuls

Nov. 13, Shantung joined the revolution

Nov. 14, Second Republic set up in the North at Chi-Fu, Shantung Province

Nov. 15, Yuan Shih-Kai arrived in Peking and assumed office as Premier

Nov. 16, Yuan announced new Cabinet. Only 1 Minister a Manchu, Liang Tung-yen, Minister of Foreign Affairs

Nov. 22, Shensi joined the revolution

Nov. 26, Regent took oath to support the Constitution

Nov. 27, Government troops recaptured Han-Yang from rebels

Nov. 28, Wuchang surrendered to rebels

Nov. 30, Armistice concluded at request of rebel General Li Yuan-hung for 3 days

Dec. 2, Capture of Nanking by rebels; Kiansu joined the revolution

Dec. 4, Armistice extended

Dec. 6, Prince Chun, Regent, forced to resign. Accepted blame for revolution

Dec. 9, Tang Shao-yi appointed by Yuan as Imperial Delegate to negotiate peace with rebels left Peking and began negotiations at Hankow on the 11th

Dec. 17, Tang Shao-yi arrived at Shanghai and began conference at which 14 provinces represented the following day

Dec. 18, Imperial family left Peking for safety

Dec. 18–31, Peace Conference at Shanghai

Dec. 20, Treaty with Russia delimited boundary with Mongolia

Dec. 23, Japanese Minister in Peking formally announced to Yuan that Japan would not recognize a Chinese Republic

Dec. 25, Dr. Sun Yat-sen arrived from Europe reaching Shanghai Dec. 27

Dec. 28, Russia requested China to resume control of Mongolia

——, Revolt of Mongolian princes. Khutukhtu (Hutukhtu) crowned Emperor of Mongolia at Urga

——, Edict issued by Yuan agreed to abide by decision of a national conference as to form of government

Dec. 29, Nanking Assembly elected Dr. Sun Yat-sen President

——, Shanghai Peace Conference resolved that a national convention must decide form of government for China

Dec. 31, Shanghai Conference proclaimed Chinese Republic, Dr. Sun Yat-sen, first President and his society, the Tung Men Hui, became the Kuomintang or Nationalist Party; F. A. Wang Chung-hui, Minister of Foreign Affairs; Chen Chin-tao, Finance; Dr. Wu Ting Fang, Justice

1912

Jan. 1, Dr. Sun Yat-sen sworn in as provisional President of Chinese Republic at Nanking at tomb of Hung-Wu founder of Ming dynasty

Jan. 3, Republican Cabinet announced, Huan Hsen appointed Prime Minister and Minister of War, and Wu Ting-fang, Chang Chien, and Chen Chin-tao members

Jan. 5, Dr. Sun Yat-sen inaugurated as President at Nanking. Manifesto to Foreign Powers announced establishment of Republic

Jan. 6, Mutiny of troops at Luan Chou 100 miles south of Peking

Jan. 8, Russia notified China that independence of Mongolia must be recognized

Jan. 9, Russian troops began to expel Chinese from Mongolia

——, Railroad held against rebels from Peking to the sea with aid of foreign troops

Jan. 11, Assembly dissolved

Jan. 17, Conference of Princes held to discuss abdication. Declared against it

Jan. 19, Ultimatum of rebels demanded abdication of the Emperor

Jan. 27, Dr. Sun Yat-sen offered to resign as President in favor of Yuan

Feb. 12, Emperor Pu Yi abdicated, ending rule of Manchu dynasty of 267 years. Edict granted power to Yuan Shih-Kai to establish a provisional Republic in conjunction with the Nanking Government

Feb. 14, Resignation of Dr. Sun Yat-sen as provisional President accepted

Feb. 15, Yuan Shih-Kai elected provisional President by Assembly at Nanking of representatives of 17 provinces

Feb. 20, General Li Yuen-hung elected commander of army and Vice-President by Assembly

Feb. 29, Revolt of Manchu troops in Peking which spread to other cities

March 7, Loan of $700,000 by group of international bankers to provisional Government

March 10, Yuan Shih-kai inaugurated President at Peking and General Li Yuen-hung, Vice-President, Tang Shao-yi, Prime Minister, appointed March 29

——, Provisional Constitution proclaimed at Nanking

March 14, Loan from Belgian bankers. Canceled April 27 because of protest of the United States, Great Britain, France, and Germany as violation of previous agreement

March 20, National Assembly granted suffrage to women property owners able to read and write

March 23, First trial by jury begun at Shanghai

April 11, Mutiny of 1,500 troops at Nanking suppressed

April 29, Advisory Council formally inaugurated at Peking

June 15, Tang Shao-yi left Peking and later resigned as Prime Minister

June 26, Lu Cheng-hsiang former Minister of Foreign Affairs became Prime Minister

June 29, Resignation of Chen Chemei, Minister of Industry and Commerce

Aug. 1, Dr. George Ernest Morrison, Peking correspondent of the London *Times*, appointed political adviser to the President of China

Aug. 12, Fatal riots at Hongkong and Tientsin

Aug. 16, Arrest and execution at Peking of rebel generals Chang Chen-wu, and Fenge Wei

Aug. 17, Protest of Great Britain against Chinese military operations in Tibet

Aug. 24, Arrival of Dr. Sun Yat-sen at Peking

Aug. 30, Loan for £5,000,000 concluded with British syndicate, the "Chinese Government 5% Gold Loan" guaranteed by revenues of salt tax

Sept. 16, Liang Ju-hao (M. T. Liang) elected Minister of Foreign Affairs

Sept. 22, Lu Cheng-hsiang resigned as Acting Prime Minister which office he had held since Aug. 19 because of absence of the Prime Minister on sick leave, Chao Ping-Chun appointed

Sept. 29, Mandate ordered suppression of secret societies

Oct. 18, Payment of Boxer indemnities resumed

Nov. 3, Russian-Mongolian Treaty of alliance signed. Russia agreed to guarantee independence in return for special commercial concessions

Nov. 17, Meeting of 110 Mongol princes at Peking protested against Russian-Mongolian Treaty

1913

Jan. 10, Elections for National Assembly held

Jan. 12, Six Power group of bankers concluded agreement for loan of $125,000,000 to China

Jan. 21, Mongolia and Tibet formed alliance for mutual protection, trade relations, and defense of Buddhism

Feb. 21, Death of the Empress Lungyii in Forbidden City

March, F. J. Goodnow, American, appointed constitutional adviser to the Government

March 18, American bankers withdrew from $125,000,-000 loan to China because of refusal of President Wilson to support loan

March 21, Sieng Chiao-jen, Kuomintang Party, who

had criticized Yuan for failure to institute a party government, shot by assassin at railroad station

April 8, First session of elected Parliament of the Republic (Kuomintang) met in Peking

April 11, Chinese Republic formally recognized by Brazil

April 21, Five Power loan of $125,000,000 formally concluded by group of bankers of Great Britain, France, Russia, and Japan

May 2, Republic formally recognized by the United States and by Mexico

May 9, Government protested against California legislation aimed against Japanese ownership of land

——, Loan formally accepted by the Government

May 30, Agreement with Russia as to Mongolia

July 10, Second revolution begun in southern provinces against Yuan

July 10–Oct. 31, Joint Committee of 60 members of the National Assembly met and drafted Constitution

July 12, Fighting between northern and southern troops in Kiangsi Province

July 15, General Huang Hsing in Kiangsi Province proclaimed commander-in-chief of "punitive expedition" against Yuan

July 18, Tsen Chun-hsuan proclaimed President by southern revolutionists

July 20, Rebels defeated on Shantung border evacuated Hsu Chow-fu

July 21, Manifesto of Dr. Sun declared for the South

July 23, Hsuing Hsi-ling elected Prime Minister by House and by Upper House a week later

——, Northern forces defended Shanghai arsenal against attack by rebels

July 27, Government troops captured Hukow forts in Kiangsi Province

Aug. 6, Dr. Sun Yat-sen fled from China on ship bound for Japan

Aug. 13, Rebels defended Woosung forts against attack until this date

Sept. 1, General Chang Hsun commanding northern troops took Nanking which was looted by soldiers

Sept. 8, Hsuing Hsi-ling appointed Prime Minister

Sept. 10, Note from Japan demanded indemnity for 3 Japanese subjects killed in taking of Nanking, and apology

Sept. 13, Government agreed to Japanese demands

Sept. 28, Formal apology to Japan made by General Chang Hsun for Nanking incident

Oct. 3, Law enacted providing for system of auditing Government accounts

Oct. 5, Japanese companies received concessions for 3 railroads in Manchuria

——, Election law promulgated

Oct. 6, Yuan Shih-kai reëlected President by National Assembly, and Li Yuan-hung, Vice-President

——, Recognition of the Government by Japan and Russia

Oct. 10, President Yuan inaugurated for second term

Oct. 25, Draft Constitution approved by constitutional convention

Nov. 4, Mandate of the President dissolved the Kuomintang Party for complicity in late rebellion and expelled its members from the National Assembly, leaving Parliament without a quorum taking 252 of 596 members from the Lower House, and 98 out of 274 from the Upper House

Nov. 5, Treaty with Russia signed by which autonomy of Outer Mongolia recognized under suzerainty of China. Both countries agreed to abstain from colonization

Nov. 10, Chino-French Bank signed contract for $30,000,000 loan to China

Nov. 13, Parliament suspended by vote of remaining members

Nov. 24, Martial law in Peking ended

Dec. 26, A Council of 7 members designated as the Administrative Council met in Peking

1914

Jan. 11, President Yuan Shih-kai dissolved Parliament and appointed committee to draft a Constitution

Jan. 26, New rules for a constitutional convention promulgated by the President

Jan. 30, Administrative Council reëstablished worship of Heaven and of Confucius

——, American Red Cross Agreement with Government for loan of $20,000,000 to undertake flood protection in Hwai River Valley in provinces of Kiangsu and Anhui

Feb. 13, Hsuing Hsi-ling dismissed as Prime Minister. Succeeded by Sun Pao-chi Minister of Foreign Affairs

March 1, Provincial assemblies dissolved

March 18, Constitutional convention opened in Peking

April 3, Press law enacted

May 1, Constitution prepared by constitutional convention promulgated by the President

May 2, Cabinet reorganized and post of Prime Minister replaced by that of Secretary of State to which office Hsu Chih-chang appointed

May 23, President Yuan separated military and civil administration in the provinces, reviving former Manchu provincial system

June 20, Council of State inaugurated with ceremony

July 2, Agreement of Government to permit extension of railroad by Germans from Kaomi near Tsingtau to Suchowfu, junction of the Tientsin-Pukow and Belgian railroads

July 3, Anglo-Russian-Chinese Convention on status of Tibet granted complete autonomy in Tibet proper and partial autonomy in eastern Tibet

July 27, Preliminary Agreement with Belgium signed for construction of railroad from Lanchowfu to Kuldja

Aug. 5, "White Wolf" bandit who had led army, looting and plundering towns in the northwestern provinces, captured and killed by Chinese official who received $50,000 reward from the Government

Aug. 6, China declared neutrality in European War

Aug. 15, Japan demanded from Germany the surrender of Kiaochau. See World War

Sept. 15, Advancement of Peace Treaty with the United States signed

Sept. 30, Agreement with Russia signed provided for establishment of Russian protectorate over Outer Mongolia. See also Mongolia

Nov. 7, Surrender of Tsingtao to Japanese and British forces. See World War

Dec. 18, Contract with British company for construction of a railroad from Shasi in Hupeh to Singyifu in Keweichow by way of Changteh and Kweiyang in Hunan

Dec. 23, Contract for 2 railroads with German companies signed (1) from Kaomi southward to Hanchwang and (2) extension of Shantung railroad from Tsinanfu to Shunteh on the Hankow railroad

Dec. 28, Japanese reopened port of Kiachou for trade

Dec. 29, New election law promulgated fixed term of President at 10 years

1915

Jan. 16, China announced abolition of military zone in Shantung

Jan. 18, Japan presented the "Twenty-one Demands" to China: Japan to succeed to all German rights in Shantung and railroad concession, control of South Manchuria, large coal and iron concessions, cession of territory to any other Power forbidden, appointment of Japanese advisers, purchase of munitions from Japan, and various other preferences in railroads and mines

Feb. 2–18, Conference with Japan on the "Twenty-one Demands"

Feb. 11, General Amnesty granted to rebels which included Dr. Sun Yat-sen

Feb. 12, China submitted formal statement on each of demands, agreeing to 12

——, Protocol of Opium Convention of 1912 signed at The Hague by representatives of China, the United States, and the Netherlands

Feb. 17, Chinese Government published complete text of the "Twenty-one Demands"

March 3, China agreed to an extension for 99 years of Japanese leases of the ports of Dalny and Port Arthur

March 23, China accepted 4 of demands as to control by Japanese of foreign concessions in southern Manchuria

April 26, Japan submitted a revised list of demands

May 1, China accepted all demands except as to Eastern Inner Mongolia and one which called for concession to Japan to construct railroads in South China

——, General Chen Yi and northern army of 10,000 men sent to Szechuan to restore order and put down revolt

May 7, Japanese ultimatum to China as to acceptance of demands reserving for future considerations those most subversive of China's sovereignty

May 8, China accepted revised 24 "Demands"

May 25, Treaties with Japan and Notes embodying "Demands" signed by which Japan acquired German rights in Shantung and additional railroad concessions, Japanese possessions in South Manchuria and Eastern Inner Mongolia recognized, China not to cede or lease any harbor, bay, or island to any other Power than Japan, and recognition of superior claims of Japanese for appointments as political, financial, and military advisers

June 7, Russo-Chinese-Mongolian Treaty confirmed Agreement of Nov. 5, 1913 for autonomy of Mongolia under suzerainty of China

July 13, Floods inundated districts in provinces of Kwang-tung, Kwangsi, and Kiangsi with loss of life and damage to property

Sept. 2, Resignation of Li Yuan-hung, Vice-President

Oct. 29, Diplomatic representatives of Great Britain, Russia, and Japan supported unofficially by the French Government requested that the Chinese postpone any action as to return to monarchical form of Government until end of the European War

Nov. 5, Vote 1,997 to 50 in favor of a monarchy

Dec. 5, Mutiny of sailors of training ship "Choa-ho" in harbor at Shanghai

Dec. 11, Yuan Shih-kai accepted invitation of the Council of State to assume the throne and ceremony of coronation set for Feb. 9 but later indefinitely postponed because of revolution which broke out in Yunnan and spread to Nanking, Fukien, and Hunan

Dec. 12, The monarchy proclaimed

——, Li Yuan-hung proclaimed President of a provisional Government at Canton

Dec. 26, Military Governor Tsai Ao of Province of Yunnan in revolt declared independence

1916

Jan. 1, Revolution against the monarchy broke out in Yunnan headed by Tsai Ao, and independence of the Province declared by the two Governors

Jan. 21, Announcement that coronation postponed sine die

Feb. 10, Revolutionists took Lu-Chow

March 16, Ultimatum of Powers signatories of Protocol of 1901 demanded cessation of hostilities in the Tientsin-Taku Bar area and of interference with foreign shipping. Accepted

March 22, Yuan Shih-kai issued proclamation that he would abandon plan for monarchy and adhere to Republic

March 27, Council of State repealed monarchical legislation and restored the Republic

March 28, Agreement with Russia signed by which Russia received permission to construct a railroad between Blagoveshschensk on the Russian-Amur frontier and Harbin and Tsitsikar in Manchuria

April 6, Canton declared independence of central Government

April 12, Province of Che-King declared independence

April 13, Province of Kiangsi declared independence

April 22, Tuan Chi-jui accepted appointment as Prime Minister and Minister of War, organized Cabinet April 24 with Lu Chen Hsing Minister of Foreign Affairs and Sun Pao Chi, Finance, to which civil authority transferred by Yuan

June 6, Death of President Yuan Shih-kai. Vice-President Li Yuan-hung assumed office as President

June 9, Revolted provinces rescinded their declaration of independence

Aug. 1, Republican Parliament convened in 1914 dissolved by Yuan Shih-kai and installed Government. Tuan Chi-jui formed a coalition Cabinet

Aug. 13, Chinese troops attacked Japanese troops at Cheng-Chiatum near Mukden

Sept. 3, Japan demanded indemnity and apology and certain rights in Inner Mongolia

Sept. 30, Government signed contract with American company for construction of 1,100 miles of railroad at cost of over $60,000,000

Oct. 31, Feng Kuo-chang elected Vice-President

1917

Jan. 5, Announcement of loan placed in the United States for $5,000,000

Jan. 23, Settlement of Cheng-Chiatun incident with Japan by exchange of Notes. China agreed to indemnity, apology, punishment of officers involved, and preferential rights in southern Manchuria and Inner Mongolia

Feb. 4, The American Minister at Peking invited China to protest against German submarine campaign and sever diplomatic relations with Germany

Feb. 16, Secret Agreement of Japan with Great Britain

as to Shantung supporting Japanese claims to German rights. Acceded to by France March 1, and Russia March 5

Feb. 28, Joint memorandum of Allied Ministers at Peking notified the Government that if diplomatic relations were severed with Germany the Powers would suspend the Boxer indemnity payments and consent to revision of customs tariff

March 1, Wu Ting Fang resigned as Minister of Foreign Affairs

March 4, The President refused to sever diplomatic relations with Germany and Premier Tuan-Chi-jui with several other Ministers resigned but resumed office

March 14, Diplomatic relations with Germany severed. German ships seized

March 15 and 16, German concessions at Hankow and Tientsin taken over by Chinese

May 23, Premier Tuan Chi-jui dismissed by the President on charge of defying Parliament and attempt to establish military despotism. Wu Ting-fang appointed Prime Minister

May 29, Announcement that military governors of several northern provinces had declared independence of the central Government

June 1, Military governors meeting at Tientsin demanded reinstatement of Tuan and declaration of war and declared 11 provinces had withdrawn from the central Government

June 2, Military governors at Tientsin set up a provisional government under dictatorship of Hsu Shih-Chang

June 7, General Chang Hsun, military governor of Anhwei, reached Tientsin, and march begun on Peking

June 12, Parliament dissolved by President Li Yuan-hung. Members proceeded to Canton

——, General Chang Hsun with private army of 40,000 arrived at Peking

July 1, *Coup d'état* of General Chang Hsun restored Manchu boy Emperor, Hsuan-Tung to the throne at Peking. The President imprisoned but escaped

July 6, Vice-President Feng Kuo-Chang assumed office as Acting President and established republican government at Nanking

July 8, Republican army rallied by Feng Kuo-Chang and Tuan Chi-jui advanced on Peking to overthrow the Empire

——, Abdication of the Emperor announced

July 12, General Chang Hsun defeated by republican army and Republic restored. Chang took refuge in the Dutch legation

July 15, Tuan Chi-jui assumed office as Premier

July 17, Li Yuan-hung refused to resume office as President

Aug. 1, Feng Kuo-Chang became Acting President for remainder of term of Yuan

Aug. 14, Declaration of war on Germany and Austria

Aug. 29, Agreement signed with group of Japanese bankers for loan of about $5,000,000 for administrative purposes

Sept. 3, 70 members of disbanded Parliament proclaimed a military government at Canton with Dr. Sun Yat-sen as commander-in-chief

Nov. 10, National Council opened at Peking

Nov. 24, Resignation of Tuan Chi-jui as Premier

Nov. 28, Province of Ninpo declared independence of central Government

Nov. 30, Wang Shih-Chen appointed Prime Minister

Dec. 4, Chinchow in Hupek declared independence of central Government

Dec. 25, New tariff promulgated covering trade with non-treaty nations; luxuries 30 to 100% *ad valorem*, "useless goods" 20–30% *ad valorem*, "useful goods" 10 to 20%, "necessary goods" 5 to 10%

Dec. 31, Cultivation of opium ended

1918

Jan. 8, Contracts with American companies for high power wireless stations in Shanghai, Peking, Canton, Hankow, and Harbin

Feb. 13, Earthquake at Swatow killed several hundred persons

Feb. 17, Revised electoral law promulgated

Feb. 21, Contract with the Mitsui Company (Japanese) for erection of high power wireless

April 12, Government troops defeated rebels at Hupeh

April 19, Government forces captured Hunan

May 1, Government forces defeated at Nanhsiung in province of Kwangtung

May 16, Secret military Agreement with Japan for coöperation in Far East against Germany

May 17, Trading with enemy countries prohibited

May 19 and 23, Naval Convention with Japan signed

June 13, Treaty with Switzerland signed the last in which China conceded extraterritorial rights

Aug. 11, New Parliament formally opened

Sept. 4, Hsu Shih-Chang elected President by Parliament (Candidate of Anfu Club favorable to Japan)

Sept. 6, Second Sino-Japanese military Convention signed

Sept. 24, Secret Agreement with Japan by which Japan to surrender Shantung Railroad to a Sino-Japanese Company. Japanese troops to be withdrawn and civil administration set up by Japan Oct. 1, 1917 abolished

Oct. 6, Canton Government declared war on the central Government

Oct. 11, Resignation of General Tuan Chi-juii, Prime Minister

Oct. 15, Hsu Shih-Chang inaugurated President

Nov. 16, Mandate of the President ordered commanders to suspend hostilities with the southern provinces and armistice was followed by conference

Nov. 17, Lu Chen-hsiang formed Cabinet which included Dr. V. K. Wellington Koo and Dr. C. T. Wang

1919

Jan., Chien Nang Hsun became Prime Minister

Jan. 18, Peace Conference opened in Paris. China represented by 2 delegates

April 30, Decision of Council of Three at Peace Conference to transfer Shantung Peninsula and Kiaochou to Japan. To be restored to China eventually

May 4, Chinese delegation at Peace Conference protested decision as to Shantung

——, Parade of 15,000 students in Peking, demonstration against Shantung decision

May 5, Agreement of Allied Powers to place embargo on arms to China preventing shipment of munitions to any faction

May 6, Decision of Cabinet to instruct delegates not to sign Treaty with Germany assigning German rights in Shantung to Japan

May 7, Students arrested on May 4, released and student strike ended but demand continued for resignation of Ministers accused of pro-Japanese activities

May 7, General strike at Shanghai and anti-Japanese boycott begun

May 12, Joint Agreement of American, British, French, and Japanese bankers for financing Chinese loans

May 16, Conference of representatives of North and South China for settlement of differences ended in failure

May 20, Student strike for dismissal of "the traitors" joined by merchants and workers

June 10, Resignation of Cabinet, "the traitors" Tsao Yu-ling, Chang Tsung-tsiang, and Lu Chung-yu. Chin Yun Peng became Prime Minister

June 28, Chinese delegation refused to sign the Treaty of Versailles because of provisions regarding Shan-tung. By the Treaty Germany renounced all treaty rights in China

July 18, Clash with Japanese soldiers at Kuanchengtze near Changchun

Aug. 8, Parliament authorized the President to issue mandate declaring end of war with Germany

Sept. 10, Peace Treaty with Austria signed. By this Treaty Austria renounced all treaty rights in China

Sept. 14, The American Minister Dr. Paul S. Reinsch resigned because of opposition to Shantung settlement

Sept. 15, Declaration of end of war with Germany

Nov. 16, Ultimatum of Chinese General Hsu forced President of Mongol Council to ask for cancelation of Mongol autonomy and annexation to China. *See* Mongolia

——, Riots at Fuchow. Chinese killed by Japanese residents

Dec. 1, Government demanded removal of Japanese consul at Fuchow, punishment of leaders of riot, and indemnity

Dec. 3, Treaty with Bolivia signed. Extra-territorial rights excluded

Dec. 15, Meeting of Political Council, the old Central Administrative Council under new name

1920

Jan., New Cabinet constituted under General Chin Yun-Peng

Jan. 20, Note from Japan stated willingness to enter into negotiations for return of Shantung

May 15, Admiral Sa Chen-peng appointed Acting Premier in place of Chin Yun-peng

May 26, Treaty of St. Germain ratified by the House and 3 days later by Senate

June 1, Treaty of friendship with Persia signed

June 4, Peace Treaty with Hungary signed

July 6, Wu Pei-fu and Tsao-Kun of Chihli dismissed from their commands by mandate of the President. Wu Pei-fu advanced with army from Hunan on Peking to displace Tuan Chi-jui and Anfu Party from control over central Government

July 16, China became original member of the League of Nations

July 28, Resignation of General Tuan Chi-jui of his command accepted by the President after his defeat by Wu Pei-fu south of Peking

Aug. 1, Payment of Russian share of Boxer indemnity suspended

Aug. 4, Chang Tso-lin and Tsao-Kun arrived at Peking

Aug. 11, Chin Yun-peng appointed Prime Minister and Minister of War

Sept., General Chen Chiung began hostilities against the Kwangsi faction at Canton and was defeated in October

Oct. 2, Russo-Asiatic Bank signed supplementary agreement with the Government as to Chinese Eastern Railroad by which one-half of the board of directors should be Chinese

Oct. 15, Formal Agreement as to loans to China signed by representatives of American, British, French, and Japanese banks for formation of new financial consortium in China

Oct. 25, In Mongolia Baron Ungern-Sternberg (anti-Bolshevik Cossack) attack on Urga repulsed by Chinese garrison

Oct. 30, Proclamation of President Hsu declared North and South China reunited and called for election for new Parliament

Dec. 16, Earthquake near Pingliang, Kansu, with great loss of life

1921

Jan. 25, The Southern Government received first diplomatic delegate from Soviet Russia at Canton

Jan. 28, Sino-Japanese military and naval agreements of 1918 and 1919 terminated

Feb. 1–3, Baron Ungern-Sternberg drove Chinese out of Urga

Feb. 25, Kingdom of Mongolia declared independent by Mongols joined with "White" Russians and Japanese

March 11, Agreement signed for China Consortium by international bankers which should monopolize all future Chinese loans

April 7, Dr. Sun Yat-sen elected President of China by extraordinary session of Parliament at Canton

May 5, Dr. Sun Yat-sen formally inaugurated President

May 20, Treaty of amity and commerce with Germany signed

July 6, Soviet forces occupied Urga and established a Red Government in Mongolia

Sept. 26, Agreement with Mexico amended Treaty of friendship, commerce, and navigation of Dec. 14, 1899 and prohibited emigration of laborers between the two countries

Oct. 12, Canton Government declared war on the Peking Government

Nov. 5, Treaty signed in Moscow between Mongolian Red Government at Urga and Russian Soviet Government

Nov. 12, Washington Conference opened. China sent delegates, Dr. Wellington Koo and others

Nov. 22, Declaration of Chinese delegation at Washington Conference as to non-alienation of Chinese territory

Dec. 10, Resolution adopted at Washington Conference regarding extraterritorialty

Dec. 14, General Chang Tso-lin arrived in Peking

Dec. 17, General Chang forced the resignation of Premier Chin Yun-peng

Dec. 24, New Cabinet formed with Liang Shi-yi Prime Minister under the protection of Chang Tso-lin

1922

Jan. 13–March 5, Seamen's strike and general strike in Hongkong

Jan. 28, Liang Shi-yi left Peking for Tientsin forced by threats of Wu Pei-fu, who charged new Cabinet with being pro-Japanese, to resign as Premier

Feb. 1, Resolution of Washington Conference as to

unification of Chinese railroads, reduction of military forces, radio stations, &c.

Feb. 1, Announcement by Mr. Balfour at the Washington Conference that Great Britain would surrender lease of Weihawei to China

Feb. 4, Treaty on Chinese territorial integrity and maintenance of the "open door" signed at Washington Conference by the United States, Great Britain, Japan, France, Italy, China, the Netherlands, Belgium, and Portugal

——, Nine Power Treaty on the Chinese customs tariff signed

——, Shantung Treaty signed provided for immediate return by Japan of former German properties and for modification of the "Twenty-one Demands"

Feb. 24, 160 vessels held in Hongkong harbor by the strike

March 8, Wireless telephone service opened between Tientsin and Peking

March 28, Agreement signed at Peking for evacuation of Japanese troops along Shantung Railroad Zone

March 31, Tariff Revision Commission under Washington Treaty of Feb. 6 held first meeting at Shanghai

April 7, Abrogation of Russo-Chinese customs Agreement of 1881

April 21, Civil war begun between General Chang Tso-lin, war lord of Manchuria, and Wu Pei-fu, lord of the Yangtze

——, Mandate of Dr. Sun Yat-sen dismissed General Chen Chiung-min from offices

April 23, The Tientsin-Pukow railroad torn up at Machang by the Wu Pei-fu forces

April 26, General Chang in alliance with Dr. Sun Yat-sen began fighting south of Peking which developed into battle with Wu Pei-fu

May 1-6, First National Labor Congress met at Canton, delegates from 200 unions

May 4, Fighting in Chihli Province ended in victory of Wu at Changsintien

May 6, President ordered arrest of Premier Liang Shih-yi and 2 other pro-Japanese Ministers

May 10, Order of the President dismissed Chang Tso-lin as Inspector-General of Manchuria

May 13, Chang proclaimed independence of North Manchuria

June 1, Resignation of President Hsu Shih-Chang forced by Wu Chow Tze-chi who became Acting Prime Minister

June 2, Li Yuan-hung former President invited to resume the presidency

June 8-16, Fighting around Chingwangtao resulted in occupation of town by forces of Wu Pei-fu

June 10, Li Yuan-hung took office as President, Chow Tse-Chi, acting Premier

June 13, New Cabinet formed, Dr. W. W. Yen, Prime Minister

June 16, Armistice concluded between Chang and Wu at Chengwangtao

June 16-17, At Canton Dr. Sun Yat-sen defeated by troops formerly under General Chen Chiung-ming in battle

June 23, Death of Dr. Wu Ting-fang

July 2, Japanese garrison withdrew from Hankow

July 31, Wang Chung-hui appointed acting Prime Minister on resignation of Yen

Aug. 1, Parliament opened, that of 1917 revived

Aug. 4, Chang Tso-lin and Tsao Kun arrived at Peking

Aug. 9, Hsu Shucheng and 8 other Anfu leaders took refuge in the Japanese legation

Aug. 9-14, Further defeat of Dr. Sun Yat-sen's generals by Chen Chiung-ming

Aug. 14, Dr. Sun escaping from Canton on British gunboat arrived at Shanghai

Sept. 2, Sino-Soviet Conference opened

Sept. 16, Japanese withdrew from Harbin

Sept. 20, Cabinet reorganized under Dr. Wang Chung-hui. Dr. Wellington Koo made Minister of Foreign Affairs

Oct. 8, General Hsu Shuhchen set up an independent government at Yenping in the province of Fukien

Oct. 12, Government troops defeated General Hsu Shuchen near Yenping

Oct. 13, Hsu Chung-chi, adherent of Sun Yat-sen, captured Foochow

Oct. 30, Civil administration of Kiaochau territory except Tsingtao transferred by Japan to China

Nov., New system of education introduced, 6 year primary course, 6 year secondary, and 4 to 6 college

Nov. 28, Cabinet resigned. Anti-reform Tuchans in control impeached Premier Wang and Dr. Wellington Koo

Nov. 30, Temporary Cabinet formed with Wang Ta-hsieh to sign Agreement with Japan

Dec. 1, Agreement with Japan by which Japan transferred all interests in Shantung

Dec. 3, General Chang Shao-T'seng appointed Prime Minister

Dec. 5, Agreement with Japan signed as to Shantung railroad

Dec. 10, Kiaochau restored by Japan on payment by China of 14,000,000 gold yen in treasury notes for Japanese improvements

Dec. 12, Wang Chen-ming appointed acting Prime Minister

Dec. 18, Yunnan and Kwangsi forces with supporters of Dr. Sun Yat-sen captured Wuchow and threatened Canton

Dec. 20, Announcement of Great Britain that further payments of Boxer indemnity would be used for mutually beneficial purposes

1923

Jan. 1, Tsingtao Railway (Shantung) formally transferred to China by Japan

Jan. 4, Cabinet appointed: Premier, Chang Shao-Tseng; Minister of the Interior, Kao Ling-Yu; Foreign Affairs, Huang Fu; Agriculture and Commerce, Li Ken-Yuan; Education, Peng Yun-Yi; Communications, Wu Yu-Ling; War, Chang Shao-Tseng; Navy, Li Ting-Hsin; Justice, Chiun Koh; Finance, Liu En-Yuan

Jan. 6, Kwangsi force and Yunnanese captured Wuchau and advanced towards Canton

Jan. 10, Chinese flag raised at Kiao-chau for first time in 24 years

Jan. 15, Chen Chiung-ming evacuated Canton retiring to Waichow on approach of troops of Dr. Sun, and government officials fled to foreign settlement, Shameen

Feb. 10, Agreement with France that further payments of Boxer indemnity be used for the Banque Industrielle and for educational purposes

Feb. 21, Dr. Sun Yat-sen reëstablished his government in Canton

March 8, Chang Shao-Tseng ousted but allowed to

return March 20 on condition of agreement to authorize and finance military expedition against Kwantung, Szechuan, and Hunan

March 10, Note to Japan requested abrogation of Treaty of 1915 containing the "Twenty-one Demands" and return of Dalny and Port Arthur. Refused by Japan

March 30, Japan passed law providing that Japanese share of Boxer indemnity be used for education and culture in China

——, British Government decision to cancel amount still due on Boxer indemnity

April 16, Kwangsi troops led by General Sheng Hung-yin attacked Yunnanese in Canton

May 3, New Trade Mark Act promulgated

May 6, Shanghai-Peking express derailed and robbed, and 300 passengers including 30 foreigners held for ransom for $1,000,000 by bandits near Lincheng, the last released June 12

May 17, The heights above Canton captured by Yunnanese troops and those of Dr. Sun defeating Kwangsi force

May 31, Provisional Agreement with Great Britain for return of Weihaiwei

June 5, Resignation of Chang Shao-T'seng Ministry. Chang fled to Tientsin

June 13–14, President Li Yuan-hung forced to resign by Tsao K'un and Wu Pei-fu and Wang Ch'eng-pin, civil governor of Chihli; fled to Tientsin

June 14, Kao Ling-Yu, Minister of the Interior, became Prime Minister

June 22, Treaty of commerce and navigation with Latvia signed

July 2, Manifesto of Dr. Sun from Canton addressed to foreign Powers requested them to withhold recognition of Peking Government

July 6, Troops of Dr. Sun took Shiuchow

July 20, Troops of Dr. Sun took Amoy

Aug. 1, Parliament of June, 1917, convened

Aug. 4, Commission for the Readjustment of Finance established to prepare a budgetary system

Aug. 10, Note presented to Peking Government signed by representatives of 17 countries including the United States demanded reparation for incident of May 6, and asked for organization of a special railroad guard under foreign officers

Aug. 18, Typhoon in Hongkong harbor caused loss of life. British submarine and crew sunk

Sept., Michael Borodin arrived from Russia to act as advisor of Kuomintang

Sept. 24, Reply of Peking Government to Note of Powers of Aug. 10 unsatisfactory

Oct. 5, Marshal Tsao Kun elected President by Parliament. Alleged that for each of the 423 votes he paid $5,000. Dr. Sun denounced election as fraud

Oct. 10, New Constitution promulgated on assumption of office by the President

Oct. 15, Reply of Peking Government accepted principal demands of Powers

Oct. 22, Death of Chow Tsu-Chi former Premier

Nov. 8, Tsao Kun inaugurated as President

Nov. 11, Dr. Sun's troops captured Waichow

Dec. 1, Dr. Sun threatened to seize customs revenues at Canton

Dec. 6, Foreign marines landed at Canton to guard custom-house and warships dispatched by Great Britain, the United States, Japan, France, Italy, and Portugal

1924

Jan. 13, New Cabinet formed with Sun Pao-chi as Prime Minister, Dr. Wellington Koo, Minister of Foreign Affairs, as approved by Parliament, Jan. 9

Jan. 21, First Congress (Kuomintang) convened at Canton, Dr. Sun Yat-sen, founder, elected President

Jan. 27, Chengtu, capital of province of Szechuan, taken

Jan. 28, Constitution of the Kuomintang adopted by Congress at Canton

March 14, Preliminary Agreement with Russia signed gave de jure recognition by China of Soviet Government

April 12, Protest of organization of Canton merchants against fiscal measures of the Government

April 28, Foreign warships withdrawn

May 3, Note of American Minister stated interest of the United States in protection of all interests in Chinese Eastern Railway, followed by Note from French Minister, May 7

May 21, Treaty with Germany signed. German property held in World War released

May 31, Eastern Chinese Railroad Agreement with Russia signed provided for recognition of Russia and gave China right to purchase railroad prior to expiration of original agreement and arranged for joint administration of the railroad by Chinese and Russians

July 2, Resignation of Premier Sun Pao-chi. Dr. Wellington Koo appointed acting Premier

July 15–Aug. 19, General strike in Canton against foreign control and concessions and boycott of French and German steamers

Aug. 9, Note presented to Diplomatic Corps by Peking Government demanded rendition of Shanghai Mixed Court

Aug. 11, The "Volunteers" organized by merchants in Canton declared general strike and martial law unless vessel with arms consigned to them released by Dr. Sun

Aug. 24, Mass meeting at Shanghai formed National Anti-Opium Association to rally to support of League of Nations efforts to secure restriction in narcotics

Aug. 26, "Labor Corps" formed in Canton by Kuomintang, later known as "Red Army"

Aug. 28, Chi Hsieh-yuan, Inspector General of Kiangsu, Kiangsi, and Anhwei, issued manifesto announcing he would begin hostilities to unify China and remove Shanghai from jurisdiction of Lu Yung-hsiang of Chekiang

Sept. 2, Sun Chuan-fang declared war on Lu Yung-hsiang

Sept. 3, Lu Yung-hsiang declared war on President Tsao Kun

Sept. 7, Chang Tso-lin of Manchuria declared war on President Tsao Kun and Wu Pei-fu

Sept. 12, Dr. W. W. Yen elected Prime Minister by Parliament

Sept. 18, Mandate of the President declared war on Chang Tso-lin and appointed Wu Pei-fu commander-in-chief of the army

Sept. 20, Separate Agreement signed at Mukden between Manchuria (Chang Tso-lin) and Russia, Russia recognizing autonomous status of Manchuria

Sept. 24, United Commercial Guilds of Kwangtung Province made public statement to overseas Chinese urging them to withdraw support from Dr. Sun because of his alliance with Communists

Oct. 9, Marshal Chi Hsieh-yuan took Sunkiang in Shanghai district

Oct. 10, Fighting begun at Canton with "Red Army." Loss by incendiary fires $50,000,000 by Oct. 20

Oct. 13, Lu Yung-hsiang, defeated in Chekiang Province, fled to Japan

——, Armistice declared

Oct. 15, The "Volunteers" in Canton defeated in battle with the "Red Army" and the city looted by Reds with loss of life and damage to property

Oct. 22–23, General Feng Yu-hsiang deserted General Wu Pei-fu, entered Peking, seized the palace in night attack, making the President a prisoner, demanding cessation of hostilities, dismissal of General Wu Pei-fu

Oct. 24, Mandate of the President ordered cessation of hostilities and dismissed Wu Pei-fu

Oct. 30, Chingwangtao occupied by forces of Chang Tso-lin

Oct. 31, Provisional Cabinet with General Huang Fu as acting Premier appointed, C. T. Wang, Minister of Foreign Affairs and Finance

Nov. 2, Resignation of President Tsao Kun. He remained a prisoner in Peking until April, 1926

Nov. 3, New Cabinet canceled the Abdication Acts of the late dynasty, depriving the ex-Emperor of his title, giving him the name of Mr. Pu-yi

Nov. 5, Soldiers of General Feng Yu-hsiang surrounded the Imperial Palace and forced young Manchu ex-emperor to sign agreement he would waive all monarchical rights, and to leave the "Forbidden City"

Nov. 10, Ten day conference begun of Generals Chang, Feng, and Marshal Tuan

Nov. 14, Wu Pei-fu who had left Tientsin Nov. 3 arrived at Nanking where Marshal Chi Hsieh proclaimed independence of the Central Government

Nov. 15, Announcement that Tuan Chi-jui would accept office as "Provisional Chief Executive"

Nov. 19, Marshal Wu Pei-fu organized an independent military government at Hankow in opposition to the Peking Government

Nov. 24, Marshal Tuan Chi-jui assumed office as "Chief Executive," supported by Chang Tso-lin

Nov. 27, General Feng Yu-hsiang named provisional Cabinet with Tuan Chi-jui as Prime Minister

Nov. 29, Pu Yi (Hsuan Tung), deposed Emperor, took refuge in Japanese legation

Dec. 9, Provisional Government recognized in joint Note by representatives of Powers signatory of the Washington Treaties on condition that all engagements of previous governments be recognized

Dec. 11, Tuan Chi-jui dismissed Chi Hsi-yuan as Inspector General of Kiangsu, Kwansi, and Anhwei and appointed Lu Yung-hsiang "Pacification Commissioner" for Kiangsu and Anhwei

Dec. 24, Formal assurance given by the Government to the Powers of recognition of engagements of previous governments

——, Tuan Chi-jui issued call for a reorganization conference

Dec. 26, Hsu Shi-yeng appointed Premier

Dec. 31, Dr. Sun Yat-sen, invited by the northern military leaders, arrived at Peking

1925

Jan. 10, Marshal Lu Yung-hsiang occupied Nanking and advanced on Shanghai

Jan. 11, Fighting at Shanghai. Marshal Chi Hsieh-yuan left in possession

Jan. 16, Forces of Chang Tso-lin under Chang Tsung-Chang attacked combined army of Sun Chuan-fang and Chi Hsieh-yuan

Jan. 17, Chang's troops commanded by Chang Tsung-Chang occupied Chinkiang

Jan. 25, Chi Hsieh-yuan's troops defeated by Chang Tso-lin forces

Jan. 28, Forces of Chang Tso-lin entered Shanghai

Feb. 1–April 21, Reorganization Conference at Peking of generals. Dr. Sun Yat-sen's Party, the Kuomintang, refused to participate

Feb. 5, General Chen Chiung-ming made attack on Canton

Feb. 7, Chinese delegates withdrew from 2d Opium Conference at Geneva

Feb. 21, The Peking Government paid $300,000 (silver) to dean of the diplomatic corps in part payment for May 6, 1923 Lincheng bandit robbery of the Shanghai-Peking express

Feb. 23, Hsuan Tung, deposed Manchu Emperor, left Peking and took up residence in Japanese concession at Tientsin

March 5, Dr. Sun Yat-sen's Party, the Kuomintang, occupied Swatow and drove out General Chen Chiung-ming

March 6, Russia notified China that Russian troops had been withdrawn from Mongolia

March 12, Death of Dr. Sun Yat-sen, leader of the Kuomintang Party

March 20, Chiang Kai-shek arrested Communists and Russians in anti-Communist raid in Canton

April 12, Agreement with France settled the "gold franc controversy." Boxer indemnity remitted for rehabilitation of Banque Industrielle which had failed in 1921

April 21, Reorganization Conference dissolved

May 1–7, Second National Labor Congress met at Canton and created a general labor union for all China

May 9, Parade of 20,000 students in Peking attempted to break into house of Chief Executive

May 15, Strikers broke into factory of Naigai Cotton Mill Company and destroyed machinery. British (Hindu) police killed one of strikers

May 27, Strike begun in Japanese mills at Tsingtao (Shantung), Japanese troops sent to establish order

May 30, Shanghai foreign (Sikh) police fired on parade of strikers and students in sympathy with strike of Chinese workers in Japanese mills, killing 9 and wounding 20

June 1, General strike declared at Shanghai accompanied by rioting

June 2 and 4, Protest of Government against shooting of Chinese by foreign police. American, British, and Italian marines landed at Shanghai to protect international settlement

June 3, Resolution of Board of Trustees of the China Foundation for the Promotion of Education and Culture that funds of Boxer indemnity remitted by the United States be applied to the development of scientific knowledge and cultural enterprises

June 6, General Yang Hsi-min, with Yunnanese army, occupied Canton beginning civil war

June 12, Kuomintang drove Yunnanese from Canton

June 19, After mass meeting in Canton under auspices of the Kuomintang circulars distributed ordering boycott of foreign goods, refusal to work for foreigners, &c.

June 20, Strike spread to Hongkong and Canton

June 23, Parade of workers, students, and citizens in Canton a demonstration against Shanghai shooting. 3 shots by unknown persons started firing on crowd by British and French machine guns, 52 killed, 117 fatally wounded

June 24, Note of Peking Government presented 14 demands to Powers as a result of the Shanghai incident asking revision of the unequal treaties

June 26, British Minister at Peking made formal protest regarding firing on British concession at Canton on June 23

——, Note from Canton Government to British and French consuls demanded compensation and surrender of Shameen

July 1, The "National Government of the Republic of China" established at Canton with Wu Hon-min (Kuomintang) as civil Governor

July 2, Commission composed of French and Italian Ministers and American Charge d'Affaires at Peking appointed to negotiate with Chinese regarding the Shanghai incident

July 4, Anti-foreign riots at Swatow

July 15, Bids on English railroad material refused in boycott of English goods

July 19, Last of Boxer indemnity remitted to China by the United States

July 24, Anti-foreign riots at Canton

July 31, Anti-foreign riots at Nanking

Aug. 12, "Strike Committee" at Canton issued regulations prohibiting access to Kwangtung ports by British and Japanese vessels

——, Fatal riots at Hongkong and Tientsin

Aug. 18, Government invited representatives of 8 Powers to meet in conference at Peking on Oct. 26

Aug. 26, Responsibility for Strike Committee regulations disowned by Canton Government

Aug. 30, Assassination of Liao Chung-kai, Minister of Finance, and political commissar of Whampoa Military Academy

Sept. 4, Powers representing the Washington Conference sent identic Notes to China declaring willingness to consider proposals for modification of treaties

Sept., Swatow occupied by Chen Chuing-min's "anti-Red army"

Sept. 5, Agreement with Belgium regulated method of payment of Boxer indemnity

Sept. 26, Anti-British strike at Shanghai ended

Sept. 28, Strike of telegraph operators for increase of wages and shorter hours

Oct. 1, Agreement with Italy settlement of Boxer indemnity

Oct. 7–27, Judicial inquiry into Shanghai affair of May 30 by Sir Henry Collen, Judge E. G. Johnson and Judge Kisaburo Sugg

Oct. 15, General Chang Tso-lin's troops under Yang Yu-ting withdrew from Shanghai as troops from Chekiang under Sun Chuan-fang advanced on city which was occupied

Oct. 19, Commercial Treaty with Austria signed

Oct. 20, Nanking surrendered to Sun Chuan-fang

Oct. 21, Statement of Wu Pei-fu at Hankow that 14 provinces had made appeal to him to take action against the Peking Government and Bolshevism and Communism

Oct. 26, Customs Tariff Conference opened in Peking

attended by representatives of Belgium, France, Great Britain, Italy, Japan, the Netherlands, Portugal, Denmark, Norway, Peru, Spain, and the United States

Nov. 1, Agreement with Italy as to method of payment of Boxer indemnity

Nov. 6, Cantonese forces under Chiang Kai-shek recaptured Swatow

Nov. 13, Agreement between Chang Tso-lin and Feng Yu-hsiang for withdrawal of Changs' troops from the vicinity of Peking

Nov. 17, General strike and boycott at Hankow

Nov. 19, Customs Tariff Conference at Peking acceded to China's demand for treaty giving unrestricted tariff rights to begin Jan. 1, 1929. The likin or provincial tariff duties to be abolished at the same time

Nov. 22, Revolt of part of Chang's troops under Kuo Sung-ling

Nov. 26, Troops of Feng Yu-hsiang occupied Peking

Dec. 6, Kuo Sung-ling began advance towards Mukden and defeated forces of Chang Tso-lin the following day near Chunchow, Manchuria

Dec. 9, Army of Feng Yu-hsiang attacked Li Ching-lin, adherent of Chang Tso-lin at Tientsin

Dec. 11, National Constitutional Drafting Committee adopted a new Constitution

Dec. 12, Li Ching-lin defeated Honan troops south of Tientsin

Dec. 17, General Feng Yu-hsiang began unsuccessful attack at Jegow, 160 miles south of Peking

——, Japanese troops as permitted by Treaty of Portsmouth entered Mukden to protect the railroad

Dec. 21, Kuo Sung-ling captured Hsinminfu

Dec. 22, Peitsang taken by forces of General Feng advancing on Tientsin

Dec. 23, Judicial commission in Shanghai affair gave decision exonerating the Shanghai Municipal Commission. $75,000 granted to families of Chinese killed and wounded, May 30

——, Chang Tso-lin victorious at Paikifu

Dec. 24, Chang Tso-lin's troops defeated and captured Kuo Sung-lin

——, General Feng Yu-hsiang captured Tientsin, defeating General Li Ching-lin at Sinminfu

Dec. 27, Kuo Sung-lin executed

Dec. 29, General Hsu Shu-cheng (Anfu) assassinated near Peking

1926

Jan. 1, Chang Tsung-lin held Manchuria and exercised suzerainty over Shantung ruled by Chang Chung Chang, Wu Pei-fu central provinces of Hupeh and Honan including city of Hankow, Sun Chuan-fang 5 provinces southeast of Shanghai, Feng Yu-hsiang Chihli including cities of Tientsin and Peking, southern provinces of Kwangsi and Kweichow held by southern Nationalists with headquarters at Canton

Jan. 2, Second triennial Kuomingtang All-Chinese Congress opened

Jan. 9, Resignation of General Feng accepted by Cabinet, and Feng appointed Special Commissioner to study industries abroad

Jan. 12–Sept. 16, Conference on Extraterritoriality met at Peking, Silas Strawn, American, chairman

Jan. 16, M. Ivanov, general manager of Chinese Eastern Railroad, refused to transport Chinese troops without payment. Train seized by Chinese

Jan. 19, Battle of Shanhaikwan. General Feng Yu-hsiang defeated Manchurian General Chang Tso-lin

Jan. 21, General Wu Pei-fu began advance from Hupeh Province towards Peking

——, M. Ivanov, manager of Chinese Eastern Railroad, arrested by Chang Tso-lin in dispute as to payment for transit of troops

Jan. 22, Ultimatum from Russia as to Chinese Eastern Railroad affair

Jan. 24, Agreement with Russia as to Chinese Eastern Railroad and Russians released

Feb. 21, Commissioner of Customs (British) at Canton with approval of foreign consuls announced closing of ports of Canton and Whampoa because of seizure of cargoes by strikers

Feb. 25, Strikers at Canton restored seized goods and ports reopened the following day

March 3, Chihli and Shantung forces associated with Fengtien party started offensive against Kuominchun near Tientsin

March 4, Peking Government denounced French Treaties delimiting frontier with Indo-China

March 8, General Feng Yu-hsiang in command of Taku forts attacked by forces of Chang Tso-lin

March 9, Foreign shipping fired on by Taku forts

March 10, Protest of Powers signatory of Boxer indemnity Treaties as to forts at Taku

March 13, Japanese destroyer fired on from Taku forts

March 18, Students riots at Peking in demonstration against the Government because of acceptance of Russian ultimatum. 40 killed by police

March 20, Premier Chia Teh-yao resigned

——, *Coup d'état* of General Chiang Kai-shek at Canton. Russian Communists and strike leaders arrested

March 22, Kuominchun forces evacuated Tientsin, retiring to Peking. Tientsin occupied by forces of Chang Tso-lin

March 23, British destroyed pirate headquarters at Bias Bay by naval and aërial bombardment

March 23–April 15, Siege of Peking by Wu Pei-fu and Chang Tso-lin who combined to drive Kuominchun forces of Marshal Feng from the city

March 30, General Sun Chuan-fang, military governor of Kiangsu Province and of Shanghai, declared independence of the 5 central provinces under his control, joining forces with Chang Tso-lin and Wu Pei-fu

April 6, Government informed Belgium of desire to revise Treaty of 1865

April 10, Army deposed President Tuan Chi-jui and released his predecessor Tsao-Kun, Wu Pei-fu invited to assume control of administration

April 15, General Feng and Kuominchun (Nationalist) forces evacuated Peking and retired northeast making his headquarters in Nankow Pass with Kalgan on Manchurian frontier as base

April 17, Resignation of Premier Chi Teh-yao

April 19, Allied troops entered Peking

April 25, Second coup d'état of Chiang this time against the moderates, C. C. Wu forced to retire to Shanghai

April 28, General Wu Pei-fu appointed General Wang Muan-Chin ruler of Peking

May 1, President Tsao Kun resigned

May 5, Borodin, returned to Canton, reached agreement with Chiang that Russians would support military expedition against the North. Communists reinstated

May 13, Dr. W. W. Yen became Prime Minister

May 23, Eugene Chen became acting Minister of Foreign Affairs, succeeding Hu Han-min

May 27, General Wu attacked Cantonese along the Kwangtung frontier

May 30, General Sun Chuan-fang organized the 5 central provinces under his control into an independent state

June 4, Revenues of salt gabelle at Tientsin taken over by local military governor

June 11, General Chiang Kai-shek assumed office as Commander-in-Chief of Nationalist army at Canton

June 21, Anti-British strike and boycott begun in Canton

June 22, Resignation of Dr. Yen, Prime Minister. Succeeded by Admiral Tu Hsi-kwei

July 10, Fengtien troops occupied Hankow Pass and Yuchan, evacuated by Kuominchun

July 12–14, The Kuominchun evacuated the Nankow position, retiring to Suiyuan

July 13, Tang Sheng-chi (Kuomintang) in alliance with Cantonese occupied Changsha, defeating forces of Wu Pei-fu

July 15, Opening of general attack on Kuominchun forces by Allies

——, General Wu ordered release of salt revenues which had been seized by his forces at Tientsin

July 15–25, Hongkong-Canton negotiations

Aug. 13, Diplomatic body approved draft Agreement for rendition of Shanghai Mixed Court

Aug. 14, Defeat of Kuominchun forces at Nankow Pass

Aug. 16, General Feng's forces (Kuominchun) withdrew from Nankow Pass and Kalgan into Fengchen Province, Shansi

Aug. 19, Chang Tso-lin's forces commanded by General Kuo occupied Kalgan

Aug. 22, Canton-Hunan forces captured Yochow

Aug. 25, Forces of General Wu Pei-fu reached Hankow from Peking

Aug. 27, Belgium declined to abolish unequal treaties until stable government in control of China

Aug. 28, Announcement by Kuomintang that General Feng Yu-hsiang, Kuominchun leader, had been admitted into Party

Aug. 31, Provisional Agreement signed for establishment of Shanghai Provisional Court to replace Shanghai Mixed Court. Published Sept. 27

Sept. 1–Oct. 11, Siege of Wuchang, Hanyang, and Hankow by Cantonese forces

Sept. 2, At Harbin Chang Tso-lin seized 11 steamers and 30 barges of Chinese Eastern Railroad

Sept. 5, Clash of British and Chinese at Wanhsien on upper Yangtse River over seizure of boats by Chinese. British fired on city

——, Canton strikers seized French oil vessel

Sept. 6, Chang Kai-shek (Cantonese) forced evacuation of Hanyang, Wu Pei-fu retreating northward

Sept. 8, Hankow surrendered to Southerners

Sept. 11, Karakhan, Soviet Minister, deported by Peking Government

Sept. 16, Report of Extra-Territorial Commission signed by representatives of the United States, Belgium, British Empire, Denmark, China, &c.

Sept. 17–Oct. 15, Series of engagements around Nanchang between Cantonese troops and troops of General Sun Chuan-fang, Nanchang, capital of Kiangsi, captured by Southerners on the 19th and retaken on the 22d

Sept. 25, Sun Chuan-fang recaptured Nanchang, threatening position of Chang Kai-shek in Canton

Oct. 2, Dr. Wellington Koo appointed acting Prime Minister and Minister of Foreign Affairs in Peking Government, Pan Fu, Minister of Finance

Oct. 10, Canton Government terminated boycott against British which had lasted 15 months

Oct. 11, Wuchang taken by Cantonese forces of Chang Kai-shek after siege of 40 days

——, New surtaxes levied by Canton Government

Oct. 12, Firing on Japanese vessel, on French vessels on the 13th, and American, and British vessels on the 14th and 19th

Oct. 15, Kuomintang Congress opened in Canton, adopted program

Oct. 16–19, Revolt of Governor Hsia Chao of Chekiang Province in favor of the Cantonese Government suppressed

Oct. 21, Peking Government demanded revision of Treaty of 1896 with Japan

Nov. 3, Declaration of diplomatic corps at Peking that they refused to recognize legality of Canton surtaxes

Nov. 5, Negotiations for revision of Treaty of commerce of 1865 with Belgium came to an end without agreement

——, Cantonese forces occupied Kiukiang, Sun Chuan-fang's army in retreat withdrew from Kiangsi Province

Nov. 6, Government announced formal abrogation of Treaty with Belgium of Nov. 2, 1865

Nov. 10, Cantonese army invested Nanking

Nov. 17, Strikes at Hankow

Nov. 18, Military council at Tientsin decided on united action against the Cantonese

Nov. 29, Resignation of Peking Cabinet because of lack of funds

Dec. 1, Political Council of the Kuomintang decided to move the Southern Government to Wuchang

Dec. 2, Chang Tso-lin became commander-in-chief of reorganized Northern army known as the Ankuochun or "tranquility restoration army"

Dec. 3, Cantonese occupied Foochow and extended power over Fukien Province

Dec. 4, Announcement of decision to terminate all the unequal Treaties and refusal to submit interpretation of Treaty of 1865 with Belgium to decision of Permanent Court of International Justice

Dec. 10, Leading members of the Southern Government now styled the Nationalist Government, including all members of the family of Dr. Sun Yat-sen, and Borodin arrived at Hankow

Dec. 18, Memorandum of British Government defined position regarding China as to surtaxes

1927

Jan. 1, Mixed Court at Shanghai formally transferred to Chinese after 15 years

——, Nationalist mandate consolidated cities of Hankow, Wuchang, and Hanyang into one city to be known as Wuhan, to be nationalist capital

Jan. 3, British concession at Hankow attacked by mob of Chinese. Dispersed by Chinese soldiers. British marines landed

Jan. 4, First meeting of Shanghai Provisional Court

——, British marines withdrawn. Chinese mob returned and stormed the British concession at Hankow

Jan. 5, French Mixed Court turned over to Chinese control

Jan. 6–7, Chinese invaded British concession at Kiukiang. British subjects evacuated

Jan. 7, British concession at Hankow evacuated by all foreigners

Jan. 11, Belgian Consul General molested at Hankow

Jan. 12, Peking Government issued mandate levying Washington surtaxes

——, Dr. Wellington Koo became Premier and Minister of Foreign Affairs, reconstituting Regency Cabinet, Pan Fu, Minister of Communications

Jan. 14, Foreign missions at Fuchow attacked and looted

Jan. 20, Washington surtaxes levied at ports by order of the President after refusal of Sir Francis Aglen, Inspector of Customs, to issue the necessary orders

Jan. 21, Decision of British Government to send 3 brigades of troops to Shanghai

Jan. 24, British business houses in Hankow reopened

Jan. 27, Announcement of State Department of the United States of readiness to enter into negotiations for new treaties with a central Government which could speak for all of China

——, British troops landed in Shanghai for protection of foreigners

Feb. 1, Surtax of 2½% and luxury surtax came into effect

——, Sir Francis Aglen, Inspector General of Customs, dismissed by Peking Government, A. H. F. Edwards appointed

Feb. 7, Representatives of the Powers in Peking protested against levy of surtaxes

Feb. 15, Belgians withdrew complaint at Hague Court against China for abrogation of Treaty in view of negotiations pending for new Treaty

Feb. 16, Forces of Marshal Sun Chuan-fang defeated by Nationalist army at Hangchow and Hangchow occupied by Nationalists on the 18th

Feb. 19, "Chen-O'Malley" Agreement signed with Great Britain provided for restoration of British concession at Hankow

Feb. 19–24, General strike at Shanghai in support of Nationalist advance

Feb. 21, Marshal Chuan-fang resigned his command in Shanghai area to Chang Tsu Tsung Chang

Feb. 22, French settlement at Shanghai shelled by Chinese Communists

Feb. 28, Seizure of Soviet steamer "Panniat Lenina" by Shantung forces and "White" Russians in army of Chang Tsung-chang and arrest of Madame Borodin and Soviet couriers off Nanking

March 2, "Chen-O'Malley" Agreement for restoration to China of British concession at Kiukiang

March 4, Retreat of troops of Chang Tsung-chang holding line south of Shanghai to Nanking begun

March 8, Rioting and looting at Wuhu

March 12, Shantung troops attempting to enter international settlement at Shanghai repulsed by British troops

March 14–21, Northern army defeated by Nationalists in a series of engagements south of Nanking, the only provinces remaining opposed to Nationalists being Shantung and Chihli controlled by Chang Tso-lin

March 15, Formal rendition of British concessions at Hankow and Kiukiang

March 21, Shanghai taken by Nationalist forces of Chiang Kai-shek, General Pi Shou-chan defending Shanghai went over to Nationalists

March 22, British troops prevented Chinese troops from entering international settlement at Shanghai
——, Chiang Kai-shek embarked from Kiukiang for Nanking leaving the Communists Eugene Chen and Borodin in control
March 23, Nanking evacuated by Northern forces and occupied by Nationalists under Cheng Chien
March 24, Southern troops (Nationalists) commanded by General Chen Chien entering Nanking attacked and looted foreign consulates. Among foreigners killed was Dr. J. E. Williams, American, vice-president of Nanking University. Bertram Giles British Consul wounded
March 29, 50 Shanghai banks and industries sent message to the United States deeply regretting the Nanking incident of March 24
April 1, Nationalist army began advance north from the Yangtse River
April 2, Russian Communist Manifesto urged the proletariat of the world to assist the Nationalist Chinese. Group of Communists reached Hankow overland from Canton
April 3, Japanese concession at Hankow attacked by a mob. Marines landed offered successful resistance
April 6, Police raided the Soviet embassy and offices in Peking. Documents seized and 16 Russians and 36 Chinese arrested, including Li Ta-Chao, professor in the National University and leader of Chinese Communist Party
April 8 (about), Nationalists defeated by Sun Chuanfang's army at Yangchow and Chuchow
April 11, Joint Note of representatives of the United States, Great Britain, Japan, France, and Italy demanded apology, reparations, and punishment of persons responsible for Nanking incident of March 24
April 12, Communists of Shanghai called general strike
April 12–13, Chiang Kai-shek forces raided Communists at Shanghai
April 13, Northern troops commanded by Marshal Sun Chuan-fang occupied Pukow
April 14, General labor union at Shanghai dissolved
April 15, Kuominchun Executive Committee at Nanking decided to set up Government in opposition to the Hankow Government of the Communists
——, Reply of Government to Note of Powers of April 11 accepted responsibility for Nanking incident
April 16, Li Cha-sum raided Communists at Canton
April 18, Chiang Kai-Shek inaugurated moderate Nationalist Government at Nanking, Dr. C. C. Wu, Minister of Foreign Affairs
——, Hankow Government declared embargo on silver
April 22, Martial law proclaimed in native city of Shanghai
April 28, Li Ta-Chao and 19 of Chinese arrested in raid of April 6 executed
——, Anti-foreign boycott begun
May 7, Serious fighting at Chumatien in Honan between forces of Chang Tso-lin and Nationalist forces from Hankow
May 10, Fighting in Kiangsi Province between Chiang Kai-shek's forces and Hankow troops
May 13, C. C. Wu appointed Foreign Minister of Nanking Government in place of Eugene Chen
May 15, Pukow occupied by Chiang Kai-shek and Sun Chuan-fang forced to retire
May 17, British diplomatic representatives left Hankow
——, Fengtien forces reached Chumatien and clashed with army of Tang Sheng-chi near Yencheng on 21st

May 22, Severe earthquake in Kansu Province with great loss of life
May 26, Feng Yu-hsiang captured Loyang
May 26–30, Second battle at Chumatien. Northern troops defeated forces of Tang Shien-chih
May 28, Japan announced decision to send 2 battalions of troops to Tsingtao to defend Japanese lives and property
May 30, Chiang Kai-shek forces took Pengpu and Hsuchow (Suchow) and Mingkwang and advanced into Shantung Province
May 31, Japanese troops reached Tsingtao
June 1 and 20, Peking Government protested to Japan against sending of troops to Tsingtao as violation of Washington Treaty regarding Shantung
June 5, General Yen Hsi-san, Governor of Shansi, raised nationalist flag proclaiming adherence to the Kuomintang
June 7, Chiang Kai-shek forces took Hanchwang on Tientsin-Pukow railroad
June 9, Sun Chuang-fang defeated in Kiangsu Province. Nationalists occupied Lincheng and Tsaochuang
——, Yang Sen's advance on Hankow repulsed
June 18, At Peking Chang Tso-lin proclaimed himself Dictator and assumed title "Generalissimo of the Forces for the Suppression of Communism" and appointed new Cabinet with Pan-fu as Prime Minister on resignation of Regency Cabinet: Premier, P'an Fu; Foreign Affairs, Wang Yin-t'ai; Military and Naval Affairs, Gen. Ho Feng-lin; Interior, Shen Jui-lin; Finance, Yen Tse-p'u; Justice, Yao Chen; Education, Liu Chieh; Industry, Chang Ching-hui; Agriculture and Labor, Mo Teh-hui; Communications, P'an Fu
June 24, Joint declaration issued by Feng and Chiang demanded expulsion of extremists from the Kuomintang Party and dismissal of Borodin and other Russians
June 30, Renewed advance of Nationalists in Shantung
——, Nanking Government issued new tariff regulations, 3½% on all imports beginning July 4, and higher rates after Aug. 1, 1.30 on certain luxuries specified including tobacco, 50% on wines. Date of Sept. 1 substituted for Aug. 1 later
July 1, Declaration of boycott of Japanese goods came into effect
July 6, Japanese troops advanced from Tsingtao to Tsinan
July 8–14, Northern forces advanced down the Pukow-Tientsin railroad as far as Hsuchow
July 11, Madame Borodin who was arrested Feb. 28 released
July 14, Mrs. Sun Yat-sen announced withdrawal from the Wuhan Government and in August with Eugene Chen proceeded to Moscow
July 17, Anti-Communist coup d'état at Hankow effected by General Ho Chien
July 18, Martial law proclaimed at Hankow and Communists arrested
July 20, Northern forces defeated Nationalists near Lincheng
——, Proclamation announced likin and other taxes on goods in transit would be abolished Sept. 1
July 24, Chiang Kai-shek evacuated Hsuchow after siege and Northern forces took possession
July 27, Michael Borodin, Russian Communist, left Hankow for Chengchow returning to Russia to escape arrest by Chiang Kai-shek

July 30, General Chiang Kai-shek withdrew from Pengpu. Reoccupied by Northern troops Aug. 8

Aug. 2–3, Advance of Northern forces in Kiangsu checked at Suchow

Aug. 6, Metropolitan University created at Peking by amalgamation of the 9 government universities

Aug. 8, General Chang Fa-kwei recaptured Nanchang from "Red" army of Yeh Ting

Aug. 12, General Chiang Kai-shek resigned as commander-in-chief of the Nanking Kuomintang (Nationalist) army because of his reverses, failure of Feng to keep agreement of June 22 of coöperation, and refusal of others to obey orders

Aug. 14, Northern forces reached the Yangtse opposite Chin Kiang

Aug. 15, Hankow Government lifted the embargo on silver

Aug. 17, Advance of Sun Chuan-fang reoccupied Pukow

Aug. 22, Shansi forces occupied Fengchen

Aug. 22–23, Conference of Nanking and Hankow Kuomintang leaders at Kuling attempted reconciliation

Aug. 25, Shansi troops occupied Pingtichuan

Aug. 26, Sun Chuan-fang's troops crossed the Yangtse but were forced to retreat to Pengpu after 2 days with loss of 10,000 men

Sept. 1, Shansi troops occupied Kweiwacheng evacuated by the Kuominchun

——, Second punitive expedition of British naval forces against the pirates of Bias Bay

——, Proclamation declared duties announced June 30 and July 20 to take effect Sept. 1 were repealed

Sept. 5, Anti-Japanese riot at Mukden

Sept. 7, Nanking forces of Generals Li Tsung-jen and Ho Yen-ching recaptured Pukow

Sept. 8, Japanese troops withdrawn from Tsinan

Sept. 15, Kuomintang Conference at Nanking reconstructed the Hankow and Nanking governments

Sept. 20, New Nationalist Government formed at Nanking under a commission of five, Hu Han-min, Wang Ching-wei, Tsai Yuan-pei, Tan Yen-kai, and Li Lieh-Chun, the "September Government," C. C. Wu, Minister of Foreign Affairs, Sun Fo, Finance

Sept. 21, Attack on Japanese concession at Hankow successfully repelled

Sept. 24, Swatow captured by Red Army under Yeh Ting and Ho Lung. By Oct. 3 Li Chaisum's forces had driven them out of the city

Sept. 27, General Yen Hsi-shan (Tuchun) of Shansi attacked forces of Chang Tso-lin at Kalgan, cutting the Peking-Suiyuan railroad, forcing them to retreat

Sept. 30, Wuhan Political Council repudiated authority of Nanking Government

Oct.–Nov., Adherents of Tang Sheng-chih established government at Hankow opposed to the Nanking government, the "Nanking-Hankow War" ending with flight of Tang to Japan

Oct. 1, Nationalist Foreign Minister protested against demands of Japan in Manchuria

——, Russian Communist advisers imprisoned

Oct. 3, Advance towards Peking begun by Generals Feng Yu-hsiang and Yen Hsi-shan of Shansi Province

——, Shansi forces occupied Kalgan

Oct. 6, Nanking troops withdrew from Pukow and city reoccupied by forces of Sun Chuan-fang

Oct. 10, Forces of Chang Tso-lin attacked and defeated Shansi army near Nankow Pass

Oct. 14, Fengtien forces occupied Shihchiachuang after battle

Oct. 15, Kalgan reoccupied by forces of Chang Tso-lin

Oct. 18, Clash of Nanking and Wuhan forces at Wuhu

Oct. 20, British submarine L4 in action at Bias Bay against pirates who had seized the steamer "Irene"

Nov. 3, Attempt to renew anti-British boycott at Canton

Nov. 5, General Chiang Kai-shek, leading Nationalist army, took Kiukiang

Nov. 6, Feng Yu-hsiang advanced along the Lunghai railroad, captured Kweiteh and defeated Chang Tsung-chang's troops

Nov. 7, Conflict between "White" Russians and Soviet consulate at Shanghai

——, Chiang Kai-shek returned to Shanghai

Nov. 12, General Tang Seng Chi evacuated Hankow, setting fire to the native city as he left

Nov. 14, General Ho Ying-chin, commanding Nanking troops, took Liuhuaikuan

Nov. 15, Wang Ching-wei and General Li Chai-sum left Canton to attend Kuomintang Conference at Shanghai

——, Nanking troops entered Wuchang. Tang fled to Japan and his troops retired to Hunan

Nov. 16, Chang Fa-kuei expelled the Cantonese troops loyal to Li Chai-sum and established himself in power

——, Northern advance of Nationalist army checked at Ming-kwang by Sun Chuan-fang

Nov. 17, Nanking forces occupied Hankow

Nov. 19, Marshal Sun Chuan-fang evacuated Pengpu, withdrawing to Kuchen

Nov. 23, Group of financiers protested to the United States against loan by Morgan and Company to the South Manchurian railroad as an "imperial Japanese political and economic instrument"

Nov. 26, Chang Fa-kuei broke up Hongkong strikers' organization which had existed at Canton since 1925

Nov. 26 (about), Chang Fa-kuei finally broke up strikers' organization which had existed at Canton since 1925

Nov. 28, Sianfu, capital of Shensi, besieged since April 17, relieved by Kuominchun troops

Nov. 30, British steamer "Siangtan" boarded by pirates below Ichang, Captain Lalor held for ransom. Released Dec. 12

Dec. 1, International Tariff Revaluation Commission opened proceedings at Peking

Dec. 3, Central Committee of the Kuomintang opened session at Shanghai

Dec. 10, Ching Kai-shek again commander-in-chief of the Kuomintang army

Dec. 11, Canton seized by Communists and "Red" peasant army led by Yeh Ting

Dec. 13, Canton retaken by General Li Fu-lin after battle

Dec. 14, Commercial Treaty with Sweden signed

——, Order of Nanking Government closed all Soviet consulates in its territory

Dec. 15, Nationalist Government at Nanking broke off diplomatic relations with Russia because of activities of Russian Communists

Dec. 16, Soviet consulate at Hankow raided and Chinese and Russians arrested

——, Hsuchow occupied by forces of Nanking under General Feng Yu-hsiang

Dec. 20, Chinese Communists arrested at Hankow executed and Russians expelled

Dec. 26, Pei Chung-hsi took up military command at Hankow

Dec. 30, Li Chai-sum reëstablished in power at Canton

——, Chochow evacuated by Shansi troops following negotiations and 79 day siege of Northern forces ended

——, Soviet Consul General and his wife released from custody in Canton

1928

Jan. 9, Chiang Kai-shek announced renewal of hostilities of Nationalists against Communists and Northern armies

Jan. 21, Execution of 30 Communists as plotters of revolt

Jan. 27, Statement of T. V. Soong, Minister of Finance of the Nationalist Government at Nanking, that the Nationalist Government controled 16 of the 21 provinces of China which produced 70% of the customs revenue, the right of any other authorities to exercise control of the Customs administration or to appoint any agent to exercise such control denied

Feb. 3–10 4th Plenary session of the Kuomintang Party held at Nanking

Feb. 19, Marshal Chang Chun-chang landed at Lungkow and with support of General Chu-Yu former tuchan of Chihli began offensive against the Government. Defeated

March 5, Mandate appointed Customs Tariff Autonomy Commission

March 18, Nanking Government issued 2 mandates ordering arrest of persons responsible for the Nanking incident and enjoining general protection of lives and property of foreigners

March 30, Notes exchanged with the United States by which China expressed regret for Nanking incident of 1927 and promised compensation to be arranged by joint commission

April 17–19, Northern army of General Sun Chuanfang defeated by General Feng Yu-hsiang

April 19, Japan ordered 5,000 troops to Shantung for protection of railroad zone

April 20, Peking Government protested against Japanese troops at Tsinanfu

April 21, Nanking Government protested against Japanese troops in Shantung

April 22, Northern forces withdrew from Tsinanfu, railroad lines cut

May 1, Nationalist forces commanded by General Ho Yao-tsu entered Tsinanfu

May 3, Japanese property at Tsinanfu looted

May 3–5, Fighting in streets of Tsinanfu between Chinese and Japanese soldiers

May 9, Japanese bombarded walled city of Tsinanfu

——, Announcement of Chang Tso-lin at Peking that he was willing to leave the question of the national government to the people if they could agree on "a fair and impartial decision"

May 15, Japanese Note demanded apologies, punishment of officers for Tsinan affair and suspension of hostilities within 7 miles of the Shantung railroad

May 18, Memorandum from Japan warned China that Japan would take steps if order and peace in Manchuria threatened

May 19, Treaty of friendship and commerce with Poland signed

——, Chang Tso-lin defeated Feng Yu-hsiang

May 23, Northern army of General Sun Chuan-fang recaptured Hokien from Feng's troops

——, Resignation of Huang Fu, Nationalist Foreign Minister, and dismissal of General Cheng Chien involved in the Nanking incident of 1927

——, Dr. C. C. Wu, former Minister of Foreign Affairs of the Nationalist Government (Nanking) opened offices in Washington (U.S. of A.). Received by Secretary of State Kellogg in informal conversation

May 26, Treaty of friendship with Greece signed

May 30, Reply of Nanking Government to Japanese memorandum of May 18 warned Japan against interference in domestic affairs of China

June 3, Chang Tso-lin with his Cabinet withdrew from Peking as victorious Nationalist army advanced on the city

June 4, Train on which Chang Tso-lin was traveling bombed and Chang fatally wounded

——, Ministers of the Powers in Peking addressed Notes (identical) to Chiang Kai-shek, Feng Yuhsiang, and Yen Hsi-shan (Nationalists) asking that General Pao, Northern General, invited by the "elder statesmen" to remain to maintain order in Peking during interim period be permitted to act until he could be relieved by Nationalist troops and then be permitted to retire with his men

June 5, Advance guard of the Nationalist forces entered Peking

June 8, General Yen Hsi-shan with Shansi troops formally occupied Peking

June 9, General Chiang Kai-shek resigned as commander-in-chief

——, Act provided for settlement of labor disputes

June 12, Chinese part of Tientsin surrendered to Nationalist troops commanded by General Fu Tso-yi

June 14, C. T. Wang appointed Minister of Foreign Affairs in place of General Hwang-Fu

June 20, Death ("officially") of Chang Tso-lin. His son Chang Hsueh-liang, proclaimed Governor of Fengtien Province

June 20–30, Nationalist Economic Conference at Shanghai

June 21, Name of Peking changed to Peiping meaning "Northern Peace"

June 24, British troops arrived at Tongshan to protect lives and property of British and other foreign employees of the Kailan Mining Administration

July 2, Sum of $173,000 deposited in Bank of China in name of the District Salt Inspectors at Tientsin transferred to credit of Nationalist Government at Nanking without consent of the depositors

July 6, Nationalist leaders proceeded to tomb of Sun Yat-sen to announce to his spirit the fulfilment of his wishes, capture of Peking from northern war lords

July 7, Nationalist Government mandate stated that all "unequal treaties" which had expired were abrogated and that steps would be taken to terminate those that had not yet expired

July 8, The Government issued interim regulations subjecting nationals of Powers with whom treaties had expired to Chinese laws

July 13, Nanking Government announced termination as of July 7 of conventions of 1886, 1887, and 1895 with France as to trade on Indo-China frontier. French Note in reply denied Chinese right of abrogation

July 19, Japanese Government announced terms for settlement of Tsinan looting of property, May 3–12

July 20, C. T. Wang, Foreign Minister, notified Japan of abrogation of commercial treaty

July 24, General Chung Chen-kuo Shanti attacked and captured Chefoo

July 25, Tariff Treaty signed with the United States to become effective Jan. 1, 1929. Treaty constituted *de jure* recognition of the Nationalist Government repealing that of 1903 and recognition of Chinese tariff autonomy

Aug. 1, Message of Pope to Chinese Catholics on ending of civil war

——, Nationalist Reconstruction Committee announced that Nanking would be made the capital of China

Aug. 8–15, 5th Plenary Session of the Central Executive Committee of the Kuomintang at Nanking

Aug. 9, Sino-British Agreement as to settlement of Nanking incident of 1927

Aug. 17, Agreement with Germany concluded for reciprocity in customs

Aug. 27, Announcement compulsory military training would be introduced in colleges

Sept. 1, New criminal code and code of criminal procedure became effective

Sept. 9, General Pai Tsung-hsi commanding Kwangsi troops attacked remainder of Chihli and Shantung armies along Peking-Mudken railroad between Tientsin and Manchurian border

Oct. 2, Official announcement confirmed appointment of Mr. A. H. F. Edwardes as Inspector General of Maritime Customs and Mr. F. W. Maze, deputy Inspector General

Oct. 4, Organic law, 6 principles for guidance of people, promulgated by Nationalist Government (Kuomintang)

Oct. 7, Announcement of establishment of Central Bank of China by the Government and issue of short term loan designed to restore the currency

Oct. 9, Exchange of Notes with Italy settled Nanking incident of March, 1927

Oct. 10, General Chiang Kai-shek elected Oct. 9 inaugurated in Nanking as President of China, C. T. Wang, Minister of Foreign Affairs

Oct. 19, Conference on treaty and tariff questions opened at Nanking

Oct. 25, Cabinet appointed, Tan Yen-kai, President of the Administrative Council; T. V. Soong, Minister of Finance; C. T. Wang, Foreign Affairs; Feng Yuhsiang, War; Admiral Yang Shu-Shuang, Navy

Oct. 28, National Government issued manifesto detailing program of internal reform

Nov. 1, New Central Bank with capital of $20,000,000 (Mexican) opened at Shanghai

Nov. 11, British Consulate General reopened at Nanking

Nov. 12, Tariff autonomy Treaty with Norway signed

Nov. 18–23, Negotiations with Japanese at Nanking to settle Nanking and Tsinanfu and other incidents broke down because of refusal of Japanese to withdraw troops from Shantung

Nov. 22, Provisional Treaty of amity and commerce with Belgium signed which provided for tariff autonomy by which Belgium agreed to conditionally surrender extraterritoriality

——, Treaty of friendship and commerce with Bulgaria signed

Nov. 27, Treaty of amity and commerce with Italy signed provided for tariff autonomy

Dec. 10, New tariff schedule promulgated to go into effect Feb. 1

Dec. 11, Revolt of Communists at Canton begun

Dec. 12, Tariff Autonomy Treaty with Denmark signed

Dec. 13, Students in riot at Nanking anti-Japanese and anti-Treaty demonstration

Dec. 18, Treaty of commerce with Great Britain signed

Dec. 19, Tariff-autonomy Treaty with the Netherlands signed

——, Tariff and extra-territoriality Treaty with Portugal signed

Dec. 20, Treaty granting tariff autonomy to China signed with Great Britain

——, Tariff-autonomy Treaty with Sweden signed

——, British Minister Sir Miles Lampson formally presented credentials to Nationalist Government

Dec. 22, Tariff-autonomy Treaty with France signed

Dec. 27, Tariff-autonomy and extra-territoriality Treaty with Spain signed

Dec. 29, Manchuria hoisted Nationalist flag, formally submitting to Nationalist Government

1929

Jan. 1–25, Disbandment Conference held at Nanking

Jan. 1, President Chiang appealed to war lords to disband their armies and surrender control to central Government

——, Chang Hsueh-liang appointed chairman of Political Council of Northeast Provinces (Manchuria)

Jan. 10, F. W. Maze appointed Foreign Inspector General of Customs

Jan. 10–11, General Yang Yu-ting arrested and executed in alleged plot to establish an independent Manchuria

Jan. 18, Disbandment Conference agreed on reduction of army and central control of finances

Feb. 1, An autonomous tariff schedule came into effect. Former uniform rate of 5% replaced by highly differentiated schedule with duties ranging from 5% to 27½%

Feb. 5, Nationality law promulgated

Feb. 5–March 20, "North China Star" American newspaper suppressed by the Government

Feb. 7, Marshal Feng withdrew from Nanking for avowed purpose of application of the principle of disbandment but believed to be preparing to seize Shantung on its evacuation by Japanese troops

Feb. 9, Professor Edwin W. Kemmerer and group of experts invited by the Nationalist Government to study economic and financial rehabilitation of China arrived at Shanghai

Feb. 19, Chang Tsung-chang former military Governor (Tuchun) of Shantung landed troops at Lungkow from Darien in attempt to regain control of Shantung

Feb. 22, Nationalist and anti-Nationalist forces in battle near Shantung

Feb. 23, Military *coup d'état* of Li Tsung-jen at Changsha in Hunan Province set up General Ho Chien as head of Government deposing General Lu Tiping, appointee of Nationalist Government

March 1, From this date smoking of opium became a punishable offense

March 5, Announcement that Sir Frederick Whyte (British) had been appointed Political Advisor of the Nanking Government

March 12, Resignation of Yu-Hsiang as Minister of War. Remained neutral

March 14, Manifesto published by 13 military leaders headed by Wang Cheng-wei denouncing the Nanking Government

March 15–28, Third National Congress of Kuomintang Party at Nanking

March 21, Li Chi-shen, Kwangsi leader, ruler of Canton, arrested at Nanking and interned when he arrived at Nanking to attend the Congress and to mediate on behalf of the Wuhan generals

March 24, Agreement with Japan, settlement of Tsinan-fu incident of May, 1928, announced, provided for immediate withdrawal of Japanese troops from Shantung

March 26, Mandate against Kwangsi leaders Li Tsung-jen, Li Chaisum, and Pai Chung-hsi issued by Nanking Government. President Chiang left Nanking to take command of campaign against Wuhan-Kwangsi group

March 27, Chang Tsung-chang occupied Chefoo

March 28, Agreement with Japan, settlement of Tsinan-fu incident, signed

April 4, Nanking Government asked Japan to postpone retirement of troops from Shantung until Central Government troops could take over the region

——, Hankow evacuated by Wunan leaders and occupied the following day by forces of Chiang Kai-shek

April 14, Governor Chao Chi left Tsing-tao for Darien and control of Manchuria passed to Nanking Government

April 22, Nationalist General Liu Chen-nien defeated Chang Tsung-Chang at Ninghai

April 23, Nationalist forces under General Liu Chen-nien recaptured Chefoo

April 24, Anti-Japanese riots at Shanghai

April 26, Mandate of Nanking Government divided control of Shantung between 3 authorities

——, Arms embargo of the Powers of May, 1919 against China, never effective, canceled from this date

April 27, Note of Nanking Government to Great Britain, the United States, the Netherlands, France, Norway, and Brazil asking abolition of extra-territoriality in China. Replies from Great Britain, the United States, France, and the Netherlands, Aug. 10, Norway, Aug. 15

April 29, Provisional National Assembly met at Peking

May 2, Agreement with Japan signed settled Nanking and Hankow incidents

May 4–June 6, Ban placed on "North China Daily News"

May 6, Death of smallpox at Shanghai of Colonel Maximilian Bauer, German military advisor to General Chiang Kai-shek

May 8, Foreign Minister C. T. Wang notified the Powers that the Mixed Court Protocol of Jan., 1919 lapsed in June

May 9–18, Kwangsi forces commanded by General Huang Shao-hsiung, defeated in invasion of Kwang-tung

May 10, Armistice arranged

May 15, General Ho Chien, Governor of Hunan, supporting the National Government, occupied Kweitin, capital of Kwangsi

May 20, Japanese evacuation of Shantung completed

May 22, Li Tsung-jen and Pai Ch'ung-hsi repulsed in offensive against Canton

May 23, Feng Yu-hsiang, military ruler of Honan, Shensi, and Kansu and aspiring to rule in Shantung, in revolt against Nanking Government dismissed from all offices and expelled from the Party

——, Book I Civil Code "General Principles" issued in English translation

May 24, Government announced a punitive expedition against Marshal Feng and ordered his arrest

May 27, Police raided Russian consulates at Harbin, Manchouli, and other cities in northern Manchuria charging use of consulates by Communists for conspiracy against the Government. 39 persons arrested and documents seized

——, Resolution of Congress at Nanking expelled the Kwangsi group from the party Li Chai-sum, Li Tsung-jen and Pei Chung-hsi arrested

May 30, Japan gave *de jure* recognition to Chinese National Government

May 31, Protest of Soviet Government against raid at Harbin and other places

June 1, State funeral of Dr. Sun Yat-sen and removal of body to mausoleum built by the Government on Purple Mountain outside Nanking

June 2, Arrest of Russian Consul General from Mukden and Vice-Consul from Harbin and Russian railroad officials at frontier station at Manchouli

June 3, End of Kwangsi revolt against Nanking Government

June 20, Agreement signed with Great Britain provided for training Chinese naval cadets in England

July 5, Order for arrest of Feng canceled, his soldiers paid, and Feng sent to Europe as special investigator of foreign economics

July 10, Russian officials and employees of the Russian-owned Chinese Eastern Railway at Harbin arrested and deported and Chinese and Manchurian officials seized control of the railway, the telephone and telegraph systems, and the Soviet mercantile fleet and replaced officials with Chinese and "White" Russians on ground that Mukden Agreement of 1924 had been violated

July 13, Russian ultimatum demanded conference on Chinese Eastern Railway, release of Russian prisoners, and abrogation of acts as to railroad

July 16, Reply of Nationalist Government to Russia that a plenipotentiary was leaving to discuss all matters pending between the 2 Governments and demanded release of Chinese imprisoned in Russia

July 17, Second Russian Note to China broke off diplomatic relations

——, Regulations adopted prescribing abolition of provincial commissioners of foreign affairs as of Jan. 1, 1930

July 19, Secretary of State Stimson (American) reminded Chinese and Russian Governments of obligations under the Paris Pact for renunciation of war

July 20, China broke off diplomatic relations with Russia

July 22, Second Note to Russia affirmed desire to settle dispute by negotiation

——, Reply of both Russian and Chinese Governments declared intentions to observe Paris Pact

July 25, Clash with Russians near Manchouli

July 27, Communist army captured Changsha looting and burning the Government and private property

July 29, Troops withdrawn from frontier and 12 mile neutral zone created between troops at Manchouli and Pogranichnaya

Aug. 1, Exchange of Notes with Russia

Aug. 1–6, Disbandment Conference at Nanking agreed to reduce army

Aug. 6, General Ho Chien recaptured Changsha

——, Resignation of Finance Minister Soong because unable to balance budget because of military expenditure

Aug. 8, Shanghai municipal electric plant purchased by American company for $46,704,600 gold

Aug. 10, Note from the United States declined to accede to request of April 27 for immediate abolition of extraterritoriality on ground that China not in position to be able to guarantee justice to Americans in Chinese courts

Aug. 13, Raid of Soviet forces near Jalai Nar and Suifenho

Aug. 29, Regulations for private schools prohibited instruction in religion as a required course and provided that foreigners should not be more than one-third of the Board of Directors

Aug. 30, Soviet Government accepted proposal of China for joint declaration for settlement of question of Chinese Eastern Railway

Aug. 31, Agreement with Belgium signed by which Belgium agreed to retrocession of concession at Tientsin

Sept. 2, Colonel Kriebel (German) appointed military adviser to General Chiang Kai-shek

Sept. 9, Chinese and "White" Russians attacked Soviet forces on border (Russia cited 28 such attacks between Sept. 10 and 23)

Sept. 10, Proposal of C. C. Wu, Chinese delegate at League of Nations at Geneva, that the Assembly be authorized under Article 19 of the Covenant to advise reconsideration of treaties that had become inapplicable and dangerous. Rejected by Agenda Committee Sept. 11 but later (24th) adopted by Judiciary Committee in modified form

Sept. 16, Announcement that extraterritoriality would be terminated on Jan. 1, 1930 whether Foreign Powers affected agreed or not

Sept. 18, Commercial Treaty with Poland signed

Sept. 19, Revolt of Chang Fa-kuei with his "Ironsides" at Ichang on Yangtse River in Hupeh Province

Sept. 21, New Reorganization Party declared for Chang Kai-shek

Sept. 23, Chinese police and Japanese railroad guards in clash at Tiehling 40 miles north of Mukden

Sept. 27, Decision of American Red Cross based on report of investigation (June 15–Aug.) not to undertake famine relief

Sept. 30, Treaty of friendship with Greece signed

Oct. 3, Arrest ordered of Wang Ching-wei and the Left Reorganizationist leaders

——, Revolt of General Shih Yu-san at Pukow across the river from Nanking failed in attempt to seize the capital and retreated to Pengpu in Anhwei

Oct. 10, Book I of Code declared in force

Oct. 12, Russians defeated Chinese in Three Rivers District in renewal of border hostilities

Oct. 15, General Yen Hsi-shan, Governor of Shansi, arrested Marshal Feng Yuhsiang

Oct. 17, Revolt of military Governor of Anhwei

Oct. 18, Revolt at Wuhu on Yangtse 55 miles from Nanking

Oct. 21, Trade Union Act promulgated

Oct. 27, Kuominchun launched general attack in direction of Loyang-Chengchow

Oct. 28, Commander of Foochow garrison in south east declared independence of Fukien Province from the Nanking Government

Oct. 31, Agreement with Great Britain signed for retrocession of Chinkiang

Nov. 1, Reply of United States to Note of Sept. 5 declared willingness to enter into negotiations for the abolition of extraterritoriality

Nov. 3, Kuominchun rebels won decisive victory capturing Mihsien

Nov. 9, Mihsien recaptured by Government troops

Nov. 9–Dec. 14, Mission from the Health Organization of the League of Nations headed by Dr. L. Rajchman invited by the National Government to study the public health situation in China

Nov. 12, Mexico relinquished extraterritorial rights in China

Nov. 15, Concession of Chinkiang, Kiangsu Province, formally returned to China by British

Nov. 17, Soviet forces attacked and captured Manchouli and Jalai Nar and their garrisons

Nov. 21, Nanking forces in surprise attack captured Loyang from the Kuominchun

Nov. 24, Kuominchun armies driven back in Honan and Hupei

Nov. 26, Chang Hsueh-liang (Manchuria) accepted conditions of Soviet Notes of July 13 and 25

Nov. 27, Hailar occupied by Soviet troops

Dec. 2, Memorandum addressed to China by Governments of the United States, France, Great Britain, and Italy calling attention to Pact of Paris

Dec. 3, Protocol signed by representatives of Mukden and Soviet for reorganization of the administration of the Chinese Eastern Railroad. Approved by Nationalist Government Dec. 7

Dec. 3–7, Mutiny of Nationalist troops at Pukow led by Shi Yu-san

Dec. 4, Mutiny of troops in Anking, capital of Anhwei, who joined forces with Shi Yu-san at Pengpu

Dec. 7, Manifesto signed by Tang Sheng-chih and several northern generals denounced the Nanking Government

——, Mutiny of troops at Changchow 75 miles southeast of Nanking on railroad suppressed by loyal troops from Hankow

Dec. 9, Negotiations opened at Nanking with representatives of British, American, French, Dutch, Norwegian, and Brazilian legations

——, Railroad from Nanking to Shanghai cut by "Communist bands"

Dec. 11, Armies of Chang Fa-kuei and Kwangsi forces defeated 30 miles from Canton

Dec. 12, Kuomintang at Nanking expelled Wang Ching-wei from the Party

Dec. 13, Negotiations with Russia for settlement of differences begun at Khabarovsk, eastern Siberia

Dec. 18, General Chiang Kai-shek announced end of revolt

Dec. 20, British Note agreed on Jan. 1, 1930 as date from which gradual abolition of extra-territoriality should be regarded to have begun in principle

Dec. 21, Marshals Yen and Chang Hsueh-liang formally declared loyalty to the Nanking Government

Dec. 22, Khabarovsk Protocol signed with Russia ended dispute as to Chinese Eastern Railway restoring *status quo*

Dec. 23, Soviet forces withdrew from Manchuria

Dec. 28, Manifesto of the Government as to process of abolishment of extraterritoriality to begin Jan. 1

1930

Jan. 1, British Aide-Memoire to China regarding manifesto of Dec. 28, 1929 accepted invitation to enter into negotiations as to abrogation of extraterritoriality. American and French Notes, Jan. 2

Jan. 5, Italian Note refused to accept extraterritoriality

Jan. 25, New regulations issued for mixed court in French concession at Shanghai

Feb. 1, Tariff autonomy with Japan went into effect

Feb. 3, Shanghai Provisional Court resumed work on old basis

——, Revised law provided for government control of provinces by group of 7 to 9 councilors appointed by Nanking Government

Feb. 12, Treaty of amity and commerce with Czechoslovakia signed

Feb. 13, Yen Hsi-shan recently appointed Vice Commander-in-Chief of National army demanded retirement of General Chiang Kai-shek, Commander-in-Chief and reorganization of the Nanking Government

Feb. 17, Agreement as to reorganization of the Shanghai Provisional Court signed by representatives of the United States, Great Britain, France, the Netherlands, Norway, and Brazil to last 3 years and to become effective April 1

March 1–6, Third plenary session of the Kuomintang Central Executive Committee

Wang Ching-wei expelled from the Party

March 12, New Sino-Japanese Customs Tariff Convention signed

March 17, Law of June 1928 as to settlement of labor disputes

March 18, General Feng arrived at Sianfu, capital of Shensi Province, and resumed active command of the Kuominchun forces

——, General Yen's forces took control of the government administrative offices at Peiping displacing appointees of the Nanking Government and establishing a rival government

March 29, Report of Kemmerer Commission published by the Nationalist Government

March 30, Yuanchow in Kiangsi looted by Communist band

March 31, Shansi forces compelled retirement of Nationalist troops stationed north of Tientsin

April 2, Yen Hsi-shan formally assumed command of the northern antigovernment coalition the "National" army. Feng to be Yen's deputy and Wang Ching-wei recognized by Yen as the legal head of the Kuomintang

April 3, Announcement of China Inland Mission that no ransom money would be paid to bandits for missionaries taken captive as to do so "would endanger every foreigner in the interior of China, and place a premium on kidnapping"

April 5, Punitive expedition sent against Yen and his northern associates

April 6, Tariff Agreement with Japan signed

April 18, Convention for the rendition of Weihaiwei signed with Great Britain

April 24, Yen and Feng invited Wang Ching-wei to come to Peking

April 30, Yen Hsi-shan ordered seizure of customs revenue at Tientsin

May 1, Peiping Government established by Yen

May 6, Customs Agreement with Japan signed

May 8, Northern Alliance launched offensive against the Nanking Government on 3 fronts in Kiangsu and west Shantung and southern Hupeh

May 12, Looting of Yungyang by Communists

May 16, Commercial Treaty with France regarding Indo-China signed

May 20, Chinese Eastern Railway Conference opened at Moscow

June 4, Insurgent General Chang Fa-kuei occupied Changsha and threatened Hankow

June 10, Yochow occupied by Kwangsi forces

June 16, General Yen Hsi-shan took over Tientsin office of Chinese Maritime Customs. Bertram Lennox Simpson appointed by him Commissioner of Customs

June 17, Nationalist army defeated rebels south of Wuchang and recaptured Changsha

June 25, Northern rebels captured Tsinanfu capital of Shantung

June 27, Arbitration Treaty with the United States signed

July 4, China agreed to pay its arrears to the League of Nations in 20 annual payments

July 13, Reorganization Conference held at Peiping

July 23, Wang Ching-wei arrived at Peiping

July 28, Changsha taken by Communists who burned and looted the city and killed the inhabitants

July 31, Communists at Changsha fired on American gunboat "Palos" wounding 5 sailors

Aug. 5, Changsha reoccupied by provincial force under General Ho Chien

Aug. 15, Nationalist forces recaptured Tsinan from Northern rebels

Aug. 20, Communists burned Wusueh on the Yangtse River after robbing the inhabitants

Aug. 22, More than 100 Communists arrested in raids on Communist headquarters in Peiping and Nanking

Aug. 30, Manchurian war lord Marshal Chang Hsueh-liang occupied territory around Peiping and Tientsin notifying Nanking Government of his intervention

Sept. 9, State Council of the Northern Coalition sworn in at Peiping, Yen Hsi-shan, chairman, Wang Ching-wei, Hsieh Chih, General Feng Yu-hsiang, and General Li Tsung-jen members

Sept. 19–22, Agreement with Great Britain signed for remission of Boxer indemnity

Sept. 21, Manchurian troops occupied Tientsin

Sept. 22, Death of General Tan Yen-Kai, president of the Executive Yuan in 1929 in Shanghai

Sept. 23, Manchurian troops occupied Peiping

Oct. 1, Weihaiwei returned to China by Great Britain as according to the Agreement of April

——, Assassination of Mr. Simpson in charge of customs

Oct. 3, Administration of customs taken over by Mr. Grierson appointed by the Nanking Government and a Chinese superintendent appointed by Chiang Hsueh-liang

Oct. 6, Chengchow captured by Nanking forces from Feng Yu-hsiang

Oct. 9, Chang Hseueh-liang sworn in as Vice Commander-in-Chief of Nationalist Army

Oct. 11, Negotiations with Russia at Warsaw for settlement of Chinese Eastern Railway dispute not successful

Oct. 12, Manifesto of President Chang Kai-shek outlined 5 points of program including the eradication of communism, rehabilitation of finances, and new Constitution

Nov. 4, General Yen Hsi-shan announced his retirement from politics

Nov. 12–18, Fourth plenary session of the Kuomintang Central Executive Committee at Nanking opened by President Chiang Kai-shek

Nov. 12–23, Visit of Chang Hsueh-liang to Nanking

Nov. 15, Conference at Nanking on Chinese foreign and domestic debts attended by representatives of the United States, Great Britain, France, Belgium, the Netherlands, and Italy

Nov. 24, Negotiations with France opened regarding extraterritoriality

———, Request of Dr. C. T. Wang to Japan to relinquish concession at Hankow refused by Japan

Dec. 4–16, Conference with Russia as to settlement of disputes as to administration of Chinese Eastern Railroad again broken off without result

Dec. 22, Yen Hsi-shan sailed from Tientsin for Darien

———, Cabinet of Ministers, sworn on December 22, 1930, as follows: President of the Administrative Council, Chiang Kai Shek; Minister of Finance, T. V. Soong; Foreign Affairs, Dr. C. T. Wang; War, Ho Ying-Ching; Navy, Admiral Yang Shu-chuang; Industry, H. H. Kung; Education, Kao Lu; Railways, Sun Fo; Interior, Liu Shang Ching; Communications, Wang Peh-chun

Dec. 29, Nanking Government promulgated a new and higher tariff schedule to go into effect Jan. 1, 1931

CHOSEN

See Korea.

CHRISTMAS ISLAND

Christmas Island, annexed by Great Britain June, 1888. *See* Straits Settlements.

COCHIN CHINA

Cochin-China, the six southern provinces of the Empire of Annam in the Indo-China Peninsula, ceded to France by Treaties of June 5, 1862, after the capture of Saignon by Admiral Charner in February, and July 15, 1867 with Siam; annexation of entire 6 provinces proclaimed June 25, 1867; area estimated at 26,476 square miles, population in 1928 estimated as 4,303,418 of whom 16,062 were French, and 733 European foreigners (excluding the military forces). Saignon had a population of 130,000 of whom 12,600 were French, and 650 other Europeans, exclusive of 3,066 troops. In 1887 it was united with Cambodia, Annam, and Tonking to form the Indo-Chinese Union. *See* Indo-China, French.

COCOS OR KEELING ISLANDS

See Straits Settlements.

DAMÃO

Damão or Daman, Portuguese Colony on the coast of India about 100 miles north of Bombay on the Gulf of Cambay, occupied by the Portuguese in 1558 and finally ceded by the Marathas in 1780; total area 169 square miles.

DIU

Diu, Portuguese Island of Bombay, India, about 140 miles west of Damão, at southern extremity of the peninsula of Kathiawar, area 20 square miles; population in 1921, 13,844; came into possession of the Portuguese in 1515.

FORMOSA

Formosa (Taiwan), Japanese Island, situated 90 miles off the coast of China; area 13,892 square miles; population of 4,524,161. The Island was ceded to Japan by China by the Treaty of Shimonoseki of April 17, ratified on May 8, 1895, and Japan took formal possession on June 2, civil government beginning on March 31, 1896, after revolt of resident Chinese subdued.

Eizo Ishizuka, Governor General.

1661

The early Spanish and Dutch settlers were expelled by Chinese colonists.

1874

Oct. 31, Treaty between China and Japan gave indemnity to Japan for massacre of Japanese sailors, and Japanese troops withdrawn.

FRENCH INDIA

French India: As established by the treaties of 1814, and 1815, the French possessions in India consist of five separate colonies, which cover an aggregate of 50,803 hectares (about 196 square miles), and had on January 1, 1929, the following estimated populations:—

Pondichéry	47,626
Oulgaret	24,666
Villenour	21,236
Tiroubouvané	25,395
Bahour	20,109
Nettapacom	15,715
Modéliarpeth	14,214
Ariancoupom	19,103
Karikal	17,314
Tirnoular	9,758
Grande Aldée	7,786
Neravy	8,659
Nédounkadou	7,850
Cotchéry	6,861
Chandernagor	27,393
Mahé	11,959
Yanaon	4,816
Total	290,460

In 1929, the population of the Provinces was as follows:—Pondichéry, 188,064; Karikal, 58,228; Chandernagor, 27,393; Mahé, 11,959; Yanaon, 4,816.

See also Chandernagor; Karikal; Mahé; Pondicherry; Yanaon.

FRENCH INDO-CHINA

French Indo-China, region in the southeastern peninsula of Asia. *See also* Annam; Cambodia; Cochin-China; Tonking.

French Indo-China, with an area of about 285,-000 square miles and a population, in 1926, of 20,700,000, of whom 33,000 were European (including military forces), consists of 5 States: the Colony of Cochin-China, the Protectorates of Annam, Cambodia (including the territory around Battambang ceded by Siam in 1907), Tonking, and Laos; and Kwang-Chau-Wan, leased from China. The whole country is under a Governor-General, assisted by a Secretary-General, and each of the States has at its head an official bearing the title of Resident-Superior, except in the case of Cochin-China, which, being a direct French Colony while the others are only Protectorates, has a Governor at its head. There is a Government Council for the whole of Indo-China and a Permanent Commission of the Council. Hanoi is the capital.

Pierre Pasquier, Governor-General, Aug. 22, 1928.

M. Graffeuil, Secretary General, Nov. 4, 1928.

GEORGIA

Georgia (Georgian Socialist Soviet Republic) occupies the whole of the western part of Trans-Caucasia with an area of 26,381 square miles, population in 1926 2,660,963, and includes the Abkhasian Socialist Soviet Republic, the Ajaristan Autonomous Soviet Republic, and the Autonomous Region of Southern Ossetia. Georgia, a kingdom for 2,000 years, was known to the Romans and Greeks as Iberia, though its earliest name was Karthli or Karthveli. Georgia was conquered by one of Alexander's generals about 331 B.C., but threw off the yoke of his successors. It was subjugated to Rome by Pompey 65 B.C., but retained its own sovereigns. Christianity was introduced in the third century, and Tiridates freed the country from Persian rule. In the eighth century Georgia was subdued by Arabs, and in the eleventh century by the Seljuk Turks, and by the Mongol hordes 1220, and 1222, and 1236, freed by Alexander I in 1403. From the 14th to the 18th centuries Georgia was successively held by Persian and Turkish monarchs. Heraclius II (1783) declared himself a vassal of Russia, and his suc-

cessor George XIII surrendered his territories to the Tsar, and in 1802 Georgia became a Russian province, divided into the Governments of Tiflis and Kutais.

1917

Sept. 17, Council of the Trans-Caucasian Peoples met at Tiflis and Sept. 20 proclaimed union of Georgia, Armenia, and Azerbaijan as the Trans-Caucasian Federal Republic

Nov. 22, National Assembly elected

1918

Jan., Chief Commissary sent to Tiflis by the Petrograd Government ejected

March 3, Treaty of Brest-Litovsk awarded Georgia to Turkey

April 15, Turks occupied Batoum (Batum)

May 26, Georgia declared independence of Transcaucasian Federation which was dissolved

May 28, Agreement with Germany by which financial and military support of Germany extended to the Georgian Republic

June 4, Treaty with the Germans and Turks concluded which resulted in "friendly" occupation by the Germans

Oct. 30, Allied Armistice with Turkey ensured evacuation of Turks

Nov. 11, Allied Armistice with Germany ensured evacuation of Germans

Dec. 27, British garrison occupied Batoum (Batum)

1919

March 12, Act of Independence confirmed by Constituent Assembly

1920

May 7, Treaty of peace with Russia signed by which Russia recognized the district and port of Batoum as Georgian territory, and independence of Georgia

——, Treaty of friendship with Azerbaijan signed

July 7, British garrison evacuated Batoum and handed over the district to Georgia

Nov. 15, Georgia asked for admission to the League of Nations which was not granted

1921

Jan. 27, Supreme Council gave *de jure* recognition of the Menshevik Government

Feb. 12, Rising against the Government and invasion of Russian Soviet troops

Feb. 16, Soviet forces captured Salakhlo south of Tiflis

Feb. 22, Turkish ultimatum demanded cession of Ardahan and Artvin

Feb. 25, Soviet forces commanded by General Budenny occupied Tiflis

March 11, Turks occupied Batoum

March 14, Armistice with Russia signed and Convention

March 16, Treaty between Turkey and Russia signed by which Turkey engaged to cede Batoum back to Georgia

March 17, With help of Russians Turks ejected from Batoum

March 19, Soviet Republic proclaimed, Menshevik Government and British Mission left by sea

March 25, Turkish troops withdrawn

Oct. 13, Treaty with Turkey signed, cession of Batoum and recognition

1922

Jan. 27, Great Britain granted *de jure* recognition
March 12, Georgia united with Armenia and Azerbaijan
   forming the Trans-Caucasian Socialist Federal
   Soviet Republic
March 15–April 22, Revolt against Soviet rule

GOA

Goa, a Portuguese settlement on the western
coast of India, area 1,301 square miles, population
in 1921, 508,058. The ancient Hindu city of Goa
was famous in history, ruled by the Kadamba
dynasty from the second century A.D. to 1312,
and by Mohammedan invaders of the Deccan
from 1312 to about 1370, and was then annexed
to the Hindu kingdom of Vijayanagar. Albuquerque founded town of Old Goa in 1511. *See
also* Portuguese India.

HEJAZ

See Arabia.

HONG KONG

Hong Kong, British Crown Colony, is one of a
number of islands situated off the south-eastern
coast of China at the mouth of the Canton River,
about 91 miles south of Canton, area about 32
square miles, including islands, with about 94,000
inhabitants, exclusively Chinese. The Colony was
ceded to Great Britain by China January 20, 1841,
cession confirmed by the Treaty of Nanking in
August, 1842, and the charter bears date April 5,
1843. By a Convention signed June 9, 1898, China
leased to Great Britain for 99 years territory
adjacent to British Kowloon in the province of
Kwang-tung, including Mirs Bay and Deep Bay,
area of mainland and islands leased about 359
square miles.

The opposite peninsula of Kowloon, on the
mainland, was ceded to Great Britain by Treaty
in Oct., 1860.

Sir William Peel, Governor.

INDIA

India, the peninsula of Hindustan, bounded on
the north by the Himalayas, bounded on the
west by the Arabian Sea, and on the east the Bay
of Bengal, and includes Burma, the country on
the eastern shore of the Bay of Bengal, under
British rule, directly or indirectly. The term
British India includes only the districts subject to
British law, and does not include the Indian
States and Agencies. The Indian States are

governed by the Indian Princes, Ministers, or
Councils and the control of the British Government varies considerably in degree. The Princes
have no right to make war or peace, or to send
ambassadors to each other or to external States;
they maintain military forces within certain
limits; the sanction of the Government of India
is required before Europeans of certain classes can
be employed; and the Supreme Government can
exercise control in case of misgovernment. Within
these limits the more important Princes are
autonomous in their own territories.

BRITISH PROVINCES	AREA IN SQ. MILES (1921)	POPULATION IN 1921
Ajmer-Merwara	2,711	495,271
Andamans and Nicobars . .	3,143	27,086
Assam	53,015	7,606,230
Baluchistan [1]	54,228	420,648
Bengal	76,843	46,695,536
Bihar and Orissa	83,161	34,002,189
Bihar	42,360	23,380,288
Orissa	13,736	4,968,873
Chota Nagpur . . .	27,065	5,653,028
Bombay (Presidency) . . .	123,621	19,348,219
Bombay	77,035	16,012,342
Sind	46,506	3,279,377
Aden	80	56,500
Burma	233,707	13,212,192
Central Provinces & Berar . .	99,876	13,912,760
Central Provinces . .	82,109	10,837,444
Berar	17,767	3,075,316
Coorg	1,582	163,838
Delhi	593	488,188
Madras	142,260	42,318,985
North-West Frontier Province [1] .	13,419	2,251,340
Punjab	99,846	20,685,024
United Provinces	106,295	45,375,787
Agra	82,137	33,209,145
Oudh	24,158	12,166,642
Total Provinces	1,094,300	247,003,293

[1] Districts and Administered Territories.

Indian States and Agencies in political relations
with the Indian Government:—

STATE OR AGENCY	AREA IN SQ. MILES IN 1921	POPULATION IN 1921
Assam (Manipur) State . . .	8,456	384,016
Baluchistan States . . .	80,410	378,977
Baroda State	8,127	2,126,522
Bengal States	5,434	896,926
Bihar and Orissa States . . .	28,648	3,959,669
Bombay States (including States in the Western India Agency) .	63,453	7,409,429
Central India Agency . .	51,531	5,997,023
Central Provinces States . .	31,176	2,066,900
Gwalior State	26,357	3,186,075
Hyderabad State	82,698	12,471,770
Kashmir State	84,258	3,320,518
Madras States Agency . .	10,696	5,460,312
Mysore State	29,475	5,978,892
N.W. Frontier Province (Agencies & Tribal areas) . .	25,500	2,825,136
Punjab States Agency . .	37,059	4,416,036
Rajputana Agency . . .	128,987	9,844,384
Sikkim State	2,818	81,721
United Provinces States . .	5,949	1,134,881
Total States	711,032	71,939,187
Total India	1,805,332	318,942,480

The population (1921) of the principal towns:

Towns	Population	Towns	Population
Bombay	1,175,914	Bangalore	237,496
Calcutta (with		Karáchi	216,883
suburbs) [1]	1,132,246	Cawnpore	216,436
Madras	526,911	Poona	214,796
Hyderábád	404,187	Benares	198,447
Rangoon	341,962	Agra	185,532
Delhi	304,420	Amritsar	160,218
Lahore	281,781	Allahábád	157,220
Ahmedábád	274,007	Mandalay	148,917
Lucknow	240,566	Nágpur	145,193

[1] Including Howrah it was 1,327,547.

It is assumed that the country was occupied by an ancient pre-Dravidian race which was driven into the hills by another ancient race of a higher type from outer Asia called the Dravidians, the Indo-Aryan immigration from the north coming between 2400 and 1500 B.C.

Lord Willingdon, Viceroy and Governor General, 1931.

327 B.C. to 1748

327 B.C., Invasion of Alexander the Great; King Porus is defeated, submits and retains his kingdom

A.D. 1024, Irruptions of the Mahometans, under Mahmud Ghuzni, 1001–24; he captured Somnath

1186, Extinction of the house of Ghuzni; rule of the slave-kings of Delhi, 1206–1288; of the Kilghis and house of Toghlak, 1288–1412; of the Syuds, 1412–50; of the house of Lodi, 1450–1526

1205, Pathan, or Afghan Empire, founded

1219, Mogul invasion under Genghis Khan; he died, 1227

1397, The Mogul Tartars, under the conduct of Timour, or Tamerlane, invade Hindostan, and take Delhi; defeat the Indian army; conquer Hindostan, and butcher 100,000 of its people, 1398–99

The Cape route to India discovered by Vasco da Gama; he left Lisbon, July 8, 1497, arrived at Calicut, May 20, 1498, and returned to Lisbon, Aug. or Sept., 1499

1502, The first European settlement (Portuguese) established by him at Cochin (S. Coast)

1508, Albuquerque governor-general; dies at Goa, 1514

1519–26, Conquest of India completed by the Sultan Baber, founder of the Mogul empire

1531–56, Reign of his son Humayun

1556–1605, Reign of Akbar, greatest sovereign of Hindostan

1600, The Portuguese introduce tobacco

1602, The Dutch first visit India, 1601; establish a United East India Company

1605–27, Reign of Jehanghir

1619, Tranquebar granted to the Danes

1627–58, Reign of Shah Jehan; golden age of the Moguls

1658–1707, Aurungzebe dethrones his father and murders his brothers, 1658; reigns

1659, Rise of the Mahratta power under Sevajee; he assumes royalty, 1674; dies 1680

1664, French East India Company established

1687, Aurungzebe conquers Golconda, &c.

1702, His prosperity wanes; dies Feb. 22, 1707

1707, Bahadoor Shah succeeds; dies 1712

1713, Jehander Shah; dethroned and killed, 1718

1719, Accession of Mahomed Shah

1723, Independence of the Nizam of the Deccan

1730, Rise of the Mahratta families, Holkar and Scindiah

1739, Invasion of the Persian Nadir Shah or Kouli Khan: at Delhi he orders a general massacre, and 100,000 persons perish; carries away treasure amounting to 32,000,000l. sterling

1748, Mahomed Shah dies

[The Mogul Empire now became merely nominal, independent sovereignties being formed by petty princes. In 1761, Shah Alum II, attacking the English, was defeated at Patna, Jan. 15. In 1764, after the battle of Buxar, he was thrown upon the protection of the English, who established him at Allahabad. After the victory at Delhi in 1803, Gen. Lake restored the aged monarch to a nominal sovereignty, which descended at his death to his son, Akbar Shah. Akbar died in 1837, and was succeeded by the last King of Delhi (his son), who received a pension of about 125,000l. per annum. He joined the mutiny in 1857; was tried in 1858, and transported to Rangoon; died there, Nov. 11, 1862]

BRITISH POWER IN INDIA

1528 to 1781

1528, Attempt made to reach India by the north-east and north-west passages

1579, Sir Francis Drake's expedition

1589, Levant company's land expedition

1591, First commercial adventure from England

1600, First charter to the London company of merchants

1612, Factories established at Surat, &c.

1615, Sir Thos. Roe, first English ambassador

1653, Madras founded, 1640; made a presidency

1662, Bombay ceded to England as part of dowry of Catherine, Queen of Charles II

1664, French company established

1674, They settle at Pondicherry

1698, Calcutta purchased

1746–49, War between the English and French in India

1748, English besiege Pondicherry, the seat of the French government, without success

1751, Clive takes Arcot

1754, Peace made

Feb. 11, 1755–56, Severndroog and other strongholds of the pirate Angria taken

June 20, 1756, Capture of Calcutta by Surajah Dowla; suffocation of English in the Black hole

June 23, 1757, Calcutta retaken by Clive, Jan. 2; he defeats the Soubah at Plassey

1757, Fort William, the strongest fort in India, built

1758, French successful under Lally

1759, But lose nearly all their power

Jan. 22, 1760, The French under Lally defeated by Sir Eyre Coote near Wandewash

1763–64, Hyder Ali usurps the sovereignty of Mysore

Nov. 6, 1763, Conquest of Patna

Oct. 23, 1764, Battle of Buxar, victory of Sir Hector Monroe over troops of the Nabob of Oude

1765, The nabob becomes subject to the English

Aug. 12, 1765, Lord Clive obtains the Dewanny by an imperial grant, which constitutes the company the receivers of the revenue of Bengal, Bahar, and Orissa, and gives the British the virtual sovereignty of these countries

Nov. 12, 1766, Treaty with Nizam Ali: the English obtain the Northern Circars

Jan., 1769, Hyder Ali ravages the Carnatic

1770-71, Famine in Bengal

April 13, 1772, Warren Hastings governor of Bengal

1773, India Bill; supreme court established

1774, Treaty with Bhootan

——, Death of Clive; ungratefully treated

May 30, 1775, Accusations commence against Warren Hastings; accused of taking a bribe from a concubine of Meer Jaffier

March 11, 1776, Nuncomar, a Brahmin, accuses Warren Hastings of receiving bribes

Aug. 5, 1776, Is hanged for forgery

[Sir Elijah Impey, the judge, was censured at the time, but afterwards vindicated]

Aug. 4, 1778, Fortress of Gwalior taken by Popham

Oct. 11, 1778, Pondicherry taken

Oct. 31, 1780, Hyder Ali overruns the Carnatic, and defeats the British, Sept. 10; takes Arcot

July 1, 1781, Hyder Ali defeated by Sir Eyre Coote

Sept. 19, 1781, Warren Hastings accused of taking more bribes

1782

March, Bussy lands with a French detachment

——, War with Hyder Ali aided by the French

June 2, Hyder Ali overthrown by Coote

Dec., Death of Hyder, and accession of his son, Tippoo Sahib

1783

April, Tippoo, who had taken Cuddalore, now takes Bednore

Pondicherry restored to the French, and Trincomalee to the Dutch

Fox's India bill thrown out

1784

Pitt's India bill establishing the board of control

March 11, Ignoble peace with Tippoo

1786 to 1790

1786, Charges against Warren Hastings

Feb. 13, 1788, His trial begun

1790, War with Tippoo renewed

1791

March 21, Bangalore taken by British under Lord Cornwallis

May 15, Cornwallis defeats Tippoo at Arikera

Dec. 21, Fortress of Savandroog taken

1792

March 19, Definitive treaty with Tippoo; his two sons hostages

1793

Civil and criminal courts erected

Pondicherry again taken

1794

March 29, Tippoo's sons restored

1795

First dispute with the Burmese; adjusted by General Erskine

April 23, Warren Hastings acquitted

1798

Feb. 13, Death of Christian F. Schwartz, 50 years missionary and philanthropist, "the apostle of India," aged 71

May 17, Government of Lord Mornington, afterwards Marquis Wellesley

1799

June 22, Seringapatam stormed by Gen. Baird; Tippoo Sahib killed, May 4; Mysore divided

1800

Victories of the British; the Carnatic conquered

1802

June 4, The Nabob of Furruckabad cedes his territories to the English for a pension

Dec. 31, Important treaty of Bassein (with Mahrattas)

1803

Mahratta war. Victories of Sir Arthur Wellesley and General Lake

Sept. 23, Wellesley's great victory at Assaye

Dec., Pondicherry (restored 1801) retaken

1804

1804-05, War with Holkar

1805

April 2, Capture of Bhurtpore

Oct. 5, Lord Wellesley superseded by the Marquis Cornwallis, who dies

Nov. 23, The Mahratta chief, Scindiah, defeated by the British; treaty of peace

Dec. 24, Treaty of peace with Holkar

1806 to 1818

July, 1806, Sepoy mutiny at Vellore; 800 killed; 200 wounded

Nov. 21, 1807, Cumoona surrenders

Aug. 23, 1809, Mutiny at Seringapatam quelled

July, 1813, Act opening the trade to India

1814-15, War with Nepaul

Dec. 21, 1817, Holkar defeated by Sir T. Hislop

1817-18, Pindaree war. English successful

Jan. 6, 1818, Peace with Holkar

1824

May 5, Burmese war. The British take Rangoon

Lord Combermere commands in India

Malacca ceded, and Singapore purchased

Nov., Barrackpore mutiny, many sepoys killed

1825

Dec. 25, General Campbell defeats the Burmese near Prome

1826 to 1837

Jan. 18, 1826, Bhurtpore stormed by Combermere

Feb. 24, 1826, Peace with the Burmese

[They pay 1,000,000l. sterling, and cede a great extent of territory]

Dec. 7, 1829, Abolition of suttees, or the burning of widows

Aug. 28, 1833, Act opening the trade to India, and tea trade, &c., to China, forming a new era in British commerce

April 10, 1834, Coorg annexed; Rajah deposed

May 1, 1834, The natives admitted to the magistracy

Oct. 8, 1835, The Nawab Shumsoodden put to death for the murder of Mr. Frazer, British resident

1837–38, Severe famine
1837, Postal service begun

1838

Aug. 1, Slavery abolished
Oct. 1, Afghan war. Proclamation against Dost Mahomed

1839

April 21, The British occupy Candahar
July 23, Battle of Ghiznee; victory of Sir John (afterwards Lord) Keane
July 26, Wade forces the Khyber pass

1840

Oct. 18, English defeat Dost Mahomed
Nov. 5, Kurrock Singh, King of Lahore, dies; at his funeral his successor is killed by accident, and Dost Mahomed, next heir, surrenders to England

1841

Nov. 2, Rising against the British at Kabul; Sir Alex. Burnes and others murdered
Dec. 23, Sir Wm. Macnaghten assassinated
1841–42, Jellalabad held by Sir R. Sale

1842

Jan. 6–13, The British under a convention evacuate Kabul, placing Lady Sale, &c., as hostages with Akbar Khan; a massacre ensues of about 16,000 men, women, and children
March 1, The British evacuate Ghiznee
April 5, Sortie from Jellalabad; General Pollock forces the Khyber pass
Sept. 6, Ghiznee retaken by General Nott
Sept. 16, General Pollock enters Kabul
Sept. 21, Lady Sale and other prisoners rescued by Sir R. Shakspeare; arrive at Gen. Pollock's camp
Oct. 12, Kabul evacuated after destroying the fortifications

1843

Feb. 17, Scinde war. Ameers defeated by Sir Charles Napier at Meanee
June, Scinde annexed to the British Empire; Sir Charles Napier Governor
Dec. 29, Gwalior war. Battles of Maharajpoor and Punniar: the strong fort of Gwalior, the "Gibraltar of the East," taken

1845

Danish possessions in India purchased
Dec. 14, Sikh war.* The Sikhs cross the Sutlej River and attack the British at Ferozepore
Dec. 18, Sir H. Hardinge, after a long rapid march, reaches Moodkee; the Sikhs (20,000) make an attack; after a hard contest they retire, abandoning their guns
Battle of Ferozeshah. The British, commanded by Sir Hugh Gough, attacked the entrenchments of the Sikhs, and carried their first line of works, Dec. 21;

* Runjeet Singh, long the ruler of the Sikhs and the Punjab, lived in amity with the British. After his death, June 27, 1839, several of his successors (children and grandchildren) were in turn assassinated. During the minority of his son Dhuleep Singh, the favorite of the Maharanee, Lall Singh, ruled; and finding the army ungovernable, sanctioned the unprovoked attack on the British, as given above.

but night coming on, the operations were suspended till daybreak, when their second line was stormed by General Gilbert, and 74 guns captured. The Sikhs advanced to retake their guns, but were repulsed with great loss, and retreated towards the Sutlej, Dec. 22; and recrossed that river unmolested, Dec. 27. The British loss was reckoned at 2,415

1846

Jan. 28, Battle of Aliwal; the Sikhs defeated by Sir Harry Smith
Feb. 10, Great battle of Sobraon; the enemy defeated with immense loss by Sir Hugh Gough
Feb. 20, Citadel of Lahore occupied by Sir Hugh Gough, and the war terminates
Feb. 23, Sir R. Sale dies of his wounds received at Moodkee (Dec. 18, 1845)
March 9, Treaty of Lahore signed

1847

Jan. 13, Vizier Lall Singh deposed

1848

June 18, Lieut. Edwardes joins General Courtland, and engages the army of Moolraj, which he defeats after a sanguinary battle of nine hours, at Kennyree
Sept. 22, General Whish raises the siege of Mooltan through the desertion of Shere Singh
Nov. 22, Cavalry skirmish at Ramnuggur
Dec. 3, Shere Singh, entrenched on the right bank of the Chenab, with 40,000 men and 28 pieces of artillery; Gen. Thackwell crosses the river with 8 infantry regiments, with cavalry and cannon, Dec. 1, and attacks his left flank at Sadoolapore

1849

Jan. 13, Lord Gough attacks the enemy's advanced position; victory of Chillianwallah
Jan. 22, Unconditional surrender of the citadel of Mooltan by Moolraj
Feb. 21, Victory of Guzerat
March 7, Sir Chas. Napier appointed comm.-in-chief
March 14, The Sikhs surrender unconditionally
March 29, Formal annexation of the Punjab to the British dominions; Dhuleep Singh obtains a pension of 40,000l.
Sept., Moolraj sentenced to death for the murder of Mr. Agnew and Lieut. Anderson, Aug.; commuted to transportation for life

1850

Feb. 27, Sir Charles Napier disbands the 66th Bengal native infantry, for mutiny
March 20, Dr. Healy, of the Bengal army, and his attendants, murdered by the Affreedis
July 2, Resignation of his command in India by Sir Charles Napier

1851

Jan. 28, Burmese war. Death of Bajee Rao, ex-peishwa of the Mahrattas. [His nephew Nana Sahib's claim for continuance of the pension (80,000l.) refused]
Oct. 29, A British naval force arrives before Rangoon, in the Burman Empire, and Commodore Lambert allows the Viceroy thirty-five days to obtain instructions from Ava

1852

Jan. 4, The Viceroy of Rangoon interdicts communication between the shore and the British ships of war; and erects batteries to prevent their departure

[Commodore Lambert blockades the Irawaddy; the *Fox*, *Hermes*, &c., attacked by the batteries, destroy the fortifications, and kill nearly 300 of the enemy]

May 19, Martaban (April 5), Rangoon (April 14), and Bassein stormed by the British

July 9, Prome captured by General Godwin

Dec. 20, Pegu annexed to Indian Empire by proclamation of the Governor-General

1853

Jan., Revolution at Ava; the King of Ava deposed by his younger brother

April 16, First Indian railway opened (from Bombay to Tannah)

June, Termination of the war

Aug. 20, New India bill passed

Oct. 26, Death of General Godwin

Dec. 8, Assassination of Capt. Latter

Dec. 11, Rajah of Nagpoor dies, and his territories fall to the E. I. Company

1854

Opening of Ganges canal

First Indian postage stamp struck

1855

Feb. 3, Opening of the Calcutta railway

March 30, Treaty of friendship with Dost Mahomed of Kabul

July, Insurrection of the Sonthals

1856

May, Which is only finally suppressed

Feb. 7, Oude annexed

1857

MUTINY OF THE NATIVE ARMY

March, Mutinies in the Bengal army: at Barrackpore, &c., several regiments disbanded. On the introduction of the improved (Enfield) musket in the Indian army, greased cartridges had been brought from England. These were objected to by the native soldiers, and the issue of them was immediately discontinued by orders in Jan., 1857. A mutinous spirit however gradually arose in the Bengal native army. In March several regiments were disbanded, followed by others, till the army had lost by disbandment and desertion, about 30,000 men. On April 5, a sepoy, and on April 20, a jemadar, or native lieutenant, were executed. At the end of May, 34 regiments were lost. In April, 85 of the 3rd Bengal cavalry at Meerut refused to use their cartridges. On May 9 they were committed to gaol. On Sunday, the 10th, a mutiny in the native troops broke out; they fired on their officers, killing Col. Finnis and others. They then released their comrades, massacred many Europeans, and fired the public buildings. The European troops rallied and drove them from their cantonments. The mutineers then fled to Delhi

May 10, Mutiny at Meerut (near Delhi). The mutineers seize Delhi, commit dreadful outrages, and proclaim the King of Delhi Emperor, May 11–12, &c.

May 12, Three native regiments disbanded at Lahore by the energy of Mr. Montgomery and Brigadier Corbett, who save the Punjab

May, Martial law proclaimed by the British Lieut. Governor, J. R. Colvin

May 27, British troops under General Anson advance on Delhi: his death

May 30, Mutiny at Lucknow

June 4, Neil suppresses the mutiny at Benares, June 3; and recovers Allahabad

Mutiny spreads throughout Bengal: fearful atrocities committed

June 11, Native troops disbanded at Mooltan, which is saved

June 14, Ex-King of Oude arrested

July 1, Siege of the residency at Lucknow by the rebels, commences

July 4, Sir H. Lawrence dies of his wounds at Lucknow

July 5, Sir H. Barnard, commanding before Delhi, dies of cholera, succeeded by General Reed

July 12, General Nicholson destroys a large body of rebels at Sealcote

July 17, Cawnpore surrenders to Nana Sahib, who kills the garrison, &c., June 28; he is defeated by General Havelock, July 16; who re-captures Cawnpore

July 18, Mutinies suppressed at Hyderabad; and at Lahore, July 20

July 22, General Reed retires, and Sir Archdale Wilson takes the command before Delhi

July 25, Revolt at Dinapore: the British repulsed with severe loss at Arrah

July 31, Lord Canning's so-called "clemency" proclamation

Aug. 15, Victory of Neill at Pandoo Nuddee

Aug. 25, General Nicholson's victory at Nujuffghur [he dies Sept. 23]

Sept. 14, Assault of Delhi; taken, Sept. 20; the King captured, Sept. 21; his son and grandson slain by Colonel Hodson, Sept. 22

Sept. 16, Sir James Outram joins Havelock and serves under him

Sept. 25, 26, Havelock marches to Lucknow and relieves the besieged residency; retires and leaves Outram in command; Neill killed

Sept. 27, Colonel Greathed defeats the rebels at Bolundshohur; destroys a fort at Molaghur, Sept. 29; takes Allyghur, Oct. 5; and defeats rebels at Agra, Oct. 10

Nov. 3, Sir Colin Campbell (afterwards Lord Clyde) appointed commander-in-chief, July 11; arrives at Cawnpore

Nov. 16, Marches to Alumbagh, near Lucknow, Nov. 9; and takes Secunderabagh

Nov. 18–25, Joined by Havelock, he attacks the rebels and rescues the besieged in the residency

Nov. 24, Havelock dies of dysentery at Alumbagh

Nov. 27, General Windham (at Cawnpore) repulsed with loss in an attack on the Gwalior contingent, who take part of Cawnpore

Nov. 28, Sir C. Campbell arrives at Cawnpore, which he retakes; and defeats the Gwalior rebels, Dec. 6

Dec. 14, 17, and 27, The rebels defeated by Seaton; at Goruckpore by Rowcroft, Dec. 27; and at Futtehghur by Sir C. Campbell, Jan. 2, 1858

1858

Jan., Lucknow strongly fortified by the rebels

Jan. 27 to March 9, Trial of King of Delhi; sentenced to transportation

Feb. 11, Sir C. Campbell marches to Lucknow; the siege commences, March 8; taken by successive assaults; the enemy retreat; Hodson killed, March 14–19

March 30, General Roberts takes Kotah

April 4, Sir Hugh Rose beats the enemy severely, and takes Jhansi

April 19, General Whitelock takes Budaon

April 27, Death of Capt. Sir W. Peel, of small-pox, at Cawnpore

May 4, General Penny killed in Rohilcund

May 7, Bareilly recaptured

May 23, Sir Hugh Rose defeats the rebels several times—at Kooneh, May 11, and near Calpee, which he retakes

May 29, Victory of Sir E. Lugard at Jugdespore

June 13, The rebels seize Gwalior, the capital of Scindiah, who escapes to Agra

June 19, The rebels defeated by Sir H. Rose (the heroic Ranee of Jhansi killed), June 17; Gwalior retaken and Scindiah reinstated

Tantia Topee heads a division of the rebels

July, Rajahs of Jeypore, &c., surrender; Rohilcund and other provinces tranquillized

Aug. 14, General Roberts destroys the remains of the Gwalior rebels

Aug., Many Oude chiefs surrender

Aug. 31, An attempt of disbanded regiments to retake their arms at Mooltan, suppressed by Major Hamilton (300 killed on the spot, and 800 slain or captured afterwards)

Sept. 1, The Government of the East India Company ceases

Sept. 15, General Mitchell defeats Tantia Topee, near Rajghur

Nov. 1, Queen Victoria proclaimed throughout India—Lord Canning to be the first viceroy

Nov. 1–30, Campaign in Oude begins; several chiefs submit, others subdued

Nov. 24, At Dhooden Khera Lord Clyde (formerly Sir C. Campbell) defeats Beni Mahdo

Nov. 25, Flight of Tantia Topee—he is beaten in Guzerat by Major Sutherland

Dec. 4–11, The ex-King of Delhi sails for the Cape of Good Hope; the colonists refuse to receive him; he is sent to Rangoon

Dec. 6, Brigadier John Jacob dies at Jacobabad

1859

Jan., Enforcement of the Disarming Act in the north-west provinces

——, Rebels completely expelled from Oude; enter Nepaul

Jan. 1, The Punjab made a distinct presidency

Feb. 10, Defeat of the Begum of Oude and Nana Sahib by General Horsford

March, The new Indian tariff creates much dissatisfaction

April 2, Mann Singh surrenders

April 18, Tantia Topee taken, April 7; hanged

May 23, Sir Hope Grant defeats Nana Sahib in the Jorwah pass

June 22, Sir Chas. Wood becomes Sec. for India

Sept., An income tax bill (called "the Trades' and Professions' Licensing Bill") passes the legislative council; great meetings at Calcutta and Madras protesting against it

Oct. 1, Rajah Jey-loll Singh hanged

Oct., Nana Sahib, in force, in Nepaul on the frontiers of Oude

Dec. 24, Insurgents in Nepaul dispersed

1860

March, Paper currency determined on

March 2, Bahadoor Khan, ex-King of Bareilly, hanged for murders caused by him

July, Sir Hugh Rose takes command of the Indian army, amalgamated with the British

July 21, Lord Canning's recommendation that the adopted successors of Indian princes should be recognized agreed to by the home government

Aug. 3, Death of Sir H. Ward, new governor at Madras; and of James Wilson, Aug. 11

Nov., British troops repulsed in Sikkim

Dec., Nana Sahib, supposed to have died of jungle fever in Aug., 1858, is said to be living in Tibet

——, Agitation against the income tax suppressed at Bombay and other places

1861

Jan. 10, Mr. Samuel Laing, successor to Mr. James Wilson, arrives

Jan.–June, Famine in N.W. provinces through failure of the crops

March 31, Kootoob-ood-deen, grandson of Tippoo Sahib, murdered by his servants

June 25, Order of the "Star of India" constituted

Aug., New Indian council and new high court of judicature established

Oct., Law of property in India altered; sale of waste lands authorized

1862

Jan. 18, First meeting of new legislative council; includes several Indian Princes

March 12, Lord Elgin, new Governor-General, installed at Calcutta

July 12, High court of judicature at Bengal inaugurated

1863

Jan. 8, Sir Charles Trevelyan, new Finance Minister arrives

Oct., Rise of Ram Singh, a fanatic, in N.W. provinces

Nov. 20, Death of the Viceroy, Lord Elgin

Dec. 29, War with warlike hill tribes on the N.W. frontiers, Oct.; severe conflict, Gen. Chamberlain wounded, Nov. 20; command assumed by Major-Gen. John Garvock, who totally defeated the enemy (about 15,000) in Chamta pass, Dec. 15, 16; war ended

Dec., The Hindu religion deprived of government support

1864

Jan. 12, Sir John Lawrence, Lord Elgin's successor, assumes office

March, Excitement amongst the Hindoos on account of government suppressing funeral rites on sanitary grounds

July, Gold currency (a sovereign = 10 rupees) ordered to be introduced at Christmas

Oct. 18, Grand durbar, held by Sir John Lawrence, at Lahore; 604 native princes present

Dec. 12, War with the Bhootanese—fortress of Dhalimcote taken

1865

Feb., The Bhootanese attack on Dewangiri repulsed with severe loss, Jan. 29, evacuated by the British

March 1, Opening of the Indo-European telegraph—a telegram from Kurrachee received

March 31, W. Massey succeeds Sir C. Trevelyan as finance minister; he arrives at Calcutta

April 2, Dewangiri recaptured by Gen. Tombs

April 23, Sir Hugh Rose retires from command of the army; which is assumed by Sir Wm. Mansfield

May, Sir Charles Trevelyan's plans reversed by Sir C. Wood

July 31, Death of the able and beneficent Hon. Juggonath Sunkersett, the recognized representative of the Hindoo community

July, Negotiation with the Bhootanese

Nov. 13, Peace with the Bhootanese signed

1866

April, Settlement of the question respecting marriage of Hindoo converts

Aug.–Nov., Famine in Orissa, Bengal: about 1,500,000 perished

Oct., Relief by government

Oct. 6, Dr. Cotton, Bishop of Calcutta, accidentally drowned

1867

Dec. 29, The fierce Wagheers of Kattywar, in a night attack, are nearly exterminated; Capts. Hibbert and La Touche killed

1868

Oct., War on the N.W. frontier; the Bazotees, fanatical Mahometans, defeated by General Wilde; 30 killed and wounded; all dispersed, Oct. 4; villages burnt as punishment for outrages

Aug. 30, Death of the Begum of Bhopal, who helped the British during the mutiny

Dec. 9, The Duke of Argyll Secretary for India

1869

Jan. 12, Arrival of the Earl of Mayo, the new Viceroy, at Calcutta

March 27, Meeting of the Viceroy and Shere Ali, the Afghan sovereign, who receives a subsidy and presents

April 1, New divorce act in operation

Aug., Rise of a body of Indian religious reformers termed the Brahmo Somaj

Aug. 11, Act for the better governing of India and defining the governor-general's powers passed

1870

March, Railway between Calcutta and Bombay completed

May, Announced deficiency in the revenue; increased taxation proposed; much opposition to the income tax

Indian coinage act passed

1871

Jan. 1, Death of Sir H. Durand

Jan. 25, Sir Proby Cautley, designed Ganges canal works, &c., died, aged 68

Jan., Volunteer system proposed for India

Feb., Indian finance committee appointed

Aug. 5, Indian civil engineering college, Cooper's-hill, opened by the Duke of Argyll, Secretary for India

Nov., Much corrupt opposition to the income tax reported

Dec. 1, Military expedition under Generals Nutthall

and Bourchier, aided by the Rajah of Munnipore, against the Looshais, about Nov. 13; skirmishes

Dec. 22, Death of the Earl of Ellenborough, a late governor-general

Dec. 29, Skirmishes with the Looshais, Dec. 21, 23; they sue for peace

1872

Jan. 7–12, The King of Siam visits Calcutta

Jan. 15–17, Outbreak of the Kookas, near Loodiana, severely suppressed by commissioners Cowan and Forsyth

Jan. 28, Looshais repulsed and strongholds taken

Feb. 8, The Viceroy arrives at Rangoon, Jan. 28; on his return he visits the convict establishment in the Andaman Islands, and is assassinated at Port Blair by Shere Ali, a convict, while about to embark in the *Glasgow*

Feb. 23, Lord Napier acts as Viceroy

Feb. 28, Looshais surrender unconditionally; army returning

March 7, The Kamous tribe, while carrying off Looshai captives, defeated, and captives rescued; British returning to Calcutta

March 12, Shere Ali hanged, without confessing associates

May 3, Lord Northbrook sworn in as Viceroy

July 27, Liakat Ali, on confession, condemned to transportation for life

July, Christian marriage Bill passed

Changes in criminal procedure; compromise

1873

March 21, The income tax not renewed

About Sept. 13, 14, Riots of the Moplahs, Mahometan fanatics, on coast of Malabar, suppressed by military

Oct., New tax (road cess) reported successful

1874

Feb. 21, The Marquis of Salisbury, Secretary for India

March 30, A loan not exceeding 100,000,000*l.* for India government authorized by parliament

Sir R. Temple installed Lieut.-Gov. of Bengal in place of Sir George Campbell

June, Crisis of famine past; reported declining; much rain; good prospects

Dec., Outrages of Duffla tribes on N.W. frontier (troublesome, 1838–9; 1852; Feb., 1873); expedition against them

1875

Jan. 29, The Duffla tribes surrender and pay fine

About Feb. 24, Lieut. Holcombe and a surveying party (about 70) in Assam, massacred by Naga natives

March 15–25, Naga tribes chastised severely; the objects of the expedition accomplished

April 23, Close of inquiry into the conduct of the Gaekwar of Baroda; verdict of 3 British judges, guilty; of 3 natives, not proved; March 30; he is deposed for misgovernment by the Viceroy, and ordered to live in British India with suitable provision; proclamation that a successor be appointed

May 22, Eldest son of the Gaekwar appointed successor

May, Difficulties with Burmah

June, Mission of Sir Douglas Forsyth to Mandalay

June 3, New Gaekwar of Baroda installed

July, Establishment of a new Mahometan college for the N.W. provinces (chiefly by Ahmed Khan); announced

Oct. 11, The Prince of Wales sails for India, arrives at Bombay, Nov. 8; sails from Bombay, March 13, 1876

1876

April 12, Lord Lytton, new Viceroy, takes oath at Calcutta

May 1, Queen Victoria proclaimed Empress of India in London

Aug. 19, Vice-regal proclamation of Queen Victoria's title, "Empress of India" (to be proclaimed at Delhi, Jan. 1, 1877)

About Oct. 17, Sir John Strachey appointed financial minister; governor of N.W. provinces, Nov.

1877

Jan. 1, Proclamation of Queen Victoria as Empress of India at Delhi, by the Viceroy; also at Calcutta, Madras, and Bombay

——, Creation of the "Order of the Empire of India" announced

End of April, The raids of the Affreedis on N.W. frontiers suppressed; announced

June, Famine formidable, but energetically met

Aug. 29, 30, Disturbances on N.W. frontier; raids of the Jawakies, or Jowakies, an Affreedi tribe; chastised by expedition under Sir Rd. Pollock; again by Gen. Keyes, Nov.

Nov., Dec., Jummu, the Jawakies' stronghold, taken; they are defeated and dispersed

Dec. 31, "Imperial Order of the Crown of India," for ladies; instituted

1878

Feb. 22, The Jawakies defeated by cavalry, Feb. 15; surrender unconditionally; announced

March 14, Bill to restrain license of the native press, passed by the council at Calcutta

March, Budget; cost of famine about 3,450,000*l*.

Sept., War with Afghanistan. *See s.v.*

1879

Feb., England now holds the passes through which India is accessible by land

May 26, Treaty of peace signed at Gandamuk

Aug. 11, Indian Railways Guarantee act passed

Aug. 15, Loan of sum under 5,000,000*l*. for India; authorized by act

Sept., Mutiny and massacres at Kabul (*see* Afghanistan)

Oct., New stringent rules for newspaper correspondents with army; issued

1880

Marquis of Ripon, new Viceroy, arrives at Calcutta; Col. Gordon, his secretary

1881

Jan., Sir Donald Stewart appointed commander-in-chief of the Indian army

March, Death of Gholam Hussein Khan, able and faithful friend to the British

About May 8, War declared against the Wazaris, April 12; ends with their submission

June 27, Proposals for loan of 3,000,000*l*., issued

1882

Nov. 24, The Sirhind canal (502 miles, for irrigation) opened by the Viceroy

1883

Feb. 28, Mr. Ilbert's Criminal Procedure Amendment bill strongly opposed by all the non-official Europeans and the army throughout India; very great meeting at Calcutta

March 29, European and Anglo-Indian Defense association, Calcutta, formed; first meeting

April, An Anglo-Indian association for the natives formed in London

July, Major Baring succeeded by Sir Auckland Colvin as Finance Minister

July–Aug., High courts of Bombay and Madras favor, that of Calcutta opposes, the Ilbert bill

Dec. 21, Ilbert bill: compromise announced; Europeans allowed to claim a jury wholly or partly European

Dec. 24, Akha raids into Assam; Major Beresford's forces repulsed

1884

Jan. 8, The Akhas dispersed by Gen. Hill

Jan. 25, Ilbert bill amended and passed

About Sept. 22, Expedition to the Zhob valley to punish the Kakar Pathans for their raids into British territory

Oct. 23, They are defeated by Gen. Tanner, 56 killed

Dec. 13, Earl of Dufferin installed Viceroy at Calcutta

1885

March 11, Important Bengal tenancy Bill passed

March, Sir Donald Stewart, with 50,000 men, ordered to advance to Quetta

April 2–12, Meeting of the Ameer of Afghanistan and the Viceroy at Rawul Pindi, conference, and durbar

July 22, Proposed loan of 10,000,000*l*. May 21 *et seq.*; act passed

June 24, Lord Randolph Churchill appointed Secretary for India

July 30, Sir Frederick Roberts appointed commander-in-chief; announced

1886

Jan. 1, Upper Burmah annexed by proclamation of the Viceroy, Lord Dufferin

Jan. 29, Income-tax bill passed

About Feb. 6, Earl of Kimberley appointed Secretary for India

July, Sir Richard, aft. Viscount, Cross appointed Secretary for India

Dec. 28, National Indian congress at Calcutta, 400 delegates (Hindoos) to promote native advancement; and again early in 1887

1887

May 23, India 4% stock converted into 3½% by act

Sept., The Nizam of Hyderabad in a letter to Lord Dufferin the Viceroy, offers to present 20 lakhs of rupees for three years, total 600,000*l*., for the defense of the N.W. territories

Oct. 31, The Rajah of Kaparthala offers his army and five lakhs of rupees for the defense of India; announced

Nov., Four lakhs offered by Rajah of Nabha

——, Similar offers by other princes

——, Districts in Beloochistan annexed; announced

1888

Jan. 24, Military demonstration against Sikkim ordered

Feb. 9, Lord Dufferin, the Viceroy, announces his intention of resigning, for private reasons

Feb. 10, Tax on petroleum and increase of salt duty passed

Feb., Moderate National Indian congress at Madras recommends representative institutions, &c.

June 19, Major L. R. Battye and Captain H. B. Urmiston and five Sepoys killed by the Akozais during an exploration on British territory near Black Mountain, N.W. frontier

Sept., Black Mountain expedition, or "The Hazara Field Force," under Gen. McQueen, to avenge the outrage of June 19; organized; advance, seizure of Manakadana, Oct. 4; the enemy defeated with the loss of 200 men by Gen. Galbraith; guerrilla warfare; British success at Kotkai with slight loss, Oct. 5; villages burnt, enemy retiring; British casualties, 59 killed and wounded Oct. 9; Gen. McQueen advances Oct. 18; more villages burnt; Col. Crookshank dies of wounds, Oct. 24; the tribes submit and pay fines, Oct. 21–30; Gorapher peak of the Chaila mountains, 9,500 feet, taken by Gen. Channer, Nov. 2; return commenced, Nov. 5; final submission announced, Nov. 18

Nov. 18, Lord Dufferin at a durbar at Patiala announces the decision of the government to decline the acceptance of money from the princes; but recommends to raise the character of their armies and so to fit them to combine with the British for defense of India

Dec. 10, Installation of the Marquis of Lansdowne as Viceroy; departure of Lord Dufferin

Dec. 23, Raid of Lushais on the Chittagong border announced

Dec. 26, Native Indian congress at Allahabad (moderate and illogical) opened

1889

Jan., Fortress of Quetta, a bulwark of India, finished

Jan. 28, Raid of Chittagong hill tribes on British territory near Tipperah, 24 villages destroyed, above 100 British subjects killed and 91 carried off prisoners, announced

March 27, Sukkur bridge opened

March 29, Mr. Arthur Travers Crawford, an able commissioner for 34 years in Bombay, after a long investigation, was acquitted of serious charges of financial misconduct, but was for indiscreet borrowing dismissed the service, the sentence confirmed by Lord Cross, Secretary for India in a despatch

April, Military expedition sent to chastise the hill tribes for their raids and the murder of Lieut. Stewards; object effected; reported

July 1, Proposal for a new 4% loan (20,000,000 rupees) issued

Sept., Lord Reay's condoning the native Bombay officials, who confessed themselves guilty of bribery and corruption in relation to the Crawford case, much censured, but eventually approved by the government

Dec. 4, Tantia Bheel, robber chief of the central provinces, a kind of Robin Hood, in the Holkar territory began his career about 1874; robbed the rich and helped the poor; lately suffered much, captured about Aug. 18, convicted of murder (in 1879), about Oct. 20, executed at Jubbulpore

Dec. 26 et seq., 5th native Indian congress meets at Bombay (Mr. Bradlaugh present)

1890

Feb. 2, Military expedition of Sir R. G. Sandeman to promote commerce by opening a road through the Zhob districts, N.W. frontier, reported successful without bloodshed

March 17, Treaty with China respecting Sikkim

March 28, Prince Albert Victor of Wales received at Bombay by the Duke of Connaught and Lord Reay; Hyderabad, Nov. 15; Madras, Nov. 19; Mysore, Nov. 23; Rangoon, Dec. 20; Mandalay, Dec. 24, 1889; Calcutta, received by the Viceroy, Jan. 3, 1890; Benares, Jan. 14; Lucknow, Jan. 18; N.W. provinces, Jan. 20 et seq.; Lahore, Jan. 25; Khyber pass, Jan. 31; Delhi, Feb. 9; Bombay, March 22; embarked for home

Feb., Expeditions (organized by Gen. Gordon) to chastise the Chins and Lushais for their raids, and to form a road connecting Upper Burmah and Lower Bengal; Gen. Symons proceeds from the east, Gen. Tregear from the west, to form a junction, Jan.; the resistance generally feeble; the troops at times suffered much by disease; the Yokwa Chins submit to Gen. Symons, Jan. 10; peaceful surrender of Mongpunga or Lienpunga, a Lushai chief; construction of road proceeding; reconnaissances and skirmishes; 200 Hakas submit, two villages burnt; health of troops improved; junction of the two parties reported

About March 22, Guerilla warfare; Haka chiefs submit

March 24, The Tashon chiefs submit to Gen. Symons ' and pay fine and tribute, reported

About March 24, Major Gordon-Cumming on convoy duty, shot dead, from an ambuscade

April 13–16, Ten days' reconnaissance of Gen. Symons southward; Col. Tregear at Haka

April 20, The new road to Haka completed connecting Burmah and India; Haka and other posts garrisoned, reported

May 1 et seq., Gen. Symons and the expedition return to India

May 20, Submission of Malliam-pai chiefs to Gen. Tregear; raiding to cease, roads to be made, &c.

Aug., Increased agitation in India and England against Hindoo child marriages

Sept. 12, Eruption of the Lushais near Dalleswary river, Capt. Herbert Browne killed, reinforcements sent; reported

[Major Kennedy, a political officer, was authorized to redress grievances, reform the finance, &c., Jan., 1891]

Sept. 21, Revolution at Manipur

Sept. 21–24, Insurrection in Manipur in N.E. state; the Maharajah abdicates in favor of his brother, who had seized the palace, &c.

Sept. 23, Insurrection in Cambay with bloodshed, the nawab appeals to the British for help: they restore order, reported

Oct. 2, Lieut. Swinton killed in an attack

Oct. 22, The Black Mountain Expedition under Gen. Sir J. M. M'Queen starts; returns, Nov. 3

Oct. 30, The Zhob valley expedition under Gen. White arrives at Fort Sandeman

——, Ultimatum sent; skirmish

Nov. 12, The tribes submit, reported

Nov. 20, The Lushai party under Capt. Shakespear and Mr. Pughe advance to Jadunas village, 34 miles W. of Fort White, Nov. 6; returns successful

Dec. 9, The principal Lushai chiefs surrender unconditionally

1891

Jan. 9, The 6th National Congress of mixed character, no government officials present, Dec. 26–30, 1890;

Sir A. Scoble introduces a bill into the legislative council to raise the age of consent to marriage by girls from 10 to 12

About Jan. 22, Capt. Rundall with 200 rifles marches to Lushailand

About Jan. 30, A strong force marches against the marauding tribes of the Miranzai valley on the N.W. frontier

About Feb. 16 *et seq.*, Several tribes submit

About Feb. 24, Mukkmudin, principal chief of the Rubbia Kheyl tribe, surrenders, reported Feb. 19; the force returns

About March 15, Black Mountain Expedition, N.W., under Gen. Elles, two columns under Col. Williamson and Col. Hammond, starts about Jan. 15, crosses the frontier

March 19, The important factory Bill for the protection of women and children passed

——, After much public discussion, the "age of consent to marriage Bill" is passed by the legislative council

March, Disastrous expedition to Manipur

March 26, The Ghazis attack the Pioneers, slight loss, March 19; successful movement forward

April 5, Sharp engagement, 9 soldiers killed

April 7, Road-making party attacked, 14 sepoys killed, reported

About April 20, Bridge of boats over the Indus, broken up

May, The party ascend the Machai peak, 9,800 feet high, a few shots exchanged, April 18; difficult traveling, severe weather, April; huts to be constructed for the troops

April 12, Miranzai Valley Expedition.—Sir W. Lockhart with 7,000 men at Kohat preparing to resist the Orakzais and other tribes (Pathans and Afreedis); sudden attack of the tribes repulsed by the Punjaub infantry, reported April 12; the Samana heights held by Syed Mir Basha, a fanatical priest; the Mollahs preaching a jihad, reported

April 17, 18, Sir W. Lockhart with three columns captures some outposts, and clears the Samana ridge, Col. Cramer and Major Edgerton severely wounded; successful fighting; the enemy dispersed and villages burnt, April 19, 20; about 300 Orakzais killed, they disperse, and other tribes retreat, April 21 *et seq.*

April 22, Sir W. Lockhart advances against the very aggressive Akhel tribe; severe fighting, several villages destroyed

April, May, Samana range occupied; several tribes submit

May 3, Sir W. Lockhart advances to punish the Shekhans, April 29, their towers blown up; various tribes submit, accepting conditions

May 12, A representative meeting of delegates agrees to resolution to be sent to the Viceroy condemning Sir Joseph Pease's resolution respecting opium, adopted by the Commons, April 12

May 17, The tribes restore stolen property, and seek for peace; all opposition ceases, reported May 12; the troops ordered to return

Dec., The Black Mountain country evacuated by the British

Dec. 2, The Hunza and Nagar tribes oppose British road-making; fighting ensues near Gilgil, N. of Cashmere; a fort of Nilt, taken by Lieut.-Col. Durand who is wounded; several sepoys killed

Dec. 20–22, Further successes of Capt. Colin Mackenzie, Lieut. Manners Smith, and others near Nilt;

about 70 natives killed; other places occupied; Jafar Khan of Nagar submits; end of the war

Dec. 28–30, Seventh Indian National Congress opened at Nagpur with strong professions of loyalty

1892

Jan. 8 *et seq.*, M. Clément Thomas, Governor-General of French India, received by the Viceroy at Calcutta

Jan. 29, Death of Col. Sir Robert Grobes Sandeman

March 23, Sir Juland Danvers, able government director of Indian guaranteed railway companies for fifty years, retires

March 25, The Hunza-Nagar rising suppressed, and order restored, reported

March, April, Desultory war with the Lushai tribes, the British under Mr. M'Cabe generally successful

April 2, Famine relief works; persons employed; Madras, 48,000; Bombay, 2,000; Bengal, 17,000; Burma, 28,000; Mysore, 13,000; Rajputana, 33,000, reported

April 4, The Lushais attack the tea-estate at Boorooncherra and kill 52 coolies, reported

April, Advance of Capt. Shakespeare

April 22, Death of Gen. Sir Lewis Pelly, aged 67

May 3–29, Extensive rising of the Lushai tribes; several conflicts, villages destroyed, about April 24; several chiefs surrender to Mr. M'Cabe, about April 26; tranquillity gradually restored

May 12, 71,000 total on relief works

May 22, The Maharajah of Ulwar, enlightened and loyal, dies

May 26, His heir 10 years old; his minister assassinated, reported

May, Indian Currency association formed to promote the abolition of silver as the sole standard in India

Aug., Value of the rupee reduced to 1s. 3d.; great anxiety

——, Petition of the Currency Association to parliament respecting the depreciation of the rupee; largely signed at Calcutta, Bombay, Madras, &c.

Aug. 18, Earl of Kimberley appointed Secretary for India

Oct. 1, Expedition of 5,000 men (the Isazai field force) against the Black Mountain tribes, organized under Col. Sir W. Lockhart, marches

Oct. 8, Sir W. Lockhart occupies and destroys Baio, Oct. 5; the force returns, reported

Oct. 27, The Indian Currency committee (Lord Chancellor Herschell, Mr. Leonard Courtney, Sir Thomas Farrer, and others) meets

Nov. 10, Opposition of natives in Bengal against restriction of the jury system; ordered

Nov., Fighting on the N.W. frontier; tribes repulsed

Dec., Major-Gen. Sir George Stewart White appointed commander-in-chief in succession to Lord Roberts

About Dec. 27, The jury question referred to the home government

[A commission appointed, Feb., 1893]

Dec. 30, 31, Eighth Indian National congress meets at Allahabad; claims increased representation, &c.

1893

Jan. 6, Col. Turner occupies Bulandkhel on the Afghan borders

Jan., British intervention in Chitral

Jan. 31, Deputation of officials, respecting the depreciation of the rupee, received by the Viceroy

March 4, The tribes defeated in an attack on Chilas, a N.W. fort, with above 150 killed; Major Averell

Daniell and 22 others killed; Major Twigg in command of the garrison, July

March 28 *et seq.*, The Bengal jury commission in their report approves of the old system, and recommend the removal of the restrictions, with some amendments (this is adopted by government)

May 10, Disturbances at Keunjhar, in Orissa

June 26, Indian currency committee report received at Calcutta; Sir D. Barbour introduces a bill adopting its recommendations, suspending free coinage of silver, to accept gold for silver at the rate of 16*d.* for the rupee; a gold standard to be established; bill passed, well received

Aug. 15, Abdication of the Khan of Khelat; succeeded by his son, Mir Mahmud, reported

Aug. 20, Scheme for compensation to government servants for loss by the rate of exchange for the rupee, announced

Sept., Sir Henry Norman declines the appointment as Viceroy in succession to Lord Lansdowne

About Oct. 11, The Earl of Elgin appointed Viceroy

Dec. 21, The East India loan bill (10,000,000*l.*) passed

Dec. 27, The 9th Indian national congress meets at Lahore; 1,000 delegates present; Mr. Naoroji, M.P., president

1894

Jan. 2, Skirmish with the Abor tribesmen on the border of Assam; 7 of the military police killed at Bamjur

Jan., Dumbak and Silluk captured by Capt. Maxwell's force

Jan. 25, The Earl of Elgin arrives at Calcutta

Jan., James Fairbairn Finlay, Finance Minister

Feb. 27, Nine of the Bengal infantry, 6 police, and 8 followers, killed by the Abors at Bordak, and 19 prisoners carried off from Duffla

March 8, Villages burnt by Capt. Maxwell's force, reported

March 16, Safe arrival of Capt. Maxwell's punitive expedition at Sadiya

March 21, Revenue, 1893–4: improvement in land and railways; loss in opium and salt, reported

March, The Lansdowne hospital at Udaipur, constructed by the Maharana of the Rajput states, opened

April 12, Failure of the wheat harvest in the N. central provinces, reported

Nov., The interest on loans, &c., converted from 4 to 3½%; above 91½ millions had been converted

Nov. 3, An attack of 2,000 Mahsud Waziris on Col. A. H. Turner's delimitation party (Afghan frontier) defeated at Wano; 350 killed; British loss, Lieut. P. J. F. Macaulay and 44 men

Dec. 17, Punitive expedition under Sir Wm. Lockhart into Waziristan against the Mahsuds, and to carry out the demarcation

Dec. 21, 22, Makin destroyed; desultory fighting

Dec. 24–29, First medical congress at Calcutta; opened by the Viceroy; great improvement in public health through sanitation since 1868, reported

Dec. 26, Tenth Indian national congress opened at Madras; 1,150 delegates; Mr. Webb, M.P., president

About Dec. 27, A customs duty of 5% (abolished in 1882) on imported cotton goods, and a countervailing excise duty of 5% on certain classes of cotton goods manufactured in India, imposed by the legislative council to increase the revenue suffering by the depreciation of the rupee; bills passed

1895

Jan. 8, A gathering of about 700 tribesmen (Waziristan) surrenders to Col. Egerton

Feb. 12, Delimitation concluded of the southern border

Feb. 21, Sir Henry James's motion in the commons against the cotton duty negatived, 304–109

March 5, Sir Wm. Lockhart issues an ultimatum to the Mahsud chiefs at Wano, Jan. 21; his terms accepted

March 5, Col. Sir Henry Creswicke Rawlinson, diplomatist and Oriental scholar; born April 11, 1810; died

April 2, E. India railway, from Tarakeswar to Magra (the first constructed by native capital and engineers), opened by the Lieut.-Gov. of Bengal, Sir Chas. Elliott

About May 11, A royal commission appointed to inquire into the administration and expenditure of the Indian army; Lord Welby, chairman

June 25, Secretary of state, Lord George Hamilton

Oct., Sir Jaswant Singh Bahadur, Maharajah of Jodhpur, an able ruler

Dec., Punitive expedition against Kairuma, a hostile chief, in the N. Lushai hills

Dec. 27, The 11th Indian national congress opened at Poona; 1,600 delegates, Surendra Nath Bannerji, president

1896

Jan. 23, Bills for the revision of the cotton duties introduced by Sir James Westland; passed, Feb. 3

Jan. 29, Death of the Maharajah of Bhownugger, aged 38, a wise, enlightened ruler

March–May, Great distress through want of winter rains in N.W. and Central provinces, Rajputana, &c.; 296,000 employed on relief works

July 3, The home government decides that the Indian government shall partly support the Indian troops sent to Suakin, June 30; India protests, *Times*

Oct. 17, Sanari station, Quetta railway, attacked by Marris, massacre of the staff and men on the line; troops called out; reported

Nov. 8, Famine prospect through failure of rains, in Oudh, Punjab, N.W. and Central provinces, relief works, construction of wells, railways, &c., opened; 66,900 employed

Nov. 9, Death of Mr. M. Ghose, first native barrister

Dec. 17, The legislative council pass a bill raising the paper currency from 8 to 10 crores of rupees

Dec. 23, Appeal from the Indian government to Great Britain for aid

Dec. 28, 12th Indian national congress opened at Calcutta, 700 delegates

New relief works opened; energetic official action; total on relief, 404,200, Dec. 21; 2,000,000, Jan. 29, 1897; 4,500,000, June; 3,303,968, July 13

1897

Jan. 13, Famine relief fund organized at Calcutta

Jan. 28, Death of Gen. Sir Robt. Phayre, aged 77

Feb. 4, Indian plague bill passed at Calcutta

Feb., Epidemic diseases act, passed

Feb. 8, A loan authorized by the government for improving docks, &c., at Kidderpur

Feb., Energetic action of Sir Anthony Macdonnell in N.W. provinces and Oudh, one and a half million on relief or public works (18 distressed districts)

——, Many deaths in the central native states and Bundelkhand district; famine severe in S. Punjab, government works efficient

March 9, Plague localized in Bombay and Lower Scinde; decreasing

April, Irrigation of 3,000,000 acres by canals in N.W. provinces, announced

——, Mahomed Afzul, Afghan by birth, eminent general and diplomatist in the British service; born, 1834, died

June 10, Treacherous attack of Waziris on Mr. Gee, political officer, and his escort, at Maizar, in the Tochi valley, N.W. frontier; Lieut.-Col. A. C. Bunny, Capt. J. F. Browne, Lieuts. H. A. Cruickshank and Higginson, and 22 others killed; escort retired after 4 hours sharp fighting to Dattakhel; 50 Waziris killed

June 12–18, Extensive shocks of earthquake: widespread ruin; Calcutta and Assam; over 1,542 deaths

June 28, Monsoon and general rains reported in all affected districts; good crops expected; famine ceasing, Aug., Sept.

June, Total relief fund from all sources estimated, 1,500,000*l.*; 4,500,000 persons relieved in June; total cost to the Indian government, estimated 10,000,000*l.* sterling, Oct. 7

[Famine relief cost: 5,390,000 Rx.; against a budget estimate of 3,640,000 Rx.; for 1897–8; reported, March 20, 1898]

July 3, Tochi punitive expedition: 6,000 men under Major-Gen. Corrie Bird, Col. Egerton, and Col. Symons; proclamation issued; 50 tribesmen captured; British sentinels killed, July 6; Maizar found deserted, July 20; Sadda Khan and other chiefs, surrender conditionally, Nov. 1–14

July 22, Contagious diseases bill passed legislative council

July 29, Frontier war; Fanatical rising of the "mullah's followers" in the Swat valley, night attack on Malakand, repulsed; Major Taylor, Lieut.-Col. John Lamb, Lieut. Manley, and 13 men killed, July 26; severe fighting, rapid march of the Guides from Maidan, July 27; enemy repulsed with heavy loss

July 30, Field force (8,000) organized, under Major-Gen. Sir Bindon Blood and others

July 31, Rebels driven with great loss from the hills about Malakand

Aug. 2, Chakdara fort beşieged, July 26, by Pathans, over 3,000 killed; gallant defense (7 men killed during the siege), relieved by Gen. Meiklejohn

Aug. 9, Shabkadr fort attacked by 6,000 Afghans and Mohmands, Aug. 7; enemy routed, after a sharp fight, and brilliant cavalry charge, by Gen. Elles: Lieut.-Col. Wood, and 3 British killed

Aug. 17, Landikai occupied, after a desperate fight with 3,000 tribesmen; great heroism; Lieuts. Greaves and Maclean killed

Aug., Surrender of tribes in the Upper Swat valley, arms brought in

Aug. 24, 25, Fort Maude and other outposts in the Khyber pass, captured by the Afridis, Aug. 23; the Afridis shelled and dispersed by Gen. Westmacott's force

Aug. 25, Landi Kotal, and other small native forts, raided by Afridis, in the Khyber pass

Aug. 27, Small police posts burnt by Orakzais, E. and W. of the Samana range, Aug. 26; severe fighting in the Ublan pass, great heroism of medical officers and others

Aug.-Sept. 1, Four disturbed areas: Quetta, Kuram pass, the Orakzai, Afridi, and Mohmand hills, and the Swat valley; fines paid, and arms surrendered at Uch and Swat valley

Sept. 2, 3, 11, Enemy repulsed by Gen. Yeatman-Biggs, with heavy loss, in the Samana hills

Sept. 5, Native states offer support to the government

Sept. 14, Saraghari post on the Samana taken by the enemy (180 killed); the garrison, 21 Sikhs, died fighting to the last, Sept. 12; post recaptured by Gen. Yeatman-Biggs, forts Gulistan and Lockhart also relieved, large forces of the enemy driven back

Sept. 15, Gundab fort occupied, without opposition, by Gen. Elles, after a trying march into the Mohmand country

Sept. 16, Night attack on Gen. Jeffrey's brigade in the Rambat pass; Lieuts. Wm. E. Tompkins, A. W. Bailey, H. A. Harrington killed, Sept. 14; enemy (6,000) routed after a severe fight, Lieuts. Hughes and A. T. Crawford killed; total loss, 144

Sept. 17, Gen. Sir Wm. Lockhart appointed commander in succession to Sir George White

Sept. 18, Gen. Jeffrey drives the enemy from Damodota; Umra Khan's fort blown up, towers, &c., destroyed

Sept. 19, 20, Attacks by about 4,000 of Hadda Mullah's force on Sir B. Blood's camp at Nawagai, repulsed

Sept. 23, Gen. Elles drives the Mohmands from the Badmanai pass and captures the heights

Sept. 24, The enemy completely dispersed, flight of the 2 Mullahs

Sept. 25, Jarobi and forts, &c., destroyed by Gen. Westmacott's brigade

Sept. 25–Oct. 2, Submission of tribes in the Swat valley

Sept., The Ameer refuses help asked by the Afridis and others

Sept. 29, Punitive operations: 15 towers, &c., destroyed

Sept. 30, Agrah and Gat taken after a severe fight; enemy 2,000 strong; Lieut.-Col. O'Bryen and Lieut. Browne-Clayton and others killed

Oct. 3, Badelai in the Mohmand valley stormed, all the fortifications, &c., destroyed

Oct., Mohmand campaign (3 weeks) ended; 72 towers, 40 forts destroyed, arms captured, and fines paid

Oct. 10, Gen. Sir Wm. Lockhart arrives at Samana to command the Tirah expedition against the Afridis and Orakzais for breaking the treaty of 1881

Oct., Settlement with the Mohmands completed, arms surrendered

Oct. 18, Sir A. Palmer drives the enemy (about 8,000) from Chagru defile and Dargai heights with severe loss; Major Jennings-Bramly killed

Oct. 20, The enemy reoccupied Dargai and Chagru on the withdrawal of the troops, and were again driven from the ridge with great loss, after a desperate fight, great heroism shown, the heights won in 40 minutes by a gallant dash of the Gordon Highlanders under Lieut.-Col. Mathias, and others, through a murderous fire; Major C. B. Judge, Capts. J. G. Robinson and W. E. Smith, Lieut. A. L. Lamont, and 33 men killed

Oct., Reopening of the Indian mint for silver recommended by U.S.A. and French governments, July; declined

Oct. 30, The difficult and strongly-defended Sampagha pass captured, Capt. De Butts and 4 others killed, Oct. 29; the Arhanga pass taken

Nov. 5, Guerilla fighting; Tirah, Maidan occupied, Afridis dispersed

Nov. 7, Picket of one native officer and 35 Sikhs massacred in the Karmana defile, their retreat was cut off by a jungle fire

Nov. 8, Sixty hamlets and towers destroyed, severe loss inflicted on the enemy in the Arhanga pass

Nov. 11, Saran Sar occupied with slight resistance, but on retiring, Sir Wm. Lockhart's and Gen. Westmacott's brigades were fiercely attacked, the Northamptons and Sikhs bravely covering the withdrawal; Lieuts. A. H. Macintire, J. T. Maddell, and 18 men killed, enemy's loss severe, Nov. 9; successful reconnaissance, villages destroyed

Nov. 12 and 21, The Orakzai and Afridi jirgahs received by Sir Wm. Lockhart at Maidan, terms of submission announced

Nov. 16, General Kempster's force attacked by Zakkakhels and Akakhels in the Tseri-Kandao pass, Capt. N. A. Lewarne, Lieuts. R. E. A. Hales, G. D. Crooke, G. M. Wylie, and 25 men killed

Nov. 22–24, March of Gen. Westmacott's force to Datoi, 3 days' fighting, &c., Lieut. D. E. O. Jones killed

Nov. 26, 27, Lozaka pass cleared after a sharp fight by Gen. Gaselee's brigade, 5 killed

Nov. 29, Col. Spurgin's rearguard encounters heavy fighting over the Kotal hills, 4 killed

Dec. 1, 2, Chamkanni valley taken, villages burnt, Lieut. R. M. Battye killed, enemy routed

Dec. 8, 9, The Afridis' towers, &c., destroyed in the Waran and Rajgul valleys

Dec. 11, Gen. Lockhart's proclamation to the Afridis issued

Dec. 11, 13, Severe attacks on Gen. Kempster's rearguard, 9 killed; Lieut. West killed at Mamani

Dec. 19, Operations over in the Tirah district, forces withdrawn

Dec. 23, The heights from Fort Maude to Ali Mesjid occupied by the British

Dec. 27, Gen. Lockhart moves up the Khyber pass without opposition, Dec. 24; defeats the Madda-khels in the Alachi pass; enemy repulsed with heavy loss in the Bazar valley; Landi Kotal fort destroyed by Gen. Hammond's column

Dec. 30, Sir Henry Havelock-Allen, M.P., aged 67, son of Gen. Havelock, left his escort near the Khyber pass, killed by Afridis

Dec. 30, 31, Zakka-khel villages, &c., destroyed by Gen. Hammond's force; hard fight in the Khyber pass, 3 men killed

1898

Jan. 3, Major D. W. Hickman killed while out on convoy duty

Jan., Death, from exposure, of Gen. Yeatman-Biggs, aged 54, at Peshawar

Jan. 6, The enemy surprised and the Persai pass taken by Col. Adams

Jan. 7, The Tanga pass taken and 2 standards of the enemy, by Gen. Sir B. Blood

Jan. 17, Gen. Jeffreys receives the full submission of the Chamlawals at the Ambela pass

Jan., Guerilla warfare carried on by the Zakka-khels in the Khyber pass

Jan. 19, Government terms complied with by the Afridis and the Bonnerwals; Gen. Blood's force withdraws from Boner

Jan. 21, Sir J. Westland's currency bill (notes against gold), with a proviso, passed

Jan. 29, Successful advance of 3 columns to clear the Kajurai plain; the 4th from Mamani, attacked by Afridis in the Shin Kamar pass, Bazar valley, Lieut.-

Col. J. Haughton, Lieuts. Turing, Dowdall, Hughes, Walker, 28 Yorkshires, and 2 Sikhs killed; enemy's loss, 30

Feb. 11, Tochi expedition: 3 British officers, over 100 soldiers, 50 natives, and others, died from sickness; troops highly commended for their endurance, &c.

[Losses on the frontier: 684 British, including 43 officers, killed: 90 wounded, 12 men missing, and 1,233 native troops killed, from June 10, 1897–Feb. 7, 1898]

Mid-Feb., Operations in Mekran; enemy completely routed, at Gok Parosh, by a small force under Lieut.-Col. Mayne

Feb. 18, Sedition (press law) amendment act passed

March 4, Sir Wm. Lockhart's despatches on the Tirah campaign published

March 11, The Khyber pass reported peaceful; pass to be open from

March 12, Sir W. Lockhart gives a jirgah of all sections of the tribes their final choice of peace or war

——, Criminal procedure bill passed by the legislative council

March 16, The Ranjar dacoity gang (about 2 years' trial) finally convicted; 70 transported for life

March 21, Sir J. Westland's budget statement; he declares a silver standard, or the reopening of the mints impossible; the Viceroy refers the question to London, and defends the Indian government and army, March 28; a departmental committee of inquiry into the monetary system of India agreed to in the Commons, March 29

April 1, Payment of fines and surrender of rifles by the Afridis, completed

April, Sir Saiyid Ahmad, social reformer, eminent Mahometan friend of England, born 1817; died

April 29, Indian currency committee appointed, Sir Henry Fowler, chairman

July 1, Act passed for a loan of 10,000,000l. to meet losses by famine, plague, earthquakes, and war

Aug. 16, Fighting between the tribal forces of the Nawab of Dir and the Bajauris in the Jhandol valley; 136 Bajauris and 31 of the Dir forces killed, July 24; quiet reported

Aug. 25, Indian currency commission: evidence issued as a blue book

Oct. 1, Inland postage to be reduced from

Oct., Sir Wm. Lockhart appointed commander-in-chief

Nov. 18, Outbreak of plague in Madras and Mysore

Nov. 25, 26, The Hadda Mullah crosses the Swat river; serious fighting with native forces, losses on both sides; British reinforcements sent to Chakdara and Malakand, Dec. 1; the mullah's force defeated by native forces, Dec. 1–7; he is finally expelled from the Swat valley, and retreats into Kokistan, Dec. 10

Nov. 26, Indian plague commission, Dr. Thos. Fraser, F.R.S., president, arrives at Bombay

Dec. 16, Maharajah of Darbhangah, loyal benefactor, born 1856, died

Dec. 17, Jirgahs of all the Swat clans swear to Major Deane at Thana not to assist the Mullah in any rising

1899

Jan., Mr. J. M. Tata offers property worth 200,000l. on trust, to found an Indian university of research, and also to endow it with an annual income of 125,000 Rx.; other subscriptions promised, Dec. 31, 1878; bill drafted

Jan. 3, Lord Curzon appointed Viceroy Aug., 1898; welcomed at Calcutta

Feb. 5-8, Gomatti, a village, seized and 7 outlaws captured; 6 British killed; towers, &c., destroyed

March 1, Punitive expedition against the Chamkanni tribe for raids; 9 villages destroyed, 100 prisoners taken

March 20, Countervailing duties on imported bounty-fed sugar, passed by the council, comes into operation

April 22, Col. Sir R. Warburton, born 1842, distinguished for his able management of the Afridis and security of the Khyber pass, 1879-97, served in the Tirah expedition 1897-8, died

July 25, Indian currency commission, Aug., 1898; their report in favor of a gold standard, the sovereign to be legal tender, legal rate for the rupee to be 1s. 4d., adopted by government

Aug., New frontier policy, tribal militias substituted for regulars at frontier garrisons

Early Aug., Peaceful settlement arranged at a meeting between the Khan of Nawagai and the Nawab of Dir, after some conflicts

Sept. 15, Currency conversion act (gold made a legal tender, the rupee fixed at 16d.) passed (made permanent 1900)

Sept. 29, Raid of Bhils near Khergaum, severe fighting, many killed, reported

Dec. 13, The Viceroy holds a durbar at Lucknow

Indian famine through drought (1899-1901): severe in Bombay, Central Provinces, Punjaub, and elsewhere, began Sept., 1899; the government and its officers prompt and energetic in relieving distress and saving life; total on relief works, &c., 3,563,000, Jan., 1900; famine area, 420,000 sq. mi.; population, 62,000,000; relief fund started; 465,000 Rx. subscribed at a meeting in Calcutta, the Viceroy presiding, Feb. 16, 1900; central relief committee received about 1,000,000l. sterling; liberal gifts from abroad, about 25,000l. raised on the emperor's initiative in Germany, May; total on relief, 6,356,000, Aug. 7; declining, Sept.; 2,292,000, Oct. 16; India subscribes 32 lakhs, reported, Oct. 19

1900

Jan. 27, Loyal meeting of Hindus and Mahometans at Calcutta; speech by the Maharajah of Darbhanga, 63,000 Rs. subscribed to the Transvaal war fund

March 5, Indian plague commission reports favorably on Mr. Haffkine's inoculation system, thousands inoculated, Times

March 18, Death of Sir Wm. Lockhart, commander-in-chief, aged 59

March 19, The Maharajah of Jaipur presents 15 lakhs, in trust, towards the famine fund, to be permanent, announced

April 9, Report of the royal commission (1895) on Indian expenditure, proposed grant of 50,000l. a year to the India office, issued

April 12, Lord Curzon holds a durbar at Quetta; exhorts the chiefs to settle feuds and to stop murderous Ghazi raids, &c.

Mid April, Plague riots in Cawnpore, the segregation camp destroyed by the mob, 5 constables killed, troops called out, 10 deaths, April 11; plague regulations modified

July 26, Famine expenditure by Indian government, 13,000,000l. ann.

Aug. 2-4, The Viceroy visits the famine centers and relief works in Gujarat

Oct. 15, Government committee re the proposed sugar industry in Behar meets in Calcutta

Mid Oct.-Dec. 17, The Viceroy's tour round India, about 6,000 miles, very successful

Oct. 19, Punjab land alienation act, to prevent land passing into the hands of non-agriculturists, passed

Oct. 23, Mahsud Wazari raids on N.W. frontier frequent; Lieut. Hennessey killed

Nov. 7, Death of the Maharajah of Patiala

Dec. 1 et seq., Blockade against the Mahsuds in Waziristan

1901

Jan. 22-Feb. 2, Universal mourning on the death of the Queen-Empress Victoria

Feb. 4, The King-Emperor thanks the princes and people of India for loyalty and assistance in the S. African war

Feb.-Nov., New North-west Frontier province, Punjaub

March, Gen. Sir A. Palmer appointed commander-in-chief

March 22, The mines bill (1899), modified, passed

May 8, Indian Famine 1899-1900: commission appointed, Sir Anthony Macdonnell and others, Dec., 1900, report issued; great mortality in Gujarat and Bombay province, estimated deaths, 1,250,000; the great future problem being to relieve the pressure of the population on the soil; 5,095,590 gratuitously relieved; 6,257,940 on relief works

June 7, Indian Famine Union, to investigate cause and means of prevention, meets in London

July 18, Scheme for an imperial cadet corps of the sons of Indian princes and nobles; royal assent, reported

Aug. 6, Kashmir Kar, British post in the Gomal Pass, raided by Mahsud Waziris, 7 men killed

Aug. 16, Lord G. Hamilton's financial statement; estimated loss in W. India by 3 years' drought, 50,000,000l.; relief expenditure, 15,000,000l., met without additional taxation

Oct. 29, Jhelam irrigation canal at Rasul opened

Nov. 3, Sepoys ambushed by Waziri Mahsuds near the Gomal Pass, 24 and 6 other persons killed

Early Nov., The Viceroy tours through the North-Eastern provinces; welcomed at Manipur, Nov. 15; holds durbars at Mandalay, Nov. 27; Rangoon, Dec. 9

Nov. 13, Scientific plague commission commenced local investigation, Nov. 29, 1898; full report issued, with recommendations, Times

Nov. 14, Sir Antony Macdonnell retires from India after 36 years' eminent service

Dec. 5, 6, Punitive operations against the Mahsuds in Waziristan, 192 prisoners taken, villages, &c., destroyed, Nov. 25-27; further fighting, 7 villages and towers destroyed

Dec. 20, Nodiz fort in Mekran seized by Persian raiders, recaptured by the British; Mahomet Ali, the leader, and others, killed, 63 captured, the rest dispersed

Dec. 26-28, Indian National congress (over 5,000 present) held at Calcutta

Indian mines act (government inspection, &c.) passed

1902

Jan., Commission to report on the work of the universities and colleges, appointed

Early March, Mahsud Waziris submit, British lost 31 killed, blockade withdrawn

April 8, British force ambushed by outlaws on the Mahsud frontier, 8 killed, reported

April 17, The Berar question settled, the Nizam of Haidarabad cedes all territorial claims and receives 30 lakhs rupees annually, reported

April 22, The Rajah of Panna deposed and imprisoned for inciting to poison his uncle, the late Rajah (June, 1901), reported

April 26, Lord Curzon holds a durbar at Peshawar and explains the government policy towards the frontier tribes

June 6, Sugar duties bill (German and Austrian) passed

June, Reforms and progress in India; generous government grants reported

July 4, Swami Vivekananda, a religious reformer and denouncer of the caste system, died, aged 36

About July 6, Commission of inquiry into police reform, appointed

July 9, Loan of 150 lakhs of rupees subscribed 3 times over

Aug. 6, Blue-book report of the famine and relief operations, 1900–1902; excess mortality during 12 months' drought, 750,000, including 230,000 deaths from cholera and smallpox, issued

Aug. 12, Indian princes received by the King and Queen, London

Aug. 21, Good rains; crop reports favorable, Sept.

Aug. 29, Number on famine relief, 5,660,000; 58,000, Nov. 13

Sept. 23, Mr. Nowrojee M. Wadia offers about a million sterling to a trust for the relief of those deprived of subsistence by any sudden calamity, reported

Nov. 7, The Viceroy's tour in Central India ends; he visits Rajputana

Nov. 29, Punitive Kabul-Khel Waziri expedition for raids, &c.; prisoners captured, Gumati fort stormed and destroyed; Capt. White killed, Col. Tonnochy mortally wounded, 4 sepoys killed, Nov. 17, 18; operations closed successfully, 59 towers, &c., destroyed

Nov. 28–Dec., Lord Kitchener, commander-in-chief, arrives; army manœuvres at Delhi

Dec. 10, Death of the Rajah of Mandi

Dec. 11, Decennial missionary conference for India, Ceylon, Burma, and Arabia held at Madras

Dec. 22, Death of the Haddah Mullah, N.W. frontier

Dec. 29, State Entry of the Viceroy, the Duke and Duchess of Connaught into Delhi, 50 native princes and chiefs

Dec. 30, Indian art exhibition opened by the Viceroy

1903

Jan. 1, Coronation Durbar, King Edward VII proclaimed Emperor at Delhi (and throughout India) with great splendor and rejoicings; over 100 Indian rulers, about 600 *Mutiny* veterans, and a vast and brilliant assemblage present; 16,188 prisoners released, and many others in native states

Jan. 9, Durbar closed

Jan. 11, The Duke and Duchess of Connaught visit Peshawar, Meerut; other places, Jan. 18–19; Bombay, Jan. 19–23

Feb. 26, Increased military expenditure 17,100,000*l*., reported

Early April, Mr. Henry Phipps gives a total of 30,000*l*. for scientific research, agricultural education, and a Pasteur institute, reported

Aug. 4, Lord Curzon announces his decision to accept the offer of the home government for an extension of his term of office

Early Aug., Lord Curzon addresses strong protest to Lord Geo. Hamilton against the government proposal to charge India with the cost of the increased garrison in S. Africa

Aug. 12, The Viceroy reports prospects of crops generally good

Mid Aug., Report issued by the Irrigation commission proposing an outlay of 44 crores of rupees extending over 20 years on protective works

Aug. 13, Budget: 3,190,000*l*. surplus realized April, 1903; salt tax to be reduced 25%; exemption from income tax raised from 33*l*. to 66*l*.; available surplus after such deductions, 950,000*l*., 1903–4

Aug. 28, Death of Umra, Khan of Jandoul, reported

Mid Oct., About 20,000,000 acres irrigated in 1902; value of crops raised 28,000,000*l*., reported

Oct. 21, Total number of persons killed in 1902 by wild animals, 2,836; by snake bites, 23,166, reported

Oct. 29, Death of Rao Bahadur Moodelliar, merchant prince and philanthropist of S. India

Nov. 18–Dec. 7, Lord Curzon's tour in the Sikh states ends Nov. 11; he visits Muscat and the Persian Gulf ports

1904

End Feb., Blue-book stating the views of the government of India on preferential tariff, issued

March 21, Legislative council passes the universities bill abolishing the system of competitive examinations in favor of a system of selection of candidates on probation; native members oppose the bill

March 23, Budget 1904–5 presented: estimated revenue 80,148,600*l*.; estimated expenditure 79,229,000*l*. Important speech by Lord Curzon reviewing the five years' work of his viceroyalty; explains the frontier policy of the government, refers to the great increase of native Hindus holding civil appointments, and states that during his term of office the revenue had risen from 68,500,000*l*. in 1899 to 83,000,000*l*. in 1904, the surplus averaging 3,000,000*l*. per annum

April 30, Lord Curzon sails from Bombay for England on leave, Lord Ampthill, Governor of Madras, assuming the viceregal functions during Lord Curzon's absence

Aug. 8, Lord Curzon reappointed Viceroy

Aug. 12, Mr. Brodrick, Secretary of State for India, announces in the House of Commons the constitution of a railway board and the appointment of an extra member of the Viceroy's council to deal with commerce, and introduces a bill for this purpose

Aug. 15, Indian councils bills, 1904; royal assent

Sept. 10, King addresses to the Viceroy a telegram congratulating Col. Younghusband and the Tibet mission on the successful accomplishment of their labors (*see* Tibet)

Oct. 13, Commercial mission, nominated by the Indian chamber of commerce, leaves Bombay for Persia

Nov. 15, Death of Lord Northbrook, formerly Viceroy of India

Nov. 29, Death of Lord Harwich, under secretary for India

Dec. 13, Lord Curzon arrives at Bombay, Dec. 9; at Calcutta, and formally assumes the viceroyship

1905

Feb. 11, Lt.-Col. R. Harman, commanding S. Waziristan militia, stabbed with a bayonet and killed by a sepoy of the regiment at Wana

Early March, Important project for development of some of India's mineral resources, reported; American mining experts brought to India by late Mr. Tata are stated to have established the existence, in the Raipur district of the Central provinces, of immense qualities of an extremely rich iron ore; clue to this discovery first given by geological surveyors of the government. A company with 1,250,000*l.* capital about to be formed for the exploitation of this field

March 10, Major Carnegie of the Bombay political service killed during a lion hunt in the Gir forest

March 16, Commercial treaty between Japan and India, published

March 29, Unanimous approval of viceregal council of remissions of taxation in budget. Lord Curzon states that 13,000,000*l.* have been remitted in taxation in 7 years. British mission to Kabul, after conclusion of agreement with the Ameer, returning to India

April 4, Severe earthquake, causing great loss of life and damage to property throughout Northern India. Hill station at Dharmsala destroyed, 9 Europeans killed and 470 men of the Goorkha battalion; buildings wrecked. Many natives killed in Lahore, Amritsar, and Mussooree, 3,000 in Palampur sub-district, 10,000 in Kangra sub-district, narrow escape of Lady Curzon at viceregal lodge at Simla

April 9, 10, Further shocks at Simla

April 13, Towns of Sultanpur and Mandi wrecked by the earthquake, reported

April 24, Lieut.-Governor of the Punjab states that about 15,000 lives are estimated to have been lost by the earthquake in the seriously affected area, comprising 700 sq. miles, with a population of 250,000; nearly every building had collapsed or had been rendered uninhabitable; rough estimate of money required for generous relief 500,000 rupees (33,000*l.*); 200,000 rupees (13,000*l.*) already subscribed

April 30, 57,000 deaths from plague in week ending

May 23, 30,000*l.* collected in India for the Lieut.-Governor of the Punjab (earthquake) fund; death-roll estimated at 20,000

May 24, Plague in the Rawalpindi cantonment

End May, New treaty with Afghanistan published

June 23, Imperial government upholds Lord Kitchener's views on the military administration of Indian army; threatened resignation of Lord Curzon; modified scheme stated to be accepted by both the Indian government and Lord Kitchener, reported

June 24, Blue-book on the administration of the army in India, containing details of the controversy between Lord Curzon and the civil members of the council, and Lord Kitchener, commander-in-chief, respecting the existing system of Indian army organization, which is strongly condemned by Lord Kitchener, amounting, he declares, to a system of dual control which leaves the nominal responsibility to the commander-in-chief, but makes the military member of council "really omnipotent" in military matters. He affirms that in war it must break down, and unless disaster is courted "divided counsels, divided authority, and divided responsibility must be abolished." Lord Curzon, Sir Edmond Elles, military member, and the civilian members of the council traverse the most material of Lord Kitchener's statements of facts and record their entire disapproval of the changes Lord Kitchener declares to be indispensable to the safety of India; *see Times*

July 3, Official notification that in future the government of India will require the submission to them annually in September of a forecast of the estimated military expenditure for the ensuing year

July 19, Decision of the home government to reconstitute the provinces of Bengal and Assam announced at Simla

July 22, Agricultural prospects reported to be favorable in the east, center, and north, and fair in other parts, except in portions of Madras, South Bombay, and North Rajputana

End July, Famine relief camps established in parts of Madras; cholera; epidemic of cholera among the famine-stricken refugees; death-rate estimated officially to be 89.7 per 1,000

Aug. 7, Great meeting of protest against the partition of Bengal into two provinces held at Calcutta

Aug. 19, Resignation of Lord Curzon accepted by the King; Lord Minto, late Governor-General of Canada, appointed his successor

Aug. 20, White paper issued states that the action of the Viceroy was primarily due to a difference of opinion with the home government regarding the appointment of the first military supply member of the council of India

Aug. 25, Publication of a minute by Lord Kitchener, dated Aug. 17, justifying his repudiation of the Viceroy's summary of his proposals, coupled with Lord Curzon's minute, dated Aug. 23, in reply, published

Sept. 1, Proclamation published at Simla, bringing into effect the partition of Bengal from Oct. 16, 1905; Mr. J. B. Fuller appointed the first lieut.-governor of the new province of Eastern Bengal and Assam

Sept. 7, Secretaries of the anti-partition committee of Bengal reply to Chamber of Commerce of Manchester that the boycott of English goods had been forced by the disregard of the Indian government of public opinion and constitutional procedure in the matter of the partition of Bengal

Sept. 20, Lord Curzon attends a conference of the directors of education and delivers a farewell address, in which he traces the progress which has been made in education in India

Sept. 28, Great meetings at Calcutta to protest against the partition of Bengal, and in favor of boycotting British goods, Sept. 22; 50,000 persons take a solemn oath in the Kalighat temple, Calcutta, to carry out the boycott

Nov. 23, Sir Arthur Lawley appointed governor of Madras

Dec., Prince and Princess of Wales arrive in Calcutta

Dec. 20, New ("Curzon") bridge across the Ganges at Allahabad opened

1906

Jan. 9, Palace of the Thakur of Limri totally destroyed by fire, estimated damage to palace and town, which was also destroyed, 50 lakhs of rupees (333,000*l.*)

Jan. 24, Prince and Princess of Wales visit Rangoon, Jan. 13; arrive at Madras

Jan. 29, Prince and Princess of Wales visit Mysore

Feb. 8, Prince of Wales arrives at Haidarabad

Feb. 12, Viceroy reports continued lack of rain in the affected districts; number on relief works rises to 247,000

Feb. 15, The prince visits Benares; Lucknow, Feb. 22

Feb. 24, Lord Minto and Lord Kitchener express their complete satisfaction with Mr. Morley's decision on Indian army administration

Mar. 10, Severe earthquake in Bashahr, one of the hill states; 2 persons killed, 24 injured, and some buildings destroyed, reported

Mar. 19, Prince and Princess of Wales sail from Karachi in the *Renown* battleship, on the conclusion of their tour in India

Mar. 26, Mr. Felix Schuster appointed a member of the Indian Council in succession to Mr. T. C. Le Marchant

Mar. 31, Situation reported improved; number on the relief works falls to 388,000

May 1, Indian government decide to complete the Hindustan-Thibet road, in order to establish an unbroken link between Simla and Gantok, the new trade mart in Western Thibet

July 18, Death of Lady Curzon of Kedleston

Aug. 7, Mr. J. P. Hewett appointed Lieut.-Gov. of Agra and Oudh, reported

Sept. 3, "Coronation" of Surendra Nath Banerjee, leader of the agitation against the partition of Bengal, in Calcutta

Sept. 4, Disastrous floods, which destroy the indigo crop and the food crops and wipe out whole villages, reported from Behar

Sept. 18, Mr. Jas. Fairbairn Finlay, C.S.I., member of the council of India, appointed an ordinary member of the council of the governor-general of India in charge of the department of commerce and industry in succession to Mr. John Prescott Hewett, C.S.I., C.I.E., reported

Oct. 1, Lord Minto receives a deputation at Simla, who present an address from the Mahomedan community of India

Oct. 6, Lord Minto leaves Simla for Quetta on starting his autumn tour

Oct. 16, Anniversary of the partition of Bengal passes off quietly in Calcutta; the Mahomedans everywhere celebrated the anniversary with rejoicings

Oct. 28, Death of Sir Walter Morgan, late chief justice of Madras, aged 85

Dec. 17, Mr. John Ellis, through ill-health, resigns the office of under-secretary for India, reported

Dec. 20, Area under cotton nearly a million acres larger than last year; the output is estimated at 5,105,000 bales, which is a record, reported

About Dec. 24, Death of Mr. Ravi Yarma, Indian artist, aged 54

Dec. 29, Indian National congress opened in Calcutta; Mr. Naoroji, the president, delivers an address, in which he contends for the right of Indians, as British subjects, to govern themselves, Dec. 26; resolutions passed expressing indignation that Indians should be denied citizen rights in the Transvaal, and protesting against the alarming growth of military charges, Dec. 27; sittings concluded

1907

Jan. 2, Visit of the Ameer of Afghanistan.—Arrival at Landi Khana, on the border; at Peshawar, Jan. 3–7; at Agra, Jan. 9; review of 30,000 troops and a chapter of the Indian orders held, Jan. 12; at Aligarh, Jan. 16; at Gwalior, Jan. 18; at Delhi, Jan. 21; festival of Bakr Id celebrated, Jan. 25; at Calcutta, Jan. 28–Feb. 9; at Bombay, Feb. 12–Feb. 25; the Ameer leaves India on his return to his country; cordial

messages exchanged between the Viceroy and the Ameer, Mar. 7

Feb. 5, The trial of Lord Delamere and others, accused on a charge relating to an alleged fraudulent transfer of land, results in the acquittal of all defendants

March 12, Prince Ranjitsinhji installed as Jam of Nawanagar

April 13, 75,000 deaths from plague reported for week ended

April 17, Punjabi sedition case appeal.—Conviction upheld, but imprisonment changed from rigorous to simple; a riot in favor of the prisoners took place while they were being conveyed from the court to the gaol, several Europeans being assaulted

[The proprietor of the Punjabi had been sentenced in February to 2 years' imprisonment and a fine of 1,000 rupees (about 66*l.*), and the editor to 6 months' imprisonment and a fine of 200 rupees (about 13*l.*) for exciting hatred against the government and the European community]

April 25, Mass meeting of Mahomedans and influential natives, held at Lahore, strongly condemns the recent assaults on Europeans, criticism of their social institutions, and abusive language towards the government

May 2, Serious rioting at Rawalpindi; much property destroyed by the mob, who were dispersed by a party of armed police

May 9, Arrest and deportation of Lajpatrai, a prominent leader of sedition in the Punjab

May 11, Ordinance issued by the Viceroy for the regulation of public meetings in Eastern Bengal, Assam, and the Punjab; 7 days' written notice required before the holding of any public meeting in the proclaimed areas, and district magistrates empowered to prohibit meetings likely to promote sedition, published

——, Deaths from plague, during six weeks, numbered 451,892 to

May 20, Government of India decides to hand over the control of Manipur state to Rajah Chura Chand Singh, announced

May 22, A Hindu, who spread a report that the government had sent emissaries through the Punjab to poison the drinking wells, was sentenced to two years' rigorous imprisonment, and a fine of 500 rupees (33*l.*); an accomplice was sentenced to 18 months' rigorous imprisonment

June 17, Arrest of Mr. Dinanath, editor of the *Hindustan,* on charges of exciting and abetting disaffection in the army

——, Resignation of Lord Lamington, governor of Bombay, announced

July 22, Sir Geo. S. Clarke appointed to succeed him

July 24, Editor of the *Yugantar,* for preaching armed revolt, sentenced to one year's hard labor

Oct. 1, Mr. Keir Hardie in India; his tour condemned by the Anglo-Indian journals

Oct. 4, Rioting in Calcutta; police stoned, shops looted, and street lamps broken

1908

Jan. 20, Sir Louis Dane appointed Lieut.-Governor of the Punjab in succession to Sir Denzil Ibbetson, announced

Feb. 13, In consequence of frontier raids by the Zakka Khels, two brigades, under Maj.-Gen. Sir Jas. Willcocks, proceed to the Bazar valley to punish the rebels

Feb. 13, Serious rioting in Bombay, arising out of disputes between the Sunni and Shiah Mohamedans on the occasion of the Muharram celebrations; the police, having arrested several Sunnis, the mob demand their release and stone the police; European officers fire on the mob, killing 5 and wounding 40; order restored by the troops

Feb. 29, Submission of the Zakka Khels, Feb. 27; withdrawal of the troops begun

March 5, The estimated cost of the expedition against the Zakka Khels, from 66,600*l.* to 80,000*l.* *Times*

March 9, Great distress reported from India; the total number of persons in receipt of state relief being 1,388,818

March 11, Sir Cowasjee Jehanghir, Parsee merchant, gives 26,666*l.* for the promotion of science teaching in Bombay

April 18–19, Frontier Trouble, 1908.—Mohmand incursions—Gun-running on the coast of Mekran reported; cargoes of guns and ammunition secretly landed by native dhows at various points west of Gwadar, conveyed thence to the borders of Seistan and Afghanistan, or carried eastward and sold to tribesmen on the Indian frontier

April 20, Gatherings of Mohmands, joined by Afghans, assemble owing to the exhortations of the mullahs; a force of 1,200 men despatched from Peshawar to deal with the trouble

April 20, End of the telegraph strike which had been caused by the changes introduced into the Indian telegraph service by Mr. Newlands

April 24, General Willcocks attacks the tribesmen with all troops available; British casualties number 60, including several officers; enemy's loss estimated at 100 killed

April 27, Mohmands reported to have returned to their own country

May 1, Bomb outrage at Muzaffarpur; a bomb, thrown at the carriage in which Mrs. and Miss Kennedy were driving, kills Miss Kennedy and the coachman and fatally injures Mrs. Kennedy

May 2, Police raid certain houses and a newspaper office in Calcutta, discovering large quantities of explosives and anarchist literature; more than 30 arrests made

May 3, An Afghan lashkar, numbering 13,000 to 20,000, crosses the border and attacks Landi Kotal, renewing the attack in the evening, May 2; General Willcocks, with the third brigade, reaches Landi Kotal

May 8, Railway disaster near Moradabad; death roll officially stated to be about 120

May 9, Investigations following on the raids prove the existence of a revolutionary plot on a vast scale, and of a systematically organized "college" for instruction in the manufacture of bombs

May 9–10, The Indian government makes a remonstrance to Ameer against the participation of Afghans in the frontier outbreaks; the Ameer expresses regret that earlier information had not reached him and issues stringent orders recalling Afghan subjects. The hostile sections of the Mohmands refuse to come in to discuss the British terms and General Willcocks prepares to march an expeditionary force against them

May 10, Jirgah held by General Willcocks; the political officer announced that the government had summoned all the Mohmands, and, as all the Mohmands had not come in, the government would discuss nothing and the headmen could return to their homes

May 13, General Willcocks enters the Mohmand country and reaches Dand

May 18–19, A strong force under Maj.-Gen. Barrett proceeds in the direction of Bohai Dag to punish the Khwaezais

May 20, Gen. Willcocks and Gen. Anderson move into the Utmanzai country; in the encounter with the enemy, British casualties number 26, including 2 British officers killed; the enemy's loss exceeds 200

May 23, The Safi clans accept the government terms May 22, and Gen. Willcocks proceeds to assert supremacy over other sections of the Mohmands

May 24, Gen. Willcocks destroys the residence of the Gud Mullah, and disperses a gathering of 2,000 Utman Khel near Kargha, reported

May 25, Gen. Willcocks arrives at Mulla Killi; punishment of the Khoda Khel and the Bazai entrusted to Gen. Barrett, operating from Nahakki

May 28, Gen. Willcocks destroys the towers of the Bazai in the Khoda Khel district; the enemy offer some resistance but there are no casualties; destroys the strongholds of the Khoda Khel in the Bohai Dag, May 29

May 31, Every tribe having been fully dealt with, Lord Kitchener addresses to Gen. Sir J. Willcocks telegram of thanks and appreciation [the number killed, 52, wounded, 206; enemy loses 450 killed; Gen. Willcocks' despatch June 26]

June 8, Measures dealing with explosives and press offences passed

June 13, Muzaffarpur outrage—Khudiram Bose sentenced to death for the murder of Mrs. and Miss Kennedy by means of a bomb

June 21, A bomb thrown at a mail train at Barackpur wrecks the train and injures 3 people

June 26, Railway collision near Baroda; 15 persons killed and 270 injured

July 6, Death of Sir Harold Deane, chief commissioner in the north-west frontier province, *b.* 1854

July 17–18, Strike of 14,000 mill operatives who were guilty of some excesses which led to collisions with the police

July 22, Trial of Mr. Tilak, nationalist leader, for publishing seditious articles in the Poona weekly *Kasari*, of which he was editor, concluded; prisoner found guilty and sentenced to six years' transportation and a fine of 66*l.*

July 23, Strike of 20,000 mill-hands in Bombay

Aug. 7, The trial of 6 men, arrested at a house in Calcutta where a store of bombs and explosives was discovered by the police, concluded; 3 sentenced to seven years' penal servitude and 3 acquitted

Aug. 17, Ethiraj Surendranath Arya, convicted of uttering seditious speeches, sentenced to 5 years' transportation

Aug. 29, Trial of men concerned in the riot at Tinnivelli in March concluded; one man sentenced to 7 years' transportation, 5 others condemned to 5 years' rigorous imprisonment

Aug. 31, Narendro Nath Gossain, approver in the late bomb conspiracy, shot by two of his fellow-accused in alipur gaol

Oct. 24, Confiscation of the *Bande Mataram* newspaper under the new newspaper act

Nov. 7, Attempted assassination of Sir Andrew Fraser, Lieut.-Governor of Bengal

Nov. 9, A police inspector shot down in the street in Calcutta

Nov. 13, Statue of Queen Victoria, at Nagpur, defaced

Dec. 11, Summary jurisdiction act passed

Dec. 28, Indian national congress opens at Madras; Dr. Behari Ghose declares in his inaugural address that the whole of India was deeply grateful for Lord Morley's scheme of reform

1909

Jan. 5, Religious riots at Titaghur; the mosque attacked by Hindus, who destroy the sacred fittings and demolish the walls; troops fire on the mob; reported, Calcutta

Feb. 15, Asutosh Biswas, public prosecutor in the recent anarchist conspiracy case, shot dead in the court at Alipur, by a young Bengali, named Charan Bose, Feb. 10, who was convicted and sentenced to death

Feb. 22, Lord Minto reaches Calcutta on his return from his tour in Assam

Feb. 27, Report of the royal commission on decentralization in India issued as a blue-book

March 19, Charan Bose executed

April 1, Gen. Sir O'Moore Creagh appointed to succeed Lord Kitchener as commander-in-chief in the East Indies

May 6, Alipur conspiracy case.—Of 36 prisoners charged, 2 were sentenced to death, 7 to transportation for life, 5 to terms of penal servitude, and 22 were acquitted

May 25, India council's act receives royal assent

July 1, Sir W. Curzon-Wyllie and Dr. Cawas Lalcaca shot dead by an Indian student, named Madha Lao Dhingra, at the Imperial institute, London

July 10, Frontier raid by a gang of Khosh outlaws; British picket cut up

Sept. 6, Lord Kitchener leaves Simla

Sept. 13, Gen. Sir O'Moore Creagh, Lord Kitchener's successor, arrives at Simla

Oct. 22, 25 persons killed and 12 injured in an earthquake at Belput, on the Quetta line; the station and buildings completely destroyed; reported

Nov. 13, Attempt on the life of Lord Minto, the Viceroy, by a bomb being thrown, at Ahmedabad

Nov. 15, Details of the reform scheme published in Calcutta

Nov. 30, First elections under the reform scheme take place at Lucknow

Dec. 21, Murder of Mr. A. M. T. Jackson, Indian civil service collector, of Nasik, by a young Hindu

Dec. 27, Indian national congress opens at Lahore, Mr. Mulviya presiding

1910

Jan. 24, Inspector Shams-ul-Alam, of the Criminal Investigation Department shot dead in High Court, Calcutta by a Bengali youth; murderer executed, Feb. 21

Jan. 25, First meeting of enlarged and reconstructed Imperial Legislative Council

Feb. 9, New Press Act designed to suppress anarchical publications gave the Government authority to open postal matter suspected, and increased the list of offenses for which punishment could be imposed; a deposit required of all newspapers and presses which would be forfeited in case of conviction under the law

March 13, Arrival of the Dalai Lama in flight from Lhasa at Calcutta. *See* Tibet

March 19, Nasik murder trial of 7 Brahmans charged with complicity in the murder of Mr. Jackson on Dec. 21, 1909; Kanhere, Karve, and Deshpande sentenced to death, Soman, Joshi, and Vaidya to transportation for life, and Dattu Joshi to 2 years' imprisonment

March 26, Treaty with Bhootan signed

April 19, Execution of three persons for murder of Mr. Jackson

May 12, King George proclaimed at Simla

Aug. 6, Seditious Meetings Act renewed until March, 1911

Sept. 15–Dec. 24, Nasik conspiracy trial in Bombay; 11 prisoners discharged of 37, and the rest sentenced to various terms of imprisonment, Savarkar, the leader, sentenced to transportation for life

Sept. 30, Deaths from the plague during 12 months previous 448,319

Nov. 22, Lord Hardinge of Penhurst succeeded Lord Minto as Viceroy

1911

Jan. 3, Resolution of Legislative Council prohibited emigration of indentured Indians to Natal after July 1

Jan. 12, Rioting in Bombay between Sunni and Shiah Mohammedans at the Mohurrum, 42 persons killed and wounded

Feb. 21, Srish Chakravarty of Criminal Investigation Department shot and killed in Calcutta

March 18, Fifth decennial census gave the total population as 315,156,396 of which 243,933,178 the population of British India and 71,293,218 the native States

March 22, Seditious Meetings Act of 1907 reënacted

April 1, Constitution of new native State of Benares of December, 1910, proclaimed

June 15, 42 prisoners in Bengal conspiracy case acquitted but judgment reversed in August, 3 sentenced to life imprisonment, and 17 to 10 years

June 17, Mr. Ashe, Collector, assassinated

June 18, Sub-Inspector Raj Kumar Roy assassinated

Aug. 29, Death of the Nizam of Hyerabad at Simla

Sept. 30, Deaths from the plague during 12 months previous 713,377

Dec. 2, Arrival of King George and Queen Mary at Bombay, the first visit of a British sovereign to India

Dec. 12, Coronation durbar held by the King at Delhi at which were received the homage of the great officers of state and the ruling princes and chiefs of the Indian Empire

——, Announcement of removal of the capital from Calcutta to Delhi, reunion of Eastern Bengal to Bengal under Governor in Council, Assam a chief Commissionership

Dec. 15, Foundation stone of new government building laid by King George at Delhi

Dec. 30–Jan. 8, Visit of King George and Queen Mary to Calcutta

1912

Jan. 10, King George and Queen Mary left India for England

March 21, Factory Act became law establishing a 12-hour day for men, 10 for women, and 6 for children

April 2, The High Court delivered final judgment in Dacca conspiracy case on appeal, sentences of 14 of

34 upheld, the sentence of Pulin Behari Das reduced to 7 years and the others acquitted

Dec. 23, Bomb thrown seriously wounded Lord Hardinge, the Viceroy, making state entry into Delhi; the assassin escaped

1913

June 30, Smuts-Gandhi agreement as to Indians in South Africa. *See* South Africa

Aug. 3, Demolition of lavatory attached to mosque in Cawnpore by the order of the municipal board, taken by Mohammedans as an insult to their faith, led to serious rioting

Sept. 17, Appeal of Lord Hardinge to Legislative Council to Indian Mohammedans followed by visit to Cawnpore and settlement over the heads of the local authorities

Oct. 3, Failure of Credit Bank in Bombay caused panic on stock exchange which lasted during the month

Nov. 24, Lord Hardinge in speech expressed sympathy with the Indian "passive resisters" in their struggle in Natal against "invidious and unjust laws" and urged appointment of committee to inquire into condition of Indians in South Africa

1914

March, Har Dayal, native of Delhi and leader of Ghadr revolutionary party, arrested in California as an undesirable alien, but released on bail, forfeited bail and escaped from the country

May 21, Gurdit Singh, Sikh, with 396 Indians on the steamer "Komagatu Maru" arrived at Vancouver to test immigration laws and was not admitted. The party started on return voyage July 23 to avoid being deported

July 1, Indian Relief Act in South Africa made provision for redress of certain grievances and disabilities of Indians in South Africa, the £3 tax on ex-indentured Indians in Natal removed, and legal status given to *de facto* monogamous marriages

Aug. 4, British declaration of war on Germany

Aug. 8, Mobilization order

Aug. 19, Indian troops left for East Africa

Aug. 24, First Indian troops left India for war service in Europe

Sept. 8, Imperial Legislative Council passed resolution of loyalty and support of the British Government

Sept. 22, The "Emden" off Madras opened fire on large oil tanks of Burma Oil Company causing over $100,000 damage

Sept. 26, Indian troops landed at Marseilles

Sept. 27, The S.S. "Komagatu Maru" with some 400 Sikhs and 60 Mohammedans arrived from British Columbia *via* Hong Kong where they had been repatriated by the British Government, and started march to Calcutta but were forced to return to Baj Baj where clash with troops ended in killing of 18 Sikhs

Oct. 19, First Indian troops reached Flanders

Oct. 28, The Japanese S.S. "Tasu Maru" arrived at Calcutta bringing 173 Indian passengers mostly Sikhs from America, Japan, the Philippines, and Shanghai including Ghadr revolutionary leaders

Oct. 31, Indian troops arrived at Mombassa, East Africa

Nov. 2, Announcement of Government of India that Holy Places in Arabia and Mesopotamia should be immune from attack reassured Mohammedans

Nov. 22, British and Indian troops occupied Basra

1915

Jan. 12, Statement of Lord Hardinge that Indian troops were in 5 theaters of war, France, Egypt, East Africa, Persian Gulf, and China, and that 200,000 were overseas

Feb. 15, Announcement of mutiny among Bengalese troops

Feb. 20, Death of Gopal Krishna Gokhale, Moderate Nationalist leader (49)

Feb. 22, Retirement from Council of Sir Krishna Govinda Gupla and succeeded by Sardar Daljit Singh

March 4, Sara Bridge across the Ganges formally opened by the Viceroy inaugurating railroad passenger service across the Lower Ganges

March 19, Criminal Law Amendment Act passed to better secure the public safety and bring certain offenses to more speedy trial, the Defense of India Act of 1915

March 26, Attack of 10,000 tribesmen on Tochi repulsed, northwest frontier

April 30, Lahore sedition trial begun of conspirators led by Bhai Paramand which resulted in death sentence for 24, life transportation for 27

June 4, Annihilation of 14th Sikhs battery at Gallipoli

Aug. 14, Royal Commission on Public Service in India published report

Sept. 22, Resolution carried asked that India should be represented at Imperial Conferences

Nov. 5, Death of Sir Pherozeshah M. Mehta, bart.

Nov. 10, Ordinance empowered the Government to requisition all factories and workshops for the duration of the War and regulate sailings of British steamers from Indian ports

Dec. 4, S.S. "Colenso" sunk by enemy

Dec. 30, S.S. "Persia" sunk without warning in the Mediterranean and of 231 passengers and 270 crew, chiefly lascars, only 166 saved

1916

March 2, Death of Sir Chinubhoy Madhavlal, of Ahmed-Abad, first Hindu baronet

March 20, Announcement of Lord Hardinge, Viceroy, of intention of the Government to abolish system of Indian indentured labor in Jamaica, Trinidad, British Guiana, Fiji, and Dutch Surinam

April 4, Frederick John Napier Thesiger, 3d Baron Chelmsford, took office as Viceroy succeeding Baron Hardinge

July 9, The "Silk letters" addressed to the Mohammedan religious leader, Mahmud Hasan, describing the progress of the revolution in Kabul and India, the arrival of German and Turkish missions, and the formation of a "Provisional Government," came into the possession of the British Government. A plan was outlined for forming an "Army of God" to drive out the British by an alliance of all-Islamic rulers

Sept. 3, Mrs. Annie Besant formally established her Home Rule League

Oct., Nineteen elected members of the Imperial Legislative Council submitted a memorandum of reforms which included making the executives subject in legislation, administration, and finance to an elected legislative body

Dec. 29, and 31, Meetings of the Indian National Congress and the All-India Muslim League agreed to accept the modified scheme of the Nineteen members of the Imperial Legislative Council called the "Congress-League" scheme, the Mohammedans accepting on concession of heavy Mohammedan representation on certain of the proposed councils (the "Lucknow Compact")

1917

Jan. 26, Report of Royal Commission on Indian Public Services published

Feb. 28, Act to constitute an Indian Defense Force enrolled all European British subjects

March, Raiding Mahsud tribesmen on northwest frontier made strong demonstration against the fort at Sarwakai at instigation of the Afghans

May 13, Bomb explosion in Lawrence Garden, Lahore, failed to kill Europeans

June 16, Order issued interned Mrs. Besant and her two chief aids Messrs. Arundale and Wadia because of Home Rule propaganda activities, "violent and unconstitutional"

June 29, Imports of gold except under license prohibited from this date to ensure that all gold imported was used to strengthen the Indian currency position

July 2, The Mahsuds sued for peace and in August accepted terms offered them and surrendered all Government rifles in their possession

July 10, Resignation of A. Chamberlain as Secretary of State for India

Aug. 20, Announcement of Mr. Montagu, Secretary of State for India, in the British House of Commons, that the policy of the Government was "that of increasing the association of Indians in every branch of the administration and the gradual development of self-governing institutions with a view to the progressive realization of responsible government in India as an integral part of the British Empire," progress to be achieved by successive stages

Sept. 5, Mrs. Besant and Messrs. Arundale and Wadia released from internment on condition of abstaining from political agitation during the remainder of the period of the War

Sept. 28, Riot at Mohammedan village of Ibrahimpur in the Shahabad district of Bihar when Hindus attacked and looted the village

Sept. 30, Mob of 25,000 Hindus attacked Ibrahimpur and some neighboring villages in protest against killing of cows sacred to Hindus by Mohammedans at religious festival Bakr-Id to commemorate the episode of Abraham's contemplated sacrifice of his son

Oct. 2, Further attacks of Hindus on Mohammedans in Shahabad district

Oct. 9, Attacks of Hindus on Mohammedans in the Gaya district, over 30 villages looted

Nov. 9, Visit of Mr. Montagu to India

Nov. 29, Air Force (Constitution) Act

Dec., Indian National Congress held in Calcutta, Mrs. Besant, president, and all resolutions which proposed modification of the Congress-League scheme as the minimum demanded for Home Rule withdrawn

1918

Jan. 5, Statement of Lloyd George that the Allies were not fighting to deprive Turkey of her capital or Asia Minor or Thrace reassured Mohammedans

Feb., The United States arranged to sell India 6 million ounces of silver to relieve the serious shortage

April 23, The Pittman Act passed in the United States provided for sale of silver for export to India and 200 million ounces of silver sent to India

April 2, Telegram of the British Prime Minister appealed to the Government and people of India to redouble their efforts and be the bulwark to save Asia from German tyranny

April 22, Montagu-Chelmsford Report of this date was published July 8 of proposed constitutional reforms to be confined in first stage of advance to the major provinces where a dual form of government known as "dyarchy" recommended

April 27, Madras labor union organized

April 27-29, War Conference held at Delhi by the Viceroy to which certain ruling Chiefs were invited and delegates from the Provincial Governments representing all classes and opinions to concert measures for the successful prosecution of the War with special reference to man-power and the development of Indian resources

June, Influenza epidemic begun

Sept. 1, Special session of the Indian National Congress at Bombay pronounced the Montagu-Chelmsford Reforms disappointing and unsatisfactory and demanded a guarantee of full responsible government in the whole of India within 15 years and in the provinces within 6 years

Oct. 6, Influenza epidemic reached its height in Bombay with a maximum of 768 recorded deaths

Nov. 11, Armistice signed. India had provided 1,000,000 troops and contributed £1,000,000 towards the expenses of the War

Dec. 28, Indian National Congress at Delhi adopted resolution affirming decision of Bombay Congress condemning the Montagu-Chelmsford Scheme, and demanded immediate full provincial autonomy

Powers taken by Government to provide for a cheap supply of cotton cloth which resulted in lowering prices

1919

Feb. 6, The first Rowlatt Act (Emergency Powers) introduced by the Government

Feb. 10, The second Rowlatt Bill introduced by the Government proposing permanent changes in the Indian penal code and the code of criminal procedure, the possession of a seditious document with the intention to publish or circulate the same to be punishable with imprisonment, and other measures to be used for the purpose of checking anarchical and revolutionary crime, and the announcement was made that the first Rowlatt Bill (Emergency Powers) would remain in operation only 3 years after the end of the War

March 1, Mr. Gandhi published manifesto announcing his intention and formulating the pledge of passive resistance (satyagraha) against the Rowlatt Bills, Criminal Law Amendment Bill No. 1 and Criminal Law Emergency Powers Bill No. 2, as "unjust, subversive of the principles of liberty and justice, and destructive of the elementary rights of an individual on which the safety of India as a whole and the State itself is based . . ."

March 12, India Paper Currency Act

March 21, The Anarchical and Revolutionary Crimes Act, 1919 to take the place of the Defense of India Act expiring received the assent of the Governor General, (Rowlatt Bill, No. 1), gave Government powers for internment without trial in seditious districts and suspension of habeas corpus in emergency

March 23, Gandhi began war against the Act by proclaiming a hartal or stoppage of all work throughout India on March 30

March 30, Riots at Delhi, the mob in conflict with the police, 5 persons killed, and stopping of work at Amritsar, Mooltan, and other centers

April 6, Gandhi's second hartal celebrated in Calcutta, Bombay, Lahore, Amritsar, and nearly all the towns of the Central Punjab as day of humiliation

April 9, Gandhi disregarding orders not to enter Delhi and the Punjab stopped at railroad station on the provincial border and sent back to Bombay

April 10, Deportation of Nationalist leaders Kichlu and Satya Pal later convicted and imprisoned, caused riot at Amritsar where looting and burning and attacks on Europeans occurred, 2 Englishmen killed, the manager and assistant manager of bank which was burned and looted; riots at Lahore, Ahmedabad, Government buildings attacked, railway lines damaged, and telegraph wires cut

April 11, Hartal begun at Kasur

——, General Dyer arrived at Amritsar

April 12, Riots in the Bombay Presidency at Viramham and Nadiad, and in Calcutta and Bombay, and Lahore, and continued at Amritsar, and serious outbreak at Kasur where railway station seized and burned and the Civil Courts

April 13, At Amritsar where martial law had been in effect since the riots of April 10 and public meetings forbidden by proclamation of General Dyer that morning, a meeting of 6,000 Indians in the afternoon dispersed by troops of General Dyer who fired on mob killing nearly 400 persons and wounding about three times that number

April 14, Outbreak at Gujranwala where railway station attacked and Government buildings wrecked and burned stopped by use of aëroplanes in the absence of available troops

April 14–16, Serious riots at 14 places along the railway line in the Gujranwala district including Wazirabad, Akalgarh, Hafizabad, Ramnagar, Sheikhupura, Chuharkana, and Sangla

April 19, General Dyer issued the so-called "crawling" order at Amritsar that the lane on which a lady missionary had been brutally assaulted on April 10 should be closed during the day and any persons wishing to pass through should do so by measuring their length on the ground as Hindu pilgrims do at certain sacred places

April 22, Order of General Campbell ordered inhabitants of Gujranwala district to salaam before all British officers

May 10, Proclamation of the Viceroy announced Afghan war on India. *See also* Afghanistan

May 28, The Amir asked for terms of peace

May, Rising of Wazirs and Mahsuds raiding British districts at instigation of Afghans

July 26–Aug. 8, Peace Conference with Afghans

Aug. 8, Peace Treaty with Afghanistan signed. *See* Afghanistan

Sept. 1, Judgment delivered in Mainpuri conspiracy case, secret revolutionary organization of 50 persons working to overthrow British rule apprehended in case of robbery

Nov., At Khalifat Congress at Delhi Mr. Gandhi proposed non-coöperation for "Khalifat wrong" to Ottoman Empire

Dec. 6, Rouble Note Ordinance promulgated to suppress the circulation of Russian rouble notes brought into India in connection with Bolshevik propaganda

Dec. 18, Advance against the Mahsuds in rebellion begun

Dec. 21, Engagement with Mahsuds

Dec. 23, Proclamation of the King of royal assent to the Government of India (Amendment) Act based on the Montagu-Chelmsford Report and of clemency to political offenders in fullest measure compatible with the public safety. The new Constitution introduced a scheme of diarchy or dualized form of government for the provinces to apply to Bengal, Madras, Bombay, Bihar and Orissa, United Provinces, Punjab, Central Provinces and Assam, and Burma, and in the Central Government a Council of State and a Legislative Assembly substituted for the single Chamber of the Imperial Legislative Council

The Central Government reserved Military and Foreign Affairs, Tariffs and Customs, Railways, Posts and Telegraphs, Income tax, Currency, Public Debt, Commerce and Shipping, and legislation relating to Civil and Criminal Law, the "reserved subjects," those left entirely to the Provinces, the "transferred subjects"

——, Aliens Restriction Amendment Act

1920

Jan. 10, India became an original member of the League of Nations

Jan. 11, Severe fighting at Ahnai and Tangri with the Mahsuds

Jan. 14, Engagement with the Mahsuds in which British casualties heavy

May 3, Report of Hunter Committee on disturbances in Bombay, Delhi, and the Punjab in 1919, published

May 7, Campaign against the Mahsuds ended, the Mahsuds accepting the terms imposed

Aug. 26, Assassination of R. W. D. Willoughby, Deputy Commissioner, by Mohammedan fanatic, as part of Khalifat agitation against terms imposed on Turkey by Allies

Sept. 8, At National Congress at Calcutta Gandhi laid down his program of a passive resistance of non-coöperation with the Government

Sept. 19, Act constituted Imperial Bank of India

Sept. 22, Act constituted an Indian Territorial Force and provided for enrollment of persons other than Europeans and British subjects

——, Act constituted an auxiliary force of Europeans and British subjects

Oct. 1, Sir William Meyer entered on duties as first High Commissioner for India as provided by Act of Dec. 23, 1919

Oct. 16, Gandhi in address to meeting at Lucknow promised self-government to India within a year if the people followed non-political coöperation

1921

Jan. 1, Government of India Act of 1919 came into general operation

Jan. 8, Lord Reading appointed Viceroy to succeed Lord Chelmsford

Feb. 8, New Parliament opened at Delhi by the Duke of Connaught

Feb. 14, First meeting of new Council of State

Feb. 15, Legislative Assembly adopted resolution recommending Governor in Council to declare for principle of racial equality

Feb. 23, Council of State adopted resolution recommending that the Government of India be granted full fiscal autonomy

March 18, The sixth decennial census gave the total population as 319,075,132 of which 247,138,396 the population of British India, and 71,936,736 of the native States

April 2, Lord Reading assumed office as Viceroy

May 13, Lord Reading had interview with Gandhi with the result that the Ali Brothers published an apology for any passages in their speeches which might be interpreted as incitement to violence

June 20–Aug. 5, Imperial Conference recognized the incongruity between the position of India as an equal member of the British Empire and the existence of disabilities upon British Indians lawfully domiciled in some other parts of the Empire, and all the States except South Africa who refused to adopt resolution expressed opinion that it was desirable that rights of Indians to citizenship be recognized

July, The Khalifat Congress at Karachi adopted resolution that if the Khalifat question was not settled by Christmas a republic should be declared and the Ali brothers called on Mohammedan soldiers to desert alleging that military service under the Government was religiously unlawful

Aug. 1, Boycott of British imports begun

Aug. 20, Revolt of Moplahs due to Khalifat agitation begun at Tirurangadi, aiming to establish an independent Khalifat kingdom at Malabar, and attacked their Hindu neighbors

Sept. 14, The Wana Wazirs ended revolt signing treaty accepting terms imposed

Nov. 2, The Ali brothers, Mohammedan lieutenants of Gandhi, sentenced to imprisonment for 2 years for speeches inciting to "public mischief"

Nov. 4, The All-India Congress Committee authorized program of civil disobedience and boycott of foreign cloth

Nov. 17, The Prince of Wales landed in Bombay for visit to India, and the same day serious riots begun in Bombay which lasted nearly 3 days, 53 persons killed

Nov. 22, Indian-Afghanistan Treaty signed. *See* Afghanistan

Nov. 23, On this date civil disobedience to start at the Bardoli Taluq under Mr. Gandhi's personal direction, but this program was suspended, Mr. Gandhi announcing his intention of concentrating on production of the peaceful spirit he desired, because of the violence of the campaign of his "National Volunteers"

Dec. 6, Moplah revolt ended

Dec. 24, Indian National Congress met at Ahmedabad and gave Gandhi sole executive authority over all Nationalist activities in India

Dec. 29, The Abdullais in Central Waziristan sued for peace and ceased opposition

1922

Jan. 25, Factory Act amended provided for a 60-hour week and raised the minimum age of child workers from 9 to 12, and provided for weekly rest day

Feb. 1, Letter of Mr. Gandhi to the Viceroy threatened

to begin mass civil disobedience at Bardoli unless his program accepted

Feb. 4, Manifesto issued by Gandhi justified determination to resort to mass disobedience

——, Police post at Chauri Chaura in the United Provinces attacked by National Volunteers and peasants and 17 officers killed

Feb. 6, Letter of the Viceroy to Mr. Gandhi refused to regard his terms and warned him that civil government would be upheld

Feb. 12, Working Committee of National Indian Congress adopted resolutions deploring the murders at Chauri Chaura and calling for suspension of mass civil disobedience, the followers of Mr. Gandhi to stop all activities designed to court arrest, all processions, &c., and confine their activities to a "constructive program" to popularize the spinning campaign

Feb. 20, Outbreak at Assam

March 8, Publication in London of message of Lord Reading to Mr. Montagu, Secretary of State for India in which he urged revision of the Treaty of Sèvres with Turkey in deference to Mohammedan Indian sentiment

March 9, Resignation of Mr. Montagu as Secretary of State for India. *See* Great Britain

March 10, Arrest of Mr. Gandhi charged with sedition

March 17, The Prince of Wales ended Indian tour and embarked for the Far East

March 18, Gandhi sentenced to 6 years' imprisonment

March 29, Indian Press Act of 1910 and Newspaper Incitement to Offenses Act of 1908 repealed

April 4, Indian garrison at Wana attacked by hostile Wazirs

April 7–10, Royal Air Force bombed and machine gunned the Wazirs forcing them to raised the siege of Wana garrison

April 16, Founding of new university at Shantiniketan, Bengal by Sir Rabindranath Tagore

May, V. S. Srinivasa left India for visit to Australia, Canada, and New Zealand at request of British and Indian Governments to discuss the franchise and conditions of Indians in those countries

Sept. 2, Religious conflict at village of Guru-ka-Bagh

Sept. 4, Death of Sir Partab Singh

Sept. 27, Resolution of meeting of Mohammedans at Ahmedabad protested against British persecution of Turks

Oct. 4, Floods in northern Bengal with great loss of life followed by outbreak of cholera

Dec. 26, Indian Nationalist Congress opened at Gaya, C. D. Das, president, the "No-Changers," followers of Mr. Das controlled the meeting, Resolution adopted protesting British war with Turkey

1923

Jan. 1, C. R. Das, Moti Lal Nehru, and Ajmal Khan with other leaders announced constitution of a new Congress Khalifat-Swaraja Party for the conversion of their opponents to change in non-coöperation program, and favored dividing the country into administrative centers controlled by local, district, provincial, and All-India councils, a maximum of local autonomy, and stressed the organization of labor to support the national cause

Jan. 10, 172 prisoners in Chauri Chaura case of murders of Feb. 4, 1922 found guilty

Jan. 23, Dispatch of Lord Peel, Secretary of State for

India, to the Viceroy made public in which policy in regard to further constitutional reforms outlined as gradual as warranted by experience

Feb. 7, Defeat of Mahsuds

Feb. 23, Mines Act restricted hours of adult labor to 60 above ground and a 54 hour week below, and provided for a weekly day of rest, and prohibited the employment of children under 13, and of employment of women below ground

March 5, First Workmens Compensation Act

——, Act consolidated laws as to Government paper currency

March 16, Act created fund for improvement, and development of cotton industry

March 23, The Council voted to double the salt tax

March 26, The Assembly rejected enhanced salt tax by vote of 58 to 47

March 29, Finance Act enhancing salt tax enacted by certification of the Viceroy

April 1–June 4, Strike of 48,000 cotton operatives against reduction of wages in the Ahmedabad cotton mills

April 2, Code of Criminal Procedure Amendment Act removed racial distinctions in courts

April 8, Two British officers shot dead by Afghans near Landi Kotal in the Khyber Agency

April 11–14, Religious conflict of Hindus and Mohammedans at Amritsar suppressed by British troops

April 13, Wife of English staff officer at Kohlat murdered by an Afridi who fled to Afghanistan

April 27, Failure of Alliance Bank of Simla

April 30, Procession carrying "nationalist" flag at Nagpur stopped by police because of refusal to adhere to published route

May 4, The Governor in Council accepted the decision of the Allahabad High Court in appeal of 170 persons convicted in the Chauri Chaura murders confirmed death sentence of 19 leaders, and 110 persons sentenced to transportation for life, acquitted 38, and modified the sentences of the remainder

May 15, Failure of Amritsar National Bank

July 24, Treaty of Lausanne with Turkey signed by Allies

Aug. 16, Release from prison of Lajpat Rai, Dr. Kichlu, the Ali brothers and all non-coöperatives except Gandhi

Aug. 25–27, Religious conflicts between Hindus and Mohammedans at Sahararunpur and Gonda in the United Provinces and at Agra

Sept. 25, Indian National Congress met at Delhi and adopted resolution with permission of Gandhi (in prison) that the Nationalists should propose candidates for the Legislative Assembly and the provincial councils in order to obstruct legislation, and a boycott of British goods voted as a protest against limitation of Indian rights in Kenya Colony

Oct. 1–Nov. 8, Imperial Conference in London discussed Indian grievances

Oct. 24, Work begun on the Lloyd Barrage to make arable 6,000,000 acres of arid land in Sind

Dec. 28, Indian National Congress met at Coconada in the Madras Presidency, no agreement made between the Swarajists, and the "no-Changers" but open breach avoided

1924

Jan. 12, Appendicitis operation performed on Mr. Gandhi in prison successful

Jan. 15–March 25, Strike of 1,600,000 cotton mill workers in Bombay because usual bonus not paid because of bad trade conditions

Jan., Mr. Day, Englishman, mistaken for a high police official, killed by young Bengali anarchist

Jan. 31, Second Legislative Assembly opened by Lord Reading included 45 Nationalists out of 140 members

Feb. 4, Mr. Gandhi released from prison on account of his health, having served 2 years of a 6 year sentence

Feb. 14, Mr. Gandhi launched protest against South African Class Areas Bill

Feb. 18, Resolution demanding immediate constitutional progress and conference carried in Assembly by vote of 68 to 48

Feb. 21, The Shadidi Jatha of 500 men with object of resuming the alleged interrupted Akhand Path in Gurdwara Gangsar accompanied by Dr. Kitchlu, and Professor Gidwani were joined by mob of about 10,000 Akalis, and on refusing to disperse were fired on by the Administrator of Nabha State and police, 19 Akalis killed and 29 wounded

March 8, Conflict of cotton strikers with police in Bombay, 4 killed and 5 injured, fired on by police

March 17, Government Finance Bill rejected by Legislative Assembly by vote of 60 to 57

March 24, The Bengal Legislative Council rejected demand for salaries for Ministers

March 26, Certification of the Finance Bill by the Viceroy under 67B of the Government of India Act

June 13, Steel Protection Act the first step towards adoption of discriminating protection, duties on certain articles manufactured from steel were increased, and bounties granted on heavy steel rails, fish-plates, and railway wagons manufactured in India

June, At Bengal Provincial Conference over which Mr. Das presided resolution passed which spoke of "noble self-sacrifice" of the murderer of Mr. Day

June 27, All India Congress Committee met at Ahmedabad and conflict between the Swaraj Party of Mr. Das and Mr. Gandhi and the No-Change Party resulted in a series of compromises, a defeat for Mr. Gandhi and his program of non-violence, non-coöperation, non-Council entry, Hindu-Moslem unity, untouchables

July 15, Religious conflicts of Hindus and Mohammedans at Delhi

Aug. 26, The Bengal Council again rejected demand of Ministers for salary thus rejecting the dyarchy

Sept. 9–10, Conflicts between Hindus and Mohammedans at Kohat because of the publication and circulation of a pamphlet containing an anti-Islamic poem, the total casualties being about 155 killed and wounded followed by exodus of the entire Hindu population

Sept. 26, United Conference at Delhi attended by Hindus, Mohammedans, Parsees, Sikhs, and Christians adopted a series of resolutions aimed at ending community religious dissentions, declaring for toleration of religious beliefs, arbitration of disputes or settlement by the courts instead of force. An All-India Panchayat of 15 persons established including Christians, Hindus, Mohammedans, and Sikhs to appoint local committees to conciliate between the Hindus and Mohammedans

Oct. 25, The Bengal Ordinance promulgated by the Viceroy amended the criminal law of Bengal to deal with revolutionary violence

Nov. 21, All-Party Leaders' Conference summoned by

the Swarajists met in Bombay, passed resolution condemning the Bengal Ordinance

Dec. 24, Indian National Congress met at Belgaum, Mr. Gandhi, president, and formally adopted the pact between Mr. Gandhi and the Swarajists

1925

Jan. 1, Lord Reading opened the Legislative Assembly at Delhi, and in speech announced determination to end terrorism of criminal organizations in Bengal

Jan. 12, Murder of Mr. Abdulqudir Bawla, a prominent Moslem citizen of Bombay, shot while motoring by band of men attempting to abduct a dancing girl, Mumtaz Begum, who accompanied him and who had formerly been at the Court of Indore

Jan. 26, The Legislative Assembly agreed on bounty on steel manufactured in India during the 12 months ending Sept. 30, 1925

Feb. 3, First electric railroad in India opened in Bombay

Feb. 4, Death of the Nawab of Dir

Feb. 23, Report of the Committee on Auxiliary and Territorial Forces presented

Feb. 28, Fifty-four Indians convicted at Lahore for conspiracy against the Government, 4 sentenced to death, 9 to life imprisonment, and the others to various terms of imprisonment

March 2, Budget introduced estimated total revenue at 1,336,000,000 rupees for 1925–1926, and expenditure at 1,304,000,000

March 23, The Bengal Legislative Council refused to vote salaries for Indians appointed as Ministers of departments transferred by coalition vote of Swarajists and Independents of 69 to 63

March 25, The Government resumed charge of the administration of the transferred subjects on resignation of Ministers in Bengal Province

March 27, Death of Lord Rawlinson, Commander of Indian Army (63) at Delhi. Succeeded in office by Sir William Birdwood

March 30, Mr. C. R. Das, leader of the Swaraj Party issued manifesto publicly dissociating himself from "political assassination and violence in any shape or form"

March 31, Lord Birkenhead, Secretary of State for India, in speech on the revolutionary crimes in Bengal invited Mr. Das "to coöperate with the Government in repressing the violence which he deprecates"

April 3, Statement of Mr. Das in reply to Lord Birkenhead condemned the Bengal Act and declared himself unable to coöperate with the Government in "its present policy of repression"

April–June, Strike of employees of North Western Railway over discharge of workman for persisting in circulating petition during working hours

April 10, Lord Reading, Viceroy and Governor General, sailed for England to consult with the Secretary of State for India, and Lord Lytton, Governor of Bengal acted as Viceroy *ad interim*

April 11, Meeting of the All-India Hindu Mahasabha under the presidency of Lala Lajpatrai at Calcutta and resolutions adopted for promotion of Hindu religion and organizations included one relating to collection of funds for relief of sufferers in the Kohat riots of Sept., 1924

May 1, The Mahsuds accepted peace terms after 54 days of operations by the Royal Air Force over hostile areas which ended raiding for arms and abducting Hindus

May 1, Mr. Gandhi addressed meeting in Bombay giving his program as Hindu-Muslim unity, the removal of untouchability, and the use of the spinning wheel

May 3, Mr. Das presiding over meeting of the Bengal Provincial Conference defining independence for India stated that the Indian National Congress had always desired that India should remain within the British Empire if the Empire recognized her rights

June 13, Resolution of the Government directed that the transfer of all the transferred subjects in the province of Bengal should be suspended from this date to Jan. 21, 1927 because of rejection by provincial Council of the demand for the salaries of ministers

June 16, Death of Chit Ranjan Das, leader of the Swaraj (Home Rule) Party

June 25, The South African Color Bill passed third reading in the Assembly but rejected by Senate July. *See* South Africa

July 2, Celebration of the Moslem religious festival Bakr Id (baqarah id or cow festival), the slaughter of cows being abhorrent to Hindu religious sentiment, accompanied by riots between Hindus and Moslems in Calcutta and Allahabad

July 7, The Sikh Gurdwaras and Shrine Bill provided for bringing all Sikh religious places under control of Sikh communities and abolished the office of hereditary priest of the temple; passed by the Punjab Council

——, Speech of Lord Birkenhead on India in the British House of Lords declared that revision of the Constitution depended on creation of certain conditions and there would be no reconsideration of the 1919 Constitution until the responsible leaders of Indian thought showed evidence of a genuine desire to coöperate in making the best of the existing Constitution

July 16, Pandit Motilal Nehru elected leader of the Swaraj (Home Rule) Party to succeed Mr. Das

Aug. 6, Death of Sir Surendranath Banerjea

Aug. 25, Election of Pandit Motilal Nehru President of the Legislative Assembly (Lower House) the first Indian to hold the office

Sept. 7, "National Demand" Resolution adopted in Assembly called for Round Table Conference representative of Indian and Anglo-Indian interests to frame scheme for responsible government

Sept. 15, Resolution of Legislative Assembly extended grant of steel bounties to March 31, 1927

——, Strike of cotton operatives of Bombay begun against reduction of wages, which lasted until December

Sept. 21, Act to encourage and develop the bamboo paper industry

Sept. 27, Resolution introduced in Assembly by Sir D. Sarvadhikary recommending restriction of the cultivation of opium defeated

Sept. 28, Resolution recommending total prohibition as ultimate policy to be adopted by the Government and local option as a first step adopted in Assembly by majority of 30 votes

Oct. 29, Edward F. L. Wood afterwards Lord Irwin appointed Viceroy and Governor General to succeed the Earl of Reading in April, 1926

Nov. 2, First train passed through the Khyber Pass in extension of railroad from Jamrud to Landi Kotal

Nov. 25, Deputation to South Africa sailed to inquire into conditions of the resident Indians in that country

Dec. 1, Gazetted Ordinance suspended the levy and collection of the cotton excise duty

——, Mill owners of Bombay restored wages in cotton mills to former level ending strike

Dec. 22, Workmens' Compensation Consolidation Act passed

Dec. 24–28, Indian National Congress met at Cawnpore, Mrs. Sarojini Naidu, President, only 3 Muslims present, the Ali Brothers and Maulvi Abdul Kalam Azad. Resolution stated that work in the Legislatures should be carried on for the early establishment of full responsible Government coöperation when necessary or obstruction whichever would advance the national cause, and failing compliance of Government with Resolution of Feb. 18, 1924 all Swarajists should vacate their seats in all Legislatures. A number of delegates declared for a program of responsive coöperation

Dec. 31, Meeting of leading Indian politicians at Calcutta to further the cause of responsive coöperation

1926

Jan. 20, Legislative Assembly at Delhi opened by Lord Reading

Feb. 1, Announcement that the Government had decided to appoint a Commission of Enquiry into the alleged connection of the Maharaja Holkar of Indore with the murder of Mr. Bawla in Bombay on Jan. 12, 1925

Feb. 7, Mr. Elkins, Assistant Superintendent of Police in the Mardan subdivision of the Peshawar district, was shot dead by a tribesman he was trying to arrest near the Swat border

Feb. 8, First Trade Unions Bill passed the Assembly

Feb. 9, The Viceroy announced the creation of the Royal Indian Navy and the reconstruction of the Indian Mercantile Marine

Feb. 25, Sir Hari Singh crowned Maharaja of Jammu and Kashmir

Feb. 26, Formal abdication of the Maharaja Holkar of Indore in favor of his son Maharajadhiraja Yeshwant Rao II Holkar Bahadur

March 8, On debate on the budget the Swarajist Party left the Assembly after a speech by their leader, Pandit Motilal Nehru, in which he claimed that the Swarajists in the Central Legislature had shown the fullest coöperation of which they were capable and had helped to work the reforms for 2½ years and had received nothing in return but humiliation

March 25, Trade Union Act provided system of registration and regulations

March 27, The Secretary of State for India refused the petition of the Nizam of Hyderabad for restoration of the Berar Province leased to British Government in perpetuity in 1902

April 1, Lord Irwin, new Governor General and Viceroy, arrived in Bombay

April 3, New National Party formed at meeting in Bombay of Responsivists, Independents, and Moderates "to prepare for and accelerate the establishment of the Swaraj or full responsible Government in India, such as obtains in the self-governing dominions of the British Empire, with a due provision for the protection of the rights and interests of minorities and the backward and depressed classes," the employment of all peaceful and legitimate means to be used not including mass civil disobedience or the general non-payment of taxes, and the members to resort to responsive coöperation in the Legislatures when necessary

April 5, Riots between Muslims and Hindus in Calcutta suppressed by the police but continued during April and May in excess of murder, burning, and looting worse than in many years with more than 100 killed and a thousand injured

April 12, Murder of the Commandant of the Frontier Constabulary, E. C. Handyside

April 21, Meeting of the new Indian National Party and the old Swaraj Party headed by Pandit Motilal Nehru at Subarmati reached agreement known as the Subarmati Pact that the response made by the Government to the demand of Feb., 1924 should be considered satisfactory in the provinces if power and responsibility necessary was secured to Ministers

April 23, Agreement with Union of South Africa for Conference. *See* South Africa

May 27, Abdication of the Begum of Bhopal in favor of her son

June 1, Riot in Calcutta in which 40 persons hurt

June 4, The Bengal Government laid down rules to be observed in Calcutta as to music by religious processions prohibiting playing near buildings during hours of public worship

June 11, Announcement of the Government of decision to stop the export of opium for purposes other than medicinal and scientific within 10 years, that is by Dec. 31, 1935

June 14–15, Riots between Hindus and Muslims at Rawalpindi, largest military station in India, the worst of the year, begun by Sikh procession with band playing past the chief mosque, 16 persons killed and 90 injured, and many shops and houses burned

June 24, Religious riot in Delhi

July 1–7, Religious riots in the Pabna district of Bengal

July 5, Announcement of decision to admit women to membership in Indian Legislatures

July 9, Recognition of succession of Nawab Haji Hamidullah Khan as ruler of Bhopal succeeding his mother abdicating

July 15, Religious riot in Calcutta in which 14 persons killed and 116 injured occasioned by passage of Hindu procession with band playing past certain mosques

Aug. 23, The Swarajists who had left the Central Legislature in March returned

Aug. 27, Conflict of Hindus and Muslims in Delhi, 50 persons injured

Sept. 18, South African deputation to discuss position of Indians in South Africa arrived in Bombay

Sept., Death of Sir Pratrap Singh (76), Maharaja of Jammu and Kashmir

Oct. 19–Nov. 23, Imperial Conference in London, India represented by the Secretary of State for India, the Secretary to the Government of India, Department of Commerce, and the Maharaja of Burdwan

Nov. 13, Indian Sandhurst Committee headed by Sir Andrew Skeen, presented Report recommending progressive employment of Indians in higher ranks of the Army, and extension of facilities for training Indians

Nov. 24, Indian delegation headed by Sir Muhammad Habibullah Sahib Bahadur sailed for South Africa

Dec. 17–Jan. 11, 1927, Conference of Indians with Government of South Africa to discuss problems of Indians domiciled in South Africa. *See* South Africa

Dec. 28, Swami Shradhanand (Munshi Ram) shot dead at Delhi by a Mohammedan fanatic

Dec., Swarajists defeated in elections

Dec. 29, Indian National Conference concluded session at which revival of boycott of foreign cloth revived and non-coöperation

1927

Jan. 5, Sir Samuel Hoare, Secretary of State for Air, inaugurated the Egypt to India air service, arriving at Karachi from Cairo after flight from London, 6,300 miles in 63 flying hours

Jan. 10, Sir Harcourt Butler held durbar at Myitkyina and announced to the Kachin Chiefs of the Triangle that slavery must be abolished and slaves in that area would be liberated by the Government

Jan. 18, The new Council House at Delhi formally inaugurated by the Viceroy

Jan. 19, Delhi Session of the Legislative Assembly opened in new Council House

Jan. 31, Discovery by customs officer at Karachi of six dies for counterfeiting rupees bringing to light a conspiracy with connections in Quetta, Duzdap, Karachi, Birmingham, London, and Liverpool

Feb. 1, Bill introduced by Rai Sahib Harbilas Sarda proposed prohibition of marriage of Hindu children of girls below the age of 12 and of boys below the age of 15, the primary object to put a stop to child widowhood

Feb. 9, Resolution passed in the Council of State recommended prohibition in the local administrations under direct control of the Government of India which was amended to recommend that a policy designed to promote and ensure moderation in the use of alcoholic liquors would be adopted in said local administrations

Feb. 16, The first railway connecting India with Nepal was opened formally by the Maharajadhiraja of Nepal

Feb. 21, Announcement read in both Houses regarding settlement reached with the Union of South Africa regarding status of Indians domiciled in the Union

March 2, Religious conflict of Hindus and Mohammedans at Kulkathi in the Barisal district of Bengal, 1,000 Mohammedans opposed Hindu procession passing the mosque with music; 14 rioters killed and 7 injured by fire of the troops

March 16, Resolution of Sir Sankaran Sair asked the Council to recommend to the Governor General in Council that no further progress should be undertaken in India until the system of communal electorates had been abolished, but after discussion Resolution withdrawn

March 20, Mohammedan Conference at Delhi met to discuss system of communal electorates

March 26, Currency Act established gold standard fixing rupee at ratio of 1s. 6d.

——, British troops in expedition into upper reaches of the Irrawaddy River effected release of 4,000 slaves

March 28, Budget introduced Feb. 28 passed, called for 1,253,000,000 rupees

April 1, Report of the Indian Sandhurst Committee presented

April 5, Bill creating separate Indian Navy passed third reading in the Imperial House of Commons

April 10, Swarajists defeated in elections for Calcutta City Corporation

May 3 and 7, Riots between the 2 communities of Hindus and Mohammedans at Lahore, 27 killed and 272 injured

May 27, Conference held at Simla between representatives of the Government of India and of Indian States as to relations as to opium policy, and a committee appointed to consider the recommendation of the Government of India that opium cultivation be discontinued in the States

June 7, Report of special Tariff Board published with decisions of the Government agreeing to remove import duties on certain classes of mill stores and machinery permanently, but rejecting proposal for bounty on spinning of finer counts of yarn and increase of duty on cotton piece goods and differential duty against Japan

July 22, The Kukikhel and Zakkakhel Afridis (Mohammedan) on North West frontier expelled Hindus from their district in neighborhood of Kyber Pass

July 23, First station for commercial broadcasting opened by the Viceroy at Bombay

Aug. 6, Judgment delivered in "Rangila Rasul" case imposed sentence of imprisonment for 1 year and 6 months to one of accused for publication of scurrilous attack on the Prophet Mohammed and fine of Rs. 500, and 6 months and fine of Rs. 250 to second accused, which had an immediate pacific effect on inter-communal strife which had been increased by miscarriage of justice in similar case of publication of pamphlet, the "Rangila Rasul"

Aug. 22, Judgment given in final appeal against Jogesh Chandra Chatterji and Sachindra Nath Sanyal convicted of conspiracy in 1924 organized to establish a Federated Republic of the United States of India by armed revolution

Aug. 26, Calcutta broadcasting station opened by the Viceroy

Aug. 29, Lord Irwin's address to the Legislature discussed the situation arising from the inter-communal antagonism of Hindus and Mohammedans with between 250 and 300 persons killed in 18 months and over 2,500 injured

Sept. 4, Communal riots at Nagpur in Central Provinces in connection with a Mohammedan procession, 19 killed and 123 injured admitted to hospital

Sept. 7, Reduction of labor force in Bengal Nagpur Railway work shops of about 1,600 men caused passive resistance strike so that shops were closed Sept. 12 and not reopened until Dec. 8 when men consented to work

Sept. 22, Indian Tariff (Cotton Yarn Amendment Bill) provided for safeguarding duty on cotton yarn until March 31, 1930

Oct. 27, Unity Conference at Calcutta discussed cowslaughter of Mohammedans and music of Hindus near mosques allowing each freedom but urging avoidance of action to cause offense to each other

Nov. 8, Announcement in Parliament by Viceroy of appointment of Statutory Commission on Indian Reforms headed by Sir John Simon (appointed Nov. 26) membership limited to members of Parliament. Great resentment in India because no Indian members

Dec. 14, Visit of King Amanullah and Queen of Afghanistan

Dec. 22, Act of Imperial Parliament repealed law by which the Bishop of Calcutta as Metropolitan of India and Ceylon had been subject to "general superintendence and revision ' of the Archbishop of Canterbury

Dec. 23, Swami Shradanand, Hindu leader, assassinated by Moslem fanatic

Dec. 26, All-India National Congress opened and passed resolution covering political and religious points of issue between the 2 communities, joint electorates and concessions in favor of minorities, and a resolution declaring the goal of the Indian people was complete national independence. "Unity Resolution" in opposition to Simon Commission adopted

Dec. 27, National Liberal Federation of India opened in Bombay declared against the Simon Commission

Dec. 30, All-India Muslim League opened at Calcutta under presidency of Maulvi Muhammad Yakoob and passed resolution in favor of boycotting the Simon Commission

Dec. 31, All-India Muslim League opened at Calcutta under presidency of Maulvi Muhammad Yakoob and passed resolution in favor of boycotting the Simon Commission

——, All-India Muslim League under presidency of Sir Muhammad Shafi opened in separate session marking split of the Party in Lahore, and an All-India Committee of 30 members appointed to draw up a constitution for India

1928

Jan. 27, Trade Commission headed by D. B. Meek started for the Near East and Africa to make survey of potential markets for India cotton goods

Feb. 1, Delhi session of Legislature opened

Feb. 3, Arrival of Sir John Simon and Commission at Bombay. A hartal agreed upon in National Congress in December not successful in Bombay but riots in Madras and Calcutta to enforce stoppage of work

Feb. 6, Letter of Sir John Simon to Viceroy proposed that the Commission should take the form of a "Joint Free Conference" of 7 British Commissioners and an equal number of representatives chosen by the Indian Legislatures

——, Answer to this letter signed by prominent Indians of the Congress, Nationalist and Independent Parties in the Assembly adhered to decision to have nothing to do with the Simon Commission

Feb. 7, All-India Women's Conference opened by Lady Irwin which adopted resolutions urging necessity of compulsory education for girls

Feb. 12, "All-Parties Conference" opened at Delhi to discuss drafting of a constitution giving India full responsible government and settlement of Hindu-Muslim differences, which adjourned March 11 to meet in Bombay on May 19

Feb. 18, Resolution adopted by Legislative Assembly defeated proposal to coöperate with the Simon Statutory Commission by vote of 68 to 62. A reporter of Nationalist newspaper threw a brief case at head of Sir Basil Blackett from the gallery, stunning him but not seriously injuring him

Feb. 22, Resolution of coöperation with the Simon Statutory Commission adopted by the Council by vote of 34 to 13

Feb. 23, Resolution adopted proposed by Mr. Jayakar, leader of the Responsive Coöperators in Assembly that the Government direct that special facilities for education of the untouchables and other depressed classes in the provinces be provided and that the public services be opened to them

March 5, Passive resistance strike of railway employees for increase in wages caused closing of shops, lasted until July 10 (East Indian Railway)

——, Death of Lord Sinha, first Indian Advocate General

March 8, Announcement by Government that number of direct vacancies open to Indians at Sandhurst was increased from 10 to 50, and a further number up to 10 with the Viceroy's commission

March 27, Steel Industry Protection Act modified import duties

March 28, Rioting railway strikers at Barangachi dispersed by police

March 31, Simon Commission sailed for England from Bombay

April 11, Flight of French pilots Costes and Le Brix from Calcutta to Karachi established record for fastest flight across India

April 12, Judgment given in Duzdap coining conspiracy (counterfeiting) case sentenced Dickinson and Wheeler and 4 others to long terms of imprisonment

April 26–Oct. 6, General strike of textile workers in Bombay

June 17, Death of Sir Alexander Muddiman, Governor of the United Provinces; succeeded by Sir Malcolm Hailey

June 29, Strike on the South Indian Railway because of reduction of workmen in shops by 3,171 which became general on the railway July 19 and lasted until July 30

July 4, Jaji tribesmen raided Walai China village across the border into British territory and drove off 450 head of cattle and militia turning out to aid villagers fired on from covering party of Jajis inside Afghan territory

Aug. 16–Oct. 8, Strike in railway shops Nizam State Railways

Aug. 28, All Parties Conference at Lucknow adopted Nehru Report in favor of Dominion status for India, and in favor of separation of Sind from Bombay

Aug. 30, Independence of India League formed by son of Pandit Motilal Nehru, Pandit Jawharlal Nehru, attacking Dominion status

Sept. 4, Public Safety Bill introduced by the Government directed against Communists which was later defeated by casting vote of the President of the Assembly

Sept. 20, Mines Amendment Act restricted hours of labor and introduced a system of shifts in mines to come into effect April 7, 1930

Oct. 11, The Simon Commission arrived on second visit to India

Nov. 3, The All India Congress Committee adopted resolution repudiating Dominion status and declaring for independence of the British Empire

Nov. 17, Death of Lala Lajpat Rai, Swarajist leader

Dec. 7, Strike of employees of Oil Companies in Bombay which lasted until Feb.

Dec. 11, Sarda (Oudh) Canal formally opened in Sarda River irrigation system

Dec. 15, Death of the Raja of Panagal, leader of the Non-Brahim Party

Dec. 17, J. P. Saunders, assistant superintendent of police shot by Indian youth at Lahore

Dec. 22, All-Parties Conference at Calcutta

Dec. 23, Evacuation of Europeans and Indians from Kabul, Afghanistan begun by Royal Air Force

Dec. 28, New dock at Calcutta named after the King-Emperor opened by the Viceroy

Dec. 30, All-India Liberal Federation met at Allahabad passed resolutions according support to the Nehru Report and for immediate establishment of Dominion status

Dec. 31–Jan. 1, All-India Moslem Conference met at Delhi and adopted resolution urging a federal constitution with complete provincial autonomy with all residual powers, and that Muslim demands be met in any future constitution of India, the adoption of conditions stated would ensure Moslem control in provinces where they are in a majority, namely the Punjab, Bengal, and the North-West Frontier Province, Baluchistan and Snd, if or when these 3 latter become provinces

1929

Jan. 1, In Indian Civil Service 894 Europeans held positions and 367 Indians while according to program of reform on Jan. 1, 1939 it is estimated that there would be 715 Europeans and 643 Indians, and in Police Service 564 Europeans and 128 Indians to be 434 Europeans and 251 Indians on Jan. 1, 1939

Jan. 28, Lord Irwin, Viceroy, opened Legislative Assembly at Delhi and in speech reaffirmed the pledge of the British Government of Aug., 1917 that "all that can be done by one people to assist another to attain full national political stature" will be done to help India reach the goal of self-government

Feb. 4–5, Hindu strikers of Bombay Oil Companies began attack on Pathans employed to take their places, 17 Pathans killed and many injured, troops called to help the police restore order until Feb. 12 when conditions returned to normal, the total killed in riots 149

Feb. 25, The Royal Air Force completed evacuation of Europeans and Indians from Kabul having made 86 trips under fire from tribesmen bringing to safety 343 Indians, 57 Germans, 49 Turks, 25 Persians, 23 French, 23 British, and 19 Italians including the British, French, and Italian Legations

March 4, Gandhi arrested after riots in Calcutta but released on the following day on his own bond

March 20, Under the sedition law the police arrested about 100 Communists in different cities

March 28, The two rival sections of the All-India Muslim League reunited in meeting in Delhi, and resolution enumerating the safeguards which they wished to see incorporated in a constitution for India framed by Mr. Jinnah as counter-proposals to the Nehru Report

March 29, Workmens' Compensation Act amended

March 30, The All-India Hindu Mahasabha met at Surat and adopted resolution declaring that as the Muslim leaders had rejected the Nehru Report the Mahasabha had decided to return to original position in which it opposed special treatment in any matter to any community

March 30–April 6, Flight of the "City of Glasgow" from London to Karachi inaugurating weekly mail air service between England and India

April 2, Legislative Assembly met after Easter holidays and Mr. Patel, the President, refused to allow discussion of the Public Safety Bill because of probable reference to the Meerut conspiracy trial; this not accepted by the Government as within the powers of the President

April 2–4, Meetings of the Simon Commission and Central Committee with the Provincial Committees at Delhi which included representatives of all except the Central Provinces who refused to coöperate

April 6–Nov. 19, Unsuccessful strike of employees of Tinplate Works at Golmuri for better conditions and increase in wages

April 8, Bomb thrown from the gallery to the floor of the House injured 5 persons, the perpetrators, Bhagat Singh and Bhaktesawr Dutt arrested and sentenced to transportation for life

April 12, Trade Disputes Act enacted

——, Public Safety Bill promulgated by ordinance of the Viceroy

April 14, The Simon Commission left for England

April 16, Report of the Indian States Committee presented to the Imperial Parliament

April 26, Arrival of Jones-Williams and Jenkins from England at Karachi after non-stop flight of 4,130 miles in slightly over 50 hours establishing a new British record in long distance flying

May 23, Council of Agricultural Research established by the Government

——, King Amanulla with his wife and brother crossed the border from Afghanistan as refugees

June 9, Floods begun in Assam and Surma Valleys reached record height with great destruction of crops and property and in Burma and Bengal during the month

July 3, First court of enquiry set up under Trade Disputes Act to deal with the strike in the Bombay textile industry

Sept. 2–26, Simla Session of the Legislative Assembly

Sept. 12, Bill to amend the Code of Criminal Procedure (the Hunger Strike Bill) introduced but Government agreed to circulation of the Bill for further opinion after abandonment of hunger strike of prisoners at Lahore

Sept. 14, Death of Jatindranath Das, 23-year-old leader of Bengal Youth Movement after 61 day hunger strike in prison at Lahore

Sept. 23, The Legislative Assembly passed Child Marriage Bill third reading and the Council on the 28th and received assent Oct. 1 prohibiting marriage of boys under 18 and girls under 14

Oct. 18, Report of Indian Central Committee presented and published on the 24th recommended autonomy for the provinces and that dyarchy be introduced in the Central Government

Oct. 25, The Viceroy, Lord Irwin, arrived in India after 4 months visit in England

Oct. 31, Announcement of the Viceroy that after the Simon Commission had reported a Conference would be held of representatives of the British Government, British India, and the Indian States to formulate proposals for a new Constitution for India, and that "it is implicit in the Declaration of 1917 that the natural issue of India's constitutional progress, as there contemplated, is the attainment of Dominion Status"

Nov. 2, Manifesto of Indian leaders representing all groups in meetings at Bombay and Delhi stated that they hoped "to be able to tender . . . coöperation"

Dec. 23, The Viceroy received Mr. Gandhi, Pandit Motilal Nehru, Sir Tej Bahadur Sapru, Liberal leader, Mr. Jinnah, Moslem, and Mr. Patel, President of the Legislative Assembly to discuss the Government proposals

Dec. 23, Bomb thrown in attempt to wreck train on which Lord and Lady Irwin were returning to Delhi

Dec. 29, National Liberal Federation met at Madras, and Sir P. Sethna, President, urged all Parties to unite to secure a constitution based on Dominion Status

——, All-India National Congress met at Lahore

Dec. 31–Jan. 1, Resolution adopted by the Indian National Congress declared that the word "*Swaraj*" in Article 1 of the Congress constitution shall mean complete independence, and the Nehru Committee Report to have lapsed, the program of this Congress to be a complete boycott of the central and provincial legislatures, and the All-India Congress Committee to launch a program of civil disobedience including non-payment of taxes as soon as it deems fit, the Congress not to be represented at the proposed Round Table

1930

Jan. 20, Delhi Session of the Central Legislature opened

Jan. 26, "Independence Day" celebrated and newly devised national flag raised in all centers, riots between Communists and Nationalists, the former demanding active anti-British revolt, the latter passive resistance

Jan. 30, Committee appointed in 1928 to investigate facilities provided for Indian pilgrims proceeding on *Haj* from Calcutta, Bombay, and Karachi to the Hejaz presented report recommending a permanent standing committee

Feb. 1–13, Strike of 13,000 miners at the Kurharbaree and Serampur collieries on the East Indian Railway for increase

Feb. 4–March 31, Unsuccessful grievance strike of 20,000 members of the Great Indian Peninsula Railwaymen's Union

Feb. 28, Strike of men employed in sheds and workshops of the Nizam State Railways which ended March 18 over bonus

March 1, Legal union of the Church of England in India with Church of England terminated under law of 1927

March 3, R. N. Chawla with A. M. Engineer, passenger started flight from Karachi successfully completing trip to England in 17 days

March 4, Ultimatum of Mr. Gandhi to the Viceroy announced intention to inaugurate civil disobedience unless immediate steps taken to end British "exploitation"

March 12, Civil disobedience campaign against British rule in India as Mr. Gandhi and about 80 of his followers began march from near Ahmedabad, the home of Gandhi, for the Gulf of Cambay to make salt in violation of the law

March 21, Steel Protection Industry Act amended

March 29, Agreement at Kohat provided for return of the Shiah Orakzais to the lands held by them prior 1927 in Tirah

March 31, Indian Cotton Tariff Act passed the Legislature imposed protective duties on all classes of imported cotton piecegoods to the extent of 15 or 20% *ad valorem* according as they are of British or non-British manufacture subject to a minimum specific duty, and extended for 3 years the minimum specific duty under Cotton Yarn Amendment Act of 1927

April 1, Child Marriage Act came into effect. *See* Sept. 23, 1929

——, Riots of striking carters in Calcutta

April 4, Riots of railway strikers in Bombay, 30 injured

April 5, Gandhi and his followers arrived at Dandi on the seacoast and began making salt on the next day

April 6, Ram Das Gandhi, son of Mahatma Gandhi, and several others arrested at Dandi engaged in manufacture of salt from sea water in violation of the salt monopoly, first open breach of law

April 7, Riots of railways strikers at Bhusawal and Oorgaum, 50 injured, 1 killed

April 9, Religious riots at the holy Hindu city of Nasik, 100 casualties

April 11, Serious riots outside Bombay and Calcutta precipitated by Gandhi's salt campaign, 22 persons injured in Bombay

April 14, Pandit Jawarhalal Nehru, President of the All-India National Congress and J. M. Sen Gupta, Mayor of Calcutta arrested for abetting the manufacture of contraband salt and sentenced to 6 months imprisonment

April 15, Riots and street fighting in Calcutta, street cars burned and attacks on Europeans and police

April 16, Mob at Karachi attack court house where trials are proceeding and are fired on by police, 1 killed and many injured

April 18–19, Indian rebels attack Chittagong, Bengal, destroy railroad and police arsenal killing 7 guards and carrying off a thousand rifles. Bengal Ordinance introduced on the 19th as a result

——, Series of bomb explosions in 6 towns in Punjab

April 20, Disturbance in Patna

April 22, In Madras 50,000 Nationalists dispersed by troops

April 23, British and Indian troops in conflict with Nationalists at Peshawar because of arrest of members of provincial Congress Committee

April 25, Statement of Mr. Gandhi demanding redress of grievances and removal of salt tax

April 27, The Viceroy revived Press Act of 1910 establishing a rigorous censorship of the press and suspending practically all native papers to restrict Nationalist propaganda

May 2, Riots in Amritsar

May 3, Lord Irwin prorogued both Houses of the Legislature

May 5, Mahatma Gandhi, Nationalist leader in campaign of civil disobedience arrested at his camp at Jalapur and interned at jail in Yaravad near Poona

——, Earthquake at Burma with great loss of life and property

May 6, Riots at Delhi, Calcutta, and other cities and towns and hartal observed to protest against the arrest of Gandhi

May 8, Attack of mobs on police at Sholapur in Bombay Presidency, police stations burned, and the court house, 25 persons killed and 100 injured

May 11, Force of 4,000 Wazirs attacked Datta Khel Post

May 13, Martial law declared at Sholapur and 200 persons arrested in various parts of India for connection with riots

May 15, Attempt of Mrs. Sarojini Naidu to lead raid on the salt depot at Dharasana collapsed when she is threatened with arrest after sitting 28 hours in the road in front of a cordon of police

May 15–17, Riots at Mymsenin (Bengal)

May 18, Nationalists of Bombay raid the Government salt works at Wadala doing considerable damage, nearly 500 captured by the police and confined to barbed-wire prison pens

May 19, Nationalists conduct another raid on salt works at Wadala, 72 arrested

May 21, Raid of Nationalists on salt works at Dharasana near Bulsar result in 630 casualties and arrest of Mrs. Naidu, leader of civil disobedience campaign, Manilal, second son of Mahatma Gandhi. V. J. Patel assumed command of the civil disobedience campaign

May 23, Mrs. Naidu sentenced to 9 months in jail and Manilal Gandhi to 1 year for their revolutionary activities

May 25, Moslems combine with Hindus in attack on the Wadala salt works in Bombay, 30,000 participating, defended by police, much salt stolen and scores injured

——, Riot at Lucknow

——, Riot at Mardan near Peshawar, Mr. Murphy, assistant superintendent of police killed

May 27, 82 persons killed and 740 injured in race riots of Burmese and Indian dockers in Rangoon, Lucknow, Dacca, and Bombay

May 29, Battle of police and Nationalists supporting civil disobedience at Lucknow ended with calling out of squadron of cavalry

——, Riot in Calcutta

May 30, Death toll from riots in Rangoon arising from a strike of dock laborers and conflict of Indian and Burmese laborers rises to 174 and 1,500 injured

May 31, Cavalry break up attack on the salt pans of Dharasana

June 1–2, Battle between natives and police in Peshawur, martial law declared

June 5, Afridis advancing on Peshawur repulsed by British and Indian troops

June 9, First volume of the Report of the Simon Commission presented, published on the 13th and the second volume on the 24th, met with hostility by Nationalists

——, Disturbance at Amritsar

June 11, Meeting of 20,000 Moslems in Bombay repudiate the civil disobedience campaign

June 30, Pandit Motilal Nehru and other Nationalists arrested

July 1, 8, 9, 10, 11, 17, 19, 23, Riots in various places in connection with civil disobedience

July 8, India House in London formally opened by the King

July 9, Conciliatory speech of Lord Irwin, Viceroy, at Legislative Assembly at Simla

July 11, Followers of Gandhi in conflict with police at Bombay

Aug. 12, Royal Air Force bombed Afridi villages in retaliation for raids on Peshawar

Aug. 15, Martial law established at Peshawar

Aug. 25, Assault made on Sir Charles Tegart, Commissioner of Police, on streets of Calcutta

Aug. 29, Murder of F. J. Lowman, Inspector-General of Police, Bengal, at Dacca

Oct. 29, Pandit Nehru sentenced to 2 years' imprisonment for seditious actions

Nov. 12–Jan. 19, 1931, Round Table Conference in London opened by British Government and members of Parliament (13) and 76 Indians nominated by Lord Irwin, Viceroy (16 representing the Indian States and 60 the Provinces of British India) representing all races, religions, and castes who united in demanding responsible self-government for India, all minorities other than Sikhs acting together as one body in asserting claims and rights. The Indian princes announced willingness to enter a federated Indian government. The Conference ended with announcement of Prime Minister MacDonald of agreement of Government to federal plan and policy of placing responsibility for the government of India on central and provincial legislatures. On Nov. 20 the Brahmans and other high-caste Indians and Mohammedans agreed in writing that the "untouchables" should have political equality in proportion to their numbers in new Constitution. The Mohammedans demanded continuance of separate electorates and assurance of share in the government of Mohammedan minorities in Hindu communities. Draft Report adopted of agreement that as soon as possible an All-India Federation should be created with a responsible governing body, and that certain powers should be reserved from this central body to the British Government as to protection of minorities, fulfilment of Indian obligations to the outside world, and maintenance of peace. On Jan. 13, a letter published in the "Times" by Hindu representatives declared agreement of Hindus and Mohammedans to submit communal question to arbitration but the Sikhs refused to agree

Dec. 1, Agreement that Burma should be separated from India

Dec. 8, Raid of 3 Bengalis on Secretariat of the Government in Calcutta shot and killed Lieutenant-Colonel Simpson and wounded others

——and 12, Riots in Bombay

Dec. 19, Announcement of appointment of Viscount Willingdon to succeed Lord Irwin in April as Viceroy

Dec. 22, Revolt in Burma begun by native uprising in the Tharrawaddy District in the south

Dec. 23, At convocation of the Punjab University at Lahore the Governor Sir Geoffrey Montmorency shot and wounded by student

Dec. 31, In the 9 months since the beginning of the civil disobedience campaign in April 54,000 persons convicted of offenses and 23,000 in prison at end of year

1931

Jan. 26, Mr. Gandhi released from prison

March 5, "Delhi Pact" signed, civil disobedience to be discontinued, boycott of British goods to cease, work of Round Table Conference to be recognized, the Government to withdraw Ordinances which Nationalists had fought

April 17, The new Viceroy, Lord Willingdon, arrived in India

The following is a list of the past Governors-General of India, with the dates of their assumption of office:—

Warren Hastings	1774
Sir John Macpherson	1785
Earl (Marquis) Cornwallis	1786
Sir John Shore (Lord Teignmouth)	1793
Marquis Wellesley	1798
Marquis Cornwallis	1805
Sir Geo. H. Barlow	1805
Earl of Minto	1807
Earl of Moirs (Marquis of Hastings)	1813
Earl Amherst	1823

Lord W. C. Bentinck	1828
Lord Auckland	1836
Lord Ellenborough	1842
Sir H. (Lord) Hardinge	1844
Earl (Marquis) of Dalhousie	1848
Lord Canning	1856
Earl of Elgin	1862
Sir John (Lord) Lawrence	1864
Earl of Mayo	1869
Lord (Earl of) Northbrook	1876
Lord (Earl) Lytton	1876
Marquis of Ripon	1880
Earl (Marquis) of Dufferin	1884
Marquis of Lansdowne	1888
Earl of Elgin	1894
Lord (Marquis) Curzon of Kedleston . . .	1899
Earl of Minto	1905
Lord (Viscount) Hardinge of Penshurst . . .	1910
Lord (Viscount) Chelmsford	1916
Earl (Marquis) of Reading	1921
Lord (Baron) Irwin	1926
Lord Willingdon	1931

INDIA COMPANY, EAST

The first commercial intercourse of the English with the East Indies was a private adventure of three ships fitted out in 1591. Only one of them reached India; and, after a voyage of three years, the commander, Captain Lancaster, was brought home in another ship, the sailors having seized his own; but his information gave rise to a mercantile voyage, and the establishment of a company, whose first charter, in Dec., 1600, was renewed in 1609, 1657, 1661, 1693, and 1744. Its stock in 1600 consisted of 72,000*l.*, when it fitted out four ships. Meeting with success, it continued to trade, and India stock sold at 500*l.* for a share of 100*l.* in 1683.

1698 to 1853

Sept. 5, 1698, A new company (the "English") was chartered, and the old (the "London") suspended from trading for three years; the two were united, 1702

1704, New East India company established

1748, Privileges of the company continued till 1783

Aug., 1772, Affairs of the company were brought before parliament, and a committee exposed a series of intrigues and crimes

June, 1773, As remedial measures two acts passed (one authorized a loan of 1,000,000*l.* to the company; the other celebrated as the India bill), effected most important changes in the constitution of the company and its relations to India. A governor-general was appointed to reside in Bengal, to which the other presidencies were then made subordinate; a supreme court of judicature was instituted at Calcutta: the salary of the governor was fixed at 25,000*l.* per year; that of the council at 10,000*l.* each; and of the chief judge at 8,000*l.*; the affairs of the company were controlled; all the departments were reorganized, and all the territorial correspondence was henceforth to be laid before the British ministry

May 18, 1784, Mr. Pitt's bill appointing the Board of Control, passed

1793, The Company's Charter was renewed for 20 years

1813, Trade with India thrown open

1833, Trade to China opened; Charter renewed till 1854

1853, The government of India was continued in the hands of the Company till Parliament should otherwise provide

1858

Aug. 2, In consequence of the mutiny of 1857, and the disappearance of the company's army, the Government of India was transferred to the Crown, the Board of Control was abolished, and a Council of State for India instituted by the act 21 & 22 Vict. c. 106, which received the royal assent

Nov. 1, The Company's political power ceased on Sept. 1, and Queen Victoria was proclaimed as Queen of Great Britain and the Colonies, &c., in the principal places in India, amid much enthusiasm

1873

May 15, The company to be dissolved, June 1, 1874, and dividends redeemed, by the "East India Stock Dividend Redemption Act," passed

INDO-CHINA

Indo-China, known also as Farther India; the southeastern peninsula of Asia including the following divisions: Burma, politically attached to British India; Siam, an independent kingdom; French Indo-China, including Annam, Cambodia, Cochin China, Laos, and Tonking; the Federated Malay States; the Straits Settlements proper and the Malay states of Johore, Kedah, Perlis, Kelantan, and Trenggann. *See* French Indo-China, Siam, and the other principal states mentioned above.

IRAQ

Iraq (Mesopotamia) was freed from the Turks during the Great War. It was recognized as an independent State, to be placed under a Mandatory Power, and the mandate was allotted to Great Britain. On December 14, 1927, a treaty was signed between Great Britain and Iraq, by which the former undertook to recognize the latter as an independent State. This treaty has not yet been ratified. Great Britain is to recommend Iraq for admission to the League of Nations in 1932.

The country has an area of 177,148 square miles (the former Turkish vilayets respectively of Baghdad, 113,867 square miles, Basrah, 27,070 square miles, and Mosul, 36,211 square miles) and a population, according to the census of 1920, of 2,849,282.

Feisal, Reigning King, b. 1887, third son of Husein ibn Ali (Grand Sherif and Emir of Mecca, 1908-1916; King of the Hejaz November, 1916; and Caliph March 7, 1924; abdicated October 3, 1925) by the Sherifa Abdiya, daughter of his father's uncle, Abdulla V, Grand Sherif and Emir of Mecca,

1858–1877; Emir in Damascus October 1, 1917; proclaimed King of Syria March 20, 1920; abdicated July 28, 1920; elected and proclaimed King of Iraq August 23, 1921. Married, 1906, the Sherifa Huzayma, daughter of his father's brother, the Sherif Nazir.

1914

June 28, The Turkish Petroleum Company (British 75%, German 25%) obtained from Turkey the right to exclusive exploitation of the oil fields in the Mosul and Baghdad vilayets

Nov. 7, British troops landed in Mesopotamia. For the war in Iraq *see* World War

1916

May 9 and 16, Secret Agreement of France and Great Britain by which Great Britain to have control of the southern half of Mesopotamia, and French "zone of influence" established over vast area, including Mosul

1917

July 2, Proclamation established Small Cause Court to administer existing civil law

1918

Oct. 11, President Wilson's "Fourteen Points" published in local newspapers

Nov. 8, British occupied Mosul

——, Anglo-French declaration that their object in the War in the East is the complete and final enfranchisement of the peoples oppressed by the Turks, "national governments and administrations drawing their authority from the free choice of indigenous populations" to be established

1919

Jan. 10, The British took over the administration of Baghdad

April 18, The Berenguer-Long oil agreement between France and Great Britain, France to have the German 25% in Turkish Petroleum Company

Sept. 15, Anglo-French Convention signed as to territory in the Near East

1920

March 22, The independence of Lebanon proclaimed at Baalbek

April 24, San Remo oil Agreement between France and Great Britain modified that of Jan., 1919

April 25, Mandate for Iraq given to Great Britain by the Supreme Council

May 5, Announcement that Great Britain accepted mandate

June 2, Rising of Arabs at Tel Afar west of Mosul, 2 British officers and their staff killed

June 20, British Government announced that Iraq should be constituted an independent State under temporary mandate

July 2, Arab rising begun which lasted until December

July 12, British declaration invited formation of a committee of Ottoman deputies to elaborate electoral law

Aug. 10, Treaty of peace with Turkey signed at Sèvres recognized British mandate

Oct. 1, Sir Percy Cox, British High Commissioner, appointed Sept. 17, arrived in Iraq

Oct. 4, British troops reoccupied Hit

Oct. 13, Karbala surrendered to the British

Oct. 14, British garrison at Samawa relieved after siege of six weeks

Oct. 19, British garrison at Kufa relieved after siege of nearly three months

Nov. 20, Provisional Council of State for administration established at Baghdad headed by the Naqib of Baghdad

Dec. 23, Anglo-French Convention signed defined boundaries of mandates

Number of British officials, gazetted, 364; non-gazetted, 484; Indians, 2,035

1921

April, Sayid Talib Pasha deported by British on account of seditious activities

June 23, Faisal reached Basra

July 6, Transfer of Powers Ordinance transferred to Iraq Ministers powers executed by British authorities hitherto, supreme authority of High Commissioner unchanged

July 11, The Council of State on motion of the Naqib adopted resolution to offer Faisal, third son of the King of the Hejaz, the crown

Aug. 1, Fortnightly air mail service between Baghdad and Cairo begun

Aug. 23, The High Commissioner proclaimed Emir Faisal, King of Iraq by election of the people as result of plebiscite in which 96% of the inhabitants voted in his favor

Sept. 10, Royal decree appointed Iraqui Council, Sir Saiyid Abd-ur-Rahman, Prime Minister and Naquib al-Ashraf, Baghdad

Mesopotamia assumed its ancient name of Iraq

1922

March, Subjects of Ibn Saud from Akhwan attacked Iraq desert camel corps

March 25, Military Agreement with Great Britain signed

May 5, Treaty of Muhammara between Nejd and Kuwait defining boundaries arranged by Sir Percy Cox signed, repudiated by Ibn Saud later as too favorable to Iraq

June 18, Kurdish insurrection against British started in Suleimaniya

Sept. 5, British officials evacuated Suleimaniya

Oct. 1, Royal Air Force assumed control of imperial forces

Oct. 10, Treaty signed by Great Britain and Iraq regulating relations by which Iraq agreed to be guided by advice of the British High Commissioner in financial, military, and international affairs

Nov. 16, Cabinet resigned

Nov. 22, New Cabinet headed by Abdul Muhsin Beg al-Saadun

Nov. 30, Sheik Mahmud returned to Suleimaniya and established a Kurdish Government with permission of the Administration but immediately began negotiations with the Turks

Dec. 2, Protocols of Uqair signed amending Treaty of Muhmmara accepted by Ibn Saud

1923

Feb. 24, Mahmud's Kurd government declared suspended, aeroplane attack on Suleimaniya March 3 forcing flight of Mahmud

April 22, The Turks ejected from Ruwandez occupied by Iraq and Imperial troops

April 30, Protocol to Treaty of 1922 with Great Britain agreed that the Treaty should terminate upon Iraq becoming a member of the League of Nations and in any case not later than 4 years from the ratification of peace with Turkey (1928)

May 16, Iraq and Imperial troops occupied Suleimaniya

July 1, Railroads taken over by the Government

July 11, Mahmud who had been forced to leave Suleimaniya returned after withdrawal of Iraq garrison

July 24, Treaty of peace with Turkey signed at Lausanne by which Turkey resigned claim to Iraq, the dispute over Mosul beween Great Britain and Turkey to be settled by League of Nations unless agreed upon within 9 months

Sept. 25, Sir Henry Dobbs succeeded Sir Percy Cox as High Commissioner

Oct. 31, Draft Constitution published at Baghdad

Nov. 19, General Jafar Pasha el Askari became Prime Minister

1924

March, Raid of followers of Ibn Saud-Nejd on Iraq desert camel corps and shepherds

March 25, Agreement with Great Britain allowed Great Britain to maintain troops in Iraq until 1928, train native army and appoint administrative advisers for 15 years or longer

March 27, Constituent Assembly opened by King Faisal

June 10, All Agreements with Great Britain ratified by the Constituent Assembly

July 10, Organic law adopted by the Constituent Assembly

July 19, Iraq troops occupied Suleimaniya ending dominion of Kurdish chief, Sheik Mahmud

Aug. 2, Electoral law adopted by Constituent Assembly and Assembly dissolved

Aug. 6, Great Britain submitted Mosul question to the League of Nations

Aug., General Yasin Pasha el Hashimi became Prime Minister

Sept. 27, Mandate approved by Council of the League of Nations

Oct. 29, Great Britain and Turkey accepted boundary line proposed by League of Nations

1925

Jan. 16–March 23, League of Nations Commission of Inquiry conducted investigation at Mosul and published Report Aug. 7

March 5, Arabs attacked and robbed convoy on the Baghdad-Palmyra road; Mme. Maillard, wife of French Vice-Consul, fatally wounded

March 14, Agreement between Iraq and Turkey by which concession granted for exploitation of oil resources of vilayets of Mosul and Baghdad to the Turkish Petroleum Company

March 21, The Organic law promulgated and elections for first Parliament begun

June 19, Resignation of Yasin Cabinet

June 23, Elections completed for Parliament

June 26, Mushin Beg es Sadun formed Cabinet

July 16, First Parliament under the Constitution opened by King Faisal

Aug. 30, Agreement of Government with Anglo-Persian Oil Company

Aug. 31, Railroad from the Khanikin line to Kirkuk opened

Sept. 28, General Laidoner sent to Mosul by League of Nations to make investigation

Nov. 1–2, Agreements as to tribal relations between Iraq and Nejd signed by Ibn Saud and Sir Gilbert Clayton

Dec. 16, Award of the Council of the League of Nations gave Mosul to Iraq and defined Turco-Iraq boundary

1926

Jan. 13, Treaty with Great Britain signed extended relations for period of not more than 25 years or until Iraq became a member of the League of Nations

Jan. 18, Treaty with Great Britain accepted by Parliament

March 15, Al ul Bait University opened

May 24, Further Agreement with Anglo-Persian Oil Company

June 5, Treaty with Great Britain and Turkey defined frontiers between Iraq and Turkey

Nov. 21, General Jafar Pasha el Askari formed Cabinet

1927

April 1, Property tax law came into effect

April 5, Drilling operations of Turkish Petroleum Company begun at Palkhan, first attempt to open up Mosul oil fields with modern machinery

May, Income tax passed levied 3.63% on all incomes over $1,500

Oct. 25, King Faisal and Prime Minister Jaafar Pasha in London opened negotiation for revision of Treaty and for support of Great Britain in application for membership of League of Nations

Dec. 14, New Treaty signed with Great Britain by which Great Britain recognized the independence of Iraq and agreed to recommend Iraq for admission to the League of Nations in 1932

1928

Jan. 9, Resignation of Jafar Pasha as Prime Minister. Succeeded by Abdul Mushin Es Saadun as Prime Minister and Minister of Foreign Affairs; Interior, Abdul Aziz Qassab; Defense, General Nuri Pasha Said; Finance, Yusef Ghanina; Justice, Hikmet Suleiman; Works, Mohsen Shalash; Education, Tawfik Swaidi; Auqaf, Sheikh Ahmed Daud; Irrigation and Agriculture, Sulman Barrak

Jan. 19, First Parliament dissolved

Jan. 22, Negotiations with Great Britain broken off over appointment of army officers

May, General election gave Government 70 seats out of 88

May 28, Mixed Commission appointed under Treaty of June 5, 1926 completed delimitation of boundary

June 3, Provisional Commercial Agreement with Persia concluded

1929

Jan. 21, Resignation of Abdul Mushin as Prime Minister because of objection to Treaty with Great Britain

——, Wahabi rebels fired on party of Americans between Basra and Koweit killing American missionary Henry Bilkerd

March 2, Sir Gilbert Clayton arrived succeeding Sir Henry Dobbs as High Commissioner

April 1, Iraqui army established

April 29, Taufiq Beg Suwaidi became Prime Minister and Minister of Foreign Affairs

April 25, Recognition of Government by Persia

Aug. 11, Treaty of friendship and commerce with Persia concluded

Sept. 1, Land tax assessment law came into effect

Sept. 11, Death of Sir Gilbert Clayton, High Commissioner

Sept. 19, Abdul Mushin Es Saadun again Prime Minister

Oct. 3, Sir Francis Humphreys appointed High Commissioner

Nov. 13, Nazi Bey Suwaida became Prime Minister on death of Mushin Es Saadun who committed suicide because of criticism of his policies

Number of British officials, gazetted, 130; non-gazetted. 34; Indian officials, 53

1930

Jan. 27, Customs tariff law, came into effect Feb. 17, levied high duties on luxuries and most imported articles, local grain exempted from 1% export tax, building material and machinery exempted from import duties

Feb. 16, Civil Pensions Act promulgated

Feb. 24, Treaty of friendship, arbitration, and conciliation signed with Nejd. and mutual recognition of independence

March 9, Resignation of Naji Beg, Prime Minister

March 21, Demonstration of Popular and Nationalist parties against British

March 23, New Cabinet formed by General Nuri Pasha al Said as Prime Minister and Minister of Foreign Affairs; Interior, Jamil Bey Madfaie; Defense, General Jafar Pasha el Askari; Finance, Ali Jawdat Bey; Justice, Jamal Bey Baban; Communication and

Works, Jamil Pasha ar Rawi; Education, Hajji Abdul Hussein el Chelaby

June 30, New Treaty with Great Britain signed by which full independence of Iraq recognized, Iraq to be recommended for membership in League of Nations and membership to make independence *de facto*

July 4, Parliament dissolved to give people opportunity to express themselves on new Treaty with Great Britain

Aug. 31, Petition of Kurds of northern Iraq to League of Nations asking for independence

Sept. 11, Fighting at Suleimaniya between Kurdish nationalists and Iraq troops, 13 soldiers killed and 35 wounded

Nov. 3, Attack of Sheik Mahmud at Penjwin

Nov. 16, Parliament ratified Treaty with Great Britain

Dec. 3, Iraq troops in engagement with Sheik Mahmud troops

Dec. 3–4, Strike of railway shop employees at Baghdad against reduction of hours imposed as a measure of economy

JAPAN

The Empire consists of the five principal islands of Honshiu (mainland), Kiushiu, Shikoku, Hokkaido (Yezo), and Taiwan (Formosa); besides the Chishima (Kuriles), Sado, Oki, Awaji, Iki, Tsushima, Riukiu (Luchu Islands), Ogasawarajima (Bonin Islands), Bokoto (Pescadores) islands, the peninsula Chosen (Korea), and the southern half of the island of Karafuto (Sakhalin). Total area is shown as follows:—

PRINCIPAL ISLANDS	NUMBER OF ADJACENT SMALL ISLANDS	AREA IN SQUARE MILES	
		Principal Islands	Total with Adjacent Small Islands
Mainland	193	86,305	88,873
Shikoku	75	6,856	7,246
Kiushiu	158	13,768	16,201
Hokkaido (excluding the Chishima)	44	30,114	34,084
Chishima or Kurile Islands (31 islands)	—	6,024	3,970
Sado	—	335	329
Oki	1	130	135
Awaji	1	218	228
Iki	1	51	55
Tsushima	5	262	274
Riukiu (55 islands)	—	934	922
Ogasawarajima or Bonin Islands (20 islands)	—	27	40
Total (Japan proper)	477	145,024	152,357
Chosen (Korea)	1,018	82,926	84,949
Taiwan (Formosa)	14	13,807	13,840
Bokoto (Pescadores)	63	25	49
Karafuto (Japanese Sakhalin)	2	13,928	13,934
Grand Total	1,574	158,856	265,129

In 1925 (Census of October 1) the population of Japan proper was 59,736,822 (30,013,109 males and 29,723,713 females); of Chosen, 19,522,945; of Taiwan, 3,993,408; of Karafuto, 203,754. Total, 83,456,929.

In 1930 (Census of October 1) the total population of Japan proper was 64,447,724, and the

average number of persons per square kilometer was 168. The total population of the Japanese Empire was 91,792,639, including about 1½ million in the leased territory in Manchuria and the mandated Pacific islands. Tokio is the capital. On October 1, 1929, the number of Japanese residing abroad was 762,569 (434,310 males and

328,259 females). Of these, 73,930 men and 52,787 women were in South America; 108,639 men and 63,964 women in North America; 166,888 men and 139,059 women in Asia; 82,194 men and 71,678 women in Australasia; 2,572 men and 742 women in Europe; and 87 men and 29 women in Africa. On December 31, 1929, the number of foreigners in Japan was 38,829, of whom 29,500 were Chinese, 2,201 English, 2,098 American, 1,095 German, 485 French, 178 Portuguese, 35 Dutch, and 1,527 Russian.

Under the Treaty of Versailles Japan was appointed mandatory to the Pacific Islands, former German possessions north of the Equator which include the Marianne (Ladrone) Islands (except Guam), the Caroline Islands, the Marshall Islands. *See also* Australasia and Oceania.

The Japanese claim that their empire was founded by the first Emperor Jimmu Tenno, 660 B.C., and that the dynasty founded by him still reigns. It was revived in the year 1868 (the first year of the *Meiji*), when the now ruling (*de jure*) sovereign overthrew, after a short war, the power of the Shogun (the *de facto* sovereign), who had held the ruling power in successive families, since the twelfth century; and in 1871 the feudal system (Hoken Seiji) was entirely suppressed. The Emperor bears title of Tenno; but the appellation by which he is called in relation to external affairs is "Kotei," a word of Chinese origin. Only foreigners make use of the poetical title "Mikado."

By the Imperial House Law of February 11, 1889, the succession to the throne has been definitely fixed upon the male descendants. In case of failure of direct descendants, the throne devolves upon the nearest Prince and his descendants. The civil list is fixed at 4,500,000 yen.

CONSTITUTION AND GOVERNMENT

By the Constitution of February 11, 1889, the Emperor combines in himself the rights of sovereignty, and exercises the whole of the executive powers with the advice and assistance of the Cabinet Ministers, who are responsible to him, and are appointed by himself. There is also a Privy Council, who are consulted by the Emperor on important matters of State. The Emperor can declare war, make peace, and conclude treaties, and he exercises the legislative power with the consent of the Imperial Diet.

Hirohito, Emperor, born at Tokyo, April 29, 1901; succeeded his father, Yoshihito, December 25, 1926; married, January 26, 1924, to Princess Nagako, born March 6, 1903, daughter of H.I.H. Prince Kuninomiya (died January 27, 1929). Offspring:—Imperial Princess.—I, Princess Shigeko (Gerunomiya), born December 6, 1925. II, Princess Sachiko (Hisanomiya), born September 10, 1927; died March 8, 1928. III, Princess Kazuko (Takanomiya), born September 30, 1929. IV, a princess born on March 7, 1931.

665 B.C. to 1690

The early history is legendary till A.D. 500. Jimmu Tenno, the founder of the present dynasty, is said to have reigned B.C. 665

A.D. 201, The Empress Jingo is said to have conquered Korea

285, Korean civilization introduced

552, Introduction of Buddhism from Korea about

624, Its hierarchy established

1192 *et seq.*, Yoritomo, Shogun or generalissimo, since called by the Chinese Tycoon, usurps supreme power, the Emperor becoming the spiritual Emperor

Sanguinary wars among the chiefs during four centuries

About 1275–95, Japan visited by Marco Polo, a Venetian

[His "Maravigliose Cose" printed 1496]

1333–92, Weak rival dynasties in the north and south

About 1537–58, Japan visited by Mendez Pinto, a Portuguese

About 1543, The Portuguese establish trading settlements and introduce Jesuit missionaries who make many converts; by a fierce persecution beginning 1590, the Portuguese and their missionaries are expelled, and their converts massacred, 1637–42

1600 *et seq.*, The Dutch settlements under severe restrictions, suffered to remain for a time

1600, Tyeyasu, victorious over southern barons, establishes a strictly conservative government at Jedo

[His dynasty lasted till 1868]

About 1690, The learned Engelbert Kæmpfer visits Japan

[All foreigners rigidly excluded from Japan till 1853]

1853

July 8, An American expedition, under Commodore M. C. Perry, reaches Yeddo, and is favorably received; but remains only a few days

1854

March 31, A treaty of commercial alliance concluded with the United States

Oct. 14, A similar treaty with Great Britain

Dec. 23, Destructive earthquake; Anasaca and Simoda destroyed, Yeddo much injured

1855

Jan. 26, Treaty with Russia

1856

Nagasaki and Hakodadi opened to European commerce

1858

Aug. 19, Commercial treaty with Russia

Aug. 26, Lord Elgin visits Japan, with a present of a steamer for the Emperor, and is honorably received, July; obtains the treaty of Yeddo, opening Japan to British commerce

Sept. 16, The secular Emperor dies (aged 36)

Dec., Rutherford Alcock (afterwards Sir) appointed consul-general; envoy extraordinary, Nov., 1859

1860

May 14–June 30, A Japanese embassy visits Washington, New York, &c., United States

1861

July 5, Attack on the British embassy at Yeddo; some persons wounded

1862

June 27, Foreign ministers transfer the residence from Yeddo to Yokohama

Nov. 15, 19, The batteries and vessels of the Prince of Nagato fire on an English and a French vessel at the entrance of the straits of Simonosaki

1863

June 24, The Japanese Minister announces that the ports opened by virtue of the treaties will be closed

July 15–19, Some English, French, and American vessels bombard his forts and his vessels

Aug. 15, Reparation demanded; 100,000*l.* paid by the government; the Prince of Satsuma resists payment of 25,000*l.*, his portion; Admiral Kuper enters the bay of Kagosima, and is fired upon; whereupon he bombards the town and burns the Prince's steamers

Dec. 11, The Prince of Satsuma pays the 25,000*l.*

1864

Sept. 5, 6, The Japanese Government refuse to abide by the treaties; a combined fleet enters the straits of Simonosaki, Sept. 4; and attacks and destroys the Japanese batteries

1865

April, Sir Harry Parkes appointed to succeed Sir R. Alcock as envoy

Nov. 25, Treaties with England, France, &c., ratified

1866

Jan., Two more ports opened

Sept., Death of the Tycoon: his successor said to be favorable to foreigners

Nov. 26, Town of Yokohama and third part of European settlement destroyed by fire

1867

April 25, Yeddo and other places opened to trade, by the government

1868

Jan. 1, Osaka and Niogo opened to European commerce

Jan. 27–Feb., Insurrection of the Daimios; rivalry between the Emperor and Tycoon, Dec.; foreigners neutral

March 16, Japanese outrages on French sailors; culprits executed; further outrages punished, March 23

May 10–17, The Emperor's troops defeat the Tycoon's, who flees, Jan. 26–30; the Emperor's defeated near Yeddo

July, After long war and varying success the rebellion ends; the Emperor reëstablished

Name of the capital, Yeddo, changed to Tokio

Nov., Majority of the Emperor proclaimed

1869

Feb., His marriage, Feb. 9; another rebellion of the Tycoon's partisans

Dec., The Tycoon submits to the Emperor

1870–71

Great progress of internal improvements, and assimilation of European civilization; proposed establishment of railways, telegraphs, &c.

1872

Oct., First railway (from Yokohama to Shinagawa)

opened, June 12, to Yeddo; opened by the Emperor

Dec. 5, Japanese ambassadors received by Queen Victoria

Public library at Tokio established

1874

Feb.–April, Insurrection, through desire for war with Korea; soon suppressed

Nov., A successful expedition against Formosa to chastise savage tribes for massacring Japanese sailors, May; Chinese protest, Aug.; Japanese withdraw (*see* Formosa), announced

1875

April 14, The Emperor decrees a new constitution; 2 chambers, &c.

June 20, The Emperor opens a parliament of officials, nominated by himself, in Yeddo

1877

Sept., Insurrection of Satsuma and other clans specially against the ministry, Feb.; suppression announced

Oct. 13, Insurrection suppressed; power of the Daimios virtually suppressed; principals only punished; announced

1878

May 14, Okuto, able reforming minister of the interior, killed by six men (political motives)

July 25, Treaty of commerce with the United States

1881

Oct. 12, Imperial decree convoking a national assembly in 1890

Entirely new criminal code enforced

1882

Autumn, 53,760 primary schools and compulsory education established

1883

Oct. 18, Rev. Arthur W. Poole, consecrated Anglican bishop of Japan

Nov., All Japan to be thrown open to foreign trade, with mixed tribunals, announced

1884

April, Death of the last Tycoon

Sept., A new order of hereditary nobility instituted

Aug. 11, The national religion disestablished and freedom given to other religions

1885

Nov., Bishop Poole died July 9; succeeded by Rev. E. Bickersteth

Gradual adoption of alphabetical in place of ideographic writing by agency of the Roma-ji-Rai, or Roman Alphabet Association

Dec. 1, Decree giving enlarged power to the Prime Minister solely responsible to the Emperor

1887

Dec. 6, Death of Shimadju Saburo, ex-Prince of Satsuma

1888

Feb. 3, Completion of the translation of the Bible into Japanese celebrated

July 15–18, Volcanic eruption at Sho-Bandai-San; reported 400 persons killed

1889

Feb. 11, New constitution promulgated by the Emperor at Tokio; the Houses of Lords and Commons established; religious liberty and general freedom granted

April 13, 14, Volcanic eruption on Ishima Island, 300 houses destroyed; 170 persons killed

July 28–Aug. 3, Earthquakes at Kumamoto, 19 persons perish

Aug., The southern island of Kiushiu, embankments, &c., destroyed, July; S.E. Japan the Chikugo river rose 28½ feet above its usual level twice, 73,694 persons made destitute

Oct., Japanese commission of enquiry respecting parliamentary procedure in Europe, arrives in London

——, Japanese national banks reported highly prosperous

——, Nine non-treaty ports opened to commerce

1890

Jan. 16, Volcanic eruption of the Zoo, Bingo district, Fukuvama buried, inhabitants escaped

Jan. 24, Violent cyclone on the coast; 900 fishing boats wrecked, great loss of life

April 21, New civil code promulgated

May 12, The Emperor institutes a new order of knighthood, "the Golden Falcon," to commemorate the 2,555th anniversary of the coronation of Jimmu Tenno, the semi-mythical first sovereign of Japan, reported

July 1, First parliamentary election

Nov. 29, The first Japanese Parliament opened

1891

Feb. 18, Death of prince Sanjo, Prime Minister

Oct. 28, Very destructive earthquake on the Niphon islands; about 84,000 houses and railways, bridges, &c., destroyed; about 10,000 persons killed and 300,000 homeless; minor shocks follow; estimated loss 2,000,000*l.*

Dec. 29, Government ordinance to provide for the relief of the sufferers by the earthquake

1892

Feb. 15, Violent election riots with loss of 22 lives

March 15, The establishment of a Roman Catholic hierarchy authorized, reported

Aug. 29, New Cabinet formed by Count Ito

Dec. 20, *Yoshino,* large protected Japanese cruiser, launched at the Elswick works, Newcastle

1893

March, Continued opposition to the ministry; parliament prorogued, Feb. 3; deadlock closed by compromise, Feb. 17; Diet closed

About March 3, Increase of the navy agreed on

1894

March 1, Parliament opened, Nov. 28, 1893; great disorder; parliament dissolved, Dec. 30; general election; liberal victory

July, War with China (*see* Korea)

Aug. 22, Loan of 50,000,000 dollars authorized, Aug. 17; the nobles subscribe 80,000,000 dollars

Aug. 25, Anglo-Japanese treaty signed, July 16; ratified; the tariff modified and the foreign jurisdiction at the treaty ports to be abolished; British residents

equalized with the Japanese; treaty to come into force in 5 years

Oct. 22, Parliament opened by the Emperor with a firm speech against China; a large loan authorized, Oct. 17; session closed

——, Earthquake in Yamagata and Akita; the town of Sakata nearly destroyed, with great loss of life

Nov. 22, Treaty with United States N.A. signed

1895

May 8, Treaty of peace with China; concluded April 17 (*see* Korea); ratifications exchanged

Aug., Counts Ito, Yamagata, Oyama created marquises; others raised to dignity

1896

Feb. 28, *Yashima,* warship, launched on the Tyne at Elswick

March 31, *Fuji,* warship, launched on the Thames

April 4, Treaty of commerce, &c., with Germany, signed at Berlin

June 15–17, Kamaishi, in N. Japan, almost completely destroyed by earthquakes, about 1,000 lives lost, 150 shocks in 20 hrs.; about 20,000 persons drowned by a seismic wave, and many towns destroyed

Aug. 31, Earthquake in N.E. province, Rokugo destroyed, many deaths

Nov. 27, Great development of trade, new lines of steamers, docks, &c., constructed; reported

1898

May 7, Chinese war indemnity paid, 11,008,857*l.*

Nov. 1, *Shikishima* battleship launched at Blackwall (Thames)

Nov. 6, Count Okuma's cabinet resigns, Oct. 31; the Marquis Yamagata forms one

1899

Jan. 25, Lord Charles Beresford visits Yokohama; urges an alliance between Great Britain, Japan, Germany, and U.S.N.A., to prevent war in the Far East; leaves

March 7, Severe earthquake in Niphon, loss of life and property

March 13, *Asaki* battleship launched at Glasgow

April, Increased expenditure on the army and navy, taxes raised, expansion of commerce, &c., reported

June, Loan of 10,000,000*l.* issued in London

July 1, New press law (1897), free press restrictions removed

Aug. 3, Edict prohibited religious instruction in schools

Aug. 15, Imperial rescript issued, June 30; foreign treaties revised; Japan open to Europeans; consular jurisdiction abolished, July 17; ratified

Mid Aug., Chinese mission to treat for a treaty of alliance fails

Oct., House-tax becomes due, foreigners protest as exempt by treaty

1900

Jan., Government earthquake investigation committee appointed, 1893; catalogue issued

June 26, Mobilization of 20,000 troops ordered, owing to Chinese crisis

July 17, Eruption of Mount Adsuma, near Bandai San, 200 persons reported killed or injured

Sept. 29, Yamagata's ministry resigns, succeeded by the Marquis Ito

1895–Nov., Dr. Kitasato's new method of treating dysentery by inoculation very successful

1901

March 16, Political crisis, early March; taxation bills passed by the peers

March, Bill recognizing the titles of foreign landholders, passed

April 25, Financial panic, 20 banks suspend payment, reported

June 3, Crisis; cabinet resigns, May 3; Visct. Katsura forms a ministry

June 21, M. Hoshi Toru, liberal leader, assassinated by Iba Sotaro (sentenced to life-imprisonment, Sept. 10) in the Tokio city council

July, Baron Iwasaki buys and presents Prof. Max Müller's library (about 13,000 vols, and 81 Sanscrit MSS.) to Tokio University

Sept., The Chinese Emperor's letter apologizing for the murder of M. Sugiyama in Pekin (June 11, 1900) and expressing his gratitude to the Japanese for their "beneficent influence" and moderation, accepted by the Emperor, who hopes that reforms in China may soon be in progress by means of which "permanent peace in Asia" will be secured

Oct. 22, Sir Claude MacDonald, British Minister, arrives

Dec. 26, Budget presented, Dec. 23; withdrawn

1902

Jan. 30, Anglo-Japanese treaty of alliance signed, London (well received by France and Russia, March)

Feb. 6, Large financial improvement, reported

March 29, Issues of bonds, over 7½ million yen, for railways and public works

July 26, Insurgents defeated in S. Formosa

Aug. 13–15, Tori Shima, a small island, overwhelmed by a volcanic eruption, the inhabitants (over 150) killed

Aug. 22, General election; new system, reported satisfactory

Aug. 28, House-tax (on foreigners) dispute, referred to arbitration

Sept. 29, Typhoon at Yokohama, great loss of life, Odawara swept by a wave, about 200 drowned

Oct. 7, Japanese loan of 5,000,000l. issued, London

Early Oct., Naval expansion scheme, budget, 3,700,-000l., 1901–02, settled

Dec. 16, 28, The government's financial proposals opposed; parliament dissolved on rejecting compromise; general elections to be held, March 1, 1903

1903

Feb. 18, Death of Prince Komatsu (61) field-marshal of army in Chinese War 1894–95

March 4, General election

Early May, Consent of Korean government to grant to Japanese subjects equal whaling privileges on the eastern coast as have been granted to Russian government since 1899, including 3 stations on shore

June 4, Emperor opens the Diet, May 12; financial measures passed; the Formosan camphor monopoly extended to the whole Empire; Diet closed

June, Increasing excitement over the Manchuria question in Japan, reported

Early July, Dispute between Japan and Korea respecting the opening of Wi-ju, for which Japan presses and Korea refuses on ground of Russian objection

About July 10, Pressure put upon Korea for the opening of Wi-ju, plea that Russia objects regarded by Japan as irrelevant

July 13, Cabinet changes, the Marquis Ito closes his connection with the Seiyu-Kai, and accepts office of president of privy council, which will in future assume great importance in state affairs; the Marquis Yamagata and Count Matsugata appointed privy councillors; the Premier resumes office; end of crisis

Aug. 12, Strained relations caused by rivalry of Russia and Japan in Korea in consequence of Russian activity having secured a position on the Korean side of the Ya-lu and Tuman rivers. Russia seeks for the right to assist in the construction of a railway through Wi-ju to Seoul; Japanese proposal for a *modus vivendi* regarding Russian policy in Korea and Manchuria presented at St. Petersburg

Sept. 23, M. Hakano, Baron Kioura, and M. Kaiboba, appointed respectively Ministers of Justice, Agriculture and Commerce, and Education and Communication

Oct.–Nov., Strained relations between Japan and Russia on the question of the non-evacuation of Manchuria by the latter by Oct. 8 according to the terms of the convention, and Japanese interests in Korea

Dec. 11, Unsatisfactory reply of Russia to Japanese Korean proposals, received

Dec. 22, Japanese reply to Russian proposals, increasing tension

Dec. 28, 29, War preparations; two Argentine cruisers, *Rivadavia* and *Moreno*, completing at Genoa, bought by Japan for 1,500,000l.; imperial ordinances issued

Dec. 29, Japan obtains unlimited credit for military defense; naval and military preparations pressed forward

Dec. 31, Reported Japanese warning to the Powers that she will fight if her demands are not conceded; mobilization of troops

1904

Jan. 6, Russia vaguely states her intention to respect Japanese rights in Manchuria, but repeats her request for the neutralization of a third part of the territory of Korea

Jan. 11, Japan advises China, in view of the unfavorable reply of Russia, to maintain strict neutrality in the event of war

Jan. 13, Japanese reply states that negotiations would be continued with a time limit being imposed, and points out that Japan recognizes Russia's special interests in Manchuria and her right to protect them, but claims an "open door" in Manchuria, demands perfect equality in all respects for her subjects in that province; and absolutely declines the proposal for a diplomatic partition of Korea

Jan. 25, Ordinance issued at Tokio empowering the government to take over all private railway lines for military purposes

Jan. 30, Contracts for the construction of two battleships for the Japanese navy signed by the representatives of the Emperor's government in London; these warships to be built by Messrs. Vickers, Sons & Maxim, Ltd., and Sir W. G. Armstrong, Whitworth & Co., Ltd., respectively

Feb. 6, Negotiations with Russia on the subject of Manchuria and Korea broken off by Japan owing to Russia's dilatory diplomacy and warlike activity

Feb. 7, Russian Government announces that the Czar's minister in Tokio has been recalled in consequence of the decision of Japan to cease negotiations, and to recall the Japanese Ambassador from St. Petersburg

Feb. 8, Japanese fleet under Adm. Togo attacks the Russian warships at Port Arthur, and torpedoes the battleships *Retvisan*, *Tsarevitch*, and the cruiser *Pallada;* Japanese vessels escape without injury

——, Japanese troops land at Chemulpo, securing the Japanese position in Korea

Feb. 9, Another attack made by the Japanese fleet; Russian battleship *Poltava*, and the cruisers *Diana*, *Askold*, and *Norvik* seriously damaged

——, Russian cruiser *Variag* and gunboat *Korietz* sunk by the Japanese squadron under Adm. Uriu at Chemulpo

[For events of the war between Japan and Russia, *see* under Russo-Japanese War]

Feb. 13, Chinese Minister at Tokio addresses a note to Baron Komura, Japanese Foreign Minister, intimating the intention of China to maintain neutrality in the war

Feb. 26, National loan subscribed twice over; subscriptions promised amount to 280,000,000 yen (28,000,-000*l.*), reported

March 1, Japanese Government issues a reply to the note of Russia to the Powers (issued Feb. 22), justifying her action in commencing hostilities

——, General election concluded, having passed off quietly

——, Rescript issued by the Emperor summoning the Diet to meet in special session on March 13, the session to last ten days; principal bills to be introduced, one recommending an increase of 1½% on the land tax, another doubling the income tax

March 2, Cabinet in an extraordinary session discusses the war taxation measures to be submitted to the diet, providing for an increase of taxation of 70,000,-000 yen (7,000,000*l.*); in addition to the increases in the income and land taxes, duties to be increased on spirits and tobacco, and certain new taxes to be created

March 20, Diet opened by the Emperor in person: he states that the appeal to arms had been forced on Japan by Russia's want of sincerity; there could now be no pause until the object of the war was achieved

March 22, House of Representatives expresses itself as "thoroughly satisfied with the declaration of war"; House of Peers and House of Representatives pass cordial votes of thanks to the navy; all political parties join in supporting the government program of war taxes

March 23, Gen. Count Taro Katsura, Premier, states that the settled national policy of Japan was the establishment of permanent peace in the Far East, and the consolidation of the position of the Empire by promoting friendly relations with the Great Powers, and by respecting their legitimate rights

March 26, House of Representatives passes all the war-tax bills, except the duties on salt and silk, and reduces slightly the proposed increase on the land tax, giving an increase of 6,200,000*l.*, instead of 7,000,000*l.* as proposed by the government; Finance Minister, Baron Arasuké Soné, accepts the proposal

March 29, After settlement of the war program on the following basis: foreign and domestic loans, exchequer bonds, &c., 41,100,000*l.*; increased taxes, 6,200,000*l.*; economies and surpluses, 4,800,000*l.*; special accounts, 5,500,000*l.*; total, 57,600,000*l.*; Diet closes, having unanimously adopted a resolution that the house would not grudge supplies, and that

it trusted the ministers faithfully to discharge their high duties

May 10, Japanese Government decides to float another popular loan of 100,000,000 yen (10,000,000*l.*) at the issue price of 95, redeemable in five years, and bearing 5% interest

May 13, Prospectus issued of the Imperial Japanese Government 6% sterling loan for 10,000,000*l.* offered for subscription in London and New York at 93½%; bonds repayable April 5, 1911, with an option to the imperial Japanese government to redeem at any time after April 5, 1907, on six months' notice; American subscriptions for 25,000,000 dols. (5,000,000*l.*), close

June 28, Convention concluded with Korea, by which the Japanese acquire fishing privileges on the coasts of the three N.W. provinces of Korea for 20 years; Koreans granted similar privileges on the west central and S.W. coasts of Japan, announced

Japanese foreign trade shows a total increase of 28,000,-000 yen (2,800,000*l.*), of which 11,000,000 yen (1,100,000*l.*) are for exports, from Jan. 1 to June 30

July 17, Japanese Government present to the Chinese Minister in Tokio a scheme for the administration of Manchuria; principal clause states that Japan will govern the country with the assistance of a number of Chinese troops, reported

End July, Proclamation issued by Japanese announcing that they will assume police power in Korea in all matters affecting Japanese interests; no anti-Japanese meeting to be allowed

Aug. 14, Russian torpedo destroyer *Reshitelni* sheltering at Chifu, boarded and towed outside the harbor by the Japanese, Aug. 11; Russia lodges a strong protest with the Japanese Government for alleged violation of neutral territory

Aug., Death of Count Kawamura, the "Father of the Japanese navy" (on his decease he is raised by the Emperor to the rank of Admiral)

Aug. 19, Japanese marine association resolve to form a volunteer fleet of auxiliary cruisers

Aug. 20, Japanese Government define their attitude with regard to the seizure of the *Reshitelni* at Chifu, and declare their position on the entire question of Chinese neutrality; government contend that the agreement to respect Chinese territory outside the theater of war was broken by Russia's attempt to obtain in Chifu an asylum from attack which her home port had ceased to afford; they also deny that the *Reshitelni* was disarmed

Aug. 25, Korean Government stated to have agreed to engage Japanese nominees for advisers in the departments of finance and foreign affairs, and to have undertaken to follow their advice in all respects; extensive program of reforms to be inaugurated, Japan to lend Korea 3,000,000 yen (300,000*l.*) as the first instalment to place the finances of that country on a sound footing, and to correct the abuses of the nickel currency; Korea later on to withdraw her diplomatic and consular representatives abroad, and to entrust the care of her interests to Japanese officials, reported

Sept. 8, Exchequer bonds for 10,000,000 yen (1,000,-000*l.*), issued

Mid Sept., Strong political movement in Japan in favor of the abolition of all restrictions on the tenure of real estate by aliens, and of the remodeling of the law of mortgage for the purpose of removing obstacles to the introduction of foreign capital, reported

Sept. 23, Death of Mr. Lafcadio Hearn, a distinguished writer on Japanese subjects, and formerly lecturer on English literature at the Imperial University, Tokio

Sept. 28, Internal 5% loan of 80,000,000 yen (8,000,-000*l.*) decided upon by the government; price of issue 92

Nov. 6, Serious earthquake in Formosa, 78 persons killed, 23 injured

Nov. 13, Draft of war-tax measure government proposes to submit to the diet shows a proposed increase of import duties amounting to 1,500,000 yen (150,000*l.*) divided among a large number of articles

Nov. 21, Court of Arbitration meets at The Hague, Nov. 21, to pronounce judgment in the dispute between Japan and Gt. Britain, France, and Germany, with reference to the house-tax levied by Japan on buildings situated within the foreign concessions; the Powers interested claim that those buildings are exempt by reason of the perpetual lease under which they are held; court adjourns at the request of the Japanese delegate until Feb. 15, 1905

Dec. 1, New recruits join the colors under the conscription act

Dec. 4, Budget for 1905 presented, showing a total war revenue required of 780,000,000 yen (78,000,000*l.*), including provision of interest on outstanding loans. Of this sum the government anticipated that it would be only necessary to borrow 450,000,000 yen (45,000,000*l.*). Ordinary revenue required was about 22,000,000*l.*, making a total revenue for 1905 of 1,000,000,000 yen (100,000,000*l.*), proposals of the government unanimously voted

Dec. 12, The political parties endorse the government's scheme of increased war taxes, but reduce the land tax by 14,500,000 yen (1,450,000*l.*), making additions amounting to 4,500,000 yen (450,000*l.*) in other directions

Dec. 21, Special committee of the lower house, examining the draft of a new mining law, decide by 11 votes to 4 to recommend the abolition of all distinctions of nationality in regard to the ownership of mines, experience having proved the benefits of foreigners participating in Japanese industries

Dec. 31, Return of Admirals Togo and Kamimura to Tokio, enthusiastic reception by the people

1905

Jan. 2, Capitulation of Port Arthur

Jan. 24, H. P. Collins, a British subject of Portuguese extraction, publicly tried at Yokohama, sentenced to 11 years' hard labor on the charge of disclosing military secrets to the Russians

End March, Japanese Government 4½% loan for 30,000,000*l.* on the security of the tobacco monopoly issued in London and New York, and is subscribed for many times over

April 17, Arrangements for successfully financing the war during the current year reported to be completed

May 1, Baron Komura, Minister for Foreign Affairs, gives a banquet to Mr. H. W. Denison in honor of the 25th anniversary of his appointment as adviser to the Japanese foreign office

May 4, Popular excitement in Japan caused by the Russian Adm. Rozhdestvensky's abuse of French neutrality; Japanese Minister in Paris asks the French Government for explanations

May 15, Hague tribunal met to examine the dispute between Great Britain, France, Germany, and Japan with reference to the house tax levied by Japan in the foreign concessions, give judgment in favor of the foreign Powers

——, Grand Formosan trunk line from Ki-lung to Takau opened

May 28, News of Adm. Togo's victory in the Tsu Shima straits, May 27–28, received with great enthusiasm in Japan

June 8, Note by President Roosevelt to Japan and to Russia urging them to open direct negotiations for peace

June 10, Japanese reply to President Roosevelt's note received in Washington

June 18, Russia agrees to the nomination of Washington as the place of meeting of the Japanese and Russian plenipotentiaries for the consideration of possible terms of peace

July 1, Baron Komura and Mr. Takahire appointed as peace plenipotentiaries for Japan, and M. Muravieff (resigns owing to ill-health, M. Witte appointed in his place, July 13) and Baron Rosen for Russia, with full power to negotiate and conclude a treaty subject to the ratification of their respective governments

July 10, Japanese Government 4½% sterling loan (second series) for 30,000,000*l.* offered for subscription in London, NewYork, and Germany at 90. Loan secured on the annual net revenue of the government tobacco monopoly, subject only to the charge in favor of the prior loan of 30,000,000*l.*

July 25, Mr. Taft, U.S. Secretary for War, and party accompanying him on his visit to Japan enthusiastically received; Tokio *en fête*, the entire city decorated with flags and illuminated

——, Baron Komura and the other members of the peace commission arrive in New York

Aug. 5, Japanese and Russian envoys arrive at Oyster bay; received by Pres. Roosevelt on board the *Mayflower;* after formal introduction they are entertained at lunch by Pres. Roosevelt; plenipotentiaries arrive at Portsmouth, New Hampshire; are formally received by the local authorities, Aug. 8

Aug. 10, First meeting of the Peace Conference held at Portsmouth; Japanese present in writing their terms of peace, which M. Witte undertakes to consider and to reply to in writing

Aug. 12, Two sittings held; M. Witte hands Baron Komura the Russian reply to the Japanese proposals, accepting some, and rejecting others

——, New Anglo-Japanese treaty of alliance signed in London

Aug. 14, M. Witte intimates that Russia cannot entertain the Japanese demands for an indemnity, the cession of Sakhalin, the surrender of the interned Russian warships, and the limitation of Russia's naval strength in the Far East. Envoys proceed to discuss other proposals, and agree to the articles affecting Manchuria and Port Arthur, the former to be evacuated by both powers, and the principle of the "open door" to be recognized; the lease of Port Arthur by China to Russia to be transferred to Japan

Aug. 15, Japanese press adopt a firm tone with regard to the question of peace, and concur in expressing surprise at the moderation of the government

Aug. 18, *Impasse* between Russian and Japanese plenipotentiaries on the question of "reimbursement" of the Japanese expenses of the war; adjourned till Aug. 22

Aug. 19, Baron Rosen, at the express invitation of Pres. Roosevelt, visits him at Oyster bay, and has a long interview

Aug. 23, Meeting of plenipotentiaries; 4 of the 7 protocols drawn up are signed; conference adjourns to Aug. 26

Aug. 25, Russian foreign office, through its recognized press representatives, reiterates its official utterance that Russia will not pay an indemnity

Aug. 26, Czar's final reply to Pres. Roosevelt, who had entered into personal negotiations with the Czar with the view to bring about a solution of the deadlock in the peace negotiations, conveys an unqualified refusal to entertain the Japanese demand for an indemnity

——, M. Witte, at the meeting of the peace conference, declares that "half Sakhalin, and no indemnity" were Russia's final words; Baron Komura's proposal to adjourn the conference till Aug. 29 agreed to by M. Witte

Aug. 28, Specially summoned council of cabinet ministers and elder statesmen meet under the presidency of the Emperor at the palace, Tokio, to consider the latest and final phases of the conference at Portsmouth

Aug. 29, Peace conference meets; Japan withdraws her claim for an indemnity; Russian and Japanese plenipotentiaries agree to the following terms: no indemnity to Japan in any shape or form; the division of Sakhalin, no compensation payable to Japan; Russia defrays the expenses of Russian prisoners of war, but nothing for any other purpose; Japan withdraws her demand for the limitation of Russian naval power in the East, and her demand for the interned warships; the other terms of agreement previously agreed to (*see above*)

Sept. 1, Armistice signed by the Russian and Japanese plenipotentiaries to take effect when the treaty of peace is signed

Sept. 5, Treaty of peace between Japan and Russia signed at Portsmouth, N.H., by Baron Komura and M. Witte. Treaty contains 15 articles and 2 additional articles. Its more important provisions include the recognition by Russia of the preponderating interests of Japan in Korea; stipulate the simultaneous evacuation of Manchuria by the Russian and Japanese troops; transfer the Russian lease of Port Arthur and Dalny to Japan; make arrangements for the division between the two powers of the Manchurian railway; provide for the cession to Japan of the southern half of Sakhalin, and for the granting of fishing rights to Japanese subjects on the Siberian coasts; stipulate for the renewal of the commercial treaty between the two powers; and make provision for the exchange of prisoners, each power refunding to the other the actual cost of the maintenance of the prisoners of its nationality. The additional articles provide for the evacuation of Manchuria by both armies within 18 months after the signing of the treaty; and that the boundary limiting the parts owned respectively by Russia and Japan in Sakhalin shall be definitely marked off on the spot by a special boundary commission

——, Great dissatisfaction throughout Japan with the terms of peace; mass meeting of citizens held in the Hibiya park, Tokio; resolutions passed declaring

that the nation had been humiliated, and denouncing the terms of peace; grave rioting ensues on the police breaking up the crowd; mob attack the offices of the Kokumin, and burn the house of the Minister of the Interior, two persons killed, many injured

Sept. 5, Mass meetings to denounce the peace conditions held at Osaka, Nagoya, and Kioto; resignation of the government demanded

Sept. 6, Renewal of disturbances at Tokio; mob burn and destroy 10 Christian churches and a mission-house school; electric street-cars burnt by the rioters; 800 arrests made; barristers' associations decide to defend *gratis* all persons arrested; 6 deaths reported

Sept. 7, Imperial ordinance issued proclaiming martial law in Tokio; publication of the journals *Miyako*, *Yurozu*, and *Niroku* suspended

——, Tokio municipality pass a resolution denouncing the terms of peace, and declaring in favor of the abandonment of the treaty

——, Disorder at Kobe, a statue of the Marquis Ito pulled down and dragged through the streets

Sept. 8, Count Katsura holds an informal meeting with members of both houses of the Diet, in which he makes a full statement with regard to the peace negotiations, and points out the substantial character of the advantages gained by Japan

Sept. 11, Ministry urging the necessity of martial law in Tokio in view of the riots; crave the imperial judgment whether they should remain in office; Emperor replies advising the ministers to retain their offices

Sept. 13, Count Katsura, Premier, addresses the provincial governors, assembled at Tokio, with reference to the Peace Treaty; he urges them to assist in preserving order, and to use their efforts to direct the national energy to effect an expansion and development commensurate with the extent of the victories gained by Japan

Sept. 14, Important organization, representing 81 firms presided over by the millionaire Mr. Iwade, formed for the development of the industries and expansion of the foreign trade of Japan, especially with Korea and China, reported

——, Eleven peers, headed by Prince Nijo, present a memorial to the government criticizing the failure of the authorities to prevent the recent disturbances in Tokio

Sept. 15, Settled accounts for year ending March 31, show a surplus of 50,000,000 yen (5,000,000*l.*), the result of administrative economies and growth of revenue, reported

Sept. 16, Armistice commissioners meet at Sha-ho-tsu; protocol signed provides that hostilities shall be discontinued throughout Manchuria, and establishes a neutral zone, Sept. 13; armistice becomes effective

——, Resignation of Viscount Yoshikawa, the Minister of the Interior, tendered in consequence of the Tokio riots, accepted; Baron Kiyoura, Minister of Agriculture, appointed his successor

——, Committee of the lower house hold an investigation into the disturbances in Tokio; have an interview with the Premier and demand the abolition of martial law on the appointment of a special committee to inquire into the conduct of the police during the riots

Sept. 24, Commander Islands occupied by Japanese, who hoist their flag, reported

Sept. 25, 100 memorials presented to the throne against

the ratification of the peace treaty, to which the Emperor gives his personal consideration, reported

Oct. 4, Russo-Japanese peace treaty passed by the Privy Council

——, Martial law abrogated at Saseho, Nagasaki, Tsu Shima, and Hakodate

Oct. 6, Visit of the British China squadron, under Adm. Sir Gerald Noel, to Japan, arrives at Kobe; squadron arrives at Yokohama, Oct. 11

Oct. 10, Death of Adm. Saso of the naval instruction department

Oct. 14, Treaty of Peace signed by the Czar and Emperor

Oct. 22, Adm. Togo makes his formal public entry into Tokio to report to the Emperor the return of the Japanese fleet from the war

Oct. 24, Triumphal entry of Adm. Togo into Tokio

Nov. 17, As the result of the Marquis Ito's mission to Korea the Emperor of Korea accepts the Japanese program the main feature of which is the transfer of the control of the foreign affairs of Korea to Japan

Nov. 28, New 50,000,000l. foreign loan at 4% arranged; 25,000,000l. reserved for the conversion of the existing 6% loan; 25,000,000l. issued in London, Paris, Berlin, and New York

Nov. 29, Legations in London, Washington, Paris, Berlin, and St. Petersburg to be raised to embassies

Dec. 4, Budget for 1906 includes 80,000,000l. of war expenditure; ordinary expenditure, 23,000,000l., leaving a surplus of 1,200,000l.; government propose to redeem the war debt at the rate of 11,000,000l. yearly

Dec. 7, Marshal Oyama and his staff make a triumphal entry into Tokio; Gen. Kuroki received with similar enthusiasm

Dec. 20, New organized system for the appointment of a resident-general in Korea passed by the Privy Council

Dec. 22, Chino-Japanese treaty signed transferred all Russian rights in Manchuria to Japan. *See also* Manchuria

Dec. 28, Armored cruiser *Tsukuba*, the first entirely built in Japan, launched at Kure in the presence of the Crown Prince

Dec. 30, Admirals Togo and Kamimura arrive at Tokio and receive an enthusiastic welcome

1906

Jan. 25, M. Sakatani, Minister of Finance, states his proposal to convert war taxes amounting to 160,-000,000 yen (16,000,000l.) into permanent imposts and to establish a debt consolidation fund, for the service of which the sum of 110,000,000 yen (11,000,-000l.) is to be devoted annually in addition to the 36,000,000 yen (3,600,000l.) hitherto set apart for the same purpose; both proposals meet with strong opposition in the house; report submitted to the Diet by the finance department setting forth the actual war outlay from the outbreak of hostilities to Sept., 1905; army expenditure, 990,000,000 yen (99,000,-000l.); navy expenditure, 180,000,000 yen (18,000,-000l.); principal items under the former head include provisions 280,000,000 yen (28,000,000l.), arms 170,000,000 yen (17,000,000l.), clothing 140,000,000 yen (14,000,000l.)

Mid. Feb., House of Representatives passes the budget with a single concession on the part of the government, which consents to a reduction of 5,000,000 yen

(500,000l.) in the extraordinary expenditure on the army and navy; bill establishing the debt consolidation fund passes the house by 230 votes to 117; measure for the continuation of war taxes passes by 222 votes to 125. According to the ministerial proposals adopted by the lower house the war debt of over 182,000,000l. will be completely paid off in 1939, and the domestic debt of 57,000,000l. in 1942; bill for nationalizing the Japanese railways introduced in the Diet

March 1, Mr. Kato, Minister for Foreign Affairs, resigns office in connection with the government bill introduced for nationalizing all railways at present in private hands; the vacant portfolio is taken by the Marquis Saionji, the Premier

March 17, Terrible earthquake at Kagi, in Formosa; many hundred persons killed and injured, and a large number of buildings destroyed; estimated damage 90,000,000 yen (9,000,000l.)

March 20, Viscount Hayashi, Japanese Ambassador, leaves London

March 28, Lower House of the Diet passes the railway nationalization bill; estimated cost of the purchase of the home railways 500,000,000 yen (50,000,000l.); House of Peers passes the bill with amendments; bill again presented to the House of Representatives, and after violent opposition, the House adopts the bill as amended

April 13, Fatal earthquake in Formosa

April 23, Government redeems the balance of the hereditary pension bonds amounting to 16,000,000 yen (1,600,000l.)

April 30, Great triumphal review held at Tokio, all the forces that took part in the war represented, 45,000 troops present; the parade commanded by Marshal Oyama in the presence of the Emperor and the Crown Prince

May 21, Baron Komura accepts the post of Japanese Ambassador in London

July 18, Great floods in the central parts of Japan; railways interrupted; 6 freight cars fall into the famous Hotsu rapids; Kofu district converted into a huge lake; many casualties; losses amount to many million yen; thousand of persons take refuge in the temples and theaters. 4,000 houses flooded at Matsumoto, one river bank destroyed for a length of 2,700 ft.; copper mines under water; newspapers compelled to suspend publication; fast flowing mountain rivers rise over 20 ft. during the flood, reported

Oct. 24, A hurricane visited the south-west part of Japan; 128 coral fishing boats sunk, and about 1,000 Japanese lost

Nov. 15, New battleship, *Satsuma*, of 19,200 tons launched at Yokosuka

Dec. 1, Administration of Niu-chwang handed over to China

1907

April 3, International conference of the world's student Christian federation opens in Tokio; 500 delegates, representing 30 countries

June 10, Franco-Japanese treaty

June 13, Operations in Formosa; chief native stronghold captured

July 14, Return of Prince Fushimi to Tokio; friendly demonstration towards Great Britain held

July 30, Russo-Japanese convention, maintaining the integrity of China, signed in St. Petersburg

Sept. 9, Commercial and fishery agreements with Russia signed in St. Petersburg, July 28; ratified

Sept. 21, Final ceremony of the distribution of war rewards; Admiral Togo created a count

Oct. 1, Mr. Taft's anti-jingo speech in Tokio

Nov. 21, Launch of the armored cruiser *Ibuki*, the keel of which was laid in May

1908

Jan. 28, Count Hayashi, addressing the Diet at Tokio states that the question of emigration to Canada is definitely settled, Japan agreeing that the emigration shall be restricted within reasonable limits

March 14, The *Tatsu Maru* case settled; China promises to pay Japan 2,140*l.* for the arms which formed the cargo of the *Tatsu Maru*, which she will retain, and will pay also 1,250*l.* for demurrage. Japan agrees to adopt and enforce strict regulations to prevent the traffic in arms and ammunition from Japan to China

[The *Tatsu Maru*, a Japanese vessel, had been seized by China in Portuguese waters]

May 5, Arbitration Treaty with the United States signed

May 16, The Ya-lu forestry agreement with China signed

May 19, Two conventions with the United States, concerning "the protection of inventions, designs, trademarks, and copyrights of American citizens and Japanese subjects" in China and Korea respectively, signed

Aug. 19, Agreement with China as to Moukden-Antung Railway

Oct. 18–25, Visit of the American fleet

Nov. 30, Agreement between Japan and the United States to encourage the free and peaceful development of commerce in the Pacific between the two countries signed

1909

July 31–Aug. 1, Great fire at Osaka destroys 11,000 houses and sweeps a length of two miles

Sept. 4, The Manchurian convention, and the Korean boundary agreement with China, signed

Oct. 26, Prince Ito (born 1841) murdered by a Korean at Kharbin

1910

Jan. 21, Japan and Russia declined to agree to proposal of the Secretary of State (Knox) of the United States for neutralization of the railroads of Manchuria

April 13, Alien Land Ownership Act promulgated allowed foreigners to own land only when their own Governments granted reciprocal rights to Japanese, and this privilege restricted to persons and houses of business located in Japan. Certain districts set aside for purposes of national defense excepted

July 1, Port Arthur (Darien) thrown open to shipping of all nations

July 4, Convention with Russia signed as to interests in Manchuria, railroads, &c.

The following is the text of it:—

The Imperial Governments of Russia and Japan, being sincerely attached to the principles established by the Convention concluded between them on July 30th, 1907, and being desirous of developing the effects of this Convention with a view to the consolidation of peace in the Far East, have agreed to complete the said arrangement in the following manner:—

1. With the object of facilitating communications and developing the commerce of the nations, the two high contracting parties agree to extend to one another their friendly coöperation with a view to the improvement of their respective railway lines in Manchuria and the perfecting of the connecting services of the said lines, and to abstain from all competition prejudicial to the realization of this object

2. Each of the high contracting parties undertakes to maintain and respect the *status quo* in Manchuria resulting from all the treaties, conventions, and other arrangements concluded up to this date, either between Russia and Japan or between those two powers and China. Copies of the said arrangements have been exchanged between Russia and Japan

3. In the event of anything arising of a nature to threaten the *status quo* mentioned above the two high contracting parties shall enter each time into communication with each other with a view to coming to an understanding as to the measures they may think it necessary to take for the maintenance of the said *status quo*

July 17, The Government notified the Powers of Europe that commercial treaties would terminate at end of the year

July 23, Steamer *Tetsurei Maru* sunk off Chindo Island, Korea; 200 persons lost

Aug. 22, Agreement concluded by which Korea annexed to Japan

Aug. 29, Formal proclamation of annexation of Korea to be known by name of Chosen

Sept. 30, Regulations for government of Korea (Chosen) promulgated at Tokio

Oct. 1, General Seiki Terauchi became first Governor General of Chosen

Dec. 10, Trial of 26 Anarchists including Dr. Daijiro Kotoku and his wife in conspiracy to assassinate the Emperor on his way to attend a military review at Okayama

1911

Jan. 17, Dr. Kotoku and his wife sentenced to death, 11 others to terms of imprisonment

Jan. 24, Dr. Kokotu and wife executed

Feb., Prince Taro Katsura again Prime Minister

Feb. 21, Treaty of commerce and navigation with the United States signed. Declaration appended affirmed "Gentlemen's Agreement" providing for regulation by Japan of emigration of laborers to the United States

March, Factory law enacted dealing particularly with child labor

April 3, Treaty of trade and navigation with Great Britain signed

May 16, Treaty of amity with Spain signed

June 20, Agreement with Russia concluded for settlement of claims arising out of the war

July 13, Alliance with Great Britain of April 12, 1905 renewed for 10 years

Aug. 19, Treaty of commerce and navigation with France signed

Aug. 30, New Cabinet formed by the Marquis Saionji succeeded the Ministry of Katsura, Baron Uchida, Minister of Foreign Affairs

Sept. 28, Baron Yun Chi Ho and other Koreans in revolt sentenced to long prison terms

Nov. 24, Death of Marquis Jutaro Komura (56), statesman

1912

Jan. 16, Fire at Osaka destroyed 5,000 workmen's houses

Feb. 3, Premier Saionji submitted Admiral Saito's naval program to the Diet for expenditure of 90 million yen and providing for construction of eight super-dreadnoughts and four battle-cruisers

April 2, Death of Shiaroki Ishomoto, statesman

April, Strike of seamen

July 29, Death of Emperor Mutsuhito. Succeeded by his son Yoshihito

Sept. 13, General Nogi, hero of Port Arthur, and his wife committed suicide on the eve of the imperial funeral to follow their Emperor into death

Sept. 23, Typhoon destroyed $20,000,000 worth of property

Dec. 2, General Uyehara (Uehara) resigned from the Cabinet

Dec. 5, The Saionji Cabinet resigned on defeat by militarists of his policy of retrenchment

Dec. 14, Prince Katsura summoned to form Cabinet

Dec. 20, Prince Katsura took office as Prime Minister, Lieutenant-General Yasutsuma, Minister of War, Admiral Sato, Naval affairs

1913

Jan. 21, Interpellation against Government introduced by Seiyukai leaders, Ozaki, Yukio, and Motoda resulted in imperial decree proroguing the Diet for fortnight

Feb. 5, Diet met again but was again prorogued until the 8th and again to the 10th

Feb. 10, Riots in opposition to the Katsura Government. Several citizens killed in clash with police and many injured, buildings burned and several hundred persons arrested in Tokio. Simultaneous risings in Kobe, Osaka, Kyoto, Hiroshima, and other places

Feb. 12, Katsura Ministry resigned. Succeeded by Admiral Count Yamamoto

March 6, Disastrous fire destroyed property in business section of Yokohama

March, Trial of Koreans accused by 2 men arrested for burglary resulted in arrest of 123 men on confessions which they repudiated as obtained under torture and which no evidence supported; 6 of the accused sentenced to 10 years' penal servitude, 18 to 7 years, 39 to 6 years, and 41 to 5 years. On appeal Baron Yun Chi-ho, Yang Ki-tak, Im Chi-chung, An Tai-tuk, and Yi Seung-hun were sentenced to 6 years' penal servitude and Ok Kwan-pin to 5 years. The other 99 were acquitted (A. M. Young)

April, Kanegafuchi Spinning Company employing 40,000 persons in 36 mills reduced wages 25%

May 9, Formal protest sent to the United States against proposed anti-alien land legislation in California. See United States, May 19

June 24, Resignation of General Kikoshi, Minister of War. Succeeded by General Kusunose

June 28, Arbitration Treaty with the United States renewed

July 10, Death of Count Tadasu Hayashim, statesman

Sept. 1, At sack of Nanking, China, 3 Japanese subjects killed

Sept. 5, Assassination of Mr. Abe, Director of Political Affairs in the Foreign Office as protest against Government's weak policy towards China

Sept. 10, Note to China demanded reparation and indemnity for 3 Japanese citizens killed in the taking of Nanking

Sept. 28, Formal apology of China to Japan for Nanking incident. 800,000 yen indemnity paid

Oct. 5, Japanese companies received loan concessions for 3 railroads in Manchuria

Oct. 10, Death of Prince Katsura, former Prime Minister (66)

Nov. 21, Death of Prince Keiki Tokugawa, last of the Shoguns

Public debt of Japan $2,921,000,000

1914

Jan. 9–10, Volcanic eruption at Sakurashima Island in Kogoshima Bay forced 10,000 persons to emigrate

Jan. 14, Death of Count Yuko Ito

Feb. 3, Introduction of Bill in Diet by Mr. Takagi for prevention of judicial torture

Feb. 16, Death of Viscount Shuzo Aoki (69), former Minister of Foreign Affairs

March 23, Resignation of Yamamoto and his Cabinet on defeat of large naval appropriation because of scandals as to bribery and corruption in contracts

——, Parliament prorogued

April 9, Death of the Empress-Dowager (Haruko, widow of the Emperor Mutsuhito)

April 16, New Cabinet formed by Count Okuma with program calling for economy, reform, and establishment of true constitutionalism, Baron Kato, Minister of Foreign Affairs, Admiral Yashiro, and General Oka took over Admiralty and War Offices

May, Court-martial passed sentence of 3 years' imprisonment and 409,800 yen on Vice-Admiral Matsumoto implicated in scandal over battle-cruiser "Kongo" built by Vickers. Captain Sawasaki implicated in orders for wireless telegraphy was sentenced to one year's imprisonment and fine of 11,500 yen. Mitsui Bussan Kaisha surrendered £75,000 received illegally as commission on the "Kongo"

July 30, Resignation of Okuma Cabinet but reconstructed resumed office

July, Civil courts sentenced a number of directors and officials of the Mitsui company who had bribed naval officers to get order for the cruiser "Kongo" placed with Vickers and Company for whom they were agents for up to 2 years' imprisonment

Aug. 5, Neutrality statement as to European War published

Aug. 15, Note to Germany demanded that all German warships should leave Chinese waters or proceed to Kiaochau Bay and be there dismantled; that the German forts at Kiaochau should be dismantled; that Kiaochau leased territory be transferred to Japan before Sept. 15 with a view of its retrocession to China, this ultimatum presented in accordance with Japanese obligations under the Anglo-Japanese Alliance. Reply asked for by Aug. 23. No reply received

Aug. 23, War declared by Japan on Germany. See World War

Aug. 27, Diplomatic relations with Austria severed. Vice-Admiral Kato Sadakichi announced the blockade of Kiaochau Bay

Sept. 7, War credit of $26,500,000 voted by Diet

Sept. 14, Sentence of 4 years' imprisonment and fine of 368,306 yen and 5 sen given to Rear Admiral Fujii Terugoro in naval corruption case

Oct. 17, The cruiser "Takachiko" destroyed by either mine or torpedo and 280 persons drowned

Nov. 7, General Kamio received the capitulation of German garrison at Tsingtao, capital of Shantung

Dec. 4, Japanese Minister in Peking given "Twenty-one Demands" to present China at suitable time

Dec. 25, Dissolution of House of Representatives which refused to ratify increase of 2 divisions in army

Dec. 28, Port Kiachau opened by Japanese

1915

Jan. 16, China announced abolition of military zone in Shantung

Jan. 18, The "Twenty-one Demands" presented by Japan to the Chinese Government as to concessions in Shantung, Manchuria, and Inner Mongolia, the Hanyehping Iron Company, non-alienation of territory, and provision that the Chinese Government should employ Japanese political, financial, and military advisers, police administration in important places to be jointly Japanese and Chinese, and special concessions as to building of railroads and owning land

Feb. 2–April 18, Conference on the "Twenty-one Demands"

March 3, China agreed to extension for 99 years of leases of Port Arthur and Dalny to Japan

March 25, Elections a victory for the Government giving a majority of 80 seats

April 26–May 7, Revised list of 24 "Demands" presented by Japanese at Conference

May 1, China accepted "Demands" rejecting certain clauses impairing China's sovereignty

May 6, Decree of martial law issued on the Kwang-Tung Peninsula and the South Manchurian Railroad

May 7, Ultimatum to China gave 48 hours to accept "Demands" as modified reserving for future consideration those most subversive of sovereignty of China

May 8, China accepted "Demands"

May 20, Diet opened by the Emperor

May 25, Treaties with China and Notes embodying "Demands" were signed as to Japanese rights in Shantung, Manchuria, and Eastern Inner Mongolia

June 3, Bill of impeachment of the Government presented by Hara Takashi (Seiyukai) as to foreign policy which had destroyed friendship with China essential to prosperity of Japan and seconded by Mr. Inukai (Kokuminto or Nationalist) but motion thrown out on a division

July 30, Resignation of Okuma Cabinet because Viscount Oura, Home Minister, was accused of bribery and interference with election, the purchase of votes in favor of Army Bill

Aug. 10, Okuma resumed office with reconstructed Cabinet

Sept. 21, Viscount Ishii appointed Minister of Foreign Affairs

Oct. 19, Japan signed Pact of London of Sept. 15, 1914 pledge not to conclude a separate peace

Nov. 7–10, Ceremonial enthronement of the Emperor Yoshihito at Kyoto

1916

March 15, Law of nationality amended to make possible expatriation of Japanese born abroad, and provided that Japanese woman marrying an alien loses citizenship

March 30, General Oka, Minister of War, resigned. Succeeded by General Oshima

July 3, Secret Agreement with Russia by which Japanese interests in China recognized

July 8, Insurance law enacted by which the Government insured any person up to 250 yen ($125)

Aug. 13, Chinese troops attacked Japanese at Cheng-Chiatun near Mukden

Sept. 3, Demands presented to China for apology and indemnity for incident of Aug. 13 and certain rights in Inner Mongolia

Oct. 3, Resignation of Premier Okuma on the score of age

Oct. 9, Marshal Terauchi formed Cabinet, Count Terauchi, Minister of Foreign Affairs, *ad interim*

Nov. 3, Ceremony of "installing" the Crown Prince

Nov. 21, Viscount Motono appointed Minister of Foreign Affairs

Dec. 16, Announcement that Japan would not give up German islands north of the Equator occupied

1917

Jan. 17, Battle cruiser "Tsukuba" destroyed by explosion in Yokosuka Harbor, 153 lives lost

Jan. 23, Settlement of Cheng-Chiatun incident with China announced

Jan. 25, Parliament dissolved by Emperor following attack on Ministry

Feb. 16, Note signed by Great Britain guaranteed support of Japanese claims in respect to German rights in Shantung and Pacific Islands north of the equator

March 1, France in secret Agreement gave support to Japanese claims

March 5, Russia in secret Agreement gave support to Japanese claims

April 20, Elections a victory for the Government and military group

April 23, Trading with the enemy forbidden

Oct. 1, Imperial ordinance announced establishment of civil administration in leased territory in Shantung and "railway zone"

Nov. 2, Exchange of Notes with the United States (the Lansing-Isnii Agreement) by which the United States recognized Japan's special interests in China but maintenance of territorial integrity and sovereignty of China and the principle of the "open door" pledged

Dec. 30, Arrival of Japanese warship at Vladivostok "for the protection of Japanese subjects"

1918

Feb., Suicide of Oshikawa Norikichi, manager of great steel works at Yawata in Kyushu resulted in inquiry which revealed bribery and corruption

April 23, Viscount Motono succeeded as Minister of Foreign Affairs by Baron Goto

May 16, Secret Military Agreement with China signed provided for defense of mutual interests against Soviet Russia

May 23, Secret Naval Agreement with China signed

June 18, Arrival of Prince Arthur of Connaught in Japan

Aug. 2, Decision of Government to act with the United States in intervention in Siberia. Published in Government Gazette, Aug. 3

Aug. 4, Rising of fishermen and their wives in villages

in northern province of Toyama because of high price of rice. Rice shops raided. Rioting spread to Kyoto, Kobe, and other cities

Aug. 11, Japanese force landed at Vladivostok

Aug. 17, Government decree requisitioned all stocks of rice to be put on the market at reasonable prices

Aug. 23, Treaty of Arbitration with the United States signed extending Convention of May 5, 1908

Sept. 24, Secret Agreement with China granted Japanese railroad concessions

Sept. 29, Fall of the Terauchi Cabinet. Succeeded by Mr. Takashi Hara, first commoner to be Prime Minister, Count Yasuya Uchida, Minister of Foreign Affairs; Lieutenant General Baron Giichi Tanaka, Minister of War

Dec. 6, Koreans appealed to the United States for aid to effect separation from Japan

Dec. 28, Sentence of imprisonment given to Takata Shinjiro, Okura Hatsumi, and Kishimoto Ryntaro in steel and iron works scandal but sentences rendered null and void by stay of execution

1919

Jan. 7, Meeting of Korean students in Tokio discussed new principle of self-determination of peoples as suitable for Korea

Jan. 18, Peace Conference opened in Paris. Japan allowed 5 representatives, her ranking delegate a member of the Supreme Council

Jan. 21, Death of former Emperor of Korea

Jan. 28, The Press warned by police not to speak of self-determination movement in Korea

Feb. 4, Japan asked China not to disclose secret agreements with Japan at the Peace Conference. Financial proposals made as to Chinese loans not accepted by China

Feb. 12, State Department of the United States announced acceptance of Japanese proposal to restore railroad traffic in Siberia

Feb. 14, Debate on subject of universal suffrage instead of limit of franchise to men over 25 paying direct tax of 3 yen ($1.50) which excluded workers. Organized demonstrations in Tokio and riots

Feb. 23, Meeting of *Eta* (pariah caste) in Tokio

March 1, Parade of Koreans past palace where dead Emperor of Korea lying in state

March 3, Funeral of the former Emperor of Korea. Korean gatherings for independence begun

March 25, Electoral Reform Act passed increased number of electors from 1,500,000 to 3,000,000

April 17, Decree authorized rewards to farmers increasing their crops of cereals and rice

April 27, Korean Republic proclaimed

April 28, Yokohama damaged by great fire

April 30, Former German rights in Shantung awarded to Japan

May 6, Pacific Islands north of equator, former possessions of Germany, awarded to Japan to be administered by mandate system by Supreme Council

May 10, General election a victory for Government party opposed to universal suffrage gained 283 seats; the Kenseikai, 108; other parties, 68

May 15, Radical revision of Korean Government agreed upon by Privy Council substitution of civil for military Government and allowance of larger powers of self-government when independence movement abandoned by Koreans. Baron Saito appointed Governor-General

June 28, Peace Treaty with Germany signed at Versailles

July 18, Clash between Chinese and Japanese soldiers at Kuanchengtze near Changchun, 18 Japanese killed

Aug. 3, Statement of Viscount Uchida denied that Japan claimed any territorial rights in China and declared intention of Japan to return Shantung in full sovereignty to China

Aug. 19, Imperial rescript promulgated new civil government plan adopted May 15 for Korea making it a Japanese province

Sept. 19–29, Strike of 15,000 employees of the Kawasaki dockyards for eight-hour day which was granted and increase of wages

Dec. 25, Declaration of Premier Hara that Japan had no territorial claims in Siberia but would oppose extension of Bolshevik rule in eastern Siberia

1920

Jan. 10, Formal peace with Germany by exchange of ratifications

Feb. 26, Dissolution of Diet by imperial decree

Feb. 29, Russian attack on Japanese garrison at Nikolaevsk, Siberia

April 2, Six demands presented by Japan to the "Partisan Government" in Siberia. Agreed to under protest, April 29

May 14, Japanese troops landed with help of icebreakers at Decastri and marched overland to relief of Japanese garrison at Nikolaevsk, Siberia

May 27, 140 survivors of garrison of 600 murdered by Bolsheviks as troops approached

June 3, Japanese troops arrived at Nikolaevsk. Japan announced occupation of Sakhalin Province until satisfaction given for this incident

July, Arrest of G. L. Shaw, British merchant in Antung, China, because of refusal to allow Japanese police from Korean side of the Yalu River to search British steamers and other interference which hindered search for Korean rebels, regarded as hostile action against Japan

July 8, Anglo-Japanese Alliance terminated

July 28, Inquiry from the United States as to Japanese occupation of North Sakhalin

Sept. 22, Official announcement that Japan would withdraw troops from Siberia

Oct. 2, Koreans attacked Japanese consulate at Hunchun in Chientao, China and burned it; 10 Japanese killed. Reprisals by the Japanese

Nov. 21, Chinese Governor's estimate as 4,000 dead and 1,000 homes of Koreans destroyed by Japanese troops in Hunchun

Dec. 9, Socialists organized a union. Meeting dispersed by police and meeting the following night

Dec. 17, Japan received as mandates from the League of Nations the former German Islands in the Pacific north of the equator, the Caroline, Marshall, and Marianas (Ladrone) Archipelagoes

Dec. 31, Population of Japan by first imperial census 55,961,140, and including Sakhalin, Formosa, and Korea, 77,005,112. Published March 1, 1921

1921

March 3, Departure of the Crown Prince for world tour

March 11, Agreement with international bankers as to Chinese loan. *See* China

March 21, Japan announced reoccupation of Nikolaievsk with Japanese civil administration after seizure of fisheries in the Amur and dispute with Far Eastern Republic

May 7, Arrival of the Crown Prince of Japan in England on visit

May 9, General meeting of the Socialists' Union broken up by the police

May 16, Gold standard established

May 28, Socialists' Union proscribed by the Government

May 31, Note from United States Government protested invasion of Russian territory by Japan and stated that the United States would not recognize any claims or titles arising from the occupation or any action which might impair existing treaty rights or the political or territorial integrity of Russia

May, Strike in the Osaka Electric Light Works

July 8, Demonstration of 25,000 in strike of the electrical workers in the Kawasaki dockyards and Mitsubishi at Okurayama Park

July 9, Demonstration of the strikers in greatest strike up to this time in Japan at Egeyama adjoining Okurayama

July 14, The Kawasaki yard declared a lockout and troops on this day brought from Himeji at request of the Governor

Aug. 9, Manifesto called strikers to return to work as there were no funds to continue the strike

Aug. 26, Conference of Darien begun to arrange for evacuation of Siberia by Japanese. *See* Russia

Sept. 7, Japanese proposals at Disarmament Conference in Washington for restoration of Kiachau to China in return for certain railroad and mining concessions to Japan. These demands rejected by Chinese

Sept. 28, Yasuda Zenjiro reported to be richest man in Japan stabbed to death by young bandit from Manchuria. The public demonstration of labor leaders at funeral of the murderer against capitalism

Oct. 14, Trial by court martial of Major Hara who assumed responsibility for looted warehouses and sale of munitions by officials. Condemned to imprisonment for 18 months with stay of execution of sentence rendering it null and void

Nov. 4, Assassination of Premier Hara

Nov. 12, Baron Koreikiyo Takahashi assumed office as Prime Minister

——, Japan represented at Washington Conference by Prince I. Tokugawa, Admiral Baron T. Kato, and Baron K. Shidehara

Nov. 17, Launching of the battleship "Kaga" celebrated as patriotic fête

Nov. 24, Crown Prince Hirohito made Regent. The Emperor had long been incapacitated by illness

Dec. 13, Four-Power Pacific Treaty replaced the Anglo-Japanese Alliance

Dec. 18, Battleship "Tosa" launched

Public debt $18,650,000

1922

Jan. 9, Death of Marquis Okuma (83)

Feb. 1, Death of Prince Yamagata one of the last of the Elder Statesmen

Feb. 4, Treaty with China signed provided for return of Kiao-chau to China, Shantung railroad to be sold to China with other German properties and concessions in the peninsula valued at 53,406,141 gold marks

Feb. 6, Japan signed Five-Power Naval Treaty which restricted maximum capital ship tonnage to 315,000 tons. *See also* p. 565

Feb. 11, "Yap Treaty" with the United States as to rights in former German Islands in the Pacific

Feb. 23, Riots in Tokio over Bill for universal suffrage caused injury to a large number of persons

March 30, Prohibition law prohibited purchase of liquor by persons under 21

April 9–May 4, Evacuation of Japanese troops from Shantung begun

April 12, Law authorized the Government to establish courts for landlords and tenants

——, The Prince of Wales arrived in Japan on visit

May 2, Premier requested resignations of Ministers of Agriculture, Interior, Railroads, and Education

June 6, Fall of Takahashi Ministry

June 11, Cabinet on non-partisan basis formed by Admiral Kato pledged to execution of the Washington Agreements

June 20, Imperial sanction given to betrothal of the Crown Prince to the Princess Nagako

July 1, Announcement of decision of Government to withdraw troops from the Far Eastern Republic

July 5, Government announced that army would be reduced

July 6, Washington Treaties ratified. Naval budget reduced by 117,000,000 yen

Sept. 4–25, Russo-Japanese Conference at Chang-chun. Japanese refused recognition of Russia and evacuation of northern Sakhalin until indemnity paid for Nikolaevsk massacre

Sept. 30, Meeting of unions to form one single union under name of Nippon Rodo Kumiai Sorengo

Oct. 26, Japanese troops completed evacuation of Siberian mainland

Nov. 23, The Nomin Remmei or Farmers' Union inaugurated

Nov. 25, Government announced retirement of 60,000 men from the army to reduce the budget

Dec. 1, Agreement with China signed supplementary to Washington Treaty

Dec. 5, Agreement with China signed as to Shantung railroad

Dec. 10, Kiao-chau returned to China on payment by China of 14,000,000 gold yen in treasury notes for Japanese improvements

Dec. 7, Treaty of commerce and navigation with Poland signed

Dec. 17, Japanese garrison withdrawn from Tsingtau

1923

Jan. 1, Tsingtao Railway (Shantung) returned to China

Feb. 4, Death of General Kuroki

March 2, Defeat of Universal Suffrage Bill

March 14, Note to China in reply to Chinese Note of March 10 refused abrogation of treaties

March 18, The Eta in 3 days battle with "patriotic ruffians" in vicinity of Nara

March 21, Bill to introduce limited jury system to go into effect in 1928 passed Upper House

April 14, Hughes-Hanihara Notes cancelled Lansing-Ishii Agreement with the United States of Nov. 1917

Aug. 23, Agreement with the United States renewed Arbitration Treaty of May 5, 1908

Aug. 24, Death of Prime Minister Kato

Aug. 28, Count Gombei Yamamoto succeeded as Premier

Aug. 31, Death of Prince Masayoshi Matsukata

Sept. 1, Great earthquake followed by tidal wave devastated Tokio, Yokohama, Yokosuka, Nagoya and wiped out many villages. The American Red Cross estimated the number of killed as 225,000 and destitute as 2,000,000. Property loss given as $1,000,000,000

——, Death of Prince Matsukata

Sept. 2, Yamamoto Cabinet reorganized

Oct. 2, Commercial Agreement with Austria concluded

Nov. 16, Treaty of commerce and navigation with Yugoslavia signed

Dec. 1, Commercial *modus vivendi* with Spain arranged replacing commercial agreement of March 26, 1909

Dec. 27, Unsuccessful attempt on life of Prince Regent by Namba Daisuke, Socialist

Dec. 29, The Cabinet resigned after attempt on life of Prince Regent

1924

Jan. 1, New Cabinet formed by Viscount Kiego Kiyoura as Premier

Jan. 14, Earthquake south of Tokio

Jan. 26, Marriage of Prince Regent Hirohito to the Princess Nagako, eldest daughter of Prince Kuni

Jan. 31, Dissolution of Diet

Feb. 11, Loan placed in the United States of $150,000,000 and in England for £25,000,000

March 10, Treaty of commerce and navigation with Siam signed

March 19, Submarine 43 with 49 men sunk off Sasebo in collision with warship "Tatusuka"

April 10, Note of Japanese Ambassador in Washington Masanao Hanihara to Secretary Hughes referred to "grave consequences which enactment of the measure" excluding Japanese immigration would bring in relations between the 2 countries

May 10, General election a defeat for the Seiyuhonto Party supporting Premier Kiyoura

May 26, United States Immigration Act abrogated the "Gentlemen's Agreement" with Japan to restrict emigration of Japanese laborers to the United States and provided for total exclusion of Japanese

May 31, Japan presented Note protesting to the United States against the new Immigration Act

June 6, Resignation of Kiyoura Ministry

June 7, Treaty of commerce with Finland signed

June 11, Viscount Kofuei Kato formed a coalition Cabinet

June 27, Treaty of commerce with Belgium concluded

July 2, Death of Prince Matsukata, last of elder group of Elder Statesmen

July 15, Nationality law passed abolished dual citizenship for Japanese born in and resident in other countries

Dec. 1, Nationality law came into effect

1925

Jan. 20–30, Visit of naval squadron at San Francisco, California

Jan. 21, Treaty with Russia signed gave *de jure* recognition of Soviet Government, resumed diplomatic relations, and renewed Treaty of Sept. 5, 1905

Japan agreed to withdraw troops from northern Sakhalin by May 15

Feb. 4, Death of Sennosuka Yokota, Minister of Justice

March 2, Manhood Suffrage Bill giving vote to all male

citizens over 30 except those receiving government support and convicts passed House

March 16, Death of Viscount Goro Miura

——, Alien land law passed by House of Peers provided that nationals of any country barring Japanese from ownership of land should receive the same treatment in Japan. Passed Lower House March 23

March 18, Fire in Tokio destroyed 3,000 houses

March 29, Manhood Suffrage Bill passed both houses raising voters from 3,000,000 to 14,000,000

April 4, Evacuation of northern Sakhalin completed by Japanese troops

——, Resignation of Takahashi, Minister of Commerce and head of the Seiyukai Party. Succeeded as head of Party by General Baron Giichi Tanaka

April 20, Air mail service inaugurated between (1) Tokio and Osaka (2) Osaka and Fukuoka (3) Sakai-Osaka-Imaharu

April 22, Peace Preservation law commonly known as the Dangerous Thoughts Bill enacted provided that those who joined or formed societies aiming at alteration of the national constitution or the form of government or repudiation of system of private ownership of property should be subject to imprisonment not exceeding 10 years

May 5, Manhood Suffrage Act promulgated abolishing tax qualification and granting suffrage to all male citizens except paupers, and certain members of army and navy and civil officials

May 15, Protocol signed with Russia completing transfer of Sakhalin to Russia

May 16, Diplomatic relations with Russia formally resumed

May 23, Severe earthquake in western Japan. Toyooka, Kinosaki, and Kumihama destroyed

May 30, Provisional Commercial Agreement with Greece signed

July 4, Commercial Treaty with Latvia signed

July 30, Resignation of Kato Cabinet on question of tax readjustment measures

——, Treaty of commerce and navigation with Great Britain signed

Aug. 1, Kato Cabinet reorganized, resumed office

Aug. 21, Strike of 50,000 employees of Japanese cotton mills in Shanghai settled with recognition of union

Sept. 18, Fire destroyed the House of Peers and House of Representatives

Oct. 1, Second census of population gave population of Japan proper as 59,736,822, of empire as 83,456,929

Oct. 30, Commercial Treaty with Czechoslovakia signed

Nov. 30, Agreement with Russia as to oil fields in northern Sakhalin under Treaty of Jan. 21

Dec. 6, First child, a daughter, born to Prince Regent Hirohito

Dec. 28, Death of Viscount Kato, the Premier (67) and of Viscount Miura

1926

Jan. 30, Reijiro Wakatsuki became Prime Minister and president of the Kenseikai Party succeeding Kato. "Lion" Hamaguchi became Home Minister

Feb. 18, After drifting a month in the Pacific 14 of crew of 33 of the steamer "Daishin Maru III" rescued by tanker "Java Arrow"

March 5, Farmer Labor Party organized at Osaka

March 26, Law passed doubled duty on wheat and increased duty on flour 50%. Tax placed on soft drinks. Subsidies granted for domestic pig iron and steel, and educational subsidies

April 7, Death of Baron Chincho Hozumi

April 12, Dr. Yusaburo Kuratomi appointed president of the Privy Council, Kiichiro Hiranuma, vice-president

April 25, Death of Prince Yi Wang, of Korea

April 28, Death of Viscount Kageaki Kawamura

April 29, Alderman Takayama assassinated and Alderman Kato stabbed by a Korean

May 24, Eruption of volcano in central Hokkaido. More than 300 persons killed

June 2, Premier Wakatsuki reorganized the Cabinet: Home Affairs, Yuko Hamaguchi (Acting), Kenzo Adachi; Foreign Affairs, Baron Kijuro Shidehara; Finance, Chokuon Kataoka (Sept., 1926); War, General Issei Ugaki; Marine, Admiral Takeshi Takarabe; Minister of Justice, Yoku Egi; Education, Ryohei Okada; Agriculture, Chuji Machida; Commerce, Ikunosuke Fujisawa; Communications, Kenzo Adachi; Railways, Viscount Kiyoshiro Inoue

June 3, Imperial ordinance to enforce revised Factory Act passed to come into effect July 1

July 1, Health Insurance Act of 1922 came into effect

July 30, Floods in Niigata district caused death of 400 persons, and destruction of land and thousands of homes. Official estimate of property loss $5,000,000

Oct. 18, Agrarian Party (Nippon Nominto) organized

Oct. 19, Death of Eki Hioki, statesman

Nov. 1, Alien Land ownership law allowing alien ownership except in areas "necessary for national defense" came into effect. Included provision making it possible to exclude from this privilege nationals of countries which did not allow Japanese to own land

Dec. 25, Death of the Emperor Yoshihito. Succeeded by the Prince Regent Hirohito, 124th Emperor in the line of Jimmu Tenno

Emigration in the year 1926-1927 16,184 of whom 8,599 went to Brazil

1927

March 7, Earthquake in district around Gulf of Wakasa 100 miles north of Osaka killed more than 3,000 persons and injured nearly 7,000. Property damage estimated at £10,000,000

March 16, Failure of Watanabe Bank of Tokio. Within a week 8 other banks closed

March 23, "Earthquake Bill" passed provided payment for emergency paper issued during the earthquake of 1923 and stopped run on banks

March 24, Japanese consulate at Nanking looted and burned when taken by Nationalist forces

March 30, Provisional commercial Agreement concluded with Persia

April 5, Failure of Susuki Company and importers and exporters with liabilities amounting to £50,000,000 followed by suspension of Taiwan Bank precipitated financial crisis

April 11, Japan joined 4 other Powers in identic Note to China regarding Nanking incident

April 17, Wakatsuki Ministry resigned

April 18, Baron Gi-ichi Tanaka headed new Ministry (Seiyu-kai Party)

——, Nakai Bank closed

April 21, Peers Bank and Fifteenth Bank suspended followed by run on other banks. Moratorium declared closing all banks for 21 days

April 28, The Cabinet approved a 500,000,000 yen Loan Bill which would guarantee the Bank of Japan

May 3, Special session of the Diet on financial situation passed Bills for rehabilitation of banks May 12

May 10, Junnosuke Inouye appointed Governor of the Bank of Japan

May 11, Japan demanded of China that consulate at Nanking be evacuated

May 13, Most banks reopened

June 1, Shinto Club of majority of the Seiyuhonto Party changed name to Rikken Minseito (Constitutional Democratic Party)

June 2, Chuzo Mitauchi succeeded Koreiyo as Finance Minister

June 29, Consul and staff returned to Nanking

July 20, Commercial Treaty with Germany signed and memo as to importation of German dyestuffs

Aug. 20, Commercial Treaty with French Indo-China signed included regulations as to residence and navigation in Annam

Aug. 30, War Office order for withdrawal of all troops from Shantung

Sept. 13, Typhoon and tidal wave wrecked towns of Kojima and Nakamura killing 719 persons. 1,850 houses destroyed

Sept. 15, Strike of laborers begun at Noda Soy Factory which lasted until April following

Sept. 17–Oct 14, Elections for the prefectural assemblies the first under the new election law gave the Seiyukai 714 seats, the Minseito 569, the Labor Party 28, and other parties 176. 50% of the electorate failed to go to the polls

Sept. 17, Bankers decided to establish new bank, the Showa Bank, for the rehabilitation of a number of the banks which failed in April

Oct. 1, Monument unveiled at Shimoda to Townsend Harris, first American envoy to Japan

Oct. 30, For the second time in history of the country the entire fleet of 172 vessels reviewed by Emperor in Yokohama Bay

Nov. 9, Death of Dr. Bunyiui Nanjio

Dec. 26, The Emperor opened the 54th session of the Diet with formal address read personally. Adjourned until Jan. 18

Dec. 30, First subway in the Far East opened from Ufo to Asakusa in Tokio a distance of one and a half miles

1928

Jan. 1, New banking law came into effect

Jan. 21, Lower House dissolved by Premier Tanaka and general election ordered

Jan. 23, Fisheries Convention with Russia signed

Feb. 20, First general parliamentary election under manhood suffrage law. The Minseito Party gained 217 seats in the House out of 464, the Seiyukai (Tanaka's Party) 221 seats according to official statement of the Diet

April 6, Toichio Araki and Ryvkichi Matsui left Tokio for round the world trip

May 3, Mr. Suzuki, Home Minister, resigned after vote of censure of Diet on April 20

May 11, Japanese troops bombarded and occupied Tsinan-fu on Shantung Railroad driving out Chinese Nationalists

May 29, Emergency law promulgated providing death penalty for Communists

May 31, Liquor Traffic Treaty with the United States signed

June 4, Strike of 50,000 seamen at Kobe for increase of wages

June 8, Unsuccessful attempt of a peasant named Okamura to kill Premier Tanaka with a dagger at station in Tokio

July 24, Commercial Agreement with New Zealand signed

Aug. 24, Arbitration Treaty with the United States signed replaced that of May 5, 1908

Sept. 27, Marriage of Prince Yasuhito elder brother of the Emperor and Miss Setsuko Matsudaira

Oct. 1, Trial by jury came into effect in limited sphere in certain cases, first actual trial by jury Oct. 23

Nov. 1 and 2, Labor demonstration and clash with police. 29 killed, 60 wounded

Nov. 10, Ceremony of enthronement of Emperor Hirohito at Kyoto

Nov. 18–23, Negotiations at Nanking with China for settlement of Nanking and Tsinanfu incidents broke down on question of withdrawal of Japanese troops from Shantung

Dec. 24, New Parliament opened. Formal opening by the Emperor Dec. 26

1929

Jan. 16, Death of Count Sutemi Chinda

Jan. 23, Commercial Agreement with Hungary signed

March 20, Provisional Commercial Agreement with Persia signed

March 22, Death of Admiral Viscount Ryokei Inouye (84)

March 23, New and higher tariff passed placed duties on lumber

March 28, Agreement with China signed settled Tsinanfu incident, Japanese forces to be immediately withdrawn from China

April 13, Death of Count Shimpei Goto (73)

May 2, Arrival of British Mission

——, Agreement signed with China settled Nanking and Hankow incidents, China to pay compensation

May 3, In Tokio Prince Henry, third son of King George, conferred upon Emperor Hirohito the garter, British highest order of knighthood. The Order of the Chrysanthemum, highest decoration in Japan, conferred on Prince Henry by the Emperor

June 10, Department of Overseas Affairs established

June 27, Ratification of the Paris Pact by the signature of the Emperor for renunciation of war

July 1, Work by women between hours of 10 P.M. and 5 A.M. became illegal

July 2, Resignation of Baron Tanaka as Premier. Succeeded by Yuko Hamaguchi (Liberal): Home Affairs, Kenzo Adachi; Foreign Affairs, Baron Kijuro Shidehara; Finance, Junnosuke Inoue; War, General Kazunari Ugaki; Marine, Admiral Jakeshi Takarabe; Justice, Viscount Chiaki Watanabe; Education, Ryuzo Tanaka; Agriculture and Forestry, Chuji Machida; Commerce and Industry, Magoichi Tawara; Communications, Matajiro Koizumi; Railways, Tasuku Egi; Overseas Affairs, Genji Matsudaira

July 15, Passenger air service inaugurated on the Tokio-Osaka-Dairen line

July 31, Exchange of Notes with Turkey effected provisional commercial agreement

Aug. 14, Death of Lieutenant General Ogawa and 7 other aviation officers in crash of plane near Tokio

Sept. 29, Death of Baron Giichi, ex-premier. Succeeded as president of the Seiyukai by Ki Inukai

Oct. 28–Nov. 8, Institute of Pacific Relations held third conference at Kyoto for discussion of extra-territoriality in China and common interests and problems

Nov. 3, Death of Katsunoskue Inouye

Nov. 6, 825 Communists arrested by police in Tokio

1930

Jan. 11, Embargo on exportation of gold placed in 1917 lifted, return to gold standard

Jan. 21, Diet dissolved

Jan. 26, Wireless service inaugurated between Nagoya and London

Jan. 27, Death of Admiral Baron Shigeto Dewa

Feb. 4, Marriage of Prince Takamatsu, younger brother of the Emperor, and Miss Kikuko Tokugawa

Feb. 20, General election a victory for the Minsei Party: Minseito (Government Party), 273; Seiyukai (Conservative Opposition), 174; Labor, 5; Other Groups, 9; Independent, 5; total 466

——, Direct wireless service with France inaugurated

March 11, Plan of Governor General Saito of Korea for autonomy of Korea submitted to Cabinet approved

March 12, Customs Tariff Convention with China signed by which Chinese tariff autonomy recognized

March 18, Crown Prince of Denmark arrived in Tokio

March 19, Commercial Agreement with Egypt signed

March 24, Completion of restoration of Tokio following destructive earthquake of 1923 formally celebrated

April 1, Strike of municipal tramway employees in Tokio for better conditions

May 20, Commercial Treaty with China

June 9, Resignation of Vice Admiral Yamanashi

June 11, Resignation of Admiral Kanji Kato, in opposition to signing of London Naval Treaty, head of Navy. Succeeded by Admiral Shoshin Taniguchi. Vice Admiral Kobayashi and Vice Admiral Nagano succeeded Vice Admiral Yamanashi and Vice Admiral Suyetsugu as Vice Minister of the Navy and assistant chief of the General staff

July 18, Typhoon, the third most destructive in history, struck Kyushiu

July 29, Japanese consulate at Changsha burned by Chinese Communists

Aug. 16, Commercial Treaty with Austria signed

Sept. 1, First legislative enactment limiting hours of labor went into effect providing for 10 hour day for miners

Oct. 2, Emperor Hirohito ratified the London Naval Treaty

Oct. 12, Commercial Treaty with Turkey signed

Oct. 21, The Government withdrew appointment of Torikichi Obata as Minister to China because of objection to appointment by Chinese because of his connection with the "Twenty-one Demands" in 1915, ending long controversy

Oct. 27, Revolt of tribesmen in Musha, Formosa and massacre of villagers

Nov. 14, Premier Hamaguchi wounded by youth, member of reactionary patriotic society

Nov. 25, Earthquake in northern part of Idzu peninsula killed over 200 persons

JOHORE

See Malay.

KARIKAL

Karikal, French Colony in India, on the southeast coast, area 53 square miles, population 58,228. The territory was promised to the French by the Raja of Tanjore in 1738 in return for services and obtained by them by force in 1739. It was captured by the English in 1760, restored in 1765, taken again in 1768, and finally restored in 1817.

KEDAH

See Malay.

KEELING ISLANDS

See Cocos Islands.

KELANTAN

See Malay.

KOREA

Korea (Chosen), a peninsula of Asia stretching southward from Manchuria, length about 600 miles, and extreme breadth 135 miles, area 85,228 square miles, population at end of 1928, 19,189,699 including 469,043 Japanese, 18,667,334 Koreans, and 53,322 foreigners, population 1930, 21,057,969. Seoul is the capital. China renounced suzerainty over Korea in 1895. By Treaty of Aug. 22, 1910 the Korean territory was formally annexed to Japan, and the name changed to Chosen.

First conquest of the country by forces of Japan in the third century. In 1597 Japanese Emperor Taikosama invaded Korea and defeated the Koreans; evacuated the following year, but a heavy tribute exacted by Japan. In 1866, 1867, and 1871 punitive expeditions, French and American, attacked coast in retaliation for murder of missionaries and adventurers trying to break down the isolation of Korea.

1876

Feb. 26, First Treaty made with Japan in which Japan acknowledged the independence of Korea, agreed to allow a Japanese resident at the capital and 3 ports opened to Japanese trade

1882

May 22, Treaty of peace and friendship with the United States signed, commercial privileges granted
July 23, Anti-foreign mob attacked the Japanese legation at Seoul; war with Japan averted by compensation and reparations

1883

Nov. 26, Treaty of commerce with Great Britain signed

1884

June 25/July 7, Treaty of commerce with Russia signed

Dec. 5, Another anti-foreign riot of Koreans and Chinese, 7 members of the Ministry killed. Peace restored about Dec. 13 by intervention of Japan

1885

Jan. 9, Convention with Japan signed, indemnity of $30,000 paid
April 18, Convention of Tientsin signed by which Japanese and Chinese troops to be withdrawn from Korea (Chinese had been in occupation since the revolt of 1882, Japanese since the revolt of 1884)
May 12–Feb. 27, 1887, British naval force occupied Port Hamilton, island off southern end of Korea

1886

June 4, Treaty with France signed

1888

Jan. 17, Korean mission to the United States presented to the President in Washington
Aug. 8, Treaty with Russia signed

1894

May, Insurrection in one of the southern provinces
June 10, Chinese troops landed on coast at request of the Emperor to aid in suppression of rebellion
June 25, Invasion of Japanese troops, Seoul occupied, to protect Japanese interests in Korea
June 27, Remonstrance of China claiming suzerainty over Korea
June 30, The King renounces all subjection to China, and calls on the Japanese for help
June, Foreign intervention to stop the war unsuccessful
July 3, Japan proposed reforms for Korea, reform to be undertaken jointly by Japan and China, rejected by Japan
July 14, Japan obtained Treaty permitting military occupation during war with China
July, Japan demands extensive reforms, and claims observance of treaty of 1885; opposed by China
July 25, Hostilities begin between China and Japan; the *Kowshing*, a British despatch boat (Capt. Galsworthy) conveying Chinese troops, attacked by Japanese warships and sunk off Asan, Capt. Galsworthy escaped to the Japanese: many killed
July 29, Japanese victories at Chan-hon and at Asan under Gen. Oshima
Aug. 4, Chinese declaration of war
Aug. 26, Japanese army increased, they hold Seöul and some provinces, guerilla warfare; treaty of alliance between Japan and Korea signed at Seöul
Aug. 30, Asan recaptured
Sept. 10, The Emperor of China transmits a justificatory circular to the Great Powers, Aug. 23; reported
Sept. 15, 16, The Chinese surrounded and defeated with great loss at Ping-Yang, on the Tatong river; Gen. Tso (Chinese) killed
Sept. 17, Great naval battle at the mouth of the Yalu river; much slaughter, 8 Chinese vessels destroyed
Oct. 9, Japanese occupy Wi-ju without resistance, reported
Oct. 14, The British proposals for mediation considered premature by the Great Powers, reported
Oct. 22, Indecisive battle near Wi-ju, great slaughter
Oct. 25, The Japanese cross the Yalu and enter Manchuria; Chinese fort taken after sharp fighting
Oct. 26, Kiu-lien-tcheng taken by Marshal Yamagata
Oct. 31, Tung-huan-tcheng surrenders

Nov. 3, Prince Kung acknowledges the defeat of China, and requests foreign intervention

Nov. 6, 7, Kinchou and Talienwan captured

Nov. 9, Chinese routed at the Namquan Pass

Nov. 20, 21, Port Arthur, a strong naval arsenal, taken by the Japanese under Marshal Oyama by storm [Great massacre of Chinese after the battle, owing to their having killed some captive Japanese, Nov. 21–26]

Nov. 25, Vigorous attack of Chinese on Marshal Yamagata's army at the Fen-Shiu pass repulsed

Nov. 28, Korean insurgents severely defeated

Dec. 2, Kinchou reoccupied by Marshal Oyama

Dec. 5, Fuchou taken without resistance

Dec. 10, 14, Chinese defeated at Kinkuahu and Yih-man-shan

Dec. 13, Hai-tcheng taken by Gen. Katsura

Dec. 19, Chinese defeated under Gen. Sung by Gen. Katsura, near Hai-tcheng

1895

Jan. 8, Rebellion of the Tonghaks: 3 towns burnt, rebels defeated, Dec. 23; again defeated

Jan. 5, Japan refuses an armistice

Jan. 7, The independence of Korea proclaimed by the King at Seöul

Jan. 10, Desolation in Manchuria; Chinese routed at Kai-phing

Jan. 18, 19, Tung-chou bombarded and taken

Jan. 20, 24, Yung-tcheng and Ning-hai occupied

Feb. 12, Bombardment of Wei-hai-wei and the island fortress Leu-kung-tau by Adm. Ito and Marshal Oyama, began, Jan. 30; fierce fighting; Adm. Ting, Gen. Chang, Capt. Liu surrender ships and forts under honors of war, and commit suicide from grief and shame (great respect shown to their memory)

Feb. 13, Adm. McClure accepts the Japanese conditions

Feb., Japanese successful advances

March 4, 6, Niu-chuang and port of Ying-kow taken after fierce fighting by Gen. Nodzu

March 9, Denshodai burnt by the Japanese; much slaughter

March 19, Li Hung Chang, Chinese Minister Plenipotentiary, with Mr. Foster, American adviser, sent to treat for peace; received by Visc. Mutsu, Japanese Minister, at Shimonoseki in Manchuria

March 24, Li Hung Chang fired at in the face by Koyama, a young Japanese, a lunatic

——, Haichow, on the Kiangsu coast, taken

March 26, The Pescadores Islands taken

March 30, Armistice (21 days) proclaimed at Tokio. *See* Formosa, March 31, 1895

April 17, Peace signed; conditions: the independence of Korea; Japan retains conquered places, the Pescadores and part of Liao-tung peninsula, Liao, and Formosa: an indemnity of 200,000,000 taels; 4 new ports opened to commerce, Li Hung Chang departs

April 23, The ministers of Russia, Germany, and France protest against the annexation of Chinese continental territory to the Japanese Empire by the treaty

May 8, Japan abandons the claim to the Liao-tung peninsula, May 6: ratifications of the treaty exchanged

May, Armistice prolonged for 5 days; negotiations proceeding

May 13, Li Yo Shun, Korean Minister, sentenced to

penal servitude for life, and 5 officials to death, for murder and treason

May 21, Government unsettled

May *et seq.*, Count Inouye employed by Japan to promote reforms

Oct. 18, Mutiny of Korean soldiers; the palace invaded by an anti-reform mob; the Queen and 2 ladies murdered, Oct. 8; H.M.S. *Edgar* ordered to Chemulpho, Oct. 13; Visct. Miura and other Japanese ministers and soldiers recalled from Seöul, reported

Nov. 30, Evacuation of the Liao-tung peninsula by the Japanese

1896

Feb. 10, 11, Insurrection at Seöul, the King and his son take refuge in the Russian legation; Russian marines landed at Chemulpho, march to Seöul

Feb. 14, Two Korean ministers executed for treason; anti-Japanese cabinet formed; Russian influence predominant

March 23, Fighting between the Japanese and rebels near Fusan; reported

May 17, Concession to work for gold granted to a Russian company; reported

Nov. 7, Russian slow policy reported successful

1897

Feb. 20, The King leaves the Russian legation for the new palace

Feb. 24, Treaty between Russia and Japan providing for the maintenance of the independence of Korea under their military protection; text published

Oct. 8, Financial improvement under Mr. M'Leavy Brown, chief commissioner (in unison with M. Alexieff, Russian); more ports open to foreign trade; reorganization of the army by the Russians, &c.; reported

Dec. 31, Six British warships arrive at Chemulpho to support Mr. M'Leavy Brown

1898

March 25, M. Alexieff and Russian drill instructors recalled, with 3,300*l.* compensation

April, Convention signed between Russia and Japan respecting Korea

July 11, Plot against the government discovered at Seöul, officials arrested, reported

Sept. 16, Attempt to poison the Emperor and Crown Prince frustrated, reported; Tim Khunyuk, interpreter at the Russian legation, executed on a false charge, his wife and others tortured, Oct. 10, 12; the Minister of Justice dismissed, Oct. 13

Nov. 23, Political riot at Seöul, 23 deaths, reported

1899

Jan., Seöul and Chemulpho railway taken over by Japan (opened July 5, 1900)

March 22, Cabinet dismissed and 2 ministers banished on account of changes in provincial offices

May, Ports (3) on the E. coast leased to Russia for 12 years

Aug., Japanese influence again paramount in Seöul

Sept. 11, Treaty of peace and friendship with China

1900

March 30, Russia obtains an exclusive settlement at Masampho harbor, agreements signed

May, Two Korean officials, under Japanese protection,

suspected of complicity in the murder of the queen (1895), tortured and put to death

Mid-June, Judicial officials punished to appease Japan

Mid-Aug., Disturbances in the north, reported

1901

April 16, Railway loan with France concluded

May, Land at Masampho leased to Japan by government

1902

Jan. 30, Anglo-Japanese agreement, the *status quo* and independence of Korea to be maintained; *see* China

1903

Jan. 8, Korea gives its adhesion to the Geneva convention

Feb. 25, Russian demand for concession to Russo-Chinese bank of the Seöul-Wi-ju railway rejected

June *et seq.*, Dispute with Japan (*see* Japan and Russia)

Aug. 11, Lease of lands and right of timber purchases at Yongampho granted to a Russian company, full access to Yalu valley and river estuary acquired, reported

Aug. *et seq.*, Russian-Japanese negotiations held in Tokio

Oct. 20, First section of Japanese railway from Seoul to Fusan opened

Oct. 27, Yongampho fortified by the Russians, reported

End Dec., Rioting at Mokpho, Dec. 13; much unrest in the south

1904

Jan. 16, Council of state advocates an alliance with China, and expresses a firm determination to maintain the independence of Korea. Resignation of Minister of Finance and Minister of the Interior, partisans of the Japanese appointed in their places; nine government departments and bureaus, including the supreme court, abolished by imperial order owing to desire of the Emperor to carry out reforms, reported

End Jan., Korea declares that it will maintain a strict neutrality in the event of war breaking out between Russia and Japan

Feb. 8, Japanese land troops at Chemulpo

Feb. 9, Japanese squadron attack and sink the Russian cruiser *Variag* and the gunboat *Korietz* in the port, troops occupy Seöul

Feb. 23, Japanese-Korean agreement, by which Japan guarantees the independence and territorial integrity of the Korean Empire, signed

Feb. 28, Japanese defeat Russian troops at Cheng-ju and occupy the town

March 10, Formal concession by Korean Government to Japan for military railway from Seöul to Wiju, signed

——, Treaty between Japan and Korea published

March 27, Marquis Ito visits Seöul on special mission to advise the Emperor as to the reform of the internal administration of the country under Japanese control; returns

April 7, Wiju occupied by Japanese troops

May, Korean Government issue a decree annulling all treaties and agreements with Russia, including the Yalu timber concessions

Aug. 22, Korean-Japanese agreement signed at Seöul; Korean government undertakes to regulate its national finances and relations with foreign powers

regulated by a Japanese financial adviser, and a foreign diplomatic adviser recommended by Japan

Dec., Government railway between Seöul and Wiju completed as far as Pingyang

1905

Jan. 1, First railroad from Seoul to Chemulpo

Jan. 18, Government, acting on advice of Mr. Megata, financial adviser, decide to prohibit the circulation of all nickels except those issued by the national mint; general reform of the currency contemplated, and the reduction of the Korean military establishment, reported

March 13, Conspiracy to induce the Emperor to repudiate the Japanese convention discovered at Seöul; conspirators arrested

April 1, Treaty with Japan by which all telegraph and telephone lines turned over to Japan

Aug. 13, Korean-Japanese treaty concluded, stipulating that Japanese shipping shall have the right to navigate all the rivers and coast of Korea; owners of vessels to have the right to lease land and to construct wharves and jetties; treaty to be operative for 15 years from date of ratification

Nov. 30, Treaty with Japan signed at Seoul, Nov. 17; made public

1906

Jan. 30, Marquis Ito, Japanese resident-general at Seoul, outlines Japan's policy to Korea in the following terms: "The national defence of Korea will be entirely undertaken by Japan; with regard to diplomacy and the introduction of internal reforms into Korea, measures will be taken only after careful consultation with the Emperor and his ministers; every possible effort will be exerted to develop agriculture as well as mining, forestry, and fishing; the most difficult, but also the most important, measure will be that designed to promote the advancement of general education in Korea . . . the work of developing the agricultural and other resources of the country, coupled with the spread of education, will, it is hoped, establish the relations between the two countries on a closer and firmer basis"

May 31, Japanese attack on insurgents at Hong-ju; the insurgents lose 69 killed and 127 made prisoners. The Japanese lost 1 killed and 2 wounded

Dec. 7, Petty revolts, caused, it is supposed, by the enforcement of the new system of transmitting the proceeds of taxation through the local post-offices under Japanese direction, reported

1907

June 22, The Emperor appointed Korean envoy to protest to the Powers against the Japanese treaties

July 18, Resignation of the Ministry

July 19, Abdication of the Emperor Yi Hiung in favor of his son

July 20, Crown Prince enthroned as Emperor, the "puppet Emperor," Chök; much rioting in Seoul

July 25, New convention signed with Japan; the administration of Korea placed under the guidance of the Japanese resident-general

July 31, Ordinance disbanding Korean troops promulgated

Aug. 1, Mutiny of a battalion against the order; 60 Koreans and 40 Japanese killed or wounded

1908

March 25, Death of Mr. D. W. Stevens, American adviser to the Korean council of state, who had been shot three days before by two Koreans

1909

Dec. 22, Yi Wan Yon, the Prime Minister, mortally stabbed by a young Korean

1910

Jan. 31, Serious outbreak of insurgents, reported from South Phongan; 20 Japanese settlers reported murdered

June 30, Edict, issued by the Emperor, delegating to the Japanese Government the police administration of the country

Aug. 22, Treaty signed by which Japan annexed Korea; promulgated, Aug. 29

Sept. 10, Japanese Imperial Ordinance provided for local government

Oct. 30, Organic regulations promulgated established Secretariat and 5 departments, with large staff of Japanese officials

1911

Sept. 28, Baron Yun Chi Ho and other revolutionists sentenced to long prison terms

1914

April 1, Foreign settlements abolished

1917

Aug. 1, Entire railroad system placed under control of South Manchuria Railway

1918

Dec. 6, Koreans appealed to the United States for aid to secure independence of Japan

1919

Jan. 7, Meeting of Korean students in Tokio discussed new principle of self-determination of peoples as suitable for Korea

Jan. 28, The Press warned by police not to publish anything on the self-determination movement in Korea

Jan. 21, Death of the former Emperor

Feb. 28, Koreans in Peking petitioned Government of the United States to support Korean independence

March 1, Parade of Koreans past palace where dead Emperor lying in state; demonstrations for independence throughout Korea begun

March 3, Funeral of the "old Emperor"

April 27, Korean nationalists proclaimed Republic

May 15, Radical revision of Korean Government agreed upon by Privy Council of Japan, substitution of civil for military government, and allowance of larger powers of self-government when independence movement abandoned by Koreans. Baron Saito appointed Governor General

Sept. 3, The Governor General issued instructions to "High Officials" as to administrative reforms

Sept. 10, Declaration of the Governor General of reforms and fair treatment of Koreans

Oct. 3, Instructions to the Provincial Governors issued as to reforms

1926

April 25, Death of Prince Yi Wang

KURIA MURIA ISLANDS

See Aden.

KUWAIT

See Arabia.

KWANG CHAU WAN

Kwang Chau Wan, territory on the coast of China, leased to France in 1898 by China for term of 99 years with full territorial jurisdiction during that period, and increased in 1899 by the addition of 2 islands in the Bay, governed as part of Indo-China, total area of leased territory 190,000 square miles, population 250,000.

KWANTUNG

Kwantung, Chinese territory in the southern part of the Liaotung Peninsula leased by Japan from China, area about 1,438 square miles, population (1927)1,147,394 of whom 909,133 are Chinese and 236,076 Japanese (exclusive of army and navy). The territory is under a Japanese Governor General, seat of administration at Dairen (Tairend).

LABUAN

The island of Labuan lies about 6 miles from the north-west coast of Borneo. It was ceded to Britain in 1846; on January 1, 1907, was incorporated with Singapore, and on December 1, 1912, was created a separate Settlement. Area 30 sq. miles; the population in 1926 was 5,641, mostly Malays from Borneo, with some Chinese traders and about 15 Europeans. Capital, Victoria, which has about 1,500 inhabitants.

LACCADIVE ISLANDS

(ATTACHED TO MADRAS PRESIDENCY, INDIA)

A group of 14 islands (9 inhabited), about 200 miles off the west or Malabar coast of the Madras Presidency. The northern portion is called the Amindivis and is attached to the collectorate of South Kánara, the remainder to the administrative district of Malabar. Population 13,633, nearly all Mohammedans.

LAOS

Laos, territory of French Indo-China, covering about a third part of the Laotian country, bounded on the north by the Chinese province of Yun-nan, on the west by the British Shan States and Siam, on the south by Cambodia and Annam, on the east by Annam, and on the northeast by Tonking, under French protection since 1893, area estimated as 103,000 square miles, and in 1929 there were nearly one million inhabitants.

LEBANON

See Syria.

MACAO

Macao, Portuguese Colony off the coast of China consisting of the island of Macao at the mouth of the Canton River and 2 small adjacent islands of Taipa and Coloâne, area, 4 square miles, population according to census of 1927, 157,175 (3,846 Portuguese, 152,738 and 591 other nationalities). Portuguese trade factories were established as early as 1557 and Macao was ceded to the Portuguese as a commercial station in 1586 in return for their assistance against pirates subject to an annual tribute paid until 1849 when the Portuguese abolished the Chinese customhouse and declared the independence of the port. By Treaty of Dec. 1, 1887 with Portugal China confirmed the perpetual inalienable occupation and government of Macao by the Portuguese.

MAHE

Mahé, French Colony in the Malabar district of Madras, India, on the west coast at the mouth of the Mahé River, area 26 square miles, population 11,959.

MALACCA

See Malay: Straits Settlements.

MALAY (FEDERATED STATES)

Malay (Federated Malay States) Perak, Selangor, Negri Sembilan (Nine States), and Pahang in the Malay Peninsula are under British protection, area approximately: Perak 7,800 square miles; Selangor, 3,150 square miles; Negri Sembilan, 2,550 square miles; Pahang, 14,000 square miles; total, 27,500 square miles.

Population.—Census 1921: Perak, 599,055 (378,902 males and 220,153 females); Selangor, 401,009 (267,165 males and 133,844 females); Negri Sembilan, 178,762 (119,569 males and 59,193 females); Pahang, 146,064 (87,892 males and 58,172 females); total 1,324,890 (853,528 males and 471,362 females). The population contained 510,821 Malays, 494,548 Chinese, 305,219 natives

of India, 5,686 Europeans, and 3,204 Eurasians. The preponderance of males over females is due to the number of Chinese and Indian immigrants. Estimated population, June 1926, 1,476,032. The largest town is Kuala Lumpur (in Selangor) with about 80,000 inhabitants.

The Governor of the Straits Settlements is *ex officio* H.M.'s High Commissioner for these States and the other Malay States in the British sphere.

High Commissioner, Sir Cecil Clementi. Chief Secretary to Government, Vacant (March, 1930).

The following are the Rulers and Residents of the four States: Ruler of Perak, H. H. Paduka Sri Sultan Iskandar Shah, ibni Idris. Resident, C. W. H. Cochrance. Ruler of Selangor, H. H. Sultan Ala'idin Sulaiman Shah, ibni Al-Marhum Raja Muda Musa. Resident, J. Lornie. Ruler of Negri Sembilan, H. H. Muhammad, ibni Al-Marhum Antah, Yang Di-Pertuan Besar, Negri Sembilan. Resident, J. W. Simmons. Ruler of Pahang, H. H. Al-Mu'tasim Bi'llah Al-Sultan Abdullah, ibni Al-Marhum Al-Sultan Ahmad Al-Maazam Shah. Resident, C. F. J. Green.

In Perak, Selangor, and Sungai Ujong, which State was subsequently amalgamated with other States to form the Confederation of Negri Sembilan, Residents appointed in 1874.

In July 1895 a Treaty was signed by the 4 rulers by which they agreed to constitute their countries a Federation to be administered under the advice of the British Government, and to the appointment of a "Resident-General of the Malay States" to control the Residents appointed to each State, the Resident-General's advice to be followed in all matters of administration other than those touching on Islam.

Perak is ruled by a dynasty claiming descent from the last Malay Sultan of Malacca. In the seventeenth century it was overrun by the Achinese, and some time after 1636 a Johore Prince, husband of a Perak Princess was sent to rule it under the title of Sultan Mudzaffar Shah. The first European settlement was made by the Dutch in 1650, who were supplanted by the British in 1795. By the Treaty of Pangkor of Jan. 20, 1874 the Perak chiefs accepted a British Resident whose advice should be "asked and acted upon upon all questions other than those touching Malay religion and customs."

Selangor: In the fourteenth century Klang, now a district of Selangor, is said to have been subject to the Javanese Empire of Majapahit. In the next century it was given to a Penghulu of the family of the Bendaharas of old Malacca, and a son of the Sultan Mansur Shah (1458–1477) of Malacca was made ruler of Jeram, near Langat. In 1718 Daeng Chelak, a Bugis Chief, who had married a Johore Princess, settled at Kuala Selangor, and about 1780 their descendant was recognized as Sultan Salehu'd-din by the Sultan of Perak. The throne has remained in the same family ever since. In 1783 the Dutch blockaded Kuala Selangor and forced recognition of the suzerainty of Holland. From 1867 to 1873 there was civil war and in 1874 the Sultan accepted a British Resident because of anarchy among the Malay Chiefs and pirates ravaging the coast.

Negri Sembilan (the Nine States) is a federation of small native States, the 4 major States of Sungai Ujong, Jelebu, Johol, and Rembau, and the 5 minor States of Ulu Muar, Jempul, Terachi, Gunong Pasir, and Inas. Sungai Ujong, the most important of the "Nine States" is mentioned in a Javanese poem in 1365 as being subject to the Javanese Empire of Majapahit. In the fifteenth century it was ruled by Chiefs of the old kingdom of Malacca. In the eighteenth century the Chiefs of the 4 major States brought a ruler from Sumatra named Raja Melewar, ancestor of the present ruler. The Chief of Sungai Ujong accepted a British Resident in 1874, Jelebu in 1883, Rembau in 1887. In 1898 the Yam Tuan of Sri Menanti was elected titular Ruler of the whole State.

Pahang is the largest State in the Peninsula with an area of 14,000 square miles, with a coast line of 112 miles. In the thirteenth century Pahang was subject to the old Sumatran Buddhist Kingdom of Sri Vijaya, later of Majapahit. In the fifteenth century Sultan Mansur Shah of Malacca captured the Ruler and married his daughter. In the eighteenth century Pahang fell under the suzerainty of the new Sultans of Johore who left a Dato' Bendahara as ruler. By Treaty of Oct. 8, 1887 with the Governor of the Straits a British agent was stationed at the capital, and in 1888 a British Resident appointed.

MALAY STATES NOT INCLUDED IN THE FEDERATION

Malay States not included in the Federation are five in number, namely, Johore, Kedah, Perlis, Kelantan, and Trengganu.

The relations of Johore with Great Britain are defined by a treaty dated December 11, 1885; and, by an amendment to this treaty made on May 12, 1914, the Sultan agreed to accept, and to act upon the advice of, a British officer called the General Adviser. The Sultan is assisted in the administration of the State by an Executive Council, and by a Legislative Council consisting of official and unofficial members.

The rights of suzerainty, protection, administration, and control of the other four States were transferred from Siam to Great Britain by the Anglo-Siamese treaty of March 10, 1909. In all four States the Rulers are assisted in the administration by State Councils, and by British Advisers appointed by the British Government.

Johore occupies the southern part of the Malay Peninsula, area 7,678 square miles, population estimated at 338,392. The Mohammedan Empire was founded by the son of the Sultan of Malacca after its conquest by the Portuguese in 1511. The history of the next 300 years is an almost uninterrupted record of wars. Hostilities with the Portuguese continued until the arrival of the Dutch in 1602, and Johore took part in the war of the Portuguese and Dutch for the possession of Malacca. By 1637 the country was practically an appanage of the Achinese kingdom. The capital was plundered and burned by Jambi in 1673, and in 1699 the last of the Malacca royal line was assassinated and the throne passed to the Bendaharas, Malacca chiefs. Later Johore was ruled by an officer of the Bugis rulers of Rio of Riouw. In 1784 the Dutch recognized the Malay Sultan, a descendant of the Bendahara chiefs, as ruler of Johore, drove the Bugis from Riau and stationed a Resident with a garrison there, the Malay Sultan and the Bugis Viceroy after some further fighting accepting the position of dependent princes. The son of the Sultan, Sultan Husain, ceded the island of Singapore to the East India Company in 1819. In 1855 the Sultan Ali was deposed, and Temenggong given the supreme rule by the British, and his son was given the title of Maharaja by Queen Victoria in 1879. After the Treaty of Dec. 11, 1885 he was allowed to assume the title of Sultan of the State and Territory of Johore. Temenggong Abubakar was succeeded in 1895 by his son, Sultan Ibrahim, the present ruler, who promulgated a written constitution.

Kedah on the west coast of the Peninsula has an area of 3,648 square miles, and population (census 1921) of 338,544 of whom 237,043 are Malays, 59,403 Chinese, 33,019 Indians, 235 Europeans, 75 Eurasians, and 8,779 other races. There are no authentic records of the early history of the State. The country was converted to Mohammedanism in the fifteenth or sixteenth century, and like the other States in the Peninsula it was at various times under the domination of Burma, Acheen, Malacca, and Siam. There is no record of the Portuguese during their occupation of Malacca (A.D. 1511–1641) having had any intercourse with Kedah. The Dutch after conquest of Malacca from the Portuguese established commandants in Kedah from 1654 to 1711. In 1619 the King of Acheen (Achin) led the rulers of Kedah and Perak into captivity. Treaties were made with the East India Company in 1768, 1791, and 1802. In 1821 Siam took possession of the fort and later of the river reasserting control, the Sultan after several unsuccessful attempts to recover his State made submission and was reinstated in 1841. In 1868 an agreement between Great Britain and Siam replaced the Treaties with the East India Company Siam not to exercise control over Setul, Perlis, and Kubang Pasu.

Setul, under Treaty of 1909 is now part of Siam (Monthon Puket) and Perlis is independent and under British possession.

Sultan Sir Abdul Hamid Halim Shah; Regent, Tunku Ibrahim

Perlis on the west coast of the Peninsula and north of Kedah has an area of 5,713 square miles and a population (census 1921) of 40,091 of whom 34,167 were Malays. Until 1821 it was subject to Kedah, made an independent State in 1841 under Syed Hussein. The present ruler, the great-great-grandson of Syed Hussein and the fourth Raja is Raja Syed Alwi.

Kelantan, on the east coast of the Peninsula, has an area estimated at 5,713 square miles and a population (census 1921) of 309,300 including 12,799 Chinese, 127 Europeans, 3,622 Indians, 286,334 Malays, and 6,396 other races. Kelantan was subject to Palembang (Sri Vijaya Kingdom) in the thirteenth century and to the Majapahit (Java) in the fourteenth century. The present ruling family dates from 1790. Siam claimed suzerainty and a royal Prince was sent as Resident Commissioner in 1892, and in 1902 a British officer in the Siamese service was received by the Raja as Adviser, office assumed July 1903. The transfer to the protection of Great Britain was formally effected July 15, 1909.

Sultan Ismail ibni Almarhum, Sultan Hohamed IV, ruler.

Trengganu lies on the eastern seaboard of the Peninsula between Pahang and Kelantan, area of about 5,500 square miles, population (census 1921) 153,456, of whom 145,523 are Malays, 7,246 Chinese, 211 Indians, 34 Europeans, 751 other nationalities. The country was subject to Palembang and Java like Kedah, Kelantan, and Pahang. The royal house is descended from the father of the non-royal Bendahara who became Sultan of Johore in 1699. British protection dates from July 14, 1909, the nominal overlordship of Siam transferred on that date. May 24, 1919 the Sultan agreed to accept a British Adviser.

Sir Suleiman Badaru'l-alam Shah, ruler.

MALDIVE ARCHIPELAGO

See Ceylon.

MANCHURIA

Manchuria, outer territory of China, lying between the province of Chihli and Mongolia and the Amur River dividing the country from Siberia, and extending from the Khingan Mountains eastward to Korea (southeast) and the Ussuri River. On the south it projects into the Yellow Sea, the Liaotung Peninsula being between the Gulf of Liaotung to the west and Korea Bay to the east; area about 363,610 square miles, and population (1927) 24,520,661.

In the tenth century the Khitans established the Liao dynasty which was overthrown 2 centuries later by the Nüchêns, the direct ancestors of the Manchus, who established the Chin dynasty, driven out by the Mongols under Jenghiz Khan in the thirteenth century, but their descendants returned to power in the middle of the seventeenth century under the leadership of Nurhachu who united the various tribes of the Tungus race, established his capital in Fengtien (now Mukden), began struggle with China which in 1644 resulted in overthrow of the Ming dynasty and rule of the Manchus in China until the revolution of 1911.

1689

Aug. 22–27, Conference of representatives of China and of Russia near Nerchinsk on the Shilka, branch of the upper Amur, which resulted in signing of the Treaty on Aug. 27, the first of China with a western nation, settled northeastern boundaries

1858

May 16/29, The Treaty of Aigun with Russia was signed, the north bank of the Amur from the Argun fork to the sea recognized as Russian; the south bank down to the Ussuri as Chinese; and the territory between the Ussuri and the sea to be held in common by the 2 Powers until there should be a final settlement of the frontier; ratified by the Emperor of China on June 2 and the Tsar on July 8

June 1/13, The Treaty of Tientsin signed by Russia with British, French, Russian, and American representatives opened the port of Newchwang at the mouth of the Laio River to foreign trade

1860

July 20, Vladivostok occupied by Russia

Nov. 14, Convention with Russia signed by which the Treaty of Aigun confirmed and China ceded the territory held in common, now the Primorsk Province. By the 2 treaties Russia deprived China of some 343,000 square miles

1895

April 17, By the Treaty of Shimonoseki between China and Japan ending war (*see* Korea, China) the southern part of the Liaotung Peninsula was ceded to Japan

April 23, The Ministers of Russia, France, and Germany presented Note to Japan protesting the cession of territory of Liaotung Peninsula by China

May 1, Reply of Japan accepted dictation of Powers as to restoration of Liaotung with the exception of Port Arthur and Kinchow

May 5, Japan accepted terms of Powers of cession of all the territory ceded to her in South Manchuria

Nov. 8, Convention with China signed by which the territory retroceded, money compensation accepted by Japan

Dec. 22, Russo-Chinese Bank (later Russo-Asiatic) chartered by Russia

1896

Sept. 8, Chinese-Russian Railway Convention signed which provided that the Russo-Chinese Bank should establish the Chinese Eastern Railway Company to construct a railroad across Manchuria, extension of the Trans-Siberian railway, concession for 80 years then to revert to Chinese Government, but right of purchase after 30 years if desired by China

1897

Dec., Russian warships occupied Port Arthur and Talienwan

1898

March 15, Russo-Chinese Convention signed, lease of Port Arthur, Talienwan (Dairen, Dalny), and adjoining territory (Kwantung), the territory Japan had been forced to retrocede in 1895, to Russia for 25 years, and railroad concessions of 1896 extended to provide for branches to Talienwan and to In-tzu

May 7, Further Agreement of China and Russia signed defined boundaries of the leased territory

July 6, Third Agreement of China with Russia as to Chinese Eastern Railway concessions, southern branch

1899

Dalny (Dairen) declared a free port open to foreign commerce

1900

June, The Governors of the Manchurian Provinces declared war on Russia in the Boxer uprising, and attacked Russians along the Amur which led to reprisals and Russian invasion

Aug. 14, The Russian Governor General of the Amur Province declared Russian annexation of the right bank of the Amur, and followed with seizure of the harbor of Newchang, and of Harbin

1902

Jan. 30, Anglo-Japanese Alliance signed declared recognition of the independence of China and Korea

April 8, "Manchurian Convention of Evacuation" signed by Russia provided for complete evacuation of Manchuria in 18 months

1903

April 5, New demands of Russia presented to China as condition of evacuation

April 8, Date fixed by Convention for second stage of Russian evacuation of Manchuria passed without further withdrawal by Russia, and Mukden Province reoccupied and troops sent to southern Manchuria

Aug. 12, Japan proposed to Russia engagement to recognize the territorial integrity of China and Korea and maintenance of the "open door" offering recognition of the special position of Russia in Manchuria if Russia would recognize that of Japan in Korea

Oct. 3, Nov. 12, 22, Dec. 11, Jan. 7 and 31, 1904, Russian counterproposals to Japan made no concessions and the Russo-Japanese war resulted beginning Feb. 8, 1904. *See* Russo-Japanese War

Oct. 8, Treaties of commerce and navigation between China and the United States and between China and Japan provided for opening of 3 Manchurian towns, Mukden, Antung, and Tatungkao as treaty ports and for foreign settlement

1905

Sept. 5, Treaty of Portsmouth ending the Russo-Japanese War provided for evacuation of Russian and Japanese troops from Manchuria, and transferred to Japan the Russian lease of the Liaotung Peninsula, including that portion of the Chinese Eastern Railway south of Changchun

Dec. 22, Treaty of Japan with China by which China confirmed transfers and assignments made to Japan by Russia in the Treaty of Portsmouth, and additional Agreement relating to Manchuria signed regulating railways. Japan granted right to extend railroad from Mukden to Antung where it connects with the Korean railway and China engaged to open 16 Manchurian towns enumerated to international residence and trade. Secret Protocol signed by which China engaged not to construct any railroad in the neighborhood or parallel to the South Manchurian Railway which might be prejudicial to that railroad

1906

June 7, Japanese Imperial Ordinance was issued sanctioning organization of the South Manchuria Railway Company

1907

March 21, Last Russian troops left Harbin

April 7, Imperial Decree abolished Manchuria as a dependency under a Tartar General and appointed a Viceroy and 3 Governors to rule the country on same basis as the 18 provinces of the Empire

April 15, Japan ceded the Hsinmintun-Mukden Railway to China

July 30, Political Convention between Russia and Japan signed, agreement to recognize independence and territorial integrity of China. Treaties signed, maintenance of *status quo*, &c.

1908

Oct. 12, Agreement between China and Japan as to Japanese telegraphs in Manchuria

1909

Sept. 4, Japan recognized Chinese sovereignty over Chientao, Korean residents under Chinese jurisdiction. *See also* China

Oct. 2, American company (Pauling and Co.) signed agreement with the Viceroy of Manchuria for construction of railroad from Chinchow to Aigun, but final agreement not signed because of protests of Japan and Russia

Dec. 14, Proposals for neutralization of railways in Manchuria by American Secretary of State to Great Britain, France, Germany, Russia, Japan, and China

1910

Jan. 21, Russia and Japan declined to accept American proposals as to railways

July 4, Convention of Japan and Russia signed, agreement to maintain and to respect the *status quo* in Manchuria and to coöperate in improvement of their respective railway lines, in joint opposition to American proposals for Chinese purchase of railroads and internationalization

1911

Sept. 2, Agreement of China with Japan permitted extension of the Peking-Mukden Railway (Chinese)

1913

Oct. 5, Exchange of Notes of China and Japan as to construction of railway lines in Manchuria and loans from Japan for construction

1915

Jan. 18, Japan presented the "Twenty-one Demands"

to China including extension of term of lease of Port Arthur and Talienwan, and the South Manchurian and Antung railway concessions, preference to Japanese capital for loans for construction of railroads in Manchuria, preference in employment of foreign advisers for Japanese, concessions as to mining areas and privileges for Japanese subjects as to leasing land, and trade in South Manchuria. *See also* China

May 25, Treaty of China with Japan signed embodied the demands as to South Manchuria

1916

March 2, Treaty of China and Japan provided for control by Japan of the Kirin-Changchun Railway

March 28, Agreement of Chinese Government with Russo-Asiatic Bank as to construction of railroad from Harbin by way of Mergen and Aigun to Blagoveschensk (460 miles)

July 3, Treaty of Russia with Japan as to coöperation in the Far East, and concurrently Russia ceded 60 miles of the Chinese Eastern Railway between Changchun and the Sungari to Japan

1917

Aug. 1, The whole of the railway system of Korea (some 1,000 miles in length) passed under management of the South Manchurian Railway

1920

Oct. 2, Agreement of China with Russo-Asiatic Bank as to Chinese Eastern Railway. *See* China

1924

May 3, Note of American Minister declared interest of the United States in protection of all interests and maintenance of the *status quo* as to the Chinese Eastern Railway, followed by Note of French Minister on May 7

May 31, Agreement with Russo-Asiatic Bank as to Chinese Eastern Railway

Sept. 7, Chang Tso-lin declared war on President Tsao Kun. For Manchuria in civil war *see* China

Sept. 30, Agreement of China and Russia signed, detailed provisions as to the Chinese Eastern Railway

1926

Jan. 24, Agreement with Russia as to Chinese Eastern Railway

1929

May 27, Chinese police raid on Russian consulates. *See* China

Dec. 3, and Dec. 22, Protocols signed as to Chinese Eastern Railway. *See* China

MONGOLIA

Mongolia, outer territory of China to the north and northwest of China proper, divided into Inner Mongolia bordering on China and Outer Mongolia bordering on Russia, a vast and indefinite territory stretching from the Khinghan Mountains on the east to the Tarbagatai Mountains on the west, wholly inland, bounded by Manchuria on the east, area about 1,875,000 square miles, population about 750,000 Mongols and about 100,000 other nationalities. The frontier with Siberia as it exists is defined by the Treaty of Kiakhta (1727), the Treaty of Peking (1860), the Protocol of Chuguchak (1864), the Treaty of St. Petersburg (1881), the Treaty of Tsitsihar (1911).

The Mongols of Central Asia became known in history with the coming of Jenghiz Khan (1162–1227) who built up a great Mongol Empire which covered most of High Asia westward from the China Sea. He was succeeded by his son Ogotai and his grandsons Mangu, Hulagu, and Kublai. Kublai Khan, the most eminent of his successors, conquered and ruled all China building his capital at Peking in 1264. He died in 1294 at the age of 78 and was succeeded by his grandson, Toghon Timur, the last Mongol Emperor of China, whose reign ended in 1368 in defeat and expulsion, the native Ming dynasty reigning, the successors of Timur, the Khakans, reigning in Mongolia. The Mongol tribes in the seventeenth century established scattered communities under different chiefs, and those tribes nearest to China submitted to the Manchu Emperor in 1644, and West Mongolia was finally conquered in 1757 by Ch'ienlung.

1911

July, Meeting of the Mongol princes at Urga sent secret mission to Russia to ask protection against dominion of the Peking Government

Aug. 28, Note of the Russian Minister stated that Russia could not remain indifferent to violent changes in the *status quo* in Manchuria

Sept. 19, Note of Chinese Minister to Russia replied that reforms in Mongolia were introduced for the commercial and industrial development of the country

Dec. 1, The Mongol princes declared independence of China and rule of the Hutukhtu, the "Living Buddha" and expelled the Chinese officials

Dec. 20, Russo-Chinese Treaty delimited frontier of Mongolia and Siberia

Dec. 28, Hutukhtu (Khutukhtu) proclaimed Khan, Emperor, at Urga

1912

Jan. 15, Mongol invasion into Manchuria seized Hailar

Jan. 18, Mongol princes seized Uliasutai, Mongolians expelling Chinese

Aug. 7, Kobdo, chief town of western Mongolia captured, the Chinese officials taking refuge in Russian Consulate

Aug. 15, Taonanfu seized, but recaptured in battle by Chinese

Oct. 21/Nov. 3, Agreement with Russia and Government of Outer Mongolia concluded, recognized the Hutukhtu (Khutukhtu) Lama as sovereign, supporting autonomy, right of Mongolia to have a national army, and exclude Chinese troops and colonists

Dec. 29, Mongol-Tibetan Treaty of alliance signed at Urga

1913

Oct., War loan of 2 million rubles granted by Russia

Nov. 5, Declaration and exchange of Notes at Peking by which Russia recognized the sovereignty of China over Outer Mongolia and China recognized the autonomy of Outer Mongolia

1914

Sept. 30, Russo-Mongolian Agreements as to railroads and telegraphs signed, Russia recognized right of Mongolia to construct railroads but plans to be determined jointly by Russia and Mongolia

1915

May 25, Sino-Japanese Treaty provided for opening of certain places in Eastern Inner Mongolia to foreign residence and trade, and exclusive mining rights in Eastern Mongolia ceded to Japan

June 7, Treaty signed by representatives of China, Russia, and Mongolia by which Outer Mongolia recognized suzerainty of China, and Russia and China the autonomy of Outer Mongolia, the latter not to have right to conclude treaties with foreign Powers except treaties of commerce, the Chinese in Outer Mongolia to be under Chinese jurisdiction, and provision made for delimitation of frontiers

1919

Nov. 16, Outer Mongolia forced by China to renounce autonomy

Nov. 22, Chinese Government declared treaties with Russia null and void

Dec. 1, Outer Mongolia placed under Chinese military administration

1920

Oct. 25, Attack of Baron Ungern-Sternberg, anti-Bolshevik Cossack, on Urga repelled by Chinese garrison

1921

Feb. 1–3, Baron Ungern-Sternberg captured Urga and drove out the Chinese, declaring the sovereignty of the Hutukhtu, and himself military adviser

Feb. 25, Independence of Outer Mongolia declared

June, Ungern-Sternberg invaded Transbaikalia where the Soviet had set up a "Red" Government and was defeated

July 6, Russian Soviet forces occupied Urga and established Soviet Government

Sept. 15, Ungern-Sternberg, who had been captured by the Russians in August, was executed

Nov. 5, Treaty with Russia signed

1924

May 31, Sino-Russian Treaty signed recognized Chinese sovereignty over Outer Mongolia

1929

Dec. 12, New independent republic proclaimed in the district of Burga with Hailar as capital

NEGRI SEMBILANO

See Malay.

NEJD

See Arabia.

NEPAL

An independent Kingdom in the Himalayas, between 26° 25′ and 30° 17′ N. lat., and between 80° 6′ and 88° 14′ of E. long.; its greatest length 500 miles; its greatest breadth about 150; bounded on the north by Tibet, on the east by Sikkim, on the south and west by British India.

The Gurkhas, a Rajput race originally from Udaipur in Rajputana, who had settled in the province of Gorkha in Nepal, overran the whole country during the latter half of the eighteenth century, and have maintained their supremacy ever since. A commercial treaty between India and Nepal was signed in 1792, and a British Resident was sent to reside at Kathmandu, but was recalled two years later. A frontier outrage, in 1814, compelled the Indian Government to declare war; and a British force advanced to within three marches of the capital. Peace was concluded and the Treaty of Sagauli signed in December, 1815. Since then the relations of the British with Nepal have been friendly. In 1854 hostilities broke out between the Nepalese and Tibetans, and in 1856 a Treaty was concluded between the Nepalese and Tibetan Governments by which the Tibetans bound themselves to pay an annual sum of Rs. 10,000 to Nepal, to encourage trade between the two countries, and that the Nepalese Representative at Lhasa should be of high rank. Besides, trade agents are maintained at Gyantse, Kuti, Kerrong, and other trade marts in Tibet.

In accordance with the treaty of Sagauli, which amongst other things provides that accredited ministers of each shall reside at the Court of the other, a British Envoy, with a small escort of Indian sepoys lives at the capital; but he does not interfere in the internal affairs of the State.

A fresh treaty was signed on December 21, 1923. By it all previous treaties, agreements, and engagements since and including the Treaty of Sagauli were confirmed, and the British and Nepalese Governments acknowledged one another's independence, internal and external.

Area about 54,000 square miles; population estimated at about 5,600,000.

The sovereign is His Majesty Maharajadhiraja Tribhubana Bir Bikram Jung Bahadur Shah Bahadur Shumshere Jung, who was born on June 30, 1906, and succeeded his father on December 11, 1911. The Prince-Royal and Heir-apparent was born on June 11, 1920. The government of Nepal is a military oligarchy. All power is in the hands of the Prime Minister, to whom it was permanently delegated by the Maharajadhiraja Surendra Bikram Shah under pressure of the Bharadars or nobles of the State in 1867. The present Prime Minister is Major-General Sir Bhim Shamsher Jang Rana, who was appointed on November 25, 1929. The office of Prime Minister is always held by a member of his family, the succession being determined by special rules.

NICOBAR ISLANDS

The Nicobar Islands are situated to the South of the Andamans, 75 miles from Little Andaman. The British formally took possession in 1869. There are twenty-one islands, nine uninhabited; total area, 635 square miles. The islands are usually divided into three groups, Southern, Central, and Northern, the chief islands in each being respectively, Great Nicobar, Camorta with Nankauri, and Car Nicobar. The Nicobarese inhabitants numbered 9,272 (5,242 males and 4,030 females) in 1921. The islanders are known to have pursued the coconut trade for at least 1,500 years. The coconut production is estimated at 15 million nuts per annum, of which some 8 million are sold by barter and exported in small native craft and Chinese junks in the form of copra. The Government is represented by a permanent Assistant Commissioner at Car Nicobar and a Tahsildar at Nankauri. The islands are attached to the Chief Commissionership of the Andamans and Nicobars.

Lieut. Col. M. L. Ferrar, Chief Commissioner at Port Blair.

OMAN

See Arabia.

PANHANG

See Malay.

PALESTINE

Palestine, the name given by Moses (*Exodus* xv., 14) and other ancient writers, to a broad strip of land on the east coast of the Mediterranean Sea, which originally included Philistia, but was afterwards limited to the part termed the land of Canaan or Israel, Judea, and the Holy Land. After being several times conquered by the Saracens, and retaken from the seventh to the tenth century, and after being the scene of the wars of the Crusades, and other conflicts, Palestine was united to the Ottoman empire by Selim I in 1516.

After its conquest in 1917–18, by the British Forces, the country remained under British Military Administration till July 1, 1920, when a Civil Administration was set up.

The country is administered by Great Britain under a Mandate, which was passed by the Council of the League of Nations on July 24, 1922, and came officially into force on September 29, 1923.

This provides for the Balfour Declaration of November 2, 1917, to the effect that "His Majesty's Government view with favor the establishment in Palestine of a national home for the Jewish people, and will use their best endeavors to facilitate the achievement of that object, it being clearly understood that nothing shall be done which may prejudice the civil and religious rights of existing non-Jewish communities in Palestine, or the rights and political status enjoyed by Jews in any other country."

The natural and historic boundaries of Palestine run from the desert on the east, along the slopes of Mount Hermon over to the Litani on the west, where the Lebanon and Anti-Lebanon first break into a series of elevated plateaux, and thence over to the Mediterranean coast, and on the south from the Gulf of Akaba across the Desert of Sinai.

For the present political boundaries, *see* THE STATESMAN'S YEAR BOOK, 1928, p. 185.

Palestine under British Mandate is about 10,000 square miles in extent. The population, taken by official census on October 23, 1922, was 757,182, of whom 590,890 were Moslems, 83,794 Jews, 73,024 Christians, 7,028 Druzes, 163 Samaritans, 265 Bahais, and the remainder Sikhs, Hindus, and Metawilehs. The estimated population on June 30, 1930, was 588,849 Moslems, 162,467 Jews, 82,590 Christians, and 9,226 persons of other religions, making a total of 843,132, excluding about 103,000 nomads.

The country is at present divided into two districts: Southern (Jaffa), and Northern (Haifa); and the Jerusalem division.

The chief town, Jerusalem, which had been in Moslem hands since 1244, and under Turkish rule since 1517, surrendered on December 9, 1917. Its population in 1922 was 62,678. The population figures for the other principal towns at the 1922 census were: Jaffa, 47,709; Tel-Aviv, 36,754; Haifa, 24,634; Gaza, 17,480; Nazareth, 7,424; Nablus, 15,947; Safed, 8,761; Tiberias, 6,950; Hebron, 16,577; Ramleh, 7,312; Bethlehem, 6,658; Lydda, 8,103; Acre, 6,420. There was an appreciable increase in Jewish immigration during 1929. Total immigrants (1929), 6,566; Jewish immigrants, year ended December 31, 1929, numbered 2,453 men, 1,937 women, and 859 children—while Jewish emigrants in the same period numbered 1,746.

1916

April 26, Secret Agreement of Great Britain, France, and Russia by which Asiatic Turkey to be partitioned and Palestine to be placed under an international régime (Sykes-Picot)

May 9, Secret Agreement of France and Great Britain by which the ports of Haifa and Akka in Palestine to be assigned to Great Britain and the international régime in Palestine reaffirmed

1917

March 24, British invasion begun. *See* World War

Nov. 2, Declaration of Balfour in letter to Lord Roths-
child. *See* p. 879
Dec. 9, The British entered Jerusalem and military
administration begun
Dec. 11, General Allenby made formal entry into
Jerusalem by the Jaffa Gate

1918

April 4, Zionist Commission headed by Dr. Haim Weiz-
mann arrived in Jaffa and took over relief work
June 24, Proclamation organized the courts
July 24, Cornerstones of Hebrew University laid in
Jerusalem by Dr. Weizmann and others in formal
ceremony attended by General Allenby and 6,000
persons
———, Law Courts reopened
Nov. 1, Proclamation prohibited land transfer in sanjak
of Jerusalem
Nov. 30, Agricultural loans ordinance promulgated

1919

Feb. 6, Arab claims presented to the Peace Conference
by Emir Faisal. *See* Arabia
Feb. 27, Submission of the Zionist demands to the
Peace Conference by Dr. Weizmann

1920

April 4–5, Riots started in Jerusalem by a Jew throwing
a stone at the sacred flag of the Hebron Mosque
carried in procession by Arabs in annual national
festival of Nebi Musa; 5 Jews and 4 Moslems killed
and 211 Jews, 22 Moslems, and 2 Christians wounded
April 25, Supreme Council awarded mandate for
Palestine to Great Britain at the San Remo Con-
ference
July 1, Military administration replaced by civil gov-
ernment, Sir Herbert L. Samuel becoming first High
Commissioner
July 8, Amnesty granted released Vladimir Jabotinsky
arrested in connection with the riots of April 4–5
July 19, Censorship abolished
Aug. 10, Treaty of Sèvres confirmed British mandate
Aug. 26, Immigration ordinance issued
Aug. 31, Advisory Council composed of 4 Moslems,
3 Christians, and 3 Jews
Sept., Transfer of land ordinance promulgated allowed
sales under certain restrictions; amended April 4
and Dec. 8, 1921
Dec. 23, Franco-British Convention defined boundaries
between Palestine and Syria

1921

Feb., Arab Congress held at Haifa protested against
Balfour declaration and demanded a legislative
assembly elected by Arabs
May 1–3, Anti-Jewish riots in Jaffa, 3 Arabs and 27
Jews killed, and 104 Jews and 34 Arabs wounded
May 5, Arabs attacked the Jewish agricultural settle-
ments 10 miles north of Jaffa
May 6, Armed Arabs attacked the Jewish villages of
Rehoboth and Hedera
May 14, Immigration temporarily suspended
Dec. 15, Collective Punishment ordinance enabled the
District Commissioner to levy and collect fines from
all or part of the inhabitants of any village if he has
reason to believe that the inhabitants of the area
committed an offense (the culprit being unknown)
or caused loss or damage, &c.

1922

Feb. 3, Anglo-French Agreement signed as to boundary
between Palestine and Syria
May 9, Agreement signed by Great Britain and the
United States regarding Palestine mandate
June 3, Great Britain reaffirmed the Balfour declara-
tion
July 24, British mandate for Palestine approved by
the League of Nations
Aug. 10, "Palestine Order in Council" issued by Great
Britain provided organic law
Sept. 1, Palestine Order in Council came into effect
Sept. 11, British mandate proclaimed in Jerusalem
Sept. 16, Resolution adopted by the Council of the
League of Nations at suggestion of British Govern-
ment declared certain provisions of the mandate
not applicable to Transjordan
Oct. 23, Census gave population as 757,182, of whom
590,890 were Moslems, 72,024 Christians, 7,028
Druzes, 163 Samaritans, 265 Bahais, and the re-
mainder Sikhs, Hindus, and Metawilehs

1923

May 26, Declaration of British Government in Palestine conferred rights of autonomous administration
in Transjordan
Sept. 29, British mandate for Palestine came into legal
effect
Nov. 25, Syro-Palestine Congress petitioned the League
of Nations to set aside mandates
Dec. 2, Legislative Council appointed by the High
Commissioner composed of government officials, and
representatives of Jews, Moslems, and Christians

1924

May 1, The territory around Lake Huleh as far north
as Baneas transferred to Palestine according to Anglo-
French Convention of 1922
Dec. 3, American-British Palestine Mandate Convention signed
11,581 Jewish immigrants entered the country

1925

March 25, Lord Balfour arrived at Jerusalem
April 1, Hebrew University in Jerusalem opened by
Lord Balfour
July 1, Field Marshal Herbert O. C. Plumer succeeded
Sir Herbert Samuel as High Commissioner
Aug. 25, Field Marshal Lord Plumer arrived in Jeru-
salem
Sept. 1, Immigration Ordinance replaced that of 1920
Dec. 31, Jewish immigrants during the year 33,801,
emigrants 2,151

1926

Feb. 2, Treaty of friendship with Syria signed
March 30, General strike of Arabs in Palestine protest
against the French administration in Syria

1927

Jan. 2, Death of Tel Aviv of Usher Ginzberg, "Ahad
Ha'am" philosopher of Zionism
July 11, Earthquake in which 269 persons killed and
800 injured in towns of Nablus, Ramleh, Lydda, and
Salt
Nov. 1, New coinage based on English pound sterli__

introduced, the units 1,000 mils worth about 2.5 cents

Nov. 13, Announcement that the offer of $2,000,000 of John D. Rockefeller, Jr. for museum of Palestinian archæology in Jerusalem had been accepted

1928

June 21, Provisional Commercial Agreement with Egypt signed

July 6, Sir John Robert Chancellor appointed High Chancellor

Sept. 24, During service at Wailing Wall on Jewish Day of Atonement a screen separating men and women at prayer removed by English police in accordance with order in answer to complaints of Moslems of transgression of their rights of property, which aroused Jews throughout the world to great indignation, the act compared with the attempt of Pontius Pilate to bring the Roman Eagle into the Temple 1,900 years before

Nov. 19, British White Paper issued declared the Wall was sacred to the Jewish community and also to the Moslems whose legal property it was, and that the Jews might "bring to the Wall only those appurtenances of worship which were permitted under the Turkish régime"

Dec. 31, Jewish immigrants during the year numbered 2,178, emigrants 2,168; total immigrants 3,086

1929

June 30, Total population estimated as 816,064, 572,443 Moslems, 154,330 Jews, 80,225 Christians, and 9,066 persons of other religions

Aug. 15, Celebration of Jewish fast day at Wall disturbed by building of Moslems immediately around their praying place

Aug. 16, Jewish demonstration at Wall followed in a few days by counter Moslem demonstration

Aug. 23, Arab mobs began attack on Jews which continued for a week

Aug. 24, Martial law declared

———, Arabs laid waste Jewish agricultural villages of Motza, Artuf, Hulda, and Beer Tuvia

Aug. 25, Arab attack on Jewish quarters at Hebron, 50 Jews killed and one hundred seriously wounded

Aug. 29, The High Commissioner arrived from leave in England

Sept. 1, Proclamation of the High Commissioner on state of the country which angered the Arabs who issued counter-proclamations

Oct. 11, The High Commissioner issued provisional orders as to procedure at the Wailing Wall

Oct. 16, General strike of Arabs against rulings as to Wailing Wall

Oct. 24, Commission of Enquiry headed by Sir Walter Shaw sent by the British Government arrived in Palestine and began hearings which lasted until December as to the riots

———, Sheik Taleb Maraka on trial charged with instigating massacre at Hebron found guilty and sentenced to imprisonment for 2 years and fine of $250 but released on bail pending appeal, and 2 Arabs sentenced to death for murder at Safed and 12 others to life imprisonment

Oct. 27, All Arab Congress met in Jerusalem and made declaration that Palestine could not have peace unless the Balfour declaration of November, 1917 was abolished

Dec. 31, Jewish immigrants during the year 2,453, emigrants 1,746; total immigration 6,566

1930

Jan. 23, Decision of Commission of Enquiry acquitted 12 Arabs of murder in riots in Aug., 1929

Feb. 5, Hinkas, Jewish policeman, found guilty of the murder of 5 Arabs on Aug. 25, 1929 and sentenced to death

March 20, 5 Arabs sentenced to death for murder of 4 Jews in Hebron in August, 1929

March 31, Report of Shaw Commission of Enquiry published stated cause of riots of August, 1929 Arab hostility to Jews, disappointment in their national and political aspirations and fear of economic future and purchase of land by Jews, not hostility to British administration

May 12, British Government rejected demand of Arab delegation for parliamentary government, a national executive responsible to an elected legislature, and stopping of Jewish immigration and land purchase

May 17, Announcement of Government of restriction of Jewish immigration under Labor Schedule pending survey of immigration and 2,300 permits indefinitely suspended

May 20, Sir John Hope-Simpson, sent by British Government to investigate questions of land, immigration, and unemployment, arrived in Palestine

May 22, General strike of Jews as protest against suspension of immigration by the British Government

June 3–21, Commission of the Permanent Mandates Commission of the League of Nations held hearings in Palestine, an inquiry into the race riots of August, 1929

Aug. 25, Report of League of Nations Commission presented charged Great Britain with inadequate police and military protection in Palestine and for the most part confirmed findings of British White Paper of 1928 but Moslems should not be permitted to build or repair buildings adjacent to the Wall to encroach on the pavement and impair access to Jews or involve interference with the Jews during their prayers, or carry out the practice of the Zikr close to the pavement during Jewish devotions

Oct. 20, Report by Sir John Hope-Simpson published and White Paper on policy in Palestine emphasized the obligation of the Mandatory toward the non-Jewish population and gave the impression that Jewish development must be checked, that Jews must not acquire more land while Arabs were landless and must not immigrate so long as Arabs were unemployed

———, Resignation of Dr. Weizmann as head of the Zionist Organization after publication of White Paper because of policy of the Government

Nov. 1, Mass meetings in Palestine protesting against new British policy

Nov. 17, Statement of the Prime Minister in answer to attack on policy in House of Commons by Lloyd George that there was no change of policy but that "the development of Palestine must be continued under conditions which would make the harmony between Jew and Arab closer, so that the Arab may continue to enjoy the benefits he has already received from Jewish immigration and capital, and the Jew may see Palestine becoming more and more the complete embodiment of his ideal"

PENANG

Penang, island and town in British Crown Colony of Straits Settlements, area 188 square miles, 15 miles long and 19 broad, situated off the west coast of the Malay Peninsula in 50° N. Lat. and at entrance of Straits of Malacca. Founded July 17, 1786, ceded to the East Indian Company by the Sultan of Kedah. *See also* Malay (includes Province Wellesley and the Dindings).

PERAK

See Malay.

PERIM ISLAND

See Aden.

PERLIS

See Malay.

PERSIA

Persia, a kingdom of southwestern Asia, extending north from the Persian Gulf and Gulf of Oman to the Caspian Sea and Russia, and east from Irak and Turkey to Afghanistan and India.

Persia, which has an area of about 628,000 square miles, lies between 25° and 40° north latitude and between 44° and 63° 30′ east longitude. A vast portion of this area is an absolute desert, and the population is everywhere so scanty as not to exceed, on the average, 13–14 inhabitants to the square mile.

The population is estimated at 10 millions, but all figures are largely conjectural. It is estimated that the country contains some three million nomads. Of these, 260,000 are Arabs, 720,000 Turks, 675,000 Kurds and Leks, 20,700 Baluchis and Gipsies, 234,000 Lurs. These figures, however, are merely round numbers, and estimates vary.

The principal cities of Persia are: Teheran (the capital) and district, with 350,000 inhabitants; Tabriz, 180,000; Isfahan, 100,000; Meshed, 85,000; Resht, 80,000; Kerman, 40,000; Kermanshah, 40,000; Shiraz, 35,000; Yezd, 30,000; Barfurush, 30,000; Hamadan, 30,000; Kazvin, 30,000; Kum, 25,000; Sultanabad, 20,000; Kashan, 15,000; and Mohammerah, 10,000.

Reza Khan Pahlevi, Shah, reigning King, publicly proclaimed Dec. 16, 1925, succeeding Shah, Sultan Ahmad, deposed.

559 B.C to 1829

559, Cyrus revolts against the Medes, and becomes king of Persia; overthrows the Medo-Babylonian monarchy, about 557; conquers Asia Minor about 548; becomes master of the east, 536; killed in a war with the Massagetæ, B.C. 529

525, Cambyses, his son, King, 529; conquers Egypt

517, The false Smerdis killed; Darius Hystaspes King, 521; conquers Babylon

498, Conquest of Ionia; Miletus destroyed

490, Darius equips a fleet of 600 sail, with an army of 300,000 soldiers to invade the Peloponnesus, which is defeated at Marathon

480, Xerxes (King, 485); recovers Egypt, 484; enters Greece in the spring at the head of an immense force; battle of Thermopylæ

——, Xerxes enters Athens, after having lost 200,000 of his troops, and is defeated in a naval engagement off Salamis

Sept. 22, 479, Persians defeated at Mycale and Platæa

470, Cimon, son of Miltiades, with a fleet of 250 vessels, takes several cities from the Persians, and destroys their navy, consisting of about 340 sail, near Cyprus

469, His victories at the Eurymedon

465, Xerxes is murdered in his bed by Artabanus

458, Artaxerxes I Longimanus, King, 465; marries Esther

424, Xerxes I King, slain by Sogdianus, 425; who is deposed by Darius II, Nothus

401, Artaxerxes II Mnemon, King, 405; battle of Cunaxa, Cyrus the younger killed

——, Retreat of the 10,000 Greeks

399, War with Greece; invasion of Persia, 396

387, Peace of Antalcidas. Antalcidas the Lacedæmonian made peace with Artaxerxes of Persia, on behalf of Greece, but principally in favor of Sparta, giving up the cities of Ionia to the King

359, Artaxerxes III (Ochus) kills all his relations at his accession

338, He is killed by his minister Bagoas, and his son, Arses, made King

336, Bagoas kills him and sets up Darius III, Codomanus, by whom he himself is killed

334, Alexander the Great enters Asia; defeats the Persians at the river Granicus; near Issus, 333; at Arbela, 331

330, Darius III treacherously killed by Bessus

323, Alexander dies at Babylon; when his empire was divided, Persia with Syria was allotted to Seleucus Nicator, whose successors, the Seleucidæ, ruled Persia, till it was conquered by the Parthians, led by Arsaces I, the founder of the dynasty of the Arsacidæ about 250; his successors ruled till the Persian revolt, A.D. 226

A.D. 226, Artaxerxes I founds the Sassanides dynasty; restores Kingdom of Persia

227, Religion of Zoroaster restored and Christianity persecuted

240, Artaxerxes murdered; succeeded by Sapor I; Armenia becomes independent under Chosroes

260, Sapor conquers Mesopotamia, 258; repels the Romans and slays the Emperor Valerian

272, Sapor assassinated; succeeded by Hormisdas I; who favors the Manichees

273, Varanes I (Baharam) persecutes them and the Christians

277, Varanes II defeated by the Emperor Probus; makes peace

283, Persia invaded by the Emperor Carus, who conquers Seleucia and Ctesiphon

293, Varanes III; Narses, 294

298, The Emperor Galerius conquers Mesopotamia, &c.

——, Peace with Diocletian

301 or 303, Hormisdas II King

About 303, Ormuz built

337–360, Sapor II King, 309; proscribes Christianity,

326; makes war successfully with Rome for the lost provinces

363, The Emperor Julian invades Persia; slain near the Tigris, June 26; his successor Jovian purchases his retreat by surrendering provinces

372, Sapor annexes Armenia, 365; and Iberia, 366; makes peace with Rome

380, Artaxerxes II King; Sapor III, 385

386, Armenia and Iberia independent

390, Varanes IV; Yezdejird I, 404; conquers Armenia, 412

420, Varanes V, persecutes Christians; conquers Arabia Felix, 421; makes peace with the Eastern Empire for 100 years, 422

428, Armenia again united to Persia

430–2, Wars with Huns, Turks, &c.

440, Yezdejird II, King; Hormisdas III, 457; civil war, 458–86; Feroze, King, 458; Pallas, 484; Kobad, 486; Jamaspes, 497; Kobad again, 497

531–79, His son, Chosroes I, King; long wars with Justinian and his successors, with various fortune

541–2, Successful campaigns of Belisarius

590, Hormisdas IV continues the war; degrades his general, Baharam, who deposes him; but is eventually defeated

591, Chosroes II; renews the war with success, 603; Egypt and Asia Minor subdued, 614–6

627, Chosroes totally defeated by the Emperor Heraclius, who advances on Persia

628, Chosroes put to death by his son, Siroes; Artaxerxes III, King, 629; Purandokt, daughter of Chosroes, reigns, 630; Shenendeh, her lover, 631; Arzemdokt, her sister, 631; Kesra, 631; Ferokhdad, 632; Yezdejird III, 632

642, Persia invaded by the Arabs; the king flees, 641; is betrayed to them and is put to death, and his army exterminated

661, Persia becomes the seat of the Shiite or Fatimite Mahometans

813, The Taherite dynasty established; the Sofferide, 872; the Samanide, 902

1038, Persia subdued by Togrul Beg and the Seljukian Turks; who are expelled, 1194; subdued by Genghis Khan and the Mongols, 1223

1345, Bagdad made the capital

1388, The poet Hafiz died about

1399, Persia invaded by Timour, 1380; ravaged by him

1414, The poet Jami born

1501, Persia conquered by the Turcomans, 1468, who are expelled by the Shiites, who establish the Sophi dynasty under Ismail I

1590, Ispahan made the capital

1638, The Turks take Bagdad; great massacre

1783, Georgia revolts to Russia

1796, Teheran made the capital

1826–9, War with Russia

1856

Nov. 1, Rupture with England through the Persians taking Herat, Oct. 25; war declared

Dec. 8–10, Persians defeated; Bushire taken

1857

Feb. 8, General Outram defeats the Persians at Kooshab; and at Mohammerah, March 26

April 14, Peace ratified at Teheran

July, Herat given up by the Persians

1865

Railways in process of formation

1867

Electric telegraph introduced

1871

July–Oct., Great sufferings through three years, drought, accompanied by fever and cholera; about 16,000 persons perished at Ispahan, &c.

1872

July 25, Concession to Baron Julius de Reuter to make railways, waterworks, &c., for 70 years, with great power

1873

April 19, The Shah starts to visit Europe; arrives at St. Petersburg, May 22; at Berlin, May 31; at Brussels, June 16; at London, June 18; at Paris, July 5; at Turin, July 25; at Vienna, July 30; at Constantinople, Aug. 19; returned to Teheran, Sept. 23

1878

Aug. 9, The Shah visits Europe in summer; returned to Teheran

1880

Oct.–Dec., Rebellious incursions of the Kurds suppressed after much bloodshed

1886

Jan., The Russians attack the Shohsovan tribes going into winter quarters, killed about 80

1888

June 25, First railway constructed in Persia from Teheran to Shah-Abdul-Azim opened

Sept. 9, The river Karun decreed open to all nations by the intervention of England

1889

The Shah visits Europe; at St. Petersburg, May 23–26; Berlin, June 9; Amsterdam, June 16; Antwerp, June 22; at Windsor, July 2; visits Birmingham and other places, July 7–29; Paris, July 30; Munich, Aug. 19; Vienna, Aug. 23; Budapesth, Aug. 26; returns to Teheran, Oct. 20

Oct. 23, Imperial Bank of Persia established (concession to Baron Julius de Reuter, Jan. 30)

1891

Dec. 14, Great opposition of the priests and people to the monopoly of the Imperial tobacco régie (corporation); the monopoly abolished in the interior, Dec. 19; by a proclamation, Dec. 27

1892

April, Complete abolition of the monopoly demanded, Jan. 4, granted Jan. 7; compensation to the company to be paid

About May 16, The Russian Government offer to lend 500,000l. to pay the compensation to the tobacco corporation, reported April 23; the offer declined; a loan from the Imperial Bank of Persia, London, accepted

1893

Nov. 17, Great earthquake at Kuchan, 12,000 deaths, reported

1894

March 2, The coinage and importation of silver suspended

1895

Jan. 17–22, Kuchan rebuilt; again destroyed by earthquake; 11,000 lives lost

Feb., Delimitation of the Russo-Persian frontier settled by commission

1896

Jan. 2, Zanjabad and several other villages partially destroyed by an earthquake, 300 deaths

Jan. 5, Goi completely destroyed, 800 deaths

May 2, Assassination of the Shah, May 1 (Mirza Reza, the murderer, executed at Teheran, Aug. 12); succeeded by Muzaffer-ed-Deen, recognized by the Powers

1897

Jan. 10, 11, Earthquake with loss of life in the island of Kishim, 1,400 deaths

Dec.-Jan., Mr. Graves, of the telegraph department, murdered and his camp looted at Karwan; Indian troops sent to Jask; Shaki Mahomed, the murderer, executed at Jask, May 31, 1898

1898

Jan. 24, The *Baluchistan* steamship, of London, conveying arms, &c., seized by H.M.S. *Lapwing*, off Muscat

1899

Nov. 15, 16, Great fire at Resht, damage, abt. 100,000*l*.

1900

Jan. 30, Financial agreement with Russia, 5% gold loan of 22,500,000 roubles issued by the Persian government to the Loan Bank of Persia

July 17, The Shah received by the Czar at St. Petersburg; at Paris, July 28 (shot at by Salsou, Aug. 2); leaves, Aug. 11; returns, Oct. 27

1901

May 28, Anglo-Persian Oil Company established

1902

April 8, New loan of 10,000,000 roubles, entitled 5% Persian gold loan, reported

The Shah visits Europe—at Cracow, May 12; in Rome, May 22; at Dover, Aug. 17; London, Aug. 18; at Paris, Aug. 25–Sept. 14; Berlin, Sept. 15; with the Czar at Kursk, Sept. 17, 18

Sept. 6, Raiding dhows captured by H.M.S. *Lapwing* off Koweit; enemy lost about 24, 1 British killed

Dec. 27, Scheme of financial reform with corporation of Belgian experts determined upon by Persian Government, announced (*Cologne Gazette*)

Dec. 30, Concession for construction of new road from Tabriz to Kazvin, granted to Russian bank at Teheran; detrimental to British trade in northern Persia

1903

Feb. 14, Russo-Persian commercial agreement ratified by the Czar. Provides *ad valorem* duties of treaty of 1828 shall be superseded by specific duties, the majority of export duties to be abolished; farming of taxes to be entirely abolished; customs stations to be established, and provisions relating to customs and traffic and toll dues; reported to come into operation

May, Commercial convention with Great Britain, continuing the most-favored nation clause, ratified

Early Sept., Sudden and suspicious death of the Hakino-el-Mulk, one of the principal rivals of the grand vizier

Sept. 29, Banishment of the Grand Vizier, the Atabey Azam, Sept. 15; succeeded by the Ain-ed-Dowleh, cousin and son-in-law of the Shah, stated to be hostile to foreigners, reported

1904–5

British-Indian commercial mission visits Persia during the winter

1906

Jan. 23, The Persian Government refused to ratify the protocol of the commission for the division of the waters of the Helmaud between Afghanistan and Seistan, and communicated its decision to the British commission, reported

March 15, Russian consulate established at Bandar Abbas

April 4, British consul assaulted by a crowd instigated by Kukuma, a Persian doctor, against the European doctors who had begun to take sufferers from the plague from their houses to the hospital, which was demolished by the crowd; British consulate attacked; reported

April 9, Dr. Sven Hedin, the Swedish explorer, arrived at Seistan after a journey *via* Jandak, Turoot, Khur, Tabbas, Naibaud-ad-Neh, in the course of which he crossed the Dasht-i-Kavir, the great salt desert, three times

April 11, Riot at Meshed in N. Persia, 3 persons killed

July 11–13, Riot of divinity students at Teheran

July 22, More than 800 persons, fearing persecution, take refuge in the British Legation at Teheran

Aug. 1, The Grand Vizier, Ain-ed-Dauleh, dismissed by the Shah, July 30; Munshir-ed-Dauleh, while retaining the portfolio of Foreign Affairs, appointed Grand Vizier

Sept. 11, The Shah signs the reforms ordinance; Ain-ed-Dauleh sent away and business resumed

Sept. 14, Ala-es-Saltaneh appointed Minister for Foreign Affairs, and Muhtasham-es-Saltaneh Minister to Gt. Britain

Sept. 20, Regulations for election to the Persian parliament promulgated; all Persians of the male sex, able to read and write, between the ages of 30 and 70, not in the service of the state, and who have never been convicted, are entitled to vote. Persia is divided into 12 electoral districts, each returning from 6 to 19 deputies; Teheran forms a separate and 13th division, returning 60 deputies

Oct. 7, Sanieh-ed-Dauleh, ex-minister of commerce, elected president of the Persian national assembly, which was opened

End Oct., The ministry, having brought forward a motion in parliament declaring the necessity for a large foreign loan, the house decided to authorize the foundation, without foreign support, of a national bank, which should receive the state revenues and meet the state expenditure

Dec. 30, Constitution signed by the Shah

1907

Jan. 1, The revised constitution presented by the

Grand Vizier to the national assembly at Teheran, accepted

Jan. 8, Muzaffer-ed-Din Shah died

Jan. 19, Mahomed Ali Mirza crowned at Teheran

Jan. 20, A tax of 12½% on government salaries abolished by the new Shah

Feb. 6, Concession for the national bank, signed

March 17, Resignation of Zill-es-Sultan, governor of Ispahan, and uncle of the Shah, accepted; Nizam-es-Sultaneh appointed to succeed

March 18, Resignation of Mushir ed Dauleh, Grand Vizier, accepted by the Shah

April 30, Dismissal of the Minister of the Interior voted almost unanimously

May 2, Amin-es-Sultan, former Grand Vizier, president of the council and Minister of the Interior

May, A law provides for the election of rural and town councils. In these elections practically all subjects have a right to vote, and the councils will be in direct communication with the National Council

June 8, Defeat of the Salar-ed-Dauleh near Nihatend; the Prince retreated with heavy losses

June 23, Salar-ed-Dauleh took refuge at the British consulate at Kermanshah, June 19, but surrendered

Aug. 15, A Turkish force entered Persian territory, Aug. 4; Gen. Samsam and other Persian officers killed by Turks after being taken prisoners

Aug. 31, Assassination of Amin-es-Sultan, Premier

——, Great Britain and Russia agreed between themselves to limit the spheres of their respective interests in Persia to the Persian provinces adjoining the Russian frontier on the one hand, and the British frontier on the other. The two Powers respect the integrity and independence of Persia, but, at the same time, contemplate the possible necessity of financial control in conformity with the principles of the agreement. The approximate area, population, and customs revenue of each of the three spheres are given as follows:—

	Area Sq. Miles	Popu- lation	Net Revenue Customs (1913–14)
			£
British sphere . .	137,000	690,000	38,897
Russian sphere . .	305,000	6,900,000	668,264
Neutral sphere . .	188,000	1,910,000	135,131

Sept. 9, New cabinet of eight responsible ministers appointed

Oct. 4, Ala-es-Sultaneh reappointed Foreign Minister in place of Saad-ed-Dowleh, resigned

Oct. 11, New constitution, signed by the Shah, limiting sovereign prerogatives and ecclesiastical authority, granting liberty of conscience, of the person, of education, and of the press

Oct. 24, The cabinet dismissed by the Shah, Oct. 22; a new cabinet formed with Nasir-el-Mulk as Premier

Dec. 14, Resignation of the ministry; fighting between the nationalists and royalists; Teheran reported in a state of siege

Dec. 19, New cabinet formed; Nizam-es-Sultaneh, Premier and Minister of Finance

Dec. 22, Stipulations, submitted to the Shah, accepted by him

1908

Jan. 26, Frontier dispute with Turkey; Prince Firman reports that he has evacuated Suj Bulak without

resistance and has retired to Miandoab; Turkish troops enter Suj Bulak

Feb. 22, Suj Bulak evacuated by the Turks under Fazyl pasha

Feb. 28, Attempted assassination of the Shah in the streets of Teheran; three bombs, thrown at the royal carriage, kill 12 persons and injure 42, besides some horses; the Shah, who was unhurt escaped to the palace on foot

April 5, Resignation of the cabinet

April 7, Several persons, including one Russian subject, suspected of having bombs in their possession arrested

April 28, Rebellion of Kurds round Urumiah; 36 villages pillaged and 2,000 inhabitants killed, reported

May 2, Resignation of the cabinet

May 7, The Shah reappoints the Nizam-es-Sultaneh cabinet

June 4, The Shah unexpectedly leaves Teheran

June 21, Martial law proclaimed; Colonel Liakhoff appointed to the chief command

June 22, Collision between the Shah's forces and the anjumans; heavy casualties reported among the nationalists

June 23, First Parliament dissolved

July 11, The Shah apologizes to Great Britain because certain subordinate officials committed acts of disrespect towards the Legation

July 13, Death of Prince Malcolm Khan, born 1832

July 23, New ministry formed with Mushir-es-Sultaneh as Premier

Aug. 21, Suj Bulak again occupied by Turkish troops; news confirmed

Sept. 11, Renewed fighting at Tabriz by Ain-ed-Dowleh; success of the nationalists

Oct. 3, All Ottoman troops withdrawn from territory recognized as Persian, reported

Oct. 14, Ain-ed-Dowleh dismissed; Prince Firman Firma appointed to the chief command of the forces acting against Tabriz, reported

Nov. 14, Martial law proclaimed in Teheran

Nov. 22, The Shah issues a rescript in which he abolishes the constitution

Nov. 23, The rescript withdrawn

1909

Jan. 23, Earthquake in the province of Luristan; between 5,000 and 6,000 lives lost

Feb. 9, Outbreak of revolutionary disturbances reported from Resht, Maku, and other places

Feb. 16, Shua-es-Sultaneh, brother of the Shah, kidnapped at Resht by revolutionaries, who demand a ransom of 1,000l.

March 18, Nationalists take possession of the customhouse at Bandar Abbas, depose the governor, and substitute another official

April 10, Party of bluejackets landed at Bushire owing to looting by the Tangistani tribesmen

April 13, The Tangistanis evacuate Bushire, but Syed Morteza, their chief, continues to occupy the customs and appropriate the receipts. 800 brigands rob and murder the inhabitants of Aminabad and Yezdikhast (80 miles south of Ispahan). Kerman practically shut off from the outside world by robber bands, reported

April 20, Nationalist forces in Tabriz make a sortie; Mr. Baskerville, American missionary, killed

——, The Shah announces an armistice and instructs

Ain-ed-Dowleh to give every facility to the foreign representatives for procuring provisions

April 22, Reported that the Shah did not transmit the notification of the armistice to Samad Khan, leader of the tribal forces blockading Tabriz, who seized an important nationalist position

April 26, The advance guard of the Russian expedition, escorting a train of provisions, leaves the frontier

April 29, The Shah dismisses his Prime Minister and Minister for War and appoints his uncle, Naib-es-Sultaneh, to these portfolios

——, The Russian troops arrive on the outskirts of Tabriz

May 4, Nationalists attack the garrison of Kasim, of whom 20 were killed and 100 surrendered

May 5, Proclamation issued by the Shah according a constitution to the people, and adding that the elections should be completed by July 19

May 9, Political amnesty granted

May 30, Ain-ed-Dowleh appointed governor of the province of Azerbaijan

June 10, Disorders at Meshed; anti-Russian demonstration reported

June 23, Fighting between the cossacks and revolutionaries

July 1, The Shah signed revised ordinance as to elections

July 13–16, The nationalists enter Teheran, July 13; desultory fighting continues in the streets

July 16, The Sultan declared deposed by the extraordinary national council, and his son, Sultan Ahmed Mirza, aged 11, appointed to succeed him

July 31, Sheikh Fazil-ullah, reactionary, hanged in Teheran

Sept. 1, General amnesty proclaimed

Nov. 2, Ardebil beseiged by the Shahsevan and Karadaghi tribes who take up arms for the ex-Shah, about

Nov. 5, The rebels capture Ardebil

Nov. 15, The Mejliss formally opened by the Shah

Nov. 24, 250 brigands of the Kuhgelu tribe attack the escort of the Russian consul-general near Shiraz; 12 men were killed by the brigands

1910

Feb. 5, Ala-es-Sultaneh, Foreign Minister, being unable to offer an adequate explanation of his inaction in the matter of procuring the departure of the Russian troops, his dismissal was unanimously voted

March 19, Muavin-ed-Dowlah appointed Foreign Minister

July 2, Government troops defeated by Kurds

July 11, Resignation of the Sipahdar and Sardar Assad; Mustaufi el Mamalik entrusted with the formation of a ministry

July 15, Syed Abdullah murdered

Aug. 7, The Fidais refused to deliver up their arms to the government troops and fighting began in Teheran; the government's casualties were 12 killed and wounded; the Fidais lost about 30 killed and wounded, and 300 prisoners were taken; Satar Khan was wounded

Aug. 19, German-Russian Agreement as to railroads in Persia. See also Germany

Sept. 22, Death of Azad-el-Mulk, the regent, aged 76

Sept. 24, Nasr-el-Mulk elected regent

1911

Feb. 2, Parliament authorized employment of American financial adviser

Feb. 4, Minister of Finance killed by Armenians on streets of Teheran

March 4, Nasir-el-Mulk took oath of office as Regent

March 12, New Cabinet formed headed by Sepahdar Azam (Sipah Salar); Sardar Asad, Minister of the Interior

May 1, British loan passed by the Mejliss (Parliament)

May 21, Announcement that Persian-Turkish Boundary Conference at Constantinople would submit points in dispute to the Hague Court

June 13, W. Morgan Shuster, American financial adviser, arrived and made Treasurer-General of Persia

——, Law conferred plenary powers in fiscal matters on Treasurer-General

June 17, The ex-Shah Mohammed Ali landed at Gumesh Tepe on the Caspian in attempt to regain the throne and was joined by his brother Salar-ed-Dowleh who appeared at Kurdistan with force of several thousand Turcomans

July 6, Major C. B. Stokes invited by Mr. Shuster to organize a treasury gendarmerie. His appointment protested by Russia

July 26, New Cabinet headed by Samsam-es-Sultaneh

July 29, Government set reward of $100,000 on head of ex-Shah

July 31, Russian Government asked for resignation of Morgan Shuster after interference with Russian Cossacks sent to prevent confiscation of property of Shu'a es-Sultaneh, brother of the ex-Shah because he was said to owe money to the Russian Bank

Aug. 19, Agreement of Russia and Germany as to Bagdad Railroad, the German line to be connected with railroads in Persia, Germany recognizing Russian interests in Persia

Sept. 5, Decisive victory of government troops against forces of the ex-Shah near Teheran; Arshad-ed-Dowleh, rebel chief captured and shot the next day

Sept. 28, Forces of Salar-ed-Dowleh defeated at Baghishah fell back to Hamadan

Oct. 6, Hamadan occupied by Government troops

Oct. 15, Final refusal of Russian Government to allow appointment of Stokes

Oct. 29, Persian rebels aided by Russians defeated government troops near Bender-Gez

Nov. 16, Shuster refused to yield to Russia and Russian troops ordered to Persia

Nov. 17, Russian ultimatum demanded dismissal of Mr. Shuster

Nov. 19, Diplomatic relations broken off between Russia and Persia

Nov. 29, Russian Government presented second ultimatum demanding dismissal of Mr. Shuster

——, Cabinet reconstituted

Dec. 1, Russian advance on Teheran ordered on refusal to dismiss Shuster

Dec. 14, Major Stokes left Teheran ordered to return to India

Dec. 24, Nazir-el-Mulk, Regent, dissolved the Mejlis and accepted Russian demands

Dec. 25, The Cabinet dismissed Shuster and his colleagues

1912

Jan. 11, Mr. Shuster left Persia for the United States; his successor as financial adviser, M. Mornard, a Belgian

Feb. 23, Persia accepted Anglo-Russian offer of Feb. 19 for loan of $1,000,000 at 7%

March 5, Persian-Turkish Boundary Commission began meetings at Constantinople

March 11, Ex-Shah Mohammed Ali sailed from Petrovsk for Russia

June 11, The Regent left Persia, a virtual abdication

June 24, Formal opening of School for gendarmerie at Yusufabad

July 17, Russian troops in Persia numbered about 12,000

Oct. 7, Troops who had deserted to Salar-ed-Dowleh defeated near Kermanshah

1913

Jan. 16, Ala-es-Sultaneh succeeded Samsun-es-Sultaneh as Prime Minister

July 15, Agreement with Turkey as to boundary signed

July 29, Anglo-Turkish Convention for establishing a commission to improve navigation of the Shatt-el-Arab River boundary of Persia and Iraq

Sept., Return of the Regent from Europe

Dec. 30, Proclamation fixed date of election for Parliament in following summer

1914

March 28, Constituent Assembly inaugurated at Bagdad

July 21, Ahmed Mirza crowned Shah at Teheran

Aug. 14, British Admiralty purchased stock in Anglo-Persian Oil Company

Aug. 19, Mustaufi-ul-Mamalek formed Cabinet

Sept. 1, Resignation of M. Mornard, Belgian financial adviser; succeeded by M. Heynssen who resigned in April, 1915

Nov. 1, Declaration of neutrality in World War

Nov. 4, Persia declined to join Turkey in World War

1915

Jan. 5, Russians evacuated Tabriz which was taken by Turks Jan. 7 and by Russians Jan. 30. *See* World War for battles in Persia

March 4, Mochir ed Douleh, Prime Minister

April 27, Ain ed Douleh appointed Premier

May, M. Leleux appointed Treasurer General

Aug. 18, Mustaufi ul Mamalek appointed Premier

Sept. 2, British Consul-General attacked and wounded at Ispahan

Sept. 9, British Vice-Consul at Shiraz killed

Nov. 10, Swedish officered gendarmerie in affiliation with Germans arrested the members of the British colony at Shiraz and imprisoned the men

Nov. 13-14, The Austrian, German, and Turkish Ministers left Teheran and the Shah refused to accompany them

Dec. 11, Russians occupied Hamadan

Dec. 25, Firman Firma appointed Premier

1916

March 6, Sipar Salar Azam, Prime Minister

March 7, Railroad opened from Julfa to Tabriz

March, M. Hynssens reappointed Treasurer General

Aug. 29, Vossuq ed Douleh appointed Prime Minister

1917

June 6, Ala es Sultaneh appointed Prime Minister

1918

Jan. 19, Mostowfic (Mustaufi) Mamalek, Prime Minister

May 3, Samsam es Sultaneh appointed Premier

Aug. 7, Vossough-ed-Dowleh, Prime Minister

1919

Aug. 9, Anglo-Persian Agreement signed provided for loan to Persia of £2,000,000 at 7% for 20 years, Great Britain to supply military advisers and other experts and equip army to preserve order in Persia

Oct. 23, Last stronghold of rebel Kutchuk Khan captured and he was captured later and executed

Nov. 21, Persia adhered to Covenant of the League of Nations

Nov. 27, Treaty of Neuilly between the Allied Powers and Bulgaria gave Persia free access to the Black Sea

1920

Jan. 10, Persia became a member of the League of Nations

March 21, Commercial Convention with Great Britain modified that of Feb. 9, 1903

May 18, The Bolsheviks invading Persia took Enzeli and occupied Resht where a provisional Government was formed under Kuchik Khan

May 21, Persia appealed to the League of Nations for protection against the Bolsheviks

June 1, Treaty of friendship with China signed

June, Mushir-ed-Dowleh succeeded Voussough-ed-Dowleh as Prime Minister

Nov., Sipahdah-i-Azim became Prime Minister

1921

Jan. 18, Withdrawal of British troops from northern Persia, former Russian sphere, begun

Feb. 20, Sartip, Reza Khan Pahlavi, patriot, with Cossack troops from the Kazvin garrison marched on the capital to set up a strong government and protect Teheran from Soviet attack

Feb. 21, *Coup d'état* of Reza Khan seized capital and overthrew the Government and set up Saiyid Zia-ud-Din as Prime Minister

Feb. 26, Treaty of friendship with Russia signed gave *de jure* recognition canceled Persian debts and gave up Russian concessions in Persia

Feb. 27, The Anglo-Persian Convention of Aug. 9, 1919 denounced

March 1, Saiyid Zia-ud-Din formed Cabinet

March 2, Treaty with Russia canceled all loans

April 3, Saiyid Zia-ud-Din resigned as Premier and left the country

June 4, Qavam-es-Sultanah appointed Prime Minister but Reza Khan, the Minister of War, the ruler of Persia

June 22, Treaty with Afghanistan signed of diplomatic and consular relations

July 26, Lord Curzon announced British withdrawal from Persia

Sept. 29, Armitage Smith, British Controller of Finance, withdrawn

Nov. 28, Death of Sir Abdul Baha Abbas el Bahai

Dec. 12, Treaty of peace and friendship and frontiers with Turkey signed

1922

June 21, The Mejliss (Parliament) met for the first time since 1915

Aug. 15, Agreement signed by which Dr. A. C. Millspaugh (American), became Administrator General of the finances of Persia

Nov. 18, Dr. Millspaugh arrived at Teheran

1923

Jan. 27, Resignation of Ministry of Qavam-es-Sultaneh

Feb. 15, New radical national Cabinet formed by Mustanfi-ul-Mumalik

May 12, Provisional Commercial Agreement with Egypt signed

May 25, Great earthquake in northeast Persia

May 29, Cabinet of Mustanfi-ul-Mumalik defeated, resigned

June 17, Mushir-ed-Dowleh formed Cabinet

Oct. 24, Mushir-ed-Dowleh resigned and Sardar Sepah formed Cabinet

Oct., The Shah fled to Europe

Oct. 29, Reza Khan appointed himself Prime Minister

1924

March 15, Meeting of Cabinet and notables asked Reza Khan to declare in favor of a republic

April 1, Reza Khan proclaimed that the establishment of a republic would be contrary to religion

July 18, Major Robert W. Imbrie, American Vice-Consul, murdered by mob of religious fanatics as he tried to take a photograph of a shrine during a religious ceremony

Aug. 11, Commercial Treaty with Russia signed

Aug. 30, Cabinet reconstituted

Oct. 2, One person executed for Imbrie murder and Nov. 2, 2 more

Dec. 6, Shaik Khazal Khan, independent Chief of Mohammerak, capitulated to Reza Khan and was granted an amnesty

1925

March 10, Parliament passed a compulsory enlistment Bill

March 15, Treaty of friendship and commerce with Poland signed

April 4, Persia joined Russian Peace Pact

April 17, Provisional Commercial Agreement with Greece signed

April 19, Shaik Khazal Khan arrested on board his yacht and made a political prisoner

Aug. 16, Turcomans defeated by Persian troops

Aug. 26, Decree of the Government prohibited public smoking of opium

Sept. 21, Intention of the Shah to return published in newspapers

Sept. 22-23, Bread riots in Teheran

Oct. 31 The National Assembly adopted resolution to depose the Shah and the Kajar dynasty and Reza Khan made Regent, and Constituent Assembly called

Nov. 1, The former Crown Prince left Teheran

Dec. 13, Reza Khan elected hereditary Shah by the Constituent Assembly

Dec. 15, Reza Khan took oath to defend the Constitution

Dec. 16, Reza Khan publicly proclaimed

Dec., Mirza Mohammed Ali Khan Froughy appointed Prime Minister

1926

Feb. 25, The Shah appointed his eldest son, Shahpur Mohammed Riza Valiahd, Crown Prince

April 22, Treaty of peace and neutrality with Turkey signed

April 25, Reza Khan crowned at Teheran

June, Resignation of Mirza Mohammed Ali Khan Froughy. Succeeded by Mirza Hassan Khan Mostofi-el-Mamalek

July 24, Mutiny of troops in Khorassan finally suppressed by troops from Teheran

1927

Jan. 30, Prime Minister Mostofi-el-Mamalek resigned because of concession made to Anglo-Persian Oil Company without consulting Parliament

Feb. 8, Mirza Hassan Khan Mostofi-el-Mamalek returned to office reconstituting Cabinet: Foreign Affairs, Ali Ghuli Khan Ansari (Moshaver el Mamalek); Interior, Mirza Mehdi Khan Fatemy; Finance, Prince Firouz Mirza Firouz; War, Mirza Mohamed Ali Khan Forooghi (Zoka ul Mulk); Public Works, Nahdighirli Khan Hedayat (Mokhber es Saltaneh); Justice, Mirza Ali Akbar Khan Davar

March 19, Treaty of friendship and commerce with Poland

March 30, Provisional Commercial Treaty with Japan signed

April 26, The Shah notified all foreign governments that capitulations would be abolished May 10, 1928

May 10, Treaty of commerce and navigation with Germany of June 11, 1873 denounced by Persia

May 28, Cabinet resigned

June 2, New Cabinet formed by Mehdigholi Khan Hedayat (Mokhber es Saltaneh): Foreign Affairs, Ali Gholi Khan Ansari (Moshaver-el-Mamalek); Interior, Mirza Hussein Khan Samiyi (Adib-es-Saltaneh); Finance, Prince Firouz Mirza Firouz (Nusret-ed-Dowleh); War, Jaafar Gholi Khan Assad; Justice, Mirza Ali Akbar Khan Davar; Public Works, Abdullak Khan Tahmaspi (Amir Lashkar); Education, Yaha Khan Charagozloo (Jan., 1928); Post and Telegraphs, Mirza Ghassem Khan Sar

July 25, Dr. Millspaugh, American Administrator-General of Finances refused to accept new contract restricting his powers

Aug. 3, Dr. Millspaugh left Teheran

Oct. 1, Five year Pact with Russia signed of commerce, customs, and neutrality

——, Note from Turkish Government protested against marauding bands and demanded release of prisoners taken by Kurds

Oct. 6, Reply to Turkish Government explained incident and protested Turkish violation of Persian territory

Nov. 22, Note to British Government claimed sovereignty over Bahrein Islands protesting terms of Treaty of Jeddah of May 20 as between Great Britain and the Wahabi King

Nov. 28, Security Pact with Afghanistan signed

1928

March 10, Earthquake at Nehandan

April, Dr. Lindenblatt, German, appointed Administrator-General of Finances with reduced powers

April 14, Treaty of friendship and commerce with Poland signed

May 10, Abrogation of the capitulations proclaimed in force and new customs tariff

——, Provisional Commercial Agreement with Great Britain signed

May 11, Provisional Commercial Agreement with France signed

May 14, Note to Germany promised most favored nation commercial Treaty

May 15, Provisional Commercial Agreement with Belgium signed
——, Note to the United States promised most favored nation commercial Treaty
May 31, Frontier traffic Convention with Russia signed
June 3, Provisional Commercial Agreement with Iraq
June 15, Protocol with Turkey signed supplement to Treaty of April 22, 1926
June 17, Provisional Commercial Agreement with Austria signed
June 21, Commercial Agreements with Czechoslovakia and the Netherlands signed
June 25, Commercial Agreement with Italy signed
Aug. 10, Commercial Agreement with Sweden signed
Aug. 28, Commercial Agreement with Switzerland signed
Sept. 8, Commercial Agreement with Denmark signed
Sept., New National Bank opened

1929

Jan. 5, The Government protested British passport regulations for Persian subjects visiting Bahrein Islands and again asserted sovereignty over the Islands
Jan. 15, Treaty of friendship with Latvia signed
Feb. 17, Convention of friendship and commerce with Germany signed
March, Cabinet: Mehdi Quli Khan Hedayat (Mokhber es Saltaneh), Prime Minister; Foreign Affairs, Mirza Mohamed Ali Khan Farrughi (Zoka-ul-Mulk); Interior, Mirza Hussein Khan Samiyi (Adib-es-Saltaneh); Finance, Mirza Mohammed Ali Khan Farzin; War, Jaafar Gholi Khan Assad; Justice, Mirza Ali Akbar Khan Davar; Public Works, General Kerim Agha Khan Buzurjmihri; Education, Yahya Khan Qaragozlou; Post and Telegraphs, Mirza Ghassem Khan Sur
March 10, Customs Agreement with Russia signed
March 22, Metric system adopted
April 10, Frontier delimitation Treaty with Turkey signed
May 1–2, Earthquake in Khorassan, 88 villages destroyed
May 2, Strike of employees of Anglo-Persian Oil Company suppressed by troops
May 3, Ali Khan, acting Chief of Kashgais presented demands of united tribes
May 10, Treaty of commerce with Sweden signed and with France
May 15, Treaty of amity and commerce with France signed
May 23, Treaty of amity and commerce with Belgium signed
July 4, Adherence to Russian Peace Pact of Feb. 9
Aug. 11, Convention with Iraq signed
Sept. 5, Treaty of friendship with Italy signed
Sept. 7, Nationality law enacted

1930

Jan. 13, Treaty of friendship with Lithuania signed
Feb. 27, Death of deposed Shah Ahmed Mirza at Neuilly, France
March 12, Treaty of friendship with the Netherlands signed
March 16, Protest against allotment of Bahrein Islands to Great Britain filed with League of Nations
March 18, Law adopted gold standard the gold *rial* containing 100 *dinars* the new standard of value

May 8, Treaty of friendship and commerce with Norway signed
July 23–24, Protest to Great Britain and League of Nations as to British oil concessions in Bahrein Islands
Aug. 21, Election for the Mejliss
Oct. 21, Supplementary Nationality law passed to that of Sept., 1929
Oct. 29, Treaty of friendship and commerce with Czechoslovakia signed
Dec. 16, New Mejliss opened

A.D.	SHAHS

1502. Ismail or Ishmael: conquers Georgia, 1519
1523. Tamasp or Thamas I
1576. Ismail II Meerza
1577. Mahommed Meerza
1585. Abbas I the Great; made a treaty with the English, 1612; died in 1628
1628. Shah Sophi
1641. Abbas II
1666. Shah Sophi II
1694. Hussein; deposed
1722. Mahmoud, chief of the Afghans
1725. Ashraff the Usurper; slain in battle
1730. Tamasp or Thamas II; recovered the throne of his ancestors from the preceding
[Thamas-Kouli-Khan, his general, obtained great successes in this and the subsequent reigns]
1732. Abbas III, infant son of Tamasp, under the regency of Kouli-Khan, who afterwards caused himself to be proclaimed king as
1736. Nadir Shah (the victorious king); conquers India, 1739; assassinated at Khorassan by his nephew
1747. Shah Rokh
1751. [Interregnum]
1759. Kureem Khan
1779. Many competitors for the throne, and assassinations till—
1795. Aga-Mahommed Khan obtains the power, and founds the Turcoman dynasty; assassinated, 1797
1798. Futteh Ali-Shah
1834. Mahommed-Shah, grandson of Futteh; died, Sept. 10, 1848
1848. Nasr-ul-Deen, or Nasr-ed-Deen, son; born, April 4, 1829; said to be an able prince and friendly to Britain, visited Europe, 1873, 1878, and 1889; shot in a mosque near Teheran by Mirza Reza, said to be a Babi fanatic, May 1, 1896
1896. Muzaffer-ed-Deen, son, born March 25, 1853; died, Jan. 8, 1907. Heir: son, Ali Mirza Itezad-es-Sultaneh, born 1872
1907. Mohammed Ali Mirza
1909. Ahmed Mirza, born 1898
1925. Reza Khan Pahlevi

PONDICHERRY

Pondicherry, the chief possession of the French in India, situated on the western coast, 122 miles south of Madras, area 113 square miles, population 188,064. Pondicherry was established in 1683 by François Martin on site of a village given him by the Governor of Gingee. It was taken by the Dutch in 1693, restored in 1697 at the Peace of

Ryswick, besieged by the English Admiral Boscawen in 1748, taken by Colonel Eyre Coote from Lally in 1761 but restored to the French in 1763, taken again by Sir Hector Munro in 1778, restored in 1783, recaptured by the English Aug. 23, 1793, restored to the French by the Treaty of Amiens in 1802 retaken in 1803, and restored to the French in 1816.

PORTUGUESE INDIA

See Damão; Diu; Goa.

RUSSIA IN ASIA

Russia in Asia comprises Siberia including the Far Eastern Region, Central Asia, including the Uzbek Socialist Soviet Republic, the Turkoman Socialist Soviet Republic, the Tajik Socialist Soviet Republic, the autonomous regions of Kara-Kalpakia and Kirghizia (Kara-Kirghizia) and regions north of Tashkent included in the autonomous Kaizak Republic, and the Trans-Caucasian Socialist Federation of Soviet Republics including Armenia, Georgia, and Azerbaijan (*see also* names of countries).

Turkestan (Soviet Central Asia) was conquered by the Russians about 60 years ago. In 1866 Tashkent was occupied and in 1868 Samarkand, and subsequently further territory was conquered and united with Russian Turkestan. In the 70's Bokhara was subjugated, the Emir, by the agreement of 1873 recognizing the suzerainty of Russia. In the same year Khiva became a Vassal State to Russia. Until 1917, Russian Central Asia was divided politically into the Khanate of Khiva, the Emirate of Bukhara, and the Governor-Generalship of Turkestan.

After the outbreak of the Revolution various political parties contended for power in Turkestan. In the summer of 1919 the authority of the Soviet Government became definitely established in these regions, and subsequently the native dynasties in Khiva and Bukhara were expelled. The Khan of Khiva was deposed in February 1920, and a People's Soviet Republic was set up, the mediæval name of Korezm being revived. In August 1920 the Emir of Bukhara suffered the same fate, and a similar régime was set up in Bukhara. The former Governor-Generalship of Turkestan was formally constituted an Autonomous Socialist Soviet Republic within the R.S.F.S.R. on April 11, 1921.

In the autumn, 1924, a decision was accepted by the Congresses of the Soviets of Turkestan, Bokhara, and Khiva Republics to redistribute the territories of these Republics on a national basis; at the same time Bokhara and Khiva became Socialist Republics. As a result of the redistribution completed in May, 1925, the New States of Uzbekistan, Turkmenistan, and Tajikistan and several Autonomous Regions were established. The remaining districts of Turkestan populated by Kaizaks (Kirghiz) were reunited to Kazakstan.

The Autonomous Kirghiz Socialist Soviet Republic (sometimes called Kaizakistan), comprising the Governments of Uralsk, Turgai, Akomlinsk, and Semipalatinsk, had already been created within the R.S.F.S.R. (August 26, 1920). To this Republic were added the parts of the former Governorship of Turkestan inhabited by a majority of Kirghiz, and comprising the greater parts of the old Provinces of Sir Daria and Semirechinsk, together with the eastern part of Ferghana and the foothills of the Pamirs. Area, 94,956 sq. miles. Within this Autonomous Kirghiz Republic, two Autonomous Regions were established, in the interests of distinct sub groups of Kirghiz tribesmen, that of Kara-Kalpakia, extending southeast of the Sea of Aral, and Kara-Kirghizia, covering most of the old Semirechinsk Province. The remaining parts of Russian Turkestan, with the territories of the old native states of Khiva and Bukhara and the Trans-Caspian Province, constitute the two Socialist Soviet Republics of Uzbekistan and Turkmenistan. In October, 1924, the Central Executive Committee of the U.S.S.R. decided to admit these two Republics to membership of the Union, a decision which was confirmed by the Third Union Congress of Soviets in May, 1925.

RUSSO–JAPANESE WAR

The war between Japan and Russia was due to three principal causes: the rights of the Japanese in Manchuria; the independence of Korea; and the independence of China, all these interests being imperiled by the rapid extension of the Russian power. The conflict between China and Japan, 1894–95, resulted in the recognition by China of the independence of Korea, and the cession to Japan of Port Arthur and the Liao-tung peninsula; the latter advantage was, however, lost to Japan by the action of Russia, supported by France and Germany, on the ground that its possession by the Japanese would "constitute a perpetual menace to the capital of China, and render the independence of Korea illusory." Japan failed in her attempt to obtain pledges from Russia that neither Port Arthur nor the Liao-tung peninsula would be occupied by the forces of that power; assurances were, however, given "that Russia had no designs whatever on Manchuria"; but Russia refused to embody these assurances in a treaty on the ground that to do so would be an imputation on her *bona fides*. In 1898, Russia obtained from China a lease over Port Arthur and Ta-lien-wan, together with railway concessions (granted March 23); Russian forces were landed (March 28), the Trans-Siberian railway was rapidly extended south to Port Arthur, fortifications were erected, garrisons established, and Manchuria treated as if it were virtually a Russian province. In return for her support given to China after the relief of Pekin, 1900, Russia sought, but unsuccessfully, to obtain a convention securing her special rights in Manchuria, and ultimately agreed to evacuate two provinces of Manchuria on Oct. 8, 1903. The promised evacuation was not carried out, and on Oct. 30, 1903, Russian troops reoccupied Mukden, and a great number of troops were sent into Manchuria. This action of Russia in maintaining her occupation of Manchuria, notwithstanding her treaty with China and the repeated assurances given to the powers by Russia, together with aggressive action on the Ya-lu in Korean territory, caused great apprehension to Japan, as threatening the independence of Korea and the safety of Japan, especially if Manchuria were annexed by Russia. In a despatch dated July 28, 1903, M. Kurino, the Japanese Minister at St. Petersburg, was instructed by Baron Komura, Japanese Foreign Minister, "to approach the Russian Government in a spirit of conciliation and frankness, with a view to the conclusion of an understanding" on these questions, and "to a definition of their respective interests in those regions." The Japanese proposals were stated in the following terms in a despatch from Tokio, dated Aug. 3, 1903:—

I. A mutual agreement to respect the independence and territorial integrity of the Chinese and Korean Empires, and to maintain the principle of equal opportunity for the commerce and industry of all nations in those countries

II. Reciprocal recognition of Japan's preponderating interests in Korea and Russia's special interests in railway enterprises in Manchuria, and of the right of Japan to take in Korea and of Russia to take in Manchuria such measures as may be necessary for the protection of their respective interests as above defined, subject, however, to the provisions of Article I

III. Reciprocal undertaking on the part of Russia and Japan not to impede the development of those industrial and commercial activities respectively of Japan and Russia in Korea and of Russia in Manchuria, which are not inconsistent with the stipulations of Article I

IV. Reciprocal engagement that in case it is found necessary to send troops by Japan to Korea, or by Russia to Manchuria, for the purpose either of protecting the interests mentioned in Article II, or of suppressing insurrection or disorder calculated to create international complications, the troops so sent are in no case to exceed the actual number required, and are to be forthwith recalled as soon as their missions are accomplished

V. Recognition on the part of Russia of the exclusive right of Japan to give advice and assistance in the interest of reform and good government in Korea, including necessary military assistance

The following counter proposals were submitted on behalf of Russia, Oct. 3, 1903:—

I. Mutual engagement to respect the independence and territorial integrity of the Korean Empire

II. Recognition by Russia of Japan's preponderating interests in Korea, and of the right of Japan to give advice and assistance to Korea tending to improve the civil administration of the Empire without infringing the stipulations of Article I

III. Engagement on the part of Russia not to impede the commercial and industrial undertakings of Japan in Korea, nor to oppose any measures taken for the purpose of protecting them, so long as such measures do not infringe the stipulations of Article I

IV. Recognition of the right of Japan to send for the same purpose troops to Korea, with the knowledge of Russia, but their numbers not to exceed that actually required, and with the engagement on the part of Japan to recall such troops as soon as their mission is accomplished

V. Mutual engagement not to use any part of the territory of Korea for strategical purposes, nor to undertake on the coasts of Korea any military works capable of menacing the freedom of navigation in the straits of Korea

VI. Mutual agreement to consider that part of the territory of Korea lying to the north of the 30th parallel as a neutral zone, into which neither of the contracting parties shall introduce troops

VII. Recognition by Japan of Manchuria and its littoral as in all respects outside her sphere of interest.

The proposal of Russia that Manchuria should be regarded as outside the Japanese sphere of interest was, in view of the important political and commercial interests of Japan in that country, rejected by Japan, Oct. 30, 1903; other amendments, including one relating to a neutral zone, in Manchuria as well as in Korea, were proposed by Japan. Russia, in response to the protest of the Japanese government respecting the delay of the Russian government in replying to its communication, reaffirmed the proposals of Oct. 3, but omitting Article VII, Dec. 11, 1903. In reply, Dec. 21, 1903, the Japanese Government stated that Russia's exclusion of Manchuria from the negotiations nullified them entirely, the negotiations having been expressly undertaken to remove every cause for misunderstanding respecting both Korea and Manchuria; Russia was asked to reconsider the question; the neutral-zone clause to be omitted. The Russian Government reply, Jan. 6, 1904, proposing to insert the following article in the agreement, "Recognition by Japan of Manchuria and its littoral as being outside her sphere of interests, while Russia within the limits of that province will not impede Japan or other powers in the enjoyment of rights and privileges acquired by them under existing treaties with China, exclusive of the establishment of settlements." This article was subject to the understanding that the articles respecting a neutral zone, and the prohibition of Korean territory for strategical purposes, were conceded by Japan. The final proposals of the Japanese Government were presented to Russia, Jan. 13, 1904, and comprised the following modifications of the Russian terms:—

I. The elimination from Article V of the words "not to use any part of the territory of Korea for strategical purposes"

II. The elimination from Article VI as to a neutral zone

III. The acceptance of the final Article concerning Manchuria, provided that Russia agreed to respect the territorial integrity of China in Manchuria; not to impede Japan or other Powers, within the limits of Manchuria, in the enjoyment of rights and privileges acquired by them under the existing treaties with China; to recognize Korea and its littoral as being outside the Russian sphere of influence

IV. The recognition by Japan of Russia's special interests in Manchuria, and of the right of Russia to take measures necessary for the protection of those interests

Owing to the dilatory tactics of Russia the patience of

the Japanese Government became exhausted, and becoming convinced that no hope existed of a peaceable settlement of the questions at issue, and having regard also to the preparations being made with both her army and navy by Russia, the Japanese Government at Tokio announced, Feb. 6, 1904, through their minister at St. Petersburg, the breaking off of diplomatic relations with Russia. The Emperor issued, Feb. 10, an imperial rescript, giving the Japanese statement of the case against Russia, and declared war against Russia

1904

Feb. 8, Japanese fleet under Adm. Togo attacks the Russian fleet lying outside Port Arthur, and torpedoes the battleships *Retvisan* and *Tsarevitch* and the cruiser *Pallada*, midnight

Feb. 9, Russian cruiser *Variag* and gunboat *Korietz* sunk by a Japanese naval squadron under Adm. Uriu, which had escorted a number of transports and landed a Japanese force at Chemulpo

Feb. 14, Attack on Port Arthur by Japanese torpedo-boats, the Russian cruiser *Boyarin* torpedoed

Feb. 21, Gen. Kuropatkin, Minister of War, appointed commander-in-chief of the Russian forces in Manchuria

March 6, Adm. Kamimura bombards Vladivostok

March 28, Japanese advance in Korea; defeat Russians at Cheng-ju, and capture town

April 6, Gen. Kuroki, commanding the first Japanese army, 45,000 strong, advances on Wi-ju; Russians retreat across the Ya-lu

April 13, Russian squadron decoyed out of Port Arthur by the Japanese fleet; Adm. Makaroff discovers the trap laid for him, and while returning to the harbor the Russian battleship *Petropavlovsk* strikes a mine and founders; Adm. Makaroff, the famous Russian artist Verestchagin, and 700 officers and men, drowned; 80 saved, including the Grand Duke Cyril

April 26, Raid by the Vladivostok squadron off N.E. Korea; Japanese *Goyo Maru* sunk by the Russians, April 25; and also a Japanese transport ship, *Kiushiu Maru*, sunk with 200 soldiers on board who refuse to surrender

April 26, Battle of the Ya-lu.—Imperial guards and 2nd division of Japanese army under Gen. Kuroki attack the Russians on the islets of the Ya-lu and occupy them; Russians retreat to Kiu-lien-cheng; 2 gunboats, 2 torpedo-boats, and 2 steamers, detached from the Japanese Hosoya squadron, ascend the Ya-lu and silence the enemy on Antzushan, April 27; Kuroki's army crosses the river and advances on Hushan, April 29; Japanese artillery silence the Russian guns on a hill N.W. of Yuskukon; all the Japanese divisions advance and storm the heights, extending to Kiu-lien-cheng to N. of Matton and Yuskukon; 2nd and 12th divisions and the Japanese imperial guards advance by three roads, pushing the Russians before them; line from Antung to Liushukon captured; Russians surrounded on three sides by imperial guards, fight bravely, but are forced to retreat, losing 20 guns; Japanese reserve corps advance to the Liau-yang road; Russian retreat to Feng-hwang-chenn; Russians lose 28 guns and a large quantity of rifles and ammunition; Russian losses 1,363 killed, 613 taken prisoners; Japanese, 318 killed, 783 wounded, May 1

May 3, Port Arthur temporarily blocked for battleships and cruisers by the sinking of 8 merchant steamers by Japanese fleet

May 15, Japanese cruiser *Yoshino*, with 235 officers and men, rammed and sunk by the cruiser *Kasuga* during a dense fog off Port Arthur, 90 of the crew of the *Yoshino* saved

——, Japanese battleship *Hatsuse*, striking a mine 20 miles S.E. of the harbor entrance to Port Arthur, founders with 61 officers and 378 men; 300 saved

May 26, Battle of Kin-chau.—Japanese army, under Gen. Oku, advances southward on the isthmus leading to Port Arthur, and, supported by the fleet under Adm. Togo, engages the Russians at Kin-chau, on the W. of the Kwan-tung peninsula, and by night marches and seizing with great gallantry, in spite of the Russian batteries, such positions as the line of advance afforded, captures the town, obstinately defended by the Russians, after five hours' desperate fighting, May 25; the forts of Nanshan (where the Russians had 70 guns in position, and surrounded by several lines of shelter trenches, below which were wire fences and mines, interspersed with quick-firing guns) carried by assault; Russians driven back in disorder; 68 cannon and 10 machine guns captured; Japanese losses, 739 killed, 3,456 wounded; 500 Russians left dead on the field; land investment of Port Arthur thus opened

June 8, Third Japanese army, under Gen. Nodzu, which was landed at Ta-ku-shan and at Tsing-tui-tse, coöperates with Gen. Kuroki; both armies advance and occupy Siu-yen, which commanded the road to Hai-cheng

June 15, Battle of Telissu (or Wa-fang-kau).—Japanese army under Gen. Oku assumes the offensive against the Russian force under Gen. Stackelberg sent south from Ta-shih-chiao to impede the Japanese movements in the Liao-tung peninsula. Main Japanese body advances northward in two columns along the railway lines, and expels the Russians from the E. of Wa-fang-tien; the Russian forces make a stand on the line from Lung-wang-mio to Ta-fang-shen; Japanese, after a heavy cannonade, occupy the line from Panchiaton to Yuhoton, June 14; Russian force of two and a half divisions, occupying a position from Ta-fang-shen to Chengtinshan, near Telissu, attacked by the Japanese, who surround the enemy near Telissu, and after severe fighting completely rout the Russians; Russian losses, 1,854 killed, 6 guns captured, and 300 prisoners; Japanese, 217 killed, 946 wounded

June 16, The Vladivostok squadron makes a raid and sinks the Japanese transports *Hitachi Maru* and *Sado Maru*, June 15; captures the British ss. *Allanton* (released, Oct. 22)

June 23, Marshal Oyama appointed commander-in-chief of the Japanese forces with Lt.-Gen. Kodama as chief of the staff

June 26, Land attack on Port Arthur by Japanese, who capture some outer defenses

June 30–July 1, Vladivostok squadron bombards Gen-san, and successfully escapes from the Japanese fleet under Adm. Kamimura

July 3–5, Severe fighting at Port Arthur by land and by sea

July 4–6, Russian volunteer fleet cruisers *Peterburg* and *Smolensk*, flying the Russian commercial flag, pass the Bosphorus and the Dardanelles, and commence operations as warships in the Red Sea

July 13, British ss. *Crewe Hall* and *Menelaus* stopped by the volunteer cruisers off Jiddah, allowed to proceed, July 12; P. & O. steamer *Malacca*, carrying ammunition for the British navy to Shanghai and Hongkong, seized by the *Peterburg* and taken as a prize (released after strong protests by the British Government)

July 15, Japanese mails of the German liner *Prinz Heinrich* seized by the Russian volunteer cruiser *Smolensk* (German Government protests and mails are sent on by British ss. *Persia*)

July 23, Russians arm as cruisers 4 Hamburg-American liners and a liner of the North German Lloyd mercantile fleet, and despatch them with sealed orders from Libau

July 24, Gen. Kuroki dislodges the Russians from their advanced positions on the northern route from Saimatse to Liao-yang, and captures Hai-ho-yen; Russians retreat in disorder on An-ping; Gen. Oku, commanding the second Japanese army, attacks the Russians outside Ta-shih-chiao; Russian positions all taken and the enemy forced back and pursued towards Ta-shih-chiao, which is occupied by Gen. Oku; Japanese losses, 1,071 killed and wounded; Russian losses, 2,000, July 25

July 26–30, Port Arthur attacked by Japanese forces; severe fighting, Wolf hill captured; Russian loss, 1,540 killed and wounded; Japanese losses stated to be 10,000

July 27, German ss. *Arabia* seized by Russian cruisers, July 22, and taken to Vladivostok (released, Aug.); another German ss., the *Thea*, sunk by cruisers, July 24; another German ss., the *Scandia*, seized (afterwards released), July 24; British ss. *Knight Commander* sunk by the cruisers, July 24; *Calchas* (British ss.) seized and taken to Vladivostok (released, Sept. 13 after confiscation of the cargo, which was consigned to Japan), July 25; two other British vessels, the *Andora*, seized, July 25, and the *Formosa* (afterwards released), July 26; German ss. *Holsatia*, seized and released

July 31–Aug. 1, General advance by Japanese forces; severe fighting 25 miles from Liao-yang; Russians, driven from their positions, retreat towards An-ping and Tang-ho-yen; Russian force occupying strongly entrenched heights round To-mu-cheng retreat on Hai-cheng, which they evacuate; Japanese loss, 1,806 killed and wounded; Russian losses over 2,000, 8 guns captured

Aug. 3, Russians at Port Arthur driven back from their outer lines to inner defenses

Aug. 10, Russian fleet, exposed to the fire of the Japanese guns on Wolf hill (captured, July 30), make an attempt, under Adm. Vitoft, to escape from Port Arthur, all the fleet, with the exception of the cruiser *Bayan*, steam out of the harbor and are encountered by the Japanese fleet under Adm. Togo (in the action Adm. Vitoft is killed)

Aug. 11, The Russian battleships *Retvisan*, *Poltava*, *Sevastopol*, *Pobieda*, and *Peresviet*, the cruiser *Pallada*, and 3 torpedo-boat destroyers, regain the harbor of Port Arthur under Rear-Adm. Prince Ukhtomsky (the battleship *Csarevitch*, the cruiser *Novik* and 3 torpedo-boat destroyers escape to Tsin-tao and are disarmed)

Aug. 19–24, Fierce attack on Port Arthur

Aug. 24, Battle of Liao-yang.—Japanese forces immediately after the cessation of the heavy rains resume the land campaign with energy, and begin their advance on the Russian positions S. of Liao-yang from An-shan-chan to Hun-sha-ling on the right bank of the Tang-ho, and thence to Tai-tse; severe fighting between Japanese under Gen. Kuroki and the Russians near An-ping; the strongly fortified Russian positions at Kung-chang-ling carried by assault, Aug. 25; and at Hung-sha-ling, 8 guns captured, Aug. 26; division from the third army, sent by Gen. Nodzu to assist the first army on Gen. Kuroki's left flank, encounters a strong rear-guard left by the Russians at An-shan-chan under Maj.-Gen. Kontkovsky; Russians stubbornly resist, but are driven back by the Japanese; during the retreat Maj.-Gen. Kontkovsky is killed, 8 field guns are captured from the Russians, and An-shan-chan is occupied by the victors, Aug. 28; S. of Liao-yang 2nd and 3rd Japanese armies advance against the Russians and open fire on the enemy established in the Liao-yang position, the Russian military capital of S. Manchuria, situated on the railway at the junction of the two main roads, leading respectively to Korea and Port Arthur, and containing all the magazines of the field army, with stores, ammunition, hospitals, and other establishments necessary for the continuous activity of an army in the field, Aug. 29; Japanese artillery open a severe and continuous cannonade on the Russian positions, the Russian front extending from Hsinlitun, through Shou-shan, Menchafang, and Yayuchi, to the junction of the rivers Tang-ho and Tai-tse; left column of the 1st Japanese army attack the Russian position at Menchafang and Yayuchi; the enemy, reinforced, repel the attack; column of the 3rd Japanese army attack the Russian center near Weijago, with at first some success; Russians, reinforced to 2 divisions and 50 guns, come out from Liao-yang and make a fierce counter-attack; Japanese aided by part of the 1st army, repulse the Russians and establish themselves securely near Weijago: 2nd Japanese army and the main body of the 3rd army assail the Russians from Hsinlitun to Shou-shan-pao; 2nd army occupy Ta-chao-chai-tai, and attack the W. front of Shou-shan, where 100 Russian guns were in position, but without result; 1st army crosses the river Tai-tse, near Chien-tao-jau, Aug. 30; 2nd and 3rd Japanese armies resume their attack on Shou-Shan, and after a fierce struggle drive out the Russians, and turn some heavy guns (captured) on the Russians on the railway station in Liao-yang; whole of the Russian right falls back to the river in great confusion, but pursuit by Japanese checked by a second line of defensive works constructed round the town and station, and by the fire of troops held in reserve on a hill N.E. of Mu-chwang; 1st Japanese army attacks the Russian position at Hei-ying-tai, and captures Sy-kwan-tun, Sept. 1; Gen. Kuropatkin assembles troops N. of the river, attacks Gen. Kuroki, and after a desperate conflict recaptures Sy-kwan-tun and the whole of the heights W. of it; Gen. Kuroki, reinforced, repels an onslaught made on his right by a column under Gen. Orloff, and gains possession of Sy-kwan-tun; 1st Siberian army corps, which had suffered heavy losses, driven to the west, Sept. 2; order for general retreat of the Russians given by Gen. Kuropatkin, and collects a part of his shattered army at Yen-tai, Sept. 3; rear-guard at Liao-yang, which had held off the Japanese southern forces for 3 days, burns its stores and bridges, and retreats from the town; Russian losses estimated 4,000 killed, 12,000 wounded (Russian official statement, 1,810 killed, 10,811 wounded, 1,212 left on the field); Japanese, 17,539 killed and wounded; estimated strength of the armies, Russian about 150,000; Japanese about 200,000, Sept. 4

Sept. 3, British Government protests strongly to Russian Government respecting the stopping and seizure of British ships by the *Smolensk* and *Peterburg*; Russian Government requests the British Government to despatch British cruisers to search for the two cruisers, and inform them that by order of the Czar they are to cease stopping vessels in their search for contraband goods, Aug. 26; *Smolensk* and *Peterburg* met with near Zanzibar, and the Czar's order communicated

Sept. 19–30, Port Arthur attacked by Japanese

Oct. 2, Battle of the Sha-ho.—Gen. Kuropatkin issues an order of the day, intimating that he is about to take the offensive; Russians advance southwards on both sides of the railway and occupy Ben-tsia-putse and Sha-ho station, 15 miles S. of Mukden; Russian infantry brigade and 2,000 cavalry with 2 guns cross the Tai-tse river and cut the Japanese communications, which were subsequently restored, Oct. 9; 2 Japanese positions at Pen-hsi-hu captured (retaken, Oct. 10); Russian attack on Hsen-chang begun, Oct. 7, repulsed, Oct. 9; counter-attack begun by Marshal Oyama, Oct. 11; Russian offensive movement checked, left wing of the army withdrawn, Oct. 13; center retires under attack by Gen. Nodzu across the Sha-ho; fierce struggle on the Russian right around Sha-ho-pau, Russians sustain heavy losses in men and guns, Oct. 13–14; Sha-ho-pau and Li-mun-tun captured by Japanese under Gen. Oku, the Russians driven back at every point, Oct. 15; Japanese force surprised and enveloped by Russians near Liun-yan-tun, and loses 14 guns, Oct. 16

[Russian loss in battle of the Sha-ho, 13,333 left dead on the field, 709 prisoners—total Russian casualties estimated at about 60,000 killed and wounded; Japanese, 15,879 killed and wounded; Japanese capture 45 guns, 5,474 rifles and a great quantity of ammunition]

Oct. 21, Baltic fleet, under Adm. Rozhdestvensky, fire upon British North Sea trawlers fishing on the Dogger Bank (*see* England)

Oct. 25, Adm. Alexieff relieved of his position and duties as commander-in-chief of the Russian forces in the Far East, but retains his position as Viceroy; Gen. Kuropatkin appointed his successor

Oct. 25–29, Heavy bombardment with large siege and naval guns of forts Erhlungshan, Sungshushan, and East Keekwanshan, Port Arthur, by the Japanese, many guns of the forts dismounted

Nov. 16, Russian torpedo-boat destroyer *Raztoropni* escapes with despatches from Port Arthur during a snowstorm, arrives at Chifu, and is blown up by her commander

Nov. 26, General attack by Japanese on the center of the permanent forts and 203 Mètre hill, commanding the dockyard and harbor; simultaneous attack on forts Erhlungshan and Sungshushan is unsuccessful

Nov. 30, 203 Mètre hill captured

Dec. 3, Japanese naval brigade bring up heavy siege guns to 203 Mètre hill, and from that eminence commence the bombardment of the harbor of Port Arthur with 11 in. shells, inflicting damage on the Russian war vessels

Dec. 3, Supreme prize court at St. Petersburg declares the sinking of the British ss. *Thea* not justified; cargo of flour on the British ss. *Arabia* declared not contraband of war, decision of prize court at Vladivostok reversed

1905

Jan. 1, Four Russian torpedo-boat destroyers escape from Port Arthur to Chefu with despatches and a number of soldiers on board

——, Adm. Rozhdestvensky, with the Baltic squadron, arrives off Madagascar

Jan. 2, Terms of the capitulation of Port Arthur signed; they provided that the whole fortress, ships, arms, and other property of the Russian Government should be surrendered, and that soldiers, sailors, volunteers, and other officials were to be prisoners, but officers were to be allowed to retain their arms and return to Russia on parole not to take further part in the war

——, In anticipation of surrender the Russians blow up the East Keekwanshan and Q forts, and almost all their warships and steamers

Jan. 4, Forts at Port Arthur delivered up by the Russians to the Japanese

Jan. 5, Meeting of Gen. Nogi and Gen. Stössel at Plum Tree Cottage, in the village of Shui-shi-ying

Jan. 6, Gen. Stössel gives his parole; Russian prisoners march out of Port Arthur

Jan. 25, Dr. Morrison, correspondent of the *Times* at Pekin, after visiting Dalny and Port Arthur, by permission of the Japanese headquarters, records his opinion that the surrender of Port Arthur by Gen. Stössel was not justified by the condition of the fortress, and strongly condemns the Russian capitulation in view of the fact that 25,000 able-bodied soldiers, well clad and well nourished, and capable of making a sortie, were found by the Japanese in the fortress; that there was ample food for three months; that there was fuel in abundance, 70,000 tons of coal being stored in the dockyard, besides large quantities of firewood; that there was no serious failure of ammunition; that the number of buildings destroyed or injured in Port Arthur was comparatively small, the Japanese having directed their fire on the docks, workshops, and the ships in the harbor. Of the 14,000 cases in the hospital from all classes of the population, only a small proportion were wounded. In Dr. Morrison's opinion, "no more discreditable surrender has been recorded in history." He states that the heart and soul of the defense was Gen. Kondrachenko, who was killed Dec. 18, 1904, and that but for him Gen. Stössel would have capitulated some weeks earlier

——, Battle of Hei-koa-tai.—The Russian second army, 85,000 strong, with 350 guns, under Gen. Gripenberg, crosses the frozen river Hun-ho, and attacks the Japanese left; village of Hei-koa-tai captured by the Russians; Sandepu, bravely defended by a small force of Japanese, in spite of a fierce conflict, in which the Russians sustain heavy losses; left position strengthened by Marshal Oyama, who assumes the offensive, and after a long struggle, Jan. 27, drives the Russians across the Hun-ho; estimated losses—Russian, 10,000; Japanese, 7,000, Jan. 29

Feb. 15, Third Baltic squadron under Adm. Nebogatoff leaves Libau

Battle of Mukden.—The Japanese forces comprised the third army, under Gen. Nogi, on the left (looking northward); the second army, under Gen. Oku, to the right of the third army; the fourth army, under Gen. Nodzu, in the center; the first army, under Gen. Kuroki, on the right; and the right flank detachment of reservists under Gen. Kawamura. The Japanese line extended nearly 100 miles from W. to E., under the direction of Marshal Oyama. The Russian forces comprised the second army under Gen. Kaulbars (looking southward); the center under Gen. Bilderling; and the first army under Gen. Linevitch, with a detachment under Gen. Rennenkampf, the whole commanded in chief by Gen. Kuropatkin.

The general idea of the Japanese operations was the threatening of the Russian left under Gen. Linevitch, the real object the attack on the Russian right and an extended out-flanking movement. Gen. Kuropatkin (whose forces were about 400,000 men and 1,500 guns, with a strongly entrenched position on the S. and S.E. of Fushan, 26 miles east of Mukden), misled by the Japanese attack on his left, where his strongest forces were placed, failed to realize the true Japanese objective, until too late to readjust his forces. (For convenience of reference this battle, one of the greatest of modern times, is divided into 5 sections, representing the successive stages of the conflict.)

Feb. 19–28, I. The Japanese commence offensive operations on the Russian left by the advance of Gen. Kawamura over the frozen roads and rivers, Feb. 19; he gains the Ching-ho-cheng defile, the Tai-tse river having been crossed, and a fierce conflict waged for two days with the Russians, who are driven out of their entrenchments, Feb. 24; Japanese first army, under Gen. Kuroki, moves forward from the Pen-hsi-hu district upon Kao-tu-ling, and forces the Russians from their advanced positions about 10 miles N. and N.W. of Pen-hsi-hu; the fourth army, under Gen. Nodzu, advances on the Sha-ho, gaining ground and threatening the Russian position, with the result that Gen. Kuropatkin's attention was directed to the defense of his center and left

Feb. 28–March 4, II. Gen. Oku, with the Japanese second army, advances and deploys between the Sha-ho and the Hun; Gen. Nogi, with the third army on the left of Gen. Oku, rapidly marches between the Hun and the Liao in a northerly direction, overcoming all the counter-attacks of the Russians, Feb. 28. Gen. Kuropatkin becomes aware of this movement, March 1, but measures taken by him proved to be inadequate and too late, his forces being driven back in the night towards Mukden; Gen. Nogi begins his turning movement on the west, between the Hun and Liao rivers, marching rapidly in a northerly direction, Feb. 26; advances at first without encountering opposition, marches nearly due N. to Hsin-min-lun, 33 miles west of Mukden, March 1; swinging round, Gen. Nogi marches eastward on a front of 15 miles, keeping touch with Gen. Oku, at Lik-wan-pau, and pushing towards the railway; second Russian army, under Gen. Kaulbars, is forced to face westward on a line running from Machiapu to N.N.E.; the fourth and first Japanese armies, under Generals Nodzu and Kuroki respectively, make sustained efforts to pre-

vent the Russian troops from withdrawing in the center and the left to meet the decisive attack

March 5–8, III. Russian army by March 5 was held fast in the center, driven back on the left and completely turned on the right, Gen. Kuroki having forced the left of the Russian entrenchments on the Sha-ho, March 5; Russian reserves attack Gen. Oku and penetrate a short distance along the Hsin-min-tun road, but are then repulsed, March 5; Gen. Nodzu dislodges the Russians from their earthworks S. of the Sha-ho, March 2–6; Gen. Nogi's line extends its envelopment of the Russian forces to the N. of Mukden; the fortified positions of Machuntun and Tita, S. and S.E. of Fushan, reached by Gen. Kawamura, Feb. 28, are the scene of a desperate conflict, Gen. Kuropatkin bringing up his reserves to these positions; after 8 days of fierce fighting the Japanese take Machuntun, March 8; Gen. Kuropatkin decides to withdraw his center and left behind the Hun and attack Generals Oku and Nogi with all available forces from the armies of Generals Kaulbars and Bilderling, March 8; railway N. of Mukden cut by the Japanese under Gen. Nogi

March 8–9, IV. Russian first army under Gen. Linevitch effects its retreat to the line of the Hun without serious loss, and takes up a defensive position there; situation of the Russian army at Mukden becomes most critical, owing to the exhaustion of the second Russian army under Gen. Kaulbars, and the arrival at Mukden of the third army under Gen. Bilderling, which causes a great accumulation of troops in a confined space and their exposure to the concentrated fire of the Japanese, who draw in upon the town from all sides except the N.E.; a gallant attempt is made by Gen. Kuropatkin, who leads an attack of 65 battalions, checking the advance of Generals Oku and Nogi, March 9; Gen. Nodzu, having crossed the Sha-ho, sweeps on to the Hun, and penetrates the Russian line; Kuisan, E. of Mukden, occupied by the Japanese on the north, while Gen. Nogi fights to establish himself across the line of the Russian retreat, March 9; Gen. Kuropatkin, to avoid the destruction or capture of the second and third Russian armies, gives the order for a general retreat, March 9; Tita taken by the Japanese, March 9, and the Russians in this part of the field fled to the N. of Fushan

March 10–12, V. General Nodzu crosses the Hun, March 10; Japanese occupy Mukden, March 10; a large number of the Russian troops, owing to the enveloping character of the Japanese attacks, are unable to escape; Gen. Nogi occupies the line of the Puho directly across the main line of retreat and astride all the roads leading from Mukden to the N.; the remnant of the Russian army escapes over the hills in disorder, Gen. Linevitch alone retaining his formations, and showing a bold front against Gen. Kuroki, March 10; Fushan position carried by the Japanese, and the Russians retire towards Tieling, March 10; parties of Russians in the adjacent villages and positions around Mukden continue to offer resistance, but are driven from all the country 26 miles N. of Mukden, and the Russians, broken and routed, flee in great disorder to Tie-line, March 12

(Russian loss, 30,000 killed, 100,000 wounded, 50,000 prisoners; Japanese casualties, 52,500 killed and wounded. Immense captures of prisoners, arms, ammunition, provisions, &c.)

March 16, Adm. Rozhdestvensky's fleet leaves French waters

April 26, The Japanese expostulate with the French Government that the Russians are using this station as a naval base; as a result the Russian fleet leaves Kamranh bay under pressure from France, and goes to Hon-Kohe bay

May 27–28, Battle of Tsu Shima.—This, the greatest naval battle since Trafalgar (Oct. 21, 1805), was fought when the Russian Baltic fleet, under Adm. Rozhdestvensky, entering the Straits of Tsu Shima, between Korea and Japan, was attacked by the Japanese fleet under Adm. Togo, and practically annihilated. A fog at first prevailed, when Adm. Rozhdestvensky's main fleet, steaming in two columns, the battleships to starboard and cruisers to port, drew up to Tsu Shima in the forenoon of May 27. The fog cleared in the afternoon, when the Russian fleet was sighted by the Japanese scouts. Immediately on receiving the report that the Russian fleet was in sight the combined squadrons of the Japanese started for attack, and met the Russian squadron near Okimo Shima, to the S.E. of Tsu Shima. The battle began between 2 and 3 P.M., a strong breeze blowing and a high sea running. Before the engagement commenced Adm. Togo signaled from the flagship *Mikasa* to the Japanese fleet: "The fate of the Empire depends on this effort. Let every man do his utmost." Although inferior in the number of their battleships the skilful tactics and superior range of their guns gave the Japanese the superiority, and enabled them to inflict a crushing defeat on the Russians. The battle lasted until the afternoon of May 28, and included a general engagement, and a torpedo attack on the night of May 27, breaking up the defeated Russian fleet. The *Kniaz Souvaroff*, the flagship of Adm. Rozhdestvensky, was blown up; the Admiral himself, seriously wounded, was rescued by a Russian torpedo-boat destroyer (afterwards captured), and taken prisoner; Adm. Fölkersahm was killed in the conning tower of the *Oslyabya*; and Rear-Adm. Nebogatoff was taken prisoner; 21 of the ships of the Russian fleet were sunk, *viz.*, the battleships *Kniaz Souvaroff*, *Borodino*, *Oslyabya*, *Alexander III*, *Navarin*, and *Sissoi Veliky*; the cruisers *Dimitri Donskoi*, *Admiral Nakhimoff*, *Svietlana*, *Vladimir Monomakh*; a coast defence ship the *Admiral Oushakoff*; the special service ships *Russi Ural*, *Anastny*, *Kamtchatka*, and the *Ilutish*; and 5 torpedo-boat destroyers. 5 Russian ships were captured—the battleships *Nikolai I* and the *Orel*; the coast defense ships *Admiral Apraxine* and *Admiral Seniavin*; and 1 torpedo-boat destroyer. 9 Russian ships escaped; 5 cruisers, of which number the *Aurora*, *Jemchug*, and *Oleg* (with Adm. Enquist on board wounded) escaped to Manilla, and were interned; the *Almaz* succeeded in reaching Vladivostok; the *Izumrud* was wrecked in Vladimir bay; 2 special service ships escaped to Shanghai, 1 torpedo-boat destroyer to Shanghai, and another to Vladivostok. The Russian loss is estimated at 4,000 killed or drowned; 7,282 officers and men taken prisoners. The Japanese in the engagement lost 3 torpedo boats, 116 officers and men were killed and 538 wounded; the Japanese flagship *Mikasa* sustained the heaviest losses

May 31, Japanese navy department, the necessity for secrecy no longer existing, announce the loss of the battleship *Yashima* by striking a mine while blockading Port Arthur, May 15, 1904, and other naval losses hitherto withheld, *i.e.*, the torpedo-boat destroyer *Akatsuki*, sunk by a mine while engaged on blockading duty before Port Arthur, May 17; the gunboat *Oshima* sunk after a collision while coöperating with the army off the Liao-tung peninsula, May 17; the t.-b.-d. *Hayatori*, mined and sunk while blockading Port Arthur, Sept. 3; the gunboat *Atago* sunk by striking a rock before Port Arthur, Nov. 6; the cruiser *Takasago* mined and sunk while blockading Port Arthur, Dec. 12, 1904

June 5, British India Co. ss. *Ikonia*, with mails and rice from Hong-Kong, sunk by Russian cruiser

June 8, President of the United States addresses an identical Note to the Russian and Japanese Governments in which, for the welfare of mankind, he urges, them to negotiate for peace

Replies received at Washington both favorable to the proposal—that of Japan, June 10, the Russian, June 13

June 16, Various engagements in the Kang-pin district between the Japanese and Russian cavalry, the latter, 5,000 strong with 20 guns; the Japanese attack and capture Liao-yang-wo-peng, and afterwards occupy Lo-chung-pu, driving the Russian cavalry before them and inflicting severe losses

June 18, British ss. *St. Kilda* stopped and searched by the Russian Volunteer cruiser *Dneiper*, 60 miles N. of Hong-Kong, while on a voyage from Hong-Kong to Japan, June 4, and sunk the following day; strong protests by the British Government to the Russian Government

June 22, Severe fight between Japanese troops and a force of 3,000 Russians, N.W. of Nan-shan-chen-tse; part of the Russians offer a stubborn resistance, but eventually are driven northward in disorder, losing 200 men killed and wounded

——, Danish ss. *Prinsesse Marie* sunk by Russian cruiser *Terek*

July 1, M. Muravieff and Baron Rosen appointed peace plenipotentiaries for Russia, and Baron Komura and Mr. Takahira for Japan, with power to conclude a treaty subject to the ratifications of their governments

July 8, Japanese torpedo-boat destroyers of Adm. Kamimura's squadron appear off Sakhalin and attack several points, July 7; Russian batteries at Korsakvosk return the fire; ultimately the commander orders the coast guns to be blown up and all the government buildings to be burnt, and retires northward

July 10, Two Japanese cruisers and 4 torpedo-boats with troops on board despatched to Kondo promontory (S.W. Sakhalin) and after a demonstrative bombardment land a naval detachment and occupy the promontory

July 19, M. Witte, appointed peace commissioner in place of M. Muravieff, leaves St. Petersburg for Washington *via* Paris

July 22, M. Witte has an interview with the French Prime Minister and President in Paris

Aug. 5, President Roosevelt meets the peace commissioners on board the U.S. naval yacht *Mayflower* in Oyster bay

Aug. 10, Peace commissioners meet at Portsmouth, New Hampshire, U.S.; Japanese terms of peace submitted in writing

Aug. 12, Russian terms in writing submitted

Aug. 29, Many of the Japanese terms were accepted, but Russia firmly rejected the Japanese proposals for a war indemnity, the limitation of Russia's naval forces in the Far East, the surrender of the Russian ships interned in foreign ports, and the cession of Sakhalin; a deadlock resulted; President Roosevelt intervenes and addresses a direct personal appeal to the Czar; ultimately the Japanese commissioners, acting under instructions from Tokio, withdraw their demand for an indemnity, the limitation of Russian naval power in the Far East, the surrender of the interned ships, and offer to cede half of the island of Sakhalin; on these terms an agreement was arrived at

Sept. 5, Peace Treaty signed

The following are the principal articles of the Treaty of Peace:—

Article II.—His majesty the Emperor of Russia recognizes the preponderant interest, from political, military, and economic points of view, of Japan in the empire of Korea, and stipulates that Russia will not oppose any measures for its government, protection, or control that Japan will deem necessary to take in Korea in conjunction with the Korean Government; but Russian subjects and Russian enterprises are to enjoy the same status as the subjects and enterprises of other countries

Article III.—It is mutually agreed that the territory of Manchuria shall be simultaneously evacuated by both Russian and Japanese troops. All rights acquired by private persons and companies shall remain intact.

Article IV.—The rights possessed by Russia in conformity with the lease to Russia of Port Arthur and Dalny, together with the land and waters adjacent, shall pass over entirely to Japan, but the properties and rights of Russian subjects are to be safeguarded and respected

Article V.—The Russian and Japanese Governments engage themselves reciprocally not to put any obstacles in the way of the general measures, which shall be alike for all nations that China may take for the development of the commerce and industry of Manchuria

Article VI.—The Manchurian railway shall be operated jointly between the Russians and the Japanese at Kouangtchengtse. The respective portions of the line shall be employed only for commercial and industrial purposes. In view of Russia keeping her line with all the rights acquired by her convention with China for the construction of the railway, Japan acquires the mines in connection with such section of the lines which falls to her. The rights of private parties or private enterprises, however, are to be respected. Both parties to this treaty remain absolutely free to undertake what they may deem fit on the expropriated ground

Article VII.—The Russians and the Japanese engage to make a junction of the lines which they own at Kouangtchengtse.

Article VIII.—It is agreed that the lines of the Manchurian railway shall be worked with a view to ensuring commercial traffic between them without obstruction.

Article IX.—Russia cedes to Japan the southern part of Saghalin Island as far north as the fiftieth degree of north latitude, together with the island depending thereon. The right of free navigation is assured in the bays of La Perouse and Tartary

Article XI.—Russia shall make an agreement with Japan, giving the Japanese subjects the right to fish in Russian territorial waters in the seas of Japan, Okhotsk, and Behring

Article XIII.—The Russians and Japanese reciprocally engage to exchange prisoners of war, paying the real cost of the keep of the same, such cost to be supported by documents

Sept. 13, Russian and Japanese armistice commissioners meet at Sha-ho-tsu and sign the protocol providing for the cessation of hostilities between the two armies in Manchuria

Oct. 14, Treaty of peace signed

Minor engagements on sea and shore were of almost daily occurrence throughout the war, and are not all included in the preceding records

According to the *Times* correspondent writing from Tokio under date July 4, 1905, the following are the casualties in the war, made after careful examination of the figures published:—

Russia, casualties—army, 314,779; navy, 6,000; prisoners, 67,701; total, 388,480

Japan—army, 163,086; navy, 3,670, prisoners, 646; total, 167,402

Naval Losses

Russia, 12 battleships sunk, 2 battleships captured, 1 battleship interned, 5 armored cruisers sunk, 1 coast defence ship sunk, 2 coast defence ships captured, 6 cruisers sunk, 5 cruisers interned, 33 other ships and torpedo-boat destroyers sunk, 3 captured, 13 interned

Japan, 2 battleships sunk, 4 cruisers sunk, 6 other ships and topredo-boat destroyers sunk

(*See also* Russia and Japan)

SAKHALIN

Sakhalin, an island in the North Pacific off the eastern coast of Siberia, 600 miles long and from 16 to 105 miles broad, area 24,560 square miles, separated from Japan by the narrow strait of Soya. By the Treaty of Portsmouth of 1905 the part south of 50° N. Lat. became Japanese and that to the north Russian.

SELANGOR

See Malay.

SIAM

Siam (Muang Thai) an independent kingdom of southeastern Asia in the Indo-Chinese Peninsula, with an area of 200,149 square miles, about 45,000 being in the Malay Peninsula, population 11,506,-207: Siamese, 10,493,304; Chinese, 445,274; Indians and Malays, 379,618; Cambodians, 60,668; Annamites, 5,321; Shans, 27,505; Burmese, 4,880; Europeans and Americans, 1,920; Japanese, 295; other nationalities, 87,422. Bangkok is the capital.

Prajadhipok succeeded to the throne on the death of his brother Rama VI on Nov. 26, 1925, being the seventh monarch of the present reigning dynasty,

The Portuguese established trade with Siam in 1511 and the Dutch about 1604

1826

June 20, Treaty of friendship and commerce with England

1833

March 20, Treaty of amity and commerce with the United States signed

1855

April 18, Treaty of friendship with England signed

1856

May 29, Second Treaty of amity and commerce with the United States signed
Aug. 15, Treaty of friendship with France signed

1858

May 21, Treaty of commerce with Denmark

1859

Feb. 10, Treaty of commerce with Portugal

1860

Dec. 17, Treaty of commerce with Holland

1862

Feb. 7, Treaty of commerce with Germany

1867

July 15, Treaty with France signed by which Siam recognized the French Protectorate over Cambodia
Dec. 17 and 31, Treaty of commerce with the United States of 1856 modified

1868

May 18, Treaty of commerce with Sweden and Norway
Aug. 29, Treaty of commerce with Belgium
Oct. 1, King Chulalonkorn succeeded his father, Mongkout
Oct. 3, Treaty of commerce with Italy

1869

May 7, Treaty of commerce with Austria-Hungary

1870

Feb. 23, Treaty of commerce with Spain

1874

May 8, A political Constitution decreed

1883

July 14, Telegraph communication with France opened
Aug. 25, Annam became a French Protectorate
Sept. 3, Treaty with Great Britain by which International Court established

1893

April 11, Bankok-Paknam Railroad opened by the King
May 3, Conflict between Franco-Annamite troops and Laotian tribes on the Mekong River district claimed by France as part of Annam
June 5, After murder of French Inspector Grosgurin France occupied Stungtreng and Khong demanding reparation

June 13, The French occupied Samit
July 13, Siamese troops in engagement with French troops
July 26–Aug. 2, Blockade of coast by French gunboats ended by acceptance of French ultimatum of reparation and cession of territory by Siam
Oct. 3, Convention with France signed by which Siam renounced left bank of the Mekong River and islands in the River and paid an indemnity; France continued occupation of Chantabun

1895

Jan. 10, Royal decree created a Legislative Council

1896

Jan. 15, Anglo-French Convention guaranteed the independence of Siam

1897

March 27, First half of railroad from Bankok to Khorat opened by the King; completed in 1901
June 3–Dec. 16, Visit of the King to capitals of Europe

1898

Feb. 25, Treaty of commerce with Japan

1899

June 23, Treaty of commerce with Russia

1902

July 23, Shan rebellion in the north, troops defeated
July 25, Pray captured, Siamese massacred
Aug. 24, The British Consul from Nan persuaded the Shans to leave Pray and give up other positions
Oct. 7, Treaty with France; Chantabun restored but France secured Melupré, Bassac, and other territory. Not ratified

1904

Feb. 13, New Treaty with France modified that of 1893; Chantabun finally evacuated by the French and neutral zone along the Mekong renounced, Siam ceding provinces of Bassac, Melupré, and the remainder of Luang Prabang, all on the right bank of the Mekong, and the maritime district of Krat
April 8, Anglo-French Agreement delimited spheres of influence in Siam, both Powers disclaiming all intention of annexation of Siamese territory

1907

March 23, Further Treaty with France by which Siam gave up Battam, Siemrap, and Sisophon and received in return Krat and Dansai ceded in 1904; extraterritorial rights of France modified

1909

March 10, Treaty with Great Britain signed by which British extraterritorial rights in Siam modified and cession of Kelantan, Trengannu, and Kedah to Great Britain

1910

Oct. 3, Death of King Rama V (Chulalongkorn I). Succeeded by his son as Rama VI (Vajiravudh) crowned Dec. 2

1911

Population 8,266,403

SIAM

1913

March 15, Treaty with Denmark, extraterritorial jurisdiction abolished

April 1, Siamese Treasury Savings Bank opened

1917

July 22, Siam declared war on Germany and Austria-
Hungary, seized German vessels, and interned enemy
aliens

1918

Aug., Military mission sent to Europe, and military
contingent landed in Marseilles including motor
ambulance transport, and an aviation corps

1919

June 28, Siam representatives at the Peace Conference
signed the Treaty of Versailles; Germany recognized
that all treaties, agreements and rights and privileges
including rights of extraterritorial jurisdiction terminated as from July 22, 1917, German property
in Siam except diplomatic residences and offices became the property of the Siamese Government

1920

Jan. 10, Siam became an original member of the League
of Nations

Dec. 16, Treaty with the United States modified former
Treaties

1922

South Prasak Canal Project irrigating central Siam
plain completed

1924

Feb. 28, Provisional Economic Agreement with Germany signed

March 10, Treaty of commerce and navigation with
Japan signed

1925

Feb. 14, Treaty of commerce and navigation with
France signed, Protocol as to jurisdiction applied to
French citizens in Siam, and Special Convention reg-
ulating relations with French Indo-China

June 8, Treaty of friendship, commerce, and navigation
with the Netherlands signed and Jurisdiction Protocol

July 14, Treaty of friendship, commerce, and navigation and Jurisdiction Protocol with Great Britain
signed

Sept. 1, Treaty of friendship, commerce, and navigation
with Denmark signed

Nov. 26, Prajadhipok of Sukhodaya succeeded to the
throne on the death of his brother Rama VI

Dec. 19, Treaty of commerce with Sweden signed

1926

April 1, Siamese dominions divided into 14 circles
(Monthons) of which 13 have each a Lord-Lieutenant deriving authority direct from the King, and
having under him subordinate governors over various
parts of his circle. The circle of Bankok which includes the capital is under control of a Lord Prefect

May 9, Treaty of friendship, commerce, and navigation
and Jurisdiction Protocol with Italy signed

July 13, Treaty of friendship and commerce signed
with Belgium and Luxemburg

July 16, Treaty of friendship, commerce, and navigation with Norway signed

1927

March 25, The last of the consular courts closed and
2 days later a new customs tariff, controlled no
longer by Treaty limitations, went into effect

1928

Jan. 25, Notes exchanged with Great Britain regarding
the Mekong River

Oct. 27, Arbitration Treaty with the Netherlands

SIBERIA

Siberia, administrative division of Asiatic Russia, extending from the Arctic Ocean on the north
to the Mongolian border on the south, area
4,028,615 square kilometers, population 11,069,-
550, capital Novo-Sibirsk, with a population of
120,701. Other large cities are Omsk, with population of 161,475, Tomsk and Irkutsk with population of approximately 100,000 each. The conquest of Siberia was begun in 1580 by Yermak, a
Cossack. In 1710 Peter the Great began to send
prisoners there. *See* Russia.

SINGAPORE

See Malay; Straits Settlements.

SOKOTRA

Sokotra Island (Habidu *alias* Taharida) off the
coast of Africa about 150 miles northeast of Cape
Guardafui came under British protection by
Treaty with The Sultan April 23, 1886, attached
to Aden; area 1,382 square miles, population about
12,000.

SOVIET CENTRAL ASIA

See Russia, in Asia.

STRAITS SETTLEMENTS

Straits Settlements, on the Malay Peninsula, a
British Crown Colony, comprise Singapore, Penang (including Province Wellesley and the Dindings), and Malacca. Malacca is one of the oldest
European settlements in the East, having been
occupied by the Portuguese in 1511, and held by
them until driven out by the Dutch in 1641. It
was transferred to the English March 17, 1824 by
Treaty with Holland in exchange for the British
settlements in Sumatra. Penang was the first
British settlement in the Malay Peninsula, having
been ceded to the East India Company in 1786.
Singapore was important in the fourteenth century, but was destroyed by the Javanese in 1377,
and was almost uninhabited until 1819, when it

was ceded by the Johore princes. In 1826 these three settlements were incorporated under one government, which was transferred from the control of the Indian Government to that of the Secretary of State for the Colonies on April 1, 1867. The Cocos Islands were placed under the Straits Settlements in 1886, and Christmas Island in 1889. On January 1, 1907, the boundaries of the Colony were extended so as to include the Colony of Labuan.

The total area of the colony, with dependencies, is about 1,600 square miles. Singapore is an island about twenty-seven miles long by fourteen wide, with an area of 217 square miles, separated from the southern extremity of the Malay Peninsula by a strait three-quarters of a mile in width. A number of small islands adjacent form part of the settlement. The seat of government is the town of Singapore, at the southeastern point of the island. Penang is an island of 108 square miles, off the west coast of the Malayan Peninsula, and at the northern entrance of the Straits of Malacca. On the opposite shore of the mainland, distant from two to ten miles, is Province Wellesley, a strip of territory forming part of the Settlement of Penang, averaging eight miles in width, and extending forty-five miles along the coast, including ten miles of territory to the south of the Krian; total area 280 square miles. The chief town of Penang is George Town. Off the coast of Perak is the small island of Pangkor, which, together with a strip of the mainland, is British territory, the whole being known as the Dindings. Malacca is on the western coast of the peninsula between Singapore and Penang—about 110 miles from the former and 240 from the latter; it is a strip of territory 42 miles in length, and from eight to 25 miles in breadth, with an area of 720 square miles.

The population, according to the census of 1921, was 883,769 (558,741 males and 325,028 females). The estimated population for 1928: Singapore and Labuan Island, 559,270; Penang, 342,023; Malacca, 194,342; grand total, 1,095,635. See Malay.

The Governor of the Straits Settlements is also High Commissioner for the Malay States, and British Agent for British North Borneo and Sarawak.

Sir Cecil Clementi, Governor, January, 1930.

SUMATRA (DUTCH EAST INDIES)
See pp. 950, 956.

SYRIA

Syria (Republic), former province of Turkey-in-Asia, has been recognized as an independent State to be placed under a Mandatory Power. By decision of the Supreme Council of the Allied Powers at San Remo (April 25, 1920), France has been assigned the Mandate for Syria, which was confirmed by the League of Nations on July 24, 1922 (Declaration of London). The capital is Damascus.

Area and Population.—Syria under the Mandate is bounded by the Mediterranean on the west, by Palestine on the south, by Mesopotamia on the east, and by Turkey on the north.

The Anglo-French agreement of Dec. 23, 1920, defines the frontier between Syria and Mesopotamia and Palestine, and also the southern boundary of Syria. The eastern frontier of Syria runs up the Tigris as far as Jeziret-ibn-Omar, when it joins the Turkish frontier laid down in the Convention of London of March 7, 1921, confirmed by the Treaty of Angora, October 21, 1921. The section of the southern frontier between Ras Nakura and the valley of Garmonk was ratified by the two governments on March 7, 1923.

The frontier between Syria and Turkey has been fixed by the Franco-Turkish Treaty of October 21, 1921.

The country was originally organized into 5 territories (*états*), but since January 1, 1925, two of these, *viz.*, Damascus and Aleppo, were united to form the single territory of Syria (Sanjaks of Hama, Homs, Damascus, Hauran, Aleppo, Alexandretta, and Deir ez Zor). The remaining territories are those of the Alaouite (Sanjaks of Latakia and Tartons); of the Great Lebanon (Sanjaks of North Lebanon, Mount Lebanon, South Lebanon, and Bekaa); of Jebel Druze (south of Hauran).

The Great Lebanon was proclaimed a State on September 1, 1920. It has the following frontiers: North, the Nahr-el-Chebir; south, the frontier of Palestine; west, the coast; and east, the heights of Anti-Lebanon. Beirut is the seat of the Government. The national flag is the French Tricolor with a cedar superimposed on the white ground. There is one Legislative Assembly.

The autonomous Sanjak of Alexandretta, set up Jan. 1, 1925 is a part of the Syrian Republic.

The Government of Latakia was established on May 14, 1930. Capital, Latakia.

The Government of Jebel Druze has its seat at El Suweda.

The total area of Syria subject to the French Mandate may be estimated at 60,000 square miles. The total population of this area in 1929 was 2,831,622. The population of the 4 territories was as follows: Syria, 1,696,638; Lebanon, 862,618 (of whom 342,388 were Christians and 292,247 Moslems); Alawiyya, 286,920; and Jebel Druze, 51,780. The bulk of the population of Syria is of Arabic origin, and Arabic is the prevailing language, with many dialectical varieties. But there is a large influx of foreign elements, including Turks, Turkomans, Kurds, Circassians, Armenians, Persians, Jews, and a certain number of Europeans. The principal towns are Damascus, population 193,912; Aleppo, 177,313; Beirut, 134,655; Homs, 52,792; Hama, 39,960; Tripolis, 37,260; Antioch, 28,000; Latakia, 21,404; Alexandretta, 13,997; and Zahlah in Lebanon, 20,985.

M. Henri Pansot, High Commissioner, October 12, 1926.

1915

March 17, French claim to Syria lodged with the British Government

July 14, Letter of Sherif Hussein of Mecca to Sir Henry McMahon, British High Commissioner in Egypt asked for recognition of independence of Arab countries with boundary statement which included Syria. *See* Arabia

1916

May 9 and 16, Secret Agreement between Great Britain and France by which France promised Syrian coast from Alexandretta to Tyre, the interior consisting mainly of the provinces of Aleppo, Damascus, Deir-ez-Zon, Mosul, and Urfa to be part of independent Arab State

1917

June 11, British statement to 7 Syrians of Cairo, assurance that Arabian States freed by military action of their inhabitants should remain independent

1918

Oct. 1, Damascus occupied by British and Arabs. *See also* World War

Oct. 5, Beirut taken by French squadron and occupied by British troops on the 7th. General Allenby set up an administration of Occupied Enemy Territory and Emir Faisal proclaimed the Syrian State with capital at Damascus in the name of his father, King of the Hejaz; the eastern division with administration at Damascus headed by Ali Riza Pasha er Rikabi, the Lebanon and north under French officers with government at Beirut headed by Colonel P. de Piepape

Oct. 20, Franco-British Convention as to administration of occupied territory

Oct. 31, Armistice with Turkey came into effect with the Allies in complete occupation of Syria

Nov. 8, Joint declaration of Great Britain and France published that their object in the War in the East to enfranchise peoples oppressed by the Turks and establish national governments in territories liberated by the Allies

Nov. 17, Emir Faisal left Syria for Paris to represent his father King Hussein of the Hejaz at the Peace Conference and was received as the guest of France

Nov. 10, Emir Faisal arrived in London and was decorated by the King on the 12th for his services in the War in the cause of the Allies

1919

Feb. 6, Emir Faisal presented claims for Arab State at the Peace Conference

June 25, American (King-Crane) Commission sent by President Wilson to Syria arrived at Damascus and later reported that a French mandate would be unacceptable to the people

July 2, Congress at Damascus representing Moslems, Christians, and Jews asked for independence and if that not granted a mandate of the United States or Great Britain as second choice

Sept. 15, Anglo-French military Convention gave the French control of the west coast after Nov. 1, the interior remained under administration of Faisal but transferred from British to French control

Oct. 9, General H. J. E. Gouraud appointed High Commissioner for France in Syria

Nov. 4, Withdrawal of British army of occupation from the north and west begun

Nov. 18, General Gouraud, French High Commissioner, arrived at Beirut

Dec. 11, Ramadhan ibn Shalash, Arab governor of Raqqa, with Kurdish chief, Ibrahim Pasha Milli, instigated by Turks attacked Deir ez Zor still occupied by British

Dec. 21, Compulsory military service reintroduced

Dec. 25, First fighting between Arabs and French at Baalbek

1920

March 8, Syrian National Congress met at Damascus and declared for "the complete independence of Syria, without any form of foreign interference"

March 11, Faisal proclaimed King by National Congress of Syria including the Lebanon and Palestine

March 15, French and British Governments united in refusal to recognize the kingdom

March 20, Arab Nationalists seized Antioch from French troops

April 1, Turks attacked Aintab in the north which was relieved by French troops April 15–16

April 25, Supreme Council assigned mandate for Syria and the Lebanon to France

April 28, French troops withdrawn from Aintab and Turks began new siege two days later

May 1, Standard currency of the Syrian pound equal to 20 French francs introduced

May 22, Aintab again relieved by French troops

May 29, French concluded armistice with Turks at Aintab but later were attacked again and relieved for third time Aug. 11

June, Riza Pasha Cabinet succeeded by Hashim Bey Attassi

July 14, General Gouraud, French High Commissioner, sent an ultimatum to King Faisal demanding acceptance of the French mandate, of the new currency, the removal of obstacles to use of the Rayaq-Aleppo railway by French troops, abolition of conscription, and punishment of offenders against the French

July 20, Faisal accepted French terms within time limit and prorogued the National Congress; General Gouraud claimed that he had not received the acceptance and imposed new and harsher ultimatum

July 22, Hostilities begun between French troops and Arab Nationalists who acted against the orders of Faisal

July 23, French troops occupied Aleppo

July 24, French troops defeated the Arabs at Meiselun

July 25, French troops occupied Damascus and General Goybet issued proclamation dethroning Faisal who took refuge in Palestine

Aug. 4, Faisal left Haifa for Europe

Aug. 10, Treaty of peace with Turkey signed at Sèvres recognized French mandate and independence of Syria

Aug. 20, Bedouins stopped train at Khirbet el Ghazali and murdered the Syrian Prime Minister, Ala ed

Din er Rubi, the Minister of the Interior, and the President of the Council of State

Sept. 1, The Great Lebanon proclaimed State by the High Commissioner, and the States of Alaouite, Aleppo, and Damascus, Governors appointed, French for the Great Lebanon and Alaouite State, and Syrian for Aleppo and Damascus

Dec. 23, Anglo-French Convention defined boundaries with Palestine and Iraq

Dec. 20, The Druses met at Suwayda (Suweida) and drafted charter of 12 conditions under which they would recognize the French mandate. *See* March 4, 1921

1921

Feb. 10, Aintab finally recovered from the Turks

May 1, Assembly of notables elected Salim Pasha Al-Atrash governor

March 4, Jebel Druze recognized as an autonomous State under French supervision but independent of Damascus, by Treaty of General Gouraud with Druse chiefs and was officially proclaimed in April, 1922

July 24, The house of Salim bombed by French airplanes after his capture from the French of the man who had attempted assassination of General Gouraud in June and had taken refuge as a suppliant with Salim and had been arrested by the French

Oct. 4, Decree reëstablished common courts and Nov. 16 mixed tribunals which were never put into effect because of opposition

Oct. 20, Franco-Turkish Nationalist Agreement signed in which Turkey gave up claim to Syria in mandated areas and boundary agreed upon

1922

Feb. 3, Anglo-French Convention fixed boundaries to become effective March 10, 1923

April 5, State of Jebel Druze officially proclaimed

June 22, Syrian Federation of the three States of Damascus, Aleppo, and the Alaouite proclaimed, Statute of Federation signed June 28

July 24, French mandate for Syria confirmed by the League of Nations

Oct. 25, Announcement of resignation of General Gouraud as High Commissioner

1923

March 4, Alexandretta set off from Aleppo and Damascus as a new State

March 7, Further Franco-British boundary settlement

April 20, General Maxim Weygand appointed French High Commissioner to succeed General Gouraud

May 5, Amnesty granted to Salim

July 7, Decree as to courts, French magistrates to sit with native magistrates in cases of foreigners tried

Sept. 29, Mandate came into legal effect

Nov. 25, Syro-Palestine Congress petitioned the League of Nations to set aside the mandates for Syria, the Lebanon, and Palestine

1925

Jan. 1, Damascus and Aleppo united to form single State known as Syria by decree of High Commissioner of Dec. 5, 1924

Jan. 2, General Sarrail, French High Commissioner, replaced General Weygand

Jan. 10, Martial law in force since 1914 abolished

Jan. 12, The High Commissioner dissolved the Council of Great Lebanon and called for election of a new one appointing M. Cayla, a Frenchman, as Governor

Feb. 9, The Peoples' Party formed with permission of the High Commissioner

April 2, Agreement of France with Turkey gave Turkish population of Alexandretta a large measure of autonomy

April 9, Riot at Damascus on occasion of visit of Lord Balfour

June 5, The Peoples' Party at opening session adopted nationalist program

July 11, General Sarrail summoned Druse notables for conference and arrested and exiled three of them

July 18, Druse insurrection broke out against French rule led by Sultan Pasha

July 20, Sultan Pasha took Salkhad and July 22 invested Suwayda

Aug. 2, French force commanded by General Michaud attacked and routed by Druses at Mezraa in attempt to relieve French garrison at Suwayda

Aug. 20, Sultan Pasha Atrash, Druse leader, refused French offer of autonomy for State of Jebel Druse with Druse government and demanded independence of all Syria

Aug. 24, March of 1,500 Druses and Arabs on Damascus prevented by appeal of the leaders of the Peoples' Party to Sultan Pasha

Aug. 26, Druses took Der ez Zor

Sept. 24, General Gamelin who had replaced General Michaud, recalled, attacked Suwayda and succeeded in capturing the town and relieving the French garrison

Oct. 4, Nationalists seized city of Hama

Oct. 7, Arabs and Bedouins attacked Aleppo but were unable to enter the city

Oct. 12, French troops returning from raid against brigands exposed bodies of 24 persons killed and 115 prisoners in the public square at Damascus taken in the districts in which the bandits operated

Oct. 17, French soldiers in Damascus attacked

Oct. 18, General Sarrail began bombardment of Damascus which lasted 48 hours when a band of rebels led by Hasan Kharrat from the Ghutah entered the city

Oct. 20, The bombardment stopped after the Syrian Government and the President of the municipality of Damascus had agreed to imposition of a fine of $440,000 in gold and a levy of 3,000 rifles

Oct. 30, General Sarrail recalled by the French Government

Nov. 6, Henri de Jouvenel appointed High Commissioner and arrived at Beirut, Dec. 2

Nov. 25, Martial law declared in Damascus and the Hauran

Dec. 5, Hasbayya recaptured by the French troops in South Lebanon

Dec. 21, Resignation of President Bereket Subhi Bey

Dec. 22, Conference of representatives of rebel groups with the new High Commissioner, M. de Jouvenel after failure of the Amir Amin Arslan sent by him to Jebel Druze, also without result

Dec. 23, M. de Jouvenel offered presidency to Shaykh Tajii d'Din

1926

Jan. 6, Shaykh Tajii d'Din elected President

Feb. 2, Treaty of friendship with Palestine signed

Feb. 9, General Andrea made military Governor and Pierre Alype delegate of High Commissioner at Damascus

April 25, Suwayda which had been abandoned in September recaptured by the French

May 7, Druses again invaded Damascus

May 8–9, Damascus again bombarded by French artillery and aircraft with great loss of life and damage to property

May 23, Great Lebanon formally proclaimed a republic and a constitution promulgated and Charles Debbas elected President

May 30, Franco-Turkish Treaty defined boundaries, and guaranteed Syria against Turkish raids

June 3, Salkhad recaptured by the French

July 18, General Andrea began advance into the Ghuta from Damascus for punishment of villages where rebels had been harbored and over 1,500 persons killed, chiefly non-combatant peasants

July 21, Fighting outside Damascus

Aug. 20, French troops occupied Majdal Shams after bombardment from the air

Aug. 22, French troops occupied Qalaat Jandal

Aug. 24, Rebels in attack reached inner defenses of Damascus

Oct. 12, Henri Ponsot arrived to replace M. de Jouvenel as High Commissioner

Nov. 15, Draft Constitution prepared in Paris read to Permanent Mandates Commission

1927

June, Druse rebellion ended with submission of a number of chiefs, Sultan Pasha and about 600 of his followers withdrew to Transjordan

July 26, Statement of policy of new High Commissioner, M. Ponsot published promised to encourage the political development of the States

Oct. 12, The Parliament of Great Lebanon consented under protest to the modification of the constitution granted in 1926, the senate to be abolished and third of the chamber to be nominated by the Lebanese Government instead of being elected by popular vote

Oct. 25, Nationalist declaration a reply to declaration of M. Ponsot of July 26, noting the omissions in that document and stressing desire of Syria for independence and self-governing institutions

Dec. 14, Foreign affairs committee of the Senate in France passed a resolution asking that definite proposals for the future administration of Syria should be put forward

1928

Jan. 10, Decision of Delimitation Commission as to boundary between Nisibin and Jeziret Ibn'Umar

Feb. 11, Resignation of Ahmed Nami Bey as president of the Syrian State

Feb. 16, Siege of Damascus raised by High Commissioner, political prisoners released

Feb. 17, Sheikh Tajeddin became head of a provisional Government

March 20, Election law proclaimed gave franchise to all citizens over 21

April 10 and April 24, Elections held for Constituent Assembly in all States except Jebel Druze

June 9, Constituent Assembly met at Damascus and drafted constitution which was not accepted by the High Commissioner because it ignored the existence of the mandate. Constitution adopted Aug. 7

Aug. 12, The High Commissioner prorogued the Constituent Assembly for 3 months because of refusal to withdraw constitution

Dec. 17, Martial law abrogated in Damascus

1929

Feb. 5, The Constituent Assembly adjourned *sine die* by the High Commissioner because of refusal to include article in constitution as to mandate

April 4, Strike of university students at Damascus because of proposal of the Government to reduce the appropriation for education

April 13, The High Commissioner granted request of delegation of students not to reduce government appropriation to education

May 27, Charles Debbas elected for second 3 year term as President of Lebanon

June 22, Frontier between Syria and Turkey (Nisibin-Jeziret ibn Omar) settled by Treaty

1930

May 14 and 22, Constitution promulgated by the High Commissioner, Henri Ponsot, made Syria a republic with a parliament elected for 4 years and a president elected by parliament for 5 years

——, Government of Latakia established

Oct. 25, Meeting of insurgents at Nabk

TAJIKISTAN

The Tajik Soviet Socialist Republic was formed from the former regions of Bokhara and Turkestan where the population consisted mainly of Tajiks. Its equality with the other six republics of the Soviet Union was established on October 17, 1929.

Tajikistan is situated between 39° 40′ and 36° 40′ N. latitude and 67° 20′ and 75° E. longitude, north of the Oxus. On the west and north it is bordered by Uzbekistan and by the autonomous Republic of the Kirghiz; on the east by Chinese Turkestan and on the south by Afghanistan.

The Tajiks speak an Iranian dialect, little different from Persian, and they are considered to be the descendants of the original Aryan population of Turkestan. Unlike the Persians, the Tajiks are mostly Sunnis.

The area of the territory is 145,100 square kilometers (56,608 square miles), and the population on January 1, 1930, was 1,150,000. The capital is Stalinabad (formerly Dushambe).

TIBET

Tibet, a dependency of China, the highest country in the world, plateaus averaging over 16,000 feet above sea level, mountain peaks at 20,000 to 24,600 feet, the passes at 16,000 to 19,000 feet, bounded on the north by the Chinese province of Sin-Kiang, on the northeast by Kuhu-nor, on the east by Chwanben, on the west by Kashmir, and Ladakh, and on the south by India, Nepal, and Bhutan, area 463,200 square miles with population estimated at between 1,500,000 and 6,000,-000. Lhasa, the capital, has from 15,000 to 20,000 inhabitants. Buddhism was introduced from India in 622 by Srongtsan Gampo, the reputed founder of Lhasa. About 1250 Kublai Khan extended his dominions into east Tibet and is said to have invested Phagspa, a Sakya lama with sovereign power beginning the temporal dominion of the Sakya lamas and suzerainty of Chinese Emperors. The head of the Government is the Dalai Lama.

1890

March 17, A Convention signed with Great Britain at Calcutta settled boundary with Sikkim

1893

Dec. 5, Trade Convention with Great Britain signed opened a trading post at Yatung on the Tibetan side of frontier with Sikkim, and an Indian official and a Chinese official stationed there

1903

July, Mission under Colonel Younghusband sent by Indian Government to meet Tibetan and Chinese officials to discuss trade relations and foreign relations reached Kanba Jong

1904

Jan. 19, Colonel Younghusband visited Tibetans encamped at Quru; they refuse to observe conditions of the Treaties and demand withdrawal of British expedition, Jan. 29

March 31, British mission advancing into Tibet attacked by Tibetans

April 8, Tibetans defeated and mission forced passage through the Red Idol gorge

April 11, British mission arrived at Gyangtse after fighting at Khangma, and receives surrender of fort

Aug. 3, British troops arrive at Lhasa after many engagements with Tibetans

Sept. 7, Treaty with Great Britain signed at Lhasa by which Tibet undertook to carry out former agreements as to boundaries, and tariff, to open trade marts at Gyantse and Gartok as well as Yatung, abolish trade dues with India, not to alienate Tibetan territory to any foreign Power, or permit foreign intervention in Tibetan affairs, or grant concessions to foreign Power, and indemnity of £500,000

1906

April 27, Convention of China with Great Britain by which China adhered to the Lhasa Convention, and undertook not to permit any foreign Power to interfere with the territory or internal administration of Tibet, and Great Britain engaged not to annex Tibetan territory or interfere in the administration of Tibet

1907

Aug. 31, Anglo-Russian Convention signed, recognition of previous treaties by Russia, Great Britain and Russia agreed not to enter into negotiations with Tibet except through the Chinese Government, nor to send representatives to Lhasa, and exchange of Notes agreed to forbid scientific expeditions for term of 3 years

1908

March 9, Decree promulgated program of reform and of modern improvements for Tibet

April 20, New trade Agreement with Great Britain signed

Sept. 28, The Dalai Lama, who had fled to Outer Mongolia in 1904 on approach of the British mission, summoned to Peking, reached there, and then returned to Tibet

1910

Feb. 12, The Dalai Lama fled from Tibet to India on approach of Chinese military expedition from Szechuan under General Chun Ling

Feb. 23, Chinese troops occupied Lhasa

Feb. 25, Imperial decree deposed the Dalai Lama

March 12, Note of Great Britain to China as to administrative changes in Tibet prejudicial to Sikkim, Nepal, and Bhutan

March 24, The Dalai Lama received by the Viceroy of India at Calcutta

1912

April 21, Mandate of President Yuan declared Tibet a province of China

May 24, Note of Great Britain asked that assurance be given that the *status quo* in Tibet be maintained

June, The Tibetans drove the Chinese from Lhasa

July, Punitive Chinese military expedition began march on Lhasa from Szechuan

Aug. 12, Peace concluded with China at Lhasa, and 1,500 Chinese troops allowed to leave the country by the Indian route

Aug. 17, Memorandum of Great Britain to China recognized Chinese suzerainty over Tibet but denied right of China to interfere with internal administration and maintain large numbers of Chinese troops in the country

Oct. 28, Presidential mandate restored the titles of the Dalai Lama

1913

Jan. 11, Treaty of alliance with Outer Mongolia, in preamble declared independence of China of the 2 States

Jan. 23, The Dalai Lama returned to Lhasa

Oct. 13, Conference of Tibetans with representatives of China and Great Britain opened at Simla to settle boundaries of Tibet with China

1914

March 24–25, Exchange of Notes settled boundary with China

April 27, Convention with China signed; boundary arrangements repudiated by Chinese Government but accepted by Tibet and Great Britain. Tibet divided into Outer and Inner Tibet, suzerainty of China recognized, but China not to convert the country into a province or send troops into Outer Tibet or establish colonies; regulations of previous treaties as to foreign control, concessions, &c., reaffirmed

TONKING

Tonking, province of French Indo-China, brought under French protectorate by Treaty of June 6, 1884, bounded by Chinese provinces of Kwangsi and Yunnan, British Upper Burma,

Laos, Annam, and the Gulf of Tonking; area, 40,530 square miles; population in 1926, 7,401,912, including 9,143 Europeans. Treaty with Annam of Aug. 25, 1883, by which Annam recognized French protectorate after defeat of Annam forces and the "Black Flags," Chinese Canton rebels who had taken refuge in the country, Aug. 7, and capture of the Hué forts, Aug. 18–20. Treaty with China of June 9, 1885, by China recognized French protectorate.

TRANSCAUCASIAN REPUBLIC

Transcaucasian Socialist Federated Soviet Republic includes the former states of Azerbaijan, Armenia, and Georgia, bounded on the north by the Caucasian Mountains separating it from Northern Caucasia; on the west, the Black Sea; on the south, mountains, steppes, and rivers which divide it from Persia; on the east the Caspian Sea. The area of the Republic is 71,255 square miles, population in December, 1926, 5,850,692 as follows: Georgians, 33, Armenians, 24.1, Turko-Tartars, 23.1, Russians, 4.6, Ossetins, 1.7, Abkhazians, .8, others 12.3 per cent.

1917

Sept. 20, Council of peoples of Transcaucasia met at Tiflis and declared the Federal Republic of Transcaucasia founded within the Russian dominions, including Armenia, Georgia, and Azerbaijan

1918

May 26, The Federal Council dissolved, the three republics declaring independence. *See* Armenia, Georgia, Azerbaijan

Oct. 30, Under terms of the Armistice the Turks evacuated Transcaucasia

Nov. 11, Terms of Armistice ensured evacuation of Germans

1919

Aug. 19, British forces evacuated all of Transcaucasia except Batoum

1920

July 7, British forces withdrawn from Batoum. *See also* Georgia

1922

March 12, The Republics of Armenia (Erivan), Georgia, and Azerbaijan signed Agreement establishing the Transcaucasian S.S.S.R. in alliance with but independent of Russia

1923

July 6, The Transcaucasian Republic became a constituent member of the Union of Socialist Soviet Republics giving up its independence

TRANSJORDAN

This territory, which roughly corresponds to the area of the old Seljuk Kingdom of Kerak and of the Lordship of Montreal or Oultrejourdain in the Latin Kingdom of Jerusalem, is governed by a local Arab Administration under His Highness the Amir Abdullah Ibn Hussein, born in Mecca, 1882, second son of ex-King Hussein of the Hejaz and elder brother of King Feisal of Iraq, who became its ruler in April, 1921, and is assisted by an Executive Council. The country is covered by the Palestine Mandate, but the clauses relating to the establishment of a national home for the Jews are expressly excluded from operation therein.

1920

April 25, Supreme Council awarded mandate for Palestine and Transjordan to Great Britain

1921

April 1, Abdullah, second son of King Hussein, appointed ruler, began reign

1922

July 24, British mandate for Transjordan included in Palestine mandate approved by League of Nations; clauses relating to establishment of a national home for the Jews expressly excluded. *See* Palestine, Sept. 16

1923

May 26, Announcement of British Government of recognition of autonomy of Transjordan under the Amir Abdullah subject to approval of the League of Nations

1928

Feb. 20, Treaty with Great Britain signed provided for autonomous Government under the mandate

TRENGGANU

See Malay.

TURKESTAN

See Russia.

TURKEY

Turkey, Republic since 1923, occupying the peninsula of Asia Minor on the extreme west of Asia, bounded on the north by the Black Sea, on the west by the Aegean, and on the south by the Mediterranean, Syria, and Iraq, and on the east and north-east by the Transcaucasian Federation (Armenia and Georgia) and Persia. Turkey also includes a district in Europe of about 8,819 square miles in which the cities of Istanbul (Constantinople) and Adrianople are situated, and some islands off the coast. The total area is estimated as 762,736 square kilometers or 294,416 square miles excluding marshes and lakes, and by a general census taken for the first time in the history of the country, the total population was stated as of Oct. 28, 1927, 13,648,270, of whom 6,563,879 were men and 7,084,391 women; the population of Constantinople was 673,029, of Smyrna, 153,845, of Angora as determined by the Treaties, 74,784,

Adrianople, 34,669. The series of wars, Turco-Italian War of 1911–1912, the Balkan Wars of 1912–1913, and the World War of 1914–1918 caused the break up of the old Ottoman Empire, the acquisition by Italy and the Balkan States of considerable portions of the territories which constituted it, and the creation of new States or mandated territories, *viz.*, Albania, Syria, Iraq, Palestine, and loss of Turkish sovereignty over Cyprus, Egypt, and the various States of Arabia. The Treaty of Peace between the Allied Powers and Turkey signed at Lausanne July 24, 1923, defined the European frontier of the new Turkey and to some extent her Asiatic frontiers.

The present territories of Turkey as determined by the Treaties are as follows:

1. Constantinople and Eastern Thrace up to a line running roughly East and West from the mouth of the River Resvaya to a point North of Adrianople, whence the boundary takes a generally Southerly direction, determined for the most part by the River Maritza, but includes in Turkey a portion of the territory West of that river in the neighborhood of Adrianople.

2. The whole of Asia Minor, comprised within the Caucasian frontier defined by the Treaty of Kars, which leaves Kars, Artwin, and Ardahan to Turkey, the Northern portion of the old Turco-Persian frontier, a boundary line between Turkey and Iraq, as determined by the Treaty signed at Angora in June, 1926, whereby Mosul was ceded to Iraq, and a boundary line between Turkey and Syria running from Jezira-ibn-Omar on the Tigris to a point on the Gulf of Alexandretta immediately South of Payas.

3. Imbros, Tenedos, and Rabbit Islands.

In April, 1920, a Provisional Government was formed at Angora headed by Mustapha Kemal Pasha which in Nov., 1922, deposed the Sultan, abolished the office, and named a Caliph without temporal power, and took over the administration of the Government at Constantinople. On March 3, 1924, the Khaliphate (Caliphate) was abolished. On Oct. 29, 1923 the Turkish Republic was proclaimed, and Ghazi Mustapha Kemal Pasha elected President.

Mustapha Kemal Pasha, President.

1065 to 1803

1065–68, Alp Arslan and the Turks conquer Armenia and Georgia

1074–84, Asia Minor conquered; Jerusalem taken, 1076

1288, Soliman Shah drowned in the Euphrates, while on the march; his son Ertoghul, granted territories near Angora, dies

1299, Osman, or Othman, his son, Emir of the Sultan of Iconium, whose followers were named Osmanlis, founded the Ottoman Empire at Prusa, Bithynia, by policy and conquest

1330, Organization of Janissaries by Orcan about ——, Nicæa conquered; and the Morea, 1346

1361, The Turks enter Thrace, and take Adrianople

1362, Amurath I remodels the Janissaries

1389 *et seq.*, Bajazet I overruns provinces of the Eastern Empire

Sept. 28, 1396, He defeats Sigismund of Hungary at Nicopolis

July 28, 1402, He besieges Constantinople; but is interrupted by the approach of Tamerlane (or Timour), by whom he is defeated and made prisoner, at Ancyra

1430, Macedonia annexed

Nov. 10, 1444, Ladislas of Hungary defeated and slain at Varna by Amurath

Oct., 1448, Amurath defeats John Huniades at Kossova

1450, The Turks, invading Hungary, repelled by Huniades

May 29, 1453, Constantinople taken by the Turks under Mahomet II, which ends the Eastern Roman Empire

July, 1456, Belgrade relieved by Huniades' victory over the Turks

1456–60, Greece subjected to the Turks (*see* Greece)

1480, The Turks take Otranto, diffusing terror throughout Europe

1512, Selim I raised to the throne by the Janissaries; murders his father, brothers, &c.

1514, He takes the islands of the Archipelago

1515, He overruns Syria

Aug., 1516, Gains Egypt by defeat of Mamelukes

Aug., 1521, Solyman takes Belgrade; and Rhodes, Dec., 1522

Aug. 29, 1526, Defeats Hungarians at Mohatz

Oct., 1529, Repulsed before Vienna

1533, Peace with Austria

Aug., 1571, Cyprus taken from the Venetians

Oct. 7, 1571, Great battle of Lepanto; combined fleets of Spain, Venice, Genoa, Malta, and Pius V under John of Austria defeated the Turks

1579, Treaty of commerce with England

1585, Turks driven out of Persia by Shah Abbas

1606, Great fire in Constantinople

1637, War with the Cossacks, who take Azof

1638, The Turks defeat the Persians and take the city of Bagdad

1669, Candia (Crete) taken from Venice, after a 24 years' siege

Sept. 12, 1683, Vienna besieged by Mahomet IV but relieved by John of Poland

Jan. 26, 1699, Peace of Carlovitz

1703, Mustapha II deposed by Janissaries

1715, The Morea retaken by the Turks

1716, The Turks defeated at Peterwardein

1717, They lose Belgrade; and their power declines

1732, Peace of Erivan (with Persia)

1739, Belgrade taken from Austria; and Russia relinquishes Azof

1745, The Turks defeated at Kars

1749, Insurrection of Wahabees

1770, Great sea-fight in the channel of Scio; the Russian fleet defeats the Turkish

Jan., 1784, The Crimea ceded to Russia

1787–91, Disastrous war with Russia and Austria, the Turks lose more than 200,000 men

1791, Cession of Oczacow

1798, War with the French, who invade Egypt

1803, Insurrection of Mamelukes at Cairo

1807

Jan. 7, War against Russia and England

Feb. 19, Passage and repassage of the Dardanelles effected by the British fleet, but with great loss
May 25, Murder of Hali Aga

1808

The Janissaries massacre the newly discipiined troops

1809

The Russians defeated at Silistria

1812

May 28, Treaty of Bucharest between Russia and Turkey, the Pruth River made boundary line
Aug. 9, A caravan consisting of 2,000 souls, returning from Mecca, destroyed by a pestilential wind in the deserts of Arabia; 20 saved

1818 to 1820

1818–19, Subjugation of the Wahabees in Arabia
1820, Ali Pacha of Janina, in Greece, declares himself independent

1821

March 6, Insurrection in Moldavia and Wallachia
April 23, Persecution of Christians, March 6; the Greek patriarch killed at Constantinople
[For the events in connection with the independence of Greece, see Greece]

1822

April 11, Massacre at Scio (Chios)

1824

Oct. 6, Sea-fight near Mitylene; Turks defeated

1826

June 14–16, Insurrection of the Janissaries at Constantinople; they are suppressed and massacred
Aug. 30, 6,000 houses burnt at Constantinople

1827

Oct. 20, Battle of Navarino; the Turkish fleet destroyed by the fleets of England, France, and Russia

1828

Jan. 5, Banishment of 132 French, 120 English, and 85 Russian settlers from the Empire
April 26, War with Russia
June 19, Capitulation of Brahilow
June 23, Surrender of Anapa
July 20, Eminences of Shumla taken by Russians
Aug. 5, Czar Nicholas arrives before Varna
Aug. 24, Battle of Akhalzic
Sept. 9, Fortress of Bajazet taken
Sept. 26, The Sultan proceeds to the camp with the sacred standard
Oct. 1, Dardanelles blockaded
Oct. 11, Surrender of Varna
Oct. 16, Russians retreat from Shumla
Oct. 30, Surrender of the castle of the Morea to the French
Nov. 10, Siege of Silistria raised by Russians

1829

June 11, Victory of the Russians at Kuleftscha
July 2, Battle near Erzeroum
Aug. 29, Adrianople is entered by the Russians, Aug. 20; armistice agreed on
Sept. 14, Treaty of peace at Adrianople

1830

April 25, The Porte acknowledges the independence of Greece

1831

Aug. 19, New military "order of glory" (Nischan) founded

1832

July 2, St. Jean d'Acre taken by Ibrahim Pacha, son of Mehemet Ali
Dec. 21, He defeats the army of the Sultan at Konieh

1833

Jan., Ibrahim Pacha marches within eighty leagues of Constantinople, and the Sultan asks the aid of Russia
April 3, The Russians enter Constantinople
July 8, Treaty with Russia, offensive and defensive

1838

Aug. 16, Treaty of commerce with England, concluded by Lord Ponsonby, ratified

1839

Nov. 3, Hatti-sherif promulgated decreeing many reforms, termed the Tanzimat (regulations); again, at Rhodes, Jan. 6, 1840; again 1844

1849

June, Christians admitted to office in Turkey
Sept. 16, The Turkish Government refuses to surrender the Hungarian and Polish refugees on the joint demand of Russia and Austria
[The Porte (countenanced by England) firmly resists this demand]
Nov. 12, Russia suspends intercourse with the Porte
Nov. 13, The British fleet, under Sir W. Parker, anchors in Besika bay

1850

Jan., Diplomatic relations between Russia and the Porte resumed, Dec. 31, 1849; the latter sending the refugees to Konieh

1851

Jan., Turkish Croatia in a state of rebellion

1852

Feb. 13, Treaty with France respecting the holy places
Aug., Imperial order of Medjidie founded

1853

April 19, Prince Menschikoff repairs to Constantinople as Russian negotiator, Feb. 28; his peremptory demands rejected
May 21, Reschid Pacha becomes Foreign Minister; the ultimatum being rejected, Menschikoff quits Constantinople
June 6, Hatti-sherif issued, confirming the rights of the Greek Christians
June 26, Russian manifesto against Turkey
July 2, Russian army crosses the Pruth
Sept. 26, Grand national council—war to be declared if the principalities are not evacuated
Oct. 5, War declared against Russia
    [See Russo-Turkish War]
Commencement of national debt

1854

Jan. 27, Insurrection in Epirus and Albania, favored by the Greek Government at Athens—Hellenic Empire proclaimed

March 14, Volunteers from Athens join it

March 28, Rupture between Greece and Turkey

[Several conflicts ensue with varied success]

April 25, Osman Pacha storms Peta, the central point of the insurrection

May 25 and 26, English and French Governments, after many remonstrances, send troops, which arrive at the Piræus; the King of Greece submits, and promises strict neutrality: the Greek volunteers are recalled

June 14, Convention between Turkey and Austria

June 18, Abdi Pacha and Fuad Effendi take the intrenched camp at Kolampaka, and the insurrection shortly after ceases

Sept., The Russians retire from the principalities, which are thereupon occupied by the Austrians

1855

Aug., Turkish loans

1856

Feb. 18, Firman authorizing free exercise of religion

March 30, Peace with Russia by Treaty of Paris by which Black Sea opened to ships of all nations

April 15, Great Britain, France, and Austria guarantee integrity of Turkish Empire

1857

March, Austrians quit the principalities

July, Misunderstanding among the allied powers respecting Moldavian elections, which are annulled

1858

June 15, Massacre of Christians at Jedda

July 12, Lord Stratford de Redcliffe, English Ambassador at Constantinople, succeeded by Sir H. Lytton Bulwer; accredited

July, Indecisive conflicts in Montenegro between the natives and the Turks

Aug., Turkish financial reforms begun

Sept. 19, The first Turkish railway opened (from Aidan to Smyrna)

Oct., Base coinage called in; a fictitious Turkish coinage begun at Birmingham suppressed

Nov. 8, The allied Powers determine the Montenegrin boundaries

1859

Feb. 5 and 7, Prince Alexander Cousa elected Hospodar of both Moldavia and Wallachia

[The Porte at first objects, but afterwards accedes to the double election]

May, Telegraph completed between Aden and Suez

Sept. and Oct., Conspiracy against the Sultan, Sept. 17; his brother implicated; several condemned to die; reprieved

Oct., Great agitation for financial reform

1860

June, Alleged ill treatment of Christians in Turkey; proposed intervention of the great powers, May 5; the Turkish Government promises investigation and redress, May 30; all the Powers satisfied except Russia

——, War between the Druses and Maronites in Lebanon; massacres

July 9–11, Massacre of Christians at Damascus, Syria

Aug. 2, Convention on behalf of the great Powers at Paris; armed intervention of the French agreed to

1861

Feb. 24, Inundations at Galatz; loss about 175,000*l.*

March, Christians revolt in the Herzegovina, aided by the Montenegrins

April, Great need of financial reform: the British ambassador, Sir H. Lytton Bulwer, proposes a scheme

June 5, Discussion respecting the French occupation of Syria; it ceases

June 25, Death of the Sultan, Abdul-Medjid; accession of Abdul-Aziz, his brother

July, Economical reforms begun; Fuad Pacha made president of the council

Sept., Imperial order of knighthood (Osmaneh) to include civil as well as military persons, founded

Oct., Imperial guard reorganized

1862

March, He puts forth a budget; treaties of commerce with Sweden, Spain, &c.

May, A Turkish loan (8,000,000*l.*) taken up in London

Oct., Secularization of the property of the mosques (value about 3,000,000*l.*) said to be determined on

Sept. 23, Insurgents in the Herzegovina submit; peace made with Montenegro

Oct. 7, Dispute with Serbia (*see s.v.*) settled

1863

Jan. 28, A new bank established

1864

April, Great immigration of the Caucasian tribes

1865

Aug., Financial reforms; conversion and verification of the Turkish debt

Sept. 21, Fuad Pacha proposes confiscation of the property of the mosques: opposition of the Sheikh-ul-Islam

Dec. 30, Revolt of the Maronites under Joseph Karam

Revolution in Bucharest

1866

Aug., Insurrection in Crete (*See* Crete)

1867

Jan., European Turkey very unsettled

——, Maronite revolt, under Joseph Karam, suppressed; his flight; Turks leave, March 28

March 31, The recommendation of the European Powers to the Sultan to give up Crete finally declined

April 2, Destruction of the dockyards in the Golden Horn by fire

July 1–12, The Sultan, with his son and nephew, visits Paris; arrives at Buckingham Palace, London, July 12; sails from Dover, July 23; at Vienna, July 27–Aug. 1; returns to Constantinople, Aug. 7

Sept. 4, The Sultan declines the proposition of Russia for the suspension of hostilities in Crete, and an international commission

1868

May 18, Meeting of the new council of state (including Jews and Christians), with legislative, but not executive, functions

Dec., Dispute with Greece for intervention in the Cretan insurrection; *see* Greece

1869

Feb., Fuad Pacha (formerly grand vizier) dies
June, Memorial of the Porte to the European Powers desiring the abolition of the consular jurisdictions termed "capitulations"
Aug., The Khedive or Viceroy of Egypt censured for assuming sovereign powers encroaching on those of the Sultan
Oct., System of compulsory education promulgated
Nov. 16, Inauguration of the Suez Canal
Dec., The Khedive submits to the Sultan

1870

April, Modification of the "capitulations"
Oct. 21, Reported treaty between Turkey and Greece to resist European aggression in the East
Oct. 31, Russia repudiates the treaty of Paris, 1856
Nov. 15, A note delivered to the Porte (*see* Russia)
About Dec. 3, The Sultan agrees to a conference on the Black Sea question alone

1871

March 13, The Black Sea question settled by the conference at London (*see* Russia)
April 18, Omar Pacha, general, dies
May, Insurrection in Yemen, subdued
Oct. 25, Tunis made an integral part of the Empire, by decree

1872

About July 30, Mahmoud Pacha, Grand Vizier, having made enemies through dismissing foreign employés, &c., is dismissed and replaced by Midhat Pacha
Oct. 19, Midhat Pacha, who favored Austria, dismissed; replaced by Mehemet Ruchdi

1873

June 17, The Roumelian railway connecting Constantinople, Adrianople, &c., opened
Oct., Inability to raise a loan: the Sultan gives up a large sum; great financial reforms proposed
Nov., Turkish aggressions on South Arabia checked by Great Britain

1874

About Oct. 5, The Sultan ill; he recognizes his nephew Murad as successor
Oct. 20, Austria, Germany, and Russia inform Turkey that they consider they have the right to conclude separate treaties with Rumania
Oct. 28, *Mésondivé* or *Mesoudiyé*, Turkish ironclad, launched at Blackwall
Turkish debt 3,000,000*l*. in 1854; 180,000,000*l*.

1875

July–Aug., Insurrection in Herzegovina; great excitement in Bosnia, Serbia, and Montenegro
Sept.–Nov., Remonstrances of British and Russian Ambassadors with the government respecting expenditure and treatment of Christian subjects
Oct. 6, Decree (in consequence of the deficit of 5,000,-000*l*. in the budget) that for 5 years half the interest on the debt be paid in cash and half in 5% bonds
Oct. 7, Circular note remitting taxes and promising economical and commercial reform; another stating object of the government to stop onerous loans, develop the resources of the empire, &c., Oct. 20
Dec., Firman issued; ordering great reforms, equality of rights to Christians, &c.
Dec. 30, Note of Andrassy, Austrian Minister, respecting reforms, adopted by Germany and Russia, Jan.; by Great Britain, Jan. 18; transmitted to the Porte, about Feb. 7, agreed to, Feb. 10, 1876

1876

May, Insurrection in Bulgaria, promoted by foreign agitators, May 1, 2; quickly suppressed by troops sent May 7; about 65 villages burnt by the Bashibazouks and other Turkish troops; several towns destroyed; about 15,000 persons killed; atrocious cruelties to women and children; a few Turks killed by Bulgarians in self-defense (report by Mr. Schuyler, *see below*)
May 10 *et seq.*, Riots at Constantinople; the softas, fanatical students, and others, demand reforms; their cry, "Turkey for the Turks"; ministerial changes; Europeans much alarmed
May 26, British fleet arrives in Besika Bay
May 30, Meeting at Berlin of ministers of Austria, Germany, and Russia; they agree to a note to Turkey, requiring an armistice of two months, and other measures, May 11, 12; the note accepted by France and Italy, not by Great Britain, May 19; not presented through the revolution
May 30 *et seq.*, The Grand Vizier Mehemet Ruchdi, Hussein Avni, and Midhat Pacha, request the Sultan to give up some of his treasure to save the nation from ruin; he refuses and is deposed, May 29; his nephew proclaimed as Murad V; joyfully accepted by the people, and recognized by the western Powers
June 4, Abdul-Aziz recognizes Murad; said to have committed suicide (decided, by trial, to have been murdered; *see below*, June, 1881)
June 15, Assassination of Hussein Avni, the War Minister, Raschid Pacha, the Foreign Minister, and others, by Hassan, a disgraced Circassian officer, who is hanged, June 17
July 2, Declaration of war by Serbia, July 1; by Montenegro
July 3, Tchernayeff and Serbians enter Turkey; battle at Saitschar or Zaicar; Turks said to have the advantage
July 6; Severe conflict of Turks with Serbians at Yavor, near Novi Bazar; with Montenegrins at Nevesinje, July 27
July 28, Mukhtar Pacha defeated by Prince Nikita at Urba or Urbitza in Herzegovina
——, Issue of paper money announced
Aug. 7, Several days' conflict; the Turks enter Serbia, and capture Gurgosavatz; Serbians retreat
Aug. 9, Advance of the Turks under Abdul-Kerim Pacha upon Alexinatz; severe fighting
Aug. 10, Turkish barbarities in Bulgaria reported by *Daily News*' correspondent, substantiated by report of Mr. Schuyler, the American commissioner from Constantinople, dated
Aug. 14, Asserted victory of Prince Nikita at Medun, near Kutchi, about
About Aug. 24, Serbia invites the mediation of the guaranteeing powers
Aug. 31, Murad V deposed on account of bad health; his brother Abdul-Hamid II proclaimed

Sept. 1, 2, Serbians said to be severely beaten before Alexinatz; continued indecisive fighting

Sept. 3, 4, The great Powers propose an immediate armistice, the restoration of the *status quo ante bellum*, payment of an indemnity by Serbia, &c.; memorandum presented

Sept. 16, Prince Milan proclaimed King by the army at Deligrad; disapproved

About Sept. 17, Armistice till Sept. 25 agreed to

Sept. 19, Report of Mr. Baring, the British commissioner in Bulgaria, published

[It establishes the facts "that a ferocious Mussulman soldiery, in revenge for a feeble and abortive insurrection, were let loose on the inhabitants of a large province; that the population were barbarously massacred, men, women, and children included; and that during the storm of savage fury crimes of all descriptions and outrages unmentionable were perpetrated on the inhabitants."—*Times*]

Sept. 21, Firm incisive despatch from Lord Derby to Sir H. Elliot, referring to Mr. Baring's report, proposing longer armistice, &c.

Sept. 26, The Porte receives the propositions of the six great Powers

Sept. 26, 27, Serbia rejects the renewal of the armistice; Tchernayeff and army dominant; fighting renewed

Sept. 27, Lord Derby informs the deputation from the city of London that, in regard to the Eastern question, the Government is laboring for local self-government for the Turkish provinces in Europe, equal treatment of Mahometans and Christians, better administration for both, security for life and property, and effectual guarantees against repetition of outrages

Sept. 28, 29, Serbian attacks on the Turks near Alexinatz severely repulsed

Oct. 2, In reply to the great Powers the Porte declines an armistice, opposes administrative autonomy to the provinces as impracticable, proposes a senate, and guarantees incisive reforms

Oct. 13, Montenegrin victory at Danilograd

Oct. 14, Turkey's proposal of an armistice for 6 months, Oct. 10; declined by Russia, who proposes 4 to 6 weeks, longer being injurious to commerce, &c.

Oct. 15–19, Continued fighting, generally unfavorable to Serbians

Oct. 16–19, Alexinatz bombarded

Oct. 19–24, Result of fighting very favorable to Turks

About Oct. 23, Alleged conspiracy at Constantinople against the reform ministry; many arrests

Oct. 19–24, Important Turkish successes in the valley of the Morava

Oct. 20, Medun surrenders to Montenegrines

Oct. 21, Krevet taken by Turks

Oct. 29, Serbians and Russians defeated; armies under Tchernayeff and Horvaritch divided, Oct. 19–24; Djunis taken by Turks; Deligrad untenable; severe Russian loss

Oct. 31, Alexinatz captured by Turks; Russian ultimatum given, demanding 6 weeks' armistice within 48 hours, dated

Nov. 1, Armistice for two months signed

——, Deligrad captured by Turks, now virtually masters of Serbia

Nov. 4, Deligrad evacuated by Turks; farewell address of Tchernayeff to officers, exhorting to constancy

Nov. 10, Czar's speech at Moscow; he will act independently if guarantees are not obtained

Marquis of Salisbury appointed special ambassador for conference at Constantinople; he arrives at Paris, Nov. 18; Berlin, Nov. 20; Vienna, Nov. 24; Rome, Nov. 29; Constantinople, Dec. 5

Dec. 8, Alleged abortive conspiracy to restore Murad

Dec. 12, Preliminary meetings of conference of representatives of six great Powers begin (Great Britain, Russia, Austria, Germany, France, and Italy)

Dec., Armistice extended to Feb., 1877

Dec. 23, New political constitution proclaimed: (chief provisions: indivisibility of the empire; the sultan supreme; individual liberty; freedom of all creeds, of the press, and of education; equal legal taxation; a senate and two chambers; general elections by ballot every fourth year; irremovable judges, &c.)

——, Opening of the conference

Dec. 27, Financial decree of Oct. 6, 1875, abrogated

Dec. 28, Armistice extended to March 1

1877

Jan. 18, The great national council of Turkey rejects the propositions of the conference; it closes, Jan. 20; chief ambassadors leave soon after Jan. 22

About Jan. 26, Negotiations for peace opened with Serbia and Montenegro

Feb. 5, Midhat Pacha, the Grand Vizier, dismissed and banished; succeeded by Edhem Pacha; reforms to go on

About Feb. 7, Gortschakoff's circular to great Powers, inquiring what they intend to do, signed Jan. 19; published

Early in Feb., Protocols of the conference published in *Times*, &c.

Feb. 20, In Turkey "there is no aristocracy, no governing class; no organised democracy; no representative government" (Marquis of Salisbury)

March 1, Peace with Serbia signed

March 19, First Turkish parliament opened: 30 senators, 90 deputies; speech from the Sultan read

March, Gen. Ignatieff visits Berlin, Paris, London, Vienna, &c.

March 31, Protocol signed for six Powers: principles—to wait for Turkish reforms and watch; conditional disarmament in Russia and Turkey (voidable under certain conditions)

April, Protocol rejected by Turkey, April 12; justificatory circular sent to the Powers; Mr. Layard sent as temporary ambassador to Turkey

April 13, Insurrection of Mirdites or Miridites, April; armistice with Montenegro not renewed

About April 24, Arrival of Mr. Layard as ambassador, at Constantinople; he affirms the neutrality of Great Britain

April 24, War declared by Russia (*see* Russo-Turkish war, 1877)

About May 28, A jihad or holy war against Russia propounded by the Sheikh-ul-islam

May *et seq.*, Suleiman Pacha successful in Montenegro; relieves Nicksics, besieged

June, Miridite leaders captured

July, Protests against alleged Russian atrocities

Aug., Bosnian revolt reported to be ended

Nov. 26, Proclamation for increase of army by 150,000 —Christians and others to serve

About Nov. 27, The Sultan issues a rather vague proclamation of amnesty to Bulgaria

Dec. 12, Surrender of Plevna, Dec. 10; circular note to the great Powers requesting mediation

1878

Jan. 5, 6, 7, The ministry censured, resigns; still holds office; Suleiman dismissed; crisis

Feb. 13, British fleet enter the Dardanelles without permission of the Sultan

Feb., March, Insurrection in Crete, Thessaly, Epirus, &c. (*see* Greece)

March 17, Treaty of peace with Russia signed at San Stefano, March 3; ratified at St. Petersburg

April, Insurrection near Rhodope, in Roumelia, against Russians going on

May 20, Insurrection (said doubtfully to be in favor of the ex-Sultan Murad) in Constantinople, suppressed; Ali Suavi, a softa and fanatical reformer, with others, killed

May 30, Secret agreement between the Marquis of Salisbury and Count Schouvaloff, Russian Ambassador

June 4, Secret British convention with Turkey (defensive alliance): if by the Treaty of Berlin, Russia acquires Kars, Ardahan, or Batoum, Great Britain is to join the Sultan in arms in defending his dominions, he engaging to reform his government; Cyprus to be held by Great Britain till Russia returns its acquisitions

July 3, Cyprus ceded to Great Britain

July 13, Berlin conference meets, June 13

Aug. 4, Ratification of the Treaty of Berlin

Aug., Trial of Suleiman Pacha for misconduct during the war begun

——, The Turks said to be grossly ill-treated in Bulgaria, and other surrendered places

Aug. 8, Safvet Pacha's circular to foreign Powers refusing to recognize Greek proposal for annexation of Crete, Thessaly, &c.

Sept. 6, Murder of Mehemet Ali Pacha at Ipek, near Scutari, by Albanian rioters

Sept. 12, Albanian leaders with 40,000 men said to be ruling from Janina to Montenegro

Oct. 24, The Sultan accepts the reforms proposed by the British Government; announced

Dec. 4, Suleiman Pacha sentenced to degradation and imprisonment, Dec. 2; absolved by the Sultan

1879

Feb. 8, Definitive treaty of peace with Russia, signed

March, British fleet leaves the sea of Marmora

May 26, Definitive treaty with Austria, published

July, Aug., The Russians evacuate Turkey

Early in Nov., Pressure for reforms put upon the government by the British; Admiral Hornby and the fleet enter Turkish waters; quit

Nov. 18, Baker Pacha appointed inspector-general of gendarmerie in Asia Minor, announced

Dec. 31, Official relations with Great Britain temporarily suspended on account of the imprisonment of Dr. Köller, a German missionary, and Ahmed Tewfik, who assisted him in translations   .

1880

Jan. 1–10, Successful intervention of Sir A. H. Layard

Jan. 30, Note of Savas Pacha to the Powers acknowledging corruptions in judicial affairs and promising efficient reforms (in *Times*)

About March 24, Col. and Mrs. Synge (distributors of relief to Mussulmans) captured by Greek brigands, near Salonica, about Feb. 19; released for 10,000*l.*

June 12, Identic note from European Powers, June 11; given in

July 10, Osman Pacha, War Minister, dismissed

July, Naval demonstration by the European Powers at Dulcigno, suggested by Earl Granville

July 15, Collective note of the Berlin Conference presented

Aug. 3, Collective note from the Powers urging cession of Dulcigno, &c., to Montenegro, and proposing to aid the Prince in taking possession

Sept. 15, A final note from the Powers respecting cession of Dulcigno to Montenegro, delivered

Sept. 20, Admiral Beauchamp Seymour, commander of combined fleet at Ragusa, sent to make a demonstration near Dulcigno

About Sept. 27, The Sultan refuses to surrender Dulcigno; the French decline to partake in attack on the town

Oct. 3, Note from the Sultan limiting his concessions and resisting coercion; presented

Nov. 26, Immediate cession of Dulcigno ordered by the Sultan, about Oct. 23; effected

Dec. 4, The combined fleet disperses

Dec. 14, Note from the Sultan to the powers respecting the Greeks' arming

1881

Early in Jan., Circular from the Powers recommending arbitration, Dec. 24, 1880; declined by Turkey and Greece

About Jan. 15, Circular from Turkey proposing conference at Constantinople, &c.

March 30, Conference at Constantinople; agreement between Turkey and the Powers; proposals referred to Athens

About April 8, Mr. Henry Suter, engaged in mines, seized by brigands at Cassandra, in Salonika

May, Rebellion in Albania (*see s.v.*) suppressed

——, The Sultan protests against French invasion of Tunis (*see s.v.*)

——, Turkey protests against the Tunis treaty of May 12

May 23, Mr. Suter's release for 15,000*l.* ransom announced

May 24, Convention between Turkey and Greece arranged at Constantinople settling frontiers; Thessaly ceded by Turkey

June 27, 28, Trial of Midhat Pacha and others for murder of the late Sultan Abdul-Aziz; convicted; Mustapha Fahri Bey and Hadj Mehmed actual assassins; others, Mahmoud and Nouzi Pachas, the Sultan's brothers-in-law, Midhat Pacha, and others accomplices

June 29, Sentence; death to all, except two subordinates to imprisonment

July 2, Turco-Greek Convention ceding Thessaly to Greece, signed at Constantinople

July 31, The trial of Midhat and others said to be a mockery; punishment commuted to exile on intercession of the British Government; announced

Aug. 15, The captors of Mr. Suter taken in Greece

Dec. 28, Decree signed for a satisfactory settlement of the national debt

1882

Feb. 16, Capt. Selby, R.N., wounded by Albanians at Artaki, announced; died, Feb. 20

March 26, Mehemet Ruchdi Pasha dies

May 6, Russian-war indemnity convention ratified

About July 11, Sultan protests against bombardment of forts at Alexandria (*see* Egypt)

Aug. 29, Protractive negotiations respecting a military convention; agreed to

About Nov. 28, Alleged conspiracy of Fuad Pasha and others to dethrone the Sultan

Nov., Frontier disputes with Montenegro

1883

About Jan. 23, Turkish note to the Powers against British Egyptian circular

Dec. 29–Jan. 3, 1884, Difficulties with the Greek church respecting political reforms; resignation of the Œcumenical patriarch Yoachim II; not accepted; conciliation proposed

1884

Jan. 9, Resignation maintained

April, Amicable settlement of dispute, announced

May, Death of Midhat Pasha, great statesman and reformer in exile, aged 62

Aug., Circular to the six great Powers announcing the stoppage of the post offices in Constantinople, July 20, resisted; the Turkish arrangements fail, and are withdrawn

Oct. 12, Petitions to the Sultan from Macedonia respecting Turkish atrocities signed

1885

Jan., Hassan Fehmy Pasha sent to London to confer on the Egyptian question; his proposals not received

About Feb. 23, Turkey protests against Italian occupation of Massowah on the Red Sea

July 9, New tariff with England signed

About Sept. 22, Revolution in Roumelia, Sept. 18; firm Turkish note to the Powers

Oct. 14, Conference of ambassadors, Oct. 4; the ambassadors present a collective note condemning the revolution in Roumelia as breaking the Treaty of Berlin

Oct. 19, Turkey asks assistance of the Powers to settle the Roumelian affair

Nov. 11, Conference of ambassadors at Constantinople, Nov. 5; collective declaration for maintenance of *status quo ante*, About Nov. 7; division of opinion as to enforcement

1886

March 13, The Sultan ratifies the treaty between Bulgaria and Serbia

June 19, Hobart Pasha, Turkish admiral, dies, aged 64

1887

Sept. 26, Four English gentlemen captured near Smyrna by brigands who demand 3,000*l*. ransom, Sept. 24; released by payment of a ransom of 750*l*.

1888

Aug. 12–14, Direct railway communication between London and Constantinople *via* Dover and Calais in 94 hours; first train from Vienna

Oct., The Government contracts a loan for 1,350,000*l*. from the "German" bank; consequent rupture with the Ottoman Bank, its usual financial agent

Oct. 6, Concession granted for Anatolian Railroad, first of German enterprises in Turkey, opened to Angora, Jan., 1893

1889

Oct. 28, The Ottoman Bank, Sir Edgar Vincent, director, lends the Sultan 150,000*l*., reported

Nov. 23 *et seq*., Trial of Moussa Bey, *see* Armenia

Nov. 2, The German Emperor and Empress received by the Sultan at Constantinople

1890

April 30, New 5% conversion loan at 93, successfully effected by the Grand Vizier, aided by Sir Edgar Vincent; agreement signed

About May 15, The Russian Government demands payment of the arrears of the Russo-Turkish war indemnity

June, Troubles in Old Serbia by bands of Arnauts; severe fight, with much slaughter

About June 18, Turkey defers payment of indemnity till Nov., Russia demands immediate payment; note sent

June 22, British cotton and woolen yarn-spinning factory opened at Constantinople

For Armenian troubles *see* Armenia, 1889–90

1891

About Feb. 4, Arnaut revolt in Old Serbia; the government buildings in Drenitza burnt, reported

Feb. 12, Death of Musurus Pasha, diplomatist, aged 84; 33 years ambassador in London

About May 14, The Arnauts again attack the Christians in Old Serbia, who bravely resist, but are defeated with loss

June 4–8, Railway train at Tcherkesskeni, near Constantinople, attacked by brigands; two persons killed; five carried off for ransom, June 1; active measures taken by the Porte, June; captives liberated

Aug. 12, M. Eugène de Raymond, sub-manager of a vineyard company captured by brigands at Ormoudja, Aug. 7; ransomed by the Sultan

1892

Jan. 27, Payment of the war indemnity resumed

Oct. 18, The Russian Government remonstrates against the reception of M. Stamboloff, the Bulgarian Premier, Aug. 18 *et seq*.; the Porte replies courteously that this is not a violation of the treaty of Berlin

About Nov. 7, Russia again demands payment of war indemnity

1893

Feb. 15, German Anatolian Railway Company granted concession for branch from Eski Shehr to Konia which was opened in 1896

1894

July 10, 11, Earthquake at Constantinople, &c.

Dec. 9, Diplomatic relations with the Powers suspended in relation to Armenia (*see s.v.*)

1895

June 10, The great Powers demand the disarmament of the Beduin and indemnity for the attacks at Jedda

June 17, Reply of the Porte accepting in principle the proposed reforms, but objecting to supervision of the Powers

June 29, A commission appointed for reforms in Armenia; Turkhan Pasha to be inspector of certain provinces

July 20, Shakir Pasha appointed to supervise the carrying out of reforms in Armenia

July 31, Approved by the Powers

Aug. 19, The Porte rejects the control of the Powers in the administration of Armenia, reported; and appeals to France and Russia against England, without effect, about Aug. 29; the Porte communicates some concessions, Sept. 7

Sept. 30, Oct. 1, An Armenian demonstration at Constantinople resisted by the mob and police with much cruelty; 172 killed; churches filled with Armenian destitute refugees; a fierce fight at Scutari; massacre of Armenians at Pera; the ambassadors of 6 powers remonstrate with the Porte; 95 corpses delivered up to the patriarchate, Oct. 6; conflicts and massacre of 800 Armenians at Trebizond, by Turkish soldiery, Oct. 8; refugees quit the churches, under protection of the dragomans, Oct. 10–12; over 700 killed, injured and missing during the riots; British fleet at Lemnos, reported, Oct. 10

Oct. 9, Armenians attacked by Mahometans at Ak Hissar, 45 killed

Oct. 17, 20, Armenian reform scheme accepted and decreed by the Porte

Oct. 18, Decree authorizing the conversion of the 5% customs loan into 4%

Nov. 5, The ambassadors urgently demand that immediate measures be taken to suppress anarchy and bloodshed

Nov. 16, Gradual formation of the Constitutional party, desiring reform, rational government, &c.; their views published

Nov. 18, Extra powers and forces granted by the Powers to their ambassadors, for the defense of Christians

Nov., Insurrection in Arabia

Dec. 14, The Sultan, after delay, accedes to the entrance of extra foreign despatch boats, Dec. 10; martial law decreed

1896

Jan., Many Armenians in Constantinople released, Dec. 21, 1895; 182 arrests for disaffection to the Sultan

Jan.–May, Circulation of British journals prohibited

Feb. 18, Contract for a loan of 3,000,000l. sanctioned by the Porte

April 28, Scheme for administrative reform in European provinces, published

April, Despatches of vice-consul Fitzmaurice describing the atrocities and misery at Orfa, and other places, in Armenia, received at Constantinople

May 7–15, Successful intervention of Sir Philip Currie, British Ambassador, and the other ambassadors regarding the forced conversions of Armenians at Biredjik, and elsewhere

May 16, Increased persecution of Armenians in Constantinople; many Turkish students sentenced to 10 years' penal servitude for aiding the Armenians at Zeitun

June 20, Conference of ambassadors respecting Crete; the Porte accedes to all their recommendations, conditionally, July 3; again, Aug. 25

Aug. 26, The Armenian revolutionary committee, with the view of inciting the ambassadors to more active measures on behalf of the Armenians, take possession of the Ottoman bank at Constantinople. Dynamite and bombs were secretly introduced into the building

by a band of about 25 armed men; and at 1.30 P.M. revolvers were fired and bombs thrown, many gendarmes and 5 of the conspirators were killed; the staff of the bank took refuge in the upper rooms, from which Sir Edgar Vincent, the governor, and several directors, escaped by a balcony. The conspirators, after threatening to destroy the building if their demands were not granted, sent a message to the palace, where Sir Edgar Vincent and others were consulting, offering to surrender, if permitted to leave the country; their terms were agreed to; and 15 of them were taken on board Sir Edgar Vincent's yacht at night. Thence they were conveyed to Marseilles

Aug. 26–30, A great massacre of Armenians (estimated between 5,000 and 6,000) by Mahometans ensued

Aug. 29, Remonstrance of the ambassadors to the Sultan respecting the conduct of the troops in promoting the massacres; British and foreign marines landed to protect the embassies, &c.

Aug. 30, Judicial committee of inquiry appointed, 400 persons arrested

Aug. 31, The embassies abstain from celebrating the Sultan's accession; collective note to the Porte, respecting the massacres; the Porte replies, denying the truth of their statements, Sept. 12

Sept. et seq., Extraordinary tribunal appointed for the trial of the rioters, Sept. 3; many Armenians transported; some Mahometan murderers acquitted

Sept., Bomb factory discovered at Scutari, 2 leaders and 14 of the Armenian revolutionaries arrested

Sept. 15, Disorder and panics at Constantinople, trade paralyzed, foreign merchants ruined; collective note from the embassies to the Porte

Sept. 16, Repression of the "Young Turkey" party, arrests and deportation in Constantinople

Sept. 26 et seq., 3,000 Armenian refugees leave under consular assistance up to Sept. 19; exodus of all races continues

Sept. 29, Extraordinary tribunal condemns Mahometan murderers to 15 years' imprisonment; Armenians suspected of having taken part in the Armenian coup at the bank sentenced to death

Oct. 1, Armenian circular letter of complaint received by the embassies

Oct. 9, Continued arrests and injustice to Armenians; the Porte demands the right to search foreign vessels for Armenians, Oct. 6; rejected by the embassies

Oct. 10, The ambassadors complain to the Porte of the non-execution of its promises to Crete

——, Decree ordering the return of Armenian emigrants under pain of confiscation of property, &c.

Oct., Note from the Italian Embassy to the Porte demanding an indemnity for the massacre of an Italian at Constantinople and Father Salvatore in a convent near Marash in 1895, early

Oct. 12, The Austrian Embassy demands the punishment of those in command of the soldiers who murdered M. Zlatko and an indemnity of 6,000l.; paid, Oct. 22

Oct. 21, Poll tax, &c., on Mahometans decreed

Nov. 19, French intervention; release of innocent Armenians in Constantinople and provinces ordered; the Vali of Diarbekr dismissed; execution of reforms in Armenia, &c., promised, Nov. 7; delayed

Dec. 6, Manifesto issued by the "Ottoman liberal committee" denounces the Sultan, and demands the restoration of the constitution of 1876

Dec. 6, Anglo-Russian agreement concerning the execution of reforms in Turkey, announced

Dec. 15, Recall of Saadeddin Pasha from Crete, granted on demand of the ambassadors

Dec. 21, Amnesty to Armenians and Mahometans; death sentences to 100 Armenians commuted to imprisonment

Dec. 26, Sir Edgar Vincent's financial report to the Sultan on the revenue and expenditure (with recommendations); shows a yearly deficit since 1890 of 1,000,000т.

1897

Jan., Col. Mazhar Bey acquitted at Marash of the murder of Father Salvatore; new trial ordered by the Sultan at Aleppo; sentenced to life imprisonment, March 3

Jan. 20, Iradé issued accepting the demands of the Armenian patriarch with certain modifications

Feb. 6, Arrests of Armenians in Constantinople recommenced

March 2, Collective note from the six Powers presented to the Porte, and the Porte calls on the Powers to abide by the treaty of Paris, 1856

March 5, The Porte agrees to the establishment of Cretan autonomy

March, Disturbed condition of Asia Minor, bloodshed at Everek and Tokat

March 22, Mobilization of the fleet in the Bosphorus

April 5, The Powers declare that the aggressor on the Greek frontier in case of conflict shall be held responsible and shall derive no advantage

April 17, War declared against Greece

Sept. 18, Peace preliminaries signed at Constantinople

Oct., Sir R. Hamilton Lang appointed director-general of the Ottoman Bank at Constantinople

Oct. 23, Peace conferences at Constantinople, 8 articles agreed to; the Turkish protocol accepted, Dec. 2

Nov. 15–18, Rupture between Austria and Turkey concerning the severe ill-usage of Herr Brazzifolli, agent for the Austrian-Lloyd at Mersina, Asia Minor, Oct.; reparation promised by the Porte but delayed; ultimatum

Nov. 18, Full submission of Turkey

Nov. 29, Indemnities claimed by the Powers for injuries to their subjects during the troubles in Anatolia and Constantinople

Dec. 16, Treaty of peace signed at Constantinople, Dec. 4; ratified by the Sultan

Dec. 23, Memorial presented by the Armenian patriarch to the Sultan

1898

March 27, The Sultan demands the application of autonomy to Crete as existing in Lebanon and Samos, with a Christian governor (Ottoman subject)

May 6, Collective note from the Powers notifying the evacuation of Thessaly from May 6, the Greek war indemnity to be completed after the evacuation; presented to the Porte

May 18, Note to the Porte from the British Embassy complaining of grievances of British merchants, &c.; some compensation paid, July

May 31, Turco-Greek frontier settled, the foreign delegates return to Volo

June 13, Russian note to the Porte demands the repatriation of 40,000 Armenians in the Caucasus

June 30, Russian note demanding payment of the arrears of the Russo-Turkish war indemnity, presented May; 300,000т. paid, the rest guaranteed by the Ottoman Bank

July 18, The Porte refuses compensation for losses suffered by British, French, and Italian subjects during the massacres in Constantinople

Oct. 18–22, Visit of the German Emperor

Dec. 22, Ghani Bey, Albanian Col. and the Sultan's aide-de-camp, shot at Pera by Hafyz Pasha

1899

June 12, Kurdish outrages, the superior of the Pirnaschen monastery and 2 monks assassinated, Seronk and 5 villages burnt, many killed, reported

July 29, Russian note demanding cessation of frontier raids, often assisted by Hamidian cavalry

Oct. 26, Sir Nicholas O'Conor's (British Ambassador) proposals regarding the quay arrangement agreed to by the Porte

Nov. 27, Mahomedan officials banished to Yemen for sedition, and many Young Turks arrested

End Nov., Baghdad railway concession granted to a German syndicate

Dec. 14, Flight of Mahmud Pasha

1900

Jan. 30, 31, Italian ultimatum to the Porte, demanding the restoration of a kidnapped Italian girl, promptly acceded to

March 31, Russian demands for railway concessions in Asia Minor; accepted by the Porte

April 4, 5, Death of Osman Pasha

May 27, April 7 and 18, The Powers protest against proposed increase of the customs duties

June 23, Manifesto by the Young Turks, urging the powers to put an end to the Sultan's régime, presented to the embassies

Mid Aug., Major Maunsell, British vice-consul at Van, attacked and robbed by Turks

Sept. 6, Kurds defeated by Turks at Elk, reported

Sept., 11 Armenian relief agents pardoned, due to British intervention

Oct. 3, Russian note demands punishment of Kurds who attacked their vice-consul at Erzerum

Oct. 22, Armenian persecution continues, arrests daily, many released through Russian intervention

Dec. 22, 31, Greek notes respecting the frequent murders of Greeks in Macedonia, indemnity demanded

1901

May 23, The Porte seizes foreign mail-bags, May 5; regular service resumed after negotiations

July 10, America claims $95,000 for losses in Armenia, April; again, June 23; paid, reported

Early Aug., Settlement of monetary claims demanded by French bankers in the quays company

Nov. 4, French ultimatum presented

Nov. 7, Adm. Caillard's fleet seizes the custom-houses at Mytilene

Nov. 7, 11, French demands conceded by the Porte, ratified by the Sultan; relations resumed

Nov. 9, Death of Halil Rifat Pasha, aged 94

Nov. 10, Austro-Hungarian affairs settled

Nov. 12, British claim for 16,000l., respecting the Sariyeri mines, paid

Dec., Mubarakh, Sheikh of Koweyt in the Persian Gulf, shakes off the Turkish yoke

1902

Feb. 23, Miss Stone, an American missionary, and Mme. Tsilka kidnapped by brigands in Macedonia, Sept., 1901; ransomed by subscription and released

March 6, Collective note (British, French, Russian, and Italian) protesting against hindrances to commerce, &c., in Crete

March 18, First concession for Bagdad Railroad

June 5, Marshal Fuad Pasha (loyal and honorable) charged with conspiracy, March; sentenced to life-imprisonment by iradé issued (fate unknown)

July 2, M. Rouvier's project for the unification of the Ottoman debt with British, French, and German syndicates, adopted; iradé issued, Aug. 2

July 12, The Porte demands the suppression of Cretan money with Prince George's effigy

July 15, Budget statement: advance of about 3 millions needed

July 24, Commission appointed to consider reforms, &c., for Macedonia; report issued

Aug. 30, Afium Karahissar, a commercial town in Anatolia, nearly destroyed by fire, reported

Oct. 13, Circular note to the Powers asserting the bad frontier supervision by Bulgaria, Oct. 12; satisfactory replies received

Oct. 30, Frequent violations of the Aden frontier, Sir Nicholas O'Conor's demand for the withdrawal of Turkish troops agreed to

Nov., Dec. 10, 13, The Powers urge effective reforms in Macedonia; Sir Nicholas O'Conor again calls attention to the reports of cruelty by the Turks, Dec. 30

Dec. 29, Italian indemnity, 12,000l. for losses, in 1896; paid

1903

Jan., British Embassy protests against the passage of Russian torpedo boats through the Dardanelles; afterwards dropped

Feb. 10, Turco-German convention for Konia-Baghdad railway concluded

Mid Feb., Austro-Russian reform scheme for Macedonia; accepted by the Powers; presented to the Porte, and agreed to by the Sultan, Feb. 21, 23; ordered to be applied also to 6 Rumelian vilayets, Feb. 25

March 5, Revised Bagdad Railway Convention superseded that of March, 1902; Turco-German control continued

March, Sultan orders the application of the Austro-Russian reforms to all six Rumelian vilayets

March 27, Violent revolt of Albanians against the reform scheme; Sultan promises to deal firmly with the revolutionaries

March 31, Attack by an Albanian soldier, Ibrahim, on M. Stcherbina (who died by his injuries, April 10), the Russian consul at Mitrovitza

April 3, Russian and Austrian Ambassadors urge the immediate military occupation of all the Albanian centers, to which the Sultan promises compliance

Earthquake in the vilayet of Van

April 28, Turkish note addressed to the Bulgarian government by the Porte respecting the dynamite outrages by Bulgarians

May 6, Serious outbreak at Monastir

Mid May, Bulgarian Government opens direct negotiations on the Macedonian question

June 2, Imperial iradé promulgated approving of scheme of Ottoman Bank for unification of debt

End June, Turkish forces occupy strategic positions in Kossovo, Monastir, and Adrianople districts; Bulgaria calls the attention of the great Powers to this occupation

July 27, First section of Bagdad railway begun at Konia

End July, Circular issued by the Porte on the subject of Macedonia to its representatives abroad

Aug. 8, Russian consul at Monastir, M. Roskowsky, shot dead by a gendarme; full satisfaction demanded by the Russian Ambassador

Sept. 18, The Sultan expresses regret to the Russian Ambassador for excesses committed by the Turkish troops, and states that orders had been given to prevent their recurrence; iradé issued purporting to embody the reforms for Macedonia already communicated verbally to the Bulgarian Government; instructions given to Hilmi Pasha to carry out reforms without delay and ordering punitive measures against the Bulgarians to be discontinued

Oct. 17, Refusal of the Sultan to receive the identical note; iradé issued stating the resolution of his ministers with respect to reforms in Macedonia and relief for refugees

Oct. 22, Austro-Russian instructions for the execution of the reforms in Macedonia presented to the Sultan. The chief items are: the appointment of Austrian and Russian civil agents to direct the inspector-general; the reorganization of the gendarmerie by a foreign general in the service of the Porte assisted by officers of the Great Powers; the changing of the territorial division of the administrative districts to facilitate a more regular grouping of the various nationalities; mixed commission to be appointed in the chief towns composed of an equal number of Christian and Mohammedan delegates; the reorganization of administrative and judicial institutions, and the dismissal of the second-class reserves or Ilavehs and Bashi-Bazouks; these reforms to be carried without delay by the Turkish Government (additions made subsequently by Austria and Russia reserving their right to increase their consular establishment in Macedonia, and to demand an amnesty for the insurgents)

Oct. 25, First section of Berlin to Bagdad Railway from Konia to Bulgurlu opened

Nov. 3, British, French, German, and Italian embassies receive instructions from their governments to support the scheme; reply of the Porte (practically a rejection of the scheme)

Nov. 10, Pressure put by Austrian and Russian ambassadors on the Porte to accept the scheme

Nov. 25, The Porte assents to all points of the amended scheme, but stipulates that anything in its application calculated to humiliate Turkey shall be avoided

1904

Jan. 2, Emilio di Giorgis, Lt.-Gen. of the Italian army, appointed to take command of the gendarmerie under the reform scheme for Macedonia

Jan. 28, The Porte, in a note addressed to Austria-Hungary and Russia, defines its acceptance of the terms laid down by the Powers, and stipulates that the subordinates of the two civil agents should be accompanied in their official journeys of investigation by Turkish officials, and that reforms found to be necessary should be executed by the inspector-general after the sanction and on receipt of instructions by the Porte; conditions rejected by Austria-Hungary and Russia

March 3, New scheme drawn up by the foreign officers communicated to the Porte, Feb. 29; rejected by the Porte on the ground that it violated the sovereign rights of the Sultan

March 19, Counter-proposals made by the Porte to Austria-Hungary and Russia, March 17; these are rejected, the ambassadors of the two powers claiming that Gen. di Giorgis should be invested with efficient powers for the organization and control of the gendarmerie, the officers of which were not to exceed 60 in number

March 25, Porte objects to the number of foreign officers demanded by the foreign Powers, and claims that their number should not exceed 25 to be concerned with the duties of surveillance and reorganization, Turkish officers to retain the effective command

April 1, Ambassadors of the two powers, while maintaining their demand for 60 foreign officers, consent to commence their work with 25, and further insist that their demands of Feb. 29 and March 19 be at once accepted by the Porte

April 8, Agreement between the Porte and Bulgaria, by which the latter agreed to prevent the formation of insurrectionary bands and revolutionary committees in Bulgarian territory and Turkey undertook to apply the reform scheme formulated with Austria-Hungary and Russia

April 16, Gen. di Giorgis arrives at Salonika

April, Outrages by Kurds in villages near Mush, and massacres in the Susan district (*see* Armenia), during

July 26, Austria-Hungary and Russia declare their intention of increasing the number of the gendarmerie officers, to which the Porte objects; Gen. di Giorgis opposes the increase

Aug. 29, Death of the ex-Sultan Amurath V (Murad), deposed for bad health, Aug. 31, 1876, after a reign of three months

Early Oct., Macedonian Inner Organization issue a memorandum on the situation, stating that they would continue the struggle with Turkey until international military intervention had superseded Turkish rule in Macedonia

Dec. 26, The Porte subsequently consents to admit 13 new officers, in addition to the 25 previously appointed, on certain conditions

1905

Jan. 21, Scheme for financial reform in the three vilayets of Macedonia promulgated by Austria-Hungary and Russia, to be carried out under the supervision of the two civil agents; objections urged by the other powers, including Gt. Britain, to the control proposed to be vested in the representatives of Austria-Hungary and Russia

Feb. 19, Terrible excesses committed by Turkish troops in their search for arms at Kukliteh

Feb., Rising in Yemen; defeat of Turkish troops: insurgents capture Sanaa, April 20

April 26, Aden boundary dispute between Turkey and Gt. Britain settled

May 2, Cretan agitation for union with Greece during March *et seq.* (*see* Crete); Cretan assembly proclaims its union with Greece, April 20; Greek flag hoisted

on Government house at Canea, but lowered by British troops

May 8, The Powers insist on the international control of the finances of Macedonia

May, Bulgarians attacked and massacred by Greek bands in the southern district of Salonika and Monastir, during

July 21, Attempted assassination of the Sultan in Constantinople, by means of a bomb; several persons killed and injured

July 31, Representatives of the six Powers sign a note to the Porte demanding the adoption of the scheme of international financial control

End Aug., Sanaa captured from the insurgents by Turkish troops, and rebellion quelled

Sept. 25, Diplomatic note to the Porte informing the government that the international financial commissioners would arrive at Salonika on Oct. 1 to undertake the financial control of the three vilayets

Nov. 22, Strained relations between the Sultan and the Powers, the former refusing to recognize the financial commissioners, on the ground that their appointment was a violation of the sovereign rights of the Sultan; the Sultan still remaining obdurate in his refusal, a naval demonstration was ordered by the Powers, the combined fleets arrived at Mitylene, and landed a force which occupied the custom house, &c.; the Turkish troops retired, Nov. 25

Dec. 5, Lemnos occupied by the international squadron, which also prepares to occupy Tenedos and Smyrna

Dec. 6, Porte proposes that the financial delegates should be nominated for a term of two years, and should have the designation of "specialists," forming a Turkish commission under the presidency of Hilmi Pasha, a Turkish member to be added to the commission, reported

Dec. 9, Powers make certain concessions to the objections offered by Turkey in respect of the international financial control of Macedonia

Dec. 16, Porte accepts the final draft of the international financial control scheme; the naval demonstration ends

1906

Jan. 8, Death of Ahmed Nazif Pasha, and appointment of Zia Bey as Minister of Finance

March 23, Redvan Pasha, prefect of Constantinople, assassinated

May 3, British ultimatum to Turkey in the dispute respecting Tabah, in the Sinai peninsula

May 9, Situation of the Turkish troops at Sanaa reported to be almost hopeless in consequence of the non-despatch of reinforcements demanded by Marshal Ahmed Feizi Pasha

——, Death of Abeddin Pasha, formerly Foreign Minister

May 14, Porte announces its full acceptance of the British demands regarding the Egyptian frontier; Turkish garrison withdrawn from Tabah

July 5, American ministry in Constantinople raised to the status of an embassy

——, Serious collision between Turkish and Persian troops consequent on a Turkish advance into Persian territory

July 21, An attempt on the life of the Sultan; Edward Joris, with others, condemned to death (released by the Sultan as an act of clemency, Dec. 22, 1907)

Oct. 1, Sultan gives way to Great Britain's demand for

a straight line of demarcation from Akabah to Rafah, and the Turkish force stationed at Kuseimeh was withdrawn, Sept. 25; agreement signed in Cairo

Oct. 11, Severe fighting between Turkish troops and tribesmen in the Azir district of Arabia, reported

Oct. 25, Mahomedan riot at Erzerum; chief of police killed

Oct. 27, Persians at Kerbela beg protection from British vice-consul against Turkish misrule

Oct. 31, British and Russian embassies in Constantinople offer to the Porte separately, and in a friendly spirit, their good offices for an equitable settlement of the frontier dispute with Persia, reported

Nov. 9, Imperial iradé issued, sanctioning the Mazbata drawn up by the council of ministers on the 4th inst. with reference to the 3% increase in the customs

Nov. 17, Strained relations between the Porte and the Greek patriarchate, reported

1907

Jan. 12, New Turco-Bulgarian commercial agreement signed

Feb. 16, Fehim Pasha, chief of the secret police at Yildiz, attempts to blackmail a merchant engaged in British trade and to sequestrate the cargo of a vessel destined for Hamburg; British and German embassies intervene, Jan. 24; Fehim is exiled

Feb. 24, Death of Vice-Admiral Sami Pasha, prefect of the port of Constantinople, in suspicious circumstances, reported

March 29–April 2, Damage to property at Bitlis by earthquake; four casualties reported

April 19, Porte sends communication to the ambassadors, in reply to their collective note of April 10, agreeing to certain points of Gen. di Giorgis's program for rendering the Macedonian gendarmerie more effective

April 25, The protocol with reference to 3% increase of the Turkish customs duty, demanded by the Porte in order to supply the funds needed for Macedonian reforms, signed in Constantinople

June 5, Turkish force defeated by Arabs near Sana, reported

June 25, The increase of customs duties from 8 to 11% comes into force

Dec. 21, Death of Musurus Pasha, Turkish Ambassador in London

1908

Feb. 22, Suj Balak evacuated by the Turkish troops

April 20, The Porte yields to the demands of Italy, and consents to the opening of Italian post-offices within the Ottoman Empire

June 2, Concession for extension of Berlin to Bagdad Railway from Bulgurlu to Aleppo

July 7, General Shemsi Pasha shot at Monastir

July 24, The Sultan issues an iradé restoring the constitution of 1876

July 25, General amnesty proclaimed in Constantinople

Aug. 5, Death of Fehim Pasha while trying to avoid arrest

Aug. 6, New ministry formed with Kiamil Pasha as Grand Vizier

Aug. 17, Sudden death of Redjib Pasha, Minister of War; buried

Sept. 1, Opening of the Hejaz railway from Damascus to the Holy city

Oct. 1, Death of Ibrahim Pasha, Kurdish rebel leader

——, Strikers on the Smyrna-Aidin railway, derail a train, Sept. 30; collision with the troops

Oct. 5, Bulgaria proclaims its independence

Oct. 7, Austria-Hungary proclaimed annexation of Bosnia and Herzegovina

——, Crete proclaimed union with Greece

Oct. 18, Kurdish atrocity reported from Viranshehr; 76% of the population which is Christian massacred by troops and Kurds

Oct. 28, Mutiny of the officers of the 7th guard regiment on being ordered to Jeddah

Dec. 2, General Ismail Maher Pasha assassinated

Dec. 17, The Sultan opens the new parliament

1909

Feb. 13, Fall of Kiamil Pasha; Hussein Hilmi Pasha appointed Grand Vizier

Feb. 26, Protocol signed between Austria-Hungary and Turkey recognized annexation of Bosnia and Herzegovina, and provided for payment of $10,800,-000 indemnity by Austria-Hungary to Turkey, and for religious freedom to Mohammedans who remained in the province

April 6, Hassan Fehmi Effendi, editor of the *Serbesti*, assassinated

April 13, Military revolt in Constantinople; fall of the ministry and the committee of union and progress; the first army corps, backed by the Jemiyet-i-Mohammedieh (league of Mahomed) sieze the parliament-house and the telegraph offices; Emir Mahomed Arslan mortally wounded by the troops, and Nazim Pasha, Minister of Justice, killed on his way to Pera

April 14, Hilmi Pasha resigns; Abdul Hamid accepts the resignation of the cabinet and grants an amnesty to the troops; new cabinet formed with Tewfik Pasha as Grand Vizier

——, Mahmud Shevket, commander of the third army corps, mobilizes the troops at Salonika and advances on Constantinople reëstablishing order

April 15, Nazim Pasha appointed commander of the first army corps and Assistant Minister of War

April 19, Turco-Bulgarian protocol. (*See* Bulgaria)

April 23, Mahmud Shevket issues a proclamation promising pardon to all soldiers guilty of mutiny during the recent events, on condition that they make their submission; otherwise they should be mercilessly punished

April 24, Constantinople taken; Shevket Pasha enters the city, only the mutinous troops at Tashkishba, and other barracks in Pera, offer resistance to the army of occupation; these barracks were bombarded and destroyed and their garrisons forced to surrender—Galata, Pera, and Stambul occupied by the Macedonian army

April 27, Abdul Hamid II deposed; his younger brother succeeds under the name of Mahomed V

April 28, The ex-Sultan departs for Salonika

May 1, Tewfik Pasha reappointed to the grand vizierate, with Ferid Pasha as Minister of the Interior and Salih Pasha as Minister of War

May 3, 13 leaders of the mutiny hanged

May 5, Tewfik Pasha resigns; Hilmi Pasha appointed Grand Vizier, with Ferid Pasha, Interior, and Salih Pasha, War

May 12, 22 persons, implicated in the mutiny of April 13, executed

May 13, Tewfik Pasha appointed Ambassador to England

Massacres at Adena. (*See* Albania)

May 31, Turkish regulars occupy Persian territory at Suj Bulak, reported

June 22, Turkish reverse in Albania, reported

Dec. 17, Death of F. M. Edhem Pasha, commander of the Turkish army in the war with Greece, born 1851

Dec. 28, Resignation of Hilmi Pasha and the cabinet accepted by the Sultan

Dec. 30, Hakki Bey succeeds Hilmi Pasha

1910

Jan. 6, Note addressed to Great Britain, France, Russia, and Italy protested against Cretan Government decision to require officials to take the oath to the King of the Hellenes and to have the courts recognize and apply the Greek code

Jan. 9, Hakki Bey, new Grand Vizier, arrives in Constantinople

Jan. 12, New Cabinet announced under Hakki Pasha, Grand Vizier

Jan. 19, The Chiragan-palace, Constantinople, burnt down

March 21–28, King Ferdinand of Bulgaria and Queen Eleonora at Constantinople on a visit to the Sultan

April 2, King Peter of Serbia arrives at Constantinople

April 3, Turkish troops in clash with Albanians in Prishtina district

May 8, Copyright Act passed

May 12, 35,000 troops in Albania to suppress revolt. *See* Albania

May 19, Convention with Tunis signed as to frontier with Tripoli

July 11, Cretan Government announced submission to ultimatum of Powers of July 8 as to seating of Moslem delegates without requirement to take the oath

July 19, Arrest of Dr. Riza Nur with others charged with plot to overthrow Government

Aug. 31, American religious educational and benevolent institutions exempted from Ottoman law and permitted to hold land

Oct. 23, Anti-British demonstrations at Constantinople by Moslems

1911

Jan. 11 and Nov. 27, Agreements with Germany signed as to abolition of capitulations

April 3, Turkish troops defeated Albanian insurgents at Scutari

May 21, Agreement announced that Persian-Turkish Boundary Conference at Constantinople would submit points in dispute to Hague Court

July, Foreign loan of $175,000,000 negotiated in France

July 10, Assassination of Zeki Bey, Chief Secretary Public Debt Administration

July 23, Fire devastated 2 square miles in Stamboul district of Constantinople. More than 5,000 houses destroyed

Sept. 25, Protest of Italian Government as to treatment of her nationals in Tripoli presented

Sept. 28, Italy presented ultimatum to Turkey

Sept. 29, Cabinet of Hakki Bey resigned. Note to Italy conciliatory. *See* Italy

——, Turkey declared war on Italy, and Italy on Turkey

——, Italy began war on Turkey. *See* Libya and Italy

Sept. 30, Note to Powers asked intervention

Oct. 4, New Cabinet chiefly of Young Turk party organized under Said Pasha

Oct. 5, Tripoli surrendered to Italy

Nov. 2, Provisional commercial agreement with Bulgaria for one year signed

Nov. 8, Turkey protested to Powers against Italian annexation of Tripoli

Nov. 25, Extension until June 25, 1914 of German-Ottoman Treaty of commerce and navigation signed

Dec. 17, Sir Edward Crawford appointed Financial and Economic Adviser to the Government

Dec. 30, Resignation of Said Pasha Cabinet

1912

Jan. 3, Said Pasha reappointed Premier, reorganized Cabinet

Jan. 7, 7 Turkish gun boats sunk by Italians in naval engagement off Kounfiuda on Red Sea

Jan. 16, Seizure of French steamer "Carthage" by Turks

Jan. 18, Chamber of Deputies dissolved by Imperial decree

——, French steamer the "Manouba" seized

Jan. 20, Gargaresh occupied by Italians

Feb. 10, Work on Bagdad Railway east from Aleppo begun

March 5, Persian-Turkish Boundary Commission began sessions at Constantinople

April 16, Powers addressed Note to Turkey proposing mediation in war with Italy

April 18, Dardanelles closed

April 23, Bu Kemmesh occupied by Italians

——, Italian warship seized Turkish Island of Stampalia near entrance of the Dardanelles

——, Turkey accepted mediation of Powers on condition sovereign rights of Turkey be maintained and Italians evacuate Tripoli

May 17, Turkish garrison at Rhodes surrendered to Italians

May 18, Dardanelles reopened

July 9, Resignation of Mahmud Shevket Pasha, Minister of War

July 17, Resignation of Prime Minister Said Pasha on account of "internal dissentions"

July 21, Ghazi Mukhtar Pasha formed Cabinet, General Nazim Pasha, Minister of War

Aug. 2, Bulgarians at Kolschana massacred by Mohammedans

Aug. 5, Parliament dissolved and martial law declared

Aug. 16, Massacre of Albanian Christians near Montenegro frontier by Turks

Aug. 21, Resignation of Hilmi Pasha, Minister of Justice (Young Turk)

Aug. 27, Massacre of native Christians by Turks at Sienitza

Sept. 17, Arab attack on Derna repulsed. *See* Libya

Sept. 20, Armenian Patriarch of Greek Church resigned because of persecution of Armenians

Oct. 1, General mobilization of land and naval forces ordered

Oct. 6, Government announced intention to introduce administrative reforms in European provinces in attempt to avert war and intervention by Powers

Oct. 8, First Balkan war begun. Montenegro declared war on Turkey. *See also* Balkan Wars

——, Note of Russia and Austria in name of six Powers under Treaty of Berlin demanded reforms but stated in case of war they would not permit modifications of territory

Oct. 13, Governments of Greece, Serbia, and Bulgaria issued ultimatum demanding reforms, the guarantee of "the ethnic autonomy of the nationalities of the Empire" and immediate demobilization of Turkish army in Balkans

Oct. 14, Turkey declined to allow intervention of the Powers to obtain reforms

Oct. 15, Protocol of peace with Italy signed at Ouchy

——, Diplomatic relations with Bulgaria, Serbia, and Greece severed

Oct. 17, Bulgaria, Serbia, and Greece declared war on Turkey and Turkey declared war on Bulgaria and Greece

Oct. 18, Treaty of peace with Italy signed at Lausanne. Tripoli and Cyrenaica ceded to Turkey and evacuation of troops respectively agreed upon

Oct. 23, Turkish Petroleum Company founded of which Deutches Bank as assignee of Bagdad Railroad held 25%, National Bank of Turkey, 47.5%, and Anglo-Saxon Petroleum Company, 22.5%

Oct. 29, Ghazi Mukhtar, Prime Minister, resigned

Oct. 30, Kiamil Pasha succeeded as Prime Minister

Nov. 4, Turkey appealed to the Powers for intervention

Nov. 14, Proposals for mediation made by the Powers

Nov. 19, Joint note of Greece, Serbia, and Bulgaria to Turkey agreed to an armistice offering terms

Nov. 21, Turkey rejected conditions of armistice and fighting resumed

Nov. 28, Declaration of independence of Albania. *See* Albania

Dec. 3, Armistice at Chatalja lines concluded by Balkan States except Greece

Dec. 8, Young Turks leaders released from prison

Dec. 16, Peace Conference opened in London

Dec. 23, Allies demanded cession of Turkey in Europe from Rodost on Sea of Marmora to Cape Malatra on Black Sea except Gallipoli Peninsula

1913

Jan. 1, Turkey offered to cede Allies all Turkey in Europe west of line from Enos on Ægean Sea to Midia on Black Sea except Adrianople

Jan. 17, Collective Note of Powers to Turkey. *See* Balkan Wars

Jan. 22, National Assembly decided to accept conditions of peace offered by Powers

Jan. 23, *Coup d'état* of Young Turks led by Talaat Bey and Enver Bey overthrew the Government of Kaimil Pasha. Mahmud Shevket Pasha made Grand Vizier

Hussein Nazim Pasha assassinated, Reshid Bey and Sadik Bey imprisoned

Jan. 29, Allies denounced armistice and hostilities reopened at Adrianople and Chatalja

Jan. 30, Note to Powers offered further concessions

Feb. 1, London Conference broken up with no agreement

March 1, Turkey again requested mediation of Powers

April 1, Turkey accepted terms of peace proposed by Powers

April 20, Armistice signed between Turkey and the Balkan Allies except Montenegro

April 30, Reply of Montenegro to the Powers in regard to evacuation of Scutari

May 20–June 10, Second Peace Conference in London

May 30, Treaty of London signed between Turkey and Bulgaria, Greece, Montenegro, and Serbia. Turkey surrendered Crete and all European territory west

of the Enos-Midia line. Delimitation of Albanian frontiers and disposition of the Ægean Islands left to future settlement

June 11, Assassination of Mahmud Shevket Pasha

June 17, Prince Said Halim appointed Grand Vizier and General Izzet Pasha, Minister of War

June 30, Second Balkan War begun. *See* Balkan Wars

July 15, Agreement concluded on delimitation of the Turko-Persian frontier. Commission to be appointed of representatives of Turkey, Great Britain, and Russia to mark the boundaries

July 20, The Turks took and reoccupied Adrianople

July 29, Anglo-Turkish Convention to establish commission to improve navigation of Shatt-el-Arab River, Persian boundary

Sept. 17, Official announcement of agreement with Bulgaria as to frontiers

Sept. 29, Treaty of Constantinople signed with Bulgaria. Turkey retained Adrianople, Kirk Kilisse, and Dimotika

Oct. 6, Law made education compulsory for children from 7 to 16

Oct. 12, Collective Note from Germany, Austria, Great Britain, France, and Russia addressed to Ottoman Government

Oct. 14, Accord signed for settlement of French claims against Turkey. Accord signed relating to Greece, concessions, &c.

Oct. 22, Commission appointed of Turks and foreigners to examine modifications necessary in the capitulations

Oct. 27, Agreement with Russia signed respecting the Government of Armenia and railroad concessions

Nov. 14, Treaty with Greece signed at Athens by which Greece was given Crete and Ægean Islands except Tenedos, Imbros, and the Dodecanese Islands under Italian occupation

——, Death of Kiamil Pasha, former Grand Vizier

Dec. 14, General Liman von Sanders heading German military mission arrived at Constantinople

1914

Jan. 8, German General Liman von Sanders appointed commander of the first army corps. Enver Pasha (no longer Bey) appointed Chief of Staff with German aides

Feb. 8, Plan of reforms as to Armenia worked out by Powers accepted and promulgated

Feb. 14, Note to Powers insisted on possession of Chios and Mytilene and restitution by Greece of Imbros, Tenedos, and Castllorizzo

Feb. 15, Secret agreements of France with Germany whereby Germany left free to carry on Berlin to Bagdad railway

Feb. 28, Death of "Kutchuk" Said, former Grand Vizier

March 14, Final Treaty of peace with Serbia signed

March 19, British Government acquired controlling interest in Turkish Petroleum Company

April 28, Announcement of accord with Russia respecting duties and admission of Russian delegates into the Ottoman Public Debt Council to go into effect with consent of Powers

May 2, Treaty of commerce with Germany and additional conventions respecting customs extended for one year

June 15, Agreement between Great Britain and Germany as to the Bagdad railway

July 3, Announcement that Bagdad Railroad would terminate at Basra

Aug. 2, Secret alliance with Germany concluded

Aug. 3, British Admiralty sequestered 2 ships building for Turkish navy in England

Aug. 11, Announcement that Turkey had bought the "Goeben" and the "Breslau"

Aug. 14, Entente Allies offered to respect integrity of Turkey if she remained neutral

Aug. 27, Liman Pasha appointed commander-in-chief of the army

Sept. 9, Turkey announced abolition of capitulations for all foreigners

Sept. 10, Protest of Powers against abolition of capitulations

Sept. 27, Dardanelles closed by order of Colonel Weber, German officer

Oct. 29, France, Great Britain, and Italy severed diplomatic relations

——, Turkish torpedo boats raided Odessa, sunk Russian gunboat and damaged French and German ships beginning war

Oct. 30, Russia declared war on Turkey

Nov. 4, Great Britain annexed Island of Cyprus

——, Tewfik Pasha, ambassador in London applied for his passports and stated war had begun

Nov. 5, Great Britain and France declared war on Turkey

Nov. 6, Turkey severed diplomatic relations with Belgium

Nov. 11, The Sublime Porte declared a *jihad* (holy war) against the Entente Allies

Nov. 14, Official Note explained entrance into War

Nov. 16, Shot fired into launch of the U.S.S. "Tennessee"

Dec. 18, British protectorate proclaimed in Egypt

1915

Jan. 8, Serbia declared war against Turkey

Jan. 11, Further alliance with Germany signed

Feb. 19 (March 4), Secret Allied Agreement regarding Constantinople, the Straits and Persia

April 26, Pact of London by which Turkish territories partitioned, Italy to receive sovereignty over Dodecanese Islands, the Province of Adalia, Libya; England, Mesopotamia with Bagdad and 2 ports on Syrian coast; France to have Syria and Adana vilayet; Russia to have Trebizond, Erzerum, Bitlis, Van, and part of Kurdistan; Arabian State to be formed

Aug. 21, Italy declared war against Turkey

Sept. 16, Talaat Pasha, Minister of the Interior, ordered that "an end must be put to their (the Armenians') existence, however tragic the measures to be taken, and no regard must be paid to either age or sex, or to conscientious scruples." Deportations followed

Sept. 22, Dede Agatch Agreement with Bulgaria, cession of territory to Bulgaria

1916

Jan. 8, Last British and French troops evacuated the Gallipoli Peninsula

Feb. 14, Bill passed extended military service to age of 50 and exacted payment for those excused

March 16, New German loan to Turkey of 20 million pounds

April 26, Franco-Russian Treaty for partition of Turkey. *See* p. 453

April 27, Halil Bey, Minister of War, announced the replacement of Italy by Turkey in the Triple Alliance "on equal terms"

May 9–16, Sykes-Picot Agreement. *See* World War

June 9, Hussain ibn Ali, Sherif of Mecca, declared independence of the Ottoman Empire

June 27, The Sherif of Mecca proclaimed new State of Arabia

Aug. 30, Turkey declared war against Rumania

Sept. 21, French and Italian troops withdrew from neutral zone

Sept. 23 and 25, Turkish troops entered Chanak neutral zone held by British troops only but withdrew

Dec. 26, Reply of Government to note of President Wilson of Dec. 18. *See* World War

1917

Jan. 1, Government announced abrogation of the Treaty of Paris of March 10, 1856 and the Treaty of Berlin of Aug. 3, 1878

Feb. 4, Grand Vizier Said Halim succeeded by Talaat Bey. Enver Pasha became Minister of War, Ahmed Nessimi Bey, Foreign Affairs

——, Law established universal military service between ages of 20 and 45

April 17, St. Jean de Maurienne Agreement by which Italy granted possession of southern half of Anatolia including cities of Adalia, Konia, and Smyrna

April 20, Turkey severed diplomatic relations with the United States

July 8, Greece severed diplomatic relations with Turkey

July 31, Germany notified Turkey and Bulgaria that she would assume all expenses incurred by those countries in the campaign of 1917–1918

Nov. 27, Treaty with Germany signed as to war agreements and abolition of Capitulations

1918

Jan. 5, Announcement of Lloyd George that Allies had no intention of molesting the Turkish "homelands," the Straits to be internationalized

Feb. 9, Peace Treaty with the Ukraine signed by Central Powers including Turkey

Feb. 10, Death of Abdul Hamid II, deposed Sultan

March 3, Brest-Litovsk Treaty signed. *See* World War

April 2, Turkish ambassador presented credentials to Russian Soviet Republic

April 13, Armenia and Georgia refused to recognize cession of territory of Brest-Litovsk Treaty and the Turkish military occupation. Fighting in Batum, Kars, and Ardahan

May 11, Peace Treaty with Finland signed

May 30, Treaty with Austria signed by which Austria pledged not to sign any peace which would restore the Capitulations

June 8, Georgia and Armenia signed peace treaties with Turkey

July 3, Death of Mohammed V, Sultan

July 4, Valud Ed-din (Vahideddin) proclaimed Sultan as Mohammed VI

July 28, Kars, Batum, and Ardahan by plebiscite decided to unite with Turkey

Aug. 19, Commercial Treaty with Azerbaijan signed

Oct. 4, Talaat Bey, Grand Vizier and Enver Pasha, Minister of Foreign Affairs resigned and fled from the country

Oct. 5, Russia abrogated the Treaty of Peace with Turkey

Oct. 8, Turkish emissaries sent from Smyrna on a peace mission

Oct. 12, Peace Note from Turkey delivered to President Wilson Oct. 14

Oct. 20, New Cabinet formed, Tewfik Pasha, Grand Vizier, Izzet Pasha, Premier

Oct. 30, Turks signed armistice at Mudros to go into effect at noon Oct. 31

Dec. 8, Allied Military Administration established in Constantinople under direction of British Vice-Admiral

1919

March 7, New Cabinet formed, Damad Kerid Pasha, Grand Vizier and Foreign Affairs; General Shevket Torgut, Minister of War

April 12, Execution of Kiamil Mahmud Pasha charged with massacre of Armenians at Yozghad where he was Governor

April 28, Ottoman delegation to Paris Peace Conference headed by Damad Ferid Pasha left Constantinople and proceeded to Berne, Switzerland where they remained until sent for

April 29, Italian forces landed at Adalia

May 14, Greeks landed at Smyrna in accordance with mandate protected by British and French fleets

May 21, M. Sterghiades arrived at Smyrna as High Commissioner

June 17, Request of Turkish Delegation at Peace Conference for a hearing. Not granted

June 19, Amasia Protocol signed

July 4, Turkish delegation left Paris Peace Conference for Constantinople without a formal hearing

July 11, Mustapha Kemal Pasha outlawed by the Ottoman Government

July 23, Nationalist Congress presided over by Mustapha Kemal Pasha met at Erzerum

July 29, Agreement of Greece and Italy as to Greek and Italian interests in Rhodes, the Dodecanese, and the Meander Valley

Aug. 8, Turks proclaimed *jihad* against Greeks landed at Panderma

Aug. 24, First meeting of Commission of Inquiry sent to Smyrna by Governments of the Principal Allied Powers and the United States

Aug. 28, Rear Admiral Bristol, U.S.N., appointed American High Commissioner at Constantinople

Sept. 4, Nationalist Congress met at Sivas

Sept. 9, Declaration of the Congress of Sivas

Sept. 13, Signing of the National Pact charter and program of 6 articles by Mustapha Kemal and his party

Oct. 5, Damad Kerid Ministry replaced by an Ali Riza Ministry as a result of seizure of Konieh railroad center in Asia Minor by Nationalists

Oct. 7, Mustapha Kemal Pasha telegraphed to Ottoman Government the peace terms formulated at the Congresses of Erzerum and Sivas

1920

Jan. 11, Ottoman Parliament opened at Constantinople

Jan. 21, French garrison at Marash attacked by Nationalists

Jan. 28, Nationalist Pact, "Declaration of independence of the New Turkey," adopted by Ottoman Parliament at Constantinople

Feb. 9, French garrison evacuated Marash. Massacre of Armenian civilians

Feb. 18, British High Commissioner at Constantinople made official announcement that the Allies had decided not to deprive Turkey of Constantinople

March 2, Ministry resigned. Succeeded by Salih Pasha as Grand Vizier

March 16, Constantinople occupied by Allied military and naval forces. Nationalist leaders including Rauf Bey and Kara Vasif Bey arrested. Prominent Turks deported to Malta

April 6, New Cabinet headed by Damat Kerid Pasha

April 10, French garrison at Urfa massacred

April 23, Nationalist Assembly met at Angora stated adherence to National Pact, and formed a provisional Government. Mustapha Kemal Pasha elected President

April, Military Convention concluded by Kemalists with Soviet Russia

April 24, Share of Deutches Bank (25%) in Turkish Petroleum Company transferred to French group

May 6, Turkish delegation arrived at Paris to receive Treaty from Allied Powers

May 11, Draft Treaty of Sèvres given to delegation representing the Ottoman Government at Constantinople. Allowed one month for consideration. *See* Peace Conference

June 19–25, British naval forces occupied Mudania

June 22, Greek army began offensive against Nationalist forces in Turkey with permission of Allied Powers

June 24, Greeks defeated Turks at Alashehr and took the city

June 30, Publication of Constantinople Governments proposals to the Allied Draft Treaty

July 2, Fall of Balikesri to the Greeks

July 19, Allied ultimatum to Turkey demanded signature of Treaty

July 25, Adrianople evacuated by Tja fer Tayar, surrendered to the Greeks

Aug. 10, Turks signed the Treaty of Sèvres. *See* p. 563

——, Secret Pact of Sèvres signed by Great Britain, France, and Italy, defined Italian and French spheres of influence in Asiatic Turkey

Aug. 29, Greek forces occupied Ushaq

Oct. 15, Turks captured Hajin, and Cilicia in invasion of Armenian Republic of Erivan. Many Armenians massacred

Oct. 21, Turks took Kars

——, Tewfik Pasha took office as Premier

Nov. 7, Turco-Armenian armistice signed

Dec. 3, Turco-Armenian Peace Treaty signed at Alexandropol reducing Armenia to district of Erivan and Lake Gokcha

Dec. 23, Senate ratified Sèvres Treaty

1921

Jan. 20, Mustapha Kemal Pasha issued Fundamental Law. Legislative and executive authority vested in the National Assembly at Angora

Jan. 22, Porte Agreement signed established interallied control of all disbursements and revenues

Jan. 27, Official announcement of acceptance of invitation of Supreme Council to Near East Conference in London

Jan. 30, Chamber of Deputies voted to ratify Sèvres Treaty

Feb. 3, Resignation of Angora Foreign Minister Ahmed Mukhtar Pasha. Succeeded by Bekir Sami Bey

Feb. 8, Angora Government decided to send a separate mission to the London Conference

Feb. 21–March 14, London Conference. *See* p. 564

March 1, Treaty signed at Moscow between Kemalists and Afghanistan establishing diplomatic relations and providing for mutual assistance in event of attack by a third power

March 9, Secret Agreement of London between the French and the Kemalists as to immediate cessation of hostilities, evacuation of Cilicia, exchange of prisoners, protection of Armenians, &c. Not ratified

March 12, Secret Agreement of London between the Italians and the Kemalists as to conditions of Italian zone of influence in Turkey and withdrawal of Italian troops from Ottoman territory. Not ratified

March 13, Treaty of commerce with Italy signed

March 15, Former Grand Vizier Talaat Pasha assassinated in Berlin by Armenian student

March 16, Kemalist-Soviet Russia Treaty by which Turkey engaged to cede Batum back to Georgia. Territory of Turkey recognized as that stated in Nationalist Pact. Ratified May 13, by Angora Government

March 19, Russian ultimatum to Turkey demanded evacuation of Batum

March 22, New Angora Cabinet: Fevzi Pasha, Grand Vizier and Minister of War; Youssov Kemal Bey, Foreign Affairs

March 23, New Greek offensive against Turkey to enforce Sèvres Treaty in Asia Minor. *See* Greece

Oct. 13, Treaty of Kars between the Kemalist Government and the Caucasian Soviet Republics signed constituted recognition of Armenia, Azerbaijan, and Georgia. The region of Nakhichevan constituted as an autonomous territory under the protection of Azerbaijan, and Turkey ceded Batum to Georgia

Oct. 20, Franco-Turkish Nationalist Agreement ending hostilities provided for evacuation of Cilicia and other territory respectively occupied

Nov. 28, Evacuation of Cilicia by French troops begun

Dec. 12, Treaty of peace and frontiers with Persia signed

1922

Jan. 1, Kemal Pasha announced that the Nationalist Government at Angora did not recognize the authority of the Sultan as superior to that of the Turkish people

Jan. 2, Treaty of friendship between Kemalists and Ukrainia recognized independence of Ukrainia

Jan. 20, Mustapha Kemal ordered all Greek residents of Konieh deported to Erzerum

March 22–April 15, Foreign Ministers of England, France, and Italy met in Paris to discuss Græco-Turkish problems and demands of Nationalists for Treaty revision

March 23, Proposals of Powers for armistice

March 26, Conference of English, French, and Italian Foreign Ministers in Paris ended with signing of terms for revision of Sèvres Treaty

March 26, Supreme Council proposed peace terms to Governments of Greece and the Turkish Governments at Constantinople and Angora

March 31, Imperial Ottoman Government secret Agreement with Italy

April 5, Angora Government accepted armistice terms with reservations as to Anatolia

April 8, Constantinople Government accepted armistice terms with reservations regarding Thrace

April 15, Allied High Commissioners reply to Angora refusing to evacuate Anatolia

April 23, Angora Government informed Allies it would agree to preliminary discussion of peace terms

April 24, Agreement concluded between Italy and Russia regarding concessions for railways, mines, and public works in Asia Minor

May 18, Proclamation of neutrality and designation of a neutral zone by the three Allied High Commissioners at Constantinople

June 26, Kemalist Government recognized by Persia

July 12, Angora Assembly elected new commissars

——, Rauf Bey elected Prime Minister

July 25, Djemal Pasha killed by 2 Armenians at Tiflis

July 27, Greeks threatened occupation of Constantinople. Opposed by Powers. Greeks acquiesced July 29

July 30, Greek High Commissioner in Smyrna proclaimed autonomy of Anatolian territory occupied by Greeks with Smyrna as capital

Aug. 26, Turkish offensive begun. *See* Greece

Sept. 2, Turks entered Ushaq and captured Greek General Tricoupis and his staff

Sept. 9, Advance Turkish cavalry entered Smyrna

Sept. 11, Mustapha Kemal with main army entered Smyrna

Sept. 13, Fire broke out in Smyrna foreign quarter which destroyed the city and rendered 10,000 homeless. Incendiarism charged to Armenians, Greeks, and Turks by equally authentic sources

Sept. 15, Appeal of Lloyd George, British Prime Minister, to the Dominions, Balkan States, and France against Turkey

Sept. 16, British troops landed at Chanaq on Ægean Sea to protect neutrality of the Straits

Sept. 19, Premier Poincaré announced that France was not prepared to use force and advised British withdrawal from Chanaq

——, Mustapha Kemal advised Paris that he would make no attack on neutral zone if Allies would guarantee immediate restoration to Turkey of Adrianople, Constantinople, and East Thrace to Maritza River

Sept. 23, Joint Note of France, Great Britain, and Italy requested an armistice. Terms of Mustapha Kemal acceptable on condition Turkey respect neutrality of Straits zone to be placed under guard of League of Nations

Sept. 26–29, 146,700 refugees evacuated from Smyrna

Sept. 29, Angora Government accepted invitation to peace conference and suggested preliminary armistice convention. Requested Greece to evacuate Thrace within 8 days

Oct. 3–11, Armistice Conference at Mudania on Sea of Marmora of Allied Generals with representatives of Mustapha Kemal and Greece

Oct. 8, Note of Angora Government to Ottoman Public Debt Administration and Ottoman Bank repudiated all treaties, conventions, and decisions made without consent of the National Assembly since March 16, 1920

Oct. 11, Mudania Armistice Convention signed. Eastern Thrace and Adrianople to be given up to the "Grand National Assembly of Turkey" to come into effect at midnight Oct. 14–15. Hostilities between Greeks and Turks to cease and Greek troops to be withdrawn behind specified lines

Oct. 13, Military Convention signed at Mudania

Oct. 19, Refet Pasha appointed by Angora as Governor of Eastern Thrace arrived at Constantinople

Oct. 26, Invitations issued to Conference at Lausanne to revise Sèvres Treaty

Nov. 1, Grand National Assembly at Angora announced that "The Khalifate will continue to be exercised by the Osman family, but the Assembly will choose a Prince whose moral qualities, talent and conduct suit him for the choice" . . . Abdul Mejid named Caliph but without temporary power

Nov. 1, Angora Government deposed Mohammed VI and abolished Sultanate. Republic proclaimed

Nov. 2, Defensive alliance with Afghanistan signed

Nov. 5, Refet Pasha announced that Constantinople Government had ceased to exist. Archives of Sublime Porte transferred to Angora. Allied High Commissioners accepted new conditions but refused to evacuate the city

Nov. 16, National Assembly accused Mohammed VI of treason and ordered him and his Cabinet placed on trial

Nov. 17, Mohammed VI, former Sultan, embarked for Malta on British warship

Nov. 19, Abdul Mejid Effendi, second son of the late Sultan Aziz and cousin of Mohammed VI was elected Supreme Khalif of the Moslems

Nov. 20, First Lausanne Conference opened

Nov. 23, Mohammed VI declared deposed

Nov. 24, Abdul Mejid Effendi invested with Sacred Mantle of the Prophet Mohammed

Nov. 25, French evacuated Adrianople

Dec. 1, Allies approved plan of Dr. Nansen sent by League of Nations to investigate refugee problem to exchange Greeks in Turkey for Turks in Greece

1923

Jan. 30, Græco-Turkish Agreement respecting exchange of populations signed at Lausanne, and Agreement as to prisoners of war

Feb. 4, Lausanne Conference ended because of Turkish refusal to accept terms proposed

Feb. 17, Turkish Economic Congress at Smyrna

March 6, Grand National Assembly rejected Lausanne draft Treaty

March 8, Turkish counter-proposals sent to Allies

April 4, Death of Abbas Hilmi Pasha former Grand Vizier in Vienna

April 10, Grand National Assembly approved the Chester concessions of oil fields and construction of railroads to American company headed by Rear Admiral Colby M. Chester in Anatolia, almost 3,000 miles

April 11, France protested against granting of Chester concessions

April 15, Proclamation of the ex-Sultan of Turkey to Moslems called on them to disregard Act of Angora Government separating the Sultanate and the Khalifate

April 16, Grand National Assembly at Angora passed law making it an act of high treason to attempt to restore former authority of Sultan

April 23, Second Lausanne Conference opened

May 2, Arrest of Bolshevist agents in Constantinople

May 15, British syndicate bought controlling interest of Eastern Railway Bank of Zurich holding company of Anatolian Railroad link in Berlin to Bagdad project and Deutsche Bank holding company of Bagdad Railway

May 21, Death at Mecca of Durr Zadah Abdullah Effendi former Sheik Ul Islam

May 26, Agreement signed by Turkey and Greece to submit oil dispute to a mixed commission

July 23, Treaty of friendship, and juridical Convention with Poland signed

July 24, Treaty of Lausanne signed replaced Treaty of Sèvres, and ended Græco-Turkish war. Turkey recognized as a sovereign national State. Capitulations abolished, Turkey relieved of payment of reparations. Provided for protection of non-Moslem minorities, freedom and demilitarization of the Straits, exchange of Greek inhabitants in Turkey for Turkish inhabitants of Greece. Turkey surrendered claims to Hejaz, Palestine, Mesopotamia (Iraq), Syria, the Dodecanese, Cyprus, Egypt, and Tripoli; Turkey received Smyrna, Turkish Armenia, Cilicia, Anatolia, Adalia, Constantinople, Gallipoli, Adrianople, and eastern Thrace

Aug. 6, Treaty of amity, commerce, and navigation, with the United States signed

Aug. 13, Mustapha Kemal Pasha reëlected President of the Grand National Assembly

Aug. 23, Treaty of Lausanne ratified by the Grand National Assembly vote of 215 to 235

——, Evacuation of Constantinople by Allies begun

Oct. 2, Occupation of Anatolia ended by Allies

Oct. 6, Turkish troops occupied Constantinople evacuated by Allied troops

Oct. 14, Angora voted the Turkish capital by the Assembly

Oct. 29, Declaration of the Turkish Republic. Ghazi Mustapha Kemal Pasha chosen the first President and General Ismet Pasha the first Premier

Oct. 30, Grand National Assembly passed resolution against the Sultan-Caliph

——, First Republican Cabinet headed by General Ismet Pasha

Nov. 3, Patriarch Metaxakis deposed by Holy Synod of Constantinople

Nov. 4, Re-fet Pasha took over administration of Constantinople in name of the Grand National Assembly and Ottoman Empire ceased to exist

Nov. 25, Syro-Palestine Congress petitioned League of Nations to set aside the mandates for Syria, the Lebanon, and Palestine

Dec. 6, The Metropolitan of Chalcedon elected Patriarch

Dec. 11, "Anti-revolutionary" court established at Constantinople

Dec. 13, New Œcumenical Patriarch, Gregorius VII, enthroned at the Phanar

Dec. 18, Turkish Minister of Public Works announced that the Chester concessions were annulled because of failure to begin construction of railroad within time specified

——, Treaty of friendship with Hungary signed

1924

Jan. 28, Treaty of friendship, commerce, and navigation with Austria signed

March 3, Angora Assembly voted abolition of Caliphate and expulsion of Caliph and all members of the House of Osman. All educational and scientific institutions including religious colleges placed under the Department of Public Instruction

——, Treaty of friendship and consular and commercial Agreement with Germany signed

March 15, All religious schools in Constantinople closed
April 20, Constitution adopted by Angora Assembly
May 19–June 5, Conference of English and Turkish representatives as to Mosul frontier
May 31, Treaty of friendship with Sweden signed
June 24–July 13, 15 prominent Turks tried for conspiracy to kill Kemal Pasha. Hanged morning after sentence of death pronounced
Aug. 6, Treaty of Lausanne came into effect
Aug. 16, Treaty of friendship and conciliation with the Netherlands
Sept. 14, Raid of Turkish irregular troops on Mosul vilayet
Sept. 27, Treaty of friendship with Spain signed
Oct. 11, Treaty of friendship with Czechoslovakia signed
Oct. 29, Great Britain and Turkey accepted boundary line adopted by Council of League of Nations for Iraq
Nov. 21, Ministry of General Ismet Pasha resigned
Nov. 22, New Ministry of Fethi Bey succeeded Ismet Pasha
Dec. 1, Treaty of friendship and commerce with Estonia

1925

Jan. 26, Treaty of friendship with Denmark signed
Jan. 30, Deportation of Constantinos VI, Patriarch of Orthodox Greek Church, from Constantinople on ground that he was an "exchangeable" Greek
Feb. 13, Revolt against Government began in Kurdistan led by Sheik Said to restore the Caliphate
March 3, Fall of Angora Cabinet of Fethi Bey. Succeeded March 5 by Ismet Pasha
March 5, Announced that Kurds had taken Arghana, important mining center
March 7, Rebels repulsed in decisive engagement at Diyarbekr
March 11, Decision of Permanent Court respecting compulsory exchange of nationals accepted by Turkey and Greece
March 14, Turkish Petroleum Company received from Iraq Government concession to exploit oil resources of vilayets of Mosul and Bagdad for 75 years. 7 American oil companies admitted to participate with Europeans
April 2, Agreement with France by which the Turkish population of Alexandretta was accorded a large measure of autonomy within the mandated territory of Syria
April 5, Rebels compelled to evacuate 3 vilayets of Arghana
April 16, First section of railroad between Angora and Yozgad opened
April 28, Announcement of end of revolt. Sheik Said and other leaders had been captured in the middle of the month
May 1, Martial law abrogated
May 2, Treaty of friendship with Norway signed
May 19, Patriarch Constantine VI announced his resignation
May 25, Sentence of death pronounced against former senator Seyyid Abdul Kadir and his son Mehmed Char for participation in Kurd revolt
June 21, Agreement with Greece signed as to exchange of populations and rights of nationalities
June 29, Sheik Said and 21 others involved in Kurd revolt hanged

July 13, Election of Manager Basil Georgiadas, Metropolitan of Nicæa, as Greek Patriarch, to be known as Basil III
Aug. 6, Treaty of amity and commerce with the United States signed
Aug. 13, Mustapha Kemal Pasha issued decree proclaiming divorce from his wife, Latife Hanoum, effective, Aug. 5
Sept. 2, Decree made wearing of hats instead of fez compulsory for civilian officers
Sept. 4, Government closed Dervish monasteries and abolished titles dervish and sheik and imposed European dress on civil officials
Oct. 18, Treaty of friendship with Bulgaria signed
Oct. 28, Treaty of peace and friendship with Yugoslavia signed
Nov. 25, Treaty of commerce with Sweden
Nov., Law abolished the fez and ordered wearing of hats
Dec. 13, Provisional Commercial Agreement with Germany signed
Dec. 16, Mosul awarded to Iraq by Council of the League of Nations. Turkey refused to accept the award. Council defined the Turco-Iraq frontier
Dec. 17, Treaty of friendship and mutual neutrality with Russia signed

1926

Jan. 13, Treaty with Great Britain signed at Bagdad respecting Iraq
Jan. 15, Turkey adopted French criminal Code
Feb. 17, Assembly adopted new civil code based on that of Switzerland
Feb. 26, Provisional Commercial Convention with the United States signed
March 18, Turkish women admitted to the practice of law
March 22, Provisional Commercial Agreement with Denmark signed
April 17, Provisional Commercial Agreement with Egypt
April 22, Treaty of neutrality and conciliation with Persia concluded
May 15, Treaty of commerce with Sweden
May 16, Death of ex-Sultan Mohammed VI at San Remo
May 29, German commercial Code adopted
June 2 and Oct. 19, Provisional Commercial Agreement with Finland
June 5, Treaty with Great Britain and Iraq signed added Mosul to Iraq and rectified frontier of Iraq in favor of Turkey
June 7, Resignation of Ziwar Pasha as Premier. Succeeded by Adly Yeghen Pasha
June 18, Arrests made disclosed plot to kill President Kemal Pasha led by former deputy Hurscheid Bey which involved a large number of deputies and ex-deputies
July 1, Government decree brought into effect enforcement of regulations reserving all coastal trade to Turkish ships
Aug. 10, Judicial Convention with Italy signed
Aug. 11, Provisional Commercial Agreement with the Netherlands
Aug. 12, All foreign Chambers of Commerce closed illegal under new law that only 1 Chamber of Commerce and that Turkish might exist. Modified later on protest of foreigners, that they might remain open but must change their names

Aug. 23, Capture of Abdul Kadir Bey at Bulgarian frontier. Involved in plot to assassinate the President

Aug. 26, Javid Bey, Nazim Bey, Hilmi Bey, and Nail Bey, former members of the Committee of Union and Progress hung on charge of plotting against life of President Kemal Pasha

Aug. 28, Provisional Commercial Agreement with Bulgaria signed

Aug. 31, Abdul Kadir Bey, former governor of Angora, hanged

Sept. 1, New civil Code came into effect. Made civil marriage obligatory

Sept. 2, Proposal to French Government to submit indemnity for sinking of the "Lotus" to Permanent Court of International Justice. Accepted Sept. 4

Sept. 15, Trial of Lieutenant Desmons resulted in sentence of 60 days in prison and his company fined £5,000 (Turkish) for benefit of families of French sailors who lost lives when the "Lotus" was sunk

Sept. 30, Treaty of commerce with Czechoslovakia signed

Oct. 13, Commercial Agreement with Norway

Oct. 19, Commercial Agreement with Finland

Oct. 29, Treaty of commerce with Germany signed

Dec. 1, Agreement with Greece as to disposal of property of refugees which had been abandoned

Dec. 5, The Vale of Trebizond in Council forbade women wearing the veil

1927

Jan. 7, Strike of 5,000 bargemen in Constantinople

Jan. 12, Treaty of commerce with Germany signed

Jan. 18, United States Senate rejected Treaty with Turkey signed Aug. 6, 1923

Feb. 17, Exchange of Notes with the United States renewed diplomatic and consular relations and established commercial *modus vivendi*

Feb. 24, Commercial Agreement with Sweden

March 7, "Tribunals of Independence," special courts for trial of persons accused of plotting against the Government abolished

March 11, Commercial Treaty with Russia signed

March 25, Consular Convention with Poland signed

May 31, Commercial Treaty with Czechoslovakia signed

Aug. 1, Order for expulsion from this date of 2,000 "White" Russians in Constantinople unless they should adopt Turkish nationality. Time later extended

Aug. 28, Commercial Treaty with Belgium signed

Sept. 2, Election for Assembly. Mustapha named all candidates for office of Deputy and list then voted on by all males over 18. New Assembly included a large proportion of trained experts in economic, financial, agricultural, and other professional fields

Sept. 15, Battle between police and band of Armenians with object of assassination of Kemal Pasha

Oct. 4, Government sent Note protesting to Persia regarding bandits who crossed frontier and fought Turkish police at Bayezid

Oct. 14, Commercial Agreement with Finland

Oct. 15, Speech of President Kemal Pasha before the Assembly of the People's Party at Angora a review of the history of Turkey since 1919 approximating 40,000 words which took 36 hours and 30 minutes to deliver over period of several days

Oct. 28, Census taken for first time in history. The entire population with exception of census officials, a few doctors, and journalists confined within their homes and ships crews on ships in harbor for 24 hours while census taken. Result announced Nov. 4 gave population as approximately 14,000,000

Nov. 1, New National Assembly met and unanimously elected Mustapha Kemal Pasha President

Nov. 3, New Cabinet formed headed by General Ismet Pasha, Tewfik Rushdi Bey, Foreign Affairs

Nov. 7, 3 members of band of Haji Sami Circassian leader sentenced to death for plotting the assassination of the President. Hanged Jan. 18, 1928

Nov., During the month 47 persons arrested with leader Shefik Husni charged with attempt to spread communism in Turkey

Dec. 6, Announcement that martial law would be abolished and a civilian administration gradually introduced in eastern vilayets

1928

Jan. 10, Decision of Delimitation Commission as to boundary between Nisibin and Jeziret Ibn'Umar. Not accepted by Turkey. Accepted by Syria

Jan. 19, Committees of Assembly gave decision that Ihsan Bey, Dr. Fikret Bey, and Colonel Omar Nazim Bey had violated laws and had received a commission of 5% of the cost of repairing the cruiser "Yawuz" (formerly the "Goeben") from French company and from purchasing a floating dock

Feb. 10, Supreme Court began trial of Ishan Bey, former Minister of Marine, and 13 others charged with fraud in connection with naval contracts

Feb. 12, Treaty of commerce and navigation with Bulgaria signed

Feb. 16, Soviet Arcos Corporation dissolved after trial of Communists some of whom were in its employ

Feb., Trial of 3 American teachers of the American School for Girls at Brusa closed for dissemination of religious propaganda received sentences of 3 days' imprisonment and 3 Turkish pounds ($13.20)

March 31, Earthquake at Smyrna killed 68 persons and rendered thousands homeless

April 9, Decree of Assembly annulled clause in Constitution which stated the religion of the State to be Islam

April 19, Arbitration Treaty with the United States

May 25, Treaty of peace and friendship with Afghanistan signed

May 28, Treaty of commerce and navigation with Latvia signed

May 30, Pact of arbitration, neutrality, judicial regulation, and conciliation with Italy signed

June 13, Agreement for regulation of the Ottoman public debt signed in Paris

June 15, Pact with Persia signed

July 25, Treaty of commerce with the Netherlands replaced that of 1926

Aug. 6, Four Treaties with Russia signed as to frontier communications, pasture rights, &c., settlement of disputes as to inspection of cattle

Sept. 16, Second trial of American teachers at Brusa for alleged Christian propaganda contrary to law

Nov. 3, Latin alphabet substituted for Arabic characters

Nov. 28, First Turkish woman lawyer pleaded case in court

Dec. 1, National Assembly ratified Agreement of June 13 between Government and representatives of foreign bondholders

Dec. 1, Government order required newspapers to be printed in Latin alphabet after this date

1929

Jan. 1, New Nationality law came into effect. All children of foreigners born after this date to be considered Turks, to decide at 18 whether they will remain Turks or adopt nationality of parents. Turkish women who marry foreigners remain Turks

——, Law came into effect obliged all persons between ages of 16 and 40 to go to schools to be taught the Latin alphabet

Jan. 4, Treaty of friendship with Uruguay signed

Jan. 5, Treaty of friendship, conciliation, and arbitration with Hungary signed

Jan. 22, Fire in Tavala suburb of Constantinople destroyed 400 houses

Feb. 12, Leon Trotsky exiled from Russia arrived in Constantinople

Feb. 27, Turkey adhered to Russian Pact of Feb. 9

March 6, Treaty of neutrality, conciliation, and arbitration with Bulgaria signed

April 10, Frontier delimitation Treaty with Persia signed

April 16, Nationality Act modified

May 16, Arbitration Treaty with Germany signed

June 1, Made compulsory to use Latin Alphabet on law reports, balance sheets, and acts of marriage

June 11, Treaty of commerce with Rumania signed

June, New tariff enacted to take effect Sept. 1. Increased most duties about 25%

June 22, Franco-Turkish Agreement as to boundary of Syria and other frontier matters

July 2, Provisional Commercial Agreement with Great Britain signed

July 3, Accession of Turkey to Litvinov Protocol

July 10, Announcement that negotiations with Greece as to exchange of populations broken off

July 19, Fire wiped out old quarter of Angora

Aug. 3, Treaty of friendship with Egypt

Aug. 20, New penal Code based on that of Germany came into effect

Aug. 29, Most favored nation commercial Treaty with France signed

Sept. 4, Imprisonment for debt abolished

Sept. 11, Treaty of commerce with Sweden signed

Sept. 28, Death of Œcumenical Patriarch Basil III

Oct. 1, Treaty of commerce and navigation with the United States signed

——, New tariff came into effect increasing duties

Oct. 4, Albania broke off diplomatic relations because no Minister sent to Albania since accession of King Zog

Oct. 7, Photios Maniatis elected Patriarch

Oct. 12, Visit of British squadron commanded by Admiral Field

Dec. 17, Treaty of neutrality and friendship with Russia signed

——, Treaty of friendship and neutrality with France signed amplified Pact of 1925

1930

Jan. 3, Treaty of friendship, conciliation, and arbitration with France signed

March 1, Most favored nation Treaty of Commerce with Great Britain signed

March 27, Law authorized grant of subsidies to newspapers approved by the Government for period of 3 years on account of introduction of Latin alphabet

April 28, Arbitration and conciliation Agreement with Spain signed

April 29, Two women appointed as associate judges in equity courts at Ankara

May 27, Most favored nation Treaty of Commerce with Germany signed

May 28, Announcement of substitution of name Istanbul for Constantinople

May 31, Payment of tolls ceased at Gallata bridge at midnight (Angora) and Istanbul (Constantinople)

June 1, Law prohibiting the use of Arabic characters in writing or printing Turkish became effective

June 10, Agreement with Greece signed as to refugees and exchanged populations

——, Kurdish raids from Persia near Mount Ararrat begun. Frontier closed

July 13, Announcement of Government that Mount Ararat Kurdish revolt suppressed

Aug. 21, Turco-Italian Mixed Court declared itself incompetent to decide on claims of heirs of former Sultan Abdul Hamid II to properties in Libya valued at from $50,000,000 to $80,000,000

Aug. 31, Railroad opened from Angora to Sivas

Sept. 17, Treaty of friendship with Lithuania signed

Sept. 24, Visit of Dr. Tewfik Rushdi Bey, Minister of Foreign Affairs to Russia

Sept. 27, Cabinet reconstructed

Oct. 12, Treaty of commerce with Japan concluded

Oct. 30, Treaty of neutrality, arbitration, and conciliation signed with Greece and Treaty of commerce and Protocol limiting naval armaments

Nov. 22, Hearings begun at Anglo-Turkish Arbitration Court at Istanbul in case of heirs of Abdul Hamed II against British Government for restoration of properties in Iraq, Cyprus, Egypt, and Palestine valued at $60,000,000

Nov. 25, Turkey paid one-third of about $5,000,000 due under Paris Agreement of 1928 as to pre-War debt

Dec. 23, Revolt headed by Mehemet (dervish) begun in village of Menemen against wearing of hats and new Latin alphabet suppressed

Dec. 26, Cabinet reconstructed: President of the Council, General Ismet Pasha; Interior, Shukri (Şükrü) Kaya Bey; Finance, Mustafa Abdul Halik Bey; Public Works, Hilmi Bey; Foreign Affairs, Dr. Tevfik Rushdi (Rüştü) Bey; Justice, Yusuf Kemal Bey; Education, Essad (Esat) Bey; Public Health, Dr. Refik Bey; National Economy, Mustafa Şerif Bey; National Defense, Zekâi Bey

Dec. 31, Martial law proclaimed in Menemen

TURKISH SULTANS

1299–1301. Othman, Osman, or Ottoman, founded the empire, retained the title emir, but rules despotically

1326. Orchan, son, took the title "sultan"

1360. Amurath (or Murad) I; stabbed by a soldier, of which wound he died

1389. Bajazet I, Ilderim, son; defeated by Tamerlane, and died imprisoned

1403. Solyman, son: dethroned by his brother

1410. Musa-Chelebi: strangled

1413. Mahomet I, son of Bajazet

1421. Amurath II, son

1451. Mahomet II, son: took Constantinople, 1453

1481. Bajazet II, son

1512. Selim I, son

1520. Solyman I or II, the Magnificent, son
1566. Selim II, son
1574. Amurath III, son: killed his five brothers; their mother, in grief, stabbed herself
1595. Mahomet III, son: strangled all his brothers, and drowned his father's wives
1603. Ahmed (or Achmet) I, son
1617. Mustapha I, brother: deposed by the Janissaries and imprisoned
1618. Osman II, nephew; strangled by Janissaries
1622. Mustapha I again: again deposed, sent to the Seven Towers, and strangled
1623. Amurath IV, brother of Osman II
1640. Ibrahim, brother: strangled by the Janissaries
1648. Mahomet IV, son: deposed by
1687. Solyman II or III, brother
1691. Ahmed (or Achmet) II, son of Ibrahim, nephew
1695. Mustapha II, eldest son of Mahomet IV: deposed
1703. Ahmed (or Achmet) III, brother: deposed, and died in prison in 1736
1730. Mahmud I (or Mahomet V), son of Mustapha II
1754. Osman III, brother
1757. Mustapha III, brother
1774. Abdul-Ahmed or Hamid I (or Achmet IV) brother
1789. Selim III, son of Mustapha III; deposed by the Janissaries
1807. Mustapha IV, son of Abdul-Ahmed; deposed, and, with the late sultan Selim, murdered
1808. Mahmud II, or Mahomet VI, brother
1839. Abdul-Medjid (son), July 2 (born April 23, 1823); died June 25, 1861
1861. Abdul-Aziz, brother, born Feb. 9, 1830, deposed May 29; alleged suicide June 4, 1876 (*see* 1881)
1876. Amurath V (Murad) son of Abdul-Medjid, born Sept. 21, 1840; proclaimed May 30; deposed for bad health, Aug. 31; died Aug. 29, 1904
———. Abdul-Hamid II, brother, Aug. 31, born Sept. 22, 1842; deposed, April 27, 1900
1909. Mahomed V, brother, born 1844; succeeds, April 27, 1909; died July 3, 1918
1918. Mohammed VI, brother, Vahid-ed-Din (Valud-ed-din); declared deposed Nov. 23, 1922

TURKMENISTAN

(TURKOMAN SOVIET SOCIALIST REPUBLIC)

The Turkoman Soviet Socialist Republic was formed in February, 1925, and covers the territory of the former Trans-Caspian Region of Turkestan, the Charjiui vilayet of Bokhara, and a part of Khiva situated on the right bank of the Oxus. In May, 1925, the Turkoman Republic entered the Soviet Union as one of its Constituent Republics. It is bounded on the north by the Autonomous Kaizak Republic (Kirghizia), by Persia and Afghanistan on the south, by the Uzbek Republic on the east and the Caspian Sea on the west.

The principal Turkoman tribes are the Tekkés of Merv, and the Tekkés of the Attok, the Ersaris, Yomuds, and Goklans. All speak closely related varieties of Jagatai Turkish, and they are Sunni Mohammedans. The country passed under Russian control in 1881, after the fall of the Turkoman stronghold of Gök-Tépé.

The area of Turkmenistan is 491,200 square kilometers (189,603 square miles), and its population 1,030,549. The Turcomans form about 70% of the population and the Uzbeks about 16%.

The capital is Ashkabad (Poltaratsk), and other large towns are Merv, Charjiui, Kerki, Tashauz.

UZBEKISTAN

The Uzbek Soviet Socialist Republic was formed on December 5, 1924, from lands formerly included in Turkestan, Bokhara, and Khorezm. It includes a large part of the Samarkand region, the southern part of the Sir-Darya, Western Fhergana, the Western Plains of Bokhara, and the Uzbek regions of Khorezm. In May, 1925, Uzbekistan, by the decision of the Congress of Soviets of the U.S.S.R., was accepted as an equal member into the Soviet Union.

Uzbekistan lies between 36° 40′ N. latitude and 59° 50′–75° E. longitude. It is bordered on the north by the Kazak Autonomous Republic, on the east by the Kirghiz Autonomous Republic and Chinese Turkestan, on the south by Afghanistan, and on the west by the Turkoman Soviet Socialist Republic.

The area is 195,246 square kilometers (174,686, square miles). The population on January 1, 1930 of Uzbekistan (excluding Tajikistan) was 4,584,-911, of whom about one-fifth lived in towns. The capital of the Republic is Tashkent (population on January 1, 1930, 702,000); other important cities are Bokhara, Khiva, Andijan, Kokand, Namanghan, Samarkand.

The Uzbeks, who form the majority of the population over the area of the old States of Khiva and Bokhara, and the Provinces of Samarkand and Ferghana, were the ruling race in Central Asia, until the arrival of the Russians during the third quarter of the nineteenth century. The several native States over which Uzbek dynasties formerly ruled were founded in the fifteenth century upon the ruins of Tamerlane's empire. The Uzbeks speak Jagatai Turkish, which is clearly related to Osmanli and Azerbaijan Turkish, and are Sunni Mohammedans.

YANAON

Yanaon, French territory in Madras, India; area 5 square miles; population, 4,816 (1929).

YEMEN

See Arabia.

AUSTRALASIA AND OCEANIA

Australasia (Southern Asia) includes Australia with Papua, Norfolk Island, and Tasmania, New Zealand, and adjacent islands, and Fiji, the Bismarck Archipelago, New Caledonia, and New Hebrides. Australasia is a division of Oceania but the name is loosely used as the equivalent of Oceania comprising the "oceanic" Pacific islands as distinguished from the coastal archipelagoes. Oceania is, according to many geographers the fifth division of the world, comprising all the Pacific islands classified as to races found in occupation when Europeans first entered these regions as Melanesia, Micronesia, and Polynesia: Melanesia, the islands in the western and south-central area including New Guinea, the Louisiade, Solomon, Santa Cruz, New Hebrides, New Caledonia, Loyalty, and Fiji islands; Micronesia, the islands north and somewhat east of Melanesia including the Marianas, Palau (Pelew), Caroline, Marshall, and Gilbert islands; Polynesia, the eastern islands including Hawaii, the Ellice, Phœnix, Union, Manihiki, Marquesas, Cook, Society, Tubuai, and Tuamotu groups.

AUSTRALIA

Australia is the smallest continent and the largest island on the globe with total area of 2,974,581 square miles, lying southeast of Asia at a distance of 1,800 miles between the Indian and Pacific Oceans, and is situated wholly in the southern hemisphere. The Dutch historian, Wytfliet, in 1597 described the "Terra Australis" as the most southern lands, and North West Australia appeared on Dieppe maps about 1536. The first discoverer of Australia was the captain of the *Duyfhen* (Dove) Dutch navigator from Java in 1606 who entered the Gulf of Carpentaria and reached Cape Keerweer, followed by Dirck Hartog in 1616, Edel and Houtman in 1619 followed by others, and the name New Holland given to the west coast. The first English navigator to visit Australia was William Dampier in 1688. Captain Cook sighted the eastern coast April 19, 1770 at Cape Everard, Botany Bay, April 28, named for the variety of new plants obtained there and took formal possession of the land for Great Britain, and proceeded northward examining the east coast from Tasmania to Torres Straits. In 1792 A. J. d'Entrecasteaux touched at more than 300 points on the south and west coasts. In Jan., 1788, Commodore Philip, commissioned to found a penal colony, founded the city of Sydney, which he named Port Jackson. In 1824 the name New Holland changed to Australia.

The Commonwealth of Australia, consisting of the six colonies (now denominated Original States) of New South Wales, Victoria, Queensland, South Australia, Western Australia, and Tasmania, was proclaimed on January 1, 1901. Canberra is the federal capital.

On September 1, 1906, the administration of Papua was transferred to the Commonwealth (*see* Papua, p. 954). Other dependency of Australia, Norfolk Island.

Mandated territories assigned to Australia are the Bismarck Archipelago, the Solomon Islands, and New Guinea.

Sir Isaac Alfred Isaacs, Governor General.

STATES AND TERRITORIES	AREA	POPULATION [1] (CENSUS—APRIL 4, 1921)		ESTIMATED JUNE 30, 1929
			Per 100 Sq. Miles	
	Sq. Miles			
New South Wales	309,432	2,100,371	679	2,462,421
Victoria	87,884	1,531,280	1,742	1,767,539
Queensland	670,500	755,972	113	927,092
South Australia	380,070	495,160	130	579,415
Western Australia	975,920	332,732	34	411,734
Tasmania	26,215	213,780	815	212,512
Northern Territory	523,620	3,867	0.7	4,170
Federal Capital Territory	940	2,572	274	8,336
Total	2,974,581	5,435,734	183	6,373,219

[1] Excluding full blood aboriginals. These are estimated to number about 60,000. The nomadic habits of the tribes in the wild state render close computation difficult.

1788

Jan., Captain Arthur Phillip, commissioned to found a penal colony, and the first Governor, landed at Botany Bay after eight months voyage from England
Jan. 26, The present city of Sydney founded which Captain Phillip named Port Jackson
October, Colony founded at Norfolk Island

1792

Resignation of Governor Phillip broken in health. Succeeded by Lieutenant Governors Grose and Paterson

1795

Sept., Captain John Hunter, new Governor, arrived (1795–1800)

1797

John Macarthur imported merino sheep from the Cape and began the sheep breeding which eventually made Australia a solvent nation

1798

Discovery of Bass's Straits by Bass and Flinders

1800

Captain Philip G. King, Governor (1800–1806)
Grant, 1800, and Flinders survey the coasts of Australia (1801–5)

1804

Insurrection of Irish convicts, chiefly political offenders, quelled

1806

William Bligh, Governor, captain of the "Bounty" whom the mutineers set adrift in a small boat 3,300 miles from the Timor in 1789

1808 to 1834

1808, Governor Bligh for his tyranny deposed and sent home
1809, Superseded by Governor Macquarie
1813, Expeditions into the interior by Wentworth, Lawson, Bloxland; Oxley, &c., 1817–1823
1821, Population, 29,783 (three-fourths convicts)
1829, West Australia formed into a province
——, Legislative council established
1828–31, Sturt's expeditions into South Australia
1831–36, Sir T. Mitchell's expeditions into E. Australia
Aug., 1834, South Australia erected into a province

1835

Sept., First Roman Catholic bishop (Polding) arrives
Nov., Port Phillip (now Victoria) colonized

1836

June, First Church of England bishop of Australia (Broughton) arrives
Dec., Colony of South Australia founded
1836–7, Eyre's expedition overland from Adelaide to King George's Sound

1837

April, Melbourne founded
1837–39, Capt. Grey explores N.W. Australia

1839

Count Strzelecki explored New South Wales and Tasmania, 1838–43; discovered gold-fields in Bath-

urst, Wellington, &c. (kept secret by Sir George Gipps)
Suspension of transportation

1840

Strzelecki explores the Australian Alps; discovers Gipps' land; Eyre explores west Australia

1841

1841–46, Great exertions of Mrs. Chisholm; establishment of "Home for Female Emigrants"
Census—87,200 males; 43,700 females

1842

Numerous insolvencies
Incorporation of city of Sydney

1843 to 1846

1843, Landor and Lefroy explore Western Australia
1845, Sturt proceeds from South Australia to the middle of the continent
1846, Census (including Port Phillip)—114,700 males; 74,800 females

1847

Kennedy's 1st expedition, Aug. 13; killed Nov. 13, 1848

1848

April 3, Dr. Leichhardt's expedition leaves Moreton bay, Aug., 1844; arrives at Port Essington, Dec. 17, 1845: starts again, not heard of after
1848, 1855–58, A. C. Gregory, accompanied by Ferdinand von Mueller as botanist explored the north and interior

1849

Great agitation against transportation, which had been revived by Earl Grey

1850

Port Phillip erected into a separate province as Victoria

1851

Feb. 12, Gold discovered by Edward Hargreaves
Census—males, 106,000; females, 81,000 (exclusive of Victoria, 80,000)

1853

March, Mints established
Transportation ceased

1858

July, Death of Archdeacon Cowper (aged 80), after about fifty years' residence
1858–62, J. M'Douall Stuart's expeditions

1859

Dec. 4, Queensland made a province

1860

Aug., Expedition into the interior under Mr. Landells organized
Aug. 20, Robert O'Hara Burke, Wm. John Wills, and others, start from Melbourne

1861

Nov., Burke, Wills, and two others, cross the Australian continent to the gulf of Carpentaria; all perish on their return, except John King, who arrives at Melbourne

1861–62, Stuart, M'Kinlay, and Landsborough cross Australia from sea to sea

1865

Jan. 26, Cessation of transportation to Australia in three years announced amid much rejoicing

April, Morgan, a desperate bushranger and murderer, surrounded and shot

April 19, Boundary disputes between New South Wales and Victoria, summer 1864; settled amicably

1866

Jan., Total population of Australia, exclusive of natives, 1,298,667

1867

March, Meeting of ministers from the Australian colonies at Melbourne to arrange postal communication with Europe

Nov., Exploration of South Australia; Capt. Cadell discovers mouth of the river Roper, and fine pastoral country, lat. 14° S.

1871

July 13, Despatch from Lord Kimberley objecting to the complex tariffs between the Australian colonies

Sept. 27, Meeting of delegates from New South Wales, Victoria, South Australia, and Tasmania; they object to imperial interference with their mutual fiscal arrangements

1883

June, Completion of the direct railway between Melbourne and Sydney

Gradual formation of a defensive Australian fleet and army

Dec. 6, The Intercolonial conference of delegates on proposed annexation of New Guinea, at Sydney, recommended; and the formation of an Australasian federal council, Dec. 7; closes Dec. 8

1884

Jan. 1, Canon Barry consecrated Bishop of Sydney and Metropolitan of Australia

Jan., Mr. Charles Winnicke's exploring party mapped 40,000 miles of unknown country, announced

About Nov. 1, Victoria, Tasmania, and Queensland accept the scheme of federation, Aug.; opposed by New South Wales

Dec. 11, Lord Derby's dispatch deferring consideration of the federal scheme

Dec., Several states protest against the German annexations in New Guinea, &c.

1885

Jan., British flag hoisted on Woodlark and other islands

Feb., The Australian colonies proffer military contingents for the Soudan

Aug. 14, Federal council of Australasia act passed

Dec. 9, Federation of the Australasian Colonies, except New South Wales and New Zealand, completed. The formal opening of the council took place at Hobart, Jan. 25, 1886. The council met at Hobart on Jan. 16–19, 1888; again Jan. 29–Feb. 4, 1889

1888

June 14–16, Australasian Conference requests the British Government to treat with China for restriction of Chinese immigration, but recommends immediate local action

Aug. 13, Imperial defense: an act for defraying the expenses of carrying into effect an agreement for naval defense with the Australasian colonies, and providing for the defense of certain ports and coaling stations, and for making further provision for imperial defense, passed. Changes made by the Finance Act of July, 1894

1890

Feb. 5, Australian warships launched at Newcastle-on-Tyne; *Pelorus*, Nov. 25, 1889, *Persia*

Feb. 6, Conference of delegates from all the Australian colonies at Melbourne to consider a scheme of Australasian federation and federal defense; Mr. Duncan Gillies elected chief representative

Feb. 13, Sir H. Parkes' motion for the union of the colonies under one government unanimously adopted

Feb. 14, Loyal address to the Queen voted, and the meeting of a national convention in 1891 agreed to

1891

Jan. 1, Mr. Goschen's plan for uniform colonial postage (2½d.) accepted by all the colonies, reported May–June, 1890, to begin

Jan. 20–24, The federal council meets at Hobart; Victoria, Queensland, and Tasmania represented; an address to the Queen respecting trade voted

March 2, National Australasian Federation Convention, chief delegates: New South Wales, Sir Henry Parkes; Victoria, Hon. James Munro; Queensland, Sir Samuel Griffith; South Australia, Hon. Thomas Playford; Tasmania, Hon. P. O. Fysh; New Zealand, Sir George Grey; Western Australia, Hon. John Forrest; Sir Henry Parkes elected president; Sir Samuel Griffith, vice-president; meeting in the legislative chamber, Sydney, 11 A.M. At the evening banquet, principal toast, "One people, one destiny"

April 1, The title, the "Commonwealth of Australia," adopted by the convention (26 to 13)

July 21, The federal constitution adopted, April 9, to be accepted by the several colonies and confirmed by the British parliament. The Victoria parliament requires the title to be changed from "Commonwealth" to "Federation"

1892

March 14, Mr. David Lindsay, commander of the exploring expedition in N. and Central Australia, fitted out by Sir Thomas Elder, arrives at Esperance bay, Oct. 14, 1891; members resign; reported Jan. 13, and the expedition is suspended, reported

Nov. 1, The Commonwealth bill passed in South Australia, about

Autumn, Committee to consider Australasian federation appointed, Lord Brassey chairman, Mr. Arnold-Forster, Lord Lamington, Lord Playfair, Lord Reay, Sir Charles Tupper, and others, reported

1893

Feb. 3, The federal council meets at Hobart, Jan. 26; the commonwealth bill approved; closed

May 27, Twelve Australian banks stop payment.

reported May 17, 1893; conference of colonial premiers at Melbourne; a common action adopted

July 31, The Australian Federation conference opened at Sydney

1895

Jan. 23, The Australasian federation league meets at Melbourne; chairman, Sir John Madden, Chief Justice of Victoria; federation of the states approved

Jan. 30, A conference of premiers at Hobart, Jan. 29; resolution adopted; a convention of 10 delegates from each colony proposed; charged to frame a federal constitution to be submitted to the Queen after approval by the colonies

Jan. 31, Australasian federal council opened at Hobart by Visc. Gormanston, Governor of Tasmania

1896

Jan. 12, All the Australian governments telegraph their approval to Lord Salisbury of the action of his government with regard to the Transvaal (see s.v.) and promise support

Dec., The Horn scientific expedition to Central Australia, May, 1894; returned in Aug., report issued

1897

Jan. 26 et seq., Australian federal council meets at Hobart, Sir John Forrest president

Feb. 2–4, Conference of premiers at Hobart

March 22, Australian federal convention meets at Adelaide, Mr. C. C. Kingston (S. Australia) elected president; delay allowed to Queensland

April 23, New constitution adopted; constitutional, finance, and judiciary committees appointed, March 31; draft constitution bill presented by Mr. Barton, April 12; carried

Nov. 27, The Australasian federation enabling act approved Feb. 6, 1895; amendment bill passed at Sydney, reported

1898

March 16, Federal convention meets at Sydney, Sept. 2–24, 1897; final session at Melbourne, Jan. 20; the federation (commonwealth) bill, adopted

1899

Jan. 25, Federal demonstration at Melbourne, on the anniversary of the foundation of Australia

Jan. 28–Feb. 2, Premiers' conferences on federation, in Melbourne, result in agreement

Aug., Australian naval conference in favor of a naval reserve, &c., at Melbourne

Sept., Address to the Queen from all legislatures, except Western Australia, praying for the adoption of the commonwealth bill and the grant of a federal constitution

Dec. 16–Feb., 1901, Loyal support of the Imperial government in the S. African war; contingents sent

1900

Jan. 24 and April 19, Premiers' conference on proposed amendments to the federation bill at Sydney

March 27, Federal delegates received by the Queen at Windsor

May 14, Commonwealth bill introduced into the Commons

July 9, Commonwealth of Australia Constitution Act, uniting the 6 Australasian colonies (New Zealand excepted), royal assent given

End July, Commonwealth bill adopted by a referendum, in W. Australia, federation completed

Dec. 15, Lord Hopetoun appointed Gov.-Gen., July 14; arrived at Sydney

Dec. 30–Jan., 1901, First federal cabinet formed: Mr. Edmund Barton, Premier (June 26, 1902) and Minister for External Affairs; Mr. Deakin, Att.-General; Sir W. Lyne, Home; Sir Geo. Turner, Treasurer; Mr. Kingston, Commerce; Mr. Dickson, Defense (Knt. Jan. 1, died Jan. 10, 1901); Sir John Forrest, Defense; J. Drake, Postmaster-Gen.

1901

Jan. 1, Lord Hopetoun installed Governor-Gen. of the Commonwealth at Sydney

March 29, 30, Elections for the first Commonwealth parliament

May 9, The first Parliament consisting of the (King) represented by the Governor-General Lord Hopetoun, a senate or upper-house, composed of 6 senators from each of the 6 states (elected for 6 years), and a house of representatives (more varied) composed of 75 members, total 111, opened in state by the Duke and Duchess of Cornwall, in the exhibition building at Melbourne

——, Sir R. Baker elected President of the Senate and Mr. F. W. Holder Speaker of the House of Representatives; the Houses then adjourned

May 21, The federal parliament meets, Melbourne

Oct. 8, Sir George Turner's budget, high tariff bill, new duties, partly fixed and partly ad valorem, on tea, sugar, alcohol, and tobacco, introduced

Nov. 15, Immigration restriction bill read, third time, in the House of Representatives, Oct. 9; read second time in the Senate

Nov. 27, Mr. Reid's motion of want of confidence on the tariff proposals rejected, after 27 hours' debate, 39–25, Nov. 1; midnight sittings on the tariff bill, 33 hours

1902

May, Lord Hopetoun's resignation accepted

May 15, 16, Conference of state premiers at Melbourne

Mid May, Lord Hopetoun resigns; created Marquis of Linlithgow, June 26; sends farewell letters and thanks to the Australian people; leaves Brisbane, July 16; succeeded by Lord Tennyson for 1902–03, July 17

Aug. 26, Enormous loss of sheep and lambs through the drought, reported

Sept. 7, Day of humiliation and prayer for rain

Sept. 9, Commonwealth tariff bill passed by the Senate

Sept. 10, 11, General rainfall reported

1903

April 15, Conference of premiers, Sydney

Mid Aug., Resignation of Mr. Kingston, Home Minister, succeeded by Sir Wm. Lyne, rearrangement in ministry

——, Lord Northcote appointed to succeed Lord Tennyson in Dec., announced

Aug. 25, Senate passed the Naval Agreement bill, 20,000l. yearly for 10 years to Imperial navy

——, High court established by royal assent

Sept. 9, Defeat of Government on an amendment to the Conciliation bill

Sept. 10, Sir E. Barton announces bill dropped for the session

Sept. 24, Sir Samuel Griffith appointed federal chief justice, with Sir E. Barton and R. O'Connor judges of the high court; Sir E. Barton resigns the premiership, ministry reconstructed by Mr. Deakin, reported

Oct. 22, Parliament prorogued

Dec. 16, Elections for new federal parliament; increase of the Labor Party, the strength of the parties in the last and new parliament being, Senate: Ministerialists 12, new 6; Opposition 16, new 13; Labor Party 8, new 17. House of Representatives: Ministerialists 32, new 27; Opposition 27, new 26; Labor Party 16, new 29. Owing to representation being governed by population, which, since the previous election, has increased, the House of Representatives has now 7 more members, the members being 82 instead of 75

1904

Jan. 21, Lord Northcote, new governor-general, arrives at Melbourne, and is sworn in

Feb. 5, Conference between the federal treasurer and state treasurer opens; principal subjects of discussion, the proposed transfer of the state debts to the Commonwealth and the best method of encouraging immigration

Feb. 13, Dr. Deakin, Premier, at the conference of state treasurers, calls attention to the deficiency of population; he offers suggestions for advertising the attractions of Australia, and impresses the fear that labor influence, as in the Immigration Restriction Act, had an unfavorable effect

Feb. 19, Mr. Deakin, Federal Premier, addressing the conference of state treasurers, makes proposals for the encouragement of immigration from Great Britain; conference unable to come to terms regarding the assumption of state debts by the Commonwealth, owing to divergent views of the different states

March 2, Federal parliament opens; Lord Northcote, Governor-General, in his speech from the throne says, that preferential trade would secure to Australia an immense stable market, and refers to the necessity of encouraging immigration and to the appointment of a high commissioner

March 3, Mr. Deakin in the house declares the Government's readiness to support Great Britain, even to the point of sacrifice, as regards tariffs in order to obtain reciprocal preferences from the mother country

March 22, Iron bounties bill introduced in the House by Sir Wm. Lynn, Minister of Trade and Customs

April 21, Federal government defeated in House of Representatives by 38 votes to 29, on an amendment by Mr. Fisher of the Labor Party, making the arbitration bill applicable to state employés

April 26, Resignation of Mr. Deakin, succeeded by Mr. Watson, who forms a labor ministry; all members of the cabinet, except Mr. Higgins, Attorney-Gen., members of the Labor Party; arbitration bill proceeded with, clauses being added, making it applicable to railway employés and other Commonwealth state servants

May 18, Parliament adjourns until

——, Mr. Watson, Premier, announces in the House of Representatives the general program of the government and its legislative program, which includes the resumption of the arbitration bill with clauses including state employés, a capital site bill, and a

bill for appointing a high commissioner in London; measures would also be introduced for federal old age pensions, and the establishment of state control over the tobacco trade

June 1, House of Representatives by 36 votes to 24 agrees to Mr. Watson's amendment to include railway servants in the scope of the arbitration bill

July 19, Watson government defeated by 26 votes to 22 on a motion to insert a clause in the arbitration bill to include oversea shipping

Aug. 9, House of Representatives select Dalgety, in the Bombala district of New South Wales, 286 miles south of Sydney, on the Snowy river, for the federal capital

Aug. 12, Government defeated by 36 votes to 34 on motion to recommit a clause in the arbitration bill giving preference to trade unionists; resignation of Mr. Watson, who unsuccessfully makes a request to the Governor-General for a dissolution

Aug. 17, Mr. Reid forms a cabinet, himself as Premier and Minister of Internal Affairs; Sir Geo. Turner as Treasurer

Sept. 7, Mr. Reid states that the Government would respect the people's decision in favor of fiscal peace, and would await some definite proposal from the imperial government respecting preference; the conciliation bill would be taken up at stage left by the late ministry; the appointment of a high commissioner would be left over until next session

Nov. 25, Scheme of national defense, providing for a council of defense to include expert members with consultative powers, supervising naval and military administrative boards, the latter being separate from the executive command, passes House of Representatives

1905

Feb. 17, Conference of federal and state ministers at Hobart concludes its sittings. States by majority of 4 to 2 (Queensland and New South Wales) accept Sir George Turner's modified proposals with regard to state debts, whereby the Braddon clause is to be extended for 30 years from 1911, and the whole of the state debts are to be taken over by the Commonwealth whenever arrangements can be made, all future loans to be raised through the Commonwealth Government; states to be at liberty to raise loans within the Commonwealth. Decisions of conference to be ratified by the legislators of the states before actually coming into force

July 5, New commonwealth cabinet formed by Mr. Deakin, Prime Minister and Minister of External Affairs, Mr. Isaacs, Attorney-General, Sir J. Forrest, Treasurer

Nov. 10, Bills to amend the immigration laws, with special reference to Hindoos and Japanese, introduced by the Premier

Nov. 23, Federal House of Representatives discuss and adopt, by 30 votes to 20, the closure proposals of the Government, to carry certain clauses in the government's trade marks bill, which provides that goods shall be labeled, so as to indicate those made wholly by trade union labor

1906

Jan. 1, The different states having agreed to prohibit the sale and growth of opium, the Commonwealth Government prohibits the importation of the drug, except for medicinal purposes

Jan. 15, Total value of the wool clip for 1905 estimated at 18,500,000*l.*, an increase of 3,000,000*l.* as compared with that of 1904

March 1, Return of the electoral census taken Dec. 11, 1905, shows the population of the Commonwealth 4,002,893; New South Wales, 1,483,393; Victoria, 1,214,098; Queensland, 506,935; South Australia, 372,768; Western Australia, 247,072; Tasmania, 178,627, reported

Mid. March, Report of the Federal navigation commission strongly favors preferential treatment of British ships if carrying British goods, or manned by British sailors, issued

April 5, Conference of Australian premiers opened at Sydney (Western Australia not represented); resolutions passed favorable to the promotion of immigration

April 13, Immigrants into Australia during 1905 numbered 48,836, and the emigrants from numbered 46,620, an excess in arrivals of 2,216

May 21, Visit of the Japanese squadron

July 2, Trade marks act, 1905, came into operation

July 11, New mail contract between the Commonwealth Government and Sir Jas. Laing and Sons, of Sunderland; the yearly subvention to be 125,000*l.*, with an increase for acceleration

July 12, Wireless telegraphy inaugurated by the Marconi Company between Victoria and Tasmania

Sept. 5, Anti-trust bill passed by the Senate

Sept. 13, The Commonwealth House of Representatives approves the preferential tariff treaty with New Zealand

Sept. 25, The Federal House of Representatives passed a resolution to the effect that preference should only be given to British goods which are brought to Australia by British ships and manned by white labor

Oct. 9, South African preference treaty passed by the Federal Senate

Oct. 12, Parliament prorogued

Oct. 22, Great disappointment expressed in Sydney regarding the New Hebrides convention, and the Federal Government disclaims responsibility for the results. Sydney traders declare that the convention establishes French predominance at all the strategically important places, and endangers the British trade route between America and Australia

Nov. 23, Repatriation of the Kanakas.—Arrangements were made in August, to take place in September, and two shipments of Kanakas to the Solomon Isles were reported to have landed safely, while a third was on its way to the Solomon Isles and the New Hebrides

Nov. 30, Elections for the Legislative Assembly take place

Dec. 18, The final results of the elections to the Federal House of Representatives were as follows:—Deakinites, 19; Reidites, 16; Labor, 26; Anti-Labor, but supporting Mr. Deakin's policy, 14; announced

1907

Jan. 16, Exhibition of Australian products opened at Melbourne by the Governor-General

Feb. 15, Federal Premier gives permission for the importation of 1,000 Italians into Queensland to take the place of the Kanaka laborers on the N. Queensland sugar plantations now being repatriated

Feb. 20, Federal parliament opened in Melbourne by the Governor-General

Apr. 27, The 137th anniversary of Capt. Cook's landing in Australia celebrated in Sydney

May 26, Conference of state premiers for the purpose of reaching an agreement regarding the financial relations of the states and the Commonwealth and the problem of the states' debts, opened

June 19, Mr. Deakin and Sir Wm. Lyne arrive at Freemantle on their return from England

July 3, Federal parliament opened

July 30, Resignation of Sir John Forrest, Federal Treasurer

Aug. 8, New tariff proposals announced

Dec. 20, Bill finally passed by parliament authorizing the transfer of the northern territory of S. Australia to the Commonwealth

1908

Feb. 29, Death of Lord Linlithgow, first Governor-General of the Commonwealth, born 1860

March 19, Lord Dudley appointed Governor-General in succession to Lord Northcote

April 28, Conference of Australian state premiers assembles in Melbourne

June 10, The old age pensions bill passed

Visit of the American battleship fleet during its all-world cruise—at Auckland, Aug. 9–15; Sydney, Aug. 20–27; Melbourne, Aug. 29–Sept. 5; Albany, Western Australia, Sept. 11–18

Sept. 6, Lord Dudley arrives at Brisbane

Sept. 16, Parliament opened by Lord Dudley, who in his speech said that recent decisions of the high court necessitated an amendment of the constitution relating to the so-called "new protection"

Nov. 12, New cabinet formed in which Mr. Fisher, leader of the Labor Party in the federal parliament takes the offices of Premier and Treasurer

1909

March 5–12, Conference of Australian premiers opened at Hobart town

April 15, Old Age Pension Act proclaimed

May 23, Collapse of the Broken Hill strike, which lasted over 20 weeks and was estimated to have cost altogether 500,000*l.*, including 280,000*l.* in wages. The Port Pirie miners' unions decide to return to work on the terms of the Arbitration Court's award

May 26, Federal parliament opened by Lord Dudley, the Governor-General

May 27, Defeat of the Fisher Ministry

June 2, Resignation of the Fisher Ministry; Mr. Deakin undertakes the formation of a new cabinet

June 10, The Commonwealth's offer of a Dreadnought accepted by the Imperial Government

1910

End Jan., Death of Sir Chas. Todd, superintendent of telegraphs and government astronomer in South Australia from 1855 to 1906, aged 83

Feb. 9, The *Paramatta*, the first of three torpedo boat destroyers, built on the Clyde for the Australian Government, launched from the Fairfield yard at Govan

(Sydney) Feb. 18, Lord Kitchener issues his report on Australian defense. Lord Kitchener recommends the establishment of an army of a peace strength of 80,000, divided into a garrison force of 40,000 and a mobile force of 40,000, all to be enrolled, equipped and organized in the same way. The army will consist of 84 infantry battalions, 28 light horse regiments, 224 guns, 14 engineer companies, and departmental troops in proportion. This force will be provided from trained men of from 19 to 25 years of age. Trained men of 18 and 19 years old, and of 25 and 26 years old, are to be called up in war time, and to raise the strength of the force to 107,000. In addition to the training provided for by the new Defense Act, there will be six clear days' training, not including Sundays, every year for the men between 20 and 25 years of age. For the purposes of organization and training, the country must be divided into areas, each providing a definite proportion of the fighting unit, in charge of a permanent instruction officer. Ten areas will make a group, under a superior officer, who will be a brigade major in war-time. The whole of Australia is to be divided into 215 areas. The officer in command of the area will be the keystone of the citizen force. A military staff college is also recommended

Feb. 19, Third Parliament dissolved

Feb. 26, H. C. Reid appointed High Commissioner for Australia in London

March, End of the coal strike; work began

March 31, Dr. Wright, archbishop of Sydney, elected primate of Australia

April 1, Death of Bishop Barry, a former primate, aged 84

April 9, Launch of the torpedo-boat destroyer *Yarra*, second unit of the fleet of the Australian Commonwealth, at Dumbarton

April 13, The general election for the Commonwealth resulted in a victory for the Labor Party: Labor, 44 seats; Fusionists, 29; Independent Liberals, 2; referendum on constitutional amendment on financial relations between the Commonwealth and the States accepted providing that State public debts could be taken over by the Commonwealth if incurred even after the establishment of the Commonwealth, and the second proposal relating to allocation of customs and excise revenue between the Commonwealth and the States was rejected

April 19, Resignation of Mr. Deakin

April 29, The Fisher Ministry, with Mr. Fisher Prime Minister and Treasurer, formed

Acts for the government of Australia, 10 Geo. IV c. 22, May 14 (1829), 6 & 7 Will. IV c. 68, Aug. 13 (1836), 13 & 14 Vict. c. 59, Aug. 5 (1850). Act for regulating the sale of waste lands in the Australian colonies, 5 & 6 Vict. c. 36, June 22 (1842)

July 1, Fourth Parliament opened

Nov. 17, Land Tax Act placed assessment on unimproved values

Nov. 25, Emigration Act provided regulations as to young persons and aboriginal natives

——, Naval Defense Act

1911

Jan. 1, Northern Territory formally passed under control of the Commonwealth according to Agreement of Dec. 7, 1907, passing from jurisdiction of South Australia

Feb. 16, Act established the University of Western Australia which was opened in March

March 14, University of Queensland opened at Brisbane

April 3, Decennial census gave total population as 4,455,005

April 4, The first war ship built in Australia, the "Warrego" launched at Sydney

April 26, Referendum to extend the powers of the Commonwealth defeated in rejections of amendments to the Constitution as to trade and commerce, control of corporations, labor and employment, and control of monopolies

May 1, Adoption of penny postage to all parts of the British Empire adopted

July 1, Compulsory military and naval training inaugurated

July 31, Thomas, Baron Denman inaugurated Governor General

Oct. 25, Battleship "Australia" launched on the Clyde; arrived in Australia, June, 1913

1912

June 20, Motion of censure of financial policy of the Government defeated by vote of 35 to 25

Oct. 9, Maternity Act allowed a bonus paying a maximum of £5 for every child of white parents born in Australia

Dec. 24, Commonwealth Employment Compensation Act

1913

Jan. 20, Commonwealth Bank opened at Sydney

March 12, Foundation stone of new Federal Capital at Canberra laid by Lord Denman, Governor General

April 23, Parliament dissolved

May 31, General election resulted in a Liberal majority in the House but not in the Senate; referendum again defeated amendments to Constitution

June 24, Joseph Cook formed a Cabinet

July 9, Fifth Parliament opened

July 24, Foundation stone of Australia House, the Commonwealth headquarters in London laid by the King

Sept. 15, First sod of Trans-Australian railway from Port Augusta, South Australia, to Kalgoorlie, Western Australia, turned by the Governor General

1914

May 18, Sir Ronald Craufurd Munro Fergusson took office as Governor General

July 30, Both Houses of Parliament dissolved

Aug. 4, Great Britain declared war on Germany. *See* World War

Aug. 6 and 10, Exports of certain articles prohibited including copper and tin

Aug. 10, Navy placed at disposal of British Admiralty

Aug. 11, Australian troops landed at Simpsonhafen, New Britain

Aug. 19, Australian force left Sydney to seize German wireless stations and occupy German territory in the Pacific

Sept. 17, Election gave Labor Party, 42; Liberals, 32; Independents, 1

——, Third Fisher Government formed

Oct. 8, Sixth Parliament opened

Oct. 10, Conciliation and Arbitration Act of Dec. 15, 1904 amended and again on Dec. 7

Oct. 17, First Australian units embarked for France

Oct. 23, Act prohibited trading with the enemy

Oct. 29, War Precautions Act gave Government authority to deal with commerce during War

Nov. 1, Australian troops left for Egypt, disembarking at Alexandria Dec. 3

Nov. 6, German Island of Nauru occupied

Nov. 9, German cruiser "Emden" captured at Cocos Island by H.M.A.S. "Sydney"

Nov. 26, Trading with the Enemy Act amended

Dec. 21, War Pensions Act passed and Defense Act amended

1915

Feb. 17, The H.M.A.S. "Australia" joined the Grand Fleet

April 25–Dec. 19, Gallipoli campaign. *See* World War

Aug., First war loan at 4½%

Sept. 13, Act imposed a progressive tax on incomes

Sept. 17, New South Wales passed Meat Supply Act for imperial use

Oct. 26, Andrew Fisher, Prime Minister, resigned to become High Commissioner for Australia in London

Oct. 27, W. Morris Hughes became Prime Minister and Attorney General; Hugh Mahon, External Affairs; King O'Malley, Home Affairs; W. Webster, Postmaster-General; G. F. Pearce, Defense; F. G. Tudor, Trade and Customs; J. A. Jensen, Navy; W. G. Higgs, Treasurer; A. Gardiner, Vice-President of the Executive Council; E. J. Russell, Assistant Minister

1916

March 21, First Australian Corps began landing in France, the Second, June 7, the Third, Nov. 22

Oct. 27, Resignation of Mr. Higgs, Mr. Gardiner, and Mr. Russell from the Cabinet as protest against conscription

Oct. 28, Referendum defeated conscription by majority of 72,476 votes

Nov. 16, At meeting of Labor Party a resolution adopted withdrawing confidence from the Prime Minister, and Mr. Hughes walked out followed by 24 members who approved his conscription policy

Nov. 17, Hughes formed second Cabinet after resignation of anti-conscriptionist Ministers

Record wheat harvest for the year of 180,000,000 bushels

1917

Feb. 16, Commonwealth Shipping Board established

Feb. 17, National War Government formed by Mr. Hughes, a coalition Cabinet including Joseph Cook

May 5, Elections gave Government a reduced majority

June 14, Seventh Parliament opened

July 27–Sept. 19, Strike of Amalgamated Society of Engineers refusing to work under card system of checking individual work settled by allowing access to cards

July 30, Wharf laborers at Victoria began strike which extended to other States and seriously affecting shipping

Sept. 22, War Profiteering Act passed

Oct. 17, Railroad between Port Augusta and Kalgoorlie completed connecting South and West Australia

Dec. 20, Second referendum on question "Are you in favor of the proposal of the Commonwealth Government for reinforcing the Australian imperial force overseas?" defeated by negative majority of 166,588

1918

Jan. 9, Resignation of National War Cabinet of Mr. Hughes but reconstituted the following day: Prime Minister and Attorney-General, W. M. Hughes;

Navy, Sir J. Cook; Public Works and Railways, L. E. Groom; Home and Territories, P. McM. Glynn; Postmaster-General, W. Webster; Defense, G. F. Pearce; Customs, M. Greene; Treasurer, W. A. Watt; Vice-President of the Executive Council, E. J. Russell; Repatriation, E. D. Millen; Honorary Ministers, A. Poynton, Mr. Wise, Mr. Orchard

Jan. 10, Conscription referendum against defeated draft, vote 945,000 in favor and 1,121,000 against

May, Australian troops in France formed into an Army Corps commanded by Lieutenant General Sir John Monash

June 30, Census gave total population as 4,980,565 not including aborigines variously estimated from 75,000 to 100,000

Sept. 3, Death of John Forrest, 1st baron of Bunbury at sea

Sept. 12, Death of Sir George H. Reid

Nov. 11, Armistice with Germany signed. Australia sent 329,883 troops over seas, and casualties of this force reached 314,078

Nov. 20, Resolution adopted by Parliament opposed return of colonies to Germany and insisted that Australia should be consulted as to their disposal

Nov. 21, Commonwealth Electoral Act consolidated and amended election laws

1919

April 3, Riots at Brisbane, Queensland where Russian Bolshevists attacked police and soldiers

May 7, Supreme Council assigned mandate for German possessions in the Pacific south of the equator except German Samoa to Australia, Nauru Island to Great Britain

May 15, Australian Workers' Union published a manifesto condemning the Workers' Industrial Union as an imitation of the American I.W.W.

July 2, Agreement signed with Great Britain and New Zealand for the administration of Nauru Island

——, Commercial Activities Act provided for continuation of war regulations as to dairy products, sugar, wool, flax, &c.

July 13, Seamens' strike in Melbourne and Sydney

Sept. 10, Australia ratified the Treaty of Versailles

Oct. 7, Death of Alfred Deakin, former Prime Minister

Oct. 10, Bill for alteration of the Constitution to provide for nationalization of monopolies passed Parliament

Oct. 28, Treaty of Versailles Act enabled provisions of Treaty to be carried out

——, Nauru Island Agreement Act approved Agreement of July 2

Nov. 12–Dec. 10, Prize of £10,000 offered by the Australian Government for first airplane flight from Great Britain to Australia within maximum time won by flight of Captain Sir Ross Smith from Hounslow aërodrome, England to Port Darwin, Australia in 27 days, 20 hours, and 20 minutes, about 11,500 miles

Dec. 13, Election gave Liberal and Nationalist Labor parties 35 seats, and Farmers' Party 11, while Labor and other anti-government groups received only 29

Dec. 19, Referendum regarding constitutional extension of Commonwealth powers in legislation and the nationalization of monopolies defeated both proposals

1920

Jan. 6, Death of Sir Edmund Barton, first Prime Minister

Jan. 10, Australia became original member of the League of Nations

Feb. 26, Eighth Parliament opened

March 25, Resolution as to tariff adopted increased duties on goods which could be manufactured in Australia

May 19, Act made provision for repatriation of Australian soldiers

May 26, Arrival of the Prince of Wales on visit to Australia

Aug. 9, Death of Sir Samuel Griffith, former chief justice

Sept. 13, Industrial Peace Acts signed; amended Dec. 2

Sept. 30, New Guinea Act made provision for acceptance of mandate

Oct. 6, Henry William, Baron Forster of Lepe took office as Governor General

Oct. 11, Arbitration (Public Service) Act amended Act of Dec. 15, 1904

Dec. 2, Aliens Registration Act passed

——, Nationality Act passed and Immigration Act amended

Dec. 17, Mandate of Australia for German New Guinea (Kaiser Wilhelm Land), the Bismarck Archipelago, part of the Solomon Islands and other former German South Pacific Islands confirmed and defined by the Council of the League of Nations

1921

April 4, Census gave population total 5,435,734 excluding full blood aboriginals estimated as about 60,000

May 9, Civil administration established in New Guinea, and other islands under mandate

July 12, Death of Harry G. Hawker, airman, killed in crash

Oct. 5, Death of John Storey, former Premier of New South Wales

Dec. 15, Tariff Act established a Tariff Board and provided for preference to goods produced in and shipped from the United Kingdom to Australia and for reciprocal tariff agreements with other countries

Dec. 16, Commonwealth Conciliation and Arbitration Act amended

Dec. 21, Hughes Cabinet reconstructed

1922

Jan. 10, Labor unions voted in favor of merger into one union

Feb. 9, Australia's single battle cruiser placed on reserve as a result of the Washington Conference Agreements and crew of 450 men dismissed

Feb. 22, Economic Conference of representatives of capital and labor at Sydney failed to reach agreement

April 6, First air route established between Derby and Geraldton, West Australia

Aug. 22, Prime Minister Hughes returned from visit to England

Sept. 1, Reciprocal tariff Agreement between Australia and New Zealand came into effect

Oct. 18, Superannuation Benefit Act amended

Nov. 6, Parliament dissolved

Dec. 10, Elections gave Nationalists (Hughes) 27 seats in House, Labor 29, and the Liberal Country Party 14, leaving the Government without a majority

1923

Feb. 3, Resignation of Premier Hughes

Feb. 9, Stanley Melbourne Bruce formed a Cabinet, the "Bruce-Page" administration, under agreement that Dr. Page, Treasurer, should act as Prime Minister in the absence of Mr. Bruce and the Nationalists to have 6 seats and the Country Party 5

Feb. 23, Death of John Greeley Jenkins, former Prime Minister of South Australia

Feb. 28, Ninth Parliament opened

March 23, Special Federal Tribunal at Sydney rejected demands of coal operators of New South Wales, Victoria, Queensland, and Tasmania for reduction of miners wages by one-third

Sept. 1, Air Force Act established regulations for government and organization of Royal Australian Air Force

——, Invalid and Old Age Pension Act amended

Oct. 30, Police strike at Melbourne, troops called out and special constables enrolled

1924

March 13, Decision of British Government not to proceed with naval base at Singapore a disappointment to Australians who regarded it as protection against the Japanese

April 12, H.M.A.S. "Australia" sunk in accordance with provisions of Washington Treaty

April 13, Death of Sir Walter Jeans, banker

July 25, Bill providing for compulsory voting in Federal elections passed third reading in House of Representatives

Oct. 8, Bankruptcy Act passed

1925

Jan. 12, Riots in Sydney because of activities of Shipping Labor Bureau to protect strike breakers during shipping strike

Feb. 28, Shipping Labor Bureau in Sydney abolished as demanded by trade unions

April 6, Prohibition referendum in West Australia defeated prohibition by 64,377 votes against to 35,806 in favor

April 8, Migration Agreement with Great Britain signed by which the Imperial Government to facilitate the settlement of 450,000 persons within 5 years

July 1, New silver currency put into circulation

Aug. 6, Seamen's strike ended

Aug. 21, Strike of British seamen in Australian ports against wage reduction which was joined by Australians in a sympathetic strike

Sept. 23, Immigration Restriction Act amending Act of 1901

——, Customs Act amended

Sept. 26, Invalid and Old Age Pension Act of June 10, 1908 amended

——, Electoral Act gave all native and naturalized residents the franchise including Indians

Oct. 3, Parliament dissolved

Oct. 8, John Lawrence, Baron Stonehaven, took office as Governor General

Oct. 13, Compulsory conference in seamen's strike

Oct. 31, Police strike

Nov. 14, Election a victory for the Nationalists and Country Party led by Premier Bruce

Nov. 29, Seamen's strike ended, strikers accepting terms and reduction of wages

Dec. 3, Announcement of removal of ban against immigration from Germany, Austria Hungary, Bulgaria, and Turkey

1926

Jan. 13, Tenth Parliament opened

March 16, Commonwealth Crimes Act (Amendment) passed over opposition of Labor

April 1, The Customs Tariff (Papua and New Guinea Preference) came into effect

——, Labor Party Conference at Sydney

June 30–Oct. 1, Flight of Alan Cobham from London to Australia and return, 28,000 miles

July 1, Reciprocal Customs Tariff with the Union of South Africa repealed

Aug. 16, Old Age Pension Act amended

Sept. 4, Referendum vote defeated constitutional amendments to give the Commonwealth power to regulate industry and commerce and to carry on public services in event of their interruption or threat of interruption

1927

Feb. 28, Commonwealth Arbitration Court reduced hours in engineering industry from 48 hours to 44

March 22, Major General Sir G. de L. Ryrie appointed to succeed Sir Joseph Cook as High Commissioner in London

April 8, States Grants Act abolished the per capita payments of the States to the Commonwealth as from June 30

April 16, Election a victory for the "Pact" (Liberal and Country) gaining 26 seats in House out of 46

May 9, Parliament opened by the Duke of York representing the King at the new capital, Canberra

Sept. 1–10, Strike of railroad employees in Queensland, all workers dismissed from service by proclamation of the Railway Commissioner because of the hostility of the union, but reinstated on signing agreement to obey regulations

Nov. 21–Dec. 7, Strike of dock workers in dispute between ship-owners organization and Waterside Workers Federation resulted in complete tie up of shipping

Dec. 27, Bank (Savings Bank) Amendment Act

1928

Feb. 7, Solo flight of Bert Hinkler from London, England to Port Darwin, 12,000 miles flying time 15½ days establishing record

Feb. 12, Industrial Peace Conference called by the Prime Minister

March 28, Speech of William Morris Hughes, former Premier, an attack on Italian immigration

May 15, Strike of ships cooks tied up 13 coast vessels

May 31–June 9, Captain Charles Kingford-Smith in monoplane "Southern Cross" began transpacific flight from California. See United States

June 9, The "Southern Cross" arrived at Brisbane from Suva, Fiji Islands, 1,762 miles in 19 hours and 18 minutes, entire flying time from the United States 81 hours and 19 minutes for 7,435 miles

June 13, The "Southern Cross" flew to Sydney and Melbourne

Sept. 1, Compulsory referendum vote in New South Wales and the Federal Territory defeated prohibition

Oct. 9, Parliament dissolved

Nov. 17, Election reduced Government majority

Nov. 21, Government resigned

Nov. 29, Cabinet reorganized

1929

March 2, Strike of miners in coal fields against reduction of wages in northern New South Wales which lasted until June, 1930

March 18, Tariff Board Act amended

March 25, Soldiers Repatriation Act amended

March 30, Death of Sir George Knibbs, statistician

March 31, Captain Kingsford Smith left Australia for England in the "Southern Cross" and was forced down in Australian desert but rescued after 12 days

May 31, Royal Commission appointed to investigate coal strike

June 25, Captain Charles Kingsford Smith began flight from Australia to England ending trip July 10, 12,000 miles in 12 days, 21 hours, and 18 minutes flying time

Aug. 9, Most-favored-nation commercial Treaty with Spain

Sept. 10, Bruce Government defeated on proposal to abolish Federal system of compulsory industrial arbitration

Sept. 16, Parliament dissolved

Oct. 10–19, Flight of Captain Kingsford Smith from England to Port Darwin, Australia

Oct. 12, Election a victory for Labor and defeat of Bruce Government; Labor, 46 seats; Nationalist, 14; Country Party, 10; Independent, 4; Country Party Progressive, 1

Oct. 21, Bruce Cabinet resigned

Oct. 22, James Henry Scullin formed Labor Cabinet as Prime Minister, and Minister for External Affairs and Industry; E. G. Theodore, Treasurer; A. Blakeley, Home Affairs; A. E. Green, Defense; Frank Brennan, Attorney General; J. A. Lyons, Postmaster General; Frank Anstey, Health and Repatriation; J. E. Fenton, Trade and Customs

Nov. 1, From this date the constitution of the forces for defense on a voluntary basis adopted instead of universal compulsory training in force since 1911

Nov. 20, Twelfth Parliament opened

Dec. 6, Miners rejected terms agreed upon by leaders

Dec. 16–17, 8,000 miners attacked strike breakers in mine in New South Wales kept open by the Government with voluntary labor

1930

Jan. 10, Mob of 3,000 union miners attacked strike breakers at Rothbury colliery New South Wales

Jan. 17, Agreement signed with Germany regarding liquidation of German property

March 12, Federal Parliament opened

April 1, Douglas Antarctic expedition reached Adelaide from the Antarctic

May 5–May 24, Solo flight of Miss Amy Johnson from England to Port Darwin, Australia, the first woman to make flight from England, 10,400 miles in less than 20 days

May 9–July 7, Strike of engineers at Electricity Commission Works, Victoria as protest against metal trade award by Commonwealth Court

June 23, Major Charles Kingsford Smith took off from Portmarnock, Ireland in monoplane "Southern Cross" at 11.27 P.M. and arrived at Harbor Grace, Newfoundland, June 25 at 6.56 A.M.

June 26, Major Kingsford Smith left Harbor Grace at 4 A.M. and arrived at Roosevelt Field, Long Island at 7.30 P.M.

July 4, Major Kingsford Smith landed at Oakland, California completing trip around the world begun May 31, 1928

——, Report of Royal Commission on purchase of Mungana mines found E. G. Theodore, Treasurer of the Commonwealth and former Premier of Queensland with 3 others guilty of fraud. E. G. Theodore resigned from the Cabinet

July 15–Aug. 12, Strike of shearers in New South Wales against reduction of wages

July 18, Bankruptcy Act of 1924 amended

Aug. 9, Superannuation Act amended

Aug. 14, Commonwealth Employees Compensation Act repealed that of 1912

Aug. 15, Award of Commonwealth Court of Conciliation and Arbitration reducing wages accepted

Aug. 18, Sales Tax Assessment Act placed tax on certain goods imported

——, Commonwealth Conciliation and Arbitration Act of 1904 amended

Oct. 3, Arthur Herbert Tennyson, Baron Somers, became Acting Governor General

Oct. 19, Major Charles Kingsford Smith reached Australia from England in the record flying time of 9 days and 23½ hours which was 5 days and 2½ hours better than the previous record

Nov. 8–Dec. 8, Strike of slaughtermen and employees of abattoirs against enforcement of 48 hour Act

Nov. 14, Strike of shearers begun in August in West Australia against reduction of wages ended

Nov. 29, Immigration Act amended

Dec. 2, Sir Isaac Alfred Isaacs, native-born Australian appointed Governor General to succeed Lord Stonehaven

NEW ZEALAND

New Zealand, British Dominion, consists of 3 principal islands, called respectively the North, the South and Stewart Islands, and attached islands, dependencies Chatham Islands, Auckland Islands, Cook Islands, Kermadec Islands, Ross Dependency, Union Islands (Tokelau). Small uninhabited outlying islands within the boundaries of New Zealand are: Campbell Island, the Three Kings Islands, the Bounty Islands, and the Snares Islands. The former German Samoan Islands now the Territory of Western Samoa, including Savaii and Upolu were assigned under mandate from the League of Nations dated Dec. 17, 1920, to be administered by New Zealand. New Zealand is about 1,200 miles east of Australia, area excluding the annexed islands is 103,722 square miles; North Island, 44,281 square miles; South Island, 58,092; Stewart Island, 670 square miles; Chatham Islands, 372 square miles; outlying islands, 307 square miles. The area set aside for native lands for the aboriginal inhabitants, the Maoris is 4,627,353 acres. The estimated population June 30, 1930, was 1,490,405, inclusive of Maoris, 67,311, but exclusive of inhabitants of Cook and other annexed Islands,

14,584, of the Tokelau Islands, 999, and of Western Samoa (mandated territory), 44,719. The population of North Island (census, 1926), 831,813, South Island (including Stewart and Chatham Islands, 512,656. Wellington on North Island is the capital.

New Zealand was discovered by the Dutch navigator, Abel Jansen Tasman Dec. 13, 1642, and was believed to be part of a southern continent. Captain Cook on his first voyage to the southern seas sighted the east coast of North Island Aug. 24, 1769 and coasted the island, anchoring in "Poverty Bay" Oct. 8, which he named because of his inability to get supplies, leaving it Oct. 11 and naming Portland Island as he sailed south, and Hawkes Bay, Cape Kidnappers, turning north at cape he named Cape Turnagain Oct. 17, and which he returned to four months later after he had circumnavigated North Island. Oct. 30 he named East Cape, and Hick's Bay, and at bay he named Mercury Bay on account of the transit of Mercury having been observed there he landed and took possession in the name of George the III for Great Britain. Jan. 16, 1770 he came to anchor in Ship Cove on south side of the Straits ever since known by his name as the discoverer, and again landed to take possession at place he named Queen Charlotte's Sound. On Feb. 23 he sighted the northwest point of South Island which he later named Cape Farewell when he left the country March 31. During 1769 de Surveille explored North Island but was not seen by Captain Cook. On Jan. 29, 1840, Captain Hobson landed in the Bay of Islands authorized to make treaties with the native chiefs and take possession for Queen Victoria. Treaties were made with chiefs ceding the lands on Feb. 6, the Treaty of Waitangi, and the Treaty was signed by 512 chiefs within 6 months. The country was at first a dependency of New South Wales, but was separated by Letters Patent in April, 1842. By Order in Council the Colony became a Dominion Sept. 26, 1907.

Lord Bledisloe, Governor General and Commander-in-Chief.

1839

The New Zealand Company founded for colonization, and the first settlements made in the neighborhood of Cook's Strait at Petone in the Hutt Valley, and at Te Aro (later known as Wellington) on the western shores of Port Nicholson

1840

Foundation of Auckland; Nelson and Taranaki (or New Plymouth), 1841; Otago, 1848; Canterbury, 1850

1847

Dec. 29, A charter, founded upon an act passed in 1846, creating powers, municipal, legislative, and administrative

1848

Dec. 20, This charter was not acted on; a legislative council opened by the Governor

1850 to 1859

1850, New Zealand company relinquish charter
1850-3, Settlement of Canterbury, South island, founded (capital Christchurch)
1852, New constitution granted
1857, Constitution modified
New bishoprics established: Christchurch, 1856; Nelson and Wellington, 1858; Waiapu, 1859

1860

March, Insurrection of the natives (Maoris) under a chief named William King (Wirrimu Kingi), arising out of disputes respecting the sale of land; the Bishop Selwyn and others consider the natives unjustly treated
March 14-28, Indecisive actions between the militia and volunteers and the Maoris
June 30, War breaks out at Taranaki; the British repulsed with loss
Aug. 3, Australian troops sent to New Zealand, under Gen. Pratt, land
Sept. 10, 19, Oct. 9, 12, Indecisive actions
Nov. 6, Gen. Pratt defeats the Maoris at Mahoetahi, and destroys their fortified places
Nov. 22, New Zealand colonists in England justify the conduct of the Governor
Dec. 29, The Maoris defeated; Jan. 23, Feb. 24, March 16-18, 1861

1861

March 19, The war ends: surrender of natives
June, Gold discovered at Otago, &c.
July, A native sovereignty proclaimed; 5,000 British soldiers in the island

1863

May 4, Natives attack a military escort and kill 8 persons
July 17, Waikato tribe driven from a fort
Aug., War spreads; natives construct rifle pits
Sept., Proposed confiscation of Waikato lands
Nov. 20, Gen. Cameron severely defeats the Maoris at Rangariri
Dec. 9, Continued success of Gen. Cameron; capitulation of the Maori king

1864

April 29, British attack on Galepa (the gate pah) repulsed with loss of officers and men
July, Loan of 1,000,000*l.* to New Zealand; guaranteed by parliament
Aug., Several tribes submit
Sept., Maori prisoners escape and form the nucleus of a new insurrection
Oct. 25, Sir George Grey issues proposals of peace
Nov. 24, Change of ministry and policy; seat of government to be removed from Auckland to Wellington on Cook's Strait

1865

Jan. 25, Maoris' attack on Cameron severely defeated; again, Feb. 25
March 2, Outbreak of the Pai Mariri or Hau-hau heresy, a compound of Judaism and paganism, amongst the Maoris; the Rev. C. S. Volkner mur-

dered and many outrages committed; proclamation of Governor Sir George Grey against it; it is checked by the agency of a friendly native chief We-tako, April
May 25, William Thompson, an eminent chief, surrenders on behalf of the Maori king
Aug., The Hau-haus beaten in several conflicts; the governor proclaims peace, Sept. 2; British troops about to leave, Sept. 15
Oct., The Marsoi treacherously kill the envoys of peace

1866

Bishopric of Dunedin, Otago, founded
Jan., General Chute subdues the Hau-haus
May 17, Murderers of Mr. Volkner executed
July 3, Governor announces cessation of the war
Dec. 28, Death of Wm. Thompson, the Maori chief

1868

Act relating to the government of New Zealand passed in the British parliament
July 4, Te Kooti, a chief, and about 150 Maori convicts, escape from Chatham island to the mainland; they repulse troops sent against them, Sept. 7; massacre the whites at Poverty bay, Nov. 10
Sept. 23, Geo. Samuel Evans (an eminent colonist, 1838-39) dies

1869

Jan. 5, Te Kooti and the rebels defeated by Col. Whitmore; 130 Maoris killed
Feb. 12, Massacre of settlers at Taranaki
Sept., Change of ministry; Hon. Mr. Fox's proposal to pay for British troops declined by the home government
Oct., Te Kooti, thrice defeated by the colonists and friendly natives, a fugitive
Oct. 7, Despatch from Earl Granville, insisting on the withdrawal of the British troops (18th regiment) causes much dissatisfaction
Nov. 8, Friendly interview between Mr. McLean and the Maori king's minister
1869-70, Increased demand for the New Zealand fibrous plant, *Phormium tenax*

1870

Jan. 22, Departure of the last British troops
Feb. 5, Te Kooti, refusing to surrender at discretion, Jan. 24, narrowly escapes
July 31, Te Kooti's party attacked and dispersed
Aug., Political union of the islands effected
Dec. 28, Murder of Mr. Todd, surveyor, by Maoris

1871

Nov., Te Kooti reported as living by plunder; acting as a fanatical potentate
University with three colleges established in

1872

March, Friendly meeting of Mr. McLean with Wirrimu Kingi and other chiefs, who submit to the British Government

1875

Feb., The Maori king (Tawhiao) submits to the British Government

1879

May 25, Disputes with the Maoris; they expel British settlers near New Plymouth, Taranaki; and plough the land

June 22, The settlers recover their land by force

Great influence of Erueti, now Te Whiti, a fanatical Christian Maori, aged 45; he supports Maori claims, but checks bloodshed

1881

Nov. 6, Te Whiti arrested for sedition, announced

Nov. 8, He counsels passive resistance

Nov. 17, 124 arrests, announced

Dec. 3, Difficulty peaceably settled, announced

1882

Sept. 7, Several Maori chiefs in London; received by the Prince of Wales, Aug. 17; sail for home

1883

March 8, Release of Te Whiti, John, and others

About May 7, Mahuki and 20 others sentenced to imprisonment for outrages

Dec., Communication between New Zealand and the Thames by steamers; time reduced to 40 days (14,000 carcases of sheep brought)

1884

June 2, Tawhaio, the Maori king, arrives in London; appeals for redress, referring to the treaty of Waitangi (1840), July 22; sails from Gravesend, Aug. 20

Aug. 30, Mr. H. A. Atkinson forms a ministry, Aug. 28; resigns

1886

March 12, Lieut. Bryce, colonial native minister, v. G. W. Rusden, for gross libel in "History of New Zealand," charging him with cruelty, &c., to the Maoris; damages awarded, 5,000l.

May, The Maori king reconciled, sits in the legislative council

June 9, 10, Destructive volcanic eruption of Tarawera mountain; about 60 miles of beautiful fertile country desolated by showers of lava, hot cinders, and mud; about 100 persons killed; Wairoa destroyed

July, Maori incursions on European lands

1889

July 27, The debate on the Representation bill to increase the number of country members of parliament at Wellington lasted 76 hours, adjourned; amicable arrangement between town and country parties, July 29

About Nov. 26, International exhibition at Dunedin opened

Dec., Rev. A. B. Suter, Bishop of Nelson, declared primate

1890

Sept. 5, A shipping strike begun at Wellington, ended, Oct. 31

Sept. 10, Women authorized to serve in parliament and to vote at elections, Sept. 4; the bill rejected by the legislative council

1892

May, Tawhaio, the 2nd Maori king, accepts a pension

May 26, Two Americans, Messrs. Witham and Webster's old claim for compensation for seizure of land,

purchased from native chiefs; the Senate of U.S.A. recommend arbitration

Sept. 26, Disagreement between the Earl of Glasgow, the Governor, and the Ministry, who desire the appointment of 12 additional members of the legislative council; the matter referred to the home government, about Aug. 23, which agrees with the ministry

Oct., The Maoris' petition for a separate representative council declined

1893

May 1, Death of Mr. J. Ballance, the Premier; succeeded by Mr. Richard J. Seddon

Sept. 10, Act passed conferring the elective franchise on women

Nov. 29, General election; victory of the Government, reported

1894

May 7, The New Zealand loan and mercantile agency company, established 1865; misunderstandings about debentures; counsel consulted; advice not acted on, 1879–80; new debentures issued, 1892; petition to chancery for reconstruction of the company granted conditionally, April 11, 1894; examination of the directors and officers before Mr. Justice Vaughan Williams, chancery division, April 13–27; his statement respecting the evidence; the directors collectively, including Mr. Mundella, Sir John E. Gorst, and Sir James Fergusson, severely censured for reticence as to the unsecured condition of the early debenture-holders and the financial condition of the company, for misleading balance-sheets and reports, and for payments of dividends not justified, &c.

May 21, In the case of Mr. Buckley, Attorney-General of New Zealand, v. Mr. Worley B. Edwards, a puisne judge, the judicial committee of the privy council decided that the appointment of a judge is not valid unless the payment of his salary is previously secured by statute

Aug. 27, Death of Tawhiao, King of the Maoris

1895

Aug. 3, Death of Justice Christopher Wm. Richmond, statesman, aged 74

Sept. 3, Bill embodying the recommendations of the committee on the affairs of the New Zealand Bank passed

1896

July 20, Mr. Watson, president of the Bank of New Zealand, refusing to give evidence; pays 500l. fine

Sept. 3, Asiatics exclusion bill passed

Oct., A committee of the legislative council issue their report on the banking legislation, 1894 and 1895, and exonerate the government from corruption, and declare the Bank of New Zealand to be in a stable condition, Sept.; reorganization recommended

Oct. 18, The Banking bill abandoned by parliament, session closed, reported

1897

Nov. 17, Parliament opened, important measures proposed by Earl of Ranfurly, Governor, Sept. 23; eight hours' day and labor bills passed

1898

Abt. March 12, Death of Prof. Kirk, eminent botanist, conservator of forests (1886)

Sept., Death of Sir George Grey

Oct. 15, Municipal franchise reform act passed

Nov. 1, Old-age pensions act passed (amended 1900–1901)

Dec., Difficulty with Austrian emigrants, great distress

1899

Feb. 10, The Rev. Wm. Colenso, F., missionary and naturalist, died, aged 87

March 13, Sir Julius Vogel, ex-Premier, great financier, born 1835, died

April 13, Divorce bill passed, 1898; royal assent

April, Victoria university college opened in Wellington

1900

Jan. 20, Great enthusiasm on the departure of troops for S. Africa

Oct., Pacific islands visited by Lord Ranfurly (Cook, Savage, and Suwarrow formally annexed, June, 1901)

1901

End March, Death of Dean Jacobs, an influential churchman and writer

Aug., Royal commission on federation, report unanimously against it

Oct. 12, Arbitration and conciliation bill read third time in the representatives

1902

Feb. 8, March 12, Departure of the 8th and 9th contingents (total sent during the war, 6,700 officers and men, 6,620 horses)

June 27, Dr. Cowie, bishop of Auckland and primate, died

July 8, Maori councils (local self-government) act of 1901, reported successful

1903

Feb.–July, Dispute between the judges and the executive respecting precedence, &c.

May 22, Mahuta, the Maori king, appointed a member of the legislative and executive councils

June 30, Parliament opened; governor states that fiscal changes and amendment of the constitution of the privy council are necessary

Oct. 16, 1,000,000*l.* loan bill for public works passes the House of Representatives, money to be raised in the colony

Nov. 12, Naval defense bill, providing for annual sum of 40,000*l.* towards the maintenance of the Australian squadron, introduced Oct., passed

Nov. 20, Preferential (British goods) trade bill passes the House of Representatives, 50–16, and legislative council unanimously; 15,000*l.* voted by House of Representatives to Victoria Memorial in London, 27,000*l.* additional as subsidy to S. African steam service, and 5,000*l.* to promote the sale of New Zealand meat in England

1904

Feb. 19, Resolution passed at important naval defense meeting at Dunedin urges the government of New Zealand to consider measures of naval coöperation

Feb. 27, Lord Ranfurly, Governor, presides at a meeting in Wellington, held under the auspices of the Navy League; Mr. Seddon, Premier, speaks in support of the league; resolution in favor of increased naval coöperation carried unanimously

March 2, New steamship service inaugurated between Glasgow and New Zealand ports by the Tysen line

Mid April, Annual congress of trades council delegates resolve to urge the government to establish ironworks and shipbuilding yards, and to nationalize the marine, coastal, and intercolonial services; congress decides to form an independent labor party

June 28, Parliament opens; legislation promised includes measures dealing with electoral questions, licensing, and trusts

Sept. 13, Legislative council adopts the government motion regretting the introduction of Chinese labor in the Transvaal without the previous sanction by vote of the white population

Dec. 11, Death of Bp. Hadfield, formerly primate of New Zealand

Dec. 13, Capt. Seddon, son of the Premier, brings an action against Mr. Taylor, a member of the New Zealand parliament, for alleged slanderous statements regarding his conduct in the Boer war; trial began; case ends, each party paying its own costs, end Feb., 1905

1905

Early March, New political labor league of ultra-socialistic tendencies, and expressing dissatisfaction with the government, reported in course of formation throughout the colony

Mid April, In the case of Clifford *v.* the Minister of Lands, in which the plaintiff claimed 335,000*l.* for the Haxbourne estate, taken compulsorily under the land for settlements act, the compensation court, after two trials, awards 181,600*l.;* annual conference of the delegates of the N. Zealand trades and labor councils unanimously resolved to urge the government to establish state industrial works of various kinds, and also to nationalize all sources of mineral wealth and to restrict the importation of contract labor

May 25, Statement published showing the result of recent legislation in the colony in respect of preferential trade

June 2, Mr. Seddon in a speech declares that the events in the Far East constitute an argument for increasing the contribution to the navy; if N. Zealand's contribution were increased to 90,000*l.*, and Australia's to 200,000*l.*, they would have a better and more efficient squadron

June 27, Parliament opened; Gov.-Gen. states that the government is negotiating to acquire land for closer settlement, and near cities for workmen's homes; measures promised include raising of old-age pensions to 10*s.* per week; restriction on rate of interest for loans; utilization of natural waters for motive power; and the expedition of the construction of railways to promote settlement

Mid Oct., House of Representatives pass bill for a loan of 1,000,000*l.* for railway and public works; also a naval defense bill based on the recommendations of the Admiralty

Nov. 3, Mr. Seddon, Premier, announces the intention of the Government to reduce indirect taxation as a step towards a free breakfast-table; to reduce the duty on tobacco, and to increase the graduated land-tax; he declares that the Japanese would not be allowed to come to New Zealand

1906

April, Freight war begun between the various shipping companies trading between New Zealand and England, early

April 13, Sale of state-mined coal begun by the government

———, Number of immigrants into the colony, during 1905, exceeded the number of emigrants from, by 9,302

June 10, Sudden death of Mr. Seddon, the Premier

June 25, Census returns show that the total white population of New Zealand numbers 890,000, an increase in the last five years of 117,000

July 19, Death of Sir Walter Lawry Buller, formerly native commissioner and magistrate

Aug. 6, Death of G. M. Waterhouse, Premier in 1872, b. 1824

Aug. 21, Parliament opened at Wellington by the Governor

Oct. 8, Monument to Captain Cook unveiled at Poverty Bay, the spot in N.Z. where he first landed

Oct. 22, Penny postage established between the United States and N.Z., announced

Nov. 23, Dr. Findlay appointed Attorney-General and Colonial Secretary, in succession to the late Colonel Pitt; the Premier takes the portfolio of Defense

Nov. 23, Shipping war between the lines trading between Gt. Britain and N.Z., reported at an end

1907

March 14, Death of the Ven. Sam. Williams, Archdeacon of Waiapu, b. 1822

March 16, Strike of slaughtermen terminated; the strikers, though ignoring the arbitration court, secured nearly all their demands

End June, Death of Sir John Hall, Premier 1879–82, b. 1824

June 26, Return of Sir Jos. Ward from England

June 27, Parliament opened at Wellington; speech from the throne announced the consent of the home government to advise the King to raise the status of N. Zealand to that of a dominion

July 16, The budget introduced by Sir J. Ward in the House of Representatives; increase in the land tax and reductions in other taxes announced; revenue for the year estimated at 8,200,000l.

Sept. 10, Royal proclamation issued declaring that the colony of N. Zealand from the 26th inst. shall be called the Dominion of New Zealand

Dec. 11, Parliament buildings burned

1908

Jan. 16, Exports from N. Zealand in 1907 amounted to 20,000,000l., creating a record; the value of imports was 17,000,000l.

April 28, Revenue for the past year reached the record sum of 9,063,989l.; expenditure, 8,213,965l.; surplus, 800,000l.; which was transferred to the public works account

May 11, Strike of miners, employed by the Blackball company, settled

June 29, Parliament reopened

July 14, Maori congress, representing the native race, opened at Wellington

Aug. 9–15, Visit of the American battleship fleet to Auckland

Sept. 21, Statistics published show enormous progress made by the colony in half a century; population, which in 1858 was 59,000, is now 930,000; value of imports and exports in the same period rose from 1,574,000l. to 37,300,000l. *Times*

Oct. 2, Naval bill to increase New Zealand's naval subsidy from 40,000l. to 100,000l. passed the upper house

Oct. 9, Mr. W. Hall-Jones appointed high-commissioner in London

1909

Jan. 27, Labor troubles with the Auckland mineowners settled

March 10, Eruption of the Ngauruhoe volcano

March 22, The Government decides to defray the cost of building and arming a first-class battleship to be presented to the British Government

March 24, The offer accepted by the British Government

March 31, The population estimated at 1,028,000

1910

Feb. 28, Volunteer system in New Zealand terminates; the new Defense act, under which the volunteers are absorbed into the territorial force, with its compulsory service, begins, March 1

May 5, Sir Joseph Ward, Prime Minister, announced decision of the Government to carry out Lord Kitchener's recommendations to increase period of compulsory military training from 12 to 25 years, and make peace establishment army 20,000 trained men, and citizen army of 80,000

June 8–22, Sir Robert Stout, Chief Justice, Administrator

June 22, John Poynder Dickson-Poynder, Baron Islington, assumed office as Governor General

July 20, Strike of coal miners at Paparoa

Sept. 28, Public Debt Extinction Act provided for creation of sinking funds for the extinction of the public debt in 75 years

Nov. 2, Defense Amendment Act embodied Lord Kitchener's recommendations

Nov. 21, National Provident Fund Act established a voluntary scheme of old age and other annuities for protection of the family, the State to subsidize to the extent of one-fourth of the contributions

———, Licensing Amendment Act made a three-fifths vote a condition of prohibition

Dec. 3, Workers Dwellings Act provided for better housing

1911

July 1, Armored battle cruiser "New Zealand" built as a gift to the Imperial Government was launched

Oct. 28, Patent and Trade Marks Act

———, Widows' Pension Act granted a pension to indigent widows for each child under 14

———, Industrial and Conciliation Act of 1908 amended

Nov. 20, Parliament dissolved

Dec. 7, General election and referendum vote on prohibition; Government (Liberals) 37 seats, Opposition (Reform Party), 37; Labor, 4; Independents, 2; prohibition defeated

1912

Feb. 15, Eighteenth Parliament opened

Feb. 27, No confidence vote rejected by the casting vote of the Speaker

March 28, Sir Joseph Ward resigned as Prime Minister and was succeeded by Thomas Mackenzie

May 13–Nov. 30, Strike of gold miners at Waihi which ended in defeat

July 6, The Mackenzie Government defeated on vote of confidence

July 10, The Mackenzie Government resigned ending Liberal rule of 21 years

——, William Ferguson Massey, leader of the Reform Party, formed Cabinet as Prime Minister and Minister of Lands, Agriculture, and Labor; James Allen, Finance, Defense, and Education; W. H. Herries, Railways and Native Affairs; William Fraser, Public Works and Mines; A. L. Herdman, Attorney General; Justice M. B. Fisher, Customs and Marine; Francis H. D. Bell, Internal Affairs and leader of the Legislative Council; R. H. Rhodes, Postmaster-General and Public Health; and Maui Pomare, member representing the native race

Oct. 12, Battleship "New Zealand" commissioned

Nov. 7, Land Act provided for purchase of Crown "settlement lands"

——, Education Act of 1908 amended

——, Aged and Infirm Persons Protection Act

——, Public Service Acts regulated public service and provided for superannuation allowances

Dec. 19, The Earl of Liverpool took office as Governor

1913

Oct. 3, Act amended Industrial Conciliation and Arbitration Act of 1908

Oct. 18, Strike of shipwrights union in Wellington

Oct. 22, Strike of Wellington Waterside Workers Union in sympathy with shipwrights which spread to other ports and to the coal mines

Nov. 10, General strike declared

Nov. 22, Copyright Act passed

Dec. 11, Naval Defense Act provided for the establishment of a New Zealand Naval Force to be raised and maintained by voluntary enlistment which in time of war was to be at the disposal of the British Admiralty

Dec. 15, Act provided for investigation of labor disputes placing check on unions not registered under the Arbitration Act

Dec. 20, Strike ended in defeat declared off except in mines where strike continued for another month

1914

Aug. 3, Proclamation placed naval force under British Admiralty and called out naval reserves before the declaration of war by Great Britain

Aug. 5, Declaration of war of Aug. 4 by Great Britain on Germany read in Wellington from the steps of Parliament House by Lord Liverpool

—— and 7, Amendments to Banking Act of 1908 empowered the Governor in Council to make banknotes legal tender

Aug. 6, Message received from the Imperial Government asked that German wireless at Samoa be seized

Aug. 7, Cable offering services of an expeditionary force accepted by Great Britain Aug. 12

Aug. 10, Regulation of Trade and Commerce Act gave the Government authority to fix maximum prices, to prohibit exportation and to suspend or modify the Labor laws

Aug. 14, Mortgages Extension Act restrained a mortgagee from calling in or exercising his power of sale except by permission of court

Aug. 15, New Zealand force left Wellington for German Samoa

Aug. 26, Wheat sold at 5s. per bushel a rise of 25% since Aug. 1, and flour at £12 per ton a rise of 20%

Aug. 29, New Zealand force landed at Apia, German Samoa

Aug. 30, German Samoa declared annexed to the British Crown

Oct. 15, Main army left Wellington for Western Australia to join transports bound for Egypt

Nov. 2, War Regulations Act authorized the Governor in Council to make regulations prohibiting acts "injurious to the public safety, the defense of New Zealand, or the effective conduct of the military or naval operations of His Majesty during the present war "

——, Trading with the Enemy prohibited

Nov. 5, Legislative Council Act provided for the popular election of a Council of 40 members but its operation suspended by an amending Act

——, Education Act amended provided for establishment of a Department of Education

Nov. 20, Parliament dissolved

Nov. 30, First New Zealand ship the "Maunganui" entered the Suez Canal

Dec. 3, New Zealand forces disembarked at Alexandria. For campaign *see* World War

Dec. 10, Election resulted in Government majority: Reform Party, 41 seats; Liberals (Opposition), 32; Labor, 7

Dec. 14, Second force left New Zealand

1915

Jan. 8, Proclamation fixed maximum price of wheat at 5s. 9d. per bushel

Feb. 8, All restrictions on sale of wheat and flour removed

Feb. 14, Third expeditionary force left New Zealand

April 17, Fourth expeditionary force left New Zealand

April 25–Dec. 19, Gallipoli campaign. *See* World War

March 3, Department of Imperial Government Supplies constituted to control purchases of frozen meat which from this date was commandeered for purchase by the Imperial Government

June 24, Nineteenth Parliament opened

June 30, Public Revenues Amendment Act under which the Government asked for immediate authorization to borrow £10,000,000 which was granted

Aug. 4, Announcement of union of 2 chief political parties to form War Cabinet

Aug. 12, National Cabinet formed by Prime Minister Massey (Reform) as Prime Minister, Lands, and Labor; Sir Joseph G. Ward (Liberal), Finance and Postmaster-General; James Allen (Reform), Defense; W. H. Herries (Reform), Railways and Native Affairs; A. L. Herdman (Reform), Attorney-General; R. McNab (Liberal), Justice and Marine; William Fraser (Reform), Public Works; G. W. Russell (Liberal), Internal Affairs and Public Health; Sir Francis H. D. Bell (Reform), leader of the Legislative Council; A. M. Myers (Liberal), Customs, Munitions, and Supplies; W. D. S. Macdonald (Liberal), Agriculture and Mines; J. A. Hanan (Liberal), Education; Mauri Pomare (Reform), Cook and other Islands and member of the Executive Council representing the native race

Aug. 14, Expeditionary force left New Zealand

Aug. 15, First War Pensions Act passed

Sept. 20, Scheelite commandeered by Department of Imperial Government Supplies

Oct. 11, Act made provision for raising additional expeditionary force for service abroad

Oct. 11, Miners' Pthisis Act provided for allowance to miners who had contracted the disease

Oct. 12, Cost of Living Act provided for establishment of Board of Trade

Oct. 15, Discharged Soldiers' Settlement Act provided for settlement of returned soldiers on the land

Nov. 4, Cheese commandeered by the Department of Imperial Government Supplies

Dec. 27, New Zealand troops from Gallipoli arrived in Egypt to take part in Sinai and Palestine campaigns

1916

March, Board of Trade established under Cost of Living Act of 1915 to advise the Government on the development and protection of trade, industry, and commerce, fix prices, &c.

March 20, New Zealand Division transferred to western front. *See* World War

May 17, New Zealand Branch of British Red Cross Society established

Aug. 1, Military Service Act established conscription for the period of the World War

Aug. 7, Act placed tax of 45% on excess profits arising during the War, and authorized loan of £16,000,000

Sept. 1, First war loan issued, 4½% bonds redeemable in 15 years

Oct. 13, Maximum prices for butter for local consumers placed at 1s. 4d. per pound, and export of butter and cheese prohibited except under license

Nov. 23, First ballot under conscription taken

Dec. 1, Wool commandeered for the Imperial Government at fixed price 55% above that of 1913–14

1917

Jan. 18, Order in Council fixed price of milk in Wellington at 10½d. per gallon wholesale, the winter price higher

Jan. 25, Two State meat shops opened at Auckland which were closed at the end of the year when meat prices accepted by trade

Feb. 5, Sheepskins commandeered for the Imperial Government

March 12, Order in Council commandeered all hides and calf skins for the Imperial Government

April, Coal strike

May 11, Governor granted style of Governor General by letters patent

June 28, The Earl of Liverpool, assumed title of Governor General

Sept. 15, Finance Act increased land tax 50% and tax increased on incomes over £300 from 6d. to 1s. 3d.; for incomes exceeding £2,400, 1s. 4d. to a maximum of 7s. 6d. on incomes exceeding £6,700, and for companies from 1s. to 2s. 3d., and additional revenue obtained from stamp taxes, customs duties, amusement taxes, railway fares, and freights

Oct. 4–12, New Zealand Division took prominent part in operations north east of Ypres. *See* World War

Oct. 31, Land law amended as to Crown and other lands

Nov. 20, Requisition of exportable surplus butter for the Imperial Government begun

Dec. 22, Order in Council prohibited private dealing in wheat and provided for Government purchase of crop

1918

Feb. 4, Resignation of Mr. Herdman from Cabinet to become Supreme Court judge, Mr. H. D. Guthrie (Reform) succeeded him

Feb. 10, Order in Council prohibited export of potatoes

Feb., Prices of bacon and ham fixed at price as of Dec. 1, 1917

March 4, Price of bread fixed at 9½d. in Christchurch and Dunedin and at 10d. in Auckland and Wellington

April 16, Maximum wholesale price of butter for the local consumer fixed at 1s. 5d. and retail 1s. 8d.

June 26, The steamer "Wimmera" sunk by enemy mine off New Zealand coast

Aug. 6, Price of timber fixed for local use and regulations provided for gradual diminution of export to protect national forests

Oct. 12, Prime Minister Massey and Sir Joseph Ward returned from England and attendance at Imperial Conference

Nov. 5, Act restricted entry of undesirable immigrants

Nov. 11, Armistice signed. New Zealand sent 100,444 soldiers and nurses over seas, the total number of men provided was 124,211 of whom 91,941 were volunteers

Dec. 10, Licensing Amendment Act abolished local option established in 1893 and provided for a special poll on national prohibition and for triennial polls on the 3 alternatives of license, prohibition without compensation, and state purchase and control

Dec. 12, Mr. Massey and Sir Joseph Ward left New Zealand to attend the Peace Conference. During absences of the Prime Minister Sir James Allen was acting Premier

1919

Jan., Visit of French mission headed by General Pau

April 10, Referendum on prohibition resulted in 264,189 for license, and 253,827 for prohibition with compensation

May 7, Supreme Council awarded the mandate for German Samoa to New Zealand

July 2, Agreement signed with Great Britain and Australia for the administration of Nauru Island under British mandate

Aug. 13, Proclamation abolished the Expeditionary Force

Aug. 19, Amending regulations regarding timber for exportation as to maximum quantities

Aug. 21, Dissolution of National Ministry

Aug. 23–Oct. 2, Visit of Viscount Jellicoe, Admiral of the Imperial Fleet on naval mission

Aug. 25, Massey Cabinet took office

Sept. 2, Treaty of Versailles ratified

Oct. 6, Regulations gazetted provided for sale of standardized boots under Board of Trade for those who cared to take advantage of the offer on account of high prices

Oct. 29, Women made eligible for seats in Parliament with passage of Bill by Legislative Council

Nov. 27, Parliament dissolved

Dec. 17, Election gave Reform Party (Government) 47 seats: Liberal (Opposition), 20; Labor, 8; Independent Labor, 2; Independent, 3; Sir Joseph Ward defeated in a constituency which had returned him to Parliament for 32 years

——, Referendum on prohibition resulted in 241,251 for License, 32,261 for State purchase and control, and for prohibition, 270,250, but as no absolute majority secured no change made

1920

Jan. 10, New Zealand became original member of the League of Nations

Feb. 11, Control of prices of bacon and ham ended

March 11, Imperial Order in Council authorized Dominion Parliament to legislate for Samoa

April 24–May 22, Visit of the Prince of Wales

April 29–May 1, Strike of railwaymen for increase which ended with reference of claims to arbitration with resulting concessions

June 17, Maximum price for butter to local consumer 1s. 4¾d. per pound wholesale, retail 1s. 9d.

June 24, Ministry reconstructed: W. F. Massey, Prime Minister, Finance, and Railways; Sir William H. Herries, Native Affairs and Labor; Sir William Fraser, Mines; Sir Francis H. D. Bell, Attorney General and leader of Legislative Council; D. H. Guthrie, Lands and Repatriation; W. Nosworthy, Agriculture and Immigration; J. G. Coates, Public Works and Postmaster General; E. P. Lee, Justice and External Affairs; C. J. Anderson, Internal Affairs; and Maui Pomare, Cook and other Islands, and member of Executive Council representing native race

——, Twentieth Parliament opened

July 8–Sept. 26, Sir Robert Stout, Chief Justice, Administrator acting as Governor General

Aug. 31, Death of W. D. S. Macdonald, Liberal leader

Sept. 27, Viscount Jellicoe of Scapa assumed office as Governor General

Oct. 18, Order in Council fixed maximum price of butter at 1s. 11½d. per pound wholesale and 2s. 3d. retail

Nov. 9, Immigration Restriction (Amendment) Act

Nov. 11, Act passed empowered Commonwealth Arbitration Court to review industrial awards taking into consideration the cost of living

Dec. 17, Mandate over Western Samoa (former German) confirmed by the Council of the League of Nations, the mandate including Savaii and Upola Islands

1921

Feb. 15, The increase of food prices over the level of July 75.05%

March 1, Death of Sir James Prendergast, former Chief Justice

March 14, Order in Council constituted Naval Board charged with control of all matters relating to the Naval Forces

March 21, Order in Council fixed maximum prices of timber in accordance with price lists approved by Board of Trade

April 17, Census gave total 1,218,270 white population, and about 49,000 Maori aborigines

Dec. 7, Act provided for government of Samoa

Dec. 9, New Customs Tariff approved by House increased taxes on luxuries

World record export of butter and cheese, 20,000,000 pounds

1922

Feb. 11, Meat Export Control Act established Board to control industry

April 25, Anzac Day observed as a national holiday as a Sunday

Sept. 1, Reciprocal Tariff Agreement with Australia came into effect

Oct. 31, Workmen's Compensation Act

Nov. 10–Jan. 23, 1923, Strike of ship workers against award of Commonwealth Arbitration Court

Nov. 15, Parliament dissolved

Dec. 7, Election gave Reform Party 38 seats; Liberals and Independent Liberals, 25; and Labor, 17

1923

Feb. 8, Twenty-first Parliament met

Feb. 28, Flour subsidy ended

June 26, D. H. Guthrie succeeded as Minister of Railways, Lands, &c., by J. G. Coates, and E. P. Lee as Minister of Justice by C. J. Parr

July 30, The Ross Dependency proclaimed a British Settlement and placed under jurisdiction of the Governor General of New Zealand by Order in Council

Aug. 6, The Otira tunnel (Arthur's Pass) officially opened establishing direct railroad connection between the east and west coasts

Aug. 28, Dairy-produce Export Control Act established Board to control the industry

Aug. 29, Apprentices Act superseded the Master and Apprentice Act of 1865 placing employment of apprentices under Court of Arbitration and Apprentice Committees to be set up in the various industries and localities

Liquor referendum vote taken gave 290,566 for prohibition, 272,443 for continuance of non-prohibition system, and 34,261 for State supervision and control

1924

March 13, Decision of Imperial Government not to proceed with construction of naval base at Singapore caused much dissatisfaction

April 21–29, Unsuccessful strike of railroad men against longer hours and for a wage increase

Oct. 29, Land Transfer Act made registration of land titles compulsory and brought under Land Transfer Act of 1916 land heretofore alienated from Crown

Nov. 26–Dec. 12, Sir Robert Stout, Chief Justice, Administrator ad interim

Dec. 13, General Sir Charles Fergusson, bart. assumed office as Governor General

1925

March 1, Embargo placed on importation of wheat and flour

March 12, Strike of miners against coöperative contract system

May 10, Death of W. F. Massey, Prime Minister

May 14–May 30, Sir Francis Henry Dillon Bell, Prime Minister ad interim

May 30, Joseph Gordon Coates took office as Prime Minister

Oct. 14, Parliament dissolved

Nov. 4, Election gave Government a majority: Reform Party (Government), 55 seats; Liberals and Independent Liberals, 11; Labor, 13; Independent, 1; prohibition defeated by referendum vote

Dec. 14, Private dealing in wheat prohibited

1926

Jan. 14, Private importation of wheat prohibited

Feb. 11, Administration of Union Islands (Tokelau), formerly part of the Gilbert and Ellice Islands Colony, transferred to the jurisdiction of New Zealand to be administered by the Administrator of Western Samoa

Feb. 23, The Government agreed to free market for wheat with duties at 1s. 2½d. per bushel for wheat,

£3 per ton of flour, and £1 per ton on bran and pollard

Feb. 28, Prohibition of private dealing in wheat and of private importation revoked

April 20, Decision of Government that no permits to Chinese for residence in New Zealand should be granted for one year

May 23, Special Prime Minister's Department created under control of F. D. Thomson

——, Cabinet reconstituted, J. G. Coates, Prime Minister and Minister of Railways, Public Works, and Native Affairs; D. H. Guthrie and Sir F. H. D. Bell, without Portfolio; W. D. Stewart, Attorney General, Finance, and Stamp Duties; William Nosworthy, Immigration, Post Master General, Telegraphs, External Affairs; A. D. McLeod, Industries and Commerce, Lands; Sir R. H. Rhodes, without Portfolio, leader of the Legislative Council; Sir M. Pomare, Cook Islands and member representing Native Race; F. J. Rolleston, Attorney General, Justice, and Defense; R. A. Wright, Education; K. S. Williams, Public Works; O. J. Hawken, Agriculture; R. F. Bollard, Internal Affairs

June 16, Twenty-second Parliament opened

Sept. 1, From this date the Dairy Export Control Board exercised absolute control of sales in all dairy produce and export to Great Britain and North America

Sept. 9, Workmen's Compensation Act amended raising the limits of compensation

——, Family Allowance Act granted 2s. a week for each child under 14 to families of the poorest class

Sept. 11, Mining law enacted

Dec. 16, Announcement of agreement with Great Britain by which assisted settlers to receive the benefit of large reductions in boat transportation rates

1927

Feb. 22, March 22, Visit of the Duke and Duchess of York

March 14, Dairy Export Control Board reversed policy of 1926 exercising now only limited control and rescinding all resolutions dealing with fixing of prices

April 24, Announcement that New Zealand would contribute £100,000,000 toward naval base at Singapore

July, Petition signed by 145 native Samoan chiefs protested against administration

Aug. 5, Samoan Amendment Act gave Administration power to deal with persons hindering the Government in performance of its duties under the mandate

Sept. 5, Commission appointed to inquire into the situation and administration of Samoa; report issued later vindicated administration

Oct. 20, Industrial Arbitration Bill introduced abolishing permanent representation of employers and employees in arbitration courts and substitution of representatives from each industry in given disputes rejected because of clause exempting dairy and farm industry from its operation

Oct. 21, Appeal of 2 Samoan chiefs against sentence of banishment imposed dismissed by the Supreme Court

Oct. 25, Customs Tariff revised increased preference granted to goods of British origin, a large number of items such as earthenware, table china, linen, cement, and corrugated iron placed on free list as from Great

Britain, and duty on British cotton yarns removed, and duty on unassembled motor cars reduced to 5%

Nov. 21, L. S. Amery, Secretary of State for Dominions, reached Auckland from Australia

1928

March 22, Colonel Stephen S. Allen appointed Administrator of Western Samoa

March 27, Industrial Conference at Sydney

July 24, Commercial Agreement with Japan signed, New Zealand's first Treaty with a foreign Power

Oct. 18, Parliament dissolved

Nov. 14, Election a defeat for the Government: Reform Party, 28; United Party (Liberals), 29; Labor, 19; Independent, 4

——, Vote for prohibition 294,453, for State purchase and control 64,276, for national continuance 373,692

Dec. 4, Twenty-third Parliament opened

Dec. 7, Coates Ministry resigned

Dec. 10, Sir Joseph George Ward formed Cabinet (United Party) as Prime Minister, Minister of Finance and of Stamp Duties, and External Affairs; George W. Forbes, Lands and Agriculture; Thomas M. Wilford, Justice and Defense; Sir Apirana Turupa Ngata, Cook Islands and Native Affairs; Harry Atmore, Education; William A. Veitch, Labor and Mines; E. A. Ransom, Public Works; W. B. Tavener, Customs, and Commissioner of State Forests; James B. Donald, Telegraphs and Postmaster-General; P. A. de la Perrelle, Internal Affairs; John G. Cobbe, Industries and Commerce, Marine, and Immigration; A. J. Stallworthy, Health; T. K. Sidey, Attorney General

1929

Jan., A £7,000,000 loan at 4½% was floated at 95 in London

June 17, Severe earthquake damaged the west coast, the most disastrous ever experienced in New Zealand

Dec. 1, Lord Bledisloe appointed Governor General

1930

Jan. 14, The Mau (Samoan League) was proclaimed a seditious organization

April 9, The Byrd Antarctic Expedition was officially entertained by the Government at Wellington

May 15, Resignation of the Prime Minister, Sir J. G. Ward due to ill health

May 28, George William Forbes took office as Prime Minister and Minister of Finance, External Affairs, Customs and Stamp Duties; E. A. Ransom, Lands and Commissioner of State Forests; W. A. Veitch, Railways; W. B. Tavener, Public Works and Transport; P. A. de la Perrelle, Industries and Commerce and Internal Affairs; J. G. Cobbe, Defense and Justice; S. G. Smith, Labor and Immigration; J. B. Donald, Telegraph and Marine and Postmaster-General; Sir A. Ngata, Cook Islands and Native Affairs; A. J. Stallworthy, Health; A. J. Murdoch, Agriculture and Mines; H. Atmore, Education; R. Masters, Minister without Portfolio

July 7, Death of Sir Joseph G. Ward (74)

Aug. 18, Tariff Act gave increased preference to goods of British origin, and increased duties on American goods; automobiles, cigars, cigarettes, increased and gasoline tax

Oct. 11, Unemployment Insurance Act passed

PACIFIC ISLANDS

Admiralty Islands. *See* Bismarck Archipelago.

Auckland Islands, 50° 31' S., 166° 19' E., 200 miles S. of Stewart Island. Area of largest about 330 square miles. Uninhabited. The New Zealand Government maintains a depot of provisions and clothing for the use of shipwrecked mariners on the largest island of the group.

Baker Island. *See* Phœnix Islands.

Bali, one of the Lesser Sunda Islands of the Dutch East Indies, situated east of Java, and with Lombok forming a Residency (1882). Area of Bali, 2,095 square miles, population (1925) 946,387; area of Lombok, 3,126 square miles, population, 599,544. The Dutch established relations with Bali as early as 1597, but it was not until 1839 that Dutch sovereignty was acknowledged by the native rulers and revolts prevented establishment of Dutch rule until 1849. The revolts of 1906 and 1908 led to direct Dutch government over the entire island, the Raja of Bangli being recognized as a stadtholder. His successors rule under the Dutch in Bangli and Gianjar as regents, and Karang Asen has its stadtholder. The Dutch East India Company made a Treaty with the native rulers of Lombok in 1675. Mataram accepted Dutch suzerainty in 1843, but rejected it in 1872, and was conquered by the Dutch in 1894, appealed to by the Sassak population, oppressed. All of Lombok is now under direct Dutch rule.

Bismarck Archipelago, islands lying north and northeast of New Guinea, included in former German New Guinea, and now under Australian mandate. *See also* New Guinea. In November, 1884, a German Protectorate was declared over the New Britain Archipelago and several adjacent groups of islands, and in May, 1885, they were renamed the Bismarck Archipelago. The Archipelago lies between 141° 30' and 156° east longitude, and the Equator and 8° south latitude. The chief islands are New Britain, area 10,000 square miles; New Ireland, area 3,000 square miles; Lavongai (late New Hanover), 530 square miles; Duke of York Islands, area 22 square miles; the Admiralty Islands (principal island, Manus), area 600 square miles. The other groups included in this Archipelago are Mussau Islands, Gardner Islands, Nuguria, Nissan Island, the Vitu Islands, Umboi Islands, Hermit Islands, Ninigo Group, Kaniet and Sae Islands. In these various groups there are upwards of 100 small islands. The native population of the Archipelago in 1925 of areas patrolled was 135,600.

New Britain, the largest island of this group, is a long island of crescent shape lying east and west. It has a mean breadth of 50 miles and a length of 300 miles. The island is practically un-

developed except for the Gazelle Peninsula in the north, four plantations on the northern coast, and six plantations on the southern coast, west of Henry Reid Bay. A Government station, named Gasmata (non-indigenous population 16), has been established about midway along the southern coast. Talasea (non-indigenous population 34) is situated on the north coast. The interior of the island is little known. The native population within explored areas in 1926 was 81,859.

New Ireland, the second in size and importance of the Bismarck Archipelago, is situated north of New Britain, from which it is separated by St. George's Channel. The chief town is Kavieng (non-indigenous population, 356), at the northwest extremity of the island. The only other town is Namatanai (non-indigenous population, about 148), on the south-east coast.

The Admiralty Islands are the most important of the small groups. The chief island is Manus, sometimes called Great Admiralty Island. The chief town is Lorengau (population, including district, about 40) on the north-east coast. The native population of the group in 1925 was 13,800. Coconuts are the chief article of cultivation, and there are valuable pearl and other shell fisheries.

Borneo, island of the Malay Archipelago, area 293,496 square miles. The first account of the island was given by the survivors of the Magellan expedition. After Magellan's death in the Philippines the ships of the expedition visited Borneo and stayed at Brunei, then the center of a wealthy kingdom. Early Dutch and English factories were established and abandoned. In the early nineteenth century the Dutch obtained concessions from the Sultan of about half his kingdom, and are in present possession of the larger and more valuable part of the Island. Dutch Borneo is a Residency of the Dutch East Indies. *See s.v.* North Borneo, Sarawak, on the northwest coast, and Brunei between North Borneo and Sarawak are British protectorates. Treaty of June 20, 1891, settled boundaries between Dutch and English territory.

British North Borneo, the northern part of the Island, has an area of about 31,106 square miles, population (1921 census), 257,804, consisting mostly of Mohammedan settlers on the coast and aboriginal tribes inland: the Europeans numbered 533; Eurasians, 213; Chinese, 37,856; Malays, 20,263. The number of natives was 197,058. The most numerous are the Dusuns, 112,287; the Muruts, 37,447; and the Bajaus, 33,070. Chief towns, Sandakan (population 11,936), on the east coast, and Jesselton, on the west coast.

The territory is under the jurisdiction of the British North Borneo Company, being held under grants from the Sultans of Brunei and Sulu (Royal Charter in 1881). It is administered by a Governor (appointed with the approval of the

Secretary of State) in Borneo, and a Court of Directors in London, appointed under the Charter. On May 12, 1888, the British Government proclaimed a formal protectorate over the State of North Borneo. In 1898 certain border lands were acquired.

A. F. Richards, Governor.

Brunei has an area of about 2,500 square miles and population (1921 census), 25,454; (Europeans, 35; Malays and Bornean races, 23,938; Chinese, 1,434; Indians, 37; others, 10). The Sultanate was formerly a great and powerful State and in the early years of the 16th century the authority of its rulers extended over the northern part of the Island, over the Sulu Islands, and part of the Philippines. Cessions of territory have reduced the Sultan's territory to the town and district of Brunei and some outlying districts, of which the most important are Tutong, Belait, and Temburong. In 1888 Brunei was placed under British protection, and by Treaty of Jan. 2, 1906, the Sultan agreed to hand over the administration to a British resident.

Sarawak has an area of about 50,000 square miles with a population of about 600,000. In September, 1841, the Sultan of Brunei ceded this district, then 7,000 square miles, to Sir James Brooke, English officer, in return for his services in helping to suppress a rebellion. In 1861, 1882, 1884, and 1890 further cessions of territory were made to Sarawak. In 1863 Sarawak was recognized by the British Government as an independent State and March 17, 1888 a treaty was concluded by which British protection given, the British Government to control the foreign relations but the internal administration entirely in the hands of the Rajah. Sir Charles Johnson Brooke succeeded his uncle as Rajah June 11, 1868, and was succeeded by his son, Sir Charles Vyner Brooke, May 17, 1917.

Caroline Islands, former German possessions north of the Equator, under mandate of Japan, consist of about 500 coral islets. Ponapé, the largest is 134 square miles in area; Yap, 80 square miles; Kusaie (Ualan), 42 square miles; the total group about 550 square miles. Ponapé has 2,286 inhabitants; Yap; 7,332; and Parao, 7,257; the population mainly of Malay origin with some Chinese and Japanese.

Celebes, one of the Greater Sunda Islands in the Dutch East Indies, east of Borneo, and separated from that island by the Strait of Macassar, area about 70,000 square miles. Discovered by the Portuguese (1512) who were displaced by the Dutch expedition of Cornelis Speelman in the seventeenth century at Macassar (1666).

Chatham Islands, dependency of New Zealand 43° 50' S., 177° W., 536 miles E. of New Zealand.

Area 375 square miles; population (April, 1926) 562 (268 Europeans and 294 Maoris and Moriorises).

Christmas Island. *See* Gilbert and Ellice Islands.

Clipperton Island, French possession in 10° 17' N. Lat. and 109° 13' W. Long., 670 miles southwest of the Mexican port of Acapulco, and also claimed by Mexico. It is 2 to 3 miles in diameter and uninhabited.

The **Cocos** or **Keeling Islands,** a group of about twenty small coral islands. Latitude 12° 5' S. and Longitude 96° 53' E., 581 miles distant from Java Head (S. 56° W.), and 1,161 miles from Singapore (S. 30° W.). The largest is 5 miles by ¼ mile. They were declared a British Possession in 1857, were placed by Letters Patent of October 13th, 1878, under the control of the Governor of Ceylon, and by Letters Patent of February 1st, 1886, under the Governor of the Straits Settlements. In 1903 they were annexed to the Straits Settlements and incorporated with the Settlement of Singapore. Estimated population, 800.

Cook Islands (Hervey Islands) were declared to be under British protection in Oct., 1888, by Captain Bourke of H.M.S. "Hyacinth" and Te Au-o-Tu, Manuae, and Takutea (at that time known as the Hervey group) by Commander Nicolls of H.M.S. "Coromant" in June, 1889. The Islands were annexed to New Zealand June 11, 1901 with Niue and other South Pacific Islands. They lie between 8° and 23° S. lat., 157° and 170° W. long. The names of the islands with their populations (1926) are as follows:—

	POPULATION
Cook Islands—	
Rarotonga	3,906
Mangaia	1,249
Atiu	933
Aitutaki	1,431
Mauke (Parry Is.)	511
Mitiaro	238
Hervey Islands	23
Niue (Savage Is.)	3,795
Palmerston Is.	90
Penrhyn (Tongareva)	395
Manahiki	416
Rakaanga	327
Danger (Pukapuka)	526
Suwarrow	—
Total	13,833

Total area of the Cook and other islands about 280 square miles.

Rarotonga is 20 miles in circumference; Atiu, 20 miles; Aitutaki, 21 miles; Niue (or Savage Island), 40 miles. Laws for the Cook Islands have been made since 1890 by a general Legislature, and are administered by an Executive Council, of which the Arikis, or native chiefs, are members. At Rarotonga and Niue there are (New Zealand) Resident Commissioners, whose approval is required for all enactments. The customs tariff of New Zealand is enforced.

Dutch East Indies, Dutch East Indies form the territory of Netherlands India.

Dr. A. C. D. de Graeff, Governor General.

The Philippines and New Guinea are sometimes included in Malay archipelago.

—		AREA: ENGLISH SQUARE MILES	POPULATION DEC. 31, 1927
Java and Madura		50,811	37,433,760
Island of Sumatra { Sumatra, West Coast		18,029	1,613,399
Tapanoeli		14,760	905,320
Sumatra, East Coast		36,100	1,227,817
Benkoelen		9,995	281,215
Lampongs		10,914	258,891
Palembang		33,173	872,552
Djambi		18,719	201,731
Atjeh		21,448	802,661
Riau-Lingga Archipelago		12,506	236,569
Bangha		4,549	169,281
Billiton		1,873	71,276
Borneo, West District		56,838	717,004
Borneo, South and East Districts		149,972	1,105,422
Island of Celebes { Selebes		48,061	2,539,610
Manado		24,618	909,164
Molucca Islands { Amboina		17,372	359,181
Ternate		12,796	284,818
New Guiné		160,692	—
Timor Archipelago		26,410	1,168,246
Bali and Lombok		4,072	1,586,652
Approximate total		733,715	52,824,569

Ellice Islands. *See* Gilbert and Ellice Islands.

Fanning Islands. *See* Gilbert and Ellice Islands.

Fiji Islands, British Colony, archipelago of some 250 islands lying between Lat. 15° and 22° S. and Long. 178° W. and 177° E. distant from Sydney about 1,700 miles and from Auckland 1,100 miles. There are eight main groups: (1) The Ono group, 6 islets in extreme south, (2) the Lakemba group of about 33 islands, (3) the Exploring Islands, about 10 islets of which Vanua Mbalavu is the largest, (4) Lomai Viti or Inner Fiji, about 12 or more scattered islands in the Koro Sea, (5) Vanua Levu, Taveuni, and the Ringgold Islands, (6) Viti Levu and the adjacent islands, (7) Kandavu, and (8) the Yasawa, the last 3 groups often called the Western or Leeward Islands, and the Lakemba and Exploring Islands are often grouped together as the Windward Islands, Eastern or Lau group. The Island of Rotuma, is included as a dependency, including all islands between 12° and 15° S. and between 175° and 180° E., added to the Colony in 1880, area 7,083 square miles. The largest of the Fiji group is Viti Levu, area 4,053 square miles, the next Vana Levu, area 2,130 square miles. On December 31st, 1929, the population of the Colony, including Rotuma, was estimated at 180,005; Europeans, 4,726 (2,539 males, 2,187 females); Fijians, 91,711 (47,243 males, 44,468 females); Indians, 73,121 (43,859 males, 29,262 females); Chinese, 1,464 (1,352 males, 112 females); half-castes, 3,281 (1,697 males, 1,584 females); others, 5,632 (3,598 males, 2,034 females). Suva, the capital, is on the south coast of Viti Levu; European population (census of April 24, 1921), 1,443, suburbs, 298, total, 1,741.

The Fiji Islands were discovered by Tasman in 1643 and visited by Captain Cook in 1769. The sovereignty was ceded to Great Britain on October 10, 1874. The Constitution is regulated by Letters Patent of February 9, 1929.

Sir Murchison Fletcher, Governor of Fiji and High Commissioner for the Western Pacific.

Gambier Islands made a French Protectorate in 1844 lie at the southeastern end of the Tuamotu Archipelago, grouped with the Tubuai and Rapa islands as the Gambier Administration, the Gambier group (of which Mangareva is the principal) having six square miles of area and 501 inhabitants; the Tubuai (or southern) Islands, of which Rurutu is the largest, Raivavae (or Vavitu), Rimatara, and, far to the south, Rapa, having together an area of 115 square miles and 3,170 inhabitants; Makatea, 1,086 inhabitants; Island of Maiao, 81 inhabitants. The total area of the Establishments is estimated at 1,520 square miles, and their population, according to the census of 1926, was 35,862, of whom 29,644 were natives. There were 870 French, 217 English, and 3,989 Chinese. In 1903 it was decreed that separate islands or groups should no longer be regarded as distinct Establishments, but that all should be united to form a homogeneous colony.

Gilbert and Ellice Islands Colony (British). The islands in this group were proclaimed as Protectorates in May 27 and Sept. respectively 1892 and annexed (at the request of the native Governments) as Gilbert and Ellice Islands Colony, on November 10, 1915. The Colony includes several groups of islands. (1) The *Ellice Islands,* between 5° 30′ and 11° 20′ S. lat., and 176° and 180° E. long. (population June 30, 1926, 3,582). The principal islands are Funafuti,

Nukufetau, Vaitupu, Nui (or Netherland), Niutao (or Lynx of Speiden), Nanumaga (or Hudson), Nanumea (or St. Augustine), Nukulaelae (or Mitchell); Nurakita; area of group, 14 square miles. (2) *Fanning Island*, 3° 50′ N., 159° W.; area 15 square miles; *Washington Island*, 4° 40′ N., 160° 20′ W., area 6 square miles, population of the two islands, June 30, 1926, 491, including 41 Europeans; and *Ocean Island* (population June 30, 1926, 2,386, including 96 Europeans and 397 Asiatics). The last-named island is the Colony headquarters. It is situated 0° 52′ S., and 169° 35′ E., is six miles in circumference, and was annexed by Great Britain in 1901. The island is exceedingly rich in high-grade phosphate, which is worked by the British Phosphate Commission who purchased the rights of the Pacific Phosphate Company in 1921. A wireless station on the island maintains telegraphic communication *via* Fiji and Australia. (3) *Christmas Island*, situated roughly 2° N. lat., and 157° W. long., discovered by Cook in 1777, annexed by Great Britain in 1888, and included in the Colony in November, 1919, is the largest atoll in the Pacific, being over 100 miles in circumference. It is leased to the Central Pacific Coconut Plantations, Ltd., for a term of 87 years from January 1, 1914. Population 1922, European, 4, Tahitians, 28. (4) The *Gilbert Islands* on the equator (population 1926, 23,410). The principal islands are Butaritari, Makin, Tarawa, Abaiang, Marakei, Maiana, Abemama, Kuria, Aranuka, Nonouti, Tabiteuea, Beru, Nukunau, Onotoa, Tamana, and Arorae. Area, 166 square miles; population at 1921 census: 264 Europeans, 29,285 Pacific Island natives, and 348 Asiatics; total, 29,897.

Guam, situated at the southern extremity of the Mariana Archipelago, in latitude 13° 26′ N., longitude 144° 43′ E., is the largest island of that group. It was ceded by Spain to the United States by the Treaty of Paris (December 10, 1898). It is under the jurisdiction of the Navy Department of the United States, and has been designated as a Naval Station for the purposes of government and protection. A garrison of marines and a shore naval force are maintained here.

The length of the island is 32 miles, the breadth from 4 to 10 miles, and the area 210 square miles. Agaña, the seat of Government, is about eight miles from the anchorage in Apra Harbour. The port of entry is Piti. The number of inhabitants (exclusive of the military establishment and non-native residents) on June 30, 1930 was 19,139, of whom 17,437 were classed as "natives." *See also*, United States Dependencies.

Hawaii. The Hawaiian Islands lie in the North Pacific Ocean, between 18° 54′ and 22° 15′ north latitude, and 154° 50′ and 160° 30′ west longitude, about 2,020 miles south-west of San Francisco. The Hawaiian Islands (formerly known as the Sandwich Islands), celebrated in August, 1928, the 150th anniversary of their discovery by Captain James Cook, the English navigator. The Islands formed during the greater part of the nineteenth century an independent kingdom, but in 1893 the reigning Queen, Liliuokalani (died November 11, 1917), was deposed and a provisional government formed; in 1894, a Republic was proclaimed, and in accordance with the request of the people of Hawaii expressed through the Legislature of the Republic, and a resolution of the United States Congress of July 6, 1898 (signed July 7 by President McKinley), the Islands were on August 12, 1898, formally annexed to the United States. On June 14, 1900, they were constituted as the Territory of Hawaii. The Organic Act has since been amended several times.

The total area of the islands is 6,454 square miles. The principal islands of the group are Hawaii, 4,015; Maui, 728; Oahu, 598; Kauai, 547; Molokai, 261; Lanai, 139; Niihau, 97; Kahoolawe, 69. According to the census of 1930, the total population of the islands numbered 368,336, an increase of 112,424, or 43.8% since 1920. The capital, Honolulu, on the Island of Oahu, has a population of 137,582 according to 1930 census, and Hilo, 19,468.

The estimated number of Hawaiians on June 30, 1929, was 20,479, and 27,285 part-Hawaiians. There are estimated to be 25,211 Chinese, 137,407 Japanese, 29,717 Portuguese, 63,869 Filipinos, 6,923 Porto Ricans, 1,851 Spanish, 38,006 Americans, British, Germans, and Russians, 6,393 Koreans, 508 others. Large numbers from the various racial groups were born in the Islands, and are American citizens. *See also* United States Dependencies.

Lawrence M. Judd, Governor, 1929–1933.

Hoorn Islands (Futuna and Alofa). *See* New Caledonia.

Huon Islands. Discovered by the French in 1791. *See* New Caledonia.

Jarvis Island British "Line" Island, on the Equator, 159° W., area 1½ square miles, population 30.

Java, island of the Malay Archipelago (Dutch East Indies) seat of the Dutch Colonial Government, area 48,504 square miles; area of Madura, adjacent and associated island, 1,732; and of the smaller islands administratively included in Java, 1,416, making a total of 50,970 square miles. The more important of the small islands are Pulau Panaitan (Princes Island) 47 square miles, the Thousand Islands, the Karimon Java Archipelago, Bavian (Bawian), Sapudi and Kangean archipelagoes. Batavia is the capital of Java and of the Dutch East Indies, population 290,408. The

Portuguese discovered the Island in 1511. The Dutch arrived in 1595 and the first Dutch Governor (1610) built a fort in the region of the present Batavia, 1619. In 1677 the principality of Jakarta was ceded to them, the Preanger in 1705, and by 1745 Dutch sovereignty was recognized over the entire northeast coast after repeated conflicts with the natives, and in 1755 the States of Surakarta and Jokjakarta acknowledged Dutch rule. The kingdom of Bantam was subjugated in 1808. The Island capitulated to the British Sept. 18, 1811, and was restored in 1816 under Treaties of 1814 and 1815.

Kaiserwilhelms Land, former German New Guinea. *See* New Guinea.

Keeling Islands. *See* Cocos Islands.

Kermadec Islands, 36° S., 178° 30′ W., 600 miles N.N.E. of New Zealand, dependency of New Zealand. Area 15 square miles. Now uninhabited. The largest of the group is Raoul or Sunday Island, 20 miles in circuit; Macaulay Island is 3 miles in circuit.

Labuan lies about 6 miles from the north-west coast of Borneo. It was ceded to Britain in 1846; on January 1, 1907, was incorporated with Singapore, and on December 1, 1912, was created a separate Settlement. Area 30 sq. miles; the population in 1928 was 5,904, mostly Malays from Borneo, with some Chinese traders and about 26 Europeans; in 1929 was 6,029—4,180 Malays, and 1,607 Chinese. Capital, Victoria, which has about 1,500 inhabitants.

Ladrone Islands. *See* Marianne Islands.

Leeward Islands (Iles sous le Vent) western islands of the Society Group of the French settlements including Raiatéa, Tahaa, Huahiné, Bora Bora, Motu Iti (Tubai), Maura (Maupiti), Mopihaa, Fenua Ura or Scilly, and Bellingshausen or Motu one, the most important, Huahiné (population 1,283), Raiatéa and Tahaa (population 4,307, and Bora Bora and Maupiti (population 4,307). For British group *see* West Indies.

" Line Islands," term applied to a number of small islands lying north of the Society Islands and widely scattered a few degrees north and south of the Equator.

Lord Howe Island, dependency of State of New South Wales, situated about 436 miles northeast of Sydney, area 3,220 acres, measuring about 5½ miles by one mile; discovered Feb. 17, 1788 by Lieutenant H. L. Ball.

Lord Howe Islands or Ontong Java. *See* Solomon Islands.

Louisiade Archipelago (Papua, New Guinea) discovered by the Spanish expedition of Mendaña from Peru in 1605, Torres, the pilot coasting south of New Guinea; named by de Bougainville in 1786 after Louis XIV.

Loyalty Islands, French possessions, lie parallel to New Caledonia at a distance of about 70 miles of which they are a dependency. The chief islands are Maré, Lifou or Chabrol, and Uvéa, total area 800 square miles. Annexed by France 1864.

Madura Island. *See* Java.

Malay Archipelago. *See* Dutch East Indies.

Malden Island, British " Line " Island, 4° S. Lat., 155° W. Long., area 35 square miles.

The **Marianne** (or **Ladrone**) **Islands,** former German possessions now under mandate of Japan are situated in about 12° to 21° N. and 145° E. The largest island, Guam, was ceded to the United States in 1898 (*see* Guam). The islands passed from Spanish to German possession Oct. 1, 1899 for payment of £840,000. Sipan is the seat of Government. The total area is 245 square miles excluding Guam. The Japanese population of the Islands was 16,202 Oct. 1, 1899, and the native, 48,617. They were discovered by Magellan in 1521 and named Islands of the Thieves (*Islas de los Ladrones*) and received the name *Las Marianas* in 1688 in honor of Maria Anna of Austria, widow of Philip IV of Spain. Of the northern group of 10 volcanic islands Agrigan, Anatahan, Alamagan, and Pagan are inhabited, and of the southern group of 5 islands, Rota, Guam, Aguijan, Tinian, and Saypan all are inhabited save Aguijan.

Marquezas Islands (French) lie north of the Tuamotu Archipelago extending over 250 miles from southeast to northwest, and comprise 11 islands in 2 groups, with total area of 480 square miles, and 2,255 population, the largest islands being Nukahiva in the northwest group (186 square miles) and Hivoa in the southwest group (154 square miles). The southeast islands were discovered in 1595 by Alvaro Mendaña, Spaniard, and were rediscovered by Captain Cook in 1774. The northwestern group were sighted by the American Captain Ingraham in 1791, and by the French Captain Marchand in the later same year. In May 1842 Admiral Dupetit-Thouars took formal possession for France.

Marshall Islands, former German possessions included in German New Guinea, now administered by Japan under mandate of League of Nations, are divided in 2 groups, the northeast line, with 15 islands is called Ratack (Radak), and the southwestern group, 18 islands, Ralik, area estimated as 160 square miles, population 303 Japanese, 19 foreigners, and 9,356 natives. The chief island and administrative center is Jaluit. The islands were probably visited by de Saavedra in 1529, Captain Wallis visited the group in 1767, and Captains Marshall and Gilbert explored the islands in 1788. They were annexed by Germany in 1885. Nauru or Pleasant Island, lying to the southwest, was included in the German administration.

Moluccas or **Spice Islands** (Malay Archipelago) in a wide sense include all the Dutch East Indies, and in narrow sense (*see* Dutch East Indies) Amboina, Ternate, and Dutch New Guinea. The name is said to be derived from the Arabic for " king." Amboina and Banda were discovered by the Portuguese about 1511, and claimed by the Spaniards after voyage of Magellan for Spain (1519–21) under the Treaty of Tordesillas (1494) but sold to the Portuguese in 1529. The Dutch made treaty with the Sultan of Ternate and chiefs of Amboina by which they were able to dispossess the Portuguese, and in 1683 they declared all contracts with the Sultan of Ternate null and void, and assumed the sovereignty of the Moluccan Islands. Treaty with England in 1619 by which England to share in the trade, and March 17, 1824 Treaty between Great Britain and the Netherlands defined territories and made commercial arrangements. Amboina under English rule 1796–1802.

Nauru Island, lying 26 miles south of the Equator, area 5,396 acres, is about 4,000 miles from the nearest Marshall Islands, annexed by Germany in October, 1888, it was surrendered to Australian forces in 1914, and is administered by Great Britain under mandate dated Dec. 17, 1920, conferred on the British Empire, and approved by the League of Nations. Great Britain, Australia, and New Zealand agreed in July, 1919 that Australia should appoint the first Administrator for a term of 5 years, and thereafter the Administrator was to be appointed as the three Governments should decide. Population April 1, 1930: 147 Europeans, 1,411 Nauruans, 16 other Pacific islanders, and 1,110 Chinese; total 2,684.

New Britain. *See* Bismarck Archipelago.

New Caledonia, French Colony, in the southwestern Pacific, about 900 miles from Australia, has a total length exceeding 248 miles and an average breadth of 31 miles, an area of 8,548 square miles, population in 1926, 51,816, of whom 14,893 were free, 1,281 of convict origin, and 27,490 Melanesians and Polynesians. On July 1, 1930 the native population was 27,777, Nouméa, the capital, 10,226 inhabitants (1926) of whom 6,430 were free. Captain Cook discovered the Island in 1774 touching at Balade (original name of the Island), and it was visited by the French expedition of d'Entrecasteaux in 1793. After an incident with the natives in 1851 the Island was formally annexed by France in " 1853 to assure France in the Pacific the position demanded by its naval interests, military and commercial, and to afford the opportunity of putting in force the

Government's views with regard to the treatment of criminals " (*Moniteur*, Feb. 14, 1854).
Dependencies of New Caledonia are:
1. The Isle of Pines, 30 miles to the south-east, with an area of 58 square miles and a population of about 600.
2. The Wallis Archipelago, northeast of Fiji, with an area of 40 square miles and about 4,500 inhabitants. The islands were placed under the French protectorate in 1842. There is a French Resident, and the archipelago is in regular communication with Nouméa. Budget for 1927, 298,640 francs.
3. The Loyalty Islands, 60 miles east of New Caledonia, consisting of 3 large islands, Maré, Lifou, and Uvéa, and many small islands with a total area of about 800 square miles. The chief culture in the islands is that of coconuts; the chief export, copra and rubber.
4. The Huon Islands, 170 miles north-west of New Caledonia, a most barren group.
5. Futuna and Alofi, south of the Wallis Islands, with about 1,500 inhabitants, discovered by the Dutch in 1616 were annexed by France in 1888.
M. Guyon, Governor (M. Thaly, Acting)

New Guinea, next to Australia, New Zealand, and Greenland, the largest island in the world, has an area of 312,329 square miles. It is separated from Australia by the Torres Strait and the Arafura Sea. The Island was discovered in 1511 by Antonio de Abrea, Portuguese navigator, was visited by Jorge de Meneses in 1526 and named Papua, the name New Guinea given by Ynigo Ortiz de Retez who landed on the north coast in 1546. The East India Company (English) annexed New Guinea in 1793; the Dutch annexed some parts of the west coast in the eighteenth century, in 1828 established a fort at Triton Bay and took possession of the southwest coast, and after 1848 claimed the whole island to the west of 141° E. long. as suzerains of the Sultan of Tidore. Captain Moresby discovered Port Moresby in 1873 and provisionally annexed east New Guinea, but the provisional annexation was annulled in spite of protests of Australians. The Government of Queensland annexed it to the British Empire April 4, 1883, but the annexation was repudiated by Lord Derby.
In Nov., 1884, the German New Guinea Colonization Company which had been formed in May, raised the German flag at several places on the northern shore not claimed by the Dutch, and on Dec. 23, 1884 Bismarck notified the Powers of the annexation of the north-east coast and adjacent islands. The British Protectorate was proclaimed by Commodore Erskine Nov. 6, 1884 over the south-east coast of New Guinea and the adjacent islands, and the territory was annexed to the British Crown Sept. 4, 1888. The boundaries were settled by Anglo-German Convention of April 25,

1885, and Anglo-Netherlands Convention of May 16, 1895.

The former *German New Guinea* was assigned by the League of Nations Dec. 17, 1920 to Australia to be administered as mandated territory. German New Guinea was the name given to all those territories held by Germany in the Western Pacific which were governed from Rabaul, the capital of these Possessions. It included: Kaiserwilhelmsland, Bismarck Archipelago, the German Solomon Islands, Nauru, the Caroline Islands, the Marshall Islands, and the Marianne or Ladrone Islands (excepting the Island of Guam). These Possessions were occupied by an Australian Force on September 12, 1914. The islands north of the Equator, namely, the Marshall, Caroline, Pelew, and Ladrone (Marianne) Islands, are now administered by Japan as mandatory. Those south of the Equator, namely, the Bismarck Archipelago, those of the Solomon Islands formerly owned by Germany, and (late) German New Guinea, are assigned to Australia, German Samoa to New Zealand, and Nauru, a small islet just south of the Equator, to the British Empire. Kaiserwilhelmsland, the northern section of southeast New Guinea included Manam, Karkar, Long, Bagabag, Schouten, Le Maire, and some smaller islands. It has an area of 70,110 square miles with population estimated in 1929 as 456,941 natives, 1,808 British, 1,253 Chinese, 213 Dutch, 328 German, 45 Japanese, 106 American, total non-indigenous population, 3,928. The seat of government is Rabaul, New Britain. Civil administration established by Australia May 9, 1921. Brigadier General E. A. Wisdom, Administrator.

Dutch New Guinea comprises the entire western half of the Island with an area of 151,789 square miles (160,692 also given) with population estimated at 195,460 of whom 237 are Europeans or Eurasians. It is included in the Dutch East Indies, Molucca Group. *See* p. 950. Expedition of Le Maire and Schouten landed on New Guinea in 1616, made treaty with the Rajah of Onin in 1678.

British New Guinea the southeastern part of the island is named Papua. The area is 90,540 square miles of which about 87,786 are the mainland and 2,754 miles the islands of the d'Entrecasteaux and Luoisdale groups and all islands between 8° and 12° S. Lat. and 141° and 155° E. Long. On June 30, 1930 the population was as follows: Europeans, 1,525; Papuans (estimated) 275,000. In 1901 the Government of Australia agreed to take over New Guinea as a territory, the political transfer being completed by the Papua Act of Nov. 1905. On Sept. 1, 1906 a proclamation issued by the Governor General of Australia declared that British New Guinea was to be known henceforth as the territory of Papua.

Sir J. H. P. Murray, Lieutenant Governor and Judge.

New Hebrides Group lies roughly 500 miles west of Fiji and 250 miles north-east of New Caledonia, and about 1,000 miles from the coast of Australia, estimated area 5,700 square miles. The group is under joint administration of Great Britain and France as provided for by Anglo-French Convention of Nov. 16, 1887 supplemented by a joint declaration of Jan. 26, 1888 which created a Joint Naval Commission with limited powers for government, and the Commission to settle land claims established by Anglo-French Declaration of April 8, 1904, and finally the Condominium established by Anglo-French Convention of Feb. 27, 1906 formally confirmed by a Convention of Oct. 20, 1906 followed by regulations for Mixed Tribunal May 17, 1907, each Power retaining separate jurisdiction and control of its own citizens and subjects, and regulation of native affairs by the High Commissioners jointly. A Protocol signed in London Aug. 6, 1914 to replace the Convention of 1906 ratified March 18, 1922 guaranteed interests of British, French, and natives, fixed conditions of land-holding, and provided for regulation of recruitment of native labor. The population of the New Hebrides to which are attached the Banks and Torres Islands is estimated as 66,671, natives about 60,000, British nationals 205, French nationals 779, foreigners 86, Asiatics and Protected French Subjects (mostly coolies under indenture) 5,601. The largest islands are Espiritu Santo, 1,900 square miles; Malekula, 980 square miles; Eromanga, 429 square miles; and Vanua Lava, 136 square miles. The Torres or Vava (Ababa) group are 5 small islands, the Banks group include Vanua Lava, Gaua (Santa Maria), and several small islands, the northern New Hebrides include Espiritu Santo (Marina), Malekula, Epi, Efate (Vaté or Sandwich), Ambrym, Aragh or Pentecost, Aurora (Maiwo), and several smaller islands, and the southern New Hebrides widely scattered include Eromanga, Tana (Aipera) Aneityúm, and several small islands. The areas under cultivation are British, 8,685 acres, French 35,500 acres producing cotton, coconuts, and coffee chiefly. Discovered by Pedro Fernandes de Queiros, Portuguese pilot of Mendaña in 1606.

Sir A. G. M. Fletcher, British Higher Commissioner.

M. Guyon, French High Commissioner.

G. A. Joy, British Resident Commissioner.

M. Thaly (Acting) French Resident Commissioner.

New Ireland. *See* Bismarck Archipelago.

Norfolk Island, the principal of 3 small islands lying 930 miles east-northeast of Sydney, Australia, the other islets being Phillip and Nepean Islands, total area about 15 square miles, formerly a part of the Colony of New South Wales but now administered by the Commonwealth Government. They were discovered by Captain Cook in 1774. Population in 1927, 853.

Ocean Island or **Banaba** is the seat of government of the Gilbert and Ellice Island Colony, annexed to this Colony by Order in Council of Jan. 27, 1916 with Fanning and Washington Islands. *See* Gilbert and Ellice Islands.

Palau (Pelew) **Islands** are the Western Carolinas with Palau and Yap as administrative centers. The largest islands of the 26 are Babeltop, Uruktapi, Korror, Angaur, Peleliu, and Eimalk, total area, 175 square miles, and the population, 6,361 (5,754 natives). The islands were sighted in 1543 by Ruy Lopez de Villalobos. Germany bought the islands from Spain in 1899. After the World War they came under mandate of Japan. *See* Caroline Islands and Yap.

Palmyra, British "Line" Island in 6° N., 162° 30′ W., area 1½ square miles. Claimed by the United States.

Papua. *See* New Guinea, British.

Paumoto Archipelago. *See* Tuamoto Islands.

Philippine Islands, archipelago of 7,083 islands and islets, area 114,400 square miles, a group of the Malay Archipelago, extending almost due south from Formosa to Borneo and the Moluccas. They were ceded by Spain to the United States by Treaty of peace of April 11, 1899. Only 466 have areas of one square mile or over. 11 have total area of over 1,000 square miles, Luzon, with area of 40,814 square miles; Mindanao, 36,906 square miles; Samar, 5,124 square miles; Negros, 4,903 square miles; Palawan, 4,500 square miles; Panay, 4,448 square miles; Mindoro, 3,794 square miles; Leyte, 2,799 square miles; Cebu, 1,695 square miles; Bohol, 1,534 square miles; and Masbate, 1,255 square miles.

The total population, according to the Philippine Census of 1918, is 10,314,310, chiefly of Malay race, 91% of whom are Christians, and only 932,953, or 9% are Moros and Pagans, though these are fast taking advantage of the all-pervading system of public schools. The population of Manila, the capital and the leading commercial and industrial center, is 285,306, of whom 259,437 are Filipinos, 17,760 Chinese, 1,612 Japanese, 2,916 Americans, 2,050 Spaniards, 664 English, 201 Germans, 121 French, 71 Swiss, and the rest of other nationalities.

Other towns with their estimated present population, including suburbs, are: Iloilo on Panay, 67,143; Cebu on Cebu, 86,152; Legaspi (formerly Albay), 33,048; Laoag, 40,879; Vigan, 19,939; Naga, 9,468 (all on Luzon); and Zamboanga on Mindanao, 47,302. Baguio, in the Mountain Province, is the summer capital, corresponding to

Simla in India, and has a population of 8,449. *See also* United States Dependencies.

Dwight F. Davis, Governor General.

Phœnix Islands (British), between 2° 30′ and 4° 30′ S. lat., and 171° and 174° 30′ W. long. Eight islands: Mary, Enderbury, Phœnix, Birney, Gardner, McKean, Hull, Sydney; area of group, 16 square miles, population, 59. All except McKean and Enderbury Islands are leased to the Samoa Shipping and Trading Company for 87 years from Jan. 1, 1914.

Pitcairn Island (British) in 25° 5′ S., 130° 5′ W. Long. nearly equidistant from Australia and America. It was discovered by Carteret in 1767 but remained uninhabited until 1790, when it was occupied by the mutineers of the British ship "Bounty," 9 sailors, 6 Tahitian men, and 12 Tahitian women, who were discovered there in 1808, annexed by Great Britain in 1838. Pitcairn Island has area of 2 square miles. The islands of Henderson, Ducie, and Oeno were annexed in 1902, total area of islands about 10 square miles. Population in 1914 was 140, 35 adult males, 39 adult females, and 66 children.

Ross Dependency. The coasts of the Ross Sea, with the adjacent islands and territories, between 160° East longitude and 150° West longitude, and south of the 60th degree of latitude, were proclaimed a British Settlement and placed under the jurisdiction of the Governor-General of New Zealand by Order-in-Council of July 30th, 1923.

Rotumâ. *See* Fiji Islands.

Sakhalin, in the North Pacific. *See* p. 897.

Samoa, is a group of islands in the Western Pacific, lying in 13½° to 14° S. lat., and 168° to 173° W. long. The islands are some 130 miles N. of Tonga and between 400 and 500 miles N. E. of Fiji. The group consists of nine islands, in addition to rocks and islets. They are all, with the exception of Rose Island, of volcanic formation, and are, for the most part, surrounded with coral reefs. The four largest islands are Savaii, Upolu, Tutuila and Tau, in the Manu'a Group. By the Anglo-German Agreement of November 14, 1899, ratified by the United States in January, 1900, Great Britain renounced all rights over the islands in favor of Germany as regards Savaii, Upolu, Apolima, and Manono, and in favor of the United States as regards Tutuila and other islands.

The former German Samoan Islands, now the Territory of Western Samoa, include Savaii and Upolu, the largest of the Samoan or Navigators' Islands.

On August 29, 1914, the British occupied German Samoa. By the Treaty of Peace, 1919, Germany surrendered her possessions abroad, and Samoa is assigned under a mandate dated December 17, 1920, from the League of Nations to His Majesty the King in right of his Dominion of New Zealand, which has been empowered to govern Western Samoa. The military training of the natives, except for local police or defense purposes, is prohibited, and no naval or military base or any fortifications may be established.

The civil administration was inaugurated on May 1, 1920.

Savaii has an area of about 700 square miles; Upolu has an area of approximately 430 square miles. Several adjacent islets were included in the German dependency. The port of Apia is in Upolu. The inhabitants of the islands are Polynesians, professing Christianity (Protestants, Catholics, and Mormons). Population of Western Samoa, as recorded at December 31, 1929, was:— Europeans and half-castes, 2,749; Samoan natives, 40,722; Chinese laborers under contract, 955; other islanders, 145: total 44,571.

The Dutch were the first to visit the Islands, Jacob Roggeveen; the French, Louis de Bougainville, explored the Islands in 1768, and La Pérouse in 1787. A British war vessel arrived in 1791. In 1847, 1853, and 1861 respectively, Great Britain, the United States, and Germany appointed representatives. In 1872 the harbor of Pago Pago was ceded to the United States as a coaling station. For further history *see* United States Dependencies.

Sandwich Islands. *See* Hawaiian Islands.

Santa Cruz Islands (Queen Charlotte) comprise a dozen islands lying east by south of the British Solomon Islands, and are included in the British Protectorate of the Solomon Islands, total land area about 380 square miles. Santa Cruz or Ndeni, 200 square miles, is the largest, Vanikolo, the next largest is less than half this size.

Sarawak. *See* Borneo.

Society Islands (French) number 14 and are divided into the Windward (eastern) group, and the Leeward (western) group. The principal islands in the Windward group are Tahiti, with area of 402 square miles, Moorea (Aimeo), Mehetia, Tubuai, Manu, and Tetiaroa. The Leeward group includes Raiatea, Tahaa, Huahine, Bora Bora, Motu Iti (Tubai), Maurua (Maupiti), Mopihaa, Fenua Ura or Scilly, and Bellingshausen or Motu One. Tahiti had population of 8,585 inhabitants (1926). The town of Papeete on the Island of Tahiti is the center of government for French Oceanica. Tahiti was first discovered June–July, 1767, by Captain Wallis in H.M.S. "Dolphin," was visited in 1768 by the Frenchman Bougainville, and in 1769 by Captain Cook. French Protectorate declared Sept. 9, 1842, and Tahiti made a French Colony in 1880. By Treaty of Dec. 24, 1885, Germany renounced claims to Windward Islands.

Solomon Islands, archipelago in the western Pacific under British Protectorate. The former German Solomon Islands were assigned to Australia in 1920 under mandate of the League of Nations, total land area 17,000 square miles. The islands were discovered by the Spaniard, Alvaro Mendaña in 1567 who named them after King Solomon in anticipation of their natural riches, and the 3 large islands of San Cristoval, Guadalcanal, and Ysabel. Philip Carteret rediscovered the islands in 1767 and annexed by means of lead plates, and in 1768 Louis de Bougainville discovered the 3 northern islands, Buka, Bougainville, and Choiseul. The French explorer, J. F. de Surville visited the islands in 1769, Lieutenant Shortland in 1788, d'Entrecasteaux in 1792 and 1793, and Dumont d'Urville in 1838. In October, 1885, Lieutenant Rötter raised the German flag at Choiseul. By Franco-German Agreement of Dec., 1885, and Anglo-German Agreement of April 6, 1886, the German sphere in the Pacific was recognized and defined. In the Samoa Convention of Nov. 14, 1899, Germany ceded islands east and southeast of Bougainville to Great Britain. The German Solomon Islands were added to the sphere of New Guinea in 1886 and in 1914 consisted of the Islands of Bougainville, Buka, and adjacent islands, including Nuguria, Nissan, Kilinailau, Tauu (Mortlock), and Nukumanu (Tasman) Islands. Bougainville has an area of 3,880 square miles, and a native population (of areas patrolled in 1929) of 28,822, and Buka an area of 190 square miles, and a native population, including adjacent islands, 1929, 7,570. Other smaller islands in this group have a total area of 30 square miles and a native population in 1929 of 2,227. They were occupied by Australians in 1914. *See* World War.

British Solomon Islands, about 8° S. and 160° W., are Guadalcanar, Malaita, Ysabel, San Cristoval, New Georgia, Choiseul, Shortland, Mono (or Treasury), Vella Lavella, Ranongo, Gizo, Rendova, Russell, Florida, Rennell, and numerous small islands (the Lord Howe Group or Ontong Java, the Santa Cruz Islands, Tucopia and Mitre Islands, and the Duff, or Wilson Group, are also included in the Solomon Islands Protectorate). The total area of land and sea included in the British Solomon Islands Protectorate boundaries is approximately 375,000 square nautical miles. Population (in December, 1929), Europeans, 447; Aliens, 241; native population, about 150,000. They are under British Protection. The British Protectorate was declared over the southern Solomons in 1893 and the other Solomons in 1900.

Starbuck, British " Line" Island, 5° 30' S. Lat., 155° W. Long., area 1 square mile, uninhabited.

Sumatra lies between 5° 39' north and 5° 57' south Lat., so that the Equator divides it into 2 nearly equal parts, total area 167,954 square miles; the most westerly, and after Borneo, the largest of the Sunda Islands in the Malay Archipelago. It is separated from Java by the Sunda Straits, and from the Malay Peninsula by the Malacca Straits. The Dutch expedition of Cornelis Houtman (April 2, 1595–Aug. 20, 1597) reached Sumatra Jan. 1, 1596. A Dutch East India Company trade factory was established in Palembang and concluded a trade treaty in 1662, and a trade treaty with the Sultan of Menangkagau in 1664. In 1685 the English established a trade factory at Benkulen, and in 1781 captured all the Dutch possessions on the west coast which were restored by the Treaty of Versailles in 1783, captured again in 1795 and restored in 1814 by the Treaty of London. By a Treaty of March 17, 1824, the English ceded Benkulen to Holland and retired from Sumatra, the entire coast except Atjeh then under Dutch rule, and the Sultanate of Palembang was abolished in 1825, and the inland districts conquered; the Achinese finally conquered in Dec., 1907, after long war which began in March, 1873, and was carried on in one form or another until the Sultan surrendered and was deported.

Sunda Islands, name given to the islands from the Malay Peninsula to the Moluccas, including the Great Sunda Islands—Sumatra, Java, Borneo, Celebes, Banka, and Billington, and the Lesser Sunda Islands—Bale, Lombok, Sumbawa, Flores, Sumab, Timor, &c. *See* Dutch East Indies.

Tahiti, the largest and most important of the French Society Islands. *See* Society Islands.

Tasmania, the smallest State of the Australian Commonwealth, is an island at the southern extremity of the continent of Australia, from which it is divided by Bass' Straits, 120 miles wide, Victoria being on the other side of the Straits. It was discovered by Abel Jans Tasman, Dutch navigator, Nov. 24, 1642, and by him named Van Diemen's Land, the name by which it was known to 1853, after his patron, Van Diemen. The area of the State is 26,215 square miles including Macquarie Island (170 square miles). The adjacent islands are 55 in number, most of them in Bass' Straits, the chief are the Furneaux group (including Flinders Island), Robbins Island, King Island, Bruny Island, on the south, and Maria Island on the east coast. In 1803 a penal settlement was founded by Lieutenant Bowen sent by Governor King from New South Wales. In 1825 the Colony was made independent of New South Wales, Colonel Arthur appointed Governor. In 1853 it ceased to be a penal settlement and the name was changed to Tasmania. Act of the Imperial Parliament of May 1, 1855 granted a Constitution.

Timor (Malay Archipelago) largest of the Lesser Sunda Islands; divided between Portugal and the Netherlands. The Portuguese obtained possession of the Island early in the 16th century; it was visited by Magellan 1521; the Dutch landed in 1613, settled at Kupang, western part of Island, in 1618, and have held entire western part of Island since 1769, making treaties of alliance with the native chiefs in 1756. During the English occupation of Java (1811–1816) Timor was held by the English. Portuguese Timor is the northeastern part of the Island with a small enclave in the south (Ocussi-Ambeno) and the adjacent islands of Pulo Cambing (Kambing) and Pulo Jako (area of 7¼ square miles), total area, 7,300 square miles, population in 1926, 451,604. Dutch Timor is the southwestern half of the Island, and with Sumba, Flores, the Alor and Solor Isles, Savu, and Rotti, forms the Residency of Timor and Dependencies of the Dutch East Indies, area about 5,000 square miles, population about 360,000, including the dependencies, 1,143,626. The division of the Island was made by Treaty of April 20, 1859 settling the boundaries between Dutch and Portuguese territory, Portuguese claims in Flores, Solor, and Alor groups ceded to the Netherlands, and by later Boundary Conventions of June 10, 1893 with Declaration of July 1, and Oct. 1, 1904, ratified in 1908 and finally brought into effect by arbitration award of June 25, 1914, of M. Lardy, Swiss member of the Hague Court of Arbitration who decided in favor of the Dutch claims as to frontier of the Ocussi enclave.

Tokelau Islands. *See* Union Islands.

Tonga or **Friendly Islands,** British Protectorate, about 100 islands southeast of the Fiji in 3 groups called respectively Tongatabu, Haapai (Haabai), and Niuafoou, total area about 385 square miles. The only large islands are Tongatabu (area about 125 square miles), Vavua, and Eua. Tongabatu is about 1,000 miles from Auckland, Sydney. They were discovered by the Dutch navigator, Abel Janszoon Tasman, Jan. 19–25, 1643. In 1616 Jacob Lemaire and William Cornelis Schouten reached the island of Niuatobutabu (Keppel Island) which is politically included in this group. Samuel Wallis visited the islands in 1767, and Captain Cook in 1773 and 1777. In 1799 a native revolt began which was finally put down by the rule of Taufaahau who became king in 1845 as George Tubou I. He was succeeded in 1893 by his great-grandson under the same title, and on the death of George II (1918) his daughter, Salote succeeded as Queen. In accordance with the Declaration of Berlin of April 6, 1886, the Tonga Islands were a neutral region, but Anglo-German Treaty of Nov. 14, 1899 made them practically a British Protectorate. A Treaty of friendship between Tonga and Great Britain was amended June 2, 1891, and replaced by new Treaty of May 18, 1900 which formally accepted British protection, proclaimed May 19.

Tuamotu Archipelago (French), known formerly as the Paumoto Archipelago, includes about 80 small coral islands, the northern islands lying between the Society and the Marquesas Islands, total land area 330 square miles, population, 4,276. The principal islands are Fakarava, Anaa, Kaukura, Rahiroa (Rangiroa), and Makatea in the northwestern part of the archipelago. The seat of the French Resident is Fakarava. The first discoverer of the islands was Pedro Fernandez Quiros in 1606. France assumed a protectorate in 1844, and annexed the islands in 1881. They form part of the dependency of Tahiti.

Tubai or **Austral Islands** (French) lie south of the Society Islands, 7 islands with total area of 115 square miles. Captain Cook visited Rurutu in 1769, and Tubuai in 1777. Rapa was discovered by Vancouver in 1791. The islands are united to the Gambier Administration, and dependent on Tahiti. *See* Gambier Islands.

Union Islands (Tokelau), British Protectorate, 1889, formerly part of the Gilbert and Ellice Islands Colony, have been transferred to the jurisdiction of New Zealand, February 11, 1926, and are administered by the Administrator of Western Samoa. They lie between 8° 30′ and 11° S. lat., and 171° and 172° W. long. (population 1926, 1,033), and comprise five clusters of islets, the principal of which are Fakaofo or Bowditch, Nukunono or Duke of Clarence, Atafu or Duke of York; area of group, 7 square miles.

Van Diemen's Land. *See* Tasmania.

Wallis Archipelago (French) dependency of New Caledonia. *See* New Caledonia.

Washington Island. *See* Gilbert and Ellice Islands.

Windward Islands. *See* Society Islands.

Yap, island of the Caroline group, former German possession, the seat of administration for the western Carolinas, with the Palau and Mariana Islands, and important cable station, situated south of Japan and east of the Philippines in Lat. 9° 35′ N., Long. 138° 15′ E. On May 7, 1919 Japan was given mandate over this island with other German islands north of the Equator, mandate confirmed by the League of Nations Dec. 17, 1920. The United States made reservation to the Four Power Treaty signed Dec. 13, 1921, and repeated in connection with the Supplemental Agreement of Feb. 6, 1922, protesting against Japanese mandate proposing that the island should be internationalized for cable purposes. By the Treaty between the United States and Japan signed Feb. 11, 1922 the United States consented to the administration by Japan, the United States granted equality with Japan or any other nation as to cable and radio-telegraph service.